CAM

Learner's
Dictionary
English–Turkish

CAMBRIDGE
UNIVERSITY PRESS

CAMBRIDGE UNIVERSITY PRESS

Cambridge, New York, Melbourne, Madrid, Cape Town, Singapore, São Paulo, Delhi

Cambridge University Press
The Edinburgh Building, Cambridge CB2 8RU, UK

http://www.cambridge.org
Information on this title: www.cambridge.org/9780521736435

First published 2009

Printed in Italy by L.E.G.O. S.p.A.

A catalogue record for this publication is available from the British Library

ISBN 978-0-521-73643-5 paperback

Türkçe Yarı İki Dilli Versiyon Redaksiyon Ekibi

Yönetici Redaktör
Stella O'Shea

Uzman Redaktör
Melissa Good

Türkçe Çevirmen
Hidayet Tuncay

Türkçe Redaktör
Sibel Sagner

Çalişma Sayfalarin, Türkçe Çevirmeni ve Redaktöry
Ferhat Kenan Kunduh, Enel Soyu (First Edition Translations Ltd Cambridge)

Sıkça Rastlanan Öğrenci Notları
Diane Nichols

Duzeltmenler
Nathalie Horner
Jill Leatherbarrow
Kayhan Mutlu
Pinar Ussakli
Ilkay White

Proje Yöneticisi (CD-ROM)
Dorota Bednarczyk-Krajeweska

Geliştirici (CD-ROM)
Alison Mitchell

Sistem ve Network Yönetim
Dominic Glennon
Daniel Perrett

Bütünce
Ann Fiddes, Global Corpus Manager
Julie Sontag, Corpus Administrator
Nathalie Horner, Corpus Assistant

Prodüksiyon
Clive Rumble

v

İçindekiler

Giriş

Cambridge Learner's Dictionary'nin yeni, güncelleştirilmiş baskısına (3. baskı) hoş geldiniz Elinizde, birçok nedenle orta ve ortanın üstü seviyelerde İngilizce öğrenen Türk öğrenciler için mükemmel olarak tasarlanmış bir sözlük bulunmaktadır.

Kelimelerin açık anlamları (tanımlar)
Kelimelerin anlamlarını bilmeniz gerekir. Kelime açıklamalarımız kısa, açık ve doğrudur. Tanımlarımızda sadece anlayacağınız basit İngilizce kullanır.

Dilbilgisinde yardım
İngilizceyi doğru şekilde konuşabilmek ve yazabilmek istiyorsunuz. Dilbilgisi ile ilgili bilgilerimiz açık, faydalı ve yanlışlardan nasıl kaçınacağınızı gösterecek şekilde sunulmuştur.

Kulağa doğal gelen örnekler
Kelimeleri nasıl kulağa doğal gelecek şekilde kullanacağınızı bilmek istiyorsunuz. Bu sözlük 27.000'den fazla örnek içermektedir. Bunlar bir kelimenin içinde en çok söylendiği veya yazıldığı bağlam ile sıklıkla birlikte kullanıldığı kelime türlerini gösterirler.

Kelime ortakları (eş dizimliler)
A good buy ve a big decision gibi sıklıkla birlikte söylenen veya yazılan kelimelere kelime ortakları veya eş dizimliler denir. Akıcı ve kulağa doğal gelen bir İngilizce üretmek için en önemli beceri belki de doğru kelimelerin bir araya nasıl getirileceğini bilmektir. Bu sözlük kelime ortakları hakkında bu seviyedeki diğer tüm sözlüklerden daha fazla bilgi içerir.

Anahtar kelimeler
Öğrenilmesi en önemli kelimelerin hangileri olduğunu bilmek istiyorsunuz. İngilizce dilindeki en önemli 2000 kelime mavi renkle ve yanlarında bir anahtar simgesi o→ ile gösterilmiştir.

Yeni kelimeler
İngilizce sürekli olarak değişmektedir. Bu sözlüğün teknoloji, moda ve müzik gibi alanlardaki yeni kelimelerle gerçekten güncel olduğundan emin olabilirsiniz.

Kendi kendine çalışma

Kendi kendinize İngilizce çalışabilmek istiyorsunuz. Bu sözlükte, öbek fiiller ve heceleme gibi konularda birçok açık ve yararlı bilgilerin olduğu 59 sayfalık *Ekstra yardım sayfalarını* içeren bir orta bölüm vardır. Ayrıca kelime dağarcığınızı genişletmenize yardımcı olmak için tam renkli 16 sayfa dolusu resim ve fotoğraf da bulunmaktadır.

Cambridge International Corpus ve Cambridge Learner Corpus

Yukarıda anlatılan özelliklerin tümü, *bir milyarı* aşkın İngilizce kelimenin derlemesi olan *Cambridge International Corpus* kullanılarak yaratılmıştır. Sadece Cambridge sözlükleri bu muhteşem kaynak kullanılarak üretilir. Bizim bütüncemizdeki İngilizce, gazeteler, en iyi satan romanlar, web siteleri, dergiler, TV programları ve kişilerin günlük konuşmalarının kayıtları gibi birçok yerden gelir. Bu dilin bütününü çok büyük bir veri tabanında saklıyor ve İngilizcenin gerçekten nasıl kullanıldığını görmek için kullanıyoruz. Sözlükte söylediğimizin doğru olduğundan emin olmamız için gereken kanıtı bize bu bütünce verir.

Sahip olduğumuz diğer bir değerli araç da *Cambridge Learner Corpus* olup, dünyanın her yerindeki Cambridge ESOL İngilizce sınavlarına giren öğrencilerin yazdığı sınav yazıları derlemesidir. Bu öğrenci bütüncesi hangi kelimelerin Türk öğrenciler için sorun yarattığını gösterir. Bu da, Türk öğrenciler için yararlı bilgileri, *Sıkça Rastlanan Öğrenci Yanlışları Notları* şeklinde sizin bunlardan kaçınmanıza yardımcı olmak için ekleyebilmemiz anlamına gelir.

Sözlüğün beraberinde verilen CD-ROM'da, sözlükteki her kelime Türkçe karşılıklarıyla beraber verilmiştir. Bunların dışında ekstra olarak kelimelerin Britanya ve Amerikan aksanlı telaffuzları, başka benzeri olmayan ve sözlükte kullanılan her bir kelimenin eş anlamlısını veya konu listesini veren SMART eş anlamlılar sözlüğünü, fiil eklerinin bilgilerini, alıştırma ve çalışma sayfalarını ve Türk öğrencilerin en çok yaptıkları hataları gösteren bilgiler bulunmaktadır. (ayrıntılı bilgi için bkz. CD-ROM kullanım kılavuzu)

Siz ve diğer Türk öğrencilerin *Cambridge Learner's Dictionary*'yi zevkle kullanacağınızı biliyoruz. Kullanın ve İngilizcenizin gelişmesini görün.

Dünyanın en gözde öğrenci sözlüğünü ziyaret edin.

http://dictionary.cambridge.org

Bu sözlük nasıl kullanılır

Kelime bulmak

Her bir giriş, kelimenin kök biçimi ile başlar.

language /ˈlæŋgwɪdʒ/ *noun* **1** [COMMUNICATION] [U] communication between people, usually using words **dil, lisan** *She has done research into how children acquire language.* **2** [ENGLISH/SPANISH/JAPANESE ETC] [C] a type of communication used by the people of a particular country **bir ülkede konuşulan dil, lisan** *How many languages do you speak?* **3** [TYPE OF WORDS] [U] words of a particular type, especially the words used by people in a particular job **belli bir işe ait özel dil, lisan, mesleki dil** ○ *the language of business* **4** [COMPUTERS] [C, U] a system of instructions that is used to write computer programs **bilgisayar dili** ⊃See also: **body language, modern languages, second language, sign language.**

İki ayrı kelimeden oluşan kelimeler (birleşikler) alfabetik olarak sıralanmıştır. Vurgu işaretleri (ˈ) kelimenin hangi kısmının kuvvetlice söyleneceğini gösterir.

ˈlanguage laˌboratory *UK* (*US* ˈlanguage ˌlaboratory) *noun* [C] a room in a college or school where you can use equipment to help you practise listening to and speaking a foreign language **dil laboratuvarı**

Bir kelime başka şekilde hecelenebiliyorsa veya bunun için başka bir kelime varsa, bu gösterilmiştir.

dialogue (*also US* **dialog**) /ˈdaɪəlɒg/ *noun* [C, U] **1** the talking in a book, play, or film **karşılıklı konuşma, diyalog 2** a formal discussion between countries or groups of people **ülkeler/kişiler arası karşılıklı diyalog/görüşme**

İki kelime aynı yazılışa sahip, fakat konuşmanın farklı kısımlarına aitse (örneğin isim ve fiil gibi) bunların farklı girişleri vardır.

interface¹ /ˈɪntəfeɪs/ *noun* [C] **1** a connection between two pieces of electronic equipment, or between a person and a computer **ara birim, arayüz** *a simple user interface* **2** a situation, way, or place where two things can come together and have an effect on each other **çıkış noktası** *the interface between technology and tradition*

interface² /ˈɪntəˌfeɪs/ *verb* [I, T] to communicate with people or electronic equipment, or to make people or electronic equipment communicate **kişilerle/elektronik araçlarla iletişim kurmak/kurdurmak** *We use email to interface with our customers.*

Ana kelimeden türemiş kelimeler girişin sonunda gösterilmiştir. Bir kelime düzenli kalıpla oluşturulmamışsa veya anlamını tahmin etmek kolay değilse bunun kendisine ait bir açıklaması bulunur. 881. sayfadaki Kelime Başlangıç ve Sonlarına bakınız.

fluent /'fluːənt/ *adjective* **1** able to use a language naturally without stopping or making mistakes **akıcı konuşan; bir dili akıcı/hatasız kullanan** *She is fluent in six languages.* **2** produced or done in a smooth, natural style **akıcı** *Hendrik speaks fluent English.* ● **fluency** /'fluːənsi/ *noun* [U] **akıcılık** ● **fluently** *adverb* **akıcı bir şekilde**

Bir girişin anlaşılması

Bir kelimenin birden fazla anlamı varsa en sık kullanılan anlamı önce gösterilmiştir.

Birkaç anlamı olan kelimeler için aradığınız anlamı bulmanıza yardımcı olacak **KILAVUZ KELİMELER** vardır.

Cambridge International Corpus'a dayalı örnek cümleler kelimelerin tipik durumlarda nasıl kullanıldıklarını gösterir.

voice¹ /vɔɪs/ *noun* **1** SOUNDS [C] the sounds that you make when you speak or sing **ses** *I could hear voices in the next room.* ○ *Jessie has a beautiful singing voice.* ○ *Could you please* ***keep your voices down*** (= speak more quietly)? ○ *He* ***raised his voice*** (= spoke more loudly) *so that everyone could hear.* **2** ***lose your voice*** to become unable to speak, often because of an illness **sesini kaybetmek** *She had a bad cold and was losing her voice.* **3** OPINION [C] someone's opinion about a particular subject **fikir, düşünce** *The programme gives people the opportunity to make their voices heard.* **4** PERSON [no plural] someone who expresses the opinions or wishes of a group of people **sözcü, temsilci, konuşmacı** *It's important that students have a voice on the committee.* ○ See also: **the passive.**

Her kelime, bir cümle öğesi etiketine sahiptir (örneğin *noun, verb, adj*). Kelime türleri listesi için ön kapağın içine bakınız.

Dilbilgisi etiketleri bir kelimenin nasıl kullanıldığını gösterir. Sayfa xiii'deki dilbilgisi etiketlerine bakınız.

say¹ /seɪ/ *verb* [T] says, *past* said **1** WORDS to speak words **söylemek, demek** *"I'd like to go home," she said.* ○ *I couldn't hear what they were saying.* ○ *How do you say this word?* **2** TELL to tell someone about a fact, thought, or opinion **söylemek, belirtmek, ifade etmek** [+ question word] *Did she say where she was going?* ○ [+ (that)] *The jury said that he was guilty.* **3** INFORMATION to give information in writing, numbers, or signs **bilgi vermek, göstermek, belirtmek** *My watch says one o'clock.* ○ *What do the papers say about the election?* **4** ***say sth to yourself*** to think something but not speak **düşünmek, kendi kendine demek** *"I hope she likes me," he said to himself.*

Bu simge öğrenilmesi önemli çok sık kullanılan kelimeleri gösterir.

Söyleyişler International Phonetic Alphabet (IPA)'i kullanır. Bu simgelerin bir listesi sözlüğün arka kapağının içindedir. En zor simgeler her sayfanın sonunda ayrıca açıklanmıştır. Söyleyiş sisteminin bir açıklaması sayfa xvı'dadır.

Kelimelerin düzensiz çekimleri de açıkça gösterilmiştir. Düzensiz fiil çekimlerinin bir listesi 878. sayfada ve düzenli çekimlerin açıklaması da 876. sayfada bulunmaktadır.

Bu etiketler bir kelimenin ne zaman Britanya İngilizcesinde, ne zaman Amerikan İngilizcesinde kullanıldığını gösterir. Bu etiketlerin sayfa xv'deki açıklamasına bakınız.

Bu etiketler bir kelimenin ne kadar resmi, resmi olmayan v.b. olduğunu söyler. Tüm bu etiketlerin sayfa xv'deki açıklamasına bakınız.

Bir kelime hakkında daha fazla bilgi öğrenmek

İç göndermeler zıtlar, resimler, çalışma sayfaları ve deyimler gibi ilgili bilgileri nerede bulacağınızı gösterir.

speak (spi:k) *verb past tense* **spoke**, *past participle* **spoken** **1** [I] to say something using your voice **konuşmak** *to speak loudly/quietly* ○ *There was complete silence - nobody spoke.* **2 speak to sb** *mainly UK (mainly US* **speak with sb)** *to talk to someone* **biriyle konuşmak** *Could I speak to Mr Davis, please?* ○ *Have you spoken with your new neighbors yet?* **3 speak about/of sth** to talk about something **bir şey hakkında konuşmak** *He refused to speak about the matter in public.* **4 speak English/French/German, etc** to be able to communicate in English/French/German, etc **yabancı dil konuşmak** *Do you speak English?* **5** [I] to make a speech to a large group of people **konuşma yapmak** *She was invited to speak at a conference in Madrid.* **6 speak for/ on behalf of sb** to express the feelings, opinions, etc of another person or of a group of people **birisi adına konuşmak** *I've been chosen to speak on behalf of the whole class.*

chat¹ /tʃæt/ *verb* [I] **chatting**, *past* **chatted** to talk with someone in a friendly and informal way **sohbet etmek, çene çalmak, hoş beş etmek, yarenlik etmek, (argo) lakırdamak** *I wanted to chat to you about the party on Saturday.*
chat sb up *phrasal verb UK informal* to talk to someone in a way that shows them that you are sexually attracted to them **konuşarak tavlamak, ilşki kurmaya çalışmak, (argo) asılmak, konuşarak arkadaşlık kurmak**

ask /ɑːsk/ *verb* **1** QUESTION [I, T] to say something to someone as a question which you want them to answer **sormak** [+ two objects] *Can I ask you a few questions?* ○ *I asked him about his hobbies.* ○ [+ question word] *I asked why the plane was so late.* See Common learner error at **question**. **2** WANT SOMETHING [I, T] to say something to someone because you want them to give you something **istemek, dilemek** *He's asked for a bike for his birthday.*

Sıkça birlikte kullanılan kelimeler
(eş *dizimliler veya kelime*
ortakları) örneklerde koyu yazı ile
gösterilmiştir.

communicate /kə'mjuːnɪkeɪt/ *verb* [I, T] **1** to share information with others by speaking, writing, moving your body, or using other signals **iritbatta olmak, bağlantı kurmak, haberleşmek** *We can now communicate instantly with people on the other side of the world.* **2** to talk about your thoughts and feelings, and help other people to understand them **iletişim kurmak, kendini anlatmak/anlaşılmasını sağlamak** *He can't communicate with his parents.*

Bazı kelimeler bir deyimin parçası
olarak kullanılır. Bu, tanımın başında
açık olarak gösterilmiştir.

Öbek fiiller, fiil girişinden sonra
alfabetik sırada gelir.

spell[1] /spel/ *verb past* **spelled** or *also UK* **spelt 1** [T] to write down or tell someone the letters which are used to make a word **hecelemek, harf harf söylemek** *How do you spell that?* ○ *Her name's spelt S-I-A-N.* **2** [I] If you can spell, you know how to write the words of a language correctly. **yazım kurallarına göre yazmak** *My grammar's all right, but I can't spell.* **3 spell disaster/trouble, etc** If something spells disaster, trouble, etc, you think it will cause something bad to happen in the future. **felâket/sorun/kötülük getirmek; kötülüğe neden olmak; berbat etmek** *The new regulations could spell disaster for small businesses.*
spell sth out *phrasal verb* to explain something in a very clear way with details **ayrıntıyla açıklamak, açıkça anlatmak** *They sent me a letter, spelling out the details of the agreement.*

Bazı kelimeler bir deyimin parçası
olarak kullanılır. Bunlar, girişin
sonunda koyu yazı ile gösterilmiştir.

message[1] /'mesɪdʒ/ *noun* [C] **1** a piece of written or spoken information which one person gives to another **ileti, haber, mesaj** *Did you get my message?* ○ *I left her several messages, but she hasn't returned my call.* **2** the most important idea of a film, book, etc **(film, kitap, vs.) verilmek istenen duygu ve düşünce, mesaj** *The book conveys a complex message.* **3 get the message** *informal* to understand what someone wants you to do by their actions **söylenen şeyi anlamak, mesajı almak** *Don't return any of his calls - he'll soon get the message and leave you alone.*

Tüm açıklamalarımızda basit
kelimeler kullanılmıştır. Alışılmıştan
daha zor kelimeler kullanmak
zorunda kaldığımız yerde o kelime
parantez içinde açıklanmıştır.

express[1] /ɪk'spres/ *verb* [T] to show what you think or how you feel using words or actions **ifade etmek** *I'm simply expressing my opinion.* ○ [often reflexive] *You're not expressing yourself (= saying what you mean) very clearly.*

Kutulardaki bilgiler

Bu Word Partner kutuları sıkça birlikte söylenen veya yazılan ve genellikle "eş dizimliler" veya "kelime ortakları" denen kelimeler hakkında bilgiler vermektedir. Sözlükte bu kutulardan 1000'den fazlası bulunmaktadır.

text message .... İLE BİRLİKTE KULLANILAN KELİMELER

get/send a text message ● a text message **saying** sth ● a text message **from/to** sb

Bu thesaurus kutuları aynı veya benzer anlamlı tüm farklı kelimeleri gösterir. Sözlükte bu kutulardan 80 tanesi bulunmaktadır.

talk .... BAŞKA BİR DEYİŞLE

En sıklıkla kullanılan alternatifler **speak** ve **say** fiilleridir. *Could you* **speak** *more quietly, please?* ● *I couldn't hear what they were* **saying**.
chat fiili veya **have a chat** söylemi iki kişinin arkadaşça bir ortamda sohbet ettiklerini belirtir. *We were just* **chatting** *about the party on Saturday.* ● *Give me a call and we'll* **have a chat**.
Eğer kişiler önemli olmayan konularda uzun süreyle konuşuyorlarsa, **chatter**, **natter** (gayri resmi), ve **have a natter** ifadeleri kullanılabilir. *She spent the morning* **chattering** *away to her friends.* ● *We* **had a long natter** *over coffee.*
Eğer kişi bir olay hakkında çok uzun süreyle artık bıktırıcı bir şekilde konuşuyorsa, **go on** deyimi kullanılabilir. *He's always* **going on** *about how much he hates his work.*
Eğer kişi bir şey hakkında şikayet ettiğinden dolayı kısık sesle konuşuyorsa, **mumble** ve **mutter** fiilleri kullanılabilir. *She walked past me,* **muttering** *to herself.* ● *He* **mumbled** *something about it being a waste of time.*
Eğer kişi diğer insanların duymaması için çok kısık sesle konuşuyorsa, **whisper** fiili kullanılabilir. *What are you two girls* **whispering** *about?*

Cambridge Learner Corpus'a dayalı Common Learner Error notları Türk öğrenciler için sıklıkla sorun yaratan kelimeler hakkında bilgi verir.

YAYGIN HATALAR

plan
Dikkat! Fiil sonlarını kontrol ediniz. Çoğu Türk öğrenci, **plan** fiilini geçmiş zamanda kullanırken hata yapmaktadır. **Plan** fiilinin 2. ve 3. halleri **planned** şeklindedir. Fiilin -ing formu **planning** şeklindedir.

Bu sözlüğün kullanımı hakkında daha fazla bilgi

Dilbilgisi etiketleri

Bir kelimenin *her zaman* belirli bir dil bilgisi biçiminde kullanılması zorunluysa, o biçim girişin veya anlamın başında gösterilmiştir. Sıkça rastlanan ve tipik olan fakat *her zaman* kullanılmayan kalıplar, nasıl kullanıldıklarını gösteren örnek cümlelerin yanında verilmiştir.

İsimler

C	sayılabilen isim	pencil, friend, house
U	sayılamayan isim, çoğulu yoktur	water, advice, health
C, U	isim, hem sayılabilen hem de sayılamayan isim olabilir	Ability, quantity, exercise ▶ *You should take some **exercise**.* ▶ *I do my **exercises** every morning.*

⮑ ayrıca Orta 20'deki Extra help sayfasındaki **Sayılabilen ve sayılamayan isimlere** bakınız

group	bir insan veya cansız grubundan söz eden ve hem tekil hem de çoğul fiil ile kullanılabilen grup isim	government, class, team ▶ *The French **team are** European champions.* ▶ *His **team is** top of the league.*
plural	çoğul isim, çoğul fiil ile kullanılır	trousers, scissors, pliers
no plural	a veya an ile kullanılabilen fakat çoğulu olmayan isim	rush, vicious circle, wait ▶ *Sorry, I'm in **a rush**.*
usually plural	genellikle çoğul biçimde kullanılan isim	statistics, resources, regulations
usually singular	genellikle tekil biçimde kullanılan isim	mess, range, world

Fiiller

I	geçişsiz fiil, nesnesi yoktur	sleep, glance, fall ▶ *Anna's **sleeping**.*
T	geçişli fiil, nesnesi olması zorunludur	cure, hit, catch ▶ *Fiona **hit** her **sister**.*
I, T	hem geçişsiz hem de geçişli olabilen fiil	sing, explain, drive ▶ *I always **sing** in the bath.* ▶ *He **sang** a love **song**.*
+ two objects	iki nesnesi olan çift geçişli fiil	give, send, lend ▶ *She **gave me** the **keys**.*
often passive	sıklıkla edilgen olarak kullanılan fiil	allow ▶ *Smoking **is not allowed** in the restaurant.*
often reflexive	sıklıkla bir dönüşlü adıl ile birlikte kullanılan fiil (myself, yourself, herself v. b.)	defend ▶ *He can **defend** himself.*

Bir fiil veya fiillin anlamı *her zaman edilgen* (örneğin inundate, demote, affiliate) veya *her zaman dönüşlüyse* (örneğin brace, ingratiate, steel), dil bilgisi kalıbının tümü girişin başında gösterilmiştir.

Bazı fiiller veya fiil anlamlarını **her zaman bir belirteç veya ilgeç izler** (örneğin creep, flick, trickle). Bu olduğunda kullanılan belirteç ve ilgeçlerin sıkça rastlanan örnekleri giriş veya anlamın başında gösterilmiştir.

➲ ayrıca Orta 27'deki Extra help sayfasındaki **Fiil kalıplarına** bakınız

Sıfatlar

always before noun	niteleme sıfatı, her zaman isimden önce gelir	major, basic, staunch ▶ *a staunch supporter*
never before noun	yüklemcil sıfat, **be, seem, feel** gibi fiillerle kullanılır	afraid, ready, done ▶ *She's afraid of water.*
always after noun	her zaman sıfatı doğrudan ismin ardından kullanılır	galore, proper, incarnate ▶ *the devil incarnate*

Diğer dil bilgisi kalıpları

Aşağıdaki kalıplar isimlere, sıfatlara ve fiillere gönderme yapabilir:

+ that	kelimeyi bir **that clause** takip eder ve **that** eklenmesi zorunludur	boast, assertion, evident ▶ *It was evident from her voice that she was upset.*
+ (that)	kelimeyi bir **that clause** takip eder fakat **that** kullanılması zorunlu değildir	hope, amazed, doubt ▶ *I hope that the bus won't be late.* ▶ *I hope the bus won't be late.*
+ doing sth	kelimeyi –ing biçiminde bir fiil takip eder	enjoy, busy, difficulty ▶ *I enjoy going to the beach.*
+ to do sth	kelimeyi bir mastar fiil takip eder	confidence, careful, decide ▶ *I didn't have the confidence to speak up.*
+ for/of, etc + doing sth	kelimeyi bir ilgeç (örneğin for/of) ardından da –ing biçiminde bir fiil takip eder	apologize, idea, guilty ▶ *She apologized for being late.*
+ question word	kelimeyi bir soru kelimesi (örneğin **who, what, how**) takip eder	ask, certain, clue ▶ *I'm not certain who to ask.*
used in questions and negatives	kelime sorularda ve olumsuz cümlelerde kullanılır	mind, much, yet ▶ *Do you mind if I come in?* ▶ *I haven't seen him yet.*

Kullanım etiketleri

informal	tanıdığınız kişilerle konuşurken veya iletişim kurarken kullanılmakla beraber, normalde ciddi yazılarda kullanılmaz	brainy, freebie, goalie
formal	kişilerle hukuk veya iş hakkında ciddi yazışmalar veya iletişim kurmak için kullanılır	examination, moreover, purchase
very informal	iyi tanıdığınız kişilerle konuşurken kullanılmakla beraber, normal yazışmalarda kullanılmaz. Bu kelimelerin bazıları kişileri gücendirebilir ve bu durum girişte açıklanmıştır.	prat, barf, crap
spoken	konuşmada kullanılan bir kelimenin yazılış şekli	yeah, hey, eh
humorous	komik olmak veya şaka yapmak için kullanılır	couch potato, snail mail
literary	sıradan konuşmada değil kitaplarda ve şiirlerde kullanılır	beloved, slumber, weep
old-fashioned	modern İngilizcede kullanılmaz – bu kelimelerin kitapların yanısıra, yaşlılar tarafından veya komik olmak için kullanıldığını görürsünüz	gramophone, spectacles, farewell
trademark	bir şirket tarafından üretilen bir ürünün adı. Bazen bir ticari marka genel bir kelime olarak kullanılır	Coke, Hoover, Sellotape

UK/US etiketleri

Bu sözlükteki tanım ve örneklerde kullanılan heceleme Britanya İngilizcesidir. Bununla beraber Amerikan İngilizcesi de anlaşılır biçimde açıklanmış ve Britanya İngilizcesi ile Amerikan İngilizcesi arasında farkın olduğu yerlerde bu durum gösterilmiştir.

UK	sadece Britanya İngilizcesinde kullanılır	pavement, petrol station
US	sadece Amerikan İngilizcesinde kullanılır	sidewalk, gas station
mainly UK	çoğunlukla Britanya İngilizcesinde kullanılmakla beraber, bazen Amerikan İngilizcesinde de kullanılır	lecturer, rubbish, nightdress
mainly US	çoğunlukla Amerikan İngilizcesinde kullanılmakla beraber, bazen Britanya İngilizcesinde de kullanılır	movie, apartment, semester
also UK	Britanya İngilizcesinde de kullanılabilecek başka bir kelime	truck (*also UK* lorry) ■ **truck** Britanya ve US İngilizcelerinde kullanılır **lorry** Britanya İngilizcesinde de kullanılır
also US	Amerikan İngilizcesinde de kullanılabilecek başka bir kelime	railway (*also US* railroad) ■ **railway** Britanya ve US İngilizcelerinde kullanılır **railroad** US İngilizcesinde de kullanılır

➲ ayrıca sayfa Orta 38'deki Extra help page **UK ve US İngilizcesine** bakınız

Söyleyiş

Tüm söyleyişler International Phonetic Alphabet'i kullanır. Sesbilgisi simgelerinin bir listesi sözlüğün arka kapağının içindedir. Örneğin /p/, /s/, /k/, gibi birçok sesbilgisi sembollerinin sesleri, benzedikleri harfin en çok rastlanan söylenişinin aynısıdır. Böyle olmayanlar sözlükteki her sayfanın dibinde açıklanmıştır. Birden fazla söyleyişin gösterildiği yerlerde, daha sıkça rastlanan ilktir, fakat her ikisi de sıklıkla kullanılır.

Britanya ve Amerikan söyleyişleri

Çoğu kelimeler Britanya ve Amerikan İngilizcelerinde kabul edilen, sadece bir söyleyişle verilmiştir. Britanya ve Amerikan İngilizceleri arasında bazı alışılagelmiş farklılıklar olup bunlar her kelime için gösterilmemiştir.

Bunların başlıcaları:

1 **Hard** veya **teacher** kelimelerindeki r harfi Amerikan İngilizcesinde söylenir ancak Britanya İngilizcesinde söylenmez.

2 **Later** ve **butter** kelimelerindeki t ve tt, Amerikan İngilizcesinde neredeyse bir /d/ sesi gibi yumuşak biçimde söylenir.

Britanya ve Amerikan söyleyişleri arasında büyük farklılıklar olduğunda her iki biçim de gösterilir. Amerikan söyleyişinden önce simge ⓤ gösterilmiştir, örneğin **schedule** /ˈʃedjuːl ⓤ ˈskedʒuːl/

Vurgu kalıpları

Vurgu kalıpları kelimeyi söylerken hangi kısmını vurgulamanız gerektiğini gösterir.

/'/ bir kelimedeki ana vurguyu gösterir. Örneğin **picture** /ˈpɪktʃəʳ/ kelimesinde ilk kısmı, **deny** /dɪˈnəɪ/ kelimesinde ise ikinci kısmı vurgulamalısınız ikinci kısım.

/ˌ/ bir kelimedeki en önemli ikinci vurguyu gösterir. Örneğin **submarine** /ˌsʌbməˈriːn/, kelimesinde ana vurgu kelimenin son kısmındadır fakat kelimenin ilk kısmını da hafifçe vurgulamalısınız.

Bileşik kelimelerin (iki veya daha fazla ayrı kelimeden oluşturulmuş kelimeler) vurgu kalıpları üzerlerinde gösterilmiştir. Örneğin **de_signer_baby**, kelimesinde ana vurgu kelimenin son kısmındadır fakat kelimenin ilk kısmını da hafifçe vurgulamalısınız.

Güçlü ve zayıf biçimler

Sıkça rastlanan bazı kelimelerin (örneğin and, them, of) güçlü ve zayıf biçimleri vardır. Zayıf biçimlerine daha sık rastlanır.

Örneğin 'I saw them leave.', cümlesinde zayıf /ðəm/ biçimi kullanılır.

Güçlü biçim, kelimeyi vurgulamak istediğinizde kullanılır. Örneğin 'They said they saw me, but I didn't see them.', cümlesinde güçlü /ðem/ biçim kullanılır.

Düzenli çekimler

Düzenli olmayan (alışılmış şekilde biçimlenmemiş) tüm çekimler (örneğin çoğullar, geçmiş zaman) kelime girişinde gösterilmiştir. Çekimleri biçimlendirmenin düzenli yolu aşağıda gösterilmiştir.

İsimler

Çoğu isimler çoğullarını –s ekleyerek biçimlendirirler
▶ chair, chairs   ▶ plate, plates

s, –ss, –ch, –x, ve –z, ile biten isimler çoğullarını –es ekleyerek biçimlendirirler
▶ mass, masses   ▶ match, matches

Bir ünsüz harf (örneğin. m, t, p) + –y ile biten isimler çoğullarını –y'yi çıkarıp –ies ekleyerek biçimlendirirler
▶ baby, babies   ▶ university, universities

Sıfatlar

Bir kişi veya bir şeyin, başka bir kişi veya şeye göre belirli bir niteliğin daha fazlasına sahip olduğunu göstermek için, sıfatların karşılaştırmalı biçimi kullanılır. Düzenli karşılaştırmalı biçim yaratmak için, ya sıfatın sonuna -er ekler veya kendisinden önce more kelimesini kullanırsınız.

Bir kişi veya bir şeyin, başka bir kişi veya şeye göre belirli niteliğin daha fazlasına sahip olduğunu göstermek için sıfatların üstünlük dereceli biçimi kullanılır. Düzenli üstünlük dereceli biçim yaratmak için, ya sıfatın sonuna -est ekler veya kendisinden önce most kelimesini kullanırsınız.

Tek heceli sıfatlar karşılaştırmalı ve üstünlük dereceli biçimlerini –er ve –est ile oluştururlar.
▶ small, smaller, smallest

İki heceli sıfatların tümü karşılaştırmalı ve üstünlük dereceli biçimlerini –more ve –most ile oluşturabilirler.
▶ complex, more complex, most complex

Bazı iki heceli sıfatlar –er ve –est de kullanabilirler. Bunların en sıkça rastlananları:
▪ y ve –ow ile biten sıfatlar,
▶ happy, noisy, shallow
▪ -le ile biten sıfatlar,
▶ able, noble, simple
▪ diğer bazı sıkça rastlanan iki heceli sıfatlar,
▶ common, cruel, handsome, pleasant, polite, quiet, solid, wicked

Üç heceli sıfatlar karşılaştırmalı ve üstünlük dereceli biçimlerini genellikle –more ve –most ile oluştururlar.
▶ beautiful, more beautiful, most beautiful

–er, –est biçimlerini kullanırken sıfat –e ile bitiyorsa sonunu eklemeden önce –e'yi çıkarın
▶ pale, paler, palest

Sıfat –y ile bitiyorsa sonunu eklemeden önce bunu –i'ye dönüştürün
▶ happy, happier, happiest

Fiiller

Düzenli fiillere aşağıdaki sonlar eklenir:

–s, –ss, –ch, –x, ve –z ile biten fiillere 3. tekil şahıs için –s, veya –es ekleyin

geniş zaman sıfat fiili için –ing ekleyin

geçmiş zaman ve geçmiş zaman sıfat fiili için –ed ekleyin
▶ pack, packs, packing, packed

–e ile biten fiiller için geniş zaman sıfat fiili, geçmiş zaman ve geçmiş zaman sıfat fiili sonu eklemeden önce –e'yi çıkarın.
▶ hate, hates, hating, hated

–y ile biten fiillerde üçüncü tekil şahıslar için –y'yi çıkarıp –ies ve, geçmiş zaman ile geçmiş zaman sıfat fiili için –ied ekleyin.
▶ cry, cries, crying, cried

A, a /eɪ/ the first letter of the alphabet **alfabenin ilk harfi**

o━ **a** (also **an**) strong form /eɪ/ weak form /ə/ determiner **1** BEFORE NOUN used before a noun to refer to a single thing or person but not a particular thing or person or not one that you have referred to before **belirsiz tanım artıkeli** I need a new car. ○ I saw a woman speaking to him. **2** ONE one before a hundred dollars ○ a dozen eggs **3** EVERY/EACH every or each **her veya herbiri** A child needs love. ○ Take one tablet three times a (= each) day. **4** TYPE used to say what type of thing or person something or someone is **bir şeyin veya birinin ne tür bir kişi ya da şey olduğunu belirtir** It's a guinea pig. ○ She's a doctor. **5** AN ACTION used before some action nouns when referring to one example of the action **eylem bildiren isimlerden önce kullanılır** I'm just going to have a wash. ○ Take a look at this. **6** TWO NOUNS used before the first of two nouns that are often used together **çoğunlukla birlikte kullanılan iki isim olduğunda ilk isimden önce kullanılır** a cup and saucer **7** AMOUNTS used before some phrases saying how much of something there is **bir şeyin ne kadar kaldığını bildiren bazı ifadelerden önce kullanılır** a few days ○ a bit of sugar **8** NAME used before a person's name when referring to someone you do not know **bilinmeyen birine işaret etmek için o isimden önce kullanılır** There's a Ms Leeming to see you.

YAYGIN HATALAR

a or **an**?

Dikkat: Doğru kelimeyi seçim **a** tanım ekini sesli harfle başlamayan kelimeler ile kullanın: a car, a teacher, a school **an** tanım ekini a-e-i-o-u gibi sesli harflerden önce veya bu seslerden önce kullanın: an orange, an elephant, an hour

a- /eɪ/ prefix not, without **olumsuzluk öneki; -sız, siz** atypical ○ amoral

aback /əˈbæk/ adverb **be taken aback** to be very surprised or shocked **çok şaşırmış olmak, şoke olmak** I was rather taken aback by her honesty.

abacus /ˈæbəkəs/ noun [C] a square object with small balls on wires, used for counting **üzerinde küçük boncuklar dizili sayı sayma aracı, abaküs**

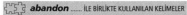
     abandon .... İLE BİRLİKTE KULLANILAN KELİMELER

be forced to abandon sth ● abandon an **attempt/ effort/idea/plan/search**

abandon /əˈbændən/ verb [T] **1** to leave someone or something somewhere, sometimes not returning to get them **birşeyi, birini geri dönmemek koşuluyla bırakmak, terketmek** They were forced to abandon the car. **2** to stop doing something before it is finished, or to stop following a plan, idea, etc **bir fikri, planı izlemeyi bırakmak ya da bir şeyi bitirmeden vazgeçmek** The match was abandoned because of rain. ● **abandoned** adjective **terkedilmiş** ● **abandonment** noun [U] **terk**

abate /əˈbeɪt/ verb [I] formal to become less strong **zayıf düşmek, güçsüzleşmek** By the weekend, the storms had abated.

abattoir /ˈæbətwɑːʳ/ UK (UK/US **slaughterhouse**) noun [C] a place where animals are killed for meat **mezbahane, hayvan kesim yeri**

abbey /ˈæbi/ noun [C] a group of buildings that is a home for monks or nuns (= religious men or women who live separately from other people) **manastır**

abbreviate /əˈbriːvieɪt/ verb [T] to make a word or phrase shorter **bir ifadeyi, sözcüğü kısaltmak** The word 'street' is often **abbreviated to** 'St'.

abbreviation /əˌbriːviˈeɪʃᵊn/ noun [C] a shorter form of a word or phrase, especially used in writing **kısaltma** A doctor is often called a 'GP', an **abbreviation for** 'general practitioner'.

abdicate /ˈæbdɪkeɪt/ verb **1** [I] If a king or queen abdicates, they choose to stop being king or queen. **tahtı terketmek, görevden vazgeçmek 2 abdicate responsibility** formal to decide not to be responsible for something any more **bir şeyin sorumluluğunu daha fazla üslenmemek** ● **abdication** /ˌæbdɪˈkeɪʃᵊn/ noun [C, U] **vazgeçmek, terk**

abdomen /ˈæbdəmən/ noun [C] formal the lower part of a person or animal's body, containing the stomach and other organs **karın boşluğu, karın** ● **abdominal** /æbˈdɒmᵊnᵊl/ adjective to do with the abdomen abdominal pains

abduct /əbˈdʌkt/ verb [T] to take someone away illegally **zorla kaçırmak** He was abducted by a terrorist group. ● **abduction** /əbˈdʌkʃᵊn/ noun [C, U] formal **tahttan vazgeçme**

aberration /ˌæbəˈreɪʃᵊn/ noun [C] formal a temporary change from what usually happens **geçici sapma, doğru yoldan ayrılma**

abet /əˈbet/ verb **abetting**, past **abetted** ⊃See aid² and abet (sb).

abhor /əbˈhɔːʳ/ verb [T] **abhorring**, past **abhorred** formal to hate something or someone very much **nefret etmek, iğrenmek** ● **abhorrence** /əbˈhɒrᵊns/ noun [U] formal **tiksinti**

abhorrent /əbˈhɒrənt/ adjective formal morally very bad **iğrenç, nefret uyandıran, ahlak dışı** an abhorrent crime

abide /əˈbaɪd/ verb **can't abide sb/sth** to strongly dislike someone or something **aşırı derecede nefret etmek, hoşlanmamak** I can't abide rudeness. **abide by sth** phrasal verb to obey a rule **kurallara uymak, itaat etmek** Staff who refused to abide by the rules were fired.

abiding /əˈbaɪdɪŋ/ adjective [always before noun] An abiding feeling or memory is one that you have for a long time. **kalıcı, var olan, sürekli** My abiding memory is of him watering his plants in the garden. ⊃See also: law-abiding.

     ability .... İLE BİRLİKTE KULLANILAN KELİMELER

have/lack/possess ability ● innate/remarkable/ uncanny ability

o━ **ability** /əˈbɪləti/ noun [C, U] the physical or mental skill or qualities that you need to do something **fiziksel veya zihinsel yetenek, kabiliyet, güç** athletic/academic ability ○ [+ to do sth] He had the ability to explain things clearly. ○ The report questions the technical ability of the staff. ⊃Opposite inability ⊃Compare disability.

A

abject /'æbdʒekt/ *adjective* **1 abject misery/poverty/ terror, etc** when someone is extremely unhappy, poor, afraid, etc **perişan, sefil, umutsuz, zavallı 2** showing that you are very ashamed of what you have done **ezik, mahcup, pişman, utanmış** *an abject apology*

ablaze /ə'bleɪz/ *adjective* [never before noun] burning strongly **alevler içinde yanma, yanan**

○━**able** /'eɪbl/ *adjective* **1 be able to do sth** to have the ability to do something or the possibility of doing something **bir şeyi başarmak, yapma yeteneğine sahip olmak, yapabilmek** *He'll be able to help you.* ⊃Opposite **be unable to do sth. 2** clever or good at doing something **becerikli, zeki ve bir şeyi yapmada iyi** *She's a very able student.* ● **ably** *adverb Robson, ably assisted by Anderson, has completely rebuilt the team.*

able-bodied /ˌeɪbl'bɒdɪd/ *adjective* having all the physical abilities that most people have **herkesin sahip olduğu fiziksel yeteneklere sahip olmak**

abnormal /æb'nɔːməl/ *adjective* different from what is normal or usual, in a way which is strange or dangerous **garip, anormal, farklı** *abnormal behaviour/weather* ○ *They found **abnormal levels** of lead in the water.* ● **abnormally** *adverb **abnormally** high temperatures* **anormal bir şekilde**

abnormality /ˌæbnɔː'mælətɪ/ *noun* [C, U] something abnormal, usually in the body **bilhassa vücutta görülen anormallik** *a genetic abnormality*

aboard /ə'bɔːd/ *adverb, preposition* on or onto a plane, ship, bus, or train **uçak, gemi, otobüs veya trene doğru, trende olma** *Welcome aboard flight BA109 to Paris.*

abode /ə'bəʊd/ *noun* [C] *formal* a home **konut, ev, ikametgâh**

abolish /ə'bɒlɪʃ/ *verb* [T] to officially end something, especially a law or system **kanun veya bir sisteme son vermek, yürürlükten kaldırmak** *National Service was abolished in Britain in 1962.* ● **abolition** /ˌæbə'lɪʃən/ *noun* [U] *the abolition of slavery* **iptal**

abominable /ə'bɒmɪnəbl/ *adjective* extremely bad **berbat, oldukça kötü** *abominable behaviour* ● **abominably** *adverb* **iğrenç bir şekilde**

Aboriginal /ˌæbə'rɪdʒənl/ *adjective* relating or belonging to the original race of people who lived in Australia **Avustralya yerlilerinden olan, yerli** ● **Aborigine** /ˌæbə'rɪdʒɪni/ *noun* [C] an Aboriginal person **yerli, Aborijin**

abort /ə'bɔːt/ *verb* [T] **1** to stop a process before it has finished **bitmeden önce durdurmak, son vermek** *The take-off was aborted due to bad weather.* **2** to end a pregnancy that is not wanted using a medical operation **kürtaj yapmak**

abortion /ə'bɔːʃən/ *noun* [C, U] a medical operation to end a pregnancy when the baby is still too small to live **kürtaj** *She had an abortion.*

abortive /ə'bɔːtɪv/ *adjective* [always before noun] An abortive attempt or plan fails before it is complete. **sonuçsuz, beyhude, boş**

the ABO system /ˌeɪbiː'əʊsɪstəm/ *noun* the system that divides human blood into four main groups called A, B, AB and O **kan gruplarını A,B, AB ve O olarak dört ana grupta toplayan sistem.**

abound /ə'baʊnd/ *verb* [I] *formal* to exist in large numbers **çok sayıda olmak, sayıca fazla olmak** *Rumours abound about a possible change of leadership.*

○━**about¹** /ə'baʊt/ *preposition* **1** [SUBJECT] relating to a particular subject or person **hakkında, ile ilgili** *a book about the Spanish Civil War* ○ *What was she talking about?* **2** [DIRECTION] *UK* (*US* **around**) to or in different

parts of a place, often without purpose or order **bir yerde ya da orada rastgele bulunma, oralarda olma** *We heard someone moving about outside.* **3 what/ how about ...?** **a** [SUGGESTION] used to make a suggestion **öneride bulunmak** *How about France for a holiday?* **b** [OPINION] used to ask for someone's opinion on a particular subject *...ne dersin? .... sence nasıl olur? What about Ann - is she nice?*

○━**about²** /ə'baʊt/ *adverb* **1** [APPROXIMATELY] used before a number or amount to mean approximately **yaklaşık olarak** *It happened about two months ago.* **2** [DIRECTION] *UK* (*US* **around**) to or in different parts of a place, often without purpose or order **bir yerde ya da orada rastgele bulunma, oralarda olma** *She's always leaving her clothes lying about.* **3** [NEAR] *UK* (*US* **around**) If someone or something is about, they are near to the place where you are now. **oracıkta, hemen yanıbaşında, neredeyse** *Is Kate about?* **4 be about to do sth** to be going to do something very soon **bir şeyi yapmak üzere olmak** *I stopped her just as she was about to leave.*

○━**above¹** /ə'bʌv/ *adverb, preposition* **1** [HIGHER POSITION] in or to a higher position than something else **yukarıya, üste doğru** *There's a mirror above the washbasin.* ○ *I could hear music coming from the room above.* **2** [MORE] more than an amount or level **üstünde, fazlasıyla, ziyadesiyle** *It says on the box it's for children aged three and above.* ○ *Rates of pay are above average.* **3** [RANK] in a more important or advanced position than someone else **üstünde, idarece yukarıda olan, amir konumunda** *Sally's grade above me.* **4** [TOO IMPORTANT] too good or important for something **bir şey için çok önemli ve iyi olan, fevkinde olan** *No one is above suspicion in this matter.* **5 above all** most importantly **en önemlisi** *Above all, I'd like to thank everyone.*

above² /ə'bʌv/ *adjective, adverb* higher on the same page **sayfa başında, tepesinde, sayfanın üst tarafında** *the above diagram* ○ *the address shown above*

a‚bove 'board *adjective* [never before noun] honest and legal **dürüst ve yasal** *We hired a lawyer to make sure the agreement was all above board.*

abrasive /ə'breɪsɪv/ *adjective* **1** An abrasive substance is rough and can be used for rubbing surfaces, to make them clean or smooth. **temizleyici, yüzey temizleyici 2** speaking or behaving in a rude and unpleasant way **kaba saba konuşma ya da davranma** *an abrasive manner*

abreast /ə'brest/ *adverb* **1 keep (sb) abreast of sth** to make sure that you or someone else knows about the most recent changes in a subject or situation **birini bir konu, gelişme hakkında bilgilendirmek, bilgi sahibi olmak** *I'll keep you abreast of any developments.* **2 two/three/four, etc abreast** If people who are moving are two/three, etc abreast, that number of people are next to each other, side by side. **yan yana, bir hizada** *They were cycling four abreast, completely blocking the road.*

abridged /ə'brɪdʒd/ *adjective* An abridged book or other piece of writing has been made shorter. **kısaltılmış** ⊃Opposite **unabridged.** ● **abridge** /ə'brɪdʒ/ *verb* [T] **kısaltmak**

┌─────────────────────────────────────┐
│ **abroad** .... İLE BİRLİKTE KULLANILAN KELİMELER │
└─────────────────────────────────────┘

go/live/travel/work abroad ● **a holiday/trip** abroad

○━**abroad** /ə'brɔːd/ *adverb* in or to a foreign country **yabancı, dış ülke** *He goes abroad a lot with his job.*

abrupt /ə'brʌpt/ *adjective* **1** sudden and not expected **ani, aniden, beklenmedik anda** *Our conversation came to an abrupt end.* **2** dealing with people in a quick way that is unfriendly or rude **önemsizmiş gibi davranma, umursamama, kaba davranış** *She has a* *rather abrupt manner.* ● **abruptly** *adverb* **ani bir şekilde**

abscess /'æbses/ *noun* [C] a painful, swollen area on the body which contains a yellow liquid **vücudun yaralı bir yerinde su toplanması, apse**

abscond /əb'skɒnd/ *verb* [I] *formal* to leave somewhere suddenly without permission because you want to escape, or because you have stolen something **izinsizce kaçmak, ayrılmak, sıvışmak**

⊡⊡⊡ absence ...... İLE BİRLİKTE KULLANILAN KELİMELER

a lengthy/long/prolonged absence ● an absence from sth ● during/in sb's absence

absence /'æbsəns/ *noun* **1** [C, U] a time when you are not in a particular place **yok olan, mevcut olmayan** *Lisa will be acting as manager in Phil's absence* (= while Phil is not here). ○ *A large number of absences from work are caused by back problems.* **2** [U] when something does not exist **yok olma, bir şeyin, birinin yokluğu, var olmayışı** *In the absence of any proof, it is impossible to accuse her.*

absent /'æbsənt/ *adjective* not in the place where you are expected to be, especially at school or work **yok, orada değil, mevcut değil** *He has been absent from school all week.*

absentee /,æbsən'tiː/ *noun* [C] someone who is not in a place where they should be **olmayan kişi** ● **absenteeism** *noun* [U] when someone is often absent from work or school **devamsızlık**

absently /'æbsəntli/ *adverb* without thinking about what you are doing **düşünmeden, rastgele** *He stared absently at the television screen.*

absent-minded /,æbsənt'maɪndɪd/ *adjective* often forgetting things **unutkan** ● **absent-mindedly** *adverb* **dikkatsizce** ● **absent-mindedness** *noun* [U] **dikkatsizlik**

absolute /'æbsəluːt/ *adjective* [always before noun] **1** complete **tam, olması gerektiği gibi** *absolute power/control* ○ *The party was an absolute disaster.* **2** definite **kesin, belli** *There was no absolute proof of fraud.*

o~**absolutely** /,æbsə'luːtli/ *adverb* **1** completely **tamamiyle** *The food was absolutely delicious.* ○ *There's absolutely nothing* (= nothing at all) *left.* **2** used to strongly agree with someone **kesinlikle,** *"Do you think it helped his career?" "Absolutely."* **3 Absolutely not.** used to strongly disagree with someone or to agree with something negative **kesinlikle hayır, kesinlikle öyle değil anlamında** *"Are you suggesting that we should just ignore the problem?" "No, absolutely not."*

absolve /əb'zɒlv/ *verb* [T] *formal* to formally say that someone is not guilty of something, or to forgive someone **aklamak, temize çıkarmak, suçsuzluğunu ispat etmek**

absorb /əb'zɔːb/ *verb* [T] **1** [LIQUID] If a substance absorbs a liquid, it takes it in through its surface and holds it. **emmek, içine çekmek** *The fabric absorbs all the moisture, keeping your skin dry.* **2 be absorbed in sth** to give all your attention to something that you are doing **bütün dikkatini bir şeye vermek, yoğunlaşmak** *Simon was so absorbed in his computer game, he didn't notice me come in.* **3** [REMEMBER] to understand and remember facts that you read or hear **gerçekleri anlamak ve hatırlamak** *It's hard to absorb so much information.* **4** [BECOME PART OF] If something is absorbed into something else, it becomes part of it. **bir şeyi içine sindirmek, kabullenmek, onun bir parçası olmak** *The drug is quickly absorbed into the bloodstream.*

absorbent /əb'zɔːbənt/ *adjective* An absorbent substance can take liquids in through its surface and hold them. **soğurgan, emici, temizleyici**

absorbing /əb'zɔːbɪŋ/ *adjective* very interesting **çok ilginç** *an absorbing book/game*

abstain /əb'steɪn/ *verb* [I] **1** *formal* to not do something that you enjoy because it is bad or unhealthy **çok istediği bir şeyden uzak durmak, mahrum kalmak** *The doctor suggested that he abstain from alcohol.* **2** to choose not to vote for or against something **uzak durmak, tarafsız kalmak, hiç bir şekilde oy vermemek** *63 members voted in favour, 39 opposed and 5 abstained.* ● **abstention** /əb'stenʃ³n/ *noun* [C, U] **çekimserlik**

abstinence /'æbstɪnəns/ *noun* [U] *formal* when you do not do something that you enjoy because it is bad or unhealthy **mahrum olma, uzak durma, kaçınma**

abstract /'æbstrækt/ *adjective* **1** relating to ideas and not real things **soyut** *an abstract concept* **2** Abstract art involves shapes and colours and not images of real things or people. **gerçek nesne ve kişilerin imgelerinden çok renk ve şekilleri içeren soyut sanat**

absurd /əb'zɜːd/ *adjective* very silly **çok saçma, aptalca** *an absurd situation/suggestion* ● **absurdity** *noun* [C, U] **saçmalık** ● **absurdly** *adverb* **saçma bir şekilde**

abundance /ə'bʌndəns/ *noun* [U, no plural] *formal* a lot of something **çok, gereğinden fazla olan, aşırı** *an abundance of flowers* ○ *There was food in abundance* (= a lot of food).

abundant /ə'bʌndənt/ *adjective* existing in large quantities **aşırı, çok fazla** *an abundant supply of food* ● **abundantly** *adverb* **bolca**

abuse¹ /ə'bjuːs/ *noun* **1** [WRONG USE] [C, U] when something is used for the wrong purpose in a way that is harmful or morally wrong **istismar etme, kötüye kullanma** *drug/alcohol abuse* ○ *abuse of public money* **2** [VIOLENCE] [U] violent, cruel treatment of someone **kaba ve çirkin davranma** *child abuse* ○ *sexual abuse* **3** [LANGUAGE] [U] rude and offensive words said to another person **başkasına kaba ve aşağılayıcı söz söyleme, küfretme** *Rival fans shouted abuse at each other.*

abuse² /ə'bjuːz/ *verb* [T] **1** [VIOLENCE] to treat someone cruelly and violently **birine kaba ve vahşice davranmak** *He was physically abused by his alcoholic father.* **2** [WRONG USE] to use something for the wrong purpose in a way that is harmful or morally wrong **kötüye kullanmak, istismar etmek** *to abuse alcohol* **3** [LANGUAGE] to say rude and offensive words to someone **aşağılayıcı ve kaba söz söylemek** *The crowd started abusing him.* ● **abuser** *noun* [C] **kötü davranan**

abusive /ə'bjuːsɪv/ *adjective* saying rude and offensive words to someone **birine kaba ve aşağılayıcı söz söyleme, davranma** *an abusive phone call*

abysmal /ə'bɪzm³l/ *adjective* very bad, especially of bad quality **çok kötü, berbat, adi** *the team's abysmal performance last season* ● **abysmally** *adverb* **çok kötü kalitede/durumda olan**

abyss /ə'bɪs/ *noun* **1** [C] a very bad situation which not improve **hiç iyiye gitmeyen kötü bir durum** [usually singular] *The country is sinking into an abyss of violence and bloodshed.* **2** *literary* a very deep hole **çok derin çukur, inanmaz çukura**

abyssal /ə'bɪs³l/ *adjective* found at the bottom of deep oceans (= big seas) **okyanus çukuru, derin çukur**

AC /,eɪ'siː/ *noun* [U] *abbreviation for* alternating current: electrical current which regularly changes the direction in which it moves **değişken elektrik akım** ⊃Compare DC.

A

.ac /ˌdɒtˈæk/ *internet abbreviation for* academic institution: used in some internet addresses for organizations such as universities **internet adreslerinde akademik bir kuruluşu simgeleyen uzantı imgesi**

academia /ˌækəˈdiːmiə/ *noun* [U] the people and organizations, especially universities, involved in studying **öğrenimle ilgili, bilhassa üniversiteler ve orada çalışan insanlar topluluğu**

academic¹ /ˌækəˈdemɪk/ *adjective* **1** [EDUCATION] related to education, schools, universities, etc **eğitime ilişkin, akademik** *academic ability/standards* ○ *It's the start of the academic year.* **2** [SUBJECTS] related to subjects which involve thinking and studying and not technical or practical skills **teknik ve pratik becerilerden çok düşünce ve çalışmayı içeren konulara ilişkin** *academic subjects* **3** [CLEVER] clever and good at studying **zeki ve eğitimde iyi, eğitime düşkün 4** [NOT REAL] If what someone says is academic, it has no purpose because it relates to a situation that does not exist. **soyut, kuramsal, pratiğe dayanmayan** *The whole discussion is academic since management won't even listen to us.* ● **academically** *adverb* **akademik açıdan**

academic² /ˌækəˈdemɪk/ *noun* [C] someone who teaches at a university or college, or is paid to study there **akademik personel, üniversite hocası**

academy /əˈkædəmi/ *noun* [C] **1** a college which teaches people the skills needed for a particular job **belirli bir alanda gerekli olan becerileri öğreten kurum, akademi** *a military academy* **2** an organization whose purpose is to encourage and develop an art, science, language, etc **bilim, sanat ve dil benzeri konularda eğitim sağlayan ve teşvik eden kurum** *the Royal Academy of Music*

accelerate /əkˈseləreɪt/ *verb* **1** [I] to start to drive faster **hızını artırmak, gaza basmak 2** [I, T] to start to happen more quickly, or to make something start to happen more quickly **hızlandırmak, daha da hızlı hale getirmek** *Inflation is likely to accelerate this year.* ● **acceleration** /əkˌseləˈreɪʃᵊn/ *noun* [U] **hızlanma**

accelerator /əkˈseləreɪtəʳ/ *noun* (*also US* **gas pedal**) *noun* [C] the part of a car which you push with your foot to make it go faster **gaz pedalı** ➲Orta kısımdaki renkli sayfalarına bakınız.

accent /ˈæksᵊnt/ *noun* [C] **1** [PRONUNCIATION] the way in which someone pronounces words, influenced by the country or area they come from, or their social class **aksan** *an American accent* ○ *a French accent* **2** [WRITTEN MARK] a mark above a letter to show you how to pronounce it, for example (à) and (é) **bazı harflerin üzerinde nasıl telaffuz edileceğini gösteren işaret, aksan 3** [WORD EMPHASIS] the word or part of a word that you emphasize when you are speaking **konuşurken vurgulanan kelime ya da bir bölümü** *In the word 'impossible' the accent is on the second syllable.* **4 the accent on sth** particular importance or attention that you give to something **bir şeye verilen/gösterilen özel önem, itina** *a wonderful menu with the accent on fresh fish*

accentuate /əkˈsentʃueɪt/ *verb* [T] to emphasize something so that people notice it **başkalarının farketmesini sağlamak için vurgulamak** *make-up to accentuate the eyes*

o~**accept** /əkˈsept/ *verb* **1** [AGREE] [I, T] to agree to take something that is offered to you **almak, kabul etmek** *to accept an invitation/offer* ○ *He won't accept advice*

from anyone. **2** [ADMIT] [T] to admit that something is true, often something unpleasant **genelde hoş olmayan bir şeyin doğru olduğunu kabul ve itiraf etmek** [+ (that)] *He refuses to accept that he's made a mistake.* **3** [ALLOW TO JOIN] [T] to allow someone to join an organization or become part of a group **birini bir kuruluşa kabul etmek, katılımına izin vermek** *She's been accepted by two universities.* **4 accept responsibility/blame** to admit that you caused something bad that happened **sorumluluğu kabul etmek, suçlamayı üstlenmek** *The company has now accepted responsibility for the accident.* **5** [UNDERSTAND] [T] to understand that you cannot change a very sad or unpleasant situation **bir durumu olduğu gibi kabullenmek** *The hardest part is accepting the fact that you'll never see that person again.*

acceptable /əkˈseptəbl/ *adjective* **1** good enough **yeteri derecede iyi, kabul edilebilir.** *work of an acceptable standard* ○ *We still hope to find a solution which is acceptable to both sides.* **2** allowed or approved of **izin verilebilir veya tasdik edilebilir, kabullenilebilir** *Smoking is less and less socially acceptable.* ➲Opposite **unacceptable.** ● **acceptability** /əkˌseptəˈbɪləti/ *noun* [U] **kabul edilebilirlik**

acceptance /əkˈseptəns/ *noun* [C, U] when you accept something **kabul, onama** *his acceptance of the award* ○ *There is a growing public acceptance of alternative medicine.*

accepted /əkˈseptɪd/ *adjective* agreed or approved by most people **çoğu kimse tarafından kabul gören, onaylanan** *an accepted spelling*

access¹ /ˈækses/ *noun* [U] **1** when you have the right or opportunity to use or see something **bir şeye ulaşım hakkı, fırsatı** *I don't have access to that kind of information.* ○ *Do you have Internet access?* **2** the way in which you can enter a place or get to a place **bir yere girme ya da ulaşma biçimi** *The only access to the village is by boat.*

access² /ˈækses/ *verb* [T] to find or see information, especially using a computer **bilgisayarı kullanarak bilgiye ulaşmak** *You can access the files over the Internet.*

accessible /əkˈsesəbl/ *adjective* **1** easy to find or reach **kolay ulaşılabilir, elde edilebilir** *Information such as this is freely accessible to the public.* ○ *The hotel is in a quiet but easily accessible part of the resort.* ➲Opposite **inaccessible.** **2** easy to understand **kolay anlaşılabilir** *They are attempting to make opera accessible to a wider audience.* ● **accessibility** /əkˌsesəˈbɪləti/ *noun* [U] **ulaşılabilirlik**

accessory /əkˈsesᵊri/ *noun* [C] **1** something extra which is not necessary but is attractive or useful **takı, aksesuar** [*usually plural*] *bathroom accessories* ○ *computer accessories* **2** *formal* someone who helps a criminal to commit a crime **suç ortağı, yardakçı** *an accessory to murder*

'access proˌvider *noun* [C] a company that makes you able to use the Internet, so that you can use email and see or show documents **internete ulaşım olanağı sağlayan şirket**

o--**accident** /ˈæksɪdᵊnt/ *noun* [C] **1** something bad which happens that is not intended and which causes injury or damage **kaza** *a car/traffic accident* ○ *She had an accident in the kitchen.* ○ *I didn't mean to spill his drink. It was an accident.* **2 by accident** without being intended **kazara, istemeden** *I deleted the wrong file by accident.*

accidental /ˌæksɪˈdentᵊl/ *adjective* not intended **kazara, istemeden olan, meydana gelen** *accidental damage* ● **accidentally** *adverb She accidentally knocked over a glass of red wine.* **tesadüfen**

accident-prone /ˈæksɪdᵊntˌprəʊn/ *adjective* Someone who is accident-prone often has accidents. **sürekli kazaya sebep olan, sakar**

acclaim /əˈkleɪm/ *noun* [U] praise from a lot of people **alkış, övgü** *international/critical acclaim*

acclaimed /əˈkleɪmd/ *adjective* praised by a lot of people **övülen, alkışlanan** *the acclaimed singer and songwriter*

acclimatize (*also UK* -ise) /əˈklaɪmətaɪz/ *verb* [I, T] to start to feel happy with the weather, the way of life, etc in a new place, or to make someone do this **yeni bir iklime, ortama alışmak, alıştırmak, uyum sağlamak** ● **acclimatization** /əˌklaɪmətaɪˈzeɪʃᵊn/ *noun* [U] **yeni yaşam koşullarına alışma**

accolade /ˈækəleɪd/ *noun* [C] *formal* a prize or praise given to someone because they are very good at something **başarıdan dolayı ödüllendirme ya da övgü**

accommodate /əˈkɒmədeɪt/ *verb* [T] **1** [HAVE SPACE FOR] to have enough space somewhere for a number of things or people **eşya veya insanlar için yeteri kadar yer, alan sağlamak** *We need more roads to accommodate the increase in traffic.* **2** [HELP] to do what someone wants, often by providing them with something **bir şeyler sağlayarak birinin istediği şeyleri yapmak** *He requires special equipment and, where possible, we've accommodated those needs.* **3** [GIVE A HOME] to provide someone with a place to live or stay **birine kalacak veya yaşayacak yer sağlamak** *The athletes will be accommodated in a special Olympic village.*

accommodating /əˈkɒmədeɪtɪŋ/ *adjective* willing to change your plans in order to help people **başkalarına yardım etmek için planlarda değişiklik yapma isteği**

accommodation /əˌkɒməˈdeɪʃᵊn/ *noun* [U] (*also US* accommodations [plural]) a place where you live or stay **ikametgah, yaşanan veya kalınan yer** *rented accommodation* ○ *The price includes travel and accommodation.*

YAYGIN HATALAR

accommodation
Dikkat: Yazılışına dikkat edin. **Accommodation** Türk öğrencileri tarafından en çok yanlış yazılan 10 kelimeden biridir. Unutmayın: Kelimenin doğru yazılımında **cc** ve **mm** vardır.

accompaniment /əˈkʌmpᵊnɪmənt/ *noun* **1** [C] *formal* something that is nice to eat or drink with a particular food or drink **yiyecek ve içeceklerin birbiri ile yemesindeki uyum** *salmon with an accompaniment of green salad* **2** [C, U] music that is played with the main instrument or with a singing voice **ana enstrümana ya da şarkı söyleyen kişiye eşlik eden müzik** *a song with piano accompaniment*

accompany /əˈkʌmpᵊni/ *verb* [T] **1** [GO WITH] *formal* to go somewhere with someone **birine eşlik etmek** *We accompanied her back to her hotel.* **2** [HAPPEN TOGETHER] to happen or exist at the same time as something else **aynı**

anda olmak ya da bulunmak *The teachers' book is accompanied by a video cassette.* **3** [MUSIC] to play a musical instrument with someone else who is playing or singing **ana enstrümana ya da şarkı söyleyen kişiye enstrüman çalarak eşlik etmek**

accomplice /əˈkʌmplɪs/ *noun* [C] someone who helps a criminal to commit a crime **suçortağı, yardakçı**

accomplish /əˈkʌmplɪʃ/ *verb* [T] to succeed in doing something good **başarmak, üstesinden gelmek** *I feel as if I've accomplished nothing all day.*

accomplished /əˈkʌmplɪʃt/ *adjective* having a lot of skill in art, music, writing, etc **sanat, müzik ve yazıda beceri sahibi olmak** *an accomplished musician/painter*

accomplishment /əˈkʌmplɪʃmənt/ *noun* **1** [U] when you succeed in doing something good **büyük başarı** *Finishing the course gave me a great sense of accomplishment.* **2** [C] *formal* a skill in art, music, writing, etc **sanat, müzik ve yazıda büyük başarı**

accord¹ /əˈkɔːd/ *noun* **1 of your own accord** If you do something of your own accord, you choose to do it and no one else forces you. **kendi isteğiyle, kendi rızasıyla, isteyerek** *Luckily, she left of her own accord.* **2** [C] an official agreement, especially between countries **ülkeler arasındaki resmi antlaşma** *a peace/trade accord*

accord² /əˈkɔːd/ *verb* [T] *formal* to treat someone specially, usually by showing respect **birine saygı göstermek, saygın davranmak, öyle muamele etmek** *respect accorded to doctors*

accordance /əˈkɔːdᵊns/ *noun formal* **in accordance with sth** agreeing with a rule, law, or wish ...**doğrultusunda, uyarınca, uygun olarak** *Both companies have insisted that they were acting in accordance with the law.*

accordingly /əˈkɔːdɪŋli/ *adverb* in a way that is suitable **ona göre, öyle, ...uygun şekilde** *We'll wait until we hear the decision and act accordingly.*

o--**according to** /əˈkɔːdɪŋtuː/ *preposition* **1** as said by someone or shown by something ...**e, ya göre** *According to our records, she was absent last Friday.* **2** based on a particular system or plan **husısı bir plan ya da sisteme göre** *Children are allocated to schools according to the area in which they live.*

accordion /əˈkɔːdiən/ *noun* [C] a musical instrument with a folding centre part and keyboards at both ends, which you play by pushing the two ends together **akordiyon**

accost /əˈkɒst/ *verb* [T] If someone you do not know accosts you, they move towards you and start talking to you in an unfriendly way. **yabancı birinin yanına gidip dostça olmayan tarzda konuşmak**

🧩 *account* ...... İLE BİRLİKTE KULLANILAN KELİMELER

1 give an account of sth ● a **brief/detailed/full** account ● an **eye-witness/first-hand** account ● an account **of sth**
2 close/open an account ● have an account [name of bank] ● a **joint/personal/savings** account ● an account **holder/number**

account¹ /əˈkaʊnt/ *noun* [C] **1** [REPORT] a written or spoken description of something that has happened **olup bitenlerin sözlü ya da yazılı açıklaması** *They gave conflicting accounts of the events.* **2** [BANK] (*also bank account*) an arrangement with a bank to keep your money there and to let you take it out when you need **banka hesabı** *I paid the money into my account.* **3** [SHOP] an agreement with a shop or company that allows you to buy things and pay for them later **şirket ya da mağazalarla yapılan vadeli alışveriş sözleş-**

mesi **4 take sth into account; take account of sth** to consider something when judging a situation **dikkate almak, hesaba katmak** *You have to take into account the fact that he is less experienced when judging his performance.* **5 on account of sth** *formal* because of something ...**yüzünden, sebebiyle** *He doesn't drink alcohol on account of his health.* **6 by all accounts** as said by a lot of people **her şeye rağmen, bütün söylenenlere rağmen** *The party was, by all accounts, a great success.* **7 on my account** just for or because of me **bu yüzden veya benim yüzümden** *Please don't change your plans on my account.* **8 on no account; not on any account** UK not for any reason or in any situation **hiç bir surette, asla, hiç bir şekilde** *On no account must these records be changed.* ⊃See also: **checking account, current account, deposit account.**

account² /əˈkaʊnt/ *verb*
account for sth *phrasal verb* **1** to be part of a total number of something **bir bütünün parçası olmak, bir bölümünü oluşturmak** *Oil accounts for 40% of Norway's exports.* **2** to be the reason for something, or to explain the reason for something **açıklamak, izah etmek**, *She was asked to account for the missing money.*

accountable /əˈkaʊntəbl/ *adjective* [never before noun] having to be responsible for what you do and able to explain your actions **sorumlu, açıklayıcı olabilme** *Hospitals must be held accountable for their mistakes.* ○ *Politicians should be accountable to the public that elects them.* ⊃Opposite **unaccountable.** • **accountability** /əˌkaʊntəˈbɪləti/ *noun* [U] **mesuliyet**

accountancy /əˈkaʊntənsi/ UK (US **accounting**) *noun* [U] the job of being an accountant **muhasebe**

accountant /əˈkaʊntənt/ *noun* [C] someone whose job is to keep or examine the financial records of a company or organization **muhasebeci**

accounts /əˈkaʊnts/ *noun* [plural] an official record of all the money a company or organization has received or paid **banka hesapları**

accreditation /əˌkredɪˈteɪʃ°n/ *noun* [U] official approval of an organization **akreditasyon, kredibilitesi olması** • **accredited** /əˈkredɪtɪd/ *adjective* officially approved **resmen onaylanmış olan**

accumulate /əˈkjuːmjəleɪt/ *verb* [I, T] to increase in amount over a period of time, or to make something increase over a period of time **biriktirmek, artırmak, tasarruf etmek** *The chemicals accumulate in your body.* • **accumulation** /əˌkjuːmjəˈleɪʃ°n/ *noun* [U] **birikim**

accuracy /ˈækjərəsi/ *noun* [U] how correct or exact something is **doğruluk, güvenilirlik** *The new system should help to improve the accuracy of weather forecasts.*

accurate /ˈækjərət/ *adjective* correct or exact **doğru, tam** *accurate information/measurements* ○ *She was able to give police a fairly accurate description of the man.* ⊃Opposite **inaccurate.** • **accurately** *adverb* **doğru bir şekilde**

⟨⟩ *accusation* ...... İLE BİRLİKTE KULLANILAN KELİMELER

make an accusation • **deny/dismiss/face/reject** an accusation • a **false/wild** accusation • accusations **of** sth • an accusation **against** sb • an accusation **by/from** sb

accusation /ˌækjʊˈzeɪʃ°n/ *noun* [C] when you say that someone has done something bad **suçlama** *He made a number of accusations against his former colleagues.*

◦┅**accuse** /əˈkjuːz/ *verb* [T] to say that someone has done something bad **suçlamak** *He was falsely accused of murder.* ○ [+ of + doing sth] *She accused Andrew of lying to her.* • **accuser** *noun* [C] **suçlayan**

the accused /əˈkjuːzd/ *noun formal* the person or people who are accused of a crime in a court of law **suçlanan**

accusing /əˈkjuːzɪŋ/ *adjective* showing that you think someone is responsible for something bad **suçlayan** *Why are you giving me that accusing look?* • **accusingly** *adverb* *She looked at me accusingly.* **suçlayıcı bir şekilde**

accustom /əˈkʌstəm/ *verb*
accustom yourself to sth/doing sth *phrasal verb* to experience something often enough for it to seem normal to you **kendini bir şeye/bir şeyi yapmaya alıştırmak**

accustomed /əˈkʌstəmd/ *adjective* **accustomed to sth/doing sth** If you are accustomed to something, you have experienced it often enough for it to seem normal to you. **bir şeye/bir şeyi yapmaya alışık olmak** *I've worked nights for years now so I've grown accustomed to it.*

ace¹ /eɪs/ *noun* [C] **1** a playing card with one symbol on it, that has the highest or lowest value in many games **iskambil oyununda as, birli 2** when the first shot by a tennis player is too good for the other player to hit back **teniste karşı tarafın çeviremediği, servis ile tek vuruşta alınan sayı**

ace² /eɪs/ *adjective informal* very good **çok iyi**

ache¹ /eɪk/ *noun* [C] a feeling of pain over an area of your body which continues for a long time **ağrı** *There's a dull ache in my right shoulder.* ⊃See also: **stomach ache.**

ache² /eɪk/ *verb* [I] If a part of your body aches, it is painful. **ağrımak** *My legs ache after all that exercise.*

◦┅**achieve** /əˈtʃiːv/ *verb* [T] to succeed in doing something good, usually by working hard **başarmak** *I've achieved my ambition* ○ *I've been working all day but I feel I've achieved nothing.* • **achievable** *adjective* possible to achieve **başarılabilir** *achievable goals* • **achiever** *noun* [C] *He's from a family of high achievers* (= very successful people). **başaran**

⟨⟩ *achievement* ...... İLE BİRLİKTE KULLANILAN KELİMELER

a **great/notable/outstanding/remarkable** achievement • sb's **crowning** achievement • a **sense of** achievement

achievement /əˈtʃiːvmənt/ *noun* **1** [C] something good that you achieve **başarı** *This film is his greatest achievement to date.* **2** [U] when you succeed in doing something good, usually by working hard **üstün başarı** *You get such a sense of achievement when you finish the course.*

acid¹ /ˈæsɪd/ *noun* [C, U] one of several liquid substances with a pH of less than 7 which react with other substances, often burning or dissolving them **asit** *hydrochloric acid*

acid² /ˈæsɪd/ *adjective* **1** (also **acidic** /əˈsɪdɪk/) containing acid, or having similar qualities to an acid **asitli** *acid soil* ○ *an acid smell/taste* **2** **acid remark/comment,** etc an unkind remark that criticizes someone **nazik olmayan eleştirel ifade, söz, yorum**

acid ˈrain *noun* [U] rain that contains chemicals from pollution and damages plants, etc **asit yağmuru**

⟨⟩ *acknowledge* ...... İLE BİRLİKTE KULLANILAN KELİMELER

be **generally/widely/universally** acknowledged • acknowledge sb/sth **as/to be** sth

acknowledge /əkˈnɒlɪdʒ/ *verb* [T] **1** ACCEPT to accept that something is true or exists **kabul etmek, doğruluğunu ikrar etmek** [+ (that)] *He acknowledged that there was a problem.* **2** LETTER to tell someone, usually in a letter, that you have received something they sent you **alındı yazısı göndermek** *Send a letter acknowledging receipt of his application.* **3** [SAY HELLO] to let someone know that you have seen them, usually by saying hello **birine gülümseyerek ve selamlayarak tanıdığını belirtmek** *She didn't even acknowledge my presence.*

acknowledgement (*also* acknowledgment) /əkˈnɒlɪdʒmənt/ *noun* **1** [ACCEPT] [C, U] when you accept that something is true or exists **kabul, onay, tasdik** *There was no acknowledgement of the extent of the problem.* **2** [LETTER] [C] a letter telling you that someone has received something that you sent them **alındı yazısı 3** [BOOK] [C] something written at the front of a book by the author to thank people who have helped them **kitabın ilk sayfasında yazar tarafından yazılan teşekkür yazısı** [usually plural] *His name appears in the acknowledgements.*

acne /ˈækni/ *noun* [U] a skin problem that young people often have that causes spots on the face **sivilce, akne**

acorn /ˈeɪkɔːn/ *noun* [C] an oval nut which grows on oak trees **meşe palamudu**

acoustic /əˈkuːstɪk/ *adjective* **1** [always before noun] An acoustic musical instrument does not use electricity. **elektrik gerektirmeyen akustik müzik aleti** *an acoustic guitar* **2** relating to sound and hearing **ses ve işitmeyle ilgili**

acoustics /əˈkuːstɪks/ *noun* [plural] the way in which the shape of a room affects the quality of sound **bir odanın akustik/ses yansıtma yapısı** *The acoustics of the hall were terrible.*

acquaintance /əˈkweɪntəns/ *noun* [C] someone who you know but do not know well **tanıdık, bildik, aşina** *He's just a business acquaintance.*

acquainted /əˈkweɪntɪd/ *adjective* [never before noun] *formal* **1** If you are acquainted with someone, you have met them but do not know them well. **tanınan, bilinen** *We're already acquainted - we met at Elaine's party.* **2 be acquainted with sth** to know about something **birine aşina olmak, bilmek, tanımak** *I'm afraid I'm not yet acquainted with the system.*

acquiesce /ˌækwiˈes/ *verb* [I] *formal* to agree to something, often when you do not want to **kabullenmek, istemeden razı olmak, ses çıkarmamak ● acquiescence** *noun* [U] *formal* **kabul, rıza**

acquire /əˈkwaɪər/ *verb* [T] **1** to get something **elde etmek** *I managed to acquire a copy of the report.* **2** to learn something **bir şeyi öğrenmek, edinmek** *to acquire knowledge/skills*

acquisition /ˌækwɪˈzɪʃən/ *noun* **1** [U] the process of learning or getting something **edinim** *children's acquisition of language* **2** [C] something that you get, usually by buying it **genellikle satın alarak elde etme** *And the hat - is that a recent acquisition?*

acquit /əˈkwɪt/ *verb* [T] **acquitting,** *past* **acquitted** If someone is acquitted of a crime, a court of law decides that they are not guilty. **temize çıkarmak, aklanmak, beraat etmek** [often passive] *Both men were acquitted of murder.*

acquittal /əˈkwɪtəl/ *noun* [C, U] when a court of law decides that someone is not guilty of a crime **beraat, suçsuzluk, aklanma, aklama**

acre /ˈeɪkər/ *noun* [C] a unit for measuring area, equal to 4047 square metres **hektar**

acrid /ˈækrɪd/ *adjective* An acrid smell is unpleasant and causes a burning feeling in your throat. **keskin, boğazı yakan koku**

acrimonious /ˌækrɪˈməʊniəs/ *adjective* involving a lot of anger, disagreement, and bad feelings **uyuşmazlık, kötü hisler ve bir çok tehlikeyi barındıran** *an acrimonious divorce ● acrimony* /ˈækrɪməni/ *noun* [U] angry, bad feelings between people **insanlar arasındaki kötü hisler ve kızgınlık, husumet**

acrobat /ˈækrəbæt/ *noun* [C] someone who entertains people by performing difficult physical acts, such as walking on a wire high above the ground **akrobat ● acrobatic** /ˌækrəˈbætɪk/ *adjective* akrobatik **● acrobatics** /ˌækrəˈbætɪks/ *noun* [plural] the actions of an acrobat **akrobatik hareketler**

acronym /ˈækrəʊnɪm/ *noun* [C] a word made from the first letters of other words **kelimelerin baş harflerinden yapılan kelime, akronim** *AIDS is the acronym for 'acquired immune deficiency syndrome'.*

o-*•**across** /əˈkrɒs/ *adverb, preposition* **1** [SIDES] from one side of something to the other **karşıdan karşıya** *I was walking across the road.* ○ *They've built a new bridge across the river.* **2** [OPPOSITE] on the opposite side of **karşı tarafta** *There's a library just across the street.* **3** [MEASURE] used after a measurement to show how wide something is **bir uçtan öbür uca, geniş** *The window measures two metres across.*

acrylic /əˈkrɪlɪk/ *noun* **1** [U] a type of cloth or plastic produced by chemical processes **akrilik 2** [C, usually singular] a type of paint **akrilik boya ● acrylic** *adjective* **akrilikten yapılma** *acrylic paints*

o-*•**act**[1] /ækt/ *verb* **1** [BEHAVE] [I] to behave in a particular way **davranış göstermek, harekette bulunmak** *to act responsibly* ○ *Jeff's been acting strangely recently.* ○ *Stop acting like a child!* **2** [DO SOMETHING] [I] to do something, especially in order to solve a problem **bir problemi çözmede girişimde bulunmak** *We have to act now to stop the spread of this disease.* **3** [PERFORM] [I, T] to perform in a play or film **bir film ya da oyunda oynamak** *He's acted in a number of successful Hollywood films.*

act as sth *phrasal verb* **1** to do a particular job, especially one you do not normally do **normalde yapmadığı bir işi yapmak, ... olarak görev yapmak** *He was asked to act as an adviser on the project.* **2** to have a particular effect ... **gibi etki yapmak** *Caffeine acts as a stimulant.*

act sth out *phrasal verb* to perform the actions and words of a situation or story **rol yapmak, bir hikaye veya durumu rol yaparak sergilemek** *The children acted out a verse from their favourite poem.*

act up *phrasal verb* If someone, especially a child, acts up, they behave badly. **yaramazlık yapmak, kötü davranmak**

act .... İLE BİRLİKTE KULLANILAN KELİMELER

an act **of** sth ● **commit** an act ● a **barbaric/cowardly** act ● a **criminal/terrorist** act

act[2] /ækt/ *noun* **1** [DO] [C] something that someone does **eylem** *an act of terrorism/kindness* **2** [LAW] [C] a law made by a government **kanun** *an act of Congress/Parliament* **3** [THEATRE] [C] one of the parts a play is divided into **tiyatro oyununda perde** *Her character doesn't appear until Act 2.* **4** [PERFORMERS] [C] one or several performers who perform for a short while in a show **oyun** *a comedy double act* **5** [FALSE BEHAVIOUR] [no plural] behaviour which hides your real feelings or intentions **gerçek duygu ve niyetleri gizleyen davranış, ...mış gibi yapma** *Was she really upset or was that just an act?* **6 in the act (of doing sth)** doing something wrong **bir şeyi yanlış/hatalı yapma** *I caught him in the act of opening one of my letters.* **7 get your act together** *informal* to organize your activities so that you can make progress **ilerleme kaydetmek için faaliyetleri**

A

organize etmek, sıraya koymak, düzenlemek ● **8 get in on the act** *informal* to become involved in something successful that someone else has started başarıyla yapılmaya devam eden bir şeye dahil olmak, katılmak

acting¹ /'æktɪŋ/ *adjective* **acting chairman/director, etc** someone who does a job for a short time while the person who usually does it is not there **vekil başkan, idareci, müdür vb.**

acting² /'æktɪŋ/ *noun* [U] the job of performing in plays and films **oyunlarda ve filmlerde gösteri yapma** *He's trying to get into acting.*

⊶**action** /'ækʃᵊn/ *noun* **1** [DO] [C, U] something that you do **hareket, eylem** *She has to accept the consequences of her actions.* ○ *We must take action* (= do something) *before the problem gets worse.* ○ *So what do you think is the best course of action* (= way of dealing with the situation)? ○ *It was the first time I'd seen firemen in action* (= doing a particular activity). **2** [ACTIVITY] [U] things which are happening, especially exciting or important things **aksiyon, hareket, heyecan uyandıran şeyler** *He likes films with a lot of action.* ⊅Opposite **inaction. 3 out of action** damaged or hurt and not able to operate or play sports **bozuk, kullanım dışı, hasarlı, işlevsiz** *They've got three players out of action.* **4 legal action** a legal process in a court **yasal işlem** *They are planning to take legal action against the company.* **5** [FIGHTING] [U] fighting in a war **savaş, mücadele** *He was killed in action* (= while fighting). **6** [PROCESS] [no plural] a movement or natural process **hareket veya tabii işlem** *The rocks are smoothed by the action of water.* ⊅See also: **industrial action**, be all **talk²** (and no action).

action-packed /'ækʃᵊn,pækt/ *adjective* An action-packed film or story has a lot of exciting events. **heyecan verici, aksiyon sahneleri bol hikaye ya da film**

‚action 'replay *UK* (*US* **instant replay**) *noun* [C] when part of a film of a sporting event is shown again, often more slowly **yavaş çekimde tekrar gösterme**

activate /'æktɪveɪt/ *verb* [T] to make something start working **harekete geçirmek** *The alarm can be activated by a laser beam.*

⊶**active** /'æktɪv/ *adjective* **1** [INVOLVED] very involved in an organization or planned activity **planlı bir eylemde aktif, görevli** *He played an active role in the campaign.* **2** [BUSY] doing a lot of things, or moving around a lot **aktif, yerinde duramayan** *Even at the age of 80 she's still very active.* **3** [GRAMMAR] An active verb or sentence is one in which the subject of the verb is the person or thing doing the action. For example 'Andy drove the car.' is an active sentence. **etken yapı** ⊅Compare **passive. 4** [VOLCANO] An active volcano could throw out rocks, fire, etc at any time. **faal (yanardağ)**

actively /'æktɪvli/ *adverb* in a way that causes something to happen **faal olarak, aktif bir şekilde** *He actively encourages me to spend money.*

activist /'æktɪvɪst/ *noun* [C] someone who tries to cause social or political change **sosyal ve siyasi değişikliğe olmasına çabalayan kişi** *a political activist* ● **activism** *noun* [U] **politik durumları değiştirmek için ortalığı ayağa kaldırma**

┌─────────────────────────────────────┐
│ 🔳 **activity** .... İLE BİRLİKTE KULLANILAN KELİMELER │
│   │
│ **do/perform** an activity ● **frantic/strenuous** activity │
│ ● **outdoor/leisure** activity ● **a flurry of** activity │
└─────────────────────────────────────┘

⊶**activity** /æk'tɪvəti/ *noun* **1** [EVENT] [C] something which you do for enjoyment, especially an organized event **faaliyet** *The centre offers a range of activities, such as*

cycling, swimming, and tennis. **2** [WORK] [C, U] the work of a group or organization to achieve an aim **eylem, faaliyet** *criminal/terrorist activities* **3** [MOVEMENT] [U] when a lot of things are happening or people are moving around **faaliyet, değişik hareketler** *There was a sudden flurry of activity* (= short period of activity) *at the back of the hall.* ⊅Opposite **inactivity.**

⊶**actor** /'æktə^r/ *noun* [C] someone, especially a man, whose job is to perform in plays and films **aktör, erkek oyuncu**

⊶**actress** /'æktrəs/ *noun* [C] a woman whose job is to perform in plays and films **aktris, bayan oyuncu**

⊶**actual** /'æktʃuəl/ *adjective* **1** real, not guessed or imagined **gerçek** *We were expecting about fifty people, though the actual number was a lot higher.* **2 in actual fact** *UK* really **hakikaten** *It was due to start at ten, but in actual fact, it didn't begin until nearly eleven.*

⊶**actually** /'æktʃuəli/ *adverb* **1** [TRUTH] used when you are saying what is the truth of a situation **gerçekten** *He didn't actually say anything important.* **2** [SURPRISE] used when you are saying something surprising **doğruya** *She sounds English but she's actually Spanish.* ○ *Did you actually meet the president?* **3** [MISTAKE] mainly *UK* used when you are disagreeing with someone or saying no to a request **doğrusunu söylemek gerekirse** *"You didn't tell me." "Actually, I did." ○ "Do you mind if I smoke?" "Actually, I'd rather you didn't."*

acumen /'ækjəmən/ *noun* [U] the ability to make good judgments and decisions **yerinde ve doğru karar verebilme yeteneği** *business/political acumen*

acupuncture /'ækjʊpʌŋktʃə^r/ *noun* [U] a way of treating pain or illness by putting thin needles into different parts of the body **akupunktur**

acute /ə'kju:t/ *adjective* **1** [EXTREME] An acute problem or negative feeling is extreme. **şiddetli, çok fazla, akut** *There's an acute shortage of medical staff.* ○ *acute pain* ○ *acute anxiety* **2** [ANGLE] An acute angle is less than 90 degrees. **dar (açı) 3** [QUICK TO NOTICE] quick to notice or understand things **(anlayışı/algılaması) keskin, kuvvetli, güçlü** *an acute mind* ○ *Dogs rely on their acute sense of smell.*

acutely /ə'kju:tli/ *adverb* very strongly **çok güçlü bir şekilde** *I was acutely aware of how Alex felt about the situation.*

AD /,eɪ'di:/ *abbreviation for* Anno Domini: used to show that a particular year came after the birth of Christ **milattan sonra** *1066 AD*

ad /æd/ *noun* [C] an advertisement **ilan** ⊅See also: **classified ad.**

adamant /'ædəmənt/ *adjective* very sure of what you think and not willing to change your opinion **inatçı, dik başlı, dediğim dedikçi, sert** [+ (that)] *They are adamant that they have not broken any rules.* ● **adamantly** *adverb* **kararlı bir şekilde**

Adam's apple /,ædəmz'æpl/ *noun* [C] the lump in a man's throat that you can see moving up and down when he speaks or swallows **Adem elması, erkek boğazında konuşurken inip çıktığı görülebilen kıkırdak gırtlak çıkıntısı, hançere**

adapt /ə'dæpt/ *verb* **1** [CHANGE BEHAVIOUR] [I] to change your behaviour so that it is suitable for a new situation **uyum sağlamak, uymak** *It takes time to adapt to a new working environment.* **2** [CHANGE SOMETHING] [T] to change something so that it is suitable for a different use or situation **bir şeyi yeni bir duruma veya kullanıma uydurmak, uymasını sağlamak** *Courses have to be adapted for different markets.* **3** [BOOK] [T] to change a book or play so that it can be made into a film or television programme **uyarlamak** *Both novels have been adapted for television.*

adaptable /ə'dæptəbl/ *adjective* able to change to suit different situations or uses **uydurulabilir, değiştirilebilir** ● **adaptability** /əˌdæptə'bɪləti/ *noun* [U] **değişkenlik**

adaptation /ˌædæp'teɪʃⁿn/ *noun* **1** [C] a film, television programme, or play which has been made from a book **uyarlama 2** [C, U] the process or act of changing to suit a new situation **yeni bir duruma uydurma/uyma** *Evolution occurs as a result of adaptation to new environments.*

adapter (*also* adaptor) /ə'dæptər/ *noun* [C] something that is used for connecting two or more pieces of electrical equipment to an electrical supply **akım değişimine uyumlu hale getiren cihaz, adaptör**

○-**add** /æd/ *verb* **1** [PUT WITH] [T] to put something with something else **ilave etmek, katmak** *Add the eggs to the cream.* **2** [INCREASE] [I, T] to increase an amount or level **seviyesini veya miktarını artırmak** *Then there's the service charge which adds another ten percent to the bill.* **3** [SAY MORE] [T] to say another thing **sözle ilavede bulunmak** [+ that] *She said she liked him but added that he was difficult to work with.* **4** [CALCULATE] [T] to put two or more numbers or amounts together to get a total **rakamları toplamak** ⊃See also: add **insult²** to injury.

add (sth) up *phrasal verb* to put numbers together in order to reach a total **toplayarak artırmak, toplama ulaşmak** *When you add up everything we've spent, it's cost well over £200.*

not add up *phrasal verb informal* If something does not add up, you cannot believe it is true **doğru olduğuna inanmamak, doğruluk payı olmamak** *She gave me an explanation but somehow it doesn't add up.*

adder /'ædər/ *noun* [C] a small, poisonous snake **küçük zehirli bir yılan**

addict /'ædɪkt/ *noun* [C] **1** someone who cannot stop taking a drug **tiryakilik, müptela olma** *a heroin/drug addict* **2** *informal* someone who likes something very much and does it or has it very often **tiryaki, bir şeye müptela olan** *a TV/computer game addict*

addicted /ə'dɪktɪd/ *adjective* **1** not able to stop taking a drug **uyuşturucu bağımlılığı olan** *He later became addicted to heroin.* **2** *informal* liking something very much and doing or having it too often **bir şeye bağımlılığı olan** *He's addicted to chocolate/football.*

addiction ...... İLE BİRLİKTE KULLANILAN KELİMELER

fight/have/suffer from an addiction ● alcohol/drug/gambling addiction ● addiction to sth

addiction /ə'dɪkʃⁿn/ *noun* [C, U] when you cannot stop doing or taking something because you are addicted to it **bağımlılık**

addictive /ə'dɪktɪv/ *adjective* If something is addictive, it makes you want more of it so that you become addicted. **bağımlılığı artıran** *Tobacco is highly addictive.*

addition /ə'dɪʃⁿn/ *noun* **1 in addition (to sth)** added to what already exists or happens, or more than you already do or have **ilave olarak, ayrıca** *In addition to teaching, she works as a nurse in the holidays.* **2** [U] the process of adding numbers or amounts together in order to get a total **toplama 3** [C] a new or extra thing which is added to something **ilave** *Defender Matt Smith is the latest addition to the team.*

additional /ə'dɪʃⁿnəl/ *adjective* extra to what already exists **ilaveten, ekstra** *We plan to take on an additional ten employees over the next year.* ● **additionally** *adverb* **ek olarak**

additive /'ædɪtɪv/ *noun* [C] a chemical which is added to food in order to make it taste or look better or to keep it fresh **katkı maddesi**

add-on /'ædɒn/ *noun* [C] a piece of equipment that can be connected to a computer to give it an extra use **bilgisayara ilave kullanım olanağı sağlamak için takılan cihaz**

address ...... İLE BİRLİKTE KULLANILAN KELİMELER

give sb your address ● your business/home/work address ● a change of address

○-**address¹** /ə'dres/ ⓤⓢ /'ædres/ *noun* [C] **1** [BUILDING DETAILS] the details of where a building is, including the building number, road name, town, etc **adres 2** [ELECTRONIC] a series of letters, signs, or numbers used to send email to someone or to reach a page of information on the Internet **internet adresi** *an email/web address* **3** [SPEECH] a formal speech to a group of people **resmi konuşma, hitap** ⊃See also: forwarding address, public address system.

YAYGIN HATALAR

address

Dikkat: Yazılışına dikkat edin. **Address** Türk öğrencileri tarafından en çok yanlış yazılan 10 kelimeden biridir. Unutmayın: Kelimenin doğru yazılımında dd ve ss vardır.

address² /ə'dres/ *verb* [T] **1** [BUILDING DETAILS] to write a name or address on an envelope or parcel **adres yazmak** *A parcel arrived addressed to Emma.* **2** [DEAL WITH] to deal with a problem **bir sorunla ilgilenmek** *We have to address the issue/problem before it gets worse.* **3** [SPEAK] *formal* to speak to someone, or to give a speech to an audience **biriyle konuşmak veya dinleyici kitlesine hitap etmek** *Today she will be addressing a major conference in London.* **4 address sb as sth** *formal* to give someone a particular name or title when you speak or write to them **konuşurken veya yazarken birine özel bir isim ya da ünvan vermek** *Do you think I should address him as 'Mr Benson' or 'Albert'?*

a'ddress ˌbook (*US* 'address ˌbook) *noun* [C] **1** a computer document that keeps a list of names and email addresses **isim ve adresleri barındıran bilgisayar dokümanı 2** a book in which you keep a list of names and addresses **adres defteri**

adept /æ'dept/ *adjective* good at doing something difficult **zor olan şeyleri yapmada başarılı** *She's very adept at dealing with the media.*

adequate /'ædɪkwət/ *adjective* **1** enough **yeter, kâfi** *I didn't have adequate time to prepare.* **2** good enough, but not very good **yeteri kadar iyi, fakat çok iyi değil** *The sound quality isn't exceptional but it's adequate for everyday use.* ⊃Opposite inadequate. ● **adequately** *adverb* **Make sure you are adequately equipped for the journey. yeterli şekilde**

adhere /əd'hɪər/ *verb* [I] *formal* to stick to a surface **yapışmak**

adhere to sth *phrasal verb* to obey a rule or principle **bir kural veya ilkeye itaat etmek, bağlı olmak** *We always adhere strictly to the guidelines.*

adherence /əd'hɪərⁿns/ *noun* [U] *formal* when someone obeys a set of rules or principles **bağlılık, itaat** ● **adherent** *noun* [C] *formal* someone who obeys a particular set

A

of rules, principles, etc **bağlı, itaatkâr, kural ve ilke-lere uyan kişi**

adhesive /əd'hi:sɪv/ *noun* [C] a substance used for sticking things together **yapışkan, yapıştırıcı** ● **adhesive** *adjective* **yapışkan**

ad hoc /ˌæd'hɒk/ *adjective* not regular or planned, but happening only when necessary **düzenli ve planlı olmayan, fakat sadece gerektiğinde olan** *We meet on an ad hoc basis.*

adjacent /ə'dʒeɪsᵊnt/ *adjective formal* If two things are adjacent, they are next to each other. **yanyana, bitişik, ilişik** *The fire started in an adjacent building.* ○ *They live in a house adjacent to the railway.*

o͙**adjective** /'ædʒɪktɪv/ *noun* [C] a word that describes a noun or pronoun. The words 'big', 'boring', 'purple', and 'obvious' are all adjectives. **sıfat** ● **adjectival** /ˌædʒɪk'taɪvᵊl/ *adjective* containing or used like an adjective **sıfat içeren veya sıfat gibi kullanılan** *an adjectival phrase*

adjoining /ə'dʒɔmɪŋ/ *adjective* next to and joined to something **yanıbaşında olan ve bir şeye bağlı olan** *an adjoining room*

adjourn /ə'dʒɜ:n/ *verb* [I, T] *formal* to stop a meeting, especially a legal process, for a period of time or until a later date **ertelemek, ara vermek, kesmek, ertelenmek** *The judge adjourned the case until March 31.* ● **adjournment** *noun* [C] **erteleme**

adjudicate /ə'dʒu:dɪkeɪt/ *verb* [I, T] *formal* to make an official judgment or decision about a competition or disagreement **bir yarışma veya uyuşmazlık konusunda karar vermek, hükmetmek, hükme bağlamak** *Occasionally, he has to adjudicate on a pensions matter.* ● **adjudication** /əˌdʒu:dɪ'keɪʃᵊn/ *noun* [U] **karar** ● **adjudicator** *noun* [C] **hakem**

adjust /ə'dʒʌst/ *verb* **1** [T] to change something slightly so that it works better, fits better, or is more suitable **ayarlamak** *You can adjust the heat using this switch here.* ○ *The figures need to be adjusted for inflation.* **2** [I] to change the way you behave or think in order to suit a new situation **yeni bir duruma ayak uydurmak, uyum sağlamak** *They found it hard adjusting to life in a new country.*

adjustable /ə'dʒʌstəbl/ *adjective* able to be changed slightly in order to suit different people or situations **ayarlanabilir** *an adjustable seat*

adjustment /ə'dʒʌstmənt/ *noun* [C, U] a slight change that you make to something so that it works better, fits better, or is more suitable **ayarlama** *We've made a few adjustments to the schedule.*

ad lib /ˌæd'lɪb/ *verb* [I, T] to speak in public without having planned what to say **rastgele, hazırlıksız, irticalen konuşmak** *I had no script so I had to ad lib.*

admin /'ædmɪn/ *noun* [U] *UK short for* administration **idare, yönetim**

administer /əd'mɪnɪstə^r/ *verb* [T] **1** to organize or arrange something **idare etmek, düzenlemek** *The fund is administered by the Economic Development Agency.* **2** *formal* to give medicine or medical help to someone **birine tıbbi yardımda bulunmak** *to administer first aid*

administration /ədˌmɪnɪ'streɪʃᵊn/ *noun* **1** [U] the work of organizing and arranging the operation of something, such as a company **bir şirket idaresi, yönetimi** *The job involves a lot of administration.* **2** [C] *mainly US* the president and politicians who govern a country at a particular time, or a period of government **idare, yönetim dönemi, iktidar dönemi** *the Bush administration*

administrative /əd'mɪnɪstrətɪv/ *adjective* relating to the organization and management of something **idare ve yönetimle ilgili** *The work is largely administrative.*

administrator /əd'mɪnɪstreɪtə^r/ *noun* [C] someone who helps to manage an organization **idareci, yönetici**

admirable /'ædmᵊrəbl/ *adjective* If something is admirable, you respect or approve of it. **hayranlık uyandıran, duyulan** *He has many admirable qualities.* ● **admirably** *adverb* **takdire şayan bir şekilde**

admiral /'ædmᵊrəl/ *noun* [C] an officer of very high rank in the navy **amiral**

express/feel/have admiration ● enormous/great/grudging/profound admiration ● admiration for sb

admiration /ˌædmə'reɪʃᵊn/ *noun* [U] when you admire someone or something **hayranlık** *My admiration for him grows daily.*

admire /əd'maɪə^r/ *verb* [T] **1** to respect or approve of someone or something **hayran olmak, gıbta etmek, saygı duymak** *You have to admire him for being so determined.* **2** to look at something or someone, thinking how attractive they are **hayranlığını belli ederek bakmak, gözünü alamamak** *We stood for a few minutes, admiring the view.* ● **admirer** *noun* [C] **hayran**

admissible /əd'mɪsəbl/ *adjective formal* allowed or acceptable, especially in a court of law **yasal olarak kabul edilebilir, izin verilebilir** *admissible evidence*

admission /əd'mɪʃᵊn/ *noun* **1** MONEY [U] the money that you pay to enter a place **giriş ücreti** *Art exhibition - admission free.* **2** TRUTH [C] when you agree that you did something bad, or that something bad is true **itiraf, suçu kabul etme** *This is, by her own admission, lazy.* ○ *His departure was seen by many as an admission of guilt.* **3** PERMISSION [C, U] when someone is given permission to enter somewhere or to become a member of a club, university, etc **kayıt ve kabul etme** *She's applied for admission to law school.*

Eğer kişi kötü bir olayın doğruluğunu kabul ediyorsa **accept** ve **acknowledge** fiilleri kullanılabilir. *I accept that things should have been done differently.* ● *He refuses to acknowledge the problem.*
Eğer kişi kötü bir şey yaptığını itiraf ediyorsa **confess** fiili kullanılır. *Rawlinson finally confessed to the murder.*
Own up, fess up ve **come clean** söylemleri kişinin kötü bir şey yaptığını itiraf ettiği durumlarda kullanılabilir. *I decided to come clean about the broken vase.* ● *Come on, own up - who's eaten the last sandwich?*

o͙**admit** /əd'mɪt/ *verb* **admitting**, *past* **admitted** **1** [I, T] to agree that you did something bad, or that something bad is true **itiraf etmek** [+ doing sth] *Both men admitted taking illegal drugs.* ○ [+ to + doing sth] *She admitted to stealing the keys.* ○ *I was wrong - I admit it.* ○ [+ (that)] *He finally admitted that he couldn't cope.* **2** [T] to allow someone to enter somewhere, especially to take someone who is ill into hospital **kabul etmek, hastayı kabul etmek** *UK to be admitted to hospital/ US to be admitted to the hospital* ○ *It says on the ticket 'admits 2'.*

admittance /əd'mɪtᵊns/ *noun* [U] permission to enter a place **izin, müsaade**

admittedly /əd'mɪtɪdli/ *adverb* used when you are agreeing something is true although you do not want to **kabul etmek gerekir ki ...** *Admittedly I was partly to blame but it wasn't all my fault.*

admonish /ədˈmɒnɪʃ/ *verb* [T] *formal* to gently tell someone that they have done something wrong **hafif bir dille azarlamak, uyarmak, ikaz etmek**

ado /əˈduː/ *noun* **without further/more ado** without waiting any more **artık daha fazla beklemeden, hemen**

adolescence /ˌædəlˈesəns/ *noun* [U] the period of time in someone's life between being a child and an adult **gençlik, buluğ çağı, ergenlik**

adolescent /ˌædəlˈesənt/ *noun* [C] a young person who is between being a child and an adult **ergen, genç, buluğ çağına ermiş kişi** ● **adolescent** *adjective* **ergen**

adopt /əˈdɒpt/ *verb* **1** [I, T] to legally become the parents of someone else's child **evlat edinmek 2** [T] to accept or start using something new **yeni bir şeyi kullanmaya başlamak veya kabul etmek** *We've adopted a new approach.* ● **adopted** *adjective* an adopted son **evlat edinilmiş** ● **adoption** /əˈdɒpʃən/ *noun* [C, U] **evlat edinme**

adorable /əˈdɔːrəbl/ *adjective* very attractive, often because of being small **bilhassa küçük olduğu için çok çekici olan, minyon** *an adorable little boy*

adore /əˈdɔːr/ *verb* [T] **1** to love someone and have a very good opinion of them **birini çok sevmek ve hakkında iyi kanaate sahip olmak** *Sarah adored her father.* **2** to like something very much **bir şeyden çok haz almak, çok sevmek** *I adore travelling.* ● **adoration** /ˌædəˈreɪʃən/ *noun* [U] **hayranlık**

adorn /əˈdɔːn/ *verb* [T] *formal* to decorate something **süslemek, bezeme etmek** *The room was adorned with flowers.* ● **adornment** *noun* [C, U] **süsleme**

adrenalin (*also* adrenaline) /əˈdrenəlɪn/ *noun* [U] a substance that your body produces when you are angry, excited, or frightened which makes your heart beat faster **adrenalin, salgı**

adrift /əˈdrɪft/ *adjective* **1** [never before noun] If a boat is adrift, it floats around in the water and is not tied to anything. **denizde, suda sürüklenen, akıntıya kapılan 2 come adrift** to become loose and not joined to anything **başıboş olmak, hiç bir şeyle bağlantısı olmamak, terk edilmiş olmak** *A few bricks in the garden wall had come adrift.*

adulation /ˌædjʊˈleɪʃən/ *noun* [U] great praise and admiration for someone, often which they do not deserve **haketmediği halde birine gösterilen hayranlık ve övgü**

o⇥**adult¹** /ˈædʌlt/, /əˈdʌlt/ *noun* [C] a person or animal that has finished growing and is not now a child **yetişkin, erişkin kişi ya da hayvan**

adult² /ˈædʌlt/, /əˈdʌlt/ *adjective* **1** [NOT A CHILD] having finished growing **yetişkin, erişkin** *an adult male rat* **2** [RELATING TO ADULTS] [always before noun] for or relating to adults **yetişkinlere ilişkin, yetişkin için** *adult education* ○ *adult life* **3** [SEXUAL] Adult books, films, etc. show naked people or sexual acts and are not for children. **yetişkin kitabı, film ve seks içeren**

adultery /əˈdʌltəri/ *noun* [U] sex between a married person and someone who is not their husband or wife **zina, yasak aşk, evlilik dışı ilişki** ● **adulterous** *adjective* **zina yapan**

adulthood /ˈædʌlthʊd/ US /əˈdʌlthʊd/ *noun* [U] the part of your life when you are an adult **erişkinlik, yetişkinlik**

medical/scientific/technological advances ● a major advance ● advances **in** sth

advance¹ /ədˈvɑːns/ *noun* **1 in advance** before a particular time **önceden** *You need to book your ticket at least 14 days in advance.* **2** [PROGRESS] [C, U] new discoveries and inventions **yeni keşifler ve icatlar** *technological/scientific advances* **3** [MONEY] [C] a payment given to someone before work has been completed, or before the usual time **avans, önceden ödenen para, ödeme 4** [FORWARD] [C] a movement forward, especially by an army **ordunun ileri hareketi**

advance² /ədˈvɑːns/ *verb* **1** [I, T] to develop or progress, or to make something develop or progress **geliştirmek, ilerletmek** *He moved to New York with hopes of advancing his career.* **2** [I] to move forward to a new position, especially while fighting **muharebede yeni bir mevziye doğru ilerlemek** *Rebel soldiers advanced on the capital.*

advance³ /ədˈvɑːns/ *adjective* [always before noun] happening or ready before an event **önceden olan** *advance planning/warning* ○ *an advance booking*

advanced /ədˈvɑːnst/ *adjective* **1** having developed or progressed to a late stage **gelişmiş, bir üst aşamaya çıkmış** *advanced technology* ○ *The disease was at an advanced stage.* **2** at a higher, more difficult level **ileri düzeyde, ileri** *an advanced English course*

advancement /ədˈvɑːnsmənt/ *noun* [C, U] progress **ilerleme** *career advancement* ○ *technological advancements*

advances /ədˈvɑːnsɪz/ *noun* **sb's advances** things that someone says and does to try to start a sexual relationship with someone **biriyle cinsel birlikteliği başlatmak için birinin söylediği şeyler**

a big/enormous/main/major advantage ● an unfair advantage ● take advantage of sth ● the advantage of sth

o⇥**advantage** /ədˈvɑːntɪdʒ/ *noun* [C, U] **1** something good about a situation that helps you **avantaj** *One of the advantages of living in town is having the shops so near.* **2** something that will help you to succeed **üstünlük** *These new routes will give the airline a considerable advantage over its competitors.* ○ *If we could start early it would be to our advantage* (= help us to succeed). ⊃Opposite **disadvantage. 3 take advantage of sth** to use the good things in a situation **bir şeyden fayda/avantaj sağlamak** *I thought I'd take advantage of the sports facilities while I'm here.* **4 take advantage of sb/sth** to treat someone badly in order to get what you want **birinden/birşeyden çıkar elde etmek/çıkarını gözetmek**

advantageous /ˌædvənˈteɪdʒəs/ *adjective* helping to make you more successful **fayda, avantaj sağlayan**

advent /ˈædvent/ *noun* **1 the advent of sth** the start or arrival of something new **yeni bir şeyin ortaya çıkması ya da başlaması** *the advent of the Internet* **2 Advent** the religious period before Christmas (= a Christian holiday) in the Christian year **noelden önceki dini dönem, noel arefesi**

have an adventure ● be looking for adventure ● a big/exciting adventure ● an adventure holiday/playground

o⇥**adventure** /ədˈventʃər/ *noun* [C, U] an exciting and sometimes dangerous experience **macera** *It's a film about the adventures of two friends travelling across Africa.* ● **adventurer** *noun* [C] **maceracı**

adventurous /əd'ventʃⁿrəs/ *adjective* **1** willing to try new and often difficult things **maceracı, macera arayan** *I'm trying to be more adventurous with my cooking.* **2** exciting and often dangerous **macera yaratan, heyecan veren** *He led an adventurous life.*

oᴛ **adverb** /'ædvɜːb/ *noun* [C] a word that describes or gives more information about a verb, adjective, phrase, or other adverb. In the sentences 'He ate quickly.' and 'It was extremely good.', 'quickly' and 'extremely' are both adverbs. **zarf**

adversary /'ædvəsⁿri/ *noun* [C] *formal* someone who you are fighting or competing against **hasım, düşman, rakip**

adverse /'ædvɜːs/ *adjective formal* **1 adverse conditions/effects/impact** things that cause problems or danger **tehlike ve probleme neden olan olumsuz koşullar, etkiler** *adverse weather conditions* ○ *Pollution levels like these will certainly have an adverse effect on health.* **2 adverse comment/publicity/reaction, etc** something negative that is said or written about someone or something **olumsuz yorum, tepki, kanaat** ● **adversely** *adverb* **muhalif bir şekilde**

adversity /əd'vɜːsəti/ *noun* [C, U] *formal* an extremely difficult situation **son derece zor bir durum, güçlük, sıkıntı** *She showed a great deal of courage in adversity.*

advert /'ædvɜːt/ *noun* [C] *UK* an advertisement **ilan**

advertise /'ædvətaɪz/ *verb* **1** [I, T] to tell people about a product or service, for example in newspapers or on television, in order to persuade them to buy it **ilan etmek, duyurmak, reklam yapmak** *Companies are not allowed to advertise cigarettes on television any more.* **2** [I] to put information in a newspaper or on the Internet, asking for someone or something that you need **ilan vermek** *The university is advertising for administrative staff.* ● **advertiser** *noun* [C] a company that advertises things **ilan, reklam şirketi**

advertisement /əd'vɜːtɪsmənt/ ⑤ /ˌædvər'taɪzmənt/ *noun* [C] a picture, short film, song, etc which tries to persuade people to buy a product or service **resim, film, şarkı ve benzeri ilanlar** *a newspaper/television advertisement*

YAYGIN HATALAR

advertisement

Dikkat: Yazılışına dikkat edin. **Advertisement** Unutmayın: Kelimenin doğru yazılımına s harfinden sonra e vardır.

---

oᴛ **advertising** /'ædvətaɪzɪŋ/ *noun* [U] the business of trying to persuade people to buy products or services **reklam yapma, duyurma, ilan etme** *an advertising agency*

---

advice ...... İLE BİRLİKTE KULLANILAN KELİMELER

ask for/give/offer/provide/seek advice ● take sb's advice ● bad/conflicting/expert/good advice ● advice on/about sth ● a piece of advice

---

oᴛ **advice** /əd'vaɪs/ *noun* [U] suggestions about what you think someone should do or how they should do something **öğüt, tavsiye, öneri** *She asked me for advice about writing a book.* ○ *There's a booklet giving advice on how to set up your own club.* ○ *I took your advice* (= did what you suggested) *and went home early.* ○ *Can I give you a piece of advice?*

advisable /əd'vaɪzəbl/ *adjective* [never before noun] If something is advisable, it will avoid problems if you do it. **tavsiye edilebilir, önerilebilir** *It is advisable to book seats at least a week in advance.*

oᴛ **advise** /əd'vaɪz/ *verb* **1** [I, T] to make a suggestion about what you think someone should do or how they should do something **öğüt vermek** [+ to do sth] *His doctor advised him to take time off work.* ○ *They advise the government on environmental matters.* ○ *The government is advising against travelling in the area.* ○ [+ that] *They're advising that children be kept out of the sun altogether.* **2** [T] *formal* to give someone official information about something **tavsiyede, öneride bulunmak** *They were advised of their rights.*

adviser (*also* advisor) /əd'vaɪzə^r/ *noun* [C] someone whose job is to give advice about a subject **danışman** *a financial adviser*

advisory¹ /əd'vaɪzⁿri/ *adjective* **advisory committee/panel/board, etc** a group of people whose purpose is to give advice **danışma komitesi, kurulu**

advisory² /əd'vaɪzⁿri/ *noun* [C] *US* an official announcement that contains advice, information, or a warning **öğüt, bilgi ve uyarı içeren resmi duyuru** [usually plural] *weather/travel advisories*

advocate¹ /'ædvəkeɪt/ *verb* [T] to express support for a particular idea or way of doing things **savunmak, desteklemek** *I certainly wouldn't advocate the use of violence.* ● **advocacy** /'ædvəkəsi/ *noun* [U] when someone advocates something **savunma, destekleme**

advocate² /'ædvəkət/ *noun* [C] **1** someone who supports a particular idea or way of doing things **savunan, destekleyen, arka çıkan** *He has always been an advocate of stricter gun controls.* **2** *UK* a lawyer who defends someone in court **avukat**

A&E /ˌeɪənd'iː/ *UK* (*US* emergency room) *noun* [C, U] abbreviation for Accident and Emergency: the part of a hospital where people go when they are injured or ill and need treatment quickly **acil servis, kazalar için acil servis bölümü**

aerial¹ /'eəriəl/ *UK* (*US* antenna) *noun* [C] a piece of metal that is used for receiving television or radio signals **anten, tv veya radyo alıcısı** ↪Orta kısımdaki renkli sayfalarına bakınız.

aerial² /'eəriəl/ *adjective* [always before noun] in or from the air, especially from an aircraft **hava ile ilgili havadan gelen, bilhassa uçak** *an aerial photograph/view*

aerobic /eə'rəʊbɪk/ *adjective* **1** Aerobic exercise is intended to make your heart stronger. **kalbi güçlendiren bir ekzersiz türü 2** needing or using oxygen **oksijene gereksinim duyan veya kullanan**

aerobics /eə'rəʊbɪks/ *noun* [U] physical exercises that you do to music, especially in a class **topluca müzik eşliğinde yapılan fiziksel ekzersiz** *She goes to aerobics* (= to aerobics classes).

aerodynamic /ˌeərəʊdar'næmɪk/ *adjective* having a shape that moves quickly through the air **havanın sürtünme etkisini azaltan biçimde tasarlanan** ● **aerodynamics** *noun* the study of how objects move through the air **nesnelerin havada hareketinin çalışılması**

aeroplane *UK*, **airplane** *US*

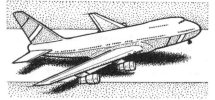

aeroplane /'eərəpleɪn/ *UK* (*US* airplane) *noun* [C] a vehicle that flies and has an engine and wings **uçak**

aerosol /'eərəsɒl/ *noun* **aerosol** [C] a metal container that forces a liquid out in small drops when you press a button sıkıldığında sıvıyı zerrecikler şeklinde fışkırtan metal kutu, sprey

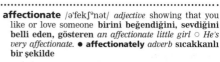

aerospace /'eərəʊspeɪs/ *noun* [U] the design and production of aircraft uçak tasarım ve üretim

aesthetic (*also US* esthetic) /es'θetɪk/ *adjective* relating to beauty and the way something looks **estetik** *the aesthetic appeal of cats* ● **aesthetically** *adverb* **estetik, uyumlu bir şekilde**

aesthetics (*also US* esthetics) /es'θetɪks/ *noun* [U] the study of beauty, especially in art **estetik ilmi**

AFAIK *internet abbreviation for* as far as I know: used when you believe that something is true, but you are not completely certain **bildiğim kadarıyla ...**

afar /ə'fɑːʳ/ *adverb literary* **from afar** from a long distance **uzun mesafeden, uzaktan, uzaklardan** *He had admired her from afar.*

affable /'æfəbl/ *adjective* pleasant and friendly **güzel, hoş, cana yakın, içten**

affair /ə'feəʳ/ *noun* **1** [C] a situation or set of related events, especially bad ones **bilhassa kötü olay, hadise** *The government's handling of the affair has been widely criticized.* **2** [C] a sexual relationship between two people when one or both of them is married to someone else **yasak cinsel ilişki (evli olmayan iki kişi arasında)** *He's been having an affair with a woman at work.* **3 be sb's affair** If something is your affair, it is private and you do not want anyone else to be involved or know about it. **şahsi mesele, kişisel konu** ⊃See also: love affair.

affairs /ə'feəz/ *noun* [plural] situations or subjects that involve you **birinin bulaştığı konu ve durumlar** *He refused to discuss his financial affairs.* ⊃See also: current affairs, state of affairs.

◦⁻**affect** /ə'fekt/ *verb* [T] **1** to influence or something, or cause them to change **etkilemek veya değişimine sebep olmak** *It's a disease which affects many older people.* **2** to cause a strong emotion, especially sadness **duygusal olarak üzülmesine, hissetmesine sebep olmak, etkilemek** [often passive] *I was deeply affected by the film.*

affectation /ˌæfek'teɪʃᵊn/ *noun* [C, U] a way of speaking or behaving that is not natural to someone **birine yakışmayan şekilde konuşma ya da davranma biçimi**

affected /ə'fektɪd/ *adjective* behaving or speaking in a way that is not natural or sincere **samimi ve alışılmış olmayan biçimde konuşan veya davranan**

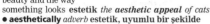
🔲🔲🔲 **affection** .... İLE BİRLİKTE KULLANILAN KELİMELER

show affection ● affection for sb ● a display/show of affection

affection /ə'fekʃᵊn/ *noun* [C, U] a feeling of liking or loving someone **sevgi, şefkât, düşkünlük, beğeni** *Ann's affection for her grandfather was obvious.*

affectionate /ə'fekʃᵊnət/ *adjective* showing that you like or love someone **birini beğendiğini, sevdiğini belli eden, gösteren** *an affectionate little girl* ○ *He's very affectionate.* ● **affectionately** *adverb* **sıcakkanlı bir şekilde**

affiliate /ə'fɪlieɪt/ *verb* **be affiliated to/with sth** to be officially connected to, or a member of, a larger organization **resmi olarak büyük bir kuruluşa bağlı olmak, ilişkili veya üyesi olmak** *a college affiliated to the University of London* ● **affiliation** /əˌfɪli'eɪʃᵊn/ *noun* [C, U] **bağlı olma durumu**

affinity /ə'fɪnəti/ *noun* **1** [no plural] a feeling that you like and understand someone or something **yakın ilgi, alaka** *She seems to have a natural affinity for/with water.* **2** [C, U] a similarity **benzerlik** *There are affinities between this poem and some of his earlier work.*

affirm /ə'fɜːm/ *verb* [T] *formal* to say that something is true **kabul etmek, doğruluğunu kabul etmek** *He gave a speech affirming the government's commitment to education.* ● **affirmation** /ˌæfə'meɪʃᵊn/ *noun* [C, U] **onay**

affirmative /ə'fɜːmətɪv/ *adjective formal* In language, an affirmative word or phrase expresses the meaning 'yes'. **olumluluk içeren ifade veya kelime** *an affirmative answer*

affix /'æfɪks/ *noun* [C] a group of letters that you add to the beginning or the end of a word to make another word. In the word 'non-alcoholic', 'non-' is an affix. **kelimelerin önüne veya sonuna getirilen ekler, ek** ⊃Compare prefix, suffix.

afflict /ə'flɪkt/ *verb* [T] *formal* If an illness or problem afflicts you, it makes you suffer. **acı vermek, musallat olmak, üzmek, acı çekmek** [often passive] *a country afflicted by civil war* ● **affliction** /ə'flɪkʃᵊn/ *noun* [C, U] something that makes you suffer **acı, dert, sıkıntı, üzüntü, bela**

affluent /'æfluənt/ *adjective* having a lot of money **varlıklı, zengin, hali vakti yerinde** *affluent families/ neighbourhoods* ● **affluence** /'æfluəns/ *noun* [U] **bolluk**

◦⁻**afford** /ə'fɔːd/ *verb* [T] **1 can afford** to have enough money to buy something or enough time to do something **altından kalkabilmek, üstesinden gelebilmek, alabilmek** *I can't afford a new computer.* ○ [+ to do sth] *Can we afford to go away?* ○ *I'd love to come out but I can't afford the time.* **2 can afford to do sth** If you can afford to do something, it is possible for you to do it without causing problems. **halledebilmek, yapabilmek, sorunsuzca çözebilmek** *We can't afford to take that risk.*

affordable /ə'fɔːdəbl/ *adjective* cheap enough for most people **alınabilir, kelepir, herkesin alabileceği türden, makul** *affordable housing/prices*

affront /ə'frʌnt/ *noun* [C] something that is offensive or insulting to someone **gücendiren, kıran, küstüren** *He regarded the comments as an affront to his dignity.*

afield /ə'fiːld/ *adverb mainly UK* **far/further afield** away from the place where you are **uzakta, yaşanılan yere uzak** *We hired a car so we could travel further afield.*

afloat /ə'fləʊt/ *adjective* **1** floating on water **suda yüzen** **2 stay afloat** to have enough money to continue a business **işini devam ettirebilecek kadar paraya sahip olmak, zar zor sürdürmek** *Many small business are struggling to stay afloat.*

afoot /ə'fʊt/ *adjective* [never before noun] being planned, or happening now **planlanan veya olup bitmekte** *There are plans afoot to launch a new radio station.*

A

afraid ...... BAŞKA BİR DEYİŞLE

Afraid anlamına gelen diğer kelimeler **frightened** ve **scared** şeklindedir. *He's **frightened** that the other children will laugh at him.* ● *Gerry has always been scared of heights.*

Eğer kişi gerçekten çok korktuysa, durumu belirtmek için **petrified, terrified, panic-stricken**, veya çok gayri resmi olarak **scared to death** söylemleri kullanılabilir. *I'm **terrified** of flying.* ● *She was panic-stricken when her little boy disappeared.* ● *He's **scared to death** of having the operation.*

Eğer kişi duyduğu endişeden dolayı bir şeyden korkuyorsa, kişinin hislerini belirtmek için **anxious, concerned, nervous** veya **worried** sıfatları kullanılabilir. *I'm **worried** that something will go wrong.* ● *All this waiting is making me feel **anxious**.*

Eğer kişi gelecekte olabilecek olan bir şey hakkında endişe duyuyorsa, kişinin duygularını belirtmek için **apprehensive** veya **uneasy** sıfatları kullanılabilir. *He's a bit **apprehensive** about living away from home.*

○╸**afraid** /ə'freɪd/ *adjective* [never before noun] **1 I'm afraid** used to politely tell someone bad news or to politely disagree with someone korkarım ki ..., maalesef, galiba *We haven't got any tickets left, I'm afraid.* ○ [+ (that)] *I'm afraid that I've broken your vase.* **2** frightened korkmuş, ürkmüş *She's **afraid** of water.* **3** worried that something bad might happen korku uyandıran, endişe veren [+ (that)] *Many people are **afraid** that they might lose their jobs.* ○ [+ of + doing sth] *He was **afraid** of upsetting Clare.*

afresh /ə'freʃ/ *adverb* If you do something afresh, you do it again in a different way. yeniden, tekrar, bir kez daha *Juan tore up the letter he was writing and started **afresh**.*

African /'æfrɪkən/ *adjective* relating or belonging to Africa Afrika'ya ait, Afrika'dan *African art/music* ● **African** *noun* [C] someone from Africa Afrikalı

African-American /ˌæfrɪkənə'merɪkən/ (*also* Afro-American /ˌæfrəʊə'merɪkən/) *adjective* relating or belonging to American people whose families came from Africa in the past Afrika kökenli Amerikalı, *the African-American community* ● **African-American** (*also* Afro-American) *noun* [C] Amerika'da yaşayan fakat kökleri Afrika'da olan *a 25-year-old African-American*

Afro-Caribbean /ˌæfrəʊkærɪ'bi:ən/ *adjective* UK relating to people from the Caribbean whose families originally came from Africa Afrika asıllı Karayipliler *Afro-Caribbean art/music*

○╸**after¹** /'ɑ:ftər/ *preposition* **1** TIME/EVENT when a time or event has happened sonra *We went swimming after lunch.* ○ *Let's get the shopping. **After that**, we can have coffee.* **2** IN PLACE/ORDER following in place or order peşpeşe *H comes after G in the alphabet.* **3** TIME US (UK/US past) used to say how many minutes past the hour is geçe *It's five after three.* **4** BECAUSE OF used as a result of something that happened *... den dolayı I'll never trust her again after what she did to me.* **5** DESPITE despite ... rağmen *I can't believe he was so unpleasant after you gave him so much help.* **6** FOLLOW following someone or something peşinden *We ran after him, but he escaped.* **7 after 5 minutes/2 weeks, etc** when five minutes, two weeks, etc have passed 5 dakika/2 hafta vs. sonra **8 day after day/year after year, etc** continuing for a long time, or happening many times gün be gün, yıldan yıla vs. *I'm bored with going to school day after day.* **9** NAMED FOR used when giving someone or something the same name as another person or thing birinin adını verme *It was called the Biko building, after the famous South African.* **10 after all a** NOT EXPECTED used to say that something

happened or was true although you did not expect it to happen or be true rağmen *Helen couldn't come to the party after all.* **b** EMPHASIZE TRUTH used to add information that shows that what you have just said is true bunun dışında, ötesinde, ayrıca *You can't expect to be perfect - after all, it was only your first lesson.* **11 be after sth** *informal* to be trying to get something peşinde olmak, elde etmeye çalışmak *What type of job are you after?* **12 be after sb** *informal* to be looking for someone birinin ardında, peşinde olmak, arıyor olmak *The police are after him.*

○╸**after²** /'ɑ:ftər/ *conjunction* at a later time than something else happens sonrasında *We arrived after the game had started.* ○ *After further discussion, we decided to call the police.*

○╸**after³** /'ɑ:ftər/ *adverb* later than someone or something else ardından, peşinden *He had the operation on Monday and I saw him the day after.*

aftermath ...... İLE BİRLİKTE KULLANILAN KELİMELER

in the aftermath of sth ● the immediate aftermath

aftermath /'ɑ:ftəmɑ:θ/ *noun* [no plural] a situation that is the result of an accident, crime, or other violent event sonraki dönem, sonrası *There are calls for tighter airport security in the aftermath of last week's bombing.*

○╸**afternoon** /ˌɑ:ftə'nu:n/ *noun* **1** [C, U] the time between the middle of the day, and the evening öğleden sonra *I played tennis on Saturday afternoon.* ○ *The train arrives at 3 o'clock in the afternoon.* ○ *What are you doing this afternoon* (= today in the afternoon)? **2 (Good) afternoon.** used to say hello to someone in the afternoon tünaydın

aftershave /'ɑ:ftəʃeɪv/ *noun* [C, U] a liquid with a pleasant smell that men put on their faces after shaving (= removing hair) traş sonrası kullanılan güzel koku

aftertaste /'ɑ:ftəteɪst/ *noun* [C] the taste that a food or drink leaves in your mouth when you have swallowed it bir şeyi yedikten sonra ağızda kalan tat, damakta kalan tat [usually singular] *a bitter/sweet aftertaste*

afterthought /'ɑ:ftəθɔ:t/ *noun* [C] something that you say or do later sonradan akla gelen fikir düşünce [usually singular] *She only asked me to the party as an afterthought.*

○╸**afterwards** /'ɑ:ftəwədz/ (*also* US afterward) *adverb* at a later time, after something else has happened sonraları, daha sonrasında *I did my homework and went swimming afterwards.*

○╸**again** /ə'gen/ *adverb* **1** once more tekrar, yine, yeniden *I'll ask her again.* ○ *I'll see you again next week.* **2** as before önceden olduğu gibi, öncesindeki gibi *Get some rest and you'll soon be well again.* **3 again and again** many times tekrar tekrar, durmaksızın, biteviye *He played the same song again and again.* **4 all over again** repeated from the beginning tekrar, yeni baştan *We had to start all over again.* **5 then/there again** used when adding a fact to something you have just said aynı konuya tekrar dönersek, öncekine ilave olarak *I failed my history test - but then again, I didn't do much studying for it.*

○╸**against** /ə'genst/ *preposition* **1** NOT AGREE disagreeing with a plan or activity karşı olma *Andrew wants to change offices but I'm against it.* ○ *There were 70 votes for the new proposal and 30 against.* **2** COMPETE competing with or opposing someone or something karşı yarışma *Liverpool is playing against AC Milan.* ○ *the fight against racism* **3** TOUCH touching something dayanan, yaslanan *Push the bed against the wall.* **4** PROTECT protecting you from something bad bir şeye karşı

koruyan, sakınan *Fresh fruit in the diet may protect against cancer.* **5** OPPOSITE DIRECTION in the opposite direction to the way something is moving **karşı taraftan, karşısında** *I was cycling against the wind.* **6 against the law/the rules** forbidden by a law or by rules **yasalara/kurallara aykırı, yasaklanmış** *It's against the law to leave young children alone in the house.* **7 against sb's advice/wishes, etc** If you do something against someone's advice, wishes, etc, you do it although they have said you should not or must not. **birinin tavsiye/ istek/arzularına karşın, bunların aksine** *He flew there against his doctor's advice.* **8 have sth against sb/sth** to have a reason not to like someone or something **bir şeye, kişiye karşı olma ya da sevmemek için bir sebebi olmak** *I've got nothing against him personally, I just don't think he's the right man for the job.*

---

age .... İLE BİRLİKTE KULLANILAN KELİMELER

reach the age of [18/60/75, etc] ● **at/from** the age of [8/ 12/60, etc] ● [8/25/70, etc] **years of** age ● **at** sb's age ● **an** age **limit**

---

o-*age¹ /eɪdʒ/ *noun* **1** HOW OLD [C, U] the number of years that someone has lived, or that something has existed **yaş** *The show appeals to people of all ages.* ○ *She left India* **at the age of** *12.* ○ *Children under 10* **years of** *age must be accompanied by an adult.* **2** HISTORY [C] a period of history **çağ** *the Ice Age* ○ *We're living in the* **age of** *electronic communication.* **3** OLD [U] when something is old **yaş, eski şey/kişi** *Some wines improve* **with age.** **4 under age** too young to do something legally **reşit olmayan, çok genç, yaşı tutmayan** ⊃See also: **the Middle Ages, old age.**

age² /eɪdʒ/ *verb* [I, T] UK **ageing**, US **aging**, *past* **aged** to become older or to make someone seem older **yaşlanmak, eskimek** *Dad has aged a lot recently.*

aged¹ /eɪdʒd/ *adjective* having a particular age **yaşlı, yaşlanmış** *They have one daughter, aged three.* ⊃See also: **middle-aged.**

aged² /ˈeɪdʒɪd/ *adjective* old **eski, eskimiş** *an aged dog* ○ *improved health care for the aged*

'age ˌgroup *noun* [C] people of a particular age **yaş grubu** *job training for people in the 16-24 age group*

ageing¹ UK (US **aging**) /ˈeɪdʒɪŋ/ *adjective* becoming older **yaşlanan, eskiyen** *an ageing population*

ageing² UK (US **aging**) /ˈeɪdʒɪŋ/ *noun* [U] the process of becoming older **yaşlanma, eskime** *the ageing process*

'age ˌlimit *noun* [C] the age at which a person is allowed or not allowed to do something **yaş sınırı** *Eighteen is the legal age limit for buying alcohol.*

agency /ˈeɪdʒ°nsi/ *noun* [C] **1** a business that provides a service **ajans, hizmet sağlayan bir iş, büro** *an advertising agency* **2** an international organization or government department **uluslararası kurum veya devlet dairesi** *an international development agency* ⊃See also: **travel agency.**

---

agenda .... İLE BİRLİKTE KULLANILAN KELİMELER

set (= decide) the agenda ● be **off/on** the agenda ● be **at the top of/high on** the agenda ● the agenda **for** sth

---

agenda /əˈdʒendə/ *noun* [C] **1** a list of subjects that people will discuss at a meeting **gündem** *There are several items* **on the agenda.** **2** important subjects that have to be dealt with **gündemde olan konular** *The issue of rail safety is back on the political agenda.*

agent /ˈeɪdʒ°nt/ *noun* [C] **1** someone whose job is to deal with business for someone else **acente, vekil, temsilci** *a literary agent* **2** (*also* **secret agent**) someone who tries to find out secret information, especially about another

country **ajan** ⊃See also: **estate agent** *UK*, **real estate agent** *US*, **travel agent.**

ages /ˈeɪdʒɪz/ *noun* [plural] *informal* a very long time **asırlardır** *I've been waiting here for ages.* ○ *It takes ages to cook.*

aggravate /ˈægrəveɪt/ *verb* [T] **1** to make a situation or condition worse **bir durumu, şartları daha da kötüye götürmek, ağırlaştırmak, kötüleştirmek** *His comments only aggravated the problem.* **2** to annoy someone **birini rahatsız etmek, kızdırmak, sinirlendirmek** *She's starting to really aggravate me.* ● **aggravating** *adjective* **kötüleştirici** ● **aggravation** /ˌægrəˈveɪʃ°n/ *noun* [C, U] **kötüleştirme**

aggregate /ˈægrɪgət/ *noun* [C, U] a total **toplam, toplamda agrega** *UK Liverpool won 2-0* **on aggregate** (= in total).

aggression /əˈgreʃ°n/ *noun* [U] angry or violent behaviour towards someone **saldırganlık, nedensiz kavga** *an act of aggression*

aggressive /əˈgresɪv/ *adjective* **1** behaving in an angry and violent way towards another person **saldırgan, kavgacı** *aggressive behaviour* **2** using forceful methods and determined to succeed **başarılı olmak için güç kullanan, kararlı, atılgan, girişken** *an aggressive marketing campaign* ● **aggressively** *adverb* **sinirli bir şekilde**

aggressor /əˈgresər/ *noun* [C] someone who starts a fight or war with someone else **saldırganlığı, savaşı başlatan**

aggrieved /əˈgriːvd/ *adjective* upset or angry because someone has treated you unfairly **üzüntülü, incinmiş, haksızlığa maruz kalmış**

aghast /əˈgɑːst/ *adjective* **[never before noun]** very shocked **çok şaşırmış, şoke olmuş** *She looked at him aghast.*

agile /ˈædʒaɪl/ ⑩ /ˈædʒ°l/ *adjective* **1** able to move your whole body easily and quickly **atik, hızlı, çevik 2** able to think quickly in an intelligent way **zeki ve hızlı düşünebilen** *an agile mind* ● **agility** /əˈdʒɪləti/ *noun* [U] **ataklık**

aging /ˈeɪdʒɪŋ/ *noun, adjective* US spelling of ageing **yaşlanma, yaşlı**

agitate /ˈædʒɪteɪt/ *verb* [I] to argue strongly about something in order to achieve social or political changes **sosyal veya siyasi değişiklikleri kazanmak için yaygara koparmak, tartışma çıkarmak, ajite etmek** *They continued to agitate for changes in the legal system.* ● **agitator** *noun* [C] **tahrik eden**

agitated /ˈædʒɪteɪtɪd/ *adjective* very anxious or upset **çok üzgün, kızgın, endişeli** *He seemed agitated, as if something was worrying him.* ● **agitation** /ˌædʒɪˈteɪʃ°n/ *noun* [U] **tahrik etme**

AGM /ˌeɪdʒiːˈem/ *UK* (US **annual meeting**) *noun* [C] *abbreviation for* Annual General Meeting: a meeting that happens once every year in which an organization discusses the past year's activities and chooses the people who will be in charge of the organization **yıllık genel kurul toplantısı**

agnostic /ægˈnɒstɪk/ *noun* [C] someone who believes that we cannot know if God exists or not **Allah'ın varlığının bilinemezliğini savunan kişi, agnostik, bilinemezciliği savunan** ● **agnostic** *adjective* **Tanrı'nın varlığına inanmayan**

o-*ago /əˈgəʊ/ *adverb* **ten minutes/six years/a long time ago** used to refer to a time in the past **on dakika/altı yıl/ uzun bir süre önce** *They moved to London ten years ago.*

agonize (*also UK* -**ise**) /ˈægənaɪz/ *verb* [I] to spend a lot of time worrying about a decision **bir karara ilişkin**

A

uzun süre endişe duymak, kıvranmak *Lee agonized over what to buy his girlfriend.*

agonizing (*also UK* -ising) /'ægənaızıŋ/ *adjective* causing you a lot of pain or worry **kıvrandıran, acı veren, endişelendiren** *an agonizing choice*

agony /'ægəni/ *noun* [C, U] extreme suffering, either physical or mental **çok yoğun zihinsel/fiziksel ıstırap, sıkıntı** *She lay on the bed in agony.*

'agony ,aunt *noun* [C] *UK* someone who gives advice on personal problems, in a newspaper or magazine **gazete veya dergilerde kişisel sorunlarla ilgili tavsiyelerde bulunan kişi, "Güzin abla"**

○**agree** /ə'gri:/ *verb* agreeing, *past* agreed **1** [SAME OPINION] [I, T] to have the same opinion as someone **aynı fikirde olmak** *I agree with you.* ○ *She's definitely the right person for the job." "I agree."* ○ [+ (that)] *We all agreed that mistakes had been made.* ○ *We agree about most things.* **2** [SAY YES] [I] to say you will do something that someone asks you to do **birinin istediği şeyi yapacağını söylemek, kabul etmek, tamam demek** [+ to do sth] *She agreed to help him.* **3** [DECIDE] [I, T] to decide something with someone **biriyle bir şeye karar vermek, ortak karar almak** *We couldn't agree on what to buy.* ○ [+ to do sth] *They agreed to meet on Sunday.* ○ [+ (that)] *We agreed that they would deliver the sofa in the morning.* **4** [DESCRIPTION] [I] If two descriptions agree, they are the same. **aynı olduğunu görmek, uyuşmak, birbirine uymak** ⊃Opposite **disagree.**

agree with sth *phrasal verb* to think that something is morally acceptable **ahlaken bir şeyin kabul edilebilir olduğunu düşünmek** *I don't agree with hunting.*

agreeable /ə'gri:əbl/ *adjectiveformal* **1** pleasant or nice **güzel, hoş, kabul edilebilir, anlaşılabilir** *an agreeable young man* ⊃Opposite **disagreeable. 2** be **agreeable to sth** to be willing to do or accept something **bir şeyi yapmaya veya kabul etmeye istekli olmak** *If Harvey is agreeable to the proposal, we'll go ahead.* ● **agreeably** *adverb* **kabul edilebilir bir şekilde**

---
agreement ...... İLE BİRLİKTE KULLANILAN KELİMELER

reach/sign an agreement ● a draft/written agreement ● an agreement between sb
---

○**agreement** /ə'gri:mənt/ *noun* **1** [C] a promise or decision made between two or more people **antlaşma** *an international agreement* ○ *It was difficult to reach an agreement.* **2** [U] when people have the same opinion as each other **uyuşma** *Not everyone was in agreement.* ⊃Opposite **disagreement.**

agriculture /'ægrıkʌltʃər/ *noun* [U] the work and methods of growing crops and looking after animals which are then used for food **tarım, ziraat** ● **agricultural** /,ægrı'kʌltʃºrºl/ *adjective* **tarımsal**

agritourism /,ægrı'tʊərızm/ *noun* [U] the business of providing holidays for people on farms or in the countryside **tarım turizmi**

aground /ə'graʊnd/ *adverb* **run aground** If a ship runs aground, it cannot move because the water is not deep enough. **karaya oturmak, geminin karaya oturması**

ah /ɑ:/ *exclamation* **1** used to show sympathy or to show pleasure at seeing a baby or attractive animal **oooh (hayret ve hayranlık bildiren ünlem)** *Ah, you poor thing!* ○ *Ah, look at that little kitten!* **2** used to show that you have just understood something **aha (birşeyin anlaşıldığında "anladım" anlamında bir ünlem)** *Ah, now I see what you're saying!*

aha /ə'hɑ:/ *exclamation* used when you suddenly understand or find something **anında anladığını veya bulduğunu belirten nida, ünlem** *Aha! That's where I left my keys!*

○**ahead** /ə'hed/ *adjective, adverb* **1** [IN FRONT] in front **önde** *The road ahead is very busy.* ○ *Rick walked ahead of us.* **2** [FUTURE] in the future **ileride, gelecekte** *She has a difficult time ahead of her.* **3** [MORE POINTS] having more points than someone else in a competition **bir yarışmada önde, başta olan/olma** *Barcelona was ahead after ten minutes.* **4** [MORE PROGRESS] making more progress than someone or something else **birinden ya da bir şeyden daha da ileride olma** *Sue is ahead of everyone else in French.* **5 go ahead** *informal* used to allow someone to do something **hadi, tamam, devam et, başla** *"Can I use your phone?" "Sure, go ahead."* **6 ahead of time/schedule** before the time that was planned **planlanan zamanın/programın önünde olmak** *We finished the project ahead of schedule.* ⊃See also: be one step[1] ahead (of sb), be streets (**street**) ahead (of sb/sth), be ahead of your time[1].

-aholic /-ə'hɒlık/ *suffix* unable to stop doing or taking something **bir şeyi almaya veya yapmaya engel olamamak, müptelası olmak** *chocaholic* (= someone who cannot stop eating chocolate)

aid[1] /eɪd/ *noun* **1** [U] money, food, or equipment that is given to help a country or group of people **insani yardım, para, yiyecek ve malzeme yardımı** *Emergency aid was sent to the flood victims.* ○ *aid workers* **2 in aid of sb/sth** *UK* in order to collect money for a group of people who need it **...e yardım amacıyla, ... in yararına, iyiliğine** *a concert in aid of famine relief* **3 with the aid of sth** using something to help you **bir şeyin yardımıyla, desteğiyle** *She can walk with the aid of a stick.* **4 come/go to sb's aid** to come to someone and help them **birinin yardımına gitmek, koşmak** *Luckily a policeman came to my aid.* **5** [C] a piece of equipment that helps you to do something **yardım malzemesi** *teaching aids such as books and videos* ⊃See also: Band-Aid, first aid, visual aid.

aid[2] /eɪd/ *verb formal* **1** [T] to help someone **birine yardım etmek 2 aid and abet (sb)** in law, to help someone do something that is illegal **hukukta birine kanunsuz bir işte yardım ve yataklık etmek**

aide /eɪd/ *noun* [C] someone whose job is to help someone important, especially in the government **özellikle devlette önemli birinin yardımcısı, yardımcı** *a former aide to the President*

AIDS, Aids /eɪdz/ *noun* [U] *abbreviation for* acquired immune deficiency syndrome: a serious disease that destroys the body's ability to fight infection **kazanılmış bağışıklık kaybı sendromu, vücudun enfeksiyonlara karşı koymasını yok eden ve çoğunlukla cinsel temas yoluyla geçen ciddi ve bulaşıcı bir hastalık** ⊃Compare HIV.

ailing /'eɪlıŋ/ *adjective* weak or ill **zayıf, hasta, güçsüz** *an ailing company/economy*

ailment /'eɪlmənt/ *noun* [C] an illness **hastalık** *Treat minor ailments yourself.*

---
aim ...... İLE BİRLİKTE KULLANILAN KELİMELER

achieve your aim ● sb's/sth's main/ultimate aim ● the aim of sth ● with the aim of doing sth
---

aim[1] /eɪm/ *noun* **1** [C] the purpose of doing something, and what you hope to achieve **amaç, hedef** *The aim of the film was to make people laugh.* ○ [+ of + doing sth] *He went to Paris with the aim of improving his French.* **2 sb's aim** someone's ability to hit an object by throwing something or shooting at something **hedef alma,**

hedef 3 take aim to point a weapon towards someone or something **nişan almak**

aim² /eɪm/ *verb* **1 aim for/at sth; aim to do sth** to intend to achieve something **bir şeyi başarmayı hedeflemek, amaçlamak** *I aim to arrive at three o'clock.* ○ *We're aiming for a 10% increase in sales.* **2 be aimed at sb** to be intended to influence or affect a particular person or group **bir grup ya da kişiyi etkilemek, etki altına almayı hedeflemiş olmak, amaç edinmek** *advertising aimed at students* **3 be aimed at doing sth** to be intended to achieve a particular thing **belli bir şeyi başarmayı hedeflemek** *a plan aimed at reducing traffic* **4** [I, T] to point a weapon towards someone or something **silahla nişan almak, silahı bir hedefe doğrultmak** *He aimed the gun at the lion.*

aimless /'eɪmləs/ *adjective* with no purpose **amaçsız, hedefsiz, belli bir amacı olmayan** ● **aimlessly** *adverb* **amaçsızca**

ain't /eɪnt/ *informal short for* am not, is not, are not, have not, or has not. This word is not considered correct by most people. **am not, is not, are not, have not or has not gibi olumsuz yardımcı fiillerin kısaltması**

o━**air¹** /eəʳ/ *noun* **1** GAS [U] the mixture of gases around the Earth which we breathe **hava** *air pollution* ○ *He went outside to get some fresh air* (= clean, cool air). **2 the air** the space above and around things **hava, boşluk** *He fired his gun into the air.* **3** TRAVEL [U] travel in an aircraft **hava yolu** *I like travelling by air.* ○ *air safety* **4** QUALITY [no plural] a particular appearance or quality **bir şeyin görüntüsü, havası** *He has an air of authority.* **5 be on air** to be broadcasting on television or radio **yayında olmak 6 clear the air** If an argument or discussion clears the air, people feel less angry or upset after it. **havayı yumuşatmak, sakinleştirmek** ● **7 disappear/vanish into thin air** to suddenly disappear in a mysterious way **gizemli bir şekilde aniden ortadan kaybolmak** ● **8 be up in the air** If something is up in the air, no decision has been made. **kararsız olmak, belli olmamak, herhangi bir karar verilmemiş olmak** *Our plans for the summer are still up in the air.* ⊃See also: **a breath of fresh air, mid-air.**

air² /eəʳ/ *verb* **1** BROADCAST [T] to broadcast something on radio or television **radyo veya televizyon yayını yapmak 2 air your opinions/views, etc** to say what your opinions are **düşüncelerini/görüşlerini söylemek** *The meeting will give everyone a chance to air their views.* **3** ROOM [T] to make a room smell better by opening a door or window **bir yeri havalandırmak 4** CLOTHES [I, T] If clothes air, or if you air them, you hang them up with a lot of air around them. **giysileri havalandırmak**

airbag /'eəbæg/ *noun* [C] a bag in the front of a car that protects people in an accident by filling with air **hava yastığı** *passenger/twin airbags*

airbase /'eəbeɪs/ *noun* [C] a military airport **hava üssü**

airborne /'eəbɔːn/ *adjective* moving in, or carried by the air **hava ile taşınan, hareket ettirilen, hava indirme (askerlikte)** *airborne troops* ○ *an airborne virus*

'air ˌcon *noun* [U] *UK abbreviation for* air conditioning **klima, klima ile ısıtma/soğutma**

'air conˌditioner *noun* [C] a machine that keeps the air cool in a building or a car **soğutucu, klima**

'air conˌditioning *noun* [U] a system that keeps the air cool in a building or car **soğutma sistemi** ● **air-conditioned** /'eəkənˌdɪʃənd/ *adjective* having air conditioning **soğutma sistemi olan** *an air-conditioned office*

o━**aircraft** /'eəkrɑːft/ *noun* [C] *plural* aircraft a vehicle that can fly **uçabilen araç, uçak**

'aircraft ˌcarrier *noun* [C] a ship on which aircraft can take off and land **uçak gemisi**

airfare /'eəfeəʳ/ *noun* [C] the cost of a ticket to fly somewhere **uçuş ücreti**

airfield /'eəfiːld/ *noun* [C] a place where small or military aircraft can take off and land **askeri havaalanı**

'air ˌforce *noun* [C] the part of a country's military organization that uses aircraft to fight wars **hava kuvvetleri**

'air hoˌstess *UK* (*UK/US* flight attendant) *noun* [C] someone whose job is to serve passengers on an aircraft and to make sure that safety rules are obeyed **uçakta kabin görevlisi, uçuş hostesi**

'airing ˌcupboard *noun* [C] *UK* a warm cupboard where you keep sheets, clean clothes, etc **çarşaf ve temiz giysilerin korunduğu sıcak dolap**

airless /'eələs/ *adjective* An airless room does not have enough fresh air. **havasız**

airlift /'eəlɪft/ *noun* [C] when people or things are moved by aircraft because it is too difficult or too slow to travel by road **hava yolu ile taşıma** *an airlift of medical supplies* ● **airlift** *verb* [T] [often passive] *Three small children were airlifted to safety.* **hava yoluyla nakletme**

airline /'eəlaɪn/ *noun* [C] a company that provides regular flights to places **hava yolu**

airliner /'eəlaɪnəʳ/ *noun* [C] a large plane for carrying people **insan taşıma amaçlı büyük uçak**

airmail /'eəmeɪl/ *noun* [U] the sending of letters or parcels by plane **hava yolu ile gönderilen mektuplar, parseller** *an airmail letter*

airman /'eəmən/ *noun* [C] *plural* airmen a man who flies an aircraft in a country's air force **hava kuvvetleri uçuş personeli**

airplane /'eəpleɪn/ *US* (*UK* aeroplane) *noun* [C] a vehicle that flies and has an engine and wings **uçak** ⊃See picture at aeroplane.

o━**airport** /'eəpɔːt/ *noun* [C] a place where planes take off and land, with buildings for passengers to wait in **hava limanı**

'air ˌraid *noun* [C] an attack by military planes **hava taarruzu, saldırısı**

airspace /'eəspeɪs/ *noun* [U] the sky above a country that belongs to that country **hava sahası**

airstrike /'eəstraɪk/ *noun* [C] an attack by military planes **askeri jetlerce gerçekleştirilen hava taarruzu**

airtight /'eətaɪt/ *adjective* An airtight container does not allow air in or out. **hava geçirmez**

ˌair traffic conˈtroller *noun* [C] the person in an airport who tells pilots when to take off and land their aircraft **hava trafik kontrolörü, kule görevlisi**

airy /'eəri/ *adjective* An airy room or building is pleasant because it has a lot of space and air. **havadar**

aisle /aɪl/ *noun* [C] a passage between the lines of seats or goods in a plane, church, supermarket, etc **koridor, geçişler için kullanılan dar alan**

ajar /ə'dʒɑːʳ/ *adjective* [never before noun] If a door is ajar, it is slightly open. **aralık, az açık**

aka /ˌeɪkeɪ'eɪ/ *adverb abbreviation for* also known as: used when giving the name that a person is generally known by, after giving their real name **ayrıca şöyle de bilinir anlamında kısaltma** *Peter Parker, aka Spiderman*

akin /ə'kɪn/ *adjective formal* **be akin to sth** to be similar to something **bir şeye çok fazla benzemek, yakın olmak, akraba olmak**

aisle

à la carte /ˌælə'kɑːt/ *adjective, adverb* choosing food as separate items from a menu (= list of food), not as a meal with a fixed price **restoranlarda yemeklerin menü-den seçilerek sipariş edilmesi**

alacrity /ə'lækrəti/ *noun* [U] *formal* If you do something with alacrity, you do it in a very quick and willing way. **bir şeyi isteyerek ve hızlı bir şekilde yapma, hızlı ve çevikçe yapma**

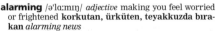

alarm ...... İLE BİRLİKTE KULLANILAN KELİMELER

an alarm **goes off/sounds** ● **set off/trigger** an alarm ● a **burglar/fire/smoke** alarm ● a **car** alarm ● an alarm **system**

alarm¹ /ə'lɑːm/ *noun* **1** [WARNING] [C] a loud noise that warns you of danger **uyandırma, ikaz, alarm** *a fire alarm* ○ *to set off an alarm* **2** [CLOCK] [C] (*also* **alarm clock**) a clock that makes a noise to wake you **çalar saat, alarm 3** [WORRY] [U] a sudden feeling of fear or worry that something bad might happen **ürperti, tedirginlik** *There's no need for alarm - it is completely safe.* **4 raise the alarm** to warn someone of a dangerous situation **birini tehlikeye karşı uyarmak, ikaz etmek** *Her parents raised the alarm when she failed to return home.* ⊃See also: **burglar alarm, false alarm.**

alarm² /ə'lɑːm/ *verb* [T] to make someone worried or frightened **birini endişelendirmek, korkutmak** *I don't want to alarm you but he really should be here by now.*

a'larm ˌclock *noun* [C] a clock that makes a noise to wake you **alarmı olan çalar saat** *I've set the alarm clock for six.*

alarm clock

alarmed /ə'lɑːmd/ *adjective* worried or frightened by something **bir şey tarafından korkutul-muş, endişelenmiş** *I was a bit alarmed at the number of people in the audience.*

alarming /ə'lɑːmɪŋ/ *adjective* making you feel worried or frightened **korkutan, ürküten, teyakkuzda bıra-kan** *alarming news*

alas /ə'læs/ *exclamation literary* used to show sadness **tüh, yazık, eyvah, vah vah**

albeit /ɔːl'biːɪt/ *conjunction formal* although ... **e,a rağ-men, olsa da, gerçi** *He tried, albeit without success.*

albino /æl'biːnəʊ/ ⑤ /æl'baɪnəʊ/ *noun* [C] a person or animal with white skin, white hair or fur, and pink eyes **beyaz tenli, kıllı ve pembe gözlü hayvan veya insan, albino**

album /'ælbəm/ *noun* [C] **1** several songs or pieces of music on a CD, a record, etc **müzik albümü 2** a book in which you keep photographs, stamps, etc **fotoğraf albümü**

alcohol /'ælkəhɒl/ *noun* [U] **1** drinks such as wine and beer that can make you drunk **şarap ve bira gibi alkollü içecekler 2** a liquid that has no colour and is in drinks that make you drunk **sarhoşluk veren madde, alkol**

alcoholic¹ /ˌælkə'hɒlɪk/ *noun* [C] someone who regu-larly drinks too much alcohol and cannot stop the habit **alkolik, ayyaş kişi**

alcoholic² /ˌælkə'hɒlɪk/ *adjective* **1** containing alcohol **alkol içeren** *alcoholic drinks* **2** [always before noun] regu-larly drinking too much alcohol and unable to stop the habit **alkol/içki bağımlısı** *She lived with her alcoholic father.*

alcoholism /'ælkəhɒlɪzᵊm/ *noun* [U] the condition of being an alcoholic **alkolizm**

alcove /'ælkəʊv/ *noun* [C] a part of a wall in a room that is further back than the rest of the wall **duvarda girinti**

ale /eɪl/ *noun* [C, U] a type of beer **bir tür bira**

alert¹ /ə'lɜːt/ *adjective* quick to notice and react to things around you **teyakkuz hali, uyanık olma hali, dik-katli** *A young dog should be alert and playful.* ○ *Teac-hers need to be alert to sudden changes in students' beha-viour.* ● **alertness** *noun* [U] **uyanıklık, dikkat**

alert² /ə'lɜːt/ *verb* [T] to warn someone of a possibly dan-gerous situation **birini muhtemel tehlikeye karşı uyarmak, ikaz etmek, tayakkuza sokmak** *Six hours later she still wasn't home so they alerted the police.*

alert³ /ə'lɜːt/ *noun* **1** [C] a warning about a possibly dan-gerous situation **uyarı, ikaz** *a bomb alert* **2 be on full/red alert** to be expecting problems and ready to deal with them **uyanık olmak, ayakta olmak, teyak-kuzda olmak, kırmızı alarm** *Police in the region were on full alert against further attacks.*

'A ˌlevel *noun* [C] in England and Wales, an exam taken at the age of eighteen, or the qualification itself **İngiltere ve Galler'de 18 yaşında girilen bir tür sınav**

algae /'ældʒiː/ *noun* [U, group] a plant with no stem or leaves that grows in or near water **su yosunu**

algebra /'ældʒɪbrə/ *noun* [U] a type of mathematics in which numbers and amounts are shown by letters and symbols **cebir**

alias¹ /'eɪliəs/ *noun* [C] a false name, especially one used by a criminal **özellikle suçlularca kullanılan sahte isim, takma ad**

alias² /'eɪliəs/ *preposition* used when giving the name that a person is generally known by, after giving their real name **asıl adı verildikten sonra takma ad kulla-nımı** *Grace Kelly, alias Princess Grace of Monaco*

alibi /'ælɪbaɪ/ *noun* [C] proof that someone was not in the place where a crime happened and so cannot be guilty **suçun meydana geldiği zaman başka bir yerde olduğunu gösteren kanıt**

alien¹ /'eɪliən/ *adjective* **1** strange and not familiar **aca-yip, ışık olunmayan** *The custom was totally alien to her.* **2** [always before noun] relating to creatures from an-other planet **yaratık gibi, uzaylı bir yaratığa ilişkin olan** *an alien spacecraft*

alien² /'eɪliən/ *noun* [C] **1** a creature from another planet **yaratık 2** *formal* someone who does not legally belong to the country where they live or work **yabancı, yaşa-dığı/çalıştığı ülkeye yasal olarak ait olmayan**

alienate /'eɪliəneɪt/ *verb* [T] **1** to make someone stop supporting and liking you **başkalaştırmak, aralarını**

açmak, uzak durmasını sağlamak *The government's comments have alienated many teachers.* **2** to make someone feel that they are different and do not belong to a group **başka olduğuna ve bir gruba ait olmadıklarına birini ikna etmek, inandırmak** *Disagreements can alienate teenagers from their families.* ● **alienation** /ˌeɪliəˈneɪʃᵊn/ *noun* [U] **yabancılaşma**

alight¹ /əˈlaɪt/ *adjective* [never before noun] mainly UK burning **yanıcı, yanan** *Vandals set the car alight* (= made it burn).

alight² /əˈlaɪt/ *verb* [I] *formal* to get out of a bus, train, etc **tren, otobüsden inmek** *He alighted from the taxi.*

align /əˈlaɪn/ *verb* **1** [T] to put things in an exact line or make them parallel **bir hizaya getirmek, dizmek, ayarlamak, hizalamak 2 align yourself with sb; be aligned with sb** to support the opinions of a political group, country, etc **bir ülke ve siyasi grubun fikirlerini desteklemek, kendini yakın hissetmek** *Many voters are not aligned with any party.* ● **alignment** *noun* [C, U] **sıra**

alike¹ /əˈlaɪk/ *adjective* [never before noun] similar **benzer, tıpkısı** *The children look so alike.*

alike² /əˈlaɪk/ *adverb* **1** in a similar way **benzer şekilde** *We think alike.* **2** used to say that two people or groups are included **ve benzeri/benzerleri** *It is a disease which affects men and women alike.*

alimony /ˈælɪməni/ *noun* [U] money that someone must pay regularly to their wife or husband after the marriage has ended **nafaka**

o▪**alive** /əˈlaɪv/ *adjective* [never before noun] **1** [NOT DEAD] living, not dead **sağ, yaşayan** *Are your grandparents still alive?* **2** [PLACE] full of activity and excitement **canlı, hareketli** *The bar was alive with the sound of laughter.* ○ *The city comes alive at night.* **3** [CONTINUING] continuing to exist **varlığı devam eden, var olmayı sürdüren** *Local people are fighting to keep the language alive.* **4 be alive and kicking/well** to continue to be popular or successful **popüler ve başarılı olmayı sürdürmek, hâlâ kendinden söz ettirmek** *Despite rumours to the contrary, feminism is alive and kicking.*

o▪**all¹** /ɔːl/ *pronoun*, *determiner* **1** [EVERY ONE] every person or thing in a group **hepsi** *We were all dancing.* ○ *I've watched all of the programmes in the series.* **2** [WHOLE AMOUNT] the whole amount of something **tamamı** *Who's eaten all the cake?* ○ *He spends all of his money on clothes.* **3** [WHOLE TIME] the whole of a period of time **zamanın tamamı** *all week/month/year* ○ *He's been studying all day.* **4** [ONLY THING] the only thing **tümü** *All I remember is waking up in hospital.* **5 at all** in any way **hiç, hiçte** *He hasn't changed at all.* ○ *UK Can I help at all?* **6 in all** in total **toplam olarak, yekün olarak** *There were twenty people at the meeting in all.*

o▪**all²** /ɔːl/ *adverb* **1** completely or very **tamamen veya çokca** *You're all wet!* ○ *I'm all excited now.* **2 all over a** in every place **her yerde** *Lee has travelled all over the world.* **b** finished **bitmiş, tamam** *It was all over very quickly.* **3 2/5/8, etc all** used to say that two players or teams have the same number of points in a game **iki oyuncu ya da takım aynı puanlara sahip olduğunda söylenir** *It was 3 all at half time.* **4 all along** from the beginning of a period of time **bir sürenin başlangıcından beri, öteden beri** *I said all along that it was a mistake.* **5 all but** almost **hemen hemen, neredeyse** *The film was all but over by the time we arrived.* **6 all the better/easier/more exciting, etc** much better, easier, etc **daha da iyi, kolay vb.** *The journey was all the more dangerous because of the bad weather.* **7 all in all** considering everything **genellikle, tümüyle, tamamen, herşeyi kapsayan şekilde** *All in all, I think she did well.*

Allah /ˈælə/ *noun* the name of God for Muslims **Allah**

allay /əˈleɪ/ *verb formal* **allay sb's concerns/fears/suspicions, etc** to make someone feel less worried or frightened, etc **birinin daha az endişelenmesini veya korkmasını sağlamak, korkularını, endişelerini, sorunlarını azaltmak** *I tried to allay his fears about the interview.*

allegation ...... İLE BİRLİKTE KULLANILAN KELİMELER

make/deny/face/investigate an allegation ● a serious allegation ● an allegation of sth ● an allegation against sb

allegation /ˌælɪˈgeɪʃᵊn/ *noun* [C] when you say that someone has done something wrong or illegal, without proof that this is true **suçlama, zan altında bırakma, iddia** *allegations of corruption* ○ [+ that] *He denied allegations that he had cheated.*

allege /əˈledʒ/ *verb* [T] to say that someone has done something wrong or illegal, but not prove it **iddia etmek, öne sürmek, kanıtsız suçlamak** [often passive] *The teacher is alleged to have hit a student.* ○ [+ (that)] *He alleges that Bates attacked him.*

alleged /əˈledʒd/ *adjective* [always before noun] believed to be true, but not proved **iddia edilen, isnat edilen, ispatlanmadan suçlu olduğuna inanılan** *an alleged attack* ● **allegedly** /əˈledʒɪdli/ *adverb* *He was arrested for allegedly stealing a car.* **söylenene göre**

allegiance /əˈliːdʒᵊns/ *noun* [U] loyalty and support **bağlılık, sadakat, destek** *To become a citizen, you have to pledge/swear allegiance to* (= say you will be loyal to) *the United States.*

allegory /ˈælɪgəri/ *noun* [C, U] a story, poem, or painting that has a hidden meaning, especially a moral one **içinde ahlaki değerlere ait gizli anlam içeren hikaye, şiir ya da tablo, allegori** ● **allegorical** /ˌælɪˈgɒrɪkᵊl/ *adjective* **içinde gizli bir mesaj veya ders olan hikayeler**

allergic /əˈlɜːdʒɪk/ *adjective* **1** [never before noun] having an allergy **alerjik, alerjisi olan** *I'm allergic to eggs.* **2** [always before noun] caused by an allergy **alerjinin sebep olduğu** *an allergic reaction*

allergy /ˈælədʒi/ *noun* [C] a medical condition in which your body reacts badly to something that you eat, breathe, or touch **alerji** *an allergy to dogs*

alleviate /əˈliːvieɪt/ *verb* [T] to make problems or suffering less extreme **hafifletmek, etkisini azaltmak** *She's been given some tablets to alleviate the pain.* ● **alleviation** /əˌliːviˈeɪʃᵊn/ *noun* [U] **iyileştirme**

alley /ˈæli/ (*also* alleyway /ˈæliweɪ/) *noun* [C] **1** a narrow road between buildings **binalar arasındaki dar yol, geçit 2 be right up sb's alley** US informal (UK be right up sb's street) to be exactly the type of thing that someone knows about or likes to do **birinin istediği veya yapmayı sevdiği gibi bir şey olmak**

alliance ...... İLE BİRLİKTE KULLANILAN KELİMELER

form an alliance ● an alliance between sb and sb ● an alliance with sb ● in alliance with sb

alliance /əˈlaɪəns/ *noun* [C] an agreement between countries or political parties to work together to achieve something **müttefiklik, ortaklık** *an alliance between France and Britain*

allied /ˈælaɪd/ *adjective* **1** [always before noun] joined by a formal agreement **müttefik olan, resmi antlaşmayla ortaklık oluşturan** *the allied powers* **2 be allied to/with sth** to be related to something **bir şeye/bir şeyle ilişkili olmak, bağlantılı olmak** *a group closely allied with the Green Party*

alligator   20   o⚬ Important words to learn

alligator /ˈælɪgeɪtəʳ/ **noun** [C] a big reptile with a long mouth and sharp teeth, that lives in lakes and rivers **timsah**

alligator

all-night /ˈɔːlnaɪt/ *adjective* lasting all night **bütün gece boyunca olan, süregelen** *Tom was tired after his all-night party.*

allocate /ˈæləkeɪt/ *verb* [T] to give some time, money, space, etc to be used for a particular purpose **ayırmak, pay ayırmak, vermek, tahsis etmek** *The government has promised to allocate extra money for health care.* ○ *More police time should be allocated to crime prevention.*

allocation /ˌæləˈkeɪʃʰn/ *noun* **1** [C] an amount of money, time, space, etc that is allocated **tahsisat 2** [U] when money, time, space, etc is allocated **tahsis etme, ayırma** *the allocation of money*

allot /əˈlɒt/ *verb* [T] **allotting,** *past* **allotted** to give someone a particular amount of something **birine birşeyin bir miktarını vermek, ayırmak** *They were allotted seats on the front row.*

allotment /əˈlɒtmənt/ *noun* **1** [C] in Britain, a small area of land that people rent and grow vegetables and flowers on **Britanya'da insanların kiralayarak üzerinde bir şeyler yetiştirdikleri küçük toprak parçası 2** [C, U] the process of sharing something, or the amount that you get **bölüşme, hisselere ayırıp paylaşma, tahsis etme**

all-out /ˈɔːlˌaʊt/ *adjective* [always before noun] complete and with as much effort as possible **tam ve mümkün olan en son çaba ile** *an all-out battle/effort*

o⚬**allow** /əˈlaʊ/ *verb* [T] **1** [GIVE PERMISSION] to give someone permission for something **müsaade etmek, izin vermek** [often passive] *Smoking is not allowed in the restaurant.* ○ [+ to do sth] *You are not allowed to use calculators in the exam.* ○ [+ two objects] *Patients are not allowed visitors after nine o'clock.* **2** [NOT PREVENT] to not prevent something from happening **bir şeyin oluşunu engelleyememek** [+ to do sth] *They have allowed the problem to get worse.* **3** [MAKE POSSIBLE] to make it possible for someone to do something **birisi için bir şeyi yapmasını temin etmek, mümkün kılmak** [+ to do sth] *The extra money will allow me to upgrade my computer.* **4** [TIME/MONEY] to plan to use a particular amount of money, time, etc for something **bir miktar para ve zamanı bir şey için kullanmayı planlamak, ayırmak** *Allow three hours for the whole journey.*

allow for sth *phrasal verb* to consider or include something when you are making plans **planlarken birşeyleri dikkate almak, göz önünde bulundurmak** *The journey should take two hours, allowing for delays.*

allowance /əˈlaʊəns/ *noun* [C] **1** money that you are given regularly, especially to pay for a particular thing **harcırah, pay, ödenek, tahsisat** *a clothing allowance* **2** an amount of something that you are allowed **birşeyin birinin kullanımına ayrılan miktarı, tahsisat, pay, hisse** *The luggage allowance is 25 kilos.* **3 make allowances for sb/sth** to remember that someone has a disadvantage which is not their fault when you are judging their behaviour or work **birinin işini ya da davranışını yargılarken onların elinde olmayan dezavantajları olduğunu hatırlamak, suçu sadece kişilere yüklememek** *They made allowances for the fact that he was ill.*

alloy /ˈælɔɪ/ *noun* [C] a metal that is a mixture of two or more metals **alaşım**

o⚬**all 'right¹** (*also* alright) *adjective* [never before noun], *adverb* **1** [GOOD] good enough, although not very good **peki, tamam, pekâla** *The hotel wasn't brilliant but it was all right.* ○ *It's a cheap wine but it tastes all right.* **2** [SAFE] safe or well **güvende, emin, iyi, sağ salim** *I'm all right thanks. How are you?* ○ *Did you get home all right last night?* **3 that's all right a** [THANKS] used as an answer when someone thanks you **bir şey değil, rica ederim** *"Thanks for cleaning the kitchen." "That's all right."* **b** [SORRY] something you say when someone says sorry to show that you are not angry **önemli değil, boş ver, aldırma, tamam** *"I'm sorry - I forgot all about it." "That's all right."*

all 'right² (*also* alright) *exclamation* used to agree to a suggestion or request **tamam, işte bu, peki, gibi bir öneri ve ricayı kabul etmek için kullanılır** *"How about going out for dinner?" "All right."*

all-time /ˌɔːlˈtaɪm/ *adjective* [always before noun] If something is at an all-time best/high/low, etc, it is the best/highest/lowest, etc it has ever been. **daima revaçta olan, her daim iyi**

allude /əˈluːd/ *verb*
allude to sb/sth *phrasal verb formal* to refer to someone or something but not directly **dolaylı yoldan birine/bir şeye atıfta bulunmak, değinmek**

allure /əˈljʊəʳ/ *noun* [U] an attractive or exciting quality **cazibe, çekicilik, büyü** *the allure of the city* ● **alluring** *adjective* attractive or exciting **cezbedici, çekici, heyecan veren** *an alluring image*

allusion /əˈluːʒʰn/ *noun* [C, U] *formal* when you refer to someone or something but not directly **ima, kinaye, taş, dolaylı yoldan dokundurma** *a play full of allusions to* Shakespeare

ally¹ /ˈælaɪ/ *noun* [C] **1** someone who supports you, especially when other people are against you **müttefik, destekleyen, arka çıkan, ortak 2** a country that has agreed to help another country, especially in a war **savaş müttefiki ülke, müttefik, dost, ortak amaçları olan ülkeler**

ally² /əˈlaɪ/ *verb*
ally yourself to/with sb *phrasal verb* to join someone and support them **birine/bir şeye yardım etmek için katılmak, müttefik olmak, ortak olmak**

almighty /ɔːlˈmaɪti/ *adjective* **1** [always before noun] very strong or forceful **güçlü, ilahi, çok kudretli** *All of a sudden I heard an almighty bang in the kitchen.* **2** having the power to do everything, like a god **ilahi, kudretli, Tanrı gibi güçlü** *Almighty God*

almond /ˈɑːmənd/ *noun* [C, U] a flat, oval nut, often used in cooking **acıbadem**

o⚬**almost** /ˈɔːlməʊst/ *adverb* **1** If something almost happens, it does not happen but it is very close to happening. **hemen hemen, neredeyse, az kalsın** *I almost missed the bus.* **2 almost always/everyone/half, etc** not always/everyone/half, etc but very close to it **nereyse herkes/yarısı/daima, bir şeyin hemen hemen tamamına yakını** *He's almost always late.*

o⚬**alone** /əˈləʊn/ *adjective,* *adverb* **1** [never before noun] without other people **yalnız** *She lives alone.* **2** [always after noun] used to emphasize that only one person or thing is involved **tek, tek kişi, sadece o** *Last year alone the company made a million dollars.* **3 leave sb alone** to stop talking to someone or annoying them **birini yal-**

nız,tek başına bırakmak, rahatsız etmemek *Leave him alone, he's tired.* **4 leave sth alone** to stop touching something **bir şeyi serbest bırakmak, dokunmamak** *Leave your hair alone!* ⊃See also: **let alone.**

○─**along¹** /ə'lɒŋ/ *preposition* **1** [DIRECTION] from one part of a road, river, etc to another **baştan sona, bir uçtan öbürüne** *a romantic walk along the beach* **2** [NEXT TO] in a line next to something long **boyunca, yan yana** *a row of new houses along the river* **3** [PARTICULAR PLACE] at a particular place on a road, river, etc **yol, nehir vb. yerlerde belli bir noktada, yerde** *Somewhere along this road there's a garage.*

○─**along²** /ə'lɒŋ/ *adverb* **1** forward **ileriye, öne doğru** *We were just walking along, chatting.* **2 be/come along** to arrive somewhere **bir yere varmak, ulaşmak** *You wait ages for a bus and then three come along at once.* **3 bring/take sb along** to take someone with you to a place **birini bir yere yanında, beraberinde götürmek** *She asked if she could bring some friends along to the party.* **4 along with sb/sth** in addition to someone or something else **ile birlikte, beraberinde, birini/birşeyi yanına alarak** *California along with Florida is probably the most popular American holiday destination.*

alongside /ə,lɒŋ'saɪd/ *adverb, preposition* **1** next to someone or something **birşeyin veya birinin yanında, yanıbaşında, ile birlikte olarak** *A car pulled up alongside ours.* **2** together with someone **biriyle birlikte, ortak, beraberce** *She enjoyed working alongside such famous actors.*

aloof /ə'luːf/ *adjective* **1** not friendly, especially because you think you are better than other people **uzak, soğuk, mesafeli** *He seems arrogant and aloof.* **2** not involved in something **bir işi olmayan, boş, ilgisiz, alakasız** *He tried to remain aloof from family arguments.*

aloud /ə'laʊd/ *adverb* in a way that other people can hear **sesli, yüksek sesle** *to laugh aloud* ○ *The author read aloud from his new book.*

alphabet /'ælfəbet/ *noun* [C] a set of letters used for writing a language **alfabe** *The English alphabet starts at A and ends at Z.*

alphabetical /,ælfə'betɪkᵊl/ *adjective* arranged in the same order as the letters of the alphabet **alfabetik sıraya göre, dizilişe göre** *Put the names in alphabetical order.* ● **alphabetically** *adverb* **alfabetik bir şekilde**

alpine /'ælpaɪn/ *adjective* [always before noun] existing in, or relating to high mountains **yüksek dağlarda var olan, oraya ait olan** *an alpine village*

○─**already** /ɔːl'redi/ *adverb* **1** now, or before a particular time in the past **zaten, çok önceden** *I've already told him.* ○ *By the time we arrived, he'd already left.* **2** used to say that something has happened earlier than you expected **çoktan, evvelce** *I'm already full and I've only eaten one course.*

○─**alright** /ɔːl'raɪt/ *adjective, adverb, exclamation* another spelling of **all right** **tamam, pekâla**

○─**also** /'ɔːlsəʊ/ *adverb* in addition **de, da, dahi, hem de** *She speaks French and also a little Spanish.* ○ *The book also has a chapter on grammar.*

altar /'ɔːltər/ *noun* [C] a table used for religious ceremonies, especially in a Christian church **bilhassa Hıristiyan kilisesinde dini törenler için kullanılan masa, sunak**

○─**alter** /'ɔːltər/ *verb* [I, T] to change, or to make someone or something change **değiştirmek, değişmesini sağlamak, değişmek** *We've had to alter our plans.*

alteration ...... İLE BİRLİKTE KULLANILAN KELİMELER

make alterations (to) sth ● a **major/minor/slight** alteration ● an alteration **in/to** sth

alteration /ɔːltᵊr'eɪʃᵊn/ *noun* [C, U] a change, or the process of changing something **değişme, değişim, düzeltme, onarım** *We've made a few alterations to the kitchen.*

alternate¹ /ɔːl'tɜːnət/ *adjective* **1 alternate days/weeks/years, etc** one out of every two days, weeks, years, etc **iki günde, ayda/yılda bir, gün/ay/yıl aşırı, münavebeli** *I work alternate Saturdays.* **2** with first one thing, then another thing, and then the first thing again, etc **sırayla, peşpeşe olan, birbirini takip eden** *a dessert with alternate layers of chocolate and cream* **3** [always before noun] *US* An alternate plan, method, etc is one that you can use if you do not want to use another one. **değişik, başka, ilave, alternatif olan** ● **alternately** *adverb* **ardı sıra**

alternate² /'ɔːltəneɪt/ *verb* **1** [I] If two things alternate, one thing happens, then the other thing happens, then the first thing happens again, etc. **birbiri peşi sıra olmak, sırayla meydana gelmek, önce biri sonra diğeri olmak** *She alternates between cheerfulness and deep despair.* **2 alternate sth with sth** to use or do one thing then another thing and then the first thing again, etc **bir şeyi diğer bir şeyle değişmeli olarak yapmak, kullanmak** *They alternate classical pieces with more modern works.* ● **alternating** *adjective* **alternating moods of anger and sadness değişken**

alternative¹ /ɔːl'tɜːnətɪv/ *noun* [C] one of two or more things that you can choose between **alternatif, iki şey arasında seçim** *It's a low-fat alternative to butter.* ○ *After the public protests the government had no alternative but to change its policy.*

alternative² /ɔːl'tɜːnətɪv/ *adjective* [always before noun] **1** (*also US* **alternate**) An alternative plan, method, etc is one that you can use if you do not want to use another one. **değişik, başka, ilave, alternatif olan** *We can make alternative arrangements if necessary.* **2** different to what is usual or traditional **alışılan ve geleneksel olandan farklı, değişik** *alternative comedy* ○ *an alternative lifestyle*

alternatively /ɔːl'tɜːnətɪvli/ *adverb* used to give a second possibility **alternatif olarak, bir başka olasılık olarak** *We could go there by train or, alternatively, I could drive us.*

al,ternative 'medicine *noun* [U] any way of trying to make an illness better that uses medicines or methods that are not normally used in Western medicine **alternatif tıp**

○─**although** /ɔːl'ðəʊ/ *conjunction* **1** despite the fact that ... **e,a rağmen, ... e karşın, ise de, olmakla beraber** *She walked home by herself, although she knew it was dangerous.* **2** but **fakat, ancak** *He's coming this evening, although I don't know exactly when.*

altitude /'æltɪtjuːd/ *noun* [C, U] the height of something above sea level **irtifa, yükseklik, deniz seviyesinden yükseklik** *flying at an altitude of 8000 metres.*

alto /'æltəʊ/ *noun* [C] a woman or boy with a low singing voice **müzikte en düşük kadın ve erkek sesi**

○─**altogether** /,ɔːltə'geðər/ *adverb* **1** [COMPLETELY] completely **tamamen** *The train slowed down and then stopped altogether.* ○ *I'm not altogether sure about the idea.* **2** [TOTAL] in total **hepsi, bütünü, toplam olarak** *There were twenty people there altogether.* **3** [GENERALLY] when you consider everything **hep beraber, hepsi, tümü** *Altogether, I'd say the party was a great success.*

aluminium /ˌæljə'mɪnɪəm/ UK (US **aluminum** /ə'lu:mɪnəm/) noun [U] a light, silver-coloured metal used for making containers, cooking equipment, and aircraft parts (symbol **Al**) **aluminyum** *aluminium cans/foil*

always ...... BAŞKA BİR DEYİŞLE

Eğer kişi **always** kelimesini tekrar eden bir şey için kullanıyorsa, bunun yerine **constantly, continually, forever, time after time** veya **all the time** söylemlerini de kullanabilir. *He's **constantly/forever** losing his keys.* ● *I'm fed up with you making excuses **all the time.*** **Invariably** kelimesi kötü olan bir durumu açıklamada **always** kelimesine göre bazen daha resmi bir söylem olabilmektedir. *The train is **invariably** late.* **Without fail** söylemi bir kişinin bir işi en zor şekliyle bile her durumda yaptığını göstermek için kullanılabilir. *He visited her every Sunday **without fail.***

o⁼**always** /'ɔ:lweɪz/ adverb **1** [EVERY TIME] every time, or at all times **her zaman, sürekli** *I always walk to work.* **2** [UNTIL NOW] at all times in the past **daima, hep olan** *We've always lived here.* **3** [FOREVER] forever **ebediyyen, her daim, sonuna dek** *I will always remember you.* **4** [MANY TIMES] again and again, usually in an annoying way **tekrar tekrar, biteviye, durmaksızın** [+ doing sth] *He's always losing his keys.* **5 can/could always do sth** used to suggest something **bir şeyi yapmayı önermek, öneride bulunmak** *You can always stay with us if you miss your train.*

Alzheimer's (disease) /'æltshaɪməzdɪˌzi:z/ noun [U] a brain disease mainly of old people which makes a person forget things and stops them from thinking clearly **daha çok yaşlılarda görülen unutkanlığa sebep olan hastalık, Alzheimer hastalığı**

o⁼**a.m.** (also **am**) /ˌeɪ'em/ used to refer to a time between 12 o'clock in the night and 12 o'clock in the day **gece 12'den öğlen 12'ye kadar olan zaman dilimi** *We're open from 9 a.m. to 5 p.m. daily.*

am strong form /æm/ weak forms /əm/, /m/ present simple I of be ... **im anlamında birinci tekil şahıs "I" yardımcı fiili**

amalgamate /ə'mælgəmeɪt/ verb [I, T] If two or more organizations amalgamate, they join to become one, and if you amalgamate them, you make them do this. **iki kurumun bir araya gelerek birlik oluşturması, tek bir çatı altında toplanmak, birlik olmak** *a decision to **amalgamate** with another school* ● **amalgamation** /əˌmælgə'meɪʃ⁰n/ noun [C, U] **birleşim**

amass /ə'mæs/ verb [T] formal to get a lot of money or information over a period of time **zamanla bir çok para ve bilgiyi bir araya getirmek, biriktirmek, sahip olmak** *He **amassed** a fortune in the diamond trade.*

amateur¹ /'æmətər/ adjective doing something as a hobby and not as your job **amatörce** *an amateur photographer*

amateur² /'æmətər/ noun [C] **1** someone who does something as a hobby and not as their job **amatör 2** someone who is not good at what they do **acemi, amatör** *I won't be giving them any more work - they're a bunch of amateurs.*

amateurish /'æmət⁰rɪʃ/ ⓤ /ˌæmə't3:rɪʃ/ adjective done without skill or attention **acemice, beceriksizce yapılan/yapılmış**

amaze /ə'meɪz/ verb [T] to make someone very surprised **birini şaşırtmak, hayrete düşürmek** *It amazes me how much energy that woman has.*

amazed /ə'meɪzd/ adjective extremely surprised **şaşırmış, hayretler içinde kalmış** *I was **amazed** at the price.* ○ [+ (that)] *I was amazed that Paul recognized me.*

amazement /ə'meɪzmənt/ noun [U] extreme surprise **hayret, şaşkınlık, şaşma** *Jana looked at him **in amazement**.* ○ *To his **amazement** they offered him the job.*

amazing /ə'meɪzɪŋ/ adjective very surprising **şaşırtan, hayrete düşüren** [+ question word] *It's amazing how many people can't read.* ● **amazingly** adverb **şaşılacak şekilde**

ambassador /æm'bæsədər/ noun [C] the main official sent by the government of a country to represent it in another country **büyükelçi, diplomat, sefir** *the French ambassador to Britain*

amber /'æmbər/ noun [U] **1** a colour between yellow and orange **kehribar kırmızısı, sarı ile portakal rengi arası bir renk 2** a hard, clear yellowish-brown substance, used for making jewellery **mücevherat yapımında kullanılan katı sarımsı kahverengi bir madde** ● **amber** adjective an amber traffic light **sarı ve turuncu arası bir renk**

ambience (also **ambiance**) /'æmbɪəns/ noun [U, no plural] the qualities of a place and the way it makes you feel **ortam, hava, ambians** *Lighting adds a lot to the ambience of a room.*

ambiguity /ˌæmbɪ'gju:əti/ noun [C, U] when something has more than one possible meaning **anlam kargaşası, çok anlamlılık, karmaşa, anlaşılmazlık** *Legal documents must be free of ambiguity.*

ambiguous /æm'bɪgjuəs/ adjective having more than one possible meaning **çok anlamlı, zor anlaşılan, karmaşık** *an ambiguous statement* ● **ambiguously** adverb **belirsiz şekilde**

ambition ...... İLE BİRLİKTE KULLANILAN KELİMELER

have an ambition ● achieve/fulfil/realize an ambition ● a burning/lifelong ambition

o⁼**ambition** /æm'bɪʃ⁰n/ noun **1** [C] something you want to achieve in your life **hırs** *My ambition is to retire at forty.* **2** [U] a strong feeling that you want to be successful or powerful **tutku, ihtiras** *My sister always had more ambition than me.*

ambitious /æm'bɪʃəs/ adjective **1** wanting to be successful or powerful **hırslı, azimli** *an ambitious young lawyer* **2** An ambitious plan will need a lot of work and will be difficult to achieve. **hırs, azim, gayret gerektiren** *This is our most ambitious project so far.*

ambivalent /æm'bɪvələnt/ adjective having two different feelings about something **çelişkili, karmaşık duygular içinde olan, kararsız, ne yapacağını bilmez halde olan** *He was ambivalent about moving to London.* ● **ambivalence** /æm'bɪv⁰ləns/ noun [U] **kararsızlık**

amble /'æmbl/ verb **amble along/around/through, etc** to walk somewhere in a slow and relaxed way **salına salına, yavaş yavaş yürümek,** *We ambled home across the fields.*

ambulance /'æmbjələns/ noun [C] a vehicle that takes people to hospital when they are ill or hurt **cankurtaran, acil hasta taşıma aracı, ambulans**

ambush /'æmbʊʃ/ verb [T] to attack a person or vehicle after hiding somewhere and waiting for them to arrive **pusu kurmak, pusu atmak, tuzak kurmak, tuzağa düşürmek** [often passive] *The bus was ambushed by a gang of youths.* ● **ambush** noun [C] *Two policemen were killed in a terrorist ambush.* **saldırı**

ambush

ameliorate /ə'miːliºreɪt/ *verb* [T] *formal* to make a problem or bad situation better **iyileştirmek, iyi duruma getirmek**

amen /ˌɑːˈmen/ *exclamation* something that Christians say at the end of a prayer **amin**

amenable /ə'miːnəbl/ *adjective* willing to do or accept something **iyi huylu, yumuşak başlı, uysal** *She may be more amenable to the idea now.*

amend /ə'mend/ *verb* [T] to slightly change the words of a document **hafif düzeltmek, değiştirmek** [often passive] *The contract has now been amended.*

amendment /ə'mendmənt/ *noun* [C, U] a change in the words of a document, or the process of doing this **düzeltme, değiştirme, küçük değişikliklerle yeniden düzenleme** *to make an amendment to the human rights law*

amends /ə'mendz/ *noun* **make amends** to do something nice for someone to show that you are sorry for something that you have done **hatalarını telafi etmek, düzeltmek, gönlünü almak, kusurunu gidermek** *I want to make amends for the worry I've caused you.*

amenity /ə'miːnəti/ ⓤ /ə'menəti/ *noun* [C] a building, piece of equipment, or service that is provided for people's comfort or enjoyment **yaşamı kolaylaştıran şeylerin tümü** [usually plural] *The campsite's amenities include a pool and three restaurants.*

American /ə'merɪkən/ *adjective* **1** relating to the United States of America **ABD'ye ait olan, Amerikalı** *an American accent* **2 North/South American** relating to one or more of the countries of North/South America **kuzey/güney Amerikalı** ● **American** *noun* [C] someone who comes from the United States of America **Amerikan vatandaşı, Amerikan uyruklu** ➲See also: Native American.

Aˌmerican ˈfootball *UK* (*US* **football**) *noun* [U] a game for two teams of eleven players in which each team tries to kick, run with, or throw an oval ball across the opposing team's goal line **Amerikan futbolu** ➲Orta kısımdaki renkli sayfalarına bakınız.

Aˌmerican ˈIndian *adjective* relating or belonging to the original race of people who lived in North America **Amerika yerlisine ait, ilişkin, kızılderili kültürüne dair** ● **American Indian** *noun* [C] **Kuzey Amerika kökenli**

amiable /'eɪmiəbl/ *adjective* pleasant and friendly **samimi, uysal, iyi huylu, yumuşak tabiatlı, iyi hoş** *an amiable young man* ● **amiably** *adverb* **dostça**

amicable /'æmɪkəbl/ *adjective formal* done in a friendly way, without arguments **dostça, dostane yapılan, tartışmasız yapılan** *an amicable agreement/divorce* ● **amicably** *adverb* **dostane bir şekilde**

amid /ə'mɪd/ (*also* **amidst** /ə'mɪdst/) *preposition formal* **1** while something else is happening **bir başka şey olurken, tam orta yerinde** *Security was increased amid fears of further terrorist attacks.* **2** among **ortasında, arasında** *a village set amid the hills*

amiss[1] /ə'mɪs/ *adjective* [never before noun] If something is amiss, there is something wrong. **kusurlu, kötü, yanlış, hatalı** *I knew something was amiss when he didn't answer the door.*

amiss[2] /ə'mɪs/ *adverb* **1 would not go amiss** *UK* If something would not go amiss, it would be useful or nice in a particular situation. **kötü, yanlış bir şey olmazsa, kusur bulunmazsa, kötüye gitmez** *A cup of coffee wouldn't go amiss.* **2 take it amiss** *UK* to feel upset by what someone says or does **yanlış anlamak, birinin yaptığını veya söylediğini ters anlamak, başka türlü yorumlamak ve bundan dolayı kötü hissetmek** *I think she might take it amiss if I left early.*

ammonia /ə'məʊniə/ *noun* [U] a liquid or gas with a strong smell, used in substances for cleaning things (formula NH_3) **temizleme maddeleri içinde kullanılan keskin kokulu sıvı ya da gaz, amoniya**

ammunition /ˌæmjə'nɪʃºn/ *noun* [U] **1** a supply of bullets and bombs to be fired from guns **cephane, mermi, mühimmat 2** facts that you can use to criticize someone **birini eleştirmek için kullanılacak gerçekler**

amnesia /æm'niːʒə/ *noun* [U] a medical condition that makes you forget things **unutkanlık hastalığı, bellek kaybı, amnezya**

amnesty /'æmnəsti/ *noun* **1** [C, U] a time when a government allows political prisoners to go free **genel af 2** [C] a time when people can give weapons or drugs to the police, or admit that they have done something illegal, without being punished **teslim olma, itirafçı olma, cezalandırılmamak koşuluyla teslim olma**

o╍**among** /ə'mʌŋ/ (*also* **amongst** /ə'mʌŋst/) *preposition* **1** [IN THE MIDDLE] in the middle of something **ikiden fazla şey arasında** *He disappeared among the crowd.* **2** [IN A GROUP] in a particular group **belli bir grubun içinde** *The decision will not be popular among students.* ○ *I'm going to give you a minute to talk amongst yourselves* (= talk to each other). **3** [ONE OF A GROUP] to be one of a small group **küçük bir gruptan olma** *He is among the top five tennis players in the country.* **4** [DIVIDE] to each one in a group **bir gruptaki kişilerden her birine** *She divided the cake among the children.*

amoral /ˌeɪ'mɒrəl/ *adjective* not caring if what you are doing is morally wrong **ahlaki değer taşımayan, ahlakdışı, ahlaksız** *an amoral person/act*

amorous /'æmºrəs/ *adjective* full of love and sexual excitement **sevdalı ve cinsel heyecanı olan, aşk ve şehvet duyan** *amorous adventures*

o╍**amount**[1] /ə'maʊnt/ *noun* [C] how much there is of something **miktar, yekun, tutar** *The project will take a huge amount of time and money.*

amount[2] /ə'maʊnt/ *verb*
amount to sth *phrasal verb* **1** to be the same as something, or to have the same effect as something **bir şeyle aynı olmak, aynı etkiyi yaratmak** *He gave what amounted to an apology on behalf of the company.* **2** to have a particular total **belli bir yekun tutmak, belli bir tutarı olmak** *goods amounting to $800*

amp /æmp/ (*also* **ampere** /'æmpeər/) *noun* [C] a unit for measuring the strength of an electric current **amper, elektrik akımının gücünü ölçen birim**

ample /'æmpl/ *adjective* **1** enough, or more than enough **yeterinden fazla, kâfi miktarda, yeterince, çok fazla** *She's had ample time to get the work done.*

A

2 large **büyük, geniş** *her ample bosom* ● **amply** *adverb* **bolca**

amplifier /'æmplɪfaɪəʳ/ *noun* [C] a piece of electronic equipment that makes sounds louder **ses gücünü artı-ran elektronik alet, amplifikatör**

amplify /'æmplɪfaɪ/ *verb* [T] **1** to make a sound louder using electronic equipment **ses gücünü, şiddetini, seviyesini artırmak 2** *formal* to make a feeling or opinion stronger or clearer **bir his veya düşünceyi daha güçlü veya açık hale getirmek, belirginleştirmek** ● **amplification** /ˌæmplɪfɪ'keɪʃᵊn/ *noun* [U] **yükselme**

amputate /'æmpjəteɪt/ *verb* [I, T] to cut off someone's leg, arm, finger, etc in a medical operation **birinin bacağını, kolunu, parmaklarını tıbbi bir ameli-yatla kesmek** *His leg was amputated at the knee.* ● **amputation** /ˌæmpjə'teɪʃᵊn/ *noun* [C, U] **kesme**

amuse /ə'mjuːz/ *verb* [T] **1** to make someone smile or laugh **eğlendirmek** *I took him an article that I thought might amuse him.* **2** to keep someone interested and help them to have an enjoyable time **ilgisini çekmek, eğlendirmek, iyi vakit geçirmelerini sağlamak** [often reflexive] *I bought a magazine to amuse myself while I was on the train.*

amused /ə'mjuːzd/ *adjective* **1** showing that you think something is funny **eğlenmiş, şaşırmış, keyif almış** *an amused smile* ○ *She was very amused by/at your comments.* **2 keep sb amused** to keep someone interested and help them to have an enjoyable time **birinin eğlenmesini sağlamak, iyi vakit geçirmesine yar-dımcı olmak** *How do you keep an eight-year-old boy amused?*

amusement /ə'mjuːzmənt/ *noun* **1** [U] the feeling that you have when something makes you smile or laugh **eğlence, keyif, eğlenti** *I watched the performance with great amusement.* ○ *To our amusement the tent collap-sed on top of them.* **2** [C, U] an enjoyable way of spending your time **keyf alınarak yapılan şey, eğlence** *I play the piano but just for my own amusement.*

a'musement ˌpark *noun* [C] a large park where you can ride on exciting machines **luna park**

amusing /ə'mjuːzɪŋ/ *adjective* making you laugh or smile **eğlendiren, keyf veren, güldüren** *an amusing letter*

○▪**an** *strong form* /æn/ *weak form* /ᵊn/ *determiner* used instead of 'a' when the next word starts with a vowel sound **bir** *an apple* ○ *an hour* ⊃See Common learner error at **a**.

anaemia *UK* (*US* anemia) /ə'niːmiə/ *noun* [U] a medical condition in which your blood does not contain enough red cells **kansızlık** ● **anaemic** *UK* (*US* anemic) /ə'niː-mɪk/ *adjective* **kansız**

anaesthetic *UK* (*US* anesthetic) /ˌænəs'θetɪk/ *noun* [C, U] a drug that makes you unable to feel pain during an operation **anestezi, ilaçla uyuşturma** *The operation is done under anaesthetic* (= using anaesthetic). ⊃See also: general anaesthetic, local anaesthetic.

anaesthetist *UK* (*US* anesthetist) /ə'niːsθətɪst/ Ⓤ /ə'nesθətɪst/ *noun* [C] a doctor in a hospital who gives anaesthetics to people **anestezist, anestezi uzmanı doktor**

anaesthetize /ə'niːsθətaɪz/ *UK* (*US* anesthetize /ə'nes-θətaɪz/) *verb* [T] to give someone drugs that make them unable to feel pain **anestezi uygulama, uyuşturma**

anagram /'ænəgræm/ *noun* [C] a word or phrase made by putting the letters of another word or phrase in a different order **bir kelimenin harflerini kullanarak başka bir kelime üretme, çevrik söz, ifade, anag-ram** *'Team' is an anagram of 'meat'.*

anal /'eɪnᵊl/ *adjective* relating to the anus (= hole where solid waste comes out of the body) **anüs ile ilgili, anal**

analogous /ə'næləgəs/ *adjectiveformal* similar in some ways **bazı hususlarda benzeşen, benzeyen** *It's often said that life is analogous to a journey.*

analogy /ə'nælədʒi/ *noun* [C, U] a comparison that shows how two things are similar **iki şeyin birbirin-den nasıl farklı olduğunu gösteren mukayese** *She draws an analogy between life's events and a game of chance.*

analyse *UK* (*US* analyze) /'ænᵊlaɪz/ *verb* [T] to examine the details of something carefully, in order to under-stand or explain it **analiz etmek, detaylı bir şekilde incelemek** *to analyse information* ○ *Blood samples were analysed in the laboratory.*

🧩 **analysis** ...... İLE BİRLİKTE KULLANILAN KELİMELER

do an analysis ● a **detailed** analysis ● an analysis **of** sth ● **send** sth **for** analysis

analysis /ə'næləsɪs/ *noun* [C, U] *plural* **analyses** /ə'nælə-siːz/ the process of analysing something **analiz, irde-leme, inceleme** *a detailed analysis* ○ *A sample of soil was sent for analysis.*

analyst /'ænᵊlɪst/ *noun* [C] someone whose job is to examine the details of a situation carefully, and give their opinion about it **analiz yapan, inceleyen, irde-leyen** *a financial/political analyst*

analytical /ˌænᵊl'ɪtɪkᵊl/ (*also* analytic) *adjective* examin-ing the details of something carefully, in order to under-stand or explain it **detaylı ve derinlemesine incele-yen, analitik, irdeleyici** *analytical skills* ○ *an analytical mind*

analyze /'ænᵊlaɪz/ *verb* [T] *US spelling of* analyse **analiz etmek**

anarchist /'ænəkɪst/ *noun* [C] someone who thinks that society should not be controlled by a government and laws **anarşist, toplumun kanunlarla idare edilme-mesi gerektiğini savunan**

anarchy /'ænəki/ *noun* [U] when there is no law or gov-ernment, or when people ignore them **anarşi, kaos** ● **anarchic** /æn'ɑːkɪk/ *adjective* **anarşik**

anatomy /ə'nætəmi/ *noun* **1** [U] the scientific study of the body and how its parts are arranged **anatomi, insan vücudunun bilimsel olarak çalışması 2** [C] the body of a person or living thing **insan ve diğer can-lıların bedeni, vücudu** [usually singular] *the female ana-tomy* ● **anatomical** /ˌænə'tɒmɪkəl/ *adjective* **anatomik**

ancestor /'ænsestəʳ/ *noun* [C] a relative who lived a long time ago **ced, ata** *My ancestors came from Ireland.* ● **ancestral** /æn'sestrᵊl/ *adjective* **geçmişteki atalara ait**

ancestry /'ænsestri/ *noun* [C, U] your relatives who lived a long time ago, or the origin of your family **soy, ced, ata, çok eski atalar** *Americans of Japanese ancestry*

anchor¹ /'æŋkəʳ/ *noun* [C] **1** a heavy, metal object that is dropped into water to stop a boat from moving **çıpa 2** *US* someone who reads the news and announcements on a

anchor

television or radio programme **televizyon ve radyoda duyuruları yapan, haberleri sunan kişi, ankorman**

anchor² /'æŋkəʳ/ *verb* **1** [BOAT] [I, T] to stop a boat from moving by dropping a heavy metal object into the water **demir atmak, demirlemek, çıpayı suya indirmek** **2** [FASTEN] [T] to make something or someone stay in one position by fastening them firmly **bir şeyin, birinin bir yerde sabit durmasını sağlamak** *We anchored ourselves to the rocks with a rope.* **3** [PROGRAMME] [T] *US* to read the news or announcements on television or radio as your job **televizyon veya radyoda haber bültenlerini sunmak**

ancient /'eɪnʃ³nt/ *adjective* **1** [always before noun] from a long time ago **eskiden olan, çok önceleri olan, eskiden** *ancient Greece/Rome* ○ *an ancient building* **2** *humorous* very old **eski, antika** *This computer is ancient.*

o⊷**and** *strong form* /ænd/ *weak forms* /ənd/, /ən/ *conjunction* **1** [JOIN] used to join two words or two parts of a sentence **ve anlamına gelen bağlaç** *tea and coffee* ○ *We were tired and hungry.* **2** [AFTER] used to say that one thing happens after another thing **sıra olan hadiseleri anlatırken sıralamada kullanılan bağlaç** *I got dressed and had my breakfast.* **3** [SO] so **böylece, böylelikle, bu nedenle** *The car wouldn't start and I had to get a taxi.* **4** [AFTER VERB] *mainly UK* used instead of 'to' after some verbs, such as 'try' and 'go' **bazı fiillerden sonra 'to' anlamında kullanılır** *Try and eat something.* **5** [NUMBERS] used when saying or adding numbers **rakamları söylemede veya toplamada kullanılır** *It cost a hundred and twenty pounds.* ○ *UK Two and three equals five.* **6** [EMPHASIZE] used between two words that are the same to make their meaning stronger **aynı iki kelime arasında anlamı daha da kuvvetlendirmek için kullanılır** *The sound grew louder and louder.*

anecdote /'ænɪkdəʊt/ *noun* [C] a short story that you tell someone about something that happened to you or someone else **kısa hikaye, anlatım** *a speech full of anecdotes* ● **anecdotal** /ˌænɪk'dəʊt³l/ *adjective* consisting of things that people have said, and not facts **gerçeklerden çok söylenenlere dayalı, aslı astarı olmayan** *anecdotal evidence*

anemia /ə'niːmiə/ *noun* [U] *US spelling of* anaemia (= a medical condition in which your blood does not contain enough red cells) **kansızlık, anemi**

anemic /ə'niːmɪk/ *adjective US spelling of* anaemic (= having anemia) **anemik, kansızlığı olan, kansız**

anesthetic /ˌænəs'θetɪk/ *noun* [C, U] *US spelling of* anaesthetic (= a drug that makes you unable to feel pain during an operation) **anestezi, uyuşturan ilaç, bayıltıcı ilaç**

anesthetist /ə'nesθətɪst/ *noun* [C] *US spelling of* anaesthetist (= a doctor who gives anaesthetics to people) **anestezist, anestezi uzmanı doktor**

anew /ə'njuː/ *adverb literary* If you do something anew, you do it again in a different way. **yeniden, farklı/yeni bir şekilde** *Moving to another city gave me the chance to start anew.*

angel /'eɪndʒ³l/ *noun* [C] **1** a spiritual creature like a human with wings, who some people believe lives with God in heaven **melek 2** a very good, kind person **melek gibi kişi, çok iyi insan** *Be an angel and get me*

angel

a drink. ● **angelic** /æn'dʒelɪk/ *adjective* very beautiful or good **çok güzel, çok iyi, anjelik** *an angelic child*

express/show anger ● **be trembling with** anger ● **in** anger ● **public** anger ● **mounting/growing** anger ● anger **at/over** sth

o⊷**anger¹** /'æŋgəʳ/ *noun* [U] a strong feeling against someone who has behaved badly, making you want to shout at them or hurt them **öfke, kızgınlık, hiddet** *public anger at the terrorist killings* ○ *He never once raised his voice in anger.*

anger² /'æŋgəʳ/ *verb* [T] to make someone angry **öfkelenmek, kızmak, hiddetlenmek** [often passive] *Students were angered by the college's decision.*

angle¹ /'æŋgl/ *noun* [C] **1** [SPACE] a space between two lines or surfaces that meet at one point, which you measure in degrees **açı** *an angle of 90 degrees* **2 at an angle** not horizontal or vertical, but sloping **dikey veya yatay değil, eğimli olarak** *He wore his hat at an angle.* **3** [WAY OF THINKING] the way you think about a situation **düşünce, bakış tarzı, biçimi** *Try looking at the problem from my angle.* **4** [DIRECTION] the direction from which you look at something **bakış açısı** *This is the same building photographed from different angles.* Ↄ*See also:* right angle.

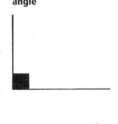

angle

angle² /'æŋgl/ *verb* [T] to aim or turn something in a direction that is not horizontal or vertical **eğimli, meyilli hale getirmek** *She angled a shot into the corner of the court.*

be angling for sth *phrasal verb* to try to get something without asking for it in a direct way **bir şeyi doğrudan istememek, dolaylı bir şekilde elde etmeye çalışmak** *Is he angling for an invitation?*

angler /'æŋgləʳ/ *noun* [C] someone who catches fish as a hobby or sport **amatör balıkçı**

Anglican /'æŋglɪkən/ *adjective* belonging or relating to the Church of England (= the official church in England) **Anglikan kilisesine mensup, Anglikan** ● **Anglican** *noun* [C] **Anglikan**

angling /'æŋglɪŋ/ *noun* [U] the sport or hobby of catching fish **amatör balıkçılık, balık tutma**

Anglo- /æŋgləʊ-/ *prefix* of or connected with Britain or England **Britanya veya İngiltere ile ilişkili veya oradan anlamında önek** *Anglo-Indian, Anglo-Saxon*

Bir kişi eğer olan bir olaydan dolayı sinirli ise, bu durumda **annoyed** veya **irritated** kelimeleri kullanılabilir. *He was a bit annoyed with her for being late.* ● *I was irritated that he didn't thank me.*

Kişinin çok sinirli olduğunu belirtmek için **furious, irate** veya **livid** sıfatları kullanılabilir. *My boss was furious with me.* ● *Hundreds of irate passengers have complained to the airline.*

Eğer bir çocuğa kızmışsanız, kendinizi **cross** kelimesiyle tanımlayabilirsiniz. *I'm* **cross** *with you for not telling me where you were going.*
Up in arms ifadesi bazen kişilerin haksız bir durumla karşı karşıya kaldıklarını düşündükleri durumlarda kullanılır. *Local people are* up in arms *over plans to close the local swimming pool.*
Eğer kişi çok ani bir şekilde sinirlenmişse, resmi bir ifade olmayan **go crazy/mad** kullanılır. *Dad went* crazy/mad *when he found out we'd broken the window.*

o⟶**angry** /'æŋgri/ *adjective* having a strong feeling against someone who has behaved badly, making you want to shout at them or hurt them **kızgın, sinirli, hiddetli, asabi** *He's really* **angry** *at/with me for upsetting Sophie.* ○ *I don't understand what he's* **angry** *about.* ● **angrily** *adverb* **sinirli bir şekilde**

angst /æŋst/ *noun* [U] a strong feeling of worry and unhappiness **aşırı mutsuzluk ve endişe** *teenage angst*

anguish /'æŋgwɪʃ/ *noun* [U] extreme suffering, especially mental suffering **şiddetli ıstırap, elem, keder, özellikle zihinsel ızdırap** *It's the anguish of knowing that I can do nothing to help.* ● **anguished** *adjective* [always before noun] *anguished parents* **kederli**

angular /'æŋgjʊlə'/ *adjective* An angular shape or object has a lot of straight lines and sharp points. **çizgili, köşeli, sivri uçları olan** *an angular face*

o⟶**animal**[1] /'ænɪmᵊl/ *noun* [C] 1 [NOT A HUMAN] something that lives and moves but is not a person, bird, fish, or insect **hayvan** *a wild animal* ○ *She's a real animal lover.* 2 [NOT A PLANT] anything that lives and moves, including people, birds, etc **yaşayan canlılar** *Are humans the only animals to use language?* 3 [CRUEL PERSON] *informal* a very cruel and violent person **hayvan gibi kimse, kaba saba kimse**

animal[2] /'ænɪmᵊl/ *adjective* [always before noun] Animal qualities and feelings relate to your basic physical needs. **hayvani, hayvan gibi** *animal passion*

animate /'ænɪmət/ *adjective formal* alive **canlı, yaşayan** ⊃Opposite inanimate.

animated /'ænɪmeɪtɪd/ *adjective* 1 showing a lot of interest and excitement **canlı, coşkulu, heyecan dolu** *an animated conversation* 2 An animated film is one in which drawings and models seem to move. **canlandırılan, canlı, canlı gibi hareket eden çizim ve modeller**

animation /,ænɪ'meɪʃᵊn/ *noun* 1 [U] interest and excitement **ilgi ve heyecan, canlılık** *She spoke with great animation.* 2 [C, U] an animated film, or the process of making animated films **animasyon, canlandırma** *computer animation*

animosity /,ænɪ'mɒsəti/ *noun* [C, U] when someone hates or feels angry towards someone else **kızgınlık, kin, öfke** *There is no animosity between the two teams.*

ankle /'æŋkl/ *noun* [C] the part of your leg that is just above your foot **ayak bileği** ⊃Orta kısımdaki renkli sayfalarına bakınız.

annex[1] /ə'neks/ *verb* [T] to start to rule or control an area or country next to your own **komşu ülkeyi veya bölgeyi kontrol veya yönetmeye başlamak** ● **annexation** /,ænek'seɪʃᵊn/ *noun* [C, U] **katma, ekleme**

annex[2] *(also UK annexe)* /'æneks/ *noun* [C] a building that is joined to a larger one **müştemilat, eklenti, küçük yapı**

annihilate /ə'naɪleɪt/ *verb* [T] 1 to destroy something completely **bir şeyi tamamen yok etmek, imha etmek** *a city annihilated by an atomic bomb* 2 *informal* to defeat someone very easily **birini kolayca yenmek,**

bertaraf etmek ● **annihilation** /ə,naɪ'leɪʃᵊn/ *noun* [U] **imha**

anniversary ...... İLE BİRLİKTE KULLANILAN KELİMELER

the [10th/50th/500th, etc] anniversary of sth ● **commemorate/mark** an anniversary ● sb's **wedding** anniversary ● anniversary **celebrations**

anniversary /,ænɪ'vɜːsᵊri/ *noun* [C] a date on which you remember or celebrate something that happened on that date one or more years ago **yıldönümü** *a wedding anniversary* ○ *the 40th anniversary of Kennedy's death* ⊃See also: silver wedding anniversary.

o⟶**announce** /ə'naʊns/ *verb* [T] to tell people about something officially or with force or confidence **duyurmak, ilan etmek, anons etmek** *The company has announced plans to open six new stores.* ○ [+ (that)] *Halfway through dinner, he announced that he was going out.*

announcement ...... İLE BİRLİKTE KULLANILAN KELİMELER

make an announcement ● a **formal/official/public** announcement ● an announcement **about/on** sth ● an announcement **by/from** sb

o⟶**announcement** /ə'naʊnsmənt/ *noun* 1 [C] something that someone says officially, giving information about something **duyuru, ilan, anons** *The Prime Minister made an unexpected announcement this morning.* 2 [no plural] when someone announces something **duyurulan, ilan edilen**

announcer /ə'naʊnsə'/ *noun* [C] someone who introduces programmes on the radio or television **anons spikeri, duyuran kimse**

annoy /ə'nɔɪ/ *verb* [T] to make someone slightly angry **kızdırmak, rahatsız etmek** *He's always late and it's starting to annoy me.*

annoyance /ə'nɔɪəns/ *noun* [U] the feeling of being annoyed **kızgınlık, rahatsızlık, huzursuzluk** *He kept losing his keys, much to the annoyance of* (= which annoyed) *his wife.*

annoyed /ə'nɔɪd/ *adjective* slightly angry **kızgın, rahatsız** *I was a bit* **annoyed** *with/at Kathy for not coming.*

annoying /ə'nɔɪɪŋ/ *adjective* making you feel annoyed **kızdıran, rahatsızlık veren, huzursuz eden** *an annoying habit/cough*

o⟶**annual**[1] /'ænjuəl/ *adjective* 1 happening or produced once a year **yıllık, yılda bir olan** *an annual meeting/report* 2 measured over a period of one year **yılda bir kez** *annual rainfall* ● **annually** *adverb* **her yıl**

annual[2] /'ænjuəl/ *noun* [C] 1 a plant which grows, produces seed, and dies within one year **yıllık bitki, ömrü bir yıl olan bitki** 2 a book produced every year containing new information about the same subject **yıllık, yılda bir çıkarılan kitap, ajanda**

annulment /ə'nʌlmənt/ *noun* [C, U] *formal* when a court says officially that a marriage or agreement does not now exist and was never legal **bir evlilik veya antlaşmayı yasal olarak fesh etme, yürürlükten kaldırma**

anomaly /ə'nɒməli/ *noun* [C] *formal* something that is unusual and that does not seem right **anormallik, olağan dışı bir şey** *There are some anomalies in the data.*

anonymity /,ænə'nɪməti/ *noun* [U] when someone's name is not given or known **isim vermeden, ismini saklayarak, gizlice** *She agreed to speak to a journalist but requested anonymity.*

anonymous /ə'nɒnɪməs/ *adjective* not giving a name **isimsiz, anonim** *an anonymous phone call* ○ *The win-*

ner has asked to **remain anonymous.** ● **anonymously** *adverb* **ismini açıklamadan**

anorak /ˈænᵊræk/ *noun* [C] *UK* **1** a jacket with a hood (= part that covers your head) that protects you from rain and cold **anorak 2** *humorous* a boring person who is too interested in the details of a hobby and who is not good in social situations **zevk için yapılan bir şeyin detayıyla uğraşan ve sosyal durumlarda iyi olmayan sıkıcı kişi, asosyal kişi**

anorexia /ˌænᵊrˈeksiə/ (*also* anorexia nervosa /ænər-ˌeksiənɜːˈvəʊsə/) *noun* [U] a mental illness in which someone refuses to eat and becomes very thin **iştahsızlık, anoreksiya, yemek yiyememek**

anorexic /ˌænᵊrˈeksɪk/ *adjective* having the illness anorexia **iştahsız, yemek yiyemeyen** ● **anorexic** *noun* [C] **anoreksik**

o➔**another** /əˈnʌðᵊr/ *pronoun, determiner* **1** one more person or thing, or an additional amount **diğeri, diğer, bir başkası, bir diğeri** *Would you like another piece of cake?* ○ *We can fit another person in my car.* **2** a different person or thing **diğer bir kişi ya da şey, öteki, diğeri, öbürü** *I'm going to look for another job.* ○ *This one's slightly damaged - I'll get you another.*

o➔**answer¹** /ˈɑːnsᵊr/ *verb* **1** [WORDS] [I, T] to speak or write back to someone who has asked you a question or spoken to you **cevap vermek, yanıtlamak** *I asked when she was leaving but she didn't answer.* ○ *I must answer his letter.* **2** [DOOR] [I, T] to open the door when someone has knocked on it or rung a bell **kapıya bakmak** *I knocked several times but no one answered.* **3** [TELEPHONE] [I, T] to pick up the telephone receiver (= part that you hold to your ear) when it rings **telefona cevap vermek, cevaplamak** *Could someone answer the phone?* **4** [TEST] [T] to write or say something as a reply to a question in a test or competition **sınavda cevap vermek, yanıtlamak, soruları cevaplamak**
answer (sb) back *phrasal verb* If a child answers back, they reply rudely to an adult. **kabaca cevap vermek, karşılık vermek**
answer for sth *phrasal verb* **1** to be responsible for something, or punished for something **bir şeyden sorumlu tutulmak veya cezalandırılmak** *Do you think parents should have to answer for their children's behaviour?* **2** **have a lot to answer for** to be the main cause of something bad which has happened *"Why is violent crime on the increase?" " Well, I think television has a lot to answer for."*

┌───┐
│ **answer** ...... İLE BİRLİKTE KULLANILAN KELİMELER │
└───┘
get/give/know/provide an answer ● **a correct/simple/wrong** answer ● **the** answer **to** sth

o➔**answer²** /ˈɑːnsᵊr/ *noun* [C] **1** [WORDS] what you say or write back to someone who has asked you a question or spoken to you **cevap, yanıt** *I asked him if he was going but I didn't hear his answer.* ○ *Please give me your answer by next week.* **2** [DOOR/TELEPHONE] When someone answers the telephone or the door **kapıya, telefona bakma** [usually singular] *I rang the bell but there was no answer.* **3** [SOLUTION] a way of solving a problem **cevap** *It's a difficult situation and I don't know what the answer is.* **4** [TEST] the correct number or information given as a reply to a question in a test or competition **yanıt, sorunun cevabı** *Did you get the answer to Question 6?*

answerphone /ˈɑːnsəfəʊn/ *UK* (*UK/US* answering machine) *noun* [C] a machine that records your message if you telephone someone and they do not answer **telesekreter, evde kimse yokken telefonu doğrudan yanıtlayan makina** *I left a message on her answerphone.*

ant /ænt/ *noun* [C] a small, black or red insect that lives in groups on the ground **karınca** ⊃See picture at insect.

antagonism /ænˈtægᵊnɪzᵊm/ *noun* [U] feelings of strong disagreement or hate **kötülük, düşmanlık, kin** *There's a history of antagonism between the two teams.*

antagonistic /ænˌtægᵊnˈɪstɪk/ *adjective* strongly disagreeing with someone or something **şiddetle karşı çıkan, hiç tasvip etmeyen, karşı olan, kötümser davranan** *He's antagonistic towards critics.*

antagonize (*also UK* -ise) /ænˈtægᵊnaɪz/ *verb* [T] to make someone angry or unfriendly towards you **birinin düşmanca, samimiyetsizce davranmasına neden olmak, kızdırmak, düşman etmek** *He's antagonized colleagues by making changes without discussing them.*

the Antarctic /ænˈtɑːktɪk/ *noun* the very cold area around the South Pole **Antartika** ● **Antarctic** *adjective* [always before noun] *Antarctic wildlife* **Antartik**

antelope /ˈæntɪləʊp/ *noun* [C] an animal like a large deer with long horns **antilop, uzun boynuzlu büyük bir geyiği andıran hayvan**

antenatal /ˌæntɪˈneɪtᵊl/ *UK* (*US* prenatal) *adjective* [always before noun] relating to pregnant women before their babies are born **doğum öncesi olan, doğum öncesi hamile kadınlara ilişkin** *an antenatal class*

antenna /ænˈtenə/ *noun* [C] **1** *plural* **antennae** one of two long, thin parts on the head of an insect or sea creature, used for feeling things **anteni, olan böcek veya deniz canlısı** **2** *plural* **antennae** or **antennas** *US* (*UK* aerial) a piece of metal that is used for receiving television or radio signals **anten, almaç** ⊃Orta kısımdaki renkli sayfalarına bakınız.

anthem /ˈænθəm/ *noun* [C] a song chosen by a country or organization to be sung on special occasions **marş** ⊃See also: national anthem.

anthology /ænˈθɒlədʒi/ *noun* [C] a book which includes stories or poems written by different people **birçok kişi tarafından yazılan şiir ve hikayelerin bir arada olduğu kitap, antoloji**

anthropology /ˌænθrəˈpɒlədʒi/ *noun* [U] the scientific study of human development and society or different societies **insanbilim, antropolji** ● **anthropologist** /ˌænθrəˈpɒlədʒɪst/ *noun* [C] **antropolog** ● **anthropological** /ˌænθrəpəˈlɒdʒɪkᵊl/ *adjective* **antropolojik**

anti- /ˈænti-/ ⟨US⟩ /ˈæntaɪ/ *prefix* **1** opposed to or against **karşı, ters, zıt anlamında önek** *anti-terrorist laws, anti-American protesters* **2** opposite of or preventing **bir şeyin karşıtı ya da önleyeni anlamında önek** *anti-clockwise movement, anti-lock brakes, anti-depressant drugs* ⊃Compare pro-.

antibiotic /ˌæntibaɪˈɒtɪk/ ⟨US⟩ /ˌæntaɪ-/ *noun* [C] a medicine which cures infections by destroying harmful bacteria **antibiyotik** [usually plural] *He is on antibiotics for an ear infection.*

antibody /ˈæntiˌbɒdi/ *noun* [C] a substance produced in your blood to fight disease **antikor**

anticipate /ænˈtɪsɪpeɪt/ *verb* [T] to expect something, or to prepare for something before it happens **merakla beklemek, ummak** *to anticipate a problem* ○ [+ that] *We anticipate that prices will fall next year.*

anticipation /ænˌtɪsɪˈpeɪʃᵊn/ *noun* [U] **1** when you are waiting for something to happen, usually with excitement **ümit, beklenti** *The children were breathless with anticipation.* **2** **in anticipation (of)** in preparation for something happening **beklentisiyle, ümidiyle** *She's even decorated the spare room in anticipation of your visit.*

A

anticlimax /ˌæntɪˈklaɪmæks/ ⓤ /ˌæntaɪ-/ *noun* [C, U] a disappointing experience, often one that you thought would be exciting before it happened or one that comes after a more exciting experience **hayal kırıklığı, düş kırıklığı, beklenen bir şeyin tam aksinin olması** *After so much preparation, the party was a bit of an anticlimax.*

anti-clockwise /ˌæntɪˈklɒkwaɪz/ *UK* (*US* **counterclockwise**) *adjective, adverb* in the opposite direction to the way the hands (= parts that point to the numbers) of a clock move **saat yönünün aksine, aksinde olan** *Turn the knob anti-clockwise.* ᗺSee picture at **clockwise**.

antics /ˈæntɪks/ *noun* [plural] unusual or bad behaviour that entertains or annoys people **maskaralık, soytarılık** *He's well known for his antics on and off the tennis court.*

anti-depressant /ˌæntɪdɪˈpresᵊnt/ ⓤ /ˌæntaɪ-/ *noun* [C] a medicine for people who are depressed (= severely unhappy) **sıkıntı, mutsuzluk ve huzursuzluğu giderici ilaç, antidepresan**

antidote /ˈæntɪdəʊt/ *noun* [C] **1 antidote to sth** an activity that stops something bad from harming you **bir şeyi birine zarar vermekten alıkoyan bir faaliyet, eylem, önleyici** *Exercise is the best antidote to stress.* **2** a substance that stops another substance from damaging your body **bir başka maddenin vücuda verebileceği zararı önleyen madde, panzehir** *a deadly poison with no antidote*

anti-oxidant /ˌæntiˈɒksɪdənt/ ⓤ /ˌæntaɪ-/ *noun* [C] **1** a substance that slows down the rate at which something decays because of oxidization (= combining with oxygen) **paslanmayı yavaşlatan ve önleyen madde, anitoksidan 2** a substance, for example a vitamin in food, that protects your body from damage **vücudu yıpranmaktan koruyan, yiyeceklerin içinde bulunan bir madde**

antipathy /ænˈtɪpəθi/ *noun* [U] *formal* a strong feeling of dislike for someone **sevmeme, hoşlanmama, hoşnut olmama, antipati** *He is a private man with a deep antipathy to/towards the press.*

antiperspirant /ˌæntɪˈpɜːspᵊrənt/ ⓤ /ˌæntaɪ-/ *noun* [C, U] a substance that prevents you from becoming wet under your arms when you are hot **terlemeyi önleyen, terlemeyi giderici**

antiquated /ˈæntɪkweɪtɪd/ *adjective* very old and not modern enough **çok eski olan, antikalaşmış, bayağı eski olan** *an antiquated system*

antique /ænˈtiːk/ *noun* [C] an object that is old, and often rare or beautiful **antika, değerli, nadir bulunan bir nesne** *His home is full of valuable antiques.* ○ *an antique shop* ● **antique** *adjective* antique furniture/china **eskiye ait, antik**

antiquity /ænˈtɪkwəti/ *noun* **1** [U] *formal* the ancient past **çok eski geçmiş, eski çağlar** *the writers of antiquity* **2** [C] an ancient object **çok eski, antika bir nesne** [usually plural] *priceless Egyptian antiquities*

anti-Semitism /ˌæntɪˈsemɪtɪzᵊm/ ⓤ /ˌæntaɪ-/ *noun* [U] when someone hates Jewish people, or treats them in a cruel or unfair way **Yahudi karşıtlığı** ● **anti-Semitic** /ˌæntɪsɪˈmɪtɪk/ *adjective* **Yahudi toplumunu sevmeyen**

antiseptic /ˌæntɪˈseptɪk/ *noun* [C, U] a substance that you put on an injury to prevent infection **enfeksiyon önleyici madde, antiseptik** ● **antiseptic** *adjective* antiseptic cream **antiseptik**

anti-social /ˌæntɪˈsəʊʃᵊl/ ⓤ /ˌæntaɪ-/ *adjective* **1** Anti-social behaviour harms or upsets the people around you. **sosyal olmayan, toplum dışı olan, topluma zararlı ya da düşman** *Increasingly, smoking is regar-* ded as an anti-social habit. **2** An anti-social person does not like being with other people. **toplum dışında olan, toplumla uyum sağlayamayan**

anti-spam /ˌæntɪˈspæm/ ⓤ /ˌæntaɪ-/ *adjective* [always before noun] used to stop people sending or receiving emails that are not wanted, especially advertisements **gereksiz elektronik gönderileri engelleyen, lüzumsuz elektronik gönderilerin gelmesini engelleyen** *anti-spam legislation*

anti-terrorist /ˌæntɪˈterᵊrɪst/ ⓤ /ˌæntaɪ-/ *adjective* intended to prevent or reduce terrorism (= the use of violence for political purposes) **terör karşıtı olan, terörü azaltmaya yönelik** *anti-terrorist laws/legislation*

antithesis /ænˈtɪθəsɪs/ *noun* [C] *plural* **antitheses** /ænˈtɪθəsiːz/ *formal* the exact opposite **karşı görüş, karşı tez, bir şeyin tam karşıtı görüş, tez, sav** [usually singular] *She is slim and shy - the antithesis of her sister.*

anti-virus /ˌæntiˈvaɪərəs/ ⓤ /ˌæntaɪ-/ *adjective* [always before noun] produced and used to protect the main memory of a computer against infection by a virus **bilgisayarın hafızasını virüs bulaşmasına karşı korumak için üretilen ve kullanılan** *anti-virus software/programs*

antler /ˈæntləʳ/ *noun* [C] a horn that looks like branches on the head of a male deer **erkek geyiğin ağaç dallarını andıran boynuzu**

anus /ˈeɪnəs/ *noun* [C] a hole where solid waste comes out of the body **makat, anüs**

┌─────────────────────────────────┐
│ **anxiety** ...... İLE BİRLİKTE KULLANILAN KELİMELER │
└─────────────────────────────────┘

a cause/source of anxiety ● feelings/levels of anxiety ● anxiety about/over sth

anxiety /æŋˈzaɪəti/ *noun* [C, U] the feeling of being very worried **endişe, korku, vesvese, tasa, kaygı** *That explains his anxiety about her health.*

anxious /ˈæŋkʃəs/ *adjective* **1** worried and nervous **endişeli, sinirli, tasalı, kaygılı** *She's very anxious about her exams.* **2** wanting to do something or wanting something to happen **bir şeyin olmasını ya da yapmayı heyecanla isteyen, bekleyen, endişe duyan** [+ to do sth] *He's anxious to get home.* ○ [+ that] *I was anxious that no one else should know.* ● **anxiously** *adverb* We **waited anxiously** by the phone. **endişeli bir şekilde**

◦▪**any¹** *strong form* /ˈeni/ *weak form* /əni/ *pronoun, determiner* **1** used in questions and negatives to mean 'some' **hiç, soru ve olumsuz cümlelerde biraz anlamında** *Is there any of that lemon cake left?* ○ *I haven't seen any of his films.* ○ *I asked Andrew for some change but he hasn't got any.* **2** one or each of a particular kind of person or thing when it is not important which **biri, herhangi biri** *Any advice that you can give me would be greatly appreciated.* ○ *Any of those shirts would be fine.*

◦▪**any²** *strong form* /ˈeni/ *weak form* /əni/ *adverb* used in questions and negatives to emphasize a comparative adjective or adverb **bir üstünlük derecesi bildiren sıfat veya zarfları vurgulamak için soru ve olumsuz cümlelerde kullanılır** *Do you feel any better?* ○ *I can't walk any faster.* ○ *She couldn't wait any longer.*

◦▪**anybody** /ˈeniˌbɒdi/ *pronoun* another word for anyone **herhangi bir kimse, herhangi biririsi**

anyhow /ˈenihaʊ/ (*also* **anyway**) *adverb* **1** [MORE IMPORTANTLY] used to give a more important reason for something that you are saying **her nasılsa, zaten** *I don't need a car and I can't afford one anyhow.* **2** [DESPITE] despite that **tüm bunlara rağmen, rağmen** *He hates carrots but he ate them anyhow.* **3** [IN CONVERSATION] used when you are returning to an earlier subject **her neyse** *Anyhow, as I said, I'll be away next week.* **4** |CHANGING STATEMENT| used when you want to slightly change something that you have just said **zaten, nasılsa, söylenen üzerinde küçük bir değişiklik yapılacağı zaman kullanılır** *Boys aren't horrible - not all of them anyhow!*

ˌany ˈmore (*also* **anymore**) *adverb* If you do not do something or something does not happen any more, you have stopped doing it or it does not now happen. **artık, bundan böyle** *This coat doesn't fit me any more.*

☞**anyone** /ˈeniwʌn/ (*also* **anybody**) *pronoun* **1** used in questions and negatives to mean 'a person or people' **herhangi bir kimse** *I didn't know anyone at the party.* ○ *Does anyone else* (= another person/other people) *want to come?* **2** any person or any people **biri, birisi, birileri** *Anyone can go - you don't have to be invited.*

anyplace /ˈenipleɪs/ *adverb US* anywhere **herhangi bir yer**

☞**anything** /ˈeniθɪŋ/ *pronoun* **1** used in questions and negatives to mean 'something' **hiçbir şey** *I haven't got anything to wear.* ○ *Was there anything else* (= another thing) *you wanted to say?* **2** any object, event, or situation **hiçbir, hiçbiri** *We can do anything you like.* ○ *Tom will eat anything.* **3 anything like** used in questions and negatives to mean 'at all similar to' **benzeyen herhangi bir şey** *Does he look anything like his brother?*

☞**anyway** /ˈeniweɪ/ (*also* **anyhow**) (*also US* **anyways** *spoken*) *adverb* **1** |MORE IMPORTANTLY| used to give a more important reason for something that you are saying **zaten, her nasılsa, her durumda, yine de** *We can drive you to the station - we go that way anyway.* **2** |DESPITE| despite that **tüm bunlara rağmen, rağmen** *He hates carrots but he ate them anyway.* **3** |IN CONVERSATION| used when you are returning to an earlier subject **her neyse** *Anyway, as I said, I'll be away next week.* **4** |CHANGING STATEMENT| used when you want to slightly change something that you have just said **zaten, nasılsa, söylenen üzerinde küçük bir değişiklik yapılacağı zaman kullanılır** *Boys aren't horrible - not all of them anyway!*

☞**anywhere** /ˈeniweər/ (*also US* **anyplace**) *adverb* **1** in or to any place **herhangi bir yere/yerde** *Just sit anywhere.* ○ *I couldn't find a post office anywhere.* **2** used in questions and negatives to mean 'a place' **soru ve olumsuz cümlelerde 'herhangi bir yere' anlamında kullanılır** *He doesn't have anywhere to stay.* ○ *Is there anywhere else you'd like to visit while you're here?* **3 anywhere near sth** used in questions and negatives to mean 'close to being or doing something' **bir şeyi yapmaya veya bir yerde olmaya' çok yakın anlamında** *The house isn't anywhere near ready.* **4 not get anywhere** *informal* to not make any progress **hiç bir yere varamamak, bir sonuç elde edememek** *I tried discussing the problem with her but I didn't get anywhere.*

☞**apart** /əˈpɑːt/ *adverb* **1** |SEPARATED| separated by a space or period of time **ayrı, ayrılmış, ayrık, başka** *Stand with your feet wide apart.* ○ *Our kids were born just eighteen months apart.* **2** |INTO PIECES| into separate, smaller pieces **küçük parçalar/ayrılan, ayırmaya doğru, ayırt edilebilecek şekilde** *My jacket is coming/falling apart.* **3 apart from a** |EXCEPT| except for ... **den başka, ayrıca, ...den gayri** *Apart from Jodie, who hurt her leg, all the children were fine.* **b** |IN ADDITION| in addition to **yanısıra, ilaveten, ayrıca buna ilave olarak** *He works a ten-hour day and that's apart from the work he does at the weekend.*

apartheid /əˈpɑːtaɪt/ *noun* [U] in the past in South Africa, a political system in which white people had power over black people and made them live separately **geçmişte Güney Afrika'da onları ayrı yaşamaya** zorlayan beyazların siyahlar üzerinde gücü olduğunu gösteren siyasi sistem, ırk ayrımcılığı

☞**apartment** /əˈpɑːtmənt/ *noun* [C] *mainly US* a set of rooms for someone to live in on one level of a building or house **daire**

aˈpartment ˌbuilding *noun* [C] *US* a building which is divided into apartments **apartman**

apathetic /ˌæpəˈθetɪk/ *adjective* not interested in anything or willing to change things **ilgisiz, duyarsız, duygusuz** *Young people today are so apathetic about politics.*

apathy /ˈæpəθi/ *noun* [U] when someone is not interested in anything or willing to change things **duyarsızlık, ilgisizlik**

ape /eɪp/ *noun* [C] a hairy animal like a monkey but with no tail and long arms **uzun kolları olan kuyruğu olmayan maymun benzeri hayvan, bir tür maymun**

ape

aperitif /əˌperəˈtiːf/ *noun* [C] a small alcoholic drink before a meal **yemekten önce alınan içki, aperatif**

aperture /ˈæpətʃər/ *noun* [C] a small hole, especially one that allows light into a camera **fotoğraf makinasının ışık almasını sağlayan küçük delik**

apex /ˈeɪpeks/ *noun* [C] the highest part of a shape **doruk, zirve, en tepe nokta** *the apex of a pyramid*

apiece /əˈpiːs/ *adverb* each **her biri** *Dolls from this period sell for £300 apiece.*

the apocalypse /əˈpɒkəlɪps/ *noun* in some religions, the final destruction of the world **kıyamet günü, dünyanın sonu**

apocalyptic /əˌpɒkəˈlɪptɪk/ *adjective* showing or describing the destruction of the world **kıyamete benzer, herşeyin yok oluşuna benzer** *an apocalyptic vision of the future*

apologetic /əˌpɒləˈdʒetɪk/ *adjective* showing or saying that you are sorry about something **pişman, özür dileyen** *an apologetic smile* ○ *She was very apologetic about missing the meeting.*

apologize (*also UK* **-ise**) /əˈpɒlədʒaɪz/ *verb* [I] to tell someone that you are sorry about something you have done **özür dilemek, pişmanlığını bildirmek** *The bank apologized for the error.* ○ *The pilot apologized to passengers for the delay.*

🧩 **apology** .... İLE BİRLİKTE KULLANILAN KELİMELER

demand/make/owe sb/**receive** an apology ● **accept** sb's apology ● **make no** apology **for** (doing) sth ● a formal/full/public apology ● an apology **for** sth ● an apology **to** sb

apology /əˈpɒlədʒi/ *noun* [C, U] something you say or write to say that you are sorry about something you have done **özür, pişmanlık bildiren söz veya yazı** *I have an apology to make to you - I opened your letter by mistake.* ○ *a letter of apology*

apostle /əˈpɒsl/ *noun* [C] one of the twelve men chosen by Jesus Christ to teach people about Christianity **havari, oniki havariden biri**

apostrophe /əˈpɒstrəfi/ *noun* [C] **1** a mark (') used to show that letters or numbers are absent (') **işareti, kesme işareti** *I'm* (= I am) *hungry.* ○ *I graduated in '98*

A

(= 1998). **2** a punctuation mark (') used before the letter 's' to show that something belongs to someone or something **bir noktalama işareti, kesme işareti** *I drove my brother's car.* ⊃See study page **Punctuation** on page Centre 33.

appal *UK* (*US* **appall**) /ə'pɔːl/ *verb* [T] **appalling**, *past* **appalled** to make someone extremely shocked or upset **şoke etmek, sarsmak, üzmek** *The amount of violence on television appals me.* ○ *We were **appalled at/by** her behaviour.* ● **appalled** *adjective* **şaşırmış**

appalling /ə'pɔːlɪŋ/ *adjective* **1** shocking and very unpleasant **şok edici, dehşet verici** *Many live in appalling conditions.* ○ *appalling injuries* **2** very bad **çok kötü, berbat** *appalling behaviour/weather* ● **appallingly** *adverb* **şaşırmış bir şekilde**

apparatus /ˌæpər'eɪtəs/ ⓊⓈ /ˌæpə'rætəs/ *noun* [C, U] *plural* **apparatus** or **apparatuses** a set of equipment or tools used for a particular purpose **aletler** *The diver wore breathing apparatus.*

apparel /ə'pærəl/ *noun* [U] *mainly US* clothes **giysiler** *children's/women's apparel*

apparent /ə'pærᵊnt/ *adjective* **1** obvious or easy to notice **aşikâr, açık, görünen** [+ that] *It soon became apparent that she had lost interest in the project.* ○ *Suddenly, for no apparent reason* (= without a reason) *he started screaming and shouting.* **2** [always before noun] seeming to exist or be true **belli, ortada, var olan** *I was a little surprised by her apparent lack of interest.*

◦~**apparently** /ə'pærəntli/ *adverb* **1** used to say that you have read or been told something although you are not certain it is true **görünen o ki, aşikâr olarak** *Apparently it's going to rain today.* **2** used to say that something seems to be true, although it is not certain **görünüşe göre, anlaşılan** *There were two apparently unrelated deaths.*

apparition /ˌæpᵊr'ɪʃᵊn/ *noun* [C] *literary* a ghost **hayalet**

╬╬╬ *appeal* .... İLE BİRLİKTE KULLANILAN KELİMELER

issue/launch/make an appeal ● an appeal for sth

appeal¹ /ə'piːl/ *noun* **1** REQUEST [C] when a lot of people are asked to give money, information, or help **ricada bulunma, isteme, yardım talep etme** *The appeal raised over £2 million for AIDS research.* **2** QUALITY [U] the quality in someone or something that makes them attractive or enjoyable **çekicilik, hoşluk, sevimlilik** *I've never understood the appeal of skiing.* **3** LAW [C] a request to a court of law to change a previous legal decision **yüksek mahkemeye başvuru, temyiz başvurusu** *He won his appeal against his jail sentence.*

appeal² /ə'piːl/ *verb* [I] **1** REQUEST to strongly request something, often publicly **talep etmek, rica etmek, istemek** *The police have appealed for more information.* ○ *They appealed to the commission to keep the hospital open.* **2** ATTRACT to attract or interest someone **çekmek, cezbetmek** *Cycling has never appealed to me.* **3** FORMALLY ASK to formally ask someone to change an official or legal decision **başvuruda bulunmak, resmen talep etmek, ricada bulunmak** *He is appealing against a ten-year prison sentence.*

appealing /ə'piːlɪŋ/ *adjective* attractive or interesting **çekici, ilgi uyandıran, cezbeden** *The idea of living in Paris is very appealing.* ● **appealingly** *adverb* **ilgi çekici şekilde**

◦~**appear** /ə'pɪər/ *verb* [I] **1** SEEM to seem to be a particular thing or have a particular quality **gibi gözükmek** *He appeared calm and relaxed.* ○ *She appeared to be crying.* ○ [+ (that)] *It appears that we were wrong about him.* **2** BE SEEN to start to be seen **görünmek, gözükmek, gözükmeye başlamak** *He suddenly appeared in the doorway.* ○ *Then a bright light appeared in the sky.*

⊃Opposite **disappear**. **3** BECOME AVAILABLE to start to exist or become available **ortaya çıkmak, var olmaya başlamak** *Laptop computers first appeared in the 1990s.* ○ *The story appeared in all the major newspapers.* **4** **appear in/ at/on, etc** to perform in a film, play, etc, or be seen in public **bir film, oyunda rol almak, toplum içinde gözükmek** *She appears briefly in the new Bond film.*

◦~**appearance** /ə'pɪərᵊns/ *noun* **1** IN PUBLIC [C] an occasion when someone appears in public **television/public appearance** ○ *He made two appearances during his brief visit.* **2** WAY YOU LOOK [no plural] the way a person or thing looks **görüntü, görünüm** *She's very concerned with her appearance.* **3** ARRIVAL [no plural] when you arrive somewhere or can be seen somewhere **gözükme, görünme** *Her appearance at the party was a surprise.* ⊃Opposite **disappearance**. **4** BECOMING AVAILABLE [no plural] when something starts to exist or becomes available **ortaya çıkma, gözükmeye başlama** *The appearance of new products on the market has increased competition.*

appease /ə'piːz/ *verb* [T] to avoid more arguments by doing what someone wants **birinin istediği gibi davranmak, huyuna suyuna gitmek, söyleneni yapmak** ● **appeasement** *noun* [U] **sakinleştirme**

appendicitis /əˌpendɪ'saɪtɪs/ *noun* [U] an illness in which your appendix becomes larger than usual and painful **apandist**

appendix /ə'pendɪks/ *noun* [C] **1** *plural* **appendixes** a small tube-shaped part inside the body below the stomach, attached to the large intestine **midenin alt kısmında küçük tüp şeklinde çıkıntı, bölüm, kör bağırsak 2** *plural* **appendices** a separate part at the end of a book, article, etc which contains extra information **kitap, makale vb. sonuna konulan ilave bilgi, ek**

╬╬╬ *appetite* .... İLE BİRLİKTE KULLANILAN KELİMELER

give sb/have an appetite ● lose your appetite ● a good/healthy/huge appetite ● loss of appetite

appetite /'æpɪtaɪt/ *noun* [C, U] **1** the feeling that makes you want to eat **iştah** *All that walking has given me an appetite.* **2 an appetite for sth** when you want something very much **bir şeyi çok arzu etme, iştahla isteme** *his appetite for adventure* **3 whet sb's appetite** to make someone want more of something **iştahını açmak, iştahını kabartmak, çok istemesini sağlamak**

appetizer /'æpɪtaɪzər/ *US* (*UK* **starter**) *noun* [C] something that you eat as the first part of a meal **iştah açıcı**

appetizing (*also UK* -ising) /'æpɪtaɪzɪŋ/ *adjective* If food is appetizing, it looks or smells as if it will taste good. **iştah açan, iştah kabartan**

applaud /ə'plɔːd/ *verb* **1** [I, T] to clap your hands to show that you enjoy a performance, talk, etc **alkışlamak, alkış tutmak** *The audience applauded loudly.* **2** [T] *formal* to approve of or admire something **beğenmek, onaylamak, takdir etmek** *Most people will surely applaud the decision.*

applause /ə'plɔːz/ *noun* [U] when people make a noise by clapping their hands to show they have enjoyed or approve of something **alkış** *There was loud applause at the end of her speech.*   **apple**

◦~**apple** /'æpl/ *noun* [C] a hard, round fruit with a green or red skin **elma** ⊃Orta kısmındaki renkli sayfalarına bakınız ⊃See also: **Adam's apple**.

applet /'æplət/ *noun* [C] a small computer program that is automatically copied on to a computer when you look at a document that needs this program to make it work **bir dokümanı incelerken bu programın çalışmasına gereksinim duyulduğunu varsayıp otomatik olarak bilgisayara kopyalanan küçük bir bilgisayar programı**

appliance /əˈplaɪəns/ noun [C] a piece of electrical equipment with a particular purpose in the home **elektrikli alet** *fridges, radios, and other **electrical appliances***

applicable /əˈplɪkəbl/ adjective affecting or relating to a person or situation **bir kişi ya da duruma ilişkin olan, etken olan, uygulanabilir** *This law is only **applicable to** people living in Europe.*

applicant /ˈæplɪkənt/ noun [C] someone who asks for something officially, often by writing **başvuran, müracaat eden kişi** *There were over fifty **applicants** for the job.*

application /ˌæplɪˈkeɪʃ°n/ noun 1 [REQUEST] [C] an official request for something, usually in writing **başvuru, müracaat** *an **application for** a bank loan* 2 [USE] [C, U] a way in which something can be used for a particular purpose **uyarlama** *This technology has many practical applications.* 3 [COMPUTER PROGRAM] [C] a computer program designed for a particular purpose **belirli bir amaç için tasarlanmış bilgisayar programı**

appliˈcation ˌform noun [C] a form that you use to officially ask for something, for example a job **başvuru formu**

applied /əˈplaɪd/ adjective **applied mathematics/science, etc** mathematics, science, or another subject which is studied for a practical use **uygulamalı matematik/fen**

apply /əˈplaɪ/ verb 1 [ASK] [I] to ask officially for something, often by writing **başvurmak, müracaatta bulunmak** *I've **applied for** a job.* ○ *He has **applied to** several companies.* 2 [AFFECT] [I] to affect or relate to a particular person or situation **belli bir durun ya da kişiyle ilişkilendirmek, etkilemek** *This law only **applies to** married people.* 3 [USE] [T] to use something in a particular situation **uygulamak, bir şeyi belli bir durum için kullanmak** *The same method can be **applied to** other situations.* 4 [ON SURFACE] [T] to spread a substance on a surface **sürmek, yaymak, bir yüzeye sürmek, uygulamak** *Apply the cream daily until the symptoms disappear.* 5 **apply yourself** to work hard **kendini bir şeye vermek, çok çalışmak** *If he doesn't apply himself, he'll never pass his exams.*

appoint /əˈpɔɪnt/ verb [T] to officially choose someone for a job **resmen atamak, görevlendirmek** *He was **appointed as** company director last year.*

appointed /əˈpɔɪntɪd/ adjective **appointed date/time/place, etc** the date, time, place, etc that has been chosen for something to happen **randevu tarihi/zamanı/yeri**

▓▒▓ appointment .... İLE BİRLİKTE KULLANILAN KELİMELER

have/make an appointment • cancel/keep/miss an appointment • an appointment with sb

o•▬**appointment** /əˈpɔɪntmənt/ noun 1 [C] a time you have arranged to meet someone or go somewhere **randevu** *a doctor's/dental appointment* ○ *I **made an appointment** with my hairdresser for next Monday.* 2 [C, U] when you officially choose someone for an important job, or the job itself **atama, görevlendirme** *the appointment of three new teachers*

apportion /əˈpɔːʃ°n/ verb [T] formal 1 to choose how much of something a person or each person should have **paylaştırmak, bölüştürmek** 2 **apportion**

blame/responsibility to say who was responsible for something bad that happened **sorumluluğu, suçu paylaştırmak**

appraisal /əˈpreɪz°l/ noun [C, U] 1 when you examine someone or something and judge how good or successful they are **değerlendirme, değerini tahmin etme, değerleme** *a critical appraisal* 2 a meeting where the manager of an employee talks to them about the quality of their work **değerlendirme toplantısı** *an appraisal scheme*

appraise /əˈpreɪz/ verb [T] to examine something and judge it **değerlendirme, değerini ortaya koyma** *We need to stop and appraise the situation.*

appreciable /əˈpriːʃəbl/ adjective formal large or important enough to be noticed **gereğinden büyük, kayda değer, fark edilebilen** *There's an appreciable difference in temperatures between the two regions.*

appreciate /əˈpriːʃieɪt/ verb [T] 1 to understand how good something or someone is and be able to enjoy them **takdir etmek** *There's no point buying him expensive wines - he doesn't appreciate them.* 2 [GRATEFUL] [T] to feel grateful for something **çok takdir etmek, müteşekkir olmak** *I'd really appreciate your help.* 3 [UNDERSTAND] [T] to understand something about a situation, especially that it is complicated or difficult **farkında olmak, anlamak, farkına varmak** [+ (that)] *I appreciate that it is a difficult decision for you to make.* 4 [INCREASE] [I] formal to increase in value **değeri artmak, değerlenmek** *Houses and antiques generally appreciate with time.*

appreciation /əˌpriːʃiˈeɪʃ°n/ noun [U] 1 [VALUE] when you understand how good something or someone is and are able to enjoy something **takdir, değerli bulma** *His appreciation of art increased as he grew older.* 2 [FEEL GRATEFUL] when you feel grateful for something **beğenme, takdir etme** *To show our appreciation, we've bought you a little gift.* 3 [UNDERSTANDING] when you understand something about a situation, especially that it is complicated or difficult **anlama, zor olan bir şeyi kavrama, halletme** *He has no appreciation of the size of the problem.* 4 [INCREASE] formal an increase in value **değerlenme, değeri artma**

appreciative /əˈpriːʃiətɪv/ adjective showing that you understand how good something is, or are grateful for something **takdir eden, değer, kıymet bilen** *an appreciative audience* • **appreciatively** adverb **müteşekkir durumda**

apprehend /ˌæprɪˈhend/ verb [T] formal If the police apprehend someone, they catch them and take them away to ask them about a crime which they might have committed. **tutuklamak, tevkif etmek**

apprehension /ˌæprɪˈhenʃ°n/ noun [U] an anxious feeling about something that you are going to do **endişe, korku, yersiz kuruntu** *It's normal to feel a little apprehension before starting a new job.*

apprehensive /ˌæprɪˈhensɪv/ adjective feeling anxious about something that you are going to do **endişeli, kaygılı, korku duyan** *He's a bit apprehensive about living away from home.*

apprentice /əˈprentɪs/ noun [C] a person who is learning a job by working for someone who already has skills and experience **çırak**

apprenticeship /əˈprentɪʃɪp/ noun [C, U] when someone learns the skills needed to do a job by working for someone who already has skills and experience **çıraklık**

o•▬**approach¹** /əˈprəʊtʃ/ noun 1 [METHOD] [C] a way of doing something **yaklaşım** *Liam has a different approach to*

A

the problem. ○ *We've decided to* ***adopt/take*** *a new* ***approach.*** **2** ASKING [C] when you speak or write to someone, often asking to buy something or offering them work **yaklaşma, bir konuda belli bir yaklaşım ortaya koyma** **3** COMING CLOSER [U] when something or someone gets nearer, in distance or time **yaklaşma, yakına gelme, zaman olarak yaklaşma** *the approach of winter* **4** PATH [C] a path or route that leads to a place **bir yere götüren yol, yaklaşım, rota**

o-**approach**[2] /ə'prəʊtʃ/ *verb* **1** COME CLOSE [I, T] to come close in distance or time **yakına gelmek, yaklaşmak** *The train now approaching platform 2 is the 5.35 to London, Kings Cross.* ○ *Christmas is fast approaching.* **2** DEAL WITH [T] to deal with something **bir şeyle ilgilenmek, alakadar olmak** *I'm not sure how to approach the problem.* **3** SPEAK TO SOMEONE [T] to speak or write to someone, often asking to buy something or offering them work **konuyu açmak, konuyu oraya getirmek** *She's been approached by a modelling agency.*

approachable /ə'prəʊtʃəbl/ *adjective* friendly and easy to talk to **yakınlaşılabilir, iletişim kurulabilir, dost canlısı, yaklaşılabilir**

o-**appropriate**[1] /ə'prəʊpriət/ *adjective* suitable or right for a particular situation or person **uygun, yerinde** *Is this film* ***appropriate for*** *young children?* ⊃Opposite **inappropriate.** • **appropriately** *adverb appropriately dressed* **düzgünce**

appropriate[2] /ə'prəʊprieɪt/ *verb* [T] *formal* to take or steal something **izinsiz almak, çalmak** • **appropriation** /əˌprəʊpri'eɪʃən/ *noun* [U] **alma veya çalma**

approval ...... İLE BİRLİKTE KULLANILAN KELİMELER

gain/get/win/receive/seek approval • **formal/full** approval • approval **for** sth

approval /ə'pru:vəl/ *noun* [U] **1** when you think that something or someone is good or right **onay, tasdik** *I don't need his approval.* ⊃Opposite **disapproval. 2** official permission **onama, tasdik, kabul yazısı, izin** *The project has now* ***received approval*** *from the government.*

o-**approve** /ə'pru:v/ *verb* **1** [T] to allow or officially agree to something **onaylamak, izin vermek, tasdik etmek** *The council has* ***approved plans*** *for a new shopping centre.* **2** [I] to think that something is good or right **kabul etmek, tasdik etmek** *I don't* ***approve of*** *smoking.* ⊃Opposite **disapprove.**

approving /ə'pru:vɪŋ/ *adjective* showing that you think something is good or right **onayan, kabul eden, tasdik eden** *an approving smile* ⊃Opposite **disapproving.** • **approvingly** *adverb* **onaylayıcı**

approx *written abbreviation for* approximately **yaklaşık olarak, tahminen**

approximate[1] /ə'prɒksɪmət/ *adjective* not completely accurate but close **yaklaşık, hemen hemen** *Do you have an approximate idea of when he's arriving?*

approximate[2] /ə'prɒksɪmeɪt/ (*also* **approximate to**) *verb* [T] *formal* to be almost the same as something **bir şeye hemen hemen tam olarak benzemek, yaklaşmak** • **approximation** /əˌprɒksɪ'meɪʃən/ *noun* [C, U] **aşağı yukarı aynı olma**

approximately /ə'prɒksɪmətli/ *adverb* close to a particular number or time although not exactly that number or time **tahminen, yaklaşık olarak** *The college has approximately 700 students.*

Apr *written abbreviation for* April **nisan**

apricot /'eɪprɪkɒt/ *noun* [C] a small, soft, orange fruit **kayısı**

o-**April** /'eɪprəl/ (*written abbreviation* **Apr**) *noun* [C, U] the fourth month of the year **nisan**

ˌ**April 'Fool's Day** *noun* 1 April, a day when people play tricks on people, then say 'April fool!' **nisan bir şaka günü**

apron /'eɪprən/ *noun* [C] a piece of clothing you wear when cooking to keep your clothes clean **önlük, mutfak önlüğü**

apron

apt /æpt/ *adjective* **1** suitable for a particular situation **uygun, isabetli, yerinde** *an apt description* **2 be apt to do sth** to often do something **bir şeyi yapma eğiliminde olmak, eğilimli olmak** *He's apt to forget his keys.* • **aptly** *adverb* **uygun bir şekilde**

aptitude ...... İLE BİRLİKTE KULLANILAN KELİMELER

have/show an aptitude **for** (doing) sth • a **natural** aptitude • an aptitude **test**

aptitude /'æptɪtju:d/ *noun* [C, U] a natural skill or an ability to do something well **yetenek, doğuştan gelen beceri, kabiliyet, yatkınlık** *He has an* ***aptitude for*** *learning languages.* ○ *an* ***aptitude test***

aquarium /ə'kweəriəm/ *noun* [C] **1** a building where fish and other water animals are kept for people to visit **akvaryum olarak tasarlanmış bina** **2** a glass container filled with water that fish are kept in **akvaryum**

Aquarius /ə'kweəriəs/ *noun* [C, U] the sign of the zodiac which relates to the period of 21 January - 19 February, or a person born during this period **kova burcu** ⊃See picture at **zodiac.**

aquatic /ə'kwætɪk/ *adjective* living or growing in water, or related to water **suda yaşayan, büyüyen, su ile ilgili** *aquatic animals*

Arab /'ærəb/ *adjective* relating or belonging to the people of the Middle East or North Africa whose families came from Arabia in the past **Arap, Arap'a ait** *Arab countries* • **Arab** *noun* [C] an Arab person **Arap soyundan gelen kişi**

Arabic /'ærəbɪk/ *noun* [U] the language used by Arab peoples **Arapça** • **Arabic** *adjective* **Arapça**

arable /'ærəbl/ *adjective* suitable for or used for growing crops **tarıma elverişli, verimli, uygun** *arable land/farming*

arbiter /'ɑ:bɪtər/ *noun* [C] **1** someone who judges what is right or helps to solve an argument **hakem 2 arbiter of fashion/style/taste, etc** someone who decides what is beautiful or stylish **moda/stil/lezzet konusunda söz sahibi, otorite**

arbitrary /'ɑ:bɪtrəri/ *adjective* not based on a system or principles and often seeming unfair **keyfi, isteğe göre düzenlenen, rastgele** *an* ***arbitrary decision*** • **arbitrarily** /ˌɑ:bɪ'treərəli/ *adverb* **keyfiyen**

arbitrate /'ɑ:bɪtreɪt/ *verb* [I, T] to officially help to solve an argument between two people or groups **kişiler arasındaki anlaşmazlığı çözmek, hakem olmak, resmen yardım etmek** • **arbitrator** *noun* [C] **hakem**

arbitration /ˌɑ:bɪ'treɪʃən/ *noun* [U] the process of solving an argument between people by helping them to agree to an acceptable solution **bir sorunu hakem aracılığı ile çözme, aracı vasıtasıyla halletme**

arc /ɑ:k/ *noun* [C] a curved line that looks like part of a circle **kemer, kavis, yay**

arcade /ɑ:'keɪd/ *noun* [C] **1** a place where you can pay to play games on machines **oyun salonu, atari salonu** *an amusement arcade* **2** a passage, especially between shops, that is covered by a roof **dükkanlar arasında üzeri kapalı geçit, pasaj, arasta** *a shopping arcade*

arch

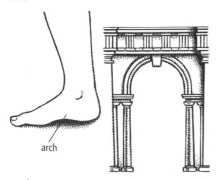

arch

arch¹ /ɑːtʃ/ *noun* [C] **1** a curved structure that usually supports something, for example a bridge or wall **köprü, duvar kemeri, kemer 2** the curved, middle part of your foot that does not touch the ground **ayağın orta kısmında yere değmeyen kavisli bölüm**

arch² /ɑːtʃ/ *verb* [I, T] to be a curved shape or make something become a curved shape **kavis vermek, kemer inşa etmek** *The bridge arched over the river.*

archaeologist (*also US* archeologist) /ˌɑːkiˈɒlədʒɪst/ *noun* [C] someone who studies archaeology **arkeolog**

archaeology (*also US* archeology) /ˌɑːkiˈɒlədʒi/ *noun* [U] the study of ancient cultures by looking for and examining their buildings, tools, and other objects **arkeoloji** ● **archaeological** (*also US* archeological) /ˌɑːkiəˈlɒdʒɪkəl/ *adjective* **arkeolojik, eskiye ait**

archaic /ɑːˈkeɪɪk/ *adjective* very old and often not suitable for today **çok eski, güncel olmayan, geçerli olmayan, tedavülden kalkmış** *an archaic law*

archbishop /ˌɑːtʃˈbɪʃəp/ *noun* [C] a priest of the highest rank in some Christian churches, responsible for a very large area **başpiskopos** *Archbishop Desmond Tutu*

archeologist /ˌɑːkiˈɒlədʒɪst/ *noun* [C] *another US spelling of* archaeologist **arkeolog**

archeology /ˌɑːkiˈɒlədʒi/ *noun* [U] *another US spelling of* archaeology **arkeoloji**

archery /ˈɑːtʃəri/ *noun* [U] a sport in which you shoot arrows **okçuluk**

architect /ˈɑːkɪtekt/ *noun* [C] someone who designs buildings **mimar**

architecture /ˈɑːkɪtektʃər/ *noun* [U] **1** the design and style of buildings **mimarlık** *modern architecture* **2** the skill of designing buildings **mimarlık becerisi** ● **architectural** /ˌɑːkɪˈtektʃərəl/ *adjective* **mimari**

archive¹ /ˈɑːkaɪv/ *noun* [C] **1** a collection of historical documents that provides information about the past, or a place where they are kept **arşiv** *the national archives* **2** a place on a computer used to store information or documents that you do not need to use often **bilgisayarda çok sık kullanılmayan bilgi ve belgelerin saklandığı yer, arşiv**

archive² /ˈɑːkaɪv/ *verb* [T] to store paper or electronic documents in an archive **arşivlemek, saklamak, depolamak**

the Arctic /ˈɑːktɪk/ *noun* the very cold area around the North Pole **Kuzey kutbuna ait** ● **Arctic** *adjective* *Arctic temperatures* **Kuzey Kutup Bölgesi**

ardent .... İLE BİRLİKTE KULLANILAN KELİMELER
an ardent admirer/fan/supporter

ardent /ˈɑːdənt/ *adjective* [always before noun] enthusiastic or showing strong feelings **coşkulu, ateşli, tutkulu** *an ardent supporter of Arsenal* ● **ardently** *adverb* **istekli bir şekilde**

arduous /ˈɑːdjuəs/ *adjective* needing a lot of effort to do **güç, çetin, çok çaba gerektiren** *an arduous journey/task*

are *strong form* /ɑːr/ *weak form* /ər/ *present simple you/we/they of* be **yardımcı fiil -iz, -siniz, -sin anlamında**

∘⊷**area** /ˈeəriə/ *noun* **1** [REGION] [C] a region of a country or city **saha, bölge** *an industrial area* ○ *a mountainous area* ○ *the London area* **2** [PART] [C] a part of a building or piece of land used for a particular purpose **alan, bina ya da toprak parçası** *a play/picnic area* **3** [SUBJECT] [C] a part of a subject or activity **bölüm, alan, konu veya faaliyetin bir parçası** *Software is not really my area of expertise.* **4** [SIZE] [C, U] the size of a flat surface calculated by multiplying its width by its length **yüzölçüm, ebat, boyut** ●See also: catchment area, no-go area.

'area ˌcode *noun* [C] a set of numbers used at the beginning of all the telephone numbers in a particular area **bölge kodu**

arena /əˈriːnə/ *noun* [C] **1** a flat area with seats around where you can watch sports and other entertainments **düz alan, saha arena, eğlence alanı** *an Olympic/sports arena* **2** in the political/public, etc arena involved in politics/the government, etc **siyasi/toplumsal alanda, sahada, konuda**

∘⊷**aren't** /ɑːnt/ **1** *short for* are not **olumsuzluk eki** *We aren't going to the party.* **2** aren't I? *short for* am I not? **değil mi?** *I am invited, aren't I?*

arguable /ˈɑːgjuəbl/ *adjective* **1** It is arguable that it is possibly true that **muhtemelen doğrudur ki** *It is arguable that the government has failed in this respect.* **2** If something is arguable, it is not certain if it is true. **tartışmalı, doğruluğu belli olmayan** *It is arguable whether this method would even have succeeded.*

arguably /ˈɑːgjuəbli/ *adverb* possibly **muhtemelen, olası bir şekilde** *He's arguably the greatest footballer in the world.*

∘⊷**argue** /ˈɑːgjuː/ *verb* arguing, *past* argued **1** [I] to speak angrily to someone, telling them that you disagree with them **tartışmak, münakaşa etmek** *My parents are always arguing about money.* ○ *Kids, will you stop arguing with each other?* **2** [I, T] to give reasons to support or oppose an idea, action, etc **bir fikri tartışmak, nedenleri öne sürmek** [+ that] *He argued that cuts in military spending were necessary.* ○ *She argued for/against tax cuts.*

argument .... İLE BİRLİKTE KULLANILAN KELİMELER
have an argument ● an argument about/over sth ● a heated/violent argument

∘⊷**argument** /ˈɑːgjəmənt/ *noun* [C] **1** an angry discussion with someone in which you both disagree **münakaşa** *They had an argument about who should do the cleaning.* **2** a reason or reasons why you support or oppose an idea, action, etc **tartışma, argüman** *There are many arguments for/against nuclear energy.*

argumentative /ˌɑːgjəˈmentətɪv/ *adjective* often arguing or wanting to argue **tartışan, tartışmaya eğilimli**

aria /ˈɑːriə/ *noun* [C] a song that one person sings in an opera **arya**

A

arid /'ærɪd/ *adjective* very dry and without enough rain for plants **kurak, çorak, çatlamış, kupkuru** *an arid region/climate*

Aries /'eəriːz/ *noun* [C, U] the sign of the zodiac which relates to the period of 21 March - 20 April, or a person born during this period **Koç burcu** ⊃See picture at **zodiac.**

arise /ə'raɪz/ *verb* [I] *past tense* **arose,** *past part* **arisen 1** If a problem arises, it starts to happen. **ortaya çıkmak, doğmak, zuhur etmek** *The whole problem arose from a lack of communication.* **2** *literary* to get up, usually from a bed **kalkmak, yataktan kalkmak**

aristocracy /ˌærɪ'stɒkrəsi/ *noun* [group] the highest social class, usually in countries which have or had a royal family **aristokrasi**

aristocrat /'ærɪstəkræt/ *noun* [C] a member of the highest social class **aristokrat** • **aristocratic** /ˌærɪstə'krætɪk/ *adjective* an *aristocratic family* **asil**

arithmetic /ə'rɪθmətɪk/ *noun* [U] when you calculate numbers, for example by multiplying or adding **matematik**

o↩**arm**[1] /ɑːm/ *noun* [C] **1** [BODY PART] the long part at each side of the human body, ending in a hand **kol** *He put his arms around her.* ○ *She was standing with her arms folded* (= with one arm crossed over the other). ⊃Orta kısımdaki renkli sayfalarına bakınız. **2 arm in arm** with your arm gently supporting or being supported by someone else's arm **kolkola, birbirini destekleyerek 3** [CLOTHES] the part of a piece of clothing that you put your arm in **elbise kolu 4** [CHAIR] the part of a chair where your arm rests **sandalye, koltuk kolu 5 twist sb's arm** *informal* to persuade someone to do something **ikna etmek, yola getirmek, bir şeyi yaptırmak** ⊃See also: **arms.**

arm (illustration label)

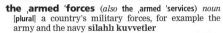

arm[2] /ɑːm/ *verb* [T] to give weapons to someone **silahlandırmak, silah vermek** *The terrorists had armed themselves with automatic rifles.* ⊃Opposite **disarm.**

armaments /'ɑːməmənts/ *noun* [plural] military weapons and equipment **askeri silah ve techizatlar** *nuclear armaments*

armband /'ɑːmbænd/ *noun* **1** [C] a strip of material worn around your upper arm **pazubandı, kola takılan bant** *a black/reflective armband* **2 armbands** *UK* two plastic tubes that you fill with air and wear round the top of your arms when you are learning to swim **yüzerken takılan kolluk**

armchair /'ɑːmtʃeər/ *noun* [C] a comfortable chair with sides that support your arms **koltuk** ⊃Orta kısımdaki renkli sayfalarına bakınız.

armed /ɑːmd/ *adjective* **1** carrying or using weapons **silahlı** *armed guards/police* ○ *an armed robbery* (= robbery where guns are used) ⊃Opposite **unarmed.** **2 armed with sth** carrying or knowing something that will be useful **donanımlı, faydalı bir şeyi bilmek, yanında bulundurmak** *I like to go to a meeting armed with the relevant facts.*

the ˌarmed 'forces (*also* **the ˌarmed 'services**) *noun* [plural] a country's military forces, for example the army and the navy **silahlı kuvvetler**

armful /'ɑːmfʊl/ *noun* [C] the amount that you can carry in your arms **kollar dolusu, kollarla taşınabilen miktar** *an armful of books*

armistice /'ɑːmɪstɪs/ *noun* [C] an agreement to stop fighting that is made between two countries **ateşkes**

armour *UK* (*US* **armor**) /'ɑːmər/ *noun* [U] metal clothing which soldiers wore in the past to protect them when fighting **zırh** *a suit of armour*

armoured *UK* (*US* **armored**) /'ɑːməd/ *adjective* covered with a protective layer of metal **zırhlı** *an armoured vehicle*

armpit /'ɑːmpɪt/ *noun* [C] the part of your body under your arm, where your arm meets your shoulder **koltuk altı** ⊃Orta kısımdaki renkli sayfalarına bakınız.

arms /ɑːmz/ *noun* [plural] **1** weapons **silahlar** *the sale of arms* **2 be up in arms** to be very upset and angry about something **kızmak, kızgın olmak, kendini kaybetmek, küplere binmek** *Local residents are up in arms over plans to close the swimming pool.*

⊞☷☷ **army** ...... İLE BİRLİKTE KULLANILAN KELİMELER

join the army • **be** in the army

o↩**army** /'ɑːmi/ *noun* [C] **1** a military force that fights wars on the ground **ordu** *the British Army* **2** a group of people that is organized to do the same job **aynı işi yapmak üzere bir araya gelen kalabalık insan topluluğu** *an army of cleaners/helpers*

aroma /ə'rəʊmə/ *noun* [C] a nice smell that usually comes from food or drink **yiyecek ve içeceklerden gelen koku, aroma** *the aroma of freshly baked bread* • **aromatic** /ˌærəʊ'mætɪk/ *adjective* having a nice smell **güzel koku veren, aromatik** *aromatic herbs*

aromatherapy /əˌrəʊmə'θerəpi/ *noun* [U] a way of making a person who is ill better by rubbing pleasant-smelling oils into the skin or allowing them to smell the oils **aromaterapi, kokularla yapılan terapi**

arose /ə'rəʊz/ *past tense of* arise **zuhur etmek, ortaya çıkmak, doğmak**

o↩**around** /ə'raʊnd/ *adverb, preposition* **1** [IN A CIRCLE] (*also UK* **round**) on all sides of something **çevresinde, çevresine** *They sat around the table.* **2** [DIRECTION] (*also UK* **round**) to the opposite direction **ters yönde, tersine, arkasına** *He turned around and looked at her.* **3** [CIRCULAR MOVEMENT] (*also UK* **round**) in a circular movement **dönerek, döner biçimde** *This lever turns the wheels around.* **4** [ALONG OUTSIDE] (*also UK* **round**) along the outside of something, not through it **boyunca, yanı boyunca** *You have to walk around the house to get to the garden.* **5** [TO A PLACE] (*also UK* **round**) to or in different parts of a place **bir yerin farklı bölgelerine, çevresine** *I spent a year travelling around Australia.* **6** [SEVERAL PLACES] (*also UK* **round**) from one place or person to another **bir yerden veya birinden öbürüne** *She passed a plate of biscuits around.* **7** [HERE] here, or near this place **buralarda, yakınlarda, yakınlara, buralara** *Is Roger around?* **8** [EXISTING] present or available **hazır, elde edilebilir, mevcut** *Mobile phones have been around for years now.* **9** [APPROXIMATELY] used before a number or amount to mean 'approximately' **yaklaşık, hemen hemen** *around four o'clock* ○ *around twenty thousand pounds* ⊃See also: throw your **weight** around.

arousal /ə'raʊzəl/ *noun* [U] when someone is sexually excited **tahrik olmuş, uyanmış, uyarılmış, cinsel istek uyanışı**

arouse /ə'raʊz/ *verb* [T] **1** to make someone have a particular feeling or reaction **harekete geçirmek** *It's a subject which has **aroused** a lot of interest.* **2** to make someone sexually excited **uyandırmak, tahrik olmak, tahrik etmek**

o⊶**arrange** /ə'reɪndʒ/ *verb* [T] **1** to make the necessary plans and preparations for something to happen **düzenlemek, planlamak, hazırlık yapmak** *to arrange a meeting* ○ *I'll **arrange for** a car to come and pick you up.* ○ [+ to do sth] *We've arranged to visit the house on Saturday afternoon.* **2** to put objects in a particular order or position **düzenlemek, yerlerine koymak, tanzim etmek** *The books are arranged alphabetically by author.*

> 🧩 **arrangement** ...... İLE BİRLİKTE KULLANILAN KELİMELER
>
> have/make an arrangement • arrangements for sth
> • alternative/necessary arrangements

o⊶**arrangement** /ə'reɪndʒmənt/ *noun* **1** [PLANS] [C] plans for how something will happen **planlama, düzenleme** [usually plural] *We're meeting tomorrow to discuss arrangements for the competition.* ○ [+ to do sth] *I've **made** arrangements to go home this weekend.* **2** [AGREEMENT] [C, U] an agreement between two people or groups **düzenleme, ayarlama, anlaşma** *We have an arrangement whereby we share the childcare.* ○ *Viewing is by prior arrangement.* **3** [POSITION] [C] a group of objects in a particular order or position **belli bir düzende duran bir grup nesne, tanzim** *a flower arrangement*

array /ə'reɪ/ *noun* [C] a large number of different things **sergi, düzenleme** [usually singular] *There is **a** vast **array** of books on the subject.*

arrears /ə'rɪəz/ *noun* [plural] money that is owed and should have been paid before **gecikmiş borç, zamanında ödenmeyen para** *mortgage/rent arrears* ○ *He is already in arrears with the rent.*

o⊶**arrest¹** /ə'rest/ *verb* [T] If the police arrest someone, they take them away to ask them about a crime which they might have committed. **tutuklamak** *He was arrested for possession of illegal drugs.*

> 🧩 **arrest** ...... İLE BİRLİKTE KULLANILAN KELİMELER
>
> make an arrest • resist arrest • be under arrest • the arrest of sb • an arrest for [murder/drugs offences, etc]

arrest² /ə'rest/ *noun* [C, U] when the police take someone away to ask them about a crime which they might have committed **tutuklama** *Police **made** 20 **arrests** at yesterday's demonstration.* ○ *He's **under arrest** (= has been arrested).* ➔See also: house arrest.

o⊶**arrival** /ə'raɪvəl/ *noun* **1** [ARRIVING] [U] when someone or something arrives somewhere **varış, geliş** *He first met Panos soon after his arrival in Greece.* ○ *There was a car waiting for him **on arrival**.* **2** [BECOME AVAILABLE] [U] when something new is discovered or created or becomes available **ortaya çıkış, keşfedilen, mevcut olan** *The town grew rapidly with the arrival of the railway.* **3** [NEW PERSON/THING] [C] a new thing or person that has arrived **yeni bir kişi veya şeyin varışı, ortaya çıkışı** *Two teachers were there to greet the **new arrivals**.*

o⊶**arrive** /ə'raɪv/ *verb* [I] **1** to get to a place **varmak, ulaşmak** *When he first **arrived in** New York, he didn't speak a word of English.* ○ *We were the last to **arrive at** the station.* ○ *A letter arrived for you this morning.* **2 arrive at an answer/decision/conclusion, etc** to find an answer to a problem or make a decision after a lot of discussion **bir sonuca/karara/cevaba ulaşmak, varmak** *We didn't arrive at any firm conclusions.* **3** to happen or start to exist **meydana gelmek, var olmaya başlamak, zuhur etmek** *Summer had finally arrived.*

arrogant /'ærəgənt/ *adjective* believing that you are better or more important than other people **kibirli, kendini beğenmiş, burnu havada, küstah, ukela** *I found him arrogant and rude.* • **arrogance** /'ærəgəns/ *noun* [U] **kibir** • **arrogantly** *adverb* **ukalaca**

arrow /'ærəʊ/ *noun* [C]   **arrow**
1 a symbol used on signs to show a direction **yön gösteren işaret, ok 2** a long, thin stick with a sharp point at one end which is fired from a bow (= curved piece of wood with a tight string fixed at both ends) **ok**

arse /ɑːs/ *UK very informal* (*US* ass) *noun* [C] a person's bottom **kıç, basen, popo**

arsenal /'ɑːsᵊnᵊl/ *noun* [C] a large collection of weapons **silah yığını, silah deposu**

arsenic /'ɑːsᵊnɪk/ *noun* [U] a chemical element that is a very strong poison (symbol As) **arsenik**

arson /'ɑːsᵊn/ *noun* [U] the crime of intentionally burning something, such as a building **kundaklama, yangın çıkarma** • **arsonist** *noun* [C] someone who commits arson **kundakçı, kundaklama yapan kişi**

o⊶**art** /ɑːt/ *noun* **1** [U] the making or study of paintings, drawings, etc or the objects created **sanat** *fine/modern art* ○ *an art exhibition/gallery* **2** [C, U] a skill in a particular activity **sanat, belli bir konuda yetenek** *the art of conversation* ➔See also: martial art, work of art.

artefact *UK* (*US* artifact) /'ɑːtɪfækt/ *noun* [C] an object, especially something very old of historical interest **tarihi ve çok eski bir sanat eseri, nesne**

artery /'ɑːtᵊri/ *noun* [C] **1** one of the tubes in your body that carries blood from your heart **atardamar 2** an important route for traffic **trafikte ana arter**

artful /'ɑːtfᵊl/ *adjective* [always before noun] showing skill **becerikli, maharet içeren, ustalık gerektiren, ustaca** *an artful use of colour* • **artfully** *adverb* **becerikli bir şekilde**

arthritis /ɑː'θraɪtɪs/ *noun* [U] an illness which causes the parts of the body where bones meet to become painful and often big **romatizma** • **arthritic** /ɑː'θrɪtɪk/ *adjective* **an arthritic hip/knee artrit**

artichoke /'ɑːtɪtʃəʊk/ *noun* [C, U] a round, green vegetable with thick, pointed leaves covering the outside **enginar**

article /'ɑːtɪkl/ *noun* [C] **1** [WRITING] a piece of writing in a magazine, newspaper, etc **makale 2** [OBJECT] an object, especially one of many **madde** *an article of clothing/furniture* **3** [GRAMMAR] in grammar, used to mean the words 'the', 'a', or 'an' **dilbilgisinde 'the', 'a', veya**

A

'an' gibi başına geldiği sözcüğü tarif eden tanım harfleri ➲See also: definite article, indefinite article.

articulate¹ /ɑːˈtɪkjələt/ adjective able to express ideas and feelings clearly in words **fikir ve hislerini kelimelerle anlatabilen, kendini ifade edebilen, açık seçik, anlaşılabilir** She's an intelligent and highly articulate young woman. ➲Opposite **inarticulate.**

articulate² /ɑːˈtɪkjəleɪt/ verb [T] formal to express ideas or feelings in words **açıklamak, kendini ifade etmek, düşünce ve duygularını rahatça ifade etmek** He articulates the views and concerns of the local community.
● **articulation** /ɑːˌtɪkjəˈleɪʃ°n/ noun [U] **telaffuz**

articulated /ɑːˈtɪkjəleɪtɪd/ adjective [always before noun] mainly UK An articulated vehicle is long and has two parts which are joined together to help it turn corners. **çekicisi olan taşıt, treylerli araç** an articulated lorry

artifact /ˈɑːtɪfækt/ noun [C] US spelling of artefact **kul yapımı, insan yapımı nesne**

artificial /ˌɑːtɪˈfɪʃ°l/ adjective **1** not natural, but made by people **yapay, insan yapımı** an artificial flower/lake ○ an artificial heart **2** not sincere **samimi olmayan, yapay, suni** ● **artificially** adverb **suni bir şekilde**

,artificial in'telligence UK (US arti,ficial in'telligence) noun [U] the study and development of computer systems which do jobs that previously needed human intelligence **yapay zekâ**

artillery /ɑːˈtɪl°ri/ noun [U] large guns, especially those fixed on wheels used by an army **top**

artisan /ˌɑːtɪˈzæn/ ⓤⓢ /ˈɑːrtəz°n/ noun [C] old-fashioned someone who does skilled work with their hands **zanaatkâr, esnaf, usta**

o╌**artist** /ˈɑːtɪst/ noun [C] someone who creates art, especially paintings and drawings **ressam**

artistic /ɑːˈtɪstɪk/ adjective **1** showing skill and imagination in creating things, especially in painting, drawing, etc **yaratıcı kabiliyeti olan, sanatkâr ruhlu** artistic talent **2** [always before noun] relating to art **sanatsal** the artistic director of the theatre ● **artistically** adverb **sanatsal olarak**

artistry /ˈɑːtɪstri/ noun [U] great skill in creating or performing something, such as in writing, music, sport, etc **sanatçılık, sanat kabiliyeti**

arts /ɑːts/ noun **1** [plural] (also US liberal arts) subjects of study which are not science, such as history, languages, etc **sanat konuları** an arts subject/degree **2 the arts** activities such as painting, music, film, dance, and literature **sanatlar** public interest in the arts ➲See also: the performing arts.

artwork /ˈɑːtwɜːk/ noun [U] the pictures or patterns in a book, magazine, CD cover, etc **sanat eseri, sanat çalışması**

arty /ˈɑːti/ (also US artsy /ˈɑːtsi/) adjective knowing a lot about art, or wanting to appear as if you do **sanattan anlarmış gibi gözüken, sanatsever gibi davranan**

o╌**as** strong form /æz/ weak form /əz/ preposition, conjunction **1 as .... as** used to compare two things, people, amounts, etc **kadar** He's not as tall as his brother. ○ She earns three times as much as I do. **2** WHILE used to describe two things happening at the same time or something happening at a particular time **iken** He was shot in the back as he tried to escape. ○ I think your opinions change as you get older. **3** FOR THIS PURPOSE used to describe the purpose, role, or appearance of something or someone **olarak, görevinde** She works as a waitress. ○ It could be used as evidence against him. **4** LIKE in the same way **aynı, benzer, eşdeş** This year, as in previous years, tickets sold very quickly. **5** IN THIS WAY

used to describe the way in which people see or think of something or someone **gibi** Most people think of nursing as a female occupation. **6** BECAUSE because **çünkü** You can go first as you're the oldest. **7 as if/as though** used to describe how a situation seems to be **sanki** It looks as if it might rain. **8 as for** used to talk about how another person or thing is affected by something ...e, a **gelince** I was pleased. As for Emily, well, who cares what she thinks. **9 as from/as of** formal starting from a particular time, date, etc **tarihi itibariyle** The new conditions are effective as of 15 May. **10 as to** formal about **hakkında, ...e, a gelince** There's no decision as to when the work might start.

asap /ˌeɪeseɪˈpiː/ abbreviation for as soon as possible **en kısa zamanda, mümkün olduğunca çabuk, mümkün olduğça hızlı**

asbestos /æsˈbestɒs/ noun [U] a soft grey-white material which does not burn easily, once used in building **asbestos**

Asbo (also ASBO) /ˈæzbəʊ/ UK abbreviation for anti-social behaviour order: an official order that a person must stop doing something bad or they might go to prison **toplum kurallarına aykırı davranmama talimatı**

ascend /əˈsend/ verb [I, T] formal to move up or to a higher position **yükselmek, yukarı çıkmak, tırmanmak**

ascendancy (also ascendency) /əˈsendənsi/ noun [U] formal a position of power, strength, or success **yükselme, tırmanma, güce ulaşma, başarıyı yakalama** in the ascendancy

ascending /əˈsendɪŋ/ adjective [always before noun] starting with the lowest or smallest and becoming greater or higher **yükselen, yukarı çıkan, başarı kazanan** They announced the results in ascending order.

ascent /əˈsent/ noun **1** CLIMB [C] when someone climbs or moves up **çıkış, yükseliş** his first ascent of the mountain **2** BECOMING SUCCESSFUL [no plural] when someone starts to become successful **tırmanış, başarı ulaşma** The book describes his rapid ascent from truck driver to film star. **3** PATH UP [C] a path or road which goes up a hill or mountain **tırmanan yol; dağı, tepeyi aşan yol** a steep ascent

ascertain /ˌæsəˈteɪn/ verb [T] formal to discover something **saptamak, tespit etmek, belirlemek** [+ question word] We are still trying to ascertain whether the fire was started deliberately.

ascribe /əˈskraɪb/ verb
ascribe sth to sth phrasal verb formal to say that something is caused by something else **birşeyi bir şeye bağlamak, atfetmek, sebebinin o olduğunu söylemek** She ascribes her success to hard work.

ash /æʃ/ noun **1** [U] the soft, grey powder which remains when something has burnt **kül** cigarette ash **2** [C] a forest tree **dişbudak ağacı**

o╌**ashamed** /əˈʃeɪmd/ adjective **1** feeling guilty or embarrassed about something you have done **utanmış, mahcup** You've got nothing to be ashamed of. ○ [+ to do sth] He was ashamed to admit his mistake. **2 be ashamed of sb** to be angry and disappointed with a family member or friend because they have behaved badly **birinden utanmak, mahcup olmak** He was so rude to Phil - I was ashamed of him.

ashes /ˈæʃɪz/ noun sb's ashes the powder that remains when a dead person's body has been burnt **bir kimsenin külleri** scatter her ashes

ashore /əˈʃɔːʳ/ adverb onto land from the sea, a river, a lake, etc **sahile, kıyıya doğru, kıyıda** We swam ashore.

ashtray /'æʃ,treɪ/ *noun* [C] a small, open container used to put cigarette ash and finished cigarettes in **kül tablası**

Asian /'eɪʒ³n/ *adjective* relating or belonging to Asia **Asyalı** *Asian culture* ● **Asian** *noun* [C] someone from Asia **Asya kökenli, Asyalı**

aside¹ /ə'saɪd/ *adverb* **1** in a direction to one side **yan tarafa, yanıbaşına, yanına** *I gave her a plate of food but she pushed it aside.* **2** If you put or set something aside, you do not use it now, but keep it to use later. **bir kenara, bir tarafa koyma, saklama** *We've put some money aside to pay for the children's education.* **3** *aside from* except for ... **den başka, haricinde, hariç, den gayri**

aside² /ə'saɪd/ *noun* [C] something which you say quietly so that not everyone can hear it, often something funny **fısıldaşma, fısıldama, fısıltıyla söylenen şey**

o─ **ask** /ɑːsk/ *verb* **1** QUESTION [I, T] to say something to someone as a question which you want them to answer **sormak** [+ two objects] *Can I ask you a few questions?* ○ *I asked him about his hobbies.* ○ [+ question word] *I asked why the plane was so late.* ⊃See Common learner error at **question**. **2** WANT SOMETHING [I, T] to say something to someone because you want them to give you something **istemek, dilemek** *He's asked for a bike for his birthday.* **3** REQUEST [I, T] to say something to someone because you want them to do something **istekte bulunmak** [+ to do sth] *They've asked me to look after their dog while they're away.* **4** INVITE [T] to invite someone to do something **ricada bulunmak** *She asked him out to lunch the next day.* **5** WANT PERMISSION [I, T] to say something to someone because you want to know if you can do something **talep etmek** *Bruce asked if he could stay with us for a few days.* ○ [+ to do sth] *She asked to leave early.* **6** PRICE [T] to want a particular amount of money for something which you sell **para talebinde, isteğinde bulunmak** *How much are you asking for it?* **7** *ask yourself sth* to think about something carefully **kendi içinde dikkatlice değerlendirmek, özenle düşünmek** *You've got to ask yourself whether it's what you really want.* **8** *ask for it/trouble informal* to behave in a way that is likely to make something unpleasant happen to you or to cause you problems **belasını istemek, kaşınmak, bela aramak** *Drinking and driving is asking for trouble.* **9** *don't ask me informal* used to tell someone that you do not know the answer to a question and that you are surprised they have asked you **bana hiç sorma, ben bilmem, bana niye soruyorsun ki?** *Don't ask me why you left your last job!* **10** *you may well ask* said to someone who has asked you a question that would be difficult or interesting to answer **sorsaydın, sorabilirsin, nereden çıktı şimdi bu soru anlamında cevaplaması zor ve ilginç bir soru soran kişiye söylenen ifade**

askew /ə'skjuː/ *adjective* [never before noun] not straight **yamuk, eğri büğrü** *The picture was slightly askew.*

asleep ...... BAŞKA BİR DEYİŞLE
Eğer kişi uyumaya başlamışsa, **fall asleep** söylemi kullanılabilir. *I fell asleep in front of the TV.*
Eğer kişi derin uykuya dalmışsa, **fast asleep** söylemi kullanılabilir. *You were fast asleep by the time I came to bed.*
Doze ve snooze fiillerinin yanısıra **have/take a nap** söylemi, özellikle gün içinde kısa süreli uyunduğunu belirtmek için kullanılır. *She's always dozing in front of the TV.* ● *Granddad was snoozing in his chair.* ● *Oliver is really tired so he's just taking a nap.*

doze off ve **nod off** (gayri resmi) deyimleri, özellikle gün içinde uyunduğunu belirtmek için kullanılır. *I must have nodded off after lunch.* ● *She dozed off during the lecture.*

o─ **asleep** /ə'sliːp/ *adjective* **1** *be asleep* to be sleeping **uykulu olmak** *The children are asleep.* ○ *I was fast/sound asleep* (= sleeping deeply). **2** *fall asleep* to start sleeping **uykuya dalmak** *He fell asleep in front of the TV.*

asparagus /ə'spærəgəs/ *noun* [U] a vegetable consisting of a long, green stem with a pointed end **kuşkonmaz**

aspect /'æspekt/ *noun* **1** [C] one part of a situation, problem, subject, etc **özellik, bir problem, konu, durumun bir bölümü, bir yönü** *His illness affects almost every aspect of his life.* **2** [U, C] the form of a verb which shows how the meaning of a verb is considered in relation to time **bir fiilin zamana ilişkin anlamının nasıl dikkate alındığını gösteren şekli**

asphalt /'æsfælt/ *noun* [U] a hard, black substance used to make roads and paths **asfalt, yol kaplama maddesi**

asphyxiate /əs'fɪksieɪt/ *verb* to die because you cannot breathe **boğulmak, boğmak** ● **asphyxiation** /əs,fɪksi'eɪʃ³n/ *noun* [U] **boğulma**

aspiration ...... İLE BİRLİKTE KULLANILAN KELİMELER
have aspirations *to do sth/of doing sth* ● *high* aspirations ● *dreams/hopes* and aspirations ● aspirations *for sth*

aspiration /,æsp³r'eɪʃ³n/ *noun* [C, U] something you hope to achieve **özlem, emel, hasretle beklenen** *The story is about the lives and aspirations of the Irish working classes.*

aspire /ə'spaɪər/ *verb aspire to sth; aspire to do sth* to hope to achieve something **bir şeyi başarmayı ümit etmek, başarmaya çalışmak, umutlanmak** *He has never aspired to a position of power.*

aspirin /'æsp³rɪn/ *noun* [C, U] *plural* **aspirin** *or* **aspirins** a common drug used to reduce pain and fever **aspirin**

aspiring /ə'spaɪərɪŋ/ *adjective* *an aspiring actor/politician/writer, etc* someone who is trying to become a successful actor/politician/writer, etc **büyük çaba, heves gösteren aktör, politikacı, yazar**

ass /æs/ *noun* [C] **1** BOTTOM *US very informal* (*UK* arse) a person's bottom **kıç** **2** PERSON *informal* a stupid person **aptal, salak, ahmak, budala** **3** ANIMAL *old-fashioned* a donkey (= animal like a small horse) **eşek**

assailant /ə'seɪlənt/ *noun* [C] *formal* a person who attacks someone **saldırgan**

assassin /ə'sæsɪn/ *noun* [C] a person who kills someone important or famous, often for money **suikastçı**

assassinate /ə'sæsɪneɪt/ *verb* [T] to kill someone important or famous **suikast yapmak** ● **assassination** /ə,sæsɪ'neɪʃ³n/ *noun* [C, U] **süikast**

assault /ə'sɔːlt/ *noun* [C, U] an attack **saldırı, hücum** *an assault on a police officer* ○ *sexual assault* ● **assault** *verb* [T] **saldırmak**

assemble /ə'sembl/ *verb* **1** [I, T] to join other people somewhere to make a group, or to bring people together into a group **toplanmak, bir araya gelmek, grup oluşturmak** *They assembled in the meeting room after lunch.* **2** [T] to build something by joining parts together **birleştirmek, toplamak, parçaları bir araya getirmek**

assembly /ə'sembli/ *noun* **1** SCHOOL [C, U] *UK* a regular meeting of all the students and teachers at a school **tüm öğrenci ve öğretmenlerin katıldığı genel toplantı** *morning assembly* **2** GROUP [C] a group of people, such as a government, who meet to make decisions, laws, etc meclis, toplantı, genel kurul *the national assembly* **3** [BUILD] [U] when you build something by joining parts together **birleştirme, toplama, bir araya getirme**

assent /əˈsent/ *noun* [U] *formal* agreement or approval **onama, onay, kabul** *Has she given her assent?* ● **assent** *verb* [I] *formal* to agree to something **kabul göstermek, onaylamak, uyuşmak**

assert /əˈsɜːt/ *verb* **1 assert yourself** to behave or speak in a strong, confident way **cesaretle, kendine güvenerek konuşmak, davranmak, iyi olduğunu göstermek** *She has to learn to assert herself.* **2 assert your authority/control/independence, etc** to do something to show other people that you have power **gücünü göstermek, yetkisini ortaya koymak 3** [T] *formal* to say that something is certainly true **iddia etmek, açıklamak, belirtmek** [+ that] *He asserts that she stole money from him.*

assertion /əˈsɜːʃ³n/ *noun* [C, U] *formal* when you say that something is certainly true **belli etme, belirtme, gösterme, bildirme, açıklama** [+ that] *I don't agree with his assertion that men are safer drivers than women.*

assertive /əˈsɜːtɪv/ *adjective* behaving or speaking in a strong, confident way **kendine aşırı güvenen, kendinden emin** *You need to be much more assertive.* ● **assertively** *adverb* **kendine güvenen bir şekilde** ● **assertiveness** *noun* [U] **emin olma hali**

assess /əˈses/ *verb* [T] to make a judgment about the quality, size, value, etc of something **değerlendirmek, değerini belirlemek** *The tests are designed to assess a child's reading skills.* ● **assessment** *noun* [C, U] **değerlendirme**

asset /ˈæset/ *noun* [C] **1** a person, skill, or quality which is useful or helps you to succeed **başarıya katkısı olan nitelik, beceri ve kişi** *He'll be a great asset to the team.* **2** something which a person or company owns which has a value **varlık, mal değeri, servet, mal** [usually plural] *The company has $70 billion in assets.*

assiduous /əˈsɪdjuəs/ *adjective formal* showing a lot of effort and determination **sebat eden, sebatkâr, kararlı ve azimli** ● **assiduously** *adverb* **gayretli ve inançlı**

assign /əˈsaɪn/ *verb* [T] to give someone a particular job or responsibility **görevlendirmek, görev vermek** [+ two objects] *UN troops were assigned the task of rebuilding the hospital.* ○ [often passive] *The case has been assigned to our most senior officer.*

assign sb to sth *phrasal verb* to give someone a particular job or place to work **birini bir şeye görevlendirmek** [often passive] *Which police officer has been assigned to this case?*

assignment /əˈsaɪnmənt/ *noun* [C, U] a piece of work or job that you are given to do **görev, ödev** *a written assignment* ○ *He's on assignment in Brazil.*

assimilate /əˈsɪmɪleɪt/ *verb formal* **1** [T] to understand and remember new information **yeni bilgiyi özümlemek, anlamak, benimsemek 2** [I, T] to become part of a group, society, etc, or to make someone or something become part of a group, society, etc **benzetmek, benzemek, bir grubun parçası olmak veya kaynaşmak** *The refugees have now assimilated into the local community.* ● **assimilation** /ə͵sɪmɪˈleɪʃ³n/ *noun* [U] **öğrenme, özümseme**

assist /əˈsɪst/ *verb* [I, T] to help **yardım etmek** *The army arrived to assist in the search.* ○ *He's assisting the police with their investigation.*

assistance /əˈsɪst³ns/ *noun* [U] *formal* help **yardım** *financial/medical assistance* ○ *Can I be of any assistance?* (= Can I help you?)

assistant /əˈsɪst³nt/ *noun* [C] **1** someone whose job is to help a person who has a more important job **yardımcı, asistan** *an administrative assistant* ○ *assistant manager* **2** a sales/shop assistant *mainly UK* someone who helps customers in a shop **tezgâhtar, mağaza çalışanı**

associate¹ /əˈsəʊʃieɪt/ *verb* [T] to relate two things, people, etc in your mind **ilişkilendirmek, bağdaştırmak** *Most people associate this brand with good quality.*

associate with sb *phrasal verb formal* to spend time with someone **ile arkadaşlık etmek, görüşmek**

be associated with sth *phrasal verb* to be related to something or caused by something **ile ilişkilendirilmek, ilişkilendirmek, bağlantısı olmak, sebep olunmak** *There are many risks associated with smoking.*

associate² /əˈsəʊʃiət/ *noun* [C] someone who you know because of work or business **işten tanıdık, bildik, iş arkadaşı** *She's a business associate of mine.*

associate³ /əˈsəʊʃiət/ *adjective* **associate director/editor/producer, etc** someone in a slightly less important position than the main person **muavin, yardımcı, müdür yardımcısı vb.**

association /ə͵səʊʃiˈeɪʃ³n/ *noun* **1** [C] an organization of people with the same interests or with a particular purpose **kuruluş, teşkilat, kurum, aynı amacı taşıyan insanların oluşturduğu birliktelik, dernek** *the Football Association* **2** [C, U] a connection or relationship between two things or people **ilişki, ortaklık, birliktelik 3** in association with working together with **ile beraber, ile birlikte, ortak olarak** *The event was organized in association with the Sports Council.* ⊃See also: savings and loan association.

assorted /əˈsɔːtɪd/ *adjective* of different types **çeşitli, muhtelif, karışık** *a box of assorted chocolates*

assortment /əˈsɔːtmənt/ *noun* [C] a group of different types of something **karışım, çeşit,** *an assortment of vegetables*

assuage /əˈsweɪdʒ/ *verb* [T] *formal* to make unpleasant feelings less strong **nahoş durumları hafifletmek, etkisini azaltmak, teselli etmek, teskin etmek** *The government tried to assuage the public's fears.*

o* **assume** /əˈsjuːm/ *verb* [T] **1** to think that something is likely to be true, although you have no proof **farzetmek, varsaymak, üstlenmek** [+ (that)] *Everything was quiet when I got home so I assumed that you had gone out.* **2 assume control/power/responsibility, etc** to take a position of control/power/responsibility, etc **sorumluluğu, kontrolü üstlenmek, üzerine almak** *He assumed the role of spokesman for the group.* **3 assume an air/expression, etc** *formal* to pretend to have a feeling that you do not have **bir havaya girmek, gibi davranmak, olduğundan farklı davranmak 4 assume a false identity/name, etc** to pretend to be someone else **başkası gibi davranmak, kendini birinin yerine koyarak davranmak** *an assumed name*

assumption ...... İLE BİRLİKTE KULLANILAN KELİMELER

make an assumption ● **be based on** an assumption ● a **basic/common/false/underlying** assumption ● **do** sth **under** the assumption **that** ● an assumption **about** sth

assumption /əˈsʌmpʃ³n/ *noun* [C] **1** something that you think is true without having any proof **zan, sanı, varsayım** *People tend to make assumptions about you when you have a disability.* ○ *These calculations are based on the assumption that prices will continue to rise.* **2 the assumption of power/responsibility, etc** *formal* when someone takes a position of power/responsibility, etc **sorumluluğu, gücü ele geçirme, gücün elde bulundurulması**

assurance /əˈʃʊərᵊns/ noun **1** [C] a promise vaat, söz, güvence, sigorta, garanti, teminat [+ that] *He gave us an assurance that it would not happen again.* **2** [U] confidence **güven, kendine güven, özgüven** *He spoke with calm assurance.*

assure /əˈʃɔːʳ/ verb [T] **1** to tell someone that something is certainly true, especially so that they do not worry **birini emin kılmak, inandırmak, garanti vermek** [+ (that)] *She assured them that she would be all right.* **2** to make something certain to happen **garanti etmek, güvence vermek** *This loan should assure the company's future.*

assured /əˈʃʊəd/ adjective **1** showing skill and confidence **güvenilir, güvenli, özgüveni olan, becerikli, emin** *an assured performance* **2 be assured of sth** to be certain to get or achieve something in the future **bir şeyden emin olmak** *They are now assured of a place in the final.* ➔See also: self-assured.

asterisk /ˈæstᵊrɪsk/ noun [C] a written symbol in the shape of a star (*), often used to mark a particular word, phrase, etc **bir şeyi belirtmek için kullanılan sembol, işaret, yıldız, asteriks**

asthma /ˈæsmə/ noun [U] an illness which makes it difficult to breathe **astım** *She had an asthma attack.* ● **asthmatic** /æsˈmætɪk/ adjective *an asthmatic child* **astıma dair**

astonish /əˈstɒnɪʃ/ verb [T] to make someone very surprised **şaşırtmak, hayrete düşürmek** *Her quick recovery has astonished doctors.*

astonished /əˈstɒnɪʃt/ adjective very surprised **şaşkın, şaşırmış** *He was astonished at her behaviour.*

astonishing /əˈstɒnɪʃɪŋ/ adjective very surprising **şaşırtan, hayrete düşüren** *It's astonishing that so many people believed his story.* ● **astonishingly** adverb **şaşırtıcı bir şekilde**

astonishment /əˈstɒnɪʃmənt/ noun [U] extreme surprise **şaşkınlık, hayret** *The others stared at him in astonishment.* ○ *To my astonishment, he started laughing.*

astound /əˈstaʊnd/ verb [T] to make someone very surprised **hayretler içinde bırakmak, çok şaşırtmak** *The speed of her recovery has astounded doctors.*

astounded /əˈstaʊndɪd/ adjective very surprised **çok şaşırmış** *I'm astounded at/by these prices.*

astounding /əˈstaʊndɪŋ/ adjective very surprising **hayrete düşüren, şaşkınlık yaratan** *an astounding success* ● **astoundingly** adverb **şaşırtıcı bir şekilde**

astray /əˈstreɪ/ adverb **1 go astray** to get lost or go in the wrong direction **kaybolmak, yoldan çıkmak, yanlış yola sapmak, yolunu kaybetmek** *One of my bags went astray at the airport.* **2 lead sb astray** to encourage someone to do bad things that they should not do **yoldan çıkarmak, kötü yola düşmesine sebep olmak, baştan çıkarmak, ayartmak, azdırmak** *He was led astray by his friends.*

astride /əˈstraɪd/ adverb If you sit or stand astride something, you have one foot on each side of it. **bacakları iki yana açık olarak**

astro- /ˈæstrəʊ-/ prefix relating to stars or outer space **uzaya ve yıldızlara ilişkin (önek)** *astronomer* ○ *astrophysics*

astrology /əˈstrɒlədʒi/ noun [U] the study of the positions and movements of stars and planets to say how they might influence people's lives **yıldızbilimciliği, müneccimlik, astroloji** ● **astrologer** noun [C] someone who studies astrology **gökbilimci** ● **astrological** /ˌæstrəˈlɒdʒɪkəl/ adjective **astroloji ile ilgili**

astronaut /ˈæstrənɔːt/ noun [C] someone who travels into space **astronot**

astronomical /ˌæstrəˈnɒmɪkᵊl/ adjective **1** An astronomical amount is extremely large. **çok fazla, görülmemiş miktarda, değerde** *astronomical prices* **2** relating to astronomy **gökbilime ilişkin, gökbilimsel** ● **astronomically** adverb **çok pahalı**

astronomy /əˈstrɒnəmi/ noun [U] the scientific study of stars and planets **gökbilimi, yıldızların ve gezegenlerin bilimsel çalışması, astronomi** ● **astronomer** noun [C] a scientist who studies astronomy **gök cisimlerini bilimsel olarak çalışan bilim adamı**

astute /əˈstjuːt/ adjective good at judging situations and making decisions which give you an advantage **kurnaz, akıllı, cin gibi, sezgileri kuvvetli, öngörüsü gelişmiş** *an astute businesswoman* ○ *politically astute* ● **astutely** adverb **zekice**

asylum /əˈsaɪləm/ noun **1** [U] when someone is allowed to stay somewhere because they are escaping danger in another country **sığınma 2** [C] old-fashioned a hospital for people with a mental illness **akıl hastanesi, tımarhane** ➔See also: political asylum.

aˈsylum ˌseeker noun [C] someone who leaves their country to escape from danger, and tries to get permission to live in another country **sığınmacı, sığınma talebinde bulunan**

asymmetrical /ˌeɪsɪˈmetrɪkᵊl/ adjective not being exactly the same shape and size on both sides **asimetrik** ● **asymmetry** /eɪˈsɪmɪtri/ noun [U] **aynı şekil ve büyüklükte olmayan**

∘ᴗ **at** strong form /æt/ weak form /ət/ preposition **1** [PLACE] used to show the place or position of something or someone **bir şeyin veya birinin konumunu, yerini göstermede kullanılır, ... de, da** *We met at the station.* ○ *She's at the library.* **2** [TIME] used to show the time something happens ... de, da, zamanında *The meeting starts at three.* **3** [DIRECTION] towards or in the direction of ... e, ... a doğru *She threw the ball at him.* ○ *He's always shouting at the children.* **4** [ABILITY] used after an adjective to show a person's ability to do something **sıfatlardan sonra bir kişinin bir şeyde başarılı, iyi olduğunu belirtir** *He's good at making friends.* **5** [CAUSE] used to show the cause of something, especially a feeling **bir şeyin sebebini belirtir, özellikle bir hissin** *We were surprised at the news.* **6** [AMOUNT] used to show the price, speed, level, etc of something **ücret, hız, seviye belirtmede kullanılır** *He denied driving at 120 miles per hour.* **7** [ACTIVITY] used to show a state or activity **bir durumu veya eylemi bildirmede** *a country at war* **8** [INTERNET] the @ symbol, used in email addresses to separate the name of a person, department, etc from the name of the organization or company **elektronik posta işaretinin '@' okunuşunu belirtir**

ate /eɪt/, /et/ past tense of eat **yemek' fiilinin geçmiş zaman hali**

atheist /ˈeɪθiɪst/ noun [C] someone who believes that there is no god **Tanrı'nın varlığına inanmayan, ateist** ● **atheism** noun [U] **Tanrının varlığına inanmama durumu**

athlete /ˈæθliːt/ noun [C] someone who is very good at a sport and who competes with others in organized events **koşucu, atlet**

athletic /æθ'letɪk/ *adjective* **1** strong, healthy, and good at sports **güçlü, atletik ve sağlıklı 2** [always before noun] relating to athletes or to the sport of athletics **atletizm ve atletlere ilişkin**

athletics /æθ'letɪks/ UK (US **track and field**) *noun* [U] the sports which include running, jumping, and throwing **atletizm sporu** ⟳Orta kısımdaki renkli sayfalarına bakınız.

-athon /-əθɒn/ *suffix* an event or activity that lasts a long time, usually to collect money for charity **uzun süre devam eden faaliyet veya eylem** *a walkathon* (= a long walk)

atlas /'ætləs/ *noun* [C] a book of maps **harita atlası** *a road atlas* ○ *a world atlas*

ATM /ˌeɪtiː'em/ *noun* [C] *mainly US abbreviation for* automated teller machine: a machine that you get money from using a plastic card **otomatik para çekme makinası**

🧩 **atmosphere** .... İLE BİRLİKTE KULLANILAN KELİMELER

create an atmosphere ● an atmosphere **of** [fear/trust, etc] ● a **family/friendly relaxed** atmosphere

atmosphere /'ætməsfɪə^r/ *noun* **1** [no plural] the feeling which exists in a place or situation **bir yerin havası, genel durumu** *a relaxed atmosphere* **2** the atmosphere the layer of gases around the Earth **atmosfer, dünyayı çevreleyen gazlardan oluşan tabaka 3** [no plural] the air inside a room or other place **kapalı bir alanın havası** *a smoky atmosphere*

atmospheric /ˌætməs'ferɪk/ *adjective* **1** [always before noun] relating to the air or to the atmosphere **hava veya atmosferle ilgili** *atmospheric conditions* **2** creating a special feeling, such as mystery or romance **gizem ve romans yaratan, farklı bir his uyandıran** *atmospheric music/lighting*

atom /'ætəm/ *noun* [C] the smallest unit that an element can be divided into **atom**

atomic /ə'tɒmɪk/ *adjective* **1** [always before noun] relating to atoms **atoma ilişkin** *an atomic particle* **2** using the energy created when an atom is divided **atom enerjisi kullanan** *atomic power/weapons*

a,tomic 'bomb (*also* 'atom ˌbomb) *noun* [C] a very powerful bomb which uses the energy created when an atom is divided **atom bombası**

a,tomic 'energy *noun* [U] energy which is produced by dividing atoms **atom enerjisi**

atop /ə'tɒp/ *preposition* US on the top of **tepesinde, üstünde, başının üstünde, en üstünde**

atrium /'eɪtriəm/ *noun* [C] *plural* **atriums** atria a large, central room with a glass roof in an office building, restaurant, etc **çatısı camla kaplı büro, lokanta vb. alışveriş mağazalarının bulunduğu geniş alan, merkezi yer**

atrocious /ə'trəʊʃəs/ *adjective* **1** extremely bad **çok kötü, acımasız, zalim** *atrocious weather* **2** violent and shocking **şiddetli ve şok edici** *an atrocious crime*

atrocity /ə'trɒsəti/ *noun* [C, U] when someone does something extremely violent and shocking **acımasızlık, şiddet, büyük kötülük** *Soldiers have been committing atrocities against civilians.*

○ᴴ**attach** /ə'tætʃ/ *verb* [T] **1** JOIN to join or fix one thing to another **tutturmak, bağlamak, iliştirmek** *She attached a photograph to her letter.* **2 attach importance/value, etc to sb/sth** to think that someone or something has importance/value, etc **bir şeye, birine, önem/değer atfetmek, vermek, öyle olduğunu düşünmek** *You attach too much importance to money.* **3** INCLUDE to include something as part of something

else **bir şeye ilave olarak dahil etmek, eklemek** *There were too many conditions attached to the deal.* ⟳See also: no strings (string¹) (attached). **4** COMPUTER to add an attachment (= computer file) to an email message **e-posta iletisine ekleme yapmak**

attached /ə'tætʃt/ *adjective* **be attached to sb/sth** to like someone or something very much **birine, birşeye bağlanmak, müptelası olmak, çok sevmek** *I've become rather attached to my old car.*

attachment /ə'tætʃmənt/ *noun* **1** FEELING [C, U] a feeling of love or strong connection to someone or something **bağlılık, birine, birşeye güçlü bağlılık hissi, düşkünlük, tutkunluk** *I wasn't aware of any romantic attachments.* **2** EMAIL [C] a computer file which is sent together with an email message **bir ileti eki** *I wasn't able to open that attachment.* **3** EQUIPMENT [C] an extra part which can be added to a piece of equipment **ek, ilave** *There's a special attachment for cleaning in the corners.*

🧩 **attack** .... İLE BİRLİKTE KULLANILAN KELİMELER

1 launch/mount an attack ● be **under** attack ● a **bomb/terrorist** attack ● an attack **on** sb/sth
2 launch/mount an attack ● **be/come under** attack ● a **personal/scathing** attack ● an attack **on** sb/sth

○ᴴ**attack¹** /ə'tæk/ *noun* **1** VIOLENCE [C, U] a violent act intended to hurt or damage someone or something **saldırı, taarruz, atılma, hücum** *a terrorist attack on the capital* **2** CRITICISM [C, U] when you say something to strongly criticize someone or something **birine eleştirel bir saldırı, bulaşma, eleştiri** *a scathing attack on the president* **3** ILLNESS [C] a sudden, short illness **nöbet, kriz, ani rahatsızlık** *a nasty attack of flu* **4** SPORT [C, U] in games such as football, when the players in a team try to score points, goals, etc **futbolda hücum, atak** ⟳See also: counter-attack.

○ᴴ**attack²** /ə'tæk/ *verb* **1** VIOLENCE [I, T] to use violence to hurt or damage someone or something **saldırmak, hücum etmek** *He was attacked and seriously injured by a gang of youths.* **2** CRITICISM [T] to strongly criticize someone or something **eleştirmek, sürekli kusur bulmak, saldırmak** *She attacked the government's new education policy.* **3** DISEASE [T] If a disease, chemical, etc attacks someone or something, it damages them. **saldırıya uğramak, kimyasal madde veya hastalığa maruz kalmak** *The virus attacks the central nervous system.* **4** SPORT [I, T] If players in a team attack, they move forward to try to score points, goals, etc. **saldırıya, hücuma geçmek, atak geliştirmek**

attacker /ə'tækə^r/ *noun* [C] a person who uses violence to hurt someone **saldırgan** *The police think she must have known her attackers.*

attain /ə'teɪn/ *verb* [T] to achieve something, especially after a lot of work **öğrenmek, elde etmek, kazanmak** *She's attained a high level of fitness.* ● **attainable** *adjective* possible to achieve **elde edilebilir, kazanılabilir, başarılabilir** ● **attainment** *noun* [C, U] when you achieve something **başarı, kazanım, hüner, beceri, marifet**

🧩 **attempt** .... İLE BİRLİKTE KULLANILAN KELİMELER

make an attempt ● a **successful/unsuccessful** attempt ● an attempt **at** sth/doing sth ● **in** an attempt to do sth

○ᴴ**attempt¹** /ə'tempt/ *noun* [C] **1** when you try to do something **teşebbüs, girişim, deneme** *This is his second attempt at the exam.* ○ [+ to do sth] *They closed the road in an attempt to reduce traffic in the city.* ○ *She made no attempt* (= did not try) *to be sociable.* **2 an attempt on**

sb's life when someone tries to kill someone **birinin hayatına kasdetmek, saldırmak, saldırıya geçmek**

○ᴧ**attempt²** /ə'tempt/ *verb* [T] to try to do something, especially something difficult **teşebbüs etmek, saldırmak, girişmek** [+ to do sth] *He attempted to escape through a window.*

attempted /ə'temptɪd/ *adjective* **attempted murder/robbery, etc** when someone tries to commit a crime but does not succeed **soygun ve cinayet girişimi**

attend...... BAŞKA BİR DEYİŞLE

Attend yerine genellikle **come/go** to kullanılır. *How many people* **came to** *the meeting?* • *He* **goes to** *church regularly.*
Make yerine bazen kişinin bir davete veya olaya yetişip yetişemeyeceği konuşulurken kullanılır. *I'm afraid I can't* **make** *the meeting this afternoon* (= I will not be able to attend).
Make it ifadesi bir yere, problemlere rağmen, varıldığında kullanılır. *The traffic was so bad we only just* **made it** *in time for the start of the film.*

attend /ə'tend/ *verb* [I, T] *formal* **1** to go to an event **katılmak, yer almak, devam etmek** *to attend a concert/meeting* **2 attend a church/school, etc** to go regularly to a particular church/school, etc **sürekli devam etmek, takip etmek**

YAYGIN HATALAR

attend

Unutmayın! Attend fiilini bir olaya veya davete katılmak anlamında kullandığınız zaman, hiçbir zaman **to** veya **at** edatları kullanılmaz. Attend **to/at** an event yanlıştır. Doğru kullanım şekli **attend an event** şeklindedir.: ~~Twenty of our staff will attend to the training course.~~ Yanlış cümle örneği

Twenty of our staff will attend the training course.

attend to sb/sth *phrasal verb formal* to deal with something or help someone **bir şeyle ilgilenmek veya birine yardım etmek**

attendance /ə'tendəns/ *noun* [C, U] **1** the number of people who go to an event, meeting, etc **katılım, devam, mevcudiyet** *falling attendance* **2** when you go somewhere such as a church, school, etc regularly **yoklama, katılım, devam** *His attendance at school is very poor.* **3 in attendance** *formal* present at an event **var, hazır, orada, mevcut** *They have doctors in attendance at every match.*

attendant /ə'tendənt/ *noun* [C] someone whose job is to help the public in a particular place **belirli yerlerde halka yardım etme amacıyla bulunan kişiler** (mağaza, otopark) *a parking attendant* ⊃See also: **flight attendant**.

attention...... İLE BİRLİKTE KULLANILAN KELİMELER

pay attention (**to** sth/sb) • **give** sth attention • **have/hold/keep** sb's attention • **careful/full/special/undivided** attention

○ᴧ**attention** /ə'tenʃ°n/ *noun* [U] **1** when you watch, listen to, or think about something carefully or with interest **dikkat** *Ladies and gentlemen, could I* **have your attention**, *please?* **2 pay attention (to sth)** to watch, listen to, or think about something carefully or with interest **dikkat etmek, can kulağıyla dinlemek, seyretmek** *You weren't paying attention to what I was saying.* **3 bring/draw (sb's) attention to sth/sb** to make someone notice something or someone **birinin dikkatini çekmek, dikkatini vermesini sağlamak** *If I could just draw your attention to the second paragraph.* **4 attract/get (sb's) attention** to make someone notice

you **birinin farketmesini sağlamak, dikkatini çekmek** *I waved at him to get his attention.* **5** treatment to deal with a problem **özen, itina, dikkat** *medical attention* ○ *This old engine needs a lot of attention.*

attentive /ə'tentɪv/ *adjective* listening or watching carefully and showing that you are interested **dikkatli, özenli, ilgili, alakadar olan** *an attentive student* • **attentively** *adverb* **dikkatlice**

attest /ə'test/ *verb* [I, T] *formal* to show or prove that something is true **bildirmek, açıklamak, göstermek**

attic /'ætɪk/ *noun* [C] a room at the top of a house under the roof **tavan arası**

attire /ə'taɪə'/ *noun* [U] *old-fashioned* the clothes that you wear **giysi, kıyafet, elbise** • **attired** *adjective* dressed in a particular way **giyinmiş, giyinik, belli bir tarzda giyinmiş** *suitably attired*

attitude...... İLE BİRLİKTE KULLANILAN KELİMELER

have/take a [positive/responsible, etc] attitude • a **casual/hostile/negative/positive** attitude • (sb's) attitude **to/towards** sth/sb

○ᴧ**attitude** /'ætɪtjuːd/ *noun* [C, U] how you think or feel about something and how this makes you behave **tavır, eda, davranış** *a positive attitude* ○ *He has a very bad attitude to/towards work.*

attorney /ə'tɜːni/ *noun* [C] *US* a lawyer **avukat** *a defense attorney* ⊃See also: **district attorney.**

○ᴧ**attract** /ə'trækt/ *verb* [T] **1** to make people come to a place or to a particular thing by being interesting, enjoyable, etc **çekmek, cezbetmek** *The castle attracts more than 300,000 visitors a year.* ○ *to* **attract** *more science graduates to teaching.* **2 attract attention/interest, etc** to cause people to pay attention/be interested, etc **dikkat çekmek, ilgisini çekmek, cezbetmek, 3 be attracted to sb** to like someone, especially sexually, because of the way they look or behave **birini cazibesine kapılmak, etkilenmek, cazip bulmak, sevmek, hoşlanmak** *I was attracted to him straight away.* **4** If something attracts a substance or object, it causes it to move towards it. **çekmek, harekete geçirmek** *Magnets attract metal.*

attraction...... İLE BİRLİKTE KULLANILAN KELİMELER

an **added/a big/the main/a major/the star** attraction • a **tourist** attraction • the attraction **of** sth • an attraction **for** sb

attraction /ə'trækʃ°n/ *noun* **1** [C] something that makes people come to a place or want to do a particular thing **çekim, cezbetme** *a tourist attraction* ○ *The opportunity to travel is one of the main attractions of this job.* **2** [U] when you like someone, especially sexually, because of the way they look or behave **cazibe, cinsel cazibe** *physical attraction*

attractive...... BAŞKA BİR DEYİŞLE

Beautiful ve lovely sıfatları genellikle **attractive** sıfatının yerine kullanılır ve hem kişi hem de cansız varlıkların tasvirinde kullanılırlar. *His wife is very* **beautiful.** • *We drove through some really* **beautiful/lovely** *countryside.* • *You look* **lovely!**
Eğer bir kişi çekiciyse, bu durumda kişi için **good-looking** ifadesi kullanılabilir. **Handsome** sıfatı erkekler için ve **pretty** sıfatı da bayanlar için kullanılır. *He's certainly very* **good-looking.** • *Your daughter is very* **pretty.**
Eğer kişi çok çekiciyse, onlar için **gorgeous** veya **stunning** ifadeleri kullanılır. *You look* **gorgeous** *in that dress!* • *Her daughter is absolutely* **stunning.**
Eğer bir şey çok çekiciyse, **breathtaking, exquisite,**

A

stunning veya **gorgeous** ifadeleri kullanılır. *The views from the window were* **breathtaking** • *These hand-made decorations are* exquisite.
Küçük boyutundan dolayı bir kişi veya şey çekici ise, **cute** veya **sweet** ifadeleri kullanılır. *He's got a really* cute *baby brother.* • *Look at that kitten - isn't she* sweet?
stylish ve **chic** sıfatları bir şeyin çekici ve modaya uygun hale getirildiğini göstermek için kullanılır. *He took me to a very* chic *restaurant.* • *Their house is very* stylish.

○ᴬ**attractive** /ə'træktɪv/ *adjective* **1** beautiful or pleasant to look at çekici, güzel, hoş, cezbedici *an attractive woman* ○ *I find him very attractive.* **2** interesting or useful ilginç, faydalı, hoşa giden, *We want to make the club* **attractive** *to a wider range of people.* ⟳Opposite unattractive. • **attractively** *adverb* ilgi çeken bir şekilde • **attractiveness** *noun* [U] çekicilik

attributable /ə'trɪbjətəbl/ *adjective* **attributable to sth** caused by something bir şeye yorulabilir, bağlanabilir *A lot of crime is attributable to the use of drugs.*

attribute¹ /ə'trɪbjuːt/ *verb*
attribute sth to sth *phrasal verb* to say that something is caused by something else bir şeyi başka bir şeye yormak, bağlamak, atfetmek *He attributes his success to hard work.*
attribute sth to sb *phrasal verb* to say that someone wrote, said, or made something bir şeyi birine atfetmek, yormak, bağlamak, maletmek *This drawing has been attributed to Picasso.*

attribute² /'ætrɪbjuːt/ *noun* [C] a quality or characteristic that someone or something has özellik, nitelik, hususiyet, karakteristik *Her hair is her best attribute.*

attributive /ə'trɪbjətɪv/ *adjective* An attributive adjective comes before the noun it describes. nitelik sıfatı ⟳Compare predicative.

aubergine /'əʊbəʒiːn/ *UK* (*US* eggplant) *noun* [C, U] an oval, purple vegetable that is white inside patlıcan ⟳Orta kısımdaki renkli sayfalarına bakınız.

auburn /'ɔːbən/ *adjective* Auburn hair is red-brown. kestane rengi, kızıla çalan kahverengi

auction /'ɔːkʃən/ *noun* [C, U] a sale in which things are sold to the person who offers the most money açıkartırma, mezat • **auction** (*also* auction off) *verb* [T] to sell something at an auction açık artırmada satma, açık artırmaya çıkarmak

auctioneer /ˌɔːkʃən'ɪər/ *noun* [C] the person who is in charge of an auction açık artırma yapan kişi

audacity /ɔː'dæsəti/ *noun* [U] showing too much confidence in your behaviour in a way that other people find shocking or rude cesurluk, yürekli davranış, kendine güveni olan *And then he had the audacity to blame me for his mistake!* • **audacious** /ɔː'deɪʃəs/ *adjective* küstah

audible /'ɔːdəbl/ *adjective* If something is audible, you can hear it. işitilebilir, kolay duyulabilen *His voice was barely audible.* ⟳Opposite inaudible. • **audibly** *adverb* duyulabilir şekilde

audience ...... İLE BİRLİKTE KULLANILAN KELİMELER

1 be in the audience • a member of the audience
2 reach an audience • sth's target audience • a wide audience

○ᴬ**audience** /'ɔːdiəns/ *noun* **1** GROUP [group] the people who sit and watch a performance at a theatre, cinema, etc dinleyici *There were a lot of children in the audience.* **2** TYPE [group] the type of people who watch a particular TV show, read a particular book, etc bir filmin ya da kitabın müdavimi, sürekli izleyen ve dinleyici

This magazine is aimed at a teenage audience. **3** MEETING [C] *formal* a formal meeting with an important person resmi bir toplantıya davet, kabul, huzura davet, kabul etme *an audience with the Queen*

audio /'ɔːdiəʊ/ *adjective* relating to the recording or playing of sound ses kaydı ve çalınmasıyla ilgili *audio equipment*

audio- /ɔːdiəʊ-/ *prefix* relating to hearing or sound (önek) duymak ya da sesle ilgili, ilişkin *audiotape*

audit /'ɔːdɪt/ *noun* [C] when an independent person examines all the financial records of a company to produce a report hesap ya da bilanço kontrolü yapan kişi • **audit** *verb* [T] kontrol etmek • **auditor** *noun* [C] denetçi

audition /ɔː'dɪʃən/ *noun* [C] when someone does a short performance to try to get a job as an actor, singer, etc oyuncu ve şarkıcı vb. konularda bir işe girmek için yapılan yetenek denemesi, kısa rol çalışması • **audition** *verb* [I] seçmelere katılmak

auditorium /ˌɔːdɪ'tɔːriəm/ *noun* [C] the part of a theatre, hall, etc where people sit to watch a performance konferans, gösteri salonu, oditoryum

Aug *written abbreviation for* August ağustos

augment /ɔːg'ment/ *verb* [T] *formal* to increase the size or value of something by adding something to it çoğaltmak, arttırmak, değerlendirmek

○ᴬ**August** /'ɔːgəst/ (*written abbreviation* Aug) *noun* [C, U] the eighth month of the year ağustos

○ᴬ**aunt** /ɑːnt/ (*also* auntie, aunty /'ɑːnti/) *noun* [C] the sister of your mother or father, or the wife of your uncle teyze, hala ⟳See also: agony aunt.

au pair /ˌəʊ'peər/ *noun* [C] a young person who goes to live with a family in another country and looks after their children, does work in their house, etc dil öğrenmek amacıyla başka ülkede aile yanında kalan, verilen işleri yapan ve onlarla yaşayan gençler (daha çok bayan)

aura /'ɔːrə/ *noun* [C] a feeling which a person or place seems to have bir yere, kişiye ilişkin his, duygu, aora *an aura of mystery*

aural /'ɔːrəl/ *adjective* relating to hearing işitmeyle ilgili

auspices /'ɔːspɪsɪz/ *noun* **under the auspices of sb/sth** *formal* with the help or support of a person or organization bir kişi ya da kuruluşun desteği, yardımıyla, ... in himayesiyle, sayesinde *The conference was held under the auspices of the Red Cross.*

auspicious /ɔː'spɪʃəs/ *adjective* If an event or time is auspicious, it makes you believe that something will be successful in the future. hayırlı, umut verici, uğurlu *an auspicious start*

austere /ɒs'tɪər/ *adjective* **1** plain, simple, and without unnecessary decorations or luxuries basit, sıradan, herhangi bir süsü ve lüksü olmayan, sade, yalın, gösterişsiz *an austere room* **2** strict or severe çetin, zor, güç *an austere woman* • **austerity** /ɒs'terəti/ *noun* [U] yalınlık

authentic /ɔː'θentɪk/ *adjective* If something is authentic, it is real, true, or what people say it is. hakiki, orijinal, gerçek *authentic Italian food* • **authentically** *adverb* orijinal, gerçek bir şekilde • **authenticity** /ˌɔːθen'tɪsəti/ *noun* [U] gerçek, orjinal

○ᴬ**author** /'ɔːθər/ *noun* [C] someone who writes a book, article, etc yazar *a popular author of children's fiction*

authoritarian /ˌɔːθɒrɪ'teəriən/ *adjective* very strict and not allowing people freedom to do what they want otoriter, disiplinli *an authoritarian leader/regime*

authoritative /ɔː'θɒrɪtətɪv/ *adjective* **1** An authoritative book, report, etc is respected and considered to be accurate. güvenilir, inanılır, o konuda söz sahibi *an authoritative guide* **2** confident and seeming to be in control of a situation hakim olan, otorite sağlayan, kendinden emin *an authoritative manner/voice*

◦━**authority** /ɔː'θɒrəti/ *noun* **1** [POWER] [U] the official power to make decisions or to control other people yetki, otorite *a position of authority* ○ [+ to do sth] *The investigators have the authority to examine all the company's records.* ○ *We need the support of someone in authority.* **2** [OFFICIAL GROUP] [C] an official group or government department with power to control particular public services yasal, resmi yetkisi olan grup veya devlet dairesi *the local housing authority* **3** [QUALITY] [U] the quality of being confident and being able to control people bilirkişi, uzman, otorite *She has an air of authority.* **4** an authority on sth someone who has a lot of knowledge about a particular subject bir konuda uzman olan, yetkili, bilirkişi olan *She is an authority on seventeenth-century English literature.* ⊃See also: local authority

authorize (*also UK* -ise) /'ɔː'θ³raɪz/ *verb* [T] **1** to give official permission for something yetkili kılmak, yetki vermek **2** be authorized to do sth to be officially allowed to do something bir şeyi yapmaya resmi yetkili olmak, söz sahibi olmak *Only managers are authorized to sign expense forms.* • **authorization** /,ɔː'θ³raɪ'zeɪʃ³n/ *noun* [U] yetki

autistic /ɔː'tɪstɪk/ *adjective* Autistic children have a mental illness which causes problems with communicating and forming relationships. otistik, zihinsel hastalığı olan • **autism** /'ɔː'tɪz³m/ *noun* [U] otizm

auto /'ɔː'təʊ/ *adjective* US relating to cars otolarla ilgili *the auto industry*

auto- /ɔː'tə/ *prefix* **1** operating without being controlled by humans 'kendi kendine çalışan' anlamında önek *autopilot* (= a computer that directs an aircraft) **2** self 'kendi' anlamında önek *autobiography* (= a book that someone writes about their own life)

autobiography /,ɔː'təʊbaɪ'ɒɡrəfi/ *noun* [C] a book written by someone about their own life yaşam öyküsü, özyaşam kitabı, detaylı öykü ve özgeçmiş • **autobiographical** /,ɔː'təʊbaɪəʊ'ɡræfɪkəl/ *adjective* Kişinin kendi hayatıyla ilgili yazdığı kitap

autograph /'ɔː'təɡrɑːf/ *noun* [C] a famous person's name, written by that person onlü birinin imzası, adı soyadı • **autograph** *verb* [T] *an autographed photo* kendi el yazısı ile imza atmak

automate /'ɔː'təmeɪt/ *verb* [T] to control something using machines and not people makinalar yardımıyla bir şeyi kontrol etmek, makineleştirmek • **automated** *adjective* *a fully automated system* otomasyon uygulanan • **automation** /,ɔː'tə'meɪʃ³n/ *noun* [U] otomasyon

automatic¹ /,ɔː'tə'mætɪk/ *adjective* **1** [MACHINE] An automatic machine works by itself or with little human control. kendi kendine çalışan, otomatik *automatic doors* **2** [CERTAIN] certain to happen as part of the normal process or system olması kesin, kaçınılmaz olan *You get an automatic promotion after two years.* **3** [REACTION] done as a natural reaction without thinking kendiliğinden, kendi kendine, doğal bir tepki olarak oluşan *My automatic response was to pull my hand away.* • **automatically** *adverb* otomakik bir şekilde

automatic² /,ɔː'tə'mætɪk/ *noun* [C] a car in which you do not have to change the gears (= parts that control how fast the wheels turn) otomatik vitesli araba

automobile /'ɔː'təməʊbiːl/ *noun* [C] US a car araba, otomobil *the automobile industry*

automotive /,ɔː'tə'məʊtɪv/ *adjective* [always before noun] relating to cars and car production araba ve araba üretimiyle ilgili, otomotiv *the automotive industry*

autonomous /ɔː'tɒnəməs/ *adjective* independent and having the power to make your own decisions kendi kendini yönetebilen, otonom, özerk *an autonomous region/state*

autonomy /ɔː'tɒnəmi/ *noun* [U] the right of a country or group of people to govern itself özerklik, otonomi *Local councils need more autonomy.*

autopsy /'ɔː'tɒpsi/ *noun* [C] a medical examination of a dead body to discover the exact cause of death otopsi

◦━**autumn** /'ɔː'təm/ *noun* (*also US* fall) *noun* [C, U] the season of the year between summer and winter, when leaves fall from the trees sonbahar *I'm starting a new job in the autumn.* ○ *autumn leaves* • **autumnal** /ɔː'tʌmnəl/ *adjective* typical of autumn sonbahara ait, sonbahara özgü

auxiliary /ɔː'ɡ'zɪliəri/ *adjective* providing extra help or support yardımcı, yardım eden *an auxiliary nurse*

au,xiliary 'verb *noun* [C] a verb which is used with another verb to form tenses, negatives, and questions. In English the auxiliary verbs are 'be', 'have', and 'do'. yardımcı fiil

avail /ə'veɪl/ *noun* to no avail without success, especially after a lot of effort beyhude, sonuçsuz, başarısız, boş yere *She sent more than 50 letters, but to no avail.*

 available ...... İLE BİRLİKTE KULLANILAN KELİMELER

be/become available • make sth available • easily/ freely/readily/widely available • be available to sb

◦━**available** /ə'veɪləbl/ *adjective* **1** If something is available, you can use it or get it. mevcut, hazır *This information is available free on the Internet.* ○ *The new drug is not yet available to the public.* **2** If someone is available, they are not busy and so are able to do something. uygun, hazır, meşgul değil, görüşmeye hazır *No one from the company was available to comment on the accident.* ⊃Opposite unavailable. • **availability** /ə,veɪlə'-bɪləti/ *noun* [U] bulunabilirlilik

avalanche /'æv³lɑːnʃ/  avalanche
noun [C] **1** when a large amount of snow falls down the side of a mountain çığ **2** an avalanche of sth a sudden, large amount of something, usually more than you can deal with çığ gibi olmak, çığ gibi gelmek, bir şeyin ani artışı, ortaya çıkışı *an avalanche of mail*

avant-garde /,æv³ŋ'ɡɑːd/ *adjective* If art, music, etc, is avant-garde, it is new and unusual in style. yeni ve alışık olunmayan tarz, avangard, öncü, yenilikçi

avarice /'æv³rɪs/ *noun* [U] formal a strong feeling that you want a lot of money and possessions para hırsı, servet/ün/şan/şöhret tutkusu, hırsı

avatar /'æv³tɑː'/ *noun* [C] an electronic image of a person that represents the computer user, especially in games bilgisayar oyunlarında kişiyi temsil eden elektronik görüntü, imaj

A

Ave *written abbreviation for* avenue **bulvar, geniş cadde** *132, Gainsborough Ave*

avenge /ə'vendʒ/ *verb* [T] *literary* to punish someone for doing something bad to you, your family, etc **öcünü almak, öç almak, acısını çıkarmak** *He swore he would avenge his brother's death.*

avenue /'ævənjuː/ *noun* [C] **1** (*written abbreviation* **Ave**) a wide road in a town or city, often with trees along it **iki tarafı ağaçlarla kaplı geniş cadde, bulvar 2** a possible way of doing or achieving something **bir sonuca, başarıya ulaştıran yol, başarıya giden yol** *We have exhausted all other avenues of treatment.*

⚬⁻**average**¹ /'ævərɪdʒ/ *adjective* **1** [USUAL] usual and like the most common type **sıradan, diğerleriyle aynı olan, vasat** *an average person* ○ *an average day* **2** [AMOUNT] [always before noun] An average amount is calculated by adding some amounts together and then dividing by the number of amounts. **ortalama miktar, ölçüde olan** *an average age/temperature* **3** [NOT EXCELLENT] not excellent, although not bad **vasat, sıradan** *The food was pretty average.*

⚬⁻**average**² /'ævərɪdʒ/ *noun* **1** [C] an amount calculated by adding some amounts together and then dividing by the number of amounts **ortalama** *They work an average of 30.5 hours per week.* **2** [C, U] the usual or typical amount **vasat, sıradan olan** *well above/below average* **3 on average** usually, or based on an average **ortalama olarak, aşağı yukarı** *Female workers earn, on average, a third less than men.*

average³ /'ævərɪdʒ/ *verb* [T] to reach a particular amount as an average **belli bir ortalamayı tutturmak, ulaşmak** *He averages about 20 points a game.*

averse /ə'vɜːs/ *adjective* **1 not be averse to sth** *UK humorous* to be happy or willing to do or have something **hevesli olmak, istekli davranmak, bir şeyi yapmaktan, sahip olmaktan dolayı mutlu olmak** *She's not averse to the occasional glass of champagne.* **2 be averse to sth** *formal* to strongly dislike something **karşı olmak, fazlasıyla nefret etmek, hoşlanmamak**

aversion /ə'vɜːʒən/ *noun* **an aversion to sth** when you strongly dislike something **bir şeye karşı duyulan aşırı isteksizlik ve hoşlanmama**

avert /ə'vɜːt/ *verb* **1 avert a crisis/disaster/war, etc** to prevent something bad from happening **bir krizi/hastalığı/savaşı önlemek, engel olmak 2 avert your eyes/face/gaze** to turn your head away so that you do not see something **kafasını başka yöne çevirmek, öbür tarafa dönmek, bakmamak**

avian flu /ˌeɪviən'fluː/ *noun* [U] bird flu: an illness that kills birds and can sometimes pass from birds to people **kuş gribi**

aviary /'eɪviˀri/ *noun* [C] a large cage for birds **büyükçe bir kuş kafesi**

aviation /ˌeɪvi'eɪʃˀn/ *noun* [U] flying aircraft or producing aircraft **havacılık** *the aviation industry*

avid /'ævɪd/ *adjective* very interested and enthusiastic **hevesli, coşkulu, istekli, gayretli** *an avid reader* • **avidly** *adverb* **ilgili ve istekli şekilde**

avocado /ˌævə'kɑːdəʊ/ *noun* [C, U] a dark green, oval fruit which is pale green inside and is not sweet **avokado**

⚬⁻**avoid** /ə'vɔɪd/ *verb* [T] **1** to stay away from a person, place, situation, etc **kaçınmak, sakınmak, uzak durmak, (argo) atlatmak, birini ekmek** *Try to avoid the city centre.* **2** to prevent something from happening **önlemek, engel olmak, karşı durmak** *Book early to avoid disappointment.* **3 avoid doing sth** to intentionally not do something **bir şeyi yapmaktan kaçınmak,**

göz ardı etmek, ihmal etmek, uzak durmak *She managed to avoid answering my question.* • **avoidable** *adjective* possible to avoid **gözardı edilebilir, ihmal edilebilir, kaçınılabilir** ↻Opposite **unavoidable.** • **avoidance** *noun* [U] when you avoid something **kaçınma, gözardı etme, sakınma**

await /ə'weɪt/ *verb* [T] *formal* **1** to wait for something **beklemek** *We are awaiting the results of the tests.* **2** If something awaits you, you will experience it in the future. **beklemek, gelecekte bir şeyin olmasını beklemek** *A surprise awaits her when she gets home.*

⚬⁻**awake**¹ /ə'weɪk/ *adjective* **1 be/lie/stay, etc awake** to not be sleeping **uyanık kalmak, uyumamak** *Is Tom awake yet?* ○ *The noise from the party kept me awake all night.* **2 be wide awake** to be completely awake **tamamen uyanık olmak**

awake² /ə'weɪk/ *verb* [I, T] *past tense* **awoke**, *past part* **awoken** *literary* to wake up, or make someone wake up **uyandırmak**

awaken /ə'weɪkən/ *verb* **1** [T] *formal* to cause an emotion, feeling, etc **bir his duyguyu uyandırmak** *The song awakened painful memories.* **2** [I, T] *literary* to wake up, or make someone wake up **uyandırmak, uyanmak**

awakening /ə'weɪkənɪŋ/ *noun* [no plural] **1** when you start to be aware of something or feel something **uyanan, farkına varan, olup biteni anlayan 2 a rude awakening** If you have a rude awakening, you have a shock when you discover the truth about a situation. **hayal kırıklığına uğrayarak uyanma, bir şeyin farkında olma**

▦ **award** ...... İLE BİRLİKTE KULLANILAN KELİMELER

present/receive/win an award • an award for sth • an awards ceremony • an award winner

award¹ /ə'wɔːd/ *noun* [C] **1** a prize given to someone for something they have achieved **ödül, başarı ödülü** *the award for best actress* ○ *to receive/win an award* **2** money given to someone because of a legal decision **para ödülü**

award² /ə'wɔːd/ *verb* [T] to officially give someone something such as a prize or an amount of money **ödül vermek** [+ two objects, often passive] *He was awarded the Nobel Prize for Physics.*

⚬⁻**aware** /ə'weəʳ/ *adjective* **1 be aware of/that** to know about something **bir şeyin farkında olmak, farkına varmak** *Are you aware of the risks involved?* ○ *She was well aware that he was married.* ↻Opposite **unaware.** **2** interested in and knowing a lot about a particular subject **farkında, haberdar** *politically/socially aware*

▦ **awareness** ...... İLE BİRLİKTE KULLANILAN KELİMELER

create/increase/raise awareness • a greater/growing/heightened/increased awareness • public awareness • an awareness about/of sth • an awareness among [parents/students, etc]

awareness /ə'weənəs/ *noun* [U] when you know about something **farkındalık, bilinçlenme, bilinç** *Environmental awareness is increasing all the time.*

awash /ə'wɒʃ/ *adjective* **be awash with sth** *UK* (*US* **be awash in sth**) to have a lot of something, often too much **bir şeyle dopdolu olmak, çalkalanmak** *The sport is awash with money.*

⚬⁻**away**¹ /ə'weɪ/ *adverb* **1** [DIRECTION] to or in a different place or situation **farklı bir yere/konuma, konumda, yerde** *Go away and leave me alone.* ○ *We'd like to move away from the town centre.* **2** [DISTANCE FROM] at a particular distance from a place **uzakta, ötede** *The* nearest town was ten miles away. ○ How far away is the station? **3** NOT THERE not at the place where someone usually lives or works **uzaklarda, başka yerlerde** Shirley's feeding the cat while we're away. **4** SAFE PLACE into a usual or safe place **bilinen veya emin bir yere** Can you put everything away when you've finished? **5 two weeks/five hours, etc away** at a particular time in the future **ik hafta/beş saat vb. sonra, ötede, uzakta** My exam's only a week away now. **6** CONTINUOUS ACTION used after a verb to mean 'continuously or repeatedly' **devamlı', 'tekrar, tekrar' anlamında** Chris was hammering away in the garden all day. **7** GRADUALLY gradually disappearing until almost or completely gone **gitgide gözden uzaklaşan, kaybolan ve tamamen yok olacak biçimde** The snow has melted away. **8** SPORT UK If a sports team is playing away, the game is at the place where the other team usually plays. **deplasmanda, evsahibi takımın sahasında** ➡See also: take your breath away, give the game¹ away.

away² /ə'weɪ/ adjective [always before noun] UK In sports, an away game is played at the place where the other team usually plays. **deplasman**

awe /ɔ:/ noun [U] **1** a feeling of great respect and sometimes fear **merak ve birazda korku içeren saygı** I was filled with awe at the sheer size of the building. **2 be in awe of sb** to feel great respect for someone **birisine çok büyük saygı duymak, hürmet göstermek** As children we were rather in awe of our grandfather.

awe-inspiring /'ɔ:ɪnspaɪərɪŋ/ adjective causing people to feel great respect or admiration **büyük hayranlık veya saygı uyandıran**

awesome /'ɔ:səm/ adjective very great, large, or special and making you feel respect and sometimes fear **saygı uyandıran, heybetli, ürkütücü, çok özel** an awesome challenge/responsibility ○ The scenery was awesome.

o⊶**awful** /'ɔ:fˀl/ adjective **1** very bad, of low quality, or unpleasant **korkunç, berbat, nahoş, kalitesiz, dehşet** an awful place ○ The film was absolutely awful. **2 an awful lot (of sth)** informal a large amount **korkunç büyük miktar, çok fazla, yeterinden çok fazla** It cost an awful lot of money.

awfully /'ɔ:fˀli/ adverb very **çok, ziyadesiyle, aşırı, müthiş, acayip** awfully difficult/good

awhile /ə'waɪl/ adverb US for a short time **kısa bir süre için** Let's wait awhile and see what happens.

o⊶**awkward** /'ɔ:kwəd/ adjective **1** DIFFICULT difficult or causing problems **çetin, zor ve sorun çıkaran, sakar** an awkward customer ○ an awkward question **2** EMBARRASSING embarrassing and not relaxed **münasebetsiz, uygunsuz, mahcup eden** an awkward pause/silence ○ I'm in an awkward situation. **3** NOT ATTRACTIVE moving in a way that is not attractive **hantal, biçimsiz, yakışıksız** His movements were slow and awkward. • **awkwardly** adverb problem yaratan **şekilde** • **awkwardness** noun [U] problem yaratan, **zor durum**

awoke /ə'wəʊk/ past tense of awake **awake fiilinin geçmiş zaman hali**

awoken /ə'wəʊkˀn/ past participle of awake **awake fiilinin 3. hali (uyanık)**

awry /ə'raɪ/ adverb **go awry** to not happen in the correct way **tersine gitmek, yolunda gitmemek** Suddenly everything started to go awry.

axe¹ (also US **ax**) /æks/ noun [C] a tool consisting of a wooden handle with a sharp piece of metal at one end, used for cutting trees or wood **balta**

axe² (also US **ax**) /æks/ verb [T] to get rid of something or someone suddenly **bir şeyden, birinden aniden kurtulmak, kesip atmak, bırakmak** The company has announced plans to axe 500 jobs.

axes /'æksi:z/ plural of axis **eksen**

axis /'æksɪs/ noun [C] plural **axes** /'æksi:z/ **1** an imaginary, central line around which an object turns **eksen 2** a line at the side or bottom of a graph (= picture showing measurements) **bir grafiğin altında veya yanında ölçümleri gösteren çizgi, hat**

axle /'æksl/ noun [C] a long metal bar which connects two wheels on a vehicle **aks, dingil**

aye /aɪ/ exclamation informal yes, used especially in Scotland and the North of England **daha çok İskoçya ve İngiltere'nin kuzeyinde kullanılan 'evet' anlamında sözcük**

B

B, b /biː/ the second letter of the alphabet **alfabenin ikinci harfi**

BA /ˌbiːˈeɪ/ *noun* [C] *abbreviation for* Bachelor of Arts: a university or college qualification in an arts (= not science) subject which usually takes 3 or 4 years of study **sanat ve sosyal bilimler alanında alınan lisans diploması**

baa /bɑː/ *noun* [C] the sound that a sheep makes **koyun sesi, mee**

babble /ˈbæbl/ *verb* [I] to talk quickly in a way which is confused, silly, or has no meaning **yarım yamalak konuşmak, bebek gibi konuşmak** ● **babble** *noun* [U] *the babble of voices* **mırıldanma, laf geveleme**

babe /beɪb/ *noun* [C] **1** *very informal* a young, attractive woman **genç, çekici kadın, bebek gibi kadın 2** *literary* a baby **bebek**

📑 baby ...... İLE BİRLİKTE KULLANILAN KELİMELER

have/be expecting/give birth to a baby ● a baby is born ● a new/newborn baby

०►**baby** /ˈbeɪbi/ *noun* [C] **1** a very young child **çok genç çocuk** *a baby girl/boy* ○ *baby clothes* ○ *Liz has had a baby.* ○ *Maria's expecting a baby* (= she is pregnant). **2** a very young animal **çok genç hayvan yavrusu** *a baby bird*

ˈbaby ˌboom *noun* [C] a time when a lot of babies are born in a particular area **doğum oranındaki artış** *the postwar baby boom*

ˈbaby ˌcarriage *noun* [C] *US* a small vehicle with four wheels for carrying a baby **bebek arabası, puset**

babyish /ˈbeɪbiɪʃ/ *adjective* Babyish behaviour is silly, like the behaviour of a young child. **çocukça, çocuk gibi**

babysit /ˈbeɪbisɪt/ *verb* [I, T] **babysitting**, *past* **babysat** to look after children while their parents are not at home **çocuk bakmak, çocuk bakıcılığı yapmak** ● **babysitter** *noun* [C] *We'd like to come, but we can't get a babysitter.* **bebek bakıcısı** ● **babysitting** *noun* [U] **bebek bakma**

bachelor /ˈbætʃ⁹ləʳ/ *noun* [C] **1** a man who is not married **bekâr 2 Bachelor of Arts/Science/Education, etc** a university or college qualification which usually takes 3 or 4 years of study, or a person who has this qualification **eğitim, fen, sanat ve sosyal bilimler alanında alınan lisans diploması**

०►**back¹** /bæk/ *adverb* **1** [RETURNING] where someone or something was before **geçmişte** *When do you go back to college?* ○ *I put it back in the cupboard.* **2** [BEHIND] in a direction behind you **geriye doğru** *Anna stepped back.* ○ *Flint leaned back in his chair.* **3** [REPLY] as a reply or reaction to something **cevap, karşılık olarak** *UK to ring back/ US to call back* ○ *I signalled to her and she waved back.* **4** [STATE] to the state something or someone was in before **geri, eski haline doğru** *Hopefully things will get back to normal again now.* ○ *I'm sure we can put it back together again* (= repair it). ○ *Try to go back to sleep.* **5** [EARLIER] at or to an earlier time **öncelere, geçmişe ya da geçmişte, öncesinde** *We first met back in 1973.* ○ *Looking back, I think we did the right thing.* **6** [AWAY FROM] in a direction away from something **uzağa, öteye, geriye doğru** *He pulled back the curtain.* **7 back and forth** (*also UK* **backwards and forwards**) in one direction, then the opposite way, then in the origi-

nal direction again many times **ileri geri, git gel, sürekli aynı yönde ve geri** *He has to travel back and forth between London and Paris every week.*

०►**back²** /bæk/ *noun* [C] **1** [NOT FRONT] the part of something that is furthest from the front or in the opposite direction to the front **arka, geri** *He wrote his number down on the back of an envelope.* ○ *I always keep a blanket in the back of the car.* **2** [BODY] the part of your body from your shoulders to your bottom **sırt** *back injuries/pain* ○ *He was lying on his back.* ᗡ*Orta kısımdaki renkli sayfalarına bakınız.* **3** [SEAT] the part of a seat that you lean against when you are sitting **oturulan sandalyenin arkası, sırtlığı** *the back of a chair* **4 back to front** *UK* with the back part of something where the front should be **arkadan öne, geriden öne doğru** *You've got your trousers on back to front.* **5 in back of** *US* behind **gerisinde, arkasında** *They sat in back of us on the plane.* **6 at/in the back of your mind** If you have a thought or idea at the back of your mind, you are always thinking about it. **kafasının gerisinde, zihninde, zihninin gerisinde** ● **7 behind sb's back** If you do something behind someone's back, you do it without them knowing, often in an unfair way. **birinin arkasından, haberi olmadan** *Have they been saying things about me behind my back?* ● **8 be glad/happy, etc to see the back of sb/sth** *UK* to be pleased when someone leaves or something ends because you did not like them **hoşlanmadığı bir şeyin bitişini, birinin gidişini görmekten memnun olmak** ● **9 be on sb's back** to remind someone again and again to do something, or to criticize someone in an annoying way **sürekli tepesinde olmak, daima hatırlatmak veya rahatsızlık derecesinde eleştirmek** ● **10 turn your back on sb/sth** to decide to stop having contact with someone or something, or to refuse to help someone **birine sırtını çevirmek, sırtını dönmek, artık yardım etmemek** *She turned her back on Hollywood and went to live in Florida.* **back**, be (like) **water¹** off a duck's back.

back³ /bæk/ *verb* **1** [T] to give support or help to a person, plan, or idea **desteklemek, yardım etmek** *He backed Mr Clark in the recent election.* **2** [T] to risk money by saying that you think a horse, team, etc will win a race, game, or competition in order to win more money if they do **çok daha fazla kazanmak için bir takımı, atı vb. desteklemek** *Many people are backing Holyfield to win the fight.* **3 back (sth) away/into/out, etc** to move backwards or drive backwards **geriye gitmek, geri çekilmek, geriye doğru sürmek** *She saw he had a gun and backed away.*

back away *phrasal verb* to show that you do not support a plan or idea any more and do not want to be involved with it **uzak durmak, bulaşmamak, karışmadığını, desteklemediğini göstermek, belli etmek** *The government has backed away from plans to increase taxes.*

back down *phrasal verb* to admit that you were wrong, or agree not to do something **geri adım atmak, hatasını kabul etmek, bir şeyi yapmamayı kabul etmek** *The council backed down over rent increases.*

back off *phrasal verb* **1** to move away from someone, usually because you are afraid **birinden uzak durmak, bulaşmamak, yakın olmamak** *I saw the knife and backed off.* **2** *mainly US* to stop supporting a plan **bir planı desteklemekten vazgeçmek, arka çıkma-**

mak *The president has backed off from a threat to expel U.N. soldiers.*

back out *phrasal verb* to decide not to do something you had planned or agreed to do **vazgeçmek, caymak, planlanan veya üzerinde anlaşılan bir şeyi yapmaktan vazgeçmek** *Nigel backed out at the last minute, so we had a spare ticket.*

back sb up *phrasal verb* **1** to support or help someone **birini desteklemek, arka çıkmak** *My family backed me up in my fight for compensation.* **2** to say that someone is telling the truth **birini sözle desteklemek, yanında olmak** *Honestly, that's exactly what happened - Claire'll back me up.*

back sth up *phrasal verb* **1** to prove that something is true **bir şeyin doğru olduğunu kanıtlamak** [often passive] *His claims are backed up by recent research.* **2** to make an extra copy of computer information **yedeklemek, bilgiyi yedeğe almak, kopyasını çıkarmak**

back (sth) up *phrasal verb* to drive backwards **geriye doğru sürmek, geri çekilmek, geri geri gitmek**

⌐**back⁴** /bæk/ *adjective* **1** [always before noun] at or near the back of something **arkada, sırtta, geride** *back door/ garden/page* ○ *I put it in the back pocket of my jeans.* **2** **back road/street** a very small road or street that goes behind or between buildings **arka cadde/yol/ sokak** ➔See also: put sth on the back burner.

backache /ˈbækeɪk/ *noun* [C, U] a pain in your back **sırt ağrısı**

backbench /ˌbækˈbentʃ/ *adjective UK* **a backbench MP/ politician, etc** a member of the government who does not have an important position **önemli konumda olmayan hükümet üyesi, milletvekili, politikacı ● backbencher** *noun* [C] a backbench politician **aktif, önemli görevi olmayan siyasetçi**

the backbenches /ˌbækˈbentʃɪz/ *noun* [plural] *UK* the place where backbench politicians sit **kabinede görev almayan milletvekillerinin oturduğu yer, mevki** *He prefers to remain on the backbenches.*

backboard /ˈbækbɔːd/ *noun* [C] in basketball (= a sport), a board behind the metal ring that you have to throw the ball through to score **basket potası, çemberin tutturulduğu arka pano** ➔Orta kısımdaki renkli sayfalarına bakınız.

backbone /ˈbækbəʊn/ *noun* [C] **1** the main or strongest part of something **belkemiği, bir şeyin ana ve en güçlü parçası** *The car industry remains the backbone of the area's economy.* **2** the line of bones down the centre of your back **omurga, belkemiği**

backdrop /ˈbækdrɒp/ *noun* [C] **1** the situation that an event happens in **bir hadisenin, olayın olduğu durum** [usually singular] *The attack took place against a backdrop of rising tensions between the two communities.* **2** the painted cloth at the back of a stage in a theatre **tiyatroda sahne gerisinde boyalı örtü, kumaş parçası**

backer /ˈbækər/ *noun* [C] someone who supports a person or plan, especially by giving them money **maddi destek sağlayarak birini, bir planı destekleyen kimse**

backfire /ˌbækˈfaɪər/ *verb* [I] If something that you do backfires, it has the opposite result of what you wanted. **olumsuz sonuç vermek, geri tepmek, umulduğu gibi olmamak**

---

background ...... İLE BİRLİKTE KULLANILAN KELİMELER

come from a [poor/different, etc] background **●** sb's **family** background

---

background /ˈbækɡraʊnd/ *noun* **1** [SOUND] [no plural] Sounds in the background are not the main sounds

you can hear. **geri taraf, arka plan** *background music/noise* ○ *I could hear a baby crying in the background.* **2** [PERSON] [C] a person's education, family, and experience of life **bir kişinin geçmişi, ailesi, eğitimi, yaşam tecrübesi** *She came from a middle-class background.* **3** [PICTURE] [C, U] the parts at the back of a picture, view, etc which are not the main things you look at **bir tablonun, resmin geri planı, zemini** *gold stars on a black background* **4** [SITUATION] [C] the situation that an event happens in, or things which have happened in the past which affect it **bir hadisenin, olayın geçmişi, oluş biçimi** [usually singular] *The talks are taking place against a background of economic uncertainty.* **5** in **the background** If a person stays in the background, they try not to be noticed. **geri planda, arka zeminde**

backhand /ˈbækhænd/ *noun* [C] when you hit a ball with your arm across your body, in sports such as tennis **teniste raketin dışarı alışveriş**

backing /ˈbækɪŋ/ *noun* [U] support, especially money, for a person or plan **destekleme, arka çıkma, yardım etme** *financial backing* ○ *The proposal has the full backing of the government.*

backlash /ˈbæklæʃ/ *noun* [C] when people react against an idea which was previously popular **önceleri meşhur olan bir düşünceye, inanışa karşı olma, karşı çıkma** [usually singular] *a backlash against the royal family*

backlog /ˈbæklɒɡ/ *noun* [C] work that should have been done earlier **birikmiş işler, önceden yapılmış olması gereken iş**

backpack /ˈbækpæk/ *noun* [C] a bag that you carry on your back **sırt çantası** ➔See picture at luggage. **● backpacking** *noun* [U] *to go* **backpacking sırt çantasıyla seyahate çıkma ● backpacker** *noun* [C] **sırt çantasıyla seyahate çıkıp istediği yeri ziyaret eden kişi**

backpack

backside /ˌbækˈsaɪd/ ⓊＳ /ˈbækˌsaɪd/ *noun* [C] *informal* the part of your body that you sit on **popo, kıç**

backslash /ˈbækslæʃ/ *noun* [C] the symbol '\', used in computer programs **bilgisayar programlarında kullanılan '\' imge** ➔Compare forward slash.

backstage /ˌbækˈsteɪdʒ/ *adverb* in the area behind the stage in a theatre where performers get ready **kulis**

backstroke /ˈbækstrəʊk/ *noun* [U] a style of swimming on your back **sırtüstü yüzme**

back-to-back /ˌbæktəˈbæk/ *adjective, adverb* **1** If two people or things are back-to-back, their backs are touching or facing each other. **sırt sırta** *They stood back-to-back.* **2** If two things happen back-to-back, one happens after the other without a pause. **arka arkaya, peş peşe** *back-to-back interviews*

backtrack /ˈbæktræk/ *verb* [I] to say that you did not mean something you said earlier **önceden söylediği şeyleri kasdetmediğini söylemek** *The government has backtracked on its promises.*

backup /ˈbækʌp/ *noun* **1** [C, U] extra help, support, or equipment which is available if you need it **destek, yardım, ilave yardım** *Medical staff are on call to provide backup in case of an emergency.* **2** [C] an extra copy of computer information **yedek, bilgisayarda bilginin yedeklemesi** *to make a backup*

backward /'bækwəd/ *adjective* **1** [always before noun] in the direction behind you **geride, arkada** *a backward glance* **2** less developed or slower to develop than normal **az gelişmiş ya da normalden az hızla gelişen** *a backward country*

⚬**backwards** /'bækwədz/ (*also* **backward**) *adverb* **1** DIRECTION towards the direction behind you **geriye doğru, arkaya doğru** *She took a couple of steps backwards.* **2** EARLIER towards an earlier time or an earlier stage of development **gelişmenin ilk safhalarına ya da başlarına doğru** *Let's start with your most recent job and work backwards.* **3** OPPOSITE ORDER in the opposite order to what is usual **alışılmış olanın akside, tersine doğru** *"Erehwon" is "nowhere" spelled backwards.* **4** WRONG WAY (*also UK* **back to front**) with the part that is usually at the front at the back **tersinden, arkasını öne** *You've got your skirt on backwards.* **5** **backwards and forwards** *UK (UK/US* **back and forth**) in one direction then the opposite way and back again many times **sürekli ileri geri, öne arkaya doğru** *I have to drive backwards and forwards between here and Ipswich every day.* **6** **bend over backwards** to try extremely hard to help or to please someone **birine yardım etmek veya memnun etmek için sıkı denemelerde bulunmak** [+ to do sth] *She bent over backwards to help him.*

backyard /ˌbæk'jɑːd/ *noun* [C] *US* the area behind a house **arka bahçe**

bacon /'beɪkⁿn/ *noun* [U] meat from a pig cut into long thin slices **domuz pastırması**

bacteria /bæk'tɪəriə/ *noun* [plural] very small living things that sometimes cause disease **bakteri** ● **bacterial** *adjective* made from or caused by bacteria **bakterinin neden olduğu, bakteriden olan** *bacterial infections*

⚬**bad** /bæd/ *adjective* **worse**, **worst** **1** NOT PLEASANT not pleasant **hoş olmayan, nahoş** *bad weather* ○ *bad news* ○ *My phone bill was even worse than I'd expected.* ○ *He's in a bad mood today.* **2** LOW QUALITY of low quality **kötü** *bad behaviour* ○ *The service was really bad.* ○ *He's always been bad at maths.* **3** SEVERE very serious or severe **çok kötü, ciddi, zor, çetin, fena** *a bad injury* ○ *the worst flooding for years* **4** NOT LUCKY not lucky, not convenient, or not happening how you would like **uygun değil, şans getirmeyen, istenildiği gibi olmayan** *It was just bad luck that she heard us.* ○ *Is this a bad time to ask?* **5** **not bad** satisfactory **fena değil, fena sayılmaz** *"There are about 10 people in a group." "Oh well, that's not bad." ○ That's not bad for such a small company.* **6** **be bad for sb/sth** to be harmful for someone or something **birisine/birşeye zarar vermek, kötü olmak** *Looking at a computer screen for too long can be bad for your eyes.* **7** **feel bad about sth/doing sth** to feel guilty or sorry about something that has happened **olan bir şeyden ötürü kendini kötü veya suçlu hissetmek** *I felt bad about letting her down.* **8** **too bad a** SYMPATHY *mainly US informal* used to say that you are sorry about a situation **fena, tüh, eyvah, kötü** *"He didn't get the job." "Oh, that's too bad."* **b** CANNOT CHANGE *informal* used to say that nothing can be done to change a situation **Çok fena, çok kötü, eyvah, ne yazık** *I know you don't want to go but it's too bad, we have to.* **9** EVIL evil, kötülük yapan, şeytanca davranan *She's a really bad person.* **10** NOT FRESH Bad food is not fresh and cannot be eaten. **bozulmuş, çürük** **11** PAINFUL [always before noun] If you have a bad arm, leg, heart, etc, there is something wrong with it and it is painful. **ağrıyan, sızlayan, kötü durumda olan** ⊃See also: bad blood, be in sb's good/bad books (book¹).

baddie /'bædi/ *noun* [C] *mainly UK informal* a bad person in a film, book, etc **kitap, film vb. kötü karakter,**

bade /bæd/ *past tense of* bid³ **bid fiilini 3. hali**

badge /bædʒ/ *noun* [C] **1** a piece of plastic, metal, etc which you wear on your clothes showing your name or the organization you work for **isimlik, isim etiketi, rozet 2** *UK* (*US* **button**) a piece of plastic, metal, etc with words or pictures on it that you wear on your clothes for decoration **kolluk, arma, rozet**

badger /'bædʒə^r/ *noun* [C] a wild animal with thick black and white fur that lives under the ground and comes out at night **porsuk, toprak altında yaşayan ve gece ortaya çıkan kalın siyah ve beyaz tüylü hayvan**

⚬**badly** /'bædli/ *adverb* **worse, worst 1** very seriously **çok ciddi bir şekilde, ciddiyetle,** *badly damaged/injured* **2** in a way that is of low quality or in an unpleasant way **fena halde, kalitesizce, hoş olmayan tarzda** *to behave badly* ○ *They played badly in the first half.*

badminton /'bædmɪntən/ *noun* [U] a sport for two or four people in which you hit a shuttlecock (= a light object with feathers) over a net **badminton**

bad-tempered /ˌbæd'tempəd/ *adjective* a bad-tempered person gets angry or annoyed easily **kötü huylu, geçimsiz** *'Sam's been bad-tempered recently, is something worrying him?'*

baffle /'bæfl/ *verb* [T] If something baffles you, you cannot understand it at all. **şaşırtmak, kafasını karıştırmak** [often passive] *The police were baffled by his disappearance.*

bag

handbag

rucksack UK, backpack US

carrier bag UK, grocery bag US

briefcase

⚬**bag¹** /bæg/ *noun* [C] **1** CONTAINER a container made of paper, plastic, etc, used for carrying things **kağıt, plastik vb. maddeden yapılmış torba** *a paper/plastic bag* ○ *He packed his bags and left.* **2** FOR WOMAN (*also* **handbag**) *mainly UK* a bag with handles in which a woman carries her money, keys, etc **çanta, bayanların eşyalarını koydukları çanta 3** AMOUNT the amount a bag contains **çanta dolusu, torba dolusu, yığınla** *It doesn't weigh more than a couple of bags of sugar.* **4** **bags of sth** *mainly UK informal* a large amount of something **çantalar, torbalar dolusu, çok, epeyce** *There's bags of room.* **5** **bags** Bags under your eyes are areas of loose or dark skin. **gözaltı torbacıkları** ⊃See also: carrier bag, let the cat out of the bag, shoulder bag, sleeping bag, tote bag.

bag² /bæg/ *verb* [T] **bagging**, *past* **bagged** *informal* to get something, especially before other people have a chance to take it **herkesten önce almak, elde etmek, ele geçirmek** *Bag us some decent seats.*

bagel /'beɪgªl/ *noun* [C] a type of bread made in the shape of a ring **yuvarlak halka şekilli bir tür ekmek** ⊃See picture at **bread**.

baggage /'bægɪdʒ/ *noun* [U] **1** all the cases and bags that you take with you when you travel **bagaj, eşya** *baggage reclaim* **2** feelings and experiences from the past that influence how you think and behave now **şu an içinde bulunulan hali de etkileyen geçmişten gelen hisler ve tecrübeler** *emotional baggage*

baggy /'bægi/ *adjective* Baggy clothes are big and loose. **geniş, bol, sarkık, asık**

bagpipes /'bægpaɪps/ *noun* [plural] a Scottish musical instrument that is played by blowing air into a bag and forcing it through pipes **tulum, İskoç müzik aleti**

baguette /bæg'et/ *noun* [C] a French-style loaf of bread that is long and thin and white **Fransız usulü ince, uzun, beyaz somun ekmeği, baget** *a ham and cheese baguette*

bail[1] /beɪl/ *noun* [U] when money is paid to a court so that someone can be released from prison until their trial **kefalet, kefalet ücreti** *He was released on bail.* ○ *She was granted bail.*

bail[2] /beɪl/ *verb* **be bailed** If someone is bailed until a particular time, they can leave prison until then if they pay money to the court. **kefaletle serbest bırakılmak**
bail sb out *phrasal verb* **1** to help a person or organization by giving them money **bir kişi ya da kuruma para ile destek olmak, yardımcı olmak** *Companies can't expect the government to keep bailing them out.* **2** to pay money to a court so that someone can be released from prison until their trial **birinin kefaletle serbest bırakılmasını sağlamak, kefalet ödemek**

bailiff /'beɪlɪf/ *noun* [C] **1** UK someone whose job is to take away things people own when they owe money **icra/haciz memuru** **2** US someone whose job is to guard prisoners in a court **gardiyan, muhafız, mübaşir**

bailout /'beɪlaʊt/ *noun* [C] mainly US when a company is given money to solve its financial problems **ticari kefalet, bir şirkete yapılan maddi yardım**

bait[1] /beɪt/ *noun* [U, no plural] **1** food that is used to try to attract fish or animals so that you can catch them **yem, olta veya kapan yemi** **2** something that you use to persuade someone to do something **birini ikna etmek için kullanılan şey, yem**

bait[2] /beɪt/ *verb* [T] **1** to put food in or on something to try to catch fish or animals **yemlemek** *a mouse trap baited with cheese* **2** to try to make someone angry by laughing at them or criticizing them **birini alaycı bir gülme ile veya eleştirerek kızdırmaya çalışmak, alay etmek**

bake /beɪk/ *verb* [I, T] to cook something such as bread or a cake with dry heat in an oven **fırında pişirmek, fırınlamak** *a baked apple* ⊃See picture at **cook**.

baked 'beans *noun* [plural] beans cooked in a tomato (= soft, round, red fruit used like a vegetable) sauce and sold in tins (= metal containers) **fırınlanmış fasulyeler**

baked po'tato *noun* [C] a potato baked and served with the skin (= outer layer) still on **fırınlanmış patates**

baker /'beɪkəʳ/ *noun* [C] someone who makes and sells bread, cakes, etc **fırıncı** *Can you call at **the baker's** and get a loaf of bread?*

bakery /'beɪkªri/ *noun* [C] a shop where you can buy bread, cakes, etc **fırın**

baking /'beɪkɪŋ/ *adjective informal* Baking weather is very hot. **kavurucu derecede sıcak olan, pişiren**

B

⟐⟐⟐ **balance** .... İLE BİRLİKTE KULLANILAN KELİMELER

1 keep/lose your balance ● knock/throw sb off balance ● sb's sense of balance
2 find/maintain/strike a balance ● redress the balance ● a delicate balance ● a balance between sth and sth

balance[1] /'bæləns/ *noun* **1** [WEIGHT] [U] when the weight of someone or something is spread in such a way that they do not fall over **denge** *I lost my balance and fell off the bike.* ○ *The force of the explosion threw him **off balance** (= it was difficult for him to stay standing).* **2** [EQUAL] [U, no plural] when the correct amount of importance is given to each thing so that a situation is successful **denge, dengeli oran, dağıtım** *We hope to **strike a balance between** police powers and the protection of citizens.* ⊃Opposite **imbalance**. **3** [FAIR] [U] when you consider all the facts in a fair way **dengede tutma, herşeyi değerlendirme, dikkate alma** *I felt his report lacked balance.* **4** **on balance** used to give your opinion after you have considered all the facts about something **herşey hesaba katılmış** *On balance, I'd prefer a woman dentist to a man.* **5** [MONEY] [C] the amount of money that you still have to pay, or that you have left to use **kalan miktar, bakiye** [usually singular] *I always pay off the balance on my credit card each month.* **6** **be/hang in the balance** If something hangs in the balance, nobody knows if it will continue to exist in the future or what will happen to it. **ortada kalmak, arada kalmak, ne yapacağını bilememek, ortada olmak, henüz belli olmamak** *After a bad year, Judd's career hung in the balance.*

balance[2] /'bæləns/ *verb* **1** [I, T] to be in a position where you will not fall to either side, or to put something in this position **dengede tutmak** *She was trying to balance a book on her head.* **2** [T] to give the correct amount of importance to each thing so that a situation is successful **dengelemek** *I struggle to balance work and family commitments.* **3** **balance the books/budget** to make sure that you do not spend more money than you get **bütçeyi dengelemek, bütçeyi dengede tutmak**
balance sth against sth *phrasal verb* to compare the advantages and disadvantages of something **bir şeyin avantaj ve dezavantajlarını kıyaslamak** *The ecological effects of the factory need to be balanced against the employment it provides.*

balanced /'bælənst/ *adjective* **1** considering all the facts in a fair way **dengeli** *a balanced discussion of his work* **2** **a balanced diet/meal** a healthy mixture of different kinds of food **dengeli beslenme/diyet yapma** ⊃See also: **well-balanced**.

balance of 'payments *noun* [no plural] mainly UK the difference between how much a country pays to other countries and how much it gets paid by other countries **ödemeler dengesi**

balance of 'power *noun* [no plural] the way in which power is divided between different people or groups **güçler dengesi** *maintaining the balance of power in the European Union*

'balance ,sheet *noun* [C] a document that shows what a company has earned and what it has spent **bilanço**

balcony /'bælkəni/ *noun* [C] **1** a small area joined to the wall outside a room on a high level where you can stand or sit **balkon** **2** the seats in an upper area of a theatre **tiyatroda balkon**

bald 50 o̅ Important words to learn

bald /bɔːld/ *adjective* **1** with little or no hair **kel, az saçı olan** *John started to go bald at an early age.* ○ *I've got a bald patch/spot.*
2 [always before noun] Bald facts or ways of saying things are very clear and are not intended to comfort you. **çıplak, gerçeğin ta kendisi** ● **baldness** *noun* [U] **kellik**

balding /ˈbɔːldɪŋ/ *adjective* becoming bald **kelleşmek, saçların dökülmesi**

baldly /ˈbɔːldli/ *adverb* If you say something baldly, you say it in a very clear way which may upset the person you are speaking to. **dosdoğru, çarpıtmadan, tüm çıplaklığıyla** *"I don't love you any more," he said baldly.*

bale /beɪl/ *noun* [C] a large amount of something such as paper, cloth, or hay (= dried grass), that is tied together so that it can be stored or moved **balya, demet, deste, denk**

baleful /ˈbeɪlfᵊl/ *adjective formal* evil or angry **kötü, kızgın, fena, kem** *a baleful look*

balk (*also UK* **baulk**) /bɔːlk/ ⑤ /bɔːk/ *verb* [I] to not want to do something that is unpleasant or difficult **kaçınmak, sakınmak, uzak durmak** *Most people balk at paying these kind of prices for clothes.*

ball

o̅ **ball** /bɔːl/ *noun* [C] **1** a round object that you throw, kick, or hit in a game, or something with this shape **top** *a tennis ball* ○ *a ball of string* **2** a large formal occasion where people dance **balo 3 have a ball** *informal* to enjoy yourself very much **eğlenmek 4 be on the ball** *informal* to be quick to understand and react to things **kolay kavrayıp hemen anlamak ve tepki vermek** ● **5 set/start the ball rolling** to begin an activity that involves a group of people **ortak bir eylemi başlatmak, ilk vuruşu yapmak** *I've started the ball rolling by setting up a series of meetings.* ⇒See also: ball game, crystal ball.

ballad /ˈbæləd/ *noun* [C] a song that tells a story, especially about love **türkü, balad**

ballerina /ˌbæləˈriːnə/ *noun* [C] a female ballet dancer **balerin, bayan bale dansçısı**

ballet /ˈbæleɪ/ ⑤ /bæˈleɪ/ *noun* **1** [DANCING] [U] a type of dancing that is done in a theatre and tells a story, usually with music **balet, erkek bale dansçısı 2** [PERFORMANCE] [C] a particular story or performance of

ballet dancing **bale 3** [DANCERS] [C] a group of ballet dancers who work together **bale dansçıları** *the Royal Ballet*

'ball ˌgame *noun* [C] **1** *US* a game of baseball (= where teams hit a ball and run round four fixed points), basketball (= where teams throw a ball through a high net), or American football **topla oynanan oyunlar 2 a whole new ball game** *informal* (*also* a different ball game) a completely different situation from how things were before **öncekinden farklı yeni bir durum, farklı bir durum** *We'd been climbing in Scotland, but the Himalayas were a whole new ball game.*

ballistic /bəˈlɪstɪk/ *adjective* **go ballistic** *informal* to suddenly become very angry **aniden kızmak, sinirlenmek, küplere binmek**

balloon

hot-air balloon

balloon¹ /bəˈluːn/ *noun* [C] a small coloured rubber bag that you fill with air to play with or to use as a decoration **balon** *Could you help me to blow up some balloons?* ⇒See also: hot-air balloon.

balloon² /bəˈluːn/ *verb* [I] to suddenly become much larger **büyümek, genişlemek, balon yapmak** *I ballooned to 14 stone when I had my second baby.*

ballot …… İLE BİRLİKTE KULLANILAN KELİMELER

hold a ballot ● a ballot on sth ● be on a ballot ● UK ballot papers ● a ballot box

ballot¹ /ˈbælət/ *noun* [C, U] a secret written vote **oylama** *to hold a ballot* ○ *She was the only candidate on the ballot* (= available to vote for). ○ *UK ballot papers* ○ *a ballot box* (= box where votes are collected)

ballot² /ˈbælət/ *verb* [T] *mainly UK* to ask people to vote in a ballot so that you can find out their opinion about something **oylamak, oylamaya sunmak** *In July he will ballot his members on how they want to proceed.*

ballpark /ˈbɔːlpɑːk/ *noun* **1** [C] *US* a place where baseball (= game where teams hit a ball and run round four fixed points) is played and watched **beyzbol alanı, sahası 2 ballpark estimate/figure** a number or amount that is not exact but should be near the correct number or amount **tahmini rakamlar, tahminler, tahmini miktar** *$3 million would be a ballpark figure for sales next year.*

ballpoint pen /ˌbɔːlpɔɪntˈpen/ *noun* [C] a pen with a very small ball in the end that rolls ink onto the paper **tükenmez kalem**

ballroom /ˈbɔːlruːm/ *noun* [C] a large room where dances are held **balo salonu**

bamboo /bæmˈbuː/ **bamboo**
noun [C, U] a tall plant with hard hollow stems, often used for making furniture **bambu, kamış**

ban¹ /bæn/ verb [T] banning, past banned to officially say that someone must not do something **resmen yasaklamak, men etmek** *A lot of people think boxing should be banned.* ○ [+ from + doing sth] *Ian's been banned from driving for 2 years.*

🧩 **ban** ...... İLE BİRLİKTE KULLANILAN KELİMELER

impose/introduce/lift a ban ● a blanket/complete/outright/total ban ● a ban on (doing) sth

---

ban² /bæn/ noun [C] an official rule that people must not do or use something **resmi yasaklama, men** *There is a ban on developing land around the city.*

banal /bəˈnɑːl/ adjective ordinary and not exciting **sıradan, hiç bir özelliği olmayan, banal** *banal pop songs*

o→ **banana** /bəˈnɑːnə/ noun [C, U] a long, curved fruit with a yellow skin **muz** ⊃Orta kısımdaki renkli sayfalarına bakınız.

o→ **band¹** /bænd/ noun [C] **1** [MUSIC] a group of musicians who play modern music together **müzik topluluğu, grup, orkestra** *a jazz band* **2** [LINE] a line of a different colour or design **şerit, çizgi, renk şeridi** *The band of lighter coloured soil marks the position of the fort.* **3** [CIRCLE] a piece of material put around something **bağ, kuşak, kayış, sargı, bandaj** *an elastic band* **4** [PEOPLE] a group of people who do something together **topluluk, grup** *the Cathedral's band of regular worshippers* **5** [PART] UK one of the groups that something is divided into **bir şeyin bölündüğü gruplardan biri** *the 20-25 age band* ⊃See also: elastic band, rubber band.

band² /bænd/ verb
band together phrasal verb to work with other people in order to achieve something **iş birliği yapmak, ortak çalışma grubu oluşturmak, imece usulü çalışmak, birleşmek, bir araya gelmek** *Companies banded together to keep prices high.* ⊃Opposite disband.

bandage¹ /ˈbændɪdʒ/ **bandage**
noun [C] a long piece of soft cloth that you tie around an injured part of the body **bandaj, sargı**

bandage² /ˈbændɪdʒ/ verb [T] to put a bandage around a wound or injury **sargı yapmak, bandajlamak**

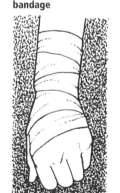

Band-Aid /ˈbændeɪd/ US trademark (UK plaster) noun [C] a small piece of cloth or plastic that sticks to your skin to cover and protect a small wound **yara bandı**

BandB /ˌbiːənˈbiː/ noun [C] abbreviation for bed and breakfast **oda ve kahvaltı**

bandit /ˈbændɪt/ noun [C] a thief who attacks people who are travelling in a wild place **haydut**

bandwagon /ˈbændˌwæɡən/ noun **get/jump on the bandwagon** to become involved in an activity which is successful so that you can get the advantages of it yourself **çıkar elde etmek için iyi giden bir eylemde yer almak, sürüye uymak** *Publishers are rushing to get on the CD-ROM bandwagon.*

bandwidth /ˈbændwɪtθ/ noun [usually singular] the amount of information per second that can move between computers connected by a telephone wire **dalga genişliği, bant aralığı**

bang¹ /bæŋ/ noun [C] **1** a sudden loud noise **patlama, infilak** *The door slammed with a deafening bang.* **2** when you suddenly hit part of your body on something hard **darbe, güm diye çıkan ses, küt diye ses** *a nasty bang on the head* informal If **3 go out with a bang** someone or something goes out with a bang, they stop existing or doing something in an exciting way. **aniden yok olmak, kaybolmak, bir şeyi yapmaktan vazgeçmek** ● **4 more bang for your buck(s)** US informal the best result for the smallest effort **küçük bir çaba karşılığı en iyi sonuca ulaşma**

bang² /bæŋ/ verb [I, T] **1** to make a loud noise, especially by hitting something against something hard **çarpmak, güm diye ses çıkarmak, çarpışmak, toslamak** *We heard the door bang.* ○ *Ben banged his fist on the desk.* **2** to hit part of your body against something hard **çarpmak, sert bir cisme çarpmak** *Ted fell and banged his head.* ⊃See also: be banging your **head¹** against a brick wall.

bang³ /bæŋ/ adverb UK informal exactly **tam olarak, doğru bir şekilde** *The books were piled up slap bang in the middle of the kitchen table.* ○ *The curtain rose bang on time.*

banger /ˈbæŋəʳ/ noun [C] UK informal **1** an old car that is in a bad condition **eski ve kötü durumda otomobil, külüstür 2** a sausage (= tube of meat and spices) **sosis**

bangle /ˈbæŋɡl/ noun [C] a circle of stiff plastic, metal, etc that people wear around the arm as jewellery **bilezik, halka**

bangs /bæŋz/ noun [plural] US (UK fringe [C]) hair that is cut short and straight at the top of someone's face **kâkül, perçem**

banish /ˈbænɪʃ/ verb [T] **1** to send someone away from a place, often as a punishment **sürgün etmek, kovmak, sürgüne yollamak** [often passive] *He was banished to a remote Alaskan island.* **2** to make yourself stop thinking about something or feeling a particular way **çıkarıp atmak, kendini bir şeyi düşünmekten, hissetmekten alı koymak** *Banish winter blues with a holiday in the sun!*

banister /ˈbænɪstəʳ/ noun [C] a long piece of wood that you can hold as you go up or down stairs **trabzan, merdiven korkuluğu**

banjo /ˈbændʒəʊ/ noun [C] a musical instrument like a guitar with a round body **bir tür gitar, banço**

o→ **bank¹** /bæŋk/ noun [C] **1** [MONEY] an organization or place where you can borrow money, save money, etc **banka** *Most banks are reluctant to lend money to new businesses.* **2** [RIVER] the land along the side of a river **nehir, ırmak kenarı, kıyısı** *We found a shady spot on the river bank.* **3** [STORE] a place where a supply of something can be kept until it is needed **banka, depo** *a blood bank* **4** [PILE] a large pile of snow, sand, or soil **yığın, küme** ⊃See also: bottle bank, merchant bank, piggy bank.

bank² /bæŋk/ verb **1** [I, T] to put or keep money in a bank **bankaya para yatırmak** *to bank a cheque* ○ *Who do you bank with?* ○ *I bank at the First National Bank.* **2** [I] When a plane banks, it flies with one wing higher than the other when turning. **dönüş yapan uçağın yan yatarak uçması**

bank on sb/sth *phrasal verb* to depend on someone doing something or something happening **güvenmek, itimat etmek, umut bağlamak** *Chrissie might arrive on time, but I wouldn't bank on it.*

'**bank a,ccount** *noun* [C] an arrangement with a bank to keep your money there and take it out when you need to **banka hesabı**

banker /'bæŋkə'/ *noun* [C] someone who has an important job in a bank **banker, bankacı**

,**bank 'holiday** *noun* [C] *UK* an official holiday when all banks and most shops and offices are closed **resmi tatil günü** *Spring bank holiday*

banking /'bæŋkɪŋ/ *noun* [U] the business of operating a bank **bankacılık**

banknote /'bæŋknəʊt/ *mainly UK* (*US* bill) *noun* [C] a piece of paper money **kağıt para, banknot**

bankrupt[1] /'bæŋkrʌpt/ *adjective* unable to continue in business because you cannot pay your debts **müflis, batkın, iflas etmiş** *He went bankrupt after only a year in business.*

bankrupt[2] /'bæŋkrʌpt/ *verb* [T] to make someone bankrupt **iflas etmek**

bankruptcy /'bæŋkrəptsi/ *noun* [C, U] when a person or organization becomes bankrupt **iflas** *Factories that continue to make losses could soon face bankruptcy.*

'**bank ,statement** *noun* [C] a piece of paper that shows how much money you have put into your bank account and how much you have taken out **hesap dökümü, dekont, banka defteri,cüzdanı**

banner /'bænə'/ *noun* [C] a long piece of cloth, often stretched between poles, with words or a sign written on it **pankart, bayrak, sancak, başlık, tepe yazısı**

'**banner ,ad** *noun* [C] an advertisement that appears across the top of a page on the Internet **internet sayfalarında tepede verilen reklam**

banquet /'bæŋkwɪt/ *noun* [C] a large formal dinner for a lot of people **ziyafet, şölen**

banter /'bæntə'/ *noun* [U] conversation which is funny and not serious **şaka, latife, alay, istahza**

baptism /'bæptɪzᵊm/ *noun* [C, U] a Christian ceremony in which water is put on someone to show that they are a member of the Church **vaftiz, vaftiz töreni**

Baptist /'bæptɪst/ *adjective* belonging or relating to a Christian group which only believes in baptism for people who are old enough to understand what it means **Baptist, bir Hıristiyan mezhebi mensubu** *the Baptist Church* ● **Baptist** *noun* [C] **vaftiz**

baptize (*also UK* -ise) /bæp'taɪz/ (US) /'bæptaɪz/ *verb* [T] to perform a baptism ceremony for someone **vaftiz etmek**

o➤**bar**[1] /bɑː'/ *noun* [C] **1** [DRINKING] a place where alcoholic drinks are sold and drunk, or the area behind the person serving the drinks **bar, meyhane** *I met him in a bar in Soho.* **2** [BLOCK] a small block of something solid **kalıp (çikolata, sabun vb.), parça** *a chocolate bar* ○ *gold bars* ↪*Orta kısımdaki renkli sayfalarına bakınız.* **3** [LONG PIECE] a long, thin piece of metal or wood **sırık, çubuk, kazık** *There were bars on the downstairs windows.* **4** [PREVENTING SUCCESS] *UK* something that prevents you doing something or having something **bariyer, engel, mania, çıta** *Lack of money should not be a bar to a good education.* **5** [MUSIC] one of the short, equal groups of notes that a piece of music is divided into **bir müzik parçasının kısa eşit nota gruplarından biri** *The band played the first few bars.* **6 the bar** lawyers (= people whose job is to know about the law and deal with legal situations) thought of as a group **baro** *Haughey was called to the bar* (= became a lawyer) *in 1949.*

7 behind bars in prison **hapiste, kodeste, mahpus, hapishanede**

bar[2] /bɑː'/ *verb* [T] **barring,** *past* **barred 1** [PREVENT] to officially prevent someone doing something or going somewhere, or to prevent something happening **engel olmak, resmen engellemek, yasaklamak, kapatmak** [+ from + doing sth] *The court barred him from contacting his former wife.* **2** [KEEP OUT] to stop someone going into a place **girmesine izin vermemek, engel olmak** *A line of policemen barred the entrance to the camp.* **3** [CLOSE] to close and lock a door or gate **kapatmak, önlemek, engellemek**

bar[3] /bɑː'/ *preposition* **1** except ... **den başka, maada, ayrıca** *I've read all her books, bar one.* **2 bar none** used to emphasize that someone or something is the best **istisnasız, ondan daha iyisi yok** *the best suspense writer going, bar none*

barbarian /bɑː'beəriən/ *noun* [C] someone who behaves in a way which shows they are not well educated and do not care about the feelings of others **barbar, acımasız, vahşi, zalim kimse**

barbaric /bɑː'bærɪk/ *adjective* violent and cruel **barbar, vahşi** *a barbaric act of violence* ● **barbarically** *adverb* **kabaca**

barbecue[1] /'bɑːbɪkjuː/ *noun* [C] **1** a party at which you cook food over a fire outdoors **açık havada piknik, mangal partisi, barbekü 2** a metal frame for cooking food over a fire outdoors **üzerinde et pişirilen büyükçe mangal**

barbecue

barbecue[2] /'bɑːbɪkjuː/ *verb* [I, T] **barbecuing,** *past* **barbecued** to cook food on a barbecue **mangal yapmak, mangalda et pişirmek** *barbecued chicken wings*

barbed wire /ˌbɑːbd'waɪə'/ *noun* [U] strong wire with short, sharp points on it to keep people out of a place **dikenli tel** *a barbed wire fence*

barber /'bɑːbə'/ *noun* [C] someone whose job is to cut men's hair **berber** *Dad goes to the barber's* (= the barber's shop) *once a month.*

'**bar ,code** *noun* [C] a row of black lines on something you buy, that a computer reads to find the price **barkod, elektronik fiyat etiketi**

bare[1] /beə'/ *adjective* **1** [NO CLOTHES] not covered by clothes **çıplak** *a bare chest* ○ *She ran out into the road in her bare feet.* **2** [NOT COVERED] not covered by anything **açık, çorak, sade** *bare floorboards* **3** [EMPTY] empty **boş** *a bare room* ○ *The cupboard was bare.* **4** [BASIC] including only the smallest amount that you need of something **gereksinim duyulan şeyin çok azı** *The report just gave us the barest facts about the accident.* ○ *Tony's salary only covers* **the bare essentials** *for the family.* ↪*See also:* with your bare hands (**hand**[1]).

bare[2] /beə'/ *verb* [T] to take away the thing that is covering something so that it can be seen **soymak, açmak, ortaya çıkarmak** *He bared his chest.* ○ *The dog bared its teeth.*

barefoot /beə'fʊt/ *adjective, adverb* not wearing any shoes or socks **çıplak ayak, çıplak ayakla** *They ran barefoot along the wet beach.*

barely /'beəli/ *adverb* only just **hemen hemen, ancak, sadece** *He was barely alive when they found him.*

barf /bɑ:f/ *verb* [I] *US very informal* to vomit **kusmak, yediklerini çıkarmak • barf** *noun* [U] **istifra**

🔲 ***bargain*** ...... İLE BİRLİKTE KULLANILAN KELİMELER

get/pick up/snap up a bargain • a bargain **price** • bargain **hunting**

bargain¹ /'bɑ:gɪn/ *noun* [C] **1** something that is sold for less than its usual price or its real value **ucuz, hesaplı alışveriş, kelepir** *At $8.95, it's a bargain.* **2** when you agree to something someone else wants so that they will agree to something you want **pazarlık** *They were prepared to strike a bargain to avoid more fighting.* **3 into the bargain** *mainly UK* as well as everything else **üstüne üstlük, üstelik, caba** *Caffeine has no good effects on health and is mildly addictive into the bargain.*

bargain² /'bɑ:gɪn/ *verb* [I] to try to make someone agree to something better for you **sıkı/kıyasıya pazarlık etmek** *Do not hesitate to bargain over the price.*

bargain for/on sth *phrasal verb* to expect or be prepared for something **herşeye hazırlıklı olmak, hesaba katmak, ummak** *We hadn't bargained on such a long wait.* ○ *The stormy weather proved to be more than anybody bargained for.*

barge¹ /bɑ:dʒ/ *noun* [C] a long, narrow boat with a flat bottom that is used to carry goods **mavna, yük gemisi**

barge² /bɑ:dʒ/ *verb informal* **barge past/through/ahead, etc** to walk somewhere quickly, pushing people or things out of the way **sağa sola çarpa çarpa, yalpalayarak hızlıca yürümek, geçip gitmek** *Fred barged through the crowd.*

barge in/barge into sth *phrasal verb* to walk into a room quickly and without being invited **bir yere bodoslama dalmak, hızlıca ve davet edilmeden girmek**

baritone /'bærɪtəʊn/ *noun* [C] a man who sings in a voice that is quite low **bariton, müzikte bir ses**

bark¹ /bɑ:k/ *noun* **1** [U] the hard substance that covers the surface of a tree **ağaç kabuğu 2** [C] the sound that a dog makes **havlama**

bark² /bɑ:k/ *verb* **1** [I] If a dog barks, it makes loud, short sounds. **havlamak 2** [I, T] to speak loudly and quickly **bir şeyi havlar gibi hızlı ve yüksek sesle söylemek** *I'm sorry, I had no right to bark at you like that.*

barley /'bɑ:li/ *noun* [U] a type of grain used for making food and alcoholic drinks **arpa**

barmaid /'bɑ:meɪd/ *UK (US bartender) noun* [C] a woman who serves drinks in a bar **barda içki servisi yapan bayan**

barman /'bɑ:mən/ *UK (US bartender) noun* [C] *plural* **barmen** a man who serves drinks in a bar **barda içki servisi yapan bay**

bar mitzvah /ˌbɑ:'mɪtsvə/ *noun* [usually singular] a religious ceremony for a Jewish boy when he reaches the age of 13 **Yahudilerde erkek çocuk 13 yaşına bastığında yapılan dini tören**

barmy /'bɑ:mi/ *adjective UK informal* crazy or silly **zıpır, kaçık, çılgın, aptal** *What a barmy idea!*

barn /bɑ:n/ *noun* [C] a large building on a farm where crops or animals can be kept **ahır, samanlık**

barometer /bə'rɒmɪtə^r/ *noun* [C] **1** a way of showing what people think or what the quality of something is **bir şeyin kalitesini veya insanların ne düşündüğünü gösteren ölçüt, gösterge** *Car sales are viewed as a barometer of consumer confidence.* **2** a piece of equipment that measures air pressure (= the force of

the air) and shows when the weather will change **barometre, basınçölçer**

baron /'bær^ən/ *noun* [C] **1** a man of high social rank in the UK and other parts of Europe **Avrupa ve Birleşik Krallık'da sosyal düzeyi yüksek kişi, üstdüzey kişi, baron 2** a man who owns or controls a lot of a particular industry **belli bir alanda endüstrinin çoğunu elinde tutan kişi** *a wealthy media baron*

baroness /'bær^ənes/ *noun* [C] a woman of the same rank as a baron or married to a baron, or a title given to a woman in the UK who has earned official respect **baronla evli ya da ona benzer şekilde aynı sosyal statüdeki kadın, barones** *Baroness Thatcher*

baroque /bə'rɒk/ *adjective* relating to the style of art, building, and music that was popular in Europe in the 17th and early 18th century, and which had a lot of decoration **17. ve 18. yüzyıl Avrupasına özgün sanat, inşaat ve müziğe ilişkin, barok**

barracks /'bær^əks/ *noun* [C] *plural* **barracks** a group of buildings where soldiers live **asker barakaları, kışla binaları**

barrage /'bær^ədʒ/ ⓤ /bə'rɑ:dʒ/ *noun* **1 a barrage of sth** a lot of questions, complaints, or criticisms **soru, şikayet ve eleştiri bombardumanı** *He faced a barrage of questions about his decision to leave the show.* **2** [C] a continuous attack with several big guns **ağır silahlarla yaylım ateşi**

barrel /'bær^əl/ *noun* [C] **1** a large, round container for storing liquids such as oil or wine **varil, fıçı 2** the tube in a gun that the bullet shoots out of **namlu**

barrel

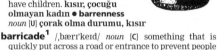

barren /'bær^ən/ *adjective* **1** Land that is barren does not produce crops. **kısır, kıraç, çorak, verimsiz toprak 2** *old-fashioned* A woman who is barren cannot have children. **kısır, çocuğu olmayan kadın • barrenness** *noun* [U] **çorak olma durumu, kısır**

barricade¹ /ˌbærɪ'keɪd/ *noun* [C] something that is quickly put across a road or entrance to prevent people from going past **siper, barikat, engel**

barricade² /ˌbærɪ'keɪd/ *verb* [T] to build a barricade somewhere **barikat kurmak, siper oluşturmak** [often reflexive] *They barricaded themselves in the building* (= built a barricade so that nobody could get to them).

🔲 ***barrier*** ...... İLE BİRLİKTE KULLANILAN KELİMELER

act as/be/create/serve as a barrier to sth • break through/overcome/remove a barrier • the biggest/ the main/a major barrier • [age/size, etc] is no barrier to sth

barrier /'bæriə^r/ *noun* [C] **1** a type of fence that prevents people from going into an area **çit, mania, bariyer** *Police erected barriers to hold back the crowd.* **2** something that prevents people from doing what they want to do **engel, set, korkuluk** *Shyness is a big barrier to making friends.* ⇒See also: crash barrier.

barring /'bɑ:rɪŋ/ *preposition* if something does not happen **haricinde, dışında, hariç** *We should arrive at about five o'clock, barring accidents.*

barrister /'bærɪstə^r/ *noun* [C] in the UK, a lawyer (= someone whose job is to know about the law and deal with legal situations) who can work in the highest courts **avukat, dava vekili, yüksek mahkemelere çıkabilen avukat**

barrow /'bærəʊ/ *UK (UK/US* **wheelbarrow**) a big, open container with a wheel at the front and handles that is used to move things, especially around in a garden **elarabası, tekerlekli araba, seyyar tezgâh**

bartender /'bɑːˌtendər/ *US (UK* **barman/barmaid**) *noun* [C] someone who serves drinks in a bar **barmen, bar görevlisi**

barter /'bɑːtər/ *verb* [I, T] to exchange goods or services for other goods or services, without using money **değiş tokuş yapmak, takas etmek, trampa yapmak, mübadele etmek**

base¹ /beɪs/ *noun* [C] **1** [BOTTOM] the bottom part of something, or the part something rests on **temel, taban, kaide** *I felt a sharp pain at the base of my thumb.* **2** [MAIN PART] the most important part of something, from which other things can develop **esas, temel, asıl** *a solid economic base* **3** [PLACE] the main place where a person lives or works, or from where they do things **çalışma ve yaşama alanı, yeri** *Keswick is an excellent base for exploring the Lake District.* **4** [ARMY] a place where people in the army or navy live and work **üs, askeri üs** *an American Air Force base* **5** [ORGANIZATION] the place where the main work of an organization is done **ana karargâh, ana merkez** *The company's European base is in Frankfurt.* **6** [SUBSTANCE] the main substance in a mixture **karışımın ana hammadesi** *paints with an oil base* **7** [BASEBALL] one of the four places in baseball that a player must run to in order to win a point **beyzbolda bir oyuncunun mutlaka ulaşması gereken noktalardan biri** **8** [CHEMISTRY] a chemical substance with a pH (= measure of how acid something is) of more than 7 **9** [MATHS] a number that is used as the most important unit in a system of counting *The binary system of counting uses base 2.* **10 be off base** *US informal* to be wrong **hatalı, yanlış olmak, kusurlu olmak** *In 1893, many of the forecasts about 1993 were way off base.* ● **11 touch/cover all the bases** *mainly US* to deal with every part of a situation or activity **her tür detayla ilgilenmek, bütün yönlerini ele almak**

base² /beɪs/ *verb* **be based at/in, etc** If you are based at/in, etc a particular place, that is the main place where you live or work. **bir yerde görevli olmak, görevlendirilmek, belli bir yerde çalışmak** *The company is based in Geneva.*
base sth on/upon sth *phrasal verb* If you base something on facts or ideas, you use those facts or ideas to develop it. **bir şeyi birşeye dayandırmak, atfetmek, dayanmak** *Her latest TV serial is based on a true story.*

oͺ**baseball** /'beɪsbɔːl/ *noun* **1** [U] a game in which two teams try to win points by hitting a ball and running around four fixed points **beyzbol 2** [C] the ball used in this game **beyzbol topu** ➔Orta kısımdaki renkli sayfalarına bakınız.

baseball cap *noun* [C] a type of hat with a long flat piece at the front to protect the eyes from the sun **beyzbol şapkası** ➔Orta kısımdaki renkli sayfalarına bakınız.

base camp *noun* [C] the place from which people go to climb mountains **ana kamp üssü**

basement /'beɪsmənt/ *noun* [C] a room or set of rooms that is below ground level in a building **bodrum**

bases /'beɪsiːz/ *plural of* basis **temel, esas, sistem**

bash¹ /bæʃ/ *verb* [T] *informal* **1** to hit someone or something hard **şiddetle vurmak, darbe indirmek** *I bashed my arm on the car door as I got out.* **2 immigrant-bashing/lawyer-bashing/union-bashing, etc** when particular groups are criticized strongly and unfairly **göçmen/avukat/sendika vs. gibi belirli grupların acımasızca ve adil olmayan bir şekilde eleştirilmesi**

bash² /bæʃ/ *noun* [C] *informal* **1** a party **parti, grup 2** a hard hit on something **darbe, vuruş** *a bash on the nose* **3 have a bash (at sth)** *UK informal* to try to do something **denemek, girişimde bulunmak** *I've never been water-skiing but I'd love to have a bash at it.*

bashful /'bæʃfᵊl/ *adjective* shy and easily embarrassed **utangaç, mahcup, sıkılgan ● bashfully** *adverb* **çekingen bir şekilde**

oͺ**basic** /'beɪsɪk/ *adjective* **1** [MAIN] [always before noun] being the main or most important part of something **temel, esas olan** *basic ideas/principles* **2** [NECESSARY] including or providing only the things that are most necessary **eses olan şeyi içeren, sağlayan** *basic training/services/skills* **3** [SIMPLE] very simple, with nothing special added **temel, ana, esas, basit, hiç bir özelliği olmayan** *My software is pretty basic.*

oͺ**basically** /'beɪsɪkᵊli/ *adverb* **1** in the most important ways **esasen, aslında, esasında** *Frazier's films are basically documentaries.* ○ *The two PCs are basically the same.* **2** used to introduce a short explanation about something **esas olarak, temel anlamda** *Basically, what he's saying is that we need more time.*

the basics /'beɪsɪks/ *noun* the most important facts, skills, or needs **en önemli gerçekler, beceriler veya gereksinimler, temel ihtiyaçlar** *the basics of computer technology*

basil /'bæzᵊl/ ⓤ /'beɪzᵊl/ *noun* [U] a herb with a sweet smell **fesleğen**

basin /'beɪsᵊn/ *noun* [C] **1** [BOWL] *mainly UK* a bowl for liquids or food **leğen, çanak** *a basin of water* **2** [BATHROOM] *UK (UK/US* **sink**) the bowl that is fixed to the wall in a bathroom, where you can wash your hands and face **lavabo 3** [LAND] a low area of land from which water flows into a river **havza, su havzası**

oͺ**basis** /'beɪsɪs/ *noun* [C] *plural* **bases** /'beɪsiːz/ **1 on a daily/monthly/regular, etc basis** how often something happens or is done **günlük/aylık/düzenli olarak, aralıklarla** *Meetings are held on a weekly basis.* **2 on a commercial/full-time/percentage, etc basis** the way something happens or is organized **ticari/tam zamanlı/yüzde vs. esasında dayalı olarak, şeklinde, biçiminde** *We will consider claims for asylum on a case by case basis.* **3** the reason for something **dayanak, bir şeyin dayandığı nokta** *Marks are awarded on the basis of progress and performance.* ○ *There is no legal basis for his claim.* **4** a situation, fact, or idea from which something can develop **bir gerçek veya fikrin çıkış noktası, durumu** *Dani's essay can serve as a basis for our discussion.*

bask /bɑːsk/ *verb* [I] to sit or lie in a place that is warm **güneşlenmek, sıcak bir yerde uzanmak** *Seals basked on the rocks.*
bask in sth *phrasal verb* to enjoy the way other people admire you **başkalarının kendisine duyduğu hayranlıktan hoşnut olmak** *They basked in the glory of victory had brought them.*

oͺ**basket** /'bɑːskɪt/ *noun* [C] **1** a container with a handle made of thin pieces of wood, wire, plastic, etc **sepet** *a shopping basket* **2** when a player throws the ball through the net in basketball **basketbolda sayı, basket** ➔See also: wastepaper basket.

oͺ**basketball** /'bɑːskɪtbɔːl/ *noun* **1** [U] a game in which two teams try to win points by throwing a ball through a high net **basketbol 2** [C] the large ball used in the game of basketball **basketbol topu** ➔Orta kısımdaki renkli sayfalarına bakınız.

bass /beɪs/ *noun* **1** [VOICE] [C] a man who sings with a very low voice **bas sesle şarkı söyleyen erkek şarkıcı, bas 2** [MUSIC] [U] the lower half of the set of musical notes müzikye bas sesleri veren nota, alçak perdeli 3 INSTRUMENT [C, U] (*also* double bass) a large, wooden musical instrument with four strings that you play while standing up or sitting on a high chair bas ses veren müzik aleti 4 GUITAR [C, U] (*also* ,bass gui'tar) an electric guitar that makes a low sound bas gitar

bassoon /bə'su:n/ noun [C] a long, wooden musical instrument that you blow through to make a low sound fagot

bastard /'bɑːstəd/ noun [C] **1** an offensive word for a man you do not like alçak, hain, cibiliyetsiz **2** *old-fashioned* an offensive word for a child whose parents are not married piç, gayri meşru çocuk

bastion /'bæstiən/ noun [C] a place, organization, etc where particular ideas or ways of doing things are protected hususi fikirlerin veya bir şeyi yapma şekillerinin saklandığı, korunduğu yer, kale, korunak *the last bastion of male chauvinism*

bat¹ /bæt/ noun [C] **1** a piece of wood used to hit the ball in some sports beyzbol sopası **2** a small animal like a mouse with wings that flies at night yarasa

bat² /bæt/ verb [I] batting, *past* batted to try to hit a ball with a bat sopayla bir topa vurmaya çalışmak *Rimmer batted well for Oxford.* ⊃See also: not bat an eyelid.

batch /bætʃ/ noun [C] a group of things or people that are dealt with at the same time or are similar in type takım, yığın, alay, bölüm, dizi, grup, küme *the university's first batch of students* ○ *Fry the aubergines in batches.*

bated /'beɪtɪd/ adjective ⊃See with bated breath.

o⌐ **bath¹** /bɑːθ/ noun [C] **1** UK (US bathtub) the container that you sit or lie in to wash your body küvet ⊃Orta kısımdaki renkli sayfalarına bakınız. **2** when you wash your body in a bath, or the water in the bath banyo [usually singular] *I'll just have a quick bath.* ○ UK *She ran herself a bath* (= filled a bath with water).

bath² /bɑːθ/ verb [I, T] UK to wash yourself or someone else in a bath banyo yapmak, yıkanmak, çimmek *Emma usually baths the kids about seven o'clock.*

bathe /beɪð/ verb **1** WASH YOURSELF [I, T] to wash yourself or someone else in a bath banyo yapmak, duş yapmak *As a rule, I bathe every day.* **2** PART OF BODY [T] to wash part of someone's body, often because it is hurt vücudun bir bölümünü temizlemek, yıkamak *Bathe your eye with cool salty water.* **3** SWIM [I] *old-fashioned* to swim yüzmek ⊃be bathed in light to look attractive in a beautiful light güzel bir ışıkta çok çekici gözükmek *The mountain was bathed in red-gold light from the setting sun.*

'bathing ,suit noun [C] a piece of clothing that you wear to swim in mayo

bathrobe /'bɑːθrəʊb/ noun [C] a soft coat that you wear before or after a bath bornoz

o⌐ **bathroom** /'bɑːθruːm/ noun [C] **1** a room with a bath, sink (= bowl for washing), and often a toilet banyo, tuvalet ⊃Orta kısımdaki renkli sayfalarına bakınız. **2 go to the bathroom** US to use the toilet tuvalete gitmek

bathtub /'bɑːθtʌb/ US (UK bath) noun [C] the container that you sit or lie in to wash your body banyo küveti ⊃Orta kısımdaki renkli sayfalarına bakınız.

bat mitzvah /,bæt'mɪtsvə/ noun [usually singular] a religious ceremony for a Jewish girl when she reaches the age of 12 or 13 **12 veya 13 yaşına ulaştığında yahudi kızları için yapılan dini tören**

baton /'bætᵊn/ US /bə'tɑːn/ noun [C] **1** STICK a thin stick used to control the rhythm of a group of musicians orkestra şeflerinin müziği idare ederken kullandığı çubuk **2** POLICE a thick stick that a police officer uses as a weapon cop **3** RACE a stick that a runner passes to the next person in a race bayrak koşusunda kullanılan değnek, çubuk, bayrak

batsman /'bætsmən/ noun [C] *plural* batsmen UK the person who is trying to hit the ball in cricket kriket sporunda sopa ile topa vuran oyuncu ⊃Orta kısımdaki renkli sayfalarına bakınız.

battalion /bə'tæliən/ noun [C] a large group of soldiers made from several smaller groups tabur

batter¹ /'bætəʳ/ noun **1** [U] a mixture of flour, milk, and often eggs used to make cakes and pancakes (= thin fried cakes), and to cover fish, etc before it is fried süt, yağ, un ve yumurta karışımı kek hamuru, pasta hamuru **2** [C] the person who is trying to hit the ball in baseball beyzbolda sopa ile topa vurmaya çalışan oyuncu ⊃Orta kısımdaki renkli sayfalarına bakınız.

batter² /'bætəʳ/ verb [I, T] to hit someone or something repeatedly very hard durmadan vurmak, dövmek, hırpalamak *If you don't open up we'll batter the door down.* ○ *Waves battered against the rocks.*

battered /'bætəd/ adjective old and not in very good condition harap olmuş, köhne, külüstür *a battered copy of her favourite novel*

battering /'bætərɪŋ/ noun [C] when someone or something is hit repeatedly, criticized strongly, or damaged badly şiddetle dövme, acımasızca eleştirme, fazlasıyla zarar verme [usually singular] *The prime minister has taken quite a battering this week.*

o⌐ **battery** /'bætᵊri/ noun **1** [C] an object that provides electricity for things such as radios, toys, or cars akü, pil, batarya *My car has got a flat battery* (= one that has no electricity left). **2** [U] *formal* the crime of hitting someone darp suçu, darp etme *assault and battery*

battery

⊞ **battle** .... İLE BİRLİKTE KULLANILAN KELİMELER

face/fight/lose/win a battle ● a bitter/long-running/uphill battle ● a legal battle ● a battle for sth ● a battle with sb/between sb and sb

battle¹ /'bætl/ noun **1** WAR [C, U] a fight between two armies in a war muharebe, savaş, çarpışma, vuruşma *the Battle of Waterloo* ○ *Her grandfather was killed in battle* (= while fighting). **2** POWER [C] when two people or groups compete against each other or have an argument about something mücadele, yarışma, çetin uğraş *a battle for control in the boardroom* **3** PROBLEMS/ILLNESS [C] a fight against something that is hurting or destroying you mücadele etme, direnç gösterme, uğraşma *a long battle against cancer* **4 fight a losing battle** to try hard to do something when there is no chance that you will succeed kaybedilmek üzere olan bir savaşı kazanmak için mücadele etmek, uğraşmak, savaşmak *I try to control what my children watch on TV, but I think I'm fighting a losing battle.*

battle² /'bætl/ *verb* [I] to try very hard to do something that is difficult **mücadele etmek, savaşım vermek, zoru başarmak için uğraşmak** *Both teams are battling for a place in the Premier League.* ○ *Throughout the campaign Johnson was battling against severe health problems.*

baulk /bɔːk/, /bɔːlk/ *UK* (*UK/US* **balk**) *verb* [I] to not want to do something that is unpleasant or difficult **hoş olmayan veya zor bir şeyi yapmayı istememek** *Most people would baulk at paying these kind of prices for clothes.*

bawl /bɔːl/ *verb* [I, T] *informal* to shout or cry loudly **haykırmak, bas bas bağırmak, feryat etmek**

bay /beɪ/ *noun* **1** [C] an area of coast where the land curves in **körfez** *a sandy bay* **2** [C] a part of a building or place that is used for a particular purpose **cumba, bölme, özel amaç için ayrılmış oda** *a parking bay* **3 keep/hold sth at bay** to prevent something unpleasant from coming near you or from happening **istenmeyen bir şeyin olmasını engellemek, uzak tutmak, engel olmak** *Gunmen kept police at bay for almost four hours.*

bayonet /'beɪənət/ *noun* [C] a knife that is fastened onto the end of a long gun **süngü**

bazaar /bə'zɑːʳ/ *noun* [C] **1** a market in Eastern countries **pazar, pazar yeri, çarşı** **2** a sale where goods are sold to raise money for a school, church, etc **hayır işleri için çeşitli eşyaların satıldığı yer, Pazar**

B&B /ˌbiːən'biː/ *noun* [C] *abbreviation for* bed and breakfast (= a small hotel or private house where you pay for a room to sleep in for the night and a meal in the morning) **otellerde oda ve kahvaltının fiyata dahil olduğunu belirten ifade**

BBC /ˌbiːbiː'siː/ *noun abbreviation for* British Broadcasting Corporation: one of the main television and radio companies in the United Kingdom **Britanya yayın kuruluşu** *a cookery programme on BBC2*

BC /biː'siː/ *abbreviation for* Before Christ: used to show that a particular year came before the birth of Christ **milattan önce** *331 BC*

o╌**be¹** *strong form* /biː/ *weak forms* /bi/, /bɪ/ *verb being, past tense* **was**, *past participle* **been** **1** used to describe or give information about someone or something **be' fiili, olmak anlamında bir şeyi tasvir etmek ya da bilgi vermek için kullanılır** *I'm sixteen.* ○ *I'm Andy.* ○ *Her mother is a teacher.* ○ *He's German.* ○ *They were very upset.* ○ *He was very ill last year.* ○ *I'm sorry I'm late.* ○ *They've been unlucky.* ○ *Be quiet!* **2 there is/there are/there was, etc** used to show that someone or something exists **bir şeyin ya da birinin var olduğunu göstermek için kullanılır** *There were about fifty people at the party.* ○ *Is there a bank near here?* **3** used to show the position of someone or something **birinin ya da bir şeyin durumunu belirtmek için kullanılır** *It's been in the cupboard for months.* ○ *She's in the kitchen.* **4 it is/it was, etc** used to give a fact or your opinion about something **bir şey hakkında düşünce veya bir gerçeği bildirmek için kullanılır** *It's not surprising that she left him.* ○ *It's a good idea to keep a spare key somewhere safe.*

be² *strong form* /biː/ *weak forms* /bi/, /bɪ/ *auxiliary verb* **1** used with the present participle of other verbs to describe actions that are or were still continuing **yardıncı fiil (am, is, are, was, were)** *Where are you going?* ○ *How long have you been sitting there?* ○ *He was standing by the window.* ○ *He's working at the moment.* **2** used with the present participle of other verbs, and sometimes after a modal verb, to describe actions that will happen in the future **modal fiiller ile ve diğer fiillerle üçüncü hallerini içeren yapıda kullanılır**

I'm going to France next week. ○ *I'll be coming back on Tuesday.* **3** used with the past participle of other verbs to form the passive **fiillerin üçüncü halleriyle edilgen yapıda kullanılır** *He was injured in a car crash.* ○ *The results will be announced next week.* **4** used in conditional sentences to say what might happen **ikinci tip şartlı cümlelerde kullanılır** *If he were to offer me the job, I'd take it.* **5** used to say that someone must or should do something **zorunluluk belirten hallerde kullanılır** *You are not to see him again.* **6** *formal* used to show that something has been organized **bir şeylerin düzenlenmiş olduğunu göstermede kullanılır** *They are to stay with us when they arrive.*

beach ...... İLE BİRLİKTE KULLANILAN KELİMELER

on the beach ● a sandy beach ● a beach house

o╌**beach** /biːtʃ/ *noun* [C] an area of sand or rocks next to the sea **plaj**

beacon /'biːkən/ *noun* [C] a light on a hill or in a tower that warns people of something or is a signal or guide **deniz feneri veya kulede parlayan işaret ışığı, uyarı ateşi**

bead /biːd/ *noun* [C] **1** a small, round ball of glass, plastic, or wood that is used for making jewellery **tespih, boncuk taneleri** *a necklace of coloured glass beads* **2** a small drop of liquid on a surface **damla, su zerrecikleri, taneleri** *beads of sweat*

beak /biːk/ *noun* [C] the hard part of a bird's mouth **gaga**

beaker /'biːkəʳ/ *noun* [C] *UK* a tall cup without a handle, usually made of plastic **büyük, ağzı yayvan bardak**

beam¹ /biːm/ *noun* [C] **1** [LIGHT] a line of light shining from something **ışın, ışık, şua, huzme** *a laser beam* ➾See picture at **light**. **2** [WOOD] a long, thick piece of wood, metal, or concrete that is used to support weight in a building or other structure **kiriş, hatıl** **3** [SMILE] *UK* a big smile **büyük bir gülümseme**

beam² /biːm/ *verb* **1** [SMILE] [I] to smile very happily **mutlu bir şekilde gülümsemek, tebessüm etmek** *The baby beamed at me.* **2** [SEND] [T] to send a television or radio signal **sinyal göndermek, yaymak** [often passive] *The match was beamed live by satellite around the world.* **3** [SHINE] [I] If the sun or the moon beams, it shines brightly. **parlak ışık saçmak**

beamer /'biːməʳ/ *noun* [C] a data projector: a machine that allows you to show words or images on a screen or wall **projeksiyon makinası, bilgi ve resimleri ışık yardımıyla yansıtmaya yarayan makina**

bean /biːn/ *noun* [C] **1** [SEED] a seed of some climbing plants, that is used as food **fasulye** *soya beans* **2** [VEGETABLE] a seed case of some climbing plants that is eaten as a vegetable **kahve, bezelye, bakla ve fasulye gibi bitkilerin yenilen taneleri** *green beans* **3** [COFFEE/CHOCOLATE] a plant seed used to make coffee and chocolate **kahve ve çikolata yapımında kullanılan kakao çekirdeği** *coffee beans* ➾See also: baked beans, runner bean.

bean curd /'biːnkɜːd/ *noun* [U] tofu (= a soft, pale food made from the soya bean plant) **soya fasulyesinden yapılan ezme, püre**

bear¹ /beəʳ/ *verb* [T] *past tense* **bore**, *past participle* **borne 1** [ACCEPT] to accept someone or something unpleasant **tahammül etmek, kaldırmak, dayanmak, katlanmak** *She couldn't bear the thought of him suffering.*

○ *I like her, but I can't bear her friends.* ○ [+ to do sth] *How can you bear to watch?* ○ *The pain was too much to bear.* **2 bear a resemblance/relation, etc to sb/sth** to be similar to someone or something **benzemek** *He bears a striking resemblance to his father.* **3** CARRY *formal* to carry something **taşımak** *He came in, bearing a tray of drinks.* **4** WEIGHT to support the weight of something **çekmek, götürmek, kaldırmak** *I don't think that chair will bear his weight.* **5 bear the responsibility/ cost, etc** to accept that you are responsible for something, you should pay for something, etc **sorumluluğu üstlenmek, maliyetine katlanmak, sonucuna razı olmak** *He must bear some responsibility for the appalling conditions in the prison.* **6** FEELING to continue to have a bad feeling towards someone **çekmek, katlanmak, tahammül etmek** *They were rude to her in the past, but she's not the kind of woman who bears grudges* (= continues to be angry). **7** HAVE CHILD *formal* to give birth to a child **doğurmak, dünyaya getirmek** *She has been told that she will never bear children.* **8** NAME to have or show a particular name, picture, or symbol **hususi bir isim, resim veya sembolü olmak, göstermek** *The shop bore his family name.* **9 bear left/right** to turn left or right **sola/sağa dönmek** *Bear right at the next set of traffic lights.* ⊃See also: bear **fruit, grin** and bear **it**.
bear sb/sth out *phrasal verb* to prove that someone is right or that something is true **birşeyin doğru, birinin haklı olduğunu ispat etmek** *The facts do not bear out his claims.*
bear with sb *phrasal verb* to be patient and wait while someone does something **sabırlı olmak, sabır göstermek, sabırla beklemek** *If you'll bear with me a moment, I'll just find your details.*

bear² /beə^r/ *noun* [C] a large, strong, wild animal with thick fur **ayı** ⊃See also: polar bear, teddy bear.

bear

bearable /ˈbeərəbl/ *adjective* If an unpleasant situation is bearable, you can accept or deal with it. **katlanılabilir, dayanılabilir, tahammül edilebilir** *Having her there made life at home more bearable for me.* ⊃Opposite unbearable.

beard /bɪəd/ *noun* [C] the hair that grows on a man's chin (= the bottom of his face) **sakal** ● **bearded** *adjective* with a beard **sakallı**

bearer /ˈbeərə^r/ *noun* [C] a person who brings or carries something **taşıyıcı,hamal** *I am sorry to be the bearer of bad news.*

bearing /ˈbeərɪŋ/ *noun* **have a bearing on sth** to have an influence on something or a relationship to something ... ile ilgili olmak, üzerinde etkisi olmak *What you decide now could have a considerable bearing on your future.*

bearings /ˈbeərɪŋz/ *noun* **1 get/find your bearings a** to find out where you are **nerede olduğunu öğrenmek, bulmak** *She looked at the sun to find her bearings.* **b** to become confident in a new situation **yeni bir durumdan emin olmak, güvenmek** *When you start a new job, it can take some time to get your bearings.* **2 lose your bearings** to become confused about where you are **nerede bulunduğunu bilmemek, yolunu yordamını şaşırmak**

beast /biːst/ *noun* [C] **1** *formal* an animal, especially a large or wild one **bilhassa büyük ve vahşi bir hayvan 2** *old-fashioned* an annoying or cruel person **kaba ve iğrenç adam, hınzır**

beastly /ˈbiːstli/ *adjective old-fashioned* unkind or unpleasant **hayvanca, kabaca, iğrenç bir şekilde, hınzırca**

∘⃛**beat¹** /biːt/ *verb past tense* **beat**, *past part* **beaten**, *also US* **beat 1** DEFEAT [T] to defeat someone in a competition **yenmek, mağlup etmek** *Our team beat Germany 3-1.* ⊃See Common learner error at **win**. **2** HIT [I, T] to hit a person or animal hard many times **dövmek, dayak atmak** *She beat the dog with a stick.* ○ *She was beaten to death.* **3** SOUND [I, T] to hit against something hard, making a continuous or regular sound **atmak, çarpmak, vurmak, düzenli darbe indirmek** *soldiers beating drums* ○ *Rain beat against the windows.* **4** GET RID OF [T] to get rid of something bad **kötü bir şeyden kurtulmak, başından atmak** *I'm determined to beat this illness.* **5** HEART [I] When your heart beats, it makes regular movements and sounds. **atmak, çarpmak, (kalp vb.) düzenli kareket etmek ve ses çıkarmak** *By the time the doctor arrived, his heart had stopped beating.* **6** BE BETTER [T] to be better than something **bir şeyden daha iyi olmak** [+ doing sth] *Being at the youth club beats sitting at home.* **7 you can't beat sth** used to emphasize that something is best **onu yenemezsin, üstesinden gelemezsin, mağlup edemezsin** *You can't beat Pedro's for a great pizza.* **8 take a lot of/some, etc beating** to be so good or enjoyable that it is hard to find anything better **daha iyisi bulunamayacak kadar iyi, hoş olmak, rakipsiz olmak, eline su dökememek, üstüne olmamak** *This ice cream takes some beating.* **9** FOOD [T] to mix food using hand, quick movements **çırpmak, karıştırmak** *Beat the egg whites until they are stiff.* **10 it beats me** *informal* something that you say when you do not understand a situation or someone's behaviour **bir anlam veremiyorum, Allah Allah, bana bir şey ifade etmiyor** *It beats me why she goes out with him.* ⊃See also: beat about the **bush**, beat/knock the (living) **daylights** out of sb, off the beaten **track¹**.
beat down *phrasal verb* If the sun beats down, it is very hot and bright. **çok sıcak ve yakıcı olmak, kavurmak**
beat sb down *phrasal verb UK* to persuade someone to charge you less for something **birini daha az para almaya ikna etmek, pazarlıkta galip gelmek**
beat sb/sth off *phrasal verb* to manage to defeat someone who is attacking you **püskürtmek, mağlup etmeyi başarmak, üstesinden gelmek**
beat sb to sth *phrasal verb* to do something before someone else does it *I was going to ask her to the party, but you beat me to it.*
beat sb up *phrasal verb* to attack someone by hitting or kicking them many times **dövmek, dayak atmak, sopa çekmek** *He beat up one of the other prisoners.*

beat² /biːt/ *noun* [C] **1** REGULAR SOUND a regular sound that is made by your heart or by something hitting a surface **kalp atışı, tık sesi** *a heart beat* ○ *the beat of a drum* **2** RHYTHM the main rhythm of a piece of music **müzikte vuruş, tını, çıkarılan her bir ses, nota, tempo** *loud music with a regular beat* **3** AREA the area of a town or city that a police officer walks around regularly **devriye** *Having more police officers on the beat* (= walking around their beat) *should help to reduce crime.*

beating /ˈbiːtɪŋ/ *noun* **1** [C] when someone hits another person hard many times **dayak 2 take a beating** to be defeated, criticized, or damaged **yenilgiye uğramak, eleştirilmek, hasar görmek** *Our team took a severe beating in the tournament.*

beautician /bjuː'tɪʃ°n/ *noun* [C] someone whose job is to improve people's appearance by treatments to their hair, skin, etc **güzellik uzmanı**

B

beautiful ...... BAŞKA BİR DEYİŞLE

Eğer kişi (kadın veya erkek) güzel ise, **attractive** veya **good-looking** sıfatları kullanılabilir. **Handsome** sıfatı erkekler için ve **pretty** sıfatı da bayanlar için kullanılır. *Her husband is really* **good-looking**. ● *Your daughter is very* **pretty**.

Eğer kişi, özellikle de bir kadın, çok güzelse, **gorgeous** veya **stunning** ifadeleri kullanılabilir. *You look* **gorgeous** *in that dress!* ● *I think she's* **stunning**.

breathtaking, lovely, gorgeous sıfatları genellikle tasvir edilen güzel bir manzaranın ifadesinda kullanılır. *The views from the window were* **breathtaking**. ● *We drove through some* **gorgeous** *countryside.*

exquisite sıfatı güzel ve narin şeylerin tasvirinde kullanılır. *They do the most* **exquisite** *hand-made decorations.*

o⁻**beautiful** /'bjuː.tɪf°l/ *adjective* **1** very attractive **güzel, hoş, latif** *a beautiful woman* ○ *beautiful scenery* **2** very pleasant **çok hoş, çok güzel** *beautiful music* ○ *It's a beautiful day* (= the sun is shining). ● **beautifully** *adverb a beautifully illustrated book* ○ *She sings beautifully.* **güzelce**

YAYGIN HATALAR

beautiful

Dikkat: Yazılışına dikkat edin. **Beautiful** Türk öğrencileri tarafından en çok yanlış yazılan 10 kelimeden biridir. Untumayın! Kelimenin doğru yazılışına **eau** ve bir tane **l** vardır.

beauty ...... İLE BİRLİKTE KULLANILAN KELİMELER

great/sheer/stunning beauty ● **natural** beauty ● **beauty products**

o⁻**beauty** /'bjuː.ti/ *noun* **1** QUALITY [U] the quality of being beautiful **güzellik** *The whole area is famous for its natural beauty.* ○ *a beauty contest* (= competition to find the most beautiful woman) **2 the beauty of sth** the quality that makes something especially good or attractive **bir şeyin güzelliği, çekiciliği** *The beauty of the plan is that it won't cost anything.* **3 a beauty product/treatment** a product or treatment to make you more beautiful **güzellik ürünü, bakımı 4** EXCELLENT THING [C] *informal* something that is an excellent example of its type **türünün en güzel örneği, güzellik** *That last goal was a beauty.* **5** WOMAN [C] *old-fashioned* a beautiful woman **güzel bir kadın**

'beauty ,salon (*also US* **'beauty ,parlor**) *noun* [C] a place where you can have beauty treatments **güzellik salonu**

'beauty ,spot *noun* [C] **1** *UK* a place in the countryside that is very beautiful **güzel bir köşe, mahal, nokta 2** a small dark mark on someone's face **güzellik beni, yüzde koyu siyah ben**

beaver /'biː.vəʳ/ *noun* [C] an animal with brown fur, a long, flat tail, and sharp teeth, which builds dams (= walls made of pieces of wood) across rivers **kunduz**

became /bɪ'keɪm/ *past tense of* become **become' fiilinin 2. hali**

o⁻**because** /bɪ'kɒz/, /bɪ'kəz/ *conjunction* used to give a reason for something **çünkü** *I phoned because I needed to talk to you.* ○ *I can't come out tonight because I've got too much homework.*

YAYGIN HATALAR

because

Dikkat: Yazılışına dikkat edin. **Because** Türk öğrencileri tarafından en çok yanlış yazılan 10 kelimeden biridir. Unutmayın! **ou** olarak yazmayın! **au** şeklinde yazın.

o⁻**because of** /bɪ'kɒzəv/, /bɪ'kəzəv/ *preposition* as a result of someone or something *... den dolayı, yüzünden, ...* **den ötürü, sebebiyle** *We got into all this trouble because of you.*

beck /bek/ *noun* **be at sb's beck and call** to be always ready and willing to do what someone wants **daima hizmetinde olmak, her zaman yardıma hazır olmak**

o⁻**beckon** /'bek°n/ *verb* **1** WAVE [I, T] to move your hand, head, etc to show someone that you would like them to come nearer **başla, elle işaret etmek, çağırmak** *She beckoned to the waiter.* **2** BE LIKELY [I] to seem very likely to happen **olacakmış, gerçekleşecekmiş gibi görünmek** *A career as a lead guitarist beckoned.* **3** BE ATTRACTIVE [I] If a place beckons, it is very attractive to you, and you want to go there. **çekmek, cezbetmek, etkilemek, çekmek** *The bright lights of London beckoned.*

o⁻**become** /bɪ'kʌm/ *verb past tense* **became**, *past part* **become 1** become available/rich/a writer, etc to begin to be something **bir şey olmaya başlamak** *They became great friends.* ○ *She wants to become a teacher when she leaves school.* ○ *This style of skirt is becoming fashionable.* **2 what/whatever became of sb/sth** something you say when you want to know what has happened to someone **ne olursa olsun** *Whatever became of your friend Harry?*

bed ...... İLE BİRLİKTE KULLANILAN KELİMELER

go to bed ● **be in/lie in/be tucked up in** bed ● **get into/get out of** bed ● **make** the bed ● be **on** the bed ● **share** a bed ● a **double/single** bed

o⁻**bed¹** /bed/ *noun* **1** FURNITURE [C, U] a piece of furniture that you sleep on **yatak** *a single/double bed* ○ *What time did you go to bed last night?* ○ *She was lying in bed when I arrived.* ○ *He had only just got out of bed.* ○ *Have you made the bed* (= tidied the bed after you have slept in it)? **2** GROUND [C] a piece of ground that is used for growing plants, especially flowers **maşala, evlek, tarh** *a flower bed* **3** BOTTOM [C] the ground at the bottom of the sea, a river, etc **dere, deniz yatağı, tabanı** *the sea bed* ◆See also: bunk beds.

,bed and 'breakfast (*also* B & B) *noun* [C] a small hotel or private house where you pay for a room to sleep in for the night and a meal in the morning **oda ve kahvaltı**

bedclothes /'bedkləʊðz/ *noun* [plural] the sheets and other pieces of cloth that cover you and keep you warm in bed **nevresim takımı**

bedding /'bedɪŋ/ *noun* [U] **1** the sheets and other pieces of cloth that cover you and keep you warm in bed **nevresim takımı, yorgan ve çarşaf takımı 2** material such as hay (= dried grass) that animals sleep on **hayvanlar için kuru ot yığınından oluşan ağılda veya açıkta yatak**

bedraggled /bɪ'drægld/ *adjective* untidy, and often wet and dirty **darma dağınık, pejmürde, kir pas içinde**

bedrock /'bedrɒk/ *noun* [U] *formal* a situation, idea, or principle that provides a strong base for something **bir şeye temel teşkil eden prensip, fikir veya durum** *Family life is the bedrock of a stable society.*

B

o⌐**bedroom** /'bedru:m/ *noun* [C] a room used for sleeping in **yatak odası**

bedside /'bedsaɪd/ *noun* [no plural] **1** the area at the side of a bed **yatak kenarı, başucu** *He was at her bedside in the hospital.* ○ *a bedside table/lamp* **2 bedside manner** a doctor's ability to make the people they are treating feel comfortable **bir doktorun hastasına sevecen yaklaşımı, rahatlatıcı tavrı** *My surgeon has a wonderful bedside manner.*

bedsit /'bedsɪt/ *noun* [C] UK a rented room where you live, sleep, and cook your meals **pansiyon, kiralık oda**

bedspread /'bedspred/ *noun* [C] a cloth cover that is put over a bed **yatak örtüsü**

bedtime /'bedtaɪm/ *noun* [C, U] the time that you usually go to bed **yatma vakti**

bee /biː/ *noun* [C] a flying insect that has a yellow and black body and makes honey (= sweet, sticky food) **arı** *the queen bee*

beech /biːtʃ/ *noun* [C, U] a large tree with a smooth grey trunk (= main, vertical part) that produces small nuts **kayın ağacı**

beef¹ /biːf/ *noun* [U] the meat of a cow **sığır eti** *roast beef* ⊃See also: ground beef.

beef² /biːf/ *verb*
 beef sth up *phrasal verb* to make something stronger or more important **güçlendirmek, daha önemli hale getirmek** *The company wants to beef up its sales force by employing new graduates.*

beefburger /'biːfˌbɜːgəʳ/ UK (UK/US **hamburger**) *noun* [C] very small pieces of meat that are pressed together into a round flat shape, cooked, and eaten between bread **ayaküstü yenilen sığır etinden yapılan yiyecek, biftekburger**

beehive /'biːhaɪv/ (*also* **hive**) *noun* [C] a special container where people keep bees **arı kovanı**

been /biːn/, /bɪn/ *verb* have **been to** to have gone to a place and come back **bir yerde kısa süreli bulunmuş olmak, bulunmak** *Have you ever been to Thailand?* ⊃Inflection of **be**.

beep /biːp/ *verb* **1** [I] If a machine beeps, it makes a short, high noise. **bip sesi çıkarmak, biplemek 2** [I, T] If a car horn (= part you press to make a warning sound) beeps or if you beep it, it makes a loud noise. **araçlarda sürücüyü ikaz eden, uyaran bip sesi, klakson sesi** *Beep the horn to let me know that you're here.* ● **beep** *noun* [C] **bip sesi**

beeper /'biːpəʳ/ (*also* UK **bleeper**) *noun* [C] a small piece of electronic equipment that you carry which makes a short high sound when someone wants to talk to you **sesle uyarı cihazı, çağrı cihazı**

o⌐**beer** /bɪəʳ/ *noun* [C, U] an alcoholic drink made from grain, or a glass or container of this drink **bira** *a pint of beer*

beet /biːt/ US (UK **beetroot**) *noun* [C, U] a round, dark red vegetable, that is usually cooked and eaten cold **pancar**

beetle /'biːtl/ *noun* [C] an insect with a hard, usually black, shiny body **çoğunlukla sert parlak ve siyah kabuksu vücudu olan bir böcek**

beetroot /'biːtruːt/ UK (US **beet**) *noun* [C, U] a round, dark red vegetable, that is usually cooked and eaten cold **pancar**

befall /bɪ'fɔːl/ *verb* [T] *past tense* **befell**, *past participle* **befallen** *formal* If something bad befalls you, it happens to you. **vuku bulmak, olmak, meydana gelmek, başına gelmek** *A dreadful misfortune has befallen the family.*

befit /bɪ'fɪt/ *verb* [T] **befitting**, *past* **befitted** *formal* to be suitable or right for someone or something **birisi veya bir şey için doğru ya da uygun olmak** *He was given a huge welcome, as befits such a hero.*

o⌐**before¹** /bɪ'fɔːʳ/ *preposition* **1** [EARLIER] earlier than something or someone **bir şeyden, birinden önce** *a week before Christmas* ○ *She arrived before me.* ○ [+ doing sth] *Think hard before accepting the offer.* **2** [IN FRONT OF] in a position in front of someone or something **bir şey ya da birinin önünde** *I've never performed this before an audience.* ○ *He stood before her, shaking.* **3** [PLACE] at a place that you arrive at first when travelling towards another place **bir yere varmadan önce** *The hospital is just before the bridge.* **4** [IN ORDER] in front of someone or something in an order or a list **listede birinden, bir şeyden önce** *P comes before Q in the alphabet.* **5** [IMPORTANCE] treated as more important than someone or something **önde gelen, önde olan, öncelikli** *They always put the children's needs before their own.* **6** [EXAMINATION] being formally examined or considered by a group **resmi olarak incelenen veya bir grup tarafından dikkate alınan** *He appeared before the court dressed in jeans.*

o⌐**before²** /bɪ'fɔːʳ/ *conjunction* **1** [EARLIER] earlier than the time when something happens **bir şey olmadan önce** *He was a teacher before he became famous.* ○ *Before I could warn him, he had fallen.* **2** [TO AVOID STH] in order to avoid something bad happening **öncesinde** *Put that stick down before you hurt someone.* **3** [UNTIL] until ... e, a kadar, ... ceye kadar *It took a few moments before I realized that he was lying.*

o⌐**before³** /bɪ'fɔːʳ/ *adverb* at an earlier time, or on a previous occasion **daha da önceden veya önceki bir fırsatta, durumda** *I've never seen her before.* ○ *We had spoken on the phone a few days before.*

beforehand /bɪ'fɔːhænd/ *adverb* before a particular time or event **önceleri, öncesinden, önceden olan** *Did you know beforehand what they had planned to do?*

befriend /bɪ'frend/ *verb* [T] *formal* to be friendly to someone, especially someone who needs support or help **yardım etmek, dostça davranmak, elinden tutmak**

beg /beg/ *verb* **begging**, *past* **begged 1** [I] to ask someone for food or money, because you do not have any **dilenmek, istemek** *Young children were begging on the streets.* **2** [I, T] to make a very strong and urgent request **yalvarmak** *She begged him for help.* ○ [+ to do sth] *I begged her not to go.* ⊃See also: I beg your **pardon²**..

began /bɪ'gæn/ *past tense of* begin **başlamak' fiilinin geçmiş zaman hali**

beggar /'begəʳ/ *noun* [C] a poor person who lives by asking other people for money and food **dilenci**

o⌐**begin** /bɪ'gɪn/ *verb* **beginning**, *past tense* **began**, *past participle* **begun 1** [START TO DO] [I, T] to start to do something **başlamak** [+ to do sth] *The children began to cry.* ○ [+ doing sth] *Have they begun building the wall yet?* ○ *She began her career as a journalist on a local newspaper.* **2** [START TO HAPPEN] [I] to start to happen **olmaya başlamak** *What time does the film begin?* **3 begin with sth** to have something at the start **bir şeye başlamak** *Local phone numbers begin with 1223.* **4 to begin with a** [AT THE START] at the start of a situation **başlamak gerekirse, başlarsak** *To begin with, the two girls got on well.* **b** [GIVE REASON] used to give the first important reason for something **ilk başta değinmek gerekirse, şununla başlarsak** *To begin with, we can't leave the children alone.*

beginner /bɪ'gɪnəʳ/ *noun* [C] someone who is starting to do or learn something for the first time **başlangıç seviyesinde olan** *I'm a complete beginner at yoga.*

o=**beginning** /bɪ'gɪnɪŋ/ *noun* [C] the first part of something or the start of something **başlangıç, ilk başlar** [usually singular] *We met at the beginning of 1998.* ○ *Things went well in the beginning.*

begrudge /bɪ'grʌdʒ/ *verb* [T] **1** to feel upset because someone has something that you would like **haset etmek, çok görmek, gıpta etmek, gözü olmak** [+ two objects] *I don't begrudge him his success.* **2** to feel upset because you have to spend money on something or spend time doing something **istemeye istemeye ödemek, cimrice davranmak, para harcamayı sevmemek** *They begrudge every penny that they have to spend on him.*

beguile /bɪ'gaɪl/ *verb* [T] *formal* to attract someone very much, sometimes in order to deceive them **aklını çelmek, kandırmak** [often passive] *I can see how people are beguiled by his charm.* ○ *a beguiling smile*

begun /bɪ'gʌn/ *past participle of* begin **başlamak' fiilinin 3. hali**

behalf /bɪ'hɑːf/ *noun* **on sb's behalf** If you do something on someone's behalf, you do it for them or instead of them. **adına, temsilen** *We are campaigning on behalf of thousands of refugees.* ○ *Will you accept the prize on my behalf?*

o=**behave** /bɪ'heɪv/ *verb* [I] **1** to do or say things in a particular way **davranmak, davranış göstermek, belli bir şekilde yapmak ya da söylemek** *to behave badly/stupidly* ○ *They are behaving like children.* **2** (*also* behave yourself) to be polite and not make a situation difficult **uslu durmak, yaramazlık yapmamak** *Try to behave.* ○ *The children can only come if they promise to behave themselves.* ⊃Opposite misbehave.

-behaved /bɪ'heɪvd/ *suffix* used after a word describing how someone behaves **... - huylu** *a badly-behaved child* ⊃See also: well-behaved.

behaviour ...... İLE BİRLİKTE KULLANILAN KELİMELER

anti-social / bad / disruptive / good / normal behaviour

o=**behaviour** UK (*US* behavior) /bɪ'heɪvjəʳ/ *noun* [U] the way that you behave **davranış, tavır** *good/bad behaviour* ○ *Did you notice anything odd about his behaviour?*

behavioural UK (*US* behavioral) /bɪ'heɪvjərəl/ *adjective* relating to behaviour **davranışla ilgili, tavıra ilişkin** *behavioural changes/problems*

behead /bɪ'hed/ *verb* [T] to cut someone's head off **kellesini/başını uçurmak, koparmak, kesmek**

beheld /bɪ'held/ *past of* behold **farkına varmak, görmek fiilinin 2. hali**

o=**behind**[1] /bɪ'haɪnd/ *preposition* **1** [BACK] at or to the back of someone or something **arkasında, arka tarafta** *Close the door behind you.* ○ *The pub is behind the train station.* **2** [LESS SUCCESSFUL] slower or less successful than someone or something **gerisinde, geride** *Our team is 3 points behind the winners.* ○ *The building work is already behind schedule* (= late). **3** [CAUSING] causing something, or responsible for something **arkasında olan, sebep olan** *What was the reason behind her decision to leave?* **4** [SUPPORTING] giving your help or support to someone **arkasında destek olan, geriden destekleyen** *The group is 100 percent behind her.* **5** [NOT AFFECTING] If a bad experience or your own bad behaviour is behind you, it does not exist or affect your life now. **her şeyin geride oluşu, kalmış olması** *He's put his criminal past behind him.*

o=**behind**[2] /bɪ'haɪnd/ *adverb* **1** [BACK] at or to the back of someone or something **gerisine, arkasına doğru** *Somebody grabbed me from behind.* **2** [SLOWER] slower or later than someone else, or the **geri-**

sinde kalan, arkada kalan *She's behind with the rent* (= is late to pay it). **3** [PLACE] in the place where someone or something was before **gerilerde, geriye doğru giden** *You go on ahead. I'll stay behind and tidy up.* ○ *When we got to the restaurant, I realized that I had left my purse behind.*

behind[3] /bɪ'haɪnd/ *noun* [C] *informal* the part of your body that you sit on **arka, kıç, popo**

behold /bɪ'həʊld/ *verb* [T] *past* beheld *literary* to see something **farkına varmak, görmek**

beige /beɪʒ/ *noun* [U] a pale brown colour **bej renk** ● **beige** *adjective* ⊃Orta kısımdaki renkli sayfalarına bakınız. **bej**

being[1] /'biːɪŋ/ *noun* **1** [C] a living person or imaginary creature **yaşayan canlı ya da hayali yaratık** *human beings* **2 come into being** to start to exist **varolmaya başlamak,** *The new law comes into being next month.* ⊃See also: well-being.

being[2] /'biːɪŋ/ *present participle of* be **olmak, be fiilinin -ing almış hali**

belated /bɪ'leɪtɪd/ *adjective* coming late, or later than expected **gecikmiş, geç kalmış, geç** *a belated attempt to win votes* ● **belatedly** *adverb* *Supermarkets have belatedly realized the purchasing power of mothers.* **gecikmiş**

belch[1] /beltʃ/ *verb* **1** [I] to make a sudden noise as air from your stomach comes out through your mouth **geğirmek 2** [T] (*also* belch out) to produce a lot of smoke, fire, gas, etc **duman, ateş, gaz vs. püskürtmek** *tall chimneys belching smoke*

belch[2] /beltʃ/ *noun* [C] the noise you make when you belch **geğirme**

beleaguered /bɪ'liːgəd/ *adjective formal* having a lot of problems **pek fazla sorunu olan, derdi tasası çok olan, dertli, sorunlu** *the beleaguered farming industry*

belfry /'belfri/ *noun* [C] the tower of a church where the bells are hung **kilisede çanların asıldığı kule, çan kulesi**

belie /bɪ'laɪ/ *verb* [T] belying, *past* belied *formal* to give a wrong idea about something **bir şey hakkında yanlış fikir vermek** *His shy manner belied his very sharp mind.*

belief ...... İLE BİRLİKTE KULLANILAN KELİMELER

a firm / mistaken / sincere / strong / widespread / widely-held belief ● have/hold a belief ● a belief in sth ● a belief that

o=**belief** /bɪ'liːf/ *noun* **1** [TRUE] [U, no plural] when you believe that something is true or real **inanç, iman** *It is a widely-held belief that smoking helps you lose weight.* ○ *She married him in the belief that he would change.* ⊃Opposite disbelief. **2** [IDEA] [C, U] an idea that you are certain is true **kanı, inanç** *religious/political beliefs* **3** [EFFECTIVE] [U, no plural] the feeling that someone or something is effective or right **güven, itimat** *a belief in social justice* **4 beyond belief** too bad, good, difficult, etc to be real **inanılması güç, inanması zor** *The evil of this man is beyond belief.*

believable /bɪ'liːvəbl/ *adjective* If something is believable, you can believe that it could be true or real. **inanılabilir** ⊃Opposite unbelievable.

o=**believe** /bɪ'liːv/ *verb* **1** [TRUE] [T] to think that something is true, or that what someone says is true **güvenmek, itimat etmek** [+ (that)] *They believe that their health has suffered because of the chemicals.* ○ *Do you believe him?* ⊃Opposite disbelieve. **2** [THINK] [T] to think something, without being completely sure **sanmak, varsaymak, farzetmek** *The murderer is believed to be in his thirties.* **3** [RELIGION] [I] to have religious beliefs **inanmak, itikat etmek, iman etmek 4 not believe your eyes/ears** to

be very surprised when you see someone or something, or when you hear what someone says **gözlerine/ kulaklarına inanamamak, çok şaşırmak** *I couldn't believe my ears when Dan said they were getting married.* **5 believe it or not** used to say that something is true although it seems surprising **ister inan, ister inanma** *He even remembered my birthday, believe it or not.*
believe in sth *phrasal verb* to be certain that something exists **bir şeye inanmak, iman etmek, tam inanç göstermek** *I believe in life after death.*
believe in sth/doing sth *phrasal verb* to be confident that something is effective or right **inanmak, doğru saymak, inancı olmak** *He believes in saying what he thinks.*

believer /bɪˈliːvər/ *noun* [C] **1** a person who has a religious belief **inanan, inançlı, imanlı 2 a firm/great/ strong, etc believer in sth/doing sth** someone who has confidence in a particular idea or way of doing things **bir şeye/şeyi yapmaya güçlü bir şekilde inanan, güvenen, güveni olan kişi** *She's a firm believer in freedom of speech.*

belittle /bɪˈlɪtl/ *verb* [T] *formal* to say that someone or something is not very important or not very good **küçültmek, küçümsemek**

bell

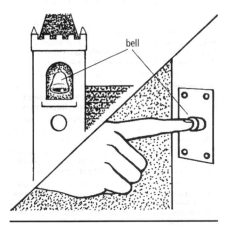
bell

o━**bell** /bel/ *noun* [C] **1** a hollow, metal object, shaped like a cup, that makes a ringing sound when you hit it **çan** *the sound of church bells ringing* **2** an electrical object that makes a ringing sound when you press a switch **zil** *Please ring the bell for attention.* **3 give sb a bell** UK *informal* to telephone someone **telefonla aramak ● 4 ring a bell** If a word, especially a name, rings a bell, you think you have heard it before. **çağrıştırmak, anımsa(t)mak, aklına getirmek, hatırla(t)mak**

belligerent /bəˈlɪdʒərənt/ *adjective* wanting to fight or argue **münakaşa eden, ağız dalaşını seven**

bellow /ˈbeləʊ/ *verb* [I, T] to shout something in a loud voice **böğürmek, yüksek sesle söylemek ● bellow** *noun* [C] **bağırma**

belly /ˈbeli/ *noun* [C] *informal* your stomach (= organ where food is digested), or the front part of your body between your chest and your legs **karın/bel bölgesi**

'belly ,button *noun* [C] *informal* the small, round, and usually hollow place on your stomach, where you were connected to your mother before birth **göbek çukuru**

o━**belong** /bɪˈlɒŋ/ *verb* **1 belong in/on/there, etc** to be in the right place **doğru yerde olmak** *That chair belongs in the dining room.* **2** [I] to feel happy and comfortable in a place or with a group of people **bir yere, bir şeye ait olmak** *I never felt that I belonged there.*
belong to sb *phrasal verb* If something belongs to you, you own it. **birine ait olmak, onun olmak** *This necklace belonged to my grandmother.*
belong to sth *phrasal verb* to be a member of a group or organization **bir gruba, kuruluşa ait olmak, mensubu olmak** *We belong to the same youth club.*

belongings /bɪˈlɒŋɪŋz/ *noun* [plural] the things that you own **şahsi eşyalar** *I took a few personal belongings with me.*

beloved /bɪˈlʌvɪd/ *adjective literary* very much loved **sevilen, sevgili, aziz**

o━**below** /bɪˈləʊ/ *adverb, preposition* **1** POSITION in a lower position than someone or something else **aşağıda** *Send your answers to the address below* (= lower on the page or on a later page). **2** LESS less than an amount or level **altında, belli bir seviyenin altında** *The temperature there rarely drops below 22°C.* ○ *His work is below average.* **3** RANK lower in rank **ast, ast rütbede, kademede olan** *Monica is a grade below me.*

o━**belt¹** /belt/ *noun* [C] **1** WAIST a long, thin piece of leather, cloth, or plastic that you wear around your waist **kemer** ➔Orta kısımdaki renkli sayfalarına bakınız. **2** AREA an area of a particular type of land, or an area where a particular group of people live **kuşak, bölge, belli bir grubun yaşadığı yöre** *the commuter belt* ○ *a narrow belt of trees* **3** MACHINE part of a machine that moves in a circle to carry objects or to make a machine work **kayış** *The car needs a new fan belt.* **4 have sth under your belt** to have already achieved, learnt, or done something important **başarı hanesine kaydetmek, çantada keklik olarak görmek** *At 18, she already has several victories under her belt.* **● 5 tighten your belt** to try to spend less money **kemerleri sıkmak** ➔See also: conveyor belt, green belt, safety belt, seat belt.

belt

belt² /belt/ *verb informal* **1 belt along/down/through, etc** UK to move very fast **çok hızlı hareket etmek** *He came belting down the street.* **2** [T] to hit someone or something very hard **vurmak, dövmek, hızlıca vurmak**
belt sth out *phrasal verb* to sing something very loudly **yüksek sesle şarkı söylemek,**
belt up *phrasal verb* UK *informal* used to tell someone to stop talking or making a noise **sesini kes', 'çeneni kapa' biçiminde uyarı** *Just belt up, would you? I'm trying to concentrate.*

belying /bɪˈlaɪɪŋ/ *present participle of* belie **yalan söylemek', 'kandırmak' fiilinin -ing hali**

bemused /bɪˈmjuːzd/ *adjective* slightly confused **biraz kafası karışmış, hafif şaşırmış** *He seemed bemused by all the attention.*

bench /benʃ/ *noun* [C] **1** a long seat for two or more people, usually made of wood or metal **bank, oturak** *a park bench* **2 the bench a** in some sports, a place where players sit when they are not playing **yedek kulübesi b** a judge in court, or judges as a group **yargıç, yargıçlar kurulu** *Please address your comments to the bench.*

benchmark /ˈbenʃmɑːk/ *noun* [C] a level of quality with which other things of the same type can be compared **kalite seviyesi** *Her performance set a new benchmark for ballet dancing.*

ᵒ⁺**bend¹** /bend/ *verb* [I, T] *past* **bent 1** to move your body or part of your body so that it is not straight **eğmek, bükmek** *He was bending over to tie his shoelaces.* ○ *Bend your knees when lifting heavy objects.* **2** to become curved, or to make something become curved **kıvrılmak, eğilmek, bükülmek** *The trees were bending in the wind.* ○ *The road bent sharply to the left.* ⊃See also: bend over **backwards**, bend/stretch the rules (**rule¹**).

░░░ **bend** .... İLE BİRLİKTE KULLANILAN KELİMELER

a sharp/tight bend ● a bend in sth

bend² /bend/ *noun* [C] **1** a curved part of something **dönemeç, viraj** *a bend in the road/river* **2 drive/send sb round the bend** *informal* to make someone very angry, especially by continuing to do something annoying **birini çileden çıkarmak, alnından kaşımak, çılgına çevirmek, küplere bindirmek, neden olmak** ⊃See also: hairpin bend.

beneath¹ /bɪˈniːθ/ *adverb, preposition* **1** under something, or in a lower position than something **altında, alt tarafta, aşağıda** *He hid the letter beneath a pile of papers.* ○ *She looked out of the window at the children playing beneath.* **2** If someone or something is beneath you, you think they are not good enough for you. **aşağıda, altta, düşük seviyede** *He thinks housework is beneath him.*

benefactor /ˈbenɪfæktəʳ/ *noun* [C] someone who gives money to help an organization or person **hayırsever, hami, yardımsever, iyilikçi**

beneficial /ˌbenɪˈfɪʃʳl/ *adjective* helpful or useful **faydalı, yararlı, hayırlı** *Exercise is beneficial to almost everyone.*

beneficiary /ˌbenɪˈfɪʃʳri/ *noun* [C] *formal* someone who receives money, help, etc from something or someone else **düşkün, yardıma muhtaç** *They were the beneficiaries of free education.*

░░░ **benefit** .... İLE BİRLİKTE KULLANILAN KELİMELER

enjoy/have/offer/reap benefits ● [the drawbacks/ risks, etc] outweigh the benefits ● great/long-term/maximum/potential/tangible benefit ● of benefit to sb

benefit¹ /ˈbenɪfɪt/ *noun* [C, U] **1** something that helps you or gives you an advantage **kâr, fayda, yarar, çıkar, kazanç** *I've had the benefit of a happy childhood.* **2** money that the government gives to people who are ill, poor, not working, etc **düşkünlere yapılan devlet yardımı** *unemployment benefit* **3 for sb's benefit** in order to help someone **birinin yararına/iyiliğine/çıkarına** *We bought the piano for the children's benefit.* **4 give sb the benefit of the doubt** to choose to believe what someone tells you even though it may be wrong or a lie **yanlış ve yalan olduğunu bilinmesine rağmen birinin söylediklerine inanmayı seçmek** ⊃See also: child benefit, fringe benefit.

benefit² /ˈbenɪfɪt/ *verb* **benefiting**, *past* **benefited 1** [I] to be helped by something **faydalı olmak, yararlı olmak** *The film benefited from the excellent acting by its stars.* **2** [T] to help someone **yardım etmek, yararına çalışmak** *The charity supports activities that directly benefit children.*

benevolent /bɪˈnevʳlənt/ *adjective formal* kind, generous, and helpful **iyiliksever, cömert, hayırsever, yardımsever** ● **benevolence** /bɪˈnevʳləns/ *noun* [U] **kibarlık**

benign /bɪˈnaɪn/ *adjective* **1** not likely to kill you **tehlikesiz, zararsız** *a benign tumour* **2** kind, or not intending to harm anyone **iyi kalpli, mülayim, nazik, halim** *a benign ruler*

bent¹ /bent/ *adjective* **1** curved and not now straight or flat **eğilmiş, bükülmüş, eğik, yamulmuş** *The metal bars were bent and twisted.* **2 bent on sth/doing sth** determined to do something or get something **bir şeyi yapmaya azmetmek, kararlı olmak** *Both parties are bent on destroying each other's chances of winning.* **3** *UK informal* not honest **namussuz, haysiyetsiz** *a bent policeman*

bent² /bent/ *past of* bend **bend¹ fiilinin geçmiş zaman hali**

bequeath /bɪˈkwiːð/ *verb* [+ two objects] *formal* to formally arrange to give someone something after you die **vasiyet etmek, vasiyetle bırakmak, miras bırakmak** *He bequeathed his art collection to the city of Glasgow.*

bequest /bɪˈkwest/ *noun* [C] *formal* money or property that you have arranged for someone to get after you die **vasiyetle bırakılan şey, miras**

berate /bɪˈreɪt/ *verb* [T] *formal* to speak angrily to someone **azarlamak, haşlamak, kızgınca konuşmak** *She berated him for being late.*

bereaved /bɪˈriːvd/ *adjective* If you have been bereaved, someone you loved has died. **birini sevdiğinden mahrum etmek, sevdiğini kaybetmek** *bereaved parents* ○ *The minister spoke quietly with the bereaved.* ● **bereavement** *noun* [C, U] *formal* **mahrumiyet, yoksun kalmak**

bereft /bɪˈreft/ *adjective formal* **1 bereft of sth** completely without something **birşeyden mahrum olmak, yosun olmak** *They were bereft of new ideas.* **2** [never before noun] alone and extremely sad **yalnız ve son derece üzgün** *She was left bereft by his death.*

beret /ˈbereɪ/ ⑥ /bəˈreɪ/ *noun* [C] a round, flat hat made of soft material **bere**

berry /ˈberi/ *noun* [C] a small, round fruit on some plants and trees **(çilek, kiraz vb.) yumuşak, küçük meyve**

berserk /bəˈzɜːk/ *adjective* **go berserk** *informal* to become extremely angry or violent **deliye dönmek, çıldırmak, aklını oynatmak, kudurmak**

berth /bɜːθ/ *noun* [C] **1** a bed on a boat or train **kuşet, yatak, ranza 2** a place for a boat to stay in a port **bir geminin, teknenin rıhtımdaki yeri, palamar**

beset /bɪˈset/ *verb* [T] *formal* If problems beset you, they cause you continuing difficulties. **rahat vermemek, muhasara etmek, huzursuz etmeye devam etmek** [often passive] *The project has been beset by problems from the start.*

beside /bɪˈsaɪd/ *preposition* **1** next to someone or something, or very near them **yanında, yanıbaşında** *She knelt beside his bed.* **2 be beside yourself (with sth)** to experience a powerful emotion **kendini kaybetmek, kendinden geçmek, çılgına dönmek** *He was beside himself with rage.*

besides¹ /bɪˈsaɪdz/ *preposition* in addition to something or someone **bundan başka, zaten, bununla birlikte** *Do you play any other sports besides football?*

besides² /bɪˈsaɪdz/ *adverb* **1** used to give another reason for something **ayrıca, bunun yanısıra** *She won't mind if you're late - besides, it's not your fault.* **2** in addition to something that you have already said **üstelik, bir de** *Besides looking after the children, she also runs a successful business.*

besiege /bɪˈsiːdʒ/ *verb* **1 be besieged by/with sb** to have lots of people asking you questions or making demands **insanlar tarafından kuşatılmak, etrafı sarılmak** *The president was besieged by reporters.* **2 be besieged by/with sth** to receive many demands or criticisms **bir çok talep ve eleştiri almak** *The radio station was besieged with calls from angry listeners.* **3** [T] to surround a place with an army in order to attack it **kuşatmak, muhasara etmek**

o-**best¹** /best/ *adjective superlative of* good: better than any other **en iyi** *She's one of our best students.* ○ *Give her my best wishes.* ○ *Susie's my best friend* (= the friend I like more than any other). ○ *What's the best way to get to Manchester from here?* ⊃See also: **second best**, the **best/greatest thing** since sliced bread.

o-**best²** /best/ *adverb superlative of* well **1** most, or more than any other **en iyisi** *Which of the songs did you like best?* **2** in the most suitable or satisfactory way **en tatminkâr ve uygun şekilde** *I sleep best with the windows open.*

best³ /best/ *noun* **1 the best** someone or something that is better than any other **en iyisi** *He's the best of the new players.* **2 at best** used to show that the most positive way of considering something is still not good **en hafifinden, en azından** ,**hiç değilse** *At best, only 50 per cent of babies born at 24 weeks will survive.* **3 at his/its, etc best** at the highest level of achievement or quality **formunda, havasında, başarısının/kalitesinin zirvesinde** *The article is an example of journalism at its best.* **4 do/try your best** to make the greatest effort possible **elinden gelen her şeyi yapmak** *I did my best to persuade him.* **5 bring out the best in sb** to cause someone's best qualities to show **birinin sahip olduğu yetenekleri** **keşfetmesine/göstermesine/ortaya koymasına sebep olmak 6 make the best of sth** to try to be positive about a situation you do not like but cannot change **oluru ile yetinmek, azına çoğuna bakmamak, bir durumu olduğu gibi kabullenmek** *Our hotel room is rather small, but we'll just have to make the best of it.* **7 for the best** If something is for the best, it seems unpleasant now, but will improve a situation in the future. **düzelme ümidiyle, daha iyi olacağına yorarak** *Divorce is always painful, but it really was for the best.* **8 at the best of times** used to show that something is not good when it is the best it can be **olsa olsa, olabileceği halde iyi olmadığını göstermek için kullanılır** *He's not exactly patient at the best of times.* **9 have the best of both worlds** to have the advantages of two different situations **her iki durumdan da avantaj sağlamak, her iki açıdan da kazançlı çıkmak** *Living in the country and working in the city you have the best of both worlds.*

,**best 'man** *noun* [no plural] a man who stands next to the man who is getting married at the marriage ceremony and helps him **sağdıç**

bestow /bɪ'stəʊ/ *verb* [T] *formal* to give someone an important present or a public reward for their achievements **bağışlamak, sunmak, vermek, bahşetmek** *He won the Nobel Peace Prize, an honour also bestowed on his colleague.*

bestseller /ˌbest'selər/ *noun* [C] a very popular book that many people have bought **en çok satılan, çok satan** ● **best-selling** *adjective* [always before noun] *best-selling authors* **en iyi satan, bir numara**

bet¹ /bet/ *verb* [I, T] **betting**, *past* **bet 1** to risk money on the result of a game, competition, etc **bahse girmek, iddiaya girmek** *He lost all his money betting on horses.* ○ [+ two objects + (that)] *I bet him a dollar that I was right.* **2 I bet** *informal* something that you say to show that you believe that something is true or will happen **iddia ediyorum, eminim ki** [+ (that)] *I bet that he's forgotten my birthday again.* **3 You bet!** *mainly US informal* used to say that you will do something with enthusiasm **elbette, ne zannettiniz** *"Are you going to Pam's party?" "You bet!"*

have/place a bet (on) sth ● put a bet on sth ● lose/win a bet

bet² /bet/ *noun* [C] **1** when you risk money on the result of a game, competition, etc **bahis, iddia** *She won her bet.* ○ *He put a bet on Manchester United winning on Saturday.* **2 a good bet** something that would be useful, clever, or enjoyable to do **yapılması faydalı, akıllıca ve hoşa giden şey** *Putting your savings in a high-interest account would be a good bet.* **3 your best bet** the best decision or choice **en iyi karar veya seçim** *Your best bet in terms of value would be the Regent Hotel.* **4 hedge your bets** to avoid choosing one particular thing or action when it is not certain which is the right choice **neyi seçeceğine karar verememek, doğruyu tahmin edememek, iki arasında seçim yapmaktan kaçınmak** *Journalists are hedging their bets on the likely outcome of the election.* ● **5 a safe bet** something that you are certain will happen **kesin tahmin** *Wheeler is a safe bet for a place on the team.*

betray /bɪ'treɪ/ *verb* [T] **1** PERSON to behave in a dishonest or cruel way to someone who trusts you **hıyanetlik yapmak, aldatmak** *When I heard what he had said about me, I felt betrayed.* **2** SECRETS If you betray your country or an organization, you give secret information to its enemies or to other organizations. **ihanet etmek, bir sırrı ifşa etmek, ele vermek 3** EMOTION to show an emotion that you were trying to hide **saklamaya çalıştığı hissini göstermek** *Her face was calm, but her hands betrayed her nervousness.*

betrayal /bɪ'treɪəl/ *noun* [C, U] when you betray someone **ihanet, ifşa, açığa vurma** *a betrayal of trust*

o-**better¹** /'betər/ *adjective* **1** *comparative of* good: of a higher quality, more effective, or more enjoyable than something or someone else **daha iyi** *Jeff's been offered a better job in the States.* ○ *The sales figures were better than expected.* ○ *Her English has got a lot better* (= improved) *recently.* **2** healthy, or less ill than before **sağlığı daha iyi, daha sağlıklı** *I feel much better.* ○ *I hope you get better soon.* **3 the bigger/brighter/hotter, etc the better** used to say that the bigger, brighter, hotter, etc something is, the more pleased you will be **ne kadar büyük/parlak/sıcak vs., o kadar iyi**

o-**better²** /'betər/ *adverb* **1** *comparative of* well: to a greater degree, or in a more successful or effective way **daha iyi biçimde, şekilde, derecede** *I'd like to get to know you better.* ○ *Helen did much better than me in the exam.* **2 he/you, etc had better do sth** used in order to say what you think someone should do **bir şeyler yapsan/yapsa iyi olur** *You'd better hurry or you'll miss the train.* **3 know better** to have enough experience not to do something stupid or something that will not achieve anything **daha iyi bilmek** *I thought she'd listen to me - I should have known better.*

better³ /'betər/ *noun* **1 for the better** If a situation changes for the better, it improves. **en azından, daha da iyiye doğru, daha iyi olsun diye** *Their relationship has changed for the better.* **2 get the better of sb** If a feeling gets the better of you, it becomes too strong to control. **birini mağlup etmek, hakkından gelmek** *Curiosity finally got the better of her and she opened the letter.*

better⁴ /'betər/ *verb* [T] to do something better than it has been done before **iyileştirmek, daha da iyi hale getirmek** *He bettered his previous best time for a marathon.*

,**better 'off** *adjective* [never before noun] **1** richer **daha zengin** *We're a lot better off now that Jane's started work again.* **2** in a better situation **daha iyi bir durumda** *Simon's such an idiot - you'd be better off with-*

out him. **3 you're better off doing sth** used to give advice **bir şeyler yapsan çok iyi olur, iyi edersin** *You're better off getting a taxi.*

B ◦**between**[1] /brˈtwiːn/ *preposition* **1** SPACE in the space that separates two places, people, or things **arasında (mesafe)** *The town lies halfway between Florence and Rome.* ○ *A narrow path runs between the two houses.* **2** TIME in the period of time that separates two events or times **arasında (zaman, süreç)** *The shop is closed for lunch between 12.30 and 1.30.* **3** INVOLVE involving two or more groups of people **arasında (iki veya daha fazla insan)** *Tonight's game is between the New Orleans Saints and the Los Angeles Rams.* **4** AMOUNT used to show the largest and smallest amount or level of something **bir şeyin en geniş ve en küçük miktarını göstermede** *Between 50 and 100 people will lose their jobs.* **5** CONNECT connecting two or more places or things **iki ya da daha fazla yer ve eşyayı birleştirmede** *There is a regular train service between Glasgow and Edinburgh.* **6** SEPARATE separating two or more things or people **iki ya da daha fazla yer ve eşyayı ayırmada** *the gap between rich and poor* ○ *What's the difference between these two cameras?* **7** SHARE shared by a particular number of people **belli sayıda insan tarafından paylaşılan** *We drank two bottles of wine between four of us.* **8** AMOUNT If something is between two amounts, it is larger than the first amount but smaller than the second. **iki miktar arasında** *The temperature will be between 20 and 25 degrees today.* **9** CHOOSE If you choose between two things, you choose one thing or the other. **iki şey arasında seçim yapmada**

between[2] /brˈtwiːn/ (*also* **in between**) *adverb* **1** in the space that separates two places, people, or things **iki yer, insan, eşyayı ayıran boşluk** *The wood is in neat piles with newspaper placed between.* **2** in the period of time that separates two events or times **iki olay veya zamanı ayıran dönemde** *There's a train at 6.15 and one at 10.30 but nothing in between.*

beverage /ˈbevərɪdʒ/ *noun* [C] *formal* a drink **içecek**

beware /brˈweər/ *verb* [I] used in order to warn someone to be careful **dikkat et, uyanık ol, farkında ol** *Beware of the dog.* ○ [+ of + doing sth] *You should beware of spending too long in the sun.*

bewildered /brˈwɪldəd/ *adjective* very confused and not sure what to do **şaşkın, afallamış, serseme dönmüş** *She looked bewildered.* ● **bewilderment** *noun* [U] *He stared at me in bewilderment.* **şaşkınlık**

bewildering /brˈwɪldərɪŋ/ *adjective* making you feel confused **sersemleten, şaşkına çeviren, afallatan** *There was a bewildering range of subjects to choose from.*

bewitch /brˈwɪtʃ/ *verb* [T] If someone or something bewitches you, you find them extremely attractive and interesting. **büyülemek, hayran bırakmak** *a bewitching smile*

◦**beyond**[1] /brˈjɒnd/ *preposition* **1** DISTANCE on the other side of something **ötede, yan tarafında** *Our house is just beyond the bridge.* **2** TIME continuing after a particular time or date **den sonra, akabinde** *A lot of people now live beyond the age of 80.* **3 beyond belief/repair/recognition, etc** impossible to believe/repair/recognize, etc **inanması/tamiri/tanınması vb. imkansız** *Steven had changed beyond all recognition.* **4** NOT UNDERSTAND *informal* If something is beyond you, you cannot understand it. **birinin algılama/anlama düzeyinin ötesinde** *It's beyond me why anyone would want to buy that house.* **5** EXCEPT except for **ayrıca, dışında, hariç** *She said very little beyond the occasional 'yes' and 'no'.* **6** INVOLVING OTHERS involving or affecting other things or people than the ones you have talked

about **mevcut olanları/bahsedilenlerin dışında** *You should try to develop interests beyond the family.*

beyond[2] /brˈjɒnd/ *adverb* **1** on the other side of something **ötesinde, öte tarafında** *From the top of the hill, we could see our house and the woods beyond.* **2** continuing after a particular time or date **belli bir zaman ve süreden sonra da devam eden** *The strike looks set to continue into March and beyond.*

bhangra /ˈbæŋɡrə/ *noun* [U] a type of pop music based on traditional music from North India and Pakistan **kuzey Hindistan ve Pakistan'a özgü geleneksel müzikten oluşan bir tür pop müzik**

bi- /baɪ-/ *prefix* two **iki' anlamında önek** *bilingual* (= speaking two languages) ○ *bimonthly* (= happening twice in a month or once every two months)

biannual /baɪˈænjuəl/ *adjective* happening twice a year **yılda iki kez olan** ⊃Compare **biennial**.

bias /ˈbaɪəs/ *noun* [C, U] when you support or oppose someone or something in an unfair way because you are influenced by your personal opinions **önyargı** *a bias towards/against private education* ○ *The news channel has been accused of bias in favour of the government.*

biased /ˈbaɪəst/ *adjective* showing unfair support for or opposition to someone or something because of your personal opinions **önyargılı** *to be biased against/towards younger workers*

bib /bɪb/ *noun* [C] a piece of cloth or plastic that is worn by young children when they are eating in order to stop their clothes getting dirty **mama önlüğü, bebe önlüğü**

bible /ˈbaɪbl/ *noun* **1 the Bible** the holy book of the Christian and Jewish religions **incil 2** [C] a copy of this book **incil kopyası 3** [C] a book or magazine that gives important information and advice about a particular subject **bir konuda önemli bilgiler içeren, veren dergi veya gazete** *'Vogue' was regarded as the fashion student's bible.*

biblical /ˈbɪblɪkəl/ *adjective* relating to the Bible **İncil'e ilişkin**

bibliography /ˌbɪbliˈɒɡrəfi/ *noun* [C] a list of books and articles on a particular subject **kaynakça, bibliyoğrafya**

bicentenary /ˌbaɪsenˈtiːnəri/ Ⓤⓢ /baɪˈsentəneri/ *UK* (*US* **bicentennial** /ˌbaɪsenˈteniəl/) *noun* [C] the day or year that is 200 years after an important event **200 yıl sonra olan gün veya yıl** *the bicentenary of Schubert's birth* ○ *bicentennial celebrations*

biceps /ˈbaɪseps/ *noun* [C] *plural* **biceps** the large muscle at the front of your upper arm **pazı**

bicker /ˈbɪkər/ *verb* [I] to argue about something that is not very important **didişmek, çekişip durmak, incir çekirdeğini doldurmayacak konularda atışmak** *They were bickering over which channel to watch.*

🧩 **bicycle** ...... İLE BİRLİKTE KULLANILAN KELİMELER

ride a bicycle ● **be on** a bicycle ● a bicycle **helmet**

◦**bicycle** /ˈbaɪsɪkl/ *noun* [C] a vehicle with two wheels that you sit on and move by turning the two pedals (= parts you press with your feet) **bisiklet** ⊃Orta kısımdaki renkli sayfalarına bakınız.

bicycle

🧩 **bid** ...... İLE BİRLİKTE KULLANILAN KELİMELER

launch/mount a bid ● **in a** (**desperate**) bid to do sth ● a bid **for** sth

bid¹ /bɪd/ *noun* [C] **1** ATTEMPT an attempt to achieve something **girişim, deneme, teşebbüs** *a successful bid for re-election* ○ [+ to do sth] *The council has banned cars from the city centre in a bid to reduce pollution.* **2** BUY an offer to pay a particular amount of money for something **fiyat teklifi, teklif, fiyat önerisi** *I made a bid of $150 for the painting.* **3** WORK an offer to do work for someone for a particular amount of money **bir iş için fiyat önerisi, götürü ücret teklifi** *We put in a bid for the stadium contract.*

bid² /bɪd/ *verb* **bidding**, *past* **bid 1** [I, T] to offer to pay an amount of money for something **fiyat teklif etmek, önermek** *They bid $500 million for the company.* **2 bid for sth; bid to do sth** to try to do or obtain something **bir şey yapmak veya elde etmek için uğraşmak, çabalamak** *Five firms have bid for the contract.*

bid³ /bɪd/ *verb* **bidding**, *past tense* **bid** or **bade**, *past participle* **bid** or **bidden bid sb farewell/goodbye/good night, etc** *literary* to say goodbye, good night, etc **birine hoşçakal/Allah'a ısmarladık/iyi geceler vs. Demek** *She bade her guests good night.*

bidder /ˈbɪdər/ *noun* [C] someone who offers to pay a particular amount of money for something **teklif sunan, fiyat teklif eden kimse** *The house will be sold to the highest bidder* (= the person who offers to pay the most).

bidding /ˈbɪdɪŋ/ *noun* [U] **1** when people offer to pay a particular amount of money for something **fiyat teklif etme, miktar önerme 2 do sb's bidding** *literary* to do what someone tells you to do **birinin söylediklerini yapmak, söyleneni harfiyen uygulamak**

bide /baɪd/ *verb* ➔See bide your time¹.

bidet /ˈbiːdeɪ/ ⑮ /bɪˈdeɪ/ *noun* [C] a small low bath that a person uses to wash their bottom and sex organs **bide, taharet oturağı, lavabosu**

biennial /baɪˈeniəl/ *adjective* happening every two years **iki yılda bir olan** ➔Compare biannual.

o⊶**big¹** /bɪg/ *adjective* **bigger**, **biggest 1** SIZE large in size or amount **büyük, kocaman, iri** *I come from a big family.* ○ *We're looking for a bigger house.* **2** IMPORTANT important or serious **önemli, ciddi** *Tonight's big game is between Real Madrid and Manchester United.* ○ *Buying that car was a big mistake.* **3 your big brother/sister** *informal* your older brother/sister **ağabey/abla 4** SUCCESSFUL *informal* successful or popular **başarılı veya meşhur** *The programme's been a big hit* (= very popular) *with young children.* **5 make it big** *informal* to become very successful or famous **başarılı veya meşhur olmak**

big² /bɪg/ *verb*
big sth/sb up *phrasal verb* [T] *informal* to praise someone or something a lot, sometimes more than they deserve **bir şeyi, birini gereğinden fazla övmek,**

ˌ**big 'business** *noun* [U] **1** an activity that makes a lot of money **çok para getiren iş, faaliyet, çalışma** *Football has become big business.* **2** large, powerful businesses **büyük, güçlü bir iş, büyük şirket**

bigot /ˈbɪgət/ *noun* [C] a bigoted person **bağnaz, darkafalı kimse**

bigoted /ˈbɪgətɪd/ *adjective* A bigoted person has very strong, unfair opinions and refuses to consider different opinions. **bağnaz, dar kafalı, ileriyi göremeyen, yeniliklere açık olmayan, yobaz, önyargılı ● bigotry** /ˈbɪgətri/ *noun* [U] when someone is bigoted **bağnazlık, önyarı, yobazlık**

big-ticket /ˈbɪgˌtɪkɪt/ *adjective* [always before noun] *US* Big-ticket items are expensive things to buy, such as cars or furniture. **araba, mobilya gibi pahalı şeyler**

o⊶**bike** /baɪk/ *noun* [C] **1** *informal short for* bicycle **bisiklet 2** *informal short for* motorbike/motorcycle (= a vehicle with two wheels and an engine) **motorsiklet**

biker /ˈbaɪkər/ *noun* [C] someone who rides a motorbike (= vehicle with two wheels and an engine) **motorsiklet kulanan kişi**

bikini /bɪˈkiːni/ *noun* [C] a piece of clothing with two parts that women wear for swimming **bikini** ➔Orta kısımdaki renkli sayfalarına bakınız.

bilateral /baɪˈlætərəl/ *adjective* involving two groups or countries **ikili, iki taraflı, iki kişi veya ülkeyi içeren** *bilateral talks/agreements/trade*

bile /baɪl/ *noun* [U] a bitter liquid made and stored in the body that helps to digest fat **safra, öd**

bilingual /baɪˈlɪŋgwəl/ *adjective* using or able to speak two languages **ikidilli, çift dil konuşabilen** *a bilingual dictionary* ○ *She's bilingual.*

pay/settle a bill ● **a bill comes to** [£100/$500, etc] ● **a bill for sth** ● **an electricity/gas/phone bill**

o⊶**bill¹** /bɪl/ *noun* [C] **1** PAYMENT a piece of paper that tells you how much you must pay for something you have bought or for a service you have had **fatura** *Have you paid the electricity bill?* **2** LAW a written plan for a law **kanun maddesi** *Parliament will vote today on whether to pass the reform bill.* **3** MONEY *US* (UK **note**) a piece of paper money **kağıt para** *a five dollar bill* **4** ENTERTAINMENT *UK* what is on at a cinema or theatre **sinemada/tiyatroda gösterimde olan 5** BEAK a bird's beak **gaga**

bill² /bɪl/ *verb* **1 be billed as sth** to be advertised with a particular description **belli bir tasvir ile reklam yapmak** *The film was billed as a romantic comedy.* **2** [T] to give or send someone a bill asking for money that they owe for a product or service **fatura etmek, faturalandırmak** *He billed us for the materials.*

billboard /ˈbɪlbɔːd/ *(also UK* **hoarding**) *noun* [C] a large board used for advertising, especially by the side of a road **reklam panosu**

billfold /ˈbɪlfəʊld/ *US* (*UK/US* **wallet**) *noun* [C] a small, flat container for carrying paper money and credit cards (= plastic cards used for paying with) **cüzdan**

billiards /ˈbɪliədz/ *noun* [U] a game in which two people try to hit coloured balls into holes around the edge of a table using long, thin sticks **bilardo**

billing /ˈbɪlɪŋ/ *noun* [U] **1** when people are sent letters to ask for payments **faturalandırma 2 star/top billing** when a particular performer is shown as the most important person in a performance **assolist, en önemli sanatçı, yıldız sanatçı**

billion /ˈbɪliən/ the number 1,000,000,000 **milyar**

billow /ˈbɪləʊ/ *verb* [I] to be moved and spread out by a current of air **dalgalanmak, sallanmak, kıpırdamak, oynamak** *Smoke billowed out of the building.*

bimbo /ˈbɪmbəʊ/ *noun* [C] *very informal* a young woman who is attractive but not intelligent **güzel, ancak zeki olmayan genç bayan**

o⊶**bin** /bɪn/ *noun* [C] **1** *UK* (*US* **trash can**) a container that is used to put waste in **çöp kovası/kutusu/bidonu** *a* *rubbish/wastepaper bin* ○ *I threw it in the bin.* ⊃Orta kısımdaki renkli sayfalarına bakınız. **2** a container for storing things **teneke kutu** *a storage bin*

binary /'baɪnᵊri/ *adjective* The binary system expresses numbers using only 1 and 0, and is especially used for computers. **bilhassa bilgisayarda 1 ve 0 rakamlarını kullanan**

bind¹ /baɪnd/ *verb* [T] *past* **bound 1** [TIE] to tie something together with string, rope, etc **bağlamak, balya yapmak, demet haline getirip bağlamak** *His hands were bound behind his back.* **2** [KEEP PROMISE] to force someone to keep a promise **birini sözünü tutmaya zorlamak, zorunlu kılmak** *His contract binds him to working a six-day week.* **3** [UNITE] to unite people **bir araya getirmek, birleştirmek** *Culture and language bind people together.* **4** [BOOK] to fasten together pages to make a book **ciltlemek**

bind² /baɪnd/ *noun* [no plural] *informal* **1** a difficult or unpleasant situation **zor ve hoş olmayan bir durum** *a financial bind* **2** *UK* a job which uses a lot of your time **bağlayıcı bir iş, zaman gerektiren uğraş** *Cleaning the bathroom is a bind.*

binder /'baɪndə^r/ *noun* [C] a strong cover for holding together pieces of paper **klasör**

binding /'baɪndɪŋ/ *adjective* A binding agreement, promise, etc cannot be broken or changed. **bağlayıcı** *It's a legally binding contract.*

binge¹ /bɪndʒ/ *noun* [C] when you eat or drink too much or spend too much money in shops **kriz, bir şeyi yapmadan durmamak**

binge² /bɪndʒ/ *verb* [I] **bingeing** or **binging** to eat too much food at one time **tıka basa yemek, silip süpürmek, aşırı yemek** *I've been bingeing on chocolate.*

'**binge ,drinking** *noun* [U] when someone drinks too much alcohol on one occasion **çok içki içmek, kör kütük sarhoş olmak** ●'**binge ,drinker** *noun* [C] **yoğun içici**

bingo /'bɪŋgəʊ/ *noun* [U] a game in which people mark numbers on a card as they are called, and the person whose numbers are called first is the winner **bir tür tombala, bingo**

binoculars /bɪ'nɒkjələz/ *noun* [plural] a piece of equipment for looking at things that are far away, made from two tubes with glass at the ends **dürbün** *a pair of binoculars*

binoculars

bio- /baɪəʊ-/ *prefix* relating to living things or human life **yaşayan canlılar ve insan hayatına ilişkin önek** *biodiversity* ○ *bioethics*

biochemical /,baɪəʊ'kemɪk^əl/ *adjective* relating to the chemistry of living things **biyokimyasal**

biochemistry /,baɪəʊ'kemɪstri/ *noun* [U] the study of the chemistry of living things such as plants, animals, or people **biyokimya** ● **biochemist** *noun* [C] a scientist who studies biochemistry **biyokimyacı**

biodegradable /,baɪəʊdɪ'greɪdəbl/ *adjective* Biodegradable substances decay naturally without damaging the environment. **çevreye zarar vermeden tabiatta kaybolabilen**

biodiesel /'baɪəʊ,di:zl/ *noun* [U] fuel used in the engines of some vehicles that is made from vegetable oil or animal fat **biyodizel**

bioethanol /,baɪəʊ'eθɑnɒl/ *noun* [U] fuel used in the engines of some vehicles that is partly made from ethanol (= a chemical that comes from sugar) **biyoetanol, bir tür dizel araç yakıtı**

biofuel /'baɪəʊ,fjʊəl/ *noun* [U] fuel produced from plant material

biographer /baɪ'ɒgrəfə^r/ *noun* [C] someone who writes the story of a particular person's life **biyografi/yaşam öyküsü yazarı**

biography /baɪ'ɒgrəfi/ *noun* [C] the story of a person's life written by another person **yaşam öyküsü, biyografi** ● **biographical** /,baɪəʊ'græfɪkəl/ *adjective* about someone's life **yaşam öyküsüne dair, ilişkin** *biographical information*

biological /,baɪə'lɒdʒɪkᵊl/ *adjective* **1** relating to the study of living things such as plants and animals **biyolojik, biyolojiyle ilgili** *biological sciences* **2** using living things or poisons made from living things **yaşayan canlılardan elde edilen zehirleri veya onların kendisini kullanan, biyolojik** *biological weapons* ● **biologically** *adverb* **biyolojik olarak**

biology /baɪ'ɒlədʒi/ *noun* [U] the study of living things **yaşayan canlılar bilimi, biyoloji** ● **biologist** *noun* [C] a scientist who studies biology **biyolog**

biometric /,baɪəʊ'metrɪk/ *adjective* using a person's characteristics, e.g. their voice or the pattern of their eyes, to prove who they are

biopsy /'baɪɒpsi/ *noun* [C] when a small number of cells are taken from a part of the body and examined to see if there is a disease **biyopsi, tetkik için vücuttan küçük bir parçanın alınması**

biotechnology /,baɪəʊtek'nɒlədʒi/ *noun* [U] the use of living cells and bacteria in chemical processes, especially in the food and medical industries **biyoteknoloji**

bioterrorism /,baɪəʊ'terərɪz^əm/ *noun* [U] when people use living things, such as bacteria, to hurt other people for political reasons **biyoterörizm, kimyasal terörizm** ● **bioterrorist** *noun* [C] **diğer kişilere zarar vermek için hastalık yayıcı girişimlerde bulunma**

bipartisan /baɪ'pɑːtɪzæn/ *adjective* involving two political parties **iki siyasi partiyi ilgilendiren** *a bipartisan agreement*

birch /bɜːtʃ/ *noun* [C, U] a tree that has thin, smooth branches **huş ağacı**

o-**bird** /bɜːd/ *noun* [C] an animal that has wings and feathers and is usually able to fly **kuş**

'**bird ,flu** (avian flu) *noun* [U] an illness that kills birds and can sometimes pass from birds to people **kuş gribi**

birdie /'bɜːdi/ *US* (*UK* shuttlecock) *noun* [C] a small object with feathers that is used like a ball in badminton (= a sport like tennis) **bedminton sporunda top gibi kullanılan ve tüyleri olan küçük nesne**

,**bird of 'prey** *noun* [C] *plural* **birds of prey** a large bird that kills smaller animals for food **yırtıcı kuş, leşle beslenen kuşlar**

bird-watching /'bɜːd,wɒtʃɪŋ/ *noun* [U] the hobby of looking at birds **kuş gözlemciliği, ornitoloji**

biro /'baɪərəʊ/ *noun* [C] *UK trademark* a type of pen that has a very small metal ball at its end and a thin tube of ink inside **tükenmez kalem**

o-**birth** /bɜːθ/ *noun* **1** give birth When a woman or an animal gives birth, she produces a baby from her body. **doğum yapmak** *She gave birth to twins.* **2** [C, U] the time when a baby is born **doğum** *a difficult birth* ○ *Write your date of birth* (= the date when you were born) *here.* **3** [U] *literary* the beginning of something **bir şeyin doğuşu, ortaya çıkışı** *the birth of modern science* **4 American/Italian, etc by birth** born in a particular place or having parents with a particular nationality **Amerika/İtalya vb. doğumlu**

'birth cer,tificate noun [C] an official document that records when and where a person was born **nüfus cüzdanı, doğum belgesi**

'birth con,trol noun [U] methods of limiting the number of children you have **doğum kontrolü**

▨▤▦ **birthday** ...... İLE BİRLİKTE KULLANILAN KELİMELER

celebrate your birthday ● **on** sb's [1st/50th/100th, etc] birthday ● a birthday **cake/card/party/present**

o→**birthday** /'bɜːdeɪ/ noun [C] the day on which someone was born, or the same date each year **doğum günü** She is celebrating her seventieth birthday. ○ Happy Birthday! ○ a birthday cake/party

birthmark /'bɜːθmɑːk/ noun [C] a mark on someone's skin that has been there since they were born **doğum lekesi, doğuştan gelen leke, iz, ben**

birthplace /'bɜːθpleɪs/ noun [C] the place where someone was born **doğum yeri**

'birth ,rate noun [C] a measurement of the number of babies born in a particular period **doğum oranı**

o→**biscuit** /'bɪskɪt/ noun [C] **1** UK (US cookie) a thin, flat cake that is dry and usually sweet **bisküvi** ⊃Orta kısımdaki renkli sayfalarına bakınız. **2** US a small, soft, round bread **küçük, yumuşak, yuvarlak ekmek**

bisexual /baɪ'sekʃuəl/ adjective sexually attracted to both men and women **her iki cinse ilgi duyan/ilgi uyandıran, biseksüel**

bishop /'bɪʃəp/ noun [C] a priest of high rank in some Christian churches **piskopos** the Bishop of Oxford

bison /'baɪsən/ noun [C] plural **bison** a large, wild animal similar to a cow with long hair **öküz, bizon öküzü**

bistro /'biːstrəʊ/ noun [C] an informal place to eat or drink, in a French style **Fransız usulü yenilen içilen yer, bistro**

o→**bit** /bɪt/ noun [C] **1** SMALL AMOUNT a small amount or piece of something **küçük parça, parçacık** I wrote it down on a bit of paper. ○ There's a little bit more pasta left. ○ My favourite bit of the film is right at the end. ○ The books are falling **to bits** (= into separate parts). **2 a bit** a SLIGHTLY slightly **biraz, birazcık** It's a bit cold in here. ○ It was a bit too expensive. **b** SHORT TIME informal a short time **çok kısa bir süre, anlık** I'll see you **in a bit**. ○ She lived in Italy **for a bit**. **3 a bit of a change/fool/problem, etc** a change, fool (= stupid person), problem, etc, but not an important or serious one **birazcık değişim/aptal/sorun vs.** I am a bit of a romantic. ○ It was a bit of a shock. **4 quite a bit** informal a lot **oldukça, çok** He does quite a bit of travelling. ○ She is quite a bit older than him. **5 a bit much** informal more than is fair, or more than you can deal with **birazcık fazla** It's a bit much to expect me to tidy up their mess. **6 bit by bit** gradually **azar azar, biraz biraz** She saved up the money, bit by bit. **7 every bit as** used to emphasize that one thing is equally good, important, etc as something else **tamamiyle, tamamı diğerleri kadar iyi, önemli** The gardens are every bit as impressive as the castle itself. **8 bits and pieces** small things or jobs which are not connected or not very important **ıvır zıvır; ufak, önemsiz şeyler** We've packed most of it up now, there are just a few bits and pieces left. **9** COMPUTER a unit of information in a computer **bilgisayarda bilgi birimi, bit 10** HORSE a piece of metal which goes in the mouth of a horse to control it **gem, atın gemi**

bit² /bɪt/ past tense of **bite** **ısırmak' fiilinin 2. hali**

bitch¹ /bɪtʃ/ noun [C] **1** very informal an offensive name for an unpleasant woman **(argo) kaltak, kancık, kahpe, şıllık 2** a female dog **dişi köpek**

bitch² /bɪtʃ/ verb [I] very informal to talk in an unkind way about people **insanlar hakkında ileri geri, nezaketsizce konuşmak, dır dır etmek** She's always bitching about her boss.

bitchy /'bɪtʃi/ adjective If someone is bitchy, they are unkind about other people. **hain, kancık, kahpe** a bitchy comment

o→**bite¹** /baɪt/ verb past tense **bit**, past participle **bitten 1** [I, T] to cut something using your teeth **ısırmak** She bit into an apple. ○ He bites his fingernails. ○ He was bitten by a dog. **2** [I] to begin to have a bad effect **etkisini göstermeye başlamak, kötü etkisi ortaya çıkmak** Higher mortgage rates are beginning to bite. ⊃See also: bite the bullet, bite the dust¹. **3 come back to bite you** If a problem will come back to bite you, it will causes more trouble for you in the future if you do not solve it now. **bir problemi küçükken çözmek, ileride çok daha fazla dert açmasını önlemek**

bite² /baɪt/ noun **1** [C] a piece taken from food when you bite it **lokma** She took a bite from her pizza. **2** [C] an injury caused when an animal or insect bites you **ısırık** mosquito bites **3 a bite** a small meal **bir lokma bir şey, küçük bir yemek** I just want to grab a bite to eat.

biting /'baɪtɪŋ/ adjective A biting wind or biting cold is extremely cold and hurts your skin. **dundurucu, bıçak gibi kesen, şiddetli**

bitmap /'bɪtmæp/ noun [C] a computer image formed from many small points on the screen

bitten /'bɪtən/ past participle of **bite** **ısırmak' fiilinin 3. hali**

bitter¹ /'bɪtər/ adjective **1** ANGRY angry and upset because of something bad which has happened that you cannot forget **kızgın, içerlemiş, çok kötü** I feel very bitter about my childhood. **2** HATE full of hate or anger **kin ve kızgınlık dolu, amansız acımasız** a bitter argument/dispute **3** SOUR having a strong, sour, usually unpleasant taste **acı tadı olan 4** COLD extremely cold **iliklere işleyen soğuk, sert soğuk** a bitter wind **5 to/until the bitter end** until something is completely finished, usually something unpleasant **sonuna dek, ölesiye, tamamen son buluncaya kadar** He was determined to stay right to the bitter end. **6** DISAPPOINTED making you feel very disappointed **kötü, üzücü, hayal kırıklığına uğramış** Losing the championship was a bitter disappointment. ● **bitterness** noun [U] **hüzün**

bitter² /'bɪtər/ noun [U] UK A type of beer with a bitter taste **siyah bira**

bitterly /'bɪtəli/ adverb **1** in a way which shows strong negative emotion such as anger or disappointment **amansız, şiddetli derecede, kızgın bir şekilde, acımasızca** We were bitterly disappointed about the decision. **2** If it is bitterly cold, the weather is extremely and unpleasantly cold. **keskin ayaz, soğuk, berbat bir kış**

bizarre /bɪ'zɑːr/ adjective very strange and surprising **garip, tuhaf, acayip** bizarre behaviour ● **bizarrely** adverb **garip bir şekilde**

o→**black¹** /blæk/ adjective **1** COLOUR being the colour of coal or of the sky on a very dark night **kara** a black jacket ⊃Orta kısımdaki renkli sayfalarına bakınız. **2** PERSON Someone who is black has the dark skin typical of people from Africa. **zenci ırkından** black athletes/Americans **3** OF BLACK PEOPLE relating to black people **siyahi** the black community **4** DRINK Black tea or coffee has no milk or cream added to it. **sade (kahve, çay) 5** HUMOUR funny about unpleasant or frightening subjects **kara (mizah)** black comedy **6** ANGRY angry **kızgın** He gave her a black look. **7** SITUATION If your situation or future is black, it is very bad. **geleceği karanlık, belirsiz**

8 black and blue covered with bruises (= marks on your skin from being hit) **yara bere, çürük içinde, yüzü gözü mosmor** ● **9 black and white** very clear or simple **açık ve net** *The issue of nuclear weapons is not black and white.* ● **blackness** *noun* [U] ⊃See also: jet-black, pitch-black. **siyahlık**

☞**black²** /blæk/ *noun* **1** [COLOUR] [C, U] the colour of coal or of the sky on a very dark night **siyah** *She always dresses in black* (= in black clothes). ⊃Orta kısımdaki renkli sayfalarına bakınız. **2** [PERSON] [C] a black person **zenci 3 in the black** If your bank account is in the black, it contains some money. **banka hesabında bakiyenin az olması 4 in black and white a** [PRINT] printed in a book, newspaper, or official document **yazı ile** *Look at the contract - it's all there in black and white.* **b** [NO COLOUR] using or seeing no colours, but only black, white, and grey **siyah beyaz** *I saw the original film in black and white.* ⊃See also: jet-black.

black³ /blæk/ *verb*
black out *phrasal verb informal* to suddenly become unconscious **aniden bayılmak, kendinden geçmek**

blackberry /'blækb³ri/ *noun* [C] a small, soft, dark purple fruit with seeds **böğürtlen**

BlackBerry /'blækb³ri/ *noun* [C] *trademark* a computer with no wires that fits in your hand and that you can use for documents, email and Internet access **kablosuz el bligisayarı** ⊃See study page The Web and the Internet on page Centre 37. ● **BlackBerry** *verb* [I] to use a BlackBerry **kablosuz el bligisayarı kullanmak**

blackbird /'blækbɜːd/ *noun* [C] a bird with black feathers and a yellow beak **karatavuk**

blackboard /'blækbɔːd/ (*also US* **chalkboard**) *noun* [C] a large board with a dark surface that teachers write on with chalk (= soft, white rock) **kara tahta** ⊃Orta kısımdaki renkli sayfalarına bakınız.

,**black 'box** *noun* [C] a small machine on an aircraft that people use to discover the reason for an aircraft accident **kara kutu**

blackcurrant /,blæk'kʌr³nt/ *noun* [C] *UK* a very small, round, sour, dark purple fruit **kuşüzümü** *blackcurrant juice/jelly*

blacken /'blæk³n/ *verb* **1** [I, T] to become black or to make something become black **karartmak, kararmak** *Storm clouds blackened the sky.* **2** [T] If you blacken someone's name, you say bad things about them. **karalamak, leke sürmek, kötülemek**

,**black 'eye** *noun* [C] an eye that has a dark circle around it because it has been hit **gözü mosmor**

,**black 'hole** *noun* [C] an area in outer space that sucks material and light into it from which it cannot escape **uzayda kara delik**

blacklist /'blæklɪst/ *verb* [T] to include someone on a list of people you think are bad or you will not deal with **kara liste oluşturmak, kara listeye almak** [often passive] *He was blacklisted by the banks and credit card companies.*

,**black 'magic** *noun* [U] magic used for evil **kara büyü**

blackmail /'blækmeɪl/ *noun* [U] when someone forces you to do something, or to pay them money, by saying they will tell another person something that you want to keep secret **şantaj** ● **blackmail** *verb* [T] [+ into + doing sth] *They used the photographs to blackmail her into spying for them.* **şantaj yapmak** ● **blackmailer** *noun* [C] **şantaj yapan kişi**

,**black 'market** *noun* [C] illegal trading of goods that are not allowed to be bought and sold or that there are not enough of for everyone who wants them **kara borsa** *the black market in heroin*

blackout /'blækaʊt/ *noun* [C] **1** [UNCONSCIOUS] when someone suddenly becomes unconscious **bayılma, baygınlık geçirme, kendinden geçme 2** [NO INFORMATION] when information is kept from people **delilleri, bilgileri karartma, bilgi kesintisi** [usually singular] *a media/news blackout* **3** [NO ELECTRICITY] a failure in the supply of electricity **elektrik kesintisi 4** [NO LIGHTS] a period during a war when no lights must show at night **savaş sırasında karartma**

blacksmith /'blæksmɪθ/ *noun* [C] someone whose job is to make things from metal, especially shoes for horses **demirci, nalbant**

bladder /'blædə'/ *noun* [C] the organ where waste liquid is stored before it leaves your body **idrar kesesi, sidik torbası, mesane** ⊃See also: gall bladder.

blade /bleɪd/ *noun* [C] **1** the flat, sharp, metal part of a knife, tool, or weapon **(bıçak, jilet, ustra vb.) ağız, uç, keskin bölüm 2** a long, narrow leaf of grass or a similar plant **bitkilerin geniş, uzun yassı yaprakları** *a blade of grass* ⊃See also: razor blade, shoulder blade.

☞**blame¹** /bleɪm/ *verb* [T] **1** to say or think that someone or something is responsible for something bad which has happened **ayıplamak, sorumlu tutmak, suçlamak** *Many people blame him for Tony's death.* ○ *Poor housing is to blame for many of their health problems.* ○ *They apologized for the delay and blamed it on technical problems.* **2 I don't blame him/them/you, etc** used to say that you understand and accept the reason for what someone is doing **onu/onları/seni/sizi suçlamıyorum, kimseyi suçlamıyorum** *"I think I'll go home early." "I don't blame you - you look really tired."*

━━━━━━━━━━━━━━━━━━━━
blame ...... İLE BİRLİKTE KULLANILAN KELİMELER

apportion blame ● **get/shoulder/take** the blame **for** sth ● **lay/put** the blame **on** sth
━━━━━━━━━━━━━━━━━━━━

blame² /bleɪm/ *noun* [U] when people say that someone or something is responsible for something bad **suç, kabahat,sorumluluk, neden** *The manager should take the blame for the team's defeat.* ○ *They put the blame on faulty equipment.*

blameless /'bleɪmləs/ *adjective* not responsible for anything bad **suçsuz, kabahatsiz** *They concluded that Lucy was entirely blameless.*

bland /blænd/ *adjective* **1** not interesting or exciting **sıkıcı, ilginç olmayan, sıradan** *bland statements* **2** If food is bland, it does not have much taste. **tatsız tuzsuz, lezzetsiz**

blank¹ /blæŋk/ *adjective* **1** with no writing, pictures, or sound **(kağıt, kaset vs.) boş, içinde hiç bir şey olmayan** *a blank page* ○ *a blank tape* ○ *The space for the date was left blank.* **2 go blank** If your mind goes blank, you suddenly cannot remember or think of something. **hafıza kaybı yaşamak, bir şey hatırlayamamak 3** showing no feeling or understanding **boş, anlamsız, hissiz** *a blank expression* ⊃See also: point-blank.

blank² /blæŋk/ *noun* **1** [C] an empty space on a piece of paper or form where information can be given **boş, kullanılmamış (kağıt)** *Just fill in the blanks.* **2 draw a blank** to be unable to get information, think of something, or achieve something **(piyangoda) boş çekmek, bilgiye ulaşamamak, bir şey düşünememek** *All their investigations have drawn a blank so far.*

,**blank 'cheque** *UK* (*mainly US* ,**blank 'check**) *noun* [C] If you give someone a blank cheque, you allow them as much money as they want or need to do something. **açık çek, bone, senet**

blanket¹ /'blæŋkɪt/ *noun* [C] **1** a thick, warm cover that you sleep under **battaniye 2** a thick layer of something **kalın tabaka** *a blanket of cloud/snow*

blanket² /'blæŋkɪt/ *adjective* [always before noun] including or affecting everything **herşeyi etkileyen veya içeren** *a blanket ban*

blanket³ /'blæŋkɪt/ *verb* [T] to completely cover something **bir şeyi tamamen kapsamak, içine almak** *The ground was blanketed with snow.*

blankly /'blæŋkli/ *adverb* without showing any emotion or understanding **boş boş, hiç bir duygu veya anlayış göstermeden** *She just stared at me blankly.*

blare /bleə^r/ *verb* [I] to make a very loud noise **şiddetli ve sert ses çıkarmak** *There was music blaring from his room.*

blasphemy /'blæsfəmi/ *noun* [U] something which you say or do that shows you do not respect God or a religion **kutsal şeylere saldırı, küfür** ● **blasphemous** /'blæsfəməs/ *adjective* expressing blasphemy **kutsalı saymayan, hürmetsiz, dini inançlara saygı duymayan**

blast¹ /blɑːst/ *noun* 1 EXPLOSION [C] an explosion **büyük patlama** *a bomb blast* 2 AIR [C] a sudden strong movement of air **rüzgarın çıkması, ani fırtına çıkması** *a blast of cold air/heat* 3 **full blast** If something is happening or working full blast, it is at its loudest, strongest, or fastest level. **tam faaliyette, tam kapasite, en üst seviyede, güçte** *The heating was on full blast.* 4 NOISE [C] a sudden loud noise **ani çıkan yüksek ses, gürültü** *a blast on the trumpet* 5 ENJOYMENT [no plural] *US very informal* an exciting and enjoyable experience **heyecan verici ve çok hoş bir deneyim** *Eric's party was a blast.*

blast² /blɑːst/ *verb* 1 NOISE [I, T] to make a very loud noise **patlamak, infilak etmek, tahrip etmek** *rock music blasting from a stereo* 2 MOVE [I, T] to move through something or to hit something with force **bir şeyin arasından hızlıca geçmek veya bir şeye hızlı ve güçlü bir darbe indirmek** *Dixon blasted the ball past the goalkeeper.* 3 EXPLODE [T] to break through rock using explosives **patlayıcılarla kayaları parçalamak** *They blasted a hole in the rock face.* 4 GUNS [T] to destroy a person or place with guns or bombs **ağır silah ve bombalarla bir yeri veya kişiyi havaya uçurmak, tahrip etmek**

blast off *phrasal verb* When a spacecraft blasts off, it leaves the ground to go into space. **(uzay aracı) fırla(t)mak, büyük bir gürültüyle kalkmak, havalanmak**

blast³ /blɑːst/ *exclamation UK* used when you are annoyed at something **lanet olsun, Allah belanı versin, Allah kahretsin** *Blast! I forgot the keys.*

blast-off /'blɑːstɒf/ *noun* [U] when a spacecraft leaves the ground **bir uzay aracının aniden havalanması, kalkışı, gürleyen bir sesle havalanması**

📦 **blatant** ...... İLE BİRLİKTE KULLANILAN KELİMELER

a blatant **attempt** to do sth ● a blatant **disregard for** sth ● a blatant **lie**

---

blatant /'bleɪt°nt/ *adjective* very obvious, with no attempt to be honest or behave well **kaba, arsız, utanmaz, pervasız, terbiyesiz** *blatant lies/racism* ● **blatantly** *adverb* **bariz bir şekilde**

blaze¹ /bleɪz/ *verb* [I] to burn or shine very brightly or strongly **parlamak, parıldama, güçlü ve çok parlak bir şekilde yanmak veya parlamak** *The sun blazed down on the dry countryside.*

blaze² /bleɪz/ *noun* [C] 1 a large, strong fire **büyük, güçlü ateş** *The blaze started in the hall.* 2 **a blaze of colour/lights etc** very bright colour, lights, etc **çok parlak renkler, ışıklar** *The tulips provided a blaze of colour outside her window.* 3 **a blaze of glory/publicity**

a lot of public attention for a short time **bir zafer gösterisi, toplumsal patlama**

blazer /'bleɪzə^r/ *noun* [C] a type of jacket, often worn as part of a school uniform **metal düğmeli bir ceket türü**

blazing /'bleɪzɪŋ/ *adjective* [always before noun] 1 very hot **çok sıcak, bunaltıcı sıcak** *a blazing log fire* 2 *UK* very angry **çok kızgın, öfkeli** *a blazing row*

bleach¹ /bliːtʃ/ *noun* [U] a strong chemical used for cleaning things or removing colour from things **ağartma, rengini giderme, temizleme, lek çıkarma,**

bleach² /bliːtʃ/ *verb* [T] to remove the colour from something or make it lighter using chemicals **ağartmak, rengini gidermek, temizlemek, lek çıkarma,** *She's bleached her hair.*

bleak /bliːk/ *adjective* 1 If a situation is bleak, there is little or no hope for the future. **umutsuz, gelecek vaad etmeyen** *The future is looking bleak for small clubs struggling with debts.* 2 If a place is bleak, it is cold, empty and not attractive. **soğuk, boş, sevimsiz, nahoş** *a bleak landscape* ● **bleakness** *noun* [U] **umutsuzluk**

bleary /'blɪəri/ *adjective* If you have bleary eyes, you cannot see clearly because you are tired or have just woken up. **mahmur, uykulu, gözleri yorgun**

bleat /bliːt/ *verb* [I] 1 to make the noise of a sheep or goat **melemek, keçi veya koyun gibi ses çıkarmak** 2 to speak or complain in a weak and annoying way **cılız, hastalıklı ve rahatsız edici bir sesle konuşmak, dert yanmak, sızlanmak** *She keeps bleating about her lack of money.* ● **bleat** *noun* [C] **meleme**

bled /bled/ *past of* bleed **kanamak' fiilinin geçmiş zaman hali**

bleed /bliːd/ *verb* [I] *past* bled to have blood coming from a cut in your body **kanamak** ● **bleeding** *noun* [U] *Try to stop the bleeding.* **kanama**

bleep /bliːp/ *noun* [C] a short, high electronic noise **kısa, yüksek elektronik ses, gürültü, bip sesi** ● **bleep** *verb* [I] **bip sesi çıkarma**

bleeper /'bliːpə^r/ *UK (UK/US* beeper) *noun* [C] a small piece of electronic equipment which you carry that makes a sound when someone wants to speak to you **sesle uyarı yapan elektronik alet, çağrı cihazı**

blemish /'blemɪʃ/ *noun* [C] a mark which spoils the appearance of someone or something **leke, iz, yara izi, kusur**

blend¹ /blend/ *verb* 1 [T] to mix two or more things together completely **karıştırmak, katıştırmak** *Blend the ingredients into a smooth paste.* 2 [I, T] to combine two or more things **iki ya da daha fazla şeyi birleştirmek** *The team blends new, young players with more mature, experienced ones.*

blend in *phrasal verb* If something or someone blends in, they look or seem the same as the people or things around them and so are not easily noticed. **kaynaşmak, karışmak, kalabalığın arasına karışmak, uyum sağlamak**

blend² /blend/ *noun* [C] a combination of two or more things **karışım, harman** *Their music is a blend of jazz and African rhythms.*

blender /'blendə^r/ *noun* [C] an electric machine for making soft foods into a smooth liquid **karıştırıcı** ⊃Orta kısımdaki renkli sayfalarına bakınız.

bless /bles/ *verb* [T] 1 to ask God to help or protect someone or something, or to make it holy **Tanrı'nın yardımını dilemek, inayet istemek, kutsamak, takdis etmek** *The priest blessed their marriage.* 2 **be blessed with sth** to be lucky enough to have something good

blessed   70   oᴑ Important words to learn

Allah'ın sevgili kulu olmak; nimetine, şansına sahip olmak *He's blessed with a wonderful singing voice.* **3 Bless you!** something you say when someone sneezes çok yaşa! **4 bless her/him/them, etc** *informal* used to show your affection for the person you are talking about onu, onları vs. birilerine ilgi göstermek, iyi davranmak, alakadar olmak *Peter, bless him, slept all the way through it.*

blessed /'blesɪd/ *adjective* [always before noun] **1** pleasant and wanted very much hoş ve çok istenen, aranan, kutsanmış *The rain was a blessed relief.* **2** holy kutsal, mukaddes, mübarek, lütuf *the Blessed Virgin Mary*

blessing /'blesɪŋ/ *noun* **1** [LUCK] [C] something which is lucky or makes you happy nimet, lütuf, kişiyi mutlu eden şey *It is a blessing that no one was hurt.* **2** [APPROVAL] [U] approval that someone gives to a plan or action razı olma, rıza göstermek, hayır dua, destek, rıza *Mr Newton has given his blessing for the plan.* **3** [RELIGION] [C, U] protection or help from God, or a prayer to ask for this takdis, dua, Tanrı'ya yakarış, yalvarma **4 a blessing in disguise** something that has a good effect, although at first it seemed that it would be bad beklenmedik lütuf, nimet ● **5 a mixed blessing** something which has both good and bad effects iyi ve kötü yönleri, etkileri olan, günahı ve sevabı olan

blew /bluː/ *past tense of* blow esmek, üflemek' fiilinin 2. hali

blight /blaɪt/ *noun* [no plural] something which has a very bad effect on something, often for a long time uzun süre kötü etkisi olmak, kabus gibi çöken etki *the blight of poverty/unemployment* ○ *He became a blight on their lives.* ● **blight** *verb* [T] to cause damage to or have a bad effect on something hasara sebep olmak, kötü etkisi olmak *Injury has blighted his career.*

oᴑ**blind** /blaɪnd/ *adjective* **1** not able to see kör, ama, gözleri görmeyen *She went blind after an accident.* ○ *This project provides guide dogs for the blind.* **2 be blind to sth** to not notice something, or not want to notice something görmezlikten gelmek, bir şeye karşı kayıtsız olmak, gözünü kapamak, gözü hiçbir şey görmemek *Drivers who speed are often blind to the risks they cause.* **3 blind panic/rage/trust, etc** an extremely strong feeling that makes you do things without thinking gözü kapalı davranma, düşünmeden hareket etme, gözünü karartmak ve yapma **4 a blind corner/bend** *UK* a bend or corner on a road that is dangerous because you cannot see cars coming around it trafikte/yolda kör nokta, dönemeç, köşe ● **blindness** *noun* [U] körlük ⊃See also: colour-blind, turn a blind eye¹ (to sth).

blind² /blaɪnd/ *verb* **1** [T] to make someone blind, either for always or for a short time gözünü kapatmak, bağlamak [often passive] *I was blinded by the car headlights.* **2 blind sb to sth** to make someone unable to understand the truth about someone or something birinin gerçeği anlamaması için gözünü kör etmek, görmesine engel olmak *Love blinded her to all his faults.*

blind³ /blaɪnd/ *noun* [C] a cover that you pull down over a window perde, kapatan şey ⊃See also: venetian blind.

‚blind 'date *noun* [C] a romantic meeting between a man and a woman who have not met before önceden tanımadığı karşı cinsten biriyle romantik buluşma

blindfold /'blaɪndfəʊld/ *noun* [C] a piece of cloth that you put over someone's eyes so they cannot see gözbağı ● **blindfold** *verb* [T] to put a blindfold on someone gözlerini bağlamak

blinding /'blaɪndɪŋ/ *adjective* **1** A blinding light is extremely bright. gözleri kör edecek derecede parlayan **2** A blinding headache (= pain in the head) is extremely painful. gözleri kör edecek kadar ağrıyan

blindly /'blaɪndli/ *adverb* **1** not able to see or not noticing what is around you körmüşcesine, gözü kapalı olarak, dikkat etmeden *Carly reached blindly for the light switch.* **2** not thinking about what you are doing körükörüne, fazla üzerinde düşünmeden *They just blindly followed orders.*

'blind ‚spot *noun* [C] **1** a difficulty in accepting or understanding a particular thing kör, belirsiz nokta, anlamakta, kabullenmede zorluk *She has a complete blind spot where relations with the press are concerned.* **2** the part of the road just behind you, that you cannot see when you are driving kör bölge, görülmesi zor alan, nokta

blink /blɪŋk/ *verb* **1** [I, T] to open and close both of your eyes quickly hızlıca göz kırpmak **2** [I] If a light blinks, it goes on and off quickly. hızlı yanıp sönmek ● **blink** *noun* [C] göz kırpma

blinkered /'blɪŋkəd/ *adjective* not willing to consider new or different ideas yeni ve farklı fikirleri kabul etmeyen, bağnaz, yeniliklere açık olmayan *a blinkered attitude*

blip /blɪp/ *noun* [C] **1** a small, temporary, and usually negative change from what usually happens geçici değişim, sapma, aksama *The rise in unemployment may just be a blip.* **2** a small spot of light on an electronic screen, sometimes with a short, high sound bip sesi

bliss /blɪs/ *noun* [U] complete happiness mutluluk, bahtiyarlık, saadet *My idea of bliss is lying on a sunny beach.* ● **blissful** *adjective* making you feel very happy mutluluk verici, saadet bahşeden *a blissful childhood* ● **blissfully** *adverb* *She seemed blissfully unaware of the chaos she had caused.* mutlu bir şekilde

blister¹ /'blɪstə{r}/ *noun* [C] a painful, raised area of skin with liquid inside, that you get if your skin has been rubbed or burned, or a similar area on a painted surface vücudun su toplaması, kabarcık, kabarma

blister² /'blɪstə{r}/ *verb* [I, T] to get or cause blisters su toplamak, kabarmak, su toplanmasına sebep olan

blistering /'blɪst{ə}rɪŋ/ *adjective* **1** [CRITICISM] using very strong criticism sivri dilli, öfkeli, zehir zemberek *a blistering attack* **2** [HEAT] extremely hot yakıcı, kavurucu, cehennem sıcağı *blistering sunshine* **3** [SPEED] extremely fast çok hızlı, aşırı süratli *The economy has grown at a blistering pace.*

blithely /'blaɪðli/ *adverb* without thinking about what might happen düşünmeksizin, kaygısız, sonunu düşünmeden *People were blithely ignoring warnings not to swim in the river.*

blitz¹ /blɪts/ *noun* [C] **1** a lot of activity to achieve something in a short time telaş, yoğun çaba ve faaliyetler, gayret *We had a cleaning blitz before my parents came home.* **2 the Blitz** bomb attacks on British cities during the Second World War 2. dünya savaşında Britanya şehirlerine yapılan hava saldırıları, bombardımanı

blitz² /blɪts/ *verb* [T] **1** to defeat someone or something completely birini, birşeyi tamamen defetmek, yenmek,; üstesinden, hakkından gelmek **2** to drop bombs on something hava bombardımanı yapmak, bombalamak, hava saldırısı gerçekleştirmek

blizzard /'blɪzəd/ *noun* [C] a storm with strong winds and snow kar fırtınası, tipi

bloated /'bləʊtɪd/ *adjective* **1** swollen because of air or liquid inside şiş, şişkin, kabarmış **2** feeling uncomfortable because you have eaten too much şişmiş, çok yemiş, tıkabasa dolu

blob /blɒb/ *noun* [C] a small amount of a thick liquid damla, leke *a blob of cream/glue* ⊃Orta kısımdaki renkli sayfalarına bakınız.

bloc /blɒk/ *noun* [C] a group of countries with similar political ideas, who work together **bir grup ülkenin aralarında oluşturdukları blok, cephe** *the communist bloc*

block

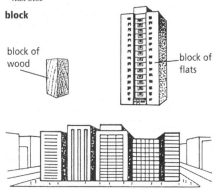

block of wood

block of flats

block¹ /blɒk/ *noun* [C] **1** [PIECE] a solid piece of something, usually in the shape of a square or rectangle **blok, engel, kütük, kalıp, kütle** *a block of ice/stone/wood* **2** [DISTANCE] *US* the distance along a street from where one road crosses it to the place where the next road crosses it **iki cadde arasında kalan bölge, mahal** *They only live two blocks away from the school.* **3** [BUILDING] a large building containing many apartments or offices **binalar grubu bir dizi bina, bloklar** *UK a block of flats* **4** [GROUP OF BUILDINGS] a square group of buildings or houses with roads on each side **her iki tarafında yol olan ve bir çok binadan oluşan binalar kümesi, blokları** *Omar took the dog for a walk round the block.* **5** [CANNOT THINK] If you have a block about something, you cannot understand it or remember it. **anlamakta güçlük, engel, bir şeye kapalı olma** *I had a complete mental block about his name.* **6** [STOP PROGRESS] something that makes it difficult to move or make progress **engel, tıkanma, tıkanıklık** **7** [AMOUNT] an amount or group of something that is considered together **birlikte düşünülen şeylerin oluşturduğu grup, küme, yığın, blok** *This block of seats is reserved.* ⊃See also: be a chip¹ off the old block, stumbling block, tower block.

block² /blɒk/ *verb* [T] [CANNOT PASS] (*also block up*) to prevent anyone or anything from passing through a place **engel olmak, bloke etmek, geçmesine izin vermemek** *A fallen tree blocked the road.* ○ *a blocked drain* **2** [STOP PROGRESS] to stop something from happening or making progress **tıkamak, engellemek, durdurmak** *The council's blocked plans for a new supermarket.* **3** [CANNOT SEE] to be between someone and the thing they are looking at, so that they cannot see **görüntüyü engellemek, iki kişi ya da şey arasında engel oluşturmak, görüşünü engellemek** *A pillar was blocking my view.*

block sth off *phrasal verb* to close a road, path, or entrance so that people cannot use it **engellemek, kapatmak, geçişe engel olmak, kesmek, tıkamak** *Police blocked off the road where the body was found.*

block sth out *phrasal verb* **1** to try to stop yourself thinking about something unpleasant **kendini kötü şeyler düşünmekten uzak tutmak, alıkoymak, engellemek, aklından silmeye çalışmak, düşünmemeye çalışmak** *I've blocked out memories of the accident.* **2** to stop light or noise passing through something

ışık veya sesin gelmesini engellemek, kesmek, durdurmak *Most sunscreens block out UVB radiation.*

blockade /blɒk'eɪd/ *noun* [C] when a government or soldiers stop goods or people from entering or leaving a place **kuşatma, abluka** *The government imposed a blockade on oil trading.* ● **blockade** *verb* [T] **kuşatma yapmak**

blockage /'blɒkɪdʒ/ *noun* [C] something that stops something else passing through **tıkanıklık** *His death was caused by a blockage in his arteries.*

blockbuster /'blɒk,bʌstəʳ/ *noun* [C] *informal* a book, film, etc that is very popular and successful **(kitap, film vs.) büyük başarı, meşhur, bomba** *a new blockbuster movie*

,block 'capitals *noun* [plural] letters in the form A, B, C, not a, b, c **büyük harfler**

blog /blɒg/ *noun* [C] (*also* **weblog**) a record of your thoughts that you put on the Internet for other people to read **başkalarının okuması için internete konulan fikirler/düşünceler** ⊃See study page **The Web and the Internet** on page Centre 36. ● **blog** *verb* [I] **internete bir konu ile ilgili fikirlerinizi yayınlamak** ● **blogger** /'blɒgəʳ/ *noun* [C] a person who writes or reads a blog **bu düşünceleri okuyan kişi**

bloke /bləʊk/ *noun* [C] *UK informal* a man **adam** *Jake's a nice bloke.*

blonde¹ (*also* **blond**) /blɒnd/ *adjective* **1** Blonde hair is pale yellow. **sarı saç 2** Someone who is blonde has pale yellow hair. **sarışın olan**

blonde² (*also* **blond**) /blɒnd/ *noun* [C] someone, especially a woman, who has pale yellow hair **sarışın**

o⟶**blood** /blʌd/ *noun* [U] **1** the red liquid that flows around your body **kan** *a blood test/sample* **2** the family or place that you come from **kan bağı** *I've got some Spanish blood in me.* **3** **be in your blood** If something is in your blood, you and other people in your family are interested in it or good at it. **kanında, doğasında, yapısında olmak** *Sailing is in my blood.* **4** **bad blood** feelings of hate between people because of things that have happened in the past **kan davası, husumet, kin, garaz, düşmanlık** ● **5** **in cold blood** in a cruel way, without showing any emotion **soğuk kanlı** *He shot three policemen in cold blood.* ● **6** **new blood** new people in an organization who will provide new ideas and energy **taze kan, yeni insanlar** ⊃See also: your own **flesh** and blood.

bloodbath /'blʌdbɑːθ/ *noun* [no plural] an extremely violent event in which many people are killed **kan gölü, katliam**

blood-curdling /'blʌd,kɜːdlɪŋ/ *adjective* extremely frightening **insanın kanını donduran, tüyler ürpertici** *a blood-curdling scream*

'blood ,donor *noun* [C] someone who gives some of their blood for ill people who need it **kan bağışında bulunan kişi**

'blood ,group *UK* (*UK/US* **blood type**) *noun* [C] one of the groups that human blood is divided into **kan grubu**

bloodless /'blʌdləs/ *adjective* achieved without killing or violence **kansız, kan akıtmadan** *a bloodless coup*

'blood ,pressure *noun* [U] the force with which blood flows around your body **kan basıncı** *high/low blood pressure*

bloodshed /'blʌdʃed/ noun [U] when people are killed or injured in fighting **kan dökme, kan davası** *Peace talks have failed to end the bloodshed in the region.*

bloodshot /'blʌdʃɒt/ adjective Bloodshot eyes are red in the part that should be white. **kan çanağı, kanlanmış, kızarmış**

'**blood ˌsport** noun [C] a sport in which animals are killed **avcılık**

bloodstained /'blʌdsteɪnd/ adjective Something that is bloodstained has blood on it. **kanlı, kan bulaşmış, kan izi olan**

bloodstream /'blʌdstriːm/ noun [no plural] the flow of blood around your body **kan dolaşımı**

bloodthirsty /'blʌd,θɜːsti/ adjective enjoying using or watching violence **kana susamış**

'**blood transˌfusion** noun [C] when blood is put into someone's body **kan nakli**

'**blood ˌtype** (also UK **blood group**) noun [C] one of the groups that human blood is divided into **kan grubu**

'**blood ˌvessel** noun [C] one of the small tubes that blood flows through in your body **kan damarı**

bloody¹ /'blʌdi/ adjective **1** covered in blood **kanlı** *bloody hands* **2** violent and involving a lot of blood and injuries **kanlı, şiddet, kan ve yara bere içeren** *a bloody war*

bloody² /'blʌdi/ adjective, adverb UK very informal used to show anger or to emphasize what you are saying in a slightly rude way **lanet olası, Allah'ın belası, kör olasıca** *I can't find my bloody keys.* ○ *We were bloody lucky to win.*

bloom¹ /bluːm/ noun **1** [C] a flower **tomurcuk, çiçek** *beautiful, pink blooms* **2 in bloom** with flowers that are open **çiçek açmış** *In June the roses are in bloom.*

bloom² /bluːm/ verb [I] **1** If a plant blooms, its flowers open. **tomurcuklanmak, çiçek açmak 2** to develop and become successful, happy, or healthy **gelişmek, başarılı, mutlu ve sağlıklı olmak** *Their romance bloomed while they were in Paris.*

blossom¹ /'blɒsᵊm/ noun [C, U] a small flower, or the small flowers on a tree or plant **çiçek, küçük çiçekler** *cherry blossom*

blossom² /'blɒsᵊm/ verb [I] **1** If a tree blossoms, it produces flowers. **çiçek açmak, çiçeklenmek 2** to develop and become successful or beautiful **büyümek, gelişip, serpilmek, güzelleşmek** *She has blossomed into a world champion.*

blot¹ /blɒt/ verb [T] **blotting**, past **blotted** to dry wet marks using soft paper or a cloth **lekeyi silmek, kurulamak, çıkarmak**
blot sth out phrasal verb **1** to stop yourself from thinking about something unpleasant **kötü bir şeyi düşünmeyi bırakmak** *I've tried to blot out memories of my relationship with Dieter.* **2** If smoke or cloud blots out the sun, it prevents it from being seen. **silmek, örtmek, kapatmak, engellemek, görüntüsünü gölgelemek**

blot² /blɒt/ noun **1** [C] a mark on something, made by ink or paint falling on it **leke 2 a blot on sth** something that spoils something else **leke, kötü iz, bir şeyi bozan leke** *The financial scandal was a blot on his reputation.*

blotch /blɒtʃ/ noun [C] a mark on something, especially your skin **leke ● blotchy** (also blotched) adjective having blotches **lekeli, leke dolu**

'**blotting ˌpaper** noun [U] thick paper used for drying wet ink **kurutma kağıdı**

blouse /blaʊz/ ⑤ /blaʊs/ noun [C] a piece of clothing like a shirt that women wear **bluz**

⚬⁼**blow**¹ /bləʊ/ verb past tense **blew**, past participle **blown**
1 WIND [I] If the wind blows, it moves and makes currents of air. **esmek** *A cool sea breeze was blowing.* **2** PERSON [I] to force air out through your mouth **üflemek** *She blew on her coffee before taking a sip.* **3 blow sth down/across/off, etc** If the wind blows something somewhere, it makes it move in that direction. **savurmak, savrulmak, uçuşturmak, uçuşmak, uçurtmak** *The storm blew trees across the road.* **4** MOVE [I] to move in the wind **uçuşmak, esmek** *branches blowing in the breeze* **5** INSTRUMENT [I, T] to make a sound by forcing air out of your mouth and through an instrument **ıslık çalmak, çalmak, üfleyerek ses çıkarmak** *Ann blew a few notes on the trumpet.* **6** MAKE [T] to make shapes out of something by blowing into it **üfleyerek şekil vermek (cam vb.)** *to blow bubbles* **7** SPEND [T] informal to spend a lot of money quickly and without considering it seriously **har vurup harman savurmak, düşüncesizce harcamak** *Lou blew all her prize money on a diamond necklace.* **8 blow it/your chance(s)** informal If you blow it or blow your chance, you lose an opportunity to do something by doing or saying the wrong thing. **yanlış sözcük kullanarak ya da yanlış yaparak bir şeyi yapma fırsatını elinden kaçırmak, her şeyi berbat etmek** *Tom blew his chances of getting the job by arriving late for the interview.* **9 blow your nose** to clear your nose by forcing air through it into a handkerchief (= piece of cloth or soft paper) **burnunu silmek, sümkürmek 10** ELECTRICITY [I, T] If a piece of electrical equipment blows, it suddenly stops working because the electric current is too strong. **(elektrikli alet) patlamak, yanarak patlamak, yanmak, sigortası atmak, ampülü yanmak vb.** ⊃See also: blow your mind¹, blow/get sth out of proportion.
blow sb away phrasal verb mainly US informal to surprise or please someone very much **birini şaşırtmak ve mutlu, memnun etmek** *a movie that will blow you away*
blow (sth) out phrasal verb If a flame blows out, or if you blow it out, it stops burning because you or the wind have blown it. **bir ateşi söndürmek, üfleyerek söndürmek**
blow over phrasal verb If a storm or an argument blows over, it ends. **bitmek (tartışma), geçmek(fırtına), dağılmak, etkisi bitmek, sönmek**
blow (sb, sth) up phrasal verb to destroy something or kill someone with a bomb, or to be destroyed by a bomb **param parça etmek, darmadağın etmek, uçurmak, yok etmek, bomba ile parçalamak, infilak etmek** *Terrorists blew up an office building in the city.*
blow sth up phrasal verb to fill something with air **şişirmek** *blow up a balloon*
blow up phrasal verb **1** If a storm or an argument blows up, it starts suddenly. **patlak vermek, birden ortaya çıkmak 2** informal to suddenly become very angry **aniden kızmak, küplere binmek, tepesi atmak**

blow² /bləʊ/ noun [C] **1** DISAPPOINTMENT a shock or disappointment **hayal kırıklığı, şok** *Losing his job was a terrible blow to him.* **2** HIT a hard hit with a hand or heavy object **darbe, vuruş** *He suffered serious blows to the head during the attack.* **3** INSTRUMENT when you blow something or blow into an instrument or other object **vurma, vuruş** *a blow on the whistle* **4 come to blows** to fight or argue **döğüşmek veya tartışmak**

blow-by-blow /,bləʊbaɪˈbləʊ/ adjective **a blow-by-blow account/description** a description of an event that gives all the details in the exact order that they happened **adım adım izah/tasvir, harfi harfine tanımlama**

blow-dry /'bləʊdraɪ/ verb [T] to dry your hair in a particular style using a hairdryer (= electrical equipment for drying hair) **kurutma makinasıyla saçlarını**

kurutmak ● **blow-dry** *noun* [no plural] *I had a cut and blow-dry.* kurulama

blown /'bləʊn/ *past participle of* blow **üflemek, esmek' fiilinin 3. hali**

blowout /'bləʊaʊt/ *noun* [C] **1** [TYRE] when a tyre suddenly explodes while a vehicle is still moving **teker patlaması 2** [MEAL/PARTY] *informal* an expensive meal or a big party **pahalı bir yemek, ziyafet veya büyük bir parti 3** [SPORT] *US informal* when one team or player beats another easily in a sport **mağlup etme, galibiyet, yenme**

bludgeon /'blʌdʒ³n/ *verb* [T] to hit someone several times with a heavy object **sopayla kıyasıya dövmek, dayak atmak** [often passive] *She was bludgeoned to death with a hammer.*

○**blue**¹ /bluː/ *adjective* **1** [COLOUR] being the same colour as the sky when there are no clouds **mavi, mavi renk** *a dark blue jacket* ➜Orta kısımdaki renkli sayfalarına bakınız. **2** [SAD] *informal* sad **üzgün, kederli 3** [SEX] about sex **müstehcen** *a blue joke/movie* ➜See also: **black**¹ and blue, once in a blue **moon**.

○**blue**² /bluː/ *noun* **1** [C, U] the colour of the sky when there are no clouds **gök mavi** ➜Orta kısımdaki renkli sayfalarına bakınız. **2 out of the blue** If something happens out of the blue, you did not expect it. **beklenmedik, damdan düşer gibi, durup dururken** *One day, completely out of the blue, I had a letter from her.*

bluebell /'bluːbel/ *noun* [C] a plant with small, blue flowers shaped like bells **yabani sümbül**

blueberry /'bluːb³ri/ *noun* [C] a small, sweet, dark blue fruit that grows on bushes **böğürtlen**

blue-chip /ˌbluː'tʃɪp/ *adjective* [always before noun] A blue-chip company or investment is considered certain to make a profit. **kâr yapan şirket, yatırım**

blue-collar /ˌbluː'kɒlə³/ *adjective* [always before noun] A blue-collar worker does physical work, especially in a factory. **işçi sınıfından olan, işçi sınıfına mensup**

blueprint /'bluːprɪnt/ *noun* [C] a plan that shows how someone will design, build, or achieve something **proje, plan** *a blueprint for political reform*

blues /bluːz/ *noun* [plural] **1** a type of slow, sad music that was developed by African-Americans **hüzünlü, yavaş bir tür müzik** *jazz and blues* **2 have/get the blues** *informal* to feel or become sad **kederlenmek, üzülmek, kendini üzgün hissetmek**

Bluetooth /'bluːtuːθ/ *noun* [U] *trademark* a technology that allows equipment such as computers and mobile phones to connect with no wires or cables **bilgisayar ve cep telefonu gibi aletlerin kablosuz olarak bağlantısını sağlayan teknolojiye verilen ad** *a Bluetooth headset*

bluff¹ /blʌf/ *verb* [I, T] to pretend you will do something or that you have knowledge, in order to force someone to do something **blöf yapmak, ... mış gibi davranmak, böyle yaparak birini ikna etmek** *He won't really leave her - he's only bluffing.*

bluff² /blʌf/ *noun* **1** [C] an attempt to bluff **blöf, numara 2 call sb's bluff** to tell someone to do the thing they say they will do, because you do not think they will do it **birinin blöfünü görmek, rest çekmek, meydan okumak**

blunder¹ /'blʌndə³/ *noun* [C] a serious and often stupid mistake **gaf, ciddi bir hata** *a series of financial blunders*

blunder² /'blʌndə³/ *verb* [I] **1** to make a serious mistake **gaf yapmak, baltayı taşa vurmak, çam devirmek 2 blunder around/into, etc** to move somewhere in a heavy way, as if you cannot see well **sağa sola çarpa**

çarpa, yalpalayarak yürümek, çarpıp geçmek, tepeleyerek yürümek *He blundered around, looking for the light switch.*

blunt¹ /blʌnt/ *adjective* **1** not sharp **kör, keskin olmayan** *a blunt knife* **2** saying exactly what you think without caring about people's feelings **pervasız, açık konuşan, lafını sakınmayan, sözünü esirgemeyen, lafının önünü sonunu hesaba katmayan, dobra dobra konuşan** *a blunt letter* ● **bluntness** *noun* [U] **sivri olmayan, kör**

blunt² /blʌnt/ *verb* [T] **1** to make a feeling less strong **bir şeyin etkisini azaltmak** *Mario's comments blunted everyone's enthusiasm.* **2** to make something less sharp **körleştirmek, köreltmek**

bluntly /'blʌntli/ *adverb* saying exactly what you think without caring about people's feelings **pervasızca, açıkça, dobra dobra, fütursuzca**

blur¹ /blɜːr/ *verb* [I, T] **blurring**, *past* **blurred 1** to make the difference between two things less clear, or to make it difficult to see the exact truth about something **bir şeyin iyi görülmemesini sağlamak, net görülmesini engellemek** *a book that blurs the distinction between reality and fiction* **2** to become difficult to see clearly, or to make something become difficult to see clearly **bulanıklaştırmak, bulanıklaşmak, net görünmemek** *soft sunlight that blurred the edges of the mountains*

blur² /blɜːr/ *noun* [no plural] something that you cannot see or remember clearly **bulanık, net olmayan, kolay seçilemeyen** *The accident happened so quickly that it's all a blur.*

blurb /blɜːb/ *noun* [C] a short description to advertise a product, especially a book **özellikle kitap gibi ürünlerin reklamını yapmak için kısa bir tanım, özgün tanım, tanıtma, reklam**

blurred /blɜːd/ *adjective* **1** (*also* **blurry** /'blɜːri/) not clear **bulanık, puslu, iyi görünmeyen, göremeyen** *a blurred photograph* ○ *blurred memories* **2** If your sight is blurred, you cannot see clearly. **bulanık gören, iyi seçemeyen** *blurred vision*

blurt /blɜːt/ (*also* **blurt out**) *verb* [I] to say something suddenly and without thinking, especially because you are excited or nervous **ağzından kaçırmak, pat diye söyleyivermek, düşünmeden sarfetmek** *"Will you marry me?" he blurted.*

blush /blʌʃ/ *verb* [I] If you blush, your face becomes red, especially because you are embarrassed. **kızarmak, yüzü kızarmak, kıpkırmızı olmak, mahcup olmak** *He blushed with shame.* ● **blush** *noun* [C] **yüzünün kızarması**

blusher /'blʌʃə³/ *UK* (*US* **blush**) *noun* [U] red powder or cream that women put on their faces in order to make them more attractive **allık** ➜See picture at **make up**.

bluster /'blʌstə³/ *verb* [I, T] to speak in a loud and angry way, often with little effect **gürültü etmek, ağız dalaşı yapmak, homurdanarak konuşmak, belli belirsiz söylemek** ● **bluster** *noun* [U] **bağırıp çağırma**

blustery /ˈblʌstˀri/ *adjective* very windy **çok rüzgarlı, fırtınalı** *a cold, blustery day*

boar /bɔːʳ/ *noun* [C] **1** a male pig **erkek domuz 2** (*also* **wild boar**) a wild pig **yaban domuzu**

board

board²

board¹ /bɔːd/ *noun* **1** ⸤WOOD⸥ [C] a long, thin, flat piece of wood **tahta, döşeme tahtası** *He nailed some boards across the broken window.* **2** ⸤SURFACE⸥ [C] a flat piece of wood, plastic, etc used for a particular purpose **levha** *an ironing board* ○ *a chopping board* **3** ⸤INFORMATION⸥ [C] a piece of wood, plastic, etc on a wall, where information can be put **pano, ilan panosu, duyuru panosu** *Have you seen the poster on the board?* **4** ⸤SCHOOL ROOM⸥ [C] a surface on the wall of a school room that the teacher writes on **yazı tahtası** *Copy down the sentences from the board.* **5** ⸤GAMES⸥ [C] a piece of wood, cardboard, etc for playing games on **oyun tahtası** *a chess board* **6** ⸤ORGANIZATION⸥ [group] a group of people who officially control a company or organization, or a particular type of business activity **kurul, komisyon, yönetim kurulu** *The board approved the sales plan.* ○ *the Gas/Tourist Board* **7 on board** on a boat, train, aircraft, etc **gemi, tren, uçak vb. araçlarda olmak 8** ⸤MEALS⸥ [U] meals that are provided when you stay in a hotel **otellerde verilen yemekler** *bed and board* ○ *How much is a single room with full board* (= all meals)? **9 across the board** affecting everyone or every part of something **herkesi, herşeyi yakından ilgilendiren, etkileyen** *Jobs are likely to be lost across the board.* ⊃See also: bulletin board, diving board, drawing board, full board, half board, ironing board.

board² /bɔːd/ *verb* **1** [I, T] to get on a bus, boat, aircraft, etc **gemi, tren, uçak vb. araçlara binmek** *He boarded the train to London.* **2** [I] If an aircraft, train, etc is boarding, passengers are getting onto it. **uçak, tren vb. araçlara binmek üzere ilerlemek, biniş kartını alarak binmek**
board sth up *phrasal verb* to cover a door or window with wooden boards **tahta levhalarla kaplamak, örtmek, gizlemek**

boarder /ˈbɔːdəʳ/ *noun* [C] **1** ⸤STUDENT⸥ *UK* a student who lives at school **yatılı öğrenci 2** ⸤PERSON⸥ *US* (*UK* **lodger**) someone who pays for a place to sleep and meals in someone else's house **pansiyoncu 3** ⸤SPORT⸥ someone who goes snowboarding (= sport where you stand on a board to move over snow) **kar üzerinde kaymak için bekleyen kişi**

ˈboard ˌgame *noun* [C] a game such as chess that is played on a board **oyun tahtası üzerinde oynana oyun (dama, satranç vb.)**

ˈboarding ˌhouse *noun* [C] a house where you pay for a room and meals **pansiyon**

ˈboarding ˌpass (*also* **ˈboarding ˌcard**) *noun* [C] a piece of paper you must show to get on an aircraft **uçak biniş kartı**

ˈboarding ˌschool *noun* [C] a school where students live and study **yatılı okul**

boardroom /ˈbɔːdruːm/ *noun* [C] a room where the people who control a company or organization have meetings **toplantı salonu, yönetim kurulu odası**

boast¹ /bəʊst/ *verb* **1** [I, T] to talk with too much pride about what you have done or what you own **böbürlenmek, gereksiz ve yersiz övünmek, şişmek, caka satmak** *I wish she would stop boasting about her exam results.* ○ [+ that] *Liam boasted that he owned two sports cars.* **2** [T] If a place boasts something good, it has it. **sahip olmak, bir yere/yerlere sahip olmak** *New York boasts some of the best museums in the world.*

boast² /bəʊst/ *noun* [C] something you are proud of and like to tell people about **övünme, böbürlenme, şişinme, caka satma**

boastful /ˈbəʊstfˀl/ *adjective* talking with too much pride **övüngen, sürekli böbürlenen, şişen** *boastful remarks*

○•**boat** /bəʊt/ *noun* **1** [C] a vehicle for travelling on water **gemi, kayık, sandal** *a fishing boat* **2 be in the same boat** to be in the same unpleasant situation as other people **aynı gemide olmak, aynı olumsuz koşullara tabi olmak, aynı kaderi paylaşmak** *She complains that she doesn't have enough money, but we're all in the same boat.* ● **3 miss the boat** to be too late to get what you want **gemiyi kaçırmak, fırsatı kaçırmak, fırsatı vaktinde değerlendirememek** *I'm afraid you've missed the boat. All the tickets have been sold.* ● **4 push the boat out** *UK* to spend a lot of money, especially when you are celebrating **para harcarken ipin ucunu kaçırmak, masraftan kaçınmamak, kutlamalarda çok masraf etmek** ● **5 rock the boat** to do or say something that changes a situation in a way that causes problems **fikir ayrılığı çıkararak işleri büsbütün berbat etmek, pişmiş aşa su katmak** ⊃See also: rowing boat.

bob /bɒb/ *verb* [I] **bobbing**, *past* **bobbed** to move up and down quickly and gently **nazikçe aşağı yukarı gidip gelmek, aşağı yukarı hareket ettirmek** *boats bobbing in the harbour*

bobby /ˈbɒbi/ *noun* [C] *UK informal old-fashioned* a police officer **polis**

ˈbobby ˌpin *US* (*UK* **hairgrip**) *noun* [C] a small, thin piece of metal, used to fasten a woman's hair in position **pigin, saça takılan ince uzun metal toka**

bode /bəʊd/ *verb literary* **bode ill/well** to be a bad or good sign for the future **(iyiye/kötüye) alamet olmak** *These religious differences do not bode well for their marriage.*

bodily¹ /ˈbɒdɪli/ *adjective* [always before noun] relating to a person's body **bir insanın bedeniyle ilgili, bedensel, fiziksel** *bodily strength*

bodily² /ˈbɒdɪli/ *adverb* If you move someone bodily, you lift or push them. **birini bedenen sarsarak, itip kakarak** *He carried her bodily out of the room.*

○•**body** /ˈbɒdi/ *noun* **1** ⸤PERSON⸥ [C] the whole physical structure of a person or animal **beden, vücut** *the human body* ⊃Orta kısımdaki renkli sayfalarına bakınız. **2** ⸤DEAD⸥ [C] a dead person **ceset** *Police found the body in a field.* **3** ⸤NOT ARMS/LEGS⸥ [C] the main part of a person or animal's body, not the head, arms, or legs **gövde** *a dog with a thin body and short legs* **4** ⸤GROUP⸥ [group] an official group of people who work together **beraber çalışan bir grup**

insan, kurul *the sport's regulatory body* **5** [MAIN PART] [no plural] the main part of something **esas bölüm, gövde** *The body of the book is about his childhood.* **6** [AMOUNT] [no plural] a large amount of information **ana bölüm, bilginin en büyük bölümü** *a body of research into AIDS* **7** [VEHICLE] [C] the main part of a vehicle **gövde, kaborta** *The body of the ship was not damaged.*

bodybuilding /ˈbɒdibɪldɪŋ/ *noun* [U] doing exercises with heavy weights to make your muscles big **vücut geliştirme** ● **bodybuilder** *noun* [C] **vücut geliştiren spor dalı**

bodyguard /ˈbɒdigɑːd/ *noun* [C] someone whose job is to protect someone **koruma, muhafız**

body ˌlanguage *noun* [U] the way you move your body, that shows people what you are feeling **vücut dili**

bog¹ /bɒg/ *noun* [C, U] an area of soft, wet ground **bataklık**

bog² /bɒg/ *verb* **bogging**, *past* **bogged** **be bogged down** *phrasal verb* to become so involved in something that you cannot do anything else **takılıp kalmak, saplanmak, bulaşmak, içinden çıkamamak, çıkmaza girmek** *Try not to get too bogged down in details.*

boggle /ˈbɒgl/ *verb* **the mind boggles** *UK informal* (US **it boggles the mind** *informal*) something you say if something is difficult for you to accept, imagine, or understand **akıl ermez, hafsala almaz, inanılmaz** *The mind boggles at the stupidity of some people.* ➔See also: **mind-boggling.**

bogus /ˈbəʊgəs/ *adjective* pretending to be real **düzmece, sahte** *a bogus doctor* ○ *bogus documents*

bohemian /bəʊˈhiːmiən/ *adjective* typical of artists, musicians, etc, who live in a more informal way than most people **bohem**

o–**boil¹** /bɔɪl/ *verb* [I, T] **1** [LIQUID] If a liquid boils, or if you boil it, it reaches the temperature where bubbles rise up in it and it produces steam. **kaynamak** *boiling water* **2** [CONTAINER] If a container of liquid boils, or if you boil it, the liquid inside it reaches the temperature where bubbles rise up in it and it produces steam. **kaynatmak** *I've boiled the kettle.* **3** [COOK] to cook food in water that is boiling **haşlamak** *Boil the pasta for 10 minutes.* ➔See picture at **cook.**
boil down to sth *phrasal verb* If a situation or problem boils down to something, that is the main reason for it. **özetleyecek olursak, hülasa, kısaltmak, özetlemek** *The problem boils down to one thing - lack of money.*
boil over *phrasal verb* **1** If a liquid that is being heated boils over, it flows over the side of the pan. **taşmak, taşırmak 2** If a difficult situation or bad emotion boils over, it cannot be controlled any more and people start to argue or fight. **galeyana gelmek, taşkınlık yapmak, çığırdan çıkmak, kontrolden çıkmak**

boil² /bɔɪl/ *noun* **1 bring sth to the boil** to heat something until it starts to produce bubbles and steam **kaynatmak** *Bring the water to the boil, then add the rice.* **2** [C] a red swollen area on the skin that is infected **çıban**

boiler /ˈbɔɪləʳ/ *noun* [C] a piece of equipment that provides hot water for a house **buhar kazanı, termosifon**

boiling /ˈbɔɪlɪŋ/ (*also* ˌboiling ˈhot) *adjective informal* very hot **kaynayan, çok sıcak** *It's boiling in here!*

ˈboiling ˌpoint *noun* [C] the temperature that a liquid boils at **kaynama noktası**

boisterous /ˈbɔɪstᵊrəs/ *adjective* noisy and full of energy **şamatacı, taşkın, ele avuca sığmayan, eyyamcı** *a boisterous child* ● **boisterously** *adverb* **gürültülü**

bold ⋅⋅⋅⋅⋅⋅⋅ İLE BİRLİKTE KULLANILAN KELİMELER
a bold **decision/move/plan/step**

bold¹ /bəʊld/ *adjective* **1** [NOT FRIGHTENED] not frightened of taking risks **atak, cüretkâr, cesur, gözükara, gözüpek** *It was a bold decision to go and live abroad.* **2** [COLOUR/SHAPE] strong in colour or shape **koyu renkli, göze çarpan** *bold colours* ○ *a bold design* **3** [LETTERS] words that are printed in bold letters are darker and thicker than normal words ● **boldly** *adverb* **cesurca** ● **boldness** *noun* [U] **cesurluk**

bollard /ˈbɒlɑːd/ *noun* [C] *UK* a short thick post in a road, used to stop cars driving somewhere **kısa kalın trafik direği**

bolster /ˈbəʊlstəʳ/ *verb* [T] to make something stronger by supporting or encouraging it **desteklemek, geliştirmek, yüreklendirmek** *Strong sales are bolstering the economy.*

bolt¹ /bəʊlt/ *noun* [C] **1** a metal bar that you push across a door or window to lock it **kapı/pencere sürgüsü 2** a small piece of metal that is used with a nut (= metal piece with a hole in the middle) to fasten pieces of wood or metal together **civata** ➔See picture at **tool** ➔See also: **nut (nut), bolts.**

bolt² /bəʊlt/ *verb* [T] **1** [FASTEN] to fasten two things together with a bolt **iki şeyi civatayla birleştirip, sıkıştırmak** *The seats in the cinema were bolted to the floor.* **2** [LOCK] to lock a door or window with a bolt **kapı ya da pencereyi sürgü ile kitlemek, mandallamak 3 bolt down/out/through, etc** to move suddenly and quickly **aniden ve hızlı hareket etmek** *The cat bolted out of the door when it saw the dog.* **4** [EAT] (*also* bolt down) to eat something very quickly **hızlıca atıştırmak, tıkınmak, çiğnemeden yutmak**

ˌbolt ˈupright *adverb* sitting or standing with your back very straight **dimdik**

bomb ⋅⋅⋅⋅⋅⋅⋅ İLE BİRLİKTE KULLANILAN KELİMELER
plant a bomb ● a bomb **explodes/goes off** ● a bomb **attack/blast** ● a bomb **scare/threat/warning**

o–**bomb¹** /bɒm/ *noun* [C] a weapon that explodes and causes damage **bomba** *The bomb destroyed several office buildings in the city.* ➔See also: **atomic bomb.**

bomb² /bɒm/ *verb* **1** [T] to attack a place using bombs **bombalamak** *The factories were bombed during the war.* **2 bomb along/down/through, etc** *UK informal* to move very quickly **hızlı bir şekilde hareket etmek, acele ile hareket etmek** *A car came bombing down the road.*

bombard /bɒmˈbɑːd/ *verb* [T] to continuously attack a place using guns and bombs **bombardıman etmek, topa tutmak** ● **bombardment** *noun* [C, U] *an aerial bombardment* **saldırı**
bombard sb with sth *phrasal verb* to give someone too much information, to ask too many questions, etc **birini bilgi ve soru yağmuruna/bombardımanına tutmak**

bomber /ˈbɒməʳ/ *noun* [C] **1** an aircraft that drops bombs **bombardıman uçağı 2** someone who puts a bomb somewhere **bombacı**

bombshell /ˈbɒmʃel/ *noun* [C] *informal* a piece of usually bad news that surprises you very much **birini şaşırtan kötü haber, şaşırtıcı bilgi, belge** *He dropped a bombshell by announcing that he was quitting the sport.*

bona fide /ˌbəʊnəˈfaɪdi/ *adjective* real and honest **hakiki, gerçek, gerçekten** *Make sure you are dealing with a bona fide company.*

bonanza /bə'nænzə/ *noun* [C] a situation in which many people are successful and get a lot of money **zengin maden damarı, büyük para/kazanç kaynağı** *The Internet is a bonanza for the computer industry.*

🔲 bond ...... İLE BİRLİKTE KULLANILAN KELİMELER
create/forge/form/strengthen a bond • a **close** bond • a bond **with** sb/**between** sb and sb

bond[1] /bɒnd/ *noun* [C] **1** an interest, experience, or feeling that makes two people feel connected **bağ, ilişki, münasebet, muhabbet, hoşlanma** *A love of opera created a bond between them.* **2** an official document from a government or company to show that you have given them money that they will pay back with a certain amount of extra money **bono, senet, mukavele, sözleşme**

bond[2] /bɒnd/ *verb* **1** [I, T] If two things bond, they stick together, or if you bond them, you make them stick together. **yapışmak, birbirine bağlanmak, bağlamak** *This glue bonds wood and metal in seconds.* **2** [I] to develop a strong relationship with someone **biriyle güçlü bir ilişki geliştirmek, oluşturmak** *Physical contact helps a mother bond with her baby.*

bondage /'bɒndɪdʒ/ *noun* [U] when someone is completely controlled by something or is a slave (= owned by the person they work for) **kölelik, tutsaklık, esaret**

bone[1] /bəʊn/ *noun* **1** [C, U] one of the hard pieces that make the structure inside a person or animal **kemik** *He broke a bone in his hand.* **2** a **bone of contention** something that people argue about **insanların üzerinde tartıştığı şey, tartışma konusu** • **3** have a **bone to pick with sb** *informal* to want to talk to someone because you are annoyed about something they have done **biriyle görülecek hesabı olmak, biriyle paylaşılacak kozu olmak** • **4** make no **bones about sth/doing sth** to say what you think or feel, without being embarrassed **tereddüt etmeden, çekinmeden, utanmadan düşündüğünü, hissettiğini söylemek** *She made no bones about her reluctance to work with me.*

bone

bone[2] /bəʊn/ *verb* [T] to remove the bones from meat or fish **kılçıklarını ayıklamak, kemiklerini ayırmak, temizlemek**

'bone ‚marrow *noun* [U] the soft substance inside bones **kemik iliği**

bonfire /'bɒnfaɪə^r/ *noun* [C] a large fire outside, often used for burning waste **işe yaramaz şeyleri yakarak oluşturulan büyük ateş**

bonkers /'bɒŋkəz/ *adjective informal* crazy **deli, aklını kaçırmış, çılgın**

bonnet /'bɒnɪt/ *noun* [C] **1** *UK* (*US* **hood**) the metal cover of a car's engine **motor kapağı** ⊃Orta kısımdaki renkli sayfalarına bakınız. **2** a hat that you tie under your face **çenenin altından bağlanan bir tür şapka, bere, İskoç beresi**

bonus /'bəʊnəs/ *noun* [C] **1** an extra amount of money that you are given, especially because you have worked hard **ikramiye, kâr payı, prim, temettü** *All employees received a bonus of £500.* **2** another pleasant thing in addition to something you were expecting **beklenile-**

nin dışında ilave verilen ikramiye, hediye, ödeme *The sunny weather was an added bonus.*

bony /'bəʊni/ *adjective* very thin, so that you can see or feel bones **kemikleri çıkmış, kemikli** *bony elbows*

boo /bu:/ *verb* [I, T] **booing**, *past* **booed** to shout the word "boo" to show that you do not like a speech, performance, etc **yuhalamak, ıslıklamak, yüksek sesle protesto etmek** • **boo** *noun* [C] **yuhlama**

boob /bu:b/ *noun* [C] *informal* **1** a woman's breast **göğüs, meme 2** a silly mistake **aptalca yapılan hata**

booby prize /'bu:bi‚praɪz/ *noun* [C] a prize that you get if you finish last in a competition **sonuncuya verilen ödül**

booby trap /'bu:bi‚træp/ *noun* [C] something dangerous, especially a bomb, that is hidden somewhere that looks safe **bubi tuzağı, iyi gizlenmiş ve şüphe uyandırmayan tuzaklı bomba** • **booby-trap** *verb* [T] [often passive] *His car was booby-trapped.* **tuzak kurmak (bomba)**

book[1] /bʊk/ *noun* **1** [C] a set of pages fastened together in a cover for people to read **kitap** *a book about animals* **2** a book of stamps/tickets, etc a set of stamps, tickets, etc that are fastened together inside a cover **makbuz demeti, koçanlı makbuz 3** [C] a set of pages fastened together in a cover and used for writing on **alıştırma kitabı** *an address book* **4** do sth **by the book** to do something exactly as the rules tell you **her şeyi kitabına, kuralına uygun yapmak** • **5** be in sb's **good/ bad books** *UK informal* If you are in someone's good books, they are pleased with you, and if you are in their bad books, they are angry with you. **birinin memnun, sevdiği/kızgın olduğu kişi olmak** ⊃See also: **cookery book**, take a **leaf[1]** out of sb's book, **phone book**, **reference book**.

book[2] /bʊk/ *verb* **1** ARRANGE [I, T] to arrange to use or do something at a particular time in the future **bir şeyi ileri de kullanılmak, yapmak üzere düzenlemek** *to book a ticket/hotel room* ○ *We've booked a trip to Spain for next month.* ○ *Sorry, the hotel is fully booked* (= has no more rooms). **2** CRIME [T] to officially accuse someone of a crime **birisini bir suçtan dolayı resmen suçlamak, suçlu olduğu hükmüne varmak** *Detectives booked him for resisting arrest.* **3** SPORT [T] *UK* If a sports official books you, they write an official record of something you have done wrong. **spor yetkilisinin yapılan yanlıştan dolayı birini kaydetmesi, kayıt altına alması** *The referee booked two players for fighting during the game.*

book in/book into sth *phrasal verb UK* to say that you have arrived when you get to a hotel **otele kayıt yaptırmak, gelişini bildirmek**

book sb in/book sb into sth *phrasal verb mainly UK* to arrange for someone to stay at a hotel **birisi için otelde yer ayırtmak, rezervasyon yaptırmak**

bookcase /'bʊkkeɪs/ *noun* [C] a piece of furniture with shelves for putting books on **kitaplık** ⊃Orta kısımdaki renkli sayfalarına bakınız.

'book ‚club *noun* [C] a group of people who meet regularly to talk about books they have read **kitap okuma kulübü**

bookie /'bʊki/ *noun* [C] *informal* someone whose job is to take and pay out money that people risk trying to guess the result of horse races, sports events, etc **müşterek bahislerde, şans oyunlarında kuponları alan ve ikramiyeleri ödeyen kişi, bahsi yöneten kişi**

🔲 booking ...... İLE BİRLİKTE KULLANILAN KELİMELER
accept/cancel/make/take a booking • an **advance** booking • a booking **for** sth • a booking **fee/form**

booking /'bʊkɪŋ/ *noun* [C, U] *mainly UK* an arrangement you make to have a hotel room, tickets, etc at a particular time in the future **rezervasyon, yer ayırtma** *advance booking*

bookkeeping /'bʊk,kiːpɪŋ/ *noun* [U] recording the money that an organization or business spends and receives **defter tutma, muhasebe, saymanlık ● bookkeeper** *noun* [C] **muhasebeci**

booklet /'bʊklət/ *noun* [C] a small, thin book that contains information **kitapçık, risale, küçük kitap, el kitabı** *The tourist office has booklets about the area.*

bookmaker /'bʊk,meɪkəʳ/ *noun* [C] a bookie **yarışlarda bahis defterini tutan kişi**

bookmark¹ /'bʊkmɑːk/ *noun* [C] **1** something you put in a book so you can find the page you want **sayfa aralığı, sayfanın yerini belirten işaret 2** an address on the Internet that you record so that you can quickly find something again **sonradan kolay bulunabilsin diye internet adresi kaydı, adres kaydı** *Add this website to your bookmarks.*

bookmark² /'bʊkmɑːk/ *verb* [T] to make a record of the address of an Internet document in your computer so that you can find it again easily **bir internet adresini sonradan kullanmak düşüncesiyle kaydetmek**

books /bʊks/ *noun* [plural] the written financial records of a business or organization **muhasebe defterleri, kayıtları**

bookseller /'bʊk,seləʳ/ *noun* [C] a person or company that sells books **kitapçı, kitap satan kişi**

bookshelf /'bʊkʃelf/ *noun* [C] *plural* **bookshelves** a shelf for holding books **kitaplık rafı, kitap rafı**

bookshop /'bʊkʃɒp/ *UK* (*US* **bookstore** /'bʊkstɔːʳ/) *noun* [C] a shop that sells books **kitapçı**

bookworm /'bʊkwɜːm/ *noun* [C] *informal* someone who enjoys reading very much **çok kitap okuyan, kitap kurdu**

boom¹ /buːm/ *noun* [C] **1** a period when there is a big increase in sales or profits **artış, patlama, satışlarda patlama, kâr artışı** *an economic boom* ○ *The 1990's saw a boom in computer sales.* **2** a loud, deep sound **parlama, infilak, gürleme, uğultu, gümbürtü** ⊃See also: **baby boom.**

boom² /buːm/ *verb* [I] **1** If something is booming, it is increasing or becoming more successful or popular very quickly. **birden meşhur olan, başarılı hale gelen, artan, çoğalan** *House prices are booming.* **2** to make a loud, deep sound, or to speak in a loud, deep voice **ani ses çıkarmak, yüksek ses çıkarmak, yüksek sesle konuşmak**

boomerang /'buːməræŋ/ *noun* [C] a curved piece of wood that comes back to you when you throw it **fırlatıldığında geri gelen hafif kıvrımlı bir tahta, bumerang, fırlatgelsin, atgelsin**

boon /buːn/ *noun* [C] something helpful that improves your life **imet, lütuf, iyilik** [usually singular] *Microwaves are a boon for busy people.*

give sb/sth a boost ● receive a boost ● a **huge/major/ massive/much-needed** boost ● a **confidence/morale** boost ● a boost to sth ● a boost **for** sb

boost¹ /buːst/ *noun* [C] something that makes you feel more confident and happy, or that helps something increase or improve **desteklemek, kendine güvenli ve mutlu olmasına yardımcı olmak** *Increased tourism was a major boost to the local economy.*

boost² /buːst/ *verb* [T] to increase or improve something **geliştirmek, artırmak** *Getting the job has boosted my confidence.*

booster /'buːstəʳ/ *noun* **1 a confidence/morale, etc booster** something that makes you feel happier or more confident **daha mutlu ve daha kendinden emin hissetmenize yardımcı olan şey 2** [C] an engine on a spacecraft that gives extra power for the first part of a flight **roket motorunun gücünü daha da artıran motor**

boot¹ /buːt/ *noun* [C] **1** a strong shoe that covers your foot and part of your leg **çizme, potin, bot** *a pair of boots* ⊃Orta kısımdaki renkli sayfalarına bakınız. **2** *UK* (*US* **trunk**) a closed space at the back of a car for storing things in **araba bagajı** ⊃Orta kısımdaki renkli sayfalarına bakınız. **3 get/be given the boot** *informal* to be told that you must leave your job **pabucu(nu) eline ver(il)mek, sepetle(n)mek, işine son ver(il)mek 4 too big for your boots** *UK informal* (*US* **too big for your britches** *informal*) behaving as if you are more important or more clever than you really are **sanki daha önemli veya daha zekiymiş gibi bir tavır takınma, kendini büyümseme,** ⊃See also: **car boot sale.**

boot² /buːt/ *verb* [T] *informal* to kick someone or something **tekmelemek, tepiklemek**

boot sb out *phrasal verb informal* to make someone leave a place or job **birinin pabucunu eline vermek, işten ayrılmaya zorlamak**

bootcut /'buːtkʌt/ *adjective* bootleg **yasadışı içki yapıp satan, içki kaçakçısı**

booth /buːð/ *noun* [C] a small area that is separated from a larger public area, especially used for doing something privately **kabin, baraka, odacık, küçük kulübe** *a telephone booth*

bootleg /'buːtleg/ (*also* **bootcut**) *adjective* bootleg trousers are wider at the bottom than at the knee **alt tarafı geniş pantolon ● bootlegs** *noun* [plural]

booty /'buːti/ *noun* [U] valuable things stolen by thieves or by an army in a war **ganimet, çapul, yağma**

booze¹ /buːz/ *noun* [U] *informal* alcoholic drinks **içki, alkollü içkiler**

booze² /buːz/ *verb* [I] *informal* to drink alcohol **alkol almak, içki içmek**

cross the border ● **across/on/over** the border ● the border **between** [France and Spain/Switzerland and Italy, etc] ● [Germany's/Syria's, etc] border **with** [France/Lebanon, etc] ● the [French/Mexican, etc] **side** of the border ● border **controls /guards**

◦━**border¹** /'bɔːdəʳ/ *noun* [C] **1** the line that separates two countries or states **sınır, serhat, hudut** *the border between France and Canada* ○ *We crossed the border from Canada into the US.* **2** a strip around the edge of something for decoration **hat, çizgi, şerit** *white plates with a blue border*

border² /'bɔːdəʳ/ *verb* [T] **1** to form a line around the edge of something **kenarına hat çekmek, çizgi çekmek, kenar çizmek** [often passive] *The fields are bordered by tall trees.* **2** to have a border with another country **sınır çizmek, sınırları belirlemek** [often passive] *Spain is bordered by France and Portugal.*

border on sth *phrasal verb* to almost be a more extreme thing **sınırları zorlamak** *Her anger bordered on aggression.*

borderline¹ /'bɔːdəlaɪn/ *adjective* If something or someone is borderline, it is not clear if they are good enough or if they will succeed. **sınırda olan, her iki kategori-**

yede girebilen *Borderline cases should take the exam again.*

borderline² /'bɔːdᵊlaɪn/ *noun* [no plural] the point where one feeling, quality, level, etc ends and another one begins **bir şeyin bitip diğerinin başladığı sınır çizgisi** *My work was on the borderline between two grades.*

bore¹ /bɔːʳ/ *verb* **1** [T] to make someone feel bored **sıkmak, canını sıkmak, usandırmak** *His war stories really bore me.* **2** [I, T] to make a hole in something hard with a tool **delmek, matkapla delmek, delik açmak**

bore² /bɔːʳ/ *noun* **1** [C] someone who talks too much about things that are not interesting **cansıkıcı/sıkıcı kimse 2** [no plural] a situation or job that annoys you because it causes difficulties or is not interesting **sıkıcı bir iş, can sıkıcı bir durum** *It's a real bore not having a car.*

bore³ /bɔːʳ/ *past tense of* bear **tahammül etmek' fiilinin 2. hali**

o▪**bored** /bɔːd/ *adjective* feeling tired and unhappy because something is not interesting or because you have nothing to do **canı sıkkın, sıkılmış, usanmış** *I'm bored with doing homework.* ○ *We were bored stiff* (= extremely bored) *in her lessons.* ● **boredom** /'bɔːdəm/ *noun* [U] when you are bored **can sıkıntısı** *I nearly died of boredom.*

boring ...... BAŞKA BİR DEYİŞLE

Bland ifadesi genellikle yiyeceklerin tarifinde kullanılır. *This sauce is really bland, it doesn't taste of anything.*
Eğer bir film, oyun, kitap veya kişi sıkıcıysa, bunun ifadesi için **dull** sıfatı kullanılır. *I find her writing a bit dull.*
Monotonous ifadesi genellikle dinlediğiniz bir şey hakkındaki söylemde kullanılır. *The teacher had a really monotonous voice and I almost fell asleep.*
Bir etkinlikten bahsederken, bazen **tedious** ifadesi kullanılır. *You have to fill in various forms, which is a bit tedious.*
Eğer bir konuşma metni veya yazı uzunluğundan dolayı sıkıcıysa, bunu **long-winded** ifadesi ile açıklayabiliriz. *He gave this really long-winded explanation about why he'd changed his mind.*

o▪**boring** /'bɔːrɪŋ/ *adjective* not interesting or exciting **sıkıcı, can sıkıcı** *a boring job* ○ *The film was so boring, I fell asleep.*

o▪**born¹** /bɔːn/ *verb* **1 be born a** When a person or animal is born, they come out of their mother's body and start to exist. **dünyaya gelmek, doğmak** *She was born in London in 1973.* ○ *an American-born writer* (= born in America) **b** If an idea is born, it starts to exist. **doğmak, (bir fikir) ortaya çıkmak**

born² /bɔːn/ *adjective* **a born actor/leader/teacher, etc** someone who has a natural ability to act, lead, teach, etc **aktör/lider/öğretmen vb. Doğmak**

born-again /,bɔːnə'gen/ *adjective* **a born-again Christian** someone who has become a very enthusiastic member of the Christian religion **hıristiyanlık dininin coşkulu bir mensubu, sanki hıristiyan doğmuş**

borne /bɔːn/ *past participle of* bear **doğmak' fiilinin hali**

borough /'bʌrə/ ⑩ /'bɜːrəʊ/ *noun* [C] a town or part of a city **kasaba, belediyelik belde**

o▪**borrow** /'bɒrəʊ/ *verb* **1** USE [T] to use something that belongs to someone else and give it back later **ödünç almak** *Can I borrow a pen please?* ○ *I borrowed the book from my sister.* **2** MONEY [I, T] to take money from a bank or financial organization and pay it back over a

period of time **borç almak, borçlanmak 3** IDEA [T] to take and use a word or idea **bir fikri, sözcüğü ödünç almak** *The English word 'rucksack' is borrowed from German.*

borrower /'bɒrəʊəʳ/ *noun* [C] someone who borrows money **ödünç alan kişi**

bosom /'bʊzᵊm/ *noun* **1** [C] a woman's breasts **göğüs 2 a bosom buddy/pal, etc** a very good friend **can dostu, candan dost, yaren**

o▪**boss¹** /bɒs/ *noun* [C] someone who is responsible for employees and tells them what to do **patron, işveren** *I'll ask my boss if I can leave work early tomorrow.*

boss² /bɒs/ (*also* boss about/around) *verb* [T] to tell someone what they should do all the time **patronluk yapmak, birine ne yapması gerektiğini söylemek** *My older brother is always bossing me about.*

bossy /'bɒsi/ *adjective* always telling other people what to do **emretmeyi seven ,sürekli emir verir gibi davranan, zorba** ● **bossiness** *noun* [U] **çok bilmişlik**

botanist /'bɒtᵊnɪst/ *noun* [C] someone who studies plants **botanikçi, bitkileri araştıran kişi, bitki bilimci**

botany /'bɒtᵊni/ *noun* [U] the scientific study of plants **bitki bilimi, botanik ilmi** ● **botanical** /bə'tænɪkəl/ (*also* botanic /bə'tænɪk/) *adjective* relating to botany **bitki bilimine ilişkin**

botch /bɒtʃ/ (*also* botch up) *verb* [T] to spoil something by doing it badly **baştan savma yapmak, üstünkörü yapmak, bir şeyi berbat etmek, yüzüne gözüne bulaştırmak** *a botched robbery*

o▪**both** /bəʊθ/ *pronoun, determiner, quantifier* **1** used to talk about two people or things **herikisi** *The children both have red hair.* ○ *Both of my sisters are teachers.* ○ *Would you like cream, ice cream, or both?* **2 both... and...** used to emphasize that you are talking about two people or things **hem ... hem de** *Both Jack and his wife are keen chess players.* ⊃See also: have the **best³** of both worlds.

o▪**bother¹** /'bɒðəʳ/ *verb* **1** ANNOY [T] to annoy someone by trying to get their attention when they do not want to see you or talk to you **taciz etmek, canını sıkmak, uğraşmak** *Sorry to bother you, but could you spare any change?* **2** WORRY [T] to make someone feel worried or upset **birini üzmek, endişeye sevketmek** *Living on my own doesn't bother me at all.* **3** DO [I, T] to make the effort to do something **uğraşmak, didinmek, çaba sarfetmek** [+ doing sth] *Don't bother making the bed - I'll do it later.* ○ [+ to do sth] *He didn't even bother to call.* **4 can't be bothered** *informal* If you can't be bothered to do something, you are too lazy or tired to do it. **hiç** *işim yoktu sanki, bana ne* [+ to do sth] *I can't be bothered to iron my clothes.* **5 not bothered** UK *informal* If you are not bothered about something, it is not important to you and does not worry you. **zahmet etme, kendini yorma, boşver, aldırma, tasalanma** *"Do you want tea or coffee?" "Either, I'm not bothered."*

bother² /'bɒðəʳ/ *noun* [U] trouble or problems **sorun, dert, tasa, problem** *"Are you sure you don't mind taking me?" "No, it's no bother, really!"*

bothered /'bɒðəd/ *adjective* [never before noun] If you are bothered about something, it is important to you and you are worried about it. **sıkılmış, canı sıkılmış, üzgün, dertli** *He's very bothered about what other people think.*

Botox /'bəʊtɒks/ *noun* [U] *trademark* Botulinum Toxin: a drug used in a person's face to make it look smooth and young **yüze sürülerek genç ve pürüzsüz görünmesini sağalayan ilaç, bilinen adıyla botoks** ● **Botox** *verb* [T] **gerdirmek**

o–**bottle**¹ /'bɒtl/ *noun* [C] a container for liquids, usually made of glass or plastic, with a narrow top **şişe** *an empty bottle* ○ *a bottle of wine* ⊃See also: **hot-water bottle.**

bottle² /'bɒtl/ *verb* [T] to put liquid into a bottle **şişelemek** [often passive] *This wine was bottled in France.* ○ *bottled beer/water*

bottle sth up *phrasal verb* to not allow yourself to show or talk about your feelings **hislerini gizlemek, bastırmak, saklamak; hakkında konuşmamak**

'**bottle ,bank** *noun* [C] *UK* a large container outside, where you can put empty bottles so that the glass can be used again **şişelerin toplandığı yer, şişe bankası**

bottleneck /'bɒtlnek/ *noun* [C] **1** something that causes a process to happen more slowly than it should **darboğaz; bir işi çıkmaza sokan, sekteye uğratan, yavaşlatan şey 2** a narrow part of a road where traffic moves slowly **trafikte dar geçit, yolun, caddenin daraldığı yer**

o–**bottom**¹ /'bɒtəm/ *noun* **1** LOWEST PART [C] the lowest part of something **dip, aşağı taraf** [usually singular] *Click on the icon at the bottom of the page.* **2** FLAT SURFACE [C] the flat surface on the lowest side of something **taban, alt kısım, alt satıh** [usually singular] *There was a price tag on the bottom of the box.* **3** LOWEST POSITION [no plural] the lowest position in a group, organization, etc **alt seviye, bir kuruluşta, grupta en alt konum, durum** *He got bad exam marks and is at the bottom of the class.* **4** SEA/RIVER ETC [no plural] the ground under a river, lake, or sea **ırmak, göl ve deniz tabanı** *Divers found the wreck on the bottom of the ocean.* **5** FURTHEST PART [no plural] the part of a road or area of land that is furthest from where you are **yolun, arazinin alt tarafı, alt ucu** *Go to the bottom of the road and turn left.* **6** PART OF THE BODY [C] the part of your body that you sit on **kıç, popo 7 be at the bottom of sth** to be the cause of a problem or situation **bir problemin, sorunun arkasında olmak, sebebi olmak 8 get to the bottom of sth** to discover the truth about a situation **bir meselenin içyüzünü/ aslını astarını öğrenmek, gerçeklere hakim olmak** ⊃See also: **rock bottom,** from **top**¹ to bottom.

bottom² /'bɒtəm/ *adjective* [always before noun] in the lowest position **en alt düzeyde, durumda** *the bottom drawer*

bottomless /'bɒtəmləs/ *adjective* **a bottomless pit** a supply, especially of money, that has no limit **limitsiz, sınırsız para desteği, nakit akışı**

the ,bottom 'line *noun* the most important fact in a situation **en önemli gerçek, asıl nokta, gerçeğin ta kendisi** *The bottom line is that if you don't work, you'll fail the test.*

bough /baʊ/ *noun* [C] *literary* a large branch on a tree **bir ağacın ana dallarından biri**

bought /bɔːt/ *past of* buy **satın almak' fiilinin geçmiş zaman hali**

boulder /'bəʊldəʳ/ *noun* [C] a very large rock **büyük kaya kütlesi**

boulevard /'buːləvɑːd/ *noun* [C] a wide road in a city, usually with trees along it **şehir içinde sıralı ağaçlarla kaplı büyük cadde, anayol, bulvar**

bounce¹ /baʊns/ *verb* **1** BALL [I, T] to hit a surface and then move quickly away, or to make something do this **vurup sıçratmak, zıplamak** *The ball bounced high into the air.* **2** JUMP [I] to jump up and down several times on a soft surface **sıçramak, zıplamak, yumuşak zemin üzerinde defalarca aşağı yukarı zıplamak** *The children loved bouncing on the bed.* **3 bounce along/ around/into, etc** to move somewhere in a happy and energetic way **bir yere doğru mutlu ve enerji dolu olarak yürümek, girmek, hareket etmek** *Sarah bounced into the room with a big smile on her face.*

4 NOT PAY [I, T] If a cheque (= piece of printed paper you write on to pay for things) bounces, or a bank bounces it, the bank will not pay it because there is not enough money in the account. **(çek) geri gelmek, geri dönmek, protesto olmak**

bounce back *phrasal verb* **1** to be successful or happy again after a failure, disappointment, etc **bir düş kırıklığı ve başarısızlıktan sonra tekrar mutlu ve başarılı olmak, eski haline dönmek, iyileşmek** *After a terrible start the team bounced back and won the game.* **2** If an email bounces back, it is returned to you because the address is not correct or there is a computer problem. **bir gönderi, elektronik posta iletisi geri gelmek, bir sorundan ötürü iletiyi dönmek**

bounce² /baʊns/ *noun* [C, U] when something bounces, or the quality that makes something able to bounce **zıplama, sıçrama, hoplama, gidip gelme**

bouncer /'baʊnsəʳ/ *noun* [C] someone whose job is to stand at the door of a bar, party, etc and keep out people who are not wanted **bar, gece kulübü görevlisi, kapıdan girmeye çalışanları sıraya sokan, düzeni sağlayan kişi, fedai, koruma**

bouncy /'baʊnsi/ *adjective* **1** happy and full of energy **enerji ve mutluluk dolu, coşkulu** *She's very bouncy and confident.* **2** able to bounce **zıplayabilen, hoplayabilen, sıçrayabilen** *bouncy balls*

bound¹ /baʊnd/ *adjective* **1 bound to do sth** certain to do something, or certain to happen **olması, yapılması kesin olmak** *You're bound to feel nervous before your driving test.* **2 bound up with sth** closely connected with something **bir şeyle çok yakın ilişkisi, balantısı olmak** *A country's culture is bound up with its language and history.* **3** [never before noun] having a moral or legal duty to do something **bir şeyi yapmak için ahlaki ve yasal zorunluğu, görevi olan, yükümlü, sorumlu** *The witness was bound by an oath to tell the truth.* **4** [never before noun] travelling towards a particular place **belli bir yere doğru seyahat eden** *He was on a train bound for Berlin.*

bound² /baʊnd/ *verb* [I] to move quickly with large steps or jumps **büyük adımlarla ve koşa zıplaya, hızlıca hareket etmek** *Guy bounded across the room to answer the phone.*

bound³ /baʊnd/ *noun* [C] a big jump **zıplama, sıçrama, sekme** ⊃See also: by/in leaps (**leap**²) and bounds.

bound⁴ /baʊnd/ *past of* bind **bağlamak' fiilinin geçmiş zaman hali**

boundary /'baʊndᵊri/ *noun* [C] **1** a line that divides two areas or forms an edge around an area **sınır, çizgi, hat, hudut, kenar** *The mountains mark the boundary between the two countries.* **2** a limit **limit, belli bir miktar** *Such violence is beyond the boundaries of civilized conduct.*

boundless /'baʊndləs/ *adjective* having no limit **limitsiz, sınırsız, sonsuza dek** *He has boundless energy/ enthusiasm.*

bounds /baʊndz/ *noun* **1** [plural] legal or social limits **yasal veya toplumsal sınırlar, limitler, mecburiyetler, zorunluklar** *They have overstepped the bounds of good taste.* **2 out of bounds** If a place is out of bounds, you are not allowed to go there. **giriş yasak, yasak bölge, girilmesine izin verilmeyen** *The staff room is out of bounds to students.*

bounty /'baʊnti/ *noun* **1** [C, U] a large or generous amount of something **cömertlik, gönlü genişlik 2** [C] an amount of money paid as a reward **ödül olarak ödenen para, ödül**

bouquet /buˈkeɪ/ *noun* [C] flowers that are tied together in an attractive way **çiçek demeti, buket**

bourbon /'bɜːbən/ *noun* [C, U] a type of American whisky (= strong alcoholic drink) **Amerikan viskisi, börbun**

bourgeois /'bɔːʒwɑː/ *adjective* typical of middle class people who are too interested in money and correct social behaviour **para ve doğru toplumsal davranış biçimiyle ilgili orta sınıf insanlar topluluğu, burjuva sınıfından olan** *bourgeois values* ● **the bourgeoisie** /ˌbɔːʒwɑːˈziː/ *noun* [group] the middle class, that owns most of society's money **toplum sermayesinin en çoğunu elinde bulunduran orta sınıf, burjuvazi**

bout /baʊt/ *noun* [C] **1** a short period of activity or illness **nöbet, hastalık nöbeti** *a bout of depression* **2** a fight in boxing **boks maçı**

boutique /buːˈtiːk/ *noun* [C] a small shop that sells fashionable clothes **moda giysiler satan küçük dükkan, butik**

bovine /'bəʊvaɪn/ *adjective* relating to cows **ineklere ilişkin**

bow¹ /baʊ/ *verb* [I, T] to bend your head or body forward in order to show respect or to thank an audience **bir grup karşısında eğilerek saygı göstermek, reverans yapmak, öne doğru eğilmek** *The actors all bowed after the performance.* ○ *We **bowed** our **heads** in prayer.*

bow out *phrasal verb* to leave a job or stop doing an activity, usually after a long time **uzun bir süreden sonra bir eylemi/bir işi bırakmak, terketmek, mesleği sona ermek** *He bowed out of politics at the age of 70.*

bow to sth/sb *phrasal verb* to do what someone else wants you to do **birinin emirlerine itaat etmek, söylediği her şeyi yapmak, birine/birşeye itaat etmek, boyun eğmek/uymak** *The government are refusing to bow to public pressure.*

bow² /baʊ/ *noun* [C] **1** when you bow **eğilme, reverans, selamlama** *The actors came back on stage and took a bow.* **2** the front part of a ship **pruva, geminin başı**

bow³ /bəʊ/ *noun* [C] **1** [KNOT] a knot with two curved parts and two loose ends, that is used to tie shoes or as decoration **fiyonk, ilmek 2** [MUSIC] a long, thin piece of wood with hair stretched between the ends, used to play some musical instruments **müzik aletlerini çalmak için kullanılan yay 3** [WEAPON] a piece of curved wood with string fixed to both ends, used for shooting arrows **ok atmaya yarayan yay**

bowel /baʊəl/ *noun* [C] the long tube that carries solid waste from your stomach out of your body **bağırsak** [usually plural] *He's got trouble with his bowels.*

☞**bowl¹** /bəʊl/ *noun* [C] a round, deep dish used for holding soup and other food **çanak, kâse, kap, çorba kâsesi** *a bowl of rice/soup*

bowl² /bəʊl/ *verb* [I, T] **1** to roll a ball along a surface as part of a game **topu yuvarlamak, bowling oyununda topu yuvarlamak 2** in cricket, to throw a ball to the person who has to hit it **kriket oyununda topa vurması gereken oyuncuya topu fırlatmak**

bowler /'bəʊlər/ *noun* [C] in cricket, the player who throws the ball so someone can hit it **krikette topu atan oyuncu** ➔Orta kısımdaki renkli sayfalarına bakınız.

bowler 'hat UK (US **derby**) *noun* [C] a round, hard, black hat worn by men, especially in the past **geçmişte erkeklerin giydiği yuvarlak, sert siyah şapka, hasket, melon şapka**

bowling /'bəʊlɪŋ/ *noun* [U] a game in which you roll a large ball along a wooden track in order to knock down bottle-shaped objects **topu yuvarlayarak dizili olan lobutları devirerek oynanan oyun, bowling**

bowls /bəʊlz/ *noun* [U] UK a game in which you roll large balls as close as possible to a smaller ball **tahta toplarla oynanan bir oyun**

bow 'tie *noun* [C] a piece of cloth around the neck in the shape of a bow that men sometimes wear, especially at formal events **papyon kravat**

☞**box¹** /bɒks/ *noun* **1** [CONTAINER] [C] a square or rectangular container **kutu** *a cardboard box* ○ *a box of chocolates/matches* ➔See picture at **container. 2** [SQUARE SPACE] [C] a small square on a page that gives you information or where you write information **kağıt üzerindeki kutucuklar** *Tick the box if you would like more details.* **3** [SMALL PLACE] [C] a small area of a theatre, court, etc that is separate from where other people are sitting **loca; tiyatro, sinema gibi yerlerde küçük bölme 4 the box** *informal* the television **televizyon** *What's on the box tonight?* ➔See also: **phone box, post box, witness box.**

box² /bɒks/ *verb* **1** [I, T] to do the sport of boxing **boks yapmak 2** [T] (*also* box up) to put something in a box **kutulamak, kutuya koymak** *We boxed up the old books.*

box sb/sth in *phrasal verb* to move so close to someone or something that they cannot move **kutulamak** [often passive] *When I returned I found that my car had been boxed in.*

boxer /'bɒksər/ *noun* [C] someone who does the sport of boxing **boksör**

boxers /'bɒksəz/ ('boxer ,shorts) *noun* [plural] loose underwear worn by men **erkek içgiyim, geniş külot** ➔Orta kısımdaki renkli sayfalarına bakınız.

boxing /'bɒksɪŋ/ *noun* [U] a sport in which two people hit each other while wearing big, leather gloves (= pieces of clothing for your hands) **boks sporu** ➔Orta kısımdaki renkli sayfalarına bakınız.

boxing

'Boxing ,Day *noun* [C, U] 26 December, a public holiday in Britain and Canada **26 Aralık noel ertesi Britanya ve Kanada'da resmi tatil günü**

'box ,office *noun* [C] the place in a theatre, cinema, etc where you buy tickets **bilet gişesi**

☞**boy¹** /bɔɪ/ *noun* **1** [C] a male child or young man **erkek çocuk** *We've got three children - a boy and two girls.* **2 the boys** *informal* a group of male friends **erkek çocuklardan oluşan bir grup** *Steve's gone out with the boys.*

boy² /bɔɪ/ (*also* oh boy) *exclamation* used when you are excited or pleased **oh be!, aman Allah'ım!; heyecan ve memnuniyet bildiren ünlem** *Boy, that was good!*

'boy ,band *noun* [C] a pop music group made up of young men who sing and dance **erkek çocukarından oluşan pop müzik grubu**

boycott /'bɔɪkɒt/ *noun* [C] when someone refuses to buy, use, or do something because they do not approve of it **boykot, direniş** *Environmental groups have called for a boycott of the company's products.* ● **boycott** *verb* [T] *Several countries boycotted the international peace talks.* **boykot yapmak**

☞**boyfriend** /'bɔɪfrend/ *noun* [C] a man or boy who someone is having a romantic relationship with **erkek arkadaş, bir kızın sevgilisi**

boyhood /'bɔɪhʊd/ *noun* [U] the part of a male's life when they are a boy **çocukluk çağı**

boyish /'bɔɪɪʃ/ *adjective* like a boy **erkek çocuğu gibi, çocukça** *boyish charm*

Boy 'Scout *UK* (*US* **'Boy ,Scout**) *noun* [C] a boy who belongs to an organization that teaches boys practical skills **yavru kurt, izci**

bra /brɑː/ *noun* [C] a piece of woman's underwear that supports the breasts **sutyen** ➲Orta kısımdaki renkli sayfalarına bakınız.

brace¹ /breɪs/ *verb* **brace yourself** to prepare for something difficult or unpleasant **kendini zor veya hoş olmayan bir durum için hazırlamak, hazırlıklı olmak** *I braced myself for bad news.*

brace² /breɪs/ *noun* [C] **1** something that supports or holds something in the correct position **gergi ,kuşak, bağ, askı** *He wore a neck brace for months after the accident.* **2** a wire object that some children wear to make their teeth straight **düzgün olması için dişe takılan tel**

bracelet /'breɪslət/ *noun* [C] a piece of jewellery that you wear around your wrist **bilezik** ➲See picture at **jewellery.**

braces /'breɪsɪz/ *UK* (*US* **suspenders**) *noun* [plural] two straps fixed to a pair of trousers that go over your shoulders and stop the trousers from falling down **pantolon askısı**

bracing /breɪsɪŋ/ *adjective* Bracing weather or a bracing activity makes you feel cold but healthy and full of energy. **canlandıran (hava), hayat katan, sağlıklı kılan (faaliyet)** *bracing sea air* ○ *a bracing walk*

bracket¹ /'brækɪt/ *noun* [C] **1** a group of people whose ages, taxes, etc are between two limits **yaşları, vergileri vs. iki sınır arasında olan bir grup insan** *Most heart attack victims are in the 45-65 age bracket.* **2** a piece of metal, wood, etc, that is fixed to a wall to support something, especially a shelf **metal, ahşap raf askısı, dayanak, destek, dirsek**

bracket² /'brækɪt/ *verb* [T] **1** to put curved lines () around words, phrases, numbers, etc to make them separate **parantez içine almak 2** to consider two or more people or things to be similar **bir tutmak, eş tutmak, benzer görmek** [often passive] *Canadian accents are often bracketed with American accents.*

brackets /'brækɪts/ (*also* **parentheses**) *noun* [plural] *UK* two curved lines () used around extra information or information that should be considered as separate from the main part **parantez işaretleri**

brag /bræg/ *verb* [I] **bragging**, *past* **bragged** to talk with too much pride about what you have done or what you own **böbürlenmek, gereksiz övünmek, yüksekten atmak, palavra sıkmak** *He's always bragging about how much money he earns.*

braid¹ /breɪd/ *noun* **1** [C] *US* (*UK* **plait**) a single piece of hair made by twisting three thinner pieces over and under each other **saç örgüsü 2** [U] a thin piece of cloth or twisted threads used for decorating clothes **kurdela, kordon, örgülü şerit**

braid² /breɪd/ *US* (*UK* **plait**) *verb* [T] to twist three pieces of hair over and under each other **saç örmek**

braille /breɪl/ *noun* [U] a system of printing for blind people, using raised patterns that they read by touching **körlere mahsus kabartma yazı, körler alfabesi**

brain /breɪn/ *noun* **1** [C] the organ inside your

brain

head that controls your thoughts, feelings, and movements **beyin** *brain damage* **2** [C] *informal* an extremely intelligent person **son derece zeki insan** [usually plural] *This university attracts some of the best brains in the country.* **3** **brains** intelligence **zekâ** *He has brains and good looks.* **4** **have sth on the brain** *informal* to think or talk about something all the time **kafasında/beyninde sürekli bir şeyler olmak, daima düşünmek, üzerinde konuşmak** *You've got football on the brain!* **5** **the brains behind sth** *informal* the person who has planned and organized something successful **bir şeyin arkasındaki beyin, yapan kişi, güç** *Anthony is the brains behind the project.*

brainchild /'breɪntʃaɪld/ *noun* **the brainchild of sb** someone's new and clever idea or invention **yeni ve zekice fikir veya icat** *The project is the brainchild of a Japanese designer.*

brainstorm /'breɪnstɔːm/ *US* (*UK* **brainwave**) *noun* [C] a sudden, clever idea **beyin fırtınası**

brainstorming /'breɪn,stɔːmɪŋ/ *noun* [U] when a group of people meet to develop new ideas **beyin fırtınası yapmak, bir araya gelip yeni fikirleri tartışmak** *a brainstorming session*

brainwash /'breɪnwɒʃ/ *verb* [T] to make someone believe something by telling them that it is true many times **beyin yıkamak** [+ into + doing sth] *Advertising often brainwashes people into buying things they do not really need.* ● **brainwashing** *noun* [U] **beyin yıkama**

brainwave /'breɪnweɪv/ *UK* (*US* **brainstorm**) *noun* [C] a sudden, clever idea **aniden akla gelen zekice bir fikir**

brainy /'breɪni/ *adjective informal* clever **akıllı, zeki**

🧩 **brake** ...... İLE BİRLİKTE KULLANILAN KELİMELER

apply/hit/slam on the brakes ● the brakes **fail**

brake¹ /breɪk/ *noun* [C] **1** the part of a vehicle that makes it stop or go more slowly **fren 2** something that stops or slows the progress of something **frenleyen, durduran şey** *High inflation has put the brakes on economic growth.*

brake² /breɪk/ *verb* [I] to make a vehicle stop or move more slowly, using its brake **fren yapmak, durdurmak**

'brake ,pedal *noun* [C] the part of a car which you push with your foot to make it go more slowly **fren pedalı** ➲Orta kısımdaki renkli sayfalarına bakınız.

✎**branch¹** /brɑːnʃ/ *noun* [C] **1** ⌈TREE⌉ one of the many parts of a tree that grows from its trunk (= main, vertical part) **dal ,kol, ağaç dalı** ➲See picture at **tree. 2** ⌈BUSINESS⌉ one of several shops, offices, etc that are part of a company or organization **şube, branş** *a bank with branches all over the country* **3** ⌈SUBJECT⌉ a part of a subject **bir konunun bölümü** *Neurology is a branch of medicine.*

branch² /brɑːnʃ/ (*also* **branch off**) *verb* [I] If a road, path, etc branches, it separates into two or more roads, paths, etc. **ayrılmak, çatallaşmak, bir kaç kola ayrılmak**
branch out *phrasal verb* to start to do something different from what you usually do, especially in your job **bir şeyi her zamanki yaptığından farklı bir biçimde yapmaya başlamak** *After working in publishing, she branched out into journalism.*

brand¹ /brænd/ *noun* [C] **1** a product that is made by a particular company **belli bir şirketin ürettiği ürün** *Which brand of toothpaste do you use?* **2** a particular type of something **marka** *a team that plays a distinctive brand of football*

brand² /brænd/ *verb* [T] **1** to describe someone or something in a way that makes them seem bad **bir şeyi, birini lekelemek, damgalamak** *The media branded* *him a liar.* **2** to burn a mark on an animal to show who owns it **dağlamak, büyük baş hayvanların kime ait olduğunu göstermek için dağlamak, damgalamak**

brandish /'brændɪʃ/ *verb* [T] to wave something in the air, especially a weapon **sallamak, savurmak** *He came running into the room, brandishing a gun.*

'brand ,name *noun* [C] the special name that a company gives to a product **marka adı**

,brand 'new *adjective* completely new **yepyeni, gıcırgıcır, hiç kullanılmamış**

brandy /'brændi/ *noun* [C, U] a strong alcoholic drink made from wine **kanyak, brendi**

brash /bræʃ/ *adjective* too confident **küstah, haddini bilmez** *a brash young businessman*

brass /brɑːs/ *noun* [U] **1** a shiny yellow metal **pirinç** *a door with a brass handle* **2** the group of musical instruments made from brass **pirinçten yapılmış müzik aletleri** *a brass band*

brat /bræt/ *noun* [C] a child who behaves badly **velet, yaramaz çocuk, afacan, haşarı çocuk, yumurcak** *a spoilt brat*

bravado /brə'vɑːdəʊ/ *noun* [U] behaviour that is intended to make people admire you for your bravery and confidence **efelik, kabadayılık,**

○ **brave**[1] /breɪv/ *adjective* showing no fear of dangerous or difficult situations **cesur, yürekli** *He died after a brave fight against cancer.* • **bravely** *adverb* **cesurca**

brave[2] /breɪv/ *verb* [T] to deal with a dangerous or unpleasant situation in a brave way **cesaret etmek, cüret etmek, yürekli davranmak, meydan okumak** *Crowds braved the cold weather to watch the game.*

bravery /'breɪvᵊri/ *noun* [U] when someone is brave **cesaret, yüreklilik, yiğitlik**

bravo /brɑː'vəʊ/ *exclamation* something you shout to show that you approve of something, for example a performance **(ünlem) bravo!, helal olsun!**

brawl /brɔːl/ *noun* [C] a noisy fight, usually in public **arbede, dalaşma, hırgür, kavga, ağız dalaşı** *a drunken brawl in a bar* • **brawl** *verb* [I] **tartışmak**

brazen /'breɪzᵊn/ *adjective* not feeling at all ashamed about your bad behaviour **arsız, yüzsüz, utanma bilmez** *a brazen cheat* • **brazenly** *adverb* **utanmadan**

BRB *internet abbreviation for* be right back: used when you stop taking part in a discussion on the Internet **internette konuşmayı kesip, kısa süre sonra döneceğini belirten kısaltma, Az Sonra Döneceğim (ASD)**

   🧩 *breach ...... İLE BİRLİKTE KULLANILAN KELİMELER*

(a) breach **of** sth • be **in** breach **of** sth • a **flagrant** breach **of** sth

breach[1] /briːtʃ/ *noun* **1** [C, U] when someone breaks a rule, agreement, or law **ihlal, bozma, çiğneme, uymama** *a policy that is in breach of international law* ○ *He was sued for breach of contract.* **2** [C] *formal* a serious disagreement between two groups, countries, etc **kopukluk uyuşmazlık, anlaşmazlık**

breach[2] /briːtʃ/ *verb* [T] to break a rule, law, or agreement **ihlal etmek, bozmak, çiğnemek, uymamak**

○ **bread** /bred/ *noun* [U] a basic food made by mixing and baking flour, water, and sometimes yeast (= substance that makes it rise) **ekmek** *a slice of bread* ○ *a loaf of white bread* ⊃See also: the best/greatest **thing** since sliced bread.

breadcrumbs /'bredkrʌmz/ *noun* [plural] very small pieces of dry bread, used in cooking **ekmek kırıntıları, galeta tozu**

bread

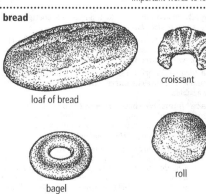

loaf of bread

croissant

bagel

roll

breadth /bretθ/ *noun* [U, no plural] **1** the distance from one side of something to the other side **genişlik** *a swimming pool with a breadth of 10 metres and a length of 50 metres* **2** **sb's breadth of experience/knowledge/ interest, etc** the great number of different things that someone has done, knows, is interested in, etc **birinin deneyim/bilgi/ilgi vs. Konularında genişliği, derinliği, yaptıkları** ⊃See also: the **length** and breadth of sth.

breadwinner /'bred,wɪnəʳ/ *noun* [C] the person who earns the money in a family **evin geçimini sağlayan kimse**

break

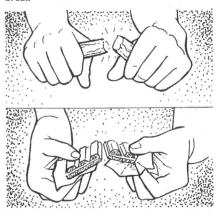

○ **break**[1] /breɪk/ *verb past tense* **broke**, *past participle* **broken 1** [SEPARATE] [I, T] to separate into two or more pieces, or to make something separate into two or more pieces **kırmak** *The vase fell on the floor and broke.* ○ *They had to break a window to get in.* **2 break your arm/leg, etc** to damage a bone in your arm/leg, etc **kolunu/bacağını kırmak** *Carolyn broke her leg in a skiing accident.* **3** [NOT WORK] [I, T] If you break a machine, object, etc, or if it breaks, it stops working because it is damaged. **bozulmak, çalışmamak, kırılmak** *Who broke the video?* **4 break an agreement/promise/rule, etc** to not do what you should do according to an agreement/ promise/rule, etc **antlaşma/söz/kural/ bozmak vb., ihlal etmek, uymamak** *Police stopped him for breaking the speed limit.* **5 break the law** to do something illegal **yasayı ihlal etmek, kanuna uymamak**

6 break the news to sb to tell someone about something unpleasant that has happened **birine tatsız/hoş olmayan bir haberi vermek, felaket tellalı olmak 7 break the silence** to make a noise, speak, etc and end a period of silence **sessizliği bozmak** *The silence was broken by a sudden knock at the door.* **8 break a habit/routine, etc** to stop doing something that you usually do **bir alışkanlık/rutin vs. vazgeçmek, bırakmak 9 break a record** to do something faster, better, etc than anyone else **rekor kırmak** *He broke the world record for the 200m.* **10** [REST] [I, T] to stop the activity you are doing to have a short rest **ara vermek, nefes almak, teneffüs yapmak, mola vermek** *Let's break for five minutes and have a drink.* **11** [BECOME KNOWN] [I, T] If news or a story breaks, or if someone breaks it, it becomes known by the public for the first time. **patlak vermek, acil haber olarak sunmak 12** [WEATHER] *UK* If the weather breaks, it changes suddenly, and usually becomes worse. **(hava) bozulmak, kötüleşmek 13** [VOICE] [I] When a boy's voice breaks, it becomes deeper and sounds like a man's voice. **erkeksi ve kalın ses çıkarmak, sesi kalınlaşmak 14** [WAVE] [I] When a wave breaks, it reaches its highest point as it moves towards the land, and then becomes flat and white. **dalga çıkmak, yükselmek 15** [STORM] [I] If a storm breaks, it starts suddenly. **(fırtına) çıkmak, meydana gelmek 16 break even** to not make money but also not lose money **17 break free/loose** to suddenly escape or become separate from something **kaçıp kurtulmak, serbest/başıboş kalmak, ayrılmak 18 dawn/day breaks** When dawn (= early morning)/day breaks, the sky becomes lighter because the sun is rising. **gün ağarmak, şafak sökmek** ⊃See also: break new ground¹, break sb's **heart,** break the **ice¹,** break the **mould¹,** break ranks (**rank¹**).

break away *phrasal verb* **1** to suddenly leave or escape from someone who is holding you **kaçıp kurtulmak, ansızın kaçmak, firar etmek, elinden kurtulmak 2** to stop being part of a group because you disagree with them **ayrılmak, grup üyesi olmaktan vazgeçmek** *Some members broke away to form a new political party.*

break down *phrasal verb* **1** [MACHINE] If a machine or vehicle breaks down, it stops working. **bozulmak, çalışmamak, kırılmak, arıza yapmak** *My car broke down on the way to work.* **2** [COMMUNICATION] If a system, relationship, or discussion breaks down, it fails because there is a problem or disagreement. **(ilişki, tartışma, sistem) bozulmak, kötüye gitmek, başarısız olmak, çalışmamak** *Their marriage broke down after only two years.* **3** [CRY] to become very upset and start crying **sinirleri boşalmak, kötü hissetmek, canı sıkılmak, yıkılmak**

break sth down *phrasal verb* to divide something into smaller, simpler parts **parçalamak, ayrıştırmak, küçük parçalara bölmek**

break in *phrasal verb* to get into a building or car using force, usually to steal something **bir yere hırsızlık amacıyla zorla girmek; sözünü kesmek, araya girmek**

break sth in *phrasal verb* to wear something new, usually shoes, for short periods of time to make them more comfortable **yeni bir şey giymek ve rahatlamak (bilhassa ayakkabı)**

break into sth *phrasal verb* **1** to get into a building or car using force, usually to steal something **bir yere/araca hırsızlık amacıyla zorla girmek; sözünü kesmek, araya girmek 2** to suddenly start doing something **ansızın bir şeyi yapmaya başlamak** *The crowd broke into a cheer when he came on stage.*

break (sth) off *phrasal verb* to separate a part from a larger piece, or to become separate from something **bir**

şeyi ayırmak, koparıp almak/ayırmak *He broke off a piece of chocolate.*

break off *phrasal verb* to suddenly stop speaking or doing something **ansızın konuşmayı kesmek, küsmek, konuşmamak** *She broke off in the middle of a sentence.*

break sth off *phrasal verb* to end a relationship **bir ilişkiyi bitirmek, son vermek** *She broke off the engagement just two weeks before the wedding.*

break out *phrasal verb* **1** If a fire, war, disease, etc breaks out, it starts suddenly. **patlak vermek, meydana gelmek, ortaya çıkmak** *A fight broke out among the crowd.* **2** to escape from prison **hapisten kaçmak, firar etmek** *to break out of jail* **3 break out in a rash/sweat, etc** to suddenly have spots or sweat (= salty liquid) appear on your skin

break through sth *phrasal verb* to force your way through something that is holding you back **(engelleri/kuşatmayı) yarıp geçmek** *Protesters broke through the barriers.*

break (sth) up *phrasal verb* to divide into many pieces, or to divide something into many pieces **parçalara ayırmak, paramparça etmek, bölmek** *The company has been broken up and sold.*

break up *phrasal verb* **1** If people break up, they stop having a relationship or stop working together. **ayrılmak, ilişkiyi sonlandırmak, yolları ayrılmak** *He's just broken up with his girlfriend.* **2** *UK* When schools or colleges break up, the classes end and the holidays begin. **sona ermek, öğretim sona ermek, tatile girmek**

break² /breɪk/ *noun* [C] **1** [STOP] when you stop an activity for a short time, usually to rest or to eat **ara, fasıla, teneffüs, dinlenme arası, paydos, mola** *a coffee/tea break* ○ *Take a break and come back after lunch.* **2** [HOLIDAY] a holiday or period of time away from work, school, etc **tatil, ara, dinlenme** *the spring break* ○ *a weekend break to Paris* **3** [OPPORTUNITY] a lucky opportunity **şanslı bir fırsat** *His big break came when he was offered a part in a TV series.* ○ *Meeting Tom was my lucky break.* **4** [DAMAGE] where something has separated in an accident **kırılma, bozulmak, darmadağın olma, kazada kopma** *a break in the bone* **5 a break with sth** when you end a relationship, connection, or way of doing something **bir ilişkiyi/bağlantıyı/yapmayı bitirme, son verme** *a break with tradition*

breakable /ˈbreɪkəbl/ *adjective* able to break easily **kolay kırılabilir** *a breakable vase*

breakage /ˈbreɪkɪdʒ/ *noun* [C, U] when something has been broken **kırılanlar, kırıklar** *The delivery company must pay for any breakages.*

breakaway /ˈbreɪkəweɪ/ *adjective* **a breakaway group/republic/region, etc** a group/region, etc that has separated itself from a larger group or region because of a disagreement **anlaşmazlık nedeniyle bir grup/bölgeden bağımsız topluluk, cumhuriyet, bölge vs.**

breakdown /ˈbreɪkdaʊn/ *noun* [C] **1** [ILLNESS] (*also* nervous breakdown) a short period of mental illness when people are too ill to continue with their normal lives **zihinsel çöküntü, yıkım olma** *to have a breakdown* **2** [FAILURE] when something such as communication or a relationship fails or ends **başarısızlığa uğrama, sonlandırma** *a breakdown in the peace talks* **3** [EXPLANATION] a short explanation of the details of something **detayların kısa dökümü, izahı, açıklaması** *I need a breakdown of the costs involved.* **4** [NOT WORKING] when a vehicle or machine stops working for a period of time **bozulma, arıza, çalışmama**

o⊷**breakfast** /ˈbrekfəst/ *noun* [C] the food you eat in the morning after you wake up **kahvaltı** *She had breakfast* *in bed this morning.* ● **breakfast** *verb* [I] ⊃See also: bed and breakfast, continental breakfast, English breakfast. **kahvaltı etmek**

break-in /'breɪkɪn/ *noun* [C] when someone forces their way into a building or car, usually to steal something **haneye/araca tecavüz, zorla girme** *There has been another break-in at the office.*

'breaking ,point *noun* [U] when a situation has become so bad that it cannot continue **kırılma noktası** *Things had become so bad at work they'd almost reached breaking point.*

breakneck /'breɪknek/ *adjective* **breakneck speed/ growth, etc** dangerously fast speed/growth, etc **tehlikeli şekilde hızlı sürat/büyüme, anormal hız/ gelişme**

breakout /'breɪkaʊt/ *noun* [C] an escape, usually from prison **firar, kaçış**

⊞ **breakthrough** ...... İLE BİRLİKTE KULLANILAN KELİMELER

make/provide a breakthrough ● a breakthrough **comes** ● a **big/crucial/major/real** breakthrough ● a **medical/scientific** breakthrough ● a breakthrough **in** sth

breakthrough /'breɪkθruː/ *noun* [C] an important discovery or development that helps solve a problem **büyük hamle, önemli buluş, ilerleme, gelişme** *a major breakthrough in the fight against cancer*

break-up /'breɪkʌp/ *noun* [C] **1** when a close relationship ends **ayrılma, dağılma, ilişkiyi bitirme** *He moved away after the break-up of his marriage.* **2** when a country, group, etc separates into several smaller parts **parçalanma, ayrılma, yeniden bir grup oluşturma, bir ülkenin parçalanması**

breast /brest/ *noun* **1** [C] one of the two soft, round parts on a woman's chest **göğüs, meme 2** [C, U] the front part of a bird's body, or the meat from this area **kuşların göğüs kısmı** *chicken breast*

breast-feed /'brestfiːd/ *verb* [I, T] *past* **breast-fed** If a woman breast-feeds, she gives a baby milk from her breast. **emzirmek, süt vermek** ● **breast-feeding** *noun* [U] **emzirme**

breaststroke /'breststrəʊk/ *noun* [U] a way of swimming in which you push your arms forward and then to the side, while you kick your legs backwards **yüzüstü yüzme**

breath /breθ/ *noun* **1** [U] the air that comes out of your lungs **nefes, soluk** *His breath smells of garlic.* **2** [C] when air goes into or out of your lungs **solunum, nefes** *She took a deep breath before she started.* **3 be out of breath** to be breathing quickly because you have been running, walking fast, etc **nefesi tükenmek, nefes nefese kalmak 4 catch your breath; get your breath back** to rest for a short time until you can breathe regularly again **nefeslenmek, soluklanmak, kendine gelmek, 5 under your breath** If you say something under your breath, you say it very quietly so that other people cannot hear it. **fısıldamak, fısıldayarak söylemek 6 hold your breath** to keep air in your lungs and not let it out **nefesini tutmak** *How long can you hold your breath under water?* **7 don't hold your breath** *humorous* something that you say in order to tell someone that an event is not likely to happen **nefesini tutma, rahat ol, kendini kasma, için ferah olsun** *He said he'd phone, but don't hold your breath.* **8 a breath of fresh air** someone or something that is new, different, and exciting **yeni bir nefes, taze soluk** ● **9 take your breath away** If something takes your breath away, you feel surprise and admiration because it is so beautiful or exciting. **nefesini kesmek, hayran bırakmak** *The*

view from the window took my breath away. ● **10 with bated breath** in an excited or anxious way **heyecanlı veya endişeli bir şekilde, endişeyle, nefes kesen** *I waited with bated breath as the results were read out.*

breathalyser /'breθəlaɪzəʳ/ *noun* [C] *UK* a piece of equipment that tests your breath to measure how much alcohol you have had **nefeste alkol muayene cihazı** ● **breathalyse** *verb* [T] *UK* to measure the alcohol in someone's body using a breathalyser **alkol muayenesi yapmak**

⚬ **breathe** /briːð/ *verb* [I, T] to take air into and out of your lungs **nefes alıp vermek** *breathe in/out* ○ *breathe deeply* ⊃See also: be breathing down sb's **neck**, not breathe a word[1].

breather /'briːðəʳ/ *noun* [C] *informal* a short rest **kısa istirahat, dinlenme** *If you start to feel tired, take a breather.*

breathing /'briːðɪŋ/ *noun* [U] when you take air into and out of your lungs **nefeslenme, nefes alıp verme** *The doctor listened to my breathing.*

'breathing ,space *noun* [U] an opportunity to stop, relax, or think about things **rahatça nefeslenecek, dinlenilecek ve kafadaki sorunları atabilecek yer, fırsat**

breathless /'breθləs/ *adjective* not able to breathe enough **nefessiz** ● **breathlessly** *adverb* **nefessiz bir şekilde**

breathtaking /'breθ,teɪkɪŋ/ *adjective* very beautiful or surprising **nefes kesen, inanılmaz** *breathtaking views* ● **breathtakingly** *adverb* **nefes kesici bir şekilde**

bred /bred/ *past of* breed **doğurmak, yavrulamak' fiilinin geçmiş zaman hali**

breed[1] /briːd/ *noun* [C] **1** a type of dog, sheep, pig, etc **köpek, koyun, domuz vb. ırk, cins, soy** *a rare breed of cattle* **2** a type of person or thing **insan soyu, eşya cinsi, türü** *a new breed of bank*

breed[2] /briːd/ *verb past* **bred** /bred/ **1** [I] If animals breed, they produce young animals. **yavrulamak 2 breed chickens/horses/rabbits, etc** to keep animals in order to produce young **yavrulamaları için tavuk/at/tavşan yetiştirmek 3 breed contempt/ ignorance, etc** to cause something to develop, especially something bad **kötü bir şeyin olmasına yol açmak, sebep olmak**

breeder /'briːdəʳ/ *noun* [C] someone who keeps animals in order to produce young animals **yetiştirici, üretici** *a dog/horse breeder*

breeding /'briːdɪŋ/ *noun* [U] **1** when animals produce young animals **üretme, yetiştirme** *the breeding season* **2** when someone keeps animals in order to produce young animals **besleme, yetiştirme** *horse breeding*

'breeding ,ground *noun* [C] **1** a place where something develops quickly, especially something bad **bilhassa kötü şeylerin çabucak çoğaldığı, ürediği yer** *This estate is a breeding ground for crime.* **2** a place where animals breed **üreme yeri, alanı**

breeze[1] /briːz/ *noun* [C] a gentle wind **esinti, meltem** *a cool breeze*

breeze[2] /briːz/ *verb informal* **breeze along/into/ through, etc** to move somewhere quickly in a confident way and without worrying **güvenli ve endişesizce bir yere dalmak, girmek, ilerlemek**

breezy /'briːzi/ *adjective* **1** with a slight wind **esintili** *a cool, breezy day* **2** happy, confident, and enthusiastic **canlı, neşeli, cıvıl cıvıl, mutlu** *a cheerful, breezy style* ● **breezily** *adverb* **serin bir şekilde**

brethren /'breðrən/ *noun* [plural] members of an organized group, especially a religious group of men **erkeklerin oluşturduğu bir (dini) grubun üyeleri**

brevity /'brevəti/ *noun* [U] *formal* **1** when speech or writing is short and contains few words **kısa söz ve ifadeler 2** when something lasts for a short time **kısalık, sadelik**

brew¹ /bru:/ *verb* **1** [T] to make beer **bira yapmak 2** [I, T] If you brew tea or coffee, you make it by adding hot water, and if it brews, it gradually develops flavour in hot water. **demlemek, yapmak, hazırlamak 3** be **brewing** If something bad is brewing, it is beginning to develop. **için için kaynamak, fokurdamak (kötü bir şey)** *There is a row brewing over the plans.*

brew² /bru:/ *noun* [C] *informal* a drink made by brewing, such as beer or tea **demlenerek/mayalanarak yapılan bir içecek**

brewer /'bru:əʳ/ *noun* [C] a person or organization that makes beer **bir imalatçısı/üreticisi/yapımcısı**

brewery /'bru:ʳri/ *noun* [C] a company that makes beer **bira imalathanesi/fabrikası**

🧩 **bribe** ...... İLE BİRLİKTE KULLANILAN KELİMELER

accept/take a bribe ● **offer** sb/**pay** a bribe ● **a cash** bribe

bribe /braɪb/ *noun* [C] money or a present given to someone so that they will do something for you, usually something dishonest **rüşvet verme** *The politician was accused of accepting bribes from businessmen.* ● **bribe** *verb* [T] [+ to do sth] *He was bribed to give false evidence at the trial.* **rüşvet vermek**

bribery /'braɪbʳri/ *noun* [U] when someone is offered money or a present so that they will do something, usually something dishonest **rüşvet** *bribery and corruption*

bric-a-brac /'brɪkə,bræk/ *noun* [U] a collection of small, decorative objects that have little value **biblo, süs eşyası, aksesuar koleksiyonu**

brick /brɪk/ *noun* [C] a small, hard, rectangular block used for building walls, houses, etc **tuğla** *a brick wall* ⊃See also: be banging your **head¹** against a brick wall.

brick

bricklayer /'brɪk,leɪəʳ/ *noun* [C] someone whose job is to build houses, walls, etc with bricks **duvar/tuğla ustası, duvarcı**

bridal /'braɪdəl/ *adjective* [always before noun] relating to a woman who is getting married, or relating to a wedding **geline ait, gelini ilgilendiren** *a bridal gown*

bride /braɪd/ *noun* [C] a woman who is getting married **gelin** *the bride and groom*

bridegroom /'braɪdgru:m/ (*also* groom) *noun* [C] a man who is getting married **damat**

bridesmaid /'braɪdzmeɪd/ *noun* [C] a woman or girl who helps the bride on her wedding day **nedime**

o━**bridge¹** /brɪdʒ/ *noun* **1** [STRUCTURE] [C] a structure that is built over a river, road, etc so that people or vehicles can go across it **köprü** *to go across/over a bridge* ○ *Brooklyn Bridge* **2** [CONNECTION] [C] something that connects two groups, organizations, etc and improves the relationship between them **birleştirici unsur, köprü** *After the war they tried to build bridges with neighbouring countries.* **3 the bridge of your nose** the hard part of your nose between your eyes **burun üs kenarı, burun kemeri 4 the bridge** the raised area of a ship where the controls are **köprü (gemi) 5** [GAME] [U] a card game for four players **briç oyun (iskambil) 6 I'll/we'll cross**

bridge

that bridge when I/we come to it. something you say when you do not intend to worry about a possible problem now, but will deal with it if or when it happens **dereyi görmeden paçaları sıvamak, zamanı gelince icabına bakarım(z), gereğini yaparım(z)**

bridge² /brɪdʒ/ *verb* **bridge the gap/gulf, etc** to make the difference between two things smaller **aradaki farkı gidermek, boşluğu doldurmak, farklılıkların üstesinden gelmek** *This course is designed to bridge the gap between school and work.*

bridle /'braɪdl/ *noun* [C] a set of straps that you put on a horse's head to control it **ata takılan gem, yular**

brief¹ /bri:f/ *adjective* **1** lasting only for a short time **kısa, öz olarak** *a brief visit* **2** using only a few words **bir kaç sözle ifade edilen** *a brief description/statement* **3 in brief** using only a few words **kısaca, özet olarak ifade edilen** *world news in brief* ● **briefly** *adverb* *They discussed the matter briefly.* **kısaca**

brief² /bri:f/ *verb* [T] to give someone instructions or information **kısa bilgi vermek, özetlemek** [often passive] *At the meeting reporters were briefed on the plans.*

brief³ /bri:f/ *noun* [C] a set of instructions or information **kısa, özet, öz bilgi** [+ to do sth] *My brief was to improve the image of the city.*

briefcase /'bri:fkeɪs/ *noun* [C] a flat, rectangular case with a handle for carrying documents, books, etc **evrak çantası, el çantası** ⊃See picture at **bag.**

briefing /'bri:fɪŋ/ *noun* [C, U] a meeting when people are given instructions or information **toplantı, kısa toplantı, bilgilendirme toplantısı, brifing** *a press briefing*

briefs /bri:fs/ *noun* [plural] underwear that you wear on your bottom **don, külot, iç çamaşırı** *a pair of briefs* ⊃Orta kısımdaki renkli sayfalarına bakınız.

brigade /brɪ'geɪd/ *noun* [C] **1** a large group of soldiers **tugay 2** *UK humorous* a group of people with a particular characteristic or interest **ekip, aynı amaçlar için bir araya gelmiş insanlar topluluğu** *the anti-smoking brigade* ⊃See also: fire brigade.

brigadier /,brɪgə'dɪəʳ/ *noun* [C] a British army officer of high rank **tuğgeneral, tugay komutanı, Büyük Britanya ordusunda yüksek rütbeli bir subay**

o━**bright** /braɪt/ *adjective* **1** [COLOUR] having a strong, light colour **parlak renkli** *bright yellow/blue* **2** [LIGHT] full of light or shining strongly **parlak, parıldayan** *bright sunshine* **3** [INTELLIGENT] intelligent **zeki, akıllı** *He's a bright boy.* **4** [HAPPY] happy or full of hope **mutlu ve umut dolu, umutlu** *She's always so bright and cheerful.* ● **brightly** *adverb* **brightly coloured** *flowers* **aydınlık bir şekilde** ● **brightness** *noun* [U] **aydınlık**

brighten /ˈbraɪtᵊn/ (also brighten up) verb [I, T] **1** to become lighter or more colourful, or to make something become lighter or more colourful **aydınlatmak, şenlenmek, keyiflenmek, aydınlanmak** A picture or two would brighten up the room. **2** to become happier, or to make someone become happier **keyiflen(dir)mek, mutlu olmak, mutlu etmek** She brightened up when she saw him.

brilliant /ˈbrɪliənt/ adjective **1** GOOD UK very good **çok iyi, harika** We saw a brilliant film. **2** CLEVER extremely clever **oldukça akıllı** a brilliant scholar **3** LIGHT full of light or colour **parlak, pırıl pırıl** The sky was a brilliant blue. ● **brilliantly** adverb **muhteşem bir şekilde** ● **brilliance** /ˈbrɪliəns/ noun [U] **iyi olma durumu, parlaklık**

brim¹ /brɪm/ verb **brimming**, past **brimmed** **be brimming with sth** to be full of something **bir şeyle dopdolu olmak, dolu dolu olmak** Her eyes were brimming with tears.

brim² /brɪm/ noun [C] **1** the flat part around the bottom of a hat **şapkanın düz olan tepe kısmı 2** the top edge of a container **bir kabın en üst kenarı** He filled my glass **to the brim**.

brine /braɪn/ noun [U] salty water, often used for keeping food from decaying **tuz suyu, salamura suyu** olives in brine

☛**bring** /brɪŋ/ verb [T] past **brought 1** to take someone or something with you when you go somewhere **götürmek/getirmek** Did you bring an umbrella with you? ○ [+ two objects] He brought me some flowers. **2 bring happiness/peace/shame, etc** to cause happiness/peace/shame, etc **mutluluk/barış/utanç getirmek, sebep olmak** Money does not always bring happiness. **3 can not bring yourself to do sth** to not be willing to do something because it is so unpleasant **bir şeyi yapmayı kendine yedirememek, istekli olmamak, içinden gelmemek** He couldn't bring himself to talk to her. ⇒See also: bring sb/sth to their knees (knee), bring sth to light¹.

bring sth about phrasal verb to make something happen **bir şeyin olmasını sağlamak** The Internet has **brought about** big changes in the way we work.

bring sth back phrasal verb **1** to return from somewhere with something **bir şeyi alıp gelmek, geri getirmek, geri vermek** [+ two objects] Can you bring me back some milk from the shop, please? **2** to make someone think about something from the past **hatırına gelmek/getirmek, hatırlamak** The photos **brought back** memories.

bring sb down phrasal verb to cause someone in a position of power to lose their job **birini alaşağı etmek, birini işinden etmek, yetkisine son vermek** This scandal could **bring down** the government.

bring sth down phrasal verb to reduce the level of something **bir şeyin düzeyini düşürmek, azaltmak** to **bring down** prices

bring sth forward phrasal verb to change the date or time of an event so that it happens earlier than planned **tarihi öne çekmek, daha yakın bir tarihe almak** I've brought forward the meeting to this week.

bring sth in phrasal verb **1** to introduce something new, usually a product or a law **genellikle bir ürün veya yasayı tanıtmak, gündeme getirmek** New safety regulations were brought in last year. **2** to earn or make money **para kazanmak, gelir elde etmek, kazanç sağlamak** The film has brought in millions of dollars.

bring sb in phrasal verb to ask someone to do a particular job **birinden bir işi yapmasını rica etmek** We need to bring in an expert to sort out this problem.

bring sth off phrasal verb to succeed in doing something difficult **zor bir görevi başarmak, üstesinden gelmek** How did he manage to bring that off?

bring sth on phrasal verb to make something happen, usually something bad **kötü bir şeyin olmasına neden olmak** [often passive] Headaches are often brought on by stress.

bring sth out phrasal verb **1** to produce something to sell to the public **bir şey üretmek, çıkarmak, piyasaya sürmek** They have just brought out a new, smaller phone. **2** to make a particular quality or detail noticeable **iyi tarafını, detayını ön plana çıkarmak** Salt can help to bring out the flavour of food.

bring sb together phrasal verb to cause people to be friendly with each other **dost/arkadaş olmalarını sağlamak, temin etmek** The disaster brought the community closer together.

bring sb up phrasal verb to look after a child and teach them until they are old enough to look after themselves **bakmak, büyütmek, yetiştirmek, bakıp büyütmek** She was brought up by her grandparents.

bring sth up phrasal verb **1** to start to talk about a particular subject **bir şeyi/konuyu/hususu gündeme getirmek, söz konusu etmek** There are several points I'd like to bring up at tomorrow's meeting. **2** UK to vomit something **kusmak, çıkarmak, yediklerini çıkarmak**

brink /brɪŋk/ noun **be on the brink of sth** to be in a situation where something bad is going to happen very soon **hemen hemen, ramak kala, neredeyse, üzere** The two countries are on the brink of war.

brisk /brɪsk/ adjective quick and energetic **faal, canlı, enerjik, süratli, çevik, hareketli** a brisk walk ● **briskly** adverb **çabuk bir şekilde**

bristle¹ /ˈbrɪsl/ verb [I] to show that you are annoyed about something **bir şeyden rahatsız olduğunu göstermek** She bristled at the suggestion that it was her fault.

bristle² /ˈbrɪsl/ noun [C, U] a short, stiff hair **kısa sert saç, kıl, tüy** ● **bristly** adjective **kıllı**

Brit /brɪt/ noun [C] informal someone who comes from Great Britain **Büyük Britanya uyruklu**

British /ˈbrɪtɪʃ/ adjective relating to Great Britain or the United Kingdom **Büyük Britanya veya Birleşik Krallığa ilişkin, ait**

the British /ˈbrɪtɪʃ/ noun [plural] the people of Great Britain or the United Kingdom **Büyük Britanya veya Birleşik Krallık halkı**

Briton /ˈbrɪtᵊn/ noun [C] someone who comes from Great Britain **Büyük Britanyalı**

brittle /ˈbrɪtl/ adjective hard but able to be broken easily **kolay kırılır, gevrek** brittle bones

broach /brəʊtʃ/ verb **broach an idea/subject/topic, etc** to begin to talk about something, usually something difficult or embarrassing **genellikle zor ve utandıran bir fikri/konuyu/hususu anlatmaya girişmek, teşebbüs etmek** I don't know how to broach the subject of money with him.

broad /brɔːd/ adjective **1** wide **geniş broad shoulders** ○ a broad smile **2 a broad range/variety, etc** a group that includes many different things or people **bir çok kişi veya şeyi kapsayan bir grup, geniş yelpaze** a broad range of subjects **3 a broad outline/picture, etc** a general description, without detail **fazla detaya girmeden genel bir tanımlama** This is just a broad outline of the proposal. **4** A broad accent (= way of speaking from a region) is very noticeable. **yaygın, kaba telaffuz 5 in broad daylight** during the day when it is light and people can see **güpe gündüz, gün ortası** He was attacked in broad daylight.

B

broadband /'brɔːdbænd/ *noun* [U] a system that allows large amounts of information to be sent very quickly between computers or other electronic equipment **geniş bant**

broadcast¹ /'brɔːdkɑːst/ *noun* [C] a television or radio programme **radyo, tv yayını** *a news broadcast* ● **broadcast** *adjective* [always before noun] relating to television or radio **radyo, tv yayınına ilişkin** *broadcast news*

broadcast² /'brɔːdkɑːst/ *verb* [I, T] *past* **broadcast**, *also US* **broadcasted** to send out a programme on television or radio **yayın yapmak** [often passive] *The concert will be broadcast live next week*. ● **broadcaster** *noun* [C] someone who speaks on radio or television as a job **tv ve radyoda sunum yapan, konuşan kişi** ● **broadcasting** *noun* [U] **televizyon veya radyo yayını**

broaden /'brɔːdən/ *verb* [I, T] **1** to increase or make something increase and include more things or people **artırmak, artmak** *We need to broaden the range of services that we offer.* ○ *Travel broadens your mind.* **2** to become wider or make something become wider **genişlemek, genişletmek** *Her smile broadened and she began to laugh.*

🧩 **broadly** ...... İLE BİRLİKTE KULLANILAN KELİMELER

broadly **in line with/similar** ● broadly **welcome** sth

broadly /'brɔːdli/ *adverb* in a general way and not including everything or everyone **genel anlamda** *The plans have been broadly accepted.*

broadsheet /'brɔːdʃiːt/ *noun* [C] *UK* a large newspaper, usually considered to be more serious than smaller newspapers **büyük bir gazete**

broccoli /'brɒkəli/ *noun* [U] a green vegetable with a thick stem **brokoli, yeşil bir sebze**

brochure /'brəʊʃər/ ⑮ /brəʊ'ʃʊr/ *noun* [C] a thin book with pictures and information, usually advertising something **broşür, el ilanı** *a holiday/travel brochure*

broil /brɔɪl/ *US* (*UK/US* grill) *verb* [T] to cook food using direct heat **direk ateşte pişirmek, ızgarada pişirmek**

broiler /'brɔɪlər/ *US* (*UK/US* grill) *noun* [C] a piece of equipment used for cooking food under direct heat **ızgara**

broke¹ /brəʊk/ *adjective informal* **1 be broke** to not have any money **beş parasız, züğürt, meteliksiz, yolsuz 2 go broke** to lose all your money and have to end your business **beş parasız kalmak, meteliğe kurşun atmak, işini kaybedip bütün parasını kaybetmek**

broke² /brəʊk/ *past tense of* break **kırmak' fiilinin 2. hali**

broken .... BAŞKA BİR DEYİŞLE

Eğer bir alet düzgün bir şekilde çalışmıyorsa, bunu belirtmek için **dead**, **defunct** veya gayri resmi olan **bust** ifadeleri kullanılabilir. *You won't be able to watch the match, the telly's bust.* ● *The phone's dead, there must be a problem with the line.*

Eğer halka açık yerlerdeki aletlerde bir bozukluk varsa, bunu belirtmek için **out of order** ifadesi kullanılır. *The coffee machine was out of order.*

Eğer bir alet çalışmıyor halde ise, resmi olmayan ortamlarda, bunu belirtmek için **have had it** veya **give up the ghost** söylemleri kullanılır. *The kettle's had it, you'll have to boil a pan of water.* ● *I can't give you a lift - my car's given up the ghost.*

o→ **broken¹** /'brəʊkən/ *adjective* **1** damaged and separated into pieces **kırık, darma dağınık, harap vaziyette** *broken glass* ↪Opposite **unbroken**. **2 a broken arm/leg, etc** an arm/leg, etc with a damaged bone **kırık kol/ bacak 3** If a machine or piece of equipment is broken,

it is not working. **bozuk, çalışmaz** *The video's broken.* **4 a broken heart** when you are very sad because someone you love has ended a relationship with you **kırık kalp 5 a broken home** a family in which the parents do not now live together **parçalanmış aile, ebebveynleri ayrılmış aile 6 a broken promise** a promise that has not been kept **tutulmayan söz, yerine getirilmeyen vaad 7 broken English/Spanish, etc** English/Spanish, etc that is spoken slowly and has a lot of mistakes in it **kırık dökük, yarım yamalak İngilizce/İspanyolca**

broken² /'brəʊkən/ *past participle of* break **kırmak' fiilinin 3. hali**

broken-down /ˌbrəʊkən'daʊn/ *adjective* not working or in bad condition **çalışmaz durumda, bozuk, atıl durumda** *a broken-down vehicle*

broken-hearted /ˌbrəʊkən'hɑːtɪd/ *adjective* very sad because someone you love has ended a relationship with you **kırık kalpli, kalbi kırık**

broker¹ /'brəʊkər/ *noun* [C] **1** (*also* **stockbroker**) someone whose job is to buy and sell shares (= equal parts of a company's total value) **komisyoncu, aracı, simsar, borsa komisyoncusu 2 an insurance/mortgage, etc broker** someone who makes other people's financial arrangements for them **emlak/sigorta vb. Komisyoncusu**

broker² /'brəʊkər/ *verb* [T] to arrange an agreement **bir antlaşmayı düzenlemek** *The peace deal was brokered by the US.*

bronchitis /brɒŋ'kaɪtɪs/ *noun* [U] an illness in your lungs which makes you cough and have problems breathing **bronşit**

bronze¹ /brɒnz/ *noun* **1** [METAL] [U] a shiny orange-brown metal **tunç, bronz 2** [COLOUR] [U] an orange-brown colour **bronz rengi 3** [PRIZE] [C] a bronze medal (= a small, round disc given to someone for finishing third in a competition) **yarışmalarda 3. olan yarışmacıya verilen madalya, bronz madalya** *He won a bronze in the 200m.*

bronze² /brɒnz/ *adjective* **1** made of bronze **bronzdan yapılmış, tunçtan yapılmış** *a bronze statue* **2** being the colour of bronze **tunç rengi**

ˌbronze 'medal *noun* [C] a small, round disc given to someone for finishing third in a race or competition **bronz madalya**

brooch /brəʊtʃ/ *noun* [C] a piece of jewellery for women which is fastened onto clothes with a pin **broş, yaka iğnesi** *a diamond brooch*

brood¹ /bruːd/ *noun* [C] a family of young birds or animals, all born at the same time **bir defada yumurtadan çıkan yavrular, bir batında doğanlar**

brood² /bruːd/ *verb* [I] to think for a long time about things that make you sad or angry **kara kara düşünmek, derin derin düşünmek, kafa yormak** *I wish he'd stop brooding about the past.*

brook /brʊk/ *noun* [C] a small stream **dere, çay, küçük akarsu**

broom /bruːm/ *noun* [C] a brush with a long handle used for cleaning the floor **süpürge** ↪See picture at **brush**.

broth /brɒθ/ *noun* [U] soup, usually made with meat **etsuyu çorba, etli çorba** *chicken broth*

brothel /'brɒθəl/ *noun* [C] a building where prostitutes (= people who have sex for money) work **genelev, hayat kadınlarının çalıştığı yer**

o→ **brother** /'brʌðər/ *noun* [C] **1** [RELATIVE] a boy or man who has the same parents as you **erkek kardeş** *an older/ younger brother* ○ *my big/little brother* **2** [MEMBER] a man who is a member of the same race, religious group, organization, etc **aynı ırk, din, grup, kurumun**

B

üyesi olan, kardeş, birader **3** RELIGION (*also* **Brother**) a monk (= man who lives in a male religious group) **din kardeşi, rahip** *Brother Paul*

brotherhood /'brʌðəhʊd/ *noun* **1** [C] a group of men who have the same purpose or religious beliefs **aynı dini inanca ve amaca ait bir grup erkek topluluğu, cemiyet, teşkilat 2** [U] friendship and loyalty, like the relationship between brothers **kardeşlik, dostluk, bağlılık, kardeşler arasındakine benzer bağlılık**

brother-in-law /'brʌðərɪnlɔː/ *noun* [C] *plural* **brothers-in-law** the man married to your sister, or the brother of your husband or wife **enişte, bacanak, kayın birader, kayınço (argo)**

brotherly /'brʌðʰli/ *adjective* [always before noun] relating to or typical of brothers **kardeşçe, kardeş gibi** *brotherly love*

brought /brɔːt/ *past of* bring **getirmek' fiilinin geçmiş zaman hali**

brow /braʊ/ *noun* [C] **1** the front part of your head between your eyes and your hair **alın, kaş** *He wiped the sweat from his brow.* **2 brow of a hill/slope** *UK* the top part of a hill or slope **bayır, sırtı, tepeye aşağı uzanan yokuş, yamaç**

○***brown** /braʊn/ *adjective* **1** being the same colour as chocolate or soil **çikolata veya toprak rengi** *a brown leather bag* ○ *dark brown hair/eyes* ➔Orta kısımdaki renkli sayfalarına bakınız. **2** having darker skin because you have been in the sun **esmer, yanmış, bronzlaşmış** ● **brown** *noun* [C, U] the colour brown **kahve rengi, kestane rengi**

brownfield /'braʊnfiːld/ *adjective UK* describes land that was used for industry and where new buildings can be built **inşaata elverişli, önceden endüstri alanı olan arazi, arsa** *a brownfield site* ➔Compare greenfield.

brownie /'braʊni/ *noun* [C] a small, square cake made with chocolate and nuts **çikolata ve fındıktan yapılan küçük kek**

browse /braʊz/ *verb* **1** INTERNET [I, T] to look at information on the Internet **internette bilgiye göz atmak, aramak** *to browse the Internet/Web* **2** READ [I] to read a book, magazine, etc in a relaxed way and not in detail **gazete, kitap vb. göz atmak, üstünkörü okumak** *She browsed through some travel brochures looking for ideas.* **3** SHOP [I] to walk around a shop and look at things without buying anything **mağazalarda alışveriş yapmaksızın aylak aylak dolaşmak** *I love browsing around bookshops.*

browser /'braʊzəʳ/ *noun* [C] **1** a computer program which allows you to look at pages on the Internet **internet tarayıcısı 2** someone who browses **tarayıcı, tarama/araştırma yapan kişi**

bruise /bruːz/ *noun* [C] a dark area on your skin where you have been hurt **yara, bere, çürük** *He suffered cuts and bruises after falling off his bike.* ● **bruise** *verb* [T] to cause someone or something to have a bruise **yaralamak, yaralanmasına sebep olmak** [often passive] *He was badly bruised in the accident.* ● **bruising** *noun* [U] **morarı**

brunette /bruːˈnet/ *noun* [C] a white woman with dark brown hair **esmer kadın**

brunt /brʌnt/ *noun* **bear/feel/take the brunt of sth** to experience the worst part of something **sıkıntısına/acısına katlanmak, çekmek, tahammül etmek** *He took the brunt of the criticism.*

brush¹ /brʌʃ/ *noun* **1** [C] an object made of short, thin pieces of plastic, wire, etc fixed to a handle and used to tidy hair, to clean, to paint, etc **fırça** *a stiff wire brush* **2** [no plural] the action of using a brush **fırçalama** *I need*

brush

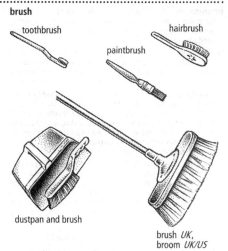

toothbrush   hairbrush
paintbrush

dustpan and brush

brush *UK*, broom *UK/US*

to give my hair a quick brush. **3 the brush of sth** when something touches you lightly **bir şeyin dokunması, huylandırması** *She felt the brush of his lips against her cheek.* **4 a brush with sth** when you experience something, or almost experience something, especially something unpleasant **hoş olmayan bir şeyi yaşama, tecrübe etme** *a brush with death*

brush² /brʌʃ/ *verb* [T] **1** to use a brush to clean or tidy something **fırçalamak** *to brush your hair/teeth* **2 brush sth away/off, etc** to move something somewhere using a brush or your hand **süpürmek, süpürüp atmak** *He brushed the snow off his coat.* **3 brush against/past sb/sth** to lightly touch someone or something as you move past them **geçerken birine hafifçe dokunmak, sürtünmek** *He brushed past me as he went up the stairs.*

brush sth aside/off *phrasal verb* to refuse to think about something seriously **bir şeyi ciddiye almayı reddetmek** *He brushed aside her suggestion.*

brush up (on) sth *phrasal verb* to improve your skills in something **becerilerini tazelemek, geliştirmek** *I'm trying to brush up on my French before I go to Paris.*

brush-off /'brʌʃɒf/ *noun informal* **give sb the brush-off** to be unfriendly to someone by not talking to them **başından atmak amacıyla soğuk davranmak, yüz vermemek**

brusque /bruːsk/ Ⓤ /brʌsk/ *adjective* dealing with people in a quick way that is unfriendly or rude **sert, nezaketsiz, umursamaz,** *a brusque manner* ● **brusquely** *adverb* **kaba bir şekilde**

brussel sprout /ˌbrʌsˈlˈspraʊt/ Ⓤ /ˈbrʌsʰlˌspraʊt/ *noun* [C] a small, green vegetable which is round and made of leaves **brüksel lahanası**

brutal /'bruːtʰl/ *adjective* very violent or cruel **zalim, vahşi, acımasız, barbar** *a brutal murder* ● **brutally** *adverb* **brutally** murdered ○ **brutally honest** acımasızca ● **brutality** /bruːˈtæləti/ *noun* [C, U] **acımasızlık**

brute¹ /bruːt/ *noun* [C] someone who behaves in a very violent and cruel way **hayvan, canavar, zalim kimse** ● **brutish** /'bruːtɪʃ/ *adjective* like a brute **hayvan gibi, hayvanlaşmış, çok kaba**

brute² /bruːt/ *adjective* **brute force/strength** great force or strength **kaba kuvvet, acı kuvvet**

BSc /ˌbiːesˈsiː/ *UK* (*US* **BS** /biːˈes/) *noun* [C] *abbreviation for* Bachelor of Science: a university or college qualification in a science subject which usually takes 3 or 4 years of study **fen bilimleri alanında lisans diploması** *He has a BSc in computer science.*

BSE /ˌbiːesˈiː/ *noun* [U] *abbreviation for* bovine spongiform encephalopathy: a disease that kills cows by destroying their brains **inekleri beyinlerini tahrip ederek öldüren bir hastalık**

BTW *internet abbreviation for* by the way: used when you write some extra information that may or may not be related to what is being discussed **sırası gelmişken, söz oraya gelmişken**

bubble[1] /ˈbʌbl/ *noun* [C] a ball of air or gas with liquid around it **hava kabarcığı** *an air bubble*

bubble[2] /ˈbʌbl/ *verb* [I] **1** If a liquid bubbles, balls of air or gas rise to its surface. **hava kabarcıkları yapmak, köpürmek, kabarmak** *The soup was bubbling on the stove.* **2** **bubble (over) with confidence/enthusiasm, etc** to be full of a positive emotion or quality **kendine güven/sevinçle coşmak,**

ˈ**bubble ˌgum** *noun* [U] a sweet that you chew and blow into a bubble **balonlu sakız**

bubbly /ˈbʌbli/ *adjective* **1** happy and enthusiastic **mutlu ve coşku dolu** *a bubbly personality* **2** full of bubbles, **köpüklü**

buck[1] /bʌk/ *noun* [C] **1** *US informal* a dollar (= US unit of money) **(argo) dolar** *It cost me twenty bucks to get a new bike lock.* **2** a male rabbit or deer **erkek tavşan, geyik** **3** **pass the buck** to blame someone or to make them responsible for a problem that you should deal with yourself **sorumluluğu üzerinden atmak, başkasına yüklemek; başkasını suçlamak**

buck[2] /bʌk/ *verb* [I] If a horse bucks, it kicks its back legs into the air. **(at) arka ayaklarıyla havaya çifte atmak**

bucket /ˈbʌkɪt/ *noun* [C] a round, open container with a handle used for carrying liquids **kova, bakraç** *a bucket of water*

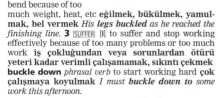

bucket

buckle[1] /ˈbʌkl/ *noun* [C] a metal object used to fasten the ends of a belt or strap **toka kopça** *a silver buckle*

buckle[2] /ˈbʌkl/ *verb* **1** [FASTEN] [I, T] to fasten a belt or strap with a buckle **bağlamak** **2** [BEND] [I, T] to bend, or to cause something to bend because of too much weight, heat, etc **eğilmek, bükülmek, yamulmak, bel vermek** *His legs buckled as he reached the finishing line.* **3** [SUFFER] [I] to suffer and stop working effectively because of too many problems or too much work **iş çokluğundan, veya sorunlardan ötürü yeteri kadar verimli çalışamamak, sıkıntı çekmek** **buckle down** *phrasal verb* to start working hard **çok çalışmaya koyulmak** *I must buckle down to some work this afternoon.*

bud /bʌd/ *noun* [C] **1** a part of a plant that develops into a leaf or a flower **tomurcuk, gonca** *In spring the trees are covered in buds.* **2** **nip sth in the bud** to stop a small problem from getting worse by stopping it soon after it starts **zamanında önlem almak, daha başlamadan**

önünü kesmek, bir problemi büyümeden önlemek ⊃See also: **taste buds.**

Buddha /ˈbʊdə/ ⓊⓈ /ˈbuːdə/ *noun* the Indian holy man on whose life and teachings Buddhism is based **Buda**

Buddhism /ˈbʊdɪzᵊm/ ⓊⓈ /ˈbuːdɪzᵊm/ *noun* [U] a religion based on the teachings of Buddha **Budizm**

Buddhist /ˈbʊdɪst/ ⓊⓈ /ˈbuːdɪst/ *noun* [C] someone who believes in Buddhism **Budist** ● **Buddhist** *adjective* a *Buddhist temple* **Budist**

budding /ˈbʌdɪŋ/ *adjective* [always before noun] starting to develop well **iyileşmeye, gelişmeye başlama** *a budding romance*

buddy /ˈbʌdi/ *noun* [C] *informal* a friend **çok yakın arkadaş, dost, yaren, kafadar, ahbap** *my best buddy*

budge /bʌdʒ/ *verb* [I, T] **1** If something will not budge, or you cannot budge it, it will not move. **kıpırda(t)mak, kımılda(t)mak** *I've tried to open the window, but it won't budge.* **2** If someone will not budge, or you cannot budge them, they will not change their opinion. **taviz vermek, fikrinden caymak, fikrini değiştirmek**

budgerigar /ˈbʌdʒᵊrɪgɑːʳ/ *noun* [C] *UK* a budgie **muhabbet kuşu**

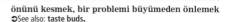

🧩 *budget* .... İLE BİRLİKTE KULLANILAN KELİMELER

have a budget of [£30 000/$5000, etc] ● be **on a tight** budget (= not have much money) ● the budget **for** sth

o⌐**budget**[1] /ˈbʌdʒɪt/ *noun* [C] **1** a plan that shows how much money you have and how you will spend it **bütçe** **2** the amount of money you have for something **bir şey için ayrılan para** *an annual budget of £30 million* **3** **the Budget** in the UK, when the government officially tells the public about its plans for taxes and spending **bütçe açıklaması, duyurusu; Birleşik Krallık'de hükümetin harcama ve vergilerle ilgili yaptığı duyuru** ● **budgetary** *adjective* [always before noun] relating to a budget **bütçeyle ilgili, bütçeye ait**

budget[2] /ˈbʌdʒɪt/ *verb* [I, T] to plan how much money you will spend on something **bütçelemek, harcamaları planlamak** *An extra £20 million has been budgeted for schools this year.*

budget[3] /ˈbʌdʒɪt/ *adjective* a budget hotel/price, etc a very cheap hotel, price, etc **çok ucuz, bütçeye uygun otel, kelepir**

budgie /ˈbʌdʒi/ *noun* [C] *UK* a small, brightly coloured bird often kept as a pet **muhabbet kuşu**

buff /bʌf/ *noun* [C] a computer/film/wine, etc buff someone who knows a lot about computers/films/wine, etc **bilgisayar/film/şarap vb. konularda çok şey bilen, uzman**

buffalo /ˈbʌfᵊləʊ/ *noun* [C] *plural* **buffaloes** or **buffalo** a large, wild animal, like a cow with horns **bufalo, boynuzlu ineğe benzer yabani hayvan** *a herd of wild buffalo*

buffer /ˈbʌfəʳ/ *noun* [C] something that helps protect someone or something from harm **tampon** *I have some money saved to act as a buffer against unexpected bills.*

ˈ**buffer ˌzone** *noun* [C] an area created to separate two countries that are fighting **tampon bölge**

buffet[1] /ˈbʊfeɪ/ ⓊⓈ /bəˈfeɪ/ *noun* [C] a meal in which dishes of food are arranged on a table and you serve yourself **açık büfe** *a cold buffet* ○ *a buffet lunch*

buffet[2] /ˈbʌfɪt/ *verb* [T] If something is buffeted by the weather, sea, etc, it is hit repeatedly and with force.

oradan oraya savurmak, beşik gibi sallamak [often passive] *The little boat was buffeted by the waves.*

'buffet ,car *noun* [C] *UK* the part of a train where you can buy something to eat or drink **restoran vagonu**

buffoon /bə'fuːn/ *noun* [C] *old-fashioned* someone who does silly things **aptal; salak, şapşal (argo)**

bug¹ /bʌg/ *noun* [C] **1** [ILLNESS] a bacteria or virus, or the illness that it causes **bakteri, virüs** *a flu/stomach bug* **2** [COMPUTER] a mistake in a computer program **bilgisayar programında hata, virüs** *This program is full of bugs.* **3** [INSECT] a small insect **küçük böcek 4** [EQUIPMENT] a small, electronic piece of equipment used to secretly listen to people talking **dinleme cihazı, böcek 5 be bitten by the bug/get the bug** *informal* to develop a strong interest or enthusiasm for a particular activity **merakını uyandırmak, merakını cezbetmek** *He's been bitten by the tennis bug.*

bug² /bʌg/ *verb* [T] **bugging**, *past* **bugged 1** to hide a piece of equipment somewhere in order to secretly listen to people talking **gizli dinleme yapmak, dinleme cihazı yerleştirmek** [often passive] *Their hotel room had been bugged.* **2** *informal* to annoy someone **canımı sıkmak, rahatsız etmek** *He's been bugging me all morning.*

buggy /'bʌgi/ *noun* [C] **1** *UK* (*US* **stroller**) a chair on wheels which is used to move small children **bebek arabası, puset 2** a vehicle with two wheels that is pulled by a horse, especially in the past **iki tekerlekli at arabası**

bugle /'bjuːgl/ *noun* [C] a small, metal musical instrument that you play by blowing into it **borazan**

∘━**build¹** /bɪld/ *verb past* **built 1** [I, T] to make something by putting materials and parts together **inşa etmek, yapmak** *build a house/wall* ○ *The bridge is built of steel and aluminium.* **2** [T] to create and develop something over a long time **kurmak, yapmak, uzun uğraşı sonucu yaratmak** *They have built a solid friendship over the years.*
build sth into sth *phrasal verb* to make something a part of something else **bir şeyi bir şeyin parçası yapmak, monte etmek, dahil etmek** *There are video screens built into the back of the seats.*
build on sth *phrasal verb* to use a success or achievement as a base from which to achieve more success **üzerine kurmak, inşa etmek**
build (sth) up *phrasal verb* to increase or develop, or to make something increase or develop **art(ır)mak, geliş(tir)mek, abartmak, büyütmek** *Traffic usually builds up in the late afternoon.*

build² /bɪld/ *noun* [C, U] the size and shape of a person's body **vücut yapısı, ölçüsü** *He's of medium build with short brown hair.*

builder /'bɪldər/ *noun* [C] someone who makes or repairs buildings as a job **inşaatçı, yapım işleriyle uğraşan kişi**

∘━**building** /'bɪldɪŋ/ *noun* **1** [C] a structure with walls and a roof, such as a house, school, etc **bina** *an office building* **2** [U] the activity of putting together materials and parts to make structures **inşaat işleri, inşa** *building materials* ⊃See also: apartment building.

'building so,ciety *UK* (*US* **savings and loan association**) *noun* [C] an organization similar to a bank which lends you money to buy a house **ev/emlak edinmek için kredi sağlayan kurum**

build-up /'bɪldʌp/ *noun* [U] **1** when something slowly increases **artış, birikim, çoğalma** [usually singular] *the build-up of traffic* **2 the build-up to sth** *UK* the period of preparation before something happens **bir şeyin hazırlık dönemi, aşaması, bir olayın oluşum öncesi**

There was a lot of excitement in the build-up to the Olympics.

built /bɪlt/ *past of* build **inşa etmek' fiilinin geçmiş zaman hali**

built-in /ˌbɪlt'ɪn/ *adjective* [always before noun] included as part of the main structure of something **üzerinde, birlikte verilen, hazır, monte edilmiş** *a computer with a built-in modem*

built-up /ˌbɪlt'ʌp/ *adjective* a built-up area has a lot of buildings **meskun, binalarla dolu**

bulb /bʌlb/ *noun* [C] **1** (*also* **light bulb**) a glass object containing a wire which produces light from electricity **ampul** *an electric light bulb* **2** a round root that some plants grow from **yumru kök, bitki soğanı** *daffodil bulbs*

bulbous /'bʌlbəs/ *adjective* large and round in an unattractive way **hatları çekici şekilde yuvarlak ve büyük** *a bulbous nose*

bulge¹ /bʌldʒ/ *verb* [I] to look larger and rounder or fuller than normal **şişkinlik/çıkıntı yapmak** *Her bags were bulging with shopping.*

bulge² /bʌldʒ/ *noun* [C] a round, raised area on a surface **şişkinlik, çıkıntı**

bulimia /bʊ'lɪmiə/ *noun* [U] a mental illness in which someone eats too much and then forces themselves to vomit **kusma hastalığı, yeme-çıkarma rahatsızlığı** ● **bulimic** *noun* [C], *adjective* **Yemek yedikten sonra yediklerini kusan kişi**

bulk /bʌlk/ *noun* **1 in bulk** in large amounts **toptan, çok miktarda** *to buy in bulk* **2 the bulk of sth** the largest part or most of something **büyük kısım** *He spends the bulk of his money on rent.* **3** [no plural] the large size of something or someone **büyüklük, iri cüsse**

bulky /'bʌlki/ *adjective* too big and taking up too much space **hantal, kaba, büyük**

bull /bʊl/ *noun* [C] a male cow **boğa** ⊃See also: be like a red rag to a bull.

bulldog /'bʊldɒg/ *noun* [C] a short, strong dog with a large head and neck **buldok köpeği**

bulldozer /'bʊlˌdəʊzər/ *noun* [C] a heavy vehicle used to destroy buildings and make the ground flat **buldozer** ● **bulldoze** *verb* [T] **buldozerle yıkım yapmak**

fire a bullet ● a bullet **flies/lodges** swh ● a **hail of** bullets ● a bullet **hole/wound**

bullet /'bʊlɪt/ *noun* **1** [C] a small, metal object that is fired from a gun **mermi, kurşun** *a bullet wound* **2 bite the bullet** to make yourself do something or accept something difficult or unpleasant **cesaretle göğüs germek, karşı durmak**

bulletin /'bʊlətɪn/ *noun* [C] **1** a short news programme on television or radio **haber bülteni** *the evening news bulletin* **2** a regular newspaper or report containing news about an organization **bülten**

'bulletin ,board *noun* [C] *US* (*UK* **noticeboard**) a board on a wall where you put advertisements and announcements **bülten/duyuru/haber panosu, tahtası** ⊃Orta kısımdaki renkli sayfalarına bakınız.

'bullet ,(point) *noun* [C] a small black circle used in writing to show separate items on a list **alt başlık/madde belirtme işareti**

bulletproof /'bʊlɪtpruːf/ *adjective* made of material that a bullet cannot go through **kurşun geçirmez** *bulletproof vests*

bullion /'bʊliən/ *noun* [U] blocks of gold or silver **külçe**

B

bullock /'bʊlək/ noun [C] a young bull (= male cow) **dana, genç boğa**

bully¹ /'bʊli/ verb [T] to intentionally frighten someone who is smaller or weaker than you **kabadayılık/zorbalık etmek, bilerek birini korkutmak, zayıf birinin üstüne üstüne gitmek** *He was bullied at school by some older boys.* ○ [+ into + doing sth] *She was bullied into leaving.* ● **bullying** noun [U] *Bullying is a problem in many schools.* **kabalık yapıp rahatsız etme**

bully² /'bʊli/ noun [C] someone who intentionally frightens a person who is smaller or weaker than them **zorba, kabadayı, kendinden daha zayıf birini bilerek korkutan kişi**

bum¹ /bʌm/ noun [C] **1** UK informal your bottom **kıç, popo 2** US informal someone who has no home and no money **berduş, çulsuz, evsiz ve parasız, meteliksiz, düşkün**

bum² /bʌm/ verb [T] **bumming**, past **bummed** very informal to ask someone for something, such as money or cigarettes, without intending to pay for them **asalak, otlakçı, başkalarının sırtından geçinen** *Hey, could I bum a cigarette?*

bum around phrasal verb informal to spend time being lazy and doing very little **tembel tembel oturarak zaman öldürmek**

bum around sth phrasal verb informal to travel to different places and not do any work **değişik yerlere seyahat etmek ve hiç çalışmamak, aylak aylak dolaşmak**

bumbag /'bʌmbæg/ UK (US **fanny pack**) noun [C] a small bag fixed to a belt that you wear around your waist **bel çantası**

bumblebee /'bʌmblbiː/ noun [C] a large, hairy bee (= flying insect) **bir tür iri yaban arısı**

bumbling /'bʌmblɪŋ/ adjective [always before noun] confused and showing no skill **karmakarışık, hiç bir işe yaramayan** *a bumbling idiot*

bummer /'bʌmər/ noun **a bummer** informal something unpleasant or annoying **hoş olmayan, rahatsız edici şey** *That last exam was a real bummer.*

bump¹ /bʌmp/ verb **1** [T] to hurt part of your body by hitting it against something hard **çarpmak, vurmak, bindirmek** *I bumped my head on the door.* **2 bump into/against sth** to hit your body, your car, etc against something by accident **kazara kafa kafaya çarpışmak, çarpmak, vurmak** *He kept falling over and bumping into things.* **3 bump along/over sth** to move in a vehicle over a surface that is not smooth **engebeli bir yerde araçla ilerlemek, gitmek** *The bus bumped along the country road.*

bump into sb phrasal verb informal to meet someone you know when you have not planned to meet them **rastlamak, tesadüfen karşılaşmak, ansızın karşılaşmak** *I bumped into an old school friend in town today.*

bump sb off phrasal verb informal to murder someone **öldürmek, haklamak**

bump² /bʌmp/ noun [C] **1** SURFACE a round, raised area on a surface **engebe, tümsek** *My bike hit a bump in the road.* **2** BODY a raised area on your body where it has been hurt by hitting something hard **şişkinlik, şişik, çıkıntı, şiş, yumru** *a nasty bump on the head* **3** MOVEMENT when something hits something hard **toslama, vuruş, çarpma** *I heard a bump upstairs.*

bumper¹ /'bʌmpər/ noun [C] a bar fixed along the front or back of a vehicle to protect it in an accident **tampon** *a front/rear bumper*

bumper² /'bʌmpər/ adjective [always before noun] bigger or better than usual **olağandan büyük ve daha iyi** *a bumper year*

'bumper ,sticker noun [C] a sign that you stick on a car, often with a funny message on it **araçlarda tamponlara yapıştırılan etiket**

bumpy /'bʌmpi/ adjective **1** SURFACE A bumpy road or surface is not smooth but has raised areas on it. **engebeli, inişli çıkışlı 2** JOURNEY A bumpy journey is uncomfortable because the vehicle moves around a lot. **sarsıntılı, sarsan, seyahatte insanın içini dışına çıkaran 3** SITUATION full of problems or sudden changes **ani değişiklikler ve sorunlarla dolu olan, sorunlu** *We had a bumpy start.*

bun /bʌn/ noun [C] **1** CAKE UK a small, round cake **küçük yuvarlak kek** *an iced bun* **2** BREAD a small, round piece of bread **çörek, küçük yuvarlak ekmek** *a hamburger/hot cross bun* **3** HAIR a hairstyle in which the hair is arranged in a small, round shape on the back of the head **topuz, saçın tepede toplanması**

🧩 **bunch** ...... İLE BİRLİKTE KULLANILAN KELİMELER

a bunch of **bananas/flowers/grapes/keys**

bunch¹ /bʌnʃ/ noun **1** [C] a number of things of the same type which are joined or held together **grup, aynı grup şeylerden oluşan deste, demet** *He handed me a bunch of flowers.* ⊃Orta kısımdaki renkli sayfalarına bakınız. **2** [C] informal a group of people **topluluk, grup** [usually singular] *His friends are a nice bunch.* **3 a bunch of sth** US informal a large amount or number of something **bir demet, bir deste** *There's a whole bunch of places I'd like to visit.*

bunch² /bʌnʃ/ verb

bunch (sb/sth) together/up phrasal verb to move close together so that you make a tight group, or to make someone or something do this **bir araya toplanmak/toplamak, grup oluşturmak, aynı amaç etrafında birleşmek** [often passive] *We were all bunched up at the back of the room.*

bunch (sth) up phrasal verb If material bunches up, or if someone bunches it up, it moves into tight folds. **demet olmak, deste deste yapmak, destelemek** [often passive] *My shirt's all bunched up at the back.*

bunches /'bʌntʃɪz/ noun [plural] UK a hairstyle in which the hair is tied together in two parts, one on each side of the head **saç topuzu, topuz**

bundle¹ /'bʌndl/ noun **1** [C] a number of things that are tied together **denk, bohça, demet, küme, yığın** *a bundle of letters/clothes* **2 a bundle of energy/nerves** informal a very energetic or nervous person **enerjik, hareketli ve sinirli kişi**

bundle² /'bʌndl/ verb **1 bundle sb into/out of/through sth** to push or carry someone somewhere quickly and roughly **birini bir yere kabaca ve hızlıca itmek, sokuşturmak, tıkıştırmak, ite kaka koymak, götürmek** *He was bundled into the back of a car and driven away.* **2** to include an extra computer program or other product with something you sell **satılan şeyin yanında başka bir ürün veya bilgisayar programı vermek**

bundle sth up phrasal verb to tie a number of things together **paket yapmak, toplamak, demet yapmak**

bundle (sb) up phrasal verb to put warm clothes on yourself or someone else **sarıp sarmalamak, sıcak giysilerle sarmak**

bung /bʌŋ/ verb **bung sth in/on, etc** UK informal to put something somewhere in a quick, careless way **gelişigüzel koyuvermek, tıkıştırmak** *Shall I bung a chicken in the oven for dinner?*

bung sth up phrasal verb UK informal to cause something to be blocked so that it does not work in the way it should **tıkanmak, kapanmak** [often passive] *The toilet was bunged up with paper.*

bungalow /ˈbʌŋɡᵊləʊ/ *noun* [C] a house that has all its rooms on the ground floor **tek katlı kır evi, bungalov**

bungee jumping /ˈbʌndʒiˌdʒʌmpɪŋ/ **(bungy jumping)** *noun* [U] the sport of jumping from a very high place while tied to a long elastic rope, so that the rope pulls you back before you hit the ground **yüksekçe yerden elastik bir halata bağlı olarak atlamak ve geri zıplamak, atlama sporu**

bungle /ˈbʌŋɡl/ *verb* [T] to do something wrong in a very careless or stupid way **bozmak, eline yüzüne bulaştırmak, berbat etmek** *a bungled robbery* ● **bungling** *noun* [U] **acemilik**

bunk /bʌŋk/ *noun* [C] a narrow bed in a ship, train, etc **kuşet, kamara yatağı, ranza**

'bunk ˌbeds *noun* [plural] two beds fixed together with one on top of the other **ranza, altlı üstlü yatak**

bunker /ˈbʌŋkəʳ/ *noun* [C] **1** an underground room where people go to be protected, especially from bombs **yer altı sığınağı, korugan 2** in golf, a hollow area filled with sand **golfte kum havuzu**

bunny /ˈbʌni/ *(also* ˈbunny ˌrabbit) *noun* [C] a child's word for 'rabbit' **çocuk dilinde tavşan**

buoy[1] /bɔɪ/ *noun* [C] a floating object used in water to mark dangerous areas for boats **şamandıra**

buoy[2] /bɔɪ/ *verb* **be buoyed (up) by sth** to feel happy or confident because of something **neşelenmek, morali yükselmek, keyfi yerine gelmek** *The team was buoyed up by their win last week.*

buoyant /ˈbɔɪənt/ *adjective* **1** [CONFIDENT] happy and confident **neşeli, keyfli, morali yüksek** *in a buoyant mood* **2** [BUSINESS] successful or making a profit **başarılı, kâr getiren, kârlı** *a buoyant economy* **3** [FLOATING] floating or able to float **yüzen, yüzebilen, su yüzeyinde kalabilen** ● **buoyancy** /ˈbɔɪənsi/ *noun* [U] **mutluluk**

ᵇᵘʳᵈᵉⁿ **burden** ...... İLE BİRLİKTE KULLANILAN KELİMELER

be/become a burden on/to sb ● carry the burden of sth ● ease/lighten/share the burden ● a heavy burden ● the burden of (doing) sth

---

burden /ˈbɜːdᵊn/ *noun* [C] something difficult or unpleasant that you have to deal with or worry about **ağır, yük, sorumluluk, zahmet, zor iş** *the burden of responsibility* ○ *I'd hate to be a burden to you when I'm older.* ● **burden** *verb* [T] to give someone something difficult or unpleasant to deal with or worry about **zahmet vermek, ağır yük yüklemek, sıkıntı vermek** *Sorry to burden you with my problems.* ● **burdensome** *adjective* **yorucu**

bureau /ˈbjʊərəʊ/ *noun* [C] *plural* **bureaux** or *US* **bureaus** **1** [OFFICE] a department or office **büro, iş yeri, ofis 2** [WRITING] *UK* a piece of furniture with drawers and a sloping top used for writing **çalışma masası, yazı masası 3** [CLOTHES] *US* (*UK* chest of drawers) a piece of furniture with drawers for keeping clothes in **kıyafetlerin konulduğu dolap, komidin**

bureaucracy /bjʊəˈrɒkrəsi/ *noun* **1** [U] complicated rules and processes used by an organization, especially when they do not seem necessary **bürokrasi, kırtasiye, gereksiz yazışma ve işlemler** *government bureaucracy* **2** [C, U] a government or organization in which there are a lot of officials in a lot of departments **devlet veya sistemin kendisi** ● **bureaucrat** /ˈbjʊərəʊkræt/ *noun* [C] someone working in a bureaucracy **devlet memuru, bürokrat** ● **bureaucratic** /ˌbjʊərəʊˈkrætɪk/ *adjective* **bürokratik**

burgeoning /ˈbɜːdʒᵊnɪŋ/ *adjective* growing very quickly **hızlı büyüyen, filiz veren** *a burgeoning population*

burger /ˈbɜːɡəʳ/ *noun* [C] a flat, round piece of food, usually made of meat, that is fried and served between pieces of bread **düz, yuvarlak ve ızgarada pişirilerek ekmek arası yenilen et, ekmekarası** *burger and fries* ○ *a veggie burger*

burglar /ˈbɜːɡləʳ/ *noun* [C] someone who gets into buildings illegally and steals things **soyguncu, hırsız**

'burglar aˌlarm *noun* [C] something that makes a noise if someone tries to get into a building illegally **hırsız alarmı**

burglarize /ˈbɜːɡləraɪz/ *verb* *US* burgle **hırsızlık yapmak, soymak**

burglary /ˈbɜːɡlᵊri/ *noun* [C, U] when someone gets into a building illegally and steals things **hırsızlık, soygun**

burgle /ˈbɜːɡl/ *UK* (*US* burglarize) *verb* [T] to get into a building illegally and steal things **soygun yapmak, soymak** [often passive] *They've been burgled twice recently.*

burial /ˈberiəl/ *noun* [C, U] when a dead body is put into the ground **defin, gömme, toprağa verme**

burly /ˈbɜːli/ *adjective* A burly man is large and strong. **iri yarı, sağlam yapılı, insan azmanı, kapı gibi**

ᴏ⚬ burn[1] /bɜːn/ *verb past* burnt *or* burned **1** [DESTROY] [I, T] to destroy something with fire, or to be destroyed by fire **yakmak, yanmak** *I burnt all his letters.* ○ *The factory burned to the ground.* ○ *He dropped his cigarette and burnt a hole in his jacket.* **2** [FLAMES] [I] to produce flames **yangın çıkarmak, yanmak** *The fire's burning well.* **3** [COOK TOO LONG] [I, T] If you burn something that you are cooking, you cook it too much and if something you are cooking burns, it cooks too much. **yemek vb. yakmak, ateşte yakarak yok etmek, dibini tutturmak, dibi tutmak** *Check the pizza - I think it's burning!* **4 burn yourself/your fingers, etc** to be hurt by fire or heat **kendini/parmağını vs. yakmak, yakarak yaralamak** *He burned his hand on the kettle.* **5** [ENERGY] [T] (*also* burn up) to use fuel to produce heat or energy **benzin yakmak** *to burn calories/fuel* **6** [COPY] [T] to copy music, information or images onto a CD **CD'ye bir şeyler kaydetmek** *He's burnt all his favourite records onto a CD.* **7** [SKIN] [I] to be very hot or sore **yanmak, kızarmak, acı ile yanmak** *Her cheeks were burning.* **8 burn with anger/hatred, etc** to feel an emotion very strongly **kızgınlıktan/nefretten yanıp tutuşmak, içi yanmak, öfkeden kudurmak, içi içini yemek**

burn (sth) down *phrasal verb* to destroy something, especially a building, by fire, or to be destroyed by fire **yanıp kül olmak, yakıp kül etmek** *Their house burnt down while they were away on holiday.*

burn out *phrasal verb* If a fire burns out, it stops producing flames because nothing remains that can burn. **için için yanarak sönmek, yavaş yavaş sönmek**

burn out *phrasal verb* to become ill or very tired from working too hard **kendini tüketmek, harap etmek, çok çalışmaktan hasta ve yorgun düşmek** *If Olivia keeps working late every night, she will burn out.*

burn (sth) up *phrasal verb* to destroy something completely, or to be destroyed completely by fire or heat **tamamen yakmak, yanıp kül olmak/etmek** *The satellite will burn up when it enters the atmosphere.*

burn[2] /bɜːn/ *noun* [C] a place where fire or heat has damaged or hurt something **yanık, yangın yeri** *She has a nasty burn on her arm.*

burner /ˈbɜːnəʳ/ *noun* **1** [C] a piece of equipment used to burn or heat something **yakmak veya ısıtmak için kullanılan araç, brülör, kazan, ocak 2 put sth on**

B

the back burner to not deal with something now, but intend to deal with it at a later time **bir şeyi ertelemek, sonraya bırakmak, bir horoz ötüm süresi kadar bekletmek**

burning /'bɜ:nɪŋ/ *adjective* **1** very hot **sıcak, alev alev yanan, kızgın, kor alev gibi** *the burning heat of the midday sun* **2 burning ambition/desire, etc** a very strong need to do something **yanıp tutuşma, güçlü bir tutku, istek, arzu 3 a burning issue/question** a subject or question that must be dealt with or answered quickly **acil çözüm veya ilgi bekleyen bir konu, sorun**

burnout /'bɜ:naʊt/ *noun* [U] *US* extreme tiredness, usually caused by working too much **yorgun, bitik, tükenmiş, harap**

burnt¹ /bɜ:nt/ *adjective* destroyed or made black by fire or heat **yanmış, kömür gibi olmuş** *burnt toast*

burnt² /bɜ:nt/ *past of* burn **yanmak' fiilinin geçmiş zaman hali**

burnt-out /ˌbɜ:nt'aʊt/ (*also* **burned-out** /ˌbɜ:nd'aʊt/) *adjective* **1** A burnt-out car or building has been almost completely destroyed by fire. **yanmış bina/araba, yangının mahvettiği araç/bina 2** *informal* tired and without enthusiasm because you have worked too hard **bitmiş, tükenmiş, yorgun, halsiz, takati kalmamış** *a burnt-out teacher*

burp /bɜ:p/ *verb* [I] to let air from your stomach come out of your mouth in a noisy way **geğirmek** ● **burp** *noun* [C] **geğirme**

burrow¹ /'bʌrəʊ/ *verb* [I] When an animal burrows, it digs a hole or passage in the ground to live in. **yuva yapmak, tünel açmak, oyuk açmak** *There are rabbits burrowing under the building.*

burrow² /'bʌrəʊ/ *noun* [C] a hole or passage in the ground dug by an animal to live in **tünel, oyuk, delik, yeraltına kazılan yuva/barınak**

burst¹ /bɜ:st/ *verb past* **burst 1** [I, T] If a container bursts, or if you burst it, it breaks suddenly, so that what is inside it comes out. **patla(t)mak, yar(ıl)mak, patlayıp param parça olmak** *A water pipe burst and flooded the cellar.* **2 burst in/out/through, etc** to move somewhere suddenly and forcefully **bir yere/yerden aniden ve zor kullanarak girmek, hareket etmek, çıkmak, geçmek** *Three masked men burst into the shop.* **3 burst into flames** to suddenly start burning **aniden tutuşmak, yanmaya başlamak 4 burst into laughter/tears, etc** to suddenly start laughing/crying, etc **birden göz yaşına boğulmak, gülmeye başlamak, ağlamak** *She burst into tears and ran away.* **5 burst open** to open suddenly and with force **pat/güm diye birden bire açılmak 6 be bursting with confidence/joy, etc** to be full of an emotion or quality **...ile dolu olmak, neşe/güven dolu olmak, duygu yüklü olmak** *She was bursting with pride.* **7 be bursting to do sth** *informal* to want to do something very much **bir şeyi yapmayı çok istemek, can atmak** *I was bursting to tell him about the party.*

burst out *phrasal verb* **1** to suddenly say something loudly **birşeyi aniden yüksek sesle söyleyivermek** *'Don't go!' he burst out.* **2 burst out laughing/crying** to suddenly start laughing/crying *I walked in and everyone burst out laughing.*

burst² /bɜ:st/ *noun* **1 a burst of sth** a sudden large amount of noise, activity, etc **gürültü, ses, eylem vb. şeylerin ani yükselişi/artışı** *a burst of applause/laughter* **2** [C] when something breaks open and what is inside it comes out **patlama, infilak**

bury /'beri/ *verb* [T] **1** to put a dead body into the ground **gömmek, defnetmek** [often passive] *He was buried next to his wife.* **2** to hide something in the ground or under something **bir şeyi toprağa gömmek, gizlemek** *buried treasure* ○ [often passive] *Two climbers were buried in the snow.* **3 bury your face/head in sth** to move your face/head somewhere where it is hidden **kafasını/yüzünü gizlemek, çevirmek, döndürmek** *She buried her face in her hands.* **4 bury yourself in sth** to give all your attention to something **bütün dikkatini bir şeye vermek, yöneltmek** *He buried himself in his work.* ➔See also: bury the **hatchet**.

∘⚬**bus** /bʌs/ *noun* [C] *plural* **buses** a large vehicle that carries passengers by road, usually along a fixed route **otobüs** *a school bus* ○ *I'll go home by bus.* ● **bus** *verb* [T] *UK* **bussing,** *past* **bussed,** *US* **busing,** *past* **bused** to take a group of people somewhere in a bus **otobüsle götürmek, taşımak** ➔See picture at **vehicle.**

bush

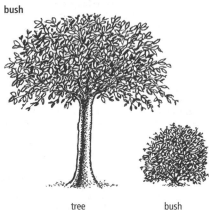

tree   bush

bush /bʊʃ/ *noun* **1** [C] a short, thick plant with a lot of branches **çalı, çalılık** *a rose bush* ○ *There was someone hiding in the bushes.* **2 the bush** wild parts of Australia or Africa where very few people live **Avustralya'nın ve Afrika'nın çok az yerleşim olan çorak toprakları 3 beat about the bush** to avoid talking about something difficult or embarrassing **lafı gevelemek, sözü döndürüp dolaştırmak, sadede gelmemek**

bushy /'bʊʃi/ *adjective* If hair or a plant is bushy, it has grown very thick. **çalılık** *bushy eyebrows*

busily /'bɪzɪli/ *adverb* in a busy, active way **meşgul bir şekilde, harıl harıl, kendini iyice kaptırmış şekilde** *He was busily writing notes.*

∘⚬**business** /'bɪznɪs/ *noun* **1** ‖TRADE‖ [U] the buying and selling of goods or services **ticaret, iş** *The shop closed last year, but now they're back in business.* ○ *We do a lot of business with China.* ○ *His company has gone out of business* (= failed). **2** ‖ORGANIZATION‖ [C] an organization that sells goods or services **işyeri, firma, ticarethane** *My uncle runs a small decorating business.* **3** ‖WORK‖ [U] work that you do to earn money **ticaret, gelir getiren iş** *She's in Vienna on business* (= working). **4 a nasty/strange, etc business** an unpleasant/strange, etc situation **nahoş/garip bir durum, iş, eylem, hadise, olay, vaka 5 be sb's (own) business** to be something private that other people do not need to know **(kendi/ şahsi) meselesi/işi olmak 6 be none of sb's business** If something is none of someone's business, they do not need to know about it, although they want to, because it does not affect them. **kimseye düşmemek, başkasını ilgilendirmemek, başkasının işi olmamak 7 mind your own business** used to tell someone in a rude way that you do not want them to ask about something private **Sana ne!', 'Sen kendi işine bak!', 'Her şeye burnunu sokma!', 'Başka işin yok mu senin!'** ↻See also: big business, show business.

'business ,class *noun* [U] a more expensive way of travelling by aircraft in which you sit in a separate part of the aircraft and are given better service **uçakta daha pahalı ve iyi servis sunulan yer uçaklarda daha çok ücret karşılığı bulunan ve daha iyi servis verilen ayrı bir bölüm**

businesslike /'bıznıslaık/ *adjective* working in a serious and effective way **iş becerir, becerikli, sistemli, pratik** *a businesslike manner*

businessman, businesswoman /'bıznısmən/, /'bıznıs,wumən/ *noun* [C] *plural* **businessmen** or **businesswomen** someone who works in business, usually in a high position in a company **işkadını/işadamı**

busk /bʌsk/ *verb* [I] UK to perform music in a public place to get money from people walking past **sokak çalgıcılığı yapmak, cadde üstünde para kazanmak için müzik yapmak** ● **busker** *noun* [C] **sokak çalgıcısı**

'bus ,station (*also UK* **coach station**) *noun* [C] a building where a bus starts or ends its journey **otobüs terminali**

'bus ,stop *noun* [C] a place where buses stop to let passengers get on or off **otobüs durağı** *I saw her waiting at the bus stop.*

bust¹ /bʌst/ *verb* [T] *past* **bust** or US **busted** *informal* 1 to break or damage something **kırmak, parçalamak** *The cops had to bust the door down to get in.* 2 If the police bust someone, they catch them and accuse them of a crime. **yakalamak, suçlamak, göz altına almak** [often passive] *He was busted for selling drugs.*

bust² /bʌst/ *noun* [C] 1 a woman's breasts, or their size in relation to clothing **meme, göğüs** *a 36-inch bust* 2 a model of someone's head and shoulders **büst** *a bronze bust of the Queen* 3 a **drug bust** when the police catch people selling or using illegal drugs **yasadışı uyuşturucu kullanna/satan kişilerin polis tarafından yakalanması**

bust³ /bʌst/ *adjective* 1 **go bust** If a business goes bust, it stops trading because it does not have enough money. **iflas etmek, batmak** *His company went bust, leaving huge debts.* 2 UK *informal* (US **busted** /'bʌstıd/) broken **bozuk, kırık, parçalanmış** *My phone's bust - can I use yours?*

bustle¹ /'bʌsl/ *verb* 1 **bustle about/around/in, etc** to move around and do things in a quick, busy way **koşuşturmak, telaş içinde sağa sola gidip gelmek** *There were lots of shoppers bustling about.* 2 **bustle with sth** to be full of people or activity **insan dolu olmak, canlı hareketli olmak, cıvıl cıvıl olmak, yaşam dolu olmak** *The town centre was bustling with people.*

bustle² /'bʌsl/ *noun* [U] people and activity **insan, telaş, faaliyet, koşuşturma** *We left the bustle of the city behind us.*

bustling /'bʌslıŋ/ *adjective* full of people and activity **hareketli, canlı, insan kaynaması** *a bustling city/ street*

bust-up /'bʌstʌp/ *noun* [C] UK *informal* a serious disagreement **ciddi anlaşmazlık/uyuşmazlık** *He left home after a big bust-up with his dad.*

o⁻**busy¹** /'bızi/ *adjective* 1 [PERSON] If you are busy, you are working hard, or giving your attention to a particular activity. **meşgul** *Mum was busy in the kitchen.* ○ [+ doing sth] *I was busy mowing the lawn.* ○ *I've got plenty of jobs to keep you busy.* ○ *He was too busy talking to notice us come in.* 2 [PLACE] A busy place is full of activity or people. **yoğun, insan ve eylem dolu olan** *a busy restaurant/ road* 3 [TIME] In a busy period you have a lot of things to do. **yoğunluk dönemi** *I've had a very busy week.* 4 [TELEPHONE] US (UK **engaged**) If a telephone line is busy, someone is using it. **meşgul, kullanılmakta olan**

busy² /'bızi/ *verb* **busy yourself** to spend time working or doing something **kendini meşgul etmek, kendine uğraşı bulmak** *We busied ourselves in the kitchen preparing dinner.*

o⁻**but¹** *strong form* /bʌt/ *weak form* /bət/ *conjunction* 1 [OPPOSITE INFORMATION] used to introduce something new that you say, especially something which is different or the opposite from what you have just said **fakat** *I'd drive you there, but I haven't got my car.* ○ *The tickets were expensive, but the kids really enjoyed it.* 2 [EXPLAINING WHY] used before you say why something did not happen or is not true **ancak** *I was going to go to his party, but I was ill.* 3 [SHOWING SURPRISE] used to show that you are surprised about what someone has just said **ama** *'Tim is leaving.' 'But why?'* 4 [CONNECTING PHRASES] used to connect 'excuse me' or 'I'm sorry' with what you say next **(özür dilemek ve araya girmek için) ama** *Excuse me, but would you mind shutting the door?*

o⁻**but²** *strong form* /bʌt/ *weak form* /bət/ *preposition* except **... nın/nin dışında, ...den başka** *Everyone but Andrew knows.* ○ *Can you buy me a sandwich? Anything but ham.* ○ *This is the last programme but one* (= the programme before the last).

but³ *strong form* /bʌt/ *weak form* /bət/ *adverb formal* only **yalnız, sadece** *We can but try.*

butcher¹ /'butʃə^r/ *noun* [C] someone who prepares and sells meat **kasap**

butcher² /'butʃə^r/ *verb* [T] 1 to kill someone in a very violent way **katletmek, delik deşik ederek öldürmek, katliam yapmak** 2 to cut an animal into pieces of meat **kasaplık yapmak, hayvan kesmek ve parçalamak**

butcher's /'butʃəz/ UK (US **'butcher ,shop**) *noun* [C] a shop that prepares and sells meat **kasap dükkânı** *I went to the butcher's to buy some sausages.*

butler /'bʌtlə^r/ *noun* [C] a man who opens the door, serves meat, etc in a large house as a job **kâhya**

butt¹ /bʌt/ *noun* 1 [BOTTOM] [C] US *informal* your bottom **kıç, popo** *He just sits on his butt all day long.* 2 [CIGARETTE] [C] the end of a cigarette that is left after it is smoked **izmarit** *There were cigarette butts all over the floor.* 3 [GUN] [C] the end of the handle of a gun **kabza, silah kabzası** *the butt of a rifle* 4 **a head butt** when you hit someone with the top, front part of your head **kafa vurma, kafa darbesi** 5 **kick sb's butt** US *informal* to punish someone or defeat someone with a lot of force **birinin kıçına tekme vurmak, cezalandırmak**

butt² /bʌt/ *verb* [T] to hit something with the top, front part of your head **kafa atmak, kafa vurmak** *He butted me in the stomach.*

butt in *phrasal verb* to interrupt or join in a conversation or activity when the other people do not want you to **izinsiz söze karışmak, lafını kesmek, müdahale**

B

etmek, nezaketsizce araya girmek *The interviewer kept butting in and wouldn't let me answer the question.*

o⇥**butter**[1] /'bʌtər/ *noun* **1** [U] a soft, pale yellow food made from cream that you put on bread and use in cooking tereyağ ⊃Orta kısımdaki renkli sayfalarına bakınız. **2 butter wouldn't melt in sb's mouth** used to say that someone looks as if they would never do anything wrong masummuş gibi görünmek, kendini çok iyi gizleyebilmek ⊃See also: peanut butter.

butter[2] /'bʌtər/ *verb* [T] to put a layer of butter on something yağ sürmek *hot buttered toast*
butter sb up *phrasal verb informal* to be very nice to someone so that they will do what you want them to do iltifat etmek, yağlamak, yağ çekmek, pohpohlamak, güzel sözlerle bir şeyi yapmaya ikna etmek

buttercup /'bʌtəkʌp/ *noun* [C] a small, bright yellow flower düğün çiçeği

butterfly /'bʌtəflaɪ/ *noun* **1** [C] an insect with large, patterned wings kelebek ⊃See picture at insect. **2 have butterflies (in your stomach)** to feel very nervous about something that you are going to do içi tir tir titremek, midesine kramplar girmek, bir şeyden dolayı aşırı endişe duymak

buttock /'bʌtək/ *noun* [C] one of the two sides of your bottom kalça, kalçanın her iki tarafı

button[1] /'bʌtᵊn/ *noun* [C] **1** a small, round object that you push through a hole to fasten clothing düğme *to do up/undo your buttons* **2** a switch that you press to control a piece of equipment bir şeyi açıp kapama düğmesi, tuş *Press the play button to listen to your recording.* ⊃See also: belly button.

button[2] /'bʌtᵊn/ *(also* button up*) verb* [T] to fasten a piece of clothing with buttons düğmelemek *Jack buttoned up his jacket.* ⊃Opposite unbutton.

buttonhole /'bʌtᵊnhəʊl/ *noun* [C] **1** a hole that you push a button through on a piece of clothing ilik, düğme iliği **2** UK a flower worn on a jacket or coat for a special occasion yakaya takılan çiçek

buxom /'bʌksəm/ *adjective* A buxom woman has large breasts. iri memeli, büyük göğüslü

o⇥**buy**[1] /baɪ/ *verb* [T] *past* bought to get something by paying money for it satın almak *I went to the shop to buy some milk.* ○ *They* bought *their house for £14,000.* ○ [+ two objects] *He bought me a camera for my birthday.*
buy into sth *phrasal verb* to believe in something inanmak, itikat etmek, kabul etmek *I don't buy into all that dieting nonsense.*
buy sb/sth out *phrasal verb* to buy part of a company or building from someone else so that you own all of it birinin elindekinin hepsini satın almak, bir binanın veya şirketin bir kısmını satın almak
buy sth up *phrasal verb* to quickly buy a lot of something, often all that is available bir şeyin mevcudunu, tamamını satın almak, kapatmak

buy[2] /baɪ/ *noun* **a good buy** when you buy something good for a cheap price iyi alışveriş, kârlı alışveriş *This coat was a really good buy.*

buyer /'baɪər/ *noun* [C] someone who buys something alıcı, alışveriş yapan kişi

buyout /'baɪaʊt/ *noun* [C] when a group of people buy the company that they work for çalıştığı şirketi satın alma

buzz[1] /bʌz/ *noun* **1** [no plural] *informal* a feeling of excitement, energy, or pleasure heyecan, coşku ve memnuniyet *He gets a real buzz from going to the gym.* **2** [C] a continuous sound like a bee makes vızıldama, vız sesi

buzz[2] /bʌz/ *verb* [I] **1** to make a continuous sound like a bee vızıldamak, arı gibi ses çıkarmak *I can hear*

something buzzing. **2** to be full of activity or excitement heyecan ve eylem dolu olmak, sürekli faal olmak, arı gibi meşgul olmak, yerinde duramamak *The crowd was buzzing with excitement.* **3 buzz about/ around, etc** to move around in a quick and busy way etrafta vızır vızır dolaşmak, sürekli koşuşturmak

buzzer /'bʌzər/ *noun* [C] a piece of electronic equipment that makes a long sound as a signal zil *to press the buzzer*

buzzword /'bʌzwɜːd/ *noun* [C] a word or expression that has become fashionable, usually in a particular subject or group of people bir konuda veya bir grup insanla ilgili olarak meşhur ve çok kullanılır hale gelen sözcük, ifade *a new political buzzword*

o⇥**by**[1] *strong form* /baɪ/ *weak forms* /bɪ/, /bə/ *preposition* **1** [DO] used to show the person or thing that does something tarafından *She was examined by a doctor.* ○ *a painting by Van Gogh* **2** [HOW] through doing or using something ile, yoluyla, vasıtasıyla *Can I pay by cheque?* ○ *We'll get there by car.* ○ [+ doing sth] *Open the file by clicking on the icon.* **3** [HOLDING] holding a particular part of someone or something ... dan tutarak, dokunarak; ...erek, arak *She grabbed me by the arm.* **4** [NEAR] near or next to someone or something yanında, yanıbaşında *I'll meet you by the post office.* ○ *A small child stood by her side.* **5** [NOT LATER] not later than a particular time or date ... e kadar, ... saatine/tarihine kadar *Applications have to be in by the 31st.* **6** [ACCORDING TO] according to ... a/a göre, uyarınca *By law you must be eighteen to purchase alcohol.* **7** [PAST] past yanından, yakınından geçerek *He sped by me on a motorcycle.* **8** [AMOUNT] used to show measurements or amounts ölçüleri ve miktarları belirtirken, ... lık, ... e ... *twelve by ten metres of floor space* ○ *Interest rates have been increased by 0.25%.* ○ *I'm paid by the hour.* **9 by accident/chance/mistake, etc** as a result of an accident/chance/mistake, etc kazara, şans eseri, yanlışlıkla, hatayla *I went to the wrong room by mistake.* **10 by day/night** during the day/night gece/gündüz **11 by day by day/little by little/one by one, etc** used in particular phrases to mean 'gradually' or 'in units of' günbegün, azar azar, birer birer *Day by day he grew stronger.*

o⇥**by**[2] /baɪ/ *adverb* past geçerek, geçip giderek, yakınından geçerek *A motorcycle sped by.*

o⇥**bye** /baɪ/ *(also* bye-bye*) exclamation* goodbye Allah'a ısmarladık!, Hoşçakal! *Bye, see you tomorrow.*

by-election /'baɪɪˌlekʃᵊn/ *noun* [C] an election in the UK to choose a new member of parliament for an area because the old one has left or died ara seçim

bygone /'baɪɡɒn/ *adjective literary* **bygone age/days/ era, etc** a time in the past geçmiş, eski çağlar/günler/dönemler

bygones /'baɪɡɒnz/ *noun* **let bygones be bygones** something that you say to tell someone to forget about the unpleasant things in the past geçmiş geçmiştir, geçmişteki kötü anıları unutalım, geçmişe sünger çekelim, (argo) geçmişe mazi diyelim

bypass[1] /'baɪpɑːs/ *noun* [C] **1** a road that goes around a town and not through it çevre yolu, şehir dışından geçen yol **2** a medical operation to make blood flow along a different route and avoid a damaged part of the heart kalp ameliyatı *a coronary/heart bypass*

bypass[2] /'baɪpɑːs/ *verb* [T] **1** to go around a place or thing and not through it çevreyi dolaşarak geçmek, direk geçişten çok dolaylı geçişi kullanmak, çevreden dolanmak *I was hoping to bypass the city centre.* **2** to avoid dealing with someone or something by dealing directly with someone or something else boş vermek, atlamak, es geçmek *They bypassed him and went straight to his manager.*

by-product /'baɪ,prɒdʌkt/ *noun* [C] something that is produced when you are making or doing something else **yan ürün** *Carbon monoxide is a by-product of burning.*

bystander /'baɪ,stændə^r/ *noun* [C] someone who is near the place where an event happens, but not directly involved in it **seyirci, civarda bulunan kişi, temaşa eden, görgü tanığı** *The gunman began firing at innocent bystanders.*

byte /baɪt/ *noun* [C] a unit for measuring the amount of information a computer can store, equal to 8 bits (= smallest unit of computer information) **bilgisayarın saklayabileceği bilgiyi ölçmek için kullanılan birim, bayt**

C

C, c /siː/ the third letter of the alphabet **alfabenin 3. harfi**

C *written abbreviation for* Celsius or centigrade: measurements of temperature **ısı ölçüm işareti, santigrat** *30°C*

c. *written abbreviation for* circa (= used before a number or date to show that it is not exact) **bir rakam veya tarihten önce kullanılan ve tam olmadığını belirten işaret** *c. 1900*

cab /kæb/ *noun* [C] **1** *informal* a taxi (= car that you pay to travel in) **taksi, ticari yolcu taşıma aracı** *We took a cab to the theatre.* ○ *a cab driver* **2** the front part of a truck where the driver sits **şoför mahalli**

cabaret /ˈkæbəreɪ/ *noun* [C, U] when someone entertains people with songs, jokes, etc in a bar or restaurant **kabare** *He's appearing in cabaret at the Café Royal.*

cabbage /ˈkæbɪdʒ/ *noun* [C, U] a large, round vegetable that consists of a lot of thick leaves **lahana**

cabbie /ˈkæbi/ *noun* [C] *informal* someone who drives a taxi (= car that you pay to travel in) **taksi sürücüsü, şoförü**

cabin /ˈkæbɪn/ *noun* [C] **1** [HOUSE] a small, simple house made of wood **ahşap kulübe** *a log cabin* **2** [SHIP] a small room to sleep in on a ship **kamara 3** [AIRCRAFT] the area where passengers sit inside an aircraft **uçakta yolcuların seyahat ettiği yer**

ˈcabin ˌcrew *noun* [C] the people on an aircraft who take care of the passengers as their job **kabin ekibi, görevlileri**

cabinet /ˈkæbɪnət/ *noun* **1** **the Cabinet** a group of people in a government who are chosen by and who advise the highest leader **kabine, bakanlar kurulu, hükümet üyeleri** *a Cabinet minister/member* **2** [C] a cupboard with shelves or drawers to store or show things in **raflı, çekmeceli dolap** *a bathroom/medicine cabinet* ↪See also: **filing cabinet.**

cable¹ /ˈkeɪbl/ *noun* **1** [WIRE] [C, U] a wire covered by plastic that carries electricity, telephone signals, etc **telefon/elektrik kablosu** *overhead power cables* **2** [ROPE] [C, U] thick wire twisted into a rope **kablo 3** [SYSTEM] [U] the system of sending television programmes or telephone signals along wires under the ground **tv ve telefon kablolarının tümü** *cable TV* ○ *This channel is only available on cable.*

ˈcable ˌcar *noun* [C] a vehicle that hangs from thick cables and carries people up hills and mountains **teleferik**

ˌcable (TˈV) (also ˌcable ˈtelevision) *noun* [U] a system of sending television pictures and sound along wires buried under the ground **kablolu televizyon yayını**

cache /kæʃ/ *noun* [C] a secret supply of something **bir şeyin gizli deposu, (argo) zula** *a cache of weapons*

cachet /ˈkæʃeɪ/ ⓤⓢ /kæʃˈeɪ/ *noun* [U] when something is admired or respected **saygınlık, hayranlık**

cacophony /kəˈkɒfəni/ *noun* [no plural] a loud, unpleasant mixture of sounds **anlaşılmaz gürültü, gürültü kirliliği**

cactus /ˈkæktəs/ *noun* [C] *plural* **cacti** /ˈkæktaɪ/ or **cactuses** a plant with thick leaves for storing water and often sharp points that grows in deserts **kaktüs, çölde yetişen dikenli bir bitki**

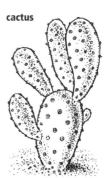
cactus

CAD /kæd/ *noun* [U] computer-aided design: the use of computers to design objects **bilgisayar destekli tasarım/çizim**

caddie /ˈkædi/ *noun* [C] someone who carries the equipment for someone playing golf **golf oyuncusunun malzemelerini taşıyan kimse, golfçü yamağı** ↪Orta kısımdaki renkli sayfalarına bakınız. ● **caddie** *verb* [I] **caddying**, *past* **caddied** to be a caddie for someone **birine yardımcı olmak, yamaklık yapmak**

cadet /kəˈdet/ *noun* [C] a young person who is training to be in a military organization, the police, etc **askeri öğrenci, harp okulu öğrencisi** *an army cadet*

caesarean (also US **cesarean**) /sɪˈzeəriən/ *noun* [C] an operation in which a baby is taken out of a woman through a cut in the front of her body **sezaryen, ameliyatla çocuk doğurma**

o⸱**cafe** (also **café**) /ˈkæfeɪ/ ⓤⓢ /kæˈfeɪ/ *noun* [C] a small restaurant where you can buy drinks and small meals **kahve, küçük lokanta, büfe**

cafeteria /ˌkæfəˈtɪəriə/ *noun* [C] a restaurant where you collect and pay for your food and drink before you eat it **kafeterya** *a school cafeteria*

caffeine /ˈkæfiːn/ *noun* [U] a chemical in coffee, tea, etc that makes you feel more awake **kafein, uyarıcı etki yapan, çay ve kahvede bulunan madde**

cage /keɪdʒ/ *noun* [C] a container made of wire or metal bars used for keeping birds or animals in **kafes** *a bird cage* ↪See also: **rib cage.**

cage

cagey /ˈkeɪdʒi/ *adjective* If someone is cagey, they are not very willing to give information, and you may think they are not honest. **ağzı sıkı, sır tutabilen, sırdaş** *He's very cagey about his past.*

cajole /kəˈdʒəʊl/ *verb* [I, T] to persuade someone to do something by being friendly or by promising them something **birini bir şey yapmaya güzellikle ikna etmek, vaatlerde bulunarak yapmasını sağlamak, aklını çelmek, ikna etmek** [+ into + doing sth] *She cajoled me into helping with the dinner.*

o⸱**cake** /keɪk/ *noun* [C, U] **1** a sweet food made from flour, butter, sugar, and eggs mixed together and baked **pasta, kek** *a chocolate/fruit cake* ○ *a piece/slice of cake* ○ *to bake/make a cake* ↪Orta kısımdaki renkli sayfalarına bakınız. **2 have your cake and eat it** to have or do two things that it is usually impossible to have or do at the same time **ne yardan ne serden vazgeçmek, her iki şeyi de yapmak; bir şeyden her iki manada kâr sağlamak** ⊃See also: the **icing** on the cake, be a **piece**¹ of cake.

caked /keɪkt/ *adjective* **be caked in/with sth** to be covered with a thick, dry layer of something **bulanmak, sıvanmak** *His boots were caked in mud.*

calamity /kə'læməti/ *noun* [C] a sudden, bad event that causes a lot of damage or unhappiness **afet, beklenmedik kötü olay**

calcium /'kælsiəm/ *noun* [U] a chemical element in teeth, bones, and chalk (= a soft, white rock) (symbol Ca) **kalsiyum**

calculate /'kælkjəleɪt/ *verb* **1** [T] to discover an amount or number using mathematics **hesaplamak** *to calculate a cost/percentage* **2 be calculated to do sth** to be intended to have a particular effect **kasıtlı olmak, kötü amaçlar için önceden tasarlanmış olmak** *His comments were calculated to embarrass the prime minister.*

calculated /'kælkjəleɪtɪd/ *adjective* based on careful thought or planning, not on emotion **hesaplanmış, her şey hesaba katılmış** *a calculated risk/decision*

calculating /'kælkjəleɪtɪŋ/ *adjective* Calculating people try to get what they want by thinking carefully and without emotion, and not caring about other people. **her şeyi hesaba katma, başkalarına aldırış etmeyen ve duygusal davranmayan, hesapçı; içten pazarlıklı** *a cold, calculating criminal*

🧩 **calculation** ...... İLE BİRLİKTE KULLANILAN KELİMELER

do/perform a calculation ● a **complex/precise/quick/rough** calculation

calculation /ˌkælkjə'leɪʃ°n/ *noun* **1** [C, U] when you use mathematics to discover a number or amount **hesaplama** *I did some quick calculations to see if I could afford to buy it.* **2** [U] when someone thinks very carefully about something without any emotion **bir şeyi en ince ayrıntısına kadar düşünüp, hesap etme**

calculator /'kælkjəleɪtər/ *noun* [C] an electronic device that you use to do mathematical calculations **hesap makinası** *a pocket calculator*

calendar /'kæləndər/ *noun* **1** [C] something that shows all the days, weeks, and months of the year **takvim 2 the Christian/Jewish/Western, etc calendar** the system used to measure and arrange the days, weeks, months and special events of the year according to Christian/Jewish/Western, etc tradition **Hıristiyan/Yahudi/Batı vs. Takvimi 3 the political/school/sporting, etc calendar** the events that are arranged during the year for a particular activity or organization **siyasi/okul/spor vs. Takvimi**

calf /kɑːf/ *noun* [C] *plural* **calves** /kɑːvz/ **1** a young cow **buzağı 2** the back of your leg below your knee **baldır** ⊃Orta kısımdaki renkli sayfalarına bakınız.

calibre UK (US **caliber**) /'kælɪbər/ *noun* [U] **1** the quality or level of ability of someone or something **bir şeyin, birisinin yetenek seviyesi veya kalitesi; kalibresi** *The calibre of applicants was very high.* **2** the measurement across the inside of a gun, or across a bullet **mermi veya silah kalibresi, ölçüsü**

CALL /kɔːl/ *abbreviation for* computer aided language learning: a way of learning languages using computers **bilgisayar destekli dil öğrenimi**

🧩 **call** ...... İLE BİRLİKTE KULLANILAN KELİMELER

make/get/take a call ● **give** sb a call ● a call **from/to** sb

◦ⁿ**call**¹ /kɔːl/ *verb* **1 be called sth** to have a particular name **belli bir isimle çağırılmak, anılmak** *a man called John* ○ *What's your dog called?* ○ *Their latest record is called "Ecstasy".* **2** GIVE NAME [+ two objects] to give someone or something a particular name **birine belli bir isim vermek, o isimle çağırmak** *I want to call the baby Alex.* **3** DESCRIBE [+ two objects] to describe someone or something in a particular way **birini,/bir şeyi hususi olarak tasvir etmek, isimlendirmek** *She called him a liar.* **4** ASK TO COME [T] to ask someone to come somewhere **çağırmak** *She called me into her office.* **5** SHOUT [I, T] (*also* **call out**) to shout or say something in a loud voice **bağırmak, seslenmek, yüksek sesle çağırmak** *I thought I heard someone calling my name.* **6** TELEPHONE [I, T] to telephone someone **telefonla aramak** *He called me every night while he was away.* ○ *Has anyone called the police?* **7** VISIT [I] (*also* **call by/in/round**) UK to visit someone for a short time **kısa ziyarette bulunmak** *John called round earlier.* **8 call an election/meeting, etc** to arrange for an election/meeting, etc to happen **bir toplantı/seçim talebinde bulunmak/ayarlamak** *The chairman has called an emergency meeting.* ⊃See also: call sb's **bluff**², call it a **day**.

call back *phrasal verb* UK to go back to a place in order to see someone or collect something **birini görmeye veya bir şeyi almaya bir yere geri gitmek** *I'll call back later to pick up the books.*

call (sb) back *phrasal verb* to telephone someone again, or to telephone someone who telephoned you earlier **birini geri aramak, aramasına yanıt vermek** *I can't talk now - I'll call you back in ten minutes.*

call for sth *phrasal verb* **1** to demand that something happens **gereksinim duymak, talepte bulunmak, gerektirmek** *to call for a ban on guns* **2** to need or deserve a particular action or quality **hak etmek, gerektirmek** *You passed your test? This calls for a celebration!*

call for sb *phrasal verb* to go to a place in order to collect someone **birini gidip almak, gidip getirmek** *I'll call for you at eight.*

call sth off *phrasal verb* **1** to decide that a planned event or activity will not happen because it is not possible, useful, or wanted now **iptal etmek, gerekli görmeyip yapmamak, vazgeçmek** *The game has been called off because of the weather.* **2** to decide to stop an activity **vazgeçmek, iptal etmek** *Police have called off the search.*

call on sb to do sth *phrasal verb* to ask someone in a formal way to do something **birinden bir şeyi resmi yoldan yapmasını istemek, ricada bulunmak** *He called on the rebels to stop fighting.*

call (sb) up *phrasal verb* mainly US to telephone someone **telefonla aramak** *My dad called me up to tell me the good news.*

call sth up *phrasal verb* to find and show information on a computer screen **bir şeyi bilgisayar ekranında görüntülemek** *I'll just call up your account details.*

be called up *phrasal verb* to be ordered to join a military organization or asked to join an official team **askere çağırılmak, askerlik için celp edilmek veya resmi bir takıma katılması istenmek** *He was called up soon after the war started.*

◦ⁿ**call**² /kɔːl/ *noun* [C] **1** TELEPHONE (*also* **phone call**) when you use the telephone **arama, telefonla arama** *Give me a call at the weekend.* ○ *I got a call from Sue this morning.* **2 a call for sth** a demand for something to happen **talep** *a call for action/peace* **3** VISIT

a short visit **kısa ziyaret** *I thought I'd pay Gary a call.*
4 SHOUT when someone shouts something **çağırma, bağırma, seslenme 5** BIRD a sound made by a bird or other animal **hayvan veya kuş sesi 6 sb's call** *informal* when someone can decide something **kendisinin kararı, karar vereceği şey** *I don't mind what we do - it's your call.* **7 call for sth** when people want or need a particular thing **talebinde bulunmak, gerektirmek** *There's not much call for interior designers round here.* **8 be on call** to be ready to go to work if you are needed, as part of your job **işe gitmeye, çalışmaya hazır olmak, emre amade olmak, her an hazır olmak 9 a close call** when something you do not want to happen nearly happens **beklenmedik bir şeyin olması, vuku bulması, meydana gelmesi, neredeyse** ●See also: be at sb's **beck and call, wake-up call.**

'call ˌcentre *noun* [C] *UK* a place where people use telephones to provide information to customers, or to sell goods or services **çağrı merkezi**

caller /ˈkɔːləʳ/ *noun* [C] **1** someone who makes a telephone call **arayan kişi, arayan** *an anonymous caller* **2** *mainly UK* someone who visits for a short time **ziyaretçi, ziyarete gelen**

call-in /ˈkɔːlɪn/ *US* (*UK* phone-in) *noun* [C] a television or radio programme in which the public can ask questions or give opinions over the telephone **dinleyici ve izleyicilerden telefonla katılması ve fikirlerini söylemesi istenen radyo veya tv programı**

calling /ˈkɔːlɪŋ/ *noun* [C] a strong feeling that you should do a particular type of work **meslek, severek yaptığı iş, görev aşkı** *She found her true calling in teaching.*

callous /ˈkæləs/ *adjective* cruel and not caring about other people **katı, duyarsız** *a callous remark* ● **callously** *adverb* **acımasızca**

◦─**calm¹** /kɑːm/ *adjective* **1** PERSON relaxed and not worried, frightened, or excited **sakin** *a calm voice/manner* ○ *Try to stay calm - the doctor will be here soon.* **2** SEA If the sea is calm, it is still and has no large waves. **sakin, dalgasız, (deniz) çarşaf gibi, durgun 3** WEATHER If the weather is calm, there are no storms or wind. **(hava) sakin, rüzgârsız, fırtınasız, durgu** ● **calmness** *noun* [U] **sükunet, sakinlik**

calm² /kɑːm/ *noun* [U] when people or conditions are calm **sükûnet, sessizlik, sakinlik, huzur, dinginlik**

calm³ /kɑːm/ *verb* [T] to make someone stop feeling upset, angry, or excited **sakinleştirmek, teskin etmek** *The police tried to calm the crowd.* ○ *a calming effect*

calm (sb) down *phrasal verb* to stop feeling upset, angry, or excited, or to make someone stop feeling this way **sakinleşmek, sakinleştirmek,** *Calm down and tell me what's wrong.*

calmly /ˈkɑːmli/ *adverb* in a relaxed way **sakin bir şekilde** *He spoke slowly and calmly.*

calorie /ˈkælᵊri/ *noun* [C] a unit for measuring the amount of energy food provides **kalori** *I try to eat about 2000 calories a day.*

calves /kɑːvz/ *plural of* calf **buzağılar**

camaraderie /ˌkæməˈrɑːdᵊri/ *noun* [U] special friendship felt by people who work together or experience something together **iş arkadaşlığı, yarenlik, iş dostluğu, ortak çaba sonucu oluşan arkadaşlık**

camcorder /ˈkæmˌkɔːdᵊʳ/ *noun* [C] a camera that you can hold in your hand and that takes moving pictures **el kamerası, görüntü kayıt cihazı**

came /keɪm/ *past tense of* come **'gelmek' fiilinin 2. hali**

camel /ˈkæmᵊl/ *noun* [C] a large animal that lives in the desert and has one or two humps (= raised parts on its back) **deve**

camel

cameo /ˈkæmiəʊ/ *noun* [C] when someone famous appears for a short time in a film or play **meşhur birinin bir film ya da oyunda kısa bir süre görünmesi** *a cameo role*

◦─**camera** /ˈkæmᵊrə/ *noun* [C] a piece of equipment used to take photographs or to make films **kamera** *a digital camera* ○ *a television camera*

cameraman /ˈkæmᵊrəmæn/ *noun* [C] *plural* **cameramen** someone who operates a television camera or film camera as their job **kameraman**

camisole /ˈkæmɪsəʊl/ *noun* [C] a piece of women's underwear for the top half of the body, with thin straps that go over the shoulders **askılı bayan iç çamaşırı, fanila** *a lace camisole* ●Orta kısımdaki renkli sayfalarına bakınız.

camouflage /ˈkæməflɑːʒ/ *noun* [U] when the colour or pattern on something is similar to the area around it making it difficult to see **kamuflaj, gizleme** *a camouflage jacket* ● **camouflage** *verb* [T] **saklamak, kamufle etmek**

camp¹ /kæmp/ *noun* **1** [C] an area where people stay in tents for a short time, usually for a holiday **kamp 2 an army/prison/refugee, etc camp** an area containing temporary buildings or tents used for soldiers/prisoners/refugees (= people forced to leave their home), etc **ordu/hapishane/sığınmacı, vs. Kampı** ●See also: base camp, concentration camp.

camp² /kæmp/ (*also* camp out) *verb* [I] to stay in a tent or temporary shelter **kamp yapmak** *We camped on the beach for two nights.*

┌───┐
│ 🔲🔲🔲 *campaign* .... İLE BİRLİKTE KULLANILAN KELİMELER │
└───┘

launch/mount/run a campaign ● a campaign **against/for** sth ● an **advertising/election** campaign

campaign¹ /kæmˈpeɪn/ *noun* [C] **1** a series of organized activities or events intended to achieve a result **kampanya, düzenlenen bir dizi faaliyetler bütünü** *an advertising/election campaign* **2** a series of military attacks **bir dizi askeri saldırı** *a bombing campaign*

campaign² /kæmˈpeɪn/ *verb* [I] to organize a series of activities to try to achieve something **kampanya düzenlemek** *to campaign against/for something* ● **campaigner** *noun* [C] *an animal rights campaigner* **seçime giren aday**

camper /ˈkæmpəʳ/ *noun* [C] **1** someone who stays in a tent on holiday **kamp yapan kişi 2** (*also* 'camper ˌvan) a vehicle containing a bed, kitchen equipment, etc that you can live in **içinde yatak, mutfak eletleri, vs. bulunduran kamp aracı, karavan**

camping /ˈkæmpɪŋ/ *noun* [U] when you stay in a tent for a holiday **kamp yapma** *We're going camping in France this summer.* ○ *a camping trip*

campsite /ˈkæmpsaɪt/ (*also* *US* campground /ˈkæmpɡraʊnd/) *noun* [C] an area where people can stay in tents for a holiday **kamp alanı, kamp yerleşim alanı**

campus /ˈkæmpəs/ *noun* [C, U] the land and buildings belonging to a college or university **yerleşke, üniver-**

C

sitenin bulunduğu alan, yer *I lived* **on campus** *in my first year.*

o⌐**can**[1] *strong form* /kæn/ *weak forms* /kən/, /kn/ *modal verb past* **could 1** ABILITY to be able to do something **yetenek, ...ebilmek, ...abilmek** *We can't pay the rent.* ○ *Can you drive?* **2** PERMISSION to be allowed to do something **izin vermede/istemede kullanılır** *You can't park here.* ○ *Can I go now?* **3** ASK used to ask someone to do or provide something **bir şeyi istemede, rica etmede kullanılır** *Can you tell her to meet me outside?* ○ *Can I have a drink of water?* **4** OFFER used to politely offer to do something **nazikçe bir şeyi teklif etmede, sunmada kullanılır** *Can I carry those bags for you?* **5** POSSIBLE used to talk about what is possible **bir olasılığı ifadede kullanılır** *You can buy stamps from the shop on the corner.* ○ *Smoking can cause cancer.* **6** TYPICAL used to talk about how someone often behaves or what something is often like **birinin zamana zaman nasıl davranabileceğini ya da bir şeyin neye benzediğini ifadede kullanılır** *She can be really rude at times.* **7** SURPRISE used to show surprise or lack of belief **sürpriz ve şaşkınlığı belirtmede kullanılır** *You can't possibly be hungry already!* ○ *Can you believe it?* ➔See study page **Modal verbs** on page Centre 22.

can[2] /kæn/ *noun* [C] **1** a closed, metal container for food or liquids **metal kutu** *a can of soup/beans* ○ *a can of paint* ➔See picture at **container**. **2 a can of worms** a situation which causes a lot of trouble for you when you start to deal with it **zor, çetin, meşakkatli bir durum** ➔See also: **trash can, watering can.**

can[3] /kæn/ *verb* [T] **canning,** *past* **canned** to put food or drink into metal containers in a factory **konservelemek, konserve yapmak** *canned tomatoes*

Canadian /kə'neɪdiən/ *adjective* relating to Canada **Kanada'ya dair, ait** ● **Canadian** *noun* [C] someone who comes from Canada **Kanada'da doğma, orada yetişmiş, oralı**

canal /kə'næl/ *noun* [C] an artificial river built for boats to travel along or to take water where it is needed **kanal, su kanalı**

canary /kə'neəri/ *noun* [C] a small, yellow bird that sings **kanarya**

cancel /'kænsᵊl/ *verb* [T] UK **cancelling,** *past* **cancelled,** US **canceling,** *past* **canceled 1** to say that an organized event will not now happen **iptal etmek** [often passive] *The meeting has been cancelled.* **2** to stop an order for goods or services that you do not now want **bir siparişi iptal etmek**
cancel sth out *phrasal verb* If one thing cancels out another thing, it stops it from having any effect. **birbirini götürmek, eşit olmak**

cancellation /ˌkænsᵊl'eɪʃᵊn/ *noun* [C, U] when someone decides that an event will not now happen or stops an order for something **iptal** *a last-minute cancellation*

Cancer /'kænsəʳ/ *noun* [C, U] the sign of the zodiac which relates to the period of 22 June - 22 July, or a person born during this period **yengeç burcu** ➔See picture at **zodiac.**

⌐⌐ **cancer** ...... İLE BİRLİKTE KULLANILAN KELİMELER

get/have cancer ● **breast/lung/prostate/skin** cancer ● cancer **of the** [liver/stomach, etc] ● cancer **patients/sufferers** ● cancer **research/treatment**

cancer /'kænsəʳ/ *noun* [C, U] a serious disease that is caused when cells in the body grow in a way that is uncontrolled and not normal **kanser** *breast/lung cancer* ○ *His wife died of cancer.* ● **cancerous** *adjective* a cancerous growth **kanserli**

candid /'kændɪd/ *adjective* honest, especially about something that is unpleasant or embarrassing **içten,**

samimi, açık kalpli *She was very candid about her personal life in the interview.* ● **candidly** *adverb* **içten**

candidacy /'kændɪdəsi/ *noun* [U] when someone is a candidate in an election **adaylık**

candidate /'kændɪdət/ *noun* [C] **1** one of the people taking part in an election or trying to get a job **aday** *a presidential candidate* **2** UK someone who is taking an exam **aday, yarışmacı, sınava katılan**

candle /'kændl/ *noun* [C] a stick of wax with string going through it that you burn to produce light **mum** ➔Orta kısımdaki renkli sayfalarına bakınız.

candle

candlelight /'kændllaɪt/ *noun* [U] light produced by a candle **mum ışığı**

candlestick /'kændlstɪk/ *noun* [C] an object that holds a candle **şamdan**

can-do /'kænˌduː/ *adjective informal* determined to deal with problems and achieve results **kararlı, azimli, göğüs geren, başarma hevesinde olan** *I really admire her can-do attitude.*

candour UK (US **candor**) /'kændəʳ/ *noun* [U] when you speak honestly, especially about something that is unpleasant or embarrassing **içtenlik, samimiyet, açık kalplilik, dürüstlük**

candy /'kændi/ *noun* [C, U] US a small piece of sweet food made from sugar, chocolate, etc **şeker** *a box of candy* ○ *a candy bar*

cane[1] /keɪn/ *noun* **1** STEM [C, U] the long, hard, hollow stem of some plants, sometimes used to make furniture **kamış 2** WALK [C] a long stick used by people to help them walk **baston, asa 3** PUNISH [C] UK a long stick used in the past to hit children at school **sopa, değnek**

cane[2] /keɪn/ *verb* [T] UK to hit someone, especially a school student, with a stick as a punishment **sopalamak, değnekle vurmak, dövmek**

canine[1] /'keɪnaɪn/ *adjective* relating to dogs **köpeklere özgü**

canister /'kænɪstəʳ/ *noun* [C] a metal container for gases or dry things **teneke kutu, bidon** *a gas canister*

cannabis /'kænəbɪs/ *mainly UK* (*mainly US* **marijuana**) *noun* [U] a drug that some people smoke for pleasure and that is illegal in many countries **esrar**

canned /kænd/ (*also UK* **tinned**) *adjective* Canned food is sold in metal containers. **konserve, konservelenmiş**

cannibal /'kænɪbᵊl/ *noun* [C] someone who eats human flesh **yamyam, insan eti yiyen** ● **cannibalism** *noun* [U] **yamyamlık**

cannon /'kænən/ *noun* [C] a very large gun, in the past one that was on wheels **(silah) top**

o⌐**cannot** /'kænɒt/ *modal verb* the negative form of 'can' **muktedir olmak' fiilinin olumsuz hali** *I cannot predict what will happen.*

cannot

Cannot her zaman tek kelime olarak yazılır. **Can not** yazmayın. **Cannot** olarak yazın.: ~~I can not believe that I won first prize.~~ Yanlış cümle örneği

I cannot believe that I won first prize.

canny /'kæni/ *adjective* clever and able to think quickly, especially about money or business **bilhassa ticaret ve**

para konusunda kafası çalışan, zehir gibi, zeki ve çabuk düşünebilen *a canny businessman*

canoe /kə'nu:/ *noun* [C] a small, narrow boat with pointed ends that you move using a paddle (= stick with a wide, flat part) kano • **canoeing** *noun* [U] the activity of travelling in a canoe kano seyahati, gezintisi

canoe

canon /'kænən/ *noun* [C] a Christian priest who works in a cathedral (= large, important church) katedralde görevli rahip *the Canon of Westminster*

'can ,opener (*also UK* tin opener) *noun* [C] a piece of kitchen equipment for opening metal food containers konserve açacağı ⊃Orta kısımdaki renkli sayfalarına bakınız.

canopy /'kænəpi/ *noun* [C] a cover or type of roof for protection or decoration tente, güneşlik, gölgelik

can't /kɑːnt/ *modal verb* **1** *short for* cannot **muktedir olmak' fiilinin kısaltılmış olumsuz hali** *I can't find my keys.* **2** used to suggest that someone should do something **bir şeyin yapılmamasını önermede kullanılır** *Can't you ask Jonathan to help?*

canteen /kæn'tiːn/ *noun* [C] a restaurant in an office, factory, or school kantin

canter /'kæntər/ *verb* [I] When a horse canters, it runs quite fast. atın dört nala koşması • **canter** *noun* [no plural] dört nala koşmak

canvas /'kænvəs/ *noun* **1** [U] strong cloth used for making sails, tents, etc kalın kumaş; branda, çadır bezi **2** [C] a piece of canvas used for a painting tuval

canvass /'kænvəs/ *verb* **1** [I, T] to try to persuade people to vote for someone in an election oy toplamak, propaganda yapmak *He's canvassing for the Labour party.* **2** [T] to ask people their opinion about something anket yapmak, nabız yoklamak *The study canvassed the views of over 9000 people.*

canyon /'kænjən/ *noun* [C] a deep valley with very steep sides kanyon

cap¹ /kæp/ *noun* [C] **1** a hat with a flat, curved part at the front kep, şapka, başlık *a baseball cap* ⊃Orta kısımdaki renkli sayfalarına bakınız. **2** a small lid that covers the top or end of something kapak, başlık ⊃See also: skull cap.

cap² /kæp/ *verb* [T] **capping**, *past* **capped 1** END to be the last and the best or worst event in a series of events bir dizi eylemde en iyisi veya en kötüsü olmak *The party capped a wonderful week.* **2** LIMIT to put a limit on an amount of money that can be borrowed, charged, etc sınırlamak, limit koymak [often passive] *The interest rate has been capped at 5%.* **3** COVER to cover the top of something örtmek, kapatmak, tepesini kapamak [often passive] *The mountains were capped with snow.*

capability /,keɪpə'bɪləti/ *noun* [C, U] the ability or power to do something yeterlik, yetenek, güç, iktidar [+ to do sth] *Both players have the capability to win this match.*

capable /'keɪpəbl/ *adjective* **1** able to do things effectively and achieve results yeterli, güçlü, muktedir *She's a very capable young woman.* **2 capable of sth/ doing sth** having the ability or qualities to be able to do something bir şeye, şeyi yapmaya muktedir ve gücü olan, yeterli olan *She was capable of great cruelty.* ⊃Opposite incapable.

capacity /kə'pæsəti/ *noun* **1** CONTAIN [C, U] the largest amount or number that a container, building, etc can hold hacim, kapasite *The restaurant has a capacity of about 200.* ○ *The stadium was filled to capacity* (= com-

letely full). **2** PRODUCE [U] the amount that a factory or machine can produce üretim miktarı, kapasitesi *The factory is operating at full capacity* (= producing as much as possible). **3** ABILITY [C] the ability to do, experience, or understand something bir şeyi yapma, anlama ve uygulama yeteneği, yetisi, kapasitesi, kavrayış, kavrama *She has a great capacity for love.* **4** JOB [C] a position or job görev, iş *He attended 100 events last year in his capacity as mayor.*

cape /keɪp/ *noun* [C] **1** a loose coat without any sleeves that is fastened at the neck pelerin **2** a large area of land that goes out into the sea burun ,denize doğru uzanan kara parçası

caper /'keɪpər/ *noun* [C] something that is done as a joke, or intended to entertain people şaka, komik şeyler, eğlence *His new movie is a comic caper.*

capillary /kə'pɪləri/ ⑤ /'kæpəleri/ *noun* [C] a very thin tube that carries blood around the body, connecting arteries to veins kılcal damar

⚬ᵂⁱ**capital¹** /'kæpɪtəl/ *noun* **1** CITY [C] the most important city in a country or state, where the government is based başkent, başşehir *Paris is the capital of France.* **2** MONEY [U] an amount of money that you can use to start a business or to make more money anapara, kapital **3** LETTER [C] (*also* ,capital 'letter) a large letter of the alphabet used at the beginning of sentences and names büyük harf ⊃See study page Punctuation on page Centre 33 ⊃See also: block capitals.

capital² /'kæpɪtəl/ *adjective* **a capital crime/offence** a crime that can be punished by death idam/ölüm cezası gerektiren suç

capitalism /'kæpɪtəlɪzəm/ *noun* [U] a political and economic system in which industry is owned privately for profit and not by the state kapitalizm, bir tür siyasi ve ekonomik sistem

capitalist /'kæpɪtəlɪst/ *noun* [C] someone who supports capitalism kapitalist • **capitalist** *adjective a capitalist society* kapitalist

capitalize (*also UK* -ise) /'kæpɪtəlaɪz/ *verb* [T] to write something using capital letters, or starting with a capital letter büyük harfle yazmak
capitalize on sth *phrasal verb* to use a situation to achieve something good for yourself yararlanmak, kendi yararına kullanmak, çıkar sağlamak *He failed to capitalize on his earlier success.*

,capital 'punishment *noun* [U] when someone is killed by the state for committing a serious crime ölüm/ idam cezası

capitulate /kə'pɪtjʊleɪt/ *verb* [I] to stop disagreeing or fighting with someone and agree to what they want teslim olmak, başkalarının boyunduruğu altına girmek, boyun eğmek • **capitulation** /kə,pɪtjʊ'leɪʃən/ *noun* [C, U] teslim

cappuccino /,kæpʊ'tʃiːnəʊ/ *noun* [C, U] coffee made with milk that has been heated with steam to produce a lot of small bubbles sütlü kahve, kapuçino

capricious /kə'prɪʃəs/ *adjective* likely to suddenly change your ideas or behaviour kaprisli

Capricorn /'kæprɪkɔːn/ *noun* [C, U] the sign of the zodiac which relates to the period of 23 December - 20 January, or a person born during this period oğlak burcu ⊃See picture at zodiac.

capsize /kæp'saɪz/ *verb* [I, T] If a boat capsizes, or if it is capsized, it turns over in the water. alabora olmak/ etmek, devrilmek, devirmek

capsule /'kæpsjuːl/ *noun* [C] **1** a small container with medicine inside that you swallow hap, kapsül **2** the part of a spacecraft that people live in **uçağın gövdesi, kabin**

captain[1] /'kæptɪn/ *noun* [C] **1** [SHIP] the person in control of a ship or aircraft **gemi kaptanı 2** [ARMY] an officer of middle rank in the army, navy, or air force **yüzbaşı (kara ve hava), albay (deniz) 3** [SPORT] the leader of a team **takım kaptanı**

captain[2] /'kæptɪn/ *verb* [T] to be the captain of a team, ship, or aircraft **kaptan olmak** *He has captained the England cricket team three times.*

captaincy /'kæptɪnsi/ *noun* [U] when someone is the captain of a team **kaptanlık**

caption /'kæpʃ³n/ *noun* [C] words written under a picture to explain it **alt yazı (resimler için)**

captivate /'kæptɪveɪt/ *verb* [T] to interest or attract someone very much **etkilemek, büyülemek** *She captivated film audiences with her beauty and charm.* ● **captivating** *adjective a captivating performance* **cezbedici**

captive[1] /'kæptɪv/ *adjective* **1** A captive person or animal is being kept somewhere and is not allowed to leave. **esir olmuş/edilmiş, tutsak edilen, 2 a captive audience/market** a group of people who have to watch something or have to buy something because they do not have a choice **tutsak edilmiş dinleyici, başka alternatifi olmayan şeyi almak zorunda olan insanlar 3 hold/take sb captive** to keep someone as a prisoner, or make someone a prisoner **tusak etmek, esir almak, tutsak edilmek**

captive[2] /'kæptɪv/ *noun* [C] someone who is kept as a prisoner **esir, tutsak**

captivity /kæp'tɪvəti/ *noun* [U] when a person or animal is kept somewhere and is not allowed to leave **esaret, tutsaklık** *lion cubs born in captivity*

capture[1] /'kæptʃəʳ/ *verb* [T] **1** [PRISONER] to catch someone and make them your prisoner **ele geçirmek, esir etmek, tutsak etmek** *Two soldiers were captured by the enemy.* **2** [CONTROL] to get control of a place with force **bir yerin kontrolünü ele geçirmek** *Rebel troops have captured the city.* **3** [GET] to succeed in getting something when you are competing against other people **elde etmek, ele geçirmek, zaptetmek** *The Green Party has captured 12% of the vote.* **4** [DESCRIBE] to show or describe something successfully using words or pictures **bir şeyi resim ve kelimeleri kullanarak tasvir etmek, göstermek** *His book really captures the spirit of the place.* **5 capture sb/sth on camera/film, etc** to record someone or something on camera/film, etc **kamera ile kaydetmek, yakalamak 6 capture sb's attention/imagination** to make someone very interested or excited **birinin ilgisini ve hayal gücünü yakalamak, heyecanlandırmak, ilgilenmesini sağlamak** *The campaign has really captured the public's imagination.* **7 capture sb's heart** to make someone love you **kendine aşık etmek, kalbini çalmak** *She captured the hearts of the nation.*

capture[2] /'kæptʃəʳ/ *noun* [U] **1** when someone is caught and made a prisoner **tutsak, mahkum, esir, tutuklu** *He shot himself to avoid capture.* **2** when someone gets control of a place with force **ele geçirme, zaptetme, el koyma** *the capture of the city by foreign troops*

🧩 car ...... İLE BİRLİKTE KULLANILAN KELİMELER

drive/park/start a car ● a car breaks down ● by car ● a car accident/crash ● a car driver

---

⚬ **car** /kɑːʳ/ *noun* [C] **1** a vehicle with an engine, four wheels, and seats for a small number of passengers **otomobil, araba** *She goes to work by car.* ○ *Where did you*

park your car? ➔Orta kısımdaki renkli sayfalarına bakınız. **2** *US* a part of a train in which passengers sit, eat, sleep, etc **vagon** *the dining car* ➔See also: **buffet car, cable car, estate car, sports car.**

caramel /'kærəm³l/ *noun* [C, U] sugar that has been heated until it turns brown and that is used to add colour and flavour to food, or a sweet made from sugar, milk, and butter **karamel**

carat (*also US* **karat**) /'kærət/ *noun* [C] a unit for measuring how pure gold is, or how much jewels (= valuable stones) weigh **karat, mücevherat değer birimi** *22 carat gold*

caravan /'kærəvæn/ *noun* [C] **1** *UK* a vehicle which people can live in on holiday and which is pulled by a car **karavan** *a caravan site* **2** a group of people with animals or vehicles who travel together across a desert **çölde birlikte seyahat eden bir grup insan**

carbohydrate /ˌkɑːbəʊ'haɪdreɪt/ *noun* [C, U] a substance in food such as sugar, potatoes, etc that gives your body energy **karbonhidrat** *You need a balance of carbo-hydrates and protein.*

carbon /'kɑːb³n/ *noun* [U] a chemical element present in all animals and plants and in coal and oil (symbol C) **karbon**

carbonated /'kɑːbəneɪtɪd/ *adjective* Carbonated drinks contain a lot of small bubbles. **gazlı (içecek)**

carbon 'copy *noun* [C] **1** a copy of a written document that is made using carbon paper (= thin paper covered in carbon) **karbon kopya 2** an exact copy of something **bir şeyin tam kopyası** *He's a carbon copy of his father.*

carbon dioxide /ˌkɑːb³ndaɪ'ɒksaɪd/ *noun* [U] a gas that is produced when people and animals breathe out, or when carbon is burned (formula CO_2) **karbondioksit**

carbon e,missions *noun* [plural] carbon dioxide and carbon monoxide made by things such as factories or cars that burn carbon and cause pollution **karbon tüketimi/emisyonu**

carbon monoxide /ˌkɑːb³nmə'nɒksaɪd/ *noun* [U] a poisonous gas that is produced by burning some types of fuel, especially petrol (= fuel for cars) (formula CO) **karbonmonoksit**

carbon 'neutral *adjective* not producing carbon emissions **karbon emisyonu üretmeyen** *a carbon-neutral fuel/home/lifestyle*

carbon ,paper *noun* [U] thin paper that is covered on one side with carbon (= a black substance) and is used for making copies of written documents **karbon kağıt**

carbon 'tax *noun* [C] a tax on oil, coal and other things which produce greenhouse gases (= gases that harm the air around the Earth) **karbon vergisi**

car 'boot sale *noun* [C] *UK* an event where people sell things they no longer want from the backs of their cars **kullanılmayan eşyaların araba bagajında satışı, araçta seyyar satış** *She spends her Sunday mornings looking for bargains at car boot sales.*

carburettor *UK* (*US* **carburetor**) /ˌkɑːbə'retəʳ/ 🇺🇸 /'kɑːbəreɪtəʳ/ *noun* [C] the part of an engine that mixes fuel and air which are then burned to provide power **karbüratör**

carcass /'kɑːkəs/ *noun* [C] the body of a dead animal **leş** *The carcasses of dead cattle littered the field.*

carcinogen /kɑː'sɪnədʒ³n/ *noun* [C] a substance that can cause cancer (= a disease when cells in your body grow in an uncontrolled way) **hücrelerin kontrolsüz büyü-mesinin neden olduğu kanseri oluşturan madde** ● **carcinogenic** /ˌkɑːsməʊˈdʒenɪk/ *adjective carcinogenic chemicals* **kanserojen**

o→**card** /kɑːd/ *noun* **1** [MESSAGE] [C] a folded piece of stiff paper with a picture on the front and a message inside that you send to someone on a special occasion **kart** *a birthday card* **2** [INFORMATION] [C] a piece of stiff paper or plastic that has information printed on it **üzerinde bilgi olan kart** *a library card* **3** [GAME] [C] (*also* playing card) one of a set of 52 pieces of stiff paper with numbers and pictures used for playing games **iskambil kağıdı** *UK a pack of cards/ US a deck of cards* ○ *We spent the evening playing cards* (= playing games using cards). **4** [PAPER] [U] *UK* thick, stiff paper **karton** **5** [WITHOUT ENVELOPE] [C] a postcard (= card with a picture on one side that you send without an envelope) **karpostal** **6** [COMPUTER] [C] a part inside a computer which controls how the computer operates **bilgisayar kartı** *a graphics/sound card* **7** **be on the cards** *UK* to be likely to happen **olması muhtemel, olası** *Do you think marriage is on the cards?* ● **8** **put/lay your cards on the table** to tell someone honestly what you think or plan to do **açık sözlü davranmak, açık olmak, dobra dobra konuşmak** ⊃See also: cash card, charge card, Christmas card, credit card, debit card, phone card, smart card, swipe card, trump card, wild card.

cardboard /ˈkɑːdbɔːd/ *noun* [U] thick, stiff paper that is used for making boxes **mukavva kartonu, mukavva kutu**

cardiac /ˈkɑːdiæk/ *adjective* [always before noun] relating to the heart **kalple ilgili, kardiyak** *cardiac surgery* ○ *cardiac arrest* (= when the heart stops beating)

cardigan /ˈkɑːdɪɡən/ *noun* [C] a piece of clothing, often made of wool, that covers the top of your body and fastens at the front **hırka** ⊃Orta kısımdaki renkli sayfalarına bakınız.

cardinal[1] /ˈkɑːdɪnᵊl/ *noun* [C] a priest with a high rank in the Catholic Church **kardinal** *Cardinal Basil Hume*

cardinal[2] /ˈkɑːdɪnᵊl/ *adjective* [always before noun] *formal* extremely important or serious **son derece önmeli ve ciddi** *One of the cardinal rules of business is know what your customer wants.*

ˌ**cardinal ˈnumber** (*also* cardinal) *noun* [C] a number such as 1, 2, 3, etc that shows the quantity of something **sıra sayılar**

o→**care**[1] /keər/ *verb* **1** [I, T] to think that something is important and to feel interested in it or worried about it **ilgilenmek, ihtimam göstermek, gözetmek** *He cares deeply about the environment.* ○ [+ question word] *I don't care how long it takes - just get the job done.* **2** [I] to love someone **aşık olmak, sevmek** *Your parents are only doing this because they care about you.* ○ *I knew that Amy still cared for me.* **3** **I/he, etc couldn't care less** *informal* used to emphasize that someone is not interested in or worried about something or someone **aldırmam(z), umursamam(z), takmam(z); umurunda olmamak, vız gelmek** [+ question word] *I couldn't care less what people think.* **4** **Who cares?** *informal* used to emphasize that you do not think something is important **Kim takar? Umurumda mı? Neden aldırayım ki?** *"Manchester United will be in the final if they win this match." "Who cares?"* **5** **Would you care for sth/to do sth?** *formal* used to ask someone if they want something or want to do something **... ile ilgilenir misin? ... yapmaya ne dersin? ...düşünür müsün? ... bakar mısın, ilgilenir misin?** *Would you care for a drink?* ○ *Would you care to join us for dinner?*

care for sb/sth *phrasal verb* to look after someone or something, especially someone who is young, old, or ill **bakımını üstlenmek, sevmek, hoşlanmak, ihtimam**

göstermek (genç, yaşlı,hasta) *The children are being cared for by a relative.*

not care for sth/sb *phrasal verb formal* to not like something or someone **hoşlanmamak, ilgi duymamak, umursamamak,** *I don't care for shellfish.*

●●●● **care** .... İLE BİRLİKTE KULLANILAN KELİMELER

take care of sb ● **need/provide/receive** care ● **constant/long-term** care ● **in/under** sb's care

o→**care**[2] /keər/ *noun* **1** [PROTECTION] [U] the process of looking after something or someone, especially someone who is young, old, or ill **bakma, ilgilenme, bakım, ilgi (genç, yaşlı, hasta)** *skin/hair care* ○ *A small baby requires constant care.* **2** [ATTENTION] [U] If you do something with care, you give a lot of attention to it so that you do not make a mistake or damage anything. **dikkat, ihtimam, özen** *She planned the trip with great care.* ○ *Fragile - please handle with care.* **3** **take care** to give a lot of attention to what you are doing so that you do not have an accident or make a mistake **özen göstermek, ihtimam göstermek** *The roads are very icy so take care when you drive home.* **4** **Take care!** *informal* used when saying goodbye to someone **Kendine iyi bak!** *See you soon, Bob - take care!* **5** [WORRY] [C] a feeling of worry **endişe, kaygı** *He was sixteen years old and didn't have a care in the world* (= had no worries). **6** **in care** *UK* Children who are in care are looked after by government organizations because their parents cannot look after them. **gözetim/bakım altında, himayesinde** *She was put/taken into care at the age of twelve.* **7** **take care of sb/sth** to look after someone or something **bakmak, ilgilenmek, ihtimam etmek** *My parents are going to take care of the house while we're away.* **8** **take care of sth/doing sth** to be responsible for dealing with something **bir şey den sorumlu olmak, bir şeyi yapmaktan sorumlu olmak** *I did the cooking while Guy took care of the washing up.* ⊃See also: intensive care.

●●●● **career** .... İLE BİRLİKTE KULLANILAN KELİMELER

begin/embark on/launch a career ● **follow/pursue** a career ● a career **in** sth ● a career **change** ● career **opportunities/prospects**

career[1] /kəˈrɪər/ *noun* [C] **1** a job that you do for a long period of your life and that gives you the chance to move to a higher position and earn more money **meslek, iş** *a successful career in marketing* **2** the time that you spend doing a particular job **meslek yaşamı** *She began her acting career in TV commercials.*

career[2] /kəˈrɪər/ *verb* **career down/into/off, etc** *UK* to move quickly and in an uncontrolled way **aşağı/yukarı rastgele koşuşturmak, koşmak** *The train careered off a bridge and plunged into the river.*

carefree /ˈkeəfriː/ *adjective* without any worries or problems **kaygısız, kayıtsız, sıkıntısız, tasasız** *a carefree childhood*

careful ...... BAŞKA BİR DEYİŞLE

Eğer kişi risklerden ve tehlikelerden uzak duruyorsa, kişiyi tanımlamak için **cautious** *She's a very* **cautious** *driver.*

Play (it) safe ifadesi riskleri engellemek anlamında kullanılır. *I think I'll* **play it safe** *and get the earlier train.*

Eğer kişi bir işi çok dikkatli bir şekilde her detayı düşünerek yapıyorsa, kişiyi tanımlamak için **meticulous, methodical,** ve **painstaking** söylemleri kullanılır. *This book is the result of years of* **meticulous/ painstaking** *research.*

o⁼**careful** /ˈkeəfºl/ *adjective* giving a lot of attention to what you are doing so that you do not have an accident, make a mistake, or damage something **dikkatli, itinalı, özenli** *careful planning/consideration* ○ *Be careful, Michael - that knife's very sharp.* ○ [+ to do sth] *We were careful to avoid the midday sun.* ● **carefully** *adverb* a *carefully prepared speech* **dikkatlice**

caregiver /ˈkeəˌɡɪvəʳ/ *US (UK* **carer)** *noun* [C] someone who looks after a person who is young, old, or ill **bakıcı, hemşire, genç, hasta ve yaşlılarla ilgilenen kişi**

careless /ˈkeələs/ *adjective* not giving enough attention to what you are doing **dikkatsiz, düşüncesiz, tasasız, kaygısız** *It was very careless of you to forget your passport.* ○ *He was fined £250 for careless driving.* ● **carelessly** *adverb* **dikkatsizce** ● **carelessness** *noun* [U] **dikkatsizlik**

carer /ˈkeərəʳ/ *UK (US* **caregiver)** *noun* [C] someone who looks after a person who is young, old, or ill **bakıcı, ilgilenen kişi, gözeten kişi**

caress /kəˈres/ *verb* [T] to touch someone in a gentle way that shows that you love them **okşamak, dokunmak, hafif hafif okşayarak sevmek, sevdiğini göstermek** ● **caress** *noun* [C] **okşayış**

caretaker /ˈkeəˌteɪkəʳ/ *noun* [C] **1** someone whose job is to look after a large building, such as a school **kapıcı, hademe, kat görevlisi, apartman görevlisi, odacı 2** *US* someone who looks after a person who is young, old, or ill **genç, yaşlı, ve hastalar için bakıcı, ihtimam gösteren, ilgilenen kişi**

cargo /ˈkɑːɡəʊ/ *noun* [C, U] *plural* **cargoes** goods that are carried in a vehicle **yük, yük eşyası** *a cargo of oil* ○ *a cargo ship/plane*

caricature /ˈkærɪkətʃʊəʳ/ *noun* [C] a funny drawing or description of someone, especially someone famous, which makes part of their appearance or character more noticeable than it really is **karikatür** ● **caricature** *verb* [T] **karikatür yapmak**

caring /ˈkeərɪŋ/ *adjective* kind and supporting other people **sevecen, şefkatli, müşfik** *She's a very caring person.*

carjacking /ˈkɑːˌdʒækɪŋ/ *noun* [C, U] the crime of attacking someone who is driving and stealing their car **araç hırsızlığı, araba hırsızlığı** ● **carjacker** *noun* [C] someone who commits the crime of carjacking **araba hırsızı**

carnage /ˈkɑːnɪdʒ/ *noun* [U] *formal* when a lot of people are violently killed or injured **katliam, toplu şekilde öldürme veya yaralama**

carnation /kɑːˈneɪʃºn/ *noun* [C] a small flower with a sweet smell that is usually white, pink, or red **karanfil**

carnival /ˈkɑːnɪvºl/ *noun* [C] **1** a public celebration where people wear special clothes and dance and play music in the roads **karnaval, cümbüş, âlem 2** *US* a place of outside entertainment where there are machines you can ride on and games that can be played for prizes **eğlence alanı, karnaval sahası, lunapark**

carnivore /ˈkɑːnɪvɔːʳ/ *noun* [C] an animal that eats meat **etobur hayvan** ⊃Compare **herbivore**. ● **carnivorous** /kɑːˈnɪvºrəs/ *adjective* eating meat **etobur**

carol /ˈkærºl/ *noun* (*also* **Christmas carol**) *noun* [C] a song that people sing at Christmas **noel ilahisi, ilahi**

carousel /ˌkærəˈsel/ *noun* [C] **1** a moving strip where passengers collect their bags at an airport **havalanındaki bagaj turnikesi 2** *mainly US* a machine that goes round and round and has toy animals or cars for children to ride on **atlıkarınca**

carp¹ /kɑːp/ *noun* [C, U] *plural* **carp** a large fish that lives in lakes and rivers, or the meat of this fish **sazan balığı**

carp² /kɑːp/ *verb* [I] to complain continually about things that are not important **sürekli kusur bulmak, şikayet etmek** *He's always carping about how badly organized the office is.*

'**car ˌpark** *UK (US* **parking lot)** *noun* [C] a place where vehicles can be parked **araç park yeri**

carpenter /ˈkɑːpºntəʳ/ *noun* [C] a person whose job is making and repairing wooden objects **marangoz, doğramacı, dülger**

carpentry /ˈkɑːpºntri/ *noun* [U] making and repairing wooden objects **marangozluk, doğramacılık**

carpet /ˈkɑːpɪt/ *noun* **1** [C, U] thick material for covering floors, often made of wool **halı** *a new living room carpet* ○ *UK fitted carpets* (= carpets that cover floors from wall to wall) **2 a carpet of sth** a thick layer of something that covers the ground **döşemeyi kaplayan sergi, yaygı, kaplama** *a carpet of snow* ● **carpet** *verb* [T] to put carpet on the floor of a room **halı sermek** *The stairs were carpeted.* ⊃See also: **the red carpet.**

carriage /ˈkærɪdʒ/ *noun* **1** [TRAIN] *UK* one of the separate parts of a train where the passengers sit **vagon** *The front carriage of the train is for first-class passengers only.* **2** [WITH HORSE] a vehicle with wheels that is pulled by a horse or **arabası 3** [GOODS] [U] *UK* the cost of transporting goods **yük taşıma/nakliye bedeli/ücreti** ⊃See also: **baby carriage.**

carriageway /ˈkærɪdʒweɪ/ *noun* [C] *UK* one of the two sides of a motorway or main road **taşıt yolu, araçlarca kullanılan yol** *the southbound carriageway* ⊃See also: **dual carriageway.**

carrier /ˈkæriəʳ/ *noun* [C] **1** [TRANSPORT] a person, vehicle, or machine that transports things from one place to another **taşıyan, taşıyıcı, nakliyeci, hamal 2** [DISEASE] a person who has a disease that they can give to other people without suffering from it themselves **hastalık taşıyan/bulaştıran kişi 3** [COMPANY] a company that operates aircraft **uçak şirketi** ⊃See also: **aircraft carrier, letter carrier.**

'**carrier ˌbag** *noun* [C] *UK* a large paper or plastic bag with handles that you are given in a shop to carry the things you have bought (**kağıt, plastik**) **alışveriş çantası** ⊃See picture at **bag.**

carrot /ˈkærət/ *noun* **1** [C, U] an orange-coloured vegetable that is long and thin and grows in the ground **havuç** ⊃Orta kısımdaki renkli sayfalarına bakınız. **2** [C] *informal* something that is offered to someone in order to encourage them to do something **ödül, teşvik eden şey, özendirme ödülü 3 carrot and stick** If you use a carrot-and-stick method, you offer someone rewards if they do something and say you will punish them if they do not. **ödül ve ceza yöntemi**

o⁼**carry** /ˈkæri/ *verb* **1** [HOLD] [T] to hold something or someone with your hands, arms, or on your back and take them from one place to another **taşımak, bir yerden bir yere götürmek** *He was carrying my bags.* **2** [TRANSPORT] [T] to move someone or something from one place to another **bir yerden bir yere taşımak** *The plane was carrying 30 passengers.* ○ *Strong currents carried them out to sea.* **3** [HAVE WITH YOU] [T] to have something with you in a pocket, bag, etc **yanında taşımak** *She still carries his photo in her purse.* **4** [DISEASE] [T] to have a disease that you might give to someone else **hastalık taşımak** *Mosquitoes carry malaria and other infectious diseases.* **5** [PART] [T] to have something as a part or a result of something **bir şeye bir parçası veya sonucu olarak sahip olmak** *All cigarette advertising must carry a government health warning.* ○ *Murder still carries the death penalty there.* **6** [SOUND] [I] If a sound or someone's voice carries, it can be heard a long way away. **sesi gür ve çok çıkmak, uzaklardan duyulmak**

7 [SUPPORT] [T] to support the weight of something **kaldır-mak, ağırlığını taşımak** *Is the ice thick enough to carry my weight?* **8** [MATHS] [T] to put a number into another column when adding numbers **9** [DEVELOP] [T] to develop something in a particular way **bir şeyi özel olarak geliştirmek** *She carried her diet to extremes.* **10 be carried** to be formally accepted by people voting at a meeting **oylama sonrası bir şeyin resmen kabul edilmesi** *The motion was carried by 210 votes to 160.* ⊃See also: carry **weight**.

be carried away *phrasal verb* to be so excited about something that you do not control what you say or do **coşmak, kendinden geçmek, heyecandan dolayı ne söylediğini kontrol edememek** *There's far too much food - I'm afraid I got a bit carried away.*

carry sth off *phrasal verb* to succeed in doing or achieving something difficult **başarılı olmak, zor bir şeyi başarmak, üstesinden gelmek** *It's not an easy part to act but he carried it off brilliantly.*

carry on *phrasal verb* to continue doing something **devam etmek, ilerlemek** [+ doing sth] *The doctors have warned him but he just carries on drinking.* ○ *Carry on with your work while I'm gone.*

carry out sth *phrasal verb* to do or complete something, especially something that you have said you would do or that you have been told to do **bir sözü yerine getirmek, yapmak, tamamlamak, başarmak, vaadi yerine getirmek** *I was only carrying out orders.*

carryall /'kæriɔːl/ *US* (*UK* holdall) *noun* [C] a large bag for carrying clothes **elbise kılıfı, askısı, torbası** ⊃See picture at **luggage**.

cart¹ /kɑːt/ *noun* [C] **1** a vehicle with two or four wheels that is pulled by an animal and used for carrying goods **at arabası (bazı yörelerde) başka hayvanlarca da çekilen 2 veya 4 tekerlekli yük taşıma arabası 2** *US* (*UK* trolley) a metal structure on wheels that is used for carrying things **araba kasası, arabanın metal yük taşıma bölümü** ⊃See picture at **trolley** ⊃See also: go-cart.

cart² /kɑːt/ *verb informal* **cart sb/sth around/away/off,** etc to take someone or something somewhere **birini, bir şeyi bir yere götürmek, taşımak**

carte blanche /ˌkɑːtˈblɑːnʃ/ *noun* [U] complete freedom to do what you want **kayıtsız şartsız egemenlik, özgürlük; tam yetki** [+ to do sth] *She was given carte blanche to make whatever changes she wanted.*

cartel /kɑːˈtel/ *noun* [C] a group of companies who join together to control prices and limit competition **pazarı ve rekâbet gücünü sınırlamak için bir araya gelen şirketler topluluğu, kartel**

cartilage /'kɑːtɪlɪdʒ/ *noun* [C, U] a strong elastic substance found where two bones connect in the human body **kıkırdak, kıkırdaksı doku**

carton /'kɑːtᵊn/ *noun* [C] a container for food and drink that is made from strong, stiff paper or plastic **mukavva kutu, mukavva, karton** *a carton of milk/fruit juice* ⊃See picture at **container.**

cartoon /kɑːˈtuːn/ *noun* [C] **1** a film made using characters that are drawn and not real **çizgi film** *Mickey Mouse and other famous cartoon characters* **2** a funny drawing, especially in a newspaper or magazine **karikatür ● cartoonist** *noun* [C] someone whose job is to draw cartoons **karikatürist**

cartridge /'kɑːtrɪdʒ/ *noun* [C] **1** a small container that is used in a larger piece of equipment and can be easily replaced **kartuş; değiştirilebilir küçük kap, kutu** *an ink cartridge* **2** a tube containing an explosive substance and a bullet for use in a gun **fişek**

cartoon

carve /kɑːv/ *verb* [I, T] **1** to make an object, a shape, or a pattern by cutting wood, stone, etc **oymak, kazımak, yontmak** *The statue was carved out of stone.* ○ *They had carved their initials into the tree.* **2** to cut a large piece of cooked meat into smaller pieces **etleri doğramak, kesip dağıtmak, dilimlemek 3 carve (out) a niche/career/role, etc for yourself** to be successful in a particular job or activity **belirli bir işte, faaliyette başarılı olmak**

carve sth up *phrasal verb* to divide something into smaller parts, in a way that people do not approve of **insanların istemediği biçimde bir şeyi küçük parçalara bölmek** *The countryside has been carved up and sold to property developers.*

carving /'kɑːvɪŋ/ *noun* **1** [C] an object or a pattern that has been carved **oyma, yontma yoluyla yapılan şey 2** [U] the activity of carving an object or pattern **oyma, yontma** *wood carving*

cascade /kæsˈkeɪd/ *verb* [I] to fall quickly and in large amounts **çağlayan, şelale gibi dökülmek, akmak, düşmek** *Water cascaded from the rocks above.* ● **cascade** *noun* [C] *literary* a large amount of something, especially something falling or hanging **şelale, çağlayan** *a cascade of golden hair*

○━**case** /keɪs/ *noun* **1** [SITUATION] [C] a particular situation or example of something **durum, hal, vaziyet, hadise, mesele** *People were imprisoned, and, in some cases, killed for their beliefs.* ○ *We usually ask for references, but in your case it will not be necessary.* ○ *The whole film is based on a case of mistaken identity.* **2** [COURT OF LAW] [C] something that is decided in a court of law **dava** *a libel/criminal/divorce case* ○ *He lost his case.* **3** [CRIME] [C] a crime that police are trying to solve **vaka** *a murder case* ○ *Police in the town have investigated 50 cases of burglary in the past month.* **4** [ILLNESS] [C] an illness, or somebody with an illness **hastalık, rahatsızlık vakası; hasta,** *4,000 new cases of the disease are diagnosed every year.* **5 be the case** to be true **doğru olmak, haklı olmak; gerçek, hakikat olmak** *Bad diet can cause tiredness, but I don't think that's the case here.* **6** [REASONS] [C] facts or reasons that prove a particular opinion **belli bir durumu kanıtlayan sebepler ve gerçekler** [usually singular] *There is a strong case for/against bringing in the new legislation.* ○ *mainly UK He put the case for more funding very convincingly.* **7** [CONTAINER] [C] a container for storing or protecting something **kasa, sandık, kutu** *a pencil case* ○ *a cigarette case* **8** [BAG] [C] *UK another word for* suitcase (= a rectangular bag or container with a handle which you use for carrying clothes in when you are travelling) **valiz, çanta 9 (just) in case** because something might happen, or might have happened ... **bilir diye, düşünce- siyle, olması halinde, durumunda, ne olur ne olmaz** *I don't think that it's going to rain, but I'll bring a raincoat just in case.* **10 in any case** used to give another reason for something that you are saying, or that you have done **ne olursa olsun, her halde, nasıl olursa olsun** *I don't want to go skiing and, in any case, I can't afford it.* **11 in that case/in which case** because that is the situation/if that is the situation **öyleyse, o takdirde, o durumda** *"Peter's coming tonight." "Oh, in that case, I'll stay in."* **12 be a case of doing sth** to be necessary to do something **bir şeyi yapmak için gerekli olmak, lüzumlu olmak** *We know that we're right. It's just a case of proving it.* **13 in case of sth** *formal* when something happens, or in preparation for when something happens **halinde, durumunda, vukuunda** *We keep a bucket of water backstage, in case of fire.* **14** [LANGUAGE] [C] any of the various types to which a noun can belong, depending on what it is doing in the sentence, usually shown by a particular ending **15 a case in point** a good example of something **bahse konu olan mesele, örnek** *Supermarkets often charge too much for goods. Bananas are a case in point.* ● **16 be/get on sb's case** *informal* to criticize someone in an annoying way because of something that they have done **birini kusurundan ötürü şiddetle eleştirmek** *She's always on my case about something.* ● **17 be on the case** *UK informal* to be doing what needs to be done **yapılması gerekeni yapıyor olmak** ⊃See also: **lower case, upper case.**

,case 'history *noun* [C] a record of what happens to a particular person **bir hastanın geçmişiyle ilgili bilgiler** *The study used case histories from 500 teenage boys.*

'case ,study *noun* [C] a report about a particular person or thing, to show an example of a general principle **durum çalışması, belli bir denek çalışması**

---
cash ...... İLE BİRLİKTE KULLANILAN KELİMELER

pay (in) cash ● [£50/$100, etc] **in** cash ● a cash **machine** ● cash **payments**
---

o⁻**cash¹** /kæʃ/ *noun* [U] **1** money in the form of coins or notes (= paper money) **nakit, peşin** *I'm taking £50 in cash.* ○ *Are you paying by cheque or cash?* **2** *informal* money in any form **nakit para, peşin para** *She's a bit short of cash at the moment.* ○ *a cash prize* ⊃See also: **e-cash, hard cash.**

cash² /kæʃ/ *verb* **cash a cheque** to exchange a cheque (= piece of paper printed by a bank and used to pay for things) for coins or paper money **çek bozdurmak**
cash in on sth *phrasal verb* to get money or another advantage from an event or a situation, often in an unfair way **...den kâr temin etmek, istifade etmek, yararlanmak** *Her family have been accused of cashing in on her death.*

cashback /'kæʃbæk/ *noun* [U] *UK* money that you can take from your bank account when you pay in a shop with a bank card **kredi kartıyla ödeme** *£50 cashback*

'cash ,card *noun* [C] *UK* a plastic card that you use to get money from a machine **makinadan para çekmek için kullanılan plastik kart**

'cash ,crop *noun* [C] a crop that is grown to be sold **para/ satış için yetiştirilen mahsul**

'cash ,desk *noun* [C] *UK* the place in a shop where you pay for the things that you buy **ödeme yeri, mağazada kasa,**

cashew /'kæʃu:/, /kə'ʃu:/ (*also* 'cashew ,nut) *noun* [C] a curved nut that you can eat **mahun fıstığı, kaju fıstığı**

cashflow /'kæʃfləʊ/ *noun* [U] the movement of money in and out of a business or bank account **nakit akışı**

cashier /kæʃ'ɪər/ *noun* [C] someone whose job is to receive and pay out money in a shop, bank, etc **kasiyer, veznedar**

'cash ma,chine (*also* UK **cashpoint**) *noun* [C] a machine, usually in a wall outside of a bank, that you can get money from using a plastic card **nakit para alınabilen makina, ATM**

cashmere /'kæʃmɪər/ ⑤ /'kæʒmɪr/ *noun* [U] a type of very soft, expensive wool **kaşmir, ince yün kumaş**

cashpoint /'kæʃpɔɪnt/ *UK* (UK/US **cash machine**) *noun* [C] a machine, usually in a wall outside a bank, that you can get money from using a plastic card **nakit para çekilebilen nokta, ATM**

'cash ,register *noun* [C] a machine that is used in shops for keeping money in, and for recording everything that is sold **kasa, alışveriş kasası**

casino /kə'si:nəʊ/ *noun* [C] a place where card games and other games of risk are played for money **gazino, kumarhane**

cask /kɑːsk/ *noun* [C] a strong, round, wooden container that is used for storing alcoholic drinks **fıçı, varil**

casket /'kɑːskɪt/ *noun* [C] **1** *UK* a small, decorated box that is used for keeping valuable objects **mücevher kutusu 2** *US* (UK/US **coffin**) a box in which a dead body is buried **tabut**

casserole /'kæsərəʊl/ *noun* **1** [C, U] a mixture of meat or beans with liquid and vegetables cooked for a long time in the oven **güveç 2** [C] (*also* 'casserole ,dish) a large, heavy container with a lid, that is used for cooking casseroles **güveç tenceresi**

cassette /kə'set/ *noun* [C] a flat, plastic case containing a long piece of magnetic material that is used to record and play sound or pictures **kaset** *a video cassette*

ca'ssette ,player *noun* [C] a machine that plays cassettes of music or sound **teyp; kaset çalar**

ca'ssette re,corder *noun* [C] a machine that is used for playing cassettes of music or sound and for recording music or sound onto cassettes **kaset kayıt cihazı**

cast¹ /kɑːst/ *verb* [T] *past* **cast 1** [ACTOR] to choose an actor for a particular part in a film or play **oyuncu seçimi yapmak** *Why am I always cast as the villain?* **2** [THROW] *literary* to throw something **fırlatmak, atmak 3** [LIGHT] *literary* to send light or shadow (= dark shapes) in a particular direction **yaymak, saçmak** *The moon cast a white light into the room.* **4 cast doubt/suspicion on sb/sth** to make people feel less sure about or have less trust in someone or something **insanların inanmamalarını/güvenmemelerini sağlamak, şüphe duymalarına neden olmak** *A leading scientist has cast doubts on government claims that the drug is safe.* **5 cast a/your vote** to vote **oy kullanmak 6 cast a spell on sb** a [ATTRACT] to seem to use magic to attract someone **birini büyülemek, gözünü kamaştırmak** *The city had cast a spell on me and I never wanted to leave.* **b** [MAGIC] to use magic to make something happen to someone **birine bir şey olması için büyü yapmak, büyü kullanmak 7** [METAL] to make an object by pouring hot metal into a container of a particular shape **döküm yapmak, kalıp çıkarmak, dökmek** ⊃See also: cast/run your/an eye¹ over sth, cast/shed light¹ on sth, cast a pall² over sth, cast a shadow¹ over sth.
cast off *phrasal verb* If a boat casts off, it leaves. **denize açılmak, yol almak, ayrılmak**

---
cast ...... İLE BİRLİKTE KULLANILAN KELİMELER

[a play/film, etc] **features** a cast ● the **cast includes** sb ● the **cast** of sth ● a **member of** the cast
---

cast² /kɑːst/ *noun* **1** [group] all the actors in a film or play **bütün oyuncu kadrosu** *The cast are in rehearsal at the moment.* **2** [C] a hard cover used to keep a broken bone in the correct position until it gets better **alçı, kırıklardan sonra yapılan alçı**

castaway /ˈkɑːstəweɪ/ *noun* [C] someone who is left on an island, or in a place where there are few or no other people, after their ship has sunk **gemisi battıktan sonra ücra bir adada tek başına kalmış kişi, terkedilmiş**

caste /kɑːst/ *noun* [C, U] a system of dividing Hindu society into social groups, or one of these groups Hint **toplumunu sosyal gruplara ayıran sistem, sınıf ayrımı, üstün sınıf** *the caste system*

castigate /ˈkæstɪɡeɪt/ *verb* [T] *formal* to criticize someone severely **acımasızca eleştirmek, cezalandırmak, şiddetle tenkit ve tekdir etmek**

cast-iron /ˈkɑːstˌaɪən/ *adjective* **1** [always before noun] able to be trusted completely, or impossible to doubt **kişiliğine çok güvenilen, güvenilir, sağlam kişilikli** *I need a cast-iron guarantee that the work will be finished on time.* **2** made of cast iron **dökme demirden, pik demirden**

ˌcast 'iron *noun* [U] a type of very hard iron **dökme demir, pik demir**

∘ **castle** /ˈkɑːsl/ *noun* [C] a large, strong building with towers and high walls, that was built in the past to protect the people inside from being attacked **kale, hisar, şato**

cast-off /ˈkɑːstɒf/ *noun* [C] a piece of clothing or other item that you give to someone because you do not want it any more **kullanılmayan giysiler, kıyafetler, döküntü** [usually plural] *This dress is another of my sister's cast-offs.*

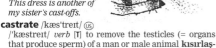

castle

castrate /kæsˈtreɪt/ ⓤ /ˈkæstreɪt/ *verb* [T] to remove the testicles (= organs that produce sperm) of a man or male animal **kısırlaştırmak, hadım etmek, iğdiş etmek** ● **castration** /kæsˈtreɪʃᵊn/ *noun* [U] **hadım etme durumu**

casual /ˈkæʒuəl/ *adjective* **1** [NOT PLANNED] [always before noun] not planned, or without particular meaning or importance **rastlantısal, tesadüfi** *a casual remark/acquaintance/meeting* **2** [RELAXED] relaxed and not seeming very interested in someone or something **kayıtsız, laubali, ilgisiz, umursamaz** *a casual manner/approach* ○ *She's much too casual about her work.* **3** [CLOTHING] Casual clothing is comfortable and not suitable for formal occasions. **gündelik, rastgele, resmi omayan, rahat 4** [WORK] [always before noun] *mainly UK* Casual work is not regular or fixed. **günlük, resmi olmayan** *casual labour/workers*

casually /ˈkæʒuəli/ *adverb* **1** in a relaxed way, or not seeming to be interested in someone or something **rahat bir şekilde** *I asked as casually as I could if she was going to be at the party.* **2** If you dress casually, you do not dress in a formal way. **gündelik olarak giyinerek, rahat giyinerek**

casualty /ˈkæʒuəlti/ *noun* **1** [INJURED] [C] someone who is injured or killed in an accident or war **malül, zayiat, kazazede, savaş veya kazada yaralanan veya ölenler** *Both sides in the conflict have promised to try to avoid civilian casualties.* **2** [BADLY AFFECTED] [C] someone or something that is badly affected by something that happens

zayiat, malül, zarar, ziyan gören *The health service has been the biggest casualty of government cuts.* **3** [HOSPITAL] [U] *UK* (*US* **emergency room**) the part of a hospital where people go when they have been injured or have urgent illnesses so that they can be treated immediately **hastanelerin acil yaralı ve hastalar için ayrılan bölümü, acil müdahale birimi**

∘ **cat** /kæt/ *noun* [C] **1** a small animal with fur, four legs and a tail that is kept as a pet **kedi 2** a large, wild animal that is related to the cat, such as the lion **kedigiller 3 let the cat out of the bag** to tell people secret information, often without intending to **bir sırrı ağzından kaçırmak, ifşa etmek, baklayı ağzından çıkarmak**

cataclysmic /ˌkætəˈklɪzmɪk/ *adjective* sudden, shocking, and violent **ani, şok eden, şiddetli** *cataclysmic changes/events*

catalogue¹ (*also US* **catalog**) /ˈkætᵊlɒɡ/ *noun* [C] **1** a book with a list of all the goods that you can buy from a shop, or of all the books, paintings, etc that you can find in a place **katalog** *a clothing catalogue* **2 a catalogue of disasters/errors/failures, etc** a series of bad events **bir dizi kötü olay, zincirleme kötü hadiseler, kötü olaylar silsilesi**

catalogue² (*also US* **catalog**) /ˈkætᵊlɒɡ/ *verb* [T] **cataloguing**, *past* **catalogued** to make a list of things, especially in order to put it in a catalogue **kataloglamak**

catalyst /ˈkætᵊlɪst/ *noun* [C] **1** someone or something that causes change **değişime neden olan kişi ya da şey** *Recent riots and suicides have acted as a catalyst for change in the prison system.* **2** a substance that makes a chemical reaction happen more quickly

catapult¹ /ˈkætəpʌlt/ *verb* **1 catapult sb/sth into/out/ through, etc** to make someone or something move through the air very quickly and with great force **havaya/da savurmak, fırlatmak** [often passive] *When the two cars collided, he was catapulted out of his seat.* **2 catapult sb to stardom/into the lead, etc** to make someone suddenly very famous/successful, etc **birini beklenmedik anda meşhur, başarılı vs. yapmak/ olmasını sağlamak**

catapult² /ˈkætəpʌlt/ *UK* (*US* **slingshot**) *noun* [C] a Y-shaped object with a piece of elastic used by children to shoot small stones **sapan, küçük taş fırlatmaya yarayan Y şeklinde çatala bağlanmış lastik**

cataract /ˈkætᵊrækt/ *noun* [C] an area of someone's eye with a disease that gradually prevents them from seeing correctly **katarakt**

catarrh /kəˈtɑːʳ/ *noun* [U] *UK* the thick substance that is produced in your nose and throat when you have a cold **balgam, sümük**

catastrophe /kəˈtæstrəfi/ *noun* [C, U] an extremely bad event that causes a lot of suffering or destruction **felaket, afet, facia, yıkıma sebep olan olay** *After the drought, the country is facing environmental catastrophe.*

catastrophic /ˌkætəˈstrɒfɪk/ *adjective* causing a lot of suffering or destruction **feci, yıkıcı**

∘ **catch¹** /kætʃ/ *verb* *past* **caught 1** [GET HOLD] [T] to stop someone or something that is moving through the air by getting hold of it **tutmak, alıkoymak** *Try to catch the ball.* ○ *She fell backwards but he caught her in his arms.* **2** [STOP ESCAPING] [T] to find and stop a person or animal who is trying to escape **bulup yakalamak, ele geçirmek** *He ran after his attacker but couldn't catch him.* ○ *Did you catch many fish today?* **3** [CRIMINAL] [T] If the police catch a criminal, they find them and take them away. **(polis) yakala(n)mak** *These terrorists must be caught.* **4** [ILLNESS] [T] to get an illness or disease **bir hastalığa tutulmak, yakalanmak** *I think I've* *caught a cold.* **5** TRANSPORT [T] to get on a bus, train, etc in order to travel somewhere **bir aracı yakalamak** *You can catch the bus from the top of the hill.* **6** DISCOVER [T] to discover someone who is doing something wrong or something secret **gizli bir şey yapanı yakalamak, (argo) enselemek** [+ doing sth] *I caught her listening outside the door.* ○ *informal You won't catch me wearing* (= I never wear) *a tie.* **7** STICK [I, T] to stick somewhere, or to make something stick somewhere **yapışmak, yapıştırmak, tutturmak** *My dress caught on the door handle as I was leaving.* **8** COLLECT [T] to collect something that is falling **düşmek üzere olan bir şeyi yakalamak** *I used a bucket to catch the drips.* **9** BE IN TIME [T] to manage to be in time to see or do something **yetişmek, yakalamak, aynı düzeye ulaşmak** *I only caught the end of the programme.* **10** HEAR [T] to hear or understand something correctly **işitmek, anlamak, doğru duymak** *I'm sorry. I didn't catch your name.* **11 catch fire** to start burning **alev almak, tutuşmak, yangın çıkmak** **12 be/get caught** to be unable to avoid something unpleasant **yakalanmak, kaçamamak** *I got caught in the rain.* **13 catch the sun** *UK* to burn your skin in the sun **güneşlenmek, bronzlaşmak** *You've caught the sun on your shoulders.* **14 catch sight of sth** to see something suddenly, often only for a short time **gözüne ilişmek/takılmak, kısa bir süre görmek** *He caught sight of himself in the mirror.* **15** HIT [T] *UK* to hit something or someone **vurmak, darbe vurmak** *The ball flew across the garden, and caught me on the chin.* ᗡSee also: catch sb's eye¹, catch sb off guard¹.

catch on *phrasal verb* **1** to become popular **meşhur olmak, popüler olmak** *I wonder if the game will catch on with young people?* **2** *informal* to understand something, especially after a long time **anlamak, kavramak, kapmak** *It took him a while to catch on to what we meant.*

catch sb out *phrasal verb UK* to trick someone so that they make a mistake **faka bastırmak, yanlış yapması için kandırmak**

catch (sb/sth) up *phrasal verb* **1** to reach someone or something that is in front of you, by going faster than them **erişmek, ulaşmak** *We soon caught up with the car in front.* **2** to reach the same level or quality as someone or something else **aynı seviyeye gelmek, ulaşmak** *She's doing extra work to catch up with the rest of the class.*

catch up *phrasal verb* to learn or discuss the most recent news **güncel haberleri öğrenmek, tartışmak** *Let's meet for a chat - I need to catch up on all the gossip.*

catch up on/with sth *phrasal verb* to do something that you did not have time to do earlier **arayı kapatmak, yakalamak, önceden yapmadığını yapmak** *After the exams, I need to catch up on some sleep.*

catch up with sb *phrasal verb* If something bad that you have done or that has been happening to you catches up with you, it begins to cause problems for you. **başı beladan kurtulmamak, yakasını bırakmamak** *I can feel the stress of the last few weeks beginning to catch up with me.*

be/get caught up in sth *phrasal verb* to become involved in a situation, often without wanting to **başını derde sokmak, istemeden bulaşmak** *How did the paper get caught up in a legal dispute?*

catch² /kætʃ/ *noun* [C] **1** WITH HANDS when someone catches something that is moving through the air **yakalama** *a brilliant catch* **2** FISH The amount of fish that someone has caught **yakalanan balık miktarı, av 3** PROBLEM a hidden problem or difficulty with something **bit yeniği, dümen, oyun, gizli amaç** *He's offering us a free flight? There must be a catch.* **4** LOCK a part on something that fastens it and keeps it closed **kilit, kanca, kopça, tutamak** *a safety catch*

Catch-22 /ˌkætʃˈtwentiˈtuː/ *noun* [C] an impossible situation: you cannot do one thing until you have done another thing, but you cannot do the other thing until you have done the first thing **içinden çıkılmaz bir durum, biri olmadan öbürünün olmadığı durum** *a Catch-22 situation*

catching /ˈkætʃɪŋ/ *adjective* [never before noun] If an illness or a mood is catching, other people can get it from you. **bulaşıcı, etkileyen, peşini bırakmayan**

catchment area /ˈkætʃmənt,eəriə/ *noun* [C] *UK* the area around a school or a hospital, where most of the students or patients come from **(hastane, okul) hizmet bölgesi, alanı**

catchphrase /ˈkætʃfreɪz/ *noun* [C] a phrase which is often repeated by a particular organization or person, and becomes connected with them **slogan, bir kurum veya kişiyle özdeşleşmiş ifade, tabir, deyim**

catchy /ˈkætʃi/ *adjective* A catchy song, tune, or phrase is easy to remember. **hatırlaması kolay, kolay hatırda kalan, hatırlanabilir**

categorical /ˌkætəˈgɒrɪkᵊl/ *adjective* If someone is categorical about what they say, they say it with force and are completely certain about it. **kesin, söylediğinin emin, arkasında duran** *a categorical assurance/denial* ● **categorically** *adverb* *They have denied categorically that they were involved in the conspiracy.*

categorize (*also UK* -ise) /ˈkætəgᵊraɪz/ *verb* [T] to divide people or things into groups of similar types **gruplara ayırmak, sınıflandırmak** *The books are categorized according to subject.*

category /ˈkætəgᵊri/ *noun* [C] a group of people or things of a similar type **sınıf, grup, kategori** *Our customers fall into two main categories: retired people and housewives.*

cater /ˈkeɪtᵊr/ *verb* [I, T] to provide and often serve food and drinks for a particular event **yiyecek ve içecek hizmetinde bulunmak, yemek servisi yapmak** *How many are we catering for at the wedding reception?*

cater for sb/sth *phrasal verb mainly UK* to provide what is wanted or needed by a particular group of people **istenileni/gereksinim duyulanı sağlamak, sunmak** *The club caters for children between the ages of 4 and 12.*

cater to sb/sth *phrasal verb* to give people exactly what they want, usually something that people think is wrong **isteğine cevap vermek, çoğunlukla yanlış olduğu düşünülen şeyi** *This legislation simply caters to unacceptable racist opinions.*

caterer /ˈkeɪtᵊrᵊr/ *noun* [C] a person or company that provides food and drinks for particular events, or for an organization **eğlence, parti ve düğün gibi faaliyetlerde yemek işlerini düzenleyen kişi veya kuruluş**

caterpillar

catering /ˈkeɪtᵊrɪŋ/ *noun* [U] providing food and drinks for people **yemek hizmeti sunan, sağlayan, ikram hizmeti** *Who did the catering for the party?*

caterpillar /ˈkætəpɪlᵊr/ *noun* [C] a small, long animal with many legs that eats leaves **tırtıl**

cathartic /kəˈθɑːtɪk/ *adjective* A cathartic

experience or event helps you to express and get rid of strong emotions. **konuşarak rahatlamayı sağlayan, içini dökebilen**

cathedral /kə'θiːdrəl/ noun [C] the largest and most important church in a particular area **katedral**

Catholic /'kæθəlɪk/ (also Roman Catholic) adjective belonging or relating to the part of the Christian religion that has the Pope (= a very important priest) as its leader **Katolik** *a Catholic priest/school* ● **Catholic** noun [C] *I think he's a Catholic.* **Katolik**

the ˌCatholic 'Church noun the Catholic religion and all the people who believe in it **Katolik Kilisesi**

Catholicism /kə'θɒlɪsɪzəm/ (also ˌRoman Ca'tholicism) noun [U] the beliefs of the Catholic religion **Katolik dini inancı**

catsup /'kætsəp/ noun [U] another US spelling of ketchup (= a thick, red sauce that is eaten cold with food) **ketçap, sos**

cattle /'kætl/ noun [plural] male and female cows, kept on a farm for their milk and meat **sığır, büyükbaş hayvan sürüsü**

catty /'kæti/ adjective informal intending to hurt someone by saying unkind things **çirkin sözlerle birini yaralayan, kaba davranan** *catty remarks*

catwalk /'kætwɔːk/ noun [C] the narrow, raised path that people walk along in a fashion show **moda gösterisinde üzerinde yürünen podyum**

Caucasian /kɔː'keɪʒən/ adjective belonging to a race of people with white or pale skin **Kafkaslı, kafkas kökenli, beyaz veya solgun benizli ırktan olan** ● **Caucasian** noun [C] a Caucasian person **Kafkas, Kafkas uyruğundan**

caught /kɔːt/ past of catch **yaklamak' fiilinin geçmiş zaman hali**

cauldron /'kɔːldrən/ noun [C] literary a large, round metal pot that is used for cooking over a fire **kazan, yemek pişirmek için büyükçe tencere, karavana**

cauliflower /'kɒlɪˌflaʊər/ noun [C, U] a large, round, white vegetable with thick, green leaves around the outside **karnabahar** ⊃Orta kısımdaki renkli sayfalarına bakınız.

ˌcause ...... İLE BİRLİKTE KULLANILAN KELİMELER

a **common/leading/probable/root** cause ● **discover/establish/identify** the cause **of** sth ● the **main** cause

o→**cause¹** /kɔːz/ noun 1 [MAKES HAPPEN] [C] someone or something that makes something happen **sebep, neden** *The police are still trying to establish the cause of the fire.* ○ *She died of natural causes.* 2 [REASON] [U] a reason to feel something or to behave in a particular way **gerekçe** *He's never given me any cause for concern.* 3 [PRINCIPLE] [C] a principle or aim that a group of people support or fight for **amaç, dava** *The money will all go to a good cause.*

o→**cause²** /kɔːz/ verb [T] to make something happen **sebep olmak** *The hurricane caused widespread damage.* ○ *Most heart attacks are caused by blood clots.* ○ [+ two objects] *I hope the children haven't caused you too much trouble.* ○ [+ to do sth] *What caused the washing machine to blow up?*

causeway /'kɔːzweɪ/ noun [C] a raised path or road over a wet area **ıslak bir bölgede geçişi sağlayan yükseltilmiş patika yol**

caustic /'kɔːstɪk/ adjective 1 A caustic remark is extremely unkind and intended to upset or criticize someone. **iğneleyici, eleştiren, acımasız, saldırgan** 2 Caustic chemicals can burn things. **yakıcı (kimyasal)**

ˌcaution ...... İLE BİRLİKTE KULLANILAN KELİMELER

advise/exercise/urge caution ● **extreme/great** caution ● do sth **with** caution ● caution **in** doing sth

caution¹ /'kɔːʃən/ noun 1 [U] great care and attention not to take risks or get into danger **dikkat, itina, özen, ihtimam, ihtiyat** *Travellers have been advised to exercise great caution when passing through the region.* ○ *I would treat anything he says with extreme caution* (= not be too quick to believe it). 2 [C] UK when a police officer or other person in authority warns you that you will be punished if you do something bad again **uyarı, ikaz** 3 **throw caution to the wind** to take a risk **risk almak, tehlikeye göğüs germek** ⊃See also: err on the side¹ of caution.

caution² /'kɔːʃən/ verb 1 [I, T] formal to warn someone of something **ikaz etmek, dikkatini çekmek** [often passive] *They were cautioned against buying shares in the company.* 2 [T] UK If police caution people, they are given a spoken warning that they will be punished next time. **uyarmak**

cautionary /'kɔːʃənəri/ adjective intended to warn or advise someone **uyaran, ikaz edici** *a cautionary tale*

cautious /'kɔːʃəs/ adjective taking care to avoid risks or danger **dikkatli, itinalı** *She is cautious about lending money to anyone.* ● **cautiously** adverb **dikkatli bir şekilde**

cavalier /ˌkævə'lɪər/ adjective formal without caring about other people or about a dangerous or serious situation **şövalye ruhlu, gözü pek, hiç bir şeyi gözü görmeyen** *a cavalier attitude*

the cavalry /'kævəlri/ noun [U, group] soldiers who fight on horses **süvariler, süvari alayı**

cave¹ /keɪv/ noun [C] a large hole in the side of a cliff (= straight, high rock next to the sea), mountain, or under the ground **mağara**

cave² /keɪv/ verb
cave in phrasal verb 1 If a ceiling, roof, or other structure caves in, it breaks and falls into the space below. **tavan çökmek, göçmek** 2 to agree to something that you were against before, after someone has persuaded you or made you afraid **razı olmak, rıza göstermek, pes etmek** *The company has finally caved in to the demands of the unions.*

caveat /'kæviæt/ noun [C] formal something you say which warns that there is a limit on a general announcement made earlier **miyadı olma, belli bir süresi olma**

cavern /'kævən/ noun [C] a large cave **büyük mağara**

caviar (also caviare) /'kæviɑːr/ noun [U] the eggs of a large fish, eaten as a food and usually very expensive **havyar**

cavity /'kævəti/ noun [C] 1 a hole or a space inside something solid or between two surfaces **oyuk, kovuk** 2 a hole in a tooth **çürük, oyuk**

cavort /kə'vɔːt/ verb [I] to jump, dance, or move about in an excited way **yerinde duramamak, heyecandan zıplamak**

cc /ˌsiː'siː/ 1 abbreviation for carbon copy: used on a letter or email to show that you are sending a copy to other people **karbon kopya, karbon kağıt** 2 abbreviation for cubic centimetre: a unit for measuring the volume of something **santi metreküp** *a 750cc motorcycle*

CCTV /ˌsiːsiːtiː'viː/ noun [U] abbreviation for closed circuit television: a system of television cameras filming in shops and public places so that people can watch and

C

protect those places **kapalı devre televizyon** *CCTV cameras*

☞**CD** /ˌsiːˈdiː/ *noun* [C] *abbreviation for* compact disc: a small disc on which music or information is recorded **CD, üzerine kayıt yapılabilen küçük disk** ⊃Orta kısımdaki renkli sayfalarına bakınız.

ˌCˈD ˌburner *noun* [C] a machine that can record information onto a CD **CD kayıt cihazı**

ˌCˈD ˌplayer *noun* [C] a machine that is used for playing music CDs **CD çalar**

CD-R /ˌsiːdiːˈɑːr/ *noun* [C] *abbreviation for* compact disc recordable: an empty compact disc for recording information only once using special computer equipment **kaydedilebilir CD**

☞**CD-ROM** /ˌsiːdiːˈrɒm/ *noun* [C] *abbreviation for* compact disc read-only memory: a CD that holds large amounts of information that can be read by a computer **salt okunur hafızası olan CD**

CD-RW /ˌsiːdiːˈdʌblju/ *noun* [C] *abbreviation for* compact disc rewritable: an empty compact disc for recording and changing information using special computer equipment **yeniden yazılabilir CD**

ˌCˈD ˌwriter *noun* [C] a CD burner **CD kaydedici/yazıcı**

cease /siːs/ *verb* [I, T] *formal* to stop **durdurmak, sona erdirmek, kesmek** [+ doing sth] *He ordered his men to cease firing.* ○ [+ to do sth] *Her behaviour never ceases to amaze me.*

ceasefire /ˈsiːsfaɪər/ *noun* [C] an agreement between two armies or groups to stop fighting **ateşkes**

ceaseless /ˈsiːsləs/ *adjective formal* continuous **aralıksız, durmaksızın, devamlı, mütemadiyyen** *the ceaseless movement of the sea* ● **ceaselessly** *adverb* **sürekli olarak**

cedar /ˈsiːdər/ *noun* [C, U] a tall, evergreen (= with leaves that do not fall off in winter) tree, or the red wood of this tree **sedir ağacı, bir tür çam**

cede /siːd/ *verb* [T] *formal* to give something such as land or power to another country or person, especially because you are forced to **zorla terketmek, devrermek, bırakmak, vazgeçmek**

ceiling /ˈsiːlɪŋ/ *noun* [C] **1** the surface of a room which you can see when you look above you **tavan 2** a limit on the amount that can be paid for something **tavan fiyat** *They have set a ceiling on pay rises.*

celeb /sɪˈleb/ *noun* [C] *informal* a celebrity (= famous person) **ünlü, meşhur biri**

☞**celebrate** /ˈseləbreɪt/ *verb* [I, T] to do something enjoyable because it is a special day, or because something good has happened **kutlamak, kutlama yapmak** *Do you celebrate Christmas in your country?*

celebrated /ˈseləbreɪtɪd/ *adjective* famous for a special ability or quality **özel yeteneği veya özelliğiyle ünlü olan** *She is celebrated for her wit.*

celebration ...... İLE BİRLİKTE KULLANILAN KELİMELER

anniversary/birthday/New Year celebrations ● be a **cause for** celebration ● sth **calls for** a celebration ● a celebration **to mark/of** sth ● **in** celebration **of** sth

celebration /ˌseləˈbreɪʃən/ *noun* [C, U] when you celebrate a special day or event **kutlama, ziyafet, eğlence** *Let's buy some champagne in celebration of her safe arrival.* ○ *You've passed? This calls for a celebration.*

celebratory /ˌseləˈbreɪtəri/ ⑤ /ˈseləbrətɔːri/ *adjective* done to celebrate something or wanting to celebrate something **kutlamaya ilişkin, kutlanan, eğlendirilen** *a celebratory dinner* ○ *in a celebratory mood*

celebrity /səˈlebrəti/ *noun* [C] a famous person **şöhret, ün**

celery /ˈseləri/ *noun* [U] a vegetable with long, pale green stems, often eaten in salads **kereviz** ⊃Orta kısımdaki renkli sayfalarına bakınız.

celestial /səˈlestiəl/ *adjective literary* relating to heaven or the sky **gökyüzüyle ilgili, göksel, cennete dair**

celibate /ˈseləbət/ *adjective* Someone who is celibate does not have sex. **inanç nedeniyle evlenmemeye yemin eden** ● **celibacy** /ˈseləbəsi/ *noun* [U] when you do not have sex **dini nedenle evlenmemeye yemin etme**

cell /sel/ *noun* [C] **1** the smallest living part of an animal or a plant **hücre, yaşayan en küçük canlı** *brain/cancer cells* **2** a small room in a prison or police station where a prisoner is kept **hücre, küçük oda, nezarethane**

cellar /ˈselər/ *noun* [C] a room under the floor of a building **mahzen, kiler** ⊃See also: **salt cellar.**

cellist /ˈtʃelɪst/ *noun* [C] someone who plays the cello **çellist, çello çalan kişi**

cello /ˈtʃeləʊ/ *noun* [C] a large, wooden musical instrument with four strings that you hold between your knees to play **çello**

Cellophane /ˈseləfeɪn/ *noun* [U] *trademark* thin, transparent material that is used for wrapping goods, especially flowers and food **selofan, ambalaj kağıdı/naylonu**

cell phone /ˈselfəʊn/ (*also* cellular phone) *noun* [C] *US* a mobile phone **cep telefonu**

cellular /ˈseljələr/ *adjective* **1** relating to animal or plant cells **hücreyle ilgili** *cellular damage* **2** [always before noun] relating to cellular phones **cep telefonuna ilişkin** *cellular companies/communications*

cellulite /ˈseljəlaɪt/ *noun* [U] fat that looks like small lumps below the skin, especially on the upper legs **selülit, vücutta biriken yağ tabakası** *I can't seem to get rid of my cellulite.*

cellulose /ˈseljələʊs/ *noun* [U] a substance in plants that is used to make some paper and plastics **selüloz, kağıt hammaddesi**

Celsius /ˈselsiəs/ (*written abbreviation* C) *noun* [U] a measurement of temperature in which water freezes at 0° and boils at 100° **santigrat**

Celtic /ˈkeltɪk/ *adjective* relating to the people of Ireland, Scotland, and Wales **İrlanda, İskoçya ve Galler halkına ilişkin/dair, Keltlere ilişkin, Keltik** *Celtic art/music*

cement[1] /sɪˈment/ *noun* [U] a grey powder used in building which is mixed with water and sand or stones to make a hard substance **çimento**

cement[2] /sɪˈment/ *verb* [T] **1** to make something such as a relationship, a belief, or a position stronger **inanç, ilişki veya bir durum vs. pekiştirmek, güçlendirmek, sağlamlaştırmak** *It was the holiday that really cemented our friendship.* **2** (*also* cement over) to cover something with cement **çimento ile yapıştırmak, çimento/beton dökmek**

cemetery /ˈsemətri/ *noun* [C] a place where dead people are buried **mezarlık, kabristan**

censor /ˈsensər/ *verb* [T] to examine books, documents, or films and remove parts of them that are offensive or not allowed by rules **sansürlemek, sansür etmek/uygulamak** [often passive] *The book was heavily censored before publication.* ● **censor** *noun* [C] **sansür**

censorship /'sensəʃɪp/ *noun* [U] when a book, film, newspaper, or other information is censored **sansür, yasak, sansür uygulaması** *political/state censorship*

censure /'senʃər/ *verb* [T] *formal* to criticize someone formally for something that they have done **kınamak, resmî yolla eleştirmek • censure** *noun* [U] *formal* eleştiri

census /'sensəs/ *noun* [C] when people in a country are officially counted and information is taken about them **nüfus sayımı**

o--**cent** /sent/ *noun* [C] a coin or unit of money with a value of $1/100$ of a dollar (= US unit of money); ¢ **sent, paranın küçük birimi, ABD dolarının yüzde biri** *The newspaper costs sixty-five cents.*

centenary /sen'ti:n°ri/ (Ⓤⓢ) /'sent°neri/ (*also US* **centennial** /sen'teniəl/) *noun* [C] the day or year that is 100 years after an important event **yüzüncü yıl dönümü, bir asır dönümü** *This year, there will be many concerts to mark the centenary of the composer's death.*

o--**center** /'sentər/ *noun, verb* US spelling of centre **merkez**

centerpiece /'sentəpi:s/ *noun* [C] US spelling of centrepiece **bir şeyin en önemli bölümü, orta süsü, masa ortasına konulan dekoratif süs**

centi-, cent- /senti-/, /sent-/ *prefix* hundred **yüz- önek** *a centimetre* ○ *a century*

centigrade /'sentɪgreɪd/ *noun* [U] a measurement of temperature in which water freezes at 0° and boils at 100° **santigrat**

centilitre /'sentɪˌliːtər/ *UK* (*US* **centiliter**) (*written abbreviation* **cl**) *noun* [C] a unit for measuring liquid, equal to 0.01 litres **santilitre**

o--**centimetre** *UK* (*US* **centimeter**) (*written abbreviation* **cm**) /'sentɪˌmiːtər/ *noun* [C] a unit for measuring length, equal to 0.01 metres **santimetre**

o--**central** /'sentrəl/ *adjective* **1** [POSITION] in or near the centre of a place or object **merkezi** *central Africa/America* ○ *The roof is supported by a central column.* **2** [ORGANIZATION] [always before noun] controlled or organized in one main place **merkezde olan, ana merkezde** *central authorities/government* ○ *the US central bank* **3** [IMPORTANT] main or most important **ana ve en önemli olan** *a central character/figure* ○ *Her role is central to the film.* **4** [CITY] in the main part of a town or city **bir şehrin ana merkezinde olan • centrally** *adverb* **merkezde**

central 'heating *noun* [U] a system of heating a building by warming air or water in one place and carrying it to different rooms in pipes **merkezi ısıtma, kalorifer**

centralize (*also UK* -ise) /'sentrəlaɪz/ *verb* [T] If a country or organization is centralized, it is controlled from one place. **merkezileştirmek, bir merkezden yönetmek/yönetilmek** [often passive] *centralized control/government* **• centralization** /ˌsentrəlaɪˈzeɪʃ°n/ *noun* [U] **merkezcilik**

o--**centre**[1] *UK* (*US* **center**) /'sentər/ *noun* **1** [MIDDLE] [C] the middle point or part of something **ortası, merkezi** *She stood in the centre of the room.* ○ *Cars are not allowed in the town centre.* **2** [PLACE] [C] a place or a building used for a particular activity **merkez, belli bir işlev için kullanılan merkez** *a health/advice centre* ○ *a centre for the homeless* **3** [BUSINESS] [C] a place where a lot of a particular activity or business takes place **iş merkezi** *an industrial centre* **4** [POLITICAL] [no plural] (*also* the centre) a political position with opinions that are not extreme **siyasette orta çizgi** *His political views are left of centre.* **5 be the centre of attention** to receive more attention than anyone or anything else **ilgi odağı**

olmak, heresin ilgisini çekmek ⊃See also: community centre, garden centre, shopping centre.

centre[2] *UK* (*US* **center**) /'sentər/ *verb* [T] to put something in the middle of an area **bir şeyi merkeze koymak, yerleştirmek**

centre around/on sb/sth *phrasal verb* to have someone or something as the main part of a discussion or activity **birini/bir şeyi tartışmanın, eylemin merkezine koymak/yerleştirmek** *The dispute centres on racial issues.*

,**centre of 'gravity** *noun* [C] *plural* **centres of gravity** the point in an object where its weight is balanced **yerçekim merkezi**

centrepiece *UK* (*US* **centerpiece**) /'sentəpi:s/ *noun* [C] **1** the most important or attractive part of something **bir şeyin en önemli/çekici bölümü** *The employment programme is the centrepiece of the government's economic strategy.* **2** a decoration that is put in the middle of a dinner table **orta süsü, masa ortasına konulan dekoratif süs**

[🧩] **century** .... İLE BİRLİKTE KULLANILAN KELİMELER

in the [17th/21st, etc] **century • the early/mid/late** [15th/19th, etc] **century • the turn of the** century (= the time around the end of one century and the beginning of the next)

o--**century** /'senʃ°ri/ *noun* [C] a period of 100 years, especially used in giving dates **yüzyıl, asır** *the twentieth century*

CEO /ˌsiːiːˈəʊ/ *noun* [C] *abbreviation for* chief executive officer: the person with the most important job in a company **bir şirkette en üst düzey yönetici**

ceramics /sə'ræmɪks/ *noun* [plural] objects that are made by shaping and heating clay **seramik • ceramic** *adjective* made by shaping and heating clay **seramikten yapılma** *a ceramic pot*

cereal /'sɪəriəl/ *noun* [C, U] **1** a plant that is grown to produce grain for food **tahıl** *cereal crops* **2** a food that is made from grain and eaten with milk, especially in the morning **tahıl gevreği, gevrek** *breakfast cereals* ⊃Orta kısımdaki renkli sayfalarına bakınız.

cerebral /'serəbrəl/ *adjective formal* **1** Cerebral films, books, etc need a lot of thought to understand them, and cerebral people think a lot. **beyinle ilgili 2** [always before noun] relating to the brain **beyine ilişkin** *cerebral arteries*

ceremonial /ˌserɪˈməʊniəl/ *adjective* relating to a ceremony **kutlamayla ilgili, törene ilişkin • ceremonially** *adverb* **törensel**

[🧩] **ceremony** .... İLE BİRLİKTE KULLANILAN KELİMELER

attend/hold a ceremony • **at** a ceremony • **an award/marriage/wedding** ceremony

ceremony /'serɪməni/ *noun* **1** [C] a formal event that is performed on important social or religious occasions **tören** *a wedding/marriage ceremony* ○ *an award ceremony* **2** [U] formal behaviour, words, and actions that are part of a ceremony **tören davranışı, ifadeleri ve hareketleri, törene dair**

o--**certain** /'sɜːt°n/ *adjective* **1** [NO DOUBT] [never before noun] completely sure of something, or knowing without doubt that something is true **kesin** [+ (that)] *I feel absolutely certain that you're doing the right thing.* ○ [+ question word] *Nobody was certain how the accident had happened.* ○ *He was quite certain about/of the thief's identity.* ⊃Opposite uncertain. **2 know/say for certain** to know something without doubt **bir şeyi kesin olarak bilmek, emin olmak** *We don't know for certain whether she's coming.* **3** [SURE TO HAPPEN] sure to happen, to do some-

c

thing, or to be true **emin, kat'i** [+ **(that)**] *It now looks certain that she will resign.* ○ [+ **to do sth**] *She is certain to do well in the exams.* ○ *How can we make certain that* (= do something to be sure that) *she sees the note?* **4** PARTICULAR [always before noun] used to refer to a particular person or thing without naming or describing them exactly **belli, besbelli, kaçınılmaz** *The museum is only open at certain times of the day.* **5 a certain** used before a noun to mean existing, but difficult to describe the exact quality or amount **kesin, belli** *He's got a certain charm.* **6 certain of** *formal* used to refer to some of a group of people or things **emin** *Certain of you already know the news.*

⚬**certainly** /'sɜ:tənli/ *adverb* **1** used to emphasize something and show that there is no doubt about it **kesinlikle, tabii** *Their team certainly deserved to win.* ○ *"Are your parents paying for dinner?" "I certainly hope so."* ○ *"Do you regret what you said?" " Certainly not!"* **2** used to agree to a request **elbette** *"Could you pass the salt, please?" "Certainly."*

certainty /'sɜ:tᵊnti/ *noun* **1** [U] when you are completely sure about something **kesinlik** *I can't say with any certainty what time she left.* **2** [C] something that is very likely to happen or cannot be doubted **kuşkusuzluk, şüphesizlik** *There are no absolute certainties in life.*

certificate /sə'tɪfɪkət/ *noun* [C] an official document that gives details to show that something is true **sertifika, belge** *a death/marriage certificate* ○ *an exam certificate* ⊃See also: **birth certificate**.

certify /'sɜ:tɪfaɪ/ *verb* [T] **1** TRUTH *formal* to say in a formal or official way that something is true or correct **sözlü ya da yazılı tasdik etmek, kabul etmek, yeterli bulmak** [+ **(that)**] *I certify that the information I have given is true.* ○ *She was certified dead on arrival at the hospital.* **2** CERTIFICATE to give someone a certificate to say that they have completed a course of study **sertifika vermek** *a certified accountant* **3** HEALTH to say officially that someone has a mental illness **resmi olarak birinin zihinsel rahatsızlığı olduğunu söylemek, bildirmek**

certitude /'sɜ:tɪtju:d/ *noun* [U] *formal* when you feel certain about something **emin olma, kesin kabul etme, eminlik**

cervix /'sɜ:vɪks/ *noun* [C] the narrow entrance to a woman's womb **rahim ağzı, dölyatağı ağzı ● cervical** /sə'vaɪkᵊl/, /'sɜ:vɪkᵊl/ *adjective cervical cancer* **rahime dair**

cesarean /sɪ'zeəriən/ *noun* [C] *US spelling of* caesarean **sezaryen, ameliyatla çocuk doğurma**

cessation /ses'eɪʃᵊn/ *noun* [C, U] *formal* when something, especially violence, stops **şiddetin sona ermesi; durma, kesilme** *the cessation of hostilities*

cf used in writing when you want the reader to make a comparison between the subject being discussed and something else **yazılan konunun başka bir konuyla mukayese edilmesi gerektiğini belirtir**

CFC /,si:ef'si:/ *noun* [C] *abbreviation for* chlorofluorocarbon: a type of gas used in some fridges (= containers for keeping food cold) and aerosols (= containers for making liquids come out in small drops), which damages the layer of gases around the Earth **kloroflorokarbon, yoğutucu gaz**

chafe /tʃeɪf/ *verb* **1** [I] to feel angry because of rules and limits **kural ve sınırlamalara kızmak, rahatsızlık duymak** *He chafed against/at the narrow academic approach of his school.* **2** [I, T] to make part of the body painful by rubbing, or to become painful because of being rubbed **kaşıyarak acıtmak, tahriş etmek**

chagrin /'ʃægrɪn/ ⓤ /ʃə'grɪn/ *noun* [U] anger or disappointment caused by something that does not happen the way you wanted it **üzen şey, kızgınlık veya hayal kırıklığı, olması istene bir şeyin olmaması halinde duyulan kızgınlık** *To his parents' chagrin, he had no intention of becoming a lawyer.*

chain

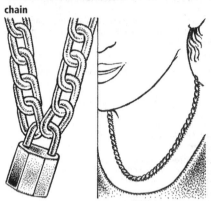

chain¹ /tʃeɪn/ *noun* **1** METAL RINGS [C, U] a line of metal rings connected together **zincir, halka** *a bicycle chain* ○ *She wore a gold chain around her neck.* ○ *The hostages were kept in chains.* **2** BUSINESS [C] a number of similar shops, restaurants, etc owned by the same company **mağazalar/lokantalar zinciri** *a chain of hotels/supermarkets* **3** EVENTS [C] a series of things that happen one after the other **peşpeşe olanlar** *His arrival set off a surprising chain of events.*

chain² /tʃeɪm/ (*also* **chain up**) *verb* [T] to fasten someone or something to someone or something else using a chain **zincirlemek, zincirle bağlamak** *I chained my bike to a lamppost.* ○ *You shouldn't keep a dog chained up like that.*

,chain re'action *noun* [C] a series of events where each one causes the next one to happen **sıralı, birbiri peşisıra olan tepki,**

chain-smoke /'tʃeɪnsməʊk/ *verb* [I, T] to smoke cigarettes one after another **hiç aralıksız, durmaksızın sigara içmek ● chain smoker** *noun* [C] **tiryaki (sigara)**

'chain ,store *noun* [C] one of a group of similar shops owned by the same company **mağazalar zinciri**

⚬**chair¹** /tʃeər/ *noun* [C] **1** FURNITURE a seat for one person, with a back, usually four legs, and sometimes two arms **sandalye** ⊃*Orta kısımdaki renkli sayfalarına bakınız.* **2** MEETING someone who controls a meeting or organization **oturum başkanı** [usually singular] *All questions should be addressed to the chair.* **3** UNIVERSITY a very important position in a university department, or the person who has this position **üniversitede önemli bir görev, bölüm başkanı** ⊃See also: **the electric chair.**

chair² /tʃeər/ *verb* [T] to control a meeting or organization **oturumu, toplantıyı yönetmek** *I've been asked to chair the committee.*

chairman, chairwoman /'tʃeəmən/, /'tʃeə,wʊmən/ *noun* [C] *plural* **chairmen** *or* **chairwomen** a man/woman who controls a meeting, company, or other organization **başkan, yönetici (bayan, erkek)**

chairperson /'tʃeə,pɜ:sᵊn/ *noun* [C] someone who controls a meeting, company, or other organization **başkan**

chalet /'ʃæleɪ/ ⓤ /ʃæl'eɪ/ *noun* [C] a small wooden house, often in a mountain area, or for people who are on holiday **dağ evi, bungalov, küçük ahşap ev, kulübe**

chalk¹ /tʃɔːk/ *noun* **1** [U] a type of soft, white rock **kireç** **2** [C, U] a small stick of chalk that is used for writing and drawing **tebeşir** *a piece of chalk* ⊃Orta kısımdaki renkli sayfalarına bakınız. **3 be chalk and cheese** *UK* If two people are like chalk and cheese, they are completely different from each other. **birbiriyle taban tabana zıt olmak, farklı olmak**

chalk² /tʃɔːk/ *verb* [T] *UK* to write something with a piece of chalk **tebeşirle yazmak**
chalk sth up *phrasal verb* to achieve something **başarmak, elde etmek** *She's chalked up five goals this season.*

chalkboard /'tʃɔːkbɔːd/ *US* (*UK/US* blackboard) *noun* [C] a large board with a dark surface that teachers write on with chalk **kara tahta, tebeşir tahtası**

chalky /'tʃɔːki/ *adjective* made of chalk, or similar to chalk **kirece benzer, kireçli**

face/pose/present/relish a challenge ● a **big/formidable/serious/tough** challenge

o-**challenge¹** /'tʃælɪndʒ/ *noun* **1** DIFFICULT [C, U] something that is difficult and that tests someone's ability or determination **birinin yetenek ve kararlılığını ölçen şey, durum** *Finding a decision that pleases everyone is the challenge which now faces the committee.* **2** INVITATION [C] an invitation to compete in a game or a fight **meydan okuma** *I'm sure Paul will race you. He never refuses a challenge.* **3** DISAGREEMENT [C] an expression of disagreement with ideas, rules, or someone's authority **birinin yetkisine, kurallar veya fikirlerine karşı durma, rakip olarak görme** *a challenge to the authority of the President*

challenge² /'tʃælɪndʒ/ *verb* [T] **1** to express disagreement with ideas, rules, or someone's authority **zora sokmak, karşı durmak, memnuniyetsizliğini dile getirmek, sorgulamak** *The election results are being challenged.* **2** to invite someone to compete in a game or fight **meydan okumak, düelloya davet etmek** *He challenged Smith to a fight.*

challenger /'tʃælɪndʒəʳ/ *noun* [C] someone who competes in a game, competition, or election, often to win a position that someone else has **rakip, meydan okuyan** *There are five challengers for the title.*

challenging /'tʃælɪndʒɪŋ/ *adjective* difficult to do in a way that tests your ability or determination **zorlayan, gayrete getiren, zora sokan** *This has been a challenging time for us all.*

chamber /'tʃeɪmbəʳ/ *noun* [C] **1** ROOM a room used for an official or special purpose **toplantı odası, oda, bölme** *a debating chamber* ○ *a burial chamber* **2** PARLIAMENT one of the groups that a parliament is divided into **parlamentoda grup** *the upper/lower chamber* **3** MACHINE/BODY a closed space in a machine or in your body **odacık, kapalı bölüm** *the left chamber of the heart* ⊃See also: gas chamber.

chambermaid /'tʃeɪmbəmeɪd/ *noun* [C] a woman whose job is to clean and tidy hotel bedrooms **oda hizmetçisi**

'**chamber ,music** *noun* [U] music that is written for a small group of musicians **oda müziği**

,**chamber of 'commerce** *noun* [C] *plural* **chambers of commerce** an organization of business people who work together to improve business in their local area **ticaret odası**

champ /tʃæmp/ *noun* [C] *informal short for* champion **şampiyon**

champagne /ʃæm'peɪn/ *noun* [U] French white wine with lots of bubbles in it which people often drink to celebrate something **şampanya**

champagne

o-**champion¹** /'tʃæmpiən/ *noun* [C] **1** a person, animal, or team that wins a competition **şampiyon** *a boxing champion* ○ *the world champions* **2** someone who supports, defends, or fights for a person, belief, or principle **savunan, savaşım veren, destekleyen** *a champion of human rights* ⊃See also: reigning champion.

champion² /'tʃæmpiən/ *verb* [T] to support, defend, or fight for a person, belief, or principle **desteklemek, mücadele etmek, savaşım vermek** *She championed the cause of free speech.*

championship /'tʃæmpiənʃɪp/ *noun* [C] **1** a competition to find the best team or player in a particular game or sport **şampiyonluk yarışı** *The world championship will be held in this country next year.* **2** the position of being a champion **şampiyonluk** *She is current holder of our tennis championship.*

a chance of sth ● a **fifty-fifty** chance ● a **fair/good/slim** chance

o-**chance¹** /tʃɑːns/ *noun* **1** POSSIBILITY [C, U] the possibility that something will happen **olasılık, şans** [+ (that)] *There's a chance that she'll still be there.* ○ *She has little chance of passing the exam.* ○ *Is there any chance of a drink?* **2** OPPORTUNITY [C] the opportunity to do something **olanak, fırsat** [+ to do sth] *I didn't get a chance to speak to you at the party.* ○ *I hope you've had the chance to look around the exhibition.* ○ *Give me a chance to prove that I can do the work.* ○ *Going on a world cruise is the chance of a lifetime* (= an opportunity which only comes once in your life). **3** LUCK [U] when something happens because of luck, or without being planned **şans, talih, kısmet** *I saw her by chance in the shop.* **4** RISK [C] a risk **risk, teklike, şans** *I'm delivering my work by hand. I'm not taking any chances.* **5 By any chance** used to ask in a polite way whether something is possible or true **Acaba? Olası mı dersin? Ne dersin? Hiç şans var mı?** *You're not Spanish by any chance, are you?* **6 stand a chance** to have a chance of success or of achieving something **başarma şansı olmak** *He stands a good chance of winning the election.* **7 chances are** it is likely **muhtemeldir ki, büyük bir olasılıkla, muhtemelen** [+ (that)] *Chances are that he'll refuse.* **8 No chance!/Not a chance!** used to emphasize that there is no possibility of something happening **İmkânsız! Olamaz! Ne mümkün! Olacak gibi değil!** *"Do you think she'd go out with me?" "No chance!"* **9 fat chance** *informal* used to say that you do not think that something is likely to happen **zayıf bir olasılık, pek mümkün değil, olası görünmüyor** *"Do you think we'll win?" "Fat chance."* ⊃See also: off-chance, outside chance.

chance² /tʃɑːns/ *verb* [T] *informal* to take a risk by doing something **göze almak, riske girmek, şansını denemek**

chance³ /tʃɑːns/ *adjective* [always before noun] A chance event is not planned or expected. **beklenmeye, planlanmamış, şans** *a chance meeting*

chancellor /'tʃɑːnsələʳ/ *noun* [C] **1** GOVERNMENT the leader of the government in some countries **(bazı ülkelerde) başbakan** *the German chancellor* **2** UNIVERSITY the person with the highest position in some universities **bazı üniversitelerde en üst seviyedeki kişi, rektör 3** [MONEY] (also ,Chancellor of the Ex'chequer) *UK* the person in the British government who makes decisions about taxes and government spending **Büyük Britanya hükümetinde maliye bakanı**

chandelier /ˌʃændə'lɪər/ noun [C] a large light that hangs from the ceiling that is made of many small lights or candles and small pieces of glass **avize**

> **change** ..... BAŞKA BİR DEYİŞLE
>
> **alter** fiili **change** fiiline alternatif olarak sıklıkla kullanılır. *We've had to* **alter** *our plans.*
> Eğer yaptığınız bir şeyi sıklıkla değiştiriyorsanız, **vary** fiilini kullanabilirsiniz. *Try to* **vary** *the children's diet a little.*
> Eğer kişi bir şeyin amacını veya görünüşünü değiştiriyorsa, bunu belirtmek için **convert** fiilini **veya turn into** deyimini kullanabilir. *We're going to* **convert** *the spare bedroom into an office.* ● *There are plans to* **turn** *his latest book* **into** *a film.*
> Eğer kişi yaptığı bir şeyden diğerine atlıyorsa, **switch** fiili kullanılabilir. *We've* **switched** *over to low fat milk.* ● *Jack has just* **switched** *jobs.*

⌐**change¹** /tʃeɪndʒ/ *verb* **1** [DIFFERENT] [I, T] to become different, or to make someone or something become different **değişmek, değiştirmek** *I hadn't seen her for twenty years, but she hadn't changed a bit.* ○ *The course changed my life.* ○ *She's* **changed** *from being a happy, healthy child* **to** *being ill all the time.* **2** [FROM ONE THING TO ANOTHER] [I, T] to stop having or using one thing, and start having or using another **değiştirmek** *The doctor has recommended changing my diet.* ○ *I'll have to ask them if they can change the time of my interview.* **3** [CLOTHES] [I, T] to take off your clothes and put on different ones **kıyafetini değiştirmek** *He* **changed out of** *his school uniform* **into** *jeans and a T-shirt.* ○ *Is there somewhere I can get changed?* **4** [JOURNEY] [I, T] to get off a bus, plane, etc and catch another, in order to continue a journey **bir vasıta değiştirmek** *I have to change trains at Bristol.* **5** [IN SHOP] [T] *UK* to take something you have bought back to a shop and exchange it for something else **bir malı değiştirmek** *If the dress doesn't fit, can I change it for a smaller one?* **6** [MONEY] [T] to get or give someone money in exchange for money of a different type **döviz bozdurmak** *Where can I change my dollars?* ○ *Can you change a £20 note for two tens?* **7** [BED] [T] to take dirty sheets off a bed and put on clean ones **çarşaf değiştirmek** *to change the bed/sheets* **8** [BABY] [T] to put a clean nappy (= thick cloth worn on a baby's bottom) on a baby **bebek bezi değiştirmek, bebeğin altını değiştirmek** ⊃See also: chop¹ and change, change hands (hand¹), change your tune¹.

change sth around/round *phrasal verb* to move objects such as furniture into different positions **mobilyaların yerini değiştirmek**

change over *phrasal verb UK* to stop using or having one thing and start using or having something else ... **e/a geçmek, dönmek; tarz/usul değiştirmek, başka bir tarza dönmek** *We've just* **changed** *over/from gas central heating* **to** *electric.*

> **change** .... İLE BİRLİKTE KULLANILAN KELİMELER
>
> **bring about / implement / make / undergo** change
> ● change **occurs/takes place** ● a **big/dramatic/ fundamental / major / radical / sweeping** change
> ● change **in/to** sth

⌐**change²** /tʃeɪndʒ/ *noun* **1** [DIFFERENCE] [C, U] when something becomes different, or the result of something becoming different **değişim** *We need to* **make** *a few* **changes to** *the design.* ○ *There is no* **change in** *the patient's condition* (= the illness has not got better or

worse). ○ *How can we* **bring about** *social* **change**? **2** [FROM ONE THING TO ANOTHER] [C, U] when you stop having or using one thing and start having or using another **değiştirme** *This country needs a* **change of** *government.* ○ *I've notified the school of our* **change of address**. **3** [NEW EXPERIENCE] [C] something that you enjoy because it is a new experience **değişiklik** [usually singular] *Going abroad for our anniversary would* **make** *a lovely* **change**. ○ *It's nice to eat together as a family* **for a change**. **4** [MONEY] [U] the money that you get back when you pay more for something than it costs **para üstü** *There's your receipt and £3 change.* **5** [COINS] [U] coins, not paper money **bozuk/ madeni/demir para** *Have you got any change for the parking meter?* ○ *Have you got change for £5* (= can you give me £5 in coins in return for paper money)? **6 a change of clothes** a set of clean clothes that you can put on if you need to take off the ones you are wearing **yedek kıyafetler, temiz giysiler 7 a change of heart** If you have a change of heart, you change your opinion or feelings about something. **tutum değiştirme, fikir değişikliği** ⊃See also: small change.

changeable /'tʃeɪndʒəbl/ *adjective* often changing, or likely to change **değişebilir, değişme olasılığı olan**

changeover /'tʃeɪndʒˌəʊvər/ *noun* [C] a change from one system or situation to another **değişim, geçiş, değiştirme, dönüş** [usually singular] *the changeover from the old computer system to the new one*

'changing ,room *noun* [C] *UK* a room in a shop where you can try clothes, or a room where you change into clothes to do sport **soyunma kabini, elbise deneme kabini; (spor) soyunma odaları**

⌐**channel¹** /'tʃænəl/ *noun* [C] **1** [TELEVISION] a television or radio station (= broadcasting company) **tv/radyo kanalı/bandı 2** [PASSAGE] a long, narrow passage for water or other liquids to flow along **kanal** *an irrigation channel* **3** [COMMUNICATION] a way of communicating with people or getting something done **iletişim kanalı** *a channel of communication* **4 the Channel** (also the ,English 'Channel) the narrow area of water between England and France **İngiltere ile Fransa arasındaki kanal, manş tüneli 5** [RIVER] a part of a river or sea that is deep and wide enough for ships to travel along **geçiş tüneli/kanalı** *a navigable channel*

channel² /'tʃænəl/ *verb* [T] *UK* **channelling**, *past* **channelled**, *US* **channeling**, *past* **channeled 1** to direct water along a particular route **suyu kanalize etmek, kanal yardımıyla götürmek** *The waste water is channelled through this pipe.* **2** to use money or energy for a particular purpose **parayı ve enerjiyi belli bir amaç için kanalize etmek, kullanmak** *We've* **channelled** *all our resources* **into** *this project.*

the ,Channel 'Tunnel *noun* the three long passages under the English Channel between England and France **Manş Tüneli, İngiltere ile Fransa'yı birbirine bağlayan üç geçişli tünel**

chant¹ /tʃɑːnt/ *verb* [I, T] **1** to repeat or sing a word or phrase many times, often shouting **yüksek sesle tekrar etmek, nakaratı söylemek** *The demonstrators* **chanted** *anti-racist slogans.* **2** to sing a religious song or prayer using a very simple tune **dini şarkı ve ilahiler söylemek**

chant² /tʃɑːnt/ *noun* [C] **1** a word or phrase that is repeated many times **aynı tempoda sürekli yinelenen söz, ifade, nakarat 2** a religious song or prayer that is sung using a very simple tune **dini şarkı veya duayı basit bir tonla söyleme, ilahi söyleme, dua okuma**

Chanukah /'hɑːnəkə/ *noun* [C, U] Hanukkah **Hanuka**

🧩 *chaos* .... İLE BİRLİKTE KULLANILAN KELİMELER

cause chaos ● **descend into/be thrown into** chaos ● **be in** chaos ● **total/utter** chaos

chaos /ˈkeɪɒs/ *noun* [U] a situation where there is no order at all and everyone is confused **kargaşa, kaos, karışıklık** *The country's at war and everything is in chaos.*

chaotic /keɪˈɒtɪk/ *adjective* in a state of chaos **kargaşaya sebep olan, karmaşık, düzensiz** *a chaotic situation*

chap /tʃæp/ *noun* [C] *UK informal* a man **adam**

chapel /ˈtʃæpəl/ *noun* [C] a small church, or a room used as a church in a building **küçük kilise, şapel**

chaperone¹ (*also* chaperon) /ˈʃæpərəʊn/ *noun* [C] an older person who goes somewhere with a younger person in order to make sure they behave well, especially a woman in the past who went with a younger woman who was not married **refakatçi, hami, koruyucu, gözetici**

chaperone² (*also* chaperon) /ˈʃæpərəʊn/ *verb* [T] to go somewhere with someone as their chaperone **birine refakat etmek, göz kulak olmak, eşlik etmek, beraber olmak**

chaplain /ˈtʃæplɪn/ *noun* [C] a priest in the army, a school, a hospital, or a prison **okul, hastane, hapishane veya ordu papazı, din görevlisi, rahip**

chapter /ˈtʃæptər/ *noun* [C] **1** one of the parts that a book is divided into **kitabın bölümleri 2** a period of time when something happens in history or in someone's life **bir insanın veya tarihin bir dönemi** *an interesting chapter in Spanish history*

🧩 *character* .... İLE BİRLİKTE KULLANILAN KELİMELER

a   colourful/lovable/shady/strong/unsavoury character ● **a real** character

o⋅**character** /ˈkærəktər/ *noun* **1** QUALITIES [C, U] the combination of qualities and personality that makes one person or thing different from others **karakter, şahsiyet, kişilik** *It's not in her character to be jealous* (= she would not usually be jealous). ○ *It would be very out of character* (= not typical) *of her to lie.* ○ *The character of the village has changed since the road was built.* **2** STORY [C] a person in a book, film, etc **kitap, film vs. de karakter, asıl kişi** *a cartoon character* **3** GOOD QUALITIES [U] qualities that are interesting or unusual **ilginç ve sıradışı özellikler** *a hotel of character* **4** PERSON [C] *informal* a particular kind of person **bir tür insan, karakter, vasıf** *an unpleasant character* **5** INTERESTING PERSON [C] an interesting or funny person whose behaviour is different from most people's **farklı özelliği/vasfı olan kişi, şahıs** *Your granny's a real character.* **6** WRITING [C] a letter, sign, or number that you use when you are writing or printing **yazıda kullanılan işaret, harf ve rakamların tümü** *Chinese characters*

characteristic¹ /ˌkærəktəˈrɪstɪk/ *noun* [C] a typical or obvious quality that makes one person or thing different from others **özellik, vasıf, karakteristik, nitelik, hususiyet** *a national characteristic* ○ *Does he have any distinguishing physical characteristics?*

characteristic² /ˌkærəktəˈrɪstɪk/ *adjective* typical of someone or something **kenidne özgü, tipik, karakteristik** *Grey stone is characteristic of buildings in that area.* ◑Opposite uncharacteristic. ● **characteristically** *adverb* **tipik**

characterization (*also UK* -isation) /ˌkærəktəraɪˈzeɪʃən/ *noun* [U] the way that people are described in a play, book, etc **tanımlama, nitelendirme**

characterize (*also UK* -ise) /ˈkærəktəˈraɪz/ *verb* [T] **1** to be typical of someone or something **belirgin özelliği olmak, simgesi olmak** [often passive] *Her behaviour in class has been characterized by rudeness and laziness.* **2** to describe or show someone or something in a particular way **bir şeyi birini hususi bir şekilde göstermek, tanımlamak, tasvir etmek** *Historians have characterized the age as a period of great change.*

charade /ʃəˈrɑːd/ ⓤ /ʃəˈreɪd/ *noun* [C] a situation which is clearly false, but where people behave as if it is true or serious **sahte, sırıtan davranış,** *The interview was just a charade.*

charcoal /ˈtʃɑːkəʊl/ *noun* [U] a hard, black substance that is produced by burning wood without much air, and that is used as fuel or for drawing **odun kömürü, mangal kömürü**

🧩 *charge* .... İLE BİRLİKTE KULLANILAN KELİMELER

make a charge ● **at no extra/free of/without** charge ● **a charge for** sth ● a charge **of** [£10/$12, etc] ● a **small** charge

o⋅**charge¹** /tʃɑːdʒ/ *noun* **1** MONEY [C, U] the amount of money that you have to pay for something, especially for an activity or a service **ücret, fiyat, tutar** *bank charges* ○ *There's no charge for children under 14.* ○ *He repaired the computer free of charge* (= it did not cost anything). **2 be in charge** to be the person who has control of or is responsible for someone or something **sorumlu olmak, mesul/yetkili olmak** *She's in charge of a team of 20 people.* ○ *Who's in charge of organizing the music for the party?* **3 take charge** to take control of or make yourself responsible for something **kontrolünü üslenmek, sorumluluğu yüklenmek** *I was happy to let her take charge of paying all the bills.* **4** CRIME [C] a formal police statement saying that someone is accused of a crime **resmi polis ithamı, suçlama tutanağı, belgesi** *to bring/press charges* ○ *She was arrested on charges of theft and forgery.* **5** ACCUSE [C] when you accuse someone of something **suçlama, itham** *This is a serious charge to make against your colleagues.* **6** ELECTRICITY [C, U] the amount of electricity that an electrical device has in it or that a substance has in it **7** ATTACK [C] an attack in which people or animals run forward suddenly **saldırı, hücum, atılma 8 reverse the charges** *UK* (*US* call collect) to make a telephone call that is paid for by the person who receives it **ödemeli arama** ◑See also: service charge.

o⋅**charge²** /tʃɑːdʒ/ *verb* **1** ASK TO PAY [I, T] to ask someone to pay an amount of money for something, especially for an activity or a service **ücretlendirmek, fiyat istemek, ücret talep etmek** [+ two objects] *They are going to charge motorists a tax to drive into the city centre.* ○ *How much do you charge for delivery?* **2** ACCUSE [T] If the police charge someone, they accuse them officially of a crime. **suçlamak, itham etmek, suçlu bulmak** [often passive] *He was charged with assault.* **3** ATTACK [I, T] to attack someone or something by moving forward quickly **saldırmak, hücum etmek, atılmak** *The bull looked as if it was about to charge.* **4 charge around/into/through, etc** to run from one place to another **oradan oraya koşuşturmak, sağa sola koşmak** *The children charged around the house.* **5** ELECTRICITY [I, T] to put electricity into something **şarj etmek**

ˈcharge ˌcard *noun* [C] a small plastic card that allows you to buy something and pay for it at a particular date in the future **taksit kartı, taksitli alışveriş kartı**

charged /tʃɑːdʒd/ *adjective* A situation or a subject that is charged causes strong feelings or arguments. **şiddetli tartışma ve hislerin oluşmasına neden olan durum** *a highly charged debate*

chariot /'tʃæriət/ noun [C] a vehicle with two wheels that was used in races and fights in ancient times and was pulled by a horse çok eskilerde yarış/savaşta kullanılan iki tekerlekli yarış/savaş arabası

charisma /kə'rızmə/ noun [U] a natural power which some people have to influence or attract people **karizma, kişilik, etkileyicilik** ● **charismatic** /ˌkærɪz'mætɪk/ adjective **karizmatik**

charitable /'tʃærɪtəbl/ adjective **1** [always before noun] A charitable event, activity, or organization gives money, food, or help to people who need it. **düşkünlere para, yiyecek ve çeşitli yardımlarda bulunan 2** kind, and not judging other people in a severe way **müşfik, anlayışlı, sevecen, merhametli** ● **charitably** adverb **bağış amaçlı**

```
       charity ...... İLE BİRLİKTE KULLANILAN KELİMELER
```
donate/give sth **to** charity ● [money, etc] **goes to** charity ● **do** sth **for** charity ● a charity **for** [homeless people/sick children, etc] ● a charity **event** (= an event to raise money for a charity)

charity /'tʃærɪti/ noun **1** [ORGANIZATION] [C, U] an official organization that gives money, food, or help to people who need it **hayır kurumu, yardım derneği, darülaceze** The raffle will raise money for charity. ○ A percentage of the company's profits go to charity. **2** [MONEY/HELP] [U] money, food, or other help that is given to people **yardım, sadaka** I won't accept charity. **3** [KINDNESS] [U] kindness towards other people **sevecenlik, hayırseverlik, merhamet, hoşgörü** an act of charity

'charity ˌshop UK (US **thrift shop**) noun [C] a shop which sells goods given by the public, especially clothes, to make money for a particular charity **yardım amaçlı özellikle kıyafet satan dükkan, mağaza**

charlatan /'ʃɑːlətⁿn/ noun [C] someone who pretends to have skills or knowledge that they do not have **şarlatan**

charm[1] /tʃɑːm/ noun **1** [C, U] a quality that makes you like someone or something **sevimlilik, çekicilik, alımlılık** The building had a certain charm. **2** [C] an object that you keep or wear because you believe that it is lucky **nazarlık, tılsım, uğur** a lucky charm

charm[2] /tʃɑːm/ verb [T] to attract someone or persuade someone to do something because of your charm **büyülemek, cezbetmek, etkisi altına almak** [often passive] We were charmed by his boyish manner.

charmed /tʃɑːmd/ adjective very lucky, or managing to avoid danger **şanslı, tehlikeyi savabilen** The young boy had led a charmed life.

charmer /'tʃɑːmə*/ noun [C] informal someone who knows how to be charming in order to attract people or persuade them to do things **etkileyici kimse, büyüleyici kimse, cazibesini kullanarak başkalarını ikna edebilen kişi**

charming /'tʃɑːmɪŋ/ adjective pleasant or attractive **alımlı, cazibeli, havalı, çekici** a charming smile/place ● **charmingly** adverb **etkileyici bir şekilde**

charred /tʃɑːd/ adjective black from having been burned **yanıp kararmış, kömür gibi olmuş, kararmış** charred wreckage

chart[1] /tʃɑːt/ noun **1** [C] a drawing which shows information in a simple way, often using lines and curves to show amounts **çizelge, tablo, grafik, çizim** a sales chart **2 the charts** an official list of the most popular songs each week **en çok satan şarkılar listesi 3** [C] a map of the sea or the sky **deniz veya gökyüzü haritası**

chart[2] /tʃɑːt/ verb [T] **1** to watch and record information about something over a period of time **bir şeyi belli bir süre izleyip kaydetmek** The documentary charted the

progress of the war. **2** to make a map of an area of land, sea, or sky **kara, deniz veya gökyüzünün haritasını yapmak, çıkarmak**

charter[1] /'tʃɑːtə*/ noun [C] a formal, written description of the principles, activities, and purpose of an organization **tüzük, yönetmelik, nizamname**

charter[2] /'tʃɑːtə*/ verb [T] to rent a vehicle, especially an aircraft **kiralamak** The holiday company chartered a plane to fly us all home.

charter[3] /'tʃɑːtə*/ adjective a **charter flight/company/ plane, etc** using aircraft paid for by travel companies for their customers **kiralık uçakla uçuş, çartır uçuşu**

chartered /'tʃɑːtəd/ adjective [always before noun] UK having the necessary qualifications to work in a particular profession **lisanslı, ehliyetli, sertifikalı** a chartered accountant/surveyor

chase

chase[1] /tʃeɪs/ verb **1** [I, T] to run after someone or something in order to catch them **kovalamak, peşinden koşmak, izlemek** The dog was chasing a rabbit. **2 chase sb/sth away/off/out, etc** to run after a person or animal to make them leave a place **kovmak, uzaklaştırmak** I chased the cat away. **3** [T] UK to try very hard to get something **elde etmeye çalışmak, peşinden koşmak** There are hundreds of graduates chasing very few jobs.

chase[2] /tʃeɪs/ noun **1** [C] when you go after someone or something quickly in order to catch them **takip, izleme, peşinden gitme** a high speed car chase **2 give chase** to go after someone or something quickly in order to catch them **birini yakalamak için peşinden gitmek, takip etmek**

chasm /'kæzⁿm/ noun [C] **1** a long, deep, narrow hole in rock or ice **derin yarık, gedik, uçurum 2** a very large difference between two opinions or two groups of people **büyük fark, uçurum, ayrılık**

chassis /'ʃæsi/ noun [C] plural **chassis** /'ʃæsiz/ the structure of a vehicle that the outer metal is fixed on to **araba şasesi, arabanın gövdesinin oturduğu ana bölüm**

chaste /tʃeɪst/ adjective not having had sex, or without sexual thoughts or intentions **iffetli, namuslu** a chaste relationship

chasten /'tʃeɪsⁿn/ verb [T] formal to make someone feel ashamed by making them understand that they have failed or done something wrong **gururunu kırmak, cezalandırmak, ıslah etmek, utandırmak, yola getirmek** [often passive] The team were chastened by their defeat. ● **chastening** adjective **küçük düşüren**

chastise /tʃæs'taɪz/ verb [T] formal to criticize or punish someone **paylamak, azarlamak**

chastity /ˈtʃæstəti/ *noun* [U] when someone does not have sex **iffet, namus**

o┅**chat**[1] /tʃæt/ *verb* [I] **chatting**, *past* **chatted** to talk with someone in a friendly and informal way **sohbet etmek, çene çalmak, hoş beş etmek, yarenlik etmek, (argo) lakırdamak** *I wanted to chat to you about the party on Saturday.*

chat sb up *phrasal verb UK informal* to talk to someone in a way that shows them that you are sexually attracted to them **konuşarak tavlamak, ilişki kurmaya çalışmak, (argo) asılmak, konuşarak arkadaşlık kurmak**

┌─────────────────────────────────────┐
│ 🧩 **chat** ...... İLE BİRLİKTE KULLANILAN KELİMELER │
└─────────────────────────────────────┘

have a chat ● **a** chat **about** sth ● **a good/little/long/quick** chat ● **a** chat **with** sb

o┅**chat**[2] /tʃæt/ *noun* [C, U] a friendly, informal conversation **sohbet, hoşbeş, lakırdı**

chateau /ˈʃætəʊ/ 🇺🇸 /ʃæˈtəʊ/ *noun* [C] *plural* **chateaux** a large house or castle in France **şato**

'**chat ˌroom** *noun* [C] a place on the Internet where you can have discussions with other people **(internette) sohbet odası**

'**chat ˌshow** *UK* (*US* **talk show**) *noun* [C] a television or radio programme where people are asked questions about themselves **ünlülerle soru cevap şeklinde yapılan söyleşi**

chatter /ˈtʃætər/ *verb* [I] **1** to talk for a long time about things that are not important **gevezelik etmek, durmaksızın konuşmak, çene çalmak 2** If your teeth chatter, they knock together because you are cold or frightened. **dişleri takır takır etmek, birbirine vurmak, takırdamak, çatırdamak** ● **chatter** *noun* [U] **sohbet**

chatty /ˈtʃæti/ *adjective* **1** liking to talk **hoşsohbet, konuşkan, geveze, çalçene, çenebaz 2** A piece of writing that is chatty has a friendly and informal style. **konşuşr gibi samimi yazılan, ifade edilen** *a chatty letter/style*

chauffeur /ˈʃəʊfər/ 🇺🇸 /ʃəʊˈfɜːr/ *noun* [C] someone whose job is to drive a car for someone else **şoför** ● **chauffeur** *verb* [T] **şoförlük yapmak**

chauvinist /ˈʃəʊvənɪst/ *noun* [C] **1** (*also* **male chauvinist**) a man who believes that men are better or more important than women **erkeklerin kadınlardan daha üstün ve iyi olduğuna inanan erkek, şovenist 2** someone who believes that their country or race is better or more important than other countries or races **kendi ırka milliyetinin başkalarından daha üstün olduğuna savunan, mutaassıp, aşırı vatansever, şoven** ● **chauvinism** *noun* [U] the beliefs and behaviour of chauvinists **mutassıplık, aşırı vatanseverlik ,aşırı milliyetçilik, şovenizm**

chav /tʃæv/ *noun* [C] *UK informal* a young person who dresses in cheap clothes and jewellery that are intended to look expensive, and who does not look clever **sahte mücevher takan ve abartılı kıyafetler/giyen çok zeki gözükmeyen**

┌─────────────────────────────────────┐
│ **cheap** ...... BAŞKA BİR DEYİŞLE │
└─────────────────────────────────────┘

Eğer bir şey çoğu kişinin satın alabileceği pahada ise, bunun belirtmek için **affordable, inexpensive** veya **reasonable** ifadeleri kullanılabilir. *There's very little* **affordable** *housing around here.* ● *They sell* **inexpensive** *children's clothes.* ● *I thought the food was very* **reasonable**.

Cut-price sıfatı bir şeyin normalden daha ucuz olduğunu belirtmek için kullanılır. *We managed to get* **cut-price** *tickets the day before the show.*

Zahmetsiz ve ucuz kullanımı olan aletler için **econo-**

mical ifadesi kullanılır. *I need a car that's reliable and* **economical**.

o┅**cheap**[1] /tʃiːp/ *adjective* **1** NOT EXPENSIVE not expensive, or costing less than usual **ucuz** *I got a cheap flight to Spain at the last minute.* ○ *It will be a lot cheaper to go by bus.* **2** PAY LESS where you have to pay less than usual or less than you expect **kelepir, umulandan daha ucuz** *Are there any cheap restaurants around here?* **3** LOW QUALITY low in price and quality **ucuz, düşük, peypaye, adi, bayağı** *cheap perfume* **4** PERSON *US* not willing to spend money **eli sıkı, cimri, para harcamayı sevmeyen**

cheap[2] /tʃiːp/ *adverb informal* **1** for a low price **ucuzca, hesaplıca** *You'll get the table cheap if you buy the chairs too.* **2 be going cheap** *UK* to be offered for sale for less money than is usual **ucuza gidiyor olmak, yok pahasına satılıyor olmak 3 not come cheap** to be expensive **ucuza gelmemek, pahalıya malolmak** *Good carpets don't come cheap.*

cheaply /ˈtʃiːpli/ *adverb* for a low price **çok ucuza, yok pahasına, kelepirmişçesine** *You can buy some goods more cheaply in America.*

cheat[1] /tʃiːt/ *verb* [I, T] to behave in a way that is not honest or fair in order to win something or to get something **hile yapmak, aldatmak, kandırmak, dürüst olmayan usullere başvurmak** *She was caught UK* **cheating in** *her French exam/ US* **cheating on** *her French exam.* ○ *He* **cheats at** *cards.*

cheat on sb *phrasal verb* to have a secret sexual relationship with someone who is not your usual sexual partner **birisine ihanet etmek; karısını/kocasını aldatmak**

cheat sb out of sth *phrasal verb* to get something that belongs to someone else by deceiving them **kandırmak, hakkını elinden almak, hile ile elde geçirmek, dolandırmak, aldatmak**

cheat[2] /tʃiːt/ *noun* [C] **1** someone who cheats **dolandırıcı, düzenbaz, dalavereci, hileci, üç kağıtçı 2** special instructions or information which someone can use to help them play a computer game more effectively **bir bilgisayar oyununu daha iyi oynayabilmek için hazırlanmış teknik bilgiler**

o┅**check**[1] /tʃek/ *verb* **1** EXAMINE [I, T] to examine something in order to make sure that it is correct or the way it should be **kontrol etmek, denetlemek, bakmak** [+ (that)] *I went to check that I'd locked the door.* ○ *Have you* **checked** *your facts?* ○ *I knelt down beside the body and* **checked for** *a pulse.* **2** FIND OUT [I, T] to find out about something **araştırmak, hakkında bilgi almak** [+ question word] *I'll check whether Peter knows about the party.* **3** ASK [I] to ask someone for permission to do something **izin istemek, müsaade etmesini istemek** *I'd like to stay overnight, but I need to* **check with** *my parents.* **4** STOP [T] to stop something bad from increasing or continuing **durdurmak, kontrol/denetim altına almak** *The government needs to find a way to check rising inflation.* **5** MARK [T] *US* (*UK* **tick**) to put a mark by an answer to show that it is correct, or by an item on a list to show that you have dealt with it **işaretlemek, kontrol işareti koymak, kontrol edildiğini göstermek 6** LEAVE [T] *US* to leave your coat, bags, or other possessions temporarily in someone's care **emanete bırakmak, birinin himayesini/gözetimine bırakmak** ➾See also: **double-check**.

check in *phrasal verb* **1** to go to the desk at an airport in order to say that you have arrived and to get the number of your seat **havalanında uçağa biniş için kayıt olmak, bagajını teslim ederek koltuk numarası almak** *We have to check in three hours before the flight leaves.* **2** to go to the desk at a hotel in order to say that

check

you have arrived, and to get the key to your room **otele kaydolmak, oda numarası ve anahtarı almak**
check sth off *phrasal verb US (UK* **tick sth off)** to put a mark next to a name or an item on a list to show that it is correct, or that it has been dealt with **kontrol edildiğini/görüldüğünü gösteren işaret koymak**
check (up) on sb/sth *phrasal verb* to try to discover how something is progressing or whether someone is doing what they should be doing **hakkında tam bir araştırma/soruşturma yapmak ve bir şeylerin nasıl gittiğini öğrenmeye çalışmak** *My boss is always checking up on me.*
check out *phrasal verb* to leave a hotel after paying your bill **otelden ayrılmak, ayrılış yapmak**
check sth out *phrasal verb* **1** [INFORMATION] *informal* to examine something or get more information about it in order to be certain that it is true, safe, or suitable **bir şeyi incelemek, hakkında bilgi edinmek, iyi ve güvende olduğundan emin olmak** *We'll need to check out his story.* **2** [GO TO SEE] *informal* to go to a place in order to see what it is like **bir yere gidip nasıl bir yer olduğunu bizzat görmek, kontrol etmek** *Let's check out that new dance club.* **3** [BOOKS] *mainly US* to borrow books from a library **kütüphaneden ödünç kitap almak**

---

check ...... İLE BİRLİKTE KULLANILAN KELİMELER

do/make a check ● a **rigorous** check ● a **final/last-minute/random/routine** check ● **safety/security** checks ● a check **of/on** sth

---

check² /tʃek/ *noun* **1** [EXAMINATION] [C] an examination of something in order to make sure that it is correct or the way it should be **kontrol, yoklama** *We do safety checks on all our equipment.* **2** [BANK] [C] *US spelling of* cheque (= a piece of paper printed by a bank that you use to pay for things) **çek 3** [RESTAURANT] [C] *US (UK* **bill)** a list that you are given in a restaurant showing how much your meal costs **hesap, fiş, hesap pusulası 4** [MARK] [C] *US (UK* **tick)** a mark (√) that shows that an answer is correct, or that you have dealt with something on a list **işareti 5** [PATTERN] [C, U] a pattern of squares of different colours **ekose; küçük, farklı renkte karelerden oluşan 6 hold/keep sth in check** to control something that could increase too quickly or become too large or powerful **durdurmak, önüne geçmek, engel olmak** *We need to keep our spending in check.* ➜See also: **rain check.**

checkbook /'tʃekbʊk/ *noun* [C] *US spelling of* chequebook (= a book of papers printed by a bank that you use to pay for things) **çek defteri**

checked /tʃekt/ *adjective* with a pattern of squares of different colours **ekoseli, kareli** *a checked shirt/tablecloth*

checkers /'tʃekəz/ *US (UK* **draughts)** *noun* [U] a game that two people play by moving flat, round objects around on a board of black and white squares **dama oyunu**

check-in /'tʃekɪn/ *noun* [C] the place at an airport where you go to say that you have arrived for your flight, or the act of going to the check-in to say that you have arrived for your flight **hava alanında kayıt yeri, varış bildirim yeri** *a check-in counter/desk*

'checking ac,count *US (UK* **current account)** *noun* [C] a bank account which you can take money out of at any time **cari hesap**

checklist /'tʃeklɪst/ *noun* [C] a list of things that you should think about, or that you must do **kontrol listesi**

checkmate /'tʃekmeɪt/ *noun* [U] the final position in the game of chess when your king cannot escape and you have lost the game **mat**

check in

checkout /'tʃekaʊt/ *noun* [C] **1** (*also US* 'checkout ,counter) the place in a large shop, especially a food shop, where you pay for your goods **kasa, kasa tezgâhı** *a supermarket checkout* **2** the place on an Internet website where you order and pay for things **internette sitesinde sipariş verilebilen ve ödeme yapılabilen yer** *After you've chosen what you want, click here to go to checkout.*

checkpoint /'tʃekpɔɪnt/ *noun* [C] a place where people and vehicles are stopped and examined **kontrol noktası** *a military/police checkpoint*

check-up /'tʃekʌp/ *noun* [C] a general medical examination to see if you are healthy **genel sağlık kontrolü; baştan aşağı kontrol** *I'm going to the doctor for a check-up.*

cheddar /'tʃedər/ *noun* [U] a type of hard, yellow cheese **kaşar peyniri**

cheek /tʃiːk/ *noun* **1** [C] the soft part of your face below your eye **yanak** *Tears ran down his cheeks.* ➜Orta kısımdaki renkli sayfalarına bakınız. **2** [U, no plural] *mainly UK* rude behaviour that shows that you do not respect someone **yüzsüzlük, küstahlık, cüretkârlık** [+ to do sth] *She had the cheek to ask me to pay for her!*

cheekbone /'tʃiːkbəʊn/ *noun* [C] one of the two bones below your eyes **elmacık kemikleri**

cheeky /'tʃiːki/ *adjective UK* slightly rude or behaving without respect, but often in a funny way **şımarık, saygısız, kaba** *He's got such a cheeky grin.* ● **cheekily** *adverb* **küstahça**

cheer¹ /tʃɪər/ *verb* **1** [I, T] to shout loudly in order to show your approval or to encourage someone **Yaşa!' 'Bravo!' gibi bir takım sözlerle yüreklendirmek, desteklemek, alkışlamak** *The crowd stood up and cheered at the end of the concert.* **2 be cheered by sth** to feel happier or encouraged because of something **neşelenmek, keyiflenmek, neşelendirmek**
cheer sb on *phrasal verb* to shout loudly in order to encourage someone in a competition **yüreklendirmek, teşvik etmek, cesaretlendirmek**
cheer (sb) up *phrasal verb* to stop feeling sad, or to make someone feel happier **neşelendirmek, mutlu etmek, keyiflendirmek** *Cheer up. It's not the end of the world.*
cheer sth up *phrasal verb* to make a place look brighter or more attractive **bir yeri güzelleştirmek, daha sevimli hale getirmek**

cheer² /tʃɪəʳ/ *noun* [C] a shout of approval or encouragement Yaşa!' 'Varol!' 'Bravo!'

cheerful /'tʃɪəfəl/ *adjective* **1** happy mutlu, neşeli, keyfli *I'm not feeling very cheerful today.* **2** bright and pleasant to look at hoş, güzel, ferah, canlı, cıvıl cıvıl *a bright and cheerful room* ● **cheerfully** *adverb* neşeli bir şekilde ● **cheerfulness** *noun* [U] neşe

cheering¹ /'tʃɪərɪŋ/ *noun* [U] shouts of encouragement and approval neşelenme, keyif alma,

cheering² /'tʃɪərɪŋ/ *adjective* Something cheering encourages you and makes you feel happier. neşelendiren, keyif veren, yüreklendiren *We received some cheering news.*

cheerleader /'tʃɪəˌliːdəʳ/ *noun* [C] a girl, especially in the United States, who leads the crowd in shouting encouragement to a team who are playing a sport kalabalıkları takımlarını desteklemek için galeyana getiren, neşelendiren kız, amigo kız

cheers /tʃɪəz/ *exclamation* **1** something friendly that you say before you start to drink alcohol with someone şerefe, şerefinize, sağlığınıza **2** *UK informal* thank you hoşçakalın, hadi eyvallah, sağol, teşekkürler

cheery /'tʃɪəri/ *adjective* bright and happy şen, keyifli, cıvıl cıvıl, neşe saçan, bıcır bıcır *a cheery wave/ smile* ● **cheerily** *adverb* mutlu ve neşeli bir şekilde

o▪ **cheese** /tʃiːz/ *noun* **1** [C, U] a food that is made from milk, is usually white or yellow, and can be either hard or soft peynir *a cheese sandwich* ➷Orta kısımdaki renkli sayfalarına bakınız. **2** **Say cheese!** something that you say to make someone smile when you are taking their photograph Gülümseyin! ➷See also: be like chalk¹ and cheese, **cottage cheese, cream cheese.**

cheesecake /'tʃiːzkeɪk/ *noun* [C, U] a sweet cake made with soft, white cheese on a biscuit base peynirli kek/ pasta

cheesy /'tʃiːzi/ *adjective informal* **1** not fashionable and of low quality moda olmayan, modası geçmiş, kalitesiz, ucuz *cheesy music* **2** **a cheesy grin** a wide smile that is not always sincere

cheetah /'tʃiːtə/ *noun* [C] a large, wild cat that has black spots and can run very fast çita

chef /ʃef/ *noun* [C] someone who is the main cook (= person who cooks) in a hotel or a restaurant şef

chemical¹ /'kemɪkəl/ *adjective* relating to chemistry or chemicals kimyasal *a chemical reaction* ○ *chemical weapons* ● **chemically** *adverb* kimyasal olarak

o▪ **chemical²** /'kemɪkəl/ *noun* [C] a basic substance that is used in chemistry or produced by chemistry kimya

chemist /'kemɪst/ *noun* [C] **1** *UK* (*US* **pharmacist**) someone whose job is to prepare and sell drugs in a shop kimyacı **2** a scientist who does work involving chemistry kimyager

chemistry /'kemɪstri/ *noun* [U] the scientific study of substances and how they change when they combine kimya bilimi, kimya

chemist's /'kemɪsts/ *UK* (*US* **drugstore**) *noun* [C] a shop where you can buy drugs, soap, beauty products, etc eczane

chemotherapy /ˌkiːməʊˈθerəpi/ (*also* **chemo** /ˌkiːməʊ/) *noun* [U] the treatment of a disease using chemicals kemoterapi, kimyevi maddeler kullanarak bir hastalığı tedavi etmek *Chemotherapy is often used to treat cancer.*

🧩 *cheque* .... İLE BİRLİKTE KULLANILAN KELİMELER

pay by cheque ● a cheque **bounces** ● **write** a cheque ● a cheque **for** [£50/£200, etc]

---

o▪ **cheque** *UK* (*US* **check**) /tʃek/ *noun* [C] a piece of paper printed by a bank that you use to pay for things çek *a cheque for £1500* ○ *Are you paying by cheque?* ➷See also: blank cheque, traveller's cheque.

chequebook *UK* (*US* **checkbook**) /'tʃekbʊk/ *noun* [C] a book of cheques çek karnesi/defteri

'**cheque ˌcard** *noun* [C] a small plastic card from your bank which you show when you write a cheque çek kartı

cherish /'tʃerɪʃ/ *verb* [T] **1** to love someone or something very much and take care of them çok sevmek, sevgiyle bağrına basmak, şefkatle davranmak **2** If you cherish an idea, hope, memory, etc, it is very important to you. bir fikir/ümit/hatıraya çok değer vermek, kıymetli bulmak

cherry /'tʃeri/ *noun* [C] a small, round red or black fruit with a large seed inside kiraz

cherub /'tʃerəb/ *noun* [C] a small child with a beautiful, round face and wings who appears in religious paintings (dini resimlerde) melek gibi çocuk, nur topu gibi çocuk

chess /tʃes/ *noun* [U] a game that two people play by moving differently shaped pieces around a board of black and white squares satranç *a chess set*

chest /tʃest/ *noun* [C] **1** the front of your body between your neck and your waist göğüs kafesi *a hairy chest* ○ *chest pains* ➷Orta kısımdaki renkli sayfalarına bakınız. **2** a strong, usually wooden, container with a lid, used for keeping things in sandık, kutu *a treasure chest* **3** **get sth off your chest** *informal* to tell someone about something that you have been worried or angry about for a long time içini dökmek, içini boşaltmak, dertleşmek

chestnut /'tʃesnʌt/ *noun* **1** [C] a nut that has a shiny, red-brown surface and is white inside, or the tree that produces these nuts kestane *roasted chestnuts* **2** [C, U] a dark red-brown colour kestane rengi ➷See also: horse chestnut.

ˌ**chest of 'drawers** *UK* (*US* **bureau**) *noun* [C] a piece of furniture with drawers for keeping clothes in şifonyer, konsol, çekmeceli dolap

chew /tʃuː/ *verb* [I, T] **1** to crush food between your teeth before you swallow it çiğnemek **2** to repeatedly bite something without swallowing it tıka basa doldurup çiğnemek *to chew gum*

chew sth over *phrasal verb* to think carefully about something, or to discuss it üzerinde iyice düşünmek, enine boyuna tartmak, kafa yormak

'**chewing ˌgum** *noun* [U] a sweet substance that you chew but do not swallow sakız, çiklet

chewy /'tʃuːi/ *adjective* Chewy food needs to be chewed a lot before you can swallow it. sakız gibi, çok iyi çiğnenmesi gereken

chic /ʃiːk/ *adjective* fashionable and attractive şık, çekici, modaya uygun, güzel *a chic restaurant*

chick /tʃɪk/ *noun* [C] a baby bird, especially a baby chicken yavru kuş, civciv

o▪ **chicken¹** /'tʃɪkɪn/ *noun* **1** [C] a bird kept on a farm for its meat and eggs tavuk **2** [U] the meat of a chicken piliç, tavuk eti *a chicken sandwich*

chicken² /'tʃɪkɪn/ *verb*

chicken out *phrasal verb informal* to decide not to do something because you are too nervous tırsmak, korkup vazgeçmek, ürküp caymak

'**chicken ˌpox** *noun* [U] a children's disease that causes a fever and red spots on the skin su çiçeği

'**chick ˌflick** *noun* [C] *humorous* a film about romantic relationships or other subjects that interest women pembe dizi, daha çok bayanların ilgisini çeken, romantik konuları işleyen film

'chick ,lit noun [U] humorous books about romantic relationships or other subjects that interest women **pembe dizi tarzında romantik konuları işleyen kitap**

chief¹ /tʃiːf/ adjective [always before noun] **1** most important **başlıca, en önemli** The wonderful weather was our **chief** reason for coming here. **2** highest in rank **şef, başkan, lider, rütbece yüksek olan** chief economic adviser to the government

chief² /tʃiːf/ noun [C] **1** the leader of a group of people **şef** tribal chiefs **2** a person who controls other people in an organization **başkan** police chiefs

,chief ex'ecutive (also chief executive officer) noun [C] the person with the most important job in a company **bir şirkette en üst düzey yönetici**

chiefly /'tʃiːfli/ adverb mainly **başlıca, en çok, esas olarak** magazines intended chiefly for teenagers

chieftain /'tʃiːftⁿn/ noun [C] the leader of a tribe (= group of people with the same language and customs) **reis, aynı dil ve gelenekleri olan kabilenin başı, şefi**

chiffon /'ʃɪfɒn/ ⑩ /ʃɪˈfɑːn/ noun [U] a soft, thin cloth used for making women's clothes **şifon kumaş**

o=**child** /tʃaɪld/ noun [C] plural **children 1** a young person who is not yet an adult **genç çocuk** an eight-year-old child ○ How many children are there in your class? **2** someone's son or daughter, also when they are adults **çocuk, evlat** Both our children have grown up and moved away. **ͻ**See also: only child.

'child a,buse noun [U] when adults treat children in a cruel or violent way **çocuk istismarı, çocukların kötüye kullanımı**

,child 'benefit noun [U] money that the British government pays every week to families with children **çocuk yardımı, Britanya hükümetinin çocuklu ailelere yaptığı haftalık yardım**

childbirth /'tʃaɪldbɜːθ/ noun [U] the process during which a baby is born **doğum** His mother died in childbirth.

childcare /'tʃaɪldkeər/ noun [U] when someone looks after children while their parents are working **çocuk bakımı**

childhood .... İLE BİRLİKTE KULLANILAN KELİMELER

spend your childhood swh/doing sth ● early childhood ● in (sb's) childhood ● a happy/lonely/unhappy childhood ● a childhood friend/sb's childhood sweetheart ● childhood memories

childhood /'tʃaɪldhʊd/ noun [C, U] the part of your life when you are a child **çocukluk**

childish /'tʃaɪldɪʃ/ adjective **1** Childish behaviour is silly, like that of a small child. **çocukça, safça ve biraz da aptalca, düşünmeden** Don't be so childish! **2** typical of a child **çocuksu, çocuğumsu, çocuk ruhlu** childish handwriting ● **childishly** adverb **çocukça** ● **childishness** noun [U] **çocukça**

childless /'tʃaɪldləs/ adjective A childless person has no children. **çocuksuz**

childlike /'tʃaɪldlaɪk/ adjective Childlike people are like children in some ways, such as trusting people or behaving in a natural way. **çocuk gibi, kolay inanan/kanan; doğal ve masum davranan**

childminder /'tʃaɪld,maɪndər/ noun [C] UK someone whose job is to look after children while their parents are working **çocuk bakıcısı**

o=**children** /'tʃɪldrən/ plural of child **çocuklar**

'child sup,port noun [U] money that someone gives the mother or father of their children when they do not live with them **çocuk yardımı, bir tür nafaka**

chili /'tʃɪli/ noun US spelling of chilli **kırmızı/yeşil acı biber**

chill¹ /tʃɪl/ verb [I, T] to become cold, or to make someone or something become cold **soğumak, soğutmak, soğuktan titremek, titretmek** Chill the wine before serving.

chill out phrasal verb informal to relax completely, or not allow things to upset you **tamamen rahatlamak, bir şeylerin kendisini üzmesine izin vermemek** Chill out, Dad - if we miss this train there's always another one.

chill² /tʃɪl/ noun **1** [COLD] [no plural] a cold feeling **üşüme, titreme** There is a definite chill in the air. **2** [FEAR] [C] a sudden frightened feeling **korkma, ani ürperti** The scream sent a chill down my spine. **3** [ILLNESS] [C] UK a cold (= common illness that makes you sneeze) that is not very bad **soğuk algınlığı, üşütme**

chilli UK (US chili) /'tʃɪli/ noun plural **chillies 1** [C, U] a small, thin, red or green vegetable that tastes very hot **kırmızı/yeşil acı biber** chilli powder **2** [U] a spicy dish of beans, meat, and chillies **acı soslu fasulye/et,**

chilling /'tʃɪlɪŋ/ adjective very frightening **ürperten, titreten, korkutucu** a chilling tale

chilly /'tʃɪli/ adjective **1** unpleasantly cold **rahatsız eden soğuk, serin, oldukça soğuk** a chilly evening **2** unfriendly **samimiyetsiz, dostça olmayan** He gave me a chilly look.

chime /tʃaɪm/ verb [I, T] If a bell or clock chimes, it rings. **vurmak, çalmak (saat)** ● **chime** noun [C] **çan sesi**

chime in phrasal verb to suddenly say something in order to add your opinion to a conversation **söze/lafa karışmak, burnunu sokmak, araya girmek, pat diye söylemek** "Quite right too!" Tonv chimed in.

chimney /'tʃɪmni/ noun [C] a wide pipe that allows smoke from a fire to go out through the roof **baca**

chimney

'chimney ,sweep noun [C] someone whose job is to clean inside a chimney, using long brushes **baca temizleyicisi**

chimpanzee /,tʃɪmpⁿnˈziː/ (also chimp /tʃɪmp/ informal) noun [C] an African animal like a large monkey **şempanze**

chin /tʃɪn/ noun [C] the bottom part of your face, below your mouth **çene ͻ**Orta kısımdaki renkli sayfalarına bakınız.

china /'tʃaɪnə/ noun [U] **1** The hard substance that plates, cups, bowls etc are made from **porselen, çini** a china teapot **2** cups, plates, etc that are made from china **porselen/çini kaplar**

chink /tʃɪŋk/ noun [C] **1** a small, narrow opening in something **yarık, çatlak 2** a short ringing sound that is made when glass or metal objects touch each other **çınlama, çın diye ses çıkarma, çınlatma**

chip¹ /tʃɪp/ noun [C] **1** [POTATO] UK (US french fry) a long, thin piece of potato that is cooked in oil **cips** [usually plural] fish and chips **ͻ**Orta kısımdaki renkli sayfalarına bakınız. **2** [IN BAG] US (UK crisp) a very thin, dry, fried slice of potato **kızarmış patates cipsi** [usually plural] barbecue-

flavoured potato chips ⊃Orta kısımdaki renkli sayfalarına bakı-nız. **3** COMPUTER a microchip (= very small part of a computer that stores information) **çip, bilgisayarda bilgi depolanan çip 4** SMALL PIECE a small piece that has broken off something **parça, yonga, kıymık** *wood chips* **5** HOLE a place where a small piece has broken off something **kırık, çentik, kırılan yer, kıymık kopan yer** *This cup has a chip in it.* **6 be a chip off the old block** *informal* to be very similar to your mother or father **annesine veya babasına çok benzemek, (deyim) hık diye burnundan düşmüş olmak ● 7 have a chip on your shoulder** *informal* to blame other people for something bad that has happened to you and continue to feel angry about it **yapılanları hazmedememek, içerlemek** *She's always had a real chip on her shoulder because she didn't go to university.*

chip² /tʃɪp/ *verb* [T] chipping, *past* chipped to break a small piece off something **kıymık halinde yontmak, çentiklemek, ucundan bir parça koparmak** *Henman may have chipped a bone in his wrist.* ○ *a chipped plate*

chip in *phrasal verb informal* to interrupt a conversation in order to say something **konuşmanın arasına girmek, sözünü kesmek** *I'll start and you can all chip in with your comments.*

chip in (sth) *phrasal verb* If several people chip in, they each give money to buy something together. **para toplamak, ortak harcamalar için para katkısında bulunmak** *We all chipped in to buy our teacher a present.*

ˌ**chip and ˈPIN** *noun* [U] a way to pay for goods and services using a credit card (= a small plastic card that allows you to buy things) and a secret number **şifre kullanarak kredi kartı ile alışveriş yapma anlamında bir deyiş**

chiropodist /kɪˈrɒpədɪst/ *UK* (*US* **podiatrist**) *noun* [C] someone whose job is to treat problems with people's feet **ayak sağlığı uzmanı**

chirp /tʃɜːp/ *verb* [I] If birds or insects chirp, they make short, high sounds. **kuşlar veya böceklerin cıvıldaması ● chirp** *noun* [C] cıvırcır ötme

chirpy /ˈtʃɜːpi/ *adjective UK informal* happy and active **mutlu, neşeli, keyfli, aktif, cıvıl cıvıl** *Why's Ben so chirpy this morning?*

chisel /ˈtʃɪzᵊl/ *noun* [C] a tool with a sharp end that you use for cutting and shaping wood or stone **keski, iskarpela** ⊃See picture at **tool.**

chivalrous /ˈʃɪvᵊlrəs/ *adjective* A chivalrous man behaves very politely towards women. **efendi, beyefendi, şövalye ruhlu ● chivalry** *noun* [U] polite behaviour towards women **kadınlara karşı kibarlık, nezaket, beyefendilik; şövalyelik**

chives /tʃaɪvz/ *noun* [plural] a plant with long, thin leaves used in cooking to give a flavour similar to onions **Frenk soğanı**

chlorine /ˈklɔːriːn/ *noun* [U] a gas with a strong smell, used to make water safe to drink and swim in (symbol Cl) **klor**

o๛**chocolate** /ˈtʃɒkᵊlət/ *noun* **1** SUBSTANCE [U] a sweet, brown food that is usually sold in a block **çikolata** *a bar of chocolate* ○ *milk chocolate* ○ *a chocolate cake* **2** SWEET [C] a small piece of sweet food covered in chocolate **çikolatalı yiyecek** *a box of chocolates* **3** DRINK [C, U] a sweet drink made with chocolate and hot milk **kakao**

˙˙˙ *choice* .... İLE BİRLİKTE KULLANILAN KELİMELER

have/make a choice ● give/offer sb a choice ●
good/informed/obvious/popular/stark/wide/

wrong choice ● a choice **between** sth ● **by** choice
● **have (no)** choice

o๛**choice¹** /tʃɔɪs/ *noun* **1** RIGHT [U, no plural] when you can choose between two or more things **seçme, belirleme** *If I had a choice, I'd give up work.* ○ *He had no choice but to accept their offer.* ○ *I'm single by choice* (= because I want to be). **2** DECISION [C] the decision to choose one thing or person and not someone or something else **seçim, tercih** *In the past women had to make a choice between a career or marriage.* **3** THINGS TO CHOOSE FROM [U, no plural] the things or people you can choose from **seçenek, çeşit, tür** *The dress is available in a choice of colours.* ○ *The evening menu offers a wide choice of dishes.* **4** CHOSEN ONE [C] the person or thing that someone has chosen **birinin seçimi, tercihi** [usually singular] *Harvard was not his first choice.* ○ *The winner got £1000 to give to the charity of her choice.* ⊃See also: **multiple choice.**

choice² /tʃɔɪs/ *adjective* [always before noun] of very good quality **tercih edilebilir, seçilebilir** *the choicest cuts of meat*

choir /kwaɪəʳ/ *noun* [group] a group of people who sing together **koro** *a school/church choir*

choke¹ /tʃəʊk/ *verb* **1** [I, T] If you choke, or if something chokes you, you stop breathing because something is blocking your throat. **nefesi tıka(n)mak, boğ(ul)mak, boğazına bir şey kaçmak** *Children can choke on peanuts.* **2** [T] (*also* **choke up**) to fill something such as a road or pipe so that nothing can pass through **tıkamak, tıkanmak** [often passive] *The roads were choked with traffic.*

choke sth back *phrasal verb* to try not to show how angry or upset you are **(kızgınlık, duygu vb.) bastırmak, göstermemeye çalışmak, kendini tutmak** *She ran to her door, choking back the tears.*

choke (sb) up *phrasal verb* to become unable to speak because you are starting to cry **ağlamaklıyken konuşamamak, tıkanmak** *I can't watch that movie without choking up.*

choke² /tʃəʊk/ *noun* [C] a piece of equipment that controls the amount of air going into a car engine **jikle, araçlarda hava akışını sağlayan/düzenleyen aygıt**

cholera /ˈkɒlᵊrə/ *noun* [U] a serious disease that affects the stomach and bowels, usually caused by dirty water or food **kolera**

cholesterol /kəˈlestᵊrɒl/ *noun* [U] a type of fat in your body that can cause heart disease if you have too much **kolesterol**

┌─────────────────────────────────┐
│ **choose** .... BAŞKA BİR DEYİŞLE │
└─────────────────────────────────┘

pick ve **select** fiilleri kişinin uzun süreli bir düşünme sürecinden sonra bir kişi veya cansız bir şey seçtiğinde kullanılır. *He's been **picked** for the school football team.* ● *We've **selected** three candidates.* Daha gayri resmi ortamlarda, bazen **go for, opt for** veya **decide on** deyimleri kullanılır. *I've **decided** on blue walls for the bathroom.* ● *I think I'll **go for** the chocolate cake.* ● *Mike's **opted for** early retirement.* **opt** ve **decide** fiilleri kişi bir şey yapmaya karar verdiğinde kullanılır. *Most people **opt** to have the operation.* ● *I've **decided** to take the job.*

o๛**choose** /tʃuːz/ *verb past tense* **chose**, *past participle* **chosen 1** [I, T] to decide which thing you want **seçmek, tercih yapmak** *I helped my sister choose a name for her baby.* ○ *They have to **choose between** earning a living or getting an education.* ○ *There were lots of books to **choose from**.* ○ *How did you choose which school to go to?* ○ *Adam was **chosen as** team captain.* **2 choose to do sth** to decide to do something **bir şeyi yapmayı seçmek, tercih etmek** *Manuela chose to take a job in Paris.*

YAYGIN HATALAR

choose

Dikkat: Fiil sonlarına dikkat edin. Birçok Türk öğrenci **choose** fiilini geçmiş zamanda veya -ing eki ile kullanırken hata yapmaktadır. **Choose** fiilini geçmiş zamanda kullanırken **chosed** veya **choosed** olarak kullanmayın. Doğru hali **chose** olarak kullanılmalıdır. **Choose** fiilinin üçüncü hali **chosen** olarak kullanılır. **Choose** fiilinin -ing hali **chosing** olarak kullanılır.

choosy /ˈtʃuːzi/ *adjective* difficult to please because of being very exact about what you like **seçici, seçici davranan, müşkülpesent** *a choosy customer*

chop

chop[1] /tʃɒp/ *verb* **chopping**, *past* **chopped** **1** [T] (*also* **chop up**) to cut something into small pieces **dilimlemek, parçalamak, kesmek, doğramak** *Chop an onion finely.* **2 chop and change** *UK informal* to keep changing your opinions, activities, or job **bir dediği bir dediğini tutmamak, sürekli karar değiştirmek**
chop sth down *phrasal verb* to cut through something to make it fall down **kesip devirmek, kesip yıkmak**
chop sth off *phrasal verb* to cut off part of something with a sharp tool **kesip koparmak**

chop[2] /tʃɒp/ *noun* [C] **1** a flat piece of meat with a bone in it **pirzola, külbastı** *a lamb chop* **2** a quick, hard hit with a sharp tool or with the side of your hand **elin tersiyle veya keskin bir aletle vurma, darbe**

chopper /ˈtʃɒpəʳ/ *noun* [C] **1** *informal* a helicopter (= aircraft with turning parts on top) **helikopter** **2** a heavy tool with a sharp edge for cutting wood, meat, etc **balta, nacak, satır**

choppy /ˈtʃɒpi/ *adjective* Choppy water has a lot of small waves. **çalkantılı, hafif dalgalı**

chopsticks /ˈtʃɒpstɪks/ *noun* [plural] thin sticks used for eating food in East Asia **özellikle Doğu Asya'da kullanılan yemek çubuğu**

choral /ˈkɔːrᵊl/ *adjective* Choral music is written for a choir (= group of people who sing). **koro için bestelenen/yazılan, koroya ait**

chord /kɔːd/ *noun* **1** [C] two or more musical notes that are played at the same time **akor** **2 strike a chord (with sb)** If something strikes a chord with you, you like it or are interested in it because it is connected with your own life or opinions. **hatırlatmak, gönül telini titretmek, hayatı ve düşünceleriyle iligili bir şeyler çağrıştırmak** ➲See also: **vocal cords**.

chore /tʃɔːʳ/ *noun* [C] a boring job that you must do **gündelik önemsiz işler, yapılması gerekli sıkıcı uğraş** *I find cooking a real chore.*

choreograph /ˈkɒriəgrɑːf/ *verb* [T] **1** to arrange an event or series of events carefully **koreografi yapmak** *a carefully choreographed publicity stunt* **2** to design the dances for a performance **bir gösterinin danslarının koreografisini yapmak** • **choreographer** /ˌkɒriˈɒgrəfəʳ/ *noun* [C] **kareograf**

choreography /ˌkɒriˈɒgrəfi/ *noun* [U] the process of designing dances for a performance **koreografi**

chorus[1] /ˈkɔːrəs/ *noun* **1** SONG [C] the part of a song that is repeated several times **nakarat** **2** SINGING GROUP [group] a large group of people who sing together **koro** **3** IN A SHOW [group] a group of dancers and singers in a show who do not have the main parts **bir gösteride ana bölümümde yer almayan şarkıcı ve dansçılar grubu** **4 a chorus of approval/demands/protest, etc** something that a lot of people say at the same time **bir grup insan tarafından aynı anda kabul/talep/protesto için söylenenler, hep birlikte söylenen, ortak söylem/tavır**

chorus[2] /ˈkɔːrəs/ *verb* [T] *UK* If two or more people chorus something, they say it at the same time. **bir çok kişi tarafından aynı anda söylemek, hepbir ağızdan söylemek**

chose /tʃəʊz/ *past tense of* choose **seçmek' fiilinin 2. hali**

chosen /ˈtʃəʊzən/ *past participle of* choose **seçmek' fiilinin 3. hali**

Christ /kraɪst/ (*also* **Jesus Christ**) *noun* the Jewish holy man believed by Christians to be the Son of God, and on whose life and teachings Christianity is based **Hazreti İsa**

christen /ˈkrɪsᵊn/ *verb* [T] to give a baby a name at a Christian ceremony and make them a member of the Christian Church **vaftiz etmek, bir çocuğa ad vermek ve Hristiyan Kilisesi üyesi yapmak** [often passive] *She's being christened in June.*

christening /ˈkrɪsᵊnɪŋ/ *noun* [C] a ceremony where someone is christened **vaftiz, vaftiz etme**

Christian /ˈkrɪstʃən/ *noun* [C] someone who believes in Christianity **Hristiyan** • **Christian** *adjective* **Hristiyan**

Christianity /ˌkrɪstiˈænəti/ *noun* [U] a religion based on belief in God and the life and teachings of Jesus Christ, and on the Bible **Hristiyanlık**

ˈChristian ˌname *noun* [C] your first name, not your family name **ilk ad**

⊶**Christmas** /ˈkrɪsməs/ *noun* [C, U] the Christian period of celebration around 25 December, when Christians celebrate the birth of Jesus Christ and people give each other presents, or the day itself **Noel** *We're going to my mother's for Christmas.* ○ ***Merry Christmas!*** ○ *Christmas dinner* ➲See also: **Father Christmas**.

ˈChristmas ˌcard *noun* [C] a decorated card that you send to someone at Christmas **Noel kartı**

ˌChristmas ˈcarol *UK* (*US* **ˈChristmas ˌcarol**) *noun* [C] a song that people sing at Christmas **Noel ilahisi/şarkısı**

ˌChristmas ˈcracker *noun* [C] a coloured paper tube with a small toy inside, that people in the UK pull open at Christmas **içinde Noel hediyesi olan renkli kağıttan tüp**

ˌChristmas ˈDay *noun* [C, U] 25 December, the day on which Christians celebrate the birth of Jesus Christ **Noel Günü**

,Christmas 'Eve *noun* [C, U] the day before Christmas Day **Noel Arifesi**

'Christmas ,tree *noun* [C] a real or artificial tree that people decorate inside their home for Christmas **Noel ağacı**

chrome /krəʊm/ *noun* [U] a hard, shiny metal that is used to cover objects **krom** *chrome bath taps*

chromosome /'krəʊməsəʊm/ *noun* [C] the part of a cell found in the nucleus, that controls what an animal or plant is like **kromozom**

chronic /'krɒnɪk/ *adjective* A chronic illness or problem continues for a long time. **müzmin, süregelen, kronik, geçmek bilmeyen, uzun süre devam eden** *a chronic shortage of nurses* ○ *chronic back pain* ● **chronically** *adverb* **süregelen, devam eden bir şekilde**

chronicle¹ /'krɒnɪkl/ *noun* [C] a written record of things that happened in the past **tarih kayıtları, tarih, geçmiş**

chronicle² /'krɒnɪkl/ *verb* [T] to make a record of something, or give details of something **her şeyi kayıt altına almak, detayıyla kaydını tutmak** *The book chronicles his life as an actor.*

chronological /ˌkrɒnə'lɒdʒɪkᵊl/ *adjective* arranged in the order in which events happened **eylemlerin oluş sırası tarih sırasına göre düzenlenmiş, kronolojik** ● **chronologically** *adverb* **sırasıyla, kronolojik olarak**

chubby /'tʃʌbi/ *adjective* pleasantly fat **tombul, tombiş, oldukça şişman** *the baby's chubby legs*

chuck /tʃʌk/ *verb* [T] *informal* to throw something **fırlatmak, atmak** *Don't just chuck your coat on the floor!*

chuck sth away/out *phrasal verb informal* to throw something away **uzaklara fırlatıp atmak, defetmek** *I chucked out all my old clothes.*

chuck sth in *phrasal verb UK informal* to stop doing something because it is boring **bir şeyi yapmaktan vazgeçmek, bırakmak, terketmek**

chuck sb out *phrasal verb informal* to force someone to leave a place **kapı dışarı etmek, kovmak, tekmeyle uzaklaştırmak** *Pierre was chucked out of school for starting a fight.*

chuckle /'tʃʌkl/ *verb* [I] to laugh quietly **katıla katıla gülmek, kıkır kıkır gülmek, kıkırdamak** ● **chuckle** *noun* [C] **kıkırdama**

chug /tʃʌg/ *verb* **chugging,** *past* **chugged chug across/along/up, etc** If a vehicle chugs somewhere, it moves slowly, making a low, regular noise with its engine. **çuf, çuf motor sesi çıkararak yavaşça ilerlemek** *a boat chugging across the lake*

chum /tʃʌm/ *noun* [C] *informal* a friend **arkadaş, dost, ahbap** ● **chummy** *adjective* friendly **samimi, dostane, içten**

chunk /tʃʌŋk/ *noun* [C] **1** a large piece of something **büyük/iri parça** *a chunk of cheese* ⊃**Orta kısımdaki renkli** sayfalarına bakınız. **2** a large part of something **büyük/iri/kocaman bölüm** *I spend a big chunk of my money on clothes.*

chunky /'tʃʌŋki/ *adjective* **1** A chunky person is short and heavy. **tıknaz, kısaboylu ve şişman 2** big, thick, and heavy **iri, kalı, ağır, kütük gibi** *chunky shoes*

∘⁻**church** /tʃɜːtʃ/ *noun* **1** [C, U] a building where Christians go to worship God **kilise** *We used to go to church every Sunday morning.* **2** [C] (*also* **Church**) one of the different groups that make up the Christian religion **mezhep,**

kilise, belli bir mezhebe ait kilise cemaati *the Anglican Church* ⊃See also: **the Catholic Church.**

churchgoer /'tʃɜːtʃˌgəʊəʳ/ *noun* [C] someone who goes to church regularly **düzenli ibadet eden/kiliseye giden kişi**

churchyard /'tʃɜːtʃjɑːd/ *noun* [C] the land around a church, often where people are buried **kilise bahçesi**

churn¹ /tʃɜːn/ *verb* **1** ⎡SURFACE⎤ [T] (*also* **churn up**) to mix something, especially liquids, with great force **çırpmak, çalkalamak** *The sea was churned up by heavy winds.* **2** ⎡STOMACH⎤ [I] If your stomach is churning, you feel sick, usually because you are nervous. **gergin olmaktan dolayı mide bulantısı/rahatsızlığı hissetmek 3** ⎡BUTTER⎤ [T] to mix milk until it becomes butter **yayık çalkalamak, sütü yağı çıkıncaya kadar çalkalamak**

churn sth out *phrasal verb informal* to produce large quantities of something very quickly **seri ve hızlı şekilde üretmek,**

churn² /tʃɜːn/ *noun* [C] **1** a container that you fill with milk and mix to make butter **yayık 2** *UK* a tall metal container for storing and transporting milk **süt depolamak ve taşımaya yarayan metal kazan, varil, bidon**

chute /ʃuːt/ *noun* [C] **1** a long thin structure that people or things can slide down **kaydırak, kayma rampası, kaydırma oluğu** *a water chute* **2** *informal short for* parachute **paraşüt**

chutney /'tʃʌtni/ *noun* [U] a mixture of fruit, vegetables, sugar, and vinegar that you eat with meat or cheese **et ve peynirle yenilen meyve, sebze, şeker ve sirkeyle yapılan bir tür turşu**

the CIA /ˌsiːaɪ'eɪ/ *noun abbreviation for* Central Intelligence Agency: the department of the US government that collects secret information about people and organizations **Merkezi Haberalma Teşkilatı, ABD gizli istihbarat kuruluşunun kısa adı**

the CID /ˌsiːaɪ'diː/ *noun abbreviation for* Criminal Investigation Department: the part of the British police force that deals with serious crimes **Suç Araştırma Bölümü; Büyük Britanya polis teşkilatının ciddi suçları araştıran bölümü**

cider /'saɪdəʳ/ *noun* [C, U] **1** *UK* a drink made from apples that contains alcohol **elma şarabı 2** *US* a drink made from apples that contains no alcohol **elma şırası**

cigar /sɪ'gɑːʳ/ *noun* [C] a thick tube made from rolled tobacco leaves, that people smoke **puro**

∘⁻**cigarette** /ˌsɪgᵊr'et/ *noun* [C] a thin tube of paper filled with tobacco, that people smoke **sigara**

cilantro /sɪ'læntrəʊ/ *US* (*UK/US* **coriander**) *noun* [U] a herb that is used in cooking **bir tür kişniş; Çin maydanozu; kişniş bitkisinin lifli kısmı**

cinder /'sɪndəʳ/ *noun* [C] a small piece of coal, wood, etc that has been burned **köz, kor**

∘⁻**cinema** /'sɪnəmə/ *noun* **1** [C] *UK* (*US* **movie theater**) a building where you go to watch films **sinema 2** [U] the art or business of making films **sinema endüstrisi** *an article about French cinema*

cinnamon /'sɪnəmən/ *noun* [U] a brown spice that is used in cooking **tarçın**

circa /'sɜːkə/ *formal* (*written abbreviation* **c.**) *preposition* used before a date to show that something happened at about that time **(tarihlerden önce) civarında** *Gainsborough's painting 'The Cottage Door' (circa 1780)*

∘⁻**circle¹** /'sɜːkl/ *noun* **1** [C] a round, flat shape like the letter O, or a group of people or things arranged in this shape **daire, yuvarlak** *We all sat on the floor in a circle.* ⊃See picture at **shape. 2** [C] a group of people with family, work, or social connections **aile, iş ve sosyal anlamda çevre** *a close circle of friends* ○ *It's a technical term used in medical circles.* **3 the circle** UK the seats in the upper area of a theatre **(sinema, tiyatro vb.) üst kısımdaki (balkondaki) oturma yerleri** ⊃See also: **inner circle, traffic circle, vicious circle.**

circle² /ˈsɜːkl/ *verb* **1** [I, T] to move in a circle, often around something **daire çizmek** *Birds circled above the trees.* **2** [T] to draw a circle around something **çevresine çizgi çizmek** *Circle the answer you think is correct.*

circuit /ˈsɜːkɪt/ *noun* [C] **1** TRACK a path, route, or sports track that is shaped like a circle **devre 2** ELECTRIC a complete circle that an electric current travels around **elektrikte devre 3** EVENTS a regular series of places or events that people involved in a particular activity go to **turnuva, peşpeşe bir şeylerin yapıldığı yerler ve yerler** [usually singular] *the tennis circuit* ⊃See also: **shortcircuit.**

circular¹ /ˈsɜːkjələr/ *adjective* **1** shaped like a circle **dairesel, yuvarlak** *a circular rug* **2** A circular journey takes you around in a circle, back to the place where you started. **başladığı yere geri getiren seyahat, gezi, başladığı güzergâhtan geçerek başladığı yere dönen** *a circular walk*

circular² /ˈsɜːkjələr/ *noun* [C] a letter or advertisement that is sent to a lot of people at the same time **aynı anda bir çok kişiye gönderilen, sirküler, genelge**

circulate /ˈsɜːkjəleɪt/ *verb* **1** INFORMATION [I] If information circulates, a lot of people hear about it. **duyurmak, yaymak, herkese ilan etmek** *Rumours are circulating that the mayor is going to resign.* **2** SEND INFORMATION [T] to give or send information to a group of people **bir grup insana bilgi göndermek ve almak** *A copy of the report was circulated to each director.* **3** MOVE [I, T] to move around or through something, or to make something move around or through something **bir şeyin etrafından dolaş(tır)mak veya içinden geç(ir)mek** *Hot water circulates through the pipes.*

circulation /ˌsɜːkjəˈleɪʃən/ *noun* **1** BLOOD [U] the movement of blood around your body **kan dolaşımı** *Exercise improves your circulation.* **2** INFORMATION [U] when something such as information, money, or goods pass from one person to another **para, bilgi ve mal dolaşımı** *Police have warned there are a lot of fake £50 notes in circulation.* **3** NEWSPAPERS [no plural] the number of copies of a newspaper or magazine that are sold each day, week, etc **(gazete, dergi vb.) tiraj**

circumcize (*also* UK -ise) /ˈsɜːkəmsaɪz/ *verb* [T] to cut off the skin at the end of a boy's or man's penis, or cut off part of a girl's sex organs **sünnet etmek, sünnet olmak ● circumcision** /ˌsɜːkəmˈsɪʒən/ *noun* [C, U] when someone is circumcised **sünnet, sünnet töreni**

circumference /səˈkʌmfərəns/ *noun* [C, U] the distance around the edge of a circle or round object **daire çevresi, çember** *The lake is 250km in circumference.*

circumspect /ˈsɜːkəmspekt/ *adjective formal* careful about things you do or say **tedbirli, itinalı, dikkatli**

circumstances .... İLE BİRLİKTE KULLANILAN KELİMELER

in/under [any/certain/difficult/normal/ etc] circumstances ● **in/under** the circumstances ● the circumstances **of/surrounding** sth ● **exceptional/normal/ unforeseen** circumstances

circumstances /ˈsɜːkəmstænsɪz/ *noun* [plural] **1** facts or events that make a situation the way it is **durumlar, koşullar, haller** *I think they coped very well under the circumstances.* ○ *We oppose capital punishment in/ under any circumstances.* **2 under no circumstances** used to say that something must never happen **ne**

olursa olsun; hiç bir şekilde/surette, asla *Under no circumstances should you approach the man.*

circumstantial /ˌsɜːkəmˈstænʃəl/ *adjective* **circumstantial evidence** information about a crime that makes you believe that something is true, but does not prove it **mevcut koşulların ortaya koyduğu delil; bir suçla ilgili henüz kanıtlanmamış ancak inandırıcı bilgi**

circumvent /ˌsɜːkəmˈvent/ *verb* [T] *formal* to find a way of avoiding something, especially a law or rule **kanun veya kural vb. kaçınmak, kaçmak, gözardı etmek**

circus /ˈsɜːkəs/ *noun* [C] a show in which a group of people and animals perform in a large tent **sirk**

cistern /ˈsɪstən/ *noun* [C] a large container to store water, especially one that supplies water to a toilet **sarnıç** ⊃Orta kısımdaki renkli sayfalarına bakınız.

citadel /ˈsɪtədəl/ *noun* [C] a strong castle that was used in the past to protect people when their city was attacked **kale, sur, hisar**

cite /saɪt/ *verb* [T] *formal* **1** to mention something as an example or proof of something else **bahsetmek, değinmek, alıntı yapmak** *The doctor cited the case of a woman who had died after taking the drug.* **2** US to order someone to go to court because they have done something wrong **mahkemeye çağırmak, mahkeme celbi göndermek** [often passive] *A local farmer was cited for breaking environmental standards.*

citizen .... İLE BİRLİKTE KULLANILAN KELİMELER

a citizen **of** [Paris/Tokyo, etc] ● your **fellow** citizens ● **decent/law-abiding** citizens

citizen /ˈsɪtɪzən/ *noun* [C] **1** someone who lives in a particular town or city **sakin, yerli** *the citizens of Berlin* **2** someone who has a legal right to live in a particular country **vatandaş, yurttaş** *My husband became a British citizen in 1984.* ⊃See also: **senior citizen.**

citizenship /ˈsɪtɪzənʃɪp/ *noun* [U] the legal right to be a citizen of a particular country **vatandaşlık, yurttaşlık** *British/French citizenship*

citrus fruit /ˈsɪtrəsˌfruːt/ *noun* [C, U] an orange, lemon, or similar fruit **turunçgiller, narenciye**

o＊**city** /ˈsɪti/ *noun* **1** [C] a large town **şehir** *the city of Boston* ○ **the city centre 2 the City** UK the part of London where the large financial organizations have their offices **Londra şehrinin ticaret merkezi** ⊃See also: **inner city.**

civic /ˈsɪvɪk/ *adjective* [always before noun] relating to a city or town and the people who live there **şehre ait, kentle ilgili** *civic leaders* ○ *The opera house was a source of great civic pride* (= people in the city were proud of it).

civil /ˈsɪvəl/ *adjective* **1** PEOPLE [always before noun] relating to the ordinary people or things in a country and not to military or religious organizations **sivillere veya şeylere ilişkin** *They married in a civil ceremony.* **2** LAW [always before noun] relating to private arguments between people and not criminal cases **medeni konularla ilgili, uygar, medeni** *a civil court* **3** POLITE polite in a formal way **kibar, nazik** *He and his ex-wife can't even have a civil conversation.*

civil engi'neering *noun* [U] the planning and building of roads, bridges, and public buildings **inşaat mühendisi**

civilian /sɪˈvɪliən/ *noun* [C] someone who is not a member of a military organization or the police **sivil, üniformasız kimse**

civility /sɪˈvɪləti/ noun [U] polite behaviour **kibarlık, nezaket**

civilization (also UK -isation) /ˌsɪvəlaɪˈzeɪʃən/ noun **1** [C, U] human society with its developed social organizations, or the culture and way of life of a society at a particular period of time **medeniyet, medeniyete sahip toplumlar** *ancient civilizations* ○ *Nuclear war could mean the end of civilization.* **2** [U] when people have an advanced and comfortable way of life **medeniyet, uygarlık** *modern civilization*

civilize (also UK -ise) /ˈsɪvəlaɪz/ verb [T] to educate a society so that it becomes more advanced and organized **medenileştirmek, uygarlaştırmak**

civilized (also UK -ised) /ˈsɪvəlaɪzd/ adjective **1** A civilized society is advanced and has well-developed laws and customs. **medeni, uygar** *A fair justice system is an important part of civilized society.* **2** polite and calm **nezih ve sakin** *Let's discuss this in a civilized manner.*

ˌcivil ˈliberties noun [plural] the freedom people have to do, think, and say what they want **vatandaşlık hakları**

ˌcivil ˈrights noun [plural] the rights that everyone in a country has **medeni haklar** *The campaign for civil rights took off in the 1960s.*

ˌcivil ˈservant noun [C] someone who works in the Civil Service **devlet memuru**

the ˌCivil ˈService noun the government departments and the people who work in them **Devlet Dairesi**

ˌcivil ˈwar noun [C, U] a war between groups of people who live in the same country **iç savaş** *The Spanish civil war lasted from 1936 to 1939.*

cl written abbreviation for centilitre (= a unit for measuring liquid) **santilitre** *a 75 cl bottle of wine*

clad /klæd/ adjective literary covered or dressed in something **giyinmiş, giyinik** *He came to the door clad only in a towel.*

o--**claim¹** /kleɪm/ verb **1** SAY [T] to say that something is true, although you have not proved it **iddia etmek, ileri sürmek** [+ (that)] *She claimed that the dog attacked her.* ○ [+ to do sth] *He claims to have seen a ghost.* **2 claim credit/responsibility/success, etc** to say that you have done or achieved something **kredi/sorumluluk/başarı talebinde bulunmak, hakkı olduğunu söylemek** *No one has claimed responsibility for yesterday's bomb attack.* ⊃Opposite **disclaim. 3** DEMAND [I, T] to ask for something because it belongs to you or you have the right to have it **talep etmek, hak iddia etmek** *She claimed $2,500 in travel expenses.* ○ *If no one claims the watch, then you can keep it.* **4** KILL [T] If an accident, war, etc claims lives, people are killed because of it. **can almak, cana malolmak** *The floods claimed over 200 lives.*

claim ...... İLE BİRLİKTE KULLANILAN KELİMELER
make a claim ● **deny/dismiss/reject** a claim ● a **false** claim ● a claim **by sb**

o--**claim²** /kleɪm/ noun [C] **1** ANNOUNCEMENT when someone says that something is true, although it has not been proved [+ (that)] *She rejected claims that she had lied.* **2** DEMAND an official demand for something you think you have a right to **talep, yasal talep** *a claim for compensation* **3** RIGHT a right to have something **hak** *You don't have any claim to the land.* **4 lay claim to sth** formal to say that something is yours or that you have done something **sahip çıkmak, sahiplenmek** **5 sb's/sth's claim to fame** a reason why someone or

something is known **birinin ya dair şeyin hak ettiği ün/şan** *My main claim to fame is meeting the President.*

clam¹ /klæm/ noun [C] a small sea creature with a shell in two parts, that you can eat **bir midye türü**

clam² /klæm/ verb **clamming**, past **clammed**
clam up phrasal verb informal to suddenly stop talking, usually because you are embarrassed or nervous **utandığı veya sinirli olduğu için içine kapanmak, suspus olmak**

clamber /ˈklæmbər/ verb **clamber into/over/up, etc** to climb somewhere with difficulty, especially using your hands and feet **sürünerek tırmanmak** *The children clambered into the boat.*

clammy /ˈklæmi/ adjective unpleasantly wet and sticky **yapış yapış, ıslak ve yapışkan** *clammy hands*

clamour¹ UK (US clamor) /ˈklæmər/ verb **clamour for sth; clamour to do sth** to ask for something continuously in a loud or angry way **kıyamet koparmak, yaygara yapmak** *Fans were clamouring for their autographs.*

clamour² UK (US clamor) /ˈklæmər/ noun [no plural] **1** a demand for something, or a complaint about something that is made by a lot of people **bir isteği yaygara koparak çözme, halletme** *the public's clamour for organic food* **2** a loud, continuous noise made by people talking or shouting **yaygara, gürltü, patırtı** *We heard the clamour of voices in the street outside.*

clamp¹ /klæmp/ noun [C] **1** a piece of equipment that is used for holding things together tightly **kelepçe, mengene 2** UK a metal cover that is put on the wheel of a car so you cannot move it if you have parked in an illegal place **lastik/teker kelepçesi**

clamp² /klæmp/ verb **1 clamp sth around/over/to, etc** to put something in a particular position and hold it there tightly **tutturmak, kelepçelemek, sabitlemek, kenetlemek** *He clamped his hand over her mouth.* **2 clamp sth onto/to/together, etc** to fasten two things together using a clamp **mengene ile sabitlemek/tutturmak 3** [T] UK to fasten a metal cover on the wheel of a car to stop it moving because it has been parked in an illegal place **yanlış park edildiğinde lastiği kelepçelemek**
clamp down phrasal verb to do something strict to try to stop or limit an activity **sıkıştırmak, baskı uygulamak, faaliyetini sınırlamak** *Local police have clamped down on teenage drinking.*

clampdown /ˈklæmpdaʊn/ noun [C] a strict attempt to stop or limit an activity **sıkıştırma, üstüne gitme, ensesinde olma** [usually singular] *a clampdown on inner city pollution*

clan /klæn/ noun [C] a large group of families who are all related to each other, especially in Scotland **klan, aşiret**

clandestine /klænˈdestɪn/ adjective formal secret and often illegal **gizli, el altından, (argo) zuladan** *a clandestine meeting*

clang /klæŋ/ verb [I, T] If something metal clangs, it makes a loud ringing sound, or if you clang it, you make it do this. **çınlamak, tınlamak** *The gate clanged shut behind me.* ● **clang** noun [C] **çınlama**

clank /klæŋk/ verb [I] If metal objects clank, they make a low noise when they touch. **şıngırdamak, metal nesnelerin temasında çıkan düşük yoğunlukta metal sesi** *The bracelets on her arm clanked as she moved.* ● **clank** noun [C] **metal cisimlerin birbirine çarptığında çıkardıkları ses**

clap

clap¹ /klæp/ *verb* **clapping**, *past* **clapped 1** [I, T] to hit your hands together, often repeatedly, especially in order to show that you enjoyed a performance **el çırpmak, alkış tutmak, el şaklatmak** *The crowd clapped and cheered for more.* **2 clap sb on the back/shoulder** to hit someone on the back or shoulder in a friendly way **sırtını sıvazlamak, birinin sırtına dostça dokunmak 3** [T] to put something somewhere suddenly **bir şeyi biryere ansızın hızla koymak, oturtmak, yerleştirmek** *She clapped her hands over her ears and refused to listen.*

clap² /klæp/ *noun* **1** [no plural] when you hit your hands together, often repeatedly **el çırpma, alkışlama, ellerini şaklatma** *Let's give our winning contestant a big clap.* **2 a clap of thunder** a sudden, loud sound that is made by thunder **gök gürlemesi**

claret /'klærət/ *noun* [U] *UK* red wine from the area of France around Bordeaux **kırmızı Bordo şarabı**

clarify /'klærɪfaɪ/ *verb* [T] to make something easier to understand by explaining it **açıklamak, izah etmek, açıklığa kavuşturmak, açıklık getirmek** *The law aims to clarify building regulations.* ● **clarification** /ˌklærɪfɪ'keɪʃᵊn/ *noun* [C, U] **netleştirme**

clarinet /ˌklærɪ'net/ *noun* [C] a musical instrument like a long, black tube, that you play by blowing into it and pressing metal keys **klarnet**

clarity /'klærəti/ *noun* [U] the quality of being clear and easy to understand **duruluk, açıklık, belirginlik**

clash¹ /klæʃ/ *verb* **1** FIGHT [I] to fight or argue **çarpışmak, çatışmak, uyuşmamak,** *Government troops clashed with rebel soldiers.* ○ *Many young people clash with their parents over what time they must be home at night.* **2** COLOUR [I] If colours or styles clash, they do not look good together. **uymamak, birbirini tutmamak** *You can't wear pink lipstick - it clashes with your dress.* **3** EVENT [I] *UK* If two events clash, they happen at the same time so that you cannot go to them both. **çatışmak, aynı zamana rastlamak** *Emma's party clashes with my brother's wedding.* **4** NOISE [I, T] to make a loud noise by hitting metal objects together **çarpışarak şangur şungur ses çıkarmak**

> **clash** ...... İLE BİRLİKTE KULLANILAN KELİMELER
>
> be **involved in** a clash ● **fierce/violent** clashes ● clashes **between** sb and sb ● a clash **with** sb ● a clash **over** sth

clash² /klæʃ/ *noun* [C] **1** FIGHT a fight or argument **çatışma, çarpışma, tartışma** *There were violent clas-*

hes *between the police and demonstrators.* **2** DIFFERENCE when ideas or qualities are very different, and this causes problems **uymama, ters düşme, çatışma, uyuşmama** *a clash of personalities* **3** SOUND a loud sound that is made when metal objects hit each other **şangır şungur ses, metal sesi** *the clash of pans in the sink*

clasp¹ /klɑːsp/ *verb* [T] to hold something or someone tightly **kavramak, sıkıca tutmak, yakalamak** *He clasped his daughter in his arms.*

clasp² /klɑːsp/ *noun* **1** [C] a small metal object that is used to fasten a bag, belt, or piece of jewellery **toka, kopça 2** [no plural] a tight hold **kavrama, tutma, yakaklam**

⚬ **class¹** /klɑːs/ *noun* **1** STUDENTS [C] a group of students who have lessons together **sınıf** *Katie and Sarah are in the same class at school.* **2** LESSON [C, U] a period of time in which students are taught something **ders** *My first class starts at 8.30.* ○ *He was told off for talking in class* (= during the lesson). **3** SOCIAL GROUP [C, U] one of the groups in a society with the same social and economic position, or the system of dividing people into these groups **zümre, tabaka, sınıf, toplumsal sınıf, toplum** *She's from a working-class background.* **4** QUALITY [C] a group into which people or things are put according to their quality **tabaka, niteliğine göre sınıflandırma** *When it comes to mathematics, he's in a different class to his peers.* ○ *second-class mail* **5** SIMILARITY [C] a group of similar or related things, especially plants and animals **tür, çeşit, tip, nevi 6** STYLE [U] *informal* the quality of being stylish or fashionable **mükemmel, klas,** *a player with real class* ➔See also: **middle class, upper class, working class.**

class² /klɑːs/ *verb* **class sb/sth as sth** to put someone or something in a particular group according to their qualities **gruplandırmak, sınıflandırmak, özelliğine göre tasnif etmek** *The tower is classed as a historic monument.*

classic¹ /'klæsɪk/ *adjective* **1** POPULAR A classic book, film, etc is one that has been popular for a long time and is considered to be of a high quality. **klasik, değerli** *the classic film 'Gone with the Wind'* **2** TRADITIONAL having a traditional style that is always fashionable **klasik, sürekli moda olan geleneksel tarzda** *a classic black jacket* **3** TYPICAL typical **tipik, kendine özgü**

classic² /'klæsɪk/ *noun* [C] a classic book, film, etc **klasik kitap, film vb.**

classical /'klæsɪkᵊl/ *adjective* **1 classical music** serious music by people like Mozart and Stravinsky **klasik müzik** *Do you prefer classical music or pop music?* **2** traditional in style **klasik** *classical and modern dance* **3** relating to ancient Greece and Rome **eski Yunan ve Roma'ya ait** *classical literature*

classically /'klæsɪkᵊli/ *adverb* **1** in a traditional style **geleneksel tarzda, klasik olarak** *a classically trained actor* **2** in a typical style **tipik bir tarzda** *a classically English tea room*

classics /'klæsɪks/ *noun* [U] the study of ancient Greece and Rome, especially the language, literature, and history **Yunan ve Roma klasikleri**

classification /ˌklæsɪfɪ'keɪʃᵊn/ *noun* [C, U] the process of putting people or things into groups by their type, size, etc, or one of these groups **tasnif, sınıflandırma, gruplandırma** *the classification of plants*

classified /'klæsɪfaɪd/ *adjective* Classified information is officially kept secret by a government. **gizli, mahrem** *classified documents/information*

classified 'ad noun [C] a small advertisement that you put in a newspaper if you want to buy or sell something **küçük ilanlar**

classify /ˈklæsɪfaɪ/ verb [T] to put people or things into groups by their type, size, etc **sınıflandırmak, ayırmak, tasnif etmek** [often passive] A third of the population has been classified as poor. ○ The books are classified by subject.

classmate /ˈklɑːsmeɪt/ noun [C] someone who is in your class at school or college **sınıf arkadaşı**

o⊷**classroom** /ˈklɑːsruːm/ noun [C] a room in a school where students have lessons **derslik, sınıf** ⊃Orta kısımdaki renkli sayfalarına bakınız.

classy /ˈklɑːsi/ adjective informal stylish and fashionable **şık, kibar, sosyetik, kaliteli**

clatter /ˈklætəʳ/ verb 1 [I] If something clatters, it makes a lot of noise when it hits something hard. **takırtı, tangırtı** 2 clatter **about/around/down, etc** to move somewhere in a very noisy way **bir yere doğru tangır, tungur hareket etmek** I could hear Sue clattering about upstairs. ● **clatter** noun [no plural] He dropped his spoon with a clatter. **tangırdama**

clause /klɔːz/ noun [C] **1** a part of a legal document **madde, fıkra, bent** a clause in a contract **2** a group of words containing a subject and a verb, that is usually only part of a sentence **cümlecik, yardımcı cümle, yan cümle** ⊃See also: relative clause, subordinate clause.

claustrophobia /ˌklɒstrəˈfəʊbiə/ noun [U] fear of being in a small or crowded place **kapalı yer korkusu**

claustrophobic /ˌklɒstrəˈfəʊbɪk/ adjective **1** feeling very anxious when you are in a small or crowded place **kapalı yerlerden korkan/bunalan/rahatsız olan 2** A claustrophobic place makes you feel anxious because it is very small or crowded. **kapalı/kasvetli/sıkıntı veren/kalabalık olan** a claustrophobic room

claw

claw¹ /klɔː/ noun [C] one of the sharp, curved nails on the feet of some animals and birds **pençe**

claw² /klɔː/ verb [I, T] If a person or animal claws something, they try to get hold of it or damage it with their nails or claws. **pençelemek, pençe atmak, tırmalamak** He clawed at the rope, trying to free himself.

claw sth back phrasal verb mainly UK to try to get back something that you had before **önceden sahip olunan bir şeyi geri almaya çalışmak** The party is desperately trying to claw back support.

clay /kleɪ/ noun [U] a type of heavy soil that becomes hard when dry, used for making things such as bricks and containers **kil** a clay pot

o⊷**clean¹** /kliːn/ adjective **1** NOT DIRTY not dirty **temiz, pak** clean hands ○ clean clothes **2** NO SEX not about sex cin-

sellik içermeyen a clean joke **3** NO CRIME showing that you have not done anything illegal **temiz, masum, suç işlememiş, vukuatsız** a clean driving licence **4** FAIR fair and honest **doğru, dürüst** a clean election/fight **5** come clean informal to tell the truth about something that you have been keeping secret **itiraf etmek, kabul etmek, gerçeği söylemek**

o⊷**clean²** /kliːn/ verb [I, T] to remove the dirt from something **temizlemek, yıkamak, süpürmek** I spent the morning cleaning the house. ⊃See also: dry clean, spring clean.

clean sth out phrasal verb **1** to take everything out of a room, car, container, etc and clean the inside of it **boşaltıp temizlemek, boşaltmak 2** informal to steal everything from a place **bir yeri soyup soğana çevirmek, tamtakır bırakmak, her şeyi çalmak**

clean (sb/sth) up phrasal verb to make a person or place clean and tidy **baştan aşağı temizlemek, tertemiz etmek, iyice silip süpürmek** We have to clean up before we leave.

clean³ /kliːn/ adverb informal used to emphasize that something is done completely **tertemiz, tamamen, temiz bir şekilde** The bullet went clean through his helmet.

clean-cut /ˌkliːnˈkʌt/ adjective Someone who is clean-cut has a tidy appearance. **düzgün, muntazam, derli toplu, eli yüzü düzgün**

cleaner /ˈkliːnəʳ/ noun **1** [C] someone whose job is to clean houses, offices, public places, etc **temizlikçi 2** [C, U] a substance used for cleaning things **temizlik ürünleri** carpet/oven cleaner **3** the cleaner's a shop where clothes are cleaned with chemicals **kuru temizleme** ⊃See also: vacuum cleaner.

cleanliness /ˈklenlɪnəs/ noun [U] the state of being clean, or the practice of keeping things clean **temizlik alışkanlığı, temizlik**

cleanly /ˈkliːnli/ adverb in a quick and tidy way **bozmadan, çabuk ile düzgünce** The branch broke cleanly away from the tree.

cleanse /klenz/ verb [T] to clean your face or an injured part of your body **temizlemek, arındırmak, yarayı/yüzü temizlemek**

cleanser /ˈklenzəʳ/ noun [C, U] a substance for cleaning, especially your face **özellikle yüz temizleme maddesi, temizleyici**

o⊷**clear¹** /klɪəʳ/ adjective **1** UNDERSTAND easy to understand **açık, anlaşılabilir** clear instructions **2** HEAR/SEE easy to hear, read, or see **net, anlaşılır, okunur, açık** These photos are very clear. ○ Can we make the sound any clearer? **3** NO DOUBT not possible to doubt **aşikâr, belli** The evidence against him was clear. ○ [+ (that)] It was clear that she was angry. ○ Ella **made it clear that** she didn't like James. **4** CERTAIN [never before noun] certain about something **emin, besbelli** Are you clear about how to get there? ○ [+ question word] I'm not very clear why she phoned. **5** NOT BLOCKED not covered or blocked by anything **ortada, açık, a** clear road ○ a clear desk **6** WITHOUT CLOUDS A clear sky does not have any clouds. **berrak, pırıl pırıl 7** TRANSPARENT easy to see through **net, belirgin, saydam** clear water ○ clear glass ⊃See also: the coast¹ is clear, crystal clear.

clear² /klɪəʳ/ verb **1** EMPTY [T] to remove all the objects or people from a place **temizlemek, kaldırmak** clear a room/shelf ○ Police cleared the building because of a bomb threat. **2** WEATHER [I] If the sky or weather clears, the clouds and rain disappear. **(hava, bulut, yağmur) açılmak, dağılmak, berraklaşmak 3** NOT GUILTY [T] to prove that someone is not guilty of something that they were accused of **temize çıkmak, aklanmak, kanun önünde masum olduğu kanıtlamak** The jury clea-

C

red him of murder. **4** MONEY [I] If a cheque (= printed paper used to pay for things) clears, the money goes from one person's bank account to another person's bank account. **hesaba geçmek/aktarmak** **5** GO OVER [T] to jump over something without touching it **üzerinden atlamak, sürtünmeden/değmeden atlamak** *The horse easily cleared the fence.* **6** GIVE PERMISSION [T] to give or get permission to do something **izin vermek/almak** *You have to **clear it with** the headteacher if you want a day off school.* ⊃See also: clear the **air**[1].

clear sth away *phrasal verb* to make a place tidy by removing things from it, or putting them where they should be **düzenlemek, her şeyi yerli yerine koymak** *The children are not very good at clearing away their toys.*

clear off *phrasal verb UK informal* used to tell someone to go away immediately **defolmak; 'Defol git!' çekip gitmesini istemek**

clear sth out *phrasal verb* to tidy a place by getting rid of things that you do not want **işe yaramayan şeyleri atarak etrafı tertipli hale getirmek, bir yeri düzeltmek**

clear (sth) up *phrasal verb* **1** *mainly UK* to make a place tidy by removing things from it or putting them where they should be **eşyaları düzenlemek, yerleştirmek, tertipli hale getirmek** *Dad was clearing up in the kitchen.* **2** to make an illness better **iyileşmek/iyileştirmek; düzeltmek** *Antibiotics will clear up the infection.*

clear sth up *phrasal verb* to give an explanation for something, or to deal with a problem or argument **bir şeyi açığa kavuşturmak, izahta bulunmak, halletmek, çözmek** *Before we sign the contract, there are a few points we should clear up.*

clear up *phrasal verb informal* If the weather clears up, the cloud and rain disappears. **gökyüzü pırıl pırıl olmak, hava açık olmak**

clear[3] /klɪəʳ/ *adverb* **1** away from something so that you are not touching it **uzakta, dokunmadan** *Stand **clear** of the doors, please.* **2 steer clear of sb/sth** to avoid someone or something because they are unpleasant or dangerous **uzak durmak, sakınmak, ilişmemek**

clear[4] /klɪəʳ/ *noun* **1 in the clear a** not responsible for a mistake or crime **temiz, masum, suçsuz, sorumlu değil b** *UK* not in a difficult situation or having problems any more **rahat, sorunsuz, zorda değil**

clearance /ˈklɪərᵊns/ *noun* [C, U] **1** PERMISSION permission from someone in authority **resmî izin, ruhsat** *The company needs to get government clearance for the deal.* **2** DISTANCE the distance that is needed for one thing to avoid touching another thing **açıklık, boşluk, iki nokta arasında geçişi sağlayan mesafe** **3** REMOVING THINGS when waste or things you do not want are removed from a place **temizleme, atılma, taşıma**

clear-cut /ˌklɪəˈkʌt/ *adjective* very certain or obvious **açık, seçik, belli, belirgin, net** *The issue is not very clear-cut.*

clearing /ˈklɪərɪŋ/ *noun* [C] a small area in the middle of a forest, where there are no trees **ormanlık alanda açıklık, boşluk**

⊶**clearly** /ˈklɪəli/ *adverb* **1** EASY in a way that is easy to see, hear, read, or understand **açık, belli, net, belirgin bir şekilde, net olarak, doğru bir şekilde** *He spoke very clearly.* **2** CERTAIN used to show that you think something is obvious or certain **açıkça, açık seçik, açık bir şekilde** *Clearly he's very talented.* **3** NOT CONFUSED If you think clearly, you are not confused. **şüphesiz, kesinlikle, apaçık**

cleavage /ˈkliːvɪdʒ/ *noun* [C, U] the area between a woman's breasts **göğüsler arasındaki boşluk, dekolte**

cleaver /ˈkliːvəʳ/ *noun* [C] a heavy knife with a large, square blade **satır, pala, nacak** *a **meat cleaver***

clef /klef/ *noun* [C] a sign written at the beginning of a line of music, that shows how high or low the notes are **(müzikte) sol anahtarı**

clemency /ˈklemənsi/ *noun* [U] *formal* when a judge, king, etc decides not to punish someone severely although they have committed a crime **şefkat, merhamet, hoşgörü**

clench /klenʃ/ *verb* [T] to close your hands or teeth very tightly, or to hold something tightly **diş/eller birbirine geçirmek/geçmek, sıkmak** *Dan **clenched his fists**.*

clergy /ˈklɜːdʒi/ *noun* [plural] priests or religious leaders **rahipler/dini liderler sınıfı** *a member of the clergy*

clergyman /ˈklɜːdʒɪmən/ *noun* [C] *plural* **clergymen** a man who is a member of the clergy **rahip, papaz**

cleric /ˈklerɪk/ *noun* [C] a member of the clergy **rahipler sınıfı üyesi**

clerical /ˈklerɪkᵊl/ *adjective* **1** relating to work done in an office **büro işlerini ilişkin, ilgili** *a clerical assistant* **2** relating to priests or religious leaders **rahipler, dini liderlere ilişkin/ait**

clerk /klɑːk/ (US) /klɜːrk/ *noun* [C] **1** someone who works in an office or bank, keeping records and doing general office work **memur, kâtip, sekreterlik işi yapan** *a bank clerk* **2** *US* someone who sells things in a shop **satış elemanı, tezgâhtar** *a store/sales clerk*

clever ...... BAŞKA BIR DEYİŞLE

Intelligent ve **smart** sıfatları genellikle **clever** sıfatına alternatif olarak kullanılır. *She's a highly* **intelligent** *woman.* • *He's one of the* **smartest** *kids in the class.*
Akıllı genç insanlar **bright** ifadesiyle de ifade edilir. *Jacob was a very* **bright** *boy.*
Brainy sıfatı gayri resmi ortamlarda genç kişilerin diğer genç kişilerden bahsederken kullandıkları bir ifadedir. *Ask Louisa to help you - she's really* **brainy**.
Çok akıllı kişiler **brilliant** veya **gifted** ifadeleriyle de tanımlanır. *William was a* **brilliant/gifted** *scholar.*

⊶**clever** /ˈklevəʳ/ *adjective* **1** able to learn and understand things quickly and easily **akıllı, zekî** *a clever student* **2** designed in an effective and intelligent way **zekice ve etkin olarak tasarlanmış** *a clever idea* ○ *a clever tool* • **cleverly** *adverb a cleverly designed toy* **akıllıca** • **cleverness** *noun* [U] **akıl**

cliché /ˈkliːʃeɪ/ (US) /kliːˈʃeɪ/ *noun* [C] something that people have said or done so much that it has become boring or has no real meaning **gerçekte bir anlamı olmayan söylenegelen ifade, söz; klişe; basmakalıp, beylik söz/ifade**

⊶**click**[1] /klɪk/ *verb* **1** SOUND [I, T] to make a short, sharp sound, or to use something to make this sound **tık/çıt/klik sesi çıkarmak/çıkartmak** *The door clicked shut behind him.* **2** COMPUTER [I, T] to press on part of a computer mouse (= small computer control) to make the computer do something **bilgisayar kullanımında 'fareyi' tıklamak, bu yolla bilgisayara komut vermek** *To start the program, **click on** its icon.* **3** PEOPLE [I] *informal* If two people click, they like each other immediately. **iki insanın birbirine kanı kaynamak, ısınmak, çabuk dost olmak** **4** IDEA [I] *informal* to suddenly understand something **şıp diye anlamak, çabuk kavramak** *Suddenly everything clicked and I realized where I'd met him.* ⊃See also: **double-click**, snap your fingers (**finger**[1]).

click[2] /klɪk/ *noun* [C] a short, sharp sound **tıkırtı, tık sesi, tık tık, çıt sesi** *the click of a switch*

client /ˈklaɪənt/ *noun* [C] someone who pays someone else for services or advice **müşteri, müvekkil/müvekkile**

clientele /ˌkliːɒnˈtel/ *noun* [group, no plural] the regular customers of a business **daimi müşteri** *The new bar aims to attract a younger clientele.*

cliff /klɪf/ *noun* [C] an area of high, steep rocks beside the sea **yamaç, yar, uçurum, sarp kayalık**

cliff

climactic /klaɪˈmæktɪk/ *adjective* [always before noun] *literary* A climactic event or time is one in which important or exciting things happen. **can alıcı/en kritik olay veya dönem, zaman**

🧩 **climate** .... İLE BİRLİKTE KULLANILAN KELİMELER

create a climate **of** [fear/trust, etc] ● **in** a climate ● **in the current/in the present** climate ● **the political/social** climate

climate /ˈklaɪmət/ *noun* **1** [C, U] the weather conditions that an area usually has **iklim, hava durumu** *a hot, dry climate* **2** [C] the situation, feelings, and opinions that exist at a particular time **ortam, hava, genel durum** [usually singular] *the political/social climate* ○ *Terrorism creates a climate of fear.*

ˈclimate ˌchange *noun* [C, U] the way the Earth's weather is changing **iklim değişimi**

climatic /klaɪˈmætɪk/ *adjective formal* relating to the weather conditions that an area usually has **iklim koşullarına ilişkin** *climatic change*

🧩 **climax** .... İLE BİRLİKTE KULLANILAN KELİMELER

build up to/come to/reach a climax ● **a dramatic/exciting/fitting/thrilling** climax ● **the climax of** sth

climax¹ /ˈklaɪmæks/ *noun* [C] the most exciting or important part of something **bir şeyin ulaştığı en önemli ve heyecan verici üst nokta, doruk/düğüm noktası** [usually singular] *The climax of her career was winning a gold medal.* ⊃Opposite **anticlimax**.

climax² /ˈklaɪmæks/ *verb* [I, T] to reach the most important or exciting part **doruk/düğüm noktasına ulaşmak/erişmek** *The festival climaxed with/in a huge fireworks display.*

o→**climb** /klaɪm/ *verb* **1** PERSON [I, T] (*also* climb up) to go up something, or onto the top of something **tırmanmak** *climb a ladder/tree/mountain* ○ *He climbed up on a chair to change the light bulb.* **2** climb into/out of/through, etc to move somewhere using your hands and legs **tırmanarak girmek/çıkmak/geçmek** *The child climbed into the back of the car.* **3** NUMBER [I] If a price, number, or amount climbs, it increases. **(fiyat, sayı, miktar) artmak, tırmanmak** *Profits climbed 11% last quarter.* **4** MOVE HIGHER [I] to move to a higher position **yükseklere/daha üst düzeylere tırmanmak** *The road climbs quite steeply.* ● **climb** *noun* [C] a *long/steep/uphill* climb **tırmanış**
climb down *phrasal verb UK informal* to change your opinion or admit that you are wrong **hatalı olduğunu kabul etmek, geri adım atmak, tükürdüğünü yalamak** *The government has been forced to climb down over the issue of increased taxes.*

climb

He climbed a tree.　　They went climbing.

climbdown /ˈklaɪmdaʊn/ *noun* [C] *UK* when someone admits that they were wrong about something or have changed their opinion **geri adım atma, hatasını kabul etme, fikir değiştirme** *an embarrassing climbdown by the government*

climber /ˈklaɪməʳ/ *noun* [C] someone who climbs mountains, hills, or rocks as a sport **dağcı, tırmanıcı**

climbing /ˈklaɪmɪŋ/ *noun* [U] the sport of climbing mountains, hills, or rocks **dağcılık, tırmanma sporu** *rock/mountain climbing* ○ *climbing boots*

clinch /klɪnʃ/ *verb* [T] *informal* **1** to finally get or win something **nihayet halletmek, çözümlemek, almak, kazanmak** *clinch a deal* **2** clinch it *informal* to make someone finally decide what to do **nihayet birinin karar vermesini sağlamak** *When he said the job was in Paris, that clinched it for me.*

cling /klɪŋ/ *verb* [I] *past* clung **1** to hold someone or something tightly, especially because you are frightened **korkudan birine/birşeye sıkı sıkıya tutunmak** *She was found clinging to the ledge.* ○ *I clung on to his hand in the dark.* **2** to stick to something **tutunmak, yapışmak** *His damp hair clung to his forehead.*
cling (on) to sth *phrasal verb* to try very hard to keep something **bir şeyi tutmaya çalışmak, sıkı sıkıya yapışmak** *He clung on to power for ten more years.*
cling to sth *phrasal verb* to refuse to stop believing or hoping for something **bir inanca/umuda sıkı sıkıya yapışmak, sarılmak** *He clung to the belief that his family were alive.*

clingfilm /ˈklɪŋfɪlm/ *UK trademark* (*US* plastic wrap) *noun* [U] thin, transparent plastic used for wrapping or covering food **yiyeceklere sarılan şeffaf yapışkan ince plastik, naylon**

clingy /ˈklɪŋi/ *adjective mainly UK* always wanting to be with someone and not wanting to do things alone **daima yanında birisiyle olmayı isteyen, yalnız yapamayan** *a clingy child*

clinic /ˈklɪnɪk/ *noun* [C] a place where people go for medical treatment or advice **klinik** *an eye/skin clinic*

clinical /ˈklɪnɪkᵊl/ *adjective* **1** [always before noun] relating to medical treatment and tests **klinik tedavi ve testlere ilişkin** *clinical trials/research* **2** only considering facts and not influenced by feelings or emotions **duygulardan çok inceleme ve araştırma sonuçlarını dikkate alan, tıbbi olarak** *a clinical approach/attitude* ● **clinically** *adverb* **clinik ortama dair**

clinician /klɪˈnɪʃ*ə*n/ *noun* [C] a doctor who treats ill people and does not just study diseases **hekim**

clink /klɪŋk/ *verb* [I, T] If pieces of glass or metal clink, they make a short ringing sound when they touch, and if you clink them, you make them do this. **çın çın diye ses çıkarmak, çınlamak** ● **clink** *noun* [C] **çarpma sesi**

clip¹ /klɪp/ *noun* [C] **1** a small metal or plastic object used for holding things together **toka, klips, kelepçe 2** a short part of a film or television programme that is shown at a different time **kısa gösterim/film; klip, parça, fragman** *They showed clips from Spielberg's new movie.* **3 a clip round the ear/earhole** *UK informal* a quick hit on the side of someone's head **birinin başına hızlıca vurma** ⊃See also: **paper clip.**

clip² /klɪp/ *verb* **clipping**, *past* **clipped 1** FASTEN [I, T] to fasten things together with a clip, or to be fastened in this way **tutturmak, tokalamak, toka takmak, takmak, klipsle tutturmak** *Clip the microphone to the collar of your jacket.* **2** CUT [T] to cut small pieces from something **kırpmak, kesmek, küçük bir parça kesmek** *Jamie was outside clipping the hedge.* **3** HIT [T] to hit something quickly and lightly **bir şeye hafif ve hızlıca vurmak** *The plane clipped a telephone line and crashed.*

clipart /ˈklɪpɑːt/ *noun* [U] small pictures which are stored on a computer and can be easily added to a document **bilgisayarda küçük resimler**

clipboard /ˈklɪpbɔːd/ *noun* [C] **1** a board with a clip at the top that holds paper in position for writing on **üzerinde kağıt tutturmacı bulunan ve yazmak için kullanılan tahta 2** an area for storing information in a computer when you are moving it from one document to another **doküman taşımda bilginin depolandığı alan**

clipped /klɪpt/ *adjective* If someone speaks in a clipped voice, their words sound quick, short, and not friendly. **hızlı, kısa ve sevimsiz konuşan/söyleyen**

clippers /ˈklɪpəz/ *noun* [plural] a tool used to cut small pieces off something **makas (tırnak, saç)** *hedge clippers*

clipping /ˈklɪpɪŋ/ *noun* [C] **1** (*also UK* **cutting**) an article or picture that has been cut out of a newspaper or magazine **dergi ve gazetelerden kesilen resim ve yazılar** *a collection of newspaper clippings about the princess* **2** a small piece that has been cut off something **bir şeyden kesilen küçük parçacık** [usually plural] *grass clippings*

clique /kliːk/ *noun* [C] a small group of people who spend a lot of time together and are unfriendly to people who are not in the group **hizip grubu, klik**

cloak /kləʊk/ *noun* **1** [C] a loose coat without sleeves that hangs down from your shoulders **pelerin, şal 2 a cloak of sth** *literary* something that is intended to cover or hide the truth of something else **perde, maske, gizlemeye yarayan örtü** *a cloak of secrecy/mystery*

cloakroom /ˈkləʊkruːm/ *noun* [C] **1** a room where you leave your coat at a theatre, school, etc **vestiyer 2** *UK old-fashioned* a toilet in a public building **umumi tuvalet/hela**

clobber /ˈklɒbər/ *verb* [T] *informal* **1** to hit someone **dövmek, pataklamak 2** to affect someone very badly **birini istenmeyen şekilde etkilemek** *a policy that has clobbered people on low incomes*

o‑**clock¹** /klɒk/ *noun* [C] **1** a piece of equipment that shows you what time it is, usually in a house or on a building **duvar saati** *She could hear the hall clock ticking.* ⊃Orta kısımdaki renkli sayfalarına bakınız. **2** *UK* a piece of equipment

in a vehicle for measuring how far it has travelled **kilometre saati** *a car with 63,000 kilometres on the clock* **3 around/round the clock** all day and all night **gece gündüz, yirmi dört saat** *Rescue teams are working round the clock to search for survivors of the earthquake.* **4 race/work against the clock** to do something as fast as you can in order to finish before a particular time **var gücüyle bitirmeye çalışmak, zamana karşı yarışmak 5 turn/put the clock back** *UK* to make a situation the same as it was at an earlier time **zamanı geriye almak, bir şeyi eski haline getirmek** ⊃See also: **alarm clock, grandfather clock.**

clock² /klɒk/ *verb*
clock sth up *phrasal verb* to achieve a particular number or amount of something **bir şeyin belli bir miktarını ve sayısını elde etmek, başarmak** *Yuri has clocked up 5,500 flying hours.*

clockwise

clockwise   anti-clockwise *UK*,
                         counterclockwise *US*

clockwise /ˈklɒkwaɪz/ *adjective, adverb* in the same direction as the hands (= parts that point to the numbers) on a clock move **saat yönünde, saat yönünde olan** ⊃Opposite **anti-clockwise** *UK*, **counterclockwise** *US*.

clockwork /ˈklɒkwɜːk/ *noun* **1** [U] a system of machinery that starts when you turn a handle or key **kurmalı, kurularak çalışan, zemberekli** *a clockwork toy* **2 (as) regular as clockwork** extremely regularly **son derece düzenli, oldukça tertipli** *The bell rang at 8 a.m., regular as clockwork.* **3 run/go like clockwork** to happen exactly as planned, with no problems **planlandığı gibi, sorunsuzca gitmek, devam etmek, olmak**

clog /klɒg/ (*also* **clog up**) *verb* [I, T] **clogging**, *past* **clogged** to fill something so that nothing can pass through it, or to be filled in this way **tıkamak, tıkanmak** [often passive] *The plughole was clogged with hair.*

clogs /klɒgz/ *noun* [plural] shoes made from wood, or shoes with a wooden sole (= bottom part) **takunya**

cloister /ˈklɔɪstər/ *noun* [C] a covered stone passage around the edges of a garden in a church or religious building **bir kilise veya mabede giriş için bahçe dışında taştan yapılmış geçit, dehliz**

clone¹ /kləʊn/ *noun* [C] **1** an exact copy of a plant or animal that scientists make by removing one of its cells **klon, yapay olarak elde edilen bitki veya hayvan kopyası** *informal* someone or something that is very similar to someone or something else **tıpatıp aynısı, benzeri, eşi**

clone² /kləʊn/ *verb* [T] to create a clone of a plant or animal **klonlamak, aynısını/benzerini yaratmak** *Scientists have already cloned a sheep.* ● **cloning** *noun* [U] *animal/human cloning* **klonlama, aynısını yapma**

o‑**close¹** /kləʊz/ *verb* [I, T] **1** DOOR/WINDOW ETC If something closes, it moves so that it is not open, and if you close something, you make it move so that it is not open. **kapatmak** *Jane closed the window.* ○ *Lie down and close your eyes.* ○ *Suddenly the door closed.*

2 [PUBLIC PLACE] If a shop, restaurant, public place, etc closes, people cannot go in it. **kapamak, kapanmak** *The supermarket closes at 8 p.m.* **3** [ORGANIZATION] (*also* **close down**) If a business or organization closes, or if someone or something closes it, it stops operating. **faaliyetine son vermek, çalışmamak** *Many factories have closed in the last ten years.* **4** [END] to end, or to end something **son vermek, kapatmak** *She closed the meeting with a short speech.*

close (sth) down *phrasal verb* If a business or organization closes down, or if someone or something closes it down, it stops operating. **bir işi, işyerini kapatmak, çalışmaya son vermek**

close in *phrasal verb* If people close in, they gradually get nearer to someone, usually in order to attack them or stop them escaping. **çevresini, etrafını sarmak, çevrelemek, kuşatmak** *Police closed in on the demonstrators.*

close sth off *phrasal verb* to put something across the entrance to a place in order to stop people entering it **önünü kapatmak, germek, geçişi engellemek, girişine engel olmak** *Police quickly closed off the area.*

∘ₐ**close²** /kləʊs/ *adjective* **1** [DISTANCE] near in distance **yakın, yanıbaşında** *His house is close to the sea.* **2** [TIME] near in time **zamanı yakın olan** *It was close to lunchtime when we arrived.* **3** [FRIENDLY] If people are close, they know each other very well and like each other a lot. **yakın, samimi, tanıdık** *close friends* ○ *I'm very close to my brother.* **4** [RELATIVE] [always before noun] A close relative is someone who is directly related to you, for example your mother, father, or brother. **akraba, anne, baba, kardeş** **5** [RELATIONSHIP] seeing or talking with someone a lot **yakın olan, biriyle sıkça görüşen** *Our school has close links with a school in China.* ○ *I'm still in close contact with my school friends.* **6 be/come close to doing sth** to almost achieve or do something **başarıya çok yakın olmak, neredeyse başarmak** *We are close to reaching an agreement.* **7 be close to sth** If someone or something is close to a particular state, they are almost in that state. **neredeyse, hemen hemen, çok yakın olmak** *She was close to tears.* **8** [COMPETITION] A close game, competition, etc is one in which people's scores are nearly the same. **sonuç/skor olarak birbirine yakın olan 9** [CAREFUL] [always before noun] looking at or listening to someone or something very carefully **yakından, dikkatli,** *On close inspection, you could see that the painting was a fake.* ○ *Keep a close watch on the children* (= watch them carefully). **10** [WEATHER] Close weather is too warm and there is not enough fresh air. **(hava) kapalı, bunaltıcı/sıcak** ● **closeness** *noun* [U] ⊃See also: a close **call²**, a close **shave²**. **yakınlık**

∘ₐ**close³** /kləʊs/ *adverb* **1** near in distance **yakınlarda/ yakında** *He stayed close to his mother.* ○ *Come a bit closer.* ○ *We walked close behind them.* ○ *There's a great beach close by* (= near). **2** near in time **kısa sürede, yakın zamanda** *The time for change is coming closer.*

close⁴ /kləʊz/ *noun* [no plural] the end of something **son, kapanış, bitiş** *They finally reached an agreement at the close of a week of negotiations.* ○ *The year was drawing to a close.*

close⁵ /kləʊs/ *noun* [C] (*also* **Close**) used in the name of a road that cars can only enter from one end **kapalı yol, kapalı şerit** *They live at 7 Kingswear Close.*

∘ₐ**closed** /kləʊzd/ *adjective* **1** [BUSINESS/SHOP] not open for business **kapalı, faal dışı, çalışmayan** *We went to the library but it was closed.* **2** [NOT OPEN] not open **kapalı, açık olmayan** *The door was closed.* ○ *Her eyes were closed.* **3** [NOT ACCEPTING IDEAS] not wanting to accept new ideas, people, customs, etc **dışa kapalı, yeni fikir, gelenek ve insanlara açık olmayan, bağnaz, kapalı** *a closed mind*

closed-circuit 'television *noun* [C, U] a system of hidden cameras that take pictures of people in public places, used to help prevent crime **kapalı devre televizyon**

close-knit /ˌkləʊs'nɪt/ *adjective* A close-knit group of people is one in which everyone helps and supports each other. **birbirine sıkı sıkıya bağlı, kopmaz, ayrılmaz** *a close-knit community*

closely /'kləʊsli/ *adverb* **1** [CAREFULLY] If you look at or listen to something closely, you look at it or listen to it very carefully. **yakından, dikkatlice 2** [CONNECTED] If two things are closely connected, related, etc, they are very similar to each other or there is a relationship between them. **ilişkili, bağlantılı, benzer** *The two languages are closely related.* ○ *I saw a cat that closely resembles ours.* **3** [VERY NEAR] in a way that is very near in distance or time **yakın zamanda, yakında (mesafe ve zaman)** *Elke came into the room, closely followed by her children.* **4** [WORK] If you work closely with someone, you work together a lot. **yakın çalışma/mesai yaparak, birlikte çalışarak, işbirliği içinde** *Nurses work closely with other medical staff.*

closet¹ /'klɒzɪt/ *US* (*UK* **wardrobe**) *noun* [C] a large cupboard for keeping clothes in **gömme dolap** ⊃See also: have a **skeleton** in the cupboard/closet.

closet² /'klɒzɪt/ *adjective* **a closet intellectual/liberal/ socialist, etc** someone who hides their true opinions or way of life **gerçek fikir ve yaşam tarzını gizleyen; kapalı, belli etmeyen**

close-up /'kləʊsʌp/ *noun* [C] a photograph of someone or something that is taken by standing very close to them **yakın çekim, yakından**

closing /'kləʊzɪŋ/ *adjective* [always before noun] The closing part of an event or period of time is the final part of it. **kapanış, son, sonlandıran** *Owen scored a goal in the closing minutes of the game.*

closure .... İLE BİRLİKTE KULLANILAN KELİMELER

face/be threatened with closure ● **save sth from** closure ● **the closure of** sth

closure /'kləʊʒəʳ/ *noun* **1** [C, U] when a business, organization, etc stops operating **faaliyetine son verme, kapanma** *factory closures* ○ *The company announced the closure of its Paris office.* **2** [U] the feeling that a sad or unpleasant experience has now finished so that you can think about it and do other things **kötü günlerin geride kalması, kapanması, kapanma, son bulma**

clot¹ /klɒt/ *noun* [C] **1** a lump that forms when a liquid, especially blood, becomes almost solid **pıhtı, kan pıhtısı 2** *UK informal* a stupid person **salak, avanak, aptal**

clot² /klɒt/ *verb* [I, T] **clotting,** *past* **clotted** to form clots, or to make clots form **pıhtılaşmak, pıhtılaştırmak**

cloth /klɒθ/ *noun* **1** [U] material made from cotton, wool, etc, and used, for example, to make clothes or curtains **kumaş, manifatura** *a piece of cloth* **2** [C] a piece of cloth used for cleaning or drying things **örtü, bez, temizlik bezi**

clothe /kləʊð/ *verb* [T] to supply clothes for someone **giydirmek**

clothed /kləʊðd/ *adjective* wearing clothes **giyinik, örtük, giymiş** *fully clothed*

clothes .... İLE BİRLİKTE KULLANILAN KELİMELER

put on/take off/wear clothes ● **change** your clothes

∘ₐ**clothes** /kləʊðz/ *noun* [plural] items such as shirts and trousers that you wear on your body **kıyafetler, giysiler, giyecekler** *She was wearing her sister's clothes.*

○ **to put on/take off your clothes** ➾Orta kısımdaki renkli sayfalarına bakınız.

clothesline /'kləʊðzlaɪn/ *noun* [C] a rope for hanging wet clothes on until they dry **çamaşır ipi**

clothes ,peg *UK* (*US* clothespin /'kləʊðzpɪn/) *noun* [C] a short piece of wood or plastic that is used to hold clothes on a rope while they dry **mandal**

clothing /'kləʊðɪŋ/ *noun* [U] clothes, especially of a particular type **giyecek** *outdoor/protective clothing*

cloud[1] /klaʊd/ *noun*

cloud

1 [C, U] a white or grey mass that floats in the sky, made of small water drops **bulut** *rain/storm clouds* **2** [C] a mass of gas or very small pieces of something floating in the air **gaz veya başka şeylerin oluşturduğu bulut** *a cloud of dust/ smoke* **3 be under a cloud** If someone is under a cloud, they are not trusted or not popular because people think they have done something bad. **gözden düşmüş, şüphe/zan altında, mimli olmak**
● **cloudless** *adjective* without clouds **bulutsuz, açık**

cloud[2] /klaʊd/ *verb* [T] **1** to make someone confused, or make something harder to understand **bulandırmak, bulanıklaştırmak** *to cloud someone's judgment/ vision* **2** [I, T] If something transparent clouds, it becomes hard to see through, and if something clouds it, it makes it hard to see through. **buğulanmak, buğulandırmak**
cloud over *phrasal verb* to become covered with clouds **bulutlarla kaplanmak, bulutlanmak**

cloudy /'klaʊdi/ *adjective* **1** When it is cloudy, there are clouds in the sky. **bulutlu** **2** A cloudy liquid is not transparent. **bulanık** *cloudy water*

clout /klaʊt/ *noun* **1** [U] power and influence over other people **nüfuz, güç ve etki** *As mayor, he has political clout.* **2** [C] *UK informal* a heavy blow made with the hand **fiske, tokat, şamar**

clove /kləʊv/ *noun* [C] **1** a small, dark-brown, dried flower that is used as a spice **karanfil** **2** one separate part in a root of garlic (= plant with a strong taste used in cooking) **bir diş sarmısak**

clover /'kləʊvə(r)/ *noun* [U] a small plant that has three round leaves and round flowers **yonca**

clown[1] /klaʊn/ *noun* [C]

clown

1 a performer who has special clothes and a painted face and makes people laugh **palyaço** **2** a silly person **soytarı, aptal**

clown[2] /klaʊn/ (*also* clown around) *verb* [I] to behave in a silly way in order to make people laugh **soytarılık etmek, aptalca davranışlar sergilemek**

🧩 **club** .... İLE BİRLİKTE KULLANILAN KELİMELER

belong to/join a club ● **a member of** a club

☞**club**[1] /klʌb/ *noun* [C] **1** ORGANIZATION an organization for people who want to take part in a sport or social activity together, or the building they use for this **kulüp** *a fitness/football club* **2** GOLF (*also* golf club) a long, thin stick used to hit the ball in golf **golf sopası** ➾Orta kısımdaki renkli sayfalarına bakınız. **3** WEAPON a heavy stick used as a weapon **sopa, kalın değnek** **4** DANCE a place open late at night where people can dance **gece kulübü** **5** clubs playing cards with black shapes like three leaves on them **(iskambil) sinek** *the ten of clubs* ➾See also: **fan club**.

club[2] /klʌb/ *verb* **clubbing**, *past* **clubbed** **1** [T] to hit a person or animal with a heavy stick **sopayla dövmek, sopa çekmek/vurmak** **2 go clubbing** *mainly UK* to go to clubs where there is music and dancing **kulübe/ dansa/eğlenceye gitmek**
club together *phrasal verb UK* If a group of people club together to buy something, they share the cost of it. **ortaklaşa almak**

clubhouse /'klʌbhaʊs/ *noun* [C] a building that the members of a club use for social activities or for changing their clothes **kulüp binası**

cluck /klʌk/ *verb* [I] to make the sound that a chicken makes **gıdaklamak** ● **cluck** *noun* [C] **gıdaklama**

clue /klu:/ *noun* [C] **1** a sign or a piece of information that helps you to solve a problem or answer a question **ipucu** *Police are searching the area for clues to the murder.* ○ *I can't remember who wrote it. Give me a clue.* **2 not have a clue** *informal* to be completely unable to guess, understand, or deal with something **hiç bir fikri olmamak** [+ question word] *I haven't a clue what you're talking about.*

,clued 'up *adjective UK* knowing all the most important information about something **bilgi sahibi, haberdar olan** *He's very clued up on the law.*

clueless /'klu:ləs/ *adjective informal* A clueless person does not know anything about a particular subject. **bilgisiz, anlayamayan, bihaber**

clump /klʌmp/ *noun* [C] a group of plants growing closely together **ağaç/bitki kümesi, topluluğu** *a clump of grass*

clumsy /'klʌmzi/ *adjective* **1** PERSON Clumsy people move in a way that is not controlled or careful enough, and often knock or damage things. **sakar, beceriksiz** **2** BEHAVIOUR If you behave in a clumsy way, you upset people because you are not careful about their feelings. **patavatsız** *a clumsy attempt to be friendly* **3** OBJECT Clumsy objects are large, not attractive, and often difficult to use. **kaba saba, hantal, kullanışsız, biçimsiz**
● **clumsily** *adverb* **sakarca** ● **clumsiness** *noun* [U] **sakarlık**

clung /klʌŋ/ *past of* cling **tutunmak, yapışmak' fiilinin geçmiş zaman hali**

cluster[1] /'klʌstə(r)/ *noun* a group of similar things that are close together **demet, salkım, küme, takım** *a cluster of galaxies*

cluster[2] /'klʌstə(r)/ *verb* **cluster around/round/together, etc** to form a close group **kümelenmek, yakın bir grup oluşturmak** *Photographers clustered round the film star.*

clutch[1] /klʌtʃ/ *verb* [T] to hold something tightly **sıkıca tutmak, kavramak, yakalamak** *She clutched a coin.*
clutch at sth *phrasal verb* to try very hard to hold something **tutmaya/kavramaya çalışmak/çabalamak** *She clutched wildly at the branch.*

clutch[2] /klʌtʃ/ *noun* **1** [C] the part of a car or truck that you press with your foot when you change gear (= part that controls how fast the wheels turn) **debriyaj, vites dişli ayracı** ➾Orta kısımdaki renkli sayfalarına bakınız. **2** [C, U] when someone holds or tries to hold something tightly **tutma, kavrama, yapışma, yakalama** **3 sb's clutches** If you are in someone's clutches, they control you, often in an evil way. **pençesinde/elinde olma**

clutter¹ /'klʌtər/ (also **clutter up**) verb [T] to cover a surface, or to fill a place with things that are not tidy or well organized **rastgele koymak, gelişigüzel/darmadağınık olarak yerleştirmek** [often passive] Every shelf is cluttered with ornaments.

clutter² /'klʌtər/ noun [U] a lot of objects that are not tidy or well organized **darmadağınıklık, öte beri ,kıvır zıvır, gereksiz şeyler** I've got too much clutter on my desk.

cm written abbreviation for centimetre (= a unit for measuring length) **santimetre**

Co 1 written abbreviation for Company (= name of business) **şirket** Williams & Co **2** written abbreviation for County (= area with own local government) **kendi bölgesel hükümeti olan ülke/memleket** Co. Wexford

co- /kəʊ-/ prefix with or together … **ile/birlikte/ortak anlamında önek** a co-author ○ to coexist

c/o written abbreviation for care of: used when you send a letter to someone who will give it to the person you are writing to … **eliyle, vasıtasıyla**

coach¹ /kəʊtʃ/ noun [C] **1** [BUS] UK a comfortable bus used to take groups of people on long journeys **otobüs, uzun yol seyahati için tasarlanmış otobüs** a coach trip **2** [PERSON] someone whose job is to teach people to improve at a sport, skill, or in a school subject **çalıştırıcı, hoca, antrenör, koç** a football/tennis coach **3** [OLD VEHICLE] a vehicle with wheels that is pulled by horses **at arabası, fayton, talaka**

coach² /kəʊtʃ/ verb [T] to teach someone so they improve at a sport, skill, or in a school subject **çalıştırmak, eğitmek, öğretmek** ● **coaching** noun [U] **yetiştirme**

'coach ,station UK (UK/US **bus station**) noun [C] a building where a bus starts or ends its journey **otobüs garajı**

coal /kəʊl/ noun **1** [U] a hard, black substance that is dug from under the ground and burnt as fuel **taş kömürü/maden kömürü** a lump of coal **2 coals** pieces of coal, usually burning **kömür ateşi, köz, kor**

coalition /kəʊə'lɪʃən/ noun [C] two or more political parties that have joined together, usually to govern a country **koalisyon hükümeti** to **form a coalition** ○ a coalition government

'coal ,mine noun [C] (also UK **colliery**) a place where people work digging coal from under the ground **kömür madeni**

coarse /kɔːs/ adjective **1** rough and thick, or not in very small pieces **kaba, büyük, iri taneli, pütürlü** coarse cloth ○ coarse breadcrumbs **2** not polite **adi, kaba saba, aşağılık, inceliktən yoksun** coarse language ● **coarsely** adverb **kalın ve kaba şeklinde**

o→**coast¹** /kəʊst/ noun [C, U] **1** the land beside the sea **sahil, kıyı, deniz kenarı** The island lies off the North African coast (= in the sea near North Africa). ○ They live on the east coast of Scotland. **2 coast to coast** from one side of a country to the other **ülkenin bir ucundan öbür ucuna 3 the coast is clear** If the coast is clear, you can do something or go somewhere because there is nobody who might see you. **etraf temiz, kimse yok, tehlikesiz, kimse görmez**

coast² /kəʊst/ verb [I] **1** to progress or succeed without any effort or difficulty **sorunsuzca ilerlemek/başarmak** Pakistan coasted to a four-wicket victory over Australia. **2** to move forward in a vehicle without using the engine, usually down a hill **yokuş aşağı aracı boşa alarak gitmek**

coastal /'kəʊstəl/ adjective situated on or relating to the coast **kıyıya ait, kıyıda olan, kıyıya ilişkin** a coastal town/resort

coastguard /'kəʊstgɑːd/ noun [C] a person or the organization responsible for preventing accidents and illegal activities in the sea near a coast **sahil güvenlik**

coastline /'kəʊstlaɪn/ noun [C, U] the part of the land along the edge of the sea **sahil şeridi** a rocky coastline

o→**coat¹** /kəʊt/ noun [C] **1** [CLOTHES] a piece of clothing with sleeves that you wear over your other clothes, especially when you go outside **palto, manto** a fur/winter coat **2** [FUR] the fur that covers an animal's body **kürk, post, hayvanın bedenini kaplayan tüy 3** [LAYER] a layer of a substance such as paint **tabaka, kaplama, boya tabakası** a coat of paint/varnish

coat² /kəʊt/ verb [T] to cover something with a thin layer of something **kaplamak, bir şey ile örtmek** Stir the rice until it is coated with butter.

'coat ,hanger noun [C] a wire, wooden, or plastic object for hanging clothes on **askı**

coating /'kəʊtɪŋ/ noun [C] a thin layer that covers the surface of something **kaplama, ince tabaka** a protective/non-stick coating

coax /kəʊks/ verb [T] to persuade someone in a gentle way **güzellikle inandırmak, güzellikle ikna etmek, gönlünü yapmak** [+ into + doing sth] She coaxed me into joining the group.

cobble¹ /'kɒbl/ verb
cobble sth together phrasal verb to make something quickly and not very carefully **çarçabuk/üstünkörü yapmak, özenmemek, baştan savma yapmak**

cobble² /'kɒbl/ noun [C] a rounded stone used on the surface of an old-fashioned road **Arnavut kaldırımı, taş kaldırım** ● **cobbled** adjective made with cobbles **kaldırım taşı kaplı** cobbled streets

cobbler /'kɒblər/ noun [C] mainly UK old-fashioned someone whose job is to make or repair shoes **ayakkabı/kundura tamircisi, ayakkabıcı**

cobblestone /'kɒblstəʊn/ noun [C] a rounded stone that is used on the surface of an old-fashioned road **kaldırım taşı**

cobra /'kəʊbrə/ noun [C] a poisonous snake that makes the skin of its neck wide and flat when it is going to attack **kobra, büyük, zehirli yılan**

cobweb /'kɒbweb/ noun [C] a structure of fine threads made by a spider (= insect with eight legs) to catch insects **örümcek ağı**

 cobweb

Coca Cola /,kəʊkə'kəʊlə/ noun [U] trademark a sweet, dark-brown drink with lots of bubbles **kola**

cocaine /kəʊ'keɪn/ noun [U] an illegal drug, often used in the form of white powder **kokain**

cock¹ /kɒk/ noun [C] an adult male chicken **yetişkin horoz**

cock² /kɒk/ verb [T] to move part of the body up or to the side **kalkmak, dikilmek, doğrulmak, … e/a doğrultmak** to cock an ear/eyebrow
cock sth up phrasal verb UK informal to do something wrong or badly **berbat etmek, bir çuval inciri berbat etmek** I really cocked up my exams.

cockerel /'kɒk⁽ə⁾rəl/ noun [C] UK a young male chicken **genç horoz**

cockney /'kɒkni/ noun **1** [U] a type of English spoken in East London **Batı Londra'da konuşulan bir tür İngi-**

lizce türü, kokni **2** [C] someone who speaks Cockney **kokni dilini konuşan**

cockpit /'kɒkpɪt/ noun [C] the part of an aircraft or racing car that contains the controls **pilot kabini, kokpit**

cockroach /'kɒkrəʊtʃ/ noun [C] a large, brown or black insect that can live in houses and places where food is prepared **hamam böceği**

cocktail /'kɒkteɪl/ noun **1** MIXTURE [C] a mixture of powerful substances **güçlü maddelerden oluşan karışım, kokteyl** *a cocktail of drugs/chemicals* **2** DRINK [C] an alcoholic drink made from two or more kinds of drink mixed together **bir çok alkollü içeceğin karşımıyla yapılan içki, kokteyl** *a cocktail bar/party* **3** DISH [C, U] a cold dish containing small pieces of food mixed together **yiyecek kokteyli/karışımı** *a prawn cocktail* ○ *fruit cocktail*

cock-up /'kɒkʌp/ noun [C] UK informal a stupid mistake or failure **aptalca yapılan kata, başarısızlık, karışıklık**

cocky /'kɒki/ adjective confident in an annoying way **kasıntı, kendini beğenmiş, kendini dev aynasında gören, ukala**

cocoa /'kəʊkəʊ/ noun [U] **1** a dark-brown powder produced from a type of bean, used to make chocolate **kakao 2** a drink made by mixing cocoa powder with hot milk **sütlü kakao**

coconut /'kəʊkənʌt/ noun [C] a very large nut with a hard, hairy shell, a white part that you eat, and liquid in the centre **Hindistan cevizi**

cocoon /kə'ku:n/ noun [C] a cover that protects some insects as they develop into adults **koza, böcek kozası**

cod /kɒd/ noun [C, U] plural cod a large sea fish which can be eaten as food **morina balığı**

code /kəʊd/ noun **1** SECRET MESSAGE [C, U] a set of letters, numbers, or signs that are used instead of ordinary words to keep a message secret **kod, şifre** *It was written in code.* ○ *They were trying to break* (= understand) *the enemy's code.* **2** TELEPHONE [C] UK (UK/US area code) a set of numbers used at the beginning of all the telephone numbers in a particular area **telefon kodu/bölge kodu 3** RULES [C] a set of rules on how to behave or how to do things **genel kurallar, kurallar manzumesi** *a code of conduct/practice* ○ *The club has a strict dress code* (= rules about what you wear). ⊃See also: **bar code, zip code.**

coded /'kəʊdɪd/ adjective written or sent in code **kodlanmış, şifreli, şifreyle yazılan/gönderilen** *a coded message/warning*

codeine /'kəʊdi:n/ noun [U] a medicine used to reduce pain **bir tür ağrı kesici, kodein**

co-ed /ˌkəʊ'ed/ ⓤⓢ /'kəʊˌed/ adjective with both male and female students **kız-erkek karışık, karma**

coerce /kəʊ'ɜ:s/ verb [T] formal to make someone do something that they do not want to do **zorlamak, mecbur etmek, cebren yaptırmak** [+ into + doing sth] *Employees said they were coerced into signing the agreement.* ● **coercion** /kəʊ'ɜ:ʃ°n/ noun [U] **zorlama**

coexist /ˌkəʊɪg'zɪst/ verb [I] If two things or groups coexist, they exist at the same time or together, although they may be very different. **farklılıklara rağmen birlikte yaşamak, bir arada olmak, birlikte bir yaşam kültürü oluşturmak** *Can science and religion coexist?* ● **coexistence** noun [U] **beraber varolma**

○✪**coffee** /'kɒfi/ noun **1** [C, U] a hot drink made from dark beans which are made into a powder, or a cup of this

drink **kahve 2** [U] the beans from which coffee is made, or the powder made from these beans **kahve taneleri** *instant coffee*

'coffee ˌtable noun [C] a low table in a room where people sit **sehpa** ⊃Orta kısımdaki renkli sayfalarına bakınız.

coffers /'kɒfəz/ noun [plural] a supply of money that a group or organization has and can spend **hazine, kasa, sandık** *government/party coffers*

coffin /'kɒfɪn/ noun (also US **casket**) noun [C] a box in which a dead body is buried **tabut** ⊃See also: the final **nail¹** in the coffin.

cog /kɒg/ noun [C] a part shaped like a tooth on the edge of a wheel in a machine, that makes another wheel turn **dişli, çark**

cogent /'kəʊdʒ°nt/ adjective A cogent argument, reason, or explanation is one which people will believe because it is clear and careful. **inandırıcı, ikna edici**

cognac /'kɒnjæk/ noun [U] good quality French brandy (= strong alcoholic drink) **kanyak**

cognitive /'kɒgnətɪv/ adjective [always before noun] formal relating to how people think, understand, and learn **anlama, kavrama, öğrenmeye ilişkin**

cohabit /kəʊ'hæbɪt/ verb [I] formal If two people cohabit, they live together and are sexual partners but are not married. **birlikte yaşamak, nikâhsız yaşamak, karı koca gibi yaşamak** ● **cohabitation** /kəʊˌhæbɪ'teɪʃ°n/ noun [U] **birlikte yaşama**

coherent /kəʊ'hɪər°nt/ adjective **1** A coherent argument, plan, etc is clear, and each part of it has been carefully considered. **tutarlı, ahenkli, kolay anlaşılır, bağdaşık, mantıklı 2** If someone is coherent, you can understand what they say. **anlaşılır, tutarlı, mantıklı** ⊃Opposite **incoherent.** ● **coherence** /kəʊ'hɪər°ns/ noun [U] **uyum, netlik** ● **coherently** adverb **uyumlu bir şekilde**

cohesion /kəʊ'hi:ʒ°n/ noun [U] when the members of a group or society are united **uyumluluk, bağlılık, birliktelik** *The country needs greater social cohesion.* ● **cohesive** /kəʊ'hi:sɪv/ adjective united and working together effectively **uyumlu, birbirine bağlı, birlikte ahenkli çalışan** *a cohesive unit/group*

cohort /'kəʊhɔ:t/ noun [C] someone who supports someone else, especially a political leader **destekçi, siyasi bir lideri destekleyen** *the prime minister's cohorts*

coil¹ /kɔɪl/ noun [C] a long piece of wire, rope, etc curled into several circles **bobin, büklüm, makara, kangal** *a coil of rope*

coil² /kɔɪl/ noun (also **coil up**) verb [I, T] to twist something into circles, or to become twisted into circles **kangal haline getirmek, çöreklenmek, bobin haline getirmek, büküp/kıvırıp rulo yapmak** *Her hair was coiled in a bun on top of her head.*

coin¹ /kɔɪn/ noun **1** [C] a flat, usually round, piece of metal used as money **madeni para** *a pound coin* **2 toss a coin** to throw a coin into the air so that it turns over several times, and see which side it lands on, often in order to make a decision **yazımı turamı atmak**

coin² /kɔɪn/ verb [T] **1** to be the first person who uses a new word or phrase **(yeni bir kelime, ifade) bulmak, uydurmak, yaratmak 2 to coin a phrase** something you say before using a common expression **denilebilir ki; tabiri caizse, diyelim ki** *Still, to coin a phrase, there is light at the end of the tunnel.*

coincide /ˌkəʊɪn'saɪd/ verb [I] **1** to happen at the same time as something else **tesadüf etmek, aynı zamana rastgelmek, çakışmak** *The band's American tour coincided with the release of their second album.*

2 When people's opinions or ideas coincide, they are the same. **uymak, uyuşmak, bağdaşmak, aynı fikirde olmak**

> *coincidence* .... İLE BİRLİKTE KULLANILAN KELİMELER

by coincidence • an **amazing/happy/remarkable/ strange/unfortunate** coincidence • **mere/pure** coincidence • **it's no** coincidence **that**

coincidence /kəʊ'ɪnsɪdəns/ *noun* [C, U] when two very similar things happen at the same time but there is no reason for it **tesadüf, rastlantı** *an amazing/strange coincidence* ○ *It was pure coincidence that we both married dentists.* • **coincidental** /kəʊ‚ɪnsɪ'dentəl/ *adjective* happening by coincidence **tesadüfi, rastlantı eseri olarak** *The similarities are coincidental.* • **coincidentally** /kəʊ‚ɪnsɪ'dentəli/ *adverb* **tesadüfi bir şekilde**

Coke /kəʊk/ *noun* [C, U] *trademark short for* Coca Cola (= a sweet, dark-brown drink with lots of bubbles) **koka kola**

Col *written abbreviation for* Colonel (= an officer of high rank in the army or air force) **albay**

cola /'kəʊlə/ *noun* [U] a sweet, dark-brown drink with lots of bubbles **kola** ⊃See also: **Coca Cola**

colander /'kʌləndər/ *noun* [C] a bowl with small holes in it used for washing food or separating water from food after cooking **kevgir, süzgeç** ⊃Orta kısımdaki renkli sayfalarına bakınız.

> *cold* ...... BAŞKA BİR DEYİŞLE

Eğer dışardaki hava soğuk veya içerideki derece düşük ise, durumu belirtmek için **bitter** veya **freezing** sıfatları kullanılır. *Wrap up warmly - it's* **bitter** *outside!* • *It's absolutely* **freezing** *in here!*
Eğer hava ve özellikle rüzgar kişiyi rahatsız edecek derecede soğuk ise, durumu belirtmek için **biting** veya **icy** sıfatları kullanılır. *A* **biting/icy** *wind blew in her face as she opened the door.*
Chilly sıfatı genellikle soğuk havayı veya düşük ısı derecesini belirtmede kullanılır. *It's a bit* **chilly** *in here - can you turn the heater on?*
Eğer ısı düşük fakat rahatsız edici değilse, **cool** ifadesi kullanılır. *That's a nice* **cool** *breeze.*
Sonbahardaki soğuk veya kış aylarındaki kuru hava bazen **crisp** ifadesiyle tanımlanır. *We walked through the forest on a* **crisp** *autumn day.*

o--**cold**[1] /kəʊld/ *adjective* **1** TEMPERATURE having a low temperature **soğuk** *cold water/weather* ○ *This soup has gone cold.* ○ *My hands are getting cold.* **2** UNFRIENDLY unfriendly or showing no emotion **duygusuz, soğuk, samimi olmayan** *a cold stare/voice* ○ *She became quite cold and distant with me.* **3** FOOD served cold **soğuk** *cold roast beef* • **coldness** *noun* [U] ⊃See also: in cold **blood**, get cold feet (**foot**[1]). **soğukluk**

> *cold* .... İLE BİRLİKTE KULLANILAN KELİMELER

catch/have a cold • a **bad/heavy/stinking** (= very bad) cold

cold[2] /kəʊld/ *noun* **1** [C] a common illness which makes you sneeze and makes your nose produce liquid **soğuk algınlığı, üşütme, üşümüş, nezle** *I've got a cold.* ○ *He caught a bad cold at school.* **2 the cold** cold weather or temperatures **soğuk hava 3 leave sb out in the cold** to not allow someone to be part of a group or activity **birini dışarda tutmak, açıkta bırakmak, eylem/ gruba dahil etmemek**

cold[3] /kəʊld/ *adverb* **1 be out cold** *informal* to be unconscious **bilinçsiz olmak, şuurunu kaybetmek, baygın bir halde olmak** *I hit my head and was out cold for two*

minutes. **2** completely and immediately **tamamen ve çabucak** *I offered him £10 but he turned me down cold.*

cold-blooded /‚kəʊld'blʌdɪd/ *adjective* showing no emotion or sympathy **soğuk kanlı, duygusuz,** *a cold-blooded killer*

cold-hearted /‚kəʊld'hɑːtɪd/ *adjective* feeling no kindness or sympathy towards other people **merhametsiz, duygusuz, acımasız**

coldly /'kəʊldli/ *adverb* in a way that is not friendly or emotional **hissizce, acımasızca, merhametsizce** *He looked at me coldly.*

colic /'kɒlɪk/ *noun* [U] When a baby has colic, it has a bad pain in the stomach. **karın ağrısı, kolik**

collaborate /kə'læbəreɪt/ *verb* [I] **1** When two or more people collaborate, they work together to create or achieve the same thing. **birlikte çalışmak, iş birliği yapmak, ortak çalışmak** *Didn't you collaborate with him on one of your books?* **2** to help people who are an enemy of your country or government **düşmanla işbirliği yapmak, ülkesinin düşmanlarıyla işbirliği yapmak, ihanet etmek** *He was accused of collaborating with the enemy.* • **collaborator** *noun* [C] **işbirliğinde bulunan**

collaboration /kə‚læbə'reɪʃən/ *noun* **1** [C, U] when two or more people work together to create or achieve the same thing, or a product of this **işbirliği, ortaklık, katılma** *The show was a result of collaboration between several museums.* **2** [U] when someone helps an enemy country or government **düşmanla işbirliği, ihanet**

collage /kɒl'ɑːʒ/ *noun* [C, U] a picture made by sticking small pieces of paper or other materials onto a surface, or the process of making pictures like this **yapıştırma resim, kolaj**

collapse[1] /kə'læps/ *verb* **1** FALL [I] When someone collapses, they fall down, usually because they are ill or weak. **düşmek, yıkılmak 2** OBJECT [I, T] to fall down or towards the inside, or to make a structure or object fall down or towards its inside **çökmek, yıkılıp dağılmak, göçmek** *The roof collapsed under the weight of snow.* **3** FALL [I] to fail to work or succeed **çalışamamak veya başaramamak** *The peace talks have collapsed.*

collapse[2] /kə'læps/ *noun* [C, U] **1** the sudden failure of a system, organization, business, etc **(sistem, kuruluş, iş vs.) çökme, yıkılma, mahvolma 2** when a person or structure becomes too weak to stand and suddenly falls **(kişi, yapı) çökme, ayakta duramama, bayılma**

collapsible /kə'læpsɪbl/ *adjective* able to be folded or made flat in order to be stored or carried **katlanabilir, açılıp kapanabilir, portatif** *a collapsible table/boat*

collar[1] /'kɒlər/ *noun* [C] **1** the part of a shirt, coat, etc that is usually folded over and goes round your neck **yaka** *a shirt collar* ⊃See picture at **jacket. 2** a narrow piece of leather or plastic that you fasten round the neck of an animal **tasma**

collar[2] /'kɒlər/ *verb* [T] *informal* to find someone and stop them going somewhere, often so that you can talk to them about something **alıkoymak, yakasına yapışmak, tutmak, yakalamak**

collarbone /'kɒləbəʊn/ *noun* [C] a bone between the base of your neck and your shoulder **köprücük kemiği**

collateral /kə'lætərəl/ *noun* [U] things that you agree to give someone if you are not able to pay back money you have borrowed from them **teminat, güvence** *I used my car as collateral for a loan.*

o--**colleague** /'kɒliːɡ/ *noun* [C] someone that you work with **iş arkadaşı**

○➤**collect¹** /kə'lekt/ *verb* **1** BRING TOGETHER [T] to get things from different places and bring them together **topla-mak, bir araya getirmek** *Police collected a good deal of information during the investigation.* ○ *Would you col-lect up the books please, Joanne?* **2** KEEP [T] to get and keep things of one type such as stamps or coins as a hobby **koleksiyon yapmak, biriktirmek, toplamak** *She collects dolls.* **3** GO TO GET [T] *UK* to go to a place and bring someone or something away from it **gidip getir-mek, uğrayıp almak** *She collects Anna from school at three o'clock.* **4** MONEY [I, T] to ask people to give you money for something, for example a charity (= organi-zation that helps people) **yardım toplamak** *I'm collec-ting on behalf of Oxfam.* **5** RECEIVE [T] to receive money that you are owed **toplamak, alacağını tahsil etmek** *You can begin to collect a pension at age 62.* **6** COME TOGETHER [I] to come together in a single place **top-lanmak, bir araya gelmek** *Journalists collected out-side the palace.* **7 collect yourself/your thoughts** to get control over your feelings and thoughts **kendini/kafasını toplamak**

collect² /kə'lekt/ *adjective, adverb US* When you tele-phone collect or make a collect telephone call, the per-son you telephone pays for the call. **ödemeli arama**

collected /kə'lektɪd/ *adjective* **1** [always before noun] brought together in one book or series of books **derlen-miş, toplanmış, kitaplaştırılmış** *His collected poems were published in 1928.* **2** showing control over your feel-ings **kendine hakim, kendini kontrol eden** *Jane was very calm and collected.*

collection .... İLE BİRLİKTE KULLANILAN KELİMELER

amass/display/have a collection ● an extensive/large/priceless/private collection

○➤**collection** /kə'lekʃᵊn/ *noun* **1** OBJECTS [C] a group of objects of the same type that have been collected by one person or in one place **aynı türden bir grup nesne, koleksiyon** *a private art collection* **2** TAKING AWAY [U] when something is taken away from a place **toplama, alma** *rubbish collection* **3** MONEY [C] an amount of money collected from several people **para veya yardım toplama, bağış, toplanan para** *We had a collection for Emily's gift.* **4** GROUP [C] a group of things or people **grup,takım, küme, derleme, anto-loji** *There's quite a collection of toothbrushes in the bathroom.*

collective¹ /kə'lektɪv/ *adjective* involving, felt by, or owned by everyone in a group **ortak, müşterek, bir-likte, hep beraber** *collective responsibility*

collective² /kə'lektɪv/ *noun* [C] a business that is owned and controlled by the people who work in it **sahipleri çalışanlardan oluşan şirket, iş**

collectively /kə'lektɪvli/ *adverb* as a group **birlikte olarak, ortaklaşa, müştereken, elbirliğiyle** *She has a staff of four who collectively earn almost $200,000.*

collector /kə'lektə'/ *noun* [C] **1** someone whose job is to collect tickets or money from people **tahsildar, topla-yıcı, bilet/para toplayan** *a tax collector* **2** someone who collects objects because they are interesting or beautiful **toplayıcı, koleksiyoncu** *a collector of modern art*

college .... İLE BİRLİKTE KULLANILAN KELİMELER

go to college ● be at college ● a college **course/lec-turer/student**

○➤**college** /'kɒlɪdʒ/ *noun* **1** EDUCATION [C, U] *UK* a place where students are educated when they are between 16 and 18 years old, or after they have finished school **kolej** *a sixth-form college* ○ *a teacher-training college*

2 UNIVERSITY [C, U] *US* a university **üniversite** **3** PART OF UNIVERSITY [C] a part of a university that has its own teachers and students **üniversitenin bağımsız bir bölümü** *Cambridge/Oxford colleges* ➜See also: com-munity college, junior college.

collegiate /kə'liːdʒiət/ *adjective* relating to or belonging to a college or its students **üniversiteyle ilgili, üniver-site öğrencisine özgü** *collegiate sports*

collide /kə'laɪd/ *verb* [I] When two objects collide, they hit each other with force, usually while moving. **çarp-mak, hareket halindeyken çarpışmak** *The car colli-ded with a van.*

colliery /'kɒljəri/ *UK* (*UK/US* coal mine) *noun* [C] a place where people work digging coal from under the ground **taş kömürü madeni, maden ocağı**

collision .... İLE BİRLİKTE KULLANILAN KELİMELER

avoid/be involved in a collision ● [a car/train, etc] in a collision with sth ● a head-on collision ● a colli-sion between sth and sth

collision /kə'lɪʒᵊn/ *noun* **1** [C] an accident that happens when two vehicles hit each other with force **çarpışma** **2 be on a collision course** If two people or groups are on a collision course, they are doing or saying things that are certain to cause a serious disagreement or fight between them. **çatışma/çarpışma/anlaşmazlık düzleminde olmak**

collocation /ˌkɒləˈkeɪʃᵊn/ *noun* [C] **1** a word or phrase that sounds natural and correct when it is used with another word or phrase **bir sözcük veya ifadenin başka sözcüklerle kullanıldığında tabii görünmesi** *In the phrase 'a hard frost', 'hard' is a collocation of 'frost', and 'strong' would not sound natural.* **2** the com-bination of words formed when two or more words are frequently used together in a way that sounds natural **tabii gözüken iki ya da daha fazla sözcüklerin uyumu, ahengi** *The phrase 'a hard frost' is a colloca-tion.*

colloquial /kə'ləʊkwiəl/ *adjective* Colloquial words or expressions are informal. **günlük konuşma dilinde, samimi; konuşma diline ait, resmi olmayan ifade ve sözcükler** *colloquial speech* ● **colloquially** *adverb* **resmi olmayan bir şekilde**

collude /kə'luːd/ *verb* [I] *formal* to do something secretly with another person or group, in order to deceive or cheat others **gizli planlar yapmak, arkasından bir şeyler çevirmek, gizlice aldatmak** *The company col-luded with competitors to fix prices.* ● **collusion** /kə'luː-ʒᵊn/ *noun* [U] *He was accused of being in collusion with the terrorists.* **hile**

colon /'kəʊlɒn/ *noun* [C] **1** a mark (:) used before a list, an example, an explanation, etc **iki nokta üst üste** ➜See study page Punctuation on page Centre 33. **2** the large intes-tine (= lower part of a person's bowels) **kalın bağırsak**

colonel /'kɜːnᵊl/ *noun* [C] an officer of high rank in the army or air force **albay**

colonial /kə'ləʊniəl/ *adjective* [always before noun] relat-ing to colonialism or a colony (= country controlled by another country) **sömürgeciliğe ait, sömürge toplu-mundan, koloni olan ülkeye ait** *colonial rule/govern-ment*

colonialism /kə'ləʊniəlɪzᵊm/ *noun* [U] the system in which powerful countries control other countries **sömürgecilik, sömürge hayatı**

colonize (*also UK* -ise) /'kɒlənaɪz/ *verb* [T] **1** to send peo-ple to live in and govern another country **sömürgeleş-tirmek, koloni haline getirmek** [often passive] *Burundi was first colonized by the Germans.* **2** to start growing or living in large numbers in a place **bir yerde koloni**

kurmak, büyük gruplar halinde yaşayıp büyümek *Weeds quickly colonize areas of cleared ground.* ● **colonist** /ˈkɒlənɪst/ *noun* [C] someone who goes to colonize a country **bir ülkeyi sömürgeleştirmeye giden kişi** ● **colonization** /ˌkɒlənaɪˈzeɪʃᵊn/ *noun* [U] **sömürgeleştirme**

colony /ˈkɒləni/ *noun* [C] **1** COUNTRY a country or area controlled in an official, political way by a more powerful country **sömürge, koloni** *a French/British colony* **2** GROUP a group of the same type of animals, insects, or plants living together in a particular place **(hayvan, böcek, bitki vb.) bir yerde beraber yaşama, koloni oluşturma/kurma** *a colony of ants* **3** PEOPLE a group of people with the same interests or job who live together **insanlar grubu, ortak amaçlar için bir araya gelmiş insanlar topluluğu** *an artists' colony*

o➤**color** /ˈkʌləʳ/ *noun, verb US spelling of* colour **renk**

colored /ˈkʌləd/ *adjective US spelling of* coloured **renkli, boyalı, boyanmış**

colorful /ˈkʌləfᵊl/ *adjective US spelling of* colourful **renkli**

coloring /ˈkʌlərɪŋ/ *noun* [U] *US spelling of* colouring **renklendirme**

colorless /ˈkʌlələs/ *adjective US spelling of* colourless **renksiz, sade**

colossal /kəˈlɒsᵊl/ *adjective* extremely large **devasa, oldukça büyük, muazzam** *colossal amounts of money*

o➤**colour¹** UK (*US* color) /ˈkʌləʳ/ *noun* **1** RED/BLUE ETC [C, U] red, blue, green, yellow, etc **renk** *Green is my favourite colour.* ○ *What colour shall I paint the kitchen?* ➋Orta kısımdaki renkli sayfalarına bakınız. **2** FILM/TV ETC [U] using or showing all the colours, not only black and white **bütün renkler** *Why didn't he shoot the film* **in colour**? **3** SKIN [U] the colour of a person's skin, which shows their race **ten rengi, derisinin rengi** FACE [U] healthy pink skin on someone's face **yüzünün rengi** *The colour drained from her cheeks.* **5** INTEREST [U] interesting or exciting qualities or parts **nitelik, ilgi çekici olma, ilginç/heyecan veren özellik** *We added your story for a bit of local colour.* **6** **with flying colours** with a very high score or with great success **büyük bir başarıyla** *He passed the entrance exam with flying colours.* ➋See also: primary colour.

colour² UK (*US* color) /ˈkʌləʳ/ *verb* **1** [I, T] to become a particular colour, or to make something a particular colour **boyamak, renklendirmek** *He drew a heart and coloured it red.* ○ *Fry the onions until they start to colour.* **2** [T] to affect what someone does, says, or feels **etkilemek** [often passive] *Her views are coloured by her own bad experiences.*

colour sth in *phrasal verb* to fill an area with colour using paint, pens, etc **bir alanı boya/renkli kalem ile boyamak**

colour-blind UK (*US* color-blind) /ˈkʌləblaɪnd/ *adjective* unable to see the difference between particular colours **renk körü**

coloured UK (*US* colored) /ˈkʌləd/ *adjective* **1** having or producing a colour or colours **renkli** *coloured lights/cloth* **2** an old-fashioned way of describing someone from a race with dark skin that is now considered offensive **siyah derili birini aşağılamada kullanılan ifade, zenci, siyah ırktan olan**

colourful UK (*US* colorful) /ˈkʌləfᵊl/ *adjective* **1** having bright colours **renkli, cıvıl cıvıl, parlak, rengarenk** *a colourful painting* **2** interesting and unusual **ilginç, ilgi çekici** *a colourful character*

colouring UK (*US* coloring) /ˈkʌlərɪŋ/ *noun* [U] **1** the colour of something, especially an animal or person's skin, hair, and eyes **cilt veya saç rengi, bir şeyin rengi** *The*

boys have their father's colouring. **2** a substance that is used to colour something **renk maddesi, boya** *food/ artificial colouring*

colourless UK (*US* colorless) /ˈkʌlələs/ *adjective* **1** without any colour **renksiz, sade, rengi olmayan** *a colourless liquid* **2** without the qualities that make someone or something interesting and unusual **renksiz, hiç bir özelliği olmayan, niteliksiz**

colt /kəʊlt/ *noun* [C] a young male horse **tay**

column

column /ˈkɒləm/ *noun* [C] **1** TALL POST a tall, solid, usually stone post which is used to support a roof or as decoration in a building **sütun, direk, kolon** *a stone/marble column* **2** NEWSPAPER a regular article in a newspaper or magazine on a particular subject or by the same writer **gazete sütunu 3** PRINT one of the blocks of print into which a page of a newspaper, magazine, or dictionary is divided **dergi, gazete veya sözlükte kolon, sütun 4** NUMBERS ETC any block of numbers or words written one under the other **altalta yazılmış sözcükler/rakamlar, sütun 5 a column of sth** something with a tall, narrow shape **bir şeyin uzun dar biçimi/direk biçiminde** *A column of smoke rose from the chimney.* **6** PEOPLE MOVING a long line of moving people or vehicles **kol, konvoy, dizi dizi/sıra sıra insan veya araçlar** *a column of refugees* ➋See also: gossip column.

columnist /ˈkɒləmnɪst/ *noun* [C] someone who writes a regular article for a newspaper or magazine **köşe yazarı** *a sports/gossip columnist*

.com /dɒtˈkɒm/ *internet abbreviation for* company: used in some Internet addresses which belong to companies or businesses **internette şirket veya işe ait olduğunu gösteren terim; şirket** *www.google.com*

coma /ˈkəʊmə/ *noun* [C] when someone is not conscious for a long time **koma halinde olan, baygın, koma** [usually singular] *She has been* **in a coma** *for over a week.*

comb¹ /kəʊm/ *noun* [C] a flat piece of metal or plastic with a row of long, narrow parts along one side, that you use to tidy your hair **tarak**

comb

comb² /kəʊm/ *verb* [T] **1** to tidy your hair using a comb **taramak 2** to search a place very carefully **karış karış aramak, didik didik etmek, altını üstüne getirmek** *Investigators* **combed through** *the wreckage.*

combat¹ /ˈkɒmbæt/ *noun* [C, U] a fight, especially during a war **muharebe, savaş, muharip** *The aircraft was shot down* **in combat**.

combat ...... İLE BİRLİKTE KULLANILAN KELİMELER

combat **crime/global warming/racism/terrorism** ● combat **the effects** of sth ● combat **a problem** ● combat **the threat of** sth ● combat **the rise in** [crime, etc]

combat² /'kɒmbæt/ *verb* [T] **combatting**, *past* **combatted**, **combating**, *past* **combated** to try to stop something unpleasant or harmful from happening or increasing **savaşmak, mücadele etmek** *new measures to combat the rise in crime*

combatant /'kɒmbət³nt/ *noun* [C] *formal* someone who fights in a war **savaşçı, muharip, mücadeleci**

combative /'kɒmbətɪv/ *adjective formal* eager to fight or argue **kavgacı, kavgayı/dalaşmayı seven**

o=**combination** /ˌkɒmbɪ'neɪʃ³n/ *noun* 1 [C, U] a mixture of different people or things **birleşim, karışım, terkip** *Strawberries and cream - a perfect combination!* ○ *We won through a combination of luck and skill.* ○ *This drug can be safely used in combination with other medicines.* 2 [C] a set of numbers or letters in a particular order which is needed to open some types of locks **şifre** *a combination lock*

o=**combine** /kəm'baɪn/ *verb* 1 [I, T] to become mixed or joined, or to mix or join things together **birleş(tir)mek, bir araya getirmek, bir araya gelmek** *My wages combined with your savings should just pay for it.* ○ *The band combines jazz rhythms and romantic lyrics.* 2 [T] to do two or more activities at the same time **aynı anda bir kaç işi yapmak** *I don't know how she combines working with studying.*

combined /kəm'baɪnd/ *adjective* [always before noun] joined together **birleşik, birlikte, beraber, ortak, müşterek** *the combined effects of poverty and disease*

combine harvester /ˌkɒmbaɪn'hɑːvɪstəʳ/ (*also* combine) *noun* [C] a large farm machine which cuts a crop and separates the grain from the stem **biçer döver makinası**

combustion /kəm'bʌstʃ³n/ *noun* [U] the process of burning **yanma, tutuşma**

o=**come** /kʌm/ *verb past tense* **came**, *past participle* **come** 1 [MOVE TOWARDS] [I] to move or travel towards a person who is speaking or towards the place that they are speaking about **gelmek** *Come and see what I've done.* ○ *Can you come to my party?* ○ *The rain came down heavily.* ○ *Here comes Adam* (= Adam is coming). 2 [ARRIVE] [I] to arrive somewhere or to go to a place **gitmek/varmak, ulaşmak, erişmek** *I'll come and see you later.* ○ [+ to do sth] *I've come to see Mr Curtis.* ○ *Dad will come for you at six.* ○ *We came to a crossroads.* 3 [GO WITH SOMEONE] [I] to go somewhere with the person who is speaking ... **ile gitmek** *Come for a walk with us.* ○ *We're going to the cinema. Do you want to come?* 4 **come after/first/last, etc** to have or achieve a particular position in a race, competition, list, etc **birinci/sonuncu olmak, sonradan/arkadan gelmek** *Our team came third.* ○ *Sunday comes after Saturday.* 5 **come past/to/up to, etc** to reach a particular length, height, or depth **belli bir safhaya ulaşmak, bir duruma gelmek** *The water came up to my waist.* 6 **come apart/off, etc** to become separated or removed from something **kopmak, sökülmek, çözülmek** *The book came apart in my hands.* ○ *The handle came off.* ○ *My shoelaces have come undone.* ○ *The door came open.* 7 **come easily/easy/naturally** to be very easy for someone **kolay gelmek, kolayına gelmek** *Singing came naturally to Louise.* 8 [HAPPEN] [I] to happen **olmak, gelmek, meydana gelmek** *Spring has come early.* ○ *The worst problems are still to come.* 9 **how come** *informal* used to ask why or how something has happened **Neden? Niçin? Nasıl olur?** *How come you didn't go to the party?* 10 **come**

and go to exist or happen somewhere for a short time and then go away **gidip gelmek** *The feeling of nausea comes and goes.* 11 [BE AVAILABLE] [I] to be available in a particular size, colour, etc **üretilmek, yapılmak, piyasaya sürülmek, satışa sunulmak, var olmak, mevcut olmak** *The table comes in three different sizes.* ○ *Furniture like this doesn't come cheap.* 12 **come to do sth** to start to do something **bir şeyi yapmaya başlamak, işe koyulmak** *I have come to rely on acupuncture.* ○ *This place has come to be known as 'Pheasant Corner'.* 13 **when it comes to sth/doing sth** used to introduce a new idea that you want to say something about **akla gelmek; ... buna/şuna gelince** *When it comes to baking cakes, she's an expert.* 14 **come to think of it** used to say that you have just thought of something **aklıma gelmişken; sahi** *Come to think of it, I've got two batteries that you can have upstairs.* ⊃See also: come to blows (blow²), I'll/We'll cross that bridge¹ when I/we come to it, come clean¹, if/when it comes to the crunch¹, (back) down to earth, come under fire¹, deliver/come up with the goods, come to grief, come/get to grips (grip¹) with sth, come to light¹, come into your/its own¹, not be/come up to scratch², come to your senses (sense¹), come/turn up trumps (trump).

come

Unutmayın! Come fiili biryere doğru hareket veya seyahat etmek anlamında kullanıldığında, ardından to edatı kullanılır:: ~~My friend came my house two weeks ago.~~ Yanlış cümle örneği

My friend came to my house two weeks ago.

come about *phrasal verb* to happen, or start to happen **olmak, meydana gelmek** *How did the idea for an arts festival come about?*

come across sb/sth *phrasal verb* to meet someone or discover something by chance **umulmadık/beklenmedik anda karşılaşmak, karşısına çıkmak, ansızın bulmak, tesadüf etmek** *I came across a lovely little restaurant in the village.*

come across *phrasal verb* 1 to seem to be a particular type of person **etki/izlenim bırakmak** *He came across as shy.* 2 If an idea or emotion comes across, it is expressed clearly and people understand it. **bir düşünceyi fikri açıkça izah etmek/açıklamak** *His bitterness comes across in his poetry.*

come along *phrasal verb* 1 [ARRIVE] to arrive or appear at a place **bir yere varmak, bir yerde gözükmek/ortaya çıkmak** *A taxi never comes along when you need one.* 2 [GO WITH SOMEONE] to go somewhere with someone **eşlik etmek, biriyle beraber gitmek** *We're going to the cinema. Do you want to come along?* 3 [EXIST] to start to exist **var olmaya başlamak, varlığı ortaya çıkmak, doğmak** *I gave up climbing when my first child came along.* 4 **be coming along** to be developing or making progress

come around *phrasal verb* 1 [VISIT] to visit someone at their house **ziyaret etmek** 2 [AGREE] to change your opinion about something, or agree to an idea or a plan that you were against **fikrini değiştirmek ve önceden karşı olduğu şeyi kabul etmek** *I'm sure she'll come around to our view eventually.* 3 [EVENT] If an event that happens regularly comes around, it happens, or is going to happen soon. **vuku bulmak, olmak, yeniden meydana gelmek** *Thanksgiving has come around again.* 4 [BECOME CONSCIOUS] to become conscious again after an accident or medical operation **bir kaza veya ameliyattan sonra kendine gelmek, ayılmak**

come back *phrasal verb* 1 to return to a place **geri gelmek, dönmek** *I've just come back from the dentist's.* 2 If a style or a fashion comes back, it becomes popular

again. **yeniden moda/meşhur/popüler olmak** *Miniskirts are coming back into fashion.*
come back to sb *phrasal verb* If something comes back to you, you remember it. **hatırlamak, hatıra gelmek** *Suddenly, the horror of the accident came back to me.*
come between sb *phrasal verb* to harm the relationship between two or more people **araya girmek, insanların arasını bozmak, nifak sokmak, aralarına girmek** *I won't let anything come between me and my children.*
come by sth *phrasal verb* to get something, especially something that is unusual or difficult to find **eline geçirmek, elde etmek, edinmek** *Cheap organic food is still difficult to come by.*
come down *phrasal verb* **1** to break and fall to the ground **yere düşmek, yıkılmak** *A lot of trees came down in the storm.* **2** If a price or a level comes down, it becomes lower. **düşmek, azalmak, düzeyi/fiyatı düşmek, ucuzlamak** *Prices always come down after Christmas.* **3** to decide that you support a particular person or side in an argument, etc **tartışmada tarafını tutmak, desteklemeye karar vermek** *The government has come down on the side of military action.*
come down on sb *phrasal verb* to punish or criticize someone **cezalandırmak, eleştirmek, yermek, şiddetle tenkit etmek** *The police are coming down hard on people for not paying parking fines.*
come down to sth/doing sth *phrasal verb* If a situation, problem, decision, etc comes down to something, then that is the thing that will influence it most. **gelip dayanmak, ... e/a dayanmak,**
come down with sth *phrasal verb informal* to get an illness **bir hastalığa yakalanmak, hasta olmak, hastalık kapmak** *I came down with the flu at Christmas.*
come forward *phrasal verb* to offer to help someone or to give information **yardım teklif etmek, bilgi vermeyi önermek** *We need witnesses to come forward with information about the attack.*
come from sth *phrasal verb* to be born, obtained from, or made somewhere **... den olmak/doğmak, elde etmek; bir yerde yapılmış/üretilmiş olmak** *She comes from Poland.* ○ *Milk comes from cows.*
come from sth/doing sth *phrasal verb* to be caused by something **bir şeyden etkilenmek; ... den olmak, sebebi olmak** *"I feel awful." "That comes from eating too many sweets."*
come in *phrasal verb* **1** ENTER to enter a room or building **içeri girmek** *Do you want to come in for a cup of tea?* **2** FASHION If a fashion or a product comes in, it becomes available or becomes popular. **yeniden moda/gündemde/elde edilebilir olmak** *Flared trousers came in during the seventies.* **3** BE RECEIVED If news, information, a report, etc comes in, it is received. **almak, ele geçmek, alınmak, ulaşmak, gelmek** *News is just coming in about the explosion.* **4 come in first/second, etc** to finish a race or a competition in first/second, etc position **5** SEA If the tide (= regular change in the level of the sea) comes in, the sea moves towards the beach or coast. **denizde dalga sahile varmak/gelmek 6** BE INVOLVED *informal* used to describe how someone is involved in a situation, story, or plan ... **de/da rolü olmak, yeri olmak, devreye girmek, parmağı olmak** *We need people to help clean up, and that's where you come in.*
come in for sth *phrasal verb* If someone comes in for criticism, praise, etc, they are criticized, praised, etc. ... **e/a uğramak, suçlanmak, eleştirilmek veya övülmek**
come into sth *phrasal verb* **1** to get money from someone who has died **mirasa konmak, mirastan pay almak, mirasa sahip olmak** *Just after I left university, I came into a bit of money.* **2 come into it** *UK informal* to influence a situation *Money doesn't come into it.*

come of sth/doing sth *phrasal verb* to happen as a result of something **bir şeyden dolayı vukua gelmek, sonucunda oluşmak, sonuçlanmak** *Did anything come of all those job applications?*
come off *phrasal verb* to happen successfully **başarıyla sonuçlanmak, başarılı olmak, etkili olmak** *His attempt to impress us all didn't quite come off.* **2 come off badly/best/well, etc** to be in a bad or good position at the end of a fight, argument, etc *She usually comes off best in an argument.* **3 Come off it!** *informal* used to tell someone that you do not agree with them or do not believe them *Oh, come off it! I saw you take it.*
come on *phrasal verb* **1** START to start to happen or work **olmaya başlamak, çalışmaya başlamak** *The heating comes on at six in the morning.* ○ *I've got a cold coming on.* **2** MAKE PROGRESS to make progress **ilerlemek, gelişmek, yol katetmek** *How's your new novel coming on?* **3 Come on!** ENCOURAGEMENT *informal* used to encourage someone to do something, to hurry, to try harder, etc **Haydi!' 'Ha gayret!' 'Haydi bakalım!' 'Hadi acele et!'** *Come on! We're going to be late.* **4** DISAGREEMENT used to tell someone that you do not agree with them, do not believe them, etc **Haydi canım sende!' 'Haydi bırakın saçmalığı!'** *Come on Bob! You made the same excuse last week.*
come out *phrasal verb* **1** BECOME AVAILABLE If a book, record, film, etc comes out, it becomes available for people to buy or see. **çıkmak, yayınlanmak, piyasaya çıkmak, basılmak** *When does their new album come out?* **2** SUN If the sun, the moon, or a star comes out, it appears in the sky. **(güneş, ay, yıldız) ortaya çıkmak, doğmak, gözükmek 3** BECOME KNOWN to become known **ortaya çıkmak, anlaşılmak, öğrenilmek, bilinmek** *The truth about him will come out in the end.* **4** SOCIAL EVENT *UK* to go somewhere with someone for a social event **biriyle katılmak/gitmek, biriyle bir davete gitmek, ilk defa bir toplantıya katılmak** *Would you like to come out for a drink?* **5** RESULT If you describe how something comes out at the end of a process or activity, you say what it is like. **olmak, bir şeye benzemek, sonuç vermek** *How did your chocolate cake come out?* **6** INFORMATION If results or information come out, they are given to people. **duyurulmak, açıklanmak, bilgi verilmek, ilan edilmek** *The exam results come out in August.* **7** BE REMOVED If dirt or a mark comes out of something, it disappears when you clean it. **(leke) çıkmak, yok olmak** *Will this red wine stain come out?* **8** PHOTOGRAPH If a photograph comes out, the picture can be seen clearly. **basılmak, resim oluşmak, resimlerin net ve iyi basılması** *The photos didn't come out very well.* **9** BE SAID If something that you say comes out in a particular way, you say it in that way. **(istenmeden) çıkmak, sözlenmek, ifade edilmek** *I wanted to tell her that I loved her, but it came out all wrong.* **10** TELL to tell people that you are homosexual (= sexually attracted to people of the same sex) **(hemcinsine ilgi duyduğunu) açık açık söylemek, açıklamak, ne olduğunu bildirmek 11 come out against/in favour of sth** to say publicly that you oppose or support something
come out in sth *phrasal verb* If you come out in a skin disease, it appears on your skin. **yüzü/derisi/cildi... ile kaplanmak, kaplı olmak**
come out of sth *phrasal verb* If something comes out of a process or event, it is one of the results. **sonuçlanmak, sonuç olarak ortaya çıkmak, ... şeklinde sonuçlanmak** *I hope something good can come out of this mess.*
come out with sth *phrasal verb* to say something suddenly that is not expected **bir şeyle birden bire ortaya çıkmak, ansızın beklenmedik şekilde söylemek**

come over *phrasal verb* **1** to come to a place, move from one place to another, or move towards someone **gelmek, ilerlemek, bir yere gitmek/taşınmak** *Are your family coming over from Greece for the wedding?* **2** to seem to be a particular type of person **başka bir tip insan gibi gözükmek/olmak** *Henry came over as a real enthusiast.*

come over sb *phrasal verb* If a feeling comes over you, you suddenly experience it. **(duygu) etkilemek, etkilenmek, kaplamak, sarmak** *I don't usually get so angry. I don't know what came over me.*

come round *phrasal verb UK* **1** VISIT to visit someone at their house **ziyaret etmek, uğramak, geçerken uğramak** *You must come round to the flat for dinner some time.* **2** AGREE to change your opinion about something, or agree to an idea or a plan that you were against **sonunda fikir değiştirip kabul etmek, dediğine gelmek 3** EVENT If an event that happens regularly comes round, it happens, or is going to happen soon. **olmak, (zamanı) gelmek** *I can't believe that winter has come round already.* **4** BECOME CONSCIOUS to become conscious again after an accident or medical operation **bir kaza veya ameliyattan sonra kendine gelmek, ayılmak**

come through *phrasal verb* **1** If information or a result comes through, you receive it. **gelmek, ulaşmak (bilgi, sonuç)** *Have the results of the tests come through yet?* **2** If an emotion comes through, other people can notice it. **açıkça görülmek, ortaya çıkmak** *His nervousness came through when he spoke.*

come through (sth) *phrasal verb* to manage to get to the end of a difficult or dangerous situation **atlatmak, kurtulmak, üstesinden gelmek** *We've had some hard times, but we've come through them.*

come to *phrasal verb* to become conscious again after an accident or medical operation **bir kaza veya ameliyattan sonra ayılmak, kendine gelmek**

come to sb *phrasal verb* If a thought or idea comes to you, you suddenly remember it or start to think about it. **hatırına gelmek, dilinin ucunda olmak, hatırlamak üzere olmak**

come to sth *phrasal verb* **1** to be a particular total when numbers or amounts are added together **yekün teşkil etmek, tutarına ulaşmak, mal olmak** *That comes to £50, please.* **2 come to a decision/conclusion/arrangement, etc** to make a decision or decide what to think about something **3** to reach a particular state or situation, especially a bad one **kötü bir duruma girmek/erişmek/ulaşmak** *You won't come to any harm.*

come under sth *phrasal verb* **1 come under attack/criticism/scrutiny, etc** to be attacked, criticized, examined, etc **2** to be controlled or dealt with by a particular authority ... **in denetiminde/kontrolünde/otoritesi altında olmak** *Water rates come under local government control.* **3** to be in a particular part of a book, list, etc **listesinde/bölümünde/altında yer almak, bulunmak, olmak** *Hairdressers come under 'beauty salons' in the Yellow Pages.*

come up *phrasal verb* **1** MOVE TOWARDS to move towards someone **birine doğru ilerlemek/gitmek** *After the concert, he came up to me to ask for my autograph.* **2** BE DISCUSSED to be discussed or suggested **sözü edilmek, ele alınmak, önerilmek** *The issue of security came up at the meeting yesterday.* **3** OPPORTUNITY If a job or opportunity comes up, it becomes available. **bir iş/fırsat çıkmak, doğmak, mevcut olmak 4** PROBLEM If a problem or difficult situation comes up, it happens. **sorun/zor bir durum zuhur etmek, olmak, meydana gelmek 5 be coming up** to be happening soon *My exams are coming up next month.* **6** SUN OR MOON When the sun or the moon comes up, it rises. **doğmak, yükselmek 7** COMPUTER If information comes up on a computer screen, it appears there. **ekranda gözükmek/çıkmak**

come up against sb/sth *phrasal verb* to have to deal with a problem or difficulty **karşılaşmak, karşı karşıya kalmak, ilgilenmek zorunda olmak** *She came up against a lot of sexism in her first engineering job.*

come up to sth *phrasal verb* to reach the usual or necessary standard **gerekli seviyeye çıkmak/ulaşmak, eski düzeye çıkmak** *This essay doesn't come up to your usual standards.*

come up with sth *phrasal verb* to think of a plan, an idea, or a solution to a problem **bir fikir/plan/çözüm ile ortaya çıkmak/ileri sürmek, öne sürmek, ortaya atmak** *We need to come up with a good scheme to make money.*

comeback /'kʌmbæk/ *noun* [C] a successful attempt to become powerful, important, or famous again **geri dönüş, dönüş, yeniden güç/iktidar kazanma, tekrar ünlü olma** *She's made a comeback with her first new album for twenty years.*

comedian /kə'mi:diən/ *noun* [C] someone who entertains people by telling jokes **güldürü sanatçısı/ustası, komedyen**

comedown /'kʌmdaʊn/ *noun* [C] *informal* a situation that is not as good as one you were in before **kötüye gidiş, eskisinden daha kötü olma** [usually singular] *Cleaning windows is a bit of a comedown after his last job.*

comedy /'kɒmədi/ *noun* [C, U] entertainment such as a film, play, etc which is funny **komedi, güldürü** *The film is a romantic comedy.*

comet /'kɒmɪt/ *noun* [C] an object in space that leaves a bright line behind it in the sky **kuyruklu yıldız**

comfort[1] /'kʌmfət/ *noun* **1** NO PAIN [U] a pleasant feeling of being relaxed and free from pain **rahatlık** *Now you can watch the latest films in the comfort of your sitting room.* **2** FOR SADNESS [U] when you feel better after being worried or sad **rahatlama, teselli** *What she said brought me great comfort.* **3** ENOUGH MONEY [U] when you have a pleasant life with enough money for everything that you need **konfor, rahatlık, müreffeh seviye** *He can afford to retire and live in comfort for the rest of his life.* **4 a comfort to sb** someone or something that helps you when you are anxious or sad **birine verilen teselli, avuntu** *The children have been a great comfort to me since her death.* **5** PLEASANT THING [C] something that makes your life easy and pleasant **lüks, konfor, hayatı kolaylaştıran şeylerin tümü** [usually plural] *Good chocolate is one of life's little comforts.* ➲Opposite **discomfort**.

comfort[2] /'kʌmfət/ *verb* [T] to make someone feel better when they are anxious or sad **rahatlatmak, teselli vermek, avutmak** ● **comforting** *adjective* *He said a few comforting words.* **rahatlatıcı**

☞**comfortable** /'kʌmftəbl/ *adjective* **1** NOT CAUSING PAIN Comfortable furniture, clothes, rooms, etc make you feel relaxed and do not cause any pain. **rahat, konforlu, huzur veren** *comfortable shoes* ○ *We had a comfortable journey.* **2** PERSON If you are comfortable, you are relaxed and have no pain. **rahat, keyfi yerinde** *Make yourself comfortable while I fetch you a drink.* ➲Opposite **uncomfortable**. **3** WITHOUT WORRIES If you are comfortable in a situation, you do not have any worries about it. **rahat, endişesiz** *I don't feel comfortable about leaving the children here alone.* **4** MONEY having enough money for everything that you need **hali vakti yerinde, yokluk çekmeyen, varlıklı, rahat** *a comfortable retirement* **5** WIN If you win a game or competition by a comfortable amount, you win easily. **zorlanmayan, rahat, endişesiz, kendinden emin** *a comfortable lead/victory* ● **comfortably** *adverb* **rahat bir şekilde**

comforter /'kʌmfətər/ *US* (*UK* duvet) *noun* [C] a cover filled with feathers or warm material, that you sleep under **yorgan, örtü**

'comfort ,zone noun [C] a situation that you know well and in which you are relaxed and confident **kendini rahat hissettiği durum/konum** *Owen thought about deep-sea diving but decided it was beyond his comfort zone.*

comfy /'kʌmfi/ adjective informal comfortable **rahatlatıcı, rahat, huzur veren**

comic¹ /'kɒmɪk/ adjective funny **komik, gülünç** *a comic actor*

comic² /'kɒmɪk/ noun [C] **1** (also **'comic ,book**) a magazine with stories told in pictures **gülmece dergisi, çizgi resimli roman 2** someone who entertains people by telling jokes **komedyen, güldürü sanatçısı**

comical /'kɒmɪkᵊl/ adjective funny in a strange or silly way **gülünç, komik, acayip** *He looked so comical in that hat.* ● **comically** adverb **komik bir şekilde**

'comic ,strip noun [C] a set of pictures telling a story, usually in a newspaper **çizgi roman, gülmece roman**

coming¹ /'kʌmɪŋ/ noun **1 the coming of sth** the arrival of something **varış, ulaşma, geliş, ortaya çıkış** *the coming of spring* **2 comings and goings** people's movements to and from a particular place over a period of time **geliş gidişler**

coming² /'kʌmɪŋ/ adjective [always before noun] a coming time or event will come or happen soon **yakında, olmak üzere** *the coming elections* ⊃See also: up-and-coming.

comma /'kɒmə/ noun [C] a mark (,) used to separate parts of a sentence, or to separate the items in a list **virgül** ⊃See study page **Punctuation** on page Centre 33 ⊃See also: inverted commas.

command¹ /kə'mɑːnd/ noun **1** [CONTROL] [U] control over someone or something and responsibility for them **komuta, kontrol** *The soldiers were under the command of a tough sergeant-major.* ○ *Jones was in command* (= the leader). **2** [ORDER] [C] an order to do something **emir, buyruk, komut, talimat 3** [KNOWLEDGE] [no plural] knowledge of a subject, especially a language **yetkinlik, hakimiyet** *She had a good command of French.* **4 be at sb's command** to be ready to obey someone's orders **emrinde olmak, emrine amade olmak 5** [COMPUTER] [C] an instruction to a computer **komut, talimat**

command² /kə'mɑːnd/ verb formal **1** [T] to control someone or something and tell them what to do **komuta etmek, yönetmek, emir komuta etmek** *He commanded the armed forces.* **2** [I, T] to order someone to do something **emretmek, buyurmak** [+ to do sth] *The officer commanded his men to shoot.* **3 command attention/loyalty/respect, etc** to deserve and get attention, loyalty, respect, etc from other people **başkalarından saygı, dikkat, bağlılık görmek, hak etmek, kazanmak**

commandeer /ˌkɒmən'dɪər/ verb [T] formal to take something, especially for military use **bilhassa askeri amaçla el koymak, almak** *The ships were commandeered as naval vessels.*

commander /kə'mɑːndər/ noun [C] an officer who is in charge of a military operation, or an officer of middle rank in the navy **komutan**

commanding /kə'mɑːndɪŋ/ adjective [always before noun] in a very successful position and likely to win or succeed **iyi durumda/her şeye hakim/üstün ve başarmak üzere olan** *He has a commanding lead in the championships.*

commandment /kə'mɑːndmənt/ noun [C] one of the ten important rules of behaviour given by God in the Bible **Hıristiyanlık'ta on emirden herhangi biri**

commando /kə'mɑːndəʊ/ noun [C] a soldier who is part of a small group who make surprise attacks **komando**

commemorate /kə'meməreɪt/ verb [T] to do something to show you remember an important person or event in the past with respect **anmak, anma töreni yapmak, anısına yapılmış olmak** *a ceremony to commemorate the battle* ● **commemoration** /kəˌmemə'reɪʃᵊn/ noun [U] *a march in commemoration of the war of independence* **anma**

commemorative /kə'memᵊrətɪv/ adjective intended to commemorate a person or event **anma törenine/anmaya ilişkin olan, törene ait olan** *a commemorative coin*

commence /kə'mens/ verb [I, T] formal to begin something **başlamak** ● **commencement** noun [C, U] formal the beginning of something **başlangıç, başlama**

commend /kə'mend/ verb [T] formal to praise someone or something **takdir etmek, övmek, methetmek** [often passive] *His courage was commended by the report.* ● **commendation** /ˌkɒmen'deɪʃᵊn/ noun [C, U] **övgü**

commendable /kə'mendəbl/ adjective deserving praise **övgüye değer, takdire mazhar olan** *She showed commendable modesty.*

comment¹ /'kɒment/ noun [C, U] **1** something that you say or write that shows what you think about something **yorum, düşünce, fikir** *He made negative comments to the press.* **2 No comment.** used to say that you do not want to answer someone's question **yorum yok, yorumsuz**

comment² /'kɒment/ verb [I, T] to make a comment **yorum yapmak, fikir beyan etmek, görüş belirtmek** *My mum always comments on what I'm wearing.* ○ [+ that] *He commented that the two essays were very similar.*

commentary /'kɒməntᵊri/ noun **1** [C, U] a spoken description of an event on the radio or television while the event is happening **naklen yayın/anlatım/bildirme** *the football commentary* **2** [U, no plural] a discussion or explanation of something **yorum, açıklama** *a commentary on American culture*

commentator /'kɒmənteɪtər/ noun [C] someone who describes an event on the radio or television while it is happening **muhabir; haber sunan/bildiren/anlatan, yorumcu** *a sports commentator*

commerce /'kɒmɜːs/ noun [U] the activities involved in buying and selling things **ticaret** ⊃See also: chamber of commerce, e-commerce.

commercial¹ /kə'mɜːʃᵊl/ adjective **1** relating to buying and selling things **ticari, ticarete ilişkin 2** intended to make a profit **kâr amacı olan, ticari** *commercial television* ● **commercially** adverb **ticari olarak**

commercial² /kə'mɜːʃᵊl/ noun [C] an advertisement on the radio or television **reklam (radyo, tv)**

commercialism /kə'mɜːʃᵊlɪzᵊm/ noun [U] when making money is the most important aim of an activity **tüccar ruhu, sadece para kazanma amacı, her şeye ticari açıdan bakma**

commercialized (also UK -ised) /kə'mɜːʃᵊlaɪzd/ adjective organized to make profits **sadece kâr/çıkar amacı güden** *Christmas has become so commercialized.* ● **commercialization** /kəˌmɜːʃᵊlaɪ'zeɪʃᵊn/ noun [U] **kar amacı gütme**

commiserate /kə'mɪzᵊreɪt/ verb [I] to express sympathy to someone who is sad or has had bad luck **acı-**

sını/derdini/sıkıntılarını paylaşmak, yakınlık göstermek, derdini dinlemek

commission¹ /kə'mɪʃ³n/ *noun* **1** GROUP OF PEOPLE [group] an official group of people who have been chosen to find out about something and say what they think should be done about it **kurul, heyet, komite, komisyon 2** PIECE OF WORK [C, U] when you arrange for someone to do a piece of work for you such as painting, writing, or making something **görev, görevlendirme, iş, yetki 3** MONEY [C, U] money given to someone when they sell something **satıştan alınan yüzde, komisyon** *The staff receive 5% commission on everything that they sell.* ○ *Many salesmen work on commission.*

commission² /kə'mɪʃ³n/ *verb* [T] to arrange for someone to do a piece of work **görevlendirmek, işini belirlemek** [+ to do sth] *I've been commissioned to write a song for their wedding.*

commissioner /kə'mɪʃənər/ *noun* [C] a member of a commission or someone with an important government job in a particular area **heyet/komite/kurul/ komisyon üyesi, murahhas üye, hükümet temsilcisi**

o‑**commit** /kə'mɪt/ *verb* [T] committing, *past* committed **1** CRIME to do something that is considered wrong, or that is illegal **(yasa dışı iş, suç vb.) işlemek, yapmak** *He was sent to prison for a crime that he didn't commit.* ○ *to commit suicide/adultery* **2** DECISION to make a firm decision that you will do something **kesin karar vermek, kendini sorumlu kılmak** *He committed himself to helping others.* **3 not commit yourself** to refuse to express an opinion about a particular subject **bir konuda fikrini açıklamayı reddetmek, söz vermemek, bağlanmamak 4** MONEY/TIME If you commit money, time, energy, etc to something, you use it to try to achieve something. **(para, zaman, enerji vb.) ayırmak, vakfetmek, sarfetmek** *The government has committed thousands of pounds to the research.*

commitment ...... İLE BİRLİKTE KULLANILAN KELİMELER

make a commitment ● **fulfil/honour/meet** a commitment ● a commitment **to** sth

o‑**commitment** /kə'mɪtmənt/ *noun* **1** PROMISE [C] a promise or firm decision to do something something **sadakat, bağlılık, kararlılık** *Players must make a commitment to daily training.* **2** LOYALTY [U] when you are willing to give your time and energy to something that you believe in **sorumluluk, yükümlülük, taahhüt** *We are looking for someone with talent, enthusiasm, and commitment.* **3** ACTIVITY [C] something that you must do that takes your time **iş, görev, eylem, sorumluluk** *I've got too many commitments at the moment.*

committed /kə'mɪtɪd/ *adjective* loyal and willing to give your time and energy to something that you believe in **bağlı, sadık, gönül vermiş, istekli** *a committed Christian* ○ *She's committed to the job.*

committee /kə'mɪti/ *noun* [group] a group of people who have been chosen to represent a larger organization and make decisions for it **komite, heyet, kurul**

commodity /kə'mɒdəti/ *noun* [C] a product that you can buy or sell **mal, ürün, emtia, meta**

o‑**common¹** /'kɒmən/ *adjective* **1** USUAL happening often or existing in large numbers **yaygın, bilinen, olağan** *Injuries are common in sports such as hockey.* ➋Opposite **uncommon. 2** SHARED belonging to or shared by two or more people or things **ortak, birlikte, paylaşılan** *a common goal/interest* ○ *English has some features common to many languages.* **3 common knowledge** something that a lot of people know **herkesin bildiği, herkesçe malum olan, genel bilgi** [+ that] *It's common knowledge that he spent time in jail.* **4** ORDINARY [always

before noun] not special in any way **yaygın, çok bilinen, sıradan** *The herbs all have common names and Latin names.* **5** LOW CLASS *UK* typical of a low social class **alelade, sıradan, kaba, adi, bayağı** *My mum thinks dyed blonde hair is really common.*

common² /'kɒmən/ *noun* **1 have sth in common** to share interests, experiences, or other characteristics with someone or something **ortak yönleri olmak, benzer tarafları olmak** *Sue and I don't have much in common.* **2 in common with sb/sth** in the same way as someone or something **gibi; ... de yaygın/görüldüğü gibi** *In common with many working mothers, she feels guilty towards her children.* **3** [C] a large area of grass in a town or village which everyone is allowed to use **mera, otlak, ortak kullanım alanı**

common 'ground *noun* [U] shared interests, beliefs, or ideas **ortak fikir/inanış/çıkar; ortak zemin/alan** *It's difficult for me to find any common ground with my dad.*

common-law /ˌkɒmən'lɔː/ *adjective* [always before noun] A common-law wife or husband is someone who is not married, but has lived with their partner for a long time as if they were married. **birlikte yaşayan, karı-koca gibi yaşayan, geleneksel kurallarla evli gibi yaşayan**

commonly /'kɒmənli/ *adverb* often or usually **sık sık, genellikle, çoğunlukla, yaygın olarak** *These caterpillars are commonly found on nettles.*

commonplace /'kɒmənpleɪs/ *adjective* [never before noun] happening often or existing in large numbers, and so not considered special or unusual **sıradan, alışılagelmiş, olağan**

the Commons /'kɒmənz/ (*also* **the House of Commons**) *noun* one of the two parts of the British parliament, with elected members who make laws **Britanya parlamentosunun üyeleri seçimle işbaşına gelen ve kanunları yapan kanadı**

common 'sense *noun* [U] the natural ability to be practical and to make good decisions **sağ duyu,** *The children shouldn't be in any danger as long as they use their common sense.*

the Commonwealth /'kɒmənwelθ/ *noun* Britain and the group of countries that used to be in the British Empire (= ruled by Britain) **Britanya milletler topluluğu**

commotion /kə'məʊʃ³n/ *noun* [U, no plural] a sudden period of noise and confused or excited movement **hengame, hır gür, koşuşturma, arbede** *He looked up to see what all the commotion was about.*

communal /'kɒmjʊn³l/ ⓤ /kə'mjuːnəl/ *adjective* belonging to or used by a group of people **ortaklaşa kullanılan, ortak** *a communal changing room*

commune /'kɒmjuːn/ *noun* [C] a group of people who live together, sharing the work and the things they own **cemaat, topluluk, komün, ortak yaşam**

communicate /kə'mjuːnɪkeɪt/ *verb* [I, T] **1** to share information with others by speaking, writing, moving your body, or using other signals **iritbatta olmak, bağlantı kurmak, haberleşmek** *We can now communicate instantly with people on the other side of the world.* **2** to talk about your thoughts and feelings, and help other people to understand them **iletişim kurmak, kendini anlatmak/anlaşılmasını sağlamak** *He can't communicate with his parents.*

communication ...... İLE BİRLİKTE KULLANILAN KELİMELER

communication **between** sb and sb ● **in** communication **with** sb ● a **means** of communication ● a **breakdown** in communication ● communication **skills** o⊷**communication** /kəˌmjuːnɪˈkeɪʃᵊn/ *noun* **1** [U] the act of communicating with other people **iletişim, haberleşme, bildirişim** *The school is improving communication between teachers and parents.* ○ *We are in direct communication with Moscow.* **2** [C] *formal* a message sent to someone by letter, email, telephone, etc **haber, ileti, mesaj, açıklama, bildiri**

communications /kəˌmjuːnɪˈkeɪʃᵊnz/ *noun* [plural] the different ways of sending information between people and places, such as post, telephones, computers, and radio **haberleşme, iletişim** *the communications industry*

communicative /kəˈmjuːnɪkətɪv/ *adjective* willing to talk to people and give them information **konuşkan, iletişime istekli**

communion /kəˈmjuːniən/ *noun* [U] (*also* Communion) the Christian ceremony in which people eat bread and drink wine, as symbols of Christ's body and blood **Hıristiyanlık'ta sadece kuru ekmek yiyerek ve şarap içerek yapılan Aşai Rabbani Ayini**

communiqué /kəˈmjuːnɪkeɪ/ ⑤ /kəˌmjuːnɪˈkeɪ/ *noun* [C] an official announcement **resmî bildiri/duyuru**

communism, Communism /ˈkɒmjənɪzᵊm/ *noun* [U] a political system in which the government controls the production of all goods, and where everyone is treated equally **Komünizm**

communist, Communist /ˈkɒmjənɪst/ *noun* [C] someone who supports communism **Komünist** ● **communist** *adjective a communist country/leader* **komünist**

community /kəˈmjuːnəti/ *noun* **1** [C] the people living in a particular area **toplum, ahali, topluluk** *a rural/small community* **2** [group] a group of people with the same interests, nationality, job, etc **halk, ahali, toplum** *the business/Chinese community*

com'munity ˌcentre UK (US **community center**) *noun* [C] a place where people who live in an area can meet together to play sport, go to classes, etc **ortak kültürel faaliyetler için kullanılan yer, dernek, lokal, sosyal tesisler**

com,munity 'college *noun* [C, U] US a two-year college where students can learn a skill or prepare to enter a university **iki yıl süreli meslek edindirmek veya üniversiteye giriş için hazırlayan yüksek okul**

com,munity 'service *noun* [U] work that someone who has committed a crime does to help other people instead of going to prison **bir suçtan dolayı hapis yatmak yerine kamu yararına yaptırılan iş/görev/hizmet**

commute /kəˈmjuːt/ *verb* [I] to regularly travel between work and home **her gün işe gidip gelmek** ● **commuter** *noun* [C] **ev iş arası seyahat eden kişi**

compact¹ /kəmˈpækt/ *adjective* small and including many things in a small space **herşeyi barındıran, derli toplu, kullanışlı, işlevsel**

compact² /kəmˈpækt/ *verb* [T] to press something together so that it becomes tight or solid **sıkıştırarak daha küçük bir yere sığdırmak, sıkılaştırmak**

compact 'disc *noun* [C] a CD (= a disc for recorded music or information) **kompak disk; yoğun kayıt diski**

companion /kəmˈpænjən/ *noun* [C] someone who you spend a lot of time with or go somewhere with **ahbap, arkadaş, yol arkadaşı** *a travelling companion*

companionship /kəmˈpænjənʃɪp/ *noun* [U] the feeling of having friends around you **dostluk, ahbaplık, arkadaşlık**

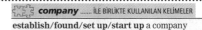 **company** .... İLE BİRLİKTE KULLANILAN KELİMELER
establish/found/set up/start up a company

o⊷**company** /ˈkʌmpəni/ *noun* **1** [BUSINESS] [C] an organization which sells goods or services **şirket, kuruluş, ortaklık** *a software/telephone company* **2** [PEOPLE] [U] when you have a person or people with you **arkadaşlık, eşlik** *I enjoy his company.* ○ *I didn't realize that you had company.* **3 keep sb company** to stay with someone so that they are not alone **arkadaşlık/eşlik etmek 4 be good company** to be a pleasant or interesting person to spend time with **iyi arkadaş/dost/ahbap olmak 5** [PERFORMERS] [C] a group of performers such as actors or dancers **grup, birlik, topluluk, kumpanya, dansçılar ve/veya sanatçılar topluluğu** *the Royal Shakespeare Company* ⊃See also: limited company.

comparable /ˈkɒmpᵊrəbl/ *adjective* similar in size, amount, or quality to something else **kıyaslanabilir, mukayese edilebilir, karşılaştırabilir** *Our prices are comparable to those in other shops.*

comparative¹ /kəmˈpærətɪv/ *adjective* **1 comparative comfort/freedom/silence, etc** a situation which is comfortable/free/silent, etc when compared to another situation or to what is usual **mukayeseli refah/özgürlük/sessizlik/sükûnet** *I enjoyed the comparative calm of his flat after the busy office.* **2** comparing similar things **karşılaştırmalı, mukayeseli** *a comparative study of two poems*

comparative² /kəmˈpærətɪv/ *noun* [C] the form of an adjective or adverb that is used to show that someone or something has more of a particular quality than someone or something else. For example 'better' is the comparative of 'good' and 'smaller' is the comparative of 'small'. **(dilbilgisi) mukayese/karşılaştırma derecesi** ⊃Compare superlative.

comparatively /kəmˈpærətɪvli/ *adverb* **comparatively cheap/easy/little, etc** cheap/easy/little, etc when compared to something else or to what is usual **nispeten ucuz/kolay/küçük vs.**

o⊷**compare** /kəmˈpeər/ *verb* **1** [T] to examine the ways in which two people or things are different or similar **mukayese etmek, kıyaslamak** *The teachers are always comparing me with/to my sister.* **2** [I] to be as good as something else **benzetmek/benzemek, karşılaştırmak, ... kadar iyi olmak** *This product compares well with more expensive brands.* **3 compared to/with sb/sth** used when saying how one person or thing is different from another ... **ile kıyasla, mukayese ederek** *This room is very tidy compared to mine.* ⊃See also: compare notes (note¹).
compare sb/sth to sb/sth *phrasal verb* to say that someone or something is similar to someone or something else **benzetmek, benzerlik bulmak**

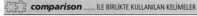 **comparison** .... İLE BİRLİKTE KULLANILAN KELİMELER
draw/make a comparison ● a comparison **between** sth and sth ● a comparison **of** sth (**with** sth) ● **by/in** comparison (**with** sth)

o⊷**comparison** /kəmˈpærɪsᵊn/ *noun* [C, U] **1** when you compare two or more people or things **mukayese, kıyaslama, karşılaştırma** *They published a comparison of schools in the area.* ○ *She's so tall that he looks tiny by/in comparison.* **2 There's no comparison.** used to say that someone or something is much better than someone or something else **kıyas götürmez, kıyaslanamaz, karşılaştırılamaz**

compartment /kəmˈpɑːtmənt/ *noun* [C] **1** one of the separate areas inside a vehicle, especially a train **odacık, kompartıman (özellikle trende)** *The first class compartment is at the front of the train.* **2** a separate part of a container, bag, etc **bölme, göz, kısım** *a fridge with a small freezer compartment*

compass /'kʌmpəs/   **compass**
noun [C] a piece of equipment which shows you which direction you are going in **pusula**

compasses /'kʌmpəsɪz/ *noun* [plural] *UK* (*US* compass [C]) a piece of equipment which is used for drawing circles **pergel**

compassion /kəm'pæʃᵃn/ *noun* [U] a feeling of sympathy for people who are suffering **şefkat, merhamet, sevecenlik**

compassionate /kəm'pæʃᵃnət/ *adjective* showing compassion **şefkatli, merhametli**

compatible /kəm'pætɪbl/ *adjective* 1 [EQUIPMENT] compatible equipment can be used together **birbirine uyan, bağdaşan, uyumlu** *This keyboard is compatible with all of our computers.* 2 [PEOPLE] If people are compatible, they like each other and are happy to spend time together. **uyumlu, kafaları birbirine uyan, iyi anlaşan** 3 [IDEAS] *formal* compatible ideas or situations can exist together **birbirine uyan durumlar/fikirler** *Such policies are not compatible with democratic government.* ● **compatibility** /kəm,pætə'bɪləti/ *noun* [U] **uyum**

compatriot /kəm'pætriət/ *noun* [C] *formal* someone who comes from the same country **vatandaş, yurttaş, hemşehri**

compel /kəm'pel/ *verb* **compelling**, *past* **compelled** *formal* **compel sb to do sth** to force someone to do something **zorlamak, cebir uygulamak, zorla yaptırmak** [often passive] *He felt compelled to resign from his job.*

compelling /kəm'pelɪŋ/ *adjective* 1 very exciting or interesting and making you want to watch, listen, etc **heyecan verici, ilgi çeken, dayanılmaz** *a compelling story* 2 If a reason, argument, etc is compelling, it makes you believe it or accept it because it is so strong. **zorunlu, kaçınılmaz, mecburi, zorlayıcı, itekleyici** *compelling evidence*

compensate /'kɒmpənseɪt/ *verb* 1 [T] to pay someone money because you are responsible for injuring them or damaging something **tazmin etmek, zararını karşılamak, tazminat ödemek, telafi etmek** *Victims of the crash will be compensated for their injuries.* 2 [I, T] to reduce the bad effect of something, or make something bad become something good **acısını telafi etmek, azaltmak** *Nothing will ever compensate for his lost childhood.*

compensation /,kɒmpən'seɪʃᵃn/ *noun* 1 [U] money that you pay to someone because you are responsible for injuring them or damaging something **tazminat** *Most of the workers have won compensation for losing their jobs.* 2 [C, U] something you get to make you feel better when you have suffered something bad **karşılık, bedel** *Free food was no compensation for a very boring evening.*

compete /kəm'piːt/ *verb* [I] 1 to take part in a race or competition **yarışmak, müsabaka etmek** *She's competing for a place in next year's Olympics.* 2 to try to be more successful than someone or something else **rekabet etmek, müsabakaya girip başarılı olmaya çalış-**

mak, çekişmek *It's difficult for small shops to compete with/against the big supermarkets.*

competent /'kɒmpɪtᵃnt/ *adjective* able to do something well **yetenekli, ehil, usta, kabiliyetli** *a competent swimmer/teacher* ● **competence** /'kɒmpɪtᵃns/ *noun* [U] the ability to do something well **ehliyet, yeterlik, yetenek, ustalık** ● **competently** *adverb* **becerikli, ehliyetli bir şekilde**

○***competition** /,kɒmpə'tɪʃᵃn/ *noun* 1 [C] an organized event in which people try to win a prize by being the best, fastest, etc **yarışma, müsabaka** *to enter a competition* 2 [U] when someone is trying to win something or be more successful than someone else **yarış, çekişme, rekâbet** *There's a lot of competition between computer companies.* ○ *Applicants face stiff competition for university places this year.* 3 **the competition** people you are competing against, especially in business **rakipler, müsabakıcılar**

competitive /kəm'petɪtɪv/ *adjective* 1 [SITUATION] involving competition **yarışmayla ilişkin, rekabete dair** *competitive sports* ○ *a highly competitive industry* 2 [PERSON] wanting to win or to be more successful than other people **hırslı, rekabeti seven, yarışma ruhu taşıyan** *She's very competitive.* 3 [PRICES/SERVICES] Competitive prices, services, etc are as good as or better than other prices, services, etc. **rekabet fiyatlarına ilişkin, ücret çekişmesi yaratan** ● **competitively** *adverb* **yarışır gibi** ● **competitiveness** *noun* [U] **rekabet gücü**

competitor /kəm'petɪtər/ *noun* [C] a person, team, or company that is competing with others **yarışmacı**

compilation /,kɒmpɪ'leɪʃᵃn/ *noun* [C] a recording, book, or film containing a collection of things from many different recordings, books, or films **derleme, bir araya getirme, derleme eser**

compile /kəm'paɪl/ *verb* [T] to collect information and arrange it in a book, report, or list **derlemek, bir araya getirmek, toplamak**

complacent /kəm'pleɪsᵃnt/ *adjective* feeling so satisfied with your own abilities or situation that you do not feel that you need to try any harder **kendi kendine yeten, halinden memnun, kayıtsız, aldırmaz** *We can't afford to become too complacent about our work.* ● **complacency** *noun* [U] when someone is complacent **kayıtsızlık, kendini beğenmişlik, kendine yeterlik** ● **complacently** *adverb* **memnun**

○***complain** /kəm'pleɪn/ *verb* [I] to say that something is wrong or that you are annoyed about something **şikayet etmek, yakınmak, dertlenmek** *Lots of people have*

complained about the noise. ○ [+ that] *He's always complaining that nobody listens to him.*

complain of sth *phrasal verb* to tell other people that something is making you feel ill **bir şeyden dertlenmek, yakınmak, şikayette bulunmak** *She's been complaining of a headache all day.*

🔲 **complaint** ...... İLE BİRLİKTE KULLANILAN KELİMELER

make/investigate/receive a complaint ● a complaint **about** sb/sth ● a complaint **against** sb ● a **formal/ official/written** complaint ● a **letter of** complaint ● have **cause for/grounds for** complaint

---

○➔**complaint** /kəm'pleɪnt/ *noun* **1** NOT SATISFACTORY [C, U] when someone says that something is wrong or not satisfactory **şikayet, itiraz** *a letter of complaint* ○ *I wish to **make a complaint**.* **2** ANNOYING THING [C] something that makes you complain **yakınma, dertlenme** *My only complaint was the lack of refreshments.* **3** ILLNESS [C] an illness **hastalık, dert, şikayet** *a stomach complaint*

complement[1] /'kɒmplɪmənt/ *noun* [C] **1** MAKE GOOD something that makes something else seem good, attractive, or complete **bütünleme, tamamlama,** *This wine is the perfect complement to the meal.* **2** TOTAL NUMBER the total amount or number of something that is needed to complete a group **hepsi, tam kadro, tam takımı** *Do we have a full complement of players for Saturday's match?* **3** GRAMMAR a word or phrase which comes after the verb and gives more information about the subject of the verb **tümleç, tamamlayıcı**

complement[2] /'kɒmplɪment/ *verb* [T] to make something else seem good or attractive **bütünlemek, tamamlamak** *The music complements her voice perfectly.*

complementary /ˌkɒmplɪ'mentᵊri/ *adjective* **1** Things which are complementary are good or attractive together. **bütünleyici, tamamlayıcı** *complementary colours/flavours* **2 complementary medicine/treatment, etc** ways of treating medical problems which people use instead of or in addition to ordinary medicine **tamamlayıcı/bütünleyici tıp/tedavi; alternatif tıp** *The clinic offers complementary therapies such as homeopathy.*

complete[1] /kəm'pli:t/ *adjective* **1** WHOLE with all parts **eksiksiz, tam, bütün, komple** *the complete works of Oscar Wilde* ○ *The report comes complete with* (= including) *diagrams and colour photographs.* **2** TOTAL [always before noun] used to emphasize what you are saying **tam, adamakıllı, iyice** *a complete waste of time* **3** FINISHED finished **bitmiş, tamamlanmış, tamam** *Our report is almost complete.*

○➔**complete**[2] /kəm'pli:t/ *verb* [T] **1** FINISH to finish doing or making something **tamamlamak, bitirmek** *The palace took 15 years to complete.* **2** MAKE STH WHOLE to provide the last part needed to make something whole **tamamlamak, bir bütünün gerekli son parçasını sağlamak** *Complete the sentence with one of the adjectives provided.* **3** WRITE to write all the details asked for on a form or other document **bir formu doldurmak, istenilen bilgileri yazmak**

○➔**completely** /kəm'pli:tli/ *adverb* in every way or as much as possible **tamamen, bütünüyle** *I completely forgot that you were coming.*

completion /kəm'pli:ʃᵊn/ *noun* [U] when something that you are doing or making is finished **sona erme, bitme, tamamlama** *The stadium is due for completion in 2008.* ○ *They will be paid **on completion of** the job.*

○➔**complex**[1] /'kɒmpleks/, /kəm'pleks/ *adjective* involving a lot of different but connected parts in a way that is difficult to understand **karmaşık, anlaşılması güç, kafa karıştıran** *complex details/issues* ○ *The situation is very complex.* ● **complexity** /kəm'pleksəti/ *noun* [C, U] when something is complex **karmaşa, kargaşa** *the complexities of life*

complex[2] /'kɒmpleks/ *noun* [C] **1** a group of buildings or rooms that are used for a particular purpose **birbirine bağlı yapılar/binalar grubu;site** *a sports/housing complex* **2** a mental problem which makes someone anxious or frightened about something **kuruntu, bir şeyden korkmaya veya birini endişeye sevkeden zihinsel sorun** *an inferiority complex*

complexion /kəm'plekʃᵊn/ *noun* [C] **1** the colour and appearance of the skin on someone's face **ten, yüz, cilt, yüzün görünümü, çehre** *a clear complexion* **2** the way something seems to be **görünüş, duruş, mahiyet** *This new information puts a completely different complexion on the situation.*

compliance /kəm'plaɪəns/ *noun* [U] *formal* when people obey an order, rule, or request **rıza, uysallık, baş eğme** *The work was done in compliance with planning regulations.*

compliant /kəm'plaɪənt/ *adjective* Compliant people are willing to do what other people want them to. **uysal, yumuşak başlı, itaatkâr**

complicate /'kɒmplɪkeɪt/ *verb* [T] to make something more difficult to deal with or understand **içinden çıkılmaz hale getirmek, karmaşıklaştırmak, güçleştirmek** *These new regulations just complicate matters further.*

○➔**complicated** /'kɒmplɪkeɪtɪd/ *adjective* involving a lot of different parts, in a way that is difficult to understand **karmaşık, zor** *a complicated problem/process* ○ *The instructions were too complicated for me.*

complication /ˌkɒmplɪ'keɪʃᵊn/ *noun* [C] **1** something which makes a situation more difficult **güçleştirme, zorlaştırma 2** a new medical problem that develops when you are already ill **hastalıkta yeni sorun, komplikasyon, rahatsızlık** *Eye problems can be a complication of diabetes.*

complicity /kəm'plɪsəti/ *noun* [U] *formal* when someone is involved in doing something wrong **suç ortaklığı, suça katılma/iştirak**

compliment[1] /'kɒmplɪmənt/ *noun* **1** [C] something that you say or do to show praise or admiration for someone **iltifat, övgü, kur, kompliman** *She was always paying him compliments.* **2 with the compliments of sb** *formal* used by someone to express good wishes when they give you something free, for example in a restaurant **müessesemizin iyi dilekleriyle; sevgi ve selamlarımızla, saygılarımızla** *Please accept this champagne with the compliments of the manager.*

compliment[2] /'kɒmplɪment/ *verb* [T] to praise or express admiration for someone **övmek, iltifat etmek, kompliman yapmak, methetmek** *He complimented me on my writing.*

complimentary /ˌkɒmplɪ'mentᵊri/ *adjective* **1** praising or expressing admiration for someone **övgü içeren, hayranlık ifade eden, övücü** *a complimentary report* **2** given free, especially by a business **ikram kabilinden, parasız, hediye olarak** *a complimentary glass of wine*

comply /kəm'plaɪ/ *verb* [I] to obey an order, rule, or request **itaat etmek, razı olmak, muvafakat etmek** *The pilot complied with instructions to descend.*

component /kəm'pəʊnənt/ *noun* [C] one of the parts of something, especially a machine **parça, unsur, eleman**

compose /kəm'pəʊz/ *verb* **1** [PARTS] [T] to be the parts that something consists of **tanzim etmek, düzeltmek, oluşturmak** [often passive] *The committee was composed of elected leaders and citizens.* **2** [MUSIC] [I, T] to write a piece of music **bestelemek, yaratmak 3 compose yourself** to make yourself calm again after being angry or upset **sakinleşmek, sükûnet bulmak, kendine hakim olmak 4** [WRITING] [T] to write a speech, letter, etc, thinking carefully about the words to use **yazmak** *Laura was composing a letter of sympathy.*

composed /kəm'pəʊzd/ *adjective* calm and in control of your emotions **sakin, kendine hakim**

composer /kəm'pəʊzə^r/ *noun* [C] someone who writes music **besteci**

composite /'kɒmpəzɪt/ *adjective* consisting of several different parts **karma, bileşik, bir çok değişik bölümden oluşan** *a composite image of the killer*

composition /ˌkɒmpə'zɪʃ°n/ *noun* **1** [PARTS] [U] the parts, substances, etc that something consists of **karışım, terkip** *the composition of the atmosphere* **2** [MUSIC] [C] a piece of music that someone has written **beste 3** [WRITING MUSIC] [U] the process or skill of writing music **müzik besteleme, yazma** *He taught composition at Yale.* **4** [WRITING] [C, U] a short piece of writing about a particular subject, done by a student **yazı, kompozisyon 5** [ARRANGEMENT] [U] the way that people or things are arranged in a painting or photograph **tasarım, çizim, yapıt, yaratma**

compost /'kɒmpɒst/ *noun* [U] a mixture of decayed leaves and plants that is added to the soil to improve its quality **yaprak ve bitkilerden oluşan doğal gübre** *a compost heap*

composure /kəm'pəʊʒə^r/ *noun* [U] when you feel or look calm and confident **sükûnet, huzur, sakinlik** *to keep/lose your composure*

compound¹ /'kɒmpaʊnd/ *noun* [C] **1** [MIXTURE] a substance that is a combination of two or more elements **bileşim, karışım, terkip** *Water is a compound of hydrogen and oxygen.* **2** [AREA] an area of land with a group of buildings surrounded by a fence or wall **etrafı duvarla çevrili arazi içinde büyük ev, malikhane, binalar topluluğu** *a prison compound* **3** [GRAMMAR] (*also* compound noun/verb/adjective) a noun, verb, or adjective that is made by two or more words used together. For example, 'golf club' is a compound. **bileşik isim**

compound² /kəm'paʊnd/ *verb* [T] to make a problem or difficult situation worse **işleri iyice kötüye götürmek, daha da berbat etmek,** *Severe drought has compounded food shortages in the region.*

compère /'kɒmpeə^r/ *noun* [C] UK someone whose job is to introduce performers on television, radio, or in a theatre **tiyatro, tv veya radyoda sanatçıları sunan kişi, sunucu, takdimci**

comprehend /ˌkɒmprɪ'hend/ *verb* [I, T] *formal* to understand **anlamak, kavramak** *I was too young to comprehend what was happening.*

comprehensible /ˌkɒmprɪ'hensəbl/ *adjective* easy to understand **kolay anlaşılabilir/kavranabilir** *Computer manuals should be easily comprehensible.*

comprehension /ˌkɒmprɪ'henʃ°n/ *noun* **1** [U] the ability to understand something **anlama/kavrama yetisi** *It's beyond my comprehension* (= I can't understand) *how anyone could be so cruel.* **2** [C, U] UK a test to see how well students understand written or spoken language **anlama-kavrama sınavı/alıştırması** *a reading comprehension*

comprehensive¹ /ˌkɒmprɪ'hensɪv/ *adjective* including everything **etraflı, kapsamlı, geniş, herşeyi içeren** *a comprehensive study of the subject* ● **comprehensively** *adverb* completely **tamamen, etraflıca** *We were comprehensively beaten in the finals.*

comprehensive² /ˌkɒmprɪ'hensɪv/ (*also* compre'hensive ˌschool) *noun* [C] a school in Britain for students aged 11 to 18 of all levels of ability **Britanya'da 11-18 yaş arası öğrencilerin gittiği okul**

compress /kəm'pres/ *verb* [T] **1** to make something smaller, especially by pressing it, so that it uses less space or time **sıkıştırmak, sıkmak, basmak, ezmek** *compressed air* ○ *The course compresses two years' training into six months.* **2** to use a special program to make information on a computer use less space **bilgisayarda bilgiyi sıkıştırarak daha az yer kaplamasını sağlayan program** ● **compression** /kəm'preʃ°n/ *noun* [U] **basınç, sıkıştırma**

comprise /kəm'praɪz/ *verb* [T] *formal* **1** to consist of particular parts or members ... **den/dan oluşmak/meydana gelmek** *The orchestra was comprised of amateur and professional musicians.* **2** to form part of something, especially a larger group **oluşturmak, meydana getirmek** *Women comprise 15% of the police force.*

compromise¹ /'kɒmprəmaɪz/ *noun* [C, U] when you agree to something which is not exactly what you want **uzlaşma, uyuşma, anlaşma, orta bir yol bulma** *We need to reach a compromise over this issue.* ○ *Decorating is usually a compromise between taste and cost.*

compromise² /'kɒmprəmaɪz/ *verb* **1** [AGREE] [I] to agree to something that is not exactly what you want **uzlaşmak, anlaşmak, orta yol bulmak** *The president may be willing to compromise in order to pass the bill.* ○ *I never compromise on fresh ingredients.* **2 compromise yourself** to do something dishonest or embarrassing that makes people stop admiring you **haysiyetine/onuruna gölge düşürmek, şerefini tehlikeye atmak 3** [BELIEFS] [T] to do something that does not agree with what you believe in **isteklerinden feragat etmek/fedakârlıkta bulunmak, istemediği halde yapmayı kabul etmek, taviz vermek** *I refuse to compromise my principles.* **4** [HARM] [T] *formal* to have a harmful effect on something **kötü etkisi olmak, tehlikeye sokmak** *The trial has been seriously compromised by sensational media coverage.*

compromising /'kɒmprəmaɪzɪŋ/ *adjective* A compromising situation, photograph, etc makes people think you have done something wrong. **yanlış anlamaya neden olan/ değişik yorumlanan** *The press printed compromising photographs of the princess and her bodyguard.*

compulsion /kəm'pʌlʃ°n/ *noun* **1** [C] a strong wish to do something, often something that you should not do **bastırılması güç istek, dürtü 2** [U] when you are forced to do something **cebren, zorlama ile** *We were under no compulsion to attend.*

compulsive /kəm'pʌlsɪv/ *adjective* **1** A compulsive habit is something that you do a lot because you want to so much that you cannot control yourself. **engellenemez, önüne geçilemez, kontrolsüz, istem dışı** *a compulsive eating disorder* **2 a compulsive eater/gambler/liar, etc** someone who is unable to stop eating/lying, etc, despite knowing that they should stop **iflak olmaz/engellenemez pis boğaz/kumarbaz/yalancı**

vs. 3 so interesting or exciting that you cannot stop reading, playing, or watching it **etkileyici, karşıkonulamaz, istek uyandıran** *This documentary about life in prison makes compulsive viewing.* ● **compulsively** *adverb* **kontrol edilemeyen bir şekilde**

compulsory /kəmˈpʌlsᵊri/ *adjective* If something is compulsory, you must do it because of a rule or law. **mecburi, zorunlu, yapılması kaçınılmaz**

◦➤**computer** /kəmˈpjuːtəʳ/ *noun* [C] an electronic machine that can store and arrange large amounts of information **bilgisayar** *We've put all our records on computer.* ○ *computer software* ➲Orta kısımdaki renkli sayfalarına bakınız.

comˌputer aided deˈsign ➲See CAD.

computerize (*also UK* **-ise**) /kəmˈpjuːtᵊraɪz/ *verb* [T] to use a computer to do something that was done by people or other machines before **önceden insan veya makina ile yapılan şeyleri bilgisayar ile yapmak; bilgisayarla donatmak** *a computerized accounts system* ● **computerization** /kəmˌpjuːtᵊraɪˈzeɪʃᵊn/ *noun* [U] **bilgisayar ortamına geçiş yapma**

comˌputer ˈliterate *adjective* able to understand and use computer systems **bilgisayar kullanmasını bilen**

computing /kəmˈpjuːtɪŋ/ *noun* [U] the study or use of computers **bilgisayar kullanma/çalışma** *a degree in computing*

comrade /ˈkɒmreɪd/ ⓤ /ˈkɑːmræd/ *noun* [C] **1** *literary* a friend, especially someone who fights with you in a war **silah arkadaşı, kader arkadaşı 2** a word used by some members of trade unions (= organizations which represent people who do a particular job) or other Socialist organizations to talk to or about each other **(sosyalist parti veya sendika üyesi) yoldaş, dost**

comradeship /ˈkɒmreɪdʃɪp/ *noun* [U] the feeling of friendship between people who live or work together, especially in a difficult situation **beraber yaşayan veya çalışan kişiler arasındaki sıkı dostluk, kader arkadaşlığı**

con¹ /kɒn/ *verb* [T] **conning**, *past* **conned** *informal* to trick someone, especially in order to take money from them **aldatmak, dolandırmak, üç kâğıda getirmek** *Thieves conned him out of his life savings.* ○ *She felt she had been conned into buying the car.*

con² /kɒn/ *noun* [C] *informal* a trick to get someone's money, or make them do what you want **alavere dalavere, dolap, dümen, üç kağıt**

ˈcon ˌartist *noun* [C] someone who tricks people into giving them money or valuable things **düzenbaz, üçkâğıtçı**

concave /ˈkɒnkeɪv/ *adjective* A concave surface curves inwards. **içbükey, içioyuk, çukur** *a concave lens*

conceal /kənˈsiːl/ *verb* [T] to hide something **gizlemek, saklamak** *The listening device was concealed in a pen.* ○ *She could barely conceal her irritation.* ● **concealment** *noun* [U] when something is hidden **gizleme, saklama**

concede /kənˈsiːd/ *verb* [T] **1** to admit that something is true, even though you do not want to **kabul etmek, kabullenmek** [+ (that)] *Even the company chairman concedes that the results are disappointing.* **2** [I, T] to allow someone to have something, even though you do not want to **rıza göstermek, teslim etmek, bırakmak, kaptırmak** *The government will not concede to rebel demands.* **3 concede defeat** to admit that you have lost a fight, argument, game, etc **mağlubiyeti/yenilgiyi kabul etmek, pes etmek**

conceit /kənˈsiːt/ *noun* [U] when you are too proud of yourself and your actions **kibir, gurur, kendinin beğenmişlik**

conceited /kənˈsiːtɪd/ *adjective* too proud of yourself and your actions **kibirli, burnu havada, kendini beğenmiş** ● **conceitedly** *adverb* **kibirli bir şekilde**

conceivable /kənˈsiːvᵊbl/ *adjective* possible to imagine or to believe **akla gelebilecek, mümkün olan, alabileceği** *every conceivable kind of fruit* ○ [+ (that)] *It is just conceivable that the hospital made a mistake.* ● **conceivably** *adverb* **akla yatan**

conceive /kənˈsiːv/ *verb* **1** [BABY] [I, T] to become pregnant **gebe/hamile kalmak 2** [IMAGINE] [I, T] to be able to imagine something **tasavvur etmek, tasarlamak, hayal edebilmek** *I cannot conceive of anything more horrible.* **3** [IDEA] [T] to think of an idea or plan **tasarlamak, planlamak, düşünüp yaratmak** *The original idea for the novel was conceived in Rome.*

◦➤**concentrate¹** /ˈkɒnsᵊntreɪt/ *verb* **1** [I] to think very carefully about something you are doing and nothing else **yoğunlaşmak, konsantre olmak, dikkatini toplamak** *Be quiet - I'm trying to concentrate.* ○ *I can't concentrate on my work. It's too noisy here.* **2** be concentrated around/in/on, etc to be present in large numbers or amounts in a particular area **bir yerde yoğunlaşma, birikmek** *Most of the fighting was concentrated in the mountains.*
concentrate on sth *phrasal verb* to use most of your time and effort to do something **dikkatini bir tek şeye yoğunlaştırmak** *She gave up her job to concentrate on writing a novel.*

concentrated /ˈkɒnsᵊntreɪtɪd/ *adjective* **1** [always before noun] using a lot of effort to succeed at one particular thing **yoğun** *a concentrated effort to finish the work* **2** A concentrated liquid has had most of the water removed. **koyulaştırılmış, konsantre, yoğunlaştırılmış** *concentrated tomato puree*

concentration .... İLE BİRLİKTE KULLANILAN KELİMELER
sth **demands/needs/requires** concentration ● **lose** concentration ● a **lapse in/of** concentration ● **your powers of** concentration

concentration /ˌkɒnsᵊnˈtreɪʃᵊn/ *noun* **1** [U] the ability to think carefully about something you are doing and nothing else **bir şeye yoğunlaşma, dikkatini toplama, konsantrasyon 2** [C, U] a large number or amount of something in the same place **yoğunluk, birikim, çokluk, fazlalık** *high concentrations of minerals*

concenˈtration ˌcamp *noun* [C] a prison where large numbers of people are kept in very bad conditions, especially for political reasons **toplama kampı**

concentric /kənˈsentrɪk/ *adjective* Concentric circles have the same centre but are different sizes. **ortak merkezli, tek merkezli**

concept /ˈkɒnsept/ *noun* [C] an idea or principle **fikir, kavram, anlayış, prensip** *the concept of free speech*

conception /kənˈsepʃᵊn/ *noun* **1** [C, U] an idea about what something is like or a way of understanding something **fikir, düşünce, kavram, algı 2** [U] when a woman or animal becomes pregnant **gebelik, hamilelik**

conceptual /kənˈseptʃuəl/ *adjective formal* based on ideas **düşünsel, fikre dayalı** *a conceptual model*

concern¹ /kənˈsɜːn/ *verb* [T] **1** [INVOLVE] to involve someone or be important to them **ilgilendirmek, alakadar etmek** *Environmental issues concern us all.* **2** [WORRY] to worry or upset someone **endişelendirmek, canını sıkmak, kaygılandırmak, tasalanmak** *What really concerns me is her lack of experience.* **3** [BE ABOUT] If a story, film, etc concerns a particular subject, it is about that subject. ...**ile ilgili olmak; ...e/a dair olmak 4 concern**

yourself to become involved with doing something **ilgilenmek, bizzat ilgilenmek** *You needn't concern yourself with the travel arrangements.*

concern .... İLE BİRLİKTE KULLANILAN KELİMELER

cause concern ● express/raise/voice concern ● grave/serious concern ● concerns about/over sth ● a matter of concern ● a cause for concern

concern² /kən'sɜːn/ *noun* **1** WORRY [C, U] a feeling of worry about something, or the thing that is worrying you **kaygı, tasa** *I have concerns about his health.* **2** IMPORTANT THING [C, U] something that involves or affects you or is important to you **ilgi, alaka, önem** *Our primary concern is safety.* **3** BUSINESS [C] a company or business **iş, şirket, kuruluş, işletme** *The perfume factory was a family concern.*

◌▪**concerned** /kən'sɜːnd/ *adjective* **1** worried **tedirgin, ürkek,** [+ that] *I am very concerned that class sizes seem to be growing.* ○ *People are becoming more concerned about what they eat.* ⊃Opposite unconcerned. **2** [never before noun] involved in something or affected by it **endişeli, tasalı, kaygılı** *A letter will be sent out to everyone concerned.* **3 as far as sb is concerned** used to show what someone thinks about something **ilgilendiği/bildiği/anladığı/düşündüğü kadarıyla** *As far as our customers are concerned, price is the main consideration.* **4 as far as sth is concerned** used to tell someone what you are talking about **dikkate alındığında, üzerinde durulduğunda, göz önüne alındığında** *As far as college is concerned, everything is fine.*

concerning /kən'sɜːnɪŋ/ *preposition* about something **ilgilendiren, alakadar eden, hakkında, ...e ait, ... ile ilgili** *I've had a letter concerning my tax payments.*

◌▪**concert** /'kɒnsət/ *noun* [C] a performance of music and singing **konser** *a pop concert*

concerted /kən'sɜːtɪd/ *adjective* [always before noun] done with a lot of effort, often by a group of people working together **ortak/elbirliği ile/birlikte yapılan** *Iceland has made a concerted effort to boost tourism.*

concerto /kən'tʃeətəʊ/ *noun* [C] a piece of music for one main instrument and an orchestra (= large group of musicians) **konçerto** *a piano concerto*

concession /kən'seʃən/ *noun* **1** AGREEMENT [C, U] something that you agree to do or give to someone in order to end an argument **ödün, taviz,** [C] *Both sides will have to make concessions.* **2** BUSINESS [C] a special right to use buildings or land or to sell a product in a particular area, or the place where that business takes place **bir arazi/bina alıp satmada/kullanmada hak, imtiyaz, işletme hakkı** *a concession to develop oil fields in the north* **3** LOW PRICE [C] UK a reduction in the price of a ticket for a particular group of people such as students, people without a job, or old people **özel indirim**

conciliation /kən,sɪli'eɪʃən/ *noun* [U] *formal* the process of trying to end an argument **uzlaştırma, arabuluculuk, barıştırma**

conciliatory /kən'sɪliətᵊri/ *adjective formal* If people behave in a conciliatory manner, they try to make people stop being angry with them. **uzlaştırıcı, arabulucu, barıştırıcı** *a conciliatory approach*

concise /kən'saɪs/ *adjective* **1** giving a lot of information clearly in a few words **özlü, kapsamlı 2** A concise book is small. **kısaltılmış, kapsamı daraltılmış, özlü** *a concise history of France* ● **concisely** *adverb* **kısa, öz bir şekilde** ● **conciseness** *noun* [U] **netlik**

conclude /kən'kluːd/ *verb* **1** END [I, T] *formal* to end something such as a meeting, speech, or piece of writing by doing or saying one last thing **bit(ir)mek, son er(dir)mek, sonuçlandırmak** *The concert concluded*

with a firework display. ○ *I would like to conclude by thanking you all for attending.* **2** DECIDE [T] to decide something after studying all the information about it very carefully **sonlandırmak, son şeklini vermek, sona erdirmek** [+ that] *The report concluded that the drug was safe.* **3** COMPLETE [T] to complete something, especially an agreement or a business arrangement **(iş anlaşması, düzenleme vb.) tamamlamak, bitirmek, sonuçlandırmak** *talks aimed at concluding the peace treaty*

concluding /kən'kluːdɪŋ/ *adjective* [always before noun] last in a series of things **sona erdiren, bitiren, sonlandıran** *Don't miss tonight's concluding episode.*

conclusion .... İLE BİRLİKTE KULLANILAN KELİMELER

draw/reach a conclusion ● come to the conclusion that ● sth leads (you) to the conclusion that

◌▪**conclusion** /kən'kluːʒᵊn/ *noun* **1** OPINION [C] the opinion you have after considering all the information about something **sonuç, nihai son** *I've come to the conclusion that we'll have to sell the car.* **2** END [C] the final part of something **son, nihai son** *the dramatic conclusion of the film* ○ *The case should finally be brought to a conclusion* (= end) *this week.* **3 in conclusion** used to introduce the last part of a speech or piece of writing **sonuç olarak, sonuç itibariyle, son olarak** *In conclusion, I would like to thank our guest speaker.* **4** ARRANGEMENT [U] when something is arranged or agreed formally **resmi sonuç, karar, antlaşma, düzenleme** *the conclusion of peace talks* **5 jump to conclusions** to guess the facts about a situation without having enough information **ani bir sonuca varmak, yeterli bilgi olmadan sonucu tahmin etmek, birden sonuç çıkarmak** ⊃See also: foregone conclusion.

conclusive /kən'kluːsɪv/ *adjective* proving that something is true **kesin** *conclusive evidence/proof* ● **conclusively** *adverb* *Tests have proved conclusively that the drugs are effective.* **kesin bir şekilde**

concoct /kən'kɒkt/ *verb* [T] **1** to invent a story or explanation in order to deceive someone **(mazeret, hikaye) uydurmak, yalan söylemek, kandırmak** *He had concocted a web of lies.* **2** to make something unusual, especially food, by mixing things together **karışım elde etmek, farklı bir karışım yapmak** ● **concoction** /kən'kɒkʃᵊn/ *noun* [C] *a concoction of meringue, ice cream, and fresh strawberries* **uydurma (hikaye)**

concourse /'kɒŋkɔːs/ *noun* [C] a large room or open area inside a building such as an airport or station **(hava alanı, istasyon vb.) yolcu bekleme salonu, büyükçe alan**

concrete¹ /'kɒŋkriːt/ *noun* [U] A hard substance that is used in building and is made by mixing sand, water, small stones, and cement (= grey powder that is mixed with water and becomes hard when it dries) **beton** *concrete blocks*

concrete² /'kɒŋkriːt/ *adjective* **1** certain or based on facts **kesin, belli, gerçeklere dayalı** *concrete evidence/proof* **2** existing in a real form that can be seen or felt **somut, elle tutulur gözle görülür** *concrete achievements/actions* ○ *concrete objects*

concrete³ /'kɒŋkriːt/ *verb* [T] UK to cover something with concrete **beton dökmek, betonla kaplamak**

concur /kən'kɜːʳ/ *verb* [I] **concurring,** *past* **concurred** *formal* to agree **anlaşmak, uyuşmak, aynı fikirde olmak** *The new report concurs with previous findings.*

concurrent /kən'kʌrᵊnt/ *adjective* happening or existing at the same time **eş zamanlı** *three concurrent prison sentences* ● **concurrently** *adverb* **aynı anda olan**

concussed /kənˈkʌst/ *adjective* [never before noun] If someone is concussed, they are suffering from concussion. **beyni sarsıntısı geçiren**

concussion /kənˈkʌʃ°n/ *noun* [C, U] a slight injury to the brain that is caused by being hit on the head and makes you feel tired or sick **beyin sarsıntısı**

condemn /kənˈdem/ *verb* [T] **1** to say very strongly that you think something is wrong or very bad **kınamak, lanetlemek, ayıplamak** *The Prime Minister was quick to condemn the terrorists.* **2** to say that a building must be destroyed because it is not safe enough for people to use **yıkım kararı almak, binayı mühürleyip kullanılmasına izin vermemek**
  condemn sb to sth *phrasal verb* **1** to say what the punishment of someone who is guilty of a serious crime will be **mahkum etmek** *He was condemned to death.* **2** to make someone suffer in a particular way **mecbur bırakmak, sıkıntı vermek, zorunlu kılmak** *Poor education condemns many young people to low-paid jobs.*

condemnation /ˌkɒndemˈneɪʃ°n/ *noun* [C, U] when you say very strongly that you think something is wrong or very bad **lanetleme, kınama, ayıplama** *widespread condemnation of the war*

condensation /ˌkɒndenˈseɪʃ°n/ *noun* [U] small drops of water that form when warm air touches a cold surface **buğu**

condense /kənˈdens/ *verb* **1** [AIR] [I, T] If hot air or a gas condenses, it changes into a liquid as it becomes colder. **sıvılaştırmak, yoğunlaş(tır)mak, sıcak gazın soğuduğunda sıvı haline gelmek 2** [WORDS] [T] to make something such as a speech or piece of writing shorter **kısaltmak, kısa ve öz yazmak/söylemek** *You need to condense your conclusion into a single paragraph.* **3** [LIQUID] [T] to make a liquid thicker by taking some of the water out of it **yoğunlaş(tır)mak** *condensed milk*

condescend /ˌkɒndɪˈsend/ *verb* **condescend to do sth** *humorous* to agree to do something even though you think you are too important to do it **kendini ona layık olmadığını düşünerek bir işi yapmak, istemiyerek de olsa yapmayı kabul etmek**
  condescend to sb *phrasal verb* to treat someone as though you are better or more important than them **üstünlük taslamak, kendini büyük görmek, tepeden bakmak**

condescending /ˌkɒndɪˈsendɪŋ/ *adjective* showing that you think that you are better or more important than someone else **başkalarını küçümseyen, kibirlenen** *a condescending smile* ● **condescendingly** *adverb* **küçümser bir tavırla**

condescension /ˌkɒndɪˈsenʃ°n/ *noun* [U] when you behave as though you are better or more important than someone else **büyüklük taslama, kibir, küçümseme, lütüf buyurma, tenezzül**

o━ condition¹ /kənˈdɪʃ°n/ *noun* **1** [STATE] [U, no plural] the state that something or someone is in **hal ,durum, konum** *My bike's a few years old but it's in really good condition.* ○ *He's in no condition* (= not well enough) *to travel.* **2** [AGREEMENT] [C] something that must happen or be agreed before something else can happen **şart, koşul** *One of the conditions of the contract is that we can't keep pets.* **3** on condition that only if **sadece … şartıyla, koşuluyla** *Visitors are allowed in the gardens on condition that they don't touch the plants.* **4** [ILLNESS] [C] an illness **rahatsızlık, hastalık** *a serious heart condition* **5 conditions** the physical situation that people are in **mevcut koşullar, şartlar** *working/living conditions* ○ *severe weather conditions*

condition² /kənˈdɪʃ°n/ *verb* [T] **1** to make a person or animal behave in a particular way by influencing the way they think **şartlandırmak, koşullandırmak,**

koşullamak [often passive, + to do sth] *The boys were conditioned to be aggressive.* **2** to put a special liquid on your hair to make it soft and healthy **saçlara şekil vermek, bakım uygulamak**

conditional /kənˈdɪʃ°n°l/ *adjective* **1** If an offer or agreement is conditional, it will only happen if something else is done first. **bir şarta/koşula bağlı, şartlı/ koşullu** *Their fee is conditional on the work being completed by January.* ➔Opposite **unconditional. 2** A conditional sentence usually begins with 'if' and says that something must be true or happen before something else can be true or happen. **şart kipi**

conditioner /kənˈdɪʃ°nər/ *noun* [C, U] a liquid that you use when you wash your hair to make it soft **saçlara şekil vere madde/sıvı**

conditioning /kənˈdɪʃ°nɪŋ/ *noun* [U] when a person or animal is made to behave in a particular way **şartlandırma, koşullandırma** *social/physical conditioning* ➔See also: **air conditioning.**

condo /ˈkɒndəʊ/ *noun* [C] *US informal short for* condominium **dairelerin sahipleri, kat malikleri olan apartman binası**

condolence /kənˈdəʊləns/ *noun* [C, U] *formal* sympathy for the family or friends of a person who has recently died **taziye, baş sağlığı dileği** *Please offer my condolences to your father.*

condom /ˈkɒndɒm/ *US* /ˈkɑːndəm/ *noun* [C] a thin rubber covering that a man wears on his penis during sex to stop a woman becoming pregnant, or to protect against diseases **prezervatif**

condominium /ˌkɒndəˈmɪniəm/ *noun* [C] *US* a building containing apartments which are owned by the people living in them, or one of these apartments **dairelerin sahipleri, kat malikleri olan apartman binası**

condone /kənˈdəʊn/ *verb* [T] to accept or allow behaviour that is wrong **müsamaha etmek, hoş görmek, onaylamak** *His comments appeared to condone drug abuse.*

conducive /kənˈdjuːsɪv/ *adjective* making something possible or likely to happen **vesile olan, yol açan, yardımcı/sebep olan** *Such a noisy environment was not conducive to a good night's sleep.*

conduct¹ /ˈkɒndʌkt/ *noun* **1** [U] the way someone behaves **davranış, hal, tavır** *a code of conduct* (= rules about how to behave) **2 conduct of sth** the way someone organizes or does something **düzenleme, idare etme, tertipleme, biçimi** *He was criticized for his conduct of the inquiry.*

╔═══════════════════════════════════════╗
  conduct .... İLE BİRLİKTE KULLANILAN KELİMELER
╚═══════════════════════════════════════╝

conduct an **experiment/an interview/an inquiry/ an investigation/research/ a survey**

conduct² /kənˈdʌkt/ *verb* **1** [DO] [T] to organize or do something **düzenlemek, yürütmek, yapmak, uygulamak** *They're conducting a survey.* **2** [MUSIC] [I, T] to stand in front of a group of musicians and control their performance (orkestra, koro vb.) **idare etmek, yönetmek 3** [HEAT] [T] If a substance conducts electricity or heat, it allows electricity or heat to go through it. (elelktrik/ısı) **iletmek, geçirmek 4 conduct yourself** to behave in a particular way **davranmak, hareket etmek** *She conducted herself with great dignity.* **5** [LEAD] [T] *formal* to lead someone to a place **götürmek, rehberlik etmek, önderlik etmek, yol göstermek** *I was conducted to a side room.*

conductor /kənˈdʌktər/ *noun* [C] **1** [MUSIC] someone who stands in front of a group of musicians or singers and controls their performance **koro/orkestra şefi 2** [BUS] *UK* someone whose job is to sell or check tickets on a

bus, train, etc **(tren, otbüs vb.) biletçi, kondüktör**
3 TRAIN *US (UK* **guard)** someone whose job is to be responsible for a train and the people who work on it **tren
şefi, kondüktör 4** HEAT a substance that allows electricity or heat to go through it **iletken, geçirgen**

cone /kəʊn/ *noun* [C] **1** a solid shape with a round or oval
base which narrows to a point, or an object which has
this shape **koni, külah** *a row of traffic* **cones 2** a container for ice cream (= sweet, frozen food) that you can
eat **külah**

confectionery /kənˈfekʃᵊnᵊri/ *noun* [U] *mainly UK*
sweet food like sweets and chocolate **şekerleme, çikolata**

confederacy /kənˈfedᵊrəsi/ *(also* **confederation** /kən-
fedəˈreɪʃᵊn/) *noun* [C] an organization of smaller groups
who have joined together for business or political purposes **ittifak, birlik, konfederasyon**

confer /kənˈfɜːʳ/ *verb* **conferring,** *past* **conferred 1** [I] to
discuss something with other people before making a
decision **fikir/görüş alışverişinde bulunmak, fikir
teatisi etmek** *I'll need to confer with my lawyers.* **2** [T]
formal to give someone something, especially an official
title, an honour, or an advantage **vermek, sunmak,
bahşetmek**

⟨⟩ conference .... İLE BİRLİKTE KULLANILAN KELİMELER

attend/hold a conference ● a conference **on** sth ● **at** a
conference ● a conference **centre** ● a **sales** conference

conference /ˈkɒnfᵊrᵊns/ *noun* [C] **1** a large, formal
meeting, often lasting a few days, where people discuss
their work, politics, subjects they are studying, etc **konferans** *the annual* **sales** *conference* **2** a small, private
meeting for discussion of a particular subject **kongre,
müzakere, toplantı** ⊃See also: **press conference.**

ˈconference ˌcall *noun* [C] a telephone call between
three or more people in different places **aynı anda üç
ve daha fazla kişi arasında yapılan çoklu görüşme**

confess /kənˈfes/ *verb* [I, T] **1** to admit that you have
done something wrong or something that you feel
guilty about **itiraf etmek** [+ to + doing sth] *The man has
confessed to stealing the painting.* ○ *Rawlinson finally
confessed to the murder.* **2** to tell a priest or God about
all the wrong things that you have done **günah çıkarmak**

confession /kənˈfeʃᵊn/ *noun* [C, U] **1** when you admit
that you have done something wrong or illegal **itiraf**
Sutcliffe has **made** *a full* **confession** *to the police.*
2 when someone tells a priest all the wrong things
they have done **günah çıkarma** *to go to confession*

confetti /kənˈfeti/ *noun* [U] small pieces of coloured
paper that you throw when celebrating something
such as a marriage **konfeti**

confidant, confidante /ˈkɒnfɪdænt/ *noun* [C] a person you can talk to about your feelings and secrets
güvenilir/emin kişi

confide /kənˈfaɪd/ *verb* [I, T] to tell a secret to someone
who you trust not to tell anyone else **güvenmek, sır-
rını vermek/açıklamak, açmak** [+ that] *Holly confi-
ded to me that she was ill.*
confide in sb *phrasal verb* to tell someone who you trust
about things that are secret or personal **açılmak, sır-
larını paylaşmak**

⟨⟩ confidence .... İLE BİRLİKTE KULLANILAN KELİMELER

1 grow in/lack/lose confidence ● sth **gives** you confidence ● **do** sth **with** confidence ● a **lack** of confidence
2 express/lose/restore confidence (in sth) ● **have**

(complete/every/little/no) confidence **in** sb/sth
● **consumer/public** confidence ● confidence **in** sth

o▲**confidence** /ˈkɒnfɪdᵊns/ *noun* **1** ABILITY [U] when you are
certain of your ability to do things well **güven, inanç,
itimat** *He's a good student, but he* **lacks** *confidence.*
○ [+ to do sth] *His training has* **given** *him the confidence
to deal with any problem that arises.* **2** TRUST [U] trusting
someone's ability or believing that something will produce good results **güvenme, itimat etme, inanma**
Kate's new to the job, but I've got **every** *confidence in
her.* **3** SECRET [C] something secret that you tell someone
sır, gizli bilgi *to exchange confidences* **4 in confidence**
If you tell something to someone in confidence, you do
not want them to tell anyone else. **sır olarak, gizli kalmak koşuluyla**

o▲**confident** /ˈkɒnfɪdᵊnt/ *adjective* **1** certain about your
ability to do things well **emin, kendinden emin** *a confident grin* ○ *He feels* **confident** *of winning.* **2** being certain that something will happen **emin olan, inanan**
[+ (that)] *Doctors are confident that she'll recover.* ● **confidently** *adverb* ⊃See also: **self-confident. kendine güvenir
bir şekilde**

confidential /ˌkɒnfɪˈdenʃᵊl/ *adjective* secret, especially
in an official situation **gizli** *These documents are
strictly confidential.* ● **confidentially** *adverb* **gizli
bir şekilde** ● **confidentiality** /ˌkɒnfɪdenʃiˈæləti/
noun [U] **gizlilik**

confine /kənˈfaɪn/ *verb* [T] to prevent someone from
leaving a place or to prevent something from spreading
kapatmak, hapsetmek, zaptetmek [often passive] *He
was confined to a prison cell for several days.*
be confined to sth/sb *phrasal verb* to only exist in a
particular area or group of people **etkili olmak, bir
yer/bir grup insana has olmak** *The flooding was confined to the basement.*
confine sb/sth to sth *phrasal verb* to limit an activity
sınırlamak, daraltmak, kapatmak, hapsetmek
Please confine your discussion to the topic.

confined /kənˈfaɪnd/ *adjective* [always before noun] A confined space is very small. **dar, kapalı**

confinement /kənˈfaɪnmənt/ *noun* [U] when someone
is kept in a room or area, usually by force **nezaretha-
nede tutulma, kapatılma, hapsedilme** ⊃See also: **solitary confinement.**

confines /ˈkɒnfaɪnz/ *noun* [plural] the outer limits or
edges of something **dış hudutları/sınırları**

confirm /kənˈfɜːm/ *verb* [T] **1** to say or show that something is true **doğrulamak, onaylamak** [+ (that)] *His
wife confirmed that he'd left the house at 8.* **2** to make an
arrangement certain **kesinleştirmek, teyit etmek**
Flights should be confirmed 48 hours before departure.
3 be confirmed to become a member of the Christian
Church at a special ceremony **(Hıristiyanlık) kiliseye
kabul edilmek/etmek**

confirmation /ˌkɒnfəˈmeɪʃᵊn/ *noun* [C, U] **1** an
announcement or proof that something is true or certain **onay, teyit, doğrulama** *You'll receive* **written confirmation** *of your reservation within five days.* **2** a special ceremony in which someone becomes a full
member of the Christian Church **kiliseye kabul
töreni**

confirmed /kənˈfɜːmd/ *adjective* **a confirmed atheist/
bachelor/pessimist, etc** someone who has behaved in
a particular way for a long time and is not likely to
change **müzmin, iflah olmaz, kesin, belli, kronik
tanrıtanımaz/bekâr/iyimser**

confiscate /'kɒnfɪskeɪt/ *verb* [T] to take something away from someone, especially as a punishment **zorla el koymak, zaptetmek** ● **confiscation** /ˌkɒnfɪ'skeɪʃ°n/ *noun* [C, U] **el koyma, alıkoyma**

conflict .... İLE BİRLİKTE KULLANILAN KELİMELER

resolve a conflict ● **be in/come into** conflict **with** sb ● a conflict **between** sb and sb ● a conflict **over** sth ● an **area of/source of** conflict

conflict¹ /'kɒnflɪkt/ *noun* [C, U] DISAGREEMENT serious disagreement **anlaşmazlık, çekişme** *The Government was in conflict with the unions over pay.* ○ *The peasants often came into conflict with the landowners.* **2** FIGHTING fighting between groups or countries **(ülke ve gruplar arsı) çatışma, mücadele, anlaşmazlık** *armed conflict* **3** DIFFERENCE when two or more different things cannot easily exist together **(iki ve daha fazla şey) çatışma, uyuşmazlık** *the conflict between science and religion* **4 a conflict of interest** a situation where someone cannot make fair decisions because they are influenced by something **çıkar çatışması**

conflict² /kən'flɪkt/ *verb* [I] If things such as beliefs, needs, or facts conflict, they are very different and cannot easily exist together or both be true. **çatışmak, uyuşmamak, anlaşamamak, beraber olamamak, çelişmek** *Her views on raising children conflict with mine.* ○ *There were conflicting accounts of how the fight started.*

conflicted /kən'flɪktɪd/ *adjective* [never before noun] confused because you have two feelings or opinions about something that are opposite **çelişen, çatışan, uyuşmayan**

conform /kən'fɔːm/ *verb* [I] to behave in the way that most other people behave **uymak, sıra harici davranış göstermemek**
conform to/with sth *phrasal verb* to obey a rule or to do things in a traditional way **uyum sağlamak/göstermek, ayak uydurmak** *All our toys conform with safety standards.*

conformity /kən'fɔːməti/ *noun* [U] **1** behaving in the way that most other people behave **uyum, uyum sağlama, ayak uydurma 2** conformity to/with sth *formal* following rules or traditional ways of doing things **bir şeye uyum gösterme; uyumlu olma**

confound /kən'faʊnd/ *verb* [T] If something confounds someone, it makes them surprised and confused, because they cannot explain it. **şaşırmak, şaşkınlık yaşamak, karıştırmak, allak bullak etmek, kafası karışmak** *The growth in the economy continues to confound the experts.*

confront /kən'frʌnt/ *verb* [T] **1** ACCUSE to tell someone something, or show them something to try to make them admit they have done something wrong **karşılaşmak, yüz yüze gelmek, yüzle(ştir)mek** *Confronted with the evidence, she broke down and confessed.* **2 be confronted by/with sth** to be in a difficult situation, or to be shown something which may cause difficulties **karşı karşıya olmak, yüz yüze olmak** *We are confronted by the possibility of war.* **3** FRIGHTEN to stand in front of someone in a frightening way **karşısına çıkmak, kork (ut)mak, tehdit etmek** *He was confronted by two masked men.* **4** DEAL WITH to see that a problem exists and try to deal with it **göğüs germek, ilgilenmek, karşı durmak, üstesinden gelmek** *First, they must confront their addiction.*

confrontation /ˌkɒnfrʌn'teɪʃ°n/ *noun* [C, U] a fight or argument **tartışma, çatışma, sürtüşme**

confrontational /ˌkɒnfrʌn'teɪʃ°n°l/ *adjective* intentionally causing fighting or an argument **çatışmaya, tartışmaya neden olan** *a confrontational style of management*

☞**confuse** /kən'fjuːz/ *verb* [T] **1** to make someone unable to think clearly or understand something **şaşırtmak, kafası karışmak** *These advertisements simply confused the public.* **2** to think that one person or thing is another person or thing **birini biriyle karıştırmak** *I don't see how anyone could confuse me with my mother!*

☞**confused** /kən'fjuːzd/ *adjective* **1** unable to think clearly or to understand something **şaşkın, aklı karışık** *Sorry, I'm completely confused.* ○ *The politicians themselves are confused about what to do.* **2** not clear **karma karışık, anlaşılması güç** *The witnesses gave confused accounts of what happened.*

confusing /kən'fjuːzɪŋ/ *adjective* difficult to understand **yanıltıcı, karmaşık, akıl karıştırıcı** *I found the instructions very confusing.*

confusion .... İLE BİRLİKTE KULLANILAN KELİMELER

sth **causes/creates/leads to** confusion ● confusion **surrounds** sth ● do sth **in confusion** ● **widespread** confusion ● confusion **about/over** sth

☞**confusion** /kən'fjuːʒ°n/ *noun* **1** NOT UNDERSTAND [C, U] when people do not understand what is happening or what they should do **karışıklık, kargaşa** *There was a lot of confusion about what was actually going on.* **2** THOUGHT [U] a feeling of not being able to think clearly **zihin karışıklığı, karmaşıklık** *He could see the confusion on Marion's face.* **3** BETWEEN SIMILAR THINGS [U] when you think that one person or thing is another **yanılgı, karıştırma 4** SITUATION [U] a situation which is confusing because there is a lot of noise and activity **karmaşa, kargaşa, belirsizlik** *In the confusion, several prisoners tried to escape.*

congeal /kən'dʒiːl/ *verb* [I] If a liquid congeals, it becomes thick and almost solid. **katılaş(tır)mak, pıhtılaş(tır)mak** *congealed fat*

congenial /kən'dʒiːniəl/ *adjective formal* pleasant and friendly **içten, samimi, cana yakın, hoş** *congenial company*

congenital /kən'dʒenɪt°l/ *adjective* Congenital diseases or problems are ones that people have from when they are born. **doğuştan olan/gelen** *congenital heart defects*

congested /kən'dʒestɪd/ *adjective* full or blocked, especially with traffic **(trafik) tıkalı, tıkanık, yoğun, sıkışık** *The roads are very congested.*

congestion /kən'dʒestʃ°n/ *noun* [U] when something is full or blocked, especially with traffic **(trafik) tıkanıklık, sıkışıklık** *traffic congestion*

conglomerate /kən'glɒm°rət/ *noun* [C] a large company that is made up of several smaller companies **holding, şirketler topluluğu**

congratulate /kən'grætʃʊleɪt/ *verb* [T] to tell someone that you are happy because they have done something good or something good has happened to them **tebrik etmek, kutlamak** *Did you congratulate Cathy on her engagement?*

congratulations /kənˌgrætʃʊ'leɪʃ°nz/ *exclamation* something that you say when you want to congratulate someone **Birini tebrik ederken söylenen şey "Kutlarım, Tebrikler"** *Congratulations on doing an outstanding job.* ○ *I hear you're getting married. Congratulations!*

congregate /'kɒŋgrɪgeɪt/ *verb* [I] to come together in a group **bir araya gelmek, toplanmak** *Young people congregated on street corners.*

congregation /ˌkɒŋgrɪ'geɪʃən/ *noun* [group] a group of people meeting to worship in church **cemaat, topluluk, ibadet için toplanmış insanlar**

congress /'kɒŋgres/ *noun* **1** [C] a large meeting of the members of one or more organizations **kongre** *an international congress on art history* **2 Congress** the group of people who make laws in the United States. Congress consists of the Senate and the House of Representatives. **(ABD) senato ve temsilciler meclisinden oluşan kongre, meclis**

congressional /kən'greʃənl/ *adjective* [always before noun] relating to the United States Congress **ABD kongresine ait** *a congressional committee*

congressman, congresswoman /'kɒŋgresmən/, /'kɒŋgres,wʊmən/ *noun* [C] *plural* **congressmen** or **congresswomen** a man or woman who is a member of the United States Congress **bay/bayan kongre üyesi**

conical /'kɒnɪkəl/ *adjective* Conical objects have a wide, round base, sloping sides and a pointed top. **koni şeklinde**

conifer /'kɒnɪfər/ *noun* [C] a tree with cones (= hard, brown, oval objects) and thin green leaves that stay green all winter **yaz kış yeşil olan kozalaklı ağaç**

conjecture /kən'dʒektʃər/ *noun* [C, U] *formal* guessing about something without real evidence **varsayım, tahmin** *Exactly what happened that night is still a matter for conjecture.* ● **conjecture** *verb* [I, T] *formal* [+ (that)] *Some people conjectured that it was an attempt to save money.* **tahminde bulunmak, varsayımda bulunmak**

conjugal /'kɒndʒʊgəl/ *adjective formal* relating to marriage **evlilikle ilgili, karı-koca ilişkisine dair**

conjugate /'kɒndʒʊgeɪt/ *verb* [T] to add different endings to a verb in order to produce all its different forms **(fiil) çekmek** ● **conjugation** /ˌkɒndʒʊ'geɪʃən/ *noun* [C, U] **fiil çekimi**

conjunction /kən'dʒʌŋkʃən/ *noun* **1** [C] A word that is used to connect phrases or parts of a sentence. For example the words 'and', 'because', and 'although' are conjunctions. **bağlaç 2 in conjunction with sth/sb** working, used, or happening with something or someone else **ile bağlantılı/ilgili olarak**

conjure /'kʌndʒər/ *verb*
conjure sth up *phrasal verb* **1** to make a picture or idea appear in someone's mind **gözünün önüne getirmek, gözünde canlandırmak** *Familiar tunes can help us conjure up memories of the past.* **2** to make something in a quick and clever way, especially food **bir şeyi maharetle hazırlamak**

conjurer /'kʌndʒərər/ *noun* [C] *another spelling of* conjuror **hokkabaz, sihirbaz**

conjuring /'kʌndʒərɪŋ/ *noun* [U] performing magic to entertain people **hokkabazlık** *a conjuring trick*

conjuror /'kʌndʒərər/ *noun* [C] a person who performs magic to entertain people **hokkabaz, sihirbaz**

conman /'kɒnmæn/ *noun* [C] a man who tricks people into giving him money or valuable things **dalaverci, dolandırıcı, üçkâğıtçı**

✛**connect** /kə'nekt/ *verb* **1** [JOIN] [I, T] to join two things or places together **birleştirmek, bağlamak** *Ferries connect the mainland with the islands.* ○ *Connect up the printer to your computer.* **2** [INVOLVE] [T] to see or show that two or more people or things are involved with each other **bağlantı kurmak, ilişkisi olmak, ilişkilendirmek** *There is no evidence to connect him with*

the crime. **3** [TRAVEL] [I] If buses, trains, aircraft, etc connect, they arrive at a particular time so that passengers can get off one and onto another. **aktarmak, aktarması olmak, bağlantılı olmak** *Can you get me a connecting flight?* **4** [TELEPHONE] [T] to make it possible for two people to talk to each other on the telephone **bağlamak, irtibatlandırma/irtibatlamak** ⟳Opposite **disconnect**.

connected /kə'nektɪd/ *adjective* **1** If people or things are connected, there is a relationship between them. **bağlantılı, ilişkili** *The hospital is connected to the University of Rochester.* ○ *He remained closely connected with the museum until his death.* ⟳Opposite **unconnected**. **2** If two things are connected, they are joined together. **bağlı** *The Red Sea is connected to the Mediterranean by the Suez Canal.* ⟳Opposite **disconnected** ⟳See also: **well-connected**.

🧩 **connection** .... İLE BİRLİKTE KULLANILAN KELİMELER

have a/no connection with sb/sth ● a close/direct connection ● a connection between sth and sth ● a connection with sth

✛**connection** /kə'nekʃən/ *noun* **1** [RELATIONSHIP] [C, U] a relationship between people or things **ilişki, ilgi, alaka** *The connection between smoking and heart disease is well known.* ○ *He denied having any connection with the terrorists.* **2** [JOINING THINGS] [C, U] something that joins things together **bağlantı, irtibat** *Many companies now offer free connection to the Internet.* **3** [TRAVEL] [C] a train, bus, or aircraft that leaves a short time after another arrives, so that people can continue their journey **aktarma (tren, uçak, otobüs)** *The train was half an hour late and I missed my connection.* **4 in connection with** used to say what something is about *...ile ilgili,* **münasebetiyle, dolayısıyla** *A man has been arrested in connection with the murder.*

connections /kə'nekʃənz/ *noun* [plural] important or powerful people who you know and who will help you **bağlantılar, nüfuzlu/güçlü tanıdıklar** *He has connections in Washington.*

connive /kə'naɪv/ *verb* [I] to work secretly to do something wrong or illegal, or to allow something wrong or illegal to happen **gizli dolap çevirmek, göz yummak, görmezden gelmek, gizli bir şeyler çevirmek** *They accused the government of conniving in drug smuggling.*

connoisseur /ˌkɒnə'sɜːr/ *noun* [C] someone who knows a lot about and enjoys good food, wine, art, etc **uzman, usta, bilgili, bir konuda uzman**

connotation /ˌkɒnə'teɪʃən/ *noun* [C, U] the feelings or ideas that words give in addition to their meanings **çağrışım, yan anlam, ima** *The word 'second-hand' has connotations of poor quality.*

conquer /'kɒŋkər/ *verb* **1** [I, T] to take control of a country or to defeat people by war **fethetmek, ele geçirmek, zaptetmek** *Peru was conquered by the Spanish in 1532.* **2** [T] to succeed in stopping or dealing with a bad feeling or a difficult problem **yenmek, başetmek, üstesinden gelmek** *He has finally conquered his fear of spiders.*

conqueror /'kɒŋkərər/ *noun* [C] someone who has conquered a country or its people **fatih, fetheden kimse**

conquest /'kɒŋkwest/ *noun* [C, U] when someone takes control of a country, area, or situation **fetih, fethetmek, zaptetmek** *the Roman conquest of Britain*

conscience /'kɒnʃəns/ *noun* **1** [C, U] the part of you that makes you feel guilty when you have behaved badly **vicdan** *a guilty conscience* ○ *My conscience is clear* (= I do not feel guilty) *because I've done nothing wrong.*

2 be on your conscience If something is on your conscience, it is making you feel guilty. **vicdanını rahatsız etmek**

conscientious /ˌkɒnʃi'enʃəs/ *adjective* always doing your work with a lot of care **titiz, dikkatli, çalışkan** *a conscientious student* ● **conscientiously** *adverb* özenli bir şekilde

conscientious objector /kɒnʃi,enʃəsəb'dʒektər/ *noun* [C] someone who refuses to work in the armed forces because they think war is wrong **vicdani retçi**

conscious /'kɒnʃəs/ *adjective* **1 be conscious of/that** to know that something is present or that something is happening **farkında/bilincinde olmak** *I'm very conscious that a lot of people disagree with me.* **2 a conscious decision/choice/effort, etc** a decision/choice/effort, etc that you make intentionally **bilinçli karar/seçim/çaba vb.** *Did you make a conscious decision to lose weight?* ↪Opposite **subconscious**. **3** awake and able to think and notice things **bilinçli, şuurlu, müdrik** *He's still conscious but he's very badly injured.* ↪Opposite **unconscious**. ● **consciously** *adverb* ↪See also: self-conscious. **farkında olarak**

-conscious /'kɒnʃəs/ *suffix* used at the end of words to mean 'thinking that something is important' **önemli/ önemseyen anlamında son ek** *a safety-conscious mother* ○ *fashion-conscious teenagers*

consciousness /'kɒnʃəsnəs/ *noun* **1** [U] when someone is awake and can think and notice things **şuur, bilinç, idrak** *He lost consciousness* (= stopped being conscious) *for several minutes.* ○ *I want to be here when she regains consciousness* (= becomes conscious again). **2** [no plural] when someone knows about something **fikir, görüş, anlayış, zihniyet** *There's a growing consciousness about environmental issues among young people.*

conscript¹ /'kɒnskrɪpt/ *noun* [C] someone who has been made to join the army **askere alınmış kimse**

conscript² /kən'skrɪpt/ *verb* [T] to make someone join the army **silah altına al(ın)mak, askere al(ın)mak** [often passive] *During World War I, he was conscripted into the Russian army.*

conscription /kən'skrɪpʃən/ *noun* [U] a system in which people are made to join the army **mecburi askerlik**

consecrate /'kɒnsɪkreɪt/ *verb* [T] to make a place or object holy in a religious ceremony **takdis etmek, kutsamak** ● **consecration** /ˌkɒnsɪ'kreɪʃən/ *noun* [U] *a consecration ceremony* **kutsama**

consecutive /kən'sekjʊtɪv/ *adjective* Consecutive events, numbers, or periods of time come one after the other. **ardışık, birbiri ardından gelen, birbiri peşi sıra olan** *the third consecutive day of rain* ● **consecutively** *adverb* **ardışık bir şekilde**

consensus /kən'sensəs/ *noun* [U, no plural] when all the people in a group agree about something **ortak mutabakat, genel görüş, oy birliği** *to reach a consensus* ○ *The general consensus is that we should wait and see what happens.*

consent¹ /kən'sent/ *noun* [U] **1** permission for someone to do something **muvafakat, müsaade, izin, rıza** *You can't come without your parents' consent.* **2 by common consent** UK used to say that everyone agrees about something **genel izinle, oy birliği ile, genel itifakla** *He is, by common consent, the most talented actor in Hollywood.*

consent² /kən'sent/ *verb* [I] to agree to do something, or to allow someone to do something **razı olmak, muvafakat etmek, izin vermek** [+ to do sth] *They eventually consented to let us enter.*

consequence ...... İLE BİRLİKTE KULLANILAN KELİMELER
face/live with/suffer the consequences ● as a consequence (of sth) ● a direct consequence ● devastating/ dire/disastrous/serious consequences ● the consequences of sth

o▪**consequence** /'kɒnsɪkwəns/ *noun* **1** [C] the result of an action or situation, especially a bad result **sonuç, netice** *The ship capsized, with disastrous consequences.* ○ *If you make him angry, you'll have to suffer the consequences.* **2 of little/no consequence** *formal* not important **önemsiz, ehemmiyetsiz** *The money was of little consequence to Tony.*

consequent /'kɒnsɪkwənt/ *adjective* [always before noun] *formal* happening as a result of something **sonuç olarak vuku bulan** *the closure of the factory and the consequent loss of 400 jobs*

consequently /'kɒnsɪkwəntli/ *adverb* as a result **sonuç itibariyle, bu nedenle, bundan dolayı** *She was the child of two models and, consequently, she was very tall.*

conservation /ˌkɒnsə'veɪʃən/ *noun* [U] **1** the protection of nature **çevre koruma** *wildlife conservation* ○ *conservation groups* **2** when you are careful not to waste energy, water, etc **doğal kaynakları koruma/muhafaza/sakınma**

conservationist /ˌkɒnsə'veɪʃənɪst/ *noun* [C] someone who believes that people should protect nature **çevre korumacı**

conservatism /kən'sɜːvətɪzəm/ *noun* [U] conservative actions and beliefs **tutuculuk, muhafazakârlık**

conservative /kən'sɜːvətɪv/ *adjective* **1** not trusting sudden changes or new ideas **tutucu, muhafazakâr** *Older people tend to be very conservative.* **2 a conservative estimate/guess** a guess about a number or amount that is probably lower than the true number or amount **ihtiyatlı/ölçülü tahmin, hesap**

Conservative /kən'sɜːvətɪv/ *noun* [C] someone who supports the Conservative Party in the UK **sağcı, sağ görüşlü, tutucu görüşleri benimseyen** *the Conservative candidate/MP*

the Con'servative ˌParty *noun* [group] one of the three main political parties in the UK **Birleşik Krallık'da üç partiden biri, Muhafazakâr Parti**

conservatory /kən'sɜːvətri/ *noun* [C] a room attached to a house that has windows all around it and a glass roof **sera, evde her tarafı camla çevrili oda**

conserve /kən'sɜːv/ *verb* [T] **1** to use something in a way that does not waste it **idareli/dikkatli/çarçur etmeden kullanmak** *Insulating the walls will help to conserve heat.* **2** to prevent harm or damage to animals or places **korumak, muhafaza etmek**

o▪**consider** /kən'sɪdər/ *verb* **1** [T] to think carefully about a decision or something you might do **enine boyuna düşünmek, dikkatle değerlendirmek** *Have you considered surgery?* ○ [+ doing sth] *We're considering buying a new car.* **2** [T] to think about particular facts when you are making a decision about something **gerçekleri dikkate almak, düşünmek** *If you buy an old house, you have to consider the cost of repairs.* **3 consider sb/ sth (to be) sth; consider that** to have a particular opinion about someone or something **birisi/bir şey hakkında özel fikirleri olmak** [often reflexive] *I don't consider myself to be a great athlete.*

considerable /kən'sɪdərəbl/ *adjective* large or important enough to have an effect **dikkate değer, önemli** *a considerable amount of money* ○ *The damage has been considerable.* ● **considerably** *adverb* Rates of pay vary considerably. **bir hayli fazla**

considerate /kənˈsɪdᵊrət/ *adjective* kind and helpful düşünceli, saygılı, anlayışlı *a polite and considerate child* ⟳Opposite **inconsiderate**.

consideration ...... İLE BİRLİKTE KULLANILAN KELİMELER

1 an **important**/the **main**/a **major** consideration ● **environmental**/**financial**/**political** considerations
2 careful/**serious** consideration ● be **under** consideration ● be **worthy of** consideration

consideration /kənˌsɪdᵊrˈeɪʃᵊn/ *noun* **1** [IMPORTANT FACT] [C] something that you have to think about when you make decisions or plans enine boyuna düşünme, dikkate alma, düşünüp taşınma *Safety is our main consideration.* **2** [CAREFUL THOUGHT] [U] when you think about something very carefully inceleme, gözden, geçirme *After careful consideration, we have decided to offer you the job.* ○ *Several options are under consideration* (= being considered). **3** [KINDNESS] [U] when you are kind to people or think about their feelings anlayış, saygı *They always treated me with consideration.* **4 take sth into consideration** to think about something when you make a decision or plan hesaba katmak, herşeyi dikkate almak, her detayı göz önünde bulundurmak

considered /kənˈsɪdəd/ *adjective* **1** [always before noun] A considered opinion or decision is based on careful thought. herşeyi ile düşünülmüş, hesaba katılmış *It is our considered opinion that he should resign.* **2 all things considered** used when you are giving your opinion about something after thinking carefully about all the facts her şey hesaba katıldı/dikkate alındı *All things considered, I think we made the right choice.*

considering /kənˈsɪdərɪŋ/ *preposition, conjunction* used for saying that you have a particular opinion about something, because of a particular fact about it bakınca, düşünülecek olursa, ...e rağmen *She's fairly fit considering her age.* ○ *Considering she'd only been there once before, she did well to find the way.*

consign /kənˈsaɪn/ *verb*
consign sb/sth to sth *phrasal verb formal* to get rid of someone or something or to put them in an unpleasant place or situation bırakmak, atmak, terketmek, kurtulmak; kötü/hoş olmayan bir konuma getirmek *They were consigned to a life of poverty.*

consignment /kənˈsaɪnmənt/ *noun* [C] an amount of goods that is being sent somewhere gönderilen/sevkedilen mallar *a ship carrying a small consignment of rice*

consist /kənˈsɪst/ *verb*
consist of sth *phrasal verb* to be formed or made from two or more things ... den oluşmak/meydana gelmek; müteşekkil olmak *a dessert consisting of fruit and cream*

consistency /kənˈsɪstənsi/ *noun* **1** [+ (that)] when someone always behaves or performs in a similar way or when something always happens in a similar way istikrar, süreklilik, tutarlılık, denge *The team has won a few matches but lacks consistency.* **2** [C, U] how thick or smooth a liquid is (sıvı) koyuluk, kıvam, yoğunluk *Beat the mixture to a smooth consistency.*

consistent /kənˈsɪstᵊnt/ *adjective* **1** always behaving or happening in a similar, usually positive, way tutarlı, istikrarlı *consistent effort/improvement* **2 consistent with sth** *formal* having the same principles as something else, or agreeing with other facts birşeyle tutarlı/uyum içinde/bağdaşık olan *His account of events is entirely consistent with the video evidence.* ● **consistently** *adverb The President has consistently denied the rumours.* düzenli olarak

consolation /ˌkɒnsəˈleɪʃᵊn/ *noun* [C, U] something that makes you feel better about a bad situation teselli, avuntu *If it's any consolation, I failed my driving test too.*

console¹ /kənˈsəʊl/ *verb* [T] to make someone who is sad feel better teselli etmek, avutmak, daha iyi hissetmesini sağlamak *I tried to console her but she just kept crying.*

console² /ˈkɒnsəʊl/ *noun* [C] an object that contains the controls for a piece of equipment kumanda düğmesi/konsolu/kolu *a video game console*

consolidate /kənˈsɒlɪdeɪt/ *verb* **1** [I, T] to make sure that you become more powerful, or that success and achievements continue strongly takviye etmek, sağlamlaştırmak, güçlendirmek *It will take him some time to consolidate his position in the banking world.* **2** [T] to combine several things, especially businesses, so that they become more effective, or to be combined in this way (iş) birleş(tir)mek, birlik oluşturmak, güçlenmek *He consolidated his businesses into one large company.* ● **consolidation** /kənˌsɒlɪˈdeɪʃᵊn/ *noun* [U] daha güçlü hale gelme

consonant /ˈkɒnsᵊnənt/ *noun* [C] a letter of the alphabet that is not a vowel ünsüz/sessiz harf

consort /kənˈsɔːt/ *verb*
consort with sb *phrasal verb* to spend time with a bad person (kötü kişilerle) ... ile vakit geçirmek/arkadaşlık etmek *They claimed he had been consorting with drug dealers.*

consortium /kənˈsɔːtiəm/ *noun* [C] *plural* **consortiums** or **consortia** an organization consisting of several businesses or banks bir çok iş veya bankanın birleşerek oluşturduğu kuruluş, konsorsiyum *an international consortium of airlines*

conspicuous /kənˈspɪkjuəs/ *adjective* very easy to notice göz önünde, göze çarpan, belli, bariz *His army uniform made him very conspicuous.* ● **conspicuously** *adverb His wife was conspicuously absent.* farkedilebilir bir şekilde

conspiracy /kənˈspɪrəsi/ *noun* [C, U] when a group of people secretly plan to do something bad or illegal komplo, gizli plan [+ to do sth] *a conspiracy to overthrow the government*

conspirator /kənˈspɪrətər/ *noun* [C] someone who secretly plans with other people to do something bad or illegal komplocu, gizli plan yapan, suikastçi

conspire /kənˈspaɪər/ *verb* **1** [I] to join with other people to secretly plan to do something bad or illegal komplo kurmak, gizli plan yapmak [+ to do sth] *He was convicted of conspiring to blow up the World Trade Center.* ○ *The king accused his advisers of conspiring against him.* **2 conspire against sb; conspire to do sth** If events or a situation conspire against you, they cause problems for you. problem olmak, bozmak, olumsuzluk yaratmak *Circumstances had conspired to ruin her plans.*

constable /ˈkʌnstəbl/ *noun* [C] a British police officer of the lowest rank Britanya'da en ast rütbede polis memuru

constant /ˈkɒnstənt/ *adjective* **1** happening a lot or all the time sürekli, devamlı *machines that are in constant use* **2** staying at the same level sabit değişmez *The temperature remained constant.* ● **constantly** *adverb He's constantly changing his mind.* sürekli olarak

constellation /ˌkɒnstəˈleɪʃᵊn/ *noun* [C] a group of stars takım yıldız, burç, yıldız kümesi

consternation /ˌkɒnstəˈneɪʃᵊn/ *noun* [U] a feeling of shock or worry şaşkınlık/korku/endişe/dehşet hissi

constipated /'kɒnstɪpeɪtɪd/ *adjective* unable to empty your bowels as often as you should **kabız(olmuş)**

constipation /ˌkɒnstɪ'peɪʃ³n/ *noun* [U] when you are constipated **kabızlık**

constituency /kən'stɪtjuənsi/ *noun* [C] an area of a country which elects someone to represent it in the government, or the people who live there **seçim bölgesi, seçim bölgesi seçmenleri/insanları**

constituent /kən'stɪtjuənt/ *noun* [C] **1** one of the parts or substances that something is made of **öğe, parça, unsur, eleman** *Methane is the main constituent of natural gas.* **2** someone who lives in a particular constituency **seçmen, bölge halkı/ahalisi**

constitute /'kɒnstɪtjuːt/ *verb* [T] to be or form something **oluşturmak, teşkil etmek, olmak, bir araya getirmek** *This defeat constitutes a real setback for their championship hopes.*

constitution /ˌkɒnstɪ'tjuːʃ³n/ *noun* [C] **1** the set of laws and principles that a country's government must obey **anayasa** *the US Constitution* **2** the state of someone's health **sağlık, sıhhat, bünye** *a strong/weak constitution*

constitutional /ˌkɒnstɪ'tjuːʃ³n³l/ *adjective* relating to the constitution of a country **anayasal, anayasaya ilişkin/ile ilgili** *a constitutional crisis*

constrain /kən'streɪn/ *verb* [T] to control something by limiting it **sınırlayarak kontrol altına almak, kısıtlamak, zorlamak, sınırlamak, baskı uygulamak** *regulations that constrain industry* ○ [often passive] *I'm constrained by decisions made in the past.*

constraint /kən'streɪnt/ *noun* [C] something that limits what you can do **sınırlama, zorlama, kısıtlama, baskı** *budget constraints* ○ *There are constraints on the medicines doctors can prescribe.*

constrict /kən'strɪkt/ *verb* **1** [T] to limit someone's freedom to do what they want to or be the way they want to **sıkmak, kısıtlamak, engellemek, sınırlandırmak, kısmen yasaklamak** *His creativity was constricted by the political regime he lived under.* **2** [I, T] to become narrower or tighter, or to make something narrower or tighter **sık(ıştır)mak, büzmek, büzüştürmek, daraltmak** *The blood vessels constricted.* ● **constriction** /kən'strɪkʃ³n/ *noun* [U] **kısıtlama**

construct /kən'strʌkt/ *verb* [T] to build something from several parts **inşa etmek, yapmak, kurmak, çatmak** *The building was constructed in 1930.*

construction /kən'strʌkʃ³n/ *noun* **1** [BUILDING WORK] [U] the work of building houses, offices, bridges, etc **inşa etme, yapma, kurma, bina etme** *railway construction* ○ *construction work* **2** [LARGE BUILDING] [C] something large that is built **inşaat, bina, yapım, yapı** *a large steel construction* **3** [WORDS] [C] The construction of a sentence or phrase is the way the words are arranged. **cümle/ifade yapısı/kurgusu**

constructive /kən'strʌktɪv/ *adjective* helpful or useful **yapıcı, yararlı, faydalı** *constructive advice/criticism* ● **constructively** *adverb* **yapıcı bir şekilde**

construe /kən'struː/ *verb* [T] **construing**, *past* **construed** to understand something in a particular way **anlam vermek, yorumlamak, kendince farklı anlamak** *Her comments could be construed as patronizing.*

consul /'kɒns³l/ *noun* [C] someone whose job is to work in a foreign country taking care of the people from their own country who go or live there **konsolos, konsül**

consular /'kɒnsjʊlə^r/ *adjective* [always before noun] relating to a consul or a consulate **konsolosa/konsolosluğa dair/ilişkin** *consular officials*

consulate /'kɒnsjʊlət/ *noun* [C] the offices where a consul works **konsolosluk** *the Cuban consulate in Mexico City*

consult /kən'sʌlt/ *verb* [T] **1** to go to a particular person or book to get information or advice **danışmak, fikir sormak/araştırmak, başvurmak** *For more information, consult your travel agent.* **2** to discuss something with someone before you make a decision **istişare etmek, müzkerre etmek, görüş alışverişinde bulunmak** *Why didn't you consult me about this?*

consultancy /kən'sʌlt³nsi/ *noun* **1** [C] a company that gives advice on subjects it knows a lot about **müşavirlik/danışmanlık/uzmanlık şirketi** *a management/recruitment consultancy* **2** [U] the activity of giving advice on a particular subject **müşavirlik, danışmanlık, uzmanlık**

consultant /kən'sʌlt³nt/ *noun* [C] **1** someone who advises people about a particular subject **danışman, müşavir, uzman** *a tax consultant* **2** UK a hospital doctor who is an expert in a particular area of medicine **mütehassıs, uzman, doktor**

consultation /ˌkɒns³l'teɪʃ³n/ *noun* **1** [C] a meeting to discuss something or to get advice **görüşme, danışma, konsültasyon** *a medical consultation* **2** [U] when you discuss something with someone in order to get their advice or opinion about it **istişare, görüşme, fikir teatisi yapılan toplantı** *After consultation with his lawyers, he decided to abandon the case.*

consultative /kən'sʌltətɪv/ *adjective* A consultative group or document gives advice about something. **danışma ile ilgili, istişari**

consume /kən'sjuːm/ *verb* [T] **1** [USE] to use something such as a product, energy, or fuel **tüketmek, bitirmek** *These lights don't consume much electricity.* **2** [EAT OR DRINK] *formal* to eat or drink something **yemek içmek 3 be consumed with/by sth** to have so much of a feeling that it affects everything you do **bunal/t)mak, sıkıntıdan patla(t)mak** *a dancer consumed by ambition* **4** [FIRE] If fire consumes something, it completely destroys it. **yakıp kül etmek**

consumer **choice/confidence/demand/protection/ spending**

consumer /kən'sjuːmə^r/ *noun* [C] someone who buys or uses goods or services **tüketici** *These price cuts are good news for consumers.*

consumerism /kən'sjuːmərɪz³m/ *noun* [U] buying and selling things, especially when this is an important part of a society's activities **tüketicilik**

consummate¹ /'kɒnsəmeɪt/ *verb* [T] to make a marriage or relationship complete by having sex **gerdeğe girmek, cinsel ilişki kurarak evliliğin gereğini yerine getirmek** ● **consummation** /ˌkɒnsə'meɪʃ³n/ *noun* [U] **mükemmelleştirme, tamamlama**

consummate² /kən'sʌmət/, /'kɒnsəmət/ *adjective* [always before noun] *formal* having great skill **becerikli, usta, işbilen** *a consummate professional* ○ *consummate ease/skill*

consumption /kən'sʌmpʃ³n/ *noun* [U] **1** the amount of something that someone uses, eats, or drinks **tüketim, tüketilen miktar** *China's total energy consumption* **2** when someone uses, eats, or drinks something **tüketim, sarf, harcama, yeme, içme, kullanma** *products sold for personal consumption*

contact¹ /'kɒntækt/ noun 1 [COMMUNICATION] [U] when you
communicate with someone, especially by speaking to
them **temas, ilişki, münasebet** *We keep in close contact with our grandparents.* ○ *Jo and I are determined
not to lose contact.* 2 [TOUCH] [U] when two people or
things are touching each other **temas, dokunma,
dokunuş** *She dislikes any kind of physical contact.*
○ *Wash your hands if they come into contact with chemicals.* 3 [PERSON] [C] someone you know who may be able
to help you because of their job or position **tanıdık,
bildik, ahbap, torpil** *business contacts* 4 [EYE] [C] *(also
contact lens)* a small piece of plastic that you put on your
eye to make you see more clearly **gözlük yerine kullanılan plastik küçük parçalar, kontak lens** ○See also:
eye contact.

contact² /'kɒntækt/ verb [T] to telephone, email or write
to someone **temas/irtibat kurmak, görüşmek,
yazışmak, konuşmak** *I've been trying to contact you
for days.*

contact

Unutmayın! Contact fiil olarak kullanıldığında ardından edat gelmez. **Contact with someone** veya **contact
to someone** yanlış kullanımlardır. Doğru hali **contact
someone** olarak kullanılmalıdır.: ~~You can contact with
me by phone or email.~~ Yanlış cümle örneği
You can contact me by phone or email.

'contact ,lens UK *(US ,contact 'lens)* noun [C] a small piece
of plastic that you put on your eye to make you see more
clearly **kontak lens**

contagious /kən'teɪdʒəs/ adjective 1 A contagious disease is one that you can get if you touch someone who
has it. **bulaşıcı, temas yoluyla geçen** 2 A contagious
feeling spreads quickly amongst people. **kolayca yayılan, fısıltı ile çabucak yayılan** *Her excitement was contagious.*

☞**contain** /kən'teɪn/ verb [T] 1 [INSIDE] If one thing contains
another, it has it inside it. **kapsamak, içermek** *a box
containing a diamond ring* 2 [PART] to have something as
a part **ihtiva etmek, içine almak** *Does this drink contain alcohol?* 3 [CONTROL] to control something by stopping it from spreading **yayılmasını engelleyerek
kontrol altına almak** *The police were
unable to contain the fighting.* 4 [EMOTION] to control your
emotions **duygularına hakim olmak** *He could barely
contain his anger.*

container /kən'teɪnər/ noun [C] an object such as a box
or a bottle that is used for holding something **kap, sandık, varil, şişe vb.**

contaminate /kən'tæmɪneɪt/ verb [T] to make something dirty or poisonous **kirletmek** *contaminated drinking water* • **contamination** /kən,tæmɪ'neɪʃⁿn/ noun
[U] **kirlilik, pislik**

contemplate /'kɒntəmpleɪt/ verb [T] to think about
something for a long time or in a serious way **üzerinde
kafa yormak, düşünmek, tasarlamak** [+ doing sth] *I'm
contemplating changing my name.* ○ *He even contempla-
ted suicide.* • **contemplation** /,kɒntəm'pleɪʃⁿn/ noun [U]
düşünme

contemporary¹ /kən'tempⁿrⁿri/, /kən'tempəri/ adjective 1 of the present time **çağdaş, modern** *contemporary music* 2 [always before noun] existing or happening at
the same time as something **çağdaş, aynı çağa ait**

a box of cereal
a bag of crisps
a carton of milk
a tube of toothpaste
a bag of peanuts
a can of drink
a tin of sardines *UK*, a can of sardines *US*
a box of chocolates
a jar of coffee
a carton of yoghurt
a tub of margarine

olan *Most contemporary accounts of the event have
been destroyed.*

contemporary² /kən'tempⁿrⁿri/, /kən'tempəri/ noun
[C] Someone's contemporaries are the people who live
at the same time as them. **çağdaş, akran, aynı çağda
yaşamış kişiler** *Shakespeare and his contemporaries*

contempt /kən'tempt/ noun 1 [U] a strong feeling that
you do not respect someone or something **küçümseme, aşağılama** *He has utter contempt for anyone
with power.* 2 **contempt of court** behaviour that is illegal because it does not obey the rules of a law court
**umursamayarak, ... hiçe sayarak, kanunları göz
ardı ederek**

contemptible /kən'temptəbl/ adjective extremely bad,
because of being dishonest or cruel **aşağılık, adi,
alçak**

contemptuous /kən'temptʃuəs/ adjective showing
contempt **aşağılayıcı, horgören, küçümseyen** • **con-
temptuously** adverb **hor görür bir şekilde**

contend /kən'tend/ verb 1 [T] formal to say that something is true **ileri sürmek, iddia etmek** [+ (that)] *His
lawyers contend that he is telling the truth.* 2 [I] to compete with someone to try to win something **yarışmak,
çekişmek, mücadele etmek, rekabet halinde olmak**
one of the groups contending for power
contend with sth phrasal verb to have to deal with a
difficult or unpleasant situation **...e karşı koymak;
hoş olmayan veya zor bir durumla baş etmek/**

uğraşmak/ilgilenmek zorunda olmak *I have enough problems of my own to contend with.*

contender /kən'tendəʳ/ *noun* [C] someone who competes with other people to try to win something **yarış-macı, müsabık** *a leading contender for an Oscar*

content¹ /'kɒntent/ *noun* [no plural] **1** the information or ideas that are talked about in a book, speech, film, etc **içindekiler, içerik** *The content of the article was controversial.* **2** the amount of a particular substance that something contains **içerik, esas** *Most soft drinks have a high sugar content.*

content² /kən'tent/ *adjective* happy or satisfied **mutlu, memnun** *Not content with second place, Jeff played only to win.* ○ [+ to do sth] *I was content to stay home and read.*

content³ /kən'tent/ *verb*
content yourself with sth *phrasal verb* to do something or have something although it is not exactly what you want **yetinmek, razı olmak, rıza göstermek** *Since it rained we had to content ourselves with playing cards.*

contented /kən'tentɪd/ *adjective* satisfied, or making you feel satisfied **tatmin olmuş, halinden memnun, hoşnut** ⊃Opposite discontented. ● **contentedly** *adverb* **tatmin olmuş bir şekilde**

contention /kən'tenʃ°n/ *noun* **1** OPINION [C] *formal* a belief or opinion **düşünce, inanç, iddia** *There's a general contention that too much violence is shown on TV.* **2** COMPETITION [U] when people or groups compete for something **rekabet, mücadele** *Johnson is back in contention for the championships.* **3** DISAGREEMENT [U] arguments and disagreements **çekişme, münakaşa, uyuşmazlık** ⊃See also: a **bone¹** of contention.

contentious /kən'tenʃəs/ *adjective* likely to make people argue **tartışmalı, çekişmeli, nizalı** *a contentious issue*

contentment /kən'tentmənt/ *noun* [U] the feeling of being happy or satisfied **kanaat, gönül rahatlığı, hoşnutluk, memnuniyet**

contents /'kɒntents/ *noun* [plural] **1** THINGS INSIDE all of the things that are contained inside something **içerik, esas** *Please empty out the contents of your pockets.* **2** INFORMATION the information or ideas that are written in a book, letter, document, etc **içindekiler, içerik** *the contents of his will* **3** BOOK a list in a book that tells you what different parts the book contains **(kitap) içindekiler bölümü** *a table of contents*

┌─ **contest** ...... İLE BİRLİKTE KULLANILAN KELİMELER ─┐
enter/be in a contest ● win a contest ● a **close** contest ● a contest **between** sb and sb ● a contest **for** sth

contest¹ /'kɒntest/ *noun* [C] a competition or election **yarışma, müsabaka**

contest² /kən'test/ *verb* [T] **1** to say formally that something is wrong or unfair and try to have it changed **itiraz etmek, karşı çıkmak** *Mr Hughes went back to court to contest the verdict.* **2** to compete for something **yarışmak, yarışmaya katılmak, müsabakaya girmek**

contestant /kən'test°nt/ *noun* [C] someone who competes in a contest **yarışmacı**

context /'kɒntekst/ *noun* [C, U] **1** all the facts, opinions, situations, etc relating to a particular thing or event **bağlam, bir konuya ilişkin tüm unsurlar** *This small battle is important in the context of Scottish history.* **2** other words that were said or written at the same time as the word or words you are talking about **bağlam, sözcüklerin birbirine ilişkin oluşturduğu**

anlam ortamı, genel sözcük bağamı *Taken out of context, her remark sounded like an insult.*

ᴏ⟋**continent** /'kɒntɪnənt/ *noun* [C] one of the seven main areas of land on the Earth, such as Asia, Africa, or Europe **kıta**

the Continent /'kɒntɪnənt/ *noun UK* the main part of land in Europe, not including Britain **Avrupa kıtası, Avrupa**

continental /ˌkɒntɪ'nent°l/ *adjective* relating to a continent **Avrupa kıtasına ilişkin** *the continental US*

Continental /ˌkɒntɪ'nent°l/ *adjective mainly UK* relating to Europe, but not Britain **Avrupa'ya ilişkin**

ˌ**continental 'breakfast** *noun* [C] a breakfast (= morning meal) consisting of fruit juice, coffee, and bread **ekmek, meyve suyu ve kahveden oluşan bir tür kahvaltı**

contingency /kən'tɪndʒənsi/ *noun* [C] **1** an event or situation that might happen in the future, especially one which could cause problems **olasılık, ihtimal, ihtiyat, ileride soruna neden olabilecek olaylar veya durumlar** *a contingency fund/plan* (= money or a plan that can be used if there are problems) **2** a **contingency fee** money that lawyers (= people who advise people about the law and deal with legal situations) charge, which is a share of what the person they represent has won **avukatlık ücreti**

contingent¹ /kən'tɪndʒ°nt/ *noun* [group] **1** a group of people from the same country, organization, etc who are part of a much larger group **heyet, delegasyon 2** a group of soldiers who are part of a larger military group **küçük askeri birlik, kıta**

contingent² /kən'tɪndʒ°nt/ *adjective* **contingent on sth** depending on something else in order to happen **bir şeye bağlı olan** *Buying the new house was contingent on selling the old one.*

continual /kən'tɪnjuəl/ *adjective* happening again and again over a long period of time **sürekli, devamlı, mütemadiyen** *I can't work with these continual interruptions.* ● **continually** *adverb* *Dad continually complains about money.* **sürekli olarak**

continuation /kənˌtɪnju'eɪʃ°n/ *noun* **1** [C] something that comes after an event, situation, or thing to make it continue or go further **devam, uzantı** *Today's meeting will be a continuation of yesterday's talks.* **2** [U, no plural] when something continues to exist, happen, or be used **devamlılık, süreklilik** *the continuation of their partnership*

ᴏ⟋**continue** /kən'tɪnjuː/ *verb* **continuing**, *past* **continued 1** [I, T] to keep happening, existing, or doing something **devam et(tir)mek, sür(dür)mek** [+ to do sth] *It continued to snow heavily for three days.* ○ [+ doing sth] *Ann continued working part-time until June.* **2** [T] to start doing or saying something again, after stopping for a short period of time **ilerle(t)mek, tekrar başlayıp devam etmek** *We'll have to continue this discussion tomorrow.* **3 continue along/down/up, etc** to go further in a particular direction **belli bir yönde ilerlemek, devam etmek**

continued /kən'tɪnjuːd/ *adjective* [always before noun] still happening, existing, or done **devam eden, aralıksız** *his continued success*

continuity /ˌkɒntɪ'njuːəti/ *noun* [U] the state of continuing for a long period of time without being changed or stopped **devamlılık, süreklilik**

continuous¹ /kən'tɪnjuəs/ *adjective* **1** happening or existing without stopping **devamlı, sürekli** *continuous pain* ○ *ten years of continuous service in the army* **2** The continuous form of a verb is used to show that an action is continuing to happen. The sentence 'He was eating lunch.' is in the continuous form. **fiillerin geçmişte ve şimdiki zaman içinde devamlılık bildirme hali** • **continuously** *adverb Their baby cried continuously all afternoon.* **hiç durmadan devam ederek**

the continuous /kən'tɪnjuəs/ *noun* the continuous form of the verb **fiillerin devam eden zaman bildirme hali**

contort /kən'tɔːt/ *verb* [I, T] If your face or body contorts, or you contort it, you twist it into a different shape, often because you are experiencing a strong emotion. **buruşturma, çarpıtma** *His face was contorted with pain.*

contour /'kɒntʊər/ *noun* [C] **1** the shape of the outer edge of something **bir şeyin dış hatları, görünüşü, silueti** *the contours of her body* **2** (*also* '**contour** ˌline**) a line on a map joining places that are at the same height (**harita**) **eşyükselti çizgileri, (çizimlerde) tesfiye eğrisi**

contra- /kɒntrə-/ *prefix* against or opposite **karşı, zıt-** anlamında önek *to contradict* (= say the opposite) ○ *contraception* (= something that is used to prevent pregnancy)

contraband /'kɒntrəbænd/ *noun* [U] goods that are brought into or taken out of a country illegally **kaçak/sirkat eşya/mal**

contraception /ˌkɒntrə'sepʃən/ *noun* [U] methods that prevent a woman from becoming pregnant **hamileliği önleme, doğum kontrolü**

contraceptive /ˌkɒntrə'septɪv/ *noun* [C] a drug or object that prevents a woman from becoming pregnant **hamileliği önleyen/doğum kontrol hapı/nesnesi**

░░░ contract ...... İLE BİRLİKTE KULLANILAN KELİMELER

enter **into**/negotiate/sign a contract • breach/break/end/terminate a contract • **in** a contract • the **terms of** a contract • a contract **between** sb and sb/**with** sb

---

o∗**contract**[1] /'kɒntrækt/ *noun* [C] a legal agreement between two people or organizations, especially one that involves doing work for a particular amount of money **sözleşme, mukavele**

contract[2] /kən'trækt/ *verb* **1** [REDUCE] [I, T] to become smaller or shorter, or to make something do this **çek (tir)mek, kısal(t)mak, küçül(t)mek** *The wood contracts in dry weather.* **2** [DISEASE] [T] *formal* to get a serious disease **hastalık kapmak, yakalanmak, bulaşmak** *She contracted malaria while living abroad.* **3** [AGREEMENT] [I, T] to make a legal agreement with someone to do work or to have work done for you **sözleşme/mukavele yapmak, imzalamak** [+ to do sth] *He's been contracted to perform in five shows.*

contract out sth *phrasal verb* to make a formal arrangement for other people to do work that you are responsible for **bir işi sözleşmeyle/mukaveleyle başkasına yaptırmak, vermek** *They've contracted out the cleaning to a private firm.*

contraction /kən'trækʃən/ *noun* **1** [MUSCLE] [C] a strong, painful movement of the muscles that a woman has when she is having a baby (**hamile**) **kasların kasılması** *She was having contractions every ten minutes.* **2** [WORD] [C] a short form of a word or group of words **kısaltma, kısaltılmış sözcükler** *'Won't' is a contraction of 'will not'.* **3** [REDUCTION] [U] when something becomes smaller or shorter **büzülme, çekme, kısalma, küçülme**

contractor /kən'træktər/ *noun* [C] a person or company that supplies goods or does work for other people **yüklenici, müteahhit, işi yapan kişi/şirket**

contractual /kən'træktʃuəl/ *adjective* relating to or stated in a contract (= legal agreement) **sözleşmeyle/mukaveleyle ilgili** *a contractual dispute*

contradict /ˌkɒntrə'dɪkt/ *verb* **1** [T] If two things that are said or written about something contradict each other, they are so different that they cannot both be true. **çelişmek, aykırı olmak, uyuşmamak, tezat yaratmak** *His account of the accident contradicts the official government report.* **2** [I, T] to say that what someone else has just said is wrong **karşı çıkmak, aksini iddia etmek**

contradiction /ˌkɒntrə'dɪkʃən/ *noun* **1** [C] a big difference between two things that are said or written about the same subject, or between what someone says and what they do **çelişki, tezat, aykırılık** *There is a clear contradiction between what she says and what she does.* **2** [U] when you say that what someone has just said is wrong **itiraz, inkar, karşı çıkma, tezat kabul etme 3 a contradiction in terms** a phrase that is confusing because it contains words that seem to have opposite meanings **yanlış anlaşılmaya sebep olabilecek tam zıt/karmaşık anlam taşıyan ifade** *An honest politician - isn't that a contradiction in terms?*

contradictory /ˌkɒntrə'dɪktəri/ *adjective* If two statements about the same subject or two actions by the same person are contradictory, they are very different. **çelişkili, birbirine zıt/aykırı**

contraption /kən'træpʃən/ *noun* [C] a machine or object that looks strange or complicated **neye benzediği anlaşılmayan makina veya nesne**

contrary[1] /'kɒntrəri/ *noun* **1 to the contrary** saying or showing the opposite **aksine, aksini** *She claimed she hadn't been involved, despite evidence to the contrary.* **2 on the contrary** used to show that the opposite of what has just been said is true **bilakis, tam tersi** *"You're a vegetarian, aren't you?" "On the contrary, I love meat."*

contrary[2] /'kɒntrəri/ *adjective* **1** opposite or very different **aksi, zıt, ters** *a contrary opinion/view* **2 contrary to sth** opposite to what someone said or thought **aksine, tersine** *Contrary to popular belief, bottled water is not always better than tap water.* **b** If something is contrary to a rule, it does not obey that rule. **zıddına, tersine**

░░░ contrast ...... İLE BİRLİKTE KULLANILAN KELİMELER

1 a complete/sharp/striking contrast • the contrast **between** sth and sth
2 in direct/marked/sharp/stark contrast (**to** sth)

---

o∗**contrast**[1] /'kɒntrɑːst/ *noun* [C, U] **1** an obvious difference between two people or things **karşılaştırma, kıyaslama, tezat, zıtlık** *The contrast between their lifestyles couldn't be greater.* ○ *The busy north coast of the island is in sharp contrast to the peaceful south.* **2 by/in contrast** used to show that someone or something is completely different from someone or something else ...**e zıt olarak; ...nin aksine** *She's quite petite, in contrast with her tall sister.*

contrast[2] /kən'trɑːst/ *verb* **1** [T] to compare two people or things in order to show the differences between them **karşılaştırmak, kıyaslamak, birbiriyle karşılaştırmak** *If you contrast his early novels with his later work, you can see how his writing has developed.* **2** [I] If one thing contrasts with another, it is very different from it. **tezat teşkil etmek, farklılıkları göstermek** *The sharpness of the lemons contrasts with the sweetness of the honey.*

contrasting /kən'trɑːstɪŋ/ *adjective* very different **çelişen, zıtlık yaratan, farklı** *contrasting colours/styles*

contravene /ˌkɒntrə'viːn/ verb [T] formal to do something that is forbidden by a law or rule **ihlal etmek, çiğnemek** ● **contravention** /ˌkɒntrə'venʃᵊn/ noun [C, U] By accepting the money, she was **in contravention of** company rules. **yasayı çiğneme**

◦**contribute** /kən'trɪbjuːt/, /'kɒntrɪbjuːt/ verb [I, T] **1** to give something, especially money, in order to provide or achieve something together with other people **katkıda/bağışta/yardımda bulunmak** I contributed $20 **towards** Andrea's present. **2** to write articles for a newspaper, magazine, or book **makale yazmak, yazarak katkıda bulunmak** She contributes to several magazines.

contribute to sth phrasal verb to be one of the causes of an event or a situation **katkısı olmak, rol oynamak, katkıda bulunmak** Smoking contributed to his early death.

◦**contribution** /ˌkɒntrɪ'bjuːʃᵊn/ noun [C] **1** something that you do to help produce or develop something, or to help make something successful **yardım, katılım** She has **made** a major contribution **to** our work. **2** an amount of money that is given to help pay for something **maddi katkı, bağış** a generous contribution to charity

contributor /kən'trɪbjʊtəʳ/ noun [C] **1** [ARTICLE] someone who writes articles for a newspaper, magazine, or book **yazı ile katkıda bulunan 2** [MONEY] someone who gives something, especially money, together with other people **destekçi, destekleyen, 3** [CAUSE] one of the causes of something **sebep, neden, faktör** Speeding is a major contributor to road accidents.

contributory /kən'trɪbjʊtᵊri/ adjective helping to cause something **yardımcı, yardım eden, katkı sağlayan**

contrive /kən'traɪv/ verb [T] formal to manage to do something difficult, or to make something happen, by using your intelligence or by tricking people **becermek, bir yolunu bulup halletmek, (argo) allem kallem edip halletmek, tasarlamak, şu ya da bu şekilde yapmak** [+ to do sth] They contrived to meet in secret.

contrived /kən'traɪvd/ adjective Something that is contrived seems false and not natural. **yapmacık, sahte, suni, tabi olmayan**

◦**control**¹ /kən'trəʊl/ noun **1** [POWER] [U] the power to make a person, organization, or object do what you want **güç, kontrol, hakimiyet** He has no control over the class. ○ The police are **in control of** the situation. ○ He **lost control** of the vehicle. **2** [RULE] [U] the power to rule or govern an area **yetki, idari hakimiyet, yönetim yetkisi** Soldiers **took control of** the airport. **3 under control** being dealt with successfully **kontrol altında** Don't worry - everything's under control. ○ I couldn't **keep** my drinking **under control**. **4 out of control** If something or someone is out of control, you cannot influence, limit, or direct them. **kontrol dışı, kontrolden çıkmış, haddini aşan 5** [RULE] [C, U] a rule or law that limits something **(kural, kanun vb.) sınırlama, tahdit** The government has introduced tighter immigration controls. **6** [CALM] [U] the ability to be calm **kendi kendini denetleme, sakinliğini koruma** It took a lot of control to stop myself hitting him. **7** [EQUIPMENT] [C] a switch or piece of equipment that you use to operate a machine or vehicle **(araç, makina vb.) açma kapama düğmesi/levyesi, kumanda kolu** Where's the volume control on your stereo? **8** [OFFICIAL PLACE] [C, U] a place where something official, usually a document, is checked **(belge, kimlik vb.) denetlenen, konrtol edilen nokta/yer** passport/immigration control **9** [IN EXPERIMENT] a person or thing that is used to compare with someone or something that

is having an experiment done on them ⊃See also: birth control, remote control, self-control.

◦**control**² /kən'trəʊl/ verb [T] controlling, past controlled **1** [MAKE SB DO STH] to make a person, organization, or object do what you want **kontrol etmek, denetlemek, ayarlamak** This switch controls the temperature. ○ Can't you control your dogs? **2** [LIMIT] to limit the number, amount, or increase of something **sınırlandırmak, bir şeyin kullanımını/miktarını/sayısını kontrol etmek** Fire crews struggled to control the blaze. **3** [RULE] to rule or govern an area **bir yeri yönetmek, idare etmek, kontrol etmek** The whole area is controlled by rebel forces. **4** [EMOTION] to stop yourself expressing strong emotions or behaving in a silly way **kendini kontrol etmek, duygularını ve davranışlarını zaptetmek** He can't control his temper.

con'trol ˌfreak noun [C] informal someone who wants to control everything about a situation and does not want other people to be involved **herşeyin kontrolünü elinde bulunduran, hakim, tekel**

controller /kən'trəʊləʳ/ noun [C] someone who directs the work of other people **kontrolör, kontrol memuru** a marketing controller

controversial /ˌkɒntrə'vɜːʃᵊl/ adjective causing a lot of disagreement or argument **tartışmalı, tartışmaya açık, nizalı, uyuşmazlık yaratan** a controversial decision/issue

---

🧩 **controversy** ...... İLE BİRLİKTE KULLANILAN KELİMELER

sth **attracts/causes/provokes/sparks** controversy ● the controversy **surrounding** sth ● **bitter/continuing/furious** controversy ● controversy **about/over** sth ● **be at the centre of** a controversy

---

controversy /'kɒntrəvɜːsi/ noun [C, U] a lot of disagreement and argument about something **tartışma, münakaşa, nizah** There is a lot of **controversy over** mobile phone towers.

conundrum /kə'nʌndrəm/ noun [C] a problem or question that is difficult to solve **çözümü güç sorun, dert, problem**

convalescence /ˌkɒnvə'lesᵊns/ noun [U] the period of time when you rest and get better after a serious illness **iyileşme süreci, nekâhet** ● **convalesce** verb [I] **nekahat döneminde olmak**

convene /kən'viːn/ verb [I, T] formal to arrange a meeting, or to meet for a meeting **topla(n)mak, bir araya gelmek, toplantı yapmak** The committee convenes three times a year.

convenience /kən'viːniəns/ noun **1** [U] when something is easy to use and suitable for what you want to do **uygunluk, kolaylık** the convenience of credit cards **2** [C] something that makes life easier **rahatlık, yaşam kolaylıkları, konfor** Fortunately, the house has every modern convenience.

con'venience ˌfood noun [C] food that can be prepared quickly and easily **çarçabuk hazırlanan yiyecek, hazır/paketlenmiş yiyecek/gıda**

con'venience ˌstore noun [C] mainly US a shop that sells food, drinks, etc, and is usually open late **büfe, geç saatlere kadar açık olan yiyecek ve içecek satan küçük dükkan**

convenient /kən'viːniənt/ adjective **1** easy to use or suiting your plans well **tam, müsait, uygun** When would be a convenient time to meet? **2** near or easy to get to **yakın, ulaşımı kolay, elverişli** The new supermarket is very convenient for me. ● **conveniently** adverb **elverişli bir şekilde**

convent /'kɒnvənt/ *noun* [C] a building where nuns (= religious women) live and pray together **rahibe manastırı**

convention /kən'venʃ°n/ *noun* 1 [MEETING] [C] a large formal meeting of people with the same interest or work **kongre, toplantı, konferans** *the Democratic Party convention* 2 [CUSTOM] [C, U] a usual and accepted way of behaving or doing something **âdet, gelenek, görenek** *In many countries it is the convention to wear black at funerals.* 3 [AGREEMENT] [C] a formal agreement between countries **resmi antlaşma, konvansiyon** *an international convention on human rights*

conventional /kən'venʃ°n°l/ *adjective* 1 Conventional people are traditional and not willing to try new ideas. **muhafazakâr, tutucu, değişime açık olmayan** 2 Conventional objects or ways of doing things are the usual ones which have been used for a long time. **geleneksel, törelere/yerleşik uygulamalara dayalı, göreneklere ilişkin** *conventional farming/medicine* 3 **conventional arms/forces/warfare, etc** not involving the use of nuclear weapons **nükleer silahların dışındaki tüm silahlar; konvansiyonel/geleneksel silahlar/güçler/savaşlar vs.** 4 **conventional wisdom** what most people believe **kamu oyu, yaygın kanı/kanaat/anlayış/inanç** ⊃Opposite **unconventional**.

conventionally /kən'venʃ°n°li/ *adverb* in a traditional way **geleneksel/göreneksel olarak** *He dressed conventionally in a suit and tie.*

converge /kən'vɜːdʒ/ *verb* [I] 1 [COME TOGETHER] If lines, roads, or rivers converge, they meet at a particular point. **birleşmek, kesişmek** 2 [FORM GROUP] to move towards a particular point and form a group there **belli bir noktada toplanmak** *The protesters converged on the town square.* 3 [BECOME SIMILAR] If ideas, interests, or systems converge, they become more similar to one another. **(fikir, ilgi, sistem) birbirine benzemek, ortak bir noktada benzeşmek** ● **convergence** *noun* [U] **birleşim noktası**

꙳꙳꙳ conversation ...... İLE BİRLİKTE KULLANILAN KELİMELER

engage in/have/join in/strike up a conversation ● **make** conversation ● a **brief/casual/long/polite/private** conversation ● a conversation **about** sth ● a conversation **between** sb and sb

---

ᴏ▪**conversation** /ˌkɒnvə'seɪʃ°n/ *noun* [C, U] a talk between two or more people, usually an informal one **konuşma, sohbet** *a telephone conversation* ○ *We had a conversation about football.* ● **conversational** *adjective* relating to or like a conversation **konuşma/sohbet ile ilgili** *a conversational style*

converse /kən'vɜːs/ *verb* [I] *formal* to talk with someone **konuşmak, sohbet etmek**

conversely /kɒn'vɜːsli/ *adverb* used to introduce something that is different to something you have just said **bunun aksine, zıddına, tam tersi olarak** *Dark lipsticks make your mouth look smaller. Conversely, light shades make it larger.*

conversion /kən'vɜːʒ°n/ *noun* [C, U] 1 when the appearance, form, or purpose of something is changed **değişim, dönüşüm** *the country's conversion to democracy* 2 when someone changes to a new religion or belief **din/inanç değiştirme** *her conversion to Christianity*

convert¹ /kən'vɜːt/ *verb* 1 [I, T] to change the appearance, form, or purpose of something **dönüştürmek, değiştirmek, döndürmek** *The old warehouse was converted into offices.* ○ *How do you convert miles into kilometres?* 2 [I, T] to change to a new religion, belief, etc, or to make someone do this **dinini değiştir(t)mek, dininden dön(dürt)mek** *When did he convert to Islam?*

convert² /'kɒnvɜːt/ *noun* [C] someone who has been persuaded to change to a different religion or belief **dinini değiştiren kimse** *a Catholic convert*

convertible¹ /kən'vɜːtəbl/ *adjective* able to be converted **dönüştürülebilen, değiştirilebilen, çevrilebilen**

convertible² /kən'vɜːtəbl/ *noun* [C] a car with a folding roof **üstü açılır araba**

convex /kɒn'veks/ *adjective* A convex surface curves out. **dışbükey** *a convex mirror/lens*

convey /kən'veɪ/ *verb* [T] 1 to communicate information, feelings, or images to someone **nakletmek, aktarmak, açığa çıkarmak, ifade etmek** *She always conveys a sense of enthusiasm for her work.* 2 to transport something or someone to a particular place **taşımak, götürmek**

conveyor belt /kən'veɪəˌbelt/ *noun* [C] a continuous moving piece of rubber or metal used to transport objects from one place to another **taşıyıcı bant**

convict¹ /kən'vɪkt/ *verb* [T] to decide officially in a court of law that someone is guilty of a particular crime **mahkûm etmek, suçlu bulmak** [often passive] *He was convicted of murder.* ○ *a convicted criminal*

convict² /'kɒnvɪkt/ *noun* [C] someone who is in prison because they are guilty of a particular crime **mahkûm, suçlu**

conviction /kən'vɪkʃ°n/ *noun* 1 [C] when someone is officially found to be guilty of a particular crime **mahkumiyet, sabıka** *He already had two convictions for burglary.* 2 [C, U] a strong opinion or belief **inanç, kanaat, itikât** *religious/moral convictions*

convince /kən'vɪns/ *verb* [T] 1 to make someone believe that something is true **ikna etmek, inandırmak** [+ that] *He tried to convince me that I needed a new car.* ○ *She convinced the jury of her innocence.* 2 to persuade someone to do something **razı etmek, ikna etmek** [+ to do sth] *I convinced her to go to the doctor's.*

convinced /kən'vɪnst/ *adjective* completely certain about something **emin, inanmış** [+ (that)] *I'm convinced that he's made a mistake.*

convincing /kən'vɪnsɪŋ/ *adjective* 1 able to make you believe that something is true or right **inandırıcı, ikna edici** *a convincing argument* 2 a **convincing win/victory** a win or victory where the person or team that wins is much better than the people they are competing against **kesin/tam/parlak zafer, galibiyet** ● **convincingly** *adverb* **ikna eder şekilde**

convoluted /'kɒnvəluːtɪd/ *adjective formal* extremely complicated and difficult to understand **son derece karmaşık ve anlaşılmaz** *a convoluted argument/story*

convoy /'kɒnvɔɪ/ *noun* [C] a group of vehicles or ships that travel together **konvoy**

convulsion /kən'vʌlʃ°n/ *noun* [C] a sudden uncontrollable movement of muscles in your body, caused by illness or drugs **ani kasılma, sarsılma, havale geçirme**

coo /kuː/ *verb* [I] cooing, *past* cooed 1 to make a soft, low sound, like a pigeon (= large, grey bird) **güvercin, kumru gibi ses çıkarmak** 2 to speak in a soft, low voice **yumuşak ve alçak sesle konuşmak**

ᴏ▪**cook¹** /kʊk/ *verb* 1 [I, T] to prepare food and usually heat it **yemek pişirmek/hazırlamak** *Who's cooking this evening?* ○ *She cooked the meat in oil and spices.* 2 [I] If food cooks, it is heated until it is ready to eat. **pişmek** *The rice is cooking.* ● **cooked** *adjective* not raw **pişmiş**
cook sth up *phrasal verb informal* to invent a story, plan, etc, usually dishonestly **uydurmak, sinsi sinsi hazırlamak, planlamak**

cook

bake

fry

boil

grill   roast

cook² /kʊk/ *noun* [C] someone who prepares and cooks food **aşçı**

cookbook /'kʊkbʊk/ (*also UK* **cookery book**) *noun* [C] a book containing instructions for preparing food **yemek kitabı**

cooker /'kʊkə^r/ *UK* (*UK/US* **stove**) *noun* [C] a piece of equipment used to cook food **üstü ocaklı fırın** *an electric cooker* ⊃See also: **pressure cooker.**

cookery /'kʊkᵊri/ *noun* [U] *UK* preparing or cooking food **yemek sanatı, mutfak sanatı, aşçılık**

ˈcookery ˌbook *UK* (*UK/US* **cookbook**) *noun* [C] a book containing instructions for preparing food **aşçılık/ yemek kitabı**

∘⁻**cookie** /'kʊki/ *noun* [C] **1** *US* (*also UK* **biscuit**) a thin, flat cake that is dry and usually sweet **kurabiye, kuru pasta** ⊃*Orta kısımdaki renkli sayfalarına bakınız.* **2** a piece of information stored on your computer which contains information about Internet documents you have looked at **bakılan internet dokümanlarına ilişkin bilginin bilgisayarda saklandığı küçük bilgi**

∘⁻**cooking** /'kʊkɪŋ/ *noun* [U] **1** preparing or cooking food **yemek pişirme** *I do most of the cooking.* **2** a style of preparing food **yemek pişirme tarzı** *vegetarian/ French cooking* ● **cooking** *adjective* [always before noun] suitable to cook with **birlikte pişirilebilen** *cooking oil/apples*

∘⁻**cool¹** /ku:l/ *adjective* **1** COLD slightly cold, but not too cold **serin, soğuk** *a cool breeze/day* ○ *cool water* **2** GOOD *informal* good, stylish, or fashionable **iyi, klas ve modaya uygun** *He looks really cool in those sunglasses.* **3** CALM calm and not emotional **sakin ve fazla duygusal olmayan, serin kanlı** *She seemed cool and confident.* **4** UNFRIENDLY unfriendly **samimi olmayan, soğuk, kayıtsız, ilgisiz 5 be cool with sth** *informal* to be happy to accept a situation or suggestion **memnuniyetle kabul etmek** *Yeah, we could leave later - I'm cool with that.* ● **coolness** *noun* [U] **serinlik**

cool² /ku:l/ *verb* [I, T] **1** to become less hot, or to make something become less hot **serinle(t)mek, soğu(t) mak** *Allow the bread to cool before slicing it.* **2** If emotions or relationships cool, or if something cools them, they become less strong. **ilişki, duygu vb. zayıfla(t) mak, etkisi azalmak, eski önemini yitirmek**

cool (sb/sth) down/off *phrasal verb* **1** to become less hot, or to make someone or something become less hot **soğumak, soğutmak** *We went for a swim to cool off.* **2** to

become calmer, or to make someone become calmer **sakinleş(tir)mek, sükûnete er(dir)mek**

cool³ /ku:l/ *noun* **1 the cool** a cool temperature **serinlik** *the cool of the early morning* **2 keep your cool** to remain calm **sakin olmak, sükûnetini korumak** ● **3 lose your cool** to suddenly become very angry **kontrolünü kaybetmek, kızmak, sinirlenmek**

cool⁴ /ku:l/ *exclamation informal* used when you like something or agree to something **Harika! İşte bu! Güzel! Çok hoş! vb. (hoşlanma ve kabul belirten) ünlem**

coolly /'ku:lli/ *adverb* without showing emotion or interest **sakin, soğukkanlı, kayıtsız, ilgisizce** *Her colleagues reacted coolly to the idea.*

coop¹ /ku:p/ *noun* [C] a cage for birds such as chickens **tavuk kümesi**

coop² /ku:p/ *verb*
coop sb up *phrasal verb* to keep a person or animal in a small area **tıkmak, tıkıştırmak, zorla yerleştirmek/ sokmak** [often passive] *We've been cooped up in a plane all day.*

co-op /'kəʊɒp/ *noun* [C] *informal short for* cooperative² **işbirliği, birliktelik, ortak çalışma**

cooperate (*also UK* co-operate) /kəʊ'ɒpᵊreɪt/ *verb* [I] **1** to work together with someone in order to achieve the same aim **işbirliği yapmak, birlikte çalışmak** *Witnesses are cooperating with detectives.* ○ *Several countries are cooperating in the relief effort.* **2** to help someone or do what they ask **birine yardım etmek, elbirliği etmek** *We can get there early as long as the children will cooperate.*

cooperation (*also UK* co-operation) /kəʊˌɒpə'reɪʃᵊn/ *noun* [U] when you work together with someone or do what they ask you **işbirliği, ortaklık, yardım** *international cooperation* ○ *The clubs work in close cooperation with the Football Association.*

cooperative¹ (*also UK* co-operative) /kəʊ'ɒpᵊrətɪv/ *adjective* **1** willing to help or do what people ask **birlikte çalışmayı seven, işbirliğine yatkın** *a cooperative and polite employee* **2** involving people working together to achieve the same aim **birlikte olan, beraber çalışan, ortaklık gerektiren** *a cooperative relationship* ● **cooperatively** *adverb* **işbirlikçi bir şekilde**

cooperative² (*also UK* co-operative) /kəʊ'ɒpᵊrətɪv/ *noun* [C] a business or organization owned and managed by the people who work in it **kooperatif**

coordinate¹ (*also UK* co-ordinate) /kəʊ'ɔ:dɪneɪt/ *verb* [T] to make different people or things work together effectively, or to organize all the different parts of an activity **etken çalışmayı düzenlemek, ayarlamak; koordine etmek, birlikte çalışmayı sağlamak/yürütmek** *My manager is coordinating the new project.*

coordination (*also UK* co-ordination) /kəʊˌɔ:dɪ'neɪʃᵊn/ *noun* [U] **1** when you organize the different parts of an activity or make people or things work together effectively **verimli/ortak çalışmayı düzenleme, koordinasyon** *The President called for closer coordination between business and government.* **2** the ability to make different parts of your body move together in a controlled way **bedensel faaliyetlerin ve uzuvların işbirliği/koordinasyon içinde çalışması** *Dancing helps develop balance and coordination.*

coordinator (*also UK* co-ordinator) /kəʊ'ɔ:dɪneɪtə^r/ *noun* [C] someone who organizes the different parts of an activity or makes people or things work together effectively **ortak çalışmaları düzenleyen, yürüten kişi, koordinatör**

cop /kɒp/ *noun* [C] *mainly US informal* a police officer **polis**

cope /kəʊp/ *verb* [I] to deal quite successfully with a difficult situation **başa çıkmak, halletmek, altından kalkmak** *How do you cope with stress?*

copier /ˈkɒpiəʳ/ *mainly US* (*UK/US* photocopier) *noun* [C] a machine which produces copies of documents by photographing them **fotokopi makinası**

copious /ˈkəʊpiəs/ *adjective* [always before noun] in large amounts **bolca, çok bol, aşırı fazla** *They drank copious amounts of wine.* ● **copiously** *adverb* **çokça**

copper /ˈkɒpəʳ/ *noun* 1 [METAL] [U] a soft, red-brown metal, used in electrical equipment and to make coins, etc (symbol Cu) **bakır** *copper wire* 2 [MONEY] [C] *UK* a brown coin with a low value **bozuk para, madeni para** 3 [POLICE] [C] *UK informal* a police officer **polis**

o▴**copy¹** /ˈkɒpi/ *noun* [C] 1 something that is made to look exactly like something else **kopya, benzer** *Always make copies of important documents.* 2 a single book, newspaper, etc of which many have been produced **nüsha, adet, baskı** *Four million copies of the book were sold in the first year.* ⊃See also: carbon copy.

o▴**copy²** /ˈkɒpi/ *verb* 1 [PRODUCE] [T] to produce something that is similar or exactly the same as something else **kopyalamak, kopyasını çıkarmak, çoğaltmak** *Copy the file onto disk.* ○ *The design was copied from the American model.* 2 [BEHAVE] [T] to behave like someone else **birinin davranışlarını taklit etmek** *He likes to copy his older brother.* 3 [CHEAT] [I, T] to cheat by looking at and using someone else's work **kopya çekmek/yapmak** *She copied his answers.*
copy sth out *phrasal verb UK* If you copy out a piece of writing, you write it out again on a piece of paper. **bir yazının kopyasını çıkarmak, kopya etmek, yazmak**
copy sb in on sth *phrasal verb* If you copy somebody in on something, you give them a copy of something, usually an email, that you have written for somebody else. **birine birisinin e-posta adresini vermek, yollamak, kopyalamak** *Please copy me in on your email to Dr White.*

copyright /ˈkɒpiraɪt/ *noun* [C, U] the legal right to control the use of an original piece of work such as a book, play, or song **telif hakkı** *The book is protected by copyright.*

coral /ˈkɒrəl/ *noun* [U] a hard, usually pink or white substance produced by a type of very small sea animal **mercan** *a coral reef*

cord /kɔːd/ *noun* [C, U] 1 thick string, or a piece of this **kalın ip, sicim** 2 (*also UK* flex) a piece of wire covered in plastic, used to connect electrical equipment to a power supply **kordon, elektrik kablosu** *an electrical cord* ○ *a telephone cord* ⊃See also: umbilical cord.

cordial /ˈkɔːdiəl/ *adjective* polite and friendly **nazik, samimi, içten** *a cordial invitation* ● **cordially** *adverb* **kibar bir şekilde**

cordless /ˈkɔːdləs/ *adjective* able to operate without an electrical cord **kordonsuz, kablosuz** *a cordless phone*

cordon¹ /ˈkɔːdᵊn/ *noun* [C] a line of police, soldiers, vehicles, etc around an area, protecting it or keeping people out **(polis, asker, araç vb.) kordon**

cordon² /ˈkɔːdᵊn/ *verb*
cordon sth off *phrasal verb* If the police, army, etc cordon off an area, they stop people from entering it. **kordon altına almak, bir bölgeyi/yeri çevrelemek**

cords /kɔːdz/ *noun* [plural] *informal* trousers made from corduroy **fitilli kadife**

corduroy /ˈkɔːdərɔɪ/ *noun* [U] thick, cotton cloth with raised parallel lines on the outside **kadife** *a corduroy jacket*

core /kɔːʳ/ *noun* 1 [IMPORTANT PART] [no plural] the most important part of a system or principle **esas, öz, ana** *core values* ○ *Better health care was at the core of the senator's campaign.* 2 [FRUIT] [C] the hard, central part of certain fruits, such as apples, which contains the seeds **orta, iç, göbek (meyve)** 3 [PLANET] [no plural] the centre of a planet **gezegenin merkezi/ortası** *the Earth's core* ⊃See also: hard core.

coriander /ˌkɒriˈændəʳ/ (*also US* cilantro) *noun* [U] a herb that is used in cooking **kişniş**

cork /kɔːk/ *noun* 1 [U] a light material obtained from the bark (= outer layer) of a particular type of tree **mantar** 2 [C] a small cylindrical piece of this material put in the top of a bottle, especially a wine bottle, to close it **şişe mantarı, tıpa**

corkscrew /ˈkɔːkskruː/ *noun* [C] a piece of equipment used for pulling corks out of wine bottles **şişe açacağı, tirbüşon**

corn /kɔːn/ *noun* [U] 1 *mainly UK* a crop of grain, or the seed from this crop used to make flour or feed animals **tahıl, ekin, tahıl tanesi** *fields of corn* 2 *US* (*UK* sweetcorn) a tall plant with yellow seeds that are cooked and eaten as a vegetable **mısır** ⊃Orta kısımdaki renkli sayfalarına bakınız.

o▴**corner¹** /ˈkɔːnəʳ/ *noun* [C] 1 [POINT] the point or area where two lines, walls, or roads meet **köşe, köşebaşı** *There was a television in the corner of the room.* ○ *The pub is on/at the corner of Ross Street and Mill Road.* 2 [PLACE] a part of a larger area, often somewhere quiet or far away **kuytu yer, köşe bucak, sakin yer** *He lives in a beautiful corner of northern California.* 3 [FOOTBALL] a kick or hit taken from the corner of the field in some games, especially football **köşe vuruşu (futbol)** 4 from/out of the corner of your eye If you see something out of the corner of your eye, you just see it, but do not look at it directly. **göz ucuyla bakma/görme** 5 around/round the corner going to happen soon **yakında olacak, kısa sürede olacak** ● 6 cut corners to do something in the quickest or cheapest way, often harming the quality of your work **baştan savma yapmak, baştan savma, üstünkörü yapmak**

corner² /ˈkɔːnəʳ/ *verb* 1 [T] to force a person or animal into a situation or place from which it is hard to escape **köşeye sıkıştırmak** *His attackers cornered him in a dark alley.* 2 **corner the market** to become so successful at selling or making a particular product that almost no one else sells or makes it **satışta başarılı olmak, tekeline almak, ele geçirmek**

cornerstone /ˈkɔːnəstəʊn/ *noun* [C] something very important that something else depends on **köşe taşı, en önemli noktası** *Freedom of speech is the cornerstone of democracy.*

cornflakes /ˈkɔːnfleɪks/ *noun* [plural] a food made from corn (= grain) and eaten with milk for breakfast (= morning meal) **mısır gevreği**

corny /ˈkɔːni/ *adjective informal* repeated so often to be interesting or funny **defalarca tekrarlanan, eski, bilinen** *a corny joke*

coronary¹ /ˈkɒrənᵊri/ *adjective* relating to the heart **kalple ilgili, koroner** *coronary heart disease*

coronary² /ˈkɒrənᵊri/ *noun* [C] a heart attack (= when the heart stops working normally) **kalp krizi, kalp sektesi**

coronation /ˌkɒrəˈneɪʃᵊn/ *noun* [C] a ceremony at which someone is officially made king or queen **(kral, kraliçe) taç giyme töreni**

coroner /'kɒrənəʳ/ *noun* [C] an official who examines the causes of someone's death, usually if it was violent or sudden **ölüm nedenini araştıran adli tıp görevlisi**

Corp *noun* [C] *written abbreviation for* corporation (=used after the name of a large company in the United States) **(kısa) şirket**

corporal /'kɔːpəʳrəl/ *noun* [C] a soldier of low rank in the army or air force **onbaşı**

‚corporal 'punishment *noun* [U] physical punishment, especially of children, usually by hitting with the hand or a stick **dayak cezası, fiziki ceza**

corporate /'kɔːpəʳrət/ *adjective* [always before noun] relating to a large company or group **büyük şirket veya gruba ilişkin** *corporate finance*

corporation /ˌkɔːpəʳ'reɪʃən/ *noun* [C] a large company or group of companies **şirket**

corps /kɔːʳ/ *noun* [C] *plural* **corps 1** a group of people involved in the same job **ekip, heyet, aynı işi yapan bir grup insan** *the press/diplomatic corps* **2** a special part of a military force **kolordu** *the Air Corps*

corpse /kɔːps/ *noun* [C] a dead person's body **ceset**

o͞»**correct¹** /kə'rekt/ *adjective* **1** accurate, or having no mistakes **doğru** *Check that you have the correct information.* ○ *Was that the correct answer?* **2** suitable for a particular situation **uygun** *correct behaviour* ○ *Have you got the correct number of players for the match?* ● **correctly** *adverb* **doğru bir şekilde** ● **correctness** *noun* [U] ⊃See also: politically correct. **doğruluk, düzgünlük**

correct² /kə'rekt/ *verb* [T] **1** [MAKE RIGHT] to make a mistake or problem right or better **düzeltmek** *The new software finds and corrects any errors on the hard disk.* **2** [IMPROVE] to improve the quality of something **kalitesini artırmak** *These contact lenses will help to correct your vision.* **3** [SHOW MISTAKE] to show someone the mistakes in something they have said or written **birinin hatasını göstermek, düzeltmek** *Our teacher normally corrects our pronunciation.*

▨▨▨ *correction* ...... İLE BİRLİKTE KULLANILAN KELİMELER

make a correction ● a **minor/small** correction ● a correction **to** sth

o͞»**correction** /kə'rekʃən/ *noun* [C, U] a change to make something right or better, or when you make such a change **düzeltme** *She made some corrections before handing in the essay.*

corrective /kə'rektɪv/ *adjective formal* intended to improve or correct something **düzeltici, geliştirici** *corrective surgery/lenses*

correlate /'kɒrəleɪt/ *verb* [I, T] If facts or pieces of information correlate, they are connected to each other and influence each other, and if you correlate them, you show their connections. **ilişkisi/bağlantısı olmak; bağlantılı/biribirine ilişkin olmak, bağlantı kurmak, ilişkisini göstermek**

▨▨▨ *correlation* ...... İLE BİRLİKTE KULLANILAN KELİMELER

a **clear/close/direct/high/strong** correlation ● a correlation **between** sth and sth

correlation /ˌkɒrə'leɪʃən/ *noun* [C] a connection between two or more things, usually where one causes or influences the other **ilişkilendirme, bağlantı kurma, karşılıklı ilişki/bağlantı** *The research showed a close correlation between smoking and lung cancer.*

correspond /ˌkɒrɪ'spɒnd/ *verb* [I] **1** to be the same or very similar **aynı/benzer olmak, birbirine uymak** *The newspaper story does not correspond with/to what really happened.* **2** to communicate with someone

by writing letters **mektuplaşmak, yazışmak, haberleşmek**

correspondence /ˌkɒrɪ'spɒndəns/ *noun* **1** [U] letters or emails from one person to another, or the activity of writing and receiving letters or emails **yazışma, haberleşme** *business correspondence* **2** [C, U] when there is a connection or similarity between two or more things **bağlantı, benzerlik, ilişki, uygunluk, mutabakat**

correspondent /ˌkɒrɪ'spɒndənt/ *noun* [C] **1** someone who reports news for newspapers, television, or radio, usually from another country **muhabir 2** someone who writes letters, usually regularly **mektup yazan kimse; mektuplaşan kişi**

corresponding /ˌkɒrɪ'spɒndɪŋ/ *adjective* [always before noun] similar or related **benzer veya ilişkili** *Draw a line between the words with corresponding meanings.*

corridor /'kɒrɪdɔːʳ/ *noun* [C] a passage in a building or train with rooms on one or both sides **koridor**

corroborate /kə'rɒbəreɪt/ *verb* [T] *formal* to say something or provide information that supports what someone says **doğrulamak, teyit etmek, kanıtlarla desteklemek** *A witness corroborated his account of the accident.* ● **corroboration** /kəˌrɒbə'reɪʃən/ *noun* [U] **onaylama**

corrode /kə'rəʊd/ *verb* **1** [I, T] If metal corrodes, or rain or chemicals corrode it, it is slowly damaged by them. **paslan(dır)mak** *Rain corroded the metal pipes.* **2** [T] to slowly damage someone or something **aşın(dır)mak, yıpranmak, yıpratmak, yavaş yavaş zarar vermek** *He was corroded by guilt.* ● **corrosion** /kə'rəʊʒən/ *noun* [U] **paslanma** ● **corrosive** /kə'rəʊsɪv/ *adjective* Acid rain is **highly corrosive. aşındırıcı**

corrugated /'kɒrəgeɪtɪd/ *adjective* [always before noun] Corrugated metal or cardboard has parallel rows of folds that look like waves. **oluklu** *a corrugated iron roof*

corrupt¹ /kə'rʌpt/ *adjective* **1** dishonest or illegal **ahlaksız, namussuz, cibiliyetsiz, hayasız, yasadışı** *a corrupt government* **2** If information on a computer is corrupt, it has been damaged or spoiled. **bozulmuş, kullanılamaz, yıpranmış** *corrupt files*

corrupt² /kə'rʌpt/ *verb* [T] **1** to make someone or something become dishonest or immoral **ahlakını bozmak, ahlakı bozulmak, yoldan çık(arıl)mak, baştan çık(ar)mak** [often passive] *He became corrupted by power and money.* **2** to damage information on a computer **bilgisaya(rı) çök(ert)mek, bilgiyi yok etmek, zarar vermek**

corruption /kə'rʌpʃən/ *noun* [U] **1** dishonest or immoral behaviour, usually by people in positions of power **ahlaki çöküntü/çürüme/kokuşma** *He was arrested for corruption and bribery.* **2** when you cause someone or something to become dishonest or immoral **ahlakını bozma, baştan çıkarma, namussuzluk, ahlaksızlık, hayasızlık** *the corruption of innocent young children*

corset /'kɔːsət/ *noun* [C] a tight piece of underwear worn by women to make themselves look thinner, especially in the past **korse**

cosmetic /kɒz'metɪk/ *adjective* **1** intended to improve your appearance **güzelleştirici, güzel görünmeyi sağlayan 2** involving only small changes or improvements that will not solve a problem **(sorunları çözmede) yüzeysel, göz boyayıcı** *Critics claimed that the changes were only cosmetic.*

cosmetics /kɒz'metɪks/ *noun* [plural] substances that you put on your face or body to improve your appearance **makyaj malzemesi, kozmetik ürünler**

cos͵metic 'surgery *noun* [U] a medical operation to make someone more attractive **güzelleşmek için yapılan tıbbi müdahale/ameliyat**

cosmic /'kɒzmɪk/ *adjective* relating to the whole universe **evrensel, kozmik** *cosmic rays*

cosmopolitan /ˌkɒzmə'pɒlɪtⁿn/ *adjective* **1** consisting of people and things from many different countries **farklı ülke insan ve kültüründen oluşan, kozmopolit** *London is a very cosmopolitan city.* **2** having experience of many different countries or cultures **farklı bir çok kültürü ve ülkeyi içinde barındıran** *a dynamic, cosmopolitan businesswoman*

the cosmos /'kɒzmɒs/ *noun* the whole universe **evren, kâinat**

cost ...... İLE BİRLİKTE KULLANILAN KELİMELER

the cost **of** sth ● **at a cost of** [£500/$1000, etc] ● the **high/low** cost of sth ● **cover** the cost of (doing) sth ● **cut/reduce** costs ● **at no extra** cost ● the cost of **living**

o▪**cost¹** /kɒst/ *noun* **1** [C, U] the amount of money that you need to buy or do something **maliyet, tutar, fiyat, eder** *The cruise ship was built at a cost of $400 million.* ○ *Software is included at no extra cost.* ○ *The cost of living* (= the cost of food, clothes, etc) *has increased.* **2** [no plural] something that you give up or lose, in order to get or achieve something **bedel** *He rescued four people at the cost of his own life.* **3 at all costs** If something must be done at all costs, it is very important that it is done. **neye malolursa olsun, ne pahasına olursa olsun** *We have to succeed at all costs.* **4 to your cost** UK because of a bad experience you have had **edindiği kötü tecrübeye dayanarak/bakarak** *An ankle injury can last a long time, as I know to my cost.*

o▪**cost²** /kɒst/ *verb past* **cost 1** [T] If something costs a particular amount of money, you have to pay that in order to buy or do it. **malolmak, tutmak, para etmek** *How much do these shoes cost?* ○ *It costs $5 to send the package by airmail.* ○ [+ two objects] *It's going to cost me a lot of money to buy a new car.* **2** [+ two objects] to make someone lose something **(birine) masraf açmak,birinin kaybetmesine yol açmak** *His lazy attitude cost him his job.*

cost³ /kɒst/ *verb* [T] to calculate the amount of money needed to do or make something **hesaplamak, paha/değer biçmek** *The building work has been costed at $30,000.*

co-star¹ /'kəʊstɑːʳ/ *noun* [C] one of two famous actors who both have important parts in a particular film **başrolü paylaşan oyuncu**

co-star² /kəʊ'stɑːʳ/ ⓤ /'kəʊstɑːr/ *verb* **co-starring,** *past* **co-starred 1** [T] If a film, play, etc co-stars two or more famous actors, they are in it. **başrolü paylaşarak oynamak, oynatmak 2** [I] to be in a film, play, etc with another famous actor **başrolü paylaşmak** *Hugh Grant co-stars with Julia Roberts in 'Notting Hill'.*

cost-cutting /'kɒstˌkʌtɪŋ/ *noun* [U] actions that reduce the amount of money spent on something **maliyet azaltıcı/düşürücü** *cost-cutting measures/strategies*

cost-effective /ˌkɒstɪ'fektɪv/ *adjective* If something is cost-effective, it achieves good results for little money. **daha düşük fiyata malolan, hesaplı, tasarruflu, ekonomik**

costly /'kɒstli/ *adjective* **1** expensive **pahalı, fahiş, masraflı** [+ to do sth] *It would be too costly to build a swimming pool.* **2** causing a lot of problems, or causing you to lose something important **pahalıya mal olan, ceremesi çok olan, bir çok sorun yaratan** *a costly mistake*

costume /'kɒstjuːm/ *noun* **1** [C, U] a set of clothes that someone wears to make them look like someone or something else, for example in a play **kıyafet, kostüm** *actors in costume* ○ *He arrived at the party dressed in a gorilla costume.* **2** [U] a set of clothes that are typical of a particular country or time in history **millî kıyafet, giysi, kostüm** *Japanese national costume* ⊃See also: swimming costume.

cosy UK (US cozy) /'kəʊzi/ *adjective* comfortable and warm **rahat, samimi, sımsıcak**

cot /kɒt/ UK (US crib) *noun* [C] a bed with high sides for a baby **beşik, bebek karyolası**

'cot ͵death UK (US SIDS) *noun* [C, U] the sudden death of a sleeping baby for no obvious reason **uykuda bebek ölümü**

cottage /'kɒtɪdʒ/ *noun* [C] a small house, usually in the countryside **kulübe, kır/dağ evi, yazlık ev**

͵cottage 'cheese *noun* [U] a soft, white cheese with small lumps in it **çökelek, lor peyniri**

cotton¹ /'kɒtⁿn/ *noun* [U] **1** CLOTH cloth or thread that is produced from the cotton plant **pamuk** *a cotton shirt/dress* **2** PLANT a plant that produces a soft, white substance used for making thread and cloth **pamuk bitkisi 3** FOR CLEANING US (UK cotton wool) a soft mass of cotton, usually used for cleaning your skin **hidrofil pamuk/cilt temizleme pamuğu** ⊃Orta kısımdaki renkli sayfalarına bakınız.

͵cotton 'wool UK (US cotton) *noun* [U] a soft mass of cotton, usually used for cleaning your skin **hidrofil pamuk/cilt temizleme pamuğu** ⊃Orta kısımdaki renkli sayfalarına bakınız.

couch¹ /kaʊtʃ/ *noun* [C] a long, comfortable piece of furniture that two or more people can sit on **kanepe, divan**

couch² /kaʊtʃ/ *verb* **be couched in/as sth** to be expressed in a particular way **belli bir dille/özgün şekilde ifade edilmek** *His explanation was couched in technical language.*

'couch po͵tato *noun* [C] UK humorous a person who is not active and spends a lot of time watching television **tv karşısında hareketsizce saatlerce oturan kişi, tembel/hareketsiz kişi**

o▪**cough¹** /kɒf/ *verb* [I] to make air come out of your throat with a short sound **öksürmek/tıksırmak**

cough sth up *phrasal verb* to make something come out of your lungs or throat by coughing **öksürerek çıkarmak, tükürmek** *Doctors were worried when she started coughing up blood.*

cough (sth) up *phrasal verb informal* to give money to someone although you do not want to **istemeyerek birine para vermek, (argo) sökülmek, ödemek**

cough² /kɒf/ *noun* [C] **1** when you cough, or the sound this makes **öksürük 2** an illness that makes you cough a lot **öksürüğe tutulma, öksürük hastalığı** *Uwe has a nasty cough.* ⊃See also: whooping cough.

o▪**could** *strong form* /kʊd/ *weak form* /kəd/ *modal verb* **1** CAN used as the past form of 'can' to talk about what someone or something was able or allowed to do **can' fiilinin geçmiş zaman hali** *I couldn't see what he was doing.* ○ *You said we could watch television when we'd finished our homework.* **2** POSSIBLE used to talk about what is possible or might happen **bir şeyin olma olasılığını anlatmada kullanılır** *The baby could arrive any day now.* ○ *This kind of crime could easily be prevented.* ○ *She could have* (= might have) *been seriously injured.* **3** ASK used to ask someone politely to do or provide something **bir şeyi nazikçe istemede veya sormada kullanılır** *Could you lend me £5?* ○ *Could I have another drink?* **4** ASK PERMISSION used to ask politely for permission to do something **naizkçe izin istemede kullanılır** *Could I speak to Mr Davis, please?* **5** SUGGEST used to make a suggestion **bir öneride/teklifte bulunmada kullanılır** *You could try painting it a different colour.* **6 I could (have)** used when you feel so happy, sad, angry, etc that you would like to do something **mutlu/ üzgün/kızgın vb. durumda bir şeyi yapma isteğinin bulunduğunu/bulunmadığını anlatmada kullanılır** *I was so grateful I could have kissed her!* ➲See study page **Modal verbs** on page Centre 22.

•━**couldn't** /'kʊd³nt/ *short for* could not **could' yardımcı fiilinin olumsuz hali** *I couldn't understand what he was saying.*

•━**could've** /'kʊdəv/ *short for* could have **geçmişte olasılık bildiren 'could have' fiilinin kısa şekli** *It could've been much worse.*

council, Council /'kaʊns³l/ *noun* [C] **1** a group of people who are elected to control a town, city, or area **meclis, encümen** *Edinburgh City Council* ○ *a council meeting* **2** a group of people who are elected or chosen to give advice or make decisions **divan, konsey, danışma kurulu** *the Medical Research Council* **3 a council house/flat** in the UK a house or flat that is owned by a city or town council and rented to people **Birleşik Krallık'da şehir veya kasaba meclisince sahip olunan ve kiraya verilen diare/ev**

'council e,state *UK* (*US* housing project) *noun* [C] a part of a city with council houses and flats (= homes owned by a council and rented to people) **şehir meclisinin/belediyenin sahip olduğu ve kiraya verilen evlerin/dairelerin bulunduğu bölge** *a Birmingham council estate*

councillor *UK* (*US* councilor) /'kaʊns³lə^r/ *noun* [C] a member of a town, city, or area council **konsey/meclis/divan/kurul üyesi**

counsel¹ /'kaʊns³l/ *noun* **1** [C] a lawyer (= someone who advises people about the law and deals with legal situations) who speaks for someone in court **avukat 2** [U] *literary* advice **nasihat, fikir, tavsiye, öğüt**

counsel² /'kaʊns³l/ *verb* [T] *UK* **counselling**, *past* **counselled**, *US* **counseling**, *past* **counseled 1** *formal* to advise someone to do something **tavsiyede bulunmak, fikir vermek, danışmanlık yapmak** [+ to do sth] *Lawyers had counselled him not to say anything.* **2** to give advice to someone who has problems **nasihat etmek, öğüt vermek**

counselling *UK* (*US* counseling) /'kaʊns³lıŋ/ *noun* [U] the job or process of listening to someone and giving them advice about their problems **danışmanlık hizmeti, müşavirlik** *a counselling service*

counsellor *UK* (*US* counselor) /'kaʊns³lə^r/ *noun* [C] someone whose job is to listen to people and give them advice about their problems **danışman, müşavir, uzman**

•━**count¹** /kaʊnt/ *verb* **1** CALCULATE [T] to see how many people or things there are **saymak, hesap etmek** *I counted the money on the table.* **2** SAY NUMBERS [I] to say numbers in their correct order **sayı saymak, sayarak hesaplamak** *Can you count to twenty in French?* **3** CONSIDER [T] to think of someone or something in a particular way **dikkatle değerlendirmek, dikkate almak** *She counted Tim as her closest friend.* ○ *You should count yourself lucky you weren't hurt.* **4** IMPORTANT [I] to be important **önemli olmak** *I believe that health and happiness count more than money.* ○ *Doesn't my opinion count for anything?* **5** INCLUDE [T] to include something or someone in a calculation **hesaba katmak, dahil etmek, hesaplarken dikkate almak** *There are 1500 people at my school, counting teachers.* **6** BE ACCEPTED [I] to be accepted or allowed as part of something **kabul edilmek, katılmak, dahil edilmek**

I've been to sixteen different countries, but I only spent half an hour in Luxembourg, so that doesn't really count.

count against sb/sth *phrasal verb* to make someone or something more likely to fail **aleyhine olmak, yararına olmamak, dezavantaj olmak, pek faydası olmamak** *She's got the qualifications for the job, but her lack of experience will count against her.*

count sb in *phrasal verb* to include someone in an activity **dahil etmek, hesaba katmak** *If you're going for a pizza, you can count me in.*

count on sb *phrasal verb* to be confident that you can depend on someone **birine güvenmek, bel bağlamak, itimat etmek** *I can always count on my parents to help me.*

count on sth *phrasal verb* to expect something to happen and make plans based on it **bir şeye bel bağlamak, beklemek, ummak** *I didn't count on so many people coming to the party.*

count sth out *phrasal verb* to count coins or pieces of paper money one by one as you put them down **birer birer sayarak destelemek, istiflemek (para)** *She counted out five crisp $20 bills.*

count sb out *phrasal verb* to not include someone in an activity **birini saymamak, hesaba katmamak, dahil etmemek**

count towards sth *phrasal verb* to be part of what is needed to complete something or achieve something **çalışmanın/başarının gerekli bir bölümünü oluşturmak** *This essay counts towards my exam result.*

count up sb/sth *phrasal verb* to add together all the people or things in a group **toplamını hesap etmek**

count² /kaʊnt/ *noun* **1** NUMBER [C] when you count something, or the total number you get after counting **hesaplama, sayma, sayım** [usually singular] *At the last count there were 410 club members.* **2 lose count** to forget how many of something there is **sayısını bilememek, hesabını şaşırmak, sayısını unutmak** *I've lost count of the number of times she's arrived late.* **3 on all/ both/several, etc counts** in all, both, several, etc parts of a situation, argument, etc **tüm, birçok, her iki durumda da/tartışmada da** *I had been wrong on both counts.* **4** RANK [C] (*also* Count) a man of high social rank in some European countries **kont 5** CRIME [C] one of the times that someone has been accused of a particular crime **bir konuda suçlamalardan herbiri; suçlama sayısı** *He was charged with two counts of assault.* ➲See also: **pollen count.**

countable noun /,kaʊntəb³l'naʊn/ (*also* 'count ,noun) *noun* [C] a noun that has both plural and singular forms **sayılabilen isim** ➲See study page **Countable and uncountable nouns** on page Centre 20.

countdown /'kaʊntdaʊn/ *noun* [C] the time just before an important event when people are counting the time until it happens **gerisayım, geriye sayma** [usually singular] *The countdown to the Olympics has begun.*

countenance¹ /'kaʊnt³nəns/ *noun* [C] *literary* the appearance or expression of someone's face **birinin yüzünün görünüşü ve ifadesi; yüz, çehre, sima**

countenance² /'kaʊnt³nəns/ *verb* [T] *formal* to accept that something should happen **bir şeyin olması gerektiğini kabul etmek** *They will not countenance building a new airport.*

counter¹ /'kaʊntə^r/ *noun* [C] **1** IN A SHOP the place in a shop, bank, etc, where people are served **tezgâh, banko** *The woman behind the counter took his money.* **2** SURFACE *US* a flat surface in a kitchen on which food can be prepared **mutfak tezgâhı 3** DISC a small disc used in some games that are played on a board **fiş, marka**

counter² /'kaʊntə^r/ *verb* [T] **1** to prevent something or reduce the bad effect that it has **kötü etkisini azalt-**

mak, etkisizleştirmek *This skin cream claims to counter the effects of sun damage.* **2** to say something to show that what someone has just said is not true **karşılık vermek, mukabelede bulunmak** *"Of course I love him," Clare countered.*

counter³ /ˈkaʊntəʳ/ *adverb* **be/run counter to sth** to have the opposite effect to something else **ters düşmek, aykırı olmak, aksine etkisi olmak** *The new road plans run counter to the government's aim of reducing pollution.*

counter- /kaʊntəʳ-/ *prefix* opposing or as a reaction to **ter-, tersine-,ter yönde-; karşılık, mukabil anlamında ön ek** *a counter-attack* (= an attack on someone who has attacked you)

counteract /ˌkaʊntəʳˈrækt/ *verb* [T] to reduce the bad effect that something else has **etkisiz hale getirmek, etkisizleştirmek, kötü etkilerini azaltmak** *drugs that counteract the side effects of sea sickness*

counter-attack /ˈkaʊntərəˌtæk/ *noun* [C] an attack that you make against someone who has attacked you in a sport, war, or argument **karşı hücum/saldırı ● counter-attack** *verb* [I, T] **karşı saldırı**

counterclockwise /ˌkaʊntəˈklɒkwaɪz/ *US* (*UK* anticlockwise) *adjective, adverb* in the opposite direction to the way the hands (= parts that point to the numbers) of a clock move **saat yönü aksine, sağdan sola doğru** ⊃See picture at **clockwise**.

counterfeit /ˈkaʊntəfɪt/ *adjective* made to look like the real thing, in order to trick people **sahte, kalp, taklit, hakiki olmayan** *counterfeit money/jewellery*

counterpart /ˈkaʊntəpɑːt/ *noun* [C] someone or something that has the same job or position as someone or something in a different place or organization **meslektaşı, karşıtı, muadili, suret, kopya**

counterproductive /ˌkaʊntəprəˈdʌktɪv/ *adjective* having the opposite effect from the one you want **ters etkili, aksine, ters tepen**

countess /ˈkaʊntɪs/ *noun* [C] a woman who has a high social rank in some European countries, especially the wife of an earl or count (= man of high social rank) **kontes** *the Countess of Abingdon*

countless /ˈkaʊntləs/ *adjective* [always before noun] very many **sayısız, pek çok, hesabı belli olmayan** *The song has been played countless times on the radio.*

o⁓**country¹** /ˈkʌntri/ *noun* **1** [C] an area of land that has its own government, army, etc **ülke, memleket** *European countries* **2 the country a** the area away from towns and cities **kır, taşra, sayfiye, şehir dışı b** the people who live in a country **millet, ulus** *The country was shocked by the President's decision.*

country² /ˈkʌntri/ *adjective* [always before noun] in or relating to the areas that are away from towns and cities **kırsal, taşraya ait** *country roads/hotels*

countryman /ˈkʌntrimən/ *noun* [C] *plural* **countrymen** someone from the same country as you **vatandaş, yurttaş**

,**country ˈmusic** (*also* ,country and ˈwestern) *noun* [U] a style of popular music from the southern and western US **ABD'nin batı ve güneyine ait pop müzik türü**

countryside /ˈkʌntrɪsaɪd/ *noun* [U] land that is not in towns or cities and has farms, fields, forests, etc **kırsal alan, taşra, şehir dışı, kırlık alan**

county /ˈkaʊnti/ *noun* [C] an area of Britain, Ireland, or the US that has its own local government **Britanya İrlanda ve ABD'de kendi bölgesel yönetimi olan eyaletten sonraki en büyük alan**

coup /kuː/ *noun* [C] **1** (*also* coup d'état /ˌkuːdeɪˈtɑː/) when a group of people suddenly takes control of a country using force **darbe** *a military coup* **2** an important achievement, often one that was not expected **beklenmedik başarı, iş** *The award is a major coup for the university.*

o⁓**couple¹** /ˈkʌpl/ *noun* **1** [no plural] two or a few **bir çift** *I went to New York with a couple of friends.* ○ *The weather has improved over the last couple of weeks.* **2** [C] two people who are married or having a romantic relationship **çift, karı koca** *a married couple*

couple² /ˈkʌpl/ *verb* **coupled with sth** combined with something else **bir şeyle bitişik, çift olmuş** *Concern about farming methods, coupled with health awareness, have led to a fall in meat consumption.*

coupon /ˈkuːpɒn/ *noun* [C] **1** a piece of printed paper that you can use to buy something at a cheaper price or to get something free **alışveriş kuponu** *Collect 10 coupons to get a free meal.* **2** a printed form in a magazine or newspaper, that you use to send for information, enter a competition, etc **gazete kuponu**

⌜⌐⌐⌐⌐ ***courage*** ...... İLE BİRLİKTE KULLANILAN KELİMELER

have the courage to do sth ● show courage ● sth takes courage ● great/immense/personal courage

courage /ˈkʌrɪdʒ/ *noun* [U] **1** the ability to deal with dangerous or difficult situations without being frightened **cesaret, yüreklilik, korkusuzluk** [+ to do sth] *She didn't have the courage to tell him the truth.* **2 pluck up courage (to do sth)** to decide to do something that you were too frightened to do before **bütün cesaretini toplayıp yapmak**

courageous /kəˈreɪdʒəs/ *adjective* brave **cesur, yürekli, korkusuz ● courageously** *adverb* **cesurca**

courgette /kɔːˈʒet/ *UK* (*US* zucchini) *noun* [C, U] a long, green vegetable which is white inside **yeşil, uzun kabak**

courier /ˈkʊriəʳ/ *noun* [C] **1** someone whose job is to take and deliver documents and parcels **kurye, haberci** **2** *UK* someone whose job is to look after people who are on holiday **rehber, kurye**

o⁓**course** /kɔːs/ *noun* **1 of course a** YES used to say 'yes' and emphasize your answer **elbette, elbet, şüphesiz, kuşkusuz** *"Can you help me?" "Of course!"* **b** OBVIOUS used to show that what you are saying is obvious or already known **herhalde, tabii** *Of course, the Olympics are not just about money.* **2 of course not** used to say 'no' and emphasize your answer **elbette/tabii ki hayır** *"Do you mind if I borrow your pen?" "Of course not."* **3** LESSONS a series of lessons about a particular subject **kurs** *She did a ten-week course in computing.* **4** PART OF MEAL [C] a part of a meal **yemek, kap, tabak** *a three-course dinner* **5** SPORT [C] an area used for horse races or playing golf **parkur, yarış pisti, golf sahası, alan** *a golf course* **6** MEDICINE [C] *mainly UK* a fixed number of regular medical treatments **tertip, kür** *a course of antibiotics* **7** ROUTE [C, U] the direction in which a ship, aircraft, etc is moving **yol, rota, seyir** *During the storm, the boat was blown off course* (= in the wrong direction). **8** ACTION [C] (*also* ,course of 'action) something that you can do in a particular situation **hal tarzı, hareket şekli, biçimi** *I think the best course of action would be to write to him.* **9 during/in/over the course of sth** during a particular time or activity **sırasında, esnasında, zarfında** *In the course of the interview she mentioned her previous experience.* **10 in due course** at a suitable time in the future **vakti gelince, uygun zamanda** *The results will be sent to you in due course.* **11** DEVELOPMENT [no plural] the way something develops, usually over a long time **gelişme, ilerleme** *Nuclear* *weapons have changed the course of modern history.* **12 in the course of time** *UK* gradually, or over a period of time **zamanla, zamanı/sırası gelince, 13 be on course for sth/to do sth** *UK* to be very likely to succeed at something **bir şeyde muhtemelen başarılı olmak 14 run its course** If something runs its course, it continues naturally until it has finished. **doğal sonucuna doğru ilerlemek, hükmünü icra etmek, olacağına varmak** ⊃See also: be on a **collision** course, **crash course**, be **par** for the course.

coursebook /'kɔːsbʊk/ *noun* [C] *UK* a book used by students when they do a particular course of study **ders kitabı**

coursework /'kɔːswɜːk/ *noun* [U] *UK* work done by students as part of their course of study **ders, çalışmalar**

∘⊶**court¹** /kɔːt/ *noun* [C, U] **1** LAW the place where a judge decides whether someone is guilty of a crime **mahkeme** *The suspect appeared in court charged with robbery.* ○ *You can take them to court* (= make them be judged in court) *if they don't pay.* **2 the court** the judge and group of people at a trial who decide whether someone is guilty of a crime **mahkeme heyeti, mahkeme kurulu 3** SPORT an area for playing particular sports **kort, oyun alanı** *a tennis/basketball court* **4** ROYAL HOUSE the official home of a king or queen and the people who live with them **kraliyet sarayı/maiyeti** ⊃See also: **High Court, the supreme court.**

court² /kɔːt/ *verb* **1** PLEASE [T] to try to please someone because you want them to support you or join you **memnun etmek, birinin desteğini istemek için onu memnun etmeye çalışmak** *Adams is being courted by several football clubs.* **2** TRY TO GET [T] to try to get or achieve something **almaya/elde etmeye çalışmak** *court investment/publicity* **3** RELATIONSHIP [I, T] *old-fashioned* to have a romantic relationship with someone you hope to marry **kur yapmak, elde etmeye çalışmak, peşinden koşmak 4 court controversy/danger/disaster, etc** to behave in a way that risks bad results **herşeyi/tehlikeyi/felaketi göze almak, göğüslemek**

courteous /'kɜːtiəs/ *adjective* polite and showing respect **kibar, saygılı, nazik • courteously** *adverb* **saygılı bir şekilde**

courtesy /'kɜːtəsi/ *noun* **1** [U] behaviour that is polite and shows respect, or a polite action or remark **nezaket, kibarlık** *The hotel treats all guests with courtesy.* ○ [+ to do sth] *He didn't even have the courtesy to thank me.* **2 (by) courtesy of sb/sth** If you have something courtesy of someone, they have allowed you to have it. **izniyle, sayesinde; (bir şeyin alınmasına izin verilmesi anlamında) alabilirsiniz, izindir** *The photograph is courtesy of the Natural History Museum.*

courthouse /'kɔːthaʊs/ *noun* [C] *plural* **courthouses** /'kɔːthaʊzɪz/ *mainly US* a building with law courts inside it **adliye sarayı, mahkeme binası**

courtier /'kɔːtiər/ *noun* [C] someone who spent a lot of time in the home of a king or queen in the past **saray mensubu/müdavimi**

court-martial¹ /ˌkɔːt'mɑːʃəl/ *noun* [C] a military court, or a trial in a military court **askeri mahkeme, divanı harp**

court-martial² /ˌkɔːt'mɑːʃəl/ *verb* [T] to judge someone in a military court **askeri mahkemede yargılanmak**

'court ˌorder *noun* [C] an instruction from a law court that someone must do or not do something **mahkeme emri**

courtroom /'kɔːtruːm/ *noun* [C] the room where a judge and other people decide whether someone is guilty of a crime **mahkeme salonu**

courtship /'kɔːtʃɪp/ *noun* [C, U] *formal* the time when people have a romantic relationship with the intention of getting married **kur yapma, uzun/kısa süreli evlilik maksadıyla yapılan flört**

courtyard /'kɔːtjɑːd/ *noun* [C] an open area by a building with walls or buildings around it **avlu,iç bahçe, hayat, taşlık**

∘⊶**cousin** /'kʌzᵊn/ *noun* [C] the child of your aunt or uncle **kuzen**

couture /kuː'tjʊər/ *noun* [U] the design, making, and selling of expensive and fashionable clothes **terzilik, pahalı ve moda kıyafetlere tasarlama, yapma ve satma**

cove /kəʊv/ *noun* [C] a place on the coast where the land curves in **koy, körfez**

covenant /'kʌvᵊnənt/ *noun* [C] a formal written agreement **mukavele, antlaşma, taahhütname, yetki belgesi**

∘⊶**cover¹** /'kʌvər/ *verb* [T] **1** PUT to put something over something else, in order to protect or hide it **örtmek, kapamak, gizlemek** *They covered him with a blanket.* ○ *He covered his face with his hands.* ⊃Opposite **uncover**. **2** LAYER to form a layer on the surface of something **(tabaka) kaplamak,** *Snow covered the trees.* ○ *My legs were covered in/with mud.* **3** DISTANCE to travel a particular distance **(mesafe) yol almak, katetmek, belli bir mesafede seyahat etmek** *We covered 700 kilometres in four days.* **4** AREA to be a particular size or area **(alan) kapsamak** *The town covers an area of 10 square miles.* **5** INCLUDE to include or deal with a subject or piece of information **içermek, kapsamak** *The book covers European history from 1789-1914.* **6** REPORT to report on an event for a newspaper, television programme, etc **anlatmak, haber/bilgi vermek (tv, gazete), röportaj yapmak** *Dave was asked to cover the Olympics.* **7** MONEY to be enough money to pay for something **(para) ödemek, karşılamak, ödemeye yetmek** *£100 should cover the cost of the repairs.* **8** FINANCIAL PROTECTION to provide financial protection if something bad happens **(mali koruma) karşılamak, masraflarını ödemek, kapsamak, yetmek** *travel insurance that covers accident and injury* ⊃See also: touch/cover all the bases (**base¹**).

cover sth up *phrasal verb* to put something over something else, in order to protect or hide it **üstünü örtmek, kaplamak**

cover (sth) up *phrasal verb* to stop people from discovering the truth about something bad **örtbas etmek, saklamak, gizlemek** *She tried to cover up her mistakes.*

∘⊶**cover²** /'kʌvər/ *noun* **1** BOOK [C] the outer part of a book, magazine, etc, that protects the pages **kitap dergi kapağı** *Her picture was on the cover of 'Vogue' magazine.* **2** PROTECTION [C] something you put over something else, usually to protect it **örtü, kapak, paravana, perde** *an ironing board cover* ○ *a lens cover* **3** FINANCIAL [U] financial protection so that you get money if something bad happens **maddi garanti, tazminat, ödeme** *The policy provides £50,000 accidental damage cover.* **4** FROM WEATHER/ATTACK [U] protection from bad weather or an attack **barınak, siper,** *They took cover under some trees until the rain stopped.* **5** FOR ILLEGAL ACTIVITY [C] something used to hide a secret or illegal activity **sırrı veya yasadışı faaliyeti gizleme, örtbas** *The club is used as a cover for a gang of car thieves.*

coverage /'kʌvᵊrɪdʒ/ *noun* [U] **1** the way a newspaper, television programme, etc reports an event or subject **tv veya gazetenin bir haberi, olayı yayınlama/sunma biçimi** *There is live coverage of the game on cable TV.* **2** *mainly US* financial protection so that you get money if something bad happens **tazminat, ödenen para, ödeme**

coveralls /ˈkʌvərɔːlz/ US (UK **overalls**) noun [plural] a piece of clothing that you wear over your clothes to keep them clean while you are working **iş tulumu, iş elbisesi**

covering /ˈkʌvərɪŋ/ noun [C] a layer that covers something **örtü, kaplama, kat, tabaka** a thick covering of snow

covering ˈletter UK (US **ˈcover ˌletter**) noun [C] a letter that you send with something to explain what it is or to give more information about it **ön yazı, üst yazı, açıklayıcı mektup**

covers /ˈkʌvəz/ noun [plural] the sheets and other layers of cloth on your bed that keep you warm **nevresim takımı**

covert /ˈkəʊvɜːt/ adjective done in a secret way **gizli, saklı** covert police operations ● **covertly** adverb **gizli bir şekilde**

cover-up /ˈkʌvərʌp/ noun [C] an attempt to prevent people finding out the truth about a crime or a mistake **örtbas etmek, hasıraltı etmek, delilleri karartmak, saklamak** Police denied accusations of a cover-up.

ˈcover ˌversion noun [C] a recording of a song already recorded by someone else **önceden yapılmış bir şarkıyı yeniden yapma** a cover version of 'Let It Be'

covet /ˈkʌvɪt/ verb [T] formal to want something very much, especially something that someone else has **gözü kalmak, imrenmek, içi gitmek, hasetlik etmek**

○*cow /kaʊ/ noun [C] **1** a large farm animal kept for milk or meat **inek 2** UK informal an offensive word for a woman **kancık, inek, şirret karı**

coward /ˈkaʊəd/ noun [C] someone who is not brave and tries to avoid dangerous or difficult situations **korkak, tabansız, ödlek**

cowardice /ˈkaʊədɪs/ noun [U] behaviour that shows that someone is not brave **korkaklık**

cowardly /ˈkaʊədli/ adjective behaving in a way that shows you are not brave **korkak, ödlek**

cowboy /ˈkaʊbɔɪ/ noun [C] **1** a man whose job is to look after cattle (= animals such as cows) in the US, and who usually rides a horse **kovboy, sığır çobanı, sığırtmaç 2** UK informal someone who does their job badly or who is dishonest in business **sorumsuz, ticarette dürüst davranmayan, üç kağıtçı, dalavereci** cowboy builders

ˈcowboy ˌboots noun [C] a type of boots with pointed toes, first worn by cowboys **kovboy çizmesi** ⊃Orta kısımdaki renkli sayfalarına bakınız.

ˈcowboy ˌhat noun [C] a type of hat with a high top and a wide lower edge, first worn by cowboys **kovboy şapkası**

cower /kaʊəʳ/ verb [I] to bend down or move back because you are frightened **korkup saklanmak, geri çekilmek, ürküp kaçmak**

co-worker /ˌkəʊˈwɜːkəʳ/ noun [C] mainly US someone that you work with **iş arkadaşı**

coy /kɔɪ/ adjective **1** not wanting to give people information about something **ketum, sır tutan, bilgi vermek istemeyen** Nigel's very coy about how much he earns. **2** pretending to be shy **sözde/göya mahcup, utangaç, utanmış gibi davranan,** a coy look ● **coyly** adverb **nazlanır gibi**

coyote /kaɪˈəʊti/ noun [C] a wild animal similar to a dog, that lives in North America **kır kurdu, köpeğe benzer vahşi bir hayvan**

cozy /ˈkəʊzi/ adjective US spelling of cosy **rahat, samimi, sımsıcak**

crab /kræb/ noun [C, U] a sea creature with ten legs and a round, flat body covered by a shell, or the meat from this animal **yengeç**

crack¹ /kræk/ verb **1** [BREAK] [I, T] to break something so that it does not separate, but very thin lines appear on its surface, or to become broken in this way **çatla(t) mak, yar(ıl)mak** The concrete had started to crack. ○ cracked dishes **2** [EGG/NUT] [T] to open an egg or nut by breaking its shell **kabuğunu kırmak 3** [HIT] [T] to hit a part of your body against something hard, by accident **kazara vurmak, çarpmak** He cracked his head on the cupboard door. **4** [SOLVE] [T] informal to solve a difficult problem **zor bir problemi çözmek** It took three months to crack the enemy's code. **5 get cracking** informal to start doing something quickly **bir şeyi yapmaya süratle başlamak 6** [LOSE CONTROL] [I] to lose control of your emotions and be unable to deal with a situation **sinir krizi geçirmek, kendinden geçmek, kontrolü kaybetmek** He finally cracked after years of stress. **7** [NOISE] [I, T] to make a sudden, short noise, or to cause something to make this noise **şırak' diye ses çıkar(t) mak, şaklamak, şaklatmak 8 crack a joke** to tell a joke **fıkra anlatmak/patlatmak/söylemek 9 not all it's cracked up to be** informal (also **not as good as it's cracked up to be** informal) not as good as people think or say **söylendiği gibi/sanıldığı kadar iyi olmamak** Being an actor isn't all it's cracked up to be.

crack down phrasal verb to start dealing with bad or illegal behaviour in a more severe way **sıkı önlemler almak, bastırmak, sindirmek** Police are **cracking down on** crime in the area.

crack up phrasal verb informal to become mentally ill **sinir krizi/buhran geçirmek**

crack (sb) up phrasal verb informal to suddenly laugh a lot, or to make someone suddenly laugh a lot **aniden kahkahaya boğ(ul)mak**

crack² /kræk/ noun **1** [LINE] [C] a line on the surface of something that is damaged **çatlak** Several cups had cracks in them. **2** [NARROW SPACE] [C] a narrow space between two parts of something or between two things **yarık, aralık, açıklık** I could see sunlight through a crack in the curtains. **3** [DRUG] [U] an illegal drug that is very harmful **esrar, uyuşturucu 4** [NOISE] [C] a sudden, short noise **darbe, vuruş** a crack of thunder **5** [JOKE] [C] an unkind joke or remark **nazik olmayan, nükte, fıkra, ifade, söz** He was always making cracks about my weight. **6 have/take a crack at sth** informal to try to do something **girişimde bulunmak, yeltenmek, denemek** I've never put up shelves before, but I'll have a crack at it. **7 the crack of dawn** very early in the morning **şafak, tanyeri, seher vakti** He gets up at the crack of dawn.

crack³ /kræk/ adjective [always before noun] of the highest quality **kaliteli, birinci sınıf, üstün özellikli** a crack regiment

announce/call for/launch/order a crackdown ● a crackdown **on** sth ● a **tough** crackdown ● a **government/police** crackdown

crackdown /ˈkrækdaʊn/ noun [C] when bad or illegal behaviour is dealt with in a very severe way, in order to stop it happening **sıkı tedbir, sert önlem** The police are having **a crackdown on** speeding.

cracker /ˈkrækəʳ/ noun **1** [FOOD] [C] a dry biscuit that you eat with cheese **kraker; ince, gevrek tuzlu bisküvi 2** [CHRISTMAS] [C] (also Christmas cracker) a coloured paper tube with a small toy inside, that people pull open at Christmas (= a Christian holiday) in the UK **patlangaç, maytap, çatapat, kestane fişeği 3** [GOOD] [no plural] UK _informal_ someone or something that is very good **iyi, çok iyi, kafa kişi**

crackle /'krækl/ _verb_ [I] to make a lot of short, dry noises **çatırdamak, hışırdamak** _A fire crackled in the hearth._
• **crackle** _noun_ [no plural] **hışırdama sesi**

cradle¹ /'kreɪdl/ _noun_ **1** BED [C] a baby's bed, especially one that swings from side to side **beşik 2** TELEPHONE the part of a telephone that holds the receiver (= the part of a telephone that you hold in your hand and use to listen and speak) **telefonda ahizenin konulduğu/asıldığı yer 3** MOBILE PHONE a small stand that holds a mobile phone **cep telefonu tutamağı/kızağı 4 the cradle of sth** the place where something started **kaynak, köken, ilk çıktığı yer** _Massachusetts, the cradle of the American Revolution_

cradle² /'kreɪdl/ _verb_ [T] to hold someone or something in a careful, gentle way **itinayla/özenle tutmak** _He cradled her in his arms._

craft¹ /krɑːft/ _noun_ **1** [C, U] an activity in which you make something using a lot of skill, especially with your hands **zanaat, al sanatı, beceri** _traditional crafts such as weaving_ **2** [C] _plural_ **craft** a boat **gemi, tekne**

craft² /krɑːft/ _verb_ [T] to make something using a lot of skill **beceriyle/maharetle yapmak** [often passive] _a bowl that was beautifully crafted from wood_

craftsman /'krɑːftsmən/ _noun_ [C] _plural_ **craftsmen** someone who uses special skill to make things, especially with their hands **zanaatkâr, usta, mahir kişi, sanatkâr** • **craftsmanship** _noun_ [U] skill at making things **zanaatkârlık, ustalık, hüner**

crafty /'krɑːfti/ _adjective_ clever at getting what you want, especially by deceiving people **hilekâr, düzenbaz, kurnaz, hilebaz** • **craftily** _adverb_ **kurnazca**

crag /kræg/ _noun_ [C] a high, rough mass of rock that sticks up from the land around it **sarp/yalçın kayalık**

cram /kræm/ _verb_ **cramming,** _past_ **crammed 1 cram sth between/in/into, etc** to force things into a small space **tıkmak, tıkıştırmak, zorla yerleştirmek/sokmak, tıka basa doldurmak** _The refugees were crammed into the truck._ **2** [I] to study a lot before an exam **sınavdan önce çok sıkı çalışmak**

crammed /kræmd/ _adjective_ completely full of people or things **sıkış tıkış, tıka basa dolu, dopdolu** _crammed commuter trains_ ○ _The room was crammed with boxes._

cramp¹ /kræmp/ _noun_ [C, U] a sudden, strong pain in a muscle that makes it difficult to move **kramp** _I've got cramp in my legs._

cramp² /kræmp/ _verb_ ⊃See cramp sb's **style¹**.

cramped /kræmpt/ _adjective_ A cramped room, building, etc is unpleasant because it is not big enough. **küçücük, daracık, dar**

cranberry /'krænbᵊri/ _noun_ [C] a small, red berry (= soft fruit) with a sour taste **ahududu, yaban mersini, keçi yemişi**

crane¹ /kreɪn/ _noun_ [C] **1** a large machine used for lifting and moving heavy things **vinç 2** a bird with long legs and a long neck **turna**

crane² /kreɪn/ _verb_ [I, T] to stretch your neck, in order to see or hear something **boynunu uzatmak**

crank /kræŋk/ _noun_ [C] **1** _informal_ someone with strange ideas or behaviour **garip fikir ve davranışları olan kişi, saplantılı kimse 2** a handle that you turn to make a machine work **manivela, kol**

cranny /'kræni/ _noun_ ⊃See every **nook** and cranny.

crap¹ /kræp/ _noun_ [U] _very informal_ a very impolite word for something that you think is wrong or bad **kötü/çirkin/ağıza alınmayacak söz/konuşma** _He was talking a lot of crap!_

crap² /kræp/ _UK (UK/US crappy /'kræpi/) adjective_ **crapper, crappest** _very informal_ a very impolite word for describing things that are very bad in quality **kötü/çirkin/ağıza alınmayacak, saçma** _a crap car/job_

⊕⊕ **crash** ...... İLE BİRLİKTE KULLANILAN KELİMELER
have/be involved in a crash • **be injured in/killed in** a crash • **the cause of** a crash • a crash **victim** • a **car/plane/train** crash

crash¹ /kræʃ/ _noun_ [C] **1** VEHICLE an accident in which a vehicle hits something **çarpışma, çarpma, kaza, taşıt/trafik kazası,** _a car/plane crash_ **2** NOISE a sudden, loud noise made when something falls or breaks **bir şeyin düştüğünde/kırıldığında çıkan ses, gümbürtü, şangırtı** _I heard a crash and hurried into the kitchen._ **3** COMPUTER when a computer or computer system suddenly stops working **bilgisayarın/bilgisayar sisteminin çökmesi 4** BUSINESS when the value of a country's businesses suddenly falls by a large amount **çökme, iflas, batma** _He lost a lot of money in the stock market crash of 1929._

crash² /kræʃ/ _verb_ **1** VEHICLE [I, T] If a vehicle crashes, it hits something by accident, and if you crash a vehicle, you make it hit something by accident. **çarpmak, kaza yapmak, düşüp parçalanmak** _The van skidded and crashed into a tree._ ○ _Rick crashed his dad's car._ **2** COMPUTER [I] If a computer or computer system crashes, it suddenly stops working. **bilgisayar/bilgisayar sistemi çökmek 3 crash against/on/through, etc** to hit something and make a loud noise **çarpıp büyük bir ses/gürültü çıkarmak** _The waves crashed against the rocks._ **4** LOUD NOISE [I] to make a sudden, loud noise **büyük bir ses çıkarmak, gümbürdemek** _Thunder crashed overhead._ **5** MONEY [I] If a financial market crashes, prices suddenly fall by a large amount. **(şirket) iflas etmek, çökmek, çözülmek**

'**crash ˌbarrier** _noun_ [C] _UK_ A fence along the middle or edge of a road for preventing accidents **refüj, yolboyunca ortaya veya kenara konulan çit, kazayı önleme amaçlı metal bariyerler**

'**crash ˌcourse** _UK (US ˌcrash 'course) noun_ [C] a course that teaches you a lot of basic facts in a very short time **hızlandırılmış yoğun kurs**

'**crash ˌhelmet** _noun_ [C] a hard hat that protects your head when you ride a motorcycle **kask, koruyucu başlık**

crass /kræs/ _adjective_ showing that you do not understand or care about other people's feelings **aptalca, ahmakça, kabaca** _a crass remark_

crate /kreɪt/ _noun_ [C] a large box used for carrying or storing things **ambalaj sandığı, kutu, büyük kutu, koli**

crater /'kreɪtəʳ/ _noun_ [C] **1** the round, open part at the top of a volcano **yanardağ ağzı, krater 2** a big hole in the ground **krater çukuru, krater** _The explosion left a crater in the road._

crave /kreɪv/ _verb_ [T] to want something very much **bir şeyi çok arzulamak/istemek; hasretini çekmek** _a child who craves affection_ • **craving** _noun_ [C] a strong feeling that you want or need a particular thing **istek, arzu, hasret** _She had a craving for chocolate._

crawl¹ /krɔːl/ *verb*
1 PERSON [I] to move on your hands and knees **emeklemek** *I crawled under the desk to plug the lamp in.* **2** ANIMAL [I] If an insect crawls, it uses its legs to move. **(böcek) tırmanmak** *There's an ant crawling up your leg.* **3** TRAFFIC [I] If traffic crawls, it moves extremely slowly. **(trafik) gıdım gıdım ilerlemek, çok yavaş ilerlemek** *We were crawling along at 10 miles per hour.* **4** TRY TO PLEASE [I] *UK informal* to try to please someone because you want them to like you or help you **yağcılık/yalakalık/dalkavukluk yapmak** *My brother is always crawling to Mum.* **5 be crawling with sb/sth** to be full of insects or people in a way that is unpleasant **insan/böcek kaynamak, aşırı kalabalık olmak, mahşer günü gibi olmak, dopdolu olmak** *The kitchen's crawling with ants.*

crawl

crawl² /krɔːl/ *noun* **1** [no plural] a very slow speed **kaplumbağa hızı** *Traffic slowed to a crawl.* **2** [U] a style of swimming in which you move your arms over your head and kick with straight legs **kolları baş üstünden hareket ettirerek ve bacakları bitişik olarak arkaya ittirerek yapılan yüzme**

crayon /'kreɪɒn/ *noun* [C] a stick of coloured wax used for drawing **mum boya**

craze /kreɪz/ *noun* [C] something that is very popular for a short time **geçici/çılgın/sezonluk moda**

crazed /kreɪzd/ *adjective* behaving in a dangerous and uncontrolled way **kudurmuş gibi, çılgın, zıvanadan çıkmış** *a crazed gunman*

○--**crazy** /'kreɪzi/ *adjective* **1** stupid or strange **aptal, acayip** *a crazy idea* ○ *I was crazy not to take that job.* **2** annoyed or angry **kızgın, çılgın** *The children are driving me crazy* (= making me annoyed). ○ *Dad went crazy when I told him what had happened.* **3 be crazy about sb/sth** to love someone very much, or to be very interested in something **sevgisinden çılgına dönmek, aşırı tutkun olmak, deli gibi sevmek** *Mia's crazy about baseball.* **4 go crazy** to become very excited about something **çılgına dönmek, aşırı heyecan duymak, deli olmak** *When he came on stage the audience went crazy.* **5 like crazy** *informal* If you do something like crazy, you do a lot of it, or do it very quickly. **çılgın gibi, deli gibi** *We worked like crazy to get everything finished.* ● **crazily** *adverb* **çılgın bir şekilde** ● **craziness** *noun* [U] **delilik**

creak /kriːk/ *verb* [I] If something such as a door or a piece of wood creaks, it makes a long noise when it moves. **gıcırdamak, gıcırtı sesi çıkarmak** *creaking floorboards* ● **creak** *noun* [C] **gıcırdama sesi** ● **creaky** *adjective* A creaky door, stair, etc creaks. **gıcırdayan, gıcırtı sesi çıkaran**

○--**cream¹** /kriːm/ *noun* **1** FOOD [U] a thick, yellowish-white liquid that is taken from milk **kaymak** *raspberries and cream* **2** FOR SKIN [C, U] a soft substance that you rub into your skin to make it softer or less painful **krem** *face/hand cream* **3** COLOUR [U] a yellowish-white colour **krem rengi 4 the cream of sth** the best people or things in a particular group **üst tabaka, en iyi şey ya da insanlar** *the cream of Milan's designers* ➸See also: ice cream.

cream² /kriːm/ *adjective* being a yellowish-white colour **krem renkli**

cream³ /kriːm/ *verb*
cream sth/sb off *phrasal verb UK* to take away the best part of something, or the best people in a group, and use them for your own advantage **(insan, eşya) kayma-**

ğını/en iyisini/en üst tabakayı almak ve kendi çıkarı için kullanmak

,cream 'cheese *noun* [U] smooth, soft, white cheese **krem peynir**

creamy /'kriːmi/ *adjective* like cream or containing cream **kremalı, kaymak kıvamında, kaymağa benzer** *creamy sauce/soup*

crease¹ /kriːs/ *noun* [C] a line on cloth or paper where it has been folded or crushed **katlama/bükme izi, kırışıklık, ütü izi**

crease² /kriːs/ *verb* [I, T] If cloth, paper, etc creases, or if you crease it, it gets a line in it where it has been folded or crushed. **kırış(tır)mak, buruş(tur)mak, katlamak** *Cotton creases very easily.*

○--**create** /kriˈeɪt/ *verb* [T] to make something happen or exist **yapmak, oluşturmak, yaratmak, meydan gelmesini sağlamak** *The project will create more than 500 jobs.* ○ *The snow created further problems.*

creation /kriˈeɪʃᵊn/ *noun* **1** PROCESS [U] when someone makes something happen or exist **ortaya konulan çalışma, kreasyon** *the creation of a new political party* **2** PRODUCT [C] something that someone has made **eser, çalışma, buluş, icat** *The museum contains some of his best creations.* **3** UNIVERSE [U] (*also* **Creation**) in many religions, when God made the universe and everything in it **yaratılış, kâinatın yaratılışı**

creative /kriˈeɪtɪv/ *adjective* good at thinking of new ideas or using imagination to create new and unusual things **yaratıcı** *Her book is full of creative ways to decorate your home.* ● **creatively** *adverb* **yaratıcı bir şekilde** ● **creativity** /ˌkriːeɪˈtɪvəti/ *noun* [U] the ability to produce new ideas or things using skill and imagination **yaratıcılık**

creator /kriˈeɪtər/ *noun* **1** [C] someone who invents or makes something **bir şeyi yapan, ortaya koyan, fikir babası, kreatör 2 the Creator** God **Tanrı, Yaratıcı, Yaradan**

creature /'kriːtʃər/ *noun* [C] anything that lives but is not a plant **yaratık** *Dolphins are intelligent creatures.*

creche /kreʃ/ *noun* [C] *UK* a place where babies and young children are looked after while their parents do something else **çocuk gündüz bakım evi, kreş**

credence /'kriːdᵊns/ *noun* **add/give/lend credence to sth** to make a story, theory, etc seem more likely to be true **bir hikaye/teori vb. gerçekmiş gibi görünmesini sağlamak, inandırmak; güven, inanç vermek/katmak** *The letters lend credence to the idea that he had an unhappy life.*

credentials /krɪˈdenʃᵊlz/ *noun* [plural] **1** skills and experience that show you are suitable for a particular job or activity **nitelik, ehliyet, beceri ve yetenekler** *academic credentials* **2** documents that prove who you are **kimlik belgesi, referans, ehliyet**

credibility /ˌkredəˈbɪləti/ *noun* [U] when someone can be believed and trusted **itibar, kredi, inanırlık, güvenirlik** *This decision has damaged the President's credibility.*

credible /'kredəbl/ *adjective* able to be trusted or believed **inanılır, güvenilir, inandırıcı** *credible evidence*

credit¹ /'kredɪt/ *noun* **1** PAYMENT [U] a way of buying something in which you arrange to pay for it at a later time **kredi, taksit** *We offer interest-free credit on all*

new cars. ○ *He bought most of the furniture on credit.*
2 [PRAISE] [U] praise that is given to someone for something they have done **takdir, övgü** *I did most of the work but Dan got all the credit!* ○ *We should give her credit for her honesty.* ○ *I can't take full credit for this meal - Sam helped.* **3 be a credit to sb/sth** to do something that makes a person or organization proud of you **övünç kaynağı olmak, medarı iftiharı olmak** *Giorgio is a credit to his family.* **4 to sb's credit** If something is to someone's credit, they deserve praise for it. **Hakkını yemeyelim; Allah için; Allah var** *To his credit, Bill never blamed her for the incident.* **5 have sth to your credit** to have achieved something **başarı hanesinde yazılı olmak, artı bir değeri olmak; bir şeyi zaten başarmış olmak** *By the age of 25, she had five novels to her credit.* **6 in credit** having money in your bank account **hesabında parası olmak 7** [MONEY] [C] an amount of money that you put into your bank account **hesaba yatırılan para** ⊃Opposite **debit**. **8** [COURSE] [C] a unit that shows you have completed part of a college course **ders kredisi**

credit² /'kredɪt/ *verb* [T] **1** to add money to someone's bank account **hesaba para yatırmak 2** to believe that something is true **inanmak, aklına getirmek, olabileceğini düşünmek** *Dean's getting married! Who would have credited it?*
credit sth to sb *phrasal verb* to say that someone is responsible for something good **maletmek; ... den ummak, beklemek** *an idea credited to Isaac Newton*
credit sb with sth *phrasal verb* to believe that someone has a particular quality **layık görmek, yakıştırmak, güvenmek, itimat etmek** *Credit me with some intelligence!*
credit sb with sth/doing sth *phrasal verb* to say that someone is responsible for something good **(iyi bir sonucun) sorumlusu kabul etmek/edilmek, maletmek, hesabına artı değer olarak kaydetmek** *She is credited with making the business a success.*

creditable /'kredɪtəbl/ *adjective* Something that is creditable deserves praise. **övgüye değer/layık, saygı duyulan** *a creditable performance*

'credit ,card *noun* [C] a small plastic card that allows you to buy something and pay for it later **kredi kartı** *He paid by credit card.*

'credit ,limit *noun* [C] the largest amount of money that a person can borrow with a credit card (= a small plastic card that allows you to buy something and pay for it later) **kredi limiti/sınırı** *a £500 credit limit*

creditor /'kredɪtər/ *noun* [C] a person or organization that someone owes money to **alacaklı, kredi veren kişi/kurum**

the credits /'kredɪts/ *noun* [plural] a list of people who made a film or television programme **(film veya tv programı) emeği geçenlerin tümü, yapım ekibi/görevlileri**

creed /kri:d/ *noun* [C] a set of beliefs, especially religious beliefs that influence your life **itikat, inançlar manzumesi**

creek /kri:k/ *noun* [C] **1** UK a narrow area of water that flows into the land from a sea or river **çay, dere, ırmak yolu 2** *mainly US* a stream or narrow river **dere, çay**

creep¹ /kri:p/ *verb past* **crept 1 creep along/in/out, etc** to move very quietly and carefully **bir yere/yerden sürünerek girmek/çıkmak/süzülmek/sıvışmak** *I crept out of the room.* **2 creep across/in/into, etc** to gradually start to exist or appear **yavaş yavaş belirmek/ortaya çıkmak/baş göstermek** *Problems were beginning to creep into their relationship.* **3 creep along/down/through, etc** to move somewhere very slowly

yavaş yavaş ilerlemek/süzülmek/sızmak *The convoy crept along in the darkness.*
creep up on sb *phrasal verb* **1** to surprise someone by moving closer to them from behind **birine arkadan sessizce yaklaşmak, şaşırtmak** *Don't creep up on me like that!* **2** If a feeling or state creeps up on you, it happens gradually so that you do not notice it. **yavaş yavaş etkilemek/baş göstermek/olmak/meydana gelmek** *Old age just creeps up on you.*

creep² /kri:p/ *noun* [C] **1** UK someone who you do not like because they are nice to people in a way that is not sincere **riyakâr, dalkavuk, yalaka 2** someone who you think is unpleasant **sevimsiz/yağcı/sevilmeyen kişi**

creeps /kri:ps/ *noun* **give sb the creeps** *informal* to make someone feel frightened or nervous **korkutmak, içini ürpertmek, tüylerini diken diken etmek,** *These old buildings give me the creeps.*

creepy /'kri:pi/ *adjective informal* strange and frightening **acayip, ürkütücü, korkutucu, ürperten** *a creepy story/person*

cremate /krɪ'meɪt/ *verb* [T] to burn a dead body **ölü yakmak ● cremation** /krɪ'meɪʃⁿn/ *noun* [C, U] the ceremony where someone is cremated **ölü yakma töreni**

crematorium /ˌkreməˈtɔːriəm/ *noun* [C] (*also US* **crematory** /'kri:mətɔːri/) *noun* [C] a place where people are cremated **ölü yakım binası, krematoryum**

crept /krept/ *past of* creep **sürünmek' fiilinin geçmiş zaman hali**

crescendo /krɪ'ʃendəʊ/ *noun* [C] when a noise or piece of music gradually gets louder **müziğin gittikçe yükselmesi/doruğa erişmesi**

crescent /'kresⁿnt/ *noun* **1** [C] a curved shape that is narrow at each end and wider in the middle **hilâl, yeni ay** *the pale crescent of the moon* **2 Crescent** used in the names of streets that have a curved shape **evlerin hilâl şeklinde tasarlanıp yerleştirldiği caddeye verilen isim** *57 Park Crescent*

crest /krest/ *noun* [C] **1** [TOP] the highest part of a hill or wave **doruk, zirve, en tepe nokta 2** [FEATHERS] the feathers that point upwards on a bird's head **ibik 3** [DESIGN] a design used as the symbol of a school, important family, etc **okul, aile) arma**

crestfallen /'krestˌfɔːlⁿn/ *adjective* disappointed or sad **mahzun, hayal kırıklığına uğramış, üzgün**

crevasse /krɪ'væs/ *noun* [C] a deep, wide crack, especially in ice **(buz) yarık, çatlak**

crevice /'krevɪs/ *noun* [C] a small, narrow crack, especially in a rock **(kaya) yarık, çatlak**

crew /kru:/ *noun* [group] **1** the people who work together on a ship, aircraft, or train **mürettebat, ekip, tayfa** *a crew member* **2** a team of people with special skills who work together **kadro, takım, ekip** *Fire and ambulance crews were at the scene.*

crewman /'kru:mæn/ *noun* [C] *plural* **crewmen** a member of the crew of a ship or aircraft **mürettebattan/tayfalardan biri**

crib /krɪb/ *US* (*UK* **cot**) *noun* [C] a bed with high sides for a baby **bebek karyolası**

cricket /'krɪkɪt/ *noun* **1** [U] a game in which two teams of eleven people try to score points by hitting a ball and running between two wickets (= sets of three wooden sticks) **kriket** *a cricket ball/bat* ⊃Orta kısımdaki renkli sayfalarına bakınız. **2** [C] an insect that jumps and makes a noise by rubbing its wings together **cırcır böceği**

cricketer /'krɪkɪtər/ *noun* [C] someone who plays cricket, especially as their job **profesyonel kriket oyuncusu**

commit a crime ● combat/reduce/fight crime ● a minor/petty/terrible/violent crime

o▪**crime** /kraɪm/ *noun* **1** [U] illegal activities **suç, cürüm** *violent crime* ○ *tough new measures to fight crime* **2** [C] something someone does that is illegal **kabahat, suç** *He committed a serious crime.* ⟳See also: war crime.

criminal¹ /ˈkrɪmɪnºl/ *adjective* **1** [always before noun] relating to crime **suça ait, suç unsuru taşıyan** *criminal activity* ○ *He has a criminal record* (= the police have an official record of his crimes). **2** *informal* very bad or morally wrong **ahlaken yanlış olan, çok kötü kabahat içeren** *It's criminal that people are having to wait so long for hospital treatment.* ● **criminally** *adverb* **suça dair**

criminal² /ˈkrɪmɪnºl/ *noun* [C] someone who has committed a crime **suçlu** *a dangerous/violent criminal*

criminologist /ˌkrɪmɪˈnɒlədʒɪst/ *noun* [C] someone who studies crime and criminals **suç ve suçluları araştıran, kriminolojist**

crimson /ˈkrɪmzºn/ *noun* [U] a dark red colour **koyu vişne rengi, çok koyu kırmızı** ● **crimson** *adjective* **vişne renginde**

cringe /krɪndʒ/ *verb* [I] **1** to feel very embarrassed about something **tedirgin olmak, utanç duymak, mahcup olmak** *Jan cringed at the sight of her father dancing.* **2** to move away from something because you are frightened **çekilmek, ürkmek, uzak durmak, korkup sinmek**

crinkle /ˈkrɪŋkl/ *verb* [I, T] to become covered in small lines or folds, or to make something become covered in small lines or folds **buruş(tur)mak, kıvırmak, kıvrıştırmak** ● **crinkly** *adjective* Something that is crinkly has crinkles in it. **buruşuk, kırışık, katlanmış**

cripple¹ /ˈkrɪpl/ *verb* [T] **1** to injure someone so that they cannot use their arms or legs **kolunu bacağını kırmak, sakat/kötürüm bırakmak** [often passive] *His son was crippled by a riding accident.* **2** to damage something very badly and make it weak or not effective **zarar vermek, çalışamaz/işe yaramaz hale getirmek** [often passive] *a country crippled by war*

cripple² /ˈkrɪpl/ *noun* [C] *old-fashioned* an offensive word for someone who cannot use their legs or arms in a normal way **kötürüm, sakat**

crippling /ˈkrɪplɪŋ/ *adjective* **1** [always before noun] A crippling illness makes someone unable to use their arms or legs in a normal way. **sakat olan, kötürüm olan, kolsuz bacaksız** **2** causing great damage **belini büken, yıkıma uğratan, yok eden**

o▪**crisis** /ˈkraɪsɪs/ *noun* [C, U] *plural* **crises** /ˈkraɪsiːz/ a situation or time that is extremely dangerous or difficult **kriz, bunalım, zor zamanlar** *an economic/financial crisis* ○ *The country's leadership is in crisis.* ⟳See also: mid-life crisis.

crisp¹ /krɪsp/ *adjective* **1** [FOOD] Crisp food is pleasantly hard. **gevrek, çıtır çıtır** *a crisp apple* ○ *crisp pastry* **2** [MATERIAL] Crisp cloth or paper money is clean and looks new, with no folds. **tertemiz, hiç kullanılmamış, yepyeni, gıcır gıcır** *a crisp linen shirt* **3** [WEATHER] Crisp weather is pleasantly cold and dry. **kuru ve soğuk hava, ayaz** *a crisp autumn day* **4** [QUICK] A crisp way of talking or behaving is quick and confident. **kendinden emin ve hızlı konuşma biçimi** **5** [IMAGE] A crisp image is very clear. **açık seçik ve net görüntü, görünüşü olan**

crisp² /krɪsp/ *UK* (*US* **chip**) *noun* [C] a very thin slice of potato that has been cooked in oil and is eaten cold

patates cipsi [usually plural] *a packet of crisps* ⟳Orta kısımdaki renkli sayfalarına bakınız.

crispy /ˈkrɪspi/ *adjective* Crispy food is pleasantly hard and easy to bite through. **kuru, gevrek, çıtır çıtır** *crispy bacon*

criss-cross /ˈkrɪskrɒs/ *verb* [I, T] If something crisscrosses an area, it crosses it several times in different directions. **bir çok kez çaprazlama geçmek** [often passive] *The forest is criss-crossed with paths and tracks.*

criterion /kraɪˈtɪəriən/ *noun* [C] *plural* **criteria** a fact or level of quality that you use when making a choice or decision **değer ölçütü, kriter** [+ for + doing sth] *We have strict criteria for deciding which students will receive a grant.*

critic /ˈkrɪtɪk/ *noun* [C] **1** someone who says that they do not approve of someone or something **muhalif, karşı görüşü savunan** *an outspoken critic of the government* **2** someone whose job is to give their opinion of a book, play, film, etc (oyun, kitap, film vs.) **a theatre/film critic**

critical /ˈkrɪtɪkºl/ *adjective* **1** [NOT PLEASED] saying that someone or something is bad or wrong **eleştirel, muhalif olan** *a critical report* ○ *He is very critical of the way I work.* **2** [IMPORTANT] very important for the way things will happen in the future **can alıcı, çok ciddi, önemli** *a critical decision* **3** [SERIOUS] extremely serious or dangerous **tehlikeli, kritik, ciddi** *The doctors said her condition was critical and she might not survive.* **4** [OPINIONS] giving judgments and opinions on books, plays, films, etc (oyun, kitap, film vs.) **eleştirel** *a critical study of Tennyson's work* ● **critically** *adverb* **eleştirel bir şekilde**

sb/sth **attracts/draws/faces/sparks** criticism ● **deflect/dismiss** criticism ● **fierce/stinging/strong** criticism ● criticism **of** sb/sth ● criticism **from** sb

o▪**criticism** /ˈkrɪtɪsɪzºm/ *noun* **1** [C, U] when you say that something or someone is bad **muhalefet, eleştiri** *Plans to close the hospital attracted strong public criticism.* **2** [U] when someone gives their judgments and opinions on books, plays, films, etc (oyun, kitap, film vs.) **eleştiri** *literary criticism*

criticize (*also UK* -**ise**) /ˈkrɪtɪsaɪz/ *verb* [I, T] to say that something or someone is bad **eleştirmek** [often passive, + for + doing sth] *The film was criticized for being too violent.*

critique /krɪˈtiːk/ *noun* [C] a report that says what is good and bad about something **eleştiri yazısı/raporu**

croak /krəʊk/ *verb* **1** [I, T] to talk or say something in a low, rough voice **boğuk bir sesle konuşmak** *"I don't feel well," he croaked.* **2** [I] If a bird or frog (= green jumping animal) croaks, it makes a deep, low sound. **(kurbağa, kuş vs.) vıraklamak, vırak vırak diye ses çıkarmak**

crochet /ˈkrəʊʃeɪ/ ⓤ /krəʊˈʃeɪ/ *verb* [I, T] to make clothes and other items using wool and a special needle with a hook at one end **tığ ile örmek, tığ işi yapmak**

crockery /ˈkrɒkºri/ *noun* [U] plates, cups, and other dishes, especially those made from clay **(bilhassa topraktan yapılmış) tabak çanak**

crocodile /ˈkrɒkədaɪl/ *noun* [C] a big reptile with a long mouth and sharp teeth, that lives in lakes and rivers **timsah**

crocus /ˈkrəʊkəs/ *noun* [C] a small yellow, purple, or white spring flower **safran, çiğdem**

croissant /'kwæsɒŋ/ ⓤ /kwɑː'sɒŋ/ *noun* [C] a soft, curved piece of bread, eaten for breakfast **ay şeklinde küçük ekmek, krosan** ⊃See picture at **bread**.

crony /'krəʊni/ *noun* [C] *informal* one of a group of friends who help each other, especially in a way that is not fair **kafadar, yandaş, yakın arkadaş** [usually plural] *He gave his cronies all the best jobs.*

crook /krʊk/ *noun* **1** [C] *informal* a criminal or someone who cheats people **üçkâğıtçı, düzenbaz, dolandırıcı** **2 the crook of your arm** the inside part of your arm where it bends **kıvrım, kavis, kolun kıvrılan bölümünün iç kısmı**

crooked /'krʊkɪd/ *adjective* **1** not straight **yamuk, çarpık, eğri büğrü** *crooked teeth* **2** *informal* not honest **haysiyetsiz, dalavereci, düzenbaz, sahtekâr** *a crooked politician*

croon /kruːn/ *verb* [I, T] to sing in a soft, low, romantic voice **yumuşak, alçak ve romantik bir sesle şarkı söylemek, mırıldanmak**

crop¹ /krɒp/ *noun* **1** [C] a plant such as a grain, fruit, or vegetable that is grown in large amounts by farmers **ürün, tahıl 2** [C] the amount of plants of a particular type that are produced at one time **ürün** *We had a record crop of grapes this year.* **3 a crop of sth** a group of the same type of things or people that exist at the same time **ortak özelliği olan bir grup insan veya aynı türden eşya** *He's one of the current crop of young Italian artists.* ⊃See also: **cash crop**.

crop² /krɒp/ *verb* **cropping,** *past* **cropped 1** CUT [T] to cut something so that it is short **kırpmak, budamak, keserek biçim vermek 2** COMPUTER [T] to cut pieces from the sides of a computer image so that it is the size you want **3** GROW [I] *UK* If a plant crops, it produces fruit, flowers, etc. **ürün vermek,**
crop up *phrasal verb* to happen or appear suddenly **ansızın zuhur etmek, baş göstermek, ortaya çıkmak** *The same old problems kept cropping up.*

cropper /'krɒpəʳ/ *noun* **1 come a cropper a** to fall over **devrilmek, yıkılmak, çökmek, düşmek** *The horse came a cropper at the first fence.* **b** to fail in an embarrassing way, or to make an embarrassing mistake **baltayı taşa vurmak, mahcup olmak, (argo) çuvallamak, başarısızlığa uğramak**

croquet /'krəʊkeɪ/ ⓤ /krəʊ'keɪ/ *noun* [U] a game played on grass, in which you hit a ball with a wooden hammer through curved wires pushed into the ground **kroket, çim üstünde oynana bir tür oyun**

o-╸**cross¹** /krɒs/ *verb* **1** FROM ONE SIDE TO ANOTHER [I, T] to go from one side of something to the other side **geçmek, karşıdan karşıya geçmek** *It's not a good place to cross the road.* **2** LINE/BORDER [I, T] to travel over a border or line into a different area, country, etc **ülkeler arası seyahat etmek** *They crossed from Albania into Greece.* **3** MEET AND GO ACROSS [I, T] If two lines, roads, etc cross, they go over or across each other. **(yollar) kesişmek 4 cross your arms/fingers/legs** to put one of your arms, fingers, or legs over the top of the other **kol/bacak/parmak çatmak, üst üste atmak, çaprazlama tutmak 5 cross yourself** to touch your head, chest, and both shoulders as a sign to God **istavroz/haç çıkarmak 6** ANIMAL/PLANT [T] to mix two breeds of animal or plant to produce a new breed **melezleştirmek, melez bir ırk elde etmek 7** MAKE SOMEONE ANGRY [T] to make someone angry by refusing to do what they want you to do **kızdırmak, söyleneni yapmayarak birini üzmek/kızdırmak** ⊃See also: I'll/We'll cross that **bridge¹** when I/we come to it., **criss-cross, double-cross**, keep your fingers (**finger¹**) crossed, cross your **mind¹**.

cross sth off (sth) *phrasal verb* to remove a word from a list by drawing a line through it **üstünü çizmek, listeden çıkarmak** *Did you cross her name off the guest list?*
cross sth out *phrasal verb* to draw a line through something that you have written, usually because it is wrong **üstünü çizmek, yanlış olanı işaretleyerek belirlemek** *Cross out that last sentence.*

o-╸**cross²** /krɒs/ *noun* **1** WOOD [C] two pieces of wood that cross each other, on which people were left to die as a punishment in the past **çarmıh 2** SYMBOL [C] an object in the shape of a cross, used as a symbol of the Christian religion **haç, Hıristiyanlıkta dini simge 3** MARK [C] a written mark (x), used for showing where something is, or that something that has been written is wrong **çarpı işareti 4 a cross between sth and sth** a mixture of two different things or people **bir şeyle/biriyle birşeyin/birinin karışımı, melez, kırma** *The dog is a cross between a terrier and a rottweiler.* **5** SPORT [C] when someone kicks or hits the ball across the field in sport, especially football **futbolda sahanın bir ucundan öbür ucuna uzun bir vuruş**

cross³ /krɒs/ *adjective* annoyed or angry **kızgın, bozuk, canı sıkkın, dargın** *Don't be cross with me!*

cross- /krɒs-/ *prefix* **1** across **karşı/ters/zıt- anlamında önek** *cross-border* **2** including different groups or subjects **çok çeşitli grup veya konuyu içeren- anlamında önek** *a cross-party committee* (= one formed from many political parties) ○ *cross-cultural*

crossbar /'krɒsbɑːʳ/ *noun* [C] **1** the post at the top of a goal in games such as football **kale üst direği 2** the metal tube that joins the front and back of a bicycle **bisikletin ön ve arkasını birleştiren demir boru**

cross-border /'krɒs,bɔːdəʳ/ *adjective* [always before noun] between different countries, or involving people from different countries **farklı ülkeleri katılımını içeren/ilgilendiren; ülkeler arası** *cross-border trade*

cross-Channel /ˌkrɒs'tʃænəl/ *adjective* [always before noun] connecting or happening between England and France **İngiltere ve Fransa'yı birleştiren, iki ülke arasında olan** *a cross-Channel ferry/route*

cross-country /ˌkrɒs'kʌntri/ *adjective* [always before noun], *adverb* **1** across fields and countryside **kır, taşra, kırsal alanda/alana ait** *cross-country running/skiing* **2** from one side of a country to the other side **ülkenin bir ucundan öbür ucuna**

cross-examine /ˌkrɒsɪg'zæmɪn/ *verb* [T] to ask someone a lot of questions about something they have said, in order to discover if it is true, especially in a court of law **çapraz sorgulama yapmak, sorguya çekmek** ● **cross-examination** /ˌkrɒsɪgˌzæmɪ'neɪʃən/ *noun* [U] **çift taraflı sorgu**

cross-eyed /krɒs'aɪd/ *adjective* A cross-eyed person has both eyes looking in towards their nose. **şaşı**

crossfire /'krɒsfaɪəʳ/ *noun* **1** [U] bullets fired towards you from different directions **çapraz ateş** *Civilians died when a bus was caught in crossfire between government and rebel troops.* **2 be caught in the crossfire** to be involved in a situation where people around you are arguing **çapraz ateşte/ateş altında kalmak**

crossing /'krɒsɪŋ/ *noun* [C] **1** WHERE PEOPLE CROSS a place where people can go across a road, river, etc **geçit, geçiş 2** SEA JOURNEY a journey across water **deniz, nehir, göl vb. yapılan yolculuk 3** WHERE LINES CROSS where roads, railways, etc cross each other **iki yolun kesiştiği yer, dört yol ağzı** ⊃See also: grade crossing, level crossing, zebra crossing.

cross-legged /ˌkrɒs'legɪd/ *adverb* **sit cross-legged** to sit on the floor with your knees wide apart and one foot over the other foot **bağdaş kurarak oturmak; bacak bacak üstünde oturmak**

,cross 'purposes *noun* **at cross purposes** If two people are at cross purposes, they do not understand each other because they are talking about different things but do not know this. **birbirinin ne dediğini düşünmeden/anlamadan konuşma**

,cross 'reference *noun* [C] a note in a book that tells you to look somewhere else in the book for more information about something **kitap içinde daha fazla bilgi için yapılan gönderme**

crossroads /'krɒsrəʊdz/ *noun* [C] *plural* **crossroads 1** a place where two roads cross each other **kavşak 2** a time when you have to make an important decision that will affect your future life **dönüm noktası** *I felt I was at a crossroads in my life.*

cross-section /'krɒssekʃᵊn/ *noun* [C] **1** a small group of people or things that represents all the different types in a larger group **farklı kültürden oluşan toplum kesiti** *a cross-section of society* **2** something that has been cut in half so that you can see the inside, or a picture of this **kesit** *a cross-section of a human heart*

crosswalk /'krɒswɔːk/ *US* (*UK* pedestrian crossing) *noun* [C] a special place on a road where traffic must stop if people want to cross **yaya geçidi**

crossword /'krɒswɜːd/ (*also* 'crossword ,puzzle) *noun* [C] a game in which you write words which are the answers to questions in a pattern of black and white squares **bulmaca**

crotch /krɒtʃ/ (*also UK* crutch) *noun* [C] the part of your body between the tops of your legs, or the part of a piece of clothing that covers this area **kasık, pantolon ağı**

crouch /kraʊtʃ/ (*also* crouch down) *verb* [I] to move your body close to the ground by bending your knees **çömelmek** *I crouched behind the chair to avoid being seen.*

crow¹ /krəʊ/ *noun* **1** [C] a large black bird that makes a loud noise **karga 2 as the crow flies** when measured in a straight line **kuş uçuşu ölçümü, dümdüz** *It's about 50 miles from London to Cambridge as the crow flies.*

crow² /krəʊ/ *verb* [I] **1** to talk in a proud and annoying way about something you have done **böbürlenmek, kabarmak, kabaca övünmek** *Donald wouldn't stop crowing about his exam results.* **2** If a cock (= male chicken) crows, it makes a loud noise, usually in the early morning. **(horoz) ötmek**

🧩 **crowd** ...... İLE BİRLİKTE KULLANILAN KELİMELER

a crowd **gathers** ● a crowd **of** [people/tourists, etc] ● **in** a crowd

---

o=**crowd¹** /kraʊd/ *noun* **1** [C] a large group of people who are together in one place **kalabalık** *A large crowd had gathered to wait for the princess.* ○ *Shop early and avoid the crowds.* **2** [no plural] *informal* a group of friends or people with similar interests **aynı amaç için bir araya gelmiş grup, topluluk** *the art/theatre crowd*

crowd² /kraʊd/ *verb* [T] **1** to stand together in large numbers **toplanmak, bir araya gelmek** *Protesters crowded the streets.* **2** to stand too close to someone **etrafında toplanmak, çevrelemek, sarmak** *Don't crowd me!*

crowd around/round (sb/sth) *phrasal verb* If a group of people crowd around or crowd around someone or something, they stand very close all around them. **başına üşüşmek, çepeçevre sarmak** *Everyone crowded around my desk.*

crowd in/crowd (sb) into sth *phrasal verb* If a large group of people crowd into somewhere, they all go

---

there and fill the place. **toplaşmak, tıkış(tır)mak, doluş(tur)mak**

crowd sb out *phrasal verb* to prevent someone or something from succeeding or existing by being much more successful than them or by being present in much larger numbers **yok etmek, rekâbetle engellemek, başarısına sekte vurmak, önlemek** *Large national companies often crowd out smaller local businesses.*

crowded /'kraʊdɪd/ *adjective* very full of people **kalabalık, tıklım tıklım** *a crowded room/train*

crown¹ /kraʊn/ *noun*

1 KING/QUEEN [C] a round object made of gold and jewels (= valuable stones) that a king or queen wears on their head **taç 2** TOP [C] the top of a hat, head, or hill **tepe, zirve, üst 3 the Crown** used to refer to the power or government of a king or queen **kraliyet, krallık** *All this land belongs to the Crown.* **4** TOOTH [C] an artificial top that is put on a damaged tooth **(diş) kaplama**

crown

crown² /kraʊn/ *verb* [T] **1** MAKE KING/QUEEN to put a crown on someone's head in an official ceremony that makes them a king or queen **taç giydirmek, taçlandırmak, kraliçe/hükümdar yapmak** [often passive] *Queen Elizabeth II of England was crowned in 1952.* **2** ON TOP *literary* to be on top of something else **tepede/zirvede olmak** *A large domed ceiling crowns the main hall.* **3** BEST PART to be the best or most successful part of something **en iyi ve en başarılı bir bölümü olmak** *a book that crowned his successful writing career*

crowning /'kraʊnɪŋ/ *adjective* [always before noun] more important, beautiful, etc than anything else **en önemli/güzel** *It was the crowning achievement of his political career.*

crucial /'kruːʃᵊl/ *adjective* extremely important or necessary **kritik, çok önemli** *a crucial decision/question* ○ *Her work has been crucial to the project's success.* ● **crucially** *adverb* **çok önemli bir şekilde**

crucifix /'kruːsɪfɪks/ *noun* [C] a model of a cross with Jesus Christ on it **çarmıha gerilmiş İsa figürü**

crucifixion /ˌkruːsə'fɪkʃᵊn/ *noun* [C, U] in the past, when someone was fastened to a cross and left to die **çarmıha gerilme/germe** *the crucifixion of Christ*

crucify /'kruːsɪfaɪ/ *verb* [T] **1** in the past, to fasten someone to a cross and leave them to die **çarmıha germek 2** *informal* to criticize someone or something in a cruel and damaging way **birini/birşeyi acımasız, kaba ve saygısızca eleştirmek** [often passive] *The film has been crucified by the media.*

crude /kruːd/ *adjective* **1** made or done in a simple way and without much skill **sıradan yapılmış; ham** *a crude device/weapon* **2** rude and offensive **kaba saba, kaba, basit** *a crude comment/remark* ● **crudely** *adverb* **kaba saba şekilde yapılmış**

,crude 'oil (*also* crude) *noun* [U] oil in its natural state before it has been treated **ham petrol**

o=**cruel** /'kruːəl/ *adjective* **crueller, cruellest** or **crueler, cruelest** extremely unkind, or causing people or animals to suffer **vicdansız, acımasız, zalim** *a cruel joke* ○ *Many people think hunting is cruel to animals.* ● **cruelly** *adverb* **acımasızca**

cruelty /'kruːəlti/ *noun* [C, U] cruel behaviour or a cruel action **acımasızlık, zulüm** *laws against cruelty to animals*

cruise¹ /kruːz/ *noun* [C] a holiday on a ship, sailing from place to place **gemi sayehati**

cruise² /kru:z/ *verb* **1** [I] to move in a vehicle at a speed that does not change **bir araçla sabit bir hızda gitmek** *The plane is cruising at 500 miles per hour.* **2** [I] to go on a cruise **gemi seyahati yapmak 3 cruise to success/victory, etc** *informal* to win a competition easily **bir yarışmayı kolayca kazanmak**

cruise 'missile UK (US 'cruise ,missile) *noun* [C] a weapon that flies through the air, and which often carries nuclear weapons **kruz füzesi; nükleer başlık taşıyan füze**

cruiser /'kru:zər/ *noun* [C] **1** a large military ship used in wars **kruvazör; büyük savaş gemisi 2** (*also* 'cabin ,cruiser) a motor boat with a room for people to sleep in **yat, kamaralı motor**

'cruise ,ship (*also* 'cruise ,liner) *noun* [C] a large ship like a hotel, which people travel on for pleasure **büyük yolcu gemisi, transatlantik**

crumb /krʌm/ *noun* **1** [C] a very small piece of bread, cake, etc **kırıntı 2 a crumb of sth** a very small amount of something **bir parça kırıntı**

crumble /'krʌmbl/ *verb* **1** [I, T] to break into small pieces, or to make something break into small pieces **ufala(n)mak, dağılmak, dağıtmak, küçük parçalara ayırmak** *Buildings crumbled as the earthquake struck.* **2** [I] If a relationship, system, or feeling crumbles, it fails or ends. (**ilişki, sistem, his vs.**) **başarısızlığa uğramak, sona ermek, darmadağın/paramparça olmak** *His first marriage crumbled after only a year.*

crummy /'krʌmi/ *adjective informal* unpleasant, or of bad quality **berbat, kalitesiz** *a crummy job* ○ *a crummy hotel*

crumple /'krʌmpl/ *verb* **1** [I, T] If something such as paper or cloth crumples, it becomes crushed, and if you crumple it, you crush it until it is full of folds. **kırış(tır)mak, buruş(tur)mak, katlamak, yamul(t)mak** *a crumpled shirt* **2** [I] If someone's face crumples, they suddenly look very sad or disappointed. **birden suratı asılmak**
crumple sth up *phrasal verb* to crush a piece of paper until it is full of folds **buruşmak, kırışmak**

crunch¹ /krʌntʃ/ *noun* **1** [C] the sound of something being crushed **garç gurç ses çıkarmak, çatır, çutur etmek** [usually singular] *the crunch of dried leaves under our feet* **2 if/when it comes to the crunch** if/when a situation becomes serious or you have to make an important decision **günü geldiğinde; hele ogün bir gelsin**

crunch² /krʌntʃ/ *verb* **1** [I, T] to make a noise by chewing hard food **çatır çutur yemek, ses çıkararak yemek** *She was crunching on an apple.* **2** [I] to make a sound as if something is being crushed **çatırdamak, çatırtı sesi çıkarmak** *The gravel crunched under our feet.*

crunchy /'krʌntʃi/ *adjective* Crunchy food is hard and makes a noise when you eat it. **kıtır kıtır, çıtır çıtır**

crusade .... İLE BİRLİKTE KULLANILAN KELİMELER

launch/mount a crusade ● be on a crusade ● a moral/personal crusade ● a crusade against/for sth

crusade /kru:'seɪd/ *noun* [C] a determined attempt to change or achieve something that you believe in strongly **savaş, mücadele ● crusader** *noun* [C] someone who is involved in a crusade **haçlı, savaşçı**

crush¹ /krʌʃ/ *verb* [T] **1** to press something so hard that it is made flat or broken into pieces **ezmek, unufak etmek** *Her car was crushed by a falling tree.* **2** to defeat someone or something completely **birini yenmek, yok etmek, dövmek** *government attempts to crush protests* ○ *a crushing defeat*

crush² /krʌʃ/ *noun* **1** [no plural] a crowd of people forced to stand close together because there is not enough room **izdiham, insan kalabalığı** *Many people fell over in the crush.* **2** [C] *informal* a strong temporary feeling of love for someone **geçici tutulma, tutku, sevdalanma** *Tim has a crush on Jennifer.*

crust /krʌst/ *noun* [C, U] **1** the hard outer surface of bread or other baked foods **kabuk 2** a hard, dry layer on the surface of something **katı dış tabaka**

crusty /'krʌsti/ *adjective* **1** unfriendly and becoming annoyed very easily **huysuz, uyuz, samimi olmayan, kolay etkilenen 2** Something that is crusty has a hard outer layer. **kabuklu** *crusty bread*

crutch /krʌtʃ/ *noun* [C] **1** a stick that you put under your arm to help you walk if you have injured your leg or foot **koltuk değneği** [usually plural] *Charles was on crutches* (= walking with crutches) *for six weeks.* **2** UK (UK/US crotch) the part of your body between the tops of your legs, or the part of a piece of clothing that covers this area **ağ, pantolon bacak arası**

crux /krʌks/ *noun* **the crux (of sth)** the main or most important part of a problem, argument, etc **düğüm noktası, can alıcı nokta**

o- **cry¹** /kraɪ/ *verb* **1** [I] to produce tears from your eyes, usually because you are sad, angry, or hurt **ağlamak** *My baby brother cries all the time.* **2** [I, T] to speak or say something loudly **bağırmak, haykırmak** *"Look at this!" cried Raj.* **⊃**See also: cry your eyes (eye¹) out, a shoulder¹ to cry on.

cry

be crying out for sth *phrasal verb informal* to need something very much **bir şey için kıvranmak, çok gereksinim duymak** *a school that's crying out for more money*

cry out (sth) *phrasal verb* to shout or make a loud noise because you are frightened, hurt, etc **(korkudan veya yaralanınca) bağırmak, haykırmak, çığlık atmak** *She cried out in terror.*

cry² /kraɪ/ *noun* **1** [C] a shout, especially one that shows that someone is frightened, hurt, etc **çığlık** *a cry of horror/joy/pain* ○ *I could hear the cries of children playing in the street.* **2** [C] a sound that a particular animal or bird makes **hayvan çığlığı/kuş sesi/ötüşü** *an eagle's cry* **3 have a cry** to produce tears from your eyes, usually because you are sad, angry, or hurt **üzgün, kızgın ve yaralı olduğunda gözlerinden yaş gelmek/ağlamak 4 be a far cry from sth** to be very different from something **alakası olmamak, çok farklı olmak** *Her luxury mansion is a far cry from the house she grew up in.*

crying /'kraɪɪŋ/ *adjective* **1 a crying need for sth** *mainly UK* a need that is very urgent **acil gereksinim, zaruri ihtiyaç** *There's a crying need for more nurses.* **2 it's a crying shame** used to say that you think a situation is very wrong **rezalet, rezillik**

crypt /krɪpt/ *noun* [C] a room under a church, especially one where people are buried (**kilise altında**) **mezar odası, sanduka**

cryptic /'krɪptɪk/ *adjective* mysterious and difficult to understand **gizemli, gizli, şifreli** *a cryptic comment/message ● cryptically adverb* gizli bir şekilde

C

crystal /'krɪstᵊl/ noun **1** ROCK [C, U] a type of transparent rock **bir tür kristal, billur kaya 2** GLASS [U] a type of high quality glass **kristal** *a crystal vase* **3** SHAPE [C] a piece of a substance that has become solid, with a regular shape **kristal, kristalleşmiş madde** *ice crystals*

,**crystal 'ball** *noun* [C] a large, glass ball that some people believe you can look into to see what will happen in the future **kristal küre**

,**crystal 'clear** *adjective* very obvious and easy to understand **billur gibi, açık seçik, apaçık** *She made her feelings crystal clear to me.*

CU *internet abbreviation for* see you: used when saying goodbye at the end of an email or text message **görüşürüz' anlamında ileti ve mektupların sonuna konulan kısaltma**

cub /kʌb/ *noun* [C] a young bear, fox, lion, etc **ayı, tilki veya aslan yavrusu**

cube¹ /kju:b/ *noun* **1** [C] a solid object with six square sides of the same size **küp** *Cut the cheese into small cubes.* ⊃See picture at **shape. 2 the cube of sth** the number you get when you multiply a particular number by itself twice **bir sayının küpü, küpünü alma** *The cube of 3 is 27.* ⊃See also: **ice cube.**

cube² /kju:b/ *verb* [T] **1** to multiply a particular number by itself twice **küpünü almak, bir sayıyı kendisiyle iki kez çarpmak** *5 cubed is 125.* **2** to cut something into cubes **küp şeklinde dilimlemek**

cubic /'kju:bɪk/ *adjective* **cubic centimetre/inch/metre, etc** a unit of measurement that shows the volume (= length multiplied by width multiplied by height) of something **santimetre/inç/metre küp** *a reservoir that holds 22 million cubic metres of water*

cubicle /'kju:bɪkl/ *noun* [C] a small space with walls around it, that is separate from the rest of a room **kabin, bölme** *a shower cubicle*

cuckoo /'kʊku:/ *noun* [C] a small bird that makes a sound like its name and puts its eggs into other birds' nests **guguk kuşu**

cucumber /'kju:kʌmbəʳ/ *noun* [C, U] a long, green vegetable that you eat raw in salads **salatalık, hıyar** ⊃Orta kısımdaki renkli sayfalarına bakınız.

cuddle /'kʌdl/ *verb* [I, T] to put your arms around someone to show them that you love them **sarılmak, kucaklamak, bağrına basmak** *Her mother cuddled her until she stopped crying.* ● **cuddle** *noun* [C] **sarılma**
cuddle up *phrasal verb* to sit or lie very close to someone **birinin yanına oturmak, sokulmak, uzanmak** *The children cuddled up to me to keep warm.*

cuddly /'kʌdli/ *adjective* soft and pleasant to hold close to you **yumuşak, şirin, insanın içine sokasının geldiği şey**

cue /kju:/ *noun* **1** ACTION/EVENT [C] an action or event that is a sign that something should happen **ipucu, işaret, olay, hareket** *The final goal was the cue for celebration.* **2** SIGNAL [C] a signal that tells someone to start speaking or doing something when acting in a play, film, etc (oyun, film vb.) **başlama işareti, replik 3 on cue** If something happens on cue, it happens at exactly the right time. **tam zamanında, tam o esnada** *Then, right on cue, Andrew appeared at the door.* **4 take your cue from sb/sth** to copy what someone else does **birinin yaptığının aynısını yapmak, taklit etmek, zeklenmek** *I took my cue from the others and left.* **5** STICK [C] a long, straight stick used to hit the balls in games like snooker (= a game played with small coloured balls on a table) **bilardo sopası, isteka**

cuff /kʌf/ *noun* [C] **1** the bottom part of a sleeve that goes around your wrist **kol ucu, kol ağzı, yen, manşet** ⊃See picture at **jacket. 2 off the cuff** If you speak off the

cuff, you do it without having planned what you will say. **hazırlıksız, irticalen, doğaçlama konuşmak; tasarlamadan, rastgele söylemek**

cuisine /kwɪz'i:n/ *noun* [U] a style of cooking **mutfak, yemek pişirme tarzı** *French/international cuisine*

cul-de-sac /'kʌldəsæk/ *noun* [C] a short road with houses which is blocked at one end **çıkmaz sokak**

culinary /'kʌlɪnᵊri/ *adjective* [always before noun] *formal* related to food and cooking **yiyecek ve yemek pişirmeyle ilgili** *culinary equipment*

cull /kʌl/ *verb* [T] to kill some of the animals in a group, especially the weakest ones, to limit their numbers **(zayıf/güçsüz hayvanları) sayılarını azaltmak için öldürmek, itlaf etmek** ● **cull** *noun* [C] **öldürme (hayvan)**
cull sth from sth *phrasal verb* to collect ideas or information from several different places **çeşitli kaynaklardan bilgi toplamak, derlemek** [often passive] *The book is culled from over 800 pages of his diaries.*

culminate /'kʌlmɪneɪt/ *verb formal* **1 culminate in/ with sth** to finish with a particular event, or reach a final result after gradual development and often a lot of effort **... ile son bulmak/sonuçlanmak; çabaları sonuç vermek; sonuca ulaşmak, doruğa ulaşmak** *His career culminated with the post of ambassador to NATO.* **2** [T] *US* to be the final thing in a series of events **bir çok eylemin en sonuncusu olmak; ... ile sonuçlanmak** *The discovery of the body culminated two days of desperate searching.* ● **culmination** /ˌkʌlmɪ'neɪʃᵊn/ *noun* [no plural] *This discovery is the culmination of years of research.* **sonuç**

culpable /'kʌlpəbl/ *adjective formal* deserving to be blamed for something bad **suçlu, kabahatli** ● **culpability** /ˌkʌlpə'bɪləti/ *noun* [U] **kabahat**

culprit /'kʌlprɪt/ *noun* [C] **1** someone who has done something wrong **suçlu, suç işlemiş kişi 2** something that is responsible for a bad situation **neden, sebep** *In many of these illnesses, stress is the main culprit.*

cult /kʌlt/ *noun* [C] **1** someone or something which has become very popular with a particular group of people **moda, tutku, heves, merak** *a cult figure/movie* **2** a religious group whose ideas are considered strange by many people **mezhep, tarikat, ibadet, ayin**

cultivate /'kʌltɪveɪt/ *verb* [T] **1** to prepare land and grow crops on it **toprağı işlemek, ekip biçmek, sürüp ekmek** *This shrub is cultivated in Europe as a culinary herb.* **2** to try to develop or improve something **bir şeyi geliştirmek, ilerletmek** *She has cultivated an image as a tough negotiator.* ● **cultivation** /ˌkʌltɪ'veɪʃᵊn/ *noun* [U] **ekim, yetiştirme**

cultivated /'kʌltɪveɪtɪd/ *adjective* A cultivated person has had a good education and knows a lot about art, books, music, etc. **müzik, sanat ve kitaplar konusunda donanımlı, bilgili, iyi eğitimli; münevver, kültürlü**

cultural /'kʌltʃᵊrᵊl/ *adjective* **1** relating to the habits, traditions, and beliefs of a society **kültürel, toplumun inanç, gelenek ve alışkanlıklarına ilişkin** *cultural diversity/identity* **2** relating to music, art, theatre, etc **sanatsal, sanata ilişkin** *cultural events* ● **culturally** *adverb* **kültürel açıdan**

o⁻**culture** /'kʌltʃəʳ/ *noun* **1** SOCIETY [C, U] the habits, traditions, and beliefs of a country, society, or group of people **kültür, toplum** *American/Japanese culture* ○ *It's a good opportunity for children to learn about other cultures.* **2** ARTS [U] music, art, theatre, literature, etc **kültür, sanat** *popular culture* **3** BIOLOGY [C, U] the process of growing things, especially bacteria (= very small living things that can cause disease), for scientific purposes, or the bacteria produced by this process **kültür, bakteri üremesi**

cultured /'kʌltʃəd/ *adjective* A cultured person knows a lot about music, art, theatre, etc. **münevver, kültürlü, iyi eğitimli**

'culture ˌshock *noun* [U] the feeling of confusion someone has when they go to a new and very different place **kültür şoku**

-cum- /kʌm/ used between two nouns to describe something which combines the two things **hem … hem de;** *… olduğu kadar;* *… olarak da a kitchen-cum-dining room* (= room which is used as a kitchen and a dining room)

cumbersome /'kʌmbəsəm/ *adjective* **1** large and difficult to move or use **kullanışsız, taşınması zor, iri ve ağır** *cumbersome safety equipment* **2** slow and not effective **hantal, ağır ve işe yaramaz** *cumbersome bureaucracy*

cumulative /'kjuːmjələtɪv/ *adjective* reached by gradually adding one thing after another **toplanarak artan, birikimli, kümülatif** *a cumulative score*

cunning /'kʌnɪŋ/ *adjective* clever at getting what you want, especially by tricking people **şeytan, kurnaz, hinoğlu hin, hilekâr** *a cunning plan/ploy* ● **cunning** *noun* [U] **kurnazlık** ● **cunningly** *adverb* **kurnazca**

cup

o▪**cup¹** /kʌp/ *noun* [C] **1** [CONTAINER] a small, round container with a handle on the side, used to drink from **fincan** *a cup of tea/coffee* **2** [SPORT] a prize given to the winner of a competition, or the name of the competition **kupa** *the World Cup* **3** [COOKING] *mainly US* a measurement of amounts of food used in cooking **ölçek** ➔See also: egg cup.

cup² /kʌp/ *verb* [T] **cupping**, *past* **cupped** to make your hands into the shape of a cup, or to hold something with your hands in this shape **avuçlamak, avucunun içinde tutmak**

o▪**cupboard** /'kʌbəd/ *noun* [C] a piece of furniture with a door on the front and shelves inside, used for storing things **dolap, büfe, mutfak dolabı** ➔Orta kısımdaki renkli sayfalarına bakınız ➔See also: have a **skeleton** in the cupboard.

curate /'kjuərət/ *noun* [C] a person who works for the Church of England and whose job is to help the vicar (= priest in a particular area) **rahip yardımcısı**

curator /kjuə'reɪtər/ *noun* [C] a person who is in charge of a museum (= a building where you can look at objects, such as art or old things) **müze müdürü, sanat galerisi müdürü**

curb¹ /kɜːb/ *verb* [T] to limit or control something **sınırlamak, denetim/kontrol altına almak** *to curb crime/ inflation*

curb² /kɜːb/ *noun* [C] **1** something which limits or controls something **denetleyen, kontrol eden** *They are*

proposing a curb on tobacco advertising. **2** *US spelling of* kerb (= the line of stones at the edge of a path next to the road) **bordür taşı, tretuvar kenarı**

curdle /'kɜːdl/ *verb* [I, T] If a liquid curdles, or if you curdle it, it gets thicker and develops lumps. **(sıvı) kesilmek, kestirmek** *Heat the sauce slowly or it will curdle.*

⟨puzzle icon⟩ **cure** .... İLE BİRLİKTE KULLANILAN KELİMELER

find/look for a cure ● a cure for sth ● the search for a cure

---

cure¹ /kjuərʳ/ *noun* [C] **1** something that makes someone with an illness healthy again **tedavi** *They are trying to find a cure for cancer.* **2** a solution to a problem **çözüm, çare, ilaç, derman**

cure² /kjuərʳ/ *verb* [T] **1** to make someone with an illness healthy again **tedavi etmek, iyileştirmek, sağlığına kavuşturmak** *Getting a better chair completely cured my back problems.* **2** to solve a problem **problemi çözmek, çare bulmak** *the fight to cure social inequality*

curfew /'kɜːfjuː/ *noun* [C] a time, especially at night, when people are not allowed to leave their homes **sokağa çıkma yasağı**

⟨puzzle icon⟩ **curiosity** .... İLE BİRLİKTE KULLANILAN KELİMELER

arouse/satisfy sb's curiosity ● (do sth) out of curiosity ● mild/natural curiosity ● curiosity about sth

---

curiosity /ˌkjʊəri'ɒsəti/ *noun* **1** [U] the feeling of wanting to know or learn about something **merak** *My curiosity got the better of me and I opened the envelope.* ○ *Just out of curiosity, how did you get my address?* **2** [C] something strange or unusual **nadir şey, antika, acayip nesne, sıradışı şey**

curious /'kjʊəriəs/ *adjective* **1** wanting to know or learn about something **meraklı** *I was curious about his life in India.* ○ *I was curious to know what would happen next.* **2** strange or unusual **garip, tuhaf, acayip** *The house was decorated in a curious style.* ● **curiously** *adverb* *She looked at him curiously.* **meraklı olarak**

curl¹ /kɜːl/ *noun* [C] something with a small, curved shape, especially a piece of hair **bukle, kıvırcık** *a child with blonde curls*

curl² /kɜːl/ *verb* [I, T] to make something into the shape of a curl, or to be this shape **bükülmek, kıvırcık şekil vermek, bukle bukle olmak** *The cat curled its tail around its body.*

curl up *phrasal verb* **1** to sit or lie in a position with your arms and legs close to your body **kıvrılmak, kıvrılıp yapmak** *She curled up and went to sleep.* **2** If something flat, such as a piece of paper, curls up, the edges start to curve up. **kenarları kıvrılmak**

curly /'kɜːli/ *adjective* shaped like a curl, or with many curls **kıvırcık, bukleli** *curly hair*

currant /'kʌrᵊnt/ *noun* [C] a small, black dried fruit used in cooking, especially in cakes **kuş üzümü**

currency /'kʌrᵊnsi/ *noun* **1** [C, U] the units of money used in a particular country **resmi para, tedavüldeki para** *foreign currency* **2** [U] when an idea is believed or accepted by many people **(fikir) geçerlilik, revaç, benimsenmişlik, yaygınlık** *This view is gaining currency within the government.* ➔See also: hard currency.

o▪**current¹** /'kʌrᵊnt/ *adjective* happening or existing now **mevcut olan, geçerli, halihazırda var olan** *What is your current address?* ● **currently** *adverb* *The factory currently employs 750 people.* **şu anda**

current² /'kʌrᵊnt/ *noun* **1** [C] the natural flow of air or water in one direction **(hava) akım, cereyan** *a current of air* ○ *dangerous/strong currents* **2** [C, U] the flow of electricity through a wire **(elektrik) akım, cereyan** *an electrical current*

current ac'count *UK* (*US* **checking account**) *noun* [C] a bank account which you can take money out of at any time **vadesiz hesap, çek hesabı**

current af'fairs *UK* (*US* **current e'vents**) *noun* [plural] important political or social events which are happening in the world at the present time **güncel olaylar**

curriculum /kəˈrɪkjələm/ *noun* [C] *plural* **curricula** or **curriculums** all the subjects taught in a school, college, etc or on an educational course **öğretim/müfredat programı/izlencesi;** *the school curriculum*

curry /ˈkʌri/ *noun* [C, U] a type of food from India, made of vegetables or meat cooked with hot spices **baharatı bol, acı Hint yemeği**

curse¹ /kɜːs/ *noun* [C] [MAGIC] magic words which are intended to bring bad luck to someone **beddua, lanet okuma** *to put a curse on someone* **2** [RUDE WORDS] a rude or offensive word or phrase **sövgü, küfür 3** [PROBLEM] something that causes harm or unhappiness, often over a long period of time **felaket, dert, bela** *Traffic is one of the curses of modern living.*

curse² /kɜːs/ *verb* [I] to use rude or offensive words **küfretmek, sövmek** *He cursed angrily under his breath.* **2** [T] to express anger towards someone or something **beddua etmek, lanet okumak** *He cursed himself for not telling David about it earlier.* **3 be cursed by/ with sth** to have something which causes problems over a long period of time **başına bela olmak; bela almak**

cursor /ˈkɜːsəʳ/ *noun* [C] a symbol on a computer screen which shows the place where you are working **imleç**

cursory /ˈkɜːsəri/ *adjective* [always before noun] *formal* done quickly and without much care **gelişigüzel, üstünkörü, acele, baştan savma** *a cursory glance*

curt /kɜːt/ *adjective* If something you say or write is curt, it is short and not very polite. **kısa, gelişigüzel, ters** ● **curtly** *adverb* **kısa ve kabaca**

curtail /kɜːˈteɪl/ *verb* [T] *formal* to reduce, limit, or stop something **durdurmak, azaltmak, kısmak, sınırlamak** *to curtail spending* ● **curtailment** *noun* [U] **kısıntı, azaltma**

curtain /ˈkɜːtᵊn/ *noun* [C] a piece of material which hangs down to cover a window, stage, etc **perde** *to draw the curtains* (= open or close them) ○ *The curtain goes up* (= the performance starts) *at 8 o'clock .* ⊃Orta kısımdaki renkli sayfalarına bakınız.

curtsey (*also* **curtsy**) /ˈkɜːtsi/ *noun* [C] a movement where a girl or woman puts one foot behind the other and bends her knees, especially to show respect to a king or queen **dizlerini kırarak ve hafifçe eğilerek selamlama, reverans yapma** ● **curtsey** *verb* [I] **reverans etmek**

curve¹ /kɜːv/ *noun* [C] a line which bends round like part of a circle **kavis, eğri, kıvrım** *a road with gentle curves*

curve² /kɜːv/ *verb* [I, T] to move in a curve, form a curve, or make something into the shape of a curve **eğilmek, kıvrılmak, bükülmek, dairevi şekil almak** *The road curves to the left.* ○ *a chair with a curved back* ⊃See picture at **flat.**

cushion¹ /ˈkʊʃᵊn/ *noun* [C] **1** a cloth bag filled with something soft which you sit on or lean against to make you comfortable **yastık, minder** ⊃Orta kısımdaki renkli sayfalarına bakınız. **2** something which protects you from possible problems **muhtemel sorunlardan koruyan, destek** *Overseas savings provide a cushion against tax rises at home.*

cushion² /ˈkʊʃᵊn/ *verb* [T] **1** to reduce the bad effects of something **kötü etkilerini azaltmak, tampon görevi yapmak** *attempts to cushion the impact of unemployment* **2** to protect something, especially part of the body, with something soft **korumak, bilhassa vücuda gelebilecek zarara yumuşak bir şeyle kaşı koymak, azaltmak** *Soft grass cushioned his fall.*

cushy /ˈkʊʃi/ *adjective informal* very easy **çok kolay** *a cushy job*

custard /ˈkʌstəd/ *noun* **1** [U] a sweet, yellow sauce made from milk and eggs, usually eaten hot with sweet food **krema, muhallebi** *apple pie and custard* **2** [C, U] a soft baked mixture made from milk, eggs, and sugar **yumurta, süt ve şekerle yapılan krema** *a custard pie/tart*

custodial /kʌˈstəʊdiəl/ *adjective* If someone is given a custodial sentence (= punishment), they are sent to prison. **gözaltında olan, tutuklu, hapis cezası alan**

custodian /kʌˈstəʊdiən/ *noun* [C] **1** *formal* a person who takes care of something valuable or important **bekçi, koruyucu, muhafız** *He's the grandson of Oscar Wilde and custodian of his private papers.* **2** *US* someone whose job is to look after a building, especially a school **bekçi, güvenlik görevlisi, okul hademesi**

custody ...... İLE BİRLİKTE KULLANILAN KELİMELER

be **awarded/given** custody (**of** sb) ● **have/win** custody (**of** sb)

custody /ˈkʌstədi/ *noun* [U] **1** the legal right to look after a child, especially when parents separate **velayet** *When they divorced, it was Nicola who* **won custody** *of their two children.* **2** when someone is kept in prison, usually while they are waiting for a trial in court **tutuklu** *He is being* **held in custody** *in Los Angeles charged with assault.* ○ *He was* **taken into custody** *by Mexican authorities.*

custom ...... İLE BİRLİKTE KULLANILAN KELİMELER

an **ancient/local/traditional** custom ● the custom **of** doing sth

custom /ˈkʌstəm/ *noun* **1** [C, U] a habit or tradition **gelenek, âdet, örf, alışkanlık 2** [U] when people buy things from shops or businesses **alışveriş, ticaret** *Free gifts are a good way of* **attracting custom.**

custom- /ˈkʌstəm/ *prefix* used before another word to mean 'specially designed for a particular person or purpose' **'özel tasarım' anlamında önek** *custom-built* ○ *custom-designed*

customary /ˈkʌstəmᵊri/ *adjective* normal or expected for a particular person, situation, or society **alışılmış, âdet olan, beklenen** [+ to do sth] *It is customary for the chairman to make the opening speech.* ● **customarily** /ˌkʌstəˈmerᵊli/ *adverb* **olağan bir şekilde**

customer /ˈkʌstəməʳ/ *noun* [C] a person or organization that buys goods or services from a shop or business **müşteri, alıcı** *a satisfied customer* ○ *Mrs Wilson is one of our regular customers.*

customise *UK* (*US* **-ize**) /ˈkʌstəmaɪz/ *verb* [T] to change something to make it suitable for a particular person or purpose **kişiselleştirmek, belli bir kişi veya amaç için değiştirmek** *Our language courses are customised to each student.*

customs /ˈkʌstəmz/ *noun* [U] the place where your bags are examined when you are going into a country, to make sure you are not carrying anything illegal **gümrük** *customs officials* ○ *to go through customs*

cut

○➤**cut¹** /kʌt/ *verb* **cutting**, *past* **cut 1** ⟨KNIFE⟩ **[I, T]** to use a knife or other sharp tool to divide something, remove part of something, or make a hole in something **kesmek** *Cut the meat into small pieces.* ○ *He cut the piece of wood in half.* ○ *I had my hair cut last week.* ○ *She cut off all the diseased buds.* **2** ⟨REDUCE⟩ **[T]** to reduce the size or amount of something **azaltmak, kısmak** *Prices have been cut by 25%.* ○ *The company is cutting 50 jobs.* **3** ⟨INJURE⟩ **[T]** to injure yourself on a sharp object which makes you bleed **kendini kesmek, yaralamak** *She cut her finger on a broken glass.* **4** ⟨REMOVE⟩ **[T]** to remove part of a film or piece of writing **(film, yazı) azaltmak, kesmek, çıkarmak** *The film was too long so they cut some scenes.* ⊃See also: cut corners **(corner¹)**, cut it/things **fine²**, have your **work²** cut out.

cut across sth *phrasal verb* **1** to go from one side of an area to the other instead of going round it **kısa yoldan/ kestirmeden gitmek** *If we cut across this field, it will save time.* **2** If a problem or subject cuts across different groups of people, all of those groups are affected by it or interested in it. **etkilenmek, ilgisini çekmek, alakadar etmek**

cut back (sth) *phrasal verb* to reduce the amount of money being spent on something **harcamaları kısmak, tasarruf etmek** *We have had to cut back on training this year.*

cut sth down *phrasal verb* to make a tree or other plant fall to the ground by cutting it near the bottom **(ağaç, bitki) kesmek, kesip devirmek**

cut down (sth) *phrasal verb* to eat or drink less of something, or to reduce the amount or number of something **daha az yemek/ içmek; azaltmak** *My doctor says I should cut down on cigarettes.*

cut sb off *phrasal verb* to stop someone speaking by interrupting them or putting the telephone down **sözünü kesmek, telefonu kapatmak** *She cut me off in the middle of our conversation.*

cut sb/sth off *phrasal verb* **1** to prevent people from reaching or leaving a place, or to separate them from other people **ayrılmasını/varmasını engellemek veya diğerlerinden ayırmak, bağlantısını kesmek**

[often passive] *The whole village was cut off by flooding.* ○ *She lives abroad and feels very **cut off from** her family.* **2** to stop providing something such as electricity or food supplies **elektrik/yiyecek sağlamayı durdurmak, kesmek** [often passive] *If we don't pay the gas bill, we'll be cut off.*

cut sth out *phrasal verb* **1** to remove something or form a shape by cutting, usually something made of paper or cloth **kesip çıkarmak, oyup almak** *She cut out his picture from the magazine.* **2** to stop eating or drinking something, usually to improve your health **sağlığını geliştirmek için bir şeyi yemekten içmekten vazgeçmek** *I've cut out red meat from my diet.* **3 Cut it out!** *informal* something you say to tell someone to stop doing something annoying **4 not be cut out to be sth/not be cut out for sth** to not have the right qualities for something *I'm not really cut out to be a nurse.*

cut out *phrasal verb* If an engine, machine, or piece of equipment cuts out, it suddenly stops working. **(motor, makina, alet) aniden durmak, çalışmamak**

cut sth/sb out *phrasal verb* to not let someone share something or be included in something **dahil etmemek, paylaşmamak, dışarda bırakmak, hariç tutmak**

cut sth up *phrasal verb* **1** to cut something into pieces **parçalara ayırmak, param parça dilimlemek 2 be cut up** *UK informal* to be very upset about something *He was very cut up when his brother died.*

cut² /kʌt/ *noun* **[C] 1** ⟨INJURY⟩ an injury made when the skin is cut with something sharp **kesik, yara, bere** *He suffered cuts and bruises in the accident.* **2** ⟨OPENING⟩ an opening made with a sharp tool **yarık, açıklık** *She made a cut in the material.* **3** ⟨REDUCTION⟩ a reduction in the number or amount of something **azaltma, kesme** *tax/job cuts* ○ *The workers were angry about the cut in pay.* **4** ⟨MEAT⟩ a piece of meat from a particular part of an animal **bir parça et** *an expensive cut of beef* **5** ⟨SHARE⟩ a share of something, usually money **(para) pay, payına düşen** *My family owns the company, so we get a cut of the profits.* **6 an electricity/power, etc cut** when the supply of something is stopped **elektrik/güç vs. Kesintisi 7** ⟨HAIR⟩ *(also* **haircut)** the style in which your hair has been cut **seç kesim şekli** ⊃See also: shortcut.

,cut and 'paste *verb* **[I, T] cutting and pasting**, *past* **cut and pasted** to move words or pictures from one place to another in a computer document **kesip yapıştırmak**

cutback .... İLE BİRLİKTE KULLANILAN KELİMELER

make cutbacks ● **drastic/severe/sharp** cutbacks ● cutbacks **in** sth

cutback /'kʌtbæk/ *noun* **[C]** a reduction of something, usually to save money **tasarruf amaçlı azaltma, düşürme, tasarruf, tenkis** *The company has made cutbacks and closed one of its factories.*

cute /kjuːt/ *adjective* **1** attractive **çekici, hoş, cana yakın, tatlı, şirin** *a cute baby* **2** *US informal* clever in a way that is annoying or rude **sevimli, hoşa giden olduğunu düşünen** *He thinks it's cute to tell dirty jokes.*

cutlery /'kʌtl°ri/ *UK (US* **silverware)** *noun* **[U]** knives, forks, and spoons **çatal-kaşık-bıçak takımı**

cutlet /'kʌtlət/ *noun* **[C]** a small piece of meat still joined to the bone **pirzola, külbastı** *a lamb cutlet*

cut-price /'kʌt,praɪs/ *mainly UK (US* **cut-rate)** *adjective* [always before noun] cheaper than usual **indirimli, ucuz, kelepir** *cut-price tickets*

cutters /'kʌtəz/ *noun* [plural] a tool for cutting something **kesici alet** *wire cutters*

cut-throat *mainly UK (also US* **cutthroat)** /'kʌtθrəʊt/ *adjective* a cut-throat business or other situation is where people will do anything to succeed and do not care if they hurt others (**iş, durum**) **acımasız, insafsız, ölesiye rekâbet olan, merhametsiz, amansız** *the cut-throat world of journalism*

cutting[1] /'kʌtɪŋ/ *noun* [C] **1** a piece cut from a plant and used to grow a new plant (**bitki**) **çelik 2** *UK (UK/US* **clipping**) an article or picture that has been cut out of a newspaper or magazine **küpür, parça, resim, yazı, bölüm**

cutting[2] /'kʌtɪŋ/ *adjective* If something you say or write is cutting, it is unkind. **incitici, kaba, üzücü, kırıcı, acı** *a cutting remark*

cutting-edge /ˌkʌtɪŋ'edʒ/ *adjective* very modern and with all the newest developments **son derece modern, en yeni gelişmeleri barındıran** *cutting-edge design/ technology*

CV /ˌsiː'viː/ *UK (US* résumé) *noun* [C] a document which describes your qualifications and the jobs you have done, which you send to an employer that you want to work for **özgeçmiş**

cwt *written abbreviation for* hundredweight (= a unit for measuring weight, equal to 50.8 kilograms in the UK and 45.36 kilograms in the US) **birleşik kallik'da 50.8 ABD'de 45.35 kilograma denk ağırlık ölçüsü, birimi**

cyanide /'saɪənaɪd/ *noun* [U] a very strong poison **siyanür, güçlü bir zehir**

cyber- /saɪbəʳ/ *prefix* relating to electronic communications, especially the Internet **bilhassa internet/elektronik iletişime ilişkin, siber- anlamında önek** *cyberspace*

cybercafe /'saɪbəˌkæfeɪ/ *noun* [C] a place where customers can buy food and drink and use computers to search for information on the Internet **internet kafe**

cyberspace /'saɪbəˌspeɪs/ *noun* [U] the Internet, considered as an imaginary area where you can communicate with people and find information **internet**

cycle[1] /'saɪkl/ *noun* [C] **1** a series of events which happen in a particular order and are often repeated **dizi, demet, bir seri olaylar zinciri** *the life cycle of a moth* **2** a bicycle **bisiklet** ⊃See also: life cycle.

cycle[2] /'saɪkl/ *verb* [I] to ride a bicycle **bisiklete binmek** ● **cycling** *noun* [U] ⊃Orta kısımdaki renkli sayfalarına bakınız.

bisiklete binme ● **cyclist** *noun* [C] someone who rides a bicycle **bisiklet sürücüsü, bisiklete binen kimse**

'cycle ˌhelmet *noun* [C] a hard hat that protects your head when you ride a bicycle **bisiklet sürücü kaskı** ⊃Orta kısımdaki renkli sayfalarına bakınız.

cyclical /'sɪklɪkᵊl/ *adjective* happening in a regular and repeated pattern **düzenli aralıklarla tekerrür eden, dönüşül** *the cyclical nature of the country's history*

cyclone /'saɪkləʊn/ *noun* [C] a violent storm with very strong winds which move in a circle **kasırga, hortum, siklon**

cylinder /'sɪlɪndəʳ/ *noun* [C] **1** a shape with circular ends and long, straight sides, or a container or object shaped like this **silindir, merdane** *an oxygen cylinder* ⊃See picture at shape. **2** a part in a car or machine's engine which is shaped like a tube, and where another part moves up and down (**araç**) **silindir**

cylindrical /sə'lɪndrɪkᵊl/ *adjective* having the shape of a cylinder **silindir biçiminde, merdane şeklinde**

cymbal /'sɪmbᵊl/ *noun* [C] a musical instrument like a metal plate which is played by being hit with a stick or another cymbal (**çalgı**) **zil**

cynic /'sɪnɪk/ *noun* [C] a cynical person **kötümser, herşeye kötü açıdan bakan, felaket tellalı**

cynical /'sɪnɪkᵊl/ *adjective* believing that people are only interested in themselves and are not sincere **iyiliğe inanmayan, kötümser bakan, olumsuz** *Many people have become cynical about politicians.* ● **cynically** *adverb* **olumsuz, inançsız bir şekilde** ● **cynicism** /'sɪnɪsɪzᵊm/ *noun* [U] cynical beliefs **kötümserlik, olumsuzculuk, sinisizm**

cyst /sɪst/ *noun* [C] a small lump containing liquid that can grow under your skin **kist, kese, yağ bezesi**

cystic fibrosis /ˌsɪstɪkfaɪ'brəʊsɪs/ *noun* [U] a serious disease which causes the lungs and other organs to become blocked **akciğer ve diğer organların tıkanmasına sebep olan ciddi bir hastalık**

czar (*also UK* tsar) /zɑːʳ/ *noun* [C] **1** a male Russian ruler before 1917 **Çar, Rus çarı 2** *informal* a powerful official who makes important decisions for the government about a particular activity **belli bir eylem için hükümet adına önemli kararları alan resmi yetkili** *a drugs czar*

D

D, d /diː/ the fourth letter of the alphabet **alfabenin dördüncü harfi**

dab /dæb/ *verb* [I, T] **dabbing**, *past* **dabbed** to touch something with quick, light touches, or to put a substance on something with quick, light touches **hızlı ve hafif hareketlerle dokunmak, sıvazlamak, ovuşturmak veya hafif ve hızlı şekilde birşeyin üzerine bir maddeyi sürmek** *She dabbed at her eyes with a tissue.* ● **dab** *noun* [C] a small amount of something **azıcık, az miktarda** *a dab of lipstick*

DAB /ˌdiːeɪˈbiː/ *noun* [U] *abbreviation for* digital audio broadcasting: an electronic system for sending radio or television information using signals in the form of numbers **DSY dijital ses yayını: rakamsal sinyalleri kullanarak tv ve radyo bilgilerini gönderen elektronik sistem**

dabble /ˈdæbl/ *verb* [I] to try something or take part in an activity in a way that is not serious **gayri ciddi olarak bir şeyi denemek ya da bir faaliyet içerisinde yer almak** *I only dabble in politics.* ○ *He dabbled with drugs at university.*

o▪**dad** /dæd/ *noun* [C] *informal* father **baba** *Can I go to the park, Dad?*

daddy /ˈdædi/ *noun* [C] a word for 'father', used especially by children **özellikle çocuklar tarafından 'baba' anlamında kullanılan sözcük; babişko**

daffodil /ˈdæfədɪl/ *noun*
[C] a yellow flower that
usually grows in spring
**fulya, genellikle
ilkbaharda açan sarı
bir çiçek**

daft /dɑːft/ *adjective UK
informal* silly **aptal,
aptalca, budala** *That's
a daft idea.*

dagger /ˈdægəʳ/ *noun* [C]
a short knife, used as a
weapon **silah olarak
da kullanılabilen, kama, kısa bıçak**

o▪**daily**[1] /ˈdeɪli/ *adjective* [always before noun], *adverb* **1** happening or produced every day or once a day **günlük, hergün ya da günde bir kez olan, yapılan** *a daily newspaper* ○ *The shop is open daily from 8 a.m. to 6 p.m.* **2** relating to one single day **tek bir güne ilişkin, günlük** *They are paid on a daily basis.* **3 daily life** the usual things that happen to you every day **günlük yaşamda olan şeyler** *Shootings are part of daily life in the region.*

daily[2] /ˈdeɪli/ *noun* [C] a newspaper that is published every day except Sunday **pazar günleri hariç her gün basılan gazete, günlük gazete**

dainty /ˈdeɪnti/ *adjective* small, attractive, and delicate **küçük, zarif, çekici, narin** *dainty feet* ● **daintily** *adverb* sevimli bir şekilde

dairy[1] /ˈdeəri/ *noun* [C] **1** a place where milk is stored and cream and cheese are made **sütün depolandığı, kaymak ve peynirin üretildiği yer 2** a company which sells milk and products made of milk **süt ve süt mamülleri satan şirket**

dairy[2] /ˈdeəri/ *adjective* [always before noun] relating to milk or products made using milk **süt ve süt ürünlerine ait, süt mamulü** *dairy products* ○ *dairy cattle*

daisy /ˈdeɪzi/ *noun* [C] a small flower with white petals and a yellow centre that often grows in grass **papatya**

dam /dæm/ *noun* [C] a strong wall built across a river to stop the water and make a lake **baraj** ● **dam** *verb* [T] **damming**, *past* **dammed** to build a dam across a river **baraj inşa etmek**

┌─ 🧩 **damage** ⋯⋯⋯ İLE BİRLİKTE KULLANILAN KELİMELER ─┐

cause/inflict/repair/suffer damage ● **extensive/permanent/serious/slight** damage ● damage **to sth**

o▪**damage**[1] /ˈdæmɪdʒ/ *noun* [U] harm or injury **zarar, ziyan, yaralama** *He suffered **brain damage** in the car crash.* ○ *The strong wind caused serious **damage to** the roof.*

o▪**damage**[2] /ˈdæmɪdʒ/ *verb* [T] to harm or break something **bir şeyi kırmak ya da zarar vermek** *Many buildings were damaged in the storm.* ○ *Smoking can seriously damage your health.* ● **damaging** *adjective* harmful **zararlı, zarar veren** *the **damaging effects** of pollution*

┌─ 🧩 **damages** ⋯⋯⋯ İLE BİRLİKTE KULLANILAN KELİMELER ─┐

award/claim/pay/seek/win damages ● **substantial** damages ● **[£400, $10,000, etc] in** damages

damages /ˈdæmɪdʒɪz/ *noun* [plural] money that a person or organization pays to someone because they have harmed them or something that belongs to them **bir kişi ya da kuruluşun bir kişiye veya ona ait olan şeylere zarar vermesinden dolayı ödediği para, tazminat** *She was awarded £400 **in damages**.*

dame /deɪm/ *noun* [C] **1** a title used in the UK before the name of a woman who has been officially respected **Birleşik krallık'da resmen tanınan bir bayana verilen asalet ünvanı** *Dame Agatha Christie* **2** *US informal* old-fashioned a woman **kadın, bayan**

damn[1] /dæm/ (*also* **damned** /dæmd/) *adjective* [always before noun] *informal* used to express anger **kızgınlık duygusunu bildirmek için kullanılan ünlem** *"Kahretsin!" He didn't listen to a damn thing I said.*

damn[2] /dæm/ (*also* **damn it**) *exclamation* used to express anger or disappointment **(lanet ederek) hiddeti ve kızgınlığı ifade etmek için kullanılır (ünlem)** *Damn! I've forgotten the tickets.*

damn[3] /dæm/ (*also* **damned** /dæmd/) *adverb informal* very **çok, çokca, epeyce** *He worked damn hard to pass that exam.*

damn[4] /dæm/ *noun* **not give a damn** *informal* to not be interested in or worried about someone or something **birisine veya bir şeye aldırış etmemek, umursamamak, dönüp bakmamak, vız gelmek** *I don't give a damn what people think.*

damn[5] /dæm/ *verb* **1 damn him/it/you, etc** used to express anger about something or someone **Allah kahretsin!, Allah belasını versin!; Yeter!** *Stop complaining, damn you!* **2** [T] to strongly criticize someone or something **birisini veya bir şeyi şiddetle eleştirmek** *He was damned by the media.*

damning /'dæmɪŋ/ *adjective* criticizing someone or something very strongly, or showing clearly that someone is guilty **yerin dibine batıran; şiddetle kötüleyen; kesin bir dille suçlayan** *damning evidence* ○ *a damning report on education standards*

damp /dæmp/ *adjective* slightly wet, usually in an unpleasant way **rutubetli ve havasız ortam** *damp clothes/grass* ○ *It was cold and damp outside.* • **damp** (*also* **dampness**) *noun* [U] when something is slightly wet **rutubet, nem**

dampen /'dæmpən/ (*also* **damp**) *verb* [T] **1** to make something less strong **bir şeyi zayıflatmak, güçsüz kılmak** *Nothing you can say will dampen her enthusiasm.* **2** to make something slightly wet **hafifce ıslatmak, nemlendirmek**

damper /'dæmpəʳ/ *noun* **put a damper on sth** to stop an occasion from being enjoyable **tatsızlaştırmak, keyfini kaçırmak** *The accident put a damper on their holiday.*

o⬝**dance¹** /dɑːns/ *verb* [I, T] to move your feet and body to the rhythm of music **dans etmek** *She's dancing with Steven.* ○ *Can you dance the tango?* • **dancer** *noun* [C] **dansçı** • **dancing** *noun* [U] **dans**

o⬝**dance²** /dɑːns/ *noun* **1** [MOVING] [C] when you move your feet and body to music **dans** *I had a dance with my dad.* **2** [STEPS] [C] a particular set of steps or movements to music **belirli bir müzik eşliğinde dans** *My favourite dance is the tango.* **3** [EVENT] [C] a social event where people dance to music **müzikli, danslı eğlence 4** [ACTIVITY] [U] the activity or skill of dancing **dans etme, dans yeteneği** *a dance school*

dandelion /'dændɪlaɪən/ *noun* [C] a yellow wild flower **kara hindiba**

dandruff /'dændrʌf/ *noun* [U] small pieces of dead skin in someone's hair or on their clothes **saç diplerinde oluşan kepek**

🧩 danger ...... İLE BİRLİKTE KULLANILAN KELİMELER

face danger • pose a danger • great/serious danger • be in danger • be in danger of sth

o⬝**danger** /'deɪndʒəʳ/ *noun* **1** [C, U] the possibility that someone or something will be harmed or killed, or that something bad will happen **tehlike** *the dangers of rock climbing* ○ *The soldiers were in serious danger.* ○ *We were in danger of missing our flight.* **2** [C] something or someone that may harm you **tehlike oluşturan kişi/şey** *Icy roads are a danger to drivers.*

dangerous ...... BAŞKA BİR DEYİŞLE

Eğer bir şey çok tehlikeliyse, bunu belirtmede **hazardous, perilous** veya **treacherous** sıfatları kullanılır. *Ice had made the roads* **treacherous**. • *Heavy rain is causing* **hazardous** *driving conditions.* • *A* **perilous** *journey through the mountains was their only escape route.* Tehlikeli olan maddeler için **harmful** veya **hazardous** ifadeleri kullanılır. *Please be aware that these chemicals are* **harmful/hazardous** *to human health.* Eğer bir şey, ortaya çıkabilecek kötü bir durumdan dolayı tehlikeli görünüyorsa, bunu belirtmede **risky** ifadesi kullanılır. *Surgery at his age would be too* **risky**.

o⬝**dangerous** /'deɪndʒ'rəs/ *adjective* If someone or something is dangerous, they could harm you. **tehlikeli** *a dangerous chemical* • **dangerously** *adverb dangerously close to the edge* **tehlikeli bir şekilde**

dangle /'dæŋgl/ *verb* **1** [I, T] to hang loosely, or to hold something so that it hangs loosely **gevşek bir şekilde asmak veya bağlamak, salla(n)mak, sark(ıt)mak** *Electrical wires were dangling from the ceiling.* **2** [T] to offer someone something they want in order to per-

suade them to do something **vaat etmek, vaatte bulunmak, ikna etmek için bir şey vaat etmek** *They dangled the possibility of a job in Paris in front of him.*

dank /dæŋk/ *adjective* wet, cold, and unpleasant **nemli, soğuk ve nahoş** *a dark, dank basement*

dapper /'dæpəʳ/ *adjective* A dapper man looks stylish and tidy. **şık, hoş, iyi giyimli erkek**

dare¹ /deəʳ/ *verb* **1 dare (to) do sth** to be brave enough to do something **cesaret etmek, cüret göstermek/etmek** *I didn't dare tell Dad that I'd scratched his car.* **2 dare sb to do sth** to try to make someone do something dangerous **tehlikeli birşeyi yapmaya zorlamak, cesaretlendirmek, teşvik etmek** *She dared her friend to climb onto the roof.* **3 Don't you dare** *informal* used to tell someone angrily not to do something **birinin bir şeyi yapmamasını kızgınca söylemek için kullanılır, kızarak ikaz etmek; Hele bir dene!; Hele bir kalkışta görelim!** *Don't you dare hit your sister!* **4 How dare she/you, etc** used to express anger about something someone has done **Ne cesaretle...!; Hangi cüretle!** *How dare you talk to me like that!* **5 I dare say** (*also* **I daresay**) used when you think that something is probably true or will probably happen **Sanırım; Galiba** *I dare say she'll change her mind.*

dare² /deəʳ/ *noun* [C] something that you do to prove that you are not afraid **cüret, cesaret** [usually singular] *She climbed down the cliff for a dare.*

daredevil /'deə,dev'l/ *noun* [C] someone who enjoys doing dangerous things **gözü pek, cesur kişi**

daren't /deənt/ *UK short for* dare not **cesaret/cüret edememek** *I daren't tell my wife how much it cost.*

daring /'deərɪŋ/ *adjective* brave and taking risks **cesur ve risk almaya hazır; gözü pek, cüretkâr** *a daring escape* • **daring** *noun* [U] **cesaret**

o⬝**dark¹** /dɑːk/ *adjective* **1** [NO LIGHT] with no light or not much light **karanlık** *It's a bit dark in here.* ○ *It doesn't get dark until 9 o'clock in the evening.* **2** [NOT PALE] nearer to black than white in colour **siyaha daha yakın, koyu renk** *dark blue/green* ○ *dark clouds* ○ *He's got dark hair and blue eyes.* **3** [PERSON] having black or brown hair or brown skin **esmer, saçı ve teni kahverengi veya siyah** *a short, dark woman with glasses* **4** [BAD] frightening or unpleasant **ürkütücü, hoş olmayan, sevimsiz, nahoş** *a dark period in human history*

o⬝**dark²** /dɑːk/ *noun* **1 the dark** when there is no light somewhere **karanlık** *He's scared of the dark.* **2 before/after dark** before/after it becomes night **gece/ karanlık öncesi veya sonrası** *She doesn't let her children out after dark.* **3 be in the dark** to not know about something that other people know about **herkesin bildiği bir konuda bilgi sahibi olmamak** *I'm completely in the dark about all this.* ⊃See also: a shot¹ in the dark.

darken /'dɑːk'n/ *verb* [I, T] **1** to become dark or make something dark **karartmak, kararmak** *the darkening sky* ○ *a darkened room* **2** If someone's mood darkens, or if something darkens it, they suddenly feel less happy. **içini karartmak, içi kararmak, tatsızlaşmak, canı sıkılmak**

darkly /'dɑːkli/ *adverb* in a frightening or mysterious way **korkutucu ve gizemli bir şekilde** *"He might not be what he seems," she said darkly.*

darkness /'dɑːknəs/ *noun* [U] when there is little or no light **karanlık** *He stumbled around in the darkness looking for the light switch.* ○ *There was a power cut and the house was in darkness.*

darling[1] /'dɑːlɪŋ/ *noun* [C] used when you speak to someone you love **sevgili, yâr** *Would you like a drink, darling?*

darling[2] /'dɑːlɪŋ/ *adjective* [always before noun] loved very much **sevgili, biricik, birtane, gözde** *my darling daughter*

darn[1] /dɑːn/ *US informal (also* **darned** /dɑːnd/) *adjective* [always before noun], *adverb* used to emphasize what you are saying, or to show that you are annoyed **ziyadesiyle; amma da, üf be; aman be** *I'm too darn tired to care.*

darn[2] /dɑːn/ *verb* [I, T] to repair a piece of clothing by sewing across a hole with thread **bir söküğü, yırtığı dikmek/diktirmek; örerek onarmak** *to darn socks*

dart[1] /dɑːt/ *noun* [C] a small arrow used in the game of darts or as a weapon **bir silah olarak ya da dart oyununda kullanılan küçük oklar** *a tranquilizer dart*

dart[2] /dɑːt/ *verb* **dart between/in/out, etc** to run or move somewhere quickly and suddenly **bir yere doğru telaşla ve aniden gitmek, koşmak, fırlamak** *A cat darted across the street.*

darts

darts /dɑːts/ *noun* [U] a game played by throwing small arrows at a round board **yuvarlak bir tahtaya küçük oklar atılarak oynanan oyun, dart**

dash[1] /dæʃ/ *verb* **1** [I] to go somewhere quickly **telaşla ve hızlıca bir yere gitmek, fırlayıp çıkmak** *She dashed downstairs when she heard the phone.* ○ *I must dash. I've got to be home by 7 p.m.* **2 dash sb's hopes** to destroy someone's hopes **birinin ümitlerini yok etmek, ümidini kırmak** *Saturday's 2-0 defeat dashed their hopes of reaching the final.* **3 dash (sth) against/on, etc** *literary* to hit or throw something with great force, usually causing damage **büyük bir hızla çarpmak, zarar vermek** *Waves dashed against the cliffs.*

dash sth off *phrasal verb UK* to write something very quickly **alelacele, çabucak not almak, çalakalem yazmak, karalamak** *She dashed off a letter to her solicitor.*

dash[2] /dæʃ/ *noun* **1** [RUN] [no plural] when you run somewhere very quickly **bir yere aceleyle koşma; fırlama** *As the rain started, we made a dash for shelter.* **2** [AMOUNT] [C] a small amount of something, often food **çoğunlukla yiyecek gibi şeylerin çok azı, birazcık** *Add a dash of milk to the sauce.* **3** [MARK] [C] a mark (—) used to separate parts of sentences **cümleyi oluşturan ifadeler arasında ayrımı sağlayan kısa çizgi** ⊃See study page Punctuation on page Centre 33.

dashboard /'dæʃbɔːd/ *noun* [C] the part facing the driver at the front of a car with controls and equipment to show things such as speed and temperature **araçların ön tarafında, hız ve ısı gibi benzer göstergelerin bulunduğu bölüm, gösterge tablosu, gösterge paneli** ⊃Orta kısımdaki renkli sayfalarına bakınız.

dashing /'dæʃɪŋ/ *adjective* A dashing man is attractive in a confident and exciting way. **kendine güvenen ve heyecan veren, şık çekici (erkek)**

🧩 **data** .... İLE BİRLİKTE KULLANILAN KELİMELER

analyse/collect data ● data **on** sth

o⊸**data** /'deɪtə/ *noun* [U] **1** information or facts about something **bilgi, veri** *financial data* **2** information in the form of text, numbers, or symbols that can be used by or stored in a computer **bilgisayarda saklanabilen yazı, rakam ve sembollerden oluşan bilgi, veri**

database /'deɪtəbeɪs/ *noun* [C] information stored in a computer in an organized structure so that it can be searched in different ways **veritabanı; farklı şekillerde ulaşılabilmesi için düzenli biçimde bilgisayara yüklenen bilgi** *a national database of missing people*

'**data pro,jector** *noun* [C] a machine that allows you to show words or images on a screen or wall **sözcük, resim ve şekilleri perde ya da duvar üzerine yansıtarak gösteren alet**

🧩 **date** .... İLE BİRLİKTE KULLANILAN KELİMELER

make/fix/set a date ● **at a future/at a later** date ● the date of sth ● sb's date **of birth**

o⊸**date**[1] /deɪt/ *noun* [C] **1** [PARTICULAR DAY] a particular day of the month or year **ay veya yılın belli bir günü, tarih** *"What's the date today?" "It's the fifth."* ○ *Please give your name, address and date of birth.* **2** [ARRANGED TIME] a time when something has been arranged to happen **tarih; bir şeyin olması için kararlaştırılan zaman** *Let's make a date to have lunch.* ○ *We agreed to finish the report at a later date.* **3 to date** *formal* up to the present time **günümüze dek** *This novel is his best work to date.* **4** [GOING OUT] a romantic meeting when two people go out somewhere, such as to a restaurant or to see a film **romantik birliktelik, buluşma, flört, randevu** *He's asked her out on a date.* **5** [PERSON] someone who you are having a romantic meeting with **flört, beraber olunan kişi, sevgili, arkadaş** *Who's your date for the prom?* **6** [FRUIT] a sticky brown fruit with a long seed inside **hurma** ⊃See also: blind date, sell-by date.

date[2] /deɪt/ *verb* **1** [MEET] [I, T] to regularly spend time with someone you have a romantic relationship with **biriyle çıkmak, romantik ilişki kurmak, buluşmak, flört etmek** *We've been dating for six months.* **2** [WRITE] [T] to write the day's date on something **tarih atmak/koymak** *a letter dated March 13th* **3** [TIME] [T] to say how long something has existed or when it was made **bir şeyin ne zaman yapıldığını, ne kadar süreyle var olduğunu bildirmek, tarihini tespit etmek** *Scientists have dated the bones to 10,000 BC.* **4** [NOT MODERN] [I, T] to stop seeming modern, or to make something not seem modern **eskimek, modası geçmek** *Clothes like these date really quickly.*

date back *phrasal verb* to have existed a particular length of time or since a particular time **geçmişte belirli bir tarihe kadar uzanmak, o tarihten buyana varolmak** *This house dates back to 1650.*

date from sth *phrasal verb* to have existed since a particular time ... **den buyana varolmak** *The castle dates from the 11th century.*

dated /'deɪtɪd/ *adjective* not modern **eskimiş, modası geçmiş** *This film seems a bit dated today.*

'date ,rape noun [C] when someone is raped (= forced to have sex when they do not want to) by someone they know, or someone they have arranged to meet **çıktığı kişinin tecavüzüne uğrama; flört tecavüzü**

daub /dɔːb/ verb [T] to put a lot of a substance like paint on a surface in a careless way, often to write words or draw pictures **sözcük yazmak ya da resim çizmek maksadıyla boya benzeri şeyi bir yüzeye sürmek, sıvamak, karalamak** The walls have been daubed with graffiti.

o▪**daughter** /'dɔːtəʳ/ noun [C] your female child **kız evlat**

daughter-in-law /'dɔːtərɪnlɔː/ noun [C] plural **daughters-in-law** your son's wife **gelin**

daunt /dɔːnt/ verb [T] If someone is daunted by something, they are worried because it is difficult or frightening. **ürkmek, bir şeyin zorluğundan ya da ürkütücü olması nedeniyle endişeye kapılmak** [often passive] I was a bit daunted by the idea of cooking for so many people.

daunting /dɔːntɪŋ/ adjective If something is daunting, it makes you worried because it is difficult or frightening. **gözü korkutan, yıldıran şey ya da görev** a daunting challenge/task

dawdle /'dɔːdl/ verb [I] to walk very slowly, or do something very slowly in a way that wastes time **sallana sallana yürümek veya zamanı boşa geçirmek için bir işi yavaş yapmak, oyalanmak** Stop dawdling! You'll be late for school!

dawn[1] /dɔːn/ noun [U] **1** the early morning when light first appears in the sky **şafak vakti, seher vakti** We woke **at dawn**. **2 the dawn of sth** literary the time when something began **bir şeyin başlama vakti** the dawn of civilization ⊃See also: the crack[2] of dawn.

dawn[2] /dɔːn/ verb [I] If a day or a period of time dawns, it begins. **bir günün ya da zaman diliminin başlaması** The day of her party dawned at last.

dawn on sth phrasal verb If a fact dawns on you, you become aware of it after a period of not being aware of it. **farkına varmak, kafasına dank etmek** [+ that] It suddenly dawned on them that Mary had been lying.

o▪**day** /deɪ/ noun **1** [24 HOURS] [C] a period of 24 hours **gün** the days of the week ○ January has 31 days. ○ I saw her the day before yesterday. **2** [LIGHT HOURS] [C, U] the period during the day when there is light from the sun **gündüz, gün boyu** a bright, sunny day ○ We've been travelling all day. **3** [WORK HOURS] [C] the time that you usually spend at work or school **iş günü** She's had a very busy day at the office. **4 the other day** a few days ago **birkaç gün önce** I saw Terry the other day. **5 day after day** every day for a long period of time **gün be gün, günlerce** Day after day they marched through the mountains. **6 one day** used to talk about something that happened in the past **bir gün** (geçmişte) One day, I came home to find my windows smashed. **7 one day/some day/one of these days** used to talk about something you think will happen in the future **elbet bir gün, gelecekte bir gün** One of these days I'll tell her what really happened. **8 days** a [PERIOD] used to talk about a particular period of time when something happened or existed **o günlerde, o günler** in my younger days b [LONG TIME] a long time **günlerce, günler boyu** I haven't seen Jack for days. **9 these days** used to talk about the present time **bu günlerde** I don't go out much these days. **10 in those days** used to talk about a period in the past **o günlerde, o zamanlar** In those days, boys used to wear short trousers. **11 the old days** a period in the past **eski günler** **12 call it a day** informal to stop doing something, especially working **özellikle işi ya da bir şeyi yapmayı sonraya bırakmak; bu günlük bu kadar; yeter** It's almost midnight - let's call it a day. ● **13 it's early**

days UK something that you say when it is too early to know what will happen **daha konuşmak için çok erken; henüz belli değil** Both teams are at the bottom of the league, but it's early days yet. ● **14 make sb's day** to make someone very happy **birisini mutlu etmek; gününü şenlendirmek** Go on, ask him to dance - it'll make his day! ● **15 save the day** to do something that solves a serious problem **ciddi bir sorunu çözmek için bir şeyler yapmak** ⊃See also: April Fool's Day, Boxing Day, Christmas Day, at the end[1] of the day, field day, Independence Day, Mother's Day, New Year's Day, open day, polling day, Valentine's Day.

daybreak /'deɪbreɪk/ noun [U] the time in the morning when light first appears in the sky **gün ağarması, tan yerinin ağarması, seher vakti**

daycare /'deɪkeəʳ/ noun [U] care provided during the day for people who cannot look after themselves, especially young children or old people **gündüz bakımı; özellikle kendisine bakamayan yaşlı ya da çocukların gün boyu bakımını sağlama** a daycare centre

daydream /'deɪdriːm/ verb [I] to have pleasant thoughts about something you would like to happen **hayal kurmak, dalıp gitmek** ● **daydream** noun [C] **hayal**

daylight /'deɪlaɪt/ noun **1** [U] the natural light from the sun **gün ışığı, gündüz** **2 in broad daylight** used to emphasize that something happens when it is light and people can see **güpe gündüz, gündüz gözüyle** He was attacked in broad daylight.

daylights /'deɪlaɪts/ noun **1 beat/knock the (living) daylights out of sb** informal to hit someone very hard many times **birine sert bir şekilde defalarca vurmak, dayak atmak** ● **2 scare/frighten the (living) daylights out of sb** informal to frighten someone very much **birini çok fazla korkutmak/ürkütmek**

,day re'turn noun [C] UK a ticket for a bus or train when you go somewhere and come back on the same day **otobüs veya tren için günü birlik gidiş dönüş bileti** a day return to Norwich

daytime /'deɪtaɪm/ noun [U] the period of the day when there is light from the sun, or the period when most people are at work **gündüz vakti, gündüz** daytime television ○ a daytime telephone number

day-to-day /ˌdeɪtə'deɪ/ adjective [always before noun] happening every day as a regular part of your job or your life **günlük, her gün olan** day-to-day activities/problems

daze /deɪz/ noun **in a daze** when you cannot think clearly because you are shocked or have hit your head **bilinçsizce, şuuru yerinde olmayarak** The survivors were walking around in a daze.

dazed /deɪzd/ adjective not able to think clearly because you are shocked or have hit your head **ne yaptığını/söylediğini bilmeyen, sersemlemiş** a dazed expression

dazzle /'dæzl/ verb [T] **1** If you are dazzled by someone or something, you think they are extremely good and exciting. **bir şeye, birine hayran olmak, etkilenmek, başını döndürmek** [often passive] I was dazzled by his intelligence and good looks. **2** If light dazzles someone, it makes them unable to see for a short time. **gözünü kamaştırmak, gözünü almak**

dazzling /'dæzlɪŋ/ adjective **1** extremely good and exciting **son derece hoş ve heyecan verici, harika, müthiş** a dazzling display/performance **2** A dazzling light is so bright that you cannot see for a short time after looking at it. **göz kamaştıran, göz alıcı** a dazzling white light

de- /di-/ *prefix* to take something away **uzağa, öteye götürme anlamında ön ek** *deforestation* (= when the trees in an area are cut down)

deacon /'di:kən/ *noun* [C] an official in some Christian churches **Hıristiyan kilisesinde resmi görevli**

o⊷**dead**[1] /ded/ *adjective* **1** NOT ALIVE not now alive **ölü, ölmüş, cansız** *She's been dead for 20 years now.* ○ *He was shot dead by a masked intruder.* ○ *There were three children among the dead.* **2** EQUIPMENT If a piece of equipment is dead, it is not working. **işe yaramaz, bitmiş** *a dead battery* ○ *The phone suddenly went dead.* **3** QUIET *informal* If a place is dead, it is too quiet and nothing interesting is happening there. **(yer, mekân) hareketsiz, cansız, sessiz, durgun, ölü 4** COMPLETE [always before noun] complete **büsbütün, tam** *We waited in dead silence as the votes were counted.* **5** BODY *mainly UK* If part of your body is dead, you cannot feel it. **hissiz, uyuşmuş (vücudun bir bölümü)** *My arm's gone dead.* **6 wouldn't be caught/seen dead** *informal* If someone wouldn't be caught dead in a place or doing something, they would never go there or do it, usually because it would be too embarrassing. **bir şeyi çok utanç vereceğini düşünerek yapmamak veya oraya gitmemek ('ölürüm de yapmam!' manasında)** [+ doing sth] *I wouldn't be caught dead wearing a bikini.* **7 drop dead** *informal* to die very suddenly **ansızın ölmek, hayatını kaybetmek, göçüp gitmek**

dead[2] /ded/ *adverb* **1** *informal* extremely or completely **son derece, tamamen, korkunç, oldukça** *UK The exam was dead easy.* ○ *US His advice was dead wrong.* **2 be dead set against sth/doing sth** to oppose something strongly **bir şeye kesinlikle karşı çıkmak, şiddetle muhalefet etmek** *My parents were dead set against us getting married.* **3 stop dead** to suddenly stop moving or doing something **ansızın/aniden durmak, harketsizleşmek**

dead[3] /ded/ *noun* **the dead of night/winter** the middle of the night/winter **kış mevsiminin/gecenin tam ortası**

deadbeat /'dedbi:t/ *noun* [C] *US informal* someone who does not pay their debts **borçlarını ödemeyen/ödeme güçlüğü çeken kişi** *a deadbeat dad*

deaden /'ded°n/ *verb* [T] to make something less painful or less strong **bir şeyin gücünü/acısını azaltmak** *She gave me an injection to deaden the pain.*

dead 'end *noun* [C] **1** a road which is closed at one end **çıkmaz sokak 2** a situation in which it is impossible to make progress **çıkışı, sonu olmayan bir durum, beyhude durum/çaba** *The peace talks have reached a dead end.* ● **dead-end** /ˌded'end/ *adjective a dead-end job/relationship* ○ *a dead-end street* **çıkmaz (sokak)**

dead 'heat *noun* [C] when two people finish a race at exactly the same time **yarışı iki kişinin aynı anda bitirmesi**

┌───┐
│ 🧩 **deadline** .... İLE BİRLİKTE KULLANILAN KELİMELER │
└───┘

set a deadline ● **meet/miss** a deadline ● a **tight** deadline ● the deadline **for** (doing) sth

deadline /'dedlaın/ *noun* [C] a time by which something must be done **bir işin bitirilmesi gereken son tarih, zaman** *to meet/miss a deadline* ○ *The deadline for entering the competition is tomorrow.*

deadlock /'dedlɒk/ *noun* [U] a situation in which it is impossible to make progress or to reach a decision **tıkanma, sonuçsuz kalma, bir karara varılamayan ya da ilerleme kaydedilemeyen durum** *The talks have reached deadlock.* ○ *There have been several attempts to break the deadlock.* ● **deadlocked** *adjective* **ilerlemeyen**

deadly[1] /'dedli/ *adjective* likely to cause death **öldürücü, amansız** ○ *a deadly virus* ○ *a deadly weapon*

deadly[2] /'dedli/ *adverb* **deadly dull/serious, etc** extremely dull/serious, etc **çok/müthiş sıkıcı/ciddi**

deadpan /'dedpæn/ *adjective* looking or sounding serious when you are telling a joke **fıkra anlatırken ciddi gözüken, renk vermeyen** *a deadpan expression*

deaf /def/ *adjective* **1** unable to hear **sağır** *Many deaf people learn to lip read.* ○ *He goes to a school for the deaf.* **2 be deaf to sth** to refuse to listen to something **dinlememek, kulaklarını tıkamak, söylenenlere itibar etmemek** ● **deafness** *noun* [U] **sağırlık** ○See also: fall on deaf ears (ear), tone-deaf. **sağırlık**

D

deafening /'def°nıŋ/ *adjective* extremely loud **kulakları sağır eden gürültü, yüksek ses** *a deafening noise*

┌───┐
│ 🧩 **deal** .... İLE BİRLİKTE KULLANILAN KELİMELER │
└───┘

agree/do/make/strike a deal ● **negotiate/sign** a deal ● a deal **between** [two people/companies, etc] ● a deal **with** sb

deal[1] /di:l/ *noun* **1** [C] an arrangement or an agreement, especially in business **(iş) anlaşma, aynı fikirde olma** *a business deal* ○ *The police refused to do/make/strike a deal with the terrorists.* **2** [C] the price you pay for something, and what you get for your money **satın alınan bir şey için ödenen miktar, değer** *I got a really good deal on my new car.* **3 a good/great deal** a lot **çok, epeyce** *A great deal of time and effort went into arranging this party.*

deal[2] /di:l/ *verb* [I, T] *past* **dealt** to give cards to players in a game **iskambil oyununda kartları dağıtmak** *Whose turn is it to deal?*
deal in sth *phrasal verb* to buy and sell particular goods as a business ... **ticaretini yapmak; alıp satmak** *a shop dealing in rare books*
deal with sth *phrasal verb* **1** to take action in order to achieve something or to solve a problem **ilgilenmek, ele almak, gereğini yapmak** *Can you deal with this gentleman's complaint?* **2** to be about a particular subject ... **ile ilgili olmak, kapsamak** *The programme dealt with teenage pregnancy.*
deal with sb/sth *phrasal verb* to do business with a person or organization ... **ile iş/alışveriş/ticaret yapmak** *I usually deal with the accounts department.*
deal with sb *phrasal verb* to meet or talk to someone, especially as part of your job **işinin gereği olarak biriyle buluşup toplantı yapmak** *She's used to dealing with foreign customers.*

dealer /'di:lər/ *noun* [C] **1** a person or company that buys and sells things for profit **tüccar, alıcı/satıcı** *a car dealer* ○ *a drug dealer* **2** a person who gives out cards to players in a game **iskambil oyununda kartları dağıtan oyuncu**

dealership /'di:ləʃɪp/ *noun* [C] a business that sells cars, usually cars made by a particular company **galeri, belli marka araçları satan şirket/firma** *a Ford/Toyota dealership*

dealings /'di:lıŋz/ *noun* [plural] activities involving other people, especially in business **iş, faaliyet, ortak işler** *Have you had any dealings with their London office?*

dealt /delt/ *past of* deal **deal' fiilinin geçmiş zaman hali**

dean /di:n/ *noun* [C] **1** an official in a college or university **dekan 2** an official in charge of a large church or group of churches **baş rahip**

○━**dear¹** /dɪəʳ/ *adjective* **1** IN LETTERS used at the beginning of a letter, before the name of the person you are writing to **sayın** *Dear Amy* ○ *Dear Mrs Simpson* ○ *Dear Sir/ Madam* **2** LIKED [always before noun] A dear person is someone who you know and like very much. **sevgili, tatlı** *my dear Peter* ○ *He's one of my dearest friends.* **3** EXPENSIVE *UK* expensive **pahalı 4 dear to sb/sb's heart** If something is dear to someone or dear to their heart, it is very important to them. **biri için değerli, sevgili, kıymetli** *The charity was very dear to his heart.*

dear² /dɪəʳ/ *exclamation* **oh dear** used to express surprise and disappointment **Eyvah! Aman Allah'ım!** *Oh dear! I forgot my keys!*

dear³ /dɪəʳ/ *noun* [C] used to address someone in a friendly way, especially a child or someone you love **canım, hayatım, cancağızım** *Don't cry, my dear.* ○ *Yes, dear?*

dearly /'dɪəli/ *adverb* very much **çok, pek fazla** *I would dearly love to visit Rome again.*

dearth /dɜ:θ/ *noun formal* **a dearth of sth** when there are not many or not enough of something available **kıtlık, azlık, yokluk** *a dearth of new homes*

🧩 **death** ...... İLE BİRLİKTE KULLANILAN KELİMELER

bleed/choke/freeze/starve to death ● be beaten/ crushed/stabbed/trampled to death ● sb's premature/sudden/tragic/untimely death ● death from sth

○━**death** /deθ/ *noun* **1** [C, U] the end of life **ölüm, ebdiyete intikal** *Do you believe in life after death?* ○ *We need to reduce the number of deaths from heart attacks.* ○ *a death threat* **2 to death** until you die **ölünceye dek/ kadar** *He was beaten to death by a gang of youths.* **3 put sb to death** to kill someone as a punishment **idam etmek, ölüm cezasıyla cezalandırmak** [often passive] *She was put to death for her beliefs.* **4 frightened/bored, etc to death** *informal* extremely frightened/bored, etc **korkudan ödü patlamak, çok korkmak, yüreği ağzına gelmek** *She's scared to death of dogs.*

deathbed /'deθbed/ *noun* **on your deathbed** very ill and going to die soon **ölüm döşeğinde**

deathly /'deθli/ *adjective, adverb* extreme in a way which is unpleasant **hiç hoş olmayan** *a deathly silence* ○ *Her face turned deathly pale.*

'**death ,penalty** *noun* [C] the legal punishment of death for a crime **ölüm/idam cezası**

,**death 'row** *noun* **on death row** in prison and waiting to be killed as a punishment for a crime **ölüm infazını bekleyen; idamı bekleyen**

'**death ,sentence** *noun* [C] legal punishment of death for a crime **ölüm cezası**

'**death ,toll** *noun* [C] the number of people who die because of an event such as a war or an accident **savaş veya kaza sonucu ölen kişi sayısı** *The death toll from the earthquake has risen to 1500.*

'**death ,trap** *noun* [C] something that is very dangerous and could cause death **ölüm tuzağı** *That old factory across the road is a real death trap.*

debase /dɪ'beɪs/ *verb* [T] *formal* to reduce the value or quality of something **değerini düşürmek, itibarını azaltmak** *They argue that money has debased football.*

debatable /dɪ'beɪtəbl/ *adjective* If something is debatable, it is not certain if it is true or not. **tartışılabilir, tartışmalı** *It's debatable whether a university degree will help you in this job.*

debate¹ /dɪ'beɪt/ *noun* [C, U] discussion or argument about a subject **tartışma, müzakere** *a political debate*

○ *There has been a lot of public debate on the safety of food.*

debate² /dɪ'beɪt/ *verb* **1** [I, T] to discuss a subject in a formal way **tartışmak, müzakere etmek** *These issues need to be debated openly.* **2** [T] to try to make a decision about something **bir konuyla ilgili karar vermeye çalışmak** [+ question word] *I'm still debating whether to go out tonight or not.*

debilitating /dɪ'bɪlɪteɪtɪŋ/ *adjective formal* A debilitating illness or problem makes you weak and unable to do what you want to do. **güçsüzleştiren, zayıf düşüren, takat bırakmayan (hastalık veya problem)** *the debilitating effects of flu*

debit¹ /'debɪt/ *noun* [C] money taken out of a bank account, or a record of this **hesaptan çekilen para** ⊃Opposite credit ⊃See also: direct debit.

debit² /'debɪt/ *verb* [T] to take money out of a bank account as a payment for something **hesaptan para çekmek** *Twenty pounds has been debited from my account.*

'**debit ,card** *noun* [C] a plastic card used to pay for things directly from your bank account **alışveriş kartı, banka kartı**

debris /'debri:/ Ⓤ /də'bri:/ *noun* [U] broken pieces of something **enkaz, moloz, kalıntı** *Debris from the aircraft was scattered over a wide area.*

🧩 **debt** ...... İLE BİRLİKTE KULLANILAN KELİMELER

be in/fall into/get into/run into debt ● get out of debt ● clear/pay off/repay /settle a debt

○━**debt** /det/ *noun* **1** [C] an amount of money that you owe someone **borç** *She's working in a bar to try to pay off her debts.* **2** [U] when you owe money to someone **borçlu olma, borç** *We don't want to get into debt.* ○ *He's heavily in debt.* **3 be in sb's debt** to feel grateful to someone who has helped you or given you something **birine şükran duymak, borçlu hissetmek, minnettar olmak**

debtor /'detəʳ/ *noun* [C] someone who owes money **borçlu**

'**debt re,lief** *noun* [U] when a bank tells a person, a company or a government that they do not have to pay back the money they owe the bank **borç iptali, borç silme**

debut /'deɪbju:/ Ⓤ /deɪ'bju:/ *noun* [C] when someone performs or presents something to the public for the first time **sahneye ilk çıkış, ilk gösteri** *She made her debut as a pianist in 1975.* ○ *This is the band's debut album.*

Dec *written abbreviation for* December **aralık ayı**

○━**decade** /'dekeɪd/ *noun* [C] a period of ten years **on yıl**

decadence /'dekəd³ns/ *noun* [U] when you do or have things only for your own pleasure or behave in an immoral way **bencillik, sadece kendi zevkini düşünme, çöküntü, ahlaki değerlere ters davranış** ● **decadent** *adjective a decadent lifestyle* **ahlaksız**

decaf /'di:kæf/ *noun* [C, U] *informal short for* decaffeinated coffee **kafeinsiz kahve, kafeini alınmış kahve** *Do you want full strength coffee or decaf?*

decaffeinated /dɪ'kæfɪneɪtɪd/ *adjective* Decaffeinated tea or coffee is made by removing the caffeine (= chemical which makes you feel more awake). **kafeinsiz**

decay /dɪ'keɪ/ *verb* [I] to gradually become bad or weak or be destroyed, often because of natural causes like bacteria or age **çürümek, çökmek** *decaying leaves* ○ *Sugar makes your teeth decay.* ● **decay** *noun* [U] when something decays **çürüme, çökme** *tooth decay* ○ *Many of the buildings had fallen into decay.*

deceased /dɪˈsiːst/ *adjective formal* **1** dead **merhum, rahmetli, ölmüş** *the deceased man's belongings* **2 the deceased** someone who has died **merhum, müteveffa** *The police have not yet informed the family of the deceased.*

deceit /dɪˈsiːt/ *noun* [U] when someone tries to make someone believe something that is not true **aldatma, düzen, hile, oyun** ● **deceitful** *adjective deceitful behaviour* **hilekar**

deceive /dɪˈsiːv/ *verb* [T] to make someone believe something that is not true **aldatmak, düzen kurmak, hile yapmak** *The company deceived customers by selling old computers as new ones.*

o⌐**December** /dɪˈsembər/ *(written abbreviation Dec) noun* [C, U] the twelfth month of the year **aralık ayı**

decency /ˈdiːsənsi/ *noun* [U] behaviour that is good, moral, and acceptable in society **edeb, dürüstlük, ahlak, haysiyet** *a sense of decency* ○ *She didn't even have the decency to tell me she wasn't coming.*

decent /ˈdiːsənt/ *adjective* **1** SATISFACTORY of a satisfactory quality or level **tatmin edici, kaliteli,** *He earns a decent salary.* ○ *I haven't had a decent cup of coffee since I've been here.* **2** HONEST honest and morally good **doğru, dürüst, ahlaklı, edepli, terbiyeli** *Decent people have had their lives ruined by his behaviour.* ○ *She should do **the decent thing** and apologize.* **3** CLOTHES [never before noun] wearing clothes **giyinik, üzerinde kıyafet olan** *Can I come in? Are you decent?* ● **decently** *adverb* **muntazam bir şekilde**

decentralize *(also UK -ise)* /diːˈsentrəlaɪz/ *verb* [T] to move the control of an organization or a government from a single place to several smaller places **kontrolü, sorumluluğu dağıtmak, merkezi yapılanmadan uzaklaşmak** ● **decentralization** /diːˌsentrəlaɪˈzeɪʃən/ *noun* [U] **merkezden yürütmeme durumu**

deception /dɪˈsepʃən/ *noun* [C, U] when someone makes someone believe something that is not true **aldatma, kandırma, dalavere, hile** *He was found guilty of obtaining money by deception.*

deceptive /dɪˈseptɪv/ *adjective* If something is deceptive, it makes you believe something that is not true. **kandıran, aldatıcı, hilekâr** *Appearances can be deceptive.* ● **deceptively** *adverb* **aldatıcı bir şekilde**

decibel /ˈdesɪbel/ *noun* [C] a unit for measuring how loud a sound is **desibel**

decide ...... BAŞKA BİR DEYİŞLE

Eğer kişi belirli bir saat veya miktardan bahsediyorsa (özellikle tarih veya fiyat gibi konularda), **fix** ve **set** fiilleri kullanılır. *The price has been* **set/fixed** *at $10.* ● *Have you* **set/fixed** *a date for the wedding?*
Eğer kişi bir plan veya tarih ile ilgili son kararını veriyorsa, bu durum için **finalize** fiili kullanılır. *We've chosen a venue, but we haven't* **finalized** *the details yet.*
Kişi bu konuda son kararını veriyorsa, bu durumda **settle** fiili ve settle on/upon deyimleri kullanılabilir. *Have you* **settled** *on a place to live yet?* ● *Right then, we're going to Spain. That's* **settled**.
make up your mind söylemi genellikle **decide** fiilinin anlamında kullanılır. *I like them both - I just can't* **make up my mind** *which one to pick.* ● *Have you* **made up your mind** *whether you're going?*
Eğer kişi iki şey arasında karar veremiyorsa, resmi olmayan durumlarda, **be torn between** something **and** something else *I'm* **torn between** *the fish pie and the beef.*

o⌐**decide** /dɪˈsaɪd/ *verb* **1** [I, T] to choose something after thinking about several possibilities **karara varmak, kararlaştırmak** [+ question word] *I haven't decided whether or not to tell him.* ○ [+ to do sth] *She's decided to take the job.* ○ [+ (that)] *The teachers decided that the school would take part in the competition.* **2** [T] to be the reason or situation that makes a particular result happen **seçim yapmak, hüküm vermek** *This match will decide the tournament.* **3 deciding factor** the thing that helps to make the final decision **karara etki eden unsur**
decide on sth/sb *phrasal verb* to choose something or someone after thinking carefully **düşünerek karar vermek, seçmek** *I've decided on blue walls for the bathroom.*

decided /dɪˈsaɪdɪd/ *adjective* [always before noun] certain, obvious, or easy to notice **karar verilen, belli, açık, belirgin** *She had a decided advantage over her opponent.* ● **decidedly** *adverb That exam was decidedly more difficult than the last one.* **kararlı bir şekilde**

deciduous /dɪˈsɪdjuəs/ *adjective* A deciduous tree has leaves that drop off every autumn. **sonbaharda yapraklarını döken**

decimal¹ /ˈdesɪməl/ *adjective* involving counting in units of 10 **ondalık** *a decimal system*

decimal² /ˈdesɪməl/ *noun* [C] a number less than one that is written as one or more numbers after a point **ondalık sayı, kesir** *The decimal 0.5 is the same as the fraction (= 1/2).* ⊃See study page **Numbers** on page Centre 30.

decimal place *UK (US 'decimal place) noun* [C] the position of a number after a decimal point **ondalık hane** *The number is accurate to three decimal places.*

decimal point *UK (US 'decimal point) noun* [C] the point (.) that is used to separate a whole number and a decimal **ondalık sayıyı ayıran nokta**

decimate /ˈdesɪmeɪt/ *verb* [T] *formal* to destroy large numbers of people or things **büyük bir bölümüne zarar vermek, yok etmek** *Populations of endangered animals have been decimated.*

decipher /dɪˈsaɪfər/ *verb* [T] to discover what something says or means **anlamak, kavramak, çözmek, sökmek** *It's sometimes difficult to decipher his handwriting.*

decision ...... İLE BİRLİKTE KULLANILAN KELİMELER

come to/make/reach a decision ● a **big/difficult/final/important/unanimous/wise** decision ● a decision **about/on** sth

o⌐**decision** /dɪˈsɪʒən/ *noun* [C] a choice that you make about something after thinking about several possibilities **karar** *She has had to **make** some very difficult decisions.* ○ [+ to do sth] *It was his decision to leave.* ○ *The committee should **come to/reach a final decision** by next week.*

decisive /dɪˈsaɪsɪv/ *adjective* **1** strongly affecting how a situation will progress or end **belirleyici** *a decisive goal/victory* **2** making decisions quickly and easily **kolay ve çabuk karar verebilen** *You need to be more decisive.* ⊃Opposite **indecisive**. ● **decisively** *adverb* **kararlı bir şekilde** ● **decisiveness** *noun* [U] **kararlılık**

deck¹ /dek/ *noun* [C] **1** SHIP/BUS/PLANE one of the floors of a ship, bus, or aircraft **(gemi, otobüs, uçak) kat, güverte** *The children like to sit on the top deck of the bus.* **2 on deck** on the top floor of a ship that is not covered **tepede, açık alanda, geminin açık üst bölmesinde** **3** CARDS *US (UK pack)* a collection of cards that you use to play a game **(iskambil) deste** **4** MACHINE a machine that you use to play records or tapes (= plastic cases containing magnetic material used to record sounds) **teyp, pikap** *a tape deck*

deck² /dek/ *verb*
be decked out *phrasal verb* to be decorated with something, or dressed in something special **donatmak, donanmak, kuşanmak** *The bar was decked out with red and yellow flags.*

deckchair /ˈdektʃeəʳ/ *noun* [C] a folding chair that you use outside **açılır kapanır iskemle, şezlong, portatif sandalye**

declaration /ˌdekləˈreɪʃ⁰n/ *noun* [C] an announcement, often one that is written and official **beyan, ilan, duyuru, bildiri** *a declaration of independence*

declare /dɪˈkleəʳ/ *verb* [T] **1** to announce something publicly or officially **duyurmak, beyan etmek** *to declare war* ○ [+ that] *Scientists have declared that this meat is safe to eat.* **2** to officially tell someone the value of goods you have bought, or the amount of money you have earned because you might have to pay tax **gümrüğe tabi mal olup olmadığını bildirmek, beyan etmek, bildirimde bulunmak** *Have you got anything to declare?*

---

decline ...... İLE BİRLİKTE KULLANILAN KELİMELER

be **in** decline • a **sharp/steady/steep** decline • a decline **in** sth

---

decline¹ /dɪˈklaɪn/ *noun* [C, U] when something becomes less in amount, importance, quality, or strength **düşüş, azalma, gerileme** *a steady decline in sales/standards*

decline² /dɪˈklaɪn/ *verb* **1** [I, T] *formal* If you decline something, you refuse it politely. **geri çevirmek, reddetmek** *She declined his offer of a lift.* ○ [+ to do sth] *He declined to comment.* **2** [I] to become less in amount, importance, quality, or strength **(miktar, önem, kalite, güç vb.) düşmek, azalmak** *Sales of records have declined steadily.*

decode /ˌdiːˈkəʊd/ *verb* [T] to discover the meaning of a message that is in code (= secret system of communication) **(şifre) çözmek**

decoder /ˌdiːˈkəʊdəʳ/ *noun* [C] a piece of equipment that allows you to receive particular television signals **şifre çözücü**

decompose /ˌdiːkəmˈpəʊz/ *verb* [I] If a dead person, animal, or plant decomposes, it decays and is gradually destroyed. **çürü(t)mek** *a decomposing body*

decor /ˈdeɪkɔːʳ/ ⑤ /deɪˈkɔːr/ *noun* [U, no plural] the style of decoration and furniture in a room or building **dekor, düzenleme**

---

decorate ...... BAŞKA BİR DEYİŞLE

Bir oda veya binanın görünümünü geliştirmek anlamında **decorate** fiiline alternatif olarak **refurbish, renovate,** ve **rewamp** fiilleri kullanılabilir. *The University library is currently being refurbished.* • *They were in the process of renovating an old barn.* • *The restaurant has recently been revamped.*
Daha gayri resmi durumlarda kullanılabilecek diğer bir seçenek ise **do up** deyimidir. *He's bought an old cottage and is gradually doing it up.*

○⁻**decorate** /ˈdek⁰reɪt/ *verb* **1** [T] to make something look more attractive by putting things on it or around it **düzenlemek, süslemek, dekore etmek** *They decorated the room with balloons for her party.* **2** [I, T] to put paint or paper on the walls or other surfaces of a room or building **duvarları süslemek, boyamak, dekore etmek** *The whole house needs decorating.* **3 be decorated** to be given a medal (= small, metal disc) as official respect for military action **madalya verilmek, nişan**

---

decorate

takılmak, ödüllendirilmek *He was decorated for bravery.*

decoration /ˌdek⁰ˈreɪʃ⁰n/ *noun* **1** [ATTRACTIVE THING] [C, U] when you make something look more attractive by putting things on it or around it, or something that you use to do this **süsleme, dekorasyon** *Christmas decorations* ○ *She hung some pictures around the room for decoration.* **2** [PAINT] [U] when the walls or other surfaces of rooms or buildings are covered with paint or paper **boyama, kağıt kaplam, badana** *This place is badly in need of decoration.* **3** [OFFICIAL RESPECT] [C] an official sign of respect such as a medal (= small, metal disc) **madalya**

decorative /ˈdek⁰rətɪv/ *adjective* making something or someone look more attractive **süsleyici, güzelleştirici** *decorative objects*

decorator /ˈdek⁰reɪtəʳ/ *noun* [C] **1** UK someone whose job is to put paint or paper on the walls and other surfaces of rooms or buildings **boya, badana ustası 2** US someone whose job is to design the appearance of rooms in houses and buildings **mimar, iç mimar, dekoratör**

decorum /dɪˈkɔːrəm/ *noun* [U] *formal* behaviour which is considered to be polite and correct **uygun ve doğru davranış**

decoy /ˈdiːkɔɪ/ *noun* [C] someone or something used to lead a person or animal to a place so that they can be caught **tuzak, yem**

---

decrease ...... İLE BİRLİKTE KULLANILAN KELİMELER

a **marked/significant/slight** decrease • a decrease **in** sth • a decrease **of** [5%/1000, etc]

---

decrease ...... BAŞKA BİR DEYİŞLE

Kişi bir miktar veya seviyeyi düşürdüğü zaman **lessen, lower, reduce** fiilleri ve bunu yanısıra **bring down** deyimi kullanılır. *They've just lowered the age at which you can join.* • *Exercise reduces the chance of heart disease.* • *They are bringing down their prices.*
Bir miktar veya seviye düştüğü zaman **drop, fall** ve **go down, come down** deyimleri kullanılır. *Unemployment has dropped/fallen from 8% to 6% in the last year.* • *Prices always come/go down after Christmas.*
Seviye veya miktar ani düşüş gösterdiğinde, **plum-**

met ve **plunge** fiilleri kullanılabilir. *Temperatures last night* **plummeted/plunged** *below zero.*
Birşeyin boyutunda küçülme gözlemlendiğinde **shrink** fiili kullanılabilir. Teknik konularda ise **contract** fiili kullanılmaktadır. *Forests have* **shrunk** *to almost half the size they were 20 years ago.* ● *As the metal cools, it* contracts.

---

decrease /dɪˈkriːs/ *verb* [I, T] to become less, or to make something become less **azalma, azaltmak; düşmek, düşürmek** *During the summer months, rainfall decreases.* ● **decrease** /ˈdiːkriːs/ *noun* [C, U] *There has been a* **decrease in** *the number of violent crimes.* ⊃Opposite increase. azalma

decree /dɪˈkriː/ *noun* [C] an official order or decision from a government or leader **kararname, emir** *a presidential/royal decree* ● **decree** *verb* [T] **decreeing**, *past* **decreed emir vermek**

o▪**decrepit** /dɪˈkrepɪt/ *adjective* old and in very bad condition **harap, yıpranmış** *a decrepit building*

decrypt /diːˈkrɪpt/ *verb* [T] to change electronic information from a secret system of letters, numbers, or symbols back into a form that people can understand **şifreyi çözerek herkesin anlayacağı bir biçimde değiştirmek**

dedicate /ˈdedɪkeɪt/ *verb* **1 dedicate your life/yourself to sth** to give most of your energy and time to something **kendini/hayatını bir şeye adamak** *She has dedicated her life to helping others.* **2 dedicate sth to sb** to say that something you have made or done is to show your love or respect for someone **bir şeyi birine ithaf etmek** [often passive] *This book is dedicated to my daughter.*

dedicated /ˈdedɪkeɪtɪd/ *adjective* **1** believing that something is very important and giving a lot of time and energy to it **kendini adamış/vakfetmiş, yoluna baş koymuş** *a dedicated teacher* **2** designed to be used for a particular purpose **ayrılmış, adanmış** *a dedicated word processor*

dedication /ˌdedɪˈkeɪʃᵊn/ *noun* **1** [U] when you are willing to give a lot of time and energy to something because you believe it is very important **adama, vakfetme** *She thanked the staff for their dedication and enthusiasm.* **2** [C] when someone says that something has been made or done to show love and respect for someone else **ithaf** *a dedication to the poet's mother*

deduce /dɪˈdjuːs/ *verb* [T] to decide that something is true using the available information **var olan bilgiyi kullanarak bir sonuca varmak, sonuç çıkarmak** [+ (that)] *From the contents of his shopping basket, I deduced that he was single.*

deduct /dɪˈdʌkt/ *verb* [T] to take an amount or a part of something away from a total **çıkarmak, indirmek, azaltmak** *The company will* **deduct** *tax* **from** *your earnings.* ○ *Marks are deducted for spelling mistakes.*

deduction /dɪˈdʌkʃᵊn/ *noun* [C, U] **1** when an amount or a part of something is taken away from a total, or the amount that is taken **indirim, azaltma, kısma, kesinti** *tax deductions* **2** when you decide that something is true using the available information **tümden gelim, sonuç çıkarım**

deed /diːd/ *noun* [C] **1** *formal* something that you do **iş, eylem, fiil** *good deeds* ○ *I judge a person by their deeds, not their words.* **2** a legal document recording an agreement, especially saying who owns something **tapu, belge, senet** [usually plural] *Where do you keep the deeds to the house?*

---

deem /diːm/ *verb* [T] *formal* to judge or consider something in a particular way **varsaymak, bir şekilde yargılamak, dikkate almak** *The book was deemed to be unsuitable for children.*

deep

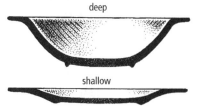

deep

shallow

o▪**deep**¹ /diːp/ *adjective* **1** ⌜TOP TO BOTTOM⌝ having a long distance from the top to the bottom **derin** *The water is a lot deeper than it seems.* **2** ⌜FRONT TO BACK⌝ having a long distance from the front to the back **enine boyuna derin, geniş, uzun** *How deep are the shelves?* **3 one metre/6 ft, etc deep** one metre/6 ft, etc from the top to the bottom, or from the front to the back **bir metre/altı fit derin** *This end of the pool is two metres deep.* **4** ⌜FEELING⌝ A deep feeling is very strong. **derin/yoğun duygu içeren** *deep affection/regret* **5** ⌜SOUND⌝ A deep sound is low. **pes, kalın, tok** *a deep voice* **6** ⌜SERIOUS⌝ serious and difficult for most people to understand **yoğun, ciddi, anlaşılması zor** *a deep and meaningful conversation* **7 a deep sleep** when someone is sleeping in a way that makes it difficult to wake them up **derin uyku 8** ⌜COLOUR⌝ A deep colour is strong and dark. **koyu** *deep brown eyes* **9 take a deep breath** to fill your lungs with air **derin bir nefes almak** *Take a deep breath and relax.* **10 deep in thought/conversation** giving all of your attention to what you are thinking or talking about, and not noticing anything else **derin düşüncelere dalmış, iyice kendini vermiş, dalmış** ⊃See also: throw sb in at the deep end¹, be in deep water¹.

o▪**deep**² /diːp/ *adverb* **1** a long way into something from the top or outside **derinine, iyice derinine** *They travelled deep into the forest.* **2 deep down** If you know or feel something deep down, you are certain that it is true, or you feel it strongly although you do not admit it or show it. **derinden, yürekten** *Deep down, I knew that I was right.* **3 go/run deep** If a feeling or a problem goes deep, it is very strong or serious and has existed for a long time. **sarpa sarmak, derine inmek, uzun süre olagelmek, gittikçe derinleşmek**

deepen /ˈdiːpᵊn/ *verb* [I, T] **1** to become deeper, or to make something become deeper **derinleş(tir)mek** *The sky deepened to a rich, dark blue.* **2** to become worse, or to make something become worse **gittikçe kötüleş(tir)mek** *a deepening crisis*

deep 'freeze UK (US 'deep ˌfreeze) *noun* [C] *another word for* freezer (= a large container in which food can be frozen and stored) **derin dondurucu**

deep-fried /ˌdiːpˈfraɪd/ *adjective* fried in a lot of oil **bol yağda kızartılmış**

deeply /ˈdiːpli/ *adverb* **1** very much **çok** *I have fallen deeply in love with her.* **2 breathe deeply** to fill your lungs with air **derin nefes almak**

deep-seated /ˌdiːpˈsiːtɪd/ (*also* deep-rooted) *adjective* strongly felt or believed and difficult to change **yerleşmiş, kök salmış, köklü, kökleşmiş** *deep-seated fears/problems*

D

deer

deer /dɪəʳ/ *noun* [C] *plural* **deer** a large, wild animal that is sometimes hunted for food and which has antlers (= long horns) if it is male **geyik**

deface /dɪˈfeɪs/ *verb* [T] to spoil the appearance of something, especially by writing or painting on it **karalamak, bozmak, yazı ya da boyayla okunmaz hale getirmek** *Several posters have been defaced with political slogans.*

default¹ /dɪˈfɔːlt/ *noun* **1** [no plural] what exists or happens usually if no changes are made **varsayılan; değişime uğramadan önceki hali 2 by default** If something happens by default, it happens only because something else does not happen. **gerekeni yapmamaktan, ihmalden** *No one else stood in the election, so he won by default.* ● **default** *adjective* [always before noun] *The default font size is 10.* **varsayılan**

default² /dɪˈfɔːlt/ *verb* [I] to not do what you have made an agreement to do, especially paying back money you have borrowed **yükümlülüğü yerine getirmemek, ihmal etmek, bilhassa bir borcu ödememek** *They have defaulted on their debt repayments.*

o***defeat¹** /dɪˈfiːt/ *verb* [T] **1** to win against someone in a fight or competition **galip gelmek** *She was defeated by an Australian player in the first round of the tournament.* **2** to make someone or something fail **yenmek, mağlup etmek** *The bill was narrowly defeated in parliament.*

defeat ..... İLE BİRLİKTE KULLANILAN KELİMELER

admit/face/suffer defeat ● a **comprehensive/crushing/humiliating/narrow** defeat

o***defeat²** /dɪˈfiːt/ *noun* **1** [C, U] when someone loses against someone else in a fight or competition **yenilgi, mağlubiyet** *The Chicago Cubs have suffered their worst defeat of the season.* **2** [no plural] when someone or something is made to fail **yenilme, başarısızlık** *the defeat of apartheid*

defeatism /dɪˈfiːtɪzʲᵊm/ *noun* [U] behaviour or thoughts that show that you do not expect to be successful **karamsarlık, yenilgi beklentisi, umutsuzluk**

defeatist /dɪˈfiːtɪst/ *adjective* behaving in a way that shows that you do not expect to be successful **başarısızlığı kabullenen, olumsuz düşüncelere sahip olan** *a defeatist attitude* ● **defeatist** *noun* [C] **yenilgiyi kabul eden**

defect¹ /ˈdiːfekt/ *noun* [C] a fault or problem with someone or something **kusur, eksik** *a birth defect* ○ *A mechanical defect caused the plane to crash.* ● **defective** /dɪˈfektɪv/ *adjective* having a fault or problem **kusurlu, eksiği olan** *defective goods*

defect² /dɪˈfekt/ *verb* [I] to leave your country or organization and go to join an enemy country or competing organization **ayrılıp karşı tarafa/düşman/rakip saflara geçmek** *He defected to the West.* ● **defection** /dɪˈfekʃᵊn/ *noun* [C, U] when someone defects **rakip tarafa geçme, ihanet eden, terkeden** ● **defector** *noun* [C] **düşman tarafına geçen**

defence ..... İLE BİRLİKTE KULLANILAN KELİMELER

mount/put up a defence ● an **effective/spirited/strong/vigorous** defence ● defence **against** sth ● [argue, etc] **in** defence **of** sth

o***defence** UK (*US* defense) /dɪˈfens/ *noun* **1** [MILITARY] [U] the weapons and military forces that a country uses to protect itself against attack **savunma, müdafaa** *Government spending on defence is increasing.* ○ *the defence minister/industry* **2** [PROTECTION] [C, U] protection, or something that provides protection against attack or criticism **savunma, koruma, müdafaa** *the body's defences against infection* ○ *She argued strongly in defence of her actions.* **3 come to sb's defence** to support someone when they are being criticized **birinin savunmasına yardım etmek, desteklemek, eleştiriler karşısında yardım etmek 4 the defence** [group] the lawyers in a court who work in support of the person who is accused of a crime **müdafaa/savunma avukatları** *He was cross-examined by the defence.* ○ *a defence lawyer* **5** [SPORT] [C, U] the part of a sports team which tries to prevent the other team from scoring points **(spor) savunma** ➋See also: **self-defence.**

defenceless UK (*US* defenseless) /dɪˈfensləs/ *adjective* weak and unable to protect yourself from attack **savunmasız, korumasız** *a small, defenceless child*

o***defend** /dɪˈfend/ *verb* **1** [PROTECT] [T] to protect someone or something from being attacked, especially by fighting **savunmak, müdafaa etmek** *The army was sent in to defend the country against enemy attack.* ○ [often reflexive] *She tried to defend herself with a knife.* **2** [SUPPORT] [T] to support someone or something that is being criticized **karşı koymak, eleştirilere karşı birini desteklemek** *The newspaper's editor defended his decision to publish the photos.* **3** [LAW] [T] to try to show in a court that someone is not guilty of a crime **mahkemede savunmak** *He has hired two lawyers to defend him in court.* **4** [SPORT] [I, T] to try to stop the other sports team from scoring points **gol olmaması için savunma yapmak 5 defend a championship/title, etc** to try to win a match or competition that you have won before **bir şampiyonluğu/ünvanı korumak** ● **defender** *noun* [C] **savunucu, savunan**

defendant /dɪˈfendənt/ *noun* [C] the person in a court who is accused of a crime **davalı, sanık**

o***defense** /dɪˈfens/ *noun US spelling of* defence **savunma, müdafaa**

defenseless /dɪˈfensləs/ *adjective US spelling of* defenceless **savunmasız, korumasız**

defensive¹ /dɪˈfensɪv/ *adjective* **1** [CRITICISM] quick to protect yourself from being criticized **savunmaya yönelik** *He's very defensive about his weight.* **2** [SPORT] mainly US A defensive player in a sports team tries to stop the other team scoring points. **savunma amaçlı 3** [ATTACK] done or used to protect someone or something from attack **savunma için kullanılan, müdafaaya yönelik** ● **defensively** *adverb* **savunur bir durumda**

defensive² /dɪˈfensɪv/ *noun* **on the defensive** ready to protect yourself because you are expecting to be criticized or attacked **savunmada; (savunma için) hazırlıklı**

defer /dɪˈfɜːʳ/ *verb* [T] **deferring,** *past* **deferred** to arrange for something to happen at a later time **tehir etmek,**

ertelemek *The payments can be deferred for three months.*

deference /'defᵊrᵊns/ *noun* [U] polite behaviour that shows that you respect someone or something **saygı, hürmet, nezaket** ● **deferential** /ˌdefᵊ'renʃᵊl/ *adjective* **saygılı**

defiance /dɪ'faɪəns/ *noun* [U] when you refuse to obey someone or something **karşı koyma, meydan okuma, itaatsizlik, hiçe sayma** *an act of defiance*

defiant /dɪ'faɪənt/ *adjective* refusing to obey someone or something **küstah, meydan okuyan, cüretkâr** *a defiant child* ● **defiantly** *adverb* **meydan okurcasına**

╔═══════════════════════════════════════╗
║ **deficiency** ...... İLE BİRLİKTE KULLANILAN KELİMELER ║
╚═══════════════════════════════════════╝

a **glaring/major/serious/severe** deficiency ● a deficiency **in** sth

deficiency /dɪ'fɪʃᵊnsi/ *noun* [C, U] **1** when you do not have enough of something **yetersizlik, kifayetsizlik** *a vitamin deficiency* **2** a mistake or fault in something so that it is not good enough **eksiklik, noksanlık** *Parents are complaining of serious deficiencies in the education system.*

deficient /dɪ'fɪʃᵊnt/ *adjective* **1** not having enough of something **yetersiz, eksik, noksan** *If you have poor night vision you may be deficient in vitamin A.* **2** not good enough **zayıf, yetersiz** *His theory is deficient in several respects.*

deficit /'defɪsɪt/ *noun* [C] the amount by which the money that you spend is more than the money that you receive **bütçe açığı** *a budget deficit*

defile /dɪ'faɪl/ *verb* [T] *formal* to spoil someone or something that is pure, holy, or beautiful **bozmak, kirletmek, lekelemek**

define /dɪ'faɪn/ *verb* [T] **1** to say exactly what something means, or what someone or something is like **tarif etmek, tanımlamak, açıklamak** *Your duties are clearly defined in the contract.* **2** to show the outer edges or shape of something **tasvir etmek, belirtmek, göstermek** *It has sharply defined edges.*

o┅**definite** /'defɪnət/ *adjective* **1** certain, fixed, and not likely to change **kesin, sabit, değişmez** *We need a definite answer by tomorrow.* **2** clear and obvious **açık seçik, aşikâr, belirgin** *There has been a definite improvement in her behaviour.*

ˌdefinite 'article *noun* [C] in grammar, used to mean the word 'the' **'belirli tanımlık' the** ⊃Compare **indefinite article.**

o┅**definitely** /'defɪnətli/ *adverb* without any doubt **kuşkusuz, kesinlikle** *This book is definitely worth reading.* ○ *"Do you want to come?" "Yes, definitely."*

definition /ˌdefɪ'nɪʃᵊn/ *noun* **1** [C] an explanation of the meaning of a word or phrase **tanım, tarif, açıklama** *a dictionary definition* **2** [U] how clear an image of something is in a photograph or on a screen **görüntünün belirginliği/açıklığı**

definitive /dɪ'fɪnətɪv/ *adjective* **1** certain, clear, and not likely to change **kesin, kat'i, açık, değişmez, sabit** *a definitive answer* **2** A definitive book or piece of work is the best of its type. **tam ve eksiksiz, en iyi, güvenilir** *the definitive guide to London* ● **definitively** *adverb* **kesin bir şekilde**

deflate /dɪ'fleɪt/ *verb* **1** [I, T] to let all the air or gas out of something, or to become emptied of air or gas **havasını in(dir)mek/boşal(t)mak** *to deflate a balloon/tyre* **2** [T] to make someone lose confidence or feel less important **havasını söndürmek, bozmak, güvenini yitirmesine sebep olmak** [often passive] *They were totally deflated by losing the match.*

deflect /dɪ'flekt/ *verb* **1** [I, T] to make something change direction by hitting or touching it, or to change direction after hitting something **yönünü değiştirmek, saptırmak, caydırmak** *The ball was deflected into the corner of the net.* **2 deflect attention/blame/criticism, etc** to cause attention/blame/criticism, etc to be directed away from you **dikkati/suçlamayı/eleştiriyi uzaklaştırmak, yönünü değiştirmek/değişmesine neden olmak** ● **deflection** /dɪ'flekʃᵊn/ *noun* [C, U] **yön değiştirme**

deforestation /diːˌfɒrɪ'steɪʃᵊn/ *noun* [U] when all the trees in a large area are cut down **ağaçtan arındırma, ormansızlaştırma**

deformed /dɪ'fɔːmd/ *adjective* with a shape that has not developed normally **biçimi bozulmuş, deforme olmuş** *deformed hands* ● **deform** /dɪ'fɔːm/ *verb* [T] **biçimini, şeklini bozmak**

deformity /dɪ'fɔːməti/ *noun* [C, U] when a part of the body has not developed in the normal way, or with the normal shape **şekil bozukluğu, sakatlık**

defraud /dɪ'frɔːd/ *verb* [T] to obtain money from someone illegally by being dishonest **dolandırmak, aldatmak, para sızdırmak**

defrost /ˌdiː'frɒst/ *verb* [I, T] **1** If food defrosts, it becomes warmer after being frozen, and if you defrost it, you make it become warmer after being frozen. **buzunu eritmek/çözmek; buzu erimek/çözülmek** *You need to defrost the fish before you can cook it.* **2** If you defrost a fridge or freezer (= machines that keep food cold), you make them warmer and remove the ice, and if they defrost, they become warmer and the ice melts. **soğutucunun buzunu çözdürmek; buzu çözülmek**

deft /deft/ *adjective* quick and showing great skill **becerikli, usta, mahir** *a deft movement/touch* ● **deftly** *adverb* **hünerli bir şekilde**

defunct /dɪ'fʌŋkt/ *adjective* not working or existing now **işlevini yitirmiş, geçerli olmayan, çalışmayan, atıl**

defuse /ˌdiː'fjuːz/ *verb* [T] **1** to make a difficult or dangerous situation calmer **yatıştırmak, zararsızlaştırmak** *He made a joke to defuse the tension.* **2** to prevent a bomb from exploding by removing the fuse (= part that starts the explosion) **bombayı/patlayıcıyı etkisiz hale getirmek**

defy /dɪ'faɪ/ *verb* **1** [T] to refuse to obey someone or something **itaati reddetmek, karşı koymak, hiçe saymak** *Some of these children openly defy their teachers.* **2 defy belief/description/explanation, etc** to be impossible to believe/describe/explain, etc **inanması/tarifi/tasviri/izahı güç olmak** *His attitude defies belief.* **3 defy sb to do sth** to tell someone to do something that you think will be impossible **meydan okumak, birine imkansız bir şeyi yapmasını söylemek** *I defy you to prove that I'm wrong.*

degenerate¹ /dɪ'dʒenᵊreɪt/ *verb* [I] to become worse **bozulmak, yozlaşmak, gittikçe bozulmak** *The protest soon degenerated into violence.* ● **degeneration** /dɪˌdʒenə'reɪʃᵊn/ *noun* [U] **kötüleşme**

degenerate² /dɪ'dʒenᵊrət/ *adjective* having low moral principles **bozulmuş, yozlaşmış, ahlaki değerlerden yoksun**

degrade /dɪ'greɪd/ *verb* [T] **1** to treat someone without respect and as if they have no value **terbiyesiz davranmak, aşağılamak, küçük düşürmek** *They think the advert degrades women.* **2** to damage the quality or condition of something **küçültmek, değersizleştirmek, alçaltmak** ● **degradation** /ˌdegrə'deɪʃᵊn/ *noun* [U] **aşağılama**

D

degrading /dɪˈɡreɪdɪŋ/ *adjective* treating people without respect and as if they have no value **aşağılayıcı/ aşağılayan, küçük düşüren** *degrading work*

⊶**degree** /dɪˈɡriː/ *noun* **1** [TEMPERATURE] [C] a unit for measuring temperature, shown by the symbol ° written after a number **sıcaklığı gösteren derece 2** [ANGLE] [C] a unit for measuring angles, shown by the symbol ° written after a number **açı gösteren derece 3** [QUALIFICATION] [C] a qualification given for completing a university course **üniversite diploması/belgesi** *She has a degree in physics.* **4** [AMOUNT] [C, U] an amount or level of something **bir şeyin miktar ve seviyesini gösteren derece** *I agree with you to a degree* (= in some ways but not completely). ⊃See also: **master**[1]'s (degree).

dehydrated /ˌdiːhaɪˈdreɪtɪd/ *adjective* not having enough water in your body **vücutta su kaybı olan, susuz kalan**

dehydration /ˌdiːhaɪˈdreɪʃən/ *noun* [U] when you do not have enough water in your body **vücutta oluşan susuzluk, su kaybı**

deign /deɪn/ *verb* **deign to do sth** to do something that you think you are too important to do **tenezzül etmek**

deity /ˈdeɪɪti/ ⓤ /ˈdiːəti/ *noun* [C] *formal* a god or goddess (= female god) **tanrı, tanrıça**

deja vu /ˌdeɪʒɑːˈvuː/ *noun* [U] a feeling that you have already experienced exactly what is happening now **bir duyguyu/hissi önceden yaşamış gibi olma** *She suddenly had a strong sense of deja vu.*

dejected /dɪˈdʒektɪd/ *adjective* unhappy and disappointed **bıkkın, bezgin, morali bozuk, hayal kırıklığına uğramış** *He looked tired and dejected.* ● **dejection** /dɪˈdʒekʃən/ *noun* [U] **mutsuzluk, hayalkırıklığı**

⊶**delay**[1] /dɪˈleɪ/ *verb* **1** [I, T] to make something happen at a later time than originally planned or expected **ertelemek** *Can you delay your departure until next week?* **2** [T] to cause someone or something to be slow or late **geciktirmek** [often passive] *I was delayed by traffic.*

delay ⋯⋯ İLE BİRLİKTE KULLANILAN KELİMELER

a **brief/short/slight** delay ● a **considerable/ lengthy/long** delay ● **cause** delays ● **experience/ face/suffer** delays

⊶**delay**[2] /dɪˈleɪ/ *noun* [C, U] when you have to wait longer than expected for something to happen, or the time that you have to wait **erteleme, gecik(tir)me** *An accident caused long delays on the motorway.*

delectable /dɪˈlektəbl/ *adjective formal* extremely nice, especially to eat **yemesi çok hoş olan, lezzetli, çok leziz**

delegate[1] /ˈdelɪɡət/ *noun* [C] someone who is sent somewhere to represent a group of people, especially at a meeting **heyet, delege, temsilci**

delegate[2] /ˈdelɪɡeɪt/ *verb* [I, T] to give someone else part of your work or some of your responsibilities **görev ve sorumlulukları dağıtmak/ vermek; yetkilendirmek**

delegation /ˌdelɪˈɡeɪʃən/ *noun* **1** [C] a group of people who have been chosen to represent a much larger group of people **heyet üyeleri, delegeler, temsilciler** *a delegation of Chinese officials* **2** [U] when you give someone else part of your work or some of your responsibilities **yetki verme, görevlendirme**

delete /dɪˈliːt/ *verb* [T] to remove something, especially from a computer's memory **silmek, yok etmek** *All names have been deleted from the report.* ● **deletion** /dɪˈliːʃən/ *noun* [C, U] **silme, silinme**

deli /ˈdeli/ *noun* [C] *short for* delicatessen **şarküteri, meze büfesi**

deliberate[1] /dɪˈlɪbərət/ *adjective* **1** done intentionally, or planned **kasdi, isteyerek, bilerek, kasıtlı** *This was a deliberate attempt by them to deceive us.* **2** careful and without hurry **sakin ve dikkatli** *Her movements were calm and deliberate.*

deliberate[2] /dɪˈlɪbəreɪt/ *verb* [I, T] to consider something carefully before making a decision **bir şeyi enine boyuna düşünmek, herşeyi dikkate almak** *They deliberated for ten hours before reaching a decision.*

⊶**deliberately** /dɪˈlɪbərətli/ *adverb* intentionally, having planned to do something **kasden, kasıtlı olarak** *He deliberately lied to the police.*

deliberation /dɪˌlɪbəˈreɪʃən/ *noun* [C, U] careful thought or talk about a subject before a decision is made **bir karara varmadan önce dikkatlice düşünme, müzakere etme** *The jury began deliberations on Thursday.*

delicacy /ˈdelɪkəsi/ *noun* **1** [FOOD] [C] a special food, usually something rare or expensive **özel bir yiyecek, çok nadir bulunan yiyecek 2** [GENTLE QUALITY] [U] the quality of being soft, light, or gentle **hassas/ince kalite 3** [EASY TO DAMAGE] [U] when something is easy to damage or break **hassas, kolay kırılır, narin 4** [NEEDING CARE] [U] when something needs to be treated very carefully **özen, ihtimam, özel ilgi** *You need to be very tactful because of the delicacy of the situation.* **5** [ATTRACTIVE] [U] when something has a thin, attractive shape **zerafet, incelik, çekicilik**

delicate /ˈdelɪkət/ *adjective* **1** [GENTLE] soft, light, or gentle **zarif, ince, hafif, yumuşak** *a delicate flavour* ○ *a delicate shade of pink* **2** [EASY TO DAMAGE] easy to damage or break **kırılgan, hassas, kolay kırılabilir** *a delicate china cup* **3** [NEEDING CARE] needing to be dealt with very carefully **hassas/özel ilgi/ihtimam isteyen** *I need to discuss a very delicate matter with you.* **4** [ATTRACTIVE] having a thin, attractive shape **zarif, ince, çekici** *delicate hands* ● **delicately** *adverb* **nazikçe**

delicatessen /ˌdelɪkəˈtesən/ *noun* [C] a shop, or a part of a shop which sells cheeses, cooked meats, salads, etc **şarküteri, meze büfesi**

delicious /dɪˈlɪʃəs/ *adjective* If food or drink is delicious, it smells or tastes extremely good. **leziz, lezzetli, nefis** *This soup is absolutely delicious.* ● **deliciously** *adverb* **lezzetli bir şekilde**

delight[1] /dɪˈlaɪt/ *noun* **1** [U] happiness and excited pleasure **sevinç, zevk, haz** *The children screamed with delight.* **2** [C] someone or something that gives you pleasure **neşe, keyif** *She is a delight to have around.*

delight[2] /dɪˈlaɪt/ *verb* [T] to make someone feel very pleased and happy **keyiflendirmek, neşelendirmek, haz vermek** *The new discovery has delighted scientists everywhere.*
delight in sth/doing sth *phrasal verb* to get a lot of pleasure from something, especially something unpleasant **zevk/keyif/haz almak** *She seems to delight in making him look stupid.*

delighted /dɪˈlaɪtɪd/ *adjective* very pleased **memnun, sevinçli, keyifli** [+ to do sth] *I'd be delighted to accept your invitation.* ○ *They are delighted with their new car.*

delightful /dɪˈlaɪtfəl/ *adjective* very pleasant, attractive, or enjoyable **hoş, zevk veren, sevimli** *We had a delightful evening.* ● **delightfully** *adverb* **harika, enfes bir şekilde**

delinquency /dɪˈlɪŋkwənsi/ *noun* [U] criminal or bad behaviour, especially by young people **özellikle gençlerde görülen suç eğilimli davranışlar**

delinquent /dɪˈlɪŋkwənt/ *noun* [C] a young person who behaves badly, usually by committing crimes **(bilhassa gençler) suçlu, suç işlemeye eğilimli genç** ● **delinquent** *adjective* **delinquent behaviour suçlu**

delirious /dɪ'lɪriəs/ *adjective* **1** speaking or thinking in a confused way, often because of a fever or drugs **(ateş ve ilaçlardan dolayı) sayıklayan, hezeyan gösteren 2** extremely happy **sevinçten çılgına dönmüş, mutluluktan uçan** *delirious fans* ● **deliriously** *adverb* **sayıklar bir durumda**

deliver /dɪ'lɪvə'/ *verb* **1** [I, T] to take things such as letters, parcels, or goods to a person or place **teslim etmek, ulaştırmak, dağıtmak** *They can deliver the sofa on Wednesday.* **2** [I, T] to achieve or do something that you have promised to do, or that people expect you to do **bir vaadi/işlemi yerine getirmek** *The company failed to deliver the high quality service that we expect.* **3 deliver a speech/talk, etc** to speak formally to a group of people **guruba konuşma yapmak, sunum yapmak** *She delivered the speech on national TV.* **4 deliver a baby** to help take a baby out of its mother when it is being born **çocuk doğurmak, doğum yapmak** ⊃See also: deliver/come up with the **goods**.

delivery /dɪ'lɪvə'ri/ *noun* [C, U] **1** when someone takes things such as letters, parcels, or goods to a person or place **(posta, paket vb.) dağıtım, teslimat** *Is there a charge for delivery?* **2** when a baby is born and comes out of its mother **doğum** *Her husband was present at the delivery.*

delta /'deltə/ *noun* [C] a low, flat area of land where a river divides into smaller rivers and goes into the sea **delta, bir kaç nehir ve kollarının oluşturduğu nehir yatağı** *the Nile delta*

delude /dɪ'luːd/ *verb* [T] to make someone believe something that is not real or true **inandırmak, kandırmak, aldatma** [often reflexive, + into + doing sth] *She deluded herself into thinking she could win.* ● **deluded** *adjective* believing things that are not real or true **aldatıcı, yanıltan, kandıran şeyler**

deluge¹ /'deljuːdʒ/ *noun* [C] **1** a very large amount of something that suddenly arrives **tufan** *They have received a deluge of complaints.* **2** a sudden, large amount of rain, or a flood **yağmur veya sel baskını, afet, tufan**

deluge² /'deljuːdʒ/ *verb* **be deluged with/by sth** to receive very large amounts of something suddenly **birşeyden aniden çok sayıda gelmesi, bastırması** *Our switchboard was deluged with calls last night.*

delusion /dɪ'luːʒ°n/ *noun* [C, U] when someone believes something that is not true **hile, aldatma, oyun, hayal** [+ (that)] *She is under the delusion that her debts will just go away.*

deluxe /də'lʌks/ *adjective* luxurious and of very high quality **çok lüks, kaliteli** *a deluxe hotel*

delve /delv/ *verb* **delve in/into/inside, etc** to search in a container to try to find something **bir şeyin içini aramak, derinlemesine aramak, içine dalmak** *He delved in his pocket and pulled out a pen.*
delve into sth *phrasal verb* to examine something carefully in order to discover more information about someone or something **derinlemesine araştırmak, incelemek, bir şeyler bulmaya, elde etmeye çalışmak** *I don't like to delve too deeply into his past.*

increase/meet/satisfy demand ● great/growing/high/steady demand ● be in demand ● demand for sth

o→**demand¹** /dɪ'mɑːnd/ *noun* **1** [U, no plural] a need for something to be sold or supplied **talep** *There's an increasing demand for cheap housing.* **2** [C] a strong request **istek, talep** *They received a final demand for payment.* **3 in demand** wanted or needed in large num-

bers **çok istenen, rağbet gören, revaçta olan** *Good teachers are always in demand.*

o→**demand²** /dɪ'mɑːnd/ *verb* [T] **1** to ask for something in a way that shows that you do not expect to be refused **dayatmak, ısrar etmek, talepte bulunmak** *I demanded an explanation.* ○ [+ that] *The survivors are demanding that the airline pays them compensation.* **2** to need something such as time or effort **gerektirmek, talep etmek, istemek** *This job demands a high level of concentration.*

demanding /dɪ'mɑːndɪŋ/ *adjective* needing a lot of your time, attention, or effort **zaman/ilgi/çaba gerektiren; talepkâr** *a very demanding job*

demands /dɪ'mɑːndz/ *noun* [plural] the difficult things that you have to do **talepler, istekler, yapmak zorunda olunan şeyler** *the demands of modern life* ○ *His new job makes a lot of demands on him* (= he has to work very hard).

demeaning /dɪ'miːnɪŋ/ *adjective* If something is demeaning, it makes you feel that you are not respected. **küçük düşüren, alçaltan, küçülten** *Some people consider beauty competitions demeaning to women.*

demeanour UK (US **demeanor**) /dɪ'miːnə'/ *noun* [C] the way that someone looks, seems, and behaves **tavır, davranış, tutum** *a quiet, serious demeanour*

demented /dɪ'mentɪd/ *adjective* mentally ill, or behaving in a very strange way without any control **deli, çılgın, aklı başında olmayan**

dementia /dɪ'menʃə/ *noun* [U] a mental illness suffered especially by old people **daha çok yaşlılarda görülen akıl hastalığı**

demi- /demi-/ *prefix* half, partly **yarım, kısmi anlamında ön ek** *demitasse* (= a small coffee cup) ○ *demigod* (= a creature that is part god and part human)

demise /dɪ'maɪz/ *noun* **1** [no plural] when something ends, usually because it has stopped being popular or successful **batma, çökme, bitiş, önemini/değerini kaybetme; gözden düşme** *the demise of apartheid* **2 sb's demise** someone's death **vefat, ölüm**

demo¹ /'deməʊ/ *noun* [C] **1** an example of a product, given or shown to someone to try to make them buy it **tanıtım gösterisi** *a software demo* **2** UK short for demonstration (= political march) **siyasi gösteri** *a student demo*

demo² /'deməʊ/ *verb* [T] to show something and explain how it works **gösteri/tanıtım yapmak; bir şeyin nasıl işlediğini göstermek** *We need someone to demo a new piece of software.*

an emerging/new democracy ● in a democracy

o→**democracy** /dɪ'mɒkrəsi/ *noun* [C, U] a system of government in which people elect their leaders, or a country with this system **demokrasi**

democrat /'deməkræt/ *noun* [C] **1** someone who supports democracy **demokrat 2 Democrat** someone who supports the Democratic Party in the US **ABD'de Demokrat Parti'yi savunan, demokrat partili** *the Democrat candidate* ⊃See also: Liberal Democrat.

democratic /ˌdemə'krætɪk/ *adjective* **1** following or supporting the political system of democracy **demokratik** *a democratic society/government* **2** where everyone has equal rights and can help to make decisions **eşitlikçi, demokratik** *a democratic discussion/debate* ● **democratically** *adverb* *a democratically elected government* **demokratik bir şekilde**

the Demo'cratic ,Party *noun* [group] one of the two main political parties in the US **(ABD) Demokrat Parti**

demolish /dɪ'mɒlɪʃ/ *verb* [T] **1** to destroy something such as a building **yıkmak, yerle bir etmek** *The factory is dangerous, and will have to be demolished.* **2** to show that an idea or argument is wrong **bir fikri çürütmek, yanlış olduğunu göstermek** *He completely demolished my argument.*

demolition /ˌdemə'lɪʃᵊn/ *noun* [C, U] when something such as a building is destroyed **yıkım, yerle bir etme** *the demolition of dangerous buildings*

demon /'diːmən/ *noun* [C] an evil spirit **cin, kötü ruh**

demonic /dɪ'mɒnɪk/ *adjective* evil **kötü, şeytani/şeytanca**

demonstrable /dɪ'mɒnstrəbl/ *adjective* Something that is demonstrable can be shown to exist or be true. **kanıtlanabilir, gösterilebilir** *a demonstrable fact* ● **demonstrably** *adverb* **kanıtlanabilir bir şekilde**

o*-**demonstrate** /'demənstreɪt/ *verb* **1** [PROVE] [T] to show or prove that something exists or is true **göstermek, kanıtlamak, ortaya koymak** [+ that] *The survey clearly demonstrates that tourism can have positive benefits.* **2** [SHOW HOW] [T] to show someone how to do something, or how something works **çalışmasını/işleyişini göstermek** *She demonstrated how to use the new software.* **3** [EXPRESS] [T] to express or show that you have a feeling, quality, or ability **kabiliyetlerini/kendini göstermek/ortaya koymak** *He has demonstrated a genuine interest in the project.* **4** [MARCH] [I] to march or stand with a group of people to show that you disagree with or support someone or something **gösteri yapmak, gösteriye katılmak** *Thousands of people gathered to demonstrate against the new proposals.*

demonstration ...... İLE BİRLİKTE KULLANILAN KELİMELER

hold/organize/stage a demonstration ● **go on/take part in** a demonstration ● **a mass** demonstration ● a demonstration **against** sth

demonstration /ˌdemən'streɪʃᵊn/ *noun* **1** [MARCH] [C] when a group of people march or stand together to show that they disagree with or support someone or something **gösteri, nümayiş, gösteri yürüyüşü** *They're taking part in a demonstration against the causes of climate change.* **2** [SHOWING HOW] [C, U] showing how to do something, or how something works **tatbikat, gösteri, tanıtım gösterisi** *We asked the sales assistant to give us a demonstration.* **3** [PROOF] [C, U] proof that something exists or is true **gösterge, kanıt, delil** *This disaster is a clear demonstration of the need for tighter controls.*

demonstrative /dɪ'mɒnstrətɪv/ *adjective* willing to show your feelings, especially your affection **duygularını gösterebilen/dışa vuran, coşkulu**

demonstrator /'demənstreɪtəʳ/ *noun* [C] a person who marches or stands with a group of people to show that they disagree with or support someone or something **bir fikrin karşıt olduğunu göstermek için büyük bir grupla gösteri yapan kişi**

demoralized (*also* UK -ised) /dɪ'mɒrəlaɪzd/ *adjective* having lost your confidence, enthusiasm, and hope **morali bozuk, cesareti kırık, demoralize olmuş** *After the match, the players were tired and demoralized.* ● **demoralizing** *adjective* making you lose your confidence, enthusiasm, and hope **cesareti kıran, morali bozan, coşkuyu azaltan** *a demoralizing defeat* ● **demoralize** /dɪ'mɒrəlaɪz/ *verb* [T] **moralini bozmak**

demote /dɪ'məʊt/ *verb* **be demoted** to be moved to a less important job or position, especially as a punishment **(ceza olarak) daha alt bir göreve getir(il)mek; rütbesini indirmek** ● **demotion** /dɪ'məʊʃᵊn/ *noun* [C, U] **indirme**

demotivated /ˌdiː'məʊtɪveɪtɪd/ *adjective* not having any enthusiasm for your work **coşku/heyecanını kaybetmek, demotive olmak,**

demure /dɪ'mjʊəʳ/ *adjective* If a young woman is demure, she is quiet and shy. **(genç kız, kadın) ağır başlı; vakur; yüzü kızaran; utanmasını bilen** ● **demurely** *adverb* **sessiz ve utangaç bir durumda**

den /den/ *noun* [C] **1** [ANIMAL'S HOME] the home of some wild animals **yabani hayvan ini, mağara** *a lions' den* **2** [ILLEGAL ACTIVITY] a place where secret and illegal activity happens **gizli buluşma yeri, kanuni olmayan şeylerin yapıldığı yer, yer altı dünyası** *a gambling den* **3** [ROOM] mainly US a room in your home where you relax, read, watch television, etc **çalışma odası**

denial ...... İLE BİRLİKTE KULLANILAN KELİMELER

issue a denial ● a **categorical/emphatic/strenuous/vehement** denial ● denial **of** sth

denial /dɪ'naɪəl/ *noun* **1** [C, U] when you say that something is not true **inkâr, yalanlama** *a denial of his guilt* **2** [U] not allowing someone to have or do something **red, kabul etmeme** *the denial of medical treatment*

denigrate /'denɪgreɪt/ *verb* [T] to criticize and not show much respect for someone or something **aşağılamak, hakaret etmek, saygı duymamak, eleştirerek küçültmek**

denim /'denɪm/ *noun* [U] thick, strong, cotton cloth, usually blue, which is used to make clothes **kot kumaşı, denim** *a denim jacket*

denomination /dɪˌnɒmɪ'neɪʃᵊn/ *noun* [C] **1** a religious group which has slightly different beliefs from other groups which share the same religion **mezhep, aynı dini paylaşan ancak kısmi inanç farklılığı gösteren grup 2** the value of a particular coin, piece of paper money, or stamp **para birimi, para, pul**

denote /dɪ'nəʊt/ *verb* [T] to be a sign of something **işareti olmak, manasına gelmek** *The colour red is used to denote passion or danger.*

denounce /dɪ'naʊns/ *verb* [T] to publicly criticize someone or something, or to publicly accuse someone of something **alenen kınamak, suçlamak** *They've been denounced as terrorists.*

dense /dens/ *adjective* **1** with a lot of people or things close together **yoğun, sıkı, kalabalık** *dense forest* **2** If cloud, smoke, etc is dense, it is thick and difficult to see through. **yoğun, koyu** *dense fog* ● **densely** *adverb* a **densely populated** area **kalabalık bir şekilde**

density /'densɪti/ *noun* [C, U] **1** the number of people or things in a place when compared with the size of the place **yoğunluk, sıklık** *The area has a high population density.* **2** the relationship between the weight of a substance and its size **(fizik) yoğunluk; bir kütlenin yoğunluğu ile hacmi arasındaki bağlantı/ilişki** *bone density*

dent[1] /dent/ *noun* [C] **1** a hollow area in a hard surface where it has been hit **çukur, göçük, girinti** *The car door had a dent in it.* **2** a reduction in something **kısma, azaltma** *The cost of repairs made a serious dent in my savings.*

dent[2] /dent/ *verb* [T] **1** to create a hollow area in the hard surface of something by hitting it **sert bir yüzeye vurarak çukurlaştırmak** *The side of the car was den-*

ted in the accident. **2** to reduce someone's confidence or positive feelings about something **birinin güvenini sars(ıl)mak, azal(t)mak** The defeat did little to dent her enthusiasm.

dental /'dentªl/ adjective relating to teeth **dişe ait/iliş-kin** dental treatment

dental floss /'dentªl,flɒs/ noun [U] a thin thread which is used for cleaning between the teeth **diş ipi**

dentist /'dentist/ noun [C] someone who examines and repairs teeth **diş hekimi, dişçi** I've got an appointment at the dentist's (= where the dentist works) tomorrow. • **dentistry** noun [U] the subject or job of examining and repairing teeth **dişçilik**

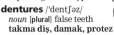 **dentist**

dentures /'dentʃəz/ noun [plural] false teeth **takma diş, damak, protez**

denunciation /dɪ,nʌnsi'eɪʃªn/ noun [C, U] when you publicly criticize someone or something, or publicly accuse someone of something **alenen suçlama, kınama**

◦ **deny** /dɪ'naɪ/ verb [T] **1** to say that something is not true, especially something that you are accused of **inkâr etmek** [+ (that)] He never denied that he said those things. ○ [+ doing sth] He denies murdering his father. **2** to not allow someone to have or do something **reddetmek, izin vermemek, yoksun bırakmak** [often passive] These children are being denied access to education.

deodorant /di'əʊdªrªnt/ noun [C, U] a substance that you put on your body to prevent or hide unpleasant smells **koku giderici sprey, deodorant**

depart /dɪ'pɑːt/ verb [I] formal to leave a place, especially to start a journey to another place **bir yerden ayrıl-mak, kalkmak, hareket etmek** The train to Lincoln will depart from platform 9. ○ He departed for Paris on Tuesday.

◦ **department** /dɪ'pɑːtmənt/ noun [C] a part of an organization such as a school, business, or government which deals with a particular area of work **bölüm, daire, departman** the sales department ○ head of the English department ⊃See also: **police department**.

departmental /,diːpɑːt'mentªl/ adjective relating to a department **bölüm, bölümü ilgilendiren** the departmental budget

de'partment ,store noun [C] a large shop divided into several different parts which sell different types of things **çok katlı alışveriş merkezi; büyük mağaza**

◦ **departure** /dɪ'pɑːtʃəʳ/ noun [C, U] **1** when someone or something leaves a place, especially to start a journey to another place **kalkış, hareket, ayrılma** the departure of flight BA117 ○ This fare is valid for weekday departures from Manchester. **2** a change from what is expected, or from what has happened before **ayrılma, sapma, değişime uğrama** This film is a major departure from his previous work.

◦ **depend** /dɪ'pend/ verb **it/that depends** used to say that you are not certain about something because other things affect your answer **belli olmaz** [+ question word] "Are you coming out tonight?" "It depends where you're going."

depend on/upon sb/sth phrasal verb **1** [NEED] to need the help of someone or something in order to exist or continue as before **bağımlı olmak, muhtaç olmak** She depends on her son for everything. ○ The city's economy

depends largely on the car industry. **2** [BE INFLUENCED BY] If something depends on someone or something, it is influenced by them, or changes because of them. **bağlı olmak, etkilenmek** [+ question word] The choice depends on what you're willing to spend. **3** [TRUST] to be able to trust someone or something to help, or to do what you expect **güvenmek, bağlanmak, itimat etmek** [+ to do sth] You can always depend on Andy to keep his promises.

dependable /dɪ'pendəbl/ adjective able to be trusted and very likely to do what you expect **güvenilir, itimat edilebilir** the team's most dependable player

dependant UK (US **dependent**) /dɪ'pendənt/ noun [C] someone, usually a child, who depends on you for financial support **bağımlı, yardıma muhtaç**

dependence /dɪ'pendəns/ (also **dependency** /dɪ'pendəntsi/) noun [U] when you need someone or something all the time in order to exist or continue as before **bağımlılık, yardıma muhtaç olma** Our society needs to reduce its dependence on the car.

dependent[1] /dɪ'pendənt/ adjective **1** needing the help of someone or something in order to exist or continue as before **bağımlı, muhtaç olan** She's completely dependent on her parents for money. **2 dependent on/upon sth** influenced by or decided by something **bağlı** The amount of tax you pay is dependent on how much you earn.

dependent[2] /dɪ'pendənt/ noun [C] US spelling of depen-dant **bağımlı, yardıma muhtaç**

depict /dɪ'pɪkt/ verb [T] to represent someone or some-thing in a picture or story **tasvir etmek** The cartoon depicts the president as a vampire. • **depiction** /dɪ'pɪkʃªn/ noun [C, U] **tanımlama**

deplete /dɪ'pliːt/ verb [T] to reduce the amount of some-thing, especially a natural supply **azaltmak, tüket-mek** Alcohol depletes the body of B vitamins. • **depletion** /dɪ'pliːʃªn/ noun [U] **azalma, düşüş**

deplorable /dɪ'plɔːrəbl/ adjective very bad or morally wrong **üzücü, esef verici, ahlaken kötü**

deplore /dɪ'plɔːʳ/ verb [T] formal to feel or express strong disapproval of something **kınamak, teessürlerini bil-dirmek, esef etmek** We deeply deplore the loss of life.

deploy /dɪ'plɔɪ/ verb [T] to move soldiers or equipment to a place where they can be used when they are needed **(asker, silah, mühimmat) konuşlandırmak** • **dep-loyment** noun [U] the deployment of nuclear weapons **yayılma, düzene geçiş**

deport /dɪ'pɔːt/ verb [T] to force a foreign person to leave a country **sınırdışı etmek, ülke dışına çıkarmak** Thousands of illegal immigrants are deported from the US every year. • **deportation** /,diːpɔː'teɪʃªn/ noun [C, U] He now faces deportation back to his native country. **sınır dışı etme, edilme**

depose /dɪ'pəʊz/ verb [T] to remove a ruler or leader from their position of power **darbeyle alaşağı etmek, tahtan indirmek, iktidarına son vermek** • **deposed** adjective the deposed president **tahttan indi-rilmiş**

pay/put down a deposit • a deposit of [£500/$300, etc] • a deposit **on** sth

deposit[1] /dɪ'pɒzɪt/ noun [C] **1** [BUYING] a payment that you make immediately when you decide to buy something, as proof that you will really buy it **kaparo, peşinat** They've **put down** a deposit on a house. **2** [BANK] an amount of money that you pay into a bank **bankaya yatırılan para** to **make a deposit 3** [SUBSTANCE] a layer of a substance that has developed from a natural or chemical process **tortu, birikinti, tabaka** *deposits of iron ore* **4** RENT an amount of money that you pay when you rent something, and that is given back to you when you return it without any damage **kiralanan yer için sonradan geri alınmak üzere ödenen güvence parası, depozito**

deposit² /dɪˈpɒzɪt/ *verb* [T] **1** PUT DOWN to put something down somewhere **yerleştirmek, koymak, biriktirmek** *He deposited his books on the table.* **2** MONEY to put money into a bank or valuable things into a safe place **bankaya para yatırmak veya değerli eşyaları bir kasaya koymak** *She deposited $150,000 in a Swiss bank account.* **3** SUBSTANCE to leave something lying on a surface, as a result of a natural or chemical process **birikinti/tortu kalmak, birik(tir)mek**

deˈposit acˌcount *noun* [C] *UK* a bank account that pays interest on the money you put into it and that you use for saving **vadeli mevduat hesabı**

depot /ˈdepəʊ/ *noun* [C] **1** VEHICLES a place where trains, trucks, or buses are kept **otobüs/tren/tır garajı** **2** GOODS a building where supplies of goods are stored **depo, cephanelik 3** STATION *US* a small bus or train station **tren veya otobüs istasyonu**

depraved /dɪˈpreɪvd/ *adjective* morally bad **ahlaken kötü** ● **depravity** /dɪˈprævəti/ *noun* [U] **ahlaksızlık**

depreciate /dɪˈpriːʃieɪt/ *verb* [I] to lose value over a period of time **değer kaybetmek, ucuzlamak; zamanla değeri azalmak** *New computers depreciate in value very quickly.* ● **depreciation** /dɪˌpriːʃiˈeɪʃən/ *noun* [U] **değer kaybı**

depress /dɪˈpres/ *verb* [T] **1** to make someone feel very unhappy, especially about the future **mutsuz etmek, canını sıkmak, keyfini/tadını kaçırmak** *This place really depresses me.* **2** to reduce the value or level of something, especially in business **azaltmak, düşürmek, rekabetle zayıflatmak (iş hayatı)** *Competition between stores has depressed prices.*

depressed /dɪˈprest/ *adjective* **1** very unhappy, often for a long time **canı sıkkın, bunalımlı, gergin, mutsuz** *She has been feeling very depressed since her marriage broke up.* **2** A depressed country, area, or economy does not have enough jobs or business activity. **(ülke, ekonomi, bölge) bunalımlı, çıkmazda olan, çöküntü içinde olan** *an economically depressed area*

depressing /dɪˈpresɪŋ/ *adjective* making you feel unhappy and without any hope for the future **kasvetli, iç karartıcı, karamsarlık veren** *The news is very depressing.*

depression /dɪˈpreʃən/ *noun* [C, U] **1** when you feel very unhappy, or a mental illness that makes you feel very unhappy **bunalım, depresyon, karamsarlık** *Nearly three million people **suffer from depression** every year.* **2** a time when there is not much business activity **ekonomik kriz, bunalım, çöküntü** *The stock market crash marked the start of a severe depression.*

deprive /dɪˈpraɪv/ *verb*
deprive sb/sth of sth *phrasal verb* to take something important or necessary away from someone or something **yoksun bırakmak, mahrum etmek** *They were deprived of food for long periods.* ● **deprivation** /ˌdeprɪˈveɪʃən/ *noun* [C, U] *sleep deprivation* **mahrum kalma**

deprived /dɪˈpraɪvd/ *adjective* not having enough food, money, and the things that you need to have a normal life **yoksun** *children from **deprived backgrounds***

dept *written abbreviation for* department (= a part of an organization or government) **bölüm, daire, departman**

a depth **of** [6 metres/8 inches, etc] ● [5cm/7 inches, etc] **in** depth ● **at/to** a depth of [5 metres/6 inches, etc]

depth /depθ/ *noun* **1** TOP TO BOTTOM [C, U] the distance from the top of something to the bottom **dikine derinlik** *The lake reaches a maximum **depth of** 292 metres.* ○ *Dig a hole 10 cm **in depth**.* ⊃See picture at **length**. **2** FRONT TO BACK [C, U] the distance from the front to the back of something **enine derinlik 3** AMOUNT [U] how much someone knows or feels about something **bilgi derinliği** *She was amazed at the depth of his knowledge.* **4 in depth** giving all the details **derinlemesine, etraflıca, ayrıntılı** *With access to the Internet, students can do their homework in greater depth.* **5 be out of your depth** to not have the knowledge, experience, or skills to deal with a particular situation or subject **bilgi ve birikimini aşmak; boyunu aşmak, bilgi ve yeteneği dışında olmak**

depths /depθs/ *noun* [plural] **1** a position far below the surface or far into something **derinlerde, derininde** *the depths of the forest* **2** the worst period of something **bir şeyin en kötü olduğu dönem, çöküş, kötüleşme dönemi** *the depths of despair*

deputy /ˈdepjəti/ *noun* [C] someone who has the second most important job in an organization **muavin, vekalet eden** *the deputy Prime Minister*

derail /dɪˈreɪl/ *verb* **1** [I, T] If a train derails, or is derailed, it comes off the railway tracks. **raydan çık(ar)mak 2** [T] If you derail plans, you prevent them from happening. **yolunda gitmemek, planlandığı gibi olmamak** ● **derailment** *noun* [C, U] **raydan çıkma (tren)**

deranged /dɪˈreɪndʒd/ *adjective* behaving in a way that is not normal, especially when suffering from a mental illness **akli dengesi yerinde olmayan**

derby /ˈdɑːbi/ ⑤ /ˈdɜːrbi/ *noun* [C] **1** *mainly UK* a type of sports competition **büyük takımların oynadığı maç, karşılaşma** *a fishing/motorcycle derby* **2 Derby** a type of horse race **bir tür at yarışı 3** *US* (*UK* bowler hat) a round, hard, black hat worn by men, especially in the past **melon şapka**

deregulate /ˌdiːˈreɡjəleɪt/ *verb* [T] to remove national or local government controls from a business **bir işten ulusal veya bölgesel hükümetin kontrolünü kaldırmak** *The government plans to deregulate the banking industry.* ● **deregulation** /ˌdiːreɡjəˈleɪʃən/ *noun* [U] **konrolü, sınırları kaldırma**

derelict /ˈderəlɪkt/ *adjective* A derelict building or piece of land is not used any more and is in a bad condition. **metruk, terkedilmiş bina/yer** *a derelict house*

deride /dɪˈraɪd/ *verb* [T] *formal* to talk about someone or something as if they are ridiculous and do not deserve any respect **alay etmek, dalga geçmek, alaya almak** *Her novel, once derided by critics, is now a classic.*

derision /dɪˈrɪʒən/ *noun* [U] when you talk about someone or something as if they are ridiculous and do not deserve respect **alay, istahza** *The novel was **greeted with derision**.*

derisive /dɪˈraɪsɪv/ *adjective* showing derision towards someone or something **alaycı, alaylı**

derisory /dɪˈraɪsəri/ *adjective* **1** so small that it seems ridiculous **çok gülünç, alay eder gibi** *a derisory sum of money* **2** cruel and making someone feel stupid **kaba, alaycı, alay eden** *derisory remarks*

derivation /ˌderɪˈveɪʃən/ *noun* [C, U] the origin of something, such as a word, from which another form has developed, or the new form itself **köken, kaynak, geldiği yer**

derivative /dɪˈrɪvətɪv/ *noun* [C] a form of something, such as a word, that has developed from another form **türemiş, türetilen**

derive /dɪˈraɪv/ *verb*
derive (sth) from sth *phrasal verb* **1** to come from or be developed from something **bir şeyi bir şeyden türetmek/türemek** *The name derives from Latin.* **2 derive comfort/pleasure, etc from sth** to get a positive feeling or advantage from someone or something *I derive great pleasure from gardening.*

dermatitis /ˌdɜːməˈtaɪtɪs/ *noun* [U] a condition which makes your skin red and painful **cilt kızarıklığı, bir tür cilt hastalığı**

derogatory /dɪˈrɒgətəri/ *adjective* showing strong disapproval and not showing any respect for someone **küçümseyici, küçültücü, aşağılayıcı, onur kırıcı, utandırıcı** *derogatory comments/remarks*

descend /dɪˈsend/ *verb* [I, T] *formal* to move or go down **alçalmak, inişe geçmek** *We descended four flights of stairs.*
be descended from sb/sth *phrasal verb* to be related to a person or creature that lived a long time ago **soyundan gelmek/türemek**

descendant /dɪˈsendənt/ *noun* [C] someone who is related to someone who lived a long time ago **soyundan gelen kimse** *She is a descendant of Queen Victoria.*

descent /dɪˈsent/ *noun* [C, U] **1** a movement down **iniş, alçalma, düşüş** *The plane began its descent into Heathrow.* **2 of Irish/French, etc descent** being related to people who lived in the past in Ireland/France, etc **İrlandalı, Fransız vb. soyundan**

☞ **describe** /dɪˈskraɪb/ *verb* [T] to say what someone or something is like **tasvir etmek, anlatmak, betimlemek, tanımlamak** *Neighbours described her as a shy, quiet girl.* ○ [+ question word] *I tried to describe what I had seen.*

🧩 **description** .... İLE BİRLİKTE KULLANILAN KELİMELER

give a description ● an **accurate/detailed/short** description ● a description **of** sth/sb

☞ **description** /dɪˈskrɪpʃən/ *noun* **1** [C, U] something that tells you what someone or something is like **tanım, anlatım, betimleme, tasvir** *I gave the police a description of the stolen jewellery.* **2 of any/every/some description** of any/every/some type **her/herhangi/bazı türlerde, çeşitlerde** *They sell plants of every description.*

descriptive /dɪˈskrɪptɪv/ *adjective* describing something, especially in a detailed, interesting way **tanımlayıcı, betimleyici**

desert[1] /ˈdezət/ *noun* [C, U] a large, hot, dry area of land with very few plants **çöl** *the Sahara Desert*

desert[2] /dɪˈzɜːt/ *verb* **1** PERSON [T] to leave someone and never come back **terketmek, He deserted his family.** **2** PLACE [T] to leave a place, so that it is empty **bir yeri terketmek** *People are deserting the countryside to work in towns.* **3** ARMY [I, T] to leave the army without permission **firar etmek, kaçmak** ● **desertion** /dɪˈzɜːʃən/ *noun* [U] **terkediş**

deserted /dɪˈzɜːtɪd/ *adjective* If a place is deserted, it has no people in it. **terkedilmiş, virane** *a deserted street*

deserter /dɪˈzɜːtər/ *noun* [C] someone who leaves the army without permission **firari**

ˌ**desert** ˈ**island** *noun* [C] a tropical island where no one lives, far from any other places **ıssız ada**

☞ **deserve** /dɪˈzɜːv/ *verb* [T] If you deserve something good or bad, it should happen to you because of the way you have behaved. **haketmek, layık olmak** *The school*

deserves praise for the way it has raised standards. ○ [+ to do sth] *He deserves to be locked up for life.* ● **deservedly** *adverb* **hakketmiş olarak**

deserving /dɪˈzɜːvɪŋ/ *adjective* If something or someone is deserving, people should help or support them. **hakeden, hakedilen, hakedilmiş** *The children's charity is a deserving cause.*

☞ **design**[1] /dɪˈzaɪn/ *noun* **1** PLANNING [U] the way in which something is planned and made **tasarım, plan** *There was a fault in the design of the aircraft.* **2** DRAWING [C] a drawing which shows how an object, machine, or building will be made **çizim, tasarım** *Engineers are working on the new designs.* **3** DECORATION [C] a pattern or decoration **desen 4** PROCESS [U] the process of making drawings to show how something will be made **taslak** *a course in art and design* ➌See also: interior design.

☞ **design**[2] /dɪˈzaɪn/ *verb* [T] **1** to draw or plan something before making it **plan çizmek, tasarlamak** *She designs furniture.* **2 be designed to do sth** to have been planned or done for a particular purpose **bir şeyin yapılmasını planla(n)mak, tasarla(n)mak** *The new law is designed to protect children.*

designate /ˈdezɪgneɪt/ *verb* [T] *formal* to choose someone or something for a particular purpose or duty **atamak, görevlendirmek** *The area has been designated as a nature reserve.* ● **designation** /ˌdezɪgˈneɪʃən/ *noun* [C, U] **tahsis, görevlendirme**

designer[1] /dɪˈzaɪnər/ *noun* [C] someone who draws and plans how something will be made **tasarımcı, tasarı/çizim yapan** *a fashion designer*

designer[2] /dɪˈzaɪnər/ *adjective* **designer jeans/sunglasses, etc** clothes or objects made by a fashionable designer **moda tasarımcısı tarafından tasarlanan nesneler/giysiler**

deˌsigner ˈ**baby** *noun* [C] a baby with some characteristics chosen by its parents and doctors using gene therapy (= the science of changing genes in order to stop or prevent a disease) **ileride doğabilecek muhtemel hastalıkları önlemek için gen tedavisi/terapisi yapılmak üzere ebeveyn ve doktorlar tarafından seçilmiş çocuk**

desirable /dɪˈzaɪərəbl/ *adjective* If something is desirable, it is very good or attractive and most people would want it. **hoş, istenebilir, arzu edilebilir** *A good education is highly desirable.* ➌Opposite undesirable.

🧩 **desire** .... İLE BİRLİKTE KULLANILAN KELİMELER

express/have a desire to do sth ● a **burning/strong** desire ● a desire **for** sth

desire[1] /dɪˈzaɪər/ *noun* **1** [C, U] a strong feeling that you want something **emel, istek, arzu, dilek** [+ to do sth] *I have no desire to have children.* ○ *There is a strong desire for peace among the people.* **2** [U] when you are sexually attracted to someone **cinsel istek/arzu**

desire[2] /dɪˈzaɪər/ *verb* [T] *formal* to want something **istemek, arzulamak** *You can have whatever you desire.*

desired /dɪˈzaɪəd/ *adjective* **the desired effect/result/shape, etc** the effect/result/shape, etc that is wanted **arzu edilen/istenen etki/sonuç/şekil** *Her medicine seems to have had the desired effect.*

☞ **desk** /desk/ *noun* [C] a table that you sit at to write or work, often with drawers **masa** ➌See also: cash desk ➌Orta kısımdaki renkli sayfalarına bakınız.

desk

desktop /'desktɒp/ *noun* [C] **1** COMPUTER SCREEN a computer screen that contains icons (= symbols that represent programs, information, or equipment) and which is usually used as a place to start and finish computer work **bilgisayar ekranı; masaüstü 2** COMPUTER (*also* **desktop computer**) a computer that is small enough to fit on a desk **masaüstü bilgisayar 3** SURFACE the top of a desk **masaüstü**

‚desktop 'publishing *noun* [U] producing finished designs for pages of books or documents using a small computer and printer (= machine for printing) **masaüstü basım**

desolate /'desᵊlət/ *adjective* **1** A desolate place is empty and makes you feel sad. **ıssız, kuş uçmaz kervan geçmez, insanı üzen ıssız mekân** *a desolate landscape* **2** lonely and unhappy **yalnız, yapayalnız, kimsesiz, mutsuz** *She felt desolate when he left.* ● **desolation** /ˌdesᵊl'eɪʃᵊn/ *noun* [U] **tenha, ıssız**

---

despair .... İLE BİRLİKTE KULLANILAN KELİMELER

abject/complete/utter despair ● **in** despair

---

despair¹ /dɪ'speəʳ/ *noun* [U] a feeling of having no hope **umutsuzluk, çaresizlik** *She shook her head in despair.*

despair² /dɪ'speəʳ/ *verb* [I] to feel that you have no hope **umutsuzluğa/çaresizliğe düşmek** *Don't despair - things will improve.* ○ [+ of + doing sth] *He had begun to despair of ever finding a job.* ● **despairing** *adjective* **umutsuz**

despatch¹ UK (UK/US dispatch) /dɪ'spætʃ/ *verb* [T] *formal* to send someone or something somewhere **göndermek, yollamak, sevketmek** *They despatched a police car to arrest him.*

despatch² UK (UK/US dispatch) /dɪ'spætʃ/ *noun* **1** [U] when someone or something is sent somewhere **sevkiyat, gönderme, yollama** *the despatch of troops* **2** [C] an official report that someone in a foreign country sends to their organization **(başka bir ülkeden gönderilen) haber, ileti, rapor, emir**

desperate /'despᵊrət/ *adjective* **1** WITHOUT HOPE feeling that you have no hope and are ready to do anything to change the situation you are in **çaresiz, her şeyi göze almış, gözü dönmüş, umutsuzluğa kapılmış** *He was absolutely desperate and would have tried anything to get her back.* **2** NEEDING SOMETHING needing or wanting something very much **çok istekli/arzulu** *By two o'clock I was desperate for something to eat.* **3** BAD A desperate situation is very bad or serious. **kritik, çok kötü, hemen hemen ümitsiz** *The economy is in a really desperate situation.* ● **desperately** *adverb* **umutsuzca** ● **desperation** /ˌdespᵊ'reɪʃᵊn/ *noun* [U] **umutsuzluk**

despicable /dɪ'spɪkəbl/ *adjective* very unpleasant or cruel **rezil ,aşağılık adi, kaba, nahoş** *a despicable act/crime*

despise /dɪ'spaɪz/ *verb* [T] to hate someone or something and have no respect for them **aşağılamak, hor görmek, küçümsemek** *The two groups despise each other.*

☞ **despite** /dɪ'spaɪt/ *preposition* **1** used to say that something happened or is true, although something else makes this seem not probable ... **e/a rağmen/karşın** *I'm still pleased with the house despite all the problems we've had.* ○ [+ doing sth] *He managed to eat lunch despite having had an enormous breakfast.* **2 despite yourself** If you do something despite yourself, you do it although you did not intend to. **arzu etmemesine rağmen**

despondent /dɪ'spɒndənt/ *adjective* unhappy and having no enthusiasm **morali bozuk, karamsar, kötümser, umutsuz** ● **despondency** *noun* [U] **mutsuzluk**

despot /'despɒt/ *noun* [C] a very powerful person, especially someone who treats people cruelly **dediğim dedikçi, zorba, despot**

dessert

dessert /dɪ'zɜːt/ *noun* [C, U] sweet food that is eaten after the main part of a meal **tatlı** *We had ice cream for dessert.*

dessertspoon /dɪ'zɜːtspuːn/ *noun* [C] UK a medium-sized spoon used for eating or measuring food, or the amount this spoon can hold **tatlı kaşığı**

destabilize (*also* UK -**ise**) /ˌdiː'steɪbᵊlaɪz/ *verb* [T] to cause change in a country or government so that it loses its power or control **istikrarsızlaştırmak, dengesini bozmak (ülke/hükümet)** *a plot to destabilize the government*

destination /ˌdestɪ'neɪʃᵊn/ *noun* [C] the place where someone or something is going **menzil, varış yeri, birinin/birşeyin gideceği/varacağı yer** *Spain is a very popular holiday destination.*

destined /'destɪnd/ *adjective* **be destined for sth; be destined to do sth** to be certain to be something or do something in the future **alnına yazılmış, mukadder olmuş, kaderinde olan** *She was destined for a brilliant future.*

destiny /'destɪni/ *noun* **1** [C] the things that will happen to someone in the future **kader, yazgı, mukadderat** *At last she feels in control of her own destiny.* **2** [U] a power that some people believe controls what will happen in the future **alın yazısı, kader, kısmet** *Nick said it was destiny that we met.*

destitute /'destɪtjuːt/ *adjective* so poor that you do not have the basic things you need to live, such as food, clothes, or money **yoksul, muhtaç, fakir** ● **destitution** /ˌdestɪ'tjuːʃᵊn/ *noun* [U] **yoksulluk**

☞ **destroy** /dɪ'strɔɪ/ *verb* [T] to damage something so badly that it does not exist or cannot be used **yıkmak, yok etmek, yerle bir etmek** *Many works of art were destroyed in the fire.*

destroyer /dɪ'strɔɪəʳ/ *noun* [C] a small, fast ship that is used in a war **muhrip, destroyer, savaş gemisi**

destruction /dɪ'strʌkʃᵊn/ *noun* [U] when something is destroyed **tahrip, yıkım, yok etme** *We are all responsible for the destruction of the forest.* ● **destructive** /dɪ'strʌktɪv/ *adjective* causing a lot of damage **yıkıcı, tahrip edici, bozguncu, zararlı, tahripkâr** *the destructive power of nuclear weapons* ➋ See also: self-destructive.

detach /dɪ'tætʃ/ *verb* [T] to take a part of something off so that it is separate **ayırmak, söküp çıkarmak**

Please complete and detach the form below and return it to the school. ● **detachable** *adjective* ayrı

detached /dɪ'tætʃt/ *adjective* **1** *UK* A detached building is not joined to another building. müstakil ev/bina **2** If someone is detached, they do not feel involved with someone or emotional about something. bağımsız, tarafsız, yansız ⊃See also: semi-detached.

detachment /dɪ'tætʃmənt/ *noun* **1** [U] when someone does not feel involved in a situation soyutlama, bağımsız kılma *He spoke with cool detachment.* **2** [C] a small group of soldiers with a particular job to do müfreze, özel görevi olan küçük askerî birlik

▨▨▨ detail .... İLE BİRLİKTE KULLANILAN KELİMELER

disclose/discuss/divulge/reveal details ● exact/full/precise/relevant details ● details about/of/on sth

∘⌐**detail**[1] /'di:teɪl/ ⓤ /dɪ'teɪl/ *noun* [C, U] **1** a fact or piece of information about something ayrıntı, teferruat, detay *Please send me details of your training courses.* ○ *She didn't include very much detail in her report.* **2** in detail including every part of something ayrıntılı/teferruatlı/detaylı olarak *He explained it all in great detail.* **3** go into detail to include all the facts about something ayrıntıya/teferruata/detaya girmek/inmek

detail[2] /'di:teɪl/ ⓤ /dɪ'teɪl/ *verb* [T] to describe something completely, giving all the facts ayrıntıyla anlatmak, detayıyla vermek, teferruata girmek

detailed /'di:teɪld/ *adjective* giving a lot of information ayrıntılı, detaylı, teferruatlı *a detailed account/description*

detain /dɪ'teɪn/ *verb* [T] to keep someone somewhere and not allow them to leave, especially in order to ask them about a crime göz altına almak, alıkoymak; tutmak *Three men were detained by police for questioning.*

detect /dɪ'tekt/ *verb* [T] to discover or notice something, especially something that is difficult to see, hear, smell, etc bulmak, ortaya çıkarmak, keşfetmek, sezmek, hissetmek, farkına varmak *This special camera can detect bodies by their heat.*

detection /dɪ'tekʃ°n/ *noun* [U] **1** when someone notices or discovers something bulma, keşfetme, belirleme, ortaya çıkarma *the early detection of cancer* **2** when the police discover information about a crime suçu/suçluyu bulma, ortaya çıkarma

detective /dɪ'tektɪv/ *noun* [C] someone, especially a police officer, whose job is to discover information about a crime dedektif, hafiye

detector /dɪ'tektə°/ *noun* [C] a piece of equipment used to discover something, especially something that is difficult to see, hear, smell, etc tarayıcı, dedektör *a smoke detector*

detente /ˌder'tɒnt/ *noun* [U] *formal* when countries become friendly with each other after a period of not being friendly uluslararası gerginliği yumuşatma, yumuşama, detant

detention /dɪ'tenʃ°n/ *noun* **1** [U] when someone is officially kept somewhere and not allowed to leave tutukla(n)ma, alıkon(ul)ma, hapsetme **2** [C, U] when a student is kept in school after the other students leave, as a punishment ders bitimi okulda kalma cezası

deter /dɪ'tɜ:°/ *verb* [T] deterring, *past* deterred to make someone less likely to do something, or to make something less likely to happen caydırmak, vazgeçirmek, yıldırmak *We have introduced new security measures to deter shoplifters.* ○ [+ from + doing sth] *Higher fuel costs could deter people from driving their cars.*

detergent /dɪ'tɜ:dʒ°nt/ *noun* [C, U] a liquid or powder that is used to clean things temizleyici/arıtıcı madde, deterjan

deteriorate /dɪ'tɪəri°reɪt/ *verb* [I] to become worse bozulmak, kötüleşmek, kötüye gitmek, kötüleşmek *Her condition deteriorated rapidly.* ● **deterioration** /dɪˌtɪəriə'reɪʃ°n/ *noun* [U] kötüleşme

▨▨▨ determination .... İLE BİRLİKTE KULLANILAN KELİMELER **D**

demonstrate/show determination ● dogged/fierce/grim/steely determination ● courage/grit/guts and determination

determination /dɪˌtɜ:mɪ'neɪʃ°n/ *noun* [U] when someone continues trying to do something, although it is very difficult azim, sebat, kararlılık *Andy Murray will need great determination and skill to win this match.*

determine /dɪ'tɜ:mɪn/ *verb* [T] **1** to discover the facts or truth about something belirlemek, saptamak, tespit etmek [+ question word] *The doctors are still unable to determine what is wrong.* **2** to decide what will happen karar vermek [+ question word] *Her exam results will determine which university she goes to.*

∘⌐**determined** /dɪ'tɜ:mɪnd/ *adjective* wanting to do something very much, and not letting anyone stop you kararlı, azimli [+ to do sth] *He's determined to win this match.*

determiner /dɪ'tɜ:mɪnə°/ *noun* [C] a word that is used before a noun or adjective to show which person or thing you are referring to. For example 'my' in 'my old car' and 'that' in 'that man' are determiners. belirleyici

deterrent /dɪ'ter°nt/ *noun* [C] something that stops people doing something because they are afraid of what will happen if they do caydırıcı/önleyici/vazgeçirici şey *They've installed a security camera as a deterrent to thieves.* ● **deterrent** *adjective a deterrent effect* caydırıcı

detest /dɪ'test/ *verb* [T] to hate someone or something very much iğrenmek, tiksinmek, nefret etmek

detonate /'det°neɪt/ *verb* [I, T] to explode or make something explode patla(t)mak, infilak et(tir)mek *The bomb was detonated safely by army officers and no one was hurt.* ● **detonation** /ˌdet°n'eɪʃ°n/ *noun* [C, U] inflak

detonator /'det°neɪtə°/ *noun* [C] a piece of equipment that makes a bomb explode bomba patlatma düzeneği

detour /'di:tʊə°/ *noun* [C] a different, longer route to a place that is used to avoid something or to visit something dolambaçlı *Several roads were closed, so we had to take a detour.*

detox /'di:tɒks/ *noun* [U] *informal* treatment to clean out your blood, stomach, etc and get rid of bad substances such as drugs vücudu zararlı maddelerden arındırma tedavisi, detoks

detract /dɪ'trækt/ *verb*
detract from sth *phrasal verb* to make something seem less good than it really is, or than it was thought to be değerini azaltmak/eksiltmek; itibarını zedelemek

detriment /'detrɪmənt/ *noun* **to the detriment of sth** causing damage to something zararına, ziyanına *He was working very long hours, to the detriment of his health.* ● **detrimental** /ˌdetrɪ'ment°l/ *adjective a detrimental effect* zararlı

devaluation /ˌdi:vælju'eɪʃ°n/ *noun* [C, U] when the value of something is reduced paranın değerini düşürme, devalüasyon yapma *the devaluation of the dollar*

devalue /ˌdiːˈvæljuː/ *verb* [T] **devaluing**, *past* **devalued**
1 to make something less valuable, especially a country's money **paranın değerini azaltmak/düşürmek** *to devalue the pound* **2** to make someone or something seem less important than they really are **değerini azaltmak/düşürmek**

devastate /ˈdevəsteɪt/ *verb* [T] to destroy or damage something very badly **yıkmak, mahvetmek, harap etmek** *A recent hurricane devastated the city.* ● **devastation** /ˌdevəˈsteɪʃ³n/ *noun* [U] **tahrip**

devastated /ˈdevəsteɪtɪd/ *adjective* **1** very shocked and upset **şaşkın, şok olmuş** *She was devastated when her husband died.* **2** completely destroyed **yıkılmış, mahvolmuş, tamamen çökmüş**

devastating /ˈdevəsteɪtɪŋ/ *adjective* **1** making someone very shocked and upset **şaşkına çeviren, şok edici, yıkıcı, perişan eden** *Despite the devastating news, no one is giving up hope.* **2** causing a lot of damage or destruction **yıkıcı, mahvedici, yok edici** *The fire has had a devastating effect on the local wildlife.*

devastatingly /ˈdevəsteɪtɪŋli/ *adverb* extremely **müthiş/şahane bir şekilde, son derece** *devastatingly funny/handsome*

➔**develop** /dɪˈveləp/ *verb* **1** CHANGE [I, T] to grow or change and become more advanced, or to make someone or something do this **gelişmek, büyümek** *The baby develops inside the mother for nine months.* ○ *He's developing into a very good tennis player.* **2** MAKE [T] to make something new such as a product **geliştirmek, büyütmek** *Scientists are developing new drugs all the time.* **3** ILLNESS [T] to start to have something, such as an illness, problem, or feeling **hastalık, problem veya bir duygu edinmek, geliştirmek** *Shortly after take-off the plane developed engine trouble.* **4** HAPPEN [I] to start to happen or exist **belirmek, ortaya çıkmak** *Further problems will develop if you do not deal with this now.* **5** FILM [T] to use special chemicals on a piece of film to make photographs appear **fotoğraf tab etmek/basmak** *I need to get my holiday photos developed.* **6** BUILD [T] to build houses, factories, shops, etc on a piece of land **imar etmek, kalkındırmak, geliştirmek**

developed /dɪˈveləpt/ *adjective* **a developed country/nation, etc** a country with an advanced level of technology, industry, etc **gelişmiş ülke/ulus** ⊃Opposite **undeveloped**.

developer /dɪˈveləpə³/ *noun* [C] a person or company that buys land and builds houses, factories, shops, etc **inşaat yatırımcısı/şirketi, imar eden, müteahhit/yüklenici**

╔═══ *development* .... İLE BİRLİKTE KULLANILAN KELİMELER

encourage/monitor/restrict development ● dramatic/major/rapid development ● in/under development

➔**development** /dɪˈveləpmənt/ *noun* **1** CHANGE [C, U] when someone or something grows or changes and becomes more advanced **ilerleme, kalkınma** *The nurse will do some tests to check on your child's development.* ○ *There have been some major developments in technology recently.* **2** MAKE [C, U] when something new is made **gelişim, büyüme** *the development of new drugs* **3** START [U] when something starts to happen or exist **ortaya çıkma, var olma** *Smoking encourages the development of cancer.* **4** BUILD [U] when new houses, factories, shops, etc, are built on an area of land **gelişme, imar** *land suitable for development* **5** BUILDINGS [C] an area of land with new houses, factories, shops, etc on it **imar olmuş/gelişmiş/büyümüş alan/bölge; imarlı bölge** *a new housing development* **6** EVENT [C] something new that happens and changes a situation **gelşme, yeni**

geliişmeler, değişime nede n olan yenilikler *Have there been any more developments since I left?* **7** PHOTOGRAPH [U] when someone makes photographs from a film **fotoğraf basımı/tab etme**

deviant /ˈdiːviənt/ *adjective* different to what most people think is normal or acceptable, usually relating to sexual behaviour **sapık (cinsel davranış)** ● **deviant** *noun* [C] **sapıklık**

deviate /ˈdiːvieɪt/ *verb* [I] to do something in a different way from what is usual or expected **yoldan çıkmak, sapmak, farklı bir yöne gitmek** *The aircraft deviated from its original flight plan.*

deviation /ˌdiːviˈeɪʃ³n/ *noun* [C, U] when something is different to what is usual, expected, or accepted by most people **sapma, yoldan çıkma, ayrılma, farklı olma** *sexual deviation*

device /dɪˈvaɪs/ *noun* **1** [C] a piece of equipment that is used for a particular purpose **alet, edavat, tertibat** *A pager is a small, electronic device for sending messages.* **2 leave someone to their own devices** to leave someone to do what they want to do **kendi kendine bırakmak, kaderiyle başbaşa bırakmak, kendine bırakmak** *With both parents out at work, the kids were often left to their own devices.*

devil /ˈdevəl/ *noun* **1 the Devil** the most powerful evil spirit, according to the Christian and Jewish religions **Şeytan 2** [C] an evil spirit **iblis, kötü ruh 3** [C] *informal* someone who behaves badly **kötü adam, kerata 4 lucky/poor, etc devil** *informal* used to describe a person who is lucky/unlucky, etc **bahtı açık/şanslı/zavallı vs. kerata 5 speak/talk of the devil** *informal* something that you say when someone you have been talking about suddenly appears **(hem olumlu/hem de olumsuz manada) iyi adam lafının üzerine gelir / iti an çomağı hazırla**

devilish /ˈdevəlɪʃ/ *adjective* evil or bad **şeytanca, kötü, berbat, pis (gülümseme)** *a devilish smile* ● **devilishly** *adverb* very **çok, hınzırca** *devilishly difficult*

devious /ˈdiːviəs/ *adjective* clever in a way that is bad and not honest **hınzır, düzenbaz** *a devious mind*

devise /dɪˈvaɪz/ *verb* [T] to design or invent something such as a system, plan, or piece of equipment **tasarlamak/tasarımını yapmak, icat etmek**

devoid /dɪˈvɔɪd/ *adjective* **devoid of sth** *formal* completely without a quality ... **(kalite vb.den) yoksun, mahrum, eksik** *His voice was devoid of emotion.*

devolution /ˌdiːvəˈluːʃ³n/ *noun* [U] when power moves from a central government to local governments **gücün merkezi hükümetten bölgesel hükümetlere devri/geçişi**

devolve /dɪˈvɒlv/ *verb*
devolve sth to sb/sth *phrasal verb formal* to give power or responsibility to a person or organization at a lower or more local level **yetkiyi/sorumluluğu daha alt düzeydeki birine/kuruma vermek, aktarmak**

devote /dɪˈvəʊt/ *verb*
devote sth to sb/sth *phrasal verb* **1** to use time, energy, etc for a particular purpose **zaman/enerji vb. belli bir amaç için vakfetmek** *She devotes most of her free time to charity work.* **2** to use a space or area for a particular purpose **bir alan/arazi ayırmak, vakfetmek, vermek** [often passive] *Most of the magazine was devoted to coverage of the royal wedding.*

devoted /dɪˈvəʊtɪd/ *adjective* loving or caring very much about someone or something **kendini vakfetmiş/adamış, bağlı, saçını süpürge eden** *She's absolutely devoted to her grandchildren.* ● **devotedly** *adverb* **sadık, bağlı bir şekilde**

devotee /ˌdevəʊˈtiː/ *noun* [C] someone who likes something or someone very much **düşkün, meraklı, hayran** *a devotee of classical music*

devotion /dɪˈvəʊʃən/ *noun* [U] **1** great love or loyalty for someone or something **düşkünlük, bağlılık, adanmışlık** *She will always be remembered for her devotion to her family.* **2** strong religious belief or behaviour **koyu dini inanç, güçlü inanç ve davranış**

devour /dɪˈvaʊəʳ/ *verb* [T] **1** to eat something quickly because you are very hungry **tıkınmak, kıtlıktan çıkmış gibi yemek 2** to read something quickly and enthusiastically **yutmak, bir çırpıda okumak**

devout /dɪˈvaʊt/ *adjective* extremely religious **dindar, dinine bağlı** *a devout Catholic/Muslim* ● **devoutly** *adverb* **dindar olarak**

dew /djuː/ *noun* [U] drops of water that form on surfaces outside during the night **çiğ**

dexterity /dekˈsterəti/ *noun* [U] skill at doing something, especially using your hands **beceri hüner, her iki elinide beceriyle kullanma** *manual dexterity*

diabetes /ˌdaɪəˈbiːtiːz/ *noun* [U] a serious medical condition in which your body cannot control the level of sugar in your blood **şeker hastalığı, diyabet** ● **diabetic** /ˌdaɪəˈbetɪk/ *adjective* **diyabetik** ● **diabetic** /ˌdaɪəˈbetɪk/ *noun* [C] someone who has diabetes **şeker/diyabet hastası**

diabolical /ˌdaɪəˈbɒlɪkᵊl/ *adjective* extremely bad **berbat, çok kötü**

diagnose /ˈdaɪəgnəʊz/ *verb* [T] to say what is wrong with someone who is ill **teşhis etmek, tanı koymak** [often passive] *She was diagnosed with/as having cancer last year.*

make a diagnosis ● a diagnosis **of** [cancer, heart disease, etc]

diagnosis /ˌdaɪəgˈnəʊsɪs/ *noun* [C, U] *plural* **diagnoses** when a doctor says what is wrong with someone who is ill **teşhis, tanı**

diagnostic /ˌdaɪəgˈnɒstɪk/ *adjective* **diagnostic methods/tests, etc** methods/tests, etc that help you discover what is wrong with someone or something **tanısal method ve testler; hata tespit yöntem ve testleri**

diagonal /daɪˈægᵊnᵊl/ *adjective* **1** A diagonal line is straight and sloping and not horizontal or vertical. **çapraz** *a tie with diagonal stripes* **2** going from the top corner of a square to the bottom corner on the other side **çapraz çizgi, köşeden köşeye, köşegen** ● **diagonally** *adverb* **köşeli bir şekilde**

draw a diagram ● a diagram **of** sth ● **in/on** a diagram

diagram /ˈdaɪəgræm/ *noun* [C] a simple picture showing what something looks like or explaining how something works **şema, şekil, diyagram**

dial¹ /daɪəl/ *noun* [C] **1** TIME/MEASUREMENT the round part of a clock, watch, or machine that shows you the time or other measurement **kadran 2** BUTTON a round part on a piece of equipment such as a television or radio that you turn to operate it, make it louder, etc **gösterge, (tv. radyo) çeşitli düğmelerin bulunduğu bölüm 3** TELEPHONE the ring of holes with numbers that you turn on the front of an old telephone **telefonda rakamların bulunduğu yer, kadran**

dial² /daɪəl/ *verb* [I, T] *UK* **dialling**, *past* **dialled**, *US* **dialing**, *past* **dialed** to make a telephone call to a particular number **telefonla aramak** *Dial 0 for the operator.*

dialect /ˈdaɪəlekt/ *noun* [C, U] a form of a language that people speak in a particular part of a country **lehçe**

'dialog ˌbox *noun* [C] a window (= a separate area on a computer screen) that appears and asks the person using the computer for information **bilgisayar ekranında çıkan diyalog/bilgi kutucuğu**

dialogue (*also US* dialog) /ˈdaɪəlɒg/ *noun* [C, U] **1** the talking in a book, play, or film **karşılıklı konuşma, diyalog 2** a formal discussion between countries or groups of people **ülkeler/kişiler arası karşılıklı diyalog/görüşme**

dial-up /ˈdaɪəlʌp/ *adjective* [always before noun] Dial-up computer systems and equipment and Internet services use a telephone connection to reach them. **(bilgisayar, cihaz, internet) telefonla bağlantı kurulabilen** ↪Compare **broadband.**

diameter /daɪˈæmɪtəʳ/ *noun* [C, U] a straight line that goes from one side of a circle to the other side and through the centre, or the length of this line **çap** *The cake was about 30 centimetres in diameter.*

diamond /ˈdaɪəmənd/
noun **1** STONE [C, U] a
very hard, transparent
stone that is extremely
valuable and is often
used in jewellery
elmas *a diamond ring*
2 SHAPE [C] a shape with
four straight sides of
equal length that join
to form two large
angles and two small
angles **baklava
deseni/biçimi/şekli**
3 BASEBALL [C] the field
where baseball is
played **beyzbol sahası**
4 diamonds playing
cards with red,
diamond shapes on
them **(iskambil) karo**
the queen of diamonds

diamond

diaper /ˈdaɪəpəʳ/ *US* (*UK* **nappy**) *noun* [C] a thick piece of paper or cloth worn by a baby on its bottom **çocuk bezi**

diaphragm /ˈdaɪəfræm/ *noun* [C] the large muscle between your lungs and your stomach that moves up and down to move air in and out of the lungs **diyafram; mide ve ciğerler arasındaki güçlü kas**

diarrhoea *UK* (*US* **diarrhea**) /ˌdaɪəˈrɪə/ *noun* [U] an illness in which your solid waste is more liquid than usual, and comes out of your body more often **ishal, cır cır**

o→**diary** /ˈdaɪəri/ *noun* [C] **1** a book containing spaces for all the days and months of the year, in which you write meetings and other things that you must remember **randevu defteri, ajanda 2** a book in which you write each day about your personal thoughts and experiences **günlük** *She kept a diary of her trip to Egypt.*

dice¹ /daɪs/ *noun* [C] *plural* **dice** a small object with six equal square sides, each with between one and six spots on it, used in games **zar** *Roll the dice to see who starts the game.*

dice

dice² /daɪs/ *verb* [T] to cut food into small, square pieces **küp şeklinde dilimlemek/kesmek** *diced onions*

dicey /ˈdaɪsi/ *adjective informal* possibly dangerous or involving a risk **tehlikeli ve risk yaratan/oluşturması muhtemel olan**

dichotomy /daɪˈkɒtəmi/ *noun* [C] *formal* the difference between two completely opposite ideas or things **ayrılık, farklılık** *the dichotomy between good and evil*

dictate /dɪkˈteɪt/ *verb* **1** [I, T] to say or read something for someone to write down **yazdırmak, dikte etmek** *Tony was busy dictating letters to his secretary.* **2** [T] to decide or control what happens **olan bitene karar verip yönlendirmek** [+ question word] *The weather will dictate where we hold the party.*

dictate to sb *phrasal verb* to tell someone what to do, often in a way that annoys them **yönlendirmek, yön vermek, emredercesine ne yapacağını söylemek,** *I'm 15 years old - you can't dictate to me any more.*

dictation /dɪkˈteɪʃən/ *noun* **1** [U] when someone speaks or reads something for someone else to write down **dikte, yazdırma 2** [C, U] when a teacher says or reads something for students to write down as a test **yazdırma sınavı, dikte alıştırması**

dictator /dɪkˈteɪtər/ *noun* [C] a leader who has complete power in a country and has not been elected by the people **diktatör** ● **dictatorial** /ˌdɪktəˈtɔːriəl/ *adjective* **diktatör**

dictatorship /dɪkˈteɪtəʃɪp/ *noun* [C, U] a country or system of government with a dictator as leader **diktatörlük, diktatörle yönetilen ülke/sitem**

o⋆**dictionary** /ˈdɪkʃənəri/ *noun* [C] a book that contains a list of words in alphabetical order with their meanings explained or written in another language **sözlük**

o⋆**did** /dɪd/ *past tense of* do **yapmak' fiilinin ikinci hali**

o⋆**didn't** /ˈdɪdənt/ *short for* did not **did not' olumsuz yardımcı fililinin kısaltılmış hali**

o⋆**die** /daɪ/ *verb* **dying,** *past* **died 1** [I] to stop living **ölmek** *Many of the refugees died of hunger.* ○ *She died from brain injuries after a road accident.* **2 be dying for sth; be dying to do sth** *informal* to very much want to have, eat, drink, or do something **bir şeyi yapmaya/bir şey için can atmak, ölmek, çok istemek, kıvranmak** *I'm dying for a drink.* **3 to die for** *informal* If something is to die for, it is extremely good. **çok arzu etmek, özlemini çekmek, uğrunda ölmek** ⊃See also: die hard².

die away *phrasal verb* If something, especially a sound, dies away, it gradually becomes less strong and then stops. **(ses) yavaş yavaş azalıp kaybolmak, dinmek**

die down *phrasal verb* If something, especially noise or excitement, dies down, it gradually becomes less loud or strong until it stops. **(heyecan gürültü) yavaşça etkisini azaltarak kaybolmak/durmak, hafiflemek, dinmek**

die off *phrasal verb* If a group of plants, animals, or people dies off, all of that group dies over a period of time. **nesli tükenmek, birer birer yok olmak**

die out *phrasal verb* to become more and more rare and then disappear completely **ortadan kalkmak, birer birer kaybolmak, gittikçe nesli tükenmek, nadir bulunur hale gelmek** *Dinosaurs died out about 65 million years ago.*

diehard /ˈdaɪhɑːd/ *adjective* [always before noun] supporting something in a very determined way and refusing to change **ölümüne, ölesiye savunma** *a diehard fan*

diesel /ˈdiːzəl/ *noun* **1** [U] fuel used in the engines of some vehicles, especially buses and trucks **dizel, mazot 2** [C] a vehicle that uses diesel in its engine **dizel araç**

diet ...... İLE BİRLİKTE KULLANILAN KELİMELER

be on/go on a diet ● follow/stick to a diet ● a special /strict diet

diet¹ /daɪət/ *noun* **1** [C, U] the type of food that someone usually eats **diyet yiyecek 2** [C] when someone eats less food, or only particular types of food, because they want

to become thinner, or because they are ill **diyet** *No cake for me, thanks - I'm on a diet.*

diet² /daɪət/ *verb* [I] to eat less food so that you become thinner **diyet yapmak**

differ /ˈdɪfər/ *verb* [I] **1** to be different **farklı/farkı olmak** *How does the book differ from the film?* ○ *These computers differ quite a lot in price.* **2** to have a different opinion **farklı düşünmek** *Economists differ on the cause of inflation.*

difference ...... İLE BİRLİKTE KULLANILAN KELİMELER

know/tell the difference ● a big/fundamental/important/obvious difference ● a difference between [sth and sth]

o⋆**difference** /ˈdɪfərəns/ *noun* **1** WAY [C, U] the way in which two people or things are not the same **fark, ayrım** *What's the difference between an ape and a monkey?* **2** QUALITY [U] when two people or things are not the same **farklı olma, benzer olmama 3** AMOUNT [C, U] the amount by which one thing or person is different from another **farklılık** *There's a big difference in age between them.* **4** DISAGREEMENT [C] a disagreement or different opinion **anlaşmazlık, uyuşmazlık** *They must try to resolve their differences peacefully.* **5 make a/any difference** to have an effect on a situation *Painting the walls white has made a big difference to this room.*

different ...... BAŞKA BİR DEYİŞLE

Eğer bir şey kişilerin beklentilerinin dışında ise, bu durum **unusual** kelimesiyle dile getirilebilir. *Carina - that's quite an* **unusual** *name.*
Alternative kelimesi bir şeyin diğerinden farklı olduğunu fakat buna rağmen onun yerine kullanılabileceğini belirtmek için kullanılır. *The hotel's being renovated, so we're looking for an* **alternative** *venue.*
Eğer bir şey diğerlerinden çok farklı ise **distinct** ve **Distinctive** kelimeleri ile ifade edilebilir. *She's got really* **distinctive** *handwriting.* ● *The word has three* **distinct** *meanings.*
Unlike edatı birbirlerinden çok farklı kişileri veya cansız şeyleri karşılaştırırken kullanılır. *Dan's actually quite nice,* **unlike** *his father.* ● *The furniture was* **unlike** *anything she had ever seen.*

o⋆**different** /ˈdɪfərənt/ *adjective* **1** not the same as someone or something else **farklı** *Jo's very different from her sister, isn't she?* ○ *UK The house is different to how I expected it to be.* **2** [always before noun] used to talk about separate things or people of the same type **başka, değişik** *I had to go to three different shops to find the book she wanted.* ● **differently** *adverb* ⊃See also: a whole new **ball game. farklı bir şekilde**

YAYGIN HATALAR

different

Dikkat: Yazılışına dikkat edin. **Different** Türk öğrencileri tarafından en çok yanlış yazılan 10 kelimeden biridir. Unutmayın! Doğru yazılışta ikinci **f** den sonra **e** var.

differential /ˌdɪfəˈrenʃəl/ *noun* [C] a difference between amounts of things **ayrım, farklılık, değişiklik** *differentials in pay/wealth*

differentiate /ˌdɪfəˈrenʃieɪt/ *verb* **1** [I, T] to understand or notice how two things or people are different from each other **ayırmak, ayrımını yapabilmek, farkını ortaya koymak, farkını anlamak** *He can't differentiate between blue and green.* **2** [T] to make someone or something different **ayırmak, farklı hale getirmek, ayırdetmek** *We need to differentiate ourselves from the competition.* ● **differentiation** /ˌdɪfərenʃiˈeɪʃən/ *noun* [U] **fark**

---

difficult .... BAŞKA BİR DEYİŞLE

Hard sıfatı genellikle **difficult** yerine kullanılır ve aynı anlama gelir. *The exam was really hard.* ● *It must be hard to study with all this noise.*

Eğer bir şeyin anlaması güç ise ve çok farklı bölüm ve seviyelerden oluşuyor ise, bu durumu belirtmek için **complicated** ifadesi kullanılabilir. *The instructions were so complicated I just couldn't follow them.*

Tricky kelimesi zor ve üstesinden gelmek için çeşitli beceriler isteyen durumlar için kullanılır. *It's quite tricky getting the bits to fit together.* ● *It's a tricky situation - I don't want to upset anyone.*

Fiddly ifadesi elle yapılan fakat çok küçük parçalardan oluştuğu için çok zorluk yaratan şeyler için kullanılır. *Repairing a watch is very fiddly.*

Awkward ifadesi problem çıkaran ve başa çıkması zor olan kişi veya cansız şeyler için kullanılır. *Dealing with awkward customers is just part of the job.* ● *Luckily, she didn't ask any awkward questions.*

Demanding çok zaman, ilgi ve gayret gerektiren anlamında kullanılır. *She has a very demanding job.* ● *Like most young children, he's very demanding.*

Challenging kelimesiyle ifade edilen bir durum zorluk içerir ve tüm becerinizi ve kararlılığınızı gerektirir. *This has been a challenging time for us all.* ● *I found the course very challenging.*

Easier said than done ifadesi gerçekleştirilmesi çok zor ve nerdeyse imkansız olan durumlar için kullanılır. *I suppose I should stop smoking but it's easier said than done.*

o⟶**difficult** /'dɪfɪkˀlt/ *adjective* **1** not easy and needing skill or effort to do or understand **zor, güç** *Japanese is a difficult language for Europeans to learn.* ○ *This game is too* **difficult for** *me.* ○ *[+ to do sth] It's difficult to think with all that noise.* **2** not friendly or easy to deal with **çetin, zor** *a difficult teenager*

🧩 **difficulty** .... İLE BİRLİKTE KULLANILAN KELİMELER

create/experience/have difficulty ● great/serious difficulty ● with/without difficulty

o⟶**difficulty** /'dɪfɪkˀlti/ *noun* **1** [U] when something is not easy to do or understand **zorluk** [+ in + doing sth] *He was* **having difficulty** *in breathing because of the smoke.* ○ *[+ doing sth] I* **had difficulty** *finding somewhere to park.* ○ *She had twisted her ankle and was walking* **with difficulty. 2** [C] something that is not easy to deal with **güçlük** *The company is having some* **financial difficulties** *at the moment.*

diffident /'dɪfɪdˀnt/ *adjective* shy and without any confidence **ürkek, kendine güveni olmayan** *a diffident young man* ● **diffidence** /'dɪfɪdˀns/ *noun* [U] **utangaçlık, güvensizlik**

diffuse /dɪ'fjuːz/ *verb* [I, T] to spread, or to make something spread over a large area, or to a large number of people **yaymak, dağıtmak**

o⟶**dig**¹ /dɪg/ *verb* **digging**, *past* **dug 1** [I, T] to break or move the ground with a tool, machine, etc **kazmak** *Digging the garden is good exercise.* **2 dig a hole/tunnel,**

dig

etc to make a hole in the ground by moving some of the ground or soil away **tünel/çukur açmak/kazmak** *They've dug a huge hole in the road.* ⊃See also: dig the/up dirt¹ on sb.

dig in/dig into sth *phrasal verb informal* to start eating food **yemeye/yemeğe başlamak** *Dig in, there's plenty for everyone.*

dig (sth) into sb/sth *phrasal verb* to press or push hard into someone or something, or to press something hard into someone or something **sokmak, daldırmak, batırmak, dürtmek, kakmak** *A stone was digging into my heel.*

dig sb/sth out *phrasal verb* to get someone or something out of somewhere by digging **kazıp çıkarmak, kazarak çıkarmak**

dig sth out *phrasal verb* to find something that you have not seen or used for a long time **araştırıp bulmak, araştırarak ortaya çıkarmak** *Mum dug out some old family photographs to show me.*

dig sth up *phrasal verb* **1** [TAKE OUT] to take something out of the ground by digging **toprağı belleyerek çıkarmak, kazıp ortaya çıkarmak** *Could you dig up a few potatoes for dinner?* **2** [BREAK GROUND] to break the ground or make a hole in the ground with a tool, machine, etc **bir alet veya makinayla toprağı kazmak, çukur açmak** *They're digging up the road outside my house.* **3** [INFORMATION] to discover information that is secret or forgotten by searching very carefully **gizli ya da unutulmuş bir şeyi dikkatli bir şekilde araştırarak ortaya çıkarmak** *See if you can dig up anything interesting about his past.*

dig² /dɪg/ *noun* **1** [REMARK] [C] something that you say to annoy or criticize someone **kinaye, dokundurma, iğneli söz, sataşma** *He was* **having a dig at** *me.* **2** [PLACE] [C] a place where people are digging in the ground looking for ancient things to study **kazı, define arama** *an archaeological dig* **3** [PUSH] [no plural] *informal* a quick, hard push **hızlı ve sert itme/dürtme** *a dig in the ribs*

digest /daɪ'dʒest/ *verb* [T] **1** to change food in your stomach into substances that your body can use **hazmetmek, sindirmek 2** to read and understand new information **anlamak, kavramak, akıl erdirmek** *You need to give me time to digest this report.* ● **digestible** *adjective* easy to digest **kolay sindirilebilir/hazmedilebilir**

digestion /daɪ'dʒestʃˀn/ *noun* [U] when your body changes food in your stomach into substances that it can use **sindirim, hazım**

digestive /daɪ'dʒestɪv/ *adjective* [always before noun] relating to digestion **sindirime ilişkin, sindirim** *the digestive system*

digger /'dɪgəʳ/ *noun* [C] a large machine that is used to lift and move soil, or a person who digs **kazıcı makina/ kişi, buldozer**

Digibox /'dɪdʒɪbɒks/ *noun* [C] *trademark* a piece of electronic equipment that allows you to watch digital broadcasts (= television sounds and pictures sent as signals in the form of numbers) on an ordinary television **dijital tv vericisi, yayın cihazı**

digit /'dɪdʒɪt/ *noun* [C] any of the numbers from 0 to 9, especially when they form part of a longer number **sayı, basamak** *a seven digit telephone number*

digital /'dɪdʒɪtˀl/ *adjective* **1** using an electronic system that changes sounds or images into signals in the form of numbers before it stores them or sends them **sayısal, dijital** *digital television* **2** A digital clock or watch shows the time in the form of numbers. **dijital, rakamları gösteren**

,digital 'camera noun [C] a type of camera that records images that you can use and store on a computer dijital kamera

dignified /'dɪɡnɪfaɪd/ adjective calm, serious, and behaving in a way that makes people respect you ciddi, vakur, ağırbaşlı, onurlu, saygı uyandıran a quiet, dignified woman

dignitary /'dɪɡnɪt³ri/ noun [C] someone with an important, official position ileri gelen/makam sahibi kimse a group of visiting dignitaries

dignity /'dɪɡnəti/ noun [U] calm and serious behaviour that makes people respect you olgunluk, vakar, ağırbaşlılık, saygınlık He behaved with great dignity and courage.

digress /daɪ'ɡres/ verb [I] to start talking about something that is not related to what you were talking about before konu dışına çıkmak, konuşulan konudan uzaklaşmak, konuyu saptırmak • digression /daɪ'ɡreʃ³n/ noun [C, U] konu değiştirme, saptırma

digs /dɪɡz/ noun [plural] UK informal a room in someone's house that you pay rent to live in kiralık oda, pansiyon

dike (also dyke) /daɪk/ noun 1 a wall built to stop water from a sea or river going onto the land set, bent 2 UK a passage that has been dug to take water away from fields su kanalı, ark

dilapidated /dɪ'læpɪdeɪtɪd/ adjective A dilapidated building or vehicle is old and in bad condition. viran, harap, yıkık dökük, hurda, hek • dilapidation /dɪ, læpɪ'deɪʃ³n/ noun [U] eski ve kötü durumda olan

dilate /daɪ'leɪt/ verb [I, T] If a part of your body dilates, or if you dilate it, it becomes wider or more open. genişle (t)mek, büyü(t)mek The drug causes your pupils to dilate. • dilation /daɪ'leɪʃ³n/ noun [U] genişleme

face/have/be in a dilemma • sth poses/presents a dilemma • a moral dilemma • a dilemma for sb • a dilemma about/over sth

dilemma /dɪ'lemə/ noun [C] when you have to make a difficult choice between two things you could do ⊶ ikilem, çıkmaz, açmaz, arada kalma She's still in a dilemma about whether she should go or not.

diligence /'dɪlɪdʒ³ns/ noun [U] when you work hard with care and effort gayret, çaba, çalışkanlık

diligent /'dɪlɪdʒ³nt/ adjective working hard with care and effort dikkatli, çalışkan, gayretli a diligent student • diligently adverb gayretli bir şekilde

dilute /daɪ'luːt/ verb [T] to make a liquid thinner or weaker by adding water or another liquid to it sulandırmak, yoğunluğunu azaltmak • dilute adjective dilute solution sulandırılmış

dim¹ /dɪm/ adjective dimmer, dimmest 1 not bright or clear loş, hafif karanlık He could hardly see her in the dim light. 2 a dim memory/recollection, etc when you can remember something slightly, but not very well belli belirsiz hatırlama, hayal meyal hafıza 3 UK informal stupid kafasız, aptal He's nice, but a bit dim. • dimly adverb a dimly lit room karanlık, loş bir şekilde

dim² /dɪm/ verb [I, T] dimming, past dimmed to become less bright, or to make something become less bright donuklaş(tır)mak, karar(t)mak He dimmed the lights and turned up the music.

dime /daɪm/ noun [C] 1 a US or Canadian coin with a value of 10 cents on sent 2 a dime a dozen mainly US informal easy to find and very ordinary istemediğin

kadar, sürüsüne bereket Millionaires are now a dime a dozen.

add/give a [new/extra, etc] dimension (to sth) • an added/extra/new dimension

dimension /,daɪ'menʃ³n/ noun [C] 1 a particular part of a situation, especially something that affects how you think or feel yön, boyut, taraf Music has added a new dimension to my life. 2 a measurement of the length, width, or height of something hacim, boyutlar

diminish /dɪ'mɪnɪʃ/ verb [I, T] to become less, or to make something become less azal(t)mak, eksil(t)mek Your pain should diminish gradually after taking these tablets.

diminutive /dɪ'mɪnjətɪv/ adjective formal extremely small minnacık, küçücük, ufacık a diminutive figure

dimple /'dɪmpl/ noun [C] a small hollow place on your skin, often one that appears on your face when you smile gamze • dimpled adjective gamzeli

din /dɪn/ noun [no plural] a lot of loud, unpleasant noise şamata, patırtı, gürültü

dine /daɪn/ verb [I] formal to eat dinner akşam yemeği yemek On Saturday we dined with friends.
dine out phrasal verb formal to eat your evening meal in a restaurant dışarda akşam yemeği yemek

diner /'daɪnər/ noun [C] 1 someone who is eating in a restaurant lokanta müşterisi 2 mainly US a small, informal restaurant esnaf lokantası, küçük ucuz lokanta

dinghy /'dɪŋi/ noun [C] a small boat bot, küçük sandal, dingi an inflatable dinghy

dingy /'dɪndʒi/ adjective dirty and not bright kirli, pasaklı, kir pas içinde, solmuş a dingy basement

'dining ,room noun [C] a room where you eat your meals in a house or hotel yemek salonu/odası

eat/have dinner • have sth for dinner

⊶dinner /'dɪnər/ noun [C, U] the main meal of the day that people usually eat in the evening akşam yemeği What's for dinner tonight?

'dinner ,jacket UK (US tuxedo) noun [C] a black or white jacket that a man wears on a very formal occasion smokin; resmi davet ve akşam yemeklerinde giyilen siyah veya beyaz ceket

dinner jacket UK, tuxedo US

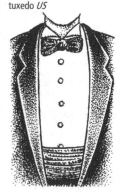

dinosaur /'daɪnəsɔːr/ noun [C] a very large animal that used to live millions of years ago dinazor

diocese /'daɪəsɪs/ noun [C] the area controlled by a bishop (= an important Christian official) piskoposluk bölgesi

dip¹ /dɪp/ noun 1 [FOOD] [C, U] a thick sauce that you can put pieces of food into before you eat them bir tür koyu sos a blue cheese dip 2 [SURFACE] [C] a lower area on a surface çukur, kuyu a sudden dip in the road 3 [AMOUNT] [C] a sudden fall in the

dinosaur

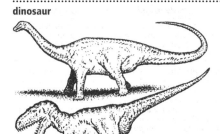

level or amount of something **ani düşüş, inme** *a dip in profits* **4** [SWIM] [C] *informal* a short swim **dalma, dalış yapma** *Let's have a quick dip in the pool before breakfast.*

dip² /dɪp/ *verb* **dipping**, *past* **dipped 1** [T] to put something into a liquid for a short time **banmak, daldırmak** *She dipped the brush into the paint.* **2** [I] to become lower in level or amount **düşmek, alçalmak, inmek** *The number of students taking sciences has dipped sharply.*

dip into sth *phrasal verb* **1** UK to read small parts of a book or magazine **(kitap, dergi) göz atmak, karıştırmak** *It's the sort of book you can dip into now and then.* **2** to spend part of a supply of money that you have been keeping **birikmiş paranın belli bir bölümünü kullanmak** *I had to dip into my savings to pay for the repairs.*

diphtheria /dɪpˈθɪəriə/ *noun* [U] a very serious disease of the throat **difteri, kuş palazı**

diphthong /ˈdɪfθɒŋ/ *noun* [C] a sound made by two vowels which are said together **iki seslinin oluşturduğu ses, diftong**

diploma /dɪˈpləʊmə/ *noun* [C] a qualification from a school, college, or university, or an official document showing that someone has completed a course of study **diploma** *a diploma in art and design*

diplomacy /dɪˈpləʊməsi/ *noun* [U] **1** dealing with the relationships between governments **diplomasi** *international diplomacy* **2** skill in dealing with people well and not upsetting them **insanlarla ilişkilerde ustalık/ beceriklilik/diplomasi** *She showed great tact and diplomacy in the meeting.*

diplomat /ˈdɪpləmæt/ *noun* [C] someone whose job is to live in another country and to keep a good relationship between their government and that country's government **diplomat**

diplomatic /ˌdɪpləˈmætɪk/ *adjective* **1** [always before noun] relating to diplomacy or diplomats **diplomatik** *diplomatic relations* **2** good at dealing with people without upsetting them **insanlarla ilişkilerde ustaca, beceriyle/diplomatça davranan** *That's a very diplomatic answer.* ● **diplomatically** *adverb* **diplomatik bir şekilde**

dire /daɪəʳ/ *adjective* very serious or bad **müthiş, ürkütücü, korkunç, ciddi** *He's in dire need of help.*

o┅**direct¹** /dɪˈrekt/, /daɪˈrekt/ *adjective* **1** [STRAIGHT] going straight from one place to another without turning or stopping **dosdoğru, dümdüz, aktarmasız** *We went by the most direct route.* **2** [NOTHING BETWEEN] with no other person or thing involved or between **doğrudan, aracısız, dolaysız** *There is a direct link between smoking*

and cancer. **3** [CLEAR] saying clearly and honestly what you think **doğrudan, ağzında gevelemeden, açık açık, açık sözlü olarak** *a direct answer* ⊃Opposite indirect.

direct² /dɪˈrekt/, /daɪˈrekt/ *adverb* going straight from one place to another without turning or stopping **dosdoğru, hiç bir yere sapmadan** *Several airlines now fly direct to Vancouver.*

direct³ /dɪˈrekt/, /daɪˈrekt/ *verb* **1** [FILM/PLAY] [T] to tell the actors in a film or play what to do **film/oyun yönetmek** *a film directed by Alfred Hitchcock* **2 direct sth against/at/towards, etc sb/sth** to aim something at someone or something **birşeyi birine/birşeye yöneltmek** *The demonstrators' anger was directed at the police.* **3** [ROUTE] [T] to show or tell someone how to get to a place **yönlendirmek, yön tarif etmek** *Can you direct me to the manager's office please?* **4** [ORGANIZE] [T] to organize and control the way something is done **yönetmek, idare etmek** *He directed the building of the new art gallery.* **5 direct sb to do sth** *formal* to officially order someone to do something **birine birşeyi yapmasını resmen emretmek, söylemek, bildirmek** *They directed us not to discuss the matter.*

¸**direct ˈdebit** *noun* [C, U] an arrangement that allows an organization to take money from your bank account at regular times to pay for goods or services **ödeme talimatı, hesaptan para çekme yetkisi veren anlaşma** *I pay my council tax by direct debit.*

> ┅┅┅ **direction** ┅┅┅ İLE BİRLİKTE KULLANILAN KELİMELER
>
> **change** direction ● **in the opposite/other** direction ● **in the right/wrong** direction ● **in the direction of** sth ● **from all/in all** directions

o┅**direction** /dɪˈrekʃⁿn/ *noun* **1** [WAY] [C] the way that someone or something is going or facing **yön, istikamet, doğrultu** *The car sped away in the direction of the airport.* ○ *I think we're going in the wrong direction.* **2 in sb's direction** towards someone **birine doğru** *She keeps looking in my direction.* **3** [DEVELOPMENT] [C] the way that someone or something changes or develops **bir şeyin gelişim veya değişim şekli, yönü, tarzı** *Our careers have gone in very different directions.* **4** [CONTROL] [U] control or instructions **talimat, yönerge** *Under his direction the company has doubled its profits.* **5** [PURPOSE] [U] knowing what you want to do **ne yapacağını bilen** *According to his teachers, he lacks direction.*

directions /dɪˈrekʃⁿnz/ *noun* [plural] instructions that tell you how to get to a place, or how to do something **talimatlar** *We stopped to ask for directions.* ○ *Just follow the directions on the label.*

directive /dɪˈrektɪv/ *noun* [C] *formal* an official instruction **yönerge, talimat, tavsiye, direktif** *The government has issued new directives on food hygiene.*

directly /dɪˈrektli/ *adverb* **1** with no other person or thing involved or between **aracısız, dosdoğru, doğrudan** *Why don't you speak to him directly?* **2 directly after/behind/opposite, etc** exactly or immediately after/behind/opposite, etc **tam, hemen karşıda/arkasında/sonra** *She was sitting directly opposite me.* **3** clearly and honestly **açık ve onurlu bir şekilde** *Let me answer that question directly.*

directness /dɪˈrektnəs/ *noun* [U] when someone is clear and honest in their speech or behaviour **davranışında ve konuşmasında dürüst/ilkeli olma** *He liked her directness and simplicity.*

¸**direct ˈobject** *noun* [C] the direct object of a transitive verb is the person or thing that is affected by the action of the verb. In the sentence 'I bought a new car yesterday.', 'a new car' is the direct object. **belirtili nesne** ⊃Compare indirect object.

director /dɪ'rektə^r/ *noun* [C] **1** an important manager in an organization or company **müdür, yönetici, idareci** *Meet the new sales director.* **2** someone who tells the actors in a film or play what to do **yönetmen** *the famous film director, Alfred Hitchcock* ⊃See also: **funeral director, managing director.**

directorate /dɪ'rekt^ərət/ *noun* [C] a part of a government or other organization with responsibility for a particular activity **genel idare/yönetim/müdürlük**

directory /dɪ'rekt^əri/ *noun* [C] a book or list of names, numbers, or other facts **rehber, kılavuz** ⊃See also: **telephone directory.**

dirt¹ /dɜːt/ *noun* [U] **1** an unpleasant substance that makes something not clean **kir, pislik, çamur, toz toprak** *You've got some dirt on your trousers.* **2** soil or rough ground **toprak** *a dirt road/track* **3 dig the/up dirt on sb** *informal* to try to discover bad things about someone to stop other people admiring them **kirli çamaşırlarını ortaya çıkarmak, gerçek yüzünü ortaya koymak**

dirt² /dɜːt/ *adverb* **dirt cheap/poor** extremely cheap/poor **son derece ucuz/kalitesiz/adi**

dirty ..... BAŞKA BİR DEYİŞLE

Eğer bir şey aşırı derecede kirli ise, durumu belirtmek için **filthy** kelimesi kullanılır. *Wash your hands before supper - they're* **filthy***!*
Eğer bir şey veya kişi kirli ve dağınık görünüyorsa, bunun ifadesi için **scruffy** veya **messy** kelimeleri kullanılabilir. *He's the typical* **scruffy** *student.* ● *Ben's bedroom is always really* **messy***.*
Eğer bir şey kirliyse ve yıkanmaya ihtiyacı varsa, **grimy, grubby** sıfatları durumun ifadesinde kullanılabilir. *Don't' wipe your* **grimy** *hands on that clean towel!* ● *He was wearing an old pair of jeans and a* **grubby** *T-shirt.*
Soiled sıfatı kirli olan şeyler (materyaller) için kullanılabilir. **Soiled** *tablecloths should be soaked in detergent.*
Eğer bir şey çok kirli ve hoş olmayan bir şekil almışsa, **squalid** sıfatı kullanılabilir. *The prisoners lived in* **squalid** *conditions.*

⊶**dirty¹** /'dɜːti/ *adjective* **1** NOT CLEAN not clean **kirli, pis** *dirty clothes* ○ *dirty dishes* **2** OFFENSIVE talking about sex in a way that some people find offensive **açık saçık, müstehcen** *dirty books/jokes* **3** DISHONEST dishonest or unfair **alçak, adi, pis, çirkin, iğrenç** *a dirty business* ⊃See also: do sb's dirty **work²**.

dirty² /'dɜːti/ *verb* [T] to make something dirty **kirletmek, pisletmek**

dis- /dɪs-/ *prefix* not or the opposite of **olumsuzluk/zıt/karşıt anlamında önek** *dishonest* ○ *disbelief* ○ *to disagree*

disability /ˌdɪsə'bɪləti/ *noun* [C, U] an illness, injury, or condition that makes it difficult for someone to do the things that other people do **özürlülük, sakatlık**

disable /dɪ'seɪbl/ *verb* [T] **1** If someone is disabled by an illness or injury, it makes it difficult for them to live in the way that most other people do. **sakatla(n)mak, sakat bırakmak** [often passive] *Some children were permanently disabled by the bomb.* **2** to stop a piece of equipment from working **etkisiz hale getirmek, bozmak, çalışmasını engellemek** *The thieves must have disabled the alarm system.*

disabled /dɪ'seɪbld/ *adjective* having an illness, injury, or condition that makes it difficult to do the things that other people do **özürlü, sakat** *They are demanding equal rights for* **the disabled***.*

disadvantage ...... İLE BİRLİKTE KULLANILAN KELİMELER

have/face a disadvantage ● a **big**/the **main**/a **major**/ a **serious** disadvantage ● a disadvantage **of/to** (doing) sth ● a disadvantage **for** sb ● the **advantages** and disadvantages **(of** sth)

disadvantage /ˌdɪsəd'vɑːntɪdʒ/ *noun* **1** [C] something which makes a situation more difficult, or makes you less likely to succeed **mahsur, sakınca, dezavantaj** *One disadvantage of living in the country is the lack of public transport.* **2 at a disadvantage** having problems that other people do not have **dezavantajlı/zararlı durumda** *Being shy puts him at a disadvantage.*

disadvantaged /ˌdɪsəd'vɑːntɪdʒd/ *adjective* Disadvantaged people are poor and do not have many opportunities. **mahrumiyette olan, yoksulluk çeken, normal yaşam koşullarına sahip olmayan** *disadvantaged children*

disaffected /ˌdɪsə'fektɪd/ *adjective* disappointed with someone or something and not supporting them as you did before **güvenini yitirmiş, küskün, hayal kırıklığına uğramış, kırgın, gayri memnun** *disaffected voters* ● **disaffection** /ˌdɪsə'fekʃ^ən/ *noun* [U] **hoşnutsuzluk, memnuniyetsizlik**

⊶**disagree** /ˌdɪsə'griː/ *verb* [I] **disagreeing**, *past* **disagreed** to have a different opinion from someone else about something **uyuşmamak, anlaşamamak** *I disagree with most of what he said.* ○ *Experts disagree about/ on the causes of the disease.*

disagreeable /ˌdɪsə'griːəbl/ *adjective formal* unpleasant **nahoş, tatsız, kötü** *a disagreeable old man*

disagreement /ˌdɪsə'griːm^ənt/ *noun* [C, U] when people have a different opinion about something or have an argument **uyuşmazlık, anlaşmazlık** *They had a disagreement about/over money.* ○ *There is a lot of disagreement among doctors on this matter.*

disallow /ˌdɪsə'laʊ/ *verb* [T] to officially refuse to accept something because the rules have been broken **reddetmek, onaylamamak, izin vermemek** *The goal was disallowed by the referee.*

⊶**disappear** /ˌdɪsə'pɪə^r/ *verb* [I] **1** NOT SEE to become impossible to see **gözden kaybolmak** *She watched him disappear into the crowd.* **2** GO to suddenly go somewhere else and become impossible to find **sırra kadem basmak, ortadan kaybolmak** *Her husband disappeared in 1991.* **3** STOP EXISTING to stop existing **ortadan kalkmak, tarih olmak** *These flowers are disappearing from our countryside.* ● **disappearance** /ˌdɪsə'pɪər^əns/ *noun* [C, U] *Police are investigating the girl's disappearance.* ⊃See also: disappear/vanish into thin **air¹**. **kayboluş**

disappoint /ˌdɪsə'pɔɪnt/ *verb* [T] to make someone feel unhappy because someone or something was not as good as they had expected **hayal/düş kırıklığına uğratmak, altüst etmek** *We don't want to disappoint the fans.*

disappointed ...... BAŞKA BİR DEYİŞLE

Eğer kişi olan bir olaydan dolayı hayal kırıklığı yaşamışsa, **disheartened** sıfatı veya resmi olmayan durumlarda **gutted** ifadesi kullanılabilir. *He was very* **disheartened** *by the results of the test.* ● *Nick's absolutely* **gutted** *that he's been dropped from the team.*
Eğer kişi verdiği sözü tutmayıp, diğer kişiyi yarıyolda bıraktıysa, durumu belirtmek için **let down** ifadesi kullanılır. *John had promised to go but he* **let** *me* **down** *at the last minute.*
Kişiye hayal kırıklığı hissettiren durumlar genellikle **letdown** ifadesiyle açıklanır. *After all that planning the party was a bit of a* **letdown***.*

Anticlimax beklenenden daha az etki yaratan ve hayalkırıklığına sebep olan bir deneyimin ifadesinde kullanılır. *After so much preparation, the party itself was a bit of an* anticlimax.

o﹣**disappointed** /ˌdɪsəˈpɔɪntɪd/ *adjective* unhappy because someone or something was not as good as you hoped or expected, or because something did not happen **hal/düş kırıklığına uğramış; sükûtu hayale uğramış** [+ (that)] *I was very disappointed that he didn't come.* ○ *I'm really disappointed in you.*

disappointing /ˌdɪsəˈpɔɪntɪŋ/ *adjective* making you feel disappointed **ümit kırıcı, düş kırıklığına uğratan** *a disappointing performance/result* ● **disappointingly** *adverb a disappointingly small audience* **hayal kırıklığına uğramış bir şekilde**

disappointment /ˌdɪsəˈpɔɪntmənt/ *noun* **1** [U] the feeling of being disappointed **hüsran, düş/hayal kırıklığı** *She couldn't hide her disappointment when she lost.* **2** [C] someone or something that disappoints you **düş/hayal kırıklığı yaratan kişi/şey** *I'm sorry I'm such a disappointment to you.*

disapproval /ˌdɪsəˈpruːvᵊl/ *noun* [U] when you think that someone or something is bad or wrong **tasdiklememe/onaylamama**

disapprove /ˌdɪsəˈpruːv/ *verb* [I] to think that someone or something is bad or wrong **tasdik etmemek/onaylamamak** *Her family disapproved of the marriage.* ● **disapproving** *adjective* showing that you think someone or something is bad or wrong **tasdik etmeyen/onaylamayan** *a disapproving look*

disarm /dɪsˈɑːm/ *verb* **1** [I, T] to give up your weapons, or to take away someone else's weapons **silahsızlandırmak, silahlardan arındırmak** *Both sides have agreed to disarm.* **2** [T] to make someone feel less angry **yumuşatmak, yatıştırmak** *His smile disarmed her.*

disarmament /dɪsˈɑːməmənt/ *noun* [U] when a country or group gets rid of some or all of its weapons **silahsızlanma** *nuclear disarmament*

disarming /dɪsˈɑːmɪŋ/ *adjective* behaving in a way that stops people feeling angry with you or criticizing you **yatıştırıcı, rahatlatıcı, yumuşatıcı** *a disarming smile*

disarray /ˌdɪsᵊrˈeɪ/ *noun* [U] when something is untidy and not organized **düzensizlik, karışıklık, başıboşluk** *The house was in complete disarray.*

🧩 **disaster** ...... İLE BİRLİKTE KULLANILAN KELİMELER

bring/cause/prevent disaster ● disaster **happens/ strikes** ● a **complete/major/terrible/unmitigated** disaster ● a **natural** disaster

o﹣**disaster** /dɪˈzɑːstəʳ/ *noun* **1** DAMAGE [C] something that causes a lot of harm or damage **felaket, âfet** *floods and other natural disasters* **2** FAILURE [C] a failure or something that has a very bad result **yıkım, felaket, şanssızlık, başarısızlık** *His idea was a total disaster.* **3** BAD SITUATION [U] an extremely bad situation **oldukça kötü bir durum** *The holiday ended in disaster.*

disastrous /dɪˈzɑːstrəs/ *adjective* extremely bad **korkunç, feci** *disastrous consequences* ○ *a disastrous week*

disband /dɪsˈbænd/ *verb* [I, T] *formal* to stop working together as a group, or to stop a group from working together **(grup çalışması) dağılmak, ayrılmak; dağıtmak, ayırmak, ortak çalılmaya son vermek**

disbelief /ˌdɪsbɪˈliːf/ *noun* [U] when you do not believe that something is true or real **inanmama, güvenmeme** *She shook her head in disbelief.*

disbelieve /ˌdɪsbɪˈliːv/ *verb* [T] to not believe someone or something **inanmamak, güvenmemek**

disc (*also US* disk) /dɪsk/ *noun* [C] **1** SHAPE a flat, round shape or object **yassı yuvarlak cisim, disk** **2** RECORDING a record or CD **plak veya CD 3** BACK a piece of cartilage (= strong material in the body) between the bones in your back **(omurgalar arasında) disk** ⊃See also: compact disc.

discard /dɪˈskɑːd/ *verb* [T] to throw something away **(işe yaramayan şeyi) atmak, ıskartaya çıkarmak** *discarded food wrappers*

discern /dɪˈsɜːn/ *verb* [T] *formal* to see or recognize something **farketmek, farkına varmak, ayırt etmek** ● **discernible** *adjective There was no discernible difference between them.* **görünür**

discerning /dɪˈsɜːnɪŋ/ *adjective* having or showing good judgment, especially about style and quality **(tarz ve kaliteyi) ayırt edebilen, anlar, anlayan** *a discerning customer/reader*

discharge¹ /dɪsˈtʃɑːdʒ/ *verb* [T] **1** to allow someone to leave a hospital or prison, or to order or allow someone to leave an organization such as the army **(hastane, hapishane, askerlik) taburcu etmek; tahliye etmek/serbest bırakmak; terhis etmek** [often passive] *She was discharged from the army yesterday.* **2** If a liquid or gas is discharged from something, it comes out of it. **(sıvı, gaz) bırakmak, salmak, çıkarmak, akıtmak**

discharge² /ˈdɪstʃɑːdʒ/ *noun* [C, U] **1** LEAVE when someone is officially allowed or ordered to leave somewhere such as a prison, hospital, or the army **(hastane, hapishane, askerlik) taburcu olma, tahliye, terhis** **2** COME OUT when a liquid or gas comes out of something **tahliye, salma, çıkarma, akma** *the discharge of carbon dioxide* **3** SUBSTANCE a liquid or gas that comes out of something **akıntı, sızıntı**

disciple /dɪˈsaɪpl/ *noun* [C] someone who follows the ideas and teaching of someone, especially of a religious leader **mürit, havari, taraftar**

disciplinarian /ˌdɪsəplɪˈneəriən/ *noun* [C] someone who is very strict and gives punishments when people break rules **disiplin uygulayan, kurallara göre davranan**

disciplinary /ˌdɪsəˈplɪnᵊri/, /ⓤ ˈdɪsəplɪmeri/ *adjective* [always before noun] relating to punishment for someone who has broken rules **disiplinle ilgili** *disciplinary action*

🧩 **discipline** ...... İLE BİRLİKTE KULLANILAN KELİMELER

enforce/establish/restore discipline ● **firm/ harsh/rigorous** discipline ● **lax/poor** discipline

discipline¹ /ˈdɪsəplɪm/ *noun* **1** CONTROL [U] when people's behaviour is controlled using rules and punishments **displin** *There should be better discipline in schools.* **2** SELF CONTROL [U] when you can control your own behaviour carefully **öz disiplin** *I don't have enough discipline to save money.* **3** KNOWLEDGE [C] *formal* a particular subject of study **belli bir çalışma konusu, bilim dalı, spor dalı** *the scientific disciplines* ⊃See also: self-discipline.

discipline² /ˈdɪsəplɪm/ *verb* [T] **1** to punish someone **ceza vermek, disipline sokmak** [often passive] *He was disciplined for missing a training session.* **2** to teach someone to behave in a controlled way **terbiye etmek, düzgün davranmayı öğretmek** [often reflexive] *You have to learn to discipline yourself.*

disciplined /ˈdɪsəplɪnd/ *adjective* behaving in a very controlled way **terbiyeli, disiplinli** *the most disciplined army in the world*

'disc jockey (*also* DJ) *noun* [C] someone who plays music on the radio or at discos **radyo ve diskoda müzik çalan kimse**

disclaim /dɪs'kleɪm/ *verb* [T] *formal* to say that you know nothing about something, or are not responsible for something **reddetmek, üslenmemek, inkâr etmek, sorumluluğu kabul etmemek** *The terrorists disclaimed responsibility for the bomb.*

disclaimer /dɪs'kleɪmə^r/ *noun* [C] when someone officially says that they are not responsible for something **yalanlama, sorumluluğu kabullenmeme**

disclose /dɪs'kləʊz/ *verb* [T] *formal* to give new or secret information to someone **ifşa etmek, açıklamak, açığa vurmak** *He refused to disclose details of the report.*

disclosure /dɪs'kləʊʒə^r/ *noun* [C, U] when someone gives people new or secret information **ifşaat, açığa vurma, açıklama**

disco /'dɪskəʊ/ *noun* [C] a place or event where people dance to pop music **diskotek, disko**

discoloured UK (US **discolored**) /dɪs'kʌləd/ *adjective* If something is discoloured, it has become a less attractive colour than it was originally. **rengi solmuş, solgun, soluk** *discoloured teeth*

discomfort /dɪs'kʌmfət/ *noun* 1 PAIN [U] slight pain **hafif ağrı, sızı** *You may feel some discomfort for a few days.* 2 MENTAL FEELING [U] when you feel slightly embarrassed or anxious **sıkıntı, hafif mahcubiyet, endişe** 3 SITUATION [C, U] a physically uncomfortable situation **zahmet, sıkıntı, eziyet**

disconcert /ˌdɪskən'sɜːt/ *verb* [T] to make someone feel confused or anxious **kafasını karıştırmak, şaşırtmak, elini ayağını dolaştırmak** [often passive] *She was disconcerted by his questions.*

disconcerting /ˌdɪskən'sɜːtɪŋ/ *adjective* making you feel confused or anxious **kafa karıştıran, elini ayağını dolaştıran** *a disconcerting silence* • **disconcertingly** *adverb* **şaşkınlıkla**

disconnect /ˌdɪskə'nekt/ *verb* [T] to separate two things that are joined or connected, especially a piece of equipment and a power supply **bağlantısını kesmek, ayırmak, irtibatını koparmak** *Switch off the machine before disconnecting it from the power supply.*

disconnected /ˌdɪskə'nektɪd/ *adjective* not joined in any way **bağlantısız, kesik, kopuk** *disconnected thoughts*

discontent /ˌdɪskən'tent/ *noun* [U] unhappiness about a situation **hoşnutsuzluk, memnuniyetsizlik** *There is growing discontent with this government.* • **discontented** *adjective* **şaşırmış**

discontinue /ˌdɪskən'tɪnjuː/ *verb* [T] **discontinuing**, *past* **discontinued** to stop producing or providing something such as a product or service **yarım/yarıda bırakmak; ara vermek; (üretim, ürün) durdurmak** [often passive] *I'm afraid this model has been discontinued.*

discord /'dɪskɔːd/ *noun* [U] disagreement between people **uyuşmazlık, anlaşmazlık, itilaf**

discount[1] /'dɪskaʊnt/ *noun* [C, U] a reduction in price **indirim, fiyat düşürme, iskonto** *They offer a 10 percent discount on rail travel for students.*

discount[2] /dɪ'skaʊnt/ *verb* [T] 1 to ignore something because you do not believe that it is true or that it will happen **ehemmiyet vermemek; hesaba katmamak, dikkate almamak; önemsememek** *You shouldn't discount the possibility of him coming back.* 2 to reduce the price of something **fiyatını düşürmek, indirim yapmak** *discounted goods/rates*

discourage /dɪ'skʌrɪdʒ/ *verb* 1 **discourage sb from doing sth** to try to persuade someone not to do something *a campaign to discourage people from smoking* 2 [T] to try to prevent something from happening **önlemeye çalışmak, önüne geçmek** *a campaign to discourage smoking* 3 [T] to make someone less confident or enthusiastic about something **cesaretini kırmak, moralini bozmak, ümidini kırmak** *I didn't mean to discourage her.* • **discouragement** *noun* [U] ⊃Opposite **encourage. cesaretin yitirilmesi**

discouraged /dɪ'skʌrɪdʒd/ *adjective* having lost your confidence or enthusiasm for something **cesareti kırılan, güvenini kaybetmiş**

discouraging /dɪ'skʌrɪdʒɪŋ/ *adjective* making you feel less enthusiastic or confident about something **cesaret kırıcı, güven kaybettiren** *discouraging results*

◦‐**discover** /dɪ'skʌvə^r/ *verb* [T] 1 FIND to find something **keşfetmek, bulmak, ortaya çıkarmak** *The body was discovered in a ditch.* 2 FIRST to be the first person to find something important **bir şeyi ilk bulan kişi olmak** *Who discovered America?* 3 GET INFORMATION to get information about something for the first time **öğrenmek, bulmak** [+ (that)] *She discovered that he had been married three times before.* ○ [+ question word] *Have they discovered what was causing your headaches?*

discoverer /dɪ'skʌvərə^r/ *noun* [C] someone who is the first person to find something important **kâşif, keşfeden, ilk bulan**

discovery ...... İLE BİRLİKTE KULLANILAN KELİMELER

make a discovery • a **chance/new** discovery • the discovery **of** sth

discovery /dɪ'skʌv^əri/ *noun* 1 [C, U] when someone discovers something **keşif, buluş** *the discovery of bones in the garden* ○ *Scientists have made some important discoveries about genetics recently.* 2 [C] something or someone that is discovered **buluş, bulma, ortaya çıkarma**

discredit /dɪ'skredɪt/ *verb* [T] to make someone or something appear bad and lose the respect of other people **kötü tarafını ortaya çıkararak herkesin önünde gözden düşürmek** *They're always looking for ways to discredit her.*

discreet /dɪ'skriːt/ *adjective* careful not to cause embarrassment or attract too much attention, especially by keeping something secret **temkinli, dikkatli ve nazik, ölçülü, sağ duyulu, ketum, ağzı sıkı** *Can I trust you to be discreet?* ⊃Opposite **indiscreet.** • **discreetly** *adverb* **gizlice**

discrepancy /dɪ'skrep^ənsi/ *noun* [C, U] when two things that should be the same are different **çelişki, farklılık** *There is a slight discrepancy between the two statements.*

discrete /dɪ'skriːt/ *adjective* separate and different **ayrı, farklı** *a word that has two discrete meanings*

discretion /dɪ'skreʃ^ən/ *noun* [U] 1 when someone is careful not to cause embarrassment or attract too much attention, especially by keeping something secret **ölçülü davranma, itidal gösterme, dikkat, ihtiyat** *You can rely on my discretion.* ⊃Opposite **indiscretion.** 2 the right to decide something **akıl, sağ duyu** *Students can be expelled at the discretion of the head teacher* (= if the head teacher decides it).

discretionary /dɪ'skreʃ^ən^əri/ *adjective* decided by officials and not fixed by rules **takdir yetkisiyle yapılan, liyakat dikkate alınarak karar verilen** *Judges have great discretionary powers.*

discriminate /dɪ'skrɪmɪneɪt/ *verb* [I] 1 to treat someone unfairly because of their sex, race, religion, etc (cinsiyet, ırk, din vb.) **ayrım/ayrımcılık yapmak, ayırt etmek** *The company was accused of discriminating against people on the basis of age.* **2** to notice a difference between two things **ayırmak, fark görmek** *Police dogs are very good at discriminating between different smells.*

discriminating /dɪˈskrɪmɪneɪtɪŋ/ *adjective* good at judging what is good quality **titiz, zevk sahibi** *a discriminating shopper*

🧩 **discrimination** ...... İLE BİRLİKTE KULLANILAN KELİMELER

face/suffer discrimination • **age/racial/sex** discrimination • discrimination **against** sb

discrimination /dɪˌskrɪmɪˈneɪʃ°n/ *noun* [U] when someone is treated unfairly because of their sex, race, religion, etc **(cinsiyet, ırk, din vb.) ayrımı/ayrımcılığı, fark gözetme, ayrım yapma** *racial/sex discrimination* ○ *discrimination against older workers*

discus /ˈdɪskəs/ *noun* [C] a round, flat, heavy object that people throw as a sport **(spor) disk**

o-**discuss** /dɪˈskʌs/ *verb* [T] to talk about something with someone and tell each other your ideas or opinions **tartışmak, görüşmek** *Have you discussed this matter with anyone else?*

🧩 **discussion** ...... İLE BİRLİKTE KULLANILAN KELİMELER

have/hold a discussion • a **heated/lengthy** discussion • a discussion **about** sth • be **under** discussion

o-**discussion** /dɪˈskʌʃ°n/ *noun* [C, U] when people talk about something and tell each other their ideas or opinions **tartışma, müzakere, görüş alış verişinde bulunma** *They were having a discussion about football.* ○ *Several ideas are still under discussion* (= being discussed).

disdain /dɪsˈdeɪn/ *noun* [U] when you dislike someone or something and think that they do not deserve any respect **küçümseme, horlama, aşağılama, hor görme** *His disdain for politicians is obvious.* • **disdainful** *adjective* *disdainful remarks* • **disdainfully** *adverb* **küçümser gibi**

🧩 **disease** ...... İLE BİRLİKTE KULLANILAN KELİMELER

be affected by/have/suffer from a disease • contract/develop a disease • cure/detect/diagnose/ treat a disease • a chronic/deadly/hereditary/ infectious disease

o-**disease** /dɪˈziːz/ *noun* [C, U] an illness caused by an infection or by a failure of health and not by an accident **hastalık, rahatsızlık** *heart disease* ○ *an infectious disease* • **diseased** *adjective* affected by a disease **hastalanmış, hastalıklı, rahatsız** *a diseased lung*

disembark /ˌdɪsɪmˈbɑːk/ *verb* [I] *formal* to leave a ship, boat, or aircraft **(uçak; gemi, tekne) inmek, karaya çıkmak, sahile çıkmak** *All passengers must disembark in Vancouver.* • **disembarkation** /ˌdɪsɪmbɑːˈkeɪʃ°n/ *noun* [U] **terketme**

disembodied /ˌdɪsɪmˈbɒdid/ *adjective* seeming not to have a body or not to be connected to a body **bedensel olmayan, bedensiz, var olmayan** *a disembodied voice*

disenchanted /ˌdɪsɪnˈtʃɑːntɪd/ *adjective* disappointed with something that you thought was good in the past **düş kırıklığına uğramış, inancını yitirmiş, (deyim) güvendiği dağlara kar yağmış** *He became disenchanted with politics.* • **disenchantment** *noun* [U] **hayalkırıklığı**

disengage /ˌdɪsɪnˈɡeɪdʒ/ *verb* [I, T] to become separated from something, or to make two things become separate **rate from each other kurtulmak, serbest bırakmak, salıvermek** *He gently disengaged his hand from hers.*

disentangle /ˌdɪsɪnˈtæŋɡl/ *verb* [T] **1** to separate someone or something that is connected to something else in a complicated way **kurtarmak, ayırmak, çıkarmak, çözmek** *He disentangled himself from her arms.* **2** to separate things such as pieces of string, hair, or wire that have become twisted together **kör düğüm olmuş bir şeyi çözmek, açmak**

disfigure /dɪsˈfɪɡər/ *verb* [T] to spoil someone's or something's appearance **güzelliğini/şeklini bozmak, biçimsizleştirmek** [often passive] *Her face was disfigured by a huge scar.*

disgrace[1] /dɪsˈɡreɪs/ *verb* [T] to make people stop respecting you or your family, team, etc by doing something very bad **itibarını kaybetmek, gözden düşmek, şerefini iki paralık etmek**

disgrace[2] /dɪsˈɡreɪs/ *noun* [U] **1** when someone does something very bad that makes people stop respecting them or their family, team, etc **ayıp, utanç, şerefsizlik, haysiyetsizlik** *They were sent home in disgrace.* **2 be a disgrace** to be very bad **çok kötü olmak** [+ that] *It's a disgrace that money is being wasted like this.* **3 be a disgrace to sb/sth** to be so bad or unacceptable that you make people stop respecting a particular group, activity, etc **yüz karası/utançkaynağı olmak; rezil etmek** *You are a disgrace to your profession.*

disgraced /dɪsˈɡreɪst/ *adjective* A disgraced person has lost other people's respect because they have done something very bad. **yüz karası, utanç kaynağı, haysiyetsiz, rezil, utanç verici** *a disgraced politician*

disgraceful /dɪsˈɡreɪsf°l/ *adjective* very bad **ayıp, utandırıcı, utanç verici, küçük düşürücü** *disgraceful behaviour* • **disgracefully** *adverb* **ayıp bir şekilde**

disgruntled /dɪsˈɡrʌntld/ *adjective* angry and upset **canı sıkkın, üzgün, bozulmuş, küskün** *Disgruntled workers have decided to go on strike.*

disguise[1] /dɪsˈɡaɪz/ *noun* [C, U] clothes and other things that you wear to change the way you look so that people cannot recognize you **kıyafet değiştirerek başkaları tarafından tanınmayı engellemek, gizlenmek** *She usually goes out in disguise to avoid being bothered by the public.* ⊃See also: a **blessing** in disguise.

disguise[2] /dɪsˈɡaɪz/ *verb* **1 disguise yourself/your voice, etc** to change your appearance/voice, etc so that people cannot recognize you **gizlenmek, saklanmak** *He managed to escape by disguising himself as a woman.* **2 be disguised as sb/sth** to be wearing clothes and other things that make you look like someone or something else **...nin kılığına bürünmek; gibi giyinmek 3** [T] to hide something such as a feeling or opinion **(fikir, his) gizlemek, saklamak, belli etmemek** *She couldn't disguise her disappointment.*

disgust[1] /dɪsˈɡʌst/ *noun* [U] a very strong feeling of dislike or disapproval **tiksinti, nefret, iğrenme** *She walked out in disgust.*

disgust[2] /dɪsˈɡʌst/ *verb* [T] If something disgusts you, it makes you feel extreme dislike or disapproval. **tiksindirmek, iğrendirmek, nefret ettirmek** *These pictures disgust me.*

disgusted /dɪsˈɡʌstɪd/ *adjective* feeling extreme dislike or disapproval of something **iğrenmiş, tiksinmiş** *I'm totally disgusted with your behaviour.*

disgusting /dɪsˈɡʌstɪŋ/ *adjective* extremely unpleasant **iğrenç, tiksinti veren, kötü, berbat** *What's that disgusting smell?*

o-**dish¹** /dɪʃ/ *noun* [C] **1** a curved container for eating or serving food from **tabak, sahan** *a baking/serving dish* **2** food that is prepared in a particular way as part of a meal **yemek** *a chicken/vegetarian dish* **3** **the dishes** dirty plates, bowls, and other objects for cooking or eating food **kapkacak, bulaşıklar** *Who's going to wash the dishes?*

dish² /dɪʃ/ *verb*
dish sth out *phrasal verb informal* to give or say things to people without thinking about them carefully **aklına geleni düşünmeden söylemek, akıl vermek**

dishcloth /'dɪʃklɒθ/ *noun* [C] a cloth used for washing dirty dishes **bulaşık bezi**

disheartened /dɪs'hɑː*t*ənd/ *adjective* disappointed or without hope **cesareti kırılmış, ümitsiz** *She was very disheartened by the results of the test.*

disheartening /dɪs'hɑː*t*ənɪŋ/ *adjective* making you feel disappointed or without hope **cesaret kırıcı, umutsuzluğa düşüren** *a disheartening experience*

dishevelled *UK* (*US* **disheveled**) /dɪ'ʃev*ə*ld/ *adjective* very untidy **darma dağınık, saçı başı dağınık, üsüt başı perişan** *dishevelled hair*

dishonest /dɪ'sɒnɪst/ *adjective* not honest and likely to lie or do something illegal **sahtekâr, yalancı, düzenbaz, namussuz** ● **dishonestly** *adverb* **dürüst olmayan bir şekilde** ● **dishonesty** *noun* [U] when someone is not honest **sahtekârlık, düzenbazlık, namussuzluk, yalancılık**

dishonour¹ *UK* (*US* **dishonor**) /dɪ'sɒnə*r*/ *noun* [U] when people stop respecting you because you have done something bad **namusuna leke sürme, onursuzluk, haysiyetsizlik, şerefsizlik** ● **dishonourable** *adjective* bad or not deserving respect **onursuz, gurursuz, haysiyetsiz** *dishonourable conduct*

dishonour² *UK* (*US* **dishonor**) /dɪ'sɒnə*r*/ *verb* [T] **1** to show no respect for someone or something by behaving badly **saygı göstermemek, şerefsizlik etmek, namusuna leke sürmek** *He felt that he had dishonoured his country.* **2** to refuse to accept or pay a cheque or a bill (= amount charged)

'**dish ,soap** *US* (*UK* **washing-up liquid**) *noun* [U] a thick liquid soap used to wash pans, plates, knives and forks, etc. **bulaşık deterjanı**

dishtowel /'dɪʃtaʊəl/ *US* (*UK* **tea towel**) *noun* [C] a cloth that is used for drying plates, dishes, etc **bulaşık kurulama bezi**

dishwasher /'dɪʃ,wɒʃə*r*/ *noun* [C] a machine that washes plates, glasses, and other kitchen equipment **bulaşık makinası** *I'll load the dishwasher.* ⊃Orta kısımdaki renkli sayfalarına bakınız.

disillusion /ˌdɪsɪ'luː*ʒ*ən/ *verb* [T] to cause someone to discover that something they believed is not true **güzünü açmasına sebep olmak, gerçeği görmesini sağlamak**

disillusioned /ˌdɪsɪ'luː*ʒ*ənd/ *adjective* feeling disappointed because something is not as good as you thought it was **düş kırıklığına/sükûtu hayale uğramış** *She says she's disillusioned with the music business.*

disillusionment /ˌdɪsɪ'luː*ʒ*ənmənt/ (*also* **disillusion**) *noun* [U] the disappointment someone feels when they discover something is not as good as they thought it was **düş kırıklığı** *There's growing disillusionment with the government.*

disinfect /ˌdɪsɪn'fekt/ *verb* [T] to clean something with a chemical that destroys bacteria **dezenfekte etmek, mikroplardan arındırmak**

disinfectant /ˌdɪsɪn'fektənt/ *noun* [C, U] a chemical substance that destroys bacteria **mikrop öldürücü, dezenfektan**

disintegrate /dɪ'sɪntɪɡreɪt/ *verb* [I] **1** to break into a lot of small pieces **parçalanıp dağılmak, paramparça olmak 2** to become much worse **dağılmak, parçalanmak** *The situation is disintegrating into total chaos.* ● **disintegration** /dɪˌsɪntɪ'ɡreɪʃ*ə*n/ *noun* [U] **parçalara ayırma**

disinterested /dɪ'sɪntrəstɪd/ *adjective* not involved in a situation and so able to judge it without supporting a particular side **yansız, kaygısız, tarafsız, çıkar kaygısı olmayan, dürüst davranan, hakkaniyet gösteren** *a disinterested observer*

disjointed /dɪs'dʒɔɪntɪd/ *adjective* having words or ideas that are not in a clear order **bölük börçük, tutarsız, kopuk, bağlantısız** *a disjointed conversation*

disk .... İLE BİRLİKTE KULLANILAN KELİMELER

save/write sth to disk ● on a disk ● disk **space**

o-**disk** /dɪsk/ *noun* [C] **1** *another US spelling of* disc **disk 2** a piece of computer equipment that records and stores information electronically **üzerine elektronik ortamda kayıp yapılabilen bilgisayar diski** *How much disk space is there?* ⊃Orta kısımdaki renkli sayfalarına bakınız. ⊃See also: floppy disk, hard disk.

'**disk ,drive** *noun* [C] the part of a computer that allows the person using the computer to store and read information from a disk **disk sürücü**

diskette /dɪ'sket/ *noun* [C] a small, flat, plastic object that you put in your computer to record and store information electronically **disket**

dislike¹ /dɪ'slaɪk/ *verb* [T] to not like someone or something **nefret etmek, sevmemek, hoşlanmamak, hazzetmemek** *Why do you dislike her so much?* ○ [+ doing sth] *I dislike ironing intensely.*

dislike² /dɪ'slaɪk/ *noun* [C, U] when you do not like someone or something **nefret, hoşlanmama, sevmeme** *a dislike of cold weather* ○ *I took an instant dislike to her* (= disliked her immediately).

dislocate /'dɪsləʊkeɪt/ *verb* [T] If you dislocate a part of your body, the bones move away from their correct position. **(kemik) çıkmak, oyna(t)mak, kaymak, yerinden çık(art)mak** *I think you've dislocated your shoulder.* ○ *a dislocated hip* ● **dislocation** /ˌdɪsləʊ'keɪʃ*ə*n/ *noun* [U] **yerinden oynatma**

dislodge /dɪ'slɒdʒ/ *verb* [T] to move something away from a fixed position **yerinden çıkartmak, zorlayıp çıkartmak**

disloyal /dɪ'slɔɪəl/ *adjective* not loyal or not supporting someone who you should support **vefasız, sadakatsiz** *I don't want to be disloyal to my friend.* ● **disloyalty** *noun* [U] *They accused her of disloyalty.* **sadakatsizlik**

dismal /'dɪzməl/ *adjective* very bad or unpleasant and making you feel unhappy **kasvetli, sıkıntılı, nahoş, iç karartan** *What dismal weather.* ○ *That was a dismal performance.* ● **dismally** *adverb* *I tried to cheer her up, but failed dismally* (= completely failed). **hüzünlü bir biçimde**

dismantle /dɪ'smæntl/ *verb* [T] **1** to take something apart so that it is in several pieces **sökmek, parçalara ayırmak, darmadağın etmek** *He's specially trained to dismantle bombs.* **2** to get rid of a system or organization **bir sistemden/kuruluştan kurtulmak**

dismay /dɪ'smeɪ/ *noun* [U] a feeling of unhappiness and disappointment **mutsuzluk, şaşkınlık, korku, endişe** *To our dismay, it started raining.*

dismayed /dɪˈsmeɪd/ *adjective* unhappy and disappointed **mutsuz, bahtsız, şaşkın** [+ to do sth] *I was dismayed to discover that he'd lied to me.*

dismember /dɪˈsmembəʳ/ *verb* [T] to cut the arms and legs off the body of a person or animal **kolunu bacaklarını kesmek, uzuvları bedenden ayırmak** *a dismembered body*

dismiss /dɪˈsmɪs/ *verb* [T] **1** NOT CONSIDER to refuse to consider an idea or opinion **ilgilenmemek, ele almamak** *The committee dismissed the idea as rubbish.* **2** MAKE LEAVE to officially make someone leave their job **ilişiğini kesmek, işten çıkar(ıl)mak, yol ver(il)mek, kov(ul)mak** [often passive] *Anyone who breaks company rules will be dismissed.* **3** ALLOW TO LEAVE to give someone official permission to leave **göndermek, gitmesine izin vermek** *The bell rang and the teacher dismissed the class.*

dismissal /dɪˈsmɪs³l/ *noun* **1** [U] when someone refuses to consider an idea or opinion **önemse(n)meme, dikkate almama** **2** [C, U] when an employer officially makes someone leave their job **çıkış verme, işten at(ıl)ma, yol ver(il)me**

dismissive /dɪˈsmɪsɪv/ *adjective* treating something as if it is not important **burun kıvıran, hafife alan, küçümseyen** *He's so dismissive of all my suggestions.* • **dismissively** *adverb* **saygısızca**

dismount /dɪˈsmaʊnt/ *verb* [I] *formal* to get off a horse or bicycle **(at, bisiklet vb.) inmek**

disobedience /ˌdɪsəʊˈbiːdiəns/ *noun* [U] when someone refuses to do what someone in authority tells them to do **itaatsizlik, başına buyrukluk, söz dinlememezlik, dik başlılık**

disobedient /ˌdɪsəʊˈbiːdiənt/ *adjective* refusing to do what someone in authority tells you to do **itaatsiz, başına buyruk, dik başlı** *a disobedient child*

disobey /ˌdɪsəʊˈbeɪ/ *verb* [T] to not do what you are told to do by someone in authority **itaat etmemek, başına buyruk davranmak, uymamak, söz dinlememek** *How dare you disobey me!*

disorder /dɪˈsɔːdəʳ/ *noun* **1** ILLNESS [C] a disease or mental problem **rahatsızlık veya zihinsel problem** *a blood disorder* **2** BAD BEHAVIOUR [U] uncontrolled, bad behaviour, especially by large groups of people **kargaşa, düzensizlik, karışıklık, patırtı gürültü** *crime and disorder* **3** NOT ORGANIZED [U] when things are untidy or confused and not organized **karmaşıklık, dağınıklık** *His financial affairs are in complete disorder.* ↪See also: **eating disorder.**

disordered /dɪˈsɔːdəd/ *adjective* confused and not organized **karışık, dağınık, düzensiz** *a disordered mind*

disorderly /dɪˈsɔːd³li/ *adjective* **1** behaving badly by being noisy or violent **serkeş, olay çıkaran, azgın, taşkın** *He was charged with being drunk and disorderly.* **2** untidy **darmadağınık, karmakarışık, düzensiz**

disorganized (*also UK* -ised) /dɪˈsɔːgənaɪzd/ *adjective* **1** not planned or organized well **plansız, düzensiz, rastgele, karışık, intizamsız** *The competition was completely disorganized.* **2** not good at planning or organizing things **düzen ve planlamada becerikli olmayan, sistemsiz**

disorient /dɪˈsɔːriənt/ (*also UK* disorientate /dɪˈsɔːriənteɪt/) *verb* [T] to make someone not know where to go or what to do **yönünü şaşırtmak, yanlış yönlendirmek**

disoriented /dɪˈsɔːriəntɪd/ (*also UK* disorientated /dɪˈsɔːriənteɪtɪd/) *adjective* confused and not knowing where to go or what to do **şaşıran, yönünü kaybeden, kay-**bolmuş, **ne yapacağını nereye gideceğini bilmeyen** *Whales become disoriented in shallow water.*

disown /dɪˈsəʊn/ *verb* [T] to say that you do not want to have any involvement or connection with someone **tanımamak, sahiplenmemek, reddetmek, inkâr etmek** *Even his parents have disowned him.*

disparage /dɪˈspærɪdʒ/ *verb* [T] to say that you think someone or something is not very good **kötülemek, aleyhinde konuşmak** [often passive] *He is often disparaged by the critics.*

disparaging /dɪˈspærɪdʒɪŋ/ *adjective* criticizing someone or something **eleştiren, kötüleyen, aşağılayan, küçük düşürücü** *disparaging remarks*

disparate /ˈdɪsp³rət/ *adjective formal* completely different **tamamen farklı** *people from disparate cultures*

disparity /dɪˈspærəti/ *noun* [C, U] *formal* difference, usually relating to the money people earn or their position **(genellikle kazanç ve konum) farklılık, fark**

dispatch[1] (*also UK* despatch) /dɪˈspætʃ/ *verb* [T] *formal* to send someone or something somewhere **göndermek, sevketmek, yollamak** *They dispatched a police car to arrest him.*

dispatch[2] (*also UK* despatch) /dɪˈspætʃ/ *noun* **1** [U] when someone or something is sent somewhere **gönderme, sevk, yollama** *the dispatch of troops* **2** [C] an official report that someone in a foreign country sends to their organization **yurtdışından gönderilen resmi rapor**

dispel /dɪˈspel/ *verb* [T] dispelling, *past* dispelled to get rid of a feeling, thought, or belief **kurtulmak, defetmek,** *He appeared on TV to dispel rumours that he was dying.*

dispensary /dɪˈspens³ri/ *noun* [C] a place where medicines are given out **dispanser, sağlık ocağı**

dispensation /ˌdɪspenˈseɪʃ³n/ *noun* [C, U] special permission to do something **özel izin, muafiyet, hariç tutma** [+ to do sth] *The court would not grant him a dispensation to visit his children.*

dispense /dɪˈspens/ *verb* [T] to give something out **vermek, dağıtmak** *a machine that dispenses drinks and snacks*
dispense with sth/sb *phrasal verb* to stop using something or someone, or to get rid of something or someone, usually because you do not need them **vazgeçmek; ... den/dan kurtulmak; ...sız/siz yapmak**

dispenser /dɪˈspensəʳ/ *noun* [C] a machine that you can get something from **(para, kahve, yiyecek) veren makina** *a cash/drink/soap dispenser*

disperse /dɪˈspɜːs/ *verb* [I, T] to separate and go in different directions, or to make something do this **dağılmak, dağıtmak; yaymak, yayılmak** *We waited until the crowds had dispersed.* • **dispersal** *noun* [U] **dağılma**

dispirited /dɪˈspɪrɪtɪd/ *adjective* unhappy and without hope **keyfi kaçmış, mutsuz ve ümitsiz, kolu kanadı kırık, çaresiz ve umutsuz**

displace /dɪˈspleɪs/ *verb* [T] **1** to take the place of someone or something **yerini almak, yerine geçmek** *Many of these workers will be displaced by modern technology.* **2** to make someone or something leave their usual place or position **yerinden etmek/çıkarmak** *The earthquake displaced thousands of people.* • **displacement** *noun* [U] **çıkarma**

display[1] /dɪˈspleɪ/ *noun* **1** ARRANGEMENT [C] a collection of objects or pictures arranged for people to look at **sergi, vitrin, sergileme, teşhir** *a display of children's paintings* **2 on display** If something is on display, it is there for people to look at. **sergide, vitrinde, teşhirde** *Many old aircraft are on display at the museum.* **3** SHOW

[C] a performance or show for people to watch **gösteri, gösterim** *a firework display* **4** [ON SCREEN] [C, U] when something is shown electronically such as on a computer screen **bilgisayar ekranı, gösterim ekranı** *The display problems might be due to a shortage of disk space.* **5 a display of affection/anger, etc** when someone behaves in a way that shows they have a particular feeling **sevgi/kızgınlık sergileme/gösterme**

display² /dɪˈspleɪ/ *verb* **1** [ARRANGE] [T] to arrange something somewhere so that people can see it **sergilemek, tezgaha koymak** *There were some family photographs displayed on his desk.* **2** [ON SCREEN] [I, T] to show something electronically such as on a computer screen **bilgisayar ekranında göstermek** *The text can be displayed and edited on screen.* **3** [FEELING] [T] to show how you feel by your expression or behaviour **bir konuda davranış göstermek** *He never displayed any interest in girls.*

displease /dɪˈspliːz/ *verb* [T] *formal* to make someone annoyed or unhappy **huzursuz etmek, memnun etmemek, gücendirmek, canını sıkmak, hoşuna gitmemek** ● **displeased** *adjective* **memnuniyetsiz**

displeasure /dɪˈspleʒər/ *noun* [U] *formal* when someone is annoyed or unhappy about something **hoşnutsuzluk, memnuniyetsizlik** *She expressed great displeasure at his behaviour.*

disposable /dɪˈspəʊzəbl/ *adjective* intended to be used only once and then thrown away **kullan at, bir kereye mahsus kullanılan, bir kullanımlık** *a disposable camera/razor*

disposable 'income UK (US dis,posable 'income) *noun* [C, U] the amount of money that you have available to spend after tax, rent and other basic things that you must pay for **zorunlu masraflardan sonra elde kalan para/gelir**

disposal /dɪˈspəʊzəl/ *noun* [U] **1** when you get rid of something, especially by throwing it away **atma, elden çıkarma** *waste disposal* ○ *the disposal of hazardous substances* **2 at sb's disposal** available for someone to use **emrine hazır/amade; kullanımına hazır** *We will have a car at our disposal for the whole trip.*

dispose /dɪˈspəʊz/ *verb*
dispose of sth *phrasal verb* to get rid of something, especially by throwing it away **atıp kurtulmak; elden çıkarmak; ...den/dan kurtulmak**

disposed /dɪˈspəʊzd/ *adjective formal* **1 be disposed to do sth** to be willing or likely to do something *I tried to tell her but she didn't seem disposed to listen.* **2 be favourably/well, etc disposed towards sth** to like or approve of something **bir şeye istekli/meyilli/lehinde vb. olmak** *She seems well disposed towards the idea.*

disposition /ˌdɪspəˈzɪʃən/ *noun* [C] the type of character someone has **karakter** *a cheerful/nervous disposition*

disproportionate /ˌdɪsprəˈpɔːʃənət/ *adjective* too large or small in comparison to something else **orantısız, küçük ya da büyük** *There are a disproportionate number of girls in the class.* ● **disproportionately** *adverb* **oransız bir şekilde**

disprove /dɪˈspruːv/ *verb* [T] to prove that something is not true **aksini ispat etmek, çürütmek**

═ **dispute** .... İLE BİRLİKTE KULLANILAN KELİMELER

have/be involved in a dispute ● **resolve/settle** a dispute ● a **bitter/long-running** dispute ● a dispute **about/over** sth

dispute¹ /ˈdɪspjuːt/ *noun* [C, U] a disagreement, especially one that lasts a long time **uyuşmazlık, anlaş-**

mazlık, çatışma *A man stabbed his neighbour in a dispute over noise.*

dispute² /dɪˈspjuːt/ *verb* [T] to disagree with something someone says **karşı çıkmak, itiraz etmek, kabul etmemek** [+ (that)] *I'm not disputing that the drug has benefits.*

disqualify /dɪˈskwɒlɪfaɪ/ *verb* [T] to stop someone from being in a competition or doing some other activity because they have done something wrong **oyun/yarışma/müsabaka dışı bırakmak, diskalifiye etmek** [often passive] *She was disqualified from the race after a drugs test.* ● **disqualification** /dɪˌskwɒlɪfɪˈkeɪʃən/ *noun* [U] **diskalifiye edilme**

disquiet /dɪˈskwaɪət/ *noun* [U] *formal* when people are anxious or worried about something **endişe, telaş, rahatsızlık** *His health has been causing disquiet.*

═ **disregard** .... İLE BİRLİKTE KULLANILAN KELİMELER

blatant/callous/flagrant/total disregard ● disregard **for/of** sb/sth

disregard¹ /ˌdɪsrɪˈɡɑːd/ *noun* [U, no plural] when someone does not care about or show any interest in someone or something **umursamama, aldırmama, önemsememe** *His behaviour shows a total disregard for other people.*

disregard² /ˌdɪsrɪˈɡɑːd/ *verb* [T] to ignore something **umursamamak, aldırmamak, dikkate almamak, önemsememek** *She chose to disregard my advice.*

disrepair /ˌdɪsrɪˈpeər/ *noun* [U] when a building is in a bad condition because someone has not taken care of it **bakımsızlık, tamire/onarıma muhtaçlık, haraplık** *The house has fallen into disrepair.*

disreputable /dɪsˈrepjətəbl/ *adjective* not respected or trusted by people **itibarını kaybetmiş, adı kötüye çıkmış, rezil rüsva, saygı uyandırmayan** *a disreputable company*

disrepute /ˌdɪsrɪˈpjuːt/ *noun* **bring sb/sth into disrepute** *formal* to cause people not to respect or trust someone or something **adını lekelemek, namına/ününe leke sürmek** *Corrupt policemen are bringing the law into disrepute.*

disrespect /ˌdɪsrɪˈspekt/ *noun* [U] when someone does not show any respect or behave politely towards someone or something **saygısızlık, kendini bilmezlik, hürmetsizlik** *a disrespect for authority*

disrespectful /ˌdɪsrɪˈspektfəl/ *adjective* being rude and not showing any respect **saygısız, kendini bilmez, hürmetsiz** *Don't be disrespectful to your mother.* ● **disrespectfully** *adverb* **saygısızca**

disrupt /dɪsˈrʌpt/ *verb* [T] to interrupt something and stop it continuing as it should **bölmek, araya girmek, sekte vurmak, engellemek** *He disturbs other children and disrupts the class.* ● **disruption** /dɪsˈrʌpʃən/ *noun* [C, U] *the disruption of services* **kesinti** ● **disruptive** *adjective disruptive behaviour* **engelleyici, rahatsız edici**

dissatisfaction /ˌdɪsˌsætɪsˈfækʃən/ *noun* [U] when you are not pleased or happy with something **tatminsizlik, hoşnutsuzluk** *He expressed his dissatisfaction with the legal system.*

dissatisfied /dɪsˈsætɪsfaɪd/ *adjective* not pleased or happy with something **tatminsiz, hoşnutsuz** *a dissatisfied customer* ○ *Are you dissatisfied with our service?*

dissect /daɪˈsekt/ *verb* [T] to cut something into pieces for scientific study **parçalara ayırmak, parça parça etmek** *We had to dissect a rat in biology.* ● **dissection** /daɪˈsekʃən/ *noun* [U] **parçalara ayırma (deney)**

disseminate /dɪˈsemɪneɪt/ *verb* [T] to spread information or ideas **(fikir, bilgi) saçmak, yaymak** *They are*

using their website to disseminate political propaganda.
● **dissemination** /dɪˌsemɪ'neɪʃᵊn/ *noun* [U] **yaymak (bilgi)**

dissent /dɪ'sent/ *noun* [U] when someone does not agree with something **görüş ayrılığı, uyuşmazlık, anlaşmazlık** *There is a lot of dissent within the Church about women priests.* ● **dissent** *verb* [I] to not agree with other people about something **aynı görüşte olmamak, uyuşmamak** ● **dissenter** *noun* [C] **muhalif**

dissertation /ˌdɪsə'teɪʃᵊn/ *noun* [C] a very long piece of writing done as part of a course of study **tez, bilimsel inceleme** *She's writing a dissertation on American poetry.*

disservice /ˌdɪs'sɜːvɪs/ *noun* [no plural] when something causes harm to someone or something **zarar, ziyan, kötülük** *Bad teaching does a great disservice to children.*

dissident /'dɪsɪdᵊnt/ *noun* [C] someone who criticizes their government in a public way **ayrılıkçı, hizipçi, muhalif** *political dissidents*

dissimilar /ˌdɪs'sɪmɪləʳ/ *adjective* different **farklı, benzemez** *Her hair is not dissimilar to yours* (= is similar to yours).

dissipate /'dɪsɪpeɪt/ *verb* [I, T] to disappear, or to make something disappear **yok etmek/olmak; gözden kaybetmek/kaybolmak** *The heat gradually dissipates into the atmosphere.*

dissociate /dɪ'səʊʃieɪt/ *verb* **dissociate yourself from sb/sth** to say that you do not have any connection or involvement with someone or something **bağlarını kesmek, ilişkisini koparmak** *He's trying to dissociate himself from his former friends.*

dissolution /ˌdɪsə'luːʃᵊn/ *noun* [U] when an organization or an official arrangement ends **dağılma, son bulma, sona erme**

dissolve /dɪ'zɒlv/ *verb* **1** [I, T] If a solid dissolves, it becomes part of a liquid, and if you dissolve it, you make it become part of a liquid. **eri(t)mek, çöz(ül)mek** *These tablets dissolve in water.* **2** [T] to end an organization or official arrangement **bir kuruluş ya da resmi antlaşmaya son vermek** *Their marriage was dissolved in 1996.* **3 dissolve into laughter/tears, etc** to suddenly start to laugh/cry, etc **ansızın ağlamaya/gülmeye başlamak**

dissuade /dɪ'sweɪd/ *verb* [T] to persuade someone not to do something **vazgeçirmek, caydırmak** [+ from + doing sth] *We tried to dissuade him from leaving.*

distance ...... İLE BİRLİKTE KULLANILAN KELİMELER
a **large/long/short/small/vast** distance ● a (short/long, etc) distance **from** [a place] ● the distance **between** sth and sth

o-- **distance**[1] /'dɪstᵊns/ *noun* **1** [C, U] the length of the space between two places or things **mesafe** *We're only a short distance from my house.* ○ *He calculated the distance between the Earth and the Sun.* ○ *Are the shops within walking distance?* **2** [no plural] somewhere that is far away, but close enough for you to see or hear the things that are there **uzaklık** *I could see Mary in the distance.* ○ *From a distance, it sounded like a bell ringing.*

distance[2] /'dɪstᵊns/ *verb* **distance yourself from sb/sth** to say or show that you are not connected or involved with someone or something **uzak durmak, uzak olmak, mesafe koymak** *She has tried to distance herself from the book.*

distant /'dɪstᵊnt/ *adjective* **1** [FAR AWAY] far away in space or time **uzak, mesafeli** *distant galaxies* ○ *the distant sound of traffic* ○ *We hope to see you in the not too dis-*

tant future. **2** [RELATIVE] A distant relative is not very closely related to you. **uzak akraba** *a distant cousin* **3** [NOT FRIENDLY] [never before noun] not friendly **soğuk, uzak, mesafeli** *She seemed cold and distant.* ● **distantly** *adverb* **distantly related uzaktan**

distaste /dɪs'teɪst/ *noun* [U] when you dislike something and think it is unpleasant **sevmeme, hoşlanmama, tiksinti** *I have developed a distaste for meat.*

distasteful /dɪs'teɪstfᵊl/ *adjective* unpleasant or offensive **tatsız, tiksindirici, nahoş** *I find this advertisement extremely distasteful.* ● **distastefully** *adverb* **hoş olmayan bir biçimde**

distil UK (US distill) /dɪs'tɪl/ *verb* [T] **distilling**, *past* **distilled** to make a liquid stronger or more pure by heating it until it changes into a gas and then changing it into a liquid again **damıtmak** *distilled water* ● **distillation** /ˌdɪstɪ'leɪʃᵊn/ *noun* [U] **damıtma** ● **distillery** /dɪs'tɪlᵊri/ *noun* [C] a place where strong alcoholic drinks are produced **içki fabrikası**

distinct /dɪs'tɪŋkt/ *adjective* **1** [DIFFERENT] different and separate **farklı, ayrı, apayrı** *This word has three distinct meanings.* **2** [HEAR/SEE] easy to hear, see, or smell **belirgin, açık** *The voices gradually became louder and more distinct.* ⊃Opposite **indistinct**. **3** [CLEAR] [always before noun] clear and certain **net, belirgin** *There's been a distinct improvement in your work.* ● **distinctly** *adverb* **farklı bir biçimde**

distinction ...... İLE BİRLİKTE KULLANILAN KELİMELER
draw/make a distinction ● a **clear** distinction ● a distinction **between** sth and sth

distinction /dɪs'tɪŋkʃᵊn/ *noun* [C, U] **1** a difference between two similar things **ayrılık, fark, ayrım** *the distinction between spoken and written language* **2** a quality or fact that makes someone or something special or different **farklılık, üstünlük, kendine has özelliği olan** *wines of distinction* ○ *He has the distinction of being the youngest player in the World Cup finals.*

distinctive /dɪs'tɪŋktɪv/ *adjective* Something that is distinctive is easy to recognize because it is different from other things. **belirleyici, fark ettiren, karakteristik** *a distinctive style of writing* ● **distinctively** *adverb* **belirgin bir şekilde**

distinguish /dɪs'tɪŋgwɪʃ/ *verb* **1** [RECOGNIZE DIFFERENCES] [I, T] to recognize the differences between two people, ideas, or things **ayırt etmek** *Children must learn to distinguish between right and wrong.* ○ *People have difficulty distinguishing Tracy from her twin sister Mary.* **2** [SHOW DIFFERENCES] [T] to make one person or thing seem different from another **belirginleştirmek, ayırt etmek, farklı kılmak** *His great skill distinguishes him from the rest of the team.* **3** [SEE/HEAR] [T] to be able to see, hear, or understand something **anlamak, seçebilmek, ayırt edebilmek** **4 distinguish yourself** to do something so well that people notice and admire you **öne çıkmak, sivrilmek, temayüz etmek** ● **distinguishable** *adjective* **ayırt edilebilir**

distinguished /dɪs'tɪŋgwɪʃt/ *adjective* famous, praised, or admired **seçkin, saygın, değerli** *a distinguished writer*

distort /dɪs'tɔːt/ *verb* [T] **1** to change the shape, sound, or appearance of something so that it seems strange **bozmak, tahrif etmek, çarpıtmak, saptırmak, biçimini bozmak** *It's a bad recording - the microphone distorted our voices.* **2** to change information so that it is not true or realistic **bilgiyi çarpıtmak, tahrifat yapmak** *Newspapers distorted the truth about their marriage.* ● **distorted** *adjective* **şekli bozulmuş** ● **distortion** /dɪs'tɔːʃᵊn/ *noun* [C, U] *a gross distortion of the facts* **tahrif, değişim**

distract /dɪ'strækt/ *verb* [T] to make someone stop giving their attention to something **dikkatini/ilgisini başka yöne çekmek, dikkatini dağıtmak** *Stop distracting me - I'm trying to finish my essay.*

distracted /dɪ'stræktɪd/ *adjective* anxious and unable to think carefully **kafası karışık, dikkati dağınık, kendini veremeyen**

distraction /dɪ'strækʃ°n/ *noun* **1** [C, U] something that makes you stop giving your attention to something else **dikkat dağıtıcı şey** *The phone calls were a constant distraction.* **2 drive sb to distraction** *UK* to make someone very annoyed

distraught /dɪ'strɔːt/ *adjective* extremely upset and unhappy **aklı başında olmayan, son derece üzgün ve mutsuz, çılgına dönmüş**

distress ...... İLE BİRLİKTE KULLANILAN KELİMELER

deep/great distress ● to sb's distress ● be in distress

distress¹ /dɪ'stres/ *noun* [U] **1** the feeling of being extremely upset or worried **elem, acı, ıstırap, keder, üzüntü, sıkıntı** *The newspaper reports caused her a great deal of distress.* **2** when someone or something is in danger and needs help **tehlikeli durum, yardım gerektiren acil durum, tehlikede olma** *an aircraft in distress*

distress² /dɪ'stres/ *verb* [T] to make someone feel very upset or worried **üzmek, acı vermek; sıkmak, endişelendirmek ● distressing** *adjective* a distressing experience **endişe verici**

distribute /dɪ'strɪbjuːt/ *verb* [T] **1** to give something out to people or places **dağıtmak, taksim etmek, paylaştırmak, vermek, tevzi etmek** *The books will be distributed free to local schools.* **2** to supply goods to shops and companies **şirket ve mağazalara ürün sağlamak/teslim etmek/dağıtmak** *The company manufactures and distributes computer equipment worldwide.*

distribution /ˌdɪstrɪ'bjuːʃ°n/ *noun* [U] when something is supplied or given out to people or places **taksim, dağıtım** *the sale and distribution of videos* **2** [U, no plural] the way something is divided and shared in a group or area **paylaşma, dağılım** *the distribution of wealth*

distributor /dɪ'strɪbjətə'/ *noun* [C] a person or organization that supplies goods to shops and companies **dağıtıcı, distribütör**

district /'dɪstrɪkt/ *noun* [C] a part of a city or country, either an official area or one that is known for having a particular characteristic or business **mıntıka, bölge, mahalle, yöre, ilçe, semt** *the fashion district of New York*

district at'torney (*abbreviation* **DA**) *noun* [C] *US* a lawyer who works for the government of a particular district **bölge avukatı**

distrust /dɪs'trʌst/ *noun* [U] when you do not trust someone or something **güvenmemek, itimat etmemek ● distrust** *verb* [T] **güvenmemek**

disturb /dɪ'stɜːb/ *verb* [T] **1** INTERRUPT to interrupt what someone is doing by making noise or annoying them **rahatsız etmek, huzurunu bozmak** *Don't disturb him, he needs to sleep.* **2** UPSET to make someone feel anxious or upset **taciz etmek, kızdırmak, rahatsızlık vermek** *Some scenes are violent and may disturb younger viewers.* **3** CHANGE to change something by touching it or moving it from its original position **karıştırmak, yerini değiştirmek, düzenini bozmak**

disturbance /dɪ'stɜːb°ns/ *noun* **1** [C, U] something that interrupts what you are doing, especially something loud or annoying **rahatsızlık, huzursuzluk 2** [C]

when people fight or shout **karışıklık, karmaşa, dalaşma**

disturbed /dɪ'stɜːbd/ *adjective* not thinking or behaving normally because of mental or emotional problems **dengesiz, (zihinsel) rahatsız/hasta, duygusal sorun yaşayan**

disturbing /dɪ'stɜːbɪŋ/ *adjective* unpleasant in a way that makes people feel anxious or upset **rahatsız edici, üzücü, huzursuz edici** *disturbing images* **● disturbingly** *adverb* **rahatsız edici bir şekilde**

disused /dɪ'sjuːzd/ *adjective* not used now **kullanılmayan, atıl** *a disused warehouse* **● disuse** /dɪ'sjuːs/ *noun* [U] when something is not used **atıl olma, kullanılmama, işe yaramama** *to fall into disuse*

ditch¹ /dɪtʃ/ *noun* [C] a long, narrow hole in the ground next to a road or field, which water can flow through **(yol boyunca) hendek, ark, su yolu**

ditch² /dɪtʃ/ *verb* [T] *informal* to get rid of someone or something that you do not need or want now **kurtulmak, başından atmak, bırakmak** *He ditched his girlfriend when she got pregnant.*

dither /'dɪðə'/ *verb* [I] to spend too much time trying to make a decision **kararsızlık yaşamak, tereddüt etmek, karar vermemek** *Stop dithering and tell me which one you want!*

ditto¹ /'dɪtəʊ/ *adverb* used to agree with something that has been said, or to avoid repeating something that has been said **ben de, al benden de okadar, aynen**

ditto² /'dɪtəʊ/ *noun* [C] a mark (") used instead of words to show that you are repeating what is written above it **den den**

ditty /'dɪti/ *noun* [C] a short, simple song **basit kısa şarkı**

diva /'diːvə/ *noun* [C] a successful and famous female singer **başarılı ve ünlü bayan sanatçı/şarkıcı**

Divali /dɪ'vɑːli/ *noun* [U] Diwali (= a Hindu festival) **bir Hint festivali**

dive

dive¹ /daɪv/ *verb* [I] *past* **dived**, *also US* **dove**, *past participle* **dived 1** JUMP IN to jump into water with your head and arms going in first **suya dalmak/atlamak** *He dived off the side of the boat into the sea.* **2** SWIM to swim under water, usually with breathing equipment **su altında dalmak, tüple dalmak 3 dive into/over/**

under, etc to move somewhere quickly **bir yere hız-lıca hareket etmek/girmek/saklanmak/gizlenmek/sokulmak** *He heard footsteps and dived under the table.* **4** [FLY] to fly down through the air very quickly **havada dalış yapmak** *Suddenly the plane dived to the ground.* **5** [VALUE] If a value or price dives, it suddenly becomes less. **değeri düşmek, fiyatı düşmek/azalmak**

dive² /daɪv/ *noun* [C] **1** [JUMP] a jump into water with your arms and head going in first **balıklama suya dalma/atlayış 2** [MOVEMENT] a quick movement somewhere **girme, saklanma, kafasını gizleme, sokulma, dalma 3** [VALUE] when the value or price of something suddenly becomes less **değerinde/fiyatında ani düşüş/azalma** *Share prices took a dive today.* **4** [PLACE] *informal* a place such as a bar which is considered to be dirty or of low quality **batakhane**

diver /ˈdaɪvəʳ/ *noun* [C] someone who swims under water, usually with breathing equipment **dalgıç**

diverge /daɪˈvɜːdʒ/ *verb* [I] **1** to be different, or to develop in a different way **(görüş, yol vb.) ayrılmak, uzaklaşmak, sapmak** *Over the years our interests have diverged.* **2** to go in different directions *At that point, the paths diverged.* ● **divergence** *noun* [C, U] **sapma, değişim gösterme**

diverse /daɪˈvɜːs/ *adjective* including many different types **çeşitli, türlü, farklı türleri barındıran** *a diverse collection of music*

diversify /daɪˈvɜːsɪfaɪ/ *verb* [I, T] If a business diversifies, it starts making new products or offering new services. **değiştirmek, farklılaştırmak, farklı alanda üretim yapmak, çeşitlendirmek** *Many designers are diversifying into casual wear.* ● **diversification** /daɪˌvɜːsɪfɪˈkeɪʃⁿn/ *noun* [U] **çeşitlendirme**

diversion /daɪˈvɜːʃⁿn/ *noun* **1** [CHANGE] [C, U] when something is sent somewhere different from where it was originally intended to go **farklı bir yere gönderme, başka bir yere yollama** *the diversion of money to other projects* **2** [ROUTE] [C] *UK* (*US* **detour**) a different route that is used because a road is closed **yönünü değiştirme, çevirme, saptırma, sapma 3** [ATTENTION] [C] something that takes your attention away from something else **(dikkatini) başka yöne çekme, dağıtma** *John created a diversion while the rest of us escaped.* **4** [ENTERTAINMENT] [C] an activity you do for entertainment or pleasure **eğlence, oyalayıcı şey, eğlencelik** *Reading is a pleasant diversion.*

diversity /daɪˈvɜːsəti/ *noun* [U] when many different types of things or people are included in something **çeşitlilik, farklılık, çok türlülük** *ethnic diversity*

divert /daɪˈvɜːt/ *verb* **1** [T] to send someone or something somewhere different from where they were expecting to go **başka yöne göndermek/saptırmak/çevirmek** *The plane was diverted to Stansted because of engine trouble.* **2 divert sb's attention/thoughts, etc** to take someone's attention away from something **dikkatini başka yöne çekmek, oyalamak**

⊶**divide** /dɪˈvaɪd/ *verb* **1** [SEPARATE] [I, T] to separate into parts or groups, or to make something separate into parts or groups **bölmek, ayırmak** *We divided up into teams of six.* ○ *Each school year is divided into two semesters.* **2 divide sth (up) among/between sb** to separate something into parts and give a part to each person in a group **taksim etmek, bölüştürmek, paylaştırmak** *The prize money will be divided equally among the winners.* **3** [PLACE] to separate a place into two areas **ikiye bölmek, ortadan ayırmak** *An ancient wall divides the city.* **4** [NUMBERS] [I, T] to calculate how many times a number can go into another number **bölme işlemi yapmak** *12 divided by 6 equals 2.*

5 [DISAGREE] [T] to cause people to disagree about something **ayrımcılık yaratmak, uyuşmamalarına sebep olmak** [often passive] *Council members were divided over plans to build a new stadium.*

dividend /ˈdɪvɪdend/ *noun* [C] an amount of money paid regularly to someone who owns shares in a company from the company's profits **kâr payı, hisse, pay**

divine /dɪˈvaɪn/ *adjective* relating to or coming from God or a god **ilahi, ulu, yüce**

diving /ˈdaɪvɪŋ/ *noun* [U] **1** the activity or sport of swimming under water, usually using special breathing equipment **dalma sporu, dalgıçlık 2** the activity or sport of jumping into water with your arms and head going in first **suya dalma/atlama** ⟳See also: **scuba diving**.

ˈ**diving ˌboard** *noun* [C] a raised board next to a swimming pool that you jump from into the water **(havuzda) sıçrama/atlama tahtası**

divisible /dɪˈvɪzəbl/ *adjective* **divisible by 2/7/50, etc** able to be divided by 2/7/50, etc **bölünebilir**

division /dɪˈvɪʒⁿn/ *noun* **1** [SEPARATED] [U] when something is separated into parts or groups, or the way that it is separated **paylaştırma, pay etme, paylaşma, bölüşme** *the equal division of labour among workers* **2** [ORGANIZATION] [C] one of the groups in a business or organization **bölüm, kısım, parça** *the sales division* **3** [DISAGREEMENT] [C, U] when people disagree about something **görüş ayrılığı, uyuşmazlık, anlaşmazlık** *a division over the issue of free medical care* **4** [CALCULATION] [U] when you calculate how many times one number goes into another number **bölme işlemi**

divisive /dɪˈvaɪsɪv/ *adjective* causing disagreements between people **ayrılıkçı, bölücü, nifak sokan, ayrımcılık yaratan** *a divisive issue*

divorce ...... İLE BİRLİKTE KULLANILAN KELİMELER

get a divorce ● **a divorce from sb** ● **divorce proceedings/rate/settlement**

divorce /dɪˈvɔːs/ *noun* [C, U] when two people officially stop being married **boşanma** *My parents are getting a divorce.* ● **divorce** *verb* [I, T] *She's divorcing her husband.* **boşanmak**

divorcée /dɪˌvɔːˈsiː/ (ᴜ) /-seɪ/ *noun* [C] a person, usually a woman, who is divorced **boşanmış kadın/kişi**

divorced /dɪˈvɔːst/ *adjective* **1** married before but not married now **boşanmış 2 get divorced** to officially stop being married **boşanmak; yasal olarak evliliğe son vermek** *My parents got divorced when I was seven.*

divulge /daɪˈvʌldʒ/ *verb* [T] to give secret or private information **ifşa etmek, bir sırrı açığa vurmak** *He would not divulge how much the house cost.*

Diwali /dɪˈwɑːli/ (*also* Divali) *noun* [C, U] a Hindu holiday in October/November that celebrates light and the new year **ekim/kasım aylarında ışığı ve yeni yıl kutlaması yapılan Hint tatili; Divali**

DIY /ˌdiːaɪˈwaɪ/ *noun* [U] *UK abbreviation for* do it yourself: when you do building, decorating, or repairs in your own home **evde küçük tamiratların yapılması fikrine dayanan faaliyet; Dekor, İnşaat Yap (DIY)**

dizzy /ˈdɪzi/ *adjective* feeling like everything is turning round, so that you feel ill or as if you might fall **başı dönen**

DJ /ˈdiːˌdʒeɪ/ (*also* disc jockey) *noun* [C] someone who plays music on the radio or at discos **disko ve radyoda müzik seçip çalan**

DNA /ˌdiːenˈeɪ/ *noun* [U] *abbreviation for* deoxyribonucleic acid; a chemical in the cells of living things which contains genetic information **genetik bilgi içeren hücre, DNA**

o▪**do¹** *strong form* /duː/ *weak form* /də/ *auxiliary verb*
1 QUESTIONS/NEGATIVES used with another verb to form questions and negative phrases **geniş zaman yardımcı fiili** *Do you need any help?* ○ *When does the next bus leave?* ○ *I don't know.* **2** MAKE QUESTION used in a phrase at the end of a sentence to make it into a question **bir ifade sonunda 'değil mi?' sorusunu yapmak için kullanılır** *Sarah lives near here, doesn't she?* ○ *That doesn't make any sense, does it?* **3** AVOID REPEATING used to avoid repeating a verb that has just been used **bir önceki cümledeki fiili kullanmamak için onun yerine kullanılır** *"I hate that song." "So do I."* ○ *My sister reads a lot more than I do.* **4** EMPHASIZE used to emphasize the main verb **ana fiilin anlamını kuvvetlendirmek için kullanılır** *He does like you, he's just shy.* ○ *Do come and visit us soon.*

o▪**do²** /duː/ *verb past tense* **did**, *past participle* **done**
1 ACTION/JOB [T] to perform an action or job **icra etmek, etmek** *Go upstairs and do your homework.* ○ *What are you doing this weekend?* ○ *What does she do?* (= What is her job?) **2** MAKE [T] to make or prepare something **yapmak, hazırlamak** *Our printer only does black and white copies.* ○ *Max's Cafe does great sandwiches.* **3 do badly/well, etc** to be unsuccessful/successful, etc **başarılı/başarısız olmak** *Sam did very well in her exams.* **4 do biology/French/history, etc** *UK* to study biology/French/history, etc **biyoloji/Fransızca/tarih çalışmak/tahsil etmek 5 do your hair/make-up, etc** to make your hair/make-up, etc look nice **saçını/makyajını yapmak 6 do sb good** to have a good effect on someone **iyi etki yapmak, iyi gelmek** *A holiday would do you good.* **7 do damage/harm, etc** to cause damage/harm, etc **zarar/hasar/ziyan vermek** *Luckily the fire didn't do much damage.* **8 will do** will be satisfactory **yetecek, kâfi gelecek/gelir** *You don't have to pay now, next week will do.* **9** SPEED [T] to travel at a particular speed **belli bir hızda ilerlemek/gitmek/seyahat etmek** *For most of the journey we were doing 70 miles an hour.*
do away with sth *phrasal verb* to get rid of something, or to stop using something **kurtulmak, halletmek, üstesinden gelmek, çözmek, ortadan kaldırmak, yok etmek** *We may do away with the school uniform soon.*
do away with sb *phrasal verb informal* to kill someone **öldürmek, icabına bakmak, yok etmek**
do sb in *phrasal verb informal* **1** to make someone extremely tired **ziyadesiyle yormak, yorgun düşürmek** *All that exercise has done me in.* **2** to attack or kill someone **saldırmak veya öldürmek**
do sth over *phrasal verb US* to do something again because you did not do it well the first time **tekrar yapmak, yeniden yapmak**
do sth up *phrasal verb* **1** *mainly UK* to fasten something **kapamak, iliklemek, örtmek** *Do your coat up. It's cold outside.* **2** to repair or decorate a building so that it looks attractive **güzelleştirmek için tadilat yapmak/dekore etmek**
do with sth *phrasal verb* used to ask where someone put something **Ne yaptın? Nereye koydun?** *What did you do with my keys?*
do with sb/sth *phrasal verb* **1 could do with sb/sth** to need or want someone or something **I could do with a few days off work.** **2 be/have to do with sb/sth** to be about or connected with someone or something *My question has to do with yesterday's homework.*
do without (sb/sth) *phrasal verb* to manage without having someone or something **...sız/siz yapabilmek, idare etmek** *Jack's the kind of player we can't do without.*

do³ /duː/ *noun* [C] *UK informal* a party **parti, eğlence** *Are you going to the Christmas do?*

docile /'dəʊsaɪl/ ⑤ /'dɑːsᵊl/ *adjective* A docile person or animal is quiet and easily controlled. **halim selim, yumuşak başlı, uysal, huysuz olmayan**

dock¹ /dɒk/ *noun* [C] **1** the place where ships stop and goods are taken off or put on **rıhtım, dok 2 the dock** *UK* (*US* **the stand**) the place in a law court where the person who is accused of a crime sits **mahkemede sanıkların oturduğu yer; sanık/suçlu locası**

dock² /dɒk/ *verb* **1** [I, T] If a ship docks, it arrives at a dock. **rıhtıma yanaşmak 2 dock sb's pay/wages** to take away part of the money you pay someone, usually as a punishment **ücretinden/maaşından ceza kesintisi yapmak; maaşının bir kısmına haciz koymak**

▷ **doctor** ...... İLE BİRLİKTE KULLANILAN KELİMELER
consult/see a doctor ● **go to** the doctor's ● a doctor's **appointment**

o▪**doctor¹** /'dɒktəʳ/ *noun* **1** [C] a person whose job is to treat people who have an illness or injury **hekim** *I have to go to the doctor's for a check-up.* **2 Doctor of Philosophy/Divinity, etc** someone who has the most advanced type of qualification from a university **doktora derecesi; bilim doktoru** ⊃See also: spin doctor.

doctor² /'dɒktəʳ/ *verb* [T] to change something, usually in a dishonest way **tahrif etmek, değiştirmek, çarpıtmak** *The photo in his passport had been doctored.*

doctorate /'dɒktᵊrət/ *noun* [C] the most advanced type of qualification from a university **doktora derecesi** *He has a doctorate in physics from Cambridge.*

doctrine /'dɒktrɪn/ *noun* [C, U] a belief or set of beliefs taught by a religious or political group **öğreti, doktrin** *Christian doctrine*

▷ **document** ...... İLE BİRLİKTE KULLANILAN KELİMELER
draw up/produce a document ● **in** a document ● a document **about/concerning/on** sth

o▪**document** /'dɒkjəmənt/ *noun* [C] **1** a piece of paper with official information on it **evrak, belge, doküman, vesika** *Please sign and return the insurance documents enclosed.* **2** a piece of text produced electronically on a computer **bilgisayarda elektronik ortamda oluşturulan belge** *How do I create a new document?*

documentary /ˌdɒkjə'mentᵊri/ *noun* [C] a film or television programme that gives facts about a real situation or real people **belgesel** *a TV documentary about the Russian Revolution*

documentation /ˌdɒkjəmen'teɪʃᵊn/ *noun* [U] **1** pieces of paper containing official information **belgeleme, belgelerle kanıtlama 2** the instructions written for a piece of computer software or equipment **bilgisayar yazılımı için yazılan talimatlar**

docusoap /'dɒkjuːsəʊp/ *noun* [C] *UK* an entertaining television programme about the lives of real people who live in the same place or who do the same thing **aynı yerde yaşayan veya aynı işi yapan insanların hayatlarını konu alan tv eğlence programı**

doddle /'dɒdl/ *noun UK* **be a doddle** *informal* to be very easy **çok kolay/çocuk oyuncağı olmak** *This computer's a doddle to use.*

dodge¹ /dɒdʒ/ *verb* **1** [I, T] to move quickly to avoid someone or something **yana çekilerek/hareket ederek kaçmak/kaçınmak/kurtulmak; sakınmak** *He managed to dodge past the security guard.* **2** [T] to avoid talking about something or doing something you should do **kurtulmak, yırtmak, es geçmek, kaytarmak; hile/oyun/kurnazlıkla atlatmak** *The minister dodged questions about his relationship with the actress.*

dodge² /dɒdʒ/ noun [C] when you avoid something, usually in a dishonest way **kaytarma, atlatma, hile/ oyun etme, kaçınma** a tax dodge

dodgy /'dɒdʒi/ adjective UK informal bad, or not able to be trusted **kötü, tehlikeli, riskli** His friend's a bit dodgy.

doe /dəʊ/ noun [C] a female deer **dişi geyik**

o͙**does** strong form /dʌz/ weak form /dəz/ present simple he/ she/it of do **yapmak' fiilinin üçüncü tekil şahıslarla kullanılan hali**

o͙**doesn't** /'dʌzⁿnt/ short for does not **yapmak' fiilinin üçüncü tekil şahıslarla kullanılan halinin olumsuz şeklinin kısaltması** Keith doesn't like mushrooms or garlic.

o͙**dog¹** /dɒg/ noun [C] an animal with fur, four legs and a tail that is kept as a pet, or trained to guard buildings and guide blind people **köpek** Let's take the dog for a walk. ⊃See also: guide dog, hot dog.

dog² /dɒg/ verb [T] **dogging**, past **dogged** to cause someone or something trouble for a long time **uzun süre sıkıntı vermek/dert açmak/sorun çıkarmak** [often passive] His football career has been dogged by injury.

dog-eared /'dɒgɪəd/ adjective If a piece of paper or a book is dog-eared, its corners are folded and torn from being touched a lot. **köşeleri kıvrılmış/yıpranmış**

dogged /'dɒgɪd/ adjective [always before noun] continuing to do or believe in something, although it is difficult **azimli, inatçı, sebatkâr, vazgeçmeyen, yılmayan, peşini bırakmayan** dogged determination ● **doggedly** adverb **inatçı bir biçimde**

doghouse /'dɒghaʊs/ noun **1** [C] US (UK kennel) a small building for a dog to sleep in **köpek kulübesi 2 be in the doghouse** If you are in the doghouse, you have done something to make people angry or annoyed with you. **kızdırmak, içerletmek, sinirlendirmek**

dogma /'dɒgmə/ noun [C, U] a belief or set of beliefs that people are expected to accept as the truth, without ever doubting them **sorgulamadan kabul edilen inançlar manzumesi** political dogma

dogmatic /dɒg'mætɪk/ adjective not willing to accept other ideas or opinions because you think yours are right **dediğim dedikçi, başka fikirleri kabul etmeyen, kestirip atan, sadece kendi fikirlerini doğru kabul eden**

dogsbody /'dɒgzbɒdi/ noun [C] UK someone who has to do boring jobs for someone else **angarya/ sıkıcı işleri yapan**

doing /'duːɪŋ/ noun **1 be sb's doing** to have been done or caused by someone **yapılmış olmak veya başkasınca sebep olunan** The problem is not all his doing. **2 take some/a lot of doing** informal to be difficult to do **çok emek/çaba gerektirmek, yapılması zor olmak** It took some doing to convince him to come.

doldrums /'dɒldrəmz/ noun **1 in the doldrums a** If a business or job is in the doldrums, it is not very successful and nothing new is happening in it. **durgun, durağan, pek fazla iş yapmayan, sinek avlayan b** UK sad and with no energy or enthusiasm **canı sıkkın, keyfi kaçık, keyifsiz**

dole /dəʊl/ verb

dole sth out phrasal verb to give something, especially money, to several people or in large amounts **dağıtmak, vermek, büyük miktarlarda dağıtmak**

the dole /dəʊl/ noun UK money that the government gives someone when they are unemployed **işsizlik parası** He's been on the dole for years.

doleful /'dəʊlfⁿl/ adjective very sad **sıkıntılı, üzüntülü, kederli** doleful eyes

doll /dɒl/ noun [C] a child's toy that looks like a small person **oyuncak bebek**

o͙**dollar** /'dɒləʳ/ noun [C] the unit of money used in the US, Canada, and some other countries; $ **dolar** a hundred dollars/$100 ○ a **dollar bill**

dollop /'dɒləp/ noun [C] a lump or mass of a soft substance, usually food **(yiyecek) topak, parça, bölüm** a dollop of cream

dolphin /'dɒlfɪn/ noun [C] an intelligent animal that lives in the sea, breathes air, and looks like a large, smooth, grey fish **yunus balığı**

domain /dəʊ'meɪn/ noun [C] a particular area, activity, or subject that someone controls or deals with **uzmanlık/ilgi/etkinlik alanı** The garden is his domain. ○ This information should be **in the public domain** (= known by the public).

do'main ,name noun [C] the part of an email or website address that shows the name of the organization that the address belongs to **e-posta veya internette isme/ şirkete tescilli adres**

dome /dəʊm/ noun [C] a curved, round roof of a building **kubbe ● domed** adjective a domed roof **kubbeli**

domestic /də'mestɪk/ adjective **1** [HOME] relating to the home and family relationships **ev/aile ilişkilerine ilişkin** domestic violence ○ What are his domestic arrangements? **2** [COUNTRY] inside one country and not international **ülke içi, dahili** a domestic flight **3** [ANIMAL] A domestic animal is kept as a pet. **evcil**

domesticated /də'mestɪkeɪtɪd/ adjective **1** A domesticated animal is kept as a pet or lives on a farm. **evcilleştirilmiş 2** A domesticated person is able or willing to do cleaning, cooking, and other jobs in the home. **evcimen, ev işi yapan, evine bağlı**

domesticity /,dɒmes'tɪsəti/ noun [U] life at home looking after a house and family **evcimenlik, evine ve ailesine bağlılık**

dominance /'dɒmɪnəns/ noun [U] power, influence, and control **egemenlik, hakimiyet, kontrol** the company's dominance in the software industry

dominant /'dɒmɪnənt/ adjective **1** main or most important **ana/esas, en önemli** Her mother was the dominant influence in her life. **2** strongest and wanting to take control **güçlü ve kontrolü elinde tutmak isteyen** a dominant older brother

dominate /'dɒmɪneɪt/ verb [I, T] **1** to control or have power over someone or something **egemen/hakim olmak; idaresi altına almak** The US continues to dominate the world politically. **2** to be the largest, most important, or most noticeable part of something **en büyük/ en önemli/en dikkate değer olmak** The cathedral dominates the skyline.

┌───┐
│ 🔾 **domination** .... İLE BİRLİKTE KULLANILAN KELİMELER │
└───┘

global/world domination ● domination **of** sth ● domination **over** sb/sth

domination /,dɒmɪ'neɪʃⁿn/ noun [U] great power and control over someone or something else **egemenlik, hakimiyet, idare** world domination

domineering /,dɒmɪ'nɪərɪŋ/ adjective trying to control people too much **hükmedici, otoriter, despotça davranan, baskıcı, zorba** a domineering mother

dominion /də'mɪnjən/ noun [U] formal the power and right to control someone or something **hakimiyet, egemenlik, idare**

domino /'dɒmɪnəʊ/ *noun* [C] *plural* **dominoes** a small, rectangular object that has spots on it, used in a game **domino** ● **dominoes** *noun* [U] a game played using dominoes **domino oyunu**

don /dɒn/ *verb* [T] **donning**, *past* **donned** *formal* to put on a piece of clothing such as a coat or hat **giymek, giyinmek**

donate /dəʊ'neɪt/ *verb* [T] **1** to give money or goods to a person or organization that needs help **bağışlamak, hibe etmek, vermek** *Four hundred new computers were donated to the college.* **2** to allow some of your blood or part of your body to be used for medical purposes **organ/kan bağışlamak**

🧩 **donation** ...... İLE BİRLİKTE KULLANILAN KELİMELER

make a donation ● a donation **of** [\$50/food/clothing, etc] ● a donation to sb/sth

donation /dəʊ'neɪʃ°n/ *noun* [C, U] when money or goods are given to help a person or organization **bağış, yardım, hibe, teberru** *Would you like to make a donation?*

⚬ **done¹** /dʌn/ *adjective* **1** finished or completed **bitirilmiş, halledilmiş, tamamlanmış** *Did you get your essay done in time?* **2** cooked enough **iyi pişmiş** *The potatoes aren't quite done yet.* ⊃See also: easier (**easy²**) said than done, **well-done**.

done² /dʌn/ *exclamation* something that you say to show that you accept someone's offer **Kabul!' 'Oldu!' 'Tamam!' 'Pekâla!'** *"I'll give you 50 pounds for the whole lot." "Done!"*

done³ /dʌn/ *past participle of* do **yapmak' fiilinin üçüncü hali**

donkey /'dɒŋki/ *noun* [C] **1** an animal that looks like a small horse with long ears **eşek, merkep 2 for donkey's years** *UK informal* for a long time **yıllardır, çoktandır**

donkey

donkey ,work *noun* [U] *UK informal* the most boring or difficult parts of a job **angarya, ayak işi, hamallık, bir işin en zor ve sıkıcı bölümü**

donor /'dəʊnə'/ *noun* [C] **1** someone who gives some of their blood or part of their body to be used for medical purposes **verici, donör, organ/kan bağışlayan kimse 2** someone who gives money or goods to a person or organization that needs help **bağışta bulunan kimse** *Ten thousand dollars was given by an anonymous donor.* ⊃See also: blood donor.

⚬ **don't** /dəʊnt/ *short for* do not **do not' fiilinin kısaltılmış hali** *Please don't talk during the exam.*

donut /'dəʊnʌt/ *noun* [C] another US spelling of doughnut (= a small, round, fried cake) **küçük, yuvarlak kızartılmış kek**

doodle

doodle /'du:dl/ *verb* [I, T] to draw little pictures or patterns on something without thinking about it **karalamak, rasgele çiziktirmek** ● **doodle** *noun* [C] **karalama (çizim)**

doom /du:m/ *noun* [U] **1** death, destruction, and other unpleasant events that cannot be avoided **kötü akibet/yazgı, ölüm, önüne geçilemez olay; kör talih** *a horrible sense of doom* **2 doom and gloom** unhappiness and feeling no hope for the future **mutsuzluk ve ümitsizlik** *Life's not all doom and gloom, you know.*

doomed /du:md/ *adjective* certain to fail, die, or have problems **alnına yazılı olan, kötü talihli, mahvolmaya/ölmeye/başarısızlığa mahkum** *Their marriage was doomed from the start.*

🧩 **door** ...... İLE BİRLİKTE KULLANILAN KELİMELER

close/open/shut/slam a door ● **knock on** a door ● **be at the** door

⚬ **door** /dɔː'/ *noun* [C] **1** the part of a building, room, vehicle, or piece of furniture that you open or close to get inside it or out of it **kapı** *Please shut the door behind you.* ○ *I can't open the door.* ○ *There's someone at the door.* **2** the space in a wall where you enter a building or room **giriş, antre, kapı aralığı** *He led us through the door to the rear of the building.* **3 behind closed doors** privately and not in public **kapalı kapılar ardında; gizliden gizliye; gizli saklı** *Most of the deals were done behind closed doors.* **4 two/three, etc doors away** in a place that is two/three, etc houses away **bir kaç ev ötede** *We live just a few doors away from the Smiths.* ⊃See also: trap door.

doorbell /'dɔː.bel/ *noun* [C] a button that you press next to a door that makes a noise to let someone know that you are there **kapı zili**

doorknob /'dɔː.nɒb/ *noun* [C] a round object on a door that you hold and turn to open or close it **kapı kolu/tokmağı**

doorman /'dɔː.mən/ *noun* [C] *plural* **doormen** a man who stands near the doors of a large building such as a hotel to watch and help the visitors **(otel) etrafı kolaçan eden ve ziyaretçilere yardım eden kapı görevlisi**

doormat /'dɔː.mæt/ *noun* [C] **1** a piece of thick material on the floor by a door used to clean your shoes before entering a building **paspas 2** *informal* someone who allows other people to treat them very badly **kendisine kötü muamele edilmesine izin veren kimse**

doorstep /'dɔː.step/ *noun* [C] **1** a step in front of the door of a building **eşik, kapı girişi 2 on your doorstep** very near to where you live **hemen yanıbaşında, çok yakında, az ilerde** *They have the Rocky Mountains on their doorstep.*

door-to-door /ˌdɔː.tə'dɔː'/ *adjective* [always before noun], *adverb* **1** going from one house or building to another **evden eve** *The hotel offers a door-to-door service to the airport.* **2** going to every house in an area **kapı kapı/ev ev dolaşarak/dolaşan** *a door-to-door salesman*

doorway /'dɔː.weɪ/ *noun* [C] an entrance to a building or room through a door **kapı aralığı, giriş** *She waited in the doorway while I ran back inside.*

dope¹ /dəʊp/ *noun informal* **1** [U] an illegal drug taken for pleasure, especially cannabis (= drug that you smoke) **esrar, uyuşturucu madde 2** [C] *US informal* a stupid or silly person **budala, aptal, salak, ahmak**

dope² /dəʊp/ *verb* **1** [T] to give a drug to a person or animal, usually so that they become sleepy **uyutucu/uyuşturucu ilaç vermek 2 be doped up** to have a lot of a drug in your body affecting your behaviour **dopink yapmak**

dork /dɔːk/ *noun* [C] *mainly US informal* a stupid or silly person **budala, aptal, salak, ahmak**

dormant /ˈdɔːmənt/ *adjective* not active or developing now, but possibly active in the future **faal olmayan, uyku hâlinde, geçici hareketsizlik** *a dormant volcano*

dormitory /ˈdɔːmɪtᵊri/ (*also* **dorm** *informal*) *noun* [C] **1** a large bedroom with a lot of beds, especially in a school **yatakhane 2** *US* (*UK* **hall of residence**) a large building at a college or university where students live **öğrenci yurdu**

dosage /ˈdəʊsɪdʒ/ *noun* [C] how much medicine you should take and how often you should take it **miktar, dozaj** *the recommended daily dosage*

🧩 dose ...... İLE BİRLİKTE KULLANILAN KELİMELER

a **high/low** dose • a **fatal/lethal** dose • a dose **of** sth

dose /dəʊs/ *noun* [C] **1** a measured amount of medicine that is taken at one time or during a period of time **doz, miktar** *What is the recommended dose?* ○ *a lethal dose* **2 a dose of** sth an amount of something, often something unpleasant (**hoş olmayan şey**) **miktar, biraz** *a dose of bad news* ● **dose** *verb* [T] to give someone a drug or medicine **ilaç/uyuşturucu vermek**

dosh /dɒʃ/ *noun* [U] *UK informal* money **para, mangır**

doss /dɒs/ (*also* **doss down**) *verb* [I] *UK informal* to sleep somewhere temporarily, such as on the floor **bulunduğu yerde uyuya kalmak, uyuklamak, şekerleme yapmak** *Can I doss at your house tonight?*
doss about/around *phrasal verb UK informal* to spend your time doing very little **zamanı çok az şey yaparak geçirmek**

dossier /ˈdɒsieɪ/ *noun* [C] a set of documents that contain information about a particular person or subject **dosya** *The officers compiled a dossier on the case.*

dot¹ /dɒt/ *noun* **1** [C] a small, round mark or spot **nokta, benek** *a pattern of blue and green dots* **2** [U] *spoken* the spoken form of '·' in an internet address **internet adresinde noktanın okunuşu** *dot co dot uk* (= .co.uk) **3 on the dot** at that exact time **tam zamanında/vaktinde** *We have to leave at 7.30 on the dot.*

dot² /dɒt/ *verb* [T] **dotting**, *past* **dotted 1** to put a dot or dots on something **nokta koymak 2** (*also* **dot around**) to be spread across an area **dağılmak, yayılmak, kaplamak** *The company has 43 hotels dotted around the UK.*

dot.com /dɒtˈkɒm/ (*also* **dotcom**) *noun* [C] a company that does most of its business on the Internet **internette şirket adresi uzantısı** *a dot.com company/millionaire*

dote /dəʊt/ *verb*
dote on sb *phrasal verb* to love someone completely and believe that they are perfect **üzerine titremek, çok sevmek/değer vermek** *She absolutely dotes on that little boy.*

doting /ˈdəʊtɪŋ/ *adjective* [always before noun] extremely loving and caring **aşırı derecede düşkün, çok seven, üzerine titreyen** *doting parents*

dotted line *noun* **1** [C] a line of printed dots on a piece of paper **noktalardan oluşan çizgi 2 sign on the dotted line** to make an agreement official by writing your name on it **imzalayarak resmi bir anlaşma yapmak**

dotty /ˈdɒti/ *adjective UK* slightly crazy **yarım akıllı, hafif kaçık** *a dotty old woman*

o⸻**double¹** /ˈdʌbl/ *adjective* **1** TWO PARTS having two parts of the same type or size **çift, iki kat** *double doors* ○ *My number is four, two, six, double two, double two* (= 426225). **2** TWICE THE SIZE twice the amount, number, or size of something **iki misli, çift olan** *a double vodka* ○ *a double hamburger* **3** FOR TWO made to be used by two people **iki kişilik** *a double bed/room*

double² /ˈdʌbl/ *verb* [I, T] to increase and become twice the original size or amount, or to make something do this **ikiye katla(n)mak; ölçü veya miktarını artırmak** *Our house has almost doubled in value.*
double (up) as sth If something doubles up as something else, it also has the purpose of that thing. **...olarak da kullanılmak, aynı işlevi görmek** *The school's gymnasium doubles up as a dining room.*
double back *phrasal verb* to turn and go back in the direction that you have come from **dönüp geldiği yöne gitmek**
double (sb) over/up *phrasal verb* to suddenly bend your body forward, usually because of pain or laughter, or to make someone do this **iki büklüm olmak/yapmak**

double³ /ˈdʌbl/ *noun* **1** [C, U] something that is twice the usual amount, number, or size **iki misli 2 sb's double** someone who looks exactly the same as someone else **ikiz, eş**

double⁴ /ˈdʌbl/ *determiner* twice as much or as many **iki kat, çift** *Our new house is double the size of our old one.*

double-barrelled *UK* (*US* **double-barreled**) /ˌdʌblˈbærəld/ *adjective* **1** A double-barrelled gun has two of the cylindrical parts that bullets come out of. **çift namlulu, çifte 2** *UK* A double-barrelled name is two names joined together. **bitişik iki isimli**

double 'bass *noun* [C] a wooden musical instrument with four strings, like a very large violin (= instrument you hold against your neck), that you play while standing up or sitting on a high chair **kemana benzer dört telli büyük ahşap müzik aleti; kontrabas**

double 'bed *noun* [C] a bed big enough for two people to sleep in **ikiz yatak**

double-breasted /ˌdʌblˈbrestɪd/ *adjective* A double-breasted jacket or coat has two sets of buttons to fasten at the front. **kruvaze ceket, çift düğmeli ceket**

double-check /ˌdʌblˈtʃek/ *verb* [I, T] to examine something again so that you are certain it is safe or correct **iki kez kontrol etmek/gözden geçirmek**

double-click /ˌdʌblˈklɪk/ *verb* [I, T] to quickly press a button twice on a mouse (= small computer control) to make something happen on a computer screen **çift tıklamak** *Double-click on the icon to start the program.*

double-cross /ˌdʌblˈkrɒs/ *verb* [T] to deceive someone who you should be helping **kazık atmak, ihanet etmek**

double-decker /ˌdʌblˈdekər/ *noun* [C] *UK* a tall bus with two levels **çift katlı otobüs** *a double-decker bus*

double-glazing /ˌdʌblˈɡleɪzɪŋ/ *noun* [U] *UK* windows that have two layers of glass to keep a building warm or quiet **çift camlı pencere**

doubles /ˈdʌblz/ *noun* [U] a game, especially tennis, in which two people play together against two other people **teniste çiftler karşılaşması**

double 'standard *noun* [C] when people are given different treatment in an unfair way **çifte standart/uygulama/muamele/işlem** [usually plural] *Critics accused the government of double standards in its policies.*

double 'take *noun* [C] when you quickly look at someone or something a second time because you cannot believe you have seen something or heard something **gözlerine inanamama; ikinci kez dikkatle bakma** [usually singular] *He did a double take when he saw her.*

doubly /ˈdʌbli/ *adverb* twice as much, or very much more **iki bakımdan; çift taraftan** *It is doubly important to drink plenty of water when it's hot.*

---

doubt ...... İLE BİRLİKTE KULLANILAN KELİMELER

express/have/raise doubts • a **nagging/serious** doubt • doubts **about** sth

---

◦⟞**doubt¹** /daʊt/ *noun* **1** [C, U] when you are not certain about something, or do not trust someone or something **şüphe, kuşku** *I have some doubts about his ability to do the job.* **2 have no doubt** to be certain **hiç şüphesiz, hiç kuşkusuz, herhalde** [+ (that)] *I have no doubt that I made the right decision.* **3 there's no doubt** it is certain **kesin, kuşkusuz, şüphesiz, su götürmez** [+ (that)] *There is no doubt that he's a good player.* **4 be in doubt** to not be certain **kuşkulanmak, şüphe duymak** *The future of the project is in doubt.* **5 cast doubt on sth** to make something seem uncertain **kuşkuya düşürmek, kuşkulu hale getirmek** *Witnesses have cast doubt on the suspect's innocence.* **6 without (a) doubt** certainly **hiç şüphesiz, kesinlikle** *She is without doubt a great musician.* **7 no doubt** used to say that something is very likely **şüphesiz, kesinlikle, kuşkusuz** *No doubt she'll spend the money on new clothes.* ⊃See also: give sb the **benefit¹** of the doubt, beyond/without a **shadow¹** of a doubt.

◦⟞**doubt²** /daʊt/ *verb* [T] **1** to feel uncertain about something or think that something is not probable **şüphelenmek, kuşku duymak, emin olmamak** [+ (that)] *I doubt that I'll get the job.* ○ *I doubt if/whether he'll win.* **2** to not believe someone or something **inanmamak, şüphelenmek** *Do you have any reason to doubt her?*

doubtful /'daʊtfᵊl/ *adjective* **1** not probable **şüpheli, kuşkulu** *It's doubtful if/whether he'll be able to come.* ○ [+ (that)] *It's doubtful that anyone survived the fire.* **2** not feeling certain about something **kesin olmayan, şüphe duyulan, belirsiz** • **doubtfully** *adverb* **şüpheyle**

doubtless /'daʊtləs/ *adverb* probably **muhtemelen, olasılık dahilinde, hiç kuşkusuz** *He will doubtless be criticized by journalists.*

dough /dəʊ/ *noun* [U] a thick mixture of flour and liquid used to make foods such as bread or pastry **hamur**

doughnut (also US **donut**) /'dəʊnʌt/ *noun* [C] a small, round, fried cake, sometimes with a hole in the middle **halka biçiminde lokma, doğnat**

doughnut

dour /dʊəʳ/, /daʊəʳ/ *adjective* unfriendly and serious **aksi, çekilmez, zıt, ters, nakıs** *a dour expression*

douse /daʊs/ *verb* [T] **1** to pour a lot of liquid over someone or something **ıslatmak, üzerine dökmek, boca etmek** *The dessert was doused with brandy and set alight.* **2** to stop a fire burning by putting a lot of water on it **yangını söndürmek** *to douse the flames/fire*

dove¹ /dʌv/ *noun* [C] a white bird, sometimes used as a symbol of peace **güvercin**

dove² /dəʊv/ *US past tense of* dive **dalmak' fiilinin ikinci hali**

dowdy /'daʊdi/ *adjective* plain and not fashionable **kılıksız, hırpani, biçimsiz**

◦⟞**down¹** /daʊn/ *adverb, preposition* **1** LOWER PLACE towards or in a lower place **altta, alta/aşağı doğru** *The kids ran down the hill to the gate.* ○ *I bent down to have a look.* **2** LEVEL/AMOUNT towards or at a lower level or amount **belli miktarın altında/altına inen** *Can you turn the music down?* ○ *Slow down so they can see us.* **3** SURFACE moving from above and onto a surface **yuka-**

rıdan bir yüzeyin üzerine doğru/üzerinde *I sat down and turned on the TV.* ○ *Put that box down on the floor.* **4** DIRECTION in or towards a particular direction, usually south **güneye doğru/güneyde; aşağı, aşağı doğru** *Pete's moved down to London.* **5 down the road/river, etc** along or further along the road/river, etc **nehir/yol boyunca** *There's another pub further down the street.* **6 note/write, etc sth down** to write something on a piece of paper **not almak/tutmak; çalakalem yazmak** *Can I just take down your phone number?* **7** STOMACH inside your stomach **midede, doğru/midede** *He's had food poisoning and can't keep anything down.* **8 be down to sb** UK to be someone's responsibility or decision **(sorumluluk/yükümlülük)** *...e düşmek, iş başa düşmek I've done all I can now, the rest is down to you.* **9 come/go down with sth** to become ill **yatağa düşmek; yatak, döşek hasta olmak** *The whole family came down with food poisoning.* **10 down under** *informal* Australia, or in Australia **Avustralya; Avustralya'da**

down² /daʊn/ *adjective* [never before noun] **1** sad **üzgün, kederli, tadı kaçmış** *What's the matter? You look a bit down today.* **2** If a computer or machine is down, it is temporarily not working. **bozuk, geçici bir süre çalışmayan** *The network was down all morning.*

down³ /daʊn/ *noun* [U] soft feathers, often used as a warm filling for bed covers **yumuşak tüy** ⊃See also: ups and downs.

down⁴ /daʊn/ *verb* [T] *informal* to drink something quickly **kafaya dikmek, bir çırpıda içmek**

down-and-out /,daʊnən'aʊt/ *adjective* If someone is down-and-out, they have no money, possessions, or opportunities. **sefil, derbeder, biçare** • **down-and-out** *noun* [C] **parasızlık, yoksulluk**

downcast /'daʊnkɑːst/ *adjective* **1** sad or disappointed **üzgün, kederli, yıkılmış 2** If someone's eyes are downcast, they are looking down. **(göz) yere/aşağı bakan**

downgrade /,daʊn'greɪd/ *verb* [T] to move someone or something to a less important position **(makam, mevki, rütbe, derece) indirmek, azaltmak, tenzili rütbe yapmak**

downhearted /,daʊn'hɑːtɪd/ *adjective* sad or disappointed **kalbi buruk, üzgün, kolu kanadı kırık**

downhill¹ /,daʊn'hɪl/ *adverb* **1** towards the bottom of a hill or slope **yokuş aşağı, tepeden aşağı** *It's so much easier cycling downhill.* **2 go downhill** to gradually become worse **gittikçe kötüleşmek, kötüye gitmek, tepetaklak olmak** *After his wife died, his health started to go downhill.*

downhill² /,daʊn'hɪl/ *adjective* **1** leading down towards the bottom of a hill or slope **yokuş aşağı** *downhill skiing* **2 be all downhill; be downhill all the way** to be much easier **oldukça kolay, çocuk oyuncağı** *From now on it will be all downhill.*

download¹ /,daʊn'ləʊd/ ⑇ /'daʊn,ləʊd/ *verb* [T] to copy computer programs, music or other information electronically using the Internet **(bilgisayarda) bilgiyi indirmek/yüklemek** *You can download this software free from their website.* ⊃See study page The Web and the Internet on page Centre 36. • **downloadable** *adjective* able to be downloaded **indirilebilir/yüklenebilir** *downloadable files/images*

download² /'daʊnləʊd/ *noun* [C] a computer program, music or other information that has been or can be downloaded **yükleme/indirme programı**

downmarket /,daʊn'mɑːkɪt/ *adjective* UK cheap and low quality **kelepir, çok ucuz, harcı âlem, ucuz ve kalitesiz**

,**down 'payment** noun [C] the first amount of money that you pay when you buy something expensive and pay over a period of time **ilk ödeme, ön ödeme, ilk taksit** *a down payment on a house*

downplay /ˌdaʊn'pleɪ/ verb [T] to make something seem less important or bad than it really is **olduğundan daha kötü ve önemsiz duruma getirmek, kötüleş- tirmek** *The report downplays the risks of nuclear power.*

downpour /'daʊnpɔːʳ/ noun [C] when it suddenly rains a lot **sağanak yağış, şiddetli yağmur**

downright /'daʊnraɪt/ adverb **downright dangerous/ rude/ugly, etc** extremely dangerous/rude/ugly, etc **son derece tehlikeli/kaba/çirkin**

downside /'daʊnsaɪd/ noun [no plural] the disadvantage of a situation **sakınca, mahsur, dezavantaj** *The downside of living in a city is all the pollution.*

downsize /'daʊnˌsaɪz/ verb [I, T] to make a company or organization smaller by reducing the number of people who work there (**şirket, kuruluş vb.) küçültmek, çalışanların sayısını azaltmak** ● **downsizing** noun [U] **küçülme (şirket)**

Down's syndrome /'daʊnzˌsɪndrəʊm/ noun [U] a con- dition that some babies are born with which affects their physical and mental development **Down send- romu**

downstairs /ˌdaʊn'steəz/ adverb on or to a lower level of a building **merdivenlerden aşağıya doğru/aşa- ğıda** *She went downstairs to see who was at the door.* ● **downstairs** adjective *a downstairs bathroom* **aşağı**

downstream /ˌdaʊn'striːm/ adverb in the direction that the water in a river is moving in **nehrin akış yönüne**

down-to-earth /ˌdaʊntuː'ɜːθ/ adjective practical and realistic **pratik ve gerçekçi, hayalci olmayan**

downtown /ˌdaʊn'taʊn/ adjective [always before noun], adverb US in or to the central part or main business area of a city **şehir merkezine/merkezinde** *down- town Chicago*

downtrodden /'daʊnˌtrɒdᵊn/ adjective treated badly and without respect from other people **ezilmiş, haksız- lığa uğramış, çiğnenmiş, ayaklar altına alınmış** *downtrodden workers*

downturn /'daʊntɜːn/ noun [C] when a business or economy becomes less successful **düşüş, işte başarı- sızlık, azalma** *There has been a sharp downturn in sales.*

downwards (also US **downward**) /'daʊnwədz/ adverb towards a lower place or level **aşağıya/alt tarafa doğru** *The river slopes downwards to the river.* ● **down- ward** adjective ⊃See also: a downward spiral. **aşağı doğru**

downwind /ˌdaʊn'wɪnd/ adjective, adverb in the direc- tion that the wind is blowing **rüzgârın esme yönüne doğru/yönünde**

dowry /'daʊri/ noun [C] money that a woman's family gives to the man she is marrying in some cultures (**bazı kültürlerde kız tarafınca erkeğe verilen) para, çeyiz, drahoma**

doze /dəʊz/ verb [I] to sleep lightly **kestirmek, şeker- leme yapmak** *Grandma was dozing in front of the TV.* **doze off** phrasal verb to gradually start sleeping, usually during the day **içi geçmek, gözleri kaymak** *He dozed off during the film.*

dozen /'dʌzᵊn/ noun, determiner **1** twelve, or a group of twelve **düzine** *There were about a dozen people at the*

party. **2 dozens** informal a lot **düzinelerce, çok** *She's got dozens of friends.* ⊃See also: a dime a dozen.

o⌐ **Dr** written abbreviation for doctor **doktor** *Dr Paul Thomas*

drab /dræb/ adjective without colour and boring to look at **renksiz, kasvetli, albenisi olmayan, sıkıcı, tek- düze drab, grey buildings**

draconian /drə'kəʊniən/ adjective very severe **çok ciddi/şiddetli** *draconian laws*

draft¹ /drɑːft/ noun **1** [C] a piece of writing or a plan that is not yet in its finished form **taslak, eskiz, müsvedde** *He made several changes to the first draft.* **2 the draft** US when people are told that they must join the armed forces **askere alma, asker celbi, celp 3** [C] US spelling of draught (= a current of cold air in a room) **hava akımı, cereyan, soğuk hava akımı**

draft .... İLE BİRLİKTE KULLANILAN KELİMELER
draft **a constitution/legislation/a letter/a proposal**

draft² /drɑːft/ verb [T] **1** to produce a piece of writing or a plan that you intend to change later **taslak hazırla- mak, müsvedde yapmak, eskiz çıkarmak** *to draft a letter* **2** to order someone to join the armed forces **askere celp etmek, askere almak/sevketmek draft sb in/draft sb into sth** phrasal verb UK to bring someone somewhere to do a particular job **birine belli bir iş yaptırmak/görev vermek için bir yere götür- mek** *Extra police were drafted in to stop the demonstra- tion.*

draftsman US (UK **draughtsman**) /'drɑːftsmən/ noun [C] plural **draftsmen** someone who draws detailed drawings as plans for something **teknik ressam**

drafty /'drɑːfti/ adjective US spelling of draughty **hava akımı olan/cereyanda kalan/olan**

drag¹ /dræg/ verb dragging, past dragged **1 drag sth/sb across/along/over, etc** to pull something or someone along the ground somewhere, usually with difficulty **birini sürüklemek, sürükleyerek götürmek** *The table was too heavy to lift, so we had to drag it across the room.* **2 drag sb along/out/to, etc** to make someone go somewhere they do not want to go **istemediği halde gitmeye zorlamak, cebir uygulamak, cebren yap- tırmak** *I have to drag myself out of bed every morning.* **3** [T] to move something somewhere on a computer screen using a mouse (= small computer control) **bilgi- sayarda mouse ile bir şeyi alıp taşımak 4** [I] (also drag on) to continue for too much time in a boring way **sıkıcı bir şekilde uzayıp gitmek, uzadıkça uzamak, kabak tadı vermek** ⊃See also: drag your feet (foot¹). **drag sb down** phrasal verb UK If an unpleasant situa- tion drags someone down, it makes them feel unhappy or ill. **canını sıkmak, hasta etmek, yatağa düşür- mek drag sb into sth** phrasal verb to force someone to become involved in an unpleasant or difficult situation **başını belaya sokmak, başına dert açmak, zorla bulaştırmak; istemeden/zorla karışmak/bulaş- mak** *I don't want to be dragged into this argument.* **drag sth out** phrasal verb to make something continue for more time than is necessary **gereksiz yere uzat- mak**

drag² /dræg/ noun **1 in drag** informal If a man is in drag, he is wearing women's clothes. **kadın kılığına girme, zenne 2 be a drag** informal to be boring and unpleasant **sıkıcı/berbat olmak; (hal) karın ağrısı olmak** *Cleaning the house is such a drag.* **3** [C] when you breathe in smoke from a cigarette **sigaradan bir fırt /nefes alma** *He took a drag on his cigarette.*

dragon /'drægⁿn/ *noun*
[C] a big, imaginary
creature which
breathes out fire
ejderha

dragon

dragonfly /'drægⁿnflaɪ/
noun [C] an insect with
long wings and a thin,
colourful body, often
seen flying near water
yusufçuk ➾See picture at
insect.

drain¹ /dreɪn/ *verb*
1 [REMOVE LIQUID] [T] to
remove the liquid from something, usually by pouring
it away **suyunu çekmek/almak** *Drain the pasta and
add the tomatoes.* **2** [FLOW AWAY] [I] If something drains,
liquid flows away or out of it. **suyu çekilerek kurumak, kurutmak** **3** [MAKE TIRED] [T] to make someone very
tired **canını çıkarmak, yormak, iflahını kesmek**
The long journey drained him. **4** [DRINK] [T] If you drain a
glass or cup, you drink all the liquid in it. **bir dikişte
içmek, nefes almadan içmek**

drain² /dreɪn/ *noun* **1** [C] a pipe or hole that takes away
waste liquids or water **pis su atık borusu/deliği** *She
poured the dirty water down the drain.* **2 a drain on sth**
something that uses or wastes a lot of money or energy
**(güç, para, zaman vb.) yük, zahmet 3 down the
drain** *informal* If money or work goes down the drain,
it is wasted. **boşa gitmek, heba olmak, çar çur
etmek/edilmek**

drainage /'dreɪnɪdʒ/ *noun* [U] the system of water or
waste liquids flowing away from somewhere into the
ground or down pipes **(su, atık su) boşaltma, tahliye,
drenaj**

drained /dreɪnd/ *adjective* If someone is drained, they
are extremely tired. **yorgun, bitkin**

drainpipe /'dreɪnpaɪp/ *noun* [C] a pipe that carries
waste water away from a building **atık su borusu, yağmur suyu borusu**

drama ...... İLE BİRLİKTE KULLANILAN KELİMELER

a drama **unfolds** • **high** drama • **human** drama

drama /'drɑːmə/ *noun* **1** [PLAY] [C] a play in a theatre or on
television or radio **oyun, piyes** *a historical drama*
2 [PLAYS/ACTING] [U] plays and acting generally **oyun, tiyatro** *modern drama* **3** [EXCITEMENT] [C, U] when something
exciting happens **heyecan verici/üzücü olay** *There
was a lot of drama in the courtroom.*

'drama ˌqueen *noun* [C] *informal* someone who gets far
too upset or angry over small problems **küçük şeylerden kolay etkilenen, dert eden kişi; çabuk öfkele-
nen/kızan kişi**

dramatic /drə'mætɪk/ *adjective* **1** [SUDDEN] very sudden
or noticeable **ani, belirgin, çarpıcı** *a dramatic
change/improvement* **2** [EXCITING] full of action and excitement **abartılı, heyecan verici, hareketli** *a dramatic
rescue* **3** [THEATRE] [always before noun] relating to plays and
acting **oyun ve tiyatroyla ilgili 4** [BEHAVIOUR] showing
your emotions in a very obvious way because you
want other people to notice you **abartan, dramatik
hale getiren, velveleci** *Stop being so dramatic!* • **dramatically** *adverb* **ani ve belirgin bir biçimde**

dramatist /'dræmətɪst/ *noun* [C] someone who writes
plays **oyun yazarı**

dramatize (*also UK* -ise) /'dræmətaɪz/ *verb* [T] **1** to make
an event or situation seem more exciting than it really
is **abartmak, dramatik hale getirmek, olduğundan
farklı göstermek** *The media tends to dramatize things.*

2 to change a story so that it can be performed as a play
oyun haline getirmek, oyunlaştırmak • **dramatiza-
tion** /ˌdræmətaɪ'zeɪʃⁿn/ *noun* [C, U] **abartı, sahneleme**

drank /dræŋk/ *past tense of* drink **içmek' fiilinin ikinci
hali**

drape /dreɪp/ *verb* **1 drape sth across/on/over, etc** to
put something such as cloth or a piece of clothing
loosely over something **sarmak, dolamak, öylesine/
rastgele örtüvermek** *He draped his jacket over the
chair and sat down to eat.* **2 be draped in/with sth** to
be loosely covered with a cloth **sarıp sarmalanmak;
sıkı sıkıya örtünmek/sarılmak** *The coffin was draped in a flag.*

drapes /dreɪps/ *noun* [plural] *mainly US* long, heavy curtains **kalın, uzun perdeler**

drastic /'dræstɪk/ *adjective* Drastic action or change is
sudden and extreme. **esaslı, ani, sert, güçlü, şiddetli,
etkili** *drastic reductions in price* • **drastically** *adverb*
Ani ve beklenmedik bir şekilde

draught¹ *UK* (*US* draft) /drɑːft/ *noun* [C] a current of cold
air in a room **cereyan, hava akımı**

draught² *UK* (*US* draft) /drɑːft/ *adjective* **draught beer/
lager, etc** a drink that comes from a large container
and not from a can or bottle **fıçı bira, büyük bira**

draughts /drɑːfts/ *UK* (*US* checkers) *noun* [U] a game that
two people play by moving flat, round objects around on
a board of black and white squares **dama oyunu**

draughtsman *UK* (*US* draftsman) /'drɑːftsmən/ *noun* [C]
plural **draughtsmen** someone who draws detailed drawings as plans for something **teknik ressam**

draughty *UK* (*US* drafty) /'drɑːfti/ *adjective* having currents of cold air blowing through **cereyanlı, hava
akımı olan** *a draughty old building*

○-**draw¹** /drɔː/ *verb past tense* **drew**, *past participle* **drawn**
1 [PICTURE] [I, T] to produce a picture by making lines or
marks, usually with a pen or pencil **çizmek** *She drew a
picture of a tree.* **2 draw sth across/back/over, etc** to
pull something or someone gently in a particular direction **çekmek, sürüklemek, sürüyerek götürmek** *He
took her hand and drew her towards him.* **3 draw into/
out/away, etc** to move somewhere, usually in a vehicle
araçla bir yere hareket etmek *The train drew into the
station.* **4 draw the curtains** to pull curtains open or
closed **perdeleri açıp kapamak 5 draw (sb's) attention to sth/sb** to make someone notice someone or
something **birinin dikkatini bir şeye çekmek** *I don't
want to draw too much attention to myself.* **6** [ATTRACT] [T] to
attract someone to a place or person **bir şeye/birine
çekmek, cezbetmek** *Thousands of tourists are drawn
to the city every year.* **7** [SPORT] [I, T] *UK* to finish a game or
competition with each team or player having the same
score **berabere kalmak, aynı puanla/skorla/
sonuçla son bulmak/bitmek** *England drew 2-2
against Italy.* **8** [TAKE OUT] [T] to take something out of a
container or your pocket, especially a weapon **silah
çekmek; çekip çıkarmak** *He drew a knife and started
threatening me.* **9 draw near/close** to become nearer in
space or time **zaman ve mekân olarak yakına gel-
mek/yakınlaşmak** *Her birthday's drawing nearer
every day.* **10 draw (a) breath** to breathe in air **nefes
almak** *She drew a deep breath and started her speech.*
11 [MONEY] [T] (*also* draw out) to take money from your
bank account **hesaptan para çekmek 12 draw to a
close/end** to be almost finished **hemen hemen bitirmek, sonuna gelmek; bitmek üzere olmak**
13 draw conclusions to make judgments after considering a subject or situation **sonuç çıkarmak, bir
sonuca varmak 14 draw a comparison/distinction**
to say that there is a similarity or difference between
two things **benzerlik/farklılık olduğunu bildir-**

mek/söylemek; karşılaştırmak; paralellik kurmak つSee also: draw a **blank**[2], draw the **line**[1] at sth, draw a **veil** over sth.

draw back *phrasal verb* to move away from someone or something, usually because you are surprised or frightened **geri çekilmek, sakınmak, geri durmak, ürkmek; korkmak**

draw sb/sth into sth *phrasal verb* to make someone or something become involved in a difficult or unpleasant situation **istenmeyen bir duruma/güçlüğe sokmak, başına dert açmak, bulaştırmak** *I'm not going to be drawn into this argument.*

draw on sth *phrasal verb* to use information or your knowledge or experience of something to help you do something **ilgili olmak, içermek, dayanmak, anlatmak, kapsamak** *His novels draw heavily on his childhood.*

draw sth up *phrasal verb* to prepare something, usually a plan, list, or an official agreement, by writing it **(plan, resmi antlaşma, liste vb.) düzenlemek**

draw[2] /drɔː/ *noun* [C] **1** *mainly UK* when a game or competition finishes with each player or team having the same score **eşit, başbaşa, aynı sonuç, berabere** *The match ended in a draw.* **2** (*also US* **drawing**) a competition that is decided by choosing a particular ticket or number **bilet ya da rakam çekilerek yapılan yarışma, piyango, kura ile belirleme** *the National Lottery draw* つSee also: the **luck** of the draw.

┌───┐
│ 🧩 **drawback** .... İLE BİRLİKTE KULLANILAN KELİMELER │
└───┘

have drawbacks ● a **big/major** drawback ● the **main/only** drawback ● a drawback **of/to/with** sth

drawback /'drɔːbæk/ *noun* [C] a problem or disadvantage **mahsur, eksiklik, sakınca, sorun** *The only drawback with this camera is the price.*

drawer /drɔːʳ/ *noun* [C] a container like a box without a lid that is part of a piece of furniture and that slides in and out **çekmece** *She opened the drawer and took out a knife.* つSee also: chest of drawers.

drawing /'drɔːɪŋ/ *noun* **1** PICTURE [C] a picture made with a pencil or pen **kalemle yapılan çizim, resim** *There were some children's drawings pinned up on the wall.* **2** ACTIVITY [U] the skill or activity of making pictures using a pencil or pen **resim/çizim yapma** *Do you want to do some drawing?* **3** NUMBER/TICKET [C] *US (UK/US* draw) a competition that is decided by choosing a particular ticket or number **kura çekme; bilet ve rakamlar seçilerek yapılan yarışma**

'drawing ,board *noun* **back to the drawing board** If you go back to the drawing board, you have to start planning a piece of work again because the first plan failed. **sil baştan, yeniden planlama/ele alma**

'drawing ,pin *UK (US* **thumbtack**) *noun* [C] a pin with a wide, flat top, used for fastening pieces of paper to a wall **raptiye**

'drawing ,room *noun* [C] *old-fashioned* a room in a large house used for sitting in and talking with guests **misafir odası, salon**

drawl /drɔːl/ *noun* [no plural] a lazy way of speaking that uses long vowel sounds **ağzını yaya yaya konuşmak, ağdalı konuşmak** ● **drawl** *verb* [I] **kelimeleri yayarak söylemek**

drawn[1] /drɔːn/ *adjective* looking very tired or ill **hasta, süzgün; bitkin gözüken** *She looked pale and drawn after the operation.* つSee also: horse-drawn.

drawn[2] /drɔːn/ *past participle of* draw **çizmek' fiilinin üçüncü hali**

drawn-out /ˌdrɔːn'aʊt/ *adjective* continuing for longer than you think is necessary **uzun, uzayan, fazla zaman alan** *long, drawn-out negotiations*

dread[1] /dred/ *verb* **1** [T] to feel worried or frightened about something that has not happened yet **dehşete kapılmak, korkmak, ödü kopmak** *I'm dreading the first day at my new school.* ○ [+ doing sth] *I dread seeing him again.* **2 I dread to think** *UK* used to say that you do not want to think about something because it is too worrying **düşünmek bile istemiyorum, konuşmak dahi istemiyorum** *I dread to think what could have happened if we hadn't been wearing seat belts.*

dread[2] /dred/ *noun* [U, no plural] a strong feeling of fear or worry **dehşet, korku** [+ of + doing sth] *a dread of being lonely*

dreadful /'dredfəl/ *adjective* extremely bad or unpleasant **berbat, korkunç, müthiş, a dreadful mistake** ○ *a dreadful man*

dreadfully /'dredfəli/ *adverb* **1** *mainly UK formal* very **korkunç şekilde, çok** *I'm dreadfully sorry.* **2** very badly **çok berbat şekilde, berbat şekilde** *The children behaved dreadfully.*

dreadlocks /'dredlɒks/ *noun* [plural] a hairstyle in which the hair is twisted together in lengths and is never brushed **çok sık örgülü saç, hiç taranmadan uzatılan saç şekli**

┌───┐
│ 🧩 **dream** .... İLE BİRLİKTE KULLANILAN KELİMELER │
└───┘

have a dream ● **in** sb's dream ● a **bad** dream ● a **recurring** dream

○**dream**[1] /driːm/ *noun* **1** [C] a series of events and images that happen in your mind while you are sleeping **rüya** *a bad dream* ○ *I had a very strange dream last night.* **2** [C] something that you want to happen although it is not very likely **hayal, rüya** *It was his dream to become an actor.* **3 be in a dream** *UK* to not notice things that are around you because you are thinking about something else **hayale dalmak, rüyada olmak 4 beyond your wildest dreams** bigger or better than anything you could imagine or hope for **hayal edebileceğinden daha büyük/iyi** ● **5 like a dream** If something or someone does something like a dream, they do it very well. **rüya gibi**

○**dream**[2] /driːm/ *verb past* **dreamed** or **dreamt 1** [I, T] to experience events and images in your mind while you are sleeping **rüya görmek** [+ (that)] *Last night I dreamed that I was flying.* **2** [I, T] to imagine something that you would like to happen **hayal etmek/kurmak** [+ of + doing sth] *I dream of living on a desert island.* ○ [+ (that)] *He never dreamed that one day he would become President.* **3 wouldn't dream of doing sth** used to say that you would not do something because you think it is wrong or silly **yapmayı kesinlikle düşünmemek, kafasına yatmamak**

dream sth up *phrasal verb* to think of an idea or plan, usually using a lot of imagination **icat etmek, uydurmak, düşünüp bulmak** *Who dreams up these new designs?*

dream[3] /driːm/ *adjective* **dream house/job/car, etc** the perfect house/job/car, etc **mükemmel/rüya gibi ev/araba/iş**

dreamer /'driːməʳ/ *noun* [C] someone who is not practical and thinks about things that are not likely to happen **hayalperest**

dreamy /'driːmi/ *adjective* **1** seeming to be in a dream and thinking about pleasant things instead of what is happening around you **hülyalı, dalgın, rüyada gibi** *She had a dreamy look in her eyes.* **2** very pleasant hayal gibi, çok hoş, harikulade *a dreamy dessert* ● **dreamily** *adverb* hayal dünyasındaymış gibi

dreary /'drɪəri/ *adjective* boring and making you feel unhappy **iç karartıcı, kasvetli, sıkıcı, mutsuz edici** *a rainy, dreary day* ○ *a dreary job*

dredge /dredʒ/ *verb* [T] to clean the bottom of a lake or river by removing dirt, plants, or rubbish **(göl, nehir vb.) dibini temizlemek**
   dredge sth up *phrasal verb* to talk about something bad or unpleasant that happened in the past **eski pislikleri ortaya dökmek, eşelemek, kirli çamaşırları ortaya çıkarmak**

dregs /dregz/ *noun* **1** [plural] the part of a drink at the bottom of a glass or other container that usually contains small solid bits **tortu, birikinti, posa, tabaka, (kahve) telve 2 the dregs of society/humanity** people who you think are extremely bad or unimportant **ayak takımı, alt tabaka**

drench /drentʃ/ *verb* [T] to make something or someone completely wet **sırılsıklam etmek, bütünüyle ıslatmak** [often passive] *He was completely drenched by the time he got home.*

◦•**dress**[1] /dres/ *verb* **1** [I, T] to put clothes on yourself or someone else **giyinmek, giydirmek** *I usually get dressed before having breakfast.* ✪Opposite **undress. 2** [I] to wear a particular type, style, or colour of clothes **giyinip kuşanmak, belli tarzda giyinmek** *Ali always dresses smartly for work.* ○ [often passive] *She was dressed in black.* **3 dress a burn/cut/wound, etc** to clean an injury and put a covering over it to protect it **bir yarayı/kesiği/yanığı temizleyip sarmak**
   dress up *phrasal verb* **1** to put on formal clothes for a special occasion **bir davet için giyinmek, kuşanmak 2** to wear special clothes in order to change your appearance, usually for a game or party **oyun veya parti için özel kıyafetler giyip görünüşünü değiştirmek** *He dressed up as Superman for the party.*

◦•**dress**[2] /dres/ *noun* **1** [C] a piece of clothing for women or girls which covers the top of the body and hangs down over the legs **bayan elbisesi** *She was wearing a short, black dress.* ✪Orta kısımdaki renkli sayfalarına bakınız. **2** [U] a particular style of clothes **elbise, giysi, giyim kuşam** *casual/formal dress* ✪See also: **fancy dress.**

dresser /'dresər/ *noun* [C] **1** *mainly US* a piece of bedroom furniture with a mirror and drawers for keeping clothes in **tuvalet masası, konsol, şifonyer 2** *UK* a piece of furniture consisting of a cupboard with shelves above for keeping plates, cups, and other kitchen equipment **vitrin, büfe, mutfak dolabı**

dressing /'dresɪŋ/ *noun* **1** [C, U] a sauce, especially a mixture of oil and vinegar for salad **sos, salata sosu 2** [C] a covering that protects an injury **sargı, bandaj, sargı bezi**

'**dressing ,gown** *UK* (*US* robe) *noun* [C] a piece of clothing, like a long coat, that you wear at home when you are not dressed **sabahlık, robdöşambır**

'**dressing ,room** *noun* [C] a room where actors or sports teams get dressed before a performance or game **soyunma/giyinme/makyaj odası, kulis**

'**dressing ,table** *noun* [C] *mainly UK* a piece of bedroom furniture like a table with a mirror and drawers **aynası ve çekmeceleri olan makyaj masası, şifonyer**

dressy /'dresi/ *adjective* Dressy clothes are suitable for a formal occasion. **resmi durumlar için uygun olan kıyafet tarzı, şık**

drew /dru:/ *past tense of* draw **çizmek' fiilinin ikinci hali**

dribble /'drɪbl/ *verb* **1** [MOUTH] [I] If someone dribbles, a small amount of liquid comes out of their mouth and goes down their face. **ağzından sıvı sızmak/akmak; salyası akmak** *Babies dribble a lot.* **2** [LIQUID] [I, T] If a liquid dribbles, it falls slowly in small amounts, and if you dribble a liquid, you pour it so it falls slowly in small amounts. **damla(t)mak** *Dribble some oil over the vegetables.* **3** [SPORT] [I, T] to move a ball along by using your hand to hit it against the ground or kicking it several times **dripling yapmak, topu kısa vuruşlarla ilerletmek** ● **dribble** *noun* [C, U] **akıntı**

dried /draɪd/ *past of* dry **kurutmak' fiilinin geçmiş zaman hali**

drier /'draɪər/ *noun* [C] *another spelling of* dryer (= a machine for drying wet things) **kurutucu**

drift[1] /drɪft/ *verb* **1 drift across/down/towards, etc** to be moved slowly somewhere by currents of wind or water **akıntıya/rüzgara kapılmak/sürüklenmek** *Smoke drifted across the rooftops.* **2 drift in/out/into, etc** to move somewhere slowly **yavaş yavaş hareket etmek/gitmek** *Guests were drifting out onto the terrace.* **3** [I] to get into a situation or job without having any particular plan **plansız, programsız balıklamasına dalmak** *He drifted into acting after university.* **4** [I] If snow or leaves drift, they are blown into piles by the wind. **(rüzgar) karı/yaprağı yığın haline getirmek, top yapmak, yığmak**
   drift apart *phrasal verb* If two people drift apart, they gradually become less friendly and the relationship ends. **gittikçe ilişkileri bozulmak; arkadaşlıkları/dostlukları sona ermek; birbirinden uzaklaşmak; yolları ayrılmak**
   drift off *phrasal verb* to gradually start to sleep **yavaş yavaş uykuya dalmak; uyuklamaya başlamak** *I drifted off during the lecture.*

drift[2] /drɪft/ *noun* **1** [C] slow, gradual movement from one place to another **yavaş yavaş, ağır hareket; hantal hareket** *the drift of people into Western Europe* **2 catch/get sb's drift** to understand the general meaning of what someone is saying **ana fikri/esas manayı/özünü anlamak 3** [C] a pile of snow or leaves that has been blown somewhere **yığıntı, birikinti, kümelenme**

drill[1] /drɪl/ *noun* **1** [TOOL] [C] a tool or machine for making holes in a hard substance **matkap** *an electric drill* ✪See picture at **tool. 2** [FOR LEARNING] [C, U] a teaching method in which students repeat something several times to help them learn it **alıştırma; tekrara dayalı bir öğretim yöntemi** *We do lots of drills to practise pronunciation.* **3 an emergency/fire, etc drill** when you practise what to do in an emergency/fire, etc **ilk yardım/yangın vb. tatbikatı 4** [SOLDIERS] [C, U] when soldiers do training for marching **askerî eğitim, talim, tatbikat**

drill[2] /drɪl/ *verb* **1** [I, T] to make a hole in a hard substance using a special tool **matkapla delik açmak/delmek; oymak; sondaj yapmak** *Billy drilled a hole in the wall.* ○ *The engineers were drilling for oil.* **2** [T] to make someone repeat something several times so that they learn it **alıştırma yaptırmak, tekrar ettirmek**

drily /'draɪli/ *adverb* another spelling of dryly (= in a serious voice but trying to be funny) **ciddi ancak komik olmaya çalışan bir ses tonuyla**

◦•**drink**[1] /drɪŋk/ *verb past tense* **drank**, *past participle* **drunk 1** [I, T] to put liquid into your mouth and swallow it **içmek** *Would you like something to drink?* ○ *He was drinking a glass of milk.* **2** [I] to drink alcohol, usually regularly **içki içmek, alkol almak** *She doesn't smoke or drink.*

drink to sb/sth *phrasal verb* to hold your glass up before drinking from it, in order to wish someone or something good luck or success **birinin/bir şeyin şerefine içmek, kutlama yapmak için içmek**
drink (sth) up *phrasal verb* to finish your drink completely **içip bitirmek, sonuna kadar içmek** *Drink up! We've got to leave soon.*

drink ...... İLE BİRLİKTE KULLANILAN KELİMELER

have a drink ● a drink **of** [water/milk, etc] ● a **hot/ cold** drink

o▴**drink²** /drɪŋk/ *noun* **1** [C] a liquid or an amount of liquid that you drink **su, içilecek şey** *a hot/cold drink* ○ *Can I have a drink of water please?* **2** [C, U] alcohol, or an alcoholic drink **içki** *Do you fancy a drink tonight to celebrate?* ➔See also: **soft drink.**

drink-driving /ˌdrɪŋk'draɪvɪŋ/ UK (US **drunk driving**) *noun* [U] driving a vehicle after drinking too much alcohol **sarhoş araba kullanmak** *He was convicted of drink-driving.*

drinker /'drɪŋkəʳ/ *noun* **1** [C] someone who regularly drinks alcohol **ayyaş, içkici, akşamcı, sürekli demlenen** *He's a heavy drinker* (= he drinks a lot of alcohol). **2 a coffee/tea/wine, etc drinker** someone who regularly drinks a particular drink **sürekli çay/ kahve/şarap içen, tiryaki**

drinking /'drɪŋkɪŋ/ *noun* [U] when someone drinks alcohol **içki içme, demlenme, alkol alma**

'**drinking ˌwater** *noun* [U] water that is safe for people to drink **içme suyu**

drip¹ /drɪp/ *verb* **dripping**, *past* **dripped 1** [I, T] If a liquid drips, it falls in drops or you make it fall in drops. **damla(t)mak, damla damla ak(ıt)mak** *There was water dripping from the ceiling.* **2** [I] to produce drops of liquid **damlamak, akmak** *The candle's dripping.*

drip² /drɪp/ *noun* **1** [DROP] [C] a drop of liquid that falls from something **damla 2** [SOUND] [no plural] the sound or action of a liquid falling in drops **damlama sesi, damla hareketi 3** [MEDICAL] [C] UK (US **IV**) a piece of medical equipment used for putting liquids into your body **damlalık** *The doctor's put him on a drip.*

o▴**drive¹** /draɪv/ *verb past tense* **drove**, *past participle* **driven 1** [CONTROL VEHICLE] [I, T] to make a car, bus, or train move, and control what it does **(araba, otobüs, tren) kullanmak/sürmek** *She's learning to drive.* ○ *He drives a red sports car.* **2** [TRAVEL] [I, T] to travel somewhere in a car, or to take someone somewhere in a car **arabayla gitmek/götürmek** *My friend drove me home last night.* **3 drive sb out/away/from, etc** to force someone to leave a place **zorla çıkarmak; kovmak; kapı dışarı etmek** *The supermarket has driven many small shops out of the area.* **4 drive sb crazy/mad/wild, etc** to make someone feel crazy, annoyed, or excited **kızdırmak, küplere bindirmek sebep olmak, kafasının tasını attırmak; rahatsız etmek; heyecanlandırmak** *That noise is driving me mad.* **5 drive sb to sth; drive sb to do sth** to make someone have a bad feeling or do something bad **kötü bir şeye/bir şey yapmaya zorlamak; itmek** *The arguments and violence drove her to leave home.* **6 drive sth into/through/towards, etc** to push something somewhere by hitting it hard **zorla iterek sokmak; itmek; sokuşturmak; tıkmak** *He drove the nail into the wall with a hammer.* **7** [MAKE WORK] [T] to provide the power or energy that makes someone or something work **enerji/azim/şevk/kuvvet vermek; itici güç olmak** [often passive] *She was driven by greed and ambition.* ➔See also: drive/send sb round the **bend²**, drive sb up the **wall.**

be driving at sth *phrasal verb* used to ask what someone really means **demek istemek, kasdetmek, demeye getirmek** *Just what are you driving at?*
drive off *phrasal verb* to leave in a car **sürüp gitmek; arabayla gitmek**

drive ...... İLE BİRLİKTE KULLANILAN KELİMELER

go for a drive

drive² /draɪv/ *noun* **1** [JOURNEY] [C] a journey in a car **sürüş, araçla yolculuk, araba gezintisi** *The drive from Boston to New York took 4 hours.* **2** [GROUND] [C] the area of ground that you drive on to get from your house to the road **ev özel araç yolu; park yerine giriş yolu** *You can park on the drive.* **3** [COMPUTER] [C] a part of a computer that can read or store information **(bilgisayar) sürücü** *a DVD drive* ○ *Save your work on the C: drive.* **4** [EFFORT] [C] when someone makes a great effort to achieve something **çaba, gayret, girişim, teşvik** [+ to do sth] *The government started a drive to improve standards in schools.* **5** [ENERGY] [U] energy and determination to achieve things **enerji, azim, şevk** *She has drive and ambition.*

drive-by /'draɪvbaɪ/ *adjective* describes something that someone does when they are inside a vehicle that is moving **araba ile geçen** *a drive-by shooting*

drive-in /'draɪvɪn/ *noun* [C] mainly US a cinema or restaurant that you can visit without getting out of your car **arabaya servis yapılabilen lokanta/arabayla girilebilen sinema**

drivel /'drɪvəl/ *noun* [U] nonsense **zırva, saçma sapan söz, lakırdı, boş laf** *He was talking complete drivel.*

driven /'drɪvən/ *past participle of* drive **'sürmek' fiilinin üçüncü hali**

driver ...... İLE BİRLİKTE KULLANILAN KELİMELER

a **bus/taxi/train/truck** driver ● the driver **of** sth

o▴**driver** /'draɪvəʳ/ *noun* [C] someone who drives a vehicle **sürücü** *a bus/train driver* ➔See also: engine driver.

'**driver's ˌlicense** US (UK **driving licence**) *noun* [C] an official document that allows you to drive a car **sürücü ehliyeti/belgesi**

drive-through /'draɪvθru:/ *noun* [C] a place where you can get a type of service by driving through, without needing to get out of your car **arabaya servis** *a drive-through restaurant*

driveway /'draɪvweɪ/ *noun* [C] the area of ground that you drive on to get from your house to the road **ev ile yol arasında araç çıkış yolu**

driving¹ /'draɪvɪŋ/ *noun* [U] when you drive a car, or the way someone drives **sürüş, araç kullanma/kullanış şekli**

driving² /'draɪvɪŋ/ *adjective* **1 driving rain/snow** rain or snow that is falling very fast and being blown by the wind **rüzgarın savurduğu hızlı yağan yağmur/kar 2 the driving force** a person or thing that has a very strong effect and makes something happen **itici güç; yüreklendirici etkisi olan kişi/şey** *She was the driving force behind the project.*

'**driving ˌlicence** UK (US **driver's license**) *noun* [C] an official document that allows you to drive a car **sürücü belgesi; şoför ehliyeti**

drizzle /'drɪzl/ *noun* [U] light rain **çiselemek, ince ince yağmak** ● **drizzle** *verb* [I] **çiselemek**

drone¹ /drəʊn/ *verb* [I] to make a continuous, low sound, like an engine **motor gibi ses çıkarmak, uğuldamak** *I could hear traffic droning in the distance.*

drone on *phrasal verb* to talk for a long time in a very boring way **monoton/sıkıcı bir ses tonuyla konuşmak** *I wish he'd stop droning on about school.*

drool /druːl/ *verb* [I] If a person or animal drools, liquid comes out of the side of their mouth. **salyası akmak**
drool over sb/sth *phrasal verb* to look at someone or something in a way that shows you think they are very attractive **hayran hayran bakmak**

droop /druːp/ *verb* [I] to hang down, often because of being weak, tired, or unhappy **sarkmak, eğilmek, çökmek** *He was tired and his eyelids were starting to droop.*

✏**drop¹** /drɒp/ *verb* **dropping**, *past* **dropped**
1 [LET FALL] [T] to let something you are carrying fall to the ground **düşürmek** *She tripped and dropped the vase.* **2** [FALL] [I] to fall **düşmek** *The ball dropped to the ground.* **3** [BECOME LESS] [I] If a level or amount drops, it becomes less. **azalmak, seviyesi düşmek** *Unemployment has*

drop

dropped from 8% to 6% in the last year. **4** [TAKE] [T] (*also* **drop off**) to take someone or something to a place, usually by car as you travel somewhere else **birini araçla götürmek; bir yere götürüp bırakmak** *I can drop you at the station on my way to work.* **5** [STOP ACTIVITY] [T] If you drop a plan, activity, or idea, you stop doing or planning it. **bırakmak, vazgeçmek** *Plans for a new supermarket have been dropped.* ○ *When we heard the news, we dropped everything* (= stopped what we were doing) *and rushed to the hospital.* **6** [STOP INCLUDING] [T] to decide to stop including someone in a group or team **kadro dışı bırakmak, ekibe almamak** *The coach dropped me from the team.* **7 drop it/the subject** to stop talking about something, especially because it is annoying or upsetting someone **cansıkıcı olduğu için konuşmaktan vazgeçmek** **8** [VOICE] [I, T] If your voice drops, or if you drop your voice, you talk more quietly. **sakin ve alçak bir sesle konuşmak** ➜See also: be dropping like flies (**fly²**).
drop by/in *phrasal verb* to visit someone for a short time, usually without arranging it before **kısa bir ziyarette bulunmak; uğramak** *I dropped in on George on my way home from school.*
drop sb/sth off *phrasal verb* to take someone or something to a place, usually by car as you travel somewhere else **birini/birşeyi götürmek; geçerken bırakmak**
drop off *phrasal verb* **1** *informal* to start to sleep **içi geçmek, uyuya kalmak** *She dropped off in front of the TV.* **2** If the amount, number, or quality of something drops off, it becomes less. **(miktarı, sayısı, kalitesi) düşmek, azalmak,** *The demand for mobile phones shows no signs of dropping off.*
drop out *phrasal verb* to stop doing something before you have completely finished **bırakmak, terketmek, vazgeçmek, tamamlamamak** *He dropped out of school at 14.*

a **big/dramatic/sharp/steep** drop ● a drop **in** sth

✏**drop²** /drɒp/ *noun* **1** [LIQUID] [C] a small, round-shaped amount of liquid **damla** *I felt a few drops of rain.* ➜Orta kısımdaki renkli sayfalarına bakınız. **2** [REDUCTION] [no plural] when the level or amount of something becomes less **düşüş, azalma, eksilme** *There has been a drop in crime*

recently. **3** [SMALL AMOUNT] [no plural] a small amount of a liquid you can drink **yudum, bir damla, fırt** *Would you like a drop more milk?* **4** [DISTANCE] [no plural] a vertical distance down from somewhere to the ground **iniş, iniş mesafesi, düşüş menzili** *It's a drop of about 50 metres from the top of the cliff.*

'drop-down ,menu *noun* [C] a pop-up menu: a list of choices on a computer screen which is hidden until you choose to look at it **kendiliğinden çıkan menü; bilgisayar ekranında seçilinceye kadar gizli kalan seçenekler listesi**

droplet /'drɒplət/ *noun* [C] a very small, round amount of liquid **damlacık**

dropout /'drɒpaʊt/ *noun* [C] **1** a student who leaves school or university before they have completely finished **okuldan ayrılan kişi; tasdikname alan kişi** *a high-school dropout* **2** someone who does not want to have a job, possessions, etc because they do not want to be like everyone else **toplum dışı kişi; başkalarına benzemeyen kişi**

droppings /'drɒpɪŋz/ *noun* [plural] solid waste from birds and some small animals **küçük hayvan dışkısı, gübre, pislik** *rabbit droppings*

drought /draʊt/ *noun* [C, U] a long period when there is no rain and people do not have enough water **kuraklık** *A severe drought ruined the crops.*

drove /drəʊv/ *past tense of* drive **'sürmek' fiilinin ikinci hali**

droves /drəʊvz/ *noun* **in droves** If people do something in droves, they do it in large numbers. **çok sayıda, epey kalabalık, büyük miktarda**

drown /draʊn/ *verb* **1** [I, T] to die because you are under water and cannot breathe, or to kill someone in this way **suda boğulmak/boğmak** *Two people drowned in a boating accident yesterday.* **2** [T] (*also* **drown out**) If a loud noise drowns the sound of something else, it prevents that sound from being heard. **gürültüye/sese boğmak** *His voice was drowned out by the traffic.*

drowning /'draʊnɪŋ/ *noun* [C, U] when someone dies because they are under water and cannot breathe **suda boğulma**

drowsy /'draʊzi/ *adjective* feeling tired and wanting to sleep **uykulu, gözünden uyku akan** *The sun was making me drowsy.* ● **drowsily** *adverb* **gevşemiş, mayışmış bir şekilde** ● **drowsiness** *noun* [U] **gevşeme**

drudgery /'drʌdʒ³ri/ *noun* [U] work that is very boring **sıkıcı ve lüzumsuz iş, angarya, istemeye istemeye yapılan iş/faaliyet**

be on/take/use drugs ● drug **abuse/addiction** ● a drug **addict/dealer/user**

✏**drug¹** /drʌg/ *noun* [C] **1** an illegal substance that people take to make them feel happy **uyuşturucu** [usually plural] *He started taking/using drugs such as heroin and cocaine.* ○ *Greg is on drugs* (= he uses drugs regularly). ○ *a drug dealer* **2** a chemical substance used as a medicine **ilaç, deva** *Scientists are developing a new drug to treat cancer.* ➜See also: hard drugs.

drug² /drʌg/ *verb* [T] **drugging**, *past* **drugged** to give someone a chemical substance that makes them sleep or stop feeling pain **ilaç vermek, uyuşturmak** *He drugged his victims before robbing them.*

'drug ,addict *noun* [C] someone who cannot stop taking drugs **uyuşturucu/ilaç bağımlısı**

drugstore /'drʌgstɔːʳ/ *US* (*UK* chemist's) *noun* [C] a shop that sells medicines and also things such as soap and beauty products **eczane; ilaç yanında sabun ve güzel-lik ürünleri de satan mağaza**

drum¹ /drʌm/ *noun* [C] **1** a round, hollow, musical instrument that you hit with your hands or with sticks **davul, trampet, dümbelek** *Anna plays the drums.* **2** a large, round container for holding substances such as oil or chemicals **büyük varil/bidon, konteyner**

drum

drum² /drʌm/ *verb* [I, T] **drumming**, *past* **drummed** to hit something several times and make a sound like a drum, or to make something do this **davul/trampet çalmak/çaldırmak** *the sound of rain drumming on the roof* ○ *She drummed her fingers nervously on the desk.*

drum sth into sb *phrasal verb* to make someone remember or believe an idea or fact by repeating it to them many times **beynine işlemek, kafasına sokmak, tekrar tekrar söyleyerek öğretmek** [often passive] *The importance of good manners was drummed into me by my father.*

drum up sth *phrasal verb* to increase interest in something or support for something **çaba göstermek, ilgiyi/desteği artırmak** *He was trying to drum up some enthusiasm for his idea.*

drummer /ˈdrʌmər/ *noun* [C] someone who plays a drum **davulcu**

drunk¹ /drʌŋk/ *adjective* unable to behave or speak normally because you have drunk too much alcohol **sarhoş** *He usually gets drunk at parties.*

drunk² /drʌŋk/ *past participle of* drink **içmek' fiilinin ikinci hali**

drunken /ˈdrʌŋkən/ *adjective* [always before noun] drunk, or involving people who are drunk **içkili, sarhoş** *a drunken man* ○ *drunken behaviour* ● **drunkenly** *adverb* **sarhoş bir şekilde** ● **drunkenness** *noun* [U] **sarhoşluk**

o╼**dry**¹ /draɪ/ *adjective* **drier, driest** or **dryer, dryest** **1** [NOT WET] Something that is dry does not have water or liquid in it or on its surface. **kuru** *dry paint* ○ *Is your hair dry yet?* **2** [NO RAIN] with no or not much rain **kurak, susuz** *a dry summer* **3** [HAIR/SKIN] Dry skin or hair does not feel soft or smooth. **(saç, cilt vb.) kuru** *My lips feel really dry.* **4** [WINE] Dry wine is not sweet. **(şarap) sek** **5** [BORING] If a book, talk, or subject is dry, it is not interesting. **(kitap, konuşma, konu vb.) yavan, kuru, sıkıcı** **6** [FUNNY] saying something in a serious way but trying to be funny **inceden inceye alaya alan, esprili, dokunduran, müstehzi** *a dry sense of humour* ● **dryness** /ˈdraɪnəs/ *noun* [U] **kuruluk**

dry² /draɪ/ *verb* [I, T] to become dry, or to make something become dry **kuru(t)mak** *He dried his hands on a towel.* ⊃See also: blow-dry.

dry (sb/sth) off *phrasal verb* to make someone or something dry, or to become dry, especially on the surface **yüzeyi/dışı kurumak/kurutmak** [often reflexive] *I dried myself off with a towel and got dressed.*

dry (sth) out *phrasal verb* to become dry, or to make something become dry **kupkuru olmak, kurutmak, kurumak**

dry (sth) up *phrasal verb mainly UK* to make plates, cups, etc dry with a cloth after they have been washed **(kap kacak) kurulamak**

dry up *phrasal verb* **1** If a supply of something dries up, it ends. **durmak, kurum** *The work dried up and he went out of business.* **2** If a river or lake dries up, the water in it disappears. **(nehir vb.) suyu çekilmek, kurumak**

,**dry 'clean** *verb* [T] to clean clothes using a special chemical and not with water **kuru temizleme** ● **dry clea-**

ner's *noun* [C] a shop where you can have your clothes cleaned this way **kuru temizleme dükkânı** ● **dry cleaning** *noun* [U] **kuru temizleme**

dryer (*also* drier) /ˈdraɪər/ *noun* [C] a machine for drying wet things, usually clothes or hair **(çamaşır, saç vb.) kurutma makinası** ⊃See also: tumble dryer.

dryly (*also* drily) /ˈdraɪli/ *adverb* If you say something dryly, you say it in a serious way but you are trying to be funny. **alay edercesine, müstehzi bir şekilde**

dual /ˈdjuːəl/ *adjective* [always before noun] having two parts, or having two of something **ikili; çift amaçlı, çift, çifte** *dual nationality*

,**dual 'carriageway** *noun* [C] *UK* a road that consists of two parallel roads, so that traffic travelling in opposite directions is separated by a central strip of land **çift yönlü yol**

dub /dʌb/ *verb* [T] **dubbing**, *past* **dubbed** **1** to give someone or something an unofficial or funny name **lakap/isim takmak** [often passive] *He was dubbed 'Big Ears' by the media.* **2** to change the language in a film or television programme into a different language **seslendirme/dublaj yapmak** [often passive] *The film was dubbed into English.*

dubious /ˈdjuːbiəs/ *adjective* **1** thought not to be completely true, honest, or legal **müphem, şüpheli, karanlık** *dubious evidence* ○ *a man with a dubious reputation* **2** not certain that something is good or true **kararsız, kuşkulu, ikircikli** *He's dubious about the benefits of acupuncture.* ● **dubiously** *adverb* **şüphe uyandıran bir şekilde**

duchess /ˈdʌtʃɪs/ *noun* [C] a woman of very high social rank in some European countries **düşes** *the Duchess of Windsor*

duck

duck¹ /dʌk/ *noun* [C, U] a bird with short legs that lives in or near water, or the meat from this bird **ördek** ⊃See also: be (like) water¹ off a duck's back.

duck² /dʌk/ *verb* **1** [I, T] to move your head or body down quickly to avoid being hit or seen **başını eğmek, eğilmek** *Billy ducked behind a car when he saw his teacher.* **2** [T] *informal* to avoid something that is difficult or unpleasant **kaytarmak, kaçmak, işine gelmediği için uzak durmak/atlatmak** *He managed to duck the issue.*

duck out of sth *phrasal verb* to avoid doing something that other people are expecting you to do **yan çizmek, (argo) su koyvermek, caymak, sakınmak, kaçmak** [+ doing sth] *She was trying to duck out of doing her homework.*

duct /dʌkt/ *noun* [C] **1** a tube in the body that a liquid substance can flow through **(vücutta) sıvının geçebi-**

leceği **kanal, tüp** *a **tear duct*** **2** *a tube or passage for air or wires that is part of the structure of a building* **(inşaat, bina vb.) kanal, boru, tüp, geçit** *a heating duct*

dud /dʌd/ *noun* [C] *something that does not work correctly* **işe yaramaz şey, bozuk, düzgün çalışmayan** ● **dud** *adjective* **bozuk**

dude /duːd/ *noun* [C] *mainly US very informal* *a man* **adam, herif** *a cool dude*

०॰**due¹** /djuː/ *adjective* **1** EVENT [never before noun] *expected or planned* **planlanan, beklenen, beklenmekte olan** [+ to do sth] *He was due to fly back this morning.* ○ *Her book is due out* (= expected to be published) *next week.* ○ *When is the baby due* (= expected to be born)? **2 due to sth** *because of something* ... **yüzünden; den dolayı, nedeniyle/sebebiyle** *The train was late due to snow.* **3** MONEY [never before noun] *Money that is due is owed to someone and must be paid.* **ödenmesi gerekli olan** *The rent is due today.* **4** DESERVE *Something that is due to you is something that is owed to you or something you deserve.* **verilmesi gerekli olan; hak edilmiş olan** *He didn't get the praise and recognition that was due to him.* **5** BEHAVIOUR [always before noun] *formal correct and suitable* **doğru, uygun, gerekli** *He was fined for driving without due care and attention.* ⊃Opposite **undue**. **6 be due for sth** *If you are due for something, it should happen very soon.* **hak etmiş, hak kazanmış, hakkı olmak, layık olmak** *I'm due for a check-up at the dentist's.*

due² /djuː/ *noun* **give sb their due** *something that you say when you want to describe someone's good qualities after they have done something wrong or after you have criticized them* **hakkını vermek/teslim etmek** *Joe's a bit slow but, to give him his due, he does work hard.*

due³ /djuː/ *adverb* **due east/north/south/west, etc** *directly east/north/south/west, etc* **(yönleri belirtirken) tam doğuya/batıya/kuzeye/güneye doğru** *sail/fly due south*

duel /ˈdjuːəl/ *noun* [C] **1** *a type of fight in the past between two people with weapons, used as a way of deciding an argument* **düello, yüz yüze meydan okuma** *He challenged him to a duel.* **2** *an argument or competition between two people or groups* **iki kişi ya da grup arasında yarış/münazara**

dues /djuːz/ *noun* [plural] *money that you must pay to be a member of an organization* **üyelik aidatı** *annual dues*

duet /djuˈet/ *noun* [C] *a piece of music for two people to perform together* **iki kişinin çalıp söylediği parça, düet**

dug /dʌg/ *past of* dig **kazmak' fiilinin geçmiş zaman hali**

duke /djuːk/ *noun* [C] *a man of very high social rank in some European countries* **dük** *the Duke of Beaufort*

dull¹ /dʌl/ *adjective* **1** BORING *not interesting* **sıkıcı, tekdüze, ruhsuz** *a dull place* ○ *a dull person* **2** NOT BRIGHT *not bright* **donuk, mat, belli belirsiz** *dull colours* ○ *dull weather* **3** SOUND *A dull sound is not loud or clear.* **boğuk, anlaşılmayan, belli olmayan** *a dull thud* **4** PAIN [always before noun] *A dull pain is not strong.* **hafif acı/ağrısı olan; müzmin şekilde ağrıyan** *a dull ache* ● **dullness** *noun* [U] **sıkıcılık** ● **dully** *adverb* **sıkıcı bir şekilde**

dull² /dʌl/ *verb* [T] *to make a feeling or quality become less strong* **his/kalite etkisini azaltmak, sönükleştirmek,** *He's on morphine to dull the pain.*

duly /ˈdjuːli/ *adverb formal* *at the correct time, in the correct way, or as you would expect* **beklendiği gibi, gereğince, hakkıyla, tam zamanında** *I ordered it*

over the Internet and within a few days, it duly arrived. ○ *I was duly impressed.*

dumb /dʌm/ *adjective* **1** *mainly US informal stupid* **aptal, gerzek** *a dumb idea/question* ○ *He's too dumb to understand.* **2** *physically unable to talk* **dilsiz, ahraz** **3** *be struck dumb* *to be unable to speak because you are so shocked or angry* **dili tutulmak, şoka girip konuşamamak** ● **dumbly** *adverb* **aptalca**

dumbfounded /ˌdʌmˈfaʊndɪd/ *adjective* *extremely surprised* **afallamış, donakalmış**

dummy¹ /ˈdʌmi/ *noun* [C] **1** BABY EQUIPMENT *UK (US pacifier)* *a small, rubber object that a baby sucks to stop it crying* **emzik** **2** STUPID PERSON *mainly US informal a stupid person* **aptal, salak** *She's no dummy.* **3** MODEL *a model of a person* **cansız manken**

dummy² /ˈdʌmi/ *adjective* [always before noun] *not real but made to look real* **yapma şey, taklit, yalancı** *dummy weapons*

dump¹ /dʌmp/ *verb* **1** [T] *to put something somewhere to get rid of it, especially in a place where you should not put it* **gizlice boşaltmak/dökmek, boca etmek** *The company was fined for illegally dumping toxic chemicals.* **2 dump sth on/in/down, etc** *to put something somewhere quickly and carelessly* **hızlıca ve dikkatsizce koymak; fırlatıp atmak** *Henri dumped his bag on the table and went upstairs.*

dump² /dʌmp/ *(also UK tip) noun* [C] **1** *a place where people take things that they do not want* **çöplük, mezbele, ardiye** *We took our old mattress to the dump.* **2** *informal a place that is dirty and untidy* **çok pis ve dağınık yer, çöplük, batakhane** *His room is a dump.*

dumpling /ˈdʌmplɪŋ/ *noun* [C] *a round mixture of fat and flour that has been cooked in boiling liquid* **lokmaya benzer pişmiş hamur topağı** *stew and dumplings*

dumps /dʌmps/ *noun* **be down in the dumps** *informal to be unhappy* **çok mutsuz olmak, ağzını bıçak açmamak, yüreğine ateş düşmek, morali bozuk olmak** *He looks a bit down in the dumps.*

Dumpster /ˈdʌmpstər/ *US trademark (UK skip) noun* [C] *a very large, metal container for big pieces of rubbish* **büyük, geniş çöp tankı/bidonu/kazanı**

dumpy /ˈdʌmpi/ *adjective informal* *short and fat* **tıknaz, bodur, kısa ve şişman**

dune /djuːn/ *(also sand dune) noun* [C] *a hill of sand in the desert or on the coast* **kum tepeciği**

dung /dʌŋ/ *noun* [U] *solid waste from a large animal* **büyük baş hayvan dışkısı; gübre, kemre**

dungarees /ˌdʌŋɡəˈriːz/ *UK (US overalls) noun* [plural] *trousers with a part that covers your chest and straps that go over your shoulders* **iş tulumu**

dungeon /ˈdʌndʒən/ *noun* [C] *a dark, underground prison, used in the past* **zindan**

dunk /dʌŋk/ *verb* [T] *to quickly put something into liquid and take it out again* **hızlıca daldırıp çıkarmak, banmak** *He dunked the roll in his soup.*

dunno /dəˈnəʊ/ *informal I dunno I do not know.* **bilmiyorum**

duo /ˈdjuːəʊ/ *noun* [C] *two people who perform together* **ikili; birlikte gösteri yapan ikili** *a comedy/pop duo*

dupe /djuːp/ *verb* [T] *to trick someone* **aldatmak, kandırmak, alavere dalavere yapmak; ketenpereye getirmek** [often passive, + into + doing sth] *He was duped into paying $4000 for a fake painting.*

duplicate¹ /ˈdjuːplɪkeɪt/ *verb* [T] **1** *to make an exact copy of something* **kopyasını/suretini çıkarmak** *The document has been duplicated.* **2** *to do something* that has already been done, in exactly the same way aynısını yapmak; tıpatıp benzerini yapmak *Ajax hope to duplicate last year's success.* ● **duplication** /ˌdjuːplɪˈkeɪʃᵊn/ *noun* [U] çoğaltma

duplicate² /ˈdjuːplɪkət/ *noun* **1** [C] something that is an exact copy of something else **kopya, suret, tekrar, benzer** *I lost my passport and had to get a duplicate.* **2 in duplicate** If a document is in duplicate, there are two copies of it. sureti/kopyası olan ● **duplicate** *adjective a duplicate key* çoğaltılmış

duplicity /djuˈplɪsəti/ *noun* [U] when you dishonestly tell different people different things **farklı kişilere farklı şeyler söylemek; iki yüzlülük; ikili oynama**

durable /ˈdjʊərəbl/ *adjective* remaining in good condition for a long time **sağlam, dayanıklı** *durable goods* ○ *a fabric that is comfortable and durable* ● **durability** /ˌdjʊərəˈbɪləti/ *noun* [U] dayanıklılık

duration /djʊəˈreɪʃᵊn/ *noun* [U] *formal* the amount of time that something lasts **süre, zaman** *The singer remained in the hotel **for the duration of** his stay in the UK.*

duress /djʊˈres/ *noun formal* **under duress** If you do something under duress, you do it because someone is forcing you to. **cebren, baskı altında, zorla** *a confession made under duress*

o⊸**during** /ˈdjʊərɪŋ/ *preposition* **1** for the whole of a period of time **esnasında, boyunca** *Emma's usually at home during the day.* **2** at a particular moment in a period of time **süresince, sırasında** *We'll arrange a meeting some time during the week.*

dusk /dʌsk/ *noun* [U] the time in the evening when it starts to become dark **gün batımı, akşam karanlığı** *As dusk fell, we headed back to the hotel.*

dust¹ /dʌst/ *noun* [U] **1** a powder of dirt or soil that you see on a surface or in the air **toz** *He drove off in a cloud of dust.* **2 bite the dust** *informal* to die, fail, or stop existing **ölmek, toprağa düşmek, yok olmak** ● **3 the dust settles** If the dust settles after an argument or big change, the situation becomes calmer. **ortalık yatışmak/düzelmek; toz bulutu dağılmak; ortalık sakinlemek; hengame yatışmak** *Let the dust settle a bit before you make any decisions about the future.*

dust² /dʌst/ *verb* [I, T] to remove dust from something **toz almak** *I tidied and dusted the shelves.*

dustbin /ˈdʌstbɪn/ *UK* (*US* **garbage can**) *noun* [C] a large container for rubbish kept outside your house **çöp bidonu/kovası/tenekesi**

duster /ˈdʌstər/ *noun* [C] *UK* a cloth used for removing dust (= powder of dirt) from furniture and other objects **toz bezi**

dustman /ˈdʌstmən/ *UK* (*US* **garbage man**) *noun* [C] *plural UK* **dustmen** someone whose job is to remove rubbish from containers outside people's houses **çöpçü**

dustpan /ˈdʌstpæn/ *noun* [C] a flat container with a handle, used with a brush for removing dirt from a floor **faraş; temizlik kovası** *Get the dustpan and brush and I'll sweep this up.* ➜See picture at **brush**.

dusty /ˈdʌsti/ *adjective* covered with dust (= powder of dirt) **tozlu; toz toprak içinde** *a dusty old chair* ○ *dusty streets*

dutiful /ˈdjuːtɪfᵊl/ *adjective* doing everything that you should in your position or job **itaatkâr, söz dinleyen; üzerine düşeni yapan** *a dutiful son* ● **dutifully** *adverb* itaatkar bir şekilde

━━━━━━━━━━━━━━━━━━━━━━━━━━━━━━━
duty .... İLE BİRLİKTE KULLANILAN KELİMELER

have/neglect/perform a duty ● a duty **to/towards** sb

o⊸**duty** /ˈdjuːti/ *noun* [C, U] **1** [RIGHT THING TO DO] something you must do because it is morally or legally right **iş, görev, sorunluluk** *a moral duty* ○ [+ to do sth] *Rail companies **have a duty** to provide safe transport.* **2** [JOB] something you do as part of your job or because of your position **görev, iş** *professional/official duties* **3 on/off duty** If a doctor, police officer, etc is on duty, they are working, and if they are off duty, they are not working. **nöbette/izinli 4** [TAX] tax that you pay on something you buy **vergi**

duty-free /ˌdjuːtiˈfriː/ *adjective* Duty-free goods are things that you can buy and bring into a country without paying tax. **gümrüksüz, gümrüğe tabi olmayan**

duvet /ˈdjuːveɪ/ Ⓤ /duːˈveɪ/ *UK* (*US* **comforter**) *noun* [C] a cover filled with feathers or warm material that you sleep under **yorgan**

DVD /ˌdiːviːˈdiː/ *noun* [C] *abbreviation for* digital versatile disc: a small disc for storing music, films and information **DVD**; üzerine film, müzik, bilgi kaydedilebilen disk *a DVD player/drive* ○ *Is this film available on DVD?*

dwarf¹ /dwɔːf/ *noun* [C] **1** an imaginary creature like a little man, in children's stories **cüce** *Snow White and the Seven Dwarves* **2** an offensive word for someone who is very short **bodur, cüce, tıknaz** ● **dwarf** *adjective* A dwarf animal or plant is much smaller than the normal size. **normal ölçülerden küçük hayvan veya bitki; bodur; minyatür**

dwarf² /dwɔːf/ *verb* [T] If something dwarfs other things, it is very big and makes them seem small. **cüceleştirmek; cüce gibi göstermek** [often passive] *The hotel is dwarfed by skyscrapers.*

dwell /dwel/ *verb* past **dwelt** or **dwelled dwell in/among/with, etc** *literary* to live somewhere **yaşamak, ikâmet etmek, oturmak**
dwell on/upon sth *phrasal verb* to keep thinking or talking about something, especially something bad or unpleasant (kötü, istenmeye şey) üzerinde durmak, uğraşmak *I don't want to dwell on the past.*

dweller /ˈdwelər/ *noun* **an apartment/city/country, etc dweller** someone who lives in an apartment/city/the country, etc **sakin, yaşayan, orada ikâmet eden**

dwelling /ˈdwelɪŋ/ *noun* [C] *formal* a house or place to live in **ev, mesken, konut, yaşanan yer**

dwindle /ˈdwɪndl/ *verb* [I] to become smaller or less **azalmak, küçülmek** *The number of students in the school has dwindled to 200.* ○ *Our savings slowly dwindled away.* ○ *dwindling supplies of oil*

dye¹ /daɪ/ *noun* [C, U] a substance that is used to change the colour of something **boya**

dye² /daɪ/ *verb* [T] **dyeing**, past **dyed** to change the colour of something by using a dye **boyamak** *He dyed his hair pink last week.*

dying /ˈdaɪɪŋ/ *present participle of* die **ölme**

dyke (*also* **dike**) /daɪk/ *noun* [C] **1** a wall built to stop water from a sea or river going onto the land **set, bent 2** *UK* a passage that has been dug to take water away from fields **kanal, ark, tahliye/boşaltma kanalı**

dynamic /daɪˈnæmɪk/ *adjective* **1** [ACTIVE] full of ideas, energy, and enthusiasm **coşku, enerji ve fikir dolu; dinamik** *a dynamic, young teacher* ○ *dynamic leadership* **2** [CHANGING] continuously changing or moving **sürekli değişen ve hareketli, yerinde duramayan** *a dynamic economy* **3** [PRODUCING MOVEMENT] A dynamic force makes something move. **canlı, itici, harekete geçiren** ● **dynamically** *adverb* enerjik bir şekilde

dynamics /daɪˈnæmɪks/ *noun* **1** [plural] the way that parts of a situation, group, or system affect each other

etki eden unsurlar, dinamikler *political dynamics*
○ *The* **dynamics** *of family life have changed greatly.*
2 [U] the scientific study of the movement of objects **nesnelerin hareketini inceleyen bilim dalı; dinamik dersi**

dynamism /'daɪnəmɪzəm/ *noun* [U] the quality of being dynamic **canlılık, hareketlilik, dinamizm**

dynamite /'daɪnəmaɪt/ *noun* [U] **1** a type of explosive **dinamit** *a stick of dynamite* **2** *informal* someone or something that is very exciting, powerful, or dangerous **heyecanlı, güçlü ve tehlikeli olan kişi/şey; dinamit gibi olan kişi/nesne** *an issue that is political dynamite*

dynasty /'dɪnəsti/ ⓤⓢ /'daɪnəsti/ *noun* [C] a series of rulers who are all from the same family **hanedan/hanedanlık** *the Ming dynasty*

dysentery /'dɪsªntªri/ *noun* [U] an infectious disease which causes severe problems with the bowels, making solid waste become liquid **dizanteri; kanlı ishal**

dysfunctional /dɪs'fʌŋkʃªnªl/ *adjective formal* not behaving, working, or happening in the way that most people think is normal **normal olarak kabul edilen şekilde olmayan/çalışmayan/davranmayan; alışılmışın dışında işlev sergileyen** *a dysfunctional family/childhood*

dyslexia /dɪ'sleksiə/ *noun* [U] a condition affecting the brain that makes it difficult for someone to read and write **(beyinde) okuma/yazma özürü; disleksi**
● **dyslexic** /dɪ'sleksɪk/ *adjective* having dyslexia **(beyin) okuma/yazma özürlü; disleksik**

E, e /iː/ the fifth letter of the alphabet **alfabenin beşinci harfi**

e- /i-/ *prefix* electronic, usually relating to the Internet **internette 'elektronik' anlamına gelen harf** *an e--ticket* ○ *e-commerce*

ᴏ⁻**each** /iːtʃ/ *pronoun, determiner* every one in a group of two or more things or people when they are considered separately **her, herbiri** *A player from each of the teams volunteered to be captain.* ○ *The bill is £36 between the four of us, that's £9 each.*

₁**each 'other** *pronoun* used to show that each person in a group of two or more people does something to the others **birbirine, birbirini** *The kids are always arguing with each other.*

eager /ˈiːɡər/ *adjective* wanting to do or have something very much **istekli, hevesli** [+ to do sth] *Sam was eager to go home and play on his computer.* ● **eagerly** *adverb an eagerly awaited* announcement **istekli bir şekilde** ● **eagerness** *noun* [U] **istek**

eagle

eagle /ˈiːɡl/ *noun* [C] a large, wild bird with a big, curved beak, that hunts smaller animals **kartal**

ᴏ⁻**ear** /ɪər/ *noun* **1** [C] one of the two organs on your head that you hear with **kulak** *The child whispered something in her mother's ear.* ⊃Orta kısımdaki renkli sayfalarına bakınız. **2** [C] the top part of some crop plants, which produces grain **başak, tahılın tepesi** *an ear of wheat/corn* **3 have an ear for sth** to be good at hearing, repeating, or understanding a particular type of sound **bir şey için kulağı iyi olmak; ...e karşı hassas olmak** *He has no ear for music.* **4 fall on deaf ears** If advice or a request falls on deaf ears, people ignore it. **önemsememek, dikkate almamak** ● **5 play it by ear** to decide how to deal with a situation as it develops **oluruna bırakmak, gidişata göre hareket etmek, bekleyip görmek** ● **6 play sth by ear** to play a piece of music by remembering the notes **bir şarkıyı ezbere çalmak, notasız kulaktan çalmak**

earache /ˈɪəreɪk/ *noun* [C, U] pain in your ear **kulak ağrısı** *I've got UK earache/ US an earache.*

eardrum /ˈɪədrʌm/ *noun* [C] a part inside your ear made of thin, tight skin that allows you to hear sounds **kulak zarı**

earl /ɜːl/ *noun* [C] a man of high social rank in the UK **kont** *the Earl of Northumberland*

earlobe /ˈɪələʊb/ *noun* [C] the soft part at the bottom of your ear **kulak memesi**

ᴏ⁻**early** /ˈɜːli/ *adjective, adverb* **earlier, earliest 1** near the beginning of a period of time, process, etc **erken, başında, başlarında** *the early 1980s* ○ *It is too early to say whether he will recover completely.* **2** before the usual time or the time that was arranged **önce, erken, erkenden** *early retirement* ○ *The plane arrived ten minutes early.* **3 at the earliest** used after a time or date to show that something will not happen before then **önce, önceden, en erken** *Building will not begin until July at the earliest.* **4 early on** in the first stage or part of something **başlangıçta, ilk zamanlarda** *I lost interest quite early on in the book.* ⊃See also: it's early days (day).

earmark /ˈɪəmɑːk/ *verb* [T] to decide that something, especially money, will be used for a particular purpose **bir kenara koymak, ayırmak, ayrılmak** [often passive] *More than $7 million has been earmarked for schools in the area.* ○ *The land is earmarked for development.*

ᴏ⁻**earn** /ɜːn/ *verb* **1** GET MONEY [I, T] to get money for doing work **para kazanmak** *She earns more than £40,000 a year.* **2 earn a/your living** to work to get money for the things you need **hayatını kazanmak; geçimini sağlamak 3** DESERVE [T] to get something that you deserve because of your work, qualities, etc **kazanmak, hak etmek, elde etmek** *As a teacher you have to earn the respect of your students.* **4** PROFIT [T] to make a profit **kâr yapmak,** *an account that earns a high rate of interest*

🧩 ***earner*** .... İLE BİRLİKTE KULLANILAN KELİMELER

high/low/top earners ● **wage** earners

earner /ˈɜːnər/ *noun* [C] **1** someone who earns money **para kazanan; kazanç sağlayan** *a high earner* **2** *UK informal* a product or service that earns you money **para kazandıran; kazanç getiren** *She has a nice little earner making curtains.*

earnest /ˈɜːnɪst/ *adjective* **1** very serious and sincere **ciddi, ağırbaşlı** *an earnest young man* ○ *an earnest effort* **2 in earnest** If something begins to happen in earnest, it really starts to happen in a serious way. **büyük bir gayret ve ciddiyetle** *The research will begin in earnest early next year.* **3 be in earnest** to be very serious about something and mean what you are saying **ciddi ve kararlı** ● **earnestly** *adverb* **dürüstçe** ● **earnestness** *noun* [U] **dürüstlük**

earring

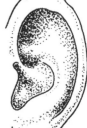

earnings /ˈɜːnɪŋz/ *noun* [plural] money that you get from working **kazanç, gelir, ücret, maaş**

earphones /ˈɪəfəʊnz/ *noun* [plural] a piece of electronic equipment that you put on your ears so that you can listen privately to radio, recorded music, etc **kulaklık**

earring /'ɪərɪŋ/ *noun* [C] a piece of jewellery that you wear on or through your ear **küpe** [usually plural] *diamond earrings*

earshot /'ɪəʃɒt/ *noun* **be out of/within earshot** If you are out of earshot, you are too far away to hear something, and if you are within earshot, you are close enough to hear something. **kulağın işiteceği/duyamayacağı/ duyabileceği uzaklıkta olmak**

o⌐**earth** /ɜːθ/ *noun* **1** [PLANET] [no plural] (*also* **the Earth**) the planet that we live on **dünya 2** [SUBSTANCE] [U] soil or ground **toprak, yer** *a mound of earth* **3** [ELECTRICAL WIRE] [C] *UK* (*US* **ground**) a wire that makes electrical equipment safer **topraklama/toprak hattı 4 cost/ charge, etc the earth** *UK informal* to cost/charge, etc an extremely large amount of money **büyük miktara malolmak; son derece fazla ücret ödemek; pahalıya malolmak 5 come (back) down to earth** to start dealing with life and problems again after you have had a very exciting time **çok keyifli bir dönemden sonra normal yaşama dönmek, problemlerle uğraşmaya başlamak ● 6 how/what/why, etc on earth?** *informal* used when you are extremely surprised, confused, or angry about something **Allah aşkına ...; Yahu ...; Acaba neden...?** *Why on earth didn't you tell me before?*

earthly /'ɜːθli/ *adjective* **1 no earthly doubt/reason/ use, etc** used to emphasize that there is not any doubt/reason/use, etc **geçerli; akla uygun; mantıklı; hiç bir şüphe/neden olmaksızın** *There's no earthly reason why you should feel guilty.* **2** *literary* relating to this world and not any spiritual life **dünyevî, maddesel** *earthly powers*

🔲 earthquake .... İLE BİRLİKTE KULLANILAN KELİMELER

an earthquake **hits/strikes** [a place] ● a **devastating/ major/massive/powerful** earthquake

earthquake /'ɜːθkweɪk/ *noun* [C] a sudden movement of the Earth's surface, often causing severe damage **deprem** *A powerful earthquake struck eastern Turkey last night.*

earthy /'ɜːθi/ *adjective* **1** referring to sex and the human body in a direct way **açık saçık konuşmaktan çekinmeyen; doğrudan cinsel içerikli konuşan** *earthy jokes* **2** similar to soil in colour, smell, or taste **topraksı, toprak gibi**

earwig /'ɪəwɪg/ *noun* [C] a small dark-brown insect with two curved parts on its tail **kulağakaçan böceği/sineği**

ease¹ /iːz/ *noun* **1** [U] If you do something with ease, it is very easy for you to do it. **kolaylık, rahatlık** *Gary passed his exams with ease.* ○ *I'm amazed at the ease with which he learnt the language.* **2 at ease** feeling relaxed and comfortable **içi rahat, huzurlu** *I felt completely at ease with him.* **3 ill at ease** feeling anxious **rahatsız, huzursuz**

ease² /iːz/ *verb* **1** [I, T] to become less severe, or to make something become less severe **hafifletmek, azaltmak** *The new road should ease traffic problems in the village.* **2 ease sb/sth back/out/up, etc** to move someone or something gradually and gently to another position **yavaşça ve ihtimamla başka bir pozisyona çevirmek, kımıldatmak; yerinden oynatmak** [often reflexive] *Tom eased himself back in his chair.*

ease off/up *phrasal verb* **1** [STOP] to gradually stop or become less **yavaş yavaş durmak veya azalmak** *The storm is easing off.* **2** [WORK LESS] to start to work less or do things with less energy **yavaşlamak** *As he got older, he started to ease up a little.* **3** [TREAT LESS SEVERELY] to start to

treat someone less severely **gevşemek, yumuşamak** *I wish his supervisor would ease up on him a bit.*

easel /'iːzᵊl/ *noun* [C] something used to support a painting while you paint it **ressam sehpası**

easel

o⌐**easily** /'iːzɪli/ *adverb* **1** with no difficulty **kolayca, kolaylıkla** *She makes friends easily.* **2** used to emphasize that something is likely **kuşkusuz, şüphesiz** *A comment like that could easily be misunderstood.* **3 easily the best/worst/biggest, etc** certainly the best/worst/biggest, etc **kesinlikle en iyi/en kötü/ en büyük**

YAYGIN HATALAR

easily
Dikkat: Çok sıklıkla yapılan kelime türetme hatası. Eğer sıfat -y ile bitiyorsa, zarfa çevirmek için -ily eklemek gerekir. **easly** olarak yazmayın. Doğru şekli **easily** olarak yazılır.

o⌐**east, East** /iːst/ *noun* **1** [U] the direction that you face to see the sun rise **doğu** *Which way's east?* **2 the east** the part of an area that is further towards the east than the rest **doğu; ...nın doğusu 3 the East** the countries of Asia, especially Japan and China **Japonya ve Çin gibi doğu ülkeleri ● east** *adjective* *New York is east of Chicago.* **doğu ● east** *adverb* towards the east **doğuya/ doğu yönüne doğru** *They sailed east.* **⊃**See also: the **Middle East.**

Easter /'iːstəʳ/ *noun* [C, U] the Christian period of celebration around Easter Sunday (= the special Sunday in March or April on which Christians celebrate Jesus Christ's return to life) **Paskalya yortusu** *the Easter holidays*

'Easter ,egg *noun* [C] a chocolate egg that people give and receive at Easter **Paskalya yumurtası**

easterly /'iːstᵊli/ *adjective* **1** towards or in the east **doğuda, doğuya doğru** *The river flows in an easterly direction.* **2** An easterly wind comes from the east. **doğudan esen** *a strong, easterly breeze*

o⌐**eastern, Eastern** /'iːstᵊn/ *adjective* [always before noun] **1** in or from the east part of an area **doğusunda, doğusundan** *eastern Europe* **2** in or from the countries of Asia **Asya** *Asya ülkelerinde/ülkelerinden Eastern philosophy* ○ *an Eastern religion*

easterner, Easterner /'iːstᵊnəʳ/ *noun* [C] *mainly US* someone from the east part of a country or area **doğulu**

,Easter 'Sunday (*also* ,Easter 'Day) *noun* [C, U] the special Sunday in March or April on which Christians celebrate Jesus Christ's return to life **mart veya nisan ayında Hıristiyanların Hz. İsa'nın hayata dönüşünü kutladıkları özel Pazar günü**

eastward, eastwards /'iːstwəd/, /'iːstwədz/ *adverb* towards the east **doğuya/doğu yönüne doğru ● eastward** *adjective* *an eastward direction* **doğuya doğru**

easy .... BAŞKA BİR DEYİŞLE

Eğer bir şeyi yapması ve anlaması kolay ise, bu durumu **simple** veya **straightforward** kelimeleri ile açıklarız. *The recipe is so **simple**, you just mix all the ingredients together.* ● *It seems like a fairly **straightforward** task.*

Eğer bir makine veya sistem kullanılması kolay bir şekilde tasarlanmışsa, durumu belirtmek için **userfriendly** ifadesi kullanılır. *This latest version of the software is much more **user-friendly**.*

Gayri resmi ortamlarda kullanılabilen ve bazı şeyleri yapmanın çok kolay olduğunu gösteren ifadeler vardır. Örneğin:...... *(UK) This machine's* a doddle *to use.* ● *My last exam was* a piece of cake. ● *Once we reached the main road the journey was* plain sailing.

o⸍**easy**¹ /'i:zi/ *adjective* **1** not difficult **kolay, basit** *an easy choice* ○ *He thought the exam was very easy.* ○ [+ to do sth] *It's easy to see why he's so popular.* **2** relaxed and comfortable **sakin, rahat** *She has a very easy manner.* **3 I'm easy** *informal* used to say that you do not mind which choice is made **Benim için farketmez; Hangisi olursa olsun** *"Would you like pizza or curry?" "I'm easy. You choose."*

easy² /'i:zi/ *adverb* **1 take it/things easy** to relax and not use too much energy **boşvermek, aldırmamak, kafaya takmak** *After his heart attack, he had to take things easy for a while.* **2 go easy on sb** *informal* to treat someone in a gentle way and not be so strict **dikkatli/nazik davranmak; fazla sıkı olmamak** *Go easy on the boy - he's only young.* **3 go easy on sth** *informal* to not eat or use too much of something **dikkatli kullanmak; bir şeyden çok fazla yememek** *Go easy on the chips, there aren't many left.* **4 easier said than done** used to say that something seems like a good idea but it would be difficult to do **demesi/söylemesi kolay**

easy-going /ˌi:zi'ɡəʊɪŋ/ *adjective* relaxed and not easily upset or worried **kaygısız, aldırış etmeyen, takmayan, kolay iletişim kurulabilen**

eat ...... BAŞKA BİR DEYİŞLE

Daha resmi bir şekilde söyleniş şekli için **consume** fiili kullanılır. *He* consumes *vast quantities of bread with every meal.*

Eğer kişi çok aç olduğundan dolayı yemeği çok çabuk yiyorsa, **devour** fiili kullanılabilir. *The children* devoured *a whole packet of biscuits.*

Bolt down, gobble up, wolf down deyimlerinin hepsi çok hızlı yemek yendiğini gösterir. *He* gobbled up *his food before anyone else had started.* ● *I gave her a plate of pasta and she* wolfed *it* down.

Scoff (scarf fiili resmi olmayan durumlarda kişinin yemeği çok hızlı yediğini gösterir. *Who* scoffed/scarfed *all the cake?*

Snack fiili ana öğünler arası yemek yemek anlamına gelir. *I've been* snacking *on biscuits and chocolate all afternoon.*

Eat out evin dışında, restoranda yemek yemek anlamına gelir. *I thought we could* eat out *tonight.*

Pick at deyimi kişinin çok az yemek yediğinde kullanılır. *He didn't feel hungry, and sat at the table* picking at *his food.*

Tuck into deyimi kişinin büyük iştah ve istekle yemek yemeğe başladığı anlamına gelir. *I was just about to* tuck into *a huge bowl of ice cream.*

o⸍**eat** /i:t/ *verb past tense* **ate**, *past participle* **eaten 1** [I, T] to put food into your mouth and then swallow it **yemek** *Who ate all the cake?* ○ *I haven't eaten since breakfast.* ○ *Let's have something to eat* (= some food). **2** [I] to eat a meal **yemek yemek** *We usually eat in the kitchen.* ᗡSee also: have your **cake and eat it**.

eat away at sb *phrasal verb* If a memory or bad feeling eats away at someone, it makes them feel more and more unhappy. **için içini yemek, içini kemirmek, sürekli düşünmek, kafaya takmak**

eat away at sth *phrasal verb* to gradually damage or destroy something **zamanla aşındırmak/zarar vermek; kemirmek**

eat into sth *phrasal verb* to use or take away a large part of something valuable, such as money or time **(para, zaman) değerli bir şeyin büyük bir bölümünü alıp götürmek veya kullanmak**

eat out *phrasal verb* to eat at a restaurant **dışarıda/restoranda yemek yemek** ᗡOrta kısımdaki renkli sayfalarına bakınız.

eat (sth) up *phrasal verb* to eat all the food you have been given **yiyip bitirmek** *Be a good boy and eat up your spinach.*

eat up sth *phrasal verb* to use or take away a large part of something valuable, such as money or time **(para, zaman) değerli bir şeyin büyük bir bölümünü alıp götürmek veya kullanmak** *Cities are eating up more and more farmland.*

eater /'i:tər/ *noun* **a big/fussy/meat, etc eater** someone who eats in a particular way or eats a particular food **(belli bir tarzda) yemek yiyen kişi**

eatery /'i:təri/ *noun* [C] *informal* a restaurant **lokanta, restoran**

'**eating di,sorder** *noun* [C] a mental illness in which someone cannot eat normal amounts of food **yemek yiyememe rahatsızlığı; düzenli yemek yiyememe**

eaves /i:vz/ *noun* [plural] the edges of a roof where it is wider than the walls **saçak; çatı saçakları**

eavesdrop /'i:vzdrɒp/ *verb* [I] **eavesdropping**, *past* **eavesdropped** to secretly listen to a conversation **gizlice dinlemek** *He stood outside the door* eavesdropping *on their conversation.* ● **eavesdropper** *noun* [C] **başkalarının konuşmalarını gizli bir şekilde dinleyen**

eBay /'i:beɪ/ *noun* [U] *trademark* a website that allows users to buy and sell things online **internet ortamında alışveriş yapılan site**

ebb¹ /eb/ *noun* **1 the ebb (tide)** when the sea flows away from the land **cezir; denizin çekilmesi 2 be at a low ebb** If someone's enthusiasm, confidence, etc is at a low ebb, it is much less than before. **durgun/cansız/kendine güveni geçmişe göre azalmak** *Staff morale is at a low ebb.* ● **3 ebb and flow** the way in which the level of something regularly becomes higher or lower in a situation **bir durumun düzensizlik arz etmesi/göstermesi** *the ebb and flow of the economy*

ebb² /eb/ *verb* [I] **1** (*also* ebb away) to gradually disappear **gözden kaybolmak, azalmak, tükenmek** *She watched her father's life slowly ebbing away.* **2** When the tide ebbs, the sea flows away from the land. **(deniz, su) çekilmek**

ebony /'eb²ni/ *noun* [U] hard black wood **abanoz**

ebullient /ɪ'bʊliənt/ *adjective* energetic, enthusiastic, and excited **enerjik, neşeli, coşkun** *an ebullient personality*

e-business /'i:bɪznɪs/ *noun* [C, U] the business of buying and selling goods and services on the Internet, or a company which does this **e-iş/ticaret**

e-cash /'i:kæʃ/ *noun* [U] money in an electronic form, used for buying goods and services on the Internet **e-nakit/para**

eccentric¹ /ɪk'sentrɪk/ *adjective* behaving in a strange and unusual way **garip/tuhaf/tipik davranan** *an eccentric professor* ○ *eccentric behaviour* ● **eccentrically** *adverb* **ilginç bir şekilde** ● **eccentricity** /ˌeksen'trɪsəti/ *noun* [U] when someone is eccentric **gariplik, tuhaflık**

eccentric² /ɪk'sentrɪk/ *noun* [C] someone who is eccentric **garip/tuhaf kişi** *a harmless eccentric*

ecclesiastical /ɪˌkli:zi'æstɪk²l/ *adjective* relating to the Christian Church **Hıristiyan kilisesine ilişkin/dair** *ecclesiastical law/history*

echelon /'eʃəlɒn/ *noun formal* **the lower/upper echelons** the people at the lower/upper level of a large organization or society **bir kuruluş veya toplumda en**

alt/üst kademedekiler *the upper echelons of government/management*

echinacea /ˌekɪˈneɪʃə/ *noun* [U] a plant that is used as a medicine, especially to help your body fight illness **kirpi otu (şifalı bir bitki)**

echo¹ /ˈekəʊ/ *verb* **echoing**, *past* **echoed** **1** [I] If a sound echoes, or a place echoes with a sound, you hear the sound again because you are in a large, empty space. **yankılanmak, eko yapmak** *Their **voices echoed** around the room.* **2** [T] to repeat something that someone else has said because you agree with it **söyleneni kabul ettiğini göstermek için tekrar etmek** *This report echoes some of the earlier research I've read.*

E

echo² /ˈekəʊ/ *noun* [C] *plural* **echoes** **1** a sound that you hear more than once because you are in a big, empty space **yankı, eko** **2** something that is very much like something else and makes you think of it **benzer, taklit** [usually plural] *There are **echoes of** Shakespeare's work in the play.*

eclectic /ekˈlektɪk/ *adjective* including many different styles and types **karma, çok çeşitli tür ve tarz içeren** *an **eclectic mix***

eclipse¹ /ɪˈklɪps/ *noun* [C] when the sun is covered by the moon, or the moon is covered by the Earth's shadow (= dark area) **güneş/ay tutulması** *a solar/lunar eclipse*

eclipse² /ɪˈklɪps/ *verb* [T] **1** to make another person or thing seem much less important, good, or famous **değerini düşürmek; önemsizleştirmek; gölgede bırakmak** [often passive] *Braque was somewhat eclipsed by Picasso.* **2** to make an eclipse of the moon or sun **güneş/ay tutulmak**

eco- /iːkəʊ-/ *prefix* relating to the environment **çevreye ilişkin anlamında ön ek** *eco-friendly cleaning products*

eco-friendly /ˌiːkəʊˈfrendli/ *adjective* describes a product that is designed so that it does not damage the environment **çevre dostu; çevreye zarar vermeyen** *eco-friendly washing powder*

ecological /ˌiːkəˈlɒdʒɪkᵊl/ *adjective* relating to ecology or to the environment **çevreye ait, ekolojik** *an ecological disaster* • **ecologically** *adverb* **ekolojik bir biçimde**

ecoˌlogical ˈfootprint *noun* [C] the amount of the earth's energy that someone or something uses **yeryüzünde var olan enerji** *You can reduce your ecological footprint by cycling more and driving less.*

ecology /iːˈkɒlədʒi/ *noun* [U, no plural] the relationship between living things and the environment, or the scientific study of this **çevrebilim, ekoloji** • **ecologist** *noun* [C] someone who studies ecology **çevrebilimci, ekolojist**

e-commerce /ˈiːˌkɒmɜːs/ *noun* [U] the buying and selling of goods and services on the Internet **e-ticaret**

o-**economic** /ˌiːkəˈnɒmɪk/, /ˌekəˈnɒmɪk/ *adjective* **1** [always before noun] relating to trade, industry, and money **ticaret/endüstri/paraya ilişkin/dair** ***economic growth*** ○ ***economic policies*** **2** making a profit, or likely to make a profit **kârlı, kâr getiren** *It's not economic to produce goods in small quantities.* ➲Opposite **uneconomic**. • **economically** *adverb The country would benefit economically.* **ekonomik olarak**

economical /ˌiːkəˈnɒmɪkᵊl/, /ˌekəˈnɒmɪkᵊl/ *adjective* not using a lot of money, fuel, etc **iktisatlı, hesaplı, ekonomik** *I need a car that's economical and reliable.* • **economically** *adverb* **ekonomik açıdan**

ˌeconomic ˈmigrant *noun* [C] a person who leaves their home country to live in another country with better work or living conditions **daha iyi iş ve yaşam koşulları için başka bir ülkeye göç eden kişi; göçmen**

economics /ˌiːkəˈnɒmɪks/ *noun* [U] the study of the way in which trade, industry, and money are organized **ekonomi/iktisat bilimi** • **economist** /ɪˈkɒnəmɪst/ *noun* [C] someone who studies economics **iktisatçı, ekonomist** ➲See also: **home economics**.

economize (*also UK* **-ise**) /ɪˈkɒnəmaɪz/ *verb* [I] to use less of something because you want to save money **iktisatlı kullanmak, hesaplı/idareli harcamak**

economy ...... İLE BİRLİKTE KULLANILAN KELİMELER

a booming/stable/strong/weak economy • the **global/local/national economy** • the economy **grows/improves/recovers/slows**

o-**economy** /ɪˈkɒnəmi/ *noun* **1** [C] the system by which a country produces and uses goods and money **ekonomi** *the German/US economy* ○ *a global economy* **2** [C, U] when someone or something does not use much money, fuel, etc **iktisat, tutumluluk** *The car's design combines comfort with economy.* ○ *UK We'll need to **make** some **economies** when I stop work.*

eˈconomy ˌclass *noun* [U] the cheapest and least comfortable seats on an aircraft **uçakta ucuz biletle seyahat edilen yer** • **eˈconomy ˌclass** *adjective, adverb* **ekonomi sınıfı**

ecosystem /ˈiːkəʊˌsɪstəm/ *noun* [C] all the living things in an area and the way they affect each other and the environment **canlılar ve çevrenin birbirine olan ilişkilerini içeren sistem; ekosistem** *Tourism is damaging the fragile ecosystem of the reef.*

ecotourism /ˈiːkəʊtʊərɪzᵊm/ *noun* [U] the business of providing holidays for people so that they can help local people and not damage the environment **ekoturizm; çevreyi koruma amaçlı turizm**

eco-warrior /ˈiːkəʊˌwɒriəʳ/ *noun* [C] someone who tries to stop activities which damage the environment **çevre savaşçısı**

ecstasy /ˈekstəsi/ *noun* **1** [U] a feeling of extreme happiness **mest olma, kendinden geçme; ayağı yerden kesilme hali** *She danced about **in ecstasy**.* **2 Ecstasy** an illegal drug that makes you feel happier and more active **yasadışı uyuşturucu hap; ekstasi**

ecstatic /ɪkˈstætɪk/ *adjective* extremely happy **mest, kendinden geçmiş; (argo) uçmuş/uçuk** • **ecstatically** *adverb* **mutluluktan deliye dönmüş bir şekilde**

ecumenical /ˌekjʊˈmenɪkᵊl/ *adjective* encouraging different types of Christian churches to unite **Hıristiyan kiliseler birliğini amaçlayan** *an ecumenical service*

eczema /ˈeksmə/ *noun* [U] a medical condition which makes areas of skin become red and dry **egzama**

o-**edge¹** /edʒ/ *noun* **1** [C] the part around something that is furthest from the centre **kenar** *Rick was sitting **on the edge of** the bed.* ○ *She ran down to the water's edge.* **2** [C] the part of a blade of a knife or tool that cuts **(bıçak vb.) ağız, keskin kenar** *a sharp/cutting edge* **3 have the edge on/over sb/sth** to be slightly better than someone or something else **burun farkıyla önde olmak, üstünlük kazanmak/sağlamak; avantajlı olmak** • **4 be on edge** to be nervous or worried **çok sinirli olmak, tepesi atmak, endişelenmek** *Sorry for shouting - I'm a bit on edge today.* • **5 take the edge off sth** to make something unpleasant have less of an effect on someone **bir şeyin kötü etkisini azaltmak/almak/gidermek; yatıştırmak** *Have an apple. It'll **take the edge off** your hunger.*

edge² /edʒ/ *verb* **1 edge (sth) up/down/past, etc** to move somewhere gradually, or to make something move somewhere gradually **ağır ağır yaklaşmak; kıyıdan kıyıdan gelmek/ilerlemek; yavaş yavaş hareket ettirmek** *She edged her way through the*

crowd of reporters. **2** [T] to put something around the edge of something else as a decoration **kenar geçirmek/yapmak** *The cloth was edged with gold.*

edgeways /'edʒweɪz/ *UK* (*US* **edgewise** /'edʒwaɪz/) *adverb* with the narrowest part going first **yandan, yanlamasına** *We should be able to get the sofa through edgeways.* ⊃See also: not get a **word**¹ in edgeways.

edgy /'edʒi/ *adjective* nervous **sinirli, asabi, gergin** *David was starting to feel a bit edgy.*

edible /'edɪbl/ *adjective* safe to eat and not harmful **yenilebilir, zararsız** *edible berries* ⊃Compare inedible.

edict /'iːdɪkt/ *noun* [C] *formal* an official order from someone in authority **resmi emir, talimat, ferman, buyruk**

edifice /'edɪfɪs/ *noun* [C] *formal* a very large building **görkemli bina, gösterişli yapı**

edit /'edɪt/ *verb* [T] to prepare text, film, etc by deciding what to include and making mistakes correct **(dergi, gazete, film vb.) basıma, yayına hazırlamak**

edition /ɪ'dɪʃ°n/ *noun* [C] **1** a book, newspaper, etc that is one of several that are the same and were produced at the same time **baskı, basım** *a new edition* ○ *The paperback edition costs £7.95.* **2** a radio or television programme that is one of a series **(radyo, tv programı) bölüm**

editor /'edɪtə'/ *noun* [C] **1** someone whose job is to prepare text, film, etc by deciding what to include and making mistakes correct **yayına hazırlayan, editör** **2** someone who is in charge of a newspaper or magazine **yayıncı, yayın müdürü, editör**

editorial¹ /ˌedɪ'tɔːriəl/ *adjective* [always before noun] **1** relating to editors or editing **yazı işleri ile ilgili** *editorial skills* **2** written by or expressing the opinions of a newspaper editor **gazeteye ilişkin editör yorumu, başyazı** *editorial pages*

editorial² /ˌedɪ'tɔːriəl/ (*US* op-ed) *noun* [C] an article in a newspaper expressing the editor's opinion **başyazı**

educate /'edʒʊkeɪt/ *verb* [T] **1** to teach someone at a school or college **öğretmek/eğitmek, eğitim vermek** [often passive] *She was educated at the Perse School.* **2** to give people information about something so that they understand it better **eğitmek** *This is part of a campaign to educate people about the dangers of smoking.*

educated /'edʒʊkeɪtɪd/ *adjective* **1** Someone who is educated has learned a lot at school or university and has a good level of knowledge. **eğitimli, tahsilli 2 an educated guess** a guess that is probably correct because you have enough knowledge about something **bilgiye/deneyime dayalı tahmin** ⊃See also: well-educated.

continue/have/provide/receive education • compulsory/good education

◦**education** /ˌedʒʊ'keɪʃ°n/ *noun* [U, no plural] the process of teaching and learning in a school or college, or the knowledge that you get from this **eğitim öğretim, tahsil** *We expect a good standard of education for our children.* • **educational** *adjective* providing education, or relating to education **eğitim/öğretim ile ilgili; eğitimsel** *the educational system* • **educationally** *adverb* ⊃See also: further education, higher education. **eğitim açısından**

eel /iːl/ *noun* [C] a long fish that looks like a snake **yılan balığı**

eerie /'ɪəri/ *adjective* unusual and slightly frightening **ürkütücü, ürkünç, ürperten** *an eerie silence* • **eerily** *adverb* **korkutucu bir biçimde** • **eeriness** *noun* [U] **ürkütücü**

have/produce an effect • an **adverse/beneficial/devastating/harmful/profound** effect • an effect on sb/sth • the effects of sth

◦**effect**¹ /ɪ'fekt/ *noun* **1** [C, U] a change, reaction, or result that is caused by something **etki, sonuç, değişim, tepki** *The accident had a huge effect on her life.* ○ *We don't know the long-term effects of this drug.* **2 in effect** used to say what the real situation is **gerçekte, aslında, doğrusu** *This means, in effect, that the plan has been scrapped.* **3 come/go into effect** to start being used **yürürlüğe girmek, kullanılmaya başlamak** *New food safety rules come into effect on Monday.* **4 take effect** to start to produce results or changes **etkisini göstermeye başlamak; sonuç vermek** *The anaesthetic takes effect in about ten minutes.* **5 to that effect** used to say that you are giving the general meaning of something but not the exact words **bu/o anlamda/mealde/manada** *He said he was bored with school or something to that effect.* **6 a sound/special/visual, etc effect** a sound, image, etc that is created artificially **ses/özel/görsel efekt** ⊃See also: side effect.

effect² /ɪ'fekt/ *verb* [T] *formal* to make something happen **sağlamak, elde etmek, meydana getirmek** *The civil rights movement effected a huge change in America.*

◦**effective** /ɪ'fektɪv/ *adjective* **1** successful or achieving the result that you want **etkili, tesirli, başarılı, sonuç veren** *effective management* ○ *What is the most effective way of teaching grammar?* **2 become/be effective** If changes, laws, etc become effective, they officially start. **resmen etkili olmaya başlamak; etkisini göstermek 3** [always before noun] used to say what the real situation is although officially it is different **gerçek, fiili** *She has effective control of the company.* ⊃Opposite ineffective. • **effectiveness** *noun* [U] **verimlilik**

effectively /ɪ'fektɪvli/ *adverb* **1** in a way that is successful and achieves what you want **etkin/etkili bir şekilde** *Teachers need to be able to communicate ideas effectively.* **2** used when you describe what the real result of a situation is **aslında, gerçeğe bakılırsa, doğrusu** *His illness effectively ended his career.*

effects /ɪ'fekts/ *noun* [plural] *formal* possessions **mal varlığı, sahip oldukları, malları, eşyaları** *my personal effects*

effeminate /ɪ'femɪnət/ *adjective* An effeminate man behaves or looks like a woman. **kadınsı, kadın gibi davranan/görünen**

efficiency /ɪ'fɪʃ°nsi/ *noun* [U] when someone or something uses time and energy well, without wasting any **verimlilik, işinin ehli olma; enerji ve zamanı iyi/verimli kullanma** *fuel efficiency* ○ *We must improve the efficiency of the industry.*

efficient /ɪ'fɪʃ°nt/ *adjective* working well and not wasting time or energy **verimli, ehil, işbilen** *an efficient person/organization* ○ *Email is a quick and efficient way of contacting people.* ⊃Opposite inefficient. • **efficiently** *adverb* **üretken, verimli bir şekilde**

effigy /'efɪdʒi/ *noun* [C] a model of a person **insan maketi, maket** *Protesters burned effigies of the president.*

make an effort • require/take effort • a big/brave/concerted/frantic/valiant effort • in an effort to do sth

◦**effort** /'efət/ *noun* **1** [C, U] an attempt to do something **gayret, çaba** [+ to do sth] *We huddled together in an* *effort to keep warm.* ○ *He was **making an effort** to be sociable.* **2** [U] the energy that you need to do something azim, enerji, coşku *I put a lot of effort into organizing the party.* ○ [+ to do sth] *It would **take** too much effort to tidy my bedroom.* **3** [U] the force that is used to make something move **4 be an effort** to be difficult or painful zor, sıkıntılı/zahmetli olmak *After his accident, walking was an effort.*

effortless /'efətləs/ *adjective* achieved without any special or obvious effort kolay, çaba gerektirmeyen, zahmetsiz *effortless grace/style* ● **effortlessly** *adverb* çaba harcamadan

effusive /ɪ'fju:sɪv/ *adjective* showing a lot of enthusiasm or approval for someone or something, often too much şakşaklayan, şakşakçı, fazla heyecan ve kabul gösteren

EFL /,i:ef'el/ *noun* [U] *abbreviation for* English as a Foreign Language: the teaching of English to students whose first language is not English Yabancı Dil olarak İngilizce; İngilizce'nin yabancı dil olarak öğretimi

ᴏ⁻ **e.g.** *(also eg)* /,i:'dʒi:/ used to give an example of what you mean meselâ, örneğin *crime writers, e.g. Agatha Christie and Ruth Rendell*

egalitarian /ɪ,gælɪ'teəriən/ *adjective formal* believing that everyone should have the same freedom and opportunities eşitlikçi

ᴏ⁻ **egg¹** /eg/ *noun* **1** FOOD [C, U] an oval object produced by a female chicken, that you eat as food yumurta *a boiled/fried egg* ⊃Orta kısımdaki renkli sayfalarına bakınız. **2** BABY [C] an oval object with a hard shell that contains a baby bird, insect, or other creature (kuş, böcek vb.yavrusu taşıyan) yumurta *The bird lays* (= produces) *its eggs in a nest.* **3** FEMALE CELL [C] a cell inside a female person or animal that can develop into a baby (kadınlarda ve dişi hayvanlardaki) yumurta **4 have egg on your face** to seem stupid because of something you have done aptallıkla suçlanan kişi olmak; yaptığından dolayı gerzek/aptal gibi görünmek ⊃See also: Easter egg, scrambled eggs.

egg² /eg/ *verb*
egg sb on *phrasal verb* to encourage someone to do something, usually something that is wrong, stupid, or dangerous teşvik etmek, tahrik etmek; kışkırtmak; (tehlikeli, aptal, yanlış şeyleri yapmaya) itmek/dürtmek *Two girls were fighting outside the club, egged on by a group of friends.*

'egg ,cup *noun* [C] a small container for holding a boiled egg while you eat it yumurtalık, yumurta kabı

eggplant /'egplɑ:nt/ *US* (*UK* aubergine) *noun* [C, U] an oval, purple vegetable that is white inside patlıcan ⊃Orta kısımdaki renkli sayfalarına bakınız.

ego /'i:gəʊ/, /'egəʊ/ *noun* [C] your opinion of yourself benlik, ego *He has a huge ego.*

egocentric /,i:gəʊ'sentrɪk/ *adjective* interested only in yourself benmerkezci

egotism /'i:gəʊtɪzᵊm/ (*also* egoism /'i:gəʊɪzᵊm/) *noun* [U] when someone thinks that they are very important and is not interested in other people bencillik, egoizm, kendini beğenmişlik ● **egotist** *noun* [C] yalnızca kendini düşünen ● **egotistic** /,i:gəʊ'tɪstɪk/ (*also* egotistical /,i:gəʊ'tɪstɪkᵊl/) *adjective* yalnızca kendini düşünen

egregious /ɪ'gri:dʒəs/ *adjective formal* extremely bad or shocking in an obvious way oldukça kötü, şok eden *an egregious example of racism*

eh? /eɪ/ *exclamation UK informal spoken* **1** used to ask someone to repeat something because you did not hear or understand it Ha? Hı? Öyle mi? (bir şeyin tekrar edilmesini istemek için kullanılır) *"You're looking tired." "Eh?" "I said, you're looking tired."* **2** used to

show interest or surprise at something Demek öyle? Öyle mi? Sue's had a baby girl, eh?

Eid /i:d/ *noun* the name of two Muslim festivals. The more important one celebrates the end of Ramadan. iki önemli İslâm bayramı; en önemlisi Ramazan Bayramı

ᴏ⁻ **eight** /eɪt/ the number 8 sekiz rakamı

ᴏ⁻ **eighteen** /,eɪ'ti:n/ the number 18 onsekiz rakamı ● **eighteenth** 18th written as a word onsekizinci

ᴏ⁻ **eighth¹** /eɪtθ/ 8th written as a word sekizinci

eighth² /eɪtθ/ *noun* [C] one of eight equal parts of something; 1/8; sekizde biri

ᴏ⁻ **eighty** /'eɪti/ **1** the number 80 seksen **2 the eighties** the years from 1980-1989 seksenli yıllar **3 be in your eighties** to be aged between 80 and 89 seksenli yaşlarda olmak ● **eightieth** 80th written as a word seksenninci

either¹ /'aɪðəʳ/, /'i:ðəʳ/ *conjunction* **either... or** used when you are giving a choice of two or more things ya *... ya da Either call me tonight or I'll speak to you tomorrow.*

ᴏ⁻ **either²** /'aɪðəʳ/, /'i:ðəʳ/ *pronoun, determiner* **1** one of two people or things when it is not important which (ikisinden) herhangi biri/biri *"Would you like red or white wine?" - "Oh, either." ○ Ask Dom or Andrew, either of them will help you.* **2** both (her) iki/ikisi *People were smoking on either side* (= at both sides) *of me.* ○ *You can use the train or the bus, either way it'll take an hour.*

ᴏ⁻ **either³** /'aɪðəʳ/, /'i:ðəʳ/ *adverb* used in negative sentences to mean that something else is also true de, da *The menu is boring and it's not cheap either.*

eject /ɪ'dʒekt/ *verb* **1** LEAVE PLACE [T] *formal* to make someone leave a place, usually using force (kuvvet kullanarak)kovmak, atmak, defetmek, kapıdışarı etmek [often passive] *He was ejected from the courtroom for shouting.* **2** LEAVE MACHINE [I, T] to come out of a machine when a button is pressed, or to make something do this bir düğmeye basınca çıkmak/çıkarmak *How do you eject the tape?* **3** LEAVE AIRCRAFT [I] to leave an aircraft in an emergency by being pushed out while still in your seat uçakta tehlike anında fırlatma koltuğuyla fırlayıp çıkmak; fırla(t)mak

eke /i:k/ *verb*
eke sth out *phrasal verb* **1** to use something slowly or carefully because you only have a small amount of it idareli/dikkatli/azar azar kullanmak; yetirmek **2 eke out a living/existence** to earn only just enough money to pay for things you need *He ekes out a living by cleaning windows.*

elaborate¹ /ɪ'læbᵊrət/ *adjective* complicated, detailed, or made carefully from many parts karmaşık, ayrıntılı, inceden inceye işlenmiş *an elaborate system/scheme* ○ *an elaborate design* ● **elaborately** *adverb* karmaşık, detaylı bir şekilde

elaborate² /ɪ'læbᵊreɪt/ *verb* [I, T] to explain something and give more details ayrıntıya girerek açıklamak/izah etmek *He wouldn't elaborate on the details.* ● **elaboration** /ɪ,læbᵊ'reɪʃᵊn/ *noun* [U] detaylandırma

elapse /ɪ'læps/ *verb* [I] *formal* If time elapses, it passes. (zaman) geçmek, geçip gitmek *Two years have elapsed since the attack.*

elastic¹ /ɪ'læstɪk/ *adjective* Something that is elastic can stretch and return to its original size. esnek, elastik *Your skin is more elastic when you are young.* ● **elasticity** /,ɪlæs'tɪsəti/ *noun* [U] the quality of being elastic esneklik

elastic² /ɪˈlæstɪk/ *noun* [U] a type of rubber that returns to its original size and shape after you stretch it **lastik, elâstikiyet**

e,lastic 'band *UK* (*UK/US* **rubber band**) *noun* [C] a thin circle of rubber used to hold things together **lastik bant**

elated /ɪˈleɪtɪd/ *adjective* extremely happy and excited **çok mutlu, coşkulu, keyifli, heyecanlı** *We were elated by/at the news.* ● **elation** /ɪˈleɪʃᵊn/ *noun* [U] **sevinç**

elbow¹ /ˈelbəʊ/ *noun* [C] the part in the middle of your arm where it bends **dirsek** ⟳Orta kısımdaki renkli sayfalarına bakınız.

elbow² /ˈelbəʊ/ *verb* [T] to push someone with your elbow, especially so you can move past them **dirsek vurmak, dirsekleyerek yol açmak** *He elbowed his way through the crowds of shoppers.*

'elbow ,room *noun* [U] space to move easily **serbestçe hareket edilebilecek alan/yer**

elder¹ /ˈeldəʳ/ *adjective* **elder brother/daughter/sister, etc** the older of two brothers/daughters/sisters, etc **daha yaşlı kız evlat/erkek, kız kardeş**

elder² /ˈeldəʳ/ *noun* **1 the elder** the oldest of two people **yaşlılar** *He's the elder of two sons.* **2 your elders** people older than you **daha büyük insanlar** *I was taught to respect my elders.* **3** [C] an important, respected, older member of a group **yaşlı/sözü dinlenen/ileri gelen/ekâbir insan**

elderly /ˈeldᵊli/ *adjective* a more polite word for 'old', used to describe people **(kibar anlamda) yaşlı, geçkin, tecrübeli** *an elderly man* ○ *Children should show respect for* **the elderly.**

eldest /ˈeldɪst/ *adjective* **eldest child/daughter/brother, etc** the oldest child/daughter/brother, etc **yaşça en büyük çocuk; kız evlat/erkek kardeş** *My eldest brother is a doctor.* ○ *Susan is* **the eldest** *of three sisters.*

e-learning /ˈiːlɜːnɪŋ/ *noun* [U] electronic learning: the business of providing courses online for students so that they can study and learn from home **e-öğrenme**

elect /ɪˈlekt/ *verb* **1** [T] to choose someone for a particular job or position by voting **oylamayla seçmek** [often passive] *She was elected to the US Senate in 2004.* ○ *He was elected president in 1997.* **2 elect to do sth** *formal* to choose to do something **bir şey yapmak için seçmek** *The child elected to stay with his mother.* ⟳See also: re-elect.

■ **election** .... İLE BİRLİKTE KULLANILAN KELİMELER
hold an election ● **run for/stand for** election ● **lose/win** an election ● an election **campaign**

o⊷**election** /ɪˈlekʃᵊn/ *noun* [C, U] a time when people vote in order to choose someone for a political or official job **seçim** *a presidential election* ○ *Who do you think will* **win the election?** ○ *Will you* **stand/run for election** *again this year?* ⟳See also: by-election, general election, re-election.

e'lection ,day *US* (*UK* **polling day**) *noun* [C] the day when people vote in an election **seçim günü**

electoral /ɪˈlektᵊrᵊl/ *adjective* [always before noun] relating to elections **seçimlere ilişkin** *the electoral system* ○ *electoral reform*

electorate /ɪˈlektᵊrət/ *noun* [group] the people who are allowed to vote in an election **seçmenler** *the British electorate*

o⊷**electric** /ɪˈlektrɪk/ *adjective* **1** EQUIPMENT Electric lights, tools, etc work using electricity. **elektrikli** *an electric light/heater* **2** SUPPLY supplying electricity **elektrik/**

enerji veren *an electric socket* ○ *electric current* **3** EXCITING full of excitement and emotion **heyecan ve duygu yüklü/dolu** *The atmosphere backstage was electric.*

electrical /ɪˈlektrɪkᵊl/ *adjective* **1** Electrical goods or equipment work using electricity. **elektrikle çalışan, elektrikli** *electrical appliances/goods* **2** relating to the production and supply of electricity **elektrikle ilgili** *an electrical engineer*

the e,lectric 'chair *noun* a chair used in parts of the US to kill a criminal using electricity **(ABD) idam cezalarında kullanılan elektrikli sandalye**

electrician /ɪˌlekˈtrɪʃᵊn/ *noun* [C] someone whose job is to put in, check, or repair electrical wires and equipment **elektrikçi**

■ **electricity** .... İLE BİRLİKTE KULLANILAN KELİMELER
generate/produce electricity ● **be operated by/be powered by** electricity ● an electricity **supply**

o⊷**electricity** /ɪˌlekˈtrɪsəti/ *noun* [U] a type of energy that can produce light and heat, or make machines work **elektrik** *The electricity has been turned off.* ○ *an electricity bill*

e,lectric 'shock *noun* [C] a sudden, painful feeling that you get when electricity flows through your body **elektrik şok**

electrify /ɪˈlektrɪfaɪ/ *verb* [T] **1** to make people who are watching something feel very excited **insanları heyecanlandırmak, harekete geçirmek** *She electrified the crowd with her fantastic performance.* **2** to supply something with electricity **elektrikli yapmak; elektriklendirmek** *an electrified railway*

electrocute /ɪˈlektrəkjuːt/ *verb* [T] to kill someone by causing electricity to flow through their body **elektrik çarpmak, elektriğe çarpılmak** [often passive] *He was electrocuted while playing on a railway line.* ● **electrocution** /ɪˌlektrəˈkjuːʃᵊn/ *noun* [U] **elektrik çarpması**

electrode /ɪˈlektrəʊd/ *noun* [C] the point where an electric current enters or leaves something such as a battery (= object which provides electricity) **elektrot**

electron /ɪˈlektrɒn/ *noun* [C] an extremely small piece of an atom with a negative electrical charge **elektron**

o⊷**electronic** /ɪˌlekˈtrɒnɪk/ *adjective* **1** Electronic equipment consists of things such as computers, televisions, and radios. **elektronik 2** Electronic music, games, etc use electronic equipment. **(müzik, oyun vb.) elektronik** ● **electronically** *adverb* **elektronik olarak**

electronics /ˌɪlekˈtrɒnɪks/ *noun* [U] the science of making electronic equipment **elektronik bilimi** *the electronics industry*

elegance /ˈelɪɡᵊns/ *noun* [U] when someone or something is stylish or attractive in their appearance or behaviour **zarafet, şıklık**

elegant /ˈelɪɡᵊnt/ *adjective* stylish or attractive in appearance or behaviour **zarif, şık, çekici, hoş** *an elegant dining room* ○ *She's a very elegant woman.* ● **elegantly** *adverb* **şık bir biçimde**

element /ˈelɪmənt/ *noun* **1** PART [C] a part of something **unsur, element** *This book has all the elements of a good detective story.* **2 an element of sth** a small amount of an emotion or quality **az bir miktar** *There's an element of truth in what she says.* **3** PEOPLE [C] a group of people of a particular type **belli tipte bir grup insan** *The disruptive element on the committee voted against the proposal.* **4** SIMPLE SUBSTANCE [C] a simple substance which cannot be reduced to smaller chemical parts **(kimya) element** *Iron is one of the elements of the Earth's crust.* **5** HEAT [C] the part of a piece of electrical equipment which produces heat **direnç/rezistans teli 6 be in your element** to be happy because you are doing what you like doing and what you are good at **sevdiği/iyi olduğu şeyi yapmaktan mutlu olmak** *I'm in my element at a children's party.*

elementary /ˌelɪ'mentᵊri/ *adjective* **1** basic **temel** *I only have an elementary knowledge of physics.* ○ *an elementary mistake* **2** relating to the early stages of studying a subject **başlangıç** *students at elementary level*

ele'mentary ˌschool US (UK **primary school**) *noun* [C] a school for children from the ages of five to eleven **ilkokul**

elements /'elɪmənts/ *noun* **the elements** the weather, especially bad weather **özellikle kötü hava** *Shall we brave the elements and go out for a walk?*

elephant

elephant /'elɪfənt/ *noun* [C] a very large, grey animal with big ears and a very long nose **fil**

elevate /'elɪveɪt/ *verb formal* **1 be elevated to sth** to be given a more important position **yükseltilmek, bir üst göreve getirilmek; daha önemli bir göreve getirilmek** *She has been elevated to deputy manager.* ○ *an elevated position* **2** [T] to move something to a higher level or height **yükseltmek** *High stress levels elevate blood pressure.* ○ *Try to keep your leg elevated.*

elevation /ˌelɪ'veɪʃᵊn/ *noun* **1** [C] the height of a place above the level of the sea **yükseklik, rakım** *The hotel is situated at an elevation of 1000m.* **2** [U] *formal* when someone or something is given a more important position **yükselme, önemli göreve gelme** *his sudden elevation to stardom*

elevator /'elɪveɪtᵊr/ US (UK **lift**) *noun* [C] a machine that carries people up and down in tall buildings **asansör**

○✺**eleven** /ɪ'levᵊn/ *the number* 11 **onbir** ● **eleventh** 11th written as a word **onbirinci**

elf /elf/ *noun* [C] *plural* **elves** a small person with pointed ears who has magic powers in children's stories **çocuk hikayelerinde sihirli güçleri olan, sivri kulaklı küçük cüsseli insan; küçük peri/cin**

elicit /ɪ'lɪsɪt/ *verb* [T] *formal* to get information or a reaction from someone **sağlamak, temin etmek** *You have to ask the right questions to elicit the information you want.*

eligible /'elɪdʒəbl/ *adjective* **1** If you are eligible to do something, you can do it because you are in the right situation. **hak sahibi, hakkı olan, uygun [+ to do sth]** *Only people over 18 are eligible to vote.* ○ *You might be eligible for a grant for your studies.* ↻Opposite **ineligible**. **2** If someone who is not married is eligible, they would be a good husband or wife because they are rich, attractive, etc. **(eş) uygun, seçilebilir, varlıklı, çekici** *an eli-*

gible young bachelor ● **eligibility** /ˌelɪdʒə'bɪləti/ *noun* [U] **uygunluk**

eliminate /ɪ'lɪmɪneɪt/ *verb* [T] **1** to remove something from something, or get rid of something **ortadan kaldırmak, gidermek** *The doctor advised me to eliminate salt from my diet.* **2** to defeat someone so that they cannot go any further in a competition **elemek, saf dışı bırakmak** [often passive] *She was eliminated after the first round of the tournament.*

elimination /ɪˌlɪmɪ'neɪʃᵊn/ *noun* **1** [U] when you eliminate someone or something **eleme, kurtulma, saf dışı etme 2** a process of elimination when you remove all possible answers to something until only one remains **cevapları/seçenekleri eleme; doğru cevabı seçme**

elite /ɪ'li:t/ *noun* [group] the richest, most powerful, or best educated group in a society **seçkin topluluğu, elit, seçkin kişiler** *a member of the elite* ○ *an elite group*

elitism /ɪ'li:tɪzᵊm/ *noun* [U] when a small group of rich, powerful, or educated people are given an advantage in a situation **seçkin kişi topluluğunun önderliği** ● **elitist** *adjective* **elitist attitudes** **toplulukta ayrıcalık sahibi olan**

elm /elm/ *noun* [C, U] a large tree which loses its leaves in winter **kara ağaç**

elocution /ˌelə'kju:ʃᵊn/ *noun* [U] the skill of speaking in a careful, clear way **hitabet, güzel konuşma sanatı**

elongated /'i:lɒŋgeɪtɪd/ US /i:'lɒŋgeɪtɪd/ *adjective* longer and thinner than usual **incecik, uzun ve sipsivri**

elope /ɪ'ləʊp/ *verb* [I] to leave home secretly with someone in order to get married **kaçmak, aşığı ile kaçmak**

eloquent /'eləkwənt/ *adjective* expressing ideas clearly and in a way that influences people **güzel konuşan, hitabeti kuvvetli** *the most eloquent speaker at the conference* ● **eloquence** /'eləkwəns/ *noun* [U] when someone or something is eloquent **güzel konuşma, güçlü hitabet** ● **eloquently** *adverb* **düzgün bir ifadeyle**

○✺**else** /els/ *adverb* **1** [IN ADDITION] in addition to someone or something **başka, başka birşey, ayrıca** *Would you like anything else to eat?* ○ *What else did he say?* **2** [DIFFERENT] different from someone or something **başka; farklı** *I don't like it here. Let's go somewhere else.* ○ *I didn't say that. It must have been someone else.* **3** [OTHER] other things or people **diğerleri, başka** *I forgot my toothbrush, but I remembered everything else.* **4 or else a** [COMPARE] used to compare two different things or situations **yoksa, aksi takdirde** *He talks to her all the time, or else he completely ignores her.* **b** [IF NOT] used to say what will happen if another thing does not happen **ya da** *We must be there by six, or else we'll miss the beginning.* **5 if all else fails** if no other plan is successful **eğer herşey başarısız olursa/tepe taklak giderse** *If all else fails, you're welcome to stay at our house.*

elsewhere /ˌels'weər/ *adverb* in or to another place **başka yerde, başka yerlere** *The report studies economic growth in Europe and elsewhere.* ○ *If we can't find it here, we'll have to go elsewhere.*

ELT /ˌiːel'tiː/ *noun* [U] *abbreviation for* English Language Teaching: the teaching of English to students whose first language is not English **İngilizce'nin yabancı dil olarak öğretimi; İngiliz Dili Öğretimi**

elucidate /ɪ'lu:sɪdeɪt/ *verb* [T] *formal* to explain something, or make it clear **izah etmek, açığa kavuşturmak, aydınlatmak**

elude /ɪ'lu:d/ *verb* [T] *formal* **1** [NOT ACHIEVE] If something that you want eludes you, you do not succeed in achieving it. **elinden kaçmak, başaramamak** *The gold medal continues to elude her.* **2** [NOT BE CAUGHT] to not be caught by someone **kaçmak, yakayı/paçayı kurtar-**

mak *He eluded the police for years before he was arrested.*
3 NOT REMEMBER If a piece of information eludes you, you
cannot remember it. **hatırına gelmemek, anımsayamamak**

elusive /ɪ'luːsɪv/ *adjective* difficult to describe, find,
achieve, or remember **tasviri/bulunması/elegeçirilmesi/başarılması/hatırlanması güç; zor bulunan**
The answers to these questions remain as elusive as ever.

elves /elvz/ *plural of* elf **periler/cinler**

'em /əm/ *informal spoken short for* them **onlar' kelimesinin kısaltılmışı**

emaciated /ɪ'meɪsieɪtɪd/ *adjective* very thin and weak
because of being ill or not eating enough food **sıska, bir
deri bir kemik, incecik**

get/send an email ● **by** email ● **in** an email ● **an** email
address/attachment

o--**email** (*also* e-mail) /'iːmeɪl/ *noun* **1** [U] a system for sending messages electronically, especially from one computer to another using the Internet **e-posta** *You can contact me by email.* ○ *What's your email address?* **2** [C, U] a
message sent electronically **e-posta iletisi** *I got an
email from Danielle yesterday.* ● **email** *verb* [T] to send a
message using email **e-posta ile ileti göndermek**

emanate /'eməneɪt/ *verb formal*
emanate from sth *phrasal verb* to come from something ...**den/dan çıkmak/kaynaklanmak** *Strange
noises emanated from the room next door.*

emancipate /ɪ'mænsɪpeɪt/ *verb* [T] *formal* to give people
more freedom or rights by removing social, legal, or
political controls that limit them **sosyal, yasal ve
siyasî denetimleri kaldırarak daha fazla özgürlük/hak tanımak** *emancipated women* ● **emancipation** /ɪˌmænsɪ'peɪʃⁿn/ *noun* [U] **serbest bırakma**

embalm /ɪm'bɑːm/ *verb* [T] to use oils and chemicals to
prevent a dead body from decaying **mumyalamak**

embankment /ɪm'bæŋkmənt/ *noun* [C] an artificial
slope built from soil or stones to stop floods, or to support a road or railway **toprak dolgu, set** *a railway
embankment*

embargo /ɪm'bɑːɡəʊ/ *noun* [C] *plural* **embargoes** an
order by a government to stop trade with another country **ambargo, ticarete yasak koyma** *an arms/oil
embargo* ○ *We will not lift* (= stop) *the trade embargo
until they end this war.*

embark /ɪm'bɑːk/ *verb* [I] to get on a ship, boat, or aircraft to begin a journey **gemiye/tekneye/uçağa binmek** ⊃Opposite **disembark.**
embark on/upon sth *phrasal verb* to start something
new or important **yeni/önemli bir şeyi başlatmak;
girişimde bulunmak** *You're never too old to embark
on a new career.*

embarrass /ɪm'bærəs/ *verb* [T] to make someone feel
ashamed or shy **utandırmak, mahcup etmek** *My
dad's always embarrassing me in front of my friends.*

embarrassed /ɪm'bærəst/ *adjective* feeling ashamed or
shy **mahcup, utanmış, sıkılmış** *She felt embarrassed
about undressing in front of the doctor.* ○ [+ to do sth] *I was
too embarrassed to admit that I was scared.*

embarrassing /ɪm'bærəsɪŋ/ *adjective* making you feel
embarrassed **mahcup eden, utandıran** *an embarrassing defeat* ○ *What has been your most embarrassing
moment?* ● **embarrassingly** *adverb* *The play was embarrassingly bad.* **utanmış bir şekilde**

acute/great/huge embarrassment ● **a source of**
embarrassment ● **the embarrassment of** doing sth

embarrassment /ɪm'bærəsmənt/ *noun* **1** [U] when you
feel embarrassed **utanç, mahcubiyet** *He blushed with
embarrassment.* ○ *Her behaviour has caused great
embarrassment to her family.* **2** [C] someone or someone that makes you feel embarrassed **utandıran/mahcup eden şey/kişi** *He is becoming an embarrassment
to the government.*

embassy /'embəsi/ *noun* [C] the official group of people
who live in a foreign country and represent their government there, or the building where they work **elçilik, elçilik görevlileri**

embedded /ɪm'bedɪd/ *adjective* **1** fixed into the surface
of something **iliştirilmiş, tutturulmuş, gömülmüş** *A
small piece of glass was embedded in his finger.* **2** If an
emotion, attitude, etc is embedded in someone or something, it is a very strong and important part of them.
iyice yerleşmiş, kökleşmiş, kemikleşmiş, bütünleşmiş; bir parçası olmuş *A sense of guilt was deeply
embedded in my conscience.*

embellish /ɪm'belɪʃ/ *verb* [T] to make something more
beautiful or interesting by adding something to it **süslemek, güzelleştirmek, ilginç hale getirmek** *He
embellished the story with lots of dramatic detail.*
● **embellishment** *noun* [C, U] **süsleme**

embers /'embəz/ *noun* [plural] pieces of wood or coal that
continue to burn after a fire has no more flames **kor,
köz**

embezzle /ɪm'bezl/ *verb* [T] to steal money that belongs
to the company or organization that you work for **zimmetine geçirmek** ● **embezzlement** *noun* [U] **hesabına
para geçirme**

embittered /ɪm'bɪtəd/ *adjective* very angry about
unfair things that have happened to you **üzülüp kızmak; haksızlığa uğradığı için üzülmek/kahrolmak**

emblazoned /ɪm'bleɪzⁿnd/ *adjective* decorated in a very
obvious way with something such as a name or a design
işlenmiş, işlemeli *Her T-shirt was emblazoned with
the company logo.*

emblem /'embləm/ *noun* [C] a picture, object, or symbol
that is used to represent a person, group, or idea **amblem, simge, işaret** *The rose is the national emblem of
England.*

embodiment /ɪm'bɒdɪmənt/ *noun* **the embodiment
of sth** If someone or something is the embodiment of
a particular idea or quality, they express or represent it
exactly. **bir şeyin somut örneği/temsilcisi/simgesi**
The mother in the story is the embodiment of evil.

embody /ɪm'bɒdi/ *verb* [T] to represent an idea or quality exactly **somutlaştırmak, tam belirgin hale getirmek** *He embodies the values of hard work and fair play.*

embrace¹ /ɪm'breɪs/ *verb* **1** HOLD [I, T] If you embrace
someone, you put your arms around them, and if two
people embrace, they put their arms around each other.
sarılmak, kucaklamak 2 ACCEPT to accept new
ideas, beliefs, methods, etc in an enthusiastic way **sorgusuz/sualsiz kabellenmek, yürekten inanmak** *We
are always eager to embrace the latest technology.*
3 INCLUDE [T] *formal* to include a number of things **bir
çok şeyi kapsamak/içermek** *The report embraces a
wide range of opinions.*

embrace² /ɪm'breɪs/ *noun* [C] when you put your arms
around someone **kucaklama, sarılma** *a passionate
embrace*

embroider /ɪmˈbrɔɪdəʳ/ *verb* **1** [I, T] to decorate cloth by sewing small patterns or pictures onto it **nakış işlemek, oya yapmak 2** [T] to add imaginary details to a story to make it more interesting **bir hikayeye daha ilginç yapmak için hayali ayrıntılar eklemek** *They accused him of embroidering the facts.*

embroidery /ɪmˈbrɔɪdᵊri/ *noun* [U] **1** the activity of sewing small patterns or pictures onto things **nakış, işleme 2** decoration on cloth made by sewing small patterns or pictures onto it **(resim, kumaş) nakış, süsleme, işleme**

embroil /ɪmˈbrɔɪl/ *verb formal* **be embroiled in sth** to be involved in an argument or difficult situation **karışmak, bulaşmak** *We don't want to become embroiled in a dispute over ownership.*

embryo /ˈembriəʊ/ *noun* [C] a human or an animal that is starting to develop in its mother's uterus **embriyon**

embryonic /ˌembriˈɒnɪk/ *adjective* starting to develop **gelişmeye başlamış, henüz ilkel** *The project is still at an embryonic stage.*

emerald /ˈemᵊrld/ *noun* **1** [C] a bright green stone used in jewellery **zümrüt 2** [U] (*also* ˌemerald ˈgreen) a bright green colour **zümrüt yeşili ● emerald** *adjective* **zümrüt**

emerge /ɪˈmɜːdʒ/ *verb* [I] **1** COME OUT to appear from somewhere or come out of somewhere **...den,dan çıkmak, görünmek, belirmek** *A figure emerged from the shadows.* **2** BECOME KNOWN to become known **belli olmak, ortaya çıkmak** *It emerged that she had lied to her employers.* **3** DIFFICULT SITUATION to reach the end of a difficult situation **zor bir durumun sonuna gelmek, üstesinden gelmek** *They emerged victorious from the fight.* **● emergence** *noun* [U] **belirme**

cope with/respond to an emergency **● a major/real** emergency **● in an** emergency

o*-**emergency** /ɪˈmɜːdʒᵊnsi/ *noun* [C] a serious or dangerous situation that needs immediate action **acil durum, acil** *You should only ring this number* **in an emergency.** ○ *an emergency exit*

e'mergency ˌbrake US (*UK* handbrake) *noun* [C] a stick inside a car that you can pull up to stop the car from moving **el freni** ⊃Orta kısımdaki renkli sayfalarına bakınız.

e'mergency ˌroom US (*UK* casualty) *noun* [C] the part of a hospital where people go when they have been injured or have urgent illnesses so that they can be treated immediately **acil durum odası**

eˌmergency ˈservices *noun* [plural] the organizations who deal with accidents and urgent problems such as fire, illness, or crime **acil durum hizmetleri**

emerging /ɪˈmɜːdʒɪŋ/ *adjective* [always before noun] starting to exist or develop **olmaya/gelişmeye/ortaya çıkmaya başlamak** *emerging economies/markets*

emigrant /ˈemɪgrənt/ *noun* [C] someone who leaves their own country to go and live in another one **göçmen**

emigrate /ˈemɪgreɪt/ *verb* [I] to leave your own country to go and live in another one **göç etmek** *We're thinking of emigrating to New Zealand.* **● emigration** /ˌemɪˈgreɪʃᵊn/ *noun* [U] **göç**

eminent /ˈemɪnənt/ *adjective* famous, respected, or important **ünlü, seçkin, güzide** *an eminent historian* **● eminence** /ˈemɪnəns/ *noun* [U] ⊃See also: pre-eminent. **ün, itibar**

eminently /ˈemɪnəntli/ *adverb formal* very **pek çok, gayet, ziyadesiyle** *He is eminently qualified for the job.*

emission /ɪˈmɪʃᵊn/ *noun* [C, U] when gas, heat, light, etc is sent out into the air, or an amount of gas, heat, light, etc that is sent out **yayma, çıkarma, emisyon** *Carbon dioxide emissions will be reduced by 20%.*

emit /ɪˈmɪt/ *verb* [T] **emitting,** *past* **emitted** to send out gas, heat, light, etc into the air **(gaz, ısı, ışık vb.) yaymak, çıkarmak** *The machine emits a high-pitched sound when you press the button.*

emoticon /ɪˈməʊtɪkɒn/ *noun* [C] an image such as :-) which looks like a face when you look at it from the side, made using keyboard symbols and used in emails to express emotions :-) **e-posta iletilerinde kullanılan imge** ⊃See study page **Emailing and texting** on page Centre 37.

display/experience/feel/show emotion **● deep/ powerful/strong** emotion

o*-**emotion** /ɪˈməʊʃᵊn/ *noun* [C, U] a strong feeling such as love or anger, or strong feelings in general **his, duygu, coşku** *He finds it hard to* **express his emotions.** ○ *She was overcome with emotion and burst into tears.*

emotional /ɪˈməʊʃᵊnᵊl/ *adjective* **1** EMOTIONS relating to emotions **hisli, duygulu, coşkulu** *a child's emotional development* **2** STRONG FEELINGS showing strong feelings, or making people have strong feelings **hissi, duygusal, içli; duygusal olan; hissi davranan** *an emotional speech* ○ *After the argument, I was feeling confused and emotional.* **3** PERSON An emotional person shows their emotions very easily or very often. **hislerini/duygularını sık ve çok kolay belli eden ● emotionally** *adverb* **hisli bir şekilde**

emotive /ɪˈməʊtɪv/ *adjective* making people feel strong emotions **duygulandırıcı, heyecanlandırıcı** *Animal experimentation is a very emotive issue.*

empathy /ˈempəθi/ *noun* [U] the ability to imagine what it must be like to be in someone's situation **bir başkasının duygularını anlayabilme, duygu sezgisi ● empathize** (*also UK* -ise) /ˈempəθaɪz/ *verb* [I] to feel empathy with someone **karşısındakinin duygularını anlamak, paylaşmak** *I think people find it easy to empathize with the main character.*

emperor /ˈempᵊrəʳ/ *noun* [C] the male ruler of an empire (= group of countries ruled by one person or government) **imparator, padişah** *Emperor Charlemagne*

emphasis /ˈemfəsɪs/ *noun* [C, U] *plural* **emphases** /ˈemfəsiːz/ **1** particular importance or attention that you give to something **önem, ehemmiyet** *Schools are starting to* **place/put** greater **emphasis on** passing exams. **2** the extra force that you give to a word or part of a word when you are saying it **vurgu, vurgulama** *The emphasis is on the final syllable.*

emphasize (*also UK* -ise) /ˈemfəsaɪz/ *verb* [T] to show that something is especially important or needs special attention **belirtmek, vurgulamak** *The government is emphasizing the importance of voting in the election.* ○ [+ that] *He emphasized that the driver was not to blame for the accident.*

emphatic /ɪmˈfætɪk/ *adjective* done or said in a strong way and without any doubt **etkili, kesin, üstüne basa basa söylenen** *an emphatic victory* **● emphatically** *adverb* **kesinlikle**

empire /ˈempaɪəʳ/ *noun* [C] **1** a group of countries that is ruled by one person or government **imparatorluk 2** a large group of businesses that is controlled by one person or company **(iş) imparatorluk** *a publishing empire*

empirical /ɪmˈpɪrɪkᵊl/ *adjective formal* based on experience or scientific experiments and not only on ideas **uygulama ve bilimsel deneye dayalı; deneysel** *empi-*

rical evidence • **empirically** *adverb* deneylere daya-
nır bir şekilde

o→**employ** /ɪmˈplɔɪ/ *verb* [T] **1** If a person or company
employs someone, they pay that person to work for
them. **iş vermek, çalıştırmak, işe almak** *The company employs 2500 staff.* ○ [+ to do sth] *They employ her
to look after their children.* **2** *formal* to use something
kullanmak *Companies employ clever tactics to persuade
us to buy their products.*

employee /ɪmˈplɔɪiː/ *noun* [C] someone who is paid to
work for a person or company **işçi, çalışan**

o→**employer** /ɪmˈplɔɪə^r/ *noun* [C] a person or company that
pays people to work for them **işveren**

employment .... İLE BİRLİKTE KULLANILAN KELİMELER

find/offer/provide/seek employment • gainful/
paid /full-time / part-time /temporary employment
• be in employment

o→**employment** /ɪmˈplɔɪmənt/ *noun* [U] **1** when someone
is paid to work for a person or company **iş, istihdam**
full-time/part-time employment ○ *It is not easy to find
employment in the countryside.* ○ *employment opportu-
nities/rights* ➔Compare unemployment. **2** *formal* the use of
something **kullanma**

empower /ɪmˈpaʊə^r/ *verb* **1** [T] to give someone the confidence, skills, freedom, etc to do something **yetki ver-
mek/tanımak; yetkilendirmek; güven kazanma-
sını sağlamak** [+ to do sth] *Education empowers people
to take control of their lives.* **2 be empowered to do sth**
to have the legal or official right to do something **bir
şey yapmaya yasal/resmî yetkisi olmak; yetkili
olmak**

empress /ˈemprəs/ *noun* [C] the female ruler, or the wife
of a male ruler, of an empire (= group of countries ruled
by one person or government) **imparatoriçe** *Empress
Josephine*

o→**empty**[1] /ˈempti/ *adjective* **1** If something is empty, it
does not contain any things or people. **boş** *an empty
house/street* ○ *empty bottles/glasses* ○ *The train was
completely empty when it reached London.* ➔See picture at
full. 2 having no meaning or value **manasız, değersiz,
boş** *an empty promise/threat* • **emptiness** *noun* [U]
boşluk

empty[2] /ˈempti/ *verb* **1** [T] (*also* empty out) If you empty a
container, or if you empty the things inside it, you
remove everything from it. **boşaltmak** *He emptied
the dirty water into the sink.* **2** [I] to become empty
boşalmak *The room emptied rapidly when the fire started.*

empty-handed /ˌempti'hændɪd/ *adjective* without
bringing or taking anything **eli boş, umduğunu bula-
mamış** *We can't go to the party empty-handed.*

emulate /ˈemjəleɪt/ *verb* [T] *formal* to try to be like someone or something that you admire or that is successful
özenip taklit etmek, öykünmek *They hope to emulate
the success of other software companies.*

emulsion /ɪˈmʌlʃ^ən/ *noun* [C, U] (emulsion paint) a water-
based paint which is not shiny when dry **plastik boya**

enable /ɪˈneɪbl/ *verb* [T] to make someone able to do
something, or to make something possible **mümkün
kılmak, imkân vermek, olanak sağlamak** [+ to do
sth] *This money has enabled me to buy a new computer.*

-enabled /ɪˈneɪb^əld/ *suffix* **1** having the necessary
equipment or system to use something **gerekli alet
veya sisteme sahip olan anlamında kullanılan son
ek** *Bluetooth-enabled mobile phones* **2** used or made possible by using a particular thing **belli bir şeyi kulla-**

narak yapmak/mümkün kılmak anlamında kullanılan son ek *voice-enabled software*

enact /ɪˈnækt/ *verb* [T] **1** to make something into a law
kanunlaştırmak [often passive] *When was this legislation enacted?* **2** *formal* to perform a story or play **bir
hikaye/oyun icra etmek, oynamak, canlandırmak**
• **enactment** *noun* [U] **kanunlaştırma**

enamel /ɪˈnæm^əl/ *noun* [U] **1** a hard, shiny substance
that is used to decorate or protect metal or clay **emaye**
2 the hard, white substance that covers your teeth (diş)
mine

enamoured *UK* (*US* enamored) /ɪˈnæməd/ *adjective* **be
enamoured of/with sb/sth** *formal* to like someone or
something very much **birini/birşeyi tutkuyla sevmek, gönül vermek**

enc (*also* encl) *written abbreviation for* enclosed: used at
the end of a business letter to show that there is something else in the envelope **zarfta bir şey var anlamında kısaltma; eklere bakınız**

encapsulate /ɪnˈkæpsjəleɪt/ *verb* [T] to express or show
the most important facts about something **özetlemek,
en önemli yönlerini/gerçekleri vurgulamak** *The
film encapsulates the essence of that period.*

encase /ɪnˈkeɪs/ *verb* **be encased in sth** *formal* to be
completely covered in something **tamamen kapla-
mak, örtmek** *The outside walls are encased in concrete.*

enchanted /ɪnˈtʃɑːntɪd/ *adjective* **1** If you are
enchanted by something, you like it very much. **büyülenmiş, kendinden geçmiş** *She was enchanted by the
Scottish landscape.* **2** affected by magic **büyülü, sihirli**
an enchanted forest

enchanting /ɪnˈtʃɑːntɪŋ/ *adjective* very nice **sihirli,
hoş, cazibeli** *What an enchanting child!*

encircle /ɪnˈsɜːkl/ *verb* [T] *formal* to form a circle around
something **sarmak, kuşatmak, çevrelemek** [often pas-
sive] *The house is encircled by a high fence.*

enclave /ˈenkleɪv/ *noun* [C] a place which is different
from the area that is around it because its people have
a different language or culture **kültür ve dil olarak
çevresinden farklı bölge** *an Italian enclave in Switzerland*

enclose /ɪnˈkləʊz/ *verb* [T] **1** to send something in the
same envelope or parcel as something else **içine koymak, iliştirmek** *I enclose a map of the area.* **2** to be all
around something and separate it from other things or
places **etrafını çevirmek, kapamak** • **enclosed** *adjective He doesn't like enclosed spaces.* **kapalı**

enclosure /ɪnˈkləʊʒə^r/ *noun* [C] a small area of land that
has a wall or fence around it **kapalı alan, etrafı çevrili
yer**

encompass /ɪnˈkʌmpəs/ *verb* [T] to include a lot of
things, ideas, places, etc **kapsamak, içermek** *Their
albums encompass a wide range of music.*

encore /ˈɒŋkɔː^r/ *noun* [C] an extra song or piece of music
that is performed at the end of a show because the audi-
ence shout for it **tekrar, bis; 'Bravo' bir daha**

encounter[1] /ɪnˈkaʊntə^r/ *verb* [T] **1** to experience something unpleasant **sevimsiz bir şeyi tecrübe etmek** *We
encountered quite a few problems at the beginning.*
2 *literary* to meet someone, especially when you do not
expect it **ansızın karşılaşmak, rastgelmek**

encounter .... İLE BİRLİKTE KULLANILAN KELİMELER

have an encounter • a chance encounter • an encounter with sb

encounter[2] /ɪnˈkaʊntə^r/ *noun* [C] a meeting, especially
one that happens by chance **karşılaşma, şans eseri
rastgelme**

⌐**encourage** /ɪnˈkʌrɪdʒ/ *verb* [T] **1** to make someone more likely to do something, or make something more likely to happen **cesaret vermek, teşvik etmek** [+ to do sth] *My parents encouraged me to try new things.* ○ *Cutting back plants will encourage growth.* **2** to give someone confidence or hope **özendirmek, körüklemek, yüreklendirmek** *My parents encouraged me when things weren't going well at school.* ⊃Opposite **discourage.** ● **encouragement** *noun* [C, U] *Children need lots of encouragement from their parents.* **destek, cesaretlendirme**

encouraged /ɪnˈkʌrɪdʒd/ *adjective* having more confidence or hope about something **yürekli, güven duyan, ümitli** *We were very encouraged by his exam results.*

encouraging /ɪnˈkʌrɪdʒɪŋ/ *adjective* making you feel more hope and confidence **yüreklendiren, cesaret veren, teşvik edici** *The team's performance was very encouraging.* ⊃Opposite **discouraging.** ● **encouragingly** *adverb* **cesaret verir şekilde**

encroach /ɪnˈkrəʊtʃ/ *verb*
encroach on/upon sth *phrasal verb* to gradually take away someone's rights, power, etc, or get control of something, often without being noticed **(haklara, güce vb.) tecavüz etmek, el uzatmak, kontrolünü ele geçirmek** *My job is starting to encroach on my family life.*

encrusted /ɪnˈkrʌstɪd/ *adjective* covered with something hard, for example dirt or stones **(üstü) taşlarla/toprakla kaplanmış/örtülü** *My trousers were encrusted with mud.*

encrypt /ɪnˈkrɪpt/ *verb* [T] to change electronic information into a secret system of letters, numbers, or symbols **elektronik bir bilgiyi gizli harf, rakam ve imgelere dönüştürmek** ● **encryption** *noun* [U] **şifreleme**

encyclopedia (*also* UK **encyclopaedia**) /ɪnˌsaɪkləˈpiːdiə/ *noun* [C] a book or a set of books containing facts about a lot of subjects **ansiklopedi**

end ...... İLE BİRLİKTE KULLANILAN KELİMELER
at the end (of sth) ● **by the** end (of sth) ● **the very** end

⌐**end**[1] /end/ *noun* **1** [FINAL PART] [no plural] the final part of something such as a period of time, activity, or story **son, nihayet, bitiş** *I'll pay you at the end of next month.* ○ *I didn't meet him until the end of the course.* ○ *a film with a twist at the end* **2** [FURTHEST PART] [C] the furthest part or final part of a place or thing **sonu, nihayeti** *They live at the other end of the street.* ○ *They were standing at opposite ends of the room.* **3** [STOP] [C] when something stops happening **son, sonlanma, nihayete erme** [usually singular] *They are calling for an end to the violence.* **4 in the end** finally, after something has been thought about or discussed a lot **sonunda, nihayetinde 5 come to an end** to finish **sona gelmek, bitirmek 6 put an end to sth** to make something stop happening **bir şeye son vermek, bitirmek** *He's determined to put an end to these rumours.* **7 bring sth to an end** to make something finish **bitirmek, bir şeyi sonuna getirmek** *The stories in the newspaper brought her career to a sudden end.* **8 no end** *informal* a lot **çok, bir hayli, ziyadesiyle** *I've had no end of trouble finding a hotel room.* **9 for hours/days, etc on end** for hours/days, etc without stopping **sürekli, aralıksız** *He waited by the telephone for hours on end.* **10** [INTENTION] [C] an intention or purpose **niyet, amaç** *She only has one end in mind.* **11 be at a loose end** to have nothing to do **yapacak bir şeyi olmamak** *Come and visit us if you're at a loose end over the weekend.* ● **12 at the end of the day** UK something that you say before you give the most important fact of a situa-

tion **sonuç olarak, neticede** *At the end of the day, what matters is that you're safe.* ● **13 at the end of your tether** (*also* US **at the end of your rope**) so tired, annoyed, or worried by something that you do not feel that you can deal with it **tahammül sınırının sonuna gelmek, artık durumla başedemeyeceğini hissetmek** ● **14 get (hold of) the wrong end of the stick** to not understand a situation correctly **tersinden/ters/yanlış anlamak** *My mum got the wrong end of the stick and thought that Jim was my boyfriend.* ● **15 make ends meet** to have just enough money to pay for the things that you need **iki yakasını bir araya getirmek** *I've taken a second job in the evenings just to make ends meet.* ● **16 not be the end of the world** If something is not the end of the world, it will not cause very serious problems. **önemli/büyük problemlere yol açmayacak olmak** *It won't be the end of the world if I don't get the job.* ● **17 be on/at the receiving end of sth** If you are on the receiving end of something, you suffer something unpleasant when you have done nothing to deserve it. **haketmediği halde bir olumsuzluktan dolayı ısdırap çeken tarafta olmak** *They are often on the receiving end of verbal abuse from angry customers.* ● **18 throw sb in at the deep end** to make someone start a new and difficult job or activity without helping them or preparing them for it **emrivaki yapmak, yeni ve zor bir şeyi yapmaya zorlamak/mecbur bırakmak** ⊃See also: **dead end, light**[1] at the end of the tunnel, **odds** and ends, the **tail**[1] end of sth, **the West End**, be at your **wits'** end.

⌐**end**[2] /end/ *verb* [I, T] to finish or stop, or to make something finish or stop **bit(ir)mek, dur(dur)mak** *What time does the concert end?* ○ *These talks do not look likely to end the war.*
end in/with sth *phrasal verb* to finish in a particular way ...ile son bulmak/sonlanmak *The evening ended in a big argument.*
end up *phrasal verb* to finally be in a particular place or situation **kendini bir yerde/durumda bulmak; boylamak; soluğu ... de/da almak** *I never thought he'd end up in prison.* ○ [+ doing sth] *He always ends up doing what Alan wants to do.* ○ *She'll end up unemployed.*

endanger /ɪnˈdeɪndʒər/ *verb* [T] to put someone or something in a situation where they might be harmed or seriously damaged **tehlikeye atmak** *He would never do anything to endanger the children's lives.*

endangered /ɪnˈdeɪndʒəd/ *adjective* **endangered birds/plants/species, etc** animals or plants which may soon not exist because there are very few now alive **nesli tükenmekte olan kuşlar/bitkiler/canlılar vb.**

endear /ɪnˈdɪər/ *verb*
endear sb to sb *phrasal verb* If a quality in someone's character, or their behaviour endears them to you, it makes you like them. **kendini sevdirmek**

endearing /ɪnˈdɪərɪŋ/ *adjective* An endearing quality is one that makes people like you. **kendini sevdiren, sevimli**

endeavour UK (US **endeavor**) /ɪnˈdevər/ *verb* **endeavour to do sth** *formal* to try very hard to do something **çok büyük çaba sarfetmek, gayret etmek** *I endeavoured to help her, but she wouldn't let me.* ● **endeavour** UK (US **endeavor**) *noun* [C, U] *human/artistic endeavour* **çaba, gayret**

endemic /enˈdemɪk/ *adjective formal* If something unpleasant is endemic in a place or among a group of people, there is a lot of it there. ...e özgü/mahsus, çokça varolan *Corruption is endemic in some parts of the police force.*

ending /'endɪŋ/ noun [C] **1** the last part of a story **hika-yenin sonu** I hope this film has a **happy ending**. **2** a part added to the end of a word **kelime sonuna yapılan ek, bitiş eki** To make the plural of 'dog', you add the plural ending '-s'.

endive /'endaɪv/ noun [C, U] a plant with bitter green leaves that are eaten in salads **hindiba bitkisi**

endless /'endləs/ adjective continuing for a long time and never finishing, or never seeming to finish **sonsuz, hiç bitmeyen** He seems to think that I have an **endless supply** of money. • **endlessly** adverb **sonsuz biir şekilde**

endorse /ɪn'dɔːs/ verb [T] formal to say publicly that you support a person or action **onaylamak, desteklemek, arka çıkmak** [often passive] The idea was endorsed by a majority of members. • **endorsement** noun [C, U] **kabul**

endow /ɪn'daʊ/ verb formal **1 be endowed with sth** to have a particular quality or characteristic ... **e/a sahip; ile donanımlı; belli bir kalite ve özelliğe sahip olmak** The country is richly endowed with natural resources. **2** [T] to give a large amount of money to a college, hospital, etc **(okul, hastane vb.) bağışta bulunmak, para bağışlamak**

end-product /'end,prɒdʌkt/ noun [C] the thing that you get at the end of a process or activity **son ürün; tüm işlemlerden geçerek en sonda elde edilen ürün**

endurance /ɪn'djʊərəns/ noun [U] the ability to keep doing something difficult, unpleasant, or painful for a long time **tahammül, dayanma gücü, sabır ve sebat gösterme** a race to test athletes' endurance

endure /ɪn'djʊər/ verb [T] formal to suffer something difficult, unpleasant, or painful **tahammül etmek, dayanmak** She's already had to endure three painful operations on her leg.

enduring /ɪn'djʊərɪŋ/ adjective existing for a long time **dayanan, tahammül edebilen, süren** the enduring popularity of cartoons

enemy ...... İLE BİRLİKTE KULLANILAN KELİMELER
have/make enemies • **arch/bitter/deadly** enemies

o͏̈**enemy** /'enəmi/ noun **1** [C] a person who you dislike or oppose **hasım, düşman** I try not to **make** any enemies. **2** [group] a country or army that your country or army is fighting against in a war **düşman devlet/ordu** enemy forces/territory

energetic /,enə'dʒetɪk/ adjective having or involving a lot of energy **canlı, enerji dolu, çalışkan, enerjik, güçlü** an energetic young woman ○ Aerobics is too energetic for me. • **energetically** adverb **enerjik bir şekilde**

energy ...... İLE BİRLİKTE KULLANILAN KELİMELER
expend/have/save/waste energy • **boundless/high/restless/surplus** energy

o͏̈**energy** /'enədʒi/ noun [C, U] **1** the power and ability to be very active without becoming tired **güç, enerji** Looking after children takes up a lot of time and energy. ○ [+ to do sth] I didn't even have the energy to get out of bed. **2** the power that comes from electricity, gas, etc **(elektrik, gaz vb.) enerji** nuclear energy ○ energy conservation ➔See also: atomic energy.

enforce /ɪn'fɔːs/ verb [T] **1** to make people obey a rule or law **(yasa, kural) yürürlüğe koymak, etkinleştirmek** It is the duty of the police to enforce the law. **2** to make a particular situation happen, or to make people accept it **sağlamak, uygulamak, yürütmek, durumu kabul ettirmek** The new teacher failed to enforce discipline. • **enforcement** noun [U] law enforcement **yürürlüğe koyma**

engage /ɪn'geɪdʒ/ verb [T] formal **1** to interest someone in something and keep them thinking about it **ilgilendirmek, meşgul etmek, dikkatini çekmek** The debate about food safety has engaged the whole nation. **2** to employ someone **iş vermek, işe almak** [+ to do sth] I have engaged a secretary to deal with all my paperwork.
engage in sth phrasal verb to take part in something **dahil olmak, karışmak, bulaşmak**
engage sb in sth phrasal verb If you engage someone in conversation, you start a conversation with them. **birini birşeye dahil etmek; biriyle bir şeyi başlatmak**

engaged /ɪn'geɪdʒd/ adjective **1** If two people are engaged, they have formally agreed to marry each other. **nişanlı** When did they get engaged? **2** UK If a telephone line or a toilet is engaged, it is already being used. **meşgul, kullanılıyor, dolu**

engagement ...... İLE BİRLİKTE KULLANILAN KELİMELER
announce/break off your engagement • your engagement **to** sb • an engagement **party/ring**

engagement /ɪn'geɪdʒmənt/ noun [C] **1** an agreement to get married to someone **nişanlılık** an engagement ring **2** an arrangement to meet someone or do something at a particular time **sözleşme, randevu, söz**

engaging /ɪn'geɪdʒɪŋ/ adjective pleasant, interesting, or attractive **çekici, hoş, ilginç** She has a very engaging personality.

engender /ɪn'dʒendər/ verb [T] formal to make people have a particular feeling or make a situation start to exist **sağlamak, inandırmak; varlığını sürdürtmek, meydan getirmek, yol açmak** We want to engender loyalty to our products.

engine ...... İLE BİRLİKTE KULLANILAN KELİMELER
start/switch on/switch off/turn off the engine

o͏̈**engine** /'endʒɪn/ noun [C] **1** the part of a vehicle that uses energy from oil, electricity, or steam to make it move **motor** a diesel/petrol engine **2** the part of a train that pulls it along **lokomotif** ➔See also: fire engine, search engine.

'engine ,driver UK (US engineer) noun [C] someone whose job is to drive a train **tren makinisti**

engineer[1] /,endʒɪ'nɪər/ noun [C] **1** someone whose job is to design, build, or repair machines, engines, roads, bridges, etc **mühendis** a mechanical/structural engineer ○ a software engineer **2** US someone whose job is to drive a train **makinist**

engineer[2] /,endʒɪ'nɪər/ verb [T] to arrange for something to happen, especially in a clever and secret way **ayarlamak, düzenlemek, tertip etmek** [often passive] She was convinced that the accident had been engineered by his enemies.

engineering /,endʒɪ'nɪərɪŋ/ noun [U] the work of an engineer, or the study of this work **mühendislik** mechanical engineering ➔See also: civil engineering, genetic engineering.

English[1] /'ɪŋglɪʃ/ noun **1** [U] the language that is spoken in the UK, the US, and in many other countries **İngilizce** American/British English ○ Do you speak English? **2 the English** [plural] the people of England **İngiliz halkı**

English[2] /'ɪŋglɪʃ/ adjective **1** relating to the English language **İngiliz diline ilişkin** an English teacher **2** relating to England **İngiltere'ye dair/ait/ilişkin** English law

,English 'breakfast *noun* [C] *UK* a dish including cooked meat and eggs, eaten as the first meal of the day **pişmiş et ve yumurtadan oluşan İngiliz usulü kahvaltı**

,English 'muffin *US* (*UK* muffin) *noun* [C] a small, round, flat bread that is often eaten hot with butter **küçük düz yuvarlak ekmek; İngiliz çöreği** ➪See picture at muffin.

engrave /ɪnˈɡreɪv/ *verb* [T] to cut words or pictures into the surface of metal, stone, etc (**metal, taş vb. üzerine) resim/sözcük kazımak/oymak** *He gave her a silver pen engraved with her name.* ● **engraver** *noun* [C] **oymacı**

engraving /ɪnˈɡreɪvɪŋ/ *noun* [C] a picture printed from an engraved piece of metal or wood **kakma, oyma, baskı, gravür**

engrossed /ɪnˈɡrəʊst/ *adjective* giving all your attention to something **bütün dikkatini veren, kendini kaptıran, dalıp giden** *He was so engrossed in what he was doing that he didn't hear the bell.*

engrossing /ɪnˈɡrəʊsɪŋ/ *adjective* very interesting, and needing all your attention **çok ilgi çekici, çok dikkat gerektiren** *an engrossing book*

engulf /ɪnˈɡʌlf/ *verb* [T] **1** to surround or cover someone or something completely **tamamen sarmak/çevrelemek; sarıp sarmalamak** [often passive] *The house was quickly engulfed in flames.* **2** to affect a place or a group of people quickly and strongly **kolayca etkilemek, etkisi altına almak** *Panic is threatening to engulf the country.*

enhance /ɪnˈhɑːns/ *verb* [T] *formal* to improve something **geliştirmek, katkıda bulunmak, zenginlik katmak, (güç, güzellik, değer vb.) arttırmak** *Winning that award greatly enhanced her reputation.* ● **enhancement** *noun* [C, U] when something is improved **gelişme, güçlenme, değer kazanma**

enigma /ɪˈnɪɡmə/ *noun* [C] someone or something that is mysterious and difficult to understand **gizem, muamma, bilmece** *She is a complete enigma to me.*

enigmatic /ˌenɪɡˈmætɪk/ *adjective* mysterious and impossible to understand completely **gizemli, muammalı, çözülmesi/anlaşılması zor**

> *enjoy ...... BAŞKA BİR DEYİŞLE*
>
> **Relish** resmi ortamlarda bir şeyden keyif alındığı anlamını vermek için kullanılır. *Jonathan always relishes a challenge.*
>
> Kişi eğer bir durum veya olaydan çok keyif aldıysa, bunu belirtmede **lap up** veya **revel in** deyimleri kullanılabilir. *He lapped up all the attention they gave him.* ● *She revelled in her role as team manager.*
>
> Eğer kişi genellikle diğer kişilerin keyif almadığı bir durumdan keyif alabiliyor ise, bunu belirtmede **delight in** deyimi kullanılabilir. *She seems to delight in making other people look stupid.*
>
> **Savour** (savor) fiili kişinin bir şeyin değerini tam anlayabilmesi için yavaş yavaş keyif aldığı durumlarda kullanılır. *It was the first chocolate he'd had for over a year, so he savoured every mouthful.*
>
> Eğer kişinin keyfi yerindeyse, gayri resmi durumlarda **have a ball** söylemi kullanılabilir. *We had a ball in Miami.*

o▪**enjoy** /ɪnˈdʒɔɪ/ *verb* [T] **1** If you enjoy something, it gives you pleasure. **hoşlanmak, sevmek, zevk almak** *I hope you enjoy your meal.* ○ [+ doing sth] *I really enjoyed being with him.* **2 enjoy yourself** to get pleasure from something that you are doing **eğlenmek, hoşça vakit geçirmek; keyfine bakmak; 'Keyfinize bakın! İyi eğlenceler!'** *Everyone eventually relaxed and began to enjoy themselves.* **3** *formal* to have or experience something

good such as success (**başarı vb.) tadını/keyfini çıkarmak** *His play enjoyed great success on Broadway.*

enjoy

Unutmayın! Enjoy fiilinin ardından edat kullanılmaz. Enjoy with veya enjoy/to something kullanımı doğru değildir. Doğru hali **enjoy something** kullanımıdır.: ~~I really enjoyed with the music festival.~~ Yanlış cümle örneği

I really enjoyed the music festival.

enjoyable /ɪnˈdʒɔɪəbl/ *adjective* An enjoyable event or experience gives you pleasure. **hoş, zevkli, sevimli** *We had a very enjoyable evening.*

enjoyment /ɪnˈdʒɔɪmənt/ *noun* [U] when you enjoy something **zevk, eğlence** *She gets a lot of enjoyment from music.*

enlarge /ɪnˈlɑːdʒ/ *verb* [I, T] to become bigger or to make something become bigger **büyü(t)mek, genişle(t)mek** [often passive] *I want to get this photo enlarged.* ○ *an enlarged liver*
enlarge on/upon sth *phrasal verb formal* to give more details about something that you have said or written **ayrıntılara girmek, detayıyla vermek**

enlargement /ɪnˈlɑːdʒmənt/ *noun* [C, U] when something is enlarged, or something that has been enlarged **büyütme, genişletmek, büyütülmüş, genişletilmiş** *I'm going to get an enlargement of this wedding photo.*

enlighten /ɪnˈlaɪtən/ *verb* [T] *formal* to give someone information about something, so that they understand a situation **aydınlatmak, bilgi vermek, açıklık getirmek** *He believes he has a duty to enlighten the public on these matters.*

enlightened /ɪnˈlaɪtənd/ *adjective* having practical, modern ideas and ways of dealing with things **aydınlanmış, modern, aydın** *an enlightened attitude*

enlightening /ɪnˈlaɪtənɪŋ/ *adjective* giving you more information and understanding about something **açıklayan, bilgi veren, bilgilendiren** *an enlightening book*

enlist /ɪnˈlɪst/ *verb* **1 enlist the help/support of sb** to ask for and get help or support from someone **birinin yardımını istemek; destek/yardım almak** *They are hoping to enlist the support of local politicians.* **2** [I] to join the army, navy, etc **askere almak; orduya katılmak**

enliven /ɪnˈlaɪvən/ *verb* [T] to make something more interesting **canlılık getirmek, daha ilginç hale getirmek** *The children's arrival enlivened a boring evening.*

en masse /ɒnˈmæs/ *adverb* If a group of people do something en masse, they do it together as a group. **ortak çalışma yaparak** *They surrendered en masse.*

enmity /ˈenməti/ *noun* [U] *formal* a strong feeling of hate **düşmanlık, aşırı nefret**

enormity /ɪˈnɔːməti/ *noun* **the enormity of sth** how big or important something is **ciddiyet, vahamet, büyüklük** *He hadn't realized the enormity of the problem.*

o▪**enormous** /ɪˈnɔːməs/ *adjective* extremely large **devasa, çok geniş/büyük, koskoca, kocaman** *This living room is enormous.*

enormously /ɪˈnɔːməsli/ *adverb* extremely **son derece, fevkalade** *an enormously popular show*

o▪**enough**[1] /ɪˈnʌf/ *pronoun, quantifier* **1** as much as is necessary **kâfi, yeterli** *They had enough fuel for one week.* ○ [+ to do sth] *Have you had enough to eat?* **2** as much or more than you want **yeter** *I've got enough work at the moment, without being given any more.* **3 have had enough** to want something to stop because it is annoying you **canına yetmek, kâfi gelmek, yetmek** *I've had enough of your excuses.* **4 that's enough** used to tell someone to stop behaving badly **Yeter! Bu kadar yeter! Kendine gel artık!**

⚬━**enough²** /ɪˈnʌf/ *adverb* **1** as much as is necessary **yeterince, oldukça** [+ to do sth] *Are you old enough to vote?* ○ *You're not going fast enough.* **2** slightly, but not very **yeteri kadar, kâfi derecede** *He's nice enough, but I don't really want to go out with him.* **3 funnily/oddly/strangely enough** although it may seem strange **acayip/saçma/komik gibi görünmesine rağmen; beklenenin aksine; yine de** *I was dreading the party, but I really enjoyed it, funnily enough.*

enquire UK (*UK/US* **inquire**) /ɪnˈkwaɪəʳ/ *verb* [I, T] to ask someone for information about something **sormak, soruşturmak, soru sormak** *"Are you staying long?" she enquired.* ○ *I'm enquiring about dentists in the area.* ● **enquirer** UK (*UK/US* **inquirer**) *noun* [C] **soruşturan**

enquire after sb *phrasal verb UK formal* to ask someone for information about someone else's health and what they are doing, in order to be polite **birini sorup soruşturmak; merak ederek sormak; halini hatırını sormak**

enquire into sth *phrasal verb formal* to try to discover the facts about something **araştırmak, soruşturmak**

enquiring UK (*UK/US* **inquiring**) /ɪnˈkwaɪərɪŋ/ *adjective* [always before noun] **1** always wanting to learn new things **araştıran, sorup soruşturan, yeni şeyleri öğrenmeye hevesli olan** *an enquiring mind* **2** An enquiring expression on your face shows that you want to know something. **sorgulayıcı, meraklı bakışlarla süzen**

🧩 **enquiry** ...... İLE BİRLİKTE KULLANILAN KELİMELER

make/receive an enquiry ● an enquiry **about** sth

enquiry UK (*UK/US* **inquiry**) /ɪnˈkwaɪəri/ *noun* **1** QUESTION [C] *formal* a question that you ask when you want more information **soru, sual** *We receive a lot of enquiries about tax issues.* **2** OFFICIAL PROCESS [C] an official process to discover the facts about something bad that has happened **soruşturma** *The hospital is holding an enquiry into the accident.* **3** ASKING QUESTIONS [U] *formal* the process of asking questions in order to get information **sorgulama, soru sorma, araştırma**

enrage /ɪnˈreɪdʒ/ *verb* [T] to make someone very angry **öfkelendirmek, hiddetlendirmek** [often passive] *Farmers are enraged by the government's refusal to help.*

enrich /ɪnˈrɪtʃ/ *verb* [T] to improve the quality of something by adding something to it **zenginleştirmek, kalitesini artırmak** [often passive] *Our culture has been enriched by the many immigrants who live here.* ● **enrichment** *noun* [U] **zenginleştirme**

enrol UK (*US* **enroll**) /ɪnˈrəʊl/ *verb* [I, T] **enrolling**, *past* **enrolled** to become or make someone become an official member of a course, college, or group **(kurs, okul, grup vb.) kaydetmek, kaydolmak; yazılmak, yazmak** *I've UK enrolled on/US enrolled in a creative writing course.* ● **enrolment** UK (*US* **enrollment**) *noun* [C, U] **kayıt**

en route /ˌɒnˈruːt/ *adverb* on the way to or from somewhere **yolda, giderken/gelirken** *We stopped in Monaco en route to Switzerland.*

ensemble /ɒnˈsɒmbᵊl/ *noun* [C] a small group of musicians or actors who regularly play or perform together **(müzik, oyuncu vb.) grup topluluk**

enshrined /ɪnˈʃraɪnd/ *verb formal* **be enshrined in sth** If a political or social right is enshrined in something, it is protected by being included in it. **kanunla korunmak; yasal olarak yer almak, yasayla güvence** altına alınmak *These fundamental human rights are enshrined in the constitution.*

enslave /ɪnˈsleɪv/ *verb* [T] *formal* to control someone and keep them in a bad situation **esir/tutsak etmek** [often passive] *These workers are enslaved by poverty.*

ensue /ɪnˈsjuː/ *verb* [I] **ensuing**, *past* **ensued** *formal* to happen after something, often as a result of it **bir şeyin sonucu olarak ortaya çıkmak** ● **ensuing** *adjective* [always before noun] *the ensuing hours/months* **ardından gelen**

en suite /ˌɒnˈswiːt/ *adjective* UK An en suite bathroom is directly connected to a bedroom. **içiçe odalar olan**

ensure /ɪnˈʃɔːʳ/ *verb* [T] *formal* to make certain that something is done or happens **temin etmek, garantiye almak, sağlamak** [+ (that)] *Please ensure that all examination papers have your name at the top.*

entail /ɪnˈteɪl/ *verb* [T] to involve something **kapsamak, gerektirmek, zorunlu kılmak** *What exactly does the job entail?*

entangled /ɪnˈtæŋgld/ *adjective* **1** involved with someone or something so that it is difficult to escape **bulaşmış, girmiş, dahil olmuş, başına dert açmış** *I don't know how I ever got entangled in this relationship.* **2** caught in something such as a net or ropes **dolaşmış, karışmış, ağlara/iplere dolanmış** *The dolphin had become entangled in the fishing net.*

⚬━**enter** /ˈentəʳ/ *verb* **1** PLACE [I, T] to come or go into a place **(yer) girmek** *The police entered by the back door.* ○ *She is accused of entering the country illegally.* **2** INFORMATION [T] to put information into a computer, book, or document **(bilgisayar) bilgiyi girmek** *You have to enter a password to access this information.* **3** COMPETITION [I, T] to take part in a competition, race, or exam, or to arrange for someone else to do this **(yarışma, sınav vb.) girmek, birini sokmak** *Are you going to enter the photography competition?* **4** ORGANIZATION [T] to become a member of a particular organization, or start working in a particular type of job **(kuruluş) girmek** *She didn't enter the legal profession until she was 40.* **5** PERIOD OF TIME [T] to begin a period of time **(zaman dilimi) girmek, başlamak** *The violence is now entering its third week.*

enter into sth *phrasal verb* to start to become involved in something, especially a discussion or agreement **(tartışmaya, anlaşmaya) girmek, dahil olmak**

enterprise /ˈentəpraɪz/ *noun* **1** BUSINESS [C] a business or organization **girişim, iş, işletme** *a state-owned enterprise* **2** PLAN [C] a difficult and important plan **önemli bir plan/eylem/işbirliği** *Putting on the concert will be a joint enterprise between the two schools.* **3** QUALITY [U] when someone is enthusiastic and willing to do something new and clever, although there are risks involved **girişkenlik, girişimcilik, cesaret** *The scheme shows imagination and enterprise.* ⟳See also: free enterprise.

enterprising /ˈentəpraɪzɪŋ/ *adjective* enthusiastic and willing to do something new, clever, and difficult **coşku ve heyecan dolu, girişken, gözüpek** *The film was made by an enterprising group of students.*

entertain /ˌentəˈteɪn/ *verb* **1** INTEREST [T] to keep someone interested and help them to have an enjoyable time **eğlen(dir)mek** *We hired a clown to entertain the children.* **2** GUEST [I, T] to invite someone to be your guest and give them food, drink, etc **davet etmek, misafir ağırlamak** *We don't entertain as much as we used to.* **3** THINK ABOUT [T] *formal* to consider or be willing to accept an idea or suggestion **düşünmek, dikkate almak, ehemmiyet vermek** *He had never even entertained the idea of her returning.*

entertainer /ˌentəˈteɪnəʳ/ *noun* [C] someone whose job is to entertain people by singing, telling jokes, etc **şarkı**

söyleyerek/fıkra anlatarak insanları eğlendiren kişi

entertaining /ˌentə'teɪnɪŋ/ *adjective* interesting and helping someone to have an enjoyable time **eğlendiren, eğlenceli, hoş** *an entertaining and informative book*

๑ᴥ**entertainment** /ˌentə'teɪnmənt/ *noun* [C, U] shows, films, television, or other performances or activities that entertain people **eğlence, şov, cümbüş** *popular entertainment* ○ *There is* live *entertainment in the bar every night.*

enthral *UK* (*US* **enthrall**) /ɪn'θrɔːl/ *verb* [T] **enthralling,** *past* **enthralled** to keep someone's interest and attention completely **büyülemek, hayran bırakmak, ziyadesiyle etkilemek** [often passive] *The children were enthralled by the circus.* ● **enthralling** *adjective* keeping someone's interest and attention completely **büyüleyen, hayran bırakan, etkileyen**

enthuse /ɪn'θjuːz/ *verb* [I] to express excitement about something or great interest in it **heyecan ve büyük ilgiyi ifade etmek, belirtmek, hayranlığını vurgulamak** *She couldn't stop enthusing about the film.*

enthusiasm /ɪn'θjuːziæᵊm/ *noun* [U] when you feel very interested in something and would very much like to be involved in it **coşku, heyecan, heves, şevk** *She has always had a lot of enthusiasm for her work.*

enthusiast /ɪn'θjuːziæst/ *noun* [C] someone who is very interested in and involved with a particular activity or subject **hevesli, meraklı, tutkun kimse** *a sports enthusiast*

enthusiastic /ɪnˌθjuːzi'æstɪk/ *adjective* showing enthusiasm **coşkulu, hevesli, heyecanlı, şevkli** *The teacher was very enthusiastic about my project.* ● **enthusiastically** *adverb* **istekli bir şekilde**

entice /ɪn'taɪs/ *verb* [T] to persuade someone to do something by offering them something pleasant **ayartmak, baştan çıkarmak, kandırmak, kanına girmek** [+ to do sth] *Supermarkets use all sorts of tricks to entice you to buy things.* ● **enticing** *adjective* Something which is enticing attracts you by offering you something pleasant. **baştan çıkaran, kandıran, ayartan, kanına giren**

entire /ɪn'taɪəʳ/ *adjective* [always before noun] whole or complete **bütün, tam, tamamı** *She spent her entire life caring for other people.*

entirely /ɪn'taɪəli/ *adverb* completely **bütünüyle, tamamıyla** *I'm not entirely convinced that it will work.*

entirety /ɪn'taɪərəti/ *noun* **in its entirety** with all parts included **bütünüyle, tam olarak, herşeyi ihtiva ederek** *This is the first time that the book has been published in its entirety.*

entitle /ɪn'taɪtl/ *verb* **1** **entitle sb to (do) sth** to give someone the right to do or have something **görevlendirmek, yetkili kılmak, bir şeyi yapmaya hakkı/yetkisi olmak, layık bulmak** [often passive] *I'm entitled to apply for citizenship.* **2** [T] to give something a particular title **başlık koymak, isimlendirmek** *a lecture entitled "Language, Learning and Literacy"*

entitlement /ɪn'taɪtlmənt/ *noun* [C, U] when you have the right to do or have something **yetkilendirme, görevlendirme, hak verme, layık bulma**

entity /'entɪti/ *noun* [C] something which exists apart from other things **varlık, mevcudiyet, birim** *They want the area recognized as a separate political entity.*

entourage /'ɒntʊrɑːʒ/ (US) /ˌɒntʊ'rɑːʒ/ *noun* [group] the group of people who travel with an important or famous person **birlikte çalışan/seyahat eden bir grup insan** *She arrived with her usual entourage of dancers and musicians.*

entrance ...... İLE BİRLİKTE KULLANILAN KELİMELER

the **back/front/main** entrance ● **at** the entrance ● the entrance **to** sth

๑ᴥ**entrance** /'entrəns/ *noun* **1** [DOOR] [C] a door or other opening which you use to enter a building or place **giriş, ana giriş** *They must have used the back entrance to the building.* ○ *I'll meet you at the main entrance.* **2** [COMING IN] [C] when someone comes into or goes into a place, especially in a way that makes people notice them **birinin giriş çıkışı** *The whole room went quiet when he made his entrance.* **3** [RIGHT] [U] the right to enter a place or to join an organization, college, etc **(üniversite, kuruluş vb. yerlere) giriş/katılma hakkı/yetkisi** *Entrance is free, but you have to pay for your drinks.*

entranced /ɪn'trɑːnst/ *adjective* If you are entranced by someone or something, you cannot stop watching them because they are very interesting or very beautiful. **büyüsüne kapılmış, kendini alamayan, etkilenmiş** *The children were entranced by the puppet show.*

entrant /'entrənt/ *noun* [C] someone who enters a competition, organization, or examination **yarışmacı, yarışmaya giren kişi**

entreat /ɪn'triːt/ *verb* [T] *formal* to try very hard to persuade someone to do something **yalvarmak, iknaya çabalamak**

entrenched /ɪn'trenʃt/ *adjective* Entrenched ideas are so fixed or have existed for so long that they cannot be changed. **değişmez, sabit, köklü, yerleşik** *These attitudes are firmly entrenched in our culture.*

entrepreneur /ˌɒntrəprə'nɜːʳ/ *noun* [C] someone who starts their own business, especially when this involves risks **müteşebbis, girişimci** ● **entrepreneurial** *adjective* **girişimci** *an entrepreneurial spirit*

entrust /ɪn'trʌst/ *verb* [T] to make someone responsible for doing something or looking after something **güvenmek, itimat etmek, emanet etmek, havale etmek** [often passive] *I was entrusted with the task of organizing the party.*

entry ...... İLE BİRLİKTE KULLANILAN KELİMELER

allow/gain/refuse entry ● entry into/to [a place]

๑ᴥ**entry** /'entri/ *noun* **1** [COMING IN] [U] when you come into or go into a place **giriş** *She was refused entry to the US.* ○ *Police gained entry by breaking a window.* **2** [JOINING/TAKING PART] [U] when you join an organization or take part in a competition **(kuruluş, yarışma vb.) giriş, katılım** *Are there lots of exams for entry into the legal profession?* ○ *an entry form* **3** [COMPETITION WORK] [C] a piece of work that you do to try to win a competition **kayıt, başvuru, katılım** *The first ten correct entries will receive a prize.* **4** [PIECE OF INFORMATION] [C] one of the pieces of information or writing that is recorded in a book such as a dictionary, or in a computer system **(sözlük, ansiklopedi, bilgisayar vb.) madde, girdi, madde başlığı** *a diary entry* **5** [ADDING INFORMATION] [U] when someone puts information into something such as a computer system **bilgi girişi** *data entry*

entwined /ɪn'twaɪnd/ *adjective* **1** twisted together or twisted around something **dolaşmış, dolanmış, arap saçına dönmüş** *Their arms were entwined.* **2** unable to be separated **kör düğüm olmuş, birbirine girmiş** *My fate is entwined with his.*

enumerate /ɪ'njuːməʳreɪt/ *verb* [T] *formal* to name each thing on a list **numaralandırmak, sıralamak, listelemek**

envelop /ɪn'veləp/ *verb* [T] to completely cover something **sarmak, sarmalamak, kuşatmak** [often passive] *The farm was enveloped in fog.*

envelope /'envələʊp/ *noun* [C] a flat paper container for a letter **zarf** ⊃Orta kısımdaki renkli sayfalarına bakınız.

enviable /'enviəbl/ *adjective* If someone is in an enviable situation, you wish that you were also in that situation. **gıpta edilecek, kıskanılacak** *She's in the enviable position of being able to choose who she works for.*

envious /'enviəs/ *adjective* wishing that you had what someone else has **kıskanç, gıpta eden** *She was envious of his successful career.* ● **enviously** *adverb* **imrenir bir şekilde**

🧩 **environment** .... İLE BİRLİKTE KULLANILAN KELİMELER

damage/harm/pollute/protect the environment

o⸚**environment** /ɪn'vaɪərⁿnmənt/ *noun* **1 the environment** the air, land, and water where people, animals, and plants live **çevre** *The new road may cause damage to the environment.* **2** [C] the situation that you live or work in, and how it influences how you feel **yaşanan/çalışılan çevre** *We are working in a very competitive environment.*

environmental /ɪn,vaɪərⁿn'mentⁿl/ *adjective* relating to the environment **çevreye ilişkin** *environmental damage* ○ *an environmental disaster* ● **environmentally** *adverb environmentally damaging chemicals* **çevresel**

environmentalist /ɪn,vaɪərⁿn'mentⁿlɪst/ *noun* [C] someone who tries to protect the natural environment from being damaged **çevreci**

en,vironmentally 'friendly *adjective* not damaging the environment **çevre dostu, çevreye uyan/zarar vermeyen** *environmentally-friendly washing powder*

envisage /ɪn'vɪzɪdʒ/ *mainly UK* (*mainly US* **envision** /ɪn'vɪʒ°n/) *verb* [T] to imagine something happening, or think that something is likely to happen **öngörmek, tahmin etmek, önceden kestirmek** *The police don't envisage any trouble at the festival.*

envoy /'envɔɪ/ *noun* [C] someone who is sent to represent their government in another country **hükümet tarafından görevlendirilen elçi, temsilci**

envy¹ /'envi/ *noun* **1** [U] the feeling that you wish you had something that someone else has **kıskançlık, gıpta, imrenme** *I watched with envy as he climbed into his brand new sports car.* **2 be the envy of sb** to be liked and wanted by someone **gıptayla bakılan, imrenilen, kıskanılan** *Her new office was the envy of the whole company.*

envy² /'envi/ *verb* [T] to wish that you had something that someone else has **gıpta etmek, kıskanmak, imrenmek** *I envy her good looks.* ○ [+ two objects] *I don't envy him that job.*

enzyme /'enzaɪm/ *noun* [C] a chemical substance produced by living cells which makes particular chemical reactions happen in animals and plants **enzim**

ephemeral /ɪ'fem°r°l/ *adjective formal* lasting for only a short time **kısa ömürlü, geçici**

epic /'epɪk/ *noun* [C] a story or film which is very long and contains a lot of action **destan** ● **epic** *adjective an epic journey* **destanı**

epidemic /,epɪ'demɪk/ *noun* [C] when a large number of people get the same disease over the same period of time **salgın, hastalık salgını** *the AIDS epidemic*

epilepsy /'epɪlepsi/ *noun* [U] a brain disease which can make someone become unconscious and have fits

(= when you shake in an uncontrolled way) **sara, epilepsi**

epileptic /,epɪ'leptɪk/ *noun* [C] someone who suffers from epilepsy **sara hastası** ● **epileptic** *adjective* **epilepsi hastası (epileptik)**

epilogue /'epɪlɒg/ *noun* [C] a speech or piece of writing that is added to the end of a play or book **son söz, son bölüm**

epiphany /ɪ'pɪf°ni/ *noun* [U] *literary* a moment when you suddenly understand or become aware of something **bir şeyin birdenbire anlaşıldığı/farkına varıldığı an**

episode /'epɪsəʊd/ *noun* [C] **1** one programme of a series shown on television **(tv dizisi) bölüm** *Did you see last week's episode of The X-Files?* **2** a single event or period of time **tek bir olay veya zaman dilimi** *an important episode in British history*

epitaph /'epɪtɑ:f/ *noun* [C] words that are written to remember a dead person, usually on the stone where they are buried **mezar taşı yazısı, yazıt**

epitome /ɪ'pɪtəmi/ *noun* **be the epitome of sth** to be a perfect example of a quality or type of thing **mükemmel bir örnek/sembol/simge/timsali olmak** *The hotel was the epitome of luxury.*

epitomize (*also UK* -ise) /ɪ'pɪtəmaɪz/ *verb* [T] to be a perfect example of a quality or type of thing **...nın/nin tam bir örneği timsali olmak; tam bir örnek oluşturmak** *She epitomizes elegance and good taste.*

epoch /'i:pɒk/ ⓤ /'epək/ *noun* [C] *plural* **epochs** a long period of time in history **çağ, devir**

eponymous /ɪ'pɒnɪməs/ *adjective* [always before noun] *literary* An eponymous character in a play, book, etc, has the same name as the title. **kitabın/oyunun ismiyle aynı adı taşıyan karakter olan**

o⸚**equal¹** /'i:kwəl/ *adjective* **1** the same in amount, number, or size **eşit, denk** *The sides are of equal length.* ○ *One metre is equal to 39.37 inches.* **2 equal opportunities/rights, etc** opportunities/rights, etc that are the same for everyone without anyone having an unfair advantage **eşit haklar/fırsatlar** ⊃Opposite **unequal.**

equal² /'i:kwəl/ *verb* [T] *UK* **equalling,** *past* **equalled,** *US* **equaling,** *past* **equaled 1** to have the same value, size, etc as something else, often shown using a symbol (=) **eşitlemek, denklemek** *Two plus two equals four.* **2** to be as good as someone or something else **eşit/denk/aynı olmak** *She equalled her own world record in the race.*

equal³ /'i:kwəl/ *noun* [C] someone who has the same ability, opportunities, or rights as someone else **aynı haklara/fırsatlara/yeteneğe sahip kişi** *The teacher treats us all as equals.*

🧩 **equality** .... İLE BİRLİKTE KULLANILAN KELİMELER

racial/sexual/social equality ● equality **between** sb and sb

equality /ɪ'kwɒləti/ *noun* [U] when everyone is equal and has the same opportunities, rights, etc **eşitlik, denklik** *racial/sexual equality* ○ *equality between men and women* ⊃Opposite **inequality.**

equalize (*also UK* -ise) /'i:kwəlaɪz/ *verb* **1** [I] *UK* to get the point in a game or competition that makes your score the same as the other team or player **sayıları/puanları/skoru eşitlemek 2** [T] to make things or people equal **eşit/denk hale getirmek**

o⸚**equally** /'i:kwəli/ *adverb* **1** [SAME DEGREE] to the same degree or level **eşit/denk/aynı şekilde** *an equally important question* ○ *She did equally well in the competition last year.* **2** [SAME AMOUNTS] into amounts or parts that are the same size **eşit/aynı dereced/boyutta** *She shared the money equally between the four children.* **3** SAME WAY If you treat people equally, you treat everyone in the same way so that no one has an unfair advantage. **eşit şekilde muamele ederek/davranarak**

'equal ,sign (*also* **'equals ,sign**) *noun* [C] the symbol =, used to show that two things are the same in value, size, meaning, etc **eşittir işareti**,

equanimity /ˌekwəˈnɪməti/ *noun* [U] *formal* the ability to react calmly, especially in difficult situations **ağırbaşlılık, itidal, temkin**

equate /ɪˈkweɪt/ *verb* [T] to consider one thing to be the same as or equal to another thing **bir tutmak, eşit saymak** *Many people equate wealth with happiness.*

equation /ɪˈkweɪʒən/ *noun* [C] when you show that two amounts are equal using mathematical symbols **eşitlik, denklik**

equator /ɪˈkweɪtər/ *noun* [U] the imaginary line around the Earth that divides it into equal north and south parts **ekvator** ● **equatorial** /ˌekwəˈtɔːriəl/ *adjective* relating to the equator **ekvatora ait, ekvatorla ilgili**

equestrian /ɪˈkwestriən/ *adjective* relating to riding horses **at binme/binciliğe ilişkin/ait/dair; at binen, atlı**

equi- /ekwɪ-/ *prefix* equal, equally **eşitlik/eşit biçimde anlamında ön ek** *equidistant* (= the same distance from two or more places)

equip /ɪˈkwɪp/ *verb* **equipping**, *past* **equipped 1 be equipped with sth** to include the things that are needed for a particular purpose **...ile donatılmış/techiz edilmiş olmak** *The new trains are equipped with all the latest technology.* **2** [T] to give someone the skills they need to do a particular thing **donatmak, techiz etmek** [+ to do sth] *The course didn't really equip me to be a journalist.*

> **equipment** ...... İLE BİRLİKTE KULLANILAN KELİMELER
> **install/operate/use** equipment ● **modern/necessary/specialist** equipment ● equipment **for** sth

o⌐**equipment** /ɪˈkwɪpmənt/ *noun* **1** [U] the things that are used for a particular activity or purpose **donatı, techizat, gereçler, aygıt** *kitchen/office equipment* ○ *electrical equipment* (= equipment that uses electricity) **2 a piece of equipment** a tool or object used for a particular activity or purpose **bir parça techizat**

> **YAYGIN HATALAR**
>
> equipment
>
> Unutmayın! **Equipment** kelimesinin çoğul hali yoktur. **Equipments** demek yanlıştır. **Equipments** olarak kullanmayın. **Equipment/some equipment** veya **pieces of equipment** doğru kullanımlardır.: ~~We need more up-to-date office equipments.~~ Yanlış cümle örneği
> *We need more up-to-date office equipment.*

equitable /ˈekwɪtəbl/ *adjective formal* treating everyone in an equal way **eşit muamele eden, hakka uygun, adaletli** *a fair and equitable voting system* ● **equitably** *adverb* **eşit bir şekilde**

equity /ˈekwɪti/ *noun* [U] *formal* when everyone is treated fairly and equally **adalet, eşitlik, dürüstlük, hakkaniyetlik** *pay equity* ↄCompare **inequity**

equivalent¹ /ɪˈkwɪvələnt/ *adjective* equal in amount, value, importance, or meaning **eşit, denk, eş değer, aynı** *The UK's Brit Awards are roughly equivalent to the Oscars.*

equivalent² /ɪˈkwɪvələnt/ *noun* [C] something that has the same value, importance, size, or meaning as something else **karşılık, eşdeğer, eşitlik, aynılık** *She won the equivalent of $5 million.*

er /ɜːr/ *exclamation UK spoken* (*US* **uh**) something that you say while you are thinking what to say next **ee..., ıı..., şeyy..., şeklinde düşünürken duraklamada çıkarılan ses, ünlem** *Well, er, I'm not too sure about that.*

ER /ˌiːˈɑːr/ *noun* [C] *US abbreviation for* emergency room: the part of a hospital where people come when they have been injured or have urgent illnesses so that they can be treated immediately **acil odası, acil**

era /ˈɪərə/ *noun* [C] a period of time in history that is special for a particular reason **çağ devir** *the Victorian era* ○ *a new era of peace*

eradicate /ɪˈrædɪkeɪt/ *verb* [T] *formal* to destroy or completely get rid of something such as a social problem or a disease **yok etmek, kökünü kazımak/kurutmak** ● **eradication** /ɪˌrædɪˈkeɪʃən/ *noun* [U] **yok etme, imha**

erase /ɪˈreɪz/ ⓤⓢ /ɪˈreɪs/ *verb* [T] to completely remove words, music, pictures, etc that are written or stored on a computer or other piece of equipment (**söz, müzik, resim vb.**) **silmek, yok etmek, gidermek** *I accidentally erased the tape she lent me.*

eraser /ɪˈreɪzər/ ⓤⓢ /ɪˈreɪsər/ *US* (*UK* **rubber**) *noun* [C] **1** a small object which is used to remove pencil marks from paper **silgi 2** an object which is used to remove marks from a blackboard (= a large dark board that teachers write on) **tahta silgisi** ↄOrta kısımdaki renkli sayfalarına bakınız.

erect¹ /ɪˈrekt/ *adjective* straight and standing up **dik, dimdik** *She stood very erect, with her hands behind her back.*

erect² /ɪˈrekt/ *verb* [T] *formal* to build or put up a structure **inşa etmek, dikmek, kondurmak** *When was this building erected?*

erection /ɪˈrekʃən/ *noun* **1** [C] when a penis becomes harder and bigger than usual **penisin dikleşmesi/kalkması; (tıp) ereksiyon 2** [C, U] *formal* when a structure is built or put up, or the building itself (**yapı, bina**) **dikme, yapma, inşa etme, yapı, bina**

erode /ɪˈrəʊd/ *verb* **1** [I, T] If soil, stone, etc erodes or is eroded, it is gradually damaged and removed by the sea, rain, or wind. (**toprak, kaya**) **deniz/yağmur/rüzgâr ile aşınmak/yok olmak/kaybolmak** [often passive] *The coastline is slowly being eroded by the sea.* **2** [T] *formal* to gradually destroy a good quality or situation **yavaş yavaş yok etmek/aşındırmak/kaybolmak** *Reports of corruption have eroded people's confidence in the police.* ● **erosion** /ɪˈrəʊʒən/ *noun* [U] *soil erosion* **erozyon**

erotic /ɪˈrɒtɪk/ *adjective* making you feel strong sexual feelings, or involving sexual love **cinsel arzu/istek uyandıran, erotik, cinsel istek/arzu ile ilgili** *an erotic film* ● **erotically** *adverb* **erotik, seksi bir şekilde**

err /ɜːr/ *verb* [I] *formal* to make a mistake or do something that is wrong **yanılmak, hata yapmak** ↄSee also: err on the **side¹** of caution.

errand /ˈerənd/ *noun* [C] a short journey in order to buy or do something for someone **basit/sıradan/ayak işi, getir götür işi** *I've got to run a few errands this morning before we go.*

errant /ˈerənt/ *adjective* [always before noun] An errant person has behaved badly. **kötü huylu, huysuz, kötü muamele eden** *an errant husband*

erratic /ɪˈrætɪk/ *adjective* often changing suddenly and not regular **düzensiz, değişken, kararsız, ne yapacağı belli olmayan** *His behaviour is becoming more and more erratic.* ● **erratically** *adverb* **değişken bir şekilde**

erroneous /ɪˈrəʊniəs/ *adjective formal* not correct **yanlış, hatalı** *an erroneous answer*

🧩 **error** ...... İLE BİRLİKTE KULLANILAN KELİMELER
make/correct an error ● a **fundamental/glaring** error ● do sth in error ● **human** error

o⌐**error** /ˈerəʳ/ *noun* [C, U] a mistake, especially one that can cause problems **yanlış, hata, kusur** *a computer error/ human error* ○ *to make an error* ○ *The documents were destroyed in error* (= by mistake) *by the police.*

erupt /ɪˈrʌpt/ *verb* [I] **1** VOLCANO If a volcano erupts, it suddenly throws out smoke, fire, and melted rocks. **lav püskürmek 2** HAPPEN to happen suddenly or violently **aniden şiddetle olan/vuku bulan** *Violence erupted in the city on Friday night.* **3** PERSON to suddenly become very excited or angry, or start to shout **patlamak, feveran etmek, birden kendinden geçmek, çılgına dönmek** *The whole stadium erupted when he scored the second goal.* ● **eruption** /ɪˈrʌpʃ°n/ *noun* [C, U] *a volcanic eruption* **patlama**

escalate /ˈeskəleɪt/ *verb* **1** [I, T] If a violent or bad situation escalates or is escalated, it quickly becomes worse or more serious. **gittikçe kötüleşmek, ciddi bir hal almak, tırmanmak/tırmandırmak, kızış(tır)mak** *The fight quickly escalated into a riot.* **2** [I] to rise or increase quickly **hızlıca yükselmek/artmak** *Airline prices escalate during the holiday season.* ● **escalation** /ˌeskəˈleɪʃ°n/ *noun* [C, U] *an escalation in violence* **yükseliş**

escalator /ˈeskəleɪtəʳ/ *noun* [C] moving stairs that take people from one level of a building to another **yürüyen merdiven** *We took the escalator down to the basement.*

escapade /ˌeskəˈpeɪd/ *noun* [C] an exciting and sometimes dangerous experience **tehlikeli macera, çılgınlık**

o⌐**escape**[1] /ɪˈskeɪp/ *verb* **1** GET AWAY [I] to succeed in getting away from a place where you do not want to be **kaçmak** *The two killers escaped from prison last night.* **2** AVOID [I, T] to avoid a dangerous or unpleasant situation **kötü/istenmeyen bir durumdan kaçınmak, kurtulmak, sakınmak** *to escape capture/ injury* **3** FORGET [T] If something such as a name escapes you, you cannot remember it. **hatırlayamamak** *The name of her book escapes me at the moment.* **4** NOT NOTICE [T] If something escapes your notice or attention, you do not notice or see it. **gözden/dikkatinden kaçmak** *Nothing that goes on in this office escapes her attention.* **5** GAS/LIQUID [I] If a gas or liquid escapes from a pipe or container, it comes out, especially when it should not. **(gaz, sıvı) kaçmak, sızmak, çıkmak** ● **escaped** *adjective an escaped prisoner* **kaçak**

🧩 **escape** ...... İLE BİRLİKTE KULLANILAN KELİMELER
attempt/make/plan an escape ● a **lucky/remarkable** escape ● an escape from sth/sb

o⌐**escape**[2] /ɪˈskeɪp/ *noun* **1** [C, U] when someone succeeds in getting out of a place or a dangerous or bad situation **firar, kaçma 2 a narrow escape** when someone almost dies or almost has a very bad experience **kılpayı kurtulma, zor kurtulma; (argo) yırtma, paçayı kurtarma 3** [U, no plural] something that helps you to forget about your usual life or problems **çıkış, kaçış, nefes alma, rahatlama, dinlenme** *I love old movies, they're such an escape from the real world.* ➔See also: **fire escape.**

es'cape ,(key) (*written abbreviation* Esc) *noun* [C] the key on a computer keyboard which allows you to leave a particular screen or program **bilgisayarda herhangi bir program ve ekrandan çıkma tuşu** *If you press the escape key, you will return to the main menu.*

escapism /ɪˈskeɪpɪz°m/ *noun* [U] entertainment or imagination that helps you to forget about your work and your problems **kaçış, nefes alma, eğlenme, hayale dalma; gerçeklerden kaçış** ● **escapist** *adjective* **gerçeklerden kaçan**

escort[1] /ˈeskɔːt/ *noun* **1** [C, U] a person or vehicle that goes somewhere with someone to protect or guard them **koruma görevlisi, eskort** *She was driven to court under police escort.* **2** [C] a person who goes with someone else to a social event, sometimes for payment **kavalye, refakatçi, eşlik eden**

escort[2] /ɪˈskɔːt/ *verb* [T] to go somewhere with someone, often to protect or guard them **eşlik etmek, refakat etmek** *He offered to escort me home.*

Eskimo /ˈeskɪməʊ/ *noun* [C, U] *plural* **Eskimos** or **Eskimo** *old-fashioned* another word for Inuit (= a group of people who live in the cold, northern areas of North America, Russia, and Greenland, or a member of this group) **Eskimo** *an Eskimo village*

ESL /ˌiːesˈel/ *noun* [U] *abbreviation for* English as a Second Language: the teaching of English to students whose first language is not English, but who live in a country where it is the main language **İkinci Dil olarak İngilizce**

o⌐**especially** /ɪˈspeʃ°li/ *adverb* **1** more than other things or people, or much more than usual **hele hele, özellikle** *He's always making comments about her appearance, especially her weight.* ○ *She's especially interested in American poetry.* **2** for one particular person, purpose, or reason **bilhassa, özellikle** *I cooked this meal especially for you.*

espionage /ˈespiənɑːʒ/ *noun* [U] the activity of discovering secret information about a country or company that is fighting or competing against you **casusluk** *industrial espionage*

espouse /ɪˈspaʊz/ *verb* [T] *formal* to support a belief or way of life **benimsemek, ilgi duyup desteklemek/ savunmak**

espresso /esˈpresəʊ/ *noun* [C, U] strong, black coffee **sert sade kahve**

🧩 **essay** ...... İLE BİRLİKTE KULLANILAN KELİMELER
do/write an essay ● in an essay ● an essay on sth

o⌐**essay** /ˈeseɪ/ *noun* [C] a short piece of writing about a particular subject, especially one written by a student **deneme, kompozisyon, fikre dayalı yazı** *He wrote an essay on modern Japanese literature.*

essence /ˈes°ns/ *noun* **1** [U, no plural] the basic or most important idea or quality of something **esas, asıl, öz, ruh, temel** *The essence of his argument is that we should not eat meat.* **2** [C, U] a strong liquid, usually made from a plant or flower, that is used to add a flavour or smell to something **(esans) öz, usare, bir şeyin özü** *vanilla essence*

o⌐**essential** /ɪˈsenʃ°l/ *adjective* **1** very important and necessary **önemli, gerekli, zaruri, elzem, hayati** *Computers are an essential part of our lives.* ○ *Fibre is essential for a healthy digestive system.* ○ [+ to do sth] *It is essential to arrive early for the show.* ○ [+ (that)] *It is absolutely essential that she gets this message.* **2** the most basic and important **temel, asıl, önemli, esas, belli başlı** *There's one essential point I think you've forgotten.*

essentially /ɪˈsenʃ°li/ *adverb* used when you are emphasizing the basic facts about something **gerçekten, aslında, esasında** *What he is saying is essentially true.*

eșsential ˈoil *noun* [C, U] a strong oil made from a plant which contains its smell or other special qualities **öz yağ, esans**

essentials /ɪˈsenʃ°lz/ *noun* [plural] the most important or necessary things **temel, esaslar, gerekli öğeler**

establish /ɪˈstæblɪʃ/ *verb* **1** START [T] to start a company or organization that will continue for a long time (**şirket, kurum) kurmak, tesis etmek, oluşturmak** [often passive] *The brewery was established in 1822.* **2 establish sb/sth as sth** to put someone or something into a successful and lasting position **başarılı ve uzun süre devam eden bir konuma getirmek; tanıtmak, kabul ettirmek** [often reflexive] *He quickly established himself as a talented actor.* **3 establish communication/relations, etc** to start having a relationship or communicating with another company, country, or organization (**şirket, ülke, kuruluş) ...ile iletişim/ilişki kurmak** *The two countries have only recently established diplomatic relations.* **4** DECIDE [T] to decide something **karar vermek, belirlemek** *Our first step must be to establish priorities for the weeks ahead.* **5** DISCOVER [T] to find out information or prove something **saptamak, bulmak, belirlemek** [+ question word] *The police are trying to establish how he died.* ● **established** *adjective* **yerleşik**

establishment /ɪˈstæblɪʃmənt/ *noun* **1** [C] an organization or business **ticari kuruluş, işyeri, kurum, tesis 2** [U] when an organization, school, business, etc is started **kur(ul)ma, tesis etme/edilme; kurup başlatılma** *the establishment of a new national bank* **3 the Establishment** the people and organizations that have most power and influence in a country **nüfuz sahibi kuruluş ve kişiler; egemen güçler; güç ve nüfuzu elinde bulunduranlar 4 the legal/medical, etc establishment** the group of people with most influence in a particular area of work or activity **hukuk/tıp vb. alanlarda söz sahibi/nüfuzlu/etkili insanlar topluluğu**

estate /ɪˈsteɪt/ *noun* [C] **1** LAND a large area of land in the countryside that is owned by one person or organization **malikâne, mülk, yurtluk** *a country estate* **2** BUILDINGS *UK* an area with a lot of buildings of the same type **aynı türden binaların bulunduğu bölge/mahal; arsa, arazi** *an industrial estate* **3** POSSESSIONS the possessions and money that someone owns when they die **ölen kimseden kalan mal varlığı; miras kalan taşınmaz ve nakit** ⊃See also: **housing estate, real estate.**

esˈtate ˌagent *UK* (*US* **real estate agent**) *noun* [C] someone who sells buildings and land as their job **emlâkçı, emlâk komisyoncusu**

esˈtate ˌcar *UK* (*US* **station wagon**) *noun* [C] a big car with a large space for bags behind the back seat **arkası geniş araba/otomobil; steyşın araba; pikap**

esteem /ɪˈstiːm/ *noun* [U] *formal* respect and admiration for someone **saygı, hürmet, değer, itibar, saygınlık** *My father was held in high esteem by everyone who knew him.* ⊃See also: **self-esteem.**

esteemed /ɪˈstiːmd/ *adjective formal* respected and admired **saygın, saygıdeğer, hürmetli** *a highly esteemed professor*

esthetic /esˈθetɪk/ *adjective another US spelling of* **aesthetic** (= relating to beauty and the way something looks) **estetik** ● **esthetically** *adverb* **estetiksel**

esthetics /esˈθetɪks/ *noun* [U] *another US spelling of* **aesthetics** (= the study of beauty) **güzelliğin bilimsel çalışması; güzellik bilimi**

an **accurate/rough** estimate ● an estimate **of** sth ● **give** sb an estimate

estimate¹ /ˈestɪmət/ *noun* [C] **1** a guess of what a size, value, amount, etc might be **tahmin** *a rough estimate* **2** a written document saying how much it will probably cost to do a job **tahmini hesap/ücret/maliyet/fiyat; fiyat teklifi** *Can you give me an estimate for the work?*

ᵒ⁼**estimate**² /ˈestɪmeɪt/ *verb* [T] to guess the cost, size, value, etc of something **tahmin etmek, tahminde bulunmak** [+ that] *They estimate that a hundred people were killed in the accident.* ○ *The number of dead is estimated at a hundred.* ● **estimated** *adjective* an estimated *cost* **tahmini**

estimation /ˌestɪˈmeɪʃ°n/ *noun* [U] your opinion of someone or something **kanı, kanaat, düşünce** *He is a total genius, in my estimation.*

estranged /ɪˈstreɪndʒd/ *adjective formal* **1** not now communicating with a friend or a member of your family, because you have argued **küsmüş, soğumuş, yabancılaşmış, dargın/kırgın 2** not now living with your husband or wife **ayrı yaşayan, arası açık, arası bozuk (eşler)** *his estranged wife* ● **estrangement** *noun* [C, U] **yabancılaşma, uzaklaşma**

estrogen /ˈiːstrədʒ°n/ Ⓤ /ˈestrədʒ°n/ *noun* [U] *US spelling of* **oestrogen** (= a chemical substance in a woman's body) **kadınlık hormonu, östrojen**

estuary /ˈestjuəri/ *noun* [C] the wide part of a river where it goes into the sea **haliç, nehir ağzı**

ᵒ⁼**etc** /etˈset°rə/ *abbreviation for* et cetera: used at the end of a list to show that other things or people could also be added to it **vb. (ve benzerleri); vs. (vesaire)**

etch /etʃ/ *verb* [I, T] to cut lines on a hard surface to make a picture or words **oyma yapmak, kakmak, kazımak**

eternal /ɪˈtɜːn°l/ *adjective* continuing forever, or seeming to continue forever **ebedî, ezelî, sonsuz, ölümsüz, hiç bitmeyen** *eternal youth* ● **eternally** *adverb I will be eternally grateful to you.* **sonsuz bir şekilde**

eternity /ɪˈtɜːnəti/ *noun* **1** [U] time that continues forever, especially after death **sonsuzluk, ölümsüzlük, ebediyet 2 an eternity** *informal* a very long time **çok uzun süre/zaman** *It seemed like an eternity until she came back.*

ethereal /ɪˈθɪəriəl/ *adjective* very delicate and light and almost seeming not to be from this world **bu dünyadan gibi görünmeyen, nazik, hoş, narin** ● **ethereally** *adverb* **bu dünyadan değilmiş gibi**

ethic /ˈeθɪk/ *noun* [no plural] a belief or idea that influences the way you think or behave **ilke, prensip, usül, ahlak, etik**

ethical /ˈeθɪk°l/ *adjective* **1** relating to what is right or wrong **ahlâki, ahlâkla ilgili** *The book raises some serious ethical questions.* **2** morally correct and good **ahlâken iyi ve doğru; dürüst, ilkeli** *He dealt with this case in a completely professional and ethical manner.* ⊃Opposite **unethical.** ● **ethically** *adverb* **ahlaki bir şekilde**

ethics /ˈeθɪks/ *noun* [plural] ideas and beliefs about what type of behaviour is morally right and wrong **ahlak/töre bilimi, etik** *a code of ethics* ○ *the ethics of genetic engineering*

ethnic /ˈeθnɪk/ *adjective* relating to a particular race of people **ırksal, ulusal kavimle ilgili, etnik** *ethnic minorities*

ethnic cleansing /ˌeθnɪkˈklenzɪŋ/ *noun* [U] the use of violence to remove everyone of a particular race or religion from a country **soykırım**

ethos /'i:θɒs/ *noun* [no plural] the ideas and beliefs of a particular person or group **yaşam felsefesi**

e-ticket /'i:ˌtɪkɪt/ *noun* [C] a ticket, usually for someone to travel on an aircraft, that is held on a computer and is not printed on paper **e-bilet**

etiquette /'etɪket/ *noun* [U] rules about what is polite and correct behaviour **görgü kuralları; adabı muaşeret kaideleri**

etymology /ˌetɪ'mɒlədʒi/ *noun* [U] the study of the history and origin of words and their meanings **kökenbilim, etimoloji** ● **etymological** /ˌetɪmə'lɒdʒɪkəl/ *adjective* **etimoloji ile ilgili** ● **etymologically** *adverb* **etimolojik açıdan**

the EU /ˌi:'ju:/ *noun abbreviation for* the European Union: a European political and economic organization that encourages business and good relationships between the countries that are members **Avrupa Birliği (AB)**

euphemism /'ju:fəmɪzᵊm/ *noun* [C, U] a polite word or phrase that is used to avoid saying something embarrassing or offensive **örtmece, ayıp/çirkin şeylerin daha uygun/usturuplu şekilde söylenmesi** *'Passed away' is a euphemism for 'died'.* ● **euphemistic** /ˌju:fə'mɪstɪk/ *adjective* **üstü kapalı (söz)** ● **euphemistically** *adverb* **üstü kapalı bir şekilde**

euphoria /ju:'fɔ:riə/ *noun* [U] a feeling of extreme happiness and excitement **mutluluk duygusu, sevinçli heyecan, coşku** ● **euphoric** /ju:'fɒrɪk/ *adjective* **mutlu ve heyecanlı**

euro /'jʊərəʊ/ *noun* [C] a unit of money used in European countries that belong to the European Union (= a European political and economic organization); € **avro, Avrupa Birliği para birimi**

Euro- /jʊərəʊ-/ *prefix* relating to Europe **Avrupaya ait; Avrupayla ilgili anlamında ön ek** *Europop* (= pop music from Europe)

European /ˌjʊərə'pi:ən/ *adjective* relating or belonging to Europe **Avrupa'ya ait/ilişkin** *European countries/languages* ○ *the European Parliament* ● **European** *noun* [C] *Many Europeans speak English.* **Avrupa'ya dair**

the ˌEuropean 'Union (*also* the EU) *noun* a European political and economic organization that encourages business and good relationships between the countries that are members **Avrupa Birliği**

euthanasia /ˌju:θə'neɪziə/ *noun* [U] when someone who is very old or very ill is killed so that they do not suffer any more **tatlı/rahat ölüm; ötenazi** *voluntary euthanasia*

evacuate /ɪ'vækjueɪt/ *verb* [T] to move people from a dangerous place to somewhere safer **insanları tahliye etmek/boşaltmak** *The police quickly evacuated the area after the bomb threat.* ● **evacuation** /ɪˌvækju'eɪʃᵊn/ *noun* [C, U] *the evacuation of civilians from the war zone* **tahliye**

evacuee /ɪˌvækju'i:/ *noun* [C] someone who is evacuated from a place to somewhere safer **kurtarılan/tahliye edilen kişi**

evade /ɪ'veɪd/ *verb* **1** [T] to avoid something or someone, especially in a dishonest way **kaçmak, kaçınmak, kurtulmak** ○ *to evade capture* ○ *to evade paying tax* **2** *evade the issue/question, etc* to intentionally not talk about something or not answer something **kaçamak cevaplar vermek/yanıtlamak; bilerek cevaplamak; (argo) kıvırmak, es geçmek**

evaluate /ɪ'væljueɪt/ *verb* [T] *formal* to consider or study something carefully and decide how good or bad it is **değerlendirmek, değer/paha biçmek, derecesini belirlemek** ● **evaluation** /ɪˌvælju'eɪʃᵊn/ *noun* [C, U] **değerlendirme**

evangelical /ˌi:væn'dʒelɪkᵊl/ *adjective* Evangelical Christians believe that faith in Jesus Christ and studying the Bible are more important than religious ceremonies. **Hz. İsa'ya itikât ve İncil'in çalışılmasının dini törenlerden daha önemli olduğuna inanan Evangelist Hıristiyanların inancını benimseyen**

evaporate /ɪ'væpᵊreɪt/ *verb* **1** [I, T] If a liquid evaporates or is evaporated, it changes into gas or vapour (= very small drops of water). **buharlaş(tır)mak 2** [I] If feelings evaporate, they disappear. **(duygular) uçup gitmek, yok olmak, buharlaşmak** ● **evaporation** /ɪˌvæpə'reɪʃᵊn/ *noun* [U] **buharlaşma**

evasion /ɪ'veɪʒᵊn/ *noun* [C, U] when you avoid something, especially in a dishonest way **bilerek kaçınma, sakınma, kaçma** *tax evasion*

evasive /ɪ'veɪsɪv/ *adjective* **1** trying to avoid talking about something **kaçamaklı, kesin olmayan, kaçamak** *He was very evasive about his past.* ○ *an evasive answer* **2** *take evasive action* to do something to avoid an accident or bad situation **kaçınmak, sakınarak uzak durmak; atlatmak** ● **evasively** *adverb* **kaçınırcasına** ● **evasiveness** *noun* [U] **kaçınma**

eve /i:v/ *noun* **1 Christmas Eve/New Year's Eve** the day or night before Christmas Day/New Year's Day **Noel/Yeni Yıl arifesi 2 the eve of sth** the time just before something important happens **önemli bir şeyin olmasından hemen öncesindeki zaman** *They were married in Washington on the eve of the Second World War.*

even¹ /'i:vᵊn/ *adjective* **1** FLAT flat, level, or smooth **düz, bir hizada, bir düzeyde/seviyede, engebesiz** *Find an even surface to work on.* ⊃Opposite **uneven**. **2** NOT CHANGING An even temperature or rate is regular and does not change very much. **sabit, değişmez 3** NUMBER An even number is a number which can be exactly divided by two, for example four, six, or eight. **(rakam) çift** ⊃Opposite **odd. 4** MONEY *informal* not now owing someone money **eşit, alacak vereceği olmayan** *If you pay for my cinema ticket, we'll be even.* **5** COMPETITION An even race or competition is one that both players, teams, or people involved have an equal chance of winning. **eşit şansı olan 6 get even (with sb)** *informal* If you get even with someone who has done something bad to you, you do something bad to them. **ödeşme, acısını çıkarmak, öcünü/intikamını almak**

○┉**even²** /'i:vᵊn/ *adverb* **1** used to emphasize something that is surprising **hatta, bile, ...de/da, ...dahi** *Everyone danced, even Mick.* **2 even better/faster/smaller, etc** used when comparing things, to emphasize the difference **daha bile; daha da** *I think Alex is going to be even taller than his father.* **3 even if** used to emphasize that a particular situation would not change what you have just said *...so even if* **I** *would never eat meat, even if I was really hungry.* **4 even though** although **her nekadar...da, ...olsa bile, ...rağmen** *He still smokes, even though he's got asthma.* **5 even so** used to emphasize that something surprising is true despite what you have just said **öyle de olsa, öyle olmasına karşın, buna rağmen, yine de** *Car prices have gone down a lot, but even so, we couldn't afford to buy one.*

even³ /'i:vᵊn/ *verb*
even (sth) out *phrasal verb* to become equal, or to make something equal **düzel(t)mek, düzleş(tir)mek; eşitle (n)mek, dengele(n)mek** *Sometimes I pay and sometimes Tom does - it usually evens out in the end.*

┌─────────────────────────────────────┐
   evening .... İLE BİRLİKTE KULLANILAN KELİMELER

this/tomorrow/yesterday evening ● **in the** evening
└─────────────────────────────────────┘

○┉**evening** /'i:vnɪŋ/ *noun* **1** [C, U] the part of the day between the afternoon and the night **akşam** *Are you* *doing anything **this evening**?* ○ *I go to band practice on Monday evenings.* ○ *We usually eat our main meal **in the evening**.* **2 (Good) evening.** something that you say when you meet someone in the evening **iyi akşamlar!**

evenly /ˈiːvənli/ *adverb* **1** into equal amounts, or in a regular way **muntazam bir şekilde; eşit olarak** *They decided to divide the prize money evenly between them.* **2 evenly matched** Two people or teams who are evenly matched are equally good, or have an equal chance of winning. **eşit olarak eşleşmiş/eşleşen; kazanma şansı eşit olan**

╔═════════════════════════════════════╗
║ **event** ...... İLE BİRLİKTE KULLANILAN KELİMELER ║
╚═════════════════════════════════════╝

an event **happens/occurs/takes place ● witness** an event ● a **dramatic/major/rare/tragic** event ● **recent** events

ᴼ⁻**event** /ɪˈvent/ *noun* [C] **1** something that happens, especially something important or unusual **olay** *Local people have been shocked by **recent events** in the town.* **2** a race, party, competition, etc that has been organized for a particular time **karşılaşma; parti; yarışma** *a social/sporting event* **3 in the event** *UK* used to emphasize what did happen when it was not what you had expected *...olduğunda/gerçekleştiğinde In the event, we didn't need the extra money.* **4 in the event of sth** *formal* if something happens *...olursa/olduğunda; durumunda/halinde; vuku bulduğunda An airbag could save your life in the event of an accident.* **5 in any event** whatever happens **her ne olursa olsun; her halükârda; her ne pahasına olursa olsun** *I'm not sure if I'm coming on Friday, but in any event, I'll see you next week.* ➔See also: **non-event.**

eventful /ɪˈventfºl/ *adjective* full of interesting or important events **olaylı, hâdiseli, hareketli** *a very eventful day/journey*

eventual /ɪˈventʃuəl/ *adjective* [always before noun] happening or existing at the end of a process or period of time **sonuç olarak gerçekleşen, nihaî** *the eventual winner of the competition*

ᴼ⁻**eventually** /ɪˈventʃuəli/ *adverb* in the end, especially after a long time **er geç, sonunda, nihayet** *We all hope that an agreement can be reached eventually.*

ᴼ⁻**ever** /ˈevəʳ/ *adverb* **1** at any time **şimdiye kadar; herhangi bir zamanda** *Have you ever been skiing?* ○ *No one ever calls me any more.* **2 better/faster/happier, etc than ever** better/faster/happier, etc than at any time before **öncesinden/evvelinden daha mutlu/hızlı/iyi vs. 3 hardly ever** almost never **neredeyse hiç; hiç denecek kadar az** *We hardly ever go out these days.* **4 ever since** always since that time *...den/dan beri, hep We met at school and have been friends ever since.* **5 ever so/ever such** a *UK* very/a very **çok, öylesine** *She's ever so pretty.* **6 for ever** *UK (UK/US* **forever)** always in the future **hep, her zaman, daima; ebediyen, sonsuza dek** *I'm not going to live here for ever.* **7 ever-changing/growing/increasing, etc** always changing/growing/increasing, etc **daima değişen; gelişen/artan vs.**

evergreen /ˈevəɡriːn/ *adjective* An evergreen plant has green leaves that do not fall off in winter. **yaprak dökmeyen ● evergreen** *noun* [C] a plant with leaves that do not fall off in winter **yaprak dökmeyen ağaç**

everlasting /ˌevəˈlɑːstɪŋ/ *adjective* continuing for a long time or always **ölümsüz, sonsuza dek, ebedî, daima** *everlasting love*

evermore /ˌevəˈmɔːʳ/ *adverb literary* always in the future **herzaman, sonsuza kadar**

ᴼ⁻**every** /ˈevri/ *determiner* **1** [EACH] each one of a group of people or things **her, her biri** *He knows the name of*

every child in the school. ○ ***Every one** of the paintings was a fake.* **2** [HOW OFTEN] used to show that something is repeated regularly **her, her defasında** *He goes to Spain every summer.* **3** [POSSIBLE] as much as is possible **mümkün olan her...** *I'd like to wish you **every success** in your new job.* ○ ***Every effort** is being made to rectify the problem.* **4 every now and then/every so often** sometimes, but not often **ara sıra, bazı bazı, zaman zaman** *We still meet up every now and then.* **5 one in every five/ten, etc** used to show how many people or things in a group are affected by or involved in something **her beş/on kişi/şeyden vs. biri**

ᴼ⁻**everybody** /ˈevriˌbɒdi/ *pronoun another word for* everyone **herkes, el âlem**

everyday /ˈevrideɪ/ *adjective* [always before noun] normal, usual, or happening every day **hergün** *Computers are now part of everyday life.*

╔═══════════════════════════════╗
║ **YAYGIN HATALAR** ║
╚═══════════════════════════════╝

everyday

Unutmayın! **Everyday** sıfattır ve isimden önce kullanılır. Birşeyin hangi sıklıkta olduğundan bahsetmek için, **everyday** olarak kullanamayın. Doğru yazılışı **every day** kullanımıdır: ~~I try to read English newspapers everyday.~~ Yanlış cümle örneği

I try to read English newspapers every day.

ᴼ⁻**everyone** /ˈevriwʌn/ *(also* **everybody)** *pronoun* **1** every person **herbiri** *Everyone agreed with the decision.* **2 everyone else** every other person **herkes, cümle âlem** *Everyone else was wearing jeans.*

everyplace /ˈevripleɪs/ *adverb US another word for* everywhere **her yer**

ᴼ⁻**everything** /ˈevriθɪŋ/ *pronoun* **1** all things or each thing **her şey** *They lost everything in the fire.* ○ *What's the matter Nick, is everything all right?* **2 everything else** all the other things **diğerleri, öteki şeyler** *The meat tasted strange, but everything else was okay.* **3 be/mean everything** to be the most important part of someone's life **hayatta en önemli şey olmak; herşey demek** *His children mean everything to him.* ○ *Money isn't everything.*

ᴼ⁻**everywhere** /ˈevriweəʳ/ *adverb* in or to every place **heryere/heryerde** *I've looked everywhere, but I still can't find that letter.*

evict /ɪˈvɪkt/ *verb* [T] to legally force someone to leave the house they are living in **boşaltmaya zorlamak, zorla tahliye etmek, çıkarmak** *They were evicted after complaints from their neighbours.* ● **eviction** /ɪˈvɪkʃºn/ *noun* [C, U] **tahliye**

╔═════════════════════════════════════╗
║ **evidence** ...... İLE BİRLİKTE KULLANILAN KELİMELER ║
╚═════════════════════════════════════╝

compelling/conclusive/hard/scientific/strong evidence ● **evidence of sth**

ᴼ⁻**evidence** /ˈevɪdºns/ *noun* [U] **1** something that makes you believe that something is true or exists **kanıt** *evidence of global warming* ○ [+ that] *There is no scientific evidence that the drug is addictive.* **2** information that is given or objects that are shown in a court of law to help to prove if someone has committed a crime **delil** *He was arrested despite the lack of evidence against him.* **3 give evidence** *UK* to give information and answer questions in a court of law **delil göstermek, kanıt vermek** *She was called to give evidence at his trial.* **4 be in evidence** *formal* to be noticeable **gözönünde/görünürde/meydanda olmak**

evident /ˈevɪdºnt/ *adjective formal* obvious to everyone and easy to see or understand **açık, aşikâr, belli, mey-**

danda, ortada [+ that] *It was evident from his voice that he was upset.* ⶽSee also: self-evident.

evidently /ˈevɪdᵊntli/ *adverb* **1** used to say that something can easily be noticed **belli ki; şurası açık ki/meydanda ki** *He evidently likes her.* **2** used to say that something seems probable from the information you have **su götürmez, açık olarak, besbelli** *The intruder evidently got in through an open window.*

evil¹ /ˈiːvᵊl/ *adjective* very cruel, bad, or harmful **fena, kötü, berbat, kem** *an evil monster*

evil² /ˈiːvᵊl/ *noun* [C, U] something that is very bad and harmful **kötülük, şer, zararlı** *The theme of the play is the battle between good and evil.* ⶽSee also: the lesser of two evils.

evocative /ɪˈvɒkətɪv/ *adjective* making you remember or imagine something that is pleasant **anımsatan, akla getiren, hayalini uyandıran** *evocative music* ○ *evocative of the sea*

evoke /ɪˈvəʊk/ *verb* [T] to make someone remember something or feel an emotion **anımsatmak, aklına getirmek, hissettirmek** *The story evoked memories of my childhood.*

evolution /ˌiːvəˈluːʃᵊn/ *noun* [U] **1** the way in which living things gradually change and develop over millions of years **evrim** *Darwin's theory of evolution* **2** a gradual process of change and development **gelişim, değişim, evrim, tekâmül** *the evolution of language* ● **evolutionary** *adjective* **evrimsel**

evolve /ɪˈvɒlv/ *verb* **1** [I] to develop from other forms of life over millions of years **yıllar içinde diğer canlı türlerinden türeyerek gelişmek** **2** [I, T] to develop or make something develop, usually gradually **zamanla/yavaş yavaş/tedricen gelişmek, geliştirmek** *rapidly evolving technology*

ewe /juː/ *noun* [C] a female sheep **koyun**

ex /eks/ *noun* [C] *informal* someone who used to be your husband, wife, or partner **eski, ilk, önceki (koca, eş, ortak vb.)** *My ex and his new wife live abroad.*

ex- /eks-/ *prefix* from before **önce/öncesinde/önceden anlamında önek** *an ex-boyfriend* ○ *an ex-boss*

exacerbate /ɪɡˈzæsəbeɪt/ *verb* [T] to make something worse **kötüleştirmek; olumsuz etkisini artırmak, daha kötü hale getirmek** *Sunny weather exacerbates the effects of pollution.*

o⊷**exact¹** /ɪɡˈzækt/ *adjective* completely correct in every detail **tam doğru, kesin** *I'm afraid I can't give you the exact details of the show yet.* ○ *They've lived here a long time - 25 years to be exact.* ● **exactness** *noun* [U] **netlik**

exact² /ɪɡˈzækt/ *verb* [T] *formal* to demand and get something from someone **talep etmek, istemek, almak**

exacting /ɪɡˈzæktɪŋ/ *adjective* needing a lot of effort and attention **çaba özen gerektiren, titizlik isteyen** *an exacting training schedule*

o⊷**exactly** /ɪɡˈzæktli/ *adverb* **1** COMPLETELY CORRECT used when you are giving or asking for information that is completely correct **çok doğru, tamam** *What exactly seems to be the problem?* ○ *The train got in at exactly ten o'clock.* **2** EMPHASIS used to emphasize what you are saying **tam, tamamen, tam anlamıyla, tam olarak** *I found a dress that's exactly the same colour as my shoes.* **3** AGREEMENT something that you say when you agree completely with someone **tamam, pekâla, doğru; katılıyorum** *"Surely they should have told us about this problem sooner?" "Exactly."* **4** not exactly used to say that something is not completely true **pek sayılmaz, doğru diyemem, tam değil** *"Do you live here?" "Not exactly, I'm staying with friends."* **5** not exactly easy/new/clear, etc *informal* used to say that a description is completely

untrue **tam olarak kolay/yeni/temiz vs. değil** *Let's face it, we're not exactly rich, are we?*

exaggerate /ɪɡˈzædʒᵊreɪt/ *verb* [I, T] to make something seem larger, better, worse, etc than it really is **abartmak, mübalağa etmek** *Don't exaggerate - it didn't cost that much!*

🧩 **exaggeration** ...... İLE BİRLİKTE KULLANILAN KELİMELER

a **gross/slight** exaggeration ● an exaggeration **of** sth

exaggeration /ɪɡˌzædʒᵊrˈeɪʃᵊn/ *noun* [C, U] when you describe something as larger, better, worse, etc than it really is **abartı, mübalağa** *a gross exaggeration of the facts*

exalted /ɪɡˈzɔːltɪd/ *adjective formal* very highly respected, or with a very high position **(rütbe, mevki vb.) bir hayli saygın, yüksek**

🧩 **exam** ...... İLE BİRLİKTE KULLANILAN KELİMELER

do (UK) sit/take an exam ● fail/pass an exam ● exam results

o⊷**exam** /ɪɡˈzæm/ *noun* [C] **1** an official test of how much you know about something, or how well you can do something **sınav, imtihan** *a maths exam* ○ *to fail/pass an exam* ○ *UK to sit/ UK/US to take* (= do) *an exam* **2** US a series of medical tests **muayene, tıbbi tetkik** *an eye exam*

examination /ɪɡˌzæmɪˈneɪʃᵊn/ *noun* **1** [C, U] when someone looks at something very carefully **inceleme, tetkik** *a medical examination* ○ *a close examination of the facts* **2** [C] *formal* an exam **sınav, imtihan** *a written examination*

examine /ɪɡˈzæmɪn/ *verb* [T] **1** LOOK AT to look at someone or something very carefully, especially to try to discover something **incelemek, tetkik etmek** *She picked up the knife and examined it closely.* ○ *He was examined by a doctor as soon as he arrived.* **2** TEST *formal* to test someone to see how much they know or how well they can do something **sınav/imtihan yapmak** *You'll be examined in three main areas: speaking, listening, and reading comprehension.* **3** CONSIDER to consider a plan or an idea carefully **araştırmak, soruşturmak, incelemek** *They have called a special meeting to examine the proposal.* ⶽSee also: cross-examine.

examiner /ɪɡˈzæmɪnər/ *noun* [C] someone who tests how much you know about something, or how well you can do something **imtihan eden/sınav yapan kişi**

🧩 **example** ...... İLE BİRLİKTE KULLANILAN KELİMELER

a **classic/good/prime** example ● an example **of** sth

o⊷**example** /ɪɡˈzɑːmpl/ *noun* **1** [C] something that is typical of the group of things that you are talking about **örnek, misal, numune** *This is a good example of medieval Chinese architecture.* **2** for example used to give an example of what you are talking about **örneğin, meselâ, söz gelimi** *Some people, students for example, can get cheaper tickets.* **3** [C] someone or something that is very good and should be copied **örnek, model; örnek/model alınacak kişi/şey** *He is a very good example to the rest of the class.* **4** set an example to behave in a way that other people should copy **misal teşkil etmek, örnek olmak**

exasperate /ɪɡˈzæspᵊreɪt/ *verb* [T] to annoy someone a lot **öfkelendirmek, çileden çıkarmak, sinirlendirmek, sabrını taşırmak**

exasperated /ɪɡˈzæspᵊreɪtɪd/ *adjective* extremely annoyed **sonuç olarak gerçekleşen, son derece sinirli, çileden çıkmış** *He's become increasingly exasperated with the situation.*

exasperating /ɪɡˈzæspᵊreɪtɪŋ/ *adjective* extremely annoying **asap/sinir bozucu, çileden çıkaran**

exasperation /ɪɡˌzæspəˈreɪʃᵊn/ *noun* [U] when you feel extremely annoyed with someone or something **hiddet, öfke, kızgınlık**

excavate /ˈekskəveɪt/ *verb* [I, T] to dig in the ground, especially with a machine, or to look for objects from the past **kazı/hafriyat yapmak** *These Roman coins were excavated from a site in Cambridge.* ● **excavation** /ˌekskəˈveɪʃᵊn/ *noun* [C, U] **kazı**

exceed /ɪkˈsiːd/ *verb* **1** [T] to be more than a particular number or amount **geçmek, aşmak, ihlal etmek** *Sales have exceeded $1 million so far this year.* **2 exceed the speed limit** to drive faster than you are allowed to according to the law **hız sınırını ihlal etmek/aşmak**

exceedingly /ɪkˈsiːdɪŋli/ *adverb formal* very **son derece, fazlasıyla, çok** *He was clever, attractive, and exceedingly rich.*

excel /ɪkˈsel/ *verb* **excelling**, *past* **excelled** *formal* **1** [I] to be very good at something **bir şeyde çok iyi/mükemmel olmak, üstün/ilerde olmak** *Paula always excelled in languages at school.* **2 excel yourself** to do something better than you usually do **kendini aşmak, çok mükemmelleşmek**

☞**excellent** /ˈeksᵊlᵊnt/ *adjective* very good, or of a very high quality **çok iyi, mükemmel, yüksek düzeyde** *That was an excellent meal.* ● **excellently** *adverb* **mükemmel bir şekilde** ● **excellence** /ˈeksᵊlᵊns/ *noun* [U] **mükemmelliyet**

☞**except** /ɪkˈsept/ *preposition, conjunction* not including a particular fact, thing, or person ...**den başka**; ...**in/ın dışında**; ...**hariç** *The boat sails from Oban every day except Sunday.* ○ *Everyone passed the exam except for Rory.* ○ [+ (that)] *So nothing changed, except that Anna saw her son less and less.*

excepted /ɪkˈseptɪd/ *adjective* [always after noun] *formal* not included **hariç**; ...**den başka**; ...**in/ın dışında olan** *Everybody who was asked, myself excepted, said no.*

excepting /ɪkˈseptɪŋ/ *preposition* not including ...**in/ın haricinde**; ...**den/dan başka**

exception /ɪkˈsepʃᵊn/ *noun* **1** [C, U] someone or something that is not included in a rule, group, or list **istisna, hariç tutma** *There are exceptions to every rule.* ○ *I like all kinds of movies, with the exception of horror films.* ○ *All our pupils, without exception, have access to the Internet.* ○ *Her films are always popular and this one is no exception.* **2 make an exception** to not treat someone or something according to the usual rules **ayırım yapmak, fark gözetmek** *They don't usually take cheques, but they said they'd make an exception in my case.* **3 take exception to sth** *formal* to be annoyed or insulted by something **incinmek, gücenmek, hoşlanmamak**

exceptional /ɪkˈsepʃᵊnᵊl/ *adjective* **1** extremely good **ender, müstesna, olağanüstü** *an exceptional student* **2** very unusual and not likely to happen very often **olağan dışı, istisnai, ender rastlanan, nadir görülen** *Visitors are only allowed in exceptional circumstances.* ● **exceptionally** *adverb* *an exceptionally gifted pianist* **sıra dışı şekilde iyi**

excerpt /ˈeksɜːpt/ *noun* [C] a short piece from a book, film, piece of music, etc (**kitap, film, müzik) alıntı, aktarma, iktibas**

excess¹ /ɪkˈses/ *noun* **1** [U, no plural] more of something than is usual or needed **aşırılık, bolluk** *An excess of oil on the markets has caused prices to fall sharply.* **2 in excess of sth** more than a particular amount or level ...**den/dan daha fazla** *He earns in excess of £60,000 a year.* **3 do sth to excess** to do something too much **bir şeyi**

ifrata/aşırıya kaçarak yapmak, aşırı derecede yapmak *He occasionally has a beer, but he never drinks to excess.*

excess² /ɪkˈses/ *adjective* [always before noun] more than is usual or allowed **fazla, fazladan, ek** *We had to pay £10 for excess baggage.*

excesses /ɪkˈsesɪz/ *noun* [plural] extreme, harmful, or immoral actions or behaviour **taşkınlıklar, aşırılıklar, ahlak dışılıklar**

excessive /ɪkˈsesɪv/ *adjective* more than is necessary or wanted **aşırı, ölçüsüz, istenmediği kadar** *They accused the police of using excessive force.* ● **excessively** *adverb* **fazla miktarda**

exchange¹ /ɪksˈtʃeɪndʒ/ *noun* **1** GIVING [C, U] when you give something to someone and they give you something else **değiş tokuş, alışveriş** *an exchange of ideas/information* ○ *They were given food and shelter in exchange for work.* **2** STUDENTS [C] an arrangement by which students and teachers from one country go to stay with students and teachers in another **öğrenci değişimi 3** CONVERSATION [C] a short conversation or argument **karşılıklı kısa bir konuşma** *There were angry exchanges between the police and demonstrators.* ⊃See also: the stock exchange.

exchange² /ɪksˈtʃeɪndʒ/ *verb* **1** [T] to give something to someone and receive something similar from them **değiş tokuş etmek, değiştirmek, alıp vermek** *It's traditional for the two teams to exchange shirts after the game.* **2** [T] to take something back to the shop where you bought it and change it for something else (**ürün) başka bir ürünle değiştirmek** *Could I exchange this shirt for a larger size?* **3 exchange looks/smiles/words, etc** If two people exchange looks, smiles, words, etc, they look at each other/smile at each other/talk to each other, etc. **karşılık bakışmak/gülümsemek/laflamak/söz etmek**

ex'change ˌrate *noun* [C] the amount of another country's money that you can buy with a particular amount of your own country's money **döviz kuru**

excise /ˈeksaɪz/ *noun* [U] government taxes that must be paid on some things that are made or sold in a particular country **üretim/tüketim vergisi**

excitable /ɪkˈsaɪtəbl/ *adjective* easily becoming excited **hemen/kolay heyecanlanan** *a very excitable child/puppy*

excite /ɪkˈsaɪt/ *verb* [T] **1** to make someone feel very happy and enthusiastic **mutlu etmek, heyecanlandırmak** *Try not to excite the children too much.* **2** *formal* to cause a particular reaction in someone **uyandırmak, harekete geçirmek, tahrik etmek** *This product has excited a great deal of interest.*

☞**excited** /ɪkˈsaɪtɪd/ *adjective* feeling very happy and enthusiastic **heyecanlı, heyecanlanmış** *happy, excited faces* ○ *The children are getting really excited about the party.* ● **excitedly** *adverb* **heyecanlı bir şekilde**

┌─────────────────────────────────────┐
│ **excitement** .... İLE BİRLİKTE KULLANILAN KELİMELER

cause/feel excitement ● excitement **mounts** ● **great/wild** excitement ● excitement **about/at/over** sth

☞**excitement** /ɪkˈsaɪtmənt/ *noun* [U] when people feel very happy and enthusiastic **heyecan, coşku** *The competition is causing a lot of excitement.*

┌─────────────────────────────────────┐
│ *exciting* .... BAŞKA BİR DEYİŞLE

Eğer bir olay tüm dikkatinizi toplayabilecek kadar ilgi çekiciyse, bunu ifadesinde **gripping** veya **riveting** kelimeleri kullanılabilir. *The book was gripping - I couldn't put it down.* ● *I found the film absolutely* **riveting.**

Spor ve açık alanda yapılan heycan verici aktiviteler için **exhilarating** ifadesi kullanılabilir. *I find skiing absolutely* **exhilarating**.
Action-packed sıfatı birçok heycan verici olayı içinde barındıran hikayeler veya zaman süreci için kullanılır. *We had an* **action-packed** *weekend in Berlin.*
● *The film is described as 'an* **action-packed** *thriller'.*
Heycan verici bir atmosfer **electric** ifadesiyle tanımlanabilir: *The atmosphere backstage was* **electric**.
Vibrant kelimesi genellikle heycan verici yerleri tanımlamak için kullanılır. *This is one of Europe's most* **vibrant** *cities.*

o⌐exciting /ɪkˈsaɪtɪŋ/ *adjective* making you feel very happy and enthusiastic **heyecan verici, coşkulandırıcı** *an exciting football match* ○ *You're going to Africa? How exciting!*

exclaim /ɪksˈkleɪm/ *verb* [I, T] to say something suddenly and loudly because you are surprised, annoyed, excited, etc **haykırmak, bağırmak, hayretini ifade etmek, çığlık koparmak/atmak** *"How terrible!" she exclaimed.*

exclamation /ˌekskləˈmeɪʃ³n/ *noun* [C] something that you say loudly and suddenly because you are surprised, angry, excited, etc **çığlık, bağırış, haykırma** *an exclamation of delight*

excla'mation ˌmark (*also US* **excla'mation ˌpoint**) *noun* [C] a mark (!) used at the end of a sentence that expresses surprise, excitement, or shock, or that is a greeting or an order **ünlem işareti (!)** ⊃See study page **Punctuation** on page Centre 33.

exclude /ɪksˈkluːd/ *verb* [T] **1** KEEP OUT to not allow someone or something to take part in an activity or enter a place **hesaba katmamak, hariç tutmak** [often passive] *Women are still* **excluded from** *the club.* **2** NOT INCLUDE to intentionally not include something **sokmamak, men etmek, dahil etmemek** *The insurance cover excludes particular medical conditions.* **3** POSSIBILITY to decide that something is certainly not true or possible **doğru olmadığına/ihtimal dışı olmadığına karar vermek; hariç tutamamak** *We can't exclude the possibility that he is dead.*

excluding /ɪksˈkluːdɪŋ/ *preposition* not including ... **den/dan başka; dışında, hariç; içermeyen** *That's $600 per person for seven days, excluding travel costs.*

exclusion /ɪksˈkluːʒ³n/ *noun* **1** [C, U] when someone or something is not allowed to take part in an activity or to enter a place **men etme, sokmama, hariç tutma, katmama** *the exclusion of disruptive pupils* ⊃Opposite **inclusion**. **2 to the exclusion of sth** If you do something to the exclusion of something else, you do it so much that you have no time to do anything else. **...i/ı hariç tutarak, dışta bırakarak; ...den/dan başka**

exclusive¹ /ɪksˈkluːsɪv/ *adjective* **1** expensive and only for people who are rich or of a high social class **pahalı, zengin ve yüksek sosyal sınıf için olan, özel ve pahalı, seçkin, kibar** *an exclusive private club* **2 exclusive of sth** not including something **hariç tutarak, hesaba katmaksızın, dışta bırakarak, hariç** *The price of the meal is exclusive of drinks.* ⊃Opposite **inclusive**. **3** not shared with another person, organization, newspaper, etc **kişiye özel,** *an exclusive interview*

exclusive² /ɪksˈkluːsɪv/ *noun* [C] a news story that appears in only one newspaper or on one television programme **bir tv kanalına/gazeteye özel**

exclusively /ɪksˈkluːsɪvli/ *adverb* only **yalnızca, sadece, tamamen** *an exclusively female audience*

excrement /ˈekskrəmənt/ *noun* [U] *formal* solid waste that comes out of the bottom of a person or animal **dışkı**

excrete /ɪkˈskriːt/ *verb* [I, T] to get rid of waste substances from the body **(dışkı, idrar, ter vb.) boşaltmak, çıkarmak, vücuttan atmak** ● **excretion** /ɪkˈskriːʃ³n/ *noun* [C, U] **idrar**

excruciating /ɪkˈskruːʃieɪtɪŋ/ *adjective* very bad or painful **çok acı veren, dayanılmaz, çekilmez, ıstırap/azap veren** *Her illness causes her* **excruciating** *pain.* ● **excruciatingly** *adverb* an **excruciatingly** *embarrassing situation* **acı verir şekilde**

excursion /ɪkˈskɜː³n/ *noun* [C] a short journey made by a group of people for pleasure **gezi, gezinti, seyahat** *We've booked to go on an* **excursion** *to Pompeii.*

excusable /ɪkˈskjuːzəbl/ *adjective* easy to forgive **bağışlanabilir, affedilebilir** ⊃Opposite **inexcusable**.

excuse¹ /ɪkˈskjuːz/ *verb* [T] **1** FORGIVE to forgive someone for something that is not very serious **affetmek, bağışlamak** *Please excuse my appearance, I've been painting.* ○ [+ for + doing sth] *She asked him to excuse her for being so rude.* **2** NOT DO to say that someone does not have to do something that they usually have to do **görevden affetmek, muaf/hariç tutmak** *Could I be excused from football training today?* **3** EXPLAIN to be given as a reason for someone's bad behaviour, so that it does not seem so bad **sebebini açıklamak, izah etmek; sebep olarak göstermek** *Nothing can excuse what he did.* **4 excuse me a** ATTRACTING ATTENTION used to politely get someone's attention **Affedersiniz!, Özür dilerim!, Pardon!** *Excuse me, does this bus go to Oxford Street?* **b** SAYING SORRY used to say sorry for something that you do without intending to **Çok özür dilerim!, Affedersiniz!, Kusura bakmayın!** *Oh, excuse me, did I take your seat?* ● **excusable** *adjective* **affedilir**

excuse .... İLE BİRLİKTE KULLANILAN KELİMELER

have/make/offer/think up an excuse ● a **feeble/ good** excuse

o⌐excuse² /ɪkˈskjuːs/ *noun* [C] **1** a reason that you give to explain why you did something wrong **mazeret, gerekçe, neden, sebep** [+ for + doing sth] *I hope he's got a good excuse for being so late.* **2** a false reason that you give to explain why you do something **bahane, sudan sebep/gerekçe, özür** *Nick was just looking for an excuse to call her.*

execute /ˈeksɪkjuːt/ *verb* [T] **1** to kill someone as a legal punishment **idam etmek; (ölüm hükmünü) infaz etmek** *He was executed for murder.* **2** *formal* to do something, such as follow a plan or order **yapmak, icra etmek, yerine getirmek** *to execute a deal/plan*

execution /ˌeksɪˈkjuːʃ³n/ *noun* **1** [C, U] when someone is killed as a legal punishment **idam, infaz** [U] when you do something, such as follow a plan or order **yapma, icra etme, yerine getirme** *He was killed in* **the execution** *of his duties as a soldier.*

executioner /ˌeksɪˈkjuːʃ³nər/ *noun* [C] someone whose job is to execute criminals **cellât**

executive¹ /ɪgˈzekjətɪv/ *adjective* [always before noun] **1** relating to making decisions and managing businesses **yönetim, icra, karar vermeye ilişkin/dair** *an executive director* **2** suitable for people who have important jobs in business **pahalı ve şık; üst düzey iş adamları için uygun** *Peter always stays in the executive suite.*

executive² /ɪgˈzekjətɪv/ *noun* **1** [C] someone who has an important job in a business **yönetici, idareci** *a company executive* **2 the executive** *mainly UK* the people who have the power to make decisions in an organization **yürütme/icra organı**

exemplary /ɪɡˈzemplᵊri/ *adjective formal* very good and suitable to be copied by people **örnek alınacak, mükemmel** *Sarah's behaviour is always exemplary.*

exemplify /ɪɡˈzemplɪfaɪ/ *verb* [T] *formal* to be or give a typical example of something **örnek vermek, örnekle açıklamak, örnek olmak**

exempt¹ /ɪɡˈzempt/ *adjective* [never before noun] with special permission not to have to do something or pay something **muaf, hariç tutulmak, ayrı tanınmış** *The first £4,000 that you earn is exempt from tax.*

exempt² /ɪɡˈzempt/ *verb* [T] *formal* to officially say that someone does not have to do something or pay for something **muaf/bağışık tutmak, ayrıcalık tanımak** [often passive] *Students are exempted from payment.*
● **exemption** /ɪɡˈzempʃᵊn/ *noun* [C, U] **muafiyet**

---

exercise ...... İLE BİRLİKTE KULLANILAN KELİMELER

do/get/take exercise ● daily/gentle/regular/strenuous exercise ● a form of exercise

---

exercise

⚬**exercise¹** /ˈeksəsaɪz/ *noun* 1 [PHYSICAL ACTIVITY] [C, U] physical activity that you do to make your body strong and healthy **idman, egzersiz, spor, beden eğitimi, jimnastik** *Swimming is my favourite form of exercise.* ○ *Let's do some stretching exercises to start with.* 2 [TEST] [C] a piece of written work that helps you learn something **alıştırma** *For your homework, please do exercise 3 on page 24.* 3 [ACTIVITY WITH PURPOSE] [C] an activity which is intended to achieve a particular thing **uygulama, prova, faaliyet** *The whole point of the exercise was to get people to share their ideas.* ○ *a team-building exercise.* 4 [MILITARY] [C] a set of actions that a group of soldiers do to practise their skills **askerî tatbikat, manevra, talim** *The cadets are out on military exercises.* 5 [USE] [U] *formal* the use of something such as a power or right **kullanma, tatbik etme**

exercise² /ˈeksəsaɪz/ *verb* 1 [I, T] to do physical activities to make your body strong and healthy **idman/spor/egzersiz yapmak** *I try to exercise every day.* 2 [T] *formal* to use a power, right, or ability **yapmak, uygulamak; gücü/hakkı/yeteneği kullanmak** *You should always exercise your right to vote.*

exert /ɪɡˈzɜːt/ *verb* 1 [T] to use something such as authority, power, influence, etc in order to make something happen **(yetki, güç, nüfuz vb.) uygulamak, kullanmak, tatbik etmek** *My parents exerted a lot of pressure on me to do well at school.* 2 **exert yourself** to use a lot of physical or mental energy to do something **zorlamak, çaba sarfetmek, çabalamak, kendini zorlamak** *She was too ill to exert herself much.*

exertion /ɪɡˈzɜːʃᵊn/ *noun* [C, U] when you use a lot of physical or mental energy to do something **gayret, çaba, zorlama, güç kullanma/harcama** *I get out of breath with any kind of physical exertion.*

exhale /eksˈheɪl/ *verb* [I, T] *formal* to send air out of your lungs **nefes vermek** ⊃Opposite inhale.

exhaust¹ /ɪɡˈzɔːst/ *verb* [T] 1 [SUPPLY] to finish all of the supply of something **tüketmek, kullanmak, bitirmek** *How long will it be before the world's fuel supplies are exhausted?* 2 [TIRED] to make someone very tired **yormak, tüketmek, bitkin/bitap düşürmek** 3 [SUBJECT] to say everything possible about a subject **tümüyle ele almak, enine boyuna görüşmek** *We seem to have exhausted that topic of conversation.*

exhaust² /ɪɡˈzɔːst/ *noun* 1 [U] the waste gas from a vehicle's engine **egzoz gazı** *exhaust fumes* 2 [C] (*also* exhaust pipe) *mainly UK* the pipe that waste gas from a vehicle's engine flows through **egzoz borusu** ⊃Orta kısımdaki renkli sayfalarına bakınız.

exhausted /ɪɡˈzɔːstɪd/ *adjective* very tired **çok yorgun, bitkin**

exhausting /ɪɡˈzɔːstɪŋ/ *adjective* making you feel very tired **yorucu, yıpratıcı, bitkin düşüren** *What an exhausting day!*

exhaustion /ɪɡˈzɔːstʃᵊn/ *noun* [U] when you are extremely tired **bitkinlik, yorgunluk, tükenmişlik** *The tennis star was suffering from exhaustion.*

exhaustive /ɪɡˈzɔːstɪv/ *adjective* complete and including everything **tam, etraflı, ayrıntılı, herşeyi içeren** *an exhaustive account of the incident*

ex'haust ˌpipe *mainly UK* (*also US* tailpipe) *noun* [C] the pipe that waste gas from a vehicle's engine flows through **egzoz borusu**

exhibit¹ /ɪɡˈzɪbɪt/ *verb* 1 [I, T] to show objects such as paintings to the public **sergilemek, sergilenmek** *She's exhibiting her roses at the local flower show.* 2 [T] *formal* to show a feeling, quality, or ability **belli etmek, göstermek** *The crew exhibited great courage when the plane crashed.*

exhibit² /ɪɡˈzɪbɪt/ *noun* [C] an object such as a painting that is shown to the public **sergilenen eşya/parça, eser** *a museum exhibit* ● **exhibitor** *noun* [C] someone who shows something that they own or have made to the public **sergileyen, sergici, sergi açan kişi**

exhibition /ˌeksɪˈbɪʃᵊn/ *noun* 1 [C, U] when objects such as paintings are shown to the public **sergi, gösterime sunma, gösterilme** *There's a new exhibition of sculpture on at the city gallery.* ○ *an exhibition centre* 2 [C] when someone shows a particular skill or quality that they have to the public **sergileme, ortaya koyma, gösterme**

exhibitionist /ˌeksɪˈbɪʃᵊnɪst/ *noun* [C] someone who tries to attract attention to themselves with their behaviour **sergileyen, gösteren, dikkatleri çekmeye çalışan kişi** ● **exhibitionism** /ˌeksɪˈbɪʃᵊnɪzᵊm/ *noun* [U] behaviour which tries to attract attention **gösterişçilik, gösteriş merakı**

exhilarated /ɪɡˈzɪləreɪtɪd/ *adjective* very excited and happy **heyecanlı, keyifli, mutlu**

exhilarating /ɪɡˈzɪləreɪtɪŋ/ *adjective* making you feel very excited and happy **keyif veren, heyecanlandıran** *There's nothing more exhilarating than water-skiing.*

exhilaration /ɪɡˌzɪləˈreɪʃᵊn/ *noun* [U] when you feel very excited and happy **neşe, coşku, heyecan**

exhort /ɪɡˈzɔːt/ *verb* [T] *formal* to strongly encourage someone to do something **zorlamak, şiddetle tavsiye etmek, teşvik etmek ● exhortation** /ˌeɡzɔːˈteɪʃᵊn/ *noun* [C, U] **cesaretlendirme**

exile /ˈeksaɪl/, /ˈeɡzaɪl/ *noun* **1** [U] when someone has to leave their home and live in another country, often for political reasons **sürülme, sürgün** *He spent the war years* **in exile** *in New York.* ○ *The King was forced* **into exile.** **2** [C] someone who is forced to live in another country **sürülmüş/sürgün kimse** *She lived the rest of her life as an exile in the UK.* ● **exile** *verb* [T] to force someone to leave their home and live in another country, often for political reasons **sürmek, sürgüne göndermek ● exiled** *adjective* **sürgüne yollanmış**

ɔ⇥**exist** /ɪɡˈzɪst/ *verb* [I] **1** to be real or present **var olmak, mevcut/gerçek olmak, bulunmak** *Poverty still exists in this country.* **2** to live in difficult conditions **zor şartlarda yaşamını sürdürmek** *You can't exist without water for more than a week.*

🧩 **existence** ...... İLE BİRLİKTE KULLANILAN KELİMELER

come into/go out of existence ● **be in** existence ● **the** existence **of** sth

existence /ɪɡˈzɪstᵊns/ *noun* **1** [U] when something or someone exists **varlık, var oluş, mevcudiyet** *She never doubted* **the existence of** *God.* ○ *The theatre company that we started is still* **in existence** *today.* ○ *When did the Football League* **come into existence** (= begin to exist)*?* **2** [C] a particular way of life **hayat, yaşam, varlık** *We could have a much more peaceful existence in the countryside.*

existing /ɪɡˈzɪstɪŋ/ *adjective* [always before noun] which exist or are used at the present time **varolan, yaşayan** *Existing schools will have to be expanded to accommodate the extra students.* ➔See also: pre-existing.

ɔ⇥**exit¹** /ˈeksɪt/ *noun* [C] **1** DOOR the door or gate which you use to leave a public building or place **çıkış** *a fire exit* ○ *an emergency exit* **2** LEAVING when someone leaves a place **çıkma, ayrılma** *Sue made a quick exit when she saw Mick come in.* **3** ROAD a road which you use to leave a motorway (= wide, fast road) or roundabout (= place where three or more main roads meet) **sapak, çıkış, yan yola geçiş** *Take the third exit at the next roundabout.*

exit² /ˈeksɪt/ *verb* [I, T] **1** to stop using a program on a computer **bilgisayarda programdan çıkmak** *Press escape to exit the game.* **2** *formal* to leave a place or a competition **çıkmak, ayrılmak**

'**exit ˌstrategy** *noun* [C] a plan that you use to get out of a difficult situation **zor bir durumdan çıkış stratejisi/ planı** *A good politician will plan his exit strategy before announcing his retirement from office.*

exodus /ˈeksədəs/ *noun* [no plural] when a large number of people all leave a place together **toplu çıkış, insan güruhu, kalabalık topluluk** *There has been* **a mass exodus** *of workers from the villages to the towns.*

exonerate /ɪɡˈzɒnᵊreɪt/ *verb* [T] *formal* to say that someone is not guilty of doing something that they have been blamed for **suçsuz bulmak, temize çıkarmak, muaf tutmak** [often passive] *He was* **exonerated of** *all blame by the investigation.* ● **exoneration** /ɪɡˌzɒnᵊˈreɪʃᵊn/ *noun* [U] **beraat, tahliye**

exorbitant /ɪɡˈzɔːbɪtᵊnt/ *adjective* Exorbitant prices or costs are much too high. **fahiş, aşırı yüksek, (fiyatlar) el yakan**

exorcism /ˈeksɔːsɪzᵊm/ *noun* [C, U] when an evil spirit is exorcized **(kötü) ruh çıkarma/kovma**

exorcize (*also UK* -ise) /ˈeksɔːsaɪz/ *verb* [T] **1** to make evil spirits leave a person or place by saying special prayers and having a special ceremony **(kötü) ruh çıkarmak/ kovmak 2** to get rid of something such as a bad memory **kötü hatıra vb. şeylerden kurtulmak, silmek, defetmek** *She moved to Paris to try to exorcize the past.*

exotic /ɪɡˈzɒtɪk/ *adjective* unusual, interesting, and often foreign **alışılmışın dışında, yabancı, ekzotik** *exotic fruits*

expand /ɪkˈspænd/ *verb* [I, T] to increase in size or amount, or to make something increase **genişle(t)mek, büyü(t)mek** *We are hoping to expand our range of products.*

expand on sth *phrasal verb* to give more details about something that you have said or written **açmak, ayrıntıya yer vermek** *She mentioned a few ideas, but she didn't expand on them.*

expanse /ɪkˈspæns/ *noun* [C] a large, open area of land, sea, or sky **(kara, deniz, hava) açıklık, geniş alan** *a vast expanse of water*

expansion /ɪkˈspænʃᵊn/ *noun* [U] when something increases in size or amount **genişleme, büyüme, gelişme** *the rapid expansion of the software industry*

expansive /ɪkˈspænsɪv/ *adjective formal* very happy to talk to people in a friendly way **samimi, içten, konuşkan** *He was in an expansive mood on the night of the party.*

expatriate /ɪkˈspætriət/ (*also UK* expat /ˌekˈspat/ *informal*) *noun* [C] someone who does not live in their own country **ülkesinin dışında yaşayan kişi ● expatriate** *adjective* **göç eden**

ɔ⇥**expect** /ɪkˈspekt/ *verb* **1** [T] to think that something will happen **ummak, beklemek** [+ to do sth] *He didn't expect to see me.* ○ [+ (that)] *I expect that she'll be very angry about this.* **2 be expecting sb/sth** to be waiting for someone or something to arrive **gelmesini/varmasını bekliyor olmak/ummak** *I'm expecting a letter from my sister.* **3** [T] to think that someone should behave in a particular way or do a particular thing **talep etmek, beklemek, ummak** [+ to do sth] *You will be expected to work some weekends.* **4 I expect** *mainly UK informal* used to show that you think that something is likely to be true **Umarım** *I expect Isabel's told you about me?* ○ *"Will you be coming to the party?" "I expect so."* **5 be expecting** to be going to have a baby **çocuk bekliyor olmak** *I'm expecting my first baby in May.* ➔See Common learner error at **wait**.

expectancy /ɪkˈspektᵊnsi/ *noun* [U] when you think that something pleasant or exciting is going to happen **beklenti, umut** *An air of expectancy filled the room.* ➔See also: life expectancy.

expectant /ɪkˈspektᵊnt/ *adjective* **1** thinking that something pleasant or exciting is going to happen **heyecanla bekleyen/uman, bekleyiş içinde olan** *the children's expectant faces* **2 an expectant mother/ father, etc** someone who is going to have a baby soon **çocuk bekleyen anne/baba ● expectantly** *adverb* **beklentisi olarak**

🧩 **expectation** ...... İLE BİRLİKTE KULLANILAN KELİMELER

have high/have low expectations ● **live up to/meet** (sb's) expectations ● **expectations of** sth

expectation /ˌekspekˈteɪʃᵊn/ *noun* **1** [C] when you expect good things to happen in the future **umut** [usually plural] *The holiday* **lived up to** *all our expectations* (= was as good as we expected). ○ *My parents* **had high expectations** *for me* (= expected me to be successful). **2** [C, U] when you expect something to happen **bir**

E

şeyin olmasını bekleme/umma *He had gone away and there was no **expectation of** his return.*

expedient¹ /ɪkˈspiːdiənt/ *adjective formal* An expedient action achieves a useful purpose, although it may not be moral. **(ahlakî olmasa da) işine gelen, yararına olan, uygun** *It might be expedient not to pay him until the work is finished.* ● **expediency** /ɪkˈspiːdiənsi/ *noun* [U] when something is expedient **işine gelme, çıkarına olma** *an issue of political expediency*

expedient² /ɪkˈspiːdiənt/ *noun* [C] *formal* a useful or clever action **işine gelen/çıkarına olan hareket**

expedite /ˈekspɪdaɪt/ *verb* [T] *formal* to make an action or process happen more quickly **hızlandırmak, çabuklaştırmak**

expedition /ˌekspɪˈdɪʃⁿn/ *noun* [C] an organized journey, especially a long one for a particular purpose **planlı/amaçlı gezi, inceleme/araştırma gezisi** *Peary led the first **expedition** to the North Pole.* ○ *a shopping **expedition***

expel /ɪkˈspel/ *verb* [T] **expelling**, *past* **expelled 1** to make someone leave a school, organization, or country because of their behaviour **atmak, sürmek, sınır dışı etmek, kovmak** [often passive] *He was expelled from school for hitting another student.* **2** *formal* to force air, gas, or liquid out of something **(gaz, hava, sıvı) çıkmaya zorlamak, çıkarmak, dışarı atmak**

expend /ɪkˈspend/ *verb* [T] *formal* to use effort, time, or money to do something **harcamak** [+ doing sth] *You expend far too much energy doing things for other people.* ○ *Governments expend a lot of resources on war.*

expendable /ɪkˈspendəbl/ *adjective* If someone or something is expendable, people can do something or deal with a situation without them. **değersiz, gözden çıkarılabilir, önemsiz, kolay harcanabilir** *He considers his staff as temporary and expendable.*

expenditure /ɪkˈspendɪtʃəʳ/ *noun* [U] *formal* **1** the total amount of money that a government or person spends **harcama, masraf** *The government's annual expenditure on arms has been reduced.* **2** when you use energy, time, or money **harcama, tüketim, kullanım**

☛expense /ɪkˈspens/ *noun* **1** [C, U] the money that you spend on something **masraf** *You have to **pay** your own medical **expenses**.* ○ *He eventually found her the car she wanted, **at great expense** (= it cost him a lot of money).* **2 at the expense of sth** If you do one thing at the expense of another, doing the first thing harms the second thing. **pahasına** *He spent a lot of time at work, at the expense of his marriage.* **3 at sb's expense a** If you do something at someone's expense, they pay for it. **...nın/nin hesabına** *We went on holiday at my father's expense.* **b** in order to make someone look stupid **birini aptal yerine koyarak/salak muamelesi yapan** *Stop making jokes at my expense.*

expenses /ɪkˈspensɪz/ *noun* [plural] money that you spend when you are doing your job, that your employer will pay back to you **masraflar, harcamalar** *travel expenses* ○ *They pay us two hundred pounds a week, plus expenses.*

☛expensive /ɪkˈspensɪv/ *adjective* costing a lot of money **pahalı** *expensive jewellery* ○ [+ to do sth] *It's too expensive to go out every night.* ⊃Opposite **inexpensive**. ● **expensively** *adverb* expensively dressed **pahalı bir şekilde**

🧩 **experience** ...... İLE BİRLİKTE KULLANILAN KELİMELER

gain/have/lack experience ● **good/previous/useful/wide** experience ● experience **in/of** sth ● **from** experience ● **in my** experience

☛experience¹ /ɪkˈspɪəriəns/ *noun* **1** [U] knowledge that you get from doing a job, or from doing, seeing, or feel-

ing something **tecrübe/deneyim** *Do you have any **experience of** working with children?* ○ *He knows from experience not to play with fire.* ○ *In my experience, people smile back if you smile at them.* **2** [C] something that happens to you that affects how you feel **yaşanan/hissedilen şey** *My trip to Australia was an experience I'll never forget.*

experience² /ɪkˈspɪəriəns/ *verb* [T] If you experience something, it happens to you, or you feel it. **yaşamak, tecrübe etmek, hissetmek** *It was the worst pain I had ever experienced.* ○ *We experienced a lot of difficulty in selling our house.*

experienced /ɪkˈspɪəriənst/ *adjective* having skill and knowledge because you have done something many times **tecrübeli, deneyimli** *Karsten's a very experienced ski instructor.* ⊃Opposite **inexperienced**.

🧩 **experiment** ...... İLE BİRLİKTE KULLANILAN KELİMELER

conduct/do/perform an experiment ● an experiment **on** sth

☛experiment¹ /ɪkˈsperɪmənt/ *noun* [C] a test, especially a scientific one, that you do in order to learn something or discover if something is true **deney** *to **conduct/do/perform** an experiment* ○ *They're conducting experiments on hamster cells to test the effects of the drug.*

experiment² /ɪkˈsperɪment/ *verb* [I] **1** to try something in order to discover what it is like **denemek** *Did he ever experiment with drugs?* **2** to do an experiment **deney yapmak** *Experimenting on mice can give us an idea of the effect of the disease in humans.* ● **experimentation** /ɪkˌsperɪmenˈteɪʃⁿn/ *noun* [U] **deney**

experimental /ɪkˌsperɪˈmentⁿl/ *adjective* relating to tests, especially scientific ones **deneysel; deneye dayalı** ● **experimentally** *adverb* **deneysel**

☛expert¹ /ˈekspɜːt/ *noun* [C] someone who has a lot of skill in something or a lot of knowledge about something **uzman, usta, bilir kişi** *He's an expert on Japanese literature.*

expert² /ˈekspɜːt/ *adjective* [always before noun] having a lot of skill in something or knowing a lot about something **bilgili, usta, uzman, iyi bilen** *I need some expert advice on investments.* ○ *What's your expert opinion?* ● **expertly** *adverb* He carved the roast expertly. **bilir kişi gibi**

expertise /ˌekspɜːˈtiːz/ *noun* [U] skill **beceri, ustalık, maharet, uzmanlık** *the technical expertise of the engineers*

expire /ɪkˈspaɪəʳ/ *verb* [I] If a legal document or agreement expires, you can no longer use it. **süresine kullanılmak, süresi dolmak, sona ermek** *Your contract expired six months ago.*

expiry /ɪkˈspaɪəri/ *noun* [U] *UK* the end of a period when something can be used **son kullanma, sona erme, bitim** *What's the expiry date on your passport?*

explain ...... BAŞKA BİR DEYİŞLE

Eğer kişi bir konuyu diğer bir kişiye anlamasını kolaylaştıracak şekilde anlatıyorsa, bu durum için **clarify** fiili kullanılabilir. *Let me just **clarify** what I mean here.*

define fiili bir şeyin anlamını / tanımımı vermek için kullanılır. *Your responsibilities are clearly **defined** in the contract.*

Eğer bir şey yazılı olarak net bir şekilde anlatıldıysa, bu durumu belirtmek için **set out** deyimi kullanılabilir. *Your contract will **set out** the terms of your employment.*

Eğer bir şey çok detaylı bir şekilde anlatılıyor ise, durumu belirtmede **spell out** deyimi kullanılır. *They sent me a letter, **spelling out** the details of the agreement.*

o→**explain** /ɪkˈspleɪn/ *verb* [I, T] to make something clear or easy to understand by giving reasons for it or details about it **izah etmek, açıklamak, anlatmak** [+ question word] *Can you explain why you did this?* ○ *Can you explain to me how this mobile phone works?* ○ [+ (that)] *He explained that he was going to stay with his sister.* ● **explaining** *noun* [U] when you have to explain or give a good reason for your actions **açıklama, izah, bildirme, neden gösterme** *You'll have a lot of explaining to do when dad finds out what happened.*

🧩 **explanation** .... İLE BİRLİKTE KULLANILAN KELİMELER

demand/give/have/offer an explanation ● a clear/possible/satisfactory/simple explanation ● an explanation for sth

o→**explanation** /ˌekspləˈneɪʃ³n/ *noun* [C, U] the details or reasons that someone gives to make something clear or easy to understand **açıklamalar, izahlar, detay veya nedenler** *What's your explanation for the team's poor performance?* ○ *Could you give me a quick explanation of how it works?*

explanatory /ɪkˈsplænət³ri/ *adjective* giving an explanation about something **açıklayıcı, izah edici,** *There are explanatory notes with the diagram.* ⊃See also: self-explanatory.

expletive /ɪkˈspliːtɪv/ ⓤ /ˈeksplətɪv/ *noun* [C] *formal* a swear word (= word which people think is rude or offensive) **küfür, sövgü**

explicable /ɪkˈsplɪkəbl/ *adjective formal* Something that is explicable can be explained. **açıklanabilir, izah edilebilir** ⊃Opposite inexplicable.

explicit /ɪkˈsplɪsɪt/ *adjective* **1** clear and exact **açık seçik, tam ve belirgin** *She was very explicit about her plans.* ○ *He made no explicit references to Tess.* **2** showing or talking about sex or violence in a very detailed way **(cinsel konular) açık saçık, ulu orta** *a sexually explicit film* ● **explicitly** *adverb She explicitly stated* that she did not want her name to be revealed. **açıkça**

o→**explode** /ɪkˈspləʊd/ *verb* **1** [I, T] If something such as a bomb explodes, it bursts (= breaks suddenly from inside) with noise and force, and if you explode it, you make it burst with noise and force. **patla(t)mak, infilâk et(tir)mek** *One of the bombs did not explode.* **2** [I] to suddenly start shouting because you are very angry **aniden çığlık atmak, bağırmak, küplere binmek**

exploit¹ /ɪkˈsplɔɪt/ *verb* [T] **1** to pay or reward someone enough for something **sömürmek, hakkını vermemek** [often passive] *I felt as though I was being exploited.* **2** to use or develop something for your advantage **kullanmak, yararlanmak** *We are not fully exploiting all the resources that we have.* ● **exploitation** /ˌeksplɔɪˈteɪʃ³n/ *noun* [U] *the exploitation of child workers* **istismar**

exploit² /ˈeksplɔɪt/ *noun* [C] something unusual, brave, or interesting that someone has done **kahramanlık, macera, serüven, ilginç şey** [usually plural] *Have you heard about her amazing exploits travelling in Africa?*

exploratory /ɪkˈsplɒrət³ri/ *adjective* done in order to discover or learn about something **araştırmacı, araştırıcı, inelemeye yönelik/dayalı** *an exploratory expedition* ○ *an exploratory operation*

explore /ɪkˈsplɔːr/ *verb* **1** [I, T] to go around a place where you have never been in order to find out what is there **keşfetmek; inceleme/araştırma yapmak** *The children love exploring.* ○ *The best way to explore the countryside is on foot.* **2** [T] to think about something very carefully before you make a decision about it **karar vermeden önce derinlemesine araştırmak/incelemek** *We're exploring the possibility of buying a holiday home.* ● **exploration** /ˌekspləˈreɪʃ³n/ *noun* [C, U] *She's always loved travel and exploration.* **keşif**

explorer /ɪkˈsplɔːrər/ *noun* [C] someone who travels to places where no one has ever been in order to find out what is there **kâşif, araştıran, keşfeden, inceleme yapan**

o→**explosion** /ɪkˈspləʊʒ³n/ *noun* [C] **1** when something such as a bomb explodes **patlama, infilak** *Forty people were killed in the explosion.* **2** when something increases suddenly by a large amount **ani patlama/artış** *the recent population explosion*

explosive¹ /ɪkˈspləʊsɪv/ *adjective* **1** An explosive substance or piece of equipment can cause explosions. **patlayıcı** *The explosive device was hidden in a suitcase.* **2** An explosive situation or subject causes strong feelings, and may make people angry or violent. **insanların kızgınlık ve hiddetlenmesine sebep olan; yaralayıcı, etkileyici** *a highly explosive political issue*

explosive² /ɪkˈspləʊsɪv/ *noun* [C] a substance or piece of equipment that can cause explosions **patlayıcı madde/düzenek**

exponent /ɪkˈspəʊnənt/ *noun* [C] someone who supports a particular idea or belief, or performs a particular activity **taraftar, savunucu, yandaş, mürit** *The early exponents of votes for women suffered greatly.*

export¹ /ˈekspɔːt/ *noun* **1** [C] a product that you sell in another country **ihracat; dış satım** *Scottish beef exports to Japan* **2** [U] the business of sending goods to another country in order to sell them there **ihraç malı; dış satım ürünü** *the export of industrial goods* ⊃Opposite import.

export² /ɪkˈspɔːt/ *verb* [I, T] **1** to send goods to another country in order to sell them there **ihrac etmek; ihracat yapmak** *Singapore exports large quantities of rubber.* ⊃Opposite import. **2** If you export information from a computer, you copy it to another place. **bilgisayarda bilgiyi başka bir yere taşıyıp kopyalamak** ● **exporter** *noun* [C] *Brazil is the world's largest exporter of coffee.* **aktarım, kopyalama (bilgi)**

expose /ɪkˈspəʊz/ *verb* [T] **1** HIDDEN THING to remove what is covering something so that it can be seen **açığa/meydana çıkarmak** *Our bodies need to be exposed to sunlight in order to make vitamin D.* **2** BAD THING to make public something bad or something that is not honest **foyasını ortaya dökmek, açığa vurmak, ortaya çıkarmak** *The review exposed widespread corruption in the police force.* **3** be exposed to sth to experience something or be affected by something because you are in a particular situation or place **maruz kalmak, etkilenmek** *It was the first time I'd been exposed to violence.* **4** PHOTOGRAPHY to allow light to reach a piece of camera film in order to produce a photograph **ışığa tutmak**

exposed /ɪkˈspəʊzd/ *adjective* having no protection from bad weather **açık, korunmasız** *an exposed cliff*

exposure /ɪkˈspəʊʒər/ *noun* **1** EXPERIENCING [U] when someone experiences something or is affected by it because they are in a particular situation or place **karşı karşıya kalma, maruz kalma** *There is a risk of exposure to radiation.* ○ *Many young children now have exposure to computers in the home.* **2** MAKING PUBLIC [C, U] when something bad that you have done is made public **ortaya çıkarma, ifşaat, teşhir** *She was threatened with exposure by a journalist.* **3** MEDICAL [U] a serious medical condition that is caused by being outside in very cold weather **soğuktam kaynaklanan ciddi tıbbi durum, soğuktan donma** **4** PHOTOGRAPH [C] a single photograph on a piece of film **poz, kare** *This film has 24 exposures.*

expound /ɪk'spaʊnd/ *verb* [I, T] *formal* to give a detailed explanation of something **açıklamak, belirtmek, ayrıntı vermek** *He's always expounding on what's wrong with the world.* ○ *She uses her newspaper column to expound her views on environmental issues.*

๐━**express¹** /ɪk'spres/ *verb* [T] to show what you think or how you feel using words or actions **ifade etmek** *I'm simply expressing my opinion.* ○ [often reflexive] *You're not expressing yourself* (= saying what you mean) *very clearly.*

express² /ɪk'spres/ *adjective* **1 an express service/ train, etc** a service/train, etc that is much faster than usual **hızlı servis/tren vb.** *an express train* ○ *an express service* **2 an express aim/intention/purpose, etc** a clear and certain aim/intention/purpose, etc **açık seçik amaç/niyet/maksat** *You came here with the express purpose of causing trouble.*

express³ /ɪk'spres/ (*also* ex'press ˌtrain) *noun* [C] a fast train **hızlı/ekspres tren** *I took the express to London.*

๐━**expression** /ɪk'spreʃ°n/ *noun* **1** [LOOK] [C] the look on someone's face showing what they feel or think **yüz ifadesi** *your facial expression* ○ *He had a sad expression on his face.* **2** [PHRASE] [C] a phrase that has a special meaning **özel anlamı olan ifade, deyim** *'A can of worms' is an expression meaning a difficult situation.* **3** [SHOWING THOUGHTS] [C, U] when you say what you think or show how you feel using words or actions **ifade, anlatım** *As an expression of our disapproval, we will no longer use his shop.*

expressive /ɪk'spresɪv/ *adjective* showing your feelings **anlamlı, dokunaklı, duygulu** *a very expressive face*

expressly /ɪk'spresli/ *adverb formal* **1** If you say something expressly, you say it in a clear way, so that your meaning cannot be doubted. **açıkça, açık ve net şekilde** *I expressly stated that I did not want any visitors.* **2** If something is expressly for a particular reason or person, it is for that reason or person only. **özel olarak, bilhassa** *The picture was painted expressly for me.*

expressway /ɪk'spresweɪ/ *US* (*UK* **motorway**) *noun* [C] a long, wide road, usually used by traffic travelling fast over long distances **karayolu, otoyol**

expulsion /ɪk'spʌlʃ°n/ *noun* [C, U] when someone is made to leave their school, organization, or country because of their behaviour **uzaklaştırma, kovma, çıkarma** *They threatened him with expulsion from school.*

exquisite /ɪk'skwɪzɪt/ *adjective* very beautiful or perfect **harika, enfes** *a garden of exquisite flowers* ● **exquisitely** *adverb an exquisitely dressed woman* **mükemmel bir şekilde**

extend /ɪk'stend/ *verb* **1** [MAKE BIGGER] [T] to make something bigger or longer **uzatmak, genişletmek** *We're going to extend our kitchen.* **2** [MAKE LAST] [T] to make an activity, agreement, etc last for a longer time **uzatmak, uzamak, sarkmak, daha uzun süre sürmesini sağlamak** *They have extended the deadline by one week.* **3 extend from/into/over, etc** to continue or stretch over a particular area of land or period of time **uzanmak, içlerine doğru girmek, ilerlemek (zaman dilim, alan)** *Will the building work extend into next week?* **4** [STRETCH OUT] [T] to stretch out a part of your body **(elini, kolunu, bacağını vs.) uzatmak** *She smiled and*

extended her hand. **5 extend an invitation/thanks, etc to sb** *formal* to give someone an invitation/thanks, etc **sunmak, iletmek, göndermek, vermek, arzetmek** *I'd like to extend a warm welcome to our guests.*

extension /ɪk'stenʃ°n/ *noun* [C] **1** [PART OF A BUILDING] a new room or rooms that are added to a building **ek oda/bina/uzantı** *You could build an extension onto the back of the house.* **2** [EXTRA TIME] extra time that you are given to do or use something **ilave zaman, uzatma süresi** *You might be able to get an extension on your visa.* **3** [TELEPHONE] a telephone that is connected to the main telephone in an office or other large building **(telefon) dahili hat** *Call me on extension 213.*

extensive /ɪk'stensɪv/ *adjective* large in amount or size **büyük, geniş, geniş çaplı** *an extensive art collection* ○ *The hurricane caused extensive damage.* ● **extensively** *adverb I have travelled extensively in Europe.* **kapsamlı bir şekilde**

extent /ɪk'stent/ *noun* **1** [no plural] the size or importance of something **ölçü, derece, mertebe, önem, miktar** *They are just beginning to realize the full extent of the damage.* ○ *Her face was injured to such an extent* (= so much) *that he didn't recognize her.* **2 to some extent/to a certain extent** in some ways **bir dereceye kadar, belli bir ölçüye/dereceye kadar** *I was, to some extent, responsible for the accident.*

exterior /ɪk'stɪəriə^r/ *noun* [C] the outside part of something or someone **dış, dış cephe/yüzey** [usually singular] *The exterior of the house was painted white.* ● **exterior** *adjective* [always before noun] *an exterior wall* ⊃Opposite interior. **dış**

exterminate /ɪk'stɜ:mɪneɪt/ *verb* [T] to kill a large group of people or animals **topluca yok etmek, kökünü kazımak, imha etmek** ● **extermination** /ɪkˌstɜ:mɪ'neɪʃ°n/ *noun* [C, U] **imha**

external /ɪk'stɜ:n°l/ *adjective* **1** relating to the outside part of something **harici, dış** *the external walls of the house* ○ *The ointment is for external use only* (= it must not be put inside the body). **2** coming from or relating to another country, group, or organization **dışarıdan/ hariçten gelen, dışarıya ait** *All exams are marked by an external examiner.* ⊃Opposite internal. ● **externally** *adverb* **dış bölüm ile ilgili**

extinct /ɪk'stɪŋkt/ *adjective* If a type of animal is extinct, it does not now exist. **nesli yok olmuş, soyu tükenmiş**

extinction /ɪk'stɪŋkʃ°n/ *noun* [U] when a type of animal no longer exists **yok olma, soyu/nesli tükenme** *Many species of animal are threatened with extinction.*

extinguish /ɪk'stɪŋgwɪʃ/ *verb* [T] *formal* to stop something burning or giving out light **söndürmek** *The fire took two hours to extinguish.*

extinguisher /ɪk'stɪŋgwɪʃə^r/ (*also* fire extinguisher) *noun* [C] a piece of equipment shaped like a tube, which is used to spread a substance onto a fire to stop it burning **yangın söndürme tüpü; yangın söndürücü**

extol /ɪk'stəʊl/ *verb* [T] **extolling**, *past* **extolled** to say that you think that something is very good **övmek, yüceltmek, göklere çıkarmak** *He always extols the virtues of* (= praises) *French cooking.*

extort /ɪk'stɔ:t/ *verb* [T] to get money from someone by saying that you will harm them **tehditle almak, zorla el koymak, gözünü korkutarak parasını almak** ● **extortion** /ɪk'stɔ:ʃ°n/ *noun* [U] **zorbalık, şantaj**

extortionate /ɪkˈstɔːʃᵊnət/ *adjective* Extortionate prices or costs are very high. **(fiyatlar, ücretler) fahiş, çok yüksek, aşırı, çok fazla**

o—**extra**[1] /ˈekstrə/ *adjective* more, or more than usual **fazla, fazladan, ek, ilave, ekstra** *Can I invite a few extra people?* ○ *She's been babysitting to earn some extra cash.*

> **extra** ...... İLE BİRLİKTE KULLANILAN KELİMELER
> an **added/hidden/optional** extra

extra[2] /ˈekstrə/ *noun* [C] **1** something that costs more when you buy goods or pay for a service **ekstra** *The hi-fi comes with **optional extras** such as headphones and remote control.* **2** an actor in a film who does not have a main part and usually plays someone in a crowd **figüran**

extra[3] /ˈekstrə/ *adverb* more than usual **fazladan, ilaveten** *Do you get paid extra for working late?*

extra- /ekstrə-/ *prefix* outside of or in addition to **hariçten, ilave, ek anlamında ön ek** *extracurricular activities* (= activities that are in addition to the usual school work)

extract[1] /ɪkˈstrækt/ *verb* [T] *formal* **1** to take something out, especially using force **çekmek, çekip çıkarmak, sökmek** *He's going to the dentist's to have a tooth extracted.* **2** to get the money, information, etc that you want from someone who does not want to give it to you **elde etmek, zorla almak/koparmak** *They were not able to extract a confession from her.*

extract[2] /ˈekstrækt/ *noun* [C] **1** a particular part of a book, poem, etc that is chosen so that it can be used in a discussion, article, etc **bölüm, parça** *The teacher read out **an extract from** 'Brave New World'.* **2** a substance taken from a plant, flower, etc and used especially in food or medicine **(bitki, vb.)** ...**den çıkarılan/elde edilen öz, yağ** *pure vanilla extract*

extraction /ɪkˈstrækʃn/ *noun* **1** [C, U] when something is taken out, especially using force **çıkarma, çıkarılma, çekme, çıkarma 2** of Chinese/Italian, etc **extraction** having a family whose origin is Chinese, Italian, etc **köken, soy sop, kökenden/soyundan olma**

extradite /ˈekstrədaɪt/ *verb* [T] to send someone back to the country where they are accused of a crime, so that a court there can decide if they are guilty **(suçlu) iade etmek, kendi ülkesine geri göndermek** [often passive] *The suspects were extradited to the UK.* ● **extradition** /ˌekstrəˈdɪʃn/ *noun* [C, U] **suçlu kişilerin iadesi**

extraneous /ɪkˈstreɪniəs/ *adjective* not directly connected to something **alâkasız, ilgisi olmayan, konu dışı** *extraneous information/noise*

extraordinary /ɪkˈstrɔːdᵊnᵊri/ *adjective* very special, unusual, or strange **görülmemiş, alışılmamış, olağan dışı, garip** *an extraordinary tale of courage* ○ *She was an extraordinary young woman.* ● **extraordinarily** *adverb* *Their last album was extraordinarily successful.* **sıra dışı bir şekilde**

extravagant /ɪkˈstrævəgənt/ *adjective* **1** costing too much or spending a lot more money than you need to **savurgan, müsrif** *the extravagant lifestyle of a movie star* **2** too unusual and extreme to be believed or controlled **alışılandan çok farklı, abartılı, ölçüsü kaçmış** *the extravagant claims made by cosmetics companies* ● **extravagance** /ɪkˈstrævəgəns/ *noun* [C, U] when someone or something is extravagant **savurganlık, müsriflik, israf** ● **extravagantly** *adverb* **savurgan bir şekilde**

extravaganza /ɪkˌstrævəˈgænzə/ *noun* [C] a large, exciting, and expensive event or entertainment **büyük/pahalı/heyecan verici olay/eğlence** *a three-hour extravaganza of country music*

extreme[1] /ɪkˈstriːm/ *adjective* **1** [SERIOUS] the most unusual or most serious possible **aşırı, en uçta, uç** *extreme weather conditions* ○ *In extreme cases, the disease can lead to blindness.* **2** [VERY LARGE] very large in amount or degree **çok büyük, fazla** *extreme pain* ○ *extreme wealth* **3** [OPINIONS] having such strong opinions or beliefs that most people cannot agree with you **aşırı uçta, uçuk, ekstrem, aşırı, müfrit** *extreme views* ○ *the extreme right* **4** [FURTHEST] [always before noun] at the furthest point of something **en uçta, aşırı noktada** *in the extreme south of the island*

extreme[2] /ɪkˈstriːm/ *noun* [C] the largest possible amount or degree of something **aşırı miktar/nokta, uç** *Anna's moods went **from one extreme to another*** (= first she was very happy, then she was very unhappy). ○ *Coach Wilson **took** our training **to extremes*** (= made us train extremely hard).

o—**extremely** /ɪkˈstriːmli/ *adverb* very, or much more than usual **son derece, çok, aşırı** *extremely beautiful*

ex,treme ˈsports *noun* [C, U] a game or activity which people do that is dangerous **tehlikeli sporlar** *extreme sports such as bungee jumping and snowboarding*

extremist /ɪkˈstriːmɪst/ *noun* [C] someone who has such strong opinions or beliefs that most people cannot agree with them **aşırı uç, fanatik, aşırı uçta görüşleri olan** ● **extremism** /ɪkˈstriːmɪzᵊm/ *noun* [U] **aşırılık** ● **extremist** *adjective* **aşırı uçlarda olan**

extremities /ɪkˈstremətiz/ *noun* [plural] the end parts of your body such as your hands and feet **eller ve ayaklar, uç kısımlar**

extremity /ɪkˈstreməti/ *noun formal* **1** [C] the part of something that is furthest from the centre **uç kısım, en uç uzantı** *at the north-west extremity of Europe* **2** [U] when a feeling is very strong or a bad situation very serious **aşırı/ güçlü davranış, fikir veya duygu**

extricate /ˈekstrɪkeɪt/ *verb* **extricate yourself from sth** to get yourself out of a difficult situation or unpleasant place **zor bir durumdan çıkmayı başarmak** *I didn't know how to extricate myself from such an embarrassing situation.*

extrovert /ˈekstrəvɜːt/ *noun* [C] someone who is very confident and likes being with other people **dışadönük kişi, kendine güveni olan kişi** つOpposite **introvert.** ● **extrovert** *adjective* *an extrovert personality* つOpposite **introverted. dışa dönük kişi**

exuberant /ɪgˈzjuːbᵊrᵊnt/ *adjective* full of happiness, excitement, and energy **canlı, hareketli, taşkın, coşkulu** *a warm and exuberant personality* ● **exuberance** /ɪgˈzjuːbᵊrᵊns/ *noun* [U] **neşe**

exude /ɪgˈzjuːd/ *verb* [T] If you exude love, confidence, pain, etc, you show that you have a lot of that feeling. **(sevgi, güven, acı vs.) akmak, taşmak, yayılmak, çokça var olmak**

exult /ɪgˈzʌlt/ *verb* [I] to show great pleasure, especially at someone else's defeat or failure **(birinin yenilgisine/başarısızlığına) çok sevinmek; (argo) göbek atmak; bayram etmek** *She seems to exult in her power.* ● **exultation** /ˌegzʌlˈteɪʃᵊn/ *noun* [U] **başkasının başarısızlığından haz alma**

o—**eye**[1] /aɪ/ *noun* **1** [SEEING] [C] one of the two organs in your face, which you use to see with **göz** *Sara has black hair and brown eyes.* ○ *She **closed** her **eyes** and drifted off to sleep.* **2** [NEEDLE] [C] the small hole at the end of a needle, that you put the thread through **iğne deliği 3 have an eye for sth** to be good at noticing a particular type of thing **bir şeyi gözlemlemede çok iyi olmak** *Your son has a very good eye for detail.* **4 keep your/an eye on sb/**

sth to watch or look after someone or something **göz kulak olmak, bakmak, sahip çıkmak** *Could you keep an eye on this pan of soup for a moment?*
5 have your eye on sth *informal* to want something and intend to get it **bir şeyde gözü olmak** *Jane's got her eye on that new advertising job.* **6 can't keep/take your eyes off sb/sth** to be unable to stop looking at someone or something because they are so attractive or interesting **gözlerini/kendini alamamak; çok etkilenmek** *He couldn't take his eyes off her all night.* **7 lay/set eyes on sb/sth** to see someone or something for the first time **bir şeyi ilk defa görmek** *They fell in love the moment they laid eyes on each other.* **8 look sb in the eye/eyes** to look at someone in a direct way, without showing fear or shame **doğrudan gözünün içine bakmak; gözlerini kaçırmamak** *Look me in the eye and say that you didn't steal it.* **9 in sb's eyes** in someone's opinion **görüşüne/fikrine göre** *In my parents' eyes, I'll always be a child.* **10 cast/run your/an eye over sth** *UK* to look at something quickly, often in order to give your opinion about it **hızlı bir göz gezdirmek; şöyle bir bakmak** *Would you cast an eye over our work so far?* ● **11 catch sb's a** GET SOMEONE'S ATTENTION to get someone's attention by looking at them **(birinin) gözüne çarpmak; bakışlarını yakalamak** *I tried to catch her eye, but she had already turned away.* **b** BE NOTICED to be attractive or different enough to be noticed by people **göze çarpmak, dikkatini çekmek** *It was the colour of his jacket that caught my eye.* ● **12 cry your eyes out** If someone cries their eyes out, they cry a lot about a problem or situation. **ağlamaktan gözleri kan çanağına dönmek, çok göz yaşı dökmek** ● **13 keep your eyes open/peeled (for sb/sth)** to watch carefully for someone or something **gözlerini açmak; dikkatli olmak; kuş uçurtmamak** *Keep your eyes peeled, he should be here any minute.* ● **14 keep an eye out for sb/sth** to watch carefully for someone or something to appear **bakmak, bakınmak** *Keep an eye out for the delivery van.* ● **15 see eye to eye (with sb)** If two people see eye to eye, they agree with each other. **anlaşmak, uyuşmak, aynı fikirde/görüşte olmak** ● **16 turn a blind eye (to sth)** to choose to ignore something that you know is wrong or illegal **göz yummak, görmezden gelmek** ● **17 with your eyes open** knowing about all of the problems that could happen if you do

eye

something **bile bile, göz göre göre** *I went into this marriage with my eyes open.* ⊃See also: **black eye.**

eye² /aɪ/ *verb* [T] **eyeing**, *also US* **eying**, *past* **eyed** to look at someone or something with interest **süzmek, (argo) kesik kesik bakmak; ilgi ile bakmak** *The two women eyed each other suspiciously.*

eyeball /'aɪbɔːl/ *noun* [C] the whole of the eye, that has the shape of a small ball **göz yuvarı**

eyebrow /'aɪbraʊ/ *noun* [C] the thin line of hair that is above each eye **kaş** ⊃Orta kısımdaki renkli sayfalarına bakınız.

eye-catching /'aɪˌkætʃɪŋ/ *adjective* attractive, interesting, or different enough to be noticed **göze çarpan, ilginç, çekici, kolay görülebilen** *an eye-catching poster*

'eye ˌcontact *noun* [U] *UK* If two people make eye contact, they look at each other at the same time. **göz teması**

-eyed /aɪd/ *suffix* used at the end of a word describing a person's eyes **...gözlü** *Both sisters are brown-eyed.* ⊃See also: **cross-eyed, wide-eyed.**

eyelash /'aɪlæʃ/ *(also* lash*) noun* [C] one of the short hairs that grow from the edge of your eyelids **kirpik** [usually plural] *false eyelashes*

eyelid /'aɪlɪd/ *noun* [C] **1** the piece of skin that covers your eye when you close it **göz kapağı 2 not bat an eyelid** to not react to something unusual **olağan dışı bir duruma tepki göstermemek, umrunda olmamak**

eyeliner /'aɪˌlaɪnə'/ *noun* [C, U] a coloured substance, usually contained in a pencil, which you put in a line above or below your eyes in order to make them more attractive **göz kalemi, sürme** ⊃See picture at **make up.**

eye-opener /'aɪˌəʊp°nə'/ *noun* [C] something that surprises you and teaches you new facts about life, people, etc **insanın gözünü açan/yeni bazı gerçekleri öğreten olay/şey; ibret, göz açan şey** *Living in another country can be a real eye-opener.*

eyeshadow /'aɪʃædəʊ/ *noun* [C, U] a coloured cream or powder which you put above or around your eyes in order to make them more attractive **göz farı**

eyesight /'aɪsaɪt/ *noun* [U] the ability to see **görme yeteneği** *My eyesight is getting worse.*

eyesore /'aɪsɔː'/ *noun* [C] a building, area, etc that looks ugly compared to the things that are around it **göz estetiğini bozan şey/görüntü; görsel kirlilik**

eyewitness /ˌaɪ'wɪtnɪs/ *(also* witness*) noun* [C] someone who saw something such as a crime or an accident happen **görgü tanığı, şahit** *Eyewitnesses saw two men running away from the bank.*

F, f /ef/ the sixth letter of the alphabet **alfabenin altıncı harfi**

F *written abbreviation for* Fahrenheit (= a measurement of temperature) **Fahrenheit, ısı ölçüm birimi** *a body temperature of 98.6 °F*

FA /ˌefˈeɪ/ *noun abbreviation for* Football Association: the national organization for football in England **Futbol Birliği; İngiltere'de ulusal futbol teşkilatı** *the FA Cup*

fable /ˈfeɪbl/ *noun* [C] a short, traditional story, usually involving animals, which is intended to show people how to behave **hayvan masalı, alegorik hikaye, fabl** *Aesop's fables*

fabric /ˈfæbrɪk/ *noun* **1** [C, U] cloth **kumaş, dokuma, bez** *a light/woollen fabric* **2 the fabric of sth a** the basic way in which a society or other social group is organized **bir şeyin yapısı, toplumun yapısı** *The family is part of the fabric of society.* **b** *UK* the walls, floor, and roof of a building **bir binanın çatı duvar ve döşemesi**

fabricate /ˈfæbrɪkeɪt/ *verb* [T] to invent facts, a story, etc in order to deceive someone **uydurmak, yalan düzmek** *He claims that the police fabricated evidence against him.* ● **fabrication** /ˌfæbrɪˈkeɪʃᵊn/ *noun* [C, U] **uydurma (hikaye)**

fabulous /ˈfæbjələs/ *adjective* extremely good **mükemmel, harika, oldukça iyi, inanılmaz** *They've got a fabulous house.* ○ *We had an absolutely fabulous holiday.* ● **fabulously** *adverb* extremely **oldukça** *Her family is fabulously wealthy.*

facade (*also* façade) /fəˈsɑːd/ *noun* [C] **1** a false appearance **yanıltıcı/aldatıcı görünüm** *Behind that amiable facade, he's a deeply unpleasant man.* **2** the front of a large building **bir binanın ön cephesi/yüzü** *the gallery's elegant 18th century facade*

o⊶**face¹** /feɪs/ *noun* **1** [C] the front part of the head where the eyes, nose, and mouth are, or the expression on this part **yüz, surat, çehre, sima** *She's got a long, thin face.* ○ *I can't wait to see her face when she opens the present.* **2 make a face** (*also* UK **pull a face**) to show with your face that you do not like someone or something **surat yapmak, yüz çevirmek** *The baby made a face every time I offered her some food.* **3 make faces** to make silly expressions with your face in order to try and make people laugh **komiklik yapmak ve eğlendirmek için yüzünü gözünü oynatmak** **4 sb's face falls/lights up** someone starts to look disappointed/happy **yüzü düşmek; hayal kırıklığına uğramak; mutlu/üzgün görünmeye başlamak** *His face fell when I said that she wasn't coming.* **5 to sb's face** If you say something unpleasant to someone's face, you say it to them directly, when you are with them. **yüzüne karşı; uluorta; doğrudan kendisine; açıkça** *If you've got something to say, say it to my face.* **6** the front or surface of something **yüz, yüzey, cephe** *the north face of the cliff* ○ *a clock face* **7 in the face of sth** while having to deal with a difficult situation or problem **bir şeye rağmen/karşın; ...karşısında; ...koşullar altında** *She refused to leave him, in the face of increasing pressure from friends and family.* **8 on the face of it** used when you are describing how a situation seems on the surface **görünüşe bakılırsa** *On the face of it, it seems like a bargain, but I bet there are hidden costs.* **9 keep a straight**

face to manage to stop yourself from smiling or laughing **gülmek veya gülümsemekten kendini alıkoyabilme, surat asma** *I can never play jokes on people because I can't keep a straight face.* ● **10 lose/save face** to do something so that people stop respecting you/still respect you **saygınlığını/itibarını yitirmek; onurunu kurtarmak** *He seemed more interested in saving face than telling the truth.* ⊃See also: have **egg¹** on your face, a **slap²** in the face.

o⊶**face²** /feɪs/ *verb* [T] **1** DIRECTION to be or turn in a particular direction **yüzünü birine doğru çevirmek/dönmek** *The room faces south.* ○ *She turned to face him.* **2** PROBLEM If you face a problem, or a problem faces you, you have to deal with it. **karşı karşıya olmak, karşısına sorun olarak çıkmak** [*often passive*] *This is one of the many problems faced by working mothers.* **3 can't face sth/doing sth** to not want to do something or deal with something because it is so unpleasant **göze alamamak, cesaret edememek** *I had intended to go for a run, but now I just can't face it.* **4** ACCEPT to accept that something unpleasant is true and start to deal with the situation **kabul etmek; varlığını tanımak** *She's going to have to face the fact that he's not coming back to her.* **5 let's face it** something that you say before you say something that is unpleasant but true **durumu tüm çıplaklığı ile /olduğu gibi kabul etmek** *Let's face it, none of us are getting any younger.* **6** PUNISHMENT If you face something unpleasant, especially a punishment, then it might happen to you. **göğüs germek, katlanmak** *If found guilty, the pair face fines of up to $40,000.* **7** DEAL WITH to deal with someone when the situation between you is difficult **ilgilenmek, davranmak, karşısına çıkmak** *How can I face him now that he knows what I've done?* **8** COMPETITION to play against another player or team in a competition, sport, etc **karşı karşıya gelmek; oynamak; kaşılaşmak (spor/yarışma)** *We face Spain in the semifinal.* ⊃See also: face the **music**.
face up to sth *phrasal verb* to accept that a difficult situation exists **kabullenmek**

facelift /ˈfeɪslɪft/ *noun* [C] **1** medical treatment which makes the skin of your face tighter so that you look younger **yüz gerdirme ameliyatı, estetik ameliyat** *She looks like she's had a facelift.* **2** when you improve a place and make it look more attractive **güzelleştirme, düzenleme, bakım onarım** *The council is planning a £6 million facelift for the old harbour area.*

facet /ˈfæsɪt/ *noun* [C] one part of a subject, situation, etc that has many parts **yön, taraf** *She has many facets to her personality.*

facetious /fəˈsiːʃəs/ *adjective* trying to make a joke or a clever remark in a way that annoys people **(yorum, şaka, söz vb.) rahatsız edici**

face-to-face /ˌfeɪstəˈfeɪs/ *adjective, adverb* directly, meeting someone in the same place **yüz yüze, doğrudan, karşılıklı** *We need to talk face-to-face.* ○ *She came face-to-face with the gunman as he strode into the playground.*

‚face ˈvalue *noun* **take sth at face value** to accept the way that something first appears without thinking about what it really means **görünüşe bakarak değerlendirmek, görünüşe aldanmak; görüntüye kanmak** *You can't just take everything you read in the papers at face value.*

facial /'feɪʃ°l/ *adjective* of or on the face **yüze ait, çehre ile ilgili** *facial expressions/hair*

facile /'fæsaɪl/ ⑩ /'fæsəl/ *adjective formal* A facile remark is too simple and has not been thought about enough. **yüzeysel; rastgele, basit, kolay**

facilitate /fə'sɪlɪteɪt/ *verb* [T] *formal* to make something possible or easier **mümkün kılmak, kolaylaştırmak, yardımcı olmak** *I will do everything in my power to facilitate the process.*

🧩 **facilities** ...... İLE BİRLİKTE KULLANILAN KELİMELER
offer/provide facilities ● facilities for sb/(doing) sth ● sports facilities

facilities /fə'sɪlətiz/ *noun* [plural] buildings, equipment, or services that are provided for a particular purpose **tesisler, hizmet alanları, belli bir amaç için sağlanan bina, tesis ve hizmetler** *sports/washing facilities* ○ *childcare facilities*

facility /fə'sɪləti/ *noun* [C] **1** a part of a system or machine which makes it possible to do something **bir makina ya da sistemin bir bölümü; çalışmayı sağlayan/bir şeyi mümkün kılan unsurlar** *This phone has a memory facility.* **2** a place where a particular activity happens **tesis, bina, yer** *a new medical facility*

🧩 **fact** ...... İLE BİRLİKTE KULLANILAN KELİMELER
accept/face up to/establish/explain/ignore a fact ● the fact remains ● an important/interesting/simple/undeniable fact ● the facts about sth ● know for a fact

o⸱**fact** /fækt/ *noun* **1** [TRUE THING] [C] something that you know is true, exists, or has happened **gerçek, olgu, hakikat** *I'm not angry that you drove my car, it's just the fact that you didn't ask me first.* ○ *No decision will be made until we know all the facts.* ○ *He knew for a fact* (= was certain) *that Natalie was lying.* **2** [REAL THINGS] [U] real events and experiences, not things that are imagined **gerçek olay ve tecrübeler** *It's hard to separate fact from fiction in what she says.* **3 in fact/in actual fact/as a matter of fact a** [EMPHASIZING TRUTH] used to emphasize what is really true **aslını sorarsanız; doğrusu; doğruyu söylemek gerekirse** *I was told there were some tickets left, but in actual fact they were sold out.* **b** [MORE INFORMATION] used when giving more information about something **işin doğrusu; hülasa** *"Is Isabel coming?" "Yes. As a matter of fact, she should be here soon."* **4 the fact (of the matter) is** used to tell someone that something is the truth **gerçek şu ki...; aslını sorarsan** *I wouldn't usually ask for your help, but the fact is I'm desperate.* **5 the facts of life** details about sexual activity and the way that babies are born **(doğum, çocuk yapma, cinsellik vb.) yaşamın değişmeyen gerçekleri; asıl bilinmesi gerekenler; cinsel bilgiler**

faction /'fækʃ°n/ *noun* [C] a small group of people who are part of a larger group, and oppose the ideas of everyone else **ayrılıkçılık, hizip, topluluk içinde anlaşmazlık**

o⸱**factor** /'fæktər/ *noun* [C] **1** one of the things that has an effect on a particular situation, decision, event, etc **etmen, unsur, etken, faktör** *Money was an important factor in their decision to move.* **2** a number that another larger number can be divided by exactly **(matematik) çarpan** *5 is a factor of 10.*

o⸱**factory** /'fæktªri/ *noun* [C] a building or group of buildings where large amounts of products are made or put together **fabrika** *a textile factory*

factual /'fæktʃʊəl/ *adjective* using or consisting of facts **gerçeklere/olgulara dayanan** ● **factually** *adverb factually correct/incorrect* **gerçek olan**

faculty /'fæk°lti/ *noun* **1** [C] a natural ability to hear, see, think, move, etc **kabiliyet, yeti 2 the English/law/science, etc faculty** a particular department at a college or university, or the teachers in that department **fakülte; fakülte öğretim elemanları 3 the faculty** US all of the teachers at a school or college **öğretmenler/öğretim elemanları**

fad /fæd/ *noun* [C] something that is fashionable to do, wear, say, etc for a short period of time **geçici bir moda, heves, ilgi (kısa süreli)** *the latest health fad*

fade /feɪd/ *verb* **1** [I, T] If a colour or a sound fades, or if something fades it, it becomes less bright or strong. **solmak, rengi atmak** *The music began to fade.* ○ *The walls had been faded by the sun.* **2** [I] (*also* fade away) to slowly disappear, lose importance, or become weaker **yavaş yavaş kaybolmak/önemini yitirmek; gittikçe zayıflamak** *With time, memories of that painful summer would fade away.*

faeces UK (US feces) /'fiːsiːz/ *noun* [plural] *formal* solid waste that comes out of the bottom of a person or animal **dışkı**

fag /fæg/ *noun* [C] UK *informal* a cigarette **sigara**

Fahrenheit /'fær°nhaɪt/ (*written abbreviation* F) *noun* [U] a measurement of temperature in which water freezes at 32° and boils at 212° **suyun 32 derecede donduğuu ve 212 derecede kaynadığını gösteren ısı ölçüm birimi, Fahrenheit**

o⸱**fail¹** /feɪl/ *verb* **1** [NOT SUCCEED] [I] to not be successful **başarısız olmak** *Dad's business failed after just three years.* ○ *She keeps failing in her attempt to lose weight.* **2 fail to do sth** to not do what is necessary or expected **başaramamak, üstesinden gelememek** *John failed to turn up for football practice yesterday.* **3** [EXAM] [I, T] to not pass a test or an exam, or to decide that someone has not passed **sınavı başaramamak, başarısızlığına karar vermek** *I'm worried about failing my driving test.* **4** [STOP WORKING] [I] to stop working normally, or to become weaker **normal olarak çalışmamak; gittikçe zayıflamak** *Two of the plane's engines had failed.* **5** [NOT HELPING] [T] to stop being helpful or useful to someone when they need you **yardım edememek, faydalı olamamak** *The government is failing the poor and unemployed.* **6 I fail to see/understand** used to show that you do not accept something **kabullenememek, anlayamamak** [+ question word] *I fail to see why you cannot work on a Sunday.*

fail² /feɪl/ *noun* **without fail** If you do something without fail, you always do it, even when it is difficult. **muhakkak, kesinlikle, hiç aksatmadan** *I go to the gym every Monday and Thursday without fail.*

failing¹ /'feɪlɪŋ/ *noun* [C] a bad quality or fault that someone or something has **kusur; kötü kalite** *Despite one or two failings, he's basically a nice guy.*

failing² /'feɪlɪŋ/ *preposition* **failing that** if something is not possible or does not happen **aksi takdirde; durumda; olmazsa şayet** *Our goal is to move out by January, or failing that, by March.*

🧩 **failure** ...... İLE BİRLİKTE KULLANILAN KELİMELER
admit/end in failure ● be doomed to failure ● an abject/complete/humiliating/total failure

o⸱**failure** /'feɪljər/ *noun* **1** [NO SUCCESS] [U] when someone or something does not succeed **başarısızlık** *Their attempt to climb Everest ended in failure.* **2** [PERSON/ACTION] [C] someone or something that does not succeed **fiyasko, başarısız** *All my life I've felt like a failure.* **3 failure to**

do sth when you do not do something that you must do or are expected to do **üstesinden gelememe, becerememe, başaramama** *Failure to pay within 14 days will result in prosecution.* **4** NOT WORKING [C, U] when something does not work, or stops working as well as it should **yetmezlik, yokluk, kesinti** *heart failure* ○ *All trains were delayed due to a power failure.*

faint[1] /feɪnt/ *adjective* **1** slight and not easy to notice, smell, hear, etc **belli belirsiz, zayıf, zor duyulan/farkedilen** *a faint smell of smoke* ○ *faint laughter coming from next door* **2 feel faint** to feel very weak and as if you might fall down **bayılmak üzere olmak; halsiz hissetmek** *Seeing all the blood made me feel faint.* **3 faint hope/praise/chance, etc** very little hope, praise, chance, etc **küçük umut/övgü/şans vs.** *a faint hope of winning the gold medal* **4 not have the faintest idea** used to emphasize that you do not know something **en küçük bir fikri/düşüncesi olmamak** [+ question word] *I haven't the faintest idea what you're talking about.*

faint[2] /feɪnt/ *verb* [I] to suddenly become unconscious for a short time, usually falling down onto the floor **bayılmak, kendinden geçmek** *She fainted with exhaustion.*

faintly /ˈfeɪntli/ *adverb* slightly **belli belirsiz, hafif** *faintly embarrassed*

o⌐**fair**[1] /feər/ *adjective* **1** EQUAL treating everyone in the same way, so that no one has an advantage **âdil, hakkaniyetli, kurallara uygun, adilane, dürüstçe** *a fair trial* ○ *That's not fair. You always go first!* **2** RIGHT acceptable or right **doğru kabuledilebilir** *a fair deal* ○ *We'd like to move abroad, but it's just not fair on the children.* ⊃Opposite **unfair. 3** HAIR/SKIN having pale skin or a light colour of hair **solgun; açık renk saçlı, açık renkli** *a boy with fair hair and blue eyes* ⊃Opposite **dark. 4 a fair amount/distance/size, etc** quite a large amount, distance, size, etc **oldukça büyük miktar/mesafe/ebat/ölçü vb.; epeyce** *There's still a fair bit of work to be done on the house.* **5** WEATHER sunny and not raining **(hava) açık, güzel,** *Tomorrow will be fair, with some early morning frost.* **6** AVERAGE not very good but not very bad **makul, ne iyi ne kötü** *He has a fair chance of winning.* **7 fair enough** *UK informal* used to say that you agree, or think that something is acceptable **Tamam!, Pekâlâ!, Anlaşıldı!** *"He'll only work on Sunday if he gets paid extra." "Fair enough."* ⊃See also: fair **play**[2], have your (fair) **share**[2] of sth.

fair

fair[2] /feər/ *noun* [C] **1** an event outside where you can ride large machines for pleasure and play games to win prizes **panayır, fuar, eğlence alanı 2** an event where people show and sell goods or services relating to a particular business or hobby **fuar alanı, fuar** *a trade fair*

fair[3] /feər/ *adverb* **1 play fair** to do something in a fair and honest way **adil/dürüst/ilkeli oyun 2 fair and square** in an honest way and without any doubt **dürüst/ilkeli ve kuşkusuz** *We won the match fair and square.*

fairground /ˈfeəɡraʊnd/ *noun* [C] an outside area that is used for fairs **panayır alanı**

fair-haired /ˌfeəˈheəd/ *adjective* having a light colour of hair **açık renk saçlı** *a fair-haired child*

o⌐**fairly** /ˈfeəli/ *adverb* **1** more than average, but less than very **oldukça; normalden biraz fazla, çoktan az** *a fairly big family* ○ *fairly quickly* **2** done in a fair way **adilce, hakkaniyetle, adil** *treating people fairly*

fairness /ˈfeənəs/ *noun* [U] when you treat everyone in the same way, so that no one has an advantage **adil olma, dürüstlük, iyilik, doğruluk, hakkaniyet**

‚**fair ˈtrade** *noun* [U] a way of buying and selling products that makes certain that the original producer receives a fair price **adil/dürüst ticaret/alışveriş** *fair trade coffee/chocolate* ⊃Compare free trade. ● **fairly traded** *adverb*

fairy /ˈfeəri/ *noun* [C] a small, imaginary creature that looks like a person with wings, and has magic powers **peri**

fairy

fairytale /ˈfeəriteɪl/ *adjective* [always before noun] happy and beautiful, like something in a fairy tale **peri gibi, mutlu ve güzel** *a fairytale romance/ wedding*

‚**fairy ˌtale** *noun* [C] a story told to children which involves magic, imaginary creatures, and a happy ending **peri masalı**

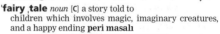 **faith** ...... İLE BİRLİKTE KULLANILAN KELİMELER

have/lose faith ● sb's faith in sb/sth

faith /feɪθ/ *noun* **1** TRUST [U] the belief that someone or something is good, right, and able to be trusted **güven, itimat** *Have faith in me. I won't let you down.* **2** STRONG BELIEF [U] strong belief in a god or gods **inanç, itikat** *Throughout her illness, she never lost her faith in God.* **3** RELIGION [C] a religion **din** *the Jewish and Christian faiths* **4 in good faith** If you act in good faith, you believe that what you are doing is good, honest, or legal. **iyi niyetle**

faithful /ˈfeɪθfəl/ *adjective* **1** RELATIONSHIP If your husband, wife, or partner is faithful, they do not have a sexual relationship with anyone else. **sadık, vefalı** *a faithful husband* ○ *They remained faithful to each other throughout their long marriage.* **2** LOYAL always loyal **daima bağlı, sadık** *his trusted and faithful servant* **3** NOT CHANGED not changing any of the original details, facts, style, etc **aslına uygun, doğru, eksiksiz** *Does the film adaptation stay faithful to the novel?* ⊃Opposite **unfaithful.** ● **faithfulness** *noun* [U] **sadakat**

faithfully /ˈfeɪθfəli/ *adverb* **1** in a faithful way **sadakatle, aslına uygun şekilde 2 Yours faithfully** used to end a formal letter to someone whose name you do not know **'Saygılarımla' anlamında resmi mektupların sonunda kullanılır**

fake[1] /feɪk/ *adjective* not real, but made to look or seem real **sahte, taklit** *fake fur* ○ *a fake passport*

fake[2] /feɪk/ *noun* [C] **1** a copy of something that is intended to look real or valuable and deceive people **sahte, taklit** *Experts say that the painting is a fake.* **2** someone who pretends to have particular skills or qualities so that they can deceive people or get their admiration **sahtekar, üç kağıtçı, dürüst olmayan**

fake³ /feɪk/ *verb* [T] **1** to copy something in order to deceive people **sahtesini yapmak, taklit etmek** *faked documents* **2** to pretend that you have a particular feeling or emotion **numara yapmak; sanki öyleymiş gibi davranmak, rol yapmak** *He said he was feeling sick, but he was just faking it.*

falcon /ˈfɔːlkᵊn/ *noun* [C] a large bird that eats small animals and is often taught to hunt by people **şahin**

o⁻**fall¹** /fɔːl/ *verb* [I] *past tense* **fell**, *past participle* **fallen** **1** [MOVE DOWN] to move down towards the ground **aşağı düşmek** *Huge drops of rain were falling from the sky.* ○ *By winter, all the leaves had fallen off the trees.* **2** [STOP STANDING] to suddenly go down and hit the ground without intending to **yere düşmek** *She fell off her bike and broke her arm.* **3** [BECOME LESS] to become less in number or amount **sayısı/miktarı düşmek/azalmak** *Housing prices have fallen by 15% since last year.* ○ *Temperatures are expected to fall from 15°C to 9°C.* **4** [BECOME WORSE] to become worse, or start to be in a bad situation or condition **gittikçe kötüleşmek; kötüleşmeye/berbat bir hal almaya başlamak** *Education standards are continuing to fall.* ○ *Empty for 30 years, the building had fallen into ruin* (= become very damaged). **5 fall asleep/ill/still, etc** to start to sleep/become ill/become quiet, etc **uykuya dalmak, hasta olmaya başlamak, sessizleşmek** *I fell asleep on the sofa watching TV.* **6 darkness/night falls** *literary* used to say that it is becoming dark **gece/karanlık çökmek** **7** [LOSE POWER] to lose power and start to be controlled by a different leader **iktidardan düşmek, gücü düşmek, başkasının hükmü altına girmeye başlamak** *In 1453 the city fell to the Turks.* **8** [HANG DOWN] to hang down **sarkmak, aşağı doğru sallanmak** *Her long blonde hair fell softly over her shoulders.* ⊃*See also:* fall on deaf ears (ear), fall flat³, fall foul¹ of sb/sth, go/fall to pieces (piece¹), fall into place¹, fall prey¹ to sth, fall by the wayside.

fall apart *phrasal verb* **1** to break into pieces **param-parça olmak, parçalanıp dağılmak** *My poor old boots are falling apart.* **2** to start having problems that you cannot deal with **altından kalkamayacağı sorunlar yaşamaya başlamak** *Their relationship fell apart after they moved to Detroit.*

fall back on sb/sth *phrasal verb* to use someone or something when other things have failed, or when there are no other choices **çaresizlikten kullanmak; ...e/a muhtaç olmak; başvurmak; duçar olmak** *We've been saving up the past few years, to have something to fall back on.*

fall behind *phrasal verb* to not do something fast enough, or not do something by a particular time **bir programın gerisinde kalmak, yetiştirememek** *Lucy's been falling behind in her homework again.*

fall for sb *phrasal verb* to suddenly have strong, romantic feelings about someone **gönlünü kaptırmak, aşık olmak**

fall for sth *phrasal verb* to be tricked into believing something that is not true **kanmak, aklı çelinmek, inanmak, üç kağıda gelmek** *He told me he owned a mansion in Spain and I fell for it.*

fall in *phrasal verb* If a roof or ceiling falls in, it drops to the ground because it is damaged. **(çatı, tavan) çökmek**

fall off *phrasal verb* If the amount, rate, or quality of something falls off, it becomes smaller or lower. **değeri/miktarı/oranı düşmek, azalmak** *Demand for new cars is falling off.*

fall on sth *phrasal verb* to happen on a particular day or date **belli bir günde/tarihte olan/meydana gelen** *New Year's Day falls on a Tuesday this year.*

fall out *phrasal verb UK* to argue with someone and stop being friendly with them **münakaşa etmek/tartışmak, küsmek, arası bozulmak** *Have you and Sam fallen out with each other again?*

fall over *phrasal verb* If someone or something falls over, they fall to the ground or onto their side. **yüz üstü ya da yanlamasına düşmek; boylu boyunca yere uzanmak** *The fence fell over in the wind.* ⊃Orta kısımdaki renkli sayfalarına bakınız.

fall through *phrasal verb* If a plan or agreement falls through, it fails to happen. **(plan, anlaşma) başarısız olmak**

fall ...... İLE BİRLİKTE KULLANILAN KELİMELER

a **dramatic/sharp/steep** fall ● a fall **in** sth

o⁻**fall²** /fɔːl/ *noun* **1** [AMOUNT] [C] when the number or amount of something becomes smaller **düşüş, azalma, küçülme** *There's been a sharp fall in prices.* **2** [MOVEMENT] [C] when someone or something moves down to the ground **düşme** *a heavy fall of snow* **3** [SEASON] [C, U] *US* (*UK/US* **autumn**) the season of the year between summer and winter, when leaves fall from the trees **sonbahar** *He started a new job in the fall.* **4** [DEFEAT] [no plural] when a city, government, leader, etc loses power or control **(lider, hükümet, şehir vb.) düşme, gücünü kaybetme** *the fall of communism*

fallacy /ˈfæləsi/ *noun* [C, U] a belief that is not true or correct **yanılgı, yanlış kanı, safsata** *It's a fallacy that problems will disappear if you ignore them.*

fallen /ˈfɔːlən/ *past participle* of fall **'düşmek' fiilinin üçüncü hali**

fallible /ˈfæləbl/ *adjective* able to make mistakes **hata yapabilir, yanılabilir** *We place our trust in doctors, but even they are fallible.* ⊃Opposite infallible. ● **fallibility** /ˌfæləˈbɪləti/ *noun* [U] **hata yapılabilirlik**

fallout /ˈfɔːlaʊt/ *noun* [U] the radiation (= powerful and dangerous energy) from a nuclear explosion **ışın/nükleer enerji serpintisi, nükleer patlamadan kaynaklanan radyoaktif yayılma**

fallow /ˈfæləʊ/ *adjective* If land is left fallow, it is not planted with crops, in order to improve the quality of the soil. **nadasa bırakılmış, ekilmemiş**

o⁻**false** /fɔːls/ *adjective* **1** [NOT TRUE] not true or correct **yalan, yanlış, asılsız** *a false name* ○ *Many rumours about her life were later proved to be false.* **2** [NOT REAL] not real, but made to look or seem real **sahte, taklit** *false teeth* ○ *false documents* **3** [NOT SINCERE] not sincere or expressing real emotions **yapmacık, sahte, aldatıcı** *false promises* ● **falsely** *adverb* **hatalı bir şekilde, gerçek olmayan**

false a'larm *noun* [C] an occasion when people believe that something dangerous is happening, but it is not **sahte alarm, yanlış uyarı** *Fire engines rushed to the scene, but it was a false alarm.*

falsehood /ˈfɔːlshʊd/ *noun* [C] *formal* a lie **yalan, yanlışlık**

false 'start *noun* [C] an occasion when you try to start an activity, event, or process, but fail and have to stop **başarısız girişim/başlangıç, yanlış teşebbüs** *The after-school club finally opened this term, after several false starts.*

falsify /ˈfɔːlsɪfaɪ/ *verb* [T] to change important information, especially in documents, in order to deceive people **önemli belgelerde tahrifat yapmak, değiştirmek**

falter /ˈfɔːltəʳ/ *verb* [I] **1** to stop being confident, powerful, or successful **gücünü kaybetmek, başarılı olamamak, bocalamak** *In the late 1980s his career began to falter.* **2** to pause, make mistakes, or seem weak when you are talking or moving **tereddüt etmek, duraksa-**

mak, hata yapmak, kekelemek, kem küm etmek *Her voice didn't falter once during the ceremony.* ○ *a few faltering steps*

fame /feɪm/ *noun* [U] when you are known by many people because of your achievements, skills, etc **ün, nam, şan, şeref** *fame and fortune* ○ *She first rose to fame as a pop star at the age of 16.* ⊃See also: sb's/sth's **claim**² to fame.

famed /feɪmd/ *adjective* famous, especially for having particular qualities **ünlü, meşhur, tanınmış** *It is a city famed for its ski slopes and casinos.*

o⁻**familiar** /fə'mɪliə^r/ *adjective* **1** easy to recognize because of being seen, met, heard, etc before **bildik, tanıdık, aşina** *It's nice to see a few familiar faces* (= people that I recognize) *around here.* ○ *This street doesn't look familiar to me.* **2 be familiar with sth** to know about something or have experienced it many times before **aşina olmak, bilmek, tanımak** *Anyone who's familiar with his poetry will find the course easy.* ⊃Opposite unfamiliar. **3** friendly and very informal **samimi, arkadaşça** *He doesn't like to be too familiar with his staff.*

familiarity /fə,mɪli'ærəti/ *noun* [U] **1** a good knowledge of something, or experience of doing or using it **aşinalık, bildik olma, yeterli bilgi/deneyim sahibi olma** *Her familiarity with computers is very impressive.* **2** friendly and informal behaviour **laubalilik, senli benlilik, teklifsizlik, sululuk**

familiarize (*also UK* -ise) /fə'mɪli°raɪz/ *verb* **familiarize sb/yourself with sth** to teach someone more about something new, or try to understand more about it yourself **tanıtmak, bilgilendirmek, aşina duruma getirmek, alıştırmak** *We spent a few minutes familiarizing ourselves with the day's schedule.*

have/raise/start/support a family ● a **big/close/ happy** family ● your **close/extended/immediate** family

o⁻**family** /'fæm°li/ *noun* **1** RELATED PEOPLE [group] a group of people who are related to each other, such as a mother, a father, and their children **aile, soy** *Her (UK) family are/ (US) family is originally from Ireland.* ○ *a family business* **2** CHILDREN [C] the children in a family **ailede çocuklar** [usually singular] *Single parents have to raise a family on their own.* ○ *Paul and Alison are hoping to start a family soon.* **3** PLANTS/ANIMALS [C] a group of similar types of plants or animals that are related to each other **familya, topluluk, bir grup bitki/hayvan**

'**family ,name** *noun* [C] the name that is used by all the members of a family **soyisim/soyadı**

,**family 'planning** *noun* [U] controlling how many children you have by using contraceptives (= pills or objects that prevent a woman from becoming pregnant) **aile planlaması**

,**family 'tree** *noun* [C] a drawing that shows the relationships between the different members of a family, especially over a long period of time **soy ağacı**

famine /'fæmɪn/ *noun* [C, U] when people living in a particular area do not have enough food for a long time causing suffering and death **açlık, kıtlık**

o⁻**famous** /'feɪməs/ *adjective* known or recognized by many people **meşhur, ünlü, tanınmış** *a famous actress* ○ *New York is a city famous for its shopping and nightlife.* ⊃See also: world-famous.

famously /'feɪməsli/ *adverb* **1 get on famously (with sb)** to have a very friendly relationship with someone **biriyle samimi/ arkadaşça ilişki içinde olmak 2** in a way that is famous **tanınmış bir şekilde, meşhurca, ünlü olarak**

a **big/huge** fan ● a **fan of** sb/sth ● **football/soccer** fans

o⁻**fan**¹ /fæn/ *noun* [C] **1** someone who admires and supports a famous person, sport, type of music, etc **hayran, taraftar,** *More than 15,000 Liverpool fans attended Saturday's game.* ○ *He's a big fan of country music.* **2** something that is used to move the air around so that it feels cooler, such as a machine or an object that you wave with your hand **yelpaze, pervane, vantilatör** *an electric fan*

fan

fan² /fæn/ *verb* [T] **fanning,** *past* **fanned** to move the air around with a fan or something used like a fan, to make it feel cooler **havalandırmak, yelpazelemek** [often reflexive] *The spectators sat in the bright sun, fanning themselves with newspapers.*

fan out *phrasal verb* If a group of people fan out, they move out in different directions from a single point. **bir noktadan değişik yönlere dağılmak**

fanatic /fə'nætɪk/ *noun* [C] someone whose interest in something or enthusiasm for something is extreme **bağnaz/tutucu kimse, yobaz, mutaassıp, fanatik** ● **fanatical** *adjective* extremely enthusiastic about something **aşırı, fanatik, gereğinden fazla heyecan/coşku gösteren** *She's fanatical about football.* ● **fanaticism** /fə'nætɪsɪz°m/ *noun* [U] **fanatism**

fanciable /'fænsiəbl/ *adjective* UK *informal* sexually attractive **cinsel cazibeli/çekici**

fanciful /'fænsɪf°l/ *adjective* Something that is fanciful comes from someone's imagination and so is probably not true or real. **hayalci, hayalperest, düşsel, gerçek dışı** *a fanciful story*

'**fan ,club** *noun* [C] an organization for the people who support and admire a particular singer, actor, sports team, etc **taraftar kulübü**

fancy¹ /'fænsi/ *verb* [T] **1** WANT UK to want to have or do something **düşlemek, arzu etmek, canı çekmek, istemek** *Do you fancy a drink?* ○ [+ doing sth] *We fancy going to the Caribbean for our holiday.* **2** PERSON UK *informal* to feel sexually attracted to someone **cinsel olarak çekici/cazibeli bulmak/olmak** *I fancied him the first time I saw him.* **3 fancy (that)!** UK *informal* used to show that you are surprised or shocked by something **Ooo!, Bak sen!, Vay vay vay!** [+ doing sth] *Fancy seeing you here!* **4** THINK *formal* to think that something is true **zannetmek, sanmak, farzetmek** [+ (that)] *I fancy that he was smiling, but I can't be sure.*

fancy² /'fænsi/ *adjective* **1** Fancy things and places are expensive and fashionable. **pahalı, moda olan** *a fancy restaurant* **2** with lots of decoration, or very complicated **süslü, karmaşık, şaşaalı** *fancy cakes*

fancy³ /'fænsi/ *noun* **1 take a fancy to sb/sth** to start to like someone or something a lot **birinden/birşeyden**

çok hoşlanmaya başlamak, beğenmek, sevmek *Marina had taken a fancy to her.* **2 take sb's fancy** If something or someone takes your fancy, you find them interesting or attractive. hoşuna gitmek, ilginç gelmek, enteresan ve çekici bulmak *We can go anywhere that takes your fancy.*

,fancy 'dress *noun* [U] *UK* special clothes that people wear for a party, which make them look like a different person karnaval kıyafeti, balo elbisesi *a fancy dress party*

fanfare /'fænfeə^r/ *noun* [C] a short, loud tune played on a trumpet (= metal musical instrument) to announce an important person or event önemli bir olay veya kişiyi duyuran trampet sesi, boru sesi, fanfar

fang

fang

fang /fæŋ/ *noun* [C] a long, sharp tooth of an animal such as a dog or a snake uzun/sivri/keskin/zehirli diş

'fanny ,pack *US* (*UK* bumbag) *noun* [C] a small bag fixed to a belt that you wear around your waist bel çantası

fantasize (*also UK* -ise) /'fæntəsaɪz/ *verb* [I, T] to imagine something that you would like to happen, but is not likely to happen düşlemek, hayal etmek, düş kurmak *We used to fantasize about becoming famous actresses.*

fantastic /fæn'tæstɪk/ *adjective* **1** [GOOD] *informal* very good harika, şahane *I've had a fantastic time.* **2** [LARGE] *informal* A fantastic amount or number of something is very large. çok fazla, çok büyük, müthiş *They're making fantastic amounts of money.* **3** [STRANGE] very strange and probably not true garip, inanılmaz, gerçeklerden uzak, düşsel *fantastic stories about monsters and witches*

fantastically /fæn'tæstɪk^əli/ *adverb* extremely inanılmaz, oldukça, olağanüstü, hayrete düşürücü *fantastically rich*

fantasy ...... İLE BİRLİKTE KULLANILAN KELİMELER
have fantasies **about/of** (doing) sth ● a fantasy **world**

fantasy /'fæntəsi/ *noun* [C, U] a situation or event that you imagine, which is not real or true fantazi, hayal ürünü şey, rüya

FAQ /,efer'kju:/ *noun* [C] *abbreviation for* frequently asked question: something that many people ask when they use the Internet or a computer program, or a file (= collection) of these questions with their answers **(internet, bilgisayar) Sıkça Sorulan Sorular (SSS)**

o▪**far**¹ /fɑː^r/ *adverb* farther, farthest or further, furthest **1** used to talk about how distant something is uzak, uzakta, uzağa, uzaktan *It's the first time I've been so far away from home.* ○ *How far is it to the supermarket?* ○ *Bournemouth is not far from Poole.* ○ *In the summer the herds move farther north.* **2** a long time uzun süre *How far back can you remember?* ○ *We need to plan further ahead.* **3** far better/cheaper/more, etc much better/cheaper/more, etc çok daha iyi/ucuz/fazla vs. *Young people are far more independent these days.* **4** far too difficult/expensive/late, etc much too difficult/expensive/late, etc çok fazla zor/pahalı/geç vs. *His trousers were far too tight.* **5** as far as I know *informal* used to say what you think is true, although you do not know all the facts bildiğim kadarıyla *As far as I know, they haven't reached a decision yet.* **6** as far as sb is concerned used to say what someone's opinion is bana/ona kalırsa *As far as I'm concerned.* **7** as far as sth is concerned used to say what you are talking about dikkate alındığında/göz önüne alındığında *As far as sport's concerned, I like tennis and football.* **8** by far used to emphasize that something is the biggest, the best, etc kat kat, çok daha *This is his best film by far.* **9** far from sth certainly not something tam tersine, aksine, bilakis *The situation is far from clear.* **10** far from doing sth certainly not doing something ...tan/den öte; ...nın da ötesinde, ... cağına/ceğine *Far from being pleased, he was embarrassed by the praise.* **11** far from it *informal* used to tell someone that something is certainly not true alakası yok, hiç, hiç bir şekilde, katiyen *He's not handsome - far from it.* **12** as far as possible as much as is possible mümkün olduğu kadar *We try to buy organic food as far as possible.* **13** go so far as to do sth to take the extreme action of doing something elinden geldiği kadar, yapabileceği kadar *He even went so far as to stop her using the telephone.* **14** go too far to behave in a way that upsets or annoys other people çok ileri gitmek, haddini bilmemek/aşmak **15** how far used to talk about how true something is Ne kadar? Ne kadarını? *How far do politicians represent the views of ordinary people?* **16** so far until now şu ana dek/kadar/değin *So far, we haven't made much progress.* **17** so far so good *informal* used to say that something has gone well until now şu ana dek her şey yolunda; her şey iyi gidiyor **18** not go (very) far If something such as money does not go far, you cannot do very much with it. iş görmez, yeterli olmaz, faydası olmaz *£1 doesn't go very far these days.*

o▪**far**² /fɑː^r/ *adjective* farther, farthest or further, furthest **1** [always before noun] describes the part of something that is most distant from you or from the centre uzak, ötede, uzakta, ötede *His office is at the far end of the corridor.* ○ *They live in the far south of the country.* **2** the far left/right used to describe political groups whose opinions are very extreme aşırı sağcı/solcu ⊃See also: be a far cry² from sth.

faraway /,fɑːrə'weɪ/ *adjective* **1** [always before noun] *literary* a long distance away uzak, uzakta, ötelerde *faraway places* **2** a faraway look/expression an expression on someone's face that shows that they are not thinking about what is happening around them uzaklara dalmış, dalgın, hülyalı, dalıp uzaklara gitmiş *He had a faraway look in his eyes.*

farce /fɑːs/ *noun* **1** [no plural] a serious event or situation that becomes ridiculous because it is so badly organized kötü düzenlemeden dolayı komediye dönen ciddi olay/durum, ele yüze bulaştırılan ve komik duruma düşürülen olay *The meeting was a complete farce.* **2** [C] a funny play in which a lot of silly things happen kaba güldürü, basit güldürü, tuluat ● farci-

cal /ˈfɑːsɪkᵊl/ *adjective* like a farce **gülünç, saçma, tuhaf, basit güldürü**

🧩 **fare** ...... İLE BİRLİKTE KULLANILAN KELİMELER

a **return/single** fare ● the fare **to** [Seattle/Moscow, etc]

fare¹ /feəʳ/ *noun* [C] the price that you pay to travel on an aircraft, train, bus, etc **taşıt ücreti, bilet ücreti, yol parası** *air/train fares*

fare² /feəʳ/ *verb formal* **fare well/badly/better, etc** used to say how well or badly someone or something does in a particular situation **iyi/kötü/çok daha iyi yapmak, olmak, gitmek** *All the children fared well in the exams.*

farewell /ˌfeəˈwel/ *exclamation old-fashioned* goodbye **Allaha ısmarladık!; Hoşça kalın!; Elveda! ● farewell** *noun* [C] when someone says goodbye **elveda deme, veda etme** *a sad farewell ○ a farewell party*

far-fetched /ˌfɑːˈfetʃt/ *adjective* difficult to believe and not likely to be true **inanması güç, abartılı, imkânsız, mübalağalı** *The idea is not as far-fetched as it might sound.*

🧩 **farm** ...... İLE BİRLİKTE KULLANILAN KELİMELER

on a farm ● farm **workers** ● farm **animals**

farm

o--**farm¹** /fɑːm/ *noun* [C] an area of land with fields and buildings that is used for growing crops and keeping animals as a business **çiftlik** *a dairy farm ○ farm animals/buildings*

farm² /fɑːm/ *verb* [I, T] to grow crops or keep animals as a business **çiftçilik/rençperlik yapmak** *Only 2% of the country's farmland is farmed organically.*

o--**farmer** /ˈfɑːməʳ/ *noun* [C] someone who owns or looks after a farm **çiftçi, rençper**

farmhouse /ˈfɑːmhaʊs/ *noun* [C] *plural* **farmhouses** /ˈfɑːmhaʊzɪz/ the house on a farm where the farmer lives **çiftlik evi**

farming /ˈfɑːmɪŋ/ *noun* [U] working on a farm or organizing the work there **çiftçilik, rençperlik**

farmland /ˈfɑːmlænd/ *noun* [U] land which is used for or suitable for farming **çiftlik arazisi**

farmyard /ˈfɑːmjɑːd/ *noun* [C] an area of ground with farm buildings around it **çiflik avlusu, çiftlik binalarının bulunduğu alan**

far-off /ˌfɑːrˈɒf/ *adjective literary* a long distance away or a long time in the past or future **çok uzak, çok eski** *far-off lands*

far-reaching /ˌfɑːˈriːtʃɪŋ/ *adjective* Far-reaching acts, events, or ideas have very big effects. **geniş kapsamlı, büyük alana etki eden** *far-reaching changes in the education system*

farsighted /ˈfɑːˌsaɪtɪd/ *US* (*UK* **long-sighted**) *adjective* able to see objects which are far away, but not things which are near to you **uzağı iyi görebilen, hipermetrop**

fart /fɑːt/ *verb* [I] *very informal* to release gas from the bowels through the bottom **gaz çıkarmak ● fart** *noun* **gaz çıkarma**

farther /ˈfɑːðəʳ/ *adjective, adverb comparative of* far: more distant **daha uzağa/uzakta; daha ötede/öteye** *I couldn't walk any farther.*

farthest /ˈfɑːðɪst/ *adjective, adverb superlative of* far: most distant **en uzağa/uzakta; en ötede/öteye** *They walked to the farthest edge of the garden.*

fascinate /ˈfæsɪneɪt/ *verb* [T] to interest someone a lot **büyülemek, hayran bırakmak** *Science has always fascinated me.*

fascinated /ˈfæsɪneɪtɪd/ *adjective* extremely interested **büyülenmiş, hayran olmuş** *They were absolutely fascinated by the game.*

fascinating /ˈfæsɪneɪtɪŋ/ *adjective* extremely interesting **büyüleyen, hayran bırakan** *I found the movie fascinating.*

fascination /ˌfæsɪˈneɪʃᵊn/ *noun* [U, no plural] when you find someone or something fascinating **cazibe, çekicilik, büyüleyicilik** *Her fascination with fashion started at an early age.*

fascism, Fascism /ˈfæʃɪzᵊm/ *noun* [U] a political system in which the government is extremely powerful and controls people's lives **faşizm; devletin insanların yaşamında herşeye hakim olduğu siyasî sistem**

fascist /ˈfæʃɪst/ *noun* [C] **1** (*also* **Fascist**) someone who supports fascism **faşist 2** someone who you do not like because they try to control other people's behaviour **baskıcı, kontrol altına almayı seven, faşist ● fascist** *adjective a fascist dictator/regime* **faşist**

🧩 **fashion** ...... İLE BİRLİKTE KULLANILAN KELİMELER

be **in** fashion ● **come into/go out of** fashion ● a fashion **for** sth

o--**fashion¹** /ˈfæʃᵊn/ *noun* **1** STYLE [C, U] the most popular style of clothes, appearance, or behaviour at a particular time **moda** *Long hair is back in fashion for men.* ○ *Fur coats have gone out of fashion.* **2** BUSINESS [U] making and selling clothes **kıyafet üretip satma** *the fashion industry* **3** WAY [no plural] the way in which someone does something **biçim, şekil, tarz, üslup, stil** *He told the story in a very amusing fashion.*

fashion² /ˈfæʃᵊn/ *verb* [T] *formal* to make something **yapmak, biçim/şekil vermek** *jewellery fashioned from recycled metal*

fashionable /ˈfæʃᵊnəbl/ *adjective* popular at a particular time **moda, modaya uygun** *fashionable clothes* ○ [+ to do sth] *It's no longer fashionable to smoke.* ᴐOpposite **unfashionable. ● fashionably** *adverb fashionably dressed* **moda ile ilgili**

fast ...... BAŞKA BİR DEYİŞLE

Eğer **fast** kelimesini sıfat olarak kullanmak istiyorsanız, buna bir alternatif olarak **quick** kelimesi kullanılabilir. *I tried to catch him, but he was too quick for me.*
Eğer bir şey hiç beklenmeden çok hızlı yapıldıysa, **prompt** veya **speedy** sıfatları kullanılabilir. *A prompt reply would be very much appreciated.* ● *He made a speedy recovery.*

Eğer bir şey çok dikkatli düşünmeden ve çok hızlı bir şekilde yapıldıysa, **hasty** ve **hurried** sıfatları kullanılabilir. *I don't want to make a* **hasty** *decision.* ● *We left early after a* **hurried** *breakfast.*

Hızlı yürüyüş genellikle **brisk** kelimesiyle ifade edilir. *We took a* **brisk** *walk through the park.*

Rapid sıfatı genellikle hızlı gelişim ve değişimi ifade etmekte kullanılır. *The 1990's were a period of* **rapid** *change/growth.*

Fast kelimesini zarf olarak kullanmak istiyorsanız, bu durumda **quickly** bir alternatif olarak kullanılabilir. *The problem needs to be sorted out as* **quickly** *as possible.*

Eğer kişi bir şeyi çok hızlı yapıyorsa, resmi olmayan ortamlarda, durumun ifadesi için **in a flash** veya **like a shot** söylemleri kulanılabilir. *I'll be back in a* **flash**. ● *There was an almighty crash and he got up* **like a shot**.

✪**fast¹** /fɑːst/ *adjective* **1** moving, happening, or doing something quickly **hızlı, süratli, çabuk** *fast cars* ○ *a fast swimmer* ○ *Computers are getting faster all the time.* **2** [never before noun] If a clock or watch is fast, it shows a time that is later than the correct time. **ileri; (zaman) ileri giden** ⊃See also: a fast **track¹** (to sth).

✪**fast²** /fɑːst/ *adverb* **1** moving or happening quickly **hızlıca, süratle, çabucak, ivedi, acilen** *We ran as fast as we could.* ○ *You'll have to act fast.* **2 fast asleep** completely asleep (= sleeping) **derin uykuda, derin uykuya dalmış 3** in a firm or tight way **sıkı sıkıya, sıkıca, sağlamca** *He tried to get away, but she held him fast.* ⊃See also: **thick¹** and fast.

fast³ /fɑːst/ *verb* [I] to eat nothing, or much less than you usually eat for a period of time **oruç tutmak** ● **fast** *noun* [C] **oruç**

✪**fasten** /ˈfɑːsᵊn/ *verb* **1** [I, T] to close or fix something together, or to become closed or fixed together **bağlamak, tutturmak; bağlanmak, tutturulmak** *Fasten your seat belts.* ○ *This dress fastens at the side.* **2 fasten sth on/to/together, etc** to fix one thing to another **bağlamak, tutturmak, sabitlemek** *He fastened the rope to a tree.* ⊃Opposite **unfasten.**

fastener /ˈfɑːsᵊnəʳ/ *noun* [C] something that is used to close or fix things together **çıt çıt, bağ, toka, kopça**

,**fast 'food** *noun* [U] hot food that can be served very quickly in a restaurant because it is already prepared **ayaküstü yenilen yemek** *fast food restaurants*

fast-forward /ˌfɑːstˈfɔːwəd/ *verb* [I, T] If you fast-forward a recording, or if it fast-forwards, you make it play at very high speed so that you get to the end more quickly. **hızlı sarmak, hızlı çalmak** ● **fast-forward** *noun* [U] **ileri sarma (teyp)**

fastidious /fæsˈtɪdiəs/ *adjective* Someone who is fastidious wants every detail of something to be correct and perfect. **zor beğenir, titiz, müşkülpesent,**

✪**fat¹** /fæt/ *adjective* **fatter, fattest 1** Someone who is fat weighs too much. **şişman, şişko** *She eats all the time but never gets fat.* **2** thick or large **kalın, büyük, iri** *a fat book* ⊃See also: fat **chance¹**.

fat² /fæt/ *noun* **1** [U] the substance under the skin of people and animals that keeps them warm **yağ, yağ tabakası** *body fat* **2** [C, U] a solid or liquid substance like oil that is taken from plants or animals and used in cooking **(bitkisel/hayvansal) yemeklik yağ** *animal/vegetable fat* ⊃See also: saturated fat.

fatal /ˈfeɪtᵊl/ *adjective* **1** A fatal accident or illness causes death. **ölümcül, ölümle sonuçlanan** *a fatal car crash* **2** Fatal actions have very bad effects. **talihsiz, kötü sonuçlar doğuran, tehlikeli** *a fatal error* ● **fatally** *adverb* **fatally injured** **ölümcül**

fatalism /ˈfeɪtᵊlɪzᵊm/ *noun* [U] the belief that people cannot change events, and that bad events cannot be avoided **kadercilik, yazgıcılık** ● **fatalistic** /ˌfeɪtᵊlˈɪstɪk/ *adjective* **kötü olayların önlenemiyeceği düşüncesi**

fatality /fəˈtæləti/ *noun* [C] *formal* the death of a person caused by violence or an accident **kaza/şiddet sonucu ölüm/can kaybı**

'**fat ,cat** *noun* [C] someone who has a lot of money, especially someone in charge of a company **para babası, çok zengin, patron**

fate .... İLE BİRLİKTE KULLANILAN KELİMELER

suffer a fate ● **decide/seal** sb's fate ● [suffer] **the same/a similar** fate

fate /feɪt/ *noun* **1** [C] what happens to someone, especially when it is something bad **son, akıbet, ölüm** *His fate is now in the hands of the jury.* **2** [U] a power that some people believe decides what will happen **kader, kısmet, talih, yazgı, alın yazısı** *I believe it was fate that caused us to meet again.* ⊃See also: **quirk** of fate.

fated /ˈfeɪtɪd/ *adjective* [never before noun] If something that happens or someone's actions are fated, they are decided by a power that controls events, and cannot be avoided. **mukadder, alnına yazılmış** [+ to do sth] *I seem fated to meet him wherever I go.* ⊃See also: **ill-fated.**

fateful /ˈfeɪtfᵊl/ *adjective* A fateful event has an important and usually bad effect on the future. **geleceği belirleyen, çok önemli, geleceği etkileyen, tarihi öneme haiz** *a fateful decision*

✪**father¹** /ˈfɑːðəʳ/ *noun* **1** [C] your male parent **baba 2 Father** The title of some Christian priests **peder, papaz (efendi)** *Father O'Brian* **3 the father of sth** the man who invented or started something **bir şeyi ilk keşfeden/başlatan/kurucu/babası** *Descartes is known as the father of modern philosophy.*

father² /ˈfɑːðəʳ/ *verb* [T] *formal* to become a male parent **baba olmak** *He fathered three children.*

,**Father 'Christmas** *noun* [no plural] *UK* a kind, fat, old man in red clothes who people say brings presents to children at Christmas **Noel Baba**

'**father ,figure** *noun* [C] an older man who gives you advice and support like a father **babacan insan, baba**

fatherhood /ˈfɑːðəhʊd/ *noun* [U] being a father **babalık**

father-in-law /ˈfɑːðərɪnlɔː/ *noun* [C] *plural* **fathers-in-law** the father of your husband or wife **kayınpeder, kayınbaba**

fathom¹ /ˈfæðəm/ *(also UK* **fathom out)** *verb* [T] to be able to understand something after thinking about it a lot **(bir şeyin iç yüzünü) kavramak, öğrenmek, anlamak** [+ question word] *No one could fathom why she had left so early.*

fathom² /ˈfæðəm/ *noun* [C] a unit for measuring the depth of water, equal to 1.8 metres **kulaç**

fatigue /fəˈtiːg/ *noun* [U] when you feel very tired **bitkinlik, aşırı yorgunluk** ● **fatigued** *adjective* **yorgun**

fatigues /fəˈtiːgz/ *noun* [plural] special clothes that soldiers wear when they are fighting or working **asker üniforması, kamuflaj elbisesi**

fatten /ˈfætᵊn/ *verb* [T] to make animals fatter so that they can be eaten **semir(t)mek, şişmanla(t)mak**
fatten sb/sth up *phrasal verb* to give a thin person or animal lots of food so that they become fatter **semirtmek, iyi beslemek, şişmanlatmak**

fattening /ˈfætᵊnɪŋ/ *adjective* Fattening food can make you fat. **şişmanlatan** *I don't eat chips, they're too fattening.*

fatty /ˈfæti/ *adjective* Fatty foods contain a lot of fat. **yağlı**

fatuous /ˈfætjuəs/ *adjective* very stupid and not deserving your attention or respect **anlamsız, saçma, yersiz** *a fatuous comment/remark*

faucet /ˈfɔːsɪt/ *US* (*UK/US* tap) *noun* [C] an object at the end of a pipe which you turn to control the flow of water **musluk** ◆See picture at **tap** ◆Orta kısımdaki renkli sayfalarına bakınız.

---

fault ... İLE BİRLİKTE KULLANILAN KELİMELER

all entirely sb's fault • **it's** sb's **own** fault • **be at** fault

---

o⸱**fault¹** /fɔːlt/ *noun* **1** sb's **fault** If something bad that has happened is someone's fault, they are responsible for it. **birinin yanlışı hatası kusuru yanılgısı** *She believes it was the doctor's fault that Peter died.* **2 at fault** responsible for something bad that has happened **kabahatli, hatalı, kusurlu** *I was at fault and I would like to apologize.* **3** [C] something that is wrong with something or with someone's character **yanılgı, hata, kusur, yanlış** *The car has a serious design fault.* **4 find fault with** sb/sth to criticize someone or something, especially without good reasons ...den/dan **yakınmak, şikayet etmek, eleştirmek**

fault² /fɔːlt/ *verb* [T] to find a reason to criticize someone or something **hata/kusur/yanlış/kabahat bulmak, eleştirmek** *I can't fault the way that they dealt with the complaint.*

faultless /ˈfɔːltləs/ *adjective* perfect, or without any mistakes **kusursuz, hatasız, mükemmel** *a faultless performance*

faulty /ˈfɔːlti/ *adjective* not working correctly **bozuk, arızalı, hatalı** *faulty brakes/wiring*

fauna /ˈfɔːnə/ *noun* [group] all the animals that live in a particular area **(belli bir bölgede yaşayan) hayvanların tümü, fauna, direy** *the flora and fauna of the area*

favour¹ *UK* (*US* favor) /ˈfeɪvəʳ/ *noun* **1** [HELP] [C] something that you do to help someone **iyilik, lütuf** *Could you do me a favour please?* ○ *I wanted to ask you a favour.* **2 be in favour of sth** to agree with or approve of a plan or idea ...den/dan **yana olmak, taraftarı/detekçisi olmak** *Most people are in favour of reducing traffic in cities.* **3 in favour of** sb/sth If you refuse or get rid of someone or something in favour of someone or something else, you choose them instead. ...nin/nın **yararına/lehine** *They dropped him from the team in favour of a much younger player.* **4 in** sb's **favour** **a** [ADVANTAGE] If something is in your favour, it helps you to win or succeed. **(birinin) lehine/lehinde** *Both sides have strong arguments in their favour.* **b** [WINNING] If a game, vote, or judgment is in someone's favour, they win. ...in/ın **lehine/yararına** *The final score was 16-10 in England's favour.* **5** [LIKE] [U] *formal* when people like something or someone **beğeni, ilgi, alaka** *Her work never found favour among the critics.* **6 be in favour/out of favour** to be popular/unpopular **gözde olmak/gözden düşmek, hâlâ beğenilen/beğenilmemek** *He has fallen out of favour recently.*

favour² *UK* (*US* favor) /ˈfeɪvəʳ/ *verb* [T] **1** to choose or prefer one possibility **beğenmek, desteklemek, olumlu bakmak** [often passive] *These are the running shoes favoured by marathon runners.* **2** to act unfairly by treating one person better than another **taraflı davranmak, kollamak, lehinde davranmak, kayırmak** *She always felt that her parents favoured her brother.*

favourable *UK* (*US* favorable) /ˈfeɪvᵊrəbl/ *adjective* **1** showing that you like or approve of someone or something, or making you like or approve of them **müsbet, lehte, olumlu** *She made a very favourable impression on us.* **2** making something more likely to be successful **uygun, elverişli, olumlu, müsait** *favourable weather conditions* ◆Opposite **unfavourable**. • **favourably** *adverb* **müsait, uygun bir şekilde**

o⸱**favourite¹** *UK* (*US* favorite) /ˈfeɪvᵊrət/ *adjective* [always before noun] Your favourite person or thing is the one that you like best. **gözde, favori, çok beğenilen/tutulan** *What's your favourite band?*

favourite² *UK* (*US* favorite) /ˈfeɪvᵊrət/ *noun* [C] **1** a person or thing that you like more than all others **favori/gözde biri ya da şey** *These chocolates are my favourites.* **2** the person or animal that is most likely to win a competition **favori, önde/iyi/kazanması muhtemel olan** *The Dallas Cowboys are now favourites to win.*

favouritism *UK* (*US* favoritism) /ˈfeɪvᵊrətɪzᵊm/ *noun* [U] unfairly treating one person or group better than another **iltimas, adam kayırma/tutma, kayırmacılık**

fawn¹ /fɔːn/ *noun* **1** [C] a young deer **yavru geyik, geyik yavrusu** **2** [U] a light brown colour **açık kahverengi**

fawn² /fɔːn/ *verb*
fawn on/over sb *phrasal verb* to praise someone or be nice to someone in a way that is false in order to get something or to make them like you **yalakalık yapmak, yaltaklanmak, dalkavukluk yapmak, (argo) kıçını yalamak**

fax¹ /fæks/ *noun* **1** [DOCUMENT] [C] a document that is sent or received using a special machine and a telephone line **belgegeçer iletisi** *I got a fax from them this morning.* **2** [SYSTEM] [U] the system of sending or receiving documents using a special machine and a telephone line **belgegeçerle belge gönderme/alma** *Some products can be ordered by fax.* **3** [MACHINE] [C] (*also* 'fax machine) a machine that is used to send and receive faxes **belgegeçer/faks** ◆Orta kısımdaki renkli sayfalarına bakınız.

fax² /fæks/ *verb* [T] to send documents using a fax machine **belgegeçerle/faksla ileti göndermek** [+ two objects] *Can you fax me a price list?*

the FBI /ˌefbiːˈaɪ/ *noun abbreviation for* the Federal Bureau of Investigation: one of the national police forces in the US that is controlled by the central government **Federal Soruşturma Bürosu** *He is wanted by the FBI for fraud.*

---

fear ... İLE BİRLİKTE KULLANILAN KELİMELER

allay/calm/cause/heighten fear • **hold** no fear for sb • **great/morbid/widespread** fear • fear **of** sth

---

o⸱**fear¹** /fɪəʳ/ *noun* **1** [C, U] a strong, unpleasant feeling that you get when you think that something bad, dangerous, or frightening might happen **korku, endişe** *She was trembling with fear.* ○ *Unlike the rest of us, Dave had no fear of snakes.* ○ [+ (that)] *There are fears that the disease will spread to other countries.* **2 for fear of** sth/doing sth because you are worried about something/doing something **birşey/birşeyi yapma korkusu/endişesi** *I didn't want to move for fear of waking her up.*

fear² /fɪəʳ/ *verb* [T] **1** to be worried or frightened that something bad might happen or might have happened **korkmak, ürpermek, endişelenmek** [+ (that)] *Police fear that the couple may have drowned.* **2** to be frightened of something or someone unpleasant **kaygılanmak, endişe duymak, korkmak** *Most older employees fear unemployment.* **3 fear the worst** If you fear the worst, you are frightened that an unpleasant situation will become much worse. **en kötüsü olmasından kormak/endişe duymak** *When there was no sign of the children, rescuers feared the worst.*

fear for sth/sb *phrasal verb* to be worried about something, or to be worried that someone is in danger **birinden/birşeyden ürpermek/kormak/endişe duymak; kaygı duymak** *Her parents fear for her safety* (= worry that she may not be safe).

fearful /ˈfɪəfəl/ *adjective formal* **1** frightened or worried **korkmuş, korku içinde, endişeli** [+ of + doing sth] *Many women are fearful of travelling alone.* **2** [always before noun] *UK* very bad **korkunç, çok fena** *Nigel has a fearful temper.* ● **fearfully** *adverb* **korku dolu**

fearless /ˈfɪələs/ *adjective* not frightened of anything **korkusuz, gözüpek, pervasız** *a fearless fighter* ● **fearlessly** *adverb* **korkusuzca**

fearsome /ˈfɪəsəm/ *adjective* very frightening **ürkütücü, dehşet verici, korkunç** *a fearsome opponent*

feasible /ˈfiːzəbl/ *adjective* possible to do **yapılabilir, gerçekleştirilebilir, uygulanabilir, mümkün, olanaklı** *a feasible plan* ○ [+ to do sth] *It may be feasible to clone human beings, but is it ethical?* ● **feasibility** /ˌfiːzəˈbɪləti/ *noun* [U] **olasılık**

feast¹ /fiːst/ *noun* [C] a large meal, especially to celebrate something special **şölen, ziyafet** *a wedding feast*

feast² /fiːst/ *verb*
feast on sth *phrasal verb* to eat a lot of food and enjoy it very much **tıka basa yemek, ne bulursa yemek, tıkınmak** *We feasted on fried chicken, ice cream, and chocolate cake.*

feat /fiːt/ *noun* **1** [C] an act or achievement that shows great skill or strength **olağanüstü başarı, büyük ustalık, kahramanlık, yüreklilik, yiğitlik, marifet** *The Eiffel Tower is a remarkable feat of engineering.* **2 be no mean feat** used when you want to emphasize that an act or achievement is very difficult **imkansız olmak, zor/başarması zor olmak, bir şeyin öğrenilmesi/başarılması artık birinden geçmiş olmak** *Learning to ski at 60 is no mean feat!*

feather /ˈfeðər/ *noun* [C] one of the soft, light things that grow from and cover a bird's skin **tüy, kuş tüyü** ● **feathery** *adjective* like feathers **tüylü, tüylerle kaplı** *feathery leaves*

🧩 **feature** .... İLE BİRLİKTE KULLANILAN KELİMELER

a **distinguishing/important/notable** feature ● a **redeeming** feature ● a feature **of** sth ● a **new** feature

◦←**feature¹** /ˈfiːtʃər/ *noun* [C] **1** PART a typical quality, or important part of something **özellik, nitelik, hususiyet** *This phone has several new features.* **2** FACE Someone's features are the parts of their face that you notice when you look at them. **(yüzdeki) belirgin özellik, dikkat çeken kısım** *His eyes are his best feature.* **3** NEWSPAPER a special article in a newspaper or magazine, or a special television programme **(belli bir konuda) dergi gazete veya tv programında özel makale/yazı** *a double-page feature on global warming*

feature² /ˈfiːtʃər/ *verb* [T] to include someone or something as an important part **birini/birşeyi önemli bir bölüme dahil etmek/yer vermek** *a new movie featuring Bruce Willis*
feature in sth *phrasal verb* to be an important part of something **bir şeyin önemli bir kısmı/bölümü olmak**

'feature ˌfilm *noun* [C] a film that is usually 90 or more minutes long **90 dakika veya daha uzun film**

◦←**February** /ˈfebruəri/ (*written abbreviation* **Feb**) *noun* [C, U] the second month of the year **Şubat ayı**

feces /ˈfiːsiːz/ *noun* [plural] *US spelling of* **faeces dışkı**

feckless /ˈfekləs/ *adjective* A feckless person is not willing to work or take responsibility for their actions. **mıymıntı, sorumsuz ve beceriksiz, zayıf karakterli**

fed /fed/ *past of* feed **'beslemek' fiilinin ikinci hali**

federal /ˈfedərəl/ *adjective* [always before noun] **1** relating to the central government, and not to the government of a region, of some countries such as the United States **federal, birleşik** *the federal government* ○ *a federal agency/employee* **2** A federal system of government consists of a group of regions that is controlled by a central government. **federal sisteme ait; merkezî hükümet tarafından kontrol edilen bir grup bölge hükümetlerinden oluşan sistem**

ˌfederal 'holiday *US* (*UK/US* national holiday) *noun* [C] a day when most people in a country do not have to work **federal tatil**

federalism /ˈfedərəlɪzəm/ *noun* [U] a political system in which separate states are organized under a central government **merkezî hükümetin başkanlığında oluşan ayrı hükümetlerin oluşturduğu siyasi sistem** ● **federalist** *noun* [C] someone who supports federalism **federalizmi destekleyen**

federation /ˌfedərˈeɪʃən/ *noun* [C] a group of organizations, countries, regions, etc that have joined together to form a larger organization or government **federasyon, kuruluşlar/ülkeler/bölgeler birliği** *the International Tennis Federation*

ˌfed 'up *adjective informal* [never before noun] annoyed or bored by something that you have experienced for too long **bıkmış, bıkkın, usanmış, bezmiş** *I'm fed up with my job.*

fee /fiː/ *noun* [C] an amount of money that you pay to do something, to use something, or to get a service **ücret** *an entrance fee* ○ *university fees*

feeble /ˈfiːbl/ *adjective* **1** extremely weak **zayıf, halsiz, dermansız, güçsüz** *She became too feeble to get out of bed.* **2** not very good or effective **etkin ve iyi olmayan, zayıf, yavan, soğuk, aptalca** *a feeble argument/excuse* ● **feebly** *adverb* **güçsüz bir durumda**

◦←**feed¹** /fiːd/ *verb past* **fed 1** GIVE FOOD [T] to give food to a person, group, or animal **beslemek, yedirmek, karnını doyurmak** *I fed Simone's cat while she was away.* **2** EAT FOOD [I] If an animal or a baby feeds, it eats. **yemek, beslenmek, karnını doyurmak** *The caterpillars feed on cabbage leaves.* **3** SUPPLY [T] to supply something such as information to a person or a machine, especially in a regular or continuous way **vermek, beslemek, sağlamak** *We fed them false information about our plans.* ⊃See also: **breast-feed.**

feed² /fiːd/ *noun* **1** [U] food for animals that are not kept as pets **besin, yiyecek, yem** *cattle/chicken feed* **2** [C] *UK* (*US* feeding) a meal for a baby or an animal **bebek/hayvan yiyeceği/maması** *He has three feeds during the night.*

🧩 **feedback** .... İLE BİRLİKTE KULLANILAN KELİMELER

get/give/provide feedback ● **negative/positive** feedback ● feedback **on** sth ● feedback **from** sb

feedback /ˈfiːdbæk/ *noun* [U] an opinion from someone about something that you have done or made **geribildirim, geri besleme** *positive/negative feedback* ○ *We've had lots of feedback on these new products from our customers.*

◦←**feel¹** /fiːl/ *verb past* **felt 1** EXPERIENCE [I, T] to experience an emotion or a physical feeling **hissetmek, hissini duy**

mak *You shouldn't feel embarrassed about making a mistake.* ○ *I felt a sharp pain in my side when I stood up.* ○ *"Are you feeling better?" "Yes, thanks, I feel fine now."* **2 feel better/different/strange, etc; feel like/ as if** If you describe the way a place, situation, or object feels, you say how it seems to you, or what your experience of it is like. **daha iyi/farklı/acayip vb. hissetmek; sanki öyle hissetmek, ...gibi hissetmet** *It felt strange to see him again after so long.* ○ *The house feels empty without the children.* ○ *This shirt feels tight under my arms.* ○ *I feel as if I've known you for ages.* **3 feel like sb/sth** to seem to be similar to a type of person, thing, or situation **birine/bir şeye benzemek; ...nın gibi görünmek** *My feet feel like blocks of ice.* ○ *I felt like a fool when I saw what everyone else was wearing.* **4** OPINION [I, T] to think something or have an opinion **hissetmek, inanmak, fikrine kapılma, düşünmek** [+ (that)] *I feel that he's the best person for the job.* ○ *Do you feel strongly* (= have strong opinions) *about it?* **5** TOUCH [I, T] to touch something, especially with your hands, in order to examine it **dokunarak hissetmek/ incelemek** *He felt her ankle to see if it was broken.* **6 feel like sth/doing sth** to want something, or want to do something **bir şeyi yapmayı canı istemek/canı çekmek** *I feel like some chocolate.* ○ *Jane felt like crying.* **7** BE AWARE [T] to be aware of something **farkına varmak, hissetmek, duymak** *You could feel the tension in the room.* ○ *I could feel them watching me.* ⊃See also: feel free¹, feel the pinch², be/feel under the weather¹.

feel for sb *phrasal verb* to feel sorry for someone because they are very unhappy, or in a difficult situation **birine acımak, sempati duymak, üzülmek, üzüntü duymak**

feel² /fiːl/ *noun* **1** [no plural] the way that something seems, or feels when you touch it **(dokunulduğunda) bir şeyin verdiği his, duygu** *I love the feel of silk against my skin.* ○ *His art has a very modern feel to it.* **2 a feel for sth** *informal* the ability to do something or use something well **bir şeyi iyi kullanma/ yapma yeteneği/hissi** *Once you get a feel for it, using the mouse is easy.* ○ *Claire has a feel for this kind of work.*

feel-good /ˈfiːlɡʊd/ *adjective* causing happy feelings about life **iyi his veren, mutlu eden, hayata bağlayan** *a feel-good story*

feeling ...... BAŞKA BİR DEYİŞLE

Feeling kelimesinin bir diğer alternatif kullanımı **emotion** kelimesiyle ifade edilir. *He finds it hard to express his* **emotions**.

Pang veya **stab** kelimeleri ani, kuvvetli ve kötü bir duygunun ifadesi için kullanılır. *Amelia felt a sharp* **pang** *of jealousy when she saw her.* ● *He felt a* **stab** *of regret as he looked at his son.*

Az miktarda hissedilen kötü bir duygunun ifadesi için **tinge** kelimesi kullanılır. *It was with a* **tinge** *of sadness that she finally said goodbye.*

o▪**feeling** /ˈfiːlɪŋ/ *noun* **1** EMOTION [C, U] emotion **his, duygu** *guilty feelings* ○ *a feeling of joy/sadness* ○ *Her performance was completely lacking in feeling.* **2** PHYSICAL [C, U] when you feel something physical **duyu** *I had a tingling feeling in my fingers.* ○ *Pablo lost all feeling* (= could not feel anything) *in his feet.* **3** OPINION [C] an opinion or belief **fikir, inanç, düşünce, his** *My feeling is that we should wait until they come back.* **4 have/get a feeling (that)...** to think that something is likely... **Bir şeyin kanısını/sezgisini/düşüncesini taşımak; kanısına hissine sahip olmak** *I had a feeling he'd be there.* ○ *I get the feeling that he doesn't like me.* **5 bad/ill feeling** when people are upset or angry with each other **kızma, gücenme, hiddet, öfke**

---

feelings ...... İLE BİRLİKTE KULLANILAN KELİMELER

express/hide/show your feelings ● **hurt** sb's feelings ● a **funny / horrible / nasty / wonderful** feeling ● **mixed/strong** feelings

feelings /ˈfiːlɪŋz/ *noun* **1** [plural] Your feelings are your beliefs and emotions. **inançlar, duygular, hisler** *You can't hide your feelings from me.* **2 hurt sb's feelings** to make someone feel unhappy **birinin duygularını/ hislerini incitmek; mutsuz etmek**

feet /fiːt/ *plural of* foot **ayaklar**

feign /feɪn/ *verb* [T] *formal* If you feign an emotion, illness, etc, you pretend to have it. **yapar gibi görünmek, yalandan yapmak, yapıyormuş gibi davranmak, numara yapmak** *He feigned illness to avoid having to work.*

feisty /ˈfaɪsti/ *adjective* active, confident, and determined **hareketli, emin, kararlı, azimli** *a feisty young woman*

feline /ˈfiːlaɪn/ *adjective* relating to cats, or like a cat **kedigillerden olan, kedi gibi**

fell¹ /fel/ *verb* [T] **1** to cut down a tree **ağaç kesmek 2** to knock someone down **düşürmek, yere sermek** *He was felled with a single punch.*

fell² /fel/ *past tense of* fall **'düşmek' fiilinin ikinci hali**

fella (*also* feller) /ˈfelə/ *noun* [C] *informal* a man **adam**

fellow¹ /ˈfeləʊ/ *noun* [C] **1** MAN *old-fashioned* a man **adam, herif, insan, ahbap, dost, arkadaş** *a big fellow with broad shoulders* **2** COLLEGE someone whose job is to teach or study a particular subject at some colleges or universities **üniversitede belli bir konuda çalışan veya öğreten hoca veya öğrenci** *She's a research fellow at St Peter's college.* **3** MEMBER a member of an official organization for a particular subject or job **üye**

fellow² /ˈfeləʊ/ *adjective* **fellow countrymen/students, etc** used to describe people who share your interests or situation **hemşehri, memleketli, arkadaş, dost** *She's earned enormous respect from her fellow artists.*

fellowship /ˈfeləʊʃɪp/ *noun* **1** JOB [C] a job teaching or studying a particular subject at some colleges or universities **üniversitede belli bir konuda/konuyu çalışma veya öğretme** *a research fellowship at Harvard* **2** FEELING [U] a friendly feeling among people **arkadaşlık, dostluk 3** GROUP [C] a group of people who share the same interests or beliefs **dernek, kurum, birlik, cemiyet**

felon /ˈfelən/ *noun* [C] someone who is guilty of a serious crime in the US (ABD) **ağır ceza suçlusu, cürüm işleyen kişi** *a convicted felon*

felony /ˈfeləni/ *noun* [C, U] a serious crime in the US **ağır suç, cürüm** *to commit a felony*

felt¹ /felt/ *noun* [U] a soft, thick cloth that is made from wool, hair, or fur that has been pressed together **keçe**

felt² /felt/ *past of* feel **'hissetmek' fiilinin ikinci hali**

felt-tip 'pen *noun* [C] a pen with a point made of soft material, usually with brightly coloured ink for colouring pictures **keçe uçlu kalem**

o▪**female¹** /ˈfiːmeɪl/ *adjective* belonging to or relating to women, or to the sex that can produce eggs or have babies **dişi** *a female athlete/employee* ○ *a female butterfly/elephant* ○ *Is it male or female?*

female² /ˈfiːmeɪl/ *noun* [C] a person or animal that belongs to the sex that can produce eggs or have babies **kız, kadın, dişi** *Our dog's just had puppies - three males and two females.*

feminine /ˈfemɪnɪn/ *adjective* **1** showing qualities that people generally think are typical of women **dişi, kadı-**

nımsı, kadına özgü, kadına yaraşır *a feminine voice* ○ *feminine beauty* **2** in some languages, belonging to a group of nouns or adjectives that have the same grammatical behaviour. The other groups are 'masculine' and 'neuter'. **bazı dillerde benzer dilbilgisi özellikleri gösteren bir grup isim ve sıfatlara ait olan; dişil**

femininity /ˌfemɪˈnɪnəti/ *noun* [U] when someone shows qualities that people generally think are typical of women **dişilik, kadınlık; kadınlık özelliği**

feminism /ˈfemɪnɪzᵊm/ *noun* [U] the belief that women should have the same economic, social, and political rights as men **kadın haklarını savunma inancı** ● **feminist** *noun* [C] someone who supports feminism **kadın hakları savunucusu** *a radical feminist* ● **feminist** *adjective feminist literature* **feminist**

fence¹ /fens/ *noun* [C]   **fence**
1 a wood, wire, or metal structure that divides or goes around an area **çit** *a garden/ electric fence* **2 sit on the fence** to wait before you choose between two possibilities **tarafsız kalmak, suya sabuna dokunmamak, çekimser kalmak** ⊃See also: picket fence.

fence² /fens/ *verb* [I] to take part in the sport of fencing **eskrim yapmak**
fence sth in *phrasal verb* to build a fence around an area **etrafını çitle çevirmek/kapatmak**
fence sth off *phrasal verb* to separate one area from another by building a fence **araya çit çekmek, çitle ayırmak**

fencing /ˈfensɪŋ/ *noun* [U] **1** the sport of fighting with thin swords (= weapons like long knives) **eskrim, eskrim sporu 2** fences, or the material that is used to make them **çit yapım malzemesi**

fend /fend/ *verb*
fend for yourself *phrasal verb* to take care of yourself without help **kendi başının çaresine bakmak, ayakları üzerinde durmayı öğrenmek**
fend sb/sth off *phrasal verb* to defend yourself against someone or something that is attacking you or annoying you **savuşturmak, defetmek, kurtulmak, geçiştirmek, atlatmak** *They managed to fend off their attackers with rocks and sticks.*

fender /ˈfendəʳ/ *noun* [C] **1** CAR US (UK wing) one of the parts at each corner of a car above the wheels **çamurluk 2** BICYCLE US (UK mudguard) a curved piece of metal or plastic fixed above a wheel of a bicycle or motorcycle to prevent water or dirt from hitting the legs of the person who is riding it **bisiklet/motorsiklet çamurluğu 3** FIREPLACE UK a low, metal structure around an open fireplace which stops the coal or wood from falling out **ocak, şömine çerçevesi**

feng shui /ˌfʌŋˈʃweɪ/ *noun* [U] an ancient Chinese belief that the way your house is built and the way that you arrange objects affects your success, health, and happiness **eski Çin'de evin inşa biçimi ve eşyaların düzenlenme şeklinin başarı, sağlık ve mutluluğa etki edeceği inancı**

fennel /ˈfenᵊl/ *noun* [U] a plant whose base can be eaten, and whose leaves and seeds are used as a spice in cooking **rezene, dereotu**

ferment¹ /fəˈment/ *verb* [I, T] If food or drink ferments, or if you ferment it, the sugar in it changes into alcohol because of a chemical process. **mayalanmak, mayalamak** *wine fermenting in barrels* ● **fermentation** /ˌfɜːmenˈteɪʃᵊn/ *noun* [U] **mayalanma**

ferment² /ˈfɜːment/ *noun* [U] *formal* excitement or disagreement caused by change or a difficult situation **heyecanlanmak, telaşlanmak**

fern /fɜːn/ *noun* [C] a green plant with long stems, narrow leaves like feathers, and no flowers **eğreltiotu**

fern

ferocious /fəˈrəʊʃəs/ *adjective* extremely angry, violent, or forceful **vahşi, yırtıcı, canavar, hiddetli, sert, acımasız** *a ferocious dog* ○ *a ferocious attack*
● **ferociously** *adverb* **kızgın ve vahşi bir şekilde**

ferocity /fəˈrɒsəti/ *noun* [U] extreme violence or force **canavarlık, vahşilik, gaddarlık** *a storm of incredible ferocity*

ferret¹ /ˈferɪt/ *noun* [C] a small animal with a long, thin body that is sometimes used to hunt rabbits **dağ/yaban gelinciği**

ferret² /ˈferɪt/
ferret sth out *phrasal verb* to find something after searching carefully for it **bulup çıkarmak, meydana çıkarmak**

Ferris wheel /ˈferɪsˌwiːl/ *noun* [C] an entertainment consisting of a large wheel that turns slowly with seats for people to sit in **dönme dolap**

ferry¹ /ˈferi/ *noun* [C] a boat that regularly carries passengers and vehicles across an area of water **feribot, araba vapuru** *a car/passenger ferry*

ferry² /ˈferi/ *verb* [T] to regularly carry passengers or goods from one place to another in a vehicle **yolcu taşımak**

fertile /ˈfɜːtaɪl/ Ⓤ /ˈfɜːrtᵊl/ *adjective* **1** Fertile land or soil produces a lot of healthy plants. **verimli, bereketli, mümbit 2** If people or animals are fertile, they are able to have babies. **doğurgan 3 fertile ground (for sth)** a situation or place where an idea, activity, etc is likely to succeed **verimli, bereketli, mümbit, semereli 4 a fertile imagination** If someone has a fertile imagination, they have lots of interesting and unusual ideas. **yaratıcı, üretken** ● **fertility** /fəˈtɪləti/ *noun* [U] **verim, doğurganlık**

fertilize (*also UK* -ise) /ˈfɜːtɪlaɪz/ *verb* [T] **1** to cause an egg to start to develop into a young animal or baby by combining it with a male cell **dölle(n)mek, tohumla (n)mak** *Once an egg is fertilized it becomes an embryo.* **2** to put a natural or chemical substance on land in order to make plants grow well **tabii veya kimyevi gübre vermek, gübrelemek** ● **fertilization** /ˌfɜːtɪlaɪˈzeɪʃᵊn/ *noun* [U] **tüp bebek yapma işlemi**

fertilizer (*also UK* -iser) /ˈfɜːtɪlaɪzəʳ/ *noun* [C, U] a natural or chemical substance that you put on land in order to make plants grow well **tabii veya kimyevi gübre**

fervent /ˈfɜːvᵊnt/ *adjective* showing sincere and enthusiastic beliefs or feelings **gayretli, ateşli, coşkun,**

heyecanlı *a fervent supporter of animal rights* ● **fervently** *adverb* içtenlikle

fervour UK (US fervor) /ˈfɜːvəʳ/ *noun* [U] extremely strong beliefs or feelings **son derece güçlü hisler veya inançlar** *religious/patriotic fervour*

fess /fes/ *verb*
fess up *phrasal verb informal* to admit that you have done something bad **suçu/hatayı/kusuru kabul etmek, itiraf etmek** *He eventually fessed up to having spilt coffee on it.*

fest /fest/ *noun* **a beer/film/jazz, etc fest** a special event where people can enjoy a particular activity or thing **film/caz festivali/eğlencesi**

fester /ˈfestəʳ/ *verb* [I] **1** If a bad feeling or situation festers, it becomes worse over a period of time. **bozulmak, daha da kötüye gitmek** *Hatred between the two groups has festered for years.* **2** If an injury festers, it becomes infected. **(yara) azmak, iltihaplanmak, cerahat toplamak** *a festering wound*

festival /ˈfestɪvəl/ *noun* [C] **1** a series of special events, performances, etc that often takes place over several days **festival, bayram, şenlik** *a dance/music festival* ○ *the Berlin Film Festival* **2** a special day or period when people celebrate something, especially a religious event **bayram, dinî festival** *the Jewish festival of Hanukkah*

festive /ˈfestɪv/ *adjective* happy and enjoyable because people are celebrating **şen, şenlikli, neşeli** *a festive mood/occasion* ○ *What are you doing for the festive season* (= Christmas)? ● **festivity** /fesˈtɪvəti/ *noun* [U] when people are happy and celebrating **eğlence, cümbüş, şenlik**

festivities /fesˈtɪvətiz/ *noun* [plural] events that people organize in order to celebrate something **bayramlar, eğlenceler, kutlamalar**

festoon /fesˈtuːn/ *verb* [T] to cover something with objects, especially decorations **süslemek, çiçek ve süslerle bezemek** [often passive] *The balcony was festooned with flags and ribbons.*

fetch /fetʃ/ *verb* [T] **1** to go to another place to get something or someone and bring them back **gidip almak/getirmek** *Can you fetch my glasses from the bedroom?* **2** If something fetches a particular amount of money, it is sold for that amount. **...e/a satılmak; etmek, malolmak** *The painting is expected to fetch $50,000 in the auction.*

fetching /ˈfetʃɪŋ/ *adjective* attractive **hoş, çekici, alımlı** *That scarf looks rather fetching on you.*

fête /feɪt/ *noun* [C] **1** UK an event that is held outside and includes competitions, games, and things for sale **açık hava eğlencesi, şölen, cümbüş** *a village fête* **2** US a special event to celebrate someone or something **özel kutlama/eğlence** ● **fête** *verb* [T] to publicly celebrate someone, often by having a special party **şölen düzenlemek, eğlence tertip etmek, ağırla(n)mak** [often passive] *She was fêted by audiences all over the world.*

fetish /ˈfetɪʃ/ *noun* [C] **1** a strong sexual interest in something unusual **uygun olmayan şeylere duyulan aşırı cinsel istek** *a rubber fetish* **2** something that someone spends too much time thinking about or doing **tapınırcasına sevilen/hürmet edilen şey, fetiş** *a fetish for cleanliness*

fetus /ˈfiːtəs/ *noun* [C] US spelling of foetus (= a young human or animal that is still developing inside its mother) **cenin, dölüt** ● **fetal** /ˈfiːtəl/ *adjective* US spelling of foetal **cenine ait**

feud ...... İLE BİRLİKTE KULLANILAN KELİMELER

a **bitter/long-running** feud ● a **family** feud ● a feud **with** sb/**between** sb and sb

feud /fjuːd/ *noun* [C] a serious and sometimes violent argument between two people or groups that continues for a long period **kan davası; bitmek bilmeyen husumet,** ● **feud** *verb* [I] *The families have been feuding for years.* **kavga**

feudal /ˈfjuːdəl/ *adjective* relating to a social system in the past in which people worked and fought for a lord (= a man of high rank) in exchange for land and protection **feodal, derebeylikle ilgili, toprak ağalığına ilişkin** ● **feudalism** *noun* [U] feodalizm

fever ...... İLE BİRLİKTE KULLANILAN KELİMELER

develop/have/run a fever ● a **high** fever

fever /ˈfiːvəʳ/ *noun* **1** [C, U] when someone's body temperature rises because they are ill **ateş** *a high/slight fever* **2** [U] when people are very excited about something **heyecanlı ruh hali** *Election fever has gripped the nation.* ⊃See also: glandular fever, hay fever.

feverish /ˈfiːvərɪʃ/ *adjective* **1** having a fever **ateşli** *I feel a bit feverish.* **2** Feverish activity is done quickly, often because of excitement or fear. **heyecanlı, telaşlı, coşkulu, ateşli** *The rescuers worked at a feverish pace.* ● **feverishly** *adverb* They worked feverishly to put out the fire. **ateşli bir şekilde**

fever ˌpitch *noun* **reach fever pitch** If emotions reach fever pitch, they become so strong that they are difficult to control. **duyguları en üst düzeye çıkmak, aşırı duygulanmak; kontrol dışı duygulanmak**

o→few /fjuː/ *quantifier* **1** a few some, or a small number of **birkaç** *It'll be here in a few minutes.* ○ *I met a few of the other employees at my interview.* **2** quite a few/a good few quite a large number of **epeyce çok, bir hayli, pek çok** *Quite a few people have had the same problem.* **3** not many, or only a small number of **(pek az) sayıda, az miktarda** *We get few complaints.* ○ *Few of the children can read or write yet.* ○ *Very few people can afford to pay those prices.* **4** few and far between not happening or existing very often **çok fazla sıklıkla olmayan; nadiren meydana gelen** *Opportunities like this are few and far between.*

fiancé /fiˈɑːnseɪ/ *noun* [C] A woman's fiancé is the man that she has promised to marry. **(erkek) nişanlı**

fiancée /fiˈɑːnseɪ/ *noun* [C] A man's fiancée is the woman that he has promised to marry. **(bayan) nişanlı**

fiasco /fiˈæskəʊ/ *noun* [C] a complete failure, especially one that embarrasses people **bozgun, hezimet, başarısızlık, fiyasko** *My last dinner party was a complete fiasco.*

fib /fɪb/ *noun* [C] *informal* a small lie that is not very important **küçük/zararsız yalan** *Don't tell fibs.* ● **fib** *verb* [I] fibbing, *past* fibbed to say something that is not true **masum/beyaz/zararsız yalan söylemek**

fibre UK (US fiber) /ˈfaɪbəʳ/ *noun* **1** CLOTH [C, U] cloth made from thin threads twisted together **lif, elyaf** *Man-made fibres like nylon are easy to wash.* **2** THIN THREAD [C] one of the thin threads that forms a substance such as cloth **lif** *The fibres are woven into fabric.* **3** FOOD [U] the substance in plants which cannot be digested and helps food pass through your body **bitkisel lif** *Broccoli is a good source of fibre.* **4** BODY [C] a structure like a thread in your body **vücuttaki lif** *muscle/nerve fibres*

fibreglass UK (US fiberglass) /ˈfaɪbəɡlɑːs/ *noun* [U] a strong, light material made by twisting together glass or plastic threads **cam elyafı, cam pamuğu, fiberglas**

fickle /ˈfɪkl/ *adjective* Someone who is fickle often changes their opinion about things. **kararsız, değişken, sürekli fikir değiştiren**

F

fiction /ˈfɪkʃ³n/ *noun* **1** [U] literature and stories about imaginary people or events **hayal mahsulü roman/edebiyat** *What's the best-selling children's fiction title?* ⊃Opposite **nonfiction**. **2** [U, no plural] something that is not true or real **gerçek olmayan, hayal mahsulü şey** ⊃See also: **science fiction**.

fictional /ˈfɪkʃ³n³l/ *adjective* existing only in fiction **sadece romanlarda olan, hayalî, düşsel, kurgusal** *a fictional character*

fictitious /fɪkˈtɪʃəs/ *adjective* invented and not real or true **uydurma, hayal mahsulü, hayali, kurgusal** *a fictitious name*

fiddle¹ /ˈfɪdl/ *verb* [T] UK *informal* to change something dishonestly in order to get money **üzerinde hile yapmak/oynamak; değiştirmek, ayarlamak** *She was fired for fiddling her travel expenses.*
fiddle (about/around) with sth *phrasal verb* **1** to touch or move things with your fingers because you are nervous or bored **...ile oynayıp durmak/oyalanmak; sürekli ellerinde bir şeylerle meşgul olmak** *Stop fiddling with your hair!* **2** to make small changes to something to try to make it work **bir şeyi kurcalayarak çalıştırmak, oynamak** *He fiddled with the wires to get the radio working again.*

fiddle² /ˈfɪdl/ *noun* [C] **1** *informal* a violin (= a wooden musical instrument with strings) **keman 2** UK a dishonest way to get money **oyun, düzen, katakulli, hile** *a tax fiddle*

fiddler /ˈfɪdlə³/ *noun* [C] someone who plays the violin (= a wooden musical instrument with strings) **kemancı**

fiddly /ˈfɪdli/ *adjective* UK difficult to do because the parts involved are small **dikkat isteyen/gerektiren, incelik gerektiren** *Repairing a watch is very fiddly.*

fidelity /fɪˈdeləti/ *noun* [U] loyalty, especially to a sexual partner **bağlılık, sadakat, vefa** ⊃Opposite **infidelity**.

fidget /ˈfɪdʒɪt/ *verb* [I] to keep making small movements with your hands or feet because you are nervous or bored **kıpır kıpır danmak, yerinde duramamak, endişeyle orasını burasını oynatmak/eline koluna hakim olamamak** *She fidgeted all the way through the job interview.* ● **fidgety** *adjective* **yerinde duramayan**

○ **field**¹ /ˈfiːld/ *noun* **1** [LAND] [C] an area of land used for growing crops or keeping animals **tarla, otlak, mera, çayır** *a wheat field* ○ *a field of cows* **2** [SPORT] [C] an area of grass where you can play a sport **futbol sahası** *a football field* **3** [AREA OF STUDY] [C] an area of study or activity **çalışma alanı/sahası** *He's an expert in the field of biochemistry.* **4** [IN RACE/BUSINESS] [no plural] the people who are competing in a race, activity, or business **yarışma/faaliyet/iş alanı/sahası** *We lead the field in genetic research.* **5** a **gas/oil field** an area of land containing gas or oil **petrol/gaz sahası 6** a **gravitational/magnetic field** an area affected by a particular physical force **yerçekimi/manyetik alan** ⊃See also: **paddy field**, **playing field**.

field² /ˈfiːld/ *verb* **1** [I, T] to try to catch or stop a ball after it has been hit in a game such as cricket or baseball **kriket ve beyzbol oyununda topu yakalamaya çalışmak** *Are we fielding or batting?* **2** [T] to send out a team or player to play in a game **takım ve oyuncuları sahaya sürmek** *Brazil fielded a strong team in the World Cup.* **3 field questions/telephone calls** to answer or deal with questions or telephone calls **sorulara/telefon aramalarına cevap vermek, bakmak**

field day *noun* **have a field day** to have the opportunity to do a lot of something you want to do, especially to criticize someone **çok başarılı bir gün geçirmek;**

hayatının gününü geçirmek *The press had a field day when they found out about the scandal.*

fielder /ˈfiːldə³/ *noun* [C] a player who tries to catch or stop the ball in games such as cricket or baseball **kriket ve beyzbolda topu yakalamaya/durdurmaya çalışan oyuncu**

field hockey US (UK **hockey**) *noun* [U] a team game played on grass where you hit a small ball with a long, curved stick **çim hokeyi**

field marshal UK (US **field marshal**) *noun* [C] an officer of the highest rank in the British army **mareşal; Britanya ordusunda en yüksek rütbeli subay**

fiend /fiːnd/ *noun* [C] **1** an evil or cruel person **çok kötü/gaddar/canavar kişi 2** someone who is very interested in a particular thing **bir şeyin aşırı düşkünü/tiryakisi/meraklısı/hastası**

fiendish /ˈfiːndɪʃ/ *adjective* **1** evil or cruel **acımasız, zalim, gaddar** *a fiendish attack* **2** very difficult or complicated **çok güç, müthiş zor ve karmaşık** *a fiendish crossword* ● **fiendishly** *adverb mainly UK* extremely **şeytancasına, çok, alabildiğine, son derece** *fiendishly clever/difficult*

fierce /fɪəs/ *adjective* **1** violent or angry **şiddetli, hiddetli, kızgın, vahşi, azgın** *a fierce attack* ○ *a fierce dog* **2** very strong or powerful **güçlü, şiddetli, kıvılcı, müthiş** *fierce winds/storms* ○ *There is fierce competition between car manufacturers.* ● **fiercely** *adverb* **kızgın ve vahşi bir şekilde**

fiery /ˈfaɪəri/ *adjective* **1** showing strong emotion, especially anger **ateşli, heyecanlı, coşkun** *a fiery temper* **2** bright or burning like a fire **ateş rengi, alev kırmızısı** *a fiery sunset*

○ **fifteen** /ˌfɪfˈtiːn/ the number 15 **onbeş** ● **fifteenth** 15th written as a word **onbeşinci**

fifth¹ /fɪfθ/ 5th written as a word **beşinci**

fifth² /fɪfθ/ *noun* [C] one of five equal parts of something; 1/5; **beşte biri**

○ **fifty** /ˈfɪfti/ **1** the number 50 **elli 2** the **fifties** the years from 1950 to 1959 **elliler 3** be **in your fifties** to be aged between 50 and 59 **ellilerinde olmak** ● **fiftieth** 50th written as a word **ellinci**

fifty-fifty /ˌfɪftiˈfɪfti/ *adjective, adverb informal* **1** shared equally between two people **yarı yarıya** *Let's divide the bill fifty-fifty.* **2** a **fifty-fifty chance** If something has a fifty-fifty chance, it is equally likely to happen or not to happen. **eşit şans, yarı yarıya şans** *We have a fifty-fifty chance of winning the match.*

fig /fɪɡ/ *noun* [C] a dark, sweet fruit with lots of seeds, that is often eaten dried **incir**

fig. *written abbreviation for* figure (= a picture or drawing in a book or document, usually with a number) **'figure' şekil sözcüğünün kısaltılmışı** *See fig. 1.*

○ **fight**¹ /faɪt/ *verb past* fought **1** [USE FORCE] [I, T] When people fight, they use physical force to try to defeat each other. **uğraşmak, savaşmak, mücadele etmek** *Two men were arrested for fighting outside a bar.* ○ *Sam's always fighting with his little brother.* **2** [JOIN WAR] [I, T] to take part in a war **savaşmak, mücadele etmek, çarpışmak** *Millions of young men fought in World War I.* **3** [ARGUE] [I] to argue **tartışmak, kavga etmek 4** [TRY TO STOP] [I, T] to try hard to stop something bad happening **mücadele etmek, savaşım vermek, engellemeye çalışmak** *He fought against racism.* ○ *New measures have been introduced to fight crime.* **5** [TRY TO ACHIEVE] [I] to try hard to achieve something you want or think is right **mücadele etmek, başarmaya çalışmak, savunmak** *They are fighting for their freedom.* ○ [+ to do sth] *He had to*

fight very hard to keep his job. **6 be fighting for your life** to be trying very hard to stay alive when you are very ill or badly injured **hasta veya yaralıyken hayat mücadelesi vermek** ⊃See also: fight a losing **battle**[1].
fight back *phrasal verb* to defend yourself when someone or something attacks you or causes problems for you **dövüşerek kendini savunmak, karşı koymak**

___
fight ...... İLE BİRLİKTE KULLANILAN KELİMELER

a fight **with** sb ● **have/get into/pick/start** a fight ● **lose/win** a fight
___

○━**fight**[2] /faɪt/ *noun* [C] **1** PHYSICAL FORCE when people use physical force to hurt or attack others **dövüş, kavga** *He's always getting into fights.* **2** EFFORT a determined effort to achieve or stop something **mücadele, savunma, kararlı çaba** *She was very active in the fight against drugs.* ○ *Join us in our fight for freedom!* ○ [+ to do sth] *This year has brought some good news in the fight to save the whales.* **3** ARGUMENT an argument **tartışma, münakaşa** *I don't want to have a fight over this.* **4** SPORT a boxing competition **boks karşılaşması**

fighter /'faɪtər/ *noun* [C] **1** (*also* 'fighter ,plane) a fast military aircraft that can attack other aircraft **savaş uçağı; jet; avcı uçağı** *a fighter pilot* **2** someone who fights in a war or as a sport **dövüşçü, mücadeleci, savaşçı, boksör**

fighting /'faɪtɪŋ/ *noun* [U] when people fight, usually in a war **savaşma, muharebe etme, çarpışma** *Thousands of civilians were killed in the fighting.*

figment /'fɪgmənt/ *noun* **a figment of sb's imagination** something that someone believes is real but that only exists in their imagination **hayali şey, uydurma şey; var olduğuna inanılan hayali şey**

figurative /'fɪgʲrətɪv/ *adjective* **1** A figurative meaning of a word or phrase is a more imaginative meaning developed from the usual meaning. **mecazi 2** Figurative art shows people, places, or things in a similar way to how they look in real life. **insanı, yeri, şeyleri gerçeğine benzer şekilde gösteren, mecazi** ● **figuratively** *adverb* **mecazi şekliyle**

___
figure ...... İLE BİRLİKTE KULLANILAN KELİMELER

a **key/leading/major/prominent** figure ● a **public** figure
___

○━**figure**[1] /'fɪgər/ *noun* [C] **1** SYMBOL a symbol for a number **sayı, rakam** *Write down the amount in words and figures.* ○ *He's now being paid a six-figure salary.* **2 single/ double, etc figures** numbers from 0 to 9/numbers from 10 to 99, etc **tekli/çiftli sayılar, iki haneli sayılar/rakamlar 3** AMOUNT a number that expresses an amount, especially in official documents **miktar, sayı, rakam** *Government figures show a rise in unemployment.* **4** TYPE OF PERSON a particular type of person, often someone important or famous **bilhassa önemli/meşhur kişi/şahsiyet** *a mysterious figure* ○ *Lincoln was a major figure in American politics.* **5** PERSON a person that you cannot see clearly **karaltı, insan figürü** *I could see two figures in the distance.* **6** BODY SHAPE the shape of someone's body, usually an attractive shape **insan bedeni, çekici insan vücudu, boy pos, endam** *She's got a good figure for her age.* **7** PICTURE (*written abbreviation* **fig.**) a picture or drawing in a book or document, usually with a number **kitap veya belgelerde sayılarla gösterilen resim ve çizimler, resim, şekil, desen** *Look at the graph shown in Figure 2.* ⊃See also: **father figure.**

figure[2] /'fɪgər/ *verb* **1** [I] to be a part of something, or to appear in something **bir şeyin parçası olmak; bir şeyde gözükmek** *Love figures in most pop songs.* **2** [T] to decide something after thinking about it **düşündük-**

ten sonra karar vermek; hesaplamak [+ (that)] *I figured that it was time to tell her the truth.* **3 that/it figures** *informal* something you say when you expected something to happen **...nin özelliği olmak; ...ın niteliği olmak, rol oynamak** *"I've run out of money, Mum." "That figures."*
figure sth/sb out *phrasal verb* to finally understand something or someone after a lot of thought **halletmek, çözmek, hesaplayarak bulmak** [+ question word] *I never could figure out what she saw in him.*

figurehead /'fɪgəhed/ *noun* [C] a leader who has no real power **sözde mevkî sahibi kimse, kukla, göstermelik kimse**

,figure of 'speech *noun* [C] *plural* **figures of speech** words that are used together in an imaginative way to mean something different from their usual meaning **benzetme, yan anlamalı söz, mecaz**

___
file ...... İLE BİRLİKTE KULLANILAN KELİMELER

1 hold/keep a file **on** sb/sth
2 close/create/download/open/save a file
___

○━**file**[1] /faɪl/ *noun* **1** INFORMATION [C] a collection of information and documents about someone or something **dosya, klasör** *The school keeps files on all its pupils.* **2** COMPUTER [C] a piece of text, a picture, or a computer program stored on a computer **tek bir isim altında depolanan bilgi bütünü, dosya** *Do you want to download all these files?* **3** CONTAINER [C] a box or folded piece of thick paper used to put documents in **karton dosya** *He keeps all his bank statements in a file.* ⊃Orta kısımdaki renkli sayfalarına bakınız. **4 on file** If information is on file, it is recorded and stored somewhere. **dosyalanmış, dosyalanıp kayda geçmiş 5** TOOL a small tool with a rough edge that is used to make a surface smooth **törpü** *a nail file* **6 in single file** in a line with one person following the other **tek sıra halinde** ⊃See also: the **rank**[1] and file.

file[2] /faɪl/ *verb* **1** PAPER [T] (*also* file away) to put documents into an ordered system of boxes or files where you can easily find them again **dosyalamak** *She filed all her tax returns under T.* **2** LAW [T] (*also* file for) to officially state that you are going to take someone to court **mahkemeye vermek, müracaat etmek, dilekçe vermek** *The police filed charges against the suspect.* ○ *His wife's filing for divorce.* **3** RUB [T] to rub something with a rough tool in order to make it smooth **eğelemek, törpülemek 4 file along/into/through, etc** to walk somewhere in a line, one behind the other **tek sıra halinde yürümek** *The audience slowly filed back to their seats.*

'file ex,tension *noun* [C] a dot followed by three letters, such as .doc or .jpg, that forms the end of the name of a computer document and shows what sort of document it is **dosya adı uzantısı**

'file ,sharing *noun* [U] the activity of putting a file onto a special place on your computer so that many other people can copy it, look at it, or use it by using the Internet **bilgisayar ortamında ortak kullanıma sunulan paylaşım dosyası** ⊃See study page **The Web and the Internet** on page Centre 36.

filet /fɪ'leɪ/ *noun* [C] *another US spelling of* fillet (= a piece of meat or fish with the bones taken out) **kemiksiz et/ balık**

'filing ,cabinet (*also US* 'file ,cabinet) *noun* [C] a piece of office furniture with deep drawers for storing documents **dosya/evrak dolabı** ⊃Orta kısımdaki renkli sayfalarına bakınız.

⊶**fill¹** /fɪl/ *verb* **1** [MAKE FULL] [I, T] (*also* **fill up**) to make a container or space full, or to become full **doldurmak** *He filled the bucket with water.* ○ *I made a drink while the bath was filling.* **2** [TAKE SPACE] [T] If people or things fill a place, there are a lot of them in it. **dolmak** *The streets were filled with tourists.* ○ *Dark clouds filled the sky.* **3** [BE NOTICEABLE] [T] If light, sound, or a smell fills a place, you can easily notice it. **ışık/ses/koku ile dolmak** *The smell of smoke filled the room.* **4 fill sb with anger/joy/pride, etc** to make someone feel very angry/happy/proud, etc **birini kızdırmak/mutlu etmek/gururlandırmak** *The thought of losing him filled her with fear.* **5 fill a post/position/vacancy** to take a new job **bir görevi üstlenmek/yeni bir işe girmek** *They still haven't found anyone to fill the vacancy.* **6 fill a need/gap/demand** to provide something that people need or want **bir gereksinimi/boşluğu/talebi gidermek, doldurmak**

fill sth in/out *phrasal verb* to write the necessary information on an official document **form doldurmak** *to fill in a form/questionnaire*

fill (sth) up *phrasal verb* to become full, or to make something become full **dolmak, doldurmak** *The restaurant soon filled up with people.*

fill² /fɪl/ *noun* **your fill** as much of something as you want or need **yeteri kadar, istediği kadar** *I've had my fill of living in the city.*

fillet (*also US* **filet**) /'fɪlɪt/ (US) /fɪ'leɪ/ *noun* [C] a piece of meat or fish with the bones taken out **kemiksiz et/balık**

filling

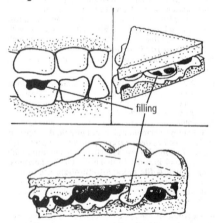

filling

filling¹ /'fɪlɪŋ/ *noun* **1** [C, U] food that is put inside things such as cakes, pastry, pieces of bread, etc **dolgu malzemesi, iç** *What sort of filling do you want in your sandwich?* **2** [C] a hard substance that fills a hole in a tooth **(diş) dolgu**

filling² /'fɪlɪŋ/ *adjective* Food that is filling makes your stomach feel full. **(yiyecek) tokluk hissi veren** *This soup is very filling.*

'filling ,station *noun* [C] a petrol station (= place where you can buy fuel for your car) **benzinlik**

🧩 *film* ...... İLE BİRLİKTE KULLANILAN KELİMELER

make a film ● a film **about** sb/sth ● **in** a film ● a **horror** film ● a **classic** film ● the film **industry**

⊶**film¹** /fɪlm/ *noun* **1** [PICTURES] [C] (*also US* **movie**) a story shown in moving pictures, shown at the cinema or on television **film** *'Titanic' was one of the most popular Hollywood films ever made.* **2** [MATERIAL] [C, U] special thin plastic used for making photographs or moving pictures, or a length of this **fotoğraf filmi** *I need to buy another roll of film.* **3** [LAYER] [no plural] a thin layer of something on a surface **ince tabaka, zar** *A thick film of dust covered the furniture.*

film² /fɪlm/ *verb* [I, T] to record moving pictures with a camera, usually to make a film for the cinema or television **film çekmek** *Most of the scenes were filmed in a studio.* ● **filming** *noun* [U] **filme çekme**

film-maker *UK* (*US* **filmmaker**) /'fɪlmmeɪkə^r/ *noun* [C] someone who makes films for the cinema or television **film yapımcısı**

'film ,star *noun* [C] a famous cinema actor or actress **film yıldızı**

filter¹ /'fɪltə^r/ *verb* **1** [T] to pass a liquid or gas through a piece of equipment in order to remove solid pieces or other substances **süzmek, süzgeçten geçirmek, elemek** *The water was filtered to remove any impurities.* **2 filter down/in/through, etc** to gradually appear or become known **giderek ortaya çıkmak/meşhur hale gelmek** *News is filtering in of an earthquake in Mexico.*

filter sth out *phrasal verb* to remove a particular substance from a liquid or gas **...den/dan arındırmak, süzmek**

filter² /'fɪltə^r/ *noun* [C] a piece of equipment that you pass a liquid or gas through in order to remove particular substances **süzgeç, filtre** *a coffee filter*

filth /fɪlθ/ *noun* [U] **1** thick and unpleasant dirt **kir, pislik** *His clothes were covered in filth and mud.* **2** offensive language or pictures, usually relating to sex **kötü söz, küfür, açık saçıklık, müstehcen yazı veya resimler**

filthy /'fɪlθi/ *adjective* **1** extremely dirty **çok pis/kirli** *Wash your hands, they're filthy!* **2** rude or offensive **açık saçık, müstehcen** *filthy language/jokes* ○ *Smoking is a filthy habit.*

fin /fɪn/ *noun* [C] a thin, triangular part on a fish, which helps it to swim **yüzgeç**

⊶**final¹** /'faɪn^əl/ *adjective* **1** [always before noun] last in a series or coming at the end of something **son, final, sonuncu** *the final paragraph* ○ *They scored a goal in the final minute.* **2** If a decision, agreement, or answer is final, it will not be changed or discussed any more. **son, nihai** *The committee's decision is final.* ➔See also: **the final nail¹ in the coffin, the final/last straw.**

final² /'faɪn^əl/ *noun* **1** [C] the last part of a competition to decide which person or team will be the winner **final** *the European Cup Final* ○ *The finals will be shown on TV.* **2 finals** exams taken at the end of a university course **final sınavları**

finale /fɪ'nɑːli/ *noun* [C] the last part of a show, event, or piece of music **bitiş, final**

finalist /'faɪn^əlɪst/ *noun* [C] a person or team in the last part of a competition **finalist**

finalize (*also UK* **-ise**) /'faɪn^əlaɪz/ *verb* [T] to make a final and certain decision about a plan, date, etc **bitirmek, sona erdirmek, son şeklini vermek** *to finalize arrangements/details*

⊶**finally** /'faɪn^əli/ *adverb* **1** [AFTER A LONG TIME] after a long time or some difficulty **en sonunda, nihayet** *After months of looking, he finally found a job.* **2** [LAST POINT] used to introduce the last point or idea **son olarak, sonuç itibariyle, netice olarak** *Finally, I'd like to thank everyone for coming this evening.* **3** [CERTAINLY] in a way that will not be changed **kesinlikle, kat'i olarak** *The date of the wedding hasn't been finally decided yet.*

finance[1] /ˈfaɪnæns/ *noun* **1** [U] the control of how large amounts of money should be spent **maliye, maliyecilik 2** [U] the money that is needed to support a business **gerekli para, finansman** *Who put up the finance for the project?* **3** sb's **finances** the money which a person, company, or country has **mali durum, para/nakit durumu** *You must learn how to manage your own finances.*

finance[2] /ˈfaɪnæns/ *verb* [T] to provide the money needed to do something **parasal kaynak sağlamak** *Who's financing the project?*

◦━**financial** /faɪˈnænʃ[ə]l/ *adjective* relating to money or how money is managed **mali, parasal** *a financial adviser* ○ *She's having some financial difficulties at the moment.* ● **financially** *adverb Many students are still financially dependent on their parents.* **finansal olarak**

finch /fɪnʃ/ *noun* [C] a small singing bird with a short beak **ispinoz kuşu**

---

find ...... BAŞKA BİR DEYİŞLE

Find fiiline bir alternatif olarak **discover** fiili kullanılabilir. *The victim's wallet was discovered in a ditch.* ● *I finally* **discovered** *the letters in a drawer.*

Eğer bir kişi bir diğerinin veya bir şeyin tam yerini tespit ederse, resmi olmayan durumlarda **locate** fiili kullanılabilir. *Police are still trying to* **locate** *the suspect.*

Eğer kişi bir şeyin gizli veya saklanmış olduğunun farkına varırsa, bu durumu belirtmede **uncover** ve **unearth** fiilleri kullanılabilir. *Reporters* **uncovered/unearthed** *evidence of corruption.*

Come across ve **stumble across/on** deyimleri kişi bir şeyi şansa bulduğu zaman kullanılır. *I* **stumbled on** *these photographs when I was cleaning out my desk.* ● *We* **came across** *a lovely little restaurant in the village.*

Eğer kişi bir şeyi çok dikkatli aramalardan sonra bulduysa, bu durumda **trace** fiili veya resmi olmayan durumlarda **track down** deyimi kullanılabilir. *Police have so far failed to* **trace/track down** *the missing woman.*

◦━**find**[1] /faɪnd/ *verb* [T] *past* **found 1** [DISCOVER WHEN SEARCHING] to discover something or someone that you have been searching for **bulmak** *I can't find my glasses and I've looked everywhere.* ○ *Police found the missing girl at a London railway station.* ○ [+ two objects] *Has he found himself a place to live yet?* **2** [DISCOVER BY CHANCE] to discover something or someone by chance **bulmak, anlamak** *The body was found by a man walking his dog.* **3** [BECOME AWARE] to become aware that something exists, or has happened **öğrenmek, farkına varmak** *I came home to find that my cat had had kittens.* **4 find the energy/money/time, etc** to have or get enough energy/money/time, etc to do something **bir şeyi yapmak için enerji/para/zaman bulmak** *Where do you find the energy to do all these things?* **5 find sb/sth easy/boring/funny, etc** to think or feel a particular way about someone or something **kolay/sıkıcı/saçma/komik bulmak** *I still find exams very stressful.* **6 find yourself somewhere/doing sth** to become aware that you have gone somewhere or done something without intending to **kendini bir yerde bir şey yapıyor bulmak; tam ortasında bulmak** *I suddenly found myself making everyone's lunch.* **7 be found** to exist or be present somewhere **bulunmak** *Vitamin C is found in oranges and other citrus fruit.* **8 find sb guilty/not guilty** to judge that someone is guilty or not guilty in a law court **suçlu/suçsuz bulmak** [often passive] *She was found guilty of murder.*

find (sth) out *phrasal verb* to get information about something, or to learn a fact for the first time **araştırıp**

ortaya çıkarmak, öğrenmek *I must find out the train times.* ○ [+ question word] *Peter was shocked when he found out what we had done.*

find[2] /faɪnd/ *noun* [C] something or someone valuable, interesting, or useful that you discover **buluş, buluntu, keşif** [usually singular] *This hotel was a real find.*

finding /ˈfaɪndɪŋ/ *noun* [C] a piece of information that has been discovered as a result of an official study **bulgu, netice, sonuç** [usually plural] *The findings of this research will be published next year.*

◦━**fine**[1] /faɪn/ *adjective* **1** [WELL] well, healthy, or happy **hoş, güzel, mükemmel** *"How are you?" "I'm fine thanks. And you?"* ○ *I had a cold last week, but I'm fine now.* **2** [GOOD] good or good enough **iyi, yeteri kadar iyi** *"Is the soup hot enough?" "Yes, it's fine."* **3** [EXCELLENT] excellent, or of very good quality **mükemmel, kaliteli, harikulade** *fine wines* ○ *He's a fine musician.* **4 (that's) fine** used to agree with a suggestion, idea, decision, etc **uygun, iyi, tamam** *"Shall we meet at 8 o'clock?" "Yes, that's fine by me."* **5** [THIN] thin or made of very small pieces **çok ince taneli, toz gibi** *fine, brown hair* ○ *fine sand* **6** [SUNNY] mainly UK sunny and not raining **güzel, güneşli, açık** *If it's fine, we could have a picnic.* **7 the finer details/points, etc of sth** the more detailed or more difficult parts of an argument, idea, etc **(düşünce, tartışma) daha detaylı/en zor/hassas noktalar**

fine[2] /faɪn/ *adverb informal* **1** very well or without any problems **çok iyi bir şekilde; hiç problemsiz** *"How did your exam go?" "It went fine thanks."* **2 cut it/things fine** to leave yourself only just enough time to do something **yeterli, kâfi, bir şey için yeterli zamanı olmak** *Twenty minutes to get to the station? That's cutting it a bit fine!*

fine[3] /faɪn/ *verb* [T] to make someone pay an amount of money as a punishment for breaking a law or rule **para cezası kesmek, para cezasına çarptırmak** [often passive] *He was fined £500 for dangerous driving.*

  ▨ **fine** ...... İLE BİRLİKTE KULLANILAN KELİMELER

face/get/receive a fine ● pay a fine ● a heavy/hefty/stiff fine ● a parking fine

---

fine[4] /faɪn/ *noun* [C] an amount of money that you must pay for breaking a law or rule **para cezası** *a parking fine* ○ *The court gave her two weeks to pay the fine.*

finely /ˈfaɪnli/ *adverb* **1** into small pieces **çok küçük, ince, hassas parçacıklar şeklinde** *Finely chop the garlic.* **2** very exactly **tam olarak** *a finely tuned machine*

◦━**finger**[1] /ˈfɪŋɡə[r]/ *noun* [C] **1** one of the five, long, separate parts at the end of your hand, including your thumb **parmak** ⟲Orta kısımdaki renkli sayfalarına bakınız. **2 have green fingers** UK (US **have a green thumb**) to be good at gardening and making plants grow well **bahçe işlerinde/bahçıvanlıkta iyi olmak** ● **3 keep your fingers crossed** *informal* to hope that things will happen in the way that you want them to **ümit etmek, ümidini kesmemek, ummak** *Let's keep our fingers crossed that it doesn't rain.* ● **4 not lift a finger** *informal* to not help someone do something, usually because you are too lazy **parmağını bile kıpırdatmamak/kılını kıpırdatmamak** *He never lifts a finger to help with the housework.* ● **5 put your finger on sth** to understand exactly why a situation is the way it is **durumun ne olduğunu tam olarak anlamak/farketmek** *Something was wrong, but I couldn't put my finger on it.* ● **6 snap your fingers** (also UK **click your fingers**) to press your thumb and middle finger together until the finger hits your hand and makes a short sound **parmaklarını çıtlatmak** ⟲See also: index **finger**.

finger² /'fɪŋgəʳ/ *verb* [T] to touch or feel something with your fingers **parmakla dokunmak/hissetmek**

fingernail /'fɪŋgəneɪl/ *noun* [C] the hard, thin part on the top of the end of your finger **tırnak**

fingerprint /'fɪŋgəprɪnt/ *noun* [C] the mark made on something by the pattern of curved lines on the end of someone's finger **parmak izi** *The police found finger-prints all over the murder weapon.*

fingertip /'fɪŋgətɪp/ *noun* **1** [C] the end of your finger **parmak ucu 2 at your fingertips** If you have something at your fingertips, you can get it and use it very easily. **parmalarının ucunda; kolayca ulaşılabilen; hazır, dokunabilecek kadar yakın** *He had all the information he needed at his fingertips.*

---
finish ...... BAŞKA BİR DEYİŞLE

End fiili durmak anlamında kullanıldığı zaman bu kelimeye bir alternatif olarak **finish** fiili kullanılabilir. *What time does the concert* **end**?
Eğer kişi bir işi yapmayı bitirdiyse, durumu belirtmede **complete** fiili kullanılır. *Have you completed all the questions?* ● *The project took 5 years to* **complete**.
Eğer kişi özellikle yemeği veya bir işi çok çabuk bitirmişse, resmi olmayan ortamlarda durumun ifadesinde **polish off** deyimi kullanılabilir. *He's just* **polished off** *two huge bowls of pasta*.
wind up deyimi bir aktivitenin yavaş yavaş bittiğini gösterir. *It's time to* **wind up** *the game now.*

finish¹ /'fɪnɪʃ/ *verb* **1** [COMPLETE] [I, T] to complete something, or come to the end of an activity **bitirmek, bitmek** *When I finish my homework, can I watch TV?* ○ [+ doing sth] *Have you finished reading that book yet?* **2** [END] [I] to end **sona erdirmek, sona ermek** *The meeting should finish at five o'clock.* **3** [USE COMPLETELY] [T] (*also* **finish off**) to eat, drink, or use something completely **bir şeyi tamamen bitirmek; içmek** *They finished their drinks and left the bar.* **4 finish first/second, etc** to be in the first/second, etc winning position at the end of a race or competition **birinci/ikinci olmak**
finish sth off *phrasal verb* **1** to complete the last part of something that you are doing **tamamlamak, son rötuşları yapmak** *I have to finish off this report by Friday.* **2** to eat, drink, or use the last part of something **sonuna kadar bitirmek; kalanını yiyip/içip bitirmek** *Would you like to finish off the pizza?*
finish up *phrasal verb mainly UK* to finally be in a particular place, state, or situation, usually without having planned it **bilhassa planlamadan belli bir yere/duruma/konuma varmak/ulaşmak** *I only went for two days, but finished up staying for a week.*
finish with sth *phrasal verb* to stop using or needing something **...ile işi bitmek; ...e/a ihtiyacı kalmamak** *Have you finished with the newspaper?*
finish with sb *phrasal verb UK* to stop having a romantic relationship with someone **bir ilişkiyi bitirmek, flörte/görüşmeye son vermek; ayrılmak; görüşmemek**

finish² /'fɪnɪʃ/ *noun* [C] **1** the end of a race, or the last part of something **varış, bitiş, son, bitim** *a close/exciting finish* ○ *I enjoyed the film from start to finish.* **2** the way the surface of something feels or looks **cila, perdah, boya, son şekli** *The table has a smooth, shiny finish.*

finished /'fɪnɪʃt/ *adjective* **1** completed **bitmiş, tamamlanmış** *How much does the finished product cost?* つOpposite **unfinished**. **2 be finished** If you are finished, you have completed something. **bitmiş, son bulmuş** *I hope I'll be finished before 5 p.m.*

fir /fɜːʳ/ (*also* 'fir ˌtree) *noun* [C] a tree with thin, straight leaves shaped like needles that do not fall in winter **köknar, köknar ağacı**

---
fire ...... İLE BİRLİKTE KULLANILAN KELİMELER
---

put out/start a fire ● a fire **breaks out/burns/rages** ● **be on** fire ● **catch** fire

fire

fire¹ /faɪəʳ/ *noun* **1** [FLAME] [U] heat, light, and flames that are produced when something burns **ateş, ısı 2 catch fire** to start burning **tutuşmak, yanmaya başlamak, alev almak** *The car crashed and caught fire.* **3 on fire** burning **yanmakta, alev almış, alevler içinde** *That house is on fire.* **4 set fire to sth; set sth on fire** to make something start burning, usually to cause damage **ateşe vermek, tutuşturmak, yakmak** *Enemy troops set fire to the village.* **5** [EVENT] [C] when something burns in a way that causes damage and cannot be controlled **yangın** *Three people were killed in the fire.* ○ *It took the firefighters two hours to put the fire out* (= stop it burning) **yangın 6** [NATURAL HEAT] [C] a pile of wood, coal, etc that is burning to produce heat **ateş** *We sat by the fire.* ○ *They put up the tents and lit a fire.* **7 an electric/gas fire** UK a piece of equipment that uses electricity/gas to heat a room **elektrikli/gazlı ısıtıcı 8** [SHOOTING] [U] the shooting of guns and other weapons **atış, ateş etme, ateş** *The soldiers opened fire* (= started shooting). **9 come under fire** to be criticized **eleştirilmek**, *The government has come under fire for closing the hospital.*

fire² /faɪəʳ/ *verb* **1** [I, T] to shoot a bullet from a gun **ateş etmek** *She fired three shots at him.* **2** [T] *informal* to tell someone they must leave their job **işten çıkarmak, kovmak, yol vermek** [often passive] *I was fired for being late.* **3 fire sb's imagination** to make someone very excited or interested in something **birinin hayal gücünü harekete geçirmek/alevlendirmek 4 fire questions at sb** to ask someone questions quickly one after the other **soru bombardımanına/yağmuruna tutmak**
fire sb up *phrasal verb* to make someone excited or angry **birini alevlendirmek/kızdırmak; heyecanlandırmak/hiddetlendirmek**

'fire aˌlarm *noun* [C] a device such as a bell that warns the people in a building that the building is on fire **yangın alarmı** *If you hear the fire alarm, you must leave the building immediately.*

firearm /'faɪərɑːm/ *noun* [C] a gun that you can carry easily **ateşli silah, tabanca**

'fire briˌgade UK (US 'fire deˌpartment) *noun* [C] an organization of people whose job is to stop fires burning **itfaiyeciler, itfaiye teşkilatı**

'fire ˌengine *noun* [C] a vehicle for carrying firefighters and equipment for stopping large fires **itfaiye aracı/arabası**

'fire esˌcape *noun* [C] a set of metal stairs on the outside of a building which allows people to leave if there is an emergency **yangın çıkışı, acil çıkış**

ʹfire exˌtinguisher *noun* [C] a piece of equipment kept inside buildings which is used to stop small fires **yangın söndürücüsü**

firefighter /ʹfaɪəfaɪtər/ *noun* [C] someone whose job is to stop fires burning **itfaiye eri**

fireman /ʹfaɪəmən/ *noun* [C] *plural* **firemen** a man whose job is to stop fires burning **itfaiyeci**

fireplace /ʹfaɪəpleɪs/ *noun* [C] a space in the wall of a room where you can have a fire, or the structure around this space **şömine, ocak** ⊃Orta kısımdaki renkli sayfalarına bakınız.

fireside /ʹfaɪəsaɪd/ *noun* [U] the area next to a fireplace **şömine yanı/başı**

ʹfire ˌstation *noun* [C] the building where fire engines are kept, and firefighters wait for emergencies **itfaiye merkezi**

firewall /ʹfaɪəwɔːl/ *noun* [C] a system that controls what information can be sent from your computer using the Internet **internette başkalarının bilgilere ulaşmasını/görmesini engelleyen sanal duvar/sistem**

firewood /ʹfaɪəwʊd/ *noun* [U] wood that is used for burning on a fire **odun, yakacak odun**

🔲 **firework** ...... İLE BİRLİKTE KULLANILAN KELİMELER

let off/set off a firework ● a firework(s) **display**

---

fireworks

firework /ʹfaɪəwɜːk/ *noun* [C] a small object that explodes to produce a loud noise and bright colours and is often used to celebrate special events **havai fişek** *a firework display*

ʹfiring ˌsquad *noun* [C] a group of soldiers who are ordered to shoot and kill a prisoner **idam mangası**

firm¹ /fɜːm/ *adjective* 1 [NOT SOFT] not soft, but not completely hard **katı, sert, sağlam** *A firm bed is better for your back.* 2 [FIXED] [always before noun] certain or fixed and not likely to change **sabit, oynamaz** *We don't have any firm plans for the weekend yet.* ○ *I'm a firm believer in equal rights.* 3 [STRONG] strong and tight **sıkı, güçlü** *a firm handshake/grip* 4 [STRICT] strict and making certain that people do what you want **katı, sözü geçen, tavizsiz** *You've got to be firm with children.* ● **firmly** *adverb* **sıkıca** ● **firmness** *noun* [U] **sıkılık**

🔲 **firm** ...... İLE BİRLİKTE KULLANILAN KELİMELER

run/set up a firm ● a firm of [solicitors, accountants, etc]

---

firm² /fɜːm/ *noun* [C] a company that sells goods or services **firma, şirket** *a law firm*

o→first¹ /fɜːst/ *adjective* 1 [BEFORE] coming before all others **ilk** *Who was the first person to arrive at the party?* ○ *He was nervous on his first day at school.* ○ *They went abroad last year for the first time since having children.* 2 [NUMBER] 1st written as a word **birinci** 3 [IMPORTANT] most important **ilk ve tek, en önemli** *Sheila won first prize in the photo competition.* ⊃See also: in the first **place¹**.

o→first² /fɜːst/ *adverb* 1 [BEFORE] before everything or everyone else **ilk olarak; önde gelen** *I can go to the cinema, but I've got to do my homework first.* ○ *Jason came first in the 400 metres* (= he won). 2 [FIRST TIME] for the first time **ilk defa; ilkinde** *I first heard the song on the radio.* ○ *He first started playing the piano at school.* 3 **at first** at the beginning of a situation or period of time **ilk başta, en başta** *At first I thought she was unfriendly, but actually she is just shy.* 4 **first; first of all a** [BEGINNING SENTENCE] used to introduce the first idea, reason, etc in a series **ilk olarak; her şeyden önce** *First, I think we have to change our marketing strategy.* **b** [BEFORE EVERYTHING] before doing anything else **ilk başta, ilk önce; öncelikle** *First of all check you have all the correct ingredients.* 5 **come first** to be the most important person or thing **önde gelen, önemli** *Her career always comes first.* 6 **put sb/ sth first** to consider someone or something to be the most important thing **ilk sıraya koymak, önemsemek** *Most couples put their children first when sorting out their problems.* 7 **First come, first served.** something you say when there is not enough of something for everyone and only the first people who ask for it will get it **ilk gelen alır; sırası gelen alır; sırayla**

o→first³ /fɜːst/ *noun, pronoun* 1 **the first** the first person, people, thing, or things **ilk kişi/insanlar/şey/şeyler** *Hillary and Norgay were the first to climb Everest.* 2 **be a first** to be something that has never happened before **bir ilk olmak** *Man walking on the moon was a first in space history.* 3 [C] the highest exam result that you can achieve at the end of a university course in the UK **(İngiltere) üniversiteyi birincilikle bitirme**

ˌfirst ʹaid *noun* [U] basic medical treatment that you give someone who is ill or injured in an emergency **ilk yardım** *The policeman gave him first aid before the ambulance arrived.*

first-class /ˌfɜːstʹklɑːs/ *adjective* 1 relating to the best and most expensive available service, especially when travelling or sending something somewhere **birinci sınıf; yüksek hizmet verilen** *a first-class ticket* ○ *a first-class stamp* 2 of very good quality **birinci kalite/ sınıf** *It was a first-class restaurant.* ● **first class** *adverb* *How much is it to send this letter first class?* **en iyi kalite**

ˌfirst ʹfloor *noun* [no plural] 1 *UK* the level of a building directly above the ground level **birinci kat** 2 *US* (*UK* **ground floor**) the level of a building on the same level as the ground **giriş/zemin katı**

firsthand /ˌfɜːstʹhænd/ *adjective, adverb* experienced, seen, or learnt directly **ilk el; ilk elden** *Police heard firsthand accounts of the accident from witnesses.* ○ *firsthand experience*

ˌfirst ʹlanguage *noun* [C] the language that someone learns to speak first **ana dil** *Madeleine's first language is French, but she also knows English and German.*

firstly /ʹfɜːstli/ *adverb* used to introduce the first idea, reason, etc in a series **ilk olarak; ilk sırada** *The aim of this activity is firstly to have fun, and secondly to keep fit.*

ʹfirst ˌname *noun* [C] the name that people who know you call you and that comes before your family name **ilk isim**

the ˌfirst ʹperson *noun* the form of a verb or pronoun that is used when people are speaking or writing about themselves. For example, 'I' and 'we' are first person pronouns. birinci tekil/çoğul şahıslar/zamirler ('I' ve 'we')

first-rate /ˌfɜːstˈreɪt/ *adjective* extremely good **birinci sınıf; en üstün nitelikli** *a first-rate team/writer*

fiscal /ˈfɪskᵊl/ *adjective* relating to government money, especially taxes **mali, parasal**

○‑**fish¹** /fɪʃ/ *noun plural* fish *or* fishes **1** [C] an animal that lives only in water and swims using its tail and fins (= thin, triangular parts) **balık** *Are there any fish in the pond?* **2** [U] fish eaten as food **(yemek) balık** *fish and chips* ⊃Orta kısımdaki renkli sayfalarına bakınız.

fish² /fɪʃ/ *verb* [I] to try to catch fish **balık tutmak** *They're fishing for tuna.*

fish sth out *phrasal verb informal* to pull or take something out of a bag or pocket, especially after searching **(cepten, çantadan) bulup/çekip çıkarmak**

fisherman /ˈfɪʃəmən/ *noun* [C] *plural* fishermen someone who catches fish as a job or as a hobby **balıkçı**

fishing /ˈfɪʃɪŋ/ *noun* [U] the sport or job of catching fish **balıkçılık** *Dad loves to go fishing.*

ˈfish ˌslice *noun* [C] *UK* a kitchen tool with a wide, flat end used for lifting and serving food **yemek servisinde kullanılan geniş düz uçlu mutfak gereci; spatula** ⊃Orta kısımdaki renkli sayfalarına bakınız.

fishy /ˈfɪʃi/ *adjective* **1** smelling or tasting like fish **balığımsı, balık gibi 2** making you feel that someone is lying or something dishonest is happening **şüpheli, kuşkulu, içinde bit yeniği olan** *His story sounds a bit fishy to me.*

fist /fɪst/ *noun* [C] a hand closed into a ball with the fingers and thumb curled tightly together **yumruk** *He banged his fist down angrily on the table.*

fist

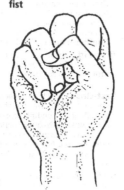

○‑**fit¹** /fɪt/ *verb* fitting, *past* fitted **1** [RIGHT SHAPE] [I, T] to be the right shape or size for someone or something **uymak, tam ölçüsünde olmak** *These trousers don't fit any more.* ○ *I can't find a lid to fit this jar.* **2 fit (sth) in/through/ under, etc** If people or things fit somewhere, or if you can fit them somewhere, that place is big enough for them. **sıkıştırmak, yerleştirmek, uydurmak** *How many people can you fit in your car?* ○ *This radio is small enough to fit into my pocket.* **3** [PUT] [T] *mainly UK* to put or fix something somewhere **uydurmak, koymak, yerleştirmek** *You ought to fit a smoke alarm in the kitchen.* **4** [SAME] [I, T] to be the same as or like something **uygun olmak, uymak, aynı olmak** *She seems to fit the police description.* **5** [SUITABLE] [T] to be suitable for something **bir şey için uygun/uyumlu olmak** *The punishment should fit the crime.*

fit in *phrasal verb* to feel that you belong to a particular group and are accepted by them **uyum sağlamak, uyuşmak; kabul görmek, kabul edilmek** *He doesn't fit in with the other pupils in his class.*

fit sb/sth in *phrasal verb* to find the time to see someone or do something **bir şeyi/birini görmeye zaman ayırmak/bulmak** *The dentist can fit you in on Tuesday morning.*

fit in with sth *phrasal verb* If one activity or event fits in with another, they exist or happen together in a way that is convenient. **bir şey diğerine uymak, beraber iyi gitmek, uyum içinde olmak** *The party is in early June. How does that fit in with your holiday plans?*

fit² /fɪt/ *adjective* fitter, fittest **1** of a good enough quality or suitable type for a particular purpose **uygun, elverişli, kaliteli** [+ to do sth] *Is this water fit to drink?* ○ *She's not in a fit state to drive.* **2** healthy, especially because you exercise regularly **sağlığı yerinde, sağlıklı, bakımlı, formda** *He's very fit for his age.* ⊃Opposite unfit. **3 do sth as you see/think fit** to do something that you feel is the right thing to do, although other people might disapprove **uygun olan/olduğunu düşündüğü şeyi yapmak,** *You must spend the money as you see fit.*

fit³ /fɪt/ *noun* **1 a good/loose/tight, etc fit** when something fits someone or somewhere well, loosely, tightly, etc **iyi/bol/sıkı vb. uyum/olma** *These shoes are a perfect fit.* **2** [C] a sudden, uncontrolled period of doing something or feeling something **ani/kontrolsüz davranış/his** *a coughing fit* ○ *I hit him in a fit of anger.* **3** [C] a short period of illness when someone cannot control their movements and becomes unconscious **kriz, nöbet, beklenmedik durum** *to have an epileptic fit* **4 have a fit** *informal* to become extremely angry **küplere binmek, hiddetlenmek, çılgına dönmek**

fitful /ˈfɪtfᵊl/ *adjective* stopping and starting and not happening in a regular or continuous way **kesik kesik, düzensiz olan, arada bir gelip giden** *fitful sleep* ● **fitfully** *adverb* **düzensiz bir şekilde**

fitness ...... İLE BİRLİKTE KULLANILAN KELİMELER

improve your fitness ● sb's fitness **level(s)** ● a fitness **programme/regime/test** ● **physical** fitness

fitness /ˈfɪtnəs/ *noun* [U] **1** the condition of being physically strong and healthy **zindelik, form, sağlık** *physical fitness* **2** the quality of being suitable for a particular purpose, job, course of study, etc **(iş, çalışma konusu, belli bir amaca) uygunluk, yerindelik** *The purpose of the exercise is to judge a soldier's fitness for combat.*

fitted /ˈfɪtɪd/ *adjective* **1** *UK* made or cut to fill a particular space exactly **tam uydurulmuş, gömme, monte edilmiş, döşenmiş** *fitted carpets/kitchens* **2** Fitted clothes fit tightly to your body. **ölçüye göre kesilmiş, bedene uydurulmuş, kalıp gibi** *a fitted jacket*

fitting /ˈfɪtɪŋ/ *adjective* suitable or right for a particular situation **uyan, uygun** *The promotion was a fitting reward for all his hard work.*

fittings /ˈfɪtɪŋz/ *noun* [plural] *mainly UK* **1** parts that are fixed to a piece of furniture or equipment **(mobilya, sıhhi tesisat, alet edavat vb.) parçaları, uygun malzemeler, tertibat** *a circular bath with gold fittings* **2** things that are fixed to the walls, floors, and ceilings inside a house but that can be moved **evde duvar, döşeme ve tavana takılanlar, asılanlar, konulanlar**

○‑**five** /faɪv/ the number 5 **beş**

fiver /ˈfaɪvᵊr/ *noun* [C] *UK informal* a piece of paper money worth £5 **5 sterlinlik kağıt para** *You owe me a fiver.*

five-star /faɪvˈstɑːr/ *adjective* describes a hotel or resort of very high quality **(otel, lokanta vb.) beş-yıldızlı**

○‑**fix¹** /fɪks/ *verb* [T] **1** [REPAIR] to repair something **tamir etmek, onarmak** *My watch is broken - can you fix it?* **2** [DECIDE] to decide a certain and exact date, price, plan, etc **(plan, tarih, fiyat vb.) tam ve kesin olarak belirlemek, kararlaştırmak** *Let's fix a day to have lunch together.* ○ *The price has been fixed at $10.* **3 fix sth**

onto/to/under, etc to fasten something in a particular place **tutturmak, takmak, monte etmek, asmak, yerleştirmek** *They fixed the bookcase to the wall.* **4** [PREPARE] to prepare a drink or meal **içki/yemek hazırlamak** [+ two objects] *I'll fix you a sandwich.* **5** [CHEAT] to do something dishonest to make certain that a competition, race, or election is won by a particular person **şike yapmak, hile yapmak/karıştırmak** [often passive] *People are saying that the elections were fixed.*

fix sth up *phrasal verb* **1** *UK* to arrange a meeting, date, event, etc **toplantı/randevu/olay vb. düzenlemek, tespit etmek, ayarlamak, belirlemek** *Can we fix up a date for the next meeting?* **2** to repair or change something in order to improve it **tamir etmek, daha iyi hale getirmek, onarmak** *Nick loves fixing up old cars.*

fix sb up *phrasal verb* to provide someone with something that they need **temin etmek, sağlamak** *My uncle has fixed me up with a summer job.*

fix² /fɪks/ *noun* **1 a quick fix** a way of solving a problem easily **hızlı çözüm; kolay çare bulma** *There is no quick fix for unemployment.* **2 be in a fix** to be in a difficult situation **köşeye sıkışmak, sıkışık durumda olmak, zor durumda olmak** *I'm in a fix and need your help.* **3** [C] *informal* an amount of an illegal drug or something that you want very much **yasadışı bir şeyden veya uyuşturucudan bir miktar** *Cath needs her fix of chocolate every day.*

fixation /fɪkˈseɪʃⁿn/ *noun* [C] a very strong interest in a particular person or thing **aşırı ilgi, saplantı, tutku, sabit bir davranış** *She's got an unhealthy fixation with her weight.*

fixed /fɪkst/ *adjective* **1** decided already and not able to be changed **sabit, değişmez, kararlaştırılmış, belirlenmiş** *a fixed price* ○ *Is the date of the wedding fixed yet?* **2** fastened somewhere and not able to be moved **tutturulmuş, sabit, oynamaz, monte edilmiş**

fixture /ˈfɪkstʃəʳ/ *noun* [C] **1** a piece of furniture or equipment that is fixed inside a house or building and is usually sold with it **sabit eşya, demirbaş, ev eşyası** [usually plural] *It comes with the usual fixtures and fittings.* **2** *UK* a sports event that is arranged for a particular day **spor karşılamaları programı, fikstür**

fizz /fɪz/ *noun* [U] bubbles of gas in a liquid or the sound that they make **kabarcık, foşurdama, köpürük** ● **fizz** *verb* [I] **fışırdamak** (içecek)

fizzle /ˈfɪzl/ *verb*
fizzle out *phrasal verb* to gradually end in a disappointing way **iyi başlayıp kötü bitmek, fos çıkmak, fiyaskoyla sonlanmak** *Their relationship soon fizzled out when they got back from holiday.*

fizzy /ˈfɪzi/ *adjective* A fizzy drink has lots of bubbles of gas in it. **kabarcıklı, baloncuklu** **fizzy**

flabbergasted /ˈflæbəgɑːstɪd/ *adjective informal* extremely surprised **şaşırmış, şaşkın, hayretler içinde**

flabby /ˈflæbi/ *adjective* having too much loose fat on your body **yağlı, gevşek, güçsüz, gevşek kaslı, sarkık** *etli flabby arms/thighs*

flag¹ /flæg/ *noun* [C] a piece of cloth with a special design and colours, that is fixed to a pole as the symbol of a country or group **bayrak** *the French flag* ○ *There was a flag flying above the castle.*

flag² /flæg/ *verb* [I] **flagging**, *past* **flagged** to become tired or less interested in something **durgunlaşmak, gevşemek, ilgisi azalmak** *The players started to flag towards the end of the game.*
flag sth down *phrasal verb* to make a vehicle stop by waving at the driver **el sallayarak bir aracı/sürücüyü durdurmak**

flagrant /ˈfleɪgrənt/ *adjective* shocking because of being so obviously wrong or bad **kasti, ahlaksız, usulsüz, gün gibi ortada, apaçık** *a flagrant disregard for the law* ● **flagrantly** *adverb* **çok belirgin**

flagship /ˈflægʃɪp/ *noun* [C] a product or service that is the best and most admired that a company has **amiral gemisi, bir şirketin en iyi ve sevilen ürünü/hizmeti**

flail /fleɪl/ (*also* flail about/around) *verb* [I, T] to wave or move your arms and legs about energetically and in an uncontrolled way **çırpınmak, sallanmak** *The wasp came towards us and Howard started flailing his arms around.*

flair /fleəʳ/ *noun* **1** [no plural] a natural ability to do something well **yetenek, yeti, kabiliyet** *She has a flair for languages.* **2** [U] doing something in an exciting and interesting way **zarafet, özgünlük, incelik** *He played with great imagination and flair.*

flak /flæk/ *noun* [U] *informal* criticism **eleştiri, tenkit** *The government took a lot of flak for breaking its election promises.*

flake¹ /fleɪk/ *noun* [C] a small, flat, thin piece of something **ince tabaka, parçacık, tane** *flakes of paint/snow*

flake² /fleɪk/ *verb* [I] to come off in small, flat, thin pieces **soyulmak, kıymık/yonga şeklinde tabaka tabaka çıkmak** *The paint was flaking off the walls.* ● **flaky** *adjective* coming off easily in small, flat, thin pieces **yonga/kıymık, ince tabaka biçiminde** *dry, flaky skin*

flake off

flamboyant /flæmˈbɔɪənt/ *adjective* **1** A flamboyant person is loud, stylish, and confident. (kişi) **çalımlı, gösterişli, havalı** *a flamboyant pop star* **2** Flamboyant clothes or colours are very bright and noticeable. (kıyafet) **gözalıcı, frapan** ● **flamboyance** /flæmˈbɔɪəns/ *noun* [U] **süs**

flame ...... İLE BİRLİKTE KULLANILAN KELİMELER
be in flames ● **burst into/go up in** flames ● flames **spread**

flame¹ /fleɪm/ *noun* [C, U] **1** hot, bright, burning gas produced by something on fire **alev** *Smoke and flames were pouring out of the burning factory.* ○ *The whole building was soon in flames* (= burning). ○ *The car crashed and burst into flames* (= suddenly started burning). **2** an angry email or message in a chat room, etc. **öfkeyle yazılmış ileti/e-posta**

flame² /fleɪm/ *verb* [I, T] to send an angry email to someone **birine kızgınlık dolu e-posta göndermek**

flaming /ˈfleɪmɪŋ/ *adjective* [always before noun] **1** [BURNING] burning with a bright light **parlak, alev alev yanan** *a* *flaming building* **2** BRIGHT very bright in colour or light **parlak, parıl parıl** *flaming red hair* **3** ANNOYED *UK informal* used to emphasize something when you are annoyed **Körolası!** *What a flaming idiot!*

flamingo /flə'mɪŋɡəʊ/ *noun* [C] a large bird with long, thin legs and pink feathers that lives near water in some hot countries **flamingo; ince uzun bacaklı pembe tüyleri olan büyük kuş**

flammable /'flæməbl/ (*also* **inflammable**) *adjective* Flammable liquids, gases, or materials burn very easily. **yanıcı, kolay yanan**

flan /flæn/ *noun* [C, U] a round, open pastry base filled with something such as fruit, or cheese and vegetables **börek, çörek** *cheese and onion flan*

flank[1] /flæŋk/ *verb* **be flanked by sb/sth** to have someone or something at the side or at each side **her iki tarafında birileri olmak; yanlarında birileriyle yürümek** *The President was flanked by police officers.*

flank[2] /flæŋk/ *noun* [C] **1** the side of the body of an animal or person from the chest to the hips **böğür, yan** **2** the side of an army when it is ready to fight (**ordu**) **yan kanat**

flannel /'flænºl/ *noun* **1** [U] soft, warm cloth for making clothes **yumuşak yünlü kumaş, flanel, pazen** *flannel pyjamas* **2** [C] *UK* (*US* **washcloth**) a small cloth that you use to wash your face and body **yüz ve vücut yıkamada kullanılan havlu/bez, lif** ⊃Orta kısımdaki renkli sayfalarına bakınız.

flap[1] /flæp/ *noun* **1** [C] a piece of cloth or material fixed along one edge to cover or close an opening **kanatlı kapak/örtü** **2** [C, U] *US* when someone is worried or excited, or a situation that causes them to feel this way **telaş, endişe, vesvese** *The President's remarks caused a huge flap.* **3 be/get in a flap** *mainly UK informal* to be or become worried or excited **telaşlanmak, endişelenmek**

flap[2] /flæp/ *verb* **flapping**, *past* **flapped** **1** WINGS [T] If a bird flaps its wings, it moves them up and down. (**kanat vb.**) **çırpmak, aşağı yukarı sallamak** **2** MOVE [I] If something such as cloth or paper flaps, the side that is not fixed to something moves around, especially in the wind. (**rüzgârda**) **sallanmak, yalpalanmak** *The curtains were flapping around in the breeze.* **3** WORRY [I] *UK informal* to become worried or excited about something **telaşlanmak, vesveselenmek, endişelenmek, heyecanlanmak** *Don't flap! We've got plenty of time to get to the airport.*

flare[1] /fleə^r/ (*also* **flare up**) *verb* [I] **1** If something bad such as anger or pain flares up, it suddenly starts or gets worse. **gittikçe/aniden kötüleşmek, artmak, daha da kötüye gitmek** *Violence flared up between football fans yesterday.* **2** to suddenly burn brightly, usually for a short time (**ateş**) **birden alevlenmek, parlamak** *The rocket flared in the sky and disappeared into space.*

flare[2] /fleə^r/ *noun* [C] **1** a piece of safety equipment that produces a bright signal when you are lost or injured **işaret fişeği, acil durum işaret ışığı** **2** a sudden, bright light **parlama, alev, parlak ışık**

flared /fleəd/ *adjective* wide at the bottom (**etek**) **evaze; (pantolon) bol/ispanyol paçalı** *flared trousers*

flash[1] /flæʃ/ *verb* **1** [I, T] to shine brightly and suddenly, or to make something shine in this way (**ışık**) **birden parla(t)mak, şimşek gibi çakmak, ışıldamak, parıldamak** *The doctor flashed a light into my eye.* ○ *Lightning flashed across the sky.* **2** [I, T] (*also* **flash up**) to appear for a short time, or to make something appear for a short time **kısa bir süre görünüp kaybolmak; kısa bir süre görünmek; parlamak** *An icon flashed up on*

the screen. **3 flash by/past/through, etc** to move somewhere fast **yıldırım gibi geçip gitmek; hızlıca geçmek** *The motorcycle flashed past us and around the corner.* **4 flash (sb) a look/smile, etc** to look/smile, etc at someone quickly **hızlı bir bakış/gülümseme vb. göstermek/atmak** *She flashed him a smile as he came in.*

flash back *phrasal verb* If your mind or thoughts flash back to something that happened in the past, you suddenly remember it. **geçmişe dönmek, anılara geri dönmek, geri dönüş yaparak olayları tekrardan hatırlayıp anlatmak**

flash[2] /flæʃ/ *noun* **1** BRIGHT LIGHT [C] a sudden bright light **ani ışık/parıltı, ışık çakması/yanması** *The bomb exploded in a flash of yellow light.* **2** CAMERA [C, U] a piece of camera equipment that produces a bright light when you take a photograph in a dark place **flaş; fotoğraf makinası/kamera ışığı** **3** SUDDEN EXPERIENCE [C] a sudden experience of something such as a feeling or idea **bir his ve fikrin ani oluşması; birden bire akla gelme** *a flash of anger* ○ *I had a flash of inspiration.* **4 in a flash** immediately, or very quickly **acilen, anlık, çok hızlı** *I'll be back in a flash.* **5 a flash in the pan** a sudden success that does not continue **anlık/geçici bir başarı**

flashback /'flæʃbæk/ *noun* [C] **1** when you suddenly remember something that happened in the past, usually something bad **geçmişe dönüş** **2** part of a film or book that goes back in time to something that happened before the main story began **bir fiil ya da kitapta esas konuya girmeden geçmişe yolculuk**

flashlight /'flæʃlaɪt/ *US* (*UK* **torch**) *noun* [C] an electric light that you can hold in your hand **el feneri**

flashy /'flæʃi/ *adjective* looking too bright, big, and expensive, in a way that is intended to get attention **parlak, şaşalı, pahalı; dikkat çeken, göz kamaştırıcı, cafcaflı** *flashy gold jewellery*

flask

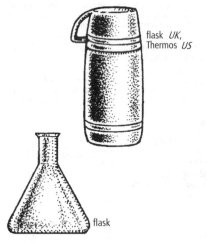

flask *UK*, Thermos *US*

flask

flask /flɑːsk/ *noun* [C] **1** HOT DRINKS *UK* (*UK/US* **Thermos**) a special container that keeps drinks hot or cold **termos** *a flask of coffee* **2** ALCOHOL a flat bottle that is used to carry alcohol in your pocket **düz şişe; kanyak şişesi** **3** SCIENCE a glass container with a wide base and a narrow opening used in science **altı geniş üstü dar deney tüpü/şişesi**

🧩 **flat** ...... İLE BİRLİKTE KULLANILAN KELİMELER

in a flat • a block of flats • a one-bedroom/two-bedroom flat • a basement flat

o⊶**flat¹** /flæt/ *mainly UK* (*mainly US* apartment) *noun* [C] a set of rooms to live in, with all the rooms on one level of a building **daire, apartman dairesi** *a large block of flats*

flat

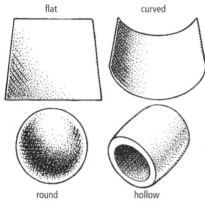

flat   curved

round   hollow

o⊶**flat²** /flæt/ *adjective* **flatter, flattest 1** SMOOTH smooth and level, with no curved, high, or hollow parts **düz, pürüzsüz** *a flat surface* ○ *The countryside around here is very flat.* **2** WITHOUT EMOTION without any energy, interest, or emotion **sıkıcı, cansız, duygusuz** *Her voice sounded very flat.* **3** WITHOUT AIR If a tyre is flat, it does not contain enough air. **(lastik) patlak, havasız 4** WITHOUT GAS If a drink is flat, it does not contain enough bubbles of gas. **gazı kaçmış, gazsız 5** WITHOUT POWER *UK* If a battery (= object which provides electricity) is flat, it does not contain any more electrical power. **(pil, akü) boşalmış, bitik, deşarj olmuş 6 a flat price/rate, etc** a price/rate, etc which is the same for everyone and does not change **düz fiyat, değişmez oran, sabit, standart** *He charges a flat rate of £15 an hour.* **7 B flat/E flat, etc** the musical note that is between the note B/E, etc and the note below it **esas notadan daha aşağı bir notada 8** TOO LOW A flat musical note sounds unpleasant because it is slightly lower than it should be. **düz, düz nota; olması gerekenden çok daha az seviyede düşük nota 9** LOW Flat shoes do not raise your feet far from the ground. **düz, tabansız, dümdüz, yayvan**

flat³ /flæt/ *adverb* **flatter, flattest 1** in a horizontal or level position on a surface **düz, yatay durumda** *She spread the cloth flat across the kitchen table.* **2 flat out** using all your energy or effort **son sürat, tamgaz, tam hızla, son sürat, olanca hızıyla** *We've all been working flat out to finish the project on time.* **3 in 5 minutes/30 seconds, etc flat** in exactly and only 5 minutes, 30 seconds, etc **tam olarak 5 dakikada/30 saniyede vs.** *He showered and got dressed in 10 minutes flat.* **4 fall flat** If an event or joke falls flat, it fails to have the effect that you wanted, such as making people laugh. **boşa çıkmak, beklenen etkiyi göstermemek/yaratmamak; ilgi uyandırmamak**

flatly /ˈflætli/ *adverb* **1 flatly deny/refuse, etc** to say something in a direct and certain way **külliyen inkâr etmek/reddetmek; açıkça/kesinlikle/tamamen söylemek** *He flatly refused to answer our questions.*

2 without showing any emotion or interest **herhangi bir hissiyat veya alaka göstermeksizin** *"He's gone," she said flatly.*

flatmate /ˈflætmeɪt/ *mainly UK* (*US* roommate) *noun* [C] someone who you share a flat with **ev arkadaşı**

flatpack /ˈflætpæk/ *adjective* used to describe furniture that is sold in pieces inside a flat box, ready to be put together **paketlenmiş; kurulmaya hazır paketlenmiş** *a flatpack table*

flat-screen TV *noun* [C] a type of television with a screen that is very thin and shows a very clear picture **düz ekran televizyon**

flatten /ˈflætᵊn/ *verb* [I, T] to become flat or to make something become flat **düzleşmek/düz hale gelmek/düzleştirmek** *Roll out the dough into balls and flatten them slightly.*

flatter /ˈflætəʳ/ *verb* **1** [T] to say nice things to someone in order to make them feel attractive or important, sometimes in a way that is not sincere **övmek, methetmek, övgüler/methiyeler düzmek; (argo) pohpohlamak, yağ çekmek** *The interviewer flattered him about his recent work.* **2 be flattered** to feel very pleased and proud **mutlu/gururlu hissetmek; gururu okşanmak, hoşa gitmek** *She was flattered by his attention.* **3** [T] to make someone look more attractive than usual **olduğundan güzel göstermek** *That new hairstyle really flatters you.* **4 flatter yourself** to believe something good about yourself, although it might not be true **kendini bir şey sanmak, kendini beğenmek; hayaline kapılmak, kendini inandırmak** *He flatters himself that he's a good driver.*

flattering /ˈflætᵊrɪŋ/ *adjective* making you look more attractive than usual **olduğundan daha çekici/güzel/farklı gösteren, çok yakışan** *a flattering picture*

flattery /ˈflætᵊri/ *noun* [U] when you say nice things to someone, often because you want something from that person **övgü, pohpohlama, dalkavukluk, yağcılık**

flaunt /flɔːnt/ *verb* [T] to make your success, money, beauty, etc very obvious so that people notice it and admire you **gösteriş yapmak, caka satmak, böbürlenmek** *Although he's a millionaire, he doesn't flaunt his wealth.*

🧩 **flavour** ...... İLE BİRLİKTE KULLANILAN KELİMELER

have a [mild/spicy/strong, etc] flavour • a delicate/delicious flavour

flavour¹ *UK* (*US* flavor) /ˈfleɪvəʳ/ *noun* **1** [C, U] the taste of a particular type of food or drink **tat, lezzet** *We sell 50 different flavours of ice cream.* ○ *Add some salt to give the soup more flavour.* **2** [no plural] a particular quality or style that something has **kendine has tarz veya kalite, belli bir nitelik, çeşni** *London has a very international flavour.*

flavour² (*US* flavor) /ˈfleɪvəʳ/ *verb* **1** [T] to give a particular taste to food or drink **lezzetlendirmek, tat vermek, çeşni katmak** [often passive] *This sauce is flavoured with garlic and herbs.* **2 cheese/chocolate, etc - flavoured** tasting of cheese/chocolate, etc **peynir/çikolata vb. tadında** *lemon-flavoured sweets*

flavouring *UK* (*US* flavoring) /ˈfleɪvᵊrɪŋ/ *noun* [C, U] something that is added to food or drink to give it a particular taste **tat verici/lezzetini artırıcı şey/tat/çeşni**

flaw /flɔː/ *noun* [C] a mistake or bad characteristic that stops someone or something from being perfect **zaaf, zayıflık, kusur, hata** *There's a flaw in your reasoning.*
• **flawed** *adjective a flawed argument* **hatalı**

flawless /ˈflɔːləs/ *adjective* with no mistakes or bad characteristics **kusursuz, hatasız, mükemmel** *a flawless complexion* ● **flawlessly** *adverb* **hatasız**

flea /fliː/ *noun* [C] a small, jumping insect that lives on animals or people and drinks their blood **bit**

'**flea ˌmarket** *noun* [C] a market where you can buy old or used things cheaply **bit pazarı**

fleck /flek/ *noun* [C] a mark, or a very small piece of something **benek, leke** *His shirt was covered in flecks of paint.*

fledgling /ˈfledʒlɪŋ/ *adjective* [always before noun] A fledgling company, country, or organization is new and not yet developed. **deneyimsiz, çiçeği burnunda, çok yeni, acemi, henüz gelişmemiş** *a fledgling democracy*

flee /fliː/ *verb* [I, T] **fleeing**, *past* **fled** to leave a place quickly because you are in danger or are afraid **sıvışmak, kaçıp gitmek, kaçmak, tüymek** *Police think the suspect has now fled the country.*

fleece /fliːs/ *noun* [C, U] **1** a warm, soft, light jacket, or the material used to make it **kaşe ceket, kaşe kumaş** **2** the thick covering of wool on a sheep **yapağı, yün, koyun postu**

fleet /fliːt/ *noun* [C] **1** a group of ships, or all of the ships in a country's navy **gemi filosu; (deniz kuv.) savaş gemisi filosu, donanma 2** a group of vehicles that are owned and controlled by one person or organization **filo** *a fleet of aircraft/cars*

flesh /fleʃ/ *noun* [U] **1** the soft part of a person's or animal's body between the skin and bones **et 2 in the flesh** in real life and not on television or in a film **gerçek yaşamda, canlı; tv'de filmde olmayan** *She looks much taller in the flesh.* **3** the soft part of a fruit or vegetable which you can eat **(meyve, sebze) etli kısmı 4 your own flesh and blood** a member of your family **kendi kanından/canından; akrabası veya aile efradından** ● **fleshy** *adjective* fat or thick, or with a lot of flesh **etli, dolgun, tombul**

flew /fluː/ *past tense of* fly '**uçmak' fiilinin ikinci hâli**

flex¹ /fleks/ *verb* [T] to bend a part of your body so that the muscle becomes tight **eğmek, bükmek, germek**

flex² /fleks/ UK (UK/US cord) *noun* [C, U] a piece of wire covered in plastic, that is used to connect electrical equipment to a power supply **kordon, kablo, elektrik kablosu**

flexible /ˈfleksɪbl/ *adjective* **1** able to change or be changed easily according to the situation **esnek, içinde bulunduğu duruma göre hareket edebilen, değişen/değiştirilebilen** *I'd like a job with more flexible working hours.* **2** A flexible substance can bend easily without breaking. **esnek, elastikî, eğilebilir** ● **flexibility** /ˌfleksɪˈbɪləti/ *noun* [U] **esneklik**

flick¹ /flɪk/ *verb* **1 flick sth into/off/over, etc** to move something somewhere suddenly and quickly through the air, usually with your fingers **bir şeyi parmaklarla hızlı hızlı çevirmek** *He quickly flicked the crumbs off the table.* **2 flick down/out/towards, etc** to make a sudden, quick movement somewhere **bir yere doğru ani ve hızlı hamle yapmak/hareket etmek** *His eyes flicked between her and the door.* **3 flick a switch** to move a switch in order to make electrical equipment start or stop working **(elektrikli alet) açma kapama düğmesini çevirmek**
flick sth on/off *phrasal verb* to move a switch in order to make electrical equipment start/stop working **bir şeyi çalıştırmak/durdurmak için düğmeyi açıp kapatmak**

flick through sth *phrasal verb* to look quickly at the pages of a magazine, book, etc **dergi/kitap sayfalarını rastgele hızlıca çevirerek bakmak**

flick² /flɪk/ *noun* [C] a sudden, quick movement **ani çabuk hareket** *With a flick of her wrist, she threw the pebble into the water.*

flicker¹ /ˈflɪkəʳ/ *verb* [I] **1** to shine with a light that is sometimes bright and sometimes weak **pır pır ederek yanmak, titreyerek yanmak; yanıp sönmek** *a candle flickering in the window* **2** to appear for a short time or make a sudden movement somewhere **gözüküp kaybolmak; bir ortaya çıkıp bir kaybolmak** *A smile flickered across her face.*

flicker² /ˈflɪkəʳ/ *noun* [no plural] **1** when a light is sometimes bright and sometimes weak **titrek ışık/alev** *the soft flicker of candlelight* **2** a slight, brief feeling or expression of an emotion **ürperti, titreme, belli belirsiz duygu, anlık duygu** *a flicker of hope*

flier (*also* flyer) /ˈflaɪəʳ/ *noun* [C] **1** a small piece of paper advertising a business, show, event, etc **el ilanı 2** someone who flies, especially a passenger on an aircraft **uçak yolcusu; uçakla seyahat eden**

flies /flaɪz/ UK (UK/US fly) *noun* [plural] the part where trousers open and close at the front **pantolon fermuarı**

flight ...... İLE BİRLİKTE KULLANILAN KELİMELER

on a flight ● a flight from/to [Paris/Tokyo, etc] ● a long-haul/short-haul flight

oᴹ **flight** /flaɪt/ *noun* **1** [JOURNEY] [C] a journey in an aircraft **uçak seyahatı** *The flight to Chicago took 4 hours.* **2** [AIRCRAFT] [C] an aircraft that carries passengers from one place to another **uçuş** *Flight 102 is ready for boarding at Gate 3.* **3** [MOVEMENT] [U] when something flies or moves through the air **uçma** *an eagle in flight* **4 a flight of stairs/steps** a set of stairs **merdivenler/basamaklar dizisi**

'**flight atˌtendant** *noun* [C] someone whose job is to look after passengers on an aircraft **kabin görevlisi**

flimsy /ˈflɪmzi/ *adjective* **1** thin and not solid or strong **ince, hafif, çürük** *a flimsy cardboard box* **2** A flimsy argument, excuse, etc is weak and difficult to believe. **zayıf/uyduruk/tutarsız/baştan savma tartışma/mazeret** *I'm sick of his flimsy excuses for being late.*

flinch /flɪnʃ/ *verb* [I] **1** to make a sudden movement backwards because you are afraid or in pain **irkilmek, çekinmek, ürkmek** *She didn't flinch when the nurse cleaned the wound.* **2** to avoid doing something that is unpleasant **uzak durmak, kaçmak, sakınmak** *Nick never flinches from difficult decisions.*

fling¹ /flɪŋ/ *verb* *past* **flung fling sth around/across/down, etc** to throw or move something suddenly and with a lot of force **fırlatıp atmak, savurmak, atmak** *She flung her arms around his neck.*

fling² /flɪŋ/ *noun* [C] **1** a sexual relationship that is short and not serious **kaçamak, çapkınlık, kısa süreli ilişki** *She had a fling with someone last summer.* **2** a short period of time when you have a lot of enjoyment or pleasure **çılgınca eğlenme, kurtlarını dökme** *This is my last fling before the exams.*

flint /flɪnt/ *noun* [C, U] a very hard, grey stone that can be used to produce a flame **çakmak taşı**

flip /flɪp/ *verb* **flipping**, *past* **flipped 1** [I, T] to turn or make something turn onto a different side, or so that it is the wrong way up **döndürmek, dönmek, ters yöne döndürmek** *to flip a coin/pancake* ○ *The boat flipped right over.* **2** [I] *informal* to become uncontrollably angry, crazy, or excited **kontrolden çıkmak, çılgına**

dönmek, heyecana kapılmak *Dad completely flipped when he saw the car.*
flip through sth *phrasal verb* to look quickly at the pages of a magazine, book, etc **dergi, kitap vb. hızlıca bakmak, göz gezdirmek**

'**flip ˌchart** *noun* [C] large pieces of paper attached to a board on legs, which you write or draw on when you are talking to a group of people **üzerinde büyük kağıtların bulunduğu konferans tahtası; yazım/çizim şövalesi**

flip-flop /ˈflɪpˌflɒp/ (*US also* **thong**) *noun* [usually plural] a type of shoe, often made of rubber, with a V-shaped strap in between the big toe and the toe next to it **tokyo terlik** ⊃Orta kısımdaki renkli sayfalarına bakınız.

flippant /ˈflɪpənt/ *adjective* without respect or not serious **saygısız, küstah, ciddiyetsiz** *a flippant remark*
● **flippantly** *adverb* **saygısızca** ● **flippancy** /ˈflɪpənsi/ *noun* [U] **saygısızlık**

flipper /ˈflɪpər/ *noun* [C] **1** a part like a wide, flat arm without fingers that some sea animals use for swimming **balık kanadı, yüzgeç 2** a long, flat, rubber shoe that you use when swimming under water **palet**

flipping /ˈflɪpɪŋ/ *adjective* [always before noun] *UK informal* used to emphasize something, or to show slight anger **vurgulayan, hafif kızgınlık gösteren** *Where are my flipping keys?*

the ˈflip ˌside *noun* the opposite, less good, or less popular side of something **bir şeyin tersi/daha az bilinen/daha az iyi tarafı**

flirt¹ /flɜːt/ *verb* [I] to behave as if you are sexually attracted to someone, usually not in a very serious way **fingirdeşmek, flört etmek, kur yapmak** *She was flirting with a guy at the bar.*
flirt with sth *phrasal verb* **1** to be interested in an idea, activity, etc but not seriously, or for only a short time **bir şeyle öylesine ilgilenmek; kafasından geçirmek; ilgileniyormuş gibi görünmek** *He flirted with the idea of becoming a priest.* **2 flirt with danger/disaster, etc** to risk experiencing something bad ● **flirtation** /flɜːˈteɪʃən/ *noun* [C, U] **ilgi**

flirt² /flɜːt/ *noun* [C] someone who often flirts with people **flört eden kimse**

flirtatious /flɜːˈteɪʃəs/ *adjective* behaving as if you are sexually attracted to someone, usually not in a very serious way **cilveli, fıkırdak, tahrik edici**

flit /flɪt/ *verb* **flitting**, *past* **flitted flit about/around/in and out, etc** to fly or move quickly from one place to another **uçuşmak, sağa sola hızlıca uçmak/hareket etmek** *Birds were flitting from tree to tree.*

float¹ /fləʊt/ *verb* **1** LIQUID [I, T] to stay on the surface of a liquid instead of sinking, or to make something do this **yüzmek, suyun üstünde kalmak, batmadan durmak** *I like floating on my back in the pool.* **2** AIR [I] to stay in the air, or move gently through the air **havada kalmak; havada süzülmek** *A balloon floated across the sky.* **3** BUSINESS [I, T] to start selling a company's shares to the public **şirket hisselerini halka arz etmek/satmaya başlamak 4 float sb's boat** *informal* to interest someone **ilgilendirmek, ilgisini çekmek** *Georgia likes William, but he just doesn't float my boat.*

float² /fləʊt/ *noun* [C] **1** VEHICLE a large, decorated vehicle that is used in public celebrations **toplumsal kutlamalarda kullanılan süslü büyük araç; tören geçit aracı 2** WATER an object that floats on water, used in fishing or when learning to swim **yüzme öğrenirken veya balık tutarken kullanılan nesne, mantar 3** BUSINESS when you float a business **iş yapma; iş**

flock¹ /flɒk/ *noun* [group] **1** a group of birds or sheep **kuş sürüsü** *a flock of geese* **2** a group of people led by one

float

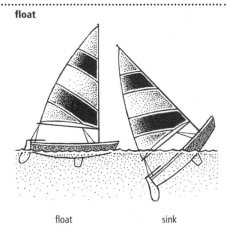

float   sink

person **birisi tarafından önderlik edilen bir grup insan; insan topluluğu** *a flock of children/visitors*

flock² /flɒk/ *verb* [I] to move or come together in large numbers **akın etmek; akın akın gitmek; hücum etmek** *Tourists are flocking to the beaches.* ○ [+ to do sth] *People flocked to hear him speak.*

flog /flɒg/ *verb* [T] **flogging**, *past* **flogged 1** to hit someone repeatedly as a punishment with something such as a stick **sopa ile dövmek, kamçılamak, dayakla cezalandırmak 2** *UK informal* to sell something quickly or cheaply **çarçabuk satmak; ucuz şekilde elden çıkarmak** *I had to flog the car to pay my bills.*
● **flogging** *noun* [C, U] **dayak cezası**

flood

flood¹ /flʌd/ *verb* [I, T] **1** If a place floods or is flooded, it becomes covered in water. **sel basmak, sular altında kalmak** [often passive] *The town was flooded when the river burst its banks.* ○ *I left the taps running and flooded the bathroom.* **2** To fill or enter a place in large numbers or amounts **dolmak, doldurmak, taşmak; tıka basa doldurmak** *Light flooded the room.* ○ *Shoppers flooded into the store.* ● **flooding** *noun* [U] *There is widespread flooding in the South.* **sel**
be flooded with sth *phrasal verb* to receive so many letters, telephone calls, etc that you cannot deal with them **çok sayıda telefon/mektup almak, çok miktarda gelmek; yağmak**

catastrophic/devastating floods • flood damage/
victims/warnings

flood² /flʌd/ noun **1** [C] when a lot of water covers an
area that is usually dry, especially when a river
becomes too full **sel baskını 2** [C] a large number or
amount of things or people that arrive at the same
time **baskın, çokça gelme, yığınla olma, bolluk,
çokluk, sel gibi** *a flood of letters/calls* **3 in floods of
tears** *UK* crying a lot **sel gibi göz yaşı**

floodgates /ˈflʌdɡeɪts/ noun **open the floodgates** to
make it possible for a lot of people to do something
**önünü açmak, fırsatlar sunmak, mümkün kılmak;
kapıları açmak; salıvermek**

floodlights /ˈflʌdlaɪts/ noun [plural] powerful lights
used to light up sports fields or the outside of buildings
at night **bina dışı ve spor sahalarını aydınlatan pro-
jetörler; stad ışıkları; aydınlatma spotları** • **floodlit**
/ˈflʌdlɪt/ adjective lit up by floodlights **projektörlerle/
spotlarla aydınlatılan**

floor¹ /flɔːʳ/ noun **1** [SURFACE] [C] a surface that you walk on
inside a building **döşeme, zemin** *a wooden/tiled floor*
○ *I must sweep the kitchen floor.* **2** [BUILDING] [C] a particular
level of a building **yer, zemin, döşeme** *the second/third
floor* **3** [BOTTOM] [no plural] the ground or surface at the
bottom of something **taban, zemin, yer** *the forest/sea
floor* **4** [AREA] [C] an area where a particular activity happens **alan, yer** *a dance floor* ➔See also: **first floor, ground
floor, shop floor.**

floorboard /ˈflɔːbɔːd/ noun [C] a long, narrow, flat board
that forms part of a wooden floor in a building **parke,
zemin döşemesi, ahşap döşeme**

flooring /ˈflɔːrɪŋ/ noun [U] the material used to make or
cover a floor **döşeme, yer kaplama** *vinyl flooring*

flop¹ /flɒp/ verb [I] **flopping**, past **flopped 1 flop down/
into/onto, etc** to fall or sit somewhere suddenly in a
heavy or relaxed way **pat diye/lök gibi düşmek/otur-
mak** *He flopped down on the sofa.* **2** to hang loosely **gevşek şekilde asmak, sallandırmak** *Her hair kept flopping in her eyes.* **3** *informal* If a film, product, plan, etc
flops, it is not successful. **(film, ürün, plan vb.) başarısızlığa uğramak, düşmek, fiyaskoyla sonuçlanmak**

flop² /flɒp/ noun [C] *informal* **1** something that is not a
success **fiyasko, başarısızlık** *The party was a bit of a
flop.* **2** a movement towards the ground, or the noise
someone or something makes as they fall down **yere
düşme, pat diye çöküverme, düşme/vurma/
çarpma/çökme sesi** *She fell onto the bed with a flop.*

floppy /ˈflɒpi/ adjective soft and loose or hanging down
loosely **sarkık, gevşek** *floppy hair* ○ *a floppy hat*

floppy 'disk (also **floppy**) noun [C] a small disk inside a
flat, square piece of plastic used in the past for storing
information from a computer **bilgisayar diski**

flora /ˈflɔːrə/ noun [U, group] the plants that grow naturally in a particular area **bitki örtüsü, flora** *Scotland's
flora and fauna*

floral /ˈflɔːrəl/ adjective [always before noun] made from
flowers or relating to flowers **çiçeklerden yapılmış;
çiçeklere ilişkin** *a floral arrangement/pattern*

florist /ˈflɒrɪst/ noun [C] **1** someone who sells and
arranges flowers in a shop **çiçekçi, çiçek satıcısı
2** (also **florist's**) a shop that sells flowers **çiçekçi dükkânı**

flotation /fləʊˈteɪʃⁿn/ noun **1** [C, U] when a company's
shares are sold to the public for the first time **şirket
hisselerinin ilk defa halka arzı/satışı 2** [U] when

something or someone floats on or in liquid **yüzme,
su üstünde kalma; batmamak**

flounder /ˈflaʊndəʳ/ verb [I] **1** [MOVEMENT] to make wild
movements with your arms or body, especially because
you are trying not to sink **batmamak için çırpınmak,
debelenmek 2** [NOT KNOW] to not know what to do or say
**bocalamak, ne söyleyeceğini/yapacağını bilme-
mek** *When he resigned, the team was left floundering.*
3 [FAIL] If a relationship, organization, or plan flounders,
it fails or begins to experience problems. **düşe kalka
bata çıka ilerlemek; sorunlar yaşamaya başlamak;
iyi gitmemek; sorunlar yaşamak** *By 1993 his marriage was floundering.*

flour /flaʊəʳ/ noun [U] a powder made from grain that is
used to make bread, cakes, and other food **un**

flourish¹ /ˈflʌrɪʃ/ verb **1** [I] to grow or develop well **serpilmek, büyümek, gelişmek** *a flourishing tourist
industry* **2** [T] to wave something around in the air **bir
şeyi havada sallamak; dikkat çekmek/işaret vermek için sallamak**

flourish² /ˈflʌrɪʃ/ noun [no plural] when someone does
something in a special and noticeable way **çalım,
fiyaka, caka, gösteriş** *The waiter handed me the menu
with a flourish.*

flout /flaʊt/ verb [T] to intentionally not obey or accept
something **takmamak, hiçe saymak, aldırış etmemek, bilerek kabul etmemek** *to flout the law/rules*

flow¹ /fləʊ/ verb [I] **1** If something such as a liquid flows,
it moves somewhere in a smooth, continuous way.
akmak *The river flows from the Andes to the ocean.* **2** If
words, ideas, or conversations flow, they continue in an
easy and relaxed way without stopping. **(kelimeler,
fikirler, konuşmalar vb.) su gibi akmak, akıver-
mek, dökülmek** *At dinner, the conversation flowed
freely.*

flow² /fləʊ/ noun **1** [no plural] when something such as a
liquid moves somewhere in a smooth, continuous way
akma *the flow of blood* ○ *the flow of information* **2 go
with the flow** *informal* to do or accept what other
people are doing because it is the easiest thing to do
**kolay olduğu için başkalarının yaptığını yapmak/
kabul etmek** *Just relax and go with the flow!* ➔See also:
ebb¹ and flow.

a bouquet of /bunch of flowers • wild flowers • cut/
fresh flowers • dried flowers

flower¹ /flaʊəʳ/ noun **1** [C] the attractive, coloured part
of a plant where the seeds grow **çiçek** *a bunch of
flowers* **2** [C] a type of plant that produces flowers
çiçek *spring/wild flowers* **3 be in flower** When plants
are in flower, they have flowers on them. **çiçekli, çiçeği
olmak 4 the flower of sth** *literary* the best part of
something **en iyi/güzel kısmı** *the flower of our nation's
youth*

flower² /flaʊəʳ/ verb [I] to produce flowers **çiçek
açmak, çiçeklenmek** *These pansies flower all summer.*

'flower ,bed noun [C] an area of soil in a garden that you
grow flowers in **tarh, çiçek tarhı**

flowery /ˈflaʊəri/ adjective **1** (also **flowered** /flaʊəd/)
decorated with a pattern of flowers **çiçekli, çiçek
desenleri ile süslü/bezenmiş** *a flowery dress*
2 Flowery language contains unnecessarily complicated and unusual words. **(dil) ağdalı, gösterişli, tumtu-
raklı**

flowing /ˈfləʊɪŋ/ adjective **1** hanging down in a long,
loose way **gevşek ve uzun şekilde sarkık, sarkan**
flowing robes/hair **2** produced in a smooth, continuous,
or relaxed style **akıcı; düzgün, devamlı** *flowing lines*

flown /fləʊn/ *past participle of* fly '**uçmak' fiilinin üçüncü hâli**

fl oz *written abbreviation for* fluid ounce (= a unit for measuring liquid) **sıvı ölçer; sıvı ölçüm birimi**

flu /fluː/ *noun* [U] an illness like a very bad cold, that makes you feel hot and weak **grip** *I had the flu last week.*

fluctuate /'flʌktʃueɪt/ *verb* [I] to keep changing, especially in level or amount **değişmek, değişimi sürdürmek** *Oil prices have fluctuated wildly in recent weeks.*
● **fluctuation** /ˌflʌktʃu'eɪʃᵊn/ *noun* [C, U] *fluctuations in house prices* **dalgalanma**

fluent /'fluːənt/ *adjective* **1** able to use a language naturally without stopping or making mistakes **akıcı konuşan; bir dili akıcı/hatasız kullanan** *She is fluent in six languages.* **2** produced or done in a smooth, natural style **akıcı** *Hendrik speaks fluent English.*
● **fluency** /'fluːənsi/ *noun* [U] **akıcılık** ● **fluently** *adverb* **akıcı bir şekilde**

fluff¹ /flʌf/ *noun* [U] small, loose bits of wool or other soft material **hav, hav yumağı, tüy** *There's a piece of fluff on your jacket.*

fluff² /flʌf/ *verb* [T] *informal* to fail to do something successfully **bir şeyi başarıyla yapmamak, başarısız olmak; eline yüzüne bulaştırmak** *I had a great chance to score but I fluffed it.*
fluff sth out/up *phrasal verb* to make something appear bigger or fuller by hitting or shaking it so that it contains more air **kabartmak, tüylerini kabartmak** *I'll fluff up your pillows for you.*

fluffy /'flʌfi/ *adjective* made or covered with soft fur or cloth **tüylü, kabarık** *a fluffy toy*

fluid¹ /'fluːɪd/ *noun* [C, U] a liquid **sıvı** *cleaning fluid* ○ *Drink plenty of fluids.*

fluid² /'fluːɪd/ *adjective* **1** [LIQUID] able to flow easily like liquid **akıcı, akışkan 2** [CHANGING] likely or able to change **değişken** *a fluid situation* **3** [SMOOTH] smooth and continuous **düzgün, devamlı** *fluid movements*

fluid 'ounce (*written abbreviation* fl oz) *noun* [C] a unit for measuring liquid, equal to 0.0284 litres in the UK and 0.0296 litres in the US **sıvı ölçüm birimi (Birleşik kallık 0.0284 liter; ABD 0.0296 litreye eşit)**

fluke /fluːk/ *noun* [C, U] something good that happens only because of luck or chance **şans** *That first goal was just a fluke.*

flume /fluːm/ *noun* [C] a large tube for people to slide down at a swimming pool **havuz kaydırağı**

flung /flʌŋ/ *past of* fling '**fırlatmak, savurmak' fiilinin ikinci hali**

fluorescent /flɔː'resᵊnt/ *adjective* **1** Fluorescent lights are very bright, tube-shaped, electric lights, often used in offices. **floresan 2** Fluorescent colours, clothes, etc are very bright and can be seen in the dark. **fosforlu, parlak, parlayan** *fluorescent pink* ○ *a fluorescent jacket*

fluoride /'flɔːraɪd/ *noun* [U] a chemical that helps to prevent tooth decay **florür** *fluoride toothpaste*

flurry /'flʌri/ *noun* [C] **1** a sudden, short period of activity, interest, or excitement **telaş, dalga, debdebe** *a flurry of phone calls* **2** a sudden, short period of snow and wind **sağanak**

flush¹ /flʌʃ/ *verb* **1** [I, T] If you flush a toilet, or if it flushes, its contents empty and it fills with water again. **sifonu çekmek 2 flush sth away/down/out, etc** to get rid of something by pushing it somewhere with lots of water, such as down a toilet **su ile temizlemek, akıtmak 3** [I] If you flush, your face becomes red

and hot, usually because you are embarrassed or angry. **yüzü kızarmak, mahcup olmak, bozulmak**
flush sb/sth out *phrasal verb* to force a person or animal to come out from where they are hiding **girdiği yerden zorla çıkarmak, çıkmaya zorlamak**

flush² /flʌʃ/ *noun* [C] **1** when your face becomes hot and red **yüz kızarması, mahcubiyet** *a hot flush* **2** a flush of excitement/pleasure, etc a sudden feeling of excitement/pleasure, etc **ani heyecan/telaş/coşku vb. fışkırması**

flush³ /flʌʃ/ *adjective* [never before noun] **1** at the same level as another surface **aynı hizada/seviyede/düzlemde olan** *I want the door flush with the wall.* **2** *informal* rich **zengin, varlıklı** *flush with cash*

flustered /'flʌstəd/ *adjective* upset and confused **canı sıkkın, telaşlı, karmakarışık, endişeli** *She arrived very late, looking flustered.*

flute /fluːt/ *noun* [C] a musical instrument in the shape of a tube that is held out to the side and played by blowing across a hole near one end **flüt**

flutter¹ /'flʌtər/ *verb* **1** [I, T] to move quickly and gently up and down or from side to side in the air, or to make something move in this way **dalgalan(dır)mak, çırpmak; sağa sola aşağı yukarı salla(n)mak** *The flag was fluttering in the breeze.* **2 flutter about/around/down, etc** to move somewhere quickly and gently, usually without any particular purpose **rastgele/amaçsızca sallanmak/sağa sola hareket etmek** *There were several moths fluttering around the light.*

flutter² /'flʌtər/ *noun* [C] **1** [MOVEMENT] a quick, gentle movement **çırpma, sallanma, kıpırdanma** *the flutter of wings* **2** [EMOTION] a state of excitement or worry **telaş, endişe, heyecan** *a flutter of excitement* **3** [RISK MONEY] *UK informal* when you risk money on the result of a game, competition, etc **bahis, bahse girme, yarış oyununa para yatırma**

flux /flʌks/ *noun* [U] continuous change **sürekli değişim gösterme hali, fokur fokur kaynama; kıpırdanma** *The housing market is still in a state of flux.*

o⌐**fly¹** /flaɪ/ *verb past tense* **flew**, *past participle* **flown**
1 [MOVE THROUGH AIR] [I] When a bird, insect, aircraft, etc flies, it moves through the air. **uçmak** *The robin flew up into a tree.* ○ *The plane was flying at 5000 feet.*
2 [TRAVEL] [I] to travel through the air in an aircraft **uçakla seyahat etmek, uçmak** *I'm flying to Delhi tomorrow.* **3** [CONTROL AIRCRAFT] [I, T] to control an aircraft **uçurmak** *She learned to fly at the age of 18.* **4** [TAKE/SEND] [T] to take or send people or goods somewhere by aircraft **uçakla/hava yoluyla göndermek** [often passive] *She was flown to hospital by helicopter.* **5 fly along/down/past, etc** to move somewhere very quickly **bir yere uçarak/hızlıca gitmek** *He grabbed some clothes and flew down the stairs.* **6 send sb/sth flying** to cause someone or something to move through the air suddenly, usually in an accident **bilhassa kazada havada uçmak/uçuşmak; havaya fırlamak 7** [LEAVE] *UK* to leave suddenly **uçar gibi çıkmak; hızlıca ayrılmak** *I must fly - I'm late for work.* **8 let fly (at sb/sth)** *mainly UK informal* to start shouting angrily or attacking someone **bas bas bağırmak, saldırmak, üzerine yürümek, saldırmak 9** [TIME] [I] If time flies, it passes very quickly. **uçup gitmek, süratle geçmek 10** [FLAG] [I, T] If you fly a flag, or a flag is flying, it is fixed to a rope or pole and raised in the air. **bayrağı dalgalandırmak, bayrak dalgalanmak** ● **flying** *noun* [U] *Ben's afraid of flying.* ⊃See also: as the **crow¹** flies, fly off the **handle²**. **uçan, uçuş**

fly about/around *phrasal verb* If ideas or remarks are flying about, they are being passed quickly from one person to another and causing excitement. **söylenti**

dolaşmak, balon uçurmak, sözcükler havada uçuşmak *All kinds of rumours are flying around about the
school closing.*
fly into a rage/temper *phrasal verb* to suddenly
become very angry **aniden parlamak, küplere binmek, tepesi atmak, saldırganlaşmak**

fly² /flaɪ/ *noun* **1** [C] a small insect with two wings **sinek**
There was a fly buzzing around in the kitchen. ⊃See picture at **insect**. **2** [C] (*also* **flies** [plural]) the part where
trousers open and close at the front **pantolon fer-
muarı** *a button/zip fly* **3 fly on the wall** If you say
that you would like to be a fly on the wall in a certain
situation, you mean that you would like to be there secretly to see and hear what happens. **gözetliyor olmak,
gizlice saklanıp gözetlemek; tepesinde olmak** • **4 a
fly-on-the-wall documentary/film** a television programme or film in which people do not act but are
recorded in real situations, sometimes without knowing **gizli kamerayla kayıt/çekim yapmak** • **5 be
dropping like flies** to be dying or becoming ill in
large numbers **telef olmak/etmek, topluca ölmek/
hastalanmak** • **6 wouldn't hurt a fly** If you say that
someone wouldn't hurt a fly, you mean that they are
very gentle and would never do anything to injure or
upset anyone. **karıncayı bile incitemez, merhametli
olmak; başkalarını üzmekten uzak durmak**

flyer (*also* **flier**) /ˈflaɪər/ *noun* [C] **1** a small piece of paper
advertising a business, show, event, etc **el ilanı** *She's
handing out flyers in the shopping centre.* **2** someone
who flies, especially a passenger on an aircraft **uçak
yolcusu; uçakla seyahat eden** *a frequent flyer* ⊃See
also: **high-flyer**.

flying /ˈflaɪɪŋ/ *adjective* [always before noun] **1** A flying
creature or object moves or is able to move through
the air. **uçan, uçabilen** *flying ants* **2 a flying visit** *UK*
a very brief visit **çok kısa ziyaret, ayak üstü uğrama**
⊃See also: with flying colours (**colour¹**).

flyover /ˈflaɪˌəʊvər/ *UK* (*US* **overpass**) *noun* [C] a bridge
that carries a road over another road **üst geçit**

FM /ˌefˈem/ *noun* [U] *abbreviation for* frequency modula-
tion; a system of radio signals used for broadcasting
programmes **radyo istasyonu, FM istasyonu**

foal /fəʊl/ *noun* [C] a young horse **tay, kısrak**

foam /fəʊm/ *noun* [U] **1** [BUBBLES] a mass of small, white
bubbles on the surface of a liquid **köpük 2** [PRODUCT] a
thick substance of small, white bubbles used as a cleaning or beauty product **güzellik ve temizlik amaçlı
kullanılan köpük** *shaving foam* **3** [FILLING] a soft substance used to fill furniture and other objects **sünger,
kauçuk**

focal point /ˈfəʊkəlˌpɔɪnt/ *noun* [no plural] the thing that
attracts most of your attention or interest in a place,
picture, etc **odak noktası; en ilgi çekici nokta** *The
fireplace is the focal point of the room.*

focus¹ /ˈfəʊkəs/ *verb* focusing, *past* focused **1** [T] If you
focus a camera or something else that you look through,
you make small changes to it until you can see something clearly. **odaklanmak, bir şeye yoğunlaşmak
2** [I, T] If you focus your eyes, or your eyes focus, they
change so that you can see clearly. **bir noktada yoğun-
laş(tır)mak** *Give your eyes time to focus in the darkness.*
focus (sth) on sth *phrasal verb* to give a lot of attention
to one particular subject or thing **bir şeye yoğunlaşmak; tüm dikkatini oraya vermek, odaklamak** *The
research focused on men under thirty.*

focus ...... İLE BİRLİKTE KULLANILAN KELİMELER

be **the focus of** sth • the focus is **on** (doing) sth

focus² /ˈfəʊkəs/ *noun* **1 the focus of sth** the person or
thing that is getting most attention in a situation or
activity **odak noktası olan şey/kişi** *the focus of our
attention* ○ *He is the focus of a police investigation.* **2** [U]
when you give special attention to something **odak-
lanma, yoğunlaşma** *Their main focus must be on reducing crime.* **3 in focus** If an image is in focus, you are
able to see it clearly. **odak noktasında; açık seçik
görülebilir konumda 4 out of focus** If an image is
out of focus, you are not able to see it clearly. **görüş
dışında; görülemez, ayarsız, odak noktası dışında**

focus group *noun* [group] a group of people who are
brought together to discuss what they think about
something such as a new product **yeni bir ürün konusunda görüşlerini almak üzere oluşturulmuş inceleme grubu,**

fodder /ˈfɒdər/ *noun* [U] food such as dried grass for animals that are kept on farms **saman, ot, kuru ot** *cattle
fodder*

foe /fəʊ/ *noun* [C] *literary* an enemy **düşman, hasım**

foetus *UK* (*US* fetus) /ˈfiːtəs/ *noun* [C] a young human or
animal that is still developing inside its mother **cenin**
• **foetal** *UK* (*US* fetal) /ˈfiːtəl/ *adjective* **foetal development** fetus ile ilgili

fog ...... İLE BİRLİKTE KULLANILAN KELİMELER

fog descends • fog clears/lifts • dense/heavy/thick
fog

fog /fɒg/ *noun* [U] thick cloud just above the ground or
sea that makes it difficult to see **sis**

foggy /ˈfɒgi/ *adjective* **1** with fog **sisli** *a foggy day* **2 not
have the foggiest (idea)** *informal* to not know any-
thing about something **en küçük bir fikri olmamak;
hiç bir şey bilmiyor olmak** [+ question word] *I haven't
the foggiest idea what you're talking about.*

foible /ˈfɔɪbl/ *noun* [C] a slightly unusual or annoying
habit **garip/ilginç alışkanlık** [usually plural] *Married
couples must learn to accept each other's little foibles.*

foil¹ /fɔɪl/ *noun* **1** [U] metal made into very thin sheets
like paper and used mainly for covering food **folyo,
aluminyum folya** (UK) *aluminium foil* / (US) *aluminum
foil* **2 a foil for sb/sth** a person or thing that shows or
emphasizes how different someone or something else is
farklılığı belirten/ortaya koyan şey ya da kişi

foil² /fɔɪl/ *verb* [T] to stop a crime, plan, etc from succeeding, or to stop someone doing what they want to do
engellemek, planını bozmak; işine çomak sokmak
[often passive] *The plot was foiled by undercover police officers.*

fold¹ /fəʊld/ *verb* **1** [MATERIAL] [T] If you fold paper, cloth,
etc, you bend it so that one part of it lies flat on top of
another part. **katlamak** *He folded the letter in half.*
2 [FURNITURE] [I, T] (*also* fold up) to make something such
as a chair or table smaller or flatter by closing it or
bending it together (sandalye, masa) **katlamak** *a folding chair* ⊃Opposite unfold. **3** [BUSINESS] [I] *informal* If a
business folds, it fails and is unable to continue. **(iş,
işyeri) kapanmak** *The magazine folded last year.*
4 fold your arms to bend your arms across your
chest, with one crossing over the other **kollarını
göğüs hizasında katlamak, birleştirmek** *He sat
with his arms folded.*

fold² /fəʊld/ *noun* [C] **1** a line or mark where paper,
cloth, etc was or is folded **kat izi/yeri** *Make a fold
across the centre of the card.* **2** a thick part where something folds or hangs over itself **kıvrım yeri** [usually plural]
folds of skin/fabric

folder /ˈfəʊldər/ *noun* [C] **1** a piece of plastic or thick
paper folded down the middle and used to store loose

papers **dosya** ⊃Orta kısımdaki renkli sayfalarına bakınız. **2** a place on a computer where particular files (= documents, pictures, etc) are kept **(bilgisayar) dosya**

foliage /ˈfəʊliɪdʒ/ noun [U] the leaves on a plant **bitki/ağaç yaprakları**

folk¹ /fəʊk/ noun **1** [plural] UK informal (US **folks**) people **insanlar, halk** country folk ○ old folk **2** sb's **folks** informal someone's parents **anne baba, ebeveynler** We always spend Christmas with my folks. **3** [U] folk music **halk türküsü, halk müziği**

folk² /fəʊk/ adjective **folk art/dancing, etc** the traditional style of art, dancing, etc among a particular group of people **geleneksel halk sanatı/dansı, folklör**

'folk ˌmusic noun [U] music written and played in a traditional style **halk müziği**

∘**follow** /ˈfɒləʊ/ verb **1** [GO] [I, T] to move behind someone or something and go where they go, sometimes secretly **takip etmek, peşinden gitmek, izlemek** She followed me into the kitchen. **2** [HAPPEN] [I, T] to happen or come after something **sonradan olmak/meydana gemek, peşinden gelmek** There was a bang, **followed by** a cloud of smoke. **3 follow a path/road, etc** to travel along a path/road, etc **belli bir yolda güzergâhta vs. seyahat etmek; o güzergâhı izlemek** Follow the main road down to the traffic lights. **4 follow instructions/orders/rules, etc** to do what the instructions/orders/rules, etc say you should do **talimat/emir/kuralları takip etmek, izlemek/yerine getirmek** I followed your advice and stayed at home. **5 follow sb's example/lead** to copy someone's behaviour or ideas **birini izlemek/örnek almak/taklit etmek 6** [UNDERSTAND] [I, T] to understand something **anlamak, kavramak, takip etmek** Could you say that again? I didn't quite follow. **7** [BE INTERESTED] [T] to be interested in an event or activity (eylem/faaliyet vb.) **takip etmek, izlemek, ilgilenmek** I followed the trial closely. **8 as follows** used to introduce a list or description **aşağıdaki gibi; şunlardır 9 it follows that** used to say that if one thing is true, another thing will also be true **...de/da doğrudur; takip edenler de doğru kabul edilir** He's big, but it doesn't follow that he's strong. ⊃See also: follow in sb's footsteps (**footstep**), follow **suit¹**.

follow on phrasal verb mainly UK to happen or exist as the next part of something **ardından gelmek, sonucunda olmak, ...den/dan oluşarak ortaya çıkmak** This report follows on from my earlier study.

follow sth through phrasal verb to do something as the next part of an activity or period of development, usually to make certain that it is completed or successful **bir işi sonuna kadar takip etmek, peşini bırakmamak**

follow sth up phrasal verb to discover more about a situation or take further action in connection with it **araştırmak, sonucunu araştırmak**

follower /ˈfɒləʊəʳ/ noun [C] someone who believes in a particular person or set of ideas **taraftar, mürit, takipçi** a follower of Jesus

following¹ /ˈfɒləʊɪŋ/ adjective **1 the following day/morning, etc** the next day/morning, etc **ertesi gün/sabah vs. 2 the following** what comes next, often used to introduce a list, report, etc **şunları; aşağıdakileri** The following is an extract from her diary: Today I stayed in bed all day.

following² /ˈfɒləʊɪŋ/ noun [no plural] a group of people who follow a leader, sport, etc, or admire a particular performer **peşinden gitme, hayranı olma, sıkı takipçisi olma; müridi olma** He has a large and loyal following.

following³ /ˈfɒləʊɪŋ/ preposition after or as a result of **sonrasında, sonucunda, arkasından** He died on October 23rd, following several years of illness.

follow-up /ˈfɒləʊʌp/ noun [C] something that is done to continue or complete something that was done before **devamı, devamında olan, (kurs, ders, eğitim vb.) tamamlayıcı/bütünleyici olan** a follow-up meeting

fond /fɒnd/ adjective **1 be fond of sb/sth** to like someone or something **sevmek, düşkün olmak; müptelası olmak** to be fond of animals/music ○ [+ doing sth] He's not very fond of dancing. **2** [always before noun] expressing or causing happy feelings **hoş, güzel, hoşa giden, mutlu eden** fond memories **3 a fond hope/belief, etc** something that you wish were true, but probably is not **muhtemelen gerçek olmayan ancak olması arzu edilen ümit/inanç 4** [+ doing sth] He's not very fond of dancing. **•fondly** adverb keyif alırcasına **•fondness** noun [C, U] We both **have a fondness for** cricket. **meraklısı olma durumu**

fondle /ˈfɒndl/ verb [T] to touch and rub part of someone's body, in a loving or sexual way **okşamak**

font /fɒnt/ noun [C] **1** a set of letters and symbols that are printed in a particular design and size **yazı karakteri** What size font are you using? **2** a container in a church which holds the water for a baptism (= Christian ceremony) **vaftiz törenlerinde kullanılan içinde su bulunan kap, sunak**

food .... İLE BİRLİKTE KULLANILAN KELİMELER

cold/hot/savoury/sweet food ● baby/cat/dog food ● canned/frozen/organic/processed food

∘**food** /fuːd/ noun [C, U] something that people and animals eat, or plants absorb, to keep them alive **yiyecek, besin, gıda** baby/dog food ○ His favourite food is pizza. ⊃Orta kısımdaki renkli sayfalarına bakınız. ⊃See also: fast food, junk food.

foodie /ˈfuːdi/ noun [C] informal someone who loves food and knows a lot about it **yiyecekleri çok seven hakkında çok şey bilen kişi**

'food ˌmile noun [C] a unit for measuring how far food travels from where it is made or grown to where it is eaten **yiyeceklerin üretildiği ve tüketildiği yerler arasındaki mesafeyi ölçüm birimi** People are becoming more concerned about how many food miles their produce has travelled.

'food ˌpoisoning noun [U] an illness caused by eating food containing harmful bacteria **gıda zehirlenmesi**

'food ˌprocessor noun [C] a piece of electrical equipment with a sharp blade, for cutting and mixing food **mutfak robotu** ⊃Orta kısımdaki renkli sayfalarına bakınız.

foodstuff /ˈfuːdstʌf/ noun [C] formal a substance used as food or to make food **gıda maddesi/ürünü** [usually plural] They need basic foodstuffs like rice and corn.

fool¹ /fuːl/ noun **1** [C] a stupid person **aptal, budala** I was a fool to trust him. **2 make a fool (out) of sb** to try to make someone look stupid intentionally **alay etmek, küçük duruma düşürmek, maskara etmek/olmak, aptal yerine koymak** She was always trying to make a fool out of me in front of my friends. **3 make a fool of yourself** to behave in a silly or embarrassing way **kendini maskara etmek, rezil olmak** I got drunk and started singing and making a fool of myself. **4 act/play the fool** UK to behave in a silly way, usually in order to make people laugh **maskaralık yapmak, aptalca davranmak** Joe is always playing the fool in class.

fool² /fuːl/ verb **1** [T] to trick someone **kandırmak, aldatmak** Don't be fooled by his appearance. ○ [+ into + doing sth] He fooled the old man into giving him the money. **2 you could have fooled me** informal something that you say when you do not believe what someone says about something that you saw or experienced yourself **beni kandırdın, öyle olduğuna inanmıştım** *"I wasn't cross." "Really? You could have fooled me."*

fool around/about *phrasal verb* to behave in a silly way or have a good time **oynamak, oyalanmak, kendini oyalamak** *Stop fooling around - this is serious!*

fool with sb/sth *phrasal verb mainly US* to deal with someone or something that could be dangerous in a stupid or careless way **aptalca davranmak, alay etmek, dalga geçmek**

foolhardy /ˈfuːlˌhɑːdi/ *adjective* taking or involving silly and unnecessary risks **çılgın, atak, cesur, gözükara, delidolu** *a foolhardy decision*

foolish /ˈfuːlɪʃ/ *adjective* silly and not wise **aptal, akılsız** [+ to do sth] *It would be foolish to ignore his advice.* ● **foolishly** *adverb* **aptalca** ● **foolishness** *noun* [U] **aptallık**

foolproof /ˈfuːlpruːf/ *adjective* A foolproof method, plan, or system is certain to succeed and not fail. **kusursuz, şaşmaz, sağlam, güvenilir**

⇒**foot¹** /fʊt/ *noun* **1** [C] *plural* **feet** one of the two flat parts on the ends of your legs that you stand on **ayak** *bare feet* ○ *He stepped on my foot.* ⊃Orta kısımdaki renkli sayfalarına bakınız. **2** [C] *plural* **foot** or **feet** (*written abbreviation* **ft**) a unit for measuring length, equal to 0.3048 metres or 12 inches **12 inç veya 0.3048'e eşit bir ölçü birimi** *Alex is about 6 feet tall.* ⊃See study page **Measurements** on page Centre 31. **3** the foot of sth the bottom of something such as stairs, a hill, a bed, or a page (**merdiven, tepe, yatak, sayfa vb.**) **taban, alt, alt ucu** *Put the notes at the foot of the page.* **4 on foot** If you go somewhere on foot, you walk there. **yayan, yürüyerek, piyade 5 be on your feet** to be standing and not sitting **dikilmek, ayakları üzerinde olmak, ayakta durmak** *I'm exhausted, I've been on my feet all day.* **6 put your feet up** to relax, especially by sitting with your feet supported above the ground **ayaklarını havaya kaldırarak yatıp uzanmak 7 set foot in/on sth** to go into a place or onto a piece of land **bir yere/araziye girmek** *He told me never to set foot in his house again.* **8 get/rise to your feet** to stand up after you have been sitting **ayakları üzerinde doğrulmak, dikilmek, kalkmak** *The audience rose to their feet.* **9 drag your feet** to deal with something slowly because you do not really want to do it **ayaklarını sürümek, direnmek, direnç göstermek** ● **10 get cold feet** to suddenly become too frightened to do what you had planned to do, especially something important (**önemli bir şeyi yapmadan önce**) **eli ayağı buz kesmek, çok korkmak/çekinmek** ● **11 get/start off on the wrong foot** to start a relationship or activity badly **yanlış bir başlangıç yapmak; kötü başlamak** *He got off on the wrong foot with my parents by arriving late.* ● **12 not put a foot wrong** *UK* to not make any mistakes **yanlış adım atmamak, hata yapmamak** ● **13 put your foot down** to tell someone in a strong way that they must do something or must stop doing something **dayatmak, diretmek, karşı çıkmak** ● **14 put your foot in it** *UK* (*US* **put your foot in your mouth**) to say something silly or embarrassing, without intending to **pot kırmak, çam devirmek** ● **15 stand on your own two feet** to do things for yourself without wanting or needing anyone else to help you **iki ayağı üzerinde durabilmek, başkasının yardımı olmadan başarabilmek**

foot² /fʊt/ *verb* **foot the bill** to pay for something **faturayı ödemek, ceremeyi çekmek, ödemek** *Why should taxpayers have to foot the bill?*

footage /ˈfʊtɪdʒ/ *noun* [U] film of an event **bir hadisenin filmi** *news/TV footage*

⇒**football** .... İLE BİRLİKTE KULLANILAN KELİMELER

play football ● **a** football **club/match/player/team** ● **a game of** football

⇒**football** /ˈfʊtbɔːl/ *noun* **1** UK GAME [U] *UK* (*UK/US* **soccer**) a game in which two teams of players kick a round ball and try to score goals **futbol** *a game of football* ○ *a football match/team* ⊃Orta kısımdaki renkli sayfalarına bakınız. **2** US GAME [U] *US* (*UK* **American football**) a game in which two teams of players try to kick, run with, or throw an oval ball across each other's goal line **futbol** ⊃Orta kısımdaki renkli sayfalarına bakınız. **3** BALL [C] a large ball for kicking, especially in football **futbol topu** ● **footballer** *noun* [C] *UK* someone who plays football, especially as their job **futbol oyuncusu** ● **footballing** *adjective* [always before noun] relating to or playing football **futbolla/futbol oyunu ile ilgili** *his footballing career*

foothills /ˈfʊthɪlz/ *noun* [plural] the lower hills next to a mountain or line of mountains **küçük tepeler, tepecikler**

foothold /ˈfʊthəʊld/ *noun* [C] **1** a place where it is safe to put your foot when you are climbing (**dağcılıkta**) **ayak basılacak yer 2** a safe position from which you can make more progress, for example in business **sağlam yer, emin durum/konum** *We are still trying to gain a foothold in the Japanese market.*

footing /ˈfʊtɪŋ/ *noun* **1** [no plural] when you are standing on a surface firmly **denge** *I lost my footing and fell.* **2 be on an equal/firm, etc footing** to be in an equal/safe, etc position or situation **dengede/sağlam konumda/durumda olmak**

footnote /ˈfʊtnəʊt/ *noun* [C] extra information that is printed at the bottom of a page **dipnot**

footpath /ˈfʊtpɑːθ/ *noun* [C] *mainly UK* a path or track for people to walk along, especially in the countryside **patika, keçi yolu** *a public footpath*

footprint /ˈfʊtprɪnt/ *noun* [C] **1** a mark made by a foot or shoe **ayak izi** [usually plural] *The police found some footprints in the mud.* **2** the amount of space on a surface that something needs, especially a computer **yer, kaplama alanı, bilgisayarın kapladığı alan** ⊃Compare **ecological footprint.**

footstep /ˈfʊtstep/ *noun* **1** [C] the sound of a foot hitting the ground when someone walks **ayak sesi** [usually plural] *I heard footsteps behind me and quickly turned round.* **2 follow in sb's footsteps** to do the same job or the same things in your life as someone else, especially a member of your family **özellikle aileden birini yakından takip etmek, yaptığı her şeyin aynısını yapmak, izinden gitmek** *He followed in his father's footsteps and became an actor.*

footwear /ˈfʊtweər/ *noun* [U] shoes, boots, and other things that you wear on your feet **ayağa giyilen her tür giyecek, ayakkabı**

⇒**for¹** *strong form* /fɔːr/ *weak form* /fər/ *preposition* **1** GIVEN/USED intended to be given to or used by someone or something (**verilen/kullanılan**) **için** *I've bought a few clothes for the new baby.* ○ *parking for residents only* **2** PURPOSE having a particular purpose (**amaç**) **belli bir amaç için** *a cream for dry skin* ○ *What are those large scissors for?* **3** BECAUSE OF because of or as a result of something **yüzünden, den dolayı; ...dığı için** [+ doing sth] *I got fined for travelling without a ticket.* ○ *Scotland is famous for its spectacular countryside.* **4** TIME/DISTANCE used to show an amount of time or distance (**zaman, mesafe**) **süresince, mesafesince** *We drove for miles* before we found a phone box. ○ *I've been living with my parents for a few months.* **5** GET in order to get or achieve something **(elde etmek/almak) için; başarmak için** *I've sent off for an application form.* ○ *We had to wait for a taxi.* **6** HELP in order to help someone **yardım için/amacıyla** *I'll carry those bags for you.* **7** OCCASION on the occasion of **vesilesiyle, münasebetiyle** *We're having a party for Jim's 60th birthday.* **8** AT A TIME at a particular time **(belli bir zaman) için, süresince** *I've booked a table for 9 o'clock.* **9** IN EXCHANGE in exchange for something, especially an amount of money **(para, döviz) bozdurmak için** *How much did you pay for your computer?* ○ *I'd like to change it for a smaller one.* **10** SUPPORT supporting or agreeing with someone or something **(destekleme) lehinde olarak, onun için** *Who did you vote for?* ○ *There were 16 people for the motion and 14 against.* **11** REPRESENT representing or working with a country, organization, etc **(temsilen) adına, için** *He plays football for Cambridge United.* ○ *She works for a charity.* **12** TOWARDS towards or in the direction of **...e/a doğru; yönünde** *Just follow the signs for the airport.* **13** COMPARE when compared to a particular fact **(kıyas) ...e/a göre; mukayese edildiğinde** *She's quite tall for her age.* **14** MEANING meaning or representing something **anlamında, (sözcük ve ifade) için karşılık** *What's the German word for 'cucumber'?* **15** RESPONSIBILITY used to say whose responsibility something is **sorumluluğunda, kararı için** *I can't tell you whether you should go or not - that's for you to decide.* **16 for all** despite **rağmen** *For all her qualifications, she's useless at the job.* **17 for all I care/know** used to say that a fact is not important to you **aldırmam, umursamam, beni bağlamaz, önemli değil** *He could be married by now, for all I care.* **18 for now** used to say that something should happen or be done now but can be changed later **şimdilik** *Just put everything on the table for now.* **19 be for it** UK informal (UK/US **be in for it**) to be in trouble **başı belada olmak** *If Hilary finds out I'll be for it!*

forage /ˈfɒrɪdʒ/ verb [I] to move about searching for things you need, especially food **yiyecek vb. araştırmak, karnını doyurmak için gezinmek** *Chimpanzees spend most of the day foraging for fruit, leaves, and insects.*

foray /ˈfɒreɪ/ noun [C] when you try to do something that is not familiar to you, or go somewhere different, for a short time **giriş, girişim, akın, yağma, baskın** *In 2004, she made her first foray into politics.*

forbid /fəˈbɪd/ verb [T] **forbidding**, *past tense* **forbade**, *past participle* **forbidden** **1** to order someone not to do something, or to say that something must not happen **yasaklamak, men etmek** [+ to do sth] *I forbid you to see that boy again.* ○ [often passive, + from + doing sth] *He is forbidden from leaving the country.* **2 God/Heaven forbid!** something you say when you hope that something will not happen **Allah korusun!, Maazallah!, Olmaz inşallah!** [+ (that)] *God forbid that he should die during the operation.* ● **forbidden** adjective not allowed by an official rule **yasaklanan, men edilen** *Smoking is strictly forbidden in this area.*

forbidding /fəˈbɪdɪŋ/ adjective looking unpleasant, unfriendly, or frightening **ürkütücü, hoş olmayan, berbat** *a cold and forbidding landscape*

🧩 **force** .... İLE BİRLİKTE KULLANILAN KELİMELER

exert/use force ● **brute/sheer** force ● **do sth by** force ● **the force of** sth

ᴏ⚬**force¹** /fɔːs/ noun **1** POWER [U] physical power or strength **güç, zorlama** *The force of the explosion shattered every window in the street.* ○ *The army has seized power by*

force. **2** ORGANIZED GROUP [C] a group of people organized to work together for a particular purpose, for example in military service **kuvvet, belli bir amaç için oluşturulmuş güç** *the Royal Air Force* ○ *a skilled* **work force 3** INFLUENCE [C, U] power and influence, or a person or thing that has it **güç, etki, kuvvet** *the forces of good/evil* **4 in/into force** If a law, rule, etc is in force, it is being used, and if it comes into force, it starts to be used. **yürürlükte, kullanımda, etkin durumda** *The new law came into force in April.* **5 be out in force** to be somewhere in large numbers **çok sayıda toplanmak, kalabalık olmak** *Photographers were out in force at the palace today.* **6 a force to be reckoned with** a very powerful person or organization **güçlü/yetkili/nüfuzlu kişi veya kurum** ● **7 join forces** When two people or groups join forces, they act or work together. **güçleri birleştirmek; güç birliği yapmak** *She joined forces with her sister-in-law to set up a restaurant.* ➔See also: **air force, the armed forces, market forces, police force, task force.**

ᴏ⚬**force²** /fɔːs/ verb [T] **1** to make someone do something that they do not want to do **zorlamak, zorla yaptırmak** [+ to do sth] *The hijacker forced the pilot to fly to New York.* ○ [often passive] *She was forced out of the race by a knee injury.* **2** to make an object move or open by physical strength or effort **itmek, itelemek, zorla açmak, hareket ettirmek** *They had to force the lock.* ○ *She forced the window open.*

forceful /ˈfɔːsfᵊl/ adjective expressing opinions strongly and demanding attention or action **güçlü, etkileyici** *a forceful manner/personality* ● **forcefully** adverb *to argue forcefully* **şiddetli bir şekilde**

forcible /ˈfɔːsəbl/ adjective A forcible action is done using force. **zor kullanarak, zorla** *forcible entry/arrest* ● **forcibly** adverb *Thousands of people were forcibly removed from their homes.* **zoraki**

fore /fɔːʳ/ noun **to the fore** in or to an important or popular position **ön plana, ön planda** *The band first came to the fore in the late 1990s.*

forearm /ˈfɔːrɑːm/ noun [C] the lower part of your arm between your hand and your elbow (= the place where it bends) **bilekle dirsek arasındaki kısım**

foreboding /fɔːˈbəʊdɪŋ/ noun [U, no plural] a feeling that something very bad is going to happen **içe doğma, sezi, önsezi** *a sense of foreboding*

🧩 **forecast** ...... İLE BİRLİKTE KULLANILAN KELİMELER

a forecast **of** sth ● an **economic** forecast ● a **gloomy** forecast

forecast¹ /ˈfɔːkɑːst/ noun [C] a report saying what is likely to happen in the future **tahmin, tahmin raporu** *economic forecasts* ➔See also: **weather forecast.**

forecast² /ˈfɔːkɑːst/ verb [T] *past* **forecast** or **forecasted** to say what you expect to happen in the future **tahmin etmek, öngörmek** *In 2001 a serious earthquake was forecast for the area.* ● **forecaster** noun [C] *a weather forecaster* **tahmin eden**

forecourt /ˈfɔːkɔːt/ noun [C] UK a large area with a hard surface at the front of a building **avlu, bir binanın önündeki ser zemin** *a garage forecourt*

forefather /ˈfɔːˌfɑːðəʳ/ noun formal **sb's forefathers** someone's relatives who lived a long time ago **uzun süre önce yaşamış akrabalar**

forefinger /ˈfɔːˌfɪŋɡəʳ/ noun [C] the finger next to your thumb **işaret parmağı**

forefront /ˈfɔːfrʌnt/ noun **be at/in the forefront of** sth to have an important position or job in an area of activity **ön sırada/önlerde olmak, önemli bir mevkide**

olmak *The company is at the forefront of developing new technology.*

forego /fɔː'gəʊ/ *verb* [T] **foregoing,** *past tense* **forewent,** *past part* **foregone** *another spelling of* forgo (= to decide not to have or do something you want) **vazgeçmek, feragat etmek, fedakârlık etmek**

foregone con'clusion *noun* [no plural] a result that is obvious before it happens **önceden bilinen sonuç, belli sonuç** [+ (that)] *It was a foregone conclusion that he'd go into politics.*

the foreground /'fɔː'graʊnd/ *noun* **1** the area of a view or picture which seems closest to you (**resim, manzara) ön plan; ön taraf** *There's a seated figure in the foreground of the painting.* **2** the subject or person that people give most attention to **önemsenen kişi/konu** *Environmental issues have recently moved to the foreground.*

forehand /'fɔːhænd/ *noun* [C] when you hit the ball in sports such as tennis with your arm held out on the side that you hold the racket (= object to hit balls with) **içvuruş** *a forehand volley*

forehead /'fɔːhed/ *or* 'fɒrɪd/ *noun* [C] the part of your face between your eyes and your hair **alın** ⊃Orta kısımdaki renkli sayfalarına bakınız.

⚬⁻**foreign** /'fɒrɪn/ *adjective* **1** belonging to or coming from another country, not your own **yabancı** *a foreign language/student* ○ *foreign cars/films* **2** [always before noun] relating to or dealing with countries that are not your own **yabancı ülkeyle ilişkin/ilgili** *foreign policy* ○ *the Foreign Minister* **3** be foreign to sb to be something you know nothing about or do not understand **yabancı olmak, anlamamak, bildik gelmemek** *The concept of loyalty is completely foreign to him.*

foreigner /'fɒrɪnər/ *noun* [C] someone from another country **yabancı, el**

foreman /'fɔːmən/ *noun* [C] *plural* **foremen** someone who leads a group of workers **ustabaşı** *a factory foreman*

foremost /'fɔːməʊst/ *adjective, adverb formal* most important **önde gelen, en önemli** *He's one of the country's foremost experts on military law.*

forename /'fɔːneɪm/ *noun* [C] *UK formal* your first name, which comes before your family name **ilk isim**

forensic /fə'rensɪk/ *adjective* [always before noun] relating to scientific methods of solving crimes **adli, mahkemeye ait; suçların bilimsel araştırma yöntemine dair** *forensic evidence/medicine* ○ *a forensic scientist*

forerunner /'fɔːˌrʌnər/ *noun* [C] an earlier, less developed example **öncü, ilk, az gelişmiş modeli** *the forerunner of the modern car*

foresee /fɔː'siː/ *verb* [T] **foreseeing,** *past tense* **foresaw,** *past part* **foreseen** to expect a future situation or event **öngörmek, tahmin etmek** *I don't foresee any problems in the future.*

foreseeable /fɔː'siːəbl/ *adjective* **for/in the foreseeable future** as far in the future as you can imagine **tahmin edilebilir/öngörülebilir gelecekte/gelecek için** *Prices will remain high for the foreseeable future.*

foreshadow /fɔː'ʃædəʊ/ *verb* [T] *formal* to show or warn that something bigger, worse, or more important is coming **olacakları önceden göstermek/uyarmak; belirti/işaret vermek**

foresight /'fɔːsaɪt/ *noun* [U] when you know or can judge what will happen or what you will need in the future **ileri görüş, sezgi** *She had the foresight to book her flight early.*

foreskin /'fɔːskɪn/ *noun* [C, U] the loose skin that covers the end of a penis **penisin uç kısmını kapatan yumuşak deri, sünnetlik kısım**

⚬⁻**forest** /'fɒrɪst/ *noun* [C, U] a large area of trees growing closely together **orman** *pine forest* ● **forested** *adjective* covered by forest **ormanlık, ağaçlarla kaplı** *heavily forested areas*

forest

forestall /fɔː'stɔːl/ *verb* [T] to prevent something from happening by taking action before it does ... **den/dan önce hareket edip önlemek, ...den/dan önce davranmak** *to forestall an attack/crisis*

forestry /'fɒrɪstri/ *noun* [U] the work of looking after or making forests **ormancılık**

foretell /fɔː'tel/ *verb* [T] *past* **foretold** *formal* to say what is going to happen in the future **önceden bilebilmek/görmek, tahminde bulunabilmek**

forever /fə'revər/ *adverb* **1** [IN FUTURE] for all time in the future **ebediyen, daima, sonsuza dek** *I'll love you forever.* **2** [A LONG TIME] *informal* used to emphasize that something takes a long time **sürekli, ebedî olarak, çok uzun zaman** *The journey home took forever.* **3** [OFTEN] used to emphasize that something happens often **her zaman, boyuna, sürekli olarak** *She is forever helping people.*

foreword /'fɔːwɜːd/ *noun* [C] a short piece of writing at the front of a book that introduces the book or its writer **önsöz**

forfeit /'fɔːfɪt/ *verb* [T] to lose the right to do something or have something because you have done something wrong **hakkını yitirmek/kaybetmek; yoksun kalmak** *They have forfeited the right to live in society.*

forgave /fə'geɪv/ *past tense of* forgive **'affetmek' fiilinin ikinci hali**

forge[1] /fɔːdʒ/ *verb* [T] **1** to make an illegal copy of something in order to deceive people **sahtesini yapmak, kalpazanlık yapmak, taklit etmek** *a forged passport* **2** to develop a good relationship with someone or something **iyi bir ilişki kurmak/geliştirmek** *The group forged friendships that have lasted more than twenty years.*

forge ahead *phrasal verb* to suddenly make a lot of progress with something **ilerleme kaydetmek, gittikçe ileriye gitmek** *The organizers are forging ahead with a programme of public events.*

forge[2] /fɔːdʒ/ *noun* [C] a place where metal objects are made by heating and shaping metal **demirhane; haddehane**

forgery /'fɔːdʒəri/ *noun* **1** [C] an illegal copy of a document, painting, etc **sahte, taklit 2** [U] the crime of making an illegal copy of something **kalpazanlık, sahtekârlık**

forget ...... BAŞKA BİR DEYİŞLE

Slip someone's mind söylemi (resmi olmayan durumlarda) kişinin yapması gereken şeyi unuttuğunu belirtmek için kullanılır. *I meant to tell you that he'd phoned, but it completely slipped my mind.*

On the tip of your tongue söylemi, kişinin bir kelimeyi unuttuğunu fakat çok kısa bir zaman içersinde

hatırlayacağını belirtmek için kullanılır. *Oh, what was that film called? - it's* on the tip of my tongue.
Eğer kişi bir ismi hatırlayamıyorsa, durumu belirtmek için **escape** fiilini kullanır. *The name of her book* escapes *me at the moment.*

o-***forget** /fə'get/ *verb* **forgetting**, *past tense* **forgot**, *past participle* **forgotten 1** [NOT REMEMBER] [I, T] to be unable to remember a fact, something that happened, or how to do something **unutmak** *I've forgotten his name.* ○ [+ (that)] *Don't forget that Lucy and John are coming this weekend.* ○ *He'd completely forgotten about their quarrel.* ○ [+ question word] *You never forget how to ride a bike.* **2** [NOT DO] [I, T] to not remember to do something **hatırlamamak** [+ to do sth] *Dad's always forgetting to take his pills.* **3** [NOT BRING] [T] to not bring something with you because you did not remember it **getirmeyi unutmak** *Oh no, I've forgotten my passport.* **4** [STOP THINKING] [T] (*also* **forget about**) to stop thinking about someone or something **birini/birşeyi unutmak, hatırdan çıkarmak, artık düşünmemek** *I'll never forget him for as long as I live.* **5 forget it** used to tell someone not to worry about something as it is not important **boş ver, unut gitsin; önemli değil 6 I forget** used instead of 'I have forgotten' **Unuttum** *I forget when we last saw him.* **7 forget yourself** to do or say something that is not acceptable in a particular situation **kendini kaybetmek, tepesi atmak** *She completely forgot herself and started screaming at him.*

forgetful /fə'getfºl/ *adjective* often forgetting things **unutkan** *She's 84 now and getting a bit forgetful.* ● **forgetfulness** *noun* [U] **unutkanlık**

o-***forgive** /fə'gɪv/ *verb past tense* **forgave**, *past participle* **forgiven 1** [I, T] to decide not to be angry with someone or not to punish them for something they have done **affetmek, bağışlamak** *I've apologized, but I don't think she'll ever forgive me.* ○ [often reflexive] *Mike would never forgive himself if anything happened to the children.* ○ [+ for + doing sth] *Jane never forgave her mother for lying to her.* **2 forgive me** used before you ask or say something that might seem rude **affedersiniz, bağışlayın; afedersiniz** *Forgive me for asking, but how much did you pay for your bag?* **3 sb could be forgiven for doing sth** used to say that you can understand if someone might think, believe, or do something **affedilebilir, hoşgörülebilir, mazur görülebilir, bağışlanır**

┌─────────────────────────────────────┐
│ **forgiveness** .... İLE BİRLİKTE KULLANILAN KELİMELER │
└─────────────────────────────────────┘
ask (for)/beg (for) forgiveness ● forgiveness **for** sth

forgiveness /fə'gɪvnəs/ *noun* [U] when you forgive someone for something they have done **bağışla(n)ma, affetme, affedilme**

forgiving /fə'gɪvɪŋ/ *adjective* ready to forgive someone for something they have done **bağışlayıcı, affedici, hoşgören**

forgo /fɔː'gəʊ/ *verb* [T] **forgoing**, *past tense* **forwent**, *past participle* **forgone** *formal* to decide not to have or do something, although you want to have it or do it **vazgeçmek, feragat etmek, fedakârlık etmek** *She had to forgo her early ambition to be a writer.*

forgot /fə'gɒt/ *past tense of* forget **'unutmak' fiilinin ikinci hali**

forgotten /fə'gɒtən/ *past participle of* forget **'unutmak' fiilinin üçüncü hali**

o-***fork¹** /fɔːk/ *noun* [C] **1** [FOOD] a small object with three or four points and a handle, that you use to pick up food and eat with **çatal** *a knife and fork* **2** [DIGGING] a tool with a long handle and three or four points, used for digging and breaking soil into pieces **kazmak ve oymak için kullanılan çatal** *a garden fork* **3** [ROAD] a place where a

road or river divides into two parts **yol ayrımı, çatal**, **çatal ağız** *Turn right when you reach a fork in the road.*

fork² /fɔːk/ *verb* [I] If a road or river forks, it divides into two parts. **çatallaşmak, bölünmek**

fork sth out *phrasal verb UK* (*US* **fork sth over**) *informal* to pay or give money for something, especially if you do not want to **(para) bayılmak, zorla ödemek, vermek**

forlorn /fə'lɔːn/ *adjective* lonely and unhappy **terkedilmiş, yalnız ve mutsuz** *The captured soldiers looked forlorn and helpless.* ● **forlornly** *adverb* **yalnız bir şekilde**

o-***form¹** /fɔːm/ *noun* **1** [TYPE] [C] a type of something or way of doing something **biçim, şekil, görüntü** *Swimming is the best form of exercise.* **2** [PAPER] [C] a printed document with spaces for you to write information **form, başvuru fişi, çizelge, cetvel** *Please fill in/out the form using black ink.* **3 the form of sth** the particular way in which something exists **oluş biçimi, şekli, varoluş şekli** *The novel is written in the form of a series of letters.* **4** [SPORT] [U] In sport, someone's form is how well or badly they are performing. **sporda form/başarı** *The team seems to have lost its form lately.* **5 be in/on/off form** *UK* If someone is in form or on form, they are feeling or performing well, and if they are off form they are not feeling or performing well. **formda olmak/olmamak** *Harry was on good form last night.* **6** [SCHOOL GROUP] [C] *UK* (*US* **grade**) a school class or group of classes for students of the same age or ability **sınıf, grup** *He's in the third form.* **7** [SHAPE] [C] the body or shape of someone or something **şekli, formu, görüntüsü 8** [GRAMMAR] [C] a way of writing or saying a word that shows if it is singular or plural, past or present, etc **sözcük biçimi/şekli/formu** *The plural form of 'sheep' is 'sheep'.* ➾See also: application form, sixth form.

o-***form²** /fɔːm/ *verb* **1** [BEGIN] [I, T] to begin to exist, or to make something begin to exist **oluşturmak, kurmak, oluşmak** [often passive] *We are learning more about how stars are formed.* **2** [SHAPE] [I, T] to take or to make something take a particular shape **biçim vermek; şeklini almak; biçim vermek; biçimlendirmek** *Form the dough into little balls.* **3** [COMBINE] [T] to make something by combining different parts **oluşturmak, bir araya getirmek, birleştirmek** *In English you form the present participle by adding -ing to the verb.* **4** [START] [T] to start an organization or business **bir kurumu/işi başlatmak/oluşturmak** *Brown formed her own company eleven years ago.* **5** [BE] [T] to be the thing talked about or be part of it **bahsedilen şey ya da parçası olmak** *The Alps form a natural barrier between Italy and Switzerland.* **6 form an opinion/impression, etc** to begin to have a particular opinion or idea about something because of the information you have **fikir/izlenim oluşmak/oluşturmak**

o-***formal** /'fɔːmºl/ *adjective* **1** [SERIOUS] used about clothes, language, and behaviour that are serious and not friendly or relaxed **resmî** *a formal dinner party* **2** [OFFICIAL] [always before noun] public or official **kamusal/resmî** *a formal announcement/apology* **3** [IN SCHOOL] [always before noun] Formal education, training, etc happens in a school or college. **formal/resmî/olması gereken eğitim** *Tom had little formal schooling.*

formality /fɔː'mæləti/ *noun* **1** [C] something that the law or an official process says must be done **merasim, usül, formalite** *There are certain legal formalities to be completed.* **2** [U] formal and polite behaviour **resmî ve nazik tavır** *the formality of a royal funeral*

formally /'fɔːməli/ *adverb* **1** officially **resmî olarak** *The deal will be formally announced on Tuesday.* **2** in

format 296 o﹡ Important words to learn

a polite way **nazik bir şekilde, nezaketle** *They shook hands formally.*

format¹ /ˈfɔːmæt/ *noun* [C] the way something is designed, arranged, or produced **biçim, genel düzen, şekil, boyut** *This year's event will have a new format.*

format² /ˈfɔːmæt/ *verb* [T] *formatted* **1** to prepare a computer disk so that information can be stored on it **bilgisayarda bir diski biçimlendirmek/formatlamak 2** to organize and design the words on a page or document **bir sayfayı/belgeyi formatlamak/oluşturmak/düzenlemek**

formation /fɔːˈmeɪʃən/ *noun* **1** [U] the development of something into a particular thing or shape **oluş, oluşum** *the formation of a crystal* **2** [C, U] when something has a particular shape or things are arranged in a particular way **konum, düzen, tertip** *rock/cloud formations* ○ *The planes flew overhead in formation* (= in a pattern).

formative /ˈfɔːmətɪv/ *adjective* relating to the time when your character and opinions are developing **biçimlendirici, şekil verici, oluşuma veya gelişmeye ait** *She spent her formative years in New York.*

former /ˈfɔːməʳ/ *adjective* [always before noun] happening, existing, or true in the past but not now **önceki, geçmiş, sabık** *the former Soviet Union* ○ *former President Bill Clinton*

the former /ˈfɔːməʳ/ *noun* the first of two people or things that have just been talked about **ilki, birincisi, bir evvelki**

formerly /ˈfɔːməli/ *adverb* in the past **önceleri, eskiden, geçmişte, vaktiyle** *The European Union was formerly called the European Community.*

formidable /ˈfɔːmɪdəbl/ *adjective* **1** Someone who is formidable is strong and a bit frightening. **ürkütücü, müthiş, heybetli, yaşılacak, olağanüstü** *a formidable woman* **2** difficult and needing a lot of effort or thought **başedilmez, yenmesi güç, zorlu** *a formidable task*

formula /ˈfɔːmjələ/ *noun* [C] *plural* **formulas** or **formulae** **1** [METHOD] a plan or method that is used to achieve something **plan, çözüm yolu, yöntem** *There's no magic formula for success.* **2** [RULE] a set of letters, numbers, or symbols that are used to express a mathematical or scientific rule **formül, tertip, tarife, reçete 3** [LIST] a list of the substances that something is made of **tarif, formül**

formulate /ˈfɔːmjəleɪt/ *verb* [T] **1** to develop all the details of a plan for doing something **planı ayrıntısıyla geliştirmek, şekillendirmek** *They formulated a plan to save the company.* **2** to say what you think or feel after thinking carefully **açık seçik anlatmak, biçimlendirmek, özlüce tarif etmek, düşünüp bulmak** *to formulate an answer/reply* ● **formulation** /ˌfɔːmjəˈleɪʃən/ *noun* [C, U] **düzenleme**

forsake /fəˈseɪk/ *verb* [T] *past tense* **forsook**, *past participle* **forsaken** *formal* **1** to leave someone, especially when they need you **bırakıp gitmek, terketmek, yüzüstü bırakmak** *He felt he couldn't forsake her when she was so ill.* **2** to stop doing or having something **...den/dan vazgeçmek, terketmek; yapmaktan/sahip olmaktan vazgeçmek** *He decided to forsake politics for journalism.*

fort /fɔːt/ *noun* [C] a strong building that soldiers use to defend a place **kale, hisar**

forth /fɔːθ/ *adverb literary* out of a place or away from it **dışarı, dışarıya, ileri, ileriye** *The knights rode forth into battle.*

forthcoming /ˌfɔːθˈkʌmɪŋ/ *adjective* **1** [SOON] [always before noun] *formal* going to happen soon **yakında, gele-** cekte, önümüzdeki *the forthcoming election/visit* **2** [OFFERED] [never before noun] If money or help is forthcoming, it is offered or given. **telif edilen/verilen/hazır para, elde, cepte** *He insisted that no more money would be forthcoming.* **3** [WILLING] [never before noun] willing to give information **bilgi vermeye hazır, yardımsever, yardıma hazır** *Elaine wasn't very forthcoming about her love life.*

forthright /ˈfɔːθraɪt/ *adjective* saying what you think honestly and clearly **dobra dobra, direkt, açık sözlü, lafını sakınmayan** *They dealt with all our questions in a very forthright manner.*

forthwith /ˌfɔːθˈwɪθ/ *adverb formal* immediately **derhal, hemen, gecikmeksizin** *to cease forthwith*

fortifications /ˌfɔːtɪfɪˈkeɪʃənz/ *noun* [plural] strong walls, towers, etc that are built to protect a place **tahkimat**

fortify /ˈfɔːtɪfaɪ/ *verb* [T] **1** to build strong walls, towers, etc around a place to protect it **tahkim etmek, sağlamlaştırmak, güçlendirmek** *a fortified city/town* **2** to make someone feel stronger physically or mentally **ruhen ve fiziken güçlü kılmak; güçlü hissetmesini sağlamak, güçlendirmek** *She had a sandwich to fortify herself before going on.*

fortitude /ˈfɔːtɪtjuːd/ *noun* [U] *formal* when you are brave and do not complain about pain or problems **metanet, dayanıklılık, yüreklilik**

fortnight /ˈfɔːtnaɪt/ *noun* [C] *UK* two weeks **onbeş günlük zaman/mühlet** [usually singular] *a fortnight's holiday* ○ *We usually get together about once a fortnight.* ● **fortnightly** *adverb UK* happening every two weeks **iki haftada bir olan; onbeş günlük** *a fortnightly meeting*

fortress /ˈfɔːtrəs/ *noun* [C] a castle or other strong building built to defend a place **büyük kale, müstahkem mevki, hisar**

fortunate /ˈfɔːtʃənət/ *adjective* lucky **şanslı, talihli** [+ to do sth] *I'm very fortunate to be alive.* ○ *It was fortunate that someone was available to take over.* ➋Opposite **unfortunate.**

o﹡**fortunately** /ˈfɔːtʃənətli/ *adverb* happening because of good luck **Allahtan; neyse ki; iyi ki; bereket versin** *Fortunately, no one was hurt in the accident.* ➋Opposite **unfortunately.**

🔲 *fortune* .... **İLE BİRLİKTE KULLANILAN KELİMELER**

cost/earn/make/spend a fortune ● a **personal** fortune ● **the family** fortune

fortune /ˈfɔːtʃuːn/ *noun* **1** [C] a lot of money **varlık, servet, zenginlik, bol para** *She made a fortune selling her story to the newspapers.* **2** [C, U] the good or bad things that happen to you **talih, şans, başa gelen iyi ya da kötü şeyler** [usually plural] *The family's fortunes changed almost overnight.* **3 tell sb's fortune** to say what is going to happen to someone in the future **fal açmak, fal bakmak**

fortune-teller /ˈfɔːtʃuːnˌteləʳ/ *noun* [C] someone who tells you what will happen to you in the future **falcı**

o﹡**forty** /ˈfɔːti/ the number 40 **kırk** ● **fortieth** 40th written as a word **kırkıncı**

forum /ˈfɔːrəm/ *noun* [C] **1** a situation or meeting in which people can exchange ideas and discuss things **toplu tartışma, forum, açık oturum** *a forum for debate/discussion* **2** an area of a website where people go to discuss things

o﹡**forward¹** /ˈfɔːwəd/ (*also* **forwards**) *adverb* **1** [DIRECTION] towards the direction that is in front of you **ileri, ileriye doğru** *She leaned forward to make sure I could hear* *her.* **2** FUTURE towards the future **geleceğe/atiye doğru** *I always* **look forward**, *not back.* **3** PROGRESS used to say that something is making good progress **gelişmiş, gelişen, ileri** *This is a big* **step forward** *for democracy.*

forward² /ˈfɔːwəd/ *adjective* **1 forward motion/movement, etc** movement towards the direction that is in front of you **ileriye doğru hareket/hamle 2 forward planning/thinking, etc** when you plan or think about something for the future **ileri/gelecek planlama/düşünme vb. 3** Someone who is forward is too confident or too friendly with people they do not know. **samimi, cana yakın, iyi davranan**

forward³ /ˈfɔːwəd/ *verb* [T] to send a letter, email, etc that you have received to someone else **yeni adrese göndermek** *Could you forward my mail to me while I'm away?* ⊃See also: **fast-forward.**

forward⁴ /ˈfɔːwəd/ *noun* [C] a player in a sport such as football who plays near the front and tries to score goals **futbolda ileri oyuncusu; forvet**

forwarding aˈddress *noun* [C] a new address that letters and parcels should be sent to **bir sonraki/yeni adres**

forward-looking /ˈfɔːwədlʊkɪŋ/ *adjective* planning for the future and using new ideas or technology **ileriye bakan, geleceği planlayan/şekillendiren; yeni fikir ve teknolojiyi kullanmayı planlayan** *a forward-looking plan/policy*

forwards /ˈfɔːwədz/ *adverb* another word for forward **öne/ileriye doğru, ileri**

ˈforward ˌslash (*also* slash) *noun* [C] the symbol '/', used in Internet addresses and used to show where on a computer files are kept **internet adresinde kullanılan '\' işareti** ⊃Compare backslash.

forwent /fɔːˈwent/ *past tense of* forgo **vazgeçmek, feragat etmek, 'fedakârlık etmek' fiilinin ikinci hali**

fossil /ˈfɒsᵊl/ *noun* [C] part of an animal or plant from thousands of years ago, preserved in rock **fosil**

ˈfossil ˌfuel *noun* [C, U] a fuel such as coal or oil that is obtained from under the ground **kömür veya petrol enerjisi**

foster¹ /ˈfɒstəʳ/ *verb* [T] **1** to encourage a particular feeling, situation, or idea to develop **(fikir, durum, his) gelişmesine yardımcı olmak** *The growth of the Internet could foster economic development worldwide.* **2** to look after a child as part of your family for a time, without becoming their legal parent **(çocuğu) öz babası gibi beslemek, büyütmek**

foster² /ˈfɒstəʳ/ *adjective* **1 foster home/mother/parent, etc** the home where a child who is fostered lives, or the person or people who foster a child **yetimhane, evlatlık babası/annesi 2 foster child/daughter/son, etc** a child who is fostered **evlatlık çocuk; evlatlık kız evlat/erkek evlat**

fought /fɔːt/ *past of* fight **döğüşmek' fiilinin ikinci hali**

foul¹ /faʊl/ *adjective* **1** very dirty, or with an unpleasant smell **çok pis/kirli, kötü kokan** *the foul smell of rotting fish* **2** very bad or unpleasant **iğrenç, tiksindirici** *foul weather* ○ *She's in a foul mood.* **3 foul language/words** very rude and offensive words **küfürlü, küfür dolu dil/sözcükler 4 fall foul of sb/sth** *UK* to do something which causes you to be in trouble **başı derde girmek; başı belaya girmek; başına dert açmak**

foul² /faʊl/ *verb* **1** [T] to make something very dirty **pisletmek, kirletmek** *The beaches had been fouled by dogs.* **2** [I, T] to do something that is against the rules in a sport **faul yapmak, kural dışı hareket etmek** *He was fouled as he was about to shoot at goal.*

foul sth up *phrasal verb informal* to spoil something completely **yüzüne gözüne bulaştırmak, bozmak, berbat etmek** *The travel company completely fouled up our holiday.*

▢▢▢ **foul** ...... İLE BİRLİKTE KULLANILAN KELİMELER

commit a foul ● a foul **against/on** sb

foul³ /faʊl/ *noun* [C] something that someone does in a sport that is not allowed by the rules **faul, kural dışı hareket**

ˌfoul ˈplay *noun* [U] when someone's death is caused by a violent crime **cinayet, süikast** *Police do not suspect foul play at present.*

found¹ /faʊnd/ *verb* [T] **1** to start an organization, especially by providing money **kurmak, oluşturmak, tesis etmek** *The company was founded in 1861.* **2** to base something on a set of ideas or beliefs **dayanmak, temel teşkil etmek, belli bir inanca ve fikre dayandırmak** [often passive] *a society* **founded on** *principles of equality*

found² /faʊnd/ *past of* find **'bulmak' fiilinin ikinci hali**

foundation /faʊnˈdeɪʃᵊn/ *noun* **1** IDEA [C] the idea or principle that something is based on **temel, esas, asıl** *Jefferson's document* **formed the foundation** *of a new nation.* **2** STARTING [U] when an organization, state, or country is established **kurma, kuruluş, tesis** *the foundation of a new state* **3** ORGANIZATION [C] an organization that gives money for a particular purpose **vakıf** *the Mental Health Foundation* **4 foundations** [plural] *UK* (*US* foundation [C]) the part of a building, road, bridge, etc that is under the ground and supports it **temel** *concrete foundations* **5** MAKE-UP [U] make-up that is worn all over the face to give it a smooth appearance **makyaj, fondöten 6 be without foundation; have no foundation** If something is without foundation, there is no proof that it is true. **hiç bir temele/esasa dayanmayan, temelsiz, asılsız, kanıtı olmayan** *The allegations are completely without foundation.* **7 lay the foundation(s) for/of sth** to provide the conditions that make it possible for something to happen **gerekli şartları/temeli oluşturmak** *His reforms laid the foundation of future greatness.*

founˈdation ˌcourse *UK* (*US* introductory course) *noun* [C] a college or university course on a subject that students take to prepare them for a more advanced course on that subject **temel dersler, hazırlık dersleri/programı/kursu**

founder /ˈfaʊndəʳ/ *noun* [C] someone who establishes an organization **kurucu**

foundry /ˈfaʊndri/ *noun* [C] a place where metal or glass is melted and made into objects **dökümhane**

fountain /ˈfaʊntɪn/ *noun* [C] a structure that forces water up into the air as a decoration **fiskiye**

ˈfountain ˌpen *noun* [C] a pen that you fill with ink **dolma kalem**

o⊶**four** /fɔːʳ/ the number 4 **dört rakamı**

four-by-four /ˌfɔːbaɪˈfɔːʳ/ a four-wheel drive **dörtçeker**

fours /fɔːz/ *noun* **on all fours** with your hands and knees on the ground **elleriyle dizleri üzerinde**

foursome /ˈfɔːsəm/ *noun* [C] a group of four people **dörtlü grup, dörtlü** *We could go out as a foursome.*

o⊶**fourteen** /ˌfɔːˈtiːn/ the number 14 **ondört** ● **fourteenth** 14th written as a word **ondördüncü**

fourth¹ /fɔːθ/ 4th written as a word **dördüncü**

fourth² /fɔːθ/ *US* (*UK/US* quarter) *noun* [C] one of four equal parts of something; $1/4$ **dörtte bir**

Fourth of Ju'ly (*also* **Independence Day**) *noun* [U] 4 July, a national holiday in the US to celebrate the country's freedom from Great Britain in 1776 **Dört Temmuz, (ABD) Bağımsızlık Günü**

four-wheel 'drive (*written abbreviation* **4WD**) *noun* [C] a vehicle with an engine that supplies power to all four wheels so that it can drive easily over rough ground **dörtçeker araç; arazi aracı, jip** ● **four-wheel 'drive** *adjective a four-wheel drive car* **Dörtçeker**

fowl /faʊl/ *noun* [C] *plural* **fowl** or **fowls** a bird that is kept for its eggs and meat, especially a chicken **kümes hayvanı**

fox /fɒks/ *noun* [C] a wild animal like a dog with red-brown fur, a pointed nose, and a long thick tail **tilki**

foyer /ˈfɔɪeɪ/ ⑤ /ˈfɔɪər/ *noun* [C] a room at the entrance of a hotel, theatre, cinema, etc **fuaye, lobi**

fracas /ˈfrækɑː/ ⑤ /ˈfreɪkəs/ *noun* [no plural] a noisy fight or argument **gürültü, kavga, tantana**

🧩 fraction .... İLE BİRLİKTE KULLANILAN KELİMELER

a **minute/small/tiny** fraction of sth ● **a fraction of** sth

---

fraction /ˈfrækʃᵊn/ *noun* [C] **1** a number less than 1, such as ½ or ¾ **kesir** ⊃See study page **Numbers** on page Centre 30. **2** a very small number or amount **çok küçük miktar, küçük/küçük bölüm** *a fraction of a second* ● **fractionally** *adverb* by a very small amount **çok küçük ölçüde, az bir farkla** *Harry is fractionally taller than Ben.*

fracture /ˈfræktʃəʳ/ *verb* [T] to break something hard such as a bone, or a piece of rock **kırılmak, çatlamak** *She's fractured her ankle.* ● **fracture** *noun* [C] **çatlak**

fragile /ˈfrædʒaɪl/ ⑤ /ˈfrædʒᵊl/ *adjective* **1** easily broken, damaged, or destroyed **kırılgan, kolay ve çabuk kırılan** *a fragile china cup* ○ *a fragile economy* **2** physically or emotionally weak **duygusal ve fiziksel olarak zayıf, kırılgan** *a fragile little girl* ● **fragility** /frəˈdʒɪləti/ *noun* [U] **kırılganlık**

fragment¹ /ˈfrægmənt/ *noun* [C] a small piece of something **kırıntı, küçük/ufak parça** *fragments of pottery*

fragment² /frægˈment/ *verb* [I, T] to break something into small parts, or to be broken in this way **küçük küçük parçalara ayırmak; param parça olmak; parçalanmak** *The opposition has fragmented into a number of small groups.* ● **fragmented** *adjective a fragmented society* **parçalanmış, bölünmüş**

fragrance /ˈfreɪɡrəns/ *noun* [C, U] **1** a pleasant smell **güzel koku, rayiha** *the delicate fragrance of roses* **2** a substance which people put on their bodies to make themselves smell nice **güzel koku, koku, parfüm** *a new fragrance for men*

fragrant /ˈfreɪɡrənt/ *adjective* with a pleasant smell **güzel kokulu** *fragrant flowers*

frail /freɪl/ *adjective* not strong or healthy **zayıf, çelimsiz, güçsüz** *a frail old lady*

frailty /ˈfreɪlti/ *noun* [C, U] when someone is physically or morally weak **fiziksel/ahlakî zayıflık, sünepelik; karakter zayıflığı, zaaf**

frame¹ /freɪm/ *noun* [C] **1** PICTURE a structure that goes around the edge of something such as a door, picture, window, or mirror **çerçeve, kasa** *a picture frame* ○ *a window frame* **2** STRUCTURE the basic structure of a building, vehicle, or piece of furniture that other parts are added onto **iskelet, kasnak, kafes** *a bicycle frame* **3** BODY the shape of someone's body **vücut, yapı, beden** *his large/small frame* **4 frame of mind** the way someone feels at a particular time **ruhsal durum, ruh hali** *She was in a much more positive frame of mind today.*

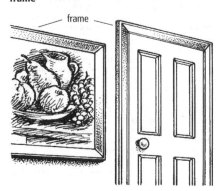

frame

frame² /freɪm/ *verb* [T] **1** PICTURE to put something such as a picture into a frame **çerçeveye koymak, çerçevelemek** *I'm going to frame this and put it on the wall.* **2** EDGE to form an edge to something in an attractive way **çerçevelemek, fon oluşturmak** *Dark hair framed her face.* **3** CRIME to intentionally make it seem as if someone is guilty of a crime **komplo kurmak, suçlu duruma düşürmek, yalan yere suçlamak** [often passive] *He claimed he had been framed by the police.* **4** EXPRESS *formal* to express something choosing your words carefully **sözcükleri dikkatle seçerek ifade etmek/anlatmak/açıklamak** *I tried to frame a suitable reply.*

frames /freɪmz/ *noun* [plural] the plastic or metal structure that holds together a pair of glasses **cam çerçevesi, kasa**

🧩 framework .... İLE BİRLİKTE KULLANILAN KELİMELER

create/develop/establish/provide a framework ● a framework **for** (doing) sth

---

framework /ˈfreɪmwɜːk/ *noun* [C] **1** a system of rules, ideas, or beliefs that is used to plan or decide something **temel yapı, iskelet, düzen, sistem** *a legal framework for resolving disputes* **2** the basic structure that supports something such as a vehicle or building and gives it its shape **şasi, kaburga, kafes, iskelet**

franchise /ˈfrænʃaɪz/ *noun* **1** [C] the right to sell a company's products or services in a particular area using the company's name **acentelik, bayilik, bir şirketin malını aynı ismi kullanarak satma hakkı; özel pazarlama hakkı** *a fast food franchise* **2** [U] the legal right to vote in elections **oy kullanma hakkı**

frank /fræŋk/ *adjective* speaking honestly and saying what you really think **samimi, içten, dürüst, açık yürekli** *a full and frank discussion* ○ *To be frank, I don't really want to see him.* ● **frankness** *noun* [U] **açık sözlülük**

frankfurter /ˈfræŋkfɜːtəʳ/ *noun* [C] a long, thin sausage (= tube of meat and spices), often eaten with bread **bir tür çeşnili Alman sosisi**

frankly /ˈfræŋkli/ *adverb* in an honest and direct way **dürüst şekilde, açıkça, açık yüreklilikle, dobra dobra** *Quite frankly, I think you're making a big mistake.*

frantic /ˈfræntɪk/ *adjective* **1** done in a fast and excited way and not calm or organized **telaşla/heyecanla/düzensiz şekilde yapılmış, rastgele ele alınmış** *a frantic search* **2** very worried or frightened **çılgın, kendinden geçmiş, çileden çıkmış** *frantic calls for help*

○ *I got home to find Joe frantic with worry.* ● **frantically** *adverb Laura was searching frantically for her keys.* **çılgınca**

fraternal /frəˈtɜːnᵊl/ *adjective* like or relating to a brother **dostça, kardeşçe**

fraternity /frəˈtɜːnəti/ *noun* **1** [U] a feeling of friendship between people **birlik, beraberlik, kardeşlik 2** [C] in the US, a social organization of male college students **(ABD)** **erkek üniversite öğrencilerinden oluşan birlik, dernek, cemiyet**

🧩 **fraud** ...... İLE BİRLİKTE KULLANILAN KELİMELER

commit fraud ● a fraud **case/charge/investigation**

fraud /frɔːd/ *noun* **1** [U] when someone does something illegal in order to get money **dolandırıcılık, düzenbazlık, sahtekârlık** *credit card fraud* **2** [C] someone who deceives people by pretending to be someone or something that they are not **sahtekâr, hilebaz, düzenbaz, dolandırıcı**

fraudulent /ˈfrɔːdjələnt/ *adjective formal* dishonest and illegal **aldatıcı, sahte, hileli** *fraudulent insurance claims* ● **fraudulently** *adverb* **hileli bir şekilde**

fraught /frɔːt/ *adjective* **1 fraught with danger/difficulties, etc** full of danger/difficulties, etc **tehlike/güçlük vs. dolu/yüklü** *The present situation is fraught with danger.* **2** *mainly UK* causing worry, or feeling worried **kaygılı, gergin** *a fraught silence*

fray¹ /freɪ/ *verb* **1** [I, T] If material or clothing frays, or if it is frayed, the threads at the edge break and become loose. **tel tel olmak, yıpra(t)nmak, eski(t)mek, 2** [I] If your temper (= mood) frays or your nerves fray, you gradually become annoyed or upset. **sinirleri yıpra(t)nmak/harap olmak/ etmek** *After hours of waiting, tempers were beginning to fray.*

fray² /freɪ/ *noun* **enter/ join, etc the fray** to start taking part in an argument or fight **tartışma, kavga, arbedeye girmek/başlamak** *The time had come for the US to enter the fray.*

fray

freak¹ /friːk/ *noun* [C] **1** *informal* someone who is very interested in a particular subject or activity **düşkün/ meraklı kimse; ilginç konularla ilgilenen kimse, eksantrik kimse** *My brother's a bit of a computer freak.* **2** someone who looks strange or behaves in a strange way **tuhaf/garip/acayip kimse** *They made me feel like a freak.*

freak² /friːk/ *adjective* **a freak accident/storm, etc** A freak event is one that is very unusual. **anormal/ tuhaf/alışılmamış kaza/fırtına vb.**

freak³ /friːk/ (*also* **freak out**) *verb* [I, T] *informal* to suddenly become very angry, frightened, or surprised, or to make someone do this **aniden kızmak/kızdırmak; ürkmek/ürkütmek; şaşırmak/şaşırtmak** *I hated that film, it totally freaked me out.*

freckle /ˈfrekl/ *noun* [C] a very small, brown spot on your skin from the sun **çil; güneşin oluşturduğu çiller** ● **freckled** *adjective* **çilli**

o--**free¹** /friː/ *adjective* **1** NOT CONTROLLED able to live, happen, or exist without being controlled by anyone or anything **serbest, bağımsız** *free trade* ○ *a free society* ○ [+ to do sth] *People should be free to say what they think.* **2** NO COST not costing any money **ücretsiz, bedava** *a free sample of perfume* ○ *Entry is free for children under 12.* ○ *The unemployed get their prescriptions free of charge.* **3** NOT A PRISONER not in prison or in a cage **hür, özgür, tutsak olmayan** *He opened the cage and set the birds free.* **4** NOT BUSY not busy doing anything **boş, meşgul olmayan** *Are you free this evening?* ○ *I don't have much free time.* **5** NOT USED not being used by anyone **serbest, boşta, kullanılmayan** *Is this seat free?* **6 free from/of sth** not containing or having anything harmful or unpleasant **...den/dan arındırılmış; zararlı madde içermeyen** *a life free from pain* **7 feel free** something that you say in order to tell someone that they are allowed to do something **Rahat ol!, Tabii buyrun, 'Hiç tereddüt etmeyin'** [+ to do sth] *Please feel free to ask questions.* ➲See also: **duty-free**, a free **hand¹**, free **rein**, tax-free, toll-free.

free² /friː/ *adverb* **1** without cost or payment **para ödemeden, ücretsiz olarak, bedava** *Children under five travel free.* ○ *He offered to do it for free.* **2** in a way that is not tied, limited, or controlled **başıboş/serbest/ çözülü şekilde** *She broke free from his grasp and ran away.*

o--**free³** /friː/ *verb* [T] **freeing**, *past* **freed 1** ALLOW TO LEAVE to allow someone to leave a prison or place where they have been kept **serbest bırakmak, salıvermek, tahliye etmek** *The last hostages were finally freed yesterday.* **2** GET OUT to get someone out of a situation or place that they cannot escape from **kurtarmak, çıkarmak** *Firefighters worked for two hours to free the driver from the wreckage.* **3** TAKE AWAY to help someone by taking something unpleasant away from them **kurtulmasına yardım etmek** *The book's success freed her from her financial worries.* **4** MAKE AVAILABLE (*also* **free up**) to make something available for someone to use **yer açmak, sağlamak** *I need to free up some space for these files.*

-free /friː/ *suffix* used at the end of words to mean 'without' or 'not containing' **...sız/siz/den/den arınmış/ içermeyen anlamında sonek** *sugarfree gum* ○ *an interest-free loan*

freebie /ˈfriːbi/ *noun* [C] *informal* something that you are given, usually by a company, and do not have to pay for **eşantiyon, ücretsiz dağıtılan**

Freecycle /ˈfriːsaɪkl/ *verb* [I, T] *trademark* to use a local Freecycle email group to give away things that you do not want now **fazla şeyleri vermek için bölgesel serbest dolaşım e-posta grubunu kullanmak** ● **freecycler** *noun* [C] **ihtiyacınız olmayan şeyleri verebileceğiniz kişilere ulaştığınız bir internet gurubu**

🧩 **freedom** ...... İLE BİRLİKTE KULLANILAN KELİMELER

be given/have the freedom to do sth ● freedom **of choice/of expression/of movement/of speech**

o--**freedom** /ˈfriːdəm/ *noun* **1** [C, U] the right to live in the way you want, say what you think, and make your own decisions without being controlled by anyone else **özgürlük, bağımsızlık** *religious freedom* ○ *freedom of choice/speech* ○ [+ to do sth] *You have the freedom to do what you want to do.* **2 freedom from sth** a situation in which you are not suffering because of something unpleasant or harmful **değişiklik, muafiyet, korunmuşluk** *freedom from fear/poverty* **3** [U] when someone is no longer a prisoner **özgürlük, hürriyet**

,free 'enterprise *noun* [U] when trade and business is allowed to operate without much control from the government **hür teşebbüs**

,free 'kick *noun* [C] a kick that a player in a football match is allowed to take after a player from the other team has broken the rules **serbest vuruş**

freelance /'fri:lɑ:ns/ *adjective, adverb* working for several different organizations, and paid according to the hours you work **serbest/bağımsız; herhangi bir kurum bağlı olmadan çalışarak** *a freelance photographer* ○ *Most of our producers work freelance.* ● **freelance** *verb* [I] **kimseye bağlı olmadan çalışmak** ● **freelancer** *noun* [C] **serbest meslek (çalışanı)**

freely /'fri:li/ *adverb* **1** without being controlled or limited **serbest bir şekilde, serbestçe, rahatça** *For the first time in months she could move freely.* ○ *Exotic foods are freely available in supermarkets.* **2** If you freely admit something, you are very willing to agree that it is true. **açıkça, özgürce itiraf ederek** *I freely admit that I was wrong about him.*

,free 'market *noun* [no plural] when the government does not control prices and trade **serbest pazar** *a free-market economy*

freephone /'fri:fəʊn/ *UK* (*US* **toll-free**) *adjective* [always before noun] A freephone number is a telephone number that you can connect to without paying. **ücretsiz telefon numarası**

free-range /ˌfri:'reɪndʒ/ *adjective* relating to or produced by farm animals that are allowed to move around outside and are not kept in cages **doğal koşullarda beslenen/üretilen** *free-range eggs*

freesheet /'fri:ʃi:t/ *noun* [C] a free newspaper **ücretsiz gazete**

,free 'speech *noun* [U] the right to express your opinions in public **konuşma/ifade özgürlüğü**

,free 'trade *noun* [C] a way to buy and sell products between countries, without limits on the amount of goods that can be bought and sold, and without special taxes on the goods **serbest ticaret** ⊃Compare **fair trade.**

freeware /'fri:weə^r/ *noun* [U] computer software that you do not have to pay for, for example from the Internet **internetten ücretsiz elde edilen bilgisayar yazılımı**

freeway /'fri:weɪ/ *US* (*UK* **motorway**) *noun* [C] a long, wide road, usually used by traffic travelling fast over long distances **ücretsiz otoyol, otoban, çevreyolu**

,free 'will *noun* **1** [U] when people choose and decide what they want to do in their own lives **özgür irade; kendi kaderini tayin etme 2 do sth of your own free will** to do something because you want to, not because someone forces you to **kendi özgür iradesiyle/baskı olmadan yapmak** *She had gone there of her own free will.*

○━**freeze¹** /fri:z/ *verb past tense* **froze**, *past participle* **frozen 1** ICE [I, T] If something freezes or is frozen, it becomes hard and solid because it is very cold. **donmak, buzlanmak, buz tutmak, dondurmak** *The river had frozen overnight.* ○ *Water freezes at 0° Celsius.* **2** FOOD [I, T] to make food last a long time by making it very cold and hard (gıda) **dondurmak, dondurarak saklamak** *You can freeze any cakes that you have left over.* **3** PERSON [I] to feel very cold **buz tutmak, çok donmak, buz kesmek** *One of the climbers froze to death on the mountain.* **4** NOT MOVE [I] to suddenly stop moving, especially because you are frightened **dona kalmak, korkudan buz kesmek** *She saw someone outside the window and froze.* **5** LEVEL [T] to fix the level of something such as a price or rate so that it does not increase (fiyat, oran) **dondurmak, sabitlemek**

freeze² /fri:z/ *noun* **1** LEVEL [C] when the level of something such as a price or rate is fixed so that it does not increase **(fiyat, oran) sabit, değişmez, dondurulmuş** *a pay freeze* **2** PROCESS [C] when a process is stopped for a period of time **belli bir süre ara verme/durdurma** *an immediate freeze on all new building in the city* **3** COLD [no plural] *informal* a period of extremely cold weather **dondurucu soğuklar**

freezer /'fri:zə^r/ *noun* [C] a large container operated by electricity in which food can be frozen and stored **derin dondurucu, dondurucu** ⊃Orta kısımdaki renkli sayfalarına bakınız.

freezing¹ /'fri:zɪŋ/ *adjective informal* very cold **dondurucu, çok üşüten, insanın iliklerine kadar işleyen** *It's absolutely freezing in here.*

freezing² /'fri:zɪŋ/ *noun* [U] the temperature at which water freezes **donma derecesi** *It was five degrees below/above freezing.*

'freezing ,point *noun* [C, U] the temperature at which a liquid freezes **donma noktası**

freight /freɪt/ *noun* [U] goods that are carried by trains, trucks, ships, or aircraft **yük, eşya, kargo**

freighter /'freɪtə^r/ *noun* [C] a large ship or aircraft that carries goods **yük gemisi, kargo uçağı**

'french ,fries *US* (*UK* **chips**) *noun* [plural] long, thin pieces of potato that have been cooked in hot oil **kızarmış patates** ⊃Orta kısımdaki renkli sayfalarına bakınız.

,French 'knickers *noun* [plural] women's loose underwear that covers all the bottom **bayan iç çamaşırı** ⊃Orta kısımdaki renkli sayfalarına bakınız.

,French 'windows (*also* ,French 'doors) *noun* [plural] a pair of glass doors that usually open into a garden **bahçe veya balkona açılan cam kapı**

frenetic /frə'netɪk/ *adjective* fast and exciting in an uncontrolled way **çılgın, coşkun, heyecanlı** *a frenetic pace* ○ *frenetic activity*

frenzied /'frenzɪd/ *adjective* wild and uncontrolled **vahşi ve kontrolden çıkmış, çılgın, kaçkın, kuduruk** *a frenzied dance*

frenzy /'frenzi/ *noun* [U, no plural] when you are so excited, nervous, or anxious that you cannot control what you are doing **çılgınlık, delilik, taşkınlık, cinnet** *She hit him in a frenzy of rage.*

frequency /'fri:kwənsi/ *noun* [C, U] **1** the number of times something happens in a particular period, or the fact that something happens often or a large number of times **sıklık, belli aralıklarla, sık sık olma** *The frequency of attacks seems to have increased recently.* **2** the rate at which a sound wave or radio wave is repeated **frekans, radyo dalgaları** *the very high frequencies of a television signal*

○━**frequent¹** /'fri:kwənt/ *adjective* happening often **sık sık, sık görülen/olan, alışılmış, olağan** *He is a frequent visitor to the US.*

frequent² /frɪ'kwent/ (US) /'fri:kwent/ *verb* [T] to go to a place often **bir yere sık sık gitmek** *a bar frequented by criminals*

○━**frequently** /'fri:kwəntli/ *adverb formal* often **sık sık** *a frequently asked question*

○━**fresh** /freʃ/ *adjective* **1** DIFFERENT new or different from what was there before **yeni, farklı** *We're looking for fresh ideas.* ○ *They decided to move abroad and* **make a fresh start.** **2** NOT OLD Fresh food has been produced or collected recently and has not been frozen, dried, etc. **taze, turfanda** *fresh fruit/vegetables* ○ *fresh bread* **3** CLEAN/COOL smelling clean or feeling pleasantly cool **hoş kokan, serin, taze, hoş** *a fresh breeze* ○ *a fresh smell* **4 fresh air** air outside buildings that is clean and cool **temiz hava** *Let's go outside and get some fresh air.* **5 fresh water** water from lakes, rivers, etc that has no salt in it **taze, turfanda 6** NOT TIRED having a lot of energy and not feeling tired **taze/temiz su** *We got up the next day feeling fresh and relaxed.* **7** SKIN Fresh skin looks healthy. **taze cilt/deri** *a fresh complexion* **8** RECENT recently made or done and not yet changed by time **yeni/taze yapılmış; değişmemiş; el değmemiş** *The memory of the accident is still very fresh in my mind.* **9 fresh from/out of sth** having just left a place **daha yeni/henüz ayrılmış, az evvel çıkmış** *The new French teacher's fresh out of college.* ● **freshness** noun [U] ⊃See also: a **breath** of fresh air. **yenilik**

freshen /ˈfreʃən/ verb
freshen up phrasal verb to quickly wash yourself so that you feel clean **yıkanıp paklanmak** *Would you like to freshen up before dinner?*
freshen sth up phrasal verb to make something look cleaner and more attractive **bir şeyi aklayıp paklamak; tertemiz hale getirmek** *A coat of paint would help to freshen this place up.*

fresher /ˈfreʃər/ noun [C] UK informal a student in the first year of university **üniversitede birinci sınıf öğrencisi**

freshly /ˈfreʃli/ adverb recently **son zamanlarda, taze, yeni** *freshly baked bread*

freshman /ˈfreʃmən/ noun [C] plural **freshmen** US a student in the first year of a course at a US college, university, or high school (= school for students aged 15 to 18) (ABD) **üniversitede ilk yıl/birinci sınıf öğrencisi**

freshwater /ˈfreʃˌwɔːtər/ adjective relating to water that is not salty **içme suyu** *freshwater fish*

fret /fret/ verb [I] **fretting**, past **fretted** to be anxious or worried **üzülmek, sıkılmak, kaygılanmak, huysuzlanmak** *There's no point in fretting about what you cannot change.* ● **fretful** adjective anxious and unhappy **sinirli, huysuz, mutsuz, gergin**

Fri written abbreviation for Friday **cuma günü**

friar /fraɪər/ noun [C] a member of a religious group of men **mensupları erkeklerden oluşan dini bir gurubun üyesi**

friction /ˈfrɪkʃən/ noun [U] **1** when a surface rubs against something, often making movement more difficult **sürtme, sürtünme 2** when people argue or disagree, often over a long period of time **sürtüşme, takışma, anlaşmazlık; dalaşma** *There's a lot of friction between my wife and my mother.*

o⌐**Friday** /ˈfraɪdeɪ/ (written abbreviation **Fri**) noun [C, U] the day of the week after Thursday and before Saturday **cuma günü** ⊃See also: Good Friday.

fridge /frɪdʒ/ noun [C] a large container that uses electricity to keep food cold **buzdolabı, dondurucu** ⊃Orta kısımdaki renkli sayfalarına bakınız.

fridge-freezer /ˌfrɪdʒˈfriːzər/ noun [C] a piece of equipment for storing food that has two parts: a fridge (= a container that keeps food cold) and a freezer (= a container that keeps food frozen) **derin dondurucusu olan buz dolabı; dondurucu ve soğutucu bölümleri ayrı buzdolabı**

fried /fraɪd/ adjective cooked in hot oil or fat **kızarmış, kızartılmış** *a fried egg* ⊃See also: deep-fried.

friend ...... İLE BİRLİKTE KULLANILAN KELİMELER
sb's **best** friend ● a **close/good** friend ● a **family** friend ● an **old** friend ● a friend **of mine**

friend ...... BAŞKA BİR DEYİŞLE
Chum, mate ve **pal** kelimeleri gayri resmi ortamlarda **friend** kelimesinin yerine kullanılabilen

kelimelerdir. *Pete was there with a couple of his **mates**.* Çok uzun süredir tanıdığınız ve sevdiğiniz bir kişi için **an old friend** tanımlaması kullanılabilir. *Rachel is one of my **oldest** friends.*
Acquaintance kelimesi tanıdığınız fakat çok samimiyetiniz olmayan kişiler için kullanılabilir. *He had a few business **acquaintances**.*
Duygularınız ve sırlarınızı paylaşabileceğiniz arkadaşınız için **confidant** ifadesi kullanılır. *Sarah was my **confidant** throughout this period and I told her everything.*
Aynı ilgi alanlarına merak duyan arkadaş topluluğu için **crowd** ifadesi kullanılabilir. *"Who was there?" "Oh, you know, Dave, Fiona and all that **crowd**."*
Resmi bir şekilde kullanılmayan **crony** kelimesi, biraradaki kişilerin birbirlerine adil olmayan bir şekilde yardım ettiklerini belirtir. *He always gives his **cronies** all the best jobs.*

o⌐**friend** /frend/ noun [C] **1** someone who you know well and like **arkadaş, dost** *Sarah's my best friend* (= the friend I like most). ○ *Gordon is a friend of mine.* **2 an old friend** someone who you have known and liked for a long time **eski bir arkadaş 3 be friends (with sb)** to know and like someone **dost/arkadaş olmak; tanışıyor olmak** *I have been friends with Jo for years.* **4 make friends (with sb)** to begin to know and like someone **arkadaş/dost olmaya başlamak** *He's shy and finds it difficult to make friends.*

o⌐**friendly¹** /ˈfrendli/ adjective **1** behaving in a pleasant, kind way towards someone **dostane, arkadaşça, dostça, içten, sıcak** *a friendly face/smile* ○ *The other students have been very friendly to us.* ⊃Opposite unfriendly. **2 be friendly with sb** to know and like someone **biriyle dost/arkadaş olmak/dostluk kurmak** ● **friendliness** noun [U] **arkadaşlık**

friendly² /ˈfrendli/ noun [C] UK a sports match that is not part of an official competition **dostluk karşılaşması/maçı**

-friendly /ˈfrendli/ suffix **1** used at the end of words to mean 'not harmful' **'zararlı değil' anlamında son ek** *environmentally-friendly detergent* **2** used at the end of words to mean 'suitable for particular people to use' **belli bir amaç veya kişi için uygun' anlamında sonek** *a family-friendly restaurant* ⊃See also: user-friendly.

friendship ...... İLE BİRLİKTE KULLANILAN KELİMELER
strike up a friendship ● a **close** friendship ● sb's friendship **with** sb ● a friendship **between** sb and sb

friendship /ˈfrendʃɪp/ noun [C, U] when two people are friends **arkadaşlık, dostluk** *a close friendship*

fries /fraɪz/ mainly US (also UK **chips**) noun [plural] long, thin pieces of potato that have been cooked in hot oil **kızarmış patates**

frieze /friːz/ noun [C] an area of decoration along a wall **duvar üzerine yapılan süsleme/dekorasyon**

frigate /ˈfrɪɡət/ noun [C] a small, fast military ship **fırkateyn, savaş gemisi**

fright /fraɪt/ noun [U, no plural] a sudden feeling of shock and fear **korku, endişe, ani ürperti/şok** *That dog gave me/a terrible fright.* ○ *She screamed in fright when she saw him.*

o⌐**frighten** /ˈfraɪtən/ verb [T] to make someone afraid or nervous **korkutmak, ürkütmek** *It frightens me when he drives so fast.* ⊃See also: scare/frighten the (living) **daylights** out of sb, scare/frighten sb out of their **wits**.
frighten sb away/off phrasal verb to make a person or animal afraid or nervous so that they go away **(insan, hayvan) korkutup uzaklaştırmak, ürkütmek**

frightened ...... BAŞKA BİR DEYİŞLE

Afraid ve scared sıfatları **frightened** sıfatının alternatifleri olarak kullanılabilirler. *She's very afraid of dogs.* ● *Gerry has always been scared of heights.*
Eğer kişi gerçekten çok korktuysa, durumu belirtmek için petrified, panic-stricken, veya çok gayri resmi olarak scared to death söylemleri kullanılabilir. *I'm terrified of flying.* ● *She was panic-stricken when her little boy disappeared.* ● *He's scared to death of having the operation.*
Eğer kişi bir durumdan dolayı endişe ettiği için korkuyorsa, afraid ve worried sıfatları kullanılabilir. *I'm afraid/worried that something will go wrong.*
Eğer kişi gelecekte olabilecek olan bir şey hakkında endişe duyuyorsa, kişinin duygularını belirtmek için apprehensive veya uneasy sıfatları kullanılabilir. *He's a bit apprehensive about living away from home.*

o⧧**frightened** /ˈfraɪt³nd/ *adjective* afraid or nervous **korkmuş, endişeye kapılmış, ürkmüş** *I've always been frightened of going to the dentist.* ○ [+ (that)] *Gerry was frightened that people would laugh at him.*

o⧧**frightening** /ˈfraɪt³nɪŋ/ *adjective* making you feel afraid or nervous **korkutan, ürküten, endişe veren** *a very frightening film* ● **frighteningly** *adverb* **korkuturcasına**

frightful /ˈfraɪtf³l/ *adjective UK old-fashioned* very bad **korkunç, ürkütücü, korku salan, müthiş** *The house was in a frightful mess.*

frightfully /ˈfraɪtf³li/ *adverb UK old-fashioned* very **çok berbat şekilde, ürkütücü olarak** *They're frightfully rich, you know.*

frigid /ˈfrɪdʒɪd/ *adjective* **1** not enjoying sexual activity, usually said about a woman **(kadın) cinsel isteksizliği/soğukluğu olan; (tıp) frijit 2** *literary* not friendly or emotional **(ilişki) pek dostane olmayan, duygusal yakınlık kurulamayan/göstermeyen**

frill /frɪl/ *noun* **1** [C] a strip of material with a lot of folds which is used to decorate the edge of cloth **fır fır 2 frills** extra things that are added to something to make it nicer or more attractive, but that are not really necessary **takıp takıştırılan ekstra/gereksiz şeyler** *a cheap, no frills airline service*

frilly /ˈfrɪli/ *adjective* with a lot of frills **fırfırlı** *a frilly dress*

fringe¹ /frɪndʒ/ *noun* [C] **1** HAIR *UK* (*US* bangs [plural]) hair that is cut short and straight at the top of someone's face **kâkül, perçem 2** DECORATION loose threads that hang along the edge of cloth as a decoration **saçak, salkım saçak 3** EDGE the outside edge of an area, group, or subject and not the main part **dışında olan, aşırı uç, dış**

fringe² /frɪndʒ/ *verb* **be fringed with sth** If a place or object is fringed with something, that thing forms a border along the edge. **çevrelenmiş/saçakları yapılmış olmak** *The river is fringed with wild flowers.*

fringe³ /frɪndʒ/ *adjective* [always before noun] not belonging to the main part of a group, activity, or subject **ayrı, ayrık, dışında, uçta olan** *fringe politics/theatre*

,fringe 'benefit *noun* [C] something extra that you get from your employer in addition to money **yan ödemeler, ilave gelirler** [usually plural] *fringe benefits such as private health care*

frisk /frɪsk/ *verb* **1** [T] to move your hands over someone's body to discover if they are hiding something such as a weapon **üstünü aramak, arama yapmak** *There were guards frisking people as they went into the building.* **2** [I] to run and jump happily like a young animal **sıçramak, oynamak, sevinçle zıplamak; (argo) kıç atmak**

frisky /ˈfrɪski/ *adjective* energetic and wanting to be active or play **oynak, canlı, enerji dolu, hoplayıp zıplayan** *a frisky puppy*

fritter /ˈfrɪtə³/ *verb*
fritter sth away *phrasal verb* to waste money or time on something that is not important **boşuna harcamak; gereksiz harcama yapmak; boşa harcamak**

frivolity /frɪˈvɒləti/ *noun* [C, U] when people are being silly and not being serious **uçarılık, ciddiyetsizlik**

frivolous /ˈfrɪvᵊləs/ *adjective* silly and not serious **uçarı, ciddiyetsiz** ● **frivolously** *adverb* **şaçma bir şekilde**

frizzy /ˈfrɪzi/ *adjective* Frizzy hair has a lot of very small, tight curls. **(saç) kıvırcık**

fro /frəʊ/ *adverb* ⊃See to³ and fro.

frog /frɒg/ *noun* [C] a small, green animal with long back legs for jumping that lives in or near water **kurbağa**

frogman /ˈfrɒgmən/ *noun* [C] *plural* **frogmen** someone whose job is to swim under water wearing a rubber suit and using special breathing equipment **dalgıç** *Police frogmen are searching the lake.*

o⧧**from** *strong form* /frɒm/ *weak form* /frəm/ *preposition* **1** STARTING PLACE used to show the place, time, or level that someone or something started at ... **den/dan** *Did you walk all the way from Bond Street?* ○ *The museum is open from 9.30 to 6.00, Tuesday to Sunday.* ○ *Prices start from £5,595.* **2** HOME used to say where someone was born, or where someone lives or works **(bir yerden) oralı, ...den/dan olan/gelen** *His mother's originally from Poland.* ○ *Our speaker tonight is from the BBC.* **3** DISTANCE used to say how far away something is ...**den/dan ötede** *Their holiday cottage is about 15 kilometres from the coast.* **4** GIVING used to say who gave or sent something to someone ...**den/dan gelme/gelen** *Have you had a Christmas card from Faye yet?* **5** REMOVING If you take something from a person, place, or amount, you take it away. ...**den/dan öteye/uzağa** *Two from ten leaves eight.* ○ *We had to borrow some money from my father to pay the bill.* **6** PRODUCED used to say where something was produced or grown **bir şeyin geldiği/üretildiği yeri göstermede kullanılır** *These vegetables are fresh from the garden.* **7** MATERIAL used to say what something is made of **bir şeyin neden mamül olduğunu/üretildiğini belirtmede kullanılır** *juice made from oranges* **8** AVOID used to show something that you want to avoid or prevent **bir şeyden uzak durmada/önlem almayı belirtmede kullanılır** *There's a bar across the front to prevent you from falling out.* **9** POSITION used to show where you are when you look at something or how you see something ...**den/dan bakıldığında/görüldüğünde anlamında** *The view from the top was absolutely breathtaking.* **10** REASON used to say why you think or believe something **bir şeye inanmada/neden öyle düşünüldüğünü belirmede kullanılır** *I guessed from her accent that she must be French.* ○ *From what I've heard, the new exam is going to be a lot more difficult.* **11** CAUSE used to say what causes something **bir şeyin neden kaynaklandığını belirtmede kullanılır** *Deaths from heart disease continue to rise every year.* ○ *He was rushed to hospital suffering from severe burns.* **12** COMPARE used when you are saying how similar or different two things, people, or places are **kıyaslama/ayrım/benzerlik belirtmede** *University is very different from school.* **13 a week/six months/ten years, etc from now** a week/six months/ten years, etc after the time when you are speaking **içinde bulunulan andan bir hafta/altı ay/on yıl sonra vb. belirtmede** *Who knows* *what we'll all be doing five years from now?* **14 from now/then, etc on** starting now/then, etc and continuing into the future **şu andan/o andan itibaren** *They were good friends from that day on.*

o--**front**[1] /frʌnt/ *noun* **1 the front a** MOST IMPORTANT SIDE the side of something that is most important or most often seen because it faces forward **ön, ön taraf** *You need to write the address clearly on the front of the envelope.* ○ *There was blood on the front of his shirt.* **b** FORWARD PART the part of something that is furthest forward **ileride, önde, ön tarafta/tarafı** *We asked to sit in the front of the plane.* ○ *He was standing right at the front.* **2 in front a** FURTHER FORWARD further forward than someone or something else **önde, ileride, ileriye doğru** *She started a conversation with the man sitting in front of her.* **b** WINNING winning in a game or competition (**yarışma, oyun**) **önde, ileride** *By half time the Italians were well in front.* **3 in front of a** NEAR close to the front part of something **önünde** *He parked the car in front of the house.* **b** SEEING/HEARING where someone can see or hear you (**görülebilecek/duyulabilecek mesafede**) **önde, önünde** *Please don't swear in front of the children.* **4** BEHAVIOUR [C] when someone behaves in a way that hides how they really feel **gerçek duygu ve hisleri gizleyerek** [usually singular] *Many parents decide to stay together, putting up a front for the children's sake.* **5** ILLEGAL ACTIVITY [C] an organization or activity that is used to hide a different, illegal activity **paravan, göstermelik olan durumda** [usually singular] *Police discovered the restaurant was just a front for a drugs operation.* **6 the front** an area of land where soldiers fight during a war **cephe/cephe hattı** *Thousands of young men were sent to the front to fight.* **7 on the business/ jobs/politics, etc front** in a particular area of activity **belli bir alanda, iş sahasında/cephesinde** *How are things on the work front at the moment?* **8** WEATHER [C] a line where warm air meets cold air affecting the weather **hava koşullarını değiştiren sıcak hava ile soğuk havanın karşılaştığı cephe/hat** *A cold front is moving across the Atlantic.*

o--**front**[2] /frʌnt/ *adjective* [always before noun] in or at the front of something **ön, ilk** *the front door/garden* ○ *the front page of the newspaper*

frontal /ˈfrʌntəl/ *adjective* **1** relating to the front of something **bir şeyin önüne/ön cephesine ilişkin 2 a frontal attack/assault** when you criticize or attack someone or something in a very strong and direct way **doğrudan ve sert biçimde saldırı/eleştiri/hücum**

frontier /frʌnˈtɪər/ *noun* **1** [C] a line or border between two countries **iki ülke arasındaki sınır, hudut 2 the frontiers of sth** the limits of what is known or what has been done before in an area of knowledge or activity **bir şeyin (bilginin, faaliyetin) sınırları/çizgileri/hatları** *the frontiers of science and technology*

,**front** ˈ**line** *noun* **1 the front line a** the place where soldiers fight in a war **muharebe/cephe hattı b** a position of direct and important influence **doğrudan ve önemli etki yaratan durum/konum; ön saflarda; ileri hatlarda** *doctors working in the front line of medicine* ● **front-line** /ˈfrʌntlaɪn/ *adjective* [always before noun] *front-line troops* **ön kısım, cephe**

front-page /ˈfrʌntˌpeɪdʒ/ *adjective* **front-page news/ story, etc** news that is very important and suitable for the front page of a newspaper (**gazete**) **ilk sayfa haberi/yorumu**

front-runner /ˌfrʌntˈrʌnər/ ⓤ /ˈfrʌntˌrʌnər/ *noun* [C] the person or organization that will most probably win something **önde giden; kazanmaya en yakın olan kişi/kuruluş**

frost[1] /frɒst/ *noun* **1** [U] a thin, white layer of ice that forms on surfaces, especially at night, when it is very cold **don, kırağı 2** [C] when the temperature is cold and water freezes **don, ayaz** *We're expecting a hard frost tonight.*

frost[2] /frɒst/ *US* (*UK/US* **ice**) *verb* [T] to cover a cake with frosting (= sweet mixture used to cover cakes) **şekerli bir karışımla kaplamak**

frostbite /ˈfrɒstbaɪt/ *noun* [U] when extreme cold injures your fingers and toes **eli ayağı buz kesme, donma, soğuktan uyuşma; soğuk ısırması**

frosted /ˈfrɒstɪd/ *adjective* Frosted glass has a special surface so that you cannot see through it. **buzlu (cam)**

frosting /ˈfrɒstɪŋ/ *US* (*UK/US* **icing**) *noun* [U] a sweet mixture used to cover or fill cakes, made from sugar and water or sugar and butter **şekerli kaplama**

frosty /ˈfrɒsti/ *adjective* **1** very cold, with a thin layer of white ice covering everything **buzlu** *a frosty morning* **2** not friendly **soğuk, buz gibi, içten olmayan** *She gave me a very frosty look.*

froth /frɒθ/ *noun* [U] small, white bubbles such as on the surface of a liquid **köpük, kabarcık ● froth** *verb* [I] **köpük çıkarmak ● frothy** *adjective* *frothy coffee* **köpüksü**

frown[1] /fraʊn/ *verb* [I] to make your face show that you are annoyed or worried by moving your eyebrows (= lines of hair above your eyes) **kaşlarını çatmak** *She frowned when I mentioned his name.*

frown on/upon sth *phrasal verb* to think that something is wrong and that you should not do it **muhalefet etmek, tavır almak, hoş karşılamamak** [often passive] *Smoking is frowned upon in many public places.*

frown[2] /fraʊn/ *noun* [C] the expression on your face when you frown **çatık kaş** *He looked at me with a puzzled frown.*

froze /frəʊz/ *past tense of* freeze '**donmak' fiilinin ikinci hali**

frozen[1] /ˈfrəʊzən/ *adjective* **1** FOOD Frozen food has been made so that it will last a long time by freezing. **donmuş, dondurulmuş (gıda/yiyecek)** *frozen peas* **2** WATER turned into ice **donmuş, buz tutmuş** *The pond was frozen and people were skating on it.* **3** PERSON *informal* extremely cold **son derece soğuk, üşüten, donduran** *Is there any heating in here? I'm frozen!*

frozen[2] /ˈfrəʊzən/ *past participle of* freeze '**donmak' fiilinin üçüncü hali**

frugal /ˈfruːgəl/ *adjective* careful not to spend very much money **tutumlu, dikkatli harcama yapan; eli sıkı**

╔══════════════════════════════════╗
║ 🧩 *fruit* ...... İLE BİRLİKTE KULLANILAN KELİMELER ║
╚══════════════════════════════════╝

dried/fresh fruit   ● **a piece of** fruit   ● fruit **juice**
● **citrus/tropical** fruit

o--**fruit** /fruːt/ *noun* **1** [C, U] something such as an apple or orange that grows on a tree or a bush, contains seeds, and can be eaten as food **meyve** *dried/fresh fruit* ○ *fruit juice* ⊃*Orta kısımdaki renkli sayfalarına bakınız.* **2 the fruit(s) of sth** the good result of someone's work or actions **bir şeyin meyveleri/başarısı/sonuçları; semeresi** *This book is the fruit of 15 years' research.* **3 bear fruit** If something that someone does bears fruit, it produces successful results. **sonuç vermek** *Our decision is just beginning to bear fruit.* ⊃See also: citrus fruit.

fruitful /ˈfruːtfəl/ *adjective* producing good or useful results **verimli, yararlı; iyi/faydalı sonuçlar veren/doğuran** *We had a very fruitful discussion.*

fruition /fruˈɪʃən/ *noun* [U] *formal* when a plan or an idea really begins to happen, exist, or be successful **gerçek-**

leşme, muradına erme, başarılı olma *The plan never really came to fruition.*

fruitless /'fru:tləs/ *adjective* not successful or achieving good results **yararsız, nafile, başarısız, iyi sonuç vermeyen** *a long and fruitless search*

fruity /'fru:ti/ *adjective* smelling or tasting of fruit **meyve aromalı/tadında/kokulu** *a fruity wine/taste*

frustrate /frʌs'treɪt/ ⑤ /'frʌstreɪt/ *verb* [T] **1** to make someone feel annoyed because things are not happening in the way that they want, or in the way that they should **düş/hayal kırıklığına uğramak; bütün hayalleri suya düşmek** *It really frustrates me when she arrives late for meetings.* **2** to prevent someone from achieving something, or to prevent something from happening **boşa çıkarmak, engellemek, planını frustrate** *They have frustrated all our attempts to find a solution to this problem.*

frustrated /frʌs'treɪtɪd/ ⑤ /'frʌstreɪtɪd/ *adjective* annoyed because things are not happening in the way that you want, or in the way that they should **hüsrana uğramış, hayalleri boşa çıkmış, umudu kırılmış** *I'm very frustrated at/with my lack of progress.*

frustrating /frʌs'treɪtɪŋ/ ⑤ /'frʌstreɪtɪŋ/ *adjective* making you feel frustrated **can sıkıcı, moral bozucu, umut kırıcı** *a frustrating situation*

frustration ...... İLE BİRLİKTE KULLANILAN KELİMELER

sheer frustration • **in** frustration • frustration **at** (doing) sth

frustration /frʌs'treɪʃ³n/ *noun* [C, U] the feeling of being annoyed because things are not happening in the way that you want, or in the way that they should **hüsran, hayal kırıklığı, bozgun** *I could sense his frustration at not being able to help.*

fry /fraɪ/ *verb* [I, T] to cook something in hot oil or fat or to be cooked in hot oil or fat **kızartmak** *Fry the onions in a little butter.* ➔See picture at **cook**.

'frying ,pan *noun* [C] a flat, metal pan with a long handle that is used for frying food **kızartma tavası** ➔Orta kısımdaki renkli sayfalarına bakınız.

ft *written abbreviation for* foot (= a unit for measuring length) **mesafe ölçü birimi, ayak**

fudge¹ /fʌdʒ/ *noun* [U] a soft sweet food made from butter, sugar, and milk **yumuşak şekerleme**

fudge² /fʌdʒ/ *verb informal* **1** [T] UK to avoid making a decision or giving a clear answer about something **oyalamak, net bir cevap vermemek, karar vermekten imtina etmek/kaçınmak** *The government continues to fudge the issue.* **2** [I, T] US to slightly cheat, often by not telling the exact truth **kandırmak, uydurmak ,hile yapmak** *He fudged on his income tax return.*

fuel ...... İLE BİRLİKTE KULLANILAN KELİMELER

fuel **bills/consumption/prices/supplies** • fuel **efficiency**

o*\ **fuel¹** /'fju:əl/ *noun* [C, U] a substance that is burned to provide heat or power **sıvı yakıt, yakacak** *The plane ran out of fuel and had to land at sea.*

fuel² /'fju:əl/ *verb* [T] UK **fuelling**, *past* **fuelled**, US **fueling**, *past* **fueled** to make people's ideas or feelings stronger, or to make a situation worse **görüşlerini ve fikirlerini desteklemek/arka çıkmak veya daha da kötüleştirmek** *Newspaper reports are fuelling fears about GM foods.*

fugitive /'fju:dʒətɪv/ *noun* [C] someone who is escaping or hiding from the police or from a dangerous situation **kaçak**

fulfil UK (US **fulfill**) /fʊl'fɪl/ *verb* **fulfilling**, *past* **fulfilled** **1 fulfil a duty/promise/responsibility, etc** to do something that you have promised to do or that you are expected to do **bir görevi/vaadi/sorumluluğu vb. yerine getirmek/yapmak** *He has failed to fulfil his duties as a father.* **2 fulfil an ambition/dream/goal, etc** to do something that you really wanted to do **bir isteği/hayali/amacı gerçekleştirmek 3 fulfil a function/need/role, etc** to do something that is necessary or useful **bir işlevi/gereksinimi/rolü vb. yerine getirmek/yapmak** *You seem to fulfil a very useful role in the organization.* **4 fulfil criteria/requirements/qualifications, etc** to have all the qualities that are wanted or needed for something **kritere/gereklilikle re/niteliklere vb. haiz/sahip olmak** *You have to fulfil certain requirements to qualify for the competition.*

fulfilled /fʊl'fɪld/ *adjective* feeling happy that you are receiving everything that you want from your life **tatmin olmuş, hoşnut** ➔Opposite **unfulfilled**.

fulfilling /fʊl'fɪlɪŋ/ *adjective* If something is fulfilling, it satisfies you and makes you happy. **tatmin edici, mutlu eden** *a fulfilling job*

fulfilment UK (US **fulfillment**) /fʊl'fɪlmənt/ *noun* [U] **1** a feeling of pleasure because you are receiving or achieving what you want **tatmin, hoşnutluk** *I hope that you'll find happiness and fulfilment in your life together.* **2** when someone does something necessary or something that they have wanted or promised to do **başarma, gerçekleştirme, yerine getirme** *Being here is the fulfilment of a lifelong ambition.*

o*\ **full¹** /fʊl/ *adjective* **1** NO MORE POSSIBLE If a container or a space is full, it contains as many things or people as possible or as much of something as possible. **dolu** *We couldn't get in, the cinema was full.* ○ *The shelves were full of books.* **2** A LOT containing a lot of things or people or a lot of something **dolu, dopdolu** *The room was full of people.* ○ *His face was full of anger.* **3** COMPLETE [always before noun] complete and including every part **tam, dolu,** *Please give your full name and address.* **4 full speed/strength/volume, etc** the greatest speed/strength/volume, etc possible **tam hız/güç/ayar** *We were driving at full speed.* ○ *She got full marks in the test.* **5 be full of yourself** to think that you are very important **dolu olmak; çok önemli olduğunu düşünmek 6 be full of sth** to be talking or thinking a lot about a particular thing **bir şeyle dopdolu olmak** *He's full of stories about his holiday.* **7** FOOD *informal* (also UK **full up**) having eaten enough food **tok, karnı doymuş, tıka basa dolu** *No more for me, thanks, I'm full.* **8 a full face/figure** a face or body shape that is large and round **ablak yüzlü, büyük ve yuvarlak yüzlü/vücutlu** ➔See also: have your hands (**hand¹**) full, be in full swing².

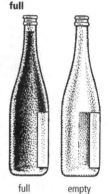

full   empty

full² /fʊl/ *noun* **1 in full** completely and with nothing missing **tamamen, tam olarak** *The speech will be published in full in tomorrow's newspaper.* **2 to the full** *mainly UK* as much or as well as possible **tam anla-**

mıyla, **sonuna kadar** *She certainly lived life to the full.*

full-blown /ˌfʊlˈbləʊn/ *adjective* completely developed **tamamen gelişmiş** *a full-blown crisis* ○ *a full-blown disease*

full ˈboard *noun* [U] *UK* when all your meals are provided in a hotel **tam pansiyon**

full-fledged /ˌfʊlˈfledʒd/ *US* (*UK* **fully-fledged**) *adjective* [always before noun] having finished developing, studying, or establishing yourself **tamamen dolu/gelişmiş; çalışmış/kendini geliştirmiş; gelişimini tamamlamış**

full-grown /ˌfʊlˈɡrəʊn/ *adjective* A full-grown person, animal, or plant has developed completely, and is not expected to grow more. **erişkin, yetişkin, tam gelişmiş** *a full-grown man*

full ˈhouse *noun* [C] when all the seats in a place such as a theatre or cinema are full **(tiyatro, sinema vb.) tam dolu, dopdolu**

full-length /ˌfʊlˈleŋθ/ *adjective* **1** a full-length book/film, etc a book/film, etc that is the usual length and not shorter **eksiksiz/tam/kısaltılmamış kitap/film** *a full-length feature film* **2** a full-length mirror/photograph, etc a mirror/image, etc that shows a person's whole body from the head to the feet **boy aynası, boy resmi 3** a full-length coat/dress/skirt, etc a long piece of clothing that reaches to your feet **upuzun elbise/etek/palto vb.**

full ˈmoon *noun* [no plural] the moon when it appears as a complete circle **dolunay**

full-on /fʊlˈɒn/ *adjective* **1** very great or to the greatest degree **çok büyük veya en büyük dercede/seviyede** *full-on luxury* **2** very serious and enthusiastic, often in a way which annoys other people **çok ciddi veya heyecanlı/coşkulu**

full-page /ˌfʊlˈpeɪdʒ/ *adjective* [always before noun] filling a complete page in a newspaper or magazine **(gazete, dergi) tam sayfa** *a full-page ad*

full-scale /ˌfʊlˈskeɪl/ *adjective* [always before noun] **1** very large or serious and involving everything that is possible or expected **geniş kapsamlı/çaplı; herşeyi içeren** *The violence has developed into a full-scale war.* **2** A full-scale model is the same size as the original thing that it is representing. **tam boy, özgün boyutta/ölçülerde**

full ˈstop *UK* (*US* **period**) *noun* [C] a mark (.) used at the end of a sentence, or to show that the letters before it are an abbreviation **nokta (.)** ➾See study page **Punctuation** on page Centre 33.

full-time /ˌfʊlˈtaɪm/ *adjective* happening or working for the whole of the working week and not only part of it **tam zamanlı** *a full-time job/course* ● **full-time** *adverb She works full-time for the council.* **tam zamanlı olarak**

☞ **fully** /ˈfʊli/ *adverb* completely **tamamen, tam olarak** *The restaurant was fully booked.* ○ *He is fully aware of the dangers involved.*

fully-fledged /ˌfʊliˈfledʒd/ *UK* (*US* **full-fledged**) *adjective* [always before noun] having finished developing, studying, or establishing yourself **tamamen gelişmiş, olgunlaşmış** *I won't be a fully-fledged doctor until after the exams.*

fumble /ˈfʌmbl/ *verb* [I] to use your hands with difficulty to try to get hold of something or find something **el yordamıyla aramak, yoklamak** *She fumbled in her bag for her glasses.*

fume /fjuːm/ *verb* [I] to be extremely angry, especially in a quiet way **öfkelenmek, sinirlenmek, küplere binmek** *A week later, she was still fuming about his behaviour.*

fumes /fjuːmz/ *noun* [plural] strong, unpleasant, and often dangerous gas or smoke **duman** *car exhaust fumes*

---
fun .... İLE BİRLİKTE KULLANILAN KELİMELER
have fun ● **good/great** fun ● **be no** fun ● **for** fun

☞ **fun¹** /fʌn/ *noun* [U] **1** enjoyment or pleasure, or something that gives you enjoyment or pleasure **eğlence, zevk** *She's great fun to be with.* ○ *Have fun!* (= enjoy yourself) ○ *It's no fun having to work late every night.* **2 for fun/for the fun of it** for pleasure and not for any other reason **eğlencesine, zevkine, zevk için 3 make fun of sb/sth** to make a joke about someone or something in an unkind way **şaka yapmak, alay etmek, dalga geçmek** *The other children at school used to make fun of his hair.*

fun² /fʌn/ *adjective* enjoyable or entertaining **eğlenceli, eğlendiren, zevk veren** *There are lots of fun things to do here.*

---
function .... İLE BİRLİKTE KULLANILAN KELİMELER
a **basic/important/primary/vital** function ● **carry out/fulfil/provide/serve** a function
---

☞ **function¹** /ˈfʌŋkʃən/ *noun* [C] **1** the purpose of something or someone **işlev** *Each button has a different function.* **2** a large, formal party or ceremony **büyük resmi davet/tören/parti** *a charity function*

function² /ˈfʌŋkʃən/ *verb* [I] to work or operate **çalışmak, işlemek,** *The operation should help his lungs to function properly again.*

function as sth *phrasal verb* to have a particular purpose **belli bir işlevi/kullanım amacı olmak** *The spare bedroom also functions as a study.*

functional /ˈfʌŋkʃənəl/ *adjective* **1** designed to be practical or useful and not only attractive **işlevsel, kullanışlı** *functional clothing* **2** operating or working correctly **çalışır durumda, işlevini yerine getiren** *The system is not yet fully functional.*

ˈfunction ˌkey (*written abbreviation* F) *noun* [C] one of the keys on a computer keyboard which has the letter F and a number on it and that makes the computer do particular jobs **(bilgisayar) işlev tuşu, F tuşu** *Press F4 to print.*

☞ **fund** /fʌnd/ *noun* **1** [C] an amount of money collected, saved, or provided for a purpose **kaynak, fon** *a pension fund* **2 funds** [plural] money needed or available to spend on something **fon, kaynaklar** *The charity closed down due to lack of funds.* ● **fund** *verb* [T] to provide money for an event, activity, or organization **para/fon ayırmak; fon sağlamak** *Who is the project funded by?*

fundamental /ˌfʌndəˈmentəl/ *adjective* relating to the most important or main part of something **temel, asıl, esas, öz, ana** *a fundamental change/difference* ○ *Training is fundamental to success.* ● **fundamentally** *adverb The world has changed fundamentally over the last century.* **esaslı bir şekilde**

fundamentalism /ˌfʌndəˈmentəlɪzəm/ *noun* [U] the belief that the traditions and rules of a religion should be followed exactly **köktencilik**

fundamentalist /ˌfʌndəˈmentəlɪst/ *noun* [C] someone who believes that the rules of their religion should be followed exactly **kökten dinci, çok dindar olan kişi** ● **fundamentalist** *adjective* **dini kuralların net ve tüm şekliyle uygulanması gerektiği inancında olan**

fundamentals /ˌfʌndəˈmentəlz/ *noun* [plural] the main principles, or most important parts of something **esasları, ana prensipleri, en önemli bölümleri**

funding 306 o--Important words to learn

funding /ˈfʌndɪŋ/ *noun* [U] money given by a government or organization for an event or activity **fon/kaynak oluşturma** *The company received state funding for the project.*

fundraiser /ˈfʌndˌreɪzər/ *noun* [C] a person or an event that collects money for a particular purpose **fon oluşturmaya/kaynak temin etmeye çalışan kişi/eylem**

fundraising /ˈfʌndˌreɪzɪŋ/ *noun* [U] when you collect money for a particular purpose **fon/kaynak oluşturma eylemi** *a fundraising event*

o--**funeral** /ˈfjuːnərəl/ *noun* [C] a ceremony for burying or burning the body of a dead person **cenaze töreni**

'funeral ˌdirector *UK* (*US* **'funeral diˌrector**) *noun* [C] someone whose job is to organize funerals and prepare dead bodies to be buried or burned **cenaze işleriyle ilgilenen kişi, cenaze levazımatçısı**

fungus /ˈfʌŋgəs/ *noun* [C, U] *plural* **fungi** or **funguses** a type of plant without leaves and without green colouring which gets its food from other living or decaying things **mantar**

funk /fʌŋk/ *noun* [U] a style of popular music with a strong rhythm that is influenced by African and jazz music **Afrika ve caz müziğinden etkilenmiş güçlü ritimleri olan bir tarz pop müzik**

funky /ˈfʌŋki/ *adjective informal* **1** fashionable in an unusual and noticeable way **kural dışı biçimde ünlü/meşhur; kolay tanınabilen** *She's got some very funky clothes.* **2** Funky music has a strong rhythm, and is good to dance to. **hareketli/hızlı ritmi olan**

funnel /ˈfʌnəl/ *noun* [C]
1 a tube with a wide part at the top that you use to pour liquid or powder into something that has a small opening **huni 2** a metal pipe on the top of a ship or train which smoke comes out of **(gemi, tren) baca**

funnel

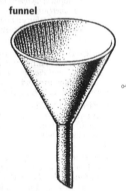

funnily /ˈfʌnɪli/ *adverb* *UK* **funnily enough** although it seems strange and surprising **işin tuhafı** *Funnily enough, I was just thinking about you when you called.*

funny ...... BAŞKA BİR DEYİŞLE

Amusing sıfatı **funny** sıfatının yerine daha resmi durumlarda kullanılabilecek bir sıfattır. *I gave her an article that I thought she would find amusing.*
Eğer bir şey çok komikse, durumu belirtmek için **Hilarious** veya (resmi olmayan) **hysterical** sıfatları kullanılabilir. *I've just read his autobiography - it's absolutely hilarious/hysterical.*
Eğer kişi akıllıca ve komik bir şekilde konuşuyorsa, kişiyi tanımlamada **witty** sıfatı kullanılabilir. *He was a very witty man.*
Comical sıfatı komik görünen bir şey veya kişi için kullanılabilir. *She looked so comical in that hat!*
Eğer kişiyi çok komik olarak nitelendirmek istiyorsanız, resmi olmayan ortamlarda **be a good laugh** ve **Be a scream** söylemlerini kullanabilirsiniz. *You'd like Amanda - she's a scream/good laugh.*

o--**funny** /ˈfʌni/ *adjective* **1** making you smile or laugh **gülünç, komik,** *a funny story* ○ *It's not funny. Don't laugh!* **2** strange or unusual and not what you expect

tuhaf, garip, komik, acayip *This chicken tastes a bit funny.*

o--**fur** /fɜːr/ *noun* **1** [U] the thick hair that covers the bodies of some animals like cats and rabbits **tüy 2** [C, U] the skin of an animal covered in thick hair and used for making clothes, or a piece of clothing made from this **kürk**

furious /ˈfjʊəriəs/ *adjective* **1** extremely angry **kızgın, öfkeli, hiddetli, celallenmiş** *He's furious at the way he's been treated.* ○ *My boss was furious with me.* **2** very energetic or fast **şiddetli, azgın, zaptedilemeyen, çok süratli** *a furious attack* ● **furiously** *adverb* **kızgınlıkla**

furlong /ˈfɜːlɒŋ/ *noun* [C] a unit of length used in horse races equal to 201 metres **at yarışlarında 201 metreye tekabül eden bir uzunluk birimi**

furnace /ˈfɜːnɪs/ *noun* [C] a container which is heated to a very high temperature and used to heat buildings, melt metal, or burn things **ocak, fırın**

furnish /ˈfɜːnɪʃ/ *verb* [T] to put furniture into a room or building **dayayıp döşemek** *They have furnished the room very simply.*
furnish sb with sth *phrasal verb formal* to provide someone with something **bir kimseye gerekli şeyleri /ihtiyaçlarını sağlamak** *Can you furnish me with any further information?*

furnished /ˈfɜːnɪʃt/ *adjective* If a room or building is furnished, there is furniture in it. **mobilyalı, dayalı döşeli**

furnishings /ˈfɜːnɪʃɪŋz/ *noun* [plural] the furniture, curtains and other decorations in a room or building **mobilya ve mefruşat**

furniture ...... İLE BİRLİKTE KULLANILAN KELİMELER

a **piece of** furniture ● **garden/office** furniture ● **antique** furniture

o--**furniture** /ˈfɜːnɪtʃər/ *noun* [U] objects such as chairs, tables, and beds that you put into a room or building **mobilya** *antique furniture*

YAYGIN HATALAR

furniture

Unutmayın! **Furniture** kelimesinin çoğul hali yoktur. **Furnitures** olarak kullanmayın. **Some furniture** veya **pieces of furniture** kullanımları doğrudur.: ~~The furnitures in the classroom are not very comfortable.~~ Yanlış cümle örneği
The furniture in the classroom is not very comfortable.

furore /fjʊəˈrɔːri/ *UK* (*US* **furor** /ˈfjʊrɔːr/) *noun* [no plural] a sudden, excited, or angry reaction to something by a lot of people **taşkınlık, kızgınlık, öfke, azgınlık** *The book caused a furore when it was published.*

furrow[1] /ˈfʌrəʊ/ *noun* [C] **1** a deep line cut into a field that seeds are planted in **tarh, bitki ekim/dikim arkı, evlek 2** a deep line on someone's face, especially above their eyes **(yüz, alın) kırışıklık, çizgi**

furrow[2] /ˈfʌrəʊ/ *verb* **furrow your brow** to make deep lines appear on your face above your eyes **yüzünü buruşturunca çizgiler oluşmak** *He furrowed his brow as he struggled to think of a solution.*

furry /ˈfɜːri/ *adjective* covered with fur or with something that feels like fur **tüylü, kürklü**

further[1] /ˈfɜːðər/ *adverb* **1** more **daha, ileri, ötede** *He refused to discuss the matter further.* ○ *Have you got any further* (= achieved any more) *with your research?* **2** *comparative of* **far**: at or to a place or time that is a longer distance away **öteye, ileriye, daha uzak/ uzakta** *Let's walk a bit further down the road.*

further² /ˈfɜːðəʳ/ *adjective* [always before noun] more or extra **daha, fazladan, ekstra** *For further details about the offer, call this number.* ○ *We will let you know if there are any further developments.*

further³ /ˈfɜːðəʳ/ *verb* [T] to make something develop or become more successful **geliştirmek, ileriye götürmek, başarılı kılmak** *He'll do anything to further his career.*

further edu'cation *noun* [U] UK education at a college for people who have left school but are not at a university **okulu yarım bırakmış olanlar için (üniversite dışında) düzenlenen resmi eğitim**

furthermore /ˌfɜːðəˈmɔːʳ/ ⓤ /ˈfɜːrðərmɔːr/ *adverb* in addition to what has just been said **dahası, ayrıca, üstelik**

furthest /ˈfɜːðɪst/ *adjective, adverb superlative of* **far**: most distant **(mesafe olarak) en ileride/ötede; en uzakta/uzağa**

furtive /ˈfɜːtɪv/ *adjective* doing something secretly, or done secretly, so that people do not notice **kaçamak, gizli; saklı gizli** *He gave her a furtive glance as soon as his wife left the room.* ● **furtively** *adverb* **gizli bir şekilde**

fury /ˈfjʊəri/ *noun* [U, no plural] extreme anger **son derece kızgınlık, hiddet, öfke** *He could hardly control his fury.*

fuse¹ /fjuːz/ *noun* [C] **1** a small object that stops electrical equipment working if there is too much electricity going through it **elektrik sigortası** *The fuse has blown. You'll have to change it.* ○ *a fuse box* **2** the part of a bomb or other explosive object that starts the explosion **bomba/patlayıcı düzeneğinde patlatıcı parça, fitil, fünye** *Light the fuse, and then stand back.*

fuse² /fjuːz/ *verb* [I, T] **1** UK If a piece of electrical equipment fuses, or if you fuse it, it stops working because there is too much electricity going through it. **sigorta atmak, sigortayı attırmak** *You've fused the lights.* **2** to join or become combined **birleş(tir)mek, kaynaş(tır)mak** *The bones of the skull are not properly fused at birth.*

fuselage /ˈfjuːzᵊlɑːʒ/ *noun* [C] the main body of an aircraft **uçak gövdesi, gövde**

fusion /ˈfjuːʒᵊn/ *noun* [C, U] when two or more things join or become combined **birleşme, kaynaşma, füzyon** *nuclear fusion* ○ *She describes her music as a fusion of folk and rock.*

fuss¹ /fʌs/ *noun* **1** [U, no plural] when people become excited, annoyed, or anxious about something, especially about something unimportant **yaygara, telaş** *What's all the fuss about?* ○ *They were making a big fuss over nothing.* **2 kick up/make a fuss** to complain about something **mesele çıkarmak, kıyamet koparmak, yaygara yapmak** *If they don't bring our food soon, I'll have to kick up a fuss.* **3 make a fuss of/over sb** to give someone a lot of attention and treat them well **hassas davranmak, üzerine titremek** *My uncle always makes a big fuss of the children.*

fuss² /fʌs/ *verb* [I] to worry too much or get too excited, especially about unimportant things **gereksiz/yersiz endişelenmek, telaşlanmak, (argo) pimpiriklenmek, vesvese yapmak, mızmızlanmak** *Please don't fuss, Mum. Everything's under control.*

fuss over sb/sth *phrasal verb* to give someone or something too much attention because you want to show that

you like them **aşırı düşkünlük göstermek, titizlenmek, üzerine titremek**

fussy /ˈfʌsi/ *adjective* **1** [NOT LIKING] only liking particular things and very difficult to please **titiz, müşkülpesent, kolay beğenmeyen** *She's a very fussy eater.* **2** [CAREFUL] too careful about unimportant details **ince detaylarda kaybolan, inciğini cinciğini düşünen, titiz, detaycı** **3** [TOO COMPLICATED] If something is fussy, it is too complicated in design and has too many details. **cicili bicili, süslü püslü**

futile /ˈfjuːtaɪl/ ⓤ /ˈfjuːtᵊl/ *adjective* certain not to have a successful effect or result **nafile, boşuna, yersiz** *a futile attempt to escape* ● **futility** /fjuːˈtɪləti/ *noun* [U] when something is futile **faydasızlık, boşunalık, beyhudelik**

futon /ˈfuːtɒn/ *noun* [C] a flat bed filled with soft material that can be used on the floor or on a wooden base, or folded into a seat **düz yatak, yer yatağı, döşek**

┌───┐
│ **future** .... İLE BİRLİKTE KULLANILAN KELİMELER │
└───┘
the **distant/foreseeable/near** future ● **plan for/predict** the future ● **in the** future

o⊶**future¹** /ˈfjuːtʃəʳ/ *noun* **1 the future a** [TIME TO COME] the time which is to come **gelecek, ati, istikbal** *He likes to plan for the future.* ○ *They hope to get married in the near future* (= soon). **b** [GRAMMAR] In grammar, the future is the form of the verb used to talk about something that will happen. **dilbilgisinde gelecek zaman 2 in future** UK (*mainly US* **in the future**) beginning from now **gelecekte, bundan sonra, ileride** *In future, I'll be more careful about who I lend my bike to.* **3** [WHAT WILL HAPPEN] [C] what will happen to someone or something in the time which is to come **gelecekte** *We need to discuss the future of the company.* **4** [SUCCESS] [U, no plural] chance of continuing to exist or succeed **geleceği** *She's got a very promising future ahead of her.*

o⊶**future²** /ˈfjuːtʃəʳ/ *adjective* [always before noun] **1** happening or existing in the time which is to come **gelecekte olacak, bundan sonra** *future plans* ○ *in future years* ○ *What will we leave for future generations?* **2 future tense** the form of the verb which is used to talk about something that will happen **gelecek zaman**

the ˌfuture ˈperfect *noun* the form of the verb which is used to show that an action will have been completed before a particular time in the future. The sentence 'I'll probably have left by then.' is in the future perfect. **gelecekte belli bir zamandan önce tamamlanacak eylemi gösteren fiil/zaman çekim; bitmiş gelecek zaman**

futuristic /ˌfjuːtʃᵊˈrɪstɪk/ *adjective* very modern and strange and seeming to come from some imagined time in the future **geleceğe ilişkin/dair, gelecekte olabilecek olan; çok fazla modern/acayip ve geleceğe ait** *a futuristic steel building*

fuzzy /ˈfʌzi/ *adjective* **1** confused and not clear **bulanık, flu, karmaşık, belirsiz, tam seçilemeyen** *We could only get a fuzzy picture on the television.* **2** covered in soft, short hairs, or material like this **kabarık, kısa yumuşak tüy benzeri şeylerle kaplı** *a fuzzy kitten* ○ *fuzzy slippers*

FYI *internet abbreviation for* for your information: used when you send someone a document or tell them something you think they should know about **bilgilerinize; bir belge gönderildiğinde ilgili kişinin dikkatini çekmek için yazılan kısaltma**

F

G

G, g /dʒiː/ the seventh letter of the alphabet **alfabenin yedinci harfi**

g *written abbreviation for* gram (= a unit for measuring weight) **gram, bir ağırlık ölçü birimi**

gabble /'gæbl/ *verb* [I, T] *UK informal* to talk quickly or in a way that people cannot understand **anlaşılmaz şekilde konuşmak, kelimeleri yuvarlamak** *He gabbled something in Italian.*

gable /'geɪbl/ *noun* [C] the top end of a wall of a building where two sloping parts of a roof meet at a point **çatı ile duvarın üst kısmının birleştiği yer**

gadget /'gædʒɪt/ *noun* [C] a small piece of equipment that does a particular job, especially a new type **alet, edavat, geçük alet** *a kitchen gadget*

Gaelic /'geɪlɪk/, /'gælɪk/ *noun* [U] a language spoken in parts of Scotland and Ireland **İrlanda ve İskoçya'nın belirli yerlerinde konuşulan dil; İrlandaca/İskoçça** ● **Gaelic** *adjective* relating to Gaelic or to the Gaelic culture of Scotland and Ireland **İskoçya ve İrlanda kültürüne özgü/ait**

gaffe /gæf/ *noun* [C] when someone says or does something embarrassing without intending to **gaf, pot kırma, bilmeden yapılan utandırıcı şey** *The minister has made a series of embarrassing gaffes.*

gag¹ /gæg/ *verb* **gagging**, *past* **gagged 1** [COVER MOUTH] [T] to fasten something over someone's mouth so that they cannot speak **ağzını tıkamak, susturmak** *The owners of the house were found bound and gagged in the cellar.* **2** [STOP INFORMATION] [T] to prevent someone from giving their opinion or giving information about something **konuşmasına izin vermemek, susturmak, engellemek** *The government is trying to gag the press over the issue.* **3** [ALMOST VOMIT] [I] to feel that you are going to vomit **midesi bulanmak** *The sight of the body made him gag.* **4 be gagging for sth** *UK informal* to want something or want to do something very much **bir şeyi/bir şey yapmayı çok arzu etmek** *I'm gagging for a coffee.*

gag² /gæg/ *noun* [C] **1** *informal* a joke or funny story **şaka, espri, komik hikâye 2** something that is fastened over someone's mouth to stop them speaking **ağız tıkacı; ağzı kapatmak için kullanılan bez, kağıt vb.**

gaggle /'gægl/ *noun* [C] a group of people, especially when they are noisy **kuru kalabalık/gürültü; gürültücü insanlar** *a gaggle of newspaper reporters*

gaiety /'geɪəti/ *noun* [U] *old-fashioned* happiness or excitement **neşe, heyecan, coşku, mutluluk**

gaily /'geɪli/ *adverb old-fashioned* in a happy way **şen şakrak bir şekilde, neşeyle, mutlu bir şekilde**

o⊷**gain¹** /geɪn/ *verb* **1** [GET] [T] to get something useful or positive **kazanmak, elde etmek** *The country gained independence in 1948.* ○ *You'll gain a lot of experience working there.* **2 gain by/from sth** to get an advantage or something valuable from something **bir şeyden yarar/çıkar elde etmek/sağlamak** *Who stands to gain from the will?* **3** [INCREASE] [T] to increase in something such as size, weight, or amount **(beden, ağırlık, miktar vb.) artmak, çoğalmak, artış göstermek** *He's gained a lot of weight in the last few months.* **4** [CLOCK] [I, T] If a clock or a watch gains, it works too quickly and shows a time that is later than the real time. **(saat) ileri gitmek** ⊃See also: gain/lose **ground¹**, get/gain the upper **hand¹**.

gain on sb/sth *phrasal verb* to get nearer to someone or something that you are chasing **yaklaşmak, sessizce sokulmak** *Quick! They're gaining on us.*

gain² /geɪn/ *noun* [C, U] **1** when you get something useful or positive **kazanç, kâr** *financial gain* **2** an increase in something such as size, weight, or amount **artma, artış, çoğalma**

gait /geɪt/ *noun* [C] someone's particular way of walking **yürüyüş tarzı** *I recognized his gait from a distance.*

gala /'gɑːlə/ ⓤ /'geɪlə/ *noun* [C] a special social event, performance, or sports competition **şenlik, kutlama, gala** *a gala concert*

galaxy /'gæləksi/ *noun* [C] a very large group of stars held together in the universe **yıldızlar kümesi, galaksi**

gale /geɪl/ *noun* [C] a very strong wind **fırtına, sert rüzgâr, bora**

gall¹ /gɔːl/ *noun* **have the gall to do sth** to be rude enough to do something that is not considered acceptable **bir şeyi yaparken küstahlık/kabalık göstermek** *I can't believe he had the gall to complain.*

gall² /gɔːl/ *verb* [T] to annoy someone **taciz etmek, rahatsızlık vermek** *What galls me is that he escaped without punishment.* ● **galling** *adjective* annoying **rahatsız edici, taciz eden** *It's particularly galling for me that she gets paid more than I do.*

gallant /'gælənt/ *adjective literary* **1** brave **cesur, yürekli** *a gallant attempt to rescue a drowning man* **2** polite and kind, especially to women **kibar, centilmen, saygılı** ● **gallantly** *adverb* **cesurca** ● **gallantry** *noun* [U] when someone is gallant **cesaret, kahramanlık; kibarlık, centilmenlik**

'gall ˌbladder *noun* [C] an organ in the body that contains a substance that helps you to digest food **safra kesesi**

gallery /'gæləri/ *noun* [C] **1** a room or building that is used for showing paintings and other art to the public **sanat galerisi; sergi salonu** *a museum and art gallery* **2** a floor at a higher level that looks over a lower floor inside a large room or building **loca, balkon, tribün** *The courtroom has a public gallery.*

galley /'gæli/ *noun* [C] a kitchen in a ship or aircraft **gemi, uçak mutfağı**

gallon /'gælən/ *noun* [C] a unit for measuring liquid, equal to 4.546 litres in the UK and 3.785 litres in the US (ABD) **4.546/(Birleşik kallik) 3.785 litreye eşit sıvı ölçüm birimi** ⊃See study page **Measurements** on page Centre 31.

gallop /'gæləp/ *verb* [I] If a horse gallops, it runs very fast. **dörtnala/doludizgin koşmak** ● **gallop** *noun* [no plural] **dört nala gidiş**

gallows /'gæləʊz/ *noun* [C] *plural* **gallows** a wooden structure used in the past to hang criminals from to kill them **darağacı**

galore /gə'lɔːʳ/ *adjective* [always after noun] in large amounts or numbers **bol bol, bolca, pek çok** *There are bargains galore at the new supermarket.*

galvanize (*also UK* -ise) /'gælvənaɪz/ *verb* [T] to make someone suddenly decide to do something **ani karar verdirmek; düşünmeden karar vermeye zorlamak** *His words galvanized the team into action.* ● **galvaniza-**

tion (*also UK* -isation) *noun* [U] **harekete geçirme, tahrik etme**

gamble¹ /'ɡæmbl/ *verb* [I, T] to risk money on the result of a game, race, or competition **kumar oynamak, şans oynamak** *He gambled away all of our savings.* ● **gambler** *noun* [C] **kumarbaz** ● **gambling** *noun* [U] **kumar**

gamble on sth *phrasal verb* to take a risk that something will happen **risk almak, riske girmek; bir şey üzerine kumar oynamak**

```
⊹⊹⊹ gamble ...... İLE BİRLİKTE KULLANILAN KELİMELER
```
take a gamble ● a gamble **backfires/pays off** ● a gamble **on** sth

gamble² /'ɡæmbl/ *noun* [C] a risk that you take that something will succeed **kumar, risk, tehlike** *Buying this place was a big gamble, but it seems to have paid off.*

```
⊹⊹⊹ game ...... İLE BİRLİKTE KULLANILAN KELİMELER
```
play a game ● **lose/win** a game ● a game **of** [chess/football, etc] ● a **computer** game

○⚬**game¹** /ɡeɪm/ *noun* **1** ACTIVITY [C] an entertaining activity or sport that people play, usually needing some skill and played according to rules **(eğlence, spor) oyun** *a computer game* ○ *Do you want to play a different game?* **2** OCCASION [C] a particular competition, match, or occasion when people play a game **oyun, yarış, yarışma** *Would you like a game of chess?* ○ *Who won yesterday's game?* **3 games** *UK* organized sports that children do at school **okulda yapılan spor** *I always hated games at school.* ○ *a games teacher* **4 the European/Commonwealth, etc Games** a special event where there are lots of competitions for different sports **Avrupa/İngiliz Milletler Topluluğu vb. oyunları/müsabakaları 5** SECRET PLAN [C] *UK informal* a secret plan **gizli plan, oyun** *What's your game?* **6** ANIMALS [U] wild animals and birds that are hunted for food or sport **spor veya yiyecek amaçlı yaban hayvan avı 7 give the game away** *UK* to spoil a surprise or joke by letting someone know something that should have been kept secret **oyunu/sürprizi/şakayı bozmak/ifşa etmek; ele vermek** ● **8 play games** to not deal with a situation seriously or honestly **bir durumla gerektiği gibi ciddi ve dürüst bir şekilde ilgilenmemek** *Someone's life is in danger here - we're not playing games.* ⊃See also: **ball game, board game, the Olympic Games, video game.**

game² /ɡeɪm/ *adjective* willing to do new things, or things that involve a risk **istekli, arzulu, gözüpek** *She's game for anything.*

Gameboy /'ɡeɪmbɔɪ/ *noun* [C] *trademark* a small machine that you play computer games on and that you can carry with you **bilgisayar oyunları oynanabilen elde taşınır oyun aleti, atari**

gamekeeper /'ɡeɪmˌkiːpər/ *noun* [C] someone whose job is to look after wild animals and birds that are going to be hunted **av hayvanı bekçisi**

gamepad /'ɡeɪmpæd/ *noun* [C] a device that you hold in your hands and use to control a computer game or video game (= a game in which you make pictures move on a screen) **bilgisayar oyunlarını uzaktan kontrol/oynatma aleti; atari kumandası**

gamer /'ɡeɪmər/ *noun* [C] someone who plays games, especially computer games **oyuncu, bilgisayar oyunu oyuncusu**

'game ,show *noun* [C] a programme on television in which people play games to try to win prizes **tv yarışma programı**

gammon /'ɡæmən/ *noun* [U] *UK* a type of meat from a pig, usually cut in thick slices **domuz jambonu**

gamut /'ɡæmət/ *noun* [no plural] the whole group of things that can be included in something **tamamı, hepsi, tümü** *The film explores the whole gamut of emotions from despair to joy.*

```
⊹⊹⊹ gang ...... İLE BİRLİKTE KULLANILAN KELİMELER
```
in a gang ● a gang **of** sth ● a gang **leader/member**

gang¹ /ɡæŋ/ *noun* [C] **1** YOUNG PEOPLE a group of young people who spend time together, usually fighting with other groups and behaving badly **çete, şebeke** *a member of a gang* ○ *gang violence* **2** CRIMINALS a group of criminals who work together **haydutlar, çete** *a gang of armed robbers* **3** FRIENDS *informal* a group of young friends **ekip, takım, grup**

gang² /ɡæŋ/ *verb*

gang up against/on sb *phrasal verb* to form a group to attack or criticize someone, usually unfairly **birini eleştirmek ve saldırmak için grup oluşturmak, çete kurmak** *Some older girls have been ganging up on her at school.*

gangly /'ɡæŋɡli/ (*also* **gangling**) *adjective* tall and thin **uzun ince, zarif** *a gangly youth*

gangrene /'ɡæŋɡriːn/ *noun* [U] the death and decay of a part of the body because blood is not flowing through it **kangren**

gangster /'ɡæŋstər/ *noun* [C] a member of a group of violent criminals **gangster, haydut, çete üyesi**

gangway /'ɡæŋweɪ/ *noun* [C] **1** *UK* a space that people can walk down between two rows of seats in a vehicle or public place **koltuk ara boşluğu, koridor, aralık 2** a board or stairs for people to get on and off a ship **lombar ağzı, dosa, bordo iskelesi**

gaol /dʒeɪl/ *noun* [C, U] *another UK spelling of* **jail** (= a place where criminals are kept as a punishment) **hapishane, kodes**

```
⊹⊹⊹ gap ...... İLE BİRLİKTE KULLANILAN KELİMELER
```
bridge/close/narrow the gap ● the gap **between** sth and sth

○⚬**gap** /ɡæp/ *noun* [C] **1** SPACE an empty space or hole in the middle of something, or between two things **aralık, açıklık, boşluk** *There's quite a big gap between the door and the floor.* ○ *The sun was shining through a gap in the curtains.* **2** DIFFERENCE a difference between two groups of people, two situations, etc **(kişi, durum) fark, ayrılık** *an age gap* ○ *This course bridges the gap between school and university.* **3** ABSENT THING something that is absent and stops something from being complete **boşluk, eksiklik** *There are huge gaps in my memory.* **4 a gap in the market** an opportunity for a product or service that does not already exist **pazar boşluğu; ürün veya hizmet eksikliği 5** TIME a period of time when nothing happens, or when you are doing something different from usual **boşluk, ara, kopukluk** *I decided to go back to teaching after a gap of 10 years.* ⊃See also: the generation gap.

gape /ɡeɪp/ *verb* [I] **1** to look at someone or something with your mouth open because you are so surprised **şaşkınlıktan ağzı açık kalmak, şaşkın şaşkın bakakalmak** *We stood there gaping in wonder at the beautiful landscape.* **2** to be wide open **ağzına/ardına kadar açık olmak**

gaping /'ɡeɪpɪŋ/ *adjective* **a gaping hole/wound, etc** a hole/wound, etc that is open very wide **çok açık yara/delik**

'gap ,year *noun* [C] *UK* a year between leaving school and starting university which you usually spend travelling or working **lise ile üniversite arasındaki seyahat ve çalışmayla geçirilen yıl**

G

gap

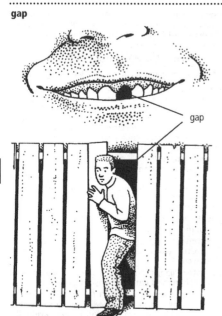

gap

G

○**garage** /'gærɑːʒ/ ⑤ /gə'rɑːʒ/ *noun* [C] **1** a small building, often built next to a house, that you can put a car in **garaj 2** a business that repairs or sells cars, and sometimes also sells fuel **oto tamirhanesi; oto alım satım komisyonculuğu**

garbage /'gɑːbɪdʒ/ *US (UK* **rubbish)** *noun* [U] **1** things that you throw away because you do not want them **çöp, işe yaramayan şeyler 2** something that you think is nonsense, wrong, or very bad quality **saçmalık, ipe sapa gelmez söz, lakırdı, palavra** *How can you listen to that garbage on the radio!*

'garbage ,can *US (UK* **dustbin)** *noun* [C] a large container for waste kept outside your house **çöp kutusu**

'garbage col,lector *US (UK* **dustman)** *noun* [C] someone whose job is to remove the waste from containers left outside houses **çöpçü, çöp toplayıcısı**

'garbage ,man *noun* [C] *US another word for* garbage collector **çöpçü**

garbled /'gɑːbəld/ *adjective* Garbled words or messages are not clear and are very difficult to understand. **karma karışık, kafa karıştıran**

○**garden** /'gɑːdən/ *noun* **1** [C] *UK (US* **yard)** an area of ground belonging to a house, often containing grass, flowers, or trees **bahçe** *the front/back garden* ○ *Dad's outside in the garden.* **2 gardens** [plural] a park or large public area where plants and flowers are grown **park, bahçe** ● **garden** *verb* [I] to work in a garden, growing plants and making it look attractive **bağ bahçe işleri yapmak, bahçecilik/bahçıvanlık yapmak**

'garden ,centre *noun* [C] *UK* a place that sells things for gardens such as plants and tools **bahçe bitkileri ve aletleri satan mağaza/dükkân**

gardener /'gɑːdənər/ *noun* [C] someone who works in a garden, growing plants and making it look attractive **bahçıvan**

gardening /'gɑːdənɪŋ/ *noun* [U] the job or activity of growing a garden and keeping it attractive **bahçecilik, bahçe işleri**

gargle /'gɑːgl/ *verb* [I] to move liquid or medicine around in your throat without swallowing, especially to clean it or stop it feeling painful **gargara yapmak**

garish /'geərɪʃ/ *adjective* unpleasantly bright in colour, or decorated too much **çok parlak, cafcaflı, janjanlı, süslü** *a garish red jacket*

garlic /'gɑːlɪk/ *noun* [U] a vegetable like a small onion with a very strong taste and smell **sarmısak** *a clove of garlic* ⊃Orta kısımdaki renkli sayfalarına bakınız.

garment /'gɑːmənt/ *noun* [C] *formal* a piece of clothing **giysi, elbise**

garnish /'gɑːnɪʃ/ *verb* [T] to decorate food with something such as herbs or pieces of fruit **garnitür** *salmon garnished with herbs and lemon* ● **garnish** *noun* [C] **donatma, süsleme**

garrison /'gærɪsən/ *noun* [C] a group of soldiers living in a particular area or building to defend it **garnizon**

garter /'gɑːtər/ *noun* [C] a piece of elastic that holds up a woman's stockings (= very thin pieces of clothing that cover a woman's foot and leg) **jartiyer**

○**gas¹** /gæs/ *noun* **1** SUBSTANCE [C, U] a substance in a form like air and not solid or liquid **gaz** *poisonous gases* **2** FUEL [U] a substance in a form like air used as a fuel for heating and cooking **hava gazı, doğal gaz, likit gaz** *(UK) a gas cooker/ (US) a gas stove* **3** CAR FUEL [U] *US (UK* **petrol)** a liquid fuel used in cars **sıvı petrol gazı; LPG** *half a tank of gas* **4** STOMACH [U] *US (UK* **wind)** gas or air in your stomach that makes you feel uncomfortable and sometimes makes noises **mide gazı 5 the gas** *US informal* the part of a car which you push with your foot to make it go faster **(araba) gaz pedalı** *step on the gas* (= drive faster). ⊃See also: natural gas, tear gas.

gas² /gæs/ *verb* [T] **gassing,** *past* **gassed** to poison or kill someone with gas **gazla zehirlemek/öldürmek**

'gas ,chamber *noun* [C] a room that is filled with poisonous gas to kill people **gaz odası**

gash /gæʃ/ *noun* [C] a long, deep wound or cut **derin yara/kesik** ● **gash** *verb* [T] **derin bir şekilde kesmek, yaralamak**

'gas ,mask *noun* [C] a cover you wear over your face to protect you from breathing poisonous gas **gaz maskesi**

gasoline /'gæsəˈliːn/ *US (UK* **petrol)** *noun* [U] *another word for* gas (= a liquid fuel used in cars) **araçlarda kullanılan gaz; likit gaz**

gasp /gɑːsp/ *verb* [I] **1** to make a noise by suddenly breathing in because you are shocked or surprised **kesik kesik/derin derin hırlayarak nefes almak; soluğu/nefesi kesilmek** *She gasped in horror as the car spun out of control.* **2** to breathe loudly and with difficulty trying to get more air **güçlükle ve hırıltıyla nefes almak; nefes darlığı çekmek** *He clutched his heart, gasping for breath.* ● **gasp** *noun* [C] *a gasp of surprise* **heyecandan nefesi kesilmek**

'gas ,pedal *US (UK/US* **accelerator)** *noun* [C] the part of a car which you push with your foot to make it go faster **gaz pedalı**

'gas ,station *US (UK* **petrol station)** *noun* [C] a place where you can buy petrol (= fuel for cars) **benzin istasyonu**

gastric /'gæstrɪk/ *adjective* relating to the stomach **mideye ait, mideyle ilgili**

gastronomic /ˌgæstrəˈnɒmɪk/ *adjective* relating to good food and cooking **yemek sanatı; lezzetli yemek pişirmeyle ilgili**

o▪**gate** /geɪt/ *noun* [C] **1** the part of a fence or outside wall that opens and closes like a door **dıskapı/ana giriş kapısı** *Please shut the gate.* **2** the part of an airport where passengers get on or off an aircraft **uçağa biniş kapısı** *The flight to Dublin is now boarding at gate 8.*

gateau /ˈɡætəʊ/ ⓤ /ɡæˈtəʊ/ *noun* [C, U] *plural* **gateaux** *UK* a large cake, usually filled and decorated with cream **kremalı pasta**

gatecrash /ˈgeɪtkræʃ/ *verb* [I, T] to go to a party or private event without an invitation **bir davete/partiye davetsizce katılmak/gitmek** ● **gatecrasher** *noun* [C] someone who gatecrashes **davetsiz misafir, zoraki davetli**

gateway /ˈgeɪtweɪ/ *noun* **1** [C] an opening in a fence or outside wall that is closed with a gate **giriş yolu 2 the gateway to sth** the way to get into something or somewhere **bir şeye giriş yolu** *the gateway to the North*

o▪**gather** /ˈgæðəʳ/ *verb* **1** ⎯MAKE A GROUP⎯ [I, T] to join other people somewhere to make a group, or to bring people together into a group **toplamak, bir araya getirmek** *Crowds of fans gathered at the stadium for the big match.* **2** ⎯COLLECT⎯ [T] to collect several things together, often from different places or people **çeşitli şeyleri bir araya getirmek/toplamak** *They interviewed 1000 people to gather data on TV viewing habits.* ○ *She gathered her things together and left.* **3** ⎯THINK⎯ [T] to think something is true because you have heard or seen information about it **bilgi toplamak, anlamak, anlam/sonuç çıkarmak** *From what I can gather, they haven't sold their house yet.* **4 gather speed/strength/support, etc** to increase in speed/strength/support, etc **hız/güç/destek kazanmak; ...ı/ı artmak**

╬╬ *gathering* ...... İLE BİRLİKTE KULLANILAN KELİMELER

at a gathering ● a gathering **of** [teachers/world leaders, etc] ● a **family** gathering

gathering /ˈgæðərɪŋ/ *noun* [C] a party or a meeting when many people get together as a group **toplantı** *a family gathering*

gaudy /ˈgɔːdi/ *adjective* unpleasantly bright in colour or decoration **cicili bicili, aşırı parlak, renkli** *a gaudy pink sweatshirt with gold embroidery*

gauge¹ /geɪdʒ/ *verb* [T] **1** to make a judgment about a situation or about what someone thinks or feels **tartmak, ölçmek, kestirmek** [+ question word] *It's impossible to gauge what her reaction will be.* **2** to measure a distance, size, or amount **ölçmek, hesaplamak**

gauge² /geɪdʒ/ *noun* [C] **1** a way of judging something such as a situation or what someone thinks or feels **ölçme, hesap, belirleme** *Street interviews aren't an accurate gauge of public opinion.* **2** a method or piece of equipment that you use to measure something **ölçme, ölçme aleti** *a fuel gauge*

gaunt /gɔːnt/ *adjective* very thin, especially because of being ill or old **zayıf, sıska (hastalık veya yaşlılıktan dolayı)** *a pale, gaunt face*

gauntlet /ˈgɔːntlət/ *noun* **1** [C] a long, thick glove (= piece of clothing for your hand) **uzun eldiven, iş eldiveni 2 run the gauntlet** to have to deal with a lot of people who are criticizing or attacking you **maruz kalmak, karşı karşıya kalmak, baş etmek zorunda olmak 3 throw down the gauntlet** to invite someone to argue, fight, or compete with you **düelloya davet etmek, meydan okumak, yarışmaya davet etmek**

gauze /gɔːz/ *noun* [U] thin, transparent cloth, especially used to cover injuries **gazlı bez, tülbent, temiz bez**

gave /geɪv/ *past tense of* give **'vermek' fiilinin ikinci hâli**

gawp /gɔːp/ *UK* (*US* **gawk** /gɔːk/) *verb* [I] to look at someone or something with your mouth open because you are shocked or surprised **şaşkınlıktan dolayı aval aval bakmak** *He just stood there gawping at me.*

o▪**gay¹** /geɪ/ *adjective* **1** homosexual **eşcinsel, homoseksüel** *Have you told your parents you're gay yet?* ○ *a gay bar/club* **2** *old-fashioned* very happy and enjoying yourself **şen şakrak, neşeli, keyifli**

gay² /geɪ/ *noun* [C] someone who is homosexual, especially a man **eşcinsellik, homoseksüellik** *equal rights for gays and lesbians*

gaze /geɪz/ *verb* **gaze at/into, etc** to look for a long time at someone or something or in a particular direction **gözlerini dikip bakmak, dik dik bakmak** *They gazed into each other's eyes.* ● **gaze** *noun* [no plural] **gözünü dikip bakma**

GB *written abbreviation for* gigabyte (= a unit for measuring the amount of information a computer can store) **bilgisayarın depolayabileceği bilginin miktarını ölçme birimi; cigabayt** *a 4 GB hard drive*

GCSE /ˌdʒiː.siː.esˈiː/ *noun* [C] *abbreviation for* General Certificate of Secondary Education: in the UK, an exam taken by students at the age of sixteen, or the qualification itself **Birleşik kallık'da onaltı yaşındaki öğrencilerin girdiği sertifika sınavı; Orta Öğretim Genel Sertifika Sınavı; ÖSS benzeri sınav** *Mary's got nine GCSEs.*

GDP /ˌdʒiː.diːˈpiː/ *noun* [U] *abbreviation for* Gross Domestic Product: the total value of goods and services that a country produces in a year **Gayri Safi Milli Üretim; bir ülkenin yıllık olarak ürettiği hizmet ve ürünlerin toplam değeri** ⊃Compare GNP.

gear¹ /gɪəʳ/ *noun* **1** [C] a set of parts in a motor vehicle or bicycle that control how fast the wheels turn **vites, dişli takımı** [usually plural] *a mountain bike with 21 gears* ○ *to change gear* **2 first/second/third, etc gear** a particular position of the gears in a motor vehicle or bicycle that controls how fast the wheels turn **birinci/ikinci/üçüncü vb. vites** *The lights turned green, but I couldn't get into first gear.* **3** [U] the clothes and equipment used for a particular purpose **elbise/donanım, alet edevat** *sports/swimming gear*

gear² /gɪəʳ/ *noun*

gear sth to/towards sb/sth *phrasal verb* to design or organize something so that it is suitable for a particular purpose, situation, or group of people **donat(ıl)mak, techiz etmek/edilmek** [often passive] *These advertisements are geared towards a younger audience.*

gear (sb/sth) up *phrasal verb* to prepare for something that you have to do, or to prepare someone else for something **hazırlamak, donatmak, hazırlıklı/donatılmış olmak** [often reflexive] *I'm trying to gear myself up for the exams.*

gearbox /ˈgɪəbɒks/ *noun* [C] the set of gears in a motor vehicle and the metal box that contains them **şanzıman, dişli/vites kutusu**

'gear ,lever *UK* (*US* **gearshift** /ˈgɪəʃɪft/) *noun* [C] a stick with a handle that you move to change gear in a vehicle **vites kolu** ⊃Orta kısımdaki renkli sayfalarına bakınız.

gearstick /ˈgɪəstɪk/ *noun* [C] *UK another word for* gear lever **vites kolu** ⊃Orta kısımdaki renkli sayfalarına bakınız.

GED /ˌdʒiː.iːˈdiː/ *noun* [C] *abbreviation for* General Equivalency Diploma: an official document in the US that is given to someone who did not complete high school (= school for students aged 15 to 18) but who has passed a government exam instead **Lise Denklik Diploması (LDD): (ABD) 15-18 yaşları arasındaki liseyi bitirememiş öğrencilerin girdiği resmi sınav**

geek /giːk/ *noun* [C] *informal* a man who is boring and not fashionable **sıkıcı ve gösterişsiz adam** ● **geeky**

adjective informal a geeky guy with a beard and glasses **sıkıcı**

geese /giːs/ *plural of* goose **kazlar**

geezer /ˈɡiːzər/ *noun* [C] *UK very informal* a man **herif, adam**

gel /dʒel/ *noun* [C, U] a thick, clear, liquid substance, especially a product used to style hair **jel, jöle** *hair gel* ○ *shower gel*

gelatine *UK* (*US* gelatin /ˈdʒelətiːn, ˈdʒelətɪn/) *noun* [U] a clear substance made from animal bones, often used to make food thicker **jelatin; hayvan kemiklerinden yapılan ve yiyecekleri pelteleştirmek için kullanılan madde**

gem /dʒem/ *noun* [C] **1** a valuable stone, especially one that has been cut to be used in jewellery **mücevher, cevher 2** *informal* someone or something that you like very much and think is very special **hazine/pırlanta gibi şey veya insan; değerli, sevilen**

Gemini /ˈdʒemɪnaɪ/ *noun* [C, U] the sign of the zodiac which relates to the period of 23 May - 21 June, or a person born during this period **ikizler burcu, ikizler burcundan olan** ⊃See picture at **zodiac.**

gender /ˈdʒendər/ *noun* [C, U] **1** the state of being male or female **cinsiyet 2** the division of nouns, pronouns, and adjectives into masculine, feminine, and neuter types **cins; isim, zamir ve sıfatların eril dişi ve nötr olarak ayrılmaları**

gene ...... İLE BİRLİKTE KULLANILAN KELİMELER

carry/have a gene ● a gene **(responsible) for** sth ● gene **therapy**

gene /dʒiːn/ *noun* [C] a part of a cell that is passed on from a parent to a child and that controls particular characteristics **gen, kalıtımsal öğe**

general¹ /ˈdʒenərəl/ *adjective* **1** NOT DETAILED not detailed, but including the most basic or necessary information **ayrıntı içermeyen, genel** *These leaflets contain some general information about the school.* ○ *I've got a general idea of how it works.* **2** MOST PEOPLE [always before noun] relating to or involving all or most people, things, or places **genel, umumi** *There seems to be general agreement on this matter.* **3** NOT LIMITED [always before noun] including a lot of things or subjects and not limited to only one or a few **yaygın, genel, geniş** *general knowledge* **4 in general a** CONSIDERING EVERYTHING considering the whole of someone or something, and not just a particular part of them **bütünü, tamamı, hemen hemen hepsi** *I still have a sore throat, but I feel much better in general.* **b** USUALLY usually, or in most situations **genellikle, umumiyetle** *In general, the weather here stays sunny.*

general² /ˈdʒenərəl/ *noun* [C] an officer of very high rank in the army or air force **general, paşa**

general anaesthetic *UK* (*US* general anesthetic) *noun* [C, U] a substance that is used to stop someone being conscious when they have an operation so that they do not feel any pain **genel anestezi**

general election *noun* [C] a big election in which the people living in a country vote to decide who will represent them in the government **genel seçim**

generalization ...... İLE BİRLİKTE KULLANILAN KELİMELER

make a generalization ● a **broad/gross/sweeping** generalization

generalization (*also UK* -isation) /ˌdʒenərəlaɪˈzeɪʃən/ *noun* [C, U] when someone says something very basic that is often true but not always true **genelleme**

generalize (*also UK* -ise) /ˈdʒenərəlaɪz/ *verb* [I] to say something very basic that is often true but not always true **genelleme yapmak, ayrıntılara girmemek**

generally /ˈdʒenərəli/ *adverb* **1** USUALLY usually, or in most situations **umumiyetle, genellikle** *I generally wake up early.* **2** AS A WHOLE considering the whole of someone or something, and not just a particular part of them **genel olarak, çoğunlukla** *The police said that the crowd was generally well-behaved.* **3** BY MOST PEOPLE by most people, or to most people **çoğu kişilerce genel kabul görerek; çoğu insana göre** *He is generally believed to be their best player.*

general practitioner (*also GP*) *noun* [C] a doctor who sees people in the local area and treats illnesses that do not need a hospital visit **pratisyen hekim**

generate /ˈdʒenəreɪt/ *verb* [T] **1** to cause something to exist **ortaya çıkarmak, oluşturmak, yaratmak** *to generate income/profit* ○ *This film has generated a lot of interest.* **2** to produce energy **enerji üretmek** *Many countries use nuclear fuels to generate electricity.*

generation /ˌdʒenəˈreɪʃən/ *noun* **1** PEOPLE [C] all the people in a society or family who are approximately the same age **nesil, kuşak** *the older/younger generation* ○ *This is the story of three generations of women.* **2** TIME [C] a period of about 25 to 30 years, the time it takes for a child to become an adult and take the place of their parents in society **25 ile 30 yaş arası nesil/kuşak dönemi** *Our family has lived in this village for generations.* **3** PRODUCT [C] a product when it is at a particular stage of development **gelişmenin belli bir safhasında olan ürün; yeni nesil ürün** *a new generation of computers* **4** ENERGY [U] the production of energy **enerji üretimi** *the generation of electricity*

the generation gap *noun* when young people and old people do not understand each other because of their age difference **nesil/kuşak farkı**

generator /ˈdʒenəreɪtər/ *noun* [C] a machine that produces electricity **elektrik enerjisi üreten makine; jeneratör**

generic /dʒəˈnerɪk/ *adjective* **1** relating to a whole group of things or type of thing **kümesel, genel 2** A generic product such as a drug is not sold with the name of the company that produced it. **(ürün) genel adı olan, üreten şirketin adı belirtilmeyen**

generosity /ˌdʒenəˈrɒsəti/ *noun* [U] the quality of being generous **cömertlik, eli açıklık**

generous /ˈdʒenərəs/ *adjective* **1** giving other people a lot of money, presents, or time in a kind way **cömert, eli açık** *a very generous man* **2** larger than usual or than expected **beklenenden fazla, bol** *a generous discount for students* ○ *a generous portion* ● **generously** *adverb* **cömert bir şekilde**

gene therapy *noun* [U] the science of changing genes (= parts of cells which control particular characteristics) in order to stop or prevent a disease **gen tedavisi/terapisi/değişimi**

genetic /dʒəˈnetɪk/ *adjective* relating to genes (= parts of cells which control particular characteristics) **genlerle ilgili/ilişkin** *a rare genetic disorder* ○ *genetic research* ● **genetically** *adverb* **genetik olarak**

genetically modified *adjective* Genetically modified plants or animals have had some of their genes (= parts of cells which control particular characteristics) changed. **(bitki, hayvan) genleriyle oynanmış; genleri değiştirilmiş**

genetic engineering *noun* [U] when scientists change the genes (= parts of cells which control particular characteristics) in the cells of plants or animals **genetik mühendisliği**

genetics /dʒəˈnetɪks/ *noun* [U] the scientific study of genes (= parts of cells which control particular characteristics) **genetik bilimi**

genial /ˈdʒiːniəl/ *adjective* kind and friendly **nazik, candan, güler yüzlü, dost canlısı**

genitals /ˈdʒenɪtᵊlz/ *noun* [plural] the sexual organs **cinsel organlar**

genius /ˈdʒiːniəs/ *noun* **1** [C] someone who is extremely intelligent or extremely good at doing something **deha, dâhi** *Einstein was a genius.* **2** [U] the quality of being extremely intelligent or extremely good at doing something **üstün yetenek, deha** *Einstein's genius*

genocide /ˈdʒenəsaɪd/ *noun* [U] the intentional killing of a large group of people who belong to a particular race or country **soykırım**

genre /ˈʒɒnrə/ *noun* [C] a type of art or writing with a particular style **(sanat, yazı) çeşit, tür, tarz, biçim** *a literary/musical genre*

gent /dʒent/ *noun* [C] *informal short for* gentleman **kibar adam, centilmen**

genteel /dʒenˈtiːl/ *adjective* very polite, especially in an artificial way **yapmacık olarak ince, kibar, nazik** ● **gentility** /ˌdʒenˈtɪləti/ *noun* [U] **kibarlık**

o→**gentle** /ˈdʒentl/ *adjective* **1** [KIND] kind and careful not to hurt or upset anyone or anything **nazik, başkalarını incitmekten çekinen, ince** *My mother was such a gentle, loving person.* **2** [NOT STRONG] not strong or severe **yumuşak, tatlı, hafif** *a mild soap that is gentle on your skin* ○ *a gentle breeze* **3** [SLOPE] A gentle slope or climb is not steep. **hafif meyilli/eğimli** ● **gently** *adverb* **kibarca** ● **gentleness** *noun* [U] **nezaket**

gentleman /ˈdʒentlmən/ *noun* [C] *plural* **gentlemen 1** a man who behaves politely and treats people with respect **kibar adam, centilmen** *He was a **perfect gentleman**.* **2** a polite word for 'man', used especially when talking to or about a man you do not know **bey, beyefendi** *There's a gentleman here to see you.*

the gents /dʒents/ *noun* [group] *UK informal* a toilet in a public place for men **erkekler tuvaleti**

o→**genuine** /ˈdʒenjuɪn/ *adjective* **1** If a person or their feelings are genuine, they are sincere and honest. **gerçek, sahi, samimi** *He shows a genuine concern for the welfare of his students.* **2** If something is genuine, it is really what it seems to be. **gerçek, samimi, içten, yapmacıksız** *a genuine gold necklace* ● **genuinely** *adverb* **hakikatten**

genus /ˈdʒiːnəs/, /ˈdʒenəs/ *noun* [C] *plural* **genera** a group of animals or plants that have the same characteristics **(hayvan, bitki) aynı tür/cins/sınıf/familya**

geo- /dʒiːəʊ-/ *prefix* relating to the earth **yeryüzüyle ilgili anlamında ön ek** *geothermal* (= of or connected with the heat inside the Earth)

geography /dʒiˈɒɡrəfi/ *noun* [U] the study of all the countries of the world, and of the surface of the Earth such as the mountains and seas **coğrafya, coğrafya bilimi** ● **geographer** *noun* [C] someone who studies geography **coğrafyacı, coğrafya bilimini çalışan kişi** ● **geographical** /ˌdʒiːəˈɡræfɪkəl/ (*also* geographic /ˌdʒiːəʊˈɡræfɪk/) *adjective* **bölgesel** ● **geographically** *adverb* **konum açısından**

geology /dʒiˈɒlədʒi/ *noun* [U] the study of rocks and soil and the physical structure of the Earth **jeoloji, yerbilimi** ● **geological** /ˌdʒiːəʊˈlɒdʒɪkəl/ *adjective* **jeolojik** ● **geologist** *noun* [C] someone who studies geology **yerbilimci**

geometric /ˌdʒiːəʊˈmetrɪk/ (*also* geometrical) *adjective* **1** having a regular shape such as a circle or triangle,

or having a pattern made of regular shapes **geometrik, şekilli 2** relating to geometry **geometriye ilişkin**

geometry /dʒiˈɒmɪtri/ *noun* [U] a type of mathematics that deals with points, lines, angles and shapes **geometri**

geriatric /ˌdʒeriˈætrɪk/ *adjective* relating to very old people **çok yaşlı insanlara ilişkin, geriatri ile ilgili** *geriatric patients* ○ *a geriatric hospital* ● **geriatrics** *noun* [U] care and medical treatment for very old people **çok yaşlı insanların bakımı ve tıbbi tedavisi; geriatri bilimi**

germ /dʒɜːm/ *noun* **1** [C] a very small living thing that causes disease **mikrop** *Wash your hands before cooking so that you don't spread germs.* **2 the germ of sth** the beginning of something **bir şeyin başlangıcı/kaynağı/tohumu** *the germ of a brilliant idea*

German 'measles (*also* rubella) *noun* [U] a disease which causes red spots on your skin **kızamıkçık**

germinate /ˈdʒɜːmɪneɪt/ *verb* [I, T] If a seed germinates or is germinated, it begins to grow. **filizlenmek, filizlendirmek** ● **germination** /ˌdʒɜːmɪˈneɪʃᵊn/ *noun* [U] **filizlenme**

gerund /ˈdʒerᵊnd/ *noun* [C] a noun made from the form of a verb that ends with -ing, for example 'fishing' in 'John loves fishing.' **fiilden türetilen isim; isim-fiil**

gesticulate /dʒesˈtɪkjəleɪt/ *verb* [I] to move your hands and arms around to emphasize what you are saying or to express something **konuşurken el kol hareketleri yapmak, jestler yapmak**

---

 gesture .... **İLE BİRLİKTE KULLANILAN KELİMELER**

a **grand/token** gesture ● a gesture **of** [friendship/goodwill, etc] ● a **nice** gesture

---

gesture¹ /ˈdʒestʃəʳ/ *noun* [C] **1** a movement you make with your hand, arm, or head to express what you are thinking or feeling **el, kol ve baş hareketi, jestler** *He made a rude gesture at the crowd.* **2** something you do to show people how you feel about a person or situation **gösterilen davranış, yapılan jest** *It would be a **nice** gesture to invite her to dinner.*

gesture² /ˈdʒestʃəʳ/ *verb* [I] to point at something or express something using your hand, arm, or head **el, kol, ve baş hareketi yapmak** *He gestured towards the window.*

o→**get¹** /get/ *verb* **getting**, *past tense* **got**, *past participle* **got** or *US* **gotten 1** [OBTAIN] [T] to obtain or buy something **elde etmek, satın almak** *I need to get some bread on the way home.* ○ [+ two objects] *I'll try to get you a ticket.* **2** [BRING] [T] to go somewhere and bring back someone or something **gidip getirmek; alıp getirmek** *Wait here while I get the car.* **3** [RECEIVE] [T] to receive something or be given something **almak, verilmek** *Did you get anything nice for your birthday?* ○ *Guy still hasn't got my email yet.* **4** [UNDERSTAND] [T] to understand something **anlamak, kavramak; çözmek** *He never gets any of my jokes.* **5 get into/off/through, etc** to move somewhere **gitmek, gelmek, varmak** *Get over here right now!* **6 get sth into/down/out, etc** to move something somewhere **getirmek, alıp getirmek, götürmek** *Could you get that bowl down from the shelf for me?* **7 get here/there/to the bank, etc** to arrive somewhere **varmak, ulaşmak, erişmek, gelmek** *What time do you normally get home from work?* **8 get sb/sth to do sth** to make someone or something do something **birine/bir şeye bir şeyi yaptırmak** *Sorry, I couldn't get the window to shut properly.* **9 get to do sth** to have an opportunity to do something **fırsatı olmak** *I never get to sit in the front seat.* **10 get ill/rich/wet, etc** to become ill/rich/wet, etc **hastalanmak, rahatsızlanmak** *We should go. It's get-*

ting late. **11 get caught/killed/married, etc** to have something done to you **yakalanmak/öldürülmek/evlenmek vs. 12 get sth painted/repaired, etc** to arrange for someone to do something for you, usually for money **tamir ettirmek, boyatmak** *I need to get my hair cut.* **13 get cancer/flu/malaria, etc** to become ill or develop an illness **hastalığa yakalanmak, rahatsızlanmak,** *I feel like I'm getting a cold.* **14 get a bus/train, etc** to travel somewhere on a bus/train, etc **binmek, bir araçla gitmek/seyahat etmek** *Maybe we should get a taxi home.* **15 get the phone/door** *informal* to answer someone calling on the telephone or waiting at the door **kapıya/telefona bakmak** *Can you get the phone?*

get about *phrasal verb UK* (*US* **get around**) **1** [TRAVEL] to travel to a lot of places **çok yeri gezmek, çokça seyahat etmek 2** [MOVE] to be able to go to different places without difficulty, especially if you are old or ill **(hasta, yaşlı) bir yere kolayca gidebilmek 3** [INFORMATION] If news or information gets about, a lot of people hear about it. **(haber, bilgi) kolayca ulaşmak; çabucak yayılmak**

get sth across *phrasal verb* to successfully communicate information to other people **bilgiyi kolayca/başarıyla iletmek/ulaştırmak; duyurmak; yaymak** *This is the message that we want to get across to the public.*

get ahead *phrasal verb* to be successful in the work that you do **başarılı olmak, başarıyı yakalamak** *It's tough for any woman who wants to get ahead in politics.*

get along *phrasal verb mainly US* (*mainly UK* **get on**) **1** If two or more people get along, they like each other and are friendly to each other. **iyi geçinmek, iyi anlaşmak** *I don't really get along with my sister's husband.* **2** to deal with a situation, especially successfully **başarıyla halletmek, ilgilenmek, başarmak, ilerlemek** *I wonder how Michael's getting along in his new job?*

get around sth *phrasal verb* (*also UK* **get round sth**) to find a way of dealing with or avoiding a problem **problemle başa çıkmak, halletmek, çözmek** *Our lawyer found a way of getting around the adoption laws.*

get around to sth *phrasal verb* (*also UK* **get round to sth**) to do something that you have intended to do for a long time **uzun zamandır yapmayı istediği bir şeyi gerçekleştirmek** *I finally got around to calling her yesterday.*

get at sb *phrasal verb UK informal* to criticize someone in an unkind way **kötü söz söylemek; üstüne üstüne gitmek; kabaca eleştirmek**

be getting at sth *phrasal verb* If you ask someone what they are getting at, you are asking them what they really mean. **ima etmek, demeye/varmaya çalışmak**

get at sth *phrasal verb* to be able to reach or get something **(bir yere) varmak, ulaşmak, erişmek**

get away *phrasal verb* **1** to leave or escape from a place or person, often when it is difficult to do this **kaçmak, uzaklaşmak, kaçıp kurtulmak** *We walked to the next beach to get away from the crowds.* **2** to go somewhere to have a holiday, especially because you need to rest **tatil yapmak üzere gitmek** *We decided to go up to Scotland to get away from it all* (= have a relaxing holiday).

get away with sth *phrasal verb* to succeed in doing something bad or wrong without being punished or criticized **kurtulmak, atlatmak, paçayı sıyırmak, (argo) yırtmak** *He shouldn't treat you like that. Don't let him get away with it.*

get back *phrasal verb* to return to a place after you have been somewhere else **geri gelmek/dönmek** *By the time we got back to the hotel, Lydia had already left.*

get sth back *phrasal verb* If you get something back, something that you had before is given to you again. **geri almak, yeniden kavuşmak/elde etmek** *I wouldn't lend him anything, you'll never get it back.*

get sb back *phrasal verb informal* to do something unpleasant to someone because they have done something unpleasant to you **karşılığını vermek, öcünü almak, kendisine yapılanın aynısını yapmak**

get back to sb *phrasal verb informal* to talk to someone, usually on the telephone, to give them some information they have asked for or because you were not able to speak to them before **sonradan aramak/ulaşmak; telefonla geri dönmek**

get back to sth *phrasal verb* to start doing or talking about something again **aynı konu veya şeye geri dönmek, tekrar değinmek/ele almak** *Anyway, I'd better get back to work.*

get behind *phrasal verb* If you get behind with work or payments, you have not done as much work or paid as much money as you should by a particular time. **zamanında ödeyememek/yapamamak; geciktirmek; gecikmek**

get by *phrasal verb* to be able to live or deal with a situation with difficulty, usually by having just enough of something you need, such as money **kıt kanaat geçinmek; yaşamın zorluklarla sürdürmek, zorluklarla başetmeye çalışmak** *I don't know how he gets by on so little money.*

get sb down *phrasal verb* to make someone feel unhappy **üzmek, moralini bozmak, huzursuz etmek** *All this uncertainty is really getting me down.*

get sth down *phrasal verb* to write something, especially something that someone has said **not almak, yazmak, not tutmak**

get down to sth *phrasal verb* to start doing something seriously and with a lot of attention and effort **yapmaya başlamak, üzerine eğilmek, ciddi şekilde ele almak** *Before we get down to business, I'd like to thank you all for coming today.*

get in *phrasal verb* **1** [ENTER] to succeed in entering a place, especially a building **girmek** *They must have got in through the bathroom window.* **2** [PERSON ARRIVING] to arrive at your home or the place where you work **işe/eve varmak/ulaşmak** *What time did you get in last night?* **3** [VEHICLE ARRIVING] If a train or other vehicle gets in at a particular time, that is when it arrives. **(tren ve diğer araçlar) varmak, gelmek, ulaşmak** *Our flight's getting in later than expected.* **4** [BE CHOSEN] to succeed in being chosen or elected for a position in a school or other organization **seçilmek, belirlenmek, seçimi kazanmak** *He wanted to go to Oxford but he didn't get in.*

get into sth *phrasal verb* **1** to succeed in being chosen or elected for a position in a school or other organization **seçilmek, belirlenmek, seçimi kazanmak 2** to become interested in an activity or subject, or start being involved in an activity **bir şeye girişmek, başlamak, bulaşmak, ilgilenmek** *How did you get into journalism?*

get into sb *phrasal verb* If you do not know what has got into someone, you do not understand why they are behaving strangely. **(birine bir şey) olmak, yapılmış olmak, neden böyle bir davranış gösterdiği anlaşılamamak**

get off (sth) *phrasal verb* **1** to leave a bus, train, aircraft, or boat **bir araçtan inmek** *We should get off at the next stop.* ↻Orta kısımdaki renkli sayfalarına bakınız. **2** to leave the place where you work, usually at the end of the day **akşam işten çıkmak** *What time do you get off work?*

Get off! *phrasal verb UK informal* something that you say in order to tell someone to stop touching someone or something **Uzak dur!', 'Dokunma!', 'Çek elini!'**

get (sb) off (sth) *phrasal verb* to avoid being punished for something you have done wrong, or to help someone avoid getting punished for something they have done wrong **(cezadan) kurtulmak, kurtarmak, atlatmak** *He got off with a £20 fine.*

get off on sth *phrasal verb informal* If you get off on something, it makes you feel very excited, especially in a sexual way. **(bilhassa cinsel yönden) heyecanlandırmak, tahrik etmek**

get off with sb *phrasal verb UK informal* to begin a sexual relationship with someone **biriyle cinsel ilişkiye girmek**

get on (sth) *phrasal verb* to go onto a bus, train, aircraft, or boat **bir araca binmek** *I think we got on the wrong bus.* ⊃Orta kısımdaki renkli sayfalarına bakınız.

be getting on *phrasal verb informal* **1** to be old **yaşlanmak 2** *mainly UK* If time is getting on, it is becoming late. **geç olmaya başlamak, zaman ilerlemek**

get on *phrasal verb mainly UK (mainly US* **get along) 1** If two or more people get on, they like each other and are friendly to each other. **iyi anlaşmak, iyi geçinmek** *I never knew that Karen didn't get on with Sue.* **2** to deal with a situation, especially successfully **bir şeyi başarıyla halletmek; ilerlemek; gitmek** *How's Frank getting on in his new job?*

get on with sth *phrasal verb* to continue doing something, especially work **yapmaya devam etmek, ilerlemek** *Get on with your homework.*

get onto sth *phrasal verb* to start talking about a subject after discussing something else **konuya dönmek, tartışmadan sonra bir şekilde belirli bir konuya gelmek** *How did we get onto this subject?*

get out *phrasal verb* **1** MOVE OUT to move out of something, especially a vehicle **araçtan inmek/çıkmak** *I'll get out when you stop at the traffic lights.* **2** DIFFERENT PLACES to go out to different places and meet people in order to enjoy yourself **gezmek, eğlenmek, yeni insanlarla tanışmak** *She doesn't get out so much now that she's got the baby.* **3** NEWS If news or information gets out, people hear about it although someone is trying to keep it secret. **(bilgi) sızmak, açığa çıkmak, ifşa olmak**

get (sb) out *phrasal verb* to escape from or leave a place, or to help someone do this **bir yerden çık(ar)mak/kaç (ır)mak** *I left the door open and the cat got out.*

get sth out of sb *phrasal verb* to persuade or force someone to tell or give you something **zorlamak, ikna etmek, ikna yoluyla yapmasını sağlamak** *He was determined to get the truth out of her.*

get sth out of sth *phrasal verb* to enjoy something or think that something is useful **(zevk, keyif) almak, tadını çıkarmak, hoşuna gitmek** *It was an interesting course but I'm not sure I got much out of it.*

get over sth *phrasal verb* **1** to begin to feel better after being unhappy or ill **kendine gelmek, iyileşmek, daha iyi hissetmeye başlamak** *It took her months to get over the shock of Richard leaving.* **2 can't/couldn't get over sth** *informal* to be very shocked or surprised about something *I can't get over how different you look with short hair.*

get sth over with *phrasal verb* to do and complete something difficult or unpleasant that must be done **(bir an evvel) yapıp kurtulmak, üstünden atmak** *I'll be glad to get these exams over with.*

get round *phrasal verb UK (US* **get around)** If news or information gets round, a lot of people hear about it. **(bilgi, haber) ortalarda dolaşmak, ağızdan ağıza yayılmak, söylenir olmak**

get round sth *phrasal verb UK (US* **get around sth)** to find a way of dealing with or avoiding a problem **üstesinden**

gelmek/kurtulmak için bir yol bulmak, bir hal çaresi bulmak**

get round sb *phrasal verb UK* to persuade someone to do what you want by being kind to them **gönlünü yapmak, güzellikle ikna etmek**

get through *phrasal verb* to manage to talk to someone on the telephone **telefonla ulaşmak, bağlantı kurmak** *I tried to ring earlier, but I couldn't get through.*

get through to sb *phrasal verb* to succeed in making someone understand or believe something **anlatabilmek, izah edebilmek, ikna edebilmek** *I just don't seem to be able to get through to him these days.*

get through sth *phrasal verb* **1** to deal with a difficult or unpleasant experience successfully, or to help someone do this **başarmak, üstesinden gelmek; bitirmesine/tamamlamasına yardımcı olmak** *If I can just get through my exams I'll be so happy.* **2** *mainly UK* to finish doing or using something **halletmek, bitirmek, tamamlamak** *We got through a whole jar of coffee last week.*

get to sb *phrasal verb informal* to make someone feel upset or angry **sinirlendirmek, üstüne gelmek, tepesine çıkmak, canını sıkmak** *I know he's annoying, but you shouldn't let him get to you.*

get together *phrasal verb* **1** to meet in order to do something or spend time together **bir araya gelmek, toplanmak** *Jan and I are getting together next week for lunch.* **2** to begin a romantic relationship **romantik bir ilişkiyi başlatmak** *She got together with Phil two years ago.*

get (sb) up *phrasal verb* to wake up and get out of bed, or to make someone do this **uyanıp yataktan kalkmak/kaldırmak** *I had to get up at five o'clock this morning.* ⊃Orta kısımdaki renkli sayfalarına bakınız.

get up *phrasal verb* to stand up **ayağa kalkmak** *The whole audience got up and started clapping.*

get up to sth *phrasal verb UK* to do something, especially something that other people think is wrong **bir şeyler karıştırmak, yaramazlık yapmak; yanlış bir şeyler yapmak** *She's been getting up to all sorts of mischief lately.*

getaway /ˈɡetəweɪ/ *noun* [C] when someone leaves a place quickly, especially after committing a crime **kaçma, kaçış, firar** *They had a car waiting outside so they could make a quick getaway.*

get-together /ˈɡettəɡeðə/ *noun* [C] an informal meeting or party **toplantı, çay, davet, parti, eğlence** *We have a big family get-together every year.*

ghastly /ˈɡɑːstli/ *adjective* very bad or unpleasant **berbat, dehşet verici, çok kötü** *a ghastly mistake* ○ *a ghastly man*

ghetto /ˈɡetəʊ/ *noun* [C] *plural* **ghettos** or **ghettoes** an area of a city where people of a particular race or religion live, especially a poor area **bir grup aynı kökten/dinden insanın yaşadığı kenar mahalle, yoksul semt, varoş, getto**

ghost /ɡəʊst/ *noun* **1** [C] the spirit of a dead person which appears to people who are alive **hayalet** *Do you believe in ghosts?* ○ *a ghost story* **2 give up the ghost** *UK humorous* If a machine gives up the ghost, it stops working completely. **tamamen bozulmak, çökmek, çalışmamak**

ghost

● **ghostly**
adjective *a ghostly figure* **ruhani**

G

'**ghost** ,**town** *noun* [C] a town where few or no people now live **terk edilmiş kasaba/şehir; kuş uçmaz kervan geçmez şehir**

ghoul /guːl/ *noun* [C] an evil spirit **kötü ruh**

GI /ˌdʒiːˈaɪ/ *noun* [C] a soldier in the US army **ABD ordusunda er/asker**

giant[1] /ˈdʒaɪənt/ *adjective* [always before noun] extremely big, or much bigger than other similar things **dev gibi, çok büyük, devasa** *a giant spider*

giant[2] /ˈdʒaɪənt/ *noun* [C] **1** an imaginary man who is much bigger and stronger than ordinary men **dev 2** a very large and important company or organization **dev şirket/kuruluş/kurum** *a media/software giant*

gibberish /ˈdʒɪbᵊrɪʃ/ *noun* [U] something that someone says that has no meaning or that cannot be understood **anlamsız söz ya da konuşma, mırıltı, homurtu**

gibe /dʒaɪb/ *noun* [C] *another spelling of* jibe (= an insulting remark) **alay edici/kırıcı/küçük düşürücü söz/ifade**

giddy /ˈɡɪdi/ *adjective* feeling as if you cannot balance and are going to fall **başı dönmüş/dönen, sersemlemiş**

⊶**gift** /ɡɪft/ *noun* [C] **1** something that you give to someone, usually for a particular occasion **armağan, hediye** *a birthday/wedding gift* **2** a natural ability or skill **doğuştan gelen/Allah vergisi kabiliyet/yetenek** *She has a gift for design.*

gifted /ˈɡɪftɪd/ *adjective* A gifted person has a natural ability or is extremely intelligent. **doğuştan aşırı zeki ve yetenekli** *a gifted athlete* ○ *a school for gifted children*

'**gift** ,**token**/,**voucher** *UK* (*US* gift certificate) *noun* [C] a card with an amount of money printed on it which you exchange in a shop for goods that cost that amount of money **hediye çeki** *a £20 gift voucher*

gig /ɡɪɡ/ *noun* [C] *informal* a performance of pop or rock music **(pop veya rock müzik) gösteri, konser**

gigabyte /ˈɡɪɡəbaɪt/ *noun* (*written abbreviation* GB) *noun* [C] a unit for measuring the amount of information a computer can store, equal to 1,000,000,000 bytes **bilgisayarın depolayabileceği bilginin miktarını ölçme birimi; cigabayt**

gigantic /dʒaɪˈɡæntɪk/ *adjective* extremely big **dev gibi, çok büyük, devasa, muazzam** *a gigantic teddy bear*

giggle /ˈɡɪɡl/ *verb* [I] to laugh in a nervous or silly way **kıkırdamak** *She started giggling and couldn't stop.* ● **giggle** *noun* [C] **kıkırdama**

gilded /ˈɡɪldɪd/ *adjective* covered with a thin layer of gold or gold paint **altın kaplı; altın suyuna batırılmış, yaldızlı** *a gilded frame/mirror*

gill /ɡɪl/ *noun* [C] an organ on each side of a fish or other water creature which it uses to breathe **solungaç**

gilt /ɡɪlt/ *noun* [U] a thin covering of gold or gold paint **altın kaplama, yaldızlı kaplama** ● **gilt** *adjective* **yaldızlı**

gimmick /ˈɡɪmɪk/ *noun* [C] something that is used only to get people's attention, especially to make them buy something **reklam hilesi; bir malın satışı için yapılan tanıtım hilesi** *a marketing/publicity gimmick* ● **gimmicky** *adjective* **ilgi çekici**

gin /dʒɪn/ *noun* [C, U] a strong alcoholic drink which has no colour **cin, bir tür alkollü içecek**

ginger[1] /ˈdʒɪndʒəʳ/ *noun* [U] a pale brown root with a strong taste used as a spice in cooking **zencefil** *ginger cake*

ginger[2] /ˈdʒɪndʒəʳ/ *adjective* *UK* Ginger hair is an orange-brown colour. **kızıl kahverengi** *She's got ginger hair and freckles.*

ginger[3] /ˈɡɪŋəʳ/ *noun* [C] *UK informal* an offensive word for a person with red hair **kızıl kafa**

gingerly /ˈdʒɪndʒᵊli/ *adverb* slowly and carefully **dikkatle, ehemmiyetle, ihtiyatla** *He lowered himself gingerly into the water.*

gipsy /ˈdʒɪpsi/ *noun* [C] *another UK spelling of* gypsy (= a member of a race of people who travel from place to place, especially in Europe) **çingene**

giraffe /dʒɪˈrɑːf/ *noun* [C] a large African animal with a very long neck and long, thin legs **zürafa**

giraffe

girder /ˈɡɜːdəʳ/ *noun* [C] a long, thick piece of metal that is used to support bridges or large buildings **kiriş, direk, payanda**

⊶**girl** /ɡɜːl/ *noun* **1** [C] a female child or young woman **kız** *We have three children - a boy and two girls.* **2 the girls** a group of female friends **kızlar, bayanlar** *I'm going out with the girls tonight.*

⊶**girlfriend** /ˈɡɜːlfrend/ *noun* [C] **1** a woman or girl who someone is having a romantic relationship with **kız/bayan/hanım arkadaş, sevgili, flört** *Have you met Steve's new girlfriend?* **2** a female friend, especially of a woman **kız arkadaş**

girth /ɡɜːθ/ *noun* [C, U] the measurement around something round, such as someone's waist **(bel veya yuvarlak bir şeyin) çevresinin ölçümü, bel ölçüsü**

gist /dʒɪst/ *noun* **the gist of sth** the main point or meaning of something without the details **bir şeyin özü ana hattı, temeli, esası**

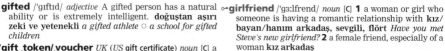

give ..... BAŞKA BİR DEYİŞLE

Offer, provide, ve **supply** fiilleri **give** fiilinin yerine sıklıkla kullanılır. *This booklet* **provides** *useful information about local services.* ● *Your doctor should be able to* **offer** *advice.* ● *The lake* **supplies** *the whole town with water.*

Donate fiili kişinin bir yardım kurumuna para veya eşya yardımı yaptığında kullanılan bir fiildir. *Four hundred pounds has been* **donated** *to the school book fund.*

Eğer birçok kişinin arasından bir kişi bir başarının gerçekleşmesi için bir katkıda bulunursa (özellikle para) bu durumun ifadesinde **contribute** fiili kullanılabilir. *I* **contributed** *twenty dollars towards Jamie's present.*

Eğer elden ele bir şey aktarılıyorsa, durumu belirtmek için **pass** ve **hand** fiilleri kullanılabilir. *Could you* **hand** *me that book, please?* ● *He* **passed** *a note to her during the meeting.*

Hand in deyimi yönetimdeki bir kişiye bir şey verildiği zaman kullanılabilen bir ifadedir. *Have you* **handed in** *your history essay yet?*

Pass on deyimi bir kişiden bir başkasına bir şey vermesini talep ettiğinde kullanılır. *Could you* **pass** *this on to Laura when you've finished reading it?*

Eğer bir ödül veya bir miktar para resmi bir şekilde veriliyorsa, **award** *veya* **present** *fiilleri kullanılabilir. She was* **presented** *with a bouquet of flowers and a cheque for £500.* ● *He was* **awarded** *the Nobel Prize for Physics.*

o━**give¹** /gɪv/ *verb past tense* **gave**, *past participle* **given**
1 PROVIDE [+ two objects] to provide someone with something **vermek** *Her parents gave her a car for her birthday.* ○ *Do you give money to charity?* ○ *Could you give me a lift to the station, please?* **2** PUT NEAR [+ two objects] to put something near someone or in their hand so that they can use it or look at it **sunmak, vermek** *Can you give me that pen?* ○ *He poured a cup of coffee and gave it to Isabel.* **3** ALLOW [+ two objects] to allow someone to have a right or an opportunity **(hak, fırsat) vermek** *We didn't really give him a chance to explain.* **4** TELL [T] to tell someone something **söylemek, anlatmak** *The woman refused to give her name.* ○ [+ two objects] *Can you give Jo a message?* **5** CAUSE [+ two objects] to cause someone to have or feel something **almasına/hissetmesine neden olmak** *I hope he hasn't given you any trouble.* ○ *This news will give hope to thousands of sufferers.* **6** ALLOW TIME [+ two objects] to allow someone or something a particular amount of time **(zaman, süre) vermek** *I'm nearly ready - just give me a few minutes.* **7** PAY MONEY [+ two objects] to pay someone a particular amount of money for something **(bir şeyin karşılığı olarak) ücret ödemek, para vermek** *I gave him £20 for his old camera.* **8** DO [T] to perform an action **(gösteri, konuşma, konferans, ders vb.) sunmak, vermek, icra etmek** *to give a cry/shout* ○ [+ two objects] *He gave her a kiss on the cheek.* **9 give sb a call/ring** to telephone someone **telefonla aramak** *Why don't you just give him a call?* **10 give a performance/speech, etc** to perform or speak in public **toplum karşısında konuşmak/gösteri yapmak/sunmak** *Tony gave a great speech.* **11 give a party** to have a party **parti vermek** *Claire's giving a birthday party for Eric.* **12** MOVE [I] to bend, stretch, or break because of too much weight **(ağır yükten dolayı) bel vermek, eğilmek, kırmak/kırılmak; genişlemek 13 give way** UK (US **yield**) to stop in order to allow other vehicles to go past before you drive onto a bigger road **yol vermek, geçmesine izin vermek**
give sth away *phrasal verb* **1** to give something to someone without asking for any money **(ücretsiz) elden çıkarmak, vermek** *They're giving away a CD with this magazine.* **2** to let someone know a secret, often without intending to **bir sırrı açıklamak, ifşa etmek, açığa vurmak** *The party was meant to be a surprise, but Caroline gave it away.*
give sth back *phrasal verb* to return something to the person who gave it to you **geri vermek, iade etmek** *Has she given you those books back yet?*
give in *phrasal verb* **1** to finally agree to what someone wants after a period when you refuse to agree **kabul etmek, direnmekten vazgeçmek, sonunda aynı noktaya gelmek** *We will never give in to terrorists' demands.* **2** to accept that you have been beaten and agree to stop competing or fighting **mağlubiyeti/yenilgiyi kabul etmek, boyun eğmek, teslim olmak**
give sth in *phrasal verb* UK to give a piece of written work or a document to someone for them to read, judge, or deal with **teslim etmek** *I have to give my essay in on Monday.*
give off sth *phrasal verb* to produce heat, light, a smell, or a gas **ısı/gaz/koku/ışık vermek/çıkarmak/yaymak** *The fire was giving off a lot of smoke.*
give sth out *phrasal verb* to give something to a large number of people **dağıtmak, vermek** *He gave out copies of the report at the end of the meeting.*
give out *phrasal verb* If a machine or part of your body gives out, it stops working correctly. **pes etmek, durmak, bitmek, tükenmek, kalmamak** *She read until her eyes gave out.*
give up (sth) *phrasal verb* **1** If you give up a habit such as smoking, or give up something unhealthy such as alcohol, you stop doing it or having it. **(sigara, alkol)** bırakmak, vazgeçmek, terk etmek *I gave up smoking two years ago.* **2** to stop doing something before you have completed it, usually because it is too difficult **yarıda bırakmak, yapmaktan vazgeçmek, caymak, tamamlamamak** [+ doing sth] *I've given up trying to help her.*
give up sth *phrasal verb* to stop doing a regular activity or job **düzenli yapılanları yapmamak, işinden vazgeçmek; işi bırakmak** *Are you going to give up work when you have your baby?*
give up *phrasal verb* to stop trying to think of the answer to a joke or question **cevabını aramaktan vazgeçmek; çözmekten vazgeçmek** *Do you give up?*
give it up for sb *phrasal verb* used to ask people to clap their hands to show that they like a performance **alkışlamasını istemek** *Ladies and gentlemen, give it up for the star of our show, Amy Jones!*
give yourself up *phrasal verb* to allow the police or an enemy to catch you **teslim olmak**
give up on sb *phrasal verb* to stop hoping that someone will do what you want them to do **birinden umidini kesmek; ...den umudu olmamak** *The doctors have given up on him.*
give up on sth *phrasal verb* to stop hoping that something will achieve what you want it to achieve **işe yarayacağını düşünmemek, ...den umudunu kesmek**

give² /gɪv/ *noun* **1** [U] when something can bend or move from its normal shape to take extra weight or size **bozulma, değişim, şekil bozukluğu 2 give and take** when people reach agreement by letting each person have part of what they want **karşılıklı anlayış/özveri/fedakârlık**

giveaway /ˈgɪvəweɪ/ *noun* **1** [C] something that is given to people free **ücretsiz dağıtım, verme, hibe olarak dağıtım 2** [no plural] something that makes it easy for people to guess something **açıklama, ifşaat, bir şeyi tahmine yarayan şey**

given¹ /ˈgɪvªn/ *adjective* **1** [always before noun] already arranged or agreed **düzenlenmiş, anlaşılmış, belirlenmiş, kararlaştırılmış, saptanmış** *They can only stay for a given amount of time.* **2 any given day/time/week, etc** any day/time/week, etc **herhangi bir gün/zaman/hafta vb.** *About 4 million women are pregnant in the US at any given time.*

given² /ˈgɪvªn/ *preposition* when you consider **belirlenen, verilen, dikkate alınan** *Given the force of the explosion, it's a miracle they survived.*

given³ /ˈgɪvªn/ *past participle of* give 'vermek' fiilinin üçüncü hâli

glacial /ˈgleɪsiəl/ ⑤ /ˈgleɪʃªl/ *adjective* [always before noun] relating to glaciers or ice **buza/buzula ait** *glacial lakes*

glacier /ˈglæsiəʳ/ ⑤ /ˈgleɪʃər/ *noun* [C] a large mass of ice that moves very slowly, usually down a slope or valley **buzul**

o━**glad** /glæd/ *adjective* [never before noun] **1** happy about something **memnun, mutlu** [+ (that)] *She's very glad that she left.* ○ [+ to do sth] *I'm so glad to see you.* **2** very willing to do something **istekli, arzulu, hevesli** [+ to do sth] *She's always glad to help.* **3 be glad of sth** *formal* to be grateful for something **müteşekkir olmak, minnettar olmak, şükran duymak** *I was glad of a few days off before going back to work.*

gladly /ˈglædli/ *adverb* willingly or happily **memnuniyetle, hay hay** *I would gladly pay extra for better service.*

glamorize (*also* UK **-ise**) /ˈglæmªraɪz/ *verb* [T] to make something seem glamorous **çekici/göz alıcı hale getirmek**

glamorous 318 o▬ Important words to learn

glamorous /ˈglæmᵊrəs/ *adjective* attractive in an exciting and special way **göz alıcı, çekici, büyüleyici** *a glamorous woman* ○ *a glamorous lifestyle*

glamour (*also US* **glamor**) /ˈglæmər/ *noun* [U] the quality of being attractive, exciting and special **çekicilik, cazibe, büyüleyicilik** *the glamour of Hollywood*

glance¹ /glɑːns/ *verb* **1 glance at/around/towards, etc** to look somewhere for a short time **göz atmak, kısa bir göz gezdirmek** *He glanced at his watch.* **2 glance at/over/through, etc** to read something quickly **hızlıca okumak, göz gezdirmek** *She glanced through the newspaper.*

glance ...... İLE BİRLİKTE KULLANILAN KELİMELER

cast / give / have a glance [at / around, etc] sb / sth ● **exchange** glances ● a **cursory/quick** glance

glance² /glɑːns/ *noun* **1** [C] a quick look **çabuk bir bakış, göz atma** *She had a quick glance around the restaurant.* **2 at a glance** If you see something at a glance, you see it very quickly or immediately. **bir bakışta, hemen, şıp diye**

gland /glænd/ *noun* [C] an organ in the body that produces a particular chemical substance or liquid **salgı bezi, salgı üreten organ**

glandular fever /ˌglændjʊləˈfiːvər/ *UK* (*US* **mononucleosis**) *noun* [U] an infectious disease that makes your glands swell and makes you feel tired **bir tür bulaşıcı beze/gudde hastalığı**

glare¹ /gleər/ *noun* **1** [U] strong, bright light that hurts your eyes **göz kamaştıran, göz alan, çok parlak** *I get a lot of glare from my computer screen.* **2** [C] a long, angry look **dik dik öfke dolu bakış 3 the glare of publicity/the media, etc** when someone gets too much attention from newspapers and television **medyanın/toplumun ilgi odağı**

glare² /gleər/ *verb* [I] to look at someone in an angry way **dik dik kızgın şekilde bakmak; gözlerini dikip bakmak**

glaring /ˈgleərɪŋ/ *adjective* **1 a glaring error/mistake/omission, etc** a very noticeable mistake or problem **çok göze çarpan hata/kusur/eksik vb.; apaçık, aşikâr, ortada olan hata veya problem 2 glaring light/sun, etc** light which is too strong and bright **göz kamaştıran/parlak ışık**

glass ...... İLE BİRLİKTE KULLANILAN KELİMELER

a **pane/sheet** of glass ● **broken** glass

o▬**glass** /glɑːs/ *noun* **1** [U] a hard, transparent substance that objects such as windows and bottles are made of **cam** *broken glass* ○ *glass jars* **2** [C] a container made of glass that is used for drinking **bardak** *Would you like a glass of water?* ➻See also: **magnifying glass, stained glass.**

glasses /ˈglɑːsɪz/ *noun* [plural] a piece of equipment with two transparent parts that you wear in front of your eyes to help you see better **gözlük** *a pair of glasses* ○ *She was wearing glasses.*

glassy /ˈglɑːsi/ *adjective* **1** A glassy surface is smooth and shiny like glass. **cam gibi, ayna gibi, pürüzsüz, pırıl pırıl 2** Glassy eyes show no expression and seem not to see anything. **(bakış) boş, donuk, anlamsız, cansız**

glaze¹ /gleɪz/ *verb* [EYES] [I] (*also* **glaze over**) If someone's eyes glaze or glaze over, they stop showing any interest or expression because they are bored or tired. **donuklaşmak, cansızlaşmak, bulanıklaşmak 2** [CLAY] [T] to cover the surface of objects made of clay with a liquid that makes them hard and shiny when they are baked **perdahlamak, cilalamak, donuklaştırmak 3** [FOOD]

glass

glasses

The window is made of glass.

[T] to put a liquid on food to make it shiny and more attractive **(yiyecek) parlatmak, daha çekici hale getirmek 4** [GLASS] [T] to put glass in a window or door **(pencere, kapı) cam takmak**

glaze² /gleɪz/ *noun* [C, U] **1** a liquid that is put on objects made of clay to make them hard and shiny when they are baked **sır, perdah 2** a liquid that is put on food to make it shiny and attractive **yiyeceklerin üzerine sürülen parlatıcı, cila, perdah, jöle vb.**

gleam¹ /gliːm/ *verb* [I] to shine in a pleasant, soft way **parıldamak, parlamak, ışıldamak** *a gleaming new car*

gleam² /gliːm/ *noun* [no plural] **1** when something shines in a pleasant, soft way **parlama, parıldama, ışıldama** *the gleam of sunlight on the frozen lake* **2** an expression in someone's eyes **gözdeki ışık, parıltı, canlılık** *She had a strange gleam in her eye.*

glean /gliːn/ *verb* [T] to discover information slowly or with difficulty **bilgiyi yavaş yavaş ve güçlükle toplamak** [often passive] *Some useful information can be gleaned from this study.*

glee /gliː/ *noun* [U] a feeling of great happiness, usually because of your good luck or someone else's bad luck **başkalarının kötü şansı veya iyi şansından dolayı duyulan mutluluk, sevinç** *Rosa began laughing with glee.* ● **gleeful** *adjective* ● **gleefully** *adverb* **neşeli bir şekilde**

glib /glɪb/ *adjective* using words in a way that is clever and confident, but not sincere **samimi olmayan ancak zeki ve kendine güvenen sözcükleri kullanma; biraz alaycı ve yapmacık**

glide /glaɪd/ *verb* **glide along/into/over, etc** to move somewhere smoothly and quietly **süzülmek, kaymak, akmak** *The train slowly glided out of the station.*

glider /ˈglaɪdər/ *noun* [C] an aircraft that has no engine and flies on air currents **planör** ● **gliding** *noun* [U] the activity of flying in a glider **planörcülük, planör uçurma** ➻See also: **hang glider, hang gliding.**

glimmer¹ /ˈglɪmər/ *noun* **1 a glimmer of happiness/hope, etc** a small sign of something good **mutluluk/ümit ışığı/kıvılcımı 2** [C] when a light shines in a weak way **titrek ışık**

glimmer² /ˈglɪmər/ *verb* [I] to shine in a weak way **titrek/cansız ışık vermek/yaymak**

catch/get a glimpse ● a brief/fleeting glimpse ● a glimpse of sb/sth

glimpse /glɪms/ *noun* [C] when you see something or someone for a very short time **anlık bakış, gözatma** *He caught/got a glimpse of her as she got into the car.* ● **glimpse** *verb* [T] to see something or someone for a very short time **gözüne ilişmek, gözüne takılmak** *She glimpsed him out of the corner of her eye.*

glint /glɪnt/ *noun* [no plural] **1** when your eyes shine with excitement or because you are going to do something bad **gözlerdeki parıldama, parıltı, coşku, heyecan belirtisi** *She had a wicked glint in her eye.* **2** when something shines or reflects light for a short time **parıltı, parıldama** ● **glint** *verb* [I] **parıldamak**

glisten /'glɪsᵊn/ *verb* [I] If something glistens, it shines, often because it is wet. **(ıslak yüzey) parlamak, ışıldamak** *Their faces were glistening with sweat.*

glitch /glɪtʃ/ *noun* [C] *informal* a mistake or problem that stops something from working correctly **hata, kusur, yanlışlık, çalışmayı engelleyen sorun** *technical glitches*

glitter¹ /'glɪtər/ *verb* [I] to shine with small flashes of light **parıldamak, ışıl ışıl yanmak** *Snow glittered on the mountains.*

glitter² /'glɪtər/ *noun* [U] **1** very small, shiny pieces of metal used for decoration **parıltılı metal, ışıltı, parıltı 2** when something seems exciting and attractive **heyecan, coşku, göz kamaştırma**

glittering /'glɪtᵊrɪŋ/ *adjective* **1** shining with small flashes of light **göz alan, parıldayan, ışıl ışıl yanan** *glittering jewels* **2** successful and exciting **başarılı, heyecan verici, göz dolduran, göz kamaştıran** *a glittering party/career*

glitz /glɪts/ *noun* [U] when something is attractive, exciting and shows money in an obvious way **çekicilik, heyecan, göz alan, şaşa, büyü, para çağrıştıran** ● **glitzy** *adjective a glitzy nightclub* **gösterişli**

gloat /gləʊt/ *verb* [I] to show pleasure at your success or at someone else's failure **kendi başarısından/başkasının başarısızlığından büyük keyif almak; 'Oh olsun!' demek; şeytanca zevk almak** *His enemies were gloating over his defeat.*

global /'gləʊbᵊl/ *adjective* relating to the whole world **küresel** *the global problem of nuclear waste* ● **globally** *adverb* **küresel**

globalization /ˌgləʊbᵊlaɪ'zeɪʃᵊn/ *noun* [U] **1** the increase of business around the world, especially by big companies operating in many countries **(iş) küreselleşme 2** when things all over the world become more similar **küreselleşme** *the globalization of fashion*

global 'warming *noun* [U] when the air around the world becomes warmer because of pollution **küresel ısınma**

globe /gləʊb/ *noun* **1 the globe** the world **dünya** *This event is being watched by 200 million people around the globe.* **2** [C] a model of the world shaped like a ball with a map of all the countries on it **küre**

globe

globule /'glɒbjuːl/ *noun* [C] a small, round mass or lump of a liquid substance **damlacık, topak** *a globule of oil*

gloom /gluːm/ *noun* [U] **1** a feeling of unhappiness and of not having any hope **kasvet, hüzün, keder** *an atmosphere of gloom* **2** when it is dark, but not completely dark **alacakaranlık**

gloomy /'gluːmi/ *adjective* **1** NEGATIVE very negative about a situation **kötümser, karamsar** *a gloomy report* **2** DARK dark in an unpleasant way **kasvetli, iç karartan** *a small, gloomy room* **3** UNHAPPY unhappy and without hope **mutsuz, umutsuz, karamsar, üzüntülü, mahzun** *a gloomy face* ● **gloomily** *adverb* **umutsuzca**

glorify /'glɔːrɪfaɪ/ *verb* [T] **1** to describe or represent something in a way that makes it seem better or more important than it really is **şişirmek, olduğundan farklı göstermek, göklere çıkarmak** *films that glorify violence* **2** to praise someone, especially God **yüceltmek, övgüler/methiyeler düzmek**

glorious /'glɔːriəs/ *adjective* **1** beautiful or wonderful **muhteşem, harika, güzel** *We had four days of glorious sunshine.* ○ *glorious colours* **2** deserving praise and respect **şanlı, şerefli, övgüye layık** *a glorious career* ● **gloriously** *adverb* **muhteşem bir şekilde**

glory¹ /'glɔːri/ *noun* [U] **1** when people praise and respect you for achieving something important **şan, şeref, ün 2** great beauty **nefes kesen güzellik, muhteşem/göz kamaştıran güzellik** *The castle has been restored to its former glory.*

glory² /'glɔːri/ *verb*
glory in sth *phrasal verb* to enjoy something and be very proud of it **gururlanmak, övünmek, keyfini çıkarmak**

gloss¹ /glɒs/ *noun* **1** PAINT [U] paint that creates a shiny surface **parlak boya, cila, parlatıcı 2** SHINE [U] shine on a surface **parlaklık, cila 3** EXPLANATION [C] a short explanation of a word or phrase in a text **kısa açıklama, küçük dipnot/bilgi**

gloss² /glɒs/ *verb* [T] to give a short explanation of a word or phrase **(sözcük, ifade) kısa bir açıklamasını vermek, izah etmek**
gloss over sth *phrasal verb* to avoid discussing something, or to discuss something without any details in order to make it seem unimportant **geçiştirmek, üstünde durmamak, önemsememek, tartışmaya değer bulmamak**

glossary /'glɒsᵊri/ *noun* [C] a list of difficult words with their meanings like a small dictionary, especially at the end of a book **(kitap, konu sonunda verilen) ek sözlük; lügatçe**

glossy /'glɒsi/ *adjective* **1** smooth and shiny **parlak ve pürüzsüz** *glossy hair* **2** Glossy magazines and pictures are printed on shiny paper. **parlak/kuşe kağıda basılmış** *a glossy brochure*

glove /glʌv/ *noun* [C] a piece of clothing which covers your fingers and hand **eldiven** *a pair of gloves* ➔Orta kısımdaki renkli sayfalarına bakınız.

'glove com,partment (*also* **glove box**) *noun* [C] a small cupboard in the front of a car, used to hold small things **torpido gözü**

glow¹ /gləʊ/ *noun* [no plural] **1** a soft, warm light **yumuşak, hoş ışık** *the warm glow of the moon* **2** when your face feels warm or appears warm and healthy **yüzünden kan damlama; sağlıklı ve sevecen görünüm** *Sam's face had lost its rosy glow.* **3 a glow of happiness/pride, etc** a strong feeling of being happy/proud, etc **güçlü mutluluk/gurur vb.hissi/duygusu; yanıp tutuşma**

glow² /gləʊ/ *verb* [I] **1** to produce a soft, warm light **yumuşak, sıcak/iç ısıtan ışık vermek** *toys which glow in the dark* **2** to have a warm and healthy appea-**

rance **sağlıklı ve içten/cana yakın/samimi görün-tüsü olmak** *Her eyes were bright and her cheeks were glowing.* **3 glow with happiness/pride, etc** to feel very happy/proud, etc **mutluluk/gurur vb. ile yanıp tutuşmak** *Glowing with pride, she showed me her painting.*

glower /'glaʊə^r/ *verb* [I] to look at someone in a very angry way **ters ters bakmak, dik dik bakmak** *The woman glowered at her husband.*

a glowing **reference/report/tribute** ● in glowing **terms**

glowing /'gləʊɪŋ/ *adjective* praising someone a lot **övgü dolu, göklere çıkaran** *She got a glowing report from her teacher.*

glucose /'glu:kəʊs/ *noun* [U] a type of sugar **glikoz**

glue[1] /glu:/ *noun* [U] a substance used to stick things together **tutkal, zamk, yapıştırıcı** *Put a bit of glue on both edges and hold them together.* ⊃Orta kısımdaki renkli sayfalarına bakınız.

glue[2] /glu:/ *verb* [T] **glueing, gluing,** *past* **glued** to stick something to something else with glue **yapıştırmak, tutturmak, zamklamak** *Do you think you can glue this vase back together?*
be glued to sth *phrasal verb* to be watching something, especially television **(tv) yerinden kıpırdamadan/ gözlerini ayırmadan seyretmek** *The kids were glued to the TV all morning.*

glum /glʌm/ *adjective* unhappy **mutsuz, üzgün, morali bozuk** *Why are you looking so glum today?* ● **glumly** *adverb* **mutsuz bir şekilde**

glut /glʌt/ *noun* [C] more of something than is needed **bolluk, çokluk** [usually singular] *There is **a glut** of houses for sale in this area.*

glutton /'glʌt^ən/ *noun* **1** [C] someone who eats too much **obur 2 be a glutton for punishment** to enjoy doing things that are unpleasant or difficult **zor ve kötü şeyleri yapmaktan zevk alıyor olmak**

gluttony /'glʌt^əni/ *noun* [U] when someone eats too much **oburluk**

gm *written abbreviation for* gram (= a unit for measuring weight) **gram**

GM /dʒi:'em/ *adjective abbreviation for* genetically modified: genetically modified plants or animals have had some of their genes (= parts of cells which control particular characteristics) changed. **(bitki, hayvan) genleriyle oynanmış; genleri değiştirilmiş** *GM foods*

GMO /ˌdʒi:em'əʊ/ *noun* [U] *abbreviation for* genetically modified organism: a plant or animal in which scientists have changed the genes (= parts of cells which control particular characteristics) **genleriyle oynanmış; genleri değiştirilmiş organizma**

GMT /ˌdʒi:em'ti:/ *noun* [U] *abbreviation for* Greenwich Mean Time: the time at Greenwich in London, which is used as an international measurement for time **Greenwich Saat Ayarı**

gnarled /nɑ:ld/ *adjective* rough and twisted, usually because of being old **boğumlu, budaklı, bükümlü, çarpık çurpuk, yamru yumru** *a gnarled tree trunk*

gnat /næt/ *noun* [C] a small flying insect that can bite you **tatarcık**

gnaw /nɔ:/ *verb* [I, T] to bite something with a lot of small bites **kemirmek, küçük küçük ısırmak** *He was gnawing on a bone.*

gnaw at sb *phrasal verb* to make someone feel more and more anxious or annoyed **birini çokça kızdır-mak/canını sıkmak/endişelendirmek/taciz etmek** *Doubt kept gnawing at him.*

gnome /nəʊm/ *noun* [C] an imaginary little man with a pointed hat **cüce, yer cücesi** *a garden gnome*

GNP /ˌdʒi:en'pi:/ *noun* [U] *abbreviation for* gross national product: the total value of goods and services produced in a country in a year, including the profits made in foreign countries **Gayri Safi Millî Hasıla** ⊃Compare GDP.

⊶**go**[1] /gəʊ/ *verb* [I] **going,** *past tense* **went,** *past participle* **gone 1** MOVE to move or travel somewhere **gitmek** *I'd love to go to America.* ○ *We went into the house.* ○ *Are you going by train?* **2** DO SOMETHING to move or travel somewhere in order to do something **bir amaç için gitmek** *Let's go for a walk.* ○ [+ doing sth] *We're going camping tomorrow.* **3** DISAPPEAR to disappear or no longer exist **gözden kaybolmak, yok olmak; yitmek** *When I turned round the man had gone.* **4 go badly/well, etc** to develop in a particular way **iyi/kötü gitmek** *My exams went really badly.* **5** CONTINUE to continue to be in a particular state **belli bir düzende/konumda devam etmek** *We won't let anyone go hungry.* **6** WORKING to work correctly **düzgün çalışmak** *Did you manage to get the car going?* **7** STOP WORKING to stop working correctly **düzgün çalışmamak, arıza yapmak, iyi gitmemek** *Her hearing is going, so speak loudly.* **8** MATCH If two things go, they match each other. **uymak, uyuşmak, birbiriyle iyi gitmek** *That jumper doesn't **go with** those trousers.* **9** TIME If time goes, it passes. **(zaman) geçmek, bitmek, yok olmak** *The day went very quickly.* **10** SONG to have a particular tune or words **(şarkı) belli bir melodisi/ezgisi ve güftesi olmak** *I can't remember how it goes.* **11** SOUND/MOVEMENT to make a particular sound or movement **belli bir ses çıkar-mak veya hareket yapmak** *My dog goes like this when he wants some food.* **12 not go there** to not think or talk about a subject that makes you feel bad **'Oraya/ona hiç değinme!', 'Sakın lafını bile etme!' 'Ne olur hiç o konuya girme!'** *"Then there's the guilt I feel about leaving my child with another woman." "Don't even go there!"*
go about sth *phrasal verb* to start to do something or deal with something **bir şeye başlamak/bir şeyle ilgilenmeye başlamak** *What's the best way to go about this?*
go after sb *phrasal verb* to chase or follow someone in order to catch them **peşinden gitmek, takip etmek, ardından takip etmek** *He ran away, but the police went after him.*
go against sth *phrasal verb* If something goes against a rule or something you believe in, it does not obey it or agree with it. **zıddına gitmek, tersine/aksine hareket etmek, kurallara uymamak** *It goes against my principles to lie.*
go against sb *phrasal verb* If a decision or vote goes against someone, they do not get the result that they needed. **aksine çıkmak, beklenen sonucu verme-mek, düşündüğünün aksine sonuçlanmak** *The judge's decision went against us.*
go ahead *phrasal verb* **1** to start to do something **yap-maya başlamak, yürütmek, ilerlemek** *We have permission to go ahead with the project.* **2** something that you say to someone to give them permission to do something **Buyrun!, Alın!, Tabi!, Hay hay!, Siz buyrun, Rica ederim!** *"Can I borrow your book?" "Yes, go ahead."* ● **go-ahead** *noun* **get/give the go-ahead**
go along *phrasal verb* **1** UK to go to a place or event, usually without much planning **öylesine uğramak, gitmek** *I might go along to the party after work.* **2** to

continue doing something **devam etmek, ilerlemek** *I'll tell you the rules as we go along.*

go along with sth/sb *phrasal verb* to support an idea, or to agree with someone's opinion **(fikir) uymak, desteklemek** *She'll never go along with this idea.*

go around *phrasal verb (also UK* **go round) 1** to be enough for everyone in a group **yetmek, kâfi gelmek, yeterli olmak** *There aren't enough chairs to go around.* **2 go around doing sth** to spend your time behaving badly or doing something that is unpleasant for other people *She's been going around telling people I'm stupid.*

go at sth *phrasal verb UK informal* to start doing something with a lot of energy and enthusiasm **istek ve gayretle bir şeyi yapmaya başlamak, girişmek, bir çırpıda bitirmek** *They're was a lot of dishes to wash so we went at it straight away.*

go away *phrasal verb* **1** LEAVE to leave a place **ayrılmak, uzaklaşmak, uzak durmak, çekip gitmek** *Go away - I'm busy.* **2** HOLIDAY to leave your home in order to spend time in a different place, usually for a holiday **tatile çıkmak, tatile gitmek için ayrılmak** *They're going away for a few weeks in the summer.* **3** DISAPPEAR to disappear **kaybolmak, yok olmak, gitmek** *That smell seems to have gone away.*

go back *phrasal verb* to return to a place where you were or where you have been before **geri gelmek, dönmek** *When are you going back to London?*

go back on sth *phrasal verb* to not do something that you promised you would do **sözünü yerine getirmemek, yapmamak, sözünde durmamak** *I never go back on my word* (= do what I said I would do).

go back to sb *phrasal verb* to start a relationship again with a person who you had a romantic relationship with in the past **yeniden başlamak, geri dönmek** *Jim's gone back to his ex-wife.*

go back to sth *phrasal verb* to start doing something again that you were doing before **geri dönmek, tekrar yapmaya başlamak** *It's time to go back to work now.*

go by *phrasal verb* **1** If time goes by, it passes. **(zaman) geçmek, geçip gitmek** *The days went by really slowly.* **2** to move past **süratle/hızlıca geçmek** *A green sports car went by.*

go by sth *phrasal verb* to use information about something to help you make a decision about the best thing to do **...göre hareket etmek/hüküm vermek; ...doğrultusunda belirlemek** *You can't go by anything she says.*

go down *phrasal verb* **1** BECOME LESS to become lower in level **düşmek, azalmak, seviyesi düşmek** *Interest rates are going down at the moment.* **2** SUN When the sun goes down, it moves down in the sky until it cannot be seen any more. **(güneş) batmak 3** COMPUTER If a computer goes down, it stops working. **(bilgisayar) çökmek, tamamen bozulmak, çalışmamak 4** REMEMBER to be considered or remembered in a particular way **hatırlanmak, unutulmamak** *This will go down as one of the most exciting soccer matches ever played.* ○ *(UK) I don't think my plan will go down well at all.*

go down with sth *phrasal verb UK informal* to become ill, usually with an illness that is not very serious **çok ciddi olmayan bir hastalığa tutulmak/yakalanmak** *Our whole class went down with the flu.*

go for sth *phrasal verb* **1** CHOOSE to choose something **seçmek** *What sort of printer are you going to go for?* **2** HAVE *informal* to try to have or achieve something **almaya/kazanmaya çalışmak/mücadele etmek, yarışmak** *He'll be going for his third straight Olympic gold medal in the 200-meter dash.* ○ *If you want it, go for it* (= do what you need to do in order to have or achieve it). **3** GET to try to get something **almaya çalışmak, uğraşmak** *He tripped as he was going for the ball.* **4** MONEY If something goes for a particular amount of money, it is

sold for that amount. **...miktara satılmak; ...e/a gitmek/mal olmak**

go for sb *phrasal verb* to attack someone **saldırmak, üzerine atılmak, hücum etmek** *He suddenly went for me with a knife.*

go in *phrasal verb* to enter a place **içeri girmek** *I looked through the window, but I didn't actually go in.*

go in for sth *phrasal verb* to like a particular activity **sevmek, hoşlanmak, haz almak** *I don't really go in for sports.*

go into sth *phrasal verb* **1** START to start to do a particular type of work **başlamak, girmek** *What made you decide to go into politics?* **2** DESCRIBE to describe, discuss, or examine something in a detailed way **açıklamak, ayrıntıya girmek** *She didn't go into any detail about the job.* **3** BE USED If an amount of time, money, or effort goes into a product or activity, it is used or spent creating that product or doing that activity. **(zaman, para, çaba) sarf etmek, vermek, harcamak, ayırmak, kullanılmak** *A lot of effort has gone into producing this play.*

go off *phrasal verb* **1** LEAVE to leave a place and go somewhere else **terk etmek, ayrılmak** *She's gone off to the pub with Tony.* **2** FOOD *UK informal* If food goes off, it is not good to eat any more because it is too old. **(yiyecek) bayatlamak, bozulmak, yenilemez hale gelmek 3** STOP If a light or machine goes off, it stops working. **kesilmek, kapanmak, durmak, çalışmamak** *The heating goes off at 10 o'clock.* **4** EXPLODE If a bomb or gun goes off, it explodes or fires. **patlamak, infilak etmek 5** MAKE NOISE If something that makes a noise goes off, it suddenly starts making a noise. **gürültü yapmak, ses çıkarmak, durup dururken çalmaya başlamak** *His car alarm goes off every time it rains.* **6 go off on one** *informal* to react angrily to something

go off sb/sth *phrasal verb UK* to stop liking someone or something **artık hoşlanmamak, haz almamak, sevmemek** *I've gone off fish recently.*

go on *phrasal verb* **1** LAST to last for a particular period of time **sürmek, devam etmek** *The film seemed to go on forever.* **2** CONTINUE to continue doing something **devam etmek, sürdürmek, sürüp gitmek** [+ doing sth] *We can't go on living like this.* **3 go on to do sth** to do something else in the future **He went on to win the final.* **4** HAPPEN to happen **olmak, meydana gelmek, vuku bulmak** *What's going on?* **5** TALK *UK* to talk in an annoying way about something for a long time **gereksiz yere sürekli aynı şeyden bahsetmek, konuşup durmak** *I wish she'd stop going on about her boyfriend.* **6** TALK AGAIN to start talking again after stopping for a short time **(konuşmaya) devam etmek, kaldığı yerden devam etmek** *He paused and then went on with his story.* **7 Go on** *informal* something that you say to encourage someone to do something **Go on, what happened next?*

go on sth *phrasal verb* to use a piece of information to help you discover or understand something **eldeki mevcut bilgiyi esas almak/göz önünde bulundurmak** *Her first name was all we had to go on.*

go out *phrasal verb* **1** LEAVE to leave a place in order to go somewhere else **dışarı çıkmak** *Are you going out tonight?* **2** LIGHT/FIRE If a light or something that is burning goes out, it stops producing light or heat. **(ışık, ampul vb.) sönmek, patlamak** *It took ages for the fire to go out.* **3** RELATIONSHIP If two people go out together, they have a romantic relationship with each other. **duygusal bir ilişki yaşamak, birlikte çıkmak, flört etmek** *I've been going out with him for a year.*

go over US to be thought of in a particular way **nasıl olacağını düşünmek, merak etmek** *I wonder how my speech will go over this afternoon.*

go over sth *phrasal verb* to talk or think about something in order to explain it or make certain that it is correct **tekrar üzerinden geçmek, bir kez daha göz atmak, tekrar ele almak** *Let's go over the plan one more time.*

go round *phrasal verb* UK (*UK/US* **go around**) **1** to be enough for everyone in a group **yetecek kadar olmak** *There aren't enough chairs to go round.* **2 go round doing sth** to spend your time behaving badly or doing something that is unpleasant for other people *She's been going round telling people I'm stupid.*

go through sth *phrasal verb* **1** EXPERIENCE to experience a difficult or unpleasant situation **zor zamanlar geçirmek, güçlükler yaşamak** *She's going through a difficult time with her job.* **2** EXAMINE to carefully examine the contents of something or a collection of things in order to find something **ayrıtısıyla ve dikkatlice incelemek** *A customs officer went through my suitcase.* **3** USE to use a lot of something **bitirmek, kullanmak** *I've gone through two boxes of tissues this week.*

go through *phrasal verb* If a law, plan, or deal goes through, it is officially accepted or approved. (**kanun, plan, anlaşma vb.**) **resmen kabul edilmek, onaylanmak**

go through with sth *phrasal verb* to do something unpleasant or difficult that you have planned or promised to do **planlanmış/vaat edilmiş/zor ve hoş olmayan bir şeyi yapmak; yapmak zorunda kalmak** *He was too scared to go through with the operation.*

go under *phrasal verb* If a company or business goes under, it fails financially. (**iş, şirket**)**batmak, iflas etmek, çökmek**

go up *phrasal verb* **1** INCREASE to become higher in level **artmak, yükselmek** *House prices keep going up.* **2** BE FIXED If a building or sign goes up, it is fixed into position. **dikilmek, yerleştirilmek, yükseltilmek** **3** EXPLODE to suddenly explode **infilak etmek, patlamak** *There was a loud bang, and then the building went up in flames.*

go without (sth) *phrasal verb* to not have something that you usually have **...sız/siz yapmak/idare etmek; ...den/dan mahrum kalmak** *They went without food for four days.*

go² /gəʊ/ *noun* [C] *plural* **goes** **1** *UK* when someone tries to do something **teşebbüs, kalkışma, girişme** *I had a go at catching a fish.* ○ *If you think you might like skiing, why don't you give it a go* (= try to do it)*?* **2** *mainly UK* someone's turn to do something **sıra, sefer, keşik** *Throw the dice Jane, it's your go.* **3 have a go at sb** *UK* to criticize someone angrily **kızgınca eleştirmek, laf etmek, tenkit etmek** *My mother's always having a go at me about my hair.* **4 make a go of sth** to try to make something succeed, usually by working hard **zoru başarmak, başarılı kılmaya çalışmak**

goad /gəʊd/ *verb* [T] to make someone angry or annoyed so that they react in the way that you want **kışkırtmak, rahatsız etmek, dürtmek** [+ *into* + doing sth] *They tried to goad us into attacking the police.*

goal .... İLE BİRLİKTE KULLANILAN KELİMELER

1 score a goal ● the **winning** goal
2 set yourself a goal ● achieve a goal

⌐⊶**goal** /gəʊl/ *noun* [C] **1** POINT a point scored in sports such as football when a player sends a ball or other object into a particular area, such as between two posts **gol** *He scored two goals in the second half.* **2** AREA In some sports, the area between two posts where players try to send the ball **(spor) kale** ○Orta kısımdaki renkli sayfalarına bakınız. **3** AIM something you want to do successfully in the future **amaç, gaye, erek** *Andy's goal is to run in the New York Marathon.*

goalie /'gəʊli/ *noun* [C] *informal short for* goalkeeper **kaleci**

goalkeeper /'gəʊl,kiː pər/ (*also US* **goaltender** /'gəʊl,tendər/) *noun* [C] the player in a sport such as football who tries to stop the ball going into the goal **kaleci, kale bekçisi** ○Orta kısımdaki renkli sayfalarına bakınız.

goalkeeper

goalpost /'gəʊlpəʊst/ *noun* [C] either of the two posts that are each side of the area where goals are scored in sports such as football **kale direği** ○Orta kısımdaki renkli sayfalarına bakınız.

goat /gəʊt/ *noun* [C] an animal with horns which is kept for the milk it produces **keçi**

gobble /'gɒbl/ (*also* **gobble up/down**) *verb* [T] *informal* to eat food very quickly **(yemek) silip süpürmek, mideye indirmek**

gobbledygook (*also* **gobbledegook**) /'gɒbldi,guːk/ *noun* [U] *informal* nonsense or very complicated language that you cannot understand **anlaşılması zor karışık ve saçma dil, söz**

go-between /'gəʊbɪ,twiːn/ *noun* [C] someone who talks and gives messages to people who will not or cannot talk to each other **aracı, ara bulucu**

goblin /'gɒblɪn/ *noun* [C] a short, ugly, imaginary creature who behaves badly **cin, gulyabani**

go-cart (*also* UK **go-kart**) /'gəʊkɑːt/ *noun* [C] a small, low racing car with no roof or windows **mini yarış arabası, gokart**

⌐⊶**god** /gɒd/ *noun* **1** **God** in Jewish, Christian, or Muslim belief, the spirit who created the universe and everything in it, and who rules over it **Allah, Rab, İlah 2** [C] a spirit, especially a male one, that people pray to and who has control over parts of the world or nature **tanrı** *the ancient Greek gods and goddesses* **3** **(Oh) (my) God!** *informal* used to emphasize how surprised, angry, shocked, etc you are **'Aman Allah'ım!', 'Aman Yarabbi!'** *Oh my God! The car has been stolen.* **4 thank God** *informal* something you say when you are happy because something bad did not happen **'Allah'a şükür', 'şükürler olsun ki!'** *Thank God nobody was hurt in the accident.*

godchild /'gɒdtʃaɪld/ *noun* [C] *plural* **godchildren** a child who has godparents (= people who take responsibility for the child's moral and religious development) **vaftiz çocuğu**

goddess /'gɒdes/ *noun* [C] a female spirit that people pray to and who has control over parts of the world or nature **tanrıça**

godfather /'gɒdfɑːðər/ *noun* [C] a man who is responsible for the moral and religious development of another person's child **vaftiz babası**

godforsaken /'gɒdfə,seɪkən/ *adjective* [always before noun] *informal* A godforsaken place is very unpleasant and usually far from other places. **kuş uçmaz kervan geçmez, kasvetli/terk edilmiş yer**

godlike /'gɒdlaɪk/ *adjective* having qualities that make someone admired and respected as if they were a god or God **üstün özelliklere sahip; saygı ve hayranlık uyandıran**

godmother /ˈɡɒdˌmʌðər/ *noun* [C] a woman who is responsible for the moral and religious development of another person's child **vaftiz annesi**

godparent /ˈɡɒdˌpeərənt/ *noun* [C] a person who is responsible for the moral and religious development of another person's child **vaftiz anne babası**

godsend /ˈɡɒdsend/ *noun* [no plural] something good which happens unexpectedly, usually when you really need it **büyük şans, devlet kuşu, nimet** *The lottery win was a godsend for her.*

goes /ɡəʊz/ *present simple he/she/it of* go **'gitmek' fiilinin 3. tekil şahıs çekim hâli**

goggles /ˈɡɒɡlz/ *noun* [plural] special glasses which fit close to your face to protect your eyes **koruyucu gözlük, dalgıç gözlüğü, büyük/koruma gözlüğü** *a pair of goggles* ⊃Orta kısımdaki renkli sayfalarına bakınız.

🧩 **going** ...... İLE BİRLİKTE KULLANILAN KELİMELER

hard/heavy/slow/tough going

going¹ /ˈɡəʊɪŋ/ *noun* **1** [DIFFICULTY] [U] how easy or difficult something is **kolay/zor** *I found the exam quite hard going.* **2** [GROUND] [U] the condition of the ground for walking, riding, etc **zeminin durumu/yapısı/elverişli olup olmadığı** **3** [LEAVING] [no plural] when someone leaves somewhere **gidiş, gidişi, ayrılış, ayrılışı** *His going came as a big surprise.*

going² /ˈɡəʊɪŋ/ *adjective* **the going price/rate, etc** the usual amount of money you would expect to pay for something **rayiç bedel/ücret, geçerli ücret/fiyat** *What's the going rate for babysitting these days?* ⊃See also: easy-going.

going³ /ˈɡəʊɪŋ/ *present participle of* go **'gitmek' fiilinin şimdiki zaman hali**

goings-on /ˌɡəʊɪŋzˈɒn/ *noun* [plural] *informal* unusual events or activities **olup bitenler, olaylar, dönen dolaplar** *strange goings-on*

go-kart /ˈɡəʊkɑːt/ *noun* [C] *another UK spelling of* go-cart (= a small, low racing car with no roof or windows) **mini yarış arabası, gokart**

☞**gold¹** /ɡəʊld/ *noun* **1** [U] a valuable, shiny, yellow metal used to make coins and jewellery (symbol Au) **altın** **2** [C, U] a gold medal (= a small, round disc given to someone for winning a race or competition) **altın madalya**

☞**gold²** /ɡəʊld/ *adjective* **1** made of gold **altından yapılmış** *gold coins* **2** being the colour of gold **altın renkli/renginde** *gold paint*

golden /ˈɡəʊldən/ *adjective* **1** being a bright yellow colour **altın sarısı** *bright golden hair* **2** *literary* made of gold or like gold **altından yapılma, altın** *a golden ring* **3** **a golden opportunity** a very exciting and valuable opportunity **altın fırsat, hayatta insanın eline bir kez geçecek fırsat**

,**golden 'wedding** *noun* [C] the day when two people have been married for 50 years **evlilikte ellinci yıl dönümü**

goldfish /ˈɡəʊldfɪʃ/ *noun* [C] *plural* **goldfish** or **goldfishes** a small, orange fish that is often kept as a pet **turuncu renkte süs balığı**

,**gold 'medal** *noun* [C] a small, round disc given to someone for winning a race or competition **altın madalya** *to win an Olympic gold medal*

'**gold ,mine** *noun* [C] **1** a place where gold is taken from the ground **altın madeni** **2** something that provides you with a lot of money **kârlı iş, altın yumurtlayan tavuk**

☞**golf** /ɡɒlf/ *noun* [U] a game on grass where players try to hit a small ball into a series of holes using a long, thin stick **golf ● golfer** *noun* [C] **golf oyuncusu** ⊃Orta kısımdaki renkli sayfalarına bakınız.

golf

'**golf ,ball** *noun* [C] a small hard white ball used for playing golf **golf topu**

'**golf ,club** *noun* [C] **1** a place where people can play golf **golf kulübü** **2** a long, thin stick used to play golf **golf sopası** ⊃Orta kısımdaki renkli sayfalarına bakınız.

'**golf ,course** *noun* [C] an area of land used for playing golf **golf sahası**

gone /ɡɒn/ *past participle of* go **'gitmek' fiilinin üçüncü hâli**

gong /ɡɒŋ/ *noun* [C] a metal disc which makes a loud sound when you hit it with a stick **gong**

gonna /ˈɡɒnə/ *informal short for* going to '...ecek, ...acak' yardımcı fiilinin kısa hali

goo /ɡuː/ *noun* [U] a thick, sticky substance **yapışkan madde**

☞**good¹** /ɡʊd/ *adjective* **better, best 1** [PLEASANT] enjoyable, pleasant, or interesting **iyi, hoş, ilginç** *a good book* ○ *Did you have a good time at the party?* **2** [HIGH QUALITY] of a high quality or level **iyi, kaliteli** *She speaks good French.* ○ *The food at this restaurant is very good.* **3** [SUCCESSFUL] successful, or able to do something well **iyi, başarılı** *Anne's a good cook.* ○ *She's very good at geography.* **4** [KIND] kind or helpful **nazik, yardımsever** *a good friend* ○ *My granddaughter is very good to me.* **5** [HEALTHY] something that you say when a person asks how you are **iyi, keyfi yerinde, güzel** *'Hi, how are you?' 'I'm good, thanks.'* **6** [POSITIVE] having a positive or useful effect **iyi gelen, işe yarayan** *Exercise is good for you.* **7** [SUITABLE] suitable or satisfactory **uygun, yerinde, yeterli** *When would be a good time to phone?* **8** [BEHAVIOUR] A good child or animal behaves well. **iyi huylu, iyi** **9** [MORALLY RIGHT] morally right **iyi ahlaklı, iyi** *a good person* ○ *He sets a good example to the rest of the class.* **10** [COMPLETE] complete and detailed **tam ve ayrıntılı** *She got a good look at the robbers.* **11** [LARGE] used to emphasize the number, amount, quality, etc of something **epey, çokça, bir hayli** *There's a good chance he'll pass the exam.* **12** [SATISFACTION] something you say when you are satisfied or pleased about something or when you agree with something **'Ne iyi!', 'Oh!', 'Hele şükür!', 'Ne güzel!'** *Oh good, he's arrived at last.* **13 Good God/grief/heavens!, etc** used to express surprise or shock **'Aman Allah'ım!', 'Aman Yarabbi!'** *Good heavens! It's already 11 p.m.* **14 a good 20 minutes/30 miles, etc** not less than 20 minutes/30 miles and probably a bit more **20 dakikadan/30 milden az olamaz/az değil** ⊃See also: be in sb's good/bad books (book¹), it's a good job, for good measure², stand sb in good stead. **15 good to go** *informal* be ready to go **gitmeye/yola çıkmaya hazır olmak** *I'll get my coat and then I'm good to go.*

good² /ɡʊd/ *noun* **1** [U] something that is an advantage or help to a person or situation **yararına, iyiliğine, çıkarına** *It's hard work, but it's for your own good.* **2 be no good/not any good** to not be useful, helpful, or valuable **hiç yararı/faydası/değeri olmamak** **3 do sb good** to be useful or helpful to someone **iyi gelmek, yardımı olmak, işe yaramak** *A holiday will do you good.* **4** [U] what people think is morally right **iyi,**

G

ahlaken doğru olan *Children don't always understand the difference between good and bad.* **5 for good** forever **temelli, ebediyen, tamamen, sonsuza kadar** *When he was 20, he left home for good.* ➲See also: do sb a/ the **world**[1] of good.

good after'noon *exclamation* something you say to greet someone when you meet them in the afternoon **'Tünaydın!', 'İyi öğleden sonralar!'**

---

goodbye ...... İLE BİRLİKTE KULLANILAN KELİMELER

kiss/say/wave goodbye ● **a final** goodbye

ᵒ⁻**goodbye** /gʊdˈbaɪ/ *exclamation* something you say when you leave someone or when they leave you **'Allah'a ısmarladık!', 'Eyvallah!', 'Hoşçakal!', 'Güle güle!'** *Goodbye Vicki! See you next week.*

good 'evening *exclamation* something you say to greet someone in the evening **'iyi akşamlar!'**

Good 'Friday *noun* [C, U] the Friday before Easter (= a Christian holiday), a day when Christians remember the death of Jesus Christ **(Paskalya öncesi) Kutsal Cuma**

good-humoured UK (US **good-humored**) /ˌgʊdˈhjuːməd/ *adjective* pleasant and friendly **neşeli, şen, candan, eğlenceli, samimi**

goodies /ˈgʊdiz/ *noun* [plural] *informal* special or nice things that you will enjoy **şekerleme, bisküvi, çikolata gibi hoşa giden şeyler** *She gave the children some sweets and other goodies.*

good-looking /ˌgʊdˈlʊkɪŋ/ *adjective* If someone is good-looking, they have an attractive face. **yakışıklı, çekici, güzel** *a good-looking woman*

good 'looks *noun* [plural] an attractive face **çekici/hoş/güzel yüz**

ᵒ⁻**good 'morning** *exclamation* something you say to greet someone when you meet them in the morning **Günaydın!, iyi sabahlar!**

good-natured /ˌgʊdˈneɪtʃəd/ *adjective* pleasant and friendly **uysal, iyi huylu, yumuşak başlı, samimi, sevecen, nazik** *a good-natured smile/crowd*

goodness /ˈgʊdnəs/ *noun* **1** [U] the quality of being good **iyilik, erdem, haslet** *She believes in the goodness of human nature.* **2 my goodness** *informal* something you say when you are surprised **Aman Yarabbi!', 'Allah Allah!', 'Tuh be!', 'Hay Allah!'** *My goodness, he's a big baby, isn't he?* **3 thank goodness** *informal* something you say when you are happy because something bad did not happen **Allah'a şükür, çok şükür, şükürler olsun** *Thank goodness that dog didn't bite you.* **4 for goodness sake** used when you are annoyed or when you want something to happen quickly **'Allah aşkın!' 'Gözünü seveyim!'** *For goodness sake, come in out of the rain.*

ᵒ⁻**good 'night** *exclamation* something you say when you leave someone or when they leave you in the evening or when someone is going to bed **'iyi geceler!'**

ᵒ⁻**goods** /gʊdz/ *noun* **1** [plural] items which are made to be sold **mal, eşya, satış amaçlı üretilmiş olan** *radios, stereos and other electrical goods* **2 deliver/come up with the goods** If you deliver the goods, you do what people hope you will do. **bekleneni yapmak**

goodwill /gʊdˈwɪl/ *noun* [U] kind, friendly, or helpful feelings towards other people **iyi niyet, hoşgörü** *He gave them a thousand pounds as a gesture of goodwill.*

goody-goody /ˈgʊdiˌgʊdi/ *noun* [C] *informal* someone who tries too hard to be good, usually to parents or teachers **iyiliksever olmaya çalışan; iyilik gösterisinde bulunan**

gooey /ˈguːi/ *adjective* soft and sticky **yapış yapış, yumuşak ve yapışkan** *a sweet, gooey sauce*

goof /guːf/ (*also* goof up) *verb* [I] US *informal* to make a silly mistake **aptalca bir hata yapmak**

goof around *phrasal verb* US to spend your time doing silly or unimportant things **aylak aylak /amaçsız dolaşmak**

goof off *phrasal verb* US to avoid doing any work **kaytarmak, yan gelip yatmak, tembellik yapmak**

goofy /ˈguːfi/ *adjective* mainly US silly **aptal, budala** *a goofy sense of humour*

Google[1] /ˈguːgl/ *noun* trademark a popular Internet search engine (= a computer program which finds things on the Internet by looking for words which you have typed in) **bilgisayar arama motoru**

Google[2] /ˈguːgl/ *verb* [T] to use the Google® search engine **Google arama motorunu kullanarak arama yapmak**

goose /guːs/ *noun* [C, U] *plural* **geese** a large water bird similar to a duck, or the meat from this bird **kaz**

gooseberry /ˈgʊzᵇᵊri/ ⓤ⑤ /ˈguːsberi/ *noun* [C] a small, sour, green fruit with a hairy skin **bektaşi üzümü**

'goose ˌpimples (*also* 'goose ˌbumps) *noun* [plural] small, raised lumps that appear on your skin when you are cold or frightened **tüylerin diken diken olması**

gore[1] /gɔːʳ/ *noun* [U] blood, usually from a violent injury **şiddetli yaralamadan oluşan kan, pıhtılaşmış kan**

gore[2] /gɔːʳ/ *verb* [T] If an animal gores someone, it injures them with its horn. **boynuzlamak, boynuzlayarak yaralamak, süsmek**

gorge[1] /gɔːdʒ/ *noun* [C] a narrow and usually steep valley **dik yamaçlı geçit, dar vadi**

gorge[2] /gɔːdʒ/ *verb* **gorge (yourself) on sth** to eat food until you cannot eat any more **patlayıncaya kadar yemek, tıka basa yemek** *She gorged herself on chocolate biscuits.*

gorgeous /ˈgɔːdʒəs/ *adjective* very beautiful or pleasant **çok güzel, hoş, harika, olağanüstü** *You look gorgeous in that dress.*

gorilla /gəˈrɪlə/ *noun* [C] a big, black, hairy animal, like a large monkey **goril**

gorse /gɔːs/ *noun* [U] a bush with yellow flowers and sharp, pointed leaves **kara çalı**

gory /ˈgɔːri/ *adjective* involving violence and blood **şiddet ve kan içeren** *a gory murder*

gosh /gɒʃ/ *exclamation* used to express surprise or shock **'Allah Allah!', 'Hay Allah!', 'Vay canına!', 'Vay anasını!', 'Aman Allah'ım!** *Gosh! I didn't realize it was that late.*

gosling /ˈgɒzlɪŋ/ *noun* [C] a young goose (= large water bird) **kaz yavrusu/palazı**

gospel /ˈgɒspᵊl/ *noun* **1** TEACHING [no plural] the teachings of Jesus Christ **incil** *to preach the gospel* **2** BOOK [C] one of the four books in the Bible that tells the life of Jesus Christ **İncil'deki dört kitaptan birisi 3 the gospel truth** something that is completely true **mutlak gerçek, asıl, esas 4** MUSIC [U] a style of Christian music, originally sung by black Americans **orijinal olarak siyahi Amerikalılarca söylenen bir tür Hıristiyan müziği**

 **gossip** ...... İLE BİRLİKTE KULLANILAN KELİMELER

a bit of/piece of gossip ● **juicy** gossip

---

gossip[1] /ˈgɒsɪp/ *noun* **1** [U] conversation or reports about other people's private lives that might or might not be true **dedikodu, söylenti, asılsız söz** *an interes-*

ting **piece of gossip** 2 [C] someone who likes to talk about other people's private lives **dedikoducu**

gossip² /'gɒsɪp/ *verb* [I] to talk about other people's private lives **dedikodu yapmak; asılsız söz/söylenti yaymak** *They were gossiping about her boss.*

'gossip ˌcolumn *noun* [C] an article appearing regularly in a newspaper giving information about famous people's private lives **dedikodu sütunu**

got /gɒt/ *past of* get **'almak' fiilinin ikinci hali**

gotta /'gɒtə/ *informal short for* got to 'got to' fiilinin kısaltılmış hâli

gotten /'gɒtªn/ *US past participle of* get **'almak' fiilinin üçüncü hâli**

gouge /gaʊdʒ/ *verb* [T] to make a hole or long cut in something **oymak, derin yarık açmak**
gouge sth out *phrasal verb* to remove something by digging or cutting it out of a surface, often violently **oymak, oyup çıkarmak**

gourmet¹ /'gʊəmeɪ/ *noun* [C] someone who enjoys good food and drink and knows a lot about it **yiyeceklerden anlayan, ağzının tadını bilen, gurme**

gourmet² /'gʊəmeɪ/ *adjective* [always before noun] relating to good food and drink **kaliteli yiyecek ve içeceğe ilişkin** *a gourmet meal*

govern /'gʌvªn/ *verb* 1 [I, T] to officially control a country **yönetmek, idare etmek** *The country is now governed by the Labour Party.* ○ *a governing body* 2 [T] to influence or control the way something happens or is done **etkilemek, belirlemek, yönlendirmek** *There are rules that govern how teachers treat children.*

governess /'gʌvªnəs/ *noun* [C] a woman employed to teach the children in a family at home **evde eğitim veren öğretmen, dadı, özel hoca**

🧩 **government** .... İLE BİRLİKTE KULLANILAN KELİMELER

bring down/elect/form/overthrow a government ● a **democratic/elected** government ● **be in** government

o⌐**government** /'gʌvªnmənt/ *noun* 1 [group] the group of people who officially control a country **hükümet** *The Government has cut taxes.* 2 [U] the method or process of governing a country **yönetme, yönetim, idare, erk** *a new style of government* ● **governmental** /ˌgʌvªn'mentªl/ *adjective* relating to government **idari, hükümete ilişkin**

governor /'gʌvªnəʳ/ *noun* [C] someone who is officially responsible for controlling a region, city, or organization **vali, yönetici, idareci, guvernör** *a prison/school governor* ○ *the Governor of Texas*

gown /gaʊn/ *noun* [C] 1 a woman's dress, usually worn on formal occasions **tuvalet, uzun elbise, gece elbisesi** *a silk gown* 2 a loose piece of clothing like a coat worn for a particular purpose **cüppe** *a hospital gown* ⊃See also: dressing gown.

GP /ˌdʒiː'piː/ *noun* [C] *abbreviation for* general practitioner: a doctor who sees people in the local area and treats illnesses that do not need a hospital visit **Pratisyen Hekim**

GPS /ˌdʒiːpiː'es/ *noun* [U] *abbreviation for* Global Positioning System: a system of computers and satellites (= equipment that is sent into space around the Earth to receive and send signals) that work together to tell a user where they are **Küresel Konumlandırma Sistemi (KKS)**

o⌐**grab¹** /græb/ *verb* [T] **grabbing**, *past* **grabbed** 1 [TAKE SUDDENLY] to take hold of something or someone suddenly **tutmak, yakalamak, kapmak** *He grabbed my arm and pulled me away.* 2 [DO QUICKLY] *informal* to

eat, do, or get something quickly because you do not have much time **hızlıca atıştırmak, çabuk çabuk yemek** *I grabbed a sandwich on the way to the station.* 3 **grab sb's attention** *informal* to attract someone's attention **dikkatini çekmek/celbetmek** 4 [TAKE OPPORTUNITY] If someone grabs a chance or opportunity, they take it quickly and with enthusiasm. (**şans, fırsat) atlamak, kaçırmamak, sarılmak, üstüne atlamak**
grab at sb/sth *phrasal verb* to try to get hold of someone or something quickly, with your hand **elle yakalamaya çalışmak, tutmak, kavramak**

grab² /græb/ *noun* 1 **make a grab for sth/sb** to try to take hold of something or someone suddenly **davranmak, sarılmak, atılmak, tutmaya/almaya/yakalamaya çalışmak** *He made a grab for the gun.* 2 **up for grabs** *informal* If something is up for grabs, it is available to anyone who wants to try to get it. **serbest, ortak kullanıma açık** *Ten free concert tickets are up for grabs.*

grace¹ /greɪs/ *noun* [U] 1 [MOVEMENT] the quality of moving in a smooth, relaxed, and attractive way **zarafet** *She moved with grace and elegance.* 2 [POLITENESS] the quality of being pleasantly polite **nezaket** *He had the grace to apologize for his mistake the next day.* 3 **with good grace** in a willing and happy way **memnuniyetle, tevekkülle** *He accepted the failure with good grace.* 4 **a month's/week's, etc grace** an extra month/week, etc you are given before something must be paid or done **fazladan verilen ay/hafta; lütuf olarak sunulan ay/hafta; ilave mühlet** 5 [PRAYER] a prayer of thanks said before or after a meal **yemeklerden önce/sonra edilen şükür duası** *to say grace*

grace² /greɪs/ *verb* [T] When a person or object graces a place or thing, they make it more attractive. **şereflendirmek, şeref vermek, teşrif etmek** *Her face has graced the covers of magazines across the world.*

graceful /'greɪsfªl/ *adjective* 1 moving in a smooth, relaxed, and attractive way, or having a smooth, attractive shape **zarif, hoş** *graceful movements* ○ *a graceful neck* 2 behaving in a polite and pleasant way **nazik, nezaketli, saygılı, hürmetli** ● **gracefully** *adverb* **nazik, hoş bir şekilde**

gracious /'greɪʃəs/ *adjective* 1 behaving in a pleasant, polite, calm way **asil, nazik, sakin, saygılı** *He was gracious enough to thank me.* 2 comfortable and with a good appearance and quality **gösterişli, debdebeli, rahat ve kaliteli, saltanatlı** *gracious homes/living* 3 **Good/Goodness gracious!** used to express polite surprise **'Aman Allah'ım!'** ● **graciously** *adverb* **nazik bir şekilde**

grade¹ /greɪd/ *noun* [C] 1 [SCORE] a number or letter that shows how good someone's work or performance is **not, derece, puan** *Steve never studies, but he always gets good grades.* ○ *(UK) Carla got a grade A in German.* 2 [LEVEL] a level of quality, size, importance, etc **derece, kalite** *I applied for a position a grade higher than my current job.* 3 [SCHOOL GROUP] *US* a school class or group of classes for students of the same age or ability **seviye, kur, seviye grubu** *My son is in fifth grade.* 4 **make the grade** to perform well enough to succeed **becermek, başarmak, yeterli başarıya ulaşmak** *He wanted to get into the team but he didn't make the grade.*

grade² /greɪd/ *verb* [T] 1 to separate people or things into different levels of quality, size, importance, etc **derecelere ayırmak, (kalite, ölçü ve önemliliğine göre) seviyelere ayırmak** *The fruit is washed and then graded by size.* 2 *US* (*UK* mark) to give a score to a student's piece of work **puanlamak, puan vermek, değerlendirmek** *to grade work/papers*

'grade ,crossing *US* (*UK* **level crossing**) *noun* [C] a place where a railway crosses a road **hemzemin geçit**

'grade ,school *noun* [C, U] *US* a school for the first six to eight years of a child's education **ilköğretim okulu**

gradient /'greɪdiənt/ *noun* [C] how steep a slope is **eğim, meyil** *a steep/gentle gradient*

o▪**gradual** /'grædʒuəl/ *adjective* happening slowly over a period of time **azar azar, yavaş yavaş** *a gradual change/improvement*

o▪**gradually** /'grædʒuəli/ *adverb* slowly over a period of time **azar azar, zamanla** *Gradually he began to get better.*

graduate¹ /'grædʒuət/ *noun* [C] **1** *UK* someone who has studied for and received a degree (= qualification) from a university **üniversite mezunu** *a science graduate* **2** *US* someone who has studied for and received a degree (= qualification) from a school, college, or university **mezun** *a high-school graduate*

graduate² /'grædʒueɪt/ *verb* **1** [I] to complete your education successfully at a university, college, or, in the US, at school (**üniversite, yüksekokul vb.**) **mezun olmak; (ABD) herhangi bir okuldan mezun olmak** *He graduated from Cambridge University in 2006.* **2 graduate to sth** to move up to something more advanced or important **dah üst/ileri bir düzeye yükselmek, ilerlemek, terfi etmek**

graduated /'grædʒueɪtɪd/ *adjective* divided into levels or stages **seviye ve safhalara ayrılmış; seviyelendirilmiş** *a graduated scale*

graduation /,grædʒu'eɪʃᵊn/ *noun* [C, U] when you receive your degree (= qualification) for completing your education or a course of study **mezuniyet** *a graduation ceremony*

graffiti

graffiti /grə'fiːti/ *noun* [U] writing or pictures painted on walls and public places, usually illegally **duvar yazısı**

graft¹ /grɑːft/ *noun* **1** SKIN/BONE [C] a piece of skin or bone taken from one part of a body and joined to another part (**kemik, deri, uzuv parçası vb.**) **yama, ek** *a skin/bone graft* **2** PLANT [C] a piece cut from one plant and joined onto another plant (**bitki, ağaç vb.**) **aşı 3** WORK [U] *UK informal* work **iş, amel** *hard graft*

graft² /grɑːft/ *verb* **1** SKIN/BONE [T] to join a piece of skin or bone taken from one part of the body to another part **yama/ek yapmak; eklemek, yamamak 2** PLANT [T] to join a piece cut from one plant onto another plant (**bitki, ağaç vb.**) **aşı yapmak, aşılamak 3** WORK [I] *UK informal* to work hard **sıkı çalışmak, çok ter dökmek**

grain /greɪn/ *noun* **1** SEED [C, U] a seed or seeds from types of grass which are eaten as food **tahıl** *grains of wheat/rice* **2** PIECE [C] a very small piece of something **tanecik, zerre** *a grain of sand/sugar* **3** QUALITY [no plural] a very small amount of a quality **azıcık, çok az miktar, zerrecik** *There isn't a grain of truth in her story.* **4 the grain** the natural direction and pattern of lines which you can see in wood or material (**ahşap, taş, kaya, mermer, demir vb.**) **damar** *to cut something along/against the grain* **5 go against the grain** If something goes against the grain, you would not normally do it because it would be unusual or morally wrong. **ilkelerine aykırı olmak, yapısına ters olmak** ⊃See also: take sth with a pinch of **salt¹**.

gram (*also UK* **gramme**) (*written abbreviation* **g, gm**) /græm/ *noun* [C] a unit for measuring weight, equal to 0.001 kilograms **gram**

o▪**grammar** /'græməʳ/ *noun* **1** [U] the way you combine words and change their form and position in a sentence, or the rules or study of this **dilbilgisi 2** [C] *mainly UK* a book of grammar rules **dilbilgisi kitabı**

'grammar ,school *noun* [C, U] **1** in the UK, a school which clever children over 11 years old can go to if they pass a special exam (**Birleşik Krallık**) **özel bir sınavı başardıktan sonra 11 yaş üzeri zeki çocukların gittiği okul 2** *US* another word for elementary school (= a school for children from the ages of five to eleven in the US) (**ABD**) **ilköğretim okulu**

grammatical /grə'mætɪkᵊl/ *adjective* relating to grammar, or obeying the rules of grammar **dilbilgisine ait/ilişkin; dilbilgisi kurallarına uyan** *grammatical rules* ○ *a grammatical sentence* ● **grammatically** *adverb* **dilbilgisi açısından**

gramme /græm/ *noun* [C] another UK spelling of gram **gram**

gramophone /'græməfəʊn/ *noun* [C] *old-fashioned* a machine for playing music **gramofon**

gran /græn/ *noun* [C] *UK informal short for* grandmother **anneanne, babaanne, büyükanne**

grand¹ /grænd/ *adjective* **1** LARGE very large and special **görkemli, büyük, heybetli** *a grand hotel* ○ *the Grand Canal* **2** IMPORTANT rich and important, or behaving as if you are **zengin ve önemli, öylemiş gibi davranan** *a grand old lady* **3** GOOD *informal* very good or enjoyable **çok iyi, harika, zevk veren**

grand² /grænd/ *noun* [C] *plural* **grand** *informal* one thousand dollars or pounds **bin dolar/pound** *The holiday cost me two grand.*

grandad /'grændæd/ *noun* [C] *another UK spelling of* granddad **dede, büyükbaba**

grandchild /'græntʃaɪld/ *noun* [C] *plural* **grandchildren** the child of your son or daughter **torun**

granddad /'grændæd/ *noun* [C] *mainly UK informal* grandfather **dede, büyükbaba**

granddaughter /'grænd,dɔːtəʳ/ *noun* [C] the daughter of your son or daughter **kız torun**

grandeur /'grændjəʳ/ *noun* [U] the quality of being very large and special or beautiful **görkem, ihtişam, heybet** *the grandeur of the hills*

o▪**grandfather** /'grænd,fɑːðəʳ/ *noun* [C] the father of your mother or father **dede, büyükbaba**

,grandfather 'clock *noun* [C] a clock in a very tall, wooden case **sarkaçlı büyük dolaplı saat**

grandiose /'grændiəʊs/ *adjective* large or detailed and made to appear important, often in an unnecessary and annoying way **görkemli, şaşaalı, tantanalı, pek gösterişli** *grandiose plans*

grandly /'grændli/ *adverb* in a very important way, or as if you are very important **önemli şekilde, sanki önemliymiş gibi**

grandma /'grændmɑː/ *noun* [C] *informal another word for* grandmother **büyükanne**

o⁻**grandmother** /'grænd,mʌðər/ *noun* [C] the mother of your mother or father **anneanne, babaanne, büyükanne**

grandpa /'grændpɑː/ *noun* [C] *informal another word for* grandfather **dede, büyükbaba**

grandparent /'grænd,peərᵊnt/ *noun* [C] the parent of your mother or father **dede veya nine, büyükbaba veya büyükanne**

grand pi'ano *noun* [C] a very large piano, usually used in public performances **kuyruklu piyano**

grand prix /,grɒn'priː/ *noun* [C] *plural* **grands prix** one of a series of important international races for very fast cars **araba yarışlarında uluslararası serilerden biri** *the Italian Grand Prix*

grand 'slam *noun* [C] when you win all the important competitions that are held in one year for a particular sport **büyük başarı, sporda önemli tüm yarışmaların tamamını kazanmış olma**

grandson /'grændsʌn/ *noun* [C] the son of your son or daughter **erkek torun**

grandstand /'grændstænd/ *noun* [C] a large, open structure containing rows of seats, used for watching sporting events **tribün**

granite /'grænɪt/ *noun* [U] a type of very hard, grey rock **granit**

granny /'græni/ *noun* [C] *informal another word for* grandmother **anneanne, babaanne, büyükanne**

grant¹ /grɑːnt/ *verb* **1** [T] *formal* to give or allow someone something, usually in an official way **vermek, tahsis etmek** [+ **two objects**] *to grant someone a licence/visa* **2** [T] *formal* to admit or agree that something is true **kabul etmek** *She's a good-looking woman, I grant you.* **3 take sb/sth for granted** to not show that you are grateful for someone or something, and forget that you are lucky to have them **doğal karşılamak, olağan kabul etmek** *Most of us take our freedom for granted.* ● **take it for granted** to believe that something is true without checking or thinking about it **...olduğu gibi kabul etmek; tabii bulmak; tartışmasız kabul etmek** [+ (that)] *I took it for granted that we'd be invited.*

🧩 **grant** ...... İLE BİRLİKTE KULLANILAN KELİMELER

apply for/get/receive a grant ● a grant for/towards sth ● a research grant

grant² /grɑːnt/ *noun* [C] an amount of money provided by a government or organization for a special purpose **ödenek, tahsisat, burs, tediye** *They received a research grant for the project.*

granule /'grænjuːl/ *noun* [C] a small, hard piece of a substance **tanecik, zerre, kırıntı, parçacık** *coffee granules* ● **granulated** /'grænjəleɪtɪd/ *adjective* **granulated sugar** **tanecik haline getirilmiş**

grape /greɪp/ *noun* [C] a small, round, green, purple or red fruit that grows in large, close groups and is often used to make wine **üzüm** *a bunch of grapes* ⊃ Orta kısımdaki renkli sayfalarına bakınız.

grapefruit /'greɪpfruːt/ *noun* [C, U] *plural* **grapefruit** or **grapefruits** a large, round, yellow fruit with a sour taste **greyfurt**

grapevine /'greɪpvaɪn/ *noun* **hear sth on/through the grapevine** to hear news from someone who heard the news from someone else **kulaktan kulağa geçmek/**

ulaşmak; başkasının başkasından duyduğunu **duymak/öğrenmek**

🧩 **graph** ...... İLE BİRLİKTE KULLANILAN KELİMELER

draw a graph ● a graph indicates/shows sth ● a graph of sth

graph /grɑːf/ *noun* [C] a picture with measurements marked on it as lines or curves, used to compare different things or show the development of something **grafik, tablo**

graph

graphic¹ /'græfɪk/ *adjective* A graphic description or image is extremely clear and detailed. **canlı, açı seçik, ayrıntılı** *The film contains graphic violence.* ● **graphically** *adverb* **çizgisel**

graphical user 'interface *noun* [C] a way of arranging information on a computer screen that is easy to understand because it uses pictures and symbols as well as words **sözcüklerin yanı sıra resim ve imgelerin de kullanımıyla anlaşılmayı kolaylaştıran bilgisayar ekranında bilginin düzenlenmesi**

graphic de'sign *noun* [U] the art of designing pictures and text for books, magazines, advertisements, etc **grafik tasarım**

graphics /'græfɪks/ *noun* [plural] images shown on a computer screen **grafik**

graphite /'græfaɪt/ *noun* [U] a soft, grey-black form of carbon used in pencils **grafit**

grapple /'græpl/ *verb*
grapple with sth *phrasal verb* to try to deal with or understand something difficult **baş etmeye çalışmak, boğuşmak, zor bir şeyi çözmeye/anlamaya çalışmak** *I had been grappling with the question for some years.*
grapple with sb *phrasal verb* to hold onto someone and fight with them **yakalayıp boğuşmak**

grasp¹ /grɑːsp/ *verb* [T] **1** to take hold of something or someone firmly **sımsıkı tutmak, yakalamak, kavramak** *He grasped my hand enthusiastically.* **2** to understand something **anlamak, manayı çözmek, kavramak** *I find these mathematical problems difficult to grasp.*
grasp at sth *phrasal verb* to quickly try to get hold of something **acele yakalayıp tutmak** *He grasped at the rope that was thrown to him.*

🧩 **grasp** ...... İLE BİRLİKTE KULLANILAN KELİMELER

have a [good/poor, etc] grasp of sth

grasp² /grɑːsp/ *noun* [no plural] **1** [UNDERSTAND] when you understand something **anlama, kavrama** *He has an excellent grasp of English.* **2** [HOLD] when you hold onto someone or something **tutma, yakalama, yapışma** *I tried to pull him out but he slipped from my grasp.* **3** [ABILITY] the ability to obtain or achieve something **başarabilme, elde edebilme** *Victory is within our grasp.*

grasping /'grɑːspɪŋ/ *adjective* wanting much more of something than you need, especially money **aç gözlü, gözü doymaz, haris** *a grasping, greedy man*

o⁻**grass** /grɑːs/ *noun* **1** [U] a common plant with narrow green leaves that grows close to the ground in gardens and fields **çimen, yeşillik, ot** *to mow/cut the grass* ○ *We lay on the grass in the sunshine.* **2** [C] a particular type of grass **çim** *ornamental grasses*

G

grasshopper /'grɑːs
ˌhɒpəʳ/ *noun* [C] a green
insect which jumps
about using its long
back legs **çekirge**

grasshopper

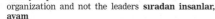

grass 'roots *noun* [plural]
ordinary people in a
society or political
organization and not the leaders **sıradan insanlar,
avam**

grassy /'grɑːsi/ *adjective* covered with grass **çimenli,
otlu, yeşillikli** *a grassy slope/meadow*

grate¹ /greɪt/ *verb* **1** [T] to break food such as cheese into
small, thin pieces by rubbing it against a grater (= kitchen tool with holes) **rendelemek** *grated cheese/carrot*
2 [I] to make an unpleasant noise when rubbing against
something **sürterek/sürtünerek ses çıkar(t)mak**
The chair grated against the floor.
grate on sb/sth *phrasal verb* If someone's voice or behaviour grates on you, it annoys you. **sinirine dokunmak, kızdırmak, sinirlendirmeye başlamak**

grate² /greɪt/ *noun* [C] a metal structure for holding the
wood or coal in a fireplace **ocak/şömine ızgarası**

grateful ...... BAŞKA BİR DEYİŞLE

Kişi bir konu ile ilgili minettar ise, bu duygusunu dile
getirmek için **appreciative** sıfatı kullanılabilir veya
aynı fikir için **appreciate** fiili kullanılabilir. *I'm
really* **appreciative** *of all the help you've given me.* • *I
really* **appreciate** *all the help you've given me.*
be glad of ifadesi başka bir alternatif olarak kullanılabilir. *We were very* **glad of** *some extra help.*
Kişinin minnettarlığını belirtmede **be indebted to**
daha resmi bir ifade olarak kullanılabilir. *I'm
indebted to my parents for all their love and support.*
Thankful ya da **relieved** sıfatları kötü bir şey meydana gelmediği için minnettarlık duyan kişinin duygularını ifade etmekte kullanılır. *I'm just* **thankful/
relieved** *that she's safe and well.*
Eğer kişi bir diğerinin yaptığı kibarlığa minnettar
ise, **touched** sıfatı kullanılabilir. *She was really*
touched *that he remembered her birthday.*

•—**grateful** /'greɪtfʰl/ *adjective* feeling or showing thanks
minnettar, müteşekkir, şükran duyan *I'm really
grateful to you for all your help.* ⊃Opposite **ungrateful.**
• **gratefully** *adverb* All donations *gratefully received.*
minnetkar bir şekilde

YAYGIN HATALAR

grateful

Dikkat! Yazılışını kontrol ediniz. **Grateful** Türk öğrencileri tarafından en çok yanlış yazılan 10 kelimeden
biridir. Unutmayın! Doğru yazılışında **ate** kullanılır.
eat kullanılmaz.

grater /'greɪtəʳ/ *noun* [C] a kitchen tool with a surface
full of holes with sharp edges, used to grate (= break
into small pieces) foods such as cheese **rende** ⊃Orta
kısımdaki renkli sayfalarına bakınız.

gratify /'grætɪfaɪ/ *verb* [T] *formal* to please someone or
satisfy their wishes or needs **sevindirmek, kıvanç
duymasını sağlamak; tatmin etmek** *I was gratified
by their decision.* ○ *a gratifying result* • **gratification**
/ˌgrætɪfɪˈkeɪʃʰn/ *noun* [U] **memnuniyet**

grating /'greɪtɪŋ/ *noun* [C] a flat structure made of long,
thin pieces of metal crossing each other over a hole in
the ground or a window **pencere parmaklığı/kafesi,
ızgara**

gratitude /'grætɪtjuːd/ *noun* [U] the feeling or quality of
being grateful **şükran, iyilik bilme, minnettarlık** *I
would like to express my deep gratitude to all the hospital
staff.*

gratuitous /grəˈtjuːɪtəs/ *adjective* unnecessary and
done without a good reason **sebepsiz, keyfi, nedensiz,
uluorta** *gratuitous violence*

gratuity /grəˈtjuːəti/ *noun* [C] *formal* an extra amount of
money given to someone to thank them for providing a
service **hizmet karşılığı verilen fazla ödeme/para;
ilave ödeme**

•—**grave¹** /greɪv/ *noun* [C] a place in the ground where a
dead body is buried **mezar, kabir**

grave² /greɪv/ *adjective* very serious **çok ciddi, vahim,
ağır başlı, vakur** *grave doubts* ○ *a grave mistake*
• **gravely** *adverb* **ciddi bir şekilde**

gravel /'grævʰl/ *noun* [U] small pieces of stone used to
make paths and road surfaces **çakıl taşı**

gravestone /'greɪvstəʊn/ *noun* [C] a stone that shows
the name of a dead person who is buried under it
mezar taşı

graveyard /'greɪvjɑːd/ *noun* [C] an area of land where
dead bodies are buried, usually next to a church
mezarlık, kabristan

gravitate /'grævɪteɪt/ *verb*
gravitate to/towards sth/sb *phrasal verb* to be
attracted to something or someone, or to move in the
direction of something or someone **cazibesine kapılmak; ...e/a doğru yönelmek/hareket etmek**

gravitational /ˌgrævɪˈteɪʃʰnʰl/ *adjective* relating to
gravity **yer çekimine ilişkin** *gravitational force*

gravity /'grævəti/ *noun* [U] **1** the force that makes
objects fall to the ground or that pulls objects towards
a planet or other body **yer çekimi** *the laws of gravity*
2 *formal* when something is very serious **ağırlık, ciddiyet, vahamet, önem** *You don't seem to realize the gravity of the situation.* ⊃See also: **centre of gravity.**

gravy /'greɪvi/ *noun* [U] a warm, brown sauce made from
the fat and liquid that comes from meat when it is being
cooked **et suyu, et suyu sosu**

•—**gray** /greɪ/ *noun* [C, U], *adjective* US spelling of grey **gri,
kül rengi**

graying /'greɪɪŋ/ *adjective* US spelling of greying (= having hair that is becoming grey or white) **(saç) kırlaşan,
grileşen, aklaşan**

graze¹ /greɪz/ *verb* **1** [EAT] [I] When cows or other animals
graze, they eat grass. **otlamak, otlatmak** *Cattle grazed
in the meadow.* **2** [INJURE] [T] *UK (UK/US* skin*)* to injure your
skin by rubbing it against something rough **sürtüp
yaralamak, sürtünmek** *I fell and grazed my knee.*
3 [TOUCH] [T] to touch or move lightly along the surface
or edge of something **sıyırıp/yalayıp geçmek, sıyırmak** *A bullet grazed his cheek.*

graze² /greɪz/ *noun* [C] *mainly UK* an injury on the surface of your skin caused by rubbing against something
sıyrık, yara bere *She has a nasty graze on her elbow.*

grease¹ /griːs/ *noun* [U] **1** a substance such as oil or fat
gres yağı, gres, koyu makine yağı 2 a substance like
thick oil that is put on parts in an engine or machine to
make them move more smoothly **makine parçalarını
yağlamaya yarayan koyu kıvamlı yağ**

grease² /griːs/ *verb* [T] to put fat or oil on or in something **yağlamak**

greasy /'griːsi/ *adjective* containing or covered with fat
or oil **yağlanmış, yağ içinde, yağlı** *greasy food/fingers*

○―**great** /greɪt/ *adjective* **1** EXCELLENT very good **mükemmel, çok iyi** *We had a great time.* ○ *I've had a great idea!* **2** IMPORTANT important or famous **önemli, ünlü, meşhur, heyecan verici** *a great statesman/novelist* **3** LARGE large in amount, size, or degree **büyük, kocaman, iri** *a great crowd of people* **4** EXTREME extreme **büyük, önemli, son derece büyük** *great success/difficulty* **5 great big/long, etc** very big/long, etc **çok büyük/uzun** *I gave her a great big hug.* **6 a great many** a large number **çok fazla, epey, bir hayli, büyük miktarda/sayıda** ● **greatness** *noun* [U] ➲See also: go to great lengths (**length**) to do sth, set great store¹ by sth, the best/greatest **thing** since sliced bread. **muhteşemlik**

great- /greɪt/ *prefix* **1 great-grandfather/-grandmother** the father/mother of your grandfather or grandmother **büyük büyük baba/anne 2 great-aunt/-uncle** the aunt/uncle of your mother or father **büyük teyze/hala/amca 3 great-grandchild/-granddaughter, etc** the child/daughter, etc of your grandson or granddaughter **büyük torun/kız torun vb. 4 great-niece/-nephew** the daughter/son of your niece or nephew **büyük yeğen/kuzen**

greatly /'greɪtli/ *adverb* very much **oldukça, çok fazla, iyice, adamakıllı, olabildiğince** *I greatly admire your paintings.* ○ *We will miss her greatly.*

greed /griːd/ *noun* [U] when you want a lot more food, money, etc, than you need **açgözlülük, tamahkârlık, hırs**

greedy /'griːdi/ *adjective* wanting a lot more food, money, etc, than you need **açgözlü, hırslı, gözünü/mal mülk/para bürümüş, açgözlü** *greedy, selfish people* ○ *They were greedy for money.* ● **greedily** *adverb* **aç gözlü bir şekilde** ● **greediness** *noun* [U] **açgözlülük**

Greek /griːk/ *adjective* relating to the culture, language, or people of Greece or ancient Greece **Yunanca, Eski Yunan'a ait**

○―**green¹** /griːn/ *adjective* **1** COLOUR being the same colour as grass **yeşil** *The traffic lights turned green.* ➲Orta kısımdaki renkli sayfalarına bakınız. **2** ENVIRONMENT [always before noun] relating to nature and protecting the environment **tabiatı/çevreyi korumaya ilişkin** *a green activist/campaigner* **3** GRASS covered with grass or other plants **yeşil, yeşillik, çimenlik** *green spaces* **4** NOT EXPERIENCED *informal* having little experience or understanding **tecrübesiz, acemi** *I was very green when I joined the company.* **5 be green with envy** to wish very much that you had something that another person has **kıskançlıktan çatlamak; hasetlik etmek** ➲See also: have green fingers (**finger¹**), **green¹**

○―**green²** /griːn/ *noun* **1** COLOUR [C, U] the colour of grass **çim/çimen rengi, yeşil** ➲Orta kısımdaki renkli sayfalarına bakınız. **2** GOLF [C] a special area of very short, smooth grass on a golf course (**golf sahası**) **düz çimenlik** *the 18th green* **3** VILLAGE [C] an area of grass in the middle of a village **çayır, çimenlik; yeşil mera**

green ˌbelt *noun* [C] an area of land around a city or town where no new building is allowed **şehir ve kasaba çevresindeki iskâna kapalı yeşil kuşak**

ˌgreen 'card *noun* [C] an official document allowing a foreigner to live and work in the US permanently (**ABD**) **çalışma ve ikâmete imkân sağlayan yeşil kart**

greenery /'griːnᵊri/ *noun* [U] green leaves, plants, or branches **yeşillik, nebat**

greenfield /'griːnfiːld/ *adjective* UK describes land where there were no buildings before, or buildings on land that have never had buildings **yeşil alan, yeşilliklerle kaplı alan** *a greenfield site* ➲Compare **brownfield**.

greengrocer /'griːnˌɡrəʊsər/ *noun* [C] UK **1 greengrocer's** a shop where you buy fruit and vegetables **manav dükkânı, zerzavat satan dükkân 2** someone who sells fruit and vegetables **manav, sebze/meyve satıcısı**

greenhouse /'griːnhaʊs/ *noun* [C] *plural* **greenhouses** /'griːnhaʊzɪz/ a building made of glass for growing plants in **sera**

the ˌgreenhouse efˌfect *noun* the gradual warming of the Earth's surface caused by an increase in pollution and gases in the air **sera etkisi**

ˌgreenhouse 'gas *noun* [C] a gas which causes the greenhouse effect, especially carbon dioxide (= a gas produced when carbon is burned) **sera etkisi yaratan gaz**

ˌgreen 'light *noun* [no plural] permission to do something **izin, müsaade** [+ to do sth] *They've been given the green light to build two new supermarkets.*

the ˌGreen ˌParty *noun* [group] a political party whose main aim is to protect the environment **Yeşiller Partisi**

greens /griːnz/ *noun* [plural] green leaves that are cooked and eaten as a vegetable **yenilebilen sebze yaprakları, yeşillikler**

greet /griːt/ *verb* [T] **1** to welcome someone **selamlamak, karşılamak, selam vermek** *He greeted me at the door.* **2** to react to something in a particular way **karşılamak, tepki verilmek/almak** [often passive] *His story was greeted with shrieks of laughter.*

greeting /'griːtɪŋ/ *noun* [C] *formal* something friendly or polite that you say or do when you meet or welcome someone **selâm**

gregarious /ɡrɪ'ɡeəriəs/ *adjective* If you are gregarious, you enjoy being with other people. **insan canlısı, topluluğu seven, sokulgan, sosyal olmaktan hoşlanan**

grenade /ɡrə'neɪd/ *noun* [C] a small bomb that is thrown or fired from a weapon **küçük bomba, silahla atılabilen/ateşlenebilen bomba**

grew /ɡruː/ *past tense of* grow **'büyümek' fiilinin ikinci hali**

○―**grey¹** UK (US gray) /ɡreɪ/ *adjective* **1** COLOUR being a colour that is a mixture of black and white **gri, kül rengi** *grey clouds* ➲Orta kısımdaki renkli sayfalarına bakınız. **2** HAIR having hair that has become grey or white **kır saçlı, ağırmış saçlı** *She went grey in her thirties.* **3** WEATHER cloudy and not bright (**hava**) **bulutlu, açık olmayan, kasvetli** *a cold, grey morning* **4** BORING not interesting or attractive **sıkıcı, çekici olmayan** *Life was grey and tedious.* **5 grey area** something which people are not certain about, usually because there are no clear rules for it **gri bölge, belli belirsiz alan/yer/bölge**

○―**grey²** UK (US gray) /ɡreɪ/ *noun* [C, U] a colour that is a mixture of black and white **gri renk** ➲Orta kısımdaki renkli sayfalarına bakınız.

greyhound /'ɡreɪhaʊnd/ *noun* [C] a thin dog with short hair that runs very fast, sometimes in races **tazı**

greying UK (US graying) /'ɡreɪɪŋ/ *adjective* having hair that is becoming grey or white **kırlaşmış, ağarmış**

grid /ɡrɪd/ *noun* **1** PATTERN [C] a pattern or structure made from horizontal and vertical lines crossing each other to form squares **birbirini yatay ve dikey çizgilerle kesen karelerden oluşan koordinat sistemi, kareler düzeni 2** POWER [no plural] a system of connected wires used to supply electrical power to a large area **elektrik şebekesi** *the National Grid* **3** MAP [C] a pattern of squares with numbers or letters used to find places on a map **karelerden ve rakamlardan oluşan koordinat sistemi**

gridlock /'grɪdlɒk/ *noun* [U] when the traffic cannot move in any direction because all of the roads are blocked with cars **trafik tıkanıklığı/sıkışıklığı**

grief /griːf/ *noun* **1** [U] great sadness, especially caused by someone's death **ıstırap, üzüntü, keder 2 Good grief!** *informal* something that you say when you are surprised or annoyed '**Vay canına!**', '**Hoppala!**', '**Vay be!**' **3 come to grief** *informal* to suddenly fail or have an accident **başı belaya girmek, kazaya/felakete uğramak, belaya çatmak ● 4 cause/give sb grief** *informal* to annoy someone or cause trouble or problems for them **kedere yol açmak, sorun yaratmak, birinin başına dert açmak**

grievance /'griːvºns/ *noun* [C] *formal* a complaint, especially about unfair behaviour **yakınma, dövünme, şikayet, dertlenme**

grieve /griːv/ *verb* **1** [I] to feel or express great sadness, especially when someone dies **acı çekmek, elem duymak, üzüntü yaşamak, yas tutmak** *He is still grieving for his wife.* **2** [T] *formal* to make someone feel very sad **elem vermek, üzmek, kederlendirmek**

grievous /'griːvəs/ *adjective formal* very serious **feci, çok ciddi, elem dolu, çok üzücü, ağır** *grievous injuries* **● grievously** *adverb* **ciddi bir şekilde**

grill[1] /grɪl/ *noun* [C] **1** (*also US* **broiler**) a piece of equipment which cooks food using direct heat from above **fırın ızgarası** ⊃*Orta kısımdaki renkli sayfalarına bakınız.* **2** a flat, metal structure used to cook food over a fire **ızgara, mangal**

grill[2] /grɪl/ *verb* [T] **1** (*also US* **broil**) to cook food using direct heat **ızgarada pişirmek, ızgara yapmak** *Grill the fish for 2 to 3 minutes on each side.* ⊃*See picture at* **cook**. **2** to ask someone questions continuously and for a long time **sorguya çekmek, sürekli soru sormak, sıkıştırmak** *I was grilled by the police for two days.*

grille /grɪl/ *noun* [C] a metal structure of bars built across something to protect it **kafes, koruyucu kafes/parmaklık, ızgara**

grim /grɪm/ *adjective* **grimmer, grimmest 1** [BAD] worrying and bad **dehşet verici, endişelendiren, korkunç, kötü** *grim news* ○ *The future looks grim.* **2** [SERIOUS] sad and serious **üzücü, ciddi, çok kötü, berbat** *a grim expression* **3** [UNPLEASANT] A grim place is ugly and unpleasant. **kasvetli, sevimsiz, iç karartıcı ● grimly** *adverb* **endişe verici**

grimace /'grɪməs/ *verb* [I] to make your face show an expression of pain or unhappiness **acı ve mutsuzluk belirtisi olarak yüzünü ekşitmek, suratını buruşturmak** *He grimaced at the bitter taste.* **● grimace** *noun* [C] **yüz ekşitme**

grime /graɪm/ *noun* [U] dirt that covers a surface **kir, pislik, kir pas** *The walls were covered in grime.* **● grimy** *adjective* covered in dirt **kirli, pis, berbat** *grimy hands*

grin /grɪn/ *verb* **grinning**, *past* **grinned 1** [I] to smile a big smile **sırıtmak, ağzı kulaklarına varmak** *He grinned at me from the doorway.* **2 grin and bear it** to accept an unpleasant or difficult situation because there is nothing you can do to improve it **sineye çekmek, yakınmadan katlanmak, sabırla tahammül etmek ● grin** *noun* [C] *She had a big grin on her face.* **gülümseme**

grind[1] /graɪnd/ *verb* [T] *past* **ground 1** to keep rubbing something between two rough, hard surfaces until it becomes a powder **öğütmek, unufak etmek** *to grind coffee* **2** to rub a blade against a hard surface to make it sharp **bilemek, keskinleştirmek 3 grind your teeth** to rub your teeth together, making an unpleasant sound **dişlerini gıcırdatmak, gıcırtı sesi çıkarmak**

grind sb down *phrasal verb* to gradually make someone lose hope, energy, or confidence **bastırmak, ümidini kırmak, ezmek, eziyet etmek, zulmetmek**

grind[2] /graɪnd/ *noun* [no plural] *informal* work or effort that is boring and unpleasant and makes you tired because it does not change **beyhude çaba/çalışma, sıkıcı ve zor iş, ömür törpüsü** *the daily grind*

grinder /'graɪndər/ *noun* [C] a machine used to rub or press something until it becomes a powder **öğütücü, değirmen** *a coffee grinder*

▓▓ **grip** ...... İLE BİRLİKTE KULLANILAN KELİMELER

loosen/release/tighten your grip ● sb's grip **on** sth

grip[1] /grɪp/ *noun* [no plural] **1** when you hold something tightly **sımsıkı tutma, kavrama** *She tightened her grip on my arm.* **2** control over something or someone **denetim, yönetim, güç, kontrol** *He has a firm grip on the economy.* **3 come/get to grips with sth** to understand and deal with a problem or situation **ile uğraşmak; ciddi olarak ele almak; anlayıp çözmeye uğraşmak/çabalamak** *It's a difficult subject to get to grips with.* **● 4 get a grip (on yourself)** to make an effort to control your emotions and behave more calmly **kendine hâkim olmak, aklını başına toplamak**

grip[2] /grɪp/ *verb* [T] **gripping**, *past* **gripped 1** [HOLD] to hold something tightly **sımsıkı tutmak, kavramak** *She gripped his arm.* **2** [INTEREST] to keep someone's attention completely **dikkatini bütünüyle çekmek** *This trial has gripped the whole nation.* **3** [EMOTION] When an emotion grips you, you feel it very strongly. **tutulmak, etkisinden kurtulamamak** [often passive] *He was gripped by fear.*

gripe /graɪp/ *verb* [I] *informal* to complain, often in an annoying way **dertlenmek, şikâyet etmek, yakınmak ● gripe** *noun* [C] **şikâyet**

gripping /'grɪpɪŋ/ *adjective* If something is gripping, it is so interesting that it holds your attention completely. **sürükleyici, etkileyici, ilgi/dikkat çekici** *a gripping story*

grisly /'grɪzli/ *adjective* very unpleasant, especially because death or blood is involved **dehşet verici, tüyler ürperten, insanın kanını donduran** *a grisly murder*

grit[1] /grɪt/ *noun* [U] **1** very small pieces of stone or sand **küçük taş, iri taneli kum, çakıl** *I've got a bit of grit in my eye.* **2** the quality of being brave and determined **cesur ve kararlı olma, azimlilik, gözü karalık**

grit[2] /grɪt/ *verb* [T] **gritting**, *past* **gritted** to put grit onto a road surface when the road has ice on it **kaygan yola kum serpmek, kumlamak** ⊃*See also:* **grit your teeth (teeth).**

gritty /'grɪti/ *adjective* **1** showing unpleasant details about a situation in a way that seems very real **çirkinlikleri örten, gerçeği saptıran, başkalaştıran** *a gritty drama* ○ *gritty realism* **2** brave and determined **cesur ve kararlı, azimli, gözü kara** *gritty determination*

groan /grəʊn/ *verb* [I] to make a long, low sound such as when expressing pain, unhappiness, etc **inlemek, inilti sesi çıkarmak** *He collapsed, groaning with pain.* **● groan** *noun* [C] **inleme**

grocer /'grəʊsər/ *noun* **1 grocer's** UK a shop that sells food and other products used in the home **bakkal dükkânı 2** [C] someone who owns or works in a grocer's **bakkal**

groceries /'grəʊsºriz/ *noun* [plural] goods bought to be used in the home such as food and cleaning products **bakkal/market alışverişi**

grocery /'grəʊsʰri/ (*also US* 'grocery ˌstore) *noun* [C] a shop that sells food and products used in the home **bakkaliye**

groggy /'grɒgi/ *adjective informal* unable to think or act quickly because you have just woken up, been ill, etc (**hastalık ve uyku nedeniyle) mahmur, henüz kendine gelememiş; düşünür hızlı hareket edemeyen** *I felt a bit groggy after the operation.*

groin /grɔɪn/ *noun* [C] the area where the legs join the rest of the body near the sexual organs **kasık** *He pulled a muscle in his groin.*

groom[1] /gruːm/ *verb* [T] **1** to prepare someone carefully for a special position or job **yetiştirmek, hazırlamak** *He's being groomed for stardom.* **2** to clean and brush an animal's fur **taramak, tımar etmek, kaşağılamak**

groom[2] /gruːm/ *noun* [C] **1** (*also* **bridegroom**) a man who is getting married **damat 2** someone who cleans and looks after horses **seyis, at bakıcısı**

groove /gruːv/ *noun* [C] a long, narrow line that has been cut into a surface **yiv, oluk**

grope /grəʊp/ *verb* **1** [I, T] to try to get hold of something with your hand, usually when you cannot see it **el yordamıyla aramak, yoklamak** *I groped in my bag for my keys.* **2 grope your way along/through, etc** to move somewhere with difficulty, feeling with your hands because you cannot see clearly **el yordamıyla ilerlemek, yolunu bulmaya çalışmak** *We groped our way through the smoke to the exit.*

grope for sth *phrasal verb* to try to think of the right words or the right way to express something **doğru sözü ve anlatım biçimini bulmaya çalışmak** *He groped for the words to tell her.*

gross[1] /grəʊs/ *adjective* **1** TOTAL A gross amount of money has not had taxes or other costs taken from it. **brüt, toplam, kesintisiz** *gross earnings/profit* **2** SERIOUS [always before noun] *formal* very serious or unacceptable **ciddi ve kabul edilemez** *gross misconduct* **3** UNPLEASANT *informal* very unpleasant **nezaketsiz, çirkin, kaba, uygunsuz** *Oh, yuck. That's really gross.*

gross[2] /grəʊs/ *verb* [T] to earn a particular amount of money as a total before tax or other costs are taken from it **brüt para kazanmak/gelir elde etmek** *The film grossed $250 million.*

grossly /'grəʊsli/ *adverb* extremely **oldukça, çok fazla, son derece** *grossly unfair/exaggerated*

grotesque /grəʊ'tesk/ *adjective* strange and unpleasant, especially in a ridiculous or slightly frightening way **biçimsiz, tuhaf, şekilsiz, uygunsuz, saçma** *a grotesque image* • **grotesquely** *adverb* **garip bir şekilde**

grotto /'grɒtəʊ/ *noun* [C] a small cave **küçük mağara**

o--**ground**[1] /graʊnd/ *noun* **1 the ground** the surface of the Earth **yeryüzü** *I sat down on the ground.* **2** SOIL [U] the soil in an area **zemin, toprak, yer** *soft/stony ground* **3** AREA [C] an area of land used for a particular purpose or activity **alan, yer, saha** *a football ground* **4** KNOWLEDGE [U] an area of knowledge, information, interest, or experience **çalışma/bilgi/ilgi/tecrübe sahası/alanı** *He had to go over the same ground several times before I understood it.* **5 break new ground** to do something that is different to anything that has been done before **çığır açmak 6 gain/lose ground** to become more/less popular and accepted **en çok/en az meşhur veya kabul edilebilir hale gelmek** *The idea is gradually gaining ground.* **7 get (sth) off the ground** If a plan or activity gets off the ground, or if you get it off the ground, it starts or succeeds. **başlatmak, başarmak, başarılı kılmak, başarılı olmak** *He worked hard at getting the project off the ground.* **8 stand**

your ground to refuse to change your opinion or move your position despite attempts to make you **diretmek, ayaklarını diremek, kararından vazgeçmemek, karşı koymak, değişime direnmek 9 suit sb down to the ground** to be exactly right or suitable for someone **tamamıyla uygun olmak; tam uymak** *That job would suit you down to the ground.* **10 be thin on the ground** to exist only in small numbers or amounts **çok az miktarda olmak; nadir/seyrek/az olmak** ⊃See also: **breeding ground, common ground.**

ground[2] /graʊnd/ *verb* **1 be grounded** If a vehicle that travels on water or in the air is grounded, it cannot or may not leave the ground. **karaya çıkmak, karada/yerde olmak; kalkamamak; kalkışı engellenmek** *The aircraft was grounded by fog.* **2 be grounded in sth** *formal* to be based firmly on something **kesinlikle bir şeye dayalı/dayanır olmak** *Fiction should be grounded in reality.*

ground[3] /graʊnd/ *past of* grind **'öğütmek' fiilinin ikinci hali**

ˌground 'beef US (UK mince) *noun* [U] beef (= meat from a cow) that has been cut into very small pieces by a machine **kıyma, çekilmiş et**

groundbreaking /'graʊndˌbreɪkɪŋ/ *adjective* based on or containing completely new ideas **çığır açan, yenilik getiren, yeni fikirler içeren** *groundbreaking research*

ˌground 'floor UK (US first floor) *noun* [C] the level of a building which is on the ground **zemin kat, giriş kat**

grounding /'graʊndɪŋ/ *noun* [no plural] knowledge of the basic facts and principles of a subject **temel eğitim/öğretim** *The course gave me a good grounding in book-keeping.*

groundless /'graʊndləs/ *adjective* Groundless fears, worries, etc have no reason or facts to support them. **asılsız, bir esasa dayanmayan, aslı astarı olmayan; mesnetsiz**

ˈground ˌrules *noun* [plural] the basic rules or principles for doing something **temel esaslar, asıl ilkeler**

grounds /graʊndz/ *noun* [plural] **1** the reason for doing or believing something **esaslar, temel unsurlar, gerekçeler, nedenler** *He resigned on medical grounds.* ○ *I refused on the grounds that* (= because) *it was too risky.* **2** the land around and belonging to a particular building or organization **sahip olunan arazi/saha/alan/toprak/yer** *We strolled around the hospital grounds.*

groundwork /'graʊndwɜːk/ *noun* [U] work or events that prepare for something that will be done or produced in the future **temel çalışma; bir şeye esas teşkil edecek çalışma ve eylemler** *The project is laying the groundwork for a new approach to research.*

ˌground 'zero *noun* [U] **1** the exact place where a nuclear bomb explodes **nükleer bombanın en son patlayacağı yer/zemin/alan/bölge 2** the place in New York City where the World Trade Center stood before it was destroyed in an attack on September 11, 2001 **New York şehrinde Dünya Ticaret Merkezi'nin 11 eylül 2001 tarihinde saldırıyla yıkılmadan önceki durduğu yer; sıfır noktası**

group ...... İLE BİRLİKTE KULLANILAN KELİMELER

form/join a group • **divide/split** sth into groups • a **large/small** group • a group **of** sth

o--**group**[1] /gruːp/ *noun* [C] **1** a number of people or things that are together in one place or are connected **grup, topluluk, küme** *She went camping with a small group of friends.* **2** a few musicians or singers who perform

together, usually playing popular music **müzik grubu**
a pop group

group² /gruːp/ *verb* [I, T] to form a group or put people or
things into a group or groups **grup/küme/topluluk
oluşturmak; bir araya gelip grup yapmak** *The children are grouped according to their ability.*

grouping /'gruːpɪŋ/ *noun* [C] a group of people or things
that have the same aims or qualities **aynı amaçlar ve
özelliklerin bir araya getirdiği bir grup insan topluluğu** *regional groupings*

grouse¹ /graʊs/ *noun* [C] **1** *plural* **grouse** a small, fat,
brown bird that some people hunt for food **bir tür keklik 2** a small complaint about something **ufak tefek
şikâyet, dertlenme**

grouse² /graʊs/ *verb* [I] to complain about something
**küçük küçük dertlenmek, şikâyet etmek, yakın-
mak**

grove /grəʊv/ *noun* [C] a small group of trees **koruluk,
ağaçlık, ağaç topluluğu** *an olive grove*

grovel /'grɒvᵊl/ *verb* [I] UK **grovelling,** *past* **grovelled,** US
groveling, *past* **groveled 1** to try very hard to be nice to
someone important so that they will be nice to you or
forgive you **aşırı derecede iyi davranıp kendini
affettirmeye çalışmak** *She grovelled to the producer
to get that part.* **2** to move around on your hands and
knees **elleri ve dizleri üzerinde sürünmek; (askerlik) yüksek sürünmek** *He was grovelling around on
the floor.*

⊶**grow** /grəʊ/ *verb past tense* **grew,** *past participle* **grown
1** [DEVELOP] [I] to develop and become bigger or taller as
time passes **büyümek, gelişmek, serpilmek** *Children
grow very quickly.* **2** [PLANT] [I, T] If a plant grows, or you
grow it, it develops from a seed to a full plant. **(bitki)
yetiş(tir)mek; büyü(t)mek** *These shrubs grow well in
sandy soil.* **3** [INCREASE] [I] to increase **artmak, çoğalmak,
büyümek, gelişmek** *The number of people living alone
grows each year.* **4 grow tired/old/calm, etc** to gradually become tired/old/calm, etc **zamanla/yavaş
yavaş yorulmak/yaşlanmak/sakinleşmek vb.** *The
music grew louder and louder.* **5** [HAIR] [I, T] If your hair or
nails grow, or if you grow them, they get longer. **(saç,
tırnak) uza(t)mak**
grow into sb/sth *phrasal verb* to develop into a particular type of person or thing **belli tarzda bir kişi gibi
gelişmek; (eşya) şekilde büyümek/gelişmek**
grow into sth *phrasal verb* If a child grows into clothes,
they gradually become big enough to wear them. **büyümek, gelişmek, irileşmek**
grow on sb *phrasal verb* If someone or something
grows on you, you start to like them. **ısınmaya başlamak, beğenmek, hoşa gitmek, sarmak** *I didn't like
her at first but she's grown on me over the years.*
grow out of sth *phrasal verb* **1** If children grow out of
clothes, they gradually become too big to wear them.
**elbisenin içine sığmamak, gittikçe kocaman
olmak/büyümek** *Adam's grown out of his shoes.* **2** to
stop doing something as you get older **yaşlandıkça
gözünde büyümek; artık yapacak gücü kendinde
bulamamak; vazgeçmek/terk etmek/bırakmak** *He
still bites his nails, but hopefully he'll grow out of it.*
grow up *phrasal verb* **1** to become older or an adult
yetişkin olmak, büyümek, gelişmek, olgunlaşmak
She grew up in New York. **2** to develop or become bigger
or stronger **büyümek, daha da güçlü ve büyük hale
gelmek** *A close friendship had grown up between them.*

grower /'grəʊəʳ/ *noun* [C] someone who grows fruit or
vegetables to sell to people **meyve sebze yetiştircisi/
üreticisi; bahçecilik yapan**

growing /'grəʊɪŋ/ *adjective* increasing **büyüyen,
artan, gelişen, çoğalan** *A growing number of people
are choosing to live alone.*

growl /graʊl/ *verb* [I] If a dog or similar animal growls, it
makes a deep, angry noise in its throat. **hırlamak**
● **growl** *noun* [C] **hırıldama**

grown¹ /grəʊn/ *adjective* **a grown man/woman** an
adult, used especially when they are not behaving like
an adult **yetişkin/erişkin adam/kadın**

grown² /grəʊn/ *past participle of* grow **'büyümek' fiilinin üçüncü hâli**

grown-up¹ /'grəʊnʌp/ *noun* [C] an adult, used especially when talking to children **yetişkin, erişkin,
reşit, olgun** *Ask a grown-up to cut the shape out for you.*

grown-up² /grəʊn'ʌp/ *adjective* with the physical and
mental development of an adult **yetişmiş, büyümüş,
gelişimini tamamlamış, reşit** *Jenny has a grown-up
son of 24.*

⟨꜑꜑꜑⟩ growth ...... İLE BİRLİKTE KULLANILAN KELİMELER

encourage/slow/stimulate/stunt   growth
●   healthy/long-term/low/rapid/slow/steady
growth ● a growth in sth

⊶**growth** /grəʊθ/ *noun* **1** [U, no plural] when something
grows, increases, or develops **büyüme, gelişme,
artma** *population growth* ○ *A balanced diet is essential
for healthy growth.* **2** [C] something that grows on your
skin or inside your body, that should not be there **şişlik,
ur, yumru**

grub /grʌb/ *noun* **1** [U] *informal* food **yiyecek, yemek
2** [C] a young, developing insect which has a fat, white
tube shape **kutçuk, tırtıl, larva**

grubby /'grʌbi/ *adjective* quite dirty **oldukça kirli, pis**
a grubby little boy

grudge¹ /grʌdʒ/ *noun* [C] a feeling of dislike or anger
towards someone because of something they have
done in the past **kin, hırs, garaz, haset, kötülük** *He
is not the type of person to bear a grudge against anyone.*

grudge² /grʌdʒ/ *verb* [T] to not want to spend time or
money or to give something to someone **esirgemek,
vermek istememek, kıyamamak, çok görmek** *He
grudged the time he spent in meetings.*

grudging /'grʌdʒɪŋ/ *adjective* done against your will, in
a way that shows you do not want to do it **isteksiz,
gönülsüz, kerhen** *He treated her with grudging respect.* ● **grudgingly** *adverb* esirgercesine, diş bileme

gruelling UK (US **grueling**) /'gruːᵊlɪŋ/ *adjective* Gruelling
activities are very difficult and make you very tired.
**çok zor, yorucu, ömür törpüsü niteliğinde, yıpra-
tan** *a gruelling bicycle race*

gruesome /'gruːsəm/ *adjective* very unpleasant or violent, usually involving injury or death **tüyler ürperten, ürkütücü, dehşet verici, korkutucu, korkunç**
a gruesome murder

gruff /grʌf/ *adjective* sounding unfriendly **kaba, hırçın, sert, soğuk, dostane olmayan** *a gruff voice*
● **gruffly** *adverb* kaba bir şekilde

grumble /'grʌmbl/ *verb* [I] to complain about something in a quiet but angry way **homur homur homurdanmak, söylenmek, dertlenmek, yakınmak, şikâyet etmek** *She's always grumbling about something.*
● **grumble** *noun* [C] şikayet

grumpy /'grʌmpi/ *adjective* easily annoyed and often
complaining **huysuz, hırçın, somurtkan, sert, aksi,**
a grumpy old man ● **grumpily** *adverb* huysuz, aksi
bir şekilde ● **grumpiness** *noun* [U] huysuzluk

grunt /grʌnt/ *verb* **1** [I, T] to make a short, low sound instead of speaking, usually when you are angry or in pain **hırıldamak, inlemek, homurdamak 2** [I] If a pig grunts, it makes short, low sounds. **(domuz) hırılda-mak, hırıltı sesi çıkarmak, inlemek ● grunt** *noun* [C] **hırıltı**

guarantee¹ /ˌɡærəˈniː/ *verb* [T] **guaranteeing**, *past* **guaranteed 1** to promise that something is true or will happen **güvence vermek, söz vermek, garanti etmek** *Every child is guaranteed a place at a local school.* ○ [+ (that)] *We can't guarantee that it will arrive in time.* **2** If a company guarantees its products, it makes a written promise to repair them or give you a new one if they have a fault. **(ürün için) yasal güvence vermek, garanti etmek**

guarantee² /ˌɡærənˈtiː/ *noun* [C, U] **1** a written promise made by a company to repair one of its products or give you a new one if it has a fault **güvence, garanti, teminat** *a three-year guarantee* ○ *I'm afraid this camera is no longer* **under guarantee**. **2** a promise that something will be done or will happen **söz verme, vaatte bulunma, garanti, güvence** [+ (that)] *There's no guarantee that it actually works.*

guard¹ /ɡɑːd/ *noun* **1** [PROTECT] [C] someone whose job is to make certain someone does not escape or to protect a place or another person **koruma, muhafız, nöbetçi, bekçi, koruyucu** *a security guard* ○ *prison guards* **2** [SOLDIERS] [no plural] a group of soldiers or police officers who are protecting a person or place **korumalar, muhafızlar; muhafız birliği; koruma gücü 3** [TRAIN] [C] (*also* **conductor**) someone who is in charge of a train **tren muhafızı/görevlisi/koruması 4** [THING] [C] something that covers or protects someone or something **siper, koruyucu aygıt/eşya, muhafaza** *a fire guard* **5 be on guard; stand guard** to be responsible for protecting a place or a person **nöbette olmak, nöbet tutmak** *Armed police stood guard outside the house.* **6 be under guard** to be kept in a place by a group of people who have weapons **gözetim/muhafaza/koruma altında olmak** *The suspect is now under guard in the local hospital.* **7 catch sb off guard** to surprise someone by doing something when they are not ready to deal with it **hazırlıksız/savunmasız yakalamak, gafil avlamak ● 8 be on (your) guard** to be ready to deal with something difficult that might happen **teyakkuzda/tetikte olmak, hazırlıklı olmak, gözünü dört açmak** *Companies were warned to be on their guard for suspicious packages.*

guard² /ɡɑːd/ *verb* [T] **1** to protect someone or something from being attacked or stolen **muhafızlık etmek, korumak, savunmak** *Soldiers guarded the main doors of the embassy.* **2** to watch someone and make certain that they do not escape from a place **nöbet tutmak, bekçilik etmek, gözlemek** *Five prison officers guarded the prisoners.*
guard against sth *phrasal verb* to try to make certain that something does not happen by being very careful **...e/a karşı önlem/tedbir almak; hazırlıklı olmak; önlemeye çalışmak** *Regular exercise helps guard against heart disease.*

guarded /ˈɡɑːdɪd/ *adjective* careful not to give too much information or show how you really feel **ihtiyatlı, dikkatli, tedbirli, ne yaptığını/yapacağını bilen** *a guarded response* **● guardedly** *adverb* **tedbirli bir şekilde**

guardian /ˈɡɑːdiən/ *noun* [C] **1** someone who is legally responsible for someone else's child **veli, vâsi** *The consent form must be signed by the child's parent or guardian.* **2** a person or organization that protects laws, principles, etc **muhafız, koruyucu, bekçi ● guardianship** *noun* [U] **bakıcılık**

guerrilla /ɡəˈrɪlə/ *noun* [C] a member of an unofficial group of soldiers fighting to achieve their political beliefs **gerilla, çeteci, yasadışı isyan/başkaldırı çete üyesi** *guerrilla warfare*

○ guess¹ /ɡes/ *verb* **1** [I, T] to give an answer or opinion about something without having all the facts **tahmin etmek, kestirmeye çalışmak, tahminde bulunmak** *Can you guess how old he is?* **2** [I, T] to give a correct answer without having all the facts **tahmin ederek bilmek, atıp tutturmak** *"You've got a promotion!" "Yes, how did you guess?"* ○ [+ (that)] *I'd never have guessed that you two were related.* **3 I guess** used when you think that something is probably true or likely **'Sanırım', 'Zannedersem', 'Galiba'** *I've known her for about 12 years, I guess.* **4 I guess so/not** used when you agree/disagree but are not completely certain about something **'Öyle sanıyorum/sanmıyorum ki'; 'Tahminime göre öyle/öyle değil' 5 Guess what?** something you say when you have some surprising news for someone **'Bak ne diyeceğim', 'Bak ne olmuş', 'Tahmin bile edemezsin'; 'Ne olduğunu tahmin edebilir misin?** *Guess what? I'm pregnant.*

🧩 **guess** ...... İLE BİRLİKTE KULLANILAN KELİMELER

have/hazard/make/take a guess **●** a **rough** guess **● at** a guess **●** a guess **as to/at** sth

guess² /ɡes/ *noun* [C] **1** an attempt to give the right answer when you are not certain what it is **tahmin, varsayım, öngörü, zan, farz etme** *How old do you think John is? Go on,* (UK) **have a guess/** (US) **take** a **guess.** ○ *At a guess, I'd say there were about 70 people there.* **2** An opinion that you have formed by guessing **tahmin, varsayılan, öngörü** *My guess is they'll announce their engagement soon.* **3 be anybody's guess** *informal* to be something that no one can be certain about **kesin olarak bilinmiyor; kimse bilmiyor; sadece bir tahmin; tahminden öteye geçemez** *What happens after the election is anybody's guess.*

guesswork /ˈɡeswɜːk/ *noun* [U] when you try to find an answer by guessing **tahmin oyunu, kestirme, tahmin**

🧩 **guest** ...... İLE BİRLİKTE KULLANILAN KELİMELER

entertain/invite/welcome guests **●** a **frequent/honoured/special/uninvited** guest

○ guest /ɡest/ *noun* [C] **1** [VISITOR] someone who comes to visit you in your home, at a party, etc **misafir, konuk, ziyaretçi** *We've got some guests coming this weekend.* **2** [HOTEL] someone who is staying in a hotel **otel müşterisi** *The hotel has accommodation for 200 guests.* **3** [TV] a famous person who takes part in a television programme or other entertainment **(tv. eğlence programı) konuk, katılımcı, davetli, konuk sanatçı** *Our special guest tonight is George Michael.* **4 Be my guest.** something you say when you give someone permission to use something or do something **'Tabii', 'Elbette', 'Buyrun', 'Rica ederim', 'Hiç çekinmeyin'**

guesthouse /ˈɡesthaʊs/ *noun* [C] a small cheap hotel **küçük otel, konukevi, pansiyon, misafirhane**

GUI /ˈɡuːi/ *noun* [C] graphical user interface: a way of arranging information on a computer screen that is easy to understand because it uses pictures and symbols as well as words **bilgisayar ekranında bilginin sözcüklerin yanı sıra resimlerle ve imgelerle tasarlanması; Grafik Kullanıcı Arayüzü (GKA)**

guidance /ˈɡaɪdəns/ *noun* [U] help or advice **önderlik, yardım, öğüt, akıl, tavsiye** *Students make choices about their future, with the guidance of their teachers.*

guide[1] /gaɪd/ *noun* [C] **1** PERSON someone whose job is to show interesting places to visitors, or to help people get somewhere **turist rehberi** *a tour guide* **2** BOOK a book that gives information about something or tells you how to do something **rehber kitapçık, el kitabı, kılavuz** *a hotel/restaurant guide* ○ *a user's guide* **3** PLAN something that helps you plan or decide what to do **örnek, model** [usually singular] *Parents use this report as a guide when choosing schools for their children.* **4 Guide** (*also* ˌGirl 'Guide) a girl who belongs to an organization in the UK that teaches practical things like living outside, and how to work as part of a team **kız izci 5 the Guides** an organization in the UK that teaches girls practical skills and how to work as part of a team (**Birleşik Krallık) kızlara pratik becerileri ve ekip çalışmasını öğreten kuruluş**

guide[2] /gaɪd/ *verb* [T] **1** to help someone or something go somewhere **rehberlik etmek, yol göstermek, öncülük etmek** *He gently guided her back to her seat.* **2** to tell someone what they should do **yönlendirmek, denetlemek** *She had no one to guide her as a teenager.*

guidebook /'gaɪdbʊk/ *noun* [C] a book that gives visitors information about a particular place **el kitabı, turist kılavuzu, rehber kitap**

'**guide ˌdog** (*also* US **seeing eye dog**) *noun* [C] a dog that is trained to help blind people **körler için eğitilmiş rehbet köpek**

⊞ guidelines ...... İLE BİRLİKTE KULLANILAN KELİMELER

draw up / issue / lay down / produce guidelines
● guidelines on sth

guidelines /'gaɪdlaɪnz/ *noun* [plural] advice about how to do something **tavsiyeler, kurallar, talimatlar** *government guidelines on tobacco advertising*

guild /gɪld/ *noun* [C] an organization of people who have the same job or interests **dernek, cemiyet, esnaf birliği, lonca, meslek kuruluşu** *the Designers' Guild*

guile /gaɪl/ *noun* [U] *formal* clever but sometimes dishonest behaviour that you use to deceive someone **hilekârlık, aldatıcılık, hilebazlık, kurnazlık**

guillotine /'gɪləti:n/ *noun* [C] a piece of equipment used to cut off criminals' heads in the past **giyotin** ● **guillotine** *verb* [T] **suçluların kafalarının koparılması**

guilt /gɪlt/ *noun* [U] **1** FEELING the strong feeling of shame that you feel when you have done something wrong **suçluluk, derin mahcubiyet** *He was overcome with guilt over what he had done.* **2** ILLEGAL the fact that someone has done something illegal **suçluluk, suç** *The prosecution must convince the jury of his guilt.* **3** WRONG the responsibility for doing something bad **kabahat, kusurluluk, yanlışlık**

guilt-ridden /'gɪltrɪdᵊn/ *adjective* feeling very guilty **çok fazla suçluluk duyan, kendini kabahatli bulan**

⁀**guilty** /'gɪlti/ *adjective* **1** ashamed because you have done something wrong **kabahatli, kusurlu** [+ about + doing sth] *I feel so guilty about not going to see them.* **2** having broken a law **suçlu** *The jury found her guilty* (= decided that she was guilty of a crime). ○ *They found him guilty of rape.* ● **guiltily** *adverb* **suçlu bir şekilde** ● **guiltiness** *noun* [U] **suçluluk**

guinea pig /'gɪniˌpɪg/ *noun* [C] **1** a small animal with fur and no tail that people sometimes keep as a pet **kobay, kobay hayvanı 2** *informal* someone who is used in a test for something such as a new medicine or product **denek, kobay kişi, üzerinde deney yapılan kişi**

guise /gaɪz/ *noun* [C] *formal* what something seems to be, although it is not **dış görünüş; zahiri görünüm, kisve, şekil, tarz, biçim** *Banks are facing new competition in the guise of supermarkets.*

guitar /gɪ'tɑ:ʳ/ *noun* [C] a musical instrument with strings that you play by pulling the strings with your fingers or a piece of plastic **gitar** *an electric guitar*

guitar

guitarist /gɪ'tɑ:rɪst/ *noun* [C] someone who plays the guitar, especially as their job **gitarist**

gulf /gʌlf/ *noun* [C] **1** a large area of sea that has land almost all the way around it **körfez** *the Arabian Gulf* **2** an important difference between the opinions or situations of two groups of people **büyük görüş ayrılığı, uçurum, önemli görüş farklılığı** *There is a growing gulf between the rich and the poor.*

gull /gʌl/ (*also* **seagull**) *noun* [C] a white or grey bird that lives near the sea and has a loud cry **martı**

gullible /'gʌlɪbl/ *adjective* Someone who is gullible is easily tricked because they trust people too much. **saftirik, kolay aldanır, bön, saf** *How could you be so gullible?*

gully /'gʌli/ *noun* [C] a narrow valley which is usually dry except after a lot of rain **dar, derin ve kurak vadi**

gulp /gʌlp/ *verb* **1** DRINK/EAT [T] (*also* **gulp down**) to drink or eat something quickly **bir dikişte yutuvermek, mideye indirmek, bütünüyle yemek** *I just had time to gulp down a cup of coffee before I left.* **2** BREATHE [I, T] to breathe in large amounts of air **derin derin nefes almak 3** SWALLOW [I] to swallow suddenly, sometimes making a noise, because you are nervous or surprised **yutkunmak, yutkunup durmak, boğazı düğümlenmek** ● **gulp** *noun* [C] *He took a large gulp of tea.* **yutkunma, yutma**

gum[1] /gʌm/ *noun* **1** MOUTH [C] the hard, pink part inside your mouth that your teeth grow out of **diş eti** [usually plural] *Protect your teeth and gums by visiting your dentist regularly.* ○ *gum disease* **2** SWEET [U] (*also* **chewing gum**) a sweet substance that you chew (= bite repeatedly) but do not swallow **sakız** *a stick of gum* **3** STICKY [U] a sticky substance like glue, used for sticking papers together **zamk, tutkal, yapıştırıcı** ⊃See also: bubble gum.

gum[2] /gʌm/ *verb* [T] **gumming**, *past* **gummed** UK to stick things together using glue **yapıştırmak, tutturmak, zamklamak**

⊞ gun ...... İLE BİRLİKTE KULLANILAN KELİMELER

point a gun at sb/sth ● fire a gun

⁀**gun**[1] /gʌn/ *noun* **1** [C] a weapon that you fire bullets out of **ateşli silah; top, tüfek, tabanca, mavzer vb. 2 jump the gun** to do something too soon, before you have thought about it carefully **ecele etmek, çabuk karar vermek, acele davranmak** ● **3 stick to your guns** *informal* to refuse to change your ideas although other people try to make you **iddiasından/fikrinden vazgeçmemek** ⊃See also: machine gun.

gun[2] /gʌn/ *verb* **gunning**, *past* **gunned**
gun sb down *phrasal verb* to shoot someone and kill them or injure them badly **silahla öldürmek/yaralamak**

gunboat /'gʌnbəʊt/ *noun* [C] a small ship used during a war **ağır silahlar taşıyan küçük savaş gemisi**

gunfire /'gʌnfaɪə^r/ noun [U] when guns are fired, or the noise that this makes **top ateşi, tüfek/tabanca ateşi**

gunman /'gʌnmən/ noun [C] plural **gunmen** a criminal with a gun **silahlı haydut, gangster**

gunner /'gʌnə^r/ noun [C] a soldier or sailor whose job is to fire a large gun **topçu, makineli tüfekçi**

gunpoint /'gʌnpɔɪnt/ noun **at gunpoint** with someone aiming a gun towards you **silah zoruyla, namlunun ucunda/menzilinde, ölüm tehdidiyle** The hostages are being held at gunpoint.

gunpowder /'gʌn,paʊdə^r/ noun [U] an explosive powder **barut**

gunshot /'gʌnʃɒt/ noun [C] when a gun is fired **silah atışı; top/tüfek/tabanca atışı; ateşli silahlarla atış** I heard a gunshot and rushed into the street. ○ **gunshot wounds** to the chest

gurgle /'gɜ:gl/ verb [I] to make a sound like bubbling liquid **lıkırdamak, lıkır lıkır ses çıkarmak** The baby was gurgling happily. ● **gurgle** noun [C] **gargara**

guru /'gu:ru:/ noun [C] **1** someone whose opinion you respect because they know a lot about a particular thing **fikirlerine itibar edilen kişi, guru, duayen, ekâbir kişi, kanaat önderi 2** a teacher or leader in the Hindu religion **Hindu dininde ruhani öğretici/lider**

gush¹ /gʌʃ/ verb [I, T] **1** If liquid gushes from an opening, it comes out quickly and in large amounts. **fışkırmak, şiddetle akmak** He ran down the street, blood gushing from a wound in his neck. **2** to praise someone so much that they do not believe you are sincere **çokça övmek, şiddetle açığa vurmak, hayranlığını abartılı bir şekilde dile getirmek** "Darling! I'm so excited!" she gushed.

gush² /gʌʃ/ noun [C] **1** a large amount of liquid or gas that flows quickly **fazla miktarda ve çok hızlı akan sıvı/gaz 2** a sudden feeling of a particular emotion **coşku, heyecan, ani duygulanma, coşkulu bir hal alma**

gust /gʌst/ verb [I] If winds gust, they blow strongly. **ani ve şiddetli esmek, bora şeklinde esmek** Winds gusting to 50 mph brought down power cables. ● **gust** noun [C] a gust of air **esinti** ● **gusty** adjective **esintili, rüzgârlı**

gusto /'gʌstəʊ/ noun **with gusto** with a lot of energy and enthusiasm **büyük bir beğeni, zevk, enerji ve coşkuyla** Everyone joined in the singing with great gusto.

gut¹ /gʌt/ noun [C] the tube in your body that takes food from your stomach to be passed out as waste **bağırsaklar, iç organlar**

gut² /gʌt/ adjective **gut reaction/feeling/instinct** a reaction/feeling, etc that you feel certain is right, although you have no reason to think so **ani/düşünmeden gösterilen tepki/his/içgüdü** I had a gut feeling that he was going to come back.

gut³ /gʌt/ verb [T] **gutting**, past **gutted 1** to remove the organs from inside a fish or other animal **bağırsaklarını/iç organlarını çıkarmak 2** to completely destroy or remove the inside of a building **bir binanın içini tamamen tahrip etmek/yıkmak; yerle bir etmek** A fire gutted the bookshop last week.

guts /gʌts/ noun [plural] informal **1** the bravery and determination that is needed to do something difficult or unpleasant **cesaret, yüreklilik, gözü karalık** It took

guts to stand up and tell the boss how she felt. **2** the organs inside a person's or animal's body **iç organlar 3 hate sb's guts** informal to dislike someone very much **aşırı derecede nefret etmek, iğrenmek, tiksinmek**

gutsy /'gʌtsi/ adjective brave and determined **cesur, kararlı, yürekli, gözü kara** a gutsy performance

gutted /'gʌtɪd/ adjective UK informal very disappointed and upset **son derece üzgün hayal kırıklığına uğramış, bezgin, bitkin** [+ (that)] Neil's absolutely gutted that he's been dropped from the team.

gutter /'gʌtə^r/ noun [C] **1** a long, open pipe that is fixed to the edge of a roof to carry water away **yağmur oluğu, su yolu, saçak boruları 2** the edge of a road where water flows away **cadde kenarında suyun akmasını sağlayan oluk, su yolu**

o┅**guy** /gaɪ/ noun informal **1** [C] a man **adam, herif** What a nice guy! **2 guys** used when you are talking to or about two or more people **arkadaşlar, sizler, dostlar** Come on, you guys, let's go home.

guzzle /'gʌzl/ verb [I, T] informal to eat or drink a lot of something quickly **açgözlü bir şekilde yemek içmek, nefes almadan silip süpürmek; hapur hupur yemek; höpür höpür içmek** Who's guzzled all the beer?

gym /dʒɪm/ noun **1** [C] a building with equipment for doing exercises **spor salonu** Nick goes to the gym three times a week. **2** [U] exercises done inside, especially as a school subject **beden eğitimi, jimnastik**

gymnasium /dʒɪm'neɪziəm/ noun [C] a gym **spor salonu**

gymnast /'dʒɪmnæst/ noun [C] someone who does gymnastics **jimnastikçi** an Olympic gymnast

gymnastics
/dʒɪm'næstɪks/ noun
[U] a sport in which you
do physical exercises
on the floor and on
different pieces of
equipment, often in
competitions
**jimnastik oyunları/
sporları yarışması**

gynaecologist UK (US
gynecologist)
/ˌgaɪnəˈkɒlədʒɪst/ noun
[C] a doctor who treats
medical conditions that
only affect women
**jinekolog; kadın
hastalıkları uzmanı**

gynaecology UK (US
gynecology)
/ˌgaɪnəˈkɒlədʒi/ noun [U]
the study and treatment
of diseases and medical
conditions that only affect women **jinekoloji; kadın
hastalıkları bilim dalı** ● **gynaecological** UK (US
gynecological) /ˌgaɪnəkəˈlɒdʒɪkəl/ adjective **jinekolojik**

gymnastics

gypsy (also UK **gipsy**) /'dʒɪpsi/ noun [C] a member of a race of people who travel from place to place, especially in Europe **çingene** a gypsy caravan

H, h /eɪtʃ/ the eighth letter of the alphabet **alfabenin sekizinci harfi**

ha /hɑː/ *exclamation* something you say when you are surprised or pleased **ha!, vay vay!, aha!, ya!**

🧩 **habit** ...... İLE BİRLİKTE KULLANILAN KELİMELER

get into/get out of the habit of doing sth ● **have/kick** a habit ● an **annoying/bad/good** habit ● **do** sth **from/out of/through** habit

---

o⁻**habit** /'hæbɪt/ *noun* **1** REGULAR ACTIVITY [C, U] something that you do regularly, almost without thinking about it **alışkanlık, huy** *He's just eating out of habit - he's not really hungry.* **2 be in/get into the habit of doing sth** to be used/get used to doing something regularly **alışkın olmak; huy/alışkanlık edinmek; düzenli olarak yapmak** *We don't want the children to get into the habit of watching a lot of TV.* **3** BAD ACTIVITY [C, U] something that you often do that is bad for your health or is annoying **kötü alışkanlık** *He has some really nasty habits.* ○ *We offer help to alcoholics who want to kick the habit.* **4** CLOTHING [C] a long, loose piece of clothing worn by some religious groups **dinî amaçlar için giyilen özel kıyafet, cüppe** *a monk's habit*

habitable /'hæbɪtəbl/ *adjective* A habitable building is in good enough condition to live in. **oturulabilir, yaşanabilir, ikamet edilebilir**

habitat /'hæbɪtæt/ *noun* [C] the natural environment of an animal or plant **doğal ortam, yaşam ortamı**

habitation /ˌhæbɪ'teɪʃⁿn/ *noun* [U] when people live in a place **oturma, ikamet** *This place is not fit for **human habitation**.*

habitual /hə'bɪtʃuəl/ *adjective* **1** usual or typical **mutat, her zamanki** *an habitual expression/gesture* **2** doing something often because it is a habit **alışkanlık** *a habitual drug user* ● **habitually** *adverb* **tipik bir şekilde**

hack¹ /hæk/ *verb* [I, T] **1** to cut something roughly into pieces **kesip parçalara ayırmak** *The victim had been **hacked to death**.* **2** to use a computer to illegally get into someone else's computer system and read the information that is kept there **başkasının bilgisayarındaki bilgilere izinsiz erişmek/ulaşmak** *Two British youths were caught **hacking into** government computers.*

hack² /hæk/ *noun* [C] *informal* someone who produces low quality writing for books, newspapers, etc **gazete ve kitap vb. yerlerde düşük kaliteli yazılar yazmak**

hacker /'hækə^r/ *noun* [C] someone who illegally gets into someone else's computer system **bilgisayar korsanı**

o⁻**had** *strong form* /hæd/ *weak forms* /həd/, /əd/, /d/ *verb* **1** *past of* have **'sahip olmak' fiilinin 2. ve 3. hali 2 be had** *informal* to be tricked or made to look silly **aldatılmak, kandırılmak** *I think I've been had - this camera doesn't work.*

haddock /'hædək/ *noun* [C, U] *plural* **haddock** a fish that lives in northern seas and is eaten as food **bir tür morina balığı, mezgit**

o⁻**hadn't** /'hædⁿnt/ *short for* had not **'had not' fiilinin kısaltılmış hali** *I hadn't seen Megan since college.*

haemophilia *UK* (*US* **hemophilia**) /ˌhiːmə'fɪliə/ *noun* [U] a serious disease in which the flow of blood from someone's body cannot be stopped when they are hurt **kanın pıhtılaşmaması hastalığı, hemofili** ● **haemophiliac** *UK* (*US* **hemophiliac**) *noun* [C] someone who has haemophilia **hemofili hastası**

haemorrhage *UK* (*US* **hemorrhage**) /'hemⁿrɪdʒ/ *noun* [C, U] when someone suddenly loses a lot of blood **yoğun kan kaybı** *a brain haemorrhage*

haemorrhoids *UK* (*US* **hemorrhoids**) /'hemərɔɪdz/ *noun* [plural] painful swollen tissue around the opening of a person's bottom **basur, hemoroit**

haggard /'hægəd/ *adjective* Someone who is haggard has a thin face with dark marks around their eyes because they are ill or tired. **çökmüş, gözlerinin altında torbalar oluşmuş, bezgin**

haggle /'hægl/ *verb* [I] to argue, especially about the price of something **sıkı pazarlık etmek** *I spent 20 minutes **haggling over** the price of a leather bag.*

ˌha 'ha *exclamation* used in writing to represent the sound someone makes when they laugh **hah hah ha!**

hail¹ /heɪl/ *noun* **1** [U] small, hard pieces of frozen rain that fall from the sky **(hava durumu) dolu halinde yağmak 2 a hail of bullets/stones/bottles, etc** a lot of bullets/stones/bottles, etc that are fired or thrown at the same time **kurşun/taş/şişe yağmuru/sağanağı**

hail² /heɪl/ *verb* **1** [T] to call or wave to someone to get their attention **seslenmek, çağırmak** *She stepped into the road and **hailed** a taxi.* **2 it hails** If it hails, small, hard pieces of frozen rain fall from the sky. **dolu yağmak**
hail sb/sth as sth *phrasal verb* to say publicly and enthusiastically that someone or something is something very good **birisini yüceltmek, övmek**
hail from *phrasal verb* to come from a particular place **bir yerden gelmek**

o⁻**hair** /heə^r/ *noun* **1** [U] the thin, thread-like parts that grow on your head **saç** *a girl with long, fair hair* **2** [C] one of the thin thread-like parts that grow on a person's or animal's skin **kıl, tüy** *My black skirt was covered in cat hairs.* **3 let your hair down** *informal* to relax and enjoy yourself **rahatlayıp keyfine bakmak, deşarj olmak** ● **4 pull/tear your hair out** to be very anxious about something **endişelenmek, kaygı duymak,** *When they still weren't home by midnight, I was pulling my hair out.* ● **5 split hairs** to argue about small details that are not important **önemli olmayan detaylar hakkında tartışmak** ⊃See also: pubic **hair**.

hairbrush /'heəbrʌʃ/ *noun* [C] a brush that you use to make your hair look tidy **saç fırçası** ⊃See picture at brush.

haircut /'heəkʌt/ *noun* [C] **1** when someone cuts your hair **saç traşı** *I really need a haircut.* **2** the style in which your hair has been cut **saç traş biçimi, kesim tarzı**

hairdo /'heəduː/ *noun* [C] *informal* the style in which someone arranges their hair **saç biçimi/tarzı/stili**

hairdresser /'heəˌdresə^r/ *noun* **1** [C] someone whose job is to wash, cut, colour, etc people's hair **kuaför, berber 2 hairdresser's** the place where you go to have your hair washed, cut, coloured, etc **kuaför berber dükkânı**

hairdryer /ˈheəˌdraɪəʳ/ noun [C] a piece of electrical equipment for drying your hair with hot air **saç kurutma makinası, fön makinası**

-haired /-ˈheəd/ suffix used after a word describing someone's hair ...**saçlı** a red-haired woman ○ a short-haired cat ⟫See also: fair-haired.

hairgrip /ˈheəgrɪp/ UK (US bobby pin) noun [C] a small, thin piece of metal, used to fasten a woman's hair in position **metal saç tokası**

hairline /ˈheəlaɪn/ noun 1 [C] the place at the top of your face where your hair starts growing **yüzün çevresinde saç başlangıç çizgisi** 2 a hairline crack/fracture a very thin line where something hard such as a bone or cup is broken **incecik/çok ince çizgi**

hairpin /ˈheəpɪn/ noun [C] a piece of metal shaped like a U, used to fasten a woman's hair in position **firkete, saç tokası**

hairpin 'bend UK (US ˌhairpin 'turn) noun [C] a bend shaped like a U on a steep road **sert viraj, keskin dönemeç, u-dönüşü**

hair-raising /ˈheəˌreɪzɪŋ/ adjective frightening but in an enjoyable way **ürkütücü, tüyleri diken diken eden** It was a rather **hair-raising journey** down the mountain road.

hairstyle /ˈheəstaɪl/ noun [C] the style in which someone arranges their hair **saç/stili/biçimi** Do you like my new hairstyle?

hairy /ˈheəri/ adjective 1 covered in hair **kıllı, tüylü** a hairy chest ○ hairy legs 2 informal frightening or dangerous **korkutucu, tehlikeli, riskli** There were some rather **hairy moments** during the race. ● **hairiness** noun [U] **kıllı olma durumu**

hajj (also haj) /hædʒ/ noun [C] plural **hajjes** or **hajes** the religious journey to Mecca which all Muslims try to make at least once in their life **tüm müslümanların inançları gereği hayatta en az bir kez Mekke'ye yaptıkları kutsal ziyaret; hac seyahati**

halal /hælˈæl/ adjective Halal meat is prepared according to Islamic law. **islami usüllere göre hazırlanan et**

hale /heɪl/ adjective **hale and hearty** healthy and full of life **sağlıklı ve yaşam dolu, zinde**

o→**half¹** /hɑːf/ noun, determiner plural **halves** 1 [C, U] one of two equal parts of something; ½; **yarısı** Rice is eaten by half of the world's population. ○ Cut the lemons into halves. ○ It'll take half an hour to get there. ○ Jenny lived in Beijing for a year and a half. 2 **break/cut/split sth in half** to divide something into two equal parts **iki eşit parçaya bölmek** Divide the dough in half and roll it out into two circles. 3 **decrease/increase, etc sth by half** to make something smaller/larger, etc by half its size **yarı yarıya azaltmak/çoğaltmak** The drug reduces the risk of stroke by half. 4 **half past one/two/three, etc** mainly UK 30 minutes past one o'clock/two o'clock/three o'clock, etc **bir/iki/üç vb. buçuk** We got back to our hotel at half past seven. 5 **half one/two/three, etc** UK informal 30 minutes past one o'clock/two o'clock/three o'clock, etc **bir/iki/üç vb. buçuk** "What time does it start?" "About half six." 6 **go halves with sb** informal to divide the cost of something with someone **masrafları paylaşmak** Shall we go halves on a present for Laura? ● 7 **half the fun/time/pleasure, etc** informal a large part of the enjoyment/time, etc **eğlencenin zamanın büyük bir bölümü** Kids today - parents don't know where they are half the time. ● 8 **not half as good/bad/exciting, etc** informal to be much less good/bad/exciting, etc than something else ...**den/dan daha iyi/kötü/heyecan verici** Her new book's not half as good as the last one.

half² /hɑːf/ adverb partly, but not completely **kısmen yarı, yarısı, yarı yarıya** half empty/full ○ Sophia is half Greek and half Spanish (= she has one Greek parent and one Spanish parent). ○ She was only half aware of what was happening.

ˌhalf 'board noun [U] mainly UK the price for a room in a hotel, which includes breakfast and dinner **yarım pansiyon**

half-brother /ˈhɑːfˌbrʌðəʳ/ noun [C] a brother who is the son of only one of your parents **üvey erkek kardeş**

half-hearted /ˌhɑːfˈhɑːtɪd/ adjective without much effort or interest **isteksiz, gönülsüz** a half-hearted attempt ● **half-heartedly** adverb **isteksizce**

half-sister /ˈhɑːfˌsɪstəʳ/ noun [C] a sister who is the daughter of only one of your parents **üvey kız kardeş**

half-term /ˌhɑːfˈtɜːm/ noun [C, U] UK a short holiday in the middle of a school term (= one of the periods the school year is divided into) **yarıyıl tatili**

half-time /ˌhɑːfˈtaɪm/ noun [U] a short period of rest between the two halves of a game **devre arası**

halfway /ˌhɑːfˈweɪ/ adjective, adverb at an equal distance between two places, or in the middle of a period of time **ortasında, yarı yolda** the halfway point ○ He was released halfway through his prison sentence.

o→**hall** /hɔːl/ noun [C] 1 (also hallway /ˈhɔːlweɪ/) a room or passage in a building, which leads to other rooms **giriş, hol, koridor** 2 a large room or building where meetings, concerts, etc are held **toplantı/konferans/konser vb. salonu** The Albert Hall ○ The disco will be held in the school hall. ⟫See also: town hall.

hallmark /ˈhɔːlmɑːk/ noun [C] 1 an official mark that is put on something made of silver or gold to prove that it is real **bir şeyin gerçek olduğunu gösteren gümüş veya altından etiket işaret; marka etiketi** 2 a quality or method that is typical of a particular type of person or thing **kişiye/eşyaya özgü ayırt edici nitelik/yöntem** Simplicity is a hallmark of his design.

hallo UK (UK/US hello) /həˈləʊ/ exclamation 1 used to greet someone **Selam!', 'Merhaba!'** Hallo, Chris, how are things? 2 used to start a conversation on the telephone **Alo!** Hallo, this is Alex.

ˌhall of 'residence UK (US dormitory) noun [C] plural **halls of residence** a building where university or college students live **öğrenci yurdu, yurt, yatakhane**

hallowed /ˈhæləʊd/ adjective 1 respected and considered important **saygın, nezih, ulu, yüce** a hallowed tradition 2 made holy by a priest **kutsanmış, takdis edilmiş** the hallowed ground of the churchyard

Halloween /ˌhæləʊˈiːn/ noun [U] the night of 31 October when children dress in special clothes and people try to frighten each other **Cadılar Bayramı**

hallucinate /həˈluːsɪneɪt/ verb [I] to see things that are not really there, because you are ill or have taken an illegal drug **hayal görmek, sanrılamak**

hallucination /həˌluːsɪˈneɪʃᵊn/ noun [C, U] when you see things that are not really there because you are ill or have taken an illegal drug **sanrı, hayal**

halo /ˈheɪləʊ/ noun [C] a gold circle of light that is shown around the head of a holy person in a painting **hale**

H

---

halt .... İLE BİRLİKTE KULLANILAN KELİMELER

bring sth to/come to a **halt** ● **an abrupt/grinding/sudden** halt

---

halt¹ /hɒlt/ noun 1 [no plural] when something stops moving or happening **durma, hareketsiz kalma** The car **came to a halt** just inches from the edge of the cliff. ○ News of the accident **brought** the party **to a halt**.

2 call a halt to sth to officially order something to stop **resmen durdurmak/durmasını istemek** *The government has called a halt to all new building in the area.*

halt² /hɒlt/ *verb* [I, T] *formal* to stop or make something stop **durmak, durdurmak** *The council ordered that work on the project should be halted immediately.*

halting /'hɒltɪŋ/ *adjective* stopping often while you are saying or doing something, especially because you are nervous **duraklayan, duraksayan; kararsız, tereddütlü** *He spoke quietly, in halting English.*

halve /hɑːv/ *verb* **1** [T] to divide something into two equal parts **iki eşit parçaya bölmek/ayırmak** *Peel and halve the potatoes.* **2** [I, T] If you halve something, or if it halves, it is reduced to half the size it was before. **bölmek, bölünmek; yarıya inmek/indirmek** *They have almost halved the price of flights to New York.*

ham /hæm/ *noun* [C, U] meat from a pig's back or upper leg **jambon, domuz pastırması** *a ham sandwich*

hamburger /'hæm₁bɜːgəʳ/ *noun* **1** [C] a round, flat shape of meat which is cooked in hot oil and eaten between round pieces of bread **hamburger** *a hamburger and fries* **2** [U] *US* (*UK* mince) beef (= meat from a cow) that is cut into very small pieces **hamburger köftesi/eti**

hamlet /'hæmlət/ *noun* [C] a very small village **küçük köy**

hammer¹ /'hæməʳ/ *noun* [C] a tool with a heavy, metal part at the top that you use to hit nails into something **çekiç** ⊃See picture at **tool.**

hammer

hammer² /'hæməʳ/ *verb* [I, T] to hit something with a hammer **çekiçle vurmak**

hammer sth into sb *phrasal verb* to repeat something to someone a lot of times until they remember it **(defalarca söyleyerek) kafasına sokmak; (tekrarlayarak) zorla öğretmek**

hammer on sth *phrasal verb* to hit something many times, making a lot of noise **yumruklamak, yumrukla vurmak, dövmek** *They were woken up by someone hammering on the door.*

hammer sth out *phrasal verb* to finally agree on a plan, business agreement, etc after arguing about the details for a long time **görüşüp karara bağlamak, enine boyuna tartışıp sonuca varmak**

hammering /'hæmᵊrɪŋ/ *noun* **1** [U] the noise made by hitting something with a hammer or hitting something hard with your hands **çekiçleme, vurma 2** [no plural] *UK informal* a very bad defeat **kötü yenilgi, berbat sonuç**

hammock /'hæmək/ *noun* [C] a large piece of cloth or strong net that you hang between two trees or poles to sleep on **hamak**

hamper¹ /'hæmpəʳ/ *verb* [T] to make it difficult for someone to do something **engellemek, sekteye uğratmak, güçleştirmek, engel olmak** *The police investigation was hampered by a lack of help from the community.*

hamper² /'hæmpəʳ/ *noun* [C] a large basket (= container made of thin pieces of wood) with a lid **kapaklı büyük ahşap sepet** *a picnic hamper*

hamster /'hæmstəʳ/ *noun* [C] a small animal with soft fur and no tail that is often kept as a pet **hemstır; tüylü, kuyruksuz küçük hayvan**

hamstring¹ /'hæmstrɪŋ/ *noun* [C] a tendon (= part that connects a muscle to a bone) at the back of the upper part of your leg **diz arkası kirişi/kordonu; veter** *a hamstring injury*

hamstring² /'hæmstrɪŋ/ *verb* [T] *past* **hamstrung** to make it difficult for a person, team, or organization to do something **zora sokmak, elini kolunu bağlamak, yapamayacak duruma getirmek**

○~**hand¹** /hænd/ *noun* **1** [ARM] [C] the part of your body on the end of your arm that has fingers and a thumb **el** *Take your hands out of your pockets.* ⊃Orta kısımdaki renkli sayfalarına bakınız. **2 take sb by the hand** to get hold of someone's hand **elini tutmak** *Bill took her by the hand and led her into the garden.* **3 hand in hand** holding each other's hand **el ele** *The young couple walked hand in hand by the lake.* **4 hold hands** to hold each other's hand **el ele tutuşmak 5 at hand** near in time or space **el altında, yakında, hazır** *Teachers are always close at hand to give help to any child who needs it.* **6 by hand** done or made by a person instead of a machine **el yapımı** *This sweater has to be washed by hand.* **7 in hand** being worked on or dealt with now **ele alınmış, elde, yapılmakta olan** *Despite the pressures we are determined to get on with the job in hand.* **8 be in sb's hands** to be in someone's control or care **birinin denetim ve gözetiminde olmak** *The matter is now in the hands of my solicitor.* **9 on hand** (*also UK* to hand) near to someone or something, and ready to help or be used when necessary **yardıma hazır, yakında, yanında** *Extra supplies will be on hand, should they be needed.* **10 at the hands of sb** If you suffer at the hands of someone, they hurt you or treat you badly. **birinin eline düşüp kötü davranış ve muameleye maruz kalmak 11** [CLOCK] [C] one of the long, thin pieces that point to the numbers on a clock or watch **yelkovan 12** [CARDS] [C] the set of playing cards that one player has been given in a game **(kağıt oyununda) eldeki kâğıtlar 13 a hand** some help, especially to do something practical **yardım** *Could you give me a hand with these suitcases?* ○ *I think Matthew might need a hand with his homework.* **14 on the one hand ... on the other hand** used when you are comparing two different ideas or opinions **bir taraftan/yandan; ... öte taraftan/yandan** *On the one hand, computer games develop many skills, but on the other, they mean kids don't get enough exercise.* **15 hands off** *informal* used to tell someone not to touch something **'Dokunma!', 'Çek ellerini!', 'Elini sürme!'** *Hands off - that's mine!* **16 change hands** to be sold by someone and bought by someone else **bir şeyin satışından dolayı el değiştirmesi** *The hotel has changed hands twice since 1982.* ● **17 a free hand** permission to make your own decisions about how you want to do something **tam yetki, hareket serbestisi** ● **18 get out of hand** to become difficult to control **kontrolden çıkmak** *It was the end of term and the children were getting a little out of hand.* ● **19 go hand in hand** If two things go hand in hand, they exist together and are connected with each other. **yakından ilişki içinde olmak, birlikte oluşmak/ortaya çıkmak** ● **20 have your hands full** to be very busy **çok meşgul olmak** *Shelley has her hands full with three kids under 5.* ● **21 get/lay your hands on sth** to find something **sağlamak, temin etmek, ele geçirmek, bulmak** ● **22 get/gain the upper hand** to get into a stronger position than someone else so that you are controlling a situation **bir üst konuma gelmek, amir olmak** *Government troops are gradually gaining the upper hand over the rebels.* ● **23 with your bare hands** without using a weapon or tool **çıplak elle, herhangi bir alet kullanmadan** ● **24 wring your hands** to press your hands together because you are upset or worried about something **(endişeden) ellerini ovuşturmak; ellerini sıkmak/kenetlemek**

hand² /hænd/ *verb* **1** [+ two objects] to give something to someone **vermek, uzatmak, sunmak** *Could you hand me that book, please?* **2 you have to hand it to sb** *infor-*

mal used when you want to show that you admire someone **hakkını teslim etmek; saygı duyduğunu göstermek** *You have to hand it to Mick, he's done a good job on that kitchen.*

hand sth back *phrasal verb* to return something to the person who gave it to you **geri vermek, teslim etmek, iade etmek**

hand sth down *phrasal verb* **1** to give toys, clothes, books, etc to children who are younger than you in your family **(oyuncak, giysi, kitap vs.) devretmek, ailenin daha küçüklerine vermek 2** to pass traditions from older people to younger ones **nesilden nesile aktarmak, babadan oğula miras kalmak** *a custom handed down through the generations*

hand sth in *phrasal verb* to give something to someone in a position of authority **teslim etmek, vermek** *Have you handed your history essay in yet?*

hand sth out *phrasal verb* to give something to all the people in a group **dağıtmak, vermek** *A girl was handing out leaflets at the station.*

hand sb/sth over *phrasal verb* to give someone or something to someone else **birini/bir şeyi teslim etmek/vermek** *The hijacker was handed over to the French police.*

-hand /hænd/ ⊃See left-hand, right-hand, second-hand.

handbag /'hændbæg/ *mainly UK (mainly US purse) noun* [C] a bag carried by a woman with her money, keys, etc inside **el çantası** ⊃See picture at **bag.**

handbook /'hændbʊk/ *noun* [C] a book that contains information and advice about a particular subject **el kitabı; kılavuz, başucu kitabı** *a teacher's handbook*

handbrake /'hændbreɪk/ *UK (US* **emergency brake**) *noun* [C] a stick inside a car that you can pull up to stop the car from moving **el freni** ⊃Orta kısımdaki renkli sayfalarına bakınız.

handcuffs /'hændkʌfs/ **handcuffs**
noun [plural] two metal rings that are joined by a chain and are put on a prisoner's wrists (= lower arms) **kelepçe**

-handed /'hændɪd/
suffix ⊃See empty-handed, heavy-handed, left-handed, red-handed, right-handed, single-handed.

handful /'hændfʊl/ *noun* **1** [C] the amount of something that you can hold in one hand **el/avuç dolusu 2 a handful of sth** a small number of people or things **çok az sayıda/bir avuç (insan, şey)** *Only a handful of people came to the meeting.* **3 a handful** *informal* someone who is difficult to control, especially a child **ele avuca sığmaz, haşarı, yaramaz, afacan**

handgun /'hændgʌn/ *noun* [C] a small gun that you can hold in one hand **elde taşınabilir/tutulabilen silah**

hand-held /'hændheld/ *adjective* describes something that is designed to be held and used easily with one or two hands **elle tutulabilen** *a hand-held computer/device*

handicap /'hændɪkæp/ *noun* [C] *old-fashioned* **1** something that is wrong with your mind or body permanently **engel, handikap** *a mental/physical handicap* **2** something that makes it more difficult for you to do something **sakatlık, özür, kusur** *I found not having a car quite a handicap in the countryside.*

handicapped /'hændɪkæpt/ *adjective old-fashioned* not able to use part of your body or your mind because it has been damaged in some way **özürlü** *mentally/physically handicapped*

handicraft /'hændɪkrɑːft/ *noun* **1** [C] an activity that involves making things with your hands and that needs skill and artistic ability **el becerisi, el sanatı 2 handicrafts** things that people make with their hands **el sanatı ürünleri, el işleri** *a sale of handicrafts*

handiwork /'hændɪwɜːk/ *noun* [U] something that someone makes or does **eser, iş, marifet** *She put down the brush and stood back to admire her handiwork.*

handkerchief /'hæŋkətʃiːf/ *noun* [C] a small piece of cloth or soft paper that you use to dry your eyes or nose **mendil**

o→**handle**[1] /'hændl/ *verb* [T] DEAL WITH **1** to deal with something **başa çıkmak, icabına bakmak, üstesinden gelmek** *He handled the situation very well.* ○ *This office handles thousands of enquiries every day.* **2** TOUCH to touch, hold, or pick up something **ellemek, dokunmak, tutmak, almak, kavramak** *You must wash your hands before handling food.* **3** BUY to buy and sell goods **alım satım işleri yapmak; ticaret yapmak** *He's been charged with handling stolen goods.*

handle

handle

handle[2] /'hændl/ *noun* **1** [C] the part of something that you use to hold it or open it **kol, kulp, tokmak** *a door handle* ○ *the handle on a suitcase* **2 fly off the handle** *informal* to suddenly become very angry **aniden çok kızmak, öfkelenmek, tepesi atmak, küplere binmek**

handlebars /'hændlbɑːz/ *noun* [plural] the metal bars at the front of a bicycle or motorcycle that you hold onto to control direction **gidon**

handler /'hændlə[r]/ *noun* [C] someone whose job is to deal with or control a particular type of thing **bakıcı, işçi, görevli** *a police dog handler*

'hand ˌluggage *noun* [U] small bags that you can carry onto an aircraft with you when you travel **el bagajı**

handmade /ˌhænd'meɪd/ *adjective* made by hand instead of by machine **el yapımı**

handout /'hændaʊt/ *noun* [C] **1** money or food that is given to people who are poor **sadaka, yardım** *Increasing numbers of people are dependent on government handouts.* **2** a copy of a document that is given to all the people in a class or meeting **el broşürü, kitapçık**

handpicked /ˌhænd'pɪkt/ *adjective* carefully chosen for a particular purpose or job **özenle seçilmiş, seçme, seçkin** *a handpicked audience*

handset /'hændset/ *noun* [C] **1** the outer part of a mobile phone **cep telefonu kapağı 2** the part of a telephone that you hold in front of your mouth and against your ear **telefon ahizesi**

H

,hands 'free *adjective* describes a piece of equipment, especially a telephone, that you can use without needing to hold it in your hand **eller kullanılmadan kullanılabilen**

handshake /'hændˌʃeɪk/ *noun* [C] the action of taking someone's right hand and shaking it when you meet or leave each other **el sıkışma, tokalaşma**

handsome /'hændsəm/ *adjective* **1** A handsome man is attractive. **yakışıklı** *tall, dark and handsome* **2 a handsome profit/sum, etc** a large amount of money **çok büyük miktarda para**

hands-on /ˌhændz'ɒn/ *adjective* physically doing something and not only studying it or watching someone else do it **bizzat yapılan, elle yapılan** *hands-on experience*

handwriting /'hændˌraɪtɪŋ/ *noun* [U] the way that someone forms the letters when they write with a pen or pencil **el yazısı**

handwritten /ˌhænd'rɪtᵊn/ *adjective* written with a pen or pencil **elle yazılmış** *a handwritten letter*

handy /'hændi/ *adjective* **1** useful or easy to use **yararlı, faydalı, kullanışlı, kolay** *a handy container/tool* **2 come in handy** *informal* to be useful at some time in the future **gelecekte yararlı olmak, işe yaramak** *Don't throw those jars away - they might come in handy.* **3** *UK informal* near to a place **el altında, kolay, kolay gidilebilir** *It's a nice house and it's handy for the station.* **4 be handy with sth** to be good at using something, usually a tool **eli yatkın, becerikli, usta, elinden iş gelir** *He's very handy with a paintbrush.*

handyman /'hændimæn/ *noun* [C] plural **handymen** someone who is good at making things or repairing them **elinden her iş gelen/eli her işe yatkın kişi; usta/becerikli kişi**

ᴏᴗ**hang¹** /hæŋ/ *verb past* **hung 1** FASTEN [I, T] to fasten something so that the top part is fixed but the lower part is free to move, or to be fastened in this way **asmak, asılmak, sallandırmak** *He hung his coat on the hook behind the door.* **2** KILL [I, T] *past also* **hanged** to kill someone by putting a rope around their neck and making them drop, or to die in this way **idam etmek, asarak idam etmek 3** IN AIR [I] to stay in the air for a long time **asılı kalmak, havada kalmak, sallanmak** *Thick fog hung over the town.* ⇨See also: be/hang in the **balance¹**, hang your **head¹** (in shame).

hang around *phrasal verb informal* (*also UK* hang about) **1** to spend time somewhere, usually without doing very much **aylak aylak dolaşmak, oyalanmak, amaçsızca gezinmek** *There's nowhere for teenagers to go, so they just hang around on street corners.* **2 hang around with sb** to spend time with someone

hang on *phrasal verb* **1** *informal* to wait for a short time **kısa süre beklemek, durmak** *Hang on - I'm almost finished.* **2** to hold something tightly **sıkıca tutmak, bırakmamak, yapışmak, sarılmak** *Hang on, we're going over a big bump here.*

hang onto sth *phrasal verb informal* to keep something **You should hang onto that - it might be worth something.**

hang out *phrasal verb informal* to spend a lot of time in a particular place or with a particular group of people **belirli yerlerde ve/veya belirli kişilerle uzun zaman geçirmek**

hang up *phrasal verb* to finish a conversation on the telephone by putting the phone down **konuşmayı bitirmek, ahizeyi yerine koymak, telefonu kapamak**

hang sth up *phrasal verb* to put something such as a coat somewhere where it can hang **asmak, askıya asmak** *You can hang up your jacket over there.*

hang² /hæŋ/ *noun* **get the hang of sth** *informal* to gradually learn how to do or use something *...in/ın yolunu/nasıl yapılacağını öğrenmek*

hangar /'hæŋə'/ *noun* [C] a large building where aircraft are kept **hangar, uçak hangarı**

hanger /'hæŋə'/ (*also* coat hanger) *noun* [C] a wire, wooden, or plastic object for hanging clothes on **askı**

'hang ˌglider *noun* [C] a structure covered in cloth that you hold onto and float through the air **planör, uçurtma**

'hang ˌgliding *noun* [U] the sport of flying using a structure covered in cloth that you hang from **planörle uçma, planörcülük**

hangover /'hæŋəʊvə'/ *noun* [C] If you have a hangover, you feel ill because you drank too much alcohol the evening before. **akşamdan kalma hali, içkiden dolayı mahmurluk**

hanker /'hæŋkə'/ *verb*

hanker after/for sth *phrasal verb* to want something very much, especially over a long period of time **arzulamak, özlemini çekmek**

hankie (*also* hanky) /'hæŋki/ *noun* [C] *informal short for* handkerchief **mendil**

Hanukkah (Chanukah) /'hɑːnəkə/ *noun* [C, U] a Jewish religious holiday lasting for eight days in December **Yahudilerin aralık ayında sekiz gün süren dini bayramı; Hanuka**

haphazard /ˌhæp'hæzəd/ *adjective* not planned, organized, controlled, or done regularly **gelişigüzel, rastgele, itinasız, lalettayin** *The whole examination process seemed completely haphazard.* ● **haphazardly** *adverb* **planlanmamış bir şekilde**

hapless /'hæpləs/ *adjective literary* having bad luck **talihsiz, bahtsız, şanssız**

ᴏᴗ**happen** /'hæpᵊn/ *verb* [I] **1** If an event or situation happens, it exists or starts to be done, usually by chance. **meydana gelmek, olmak, vuku bulmak** *Were you anywhere nearby when the accident happened?* ○ *We can't let a mistake like this happen again.* **2** to be the result of an action, situation, or event that someone or something experiences **olmak, başına gelmek, yaşamak, tecrübe etmek** *Did you hear what happened to Jamie last night?* ○ *What happens if we can't get enough tickets?* **3 happen to do sth** to do something by chance **bir şeyin tesadüfen olması** *If you happen to see Peter, say "hi" for me.* ○ *You don't happen to know her phone number, do you?* **4 as it happens; it so happens** something that you say in order to introduce a surprising fact **tesadüfen, şans eseri, rastlantı olarak** *As it happens, her birthday is the day after mine.*

happen on/upon sth/sb *phrasal verb* to find something or meet someone without planning to **tesadüfen bulmak/karşılaşmak, rastlamak, rastgelmek**

happening /'hæpᵊnɪŋ/ *noun* [C] something that happens, often a strange event that is difficult to explain **olay, vaka, olup bitenler**

happily /'hæpɪli/ *adverb* **1** HAPPY in a happy way **mutlulukla** *happily married* **2** WILLING in a way that is very willing **isteklice, severek, isteyerek** *I'd happily drive you to the airport.* **3** LUCKY having a good or lucky result **mutlulukla, sevinçle, keyifle** *Happily, the operation was a complete success.*

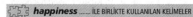

happiness ...... İLE BİRLİKTE KULLANILAN KELİMELER

find happiness

happiness /'hæpɪnəs/ *noun* [U] the feeling of being happy **mutluluk, saadet**

happy .... BAŞKA BİR DEYİŞLE

Mutlu olarak gözüken bir kiş **cheerful** olarak tanımlanabilir. *She's always very* **cheerful**. Eğer kişi herhangi birşeyden dolayı mutluysa, **pleased** veya **glad** sıfatları kullanılabilir. Bunun yanısıra eğer çok mutlularsa **delighted** sıfatı da durumu ifade eder. *He was* **pleased** *that she had come back.* ● *I was so* **glad** *to see her.* ● *They are* **delighted** *with their new car.* Eğer kişi yüksek derecede mutlu ve heyecanlı ise, kişinin durumunu ifade edebilmek için **ecstatic** veya **elated** ifadeleri kullanılabilir. *The new president was greeted by an* **ecstatic** *crowd.* ● *We were* **elated** *at the news.*

○━ **happy** /'hæpi/ *adjective* **1** PLEASED pleased and in a good mood, especially because something good has happened **mutlu, mesut** *I'm glad you've finally found someone who* **makes** *you* **happy**. ○ *Jean seems much happier now that she's moved out.* **2 happy to do sth** to be willing to do something **yapmaya istekli/gönüllü olmak** *I'd be very happy to help, if you need a hand.* **3** SHOWING HAPPINESS making you feel happy, or expressing happiness **mutlu, mesut, neşeli** *Did the book have a* **happy ending?** **4** SATISFIED satisfied and not worried **mutlu, memnun, tatmin olmuş, hoşnut** *Are you* **happy** *with your exam results?* ○ *I'm not very* **happy** *about you travelling alone at night.* **5 Happy Birthday/ New Year, etc** something friendly that you say to someone on a special day or holiday **'İyi ki doğdun!', 'Mutlu Yıllar!' vb.** *Happy Christmas!* ⊃Opposite **unhappy**.

happy-go-lucky /ˌhæpigəʊ'lʌki/ *adjective* not worried and not having any responsibilities **gamsız, kaygısız, tasasız, aldırış etmeyen, umursamayan**

'**happy ,hour** *noun* [usually singular] a period of time, usually in the early evening, when a bar (= a place where alcoholic drinks are sold and drunk) sells drinks more cheaply than usual **akşam iş çıkış saatine denk gelen ve barlarda içkilerin daha ucuza satıldığı zaman dilimi; dostlarla geçirilen mutlu zaman**

,**happy 'slapping** *noun* [U] when a group of young people attack someone and photograph their attack with mobile phones **bir grup gencin birine saldırmaları ve o anı cep telefonuyla kaydetmeleri**

harass /'hærəs/, /hə'ræs/ *verb* [T] to continue to annoy or upset someone over a period of time **taciz/tedirgin/ rahatsız etmek, bezdirmek**

harassed /'hærəst/ *adjective* tired and feeling anxious **bezmiş, tedirgin/rahatsız/huzursuz olmuş, usanmış** *harassed passengers*

🧩 ***harassment*** .... İLE BİRLİKTE KULLANILAN KELİMELER

be subjected to/suffer harassment ● racial/sexual harassment ● harassment of sb

harassment /'hærəsmənt/ *noun* [U] behaviour that annoys or upsets someone **tedirgin/rahatsız/taciz etme, bezdirme, usandırma** *sexual harassment*

harbour¹ UK (US harbor) /'hɑːbər/ *noun* [C] an area of water near the coast where ships are kept and are safe from the sea **liman**

harbour² UK (US harbor) /'hɑːbər/ *verb* [T] **1** If you harbour doubts, hopes, thoughts, etc, you feel or think about them for a long time. **(ümit, kuşku, fikir vb.) beslemek, biriktirmek, düşünmek** *He harboured dreams of one day becoming a professional footballer.* **2** to hide someone or something bad **saklamak, gizlemek** *to* **harbour** *a criminal*

○━ **hard¹** /hɑːd/ *adjective* **1** FIRM firm and stiff, and not easy to press or bend **sert, katı** *a hard surface* ○ *The seats in the waiting room were hard and uncomfortable.*

harbour

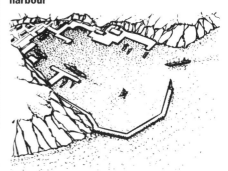

2 DIFFICULT difficult to do or understand **yapması/anlaması zor** [+ to do sth] *It must be hard to study with all this noise.* ○ *Quitting my job was the hardest decision I ever had to make.* **3** WITH EFFORT using or done with a lot of effort **çetin, zor, güç, müşkül** *the long, hard struggle* ○ *With a bit of* **hard work** *and determination we might still finish on time.* **4** UNPLEASANT full of problems and difficult to deal with **yıpratıcı, yorucu, zor, sorunlu** *My grandparents had a very hard life.* **5** NOT KIND not gentle or kind **sert, insafsız, acımasız** *She had a cold, hard look in her eyes.* **6 be hard on sb a** CRITICIZE to criticize someone too much or treat them unfairly **sert/insafsız/acımasız/merhametsiz olmak** *You shouldn't be so hard on yourself.* **b** MAKE UNHAPPY to make someone unhappy by causing them problems **mutsuz etmek, sorun çıkarmak** *Our divorce has been particularly hard on the children.* **7 be hard on sth** to damage something or make it have problems **zarar/ziyan vermek, sorun yaratmak** *Stress can be hard on any relationship.* **8 do/learn sth the hard way** to do or learn something by experiencing a lot of problems or difficulty **güçlükle/zorlukla öğrenmek/yapmak/üstesinden gelmek.** **9 give sb a hard time** *informal* to criticize someone or to treat them unfairly *He gave me a hard time about losing his keys.*

○━ **hard²** /hɑːd/ *adverb* **1** with a lot of effort **güçlükle, zorlukla** *She tried very* **hard** *but she wasn't quite fast enough.* ○ *You'll have to* **work harder***, if you want to pass this exam.* **2** with a lot of force **şiddetle, kuvvetle** *It's been raining hard all day.* ○ *She kicked the ball as hard as she could.* **3 die hard** If a belief, custom, or habit dies hard, it is very difficult to change. **(inanç, gelenek, alışkanlık) zor kaybolmak, yok olmak, değişmek** *I'm afraid that* **old habits die hard**. ● **4 hit sb hard** *UK* If a situation or experience hits you hard, it makes you so upset that you have difficulty dealing with it. **kötü vurmak, mahvetmek, sarsmak**

hardback /'hɑːdbæk/ *noun* [C] a book that has a thick, stiff cover **ciltli kitap, kalın ciltli kitap**

hard-boiled /ˌhɑːd'bɔɪld/ *adjective* A hard-boiled egg has been boiled with its shell on, until the inside is solid. **çok pişmiş/katı yumurta**

,**hard 'cash** *noun* [U] coins and paper money **nakit/ peşin para; (argo) trink para**

,**hard 'copy** UK (US 'hard ,copy) *noun* [C, U] information from a computer that has been printed on paper **basılı kağıt**

hardcore (also **hard-core**) /'hɑːdˌkɔː/ *adjective* **1** extremely loyal to someone or something, and not willing to change **yürekten bağlı; sadık, değişmeyen** *a hard-core following* **2** Hardcore magazines, films, etc show very active or offensive sexual acts. **(dergi, film) porno, açık saçık** *hardcore pornography*

hard 'core *noun* [no plural] a small group of people in society or an organization who are very active and determined not to change **ana/çekirdek kadro; esas takım** *a hard core of activists*

hard 'currency *noun* [U] money that is valuable and can be exchanged easily because it comes from a powerful country **sağlam para**

hard 'disk *noun* [C] a hard drive **(bilgisayar) ana bellek, hard disk**

'hard ,drive (*also* hard disk) *noun* [C] the part inside a computer that is not removed and stores very large amounts of information **(bilgisayar) ana bellek, esas sürücü**

hard 'drugs *noun* [plural] very strong, illegal drugs **uyuşturucu**

harden /'hɑːdᵊn/ *verb* [I, T] **1** to become hard and stiff, or to make something become hard and stiff **sertleş(tir)mek, katılaş(tır)mak** *This island is formed from volcanic lava that has hardened into rock.* **2** to stop feeling emotions about someone or something, so that you seem less kind, gentle, or weak **(duygusal olarak) sertleşmek, katılaşmak, acımasızlaşmak** *hardened criminals*

hard-headed /,hɑːd'hedɪd/ *adjective* very determined, and not willing to be influenced by your emotions **hislerine kapılmayan, kolay etkilenmeyen, kararlı** *a hard-headed manager*

hard-hearted /,hɑːd'hɑːtɪd/ *adjective* not caring how other people feel **acımasız, merhametsiz, taş kalpli, kalpsiz, zalim, insafsız**

hard-hitting /,hɑːd'hɪtɪŋ/ *adjective* A hard-hitting speech, report, article, etc is very severe or criticizes someone or something a lot. **(konuşma, rapor, makale vb.) sert, acımasız, eleştiren**

hard 'line *noun* [no plural] when someone is very strict and severe **kararlı ve çetin, azimli ve sert tutum, boyun eğmez davranış** *Judge Tucker has a reputation for taking a hard line on criminals.* ● **hardline** /,hɑːd'laɪn/ *adjective a* **hardline** *policy on illegal immigrants* **sert, aşırı**

⌐• **hardly** /'hɑːdli/ *adverb* **1** almost not, or only a very small amount **güç bela, çok az, ancak, neredeyse hiç** *I was so tired that I could hardly walk.* ○ *We've hardly ever spoken to each other.* ○ *There's hardly any food left in the fridge.* **2** used to emphasize that you think something is not likely, true, possible, etc **hiç, asla; olası bile değil** *I hardly think she'll want to talk to me now that I have a new girlfriend.*

hard-nosed /,hɑːd'nəʊzd/ *adjective* very determined, and not willing to be influenced by your emotions **azimli, kararlı, duygularından etkilenmeyen** *a hard-nosed lawyer*

hard-pressed /,hɑːd'prest/ *adjective* **1** be **hard-pressed to do sth** to not be able to do something, or have difficulty doing something **zor durumda, büyük baskı altında** *You'd be hard-pressed to find a better worker than Jeff.* **2** having problems because you are poor **maddi sıkıntı çeken, yoksul, fakir** *hard-pressed farmers*

hardship ...... İLE BİRLİKTE KULLANILAN KELİMELER

suffer hardship ● **economic/financial/physical** hardship

hardship /'hɑːdʃɪp/ *noun* [C, U] a problem or situation that makes you suffer a lot, especially because you are

very poor **zorluk, güçlük, sıkıntılı olma, çaresizlik** *They have suffered years of financial hardship.*

hard 'shoulder *UK* (*US* shoulder) *noun* [C] the area on the edge of a main road where a car can stop in an emergency **oto yolda acil durumlarda kullanılan bölüm/cep/banket**

hard 'up *adjective informal* not having enough money **eli dar/darda, para sıkıntısı içinde, maddi zorluk çeken**

hardware /'hɑːdweəʳ/ *noun* [U] **1** the machines or equipment that your computer system is made from, not the programs **(bilgisayar) donanım 2** tools and strong equipment, such as those used in the home or garden **hırdavat, alet edavat**

hard-working /,hɑːd'wɜːkɪŋ/ *adjective* doing a job seriously and with a lot of effort **çalışkan, gayretli**

hardy /'hɑːdi/ *adjective* strong enough to deal with bad conditions or difficult situations **güçlü, kuvvetli, dayanıklı, sağlam**

hare /heəʳ/ *noun* [C] an animal like a large rabbit that can run very fast and has long ears **yabani tavşan**

harem /'hɑːriːm/ ⑤ /'herəm/ *noun* [C] a group of women who live with or are married to one man in some Muslim societies, or the place where these women live **harem**

harm ...... İLE BİRLİKTE KULLANILAN KELİMELER

cause/do (sb/sth) harm ● not **come to** any harm ● **great/serious/untold** harm ● harm **to** sb

⌐• **harm¹** /hɑːm/ *noun* **1** [U] hurt or damage **zarar, ziyan** *Smoking can cause serious harm to the lungs.* ○ *Alan would never do anyone any harm.* **2** not **come to any harm** to not be hurt or damaged **hasar almamak, zarar görmemek 3** not **do any harm** to not be a bad thing to do and possibly be a good thing **zararı olmamak, zarar vermemek, yapılmasında bir mahsur olmamak** [+ to do sth] *It wouldn't do any harm to have another look.* **4 there's no harm in doing sth** used to say that something is not a bad thing to do and could possibly have a good effect **...ın/in bir zararı/sakıncası yok; zarar gelmez** *I suppose there's no harm in trying.* **5 not mean any harm** to not intend to hurt someone or damage something **zarar vermek niyetinde olmamak; üzmek istememek** *I never meant him any harm, I just wanted him to leave me alone.* **6 out of harm's way** safe from a dangerous place or situation **emniyette, emin bir yerde, güven içinde**

⌐• **harm²** /hɑːm/ *verb* [T] to hurt someone or damage something **zarar vermek, incitmek, üzmek** *Thankfully no one was harmed in the accident.*

harmful /'hɑːmfᵊl/ *adjective* causing or likely to cause harm **zararlı** *Doctors believe that smoking is harmful to your health.*

harmless /'hɑːmləs/ *adjective* **1** not able or not likely to cause any hurt or damage **zararsız** *Taken in small doses, this drug is completely harmless.* **2** not likely to shock or upset people **zararsız, zararı dokunmayan** *Their jokes seemed harmless enough.* ● **harmlessly** *adverb* **zararsız bir şekilde**

harmonica /hɑː'mɒnɪkə/ *noun* [C] a small musical instrument that you blow into as you move it across your mouth **ağız mızıkası, armonika**

harmonious /hɑː'məʊniəs/ *adjective* **1** friendly and peaceful **dostça, uyumlu** *a harmonious business relationship* **2** having or making a pleasant sound **uyumlu, ahenkli**

harmonize (*also UK* -**ise**) /ˈhɑːmənaɪz/ *verb* [I, T] **1** to be suitable together, or to make different people, plans, situations, etc suitable for each other **uyumlu hale getirmek, uyum sağlamak, bağdaş(tır)mak** *The gardens had been designed to* **harmonize with** *the natural landscape.* **2** to sing or play music in harmony **uyum içinde çalıp söylemek**

harmony /ˈhɑːməni/ *noun* **1** [U] when people are peaceful and agree with each other, or when different things seem right or suitable together **uyum** *living together in peace and* **harmony 2** [C, U] a pleasant sound in music, made by playing or singing a group of different notes together **ses/müzik uyumu**

harness¹ /ˈhɑːnɪs/ *noun* [C] **1** a set of straps fastened around a horse's body and connecting it to a vehicle that it will pull **koşum takımı 2** a set of strong, flat ropes that fasten equipment to your body or fasten you to a vehicle to prevent you from moving too much **kayış, emniyet kayışı/bağı** *All climbers must wear safety harnesses and helmets.*

harness² /ˈhɑːnɪs/ *verb* [T] **1** to put a harness on a horse, or to connect a horse to a vehicle using a harness **koşum takımı vurmak, koşmak 2** to control something so that you can use its power or qualities for a particular purpose **işe yarar hale getirmek, yararlanmak**

harp¹ /hɑːp/ *noun* [C] a large wooden musical instrument with many strings that you play with your fingers **harp, arp**

harp² /hɑːp/ *verb*
 harp on (about sb/sth) *phrasal verb* to talk about someone or something too much **dönüp dolaşıp hep aynı şeyden söz etmek, hep aynı şeyden bahsetmek, tekrarlayıp durmak, vızıldayıp durmak**

harpoon /ˌhɑːˈpuːn/ *noun* [C] a weapon with a sharp point, used especially for hunting whales (= large sea animals) **zıpkın**

harrowing /ˈhærəʊŋ/ *adjective* making you feel extremely frightened or upset **kahredici, acılı, üzücü, yürek paralayıcı** *a harrowing experience*

harsh /hɑːʃ/ *adjective* CRUEL cruel, unkind, or unpleasant in a way that seems unfair **kaba, sert, acımasız, haşin** *harsh criticism/punishment* ○ *Taking him out of the game was a bit harsh.* **2** DIFFICULT very cold, dangerous, or unpleasant and difficult to live in **zor, çok soğuk, tehlikeli, yaşanmaz** *harsh conditions* **3** STRONG too strong, bright, loud, etc **çok sert/parlak/sesli; göz kamaştırıcı, kulakları tırmalayan** *harsh chemicals* ○ *harsh lighting* ● **harshly** *adverb* **zorbalıkla** ● **harshness** *noun* [U] **zorbalık**

harvest¹ /ˈhɑːvɪst/ *noun* [C, U] when crops are cut and collected from fields **hasat, harman, ürün kaldırma 2** [C] the quality or amount of crops that are collected **hasat kalitesi/miktarı**

harvest² /ˈhɑːvɪst/ *verb* [I, T] to cut and collect crops when they are ready **hasat kaldırmak; ürün hasat etmek**

o←**has** *strong form* /hæz/ *weak forms* /həz/, /əz/, /z/ *present simple he/she/it of* have **'have' fiilinin 3. tekil şahıslar için kullanılan şekli**

has-been /ˈhæzbiːn/ *noun* [C] *informal* someone who was famous or important in the past but is now ignored **geçmişte şöhret olan fakat artık gözardı edilen, önemsenmeyen**

hash /hæʃ/ *noun* **make a hash of sth** *UK informal* to do something very badly **yüzüne gözüne bulaştırmak, bozmak, berbat etmek**

hashish /hæˈʃiːʃ/ (*also* **hash**) *noun* [U] an illegal drug that is usually smoked for pleasure **haşhaş**

o←**hasn't** /ˈhæzənt/ *short for* has not **'has not' fiilinin kısa hâli** *It hasn't rained for three weeks.*

hassle¹ /ˈhæsl/ *noun* [C, U] **1** something that is annoying because it is difficult or unpleasant to do **sıkıntı, güçlük, rahatsızlık** *I don't want to drive - it's such a hassle finding a place to park.* **2** an argument or fight **ağız dalaşı, tartışmak, ağız kavgası** *They aren't giving you any hassle, are they?*

hassle² /ˈhæsl/ *verb* [T] to annoy someone, especially by asking them something again and again **sürekli soru sorarak rahatsız /tedirgin etmek** *He's always hassling me about money.*

indecent/undue haste ● **in** sb's haste ● **do** sth **in** haste

haste /heɪst/ *noun* [U] when you are in a hurry and do something more quickly than you should **acele, telaş, koşturmaca** *In their haste to escape, they left behind all their belongings.*

hasten /ˈheɪsən/ *verb* **1** [T] to make something happen faster than usual **hızlandırmak, çabuklaştırmak 2 hasten to do sth** to hurry to do or say something **hemen/vakit kaybetmeden yapmak; çabucak yapmak** *I was not, I hasten to add, the only male there.*

hasty /ˈheɪsti/ *adjective* done very quickly, usually too quickly and without thinking enough **aceleci, telaşlı** *a hasty decision/remark* ● **hastily** *adverb* **acil bir şekilde**

o←**hat** /hæt/ *noun* [C] something you wear to cover your head, for fashion or protection **şapka** *a cowboy hat* ➔See also: **bowler hat, top hat**.

hatch¹ /hætʃ/ *verb* [I, T] If an egg hatches or is hatched, it is broken open by a baby creature such as a bird, fish, or snake being born. **civ civ çıkarmak, yavru çıkarmak, yumurtadan çıkmak 2 hatch a plan/plot, etc** to plan something secretly, especially something bad **gizli saklı planlar yapmak** *He hatched a plot to kill his wife.*

hatch² /hætʃ/ *noun* [C] a small door or opening, especially in a ship, aircraft, or spacecraft **servis penceresi, ambar kapağı, lombar ağzı** *an escape hatch*

hatchback /ˈhætʃbæk/ *noun* [C] a car that has a large door at the back, which you lift up to open **arkasında büyük kapısı olan araba; beşinci kapı**

hatchet /ˈhætʃɪt/ *noun* **1** [C] a small axe (= tool for cutting wood) **küçük balta 2 bury the hatchet** to forget about your arguments and become friends with someone again **barışıp yeniden dost olmak, aradaki kırgınlığı/dargınlığı unutmak**

o←**hate¹** /heɪt/ *verb* [T] **1** to dislike someone or something very much **nefret etmek** *They've hated each other since they were kids.* ○ [+ doing sth] *He hates going to the dentist's.* ○ [+ to do sth] *I hate to see you look so upset.* **2** used to emphasize that you are sorry you have to do something (**bir şeyi yapmak zorunda olmaktan dolayı) nefret etmek, istemeden yapmak zorunda olduğunu bildirir** *I hate to interrupt, John, but we need to leave.* ➔See also: sb's **guts**.

hate² /heɪt/ *noun* [U] when you dislike someone or something very much **nefret, tiksinme, tiksinti** ➔See also: **pet hate**.

hateful /ˈheɪtfəl/ *adjective* extremely unpleasant or unkind **iğrenç, tiksindirici, çok kötü, berbat** *She called me the most hateful names.*

deep/intense hatred ● **racial** hatred ● hatred **of** sb/sth

hatred /'heɪtrɪd/ *noun* [U] when you dislike someone or something very much **kin, nefret, düşmanlık** *He developed an intense hatred of all women.*

'hat ,trick *noun* [C] when a player or team has three successes, one after the other, especially three goals in a game **peş peşe üç gol**

haughty /'hɔːti/ *adjective* showing that you think you are much better or more important than other people **mağrur, kibirli, tepeden bakan, kendini beğenmiş** *a haughty young actress* ● **haughtily** *adverb* **kibirli bir şekilde**

haul¹ /hɔːl/ *verb* [T] to pull something somewhere slowly and with difficulty **asılıp güçlükle çekmek, sürükleyerek çekmek** *They hauled the piano into the living room.*

haul² /hɔːl/ *noun* **1** [C] an amount of something that has been stolen or that is owned illegally **yasa dışı yoldan kazanılan veya çalınan şey** *a haul of arms/drugs* **2 be a long haul** to be difficult and take a long time **uzun ve yorucu/güç olmak**

haulage /'hɔːlɪdʒ/ *noun* [U] UK the business of moving things by road or railway **nakliye/taşımacılık işi** *a road haulage firm*

haunt¹ /hɔːnt/ *verb* [T] **1** If a ghost haunts a place, it appears there often. **görünmek, ortaya çıkmak, ziyaret etmek; gözükmek** *a haunted house* **2** If an unpleasant memory or feeling haunts you, you think about or feel it often. **aklından çıkmamak, gözünün önünden gitmemek, yakasını bırakmamak** [often passive] *He was haunted by memories of the war.*

haunt² /hɔːnt/ *noun* [C] a place that someone visits often **uğrak, uğrak yeri, ziyaret yeri, sık sık gidilen yer** *Regents Park is one of my favourite haunts in London.*

haunting /'hɔːntɪŋ/ *adjective* beautiful, but in a sad way **güzel, hiç akıldan çıkmayan, kafaya takılan** *the haunting beauty of Africa*

○ⁿ**have**¹ *strong form* /hæv/ *weak forms* /həv/, /əv/, /v/ *auxiliary verb* used with the past participle of another verb to form the present and past perfect tenses **geçmişte olmuş bir olayın konuşulduğu/yazıldığı zamanda hâlâ önemli olduğunu gösteren geçmiş zaman ortaçlarıyla birlikte bileşik kipler kuran yardımcı fiil** *Have you seen Roz?* ○ *I've passed my test.* ○ *He hasn't visited London before.* ○ *It would have been better to tell the truth.* ○ *He's been working in France for two years now.* ○ *I had met his wife before.*

○ⁿ**have**² /hæv/ *modal verb* **1 have to do sth; have got to do sth** to need to do something or be forced to do something **yapmak zorunda/mecburiyetinde olmak** *I have to go to Manchester tomorrow.* ○ *Do we have to finish this today?* ○ *They've had to change their plans.* **2** used when you are telling someone how to do something **(kip) bir şeyin nasıl yapılacağını birine söylemek için kullanılır** *You've got to type in your name, then your password.* **3** used to say that you feel certain that something is true or will happen **(kip) bir şeyin olacağından veya doğruluğundan emin olduğunu belirtmek için kullanılır** *Interest rates have to come down at some point.* ○ *There's (= there has) got to be a better way of doing this.* ⊃See study page **Modal verbs** on page Centre 22.

○ⁿ**have**³ *strong form* /hæv/ *weak forms* /həv/, /əv/, /v/ *verb past* had **1** [OWN] [T] (*also* have got) to own something **sahip olmak** *I have two horses.* ○ *Laura has got beautiful blue eyes.* **2** [HOLD] [T] used to say that someone is holding something, or that someone or something is with them **bir şeyi tuttuğunu veya bir şeyin birinin yanında olduğunu bildirmek için kullanılır** *He had a pen in his hand.* ○ *She had a baby with her.*

3 [BE ILL] [T] (*also* have got) If you have a particular illness, you are suffering from it. **bir hastalığı olmak** *Have you ever had the measles?* **4** [EAT/DRINK] [T] to eat or drink something **yemek, içmek** *We are having dinner at 7 o'clock.* ○ *Can I have a drink of water?* **5 have a bath/sleep/walk, etc** used with nouns to say that someone does something **duş almak, uyku çekmek, yürüyüş yapmak vb.** *Can I have a quick shower?* ○ *Let Mark have a try.* **6 have difficulty/fun/problems, etc** used with nouns to say that someone experiences something **zorluk çekmek, eğlenmek, sorunları olmak** *We had a great time in Barcelona.* **7 have a baby** to give birth to a baby **çocuk doğurmak, bebek sahibi olmak 8 have sth done** If you have something done, someone does it for you. **bir şeyi yaptırmak/ettirmek** *I'm having my hair cut tomorrow.* ○ *We had the carpets cleaned.* **9 have had it** to be broken or not working well **kırılmak, bozulmak, iyi çalışmamak, miyadını doldurmak** *I think the car engine's had it.* ● **10 have it in for sb** to dislike someone and want to cause problems for them **birinden nefret etmek ve zarar vermek/sorun çıkarmak istemek** *She really has it in for me - I don't know what I've done to offend her.* ● **11 have it out (with sb)** to talk to someone about something they have done which made you angry, in order to try to solve the problem **sorunu çözmek için oturup konuşmak; önceden kendine yapılan ve kızdıran bir sorunu çözmek için konuşmak**

have (got) sth on *phrasal verb* to be wearing something **giyinik olmak, üzerinde elbise/kıyafet olmak** *She only had a bikini on.*

have sb on *phrasal verb* UK to make someone think that something is true, as a joke **(şaka) kandırmak, öyle olduğunu düşünmesini sağlamak** *He's not really angry - he's just having you on.*

have sth out *phrasal verb* to have something removed from your body **(diş veya başka bir organ) aldırmak; çektirmek** *I'm having two teeth out next week.*

haven /'heɪvⁿn/ *noun* [C] a safe place **sığınak, liman, güvenli yer** *a haven for wildlife*

○ⁿ**haven't** /'hævⁿnt/ *short for* have not **'have not'** fiilinin kısa hali *I haven't finished eating.*

havoc ...... İLE BİRLİKTE KULLANILAN KELİMELER

cause/create/wreak havoc ● **play** havoc **with** sth

havoc /'hævək/ *noun* [U] a very confused and possibly dangerous situation **kargaşa, keşmekeş, yıkım, büyük hasar, tahribat, zarar ziyan** *The snow has caused havoc on Scotland's roads today.*

hawk /hɔːk/ *noun* [C] a large hunting bird **şahin**

hay /heɪ/ *noun* [U] dried grass for animals to eat **saman, kuru ot**

'hay ,fever *noun* [U] an illness caused by a bad reaction to plants that some people get in the summer, especially affecting the nose and eyes **saman/bahar nezlesi**

haystack /'heɪstæk/ *noun* [C] a large pile of hay **saman/kuru ot yığını**

hazard¹ /'hæzəd/ *noun* **1** [C] something that is dangerous **tehlike, risk** *a fire hazard* ○ *a health hazard* **2 an occupational hazard** something unpleasant that sometimes happens to people who do a particular job **meslekî risk/tehlike**

hazard² /'hæzəd/ *verb* **hazard a guess** to risk guessing something **bir öneride/tahminde bulunmak; bir şeyi tahmin riskine girmek** *I don't know where he is, but I'd be willing to hazard a guess.*

hazardous /'hæzədəs/ *adjective* dangerous **tehlikeli, riskli** *hazardous chemicals*

haze /heɪz/ *noun* [U] when the air is not very clear because of something such as heat or smoke, making it difficult to see well **pus, hafif sis**

hazel /ˈheɪzʳl/ *adjective* green-brown in colour **ela** *hazel eyes*

hazy /ˈheɪzi/ *adjective* **1** If the air is hazy, it is not very clear because of something such as heat or smoke, making it difficult to see well. **puslu, sisli** *a hazy day* **2** not remembering things clearly **kafası karışık; şeyleri açık seçik hatırlayamamak** *He has only a hazy recollection of what happened.*

o¬**he** *strong form* /hiː/ *weak form* /hi/ *pronoun* used as the subject of the verb when referring to someone male who has already been talked about **(erkek) o** *"When is Paul coming?" "He'll be here in a minute."*

o¬**head¹** /hed/ *noun* [C] **1** BODY the part of your body above your neck which contains your brain, eyes, ears, mouth, nose, etc and on which your hair grows **baş, kafa, kelle; (argo) saksı** *He fell and hit his head on the table.* ⊃*Orta kısımdaki renkli sayfalarına bakınız.* **2** MIND your mind **zihin, akıl, kafa** *All these thoughts were going round in my head.* **3** ORGANIZATION the person who is in charge of an organization **başkan, şef, lider, baş** *Her father is the head of an oil company.* **4** SCHOOL *(also* ˌhead ˈteacher) UK the person in charge of a school **müdür** *You'll have to ask the head if you can have a day off school.* **5** FRONT/TOP the front or top part of something **önü, başı, tepesi, üstü** *Who is that at the head of the table?* **6 £10/$6, etc a head** costing £10/$6, etc for each person **kişi başı 10£/6$ vs. maliyet/tutar** *The meal costs £20 a head.* **7 heads** the side of a coin that has a picture of someone's head on it **tura** *Heads or tails?* **8 be banging your head against a brick wall** to do, say, or ask for something repeatedly but to be unable to change a situation **boşuna nefes tüketmek; beyhude/nafile konuşmak** ● **9 come to a head** If a problem or disagreement comes to a head, it becomes so bad that you have to start dealing with it. **dönüm noktasına gelmek; kaçınılmaz bir duruma gelmek** ● **10 go over sb's head** to be too difficult for someone to understand **birinin anlayışının dışında olmak; aşmak; anlaşılmayacak kadar zor olmak** *All this talk about philosophy went right over my head.* ● **11 go to your head** If something that you have achieved goes to your head, it makes you too proud. **şımartmak, başına vurmak, çarpmak** *Fame and fortune had gone to his head.* ● **12 hang your head (in shame)** to look ashamed or embarrassed **başı önüne eğilmek; utanç duymak; mahcup olmak** ● **13 keep your head** to stay calm in a difficult situation **soğukkanlılığını muhafaza etmek; sükûnetini korumak** ● **14 lose your head** to stop being calm in a difficult situation **paniğe kapılmak; eli ayağına dolaşmak; tepesi atmak** ● **15 raise/rear its ugly head** If a problem or something unpleasant raises its ugly head, it becomes a problem that people have to deal with. **sorun/dert/problem/olumsuzluk baş göstermek/ortaya çıkmak** ● **16 laugh/shout/scream, etc your head off** to laugh/shout/scream, etc very much and very loudly **kendinden geçerek/çılgınca gülmek/bağırmak; çığlık atmak; haykırmak vs.** ⊃*See also:* hit the nail¹ on the head, a roof over your head, off the top¹ of your head.

head² /hed/ *verb* **1 head back/down/towards, etc** to move in a particular direction **kafasını aşağı/yukarı/öne hareket ettirmek** *They headed back to the shore.* **2** LEAD [T] to lead an organization or group **yönetmek, başında olmak, sorumlu (kişi) olmak** [*often passive*] *The company is headed by a young entrepreneur.* **3** FRONT/TOP [T] to be at the front or top of something **önde/üstte olmak** *Jo headed a very short list of candidates.* **4** HIT [T] to hit a ball with your head **topa kafa**

vurmak, kafa vurmak, kafa atmak *Owen headed the ball straight into the back of the net.*
    be heading for sth *phrasal verb* to be likely to get or experience something soon **aranmak, sürüklenmek, çanak tutmak** *Those children are heading for trouble.*
    head off *phrasal verb* to start a journey or leave a place **yola koyulmak, seyahate çıkmak, ayrılmak**

headache /ˈhedeɪk/ *noun* [C] pain inside your head **baş ağrısı** *I've got a bad headache.* ⊃*See also:* splitting headache.

headhunt /ˈhedhʌnt/ *verb* [T] to persuade someone to leave their job for a job with a different company **başka bir şirkette çalışmaya ikna etmek** *She was headhunted by a rival firm.* ● **headhunter** *noun* [C] **şirketler için yönetici bulan firmalar**

heading /ˈhedɪŋ/ *noun* [C] words at the top of a piece of writing that tell you what it is about **başlık**

headlight /ˈhedlaɪt/ *noun* [C] one of the two large lights on the front of a car **(araç) far** ⊃*See picture at* light.

headline /ˈhedlaɪn/ *noun* **1** [C] the title of a newspaper story that is printed in large letters above it **manşet, başlık** *a front-page headline* **2 the headlines** the main stories in newspapers, on television, etc **tv., gazete vb. haber başlığı, haber özeti** *That story made headlines all over the world.*

headlong /ˈhedlɒŋ/ *adverb* quickly and directly **balıklama, doludizgin, çarçabuk** *The plane plunged headlong into the sea.*

headmaster /ˌhedˈmɑːstəʳ/ UK *(US* principal) *noun* [C] a man who is in charge of a school **okul müdürü**

headmistress /ˌhedˈmɪstrəs/ UK *(US* principal) *noun* [C] a woman who is in charge of a school **okul müdiresi**

ˌhead ˈoffice *noun* [usually singular] the most important office of a company, or the people who work there **ana merkez, merkez ofis** *Head office handles all complaints made against the company.*

ˌhead ˈon *adverb* **1** If two vehicles hit each other head on, the front parts hit each other as they are moving forward. **burun buruna; kafa kafaya; tokuşurcasına; bodoslama 2** If you deal with something head on, you deal with it directly, although it is difficult. **doğrudan, geri durmadan, pes etmeden, ödün vermeyerek** ● **head-on** /ˌhedˈɒn/ *adjective* a *head-on collision* **kafa kafaya**

headphones
/ˈhedfəʊnz/ *noun* [plural]
a piece of equipment
that you wear over
your ears so that you
can listen to music
without anyone else
hearing it **kulaklık** *a pair of headphones*

headphones

headquarters /ˈhedˌkwɔːtəz/ *noun* [group] *plural* **headquarters** the place from where an organization is controlled **ana karargâh, ana merkez, komuta merkezi** *police headquarters*

headset /ˈhedset/ *noun* [C] a piece of equipment that you wear over your ears so that you can hear things, especially one with a microphone (= a piece of equipment that you speak into) attached to it **mikrofonlu kulaklık** *a mobile phone headset*

,head 'start *noun* [C] an advantage that someone has over other people **üstünlük, önde olma, avantaj, avans** *Caroline's language skills should give her a head start over/on other people applying for the job.*

headstone /'hedstəʊn/ *noun* [C] a stone that shows the name of a dead person who is buried under it **mezar taşı** *The headstone was crumbling away.*

headstrong /'hedstrɒŋ/ *adjective* extremely determined **son derece kararlı, bildiğinden şaşmayan, bildiğini okuyan, dik kafalı** *a headstrong young girl*

headteacher /ˌhed'tiːtʃəʳ/ *UK* (*US* **principal**) *noun* [C] the person in charge of a school **başöğretmen, müdür** *The current headteacher will retire this year.*

headway /'hedweɪ/ *noun* **make headway** to make progress in what you are doing **ilerlemek, ileri gitmek, gelişmek** *The builders aren't making much headway with our new house.*

heady /'hedi/ *adjective* having a powerful effect on the way you feel, for example by making you feel excited **heyecan verici/veren** *a heady experience*

heal /hiːl/ (*also* **heal up**) *verb* [I, T] If a wound or broken bone heals, it becomes healthy again, and if something heals it, it makes it healthy again. **iyileş(tir)mek, düzel(t)mek** *The wound on his head had begun to heal.*
 • **healer** *noun* [C] someone who makes ill people well again using something such as prayer or magic **üfürükçü, şaklaban, sahtekâr**

▨▨ *health* ...... İLE BİRLİKTE KULLANILAN KELİMELER

damage/improve sb's health • excellent/good/ill/poor health • be in [good/bad, etc] health

◦━**health** /helθ/ *noun* [U] **1** the condition of your body **sağlık, sıhhat** *to be in good/poor health* ○ *Regular exercise is good for your health.* **2** how successful and strong something is **sağlık, sıhhat, kuvvet, canlılık** *the financial health of the business* ⊃See also: **the National Health Service.**

health-care /'helθˌkeəʳ/ *noun* [U] the set of services provided by a country or an organization for treating people who are ill **sağlık, sağlık bakımı**

'**health ˌservice** *noun* [C] *UK* the National Health Service: the system providing free medical service in the UK **ücretsiz sağlık hizmetleri; (Birleşik Krallık) Ulusal Sağlık Hizmeti**

◦━**healthy** /'helθi/ *adjective* **1** PHYSICALLY STRONG physically strong and well **sağlıklı, sıhhatli, güçlü kuvvetli, gürbüz** *Sue is a normal healthy child.* **2** GOOD good for your health **sağlığa iyi gelen** *a healthy diet* **3** SUCCESSFUL successful and strong **başarılı ve güçlü** *a healthy economy* ⊃Opposite **unhealthy.**

▨▨ *heap* ...... İLE BİRLİKTE KULLANILAN KELİMELER

a heap of sth • in a heap

heap¹ /hiːp/ *noun* **1** [C] an untidy pile of things **küme, yığın, öbek** *a heap of rubbish* **2 heaps of sth** *informal* a lot of something **çok miktarda, bir sürü, çok, epeyce** *He's got heaps of money.*

heap² /hiːp/ *verb informal* **1** [T] to put things into an untidy pile **yığmak, kümelemek, biriktirmek** *He heaped more food onto his plate.* **2 heap criticism/insults/praise, etc on sb** to criticize/insult/praise, etc someone a lot **birini eleştiri/aşağılama/övgü vs. bombardımanına tutmak**

◦━**hear** /hɪəʳ/ *verb past* **heard 1** SOUND [I, T] to be aware of a sound through your ears **işitmek** *I could hear his voice in the distance.* ○ *I can't hear - can you turn the sound up?*

2 INFORMATION [I, T] to be told some information **duymak, öğrenmek, haberi olmak** *When did you first hear about this?* ○ *Have you heard the news? Jane's back.* ○ *[+ (that)] I hear that you're leaving.* **3** LAW [T] If a judge hears a case, they listen to it in a law court, to decide if someone is guilty or not. **(mahkeme) dinlemek 4 will not hear of sth** If someone will not hear of something, they will not allow it. **...ı/i kabul etmemek; ...a/e izin vermemek/müsaade etmemek** *I wanted to pay for her meal but she wouldn't hear of it.*

hear from sb *phrasal verb* to receive a letter, telephone call, or other message from someone **telefon/mektup/ileti yoluyla haber almak** *Have you heard from Sue recently?*

have heard of sb/sth *phrasal verb* to know that someone or something exists **...ı duymuş olmak; ...dan/den haberi olmak; haberdar olmak** *I've never heard of her.*

hearing /'hɪərɪŋ/ *noun* **1** [U] the ability to hear sounds **işitme, işitme duyusu** *He lost his hearing when he was a child.* **2** [C] a meeting in a law court when a judge hears the facts of a case **duruşma, celse, oturum** *The preliminary hearing will take place next week.* **3 a fair hearing** If you get a fair hearing, someone listens to your opinion. **dinlenilme fırsatı/şansı; derdini anlatabilme fırsatı**

hearing-impaired /'hɪərɪŋɪmˌpeəd/ *adjective* A person who is hearing-impaired cannot hear or cannot hear well. **duyma özürlü** ⊃Compare **deaf.**

hearsay /'hɪəseɪ/ *noun* [U] things that people have told you and that may or may not be true **söylenti, dedikodu, aslı astarı olmayan söylem** *Everything we heard was based on hearsay and rumour.*

hearse /hɜːs/ *noun* [C] a large car that is used to take a dead body to a funeral **cenaze arabası**

▨▨ *heart* ...... İLE BİRLİKTE KULLANILAN KELİMELER

your heart beats • heart disease/failure • a heart condition/problem

heart

◦━**heart** /hɑːt/ *noun* **1** ORGAN [C] the organ inside your chest that sends blood around your body **kalp, yürek** *Isabel's heart was beating fast.* ○ *heart disease/failure* **2** CENTRE [no plural] the centre of something **merkez, orta, göbek, iç** *Her office is in the heart of Tokyo.* **3 the heart of sth** the most important part of something **özü, esası, can damarı, can evi** *We need to get to the heart of the matter.* **4** FEELINGS [C, U] someone's deepest feelings and true character **gönül, kalp, iç, öz, karakter, yapı** *She has a kind heart.* **5** SHAPE [C] a shape that is used to mean love **kalp şekli/resmi,**

kalp 6 hearts playing cards with red, heart shapes on them **kupalar (iskambil oyunu) 7 at heart** used to say what someone is really like **aslında, özünde, esasında** *I'm just a kid at heart.* **8 in your heart** used to say what you really think **kalbinin derinliklerinden, yüreğinin ta derinlerinden, dışa vurulmamış duygularından** *In his heart he felt they were wrong.* **9 with all your heart** used to say that you feel something very strongly **bütün kalbiyle, tüm içtenliğiyle, en samimi duygularıyla** *I thank you with all my heart.* **10 not have the heart to do sth** to decide not to do something that would make someone unhappy **yüreği/gönlü elvermemek, cesaret edememek, kıyamamak 11 learn/know, etc sth by heart** to be able to remember all of something **ezberleyerek öğrenmek; ezbere bilmek 12 break sb's heart** to make someone very unhappy **kalbini kırmak • 13 heart and soul** used to say that you give all your attention and enthusiasm to something **bedenen ve ruhen; bütünüyle, her şeyiyle** *She threw herself into teaching heart and soul.* ⊃See also: a **change²** of heart.

heartache /ˈhɑːteɪk/ *noun* [C, U] extreme sadness **yürek sızısı, kalp acısı**

ˈheart atˌtack *noun* [C] when someone's heart suddenly stops working correctly, sometimes causing death **kalp krizi** *I think he's had a heart attack.*

heartbeat /ˈhɑːtbiːt/ *noun* [C, U] the regular movement of the heart as it moves blood around the body **kalp atışı**

heartbreaking /ˈhɑːtˌbreɪkɪŋ/ *adjective* causing extreme sadness **yürek sızlatan/parçalayan; üzücü; kahredici** *heartbreaking news*

heartbroken /ˈhɑːtˌbrəʊkᵊn/ *adjective* If you are heartbroken, you feel extremely sad about something that has happened. **kalbi kırık, çok üzgün, acı çeken**

-hearted /-ˈhɑːtɪd/ ⊃See broken-hearted, cold-hearted, half-hearted, hard-hearted, light-hearted.

heartened /ˈhɑːtᵊnd/ *adjective* feeling happier because of something **mutlu, mesut, bahtiyar** *We all felt heartened by the news.* ⊃Opposite disheartened.

heartening /ˈhɑːtᵊnɪŋ/ *adjective* making you feel happier **mutlu eden, sevindiren, mutluluk veren** *heartening news* ⊃Opposite disheartening.

ˈheart ˌfailure *noun* [U] when someone's heart stops working, often causing death **kalp yetmezliği**

heartfelt /ˈhɑːtfelt/ *adjective* Heartfelt feelings and words are strong and sincere. **yürekten, candan, içten, samimi** *heartfelt thanks/gratitude*

hearth /hɑːθ/ *noun* [C] the floor around a fireplace **ocak/şömine çevre döşemesi**

heartily /ˈhɑːtɪli/ *adverb* **1** with a lot of enthusiasm **yürekten, coşkuyla** *We all laughed heartily at the joke.* **2** completely or very much **çok, tamamen** *I am heartily sick of the situation.*

heartland /ˈhɑːtlænd/ *noun* [C] the place where an activity or belief is strongest **merkez, orta, kalp** *the traditional heartland of the motor industry*

heartless /ˈhɑːtləs/ *adjective* cruel and not caring about other people **acımasız, kalpsiz, zalim, gaddar**

heart-to-heart /ˌhɑːttəˈhɑːt/ *noun* [C] a serious conversation between two people in which they talk honestly about their feelings **dertleşme, samimi/içten sohbet, iç dökme**

hearty /ˈhɑːti/ *adjective* **1** friendly and full of energy **neşeli ve şamatalı, arkadaşça** *a hearty laugh/welcome* **2** Hearty meals are large and satisfy you. **(yiyecek) doyurucu, bol**

▨ **heat** ...... İLE BİRLİKTE KULLANILAN KELİMELER
generate/give out heat • intense/searing heat

o⇨**heat¹** /hiːt/ *noun* **1** [HOT] [U] the quality of being hot or warm **ısı, ateş, ısı kaynağı** *the heat of summer* **2** the **heat** when it is very hot **sıcak** *I don't really like the heat.* **3** [TEMPERATURE] [U, no plural] the temperature of something **ısı, ateş** *Cook on a low heat.* **4** the **heat** US (UK the **heating**) the system that keeps a building warm **ısıtma sistemi** *Could you turn the heat up a little.* **5** [RACE] [C] a competition, especially a race, which decides who will be in the final event **eleme yarışması 6 in the heat of the moment** If you do or say something in the heat of the moment, you do or say it without thinking because you are angry or excited. **kızgınlık ve heyecan esnasında yapılan/söylenen** ⊃See also: dead heat.

heat² /hiːt/ (*also* heat up) *verb* [I, T] to make become hot or warm, or to become hot or warm **ısınmak, ısıtmak** *I'll just heat up some soup.*

heated /ˈhiːtɪd/ *adjective* **1** made warm or hot **sıcak, ısınmış 2 a heated argument/debate**, etc an angry or excited argument **kızgın, gergin, öfkeli, sinirli tartışma/münazara vb.**

heater /ˈhiːtər/ *noun* [C] a machine that heats air or water **ısıtıcı**

heath /hiːθ/ *noun* [C] an open area of land covered with wild plants and rough grass **çayırlık, fundalık, çalılık**

heather /ˈheðər/ *noun* [C, U] a small plant with purple or white flowers that grows on hills **funda, süpürgeotu**

heating /ˈhiːtɪŋ/ *UK* (*US* heat) *noun* [U] the system that keeps a building warm **ısıtma, ısınma, ısıtma sistemi/aracı** ⊃See also: central heating.

heatwave /ˈhiːtweɪv/ *noun* [C] a period of time, usually a few days or weeks, when the weather is much hotter than usual **sıcak dalgası**

heave /hiːv/ *verb* **1** [I, T] to move something heavy with a lot of effort **ağır bir şeyi zorla kaldırmak, itmek, iterek çekmek, zorla itmek** *He heaved the bag on to his shoulder.* **2** [I] to move up and down inip kalkmak, şağı yukarı hareket etmek *Her chest heaved as she started to cry.* **3 heave a sigh of relief** to breathe out loudly because you are pleased that something bad has not happened **derin bir oh çekmek, iç geçirmek; derinden iç çekmek • heave** *noun* [C] **kaldırma, çekme**

heaven /ˈhevᵊn/ *noun* [U] **1** according to some religions, the place where good people go when they die **cennet 2** *informal* something very nice that gives you great pleasure **mutlu eden şey, cennet** *This cake is absolute heaven.*

heavenly /ˈhevᵊnli/ *adjective* **1** [always before noun] relating to heaven **ilahi, cennetle ilgili, semavi** *the heavenly kingdom* **2** *informal* very nice **fevkalade, çok güzel, eşsiz, harika** *a heavenly day*

heavens /ˈhevᵊnz/ *noun* **1 the heavens** *literary* the sky **gökyüzü, sema, gök kubbe 2 (Good) Heavens!** used when you are surprised or annoyed '**Aman Allah'ım!**', '**Aman Yarabbim!**' *Heavens, what's the matter?*

heavily /ˈhevɪli/ *adverb* **1** a lot or to a great degree **şiddetle, büyük oranda, ziyadesiyle** *She's heavily involved in politics.* **2 drink/smoke heavily** to drink/smoke a lot **çok fazla sigara içmek/alkol almak 3 rain/snow heavily** to rain/snow a lot **çok fazla/yoğun yağmur/kar yağmak 4** using a lot of force **zorlukla, güçlükle; ağır ağır, zar zor** *to breathe heavily*

o⇨**heavy** /ˈhevi/ *adjective* **1** [WEIGHING A LOT] Heavy objects weigh a lot. **ağır, büyük** *heavy bags* ○ *heavy machinery/equipment* **2** [HOW MUCH] used to say how much someone or something weighs **ağır** *How heavy are you?* ○ *Oxygen is sixteen times heavier than hydrogen.*

3 A LOT large in amount or degree **yoğun, kalabalık** *heavy traffic* ○ *heavy costs* **4 a heavy drinker/smoker** someone who drinks/smokes a lot **(sigara, içki) yoğun içici 5 heavy snow/rain** when a lot of snow/rain falls **yoğun kar/yağmur 6** FORCE using a lot of force **yoğun, ağır, şiddetli** *a heavy blow* ○ *heavy breathing* **7** SERIOUS *informal* serious **ciddi, yoğun** *The discussion got a bit too heavy.* **8 heavy going** *mainly UK* too serious or difficult **çok ciddi ve zor** *I found the book very heavy going.*

heavy-handed /ˌheviˈhændɪd/ *adjective* using too much force in dealing with people **patavatsız, sakar, beceriksiz**

heavy 'metal *noun* [U] a type of very loud, modern music **çok yüksek sesle çalınan modern müzik türü**

heavyweight /ˈheviweɪt/ *noun* [C] **1** a fighter such as a boxer who is in the heaviest weight group **ağır sıklet** *the heavyweight champion of the world* **2** someone who is powerful and important **güçlü ve önemli kişi** *a political heavyweight*

Hebrew /ˈhiːbruː/ *noun* [U] the language used in the Jewish religion and in Israel **Yahudi dininde ve İsrail'de kullanılan dil; İbrani, İbranice** ● **Hebrew** *adjective* **İbranice**

hectare /ˈhekteəʳ/ *noun* [C] a unit for measuring area, equal to 10,000 square metres **10.000 metrekareye eşit yüzey ölçüm birimi; hektar**

hectic /ˈhektɪk/ *adjective* extremely busy and full of activity **telaşlı, heyecanlı, son derece yoğun, hengamesi bol** *a hectic day/week*

o▪**he'd** /hiːd/ **1** *short for* he had **'he had' fiil yapısının kısa hâli** *We knew he'd taken the money.* **2** *short for* he would **'he would' fiil yapısının kısa hâli** *No one thought he'd get the job.*

hedge¹ /hedʒ/ *noun* [C] a row of bushes growing close together, often used to divide land into separate areas **çalılıklardan oluşan çit**

hedge

hedge² /hedʒ/ *verb* [I, T] to avoid giving a direct answer **kıvır(t)mak, yan çizmek, kaçamak cevaplar vermek, gevelemek** ⊃ See also: hedge your bets (**bet²**).

hedgehog /ˈhedʒhɒg/ *noun* [C] a small animal whose body is covered with sharp points **kirpi**

hedgerow /ˈhedʒrəʊ/ *noun* [C] *UK* a row of bushes and small trees along the edge of a field or road **çalı/ağaç/fundadan oluşan çit**

heed¹ /hiːd/ *verb* [T] *formal* to pay attention to some advice or a warning **kulak asmak, ehemmiyet vermek, dikkat etmek, dinlemek, aldırmak** *Officials failed to heed his warning.*

heed² /hiːd/ *noun formal* **take heed of sth** to pay attention to something, especially some advice or a warning **...a/e önem vermek; ...a/e dikkat etmek/almak; kulak vermek**

heel /hiːl/ *noun* [C] **1** the back part of your foot **ayak topuğu** ⊃ Orta kısımdaki renkli sayfalarına bakınız. **2** the part of a shoe that is under your heel **ayakkabı topuğu** *high heels*

hefty /ˈhefti/ *adjective informal* very large **iri yarı, kocaman, çok büyük, fazla, çok miktarda** *a hefty bill/fine* ○ *a hefty woman with dyed hair*

🧩 **height** ...... İLE BİRLİKTE KULLANILAN KELİMELER

grow to/reach a height of sth ● be [3 metres, etc] **in height**

o▪**height** /haɪt/ *noun* **1** HOW TALL [C, U] how tall or high something or someone is **boy, yükseklik** *a man of average height* ○ *The tower measures 27.28 metres in height.* **2** HOW FAR UP [C, U] how far above the ground something is **yükseklik, irtifa, rakım** *The aircraft was flying at a height of about 6000 metres.* **3** TALL [U] being tall **boy, yükseklik** *People always make comments about his height.* **4 the height of sth** the strongest or most important part of something **en son derece, en üst nokta, doruk** *I met him when he was at the height of his fame.*

heighten /ˈhaɪtᵊn/ *verb* [I, T] to increase or make something increase **yüksel(t)mek; art(tır)mak; şiddetlen (dir)mek** *heightened awareness* ○ [often passive] *The book's success was heightened by the scandal.*

heights /haɪts/ *noun* **1** [plural] high places **tepe, zirve, doruk; yüksekler; yüksek yerler** *I've always been afraid of heights.* **2 new heights** when something is better or more successful than ever before **yeni zirveler; daha iyi ve başarılı olma durumu** *Our athletes have reached new heights of sporting glory.*

heinous /ˈheɪnəs/ *adjective formal* very bad and shocking **iğrenç, tiksindirici, menfur** *heinous crimes*

heir /eəʳ/ *noun* [C] a person who will have the legal right to someone's money and possessions when they die **mirasçı, varis** *He is the heir to a huge fortune.*

heiress /ˈeəres/ *noun* [C] a woman who will have the legal right to someone's money and possessions when they die **bayan varis, bayan mirasçı**

held /held/ *past of* hold **'tutmak' fiilinin 2. ve 3. hâli**

helicopter

helicopter /ˈhelɪkɒptəʳ/ *noun* [C] an aircraft which flies using long, thin parts on top of it that turn round and round very fast **helikopter**

helium /ˈhiːliəm/ *noun* [U] a gas that is lighter than air and that will not burn (formula He) **helyum gazı** *a helium balloon*

he'll /hiːl/ *short for* he will **'he will' fiil yapısının kısa hâli** *He'll be home soon.*

o▪**hell** /hel/ *noun* **1** [U] according to some religions, the place where bad people go when they die **cehennem 2** [U] *informal* an experience that is very unpleasant **cehennem azabı, çok kötü şey, büyük sıkıntı** *It's been hell working with him.* **3 the hell** *informal* used to emphasize something in a rude or angry way **'Hay Allah!', 'Kör olası!', 'Hay kör olası şeytan!', 'Lanet olası!'** *What the hell are you doing here?* **4 a/one hell**

of a *informal* used to say that someone or something is very good, big, etc **berbat, feci, bir hayli, pek çok, müthiş** *a hell of a noise* ○ *He's one hell of a tennis player.* **5 from hell** *informal* used to say that someone or something is extremely bad **cehenneme dönmüş, cehennem gibi, berbat, çok kötü** *We had the holiday from hell.* **6 like hell** *informal* very much **müthiş, feci, çok fazla, aşırı** *It's raining like hell out there.*

hellish /ˈhelɪʃ/ *adjective informal* extremely bad or unpleasant **berbat, çok kötü, korkunç** *a hellish place/journey*

☞**hello** (*also UK* **hallo**) /helˈəʊ/ *exclamation* **1** used to greet someone **'Merhaba!', 'Selâm!'** *Hello, Chris, how are things?* **2** used to start a conversation on the telephone **Alo!** *Hello, this is Alex.*

helm /helm/ *noun* **1** [C] the part that you use to direct a boat or ship (gemi) **dümen 2 at the helm** controlling a group or organization **dümende, yönetiminde, kontrolünde, idaresinde** *With Lewis at the helm we are certain of success.*

helmet

helmet /ˈhelmət/ *noun* [C] a hard hat that protects your head **çelik başlık, miğfer, kask, baret** *a cycling helmet* ➎See also: **crash helmet** ➎Orta kısımdaki renkli sayfalarına bakınız.

---

help   **BAŞKA BİR DEYİŞLE**

Aid ve **assist** fiilleri **help** fiiline alternatif olarak daha ciddi/resmi kullanılabilir. *The army arrived to* **assist** *in the search.* ● *The project is designed to* **aid** *poorer countries.*

Eğer iki veya daha fazla kişi bir şeyi başarmak amacıyla birbirine yardım ediyorsa, bu durumun ifadesi için **collaborate** veya **cooperate** fiilleri kullanılabilir. *Several countries are* **collaborating/cooperating** *in the relief effort.*

Eğer kişi bir konuyla ilgili yardım görmüş ise, durumu belirtmek için **benefit** fiili kullanılabilir. *The children have* **benefited** *greatly from the new facilities.*

Eğer kişi yardım talebinde bulunuyorsa, resmiyet taşımayan ortamlarda durumun ifadesi için **give** someone **a hand** söylemi kullanılır. *Do you think you could* **give** *me* **a hand** *with these heavy boxes?*

☞**help**[1] /help/ *verb* **1** [I, T] to make it easier for someone to do something **yardım etmek** *Thank you for helping.* ○ [+ (to) do sth] *Shall I help you to set the table?* ○ *Dad always* ***helps*** *me* ***with*** *my homework.* **2** [I, T] to make something easier or better **fayda etmek, yararı olmak, işi görmek** [+ to do sth] *When you're nervous or frightened, it helps to breathe slowly and deeply.* **3 can't/ couldn't help sth** to be unable to stop yourself doing something or to stop something happening **...dan/den kendini alamamak; elinde olmamak; ...sız/siz edememek/yapamamak** [+ doing sth] *I couldn't help thinking about what had happened.* ○ *He couldn't help it, he slipped.* **4 help yourself (to sth)** to take something, especially food or drink, without asking **(ikram vb.) kendi almak; 'Buyrun!'** *Please help yourself to some coffee.*

help (sb) out *phrasal verb* to help someone, especially by giving them money or working for them **yardım etmek; yardımda bulunmak; yardım elini uzatmak** *Carol's been helping out in the shop this week.*

---

help   İLE BİRLİKTE KULLANILAN KELİMELER

ask for/need/offer/provide/refuse help ● **a big/ great** help ● **extra/professional** help

---

☞**help**[2] /help/ *noun* **1** [U] when someone helps another person **yardım** *I was too embarrassed to* ***ask for*** *help.* ○ *Do you want any help?* **2** [no plural] something or someone that helps **yadımcı, yardım, çare, deva** *Dave has been a great help to me.* **3 with the help of sth** using something **yardımıyla, kullanarak** *We assembled the computer with the help of the manual.*

help[3] /help/ *exclamation* something that you shout when you are in danger **'imdat!'**

help desk *noun* [C] a service which provides help to the people who use a computer network (= a group of computers that share information and programs) **(ortak bilgisayar kullanım ağında) yardım masası**

helper /ˈhelpər/ *noun* [C] someone who helps another person to do something **yardımcı, muavin, asistan**

helpful /ˈhelpfʲl/ *adjective* **1** useful **faydalı, yararlı, işe yarar** *helpful advice/comments* **2** willing to help **yardımsever** *The staff here are very helpful.* ➎Opposite **unhelpful.** ● **helpfully** *adverb* **yardımseverlikle** ● **helpfulness** *noun* [U] **yardımseverlik**

helping /ˈhelpɪŋ/ *noun* [C] an amount of food given to one person at one time **bir öğün yemek, bir porsiyon yemek** *She gave me a very large helping of pasta.*

helpless /ˈhelpləs/ *adjective* not able to defend yourself or do things without help **çaresiz, âciz** *a helpless animal/child* ● **helplessly** *adverb* **umutsuzca, çaresizce**

helpline /ˈhelplaɪn/ *noun* [C] *UK* a telephone number that you can ring for help or information **yardım hattı** *If you have any questions about any of our products, just* ***call*** *our helpline.*

hem /hem/ *noun* [C] the edge of a piece of clothing or cloth that has been folded under and sewn **kıvrım kenarı, baskı, kenar** ● **hem** *verb* [T] **hemming,** *past tense* **hemmed** to sew a hem on a piece of clothing or cloth (kumaş) **kenarını bastırmak**

hem sb in *phrasal verb* to prevent someone from moving, or from doing what they want to do **hareket etmesine engel olmak; etrafını kuşatmak/çevirmek/ sarmak; kuşatılmak**

hemisphere /ˈhemɪsfɪər/ *noun* [C] one half of the Earth **yarı küre** *birds of the northern hemisphere*

hemophilia /ˌhiːməˈfɪliə/ *noun* [U] *US spelling of* haemophilia (= a serious disease in which the flow of blood from someone's body cannot be stopped when they are hurt) **kanın pıhtılaşmaması hastalığı, hemofili**

hemophiliac /ˌhiːməˈfɪliæk/ *noun* [C] *US spelling of* haemophiliac (= someone who has haemophilia) **kanı pıhtılaşmayan, hemofili hastası**

hemorrhage /ˈhemərɪdʒ/ *noun* [C, U] *US spelling of* haemorrhage (= when someone suddenly loses a lot of blood) **ani kan kaybı, kanama; hemoraji**

hemorrhoids /ˈhemərɔɪdz/ *noun* [plural] *US spelling of* haemorrhoids (= painful swollen tissue around the opening of a person's bottom) **basur, hemeroid**

hemp /hemp/ *noun* [U] a plant that is used for making rope, cloth, and the drug cannabis **kendir, kenevir**

hen /hen/ *noun* [C] a female bird, especially a chicken **tavuk**

hence /hens/ *adverb* **1** for this reason **bundan dolayı; bu yüzden/nedenle** *He's got an interview today, hence the suit.* **2 three weeks/two months, etc hence** *formal* three weeks/two months, etc from this time **şu andan itibaren üç hafta/iki ay vs.**

henceforth /ˌhensˈfɔːθ/ *adverb formal* from this time **şu andan itibaren, bundan sonra, bundan böyle** *Henceforth only English may be spoken in this classroom.*

henchman /ˈhenʃmən/ *noun* [C] *plural* **henchmen** someone who does unpleasant jobs for a powerful person

H

kötü işler için güçlü biri tarafından kullanılan adam(lar)

'hen night (also **'hen ˌparty**) noun [C] a party for women only, usually one held for a woman before she gets married **bayanlar için bekârlığa veda gecesi/partisi** ⊃Compare stag night.

hepatitis /ˌhepəˈtaɪtɪs/ noun [U] a serious disease that affects your liver (= the organ that cleans your blood) **sarılık, hepatit**

o~**her¹** strong form /hɜːʳ/ weak forms /həʳ/, /əʳ/ pronoun **1** used after a verb or preposition to refer to someone female who has already been talked about **(bayan)** onun *Where's Kath - have you seen her?* **2** used to refer to a country or ship **(ülke, gemi)** onun *God bless HMS Victoria and all who sail in her.*

o~**her²** strong form /hɜːʳ/ weak form /həʳ/ determiner belonging to or relating to someone female who has already been talked about **(bayanlar için ait/sahip olma bildirir)** onun *That's her house on the corner.* ○ *It's not her fault.*

herald¹ /ˈherəld/ verb [T] to be a sign that a particular event will happen soon **açıklamak, ilan etmek, bildirmek, işareti olmak, müjdelemek** *Thick black clouds heralded rain.*

herald² /ˈherəld/ noun [C] a sign that a particular event will happen soon **haberci, ulak, müjdeci** *A fall in unemployment was the herald of economic recovery.*

herb /hɜːb/ ⑥ /ɜːrb/ noun [C] a plant that is used in cooking to add flavour to food or used in medicines **şifalı ot/ bitki** ● **herbal** /ˈhɜːbᵊl/ adjective *herbal medicine* **bitkisel**

herd¹ /hɜːd/ noun [C] a large group of animals such as cows that live and eat together **büyükbaş hayvan sürüsü, sürü** *a herd of cattle/deer*

herd² /hɜːd/ verb [T] If people or animals are herded somewhere, they are moved there in a group. **bir araya toplamak, sürü haline getirmek** [often passive] *The passengers were quickly herded onto a bus.*

o~**here** /hɪəʳ/ adverb **1** [IN THIS PLACE] in the place where you are **burası, burayı, burada** *Does Jane live near here?* ○ *Come here!* **2** [GETTING ATTENTION] used to bring someone's attention to someone or something **işte, buraya** *Look, here's our bus.* ○ *Here, put this on.* **3 here you are/ here he is, etc** used when you see someone or something you have been looking for or waiting for **İşte!', 'Burada!', 'Buyurun!', 'İşte orada/burada!', 'İşte geliyor/ göründü!'** vb. *Here she is at last.* ○ *Here we are, this is the place.* **4** [GIVING] used when you are giving someone something **işte** *Here's a present for you.* **5 Here you are.** used when you are giving someone something **'Buyurun!', 'Buyurun burada!', 'Buyurun işte!'** *"Have you got the paper?" "Here you are."* **6** [AT THIS POINT] at this point in a discussion **şimdi, şu anda, burada, bu durumda/konumda** *I don't have time here to go into all the arguments.* **7** [ON THE TELEPHONE] used when saying who you are on the telephone **telefonda kim olduğunu belirtirken; 'Buyrun ben ...!'** *Hello, it's Tim here.* **8 here and there** in several different places but without any pattern **şurada, burada; orada, burada** *Tall trees were growing here and there.*

hereafter /ˌhɪərˈɑːftəʳ/ adverb formal from now or after this time **(hukukta) bundan böyle, gelecekte**

hereby /ˌhɪəˈbaɪ/ adverb formal with these words or this action **(resmen, resmî evrakta/işlemlerde) şimdi, bu vesileyle, bundan ötürü, bu nedenle, bunu yaparak/söyleyerek** *I hereby declare you the winner.*

hereditary /hɪˈredɪtᵊri/ adjective **1** passed to a child from its parents before birth **kalıtım, soyaçekim, irsiyet** *Depression is often hereditary.* **2** passed from parent

to child as a right **veraset, intikal, aileden gelen, atalardan geçen** *a hereditary title*

heredity /hɪˈredəti/ noun [U] the way in which mental or physical qualities pass from parent to child **kalıtım, soyaçekim, irsiyet, anne babadan geçen fizksel ve zihinsel özellikler**

heresy /ˈherəsi/ noun [C, U] a belief which is against what a group or society generally believes to be right or good **aykırı/sapkın düşünce/inanış**

heretic /ˈherətɪk/ noun [C] someone with a belief which is against what a group or society generally believes to be right or good **sapkın düşünceli/inançlı kimse/ kişi** ● **heretical** /həˈretɪkᵊl/ adjective **inançları ters düşen**

heritage /ˈherɪtɪdʒ/ noun [U] the buildings, paintings, customs, etc which are important in a culture or society because they have existed for a long time **miras, kalıtım** *our architectural/cultural heritage*

hermit /ˈhɜːmɪt/ noun [C] someone who chooses to live alone and away from other people **münzevi, inzivaya çekilmiş kişi**

hernia /ˈhɜːniə/ noun [C] a medical condition in which an organ pushes through the muscle which is around it **fıtık**

[🧩] **hero** ...... İLE BİRLİKTE KULLANILAN KELİMELER

a **local/national** hero ● an **unsung** hero

o~**hero** /ˈhɪərəʊ/ noun [C] plural **heroes 1** someone who does something brave or good which people respect or admire them for **kahraman, ilâh** *He became a national hero for his part in the revolution.* **2** the main male character in a book or film who is usually good **baş erkek karakter/oyuncu/kahraman; en önemli kişi; (halk dili) esas oğlan** *the hero of her new novel*

heroic /hɪˈrəʊɪk/ adjective **1** very brave **kahraman, cesur, yiğit** *a heroic figure* ○ *a heroic act/deed* **2** If someone makes a heroic effort to do something, they work very hard to try to do it. **kararlı, etkili, kahramanca, yiğitce** *In spite of England's heroic efforts, they lost the match.* ● **heroically** adverb **cesurca**

heroics /hɪˈrəʊɪks/ noun [plural] actions which seem brave but are stupid because they are dangerous **aptalca kahramanlık, yersiz cesaret/yüreklilik**

heroin /ˈherəʊɪn/ noun [U] a very strong drug which some people use illegally for pleasure **eroin** *a heroin addict*

heroine /ˈherəʊɪn/ noun [C] **1** the main female character in a book or film, who is usually good **baş kadın karakter/oyuncu/kahraman; en önemli kişi; (halk dili) esas kız** *the heroine of the film 'Alien'* **2** a woman who does something brave or good which people respect or admire her for **kahraman kadın, cesur/yürekli kadın**

heroism /ˈherəʊɪzᵊm/ noun [U] very brave behaviour **kahramanlık, yiğitlik** *an act of heroism*

herring /ˈherɪŋ/ noun [C, U] a small, silver-coloured fish which lives in the sea and is eaten as food **ringa, ringa balığı** ⊃See also: red herring.

o~**hers** /hɜːz/ pronoun the things that belong or relate to someone female who has already been talked about **(bayan)** ona ait, onunki *That's Ann's coat over there - at least I think it's hers.* ○ *I borrowed it from a friend of hers.*

o~**herself** /həˈself/ pronoun **1** the reflexive form of the pronoun 'she' **(bayan) kendi, kendini, kendine, kendisini, kendisine** *She kept telling herself that nothing was wrong.* **2** used to emphasize the pronoun 'she' or the particular female person you are referring to **(bayan)**

(bizzat) kendisi *She decorated the cake herself.* **3 (all) by herself** alone or without anyone else's help **kendi kendine, tek başına, kendi başına** *She managed to put her shoes on all by herself.* **4 (all) to herself** for her use only **sadece kendine ait; onun kendisine ait** *Mum's got the house to herself this weekend.*

hertz /hɜːts/ (*written abbreviation* **Hz**) *noun* [C] *plural* **hertz** a unit for measuring the frequency (= how often the wave is repeated) of a sound wave

ᴏᵐ**he's** /hiːz/ **1** *short for* he is **'He is' çekim yapısının kısa hâli** *He's my best friend.* **2** *short for* he has **'He has' çekim yapısının kısa hâli** *Sam must be tired - he's been dancing all night!*

hesitant /ˈhezɪtᵊnt/ *adjective* If you are hesitant, you do not do something immediately or quickly because you are nervous or not certain. **kararsız, tereddüt eden, duraksayan, çekingen, mütereddit** *She was hesitant about returning to her home town.* ● **hesitantly** *adverb* **kararsız bir şekilde** ● **hesitancy** *noun* [U] **kararsızlık**

hesitate /ˈhezɪteɪt/ *verb* **1** [I] to pause before doing something, especially because you are nervous or not certain **tereddüt etmek, kararsız davranmak, duraksamak, çekingen davranmak, kaçınmak, ağırdan almak** *Richard hesitated before answering.* **2 not hesitate to do sth** to be very willing to do something because you are certain it is right **tereddüt etmemek, kararsız davranmamak, çekingen davranmamak, istekli davranmak, gönüllü olmak** *They would not hesitate to call the police at the first sign of trouble.*

> ▨▨ *hesitation* .... İLE BİRLİKTE KULLANILAN KELİMELER
>
> **without** hesitation ● a **brief/momentary/ moment's/slight** hesitation

hesitation /ˌhezɪˈteɪʃᵊn/ *noun* **1** [C, U] when you pause before doing something, especially because you are nervous or not certain **tereddüt, çekingenlik, isteksizlik, gönülsüzlük, duraksama** *After a moment's hesitation, he unlocked the door.* **2 have no hesitation in doing sth** when you are very willing to do something because you know it is the right thing to do **hiç bir tereddüt göstermemek; ...dan/den hiç çekinmemek** *He had no hesitation in signing for the team.*

heterogeneous /ˌhetᵊrəʊˈdʒiːniəs/ *adjective formal* consisting of parts or things of different types **çeşitli türden; farklı türdeki şeylerden bir araya gelen** *a heterogeneous sample of people*

heterosexual /ˌhetᵊrəʊˈsekʃuᵊl/ *adjective* sexually attracted to people of the opposite sex **karşı cinse cinsel istek duyan** ● **heterosexual** *noun* [C] **karşı cinsi çekici bulan**

het up /het'ʌp/ *adjective* [never before noun] *UK informal* worried and upset **sinirli, gergin, heyecanlı, tedirgin** *Why are you getting so het up about this?*

hexagon /ˈheksəgən/ *noun* [C] a flat shape with six sides of the same length **altıgen** ● **hexagonal** /hek'sægᵊnᵊl/ *adjective* shaped like a hexagon **altı kenarlı, altıgen**

hey /heɪ/ *exclamation spoken* used to get someone's attention or to show that you are interested, excited, angry, etc **'Hey!', 'Aaa!', 'Yaa!'** *Hey, Helen, look at this!* ○ *Hey, wait a minute!*

heyday /ˈheɪdeɪ/ *noun* [no plural] the time when something or someone was most successful or popular **en parlak devir/dönem, en güzel/başarılı çağ/ dönem; en güzel günler; altın çağ** *In its heyday, the company employed over a thousand workers.*

ᴏᵐ**hi** /haɪ/ *exclamation* hello **Merhaba!, 'Selâm!'** *Hi! How's it going?*

hiatus /haɪˈeɪtəs/ *noun* [no plural] *formal* a short pause in which nothing happens or is said **sessizlik, boşluk, ara, kesinti, kopukluk**

hibernate /ˈhaɪbəneɪt/ *verb* [I] If an animal hibernates, it goes to sleep for the winter. **kış uykusuna yatmak** ● **hibernation** /ˌhaɪbəˈneɪʃᵊn/ *noun* [U] *Bears go into hibernation in the autumn.* **kış uykusuna yatma (hayvanlar)**

hiccup (*also* **hiccough**) /ˈhɪkʌp/ *noun* [C] **1** a quick noise you make in your throat when a muscle in your chest moves suddenly **hıçkırık** [usually plural] *I got hiccups from drinking too quickly.* **2** a small, temporary problem **pürüz, geçici sorun** *I'm afraid there's been a slight hiccup.*

hide

ᴏᵐ**hide¹** /haɪd/ *verb past tense* **hid**, *past participle* **hidden**
1 ▢THING▢ [T] to put something in a place where it cannot be seen or found **saklamak, gizlemek** *I hid the money in a vase.* ○ [often passive] *She kept the diary hidden in a drawer.* **2** ▢PERSON▢ [I] (*also* **hide yourself**) to go to a place where you cannot be seen or found **saklanmak, gizlenmek** *She ran off and hid behind a tree.* **3** ▢FEELING/INFORMATION▢ [T] to keep a feeling or information secret **sır olarak tutmak, saklamak, gizlemek** *He couldn't hide his embarrassment.* ○ *There's something about her past that she's trying to hide from me.*

hide² /haɪd/ *noun* [C, U] the skin of an animal which is used for making leather **post, deri**

hide-and-seek /ˌhaɪdən'siːk/ *noun* [U] a children's game in which one child hides and the others try to find them **saklambaç oyunu**

hideaway /'haɪdəweɪ/ *noun* [C] a place where you go to hide or to be alone **yalnız kalmak için kaçamak yapılan yer/mekân**

hideous /'hɪdiəs/ *adjective* very ugly **çok çirkin, iğrenç, korkunç** *a hideous monster* ● **hideously** *adverb* **çirkin bir şekilde**

hideout /'haɪdaʊt/ *noun* [C] a place where you go to hide, especially from the police or if you are in danger **saklanacak yer, gizli sığınak**

hiding /'haɪdɪŋ/ *noun* **be in hiding; go into hiding** to hide in a place, especially from the police or if you are in danger **bir yerde saklanmak, gizlenmek**

hierarchy ...... İLE BİRLİKTE KULLANILAN KELİMELER

in a hierarchy ● a hierarchy of sth

hierarchy /'haɪərɑːki/ *noun* [C] a system or organization in which people or things are arranged according to their importance **hiyerarşi, rütbe/makam/mevki/ yetki sırası/düzeni** ● **hierarchical** /ˌhaɪə'rɑːkɪkəl/ *adjective* a *hierarchical structure* **düzensel, sırasıyla**

hieroglyphics /ˌhaɪərəʊ'glɪfɪks/ *noun* [plural] a system of writing which uses pictures instead of words, especially used in ancient Egypt **hiyeroglif; resim yazı (eski Mısır)**

hi-fi /'haɪfaɪ/ *noun* [C] a set of electronic equipment for playing music, consisting of a CD player, radio, etc **üstün duyarlı ses aygıtı, müzik seti**

o⁻**high¹** /haɪ/ *adjective* **1** TALL having a large distance from the bottom to the top **yüksek** *a high building/mountain* **2** ABOVE GROUND a large distance above the ground or the level of the sea **yüksek** *a high shelf/window* ○ *The village was high up in the mountains.* **3** MEASUREMENT used to say how big the distance is from the top of something to the bottom, or how far above the ground something is ...**yüksekliğinde** *How high is it?* ○ *It's ten metres high.* **4** AMOUNT great in amount, size, or level **(miktar, ebat, seviye) yüksek, fazla, aşırı** *a high temperature* ○ *high prices/costs* ○ *The car sped away at high speed.* **5** VERY GOOD very good **(kalite, standart) çok iyi, yüksek, mükemmel** *high standards/quality* **6** IMPORTANT important, powerful, or at the top level of something **önemli, güçlü, üst seviyede, üst seviyede üst seviyede** *a high rank* ○ *Safety is our highest priority.* **7** DRUGS If someone is high, they are behaving in an unusual way because they have taken an illegal drug. **uçmuş, kafayı bulmuş, esrar çekmiş, kafası iyi** **8** SOUND A high sound or note is near the top of the set of sounds that people can hear. **(müzik, ses) yüksek, tiz, yüksek perdeden** **9 high in sth** If a food is high in something, it contains a lot of it. ...**ca/ce zengin; içinde fazla miktarda olan** *Avoid foods that are high in salt.*

o⁻**high²** /haɪ/ *adverb* **1** at or to a large distance above the ground **yükseklerde; yüksek irtifada; yukarıda; üstünde, üzerinde** *We flew high above the city.* ○ *He threw the ball high into the air.* **2** at or to a large amount or level **yükseğe, tepeye, üst seviyelere** *Temperatures rose as high as 40 degrees.*

high ...... İLE BİRLİKTE KULLANILAN KELİMELER

hit/reach a high ● an all-time/new/record high

high³ /haɪ/ *noun* [C] **1** the top amount or level which something reaches **zirve, tepe, en üst seviye** *Computer ownership has reached an all-time high* (= more people own computers than ever before). **2** a feeling of excitement or happiness **heyecan, mutluluk, sevinç, coşku**

[usually singular] *The players are still on a high from their last match.*

highbrow /'haɪbraʊ/ *adjective* A highbrow book, film, etc is serious and intended for very intelligent or well-educated people. **aydın, entelektüel; zeki ve iyi eğitimli kişiler için yazılmış/tasarlanmış**

high-class /ˌhaɪ'klɑːs/ *adjective* of very good quality **yüksek nitelikli, kaliteli, seçkin** *a high-class hotel*

High 'Court *noun* [C] the most important law court in some countries **Yargıtay; Yüksek Mahkeme** *a High Court judge*

higher edu'cation *noun* [U] education at a college or university **yüksek öğrenim**

high-flyer (*also* high-flier) /ˌhaɪ'flaɪər/ *noun* [C] someone who is very successful or who is likely to be very successful, especially in business **başarılı, gözü yükseklerde olan, hedefleri yüksek olan** ● **high-flying** *adjective* **başarılı olmaya meğilli**

high 'heels (*also* heels) *noun* [plural] women's shoes with heels raised high off the ground **yüksek topuklu ayakkabı** ● **high-heeled** *adjective* **yüksek topuklu**

the 'high ,jump *noun* a sports event in which people try to jump over a bar which gets higher and higher during the competition **(spor) yüksek atlama** ⊃Orta kısımdaki renkli sayfalarına bakınız.

highlands /'haɪləndz/ *noun* [plural] an area with a lot of mountains **dağlık bölge/arazi; yayla** *the Scottish highlands* ● **highland** /'haɪlənd/ *adjective* in or relating to the highlands **dağlık bölgeye/araziye ait; yaylaya ilişkin** *a highland village*

high-level /ˌhaɪ'levəl/ *adjective* involving important or powerful people **yüsek seviyeli, önemli ve güçlü insanları içeren** *high-level meetings/talks*

highlight ...... İLE BİRLİKTE KULLANILAN KELİMELER

highlight a danger/need/issue/problem ● highlight the need for something

highlight¹ /'haɪlaɪt/ *verb* [T] **1** to emphasize something or make people notice something **vurgulamak, dikkat çekmek, farkedilmesini sağlamak** *to highlight a problem/danger* ○ *The report highlights the need for stricter regulations.* **2** to make something a different colour so that it is more easily noticed, especially written words **üstünü renkli kalemle çizmek/belirlemek**

highlight² /'haɪlaɪt/ *noun* [C] the best or most important part of something **en önemli kısım, en ilginç bölüm** *The boat trip was one of the highlights of the holiday.*

highlighter /'haɪˌlaɪtər/ *noun* [C] a pen with bright, transparent ink which is used to emphasize words in a book, article, etc **renkli işaret kalemi** ⊃Orta kısımdaki renkli sayfalarına bakınız.

o⁻**highly** /'haɪli/ *adverb* **1** very or to a large degree **bir hayli, pek, çok, önemli derecede** *a highly effective treatment* ○ *It is highly unlikely that they will succeed.* **2** at a high level **yüksek seviyede, yüksekce** *a highly paid worker* **3 to speak/think highly of sb/sth** to have or express a very good opinion of someone or something **biriyle ilgili çok olumlu görüşleri olmak; iyi bahsetmek, övmek, iyi görüşlerini bildirmek**

Highness /'haɪnəs/ *noun* **Her/His/Your Highness** used when you are speaking to or about a royal person **Ekselansları, Majesteleri** *Thank you, Your Highness.*

high-pitched /haɪ'pɪtʃt/ *adjective* **1** A voice that is high-pitched is higher than usual. **çok tiz, yüksek perdeli** **2** describes a noise that is high and sometimes also loud or unpleasant **yüksek perdeli, çok gürültülü, kulak tırmalayan** *a high-pitched whine*

high-powered /ˌhaɪˈpaʊəd/ *adjective* very important or responsible **çok önemli, sorumlu, etkili, saygın** *a high-powered executive/job*

high-profile /ˌhaɪˈprəʊfaɪl/ *adjective* A high-profile person or event is known about by a lot of people and receives a lot of attention from television, newspapers, etc. **çok bilinen, tanınan, dikkat çeken, önemli** *a high-profile campaign/case*

high-rise /ˈhaɪˌraɪz/ *adjective* A high-rise building is very tall and has a lot of floors. **gökdelen, yüksek, çok katlı**

high ˌschool *noun* [C, U] a school in the US which children go to between the ages of 14 and 18 **lise** *I played violin when I was in high school.* ○ *a high-school student/teacher*

high ˌstreet *noun* [C] *UK* the main road in the centre of a town where there are a lot of shops **en işlek cadde, ana cadde**

high-tech (*also UK* hi-tech) /ˌhaɪˈtek/ *adjective* using or involved with the most recent and advanced electronic machines, computers, etc **ileri/yüksek teknoloji içeren** *high-tech companies/industry* ⊃Compare low-tech.

highway /ˈhaɪweɪ/ *noun* [C] *mainly US* a main road, especially between two towns or cities **otoyol, çevre yolu, şehirler arası yol**

hijack /ˈhaɪdʒæk/ *verb* [T] to take control of an aircraft during a journey, especially using violence **uçak kaçırmak** [often passive] *The plane was hijacked by terrorists.* ● **hijacker** *noun* [C] **korsan (uçak)** ● **hijacking** *noun* [C, U] **uçak kaçırma**

hike¹ /haɪk/ *noun* [C] a long walk, usually in the countryside **kır yürüyüşü**

hike² /haɪk/ *verb* [I] to go for a long walk in the countryside **kır yürüyüşü yapmak** ● **hiker** *noun* [C] **uzun yürüyüşler yapan** ● **hiking** *noun* [U] *to go hiking in the mountains* **yürüyüş**

hilarious /hɪˈleəriəs/ *adjective* extremely funny **gülmekten kırıp geçiren, gülünç, çok komik, çok eğlenceli** *They all thought the film was hilarious.* ● **hilariously** *adverb* **hilariously funny komik bir şekilde**

hilarity /hɪˈlærəti/ *noun* [U] when people laugh very loudly and think something is very funny **neşe, kahkaha, şamata, tantana**

o━**hill** /hɪl/ *noun* [C] a raised area of land, smaller than a mountain **tepe, yükselti** *They climbed up the hill to get a better view.*

hillside /ˈhɪlsaɪd/ *noun* [C] the sloping side of a hill **yamaç, etek, eğim**

hilly /ˈhɪli/ *adjective* having a lot of hills **tepelik** *hilly countryside*

hilt /hɪlt/ *noun* **to the hilt** very much or as much as is possible **tamamen, tümüyle, sonuna kadar, gittiği yere kadar** *Mark borrowed to the hilt to pay for his new car.*

o━**him** *strong form* /hɪm/ *weak form* /ɪm/ *pronoun* used after a verb or preposition to refer to someone male who has already been talked about (**erkek**) **onu/ona** *Where's Serge - have you seen him?*

o━**himself** /hɪmˈself/ *pronoun* **1** the reflexive form of the pronoun 'he' (**erkek**) **kendi, kendisi, kendini, kendisini** *John always cuts himself when he's shaving.* **2** used to emphasize the pronoun 'he' or the particular male person you are referring to (**erkek**) **zatıâli, bizzat kendisi** *Do you want to speak to Dr Randall himself or his secretary?* ○ *He made the bookcase himself.* **3 (all) by**

himself alone or without anyone else's help (**erkek**) **kendi kendine, tek başına** *Joe made that snowman all by himself.* **4 (all) to himself** for his use only **kendine özgü, sadece kendi kullanımı için** *Tim wants a desk all to himself.*

hind /haɪnd/ *adjective* **a hind foot/leg** a foot/leg at the back of an animal **arka ayak/bacak**

hinder /ˈhɪndər/ *verb* [T] to make it difficult to do something or for something to develop **engel olmak, mâni olmak, alıkoymak, güçleştirmek** [often passive] *His performance at the Olympics was hindered by a knee injury.*

hindrance /ˈhɪndrəns/ *noun* [C] something or someone that makes it difficult for you to do something **engel, mâni, mahzur** *Large class sizes are a hindrance to teachers.*

hindsight /ˈhaɪndsaɪt/ *noun* [U] the ability to understand an event or situation only after it has happened **geriye bakarak değerlendirme, sonradan farkedip anlama, sonradan farketme** *With hindsight, I should have taken the job.*

Hindu /ˈhɪnduː/ *noun* [C] someone who believes in Hinduism **Hiduizm'e inanan, Hindu** ● **Hindu** *adjective* a *Hindu temple* **Hindu**

Hinduism /ˈhɪnduːɪzᵊm/ *noun* [U] the main religion of India, based on belief in many gods and the belief that when someone dies their spirit returns to life in another body **Hinduizm; Hindistan'da bir çok tanrılı inanca dayanan ve insan öldükten sonra başka bir bedende ruhunun geri geldiğine inanılan esas din**

hinge¹ /hɪndʒ/ *noun* [C] a metal fastening that joins the edge of a door, window, or lid to something else and allows you to open or close it **menteşe, reze**

hinge² /hɪndʒ/ *verb*
hinge on sth *phrasal verb* to depend completely on something ... **a/e dayanmak/ait olmak/bağlı olmak** *Her career hinges on the success of this project.*

┌─────────────────────────────┐
│ **hint** ⋯⋯ İLE BİRLİKTE KULLANILAN KELİMELER │
│ **drop** a hint ● a **broad/heavy/subtle** hint │
└─────────────────────────────┘

hint¹ /hɪnt/ *noun* **1** [C] when you say something that suggests what you want or think, but not in a direct way **imâ** *He dropped* (= made) *several hints that he wanted a CD player for his birthday.* **2** [C] a small piece of advice **tavsiye, salık, öğüt, yararlı bilgi** *The magazine gives lots of useful hints on how to save money.* **3 a hint of sth** a small amount of something **emare, iz, belirti** *There was a hint of anger in her voice.*

hint² /hɪnt/ *verb* [I, T] to suggest something, but not in a direct way **imâ etmek** [+ (that)] *He hinted that he wants to retire next year.* ○ *She hinted at the possibility of moving to America.*

hip¹ /hɪp/ *noun* [C] one of the two parts of your body above your leg and below your waist **kalça** ⊃Orta kısımdaki renkli sayfalarına bakınız.

hip² /hɪp/ *adjective informal* fashionable **modaya uygun**

hip-hop /ˈhɪphɒp/ *noun* [U] a type of pop music with songs about problems in society and words that are spoken and not sung **müzikle konuşur gibi söylenen ve toplumun sorunlarına ilişkin bir tür pop müzik; hip-hop**

hippie /ˈhɪpi/ (*also UK* hippy) *noun* [C] someone who believes in peace and love and has long hair, especially someone who was young in the 1960s **hippi**

hippo /ˈhɪpəʊ/ *noun* [C] *short for* hippopotamus **su aygırı, hipopotam**

hippopotamus /ˌhɪpəˈpɒtəməs/ *noun* [C] *plural* **hippopotamuses** or **hippopotami** a very large animal with a thick skin that lives near water in parts of Africa **su aygırı, hipopotam**

⊶**hire¹** /haɪəʳ/ *verb* [T] **1** *UK* (*US* **rent**) to pay money in order to use something for a short time **kiralamak, kira ile tutmak** *They hired a car for a few weeks.* **2** to begin to employ someone **ücretle çalıştırmak; tutmak** *We hired a new secretary last week.*
hire sth out *phrasal verb UK* to allow someone to borrow something from you in exchange for money **kiraya/icara vermek** *The shop hires out electrical equipment.*

hire² /haɪəʳ/ *noun* [U] *UK* when you arrange to use something by paying for it **kira, icar** *The price includes flights and car hire.* ○ *Do you have bikes for hire?*

⊶**his¹** *strong form* /hɪz/ *weak form* /ɪz/ *determiner* belonging to or relating to someone male who has already been talked about **(erkek) onun, ona ait, onunla ilgili** *Alex is sitting over there with his daughter.* ○ *It's not his fault.*

⊶**his²** /hɪz/ *pronoun* the things that belong or relate to someone male who has already been talked about **(erkek) onunki** *That's Frank's coat over there - at least I think it's his.* ○ *I borrowed them from a friend of his.*

Hispanic /hɪˈspænɪk/ *adjective* relating or belonging to people whose families came from Spain or Latin America in the past **geçmişte Latin Amerika veya İspanya'dan gelenlere ait/ilişkin ● Hispanic** *noun* [C] a Hispanic person **İspanyol veya Latin Amerika asıllı**

hiss /hɪs/ *verb* **1** [I] to make a long noise like the letter 's' **tıslamak, tıs diye ses çıkarmak, ssss etmek** *The gas hissed through the pipes.* **2** [T] to speak in an angry or urgent way **tıslayarak konuşmak/fısıldamak** *"Will you be quiet," she hissed.* **● hiss** *noun* [C] a sound like the letter 's' **tıssss, ssss, tıslama**

hissy (fit) /ˈhɪsiˌfɪt/ *noun* [C] *informal* a sudden strong feeling of anger that someone cannot control **kontrolsüz ani kızgınlık, hiddet, öfke** *David, of course, threw a hissy fit when he found out.*

historian /hɪˈstɔːriən/ *noun* [C] someone who studies or writes about history **tarihçi**

historic /hɪˈstɒrɪk/ *adjective* important in history or likely to be important in history **tarihî, tarihe geçmiş, tarihî önemi olan** *historic buildings* ○ *a historic day/moment*

historical /hɪˈstɒrɪkəl/ *adjective* relating to events or people in the past, or the study of history **tarihî, tarihsel, tarihi ilgilendiren; tarih çalışmalarına ait** *a historical novel* ○ *historical documents* **● historically** *adverb* **geçmişe ait, tarihsel**

🧩 **history** .... İLE BİRLİKTE KULLANILAN KELİMELER

in sth's history ● recent history

⊶**history** /ˈhɪstəri/ *noun* **1** PAST [U] the whole series of events in the past which relate to the development of a country, subject, or person **tarih, geçmiş, ezel** *The Civil War was a terrible time in American history.* **2** SUBJECT [U] the study of events in the past **tarih** *He's very interested in modern European history.* ○ *a history book* **3 a history of sth** If you have a history of a particular problem or illness, you have already suffered from it. **geçmiş, mazi** *a man with a history of drug addiction* **4** DESCRIPTION [C] a description or record of events in the past relating to someone or something **meçmişi, mazisi, geçmiş, mazi** *The doctor read through his medical history.* ⊃See also: case history, natural history.

hit

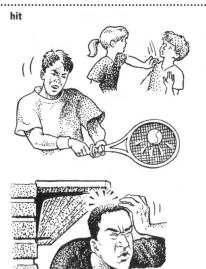

⊶**hit¹** /hɪt/ *verb* **hitting**, *past* **hit 1** HAND [T] to touch something quickly and with force using your hand or an object in your hand **vurmak, dürtmek** *She hit him on the head with her tennis racket.* **2** TOUCH [T] to touch someone or something quickly and with force, usually causing injury or damage **çarpmak, vurmak, yaralamak** *The car skidded and hit a wall.* ○ *As she fell, she hit her head on the pavement.* **3** AFFECT [I, T] to affect something badly **kötü etkilemek, berbat bir şekilde etkisi altına almak** [often passive] *The economy has been hit by high unemployment.* **4** REACH [T] to reach a place, position, or state **bir yere/konuma/duruma ulaşmak/erişmek** *Our profits have already hit $1 million.* **5** THINK [T] *informal* If an idea or thought hits you, you suddenly think of it. **(düşünce, fikir) ani acı vermek, sarsmak, üzmek, aklına gelmek/düşmek** *The idea for the book hit me in the middle of the night.* **6 hit it off** *informal* If people hit it off, they like each other and become friendly immediately. **hemen kaynaşmak, kanı kaynamak, ısınmak, iyi geçinmek, anlaşmak** ⊃See also: hit sb hard², hit the jackpot, hit the nail¹ on the head, hit the roof.
hit back *phrasal verb* to criticize or attack someone who has criticized or attacked you **karşılık vermek** *The President hit back at journalists who said he was a liar.*
hit on/upon sth *phrasal verb* to have a good idea, especially one which solves a problem **birden aklına gelmek, bulmak, keşfetmek** *We hit upon the idea of writing to the mayor to ask for his help.*

🧩 **hit** .... İLE BİRLİKTE KULLANILAN KELİMELER

a big/massive/smash hit ● a hit CD/single

hit² /hɪt/ *noun* [C] **1** SONG/FILM a very successful song, film, book, etc **(şarkı, film, kitap vb.) bir numara, liste başı, çok satan/tutmuş** *The film 'Titanic' was a big hit.* **2** PERSON/THING a popular person or thing **popüler, meşhur** *The chocolate cake was a big hit with the children.* **3** TOUCH when you touch something or when something touches you quickly and with force **çarpma, vurma, sert temas, hızlı dokunuş 4** INTERNET a request to see a document on the Internet that is then counted to calculate the number of people looking at the page **(bilgisayar) internette bir belgeye ulaşılma/görüntülenme talebi ve ulaşanların sayısı**

hit-and-miss /ˌhɪtᵊnˈmɪs/ UK (US **hit or miss**) adjective not planned, but happening by chance **gelişigüzel, rastgele, tesadüfi, şans eseri**

hit-and-run /ˌhɪtᵊnˈrʌn/ adjective A hit-and-run accident is when the driver of a vehicle hits and injures someone, but then drives away without helping. **(sürücü) vurup/çarpıp kaçan; (kaza) çarp kaç/vurkaç türü**

hitch[1] /hɪtʃ/ noun [C] a small problem **biraz aksilik, hafif sorun, ufak pürüz** The ceremony went without a hitch.

hitch[2] /hɪtʃ/ verb **1 hitch a lift/ride** to get a free ride in someone's vehicle, by standing next to the road and waiting for someone to pick you up **otostop yapmak 2** [T] (also US **hitch up**) to fasten something to an object or vehicle **bağlamak, iliştirmek, takmak, tutturmak** They hitched the caravan to the car.
hitch sth up phrasal verb to pull up a piece of clothing **yukarı çekmek**

hitchhike /ˈhɪtʃhaɪk/ verb [I] to get free rides in people's vehicles by standing next to the road and waiting for someone to pick you up **otostop yapmak** ● **hitchhiker** noun [C] **otostop yapan hişi**

hi-tech UK (UK/US **high-tech**) /ˌhaɪˈtek/ adjective using or involved with the most recent and advanced electronic machines, computers, etc **ileri/yüksek/uzay çağı teknoloji(si)**

hitherto /ˌhɪðəˈtuː/ adverb formal until now, or until a particular point in time **bu zamana kadar/değin, şimdiye kadar/değin/dek**

HIV /ˌeɪtʃaɪˈviː/ noun [U] abbreviation for human immunodeficiency virus: a virus which causes AIDS (= a serious disease that destroys the body's ability to fight infection) **insanın bağışıklık sistemini yokeden ve AIDS hastalığına sebep olan virüs**

hive /haɪv/ noun **1** [C] (also **beehive**) a special container where people keep bees **arı kovanı 2 a hive of activity** a place where people are busy and working hard **çok çalışan ve meşgul olan insanların bulunduğu yer**

HIV-positive /ˌeɪtʃaɪviːˈpɒzətɪv/ adjective If a person is HIV-positive, they are infected with HIV although they might not have AIDS. **HIV virüsü taşıyan**

hiya /ˈhaɪjə/ exclamation informal a way to say hello to someone you know well **'Selam!', 'Merhaba!'** Hiya, Mike, how are you doing?

hm (also **hmm**) /həm/ spoken something you say when you pause while talking or when you are uncertain **hımm** "Which one do you like best?" "Hmm. I'm not sure."

hoard /hɔːd/ verb [T] to collect and store a large supply of something, often secretly **gizli gizli biriktirmek/toplamak/istif etmek** He hoarded antique books in the attic. ● **hoard** noun [C] a large, secret supply or collection of something **istif, stok, biriktirme, yığma** Police found a hoard of stolen jewellery in the car.

hoarding /ˈhɔːdɪŋ/ UK (UK/US **billboard**) noun [C] a large board used for advertising, positioned by the side of a road **reklam panosu, ilan tahtası, bilbord**

hoarse /hɔːs/ adjective If you are hoarse, your voice sounds rough when you speak, often because you are ill. **boğuk, kısık, tırmalayıcı** The teacher was hoarse from shouting. ● **hoarsely** adverb **boğuk sesli bir şekilde**

hoax /həʊks/ noun [C] when someone tries to make people believe something which is not true **muziplik, oyun, şaka, işletme** The police said the bomb threat was a hoax.

hob /hɒb/ noun [C] UK the flat part on top of an oven where you heat food in pans **fırın üstü ocak** ⊃Orta kısımdaki renkli sayfalarına bakınız.

hobble /ˈhɒbl/ verb [I] to walk with small, uncomfortable steps, especially because your feet hurt **aksayarak/seke seke yürümek, topallamak**

hobby /ˈhɒbi/ noun [C] an activity that you enjoy and do regularly when you are not working **merak, uğraşı, düşkü, hobi** Do you have any hobbies?

hockey /ˈhɒki/ noun [U] **1** UK (US **field hockey**) a team game played on grass where you hit a small ball with a long, curved stick **çim hokeyi 2** US (UK/US **ice hockey**) a team game played on ice where you hit a small, hard object with a long, curved stick **buz hokeyi** ⊃Orta kısımdaki renkli sayfalarına bakınız.

hoe /həʊ/ noun [C] a garden tool with a long handle used for removing weeds (= plants you do not want) **çapa**

hog[1] /hɒg/ noun [C] mainly US a large pig **büyük besi domuzu**

hog[2] /hɒg/ verb [T] **hogging**, past **hogged** informal to use or keep all of something for yourself **kendisi için alıkoymak; tekeline/inhisarına almak ;açgözlüce kapmak** Stop hogging the newspaper! I want to read it too.

hoist /hɔɪst/ verb [T] to raise something, sometimes using a rope or machine **yukarı kaldırmak/çekmek/yükseltmek** They slowly hoisted the flag.

hold[1] /həʊld/ verb past **held 1** [IN HAND] [T] to have something in your hand or arms **elinde/kucağında tutmak** He was holding a glass of wine. ○ They were **holding hands** and kissing. **2** [KEEP IN POSITION] [T] to keep something in a particular position **belli bir konumda tutmak** Can you hold the door open please? ○ Hold your hand up if you know the answer. ○ The frame was held together with screws. **3** [ORGANIZE] [T] to organize an event **düzenlemek, yapmak** to hold talks/an election **4** [CONTAIN] [T] to contain something or to be able to contain a particular amount of something **taşımak, içermek, almak** The bucket holds about 10 litres. **5** [JOB OR QUALIFICATION] [T] to have a particular job, position, or qualification **(iş, konum, nitelik) taşımak, sahip olmak** She held the post of treasurer. **6** [COMPETITION] [T] to have a particular position in a competition **(yarışma) bir yerde olmak, belli bir konumda olmak** to hold the world record ○ to hold the lead **7** [STORE] [T] to store documents, information, etc in a particular place **(belge, bilgi vb.) depolamak, biriktirmek, düzenlemek** The documents are held in the local library. **8** [PRISONER] [T] to keep someone as a prisoner **mahkum olarak tutmak/alıkoymak/hapsetmek** Police held the suspect overnight. ○ The hijackers are **holding** them **hostage/prisoner**. **9** [ARMY] [T] If soldiers hold a place, they control it. **(askerlik) bir yeri zaptetmek, kontrol altına almak, ele geçirmek** Rebel troops held the village. **10 hold an opinion/belief/view** to believe something **düşünce/inanç/görüş sahibi olmak** They held the view that corporal punishment was good for children. **11 hold a conversation** to have a conversation **sohbet etmek 12 hold sb's attention/interest** to keep someone interested in something **dikkatini/ilgisini çekmek** The film held my attention from beginning to end. **13** [TELEPHONE] [I, T] to wait on the telephone until someone can speak to you **telefonda beklemek** Her line's busy. Would you like to hold? ○ Hold the line, please. **14** [NOT BREAK] [I] to not break **kopmamak, kırılmamak, dayanmak** The rope held. **15 Hold it!** informal used to tell someone to wait or stop doing something **'Dur!', 'Yapma!', 'Kıpırdama!', 'Durun!', 'Bekleyin!', 'Hele durun!'** Hold it! I've forgotten my coat. **16 hold shares** to own shares (= small, equal parts of the value of a company) hisse/pay sahibi olmak **17 hold your breath a** STOP BREATHING to intentionally stop breathing for a time nefesini tutmak **b** WAIT to wait for something to happen, often feeling anxious endişeyle beklemek, sabırsızlanmak **18 hold your nose** to close your nose with your fingers to avoid smelling something unpleasant burnunu tutmak/kapamak ⊃See also: hold your own¹.

hold sth against sb *phrasal verb* to like someone less because they have done something wrong or behaved badly ... a/e kullanmak; ...ın/in aleyhine kullanmak *It was his mistake, but I won't hold it against him.*

hold sb/sth back *phrasal verb* **1** to prevent someone or something from moving forward durdurmak, dizginlemek, engellemek, tutmak *The police held back the protesters.* **2** to prevent someone or something from making progress ilerlemesine engel olmak *She felt that having children would hold her back.*

hold sth back *phrasal verb* **1** to stop yourself showing an emotion kendini tutmak, duygularını belli etmemek *She couldn't hold back the tears.* **2** to not give information to someone gizlemek, söylemek istememek

hold sth/sb down *phrasal verb* **1** to stop someone moving or escaping tutmak, engel olmak, kaçmasına engel olmak, zaptetmek *It took three officers to hold down the suspect.* **2** to keep the cost of something at a low level (maliyet) aşağı çekmek, indirmek, belli bir düzeyde tutmak *to hold down prices/wages* **3 hold down a job** to keep a job *It's difficult for mothers to hold down a full-time job.*

hold off (sth/doing sth) *phrasal verb* to wait before doing something bekletmek, beklemek, ertelemek *They are holding off making a decision until next week.*

hold on *phrasal verb informal* **1** to wait beklemek, durmak *Hold on! I'll just check my diary.* **2** to hold something or someone firmly with your hands or arms sağlam tutmak, yapışıp bırakmamak *Hold on tight!*

hold onto sth/sb *phrasal verb* to hold something or someone firmly with your hands or arms sağlam tutmak, yapışıp bırakmamak *Hold onto the rope and don't let go.*

hold onto/on to sth *phrasal verb* to keep something you have elde tutmak, bırakmamak *It was a tough election, but they held onto their majority.*

hold sth out *phrasal verb* to move your hand or an object in your hand towards someone uzatmak, vermek, sunmak *She held out her glass for some more wine.*

hold out *phrasal verb* **1** If a supply of food or money holds out, you have enough for a particular period of time. dayanmak, yetmek, yeteri miktarda var olmak **2** to continue to defend yourself against an attack direnç göstermek, dayanmak, direnmek *The city is still holding out against rebel troops.*

hold out for sth *phrasal verb* to wait until you get what you want ısrarla istemek, istediğini elde edinceye kadar beklemek *I decided to hold out for a better offer.*

hold sth up *phrasal verb* to prevent something from falling down düşmesini engellemek, düşürmemek *The tent was held up by ropes.*

hold sth/sb up *phrasal verb* to make something or someone slow or late geciktirmek, yavaşlatmak, engellemek *Sorry I'm late. I got held up in traffic.*

hold up sth *phrasal verb* to try to steal money from a bank, shop, or vehicle using force (silah ve zorla) soymak, soymaya çalışmak

hold² /həʊld/ *noun* **1** WITH HANDS [C] when you hold something or someone, or the way you do this, tutuş, tutuş *Keep a tight hold on your tickets.* **2 catch/grab/take, etc hold of sth/sb** to start holding something or someone yakalayıp/kavrayıp/uzanıp/alıp vb. tutmak *He tried to escape, but I grabbed hold of his jacket.* **3 get hold of sth/sb** to obtain something, or to manage to

speak to someone elde etmek; birine ulaşmaya çalışmak; biriyle konuşmaya çalışmak *I got hold of a copy at the local library.* ○ *I rang three times, but couldn't get hold of her.* **4 on hold a** DO IN FUTURE If a plan or activity is on hold, it will not be done until a later time. beklemede *The project is on hold until we get more money.* **b** TELEPHONE waiting to speak to someone on the telephone telefonda bekleme *His secretary put me on hold.* **5 keep hold of sth** to keep something muhafaza etmek, elde bulundurmak *Keep hold of this. You might need it later.* **6 hold on/over sth/sb** power or control over something or someone kontrol, üstünlük, güç *Their company has a strong hold on the computer market.* **7** SPACE [C] an area on a ship or aircraft for storing things (gemi) ambar; (uçak) kargo, yük bölümü *a cargo hold* ⊃See also: get (hold of) the wrong end¹ of the stick.

holdall /'həʊldɔːl/ UK (US carryall) *noun* [C] a large bag for carrying clothes büyük torba, çuval, hurç, çıkın ⊃See picture at luggage.

holder /'həʊldə'/ *noun* [C] someone who officially owns something sahip, hamil *the world record holder* ○ *passport holders* ⊃See also: title-holder.

holding /'həʊldɪŋ/ *noun* [C] part of a company which someone owns hisse, pay

hold-up UK (US holdup) /'həʊldʌp/ *noun* [C] **1** something that slows you down or makes you late gecikme, tıkanıklık, sıkışıklık *There were several hold-ups on the motorway.* **2** when someone steals money from a bank, shop, or vehicle using force silahlı soygun, yol kesme, haydutluk

hole ...... İLE BİRLİKTE KULLANILAN KELİMELER

dig/fill/make a hole ● a hole in sth ● a deep hole

○-**hole¹** /həʊl/ *noun* **1** [C] a hollow space in something, or an opening in a surface delik, çukur *a bullet hole* ○ *There's a hole in the roof.* ○ *We dug a hole to plant the tree.* **2 a rabbit/mouse, etc hole** a hollow space where a rabbit/mouse, etc lives tavşan/fare deliği **3** a small, hollow space in the ground that you try to hit a ball into in a game of golf golf deliği

hole² /həʊl/ *verb*

hole up *phrasal verb informal (also be holed up)* to stay or hide somewhere gizlenmek, saklanmak, deliğe girmek

holiday ...... İLE BİRLİKTE KULLANILAN KELİMELER

book/go on/have a holiday ● a summer holiday ● be on holiday

○-**holiday¹** /'hɒlədeɪ/ *noun* **1** NO WORK [C, U] UK (US vacation) a time when you do not have to go to work or school tatil *My aunt looks after us during the school holidays.* **2** VISIT [C, U] UK (US vacation) a long visit to a place away from where you live, for pleasure tatil, seyahat *a skiing/walking holiday* ○ *Are you going on holiday this year?* **3** DAY [C] an official day when you do not have to go to school or work tatil, izin, bayram *a public holiday* ⊃See also: bank holiday, federal holiday, national holiday, package holiday. ⊃See summer holiday.

holiday² /'hɒlədeɪ/ UK (US vacation) *verb* [I] to have your holiday somewhere tatil yapmak *We usually holiday in Spain.*

holidaymaker /'hɒlədeɪˌmeɪkə'/ *noun* [C] UK someone who is away from home on holiday tatilci

holiness /'həʊlinəs/ *noun* [U] the quality of being holy mübareklik, kutsallık

holistic /həʊ'lɪstɪk/ *adjective* dealing with or treating the whole of something or someone and not just some parts tüme dayalı, tümünü içeren/kapsayan

holler /'hɒləʳ/ verb [I] US informal to shout or call loudly bağırmak, haykırmak ● **holler** noun [C] haykırış

hollow¹ /'hɒləʊ/ adjective **1** having a hole or empty space inside **kovuk, oyuk, boş** a hollow shell/tube ⊃See picture at **flat**. **2** without meaning or real feeling **boş, anlamsız, yararsız,** beyhude a hollow victory ○ a hollow laugh **3 hollow cheeks/eyes** If someone has hollow cheeks/eyes, their face seems to curve in around these areas. **yanakları/göz yuvaları çökük**

hollow

hollow² /'hɒləʊ/ noun [C] a hole or empty space in something, or a low area in a surface **çukur, oyuk, kovuk**

hollow³ /'hɒləʊ/ verb **hollow sth out** phrasal verb to make an empty space inside something **oymak, çukur açmak**

holly /'hɒli/ noun [U] a green bush with sharp, pointed leaves and small, red fruit **çoban püskülü**

Hollywood /'hɒliwʊd/ noun the centre of the US film industry **ABD film endüstrisinin merkezi, Hollywood**

holocaust /'hɒləkɔːst/ noun [C] when a very large number of people are killed and things destroyed, such as in a war or fire **büyük can ve mal kaybı, olağanüstü felaket; afet** a nuclear holocaust

hologram /'hɒləgræm/ noun [C] a photograph or image which appears to be solid and have depth when light shines on it in a particular way **hologram**

holster /'həʊlstəʳ/ noun [C] a leather container for carrying a gun on your body **tabanca kılıfı**

holy /'həʊli/ adjective **1** relating to a religion or a god **kutsal, mübarek, mukaddes** the holy city of Jerusalem **2** very religious or pure **mübarek, Tanrı'nın ve dinin hizmetinde olan** a holy man

homage /'hɒmɪdʒ/ noun **pay homage to sb** to show your respect for someone, especially by praising them in public **saygı/hürmet göstermek/sunmak; uluorta övmek/methetmek** Fans paid homage to the actress who died yesterday.

🧩 **home** ...... İLE BİRLİKTE KULLANILAN KELİMELER

go home ● be at home

o⁻**home¹** /həʊm/ noun **1** [C, U] the place where you live or feel you belong **ev, mesken** I tried to ring him, but he wasn't at home. ○ He left home (= stopped living with his family) when he was eighteen. **2** [C] a place where people who need special care live **yuva, aile ocağı** a children's home ○ My grandmother lives in a home now. **3 feel at home** to feel happy and confident in a place or situation **rahat olmak, mutlu güvende hissetmek, bulunduğu yeri yadırgamamak** After a month she felt at home in her new job. **4 make yourself at home** to behave in a relaxed way in a place, as if it was your own home **kendini evindeymiş gibi hissetmek, rahatına bakmak** Take off your coat and make yourself at home. **5 the home of sth/sb** the place where you usually find something or someone, or where they come from **bir şeyin/birinin mekânı/**

evi/bulunduğu yer France, the home of good food ⊃See also: nursing home, stately home.

o⁻**home²** /həʊm/ adverb **1** to the place where you live **eve, yuvaya** He didn't come home until midnight. ○ I went home to visit my parents. **2** at or in the place someone lives **evde, yuvada** Will you be home tomorrow evening?

home³ /həʊm/ adjective **1 sb's home address/phone number, etc** an address/telephone number, etc for the place where someone lives **ev adresi/telefonu 2** [FOR/FROM HOME] made or used in the place where someone lives **ev yapımı, evde kullanılan** home cooking ○ a home computer **3** [SPORT] relating to the place where a sporting event happens **(takım, spor) ev sahibi** The home team won 2-0. **4** [COUNTRY] relating to things in your own country **(ülke) iç işleri** home affairs

home⁴ /həʊm/ verb **home in on sth/sb** phrasal verb to give a lot of attention to something or someone **üzerinde yoğunlaşmak; bir şeye/birine çok fazla ehemmiyet/önem vermek/dikkat etmek** The report only homes in on the negative points.

homeboy /'həʊmbɔɪ/ (also homey) noun [C] mainly US informal a boy or man who is a close friend or who is from your own town **yakın arkadaş, memleketli, hemşehri**

homecoming /'həʊmˌkʌmɪŋ/ noun [C, U] when someone returns home, usually after being away for a long time **eve/yurda dönüş**

,**home eco'nomics** noun [U] a school subject in which you learn how to cook and sew **ev idaresi/ekonomisi; ev işletmesi**

home-grown /ˌhəʊm'grəʊn/ adjective **1** from your own garden **yerli, bahçeden, bahçe ürünü** home-grown vegetables **2** If someone or something is home-grown, they belong to or were developed in your own country. **yerli, ülkede yetişen, yerli malı** Our football team has many home-grown players.

homeland /'həʊmlænd/ noun [C] the country where you were born **anayurt, anavatan**

homeless /'həʊmləs/ adjective without a place to live **evsiz barksız** 10,000 people were made homeless by the floods. ○ They're opening a new shelter for the homeless. ● **homelessness** noun [U] **evsizlik**

homely /'həʊmli/ adjective **1** UK A homely place is simple, but comfortable and pleasant. **rahat ve hoş, basit** It's a small restaurant with a homely atmosphere. **2** US Someone who is homely is not very attractive. **gösterişsiz, süssüz; sevimsiz, kaknem, gudubet**

homemade (also UK home-made) /ˌhəʊm'meɪd/ adjective made at home and not bought from a shop **ev yapımı, evde yapılmış** homemade bread/cookies

homeopathy /ˌhəʊmi'ɒpəθi/ noun [U] a way of treating illnesses using very small amounts of natural substances **doğal ürünlerle tedavi yöntemi; homeopati** ● **homeopathic** /ˌhəʊmiəʊ'pæθɪk/ adjective a homeopathic remedy **bitkisel (tedavi)**

homeowner /'həʊmˌəʊnəʳ/ noun [C] someone who owns the house that they live in **ev sahibi/ev sahibesi**

'**home ,page** noun [C] the first page that you see when you look at a website on the Internet **(internet) ana sayfa, başlangıç/açılış sayfası** ⊃See study page **The Web and the Internet** on page Centre 36.

,**home 'shopping** noun [U] when someone buys goods from a magazine, a television programme, or a website **(internet, tv., dergi vb. yoluyla) alışveriş**

homesick /'həʊmsɪk/ adjective feeling sad because you are away from your home **sıla hasreti/özlemi çeken,**

H

yurt/vatan özlemi çeken ● **homesickness** *noun* [U] ev özlemi

homestead /'həʊmsted/ *noun* [C] *mainly US* a house and area of land usually used as a farm **çiftlik ve müştemilâtı**

hometown *US (UK/US* home 'town) /ˌhəʊm'taʊn/ *noun* [C] the town or city that you come from **doğduğu yer; geldiği şehir kasaba; memleket**

homeward /'həʊmwəd/ *adjective, adverb* towards home **eve doğru olan, eve doğru giden** *the homeward journey*

◦←**homework** /'həʊmwɜːk/ *noun* [U] **1** work which teachers give students to do at home **ev ödevi** *Have you done your homework yet?* **2 do your homework** to prepare carefully for a situation **ödevini iyi yapmak, iyi hazırlanmak** *It was clear that she had done her homework before the meeting.*

YAYGIN HATALAR

homework

Unutmayın! **Homework** kelimesinin çoğul hali yoktur. **Homeworks** demek doğru değildir. **Some homework** veya **pieces of homework** kullanımları doğrudur.: ~~Our new teacher gives us a lot of homeworks.~~ Yanlış cümle örneği

Our new teacher gives us a lot of homework.

homey[1] /'həʊmi/ *US (UK* homely) *adjective* A homey place is simple, but comfortable and pleasant. **sade/ basit fakat rahat, hoş**

homey[2] /'həʊmi/ *(also* homeboy) *noun* [C] *mainly US informal* a boy or man who is a close friend or who is from your own town **hemşehri; yakın arkadaş**

homicide /'hɒmɪsaɪd/ *noun* [C, U] *US* the crime of killing someone **cinayet, adam öldürme** *There were over 400 homicides in Chicago last year.* ● **homicidal** /ˌhɒmɪ'saɪdəl/ *adjective* likely to murder someone **katil ruhlu, öldürücü, ölüm saçan, adam öldürmeye meyilli** *a homicidal maniac*

homogeneous /ˌhɒmə'dʒiːniəs/, /ˌhəʊmə'dʒiːniəs/ *adjective formal* consisting of parts or members that are all the same **türdeş, aynı cinsten, homojen** *The village was a fairly homogeneous community.*

homophobia /ˌhəʊmə'fəʊbiə/ *noun* [U] hate of homosexual people **eş cinsellerden nefret etme/tiksinme** ● **homophobic** *adjective* hating homosexual people **eş cinsellerden nefret eden/tiksinen**

homosexual /ˌhəʊmə'sekʃuəl/ *adjective* sexually attracted to people of the same sex **aynı cinse ilgi duyan; aynı cinsi çekici bulan** ● **homosexual** *noun* [C] someone who is homosexual **eş cinsel; homoseksüel** ● **homosexuality** /ˌhəʊməʊˌsekʃu'æləti/ *noun* [U] the quality of being homosexual **eş cinsellik; homoseksüellik**

hone /həʊn/ *verb* [T] to improve something and make it perfect **geliştirmek, mükemmelleştirmek** *This is an opportunity for you to hone your skills.*

◦←**honest** /'ɒnɪst/ *adjective* **1** sincere and telling the truth **samimi, doğru, açık sözlü** *If you want my honest opinion, I think your hair looks awful.* **2** not likely to lie, cheat, or steal **dürüst, ilkeli, namuslu** *an honest man* ⊃Opposite **dishonest. 3 to be honest** *informal* used to express your real opinion **'Doğruyu söylemek gerekirse'** ...; **'Doğrusu** ...' *To be honest, I didn't really enjoy the party.*

honestly /'ɒnɪstli/ *adverb* **1** EMPHASIZE used to emphasize that you are telling the truth **gerçekten, hakikaten, inan olsun ki, vallahi** *Thanks, but I honestly couldn't eat another piece of cake.* **2** HONEST in an honest

way **dürüstçe, samimi bir şekilde 3** ANNOYED used to show that you are annoyed or do not approve of something **gerçekten, sahiden** *Honestly! He should have been here hours ago.*

honesty /'ɒnɪsti/ *noun* **1** [U] the quality of being honest **dürüstlük, haysiyet, namusluluk, doğru sözlülük 2 in all honesty** used when you are saying what you really think or feel about something **bütün samimiyetiyle, hakikaten** *In all honesty, I'd rather not go.* ⊃Opposite **dishonesty.**

honey /'hʌni/ *noun* **1** [U] a sweet, sticky food that is made by bees **bal** ⊃Orta kısımdaki renkli sayfalarına bakınız. **2** [C] *mainly US* a name that you call someone you love or like very much **sevgilim, canım, tatlım**

⋮⋮⋮ *honeymoon* ...... İLE BİRLİKTE KULLANILAN KELİMELER

be **on** (your) honeymoon ● a honeymoon **couple**

honeymoon /'hʌnimuːn/ *noun* [C] a holiday taken by two people who have just got married **balayı** *We went to Paris on our honeymoon.* ● **honeymooner** *noun* [C] **balayına çıkan**

honk /hɒŋk/ *verb* [I, T] to make a short sound with your car's horn (= part you press to make a warning noise) **korna çalmak** *The lorry driver honked his horn at me.*

honor /'ɒnər/ *noun, verb US spelling of* honour **şeref, namus, onur; saygı ile anmak, onurlandırmak**

honorable /'ɒnərəbl/ *adjective US spelling of* honourable **saygın, namuslu, onurlu; sayın, saygıdeğer**

honorary /'ɒnərəri/ *adjective* **1** given as a reward to show respect **fahri, onursal** *He was given an honorary degree from Cambridge University.* **2** If you have an honorary job, you are not paid for it. **şeref payesi olarak verilmiş, onursal** *the honorary chairman*

honour[1] *UK (US* honor) /'ɒnər/ *noun* **1** RESPECT [U] when people respect you because you have done what you believe is honest and right, or the quality of doing this **şeref, haysiyet, onur** *a man of honour* ○ *The soldiers fought for the honour of their country.* ⊃Opposite **dishonour. 2 in honour of sb/sth** in order to celebrate or show great respect for someone or something ...**ın/in onuruna/şerefine** *a banquet in honour of the President* **3** PRIDE [no plural] something which makes you feel proud and pleased **gurur, onur, haysiyet, şeref** [+ to do sth] *It's an honour to be team captain.* ○ [+ of + doing sth] *I had the great honour of meeting the King.* **4** REWARD [C] something that you give to someone in public to show respect for them and their achievements **şeref derecesi, onur payesi, iftihar belgesi** *She was granted the Order of Merit - one of the nation's highest honours.* **5 Her/His/ Your Honour** used when you are speaking to or about a judge **'Sayın yargıç', 'Sayın yargıçım' 6 honours** A qualification or university course with honours is of a very high level. **şeref/onur derecesi** *an honours degree*

honour[2] *UK (US* honor) /'ɒnər/ *verb* **1** [T] to show great respect for someone or something, usually in public **saygı göstermek, değer vermek, itibar etmek** [often passive] *He was honoured for his bravery.* ○ *She was honoured with an Oscar.* **2 honour an agreement/ contract/promise, etc** to do what you agreed or promised to do **(anlaşma/sözleşme/vaad) riayet etmek, uymak, tutmak, sadık kalmak, yerine getirmek** ⊃Opposite **dishonour.**

honourable /'ɒnərəbl/ *adjective UK* **1** *(US* honorable) honest and fair, or deserving praise and respect **saygın, onurlu, namuslu** *a decent, honourable man* ⊃Opposite **dishonourable. 2 the Honourable a** a title used before the name of some important government officials **sayın, saygıdeğer b** a title used in the UK before the name of certain people of high social rank **(Birleşik**

Krallık) yüksek sınıftan belli insanların isimleri önüne gelen ünvan; saygıdeğer, büyük, yüce ● **honourably** *adverb* onurlu bir şekilde

hood /hʊd/ *noun* [C] **1** a part of a coat or jacket that covers your head and neck **başlık, kukuleta, kapüşon** *a waterproof jacket with a hood* ⊃Orta kısımdaki renkli sayfalarına bakınız. **2** *US* (*UK* **bonnet**) the metal part that covers a car engine **kaput, motor kapağı** ⊃Orta kısımdaki renkli sayfalarına bakınız.

hooded /'hʊdɪd/ *adjective* having or wearing a hood **başlıklı, kukuletalı, kapüşonlu** *a hooded sweatshirt* ○ *hooded figures*

hoodie (*also* **hoody**) /'hʊdi/ *noun* [C] a sweatshirt (= a piece of clothing made of soft cotton which covers the top of your body) with a hood (= part which covers your head) **başlıklı eşofman üstü; kapüşonlu mont** ⊃Orta kısımdaki renkli sayfalarına bakınız.

hoof /huːf/ *noun* [C] *plural* **hooves** or **hoofs** the hard part on the foot of a horse and some other large animals **toynak**

hook¹ /hʊk/ *noun* **1** [C] a curved piece of metal or plastic used for hanging something on, or a similar object used for catching fish **çengel, kanca** *His coat was hanging from a hook on the door.* **2 off the hook** If a telephone is off the hook, the part you speak into is not in its correct position, so the telephone will not ring. **(telefon ahizesi) kaldırılmış, açık, yerinden çıkmış, fişi çıkmış** **3 left/right hook** when you hit someone hard with your left/right hand **sağ/sol elle darbe vurma 4 get/let sb off the hook** *informal* to allow someone to escape from a difficult situation or to avoid doing something that they do not want to do **birini beladan kurtarmak/ferahlatmak; engel olmak, sıyırmak; (argo) yırtmak**

hook² /hʊk/ *verb* **1** [T] to fasten something with a hook, hang something on a hook, or catch something with a hook **çengel ile tutturmak, kancaya asmak, kanca/çengel ile yakalamak 2 be/get hooked on sth a** to like or start to like doing something very much and want to do it all the time **aşırı düşkün olmak, tiryakisi olmak** *He's completely hooked on computer games.* **b** If you are hooked on a drug, you cannot stop taking it. **(uyuşturucu) müptelası/bağımlısı olmak** ● **hooked** *adjective* shaped like a hook **çengel/kanca biçiminde/şeklinde** *a hooked nose*

hook sth/sb up *phrasal verb* to connect a machine to a power supply or to another machine, or to connect someone to a piece of medical equipment **(makinayı) enerji kaynağına/başka bir makinaya bağlamak; (hastayı) tıbbî bir cihaza bağlamak**

hooligan /'huːlɪgən/ *noun* [C] someone who behaves badly or violently and causes damage in a public place **sokak serserisi** ● **hooliganism** *noun* [U] **serserilik, holiganlık**

hoop /huːp/ *noun* [C] a ring made of metal, plastic, or wood **çember, kasnak, halka**

hooray (*also* **hurrah**) /hʊ'reɪ/ *exclamation* something that you shout when you are happy, excited, etc or when you approve of someone or something **'Yaşa!', 'Yaşasın!' Hip, hip, hooray!**

hoot¹ /huːt/ *noun* **1** [C] a short sound made by an owl (= bird) or by a car horn (= warning equipment) **korna sesi, baykuş sesi 2 a hoot of laughter** when someone laughs loudly **yüksek sesle gülme/kahkaha atma 3** [no plural] *informal* something or someone that is very funny **komik/gülünç kimse veya şey** *The film was an absolute hoot.*

hoot² /huːt/ *verb* **1** [I, T] *mainly UK* to make a short sound with your car's horn (= part you press to make a warn-

ing noise) **korna çalmak** *The van driver hooted his horn impatiently.* **2** [I] If an owl (= bird) hoots, it makes a low 'oo' sound. **(baykuş) ötmek 3 hoot with laughter** to laugh a lot very loudly **yüksek sesle gülmek/kahkaha atmak**

Hoover /'huːvər/ *mainly UK trademark* (*UK/US* **vacuum cleaner**) *noun* [C] an electric machine which cleans floors by sucking up dirt **elektrik süpürgesi** ● **hoover** *verb* [I, T] **makineyle yerleri süpürmek**

hooves /huːvz/ *plural of* hoof **toynaklar**

hop¹ /hɒp/ *verb* [I] **hopping,** *past* **hopped 1** ONE FOOT to jump on one foot or to move about in this way **tek ayak üzerinde hoplamak/zıplamak/sıçramak; sekerek yürümek 2** ANIMAL If a small animal, bird, or insect hops, it moves by jumping on all of its feet at the same time. **(kuş, böcek) sıçramak, sekmek, hoplamak, zıplamak** *Rabbits were hopping across the field.* **3** MOVE QUICKLY *informal* to go somewhere quickly or get into or out of a vehicle quickly **sıçramak, zıplamak, atlamak; (araç) çabuk inmek/binmek** *to hop on a plane/train*

hop² /hɒp/ *noun* **1** [C] a short jump, especially on one leg **hoplama, sıçrama, sek sek 2 a short hop** *informal* a short journey or distance **bir adımlık kısa mesafe; kısa seyahat** *London to Paris is only a short hop by plane.*

o→ **hope¹** /həʊp/ *verb* **1** [I, T] to want something to happen or be true **ummak, ümit etmek, beklemek** [+ (that)] *I hope that the bus won't be late.* ○ *We had hoped for better weather than this.* ○ *"Do you think it's going to rain?" " I hope not!"* ○ *"Is he coming?" " I hope so."* **2 hope to do sth** to intend to do something **yapmaya niyetlenmek, yapmayı ümit etmek; ummak, dilemek** *Dad hopes to retire next year.*

┌───┐
hope ...... İLE BİRLİKTE KULLANILAN KELİMELER

bring / give / give up / hold out / lose / offer hope ● **fresh/great/renewed/vain** hope ● **hope of** sth/doing sth
└───┘

o→ **hope²** /həʊp/ *noun* **1** [C, U] a positive feeling about the future, or something that you want to happen **beklenti, umut, ümit** *What are your hopes and dreams for the future?* ○ [+ of + doing sth] *Young people are growing up in our cities without any hope of getting a job.* **2 sb's best/last/only hope** the best/last/only person or thing that can help you and make you succeed **en iyi/en son/tek ümidi** *Doctors say his only hope is a transplant.* **3 in the hope of/that** because you want something good to happen **umarak, umuduyla, umudu içinde** [+ of + doing sth] *She went to Paris in the hope of improving her French.* **4 pin your hopes on sb/sth** to hope that someone or something will help you to achieve what you want **umutlarını birine/birşeye bağlamak**

hopeful /'həʊpfᵊl/ *adjective* **1** feeling positive about a future event or situation **iyimser, umutlu, ümitli** *Many teenagers do not feel hopeful about the future.* ○ [+ (that)] *Police are still hopeful that they will find the missing family.* **2** If something is hopeful, it makes you feel that what you want to happen will happen. **ümit verici, umut vaat eden** *There are hopeful signs that she will make a full recovery.* ● **hopeful** *noun* someone who hopes to succeed, especially in the entertainment business **istekli/arzulu kimse; başarmaya hevesli kimse** *a young hopeful* ● **hopefulness** *noun* [U] **umut**

o→ **hopefully** /'həʊpfᵊli/ *adverb* **1** used, often at the start of a sentence, to express what you would like to happen **'Ümit ederim(z) ki, umut ederim(z) ki ...', 'Her şey yolunda giderse ...'** *Hopefully it won't rain.* **2** in a hope-

H

ful way **umutla, ümit ederek** *"Are there any tickets left?" she asked hopefully.*

hopeless /ˈhəʊpləs/ *adjective* **1** VERY BAD very bad and not likely to succeed or improve **ümitsiz, çaresiz** *a hopeless situation* ○ *They searched for survivors, but it was hopeless.* **2** NOT ABLE very bad at a particular activity **yetersiz, yeteneksiz, çok kötü, beceriksiz** *Dad's a hopeless cook.* ○ *I'm hopeless at sports.* **3** NOT POSITIVE feeling no hope **karamsar, kötümser, umutsuz, endişeli** *She was depressed and felt totally hopeless about the future.* ● **hopelessness** *noun* [U] **umutsuzluk**

hopelessly /ˈhəʊpləsli/ *adverb* extremely, or in a way that makes you lose hope **son derece; ümitsizce** *hopelessly lost* ○ *They met at university and fell hopelessly in love.*

hops /hɒps/ *noun* [plural] the flowers of a plant that are used to make beer **şerbetçi otu**

horde /hɔːd/ *noun* [C] a large group of people (insan) **kalabalık, güruh, sürü** *There was a horde of tourists outside Buckingham Palace.*

horizon /həˈraɪzᵊn/ *noun* **1** [C] the line in the distance where the sky seems to touch the land or sea **ufuk 2 broaden/expand/widen your horizons** to increase the number of things that you know about, have experienced, or can do **ufkunu genişletmek; bilgi/beceri ve deneyimlerini artırmak** *Travelling certainly broadens your horizons.* **3 on the horizon** likely to happen soon **ufukta, bekleniyor, çıkmak/görünmek üzere** *Economic recovery is on the horizon.*

horizontal/vertical

horizontal stripes

vertical stripes

horizontal /ˌhɒrɪˈzɒntᵊl/ *adjective* level and flat, or parallel to the ground or to the bottom of a page **yatay, ufki** *a horizontal line/stripe* ● **horizontally** *adverb* **yatay bir şekilde**

hormone /ˈhɔːməʊn/ *noun* [C] one of several chemicals produced in your body that influence its growth and development **hormon** ● **hormonal** /hɔːˈməʊnᵊl/ *adjective a hormonal imbalance* **hormonal**

horn /hɔːn/ *noun* [C] **1** ANIMAL one of the two hard, pointed growths on the heads of cows, goats, and some other animals **boynuz 2** EQUIPMENT a piece of equipment used to make a loud sound as a warning or signal **korna, klakson** *a car horn* ○ *The taxi driver hooted his horn.* **3** MUSIC a curved musical instrument that you blow into to make a sound **korno, boru** *the French horn*

horoscope /ˈhɒrəskəʊp/ *noun* [C] a description of what someone is like and what might happen to them in the future, based on the position of the stars and planets when they were born **yıldız falı**

horrendous /həˈrendəs/ *adjective* extremely unpleasant or bad **dehşet verici, korkunç, müthiş, berbat** *She suffered horrendous injuries in the accident.* ● **horrendously** *adverb* extremely or extremely badly **dehşet verici/korkunç/müthiş/berbat şekilde; iğrenç biçimde** *horrendously expensive*

horrible /ˈhɒrəbl/ *adjective* very unpleasant or bad **berbat, kötü, iğrenç, tiksindirici, tüyler ürpertici, dehşet verici** *What's that horrible smell?* ○ *That was a horrible thing to say to your sister.* ● **horribly** *adverb* extremely, or in a very bad or unpleasant way **dehşet verici/tüyler ürperten/iğrenç biçimde** *His plan went horribly wrong.*

horrid /ˈhɒrɪd/ *adjective* very unpleasant or unkind **korkunç, berbat, kötü, nahoş**

horrific /hɒrˈɪfɪk/ *adjective* very bad and shocking **dehşet verici, korkunç, berbat** *a horrific accident/crime* ○ *horrific injuries* ● **horrifically** *adverb* **çok kötü bir şekilde**

horrify /ˈhɒrɪfaɪ/ *verb* [T] to make someone feel very shocked **dehşete düş(ür)mek, korkutmak, aklını başından almak** [often passive] *I was horrified to hear about your accident.* ● **horrifying** *adjective* **korkunç, şaşırtıcı**

horror /ˈhɒrəʳ/ *noun* **1** [C, U] a strong feeling of shock or fear, or something that makes you feel shocked or afraid **dehşet, korku** *She watched in horror as the car skidded across the road.* **2 a horror film/movie/story** a film or story that entertains people by shocking or frightening them **korku/gerilim filmi/hikayesi**

○•**horse** /hɔːs/ *noun* [C] a large animal with four legs, which people ride or use to pull heavy things **at**

horseback /ˈhɔːsbæk/ *noun* **1 on horseback** riding a horse **at sırtında, at sürerek/binerek** *police on horseback* **2 horseback riding** US (UK horse riding) the sport or activity of riding a horse **atçılık sporu** ⊃Orta kısımdaki renkli sayfalarına bakınız.

,**horse 'chestnut** *noun* [C] a tree that produces shiny, brown nuts in thick green shells with sharp points, or one of these nuts **at kestanesi, at kestanesi ağacı**

horse-drawn /ˈhɔːsdrɔːn/ *adjective* [always before noun] A horse-drawn vehicle is pulled by a horse. **atla çekilen, at koşulan**

horseman, horsewoman /ˈhɔːsmən/, /ˈhɔːsˌwʊmən/ *noun* [C] *plural* **horsemen** or **horsewomen** a man/woman who rides horses well **(erkek/kadın) binici; süvari, atlı**

horsepower /ˈhɔːsˌpaʊəʳ/ *(written abbreviation* **hp***) noun* [U] a unit for measuring the power of an engine **beygir gücü**

'**horse ,racing** *noun* [U] the sport where people race on horses, usually to win money **at yarışı**

'**horse ,riding** UK (US 'horseback ,riding) *noun* [U] the sport or activity of riding a horse **atlı spor** ⊃Orta kısımdaki renkli sayfalarına bakınız.

horseshoe /ˈhɔːsʃuː/ *noun* [C] a U-shaped piece of metal that is nailed to a horse's foot **at nalı**

horticulture /ˈhɔːtɪkʌltʃəʳ/ *noun* [U] the study or activity of growing plants **bahçecilik, çiçekcilik, bahçıvanlık** ● **horticultural** /ˌhɔːtɪˈkʌltʃᵊrᵊl/ *adjective* relating to gardening **bahçecilik/çiçekcilik/bahçıvanlık ile ilgili**

hose /həʊz/ *noun* **1** [C] *(also UK* **hosepipe** /ˈhəʊzpaɪp/) a long pipe made of rubber or plastic and used for directing water somewhere, usually onto a garden or fire **hortum 2** [plural] *(also* **pantyhose**) US a piece of women's clothing made of very thin material that covers the legs and bottom **külotlu çorap**

hospice /'hɒspɪs/ *noun* [C] a place where people who are dying live and are cared for **düşkünler evi, onmazlar hastanesi**

hospitable /hɒs'pɪtəbl/ *adjective* A hospitable person or place is friendly, pleasant, and welcomes visitors. **misafirperver, konuksever**

hospital ...... İLE BİRLİKTE KULLANILAN KELİMELER

be **admitted to/discharged from** hospital • be (UK) **in/**(US) **in the** hospital

o-¤**hospital** /'hɒspɪtˀl/ *noun* [C, U] a place where ill or injured people go to be treated by doctors and nurses **hastane** *He was (UK)* **in hospital**/ *(US)* **in the hospital** *for two weeks.*

hospitalize (*also UK* -**ise**) /'hɒspɪtˀlaɪz/ *verb* [T] to take someone to hospital and keep them there for treatment **hastaneye kaldır(ıl)mak, hastaneye yatır(ıl)mak** [often passive] *My wife was often hospitalized for depression.*

host¹ /həʊst/ *noun* 1 PARTY [C] someone who organizes a party and invites the guests **(parti düzenleyen) ev sahibi** 2 TELEVISION [C] someone who introduces the guests on a radio or television programme **sunucu, program takdimcisi** *a talk show host* 3 PLACE [C] a country or city that provides the place and equipment for an organized event **ev sahipliği yapan ülke/kuruluş/şehir** *Australia* **played host to** *the Olympics in 2000.* 4 COMPUTERS a company that hosts websites on the Internet **internette web sitesi hizmeti sağlayan şirket/kuruluş** 5 **a host of sth** a large number of people or things **bir çok/sürü/yığın** *I've got a whole host of questions to ask you.*

host² /həʊst/ *verb* [T] 1 to be the host of an event **ev sahipliği yapmak** *to host a party/dinner* 2 to provide the computer equipment and programs that allow a website to operate on the Internet **bilgisayar malzemesi ve programları sağlamak**

hostage /'hɒstɪdʒ/ *noun* 1 [C] someone who is kept as a prisoner and may be hurt or killed in order to force other people to do something **rehine, tutsak** 2 **take/hold sb hostage** to catch or keep someone as a prisoner **rehin almak** *Two tourists were held hostage by terrorists.*

hostel /'hɒstˀl/ *noun* [C] a place like a cheap hotel, where you can live when you are away from home or have no home **han, yurt, pansiyon, misafirhane** *a hostel for the homeless* ○ *a* **student hostel** ⊃See also: youth hostel.

hostess /'həʊstɪs/ *noun* [C] 1 a woman who organizes a party and invites the guests **(parti düzenleyen) ev sahibesi** 2 a woman who introduces the guests on a television programme **tv. programlarında konukları sunan bayan** ⊃See also: air hostess.

hostile /'hɒstaɪl/ *adjective* 1 unfriendly and not liking or agreeing with something **saldırgan, düşmanca, aykırı düşünen, karşı olan, muhalif** *Some politicians were very* **hostile to** *the idea.* 2 unpleasant or not suitable for living or growing **kötü, berbat, uygun olmayan** *a hostile climate*

hostility ...... İLE BİRLİKTE KULLANILAN KELİMELER

arouse/provoke hostility • **open** hostility • hostility **to/towards** sb

hostility /hɒs'tɪləti/ *noun* 1 [U] unfriendly, angry behaviour that shows that you dislike someone **düşmanlık, düşmanca/hasımca tutum, saldırganlık** *hostility* **towards** *outsiders* 2 [U] when you strongly disagree with something or someone **karşı görüşte olma, karşı olma, muhalefet** *There is still open* **hostility to**

the idea. 3 **hostilities** [plural] *formal* fighting in a war **(savaş) çarpışmalar, çatışmalar**

o-¤**hot**¹ /hɒt/ *adjective* hotter, hottest 1 VERY WARM having a high temperature **sıcak** *a hot summer's day* ○ *a hot drink/meal* ○ *I'm too hot in this jacket.* 2 SPICY Hot food contains strong spices which cause a burning feeling in your mouth. **acı, acılı, baharatlı** *Be careful. The chilli sauce is very hot.* 3 EXCITING *informal* exciting or interesting **heyecan verici, ilginç** *Hollywood's hottest new actress* 4 **a hot issue/topic** a subject which people discuss and have strong feelings about **tartışmalı/alevli/sıcak sorun/konu** *The legalization of drugs is a hot topic.* ⊃See also: piping hot, red-hot.

hot² /hɒt/ *verb* hotting, past hotted

hot up *phrasal verb UK informal* If a situation or event hots up, it becomes more exciting and more things start to happen. **kızış(tır)mak**

hot-'air bal,loon *noun* [C] a very large balloon filled with hot air, that has a container below it where people can travel **sıcak hava balonu** ⊃See picture at balloon.

hotbed /'hɒtbed/ *noun* [C] a place where there is a lot of a particular activity, usually something bad **yatak, kaynak, yuva, mekân, yer** *The government was a* **hotbed of** *corruption.*

,**hot 'chocolate** *noun* [C, U] a hot, sweet drink with a chocolate flavour **sıcak çikolata**

'**hot ,dog** *noun* [C] a cooked sausage (= tube of meat and spices) that you usually eat inside bread **sosisli sandviç, ekmek arası sosis**

hotel ...... İLE BİRLİKTE KULLANILAN KELİMELER

at/in a hotel • a hotel **guest/room** • a **luxury** hotel

o-¤**hotel** /həʊ'tel/ *noun* [C] a place where you pay to stay when you are away from home **otel** *We spent our honeymoon* **in a** *luxury* **hotel.** ○ *a hotel room*

hotelier /həʊ'teliei/ ⓤ /həʊ'teljər/ *noun* [C] someone who owns or is in charge of a hotel **otelci, otel sahibi/yöneticisi**

hotline /'hɒtlaɪn/ *noun* [C] a telephone number that you can ring for help or information **(yardım ve bilgi için) kırmızı telefon hattı, direkt telefon hattı** *Ring our 24-hour hotline for advice.*

hotly /'hɒtli/ *adverb* 1 in an angry or excited way **kızgınlıkla, şiddetle** *He* **hotly denied** *the rumours.* 2 hotly contested If a race, election, or other competition is hotly contested, everyone is trying very hard to win it. **ciddi/çetin/zorlukla başarılmaya çalışılan yarışma**

,**hot-'water bottle** *noun* [C] a flat, rubber container that you fill with hot water to keep you warm **sıcak su şişesi/torbası, termofor**

hound¹ /haʊnd/ *noun* [C] a dog that is used when people hunt animals **tazı, av köpeği**

hound² /haʊnd/ *verb* [T] to follow someone and annoy them by asking questions or taking photographs **peşini bırakmamak; sürekli peşinde olmak** [often passive] *She is always being hounded by photographers.*

o-¤**hour** /aʊəʳ/ *noun* 1 [C] a period of time equal to 60 minutes **saat** *half an hour* ○ *It's a six-hour flight.* ○ *The job pays $5 an hour.* 2 [C] the period of time when a particular activity happens or when a shop or public building is open **(açılış kapanış veya oluş) saati** [usually plural] **working hours** ○ *Our* **opening hours** *are from 8 to 6.* ○ *I've got to go to the bank (UK) in my* **lunch hour**/ *(US)* **on my lunch hour.** 3 **hours** *informal* a long time **saatlerce** *I spent hours doing my homework.* 4 **the hour** the point when a new hour begins **saat başı** *The train leaves at two minutes past the hour.* ○ *My watch beeps* **on the** *hour.* **5 all hours** very late at night, until early morning, or almost all the time **geç saatte** *Our neighbours are up till all hours every night, playing loud music.* **6 the early/small hours** the hours between midnight and the time that the sun rises **gece yarısı ile gün doğumu arasındaki saatler** ⊃See also: **rush hour.**

hourly /'aʊəli/ *adjective, adverb* **1** happening every hour **saatte bir** *There is an hourly bus service.* **2** for each hour **saat başı** *an hourly rate/wage*

house .... İLE BİRLİKTE KULLANILAN KELİMELER

build/buy/rent/sell a house ● a detached/semi-detached/terraced house

○╸**house¹** /haʊs/ *noun plural* **houses** /'haʊzɪz/ **1** [BUILDING] [C] a building where people live, usually one family or group **ev** *a three-bedroomed house* ○ *We went to my aunt's house for dinner.* **2** [PEOPLE] [no plural] the people who live in a house **ev halkı** *The baby's screaming woke the whole house up.* **3** [PLACE FOR ACTIVITY] [C] the place where a particular business or activity happens **iş/faaliyet yapılan yer, bina** *an opera house* ○ *a publishing house* **4 the House** a group of people which makes a country's laws, or the place where they meet **meclis, kamara** *the House of Commons/Representatives* ○ *The House voted on the proposals.* **5** [THEATRE] [C] the people watching a performance or the area where they sit **seyirciler; seyirci tribünü** [usually singular] *The actors played to a full house.* **6 on the house** If food or drink is on the house in a bar or restaurant, it is free. **bedava, müesseseden, ikram** ⊃See also: **boarding house, full house, row house, terraced house, the White House.**

house² /haʊz/ *verb* [T] **1** to give a person or animal a place to live **barındırmak, yerleştirmek** *This development will house over 100 families.* **2** to provide space for something **yer temin etmek** *The museum houses a huge collection of paintings.*

house ar'rest *noun* **under house arrest** when you are kept as a prisoner in your own home **göz hapsinde olmak; cezasını evde çekmek**

houseboat /'haʊsbəʊt/ *noun* [C] a boat that people can live on **yüzer ev**

housebound /'haʊsbaʊnd/ *adjective* unable to leave your home because you are too ill or old **eve mahkum, evden dışarı çıkamayan**

household¹ /'haʊshəʊld/ *noun* [C] a family or group of people who live together in a house **hane halkı, ev, hane** *Many households own more than one television.*

household² /'haʊshəʊld/ *adjective* **1** [always before noun] connected with or belonging to a home **hane halkına/eve ilişkin** *household bills/expenses* ○ *household products/goods* **2 a household name** someone or something that everyone knows **herkesçe bilinen kimse/şey** *Her TV roles made her a household name in the UK.*

householder /'haʊshəʊldəʳ/ *noun* [C] UK someone who owns or rents a house **ev sahibi/sahibesi veya kiracı/kiralayan**

house 'husband *noun* [C] a man who takes care of the house and children while his wife or partner earns money for the family **ev erkeği**

housekeeper /'haʊsˌkiːpəʳ/ *noun* [C] someone who is paid to clean and cook in someone else's house **gündelikçi, ev temizlikçisi/hizmetçisi**

housekeeping /'haʊsˌkiːpɪŋ/ *noun* [U] the cleaning and cooking that you do in your home **ev işleri**

house (music) *noun* [U] a type of electronic pop music with a strong beat for dancing **bir tür elektronik pop müzik**

House of 'Commons *noun* [no plural] one of the two parts of the British parliament, with elected members who make laws **Avam Kamarası**

House of 'Lords *noun* [no plural] one of the two parts of the British parliament, with members who are chosen by the government **Lordlar Kamarası**

House of Repre'sentatives *noun* [no plural] a group of politicians elected by people in the US to make laws **Temsilciler Meclisi**

Houses of 'Parliament *noun* [plural] the House of Commons and the House of Lords, or the building in London where they meet **Lordlar ve Avam Kamarası; Parlamento Binası**

house warming *noun* [C] a party to celebrate moving into a new house **yeni eve ısınma/hoş geldin partisi**

housewife /'haʊswaɪf/ *noun* [C] *plural* **housewives** /'haʊswaɪvz/ a woman who stays at home to cook, clean, and take care of her family **ev hanımı/kadını**

housework /'haʊswɜːk/ *noun* [U] the work that you do to keep your house clean **ev işleri** *I can't stand doing housework.*

housing /'haʊzɪŋ/ *noun* [U] buildings for people to live in **mesken, yerleşim, iskân, ikamet** *a shortage of local housing*

housing e,state UK (US **housing de,velopment**) *noun* [C] an area with a large number of houses that were built at the same time **toplu konut**

hover /'hɒvəʳ/ *verb* [I] **1** to stay up in the air but without moving anywhere **havada belli bir yerde asılı kalmak** *A helicopter hovered overhead.* **2** If you hover, you stand and wait near someone or something. **dolanıp durmak** *A waiter hovered at the table ready to take our order.*

hovercraft /'hɒvəkrɑːft/ *noun* [C] a boat that moves across the surface of water or land supported by a large cushion (= soft container) of air **denizde ve karada gidebilen araç, hoverkraft**

○╸**how¹** /haʊ/ *adverb* **1** [WAY] used to ask about the way something happens or is done **nasıl, ne şekilde** *How did he die?* ○ *How does she manage to keep the house so tidy?* **2** [QUANTITY] used to ask about quantity, size, or age **(miktar, ebat, yaş) ne kadar, kaç** *How big is the house?* ○ *How old are they?* ○ *How much* (= what price) *was that dress?* **3** [EMPHASIZE] used before an adjective or adverb to emphasize it **ne kadar** *I was amazed at how quickly she finished.* **4** [HEALTH] used to ask about someone's health **nasıl, ne durumda** *How are you feeling today?* **5** [SITUATION] used to ask about the success or progress of a situation **(başarı ve nasıl olduğunu sorgulamada) nasıl** *How's everything going?* ○ *How was the exam?* **6 How are you?** used to ask someone if they are well and happy **'Nasılsınız?', 'Ne haber?'** *"How are you Jane?" - "Oh, not so bad thanks."* **7 How about..?** used to make a suggestion **Ne dersiniz ...?** *How about a drink?* ○ [+ doing sth] *How about going to the cinema?* **8 How come?** *informal* used to ask about the reason for something, especially when you feel surprised about it **'Niçin?', 'Nasıl?'** *"Kate's gone to the party on her own." "How come?"* **9 How strange/stupid/weird, etc. is that?** said to mean that something is strange/stupid, etc. **Ne kadar acayip/aptalca/garip vs.'** ⊃See also: **know-how.**

how² /haʊ/ *conjunction* used to talk about the way that something happens or is done **nasıl, ne şekilde** [+ to do sth] *I don't know how to turn the video on.*

o--**however**¹ /haʊˈevəʳ/ *adverb* **1 however cold/difficult/
slowly, etc** used to say that it does not make any difference how cold/difficult/slowly, etc **ne kadar (soğuk/
zor/yavaş vs.) ... olursa olsun** *We're not going to get
there in time, however fast we drive.* **2** used when you
are about to say something which is surprising compared with what you have just said **ancak, ama** *He had
always been a successful businessman. Recently, however,
things have not been going well for him.* **3** *UK* used to ask
about how something happened when the person
asking feels surprised **nasıl; nasıl oldu da** *However
did you manage to persuade her?*

however² /haʊˈevəʳ/ *conjunction* in any way **her nasıl**
However you look at it, it's still a mess. ○ *You can do it
however you like.*

howl /haʊl/ *verb* [I] **1** ANIMAL If a dog or wolf (= wild animal like a dog) howls, it makes a long, sad sound.
(köpek, yabani hayvan vb.) ulumak, ürümek
2 MAKE SOUND to make a loud sound, usually to express
pain, sadness, or another strong emotion **inlemek, feryat etmek** *He howled in pain.* ○ *The audience was how-
ling with laughter.* **3** WIND If the wind howls, it blows
hard and makes a lot of noise. **(rüzgâr) uğuldamak**
● **howl** *noun* [C] **uluma (hayvan)**

hp *written abbreviation for* horsepower (= a unit for measuring the power of an engine) **beygirgücü**

HQ /ˌeɪtʃˈkjuː/ *noun* [C, U] *abbreviation for* headquarters
(= the place from where an organization is controlled)
ana merkez, karargâh, ana komuta merkezi

hr *written abbreviation for* hour **saat**

HRH /ˌeɪtʃɑːrˈeɪtʃ/ *abbreviation for* His/Her Royal Highness: used when speaking to or about a royal person
Ekselansları, Majesteleri

HTH *internet abbreviation for* hope this helps: used when
you send someone information you think is useful,
especially when you answer a question **umarım bu
işe yarar**

HTML /ˌeɪtʃtiːemˈel/ *abbreviation for* hypertext markup
language: a way of marking text so that it can be seen
on the Internet **internette görüntülenebilmesi için
yazının belirlenmesi; HTML**

http /ˌeɪtʃtiːtiːˈpiː/ *abbreviation for* hypertext transfer
protocol: a set of instructions made by a computer program that allows your computer to connect to an Internet document **internette bir belgeye ulaşılmasını
sağlayan bilgisayar programı tarafından oluşturulan talimatlar bütünü; http (doküman transfer pro-
tokolü)**

hub /hʌb/ *noun* [C] **1** a place that is the centre of a particular activity **belli bir eylemin ana merkezi** [usually
singular] *Silicon Valley has become the **hub** of the electronics industry.* **2** the round part in the centre of a wheel
tekerlek göbeği, jant

huddle¹ /ˈhʌdl/ (*also* **huddle together/up**) *verb* [I] to move
closer to other people, or to hold your arms and legs
close to your body, usually because you are cold or frightened **sokulmak, büzülmek, yumak olmak, dertop
olmak** *They huddled around the fire to keep warm.*

huddle² /ˈhʌdl/ *noun* [C] a group of people or things that
are standing close together **kalabalık, yığın, küme,
grup, topluluk**

hue /hjuː/ *noun* [C] *literary* a colour **renk**

huff¹ /hʌf/ *verb* **huff and puff** *informal* to breathe
loudly, especially because you have been exercising
derin ve sesli nefes alıp vermek

huff² /hʌf/ *noun* **in a huff** *informal* angry with someone
incinmiş, gücenmiş, alınmış, kızgın; homurdana

homurdana *Mum's in a huff because I didn't call yesterday.*

hug¹ /hʌg/ *verb* **hug**
hugging, *past* **hugged,**
1 [I, T] to put your arms
around someone and
hold them tightly,
usually because you
love them **sarılmak,
kucaklamak** *They
hugged and kissed each
other.* **2** [T] to stay very
close to the edge of
something **bir şeyin kıyısında olmak; kıyıdan kıyıdan gitmek** *The road hugs the coast for several miles.*

hug² /hʌg/ *noun* [C] when you put your arms around
someone and hold them tightly **kucaklama, sarılma**
She gave me a big hug before she left.

o--**huge** /hjuːdʒ/ *adjective* extremely large **devasa, koca-
mak, çok büyük, çok, dünya kadar, muazzam, çok
iri** *a huge house*

hugely /ˈhjuːdʒli/ *adverb* extremely **müthiş, fevkalade, çok** *hugely popular/successful*

huh /hʌ/ *exclamation informal* used to ask a question, or
to express surprise, anger, etc **Ha!', 'Öyle mi?', 'Hı?'** *So,
you're leaving, huh?*

hull /hʌl/ *noun* [C] the main part of a ship that is mostly
under water **gemi/tekne gövdesi**

hullo *UK* (*UK/US* **hello**) /həˈləʊ/ *exclamation* **1** used to
greet someone **Selam!', 'Merhaba!'** *Hullo, Chris, how
are things?* **2** used to start a conversation on the telephone **Alo!'** *Hullo, this is Alex.*

hum¹ /hʌm/ *verb* **humming,** *past* **hummed 1** [I, T] to sing
without opening your mouth **mırıldanmak** *She hum-
med to herself as she walked to school.* **2** [I] to make a
continuous, low sound **vızıldamak, vınlamak, uğuldamak** *The computers were humming in the background.* **3** **be humming** If a place is humming, it is
busy and full of activity. **dopdolu, kaynayan, arı
kovanı gibi, ana baba günü** ● **hum** *noun* [C] a low, continuous sound **vızıltı, vınlama, uğuldama** *the hum of
traffic*

o--**human**¹ /ˈhjuːmən/ *adjective* **1** relating to people or
their characteristics **insanî, insana ait/özgü** *the
human body* ○ *human behaviour* ○ *The accident was
caused by **human error** (= a person's mistake).* **2** **be
only human** to not be perfect **mükemmel olmamak,
hata yapabilecek olmak** *Of course Tom makes mistakes - he's only human.*

human² /ˈhjuːmən/ (*also* ˌhuman ˈbeing) *noun* [C] a man,
woman, or child **insan, insanoğlu** *The disease affects
both humans and animals.*

humane /hjuːˈmeɪn/ *adjective* kind, especially towards
people or animals that are suffering **müşfik, insancıl,
sevecen, şefkatli, merhametli** *They fought for more
humane treatment of prisoners of war.* ⊃Opposite inhumane. ● **humanely** *adverb* **insanca, kibar**

humanism /ˈhjuːmənɪzᵊm/ *noun* [U] a belief system
based on human needs and values and not on a god or
religion **insanları sevme ülküsü, insancıllık, hüma-
nizm** ● **humanist** *noun* [C] **insancıl** ● **humanistic** /ˌhjuː-
məˈnɪstɪk/ *adjective* **insani**

humanitarian /hjuːˌmænɪˈteəriən/ *adjective* connected with improving people's lives and reducing suffering **insanî, insancıl, insansever** *The UN is sending
humanitarian aid to the refugees.*

humanities /hjuːˈmænətiz/ *noun* [plural] subjects that
you study which are not connected with science, such

as literature and history **beşerî ilimler, hümaniter bilimler, sosyal bilimler**

humanity /hjuːˈmænəti/ *noun* [U] **1** ALL PEOPLE all people **insanlık** *The massacre was a crime against humanity.* **2** KINDNESS kindness and sympathy towards others **insanlık, adamlık, insanı insan yapan değerler manzumesi** ⊃Opposite inhumanity. **3** BEING HUMAN the condition of being human **insanlık, insanı sevme, insancıl olma, insan sevgisi**

humankind /ˌhjuːmənˈkaɪnd/ *noun* [U] all the people in the world **tüm insanlar, insanlık**

humanly /ˈhjuːmənli/ *adverb* **humanly possible** able to be done by people **insanın yapabileceği; imkân dahilinde, yapılması mümkün** *Doctors did everything humanly possible to save her life.*

human 'nature *noun* [U] feelings, qualities, and behaviour that are typical of most people **insan tabiatı/ mizacı/huyu** *It's human nature to want to be loved.*

the ˌhuman 'race *noun* [no plural] all the people in the world **insanlık, beşeriyet, insan ırkı**

human re'sources UK (US ˌhuman 'resources) *noun* [U] the department of an organization that deals with finding new people to work there, keeping records about all the organization's employees, and helping them with any problems **insan kaynakları**

human 'rights *noun* [plural] the basic rights that every person should have, such as justice and the freedom to say what you think **insan hakları** *international laws protecting human rights* ○ *the human rights group Amnesty International*

humble¹ /ˈhʌmbl/ *adjective* **1** not proud or not believing that you are important **mütevazı, alçak gönüllü, gösterişsiz** *He's very humble about his success.* **2** poor or of a low social rank **fakir, alt sınıftan/düzeyde, önemsiz** *She rose from humble beginnings to become Prime Minister.* ● **humbly** *adverb* **mütevazi bir şekilde**

humble² /ˈhʌmbl/ *verb* [T] to make someone understand that they are not as important or special as they think they are **ezmek, burnunu sürtmek** *She was humbled by the unexpected defeat.* ● **humbling** *adjective a humbling experience* **karşıdaki kişinin kibirini kıran**

humdrum /ˈhʌmdrʌm/ *adjective* boring and ordinary **sıkıcı ve sıradan, tekdüze** *a humdrum existence*

humid /ˈhjuːmɪd/ *adjective* Humid air or weather is hot and slightly wet. **nemli, rutubetli** *a hot and humid climate*

humidity /hjuːˈmɪdəti/ *noun* [U] a measurement of how much water there is in the air **nem, rutubet**

humiliate /hjuːˈmɪlieɪt/ *verb* [T] to make someone feel stupid or ashamed **mahcup etmek, utandırmak, aşağılamak, küçük düşürmek** *How could you humiliate me in front of all my friends!* ● **humiliated** *adjective Sue felt completely humiliated.* **aşağılanmış** ● **humiliation** /hjuːˌmɪliˈeɪʃⁿn/ *noun* [C, U] **aşağılanma**

humiliating /hjuːˈmɪlieɪtɪŋ/ *adjective* making you feel stupid or ashamed **mahcup edici, onur kırıcı, küçük düşürücü, utandırıcı, aşağılayıcı** *a humiliating defeat*

humility /hjuːˈmɪləti/ *noun* [U] the quality of not being proud or not thinking that you are better than other people **alçakgönüllülük, tevazu**

humor /ˈhjuːməʳ/ *noun, verb* US *spelling of* humour **mizah, komiklik, gülünçlük (yapmak)**

humorless /ˈhjuːmələs/ *adjective* US *spelling of* humourless **mizahtan/nükteden anlamaz, çok ciddi; esprisiz**

humorous /ˈhjuːmⁿrəs/ *adjective* funny, or making you laugh **komik, gülünç, mizahî** *a humorous book* ● **humorously** *adverb* **espirili bir şekilde**

humour .... İLE BİRLİKTE KULLANILAN KELİMELER

a sense of humour ● a dry/wry humour

humour¹ UK (US humor) /ˈhjuːməʳ/ *noun* [U] **1** ABILITY the ability to laugh and recognize that something is funny **espri, mizah, espri anlayışı** *He's got a great sense of humour.* **2** FUNNY QUALITY the quality of being funny, or things that are funny **mizah, güldürü, espri** *His speech was full of humour.* **3** MOOD *formal* the way you are feeling, or your mood **mizaç, huy good humour**

humour² UK (US humor) /ˈhjuːməʳ/ *verb* [T] to do what someone wants so that they do not become annoyed or upset **huyuna suyuna gitmek, nazını çekmek, kaprislerine boyun eğmek, isteklerini yerine getirmek** *Carol applied for the job just to humour me.*

humourless UK (US humorless) /ˈhjuːmələs/ *adjective* unable to laugh and recognize when something is funny, or being without funny qualities **mizahtan/ nükteden/espriden anlamayan**

hump /hʌmp/ *noun* [C] **1** a round, raised area on a road or other surface **tümsek, yükselti, tepecik 2** a round, hard part on an animal's or person's back **(hayvan) hörgüç; (insan) kambur** *a camel's hump*

hunch¹ /hʌnʃ/ *noun* [C] a feeling or guess that something might be true, when there is no proof **önsezi, sezgi, içe doğuş** *I had a hunch that he would get the job.*

hunch² /hʌnʃ/ *verb* [I] to stand or sit with your shoulders and back curved forward **kamburunu çıkarmak; kamburunu çıkararak oturmak/durmak** *Sitting hunched over a computer all day can cause back problems.*

hunchback /ˈhʌnʃbæk/ *noun* [C] someone with a large lump on their back, which makes them lean forward

⊶**hundred** /ˈhʌndrəd/ **1** the number 100 **yüz 2 hundreds** *informal* a lot **yüzlerce, pek çok** *Hundreds of people wrote in to complain.*

hundredth¹ /ˈhʌndrədθ/ 100th written as a word **yüzüncü**

hundredth² /ˈhʌndrədθ/ *noun* [C] one of a hundred equal parts of something; 1/100 .01 **yüzde** *a hundredth of a second*

hundredweight /ˈhʌndrədweɪt/ (*written abbreviation* cwt) *noun* [C] *plural* **hundredweight** a unit for measuring weight, equal to 50.8 kilograms in the UK and 45.36 kilograms in the US **Birleşik Krallık'da 50.8 ABD'de 45.36 kilograma eşit bir ağırlık ölçüm birimi**

hung /hʌŋ/ *past of* hang **'asmak' fiilinin 2.ve 3. hali**

hunger /ˈhʌŋɡəʳ/ *noun* **1** FEELING [U] the feeling you have when you need to eat **açlık** *The children were almost crying with hunger by the time we got home.* **2** NOT ENOUGH FOOD [U] when you do not have enough food **kıtlık, açlık** *Many of the refugees died of hunger.* **3** WISH [no plural] a strong wish for something **bir şeye duyulan açlık/aşırı istek** *a hunger for success/knowledge*

'hunger ˌstrike *noun* [C, U] when someone refuses to eat in order to show that they strongly disagree with something **açlık grevi** *The prisoners went on hunger strike.*

hungover /ˌhʌŋˈəʊvəʳ/ *adjective* feeling ill after drinking too much alcohol the day before **akşamdan kalma; içkiden dolayı ertesi gün kötü hissetme**

⊶**hungry** /ˈhʌŋɡri/ *adjective* **1** wanting or needing food **aç, acıkmış** *I'm hungry. What's for supper?* **2 go**

hungry to not have enough food to eat **aç kalmak** *In an ideal world, nobody should go hungry.* **3 be hungry for sth** to have a strong wish for something **aşırı istekli/hevesli olmak** *The journalists were hungry for more details of the accident.* ● **hungrily** *adverb* **aç bir şekilde**

hunk /hʌŋk/ *noun* [C] **1** *informal* an attractive man who is often young and has a strong body **yapılı gösterişli ve çekici adam 2** a piece of something, usually large and not flat or smooth **iri parça, iri dilim** *a hunk of bread* ↪Orta kısımdaki renkli sayfalarına bakınız.

hunt¹ /hʌnt/ *verb* [I, T] **1** to chase and kill wild animals **avlamak, avlanmak** *to hunt deer/rabbits* **2** to search for something **aramak, araştırmak, bulmaya çalışmak** *The children hunted for sea shells on the beach.* ● **hunter** *noun* [C] a person who hunts wild animals **avcı**

hunt sb/sth down *phrasal verb* to search everywhere for someone or something until you find them **buluncaya kadar aramak/bulmaya çalışmak**

🔲 **hunt** .... İLE BİRLİKTE KULLANILAN KELİMELER

launch a hunt ● a hunt **for** sb/sth

---

hunt² /hʌnt/ *noun* [C] **1** a search for something or someone **arama** *a job hunt* ○ *The detective leading the hunt for the killer spoke at the news conference.* **2** when people chase and kill wild animals **av, avlanma** *a fox/deer hunt* ↪See also: witch-hunt.

hunting /'hʌntɪŋ/ *noun* [U] the sport of chasing and killing animals **avcılık** *fox-hunting*

hurdle¹ /'hɜːdl/ *noun* [C] **1** a bar or fence that people or horses jump over in a race **(at yarışı) engel, mania 2** a problem or difficulty that you have to deal with in order to be able to make progress **zorluk, sorun, engel, güçlük, zahmet** *Getting a work permit was the first hurdle to overcome.*

hurdle² /'hɜːdl/ *verb* [I, T] to jump over something, such as a bar or a fence, when you are running **engelleri aşmak, engelin üstünden aşmak** ● **hurdler** *noun* [C] **engel atlayan**

hurl /hɜːl/ *verb* **1** [T] to throw something with a lot of force, usually in an angry or violent way **fırlatmak, savurmak; fırlatıp atmak** *The demonstrators hurled stones at police.* **2** hurl abuse/insults, etc at sb to shout something at someone in a rude or angry way **hiddetle söylemek, savurmak**

hurrah (*also* hooray) /hə'rɑː/ *exclamation* something that you shout when you are happy, excited, etc, or when you approve of someone or something 'Yaşa!', 'Yaşasın!', 'Bravo!' *Hurrah! Ian's won!*

hurricane /'hʌrɪkən/ *noun* [C] a violent storm with very strong winds **kasırga, hortum, bora**

hurried /'hʌrid/ *adjective* done more quickly than normal **telaşla/aceleyle yapılmış, aceleye gelmiş** *a hurried explanation/meeting* ● **hurriedly** *adverb* **çabuk bir şekilde**

°⁻**hurry¹** /'hʌri/ *verb* [I, T] to move or do things more quickly than normal or to make someone do this **telaşla gitmek, aceleyle yapmak, acele etmek, çabuk olmak** *to hurry away/home* ○ *Please hurry, the train is about to leave.* ○ [+ to do sth] *We had to hurry to get there on time.*

hurry up *phrasal verb* to start moving or doing something more quickly **acele etmek** *Hurry up! We're going to be late.*

hurry² /'hʌri/ *noun* **1 be in a hurry** If you are in a hurry, you want or need to do something quickly. **acelesi olmak, çabuk olmak** *If you're in a hurry, it's better to take a taxi.* **2 be in no hurry; not be in any hurry** If you

are in no hurry to do something, either you do not need to do it soon or you do not really want to do it . **hiç acelesi olmamak** [+ to do sth] *They are in no hurry to sign a contract.*

°⁻**hurt¹** /hɜːt/ *verb past* hurt **1** CAUSE PAIN [T] to cause someone pain or to injure them **yaralamak, incitmek** *Simon hurt his knee playing football.* ○ [often reflexive] *She hurt herself when she slipped on an icy step.* **2** BE PAINFUL [I] If a part of your body hurts, it is painful. **acımak, ağrımak** *My eyes really hurt.* ○ [+ to do sth] *It hurts to walk on it.* **3** UPSET [I, T] to cause emotional pain to someone **canını yakmak/acıtmak, incitmek, kırmak, üzmek, kalbini kırmak** *Her comments about my work really hurt.* **4** AFFECT [T] to have a harmful effect on something **zarar vermek, zararı dokunmak** *His chances of re-election were hurt by allegations of corruption.* **5 it won't/wouldn't hurt (sb) to do sth** *informal* used to say that someone should do something **fena olmaz** *It wouldn't hurt to get there a bit earlier than usual.* ↪See also: wouldn't hurt a fly².

hurt² /hɜːt/ *adjective* [never before noun] **1** injured or in pain **yaralanmış, ağrıyan, incinmiş** *Several people were seriously hurt in the accident.* ○ *Put that knife away before someone gets hurt.* **2** upset or unhappy **üzülmüş, incinmiş, alınmış, kırılmış** *She was deeply hurt by what he said.*

hurt³ /hɜːt/ *noun* [U] emotional pain **kalp kırgınlığı, incinme, incitme, acı** *She has caused a lot of hurt.*

hurtful /'hɜːtfᵊl/ *adjective* Hurtful behaviour or remarks make someone feel upset. **incitici, ızdırap veren, kırıcı, üzücü** *hurtful comments/remarks*

hurtle /'hɜːtl/ *verb* [I] to move very quickly in a way which is not controlled and may be dangerous **hızla hareket etmek, paldır küldür ilerlemek, hızla fırlamak** *The explosion sent pieces of glass and metal hurtling through the air.*

°⁻**husband** /'hʌzbənd/ *noun* [C] the man who are married to **koca** *Janet's husband is in the Navy.*

hush¹ /hʌʃ/ *exclamation* used to tell someone to be quiet, especially if they are crying 'Sus!', 'Sakin ol!', 'Sesini çıkarma!' *It's okay. Hush now and wipe your eyes.*

🔲 **hush** .... İLE BİRLİKTE KULLANILAN KELİMELER

a hush **descends/falls** ● a **deathly** hush

---

hush² /hʌʃ/ *noun* [no plural] a period of silence **sessizlik, sükûnet, sakinlik** *A hush fell over the room.* ● **hushed** *adjective* a hushed atmosphere/crowd **sessiz, sükunetl**

hush³ /hʌʃ/ *verb* [T] to make someone be quiet **sakinleştirmek, sessiz olmasını sağlamak**

hush sth up *phrasal verb* to keep something secret, especially from the public, because it could cause embarrassment or trouble **örtbas etmek, kapatmak** *The whole affair was hushed up by the management.*

hush-hush /ˌhʌʃ'hʌʃ/ *adjective informal* If something is hush-hush, it is kept secret. **çok gizli, kizli kapaklı** *The project's all very hush-hush.*

husky¹ /'hʌski/ *adjective* **1** A husky voice is low and rough but usually sounds attractive. **(ses) boğuk, kısık, gizemli 2** *US* A husky man or boy is big and strong. **büyük güçlü kuvvetli adam/çocuk, yiğit, yapılı**

husky² /'hʌski/ *noun* [C] a large, strong dog that is used to pull heavy things across snow **Eskimo köpeği, Sibirya kurdu**

hustle¹ /'hʌsl/ *verb* **1** [T] to make someone move somewhere, especially by pushing them quickly **yaka paça/ite kaka götürmek; ite kaka götürmek; itip kakmak, iteklemek** *The security men hustled him out of* *the back door.* **2** [I, T] *informal* to try to persuade someone, especially to buy something, often illegally **(bir şeyi almak için) kanun dışı biçimde ikna etmeye çalışmak** *to hustle for business/customers*

hustle² /'hʌsl/ *noun* **hustle and bustle** busy movement and noise, especially where there are a lot of people **itiş kakış, arbede** *He wanted to escape the hustle and bustle of city life.*

hustler /'hʌslər/ *noun* [C] someone who tries to persuade people to give them what they want, especially in order to make money illegally **yasa dışı yoldan para kazanmak için insanları ikna etmeye çalışan kişi**

hut /hʌt/ *noun* [C] a small, simple building, often made of wood **kulübe, baraka** *a mountain hut*

hybrid /'haɪbrɪd/ *noun* [C] **1** PLANT/ANIMAL a plant or animal that is produced from two different types of plant or animal **melez, kırma 2** THING something, for example a machine, which is made using ideas or parts from two different things **(makina vb.) karma, karışım, bileşim 3** CAR *(also* **hybrid car)** a vehicle with an engine that uses both petrol (= a liquid fuel made from oil) and another type of energy, usually electricity **motoru benzinin yanısıra hem elektrik enerjisi hem de akü gücü ile çalışan araç ● hybrid** *adjective* **melez (hayvan, bitki)**

hydrant /'haɪdrᵊnt/ *noun* [C] a pipe, especially at the side of the road, which is connected to the water system and is used to get water to stop fires **yangın vanası/musluğu** *a fire hydrant*

hydraulic /haɪ'drɔ:lɪk/ *adjective* operated using the force of water or another liquid **hidrolik**

hydro- /haɪdrəʊ-/ *prefix* relating to water **suyla ilgili anlamında ön ek** *hydroponic* (= a method of growing plants in water)

hydroelectric /ˌhaɪdrəʊɪ'lektrɪk/ *adjective* using the force of water to create electricity **hidroelektrik** *hydroelectric power*

hydrogen /'haɪdrədʒən/ *noun* [U] a gas that combines with oxygen to form water (formula H) **hidrojen**

hydrogenated /haɪ'drɒdʒɪmeɪtɪd/ *adjective* Hydrogenated substances, for example fats, have had hydrogen added to them. ● **hydrogenation** /haɪˌdrɒdʒɪ'neɪʃᵊn/ *noun* [U]

ᕱᕱᕱ hygiene .... İLE BİRLİKTE KULLANILAN KELİMELER

standards of hygiene ● **dental/personal** hygiene

---

hygiene /'haɪdʒiːn/ *noun* [U] the process of keeping things clean, especially to prevent disease **sağlık koruma, temizlik, hijyen** *health and hygiene regulations* ○ *dental/personal hygiene* ● **hygienic** /haɪ'dʒiːnɪk/ *adjective* very clean, so that bacteria cannot spread **sıhhî, sağlıklı, temiz, hijyenik**

hymn /hɪm/ *noun* [C] a song sung by Christians in church to praise God **ilahî**

hype¹ /haɪp/ *noun* [U] when people talk a lot about something, especially in newspapers, on television, etc, and make it seem more important or exciting than it really is **medyada çok göze batan/yer alan, şişirme, çokça reklamı yapılan** *media hype* ○ *There's been a lot of hype about/surrounding his latest film.*

hype² /haɪp/ *(also* **hype up)** *verb* [T] to make something seem more important or exciting than it really is by talking about it a lot, especially in newspapers, on television, etc **şişirmek, medyada fazla gündeme getirmek, çokça sözünü etmek** *It's being hyped as the musical event of the year.* ● **hyped** *adjective* **aldatmaca**

hyper /'haɪpər/ *adjective informal* Someone who is hyper has more energy than is normal and is very excited. **çok, yüksek, aşırı, hiper**

hyper- /haɪpər/ *prefix* having a lot of or too much of a quality **çok/yüksek/aşırı anlamında ön ek** *hyperactive* ○ *hypersensitive* (= more than normally sensitive)

hyperactive /ˌhaɪpər'æktɪv/ *adjective* Someone who is hyperactive has more energy than is normal, gets excited easily, and cannot stay still or think about their work. **çok hareketli, hiperaktif** *hyperactive children* ● **hyperactivity** /ˌhaɪpᵊr'æktɪvəti/ *noun* [U] **hiperaktivite**

hyperbole /haɪ'pɜːbᵊli/ *noun* [U] *formal* when you describe something as much better, more important, etc than it really is **abartı, olduğundan farklı gösterme**

hyperlink /'haɪpəlɪŋk/ *noun* [C] text that you can click on that lets you move easily between two computer documents or two pages on the Internet **internette iki sayfa veya bilgisayar dökümanları arasında kolayca hareket etmeyi sağlayan bağlantı; yüksek hızlı bağlantı**

hypermarket /'haɪpəˌmɑːkɪt/ *noun* [C] a very large shop, usually outside the centre of town **büyük mağaza, alışveriş merkezi, hipermarket**

hypertext /'haɪpətekst/ *noun* [U] a way of joining a word or image to another page, document, etc on the Internet or in another computer program so that you can move from one to the other easily **internette veya bir başka bilgisayar programında sözcük, sayfa, belge veya imgelerin birinden diğerine geçiş yapılabilmesi için birleştirilme şekli**

hyphen /'haɪfᵊn/ *noun* [C] a mark (-) used to join two words together, or to show that a word has been divided and continues on the next line **tire (-), ara çizgi** ⊃See study page **Punctuation** on page Centre 33. ● **hyphenated** *adjective* written with a hyphen **iki tire arasında yazılmış**

hypnosis /hɪp'nəʊsɪs/ *noun* [U] a mental state like sleep, in which a person's thoughts can be easily influenced by someone else **uyutma, hipnoz** *Police placed witnesses* ***under hypnosis*** *in an effort to gain additional information.* ● **hypnotic** /hɪp'nɒtɪk/ *adjective* **hipnotic**

hypnotize *(also UK* -ise) /'hɪpnətaɪz/ *verb* [T] to place someone in a mental state like sleep, in which their thoughts can be easily influenced **uyutmak, hipnotize etmek** ● **hypnotist** *noun* [C] someone who hypnotizes people **hipnotizmacı** ● **hypnotism** /'hɪpnətɪzᵊm/ *noun* [U] when someone is hypnotized **hipnotizma, uyku**

hypochondriac /ˌhaɪpə'kɒndriæk/ *noun* [C] someone who worries about their health more than is normal, although they are not really ill **hastalık hastası, hastalık kuruntusu olan kimse, hipokondriyak** ● **hypochondria** /ˌhaɪpəʊ'kɒndriə/ *noun* [U] **hastalık hastası**

hypocrisy /hɪ'pɒkrəsi/ *noun* [C, U] when someone pretends to believe something that they do not really believe or that is the opposite of what they do or say at another time **iki yüzlülük, riyakârlık, müraîlik**

hypocrite /'hɪpəkrɪt/ *noun* [C] someone who pretends to believe something that they do not really believe or that is the opposite of what they do or say at another time **iki yüzlü/riyakâr kimse, mürai** ● **hypocritical** /ˌhɪpə'krɪtɪkᵊl/ *adjective* **iki yüzlü** ● **hypocritically** *adverb* **riyakar bir şekilde**

hypothermia /ˌhaɪpəʊ'θɜːmiə/ *noun* [U] a serious illness caused by someone's body becoming too cold **ısı kaybı/düşmesi hastalığı; hipotermia**

hypothesis /haɪ'pɒθəsɪs/ *noun* [C] *plural* **hypotheses** /haɪ'pɒθəsiːz/ a suggested explanation for something which has not yet been proved to be true **varsayım, faraziye, hipotez**

hypothetical /ˌhaɪpə'θetɪkᵊl/ *adjective* A hypothetical situation or idea has been suggested but does not yet really exist or has not been proved to be true. **farazî, varsayıma/hipoteze dayalı/dayanan**

hysteria /hɪ'stɪəriə/ *noun* [U] extreme fear, excitement, anger, etc which cannot be controlled **taşkınlık, galeyan, çılgınlık, isteri** *mass hysteria*

hysterical /hɪ'sterɪkᵊl/ *adjective* **1** If someone is hysterical, they cannot control their feelings or behaviour because they are extremely frightened, angry, excited, etc. **çılgına dönmüş, kudurmuş, taşkın, isterik, delice, duygularını kontrol edemeyen** *hysterical laughter* ○ *As soon as Wendy saw the blood, she became hysterical.* **2** *informal* extremely funny **çok komik, kahkahalara boğan, matrak** ● **hysterically** *adverb* *They all thought it was hysterically funny.* **isterik hareketlerle**

hysterics /hɪ'sterɪks/ *noun* **1** [plural] uncontrolled behaviour **sinir krizi/buhranı, isteri nöbeti 2 in hysterics** *informal* laughing so much that you cannot stop **gülme/kahkaha krizi**

Hz *written abbreviation for* hertz (= a unit of measurement used in electronics) **hertz; özellikle elektronikte her saniye tekrar eden döngü sayısını ölçmeye yarayan birimin kısa hâli**

I, i

368

I, i /aɪ/ the ninth letter of the alphabet **alfabenin dokuzuncu harfi**

o~**I** /aɪ/ *pronoun* used when the person speaking or writing is the subject of the verb **(zamir) ben** *I had lunch with Glen yesterday.* ○ *Chris and I have been married for twelve years.*

o~**ice¹** /aɪs/ *noun* [U] **1** water that has frozen and become solid **buz** *Gerry slipped on the ice and broke his arm.* ○ *I've put a couple of bottles of champagne on ice* (= in a bucket of ice to get cold). **2 break the ice** to make people who have not met before feel relaxed with each other, often by starting a conversation **havayı yumuşatmak, resmiyeti kaldırmak, buzları kırmak**

ice² /aɪs/ (*also US* **frost**) *verb* [T] to cover a cake with icing (= sweet mixture of mainly sugar) **pudra şekerli krema ile kaplamak** *an iced bun*

iceberg /'aɪsbɜːg/ *noun* [C] a very large piece of ice that floats in the sea **buz dağı** つSee also: **be the tip¹** of the iceberg.

ice 'cream *UK* (*US* **'ice ,cream**) *noun* [C, U] a sweet food made from frozen milk or cream and sugar **dondurma** *chocolate/vanilla ice cream*

'ice ,cube *noun* [C] a small block of ice that you put into drinks to make them cold **küp şeklinde buz**

'ice ,hockey (*also US* **hockey**) *noun* [U] a game played on ice in which two teams try to hit a small hard object into a goal using long curved sticks **buz hokeyi** つOrta kısımdaki renkli sayfalarına bakınız.

ice 'lolly *UK* (*US trademark* **Popsicle**) *noun* [C] a sweet, fruit-flavoured piece of ice on a small stick **saplı buzlu şekerleme**

'ice ,rink *noun* [C] an area of ice, usually inside a building, which is prepared for people to ice skate on **buz pisti**

'ice ,skate *noun* [C] a boot with a metal part on the bottom, used for moving across ice **buz pateni** ● **ice skate** *verb* [I] to move across ice using ice skates **buz pateni yapmak** ● **ice skating** *noun* [U] the activity or sport of moving across ice using ice skates **buz pateni yapma** つOrta kısımdaki renkli sayfalarına bakınız.

icicle /'aɪsɪkl/ *noun* [C] a long, thin piece of ice that hangs down from something **buz sarkıtı, saçaklardan sarkan buz**

icicles

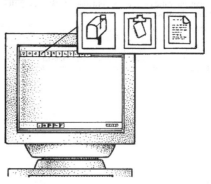

icing /'aɪsɪŋ/ *noun* [U] **1** (*also US* **frosting**) a sweet mixture used to cover or fill cakes, made from sugar and water or sugar and butter **pudra şekerli krema** *chocolate butter icing* **2 the icing on the cake** something that makes a good situation better **iyileştiren** *He was delighted to get the article published and the £100 payment was the icing on the cake.*

icon

icon /'aɪkɒn/ *noun* [C] **1** a small picture on a computer screen that you choose in order to make the computer do something **(bilgisayar) simge, imge** *Click on the print icon.* **2** a person or thing that is famous because it represents a particular idea or way of life **(kişi, şey) sembol, idol** *a cultural/fashion/national icon*

ICT /ˌaɪsiːˈtiː/ *noun* [U] *abbreviation for* information and communication technology: the use of computers and other electronic equipment to store and send information **bilgi ve iletişim teknolojisi**

icy /'aɪsi/ *adjective* **1** WITH ICE covered in ice **buzlu, kaygan, buz kaplı** *icy conditions/roads* **2** COLD extremely cold **buz gibi, müthiş soğuk** *an icy wind* ○ *icy water* **3** WITHOUT EMOTION without showing any emotion **hissiz, duygusuz, soğuk, buz gibi** *an icy look/stare* ● **icily** *adverb* **buzlu bir şekilde, hissiz bir şekilde**

o~**I'd** /aɪd/ **1** *short for* I had **I 'had' fiil yapısının kısa hâli** *Everyone thought I'd gone.* **2** *short for* I would **I 'would' fiil yapısının kısa hâli** *I'd like to buy some stamps, please.*

ID /ˌaɪˈdiː/ *noun* [C, U] *abbreviation for* identification: an official document that shows or proves who you are **kimlik** *You'll need to show some form of ID, such as a passport or driving licence.*

I'D ,card *noun* [C] an identity card **kimlik kartı**

idea .... İLE BİRLİKTE KULLANILAN KELİMELER

come up with/have an idea ● a **bad/bright/brilliant/good/stupid** idea

idea .... BAŞKA BİR DEYİŞLE

Bir şeyin nasıl yapılacağına dair fikir **plan, thought** veya **suggestion** olarak tanımlanabilir. *The plan is to hire a car when we get there.* ● *Have you got any suggestions for improvements?* ● *Have you had any thoughts on presents for your mother?*

Aniden aklınıza gelen zekice bir fikir için İngiltere'de **brainwave** Amerika'da ise **brainstorm** ifadesi kullanılır. *I wasn't sure what to do and then I had a brainwave - I could ask Anna for help.*

Theory kelimesi bir şeyi açıklamaya yönelik bir dizi fikrin tanımı için kullanılır. *He was giving a lecture on Darwin's theory of evolution.*

⊶**idea** /aɪˈdɪə/ noun **1** [SUGGESTION] [C] a suggestion or plan **öneri, fikir, plan** *"Why don't we ask George?" "That's **a good idea**."* ○ [+ for + doing sth] *Stevens explained his ideas for improving production.* ○ [+ to do sth] *It was Kate's idea to hire a car.* **2** [THOUGHT] [U, no plural] an understanding, thought, or picture in your mind **(zihindeki) anlayış, fikir, düşünce, resim** [+ of + doing sth] *Clive soon got used to the idea of having children around the house again.* ○ [+ (that)] *I don't want them to get the **idea** that we're not interested.* **3 have no idea** to not know **bir konuyla ilgili hiçbir fikri olmamak** *Beth had no idea where he'd gone.* **4** [OPINION] [C] an opinion or belief **fikir, düşünce** *My husband and I have very different ideas about school discipline.* **5** [AIM] [no plural] the aim or purpose of something **maksat, amaç** *The idea is to give local people a chance to voice their opinions.* ⊃See also: not have the foggiest (**foggy**) (idea).

ideal¹ /aɪˈdɪəl/ adjective perfect, or the best possible **uygun, mükemmel, ideal** *an ideal candidate/solution* ○ *The book is **ideal for** children aged 4 to 6.* ○ *In an ideal world, you wouldn't need to use a keyboard at all.*

ideal² /aɪˈdɪəl/ noun **1** [C] a belief about the way you think something should be **ülkü, inanç, ilke, ideal** *democratic ideals* ○ *They are committed to the ideal of equality.* **2** [no plural] a perfect thing or situation **mükemmel/ideal şey/durum** *The ideal would be to have a house in the country and a flat in the city too.*

idealism /aɪˈdɪəlɪzᵃm/ noun [U] the belief that your ideals can be achieved, often when this does not seem likely to others **idealizm** ● **idealist** noun [C] a person who believes that it is possible to achieve your ideals **idealist** ● **idealistic** /aɪˌdɪəˈlɪstɪk/ adjective **idealist olan**

ideally /aɪˈdɪəli/ adverb **1** used to describe how something would be in a perfect situation **tercihen, ideal olarak düşünüldüğünde** *Ideally, I'd like to work at home.* **2** in a perfect way **mükemmel şekilde, en uygun biçimde, tam olarak** *She seemed **ideally suited** for the job.*

identical /aɪˈdentɪkᵃl/ adjective exactly the same **tıpatıp aynı, benzer, tıpkı** *The two rooms were almost/virtually identical.* ○ *She found a dress **identical to** the one in the picture.* ● **identically** adverb **aynı şekilde, tıpatıp aynı**

iˌdentical ˈtwin noun [C] one of two babies who are born at the same time from the same egg, and look exactly the same **tek yumurta ikizi**

identifiable /aɪˌdentɪˈfaɪəbl/ adjective If someone or something is identifiable, you can recognize them and say or prove who or what they are. **kolayca tanınabilen; belli, bilinen** *clearly/readily identifiable*

┌─────────────────────────────────┐
│ **identification** .... İLE BİRLİKTE KULLANILAN KELİMELER │
└─────────────────────────────────┘
a form/a means/proof of identification

identification /aɪˌdentɪfɪˈkeɪʃᵃn/ noun [U] **1** when you recognize and can name someone or something **tanıma, teşhis, tespit** *Most of the bodies were badly burned, making identification almost impossible.* **2** an official document that shows or proves who you are **kimlik** *an identification card/number*

⊶**identify** /aɪˈdentɪfaɪ/ verb [T] **1** [RECOGNIZE] to recognize someone or something and say or prove who or what they are **belirlemek, tespit etmek; teşhis etmek** *The gunman in Wednesday's attack has been identified as Lee Giggs, an unemployed truck driver.* **2** to tell people who someone is **kimliğini belirlemek/tespit etmek** *My informant asked not to be identified.* **3** [DISCOVER] to find a particular thing or all the things of a particular group **tanımlamak, belirlemek** *You need to identify your priorities.*

identify sb/sth with sb/sth phrasal verb to connect one person or thing with another **özdeşleştirmek, öyle bilinmek/anılmak; bir tutmak** *As a politician he was identified with liberal causes.*

identify with sb/sth phrasal verb to feel that you are similar to someone, and can understand them or their situation because of this **bir tutmak, özdeşleşmek**

┌─────────────────────────────────┐
│ **identity** .... İLE BİRLİKTE KULLANILAN KELİMELER │
└─────────────────────────────────┘
cultural/national/personal identity ● **a sense of** identity

identity /aɪˈdentəti/ noun [C, U] **1** who someone is **kimlik, hüviyet** *Police are trying to **establish** the identity of a woman seen walking away from the accident.* **2** the things that make one person or one group of people different from others **belirleyici/tanımlayıcı özellik; tanımlayıcı kimlik/benlik** *cultural/national identity*

iˈdentity ˌcard noun [C] a piece of paper or a card that shows your name, photograph and information to prove who you are **kimlik kartı; hüviyet cüzdanı; nüfus kağıdı; (argo) kafa kağıdı**

ideological /ˌaɪdɪəˈlɒdʒɪkᵃl/ adjective based on or relating to a particular set of ideas or beliefs **ideolojik** *ideological conflicts/disagreements* ● **ideologically** adverb **fikir, ideoloji açısından**

ideology /ˌaɪdɪˈɒlədʒi/ noun [C, U] a set of ideas or beliefs, especially about politics **düşünce, fikirler manzumesi, ideoloji** *socialist ideology*

idiom /ˈɪdiəm/ noun [C] a group of words used together with a meaning that you cannot guess from the meanings of the separate words **deyim, tabir** ⊃See study page Idioms on page Centre 26. ● **idiomatic** /ˌɪdiəˈmætɪk/ adjective idiomatic language **deyimsel**

idiosyncratic /ˌɪdiəʊsɪŋˈkrætɪk/ adjective An idiosyncratic quality or way of behaving is typical of only one person and is often strange or unusual. **kendine özgü ama garip ve tuhaf, nev'i şahsına münhasır** ● **idiosyncrasy** /ˌɪdiəʊˈsɪŋkrəsi/ noun [C] an idiosyncratic habit or way of behaving **kişisel tuhaflık, garip alışkanlık**

idiot /ˈɪdiət/ noun [C] a stupid person or someone who is behaving in a stupid way **budala, aptal, salak** *Like an idiot, I believed him.* ● **idiocy** /ˈɪdiəsi/ noun [C, U] stupid behaviour **budalalık, aptallık** ● **idiotic** /ˌɪdiˈɒtɪk/ adjective stupid **aptalca, ahmakça, budalaca** *an idiotic grin/idea* ● **idiotically** adverb **aptalca**

idle¹ /ˈaɪdl/ adjective **1** [NOT WORKING] not working or being used **boş, atıl, işe yaramaz** *The factory has **stood idle** for over a year.* **2** [NOT SERIOUS] [always before noun] not serious or having no real purpose **gayri ciddi, gerçek amaç taşımayan, asılsız** *idle gossip* ○ *This is no idle threat.* **3** [LAZY] lazy and not willing to work **işsiz, aylak, tembel** *He knows what has to be done, he's just **bone idle** (= extremely lazy).* ● **idleness** noun [U] **başıboş gezme, işi olmama** ● **idly** adverb *We cannot **stand idly by** (= not do anything) and let this plan go ahead.* **başıboş bir şekilde**

idle² /ˈaɪdl/ verb **1** [ENGINE] [I] If an engine or machine idles, it runs slowly but does not move or do any work. **(motor) yavaş çalışmak, boşa dönmek/çalışmak** **2** [STOP WORKING] [T] US to stop someone or something working or being used, often because there is not enough work to do **durdurmak, yavaşlatmak, boşa çalıştırmak** *The closure of the plant idled about 300 workers.* **3** [TIME] [I] to spend time doing nothing **vakti boşa geçirmek, çalışmamak** *We saw her idling in the school grounds.*

idle sth away *phrasal verb* to waste time doing nothing **zamanı boşa harcamak** *I idled away a few hours watching TV.*

idol /'aɪdªl/ *noun* [C] **1** someone that you admire and respect very much **ilâh, gözde kişi, hayranlık duyulan kimse** *a pop/sporting idol* **2** a picture or object that people pray to as part of their religion **(din) tapınılan put/nesne/resim ● idolize** *(also UK -ise) verb* [T] to admire and respect someone very much **hayran olmak, taparcasına sevmek**

idyllic /ɪ'dɪlɪk/ *adjective* An idyllic place or experience is extremely pleasant, beautiful, or peaceful. **çok huzurlu ve sakin, cennet gibi, huzur dolu** *an idyllic childhood* ○ *an idyllic existence*

i.e. *(also ie)* /,aɪ'i:/ used to explain exactly what you are referring to or what you mean **yani, demek ki** *The price must be more realistic, i.e. lower.*

✎**if¹** /ɪf/ *conjunction* **1** [DEPEND] used to say that something will happen only after something else happens or is true *...sa/se ... sa/se* *We'll have the party in the garden if the weather's good.* ○ *If you eat up all your dinner you can have some chocolate.* **2** [MIGHT] used to talk about something that might happen or be true **eğer, şayet** *What will we do if this doesn't work?* **3** [WHETHER] whether **acaba; ...mı, olup olmadığı** *I wonder if he'll get the job.* **4** [ALWAYS] used to mean always or every time **her nezaman, ... dığında; eğer** *If you mention his mother, he always cries.*

if² /ɪf/ *noun* [C] *informal* something which is not certain or not yet decided **belirsizlik, bilinmezlik** *There are still a lot of ifs.* ○ *There are no ifs and buts* (= no doubts or excuses) *about it - we'll have to start again.*

iffy /'ɪfi/ *adjective informal* **1** not completely good, honest, or suitable **pek iyi/dürüst/uygun olmayan** *The milk smells a bit iffy.* **2** not certain or decided **belirsiz, kesin olmayan, henüz kararlaştırılmayan** *Simon's still kind of iffy about going to Colombia.*

igloo /'ɪglu:/ *noun* [C] a house made of blocks of hard snow **Eskimo evi, iglu, kardan ev**

igloo

ignite /ɪg'naɪt/ *verb formal* **1** [I, T] to start to burn or make something start to burn **ateşlemek, yakmak, tutuşturmak, alev almak, tutuşmak, yanmak** *A spark ignited the fumes.* **2** [T] to start an argument or fight **bir tartışma veya kavgayı başlatmak/ ateşlemek**

ignition /ɪg'nɪʃªn/ *noun* **1** [no plural] the part of a car that starts the engine **(araba) marş** *He turned the key in the ignition.* ⊃*Orta kısımdaki renkli sayfalarına bakınız.* **2** [U] *formal* when something makes something start to burn **tutuşturma, ateşleme**

ignominious /,ɪgnəʊ'mɪniəs/ *adjective formal* making you feel embarrassed or ashamed **yüz kızartıcı, küçük düşürücü, aşağılık** *an ignominious defeat* **● ignominiously** *adverb* **alçakça**

ignorance /'ɪgnªrªns/ *noun* [U] when someone does not have enough knowledge, understanding, or information **bilgisizlik, cehalet** *There is still* widespread **ignorance about** *the disease.* ○ *I was shocked by her total* **ignorance of** *world history.*

ignorant /'ɪgnªrªnt/ *adjective* **1** not having enough knowledge, understanding, or information about something **cahil, habersiz, bilgisiz** *He was a newcomer to Formula One and ignorant of many of the circuits.* **2** *UK* not polite or showing respect **görgüsüzce, cahilce, saygısız ve kaba** *an ignorant lout*

✎**ignore** /ɪg'nɔː^r/ *verb* [T] to pay no attention to something or someone **görmezden/bilmezden gelmek, gözardı etmek** *They just ignored him and carried on with the game.* ○ *We cannot afford to ignore the fact that the world's population is increasing rapidly.*

IIRC *internet abbreviation for* if I remember correctly **Eğer doğru hatırlıyorsam ...; Eğer yanlış hatırlamıyorsam ...**

il- /ɪl-/ *prefix* not **olumsuzluk öneki** *illegal* ○ *illegible*

ill ..... BAŞKA BİR DEYİŞLE

Alternatif olarak **sick** sıfatı kullanılabilir. *He was off work* **sick** *last week.*

Resmiyet taşımayan ortamlarda **poorly** ve **rough** sıfatları da kullanılabilir. *What's the matter, Sophie - are you feeling* **poorly**? *● I felt really* **rough** *after eating that curry.*

Unwell hasta anlamına gelen ve daha resmi ortamlarda kullanılan bir ifadedir. *I've felt a little* **unwell** *all week.*

Resmiyet taşımayan ortamlarda, kişinin biraz hasta olduğunu ifade etmek için **be/feel under the weather** ve **be/feel below par** söylemleri kullanılır. *I don't think I'll be coming to the party - I'm a bit* **under the weather**

✎**ill¹** /ɪl/ *adjective* **1** not feeling well, or suffering from a disease **hasta, rahatsız** *critically/seriously ill* ○ *Mark had been feeling ill for a couple of days.* **2** [always before noun] *formal* bad **kötü, berbat** *ill health* ○ *He suffered no ill effects from his fall.* ⊃See also: ill at ease¹.

ill² /ɪl/ *noun* [C] *formal* a problem **sorun, dert, bela** [usually plural] *social and economic ills*

ill³ /ɪl/ *adverb formal* **1** badly **kötü, fena** *Many of the nurses were ill prepared to deal with such badly burned patients.* **2 can ill afford (to do) sth** If you can ill afford to do something, it is likely to make things difficult for you if you do it. **durumu daha da zorlaştırmak / kötüleştirmek** *This is a match United can ill afford to lose.* **3 speak ill of sb** *formal* to say bad things about someone **...ın/in aleyhinde konuşmak; ...ı/i tenkit etmek/eleştirmek**

I'll /aɪl/ *short for* I shall/I will **'I shall/I will' fiil yapısının kısa hâli** *I'll be there at 6:00.*

ill- /ɪl-/ *prefix* in a way which is bad or not suitable **kötü, yetersiz, uygunsuz anlamında önek** *ill-prepared* ○ *an ill-judged remark*

ill-advised /,ɪləd'vaɪzd/ *adjective* not wise, and likely to cause problems in the future **akılsız, düşüncesiz, tedbirsiz ve gelecekte muhtemelen sorun çıkarabilecek**

ill-conceived /,ɪlkən'si:vd/ *adjective* badly planned or not wise **kötü planlanmış; akılsız ve tedbirsiz**

✎**illegal** /ɪ'li:gªl/ *adjective* not allowed by law **yasadışı, kanuna/yasalara aykırı** *illegal drugs/weapons* ○ [+ to do sth] *It is illegal to sell cigarettes to anyone under 16.* **● illegally** *adverb* *an illegally parked car* **kanuna aykırı bir şekilde**

il,legal 'immigrant *(also US* **il,legal 'alien)** *noun* [C] someone who goes to live or work in another country when they do not have the legal right to **yasadışı, kaçak**

illegible /ɪˈledʒəbl/ *adjective* Illegible writing is difficult or impossible to read. **okunması zor, okunaksız**

illegitimate /ˌɪlɪˈdʒɪtəmət/ *adjective* **1** An illegitimate child is born to parents who are not married to each other. **evlilik dışı çocuk, gayri meşru çocuk 2** not legal, honest, or fair **yasadışı, yasaya/kurallara aykırı; adil/dürüst olmayan** *an illegitimate use of council funds* ● **illegitimacy** /ˌɪlɪˈdʒɪtəməsi/ *noun* [U] **evlilik dışı**

ill-equipped /ˌɪlɪˈkwɪpt/ *adjective* **1** not having the necessary equipment **yetersiz, gerekli araç gereçten yoksun, kifayetsiz 2** not having the necessary ability or qualities to do something **yeterli kabiliyet ve özellikleri taşımayan** [+ to do sth] *These teachers were ill-equipped to deal with rowdy students.*

ill-fated /ˌɪlˈfeɪtɪd/ *adjective* unlucky and often unsuccessful **talihsiz, şanssız, uğursuz, kötü,** *an ill-fated expedition to the South Pole*

ill-fitting /ˌɪlˈfɪtɪŋ/ *adjective* Ill-fitting clothes do not fit well. **uymayan, üzerine oturmayan**

ill-gotten /ˌɪlˈɡɒtᵊn/ *adjective literary* obtained in a dishonest or illegal way **yasadışı yoldan elde edilen, gayri meşru** *He deposited his ill-gotten gains in foreign bank accounts.*

illicit /ɪˈlɪsɪt/ *adjective* not legal or not approved of by society **yasadışı, toplumca uygun bulunmayan, yasaya/kanuna aykırı** *an illicit love affair*

ill-informed /ˌɪlɪnˈfɔːmd/ *adjective* without enough knowledge or information **yeterli bilgi sahibi olmaksızın** *an ill-informed decision*

illiterate /ɪˈlɪtᵊrət/ *adjective* not able to read or write **okuma yazma bilmeyen, cahil**

illness ...... İLE BİRLİKTE KULLANILAN KELİMELER

cause/develop/have/recover from/treat an illness ● **a critical/minor/rare/serious/terminal** illness

◦⌐**illness** /ˈɪlnəs/ *noun* **1** [C] a disease of the body or mind **hastalık** *a serious/terminal illness* ○ *He died at the age of 83 after a long illness.* **2** [U] when you are ill **rahatsızlık**

illogical /ɪˈlɒdʒɪkᵊl/ *adjective* not based on careful thought **mantıkdışı, mantıksız, mantığa aykırı** *It would be illogical for them to stop at this stage.*

illuminate /ɪˈluːmɪneɪt/ *verb* [T] **1** to shine lights on something **aydınlatmak, ışıklandırmak** *The paintings and sculptures are illuminated by spotlights.* **2** to explain something clearly or make it easier to understand **açıklamak, aydınlatmak, ışık tutmak** ● **illumination** /ɪˌluːmɪˈneɪʃᵊn/ *noun* [C, U] *formal* **aydınlanma**

illuminating /ɪˈluːmɪneɪtɪŋ/ *adjective* giving you new information about something or making it easier to understand **aydınlatıcı, anlaşılmayı kolaylaştıran** *a most illuminating discussion*

illusion /ɪˈluːʒᵊn/ *noun* **1** [C, U] an idea or belief that is not true **hayal, hülya, kuruntu** *He had no illusions about his talents as a singer.* ○ *We are not under any illusion - we know the work is dangerous.* **2** [C] something that is not really what it seems to be **göz aldanması, yanılsama** *There is a large mirror at one end to create the illusion of more space.* ⊃See also: optical illusion.

illustrate /ˈɪləstreɪt/ *verb* [T] **1** to give more information or examples to explain or prove something **resimlemek, örneklerle anlatmak, resimlerle açıklamak** *to illustrate a point/problem* ○ [+ question word] *This new discovery illustrates how little we know about early*

human history. **2** to draw pictures for a book, magazine, etc **(kitap, dergi vb. için) resim çizmek, resimlemek, resimlerle süslemek** *an illustrated children's book*

illustration /ˌɪləˈstreɪʃᵊn/ *noun* **1** [C] a picture in a book, magazine, etc **resim, şekil** *a full-page colour illustration* **2** [C, U] an example that explains or proves something **(kitap, dergi vb.) resim, açıklayıcı örnek/resim** *This is another illustration of the power of the media.*

illustrator /ˈɪləstreɪtəʳ/ *noun* [C] a person whose job is to draw or paint pictures for books **resmeden/resimleyen kişi**

illustrious /ɪˈlʌstriəs/ *adjective formal* famous and well respected **ünlü, meşhur, şöhretli** *an illustrious career*

ill 'will *noun* [U] bad feelings between people because of things that happened in the past **kötü niyet, kin**

◦⌐**I'm** /aɪm/ *short for* I am 'I am' fiil yapısının kısa hâli

im- /ɪm-/ *prefix* not **olumsuzluk öneki** *impossible* ○ *immortal*

image ...... İLE BİRLİKTE KULLANILAN KELİMELER

create/project an image ● sb's/sth's **public** image ● an image **of** sth

◦⌐**image** /ˈɪmɪdʒ/ *noun* **1** [PUBLIC] [C, U] the way that other people think someone or something is **imaj, izlenim, fikir, intiba** *The aim is to improve the public image of the police.* **2** [PICTURE] [C] a picture, especially on film or television or in a mirror **resim, imge, görüntü** *television images of starving children* **3** [IDEA] [C] a picture in your mind or an idea of how someone or something is **görüntü, hayal** *I have an image in my mind of the way I want the garden to look.*

imagery /ˈɪmɪdʒᵊri/ *noun* [U] the use of words or pictures in books, films, paintings, etc to describe ideas or situations **tasvir, betimleme**

imaginable /ɪˈmædʒɪnəbl/ *adjective* possible to think of **tasavvur/hayal edilebilir, düşünülebilir** *ice cream of every imaginable flavour* ⊃Opposite **unimaginable**.

imaginary /ɪˈmædʒɪnᵊri/ *adjective* not real but imagined in your mind **hayalî, hayal ürünü** *The story takes place in an imaginary world.*

imagination ...... İLE BİRLİKTE KULLANILAN KELİMELER

have/lack/show imagination ● **use** your imagination ● **capture** sb's imagination ● **a fertile/vivid** imagination

◦⌐**imagination** /ɪˌmædʒɪˈneɪʃᵊn/ *noun* **1** [C] the part of your mind that creates ideas or pictures of things that are not real or that you have not seen **hayal, zihin, kafa** [usually singular] *There's nothing out here - it's just your imagination.* **2** [U] the ability to create ideas or pictures in your mind **hayal etme gücü, muhayyile, yaratıcılık** *The job needs someone with creativity and imagination.* ⊃See also: not by any **stretch²** of the imagination.

imaginative /ɪˈmædʒɪnətɪv/ *adjective* **1** Something which is imaginative is new or clever and often unusual. **yaratıcı, hayal gücüne dayanan/özgü** *an imaginative use of colour* **2** Someone who is imaginative is able to create new and interesting ideas or things. **hayal gücü kuvvetli, hayalî yaratıcı** *a highly imaginative poet* ● **imaginatively** *adverb* **hayali bir şekilde**

◦⌐**imagine** /ɪˈmædʒɪn/ *verb* [T] **1** [CREATE] to create an idea or picture of something in your mind **hayal etmek, tasavvur etmek, düşünmek, gözünde canlandırmak** [+ doing sth] *Imagine being able to do all your shopping from your armchair.* ○ [+ question word] *You can ima-*

gine how pleased I was when the letter arrived. **2** BELIEVE to believe that something is probably true **sanmak, hayal etmek** *I imagine he must be under a lot of pressure at the moment.* **3** NOT REAL to think that you hear or see something which does not really exist **hayal görmek, sanmak, zannetmek** *I can't hear anything - you must be imagining it.*

imaging /'ɪmɪdʒɪŋ/ *noun* [U] the process of producing an exact picture of something, especially on a computer screen **bilgisayar ekranında bir şeyin gerçek resmini yaratma/çizme** *computer/digital imaging*

imbalance /ˌɪm'bæləns/ *noun* [C] when two things which should be equal or are normally equal are not **dengesizlik, eşitsizlik** *There is a huge economic imbalance between the two countries.*

imbue /ɪm'bju:/ *verb* *imbuing*, *past* **imbued**
imbue sb/sth with sth *phrasal verb formal* to fill someone or something with a particular feeling, quality, or idea **belli bir duygu/kalite veya fikirle doldurmak/aşılamak** *His poetry is imbued with deep religious feeling.*

IMHO *internet abbreviation for* in my humble opinion: used when you tell someone your opinion **Benim acizane düşünceme göre ...; Benim mütevazı görüşüme göre ...**

imitate /'ɪmɪteɪt/ *verb* [T] to copy the way someone or something looks, sounds, or behaves **taklit etmek, örnek almak, benzemeye çalışmak** *She tried to imitate the way the models walked.* ● **imitator** *noun* [C] **taklitçi**

🧩 ***imitation*** ...... İLE BİRLİKTE KULLANILAN KELİMELER

a **cheap/convincing/good/pale** imitation ● an imitation **of** sb/sth

imitation /ˌɪmɪ'teɪʃᵊn/ *noun* **1** [C] a copy of something that is made to look like the real thing **taklit, yapma, sahte** *It wasn't a genuine Gucci handbag, just a cheap imitation.* ○ *imitation leather/fur* **2** [C, U] when someone copies the way another person speaks or behaves **benzetme, taklit** *He does a very good imitation of the Prime Minister.*

immaculate /ɪ'mækjələt/ *adjective* **1** perfectly clean and tidy or in perfect condition **tertemiz, fevkalâde düzenli/tertipli, pırıl pırıl** *an immaculate garden/room* **2** perfect and without any mistakes **kusursuz, mükemmel, lekesiz, tertemiz, günahsız** *an immaculate performance* ● **immaculately** *adverb* **mükemmel bir şekilde**

immaterial /ˌɪmə'tɪəriəl/ *adjective* If something is immaterial, it is not important because it does not affect a situation. **önemsiz, ehemmiyetsiz**

immature /ˌɪmə'tjʊəʳ/ *adjective* **1** not behaving in a way which is as wise and calm as people expect from someone your age **olgunlaşmamış, çocuksu** *Some of the boys are quite immature for their age.* **2** not completely developed **gelişmemiş, gelişimini tamamlamamış** *immature cells* ● **immaturity** *noun* [U] **olgun olmama**

immeasurable /ɪ'meʒᵊrəbl/ *adjective* very large or extreme and so impossible to measure **muazzam, ölçülemeyecek kadar büyük** *the immeasurable pain of losing a child* ● **immeasurably** *adverb* *His confidence has grown immeasurably since he got the job.* **ölçülemeyecek oranda, ölçüde**

☞**immediate** /ɪ'mi:diət/ *adjective* **1** WITHOUT WAITING happening or done without waiting or very soon after something else **acil, ivedi, derhal yapılması gereken** *The government has promised to take immediate action.* ○ *The drugs will have an immediate effect.* **2** IMPORTANT NOW important now and needing attention

ivedi, acil, öncelik isteyen *Our immediate concern is getting food and water to the refugees.* **3** CLOSEST [always before noun] closest to something or someone **yakın, akraba, en yakın** *Police cleared people from the immediate area following the bomb warning.* **4** the **immediate future** the period of time that is coming next **yakın gelecek 5 sb's immediate family** someone's closest relatives, such as their parents, children, husband, or wife **yakın akraba, yakın aile üyeleri, akraba hısım**

☞**immediately¹** /ɪ'mi:diətli/ *adverb* **1** now or without waiting or thinking about something **derhal, hemen** *The cause of the problem wasn't immediately obvious.* **2** next to something, or close to something in time **anıden, birden, hemen** *There are fields immediately behind the house.* ○ *Cole scored again immediately after half-time.*

immediately² /ɪ'mi:diətli/ *conjunction UK* as soon as **yapar yapmaz, olur olmaz; ...ar/er...maz/mez** *Immediately I saw her I knew something terrible had happened.*

immense /ɪ'mens/ *adjective* extremely big **muazzam, çok büyük, kocaman** *immense pressure/value* ○ *Health care costs the country an immense amount of money.*

immensely /ɪ'mensli/ *adverb* extremely **son derece, pek çok, gayet, çok** *immensely powerful/popular*

immerse /ɪ'mɜ:s/ *verb* **1 be immersed in sth; immerse yourself in sth** to be or become completely involved in something, so that you do not notice anything else **dalmak, gömülmek, kendini kaptırmak 2** [T] to put something in a liquid so that it is completely covered **daldırmak, sokmak, batırmak, gömmek** ● **immersion** /ɪ'mɜ:ʃᵊn/ *noun* [U] **daldırma**

immigrant /'ɪmɪɡrənt/ *noun* [C] someone who comes to live in a different country **göçmen, muhacir** ⊃See also: **illegal immigrant.**

immigration /ˌɪmɪ'ɡreɪʃᵊn/ *noun* [U] **1** when someone comes to live in a different country **göç** *immigration policy* **2** the place where people's official documents are checked when they enter a country at an airport, port, border, etc **(havaalanı, liman, sınır vb.) pasaport kontrol kısmı** *immigration control* ● **immigrate** /'ɪmɪɡreɪt/ *verb* [I] to come to live in a different country **bir ülkeye göç etmek**

imminent /'ɪmɪnənt/ *adjective* coming or happening very soon **çok yakın, eli kulağında, yakında, kapıda** *imminent danger*

immobile /ɪ'məʊbaɪl/ ⑤ /ɪ'məʊbᵊl/ *adjective* not moving or not able to move **sabit, kıpırdamayan, hareketsiz, kımıldamayan** ● **immobility** /ˌɪməʊ'bɪləti/ *noun* [U] **hareketsizlik**

immoral /ɪ'mɒrᵊl/ *adjective* morally wrong **ahlâka aykırı, ahlâksız, edebsiz** *immoral behaviour* ● **immorality** /ˌɪmə'ræləti/ *noun* [U] **ahlâksızlık**

immortal /ɪ'mɔ:tᵊl/ *adjective* **1** living or lasting forever **ölümsüz, ebedî, ölmez, kalıcı** *an immortal soul/love* **2** famous or remembered for a very long time **meşhur ve uzun süre unutulmayan, kalıcı** *Then he uttered the immortal line - "My name is Bond".* ● **immortality** /ˌɪmɔ:'tæləti/ *noun* [U] **ölümsüzlük**

immortalize (*also UK* -**ise**) /ɪ'mɔ:tᵊlaɪz/ *verb* [T] to make someone or something famous for a long time **ölümsüzleştir(il)mek**

immune /ɪ'mju:n/ *adjective* **1** PROTECTED [never before noun] If you are immune to a disease, you will not get it. **bağışık, direnç kazanmış** *Once you've had the virus, you are immune to it.* **2** BODY SYSTEM [always before noun] relating to the way your body fights disease **dirençli,**

korunmuş, bağışıklık gösteren *an immune deficiency/response* **3** NOT AFFECTED [never before noun] not affected by a particular type of behaviour or emotion **etkilenmez, dayanıklı, bağışıklık kazanmış** *He is immune to flattery.* **4** NOT PUNISHED [never before noun] not able to be punished or damaged by something **dokunulmazlık, muafiyet, cezalandırılmazlık** *His diplomatic passport makes him immune from prosecution.*

im'mune ˌsystem *noun* [C] the cells and tissues in your body that fight against infection **bağışıklık sistemi** [usually singular] *Vitamins help boost* (= make stronger) *your immune system.*

immunity /ɪˈmjuːnəti/ *noun* [U] when you are immune, especially to disease or from legal action **bağışıklık; dokunulmazlık, muafiyet** *diplomatic immunity* ○ *The vaccine gives you lifelong immunity to the virus.*

immunize (*also UK -ise*) /ˈɪmjənaɪz/ *verb* [T] to make a person or animal immune by giving them special medicine **aşılamak/aşılanmak; bağışık kılmak, bağışıklık sistemini güçlendirmek, bağışıklık kazan(dır)mak** *He was immunized against measles as a child.* ● **immunization** /ˌɪmjənaɪˈzeɪʃᵊn/ *noun* [C, U] *a programme of mass immunization* **bağışıklık kazandırma**

IMO *internet abbreviation for* in my opinion: used when you want to give an opinion **'Bana göre ...; Benim düşünceme göre ...; Bence ...'**

impact ...... İLE BİRLİKTE KULLANILAN KELİMELER

have/make an impact ● a **major/negative/significant** impact ● an impact **on** sth

impact¹ /ˈɪmpækt/ *noun* **1** [no plural] the effect that a person, event, or situation has on someone or something **(kişi, olay, durum vb.) etki, tesir** *Latino singers have had a major impact on pop music this year.* **2** [U] the force or action of one object hitting another **çarpma şiddeti, çarpışma, çarpma** *The missile explodes on impact* (= when it hits another object).

impact² /ɪmˈpækt/ (*also impact on/upon*) *verb* [T] mainly US to affect something or someone **etkilemek, tesir altında bırakmak** *Rising interest rates are sure to impact on the housing market.*

impair /ɪmˈpeəʳ/ *verb* [T] formal to harm something and make it less good **zarar vermek, zayıflatmak, zedelemek** [often passive] *When you're tired your judgment is impaired.* ● **impairment** *noun* [C, U] when something is impaired **sakatlık, eksiklik, zarar, ziyan, noksan, kusur** *mental/physical impairment*

impaired /ɪmˈpeəd/ *adjective* **visually/hearing impaired** unable to see or hear as well as most people **görme/duyma özürlü/kusurlu**

impale /ɪmˈpeɪl/ *verb* [T] to push a sharp object through something or someone **saplamak, batırmak, sokmak, şişlemek**

impart /ɪmˈpɑːt/ *verb* [T] formal **1** to communicate information or knowledge to someone **söylemek, aktarmak, vermek, iletmek, açığa vurmak** *I have disappointing news to impart.* **2** to give something a particular feeling, quality, or taste **katmak, kazandırmak, katmak** *Preservatives can impart colour and flavour to a product.*

impartial /ɪmˈpɑːʃᵊl/ *adjective* not supporting or preferring any person, group, plan, etc more than others **yansız, tarafsız, bîtaraf** *impartial advice* ○ *A trial must be fair and impartial.* ● **impartiality** /ˌɪmˌpɑːʃiˈæləti/ *noun* [U] when someone or something is impartial **tarafsızlık, yansızlık, adillik, adaletli olma**

impassable /ɪmˈpɑːsəbl/ *adjective* If roads or paths are impassable, vehicles cannot move along them. **geçit vermeyen, geçilemez, aşılamaz**

impasse ...... İLE BİRLİKTE KULLANILAN KELİMELER

break/reach an impasse ● an impasse **in** sth

impasse /ˈæmpæs/ ⓤ /ˈɪmpæs/ *noun* [U] a situation in which it is impossible to make any progress **açmaz, çıkmaz, kördüğüm, içinden çıkılamaz durum** *He is determined to break* (= end) *the impasse in the peace process.*

impassioned /ɪmˈpæʃᵊnd/ *adjective* showing and expressing strong emotion **tutkulu, ateşli, heyecanlı** *an impassioned plea/speech*

impassive /ɪmˈpæsɪv/ *adjective* An impassive person or face shows no emotion. **sakin, duygularını belli etmeyen, kayıtsız, aldırmaz, heyecansız** ● **impassively** *adverb* **duygusuz bir şekilde**

impatience /ɪmˈpeɪʃᵊns/ *noun* [U] when someone is impatient **sabırsızlık, tahammülsüzlük, tezcanlılık, acelecilik**

impatient /ɪmˈpeɪʃᵊnt/ *adjective* **1** easily annoyed by someone's mistakes or because you have to wait **tahammülsüz, hoşgörüsüz, toleranssız** *I do get impatient with the children when they won't do their homework.* **2** [never before noun] wanting something to happen as soon as possible **sabırsız, tahammülsüz, tezcanlı, canı tez, aceleci** *People are increasingly impatient for change in this country.* ● **impatiently** *adverb* *We waited impatiently for the show to begin.* **sabırsızca**

impeccable /ɪmˈpekəbl/ *adjective* perfect and with no mistakes **mükemmel, kusursuz, hatasız** *She speaks impeccable English.* ● **impeccably** *adverb* **impeccably dressed mükemmel bir şekilde**

impede /ɪmˈpiːd/ *verb* [T] formal to make it difficult or impossible for someone or something to move or make progress **zorlaştırmak, güçleştirmek, engellemek, sekte vurmak** *A broken-down car is impeding the flow of traffic.*

impediment /ɪmˈpedɪmənt/ *noun* [C] **1** formal something that makes it difficult or impossible for someone or something to move or make progress **engel, mânia, sekte, zorluk** *Cramped classrooms are an impediment to learning.* **2** a problem that makes speaking, hearing, or moving difficult **zorluk, güçlük, engel, sorun** *a speech impediment*

impel /ɪmˈpel/ *verb* [T] **impelling**, *past* **impelled** *formal* to make you feel that you must do something **zorlamak, sürüklemek, iteklemek, itmek** [+ to do sth] *Harry felt impelled to tell the truth.*

impending /ɪmˈpendɪŋ/ *adjective* [always before noun] An impending event will happen soon and is usually bad or unpleasant. **olması yakın, olmak üzere, eli kulağında, neredeyse** *impending disaster/doom* ○ *I've just heard about the impending departure of our chairman.*

impenetrable /ɪmˈpenɪtrəbl/ *adjective* **1** impossible to understand **anlaşılması imkânsız, anlaşılmaz, akıl ermez** *impenetrable jargon* **2** impossible to see through or go through **içinden geçilemez, içine girilemez, aşılamaz, görülemez** *impenetrable fog*

imperative¹ /ɪmˈperətɪv/ *adjective* **1** formal When an action or process is imperative, it is extremely important that it happens or is done. **zorunlu, şart, mecburi** [+ (that)] *It is imperative that I speak with him at once.* **2** An imperative form of a verb is used to express an order. In the sentence 'Stop the machine!', the verb 'stop' is an imperative verb. **(dilbilgisi) emir kipi**

imperative² /ɪmˈperətɪv/ *noun* [C] **1** something that must happen, exist, or be done **zorunluluk, mecburiyet** *a moral/political imperative* **2** the imperative form of a verb **(fiil) emir kipi**

imperceptible /ˌɪmpəˈseptəbl/ *adjective* not able to be noticed or felt **hissedilmez, fark edilmez, belli belirsiz** *She heard a faint, almost imperceptible cry.* ● **imperceptibly** *adverb* **fark edilmez bir şekilde**

imperfect /ɪmˈpɜːfɪkt/ *adjective* not perfect and with some mistakes **kusurlu, hatalı, mükemmel olmayan, aksak** *an imperfect solution* ● **imperfectly** *adverb* **mükemmel olmayan bir şekilde**

the imperfect /ɪmˈpɜːfɪkt/ (*also* the im‚perfect 'tense) *noun* The form of the verb that is used to show an action in the past which has not been completed. In the sentence 'We were crossing the road', 'were crossing' is in the imperfect. **(dilbilgisi) geçmişte süregelen ve henüz tamamlanmamış eylemleri gösteren fiil zamanı**

imperfection /ˌɪmpəˈfekʃⁿn/ *noun* [C, U] when something or someone is not perfect **zaafiyet, eksiklik, kusur, zayıflık,** *Make-up can hide small skin imperfections.*

imperial /ɪmˈpɪəriəl/ *adjective* **1** [always before noun] relating or belonging to an empire (= group of countries ruled by one person or government) or the person who rules it **imparatorluğa ait; imparator/imparatoriçe ile ilgili** *imperial rule* ○ *the imperial family* **2** The imperial system of measurement uses units based on measurements such as inches, pints, and ounces. **İngiltere'de kullanılan ağırlık/ölçüler (sistemi)**

imperialism /ɪmˈpɪəriəlɪzⁿm/ *noun* [U] **1** when one government or person rules a group of other countries **sömürgecilik/yayılmacı/emperyalist devlet/kişi** *the age of imperialism* **2** when one country has a lot of power or influence over others **sömürgecilik, yayılmacılık, emperyalizm** *cultural/economic imperialism* ● **imperialist** *adjective* relating to imperialism **sömürgecilik/yayılmacılık/emperyalizm ile ilgili**

imperil /ɪmˈperⁿl/ *verb* [T] UK imperilling, *past* imperilled, US imperiling, *past* imperiled *formal* to put someone or something in a dangerous situation **teklikeye sokmak/atmak**

imperious /ɪmˈpɪəriəs/ *adjective formal* showing that you think that you are important and expect others to obey you **amirane, otoriter, hükmeden** *an imperious manner*

impersonal /ɪmˈpɜːsⁿnⁿl/ *adjective* not being friendly towards people or showing any interest in them **soğuk, sevimsiz, kişiliksiz, başkalarına değer vermeyen, duygularını belli etmeyen** *a cold and impersonal letter*

impersonate /ɪmˈpɜːsⁿneɪt/ *verb* [T] to copy the way someone looks and behaves in order to pretend to be them or to make people laugh **...ın/in kılığına girip taklit etmek; kendine ... süsü vermek; ...nın/nin rolünü oynamak; taklidini yapmak** *Impersonating a police officer is a serious offence.* ● **impersonation** /ɪmˌpɜːsⁿnˈeɪʃⁿn/ *noun* [C, U] *He did an impersonation of Bill Clinton.* taklit ● **impersonator** *noun* [C] *an Elvis impersonator* **taklit yapan**

impertinent /ɪmˈpɜːtɪnənt/ *adjective formal* rude or not showing respect **küstah, haddini bilmez, saygısız** *an impertinent remark*

impervious /ɪmˈpɜːviəs/ *adjective* **1** not affected by something **etkilenmez, tesir altında kalmaz, dayanıklı** *She was impervious to the pain.* **2** *formal* Impervious material does not let liquid into or through it. **su vb. geçirmez** *impervious rock*

impetuous /ɪmˈpetʃuəs/ *adjective* done or acting quickly and without thinking carefully **fevrî, tez canlı, aceleci, düşünmeden hareket eden** *an impetuous outburst*

impetus ...... İLE BİRLİKTE KULLANILAN KELİMELER

give/provide [new, fresh, added, etc] impetus to sth ● the impetus behind/for sth

impetus /ˈɪmpɪtəs/ *noun* [U] **1** something that makes an activity or process happen or continue with more speed and energy **teşvik, dürtü, şevk** *His visit gave new impetus to the peace process.* **2** a physical force that makes an object start or continue to move **itici/sürükleyici güç, itme, itiş**

impinge /ɪmˈpɪndʒ/ *verb formal*
impinge on/upon sb/sth *phrasal verb* to affect or limit someone or something **etkilemek/sınırlamak, etkisi olmak** *How does your religious commitment impinge upon your professional life?*

implacable /ɪmˈplækəbl/ *adjective formal* determined not to change the strong feelings you have against someone or something **amansız, yatıştırılamaz, acımasız; yatıştırılamaz, sönmeyen, azaltılamaz** *implacable opposition/hostility*

implant¹ /ˈɪmplɑːnt/ *noun* [C] an object placed inside part of your body in an operation, to improve your appearance or treat a medical condition **(ameliyatla) yerleştirilen/dikilen şey** *breast implants*

implant² /ɪmˈplɑːnt/ *verb* [T] to place something into someone's body in a medical operation **ameliyatla yerleştirmek, koymak** *Two embryos were implanted in her womb.*

implausible /ɪmˈplɔːzəbl/ *adjective* difficult to believe or imagine **inanılmaz, inanması güç, olmayacak gibi görünen, hayali bile zor** *an implausible explanation*

implement¹ /ˈɪmplɪment/ *verb* [T] *formal* to make a law, system, plan, etc start to happen or operate **(kanun, sistem, plan vb.) uygulamaya koymak, gerçekleştirmek, etkin kılmak** *Our new computerized system will soon be fully implemented.* ● **implementation** /ˌɪmplɪmenˈteɪʃⁿn/ *noun* [U] **uygulama**

implement² /ˈɪmplɪmənt/ *noun* [C] a tool **alet, edevat, takım, araç** *a garden/farm implement*

implicate /ˈɪmplɪkeɪt/ *verb* [T] to show that someone or something is involved in something bad, especially a crime **(bilhassa suça) bulaştırmak, karıştırmak, sokmak** [often passive] *Two senior officers are implicated in the latest drugs scandal.*

implication ...... İLE BİRLİKTE KULLANILAN KELİMELER

have implications for sth ● far-reaching/profound/serious implications ● the implications of sth

implication /ˌɪmplɪˈkeɪʃⁿn/ *noun* **1** [EFFECT] a result or effect that seems likely in the future **muhtemel etki/sonuç** [usually plural] *financial/health implications* ○ *This scheme has serious implications for the local economy.* **2** [SUGGESTION] [C, U] when you seem to suggest something without saying it directly **kasdedilen mana, ima; dolaylı anlatım** *The implication was that the school had to do much better or it would be closed.* **3** [INVOLVEMENT] [U] when something or someone is implicated in something bad **suça karışma/bulaşma**

implicit /ɪmˈplɪsɪt/ *adjective* **1** suggested but not stated directly **üstü kapalı, ima yollu, imalı, gizli** *an implicit threat* ○ *We interpreted his silence as implicit agreement.* **2** complete **tam, kesin, kati, sorgusuz, kuşkusuz, şüphesiz** *implicit faith/trust* ● **implicitly** *adverb* *I trust him implicitly.* **üstü örtülü bir şekilde**

implore /ɪmˈplɔːr/ *verb* [T] *literary* to ask for something in a serious and emotional way **istirham etmek, yalvarmak, dilemek** [+ to do sth] *I implored him to let the child go.*

imply /ɪmˈplaɪ/ *verb* [T] to suggest or show something, without saying it directly **ima etmek, demek istemek, anlamına gelmek; dolaylı anlatmak, ... ın/in işareti olmak** [+ (that)] *Are you implying that I'm fat?* ○ *an implied criticism*

impolite /ˌɪmpəˈlaɪt/ *adjective formal* not polite **nezaketsiz, kaba, terbiyesiz, hadsiz**

import¹ /ɪmˈpɔːt/ *verb* [T] **1** to bring something into your country from another country for people to buy **ithal etmek; dışalım yapmak** *We import about 20 percent of our food.* **2** to copy information from one computer or computer program to another **bir bilgisayardan/programdan başka bir bilgisayara bilgiyi kopyalamak/aktarmak** *to import data* ○ *imported files* ⊃Opposite export. ● **importation** /ˌɪmpɔːˈteɪʃən/ *noun* [U] **ithalat mevzuatı** ● **importer** *noun* [C] **ithalatçı**

import² /ˈɪmpɔːt/ *noun* **1** [C] a product which is imported from another country **ithal/dışalım ürünü/malı** [usually plural] *Japanese/American imports* **2** [U] when you import goods **ithalat, dışalım** *a ban on the import of beef* ⊃Opposite export.

╔═╗ **importance** .... İLE BİRLİKTE KULLANILAN KELİMELER

central/great/major/paramount/the utmost/vital importance ● **emphasize/stress** the importance of sth ● **attach** (great) importance **to** sth ● the importance **of** sth

o╼**importance** /ɪmˈpɔːtəns/ *noun* [U] how important someone or something is **önem, ehemmiyet** *He emphasized the importance of following safety procedures.* ○ *She attaches a lot of importance to personal possessions* (= she thinks they are important).

important ...... BAŞKA BİR DEYİŞLE

Big **major, ve significant** sıfatları önemli anlamında kullanılabilir. *This is a big game tonight-if Manchester lose, they're out of the championship.* ● *This is a major decision so we'd better get it right.* ● *Did he make any significant changes to my suggestions?*
Of **note** ifadesi önemli veya ünlü kişi veya şeylerin ifadesinde kullanılır. *Did she say anything of note at the meeting?*
Önemli ve ünlü kişileri tanımlamada **eminent, prominent** veya **great** ifadeleri kullanılabilir. *Her father was an eminent historian.*

o╼**important** /ɪmˈpɔːtənt/ *adjective* **1** valuable, useful, or necessary **önemli, faydalı, gerekli, mühim** *My family is very important to me.* ○ [+ to do sth] *Listen, Donna has something important to say.* **2** having a lot of power, influence, or effect **saygın, itibarlı, önemli** *an important person/decision* ⊃Opposite unimportant. ● **importantly** *adverb* They provided hot showers and, more importantly, clean clothes. **önemli, yararlı bir şekilde**

impose /ɪmˈpəʊz/ *verb* [T] **1** to officially order that a rule, tax, punishment, etc will happen **yürürlüğe koymak, uygulamak, yüklemek** *to impose a ban/tax* ○ *The judge imposed the death penalty on both men.* **2** to force someone to accept a belief or way of living **zorla kabul ettirmek, zorlamak** *I don't want them to impose their religious beliefs on my children.*
impose on sb *phrasal verb* to ask or expect someone to do something that may give them extra work or trouble **zahmet vermek, rahatsız etmek, yük olmak, zahmete sokmak** *I hate to impose on you, but could I stay the night?*

imposing /ɪmˈpəʊzɪŋ/ *adjective* looking big and important in a way that people admire **görkemli, heybetli** *He was an imposing figure - tall and broad-chested.*

imposition /ˌɪmpəˈzɪʃən/ *noun* **1** [U] when you impose something **yürürlüğe koyma, uygulama, etkin kılma** *the imposition of a fine* **2** [C] the cause of extra work or trouble for someone else **külfet, zahmet** *It's a bit of an imposition, but could you take me to the airport?*

o╼**impossible¹** /ɪmˈpɒsəbl/ *adjective* **1** If an action or event is impossible, it cannot happen or be done. **imkânsız, olamaz, yapılamaz** *an impossible task* ○ *He finds walking almost impossible.* ○ [+ to do sth] *It was impossible to sleep because of the noise.* **2** very difficult to deal with **içinden çıkılmaz, çekilmez, zor, güç** *You're putting me in an impossible position.* ● **impossibility** /ɪmˌpɒsəˈbɪləti/ *noun* [C, U] when something is impossible **imkânsızlık, olmayacak şey, mümkün olmayan** [usually singular] *I can't do it - it's a physical impossibility.*

the impossible /ɪmˈpɒsəbl/ *noun* something that it is not possible to have or achieve **imkânsız, başarılması zor**

impossibly /ɪmˈpɒsəbli/ *adverb* extremely, in a way that is very difficult to deal with **inanılmaz derecede, son derece** *a picture of an impossibly pretty woman*

impostor (*also* imposter) /ɪmˈpɒstər/ *noun* [C] someone who pretends to be someone else in order to deceive people **sahtekâr kimse, şarlatan, dolandırıcı, üçkâğıtçı**

impotent /ˈɪmpətənt/ *adjective* **1** An impotent man is unable to have sex because his penis does not become or stay hard. **iktidarsız, cinsel gücü olmayan 2** not having the power or strength to do anything to change a situation **güçsüz, aciz, kudretsiz, zayıf, beceriksiz** *When your child is ill, you feel so impotent.* ● **impotence** /ˈɪmpətəns/ *noun* [U] **iktidarsızlık (erkek)**

impound /ɪmˈpaʊnd/ *verb* [T] If the police or someone in authority impounds something that belongs to you, for example your car, they take it away because you have broken the law. **el koymak, haczetmek, haciz yoluyla almak**

impoverished /ɪmˈpɒvərɪʃt/ *adjective formal* **1** poor or made poor **fakirleşmiş, yoksullaşmış** *an impoverished country/family* **2** made worse or weaker **kötüleşmiş, zayıflamış; daha da kötü/zayıf** *culturally/emotionally impoverished*

impractical /ɪmˈpræktɪkəl/ *adjective* **1** METHOD/IDEA Impractical ideas, methods, etc cannot be used or done easily. **(fikir, yöntem vb.) uygulanamaz, uygulanması imkânsız, zor, yapılamaz, pratik olmayan 2** PERSON Impractical people are not good at making, repairing, or planning things. **(kişi) beceriksiz, pratik olmayan, elinden iş gelmeyen 3** MATERIAL/CLOTHING not suitable for using in normal situations **uygun olmayan, normal durumlarda kullanılamaz** *I love high heels but they're rather impractical.*

imprecise /ˌɪmprɪˈsaɪs/ *adjective* not accurate or exact **belirsiz, kesin/kati olmayan, üstü kapalı** *an imprecise description*

impress /ɪmˈpres/ *verb* [T] to make someone admire or respect you **derin etki bırakmak, etkilemek, dikkatini çekmek, hayranlık uyandırmak** *I was impressed by her professionalism.* ○ *Sarah was hoping to impress him with her cooking.*
impress sth on sb *phrasal verb* to make someone understand the importance of something **kafasına sokmak, iyice anlatmak, önemini açıkça belirtmek, işlemek** *He tried to impress the importance of hygiene on them.*

impression ...... İLE BİRLİKTE KULLANILAN KELİMELER

convey/create/give/make an impression ● get an
impression ● be **under** an impression ● a **distinct/
false/favourable/indelible/lasting/misleading**
impression

o⁻**impression** /ɪmˈpreʃᵊn/ *noun* **1** OPINION [no plural] an
idea, feeling, or opinion about something or someone
izlenim, etki, initba, fikir, kanı [+ (that)] *I got/had
the impression that he was bored.* ○ *Monica gives the
impression of being shy.* ○ *Remember that it makes a
bad impression if you're late.* ○ *I think Mick was
under the impression that* (= thought that) *we were
married.* **2** COPY [C, U] when you copy the way a particular person or animal speaks or behaves, often to make
people laugh **taklit, başkasının konuşma ve hareketlerini taklit etme** *He does a brilliant impression of the
president.* **3** MARK [C] a mark left when an object is pressed into something soft **damga, mühür, iz**

impressionable /ɪmˈpreʃᵊnəbl/ *adjective* easy to influence **zayıf, kolay etkilenebilen, çabuk etki altında
kalan** *impressionable young people*

impressive /ɪmˈpresɪv/ *adjective* Someone or something that is impressive makes you admire and respect
them. **etkileyici, müthiş, unutulmaz, muazzam, hayranlık uyandıran** *an impressive performance/view*
● **impressively** *adverb* **etkileyici bir şekilde**

imprint /ˈɪmprɪnt/ *noun* **1** [C] a mark left when an object
is pressed into something soft **marka, damga, iz,
belirti** *The steps showed the imprint of his boots in the
snow.* **2** [no plural] the effect that something leaves behind
bir şeyin bıraktığı etki, iz, belirti *Much of the house
still bears the imprint of her personality.*

imprison /ɪmˈprɪzᵊn/ *verb* [T] to put someone in prison
or keep them as a prisoner **hapsetmek, hapse atmak**
[often passive] *Taylor was imprisoned in 1969 for burglary.*
● **imprisonment** *noun* [U] **hapsedilme**

improbable /ɪmˈprɒbᵊbl/ *adjective* **1** not likely to be
true or to happen **olası/muhtemel olmayan, ihtimal
dahilinde bulunmayan; olanaksız, ihtimal dışı**
2 surprising **şaşırtıcı, sürpriz, beklenmeyen, olasılık dışı** *Shirley seemed an improbable choice for a supermodel.* ● **improbably** *adverb* **olanaksız olan**

impromptu /ɪmˈprɒmptjuː/ *adjective, adverb* not
planned or prepared **hazırlıksız, önceden tasarlan-
mamış, irticalen, doğaçlama olan/yapılan; anında
yapılan** *an impromptu performance/party*

improper /ɪmˈprɒpəʳ/ *adjective formal* not correct, suitable, honest, or acceptable **yanlış, hatalı, uygun
olmayan, dürüst/kabul edilebilir olmayan; uygunsuz, yersiz, münasebetsiz** *improper conduct* ● **impro-
perly** *adverb* *The court ruled that he had acted impro-
perly.* **düzgün bir şekilde olmayan**

impropriety /ˌɪmprəˈpraɪəti/ *noun* [U] *formal* behaviour that is not correct, suitable, or honest **uygunsuz-
luk, nezaketsizlik, yakışıksızlık, münasebetsizlik**
The enquiry found no evidence of financial impropriety.

improve ...... BAŞKA BİR DEYİŞLE

Eğer bir şey kötü bir dönemden sonra iyileşme süre-
cine girmişse, durumu belirtmek için **rally** ve **recover** fiilleri kullanılabilir. *The team played badly in the
first half but* **rallied** *in the second.* ● *We are still waiting
for the economy to* **recover**.
Bir durumun iyiye gittiğini ifade etmek için **look up**
ve **pick up** deyimleri kullanılabilir. (resmi olmayan
ortamlarda) *Our financial situation is* **looking up**.
● *Business is really beginning to* **pick up**.
Work on deyimi bir şeyi geliştirmek anlamında kullanılır. *You need to* **work on** *your technique.*

Refine fiili kişinin küçük değişiklikler yaparak bir
durumu iyileştirdiğini göstermede kullanılır. *A
team of experts spent several months* **refining** *the software.*

o⁻**improve** /ɪmˈpruːv/ *verb* [I, T] to get better or to make
something better **iyileş(tir)mek, geliş(tir)mek,
ilerle(t)mek, düzel(t)mek** *Scott's behaviour has improved a lot lately.* ○ *Every year thousands of students come
to London to improve their English.* ○ *improved earn-
ings/productivity*
improve on sth *phrasal verb* to do something in a better
way or with better results than before **geliştirmek,
düzeltmek, iyileştirmek, daha ileriye götürmek** *I
hope our team can improve on last Saturday's performance.*

improvement ...... İLE BİRLİKTE KULLANILAN KELİMELER

a **continuous / dramatic / gradual / significant /
slight** improvement ● **bring about/notice/produce**
an improvement ● an improvement **in/to** sth

o⁻**improvement** /ɪmˈpruːvmənt/ *noun* [C, U] when something gets better or when you make it better **gelişme**
home improvements ○ *There's been a noticeable improvement in her work this term.* ○ *He's a definite improvement on her last boyfriend.* ○ *Sadly, her health has
shown no improvement.*

improvise /ˈɪmprəvaɪz/ *verb* [I, T] **1** to make or do something without any preparation, using only the things
that are available **ilerletme, iyileştirme, düzeltme,
geliştirme; mevcut olanaklarla yapmak** *For a football, we improvised with some rolled-up socks.* **2** to
play music or say words that you are inventing, not
reading or remembering **irticalen yapmak/çalmak/
söylemek; doğaçlamak** ● **improvisation**
/ˌɪmprəvaɪˈzeɪʃᵊn/ *noun* [C, U] **doğaçlama**

impulse ...... İLE BİRLİKTE KULLANILAN KELİMELER

resist an impulse ● sb's **first** impulse

impulse /ˈɪmpʌls/ *noun* **1** [C] a sudden feeling that you
must do something, without thinking about the results
dürtü, şevk, düşünmeden yapılan ani hareket
[usually singular] *Her first impulse was to run away.* **2 on
impulse** suddenly and without thinking first **aniden,
düşünmeden, bir anda karar vererek** *I tend to act on
impulse.* **3** [C] a short signal that carries information
through a system, for example an electrical system or
the nerves in your body **itici güç/dürtü, sinyal**

impulsive /ɪmˈpʌlsɪv/ *adjective* Impulsive people do
things suddenly, without planning or thinking carefully, but because they want to. **atak, fevrî, içinden
geldiği gibi davranan, coşkun, patavatsız** ● **impulsi-
vely** *adverb* **içten gelen bir şekilde**

impunity /ɪmˈpjuːnəti/ *noun formal* **with impunity**
without being punished **cezalandırılmadan, cezaya
çarptırılmadan** *Criminal gangs are terrorizing the
city with apparent impunity.*

impure /ɪmˈpjʊəʳ/ *adjective* not pure, but mixed with
other substances **katışık, karışık, saf olmayan**
● **impurity** *noun* [C, U] when something is impure or a
substance that is impure **saf olmayan katışık madde**

o⁻**in¹** /ɪn/ *preposition* **1** POSITION inside or towards the inside
of a container, place, or area **içinde, içine** *There's milk
in the fridge.* ○ *a shop in South London* ○ *He put his hand
in his pocket.* **2** DURING during part or all of a period of
time *...da/de We're going to Italy in April.* ○ *I started
working here in 1993.* **3** USING TIME needing or using no
more than a particular amount of time (zaman) *...
içinde/süresinde I'll be ready in a few minutes.*
4 PART OF part of something (bir şeyin içinde) *...da/*

de *Who's the woman in the painting?* ○ *There's a few spelling mistakes in your essay.* **5** JOB involved in a particular kind of job **(iş, meslek, görev vb.)** *...da/de a career in publishing/politics* **6** SUBJECT connected with a particular subject **(konu)** *...da/de alanında, sahasında a degree in philosophy* ○ *advances in medical science* **7** WEARING wearing **(kıyafet, elbise)** *...lı/li; giymiş, giyinen Do you know that man in the grey suit?* **8** EXPRESSED expressed or written in a particular way **(açıklamada)** *... ile (yaz, tamamla, doldur) Complete the form in black ink.* ○ *She spoke to him in Russian.* **9** ARRANGED arranged in a particular way **(düzenlemede)** *... şeklinde/biçiminde, şeklinde We sat down in a circle.* ○ *Is this list in alphabetical order?* **10** EXPERIENCE experiencing an emotion or condition **(deneyim, durum)** *...da/de halinde She's in a bad mood this morning.* ○ *The kitchen's in a terrible state.* **11 in all** used to show the total amount of something **toplam olarak, yekün olarak; toplam, hepsi, tamamı** *Some of the children came, so there were 15 of us in all.*

∘━**in²** /ın/ *adverb* **1** INTO A SPACE into an area or space from the outside of it **içeri, içeri doğru** *He rushed in halfway through the meeting.* ○ *Annie opened the car door and threw her luggage in.* **2** AT A PLACE at the place where a person usually lives or works **(ev, işyeri vb.) orada, içeride, evde, işte** *I phoned, but she wasn't in.* ○ *Could you ask him to ring me when he gets in?* **3** TRAIN/PLANE If a train, plane, etc is in, it has arrived at the place it was going to. **(tren, uçak vb.) gelişinde, varışında** *My train gets in at 17.54.* **4** SENT given or sent to someone official in order to be read **(gönderme) varmayı, ulaşmayı bildirmede** *Applications must be in by 28th February.* **5** TOWARDS LAND used when the sea or a ship moves close to land **(deniz, gemi vb.) karaya doğru gelmesinde kullanılır** *Let's go - the tide is coming in.* **6 be in for sth** *informal* If someone is in for a surprise, treat, shock, etc, it will happen to them soon. **başına gelecek iş olmak; sonunda muhakkak ... (olacak) olmak; başına ... gelmek** *If he thinks looking after a baby is easy, he's in for a shock.* **7 be in on sth** *informal* If you are in on something, you know about it or are involved in it. **çorbada tuzu bulunmak, rol almak** *Were you in on the surprise?* ○ *Please let me in on (= tell me) the secret.* **8** SPORT UK In cricket and similar sports, if a person or team is in, they are taking a turn to play. **(kriket vb. sporlarda) sıra elde ederek/sırayı kazanarak 9 be in for it** (*also UK* **be for it**) to be in trouble **başı belada olmak, başına gelecek iş olmak**

in³ /ın/ *adjective informal* fashionable or popular **moda, popüler,** *Pink is in this season.*

in⁴ /ın/ *noun* **the ins and outs of sth** the details of a particular subject **tüm ayrıntılar, girdisi çıktısı; bir konunun/meselenini tüm ayrıntıları** *the ins and outs of the issue*

in⁵ (*also* **in.**) *written abbreviation for* inch (= a unit for measuring length) **'inch' ölçü biriminin kısa hâli**

in- /ın-/ *prefix* not **olumsuzluk öneki; ... sız/siz** *inaccurate* ○ *insensitive*

inability /ˌɪnə'bɪləti/ *noun* [no plural] when you are unable to do something **kabiliyetsizlik, yetersizlik, güçsüzlük, beceriksizlik**

inaccessible /ˌɪnək'sesəbl/ *adjective* impossible or extremely difficult to get to **erişilemez, ulaşılamaz, ücra, çok uzak, sapa** *The plane crashed in a mountain area that was totally inaccessible to vehicles.*

inaccurate /ɪn'ækjərət/ *adjective* not correct or exact **hatalı, yanlış, doğru olmayan** *inaccurate information/figures* ● **inaccuracy** /ɪn'ækjərəsi/ *noun* [C, U]

when something is not correct or exact **yanlışlık, hata** *His book contains historical inaccuracies.*

inaction /ɪn'ækʃ⁰n/ *noun* [U] when people do not take any action, especially about a problem **atalet, hareketsizlik, harekete geçmeme, faaliyetsizlik, tembellik** *This announcement follows months of inaction and delay.*

inactive /ɪn'æktɪv/ *adjective* not active or working **hareketsiz, durgun, tembel** *Beetle grubs stay inactive underground until spring.* ● **inactivity** /ˌɪnæk'tɪvəti/ *noun* [U] when something or someone is not active or working **hareketsizlik** *a period of inactivity*

inadequacy /ɪ'nædɪkwəsi/ *noun* **1** [C, U] when someone or someone is not good enough or not of a high enough quality **yetersizlik, kalitesizlik** *feelings of inadequacy* ○ *He pointed out several inadequacies in the present system.* **2** [U] when there is not enough of something **kifayetsizlik, yetmezlik** *The basic problem is the inadequacy of our school budget.*

inadequate /ɪ'nædɪkwət/ *adjective* **1** not good enough or too low in quality **kalitesiz, yetmez** *inadequate facilities/training* ○ *Our equipment is totally inadequate for a job like this.* **2** not enough **yetersiz, kifayetsiz** *inadequate funds* ● **inadequately** *adverb* **yetersiz bir şekilde**

inadvertent /ˌɪnəd'vɜ:t⁰nt/ *adjective* not done intentionally **kasıtsız, istemeyerek** *an inadvertent error* ● **inadvertently** *adverb* *I had inadvertently picked up the wrong keys.* **kasıtsız bir şekilde**

inadvisable /ˌɪnəd'vaɪzəbl/ *adjective* likely to cause problems **tavsiye edilmez, doğru değil, sorun çıkarabilir, akıl kârı değil** *It is inadvisable for women to travel alone in this region.*

inane /ɪ'neɪn/ *adjective* very silly and annoying **anlamsız, saçma, boş, aptalca** *an inane question*

inanimate /ɪ'nænɪmət/ *adjective* not alive **cansız, ölü** *an inanimate object*

inappropriate /ˌɪnə'prəʊpriət/ *adjective* not suitable **yersiz, uygunsuz, maksada aykırı** *inappropriate behaviour* ○ *It would be inappropriate for me to comment, without knowing the facts.* ● **inappropriately** *adverb* **uygunsuzca**

inarticulate /ˌɪnɑ:'tɪkjələt/ *adjective* unable to express clearly what you feel or mean in words **derdini/düşüncesini anlatamayan, iyi konuşamayan, anlaşılmaz, açık seçik olmayan**

inasmuch as /ɪnəz'mʌtʃˌəz/ *conjunction formal* used to introduce a phrase which explains the degree to which something you have just said is true **... dığı/diği için; ... ması/mesi sebebiyle; ...dan/den dolayı** *They were strict about our appearance inasmuch as we weren't allowed to wear jewellery or make-up.*

inaudible /ɪ'nɔ:dəbl/ *adjective* impossible to hear **işitilemez, duyulamaz, duyulamayacak kadar hafif** *His voice was almost inaudible.*

inaugural /ɪ'nɔ:gjər⁰l/ *adjective* [always before noun] An inaugural speech, meeting, etc is the first one of a new organization or leader. **(konuşma, toplantı vb.) açılış, açılışa ait** *the President's inaugural address*

inaugurate /ɪ'nɔ:gjəreɪt/ *verb* [T] **1** to have a ceremony to celebrate an important person starting a new job, a new building opening, etc **törenle göreve başlamak; göreve başlama töreni yapmak** *Ronald Reagan was inaugurated in 1981.* **2** *formal* to start a new system or organization **törenle açmak** *He inaugurated a programme to fight tuberculosis.* ● **inauguration** /ɪˌnɔ:gjə'reɪʃ⁰n/ *noun* [C, U] *the inauguration of the Lord Mayor* **açılış töreni**

in-box (*also* inbox) /'ınbɒks/ *noun* [C] **1** the place on a computer where email messages are sent **e-posta iletilerinin geldiği/toplandığı bölüm**, **2** US (UK in-tray) a container where you keep letters and documents that need to be dealt with **mektup ve belgelerin toplandığı kutu**

Inc. *written abbreviation for* incorporated (= used after the name of some companies) **şirket/kuruluşu simgeleyen kısaltma** *Macmillan Inc.*

incalculable /ɪn'kælkjələbl/ *adjective* too big to measure **ölçülemeyecek kadar büyük, haddi hesabı olmayan** *The cost in human terms is incalculable.*

incapable /ɪn'keɪpəbl/ *adjective* **incapable of sth/doing sth** not able to do something or to feel a particular emotion **aciz, yeteneksiz, güçsüz** *He's incapable of controlling his temper.*

incapacitate /ˌɪnkə'pæsɪteɪt/ *verb* [T] *formal* to make someone too ill or weak to work or do things normally **iş yapamaz hâle getirmek, aciz bırakmak, felç etmek, aciz kalmak** [often passive] *He was incapacitated by illness.* • **incapacity** /ˌɪnkə'pæsəti/ *noun* [U] when you cannot do something because you do not have the ability or you are too weak **yetersizlik, acz, iş görememezlik**

incarcerate /ɪn'kɑːsəreɪt/ *verb* [T] *formal* to put and keep someone in prison **hapsetmek, hapsedilmek** [often passive] *Marks was incarcerated for robbery.* • **incarceration** /ɪnˌkɑːsə'reɪʃən/ *noun* [U] **hapsetme**

incarnate /ɪn'kɑːnət/ *adjective* [always after noun] in human form **beşer/insan şeklinde** *He was acting like the devil incarnate.*

incarnation /ˌɪnkɑː'neɪʃən/ *noun* **1** [C] a particular form of something or someone that is changing or developing **somut/canlı örnek, canlı simge, sembol, timsal** *In their new incarnation, the band have acquired a female singer.* **2 the incarnation** of the physical form of a god or quality **tanrı veya niteliğin fiziksel/canlı şekli/timsali** *the incarnation of evil/freedom* **3** [C] a particular time, in religions which believe we have many lives **bedende olma, cisimleşme, enkarnasyon, doğuş, yaşam, hayat**

incendiary /ɪn'sendiəri/ *adjective* [always before noun] designed to cause a fire **yangın çıkarıcı; yangın** *an incendiary bomb/device*

incense /'ɪnsens/ *noun* [U] a substance which burns with a strong, sweet smell, often used in religious ceremonies **tütsü, buhur**

incensed /ɪn'senst/ *adjective* extremely angry **çok kızmış, öfkelenmiş, çığırdan çıkmış**

⟨incentive ...... İLE BİRLİKTE KULLANILAN KELİMELER⟩
have/provide an incentive • an added/powerful/strong incentive • an incentive for sb

incentive /ɪn'sentɪv/ *noun* [C, U] something that encourages you to act in a particular way **teşvik, özendirme** [+ to do sth] *People had little incentive to save.* ○ *The government should provide incentives for young people to stay in school.*

inception /ɪn'sepʃən/ *noun* [no plural] *formal* the time when an organization or official activity began **başlama, başlangıç** *He has directed the project since its inception.*

incessant /ɪn'sesənt/ *adjective* continuous, especially in a way that is annoying or unpleasant **aralıksız, biteviye, ardı arkası kesilmeyen, fasılasız, devamlı** *incessant rain/noise* • **incessantly** *adverb* *The phone rang incessantly.* **sürekli bir biçimde**

incest /'ɪnsest/ *noun* [U] sex that is illegal because it is between closely related people, for example a father and daughter **yakın akraba arasında cinsel ilişki/zina, enses tilişki**

incestuous /ɪn'sestjuəs/ *adjective* **1** involving sex between people who are closely related **aile içi zina ile ilgili 2** involving a group of people who are not interested in people or things outside the group **ayrıcalık gözeten, belli bir grup dışındakilere yüz vermeyen** *Universities can be very incestuous places.*

◦-**inch¹** /ɪnʃ/ *noun* [C] **1** (*written abbreviation* in.) a unit for measuring length, equal to 2.54 centimetres **2.54 cm'ye denk uzunluk ölçü birimi, inç** ⊃See study page Measurements on page Centre 31. **2 not budge/give an inch** *informal* to refuse to change your opinions **fikirlinden vazgeçmemek, direnmek, inat etmek 3 to be every inch sth** to be a particular kind of person in every way **her şeyiyle kendine has biri olmak; tamamen, tepeden tırnağaz;** *He is every inch a gentleman.*

inch² /ɪnʃ/ *verb* **inch closer/forward/up, etc** to move somewhere slowly or by very small amounts **milim milim hareket et(tir)mek/ilerle(t)mek**

⟨incidence ...... İLE BİRLİKTE KULLANILAN KELİMELER⟩
a high/increased/low incidence • the incidence of sth

incidence /'ɪnsɪdəns/ *noun* [C] how often something happens, especially something bad **oran, nispet** [usually singular] *There's a high incidence of crime in the area.*

⟨incident ...... İLE BİRLİKTE KULLANILAN KELİMELER⟩
an incident happens/occurs • an isolated incident

incident /'ɪnsɪdənt/ *noun* [C] *formal* an event, especially one that is bad or unusual **olay, vaka, hadise, vukuat** *Police are investigating the incident.*

incidental /ˌɪnsɪ'dentəl/ *adjective* less important than the thing something is connected with or part of **öylesine, önemsiz, rastlantılı, tesadüfi** *The lyrics here are incidental to the music.*

incidentally /ˌɪnsɪ'dentəli/ *adverb* used when you say something that is not as important as the main subject of conversation but is connected to it **'Ha...', 'Sırası gelmişken ...', 'Sözü gelmişken ...', 'Aklıma gelmişken...', 'Şeyy'** *Incidentally, talking of Stephen, have you met his girlfriend?*

incinerator /ɪn'sɪnəreɪtər/ *noun* [C] a machine that is used to burn waste, especially harmful materials **çöp/atık yakma makinesi/fırın**

incipient /ɪn'sɪpiənt/ *adjective* [always before noun] *formal* just beginning **henüz başlayan, yeni başlamış/çıkmış, başlangıç aşamasındaki** *incipient wrinkles*

incision /ɪn'sɪʒən/ *noun* [C] *formal* an opening that is made in something with a sharp tool, especially in someone's body during an operation **(tıp) ameliyat yeri, yarma, kesme**

incisive /ɪn'saɪsɪv/ *adjective* showing an ability to think quickly and clearly and deal with situations effectively **hızlı ve net düşünür olası durumlarla etkin şekilde ilgilenebilen; çabuk kavrayıp çözüm üretebilen** *incisive questions*

incite /ɪn'saɪt/ *verb* [T] to do or say something that encourages people to behave violently or illegally **kışkırtmak, körüklemek, tahrik etmek, teşvik etmek** *They denied inciting the crowd to violence.* • **incitement** *noun* [C, U] when someone does or says something that incites people **kışkırtma, tahrik**

incl *written abbreviation for* including or inclusive **dahil, kapsayan, içeren**

inclination /ˌɪnklɪˈneɪʃᵊn/ *noun* [C, U] a feeling that you want to do something **eğilim, heves, merak, meyil, temayül** [+ to do sth] *She showed little inclination to leave.*

incline¹ /ɪnˈklaɪn/ *verb* [T] *formal* If you incline your head, you bend your neck so that your face bends down. **eğmek, öne eğmek**
incline to/towards sth *phrasal verb formal* to think that a belief or opinion is probably correct **bir şeye inanmaya eğilim göstermek/meyilli olmak** *I incline to the view that peace can be achieved.*

incline² /ˈɪnklaɪn/ *noun* [C] *formal* a slope **bayır, eğim, meyil** *a steep/gentle incline*

inclined /ɪnˈklaɪnd/ *adjective* [never before noun] **1** be inclined to think/believe/agree, etc to have an opinion, but not a strong opinion **düşünmeye/inanmaya/uyuşmaya meyilli olmak; eğilimi olmak** *I'm inclined to agree with you.* **2** inclined to do sth a often behaving in a particular way **eğilimli/meyilli olmak** *Tom is inclined to be forgetful.* **b** wanting to do something **gönlü istemek, eğilimi olmak, istekli olmak** *No one seemed inclined to help.* **3** artistically/technically, etc inclined having natural artistic/technical, etc ability **sanatsal/teknik kabiliyeti olan, yatkın, uygun, yetenekli** *She's very bright, but not academically inclined.*

ᴏ⟶**include** /ɪnˈkluːd/ *verb* [T] **1** to have something or someone as part of something larger or more general, such as a group, price, or process **içermek, kapsamak, içine almak** *His books include the best-selling novel 'The Foundling'.* ○ *The price includes flights and three nights' accommodation.* **2** to allow someone to take part in an activity **dahil etmek, katmak, yer vermek, katılmasına müsaade etmek** [often passive] *Local residents were included in the initial planning discussions.* ➲Opposite exclude.

ᴏ⟶**including** /ɪnˈkluːdɪŋ/ *preposition* used to show that someone or something is part of a larger group, amount, or process **içeren, dahil eden, dahil** *Fourteen people, including a prison warden, were killed.* ○ *It's £24.99, including postage and packing.*

inclusion /ɪnˈkluːʒᵊn/ *noun* [C, U] when you include someone or something, especially in a group, amount, or event **kapsama, içerme, dahil etme/edilme** *Her self-portrait was chosen for inclusion in the exhibition.* ➲Opposite exclusion.

inclusive /ɪnˈkluːsɪv/ *adjective* **1** COST An inclusive price or amount includes everything. **her şey dahil** *Prices are inclusive of flights and accommodation.* **2** NUMBERS [always after noun] including the first and last date or number stated **bildirilen ilk ve son tarihi/sayıyı içeren/kapsayan** *The course will run from October 19 to November 13, inclusive.* **3** PEOPLE Inclusive groups try to include many different types of people. **herkesi kapsayan; toplumun tüm kesimlerini içeren** *Our aim is to create a fairer, more inclusive society.* ➲Opposite exclusive.

incoherent /ˌɪnkəʊˈhɪərᵊnt/ *adjective* not using clear words or ideas, and difficult to understand **anlaşılmaz, tutarsız, açık seçik yazılmamış, abuk sabuk, ipe sapa gelmez** *His statement to the police was rambling and incoherent.* ● **incoherence** /ˌɪnkəʊˈhɪərᵊns/ *noun* [U] **anlaşılmazlık**

an **average/good/high/low/steady** income ● **earn/ have/provide** an income ● **be on** a (high/low, etc) income

ᴏ⟶**income** /ˈɪŋkʌm/ *noun* [C, U] money that you earn by working, investing, or producing goods **gelir, kazanç,**

irat *families on* **low incomes** ○ *Tourism accounts for 25% of the country's national income.*

ˈ**income supˌport** *noun* [U] in the UK, money that is paid by the government to people who have very little or no income **(Birleşik Krallık) (geliri olmayan veya çok az olan insanlara) gelir desteği, aile yardımı**

ˈ**income ˌtax** *noun* [C, U] tax that you have to pay on your income **gelir vergisi**

incoming /ˈɪnˌkʌmɪŋ/ *adjective* [always before noun] coming into a place or starting a job **gelen, varan, ulaşan, yeni, yeni seçilen/atanan** *incoming phone calls/ mail* ○ *the incoming government*

incomparable /ɪnˈkɒmpᵊrəbl/ *adjective* too good to be compared with anything or anyone else **emsalsiz, kıyas kabul etmez, kıyaslanamaz, eşsiz** *incomparable beauty*

incompatible /ˌɪnkəmˈpætəbl/ *adjective* **1** too different to exist or live together **uyumsuz, zıt, birbiriyle bağdaşmayan, uyuşmayan** *He regarded being a soldier as incompatible with his Christian faith.* **2** If equipment or software is incompatible with other equipment or software, it will not work with it. **uymayan** ● **incompatibility** /ˌɪnkəmˌpætəˈbɪləti/ *noun* [U] when two people or things are incompatible **uyuşmazlık, bağdaşmazlık, zıtlık**

incompetent /ɪnˈkɒmpɪtᵊnt/ *adjective* not able to do your job, or things that you are expected to do, successfully **yetersiz, ehliyetsiz, beceriksiz, kabiliyetsiz** *incompetent managers* ● **incompetence** /ɪnˈkɒmpɪtᵊns/ *noun* [U] **yetersizlik**

incomplete /ˌɪnkəmˈpliːt/ *adjective* not finished, or having one or more parts missing **yarım, eksik, noksan, bitmemiş, tamamlanmamış** *Decisions were made on the basis of incomplete information.* ● **incompleteness** *noun* [U] **yetersiz olma durumu**

incomprehensible /ɪnˌkɒmprɪˈhensəbl/ *adjective* impossible to understand **anlaşılması güç, anlaması/kavraması zor, akıl sır ermez** *The instructions are almost incomprehensible.* ○ *His behaviour is quite incomprehensible to me.*

incomprehension /ɪnˌkɒmprɪˈhenʃᵊn/ *noun* [U] *formal* when you do not understand something **anlayamama, kavrayamama** *She looked at him in total incomprehension.*

inconceivable /ˌɪnkənˈsiːvəbl/ *adjective* impossible to imagine **hayal bile edilemez, inanması zor, inanılmaz, akıl almaz** [+ that] *I find it inconceivable that she could be a killer.*

inconclusive /ˌɪnkənˈkluːsɪv/ *adjective* not leading to a definite decision or result **sonuçsuz, bir sonuca varmayan** *inconclusive evidence/results* ○ *The battle was inconclusive.*

incongruous /ɪnˈkɒŋgruəs/ *adjective formal* strange or not suitable for a particular situation **uygunsuz, aykırı, uyuşmaz, bağdaşmaz, tuhaf** *Bill was an incongruous sight, standing on the beach in his suit.*

inconsequential /ɪnˌkɒnsɪˈkwenʃᵊl/ *adjective formal* not important **önemsiz, ehemmiyetsiz** *inconsequential remarks*

inconsiderate /ˌɪnkənˈsɪdᵊrət/ *adjective* not caring about other people's situations or the way they feel **duyarsız, düşüncesiz, saygısız, vurdumduymaz** *It was very inconsiderate of you to keep us all waiting.*

(an) **apparent/glaring** inconsistency ● (an) inconsistency **in** sth

inconsistency /ˌɪnkən'sɪstˀnsi/ *noun* [C, U] when something is inconsistent **tutarsızlık, uyumsuzluk, aykırılık** *The report was full of errors and inconsistencies.*

inconsistent /ˌɪnkən'sɪstənt/ *adjective* **1** not staying the same in quality or behaviour **tutarsız, istikrarsız, dakikası dakikasına uymayan, kararsız** *His homework is very inconsistent.* **2** not having the same principles as something else, or not agreeing with other facts **birbirine ters düşen, uyuşmaz, aykırı** *The story Robert told his mother is totally inconsistent with what he told me.*

inconspicuous /ˌɪnkən'spɪkjuəs/ *adjective* not noticeable or attracting attention **göze çarpmaz, dikkat çekmeyen, silik** *Emma tried to make herself as inconspicuous as possible.*

incontinent /ɪn'kɒntɪnənt/ *adjective* not able to control when urine or faeces come out of your body **idrarını tutamayan, altına kaçıran**

incontrovertible /ˌɪn,kɒntrə'vɜːtəbl/ *adjective formal* certainly true **kesin, tartışılmaz, inkâr edilemez** *incontrovertible evidence/proof*

inconvenience /ˌɪnkən'viːniəns/ *noun* [C, U] when something is inconvenient, or something that is inconvenient **zahmet, rahatsızlık, sıkıntı, güçlük** *The Director apologized for any inconvenience caused.* ○ [usually singular] *Having to wait for ten minutes was a minor inconvenience.* ● **inconvenience** *verb* [T] *There were complaints from travellers inconvenienced by delays and cancellations.* **iş çıkarmak, zahmet vermek**

inconvenient /ˌɪnkən'viːniənt/ *adjective* involving or causing difficulty, such as unexpected changes or effort **zahmetli, sıkıntılı, rahatsızlık verici** *I'm sorry, I seem to have called at an inconvenient time.*

incorporate /ɪn'kɔːpˀreɪt/ *verb* [T] to include something as part of another thing **birleştirmek, katmak, dahil etmek** *He began to incorporate dance and mime into his plays.* ● **incorporation** /ɪn,kɔːpˀr'eɪʃˀn/ *noun* [U] **birlikte**

Incorporated /ɪn'kɔːpˀreɪtɪd/ (*written abbreviation* **Inc.**) *adjective* used after the name of companies which have been organized in a particular legal way **anonim şirket** *They formed their own company, Broadcast Music Incorporated.*

incorrect /ˌɪnkˀ'rekt/ *adjective* not correct **yanlış, hatalı** *His answers were incorrect.* ● **incorrectly** *adverb* *My name is spelled incorrectly on your list.* **yanlış bir şekilde**

incorrigible /ɪn'kɒrɪdʒəbl/ *adjective* having particular faults and impossible to change **düzelmez, iflah olmaz, adam olmaz, uslanmaz, yola gelmez, akıllanmaz**

Grow ve **rise** fiili **increase** fiiline alternatif olarak kullanılabilir. *The number of people living alone grows each year.* ● *Prices rose by ten percent.*
Go up deyimi fiyatların yükseldiğini ifade etmekte kullanılır. *House prices keep going up.* ● *The price of fuel has gone up by 5p a litre.*
Eğer bir şey ani ve yüksek oranda yükselme göstermişse, durumu belirtmede **escalate, rocket** veya **soar** fiilleri kullanılabilir. *Crime in the city has escalated in recent weeks.* ● *Building costs have rocketed by seventy percent.* ● *House prices have soared this year.*
Eğer kişi bir şeyin miktarı veya büyüklüğünde artış sağlıyorsa, durumu belirtmede **expand** veya **extend** fiilleri kullanılabilir. *We're hoping to expand/extend our range of products.*
Maximize fiili bir kişinin bir şeyi olabildiğince

büyütmeye çalıştığının ifadesinde kullanılır. *We need to* **maximize** *profits.*

o⊶**increase¹** /ɪn'kriːs/ *verb* [I, T] to get bigger or to make something bigger in size or amount **art(ır)mak, çoğal(t)mak** *Eating fatty food increases the risk of heart disease.* ○ *Exports of computers have* **increased** *by 15% since January.* ○ *increased demand/competition* ⊃Opposite **decrease.**

a **dramatic/sharp/significant/slight/substantial** increase ● an increase **in sth**

o⊶**increase²** /'ɪnkriːs/ *noun* **1** [C, U] when the number, size, or amount of something gets bigger **artış, çoğalma** *a price/tax increase* ○ *We are seeing an increase in standards of living.* **2 on the increase** If something is on the increase, it is happening more often. **artmakta, çoğalmakta** *Violent crime is on the increase.* ⊃Opposite **decrease.**

increasingly /ɪn'kriːsɪŋli/ *adverb* more and more **gitgide, gittikçe, gittikçe artarak** *increasingly important* ○ *Increasingly, education is seen as a right, not a privilege.*

o⊶**incredible** /ɪn'kredɪbl/ *adjective* **1** *informal* very good, exciting, or large **inanılmaz, hayret verici, hiç görülmemiş** *We had an incredible time that summer.* ○ *an incredible noise* **2** too strange to be believed **inanılmaz, akıl almaz,** *an incredible story*

incredibly /ɪn'kredɪbli/ *adverb* **1** *informal* extremely **son derece, oldukça, muazzam** *The team played incredibly well.* **2** in a way that is difficult to believe **görülmemiş, inanılması güç** *Incredibly, no one was hurt.*

incredulous /ɪn'kredjələs/ *adjective* not able to believe something **inanmaz, kuşkulu, şüpheli** *He looked incredulous when I told him the results.* ● **incredulity** /ˌɪnkrə'djuːləti/ *noun* [U] **şüphe** ● **incredulously** *adverb* **şüpheli bir şekilde**

increment /'ɪnkrəmənt/ *noun* [C] *formal* one of a series of increases **artma, artış, zam** *pay increments*

incremental /ˌɪnkrə'mentˀl/ *adjective formal* increasing by small amounts **azar azar artan/çoğalan/biriken** *incremental changes*

incriminate /ɪn'krɪmɪneɪt/ *verb* [T] to make someone seem guilty of a crime or to show that they are guilty **suçlamak, suç isnat etmek, suçlu göstermek** [often reflexive] *He refused to answer questions on the grounds that he might incriminate himself.*

incriminating /ɪn'krɪmɪneɪtɪŋ/ *adjective* Something that is incriminating makes someone seem guilty of a crime. **suçlu gösteren, suçlayan** *incriminating evidence/remarks*

incubator /'ɪŋkjʊbeɪtəʳ/ *noun* [C] a heated container that provides the right conditions for a baby born too early, or for very young birds, animals, or eggs **kuvöz, kuluçka makinesi**

incumbent¹ /ɪn'kʌmbənt/ *noun* [C] *formal* someone who has an official job, especially a political one **makam sahibi, görevli, memur, (siyasi) sorumlu, görevlendirilmiş olan** *the previous incumbent*

incumbent² /ɪn'kʌmbənt/ *adjective* **1 be incumbent on/upon sb to do sth** *formal* to be someone's duty or responsibility to do something **sorumluluğu olmak, görevi olan, üzerine düşen 2** [always before noun] holding an official job, especially a political one **...ın/in üzerine düşen; zorunlu** *the incumbent president*

incur /ɪn'kɜːʳ/ *verb* [T] **incurring,** *past* **incurred** *formal* to experience something unpleasant as a result of something you have done **maruz kalmak, uğramak,**

hedef olmak *to incur debts* ○ *I am sorry to have incurred his anger.*

incurable /ɪnˈkjʊərəbl/ *adjective* impossible to cure **tedavi edilemez, çaresi bulunamaz, devasız, iyileşmeyen** *an incurable disease*

incursion /ɪnˈkɜːʃᵊn/ *noun* [C] *formal* a sudden attack or entry into an area that belongs to other people **ani saldırı, baskın** *incursions into enemy territory*

indebted /ɪnˈdetɪd/ *adjective* **1 be indebted to sb** to be very grateful to someone **minnettar olmak, gönül borçlusu olmak, teşekkür borçlu olmak** *I'm indebted to my parents for all their support.* **2** having a debt to pay *indebted countries* • **indebtedness** *noun* [U] **borçlu olma**

indecent /ɪnˈdiːsᵊnt/ *adjective* showing or consisting of sexual behaviour, language, etc which is unacceptable to most people **açık saçık, edebe aykırı, edepsiz, çirkin** *indecent photographs* • **indecency** /ɪnˈdiːsᵊnsi/ *noun* [U] indecent behaviour, or when something is indecent **ahlaksızlık, edebsizlik, açık saçıklık, yakışıksızlık** • **indecently** *adverb* **uygunsuzca**

indecision /ˌɪndɪˈsɪʒᵊn/ *noun* [U] when you cannot make a decision **kararsızlık, tereddüt** *a moment of indecision*

indecisive /ˌɪndɪˈsaɪsɪv/ *adjective* not good at making decisions, or not producing a decision **kararsız, tereddüt eden, karar veremeyen** *She was weak and indecisive.*

indeed /ɪnˈdiːd/ *adverb* **1** [EMPHASIS] used to add emphasis after 'very' followed by an adjective or adverb **gerçekten/Sahi mi?** *For a four-year-old, her vocabulary is very good indeed.* ○ *Thank you very much indeed.* **2** [REACTION] used when someone has said something that surprises, interests, or annoys you **hakikaten, aslına bakarsan, aslında** *"She asked if you were married." "Did she, indeed?"* **3** [TRUE] used to emphasize that something is true or that you agree with it **cidden, hakikaten** *"He sounds a very interesting man." "He is indeed."* **4** [MORE] *formal* used when you say more to support or develop what has already been said **doğrusu, açıkcası, aslında** *For such creatures speed is not important, indeed it is counterproductive.*

indefatigable /ˌɪndɪˈfætɪgəbl/ *adjective formal* never becoming tired **yorulmaz, yorulmak bilmez, dur, durak bilmez** *She was indefatigable in promoting her cause.*

indefensible /ˌɪndɪˈfensəbl/ *adjective* completely wrong, and so impossible to defend or support **savunulamaz, haklı görülemez, affedilemez, bağışlanamaz** *Racism is morally indefensible.*

indefinable /ˌɪndɪˈfaɪnəbl/ *adjective* difficult to describe or explain **tarifsiz, anlatılamaz, tanımlanamaz** *an indefinable atmosphere of tension*

indefinite /ɪnˈdefɪnət/ *adjective* with no fixed time, size, end, or limit **belirsiz, tanımsız, süresiz, sonsuz, sınırsız** *an indefinite period*

inˌdefinite 'article *noun* [C] in grammar, a phrase used to mean the words 'a' or 'an' **belgisiz/belirtisiz harfi tarif** ⊃Compare definite article.

indefinitely /ɪnˈdefɪnətli/ *adverb* for a period of time for which no end has been fixed **süresiz olarak, belirsiz bir tarihe kadar** *His visit has been postponed indefinitely.*

indelible /ɪnˈdeləbl/ *adjective* **1** impossible to forget **unutulmaz, silinmez, zihinlere kazınmış** *an indelible impression/image* **2** impossible to wash away or remove **(leke vb.) çıkmaz, silinmez, sabit, yıkamakla temizlenemez** *indelible ink*

indemnity /ɪnˈdemnəti/ *noun formal* **1** [U] protection against possible damage or punishment **tazminat, ödence, ödenek, karşılama 2** [C, U] money paid or promised to you if something valuable to you is lost or damaged **teminat, tazminat, ödeme** *indemnity insurance*

indentation /ˌɪndenˈteɪʃᵊn/ *noun* [C] a mark, cut, or hole in the surface of something **çürük, çukur, delik, oyuk, girinti, çentik, bere**

independence .... İLE BİRLİKTE KULLANILAN KELİMELER
achieve/gain independence • independence from sth

∘⊷**independence** /ˌɪndɪˈpendəns/ *noun* [U] **1** when someone looks after themselves and does not need money, help, or permission from other people **özgürlük, kendi başına buyrukluk** *My parents gave me a lot of independence.* ○ *Many old people are afraid of losing their independence.* **2** when a country has its own government and is not ruled by another country **bağımsızlık, istikbal** *Mexico gained its independence from Spain in 1821.*

Indeˈpendence ˌDay (*also* Fourth of July) *noun* 4 July, a national holiday in the US to celebrate the country's freedom from Great Britain in 1776 **(ABD) 4 Temmuz Bağımsızlık Günü**

∘⊷**independent¹** /ˌɪndɪˈpendənt/ *adjective* **1** [RULE] not controlled or ruled by anyone else **bağımsız, hür** *an independent state/company* ○ *The group is independent of any political party.* **2** [NEED] not wanting or needing anyone else to help you or do things for you **serbest, özgür, ayrı, müstakil** *She's a proud, independent woman.* **3** [INFLUENCE] not influenced by anyone or anything else **özgür, kendi başına buyruk, hür** *an independent expert/study* • **independently** *adverb to operate independently* **özgür bir biçimde**

independent² /ˌɪndɪˈpendənt/ *noun* [C] a politician who does not belong to a political party **bağımsız, bağlantısız, herhangi bir siyasi partiye ait olmayan**

in-depth /ˈɪnˌdepθ/ *adjective* [always before noun] involving or considering all the details of something **her şeyi kapsayan, tam, bütün bütün** *in-depth knowledge*

indescribable /ˌɪndɪˈskraɪbəbl/ *adjective* so good, bad, large, etc that it is impossible to describe **tanımlanamaz, tarifsiz, anlatılamaz** *an indescribable feeling* ○ *indescribable agony*

indestructible /ˌɪndɪˈstrʌktəbl/ *adjective* impossible to destroy or break **yıkılamaz, dayanıklı, yok edilemez, bozulmaz**

indeterminate /ˌɪndɪˈtɜːmɪnət/ *adjective* impossible to know **meçhul, bilinmeyen, belirsiz, sınırsız** *a large woman of indeterminate age*

index¹ /ˈɪndeks/ *noun* [C] **1** [LIST] *plural* **indexes** an alphabetical list of subjects or names at the end of a book, showing on what page they are found in the text **dizin, fihrist, alfabetik sıra** *Look up 'heart disease' in the index.* **2** [INFORMATION] *plural* **indexes** a collection of information stored on a computer or on cards in alphabetical order **bilgisayar veya kartlarda bilginin alfabetik sırada toplanması 3** [SYSTEM] *plural* **indices** or **indexes** a system for comparing different values and recording changes, especially in financial markets **gösterge, endeks** *the retail price index*

index² /ˈɪndeks/ *verb* [T] to make an index for text or information, or arrange it in an index **alfabetik sıraya koymak, indekslemek, dizmek, fihrist eklemek**

'index ˌfinger *noun* [C] the finger next to your thumb **işaret parmağı**

Indian /'ɪndiən/ *noun* [C] **1** someone from India **Hintli, Hint uyruklu 2** an American Indian (= one of the original race of people who lived in North America) **Kızılderili; Amerikan yerlisi** ⊃See also: **West Indian.**

indicate /'ɪndɪkeɪt/ *verb* **1** SHOW [T] to show that something exists or is likely to be true **göstermek** [+ (that)] *Recent evidence indicates that the skeleton is about 3 million years old.* **2** SAY [T] to say something or give a signal to show what you mean or what you intend to do **göstermek, işaret etmek, belirtmek** *He has indicated his intention to resign.* **3** POINT [T] to point to someone or something **işaret ederek göstermek, belirtmek** *He indicated a man in a dark coat.* **4** SIGNAL [I, T] *UK* to show that you intend to turn left or right when you are driving **(tarafikte) işaret/sinyal vermek** *The driver turned right without indicating.*

---
indication ...... İLE BİRLİKTE KULLANILAN KELİMELER
a **clear/good/strong** indication ● an indication **of** sth

---

indication /ˌɪndɪ'keɪʃⁿn/ *noun* [C, U] **1** a sign showing that something exists or is likely to be true **belirti, işaret, iz, alamet, emare** [+ (that)] *There are strong indications that the case will be referred to the Court of Appeal.* **2** a sign showing what someone means or what they intend to do **işaret, gösterge** *Helen's face gave no indication of what she was thinking.*

indicative¹ /ɪn'dɪkətɪv/ *adjective formal* **1 be indicative of sth** to be a sign that something exists, is true, or is likely to happen **göstergesi/belirtisi/bildireni olmak** *These statistics are indicative of a widespread problem.* **2** An indicative form of a verb is used to express a fact or action. **(kip) bildiren, haber veren**

indicative² /ɪn'dɪkətɪv/ *noun* [no plural] the indicative form of a verb **bildirme/haber kipi**

---
indicator ...... İLE BİRLİKTE KULLANILAN KELİMELER
a **good/reliable/useful** indicator ● an indicator **of** sth

---

indicator /'ɪndɪkeɪtər/ *noun* [C] **1** a fact, measurement, or condition that shows what something is like or how it is changing **gösterge, belirteç, işaret** *With some goods, cost is the most reliable indicator of quality.* **2** *UK* (*US* **turn signal**) a light that flashes on a vehicle to show that the driver intends to turn right or left **(araba) (sağ, sol) sinyal** ⊃Orta kısımdaki renkli sayfalarına bakınız.

indict /ɪn'daɪt/ *verb* [T] *formal* to accuse someone officially of a crime **suçlamak, itham etmek** [often passive] *Pound was indicted for treason.*

indictment /ɪn'daɪtmənt/ *noun* **1** [C] something which shows the bad things which a person or system is responsible for **ayıp, kusur, suçlama** *The novel is a scathing indictment of the slave trade.* **2** [C, U] when someone is legally indicted, or the official document or process for doing this **(yasal) suçlama, itham**

indie /'ɪndi/ *noun* [C, U] *informal* a small independent music company or film producer **küçük, bağımsız müzik veya film yapım şirketi** *indie music/bands*

---
indifference ...... İLE BİRLİKTE KULLANILAN KELİMELER
callous/casual/cold indifference ● indifference **to/towards** sth

---

indifference /ɪn'dɪfⁿrⁿns/ *noun* [U] when you do not care about something or have any particular opinions about it **kayıtsızlık, umursamazlık** *an air of indifference*

indifferent /ɪn'dɪfⁿrⁿnt/ *adjective* **1** not caring about or interested in someone or something **kayıtsız, umursa-**

maz, vurdumduymaz, ilgisiz *They are indifferent to the plight of the unemployed.* **2** neither good nor bad **vasat, orta halli, şöyle böyle, orta karar** *an indifferent performance*

indigenous /ɪn'dɪdʒɪnəs/ *adjective* having always lived or existed in a place **yerli** *indigenous peoples* ○ *The kangaroo is indigenous to Australia.*

indigestion /ˌɪndɪ'dʒestʃⁿn/ *noun* [U] pain which you feel when your stomach is unable to digest food correctly **hazımsızlık, sindirim bozukluğu**

indignant /ɪn'dɪgnənt/ *adjective* angry because you have been treated badly or unfairly **öfkeli, içerlemiş, kızgın** *Consumers are indignant at/about the high prices charged by car dealers.* ● **indignantly** *adverb* **kızgın bir şekilde**

indignation /ˌɪndɪg'neɪʃⁿn/ *noun* [U] when someone is indignant **öfke, kızgınlık, içerleme** *His voice was trembling with indignation.*

indignity /ɪn'dɪgnəti/ *noun* [C, U] a situation which makes you lose respect or look silly, or the feeling of shame and embarrassment it gives you **hakaret, aşağılama, küçük düşürücü hareket** [+ of + doing sth] *They suffered the indignity of being searched like common criminals.*

indigo /'ɪndɪgəʊ/ *noun* [U] a blue-purple colour **çivit mavisi** ● **indigo** *adjective* **çivit mavisi**

indirect /ˌɪndɪ'rekt/ *adjective* **1** NOT CONNECTED not directly caused by or connected with something **dolaylı, endirekt, vasıtalı** *Indirect effects of the fighting include disease and food shortages.* **2** NOT OBVIOUS hidden, or not taken or given in a way that is obvious **gizli, dolaylı, doğrudan doğruya olmayan, ima yollu** *indirect taxes/costs* ○ *an indirect criticism* **3** NOT STRAIGHT not going straight from one place or person to another **dolambaçlı, dolaşık** *an indirect route* ● **indirectly** *adverb* **dolambaçlı bir şekilde**

indirect 'object *noun* [C] The indirect object of a verb with two objects is the person or thing that is affected by the result of the action of the verb. In the sentence 'Give Val some cake.', 'Val' is the indirect object. **(dilbilgisi) dolaylı tümleç** ⊃Compare **direct object.**

indiscreet /ˌɪndɪ'skriːt/ *adjective* saying or doing things which let people know things that should be secret **geveze, boşboğaz, patavatsız, düşüncesiz** *indiscreet remarks* ● **indiscretion** /ˌɪndɪ'skreʃⁿn/ *noun* [C, U] **patavatsızlık**

indiscriminate /ˌɪndɪ'skrɪmɪnət/ *adjective* not planned or controlled in a responsible or careful way **gelişigüzel, rastgele** *the indiscriminate use of pesticides* ● **indiscriminately** *adverb* *The gunman fired indiscriminately into the crowd.* **planlanmamış bir şekilde**

indispensable /ˌɪndɪ'spensəbl/ *adjective* completely necessary **elzem, çok gerekli, vazgeçilmez** *an indispensable tool/guide* ○ *She quickly became indispensable to him.*

indisputable /ˌɪndɪ'spjuːtəbl/ *adjective* obviously and certainly true **açık ve kesin, su götürmez, tartışılmaz** *an indisputable fact*

indistinct /ˌɪndɪ'stɪŋkt/ *adjective* not clear **belli belirsiz, hayal meyal, anlaşılması güç** *His words became indistinct.*

indistinguishable /ˌɪndɪ'stɪŋgwɪʃəbl/ *adjective* impossible to see or hear as different or separate **ayırt edilemez, seçilemez** *Many toy pistols are indistinguishable from real guns.*

individual¹ /ˌɪndɪ'vɪdʒuəl/ *adjective* **1** [always before noun] considered separately from other things in a group **kişisel, ferdî, şahsi** *Read out the individual let-*

ters of each word. **2** given to or relating to one particular person or thing **bireysel, tek kişilik, özel** *We deal with each case on an individual basis.*

individual² /ˌɪndɪ'vɪdʒuəl/ *noun* [C] **1** a person, especially when considered separately and not as part of a group **fert, birey, kişi, şahıs** *We try to treat our students as individuals.* **2** *informal* a person with a special characteristic, usually one you dislike **tip, karakter, kişi** *a ruthless individual*

individualism /ˌɪndɪ'vɪdʒuəlɪz³m/ *noun* [U] the quality of being different from other people **bireyselcilik**

individualist /ˌɪndɪ'vɪdʒuəlɪst/ *noun* [C] someone who likes to behave or do things differently from other people **bireyci, ferdiyetçi, kendine özgü ● individualistic** /ˌɪndɪˌvɪdʒuə'lɪstɪk/ *adjective* behaving or doing things differently from other people **kendine özgü olan, şahsi olan, şahsına özgü olan**

individuality /ˌɪndɪˌvɪdʒu'æləti/ *noun* [U] the quality of being different from others **kendine özgülük, kişilik, şahsiyet** *The houses had no character and no individuality.*

individually /ˌɪndɪ'vɪdʒuəli/ *adverb* separately and not as a group **teker teker, birer birer, ayrı ayrı** *He apologized to each person individually.*

indoctrinate /ɪn'dɒktrɪneɪt/ *verb* [T] to make someone accept your ideas and beliefs by repeating them so often that they do not consider any others **beyin yıkamak, telkin etmek, (fikir) aşılamak, kafasına sokmak** *They try to indoctrinate young people with their religious beliefs.* ● **indoctrination** /ɪnˌdɒktrɪ'neɪʃ³n/ *noun* [U] *political indoctrination* **bir fikrin aşılanması**

indoor /ˌɪn'dɔ:r/ *adjective* [always before noun] happening, used, or existing in a building **bina içi, kapalı alanda, kapalı** *an indoor swimming pool*

indoors /ˌɪn'dɔ:z/ *adverb* into or inside a building **içeriye, içeride, kapalı alana/alanda** *If you're feeling cold, we can go indoors.*

induce /ɪn'dju:s/ *verb* [T] **1** PERSUADE *formal* to persuade someone to do something **ikna etmek, inandırmak, kandırmak** [+ to do sth] *Nothing would induce me to marry that man!* **2** CAUSE *formal* to cause a particular condition **neden/sebep olmak; yol açmak** *High doses of the drug may induce depression.* **3** BABY to give a woman a drug to make her have a baby earlier than she would naturally **normal zamanından önce doğurması için ilaç vermek; erken doğum yapması için ilaç uygulamak**

inducement /ɪn'dju:smənt/ *noun* [C, U] *formal* something that someone offers you to try to persuade you to do something **teşvik, özendirme** *They offered me more money as an inducement to stay.*

induct /ɪn'dʌkt/ *verb* [T] *formal* to accept someone officially as a member of an organization **göreve getirmek, resmen kabul etmek** *He was inducted into the army in 1943.*

induction /ɪn'dʌkʃ³n/ *noun* [C, U] when someone is officially accepted into a new job or an organization **görevlendirme, atama, göreve getirme** *a two-week induction course*

indulge /ɪn'dʌldʒ/ *verb* **1** [I, T] to let yourself do or have something that you enjoy but which may be bad for you **They indulged in** *a bit of gossip.* ○ [often reflexive] *Go on, indulge yourself! Have another chocolate.* **2** [T] to let someone do or have anything they want **isteklerini yerine getirmek, şımartmak, yüz vermek** *Their children are dreadfully indulged.*

indulgence /ɪn'dʌldʒəns/ *noun* **1** [U] when you eat or drink too much or do anything you want **çok fazla yeme içme, istediğini yapma** **2** [C] something that

you do or have because you want to, not because you need it **şımarma, aklına geleni yapma** *Silk sheets are one of my indulgences.*

indulgent /ɪn'dʌldʒənt/ *adjective* If you are indulgent to someone, you give them anything they want and do not mind if they behave badly. **müsamahakâr, hoşgörülü, sabırlı** *an indulgent father* ● **indulgently** *adverb* *She smiled indulgently at her son.* ⊃See also: self-indulgent. **hoşgörülü bir şekilde**

o▪**industrial** /ɪn'dʌstriəl/ *adjective* **1** connected with industry **sanayi ile ilgili, endüstriyel** *the industrial revolution* **2** with a lot of factories **sınai, endüstriyel** *an industrial city such as Sheffield*

in'dustrial 'action *noun* [U] *UK* when workers stop working or do less work because they want better pay or conditions **daha iyi şartlara sahip olmak için iş bırakma/iş yavaşlatma eylemi**

in,dustrial es'tate *UK* (*US* industrial park) *noun* [C] an area where there are a lot of factories and businesses **sanayi bölgesi, endüstriyel alan**

industrialist /ɪn'dʌstriəlɪst/ *noun* [C] someone who owns or has an important position in a large industrial company **sanayici, fabrikatör**

industrialization /ɪnˌdʌstriəlaɪ'zeɪʃ³n/ *noun* [U] the process of developing industries in a country **sanayileşme** *Japan's rapid industrialization*

industrialized (*also UK* -ised) /ɪn'dʌstriəlaɪzd/ *adjective* Industrialized countries have a lot of industry. **sanayileşmiş** *the industrialized nations*

in'dustrial ,park *US* (*UK* industrial estate) *noun* [C] an area where there are a lot of factories and businesses **sanayi parkı/alanı/bölgesi**

in,dustrial tri'bunal *noun* [C] in the UK, a type of law court that decides on disagreements between companies and their workers **(Birleşik Krallık) iş mahkemesi; çalışanlarla şirketler arasındaki anlaşmazlıkları çözen mahkeme**

industrious /ɪn'dʌstriəs/ *adjective formal* Industrious people work hard. **çalışkan, gayretli ● industriously** *adverb* **gayretli bir şekilde**

┌─────────────────────────────────────┐
│ 🧩 **industry** .... İLE BİRLİKTE KULLANILAN KELİMELER │
└─────────────────────────────────────┘
an **important/major/thriving** industry ● an industry **booms/grows**

o▪**industry** /'ɪndəstri/ *noun* **1** [U] the production of goods in factories **üretim, mamül, mal, fabrikaların ürettiği mallar** *heavy industry* **2** [C] all the companies involved in a particular type of business **sanayi, endüstri, iş kolu, çalışma/üretim alanı** *the entertainment industry*

inedible /ɪ'nedɪbl/ *adjective* not suitable for eating **yenilmez, yenmez** *The meat was inedible.*

ineffective /ˌɪnɪ'fektɪv/ *adjective* If something is ineffective, it does not work well. **etkisiz, tesirsiz, iyi çalışmayan, randımansız ● ineffectively** *adverb* **verimli olmayan bir şekilde ● ineffectiveness** *noun* [U] **verimsizlik**

ineffectual /ˌɪnɪ'fektʃuəl/ *adjective* Ineffectual people or actions do not achieve much. **etkisiz, yeteneksiz, başarısız** *a weak and ineffectual president* ● **ineffectually** *adverb* **etkisiz bir biçimde**

inefficient /ˌɪnɪ'fɪʃ³nt/ *adjective* Inefficient people or things waste time, money, or effort, and do not achieve as much as they should. **verimsiz, yetersiz, verimli; boşuna zaman/para/çaba harcayan** *an inefficient heating system* ● **inefficiently** *adverb* **verimsiz bir şekilde ● inefficiency** /ˌɪnɪ'fɪʃ³nsi/ *noun* [C, U] **verimsizlik**

ineligible /ɪˈnelɪdʒəbl/ *adjective* not allowed to do something or have something **yetersiz, uygun görülmeyen, seçil(e)mez, uygun değil** [+ to do sth] *Foreign residents are ineligible to vote.* ○ *Non-graduates are ineligible for this position.* ● **ineligibility** /ɪˌnelɪdʒəˈbɪləti/ *noun* [U] **hak sahibi olmama durumu**

inept /ɪˈnept/ *adjective* unable to do something well **beceriksiz, yeteneksiz** *socially inept* ○ *She was totally inept at telling jokes.* ● **ineptly** *adverb* **beceriksiz bir şekilde** ● **ineptitude** /ɪˈneptɪtjuːd/ *noun* [U] **beceriksizlik**

inequality ...... İLE BİRLİKTE KULLANILAN KELİMELER
gender / racial / social inequality ● inequality **between** sb and sb

inequality /ˌɪnɪˈkwɒləti/ *noun* [C, U] when some groups in a society have more advantages than others **eşitsizlik** *inequality between the sexes*

inequity /ɪˈnekwəti/ *noun* [C, U] when something is unfair, or something that is unfair **adaletsizlik, insafsızlık** *inequities in the health care system*

inert /ɪˈnɜːt/ *adjective formal* **1** Inert substances do not produce a chemical reaction when another substance is added. **kimyasal tepkime göstermeyen** *inert gases* **2** not moving **hareketsiz, uyuşuk, eylemsiz** *Vanessa lay inert on the sofa.* ● **inertly** *adverb* **diğer bir madde ile kimyasal reaksiyona girmeyen şekilde**

inertia /ɪˈnɜːʃə/ *noun* [U] NO CHANGE when a situation remains the same or changes very slowly **hareketsizlik, cansızlık, atalet** *the inertia of larger organizations* **2** LAZY when you are too lazy to do anything **tembellik, eylemsizlik, yavaşlık, uyuşukluk, üşengeçlik** *International inertia could lead to a major disaster in the war zone.* **3** FORCE the physical force that keeps something in the same position or moving in the same direction **bir şeyin aynı durumda ve yönde durmasını sağlayan fiziksel güç**

inescapable /ˌɪnɪˈskeɪpəbl/ *adjective* An inescapable fact cannot be ignored. **kaçınılmaz, çaresiz, olması muhakkak, mukadder** *Racial discrimination is an inescapable fact of life for some people.* ● **inescapably** *adverb* **gözden kaçamayacak şekilde**

inevitable /ɪˈnevɪtəbl/ *adjective* **1** If something is inevitable, you cannot avoid or prevent it. **kaçınılmaz, çaresiz, olması muhakkak, mukadder** [+ (that)] *It was inevitable that his crime would be discovered.* **2 the inevitable** something that cannot be prevented **yazgı, mukadderat, önlenmesi mümkün olmayan** *Eventually the inevitable happened and he had a heart attack.* ● **inevitably** *adverb* *Inevitably, there was a certain amount of fighting between the groups.* **kaçınılmaz bir biçimde** ● **inevitability** /ɪˌnevɪtəˈbɪləti/ *noun* [U] **kaçınılmazlık**

inexcusable /ˌɪnɪkˈskjuːzəbl/ *adjective* Inexcusable behaviour is too bad to be forgiven. **affedilemez, kabul edilemez, hoşgörülemez, bağışlanamaz, mazur görülemez** *His rudeness was inexcusable.* ● **inexcusably** *adverb* **affedilemeyecek şekilde**

inexhaustible /ˌɪnɪɡˈzɔːstəbl/ *adjective* existing in very large amounts that will never be finished **bitmez, tükenmez, sonsuz** *The Internet is an inexhaustible source of information.*

inexorable /ɪˈneksərəbl/ *adjective formal* continuing without any possibility of being stopped **önlenemeyen, durdurulamayan** *the inexorable progress of civilization* ● **inexorably** *adverb* *These events led inexorably to war.* **durdurulması imkânsız bir şekilde**

inexpensive /ˌɪnɪkˈspensɪv/ *adjective* cheap but of good quality **ucuz fakat kaliteli** *inexpensive children's clothes*

inexperience /ˌɪnɪkˈspɪəriəns/ *noun* [U] when you do not know how to do something because you have not done it or experienced it much before **toyluk, deneyimsizlik, tecrübesizlik** *The accident was probably caused by the driver's inexperience.*

inexperienced /ˌɪnɪkˈspɪəriənst/ *adjective* without much experience or knowledge of something **toy, deneyimsiz, tecrübesiz** *Kennedy was young and inexperienced.*

inexplicable /ˌɪnɪkˈsplɪkəbl/ *adjective* so strange or unusual that you cannot understand or explain it **anlaşılmaz, açıklanması zor, esrarengiz** *To me his behaviour was quite inexplicable.* ● **inexplicably** *adverb* **açıklanamaz bir biçimde**

inextricably /ˌɪnɪkˈstrɪkəbli/ *adverb* If things are inextricably connected, they are so closely connected that you cannot separate them. **içinden çıkılamaz bir halde, karma karışık bir şekilde** *His story is inextricably linked with that of his brother.*

infallible /ɪnˈfæləbl/ *adjective* always right, true, or correct **hata yapmaz, şaşmaz, hiç yanılmaz** *infallible evidence of guilt* ○ *They're experts, but they're not infallible.* ● **infallibility** /ɪnˌfælɪˈbɪləti/ *noun* [U] **doğruluk**

infamous /ˈɪnfəməs/ *adjective* famous for being bad **adı kötüye çıkmış, kötü şöhretli, rezil, alçak** *The area became infamous for its slums.*

infancy /ˈɪnfənsi/ *noun* **1** [U] when you are a baby or a very young child **bebeklik, çocukluk, başlangıç** *Their fourth child died in infancy.* **2 in its infancy** Something that is in its infancy has only just begun to develop. **başlangıç aşamasında, emekleme çağında** *In the 1950s, space travel was in its infancy.*

infant /ˈɪnfənt/ *noun* [C] *formal* a baby or very young child **bebek, küçük çocuk**

infantile /ˈɪnfəntaɪl/ *adjective* behaving like a young child in a way that seems silly **bebekçe, çocukça, sabi gibi** *Don't be so infantile.*

infantry /ˈɪnfəntri/ *noun* [U, group] soldiers who fight on foot **piyade, piyade askeri**

infatuated /ɪnˈfætjueɪtɪd/ *adjective* If you are infatuated with someone, you feel extremely strongly attracted to them. **(delicesine) tutulmuş, kapılmış, mecnun** *As the weeks passed he became totally infatuated with her.* ● **infatuation** /ɪnˌfætjuˈeɪʃᵊn/ *noun* [C, U] **aşık olma**

infect /ɪnˈfekt/ *verb* [T] **1** DISEASE to give someone a disease **(hastalık) bulaştırmak, geçirmek** [often passive] *Thousands of people were infected with the virus.* **2** PLACE/SUBSTANCE If a place, wound, or substance is infected, it contains bacteria or other things that can cause disease. **mikrop kapmak, bulaşmak, kapmak** [often passive] *The wound became infected.* ○ *infected water/meat* ⊃Compare disinfect. **3** FEELING to make other people feel the same way as you do **etkilemek, aynı şeyleri hissetmesini sağlamak, kanına girmek** [often passive] *They became infected by the general excitement.*

∘ **infection** /ɪnˈfekʃᵊn/ *noun* [C, U] a disease in a part of your body that is caused by bacteria or a virus **enfeksiyon, hastalık** *an ear/throat infection*

infectious /ɪnˈfekʃəs/ *adjective* **1** An infectious disease can be passed from one person to another. **geçici, bulaşıcı, sârî** **2** Infectious laughter or feelings quickly spread from one person to another. **geçici, sârî** *infectious enthusiasm*

infer /ɪnˈfɜːr/ *verb* [T] **inferring**, *past* **inferred** *formal* to guess that something is true because of the information that you have **anlam/sonuç/mana çıkarmak** [+ **(that)**] *I* **inferred from** *the number of cups that he was expecting visitors.*

inference /ˈɪnfərəns/ *noun* [C] *formal* a fact that you decide is true because of the information that you have **çıkarım, sonuç, netice** *What inferences can we* **draw** *from this?*

inferior[1] /ɪnˈfɪəriər/ *adjective* not good, or not so good as someone or something else **aşağı, düşük, seviyesiz, alt, sosyal mevkisi düşük** *I've never felt* **inferior to** *anyone.* ○ *They're selling inferior products at inflated prices.* • **inferiority** /ɪnˌfɪəriˈɒrəti/ *noun* [U] when something is not as good as another thing, or when someone feels they are not as good as other people **aşağılık**

inferior[2] /ɪnˈfɪəriər/ *noun* [C] someone who is considered to be less important than other people **aşağılık kişi, adi, bayağı**

inferno /ɪnˈfɜːnəʊ/ *noun* [C] *literary* a very large hot fire **cehennem gibi yangın, büyük yangın**

infertile /ɪnˈfɜːtaɪl/ ⑤ /ɪnˈfɜːrtᵊl/ *adjective* **1** An infertile person or animal cannot have babies. **kısır 2** Infertile land is not good enough for plants to grow well there. **çorak, kıraç, verimsiz** • **infertility** /ˌɪnfəˈtɪləti/ *noun* [U] when a person or piece of land is infertile **kısırlık**

infest /ɪnˈfest/ *verb* [T] If insects, animals, weeds (= plants you do not want), etc infest a place, they cause problems by being there in large numbers. **(böcek, hayvan, ayrık otu) sarmak, sarılmak, istilaya uğramak** [often passive] *The hotel was* **infested** *with cockroaches.*

infidelity /ˌɪnfɪˈdeləti/ *noun* [C, U] when someone who is married or in a relationship has sex with someone who is not their wife, husband, or regular partner **vefasızlık, sadakatsizlik, ihanet**

infighting /ˈɪnˌfaɪtɪŋ/ *noun* [U] arguments between the members of a group **iç çekişme, iç anlaşmazlık, rekabet** *political infighting*

infiltrate /ˈɪnfɪltreɪt/ *verb* [T] to secretly join a group or organization so that you can learn more about them **sızmak, gizlice katılmak, aralarına sızmak** *A journalist managed to infiltrate the gang of drug dealers.* • **infiltration** /ˌɪnfɪlˈtreɪʃᵊn/ *noun* [C, U] **sızma, gizlice katılma** • **infiltrator** *noun* [C] **gizlice içeri sızan kişi**

infinite /ˈɪnfɪnət/ *adjective* **1** extremely large or great **pek çok, sayısız** *She took infinite care with the painting.* **2** without limits or without an end **sonsuz, sınırsız, uçsuz bucaksız** *God's power is infinite.*

infinitely /ˈɪnfɪnətli/ *adverb* very or very much **çok, çok fazla, çok daha, fersah fersah** *Travel is infinitely more comfortable now than it used to be.*

infinitive /ɪnˈfɪnətɪv/ *noun* [C] the basic form of a verb that usually follows 'to'. In the sentence 'She decided to leave.', 'to leave' is an infinitive. **mastar, fiilin ...mek/mak hali**

infinity /ɪnˈfɪnəti/ *noun* [U] **1** time or space that has no end **sonsuzluk, sınırsızlık 2** a number that is larger than all other numbers **(matematik) sonsuzluk sayısı**

infirm /ɪnˈfɜːm/ *adjective formal* weak or ill, especially because of being old **zayıf, dermansız, hâlsiz, hastalıklı**

infirmary /ɪnˈfɜːmᵊri/ *noun* [C] **1** *UK formal* used in the name of some hospitals **hastane** *Leicester Royal Infirmary* **2** *mainly US* a room in a school, prison, etc where people go when they are ill **revir**

infirmity /ɪnˈfɜːməti/ *noun* [C, U] *formal* when someone is weak and unhealthy, or the illness they have **zayıflık, dermansızlık, hâlsizlik**

inflame /ɪnˈfleɪm/ *verb* [T] to cause or increase strong emotions **kızdırmak, heyecanlandırmak** *These brutal attacks have* **inflamed passions** *in a peaceful country.*

inflamed /ɪnˈfleɪmd/ *adjective* If part of your body is inflamed, it is red and often painful and swollen. **iltihaplanmış, kızarmış, şişmiş**

inflammable /ɪnˈflæməbᵊl/ *adjective* Inflammable liquids, gases, or materials burn very easily. **yanıcı, kolay yanan**

inflammation /ˌɪnfləˈmeɪʃᵊn/ *noun* [C, U] a red, painful, and often swollen area in or on a part of your body **kızarı, kızarıklık, şişlik**

inflammatory /ɪnˈflæmətᵊri/ *adjective* intended or likely to cause anger or hate **kışkırtıcı, tahrik edici, kızdırıcı** *inflammatory statements/speeches*

inflatable /ɪnˈfleɪtəbᵊl/ *adjective* An inflatable object has to be filled with air before you can use it. **şişirilebilir** *an inflatable boat*

inflate /ɪnˈfleɪt/ *verb* **1** [I, T] to fill something with air or gas, or to become filled with air or gas **şişirmek, şişmek 2** [T] to make something such as a number, price, etc larger **(fiyat, rakam vb.) zam yapmak, artırmak, şişirmek, fahiş hâle getirmek**

inflated /ɪnˈfleɪtɪd/ *adjective* Inflated prices, costs, numbers, etc are higher than they should be. **aşırı, fahiş, yüksek**

o→ **inflation** /ɪnˈfleɪʃᵊn/ *noun* [U] the rate at which prices increase, or a continuing increase in prices **gereksiz artış, enflasyon** *low/rising inflation*

inflationary /ɪnˈfleɪʃᵊnᵊri/ *adjective* likely to make prices rise **fiyatları gereksiz artıran, enflasyona yol açan, enflasyoncu**

inflection /ɪnˈflekʃᵊn/ *noun* [C, U] **1** the way the end of a word changes to show tense, plural forms, etc **(dilbilgisi) çekim 2** the way that your voice goes up and down when you speak, for example to show that you are asking a question **tonlama, ses perdesi değişimi, sesin yükselip alçalması**

inflexible /ɪnˈfleksəbᵊl/ *adjective* **1** Inflexible rules, opinions, beliefs, etc do not change easily. **değiştirilemez** *a cold and inflexible man* **2** Inflexible materials do not bend easily. **eğilmez, bükülmez, katı, esnek olmayan** • **inflexibility** /ɪnˌfleksəˈbɪləti/ *noun* [U] **sabitlik, değişmezlik**

inflict /ɪnˈflɪkt/ *verb* [T] to make someone suffer by doing something unpleasant to them **vermek, yüklemek, uğratmak** *I would never have* **inflicted** *such suffering* **on** *you.*

in-flight /ˈɪnˌflaɪt/ *adjective* [always before noun] happening or available during a flight **uçuş esnasındaki** *in-flight entertainment*

🧩 **influence** .... İLE BİRLİKTE KULLANILAN KELİMELER

exert/have/wield influence • **bad/considerable/disruptive/good/powerful** influence • influence **on/over** sb/sth • be **under** the influence **of** sb/sth

o→ **influence**[1] /ˈɪnfluəns/ *noun* **1** [C, U] the power to affect how someone thinks or behaves, or how something develops **etki, nüfuz, sözü geçerlik** *The drug companies have a lot of* **influence on** *doctors.* **2** [C] someone or something that has an effect on another person or thing **nüfuz, etki, tesir** *His grandfather was a strong* **influence on** *him.*

o=**influence²** /'ɪnfluəns/ *verb* [T] to affect or change how someone or something develops, behaves, or thinks **etkilemek, tesir etmek, etkili olmak** *Many factors influence a film's success.* ○ [often passive] *Were you influenced by anybody when you were starting your career?*

influential /ˌɪnfluˈenʃᵊl/ *adjective* having a lot of influence **etkili, nüfuzlu, hatırlı, forslu, söz sahibi** *an influential figure in modern jazz*

influenza /ˌɪnfluˈenzə/ *noun* [U] *formal* flu (= an illness like a very bad cold, that makes you feel hot and weak) **grip**

influx /'ɪnflʌks/ *noun* [C] the arrival of a lot of people or things at the same time **doluşma, üşüşme, akın** [usually singular] *The 1990s saw an influx of foreign players into British football.*

info /'ɪnfəʊ/ *noun* [U] *informal short for* information **bilgi, haber, malûmat**

inform /ɪnˈfɔːm/ *verb* [T] **1** to tell someone about something **haber vermek, bilgi vermek, bildirmek** *If he calls me again, I shall inform the police.* ○ [+ (that)] *He informed us that we would have to leave.* **2** [+ to give someone information about something **bir şey hakkında birine bilgi vermek** [often passive] *Patients should be informed about the risks.* ○ *He keeps his parents informed of his whereabouts.*

inform against/on sb *phrasal verb* to tell the police about something illegal that someone has done **ihbar etmek**

informal /ɪnˈfɔːmᵊl/ *adjective* **1** relaxed and friendly **senli benli, rahat, samimi, teklifsiz** *an informal discussion/meeting* **2** suitable for normal situations **günlük, sıradan, her duruma uygun** *informal clothes* ○ *informal language* • **informality** /ˌɪnfɔːˈmæləti/ *noun* [U] **gayrıresmî** • **informally** *adverb* **gayrıresmî bir biçimde**

informant /ɪnˈfɔːmənt/ *noun* [C] someone who gives information to another person **bilgi veren/bildiren kişi; haber/bilgi kaynağı** *Our survey is based on over 200 informants.*

information ...... İLE BİRLİKTE KULLANILAN KELİMELER

accurate/confidential/detailed/further/useful information • **access/exchange/gather/give/ need/provide** information • information **about/on** sth

information ...... BAŞKA BİR DEYİŞLE

Çoğul bir isim olan **details** bir arada bulunan bilgileri tanımlamada kullanılır. *Please send me details of your training courses.*
Çoğul isimler olan **directions** ve **instructions** kelimeleri bir şeyin nasıl yapılacağına dair bilgi veren ifadelerde kullanılır. *Just follow the directions/instructions on the label.*
Çoğul bir isim olan **directions** bir yere nasıl gidileceğini gösteren ifade olarak da kullanılır. *We had to stop and ask for directions.*
Data kelimesi rakam veya değişkenlik göstermeyen bilgiyi tanımlamada kullanılır. *Our consultants have been collecting financial data.*
Bir konu ile ilgili yazılı bilgi **literature** olarak tanımlanır. *Some literature on our current policy is enclosed.*

o=**information** /ˌɪnfəˈmeɪʃᵊn/ *noun* [U] facts about a situation, person, event, etc **bilgi, malumat, haber** *a vital piece of information* ○ *Police are urging anyone with information about the crime to contact them.*

information
Unutmayın! **Information** kelimesinin çoğul hali yoktur. **Informations** denmez. **Informations** denmemesi gerekir. **Information, some information** veya **pieces of information** doğru kullanım şekilleridir: *I hope these informations are helpful.* Yanlış cümle örneği *I hope this information is helpful.*

infor,mation tech'nology *noun* [U] (*abbreviation* IT) the use of computers and other electronic equipment to store and send information **bilgi teknolojisi**

informative /ɪnˈfɔːmətɪv/ *adjective* containing a lot of useful facts **tanıtıcı, bilgilendiren** *a very informative lecture*

informed /ɪnˈfɔːmd/ *adjective* having a lot of information or knowledge about something **haberdar, bigi sahibi** *an informed choice/decision* ⊃See also: well-informed.

informer /ɪnˈfɔːməʳ/ *noun* [C] someone who secretly gives information to the police about a crime **ihbarcı, muhbir, jurnalci, gammazlayan, ispiyonlayan**

infraction /ɪnˈfrækʃᵊn/ *noun* [C, U] *formal* when someone breaks a rule or the law **ihlal, bozma, uymama**

infrared /ˌɪnfrəˈred/ *adjective* Infrared light feels warm but cannot be seen. **kızıl ötesi, enfraruj**

infrastructure /'ɪnfrəˌstrʌktʃəʳ/ *noun* [C] the basic systems, such as transport and communication, that a country or organization uses in order to work effectively **altyapı** [usually singular] *The country's infrastructure is in ruins.*

infrequent /ɪnˈfriːkwənt/ *adjective* not happening very often **seyrek, nadir** • **infrequently** *adverb* **nadiren**

infringe /ɪnˈfrɪndʒ/ *verb* [T] **1** *formal* to break a law or rule **bozmak, ihlal etmek, uymamak, çiğnemek** *They infringed building regulations.* **2** (*also* infringe on) to limit someone's rights or freedom **birinin hakkına, özgürlüğüne tecavüz etmek, el uzatmak** *This law infringes on a citizen's right to bear arms.* • **infringement** *noun* [C, U] *an infringement of copyright* **ihlal**

infuriate /ɪnˈfjʊərieɪt/ *verb* [T] to make someone very angry **çok kızdırmak, çileden çıkarmak, tepesini attırmak, öfkelendirmek** *What really infuriated me was the fact that he'd lied.* • **infuriating** *adjective* extremely annoying **öfkelendiren, çok kızdıran**

infuse /ɪnˈfjuːz/ *verb* **1** [T] *formal* to fill someone or something with a lot of a particular emotion or quality **telkin etmek, aşılamak** [often passive] *His work is infused with a love for tradition.* **2** [I, T] to put something into a liquid so that its taste goes into the liquid **suya bir şey katmak; (suyun) bir şey katarak tadını değiştirmek**

infusion /ɪnˈfjuːʒᵊn/ *noun* [C, U] *formal* when one thing is added to another thing to make it stronger or better **demleme, ilave etme, katma** *an infusion of cash*

ingenious /ɪnˈdʒiːniəs/ *adjective* very clever and involving new ideas, equipment, or methods **dâhice, çok akıllıca, zeki, yaratıcı** *an ingenious idea/scheme/solution* • **ingeniously** *adverb* **dâhice**

ingenuity /ˌɪndʒɪˈnjuːəti/ *noun* [U] skill at inventing things or finding new ways to solve problems **yaratıcılık; hüner, akıllılık, marifet**

ingest /ɪnˈdʒest/ *verb* [T] *formal* to eat or drink something **yemek içmek, yutmak, mideye indirmek** • **ingestion** *noun* [U] **yeme-içme**

ingrained /ɪnˈɡreɪnd/ *adjective* **1** Ingrained beliefs, behaviour, problems, etc have existed for a long time and are difficult to change. **kemikleşmiş, yerleşmiş, iyice, kökleşmiş** *For most of us, watching television is a deeply* **ingrained** *habit*. **2** Ingrained dirt has got under the surface of something and is difficult to remove. (kir) içine işlemiş

ingratiate /ɪnˈɡreɪʃieɪt/ *verb* **ingratiate yourself (with sb)** to try to make people like you by doing things to please them **(yağcılık yaparak) kendini sevdirmeye çalışmak, şirin gözükmek, maskarlık yapmak, göze girmeye çalışmak** ● **ingratiating** *adjective* Ingratiating behaviour is done to try to make people like you. **sokulgan, arkadaş canlısı, şirin gözüken, yaranmaya çalışan** *an* **ingratiating** *smile/manner*

ingratitude /ɪnˈɡrætɪtjuːd/ *noun* [U] when someone is not grateful for something **nankörlük, iyilik bilmezlik**

a **basic/essential/vital** ingredient ● an ingredient **in/of** sth

ingredient /ɪnˈɡriːdiənt/ *noun* [C] **1** one of the different foods that a particular type of food is made from **bileşimi/karışımı oluşturan madde, malzemeler 2** one of the parts of something successful **başarıya etki eden parçalardan biri; etken unsur** *Trust is an essential* **ingredient** *in a successful marriage*.

inhabit /ɪnˈhæbɪt/ *verb* [T] *formal* to live in a place **oturmak, yaşamak** [often passive] *an area inhabited by artists and writers*

inhabitant /ɪnˈhæbɪtᵊnt/ *noun* [C] someone who lives in a particular place **yaşayanlar, sakinler, oturanlar, ikâmet eden kişi** *a city with 10 million inhabitants*

inhabited /ɪnˈhæbɪtɪd/ *adjective* An inhabited place or building has people living in it. **yaşanılan, ikâmet edilen** *Is the island inhabited?*

inhale /ɪnˈheɪl/ *verb* [I, T] *formal* **1** to breathe air, smoke, or gas into your lungs **nefes almak, içine çekmek, solumak, teneffüs etmek 2** *US informal* to eat something very quickly **hızlıca yemek, yutmak** *Slow down, you're inhaling that pizza!*

inherent /ɪnˈherᵊnt/ *adjective* existing as a natural and basic part of something **kendinde/yapısında var olan; doğasında olan** *The desire for freedom is* **inherent** *in all people.* ● **inherently** *adverb There's nothing inherently wrong with his ideas.* **içten gelircesine**

inherit /ɪnˈherɪt/ *verb* [T] FROM DEAD PERSON **1** to receive possessions or money from someone who has died **miras olarak almak** *In 1842 he inherited a small estate near Liverpool.* **2** QUALITY to have the same physical or mental characteristics as one of your parents or grandparents **kalıtım yoluyla geçmek, aileden gelmek** *Miranda has inherited her father's red hair.* **3** PROBLEM If you inherit a problem, situation, or belief, it is passed on to you by someone who had it before. **başkasından geçmek/devralmak** *The mayor will inherit a city hopelessly in debt.*

inheritance /ɪnˈherɪtᵊns/ *noun* [C, U] money or possessions that someone gives you when they die **miras, kalıt, veraset** *Nick has sold off much of his inheritance.*

inhibit /ɪnˈhɪbɪt/ *verb* [T] **1** to make the progress or growth of something slower **yavaşlatmak, engellemek, dizginlemek** *a product which inhibits the growth of harmful bacteria* **2** to make it more difficult for someone to do something **güçleştirmek, zora sokmak** *Their threats* **inhibited** *witnesses* **from** *giving evidence.*

inhibited /ɪnˈhɪbɪtɪd/ *adjective* not confident enough to say or do what you want **çekingen, ürkek, sıkılgan**

have no inhibitions **about** doing sth ● **lose** your inhibitions

inhibition /ˌɪnhɪˈbɪʃᵊn/ *noun* [C, U] a feeling of embarrassment or worry that prevents you from saying or doing what you want **çekingenlik, ürkeklik, sıkılganlık, tutukluk** *The whole point about dancing is to lose all your inhibitions.*

inhospitable /ˌɪnhɒsˈpɪtəbl/ *adjective* **1** An inhospitable place is not pleasant or easy to live in because it is too hot, cold, etc. **(yer) sıcak/soğuk vs. den dolayı yaşanmaz, barınılmaz, oturulmaz** *the world's most inhospitable deserts* **2** not friendly towards people who are visiting you **misafir/konuk sevmez; soğuk**

in-house /ˌɪnˈhaʊs/ *adjective, adverb* done in the offices of a company or organization by employees of that company **yerinde yapılan/hizmetiçi olarak; kendi çalışanlarınca yapılan** *in-house training of staff*

inhuman /ɪnˈhjuːmən/ *adjective* extremely cruel **vahşi, acımasız, merhametsiz, zalim** *the inhuman treatment of prisoners*

inhumane /ˌɪnhjuːˈmeɪm/ *adjective* treating people or animals in a cruel way **insanlık dışı, insafsız, acımasız, zalim, eziyet eden** *inhumane experiments on monkeys* ● **inhumanely** *adverb* **insanlık dışı bir biçimde**

inhumanity /ˌɪnhjuːˈmænəti/ *noun* [U] extremely cruel behaviour **insafsızlık, acımasızlık, gaddarlık, barbarlık** *the inhumanity of war*

initial¹ /ɪˈnɪʃᵊl/ *adjective* [always before noun] first, or happening at the beginning **ilk, başta olan, ilk meydana gelen** *My initial reaction was one of anger.*

initial² /ɪˈnɪʃᵊl/ *noun* [C] the first letter of a name **ismin baş harfi** [usually plural] *His initials are S.G.M.*

initial³ /ɪˈnɪʃᵊl/ *verb* [T] *UK* **initialling**, *past* **initialled**, *US* **initialing**, *past* **initialed** to write your initials on something **isminin baş harflerini yazmak**

initialize /ɪˈnɪʃᵊlaɪz/ *verb* [T] to make a computer program ready to use **bilgisayar programını kullanıma hazırlamak**

initially /ɪˈnɪʃᵊli/ *adverb* at the beginning **ilk başta, ilkin, ilk olarak, başlangıçta** *The situation was worse than they initially thought.*

initiate /ɪˈnɪʃieɪt/ *verb* [T] **1** to make something begin **başlamak, başlatmak, ön ayak olmak** [often passive] *The reforms were initiated by Gorbachev.* **2** to make someone a member of a group or organization in a special ceremony, or to show someone how to do an activity **özel törenle üyeliğe almak/kabul etmek, sokmak; nasıl yapılacağını göstermek; kurallarını/esaslarını/sırlarını öğretmek** *At the age of 50, he was initiated into the priesthood.* ● **initiation** /ɪˌnɪʃiˈeɪʃᵊn/ *noun* [C, U] **başlatma**

initiative /ɪˈnɪʃətɪv/ *noun* **1** [C] a plan or activity that is done to solve a problem or improve a situation **girişim, teşebbüs** *a* **new** *government* **initiative** *to reduce crime* **2** [U] the ability to make decisions and do things without needing to be told what to do **kendi kendine karar verebilme kabiliyeti** *We need someone who can work* **on their own initiative** (= without anyone telling them what to do). **3 take the initiative** to be the first person to do something that solves a problem or improves a situation **öncü/önayak olmak, başı çekmek** *Jackson had taken the initiative and prepared a report.*

inject /ɪnˈdʒekt/ *verb* [T] **1** DRUG to put a drug into someone's body using a needle **iğne yapmak, şırınga etmek** *Phil's diabetic and has to* **inject** *himself* **with** *insulin every day.* **2** IMPROVE to add a good quality to something **(değer, kalite vb.) katmak, ilave etmek,**

eklemek *The new teacher has injected* a bit of enthusiasm *into the school.* **3** MONEY to provide a large amount of money for a plan, service, organization, etc **(para) sağlamak, vermek, temin etmek, katmak, eklemek** *The government plans to inject £100 million into schools.*

injection

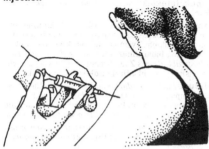

injection /ɪn'dʒekʃ°n/ *noun* **1** [C, U] when someone puts a drug into your body using a needle **iğne, enjeksiyon** *an injection of insulin* **2** [C] when a large amount of money is provided for a plan, service, organization, etc **(para) sağlama, verme, temin, katma, ekleme** *The university has welcomed the $5 million cash injection.*

injunction /ɪn'dʒʌŋkʃ°n/ *noun* [C] an official order from a court that prevents someone from doing something **mahkeme emri, resmî karar/emir** *The courts have issued an injunction to prevent the book from being published.*

⊶**injure** /'ɪndʒə^r/ *verb* [T] to hurt a person, animal, or part of your body **yaralamak, incitmek** *She injured her ankle when she fell.*

injured /'ɪndʒəd/ *adjective* hurt **yaralanmış, incinmiş** *Fortunately, no one was seriously injured in the accident.*

injury ...... İLE BİRLİKTE KULLANILAN KELİMELER

a fatal/major/minor/serious injury • cause/prevent/receive/recover from/suffer an injury • an injury to sth

⊶**injury** /'ɪndʒ°ri/ *noun* [C, U] damage to someone's body in an accident or attack **zarar, yaralanma, zedelenme, incitme** *head injuries* ○ *The passenger in the car escaped with minor injuries.* ⊃See also: add **insult**² to injury.

injustice /ɪn'dʒʌstɪs/ *noun* [C, U] a situation or action in which people are treated unfairly **adaletsizlik, haksızlık** *the fight against racial injustice*

ink /ɪŋk/ *noun* [C, U] a coloured liquid that you use for writing, printing, or drawing **mürekkep**

inkling /'ɪŋklɪŋ/ *noun* have an inkling to think that something might be true or might happen **his** *She had absolutely no inkling that we were planning the party.*

inland¹ /'ɪnlənd/ *adjective* [always before noun] Inland areas, lakes, towns, etc are a long way from the coast. **(ülke, bölge, arazi vb.) iç, içte olan; denizden uzak**

inland² /'ɪnlænd/ *adverb* towards the middle of a country and away from the coast **içlere/iç bölgelere doğru**

in-laws /'ɪnlɔːz/ *noun* [plural] *informal* the parents of your husband or wife, or other people in their family **eşlerden her birinin hısım ve akrabaları**

inlet /'ɪnlet/ *noun* [C] a narrow part of a sea, river, or lake where it flows into a curve in the land **koy, küçük körfez**

,**in-line 'skate** *noun* [C] (*also* rollerblades [plural]) a boot with a single line of wheels on the bottom, used for moving across the ground **paten, paten ayakkabısı** ⊃Orta kısımdaki renkli sayfalarına bakınız.

inmate /'ɪnmeɪt/ *noun* [C] someone who lives in a prison or in a hospital for people with mental illnesses **(hapishane, tımarhane/hastane vb.) sakin, oda arkadaşı, tutuklu**

inn /ɪn/ *noun* [C] a small hotel in the countryside **han, şehir dışında küçük otel**

innate /ɪ'neɪt/ *adjective* An innate quality or ability is one that you were born with, not one you have learned. **Allah vergisi, doğuştan gelen** *He has an innate desire to win.* • **innately** *adverb* **doğuştan gelen bir biçimde**

inner /'ɪnə^r/ *adjective* [always before noun] **1** on the inside, or near the middle of something **iç, dahili** *The monastery is built around an inner courtyard.* ⊃Opposite **outer.** **2** Inner feelings, thoughts, etc are ones that you do not show or tell other people. **(duygular, düşünceler vs.) yürekte, içte, gizli, görülmeyen, özel** *a profound sense of inner peace*

,**inner 'circle** *noun* [C] the small group of people who control an organization, political party, etc **yakın çevresi, yakın çalışma arkadaşları; beyin takımı** *The statement was made by a member of the President's inner circle.*

,**inner 'city** *noun* [C] the part of a city that is closest to the centre, often where buildings are in a bad condition and there are social problems **şehir merkezine yakın yoksul mahalle** *a plan to tackle rising crime in inner cities* • **inner-city** /'ɪnə,sɪti/ *adjective* [always before noun] *inner-city schools* **fakirlerin oturduğu mahalle**

innermost /'ɪnəməʊst/ *adjective* [always before noun] **1** Your innermost feelings, thoughts, etc are the most private ones that you do not want other people to know about. **en derindeki/gizli 2** *formal* closest to the middle of something **en içteki**

inning /'ɪnɪŋ/ *noun* [C] one of the nine playing periods in a baseball game **beyzbol oyununda 9 oyun devresinden biri**

innings /'ɪnɪŋz/ *noun* [C] *plural* innings the period of time in a game of cricket when one player or one team hits the ball **(kriket oyununda) topa vurma sırası**

innit /'ɪnɪt/ *exclamation UK very informal* used to change a statement into a question '**Değil mi?**', '**Öyle mi?**' *It's wrong, innit.*

innocence ...... İLE BİRLİKTE KULLANILAN KELİMELER

proclaim/protest/prove sb's innocence

innocence /'ɪnəs°ns/ *noun* [U] **1** when someone is not guilty of a crime **suçsuzluk, masumiyet** *She fought to prove her son's innocence.* **2** when someone does not have much experience of life and does not know about the bad things that happen **saflık, arılık, duruluk** *the innocence of childhood*

⊶**innocent** /'ɪnəs°nt/ *adjective* **1** NOT GUILTY not guilty of committing a crime **suçsuz, masum** *He claims to be innocent of the crime.* **2** NO EXPERIENCE not having much experience of life and not knowing about the bad things that happen **saf, tecrübesiz, toy** *an innocent young woman* **3** NOT DESERVED used to emphasize that someone who was hurt had done nothing wrong **hiçbir kabahati olmayan, masum** *Several innocent civilians were killed in the bombing.* **4** NOT INTENDED TO HARM not intended to harm or upset anyone **masumane, kasıtsız, üzmek/zarar vermek niyetinde olmayan** *It was an innocent mistake.* ● **innocently** *adverb* **masumca**

innocuous /ɪ'nɒkjuəs/ *adjective* not likely to upset or harm anyone **zararsız, masum, kasıtsız** *The parcel looked innocuous enough.* ● **innocuously** *adverb* **zararsızca**

innovation /ˌɪnəʊ'veɪʃ°n/ *noun* [C, U] a new idea or method that is being tried for the first time, or the use of such ideas or methods **yenilik, buluş** *the latest innovations in education*

innovative /'ɪnəvətɪv/ ⓤ /'ɪnəveɪtɪv/ *adjective* using new methods or ideas **yenilikçi, yeni fikir ve yöntemleri kullanan** *an innovative approach to programme making*

innovator /'ɪnəveɪtəʳ/ *noun* [C] someone who uses or designs new methods or products **yenilikçi**

innuendo /ˌɪnju'endəʊ/ *noun* [C, U] *plural* **innuendoes** or **innuendos** a remark that intentionally suggests something about sex, or something unpleasant about someone, without saying it directly **(cinsellik, hoş olmayan şey vs.) ima, dokundurma, kinaye, sezindirme** *The advertisement was criticized for its **sexual** innuendo.*

innumerable /ɪ'nju:m°rəbl/ *adjective* very many, or too many to count **sayısız, haddi hesabı olmayan, pek çok** *innumerable problems*

inoffensive /ˌɪnə'fensɪv/ *adjective* not likely to upset anyone or make them angry **zararsız, dokunmayan, etkilemeyen, kızdırmayan** *an inoffensive colour*

inordinate /ɪ'nɔ:dɪnət/ *adjective formal* much more than is usual or suitable **aşırı, haddinden fazla, gereğinden çok** *James seems to spend an **inordinate amount** of time on his computer.* ● **inordinately** *adverb* **aşırı bir biçimde**

inorganic /ˌɪnɔ:'gænɪk/ *adjective* not being or consisting of living things **cansız şeylerden oluşan, cansız, inorganik** *inorganic waste*

in-patient /'ɪnˌpeɪʃ°nt/ *noun* [C] someone who stays in hospital for one or more nights while they are receiving treatment **yatan hasta, tedavi amaçlı hastanede bir iki gece kalan**

input¹ /'ɪnpʊt/ *noun* 1 [IDEAS] [C, U] ideas, money, effort, etc that you put into an activity or process in order to help it succeed **katkı, girdi, yardım** *Input from students is used to develop new and exciting courses.* 2 [ELECTRICAL] [C, U] electrical energy that is put into a machine to make it work **elektrik akımı** 3 [COMPUTER] [U] information that is put into a computer **bilgisayara girilen bilgi/girdi**

input² /'ɪnpʊt/ *verb* [T] **inputting**, *past* **inputted** or **input** to put information into a computer **bilgisayara bilgi girmek**

inquest .... İLE BİRLİKTE KULLANILAN KELİMELER

hold an inquest ● an inquest **into** sth

inquest /'ɪŋkwest/ *noun* [C] a legal process to discover the cause of an unexpected death **yasal soruşturma** *There will be an **inquest into** the deaths of the three men.*

inquire *formal* (*also UK* **enquire**) /ɪn'kwaɪəʳ/ *verb* [I, T] to ask someone for information about something **sormak, soruşturmak** *If you like languages, why don't you **inquire about** French classes in your area?* ○ [+ question word] *Vronsky inquired whether the picture was for sale.* ● **inquirer** (*also UK* **enquirer**) *noun* [C] **araştırmacı** **inquire after sb** *phrasal verb UK formal* to ask someone for information about someone else's health and what

they are doing, in order to be polite **hal hatır sormak** *Jane inquired after your mother.* **inquire into sth** *phrasal verb formal* to try to discover the facts about something **araştırmak, soruşturmak** *a report inquiring into the causes of the region's housing problem*

inquiring (*also UK* **enquiring**) /ɪn'kwaɪərɪŋ/ *adjective* [always before noun] 1 always wanting to learn new things **araştırıcı, sorgulayan, öğrenmek isteyen** *an inquiring mind* 2 An inquiring expression on your face shows that you want to know something. **yüzünde sorgulayıcı bir ifade taşıyan** ● **inquiringly** *adverb* **araştırır bir şekilde**

inquiry .... İLE BİRLİKTE KULLANILAN KELİMELER

make/receive an inquiry ● an inquiry **about** sth

inquiry (*also UK* **enquiry**) /ɪn'kwaɪəri/ *noun* 1 [QUESTION] [C] *formal* a question that you ask when you want more information **araştırma** *The company has received a lot of **inquiries about** its new Internet service.* 2 [OFFICIAL PROCESS] [C] an official process to discover the facts about something bad that has happened **soruşturma** *There will be an official **inquiry into** the train crash.* 3 [ASKING QUESTIONS] [U] *formal* the process of asking questions in order to get information **soruşturma, araştırma**

inquisitive /ɪn'kwɪzətɪv/ *adjective* wanting to discover as much as you can about things **meraklı, öğrenmeye hevesli** *an inquisitive child* ● **inquisitively** *adverb* **meraklı bir biçimde** ● **inquisitiveness** *noun* [U] **araştırmacı**

inroads /'ɪnrəʊdz/ *noun* **make inroads (into/on sth)** to start to become successful by getting sales, power, votes, etc that someone else had before **satış/güç/oy elde ederek başarılı olmaya başlamak** *Women have made great inroads into the male-dominated legal profession.*

the ˌins and ˈouts *noun* all the details and facts about something **bütün ayrıntı ve gerçekler** *Tolya is someone who knows **the ins and outs** of the music industry.*

insane /ɪn'seɪn/ *adjective* 1 seriously mentally ill **deli, akli dengesini yitirmiş; çıldırmış** *a hospital for the criminally insane* 2 very silly or stupid **çok aptal, salak** *an insane decision* ● **insanely** *adverb* **akıl dışı bir şekilde**

insanity /ɪn'sænəti/ *noun* [U] 1 when someone is seriously mentally ill **delilik, çılgınlık** 2 when something is extremely stupid **aptallık, salaklık** *It would be insanity to expand the business at the moment.*

insatiable /ɪn'seɪʃəbl/ *adjective* always wanting more of something **doymak bilmeyen, açgözlü, obur, pisboğaz** *There was an **insatiable demand** for pictures of Princess Diana.* ● **insatiably** *adverb* **doymak bimez bir biçimde**

inscribe /ɪn'skraɪb/ *verb* [T] *formal* to write words in a book or cut them on an object **yazmak; kazımak** [often passive] *The child's bracelet was inscribed with the name 'Amy'.*

inscription /ɪn'skrɪpʃ°n/ *noun* [C, U] words that are written or cut in something **yazıt** *The inscription on the gravestone was almost illegible.*

o--**insect** /'ɪnsekt/ *noun* [C] a small creature with six legs, for example a bee or a fly **böcek**

insecticide /ɪn'sektɪsaɪd/ *noun* [C, U] a chemical that is used for killing insects **böcek ilacı**

insecure /ˌɪnsɪ'kjʊəʳ/ *adjective* 1 having no confidence in yourself and what you can do **kendine güveni olmayan** *a shy, insecure teenager* 2 not safe or protected

insect

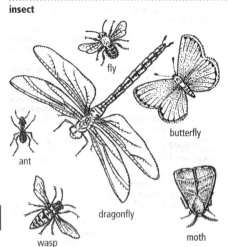

fly

butterfly

ant

dragonfly

wasp

moth

emniyetsiz, korumasız, sakat Many of our staff are worried because their jobs are insecure. ● **insecurely** *adverb* güvensiz bir biçimde ● **insecurity** /ˌɪnsɪˈkjʊərəti/ *noun* [U] güvensizlik

insensitive /ɪnˈsensətɪv/ *adjective* **1** not noticing or not caring about other people's feelings **duyarsız, vurdum duymaz, aldırışsız** *an insensitive remark* ○ *He was completely insensitive to Maria's feelings.* **2** not able to feel something, or not affected by it **hissetmeyen, etkilenmeyen** *She was insensitive to the pain.* ● **insensitively** *adverb* kayıtsız, umursamaz bir şekilde ● **insensitivity** /ɪnˌsensəˈtɪvəti/ *noun* [U] umursamazlık

inseparable /ɪnˈsepᵊrəbl/ *adjective* **1** *formal* Two things that are inseparable are so closely connected that you cannot consider them separately. **ayrılmaz, bitişik** *Rossetti's work was inseparable from his life.* **2** People who are inseparable are always together because they are such good friends. **birbirinden ayrılmaz; yakın arkadaş olan, ikiz kardeş gibi** ● **inseparably** *adverb* ayrılmaz bir şekilde

insert¹ /ɪnˈsɜːt/ *verb* [T] *formal* **1** to put something into something else **sokmak, yerleştirmek** *Insert the coin in the slot.* **2** to add something to the middle of a document or piece of writing **bir belge/yazının arasına sokmak/yerleştirmek/ilave etmek** *He inserted a new paragraph.* ● **insertion** /ɪnˈsɜːʃᵊn/ *noun* [C, U] ekleme

insert² /ˈɪnsɜːt/ *noun* [C] something that is made to go inside or into something else **araya yerleştirilen/sokulan; ilave, ek** *The leaflet is designed as an insert for a magazine.*

inshore /ˌɪnˈʃɔːʳ/ *adjective, adverb* near or towards the coast **sahile/kıyıya yakın/doğru** *inshore waters*

o⁻**inside¹** /ˌɪnˈsaɪd/ *noun* **1 the inside** the part of something that is under its surface **içi, içinde, iç kısım/taraf** *I cleaned the inside of the oven.* **2 inside out** If a piece of clothing is inside out, the part that is usually outside is on the inside. **tersyüz, içi dışında, ters** *Harry, you've got your sweater on inside out again.* **3 know sth inside out** to know everything about something **içini dışını bilmek; her şeyini bilmek**

inside² /ˌɪnˈsaɪd/ *adjective* **1** [always before noun] in or on the part of something under its surface **iç** *Put your wal-*

let in the inside pocket of your jacket. **2 inside information/knowledge, etc** information that is only known by people who are part of an organization, group, etc **gizli bilgi, sadece ilgilisinin bildiği bilgi/malumat**

o⁻**inside³** /ˌɪnˈsaɪd/ *preposition* **1** [CONTAINER] in or into a room, building, container, etc **içinde, içeride** *There were some keys inside the box.* ○ *Luckily, no one was inside the house when the fire started.* **2** [TIME] in less than a particular length of time **(zaman) içinde** *The doctor's promised to be here inside an hour.* **3** [ORGANIZATION] in an organization, group, etc and not known or happening outside it **(grup, kurum) içinde, içeride** *rumours of disputes inside the company*

o⁻**inside⁴** /ˌɪnˈsaɪd/ *adverb* **1** [CONTAINER] in or into a room, building, container, etc **içeriye, içeriye doğru** *I'm freezing, let's go back inside.* **2** [FEELING] If you have a feeling inside, people do not know about it if you do not tell them. **(duygu) içinde, kendisinde, gizli, açıkta olmayan** *She looked calm but was feeling nervous inside.* **3** [PRISON] *informal* in prison **hapiste olan**

insider /ɪnˈsaɪdəʳ/ *noun* [C] someone who knows about a business or organization because they are part of it **bir iş/kuruma ait olup hakkında çok şey bilen** *Industry insiders say they are surprised by the company's success.* ➔Compare **outsider**.

insides /ˌɪnˈsaɪdz/ *noun* [plural] *informal* your stomach **mide**

insidious /ɪnˈsɪdiəs/ *adjective* having harmful effects that happen gradually so you do not notice them for a long time **sinsi, gizlice zarar veren, saman altından su yürüten** *the insidious effects of pollution* ● **insidiously** *adverb* sinsice ● **insidiousness** *noun* [U] sinsilik

---

🧩 insight .... İLE BİRLİKTE KULLANILAN KELİMELER

gain/give/provide an insight **into** sth ● a **fascinating/rare/unique/valuable** insight

---

insight /ˈɪnsaɪt/ *noun* [C, U] the ability to understand what something is really like, or an example of this **(bir şeyin içyüzünü) anlama/kavrama yeteneği** *The book provides a fascinating insight into the world of art.*

insignia /ɪnˈsɪɡniə/ *noun* [C] *plural* **insignia** a piece of cloth or a symbol that shows someone's military rank or official position **rütbe, rozet, işaret, nişan**

insignificant /ˌɪnsɪɡˈnɪfɪkᵊnt/ *adjective* not important or large enough to consider or worry about **önemsiz, değersiz, dikkate değmez, ehemmiyetsiz** *insignificant differences* ● **insignificance** /ˌɪnsɪɡˈnɪfɪkᵊns/ *noun* [U] önemsizlik ● **insignificantly** *adverb* manasızca

insincere /ˌɪnsɪnˈsɪəʳ/ *adjective* pretending to feel something that you do not really feel, or not meaning what you say **samimiyetsiz, sahte** *an insincere apology* ● **insincerely** *adverb* içten olmayan bir şekilde ● **insincerity** /ˌɪnsɪnˈserəti/ *noun* [U] samimiyetsizlik

insinuate /ɪnˈsɪnjueɪt/ *verb* [T] to suggest that something bad is true without saying it directly **ima etmek, üstü kapalı anlatmak, sezdirmek** [+ that] *She insinuated that Perez had lied.* ● **insinuation** /ɪnˌsɪnjuˈeɪʃᵊn/ *noun* [C, U] ima

insipid /ɪnˈsɪpɪd/ *adjective* not interesting, exciting, or colourful **sıkıcı, heyecansız, yavan, tatsız, renksiz** *a dull, insipid man* ○ *The soup was rather insipid.* ● **insipidly** *adverb* yavan bir şekilde, ilginç olmayan

o⁻**insist** /ɪnˈsɪst/ *verb* [I, T] **1** to say firmly that something is true, especially when other people do not believe you **ısrar/inat etmek, direnmek, diretmek** [+ that] *Mia insisted that she and Carlo were just friends.* **2** to demand that something must be done or that you must have a particular thing **ısrar etmek, diretmek, şiddetle talep etmek** *The school insists on good behaviour from its students.* ○ [+ on + doing sth] *Frank insisted on doing all the work himself.* ○ [+ (that)] *Gerlinde insisted that I stay for dinner.*

insistence /ın'sıstᵊns/ *noun* [U] **1** when you demand that something must be done or that you must have a particular thing **diretme, ısrar** [+ that] *his insistence that his children should have a good education* ○ *Clare's insistence on a vegetarian diet caused arguments with her mother.* **2** when you say firmly that something is true, especially when other people do not believe you **inat, diretme, ısrar** [+ that] *Jane was in trouble despite her insistence that she had done nothing wrong.*

insistent /ın'sıstᵊnt/ *adjective* firmly saying that something is true or must be done **ısrarlı, diretici** [+ that] *Pedro is absolutely insistent that Sinda should be invited too.* ● **insistently** *adverb* **ısrarcı**

insofar as /ınsəʊ'fɑːr,əz/ *conjunction formal* to the degree that **...dığı/diği kadar/derecede** *The story is based insofar as possible on notes made by Scott himself.*

insolent /'ınsᵊlənt/ *adjective formal* rude and not showing respect **saygısız, küstah, terbiyesiz, kaba, çirkef** *an insolent reply* ● **insolence** /'ınsᵊləns/ *noun* [U] **küstahlık** ● **insolently** *adverb* **küstahça**

insoluble /ın'sɒljəbl/ *adjective* **1** An insoluble problem, mystery, etc is impossible to solve. **çözümlenemez, içinden çıkılamaz, halledilemez 2** An insoluble substance does not dissolve when you put it in liquid. **çözülmez, çözünmez, erimez**

insomnia /ın'sɒmniə/ *noun* [U] when you find it difficult to sleep **uykusuzluk, uyuyamazlık, uyuma güçlüğü** ● **insomniac** /ın'sɒmniæk/ *noun* [C] someone who often finds it difficult to sleep **uykusuzluk, çeken kişi zor uyur**

inspect /ın'spekt/ *verb* [T] **1** to officially visit a building or organization, in order to check that everything is correct and legal **denetlemek, teftiş etmek, araştırmak** *Schools will be inspected regularly to maintain standards.* **2** to look at something very carefully **kontrol etmek, yoklamak, gözden geçirmek** *Clara inspected her make-up in the mirror.*

inspection ...... İLE BİRLİKTE KULLANILAN KELİMELER

carry out an inspection ● an inspection **of** sth

inspection /ın'spekʃᵊn/ *noun* [C, U] **1** an official visit to a building or organization to check that everything is correct and legal **denetleme, teftiş** *Fire officers carried out an inspection of the building.* **2** when you look at something carefully **kontrol, inceleme** *On closer inspection* (= when looked at more carefully)*, the painting was discovered to be a fake.*

inspector /ın'spektər/ *noun* [C] **1** someone whose job is to check that things are being done correctly **müfettiş, denetleyici, denetçi, kontrolör** *a factory inspector* **2** a police officer of middle rank **polis müfettişi**

inspiration /,ınspᵊr'eıʃᵊn/ *noun* **1** [C, U] someone or something that gives you ideas for doing something **ilham/esin kaynağı kişi/şey** *Africa has long been a source of inspiration for his painting.* **2** [C] a sudden good idea about what you should do **ilham, esin, iyi bir fikir 3 be an inspiration to sb** to be so good that someone else admires you and is encouraged by your behaviour **ilham/esin kaynağı olmak** *The way she has dealt with her illness is an inspiration to us all.*

inspire /ın'spaıər/ *verb* [T] **1** ‾ENCOURAGE‾ to make someone feel that they want to do something and can do it **teşvik etmek, duygu aşılamak, isteklendirmek** [+ to do sth] *A drama teacher at school had inspired Sam to become an*

actor. **2** ‾FEELING‾ to make someone have a particular feeling or reaction **uyandırmak, neden olmak, telkin etmek** *Robson's first task will be to inspire his team with some confidence.* ○ *He inspires great loyalty in his staff.* **3** ‾PROVIDE IDEA‾ to give someone an idea for a book, play, painting, etc **esinlemek, ilham vermek** [often passive] *a television drama that was inspired by a true story* ● **inspiring** *adjective* giving you new ideas and making you feel you want to do something **ilham veren, şevklendiren, heyecanlandırıcı, teşvik edici** *an inspiring teacher* ○ *an inspiring book*

inspired /ın'spaıəd/ *adjective* showing a lot of skill and good ideas **yaratıcı, becerikli** *an inspired performance*

instability /,ınstə'bıləti/ *noun* [U] when a situation or someone's behaviour changes a lot and you do not know what will happen next **istikrarsızlık, dengesizlik, kararsızlık**

install (*also UK* **instal**) /ın'stɔːl/ *verb* **1** [T] ‾EQUIPMENT‾ to put a piece of equipment somewhere and make it ready to use **kurmak, tesis etmek, takmak, yerleştirmek** *The school has installed a burglar alarm.* **2** [T] ‾PERSON‾ to give someone an important and powerful job **iyi bir göreve atamak, tayin etmek, görevlendirmek** *She will be installed as Managing Director in May.* **3** ‾COMPUTER‾ [I, T] to put software onto a computer **bilgisayara yazılım programı kurmak** ● **installation** /,ınstə'leıʃᵊn/ *noun* [C, U] **yükleme, kurma**

instalment *UK* (*US* **installment**) /ın'stɔːlmənt/ *noun* [C] **1** a regular payment that you make, for example each month, in order to pay for something **taksit** *You can pay for your computer in six monthly instalments.* **2** one of the parts of a story that you can see every day or week in a magazine or on television **bölüm, tefrika** *Don't miss next week's exciting instalment.*

instance /'ınstəns/ *noun* **1 for instance** for example **mesela, örneğin, örnek olarak** *Many teenagers earn money, for instance by babysitting or cleaning cars.* **2** [C] an example of a particular type of event, situation, or behaviour **örnek, vaka** *There have been several instances of violence in the school.*

ᴏ⁻**instant¹** /'ınstənt/ *adjective* **1** happening immediately **ani, anlık, hemen olan** *The book was an instant success in the US.* **2** Instant food or drink is dried, usually in the form of a powder, and can be made quickly by adding hot water. **hazır, kulanıma hazır** *instant coffee* ⊃See also: instant replay.

instant² /'ınstənt/ *noun* [C] a moment **an, lahza** *Take a seat, I'll be with you in an instant.*

instantaneous /,ınstən'teıniəs/ *adjective* happening immediately **ani, derhal/hemen olan** *The Internet offers almost instantaneous access to vast amounts of information.* ● **instantaneously** *adverb* **ansızın**

instantly /'ınstəntli/ *adverb* immediately **hemen, derhal, anında** *A car hit them, killing them both instantly.*

instant messaging /,ınstənt 'mesıdʒıŋ/ *noun* [U] a system on the Internet which makes it possible to send messages quickly between two people using the system **internette anında ileti gönderip alma sistemi**

,**instant 'replay** *US* (*UK* action replay) *noun* [C] when part of a film of a sporting event is shown again, often more slowly **ağır çekim tekrar gösterme/oynatma**

ᴏ⁻**instead** /ın'sted/ *adverb* in the place of someone or something else **...ın/in yerine** *If you don't want pizza, we can have pasta instead.* ○ *I'm going swimming on Monday instead of Friday now.* ○ [+ of + doing sth] *Why don't you help instead of just complaining?*

instigate /'ınstıgeıt/ *verb* [T] *formal* to make something start to happen **başlatmak, ön ayak olmak** *Carolyn had instigated divorce proceedings.* ● **instigation**

/ˌɪnstɪˈɡeɪʃᵊn/ *noun* [U] teşvik ● **instigator** *noun* [C] teşvik eden

instil UK (US instill) /ɪnˈstɪl/ *verb* [T] instilling, *past* instilled to make someone have a particular feeling or idea kafasına sokmak, aşılamak, telkin etmek *He's a manager with great skill at instilling confidence in/into his players.*

instinct .... İLE BİRLİKTE KULLANILAN KELİMELER

follow/trust your instincts ● instinct tells sb sth ● sb's first/gut instinct

instinct /ˈɪnstɪŋkt/ *noun* [C, U] the way someone naturally reacts or behaves, without having to think or learn about it içgüdü, doğal eğilim [+ to do sth] *a mother's instinct to protect her children*

instinctive /ɪnˈstɪŋktɪv/ *adjective* behaving or reacting naturally and without thinking içgüdüsel, içten gelen *Her instinctive response was to fight back.* ● **instinctively** *adverb* içgüdüsel

institute¹ /ˈɪnstɪtjuːt/ *noun* [C] an organization where people do a particular kind of scientific, educational, or social work enstitü, kurum *the Massachusetts Institute of Technology*

institute² /ˈɪnstɪtjuːt/ *verb* [T] *formal* to start a plan, law, system, etc başlatmak, tesis etmek, kurmak *Major reforms were instituted in the company's finance department.*

institution /ˌɪnstɪˈtjuːʃᵊn/ *noun* [C] **1** ORGANIZATION a large and important organization, such as a university or bank kurum, kuruluş, müessese *one of the country's top medical institutions* **2** PLACE a building where people are sent so they can be looked after, for example a prison or hospital hapisane/hastane binası **3** TRADITION a custom that has existed for a long time gelenek, âdet *the institution of marriage* ● **institutional** *adjective* relating to an institution kurumsal, kuruma/kuruluşa ait, müessese ile ilgili

instruct /ɪnˈstrʌkt/ *verb* [T] **1** to officially tell someone to do something talimat vermek, emretmek, resmen söylemek [+ to do sth] *Staff are instructed not to use the telephones for personal calls.* **2** *formal* to teach someone about something öğretmek, eğitmek *She is there to instruct people in the safe use of the gym equipment.*

ͦ•͏**instruction** /ɪnˈstrʌkʃᵊn/ *noun* **1** [C] something that you have been told to do talimat direktif, emir [+ to do sth] *I had strict instructions to call them as soon as I arrived home.* **2** [U] *formal* the activity of teaching or training someone, or the information you are being taught öğretim, eğitim, bilgi, ders *religious instruction*

instructions .... İLE BİRLİKTE KULLANILAN KELİMELER

follow the instructions ● give instructions ● detailed/full instructions ● instructions on sth

instructions /ɪnˈstrʌkʃᵊnz/ *noun* [plural] information that explains how to do or use something talimatlar, teknik bilgi *Are there any instructions on how to load the software?* ○ *I just followed the instructions.*

instructive /ɪnˈstrʌktɪv/ *adjective* providing useful information öğretici, eğitici, bilgilendirici *an instructive discussion* ● **instructively** *adverb* eğitici bir biçimde

instructor /ɪnˈstrʌktər/ *noun* [C] someone who teaches a particular sport or activity öğretmen, eğitmen *a driving instructor*

ͦ•͏**instrument** /ˈɪnstrəmənt/ *noun* [C] **1** TOOL a tool that is used for doing something alet *scientific instruments* **2** MUSIC an object that is used for playing music, for example a piano or drum enstrüman, çalgı, saz **3** EQUIPMENT a piece of equipment that is used for measuring speed, light, fuel level, etc alet, aygıt, gösterge, cihaz **4** FOR ACHIEVING SOMETHING someone or something that is used for achieving something vasıta, yol, usül *The Internet is a very powerful instrument of communication.* ⊃See also: wind instrument.

instrumental /ˌɪnstrəˈmentᵊl/ *adjective* **1** be instrumental in sth/doing sth to be one of the main people or things that make something happen aracı/vasıta/yardımcı olmak *Mikan was instrumental in establishing professional basketball in the US.* **2** involving only musical instruments, and no singing (müzik) enstrümentala; sadece sazlarla çalınan

insubordinate /ˌɪnsəˈbɔːdᵊnət/ *adjective* not willing to obey rules or people in authority itaatsiz; dikbaşlı, asi ● **insubordination** /ˌɪnsəˌbɔːdɪˈneɪʃᵊn/ *noun* [U] başkaldıran

insubstantial /ˌɪnsəbˈstænʃᵊl/ *adjective* not very large, strong, or good hafif, zayıf, ince, dayanıksız *The meal was rather insubstantial.*

insufferable /ɪnˈsʌfᵊrəbl/ *adjective* extremely annoying or unpleasant dayanılmaz, çekilmez, tahammül edilmez *insufferable arrogance* ● **insufferably** *adverb* rahatsızlık veren şekilde

insufficient /ˌɪnsəˈfɪʃᵊnt/ *adjective* not enough yetersiz, kifayetsiz *insufficient information* ○ [+ to do sth] *Her income is insufficient to support a family.* ● **insufficiently** *adverb* yetersiz bir biçimde

insular /ˈɪnsjələr/ *adjective* only interested in your own country, life, etc and not willing to accept new ideas or people dışa kapalı, kendine dönük, dar görüşlü, tutucu, bağnaz ● **insularity** /ˌɪnsjəˈlærəti/ *noun* [U] dar görüşlülük, geri kafalılık

insulate /ˈɪnsjəleɪt/ *verb* [T] **1** to cover something with a special material so that heat, electricity, or sound cannot escape through it yalıtmak, izole etmek **2** to protect someone from unpleasant experiences or bad influences tecrit etmek, karantinaya almak, korumak *parents who want to insulate their children from real life*

insulation /ˌɪnsjəˈleɪʃᵊn/ *noun* [U] **1** a special material used for insulating something such as a wall, roof, or building yalıtım/izolasyon maddesi **2** when you insulate something, or when something is insulated yalıtım, yalıtma

insulin /ˈɪnsjəlɪn/ *noun* [U] a substance produced by the body that controls the amount of sugar in your blood vücudun kandaki şeker miktarını kontrol etmek için ürettiği madde, insülin

insult¹ /ɪnˈsʌlt/ *verb* [T] to say or do something to someone that is rude and offensive hakaret etmek, aşağılamak *How dare you insult me in front of my friends!* ● **insulting** *adjective* rude and offensive aşağılayan, hakaret eden; aşağılayıcı, küçük düşürücü *an insulting remark*

insult² /ˈɪnsʌlt/ *noun* [C] **1** a rude and offensive remark or action hakaret, aşağılama *They were shouting insults at each other.* ○ *His comments are an insult to the victims of the war.* **2** add insult to injury to make someone's bad situation worse by doing something else to upset them kötü bir durumu daha da kötüye götürmek

insurance .... İLE BİRLİKTE KULLANILAN KELİMELER

take out insurance ● insurance against [sickness/fire, etc] ● an insurance company/policy/premium ● car/travel insurance

insurance /ɪnˈʃʊərᵊns/ *noun* [U] an agreement in which you pay a company money and they pay your costs if you have an accident, injury, etc **sigorta** *car/travel insurance* ○ *an insurance policy*

insure /ɪnˈʃʊərˡ/ *verb* [T] to buy insurance from a company, or to provide insurance for someone **sigortalamak, sigorta etmek** *I need to get my car insured.* ○ *The policy insures you against damage and theft.*

insurmountable /ˌɪnsəˈmaʊntəbl/ *adjective formal* impossible to deal with **başa çıkılmaz, üstesinden gelinmez** *an insurmountable problem/task*

insurrection /ˌɪnsəˈrekʃˈn/ *noun* [C, U] when a group of people use force to try to get control of a government **isyan, ihtilal, başkaldırı, ayaklanma**

intact /ɪnˈtækt/ *adjective* not damaged or destroyed **sağlam, zarar görmemiş, bozulmamış, dokunulmamış** *Many of the old buildings are still intact.*

intake /ˈɪnteɪk/ *noun* [C] **1** the amount of food or drink that you take into your body **yenen/içilen miktar** [usually singular] *Reducing your salt intake can help to lower blood pressure.* **2** *UK* the group of people who start working or studying somewhere at the same time **bir iş yerinde aynı anda çalışmaya başlayan insan topluluğu** *a new intake of students*

intangible /ɪnˈtændʒəbl/ *adjective* An intangible feeling or quality exists but you cannot describe or prove it. **tanımlanamaz, kolay anlaşılamaz**

integral /ˈɪntɪɡrəl/ *adjective* necessary and important as part of something **tamamlayıcı, bütünleyici, asli, gerekli ve önemli** *The Internet has become an integral part of modern life.*

integrate /ˈɪntɪɡreɪt/ *verb* **1** [I, T] to become part of a group or society, or to help someone do this **bütünleşmek, kaynaşmak, karışmak** *After a few weeks of training he was fully integrated into the team.* **2** [T] to combine two or more things to make something more effective **bütünleştirmek, birleştirmek; entegre etmek** *plans to integrate the two schools* ● **integration** /ˌɪntɪˈɡreɪʃˈn/ *noun* [U] **katılım, bütünleşme**

integrity /ɪnˈteɡrəti/ *noun* [U] honesty and the ability to do or know what is morally right **erdem, doğruluk, dürüstlük, namusluluk** *a woman of great integrity*

intellect /ˈɪntˈlekt/ *noun* [C, U] the ability to learn and understand something, and to form ideas, judgments, and opinions about what you have learned **akıl, idrak, anlayış, zihin** *His energy and intellect are respected by many people.*

intellectual¹ /ˌɪntˈlˈlektjuəl/ *adjective* **1** using or relating to your ability to think and understand things **zihinsel, akla dayanan** *intellectual work* ○ *intellectual and physical development* **2** interested in learning and in thinking about complicated ideas **zihinsel, entelektüel** *She's very intellectual.* ● **intellectually** *adverb* **bilgi ile bağlantılı**

intellectual² /ˌɪntˈlˈlektjuəl/ *noun* [C] someone who enjoys studying and thinking about complicated ideas **aydın, münevver, entelektüel**

average/great/high/low intelligence ● **have/show/use** intelligence

o⇌**intelligence** /ɪnˈtelɪdʒˈns/ *noun* [U] **1** the ability to learn, understand, and think about things **akıl, zekâ** *a child of low intelligence* **2** secret information about the governments of other countries, or the group of people who get this information **haber, bilgi, istihbarat; istihbarat elemanları** *military intelligence* ⊃See also: artificial intelligence.

o⇌**intelligent** /ɪnˈtelɪdʒˈnt/ *adjective* able to learn and understand things easily **zeki, akıllı, çabuk ve kolay**

kavrayabilen *a highly intelligent young woman* ● **intelligently** *adverb* **akıllıca**

intelligible /ɪnˈtelɪdʒəbl/ *adjective* able to be understood **anlaşılır, açık seçik, anlaşılabilir** ⊃Opposite unintelligible.

o⇌**intend** /ɪnˈtend/ *verb* **1** [T] to want and plan to do something **niyet etmek, niyetlenmek, tasarlamak** [+ to do sth] *How long are you intending to stay in Paris?* ○ [+ doing sth] *I don't intend seeing him again.* **2** **be intended for sb; be intended as sth** to be made, designed, or provided for a particular person or purpose **ayır(ıl)mak; ... için düşün(ül)mek** *The book is intended for anyone who wants to learn more about the Internet.*

intense /ɪnˈtens/ *adjective* **1** extreme or very strong **şiddetli, yoğun** *intense heat/pain* **2** Intense people are very serious, and usually have strong emotions or opinions. **çok ciddi, ağır başlı** ● **intensely** *adverb Clare disliked him intensely.* **yoğun bir şekilde** ● **intensity** *noun* [U] **yoğunluk**

intensify /ɪnˈtensɪfaɪ/ *verb* [I, T] to become greater, more serious, or more extreme, or to make something do this **art(tır)mak, şiddetlenmek/şiddetlendirmek** *The fighting has intensified in the past week.*

intensive /ɪnˈtensɪv/ *adjective* involving a lot of work in a short period of time **yoğun** *ten weeks of intensive training* ● **intensively** *adverb* **yoğun bir şekilde**

inˌtensive ˈcare *noun* [U] the part of a hospital used for treating people who are seriously ill or very badly injured **yoğun bakım**

intent¹ /ɪnˈtent/ *noun* [U, no plural] *formal* **1** when you want and plan to do something **niyet, amaç, maksat, kasıt** [+ to do sth] *It had not been his intent to hurt anyone.* **2** **to/for all intents (and purposes)** in all the most important ways **mümkün olan her şekilde; tümüyle en önemli biçimde** *To all intents and purposes, the project was a disaster.*

intent² /ɪnˈtent/ *adjective* **1** **be intent on sth/doing sth** to be determined to do or achieve something **azimli olmak, kararlı/kendini kaptırmış olmak** *She seems intent on winning this year's tennis tournament.* **2** giving a lot of attention to something **ilgili, dikkatli** *She had an intent look on her face.* ● **intently** *adverb* **amaçlı**

announce/declare/signal your intention ● **have no intention of** doing sth

o⇌**intention** /ɪnˈtenʃˈn/ *noun* [C, U] something that you want and plan to do **niyet, maksat, kasıt, amaç, tasarı** [+ to do sth] *She announced her intention to resign.* ○ [+ of + doing sth] *I have no intention of seeing him again.*

intentional /ɪnˈtenʃˈnˈl/ *adjective* planned or intended **kasıtlı, maksatlı** *I'm sorry if I said something that offended you. It really wasn't intentional.* ● **intentionally** *adverb* **bilerek, kasıtlı**

inter- /ɪntərˈ-/ *prefix* between or among **arasında, arası anlamında bir önek** *international* ○ *an interdepartmental meeting*

interact /ɪntərˈækt/ *verb* [I] **1** to talk and do things with other people **anlaşmak, işbirliği etmek, uyuşum sağlamak** *At school, teachers say he interacted well with other students.* **2** If two things interact, they have an effect on each other. **etkileşmek, birbirini etkilemek** *We are looking at how these chemicals interact.*

interaction /ˌɪntərˈækʃˈn/ *noun* [C, U] **1** the activity of talking and doing things with other people, or the way you do this **iletişim, etkileşim; işbirliği, birliktelik** *Our work involves a lot of interaction with the cus-*

tomers. **2** when two or more things combine and have an effect on each other **etkileşim**

interactive /ˌɪntərˈæktɪv/ *adjective* **1** Interactive computer programs, games, etc involve the person using them by reacting to the way they use them. **etkileşimli, bilgi alışverişli 2** involving communication between people **kişiler arası iletişimi içeren**

intercept /ˌɪntəˈsept/ *verb* [T] to stop someone or something before they are able to reach a particular place **önlemek, yolunu kesmek, durdurmak** *Johnson intercepted the pass and went on to score the third goal.* ● **interception** /ˌɪntəˈsepʃ°n/ *noun* [C, U] **yolunu kesme**

interchangeable /ˌɪntəˈtʃeɪndʒəbl/ *adjective* If things are interchangeable, you can exchange them because they can be used in the same way. **birbirinin yerine geçebilir; birbiriyle değiştirilebilir** *interchangeable words* ● **interchangeably** *adverb* **birbiriyle değiştirilebilinir bir şekilde**

intercom /ˈɪntəkɒm/ *noun* [C] an electronic system used for communicating with people in different parts of a building, aircraft, ship, etc **dâhili haberleşme sistemi, anons sistemi** *A stewardess asked over the intercom if there was a doctor on board.*

intercontinental /ˌɪntəˌkɒntɪˈnent°l/ *adjective* in or between two continents **kıtalar arası** *an intercontinental flight*

intercourse /ˈɪntəkɔːs/ (*also* **sexual intercourse**) *noun* [U] *formal* when a man puts his penis into a woman's vagina **cinsel ilişki, ilişki**

interest ...... İLE BİRLİKTE KULLANILAN KELİMELER

develop/generate/have/show/take an interest ● a genuine/keen/passionate/strong interest ● an interest **in** sth ● be **of** interest

o⁼**interest**¹ /ˈɪntrəst/ *noun* **1** [FEELING] [U, no plural] the feeling of wanting to give your attention to something or discover more about it **ilgi, alaka** *Mark had an interest in the media and wanted to become a journalist.* ○ *After a while he simply lost interest in* (= stopped being interested) *his studies.* ○ *Bindi felt that her father didn't take much of an interest in her* (= he was not very interested). **2** [ACTIVITY/SUBJECT] [C] something you enjoy doing, studying, or experiencing **ilgi çeken/önemli şey** *We share a lot of the same interests, particularly music and football.* **3** [MONEY YOU PAY] [U] the extra money that you must pay to a bank, company, etc which has lent you money **ödenen faiz** *low interest rates* **4** [MONEY YOU EARN] [U] the money you earn from keeping your money in a bank account **faiz, kazanç 5** [QUALITY] [U] a quality that makes you think something is interesting **kalite** *Would this book be of any interest to you?* **6** [ADVANTAGE] [C, U] something that gives someone or something an advantage **yarar, çıkar, kazanç, menfaat, kâr** *A union looks after the interests of its members.* **7 be in sb's interest(s)** to help someone and give them an advantage **yararına, çıkarına** *It may not be in your interests to change jobs so soon.* **8 in the interest(s) of** sth in order to achieve a particular situation or quality ...**için; uğruna** *In the interest of safety, passengers are advised to wear their seat belts at all times.* **9** [LEGAL RIGHT] [C] *formal* the legal right to own or receive part of a building, company, profits, etc **pay, hisse** ➲See also: **self-interest, vested interest.**

interest² /ˈɪntrəst/ *verb* [T] If someone or something interests you, you want to give them your attention and discover more about them. **ilgilendirmek, ilgisini çekmek, merakını uyandırmak** *History doesn't really interest me.*

o⁼**interested** /ˈɪntrəstɪd/ *adjective* **1** [never before noun] wanting to give your attention to something and discover more about it **ilgili, meraklı** *Sarah's only interested in boys, CDs, and clothes.* ○ [+ to do sth] *I'd be interested to find out more about the course.* ➲Opposite **uninterested.** **2** [never before noun] wanting to do, get, or achieve something **ilgili, alakalı, alakadar** [+ in + doing sth] *Mark said he's interested in buying your bike.* **3 interested parties/groups** people who will be affected by a situation **ilgili, ilgili olan** ➲Opposite **disinterested.**

YAYGIN HATALAR

interested

Unutmayın! **Interested** kelimesinden sonra **in** edatı kullanılır. **Interested in** kullanımı doğrudur. **Interested about** veya **interested with something** kullanımları yanlıştır: ~~We are interested about having a holiday at your hotel.~~ Yanlış cümle örneği

We are interested in having a holiday at your hotel.

interesting ...... BAŞKA BİR DEYİŞLE

Absorbing veya **gripping** kelimeleri kişinin dikkatini yüksek seviyede çekmiş olan oyun, kitap veya filimleri tanımlamada kullanılır. *I found the book absolutely gripping - I couldn't put it down.* ● *It was a very absorbing film.*
Kendinizi alamadığınız bir oyun, televizyon programı veya bir kitap **compulsive** ifadesiyle tanımlanabilir. *I found the whole series compulsive viewing.*
Fascinating gördüğünüz veya duyduğunuz ve çok ilginç bulduğunuz şeylerin tanımında kullanılır. *The history of the place was absolutely fascinating.* ● *He's fascinating on the subject.*
Eğer bir kişi veya bir şey sahip olduğu gizemden dolayı sizde daha çok şey öğrenme isteği yaratıyorsa, **Intriguing** ifadesiyle tanımlanabilir. *It's a very intriguing situation.*

o⁼**interesting** /ˈɪntrəstɪŋ/ *adjective* Someone or something that is interesting keeps your attention because they are unusual, exciting, or have lots of ideas. **ilginç, ilgi çekici/çeken** *an interesting person* ○ *The museum was really interesting.* ○ [+ to do sth] *It'll be interesting to see what Mum thinks of John's new girlfriend.*

'**interest ˌrate** *noun* [C] the per cent of an amount of money which is charged or paid by a bank or other financial company **faiz oranı**

interface¹ /ˈɪntəfeɪs/ *noun* [C] **1** a connection between two pieces of electronic equipment, or between a person and a computer **ara birim, arayüz** *a simple user interface* **2** a situation, way, or place where two things can come together and have an effect on each other **çıkış noktası** *the interface between technology and tradition*

interface² /ˈɪntəˌfeɪs/ *verb* [I, T] to communicate with people or electronic equipment, or to make people or electronic equipment communicate **kişilerle/elektronik araçlarla iletişim kurmak/kurdurmak** *We use email to interface with our customers.*

o⁼**interfere** /ˌɪntəˈfɪər/ *verb* [I] to try to control or become involved in a situation, in a way that is annoying **karışmak, burnunu sokmak** *I know he's worried about this, but I wish he wouldn't interfere.* ○ *You shouldn't interfere in other people's business.*
interfere with sth *phrasal verb* **1** to prevent something from working effectively or from developing successfully **müdahale etmek, araya girmek, engel olmak, mani olmak** *I try not to let my dancing classes interfere with my schoolwork.* **2** If something interferes with radio or television signals, it stops you from getting

good pictures or sound. **(televizyon, radyo) yayının kaliteli gelmesini engellemek**

🧩 *interference* ...... İLE BİRLİKTE KULLANILAN KELİMELER

interference **in** sth ● interference **from** sb

---

interference /ˌɪntəˈfɪərᵊns/ *noun* [U] **1** when someone tries to interfere in a situation **müdahale, burnunu sokma, karışma** *There have been claims of too much political interference in education.* **2** noise or other electronic signals that stop you from getting good pictures or sound on a television or radio **parazit**

interim¹ /ˈɪntᵊrɪm/ *adjective* [always before noun] temporary and intended to be used or accepted until something permanent exists **geçici, muvakkat** *an interim solution* ○ *an interim government*

interim² /ˈɪntᵊrɪm/ *noun* **in the interim** in the time between two particular periods or events **iki olay arasındaki süre**

interior /ɪnˈtɪəriəʳ/ *noun* [C] the inside part of something **iç taraf, iç kısım** *the grand interior of the hotel* ⊃Opposite exterior.

in,terior de'sign *noun* [U] the job of choosing colours, designs, etc for the inside of a house or room **iç mimari** ● **interior designer** *noun* [C] someone whose job is to do interior design **iç mimar**

interjection /ˌɪntəˈdʒekʃᵊn/ *noun* [C] an exclamation or sudden expression of your feelings. For example 'Hey' in 'Hey you!' is an interjection. **ünlem**

interlude /ˈɪntəluːd/ *noun* [C] a period of time between two events, activities, etc **ara, fasıla** *a brief interlude of peace*

intermediary /ˌɪntəˈmiːdiəri/ *noun* [C] someone who works with two people or groups to help them agree on something important **aracı, arabulucu**

intermediate /ˌɪntəˈmiːdiət/ *adjective* **1** between the highest and lowest levels of knowledge or skill **ara, orta** *intermediate students* **2** between two different stages in a process **orta, orta seviyede** *intermediate steps towards achieving our goal*

interminable /ɪnˈtɜːmɪnəbl/ *adjective* lasting a very long time, in a way that is boring **bitmez, tükenmez, çok uzun** *an interminable train journey* ● **interminably** *adverb* **sonsuz bir biçimde**

intermission /ˌɪntəˈmɪʃᵊn/ *noun* [C] a short period between the parts of a play, performance, etc **ara, fasıla**

intermittent /ˌɪntəˈmɪtᵊnt/ *adjective* stopping and starting again for short periods of time **aralıklı, kesik kesik** *intermittent rain* ● **intermittently** *adverb* **aralıklı bir şekilde, sürekli olmayan**

intern¹ /ˈɪntɜːn/ *noun* [C] US **1** a young doctor who works in a hospital to finish their medical education **tıp eğitimini tamamlamak için hastanede çalışan genç hekim; stajyer hekim** **2** a student who learns about a particular job by doing it for a short period of time **stajyer öğrenci** ● **internship** *noun* [C] the time when someone is an intern **stajyerlik**

intern² /ɪnˈtɜːn/ *verb* [T] to put someone in prison for political reasons, especially during a war **savaş zamanı siyasi nedenlerden dolayı hapsetmek** ● **internment** *noun* [U] when someone is interned **hapsetme**

internal /ɪnˈtɜːnᵊl/ *adjective* **1** [INSIDE A PLACE] happening or coming from inside a particular country, group, or organization **iç, dâhili** *an internal report* ○ *internal disputes* **2** [BODY] inside your body **(beden) iç, içe ait** *internal injuries* **3** [PLACE] inside a country, building, area, etc **iç, dâhili** *an internal flight* ○ *internal walls* ⊃Opposite external. ● **internally** *adverb* **içerden**

◦ **international**¹ /ˌɪntəˈnæʃᵊnᵊl/ *adjective* relating to or involving two or more countries **uluslararası/milletlerarası/beynelmilel** *international politics* ○ *an international team of scientists* ● **internationally** *adverb* **uluslararası**

international² /ˌɪntəˈnæʃᵊnᵊl/ *noun* [C] UK a game of sport involving two or more countries, or a player in one of these games **uluslararası spor karşılaşması** *a one-day international in South Africa*

the inter,national com'munity *noun* countries of the world considered or acting together as a group **uluslararası toplum** *The international community expressed shock at the terrorist attacks.*

🧩 *the Internet* ...... İLE BİRLİKTE KULLANILAN KELİMELER

browse/surf the Internet ● on the Internet ● download sth from the Internet ● Internet **access** ● an Internet **provider/service provider**

◦ **the Internet** /ˈɪntənet/ *noun* (*also* **the Net**) the system that connects computers all over the world and allows people who use computers to look at websites (= electronic documents) **internet** *She found a lot of information on the Internet.* ○ *a company that provides cheap Internet access* ⊃See study page **The Web and the Internet** on page Centre 36.

'internet ,cafe *noun* [C] a place where customers can buy food and drink and use computers to search for information on the Internet **internet kafe**

'Internet ,dating *noun* [U] a way to meet people for possible romantic relationships, in which you look at descriptions of people on a website and arrange to meet them if you like them **İnternette tanışma/flört**

interplay /ˈɪntəpleɪ/ *noun* [U] the effect that two or more things have on each other **etkileşim, karşılıklı etkilenme** *I'm interested in the interplay between Latin and English.*

interpret /ɪnˈtɜːprɪt/ *verb* **1** [T] to explain or decide what you think a particular phrase, performance, action, etc means **yorumlamak, tefsir etmek** *His comments were interpreted as an attack on the government.* **2** [I, T] to change what someone has said into another language **çevirmek, tercüme etmek** *We had to ask the guide to interpret for us.*

interpretation /ɪnˌtɜːprɪˈteɪʃᵊn/ *noun* **1** [C, U] an explanation or opinion of what something means **yorum, tefsir** *traditional interpretations of the Bible* **2** [C] the way someone performs a particular play, piece of music, etc **(oyun, müzik vb.) yorumlama, yorum, icra** *a beautiful interpretation of Swan Lake*

interpreter /ɪnˈtɜːprɪtəʳ/ *noun* [C] someone whose job is to change what someone else is saying into another language **çevirmen, tercüman**

interrogate /ɪnˈterəgeɪt/ *verb* [T] to ask someone a lot of questions, often with great force **sorguya çekmek, sorgulamak** *Police have arrested and interrogated the two suspects.* ● **interrogation** /ɪnˌterəˈgeɪʃᵊn/ *noun* [C, U] *twelve hours of brutal interrogation* **sorgu** ● **interrogator** *noun* [C] **sorgulayan kişi**

interrogative /ˌɪntəˈrɒgətɪv/ *noun* [C] a word or sentence used when asking a question. For example 'Who' and 'Why' are interrogatives. **soru sözcüğü/kelimesi** ● **interrogative** *adjective* **soru şeklinde olan**

◦ **interrupt** /ˌɪntəˈrʌpt/ *verb* **1** [I, T] to stop someone while they are talking or doing something, by saying or doing something yourself **sözünü kesmek, lafa karışmak** *I was trying to work but the children were interrupting me.* **2** [T] to stop an action or activity, usually for a short period of time **ara vermek, yarıda kesmek** *In 1998, a leg injury interrupted his sporting career.*

a **brief/short** interruption ● **without** interruption
● an interruption **in/of** sth

interruption /ˌɪntə'rʌpʃⁿn/ noun [C, U] when an action or activity is interrupted, or something that interrupts someone or something **kesilme, ara verme; kesen, ara veren**

intersect /ˌɪntə'sekt/ verb [I, T] If two things such as lines or roads intersect, they go across each other at a particular point. **kesişmek, kesmek**

intersection /ˌɪntə'sekʃⁿn/ noun [C] US (UK **junction**) the place where two roads meet or cross each other **kavşak, kesişme noktası**

interspersed /ˌɪntə'spɜːst/ adjective **interspersed with sth** having something in several places among something else **serpiştirilmiş, belirli sıklıkla yayılmış/dağılmış** farmland interspersed with forests and lakes

interstate /'ɪntəˌsteɪt/ adjective [always before noun] relating to, or involving two or more US states **(ABD)** eyaletlerle ilgili, eyaletler arası interstate commerce/travel ○ an interstate highway

interval /'ɪntəvⁿl/ noun **1** [C] a period of time between two actions, activities, or events **ara, fasıla** After an interval of three days the peace talks resumed. **2 at intervals** repeated after a particular period of time or particular distance **aralıklarla** Patients were injected with the drug at four-hour intervals (= every four hours). **3** [C] UK (UK/US **intermission**) a short period of time between the parts of a play, performance, etc **ara, perde arası, oyun/gösteri arası, mola**

intervene /ˌɪntə'viːn/ verb [I] **1** BECOME INVOLVED to become involved in a situation in order to try to stop a fight, argument, problem, etc **araya girmek, müdahale etmek, karışmak** Government officials refused to intervene in the recent disputes. ○ [+ to do sth] Harris intervened to stop the attack. **2** INTERRUPT to interrupt someone who is talking **sözünü kesmek, lafa karışmak** "Mr Lawrence," the judge intervened, "please be silent." **3** PREVENT If something intervenes, it stops something or prevents it from happening. **durdurmak, kesmek, engellemek, araya girmek** She was going to marry Barratt but tragedy intervened.

intervening /ˌɪntə'viːnɪŋ/ adjective **the intervening months/period/years**, etc the time between two events **aradaki/aradan geçen aylar/dönem/yıllar vb.** In the intervening years, his illness had become a lot worse.

intervention /ˌɪntə'venʃⁿn/ noun [C, U] when someone intervenes, especially to prevent something from happening **müdahale, engelleme** Without medical intervention, the child would have died.

an **exclusive/frank/in-depth** interview ● **conduct/do/give/have** an interview ● an interview **with sb**

◦ **interview¹** /'ɪntəvjuː/ noun [C] **1** JOB/COURSE a meeting in which someone asks you questions to see if you are suitable for a job or course **görüşme, mülakat** I had an interview last week for a job in London. **2** NEWS a meeting in which someone is asked questions for a newspaper article, television show, etc **röportaj, mülakat** an exclusive interview with Madonna **3** POLICE a meeting in which the police ask someone questions to see if they have committed a crime **sorgulama, sorguya çekme**

interview² /'ɪntəvjuː/ verb [T] to ask someone questions in an interview **görüşme/mülakât yapmak** Police are interviewing a 43-year-old man in connection with the

murder. ○ So far we've interviewed five applicants for the Managing Director's job. ● **interviewer** noun [C] **mülakatı yapan kişi**

interviewee /ˌɪntəvjuːˈiː/ noun [C] someone who is being interviewed **mülakat, röportaj yapılan kişi**

intestine /ɪn'testɪn/ noun [C] a long tube that carries food from your stomach **bağırsak** ● **intestinal** /ˌɪntes'taɪnəl/, /ɪn'testɪnəl/ adjective relating to your intestine **bağırsaklara ilişkin**

intimacy /'ɪntɪməsi/ noun [U] when you have a very special friendship or sexual relationship with someone **samimiyet, içli dışlı olma, yakınlık**

intimate¹ /'ɪntɪmət/ adjective **1** PRIVATE private and personal **özel, kişisel, gizli, mahrem** intimate details of her family life ○ intimate conversations **2** RELATIONSHIP having a special relationship with someone who you like or love very much **yakın, candan, senli benli, her şeyi paylaşan** an intimate friend **3** SMALL If a place or event is intimate, it is small in a way that feels comfortable or private. (yer, mekân, çevre vb.) **sıcak, samimi, kısa** an intimate hotel **4** an intimate knowledge/understanding of sth when you know all of the facts about something or about how it works **tam, eksiksiz bilgi/anlayış/kavrama** ● **intimately** adverb **kişisel, özel biçimde**

intimate² /'ɪntɪmeɪt/ verb [T] formal to suggest that something is true without saying it directly **dolaylı anlatmak, ima etmek, çıtlatmak**

intimidate /ɪn'tɪmɪdeɪt/ verb [T] to intentionally frighten someone, especially so that they will do what you want **gözdağı vermek, gözünü korkutmak, yıldırmak** ● **intimidation** /ɪnˌtɪmɪ'deɪʃⁿn/ noun [U] **rahatsızlık verme**

intimidated /ɪn'tɪmɪdeɪtɪd/ adjective frightened or nervous because you are not confident in a situation **gözü korkmuş, korkmuş, yılmış, ürkmüş** Older people can feel very intimidated by computers. ● **intimidating** adjective making you feel intimidated **gözünü korkutucu, yıldırıcı, ürkütücü** I find speaking in front of a crowd very intimidating.

◦ **into** /'ɪntə/, /'ɪntu/ preposition **1** IN towards the inside or middle of something **içine, içine doğru** Stop running around and get into bed! ○ He's gone into a shop across the road. **2** CHANGE used to show when a person or thing changes from one form or condition to another **bir şeyden bir şeye dönüşünü/geçişi/değişimi belirtmede kullanılır** We're planning to turn the smallest bedroom into an office. ○ Her last novel was translated into nineteen languages. **3** ABOUT involving or about something **hakkında; ...ile ilgili** an investigation into the cause of the fire **4** TOWARDS in the direction of something or someone ...a/e doğru, yönünde/istikametinde She was looking straight into his eyes. **5** HIT moving towards something or someone and hitting them ...a/e doğru giderek/ilerleyerek çarpmayı belirtmede I backed the car into the garden wall. **6 be into sth** informal to be very interested in something **aşırı ilgi duymak/ilgili olmak/uğraşmak; tutkun/düşkün/meraklı olmak** Kate's really into classical music. **7** DIVIDE used when dividing one number by another **bölme işleminde** What's 5 into 125?

intolerable /ɪn'tɒlⁿrəbl/ adjective too bad or unpleasant to deal with or accept **tahammül edilmez, dayanılmaz, çekilmez** an intolerable situation ● **intolerably** adverb **kabul edilmez biçimde**

intolerance /ɪn'tɒlⁿrⁿns/ noun [U] when someone is intolerant **hoşgörüsüzlük, tahammülsüzlük, müsamahasızlık** religious intolerance

intolerant /ɪn'tɒlᵊrᵊnt/ *adjective* refusing to accept any opinions, beliefs, customs, etc that are different from your own **hoşgörüsüz, tahammülsüz, müsamahasız**

intonation /ˌɪntəʊ'neɪʃᵊn/ *noun* [C, U] the way your voice goes up and down when you speak **tonlama, vurgu**

intoxicated /ɪn'tɒksɪkeɪtɪd/ *adjective* **1** *formal* drunk **sarhoş, içkili, alkollü 2** *literary* very excited or enthusiastic about someone or something **sarhoş edici, baş döndürücü, heyecan verici** ● **intoxicating** *adjective* making you intoxicated **sarhoş eden** ● **intoxication** /ɪnˌtɒksɪ'keɪʃᵊn/ *noun* [U] **sarhoşluk**

intra- /ɪntrə-/ *prefix* within **içinde/iç kısmında anlamında önek** *an intranet*

intranet /'ɪntrənet/ *noun* [C] a system that connects the computers in a company or organization so that people can share information and send messages **yerel/kurumsal/iç/dâhili ağ bağlantıları**

intransitive /ɪn'trænsətɪv/ *adjective* An intransitive verb does not have an object. In the sentence 'John arrived first.', 'arrived' is an intransitive verb. **geçişsiz, nesne almayan** ➷See study page **Verb patterns** on page Centre 27. ➷Compare **transitive**.

intravenous /ˌɪntrə'viːnəs/ *adjective* Intravenous medicines or drugs are put directly into your veins (= tubes that carry your blood). **damardan, damardan zerk edilen/verilen** ● **intravenously** *adverb* **damar yoluyla**

in-tray /'ɪntreɪ/ *UK* (*US* **in-box**) *noun* [C] a container where you keep letters and documents that need to be dealt with **mektup/belge vs. kutusu/kabı** ➷Orta kısımdaki renkli sayfalarına bakınız.

intrepid /ɪn'trepɪd/ *adjective* brave and willing to do dangerous things **korkusuz, gözü kara, gözü pek, cesur** *intrepid travellers*

intricacy /'ɪntrɪkəsi/ *noun* **1 the intricacies of sth** complicated details of something **karmaşıklıklar, karmaşık ayrıntılar** *a booklet explaining the intricacies of the game's rules* **2** [U] the quality of being intricate **karmaşıklık, giriftlik, içinden çıkılmazlık** *the intricacy of the stone carvings*

intricate /'ɪntrɪkət/ *adjective* having many small or complicated parts and details **karışık, girift, içinden çıkılması zor** *an intricate pattern* ● **intricately** *adverb* **karmaşık bir biçimde**

intrigue¹ /ɪn'triːg/ *verb* [T] **intriguing,** *past* **intrigued** If someone or something intrigues you, they interest you very much. **ilgi çekmek, merak uyandırmak** *Ancient Egyptian art has always intrigued me.*

intrigue² /'ɪntriːg/ *noun* [C, U] a secret, clever plan to deceive someone or do something bad **entrika, dolap, (argo) dümen; gizli hile** *a tale of romance, intrigue, and betrayal*

intriguing /ɪn'triːgɪŋ/ *adjective* very interesting **merak uyandıran, büyüleyen, cezbeden, ilgi çekici** *an intriguing story*

intrinsic /ɪn'trɪnsɪk/ *adjective* [always before noun] An intrinsic quality or thing forms part of the basic character of something or someone. **asıl, gerçek, hakiki, esas** *Drama is an intrinsic part of the school's curriculum.* ● **intrinsically** *adverb* **içten gelen bir şekilde**

o┅**introduce** /ˌɪntrə'djuːs/ *verb* [T] **1** SOMETHING NEW to make something exist, happen, or be used for the first time **ortaya koymak, göstermek, tanıtmak, ilk kez kullanılmak** *CD players were first introduced in 1983.* ○ *We have introduced a new training schedule for employees.* **2** MEETING PEOPLE to tell someone another person's name the first time that they meet **tanıtmak, tanıştırmak,**

takdim etmek *He took me round the room and introduced me to everyone.* ○ [often reflexive] *Emma introduced herself and they shook hands.* **3** TO AN AUDIENCE to tell an audience who is going to speak to them or perform for them **(konuşmacı) sunmak, takdim etmek, anons etmek** *I'd like to introduce Rachel Elliott who is our speaker this evening.*

introduce sb to sth *phrasal verb* to help someone experience something for the first time **öğretmek, usulünü göstermek, bilgi vermek, nasıl olduğunu göstermek** *His father introduced him to the pleasures of good food.*

o┅**introduction** /ˌɪntrə'dʌkʃᵊn/ *noun* **1** SOMETHING NEW [U] when you make something exist, happen, or be used for the first time **başlatma, ortaya koyma, sunma** *the introduction of a minimum wage* **2** BOOK [C] the first part of a book or speech **giriş, sunuş, önsöz 3** BASIC KNOWLEDGE [C] a book or course which provides basic knowledge about a subject **(kitap, kurs vb.) başlangıç, ilk seviye, giriş bölümü** *an introduction to psychology* **4** FIRST EXPERIENCE [no plural] the first time someone experiences something **tanışma, başlangıç, başlama** *It was our first introduction to great poetry.* **5** FIRST MEETING [C] when you tell someone another person's name the first time that they meet **tanıştırma, takdim etme** [usually plural] *Can you do the introductions?* **6** TO AN AUDIENCE [C, U] when you tell an audience who is going to speak to them or perform for them **(konuşmacı) sunma, takdim** *My next guest needs no introduction.*

introductory /ˌɪntrə'dʌktᵊri/ *adjective* **1 an introductory chapter/essay/message, etc** a part that comes at the beginning of a piece of writing or a speech and explains what will come later **giriş bölümü/deneme yazısı/ileti vb. 2 an introductory book/course/lesson, etc** something that provides basic information about a subject **başlangıç/ilk/temel kitap/kurs/ders vb.** *an introductory course in economics* **3 an introductory discount/fare/offer, etc** something that you get when you start buying something or using a service **giriş/ilk indirim/ücret/teklif vb.**

introspective /ˌɪntrəʊ'spektɪv/ *adjective* thinking a lot about your own thoughts and feelings, in a way that is not always good for you **sürekli kendini dinleyen; hep kendi kafasındakileri düşünüp kuran; kara kara düşünen; (argo) arpacı kumrusu gibi düşünen** ● **introspection** /ˌɪntrəʊ'spekʃᵊn/ *noun* [U] **gözlem (duygu bazlı)**

introvert /'ɪntrəʊvɜːt/ *noun* [C] someone who is quiet and shy and prefers to be alone **içine kapanık kimse, içe dönük kimse** ● **introverted** *adjective* *an introverted child* ➷Opposite **extrovert**. **içe dönük**

intrude /ɪn'truːd/ *verb* [I] to become involved in a situation which people want to be private **içeri dalmak, rahatsız etmek, münasebetsiz zamanda gitmek; (argo) pat diye dalmak** *They should not have intruded on the family's grief.*

intruder /ɪn'truːdəʳ/ *noun* [C] someone who enters a place where they are not allowed to be, often to commit a crime **izinsiz girmek, zorla girmek; mütecaviz davranmak**

┌─────────────────────────────────────┐
│ **intrusion** ┄┄ İLE BİRLİKTE KULLANILAN KELİMELER │
│ an **unwarranted/unwelcome** intrusion ● an intru- │
│ sion **into/on** sth │
└─────────────────────────────────────┘

intrusion /ɪn'truːʒᵊn/ *noun* [C, U] when someone becomes involved in a situation which people want to be private **mahremiyete tecavüz, rahatsız etme, münasebetsizlik, tecavüz** *She could not bear the intrusion into her private life.*

intrusive /ɪn'truːsɪv/ *adjective* If something or someone is intrusive, they become involved in things which should be private. **tatsız, nahoş, rahatsız edici, münasebetsiz** *The magazine published intrusive pictures of the princess's family.*

intuition /ˌɪntjuˈɪʃᵊn/ *noun* [C, U] the feeling that you know something without being able to explain why **sezgi, önsezi, içe doğma** *Her approach to childcare is based on intuition.*

intuitive /ɪn'tjuːɪtɪv/ *adjective* using intuition **sezgisel, önseziye dayanan, içe doğan** *He has an intuitive understanding of animals.* ● **intuitively** *adverb* **sezgiyle**

Inuit /'ɪnuɪt/ *noun* [C, U] *plural* **Inuit** or **Inuits** a group of people who live in the cold, northern areas of North America, Russia, and Greenland, or a member of this group **Eskimo**

inundate /'ɪnʌndeɪt/ *verb* **be inundated with/by sth** to receive so much of something that you cannot deal with it **yağmak/yağdırmak, istila etmek, istilaya uğramak, bunalmak, baş edemez olmak** *Laura was inundated with flowers, cards, and other gifts.*

invade /ɪn'veɪd/ *verb* **1** [I, T] to enter a country by force in order to take control of it **istila etmek** *Portugal was invaded by the French in 1807.* **2** [T] to enter a place in large numbers **akın etmek, istila etmek, doluşmak, üşüşmek, kaplamak** *Every summer the town is invaded by tourists.* **3 invade sb's privacy** to become involved in someone's private life when they do not want you to **ihlal etmek, tecavüz etmek, bozmak**

invader /ɪn'veɪdəʳ/ *noun* [C] someone who enters a country by force in order to take control of it **istilacı**

invalid¹ /'ɪnvəlɪd/ *noun* [C] someone who is so ill that they have to be looked after by other people **hasta, özürlü, sakat, yatalak**

invalid² /ɪn'vælɪd/ *adjective* **1** An invalid document, ticket, law, etc is not legally or officially acceptable. **geçersiz, hükümsüz 2** An invalid argument is not correct. **temelsiz, çürük, dayanağı olmayan**

invaluable /ɪn'væljuəbl/ *adjective* extremely useful **son derece değerli/yararlı** *Her contacts in government proved invaluable to the company.*

invariably /ɪn'veəriəbli/ *adverb* always **her zaman, daima, hep** *The train is invariably packed.*

invasion /ɪn'veɪʒᵊn/ *noun* **1** [C, U] when an army enters a country by force in order to take control of it **istila 2 an invasion of privacy** becoming involved in someone's private life when they do not want you to **özel yaşama müdahale, özel yaşama girme; mütecaviz davranma**

⚬⟶**invent** /ɪn'vent/ *verb* [T] **1** to design or create something that has never existed before **icat etmek, bulmak** *We've invented a new game.* **2** to think of a story or explanation in order to deceive someone **(bahane, hikâye vb.) uydurmak** *She invented an excuse to leave.*

⚬⟶**invention** /ɪn'venʃᵊn/ *noun* **1** [C] something that has been designed or created for the first time **icat, buluş 2** [U] when someone designs or creates something new **icat, buluş** *the invention of printing*

inventive /ɪn'ventɪv/ *adjective* full of clever and interesting ideas **yaratıcı, bulucu, ilginç buluşları olan** *inventive designs* ● **inventively** *adverb* **yaratıcı, akılcı fikirlerle** ● **inventiveness** *noun* [U] **yaratıcılık**

inventor /ɪn'ventəʳ/ *noun* [C] someone who designs and makes new things **mucit, bulucu**

inventory /'ɪnvᵊntri/, /'ɪnvᵊntᵊri/ *noun* [C] a list of all the things that are in a place **stok listesi, sayım çizelgesi, envanter**

invert /ɪn'vɜːt/ *verb* [T] *formal* to turn something upside-down, or put something in the opposite order from how it usually is **ters yüz etmek, baş aşağı döndürmek**

inverted commas /ɪnˌvɜːtɪd'kɒməz/ *noun* [plural] *UK* a pair of marks (" ") or (' ') used before and after a group of words to show that they are spoken or that someone else originally wrote them **tırnak işaret** ⊃See study page **Punctuation** on page Centre 33.

invest /ɪn'vest/ *verb* **1** [I, T] to give money to a bank, business, etc, or buy something, because you hope to get a profit **yatırım yapmak** *He's invested over a million pounds in the city's waterfront restoration project.* **2** [T] to use a lot of time, effort, or emotions because you want to succeed **(zaman, çaba, duygu vb.) harcamak, sar fetmek** *I think she invests too much time and energy in her career.*

invest in sth *phrasal verb* to buy something because you think it will be useful **yatırım amaçlı satın almak** *Dad's decided to invest in a computer.*

investigate /ɪn'vestɪgeɪt/ *verb* [I, T] to try to discover all the facts about something, especially a crime or accident **araştırmak, soruşturmak, incelemek** *He has been questioned by detectives investigating Jenkins' murder.*

ᐤᐤ ***investigation*** .... İLE BİRLİKTE KULLANILAN KELİMELER

carry out/conduct/launch an investigation ● a **detailed/full/thorough** investigation ● an investigation **into** sth ● be **under** investigation

investigation /ɪnˌvestɪ'geɪʃᵊn/ *noun* [C, U] when officials try to discover all the facts about something, especially a crime or an accident **araştırma, soruşturma, inceleme** *Police have begun an investigation into his death.* ○ *The cause of the fire is still under investigation* (= being investigated).

investigative /ɪn'vestɪgətɪv/ ⑤ /ɪn'vestɪgeɪtɪv/ *adjective* trying to discover all the facts about something **araştırma/soruşturma/inceleme ile ilgili** *investigative journalists*

investigator /ɪn'vestɪgeɪtəʳ/ *noun* [C] someone who tries to discover all the facts about something, especially as their job **müfettiş, dedektif**

investment /ɪn'vestmənt/ *noun* **1** [C, U] the money that you put in a bank, business, etc in order to make a profit, or the act of doing this **yatırılan para, mevduat, yatırım** *Businesses need to increase their investment in new technology.* **2** [C] something that you do or have, in order to have more in the future **yatırım, yatırım yapma** *Going to college is an investment in the future.*

investor /ɪn'vestəʳ/ *noun* [C] someone who puts money in a bank, business, etc in order to make a profit **yatırımcı, mudi, yatırım yapan**

inveterate /ɪn'vetᵊrət/ *adjective* **an inveterate liar/gambler/reader, etc** someone who does something very often **uslanmaz, müptela, müzmin, kronik yalancı/kumarbaz/okuyucu**

invigorating /ɪn'vɪgəreɪtɪŋ/ *adjective* making you feel very healthy and energetic **zindeleştirici, canlandırıcı** *a long, invigorating walk* ● **invigorate** *verb* [T] to make you feel very healthy and energetic **canlandırmak, zindeleştirmek**

invincible /ɪn'vɪnsəbl/ *adjective* If someone or something is invincible, it is impossible to defeat or destroy them. **yenilmez, mağlup edilemez** *The French army seemed invincible.*

invisible /ɪn'vɪzəbl/ *adjective* Someone or something that is invisible cannot be seen. **görülmez, görünmeyen** *invisible particles called electrons* ○ *The house was* *invisible from the road.* ● **invisibility** /ɪnˌvɪzə'bɪləti/ *noun* [U] görünmezlik

accept/decline/turn down an invitation ● **an invitation to sth**

○ᶬ**invitation** /ˌɪnvɪ'teɪʃ³n/ *noun* **1** [INVITING SOMEONE] [C, U] when someone invites you to do something or go somewhere **davet, çağrı** *an invitation to dinner* ○ [+ to do sth] *He has accepted their invitation to visit China.* **2** [PIECE OF PAPER] [C] a piece of paper or card that invites someone to an event **davetiye 3** [CAUSE RESULT] [no plural] something that is likely to cause a particular result, especially a bad one **kötülüğe davetiye çıkarma** *It is an invitation to violence.*

○ᶬ**invite**¹ /ɪn'vaɪt/ *verb* [T] **1** [SOCIAL EVENT] to ask someone to come to a social event **davet etmek, çağırmak** *They've invited us to the wedding.* **2** [ASK OFFICIALLY] to officially ask someone to do something **(resmî olarak) davet etmek, rica etmek, bildirmek** [+ to do sth] *I was invited to appear on television.* **3** [REACTION] to do something that is likely to cause a particular reaction or result, especially a bad one **bir şeye davetiye çıkarmak; neden olmak, yol açmak** *Unconventional ideas often invite attack.*
invite sb in *phrasal verb* to ask someone to come into your house **evine/içeri davet etmek** *The neighbours invited us in for coffee.*
invite sb over *phrasal verb* (*also UK* **invite sb round**) to invite someone to come to your house **eve çağırmak/ davet etmek**

invite² /'ɪnvaɪt/ *noun* [C] *informal* an invitation **davet, çağrı**

inviting /ɪn'vaɪtɪŋ/ *adjective* pleasant and attractive **davetkâr, çekici, cezbedici, davet edici** *an inviting smile* ○ *The room looked cosy and inviting.* ● **invitingly** *adverb* çekici bir şekilde

invoice¹ /'ɪnvɔɪs/ *noun* [C] a list that shows you how much you owe someone for work they have done or for goods they have supplied **fatura**

invoice² /'ɪnvɔɪs/ *verb* [T] to send someone an invoice **fatura göndermek**

invoke /ɪn'vəʊk/ *verb* [T] *formal* to use a law, rule, etc to support what you are saying or doing ...**dan/den alıntı yapmak/destek almak/aktarma yapmak** *The President may invoke federal law to stop the strike.*

involuntary /ɪn'vɒlənt³ri/ *adjective* An involuntary movement or action is something you do but cannot control. **istenilmeden yapılan, irade dışı, gayriihtiyari** *an involuntary shudder* ● **involuntarily** *adverb* **istem dışı bir şekilde**

○ᶬ**involve** /ɪn'vɒlv/ *verb* [T] **1** [NECESSARY PART] If a situation or activity involves something, that thing is a necessary part of it. **gerektirmek, icap ettirmek** *The trips often involve a lot of walking.* ○ *There are a lot of risks involved.* **2** [AFFECT/INCLUDE] to affect or include someone or something in an activity **etkisi altına almak, sarmak** *an event involving hundreds of people* **3** [TAKE PART] to make someone be part of an activity or process **karışmak, bulaşmak, yer almak, bulaştırmak** *I prefer teaching methods that actively involve students in learning.*

○ᶬ**involved** /ɪn'vɒlvd/ *adjective* **1** be/get involved (in/with sth) to do things and be part of an activity or event **bulaşmak, yakından ilgilenmek** *How did you get involved in acting?* **2** be/get involved with sb to have a sexual or romantic relationship with someone **biriyle romantik veya cinsel ilişkisi olmak** *She got involved with a boy from college.* **3** complicated **karmaşık, çapraşık, anlaşılmaz** *a long and involved story*

close/direct/personal involvement ● **involvement in sth**

○ᶬ**involvement** /ɪn'vɒlvmənt/ *noun* [U] when someone or something is involved in an activity or event **katılım, iştirak, yer alma, ilgi, bağlantı** *He denies any involvement in the attack.*

inward¹ /'ɪnwəd/ *adjective* **1** [always before noun] towards the centre or the inside of something **bir şeyin içinde/ içine doğru 2 inward investment** *UK* money from foreign companies that is put into businesses in your own country **yabancı yatırım 3** [always before noun] inside your mind and not shown to other people **iç, ruhsal** *inward feelings* ⊃Opposite **outward.**

inward² /'ɪnwəd/ *adverb* (*also UK* **inwards**) *adverb* towards the inside or the centre **içeriye/içe/merkeze doğru** *The door slowly opened inward.*

inwardly /'ɪnwədli/ *adverb* in your mind without anyone else seeing or knowing **içten içe, gizliden gizliye** *She smiled inwardly.* ⊃Opposite **outwardly.**

in-your-face (*also* **in-yer-face**) /ˌɪnjə'feɪs/ *adjective informal* describes something that is done in a forceful way that intends to shock people **zorla, şok eden, göz önünde, göz göre göre** *in-your-face television advertising*

iodine /'aɪədiːn/ *noun* [U] a chemical element found in sea water, and used in some medicines (symbol **I**) **iyot, tendürdiyot**

IOU /ˌaɪəʊ'juː/ *noun* [C] *abbreviation for* I owe you: a piece of paper saying that you will pay back money you owe **borç senedi**

IOW *internet abbreviation for* in other words: used when you want to express something in a different way in order to explain it clearly **bir diğer ifadeyle; başka bir deyişle**

IPA /ˌaɪpiː'eɪ/ *noun* [U] *abbreviation for* International Phonetic Alphabet: a system of symbols for showing how words are spoken **Uluslararası Fonetik Alfabe**

iPod /'aɪpɒd/ *noun* [C] *trademark* one of a group of small electronic devices for storing and playing music **müzik kaydedip çalınabilen elektronik alet**

IQ /ˌaɪ'kjuː/ *noun* [C, U] *abbreviation for* intelligence quotient: a person's intelligence when measured by a special test **zekâ katsayısı** *a high/low IQ*

ir- /ɪr-/ *prefix* not **olumsuzluk anlamı veren önek** *irregular*

irate /aɪ'reɪt/ *adjective* extremely angry **öfkeli, kızgın** *Hundreds of irate passengers have complained on the airline.*

iris /'aɪərɪs/ *noun* [C] **1** a tall plant with purple, yellow, or white flowers **süsen, süsen çiçeği, iris 2** the coloured part of your eye **iris, göz bebeği**

Irish¹ /'aɪərɪʃ/ *adjective* relating to Ireland **İrlanda'ya ait** *Irish music/culture* ○ *Irish whisky*

Irish² /'aɪərɪʃ/ *noun* **1** [U] the language that is spoken in some parts of Ireland **İrlanda dili, İrlandaca 2 the Irish** [plural] the people of Ireland **İrlandalı**

○ᶬ**iron**¹ /aɪən/ *noun* **1** [U] a dark grey metal used to make steel (= very strong metal) and found in small amounts in blood and food (formula **Fe**) **demir** *an iron bar/gate* **2** [C] a piece of electrical equipment that you use for making clothes flat and smooth **ütü** ⊃See also: **cast iron, wrought iron.**

iron² /aɪən/ *verb* [I, T] to make clothes flat and smooth using an iron **ütülemek, ütü yapmak** *I need to iron a shirt to wear tomorrow.*

iron sth out *phrasal verb* to solve a problem or difficulty **gidermek, çözmek, çözümlemek, ortadan kaldırmak** *We're still trying to **iron** out a few problems with the computer system.*

iron³ /aɪən/ *adjective* [always before noun] extremely strong and determined **oldukça güçlü/kararlı/azimli; demir gibi** *a man of **iron** will* ⊃See also: cast-iron.

ironic /aɪəˈrɒnɪk/ *adjective* **1** saying something that you do not mean, as a joke **alaylı, alaycı, kinayeli, cinaslı, ironik** *ironic comments* **2** An ironic situation is strange because it is the opposite of what you expected. **garip, tuhaf, acayip, komik** [+ that] *It's ironic that she was hurt by the very person she's trying to help.* ● **ironically** *adverb* **şaka yoluyla**

ironing /ˈaɪənɪŋ/ *noun* [U] **1** the activity of making clothes flat and smooth using an iron (= a piece of electrical equipment) **ütü, ütüleme** *John was doing the ironing.* **2** the clothes that are waiting to be ironed, or those that have just been ironed **ütülenmeyi bekleyen/ütülenmiş kıyafetler** *a basket full of ironing*

ironing board *noun* [C] a narrow table that you use for ironing **ütü masası/tahtası**

irony /ˈaɪərəni/ *noun* **1** [C, U] a situation that is strange because it is the opposite of what you expected **tuhaflık, acayiplik, gariplik, garip tesadüf, kaderin bir cilvesi** *The irony is that now he's retired, he's busier than ever.* **2** [U] a type of humour in which people say something they do not mean **ince alay, kinaye, cinas**

irrational /ɪˈræʃ°n°l/ *adjective* Irrational feelings and actions are based on your emotions and not on good reasons. **mantıksız, saçma, akla dayanmayan, mâkul olmayan, akıl dışı** *irrational behaviour* ○ *an irrational fear of flying* ● **irrationality** /ɪ,ræʃ°nˈæləti/ *noun* [U] **mantıksızlık** ● **irrationally** *adverb* **mantıksız bir şekilde**

irreconcilable /ɪ,rek°nˈsaɪləbl/ *adjective formal* Irreconcilable beliefs, opinions, etc are so different that no agreement is possible. **bağdaşmaz/bağdaştırılamaz, zıt, ters, uzlaştırılamaz** *Irreconcilable differences led to their divorce.*

irregular /ɪˈregjələʳ/ *adjective* **1** [TIME] Irregular actions or events happen with a different amount of time between each one. **düzensiz, intizamsız, gelişigüzel** *an irregular heartbeat* ○ *They met at irregular intervals.* **2** [SHAPE] not smooth or straight, or having parts that are different sizes **düzensiz, eğri büğrü, çarpık** *an irregular coastline* **3** [GRAMMAR] not following the general rules in grammar (dilbilgisi) **düzensiz; kural dışı** *irregular verbs/plurals* **4** [BEHAVIOUR] *UK formal* slightly illegal, or not done in the usual and acceptable way **usulsüz, kurallara aykırı** *He led a very irregular life.* ● **irregularity** /ɪ,regjəˈlærəti/ *noun* [C, U] **düzensizlik** ● **irregularly** *adverb* **düzensiz bir şekilde**

irrelevant /ɪˈreləv°nt/ *adjective* not important in a particular situation **ilgisiz, konu dışı, yersiz, gereksiz** *The car had faults but these were irrelevant to the crash.* ● **irrelevance** /ɪˈreləv°ns/ *noun* [C, U] something that is irrelevant, or the quality of being irrelevant **yersizlik, gereksizlik, konu dışılık** ● **irrelevantly** *adverb* **ilgisiz, alakasız bir şekilde**

irreparable /ɪˈrep°rəbl/ *adjective* Irreparable damage, harm, injury, etc is so bad that it can never be repaired. **onarılamaz, tamir edilemez, telafisi mümkün olmayan** ● **irreparably** *adverb* **onarılamaz bir biçimde**

irreplaceable /ɪ,rɪˈpleɪsəbl/ *adjective* Someone or something that is irreplaceable is so valuable or special that you could not get another one like them. **yeri doldurulamaz, yerine yenisi konulamaz**

irrepressible /ɪ,rɪˈpresəbl/ *adjective* **1** always happy and energetic **çok neşeli ve hareketli, ele avuca sığmaz, 2** An irrepressible feeling is impossible to control. **bastırılamaz, önüne geçilemez** *an irrepressible urge to travel* ● **irrepressibly** *adverb* **keyifli, enerjik bir şekilde**

irresistible /ɪ,rɪˈzɪstəbl/ *adjective* **1** extremely attractive and impossible not to like or want **dayanılmaz, çok çekici, cezbedici** *an irresistible smile* **2** too powerful to control or ignore **karşı konulamaz, dayanılmaz** *irresistible pressure* ○ *an irresistible desire to run away* ● **irresistibly** *adverb* **karşı koyulamaz bir şekilde**

irrespective /ɪ,rɪˈspektɪv/ *adverb* **irrespective of sth** used to say that something does not affect a situation **...e/a bakmaksızın; ...ı/i hesaba katmaksızın, göz önüne almaksızın, aldırmaksızın** *Everyone should be treated equally, irrespective of skin colour.*

irresponsible /ɪ,rɪˈspɒnsəbl/ *adjective* not thinking about the possible bad results of what you are doing **sorumsuz, vurdum duymaz, mesuliyetsiz, düşüncesiz** *an irresponsible attitude* ● **irresponsibility** /ɪ,rɪ,spɒnsəˈbɪləti/ *noun* [U] **sorumsuzluk** ● **irresponsibly** *adverb* **sorumsuzca**

irreverent /ɪˈrev°r°nt/ *adjective* not showing any respect for people or traditions that are usually respected **kaba, saygısız, hürmetsiz** *irreverent humour* ● **irreverence** /ɪˈrev°r°ns/ *noun* [U] when someone or something is irreverent **saygısızlık, hürmetsizlik** ● **irreverently** *adverb* **saygısızca**

irreversible /ɪ,rɪˈvɜːsəbl/ *adjective* Something that is irreversible cannot be changed back to how it was before. **değiştirilemez, düzeltilemez, iptal edilemez, eski haline getirilemez** *Smoking has caused irreversible damage to his lungs.* ● **irreversibly** *adverb* **geriye dönüşü olmayan bir şekilde**

irrevocable /ɪˈrevəkəbl/ *adjective formal* impossible to change or stop **değiştirilemez, durdurulamaz, geriye döndürülemez** *irrevocable decisions* ● **irrevocably** *adverb* **değiştirilemez bir durumda**

irrigate /ˈɪrɪgeɪt/ *verb* [T] to provide water for an area of land so that crops can be grown **sulamak, sulama yapmak** ● **irrigation** /ɪ,rɪˈgeɪʃ°n/ *noun* [U] **sulama**

irritable /ˈɪrɪtəbl/ *adjective* becoming annoyed very easily **sinirli, asabi** *Jack's been irritable all day.* ● **irritability** /ɪrɪtəˈbɪləti/ *noun* [U] **sinirlilik** ● **irritably** *adverb* **sinirli bir şekilde**

irritant /ˈɪrɪt°nt/ *noun* [C] **1** someone or something that makes you feel annoyed **kızgınlık, öfkelendiren/kızdıran/rahatsız eden şey 2** a substance that makes part of your body hurt **kaşındırıcı/dalayıcı şey/madde, tahriş edici madde**

irritate /ˈɪrɪteɪt/ *verb* [T] **1** to annoy someone **kızdırmak, sinirlendirmek, canını sıkmak, rahatsız etmek** *His comments really irritated me.* **2** to make a part of your body hurt **tahriş etmek, kaşındırmak** *The smoke irritated her eyes.* ● **irritation** /ɪ,rɪˈteɪʃ°n/ *noun* [C, U] **sinirlendirme**

irritated /ˈɪrɪteɪtɪd/ *adjective* annoyed **rahatsız, sinirli, asabi, kızgın** *Ben began to get increasingly irritated by/at her questions.* ○ [+ that] *I was irritated that he didn't thank me.*

irritating /ˈɪrɪteɪtɪŋ/ *adjective* making you feel annoyed **rahatsız edici, kızdıran, sinirlendiren** *an irritating habit* ● **irritatingly** *adverb* **rahatsız edici bir şekilde**

is *strong form* /ɪz/ *weak form* /z/ *present simple he/she/it of* be **'be' fiilinin tekil üçüncü şahıs kullanım hâli**

Islam /ˈɪzlɑːm/ *noun* [U] a religion based on belief in Allah, on the Koran, and on the teachings of Mohammed **Müslümanlık, İslamiyet, İslamlık;**

Kur 'anı Kerim, Allah inancı ve Hz. Muhammed'in öğretilerine dayalı din/dinî inanç *The followers of Islam are called Muslims.*

Islamic /ɪzˈlæmɪk/ *adjective* related to Islam **Müslümanlığa ait, İslamlıkla ilgili** *Islamic art* ○ *an Islamic country*

o-~**island** /ˈaɪlənd/ *noun* [C] an area of land that has water around it **ada** *the Caribbean island of Grenada* ○ *the Hawaiian Islands* ● **islander** *noun* [C] someone who lives on an island **adalı, adada yaşayan kişi** ⊃See also: **desert island.**

isle /aɪl/ *noun* [C] an island, often used in the name of a particular island **ada** *the British Isles*

o-~**isn't** /ˈɪzᵊnt/ *short for* is not 'be' fiilinin tekil öznelerle kullanılan olumsuz hâli *Mike isn't coming with us.*

isolate /ˈaɪsəleɪt/ *verb* [T] to separate someone or something from other people or things **ayırmak, ayrı tutmak, tecrit etmek** *Scientists have been able to isolate the gene responsible for causing the illness.* ○ *He had been isolated from other prisoners.*

isolated /ˈaɪsəleɪtɪd/ *adjective* **1** a long way from other places **ücra yerde, uzakta bulunan, soyutlanmış** *an isolated village in the mountains* **2** alone and not having help or support from other people **yalnız, tek başına, soyutlanmış** *Kazuo felt very isolated at his new school.* **3 an isolated case/example/incident, etc** an event/action, etc that happens only once **tek, ayrı, yegâne durum/örnek/olay/hadise vb.**

isolation /ˌaɪsᵊlˈeɪʃᵊn/ *noun* **1** [U] the state of being separate from other people, places, or things **ayrılmışlık, yalnızlık, inziva** *the country's economic isolation from the rest of the world* **2 in isolation** alone or separately from other people, places, or things **tek başına, diğerlerinden ayrı olarak, müstakil, ayrı** *These poems cannot be considered in isolation.* **3** [U] a feeling of being lonely **yalnızlık, tecrit** *I had this awful sense of isolation.*

ISP /ˌaɪesˈpiː/ *noun* [C] *abbreviation for* Internet service provider: a company that connects your computer to the Internet, and lets you use email and other services **İnternet Servis Sağlayıcısı (İSS)**

🧩 *issue (noun)* .... İLE BİRLİKTE KULLANILAN KELİMELER

a **contentious/important/key/major/thorny** issue ● **address/discuss/raise/resolve** an issue ● **the** issue **of** sth

o-~**issue¹** /ˈɪʃuː/ *noun* **1** [C] an important subject or problem that people are discussing **konu, mevzu** *the issues of race and social class* ○ *political issues* ○ *Chris has raised a very important issue.* **2** [C] the newspaper, magazine, etc that is produced on a particular day **baskı, sayı, nüsha** *Have you seen the latest issue of Computer World?* **3 at issue** most important in what is being discussed **söz konusu olan, tartışılan, mevzu bahis olan** *The point at issue is what is best for the child.* **4 take issue (with sb/sth)** to disagree with what someone says or writes **birinin söylediği veya yazdığı ile uyuşmazlık/uyuşmamak** *I would take issue with you on that.* **5 have issues with sth** to often be sad, anxious, or angry because of something **bir şeyden dolayı kızgın/endişeli veya üzgün olmak** *A very high proportion of women diet frequently and have issues with their bodies.*

🧩 *issue (verb)* .... İLE BİRLİKTE KULLANILAN KELİMELER

issue an **order/statement/warning** ● issue **guidelines/instructions**

issue² /ˈɪʃuː/ *verb* [T] issuing, *past* issued **1** to say something officially **resmen bildirmek/söylemek** *The*

Prime Minister will issue a statement tomorrow. ○ *Police issued a warning about the dangers of playing near water.* **2** to officially give something to someone **resmen vermek/teslim etmek/dağıtmak** *to issue a passport/ticket/invitation* ○ *All members will be issued with a membership card.*

IT /ˌaɪˈtiː/ *noun* [U] *abbreviation for* information technology: the use of computers and other electronic equipment to store and send information **bilgi teknolojisi; bilgiyi depolamak ve göndermek için bilgisayar ve diğer elektronik aletlerin kullanımı**

o-~**it** /ɪt/ *pronoun* **1** [THING] used to refer to the thing, situation, or idea that has already been talked about **o, onu;** **bahsedilen nesne, durum veya fikre atıfta bulunmada kullanılır** *"Have you seen my bag?" "It's in the hall."* **2** [DESCRIPTION] used before certain adjectives, nouns, or verbs to introduce an opinion or description of a situation **o, onu; bir fikri veya bir durumun tasvirini belirten belli sıfat, isim veya fiillerden önce kullanılır** *It's unlikely that she'll arrive on time.* **3** [SUBJECT/OBJECT] used with certain verbs that need a subject or object but do not refer to a particular noun **o, onu; bir özne veya nesneye gereksinim duyan ancak hususi bir isme atıfta bulunmayan belli fiillerden önce kullanılır** *It costs less if you travel at the weekend.* ○ *I liked it in Scotland.* **4** [TIME/WEATHER] used with the verb 'be' in sentences giving the time, date, weather, or distances **o, onu; zâmanı, tarihi, havayı veya mesafeleri veren cümlelerde 'be' fiili ile kullanılır** *It rained all day.* ○ *What time is it?* **5** [SEEM] used as the subject of verbs such as 'seem', 'appear' and 'look' **seem', 'appear' ve 'look' fiillerinin öznesi olarak kullanılır** *It seemed unfair to leave her at home.* **6** [EMPHASIZE] used to emphasize one part of a sentence **cümlenin bir bölümünü vurgulamak için kullanılır** *It's the children I'm concerned about, not me.* **7 it's sb/sth** used to say the name of a person or thing when the person you are speaking to does not know **o'dur; konuştuğunuz kişinin bilmediği nesnenin veya kişinin adını söylemede kullanılır** *It's your Dad on the phone.*

italics /ɪˈtælɪks/ *noun* [plural] a style of writing or printing in which the letters slope to the right **italik, italik harfler; yana yatık yazı/baskı** ● **italic** *adjective* written in italics **italik, yana yatık**

itch¹ /ɪtʃ/ *verb* [I] If a part of your body itches, it feels uncomfortable and you want to rub it with your nails. **kaşınmak, kaşındırmak** *Woollen sweaters make my arms itch.* **2 be itching to do sth** *informal* to want to do something very much **şiddetle arzu etmek, can atmak, bir şeyi çok istemek** *You could tell that they were itching to leave.*

itch² /ɪtʃ/ *noun* [C] an uncomfortable feeling on your skin that makes you want to rub it with your nails **kaşıntı** *I've got an itch in the middle of my back.*

itching /ˈɪtʃɪŋ/ *noun* [U] when a part of your body itches **kaşınma** *a lotion to stop itching*

itchy /ˈɪtʃi/ *adjective* If a part of your body is itchy, it feels uncomfortable and you want to rub it with your nails. **kaşınan, kaşıntılı** *an itchy nose* ● **itchiness** *noun* [U] **kaşıntı**

o-~**it'd** /ˈɪtəd/ **1** *short for* it would 'it would' fiil yapısının kısa hâli *It'd be great if we could meet next week.* **2** *short for* it had 'it had' fiil yapısının kısa hâli *It'd taken us an hour to find Bruce's house.*

o-~**item** /ˈaɪtəm/ *noun* [C] **1** a single thing in a set or on a list **adet, kalem, parça** *the last item on the list* ○ *Various stolen items were found.* **2** a piece of news on television or radio, or in a newspaper **gazete, radyo veya tv'de**

haber *a small item on the back page of the local newspaper*

itemize (*also UK* -ise) /'aɪtəmaɪz/ *verb* [T] to list things separately, often including details about each thing **dökümünü yapmak, madde madde yazmak** *an itemized phone bill*

itinerant /aɪ'tɪnᵊrᵊnt/ *adjective* [always before noun] *formal* travelling from one place to another **gezgin, gezici, seyyar** *an itinerant preacher*

itinerary /aɪ'tɪnᵊrᵊri/ *noun* [C] a list of places that you plan to visit on a journey **gezi/yolculuk programı; güzergâh** *The President's itinerary includes visits to Boston and New York.*

ᴼ⁼**it'll** /'ɪtᵊl/ *short for* it will '**it will**' fiil yapısının kısa hâli *It'll take about twenty minutes to get there.*

ᴼ⁼**it's** /ɪts/ **1** *short for* it is '**it is**' fiil yapısının kısa hâli *"What time is it?" "It's one o'clock."* **2** *short for* it has **it has**' fiil yapısının kısa hâli *It's been a long day and I'm tired.*

ᴼ⁼**its** /ɪts/ *determiner* belonging to or relating to the thing that has already been talked about **onun, kendi, onunki** *The house has its own swimming pool.*

its or it's?

Dikkat! Çoğu Türk öğrenci bu iki kelimenin kullanımıyla ilgili hata yapmaktadırlar. **It's** it is veya it has kalıplarının kısaltılmış hâlidir.: *I love this beach because it's beautiful and clean.* **Its** aitlik gösterir. Kullanımında kesme işareti kullanılmaz. It's olarak kullanılmaz. Its şekli doğru kullanımıdır.: ~~This place is famous for it's beautiful beaches.~~ Yanlış cümle örneği
This place is famous for its beautiful beaches.

ᴼ⁼**itself** /ɪt'self/ *pronoun* **1** [REFLEXIVE] the reflexive form of the pronoun 'it' **kendi, kendisi, kendisini** *The cat licked itself clean.* **2** [EMPHASIS] used to emphasize the particular thing you are referring to **kendi, bizzat, bizzat kendisi** *The garden is enormous but the house itself is very small.* **3 (all) by itself a** [ALONE] alone **tek başına** *The dog was in the house by itself for several days.*

b [AUTOMATIC] automatically **otomatik olarak, kendiliğinden** *The heating comes on by itself.* **4 in itself** as the only thing being talked about and nothing else **aslında, haddi zatında, kendi başına düşünüldüğünde** *You've managed to complete the course - that in itself is an achievement.*

ITV /ˌaɪti:'vi:/ *noun abbreviation for* Independent Television: one of the main television companies in the United Kingdom **Özel Televizyon Kanalı; İngiltere'deki tv şirketlerinden biri** *There's a good film on ITV tonight.*

IV /ˌaɪ'vi:/ *US* (*UK* **drip**) *noun* [C] a piece of medical equipment used for putting liquids into your body **vücuda sıvı vermek için kullanılan tıbbi alet/cihaz**

I've /aɪv/ *short for* I have '**it have**' fiil yapısının kısa hâli *I've decided not to go.*

IVF /ˌaɪvi:'ef/ *noun* [U] *abbreviation for* in vitro fertilization: a treatment where a woman's egg is fertilized outside her body and put back in her body for the baby to grow **suni döllenme; bir kadının hamile kalmasını sağlamak için embriyonun kadının rahmine yerleştirme tedavisi/işlemi**

ivory /'aɪvᵊri/ *noun* [U] a hard, white substance from the tusks (= long teeth) of some animals, such as elephants (= large, grey animals) **fildişi**

ivy /'aɪvi/ *noun* [U] a dark green plant that often grows up walls **sarmaşık**

J, j /dʒeɪ/ the tenth letter of the alphabet **alfabenin onuncu harfi**

jab[1] /dʒæb/ *verb* [I, T] *jabbing, past* **jabbed** to push something quickly and hard into or towards another thing **batırmak, saplamak** *He jabbed a finger into her back.*

jab[2] /dʒæb/ *noun* [C] **1** a quick, hard push into or towards something **batırma, saplama, dürtme 2** *UK informal* an injection (= when a drug is put in your body with a needle) **iğne, aşı** *a flu jab*

jack[1] /dʒæk/ *noun* [C] **1** a piece of equipment for lifting a heavy object such as a car **kriko 2** a playing card that comes between a ten and a queen **(iskambil oyunu) vale, bacak, oğlan** *the jack of diamonds*

jack[2] /dʒæk/ *verb*
  jack sth in *phrasal verb UK informal* to stop doing something, especially a job **bırakmak, kesmek, durdurmak** *She's jacked in her job.*
  jack sth up *phrasal verb informal* to increase a price or rate suddenly and by a large amount **(fiyat, oran vs.) aniden artırmak, yükseltmek**

jackal /ˈdʒækᵊl/ *noun* [C] a wild dog that hunts in groups **çakal**

jacket

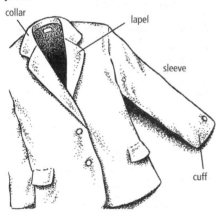

collar   lapel   sleeve   cuff

o⚬**jacket** /ˈdʒækɪt/ *noun* [C] a short coat **ceket** *a leather jacket* ⇒*Orta kısımdaki renkli sayfalarına bakınız* ⇒*See also:* **dinner jacket, life jacket, strait-jacket.**

jacket po'tato *noun* [C] *plural* **jacket potatoes** *UK* a potato that has been baked in the oven with its skin on **kumpir, fırınlanmış kabuklu patates**

jack-knife[1] /ˈdʒækˌnaɪf/ *noun* [C] *plural* **jack-knives** a knife with a blade that can be folded away into the handle **çakı**

jack-knife[2] /ˈdʒækˌnaɪf/ *verb* [I] If a large truck jack-knifes, the front part turns round to face the back in a way that is not controlled. **katlanmak, iki büklüm olmak, ikiye katlanmak**

jackpot /ˈdʒækpɒt/ *noun* **1** [C] an amount of money that is the largest prize anyone can win in a competition **büyük ikramiye 2 hit the jackpot** to be very success-

ful, especially by winning or earning a lot of money **büyük ikramiye kazanmak**

Jacuzzi /dʒəˈkuːzi/ *noun* [C] *trademark* a bath or pool that produces bubbles in the water **jakuzi**

jade /dʒeɪd/ *noun* [U] a green stone used in making jewellery **yeşim, yeşim taşı**

jaded /ˈdʒeɪdɪd/ *adjective* tired or bored with something, especially because you have done it too much **yorgun, bitkin, bezgin, usanmış**

jagged /ˈdʒægɪd/ *adjective* very rough and sharp **sivri uçlu, tırtıklı, çentikli** *jagged rocks*

jaguar /ˈdʒægjuəʳ/ *noun* [C] a large, wild cat that lives in Central and South America **jaguar**

🧩 **jail** ...... İLE BİRLİKTE KULLANILAN KELİMELER

be released from/be sent to jail ● **in** jail ● **a** jail sentence

jail[1] (*also UK* **gaol**) /dʒeɪl/ *noun* [C, U] a place where criminals are kept as a punishment **hapishane, cezaevi** *He ended up in jail.*

jail[2] /dʒeɪl/ *verb* [T] to put someone in a jail **hapsetmek, cezaevine atmak** [*often passive*] *He was jailed for two years.*

jailer /ˈdʒeɪləʳ/ *noun* [C] someone who guards prisoners in a jail **gardiyan**

jam[1] /dʒæm/ *noun* **1** [C, U] (*also US* **jelly**) a sweet food made from fruit that you spread on bread **reçel, marmelat** *a jar of strawberry jam* ⇒*Orta kısımdaki renkli sayfalarına bakınız.* **2** [C] (*also* **traffic jam**) a line of cars, trucks, etc that are moving slowly or not moving **trafikte araç sıkışıklığı** *We were stuck in a jam for hours.*

jam[2] /dʒæm/ *verb* **jamming, past jammed 1 jam sth in/ into/on, etc** to push something somewhere firmly and tightly **tıkmak, tıka basa doldurmak** *She jammed her hands into her pockets.* **2** STUCK [I, T] to get stuck or make something get stuck **tıka(n)mak, felç olmak/etmek** *The machine keeps jamming.* **3** FILL [T] to fill a place completely **tıka basa doldurmak** [*often passive*] *The streets were jammed with cars.* **4** STOP RADIO [T] to send a signal that stops a radio being able to broadcast **bozmak, karıştırmak, parazit yapmak**

jamboree /ˌdʒæmbᵊrˈiː/ *noun* [C] a big celebration or party **büyük eğlence, parti, kutlama**

Jan *written abbreviation for* January **ocak ayı**

jangle /ˈdʒæŋgl/ *verb* [I, T] If small metal objects jangle, they hit together making a ringing noise, and if you jangle them, you make them make this noise. **şıngırda(t)mak** *He was jangling his keys.* ● **jangle** *noun* [C] **tıngırdama**

janitor /ˈdʒænɪtəʳ/ *noun* [C] *US* someone whose job is to look after a building **apatman görevlisi, kapıcı** *the school janitor*

o⚬**January** /ˈdʒænjuᵊri/ (*written abbreviation* **Jan**) *noun* [C, U] the first month of the year **ocak ayı**

jar[1] /dʒɑːʳ/ *noun* [C] a glass container used for storing food **kavanoz** *a jar of jam* ⇒*See picture at* **container.**

jar[2] /dʒɑːʳ/ *verb* **jarring, past jarred** [I, T] to move suddenly, hitting something and causing pain or damage **ani hareketle incitmek, sarsmak** *The movement jarred his injured leg.*

jar on sb *phrasal verb UK* to annoy someone **sinirine dokunmak, rahatsız etmek** *Her voice jars on me.*

jargon /ˈdʒɑːgən/ *noun* [U] words and phrases used by particular groups of people that are difficult for other people to understand **mesleki sözcük dağarcığı, teknik terimler içeren özel dil** *legal jargon*

jaundice /ˈdʒɔːndɪs/ *noun* [U] a disease that makes your eyes and skin yellow **sarılık hastalığı**

jaundiced /ˈdʒɔːndɪst/ *adjective* having a negative opinion of something because of bad things that have happened to you **karamsar, şüpheci, kuşkucu** *a jaundiced view of marriage*

jaunt /dʒɔːnt/ *noun* [C] a short, enjoyable journey **gezinti, kısa seyahat**

jaunty /ˈdʒɔːnti/ *adjective* happy and confident **mutlu, neşeli, kendinden emin** *a jaunty walk*

javelin /ˈdʒævəlɪn/ *noun* **1** [C] a long, pointed stick that you throw as a sport **cirit 2 the javelin** a sport in which you throw a javelin as far as you can **cirit sporu** ⊃Orta kısımdaki renkli sayfalarına bakınız.

jaw /dʒɔː/ *noun* [C] **1** either of the two bones in your mouth that contain your teeth **çene** ⊃Orta kısımdaki renkli sayfalarına bakınız. **2 sb's jaw drops** If someone's jaw drops, their mouth opens because they are very surprised. **ağzı açık kalmak, hayrete düşmek**

jazz /dʒæz/ *noun* [U] music with a strong beat that is often played without written music **caz** *a jazz band*

jealous /ˈdʒeləs/ *adjective* **1** unhappy and angry because you want something that someone else has **kıskanç** *His new bike was making his friends jealous.* ○ *Steve has always been jealous of his brother's good looks.* **2** upset and angry because someone you love seems too interested in another person **kıskanç** *a jealous husband* ● **jealously** *adverb* **kıskanç bir şekilde**

jealousy /ˈdʒeləsi/ *noun* [U] jealous feelings **kıskançlık, haset, çekememezlik**

o▪**jeans** /dʒiːnz/ *noun* [plural] trousers made from denim (= a strong, usually blue, material) **kot pantolon, blucin** *a pair of jeans* ⊃Orta kısımdaki renkli sayfalarına bakınız.

Jeep /dʒiːp/ *noun* [C] *trademark* a strongly built vehicle with big wheels that is used for driving over rough ground **cip**

jeer /dʒɪəʳ/ *verb* [I, T] to laugh and shout insults at someone **alay etmek, yuhalamak** *The crowd outside his house jeered as he left.* ● **jeer** *noun* [C] **alay**

Jell-O /ˈdʒeləʊ/ *noun* [U] *US trademark* jelly **jöle, pelte**

jelly /ˈdʒeli/ *noun* [C, U] **1** *UK* (*US* Jell-O) a soft but solid sweet food that shakes when you move it **jöle, jel, pelte** *jelly and ice cream* **2** *US* (*UK/US* jam) a sweet food made from fruit that you spread on bread **marmelat**

jellyfish /ˈdʒelifɪʃ/ *noun* [C] *plural* **jellyfish** a sea creature with a clear body that may sting you (= put poison into your skin) **denizanası**

jeopardize (*also UK* -ise) /ˈdʒepədaɪz/ *verb* [T] to put something in a situation where there is

a risk of failing or being harmed **tehlikeye/riske sokmak/atmak** *Bad weather could jeopardize all our plans.*

jeopardy /ˈdʒepədi/ *noun* **in jeopardy** in danger of failing or being harmed **tehlikede** *If the factory closes, local jobs will be in jeopardy.*

jerk¹ /dʒɜːk/ *verb* [I, T] to move very quickly and suddenly, or to make something move like this **birdenbire yerinden fırlamak** *The truck jerked forward.*

jerk² /dʒɜːk/ *noun* [C] **1** a quick, sudden movement **fırlama, silkinme, ani hareket, sarsıntı** *a sudden jerk of the head* **2** *mainly US informal* a stupid or annoying person **aptal ve rahatsız edici kişi**

jerky /ˈdʒɜːki/ *adjective* Jerky movements are quick and sudden. **sarsıntılı, yalpalayan** ● **jerkily** *adverb* **ani, sarsıntı yaratan bir şekilde**

jersey /ˈdʒɜːzi/ *noun* **1** [C] a piece of clothing which covers the top of your body and is pulled on over your head **süeter, kazak 2** [U] soft wool or cotton cloth used for making clothes **jarse**

jest /dʒest/ *noun* **in jest** said as a joke **şaka yollu, şakadan, şaka olarak**

Jesus Christ /ˌdʒiːzəsˈkraɪst/ *noun* the Jewish holy man believed by Christians to be the Son of God, and on whose life and teachings Christianity is based **Hz isa; Hıristiyanlarca Tanrı'nın Oğlu olduğuna ve Hıristiyanlığın onun yaşamına ve öğretilerine dayandığına inanılan insan, Peygamber**

jet¹ /dʒet/ *noun* [C] **1** an aircraft that flies very fast **jet, jet uçağı** ⊃See also: jumbo jet. **2** water or gas that is forced out of something in a thin, strong line **fışkırtma, püskürtme, püskürtü**

jet² /dʒet/ *verb* [I] *jetting, past* **jetted** jet in/off, *etc* to fly somewhere in an aircraft **jetle seyahat etmek** *She jetted off to Athens for a week.*

jet-black /ˌdʒetˈblæk/ *noun* [U] a very dark black colour **simsiyah, kapkara** ● **jet-black** *adjective* jet-black hair **kapkara**

'**jet ˌengine** *noun* [C] an engine that makes an aircraft fly very fast **jet motoru**

'**jet ˌlag** *noun* [U] when you feel tired because you have just travelled a long distance on an aircraft **(uzun uçak yolculuğunun açtığı ve zaman değişimine dayalı) sersemlik, yorgunluk**

jettison /ˈdʒetɪsⁿn/ *verb* [T] **1** to get rid of something you do not want or need **işe yaramaz diye atmak, vazgeçmek** *The station has jettisoned educational broadcasts.* **2** If an aircraft or a ship jettisons something, it throws it off to make itself lighter. **(uçak, gemi) fazlalıkları atmak, fazla yükten kurtulmak**

jetty /ˈdʒeti/ *noun* [C] a wooden structure at the edge of the sea or a lake where people can get on and off boats **iskele, rıhtım, dalgakıran, mendirek**

Jew /dʒuː/ *noun* [C] someone whose religion is Judaism, or who is related to the ancient people of Israel **Yahudi, Musevi dinine inanan**

jewel /ˈdʒuːəl/ *noun* [C] a valuable stone that is used to make jewellery **mücevher, kıymetli taş**

jeweller *UK* (*US* jeweler) /ˈdʒuːələ/ *noun* [C] someone whose job is to sell or make jewellery **kuyumcu**

jewellery *UK* (*US* jewelry) /ˈdʒuːəlri/ *noun* [U] objects made from gold, silver, and valuable stones that you wear for decoration **mücevher**

Jewish /ˈdʒuːɪʃ/ *adjective* relating or belonging to the Jews **Yahudi, Yahudilerle ilgili, Yahudilere ait, Musevi dinine ait** *Jewish history/law*

jellyfish

jewellery *UK*, jewelry *US*

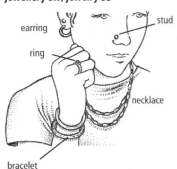

earring
stud
ring
necklace
bracelet

jibe (*also* **gibe**) /dʒaɪb/ *noun* [C] an insulting remark hakaret, küçültücü söz *He kept making jibes at me about my weight.*

jig /dʒɪg/ *noun* [C] **1** a traditional, quick dance, or the music it is danced to **oynak ve hareketli dans/ müzik 2** a piece of equipment that guides a tool for cutting and holds the object being cut

jiggle /'dʒɪgl/ *verb* [I, T] to make quick, short movements from side to side or to make something else move like this **sallamak, sallanmak**

jigsaw /'dʒɪgsɔː/ (*also* 'jigsaw ,puzzle) *noun* [C] a picture in many small pieces that you put together as a game **yapboz oyunu**

jingle¹ /'dʒɪŋgl/ *noun* [C] **1** a short song that is used to advertise a product on the radio or television **kısa reklam müziği 2** a sound made when small metal objects hit against each other **şıkırtı, şıngırtı, tıngırtı**

jingle² /'dʒɪŋgl/ *verb* [I, T] to make the sound of small metal objects hitting against each other **şıkırda(t) mak, şıngırda(t)mak, tıngırda(t)mak** *a pocket full of jingling coins*

jinx /dʒɪŋks/ *noun* [C] someone or something that brings bad luck **şanssızlık getiren kişi/şey** *There seems to be a jinx on the school.* ● **jinx** *verb* [T] **uğursuzluk getirmek**

jitters /'dʒɪtəz/ *noun* [plural] a nervous feeling **sinir, asabiyet** *Hospitals give me the jitters.*

jittery /'dʒɪtᵊri/ *adjective* nervous **sinirli, gergin, asabî** *She gets quite jittery about exams.*

Jnr *UK* (*UK/US* **Jr**) *written abbreviation for* junior (= the younger of two men in a family with the same name) **ailede aynı isimden iki erkeğin daha küçük/genç olanı**

🧩 **job** ...... İLE BİRLİKTE KULLANILAN KELİMELER

a **dead-end/full-time/good/part-time/temporary** job ● **apply for/create/do/find/get/lose** a job ● a job **as** sth

job ...... BAŞKA BİR DEYİŞLE

Daha resmi ortamlarda kullanılabilecek bir alternatif **occupation** kelimesidir. *Please fill in your name, age and occupation.*

Post ve **position** ifadeleri bir kurumun içindeki işlerin/mevkilerin ifadesinde kullanılır. *She's applied for a part-time teaching post/position.*

Career kelimesi kişinin hayatı boyunca uzun süreyle yaptığı bir iş dalının ifadesinde kullanılır. *She's had a very successful career in marketing.*

Placement veya **internship** kelimeleri kişinin bir

işi öğrenebilmek için çalışmasının ifadesinde kullanılır. *He's got a year's placement in the medical labs.*

ᴏ⁻**job** /dʒɒb/ *noun* [C] **1** PAID EMPLOYMENT the regular work that you do in order to earn money **iş** *She got a job in publishing.* ○ *Hundreds of workers could lose their jobs.* ○ *Why don't you apply for a part-time job?* **2** PIECE OF WORK a piece of work that you have to do **görev, iş** *cooking, cleaning and other household jobs* **3** RESPONSIBILITY something that is your responsibility **görev, sorumluluk** *It's my job to water the plants.* **4 make a bad/good, etc job of sth** *UK* to do sth badly/well, etc **bir şeyi iyi/kötü yapmak 5 do a good/excellent, etc job** to do something well/very well, etc **bir şeyi iyi/çok iyi yapmak** *She did a great job of organizing the event.* **6 out of a job** without a job **işsiz** *How long have you been out of a job?* **7 do the job** If something does the job, it is suitable for a particular purpose. **işi görmek, işi yapmak, işe yaramak** *Here, this knife should do the job.* ● **8 it's a good job** *UK informal* If it is a good job that something happened, it is lucky that it happened. **'iyi ki!' 'Bereket versinki!', 'Allah'tan!'** [+ (that)] *It's a good job that Jo was there to help you.* ● **9 just the job** *UK* If something is just the job, it is exactly what you want or need. **tam gereken şey/ iş, tam istenen iş**

'job de,scription *noun* [C] a list of the things you must do in your work **iş tanımı, görev tanımı/belirlenmesi**

jobless /'dʒɒbləs/ *adjective* without a job **işsiz** *young jobless people*

jobshare /'dʒɒbʃeəʳ/ *verb* [I] *UK* If two people jobshare, they do one job between them, working at different times. **iş paylaşımı** ● **jobshare** *noun* [C] *UK* **iş bölümü**

jockey /'dʒɒki/ *noun* [C] someone who rides horses in races **jokey** ⊃See also: **disc jockey.**

jog /dʒɒg/ *verb* jogging, *past* jogged **1** [I] to run slowly for exercise **koşar adım yürümek** *I jog through the park every morning.* **2** [T] to hit something gently by mistake **kazara itmek/dürtmek** *He jogged her arm.* **3 jog sb's memory** to cause someone to remember something **aklına getirmek, anımsatmak, hatırlatmak** *They hoped the photographs would jog his memory.* ● **jog** *noun* [no plural] *Let's go for a jog.* **yavaş koşu** ● **jogging** *noun* [U] **koşu**

jogger /'dʒɒgəʳ/ *noun* [C] someone who runs for exercise **koşar adım yürüyen, koşucu, yürüyüş yapan kişi**

ᴏ⁻**join¹** /dʒɔɪn/ *verb* **1** BECOME MEMBER [T] to become a member of a group or organization **girmek, üye olmak, katılmak** *He joined the army when he was eighteen.* **2** DO WITH OTHERS [T] to do something or go somewhere with someone **ortaklaşa yapmak veya birlikte gitmek, katılmak** *Would you like to join us for dinner?* **3** FASTEN [T] to fasten or connect things together **bağlamak, birleştirmek, bir araya getirmek** *Join the ends together with strong glue.* **4** MEET [I, T] to meet at a particular point **belli bir noktada buluşmak/katılmak** *The Mississippi River and the Missouri join near St Louis.* **5 join a line** (*also UK* **join a queue**) to go and stand at the end of a row of people waiting for something **sıraya/kuyruğa girmek** ⊃See also: join forces (**force¹**).

join in (sth) *phrasal verb* to become involved in an activity with other people **katılmak, yer almak, iştirak etmek** *We're playing cards. Would you like to join in?*

join up *phrasal verb* to become a member of the army or other military group **askere gitmek; asker olmak; orduya katılmak**

join² /dʒɔɪn/ *noun* [C] *UK* the place where two or more things are fastened together **bağlantı/ek yeri**

joined-up /ˌdʒɔɪnˈdʌp/ *adjective UK* **1 joined-up writing** a style of writing where each letter in a word is connected to the next one **birbirine geçmeli harflerden oluşan yazı biçimi 2 joined-up thinking** thinking about a complicated problem in an intelligent and original way, and considering everything that is connected with it **karmaşık bir sorunla ilgili olarak akıllıca ve orijinal şekilde düşünme ve en ince ayrıntıyı bile dikkate alma**

joint¹ /dʒɔɪnt/ *adjective*
[always before noun]
belonging to or done by two or more people
ortak *a joint statement* ○ *The project was a joint effort by all the children in the class.*
● **jointly** *adverb*
birlikte

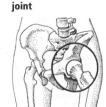
joint

joint² /dʒɔɪnt/ *noun* [C]
1 [BODY PART] a place in your body where two bones meet **eklem, eklem yeri** *the knee joint* **2** [MEAT] *UK* a large piece of meat, usually cooked in the oven **kol, but gibi büyük parça et** *a joint of beef* **3** [CONNECTION] a place where parts of a structure or machine are connected **ek, ek yeri, bağlantı yeri 4** [PLACE] *informal* a place where something is sold, especially a restaurant or bar **bir şeyin satıldığı bar/lokanta vb. yerler** *a pizza joint*

joint 'venture *noun* [C] a business activity that is done by two separate companies working together

crack/make/tell a joke ● a **dirty/sick** joke ● a joke **about** sth

○▪**joke¹** /dʒəʊk/ *noun* **1** [C] something which someone says to make people laugh, usually a short story with a funny ending **şaka, espri, fıkra** *to tell/make a joke* **2 be a joke** *informal* to not be serious or not deserve respect **şaka olmak** *The investigation was a joke.* **3 be no joke** to be serious or difficult **ciddi ve güç olmak** *It's no joke driving on icy roads.* **4 take a joke** to understand and accept a trick without becoming angry or upset **şaka kaldırmak** ↪See also: **practical joke.**

joke² /dʒəʊk/ *verb* **1** [I] to say funny things, or not be serious **şaka yapmak, fıkra anlatmak, ciddi olmamak** *She always jokes about her husband's cooking.* **2 You must be joking!/You're joking!** *informal* something you say to show that you are surprised by what someone has said, or do not believe it is true **'Şaka yapıyorsun herhalde!', 'Dalga mı geçiyorsun?'** ● **jokingly** *adverb* **şaka yaparcasına**

joker /dʒəʊkəʳ/ *noun* [C] **1** someone who likes saying or doing funny things **şakacı, şaka yapmayı/fıkra anlatmayı seven 2** one of a set of playing cards which can be used instead of another card in some games (iskambil) **joker**

jolly¹ /dʒɒli/ *adjective* happy or enjoyable **neşeli, şen şakrak, mutlu, sevinçli** *We had a jolly evening.*

jolly² /dʒɒli/ *adverb old-fashioned* very **çok, epeyce** *a jolly good idea*

jolt¹ /dʒəʊlt/ *noun* [C] **1** a sudden, violent movement **sarsıntı** *With a sudden jolt the train started moving again.* **2** an unpleasant shock or surprise **şok, nahoş sürpriz** *The reminder that he was dead gave her a jolt.*

jolt² /dʒəʊlt/ *verb* [I, T] to move suddenly and forcefully, or to make someone or something do this **sarsmak,**

sarsılmak; sarsıla sarsıla gitmek *The bus stopped suddenly and the passengers were jolted forward.*

jostle /dʒɒsl/ *verb* [I, T] to push other people in order to get somewhere in a crowd **kalabalık içinde insanları iterek gidilecek yere ulaşmak**
jostle for sth *phrasal verb* to try hard to get something **kıyasıya mücadele etmek** *Thousands of companies are jostling for business on the Internet.*

jot /dʒɒt/ *verb* [T] jotting, *past* **jotted** to write something quickly **not almak, yazmak, not etmek** *She jotted a note to Sue.*
jot sth down *phrasal verb* to write something quickly on a piece of paper so that you remember it **karalamak, not almak** *I jotted down some notes during his speech.*

journal /dʒɜːnᵊl/ *noun* [C] **1** a magazine containing articles about a particular subject **dergi** *a medical journal* **2** a book in which you regularly write about what has happened to you **günlük**

journalism /dʒɜːnᵊlɪzᵊm/ *noun* [U] the work of writing articles for newspapers, magazines, television, or radio **gazetecilik**

○▪**journalist** /dʒɜːnᵊlɪst/ *noun* [C] someone whose job is journalism **gazeteci**

journalistic /ˌdʒɜːnᵊlˈɪstɪk/ *adjective* relating to journalism or typical of journalism **gazetecilikle ilgili**

an **arduous/long/perilous/short** journey ● **begin/complete/embark on/go on/make** a journey

○▪**journey** /dʒɜːni/ *noun* [C] when you travel from one place to another **yolculuk, gezi, seyahat** *a car/train journey* ○ *We take games for the children when we go on long journeys.*

jovial /dʒəʊviəl/ *adjective* happy and friendly **neşeli, güler yüzlü, babacan, şen şakrak** *a jovial man*

joy /dʒɔɪ/ *noun* **1** [HAPPINESS] [U] a feeling of great happiness **neşe, mutluluk, sevinç** *the joy of winning* **2** [PLEASURE] [C] something or someone that makes you feel very happy **zevk, keyif, haz** *She's a joy to work with.* **3** [SUCCESS] [U] *UK informal* success **başarı** *I tried ringing for a plumber, but had no joy.*

joyful /dʒɔɪfᵊl/ *adjective* very happy, or making people feel very happy **neşeli, keyifli, sevindirici, sevinçli** *joyful news* ● **joyfully** *adverb* **keyifli bir şekilde**

joyous /dʒɔɪəs/ *adjective literary* extremely happy, or making people extremely happy **oldukça sevinçli, mutlu, keyifli, mutluluk veren** ● **joyously** *adverb* **çok mutlu bir şekilde**

joypad /dʒɔɪpæd/ *noun* [C] a gamepad **oyun aleti**

joyriding /dʒɔɪˌraɪdɪŋ/ *noun* [U] stealing cars and driving them fast and dangerously **çalıntı araba ile gezi yapma** ● **joyride** /dʒɔɪraɪd/ *noun* [C] *They took the car for a joyride.* **arabayı sahibinden izin almadan alarak, dolaşma** ● **joyrider** *noun* [C] **arabayı sahibinden izin almadan alarak dolaşan kişi**

joystick /dʒɔɪstɪk/ *noun* [C] a vertical handle you move to control a computer game, machine, or aircraft **kumanda kolu, levye**

JP /ˌdʒeɪˈpiː/ *noun* [C] *abbreviation for* Justice of the Peace: a judge in a small or local court of law **küçük mahkeme veya bölge mahkemesi yargıcı/hâkimi**

JPEG /dʒeɪpeɡ/ *noun* **1** [U] *abbreviation for* joint photographics experts group: a system for making electronic pictures use less space **elektronik resimlerin daha az alan kaplamasını sağlayan sistem 2** [C] a type of computer file (= collection of information) that contains pictures or photographs **resim ve fotoğrafları içeren bir tür bilgi toplama dosyası**

Jr (*also UK* **Jnr**) *written abbreviation for* junior (= the younger of two men in a family with the same name) **ailede aynı ismi taşıyan iki erkekten daha genç olanı** *John F. Kennedy, Jr.*

jubilant /'dʒuːbɪlənt/ *adjective* feeling or showing great happiness, usually because of a success **çok sevinçli, çok memnun, sevinçten uçan** *jubilant United supporters* ● **jubilation** /ˌdʒuːbɪ'leɪʃᵊn/ *noun* [U] a feeling of great happiness and success **büyük sevinç**

jubilee /'dʒuːbɪliː/ *noun* [C] a celebration of an important event in the past, usually one which happened 25 or 50 years ago **jübile, kutlama, yıl dönümü** *a golden jubilee* (= 50 years) ○ *a silver jubilee* (= 25 years)

Judaism /'dʒuːdeɪɪzᵊm/ *noun* [U] the religion of the Jewish people, based on belief in one God and on the laws contained in the Torah **Musevilik, Yahudilik, Musevi dini**

judge¹ /dʒʌdʒ/ *noun* [C] **1** someone who controls a trial in court, decides how criminals should be punished, and makes decisions about legal things **yargıç, hâkim** *Judge Moylan* ○ *The judge ruled that they had acted correctly.* **2** someone who decides which person or thing wins a competition **hakem** *the Olympic judges* **3 a bad/good, etc judge of sth** someone who is usually wrong/usually right, etc when they judge something **iyi/kötü vb. yargıç/hakim** *a good judge of character*

∘ᴀ**judge²** /dʒʌdʒ/ *verb* **1** [DEVELOP OPINION] [I, T] to have or develop an opinion about something or someone, usually after thinking carefully **yargıya/karara varmak, karar vermek** [+ question word] *I can't judge whether he's telling the truth or not.* ○ *You shouldn't judge people on their appearances.* ○ *He was judged guilty/insane.* **2 judging by/from** used to express the reasons why you have a particular opinion **...a/e göre, ...a/e bakılırsa, ...dan/den anlaşıldığına göre** *She must be popular judging by the number of letters that she receives.* **3** [COMPETITION] [I, T] to decide the winner or results of a competition **hakemlik etmek** *I've been asked to judge the art contest.* **4** [BAD OPINION] [I, T] to have a bad opinion of someone's behaviour, often because you think you are better than them **fikir edinip karar vermek, kanıya varmak** *What gives you the right to judge people?* **5** [GUESS] [T] to try to guess something, especially a measurement **(özellikle ölçüyü) tahmine çalışmak** *I find it difficult to judge distances.*

🧩 *judgment* .... İLE BİRLİKTE KULLANILAN KELİMELER
make/pass/reserve judgment ● **poor/good** judgment ● a **harsh/subjective** judgment ● an **error/ lapse** of judgment

∘ᴀ**judgment** (*also* judgement) /'dʒʌdʒmənt/ *noun* **1** [OPINION] [C, U] an opinion about someone or something that you decide on after thinking carefully **yargı, düşünce, fikir, kanı** *The inspector needs to make a judgment about how the school is performing.* **2** [ABILITY] [U] the ability to make good decisions or to be right in your opinions **sağduyu, anlayış, seziş; doğru karar verme yeteneği** *to have good/bad judgment* **3** [LEGAL DECISION] [C, U] an official legal decision, usually made by a judge **yargı, karar, hüküm**

judgmental (*also UK* judgemental) /dʒʌdʒ'mentᵊl/ *adjective* quick to criticize people **yargısal, eleştirel, eleştiride acele davranan**

judicial /dʒuː'dɪʃᵊl/ *adjective* relating to a court of law or the legal system **adlı, hukuki** *a judicial inquiry*

the judiciary /dʒuː'dɪʃᵊri/ *noun* all the judges in a country **yargıçlar/hâkimler**

judicious /dʒuː'dɪʃəs/ *adjective* done or decided carefully and with good judgment **makul, akla uygun, isabetli**

judo /'dʒuːdəʊ/ *noun* [U] a sport from Japan in which two people try to throw each other to the ground **judo**

jug /dʒʌɡ/ *noun* [C] a container with a handle used for pouring out liquids **sürahi, testi, güğüm** *a jug of water*

jug

juggle /'dʒʌɡl/ *verb* **1** [T] to try to do several things at once, when it is difficult to have enough time **yeterli zaman olmadığında aynı anda bir çok şey yapmaya çalışmak** *Many women have to juggle work and family.* **2** [I, T] to keep two or more objects such as balls in the air by throwing them repeatedly, usually in order to entertain people **hokkabazlık yapmak**

juggler /'dʒʌɡlər/ *noun* [C] someone who juggles objects to entertain people **hokkabaz**

∘ᴀ**juice** /dʒuːs/ *noun* [C, U] the liquid that comes from fruit or vegetables **meyve/sebze suyu** ⊃See also: orange juice.

juices /'dʒuːsɪz/ *noun* [plural] the liquid that comes from cooked meat **et suyu**

juicy /'dʒuːsi/ *adjective* **1** full of juice **sulu** *juicy apples* **2** interesting because of shocking or personal information **(şok edici veya kişisel bilgiden dolayı) meraklı, merak uyandıran, ilginç, cazip, hoş** *juicy gossip*

jukebox /'dʒuːkbɒks/ *noun* [C] a machine, usually in a bar, which plays a song when you put money into it **müzik dolabı/kutusu, para atıldığında otomatik müzik çalan alet**

∘ᴀ**July** /dʒʊ'laɪ/ *noun* [C, U] the seventh month of the year **temmuz ayı** ⊃See also: Fourth of July.

jumble¹ /'dʒʌmbl/ *noun* [no plural] a confused mixture or group of things **düzensizlik, karmakarışık yığın,** *Her handbag is a jumble of pens, make-up, and keys.*

jumble² /'dʒʌmbl/ (*also* jumble up) *verb* [T] to mix things together in an untidy way **karmakarışık etmek** [often passive] *Her clothes were all jumbled up in the suitcase.*

'jumble ˌsale *UK* (*US* rummage sale) *noun* [C] a sale of old items, especially clothes, usually to make money for an organization **yardım amaçlı kullanılmış giysi satışı; hayır işleri için satış**

jumbo /'dʒʌmbəʊ/ *adjective* [always before noun] extra large **muazzam, çok büyük, iri, kocaman** *a jumbo bag of sweets*

jumbo 'jet *noun* [C] a very large aircraft for carrying passengers **jumbo jet**

∘ᴀ**jump¹** /dʒʌmp/ *verb* **1** [INTO AIR] [I] to push your body up and away from the ground using your feet and legs **hoplamak, zıplamak, sıçramak, atlamak** *The children were jumping up and down with excitement.* ○ *I jumped over the log.* ○ *They jumped into the water.* **2 jump into/ up, etc** to move somewhere suddenly and quickly **ani ve hızla atlamak/hareket etmek/girmek** *She jumped into a taxi and rushed to the station.* **3** [GO OVER] [T] to move over something by moving up into the air **üzerinden atlamak** *The horse jumped the last fence.* **4** [INCREASE] [I, T] to suddenly increase by a large amount **(miktar) artmak, yükselmek, fırlamak** *House prices have jum-*

ped by 20%. **5** FEAR [I] to make a sudden movement because you are frightened or surprised **(korkudan, şaşkınlıktan) havaya sıçramak, zıplamak, irkilmek, hoplamak** *Her scream made me jump.* ⪢See also: get/jump on the **bandwagon**, jump to conclusions (**conclusion**), jump the **gun**¹, jump the **queue**.

jump at sth *phrasal verb* to take an opportunity to have or do something in a very willing and excited way **balıklama atlamak, dünden razı olmak, hemen kabul etmek** *He jumped at the chance to join the band.*

jump² /dʒʌmp/ *noun* [C] **1** when you push your body up into the air using your feet and legs **zıplama, hoplama, sıçrayış, atlama** *He won with a jump of 8.5 metres.* **2** a sudden increase in the amount of something (miktar) ani **artış/sıçrama/artma** *a jump in profits* ⪢See also: the high jump, the long jump.

jumper /'dʒʌmpər/ *noun* [C] **1** UK (UK/US **sweater**) a warm piece of clothing which covers the top of your body and is pulled on over your head **kazak, süveter** ⪢Orta kısımdaki renkli sayfalarına bakınız. **2** US (UK **pinafore**) a loose dress with no sleeves that is worn over other clothes such as a shirt **geniş elbise**

'jump ‚rope US (UK **skipping rope**) *noun* [C] a rope that you move over your head and then jump over as you move it under your feet **atlama ipi**

jumpy /'dʒʌmpi/ *adjective* nervous or anxious **hırçın, sinirli, diken üstünde duran, gergin, heyecanlı**

▦▦ junction ...... İLE BİRLİKTE KULLANILAN KELİMELER
the junction of sth and sth ● a **railway/road** junction ● a **busy** junction

junction /'dʒʌŋkʃən/ *noun* [C] UK the place where two roads or railway lines meet or cross each other **kavşak** *The accident happened at a busy road junction.* ⪢See also: T-junction.

juncture /'dʒʌŋktʃər/ *noun* [C]*formal* a particular point in an event or period of time **önemli an, nazik durum**

oﾐ**June** /dʒuːn/ *noun* [C, U] the sixth month of the year **haziran ayı**

jungle /'dʒʌŋɡl/ *noun* [C, U] an area of land, usually in tropical countries, where trees and plants grow close together **balta girmemiş orman**

junior¹ /'dʒuːniər/ *adjective* **1** LOW RANK low or lower in rank **ast rütbede olan, düşük rütbeli, kıdemsiz, ast** *a junior minister/senator* **2** YOUNG PEOPLE for or relating to young people **gençler için, gençlere ilişkin** *a junior tennis tournament* **3** NAME mainly US (written abbreviation **Jr**) used at the end of a man's name to show that he is the younger of two men in the same family who have the same name **ailede daha genç olan erkeğin isminden sonra kullanılır; genç olan** *Hello, I'd like to speak to Mr Anderson Junior, please.*

junior² /'dʒuːniər/ *noun* **1** be 10/20, etc years sb's junior to be 10/20, etc years younger than someone **birinden 10/20 yaş daha genç olmak** *My wife is 8 years my junior.* **2** [C] a student in their third year of study at an American college or high school (= school for 15-18 year olds) **ABD'de 15-18 yaşlarında lise veya kolejde üçüncü sınıftaki öğrenci** **3** [C] UK a child who goes to a junior school **ilköğretim okuluna giden çocuk**

'junior ‚college *noun* [C, U] a two-year college in the US where students can learn a skill or prepare to enter a university **ABD'de beceri kazandıran veya üniversiteye hazırlayan iki yıllık okul/kolej**

junior 'high school (*also* junior 'high) *noun* [C, U] a school in the US or Canada for children who are 12 to 15 years old **ortaokul**

'junior ‚school *noun* [C, U] a school in the UK for children who are 7 to 11 years old **ilkokul**

junk /dʒʌŋk/ *noun* [U] *informal* old things which have little value **değersiz eski şeyler**

'junk ‚food *noun* [U] food which is unhealthy but is quick and easy to eat **sağlıksız ama hızlı ve kolay yenilebilen yiyecek; ayaküstü atıştırılan yiyecek**

junkie /'dʒʌŋki/ *noun* [C] *informal* **1** someone who cannot stop taking illegal drugs **esrarkeş, eroinman** **2** someone who wants something or wants to do something very much **istekli/hevesli/müptela/tutkun kişi** *a publicity junkie*

'junk ‚mail *noun* [U] letters sent by companies to advertise their goods and services **reklam/tanıtım mektupları; değersiz posta**

junta /'dʒʌntə/ *noun* [C] a military government that has taken power in a country by force **cunta, askerî cunta/hükümet**

Jupiter /'dʒuːpɪtər/ *noun* [no plural] the planet that is fifth from the Sun, after Mars and before Saturn **Jüpiter; güneş sisteminin 5. gezegeni**

jurisdiction /ˌdʒʊərɪs'dɪkʃən/ *noun* [U] the legal power to make decisions and judgments **yasal yetki/selahiyet; yetki alanı** *The school is under the jurisdiction of the local council.*

juror /'dʒʊərər/ *noun* [C] a member of a jury **jüri üyesi**

▦▦ jury ...... İLE BİRLİKTE KULLANILAN KELİMELER
be on a jury

oﾐ**jury** /'dʒʊəri/ *noun* [group] **1** a group of people in a court of law who decide if someone is guilty or not **mahkeme jürisi** **2** a group of people who decide the winner of a competition **yarışma jürisi**

oﾐ**just¹** *strong form* /dʒʌst/ *weak form* /dʒəst/ *adverb* **1** ONLY only **yalnız, sadece** *I'll just have a small piece.* ○ *He just wants to win.* ○ *The film is not just about love.* **2** RECENTLY a very short time ago **az evvel, henüz, biraz önce, demin** *I've just been on a trip to France.* ○ *We've only just begun.* **3** EMPHASIS used to emphasize something you say **gerçekten, doğrusu, hakikaten, tam anlamıyla** *I just can't bear it!* **4** ALMOST NOT UK almost not **hemen hemen hiç** *This dress only just fits.* **5** EXACTLY exactly **tam olarak,** *Tim looks just like his father.* ○ *This carpet would be just right for my bedroom.* **6** ALMOST NOW now or very soon **şimdi, hemen, az sonra, neredeyse** *I'm just coming!* **7** just before/over/under, etc a little before/over/under, etc something else **sadece, yalnızca** *It costs just over $10.* ○ *She left just before Michael.* **8** just about almost **hemen hemen, neredeyse,** *I think I've remembered just about everything.* **9** be just about to do sth to be going to do something very soon **bir şey yapmak üzere olmak; bir şeyi yapmaya ramak kalmak** *I was just about to phone you.* **10** just as bad/good/tall, etc (as sb/sth) equally bad/good/tall, etc **eşit oranda, eşit olarak;** *a/e kadar* *He's just as talented as his brother.* **11** I/you/we, etc will just have to do sth used to say that there is nothing else someone can do **sadece, yalnızca, başka** *You'll just have to wait.* **12** just as at the same time as **tam o sırada, tam o anda** *She woke up just as we got there.* **13** it's just as well used to say that it is lucky that something happened **ne iyi ki, ne iyi etmişiz de, iyi ki de** *It's just as well we brought an umbrella.* ⪢See also: just the job.

just² /dʒʌst/ *adjective* fair or morally right **adil, doğru, ahlaken doğru, dürüst** *a just society* ⪢Opposite unjust.
● **justly** *adverb* **adil bir şekilde**

···

fight for/seek justice ● justice **for** sb

justice /'dʒʌstɪs/ *noun* **1** FAIR BEHAVIOUR [U] behaviour or treatment that is fair and morally correct **tarafsızlık, adalet, hakça davranış** *She tried to bring about fairness and justice for all.* ⊃Opposite injustice. **2** LAW [U] the system of laws which judges or punishes people **adalet** *the criminal justice system* **3** JUDGE [C] *US* someone who judges in a court of law **yargıç, hâkim 4 bring sb to justice** to catch a criminal and decide if they are guilty or not **adalete teslim etmek, adalet önüne çıkarmak 5 do sb/sth justice; do justice to sb/sth** to show the best or real qualities of something or someone **hakkını vermek/teslim etmek** *This postcard doesn't do justice to the wonderful scenery.*

͵Justice of the ꞋPeace *noun* [C] someone who acts as a judge in a small or local court of law **yargıç, sulh yargıcı**

justifiable /'dʒʌstɪfaɪəbl/ *adjective* having a good reason **mazur/haklı görülebilir, savunulabilir** *justifiable anger* ● **justifiably** *adverb* **açıklanabilir bir şekilde**

justification /͵dʒʌstɪfɪ'keɪʃᵊn/ *noun* [C, U] a reason for something **gerekçe, mazeret, haklı neden** *There's no justification for treating her so badly.*

justified /'dʒʌstɪfaɪd/ *adjective* fair or having a good reason **doğru, isabetli, uygun, haklı, mazur görülebilir** *justified criticism* ○ *He's perfectly justified in asking for a larger salary.* ⊃Opposite unjustified.

justify /'dʒʌstɪfaɪ/ *verb* [T] to give a good enough reason to make something seem acceptable **haklı göstermek/çıkarmak, mazur göstermek, geçerli nedeni olmak** *I don't know how they can justify those ticket prices.*

jut /dʒʌt/ *verb* **jutting**, *past* **jutted jut into/out, etc** If something juts out, it comes out further than the edge or surface around it. **çıkıntı yapmak, çıkmak, (dışarı) fırlamak** *The rocks jutted out into the sea.*

juvenile[1] /'dʒuːvᵊnaɪl/ *adjective* **1** [always before noun] by, for, or relating to young people **gençlere/çocuklara özgü/ait** *juvenile crime* **2** behaving in a silly way as if you were a young child **çocuksu, olgunlaşmamış**

juvenile[2] /'dʒuːvᵊnaɪl/ *noun* [C] especially in law, a young person **(hukuk) genç insan, çocuk**

͵juvenile deꞋlinquent *noun* [C] a young criminal **suçlu genç, suç işlemiş çocuk**

juxtapose /͵dʒʌkstə'pəʊz/ *verb* [T] *formal* to place very different things or people close to each other **(farklı eşya/kişi) yanyana koymak/yerleştirmek; zıt şeyleri bir araya getirmek** *The exhibition juxtaposes paintings with black and white photographs.* ● **juxtaposition** /͵dʒʌkstəpə'zɪʃᵊn/ *noun* [C, U] **yanyana koyma**

J

K

K, k /keɪ/ the eleventh letter of the alphabet **alfabenin onbirinci harfi**

K /keɪ/ *abbreviation for* kilobyte: a unit for measuring the amount of information a computer can store **kilobayt; bir bilgisayarın taşıyabileceği bilginin miktarını ölçen birim**

kaleidoscope /kə'laɪdəskəʊp/ *noun* **1** [C] a tube-shaped toy you look through which contains mirrors and pieces of coloured glass that make patterns **kaleydoskop; içinde ayna ve küçük renkli camlardan oluşan ve şekilleri yansıtan küçük tüp şeklinde oyuncak 2** [no plural] a mixture of different things **farklı şeylerin bileşimi, değişken** *The fashion show was a kaleidoscope of colours.*

kangaroo /ˌkæŋɡə'ruː/ **kangaroo**
noun [C] a large Australian animal that moves by jumping on its back legs **kanguru**

karat /'kærət/ *noun* [C] another US spelling of carat (= a unit for measuring how pure gold is, or how much valuable stones weigh) **karat, altının saflığını belirten ölçüm birimi**

karate /kə'rɑːti/ *noun* [U] a sport from Japan in which people fight using fast, hard hits with the hands or feet **karate**

karma /'kɑːmə/ *noun* [U] in some religions, the actions of a person in this life or earlier lives, which influence their future **bazı dinlerde, bir kişinin önceki ve şimdiki yaşamında geleceğini etkileyen hareketler**

kayak /'kaɪæk/ *noun* [C] a light, narrow boat, usually for one person, which you move using a paddle (= stick with a wide, flat part) **Eskimo kayığı • kayaking** *noun* [U] the activity of travelling in a kayak **kayıkla gitmek/seyahat etmek**

kebab /kɪ'bæb/ (*also* shish kebab) *noun* [C] small pieces of meat or vegetables cooked on a long, thin stick **kebap**

keel¹ /kiːl/ *noun* [C] a long piece of wood or metal at the bottom of a boat that helps it to balance **tekne omurgası**

keel² /kiːl/ *verb*
keel over *phrasal verb* to fall over suddenly **alabora olmak, yuvarlanmak, devrilmek**

○***keen** /kiːn/ *adjective* **1** [INTERESTED] very interested or enthusiastic **istekli, gayretli, coşkulu** *a keen golfer/photographer* ○ *He's very **keen on** travelling.* **2** [WANTING TO DO] wanting to do something very much **bir şeyi yapmaya istekli, hevesli, meraklı** [+ to do sth] *The shop is **keen** to attract new customers.* **3** [VERY GOOD] very good or well developed **çok iyi, gelişmiş** *a keen sense of smell* • **keenness** *noun* [U] **ilgi** • **keenly** *adverb* **ilgili bir şekilde**

Save fiili kişinin gelecekte kullanmak üzere bir şey sakladığının ifadesinde kullanılır. *I have some really good chocolates that I've been **saving** for a special occasion.*

Hang onto ve **hold onto** deyimleri kişinin gelecekte kullanmak üzere sakladığı bir şeyin ifadesinde kullanılır. *You should **hang/hold onto** that picture - it might be worth something.*

○***keep¹** /kiːp/ *verb past* **kept 1** [HAVE] [T] to have something permanently or for the whole of a period of time **tutmak** *You can keep that dress if you like it.* ○ *He borrowed my bike and kept it all week.* **2 keep sth in/on, etc** to regularly store something in a particular place **saklamak, bulundurmak** *I think he keeps his keys in the desk drawer.* ○ *We'll keep your application on file.* **3 keep doing sth** to continue to do something, or to do something repeatedly **ısrarla yapmaya devam etmek, sürdürmek** *I keep telling her not to leave her clothes on the floor.* ○ *He keeps hitting me.* **4 keep (sb/ sth) awake/clean/safe, etc** to remain in a particular state or make someone or something remain in a particular state **aynı durumda/konumda/şartta kalmak/kalmasını sağlamak** *He goes jogging twice a week to keep fit.* ○ *He keeps his car spotlessly clean.* **5 keep sb/sth in/inside, etc** to make someone or something stay in the same place **içerde tutmak, alıkoymak** *They will keep her at home for a few more days.* **6** [MAKE DO STH] [T] to make someone do something that stops them doing something else **meşgul etmek, oyalamak, alıkoymak** [+ doing sth] *She kept me talking for ages.* ○ *Sorry to keep you waiting.* ○ *Don't let me keep you from your work.* **7 keep a secret** to not tell anyone a secret **sır tutmak 8 keep a promise/your word, etc** to do what you have promised to do **sözünü tutmak, vaadini yerine getirmek 9 keep an appointment** to meet someone when you have arranged to meet them **randevuya gitmek/gelmek 10** [MAKE LATE] [T] to make someone arrive later than they planned **geciktirmek, alıkoymak, engel olmak** *I was expecting you at six - what kept you?* **11** [WRITE] [T] to write down something in order to remember it **not almak, bir köşeye yazmak** *to keep records/notes* **12** [FOOD] [I] If food or drink keeps, it remains fresh. **taze kalmak, bozulmamak 13** [PROVIDE MONEY] [T] to provide enough money for someone to live **bakmak, geçimini sağlamak, aileyi geçindirmek** *I can't keep a family on that salary.* **14** [ANIMALS] [T] to have and look after animals **hayvan beslemek** *Our neighbours keep pigs.* **15 keep sb going** to provide what someone needs for a short period of time **(açlık, susuzluk vs.) gidermek, bastırmak, tutmak, geçici bir süre yetmek** *Dinner is at eight, but I had an apple to keep me going.* ⮕See also: keep your **cool³**, keep a straight **face¹**, keep your **fingers** (**finger¹**) crossed, put/keep sb in the **picture¹**, keep a low **profile¹**, keep a tight **rein** on sb/sth, keep tabs (**tab**) on sb/sth, keep sb on their **toes** (**toe¹**).

keep at sth *phrasal verb* to continue to work hard at something difficult **devam etmek, peşini bırakmamak, vazgeçmemek** *Learning a language is hard but you've just got to keep at it.*

keep (sb/sth) away *phrasal verb* to not go somewhere or near something, or to prevent someone from going somewhere or near something **uzak durmak, yaklaşmamak, geride durmak** *I told them to keep away from the edge of the cliff.*

keep (sb/sth) back *phrasal verb* to not go near something, or to prevent someone or something from going past a particular place **engellemek, uzak tutmak, yaklaştırmamak** *Barriers were built to keep back the flood water.*

keep sth back *phrasal verb* to not tell someone everything you know about a situation or an event **konuyla ilgili bir şeyleri saklıyor olmak; hepsini söyleyememek** *I was sure she was keeping something back.*

keep sth down *phrasal verb* **1** to stop the number, level, or size of something from increasing **azaltmak, indirmek, düşürmek, aşağı çekmek** *I have to exercise to keep my weight down.* **2** to be able to eat or drink without vomiting **kusmadan yiyip içebilmek**

keep sb/sth from doing sth *phrasal verb* to prevent someone or something from doing something **engel/mani olmak, karşı durmak, alıkoymak, engellemek**

keep sth from sb *phrasal verb* to not tell someone about something **birinden bir şeyler gizlemek, söylememek** *Is there something you're keeping from me?*

keep sb in *phrasal verb* to make a child stay inside as a punishment, or to make someone stay in hospital **içerde kalma cezası vermek; birini zorla hastanede veya kapalı bir ortamda tutmak/alıkoymak**

keep (sb/sth) off sth *phrasal verb* to not go onto an area, or to stop someone or something going onto an area **yaklaşmamak, uzak durmak, yanaşmamak** *Keep off the grass.*

keep off (sb/sth) *phrasal verb* to stop something touching or harming someone or something **yaklaşmasına engel olmak, uzaklaştırmak, yanaştırmamak** *He put a cloth over the salad to keep the flies off.*

keep on doing sth *phrasal verb* to continue to do something, or to do something again and again **bir şeyi yapmayı sürdürmek; devam etmek** *She kept on asking me questions the whole time.*

keep on *phrasal verb* UK to continue to talk in an annoying way about something **rahatsız edici bir şekilde sürekli konuşmak** *I wish he wouldn't keep on about how much he earns.*

keep (sb/sth) out *phrasal verb* to not go into a place, or to stop someone or something from going into a place **girmesine engel olmak, sokmamak, uzak tutmak** *He locked the room and put up a sign asking people to keep out.*

keep to sth *phrasal verb* **1** to stay in one particular area **aynı yerde kalmak, orayı terketmemek** *We kept to main roads all the way.* **2** to do what you have promised or planned to do **plana bağlı/sadık kalmak; planlanan/konuşulandan ayrılmamak** *I think we should keep to our original plan.*

keep sth to sth *phrasal verb* If you keep something to a particular number or amount, you make sure it does not become larger than that. **artmasına engel olmak, bir düzeyde tutmaya çalışmak; çoğalmasına mani olmak** *I'm trying to keep costs to a minimum.*

keep sth to yourself *phrasal verb* to keep something secret and not tell anyone else about it **kendine saklamak, sadece kendisi bilmek, içinde sır olarak tutmak**

keep up *phrasal verb* **1** [SAME SPEED] to move at the same speed as someone or something that is moving forward so that you stay level with them **yetişmek, aynı seviyeye gelmek, erişmek, ulaşmak** *She was walking so fast I couldn't keep up with her.* **2** [MAKE PROGRESS] to increase or make progress at the same speed as someone or something else so that you stay at the same level as them **ileleme yaparak yetişmek, aynı hızla ilerlemeye çalışmak** *Prices have been rising very fast and wages haven't kept up.* **3** [UNDERSTAND] to be able to understand and deal with something that is happening

or changing very fast **anlamaya/kavramaya çalışmak; ne olup bittiğinden haberdar olmak; gündemi yaklamaya çalışmak** *I feel it's important to keep up with current events.*

keep sth up *phrasal verb* to not allow something that is at a high level to fall to a lower level **aynı seviyede muhafaza etmeye özen göstermek** *Make sure you eat properly - you've got to keep your strength up.*

keep (sth) up *phrasal verb* to continue without stopping or changing or to continue something without allowing it to stop or change **başetmeye çalışmak, başa çıkmak için çaba sarfetmek** *People are having difficulties keeping up the repayments on their loans.*

keep² /ki:p/ *noun* [no plural] the money needed to pay for someone to eat and live in a place **geçim için gerekli para** *He earns his keep working in a garage.*

keeper /ˈkiːpəʳ/ *noun* [C] **1** someone who looks after a place and the things, people, or animals there **bekçi, bakıcı** *a park keeper* **2** *informal short for* goalkeeper (= the player in a sport such as football who tries to stop the ball going into the goal) **kaleci**

keeping /ˈkiːpɪŋ/ *noun* **1 for safe keeping** in order to keep something safe **güvende olması için; koruma altında/güvenlikte olması için** *She put the money into a bank for safe keeping.* **2 in keeping with sth** suitable or right for a situation, style, or tradition **uyumlu, uygun olma** *The antique desk was in keeping with the rest of the furniture in the room.*

keg /keg/ *noun* [C] a large, round container used for storing beer **küçük fıçı**

kennel /ˈkenᵊl/ *noun* [C] **1** a small building for a dog to sleep in **köpek kulübesi 2** US (UK **kennels**) a place where dogs are cared for while their owners are away **köpek bakım evi**

kennel

kept /kept/ *past of* keep 'korumak' fiilinin geçmiş zaman hâli

kerb UK (US **curb**) /kɜːb/ *noun* [C] the line of stones at the edge of a pavement (= raised path that people walk on) next to the road **kaldırım kenarı**

kernel /ˈkɜːnᵊl/ *noun* [C] the part of a nut or seed inside the hard shell which you can usually eat **çekirdek**

kerosene /ˈkerəsiːn/ US (UK **paraffin**) *noun* [U] oil used for heating and in lamps (= equipment that produces light) **gaz, gaz yağı**

ketchup /ˈketʃʌp/ *noun* [U] a thick sauce made from tomatoes (= round, red fruit) that is eaten cold with food **ketçap**

kettle /ˈketl/ *noun* [C] a metal or plastic container with a lid, used for boiling water **su ısıtıcısı, çaydanlık** *Charlotte put the kettle on to make some tea.* ⊃Orta kısımdaki renkli sayfalarına bakınız.

┌─────────────────────────────────┐
│ 🔑 **key** .... İLE BİRLİKTE KULLANILAN KELİMELER │
└─────────────────────────────────┘

a bunch of/set of keys ● **the key for/to sth** ● **a car key**

◦⌐**key¹** /ki:/ *noun* [C] **1** [FOR LOCKS] a piece of metal cut into a particular shape and used for locking things such as doors, or for starting an engine **anahtar** *I've lost my car keys.* **2** [METHOD] a way of explaining or achieving something **en önemli nokta, çözüm yolu** *Hard work is the key to success.* **3** [KEYBOARD] one of the parts you press with your fingers on a keyboard or musical instrument to produce letters, numbers, or to make a sound **tuşlar 4** [MUSIC] a set of musical notes based on one particular note **müzik notaları** *the key of D major* **5** [SYMBOLS] a list which explains the symbols on a map or picture **kısaltmalar, açıklamalar 6** [ANSWERS] a list of answers to an exercise or game **cevap anahtarı** ⊃See also: under **lock²** and **key.**

key² /kiː/ *adjective* very important in influencing or achieving something **en önemli, esas, ana** *a key factor*

key³ /kiː/ *verb*
key sth in *phrasal verb* to put information into a computer or machine using a keyboard **klâvyeyi kullanarak bilgisayara/makinaya bilgi girmek**

keyboard /ˈkiːbɔːd/ *noun* [C] **1** a set of keys on a computer, which you press to make it work, or the rows of keys on a piano **klâvye** ⊃Orta kısımdaki renkli sayfalarına bakınız. **2** an electrical musical instrument similar to a piano **klâvye**

keyhole /ˈkiːhəʊl/ *noun* [C] a hole in a lock where you put a key **anahtar deliği**

keynote /ˈkiːnəʊt/ *noun* [C] the most important part of an event, idea, or speech, or something that is emphasized strongly **temel, temel kavram, ana fikir, tema** *the keynote speech/speaker*

keypad /ˈkiːpæd/ *noun* [C] a set of buttons with numbers on them used to operate a television, telephone, etc **tuş takımı**

key ˌring *noun* [C] a metal ring used for keeping keys together **anahtarlık**

kg *written abbreviation for* kilogram (= a unit for measuring weight) **kilogram'ın kısa hâli**

khaki /ˈkɑːki/ *noun* [U] a pale green-brown colour, often worn by soldiers **hâki renk; asker yeşili/hâkisi** • **khaki** *adjective* ⊃Orta kısımdaki renkli sayfalarına bakınız. **sarı ile kahverengi arası bir renk**

kibbutz /kɪˈbʊts/ *noun* [C] *plural* **kibbutzim** a place in Israel where people live and work together, often a farm or a factory **İsrail'de insanların birlikte yaşadığı ve çalıştığı yer/çiftlik/fabrika**

⌐**kick¹ /**kɪk/ *verb* **1** [I, T] to hit or move something or someone with your foot **tekmelemek** *The boys were kicking a ball back and forth.* ○ *They tried to kick the door down.* **2** [I] to move your feet and legs forwards or backwards quickly and with force **tekme atmak, tekmelemek, tepmek** *I kicked at them and screamed for help.* **3 kick yourself** *informal* to be very annoyed with yourself for doing something stupid or wrong **yaptığına çok pişman olmak; yaptığından utanmak** *I could have kicked myself for saying that.* ⊃See also: be **alive** and kicking/ well.
be kicking about/around *phrasal verb informal* If something is kicking about, it is in a particular place, but nobody is using it or paying attention to it. **kıyıda köşede unutulmuş olmak; ihmal edilmiş olmak** *We've probably got a copy of the document kicking around the office.*
kick in *phrasal verb informal* to start to be effective or to happen **etkinleşmek, olmaya/etkinleşmeye başlamak** *The new tax rate kicks in next month.*
kick off *phrasal verb* **1** When a football match or other event kicks off, it starts. **başlatmak, başlama vuruşu**

yapmak 2 *informal* to start to get angry or complain **kızmaya/yakınmaya başlamak**
kick (sth) off *phrasal verb informal* When you kick off a discussion or activity, you start it. **bir tartışmayı/ eylemi başlatmak**
kick sb out *phrasal verb informal* to force someone to leave a place or organization **kovmak, kapı dışarı etmek, atmak, defetmek** *His wife kicked him out.*

kick² /kɪk/ *noun* **1** [C] when you kick something with your foot **tekme** *He gave her a kick in the ribs.* **2** [C] *informal* a special feeling of excitement and energy **zevk, heyecan** *She gets a kick out of performing live.* **3 a kick in the teeth** used when someone treats you badly or unfairly, especially when you need or expect support **gereksinim duyarken ve destek beklerken kötü ve adil olmayan muamele görmeyi anlatmak için kullanılır** *This latest pay award amounts to a kick in the teeth.* ⊃See also: free **kick.**

kickback /ˈkɪkbæk/ *noun* [C] *US* money given to someone, especially illegally, for providing help, a job, or a piece of business **rüşvet, yasadışı yollarla ödenen/ verilen para**

kickboxing /ˈkɪkˌbɒksɪŋ/ *noun* [U] a sport in which two people fight by hitting each other with their hands and kicking each other with their feet **kikboks**

kick-off /ˈkɪkɒf/ *noun* [C, U] the time when a football match begins **futbolda başlama vuruşu**

⌐**kid¹ /**kɪd/ *noun* [C] **1** *informal* a child or young person **çocuk** *school kids* **2** a young goat **oğlak, keçi yavrusu**

kid² /kɪd/ *verb* [I, T] **kidding**, *past* **kidded 1** to make a joke, or to trick someone with a joke **şaka/espri yapmak, dalga geçmek, gırgır yapmak 2** to deceive or trick someone into believing something **kandırmak, aldatmak** [often reflexive] *You've got to stop kidding yourself. She's not coming back.*

kiddie /ˈkɪdi/ *noun* [C] *informal* a child **çocuk**

kidnap /ˈkɪdnæp/ *verb* [T] **kidnapping**, *past* **kidnapped** to take someone away using force, usually to obtain money in exchange for releasing them **adam kaçırmak** • **kidnap** *noun* [C] *a kidnap victim/attempt* **(çocuk) kaçırma** • **kidnapper** *noun* [C] **çocuk kaçıran kişi**

kidnapping /ˈkɪdnæpɪŋ/ *noun* [C, U] when someone is kidnapped **adam kaçırma**

kidney /ˈkɪdni/ *noun* [C] one of the two organs in your body which remove waste from the blood and produce urine **böbrek**

⌐**kill¹ /**kɪl/ *verb* **1** [DEATH] [I, T] to cause someone or something to die **öldürmek** *Sunday's bomb killed 19 people.* ○ *Their son was killed in a road accident.* **2 sb will kill sb** *informal* used to say that someone will be very angry with someone else **birine çok kızgınlığı belirtmek için kullanılır** *Dad will kill me for being late.* **3** [END] [T] to stop an activity or experience completely **mahvetmek, bitirmek, öldürmek; (argo) içine etmek** *His remark killed the conversation.* **4** [CAUSE PAIN] [T] *informal* to cause you a lot of pain or effort **zahmet/eziyet vermek, çok sıkıntı vermek, öldürmek, canını çıkarmak** *My feet are killing me.* ○ *It wouldn't kill you to tidy up occasionally.* ⊃See also: kill **time¹.**
kill sth/sb off *phrasal verb* to stop something or someone from existing any more **yok etmek, ortadan kaldırmak,** *Lack of funding is killing off local theatres.*

kill² /kɪl/ *noun* **1** [no plural] when an animal is killed **avlanma, öldürme 2 go/move in for the kill** to prepare to defeat someone completely or to kill them **birilerini tamamen ortadan kaldırmaya hazırlanmak; öldürmek/yok etmek için çalışmak**

killer /'kɪlə^r/ *noun* [C] someone who kills, or a disease, substance, or animal that kills **öldürücü/yok edici şey; katil, öldürücü** *Cancer and heart disease are the UK's biggest killers.* ⊃See also: serial killer.

killing /'kɪlɪŋ/ *noun* **1** [C] a murder, or when someone or something is killed **öldürme, cinayet** *the killing of civilians* **2 make a killing** *informal* to make a lot of money very quickly **vurgun vurmak, aniden çok para kazanmak; (argo) malı götürmek**

kiln /kɪln/ *noun* [C] a large oven for baking bricks and other clay objects until they are hard **tuğla ocağı/fırını**

kilo /'kiːləʊ/ *noun* [C] *short for* kilogram **kilo**

kilo- /kɪlə-/ *prefix* a thousand **bin anlamında ön ek** *a kilometre* ○ *a kilogram*

kilobyte /'kɪləʊbaɪt/ *(written abbreviation K) noun* [C] a unit for measuring the amount of information a computer can store, equal to 1024 bytes **bilgisayarın alabileceği bilginin miktarını ölçmeye yarayan 1024 bayta eşit birim**

kilogram *(also UK* kilogramme) *(written abbreviation* kg) /'kɪləʊgræm/ *noun* [C] a unit for measuring weight, equal to 1000 grams **kilogram**

o--**kilometre** *UK (US* kilometer) *(written abbreviation* km) /kɪ'lɒmɪtə^r/, /'kɪləˌmiːtə^r/ *noun* [C] a unit for measuring distance, equal to 1000 metres **kilometre**

kilowatt /'kɪləʊwɒt/ *(written abbreviation* kW) *noun* [C] a unit for measuring electrical power, equal to 1000 watts **kilovat**

kilt /kɪlt/ *noun* [C] a traditional Scottish skirt for men, made of heavy material with close vertical folds at the back **İskoçya'da erkeklerin giydiği etek; kilt, İskoç eteği**

kin /kɪn/ *noun* [plural] *formal* the members of your family **hısım, akraba** ⊃See also: next of kin.

o--**kind**[1] /kaɪnd/ *noun* **1** [C] a type of thing or person **tür, çeşit** *What kind of music do you like?* ○ *All kinds of people come to our church.* ○ *Older kids like board games and that kind of thing.* ○ *Her travel company was the first of its kind* (= the first one like it). **2 some kind of** used to talk about something when you are not sure of its exact type **bir tür/çeşit** *She has some kind of disability.* **3 kind of** *informal* used when you are trying to explain or describe something, but you cannot be exact **biraz, bir parça** *It's kind of unusual.* **4 of a kind** used to describe something that exists but is not very good **sözüm ona, sözde** *The school had a swimming pool of a kind, but it was too small for most classes to use.*

Nice ve **sweet** sıfatları **kind** sıfatının alternatifleri olarak kullanılabilir. *It was really* **nice** *of you to come.* ● *Wasn't it* **sweet** *of Heidi to call?*
Good to ifadesi, kişinin bir diğerine yardımda bulunduğunun ifadesinde kullanılır. *Jay's mother has been very* **good** *to us.*
Eğer kişi yardım etmeye gönüllü ise, kişiyi **helpful** olarak tanımlayabiliriz. *The staff here are very* **helpful**.
Caring ifadesi diğer insanlara kibar davranan ve onların mutlu ve iyi olmalarına gayret gösteren kişilerin tanımında kullanılır. *I've always thought of Mary as a very* **caring** *person.*
Mean well söylemi diğerlerine iyi davranıp yardım etmeye çalışan fakat durumu iyileştirmek için elinden bir şey gelmeyen kişilerin tanımlanmasında kullanılır. *I know my parents* **mean well**, *but I do wish they wouldn't interfere.*

o--**kind**[2] /kaɪnd/ *adjective* Kind people do things to help others and show that they care about them. **nazik, kibar, yardımsever** *Your mother was very kind to us.* ○ *It was very kind of you to come and see me.* ⊃Opposite unkind.

kinda /'kaɪndə/ *mainly US informal short for* kind of **biraz, bir parça** *I'm kinda busy right now.*

kindergarten /'kɪndəˌgɑːt^ən/ *noun* [C, U] **1** in the UK, a school for children under five **(Birleşik Krallık) ana okulu 2** in the US, a class in school for children aged five **(ABD) ana okulu sınıfı**

kind-hearted /ˌkaɪnd'hɑːtɪd/ *adjective* having a kind character **iyi kalpli, müşfik, sevecen** *a kind-hearted family man*

kindly[1] /'kaɪndli/ *adverb* **1** in a kind or generous way **nazikçe, nezaketle, kibarca** *She kindly offered to cook me lunch.* **2** *formal* used in instructions to mean 'please', usually when you are annoyed **lütfen, zahmet olmazsa, rica etsem** *Would you kindly get out of my car?* **3 not take kindly to sth** to not like something that someone says or does **hoşlanmamak, iyi karşılamamak** *He doesn't take kindly to criticism.*

kindly[2] /'kaɪndli/ *adjective old-fashioned* kind **nazik, kibar bir şekilde** *a kindly old gentleman*

kindness /'kaɪndnəs/ *noun* [C, U] when someone is kind **iyilik, sevecenlik** *Thanks for all your kindness this morning.*

o--**king** /kɪŋ/ *noun* [C] **1** RULER a male ruler in some countries **kral** *King Richard II* ○ *the kings and queens of England* **2** BEST PERSON the best or most important person in a particular activity **en iyi ve önemli kişi, kral, en iyisi** *He's the new king of pop music.* **3** PLAYING CARD a playing card with a picture of a king on it **(iskambil) papaz** *the king of spades*

kingdom /'kɪŋdəm/ *noun* **1** [C] a country with a king or queen **krallık** *the Kingdom of Belgium* **2 the animal/plant kingdom** all animals or plants considered together **hayvanlar/bitkiler âlemi/krallığı**

kingfisher /'kɪŋˌfɪʃə^r/ *noun* [C] a small, brightly coloured bird which catches fish from rivers and lakes **iskele kuşu, yalı çapkını**

king-size *(also* king-sized) /'kɪŋsaɪz/ *adjective* very big **çok büyük, en büyük boy, battal boy** *a king-size bed*

kink /kɪŋk/ *noun* [C] a bend in something long and thin **kıvrım, büklüm** *There was a kink in the cassette tape.*

kinky /'kɪŋki/ *adjective informal* involving strange or unusual sexual behaviour **tuhaf/anormal/cinsel davranış içeren**

kiosk /'kiːɒsk/ *noun* [C] a small building with a window where things like tickets or newspapers are sold **büfe, satıcı kulübesi**

kip /kɪp/ *noun* [C, U] *UK informal* a short period of sleep **kuş uykusu, kısa uyku** ● **kip** *verb* [I] **kipping**, *past* **kipped şekerleme (uyku)**

kipper /'kɪpə^r/ *noun* [C] *UK* a type of fish that has been cut open and dried over smoke **füme, ringa balığı**

o--**kiss**[1] /kɪs/ *verb* [I, T] to press your lips against another person's lips or skin to show love or affection **öpmek** *He kissed her cheek.* ○ *Len kissed Samantha goodbye at the front gate.*

kiss

K

kiss 414 ☞ Important words to learn

kneel

---

kiss ...... İLE BİRLİKTE KULLANILAN KELİMELER

give sb a kiss • **plant** a kiss **on** sb's [lips/cheek, etc] • a **lingering/passionate** kiss

kiss² /kɪs/ *noun* [C] **1** an act of kissing someone **öpüşme, öpücük** *She ran up and gave me a big kiss.* **2 give sb the kiss of life** *UK* to help to keep someone who has stopped breathing alive by blowing into their mouth **hayat öpücüğü vermek**

kit /kɪt/ *noun* **1** COLLECTION [C] a collection of things kept in a container ready for a particular use **takım, techizat** *a first-aid/tool kit* **2** CLOTHES [C, U] *UK* a set of clothes worn for sport or military service (**spor, askerî hizmette**) **spor/asker kıyafeti/forması/üniforması** *a football kit* **3** PARTS [C] a set of parts which you put together to make something **parçalar bütünü, oluşturulmak için bir araya getirilen parçaların tamamı** *He's making a model car from a kit.*

kitchen /'kɪtʃɪn/ *noun* [C] a room used to prepare and cook food in **mutfak** ➜Orta kısımdaki renkli sayfalarına bakınız.

kite /kaɪt/ *noun* [C] a toy made of paper or cloth which flies in the air on the end of a long string **uçurtma**

kitsch /kɪtʃ/ *noun* [U] decorative objects or pieces of art that are ugly, silly, or have little value **zevksiz popüler sanat süsler tasarım vb**

kitten /'kɪtᵊn/ *noun* [C] a young cat **yavru kedi**

kitty /'kɪti/ *noun* [C] an amount of money consisting of a share from everyone in a group, used for a special purpose **toplanan ortak para, fon, kasa** [usually singular] *We all put money into a kitty to pay for drinks.*

kiwi /'ki:wi:/ (*also* 'kiwi ˌfruit) *noun* [C] a small, green fruit with black seeds and brown, hairy skin **kivi**

km *written abbreviation for* kilometre (= a unit for measuring distance) **kilometrenin kısa yazılışı**

knack ...... İLE BİRLİKTE KULLANILAN KELİMELER

have/lose the knack **of** doing sth • an **uncanny** knack • a knack **for** doing sth

knack /næk/ *noun* [no plural] a special skill, or the ability to use or do something easily **hüner, marifet, yetenek, beceri, ustalık** *a knack for remembering faces* ○ *She has the knack of making people feel comfortable.*

knackered /'nækəd/ *adjective UK informal* extremely tired **bitkin, yorgun, pestili çıkmış**

knead /ni:d/ *verb* [T] to press and shape the mixture for making bread firmly and repeatedly with your hands **hamur yoğurmak**

knee /ni:/ *noun* [C] **1** the middle part of your leg where it bends **diz** *a knee injury* ➜Orta kısımdaki renkli sayfalarına bakınız. **2** the part of a pair of trousers that covers the knee **pantolonun diz kısmı 3 bring sb/sth to their knees** to destroy or defeat someone or something **dize getirmek, perişan etmek, çökertmek** *The war brought the country to its knees.*

kneecap /'ni:kæp/ *noun* [C] the round bone at the front of your knee **diz kapağı**

knee-deep /ˌni:'di:p/ *adjective* **1** reaching as high as someone's knees **diz boyu derinlikte** *knee-deep in cold water* **2 be knee-deep in sth** to have a lot of something to deal with **çok işi olmak, çok meşgul olmak** *I'm knee-deep in paperwork.*

knee-jerk /'ni:dʒɜ:k/ *adjective* **a knee-jerk reaction/response, etc** an immediate reaction that does not allow you time to consider something carefully **ani tepki göstermek, düşünmeden ve zamana vurmadan eyleme geçmek**

kneel /ni:l/ *verb* [I] *past* **knelt** or **kneeled** to go down into or stay in a position where one or both of your knees are on the ground **diz çökmek** *She knelt down beside the child.*

knew /nju:/ *past tense of* know **'bilmek' fiilinin ikinci hâli**

knickers /'nɪkəz/ *UK* (*US* panties) *noun* [plural] women's underwear that covers the bottom **kadın külotu** ➜Orta kısımdaki renkli sayfalarına bakınız.

knife¹ /naɪf/ *noun* [C] *plural* **knives** a sharp tool or weapon for cutting, usually with a metal blade and a handle **bıçak** *a knife and fork*

knife² /naɪf/ *verb* [T] to attack someone using a knife **bıçakla saldırmak, bıçaklamak** ➜See also: jack-knife.

knight¹ /naɪt/ *noun* [C] **1** a man of high social rank who fought as a soldier on a horse in the past **şövalye 2** a man who has been given the title 'Sir' by the King or Queen in the UK (**Birleşik Krallık**) **şövalye ünvanı**

knight² /naɪt/ *verb* **be knighted** to be given a knighthood **şövalye ünvanı ver(il)mek; şövalye yapılmak**

knighthood /'naɪthʊd/ *noun* [C] the title of 'Sir' given to someone by the King or Queen in the UK **şövalyelik ünvanı**

knit /nɪt/ *verb* [I, T] **knitting,** *past tense* **knitted,** *past participle* **knitted** (UK) **knit** (US) to make clothes using wool and two long needles to join the wool into rows **örmek, örgü** *She was knitting him a jumper.*

knit

knitting /'nɪtɪŋ/ *noun* [U] when something is being knitted or the thing that is being knitted **örgü, örgü örme** *She put down her knitting.*

knitwear /'nɪtweər/ *noun* [U] knitted clothes **örgü/örülmüş giysi, triko**

knob /nɒb/ *noun* **1** [C] a round handle, or a round button on a machine **tokmak, topuz** *a door knob* ○ *Turn the black knob to switch on the radio.* **2 a knob of butter** *UK* a small lump of butter **bir top yağ/tereyağ**

knock¹ /nɒk/ *verb* **1** MAKE NOISE [I] to make a noise by hitting something, especially a door, with your closed hand in order to attract someone's attention **vurmak, tıklatmak** *There's someone knocking at/on the door.* ○ *Please knock before entering.* **2** HIT [T] to hit something or someone and make them move or fall down **vurup yere yıkmak/sermek/devirmek** *He accidentally knocked the vase off the table.* ○ *I knocked over the mug.* **3** CRITICIZE [T] *informal* to criticize someone or something, often unfairly **eleştirmek, tenkit etmek, kusur bulmak** *She knocks every suggestion I make.* **4 Knock it off!** *informal* something you say when you want someone to stop doing something that is annoying you 'Kes!', 'Kes şunu!', 'Yeter artık!', 'Öff!' ⊃See also: beat/ knock the (living) daylights out of sb.

knock sth back *phrasal verb UK informal* to drink alcohol very quickly **bir biri ardısıra alkol almak/ içmek; hızlı hızlı içmek**

knock sb down *phrasal verb UK* to hit someone with a vehicle and injure or kill them **ezmek, çiğnemek, araçla çarpıp yaralamak/öldürmek** [often passive] *She was knocked down by a bus.*

knock sb/sth down *phrasal verb US* to cause someone or something to fall to the ground by hitting them **yıkmak, yere sermek, vurup düşürmek**

knock sth down *phrasal verb* to destroy a building or part of a building **yıkmak, yerle bir etmek**

knock off *phrasal verb informal* to stop working, usually at the end of a day **işi bırakmak, paydos etmek** *I don't knock off until six.*

knock sth off (sth) *phrasal verb* to take a particular amount away from something, usually a price **indirim yapmak, fiyat kırmak** *The manager knocked $5 off because it was damaged.*

knock sb out *phrasal verb* **1** to make someone become unconscious, usually by hitting them on the head **kafasına vurup bayıltmak, yere sermek, bayıltmak** *He was knocked out halfway through the fight.* **2** to defeat a person or team in a competition so they cannot take part any more **yenmek, mağlup etmek, yarış dışı bırakmak, elemek** [often passive] *The French team were knocked out in the semifinal.*

🧩 knock ...... İLE BİRLİKTE KULLANILAN KELİMELER

a **sharp** knock ● a knock **at/on** [the door/window, etc.]

knock² /nɒk/ *noun* [C] **1** a sudden short noise made when something or someone hits a surface **sert bir yere vurulduğunda çıkan tok ses** *a knock at/on the door* **2** when someone or something is hit, sometimes causing damage or injury **vurma, darbe, itme, itiş, yara bere** *a knock on the head*

knocker /ˈnɒkəʳ/ *noun* [C] a metal object fixed to the outside of a door which visitors use to knock **kapı tokmağı**

knock-on /ˌnɒkˈɒn/ *adjective UK* **a knock-on effect** When an event or situation has a knock-on effect, it causes another event or situation. **zincirleme, ard arda gelen, biri diğerini etkileyen** *Cutting schools' budgets will have a knock-on effect on teachers' jobs.*

knockout /ˈnɒkaʊt/ *noun* [C] in boxing, when one person hits the other hard and they become unconscious **nakavt, yere serme, devirme, düşürme**

🧩 knot ...... İLE BİRLİKTE KULLANILAN KELİMELER

tie a knot (in sth) ● undo/untie a knot

knot¹ /nɒt/ *noun* **1** [C] a place where pieces of string, rope, etc have been tied together **düğüm 2** [C] a unit for measuring the speed of the wind, ships, or aircraft **deniz mili; uçak, gemi veya rüzgâr hızı ölçüm birimi 3** **tie the knot** *informal* to get married **evlenmek**

knot² /nɒt/ *verb* [T] **knotting**, *past* **knotted** to tie knots in pieces of string, rope, etc **düğümlemek**

∘⁻**know¹** /nəʊ/ *verb past tense* **knew**, *past participle* **known** **1** [HAVE INFORMATION] [I, T] to have knowledge or information about something in your mind **bilmek** *"How old is she?" "I don't know."* ○ *Andrew knows a lot about computers.* ○ [+ question word] *Do you know where the station is?* ○ [+ (that)] *He knew that she was lying.*

2 [BE FAMILIAR WITH] [T] to be familiar with a person, place, or thing because you have met them, been there, used it, etc before **bilmek, görmüş/duymuş/bulunmuş/karşılaşmış olmak** *I've known Tim since primary school.* ○ *I grew up in Brussels so I know it well.* ○ *Since moving to London, I've got to know* (= become familiar with) *some nice people.* **3** [BE ABLE] [T] to be able to do something **anlamak, bilmek, yapabilmek** [+ question word] *Do you know how to ski?* ○ *I only know* (= understand and speak) *a little Spanish.* **4** **let sb know** to tell someone something **haber vermek, bildirmek, bilgilendirmek** *Let me know if you're going to the party.* **5** [GUESS CORRECTLY] [T] to guess something correctly **doğru tahminde bulunmak; doğru bilmek** *I knew she'd arrive late.* ○ *I should have known he wouldn't come.* **6** [UNDERSTAND] [I, T] to understand and agree with someone **anlayıp/bilip hak vermek, anlamak; kavramak ve hak vermek; demek istediğini anlamak** *I know what you mean about Pete - I wouldn't trust him at all.* **7** **be known as sth** to be called something **öyle bilinmek, anılmak, çağrılmak, ...ile tanınmak; ... olarak da bilinmek** *California is also known as the Sunshine State.* **8** **have known sth** to have had experience of something **bilmiş/görmüş/duymuş olmak; daha önceden deneyimi olmak** *I've never known the weather be so hot.* **9** **know better (than to do sth)** to have the intelligence or judgment not to do something **biliyor olmalıydı, bilmiş olmalı, bilmeli** *She should have known better than to eat so much. No wonder she feels sick now.* **10** **I know** a [AGREEING] used when you agree with something someone has just said **'doğru söylüyorsun!', 'Biliyorum!', 'Haklısın!'** *"It's a lovely day, isn't it?" "I know - let's hope it lasts."* **b** [NEW IDEA] used when you have an idea **'Biliyorum!', 'Ben biliyorum!', 'Bana güvenin!'** *I know - let's go to Helen's house.* **11** **you know** a used to emphasize that someone does know what you are referring to **'Bildiğiniz gibi', 'Siz de biliyorsunuz ki...'** *You know, the's the one with curly hair.* **b** something that you say while you are thinking what to say next **'Eee...', 'Biliyorsun ...'** *It's, you know, supposed to be a surprise.* **c** used to emphasize what you are saying **'Bilirsiniz', 'Herkesin de bildiği gibi'** *I'm not an idiot, you know.* **12** **as far as I know** used to say that you think something is true, but cannot be sure **'Bildiğim/bilebildiğim kadarıyla...'** *As far as I know, he's never been in prison.* **13** **you never know** used to say that something could be possible although it does not seem likely **'Asla bilemezsin...!', 'Asla tahmin bile edemezsin...!', 'Kimse bilemez...!', 'Yine de belli olmaz...!'** *You never know - you might win the lottery.* **14** **before you know it** very soon **çok yakında, kimsenin haberi olmadan** *We'll be there before you know it.* ⊃See also: know sth inside¹ out, learn/know the ropes (rope¹), know your stuff¹.

know of sth/sb *phrasal verb* to have heard of something or someone and have a little information about them **duymuş olmak, bir şekilde biliyor olmak, bilmek, tanımak** *I know of a good restaurant near the station.*

know² /nəʊ/ *noun* **be in the know** to have knowledge about something which not everyone knows **işi bilen olmak, işin içinde olmak, işin iç yüzünü/aslını bilen olmak** *People in the know were sure the film would win an Oscar.*

know-how /ˈnəʊhaʊ/ *noun* [U] practical skill and knowledge **uygulamaya yönelik teknik beceri ve ustalık; uygulama yeteneği, bir şeyi yapabilme deneyim ve bilgisi** *technical know-how*

knowing /ˈnəʊɪŋ/ *adjective* A knowing smile, look, etc shows that you know what another person is really thinking. **anlayan, anladığını gösteren, anlayışlı, bilen, farkında olan** *He gave me a knowing wink.*

knowingly /ˈnəʊɪŋli/ *adverb* **1** If you knowingly do something, you mean to do it although it is wrong. **bile bile, bilerek, kasten 2** showing that you know what another person is really thinking **biliyormuşçasına, anlayışla** *He smiled knowingly.*

🧩 knowledge .... İLE BİRLİKTE KULLANILAN KELİMELER

common/detailed/firsthand/poor/thorough knowledge ● knowledge **about/of** sth ● **have/gain/ impart** knowledge

⚬**knowledge** /ˈnɒlɪdʒ/ *noun* **1** [U, no plural] information and understanding that you have in your mind **bilgi, malumat** *He has a detailed knowledge of naval history.* ○ *He took the car without my knowledge* (= I did not know). **2 to (the best of) sb's knowledge** used to say that someone thinks that something is true, but cannot be sure **(kesin olmamakla birlikte)...nın/nin bildiği kadarıyla** *To the best of my knowledge, she's never worked abroad.*

knowledgeable /ˈnɒlɪdʒəbl/ *adjective* knowing a lot **bilgili, kültürlü, herşeyi bilen, çok bilmiş/bilen** *He's very knowledgeable about art.*

known¹ /nəʊn/ *adjective* recognized or known about by most people **bilinen, tanınan** *He's a member of a known terrorist organization.* ⟳Opposite unknown ⟳See also: **well-known.**

known² /nəʊn/ *past participle of* know **'bilmek' fiilinin üçüncü hâli**

knuckle¹ /ˈnʌkl/ *noun* [C] one of the parts of your finger where it bends **parmak eklemi/boğumu** ⟳See also: a **rap¹** on/across/over the knuckles.

knuckle² /ˈnʌkl/ *verb*
    knuckle down *phrasal verb* to start to work or study hard **sıkı çalışmaya başlamak, çok çalışmaya koyulmak**

koala /kəʊˈɑːlə/ (*also* **ko'ala ˌbear**) *noun* [C] an Australian animal like a small bear with grey fur which lives in trees and eats leaves **koala**

the Koran /kɒrˈɑːn/ ⓤ /kəˈræn/ *noun* the holy book of Islam **Kur'an-ı Kerim, İslâmiyetin kutsal kitabı**

kosher /ˈkəʊʃər/ *adjective* Kosher food is prepared according to Jewish law. **yenilmesi dinen sakıncasız, helâl; koşer, Yahudi Hukukuna göre hazırlanan yiyecek**

koala

kph *written abbreviation for* kilometres per hour: a unit for measuring speed **kilometre cinsinden saatteki hızı belirten kısaltma** *a car travelling at 100 kph*

kudos /ˈkjuːdɒs/ *noun* [U] praise and respect for what you have done **(yapılana) övgü, methiye, saygı, takdir**

kung fu /kʌŋˈfuː/ *noun* [U] a sport from China in which people fight using their hands and feet **kung fu**

Kurdish /ˈkɜːdɪʃ/ *adjective* belonging or relating to a Muslim people living in parts of Turkey, Iran, Iraq, etc **Kürt'lere ait veya onlara ilişkin; Türkiye İran ve Irak'ın belli bölümlerinde yaşayan Müslüman insanlar** ● **Kurd** /kɜːd/ *noun* [C] a Kurdish person **Kürt**

kW (*also* **kw**) *written abbreviation for* kilowatt (= a unit for measuring electrical power) **kilovat**

K

L

L, l /el/ the twelfth letter of the alphabet **alfabenin oni- kinci harfi**

l *written abbreviation for* litre (= a unit for measuring liquid) **litrenin kısa yazılışı**

lab /læb/ *noun* [C] *short for* laboratory (= a room used for scientific work) **laboratuvar**

label¹ /'leɪbᵊl/ *noun* [C] **1** [INFORMATION] a small piece of paper or other material which gives information about the thing it is fixed to **etiket** *There should be washing instructions on the label.* **2** [WORD] a word or phrase that is used to describe the qualities of someone or something, usually in a way that is not fair **damgalama, etiket- leme, adını ...a/e çıkarma** *He seems to be stuck with the label of 'troublemaker'.* **3** [MUSIC] (*also* **record label**) a company that records and sells music **müzik yapım şir- keti** *They've just signed a deal with a major record label.*

label² /'leɪbᵊl/ *verb* [T] UK **labelling**, *past* **labelled**, US **labeling**, *past* **labeled 1** to fix to a small piece of paper or other material to something which gives information about it **etiketlemek, üzerine etiket yapıştırmak/ koymak** *All food has to be labelled with 'best before' or 'use by' dates.* **2** to describe the qualities of someone or something using a word or phrase, usually in a way that is not fair **etiketleme, damgalamak, adını ...a/e çıkarmak** [often passive] *They've been unfairly labelled as criminals.*

labor /'leɪbəʳ/ *noun, verb* US *spelling of* labour **çalışma, iş, emek**

laboratory /ləˈbɒrətᵊri/ ⓤⓈ /ˈlæbrətɔːri/ *noun* [C] a room used for scientific work **laboratuvar** *research laboratories* ○ *a computer laboratory* ➔See also: **language laboratory.**

laborer /'leɪbᵊrəʳ/ *noun* [C] US *spelling of* labourer **işçi, emekçi, çalışan**

laborious /ləˈbɔːriəs/ *adjective* Laborious work is very difficult and needs a lot of effort. **büyük çaba gerekti- ren, güç, zahmetli** *a laborious task*

labors /'leɪbəz/ *noun* [plural] US *spelling of* labours 'labours' sözcüğünün bir başka yazılışı

'labor ˌunion US (UK/US **trade union**) *noun* [C] an organi- zation that represents people who do a particular job **sendika**

labour¹ UK (US **labor**) /'leɪbəʳ/ *noun* **1** [WORK] [U] work, especially the type of work that needs a lot of physical effort **çalışma, ağır iş, zahmet** *manual labour* **2** [WORKERS] [U] people who work **işçiler, emekçiler** *cheap/skilled labour* **3** [BIRTH] [C, U] the stage of preg- nancy when a woman has pain in the lower part of her body because the baby is coming out **doğum** *to be in labour/go into labour* ○ *labour pains* **4** **Labour** [group] *short for* the Labour Party **İşçi Partisi** *I voted Labour* (= for the Labour party) *at the last election.* ○ *a Labour MP* **5** *a* **labour of love** work that you do because you like it, not because you are paid for it **istek ve şevkle yapılan iş**

labour² UK *formal* (US **labor**) /'leɪbəʳ/ *verb* [I] to work hard **sıkı çalışmak, uğraşmak, çabalamak, emek harcamak** *He laboured night and day to get the house finished on time.*

labourer UK (US **laborer**) /'leɪbᵊrəʳ/ *noun* [C] a worker who uses a lot of physical effort in their job **işçi, emekçi, çalışan** *a farm labourer*

the ˈLabour ˌParty *noun* [group] one of the three main political parties in the UK (**Birleşik Krallık**) **İşçi Par- tisi**

labours (US **labors**) /'leɪbəz/ *noun* [plural] **sb's labours** work done with a lot of effort **emekler, çabalar, uğraş- lar** *He earned a mere $15 for his labours.*

lace¹ /leɪs/ *noun* **1** [U] a delicate cloth with patterns of holes **dantel, dantelâ** *a lace curtain* **2** [C] a string used to tie shoes **bağcık, kordon, bağ** *to tie/untie your laces*

lace² /leɪs/ *verb*
lace sth up *phrasal verb* to fasten something with laces **bağcıklarla bağlamak** *He laced up his boots.*
be laced with sth *phrasal verb* If food or drink is laced with alcohol or a drug, a small amount has been added to it. **bir şey ilave etmek/katmak** *coffee laced with brandy*

lacerate /ˈlæsᵊreɪt/ *verb* [T] *formal* to make deep cuts in someone's skin **derince kesmek, yarmak, yarala- mak** *a lacerated arm* ● **laceration** /ˌlæsᵊrˈeɪʃᵊn/ *noun* [C] *formal* a cut **kesik, yarık**

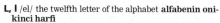 **lack** .... İLE BİRLİKTE KULLANILAN KELİMELER

a **complete/distinct/marked/total** lack of sth ● an **apparent** lack of sth

◦━**lack¹** /læk/ *noun* **lack of sth** not having something, or not having enough of something **bir şeyin eksikliği/ yokluğu** *a lack of food/money*

◦━**lack²** /læk/ *verb* **1** [T] to not have something, or not have enough of something **eksik olmak; yokluk; bir şey yetersiz olmak** *She really lacks confidence.* **2** **be lacking** If something that you need is lacking, you do not have enough of it. **bir şeyin eksik olması, yeterli miktarda olmaması** *Enthusiasm has been sadly lacking these past few months at work.* **3** **be lacking in sth** to not have a quality **eksik olmak; ...dan/den yok- sun olmak; ...sı/si yeterli olmamak** *He's totally lacking in charm of any sort.*

lacklustre UK (US **lackluster**) /ˈlækˌlʌstəʳ/ *adjective* with- out energy or excitement **heyecan/coşku/enerjiden yoksun olan; coşku ve heyecansız** *a lacklustre per- formance*

laconic /ləˈkɒnɪk/ *adjective formal* using very few words to express yourself **az ve öz, özlü, veciz** *laconic humour/wit*

lacquer /ˈlækəʳ/ *noun* [U] a clear, hard substance which is painted on wood or metal to protect it **lake, vernik**

lad /læd/ *noun* [C] UK a boy or young man **oğlan çocuğu, genç erkek** *a nice young lad* ○ *informal He's having a night out with the lads* (= his male friends).

ladder /ˈlædəʳ/ *noun* [C] a piece of equipment

ladder

which is used to reach high places, consisting of short steps fixed between two long sides **seyyar merdiven** ➔See also: the first/highest/next, etc **rung**[1] of the ladder.

laddish /ˈlædɪʃ/ *adjective UK* rude, noisy and typical of the way that young men behave in groups **kaba, şımarık, saygısız, kendini bilmez**

laden /ˈleɪdən/ *adjective* **be laden with sth** to be holding a lot of something **yüklü, eli kolu dolu; ...ile yüklü/dolu olmak** *She staggered home, laden with shopping.*

the ladies /ˈleɪdiz/ *noun* [group] *UK* a toilet in a public place for women **bayanlar tuvaleti** *Where's the ladies?*

ˈladies' ˌroom *noun* [C] *US* a room in a public place where there are women's toilets **bayanlar tuvaleti**

ladle /ˈleɪdl/ *noun* [C] a large, deep spoon, used to serve soup **kepçe** ➔Orta kısımdaki renkli sayfalarına bakınız.

◦**lady** /ˈleɪdi/ *noun* **1** [C] a polite way of saying 'woman' **hanım, hanımefendi, bayan** *There's a young lady here to see you.* ○ *Ladies and gentlemen, can I have your attention please?* **2 Lady** a title used before the name of some women of high social rank in the UK (**Birleşik Krallık**) **bayanlar için asalet ünvanı, leydi** *Lady Alison Weir*

ladybird /ˈleɪdibɜːd/ *UK* (*US* ladybug /ˈleɪdibʌg/) *noun* [C] a small flying insect which is usually red with black spots **uğur böceği**

lag[1] /læg/ (*also* time lag) *noun* [C] a period of time between two things happening (**iki şey arasındaki**) **zaman aralığı** *You have to allow for a time lag between order and delivery.* ➔See also: jet lag.

lag[2] /læg/ *verb* lagging, *past* lagged
lag behind (sb/sth) *phrasal verb* **1** to move more slowly than someone or something else so that you are behind them **geri kalmak, daha yavaş ilerlemek/gelişmek 2** to achieve less than someone or something else **daha az ilerleme kaydetmek; gerisinde kalmak** *Britain is lagging far behind the rest of Europe on this issue.*

lager /ˈlɑːɡər/ *noun* [C, U] a pale yellow beer **hafif bira** *A pint of lager, please.*

lagoon /ləˈɡuːn/ *noun* [C] a lake that contains sea water **deniz suyundan oluşan göl, deniz kulağı**

laid /leɪd/ *past of* lay 'lay' **fiilinin geçmiş zaman hâli**

laid-back /ˌleɪdˈbæk/ *adjective informal* very relaxed and not seeming worried about anything **gamsız, aldırış etmeyen, umursamayan** *a laid-back style of teaching* ○ *He's very laid-back.*

lain /leɪn/ *past participle of* lie[1] 'yalan söylemek' **fiilinin üçüncü hâli**

laissez-faire /ˌleseɪˈfeər/ *adjective* allowing things to happen and not trying to control them **başıboş, kontrolsüz, kendi hâline bırakılmış** *a laissez-faire attitude*

◦**lake** /leɪk/ *noun* [C] a large area of water which has land all around it **göl** *Lake Windermere*

lamb /læm/ *noun* **1** [C] a young sheep **kuzu** *a newborn lamb* ○ *a lamb's-wool sweater* **2** [U] meat from a young sheep **kuzu eti** *grilled lamb chops* ○ *roast leg of lamb* ➔See also: mutton dressed as lamb.

lame /leɪm/ *adjective* **1** A lame excuse or explanation is one that you cannot believe. **inandırıcı olmayan, zayıf, yetersiz** *He said he didn't go because it was raining, which is a pretty lame excuse if you ask me.* **2** A lame animal or person cannot walk because they have an injured foot or leg. **topal, aksak, bir ayağı/bacağı sakat** *a lame horse*

lament /ləˈment/ *verb* [I, T] *formal* to say that you are disappointed about a situation **yakınmak, dert yanmak, şikâyet etmek, sızlanmak** *He was lamenting the fact that so few people read fiction nowadays.*

lamentable /ˈlæməntəbl/ *adjective formal* extremely bad **berbat, yürekler acısı, perişan, acınacak** *a lamentable performance*

lamp /læmp/ *noun* [C] a piece of equipment that produces light **lamba, fener** *a table lamp* ○ *an oil lamp* ➔Orta kısımdaki renkli sayfalarına bakınız.

lamppost /ˈlæmppəʊst/ *noun* [C] a tall post with a light at the top, which you see on roads where there are houses **lamba direği**

lampshade /ˈlæmpʃeɪd/ *noun* [C] a decorative cover for an electric light **abajur** ➔Orta kısımdaki renkli sayfalarına bakınız.

LAN /læn/, /ˌelˈeɪˈen/ *noun* [C] *abbreviation for* local area network: a system that connects the computers of people who work in the same building **bölgesel alan bilgisayar ağı; aynı bina içindeki bilgisayarları birbirine bağlayan sistem** ➔Compare WAN.

◦**land**[1] /lænd/ *noun* **1** [AREA] [U] an area of ground **arazi, toprak** *agricultural land* ○ *undeveloped land* **2** [NOT SEA] [U] the surface of the Earth that is not sea **kara** *to travel over land and sea* **3** [COUNTRY] a country **ülke, memleket** *a land of ice and snow* ➔See also: no-man's land.

◦**land**[2] /lænd/ *verb* **1** [I, T] If an aircraft lands, it arrives on the ground after a journey, and if you land it, you make it arrive on the ground. (**uçak**) **inmek** *We should land in Madrid at 7 a.m.* ○ *He managed to land the helicopter on the cliff.* **2 land in/on, etc** If an object or person lands somewhere, they fall to the ground there. **yere düşmek** *She landed flat on her back.* **3** [T] to get something, usually something good **almak, elde etmek, yakalamak** *He's just landed a new job at an agency in London.*
land sb in sth *phrasal verb* to cause someone to be in a difficult situation **birinin başını derde sokmak** *His remarks have landed him in a lot of trouble with the association.*
land sb with sth *phrasal verb* If something lands you with problems, it causes problems for you. **başına bela etmek, başına kalmak** *The project's failure has landed him with debts of over £50,000.*

landfill /ˈlændfɪl/ *noun* [C] a place where waste is buried in the ground **atık/çöp/dolgu** *a landfill site*

landing /ˈlændɪŋ/ *noun* [C] **1** an arrival on the ground, usually of an aircraft or boat **karaya çıkma/iniş, inme** *They had to make an emergency landing in Chicago.* **2** the area of floor at the top of a set of stairs **sahanlık**

landlady /ˈlændˌleɪdi/ *noun* [C] a woman who you rent a room or house from **ev sahibesi; pansiyoncu bayan**

landline /ˈlændlaɪn/ *noun* [C] a telephone that is not a mobile phone **sabit telefon/telefon hattı**

landlord /ˈlændlɔːd/ *noun* [C] a man who you rent a room or house from **ev sahibi, pansiyoncu**

landmark /ˈlændmɑːk/ *noun* [C] **1** a building that you can easily recognize, especially one that helps you to know where you are **nirengi noktası, belirgin özelliği olan bina** *a historic landmark* **2** an event which is famous or important in the history of something **önemli olay, dönüm noktası** *His speech was a landmark in the history of civil rights.*

landmine /ˈlændmaɪn/ *noun* [C] a bomb which is hidden in the ground **kara mayını**

landowner /'lændəʊnəʳ/ noun [C] someone who owns a lot of land **toprak sahibi, toprak ağası** *a wealthy landowner*

landscape /'lændskeɪp/ noun [C] the appearance of an area of land, especially in the countryside **manzara, peyzaj, kır manzarası** *The cathedral dominates the landscape for miles around.*

landslide /'lændslaɪd/ noun [C] **1** when rocks and soil slide down a mountain or hill **heyelan, toprak kayması 2** an easy victory in an election **seçimde kolay elde edilen zafer, çok farklı oy üstünlüğü** *a landslide defeat/victory*

lane .... İLE BİRLİKTE KULLANILAN KELİMELER

in the [inside/fast, etc] lane ● the **fast/slow** lane

lane /leɪn/ noun [C] **1** PART part of a road or track that is separated from the other parts, usually by a painted line **şerit, kulvar** *the inside/middle/outside lane* ○ *the fast/slow lane* **2** ROAD a narrow road, usually in the countryside **patika, ara yol, kır yolu** *We drove down a winding country lane.* **3** BOATS/AIRCRAFT a route that is regularly used by boats or aircraft **rota** *It's one of the world's busiest shipping lanes.*

language .... İLE BİRLİKTE KULLANILAN KELİMELER

learn/speak a language ● foreign languages ● foul/ native/official/strong language

○-**language** /'læŋgwɪdʒ/ noun **1** COMMUNICATION [U] communication between people, usually using words **dil, lisan** *She has done research into how children acquire language.* **2** ENGLISH/SPANISH/JAPANESE ETC [C] a type of communication used by the people of a particular country **bir ülkede konuşulan dil, lisan** *How many languages do you speak?* **3** TYPE OF WORDS [U] words of a particular type, especially the words used by people in a particular job **belli bir işe ait özel dil, lisan, meslekî dil** *legal language* ○ *the language of business* **4** COMPUTERS [C, U] a system of instructions that is used to write computer programs **bilgisayar dili** ⊃See also: body language, modern languages, second language, sign language.

'language la‚boratory UK (US **'language ‚laboratory**) noun [C] a room in a college or school where you can use equipment to help you practise listening to and speaking a foreign language **dil laboratuvarı**

languid /'læŋgwɪd/ adjective literary moving or speaking slowly and with little energy, often in an attractive way **çekici bir eda ile yavaş hareket eden ve konuşan; gevşek, ilgisiz, halsiz** *a languid manner/voice*

languish /'læŋgwɪʃ/ verb [I] formal **languish at/in, etc sth** to stay in an unpleasant or difficult situation for a long time **çile çekmek, sürünmek, zorda kalmak** *to languish in jail*

lanky /'læŋki/ adjective informal A lanky person is very tall and thin. **upuzun, boylu boslu ve ince**

lantern /'læntən/ noun [C] a light that can be carried, usually with a candle inside it **fener, el feneri** *a paper lantern*

lap¹ /læp/ noun [C] **1** Your lap is the top part of your legs when you are sitting down. **kucak** *Sit on my lap and I'll read you a story.* **2** one journey around a circular race track **tur** *He's two laps behind the leaders.*

lap² /læp/ verb **lapping,** past **lapped lap against/on, etc sth** If water laps against something, it touches it gently in waves. **dalgalar şeklinde hafif hafif çarparak dokunmak/şıpırdamak; hışırdamak**
lap sth up phrasal verb informal to enjoy something very much **yalayıp yutmak/içmek; bir çırpıda bitirmek; çok hoşuna gitmek** *He loved all the attention - he was lapping it up!*

lapel /lə'pel/ noun [C] the part of a collar that is folded against the front of a shirt or jacket **klapa, yaka** *wide lapels* ⊃See picture at **jacket.**

lapse .... İLE BİRLİKTE KULLANILAN KELİMELER

a **momentary** lapse ● a lapse **in/of** sth

lapse¹ /læps/ noun [C] **1** a period of time when something fails to happen as it should **aksama, dikkat dağınıklığı, unutma, kayma** *a memory lapse* ○ *It is thought that the accident was caused by a lapse of concentration.* **2** a period of time passing between two things happening **süre, ara, aralık, fasıla** *a time lapse/a lapse of time* ○ *He turned up again after a lapse of two years.*

lapse² /læps/ verb [I] If an arrangement lapses, it stops existing because of the amount of time that has passed. **zamanı geçmek, zaman aşımına uğramak** *I've allowed my membership to lapse.*
lapse into sth phrasal verb If you lapse into something, you change to a different, and usually bad, condition. **girmek, gömülmek, düşmek** *to lapse into silence*

laptop /'læptɒp/ noun [C] a computer that is small enough to be carried around and used where you are sitting down **dizüstü bilgisayar**

laptop

○-**large** /lɑːdʒ/ adjective **1** big in size or amount **büyük, geniş, iri, kocaman, çok** *a large number of people* ○ *a large amount of money* ○ *She comes from quite a large family.* ○ *The shirt was a bit too large.* ⊃Opposite **small. 2 be at large** If someone dangerous is at large, they are not in prison. **(tehlikeli kişi/hayvan vb.) başı boş, serbest 3 sb/sth at large** people or things in general **genelde insanlar veya eşyalar** *This group is not representative of the population at large.* **4 by and large** in most situations **genellikle, tamamen, bütünüyle** *By and large, people have welcomed the changes.*

largely /'lɑːdʒli/ adverb mainly **ekseriyetle, genellikle, büyük ölçüde** *Their complaints have been largely ignored.*

large-scale /ˌlɑːdʒ'skeɪl/ adjective involving a lot of people or happening in big numbers **büyük ölçekte/ ölçüde/çapta/çaplı** *a large-scale development* ○ *large-scale redundancies*

lark /lɑːk/ noun [C] a small brown bird that is known for its beautiful singing **tarla kuşu**

larva /'lɑːvə/ noun [C] plural **larvae** /'lɑːviː/ the form of some creatures, for example insects, before they develop into a different form **kurtçuk, larva** *insect larvae*

lasagne UK (US **lasagna**) /lə'zænjə/ ⑤ /lə'zɑːnjə/ noun [U] a type of Italian food consisting of flat pieces of pasta with layers of meat and sauce in between **lazanya, arasında et ve sos olan makarna**

laser /'leɪzəʳ/ noun [C] a strong beam of light that has medical and technical uses **lazer** *a laser beam* ○ *laser surgery*

'laser ‚printer noun [C] a printer (= a machine which is connected to a computer and which produces writing or pictures) which uses a laser (= a strong beam of light) to produce very clear writing or pictures **lazer yazıcı**

lash¹ /læʃ/ verb **1** [I, T] If wind or rain lashes against something, the wind or rain is very strong and hits or blows hard against it. **(yağmur, rüzgâr vb.) çarpmak, vurmak, kamçılamak, kırbaçlamak, dövmek** *Rain lashed against the window.* **2 lash sth down/together, etc** to tie something firmly to something else **sıkıca bağlamak, sıkı sıkıya bağlamak**

lash out *phrasal verb* **1** to suddenly hit someone **vurmak, saldırmak** *He lashed out and caught her on the side of the face.* **2** to criticize someone angrily **azarlamak, çatmak, şiddetle eleştirmek** *He lashed out at the government for refusing to take action.*

lash² /læʃ/ *noun* [C] a hit with a whip (= long, thin piece of leather) **kırbaçlama, kamçılama; kamçı/kırbaç darbesi** *He was given forty lashes.*

lashes /ˈlæʃɪz/ *noun* [plural] the small hairs on the edges of your eye **kirpikler**

lass /læs/ *noun* [C] UK informal a girl or a young woman **genç kız, genç kadın** *a young lass*

o▪**last¹** /lɑːst/ *adjective, determiner* **1** MOST RECENT [always before noun] the most recent **en son, en sonuncu** *What was the last film you saw?* ○ *It's rained for the last three days.* **2** ONE BEFORE PRESENT [always before noun] The last book, house, job, etc is the one before the present one. **geçen, önceki** *I liked his last book but I'm not so keen on this latest one.* **3** FINAL happening or coming at the end **en son, son** *It's the last room on the left.* ○ *That's the last programme of the series.* ○ *I was the last one to arrive.* ○ *"How did she get on in her race?" "She was last."* **4** REMAINING [always before noun] only remaining **en son, sonuncusu** *Who wants the last piece of cake?* **5 the last person/thing, etc** the least expected or wanted person or thing **beklenen en son kişi/şey vb.** *Three extra people to feed - that's the last thing I need!* ○ *He's the last person you'd expect to see at an aerobics class.* ⊃Opposite **first** ⊃See also: be on its last legs (**leg**), the final/last **straw**, have the last **word¹**.

o▪**last²** /lɑːst/ *adverb* **1** after everything or everyone else **son, sonuncu** *I wasn't expecting to win the race but I didn't think I'd come last!* ○ *We've still got to check the figures but we'll do that last.* **2** used to talk about the most recent time you did something **en son olarak, son kez/defa** *When did you last see her?* **3 last but not least** something that you say to introduce the last person or thing on a list **son ama aynı derecede önemli olarak** *This is Jeremy, this is Cath and, last but not least, this is Eva.* ⊃Opposite **first.**

o▪**last³** /lɑːst/ *noun, pronoun* **1 the last** a person or thing that comes after all the others **son defa, en son** [+ to do sth] *We were the last to get there.* **2 the last of sth** the only part of something that remains **sonunu, en sonunu, sonuncusunu** *We've just finished the last of the wine.* **3 the day/week/year before last** the day, week, or year before the one that has just finished **sondan bir önceki/bir evvelki 4 at (long) last** finally **nihayet, sonunda,** *At last, I've found a pair of jeans that actually fit.* **5 the last I heard** used before saying a piece of information about someone that you previously heard '**En son duyduğumda/haber aldığımda/gördüğümde...**' *The last I heard, they were selling their house.*

o▪**last⁴** /lɑːst/ *verb* [I, T] **1** to continue to happen, exist, or be useful **sürmek, devam etmek** *How long will the meeting last?* ○ *We don't get much sun - enjoy it while it lasts!* ○ *The batteries only last about five hours.* **2** to be enough for a period of time **götürmek, idare etmek** *I've only got £30 to last me till the end of the month.* ○ *We've got enough food to last another week.*

last-ditch /ˌlɑːstˈdɪtʃ/ *adjective* **a last-ditch attempt/ effort** a final attempt to solve a problem that you have failed to solve several times before **en son teşebbüs, son girişim; son çare olarak baş vurulan** *a last-ditch effort to prevent war*

lasting /ˈlɑːstɪŋ/ *adjective* continuing to exist for a long time **süren, dayanan, devam eden** *lasting damage* ○ *a lasting friendship*

lastly /ˈlɑːstli/ *adverb* finally **kısacası, sözün özü, hülasa** *And lastly, I'd like to thank everyone who took part in the event.*

last-minute /ˌlɑːstˈmɪnɪt/ *adjective* done at the last possible time **son dakika, son anda yapılan** *I was just doing some last-minute preparations.*

ˈlast ˌname *noun* [C] the name that you and other members of your family all have **soyadı**

latch¹ /lætʃ/ *noun* [C] **1** a small piece of metal on a door that you move down so that the door will stay closed **kapı mandalı; kilit dili 2** a type of lock for a door that you need a key to open from the outside **mandallı kilit, sürgü, kilit**

latch² /lætʃ/ *verb*

latch on *phrasal verb informal* to begin to understand something **bir şeyi anlamaya/çakmaya başlamak** *It took me ages to latch on to what she was saying.*

o▪**late** /leɪt/ *adjective, adverb* **1** AFTER THE USUAL TIME after the usual time or the time that was arranged **geç, gecikmiş** *I was late for work this morning.* ○ *We got there too late and all the tickets had been sold.* ○ *We had a late lunch.* **2** NEAR END OF PERIOD near the end of a period of time **...ın/in sonuna doğru** *It was built in the late nineteenth century.* ○ *It was late at night.* ○ *Marsha is in her late twenties.* **3 it's late** something that you say when it is near the end of a day **geç oldu, epey gecikti** *It's late - I really should be going.* ○ *It's getting late and I'm a bit tired.* **4** DEAD [always before noun] not now alive **ölmüş, rahmetli** *the late Mrs Walker* **5 of late** *formal* recently **son zamanlarda, son dönemlerde** *We've scarcely seen him of late.*

lately /ˈleɪtli/ *adverb* recently **son günlerde, son zamanlarda** *I haven't been feeling so well lately.* ○ *Lately, I've been walking to work.*

latent /ˈleɪtᵊnt/ *adjective* A feeling or quality that is latent exists now but is hidden or not yet developed. **gizli, saklı, henüz harekete geçmemiş, henüz gelişmemiş** *latent hostility/racism*

later /ˈleɪtər/ *adjective* **1** after some time **daha sonra** *I might arrange it for a later date.* **2** more recent **en son** *I'm not so familiar with his later work.*

later (on) *adverb* after some time **daha sonra, sonra** *I'm off now - see you later.* ○ *If you're busy now we could do it later on.*

latest¹ /ˈleɪtɪst/ *adjective* [always before noun] most recent **en son, en yeni** *the latest fashions/news/technology*

latest² /ˈleɪtɪst/ *noun* **1 the latest in sth** the most recent of its type **en sonuncusu, en yenisi** *This is the latest in a series of terrorist attacks in the region.* **2 at the latest** If you tell someone to do something by a particular time at the latest, you mean they must do it before that time. **en geç** *She said to be there by 8 o'clock at the latest.*

lather /ˈlɑːðər/ *noun* **1** [U] small white bubbles that are produced when soap is used with water **köpük, sabun köpüğü 2 get into a lather** *informal* to become anxious or upset about something **endişelenmek, kızmak, canı sıkılmak**

Latin /ˈlætɪn/ *noun* [U] the language used by ancient Romans **Latince** ● **Latin** *adjective* **Latince**

ˌLatin Aˈmerican *adjective* relating or belonging to the countries of South and Central America, and Mexico **Latin Amerika; Orta Güney Amerika Meksika'ya ilişkin/ait** ● **Latin American** *noun* [C] a Latin American person **Latin Amerikalı**

Latino /lə'tiːnəʊ/ noun [C] US someone who lives in the US whose family came from Latin America ABD'de yaşayan Latin Amerikalı, Latino

latitude /'lætɪtjuːd/ noun 1 [C, U] the distance of a place north or south of the Equator (= imaginary line around the Earth's middle), measured in degrees **enlem, arz derecesi** *The latitude of Helsinki is approximately 60 degrees north.* 2 [U] *formal* freedom to do what you want **serbestlik, özgürlük, tolerans** *She should be allowed the latitude to choose the people she wants.*

latte /'lɑːteɪ/ ⑤ /'lɑːteɪ/ noun [C, U] a drink of coffee made from espresso (= strong coffee) and milk **sert kahve ve sütten yapılan içecek**

latter /'lætər/ adjective [always before noun]*formal* near the end of a period **ikinci, son** *the latter half of the twentieth century* ○ *She had moved to California in the latter part of the year.* ○ *She is now in the latter stages of the disease.*

the latter /'lætər/ noun the second of two people or things that have just been talked about **sonra söylenen, ikincisi, sonuncusu** *She offered me more money or a car, and I chose the latter.*

latterly /'lætəli/ adverb UK formal recently **son zamanlarda, yakında** *She started her career in radio, but latterly she has been working in television.*

laudable /'lɔːdəbl/ adjective formal A laudable idea or action deserves admiration, even if it is not successful. **(başarılı olmasa da) övgüye değer, takdire layık** *a laudable aim/ambition/goal*

ॱ**laugh¹** /lɑːf/ verb [I] to smile while making sounds with your voice that show you are happy or think something is funny **gülmek** *You never laugh at my jokes.* ○ *She really makes me laugh.* ○ *It's very rare that a book is so good you laugh out loud.* ○ *It was so funny, we burst out laughing* (= laughed suddenly and loudly). ➪See also: be no laughing matter¹.

laugh at sb/sth phrasal verb to show that you think someone or something is stupid **...ile alay etmek; ...ın/in hâline gülmek** *I can't go into work looking like this - everyone will laugh at me.*

laugh sth off phrasal verb to laugh about something unpleasant so that it seems less important **gülüp geçmek, umursamamak** *He was upset by the criticism though he tried to laugh it off at the time.*

laugh² /lɑːf/ noun [C] 1 the act or sound of laughing **gülme, kahkaha** *a loud/nervous laugh* ○ *At the time, I was embarrassed, but I had a good laugh* (= laughed a lot) *about it later.* 2 **be a (good) laugh** UK informal to be funny **matrak/komik olmak, gülünç olmak** *You'd like David - he's a good laugh.* 3 **for a laugh** informal If you do something for a laugh, you do it because you think it will be funny. **komiklik/espri/şaka olsun diye; eğlenmek için** *Just for a laugh, I pretended that I'd forgotten it was his birthday.*

laughable /'lɑːfəbl/ adjective If something is laughable, it is stupid and you cannot believe it or respect it. **gülünç, komik, gülünecek, tuhaf** *Most people thought his suggestions were laughable.*

'**laughing ˌstock** noun [no plural] someone who does something very stupid which makes other people laugh at them **maskara, matrak, gülünecek kimse** *If I wear this hat, I'll be the laughing stock of the party!*

┌─ **laughter** .... İLE BİRLİKTE KULLANILAN KELİMELER ─┐
burst into laughter ● **roar** with laughter ● **be in fits of** laughter

ॱ**laughter** /'lɑːftər/ noun [U] the sound or act of laughing **kahkaha, gülüş, gülme** *I heard the sound of laughter in* the room next door. ○ *The crowd roared with laughter* (= laughed very loudly).

launch¹ /lɔːnʃ/ verb [T] 1 [SEND] to send a spacecraft or bomb into the sky, or a ship into the water **(gemi) suya indirmek; (uzay aracı/bomba) uzaya fırlatmak** *to launch a rocket/satellite* ○ *to launch a boat/fleet* 2 [BEGIN] to begin an important activity **başlatmak** *to launch an attack/inquiry/investigation* 3 [NEW PRODUCT] If a company launches a product or service, it makes it available for the first time. **piyasaya sürmek, çıkarmak, sunmak** *The book was launched last February.* ○ *The airline will launch its new transatlantic service next month.*

launch into sth phrasal verb to start saying or criticizing something with a lot of anger or energy **kızgınlık ve hiddetle eleştiriye/söylemeye başlamak; atılmak, girişmek** *Then he launched into a verbal attack on her management of the situation.*

launch² /lɔːnʃ/ noun [C] 1 [SENDING] the launching of a spacecraft, ship, or weapon **uzaya fırlatma, suya indirme, silah atışı** *Poor weather delayed the space shuttle's launch.* 2 [BEGINNING] the beginning of an activity **başlama, başlangıç** *The campaign's launch was a well-publicized event.* 3 [NEW PRODUCT] the time when a new product or service becomes available **piyasaya sürme, çıkarma, sunma** *The film's launch attracted a lot of Hollywood stars.* 4 [BOAT] a large boat with a motor **büyük motorlu kayık** *a police launch*

launder /'lɔːndər/ verb [T] to hide the fact that an amount of money has been made illegally by putting the money into legal bank accounts or businesses **kara para aklamak; bir miktar parayı resmi banka hesabına veya işe yatırarak yasa dışı yollardan para kazandığı gerçeğini gizlemek** *to launder drug money* ● **laundering** noun [U] **money laundering aklama (para)**

launderette /ˌlɔːndərˈet/ UK (US **laundromat** /'lɔːndrəmæt/ trademark) noun [C] a place where you pay to use machines that wash and dry your clothes **para ile çalışan çamaşır makinalarında giysilerin yıkanıp kurutulduğu yer; çamaşırhane**

laundry /'lɔːndri/ noun [U] clothes, sheets, etc that need to be washed **kirli çamaşır** *to do the laundry* ○ *a laundry basket*

'**laundry deˌtergent** noun [C, U] US washing powder **çamaşır deterjanı**

laurels /'lɒrəlz/ noun [plural] **rest on your laurels** to be so satisfied with what you have achieved that you make no effort to improve **başarılarıyla yetinmek; başarılarıyla yetinip geliştirmek için çaba sarfetmemek** *Just because you've passed your exams, that's no reason to rest on your laurels.*

lava /'lɑːvə/ noun [U] hot melted rock that comes out of a volcano **lav**

lavatory /'lævətəri/ noun [C] formal mainly UK a toilet **tuvalet** *to go to the lavatory* ○ *public lavatories*

lavender /'lævəndər/ noun [U] a plant with purple flowers and a strong, pleasant smell **lavanta, lavanta çiçeği** *lavender oil*

lavish¹ /'lævɪʃ/ adjective showing that a lot of money has been spent **cömert, bonkör, eli açık** *a lavish meal/party* ● **lavishly** adverb *a lavishly illustrated book* **savurgan bir şekilde**

lavish² /'lævɪʃ/ verb
lavish sth on sb/sth phrasal verb to give a large amount of money, presents, attention, etc to someone or something **cömertçe vermek/dağıtmak** *They have lavished more than £6 million on the new stadium.*

break/enforce/obey/pass a law ● the law **forbids/
prohibits/requires** sth ● a law **against** sth ● be
against the law

○•**law** /lɔː/ *noun* **1 the law** the system of official rules in a
country **yasa, kanun** *You're breaking the law.* ○ *It's
against the law* (= illegal) *not to wear seat belts.* ○ *It's
their job to enforce the law.* **2 by law** If you have to do
something by law, it is illegal not to do it. **yasaya/
kanuna göre;** *yasalar/kanunlar uyarınca They
have to provide a contract by law.* **3** [RULE] [C] an official
rule in a country **yasa, kanun, hukuk** *There are laws
against drinking in the street.* ○ *They led the fight to
impose laws on smoking.* **4 law and order** the obeying
of laws in society **kanun ve nizam** *a breakdown in law
and order* **5** [SUBJECT] [U] the subject or job of understanding and dealing with the official laws of a country
hukuk *to study/practise law* ○ *a law school/firm* ○ *a
specialist in civil/criminal law* **6** [ALWAYS TRUE] [C] something that is always true in science, mathematics, etc.
kural, yöntem, kanun, yasa *the laws of nature/
physics* ○ *the law of averages/gravity* **7 lay down the
law** to repeatedly tell people what they should do, without caring about how they feel **herkese/sağa sola
emirler yağdırmak; sürekli talimatlar vermek**
*People are fed up with him laying down the law the
whole time.* ⊃See also: **brother-in-law, common-law,
daughter-in-law, father-in-law, in-laws, martial law, mother-
in-law, sister-in-law, son-in-law.**

law-abiding /ˈlɔːəˌbaɪdɪŋ/ *adjective* A law-abiding person always obeys the law. **yasalara saygılı, kanunlara
itaat eden** *a law-abiding citizen*

lawful /ˈlɔːfᵊl/ *adjective* allowed by the law **yasal,
kanuni** *He was going about his lawful business as a
press photographer.*

lawmaker /ˈlɔːˌmeɪkəʳ/ *noun* [C] US someone who
makes laws **kanun yapıcılar/hazırlayanlar** *state law-
makers*

lawn /lɔːn/ *noun* [C] an area of grass that is cut **çim, çim
alan, çimenlik** *to mow the lawn*

'lawn ˌmower *noun* [C] a machine that you use to cut
grass **çim biçme makinası**

lawsuit /ˈlɔːsuːt/ *noun* [C] a legal complaint against
someone that does not usually involve the police **dava**
The tenants have filed a lawsuit against their landlord.

○•**lawyer** /ˈlɔɪəʳ/ *noun* [C] someone whose job is to understand the law and deal with legal situations **avukat** *I
want to see my lawyer before I say anything else.*

lax /læks/ *adjective* not careful enough or not well controlled **gevşek, ihmalkâr, laçka, kayıtsız** *They seem to
have a very lax attitude towards security.*

○•**lay¹** /leɪ/ *verb past* **laid 1 lay sth down/in/on, etc** to put
something down somewhere carefully **bir yere bir
şeyi dikkatlice koymak/yerleştirmek/yatırmak**
She laid the baby on the bed. ○ *He laid the tray down on
the table.* **2** [T] to put something into its correct position
**sermek, koymak, yerleştirmek, örtmek, yaymak
vb.** *to lay a carpet* ○ *to lay bricks* **3 lay eggs** If an animal
lays eggs, it produces them out of its body. **yumurtla-
mak 4 lay the blame on sb** to blame someone, usually
when this is not fair **suçu/kabahati başkasına yüklemek; üstüne atmak; suçlamak** *You always lay the
blame on me!* **5 lay the table** UK to put plates, knives,
forks, etc on the table to prepare for a meal **yemek
masasını hazırlamak** ⊃See also: put/lay your cards (**card**)
on the table, lay the **foundation**(s) for/of sth, get/lay your hands
(**hand¹**) on sth, lay down the **law.**

lay sth down *phrasal verb* **1** to officially make new
rules, or to officially say how something must be done
**resmî kurallar koymak/belirlemek; resmen nasıl
yapılacağını söylemek/belirtmek** *The committee
has laid down guidelines for future cases.* **2** If someone
lays down their weapons, they stop fighting. **(silahları
vb.) bırakmak, savaşı/mücadeleyi/muharebeyi
durdurmak/ara vermek** *It is hoped the two sides will
lay down their arms and return to peace.*

lay into sb *phrasal verb informal* to attack or criticize
someone **pataklamak, sille tokat girişmek; verip
veriştirmek, azarlamak, acımasızca eleştirmek**
They started laying into me for no reason.

lay sb off *phrasal verb* to stop employing someone,
usually because there is no more work for them **işten
çıkarmak, işine son vermek** [often passive] *Thirty more
people were laid off last week.*

lay sth on *phrasal verb* to provide something for a
group of people **sağlamak, vermek, tertip etmek**
They're laying on free buses to and from the concert.

lay sth out *phrasal verb* **1** to arrange something on a
surface **sermek, yaymak, sergilemek,** *He'd laid his
tools out all over the kitchen floor.* **2** to explain something
clearly, usually in writing **yazarak açık biçimde izah
etmek; ayrıntılı bir şekilde yazmak** *I've just laid out
some proposals.*

lay² /leɪ/ *adjective* [always before noun] **1** involved in religious activities, but not trained as a priest **din adamı
olarak eğitilmemiş ancak dini faaliyetlerde bulunan** *a lay preacher* **2** not having special or detailed
knowledge of a subject **belli bir konuda ayrıntılı ve
özel bigisi olmayan; meslekten olmayan** *a lay
person/audience*

lay³ /leɪ/ *past tense of* lie¹ **'uzanıp yatmak' fiilinin geçmiş zaman hâli**

lay-by /ˈleɪbaɪ/ *noun* [C] UK a small area where cars can
stop at the side of a road **(yol) cep**

a layer **of** sth ● an **outer/top** layer ● a **thick** layer **of**
sth

○•**layer** /leɪəʳ/ *noun* [C] an
amount of a substance
covering a surface, or
one of several amounts
of substance, each on
top of the other
tabaka, katman, kat
the outer/top layer
○ *Place alternate layers
of pasta and meat sauce
in a shallow dish.* ○ *The
shelf was covered in a
thick layer of dust.*
● **layer** *verb* [T] [often
passive] *The potatoes are
layered with onion.*
⊃See also: the ozone layer.
katman oluşturmak

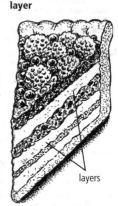

layer

layers

layman /ˈleɪmən/ (*also
layperson*) *noun* [C]
plural **laymen** someone
who does not have
special knowledge of a
subject **meslekten olmayan/deneyimsiz kişi** *Could
you please explain that in layman's terms* (= in a simple
way)?

layoff /ˈleɪɒf/ *noun* [C] the ending of someone's job by an
employer, usually because there is no more work **işten
çıkarma** [usually plural] *Several hundred more layoffs are
planned next month.*

layout /'leɪaʊt/ *noun* [C] the way that something is arranged **düzen, plan, tertip** *Do you like the layout of the kitchen?*

o⌐**lazy** /'leɪzi/ *adjective* **1** Someone who is lazy does not like working or using any effort. **tembel, haylaz** *You lazy thing!* ○ *He's too lazy to make his bed in the morning.* **2** slow and relaxed **ağır, boşvermiş, uyuşuk, yavaş, tembel** *a lazy morning/weekend* ● **lazily** *adverb* **tembel bir şekilde** ● **laziness** *noun* [U] **tembellik**

lb *written abbreviation for* pound (= a unit for measuring weight) **ağırlık ölçü birimi olan pound'un kısa yazılışı**

LCD /ˌelsiːˈdiː/ *noun* [C] *abbreviation for* liquid crystal display: a screen for showing words or pictures which uses a liquid and an electric current **sıvı kristal ekran** *LCD TV*

o⌐**lead¹** /liːd/ *verb past* **led** /led/ **1** [TAKE SOMEONE] [I, T] to show someone where to go, usually by taking them to a place or by going in front of them **öncülük etmek, götürmek, kılavuzluk etmek** *She led them down the hall.* ○ *We followed a path that led us up the mountain.* ○ *You lead and we'll follow.* ○ *I'll lead the way* (= go first to show the route). **2 lead into/to/towards, etc** If a path or road leads somewhere, it goes there. **(yol, patika) gitmek, doğru gitmek, götürmek, ulaşmak, uzanmak** *That path leads to the beach.* **3** [BE WINNING] [I, T] to be winning a game **önde olmak, kazanıyor olmak, lider durumda olmak** *They were leading by 11 points at half-time.* ○ *The Lions lead the Hawks 28-9.* **4** [BE THE BEST] [T] to be better than anyone else **herkesten daha iyi olmak, lider olmak** *I still believe that we lead the world in acting talent.* **5** [CONTROL] [T] to be in control of a group, country, or situation **yönetmek, kontrol etmek, hâkim/öncü olmak** *to lead a discussion* ○ *Is this man really capable of leading the country?* ○ *Shearer led his team to victory.* **6 lead sb to do sth** to cause someone to do or think something **yol açmak, neden olmak** *What led you to think that?* ○ *I was led to believe that breakfast was included.* **7 lead a busy/normal/quiet, etc life** to live in a particular way **belli düzende bir yaşam sürdürmek** *He was able to lead a normal life despite his illness.* **8 lead sb to a conclusion** to cause you to think that something is probably true **bir sonuca götürmek; sonuca varmasına sebep olmak** *So you thought I was leaving, did you? What led you to that conclusion?*

lead to sth *phrasal verb* to cause something to happen or exist **yol açmak, neden olmak** *A poor diet can lead to health problems in later life.*

lead up to sth *phrasal verb* to happen before an event **öncesinde olmak, yol açmak, zemin hazırlamak** *The shops are always busy in the weeks leading up to Christmas.*

o⌐**lead²** /liːd/ *noun* **1** [WINNING] [no plural] a winning position during a race or other situation where people are competing **önde olma, lider durumda bulunma** *She's in the lead* (= winning). ○ *France has just taken the lead* (= started to win). ○ *a three-goal lead* **2** [FILM/PLAY] [C] the main person in a film or play **başrol oyuncusu** *She plays the lead in both films.* **3** [DOG] [C] *UK* (*US* leash) a chain or piece of leather fixed to a dog's collar so that it can be controlled **tasma, zincir, kayış** *Dogs must be kept on a lead at all times.* **4** [ELECTRICITY] [C] *UK* (*US* cord) the wire that connects a piece of electrical equipment to the electricity supply **kordon, tal, kablo** **5** [INFORMATION] [C] information about a crime that police are trying to

solve **ipucu, bilgi, malumat** *Police are chasing up a new lead.*

lead³ /liːd/ *adjective* [always before noun] The lead performer or lead part in a performance is the main performer or part. **başrol** *the lead singer* ○ *Who played the lead role?*

lead⁴ /led/ *noun* **1** [U] a soft, heavy, grey, poisonous metal used for roofs, pipes, etc (formula **Pb**) **kurşun** *a lead pipe* ○ *lead-free petrol/gasoline* **2** [C, U] the black part inside a pencil **kurşun**

o⌐**leader** /'liːdər/ *noun* [C] **1** a person in control of a group, country, or situation **önder, lider** *a religious leader* ○ *Who's the leader of the Democratic Party in the Senate?* **2** someone or something that is winning during a race or other situation where people are competing **(yarışma) lider, önde olan** *He's fallen two laps behind the leaders.* ○ *Microsoft is a world leader in software design.*

leadership /'liːdəʃɪp/ *noun* **1** [U] the job of being in control of a group, country, or situation **liderlik, önderlik** *the leadership of the Conservative party* ○ *leadership skills/qualities* ○ *a leadership contest* **2** [group] the people in control of a group, country, or situation **liderlik, önderlik** *There is growing discontent with the leadership.*

leading /'liːdɪŋ/ *adjective* [always before noun] very important or most important **en önemli, önde gelen, esas, baş, seçkin, sivrilmiş, kalbur üstü** *He's a leading Hollywood producer.*

o⌐**leaf¹** /liːf/ *noun* [C] *plural* **leaves** /liːvz/ **1** a flat, green part of a plant that grows from a stem or branch **yaprak** *an oak leaf* ○ *a lettuce leaf* ○ *the falling leaves* **2 take a leaf out of sb's book** *mainly UK* to copy something good that someone else does **birinin yaptığını kopya etmek, kopyasını çıkarmak** ● **3 turn over a new leaf** to start to behave in a better way **yeni bir sayfa açmak, daha iyi bir davranış sergilemek**

leaf   L

leaf² /liːf/ *verb*

leaf through sth *phrasal verb* to turn the pages of a book or magazine and look at them quickly **sayfalarını karıştırmak; çabuk çabuk çevirmek** *She lay on the sofa, leafing through glossy magazines.*

leaflet /'liːflət/ *noun* [C] a piece of folded paper or a small book which contains information **kitapçık, broşür** *I picked up a useful leaflet on how to fill in tax forms.*

leafy /'liːfi/ *adjective* [always before noun] A leafy place is pleasant and quiet with a lot of trees. **bol ağaçlı, ağaçlıklı, yemyeşil, yeşili bol** *a leafy lane/suburb*

league /liːg/ *noun* **1** [C] a group of teams which compete against each other in a sport **spor ligi** *top/bottom of the league* ○ *major/minor league baseball* ○ *Who won the league championship this year?* **2 be in league with sb** to be secretly working or planning something with someone, usually to do something bad **...ile iş birliği halinde, birlikte çalışan** **3 not be in the same league as sb/sth** *informal* to not be as good as someone or something **biriyle/bir şeyle aynı seviyede olamamak; onun kadar iyi olamamak** *It's a nice enough restaurant but it's not in the same league as Rossi's.*

leak¹ /liːk/ *verb* **1** [I, T] If a liquid or gas leaks, it comes out of a hole by accident, and if a container leaks, it allows liquid or gas to come out when it should not. **sızdırmak, akmak, kaçırmak** *Water had leaked all over the floor.* ○ *The bottle must have leaked because the bag's all wet.* **2** [T] If someone leaks secret information, they intentionally tell people about it. **gizli bilgiyi sızdırmak/açığa vurmak** *Details of the report had been leaked to the press.*

leak out *phrasal verb* If secret information leaks out, people find out about it. **dışarı sızmak, açığa çıkmak, duyulmak**

leak² /li:k/ *noun* [C] **1** a hole in something that a liquid or gas comes out of, or the liquid or gas that comes out **sızıntı, akma, kaçak** *I think we may have a leak in the roof.* ○ *a gas leak* **2** the act of intentionally telling people a secret **ifşaat, sızdırma, açığa vurma, belli etme**

leakage /'li:kɪdʒ/ *noun* [U] the problem of a liquid or gas coming out of something when it should not **akıntı, sızıntı, kaçırma, kaçak**

leaky /'li:ki/ *adjective informal* Something that is leaky has a hole in it and liquid or gas can get through. **sızdıran, kaçıran; delik, yarık** *a leaky boat/roof*

⚬ **lean¹** /li:n/ *verb past* **leaned** (*also UK*) **leant** /lent/ **lean (sth) back/forward/out, etc** to move the top part of your body in a particular direction (**öne, yana, arkaya vs.) eğilmek, hamle yapmak** *She leaned forward and whispered in my ear.* ○ *Lean your head back a bit.*

lean (sth) against/on sth *phrasal verb* to sit or stand with part of your body touching something as a support **dayanmak, yaslanmak** *He leaned against the wall.* ○ *She leaned her head on his shoulder.*

lean sth against/on sth *phrasal verb* to put something against a wall or other surface so that it is supported **dayamak, yaslamak** *Lean the ladder against the wall.*

lean on sb/sth *phrasal verb* to use someone or something to help you, especially in a difficult situation (**zor durumlarda) destek almak, dayanmak, sırtını yaslamak, yaslanmak** *Her mother had always leaned on her for support.*

lean² /li:n/ *adjective* **1** thin and healthy **zayıf ama diri ve sağlıklı** *lean and fit* **2** Lean meat has very little fat on it. **yağsız, az yağlı**

leaning /'li:nɪŋ/ *noun* [C] a belief or idea **inanç, eğilim, meyil, temayül** [usually plural] *I don't know what his political leanings are.*

leap¹ /li:p/ *verb past* **leaped** or **leapt** /lept/ **1 leap into/out of/up, etc** to suddenly move somewhere **atlamak, sıçramak, hoplamak, zıplamak** *He leapt out of his car and ran towards the house.* ○ *I leapt up to answer the phone.* **2 leap off/over/into, etc** to jump somewhere **bir yere atlamak** *She leapt over the wall and disappeared down the alley.*

leap at sth *phrasal verb* to accept the chance to have or do something with enthusiasm **havada kapmak, üzerine atlamak, hemen kabul etmek, çoktan razı olmak** *I'd leap at the opportunity to work in Japan.*

🧩 leap .... İLE BİRLİKTE KULLANILAN KELİMELER

a leap **in** sth ● a leap **of** [75%/5 million, etc] ● a leap **forward**

leap² /li:p/ *noun* [C] **1** a sudden improvement or increase **ani/beklenmedik gelişme/artış; hamle, sıçrama** *There was a big leap in profits last year.* ○ *This represents a great leap forward in technology.* **2** a big jump **uzun atlama** *He finished third in the long jump with a leap of 26 feet.* **3 by/in leaps and bounds** If progress or growth happens in leaps and bounds, it happens very quickly. **hızlı artış/yükselme; büyük adımlarla ilerleme; beklenenden daha hızlı artış ve gelişme** ◑See also: **quantum leap.**

'leap ,year *noun* [C] a year that happens every four years, in which February has 29 days instead of 28 **artık yıl**

⚬ **learn** /lɜːn/ *verb past* **learned** (*also UK*) **learnt** /lɜːnt/ **1** GET SKILL [I, T] to get knowledge or skill in a new subject or activity **öğrenmek** *I learned Russian at school.* ○ *"Can you drive?" "I'm learning."* ○ *She's learned a lot about computers in the last three months.* ○ [+ to do sth] *I'm learning to play the piano.* **2** REMEMBER [T] to make yourself remember a piece of writing by reading or repeating it many times **ezberlemek** *I don't know how actors learn all those lines.* **3** UNDERSTAND [I, T] to start to understand that you must change the way you behave **öğrenmek; davranışın değiştirmesi gerektiğini kavramak** [+ (that)] *She'll have to learn that she can't have everything she wants.* ○ *The good thing is, he's not afraid to learn from his mistakes.* ◑See also: learn/know the ropes (**rope¹**).

learn or know?

Dikkat: Doğru fiili seçin! Bilinen bilgi için, **learn** fiili değil **know** fiili kullanılır.: ~~I would like to learn if your special offer will still be available in September.~~ Yanlış cümle örneği

I would like to know if your special offer will still be available in September.

learn about/of sth *phrasal verb* to hear facts or information that you did not know **duymak, haberi olmak, öğrenmek** *We only learned about the accident later.*

learned /'lɜːnɪd/ *adjective formal* Someone who is learned has a lot of knowledge from reading and studying. **bilgili, bilgin, âlim, kültürlü** *He was a very learned man.*

learner /'lɜːnər/ *noun* [C] someone who is getting knowledge or a new skill **öğrenci, acemi** *learners of English*

learning /'lɜːnɪŋ/ *noun* [U] the process of getting knowledge or a new skill **öğrenme, kavrama, bilgili olma, öğrenim** *language learning*

'learning ,curve *noun* [C] how quickly or slowly someone learns a new skill **öğrenme eğrisi/eğilimi; bir şeyin ne kadar yavaş ve hızlı öğrenildiği** *I've been on a steep learning curve since I started my new job.*

🧩 lease .... İLE BİRLİKTE KULLANILAN KELİMELER

renew/sign/take a lease ● a lease **of/on** sth

lease¹ /li:s/ *noun* [C] **1** a legal agreement in which you pay money in order to use a building or a piece of land for a period of time **kira sözleşmesi/kontratı** *We signed a three-year lease when we moved into the house.* **2 give sb/sth a new lease of life** UK (*also US* give sb/sth a new lease on life) **a** to make someone feel happy or healthy after a period of illness or sadness **hastalık ve üzüntü sonrası hayata yeniden kazandırma/yenide doğmasını sağlama** *The operation has given her a new lease of life.* **b** to improve something that was old so that it works much better **yeniden kazanmak; tekrar kullanılır/çalışır/iş görür hale getirmek**

lease² /li:s/ *verb* [T] to use a building or piece of land, or to allow someone to use a building or piece of land, in exchange for money **kiralamak, kiraya/icara vermek, kira ile tutmak** *We want to lease some office space in the centre of town.* ○ *The council eventually leased the land to a local company.*

leash /li:ʃ/ (*also UK* lead) *noun* [C] a chain or piece of leather fixed to a dog's collar so that it can be controlled **tasma, zincir, kayış**

o⊶**least**[1] /liːst/ *adverb* **1** less than anyone or anything else **en az, en az** *Which car costs least?* ○ *I chose the least expensive dish on the menu.* ○ *No one, least of all* (= especially not) *James, is going to be angry with you.* **2 at least a** as much as, or more than, a number or amount **en azından, en aşağı** *You'll have to wait at least an hour.* **b** something that you say when you are telling someone about an advantage in a bad situation **hiç değilse, hiç olmazsa** *It's a small house but at least there's a garden.* **c** used to say that someone should give a small amount of help although they do not intend to give a lot **bari, hiç olmazsa** *Even if you didn't want to send a present, you could at least have sent a card.* **d** something that you say in order to correct something you said that was wrong **daha doğrusu** *I've seen that film. At least, I saw the beginning then I fell asleep.* **3 not least** *formal* especially **hele...hiç, bilhassa, özellikle** *The whole trip was fascinating, not least because of the people I met.* **4 not in the least** not at all **hiç, zerre kadar** *I don't mind staying at home, not in the least.* ⊃See also: last[2] but not least.

least[2] /liːst/ *quantifier* **1** the smallest amount **en az, en düşük** *She earns the least money of all of us.* ○ *Jake had more experience than anyone else and I probably had the least.* **2 to say the least** used to emphasize that you could have said something in a much stronger way **en azından, abartısız, en hafif deyimiyle** *We were surprised, to say the least.*

leather /ˈleðəʳ/ *noun* [U] the skin of animals that is used to make things such as shoes and bags **deri** *a leather jacket*

o⊶**leave**[1] /liːv/ *verb past* **left** /left/ **1** GO AWAY [I, T] to go away from a place or a situation, either permanently or for a temporary period **...dan/den ayrılmak/çıkmak** *I'm leaving work early this afternoon.* ○ *What time does the bus leave?* ○ *They left for Paris last night.* ○ *"Does Trevor still work there?" "No, he left"* (= he does not work there now). ○ *She left school at 16.* **2** END RELATIONSHIP [I, T] to end a relationship with a husband, wife, or partner and stop living with them **bırakmak, terketmek, ayrılmak; ilişkiyi bitirmek** *I'll never leave you.* ○ *She left him for a younger man.* **3** NOT TAKE [T] to not take something with you when you go away from a place, either intentionally or by accident **bırakmak, yanına almamak** *Why don't you leave your jacket in the car?* ○ *She'd left a note for him in the kitchen.* ○ *That's the second umbrella I've left on the train!* **4** NOT USE ALL [T] to not use all of something **hepsini kullanmamak, bir kısmını bırakmak** *They'd drunk all the wine but they'd left some food.* ○ *Are there any biscuits left?* **5** REMAIN [T] to make a permanent mark **daimi/kalıcı iz bırakmak** *The operation may leave a scar.* **6 leave sth open/on/off, etc** to cause something to stay in a particular condition **(açık, kapalı vb.) bırakmak** *Who left the window open?* **7** DO LATER [T] to do something later that you could do immediately **ertelemek, bırakmak** *Don't leave your packing till the night before you go.* **8** GIVE [T] to arrange for someone to receive something after you die **(para, miras, mal, mülk vb.) bırakmak** *His aunt left him a lot of money.* ○ *He left the house to Julia.* **9 leave sb alone** to stop speaking to or annoying someone **yalnız bırakmak** *Leave me alone! I'm trying to work.* **10 leave sth alone** to stop touching something **dokunmamak, serbest bırakmak** *Leave your hair alone!* ⊃See also: leave someone to their own devices **(device)**, leave/make your mark[1].

leave sb/sth behind *phrasal verb* to leave a place without taking something or someone with you **unutmak, bırakmak, yanına almamak** *We were in a hurry and I think I must have left my keys behind.*

leave behind sth; leave sth behind (sb) *phrasal verb* to cause a situation to exist after you have left a place

ayrılırken arakada bir şeyler bırakmak; geride bırakmak *The army left a trail of destruction behind them.*

leave sth for/to sb *phrasal verb* to give someone the responsibility for dealing with something **birinin sorumluluğuna bırakmak/terketmek; sorumluluğu devretmek** *I've left the paperwork for you.*

leave sb/sth out *phrasal verb* to not include someone or something **dahil etmemek, dışında bırakmak** *I've made a list of names - I hope I haven't left anyone out.*

be left out *phrasal verb* If someone feels left out, they are unhappy because they have not been included in an activity. **dışlanmış hissetmek; bir kenara itilmiş hissine kapılmak** *The older children had gone upstairs to play and she felt left out.*

be left over *phrasal verb* If an amount of money or food is left over, it remains when the rest has been used or eaten. **artmak, kalmak, kullanılmamış/yenmemiş vb. olmak** *There was a lot of food left over from the party.*

annual/maternity/paternity/sick leave ● on leave ● leave **from** [work/your job, etc]

leave[2] /liːv/ *noun* [U] a period of time when you do not go to work **izin, dinlenme** *She's on maternity/sick leave.*

leaves /liːvz/ *plural of* leaf **yapraklar**

lecherous /ˈletʃ°rəs/ *adjective* A lecherous man shows too much interest in sex, in a way that is unpleasant. **şehvet düşkünü**

lecture[1] /ˈlektʃəʳ/ *noun* [C] **1** a formal talk given to a group of people in order to teach them about a subject **konuşma, konferans** *We went to a lecture on Italian art.* ○ *Do you know who's giving the lecture this afternoon?* **2** an angry or serious talk given to someone in order to criticize their behaviour **ahlâk dersi verme, eleştirme; kızgın ve ciddi konuşma** *My dad gave me a lecture on smoking last night.*

lecture[2] /ˈlektʃəʳ/ *verb* **1** [I] to give a formal talk to a group of people, often at a university **konuşma yapmak, konferans vermek** *She travelled widely throughout North America lecturing on women's rights.* ○ *For ten years she lectured in law.* **2** [T] to talk angrily to someone in order to criticize their behaviour **ahlâk dersi vermek, eleştirmek; kızgın ve ciddi konuşmak** *Stop lecturing me!* ○ *His parents used to lecture him on his table manners.*

lecturer /ˈlektʃ°rəʳ/ *noun* [C] *mainly UK* someone who teaches at a university or college **öğretim görevlisi/üyesi** *a lecturer in psychology* ○ *a senior lecturer*

led /led/ *past of* lead **'öncülük etmek' fiilinin geçmiş zaman hâli**

ledge /ledʒ/ *noun* [C] a long, flat surface that comes out under a window or from the side of a mountain **pervaz, çıkıntı, pencere altı kenarı** *The birds landed on a ledge about halfway up the cliff.*

leek /liːk/ *noun* [C, U] a long white and green vegetable that smells and tastes similar to an onion **pırasa**

leer /lɪəʳ/ *verb* [I] to look at someone in an unpleasant and sexually interested way **dik dik bakıp gözle taciz etmek, rahatsız edici şekilde bakmak** *He was always leering at female members of staff.* ● **leer** *noun* [C] **çirkin ve rahatsız edici bakış**

leery /ˈlɪəri/ *adjective* US worried and not able to trust someone **endişeli ve güvensiz; güvenemeyen** *I've gotten more leery of the media.*

leeway /ˈliːweɪ/ *noun* [U] freedom to do what you want **istediğini yapma özgürlüğü** *My current boss gives me much more leeway.*

o⁎**left¹** /left/ *adjective,* [always before noun] *adverb* on or towards the side of your body that is to the west when you are facing north **sol, sola doğru, sol tarafa** *Step forward on your left leg.* ○ *She had a diamond earring in her left ear.* ○ **Turn left** *at the end of the corridor.* ⊃Opposite **right.**

> **left (noun)** ...... İLE BİRLİKTE KULLANILAN KELİMELER
> **on** the left • the left **of** sth • be to sb's left

o⁎**left²** /left/ *noun* **1** [no plural] the left side **sol taraf** *Ned's the man sitting on my left in that photo.* ○ *Jean's house is last on the left.* **2** **the Left/left** political groups which believe that power and money should be shared more equally among people **sol, solcular, sosyalistler** *The proposals were sharply criticized by the Left.* ⊃Opposite **right.**

left³ /left/ *past of* leave **'ayrılmak' fiilinin geçmiş zaman hâli**

‚**left 'click** *verb* [I] to press the button on the left of a computer mouse (= a small piece of equipment that you move with your hand to control what the computer does) **bilgisayara komuta etmek için fare'nin sol tuşunu tıklamak**

‚**left 'field** *noun* US informal **in/from/out of left field** strange and not expected **tuhaf ve beklenmeyen** *His question came out of left field, and I didn't know what to say.*

left-hand /‚left'hænd/ *adjective* [always before noun] on the left **sol taraf** *a left-hand drive car* (= car which you drive sitting on the left-hand side) ○ *The swimming pool is on the **left-hand side** of the road.*

left-handed /‚left'hændɪd/ *adjective* Someone who is left-handed uses their left hand to do most things. **solak, sol elini kullanan** *Are you left-handed?*

leftist /'leftɪst/ *adjective* supporting the ideas of parties on the political left **solcu** *leftist politics/ideas*

leftover /'left‚əʊvə^r/ *adjective* [always before noun] Leftover food remains after a meal. **artık, artmış, kalmış** *If there's any leftover food we can take it home with us.* • **leftovers** *noun* [plural] food which remains after a meal **artan yemek, kırıntı** *We've been eating up the leftovers from the party all week.*

left-wing /‚left'wɪŋ/ *adjective* supporting the ideas of parties on the political left **sol kanat** *a left-wing newspaper* • **left-winger** *noun* [C] **sol fikirli**

leg

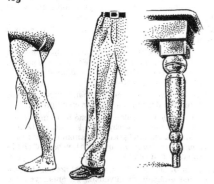

o⁎**leg** /leg/ *noun* [C] **1** PART OF BODY one of the parts of the body of a human or animal that is used for standing and walking **bacak** *He broke his leg in the accident.* ○ *There were cuts on her arms and legs.* ○ *She had bare*

legs and wore only a light summer dress. ⊃Orta kısımdaki renkli sayfalarına bakınız. **2** FOOD the meat of an animal's leg eaten as food **but** *a chicken leg* **3** FURNITURE one of the vertical parts of a chair, table, etc that is on the floor **(sandalye, masa vb.) bacağı** *a chair/table leg* **4** CLOTHES the part of a pair of trousers that covers one of your legs **(pantolon) bacağı** *He rolled up his trouser legs and waded into the water.* **5** PART OF JOURNEY one part of a journey or competition (yarışma, seyahat) **ayak, etap, menzil** *the first/second/third leg of the journey* **6 not have a leg to stand on** *informal* to have no chance of proving that something is true **destekten yoksun olmak; kuvvetli/inandırıcı kanıtı olmamak** *If you don't have a witness, you don't have a leg to stand on.* • **7 be on its last legs** *informal* If a machine is on its last legs, it will stop working soon because it is so old. **(makine) çok yıpranmış, her an bozulabilir durumda olmak** *We've had the same oven for twenty years now and it really is on its last legs.* • **8 stretch your legs** *informal* to go for a walk **yürüyüşe çıkmak, yürüyüş yapmak**

legacy /'legəsi/ *noun* [C] **1** a situation that was caused by something from an earlier time **geçmişin kalıtı, arta kalan şey** *The war has left a legacy of hatred.* **2** money or buildings, etc that you receive after someone dies **miras, kalıt, geçmişten kalan**

o⁎**legal** /'liːg^əl/ *adjective* **1** relating to the law **kanunlarla/yasalarla ilgili** *legal action/advice* ○ *the legal profession/system* **2** allowed by law **yasal, kanunî, yasaya uygun** *Is it legal to carry a handgun?* ⊃Opposite **illegal.** • **legally** *adverb* Children under sixteen are not legally allowed to buy cigarettes. **kanuni olarak**

‚**legal 'aid** *noun* [U] a system that provides free advice about the law to people who are too poor to pay for it **parasal gücü olmayanlara hukuk danışmanlık hizmeti sağlayan sistem**

legality /liː'gæləti/ *noun* [U] the legal quality of a situation or action **yasallık, yasaya uygunluk** *Some board members have questioned the legality of the proposal.*

legalize /'liːg^əlaɪz/ *verb* [T] to make something legal **yasallaştırmak, yasaya uygun hale getirmek** *How many Americans want to legalize drugs?* • **legalization** /‚liːg^əlaɪ'zeɪʃ^ən/ *noun* [U] *the legalization of abortion* **kanunlaştırma**

legend /'ledʒənd/ *noun* **1** [C, U] an old story or set of stories from ancient times **destan, efsane, menkıbe** *the legends of King Arthur* ○ *She's writing a book on Greek legend.* **2** [C] a famous person **efsane, kahraman, efsanevî kişi** *a living legend* ○ *Jazz legend, Ella Fitzgerald, once sang in this bar.*

legendary /'ledʒənd^əri/ *adjective* **1** from a legend (= old story) **efsanevî, destanımsı** *a legendary Greek hero* **2** very famous **çok meşhur, dillere destan, çok ünlü** *He became editor of the legendary Irish journal, 'The Bell'.*

leggings /'legɪŋz/ *noun* [plural] tight trousers which are made of soft material that stretches and are worn mainly by women **sıkı ve bedeni sımsıkı saran pantolon, tayt** *a pair of leggings*

legible /'ledʒəbl/ *adjective* If writing is legible, you can read it easily. **okunaklı, kolay okunabilen** ⊃Opposite **illegible.**

legion /'liːdʒən/ *noun* [C] a large group of soldiers that forms part of an army **bir ordunun belli bir bölümünü oluşturan ve genellikle gönüllü askerlerden oluşan asker grubu, lejyon**

legions /'liːdʒənz/ *noun* [plural] **legions of sb** large numbers of people **çok kalabalık insan topluluğu, sayı-**

sız, kitle, bir alay insan *He failed to turn up for the concert, disappointing the legions of fans waiting outside.*

legislate /ˈledʒɪsleɪt/ *verb* [I] If a government legislates, it makes a new law. **yasa çıkarmak, kanun yapmak** *We believe it is possible to* **legislate against** *racism.* ○ *It's hard to* **legislate for** (= make a law that will protect) *the ownership of an idea.*

▓▓▓ legislation .... İLE BİRLİKTE KULLANILAN KELİMELER

introduce/pass legislation ● a piece of legislation ● legislation on sth

legislation /ˌledʒɪˈsleɪʃⁿn/ *noun* [U] a law or a set of laws **yasalar, mevzuat** *Most people want tougher environmental legislation but large corporations continue to oppose it.*

legit /ləˈdʒɪt/ *adjective informal short for* legitimate **meşru, yasal, yasaya uygun**

legitimate /lɪˈdʒɪtəmət/ *adjective* **1** allowed by law **meşru, yasal, yasaya uygun** *Sales of illegal CDs now exceed those of legitimate recordings.* ⊃Opposite **illegitimate**. **2** A legitimate complaint or fear can be understood or believed. **yerinde, mantıklı, akla uygun, kabul edilebilir** *People have expressed legitimate fears about the spread of the disease.* ● **legitimately** *adverb* **kanuna uygun olarak**

leisure /ˈleʒəʳ/ ⒰ /ˈliːʒər/ *noun* [U] **1** the time when you are not working **boş vakit** *leisure activities* ○ *Try to spend your leisure time doing activities you really enjoy.* **2 at your leisure** If you do something at your leisure, you do it when you have the time. **boş vakitte, uygun zamanda, fırsat olduğunda** *Take it home and read it at your leisure.*

'leisure ˌcentre *noun* [C] *UK* a building with a swimming pool and places where you can play sports **spor, yüzme vb. faaliyetlerle boş vakitleri değerlendirme merkezi**

leisurely /ˈleʒəli/ ⒰ /ˈliːʒərli/ *adjective* in a relaxed way without hurrying **acelesiz, telaşsız, rahat** *a leisurely stroll*

lemon /ˈlemən/ *noun* [C, U] an oval, yellow fruit that has sour juice **limon** *a slice of lemon* ○ *lemon juice* ⊃Orta kısımdaki renkli sayfalarına bakınız.

lemon

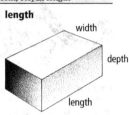

lemonade /ˌleməˈneɪd/ *noun* [C, U] **1** *UK* a cold drink with a lemon flavour that is sweet and has bubbles **limonlu gazoz 2** *mainly US* a cold drink that is made from lemon juice, water, and sugar **limonata**

o▪**lend** /lend/ *verb past* lent /lent/ **1** [+ two objects] to give something to someone for a period of time, expecting that they will then give it back to you **ödünç/borç vermek** *She lent me her car for the weekend.* ○ *I do have a bike but I've lent it to Sara.* **2** [I, T] If a bank lends money, it gives money to someone who then pays the money back in small amounts over a period. **kredi vermek** *The bank refused to lend us money for another mortgage.*
lend itself to sth *phrasal verb formal* to be suitable for a particular purpose **uygun düşmek, elverişli olmak, yaramak, müsait olmak** *The old system doesn't lend itself to mass production.*
lend sth to sb/sth *phrasal verb formal* to add a quality to something or someone **değer katmak, vermek** *We will continue to lend support to our allies.*

lender /ˈlendəʳ/ *noun* [C] a person or organization that lends money to people **ödünç veren/kredi açan kişi/ kurum vb.** *mortgage lenders*

▓▓▓ length ...... İLE BİRLİKTE KULLANILAN KELİMELER

the length **of** sth ● [20m/3cm, etc] **in** length

o▪**length** /leŋθ/ *noun*

length

width

depth

length

1 DISTANCE [C, U] the measurement or distance of something from one end to the other **uzunluk, boy** *The carpet is over three metres in length.* ○ *The length of the bay is roughly 200 miles.* ⊃See study page **Measurements** on page Centre 31. **2** TIME [C, U] the amount of time something takes **süre, müddet, zaman** *the length of a film/play/speech* ○ *Sitting still for any length of time is quite hard for most children.* **3** WRITING [C, U] the amount of writing in a book or document **(kitap, yazı vs.)** **uzunluk** *He's written books of various lengths on the subject.* **4 at length** If you talk about something at length, you talk for a long time. **uzun uzadıya, uzun bir süre, enine boyuna** *We discussed both topics at length.* **5** PIECE [C] a long piece of something **bir şeyin uzunluğu, boyu** *a length of cloth/cord/rope* **6 go to great lengths to do sth** to try very hard to achieve something **mümkün olan her şeyi yapmak, her yolu denemek, her çareye baş vurmak** *He'll go to great lengths to get what he wants.* ● **7 the length and breadth of sth** in every part of a place **her yanında, dört bir köşesinde/ köşesini** *They travelled the length and breadth of Scotland together.*

lengthen /ˈleŋθən/ *verb* [I, T] to become longer or to make something longer **uzamak, uzatmak** *lengthening waiting lists*

lengthy /ˈleŋθi/ *adjective* continuing for a long time **bitmek bilmez, çok uzun, bıktıran, uzun süren** *a lengthy discussion/process*

lenient /ˈliːniənt/ *adjective* A lenient punishment is not severe. **yumuşak, müsamahalı, hoşgörülü, mülayim** *He asked the judge to pass a lenient sentence.*

lens /lenz/ *noun* [C] **1** a curved piece of glass in cameras, glasses, and scientific equipment used for looking at things **mercek, büyüteç** ⊃See also: **contact lens, zoom lens**. **2** the part of the eye behind the pupil (= dark hole) that helps you see well

lens

lens

lent /lent/ *past of* lend **'ödünç vermek' fiilinin geçmiş zaman hâli**

Lent /lent/ *noun* [U] the religious period before Easter (= a Christian holiday), in which some Christians do not allow themselves something that they usually enjoy **dinî inanış gereği yapılan perhiz, lent** *She's given up chocolate for Lent.*

lentil /ˈlentⁿl/ *noun* [C] a very small dried bean which is cooked and eaten **mercimek** *lentil soup*

Leo /'liːəʊ/ noun [C, U] the sign of the zodiac which relates to the period of 23 July - 22 August, or a person born during this period **Aslan Burcu** ⊃See picture at **zodiac**.

leopard

leopard /'lepəd/ noun [C] a large, wild animal of the cat family, with yellow fur and dark spots **leopar**

leper /'lepəʳ/ noun [C] a person who has leprosy **cüzzamlı**

leprosy /'leprəsi/ noun [U] a serious skin disease which can destroy parts of the body **cüzzam**

lesbian /'lezbiən/ noun [C] a woman who is sexually attracted to other women **sevici, eşcinsel kadın, lezbiyen** a lesbian affair

⌐**less**¹ /les/ adverb **1** not as much **daha az** I'm trying to exercise more and eat less. ○ Plastic bottles are less expensive to produce. **2 less and less** If something happens less and less, it gradually becomes smaller in amount or not so frequent. **gittikçe daha az** I find I'm eating less and less red meat.

⌐**less**² /les/ quantifier a smaller amount **daha da az** She gets about £50 a week or less. ○ I was driving at **less than** 20 miles per hour. ○ Tuberculosis is less of a threat these days. ○ I prefer my coffee with a little less sugar.

-less /-ləs/ suffix to make a noun into an adjective meaning 'without' **...sız/siz anlamında isimleri sıfat yapan son ek** homeless people ○ a meaningless statement ○ a hopeless situation

lessen /'lesᵊn/ verb [I, T] to become less or to make something less **azalmak, azaltmak** Exercise and a healthy diet lessen the chance of heart disease.

lesser /'lesəʳ/ adjective **1** not as large, important, or of such good quality **daha az, daha küçük** The price increase was due to labour shortages and, **to a lesser extent**, the recent earthquake. ○ He faces the lesser charge of assault. **2 the lesser of two evils** the less bad of two bad things **kötünün iyisi, ehvenişer** I suppose I regard the Democratic candidate as the lesser of two evils.

lesser-known /ˌlesəˈnəʊn/ adjective not as popular or famous as something else **daha az bilinen** We stayed on one of the lesser-known Greek islands.

lesson ...... İLE BİRLİKTE KULLANILAN KELİMELER

have/take lessons ● give sb a lesson

⌐**lesson** /'lesᵊn/ noun [C] **1** a period of time when a teacher teaches people **ders saati** The best way to improve your game is to take lessons. ○ She gives French lessons. ○ Lessons start at 9 a.m. **2** an experience which teaches you how to behave better in a similar situation in the future **ders** My parents made me pay back all the money, and it was a lesson I never forgot. **3 learn your lesson** to decide not to do something again because it has caused you problems in the past **ders almak/çıkarmak; ibret almak** I'm not going out without my umbrella again - I've learnt my lesson! ● **4 teach sb a lesson** to punish someone so that they will not behave badly again **dersini vermek, haddini bildirmek, ağzının payını vermek** The next time she's late, go without her. That should teach her a lesson.

⌐**let** /let/ verb [T] **letting**, past **let 1** [ALLOW] to allow someone to do something, or to allow something to happen **birine bir şey yapması için izin vermek, bir şeyin olmasına müsaade etmek** Let them play outside. ○ Don't let the camera get wet. ○ We let a whole year go by before we tried again. **2 let sb/sth in/past/through, etc** to allow someone or something to move to a particular place **geçmesine/girmesine/geçip gitmesine izin vermek** They won't let us past the gate. ○ I won't let him near my children. ○ The roof lets in a lot of rain. **3 let's** something that you say when you are making a suggestion **hadi; ...lım/lim** Let's eat out tonight. **4 let me/us** something that you say when you are offering to help someone **(bana/bize) izin ver; (müsaadenizle) ...yım/yim/lım/lim** Let me carry your cases. **5** [BUILDING] If you let a building or part of a building, you allow someone to live there and they give you money. **kiraya vermek** I let the top floor of my house to a student. **6 Let's see/Let me see** something that you say when you are trying to remember something or calculate something **'Göreyim'/'Görelim', 'Hele bir göreyim/görelim'** Let's see - there are five people and only three beds. ○ It must have been - let me see - three years ago. **7 Let's say** something that you say when you are suggesting a possible situation or action **'Diyelim ki...', 'Meselâ/Örneğin...'** Let's say we'll meet back here in an hour. **8 let sb know (sth)** to tell someone something **söylemek, bildirmek, haber vermek, anlatmak** [+ question word] I'll let you know when we've fixed a date for the meeting. **9 let (sth) go** to stop holding something **salmak, serbest bırakmak** I let go of the rope. **10 let yourself go a** [LESS ATTRACTIVE] to allow yourself to become less attractive or healthy **kendini salmak/koyuvermek; kendini hayatın akışına bırakmak b** [RELAX] to relax completely and enjoy yourself **kendini rahat hissetmek/bırakmak, keyfine bakmak** It's a party - let yourself go! **11 let's face it** something that you say when the truth is unpleasant but must be accepted **'Olduğu gibi kabul edelim', 'Gerçekten kaçış yok'** Let's face it, we're not getting any younger. **12 let alone** used to emphasize that something is more impossible than another thing **şöyle dursun; bir şeyin başka bir şeyden daha da imkansız olduğunu vurgulamada kullanılır** You couldn't trust her to look after your dog, let alone your child. ⊃See also: let the **cat** out of the bag, let your **hair** down, get/let sb off the **hook**¹, let off **steam**¹.

let sb down phrasal verb to disappoint someone by failing to do what you agreed to do **vaadini yerine getirememek, hayal kırıklığına uğratmak, yarı yolda bırakmak** I promised to go to the party with Jane and I can't let her down.

let sb in phrasal verb to allow someone to enter a room or building, often by opening the door **girmesine izin vermek** Could you go down and let Darren in?

let yourself in for sth phrasal verb to become involved in an unpleasant situation without intending to **istemeden başına iş açmak, bulaşmak** Do you realize how much work you're letting yourself in for?

let sb off phrasal verb to not punish someone who has done something wrong, or to not punish them severely **cezalandırmamak; ...dan/den affetmek, bağışlamak** I'll let you off this time, but don't ever lie to me again. ○ The judge **let** her **off with** (= only punished her with) a fine.

let on phrasal verb to tell someone about something secret **gizli sırrı açıklamak, ifşa etmek, söylemek, yaymak** She let **on to** a friend that she'd lied in court.

let sb/sth out phrasal verb to allow a person or animal to leave somewhere, especially by opening a locked or closed door **boşaltmak, salıvermek, dışarı bırakmak**

let up *phrasal verb* If bad weather or an unpleasant situation lets up, it stops or improves. **(kötü hava/ durum vs.) düzelmek, iyiye gitmek, dinmek, kesilmek, azalmak** *I hope the rain lets up for the weekend.*

letdown /'letdaʊn/ *noun* [no plural] *informal* a disappointment **düş/hayal kırıklığı; sükûtu hayal** *After all I'd heard about the film it was a bit of a letdown when I finally saw it.*

lethal /'liːθᵊl/ *adjective* able to cause death **öldürücü**

lethargic /lə'θɑːdʒɪk/ *adjective* When you feel lethargic, you have no energy and you do not want to do anything. **uyuşuk, bitkin, halsiz, durgun ● lethargy** /'leθədʒi/ *noun* [U] the feeling of being tired and having no energy **uyuşukluk, rahavet; bitkinlik, halsizlik**

🧩 **letter** .... İLE BİRLİKTE KULLANILAN KELİMELER

get/receive/send/write a letter ● in a letter ● a letter from/to sb

o→ **letter** /'letᵊr/ *noun* [C] **1** a written message that you send to someone, usually by post **mektup** *I got a letter from Paul this morning.* **2** a symbol that is used in written language and that represents a sound in that language **harf** *the letter K* ⮕See also: covering letter.

letterbox /'letəbɒks/ *noun* [C] *UK* **1** a small hole in a door that letters are put through **mektup kutusu** **2** (*US* mailbox) a large, metal container in a public place where you can post letters **posta kutusu**

'**letter ,carrier** *US* (*UK* postman) *noun* [C] someone who takes and brings letters and parcels as a job **postacı, posta taşıyıcısı**

lettuce /'letɪs/ *noun* [C] a plant with green leaves, which is eaten in salads **marul, kıvırcık salata** ⮕Orta kısımdaki renkli sayfalarına bakınız.

leukaemia *UK* (*US* leukemia) /luː'kiːmiə/ *noun* [U] a serious disease in which a person's body produces too many white blood cells **kan kanseri, lösemi**

levee /'levi/ *noun* [C] a wall made of land or other materials that is built next to a river to stop the river from flooding (= covering everywhere in water) **nehir kenarına su baskınlarını önlemek için inşa edilen duvar; istinat duvarı**

🧩 **level** .... İLE BİRLİKTE KULLANILAN KELİMELER

the level of sth ● at a (high/low, etc) level

o→ **level¹** /'levᵊl/ *noun* [C] **1** [HEIGHT] the height of something **seviye, hiza, düzey, yükseklik** *the water level* **2** [AMOUNT] the amount or number of something **oran, düzey** *Chess requires a high level of concentration.* **3** [ABILITY] someone's ability compared to other people **bilgi/kabiliyet/yetenek düzeyi** *Students at this level need a lot of help.* **4** [FLOOR] a floor in a building **kat, yükseklik** *The store had three levels.* ⮕See also: A level, a level playing field, sea level.

level² /'levᵊl/ *adjective* **1** [never before noun] at the same height **aynı hizada, yan yana** *I got down till my face was level with his.* **2** flat or horizontal **düz, yatay** *Make sure the camera is level before you take the picture.*

level³ /'levᵊl/ *verb* [T] *UK* levelling, *past* levelled, *US* leveling, *past* leveled **1** to make something flat **tesviye etmek, düzleştirmek** *He levelled the wet cement before it set.* **2** to completely destroy a building **yerle bir etmek, yıkmak, dümdüz etmek** *Artillery fire levelled the town.* ⮕See also: A level, a level playing field, sea level.

level sth against/at sb *phrasal verb* to say that someone has done something wrong **(eleştiri, suçlama vb.) yöneltmek, eleştiride/suçlamada bulunmak** [often passive] *Charges of corruption have been levelled against him.*

level sth at sb *phrasal verb* to aim a gun at someone or something **(silah vb.) nişan almak, doğrultmak, yöneltmek, çevirmek** *He levelled the gun at my head.*

level off/out *phrasal verb* to stop rising or falling and stay at the same level **dengeyi bulmak, istikrara kavuşmak, dengelenmek** *Road deaths have levelled off since the speed limit was lowered.*

,**level 'crossing** *UK* (*US* grade crossing) *noun* [C] a place where a railway crosses a road **hemzemin geçit**

lever /'liːvᵊr/ Ⓤ /'levər/ *noun* [C] **1** a handle that you push or pull to make a machine work **kol, levye 2** a long bar that you use to lift or move something by pressing one end **manivela, kaldıraç, levye**

leverage /'liːvᵊrɪdʒ/ Ⓤ /'levərɪdʒ/ *noun* [U] the power to influence people in order to get what you want **nüfuz, etki, güç**

levy /'levi/ *verb* **levy a charge/fine/tax, etc** to officially demand money **ücret/ceza/vergi toplamak; vergilendirmek; ceza kesmek** [often passive] *A new tax was levied on consumers of luxury goods.*

lewd /luːd/ *adjective* sexual in a way that is unpleasant **müstehcen, açık saçık** *lewd comments/gestures*

liability /ˌlaɪə'bɪləti/ *noun* **1** [RESPONSIBILITY] [U] when you are legally responsible for something **yükümlülük, sorumluluk** *They have admitted liability for the damage caused.* **2** [TROUBLE] [no plural] someone or something that is likely to cause you a lot of trouble **baş belası, engel, sakınca, mahzur, ayak bağı, köstek** *Wherever we go she upsets someone - she's a real liability.* **3** [DEBT] [usually plural] a debt of a business

liable /'laɪəbl/ *adjective* **1 be liable to do sth** to be likely to do something **yatkın/olması muhtemel olmak** *He's liable to make a fuss if you wake him.* **2** legally responsible **sorumlu, yükümlü** *Corporate officials are liable for the safety of their employees.*

liaise /li'eɪz/ *verb* [I] to speak to other people at work in order to exchange information with them **fikir alışverişinde bulunmak, fikir teatisi yapmak, ortak çalışma yapmak, birlikte hareket etmek** *Our head office will liaise with the suppliers to ensure delivery.*

liaison /li'eɪzᵊn/ *noun* **1** [COMMUNICATION] [U] communication between people or groups that work with each other **irtibat, ilişki, bağlantı 2** [PERSON] [C] *US* someone who helps groups to communicate effectively with each another **irtibatı/ilişkiyi sağlayan kişi, bağlantı kuran kişi/eleman** *She served as an informal liaison between employees and management.* **3** [RELATIONSHIP] [C] a short sexual relationship between people who are not married **zina, gayrımeşru cinsel ilişki, evlilik dışı ilişki**

liar /'laɪᵊr/ *noun* [C] someone who tells lies **yalancı**

Lib Dem /lɪb'dem/ *noun* [C] short for Liberal Democrat **Liberal Demokrat**

libel /'laɪbᵊl/ *noun* [U] writing which contains bad information about someone which is not true **iftira, karalama, yalan/onur kırıcı yayın** *Tabloid magazines are often sued for libel.*

liberal /'lɪbᵊrᵊl/ *adjective* **1** accepting beliefs and behaviour that are new or different from your own **liberal; yeni ve farklı fikirlere açık ve kabul eden** *a liberal attitude* **2** Liberal political ideas emphasize the need to make new laws as society changes and the need for government to provide social services. **toplumun değişmesine paralel ve sosyal hizmetleri içeren yeni kanunlar yapılması gerekliliğini vurgulayan siyasî düşünceyi taşıyan; liberal ● liberal** *noun* [C] someone who is liberal **liberal düşünceyi benimseyen kişi**

liberal 'arts US (UK/US arts) noun [plural] subjects of study which are not science, such as history, languages, etc **liberal sanatlar**

Liberal 'Democrat noun [C] **1 the Liberal Democrats** one of the three main political parties in the UK **Liberal Demokratlar; Birleşik Krallık'daki üç ana partiden biri** He's the leader of the Liberal Democrats. **2** someone who supports the Liberal Democrats **Liberal Demokrat**

liberally /ˈlɪbᵊrᵊli/ adverb in large amounts **cömertçe, çokça, serbestçe** fruit liberally sprinkled with sugar

liberate /ˈlɪbᵊreɪt/ verb [T] to help someone or something to be free **özgürlüğüne kavuşturmak, kurtarmak, serbest bırakmak** Troops liberated the city. ● **liberation** /ˌlɪbᵊrˈeɪʃᵊn/ noun [U] the invasion and liberation of France **serbest bırakma**

liberated /ˈlɪbᵊreɪtɪd/ adjective not following traditional ways of behaving or old ideas **geleneksel davranış biçimlerini ve eski fikirleri takip etmeyen, özgür, serbest, başına buyruk; özgürlükçü** a liberated woman

liberating /ˈlɪbᵊreɪtɪŋ/ adjective making you feel that you can behave in exactly the way that you want to **özgür bırakan, serbest olmasını sağlayan, rahatlatan** Taking all your clothes off can be a very **liberating experience.**

liberty /ˈlɪbᵊti/ noun [C, U] **1** the freedom to live, work, and travel as you want to **özgürlük, hürriyet, serbestlik** Many would willingly fight to preserve their liberty. **2 be at liberty to do sth** formal to be allowed to do something **yetkili/yetki verilmiş olmak, izin verilmiş olmak, hakkı olan; yapma özgürlüğü olmak** I'm not at liberty to discuss the matter at present. **3 take the liberty of doing sth** formal to do something that will have an effect on someone else, without asking their permission **çekinmemek, bir şeyi yapma özgürlüğünü elinde bulundurmak** I took the liberty of booking theatre seats for us. ⊃See also: civil liberties.

Libra /ˈliːbrə/ noun [C, U] the sign of the zodiac which relates to the period of 23 September - 22 October, or a person born during this period **Terazi Burcu**

librarian /laɪˈbreəriən/ noun [C] someone who works in a library **kütüphaneci**

o⁓**library** /ˈlaɪbrᵊri/ noun [C] a room or building that contains a collection of books and other written material that you can read or borrow **kütüphane, kitaplık**

lice /laɪs/ plural of louse **'bit' sözcüğünün çoğulu, bitler**

licence .... İLE BİRLİKTE KULLANILAN KELİMELER

apply for/hold/issue a licence ● a licence **for** sth

licence UK (US license) /ˈlaɪsᵊns/ noun [C] an official document that allows you to do or have something **ruhsat, izin belgesi, lisans** a hunting licence ○ a marriage licence ⊃See also: driving licence, off-licence.

license /ˈlaɪsᵊns/ verb [T] to give someone official permission to do or have something **izin/ruhsat/yetki vermek** [often passive, + to do sth] Undercover agents are licensed to carry guns.

licensed /ˈlaɪsᵊnst/ adjective **1** mainly US officially approved **lisanslı, ruhsatlı, ehliyetli** a licensed physician **2** A licensed bar or restaurant is officially allowed to serve alcoholic drinks. **ruhsatlı, msaadeli**

'license ,plate US (UK number plate) noun [C] an official metal sign with numbers and letters on the front and back of a car **araba plakası** ⊃Orta kısımdaki renkli sayfalarına bakınız.

lick¹ /lɪk/ verb [T] to move your tongue across the surface of something **yalamak** to lick your lips ○ We licked the chocolate off our fingers.

lick

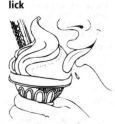

lick² /lɪk/ noun **1** [C] when you lick something **yalama, yalayış** [usually singular] Here, have a lick of my ice cream. **2 a lick of paint** UK informal If you give a wall or other surface a lick of paint, you paint it. **boyamak, yüzeye boya sürmek**

lid /lɪd/ noun [C] the top part of a container that can be removed in order to put something in or take something out **açılır kapanır kapak**

o⁓**lie¹** /laɪ/ verb [I] **lying,** past tense **lay,** past part **lain 1 lie in/on,** etc to be in a horizontal or flat position on a surface **yatmak, uzanmak** to lie in bed ○ to lie on a beach ○ to lie on your side ○ The pen lay on the desk. ○ She had lain where she fell until morning. **2 lie below/in/on/to,** etc to be in a particular place **belli bir yerde olmak, bulunmak** The river lies 30 km to the south of the city.

lie around phrasal verb **1** informal to spend time lying down and doing very little **avarelik etmek/yan gelip yatmak; tembel tembel yatmak** We spent a week by the sea, lying around on the beach. **2** If things are lying around, they are left in an untidy way in places where they should not be. **her şey dağınık olmak, darma dağınık olmak** He's always leaving money lying around.

lie back phrasal verb to lower the top half of your body from a sitting position to a lying position **uzanmak, yatmak, sırt üstü uzanmak** Lie back and relax.

lie down phrasal verb to move into a position in which your body is flat, usually in order to sleep or rest **yatmak, uzanmak** I'm not feeling well - I'm going to lie down. ⊃Orta kısımdaki renkli sayfalarına bakınız.

lie in phrasal verb UK to stay in bed in the morning later than usual **yataktan çıkmak istememek; geç kalkmak** I lay in till eleven o'clock this morning.

lie in sth phrasal verb to exist or be found in something **bir şeyde var olmak/bulunmak; ...da/de olmak** Her strength lies in her faith.

lie with sb phrasal verb If the responsibility or blame for something lies with someone, it is their responsibility. **...a/e düşmek; ...a/e ait olmak** The final decision lies with me.

o⁓**lie²** /laɪ/ verb [I] **lying,** past **lied** to say or write something that is not true in order to deceive someone **yalan söylemek/yazmak** Are you lying to me? ○ He lied about his qualifications for the job.

o⁓**lie³** /laɪ/ noun [C] something that you say or write which you know is not true **yalan, aslı astarı olmayan söz/yazı** I told a lie when I said I liked her haircut. ⊃See also: white lie.

lie-in /ˈlaɪˌɪn/ noun [no plural] UK when you stay in bed in the morning longer than usual **yatak keyfi, yataktan çıkmama, geç kalkma** I had a long lie-in this morning.

lieu /luː/ noun **in lieu of sth** formal instead of something **yerine** She took the money in lieu of the prize.

lieutenant /lefˈtenᵊnt/ ⓤⓢ /luːˈtenᵊnt/ noun [C] an officer of middle rank in the army, navy, or air force **teğmen** first/second lieutenant

🧩 **life** .... İLE BİRLİKTE KULLANILAN KELİMELER

have/lead/live a [charmed/normal, etc] life ● spend
your life (doing sth) ● an aspect/part of sb's life

o➛**life** /laɪf/ *noun plural* **lives** /laɪvz/ **1** ANIMALS/PLANTS [U]
living things and their activities **hayat, yaşam**
human/marine life ○ *Is there life in outer space?*
2 PERSON'S EXISTENCE [C] the existence of a person **hayat,**
canlı *How many lives will be lost to AIDS?* **3** TIME [C, U]
the time between a person's birth and their death
ömür, yaşam *I'm not sure I want to spend the rest of
my life with him.* ○ *Life's too short to worry about
stuff like that.* ○ *Unfortunately, accidents are part of
life.* ○ *He had a happy life.* **4** WAY OF LIVING [C, U] a way of
living **yaşam biçimi, ömür** *You lead an exciting life.*
5 family/private/sex, etc life one part of someone's
existence **aile/özel/cinsel vb. yaşam(ı)** *My private
life is nobody's business but mine.* **6** ACTIVITY [U] energy
and activity **yaşam, enerji, faaliyet, canlılık, hareket** *She was always bubbly and full of life.* ○ *I looked
through the window but couldn't see any signs of life*
(= people moving). **7** ACTIVE PERIOD [no plural] the amount
of time that a machine, system, etc exists or can be used
ömür, kullanım/çalışma süresi *Careful use will prolong the life of your machine.* **8 bring sth to life/come
to life** to make something more real or exciting, or to
become more real or exciting **canlan(dır)mak, hareket kazan(dır)mak 9 That's life.** something you say
which means bad things happen and you cannot prevent them **'Hayat bu, her şey mümkün!', 'Yaşam
bu, ne olacağını bilemeyiz!'** *You don't get everything
you want but that's life, isn't it?* **10 Get a life!** *informal*
something you say to a boring person when you want
them to do more exciting things **'Canlan biraz!',**
'Kıpırda!' *Surely you're not cleaning the house on Saturday night? Get a life!* ➜See also: the facts (fact) of life, give sb
the kiss² of life, give sb/sth a new lease¹ of life, shelf life, walk² of
life.

lifeboat /'laɪfbəʊt/ *noun* [C] a small boat that is used to
help people who are in danger at sea **kurtarma
gemisi, cankurtaran/tahliye sandalı, filika**

'**life ,coach** *noun* [C] someone whose job is to teach
people how to solve problems and make decisions in
their daily life **yaşam koçu; insanlara sorunların-
dan nasıl kurtulacağını ve doğru karar verebil-
meyi öğreten kişi**

'**life ,cycle** *noun* [C] the changes that happen in the life of
an animal or plant **yaşam döngüsü/evresi**

'**life ex,pectancy** *noun* [C, U] the number of years that
someone is likely to live **ömür, yaşam süresi**

lifeguard /'laɪfgɑːd/
noun [C] someone at a
swimming pool or
beach whose job
is to help people who
are in danger in the
water **cankurtaran**

'**life in,surance** (*also UK*
'**life a,ssurance**) *noun* [U]
a system of payments to
an insurance company
that will pay money to
your family when you
die **hayat sigortası**

'**life ,jacket** *noun* [C] a
piece of equipment that
you wear on the upper
part of your body to help
you float if you fall into
water **can yeleği**

life jacket

lifeless /'laɪfləs/ *adjective* **1** without life **cansız, ölü** *his
lifeless body* **2** without energy or feeling **donuk, cansız**
a lifeless performance

lifelike /'laɪflaɪk/ *adjective* If something is lifelike, it
looks real. **canlı gibi, sahici gibi** *a lifelike portrait/
sculpture*

lifeline /'laɪflaɪn/ *noun* [C] something that helps you
when you are in a difficult or dangerous situation
hayat bağı, can damarı, can kurtaran halatı *For a
lot of old people who live on their own, the telephone is a
lifeline.*

lifelong /,laɪf'lɒŋ/ *adjective* [always before noun] for all of
your life **ömür boyu süren** *a lifelong friend/interest*

,**life 'peer** *noun* [C] someone who has been officially
respected in the UK by being given an important title,
for example 'Lord', 'Lady' or 'Baroness' **Birleşik
Krallık'da 'Lord', 'Leydi' veya 'Barones' ünvanları
verilen ve resmen tanınan biri**

'**life ,sentence** *noun* [C] (*informal* life [U]) the punishment
of spending a very long time, or the rest of your life, in
prison **ömür boyu hapis/müebbet hapis cezası**

lifespan /'laɪfspæn/ *noun* [C] the amount of time that a
person lives or a thing exists **ömür, yaşam süresi**

lifestyle /'laɪfstaɪl/ *noun* [C] the way that you live
yaşam tarzı *a healthy lifestyle*

life-threatening /'laɪfθretᵊnɪŋ/ *adjective* likely to
cause death **yaşamı tehdit eden; muhtemelen
ölüme neden olan** *life-threatening conditions/
diseases*

lifetime /'laɪftaɪm/ *noun* [C] the period of time that
someone is alive **ömür, hayat** [usually singular] *We'll see
such huge changes in our lifetime.*

o➛**lift¹** /lɪft/ *verb* **1** UP [T] to put something or someone in a
higher position **kaldırmak, havaya kaldırmak** *Could
you help me lift this table, please?* ○ *She lifted the baby
up and put him in his chair.* **2** WEATHER [I] If fog lifts, it
disappears. **kalkmak, kaybolmak, yok olmak, dağılmak** *By noon the fog had lifted and the day turned hot.*
3 RULES [T] to stop a rule (kural) **kaldırmak** *The government had already lifted the ban on beef imports.* **4** STEAL
[T] *informal* to steal or copy something **çalmak veya
kopya etmek; yürütmek, aşırmak** *Entire paragraphs
of his thesis were lifted from other sources.* ➜See also: not lift
a finger¹.

o➛**lift²** /lɪft/ *noun* [C] **1** MACHINE *UK* (*US* elevator) a machine
that carries people up and down in tall buildings **asan-
sör** *Shall we use the stairs or take the lift?* **2** RIDE a free
ride somewhere, usually in a car **ücretsiz götürme,
arabasına alma** [usually singular] *Can you give me a lift
to the airport?* **3** MOVE when you move someone or something up to a higher position **yükseltme**

lift-off /'lɪftɒf/ *noun* [C] the moment when a spacecraft
leaves the ground **kalkış, havalanma**

ligament /'lɪgəmənt/ *noun* [C] a piece of strong tissue in
the body that holds bones together **bağ, kiriş, lif**
ankle/knee ligaments ○ *torn ligaments*

🧩 **light** .... İLE BİRLİKTE KULLANILAN KELİMELER

light shines ● a beam/ray/shaft of light ● bright
light

o➛**light¹** /laɪt/ *noun* **1** [U] the brightness that shines from
the sun, from fire, or from electrical equipment, allowing you to see things **ışık** *bright/dim light* ○ *fluores-
cent/ultraviolet light* ○ *a beam/ray of light* ○ *Light was
streaming in through the open door.* **2** [C] a device which
produces light **lamba, ışık** *car lights* ○ *to switch/turn
the light on* ○ *They must be in bed - I can't see any lights
on anywhere.* **3 a light** a flame from a match, etc used to

light

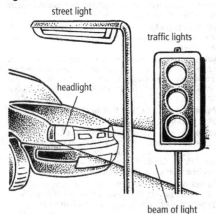

street light

traffic lights

headlight

beam of light

make a cigarette start burning **ateş** *Have you got a light, please?* **4 set light to sth** UK to make something start burning **yakmak, tutuşturmak 5 in the light of sth** (*also US* **in light of sth**) If something is done or happens in the light of facts, it is done or happens because of those facts. **ışığında; ...a/e göre/nazaran** *The drug has been withdrawn in the light of new research.* **6 bring sth to light** If information about something bad is brought to light, it is discovered. **gün ışığına çıkarmak, açığa çıkarmak** *The trial brought to light numerous contradictions in his story.* ● **7 cast/shed light on sth** to help people understand a situation **aydınlatmak, ışık tutmak** *We were hoping you might be able to shed some light on the matter.* ● **8 come to light** If information about something bad comes to light, it is discovered. **ortaya çıkmak, gün ışığına çıkmak, ortaya çıkmak** ● **9 light at the end of the tunnel** something which makes you believe that an unpleasant situation will soon end **tünelin sonundaki ışık; sıkıntıların sona ereceğini belirten işaret** ⊃See also: **green light, street light, tail light, traffic light.**

∘▪**light²** /laɪt/ *adjective* **1** NOT HEAVY not heavy **hafif** *light clothing/machinery* ○ *I can carry both bags - they're quite light.* **2** NOT MUCH small in amount **hafif, az** *light rain/snow* ○ *I only had a light lunch.* **3** NOT STRONG not strong or not forceful **zayıf, hafif, güçsüz** *a light breeze* ○ *a light embrace* **4** PALE Light colours are pale. **açık/soluk renk** *light brown/green* ○ *a light blue cardigan* **5** NOT SERIOUS easy to understand and not serious **basit, hafif, ciddi olmayan, kolay anlaşılır** *light entertainment* ○ *I'm taking some light reading on holiday.* **6 make light of sth** to talk or behave as if you do not think a problem is serious **bir şeyi hafife almak; ehemmiyet vermemek; önemsememek 7 it is light** it is bright from the sun **aydınlık, gündüz** *Let's go now while it's still light.* ● **lightness** *noun* [U] **hafiflik**

light³ /laɪt/ *verb past* **lit** or **lighted 1** [I, T] to start to burn, or to make something start to burn **yanmak, yakmak** *to light a candle/cigarette/fire* ○ *The wood was damp and wouldn't light.* **2** [T] to produce light somewhere so that you can see things **aydınlatmak** [often passive] *The room was lit by a single light bulb.* ○ *Burning buildings lit up the sky.*

light up *phrasal verb* If your face or your eyes light up, you suddenly look happy or excited. **(yüz, göz vb.) aydınlanmak, parlamak, parıldamak** *His eyes lit up when you mentioned her name.*

light (sth) up *phrasal verb* to make a cigarette, etc start burning **yakmak** *He made himself a coffee and lit up a cigarette.*

'**light ,bulb** *noun* [C] a glass object containing a wire which produces light from electricity **ampul**

light bulb

lighten /'laɪtᵊn/ *verb* **1** [I, T] If a serious situation lightens, it becomes less serious, and if something or someone lightens it, they make it less serious. **hafiflemek, hafifletmek** *Her mood lightened a bit when I asked about her holiday.* ○ *He tried to lighten the atmosphere by telling a joke.* **2 lighten the burden/load** to reduce the amount of work or trouble someone has to deal with **yükünü/sorunlarını hafifletmek/azaltmak 3** [I, T] to become less dark, or to make something less dark **aydınlatmak/aydınlanmak; ağar(t)mak** *The sun had lightened her hair.*

lighten up *phrasal verb informal* to become more relaxed and less serious **hafiflemek, rahatlamak, daha az ciddi hâle gelmek** *I wish she'd lighten up a bit.*

lighter /'laɪtəʳ/ *noun* [C] a small object that produces a flame and is used to make cigarettes start burning **çakmak**

light-hearted /ˌlaɪt'hɑ:tɪd/ *adjective* not serious **gamsız, neşeli, kaygısız, ciddi olmayan, eğlenceli** *a light-hearted remark*

lighthouse /'laɪthaʊs/ *noun* [C] *plural* **lighthouses** /'laɪthaʊzɪz/ a tall building on the coast containing a large light which warns ships that there are rocks **deniz feneri**

lighthouse

lighting /'laɪtɪŋ/ *noun* [U] the light created by electrical equipment, candles, etc **ışıklandırma, aydınlatma** *soft lighting*

lightly /'laɪtli/ *adverb* **1** gently **hafifçe, nazikçe** *He kissed her lightly on the cheek.* **2** not much **azıcık, hafifçe** *lightly cooked vegetables* **3 not do sth lightly** to think carefully about something before you do it, knowing that it is serious **hafife almadan yapmak, ciddi şekilde ele alıp dikkatlice düşünmek** *It's not a decision that I take lightly.* **4 get off lightly** (*also UK* **escape lightly**) to have less trouble or punishment than you expected **ucuz atlatmak, az bir zararla geçiştirmek**

░░ **lightning** ...... İLE BİRLİKTE KULLANILAN KELİMELER

be **struck by** lightning ● a **bolt/flash** of lightning ● **thunder and** lightning

lightning /'laɪtnɪŋ/ *noun* [U] a sudden flash of light in the sky during a storm **şimşek, yıldırım** *thunder and lightning* ○ *He was struck by lightning and killed.*

lights /laɪts/ (*also* '**traffic ,lights**) *noun* [plural] a set of red, green, and yellow lights that is used to stop and start traffic **trafik ışıkları**

lightweight /'laɪtweɪt/ *adjective* not weighing much **hafif, ince** *a lightweight jacket for the summer* ● **lightweight** *noun* [C] a sportsman such as a boxer who is not in the heaviest weight group **hafif sıklet**

∘▪**like¹** /laɪk/ *preposition* **1** SIMILAR similar to or in the same way as someone or something **benzer, gibi** *They were* *acting like children.* ○ *He looks like his father.* ○ *It sounded like Harry.* **2 What is sb/sth like?** something you say when you want someone to describe someone or something **'Neye benziyor?', 'Nasıl bir şey?', 'Nasıl biri?'** *I haven't met him - what's he like?* ○ *So what's your new dress like?* **3 What are you like?** *UK informal* used when someone has said or done something silly **'Ne yapmaya çalışıyorsun?', 'Yaptığını beğeniyor musun?', 'İyi misin?'** *You've bought another jacket? What are you like?* **4** TYPICAL If behaviour is like someone, it is typical of the way that they behave. **tam ona göre, tam ondan beklendiği gibi** *It's just like Anita to miss her train.* ○ *It's not like Tim to be late.* **5** FOR EXAMPLE for example **mesela, örneğin; gibi** *She looks best in bright colours, like red and pink.*

like ┅ BAŞKA BİR DEYİŞLE

Eğer kişi bir şeyi veya bir diğer kişiyi seviyor/beğeniyorsa, **love** ve **adore** fiilleri kullanılabilir. *I adore/ love seafood.* ● *Oliver loves animals.* ● *Kate adored her grandfather.*
Think the world of someone ve **have a soft spot for** söylemleri bir kişinin diğerini çok sevdiğini ifade edildiği durumlarda kullanılabilir. *I've always had a soft spot for Rebecca ever since she was tiny.* ● *Annabel's like a daughter to him, he thinks the world of her.*
Be fond of ifadesi kişinin bir diğerini veya bir şeyi sevmesi konusunda konuştuğu zaman kullanılır. *She's very fond of Chinese food.* ● *I think she's very fond of you.*
Grown on ve **take to/warm to** deyimleri kişinin bir diğerini veya bir şeyi sevmeye başladığı durumlarda kullanılır. *I wasn't sure about the colour at first, but it's growing on me.* ● *For some reason, I just didn't take/ warm to him.*
Take a shine to ve **take a liking to** ifadeleri kişinin bir diğerini görür görmez beğendiğinin ifadesinde kullanılır. *I think he's taken a bit of a shine to you.*

◦┅**like²** /laɪk/ *verb* [T] **1** to enjoy something or feel that someone or something is pleasant **sevmek, hoşlanmak, keyif almak** [+ doing sth] *I just like playing with my computer.* ○ [+ to do sth] *I like to paint in my spare time.* ○ *He really likes her.* ○ *What do you like about him?* ⊃Opposite dislike. **2 not like to do sth/not like doing sth** to not usually do something because you think it is wrong **bir şeyden/bir şeyi yapmaktan hoşlanmamak/zevk almamak** *I don't like to criticize her too much.* **3 would like sth** to want something **istemek, arzulamak, tercih etmek** [+ to do sth] *I'd like to think about it.* ○ *I'd like some chips with that, please.* **4 Would you like...?** used to offer someone something **'...ister misiniz?; ....arzu eder misiniz?; ...ne dersiniz?'** *Would you like a drink?* ○ [+ to do sth] *Would you like to eat now?* **5 if you like** a used to say 'yes' when someone suggests a plan **'İstersen/Dilersen/Arzu edersen'** *"Shall I come?" "If you like."* **b** used when you offer someone something **'Tabi ki', 'Nasıl istersen', 'Buyur', 'Elbette', 'Eğer isterseniz'** *If you like I could drive you there.* **6 How do you like sb/sth?** used to ask someone for their opinion **'Naşlı buldun? Nasıl buldunuz?'** *How do you like my new shoes?*

◦┅**like³** /laɪk/ *conjunction* **1** *informal* in the same way as **gibi, benzer şekilde** *Do it exactly like I told you to.* **2** *US informal* as if **sanki, gibi; ...mış/miş gibi** *He acted like he didn't hear me.*

like⁴ /laɪk/ *noun* **1** [no plural] *formal* someone or something that is similar to someone or something else **benzeri, benzeri, böyle/öyle bir şey** *Economists are predicting a depression, the like of which the world has never seen.* **2 and the like** *informal* and similar things **...ve benzeri/benzerleri; ...ve o/onlar gibi** *There's a gym that they use for dance and aerobics and the like.*

3 sb's likes and dislikes the things that someone thinks are pleasant and not pleasant **hoşlandıkları ve hoşlanmadıkları; sevdikleri ve sevmedikleri**

-like /-laɪk/ *suffix* changes a noun into an adjective meaning 'typical of or similar to' **...tipik/benzer/gibi anlamında son ek** *childlike trust* ○ *a cabbage-like vegetable*

likeable /'laɪkəbl/ *adjective* If you are likeable, you are pleasant and easy to like. **sevimli, sempatik, hoş** *a likeable character*

likelihood ┅┅ İLE BİRLİKTE KULLANILAN KELİMELER

increase/reduce the likelihood of sth ● a real/ strong likelihood ● the likelihood of (doing) sth

likelihood /'laɪklihʊd/ *noun* [U] the chance that something will happen **olasılık, ihtimal** *There's not much likelihood of that happening.*

◦┅**likely¹** /'laɪkli/ *adjective* **1** expected **muhtemel, olası, umulur, beklenir** [+ to do sth] *Do remind me because I'm likely to forget.* ○ [+ (that)] *It's likely that he'll say no.* **2** probably true **mümkün; ...acağa/eceğe benzer; ... acak/ecek gibi galiba** *the most likely explanation* ⊃Opposite unlikely.

likely² /'laɪkli/ *adverb* **1** probably **olasılıkla, muhtemeldir ki** *She'll most likely come without him.* **2 Not likely!** *UK informal* used to say that you will certainly not do something **'hiç mümkün değil!', 'Aklımdan bile geçmez!', 'Pek olası değil!'** *"So are you coming running with me?" "Not likely!"*

liken /'laɪkⁿn/
liken sth/sb to sth/sb *phrasal verb formal* to say that two people are similar or two things are similar **benzetmek; andırmak** *She's been likened to a young Elizabeth Taylor.*

likeness /'laɪknəs/ *noun* [C, U] being similar in appearance **benzerlik, benzeyiş** *There's a definite family likeness around the eyes.*

likewise /'laɪkwaɪz/ *adverb formal* in the same way ...**in gibi; ...olduğu gibi** *Water these plants twice a week and likewise the ones in the bedroom.* ○ *Watch what she does and then do likewise.*

liking /'laɪkɪŋ/ *noun* **1** [no plural] a feeling that you like someone or something **sevme, hoşlanma** *He has a liking for young women.* **2 take a liking to sb** to like someone immediately **birden sevmek/hoşlanmak/ ısınmak/kanı kaynamak** *He obviously took a liking to her.* **3 be too bright/sweet, etc for your liking** to be brighter/sweeter, etc than you like **istediğinden/ beğendiğinden daha parlak/tatlı vb. olmak** **4 be to sb's liking** *formal* to be the way that someone prefers something **zevkine göre/beğenisine uygun olmak** *Is the wine to your liking, sir?*

lilac /'laɪlək/ *noun* [C, U] a small tree that has sweet-smelling purple, pink, or white flowers **leylâk, leylâk ağacı**

lily /'lɪli/ *noun* [C] a plant with large, bell-shaped flowers that are often white **zambak**

limb /lɪm/ *noun* [C] **1** a leg or an arm of a person **kol bacak 2** a large branch of a tree **ana dal, büyük dal, kol**

lime /laɪm/ *noun* **1** FRUIT [C, U] a small, green fruit that is sour like a lemon **misket limonu 2** TREE [C] (*also* '**lime** ,tree**) a large tree that has pale green leaves and yellow flowers **ıhlamur, ıhlamur ağacı 3** SUBSTANCE [U] a white substance that is found in water and soil and is used to improve the quality of soil **kireç, kireç taşı 4** COLOUR [U] (*also* ,lime 'green) a bright colour that is a mixture of yellow and green **küf rengi; ıhlamur çiçeği rengi** ⊃Orta kısımdaki renkli sayfalarına bakınız. ● **lime** (*also* lime-green) *adjective* **limona benzer bir meyve**

the limelight /ˈlaɪmlaɪt/ *noun* attention from the public **genel ilgi, halktan gelen büyük ilgi** *She's been in the limelight for most of her career.*

limit ...... İLE BİRLİKTE KULLANILAN KELİMELER

an **age/a height/a speed/a time** limit ● **a legal/maximum/strict/an upper** limit ● **exceed/impose** a limit ● a limit **on/to** sth

☞**limit**[1] /ˈlɪmɪt/ *noun* [C] **1** the largest amount of something that is possible or allowed **(miktar) sınır, hudut, had, limit** *a time limit* ○ *Is there a **limit** on the amount of money you can claim?* ○ *There's a **limit** to how much time we can spend on this.* **2 be over the limit** *UK* to have more alcohol in your blood than is legally allowed while driving **normal alkol sınırının üstünde olmak 3 within limits** avoiding behaviour that is extreme or silly **bir dereceye kadar, belli bir yere kadar, sınırlar içinde; sınırları zorlamadan** *You can wear what you want, within limits.* **4 off limits** If an area is off limits, you are not allowed to enter it. **(bölge) yasak, (saha) girilmez** ⊃See also: speed limit.

☞**limit**[2] /ˈlɪmɪt/ *verb* [T] to control something so that it is less than a particular amount or number **sınırlamak; sınırlandırmak; ...ile yetinmek** *We'll have to limit the number of guests.*

be limited to sth *phrasal verb* to only exist in a particular area **(bir alana/bölgeye) özgü/has/mahsus olmak** *Racial problems are certainly not limited to the south.*

limit sb to sth *phrasal verb* to only allow someone a particular amount or number of something **sınırlamak, kısıtlamak** [often passive] *We're limited to two pieces of luggage each.* ○ [often reflexive] *I try to limit myself to two cups of coffee a day.*

limitation /ˌlɪmɪˈteɪʃᵊn/ *noun* [C, U] when something is controlled so that it is less than a particular amount or number **tahdit, sınırlama, kısıtlama** *the limitation of free speech* ○ *You can't write everything you want to because of space limitations.*

limitations /ˌlɪmɪˈteɪʃᵊnz/ *noun* [plural] things that someone is not good at doing **zayıf nokta, kusur, eksiklik** *Both films show her limitations as an actress.*

limited /ˈlɪmɪtɪd/ *adjective* small in amount or number **sınırlı, kısıtlı** *a limited choice* ○ *limited resources* ⊃Opposite unlimited.

limited 'company *noun* [C] a company, especially one in the UK, whose owners only have to pay part of the money they owe if the company fails financially **limited şirket**

limousine /ˌlɪməˈziːn/ (*also* limo /ˈlɪməʊ/) *noun* [C] a large, expensive car, usually for rich or important people **limuzin** *a chauffeur-driven limousine*

limp[1] /lɪmp/ *adjective* soft and weak **zayıf, takatsiz, güçsüz, bitkin** *a limp handshake* ○ *a limp lettuce*

limp[2] /lɪmp/ *verb* [I] to walk with difficulty because one of your legs or feet is hurt **topallamak, aksamak, topallayarak/aksayarak yürümek** ● **limp** *noun* [no plural] *She walks with a limp.* **topallama**

line ...... İLE BİRLİKTE KULLANILAN KELİMELER

draw a line ● a **diagonal/horizontal/straight/vertical** line

☞**line**[1] /laɪn/ *noun* **1** MARK [C] a long, thin mark **çizgi, hat** *a horizontal/straight/vertical line* ○ *Sign your name on the dotted line.* ○ *Draw a line around your hand.* **2** ROW [C] a row of people or things **kuyruk, sıra, dizi** *a line of*

trees ○ *We formed two lines, men on one side and women on the other.* **3** ROPE ETC [C] a piece of rope or wire with a particular purpose **ip, sicim, kordon, tel, olta, hat** *a clothes/fishing line* **4** TELEPHONE [C] the connection between two telephones **telefon hatları** *I've got Neil on the line for you* (= waiting to speak to you). ○ *I'll be with you in a moment - could you hold the line* (= wait), *please?* **5** WAITING [C, U] *US* (*UK* queue) a row of people waiting for something, one behind the other **kuyruk, sıra** *We were standing in line for hours to get tickets.* **6** SONG/POEM [C] a row of words on a page, for example in a song or poem **satır, dizi, mısra** *The same line is repeated throughout the poem.* **7 lines** the words spoken by an actor in a performance **oyuncunun söylediği sözler, replik, rol** *I don't know how actors remember all their lines.* **8** OPINION [C] the official opinion of an organization **resmî fikir/düşünce/anlayış/tavır** [usually singular] *the government's line on immigration* **9 along the lines of** sth based on and similar to something **gibi, şeklinde; ...lerden** *He gave a talk along the lines of the one he gave in Oxford.* **10 sb's line of reasoning/thinking, etc** your reasons for believing that something is true or right **birinin akıl yürütme/düşünme vs. biçimi/sınırı/şekli 11** PRODUCT [C] a type of product that a company sells **ürün çizgisi/serisi/yelpazesi/türü** *They're advertising a new line in garden furniture.* **12** DIRECTION [C] the direction that something moves in **hat, yol, güzergâh** *He can't kick the ball in a straight line.* **13 lines** the marks that older people have on their faces, when the skin is loose **yüzdeki çizgiler/kırışıklıklar 14** BORDER [C] *US* a border between two areas **sınır, çizgi, hat** *the New York state line* **15 be on the line** If someone's job is on the line, they may lose it. **tehlikede/kaybetmek üzere olmak 16 be in line for** sth to be likely to get something good, especially a job **...için sırada olmak; ...almaya hak kazanmış ve almak üzere olmak 17 be in line with** sth to be similar to and suitable for something **bir sırada/aynı hizada olmak; uyum halinde/uygun olmak** *a pay increase in line with inflation* **18 draw the line at** sth to never do something because you think it is wrong **yanlış olduğunu düşündüğünü yapmamaya karar almak; yapmayı reddetmek** *I swear a lot but even I draw the line at certain words.* ● **19 toe the (party) line** to do what someone in authority tells you to do although you may not agree with it **aynı fikirde olmasa da yetkilinin söylediklerini yapmak, kurallara uymak** ⊃See also: the bottom line, dotted line, front line, hard line.

line[2] /laɪn/ *verb* [T] **1** to form a row along the side of something **yana yana dizilmek, bir hizada olmak, hat oluşturmak** *Trees and cafes lined the street.* **2 be lined with** sth If a piece of clothing is lined with a material, its inside is covered with it. **astarlanmak, astar geçirmek** *a jacket lined with fur*

line (sb/sth) up *phrasal verb* to stand in a row, or to arrange people or things in a row **sıraya girmek, sırada durmak, sıraya sokmak; hizaya gelmek/getirmek** *Books were neatly lined up on the shelves.*

line sb/sth up *phrasal verb* to plan for something to happen **ayarlamak, programa almak, program yapmak; planlamak** *What future projects have you lined up?*

'line ˌmanager *noun* [C] *mainly UK* the person who manages another person in a company or business **idareci, amir, yönetici**

linen /ˈlɪnɪn/ *noun* [U] **1** an expensive cloth that is like rough cotton **keten, keten bezi** *a linen jacket* **2** pieces of cloth that you use to cover tables and beds **masa, yatak vs. örtüsü** *bed linen*

liner /'laɪnə^r/ *noun* [C] a large ship like a hotel, which people travel on for pleasure **büyük yolcu gemisi, uzun yol gemisi** *a cruise/ocean liner*

linesman /'laɪnzmən/ *noun* [C] *plural* **linesmen** in a sport, someone who watches to see if a ball goes into areas where it is not allowed **çizgi hakemi; yan hakem**

linger /'lɪŋgə^r/ *verb* [I] to stay somewhere for a long time **oyalanmak, uzun süre kalmak, eğlenmek** *The smell from the fire still lingered hours later.*

lingerie /'lɒnʒ^əri/ ⓤ /ˌlɑːnʒə'reɪ/ *noun* [U] women's underwear **kadın iç giyimi, kadın çamaşırı**

lingering /'lɪŋg^ərɪŋ/ *adjective* [always before noun] lasting a long time **uzun süren, uzun süre devam eden** *lingering doubts*

linguist /'lɪŋgwɪst/ *noun* [C] someone who is good at learning foreign languages, or someone who studies or teaches linguistics **dilbilimci**

linguistic /lɪŋ'gwɪstɪk/ *adjective* [always before noun] relating to language or linguistics **dille/dilbilimle ilgili**

linguistics /lɪŋ'gwɪstɪks/ *noun* [U] the scientific study of languages **dilbilim**

lining /'laɪnɪŋ/ *noun* [C, U] a material or substance that covers the inside of something **astar; bir şeyin üst yüzeyini kaplayan tabaka/doku** *a coat/jacket lining* ○ *the lining of the stomach*

> **link** .... İLE BİRLİKTE KULLANILAN KELİMELER
>
> **discover/establish/find** a link ● a **close/direct/ strong** link ● a link **between** sth and sth ● a link **with** sth

◦⊷**link**¹ /lɪŋk/ *noun* [C] **1** [CONNECTION] a connection between two people, things, or ideas **bağlantı, hat** *There's a direct link between diet and heart disease.* ○ *Their links with Britain are still strong.* **2** [CHAIN] one ring of a chain **halka 3** [INTERNET] (*also* hyperlink) a connection between documents or areas on the Internet **internet bağlantısı; internette alanlar ve belgeler arası bağlantı** *Click on this link to visit our online bookstore.* ⊃See study page **The Web and the Internet** on page Centre 36.

link² /lɪŋk/ *verb* [T] to make a connection between two or more people, things, or ideas **bağlamak, bağlantı kurmak/yapmak, birleştirmek** *Both men have been linked with the robberies.* ○ *The drug has been linked to the deaths of several athletes.*

link (sb/sth) up *phrasal verb* If two or more things or people link up, or if you link them up, they form a connection so that they can operate or work together. **bağla(n)mak, birleştir(il)mek** *Each house will be linked up with the new communications network.*

lion

lion /laɪən/ *noun* [C] a large, wild animal of the cat family, with light brown fur **aslan** ⊃See also: **sea lion.**

◦⊷**lip** /lɪp/ *noun* [C] **1** one of the two soft, red edges of the mouth **dudak** *He licked his lips.* ⊃Orta kısımdaki renkli say-

falarına bakınız. **2** the edge of a container that liquid is poured from **kenar, dudak**

lip-read /'lɪpriːd/ *verb* [I, T] *past* lip-read to understand what someone is saying by looking at the way their mouth moves **dudak okumak** ● **lip-reading** *noun* [U] **dudak okuma**

lip-service /'lɪpsɜːvɪs/ *noun* [no plural] **give/pay lip- service to** sth *informal* to say that you support an idea or plan, but not do anything to help it succeed **gürleyip yağmamak; sözde destek vermek, laf olsun diye desteklemek**

lipstick /'lɪpstɪk/ *noun* [C, U] a **lipstick** coloured substance that women put on their lips **ruj, dudak boyası** ⊃See picture at make up.

liqueur /li'kjʊə^r/ *noun* [C] a strong, sweet alcoholic drink which people usually drink a little of at the end of a meal **likör**

◦⊷**liquid** /'lɪkwɪd/ *noun* [C, U] a substance, for example water, that is not solid and that can be poured easily **sıvı** ● **liquid** *adjective* *liquid fuel/ nitrogen* **sıvılaşma**

liquidate /'lɪkwɪdeɪt/ *verb* [T] to close a business because it has no money left **(iş) tasfiye etmek** ● **liqui- dation** /ˌlɪkwɪ'deɪʃ^ən/ *noun* [C, U] *The store went into liquidation.* **tasfiye**

liquid-crystal display /ˌlɪkwɪdˌkrɪst^əldɪ'spleɪ/ *noun* [C] LCD **likit kristal ekran/gösterim**

liquor /'lɪkə^r/ *noun* [U] US a strong alcoholic drink **sert alkollü içki**

liquor ˌstore *noun* US (*UK* off-licence) *noun* [C] a shop that sells alcoholic drink **içki bayii, tekel bayii**

lisp /lɪsp/ *noun* [C] a way of speaking where 's' and 'z' sound like 'th' **pelteklik** ● **lisp** *verb* [I] **peltek konuş- mak**

> **list** .... İLE BİRLİKTE KULLANILAN KELİMELER
>
> **compile/draw up/make/write** a list ● a list **of** sth ● **on** a list ● a **shopping** list

◦⊷**list**¹ /lɪst/ *noun* [C] a series of names, numbers, or items that are written one below the other **liste, cetvel** *a shopping list* ○ *Is your name on the list?* ○ *Make a list of everything you need.* ⊃See also: mailing list, waiting list.

list² /lɪst/ *verb* [T] to make a list, or to include something in a list **listelemek, cetvel çıkarmak, listeye koy- mak/dahil etmek** *All participants' names are listed alphabetically.*

◦⊷**listen** /'lɪs^ən/ *verb* [I] **1** to give attention to someone or something in order to hear them **dinlemek** *What kind of music do you listen to?* ○ *She does all the talking - I just sit and listen.* ○ *You haven't listened to a word I've said.* ○ *Listen, if you need money, I'm happy to lend you some.* **2** to accept someone's advice **söz dilemek, kulak ver- mek, tavsiyeyi tutmak** *I told you she wouldn't like it but you wouldn't listen to me!*

> **YAYGIN HATALAR**
>
> **listen**
>
> Unutmayın! Duymak istediğiniz şeyi belirtmek için **to** edatını kullanınız. **Listen something** doğru kullanım değildir. **Listen to something** olarak kullanılması gerekir.: ~~I like watching television and listening music.~~
> Yanlış cümle örneği
> *I like watching television and listening to music.*

listen (out) for sth *phrasal verb* to try to hear something **kulağını dikmek, duymaya/dinlemeye çalışmak** *Could you listen out for the phone while I'm upstairs?*

listen in *phrasal verb* to secretly listen to a conversation, especially a telephone conversation **gizlice dinlemek; kulak misafiri olmak**

Listen up! *phrasal verb mainly US* something you say to tell people to listen to you *'Dinleyin!', 'Susun!' Okay, everyone, listen up! I have an announcement to make.*

listener /ˈlɪsᵊnəʳ/ *noun* [C] someone who listens **dinleyici** *The new radio station already has twelve million listeners.* ○ *She's a good listener* (= she gives you all her attention when you speak).

lit /lɪt/ *past of* light **'yakmak' fiilinin geçmiş zaman hâli**

liter /ˈliːtəʳ/ *noun* [C] *US spelling of* litre **litre**

literacy /ˈlɪtᵊrəsi/ *noun* [U] the ability to read and write **okur yazarlık**

literal /ˈlɪtᵊrᵊl/ *adjective* The literal meaning of a word or phrase is its real or original meaning. **gerçek/asıl/sözlük anlamı** *the literal meaning/sense*

literally /ˈlɪtᵊrᵊli/ *adverb* **1** having the real or original meaning of a word or phrase **kelimesi kelimesine** *They were responsible for literally millions of deaths.* **2** *informal* used to emphasize what you are saying **gerçekten, kelimenin tam anlamıyla** *He missed that kick literally by miles!*

literary /ˈlɪtᵊrᵊri/ *adjective* relating to literature, or typical of the type of language that is used in literature **edebi, edebiyatla/edebî dille ilgili** *literary criticism*

literate /ˈlɪtᵊrət/ *adjective* able to read and write **okur yazar** ⊃Opposite illiterate.

o⸱**literature** /ˈlɪtrətʃəʳ/ *noun* [U] **1** books, poems, etc that are considered to be art **edebiyat** *classical/modern literature* **2** written information about a subject **basılı/yazılı bilgi, literatür** *There is very little literature on the disease.*

o⸱**litre** UK (*US* liter) (*written abbreviation* l) /ˈliːtəʳ/ *noun* [C] a unit for measuring liquid **liter, bir sıvı ölçüm birimi**

litter .... İLE BİRLİKTE KULLANILAN KELİMELER

drop litter ● a piece of litter ● a litter bin

litter¹ /ˈlɪtəʳ/ *noun* **1** [U] pieces of paper and other waste that are left in public places **çöp, süprüntü, döküntü** **2** [C] a group of baby animals that are from the same mother and born at the same time **bir batında doğan hayvan yavruları** *a litter of kittens/puppies*

litter² /ˈlɪtəʳ/ *verb* [T] If things litter an area, they cover parts of it in an untidy way. **kirletmek, çöp atmak, pisletmek** *Clothes littered the floor.*

be littered with sth *phrasal verb* to contain a lot of something **bir çok şeyi kapsamak/barındırmak/içermek** *The whole book is littered with errors.*

o⸱**little¹** /ˈlɪtl/ *adjective* **1** SMALL small in size or amount **küçük, ufak** *a little bag/box/town* ○ *She's so little.* ○ *It costs as little as one dollar.* ○ *I might have a little bit of cake.* **2** SHORT [always before noun] short in time or distance **az, kısa** *Sit down for a little while.* ○ *Let's have a little break.* **3** NOT IMPORTANT [always before noun] not important **önemsiz, küçük, ufak** *It's only a little problem.* ○ *I'm having a little trouble with my back.* **4** YOUNG [always before noun] young and small **küçük, ufak, genç** *She was my little sister and I looked after her.*

o⸱**little²** /ˈlɪtl/ *quantifier* **1** not much or not enough **az** *He has little chance of winning.* ○ *There's so little choice.* **2 a**

little sth a small amount of something **azıcık, az bir şey** *It just needs a little effort.*

o⸱**little³** /ˈlɪtl/ *pronoun* **1** not much, or not enough **biraz, az şey** *We did very little on Sunday.* **2 a little** a small amount **biraz, bir parça** *I only know a little about my grandparents.* ○ *"More dessert?" "Just a little, please."*

o⸱**little⁴** /ˈlɪtl/ *adverb* not much or not enough **azıcık, az miktar** *It matters little.* ○ *a little-known fact*

o⸱**live¹** /lɪv/ *verb* **1** [I] to be alive **yaşamak, canlı olmak, hayatta kalmak** *She only lived a few days after the accident.* ○ *I hope I live to see my grandchildren.* **2 live at/in/near, etc** to have your home somewhere **yaşamak, ikamet etmek, yaşamını sürdürmek** *They live in New York.* ○ *We live near each other.* ○ *Where do you live?* **3** [I, T] to spend your life in a particular way **yerde yaşamak/yaşamını sürdürmek** *Many people are living in poverty.* **4 I'll never live it down!** *humorous* something you say about an embarrassing experience that other people will not forget **'Asla unutmayacağım!', 'Bu anı hiç bir zaman unutamayacağım!', 'Bu benim kulağıma küpe olsun!'**

live for sth/sb *phrasal verb* to have something or someone as the most important thing in your life **birisi/bir şey için yaşamak; hayatını adamak** *I love dancing - I just live for it.*

live on *phrasal verb* to continue to live **geçinmek, yaşamak** *She lived on well into her nineties.*

live on sth *phrasal verb* **1** Money that you live on is the money you use to buy the things that you need. *...ile yaşamak/geçimini sürdürmek* *We lived on very little when we were students.* **2** to only eat a particular type of food *...ile beslenmek/hayatını idame ettirmek* *All summer we live on hamburgers and hot dogs.*

live together *phrasal verb* If two people live together, they live in the same home and have a sexual relationship, but are not married. **birlikte yaşamak, ortak bir yaşamı paylaşmak; karı koca gibi yaşamak**

live up to sth *phrasal verb* to be as good as someone hopes **beklentilerini karşılamak; umduğu gibi olmak** *Did the trip live up to your expectations?*

live with sb *phrasal verb* to live in the same home as someone and have a sexual relationship with them although you are not married *...ile birlikte yaşamak, ortak bir yaşamı paylaşmak; karı koca gibi yaşamak*

live with sth *phrasal verb* to accept a difficult or unpleasant situation **kabullenmek, katlanmak;** *...ile yaşamayı öğrenmek* *It's a problem she's going to have to live with.*

o⸱**live²** /laɪv/ *adjective* **1** LIFE having life **canlı, yaşayan** *Millions of live animals are shipped around the world each year.* **2** ELECTRICITY A live wire has electricity in it. **akım taşıyan kablo/tel 3** BROADCAST A live radio or television programme is seen or heard as it happens. **(radyo, tv vb. program) canlı** *live coverage* ○ *a live broadcast* **4** AUDIENCE A live performance or recording of a performance is done with an audience. **(gösteri, çekmi vb.) canlı** *a live concert* **5** BOMB A live bomb has not yet exploded. **(bomba) patlamamış, aktif, faal**

live³ /laɪv/ *adverb* broadcast at the same time that something happens **naklen, canlı** *We'll be bringing the match to you live on Wednesday.*

livelihood /ˈlaɪvlihʊd/ *noun* [C, U] the way that you earn the money you need for living **geçim, rızk** *The farm is his livelihood.*

lively /ˈlaɪvli/ *adjective* full of energy and interest **canlı, ateşli, hareketli, enerji dolu** *a lively conversation/debate* ○ *a lively child* ● **liveliness** *noun* [U] **canlılık**

liver /'lɪvəʳ/ *noun* **1** [C] a large organ in your body that cleans your blood **karaciğer 2** [U] the liver of an animal that is eaten by people **(hayvan) ciğer**

lives /laɪvz/ *plural of* life '**yaşam' sözcüğünün çoğul hâli; yaşamlar**

livestock /'laɪvstɒk/ *noun* [U] animals that are kept on a farm **çiftlik hayvanları**

livid /'lɪvɪd/ *adjective* very angry **çok kızmış, öfkeli, sinirli, çılgına dönmüş**

living[1] /'lɪvɪŋ/ *noun* **1** [C] the money that you earn from your job **kazanç, geçim, geçinme** [usually singular] *to earn/make a living* ○ *What does he do for a living* (= how does he earn money)? **2 country/healthy, etc living** the way in which you live your life **kır yaşamı, sağlıklı yaşam** ⊃See also: standard of living.

living[2] /'lɪvɪŋ/ *adjective* [always before noun] **1** alive now **yaşayan, sağ** *He's probably the best known living photographer.* **2 alive yaşayan, kullanılmakta olan** *living organisms* ○ *living things* ⊃See also: beat/knock the (living) daylights out of sb, scare/frighten the (living) daylights out of sb.

'living ,room (*also UK* sitting room) *noun* [C] the room in a house where people sit to relax and, for example, watch television **oturma odası** ⊃Orta kısımdaki renkli sayfalarına bakınız.

lizard /'lɪzəd/ *noun* [C] a small animal with thick skin, a long tail, and four short legs **kertenkele**

load[1] /ləʊd/ *noun* **1** [C] something that is carried, often by a vehicle **yük** *We were behind a truck carrying a load of coal.* **2 a load/loads** *informal* a lot of something **dünya kadar, tonla, bir sürü, epey** *There were loads of people there.* ○ *Have some more food - there's loads.* **3 a load of rubbish/nonsense, etc** *UK informal* nonsense **bir sürü saçmalık; bir yığın anlamsızlık**

load[2] /ləʊd/ *verb* **1** [I, T] (*also* load up) to put a lot of things into a vehicle or machine **yüklemek, doldurmak** *Bring the car up to the door and I'll start loading up.* ○ *to load the dishwasher/washing machine* ⊃Opposite **unload. 2** [T] to put film in a camera or bullets in a gun **kameraya film takmak; silahı doldurmak**
be loaded down with sth *phrasal verb* to have too much to carry, or too much work to do **gırtlağına kadar dolu olmak; çok fazla yük yüklenmiş olmak; yapacak çok işi olmak** *I was loaded down with shopping.*
be loaded with sth *phrasal verb* to contain a lot of something **dolu/yüklü olmak** *Most fast foods are loaded with fat.*

-load /ləʊd/ *suffix* used at the end of a word to describe an amount of something that is being carried **...yük/sorumluluk/iş/görev anlamında son ek** *a truckload of soldiers*

loaded /'ləʊdɪd/ *adjective* **1** A loaded gun, or similar weapon, has a bullet in it. **(silah) dolu, patlamaya/atışa hazır, mermi ağzında 2** [never before noun] *informal* very rich **çok zengin, varlıklı**

loaded 'question *noun* [C] a question which makes you answer in a particular way **anlamlı, belli bir mana içeren, önceden ayarlanmış soru; ima içeren soru**

loaf /ləʊf/ *noun* [C] *plural* **loaves** /ləʊvz/ bread that has been baked in one large piece so that it can be cut into smaller pieces **somun ekmek** *a loaf of bread* ⊃See picture at bread.

loan ...... İLE BİRLİKTE KULLANILAN KELİMELER

apply for/repay/take out a loan ● a **bank** loan

o-- **loan**[1] /ləʊn/ *noun* **1** [C] money that someone has borrowed **borç para, ödünç para, kredi** *a bank loan*

○ *He repaid the loan within two years.* **2 be on loan** If something is on loan, someone is borrowing it. **ödünç alınmış** *Both paintings are on loan from the city museum.*

loan[2] /ləʊn/ *verb* [+ two objects] to lend something to someone **ödünç/borç/kredi vermek** *I was glad to loan my old books to her.* ○ *My dad loaned me the money.*

loath /ləʊθ/ *adjective* **be loath to do sth** *formal* to not want to do something because it will cause problems **isteksiz, gönülsüz, hevessiz olmak** *I'm loath to spend it all.*

loathe /ləʊð/ *verb* [T] to hate someone or something **iğrenmek, nefret etmek, tiksinmek ● loathing** *noun* [U] a feeling of hating someone or something **nefret, iğrenme, tiksinme**

loaves /ləʊvz/ *plural of* loaf '**somun ekmek' sözcüğünün çoğulu somun ekmekler**

lobby[1] /'lɒbi/ *noun* [C] **1** a room at the main entrance of a building, often with doors and stairs that lead to other parts of the building **lobi, giriş** *a hotel lobby* **2** a group of people who try to persuade the government to do something **(ikna) grubu, lobisi; kulis faaliyetinde bulunan kişiler** *the anti-smoking lobby*

lobby[2] /'lɒbi/ *verb* [I, T] to try to persuade the government to do something **kulis yapmak, lobi faaliyetinde bulunmak** *They're lobbying for changes to the law.*

lobster /'lɒbstəʳ/ *noun* [C, U] a sea creature that has two claws (= sharp, curved parts) and eight legs, or the meat of this animal **ıstakoz**

o-- **local**[1] /'ləʊk°l/ *adjective* relating to an area near you **yöresel, bölgesel, mahalli** *the local school/newspaper/radio station* ● **locally** *adverb* locally grown vegetables **yöresel**

local[2] /'ləʊk°l/ *noun* [C] **1** someone who lives in the area you are talking about **yerli halktan, yöre halkından olan 2 sb's local** *UK informal* a bar that is near someone's home **yakın bar, yakın ve her zaman uğrak yeri olan bar**

local anaes'thetic *UK* (*US* local anesthetic) *noun* [C, U] a substance that is put into a part of your body so that you do not feel pain there **bölgesel uyuşturma, lokal anestezi** *The procedure is carried out under local anaesthetic.*

local au'thority *noun* [group] the group of people who govern a small area of a country **mahalli idare, yerel yönetim** *Local authorities are looking for new ways to promote investment.*

local 'time *noun* [U] the official time in an area or country **mahalli/yerel saat** *We will shortly be landing in London, where the local time is 3.15.*

locate /ləʊ'keɪt/ *verb* [T] *formal* **1** to find the exact position of someone or something **yerini belirlemek/bulmak** *Police are still trying to locate the suspect.* **2 be located in/near/on, etc** to be in a particular place **belli bir konumda/yerleşmiş/kurulmuş olmak** *Both schools are located in the town.*

location .... İLE BİRLİKTE KULLANILAN KELİMELER

at/in a [remote/secret, etc] location ● the **location of** sth

location /ləʊ'keɪʃ°n/ *noun* **1** [C] a place or position **mahal, yer, konum, mevki** *They haven't yet decided on the location of the new store.* **2 on location** If a film or television programme is made on location, it is made at a place suitable to the story. **yerinde, mahallinde**

loch /lɒk/, /lɒx/ *noun* [C] a lake in Scotland **İskoçya'da bir göl** *Loch Lomond*

✐**lock¹** /lɒk/ verb **1** [I, T] to fasten something with a key, or to be fastened with a key **kilitlemek** *Did you lock the door?* ○ *If you shut the door it will lock automatically.* ⟳Opposite **unlock. 2 lock sth/sb away/in, etc** to put something or someone in a place or container that is fastened with a key **birini/bir şeyi bir yere kilitlemek/kilit altında tutmak** *She locked herself in her bedroom.* ○ *Most of my jewellery is locked away in a safe.* **3** [I] to become fixed in one position **bir şeye/yere kilitlenmek** *I tried to move forward but the wheels had locked.*
lock sb in/out *phrasal verb* to prevent someone from entering/leaving a room or building by locking the door **kilitleyerek içerde/dışarda tutmak; sokmamak; girmesine engel olmak; kapıyı üstünden kilitlemek**
lock (sth) up *phrasal verb* to lock all the doors and windows of a building when you leave it **kapıları pencereleri kapatıp kilitlemek**
lock sb up *phrasal verb* to put someone in prison or a hospital for people who are mentally ill **hapse tıkmak; hastaneye yatırmak, hastanede gözetim altında tutmak**

lock (noun) .... İLE BİRLİKTE KULLANILAN KELİMELER

fit a lock ● a lock on sth ● a safety lock

✐**lock²** /lɒk/ noun [C] **1** the thing that is used to close a door, window, etc, and that needs a key to open it **kilit** *I heard someone turn a key in the lock.* ○ *safety locks* **2** a place on a river with gates to allow boats to move to a different water level **aktarma/alavere havuzu 3 under lock and key** kept safely in a room or container that is locked **kilit altında** *I tend to keep medicines under lock and key because of the kids.*

locker /'lɒkər/ noun [C] a small cupboard in a public area where your personal possessions can be kept **(okul, spor salonu vb.) eşya dolabı** *a gym/luggage/school locker*

'**locker ,room** *noun* [C] a room where you change your clothes and leave those and other personal possessions in a locker **soyunma kabinleri ve dolapların bulunduğu oda**

locomotive /ˌləʊkə'məʊtɪv/ *noun* [C] the part of a train that makes it move **lokmotif** *a steam locomotive*

lodge¹ /lɒdʒ/ *noun* [C] a small house in the country that is used especially by people on holiday **dağ evi, kır evi, kulübe** *a hunting/mountain/ski lodge*

lodge² /lɒdʒ/ *verb* **1 lodge in/on, etc** to become stuck somewhere **saplanmak, saplanıp kalmak** *The bullet had lodged near his heart.* ⟳Compare **dislodge. 2 lodge at/ with, etc** to live in someone's home and give them money for it **pansiyoner olarak kalmak 3 lodge a claim/complaint/protest, etc** to officially complain about something **(şikâyet, protesto, iddia/talep vb.) resmen yapmak/etmek/başvurmak; ...ta/te bulunmak** *He lodged an official complaint against the officers responsible.*

lodger /'lɒdʒər/ *UK* (*US* **boarder**) *noun* [C] someone who pays for a place to sleep and meals in someone else's house **pansiyoner**

lodgings /'lɒdʒɪŋz/ *noun* [plural] *mainly UK* a room in someone's home that you pay money to live in **pansiyon odası** *temporary lodgings*

loft /lɒft/ *noun* [C] **1** the space under the roof of a house or other building **tavan arası 2** *US* the space where someone lives or works in a building that used to be a factory **eskiden fabrika olarak kullanılan bir binada yaşanan/çalışılan yer/alan**

log¹ /lɒg/ *noun* [C] **1** a thick piece of wood that has been cut from a tree **ağaç kütüğü, odun, kütük 2** a written record of events, often on a ship or aircraft **(gemi) seyir defteri/günlüğü**

log² /lɒg/ *verb* [T] **logging**, *past* **logged** to make a written record of events, often on a ship or aircraft **seyir defterine geçirmek/yazmak/kaydetmek**
log in/on *phrasal verb* to connect a computer to a system of computers by typing your name and often a password, usually so that you can start working **(bilgisayar) bağlanmak; isim girerek sisteme bağlanmak**
log off/out *phrasal verb* to stop a computer being connected to a computer system, usually when you want to stop working **(bilgisayar) sistemden çıkmak, çalışmayı bitirmek/durdurmak; sistemi kapatmak**

loggerheads /'lɒgəhedz/ *noun* **be at loggerheads (with sb)** If two people or groups are at loggerheads, they disagree strongly about something. **kavgalı olmak; çekişmek, takışmak** *He is at loggerheads with the Prime Minister over public spending.*

logic .... İLE BİRLİKTE KULLANILAN KELİMELER

the logic behind/in/of sth

logic /'lɒdʒɪk/ *noun* [U] the use of reason, or the science of using reason **mantık** *It was difficult to understand the logic behind his argument.*

logical /'lɒdʒɪkəl/ *adjective* using reason **mantıklı, mantığa uygun** *a logical choice/conclusion* ⟳Opposite **illogical.** ● **logically** *adverb* **mantıki olarak**

login /'lɒgɪn/ *noun* [C, U] a box that appears on your computer screen when you start to use a computer which is connected to a computer system **bir sisteme bağlanan bilgisayar ekranında beliren kutucuk**

logistics /lə'dʒɪstɪks/ *noun* **the logistics of sth/doing sth** the practical arrangements for something **bir şeyin etkin düzenlemesi/tertibi/yöntemi/lojistiği** *We could all use the one car but I'm not sure about the logistics of it.*

logo /'ləʊgəʊ/ *noun* [C] a design or symbol used by a company to advertise its products **amblem, arma, sembol** *a corporate logo*

loiter /'lɔɪtər/ *verb* [I] to stand in a place or walk slowly around without any purpose **amaçsız bir şekilde dolaşmak, oyalanmak** *A gang of youths were loitering outside the cinema.*

LOL *internet abbreviation for* laughing out loud: used when you think something is very funny **(internette kullanılan kısaltma) 'Çok komik/gülünç/saçma!'**

lollipop /'lɒlipɒp/ (*also UK* **lolly** /'lɒli/) *noun* [C] a large, hard sweet on a stick **saplı şeker, lolipop**

lollipop

lone /ləʊn/ *adjective* [always before noun] alone **yalnız, tek başına** *lone parents* ○ *the lone survivor*

✐**lonely** /'ləʊnli/ *adjective* **1** unhappy because you are not with other people **yalnız, kimsesiz** *She gets lonely now that the kids have all left home.* **2** A lonely place is a long way from where people live. **ıssız, kuş uçmaz kervan geçmez; gözden ırak** ● **loneliness** *noun* [U] **yalnızlık**

loner /'ləʊnər/ *noun* [C] someone who likes to be alone **yalnızlıktan hoşlanan kimse; yalnız kimse; garip** *He was always a bit of a loner at school.*

lonesome /'ləʊnsəm/ *adjective US* lonely **yalnız, garip, ıssız**

✐**long¹** /lɒŋ/ *adjective* **1** [DISTANCE] having a large distance from one end to the other **(mesafe) uzun** *long, brown hair* ○ *a long dress* ○ *It's a long way to travel to work.*

2 TIME continuing for a large amount of time (**zaman**) **uzun** *a long film/meeting* ○ *Have you been waiting a long time?* **3** HOW LONG used when asking for or giving information about the distance or time of something (**ne kadar**) **uzun, uzunlukta** *It's about three metres long.* ○ *Most of the concerts are over three hours long.* ○ *Do you know how long the film is?* **4** BOOK A long book or other piece of writing has a lot of pages or words. (**kitap,yazı vs.**) **uzun** *a long article/letter* ⊃See also: in the long/short **run**².

⊶**long**² /lɒŋ/ *adverb* **1** for a long time **uzun süre, epey zaman** *We didn't have to wait long for the train.* ○ *The band played long into the night.* **2 as long as** used when you are talking about something that must happen before something else can happen **...dığı/diği sürece; ...mak/mek şartıyla; eğer** *You can play football as long as you do your homework first.* **3 before long** soon **çok geçmeden, daha fazla geç olmadan, kısa zamanda** *He'll be home before long.* **4 long ago** If something happened long ago, it happened a great amount of time ago. **uzun süre önce, epey önce, çok evvelden** **5 no longer/not any longer** not now **artık, bundan böyle** *He no longer works here.*

long³ /lɒŋ/ *noun* [U] a large amount of time **uzun süre, uzunca bir süre** *She won't be away for long.*

long⁴ /lɒŋ/ *verb formal* **long for sth; long to do sth** to want something very much **hasretini çekmek, özlemini duymak, çok istemek, can atmak** *She longed to see him again.*

long-distance /ˌlɒŋ'dɪstⁿns/ *adjective* travelling or communicating between two places that are a long way apart **uzun mesafeli, şehirlerarası, uluslararası** *a long-distance race* ○ *a long-distance phone call*

long-haul /'lɒŋ,hɔ:l/ *adjective* [always before noun] travelling a long distance **uzun mesafe seyahat eden; uzun mesafe giden** *a long-haul flight*

longing /'lɒŋɪŋ/ *noun* [U, no plural] a feeling of wanting something or someone very much **özlem, hasret** *He gazed at her, his eyes full of longing.* ○ *a longing for his homeland* ● **longingly** *adverb* *She looked longingly at the silk dresses.* **çok isteyerek**

longitude /'lɒndʒɪtju:d/ *noun* [U] the distance of a place east or west of an imaginary line from the top to the bottom of the Earth, measured in degrees **boylam**

the 'long jump *noun* a sports event where people try to jump as far as possible (**spor**) **uzun atlama**

long-life /ˌlɒŋ'laɪf/ *adjective* UK Long-life drink or food has been treated so that it will last a long time. **dayanıklı, uzun ömürlü, uzun süre dayanan/bozulmayan** *long-life milk*

long-lost /'lɒŋ,lɒst/ *adjective* **long-lost friend/cousin, etc** a friend or relative that you have not seen for a long time **uzun zamandır/çoktan beri kayıp/ortalarda gözükmeyen arkadaş/kuzen vb.**

long-range /ˌlɒŋ'reɪndʒ/ *adjective* [always before noun] **1** relating to a time in the future **uzun vadeli/süreli** *a long-range weather forecast* **2** able to be sent long distances **uzun menzilli** *a long-range bomber/missile*

'long ,shot *noun* [C] *informal* something that is not likely to succeed **boşuna/beyhude çaba/uğraş; başarılı olması zayıf ihtimal** *It's a long shot, but you could try phoning him at home.*

long-sighted /ˌlɒŋ'saɪtɪd/ UK (US **farsighted**) *adjective* able to see objects which are far away but not things which are near to you **yakını iyi göremeyen, hipermetrop**

long-standing /ˌlɒŋ'stændɪŋ/ *adjective* having existed for a long time **uzun süre ayakta kalan, eskiden beri süregelen** *a long-standing relationship*

long-suffering /ˌlɒŋ'sʌfⁿrɪŋ/ *adjective* A long-suffering person has been very patient for a long time about all the trouble that someone has caused them. **tahammüllü, sabırlı, cefakâr, uzun süre dayanan/sabreden** *Bill and his long-suffering wife*

long-term /ˌlɒŋ't3:m/ *adjective* continuing a long time into the future **uzun vadeli** *long-term unemployment*

long-winded /ˌlɒŋ'wɪndɪd/ *adjective* If what someone says or writes is long-winded, it is boring because it is too long. **bitmek tükenmek bilmeyen, uzun uzadıya sürüp giden** *a long-winded explanation*

loo /lu:/ *noun* [C] UK *informal* toilet **tuvalet** *I'll just go to the loo.*

⊶**look**¹ /lʊk/ *verb* **1** [I] to turn your eyes in the direction of something or someone so that you can see them **bakmak** *Look at the picture on page two.* ○ *He was looking out of the window.* ○ *I looked around and there she was.* **2** [I] to try to find someone or something **bakmak, göz atmak, şöyle bir bakmak** *I'm looking for my keys.* ○ *I've looked everywhere but I can't find my bag.* **3 look nice/strange, etc; look like/as if** used to describe the appearance of a person or thing **güzel/acayip vs. gözükmek; gibi/sanki gibi gözükmek** *That food looks nice.* ○ *You look tired, my love.* ○ *Do I look silly in this hat?* ○ *He looked like a drug addict.* **4 it looks like; it looks as if** used to say that something is likely to happen **gibi gözüküyor; sanki gibi gözüküyor** *It looks like there'll be three of us.* ○ *It looks as if he isn't coming.* **5 be looking to do sth** to plan to do something **yapmayı planlamak** *I'm looking to start my own business.* **6 Look!** something you say when you are annoyed and you want people to know that what you are saying is important **'Bak!', 'Bakın!', 'Bakınız!' 'Dinle!'** *Look, I've had enough of your complaints.* ⊃See also: look the part¹.

look after sb/sth *phrasal verb* to take care of someone or something by keeping them healthy or in a good condition **bakmak, ilgilenmek, ihtimam göstermek** *Could you look after the children while I'm out?*

look ahead *phrasal verb* to think about something that will happen in the future and plan for it **ileriye bakmak; ileriyi görerek geleceği planlamak**

look at sth *phrasal verb* **1** THINK to think about a subject carefully so that you can make a decision about it **dikkatlice araştırıp incelemek** *Management is looking at ways of cutting costs.* **2** READ to read something **okumak** *Can you look at my essay sometime?* **3** EXPERT If an expert looks at something, they examine it. **araştırmak, incelemek** *Did you get the doctor to look at your knee?* **4** OPINION to consider something in a particular way **bakmak, ele almak** *If I'd been a mother I might have looked at things differently.*

look back *phrasal verb* to remember something in the past **geçmişi hatırlamak/anımsamak** *He looked back on his childhood with affection.*

look down on sb *phrasal verb* to think that someone is less important than you **küçümsemek, hor görmek, tepeden bakmak**

look forward to sth/doing sth *phrasal verb* to feel happy and excited about something that is going to happen **dört gözle beklemek; bir şeyi/yapmayı sabırsızlıkla beklemek/iple çekmek** *I'm really looking forward to seeing him.*

look into sth *phrasal verb* to examine the facts about a situation **incelemek; (nedenini) araştırmak** *They are looking into the causes of the accident.*

look on *phrasal verb* to watch something happen but not become involved in it **bakmak, seyretmek**

look on sb/sth *phrasal verb* to think about someone or something in a particular way ...**imiş gibi bakmak/görmek;** ...**muamelesi yapmak** *We look on him almost as our own son.*

Look out! *phrasal verb* something you say when someone is in danger **Dikkat et!', 'Dikkatli ol!'** *Look out - there's a car coming!*

look out for sb/sth *phrasal verb* to try to notice someone or something **dikkat etmek; hazırlıklı beklemek, gözünü dört açmak** *Look out for Anna while you're there.*

look over sth *phrasal verb* to examine something quickly **hızlıca incelemek, gözden geçirmek** *I'm just looking over what you've written.*

look through sth *phrasal verb* to read something quickly **incelemek, göz gezdirmek, gözden geçirmek** *I've looked through a few catalogues.*

look up *phrasal verb* to become better **iyileşmek, düzelmek, gelişmek** *Our financial situation is looking up.*

look sth up *phrasal verb* to look at a book or computer in order to find information (**kitap, bilgisayar vb.**) **bakmak, aramak, arayıp bulmak** *I looked it up in the dictionary.*

look up to sb *phrasal verb* to respect and admire someone **hayran olmak, saygı duymak, saymak**

look (noun) .... İLE BİRLİKTE KULLANILAN KELİMELER

have/take a look ● a close/good look ● a look at sb/sth

ꙩ⁓**look²** /lʊk/ *noun* **1** SEE [C] when you look at someone or something **bakma, bakış** [usually singular] *Take a look at these pictures.* ○ *You've got your photos back - can I have a look?* **2 have/take a look** when you try to find something **göz atma, arama, bulmaya çalışma** *I've had a look in the drawer but I can't find your passport.* **3** FACE [C] an expression on someone's face (**yüzdeki) ifade, görünüş** *She had a worried look about her.* ○ *She gave me a questioning look.* **4** FASHION [no plural] a style or fashion **görünüm, görünüş, tarz, moda** *the new look for the summer* **5 the look of sb/sth** the appearance of someone or something **görüntü, görünüm, görünüş** *I like the look of that new music programme they're advertising.* **6 sb's looks** a person's appearance, especially how attractive they are (**kişinin) görünüşü, görüntüsü, cazibesi, çekiciliği** ➜See also: good looks.

lookalike /'lʊkəlaɪk/ *noun* [C] *informal* someone who looks very similar to a famous person **benzeri, tıpkısı, aynısı** *an Elvis lookalike*

look-in /'lʊkɪn/ *noun* UK *informal* **not get a look-in** to get no chance to achieve what you want or to succeed in something **şansı/fırsatı olmamak, fırsat bulamamak** *He played so well, nobody else got a look-in.*

lookout /'lʊkaʊt/ *noun* **1** [C] a person who watches for danger and warns other people **gözcü, gözleyen, bekçi, nöbetçi, erketeci** **2 be on the lookout** to be continuing to search for something or someone **araştırmaya/gözetmeye/bulmaya çalışmaya devam etmek** *I'm always on the lookout for interesting new recipes.*

loom¹ /luːm/ *verb* [I] **1** to appear as a large, sometimes frightening shape **beklenenden/normalden çok daha büyük ve korkutucu olarak ortaya çıkmak** *Dark storm clouds loomed on the horizon.* **2** If an unpleasant event looms, it is likely to happen soon. **olması yakın vemuhtemel olmak; eli kulağında olmak, gelip çatmak** *The threat of closure looms over the workforce.*

loom² /luːm/ *noun* [C] a machine for making cloth by weaving together (= crossing over) threads **dokuma tezgâhı/makinası**

loony /'luːni/ *noun* [C] *informal* someone who behaves in a crazy way **deli/kaçık/(argo) fıttırmış/kafayı yemiş kimse** *The man's a complete loony.* ● **loony** *adjective informal* crazy **deli, kaçık, çılgın** *loony ideas*

loop¹ /luːp/ *noun* [C] a circle of something long and thin, such as a piece of string or wire **ilmik, ilmek, halka**

loop² /luːp/ *verb* **loop sth around/over, etc sth** to make something into the shape of a loop **ilmek atmak, ilmeklemek** *Loop the rope around your waist.*

loophole .... İLE BİRLİKTE KULLANILAN KELİMELER

a loophole in sth ● a legal loophole

loophole /'luːphəʊl/ *noun* [C] a mistake in an agreement or law which gives someone the chance to avoid having to do something **boşluk, kaçamak yol**

ꙩ⁓**loose** /luːs/ *adjective* **1** NOT FIXED not firmly fixed **gevşek, serbest, laçka, gevşemiş** *There were some loose wires hanging out of the wall.* ○ *One of my buttons is loose.* **2** CLOTHES large and not fitting tightly **bol, geniş** *a loose dress/sweater* **3** FREE An animal that is loose is free to move around. **başıboş, kaçmış, özgür, serbest** *Two lions escaped and are still loose.* **4** NOT EXACT not exact **rastgele, sıradan, alelusul, serbest** *It's only a loose translation of the poem.* ● **loosely** *adverb* **gevşek bir biçimde** *The film is based very loosely* (= not exactly) *on the novel.* ➜See also: at a loose end¹.

loosen /'luːsᵊn/ *verb* [I, T] to become loose or make something loose **gevşe(t)mek, laçka olmak/etmek** *He loosened his tie.*

loosen up *phrasal verb* to become more relaxed with other people **gevşe(t)mek, yumuşa(t)mak, sakinleş(tir)mek** *After a while he loosened up.*

loot¹ /luːt/ *verb* [I, T] to steal from shops and houses during a war or period of fighting **yağmalamak, talan etmek, yağma etmek** *Rioters looted the capital.*

loot² /luːt/ *noun* [U] goods which have been stolen **yağma, ganimet**

lop /lɒp/ *verb* lopping, past lopped
lop sth off *phrasal verb* to cut off something in one quick movement **kesip koparmak; bir darbede kesmek** *I lopped off the biggest branches.*

lopsided /ˌlɒp'saɪdɪd/ ⑩ /'lɒpsaɪdɪd/ *adjective* with one side lower than the other **yamuk, çarpık, eğri, dengesiz** *a lopsided grin*

loquacious /ləʊ'kweɪʃəs/ *adjective formal* talking a lot **konuşkan, çenebaz**

lord /lɔːd/ *noun* **1** [C, U] (*also* Lord) a man of high social rank, or a title given to a man who has earned official respect, in the UK **Lord, (Birleşik Krallık) bir asalet ünvanı** *Lord Lichfield* **2 the Lord** God or Christ **Tanrı, Hz. İsa 3 Good Lord!** *informal* something you say when you are surprised or angry **Aman Allah'ım!', 'Allah Allah!', 'Aman Yarabbi!', 'Vay canına!** *Good Lord! Is that the time?* ➜See also: House of Lords.

the Lords /lɔːdz/ (*also* House of Lords) *noun* [group] one of the two parts of the British parliament, with members who are chosen by the government **Lordlar Kamarası; üyeleri hükûmet tarafından seçilen Britanya parlamentosunun iki kanadından biri**

lorry /'lɒri/ UK (UK/US truck) *noun* [C] a large road vehicle for carrying goods from place to place **kamyon** ➜See picture at vehicle.

ꙩ⁓**lose** /luːz/ *verb past* lost **1** NOT FIND [T] to not be able to find someone or something **kaybetmek, yitirmek** *I've lost my passport.* ○ *She's always losing her car keys.*

2 [NOT HAVE] [T] to stop having someone or something that you had before **yitirmek, kaybetmek** *She lost a leg in a car accident.* ○ *I hope he doesn't lose his job.* ○ *He lost his mother* (= his mother died) *last year.* **3** [HAVE LESS] [T] to have less of something than you had before **bir kısmını yitirmek/kaybetmek** *She's lost a lot of weight.* ○ *He's losing his hair.* ○ *to lose your memory* **4** [NOT WIN] [I, T] If you lose a game, competition, or election, the team or person that you are competing with wins. **(oyun, müsabaka vb.) kaybetmek** *Chelsea lost by a goal.* ○ *They're losing 3-1.* ○ *They hadn't lost an election in 15 years.* **5 lose faith/interest/patience, etc** to stop feeling something good **(inanç/ilgi/sabır vb.) kaybetmek** *I'm rapidly losing interest in the whole subject.* ○ *He kept on crying and I lost my patience.* **6** [TIME] [T] If you lose a number of hours or days, you cannot work during this time. **zaman kaybetmek** *Four million hours were lost last year through stress-related illnesses.* **7** [CLOCK] [T] If a clock loses time, it goes slower than it should. **(saat) geri kalmak 8** [CONFUSE] [T] *informal* to confuse someone so that they do not understand something **aptala çevirmek; kafasını karıştırmak** *No, you've lost me there - can you explain that again?* **9** [GET RID OF] *informal* to take something away, usually because it looks bad. **ortadan kaldırmak, saklamak, çıkarıp atmak, atmak** *Lose the belt, Andrea, it looks ridiculous with that dress.* **10 lose your balance** to fall because you are leaning too much to one side **dengesini kaybetmek 11 lose count of sth** to forget the exact number **bir şeyin sayısını şaşırmak, rakamı unutmak** *I've lost count of how many times I've called her.* **12 lose your life** to die **hayatını kaybetmek; yaşamını yitirmek; ölmek** *Millions of young men lost their lives in the war.* **13 be losing it** *informal* to start to become crazy **çıldırmaya başlamak, kendini kaybetmek; (argo) kafayı yemeye başlamak** *I can't even remember my own telephone number - I think I must be losing it.* ● **14 lose it** *informal* to stop being able to control your emotions and suddenly start to laugh, shout or cry **sinirleri bozulmak, kontrolden çıkmak, kendine hakim olamamak** *I was trying so hard to stay calm but in the end I just lost it.* ↪See also: fight a losing battle¹, lose your cool³, lose/save face¹, gain/lose ground¹, lose sight¹ of sth, lose sleep² over sth.

lose out *phrasal verb* to not have an advantage that someone else has **kaybetmek, zarara uğramak, zarar görmek, mağlup olmak**

loser /'luːzə^r/ *noun* [C] **1** someone who does not win a game or competition **kaybeden/mağlup kişi, yenilen kimse** *The losers of both games will play each other for third place.* **2** *informal* someone who is not successful in anything they do **hep kaybeden/her zaman yenilgiye uğrayan kimse; kaybetmeye mahkum kişi**

╔═╗ *loss* .... İLE BİRLİKTE KULLANILAN KELİMELER

make/suffer a loss ● a loss of [$50,000/£3 million, etc]

◦┅**loss** /lɒs/ *noun* **1** [NOT HAVING] [C, U] when you do not have someone or something that you had before, or when you have less of something than before **kayıp, zayiat** *loss of income/memory* ○ *blood/hair/weight loss* ○ *job losses* **2** [MONEY] [C, U] when a company spends more money than it earns **zarar, ziyan** *Both companies suffered losses this year.* **3** [DISADVANTAGE] [no plural] a disadvantage caused by someone leaving an organization **birinin yokluğundan dolayı kurum veya kuruluşun uğradığı zarar/kayıp** *It would be a great loss to the department if you left.* **4 be at a loss** to not know what to do or say **ne yapacağını şaşırmak/bilmemek** [+ to do sth] *I'm at a loss to explain his disappearance.* **5 a sense of loss** sadness because someone has died or left **birinin kaybı veya vefatından dolayı duyulan derin**

üzüntü/keder **6** [DEATH] [C, U] the death of a person **vefat, ölüm, yokluk, kayıp** *They never got over the loss of their son.*

◦┅**lost¹** /lɒst/ *adjective* **1** [PERSON] not knowing where you are or where you should go **kaybolmuş** *I got lost on the way.* **2** [OBJECT] If something is lost, no one knows where it is. **kayıp, yitik** *Things tend to get lost when you move house.* ○ *Lost: black cat with white paws.* **3** [NEW SITUATION] not knowing what to do in a new situation **kaybolmuş, ne yapacağını bilmeyen, alışmaya çalışan** *It was his first day in the office and he seemed a bit lost.* **4 be lost without sb/sth** *informal* to be unable to live or work without someone or something **(onsuz) bir hiç olmak, işe yaramamak, iş yapamamak; (o) eli ayağı olmak** *She's lost without her computer.* **5 be lost on sb** If a joke or remark is lost on someone, they do not understand it. **anlaşılmamış olmak; etkili olmamak; boşa gitmiş olmak 6 Get lost!** *informal* an impolite way of telling someone to go away '**Kaybol!', 'Gözüm görmesin!', 'Çek git!'** ↪See also: long-lost.

lost² /lɒst/ *past of* lose '**kaybetmek' fiilinin geçmiş zaman hâli**

lost property *noun* [U] *UK* things that people have left in public places which are kept somewhere until the owners can collect them **kayıp eşya**

◦┅**lot** /lɒt/ *noun* **1 a lot; lots** a large number or amount of people or things **çok miktarda/sayıda** *There were a lot of people outside the building.* ○ *He earns lots of money.* ○ *I've got a lot to do this morning.* **2 a lot better/older/quicker, etc** much better/older/quicker, etc **çok daha iyi/yaşlı/çabuk vs.** *It's a lot better than the old system.* ○ *It's a lot quicker by train.* **3 the lot** *UK informal* all of an amount or number **tamamı, tümü, hespi** *I made enough curry for three people and he ate the lot.* **4** [GROUP] [C] *UK* a group of people or things that you deal with together **grup, bölüm, parça, yığın, parti; kişiler adamları** *I've already done one lot of washing.* **5** [AREA] [C] *US* an area of land **arazi, parsel** *a parking lot* ○ *an empty lot* **6** [SALE] [C] something being sold at an auction (= sale where things are sold to the people who pay the most) **müzayedede açık artırmaya sunulan mal/eşya/her parça** *Lot 3: a Victorian chest.* **7 sb's lot** the quality of someone's life and the type of experiences they have **(birinin) yaşamı deneyimleri yaptıkları, talih, alın yazısı** *They've done much to improve the lot of working people.*

lotion /'ləʊʃ^ən/ *noun* [C, U] a liquid that you put on your skin to make it soft or healthy **losyon** *suntan lotion* ○ *body lotion*

lottery /'lɒt^əri/ *noun* [C] a way of making money by selling numbered tickets to people who then have a chance of winning a prize if their number is chosen **piyango, bir tür şans oyunu, kumar** *the national lottery*

◦┅**loud¹** /laʊd/ *adjective* **1** making a lot of noise **gürültülü, yüksek sesli** *a loud noise* ○ *a loud voice* ○ *a loud explosion* **2** Loud clothes are too bright or have too many colours. **göz alıcı, parlak, renkli, cafcaflı; (argo) 'Ben buradayım!' diye bağıran** ● **loudly** *adverb* *She was speaking very loudly.* **yüksek sesli, göze batan**

loud² /laʊd/ *adverb* **1** loudly **yüksek sesle, gürültüyle** *Can you speak a bit louder?* **2 out loud** If you say or read something out loud, you say or read it so that other people can hear you. **başkalarının duyacağı şekilde söylenen/okunan; sesli**

loudspeaker /ˌlaʊd'spiːkə^r/ ⓤ /'laʊd.spiːkə^r/ *noun* [C] a piece of equipment used for making voices or sounds louder **hoparlör**

lounge¹ /laʊndʒ/ *noun* [C] **1** *UK* the room in a home where you sit and relax **oturma/dinlenme odası**

2 *US* a room in a hotel, theatre, airport, etc where people can relax or wait **dinlenme salonu**

lounge² /laʊndʒ/ *verb*
lounge about/around (sth) *phrasal verb* to spend your time in a relaxed way, doing very little **miskinlik etmek, tembel tembel vakit geçirmek, aylaklık etmek** *Most days were spent lounging around the pool.*

louse /laʊs/ *noun* [C] *plural* **lice** /laɪs/ a very small insect that lives on the bodies or in the hair of people or animals **bit**

lousy /ˈlaʊzi/ *adjective informal* very bad **berbat, kötü, tatsız tuzsuz keyifsiz** *lousy food/service* ○ *I felt lousy when I woke up this morning.*

lout /laʊt/ *noun* [C] a man who behaves in a rude or violent way **serseri, kaba, hödük; (argo) hıyar, dangalak, ayı**

lovable *(also* loveable*)* /ˈlʌvəbl/ *adjective* A person or animal that is lovable has qualities which make them easy to love. **sevimli, şirin, cici, hoş, cana yakın**

○• **love¹** /lʌv/ *verb* [T] **1** ROMANCE/SEX to like someone very much and have romantic or sexual feelings for them **sevmek, gönül vermek, âşık olmak** *Last night he told me he loved me.* ○ *I've only ever loved one woman.* **2** FRIENDS/FAMILY to like a friend or a person in your family very much **sevmek, şefkat ve sevgi göstermek** *I'm sure he loves his kids.* **3** ENJOY to enjoy something very much or have a strong interest in something **yürekten/taparcasına sevmek, aşırı sevmek, bayılmak, bitmek** *He loves his music.* ○ *She loves animals.* ○ [+ doing sth] *I love eating out.* **4 I'd love to** used to say that you would very much like to do something that someone is offering **'Memnuniyetle...', 'Keyifle...', 'Bayılırım!', 'Çok isterim!'** *"I wondered if you'd like to meet up sometime?" "I'd love to."*

🧩 love ...... İLE BİRLİKTE KULLANILAN KELİMELER

in love with sb • fall in love • madly in love • broterly/unconditional love

○• **love²** /lʌv/ *noun* **1** ROMANCE/SEX [U] when you like someone very much and have romantic or sexual feelings for them **aşk, sevda, sevgi, tutku** *He's madly in love with* (= he loves) *her.* ○ *I was 20 when I first fell in love* (= started to love someone). ○ *a love song/story* **2 make love** to have sex **sevişmek, cinsel ilişkide bulunmak 3** PERSON [C] someone who you like very much and have a romantic or sexual relationship with **sevgili, yâr, sevdalı** *He was my first love.* **4** FRIENDS/FAMILY [U] when you like a friend or person in your family very much **(arkadaş/aile üyeleri vb.ne duyulan) sevgi, muhabbet, aşk, düşkünlük, içtenlik** *Nothing is as strong as the love you have for your kids.* **5** INTEREST [C, U] something that interests you a lot **(bir şeye duyulan) tutku, istek, sevgi, aşk** *his love of books* **6 Love from; All my love** something you write at the end of a letter to a friend or someone in your family **'Sevgiler!', 'Sevgilerimle!', 'Gözlerinden öperim!'** *Love from Mum.* ○ *All my love, Louise.* **7** SPEAKING TO SOMEONE *mainly UK* You call someone 'love' to show affection or to be friendly. **aşkım, tatlım, hayatım, bir tanem, şekerim** *"Margot?" "Yes, love."* ○ *Two portions of chips please, love.* **8** SPORTS [U] in games such as tennis, a score of zero **(tenis vb. oyunlarda) sıfır puan** *She's leading by two sets to love.* ➔See also: a labour¹ of love.

'love af,fair *noun* [C] a romantic or sexual relationship **aşk macerası, gönül oyunu**

loveless /ˈlʌvləs/ *adjective* without love **sevgisiz, aşksız, aşktan yoksun** *She was trapped in a loveless marriage.*

'love ,life *noun* [C] the romantic relationships in a person's life **aşk hayatı** *How's your love life these days?*

○• **lovely** /ˈlʌvli/ *adjective* **1** pleasant or enjoyable **hoş, güzel, sevimli, cana yakın** *We had a lovely day together.* ○ *What lovely weather.* **2** very attractive **çekici, harika, çok hoş/güzel** *a lovely dress/house/village* ○ *You look lovely!*

lover /ˈlʌvəʳ/ *noun* **1** [C] If two people are lovers, they have a sexual relationship but they are not married. **sevgili, âşık; evli sevgililer, cinsel ilişkide bulunan sevgililer** *She had a string of lovers before her marriage finally broke up.* **2 a book/cat/dog, etc lover** someone who is very interested in books/cats/dogs, etc **(kitap, kedi, köpek vs.) düşkün seven meraklı** *She's a real cat lover.*

loving /ˈlʌvɪŋ/ *adjective* showing a lot of affection and kindness towards someone **seven, ilgi duyan, hoşlanan** *a loving relationship* ○ *a loving father* • **lovingly** *adverb* **severek**

○• **low¹** /ləʊ/ *adjective* **1** NOT HIGH near the ground, not high **alçak** *low aircraft* ○ *a low fence* **2** LEVEL below the usual level **alçak, aşağıda** *a low income* ○ *low temperatures/prices* ○ *a low number* ○ *Fish is very low in* (= has little) *fat.* **3** SOUND deep or quiet **derin, sessiz** *a low voice* ○ *a low note* **4** LIGHTS If lights are low, they are not bright. **kısık, az ışık veren** *We have very low lighting in the main room.* **5** UNHAPPY unhappy and without energy **neşesiz, keyifsiz, mutsuz** *Illness of any sort can leave you feeling low.* ➔See also: be at a low ebb¹, keep a low profile¹.

low² /ləʊ/ *adverb* **1** in or to a low position or level **düşük, alçak, aşağıda, aşağıya** *low-paid workers* ○ *Turn the deck on low.* **2** with deep notes **düşük, küçük, altta** *You can sing lower than me.*

low³ /ləʊ/ *noun* **a new/record/all-time, etc low** the lowest level **en düşük düzey/seviye; alt seviye/düzey** *Temperatures in the region hit a record low yesterday.*

low-alcohol /ˌləʊˈælkəhɒl/ *adjective* A low-alcohol drink has less alcohol in it than the normal type. **düşük alkollü** *low-alcohol beer*

low-calorie /ˌləʊˈkælᵊri/ *(abbreviation* **low-cal, lo-cal)** *adjective* A low-calorie food or drink will not make you fat because it has fewer calories (= units for measuring the amount of energy a food provides) than normal food or drink. **düşük kalorili**

low-cut /ˌləʊˈkʌt/ *adjective* describes a piece of clothing that does not cover the top part of a woman's chest **dekolte, açık, degajesi açık** *a low-cut dress*

the lowdown /ˈləʊdaʊn/ *noun informal* the most important information about something **bir şeyin içyüzü/aslı astarı/esası/özü** *Jenny will give you the lowdown on what happened at yesterday's meeting.*

lower¹ /ˈləʊəʳ/ *adjective* being the bottom part of something **daha aşağı/düşük, alt** *I've got a pain in my lower back.* ○ *She bit her lower lip.*

lower² /ˈləʊəʳ/ *verb* [T] **1** to move something to a low position **indirmek** *They lowered the coffin into the grave.* **2** to reduce the amount of something **azaltmak** *I'll join if they lower the entrance fee.*

,lower 'case *noun* [U] letters of the alphabet which are not written as capital letters, for example a, b, c **küçük harf**

low-fat /ˌləʊˈfæt/ *adjective* Low-fat foods do not contain much fat. **daha az yağlı, fazla yağ içermeyen** *low-fat cheese* ○ *a low-fat diet*

low-key /ˌləʊˈkiː/ *adjective* not attracting attention **mütevazı, sade, dikkat çekmeyen** *The reception itself was surprisingly low-key.*

lowly /'ləʊli/ *adjective* not important or respected **küçük, önemsiz,** *He took a lowly job in an insurance firm.*

low-rise /'ləʊ‚raɪz/ *adjective* describes trousers in which the top part of the trousers ends below the person's waist **(pantolon) düşük belli**

low-tech /‚ləʊ'tek/ *adjective* Something that is low-tech does not use the most recent technology. **düşük teknoloji** ⊃Compare **high-tech.**

loyal /'lɔɪəl/ *adjective* always liking and supporting someone or something, sometimes when other people do not **sadık, vefalı, hakikatli** *a loyal supporter* ○ *She's very loyal to her friends.* ⊃Opposite **disloyal.** ● **loyally** *adverb* **sadık bir biçimde**

loyalties /'lɔɪəltiz/ *noun* [plural] a feeling of support for someone **sadıklık, dostluk, samimî bağlılık** *My loyalties to my family come before work.*

loyalty /'lɔɪəlti/ *noun* [U] the quality of being loyal **sadakat, bağlılık, vefa** *Your loyalty to the company is impressive.* ⊃Opposite **disloyalty.**

lozenge /'lɒzɪndʒ/ *noun* [C] a sweet which you suck to make your throat feel better **pastil, boğaz pastili**

LP /‚el'pi:/ *noun* [C] a record that has about 25 minutes of music on each side **uzunçalar plak**

LPG /‚elpi:'dʒi:/ *noun* [U] *abbreviation for* liquid petroleum gas: a type of fuel used for heating, cooking and in some vehicles **sıvı petrol gazı**

L-plate /'elpleɪt/ *noun* [C] *UK* a red and white 'L' symbol on the car of someone learning to drive **acemi sürücü plakası**

Ltd *written abbreviation for* limited company (= used after the name of some companies) **limited şirket kısaltması** *Pinewood Supplies Ltd*

lubricant /'lu:brɪkənt/ *noun* [C, U] a liquid, such as oil, which is used to make the parts of an engine move smoothly together **makina yağı; mekanik yağ**

lubricate /'lu:brɪkeɪt/ *verb* [T] to put a lubricant on something **yağlamak** ● **lubrication** /‚lu:brɪ'keɪʃⁿn/ *noun* [U] **yağlama**

lucid /'lu:sɪd/ *adjective* **1** clear and easy to understand **açık, berrak, anlaşılması kolay** *a lucid account* **2** able to think and speak clearly **açık seçik/aklı başında düşünüp konuşabilen** *In a lucid moment, she spoke about her son.* ● **lucidly** *adverb* **anlaşılması kolay bir biçimde**

bad/beginner's/good/rotten luck ● **bring/wish** sb luck ● **curse** your luck ● a **stroke** of luck

o--**luck** /lʌk/ *noun* [U] **1** good and bad things caused by chance and not by your own actions **şans, talih** *It was just luck that I asked for a job at the right time.* ○ *Then I met this gorgeous woman and I couldn't believe my luck.* ○ *He seems to have had a lot of bad luck in his life.* **2** success **başarı** *Have you had any luck* (= succeeded in) *finding your bag?* ○ *He's been trying to find work but with no luck so far.* **3 be in luck** *informal* to be able to have or do what you want **şansı açık, şanslı, şansı yaver giden** *"Do you have any tuna sandwiches?" "You're in luck - there's one left."* **4 Good luck!** something you say to someone when you hope that they will be successful **'İyi şanslar!', 'Bol şanslar!'** *Good luck with your exam!* **5 Bad/Hard luck!** used to show sympathy when someone is unsuccessful or unlucky **'Şansa bak!', 'Vah, vah!', 'Aksilik!', 'Talihsizlik!', 'Hay Allah!'** *"They've run out of tickets." "Oh, bad luck!"* **6 the luck of the draw** If something is the luck of the draw, it is the result of chance and you have no control over it. **çekiliş sansı; çekiliş sonrası elde edilen şans** ⊃See also: a **stroke**[1] of luck.

o--**lucky** /'lʌki/ *adjective* **1** having good things happen to you **şanslı, talihli** *"I'm going on holiday." "Lucky you!"* ○ *The lucky winner will be able to choose from three different holidays.* ○ [+ to do sth] *You're lucky to have such a nice office to work in.* **2** If an object is lucky, some people believe that it gives you luck. **şans/uğur getiren** *I chose six - it's my lucky number.* ⊃Opposite **unlucky.** ● **luckily** *adverb* **şansına** *Luckily I had some money with me.* ⊃See also: **happy-go-lucky.**

lucrative /'lu:krətɪv/ *adjective* If something is lucrative, it makes a lot of money. **çok kârlı/kazançlı; kâr/kazanç getiren** *a lucrative contract/job/offer*

ludicrous /'lu:dɪkrəs/ *adjective* stupid **aptalca, çok tuhaf, gülünç, komik, mantıksız** *a ludicrous idea/suggestion* ● **ludicrously** *adverb* **aptalca**

lug /lʌg/ *verb* [T] **lugging**, *past* **lugged** *informal* to carry or pull a heavy object **sürüklemek, güçlükle taşımak** *You don't want to lug your suitcase across London.*

luggage

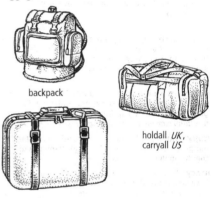

backpack

holdall *UK*, carryall *US*

suitcase

luggage /'lʌgɪdʒ/ *noun* [U] bags and cases that you carry with you when you are travelling **bagaj, yük, eşya** ⊃See also: hand luggage.

lukewarm /‚lu:k'wɔ:m/ *adjective* **1** A liquid which is lukewarm is only slightly warm. **ılık** *Dissolve yeast and one tablespoon of sugar in lukewarm water.* **2** showing little interest or enthusiasm **kayıtsız, ilgisiz, soğuk, isteksiz** *She seemed rather lukewarm about the idea.*

lull¹ /lʌl/ *verb* [T] to make someone feel calm and make them want to sleep **sakinleştirmek, uykusunu getirmek** *Soft music lulled him to sleep.*
lull sb into sth/doing sth *phrasal verb* to make someone feel safe so that you can then trick them **kandırmak amacıyla birisini yatıştırmak, teskin etmek**

lull² /lʌl/ *noun* [C] a short period of calm in which little happens **geçici sükûnet, ara, fasıla, dinme, durma** *a lull in the conversation/traffic*

lullaby /'lʌləbaɪ/ *noun* [C] a song which you sing to children to make them sleep **ninni**

lumber¹ /'lʌmbəʳ/ *verb* **lumber along/around/off, etc** to move slowly with heavy steps **hantal hantal yürümek/gitmek, ağır adımlarla ilerlemek, devrile devrile yürümek** *The bear lumbered off into the forest.*

be lumbered with sth/sb phrasal verb mainly UK to have to deal with something or someone that you do not want to **yapmak zorunda olmak, yüklenmek; angarya yüklemek** I've been lumbered with my neighbours' cat while they're away.

lumber² /'lʌmbəʳ/ US (UK **timber**) noun [U] wood that is used for building **kereste**

lumberjack /'lʌmbədʒæk/ noun [C] a person whose job is to cut down trees in a forest **oduncu, keresteci**

luminary /'lu:mɪnᵊri/ noun [C] formal a famous person who is respected for their skills or knowledge **bilgi ve yeteneklerinden dolayı saygı duyulan meşhur kimse**

luminous /'lu:mɪnəs/ adjective Something that is luminous shines in the dark. **ışıldayan, parlayan, parlak, fosforlu, ışıltılı**

lump¹ /lʌmp/ noun [C] **1** a piece of a solid substance with no particular shape **topak, parça** a lump of coal ○ You don't want lumps in the sauce. ⊃Orta kısımdaki renkli sayfalarına bakınız. **2** a hard piece of tissue under the skin caused by injury or illness **şiş, kabartı, yumru** She found a lump in her breast.

lump² /lʌmp/ verb
lump sth/sb together phrasal verb to put different groups together and think about them or deal with them in the same way **yan yana koymak, aynı kefeye koymak** American and Canadian authors tend to be lumped together.

lump 'sum noun [C] a large amount of money given as a single payment **toplu para, bir kalemde ödenen para, tek kalemde yapılan ödeme** She received a tax-free lump sum on leaving the company.

lumpy /'lʌmpi/ adjective covered with or containing lumps (= bits of solid substance) **yamru yumru, topak topak** a lumpy sauce

lunacy /'lu:nəsi/ noun [U] stupid behaviour that will have bad results **delilik, kaçıklık, çılgınlık, aptallık,** It was lunacy spending all that money.

lunar /'lu:nəʳ/ adjective [always before noun] relating to the moon **ay ile ilgili, aya ait**

lunatic /'lu:nətɪk/ noun [C] someone who behaves in a crazy way **deli, kaçık, fıttırık, üşütük, kafadan çatlak kimse** He drives like a lunatic.

lunch .... İLE BİRLİKTE KULLANILAN KELİMELER
eat/have lunch ● **have** sth **for** lunch ● **a light** lunch

ᵒᐟ**lunch¹** /lʌnʃ/ noun [C, U] a meal that you eat in the middle of the day **öğle yemeği** ⊃See also: packed lunch.

lunch² /lʌnʃ/ verb [I] to eat lunch **öğle yemeği yemek**

luncheon /'lʌnʃən/ noun [C] formal lunch **resmî öğle yemeği**

lunchtime /'lʌnʃtaɪm/ noun [C, U] the time when lunch is eaten **öğle yemeği vakti**

lung /lʌŋ/ noun [C] one of the two organs inside your chest that are used for breathing **akciğer** lung cancer

lurch /lɜ:tʃ/ verb **lurch forward/towards, etc** to suddenly move in a way that is not controlled **yalpalamak, sendelemek** The car lurched forward before hitting the tree.

lure¹ /lʊəʳ/ verb [T] to persuade someone to go somewhere or do something by offering them something exciting **ikna etmek, cezbetmek, çekmek** It seems that he was lured into a trap. ○ They had been lured to the big city by the promise of high wages.

lure² /lʊəʳ/ noun [U] the power to attract people **cazibe, çekicilik, albeni** the lure of fame/power/money

lurid /'lʊərɪd/ adjective **1** shocking in a way that involves sex or violence **cinsellik ve şiddet içeren şekilde şok edici, cazibeli** lurid details/stories **2** too brightly coloured **çok parlak renkli, baş döndüren, cinsel cazibeyi öne çıkaran** a lurid green miniskirt

lurk /lɜ:k/ verb [I] **1** to wait somewhere secretly, especially before doing something bad **pusuya yatmak, gizlenip beklemek, gizlenmek** Someone was lurking in the shadows. **2** to enter a place on the Internet and read what other people have written without them knowing you are there **e-posta tartışması için internette sohbet odasına girmek ve orada olduğu bilinmeden yazılanları okumak** ● **lurker** noun [C] **pusuya yatan kişi**

lush /lʌʃ/ adjective A lush area has a lot of healthy grass, plants, or trees. **gür, bol, bereketli**

lust¹ /lʌst/ noun [U] **1** a strong feeling of sexual attraction to someone **aşırı cinsel istek, şehvet düşkünlüğü, şehvet 2** when you want something very much **tutku, ihtiras** a lust for power

lust² /lʌst/ verb
lust after sb phrasal verb to feel strong sexual attraction for someone **aşırı cinsel istek duymak, şiddetle arzulamak**
lust after sth phrasal verb to want something very much **tutkuyla/ihtirasla istemek** to lust after fame/power

Lutheran /'lu:θᵊrᵊn/ adjective belonging or relating to a Christian group based on the teachings of Martin Luther **Marthin Luther'in öğretilerine dayalı Hıristiyan gruba ilişkin/ait; Luteran** ● **Lutheran** noun [C] **Lutheran**

luxurious /lʌgˈʒʊəriəs/ adjective very comfortable and expensive **lüks, konforlu, çok rahat ve pahalı** a luxurious hotel ○ luxurious fabrics

luxury /'lʌkʃᵊri/ noun **1** [COMFORT/PLEASURE] [U] great comfort or pleasure from expensive or beautiful things **lüks, konfor, ihtişam** to live in luxury ○ a luxury apartment/car **2** [NOT NECESSARY] [C] something expensive that you enjoy but do not need **lüks, pahalı şeyler,** It's nice to buy people the little luxuries that they wouldn't buy themselves. **3** [RARE PLEASURE] [U, no plural] something which gives you a lot of pleasure but which you cannot often do **çok zevk veren lüks/pahalı şeyler** A day off work is such a luxury.

lying /'laɪɪŋ/ present participle of lie¹,² **yalan söyleme; yalan söyleyen; yalancı**

lyrical /'lɪrɪkᵊl/ adjective expressing the writer's emotions in a beautiful way **şiirsel, kulağa hoş gelen, lirik; yazarın duygularını güzel bir biçimde dile getiren** lyrical poetry/verse

lyrics /'lɪrɪks/ noun [plural] the words of a song **güfte, şarkı sözü**

M, m /em/ the thirteenth letter of the alphabet **alfabe-nin onüçüncü harfi**

m *written abbreviation for* metre (= a unit of length) **metrenin kısa yazılışı**

MA /ˌem'eɪ/ *noun* [C] *abbreviation for* Master of Arts: a higher university qualification in an arts (= not science) subject **sosyal ve sanat alanında yüksek lisans derecesi**

ma'am /mæm/, /mɑːm/ *US short for* madam **hanımefendi, bayan** *Can I help you, Ma'am?*

mac /mæk/ *noun* [C] *UK* a coat that you wear in the rain **yağmurluk** ⊃Orta kısımdaki renkli sayfalarına bakınız.

macabre /məˈkɑːbrə/ *adjective* strange and frightening, and often connected with death **korkunç, tüyler ürpertici; ölüm korkusu veren** *a macabre story*

macaroni /ˌmækˈəˈrəʊni/ *noun* [U] pasta that is shaped like small tubes **makarna, çubuk makarna**

machete /məˈʃeti/ *noun* [C] a large knife with a wide blade **pala, maçeta**

machinations /ˌmæʃɪˈneɪʃᵊnz/ *noun* [plural] complicated and secret plans and activities **karmaşık ve gizli planlar/faaliyetler** *political machinations*

> 🔧 **machine** .... İLE BİRLİKTE KULLANILAN KELİMELER
>
> **operate/use** a machine ● **turn off/turn on** a machine ● **do sth by** machine ● a machine **for** doing sth

ᴏⱽ**machine** /məˈʃiːn/ *noun* [C] **1** [EQUIPMENT] a piece of equipment with moving parts that uses power to do a particular job **makine** *a fax machine* ○ *a coffee machine* ○ *Clothes are generally sewn by machine these days.* **2** [GROUP] a group of people all working together to achieve the same result **sistem, düzen, çark, teşkilat** *a political/war machine* **3** [COMPUTER] a computer **bilgisayar** ⊃See also: answerphone, cash machine, sewing machine, slot machine, vending machine, washing machine.

ma'chine ˌgun *noun* [C] a gun that fires a lot of bullets very quickly **makineli tüfek**

machine-readable /məˌʃiːnˈriːdəbl/ *adjective* able to be understood by a computer **bilgisayarın anlayabileceği; bilgisayarda kullanılabilen** *a machine-readable dictionary*

machinery /məˈʃiːnᵊri/ *noun* [U] **1** machines, often large machines **makine aksamı, makineler** *industrial/farm machinery* **2** the system that a group of people uses to achieve something **mekanizma, sistem, düzen** *the machinery of government*

macho /ˈmætʃəʊ/ ⓤⓢ /ˈmɑːtʃəʊ/ *adjective informal* Men who are macho emphasize their traditional male qualities, such as physical strength, and do not show emotion. **(erkek) bıçkın, haşin, sert, maço**

mackerel /ˈmækrᵊl/ *noun* [C, U] *plural* **mackerel** or **mackerels** a type of sea fish, or the meat from this fish **uskumru, uskumru balığı**

mackintosh /ˈmækɪntɒʃ/ *noun* [C] *old-fashioned* a mac **yağmurluk**

macro- /mækrəʊ-/ *prefix* large or on a large scale **büyük/büyük ölçekte anlamında ön ek** *macroeconomics* (= the study of financial systems at a national level)

ᴏⱽ**mad** /mæd/ *adjective* **1** [CRAZY] *informal* stupid or crazy **çılgın, deli, aptal** [+ to do sth] *You're mad to walk home alone at night.* **2** [ANGRY] *mainly US* angry **çılgın, çıldırmış, deli, kızgın** *Were your parents mad at you when you came home late?* **3 go mad a** [ANGRY] to become very angry **çılgına/deliye dönmek; küplere binmek** *Dad'll go mad when he finds out you took the car.* **b** [EXCITED] to suddenly become very excited **coşmak, çılgına dönmek, aniden heyecanlanmak** *When the band arrived on stage, the crowd went mad.* **4 be mad about sb/sth** *informal* to love something or someone **deli divane olmak, çok düşkün/tutkun olmak** *Jo's mad about skiing.* **5** [ILL] mentally ill **akıl hastası, deli, 6** [NOT CONTROLLED] not controlled **çılgın, kudurmuş, çılgına dönmüş** *We made a mad dash for the exit.* **7 like mad c** [QUICKLY] If you run, work, etc like mad, you do it very quickly and with a lot of energy. **deli/deliler gibi, çılgıncasına d** [PAIN] If something hurts like mad, it hurts a lot. **deliye döndüren, dünyayı zindan eden; çok acıyan**

madam /ˈmædəm/ *noun formal* **1** (*also* Madam) You call a woman 'madam' when you are speaking to her politely. **hanımefendi, bayan** *This way, madam.* **2 Madam** You write 'Madam' at the beginning of a formal letter to a woman when you do not know her name. **'Sayın Bayan'** *Dear Madam, I am writing to...*

made /meɪd/ *past of* make **'yapmak' fiilinin geçmiş zaman hâli**

-made /meɪd/ *suffix* ⊃See man-made, ready-made, self-made, tailor-made.

madhouse /ˈmædhaʊs/ *noun* [C] *informal* a place where there is a lot of uncontrolled noise and activity **tımarhane**

madly /ˈmædli/ *adverb* **1** with a lot of energy and enthusiasm **deli gibi, delicesine, çılgıncasına; enerji ve coşku dolu** *We cheered madly as the team came out onto the field.* **2 be madly in love** to love someone very much **delicesine âşık olmak**

madman, madwoman /ˈmædmən/, /ˈmædˌwʊmən/ *noun* [C] *plural* **madmen, madwomen** a crazy person **çılgın/dengesiz kimse** *He was running around like a madman.*

madness /ˈmædnəs/ *noun* [U] **1** stupid or dangerous behaviour **delilik, aptalca ve tehlikeli davranış, çılgınlık** *It would be madness to give up your job when you've just bought a house.* **2** mental illness **akıl hastalığı**

maestro /ˈmaɪstrəʊ/ *noun* [C] someone who is very good at something, especially playing music **maestro; bir şeyde özellikle müzikte çok başarılı kimse**

the mafia /ˈmæfiə/ ⓤⓢ /ˈmɑːfiə/ *noun* a large group of organized criminals **mafya** *Drug-smuggling activities have been linked to the Mafia.*

magazine

ᴏⱽ**magazine** /ˌmægəˈziːn/ *noun* [C] a thin book published every week or month, that has shiny, colourful pages

M

with articles and pictures **dergi, magazin, mecmua** *a fashion/news magazine*

maggot /'mægət/ *noun* [C] a small insect with a soft body and no legs that often lives in decaying food **kurtçuk, kurt**

⚬**magic¹** /'mædʒɪk/ *noun* [U] **1** ⟨SPECIAL POWERS⟩ special powers that can make things happen that seem impossible **büyü, sihir** *Do you believe in magic?* **2** ⟨ENTERTAINMENT⟩ clever actions intended to entertain people, often making objects appear and disappear **sihirbazlık, hokkabazlık 3** ⟨SPECIAL QUALITY⟩ a quality that makes something or someone seem special or exciting **sihir, büyü, esrar, çekicilik** *No one could fail to be charmed by the magic of this beautiful city.* **4 as if by magic** in a way that is surprising and impossible to explain **sanki sihirli bir el varmışçasına; şaşırtıcı ve açıklaması imkansız** *Food would appear on the table every day, as if by magic.* ⟳See also: **black magic.**

magic² /'mædʒɪk/ *adjective* **1** with special powers **sihirli deynekle/güçlerle** *a magic spell/wand* **2** relating to magic **büyüye/sihre ilişkin** *a magic trick* **3 magic moments** special and exciting experiences **sihirli/muhteşem anlar**

magical /'mædʒɪkᵊl/ *adjective* **1** with special powers **sihirli, büyülü** *Diamonds were once thought to have magical powers.* **2** special or exciting **büyüleyen, hayranlık uyandıran** *It was a magical night.* ● **magically** *adverb* *I knew my problems would not just magically disappear.* **büyülü**

magician /mə'dʒɪʃᵊn/ *noun* [C] **1** someone who entertains people by performing magic tricks **sihirbaz, hokkabaz 2** a character in old stories who has magic powers **büyücü**

magistrate /'mædʒɪstreɪt/ *noun* [C] a type of judge (= person who decides what punishments should be given) who deals with less serious crimes **sulh yargıcı, sulh hukuk hâkimi**

magnate /'mægneɪt/ *noun* [C] someone who is rich and successful in business **patron, kodaman, zengin, varlıklı** *a media magnate*

magnesium /mæg'niːziəm/ *noun* [U] a metallic element that burns very brightly, used to make fireworks (= explosives used to entertain people) (symbol **Mg**) **magnezyum**

magnet /'mægnət/ *noun* **1** [C] an iron object that makes pieces of iron or steel (= metal made with iron) move towards it **mıknatıs 2 be a magnet for sb** If a place or event is a magnet for people, a lot of people go there. **insanların sıkça uğradığı yer olmak; insanları kendine çeken/cezbeden yer/olay olmak** *Airports are a magnet for thieves.*

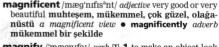

magnet

magnetic /mæg'netɪk/ *adjective* **1** with the power of a magnet **mıknatıs özelliği olan, manyetik** *a magnetic field* **2 magnetic tape/disk/storage, etc** equipment used in the past for storing information from a computer **manyetik teyp/disk/depolama aleti 3** having a character that attracts people to you **çekici, etkileyici, cazip**

magnificent /mæg'nɪfɪsᵊnt/ *adjective* very good or very beautiful **muhteşem, mükemmel, çok güzel, olağanüstü** *a magnificent view* ● **magnificently** *adverb* **mükemmel bir şekilde**

magnify /'mægnɪfaɪ/ *verb* [T] **1** to make an object look larger than it is by looking through special equipment **büyüteçle büyütmek** *The cells are first magnified under a microscope.* **2** to make a bad situation worse **berbat etmek, abartmak, büyütmek** *All your problems are magnified when you're ill.*

'magnifying ,glass *noun* [C] a piece of curved glass which makes objects look larger than they are **büyüteç**

magnitude /'mægnɪtjuːd/ *noun* [U] *formal* the large size or importance of something **büyüklük, önem, ehemmiyet** *People were still unaware of the magnitude of the problem.*

mahogany /mə'hɒgᵊni/ *noun* [U] a dark, red-brown wood used to make furniture **maun ağacı**

maid /meɪd/ *noun* [C] a woman who works as a servant in a hotel or in someone's home **(kadın) hizmetçi**

maiden¹ /'meɪdᵊn/ *noun* [C] *literary old-fashioned* a young woman who is not married **evlenmemiş genç bayan**

maiden² /'meɪdᵊn/ *adjective* **a maiden flight/voyage** the first journey of a new aircraft or ship **ilk uçuş/seyahat/sefer**

'maiden ,name *noun* [C] the family name that a woman has before she gets married **kızlık soyadı**

⚬**mail¹** /meɪl/ *noun* [U] **1** letters and parcels that are brought by post **posta 2** *mainly US* the system by which letters and parcels are taken and brought **posta servisi** *Send it by mail.* ○ *The letter is in the mail.* ⟳See also: **email, junk mail, snail mail, surface mail, voice mail.**

mail² /meɪl/ *verb* [T] *mainly US* to send a letter or parcel or email something **mektup/paket/e-posta göndermek** *Could you mail it to me?*

mailbox /'meɪlbɒks/ *noun* [C] *US* **1** a small box outside your home where letters are delivered **(ev) posta kutusu 2** (*UK* **letterbox, post box**) a large, metal container in a public place where you can post letters **(umumi) posta kutusu**

'mailing ,list *noun* [C] a list of names and addresses that an organization uses in order to send information to people **isim ve adres listesi**

mailman /'meɪlmæn/ *US* (*UK* **postman**) *noun* [C] *plural* **mailmen** a man who takes and brings letters and parcels as a job **postacı**

'mail ,order *noun* [U] a way of buying goods by ordering them from a catalogue (= book) and receiving them by post **posta ile alışveriş/sipariş**

maim /meɪm/ *verb* [T] to injure someone permanently **sakatlamak, sakat bırakmak** *Thousands of innocent people have been killed or maimed by landmines.*

⚬**main¹** /meɪn/ *adjective* [always before noun] **1** most important or largest **asıl, esas, temel** *the main problem/reason* ○ *The main airport is 15 miles from the capital.* **2 the main thing** the most important fact in a situation **önemli olan, esas olan, en önemlisi** *You're happy and that's the main thing.*

main² /meɪn/ *noun* [C] **1 gas/water main** a pipe that carries gas or water to a building **bina gaz/su girişi; ana boru, şebeke borusu 2 in the main** generally or mostly **ekseriyetle, genel anlamda, çoğunlukla** *Her friends are teachers in the main.*

'main ,course *noun* [C] the largest or most important part of a meal **ana yemek**

mainframe /'meɪnfreɪm/ *noun* [C] a large, powerful computer which many people can use at the same time **ana bilgisayar**

mainland /'meɪnlənd/ *noun* **the mainland** the main part of a country, not including the islands around it **ana kara** *A daily ferry links the islands to the mainland.* ● **mainland** *adjective* [always before noun] *mainland Britain* **kıta**

o- **mainly** /'meɪnli/ *adverb* mostly or to a large degree **çoğunlukla, başlıca, büyük oranda** *The waitresses are mainly French.*

,**main 'road** *noun* [C] a large road which leads from one town to another **ana yol** *Stay on the main road for about three miles and you'll be there.*

mainstay /'meɪnsteɪ/ *noun* **a/the mainstay of sth** the most important thing or activity **temel, asıl, en önemli unsur/eylem/faaliyet** *Cattle farming is the mainstay of the country's economy.*

the mains /meɪnz/ *noun* [group] *UK* **1** the system of pipes or wires that carries gas, water, or electricity to a building **(gaz, su, elektrik) ana hat/vana, ana giriş, ana boru, kofra** *The house isn't connected to the mains yet.* **2** the place inside a building where you can connect a machine to a supply of electricity **elektrik ana girişi** *Is the cooker turned off at the mains?*

mainstream /'meɪnstriːm/ *noun* **the mainstream** the beliefs or way of living accepted by most people **toplumca kabul gören davranış ve inançlar bütünü** *The party is now in the mainstream of politics.* ● **mainstream** *adjective* [always before noun] *mainstream culture/politics* **ana görüş**

maintain /meɪn'teɪn/ *verb* [T] **1** [NOT CHANGE] to make a situation or activity continue in the same way **sürdürmek, devam ettirmek, sağlamak** *The army has been brought in to maintain order in the region.* **2** [CONDITION] to keep a building or area in good condition **iyi bakmak, korumak, bakımını sağlamak** *A large house is very expensive to maintain.* **3** [SPEAK TRUTH] *formal* to say that you are certain something is true **iddia etmek, savunmak** [+ (that)] *He has always maintained that he is innocent.*

maintenance ...... İLE BİRLİKTE KULLANILAN KELİMELER

carry out maintenance ● **high/low** maintenance ● maintenance **of sth**

maintenance /'meɪntʰnəns/ *noun* [U] **1** the work that is done to keep something in good condition **bakım onarım** *car maintenance* ○ *I want a garden that's very low maintenance* (= easy to look after). **2** *UK* regular amounts of money that someone must pay after they have left their family so that the family still has money to live on **nafaka yol** *child maintenance*

maize /meɪz/ *UK* (*US* corn) *noun* [U] a tall plant with yellow seeds that are eaten as food **mısır**

majestic /mə'dʒestɪk/ *adjective* very beautiful or powerful in a way that people admire **görkemli, muhteşem, ihtişamlı, heybetli** *majestic scenery*

majesty /'mædʒəsti/ *noun* **1** [U] the quality of being majestic **görkem, ihtişam, haşmet** *the majesty of the pyramids* **2** **His/Her/Your Majesty** used when you are speaking to or about a king or queen **Haşmetmeap, Majesteleri** *His Majesty King Edward VII*

o- **major**¹ /'meɪdʒəʳ/ *adjective* **1** [always before noun] more important or more serious than other things or people of a similar type **ana, esas, büyük, çok önemli, ciddi** *a major problem/issue* ○ *a major city* ○ *America has played a major role in the peace process.* **2** in music, belonging to a key (= set of musical notes) which often produces a happy sound **majör** ⊃Opposite minor.

major² /'meɪdʒəʳ/ *noun* [C] **1** *US* the most important subject that a college or university student studies, or the student who is studying **ana bilim dalı, ana bilim dalı öğrencisi** *What's your major?* ○ *Diane's an English major.* **2** an officer of middle rank in the army or air force **(kara, hava) binbaşı**

major³ /'meɪdʒəʳ/ *verb*
major in sth *phrasal verb* If you major in a subject, it is the most important part of your course at a college or university. **üniversitede ana dal olarak belli bir konuda eğitim/çalışma yapmak**

majority ...... İLE BİRLİKTE KULLANILAN KELİMELER

a   **narrow/outright/overwhelming/tiny/vast** majority ● the majority **of sth** ● **in the** majority

o- **majority** /mə'dʒɒrəti/ *noun* **1** [no plural] more than half of a group of people or things **çoğunluk, ekseriyet** *The majority of people in this country own their houses.* ○ *The vast majority of smokers claim they would like to give up.* **2 be in a/the majority** to be larger than other similar groups **çoğunlukta olmak, ekseriyette olmak** *Women are in the majority in the publishing world.* **3** [C] in an election, the difference between the number of votes for the winner, and the votes for the party that came second **oy çokluğu; ekseriyet** *Labour has a strong majority.* ⊃Opposite minority.

o- **make**¹ /meɪk/ *verb* [T] *past* made **1** [CREATE] to produce or create something **yapmak, üretmek** *Shall I make some coffee?* ○ *They've made a film about her life.* **2 make a promise/remark/mistake, etc** to promise something, to say something, to do something wrong, etc **söz vermek/vaad etmek; söylemek/belirtmek; hata yapmak** *We have to make a decision today.* ○ *You're making a big mistake.* ○ *She made some useful suggestions.* **3 make sb do sth** to force someone to do something **bir şeyi yaptırmak** *You can't make me go.* **4 make sb/sth happy/sad/difficult, etc** to cause someone or something to become happy, sad, difficult, etc **birini/bir şeyi vs. mutlu etmek/üzmek/güçleştirmek** *You've made me very happy.* ○ *This is the song that made her a star.* **5** [GO TO] to be able to go to an event **varmak, ulaşmak, gitmek** *I'm afraid I can't make the meeting this afternoon.* **6** [EARN MONEY] If you make an amount of money, you earn it. **para kazanmak** *He makes £20,000 a year.* **7** [NUMBERS] If two or more numbers make a particular amount, that is the amount when they are added together. **(rakamları toplama) olmak, oluşturmak, yekün yapmak/tutmak** *That makes $40 altogether.* **8** [PERSONAL QUALITIES] [T] to have the right qualities to become a father or mother or to do a particular job **(özellik olarak baba, anne) olmak** *Andy would make a good teacher.* **9** [GIVE A JOB] [+ two objects] to give someone a particular job **(birini/birine) görev vermek, atamak, görevlendirmek, yapmak** *They made her a director of the company.* **10 make an appointment** to arrange to do something at a particular time **randevu almak** *I've made an appointment with the doctor.* **11 make the bed** to make the sheets and covers on a bed tidy **yatağı yapmak 12 make time** to leave enough time to do something although you are busy **zaman ayırmak** [+ to do sth] *You must make time to do your homework.* **13 make do (with)** to accept that something is less good than you would like **yetinmek, idare etmek** *If we can't get a bigger room we'll have to make do with this.* **14 make it a** [ARRIVE] to manage to arrive at a place **varmak, ulaşabilmek, yetişmek** *Will we make it in time for the film?* **b** [SUCCEED] to be successful **başarmak, üstesinden gelmek, halletmek** *Very few actors really make it.*

M

make for sth *phrasal verb* to move towards a place **gitmek, koyulmak, ilerlemek, yaklaşmak; ...a/e doğru yürümek** *He got up and made for the exit.*

make sth into sth *phrasal verb* to change something into something else **dönüştürmek, çevirmek** *We're going to make the spare room into an office.*

make of sb/sth *phrasal verb* If you ask someone what they make of someone or something, you want to know their opinion about that person or thing. **(kişi/şey) ... hakkında düşüncesini öğrenmek/almak, fikir sahibi olmak; anlam vermek/çıkarmak** *What do you make of this letter?*

make off with sth *phrasal verb informal* to steal something **çalıp kaçmak, aşırmak**

make sth/sb out *phrasal verb* to be able to see, hear, or understand something or someone **bir şeyi/birini anlayabilmek/işitebilmek/görebilmek** *We could just make out a building through the trees.*

make out sth *phrasal verb* to say something that is not true **uydurmak; ...mış/miş gibi söylemek; gerçeği söylememek** [+ (that)] *He made out that he'd been living in Boston all year.*

make out *phrasal verb US informal* **1** to deal with a situation, usually in a successful way **başarıyla sürdürnek/yapmak; başarıyla götürmek, ilgilenmek** *How is Jake making out in his new school?* **2** to kiss and touch someone in a sexual way **tahrik edici şekilde öpüp dokunmak**

make it up to sb *phrasal verb* to do something good for someone because you have done something bad to them in the past **telafi etmek, hatasını affettirmeye çalışmak; üzerine düşeni yapmak** *I'm sorry I missed your birthday. I'll make it up to you, I promise.*

make sth up *phrasal verb* to say or write something that is not true **yalan yanlış şeyler söylemek/yazmak; uydurmak; yakıştırmak** *I made up some story about having to go and see my sick mother.*

make up sth *phrasal verb* to form the whole of an amount **oluşturmak, meydana getirmek** *Women make up nearly 50% of medical school entrants.*

make up *phrasal verb* to become friendly with someone again after you have argued with them **barışmak, arayı düzeltmek** *Have you made up with Daryl yet?*

make up for sth *phrasal verb* to reduce the bad effect of something, or make something bad become something good **telafi etmek, gidermek, iş görmek, katkısı olmak** *I hope this money will make up for the inconvenience.*

make² /meɪk/ *noun* [C] the name of a company that makes a particular product **üretici firma/şirket adı** *I like your stereo. What make is it?*

make-believe /'meɪkbɪ,liːv/ *noun* [U] when you pretend that something is real **hayal ürünü; yapmacıklık, sahtelik** *Disneyland creates a world of make-believe.*

makeover /'meɪk,əʊvər/ *noun* [C] when you suddenly improve your appearance by wearing better clothes, cutting your hair, etc **bakım, makyaj, güzelleşme, çeki düzen** *to have a makeover*

maker /'meɪkər/ *noun* [C] the person or company that makes a product **üretici, yapımcı** *makers of top quality electrical products*

makeshift /'meɪkʃɪft/ *adjective* [always before noun] temporary and low quality **geçici ve düşük kaliteli** *makeshift shelters*

make-up, makeup /'meɪkʌp/ *noun* [U] coloured substances that a woman puts on her face in order to make herself more attractive **makyaj, yüz bakımı** *to put on/take off make-up* ○ *She doesn't wear much make-up.*

making /'meɪkɪŋ/ *noun* [U] **1** the process of making or producing something **yapım, üretim** *There's an article*

make-up

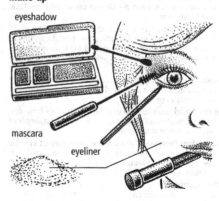

eyeshadow

mascara

eyeliner

blusher *UK*, blush *US*

lipstick

on the making of a television series. ○ *the art of film making* **2 be a sth/sb in the making** to be likely to develop into a particular thing or type of person ... **olmakta; ...olup çıkmakta; ...yapılmakta; ...a/e dönüşmekte/bürünmekte** *What we're seeing is a disaster in the making.* **3 have the makings of sth** to seem likely to develop into something **olmaya başlamak; gelişmek; ...olma niteliğine sahip olmak; ....ın/in hamurunda bulunmak** *She has the makings of a great violinist.*

malaria /mə'leəriə/ *noun* [U] a serious disease that you can get in hot countries if a mosquito (= small insect) bites you **sıtma**

○ᴀ**male¹** /meɪl/ *adjective* belonging to or relating to the sex that cannot have babies **erkek** *a male colleague* ⊃Opposite **female.**

male² /meɪl/ *noun* [C] a male person or animal **(insan, hayvan) erkek** *In 1987, 27 percent of adult males smoked.*

,male 'chauvinist *noun* [C] a man who believes that men are better or more important than women **erkek üstünlüğünü savunan erkek**

malice /'mælɪs/ *noun* [U] when you want to harm or upset someone **kasıt, kötü niyet, kötülük, hainlik, kin, garaz** *There was no malice in her comments.*

malicious /mə'lɪʃəs/ *adjective* intended to harm or upset someone **kasıtlı, kötü niyetli, kindar** *malicious gossip*

malignant /mə'lɪgnənt/ *adjective* A malignant tumour (= group of diseased cells) is one that could cause death. **habis, ölümcül, kötü**

mall /mɔːl/ *(also* **shopping mall)** *noun* [C] a large, covered shopping area **büyük kapalı alışveriş merkezi**

malleable /'mæliəbl/ *adjective* **1** easy to bend or make into a different shape **bükülebilir, her türlü şekle girebilir 2** *formal* easily influenced and controlled **kolay etkilenen/etki altına alınabilen**

mallet /'mælɪt/ *noun* [C] a tool like a hammer with a large, flat end made of wood or rubber **tokmak, çekiç** ⊃See picture at **tool.**

malnutrition /,mælnjuː'trɪʃ°n/ *noun* [U] a serious illness caused by having too little food **kötü beslenme**

malpractice /,mæl'præktɪs/ *noun* [U] when a doctor, lawyer, etc does not do one of their duties or makes a mistake at work **meslek hatası, yolsuzluk, görevi kötüye kullanma** *medical malpractice*

malt /mɔːlt/ *noun* [U] a substance made from grain that is used to make drinks, for example beer and whisky (= strong alcoholic drink) **malt**

mama /məˈmɑː/ *noun* [C] *mainly US* a child's word for 'mother' **çocuk dilinde anne**

mammal /ˈmæmᵊl/ *noun* [C] an animal that feeds its babies on milk from its body **memeli hayvan**

mammoth /ˈmæməθ/ *adjective* very large **muazzam,** *a mammoth task/project*

oʻ**man¹** /mæn/ *noun plural* **men 1** [C] an adult male human **adam** *a young/tall man* ○ *men and women* **2** [U] used to refer to both men and women **insanoğlu, ademoğlu** *Man is still more intelligent than the cleverest robot.* ⊃See also: **best man, garbage man, no-man's land,** the **man/ person, etc** in the **street.**

man² /mæn/ *verb* [T] **manning,** *past* **manned** to be present somewhere, especially in order to operate a machine **kullanmak, çalıştırmak, işletmek, idare etmek** *The emergency room is manned 24 hours a day.*

oʻ**manage** /ˈmænɪdʒ/ *verb* **1** DO SUCCESSFULLY [I, T] to do something or deal with something successfully **başarmak, becermek; ...a/ebilmek** *Will you be able to manage on your own?* ○ [+ to do sth] *Anyway, we managed to get there on time.* **2** CONTROL [T] to be in control of an office, shop, team, etc **yönetmek, idare etmek** *He used to manage the bookshop on King Street.* **3** USE TIME/MONEY [T] to use or organize your time or money **(zaman, para) kullanmak, kontrol etmek, idare etmek** *He's no good at managing his money.* **4** HAVE ENOUGH MONEY [I] to have enough money to live **geçinmek, yaşamını sürdürmek** *How can anyone manage on such a low income?*

manageable /ˈmænɪdʒəbl/ *adjective* easy to control **idare edilebilir, başa çıkılabilir** *Are they going to reduce classes to a more manageable size?*

management ...... İLE BİRLİKTE KULLANILAN KELİMELER

management **of** sth ● management **skills** ● **middle/ senior** management

oʻ**management** /ˈmænɪdʒmənt/ *noun* **1** [U] being in control of an office, shop, team, etc **idare, yönetim** *management skills/training* **2** [group] the people who are in control of an office, shop, team, etc **yönetim/idareci kadrosu** *middle/senior management*

oʻ**manager** /ˈmænɪdʒəʳ/ *noun* [C] someone in control of an office, shop, team, etc **yönetici, idareci, âmir** *a sales manager* ○ *She's the manager of the local sports club.*

managerial /ˌmænəˈdʒɪəriəl/ *adjective* relating to a manager or management **idarî, yönetsel, yönetimsel** *managerial skills*

managing diˈrector *noun* [C] *mainly UK* the main person in control of a company **genel müdür**

mandate /ˈmændeɪt/ *noun* [C] *formal* support for action given to someone by the people voting for them **(oyla verilen) hak, yetki** *The electorate have given them a clear mandate for social reform.*

mandatory /ˈmændətᵊri/ *adjective formal* If something is mandatory, it must be done. **zorunlu, mecburi, kaçınılmaz**

mane /meɪn/ *noun* [C] the long, thick hair that grows on the necks of animals such as horses or lions **(at, aslan) yelesi**

maneuver¹ *US* (*UK* manoeuvre) /məˈnuːvəʳ/ *noun* [C] **1** a movement that needs care or skill **manevra 2** a clever action, usually done to trick someone **tertip, hile,**

desise, dolap, oyun; manevra *a political/tactical maneuver*

maneuver² *US* (*UK* manoeuvre) /məˈnuːvəʳ/ *verb* [I, T] to move with care or skill **manevra yapmak** *I find big cars difficult to maneuver.*

mangled /ˈmæŋgld/ *adjective* badly crushed and damaged **paramparça olmuş, ezilmiş, hurdahaş olmuş** *a mangled body*

mango /ˈmæŋgəʊ/ *noun* [C] *plural* **mangoes** or **mangos** a tropical fruit that has a green skin and is orange inside **mango, tropik bir meyve**

manhood /ˈmænhʊd/ *noun* [U] the qualities related to being a man and not a boy **erkeklik, erlik, erişkinlik**

mania /ˈmeɪniə/ *noun* [U] extreme enthusiasm or interest **delicesine tutkunluk, düşkünlük, merak, ihtiras** *football mania*

maniac /ˈmeɪniæk/ *noun* [C] *informal* someone who behaves in an extreme or uncontrolled way **manyak, deli, çılgın** *a sex maniac* ○ *He drives like a maniac.*

manic /ˈmænɪk/ *adjective* behaving in an excited and uncontrolled way **manyakça, delice, cinnet geçirmişçesine**

manicure /ˈmænɪkjʊəʳ/ *noun* [C, U] when someone makes your hands look attractive by cleaning and cutting your nails, etc **manikür**

manifest¹ /ˈmænɪfest/ *verb* [T] *formal* to show a quality or condition **göstermek, belli etmek** [often reflexive] *Grief manifests itself in a number of different ways.*

manifest² /ˈmænɪfest/ *adjective* [always before noun] *formal* obvious **açık, aşikâr, belli, apaçık, meydanda** *her manifest lack of interest*

manifestation /ˌmænɪfesˈteɪʃᵊn/ *noun* [C, U] *formal* something which shows that a quality or condition exists **gösterge, belirti, kanıt** *one of the manifestations of the disease*

manifesto /ˌmænɪˈfestəʊ/ *noun* [C] when a political group says publicly what it intends to do **beyanname, bildirge, bildiri**

manipulate /məˈnɪpjəleɪt/ *verb* [T] to control someone or something in a clever way so that they do what you want them to do **ustalıkla idare etmek, yönlendirmek** *She knows how to manipulate the press.* ● **manipulation** /məˌnɪpjəˈleɪʃᵊn/ *noun* [U] **(negatif) yönlendirme**

manipulative /məˈnɪpjələtɪv/ *adjective* A manipulative person controls people in a clever and unpleasant way. **istediğini yaptıran; kendince yönlendiren; çıkarları doğrultusunda zekice yönlendirme yapabilen** *a devious, manipulative little boy*

mankind /mænˈkaɪnd/ *noun* [U] all people, considered as a group **insanoğlu** *the history of mankind*

manly /ˈmænli/ *adjective* having the qualities and appearance that people think a man should have **erkekçe, delikanlıca, erkek gibi** *a deep, manly voice*

man-made /ˌmænˈmeɪd/ *adjective* not natural, but made by people **insan yapısı, kul yapımı, yapay** *man-made fibres* ○ *a man-made lake*

manned /mænd/ *adjective* A place or vehicle that is manned has people working in it. **içinde insan olan** *a manned space flight*

manner .... İLE BİRLİKTE KULLANILAN KELİMELER

in a [similar/traditional/professional, etc] manner ● the manner **of** sth

oʻ**manner** /ˈmænəʳ/ *noun* [no plural] **1** the way in which a person talks and behaves with other people **tavır, hâl, konuşma şekli, tutum, davranış** *an aggressive/*

friendly manner **2** the way something happens or something is done **biçim, şekil, usül, tarz** *They dealt with the problem in a very efficient manner.*

mannerism /'mænºrızºm/ *noun* [C] something strange that someone often does with their face, hands, or voice, and that is part of their personality **kişiliğin bir parçası olan davranış biçimi; konuşma veya hareket tarzı**

manners /'mænəz/ *noun* [plural] polite ways of behaving with other people **terbiye, görgü kuralları; adabımuaşeret kuralları** *bad/good manners* ○ *table manners*

⸻ **manoeuvre (noun)** ...... İLE BİRLİKTE KULLANILAN KELİMELER

carry out/perform a manoeuvre

manoeuvre¹ *UK (US maneuver)* /mə'nu:vəʳ/ *noun* [C] **1** a movement that needs care or skill **manevra 2** a clever action, usually done to trick someone **hile, dolap, oyun** *a political/tactical manoeuvre*

manoeuvre² *UK (US maneuver)* /mə'nu:vəʳ/ *verb* [I, T] to move with care or skill **manevra yapmak** *I find big cars difficult to manoeuvre.*

manpower /'mæn,paʊəʳ/ *noun* [U] the people needed or available to do a job **insan gücü** *a manpower shortage*

mansion /'mænʃºn/ *noun* [C] a very large house **konak, köşk, malikâne**

manslaughter /'mæn,slɔːtəʳ/ *noun* [U] the crime of killing someone without intending to kill them **adam öldürme**

mantelpiece /'mæntºlpiːs/ *(also US mantel) noun* [C] the shelf above a fireplace (= place in a room where wood, etc is burned) **şömine rafı** *There was an old family photo on the mantelpiece.* ⊃Orta kısımdaki renkli sayfalarına bakınız.

mantra /'mæntrə/ *noun* [C] an idea or belief that people often say but do not think about **düşünmeden rastgele söylenen fikir veya inanış; düşünce, fikir** *the mantra of 'democratic reform'*

manual¹ /'mænjuəl/ *adjective* using your hands **elle yapılan** *manual labour/work* ○ *a manual control/gearbox* ● **manually** *adverb* **el ile yapılan**

manual² /'mænjuəl/ *noun* [C] a book that tells you how to use something or do something **el kitabı, kullanma kılavuzu**

manufacture /,mænjə'fæktʃəʳ/ *verb* [T] to produce something, usually in large numbers in a factory **üretmek, imal etmek** *Local industries manufacture plastic products, boats, and clothing.* ● **manufacture** *noun* [U] *the manufacture of computers/margarine* **üretim**

manufacturer /,mænjə'fæktʃºrəʳ/ *noun* [C] a company that manufactures something **imalatçı, yapımcı, üretici, fabrikatör** *a shoe manufacturer*

manufacturing /,mænjə'fæktʃºrɪŋ/ *noun* [U] the production of something, usually in large numbers in a factory **üretim, imalat** *car/food manufacturing*

manure /mə'njʊəʳ/ *noun* [U] solid waste from animals that is used to make plants grow well **hayvan gübresi, tabii gübre** *cow/horse manure*

manuscript /'mænjəskrɪpt/ *noun* [C] a piece of writing or music that has been written, but not published **müsvedde, el yazması kitap/müzik vs.**

o⸺**many** /'meni/ *pronoun, quantifier* **1** used mainly in negative sentences and questions to mean 'a large number of' **birçok, çok** *I don't have many clothes.* ○ *Were there many cars on the road?* ○ *I've got so many things to do this morning.* ○ *You've given me too many potatoes* (= more than I want). ○ *There aren't as many people*

here as last year. **2 how many** used in questions to ask about the number of something **kaç, kaç tane** *anlamında soru sözcüğü How many hours a week do you work?* ○ *How many do you want?* **3 as many as** used before a number or amount to show that the number or amount is large **kadar, kadar çok miktarda/sayıda** *As many as 6000 people may have been infected with the disease.* ⊃See Common learner error at **much**.

Maori /'maʊəri/ *adjective* relating or belonging to the original group of people who lived in New Zealand **Yeni Zelanda'da yaşayan yerli halka ait/ilişkin; Maori** *Maori culture* ● **Maori** *noun* [C] a Maori person **Maori, Maori yerlisi**

⸻ **map** ...... İLE BİRLİKTE KULLANILAN KELİMELER

read a map ● a **detailed** map ● a map of sth ● be (**marked**) on a map ● a **road** map

map /mæp/ *noun* [C] a picture that shows where countries, towns, roads, rivers, etc are **harita** *a road map* ○ *a large-scale map of Europe*

map

maple /'meɪpl/ *noun* [C, U] a tree that has colourful leaves in the autumn and that produces a substance like sugar **akçaağaç** *a maple leaf* ○ *maple syrup*

Mar *written abbreviation for* March **mart ayı**

mar /mɑːʳ/ *verb* [T] **marring,** *past* **marred** *formal* to spoil something **berbat etmek, bozmak, eline yüzüne bulaştırmak** *[often passive] The evening was marred by Meg's appalling behaviour.*

marathon /'mærəθºn/ *noun* [C] **1** a race in which people run for about 26 miles/42 km **maraton: 42 km. süren koşu yarışı** *the London marathon* ○ *a marathon runner* **2** a very long event **çok uzun süren ve yorucu eylem; uzun soluklu eylem** *a dance marathon*

marble /'mɑːbl/ *noun* [U] hard, smooth stone which is often used for decoration **mermer** *green/pink marble* ○ *a marble statue*

march¹ /mɑːtʃ/ *noun* [C] **1** an organized walk by a group to show that they disagree with something **protesto yürüyüşü** *to go on a march* **2** the special type of walking that soldiers do **uygun adım asker yürüyüşü; tören yürüyüşü**

march² /mɑːtʃ/ *verb* [I] **1** to walk somewhere as a group to show that you disagree with something **uygun adım toplu protesto yürüyüşü yapmak** *They marched to London to protest against health cuts.* **2** When soldiers march, they walk together with regular steps. **tören yürüyüşü yapmak 3 march off/up/down,** etc to walk somewhere fast, often because you are angry **kızgın şekilde hızlı adımlarla koşar gibi yürümek**

o⸺**March** /mɑːtʃ/ *(written abbreviation Mar) noun* [C, U] the third month of the year **mart ayı; yılın üçüncü ayı**

mare /meəʳ/ *noun* [C] a female horse **kısrak**

margarine /,mɑːdʒə'riːn/ ⑥ /'mɑːrdʒərɪn/ *noun* [U] a yellow substance made from vegetable oil which you put on bread and use in cooking **bitkisel yağ, margarin**

margin /'mɑːdʒɪn/ *noun* [C] **1** the difference between two amounts of time, money, etc, usually between people in a competition **özellikle yarışmada iki zaman/para vs. arasındaki fark, marj** *to win by a narrow/wide margin* ○ *He took third place by a*

margin *of seven minutes.* **2** an empty space down the side of a page of writing **sayfa kenarlarında bırakılan boşluk** *You can make notes in the margin.* **3 a margin of error** the amount by which a calculation can be wrong but still produce a good result **hata marjı/payı** *a margin of error of 5 percent*

marginal /ˈmɑːdʒɪnᵊl/ *adjective* small and not important **kıyıda köşede kalan, küçük ve önemsiz** *a marginal effect/improvement*

marginalize (*also UK* -ise) /ˈmɑːdʒɪnᵊlaɪz/ *verb* [T] to treat someone or something as if they are not important **birine bir şeye önemsizmiş gibi davranmak** [often passive] *The poorest countries are increasingly marginalized from the world economy.*

marginally /ˈmɑːdʒɪnᵊli/ *adverb* by a small amount **biraz, az miktarda, azar azar** *marginally more expensive*

marijuana /ˌmærɪˈwɑːnə/ *mainly US* (*mainly UK* **cannabis**) *noun* [U] a drug that some people smoke for pleasure and that is illegal in many countries **haşiş, marihuana**

marina /məˈriːnə/ *noun* [C] an area of water where people keep their boats **yat limanı, marina**

marinate /ˈmærɪneɪt/ (*also* **marinade** /ˌmærɪˈneɪd/) *verb* [T] to add a mixture of oil, wine, herbs, etc to food before cooking it **terbiye etmek, pişirmeden önce yiyeceklere baharat, şarap, yağ karışımı ilave etmek** ● **marinade** /ˌmærɪˈneɪd/ *noun* [C, U] **salamura**

marine¹ /məˈriːn/ *adjective* [always before noun] found in the sea, or relating to the sea **denize ait, denizden** *marine creatures/life* ○ *marine biology*

marine² /məˈriːn/ *noun* [C] a soldier who has been trained to fight at sea and on land **denizci, bahriyeli; deniz piyadesi** *the Marine Corps*

marital /ˈmærɪtᵊl/ *adjective* [always before noun] relating to marriage **evliliğe ait, evlilikle ilgili** *marital problems*

ˈmarital ˌstatus *noun* [U] whether or not someone is married **medeni hâli** *The form asks for personal information such as name, date of birth and marital status.*

maritime /ˈmærɪtaɪm/ *adjective* [always before noun] relating to ships and sea travel **denizciliğe ait** *a maritime museum*

⌐⌐ mark ...... İLE BİRLİKTE KULLANILAN KELİMELER

leave/make a mark ● a mark on sth ● dirty marks

o⁻**mark¹** /mɑːk/ *noun* **1** [AREA] [C] an area of dirt, damage, etc that is left on something **iz, leke, işaret** *You've got a black mark on your nose.* ○ *He's left dirty marks all over the carpet.* **2** [SCORE] [C] a number or letter that is written on a piece of work, saying how good the work is **not, puan** *She always gets good marks in English.* **3** [LEVEL] [no plural] a particular level, degree, distance, etc **seviye, düzey, mesafe** *They've just passed the 5000m mark.* ○ *Interest rates are somewhere around the seven percent mark.* **4 a mark of sth** a sign or proof that something exists **işaret, iz, belirti, gösterge** *a mark of genius* ○ *There was a minute's silence everywhere as a mark of respect.* **5 leave/make your mark** to do something that makes you successful or makes people notice you **iz bırakmak, damgasını vurmak** ● **6 On your marks. Get set. Go!** something that you say to start a running race **koşu yarışına başlama işareti** ● **7 be wide of the mark** to not be correct or accurate **doğru olmaktan çok uzak olmak; doğrunun yanından bile geçmemek** ⊃See also: **punctuation mark**, **quotation marks.**

o⁻**mark²** /mɑːk/ *verb* **1** [HAPPEN] [T] If an event marks the beginning, end, etc of something, it causes it, or happens at the same time as it. **belirlemek, işaret etmek, göstermek** *His death marks the end of an era in television.* **2** [CELEBRATE] [T] If you mark an occasion, you do something to celebrate it. **belirtmek, göstermek** *They've declared Tuesday a national holiday to mark the 10th anniversary of Independence.* **3** [SHOW A PLACE] [T] to show where something is by drawing or putting something somewhere (**çizerek**) **işaretlemek, belirtmek, göstermek** *I've marked my street on the map for you.* **4** [GIVE RESULTS] [I, T] to check a piece of work or an exam, showing mistakes and giving a letter or number to say how good it is **değerlendirmek, not vermek, puan vermek** *to mark essays* **5** [DIRTY] [T] to leave an area of dirt on something **kirli bırakmak, kirletmek**

mark sth out *phrasal verb* to show the shape or position of something by drawing a line around it **çizerek belirlemek, çizmek**

marked /mɑːkt/ *adjective* very noticeable **göze çarpan, belirgin, bariz** *belirgin, yakın There has been a marked improvement since last year.* ● **markedly** *adverb* **göze çarpan bir şekilde**

marker /ˈmɑːkəʳ/ *noun* [C] **1** (*also* ˈmarker ˌpen) a thick pen used especially for writing on boards **işaretleme kalemi** *a black felt marker* ⊃Orta kısımdaki renkli sayfalarına bakınız. **2** a sign that shows where something is **işaret, belirti**

⌐⌐ market ...... İLE BİRLİKTE KULLANILAN KELİMELER

the market is booming/is growing ● a market collapses ● the market in sth

M

market

o⁻**market¹** /ˈmɑːkɪt/ *noun* [C] **1** [SELLING PLACE] a place where people go to buy or sell things, often outside **çarşı, pazar, alışveriş yapılan açık alan** *a cattle/fish/flower market* ○ *a market stall* **2** [SHOP] *US* a supermarket (= large shop that sells food) **büyük bakkal, market 3** [BUSINESS] the buying and selling of something **alışveriş, ticaret, pazarlama** *the insurance/personal computer market* **4** [BUYING GROUP] all the people who want to buy a particular product, or the area where they live **mal satılıp alınabilecek ülke/şehir/yer; pazar, istek, talep, rağbet** *South America is our largest market.* ○ *Is there a market for* (= will people buy) *second-hand jewellery?* **5 on the market** available to buy **satılık, satılmakta, satışa arzedilmiş** *His house has been on the market for over a year.* ⊃See also: **black market, flea market, free market, niche market, the stock exchange.**

market² /'mɑːkɪt/ *verb* [T] to try to sell products using advertising or other ways of making people want to buy them **pazarlamak** *Their products are very cleverly marketed.*

marketable /'mɑːkɪtəbl/ *adjective* Marketable products or skills are easy to sell because people want them. **satılabilir, pazarlanabilir**

market 'forces *noun* [plural] the way that prices and wages are influenced by how many people want to buy a particular product and how much is available **pazar dengeleri; pazar arz talep dengeleri**

marketing /'mɑːkɪtɪŋ/ *noun* [U] the work of encouraging people to buy a product or service **pazarlama** *a career in marketing/sales and marketing*

marketplace /'mɑːkɪtpleɪs/ *noun* **1 the marketplace** in business, the buying and selling of products **pazar yeri, alışveriş, pazar** *We have to learn to compete in the international marketplace.* **2** [C] an area in a town where there is a market **pazar alanı/yeri; pazarın kurulduğu yer/mahal**

market re'search *noun* [U] the activity of finding out what people like about products and what new things they want to buy **piyasa/pazar araştırması** *a market research company*

'market ,share *noun* [C] the number of things that a company sells compared with the number of things of the same type that other companies sell **pazar payı**

markings /'mɑːkɪŋz/ *noun* [plural] the shapes and colours on an animal or bird **(hayvan veya kuş üzerinde) izler, renkler, şekiller, belirleyici özellikler**

mark-up /'mɑːkʌp/ *noun* [C] the amount by which the price of something is increased before it is sold again **fiyatı belirleyen artış miktarı; belirleyici miktar** *The usual mark-up on clothes is around 20%.*

marmalade /'mɑːm°leɪd/ *noun* [U] a sweet, soft food made with oranges or lemons and often eaten on toast (= cooked bread) **marmelât**

maroon¹ /mə'ruːn/ *noun* [U] a dark red-purple colour **kestane rengi** ● **maroon** *adjective* **kızıl kahve** ⊃Orta kısımdaki renkli sayfalarına bakınız.

maroon² /mə'ruːn/ *verb* **be marooned** to be left somewhere where you cannot get away **mahsur kalmış**

marquee /mɑː'kiː/ *noun* [C] *UK* **1** a large tent used for parties, shows, etc **büyük çadır, otağ 2** *US* a large sign over a cinema or theatre that says what films or shows are playing **sinema veya tiyatro üzerinde gösterimde olan film/gösteri tabelası/neon ışıkları**

marriage ...... İLE BİRLİKTE KULLANILAN KELİMELER

sb's marriage **breaks up/fails** ● sb's marriage **to** sb ● a **happy** marriage

๐**marriage** /'mærɪdʒ/ *noun* **1** [C, U] the legal relationship of a man and a woman being a husband and a wife **evlilik, izdivaç** *a happy marriage* **2** [C] the ceremony where people become a husband and a wife **evlenme; evlenme töreni** *a marriage ceremony/certificate*

๐**married** /'mærɪd/ *adjective* **1** A married man or woman has a wife or husband. **evli** *a married couple* ○ *She's been married to David for nearly ten years.* ○ *As far as I know, they're very happily married.* ⊃Opposite unmarried. **2 get married** to begin a legal relationship with someone as their husband or wife **evlenmek** *We got married last year.*

marrow /'mærəʊ/ *noun UK* **1** [C, U] a large vegetable which has dark green skin and is white on the inside **kabak, sakız kabağı 2** [U] (*also* **bone marrow**) the soft substance inside bones **ilik, kemik iliği**

๐**marry** /'mæri/ *verb* **1** [I, T] to begin a legal relationship with someone as their husband or wife **evlenmek** *Will you marry me?* ○ *He never married.* **2** [T] to officially make people become a husband and a wife in a ceremony **evlendirmek** *We were married by our local vicar.*

Mars /mɑːz/ *noun* [no plural] the planet that is fourth from the Sun, after the Earth and before Jupiter **Mars; güneş sistemindeki Dünya'dan sonra Jüpiter'den önce gelen gezegen**

marsh /mɑːʃ/ *noun* [C, U] an area of soft, wet land **bataklık**

marshal /'mɑːʃ°l/ *noun* [C] **1** someone who helps to organize or control a large public event **(büyük toplumsal eylem) düzenleyici, teşrifatçı, protokol görevlisi** *race marshals* **2** an important officer in police or fire departments in the US (**ABD**) **üst düzey polis müdürü, itfaiye şefi** ⊃See also: field marshal.

marshmallow /ˌmɑːʃ'mæləʊ/ ⓊⓈ /'mɑːrʃˌmæləʊ/ *noun* [C, U] a soft, white food made from sugar **lokuma benzer hafif şekerleme, marşmalov**

martial art /ˌmɑːʃ°l'ɑːt/ *noun* [C] one of the traditional Japanese or Chinese skills of fighting, done as a sport in western countries **yakın dövüş, yakın dövüş sporu**

martial law /ˌmɑːʃ°l'lɔː/ *noun* [U] the control of a country by its army instead of by its usual leaders **sıkı yönetim; askeri darbe yönetimi** *to declare martial law*

Martian /'mɑːʃ°n/ *noun* [C] in stories, someone from the planet Mars **Marslı**

martyr /'mɑːtəʳ/ *noun* [C] someone who dies for their beliefs **şehit** *a Catholic martyr* ● **martyrdom** *noun* [U] **şehitlik**

marvel¹ /'mɑːv°l/ *noun* [C] something really surprising, exciting, or good **şaşırtıcı, harika, mucize** *a marvel of modern technology*

marvel² /'mɑːv°l/ *verb* [I] *UK* **marvelling**, *past* **marvelled**, *US* **marveling**, *past* **marveled** to admire something very much **hayret etmek, şaşmak** *I'm just marvelling at your skills.*

marvellous *UK* (*US* **marvelous**) /'mɑːv°ləs/ *adjective* extremely good **olağanüstü, harikulade, fevkalade, mükemmel** *What a marvellous idea!* ● **marvellously** *UK* (*US* **marvelously**) *adverb* **mükemmel bir şekilde**

Marxism /'mɑːksɪz°m/ *noun* [U] the political and economic ideas of Karl Marx **Marksizm**

Marxist /'mɑːksɪst/ *adjective* relating to Marxism **Marksizm'e ilişkin** *Marxist ideology* ● **Marxist** *noun* [C] someone who supports Marxism **Marksist**

mascara /mæs'kɑːrə/ *noun* [U] a dark substance that you put on your eyelashes (= hairs that grow above and below your eyes) to make them look longer and thicker **rimel** ⊃See picture at make up.

mascot /'mæskɒt/ *noun* [C] a toy or a child that a person or a team takes with them to bring them luck **maskot, uğur** *He's our lucky mascot.*

masculine /'mæskjəlɪn/ *adjective* **1** having qualities that are typical of men **erkeğe ait/özgü, eril** *a masculine appearance/voice* **2** in some languages, belonging to a group of nouns or adjectives that have the same grammatical behaviour. The other groups are 'feminine' and 'neuter'. **bazı dillerde aynı dilbilgisi özelliğini gösteren bir grup isim ve sıfata ait**

masculinity /ˌmæskjə'lɪnəti/ *noun* [U] the qualities that are typical of men **erkeklik**

mash /mæʃ/ *verb* [T] to crush food until it is soft **ezmek, ezerek püre haline getirmek** *UK mashed potato/ US mashed potatoes*

mask

mask¹ /mɑːsk/ *noun* [C] a covering for the face that protects, hides, or decorates the person wearing it **maske** つSee also: **gas mask**.

mask² /mɑːsk/ *verb* [T] to prevent something from being noticed **maskelemek, gizlemek, saklamak, örtmek** *I've had to put some flowers in there to* **mask** *the smell.*

masked /mɑːskt/ *adjective* wearing a mask **maskeli** *a masked gunman*

masochism /'mæsəkɪzᵃm/ *noun* [U] when people get pleasure from being hurt **acı çekmekten zevk alma** ● **masochist** *noun* [C] someone who gets pleasure from being hurt **acı çekmekten zevk alan**

masochistic /ˌmæsə'kɪstɪk/ *adjective* getting pleasure from being hurt **acı ve eziyetten hoşlanan** *masochistic behaviour*

masonry /'meɪsᵃnri/ *noun* [U] the parts of a building that are made of bricks or stone **tuğla veya taş duvar**

masquerade /ˌmæskᵃr'eɪd/ *verb* **masquerade as sb/sth** *phrasal verb* to pretend to be someone or something **...gibi davranmak; ...kimliğine bürünmek; kılığına girmek** *She's just a teacher masquerading as an academic.*

mass¹ /mæs/ *noun* **1** [C] a solid lump with no clear shape **yığın, küme, sürü** *The sauce was now a sticky mass in the bottom of the pan.* **2 a mass of sth** a large amount or number of something **bir yığın, bir sürü, yığınlarla** *She had a mass of blond curls.* **3** [U] in physics, the amount of substance that something contains **(fizik) kütle** *One litre of water has a mass of one kilogram.* **4 masses** *informal* a large amount or number of something **epeyce, bir hayli, pek çok** *I've got masses of work to do.* **5 the masses** the ordinary people who form the largest part of society **halk kitleleri, yığınlar** *He failed to win the support of the masses.*

mass² /mæs/ *adjective* [always before noun] involving a lot of people **toplu, kitle** *mass destruction/unemployment* ○ *a mass murderer*

mass³ /mæs/ *verb* [I, T] *formal* to come together somewhere in large numbers, or make people or things do this **topla(n)mak, kitleler oluşturmak, bir araya gelmek** *Over 20,000 demonstrators massed in the town's main square.*

Mass, mass /mæs/ *noun* [C, U] a religious ceremony in some Christian churches in which people eat bread and drink wine **Aşai Rabbani Ayini, Komünyon** *to go to Mass*

massacre /'mæsəkər/ *noun* [C] the killing of a lot of people **katliam, toplu yok etme** *He ordered the massacre of over 2,000 women and children.* ● **massacre** *verb* [T] *Hundreds of civilians were massacred in the raid.* **katliam yapmak**

massage /'mæsɑːdʒ/ ⓤ /mə'sɑːdʒ/ *noun* [C, U] the activity of rubbing or pressing parts of someone's body in order to make them relax or to stop their muscles hurting **masaj** *to have a massage* ○ *She gave me a foot massage.* ● **massage** *verb* [T] *Would you massage my shoulders?* **masaj yapmak**

massive /'mæsɪv/ *adjective* very big **muazzam, iri, çok büyük, muhteşem** *a massive building* ○ *massive debts*

mass-market /ˌmæs'mɑːkɪt/ *adjective* describes something that is made to be sold to as many people as possible **toplu satış; kitle satışı için yapılmış** ●**mass ˌmarket** *noun* [C] **toplu pazar**

the ˌmass 'media *noun* [group] newspapers, television, and radio **kitle iletişim araçları**

mast /mɑːst/ *noun* [C] **1** a tall pole on a boat that supports its sails **gemi direği 2** a tall metal pole that sends out television, radio or mobile phone signals **anten direği**

master¹ /'mɑːstər/ *noun* [C] **1** [IN CHARGE] In the past, a servant's master was the man that they worked for. **efendi, sahip, patron 2** [TEACHER] *old-fashioned* a male teacher **erkek öğretmen** *the Latin master* **3** [SKILL] someone who does something very well **usta, işinin ehli, üstat, sanatkâr** *He was a master of disguise.* **4** [FOR COPYING] a document or recording from which copies can be made **ana/esas/asıl belge/kayıt vs. 5 Master of Arts/Science, etc** a higher university qualification which usually takes 1 or 2 more years of study after your first qualification, or a person who has this qualification **Sosyal/Fen Bilimleri alanında Yüksek Lisans 6 Master's (degree)** a higher university qualification **Yüksek Lisans** *to study for a Master's degree* **7 Master** *formal* a title for a boy, used before his family name or full name **küçük bey** *Master Thomas Mills*

master² /'mɑːstər/ *verb* [T] to learn how to do something well **iyice öğrenmek, hakim olmak, ustalık kazanmak** *to master a technique* ○ *He lived for several years in Italy but never quite mastered the language.*

master³ /'mɑːstər/ *adjective* [always before noun] having the skills for a particular job **beceri sahibi olan, kabiliyetli, bilgili** *a master chef/craftsman*

masterful /'mɑːstəfᵃl/ *adjective* done with great skill **ustalıkla yapılmış, beceri dolu, mükemmel** *a masterful display of golf*

mastermind /'mɑːstəmaɪnd/ *verb* [T] to plan every detail of a complicated event or activity and make sure that it happens **ustaca planlamak, zekice tasarlamak, akıllıca tertip etmek** *He allegedly masterminded both bomb attacks in the region.* ● **mastermind** *noun* [C] *It is thought he was the mastermind behind* (= the person who planned) *last year's bombing campaign.* **ustaca, zekice yapılmış plan**

masterpiece /'mɑːstəpiːs/ *noun* [C] a painting, book, or film that is generally considered to be of excellent quality **şaheser, başyapıt, en iyi eser** *'Mona Lisa' is widely regarded as Leonardo da Vinci's masterpiece.*

mastery /'mɑːstᵃri/ *noun* **1 mastery of sth** great skill or understanding of something **ustalık, maharet, beceri, hâkimiyet** *his mastery of the Japanese language* **2 mastery of/over sth** control over something **üstünlük, hakimiyet, bir konuda bilgi/kontrol sahibi olma** *The two countries battled for mastery over the region.*

masturbate /'mæstəbeɪt/ *verb* [I] to make yourself feel sexually excited by touching your sexual organs **cinsel organına dokunarak kendini tatmin etmek, mastürbasyon yapmak** ● **masturbation** /ˌmæstə'beɪʃᵃn/ *noun* [U] **mastürbasyon**

mat /mæt/ *noun* [C] **1** a piece of thick material that you put on the floor, often in order to protect it **küçük yaygı/kilim, ufak halı** *There's a mat by the door for you to wipe your feet on.* **2** a small piece of plastic or

M

other material that you put on a table so that hot plates and liquid will not damage it **nihale**

🧩 **match** ...... İLE BİRLİKTE KULLANILAN KELİMELER

play/lose/win a match ● a match **against** sb ● **in** a match

o▪**match¹** /mætʃ/ *noun* **1** GAME [C] a sports competition in which two teams or teams compete against each other **karşılaşma, müsabaka, maç** *a football/tennis match* **2** FIRE [C] a thin, wooden stick which produces a flame when you rub one end of it against a rough surface **kibrit** *a box of matches* **3** ATTRACTIVE [no plural] If something is a good match for something else, it looks attractive next to it, usually because it is the right colour. **eş, benzer, uyan, iyi giden, uyum içinde** *The curtains look nice - they're a perfect match for the sofa.* **4** RELATIONSHIP [no plural] If two people who are having a relationship are a good match, they are very suitable for each other. **(iki kişi) uyum içinde olan, birbirine yakışanlar 5 be no match for sb/sth** to not be as good as someone or something else **boy ölçüşememek, eline su dökememek, aşık atamamak, dengi olamamak** *Gibson ran well but was no match for the young Italian.*

o▪**match²** /mætʃ/ *verb* **1** BE THE SAME [I, T] If two things match, they are the same colour or type. **eşleşmek, uymak, tutmak, benzemek** *I can't find anything to match my green shirt.* ○ *Your socks don't match.* ○ *Traces of blood found on Walker's clothing matched the victim's blood type.* **2** CHOOSE [T] to choose someone or something that is suitable for a particular person, activity, or purpose **eşlemek, ...ın/in uyanını bulmak, ...ın/in uygun düşenini bulmak** *In the first exercise, you have to match the famous person to their country of origin.* **3** BE AS GOOD AS [T] to be as good as someone or something else **uymak, gitmek, yakışmak** *It would be difficult to match the service this airline gives to its customers.*
match up *phrasal verb* If two pieces of information match up, they are the same. **birbirini tutmak** *Their accounts of what happened that evening didn't match up.*
match sb/sth up *phrasal verb* to choose someone or something that is suitable for a particular person, activity, or purpose **eşleştirmek, uygun olanı/uyanı seçmek** *They look at your interests and try to match you up with someone suitable.*
match up to sth *phrasal verb* to be as good as something else **uymak, onun kadar iyi olmak** *Nothing that he wrote after this point ever matched up to his early work.*

matchbox /'mætʃbɒks/ *noun* [C] a small box containing matches **kibrit kutusu**

matching /'mætʃɪŋ/ *adjective* [always before noun] having the same colour or pattern as something else **uygun, uyumlu olan** *She wore purple shorts and a matching T-shirt.*

mate¹ /meɪt/ *noun* [C] **1** FRIEND *UK informal* a friend **arkadaş** *She's my best mate.* ○ *Pete was there with a couple of mates.* **2** TALKING TO A MAN *UK informal* You call a man 'mate' when you are speaking to him informally. **ahbap, arkadaş, dost** *Thanks, mate.* **3** ANIMAL an animal's sexual partner **eşi; dişisi/erkeği**

mate² /meɪt/ *verb* [I] When animals mate, they have sex in order to produce babies. **(hayvanlar) çiftleşmek**

o▪**material¹** /mə'tɪəriəl/ *noun* **1** SUBSTANCE [C, U] a solid substance from which things can be made **madde, malzeme** *building materials* ○ *Crude oil is used as the raw material for making plastics.* **2** CLOTH [C, U] cloth for making clothes, curtains, etc **kumaş** *Her dress was made of a soft, silky material.* **3** INFORMATION [U] the facts or ideas in a piece of writing **bir yazıdaki gerçekler ve fikirler** *I'm collecting material for an article that I'm writing.*

material² /mə'tɪəriəl/ *adjective* relating to money and possessions and not emotions or thoughts **maddî, maddesel** *the material world*

materialism /mə'tɪəriəlɪzᵊm/ *noun* [U] the belief that having money and possessions is the most important thing in life **maddecilik, materyalizm** ● **materialistic** /mə,tɪəriə'lɪstɪk/ *adjective* believing in materialism **maddeci, maddiyatçı, materyalist**

materialize (*also UK* -ise) /mə'tɪəriəlaɪz/ *verb* [I] If something does not materialize, it does not happen. **gerçekleşmek** *She was promised a promotion but it never materialized.*

materials /mə'tɪəriəlz/ *noun* [plural] the equipment that you need for a particular activity **malzeme, gereç, alet edavat, materyal** *teaching/writing materials*

maternal /mə'tɜːnᵊl/ *adjective* **1** like a mother **anne gibi, anneye özgü, anne ile/annelikle ilgili** *I've never had much of a maternal instinct* (= wish to have children). **2** [always before noun] A maternal relation is part of your mother's family. **anne tarafına ait; anne ile kan bağına ilişkin** *He's my maternal grandfather.*

maternity /mə'tɜːnəti/ *adjective* [always before noun] related to pregnancy and birth **gebelik, hamilelik** *maternity clothes*

maternity leave /mə'tɜːnəti,liːv/ *noun* [U] a period of weeks or months that a mother spends away from her usual job so that she can look after a new baby **doğum izni**

math /mæθ/ *noun* [U] *US short for* mathematics **matematik**

mathematical /,mæθᵊm'ætɪkᵊl/ *adjective* relating to mathematics **matematik ile ilgili, matematiksel** *a mathematical formula/equation* ● **mathematically** *adverb* **matematiksel**

mathematician /,mæθᵊmə'tɪʃᵊn/ *noun* [C] someone who studies mathematics **matematikçi, matematik öğrenimi yapan**

mathematics /mæθᵊm'ætɪks/ *noun* [U] *formal* the study or science of numbers and shapes **matematik, matematik bilimi**

maths /mæθs/ *noun* [U] *UK short for* mathematics **matematik**

matinée /'mætɪneɪ/ ⑮ /mætə'neɪ/ *noun* [C] an afternoon performance of a play or film **matine**

matrimony /'mætrɪməni/ *noun* [U] *formal* the state of being married **evlilik, izdivaç**

matron /'meɪtrᵊn/ *noun* [C] **1** NURSE *UK old-fashioned* a female nurse in a school, or a female nurse who is in charge of other nurses in a hospital **bayan hemşire; başhemşire 2** WOMAN *US* a married woman, especially one who is old or a widow (= woman whose husband has died) **kocası ölmüş ve tekrar evlenmiş yaşlı evli kadın 3** PRISON/SCHOOL *US* a woman who is a manager at some hospitals, schools, prisons, etc **(hastane, okul, hapishane) müdire**

matt *UK* (*US* matte) /mæt/ *adjective* not shiny **donuk, parlak olmayan, mat** *a matt photograph* ○ *matt paint*

🧩 **matter** ...... İLE BİRLİKTE KULLANILAN KELİMELER

consider/discuss/pursue/raise/resolve a matter ● **on** the matter (of sth)

o▪**matter¹** /'mætər/ *noun* **1** SUBJECT [C] a subject or situation that you need to think about, discuss, or deal with **konu, mesele, sorun** *I've been thinking about this matter for a long time.* ○ *He denied any knowledge of the matter.* ○ *To make matters worse, our car broke down!* **2** SUBSTANCE [U] the physical substances that exist in the universe **(fen) madde 3** TYPE OF THING [U] a particular type of substance or thing **madde, cisim** *vegetable matter* ○ *printed matter* **4 what's the matter** used to ask or talk about the reason for a problem 'Neyin var?', 'Sorun nedir?', 'Ne oluyor?', 'Ne oldu?' *What's the matter with your leg?* **5 there's something/nothing the matter** used to say that there is/is not a problem 'Bir sorun var/yok!', 'Bir aksilik/problem var/yok!' *There's something the matter with the washing machine.* **6 a matter of days/weeks/feet, etc** used in expressions describing how small an amount or period of time is **bir kaç gün/hafta/ayak gibi kısa bir süre/mesafeyi vurgulamada kullanılır** *The aircraft missed each other by a matter of feet.* **7 a matter of confidence/luck/waiting, etc** If something is a matter of confidence/luck/waiting, etc, that is what you need for it to happen. **güven/şans/zaman meselesi** *Learning languages is just a matter of hard work.* **8 no matter how/what/when, etc** used to emphasize that something cannot be changed **ne olursa olsun; kesinlikle; yüzde yüz; ...(nasıl/ne/ne zaman) olursa olsun** *I never manage to lose any weight, no matter how hard I try.* **9 as a matter of fact** used to emphasize that something is true, especially when it is surprising **aslında, esasında, doğruyu söylemek gerekirse, doğrusu, işin doğrusu/esası/özü** *As a matter of fact, I used to live next door to him.* **10 a matter of course** If something happens as a matter of course, it always happens as part of the normal process or system. **işin esasına uygun olarak, usulen, olağan, normal olarak** *Babies were tested for the disease as a matter of course.* **11 a matter of life and/or death** a serious situation where people could die **ölüm kalım meselesi** *Getting water to these people is a matter of life and death.* **12 it's only a matter of time** If you say that it is only a matter of time before something happens, you are sure it will happen but you do not know when. **sadece biraz zaman meselesi; an meselesi; zaman her şeyi gösterecek 13 be no laughing matter** If a subject is no laughing matter, it is serious and not something that people should joke about. **gülünecek bir husus değil; şakası yok; gayet ciddi** ⊃See also: **subject matter.**

o╼**matter²** /ˈmætə**r**/ *verb* [I] to be important, or to affect what happens **önemli olmak, olanları etkilemek** *It doesn't matter to me whether he comes or not.* ○ *"I've forgotten to bring your book back." "It doesn't matter - there's no hurry."*

matter-of-fact /ˌmætərəvˈfækt/ *adjective* not showing emotion when you talk about something **gerçekçi, hayale kapılmayan, realist** *a matter-of-fact tone/manner* ● **matter-of-factly** *adverb* **aslında!**

matting /ˈmætɪŋ/ *noun* [U] strong, rough material for covering floors **yaygı, yaygı**

mattress /ˈmætrəs/ *noun* [C] the soft, comfortable part of a bed that you lie on **döşek, minder, şilte**

mature¹ /məˈtjʊər/ *adjective* **1** completely grown or developed **olgun, kâmil, ergin, erişkin** *sexually mature* ○ *mature trees* **2** Mature people behave like adults in a way which shows they are well developed emotionally. **olgun, yetişkin** *She seems very mature for thirteen.* ⊃Opposite **immature.**

mature² /məˈtjʊər/ *verb* [I] **1** AGE to become completely grown or developed **olgunlaşmak, tamamen gelişmek, kıvamını bulmak 2** BEHAVIOUR to start to behave in a more mature way **gelişmek, olgunlaşmak, yetişmek** *Girls mature sooner than boys.* **3** MONEY If an investment (= money you have given to a bank or a company in order to make a profit) matures, you receive the money you have made from it. **faiz/yatırım geliri elde etmek**

maˌture ˈstudent *noun* [C] a college or university student who is older than the usual age **yaşı geçkin öğrenci**

maturity /məˈtjʊərəti/ *noun* [U] **1** the quality of behaving like an adult, in a way which shows that you are well developed emotionally **olgunluk, erişkinlik, yetişkinlik** *She shows remarkable maturity for a child of 13.* **2** when someone or something is completely grown or developed **büyüklük, olgunluk, gelişmişlik, erginlik** *Penguins reach maturity in late summer.*

maul /mɔːl/ *verb* [T] **1** If you are mauled by an animal, you are injured by its teeth or claws (= the sharp parts of its feet). **(hayvan tarafından) yaralanmak, parçalanmak; (hayvan) yaralamak, parçalamak** [often passive] *He was mauled by a lion.* **2** to criticize someone or something very badly **acımasızca eleştirmek; şiddetle tenkit etmek** [often passive] *His film was mauled by critics.*

mausoleum /ˌmɔːsəˈliːəm/ *noun* [C] a building where dead people are buried **anıtkabir, mozole**

mauve /məʊv/ *noun* [U] a pale purple colour **uçuk mor, leylak rengi** ● **mauve** *adjective* **leylak rengi**

maverick /ˈmævərɪk/ *noun* [C] someone who thinks and behaves in an unusual way **başına buyruk kişi, bireyci kimse; (grubun) dışında olan kimse, bağımsız** *a maverick cop/politician*

max¹ /mæks/ *adjective* **1** *informal* maximum (= the largest amount allowed or possible), often used after numbers **en yüksek, en büyük, maksimum** *The trip should take 30 minutes max.* **2 to the max** *informal* as much as possible **mümkün olduğu kadar çok; en yüksek/üst düzeye kadar** *He lived life to the max.*

max² *verb*

max out *phrasal verb informal* to use all that is available of something, especially money **bütün kaynakları sonuna kadar kullanmak** *We maxed out our credit cards when we bought all that new furniture.*

maxim /ˈmæksɪm/ *noun* [C] a phrase which gives advice **özdeyiş, düstur** *Our company works on the maxim that small is beautiful.*

maximize (*also UK* -ise) /ˈmæksɪmaɪz/ *verb* [T] to increase something as much as you can **en üst düzeye çıkarmak, artırmak; maksimum seviyeye çıkarmak** *to maximize profits*

o╼**maximum¹** /ˈmæksɪməm/ *adjective* [always before noun] The maximum amount of something is the largest that is allowed or possible. **azami, en yüksek, en büyük, maksimum** *the maximum temperature/speed* ⊃Opposite **minimum.**

ıı..... *maximum* **...... İLE BİRLİKTE KULLANILAN KELİMELER**

reach a maximum ● a maximum **of** [10/50%, etc] ● **up to** a maximum [of 10/50%, etc]

maximum² /ˈmæksɪməm/ *noun* [no plural] the largest amount that is allowed or possible **azami, en büyük miktar** *The school has a maximum of 30 students per class.*

o╼**may** /meɪ/ *modal verb* **1** used to talk about what is possibly true or will possibly happen **...a/e bilmek; ...ması/mesi mümkün olmak** *There may be other problems that we don't know about.* ○ *I think I may have a cold.* **2** *formal* used to ask or give permission **izin vermek/müsaade etmek; izin istemek; ricada bulunmak** *May I be excused, please?* ○ *You may begin.* **3 may (well) ... but** used to show that the first thing you say is not important when compared to another fact **...olabilir fakat ...dır/dir** *It may be cheap but it's not very good.* ⊃See study page **Modal verbs** on page Centre 22.

⌐**May** /meɪ/ noun [C, U] the fifth month of the year **mayıs ayı, yılın beşinci ayı**

⌐**maybe** /'meɪbi/ adverb **1** possibly **belki** *Maybe we're too early.* ○ *It could take a month, or maybe more, to complete.* **2** used to suggest something **belki, olsa olsa, muhtemel olarak** *Maybe Ted would like to go.*

mayhem /'meɪhem/ noun [U] a situation in which there is no order or control **kargaşa, arbede, karışıklık** *With five kids running around, it was complete mayhem.*

mayonnaise /ˌmeɪə'neɪz/ noun [U] a thick, cold, white sauce that is made from eggs and oil **mayonez**

mayor /meəʳ/ noun [C] the person who is elected to be the leader of the group that governs a town or city **belediye başkanı**

maze /meɪz/ noun [C] a complicated system of paths where you can easily become lost **labirent, karmaşa, karışık durum**

MB written abbreviation for megabyte (= a unit for measuring the amount of information a computer can store) **megabayt; bilgisayarın taşıyabileceği bilginin miktarını ölçme birimi** *This program needs 8 MB of hard-disk space.*

MBA /ˌembi:'eɪ/ noun [C] abbreviation for Master of Business Administration: an advanced degree in business, or a person who has this degree **İşletme/İş idaresi Yüksek Lisansı** *a Harvard MBA*

McCoy /mə'kɔɪ/ noun **the real McCoy** informal the real thing, and not a copy or something similar **gerçek şey, benzeri veya kopyası olmayan** *Cheap sparkling wines cannot be labelled 'champagne' - it has to be the real McCoy.*

MD /ˌem'di/ abbreviation for Doctor of Medicine **Tıp Doktoru**

⌐**me** /mi:/ pronoun used after a verb or preposition to refer to the person who is speaking or writing **beni, bana** *She gave me some money.* ○ *She never gave it to me.* ○ *Lydia is three years younger than me.* ○ *It wasn't me!*

meadow /'medəʊ/ noun [C] a field of grass, often with flowers **çayır, otlak, mera**

meagre UK (US **meager**) /'mi:gəʳ/ adjective not enough in amount **az, yetersiz, kıt** *a meagre ration/salary*

---
meal .... İLE BİRLİKTE KULLANILAN KELİMELER

cook/eat/have/prepare a meal ● a **[two/three, etc.] course** meal
---

⌐**meal** /mi:l/ noun [C] **1** when you eat, or the food that you eat at that time **öğün, yemek** *a three-course meal* **2 make a meal of sth** UK to spend more time and energy doing something than is necessary **...a/e gereğinden çok çaba ve zaman harcamak** *A simple apology will do. There's no need to make a meal of it!* ⊃See also: a **square²** meal.

mealtime /'mi:ltaɪm/ noun [C] when you eat **yemek, öğün/vakti/zamanı** *These days I only see him at mealtimes.*

⌐**mean¹** /mi:n/ verb [T] past **meant** /ment/ **1** MEANING to have a particular meaning **demek, anlamına gelmek** *What does 'perpendicular' mean?* ○ *The red light means stop.* **2** EXPRESS to intend to express a fact or opinion **demek istemek, kasdetmek** *I didn't mean that as a criticism.* ○ *What exactly do you mean by 'old-fashioned'?* **3 mean to do sth** to intend to do something **kasdetmek, yapmaya niyet etmek, yapmak niyetinde olmak; yapmayı tasarlamak** *I didn't mean to hurt her.* **4** RESULT to have a particular result **önemli bir sonucu olmak, anlamına gelmek** *These changes will mean better health care for everyone.* ○ *[+ (that)] It doesn't mean that you can stop working.* **5** SERIOUS to be

serious about something that you have said **söylediğinde ciddi/samimi olmak** *I'll take that sandwich away if you don't eat it properly - I mean it!* **6** IMPORTANT to have an important emotional effect on someone **önemli duygusal bir etkisi olmak** *You don't know what it means to me to get this letter.* ○ *Their support has meant a lot to us.* **7 have been meaning to do sth** to have been wanting and planning to do something **uzun süredir planlamakta/istemekte olmak** *I've been meaning to call you for weeks.* **8 be meant to do sth** If you are meant to do something, that is what you should do in order to behave correctly. **amaçlamak, tasarlamak, ...niyetiyle yapmak** *You're meant to shake the bottle first.* **9 mean well** to intend to behave in a kind way **iyi niyetli olmak** *I know my parents mean well, but I wish they wouldn't interfere.* **10 I mean a** CONTINUING SENTENCE something that people often say before they continue their sentence **'Pardon', 'Affedersiniz...'** *I mean, I don't dislike her.* **b** CORRECTING YOURSELF something that you say in order to correct yourself **'Yani...', 'Demek istiyorum ki...'** *We went there in May - I mean June.*

mean² /mi:n/ adjective **1** UNKIND unkind and unpleasant **kaba, terbiyesiz, nezaketsiz** *I thought my sister was being mean to me.* **2** NOT GENEROUS mainly UK A mean person does not like spending money, especially on other people. **cimri, pinti, hasis, eli sıkı** *He's too mean to buy her a ring.* **3** VIOLENT mainly US A mean person or animal is strong and violent, and makes people frightened. **korkutucu, ürkütücü, kaba ve vahşi** *He's a big, mean guy.* **4** GOOD [always before noun] informal very good **çok iyi, mükemmel, usta** *I make a mean spaghetti.* **5** AVERAGE [always before noun] In maths, a mean number is an average number. **(matematik) ortalama** *Their mean age at death was 84.6.* **6 no mean** used to describe something very difficult **imkânsız, çok güç/zor; henüz mümkün olmayan** *Setting up a business in two days was no mean feat* (= was a difficult thing to do).

mean³ /mi:n/ noun [no plural] formal the average **ortalama**

meander /mi'ændəʳ/ verb **1 meander along/around/through, etc** If a river, a road, or a line of something meanders, it has many curves. **(nehir, yol, hat, vb.) kıvrılmak, bükülmek** *The coast road meanders along the beach for miles.* **2 meander around/from/off, etc** to move around with no clear purpose **amaçsızca oyalanmak, oyalanarak dolaşmak, aylak aylak gezinmek** *We meandered around town for a couple of hours.*

---
meaning .... İLE BİRLİKTE KULLANILAN KELİMELER

different/hidden/precise/real/true meaning ● **convey/explain/grasp/understand** the meaning of sth
---

⌐**meaning** /'mi:nɪŋ/ noun **1** [C, U] The meaning of words, signs, or actions is what they express or represent. **anlam, mana** *The word 'squash' has several meanings.* ○ *The meaning of her gesture was clear.* **2** [U, no plural] purpose or emotional importance **gaye, duygusal önem, değer** *She felt that her life had no meaning.*

meaningful /'mi:nɪŋfᵊl/ adjective **1** USEFUL useful, serious, or important **faydalı, ciddi, önemli, manidar, anlamlı** *a meaningful discussion* **2** WITH MEANING having a clear meaning which people can understand **anlamlı, manalı, açık ve anlaşılır** *a meaningful comparison/conclusion* **3** LOOK intended to show a meaning, often secretly **gizemli, manalı, dikkate değer, manidar** *a meaningful look* ● **meaningfully** adverb **anlamlı bir şekilde**

meaningless /'mi:nɪŋləs/ adjective without any meaning or purpose **anlamsız, amaçsız, boş, beyhude,**

önemsiz *He produced yet another set of meaningless statistics.*

means ...... İLE BİRLİKTE KULLANILAN KELİMELER

(as) a means of (doing) sth ● **the means by which** sth happens/sb does sth

o→**means** /miːnz/ *noun* **1** [C] *plural* **means** a way of doing something **vasıta, yol, araç** *We had no means of communication.* ○ *It was a means of making money.* **2** [plural] money **para, varlık** *We don't have the means to buy the house.* **3 by no means; not by any means** not at all **hiç bie şekilde, asla, kat'iyen, hiç bir zaman** *I'm not an expert by any means.* **4 by all means** something that you say when you are agreeing to let someone do something 'Hay hay!', 'Elbette!', 'Şüphesiz!', 'Lütfen...!' *I have a copy of the report on my desk. By all means have a look at it.*

means-tested /ˈmiːnztestɪd/ *adjective mainly UK* If an amount of money or an activity such as education is means-tested, it is only given to people who are poor enough. **yardım edilen, eğitim yardımı verilen; yardıma muhtaç** *means-tested benefits*

meant /ment/ *past of* mean '**demek', 'anlamına gelmek' fiilinin geçmiş zaman hali**

meantime /ˈmiːnˌtaɪm/ *noun* **in the meantime** in the time between two things happening, or while something else is happening **bu arada, bu esnada, bu zaman zarfında, bu süre içinde** *Your computer won't be arriving till Friday. In the meantime, you can use Julie's.*

o→**meanwhile** /ˈmiːnˌwaɪl/ *adverb* in the time between two things happening, or while something else is happening **bu sırada, bu esnada, bu zaman zarfında, bu süre içinde** *The mother is ill. The child, meanwhile, is living with foster parents.*

measles /ˈmiːzlz/ *noun* [U] an infectious disease which covers your skin in small, red spots **kızamık** ⊃See also: German measles.

measurable /ˈmeʒᵊrəbl/ *adjective* If something is measurable, it is big enough to be measured. **ölçülebilir, farkedilebilir, görülebilir, hissedilebilir** *Extra training has led to measurable improvements in performance.* ⊃Opposite immeasurable.

o→**measure**[1] /ˈmeʒəʳ/ *verb* **1** [JUDGE] [T] to judge the quality, effect, importance, or value of something **değerini/önemini belirlemek, etkisini/kıymetini saptamak** *We will soon be able to measure the results of these policy changes.* ○ *They measured the performance of three different engines.* **2** [FIND SIZE] [T] to find the size, weight, amount, or speed of something **ölçmek, ölçüsünü almak** *I've measured all the windows.* ○ *The distances were measured in kilometres.* **3** [BE SIZE] [I] to be a certain size **belli bir ölçüde/ebatta olmak** *a whale measuring around 60 feet in length*
measure sth out *phrasal verb* to weigh or measure a small amount of something and remove it from a larger amount **miktarını belirlemek, ölçerek almak** *Use a hot spoon to measure out honey into a bowl.*
measure up *phrasal verb* to be good enough, or as good as something or someone else **uymak, ...kadar iyi/yeterli olmak, şartları karşılamak, beklenildiği gibi olmak** *He did not measure up to the requirements of the job.*

o→**measure**[2] /ˈmeʒəʳ/ *noun* **1** [C] a way of achieving something or dealing with a situation **önlem, tedbir** *This arrangement is only a temporary measure.* ○ *We must take preventative measures to stop the spread of the disease.* ○ *security measures* **2 a measure of sth** a good way of judging something **ölçü, derece, kıstas, gösterge** *Ticket sales are not necessarily a measure of*

the show's popularity. **3 a/some measure of sth** *formal* an amount of something **bir miktar, bir derceye kadar, bir ölçüde** *Bulletproof vests give some measure of protection.* **4** [U] a way of measuring something **ölçü, ölçüm, hesaplama** *The basic units of measure we use are distance, time, and mass.* **5 for good measure** as well as something you have already done or given to someone **üstelik, ayrıca, bundan başka/maada** *They stole his passport and wallet, and for good measure beat him unconscious.* ⊃See also: tape measure.

o→**measurement** /ˈmeʒəmənt/ *noun* **1** [PROCESS] [U] the process of measuring something **ölçme, ölçüm 2** [C] the size and shape of something **ölçü** *I've taken measurements of all the rooms.* **3** [WAY OF MEASURING] [U] a way of measuring something **ölçüm** *SI units are the standard units of measurement used all over the world.*

o→**meat** /miːt/ *noun* [U] muscles and other soft parts of animals, used as food **et** *I don't eat meat.* ○ *red/white meat* ⊃Orta kısımdaki renkli sayfalarına bakınız.

mecca /ˈmekə/ *noun* [no plural] a place where particular groups of people like to go because they feel happy there **herkesin gidip görmek istediği yer/mekan** *His Indiana bookstore became a mecca for writers and artists.*

mechanic /mɪˈkænɪk/ *noun* [C] someone whose job is to repair machines **tamirci, teknisyen** *a car mechanic*

mechanical /mɪˈkænɪkᵊl/ *adjective* **1** relating to or operated by machines **makinaya ait, makinayla çalışan, mekanik** *a mechanical engineer* ○ *a mechanical device* **2** If you do something in a mechanical way, you do it without emotion or without thinking about it. **düşünmeden/duygusal bağ kurmadan yapılan; mekanik, otomatik** *a mechanical performance* ● **mechanically** *adverb* **mekanik açıdan**

mechanics /mɪˈkænɪks/ *noun* [U] the study of physical forces on objects and their movement **makina bilimi**

mechanism /ˈmekənɪzᵊm/ *noun* [C] **1** a part of a piece of equipment that does a particular job **bir aletin mekanik parçası/bölümü** *The clock's winding mechanism had broken.* **2** a system for achieving something, or the way that a system works **tertibat, düzenek, sistem, mekanizma** *We need a mechanism for resolving this sort of dispute.*

mechanized (*also UK* -ised) /ˈmekənaɪzd/ *adjective* A mechanized organization or activity uses machines. **makinalaşmış, otomatik hale gelmiş** *mechanized farming/production*

medal /ˈmedᵊl/ *noun* [C] a metal disc given as a prize in a competition or given to someone who has been very brave **madalya** *a bronze medal* ○ *an Olympic medal* ⊃See also: gold medal, silver medal.

medallist *UK* (*US* medalist) /ˈmedᵊlɪst/ *noun* [C] someone who has received a medal in a sports event **madalya sahibi, madalya kazanmış** *an Olympic medallist*

meddle /ˈmedl/ *verb* [I] to try to influence people or change things that are not your responsibility **işine karışmak, burnunu sokmak, müdahale etmek** *He's always meddling in other people's business.*

the media /ˈmiːdiə/ *noun* [group] television, newspapers, magazines, and radio considered as a group **kitle iletişim araçları; görsel, işitsel ve yazılı iletişim araçları; medya** *media coverage/attention* ○ *The issue has been much discussed in the media.* ⊃See also: the mass media.

mediaeval /ˌmediˈiːvᵊl/ *adjective* another spelling of medieval (= relating to the period in Europe between about AD 500 and AD 1500) **ortaçağa ait**

median /ˈmiːdiən/ *adjective* [always before noun] relating to the middle number or amount in a series **(matema-**

tik) bir serinin ortasındaki bir rakam veya miktara ilişkin olan; **medyan** *the median age/income*

mediate /'miːdieɪt/ *verb* [I, T] to try to find a solution between two or more people who disagree about something **arabuluculuk yapmak; hakemlik etmek** *Negotiators were called in to mediate between the two sides.* ● **mediation** /ˌmiːdi'eɪʃ³n/ *noun* [U] **arabuluculuk**

mediator /'miːdieɪtə³r/ *noun* [C] someone who mediates between people who disagree about something **arabulucu, uzlaştırıcı**

medic /'medɪk/ *noun* [C] *informal* **1** a medical student or doctor **tıp öğrencisi, doktor 2** *US* someone who does medical work in a military organization **askerî kurumda tıbbî personel, sıhhiye personeli**

o╸**medical¹** /'medɪk³l/ *adjective* relating to medicine and different ways of curing illness **tıbbî, tedaviyle ilgili** *medical treatment* ○ *a medical student* ○ *She has a medical condition that makes it hard for her to work.* ● **medically** *adverb* **tıbben**

medical² /'medɪk³l/ *UK* (*US* physical) *noun* [C] an examination of your body by a doctor to find out if you are healthy **tıbbî muayene**

medicated /'medɪkeɪtɪd/ *adjective* A medicated substance contains medicine. **ilaçlı, ilaç içeren** *medicated soap*

medication /ˌmedɪ'keɪʃ³n/ *noun* [C, U] medicine that is used to treat an illness **ilaç tedavisi** *He's on medication to control his depression.*

medicinal /mə'dɪsɪn³l/ *adjective* Medicinal substances are used to cure illnesses. **tedavi edici, iyileştirici** *I keep some brandy for medicinal purposes.*

🧩 **medicine** ...... İLE BİRLİKTE KULLANILAN KELİMELER

take medicine ● a medicine **for** sth

---

o╸**medicine** /'medɪs³n/ *noun* **1** [C, U] a substance used to cure an illness or injury **ilaç, deva** *cough medicine* ○ *Have you taken your medicine today?* **2** [U] the science of curing and preventing illness and injury **tıp, tıp ilmi, doktorluk, hekimlik** *to study medicine* ○ *western/Chinese medicine*

medieval (*also* mediaeval) /ˌmedi'iːv³l/ *adjective* relating to the period in Europe between about AD 500 and AD 1500 **ortaçağa ait, ortaçağ** *medieval literature/art*

mediocre /ˌmiːdi'əʊkə³r/ *adjective* not good in quality **vasat, orta, şöyle böyle** *The acting was mediocre.* ● **mediocrity** /ˌmiːdi'ɒkrəti/ *noun* [U] **vasat olma durumu**

meditate /'medɪteɪt/ *verb* [I] **1** to think calm thoughts for a long period in order to relax or as a religious activity **tefekküre/düşünceye dalmak; meditasyon yapmak** *I meditate twice a day.* **2** *formal* to think seriously about something **enine boyuna düşünüp tartmak, ciddi ciddi düşünmek** *He meditated on the consequences of his decision.* ● **meditation** /ˌmedɪ'teɪʃ³n/ *noun* [U] *Let's spend a few moments in quiet meditation.* **meditasyon**

the Mediterranean /ˌmedɪt³r'emiən/ *noun* the sea that has southern Europe, northern Africa, and the Middle East around it, or the countries around this sea **Akdeniz** ● **Mediterranean** *adjective* a Mediterranean climate/island **Akdeniz**

o╸**medium¹** /'miːdiəm/ *adjective* in the middle of a group of different amounts or sizes **orta, vasat** *people of medium weight* ○ *She bought a medium-sized car.* ○ *The shirt comes in small, medium, and large.*

medium² /'miːdiəm/ *noun* [C] *plural* **media** or **mediums** a way of communicating or expressing something **iletişim aracı/vasıtası** *the medium of television/radio*

medicine

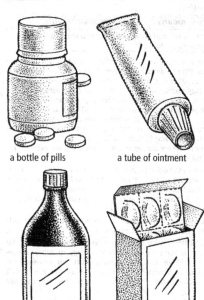

a bottle of pills   a tube of ointment

a bottle of medicine   a box of tablets

○ *The Internet has become yet another medium for marketing.*

medium-term /'miːdiəmˌtɜːm/ *adjective* continuing into the future for a time that is neither short nor long **ara dönem** *The medium-term outlook remains favourable.*

medley /'medli/ *noun* [C] a mixture of different items, especially songs **karışık, değişik şarkılardan oluşan, karma, potpori** *She sang a medley of show tunes.*

meek /miːk/ *adjective* Someone who is meek is quiet and does not argue with others. **çekingen, sıkılgan, uysal, yumuşak başlı** ● **meekly** *adverb* **uysal bir biçimde**

o╸**meet¹** /miːt/ *verb past* **met** /met/ **1** [COME TOGETHER] [I, T] to come to the same place as someone else by arrangement or by chance **buluşmak** *We met for coffee last Sunday.* ○ *I met my old English teacher while trekking in the Alps.* ○ *Each student meets with an adviser at the start of the school year.* **2** [INTRODUCE] [I, T] to see and speak to someone for the first time **tanışmak, karşılaşmak, rastlamak** *I've always wanted to meet a movie star.* ○ *"This is Helen." "Pleased to meet you."* **3** [GROUP] [I] If a group of people meet, they come to a place in order to do something. **toplanmak, toplantı yapmak, bir araya gelmek** *The shareholders meet once a year to discuss profits.* **4** [PLACE] [T] to wait at a place for someone or something to arrive **karşılamak, beklemek** *They met me at the airport.* **5** [ENOUGH] [T] to be a big enough amount or of a good enough quality for something **karşılamak, gidermek, yetmek, yeterli gelmek** *This old building will never meet the new fire regulations.* ○ *Can your product meet the needs of a wide range of consumers?* **6** [ACHIEVE] [T] to be able to achieve something **başa çıkmak, üstesin-**

den gelmek *He met every goal he set for himself.* ○ *to meet a deadline* **7** JOIN **[I, T]** to join something **birleştirmek, birleşmek** *There's a large crack where the ceiling meets the wall.* ⊃See also: make ends (**end¹**) meet.

meet up *phrasal verb* **1** to meet another person in order to do something together **buluşmak, bir araya gelmek, toplanmak** *I met up with a few friends yesterday.* **2** If roads or paths meet up, they join at a particular place. (**cadde, yol, patika, vs.**) **buluşmak, birleşmek, kesişmek, kavuşmak** *This path meets up with the main road.*

meet with sth *phrasal verb* to cause a particular reaction or result **uğramak, başına gelmek, olmak** *Both proposals have met with fierce opposition.* ○ *I trust the arrangements meet with your approval* (= I hope that you like them).

meet² /miːt/ *noun* **[C]** US a sports competition **(spor) karşılaşması, müsabaka** *a swim/track meet* ○ *His final jump set a new meet record.*

arrange/attend/chair/convene/have/hold a meeting ● an **emergency/private/recent/urgent** meeting ● a meeting **between** sb ● be **in** a meeting

o←**meeting** /ˈmiːtɪŋ/ *noun* **[C]** **1** an event where people come together for a reason, usually to discuss something **toplantı** *We're having a meeting on Thursday to discuss the problem.* ○ *He's in a meeting - I'll ask him to call you back later.* **2** UK a sporting competition **spor karşılaşması** *an international meeting*

mega- /meɡə-/ *prefix* **1** *informal* extremely **çok büyük anlamında ön ek** *megarich* (= extremely rich) **2** one million **bir milyon anlamında ön ek** *40 megabytes*

megabyte /ˈmeɡəbaɪt/ (*written abbreviation* **MB**) *noun* **[C]** a unit for measuring the amount of information a computer can store, equal to 1,000,000 bytes **megabayt; bilgisayarın taşıyabileceği bir milyon bayta eşit bilginin miktarını ölçme birimi**

megaphone /ˈmeɡəfəʊn/ *noun* **[C]** a thing that you hold in your hand and speak into to make your voice louder **megafon**

megapixel /ˈmeɡəˌpɪksˀl/ *noun* **[C]** one million pixels (= small points that form part of the image on a computer screen), used to describe the amount of detail in images made by a digital camera, computer screen, etc **megapiksel; bilgisayar ekranında ve dijital kamerada görüntüyü/imgeyi oluşturan bir milyon nokta**

megawatt /ˈmeɡəwɒt/ *noun* **[C]** a unit for measuring electrical power, equal to 1,000,000 watts **megavat; bir milyon vat'a eşit elektrik gücü ölçüm birimi**

melancholy /ˈmelənkɒli/ *adjective formal* sad **üzgün, kederli, hüzünsüz** *a melancholy expression* ● **melancholy** *noun* **[U]** *formal* a feeling of sadness **üzüntü, keder, gam**

melanoma /ˌmeləˈnəʊmə/ *noun* **[C]** a type of skin cancer (= a serious disease) that appears as a coloured mark on the skin **bir tür cilt kanseri**

melee /ˈmeleɪ/ *noun* **[C]** a situation where many people are behaving in a noisy, confused, and sometimes violent way **kargaşa, arbede, karışıklık** *In the melee his jaw was broken.*

mellow¹ /ˈmeləʊ/ *adjective* **1** pleasant and soft (**ses, renk**) **yumuşak** tatlı *a mellow voice* ○ *a mellow flavour/wine* **2** calm and relaxed (**insan**) **olgun, bilge; sakin ve rahat** *After a few drinks, he became very mellow.*

mellow² /ˈmeləʊ/ *verb* **[I, T]** to become more relaxed and gentle, or to make someone become more relaxed and

gentle **yumuşamak, yumuşatmak; hoş görülü ve temkinli hâle getirmek** *Age has mellowed him.*

melodic /məˈlɒdɪk/ *adjective* Melodic music has a pleasant tune, and melodic sounds are pleasant and like music. **ahenkli, melodik; hoş ve müzik gibi**

melodrama /ˈmeləʊˌdrɑːmə/ *noun* **[C, U]** a story in which the characters show much stronger emotions than in real life **melodram**

melodramatic /ˌmeləʊdrəˈmætɪk/ *adjective* showing much stronger emotions than are necessary for a situation **melodram kabilinden, melodramatik** *Don't be so melodramatic! It's only a scratch.*

melody /ˈmelədi/ *noun* **[C]** a song or tune **melodi**

melon /ˈmelən/ *noun* **[C, U]** a large, round, sweet fruit with a thick, green or yellow skin and a lot of seeds **kavun** ⊃Orta kısımdaki renkli sayfalarına bakınız.

o←**melt** /melt/ *verb* **1** **[I, T]** If something melts, it changes from a solid into a liquid because of heat and if you melt something, you heat it until it becomes liquid. **erimek, eritmek** *The sun soon melted the ice on the pond.* ○ *The chocolate had melted in my pocket.* ○ *melted cheese* **2** **[I]** to start to feel love or sympathy, especially after feeling angry **kızgınlıktan sonra yumuşamak, erimek; sevgi hissetmek** *When he smiles at me, I just melt.* ⊃See also: **butter¹** wouldn't melt in sb's mouth.

melt away *phrasal verb* to disappear **gözden kaybolmak, dağılmak, yok olmak** *Then I saw her and all my fears just melted away.*

melt sth down *phrasal verb* If you melt something down, especially a metal object, you heat it until it changes to liquid. (**metal**) **eritmek**

meltdown /ˈmeltdaʊn/ *noun* **[C, U]** **1** *informal* a situation of complete failure and no control **başarısızlık, kontrolden çıkma** *economic meltdown* **2** a serious accident in which nuclear fuel melts through its container and escapes into the environment **nükleer sızıntı**

'melting ˌpot *noun* **[C]** a place where people of many different races and from different countries live together **farklı ırklardan ve ülkelerden insanların bir arada yaşadığı yer; pota; kaynaşma ortamı**

o←**member** /ˈmembər/ *noun* **[C]** a person who belongs to a group or an organization **üye, aza** *family/staff members* ○ *He was a member of the university rowing club.*

ˌMember of 'Parliament *noun* **[C]** *plural* **Members of Parliament** a person who has been elected to represent people in their country's parliament **milletvekili, Parlamento üyesi**

apply for membership ● membership **of/in** sth ● a membership **card/fee**

membership /ˈmembəʃɪp/ *noun* **1** **[C, U]** the state of belonging to a group or an organization **üyelik, azalık** *I've applied for membership of the union.* ○ *a membership card/fee* **2** [group] the people who belong to a group or an organization **üyeler, azalar** *Union membership is now over three million and rising.*

membrane /ˈmembreɪn/ *noun* **[C]** a thin sheet of tissue that covers some parts inside the body in order to protect, connect or separate them **zar**

memento /mɪˈmentəʊ/ *noun* **[C]** *plural* **mementos** or **mementoes** an object that you keep to remember a person, place, or event **hatıra, yadigâr**

M

memo /'meməʊ/ *noun* [C] a written message sent from one member of an organization to another **genelge, memorandum, muhtıra, not**

memoirs /'memwɑːz/ *noun* [plural] a written story of a person's own life and experiences **hatırat, anılar**

memorabilia /ˌmemᵊrə'bɪliə/ *noun* [plural] objects relating to famous people or events that people collect **ünlü kişilere/olaylara ait eşyalar** *an auction of pop memorabilia*

memorable /'memᵊrəbl/ *adjective* If an occasion is memorable, you will remember it for a long time because it is so good. **unutulmaz, hatırlamaya değer, anılardan silinmeyecek** *a memorable performance* ● **memorably** *adverb* **hatırlanırcasına**

memorandum /ˌmemᵊr'ændəm/ *noun plural* **memoranda** *formal* a memo **genelge, memorandum, muhtıra, not**

memorial /mə'mɔːriəl/ *noun* [C] an object, often made of stone, that is built to help people remember an important person or event **anıt, abide** *a war memorial* ○ *a memorial service*

memorize (*also UK* -ise) /'memᵊraɪz/ *verb* [T] to learn something so that you remember it exactly **ezberlemek** *I've memorized all my friends' birthdays.*

‱ **memory** .... İLE BİRLİKTE KULLANILAN KELİMELER

have a bad/good memory ● have a [good, amazing, etc] memory for sth ● a photographic memory

☞ **memory** /'memᵊri/ *noun* **1** [ABILITY] [C, U] your ability to remember **bellek, hafıza** *John has an amazing memory for historical facts.* ○ *She had a photographic memory* (= was able to remember every detail). **2** [THOUGHT] [C] something that you remember **anı, hatıra** [usually plural] *I have fond memories of my childhood.* **3** [MIND] [C, U] the part of your mind that stores what you remember **hafıza, bellek, akıl** *He recited the poem from memory.* **4 in memory of sb** If you do something in memory of a dead person, you do it to show your respect or love for them. **anısına, hatırasına** *They built a statue in memory of those who died in the fire.* **5** [COMPUTING] [C, U] the part of a computer where information and instructions are stored, or the amount of information that can be stored there **(bilgisayar) bellek, hafıza; bellekteki bilgi** *You need 32 megabytes of memory to run this software.*

'**Memory** ˌ**Stick** *noun* [C] *trademark* a small electronic device designed to store information that can be put into a computer, mobile phone, etc **Hafıza Çubuğu/Kartı**

men /men/ *plural of* man **'erkek, adam', 'insan' kelimesinin çoğulu**

menace[1] /'menɪs/ *noun* **1** [C] something that is likely to cause harm **tehlike, zarar verebilecek şeyler** [usually singular] *Drunk drivers are a menace to everyone.* **2** [U] a dangerous quality that makes you think someone is going to do something bad **tehdit, göz dağı** *His eyes were cold and filled with menace.*

menace[2] /'menɪs/ *verb* [T] *formal* to cause harm to someone or something, or be likely to cause harm **zarar vermek; korkutmak; tehlike yaratabilmek** *Hurricane Bonnie continues to menace the east coast.*

menacing /'menɪsɪŋ/ *adjective* making you think that someone is going to do something bad **tehdit edici, korkutucu, ürkütücü** *a menacing gesture/voice*

mend[1] /mend/ *verb* [T] to repair something that is broken, torn, or not working correctly **tamir etmek, onarmak** *I've mended that hole in your skirt for you.*

mend[2] /mend/ *noun* **be on the mend** *informal* If you are on the mend, your health is improving after an illness. **iyileşmekte/düzelmekte/toparlanmakta olmak; iyi bir nekâhat dönemi geçiriyor olmak**

mendacious /men'deɪʃəs/ *adjective formal* not telling the truth **yalan söyleyen, sahtekâr**

menial /'miːniəl/ *adjective* Menial work is boring, and not well paid or respected. **sıkıcı, yorucu, sıradan, âdi, ucuz, saygı duyulmayan** *a menial job/task*

meningitis /ˌmenɪn'dʒaɪtɪs/ *noun* [U] a serious infectious disease that affects a person's brain and spinal cord (= the nerves in your back) **menenjit**

menopause /'menəʊpɔːz/ *noun* [U] the time, usually between the ages of 45 and 55, when a woman gradually stops having periods (= monthly blood from the uterus) **menopoz; kadınlarda 45-55 yaşlar arası âdetten kesilme zamanı**

'**men's** ˌ**room** *noun* [C] *US* a room in a public place where there are men's toilets **umumî erkek tuvaleti**

menstrual /'menstrʊəl/ *adjective* [always before noun] *formal* relating to menstruating **âdet görmeye/aybaşı olmaya dair/ilişkin** *a menstrual cycle*

menstruate /'menstrueɪt/ *verb* [I] *formal* to have a monthly flow of blood from the uterus **âdet görmek, aybaşı olmak** ● **menstruation** /ˌmenstru'eɪʃᵊn/ *noun* [U] **âdet, aybaşı**

☞ **mental** /'mentᵊl/ *adjective* [always before noun] relating to the mind, or involving the process of thinking **zihinsel, zihni, aklî** *mental health/illness* ● **mentally** *adverb a mentally ill person* **mantıken**

mentality /men'tæləti/ *noun* [C] a person's opinions or way of thinking **zihniyet, mantalite** *I can't understand the mentality of people who hunt animals for fun.*

☞ **mention**[1] /'menʃᵊn/ *verb* [T] **1** to briefly speak or write about something or someone **bahsetmek, söylemek, söz etmek, değinmek** *I'll mention your ideas to Caroline.* ○ *She didn't mention her daughter.* ○ [+ (that)] *He mentioned that he liked skydiving.* **2 not to mention** used to emphasize the importance of something that you are adding to a list **ayrıca, bir de, üstelik,... ...dan/den başka** *The resort has great hotels and restaurants, not to mention some of the best skiing in the region.*

‱ **mention (noun)** .... İLE BİRLİKTE KULLANILAN KELİMELER

deserve/get/be worth a mention ● make no mention of sth ● a brief/passing/special mention ● mention of sth

mention[2] /'menʃᵊn/ *noun* [C] a brief remark **anma, bahsetme, değinme, söz etme** *The report made no mention of the problem.*

mentor /'mentɔːʳ/ *noun* [C] *formal* an experienced person who gives help and advice to someone with less experience **akıl hocası, danışman**

☞ **menu** /'menjuː/ *noun* [C] **1** a list of food and drinks that you can order in a restaurant **yemek listesi, menü** *a lunch/dinner menu* ○ *I ordered the most expensive thing on the menu* (= available in the restaurant). **2** a list that appears on a computer screen of the choices available in a computer program **bilgisayar ekranında çıkan seçenekler listesi** *a pop-up menu*

'**menu** ˌ**bar** *noun* [C] a long, narrow area, usually at the top of a computer screen, that contains computer menus **bilgisayar ekranında bulunan seçenekler listesi**

'**menu** ˌ**option** *noun* [C] one of the choices on a computer menu **bilgisayar seçenek menüsü**

meow /miː'aʊ/ *noun* [C] *US spelling of* miaow (= the sound that a cat makes) **kedi sesi, miyav**

MEP /ˌemiːˈpiː/ *noun* [C] *abbreviation for* Member of European Parliament: a person who represents an area of a European country in the European Parliament **Avrupa Parlamento Üyesi** *the MEP for Glasgow*

mercenary[1] /ˈmɜːsᵊnᵊri/ *noun* [C] a soldier who fights for any country or organization who pays them **paralı asker**

mercenary[2] /ˈmɜːsᵊnᵊri/ *adjective* interested only in getting money or an advantage from a situation **çıkarcı, paragöz, para canlısı**

merchandise /ˈmɜːtʃᵊndaɪz/ *noun* [U] *formal* goods that are traded, or sold in shops **ticari eşya, mal, emtia** *We stock a broad range of merchandise.*

merchandising /ˈmɜːtʃᵊndaɪzɪŋ/ *noun* [U] the selling of products relating to films, television programmes, and famous people **film, tv. programı ve ünlülere ilişkin ürünlerin satışı**

merchant[1] /ˈmɜːtʃᵊnt/ *noun* [C] *formal* someone whose job is buying and selling goods, usually in large amounts **tüccar** *a wine/grain merchant*

merchant[2] /ˈmɜːtʃᵊnt/ *adjective* [always before noun] relating to trading of large amounts of goods **ticari, ticaret** *a merchant ship/seaman*

merchant 'bank *noun* [C] a bank that organizes investments in companies or lends money to them **ticaret bankası** ● **merchant banker** *noun* [C] **yatırımları ayarlayan bankacı**

mercifully /ˈmɜːsɪfᵊli/ *adverb* used to show that you are pleased that something unpleasant has been avoided **bereket versin ki** *Her illness was mercifully short.*

merciless /ˈmɜːsɪləs/ *adjective* cruel, or showing no kindness **merhametsiz, insafsız, acımasız** *a merciless attack* ○ *She was merciless in her criticism of his work.* ● **mercilessly** *adverb* **acımasızca**

Mercury /ˈmɜːkjᵊri/ *noun* [no plural] the planet that is closest to the Sun, before Venus **Merkür; Venüs'ten önce gelen ve güneşe en yakın gezegen**

mercury /ˈmɜːkjᵊri/ *noun* [U] a heavy, silver-coloured metal that is liquid at ordinary temperatures (formula Hg) **civa**

ask for/beg for/plead for mercy ● **show (no)** mercy

mercy /ˈmɜːsi/ *noun* [U] **1** kindness that makes you forgive someone, usually someone that you have authority over **merhamet, insaf** *The judge showed no mercy.* **2 be at the mercy of sth/sb** to not be able to protect yourself from something or someone that you cannot control **...ın/ın insafına kalmış; kaderi...ın/ın elinde olmak** *Farmers are often at the mercy of the weather.*

mere /mɪəʳ/ *adjective* [always before noun] **1** used to emphasize that something is not large or important **sadece, ancak, yalnız** *It costs a mere twenty dollars.* ○ *The mere thought of* (= Just thinking about) *eating octopus makes me feel sick.* **2** *the merest* used to emphasize that something is small, often when it has an important effect **ufacık...dahi** *She's upset by the merest hint of criticism.*

merely /ˈmɪəli/ *adverb* **1** used to emphasize that you mean exactly what you are saying and nothing more **sadece, yalnızca** *I'm not arguing with you - I'm merely explaining the problem.* **2** used to emphasize that something is not large, important, or effective when compared to something else **ancak, yalnızca, sadece** *The medicine doesn't make you better, it merely stops the pain.*

merge /mɜːdʒ/ *verb* [I, T] If two or more things merge, they combine or join, and if you merge two or more

things, you combine or join them. **birleş(tir)mek, kaynaş(tır)mak** *The two companies merged, forming the largest brewery in Canada.* ○ *The city's smaller libraries will be merged into a large, central one.*

merger /ˈmɜːdʒəʳ/ *noun* [C, U] when two or more companies or organizations join together **birleşme, birleştirme, kaynaştırma**

meringue /məˈræŋ/ *noun* [C, U] a light, sweet food that is made by baking the white part of an egg mixed with sugar **(yiyecek) beze**

merit[1] /ˈmerɪt/ *noun* [C, U] *formal* good qualities which deserve praise **erdem, meziyet, fazilet** *His ideas have merit.* ○ *We debated the merits of using television in the classroom.* ○ *Every application has to be judged on its own merits* (= judged by considering the qualities of each).

merit[2] /ˈmerɪt/ *verb* [T] *formal* to be important enough to receive attention or punishment **hak etmek, layık olmak** *Her crimes were serious enough to merit a prison sentence.*

mermaid /ˈmɜːmeɪd/ *noun* [C] an imaginary creature that lives in the sea and has the upper body of a woman and the tail of a fish **deniz kızı**

merry /ˈmeri/ *adjective* showing enjoyment and happiness **mutlu, şen, neşeli** *a merry laugh* ○ *Merry Christmas!* ● **merrily** *adverb* **keyifli bir şekilde**

mesh[1] /meʃ/ *noun* [C, U] material that is like a net and is made of wire, plastic, or thread **ağ, file** *a wire mesh fence*

mesh[2] /meʃ/ *verb* [I] If two or more things mesh, they are suitable for each other. **eşleşmek, uyuşmak, birbirine geçmek, kenetlenmek** *Her ideas mesh well with our plans for the future.*

make a mess ● **clean up/clear up** a mess ● **be in a mess**

o━**mess**[1] /mes/ *noun* [C] **1** UNTIDY Someone or something that is a mess, or is in a mess, is dirty or untidy. **karışıklık, dağınıklık** [usually singular] *My hair's such a mess!* ○ *The house is in a mess.* ○ *Don't make a mess in the kitchen!* **2** DIFFICULT a confused or difficult situation **zorluk, müşkül durum, dert, bela** [usually singular] *She told me that her life was a mess.* ○ *If he hadn't lied, he wouldn't be in this mess now.* **3 make a mess of sth** to damage or spoil something **berbat etmek, yüzüne gözüne bulaştırmak** *He made a mess of his first marriage.* **4** MILITARY a place where members of the armed forces eat **(kışla) yemekhane** [usually singular] *the officers' mess*

mess[2] /mes/ *verb*

mess about/around *phrasal verb informal* **1** to waste time, often by doing things that are not important **zamanı boşa geçirmek, aylak aylak durmak** *Stop messing around and do your homework!* **2** to spend time playing and doing things with no particular purpose **amaçsızca zaman öldürmek, budalalık etmek; boş/beyhude şeylerle vakit geçirmek** *I can spend hours messing around with my computer.*

mess sb about/around *phrasal verb UK informal* to treat someone badly, often by not doing something that you have promised **oyalamak; sözünü yerine getirmeyerek kötü muamele etmek**

mess about/around with sth *phrasal verb informal* to use or treat something in a careless or harmful way **oynamak, uğraşmak, kurcalamak, düşüncesizce zarar vermek** *Who's been messing around with my computer?*

M

mess sth up *phrasal verb* **1** to make something untidy or dirty **dağıtmak, karmakarışık etmek** *I hate wearing hats - they always mess up my hair.* **2** to spoil something, or to do something badly **berbat etmek, yüzüne gözüne bulaştırmak** *Don't try to cook lunch by yourself - you'll only mess it up.*

mess with sb/sth *phrasal verb informal* to become involved with someone or something dangerous **bulaşmak, karışmak, burnunu sokmak** *If you mess with drugs, you're asking for trouble.*

---
message ...... İLE BİRLİKTE KULLANILAN KELİMELER

get/leave/send/take a message ● a message for/from sb

ͦ᷄**message¹** /'mesɪdʒ/ *noun* [C] **1** a piece of written or spoken information which one person gives to another **ileti, haber, mesaj** *Did you get my message?* ○ *I left her several messages, but she hasn't returned my call.* **2** the most important idea of a film, book, etc **(film, kitap, vs.) verilmek istenen duygu ve düşünce, mesaj** *The book conveys a complex message.* **3 get the message** *informal* to understand what someone wants you to do by their actions **söylenen şeyi anlamak, mesajı almak** *Don't return any of his calls - he'll soon get the message and leave you alone.*

message² /'mesɪdʒ/ *verb* [T] to send someone an email or text message (= a written message sent from one mobile phone to another) **e-posta veya cep telefonu ile ileti/mesaj göndermek**

'message ,board *noun* [C] a place on a website where you can leave messages for other people to read **(bilgisayar) sitede ileti bırakılabilecek yer/kutucuk**

messenger /'mesɪndʒəʳ/ *noun* [C] someone who takes a message between two people **haberci, kurye, ulak**

the Messiah /məˈsaɪə/ *noun* **1** Jesus Christ **İsa Mesih** **2** the leader that Jews believe God will send them **Mesih; Yahudi inancına göre Tanrı'nın göndereceği önder**

Messrs /'mesəz/ *noun formal* a title used before the names of two or more men **Baylar** *Messrs Davis and Dixon led the discussion on tax reform.*

messy /'mesi/ *adjective* **1** untidy or dirty **darmadağınık, pis, kirli, düzensiz** *messy hair* ○ *a messy house/car* ○ *My son's bedroom is always messy.* **2** unpleasant and complicated **içinden çıkılmaz, karmakarışık, müşkül, biçimsiz, sevimsiz** *Ian's just gone through a messy divorce.*

met /met/ *past of* meet **'karşıla(ş)mak' fiilinin geçmiş zaman hâli**

metabolism /məˈtæbˀlɪzˀm/ *noun* [C] all the chemical processes in your body, especially the ones that use food **metabolizma**

ͦ᷄**metal** /'metˀl/ *noun* [C, U] a usually hard, shiny material such as iron, gold, or silver which heat and electricity can travel through **metal, maden** *scrap metal* ○ *Metals are used for making machinery and tools.* ○ *a metal sheet/bar* ● **metallic** /məˈtælɪk/ *adjective* having a quality that is similar to metal **madeni, metalik** *a metallic paint/taste* ⊃See also: **heavy metal.**

metamorphosis /ˌmetəˈmɔːfəsɪs/ *noun plural* **metamorphoses** /metəˈmɔːfəsiːz/ **1** [C] a gradual change into something very different **şekil değiştirme, değişme, metamorfoz** *The past year has seen a complete metamorphosis of the country's economy.* **2** [U] in biology, the process by which the young forms of some animals, such as insects, develop into very different adult forms **(biyoloji) değişim, başkalaşım, metamorfoz** *Caterpillars changing into butterflies is an example of metamorphosis.*

metaphor /'metəfəʳ/ *noun* [C, U] a way of describing something by comparing it with something else which has some of the same qualities **mecaz, benzetme** *She used a computer metaphor to explain how the human brain works.* ● **metaphorical** /ˌmetəˈfɒrɪkəl/ *adjective* using a metaphor **mecazi**

mete /miːt/ *verb* meting, *past* meted
mete sth out *phrasal verb formal* to punish someone **cezalandırmak, ceza vermek** [often passive] *Long jail sentences are meted out to drug smugglers.*

meteor /'miːtiəʳ/ *noun* [C] a rock from outer space which becomes very hot and burns brightly in the sky at night as it enters Earth's atmosphere (= air surrounding Earth) **göktaşı, meteor**

meteoric /ˌmiːtiˈɒrɪk/ *adjective* If the development of something is meteoric, it happens very quickly or causes great success. **baş döndürücü, hızlı, göz açıp kapayıncaya kadar olan** *a meteoric career* ○ *The band's rise to fame was meteoric.*

meteorite /'miːtiˀraɪt/ *noun* [C] a piece of rock from outer space which has fallen on Earth's surface **gök taşı**

meteorological /ˌmiːtiˀrəˈlɒdʒɪkˀl/ *adjective* [always before noun] relating to the scientific study of weather **hava tahminine ait, meteorolojik, metorolojiye ait**

meteorologist /ˌmiːtiˀrˈɒlədʒɪst/ *noun* [C] someone who studies weather, especially to say how it will be in the near future **meteoroloji uzmanı** ● **meteorology** *noun* [U] the scientific study of weather **meteoroloji**

ͦ᷄**meter** /'miːtəʳ/ *noun* [C] **1** a piece of equipment for measuring the amount of something such as electricity, time, or light **metre, sayaç** *a gas/water meter* ○ *a parking/taxi meter* **2** US spelling of metre **metre, uzunluk ölçüm birimi**

methadone /'meθədəʊn/ *noun* [U] a drug for treating people who want to stop using heroin (= an illegal drug) **esrar kullanımından vazgeçirmek için tedavide kullanılan ilaç; metadon**

methane /'miːθeɪn/ ⓤ /'meθeɪn/ *noun* [U] a gas that has no colour or smell, used for cooking and heating (formula CH₄) **metan gazı**

---
method ...... İLE BİRLİKTE KULLANILAN KELİMELER

an alternative/new/reliable/simple/traditional method ● develop/devise/use a method
---

ͦ᷄**method** /'meθəd/ *noun* [C] a way of doing something, often one that involves a system or plan **yöntem, teknik, tarz, usûl** *What's the best method of/for solving this problem?* ○ *traditional teaching methods*

methodical /məˈθɒdɪkˀl/ *adjective* careful and well organized, using a plan or system **bir yöntem dahilinde yapılmış, planlı, sistemli** *a methodical researcher* ● **methodically** *adverb* **organize edilmiş bir şekilde**

Methodist /'meθədɪst/ *adjective* belonging or relating to a Christian group that was started by John Wesley **Metodist; John Wesley'in başlattığı Hıristiyan gruba ait** ● **Methodist** *noun* [C] **Metodist**

methodological /ˌmeθədəˈlɒdʒɪkˀl/ *adjective* relating to a methodology **yöntembilime ilişkin** *methodological problems*

methodology /ˌmeθəˈdɒlədʒi/ *noun* [C, U] the system of methods used for doing, teaching, or studying something **yöntembilim; öğretim/öğrenim hayatında kullanılan yöntemler bütünü**

meticulous /məˈtɪkjələs/ *adjective* very careful, and giving great attention to detail **titiz, kılı kırk yaran, hassas, çok dikkatli** *This book is the result of meticu-*

PIECES AND QUANTITIES

a piece of . . .

tart

wood

paper

material

a slice of . . .

bread

meat

cake

a bunch of . . .

grapes

bananas

keys

flowers

a bar of . . .

soap

chocolate

a drop of . . .

oil

lumps

sugar lumps

lumps of coal

chunks of . . .

vegetables

a hunk of . . .

bread

cheese

a blob of . . .

cream

THE KITCHEN

chopping board

toaster

bread bin UK,
bread box US

tin opener UK,
can opener US

food processor

grater

oven glove

kettle

blender

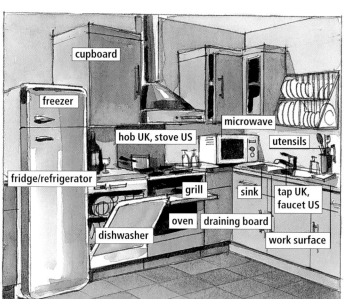

cupboard

freezer

microwave

hob UK, stove US

utensils

fridge/refrigerator

grill

sink

tap UK,
faucet US

oven   draining board

dishwasher

work surface

coffee maker

teapot

sieve

colander

scales UK, scale US

cake tin UK,
cake pan US

rolling pin

baking
tray UK,
baking
pan US

saucepan

frying pan

flan dish

whisk

ladle

fish slice UK,
spatula US

measuring spoons

THE BATHROOM

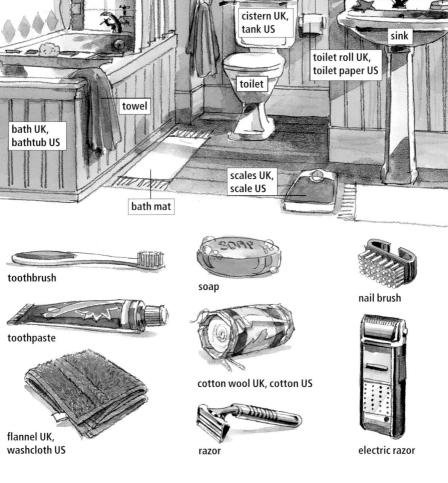

shower

bathroom cabinet UK,
medicine cabinet US

shower curtain

soap

cistern UK,
tank US

sink

toilet roll UK,
toilet paper US

toilet

towel

bath UK,
bathtub US

scales UK,
scale US

bath mat

toothbrush

soap

nail brush

toothpaste

cotton wool UK, cotton US

flannel UK,
washcloth US

razor

electric razor

THE LIVING ROOM

mirror

ornaments

picture

window

curtain

mantelpiece

bookcase

TV

windowsill

radiator

fireplace

cushion

sofa

vase

coffee table

rug

armchair

remote control

video UK, VCR US

candles

lampshade

speaker   stereo

clock

lamp

THE CLASSROOM

timetable UK, schedule US

board rubber UK, eraser US

whiteboard

blackboard

chalk

whiteboard marker

noticeboard UK, bulletin board US

teacher

pupil

pen

ruler

exercise book

textbook

file

chair

glue

Sellotape UK, Scotch tape US

rubber UK, eraser US

satchel

pencil

scissors

pencil sharpener

desk

CAR

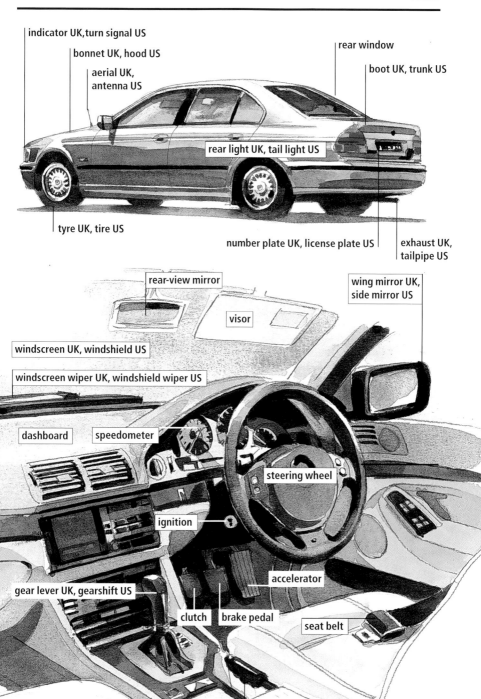

indicator UK, turn signal US

bonnet UK, hood US

aerial UK, antenna US

rear window

boot UK, trunk US

rear light UK, tail light US

tyre UK, tire US

number plate UK, license plate US

exhaust UK, tailpipe US

rear-view mirror

wing mirror UK, side mirror US

visor

windscreen UK, windshield US

windscreen wiper UK, windshield wiper US

dashboard

speedometer

steering wheel

ignition

accelerator

gear lever UK, gearshift US

clutch

brake pedal

seat belt

handbrake UK, emergency brake US

CLOTHES

jacket

cardigan

sweater

halter top

trousers UK
pants US

jeans

skirt

miniskirt

suit

salwar kameez

t-shirt

shorts

dress

pyjamas

slippers

sweatshirt

fur collar

hood

coat

mac UK
raincoat US

boots

jacket

hoodie

CLOTHES

tie

waistcoat UK
vest US

shirt

sweatshirt

gloves

scarves
(one scarf)

trousers UK
pants US

shoes

bra

cycling shorts

tracksuit UK
sweats US

boxers

briefs

bikini

swimming
trunks UK
swimsuit US

trunks

French knickers
pants UK panties US

underpants

swimming
costume UK
swimsuit US

socks

briefs

cycle helmet

camisole

tights UK

sunglasses

sun visor

belt

flip-flops

mules

trainers UK   sneakers US

baseball cap

ankle
boots

sun hat

cowboy boots

sandals

boots

FRUITS AND VEGETABLES

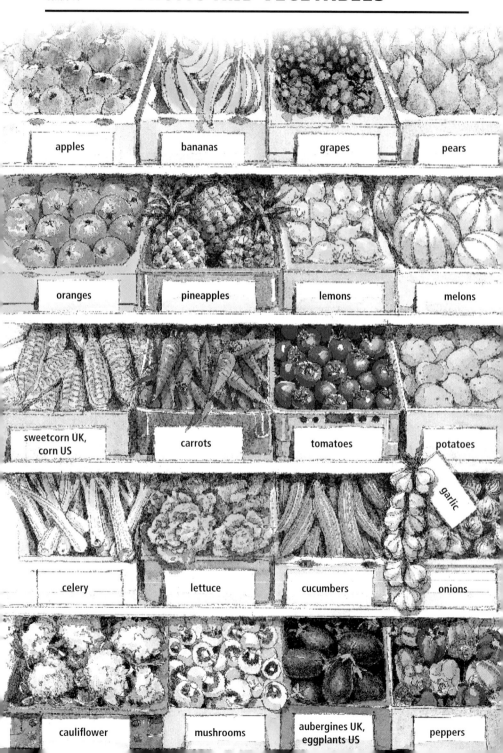

apples

bananas

grapes

pears

oranges

pineapples

lemons

melons

sweetcorn UK, corn US

carrots

tomatoes

potatoes

celery

lettuce

cucumbers

onions

garlic

cauliflower

mushrooms

aubergines UK, eggplants US

peppers

FOOD

Centre 11

roll UK,
sandwich US

sandwich UK & US

soup

biscuits UK,
cookies US

cake

salad

vegetables

pizza

rice

pasta

chips UK,
french fries US

cereal

honey

jam

crisps UK,
chips US

peanuts

egg

butter

fish

yoghurt

cheese

meat

COLOURS

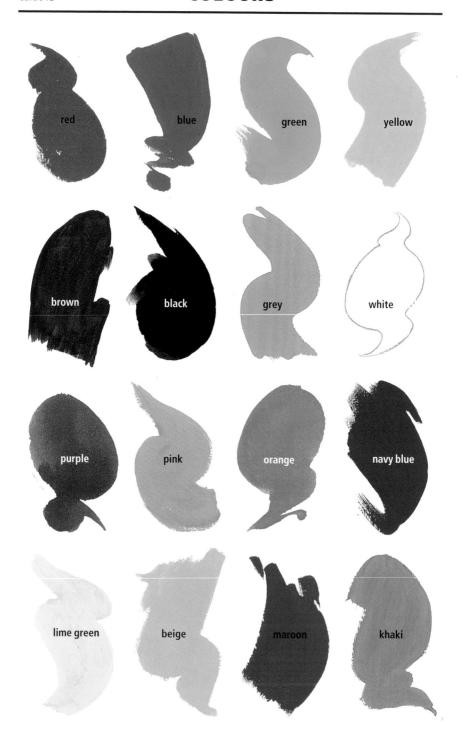

red

blue

green

yellow

brown

black

grey

white

purple

pink

orange

navy blue

lime green

beige

maroon

khaki

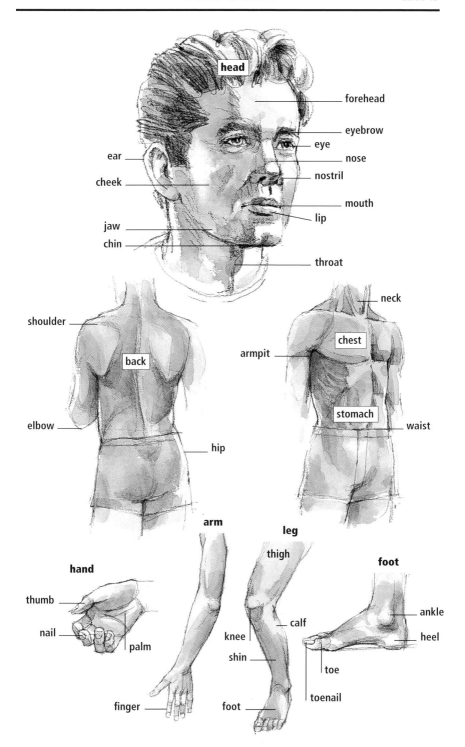

head

forehead

eyebrow

eye

nose

ear

nostril

cheek

mouth

lip

jaw

chin

throat

neck

shoulder

chest

armpit

back

elbow

stomach

waist

hip

arm

leg

thigh

hand

foot

thumb

calf

ankle

nail

knee

heel

palm

shin

finger

foot

toe

toenail

SPORTS

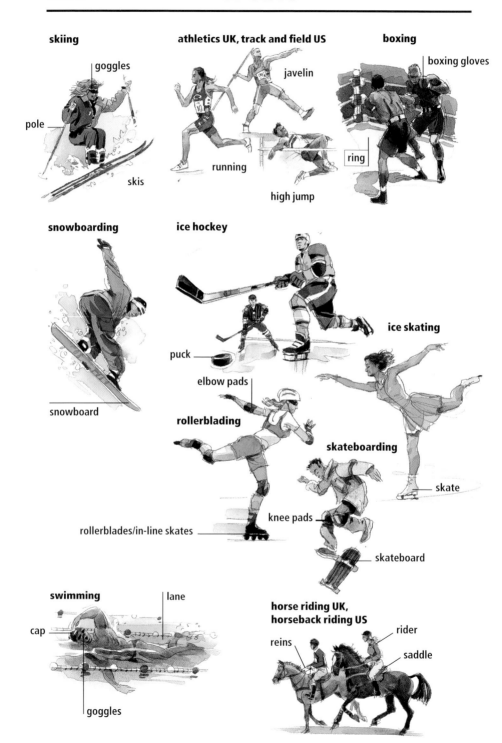

skiing

goggles

pole

skis

athletics UK, track and field US

javelin

running

high jump

boxing

boxing gloves

ring

snowboarding

snowboard

ice hockey

puck

elbow pads

ice skating

rollerblading

rollerblades/in-line skates

skateboarding

knee pads

skate

skateboard

swimming

cap

lane

goggles

horse riding UK, horseback riding US

reins

rider

saddle

SPORTS

football UK, soccer US
referee
goal
goalkeeper

American football UK, football US
helmet
goal post

rugby

golf
cup
club
caddie

basketball
backboard
basket

cricket
bowler
stumps
batsman

baseball
cap
pitcher
glove/mitt
batter

tennis
racket
net

cycling
helmet
bicycle

volleyball
net

PHRASAL VERBS

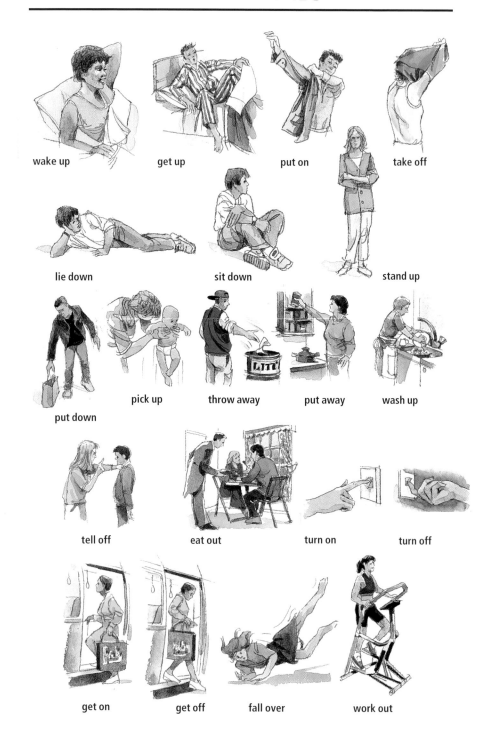

wake up

get up

put on

take off

lie down

sit down

stand up

put down

pick up

throw away

put away

wash up

tell off

eat out

turn on

turn off

get on

get off

fall over

work out

Ekstra yardım sayfaları

Çalışmanızı kontrol etmek

Bu sözlük, sıkça rastlanan yanlışlardan kaçınmanıza birçok şekilde yardımcı olabilecektir.

Common Learner Error Notları

İngilizce öğrenenler için sıklıkla sorun yaratan kelimelerin doğru olarak nasıl kullanılacağını açıklayan özel, sıkça rastlanan öğrenci yanlışları notu vardır. Bunların tümü *Cambridge Learner Corpus*'a dayalıdır.

1 Aşağıdaki cümleleri, altı çizilmiş olan kelimeye ait *Common Learner Error* notlarına bakarak düzeltin.

1 The new rule <u>affects</u> to everyone.
2 What <u>hour</u> is it?
3 It's <u>quiet</u> hot in here.
4 He did an interesting <u>speech</u>.

Dil bilgisi

Kullanmak istediğiniz kelimenin dil bilgisini her zaman kontrol edin. Tüm dil bilgisi etiketlerinin açıklamaları sayfa xiii'de olup **Sayılabilen ve sayılamayan isimler** ile **Fiil kalıpları** hakkındaki Extra help pages de size yardımcı olacaktır.

Doğru kelimelerin kullanılması

Kelimeleri kullanmanın tipik yollarını gösteren örnek cümlelere dikkatle bakınız. Bir kelime başka bir kelimeyle beraber aşırı sık olarak kullanılıyorsa buna *eş dizimli* veya *kelime ortakları* diyoruz. Bu eş dizimliler veya kelime ortakları koyu yazı ile gösterilmiştir.

2 Bu cümlelerdeki boşlukları altı çizili kelime için olan girişteki örneklere bakarak doldurun:

1 You must ___ your <u>homework</u> before you go out.
2 Shall we ___ a <u>taxi</u> to the station?
3 He has no <u>chance</u> ___ getting there on time.
4 I'm ___ rather <u>ill</u> this morning.

➲ Ayrıca bakınız Extra help pages
Sayfa Orta 33'de **Noktalama**, sayfa Orta 34'de **Heceleme**, sayfa Orta 41'de **Eş dizimliler/kelime ortağı nedir?**

3 Aşağıda PET (the Preliminary English Test) sınavına giren bir aday tarafından yazılmış bir yazı vardır. *Cambridge Learner Corpus*'tan alınmıştır. İçinde on tane yanlış vardır. Bunları bulup düzeltebilir misiniz?

The name of this place is Milan, and it is one of the most important Italian cities. You will find Milan in the north of Italy and you can get there by car, train, or plane, but about me travelling by car is the best solution. I suggest you to visit Milan not only because it's full of people but also for its historical buildings.

I decided to go in Milan because I desired seeing the Duomo, and the Castello Sforsesco, and I must say you that they are incredibles. I hope that you decide to go to Milan the next summer.

I look forward to see you very soon, with love, Luca

PS Besides in Milan there are a lots of pubs and discos where I know many interesting persons

Sınıf dili

Kelimeler hakkında soru sormak

What does 'fierce' mean?

How do you say ___ in English?

How do you spell 'castle'?

How do you pronounce this word?

What's the past tense/past participle of 'lie'?

Can you give me an example?

Could you say that again, please?

Aktiviteler hakkında soru sormak

I'm sorry, I don't understand what we have to do.

Can you repeat the instructions please?

Could you repeat that, please?

Could you speak more slowly, please?

Could I borrow a pen/pencil, etc, please?

Can you lend me a pen/pencil, please?

How long do we have to do this?

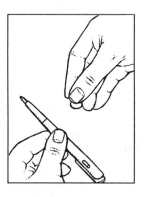

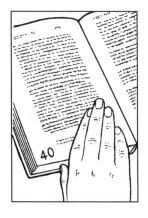

Sınıf talimatları

Open your books at page 40.

Turn to page 6.

Close your books.

Work in pairs/groups of three, four etc.

Listen to the tape, then try to answer the questions.

Write the answers on a piece of paper.

Work with your partner.

Look up these words in your dictionary.

No talking, please.

Hand in your homework as you leave.

Sayılabilen ve sayılamayan isimler

İsimler hem sayılabilen hem de sayılamayan olabilir.

Sayılabilen isimlerden önce *a/an* veya *the* bulunur ve hem tekil hem de çoğul olarak kullanılabilir.
▶ *There's a plate, three spoons and a cup on the table.*

Sayılamayan isimlerin önünde *a/an* olamaz ve şöyle kullanılamaz: çoğul olarak:
▶ *We have rice and some cheese but we haven't any wine.*

Bu sözlükte sayılabilen isimlerde [C] simgesi ve sayılamayan isimlerde [U] simgesi vardır.

1 Bu cümleler doğru mu? Altı çizilen isme bakınız.

1 We get a lot of English <u>homeworks</u>.
2 I've got some <u>sands</u> in my shoe.
3 They bought some new <u>equipment</u>.
4 Can I have some more <u>pasta</u>?
5 She carried my <u>luggages</u> to the taxi.

2 Bu cümlelerin bazılarının boşluklarında 'a' veya 'an' gereklidir. Gerekirse bunları koyunuz.

1 Why are you taking ___ umbrella? It's not raining.
2 I had ___ soup and ___ bread roll for lunch.
3 It was ___ good idea to have a party.
4 She's looking for ___ work in Madrid.
5 I often go to her for ___ advice.

10 en çok yapılan sayılamayan isim hataları

Bunlar *Cambridge Learner Corpus*'da bulunan ve orta seviye öğrencilerin 's' ekleyerek çoğullaştırmaya çalıştıkları 10 en çok rastlanan sayılamayan isim hatalarıdır. Orta seviye öğrencileri PET (the Preliminary English Test) ve FCE (the First Certificate in English) gibi sınavlara giriyorlardı.
Bu isimlerin çoğul olarak kullanılamayacaklarını aklınızda tutmaya çalışın.

1 information
2 equipment
3 advice
4 furniture
5 transport
6 homework
7 paper (= material used for writing on)
8 knowledge
9 countryside
10 stuff

Some ve *any*

Some ve any'yi çoğul sayılabilen isimlerle kullanabilirsiniz.
▶ *There are some cakes left. Are there any biscuits?*

Some ve any'yi çoğul sayılamayan isimlerle kullanabilirsiniz.
▶ *I'd like some sugar in my coffee. Is there any water in the jug?*

3 Boşlukları kutudan bir isim ile doldurunuz:

| chair | suitcase | fly | rice | furniture |
| day | weather | accidents | luggage | |

1 There's a ___ in my soup.
2 I have to buy some ___ for my new house.
3 I haven't got much ___ with me. Just this bag.
4 It's a sunny ___ today.
5 There weren't any ___ on the roads yesterday.

Much, many, a lot of, a few

Many ve **a few**'n çoğul sayılabilen isimlerle kullanabilirsiniz: ▶ *Did you take **many photographs?*** ▶ *I've got **a few friends** who live in London.*	**much**'ı sayılamayan isimlerle kullanabilirsiniz: ▶ *I haven't got **much news** to tell you.*

a lot of'u hem çoğul sayılabilen isimlerle, hem de sayılamayan isimlerle kullanabilirsiniz:
▶ *Did you take **a lot of photographs?***
▶ *I haven't **got a lot of news** to tell you.*

4 Bu cümlelerin bazı kısımlarındaki altları çizilmiş kelimelerin hangileri doğrudur? Doğru kısmı daire içine alınız.

1 Hurry up! We haven't got <u>many/a lot of</u> time.
2 I don't eat <u>much/many</u> chocolate.
3 I didn't take <u>much/many</u> photographs.
4 I don't listen to <u>much/many</u> classical music.

Hem sayılabilen hem de sayılamayan olabilen isimler.

Bazı isimler hem sayılabilen hem de sayılamayan olarak kullanılabilirler:
▶ *a fish/fish, a glass/glass, a hair/hair, a chocolate/chocolate*

Bu isimleri sayılabilen olarak kullandığımızda belirli şeylerden söz ederiz: ▶ *There are **some glasses** on the table.* ▶ *I caught **a fish** at the lake.*	Bu isimleri sayılamayan olarak kullandığımızda genel şeylerden söz ederiz: ▶ *Careful. There's broken **glass** on the floor.* ▶ *I'd like **fish** and chips for dinner.*

5 Aşağıdaki öğelere bakın. Bunlardan kaç tanesi hem sayılabilen hem de sayılamayan olarak kullanılabilir?

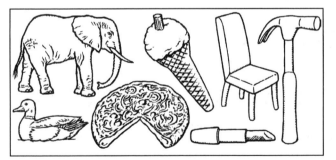

Yardımcı fiiller

Yardımcı fiil bir şeyin olası, zorunlu v.b. olduğunu göstermek için başka bir fiilden önce kullanılan fiildir, örneğin 'can', 'might', veya 'must'.
Yardımcı fiillerin kullanım ve anlamlarının bazıları.
Daha detaylı bir tanım için iyi bir dil bilgisi kitabı kullanın.

> İngilizcedeki ana yardımcı fiiller:
>
> **can   could   may   might   must   ought   shall   will   would**
>
> *Need* ve *have to*'yu da yardımcı fiil olarak kullanırız.

Aynı kelime farklı kullanım

Her yardımcı fiilin birden fazla kullanımı vardır. Örneğin, can ile olan bu iki cümleye bakın. Kullanım parantez içinde açıklanmıştır.
- ▶ *I **can** swim.* (yetenek)
- ▶ ***Can** you carry this bag for me?* (istek)

1 Bu sözlük fiilin hangi anlamının kullanıldığına karar vermenize yardımcı olur. Yardımcı fiil 'can' e bakın. Kaç anlam bulabilirsiniz?

Talimat, tavsiye, izin ve zorunluluk ifade etmek.

talimat vermek veya zorunlu olan bir şeyi söylemek için
- ▶ *You **must** wear a helmet when riding a bike.*
- ▶ *You **mustn't** smoke in here.*
- ▶ *I **have to** be at the dentist at 3 o'clock.*
- ▶ *You **needn't** shut the door.*

tavsiye vermek veya kesin bir görüş ifade etmek için
- ▶ *You **should/ought to** go to bed if you're tired.*
- ▶ *She **shouldn't** worry about me.*

izin vermek ve istemek için
- ▶ *She **can** borrow my dress.*
- ▶ ***Can/May/Could** I open the window?*

2 Soldaki cümleleri sağdaki kullanım ile eşleştirin:

1 You can borrow my camera if you like.   a instructions
2 If you feel very ill you should go to the doctor.   b permission
3 You must lock the door.   c necessary
4 You don't need to bring food – just something to drink. d advice
5 I need to make a phone call before I go out.   e not necessary

Belirlilik derecelerinin ifade edilmesi

Konuşmacıya göre otomobil John'dadır:
▶ *The car's not here – John **must** have taken it.*

Konuşmacı bunun Clare'in kız kardeşi olduğunu düşünüyor, fakat emin değil:
▶ *She **might/could** be Clare's sister. She looks very like her.*

Konuşmacı bunun mümkün olmadığını düşünüyor:
▶ *She **can't** be his mother – she's younger than me.*

Konuşmacı onun bunu yapacağından emin:
▶ *If she's promised to do it she**'ll** do it.*

Konuşmacı yağmur yağacağından emin değil:
▶ *It **might/could** rain. It's getting cloudy.*

3 Bu cümlelerdeki boşlukları sağdaki listeden bir kelime ile doldurun:

1 He ___ be a hairdresser. His hair's a mess.　　a may
2 'Do you think Joanna will call?'　　　　　　　b won't
　'Who knows? She ___ do.'　　　　　　　　　　c must
3 She ___ ever come back – I know she won't.　　d can't
4 Her hair's all wet – it ___ be raining.　　　　e might
5 'It's 1–1 and there are five minutes to play.
　We ___ still win.'

Yardımcı fiillerin biçimlendirilmesi

Yardımcı fiiller İngilizcenin diğer fiillerinden çok farklıdır:

Fiillerin biçimleri değişmez, örneğin geniş zamanın üçüncü şahsında –s yoktur.
▶ *I **can** speak Spanish and she **can** speak Portuguese.*

Bunları her zaman bir ana fiil takip eder ve kendileri ana fiil olarak kullanılamaz.
▶ *I **must make** a phone call. / We **won't wait** for you.*

Soruları biçimlendirmek için do ve did, olumsuzlar ve kısa yanıtlar kullanmaz.
▶ *'He **wouldn't** steal anything, would he?' 'Oh yes he **would**.'*

KİPSEL FİİL	KISA BİÇİM	OLUMSUZ	KISA BİÇİM
can		cannot	can't
could		could not	couldn't
may		may not	
might		might not	mightn't
must		must not	mustn't
ought to		ought not to	oughtn't to
shall		shall not	shan't
will	'll	will not	won't
would	'd	would not	wouldn't

Öbek fiiller

Öbek fiiller nedir?

Bir öbek fiili bir veya iki tane belirteç veya ilgeç takip eder.
Bazı örnekler:

get up   break down   look after   run out   look forward to

Sadece fiil ve belirteç veya ilgecin anlamını bilmekle öbek fiilin anlamını tahmin etmek genellikle mümkün değildir. Örneğin 'give up something' bir şeyi yapmayı veya kullanmayı durdurmak demektir. Bir şeyler vermekle hiçbir ilgisi yoktur.

Öbek fiillerin bulunması

Öbek fiiller, ana fiil girişinden sonra gelirler ve alfabetik sıradadırlar. Örneğin öbek fiili 'lose' fiilinin tüm anlamlarından sonra gelir.

1 Sözlükte, aşağıdaki fiillerle biçimlendirilmiş kaç tane öbek fiil bulabilirsiniz?

1 drag   2 hand   3 pack   4 make

2 Aşağıdaki cümlelerdeki boşlukları dolduracak öbek fiilleri yapmanıza yardımcı olması için sözlüğü kullanın.

1 If you carry ___ spending like that you'll have no money left.
2 I nodded ___ after lunch.
3 The brakes suddenly seized ___ .
4 It took him a long time to get ___ her death.

Şüphesiz ki fiiller sıklıkla normal anlamlarında, belirteç ve ilgeçlerle de kullanılır, örneğin:
▶ *I went into the room.*
▶ *He put the book on the shelf.*

Bunlar öbek fiiller değildir. Bunlar sadece fiillerin, belirteçlerin ve ilgeçlerin girişlerinde açıklanan normal anlamlardır.

Birden fazla anlamı olan öbek fiiller

Öbek fiillerin birden fazla anlamı vardır.
Bir öbek fiilin birden fazla anlamı olabilir.
Anlamlar sıklıkla ilintili değildir:
▶ *Just pick up the phone and ring her!* (*pick up*= kaldrmak)
▶ *She picks up languages really easily.* (*pick up*= öğrenmek)

3 Bu öbek fiillerin her biri için, her bir cümlede farklı anlamlar kullanarak, ikişer tane cümle yazın:

turn out   catch on   come under sth   fall apart

Öbek fiillerin dil bilgisi

Bazı öbek fiillerin nesneleri vardır, bazılarının yoktur ve bazen nesneleri varken bazen de yoktur. Bu, öbek fiilin sözlükteki yazılış şeklinde gösterilmiştir. Öbek fiilin yazılışı aynı zamanda nesnenin bir kişi, bir şey veya eylem olup olmadığını da gösterir.

Nesneye ihtiyacı olmayan öbek fiiller şöyle gösterilmiştir:

check in   ▶ *You need to **check in** three hours before the flight.*
drift off   ▶ *The room was so hot I could feel myself beginning to **drift off**.*

Nesneye ihtiyacı olan öbek fiiller şöyle gösterilmiştir:

pack sth in   ▶ *I **packed in** my job to go travelling.*
pack sb off   ▶ *They **packed him off** to school in Paris.*

sth'nin 'something', ve **sb'nin** 'someone' demek olduğuna dikkat ediniz.

Bir nesnenin bazen kullanılıp bazen de kullanılmadığı öbek fiiller şöyle gösterilir:

pack (sth) up   ▶ *I **packed up** all my belongings and left the house.*
                    ▶ *Could you help me **pack up**?*

Öbek fiilleri takip eden ilgeçler

Öbek fiillerin çoğunluğunu sıklıkla belirli bir ilgeç takip eder.
Bunlar sözlükte koyu harflerle gösterilmiştir.
▶ *He **dressed up** as a ghost.*

4 Bu cümlelerdeki boşlukları doğru ilgeçlerle doldurunuz.

1 She stood in ___ her boss while he was sick.
2 Just carry on ___ your work.
3 She looked back ___ her days as a student with nostalgia.
4 He's always going on ___ his car.
5 We will have to cut back ___ our spending.

Deyimler

Deyimler, içlerindeki kelimelerin alışılagelmiş anlamlarından başka anlamı olan kelime gruplarıdır. Ne anlama geldiklerini tahmin etmek genellikle mümkün değildir. Bunlar her türlü dil tiplerinde, fakat özellikle de resmi olmayan durumlarda kullanılır. Deyimlerin anlamları çoğunlukla sıradan kelimelerden daha güçlüdür. Örneğin, 'be at loggerheads with someone', 'be arguing with someone' cümlesinden daha fazla vurguya sahiptir ancak ikisinin de anlamı aynıdır.

Bu sözlükte deyimlerin bulunması

Deyimlerin çoğunluğu, deyimdeki ilk ismin girişinde bulunur.
(İsim, bir şey, kişi veya ismin yeridir.)

1 Soldaki her bir deyimin içinde bulunan ilk ismin altını çizin.
Ardından da her bir deyimi sağdaki anlamı ile eşleştirin.

1 be up to your neck in sth	a try to do something you cannot achieve
2 the final nail in the coffin	b be very busy
3 fight a losing battle	c have nothing to do
4 be at a loose end	d not laugh
5 keep a straight face	e something that causes failure

Eğer deyim bir isim içermiyorsa ilk fiil (bir şeyler yapmak için kelime) veya sıfatı (bir şeyleri tanımlamak için kelime) deneyin. Fakat bir deyim için nereye bakacağınızı bilmiyorsanız endişelenmeyin. Yanlış yere bakarsanız nereye gideceğinizi söyleyen bir ➔ bulacaksınız.

> ○⁻**breathe** /briːð/ *verb* [I, T] to take air into and out of your lungs **nefes alıp vermek** *breathe in/out* ○ *breathe deeply* ➔See also: be breathing down sb's **neck**, not breathe a word¹.

2 Aşağıdaki cümlelerin tümü vücudun bir parçasını içeren deyimler kullanır. Her bir cümleyi tamamlamak için kutudan bir vücut parçası seçin.

head	face	arm	leg	ear

1 The accident was clearly his fault – he doesn't have a ___ to stand on.
2 Most of her lecture went over my ___ .
3 Dad might lend you his camera if you twist his ___ .
4 I've never taught this class before, so I'll have to play it by ___ .
5 When I saw his hat, I could hardly keep a straight ___ .

Fiil kalıpları

Bazı fiillerin ardından bir şeyin (bir nesne) gelmesi zorunludur: ▶ *She put the cup on the table.* ▶ *Did you bring any money?*	Diğer fiiller kendilerinden sonra hiçbir şeye ihtiyaç duymazlar: ▶ *He fell.* ▶ *They don't want to stay.*
Bunlar 'geçişli' fiillerdir. Bunlar sözlükte bir [T] ile işaretlenmiştir.	Bunlar 'geçişsiz' fiillerdir. Bunlar sözlükte bir [I] ile işaretlenmiştir.

Bazı fiiller hem geçişli hem de geçişsiz olabilirler:
▶ *Did you see the moon last night?* [T]   ▶ *Can you move, please? I can't see.* [I]
▶ *Did you pay the bill?* [T]   ▶ *Have you paid?* [I]

1 Bu fiillerin geçişli, geçişsiz veya her ikisi de mi olduklarını görmek için sözlüğe bakın.

1 like	3 drive	5 tell	7 hate	9 fall
2 hear	4 smoke	6 explain	8 play	10 hit

Bazen bir fiili diğer dil bilgisi kelimeleri veya kalıplarının izlemesi gerekir, örneğin bir ilgeç, mastar fiil veya –ing ile biten bir fiil:

	I apologized to her.
[+to do sth]	*I promise to help you.*
[+ doing sth]	*Have you finished reading the newspaper?*
[+ (that)]	*He told me (that) it was safe.*

Bir fiilin ardından hangi tip dil bilgisi kullanacağınızdan emin değilseniz sözlükte kelimeye bakın. Tüm dil bilgisi düzeneklerinin tam açıklaması sayfa XIII'dedir.

2 Bu fiilleri nelerin takip ettiğini tarif edebilir misiniz? Soldaki altları çizilmiş kısımları sağdaki listede bulunan tarif ile eşleştirin.

1 He's always **complaining** that nobody listens to him.   a + **to do sth**
2 Did she **say** where she was going?   b + **two objects**
3 He doesn't **like** watching TV.   c + **that**
4 They **want** to go shopping.   d + **doing sth**
5 He **brought** me some flowers.   e + **question word**

3 Aşağıdaki dil bilgisi düzeneklerinde gösterilen bu fiillerin ve kalıpların her birisi için bir cümle yazın.

1 forget + [that]   4 start + to do sth
2 tell + question word   5 sell + two objects
3 like + doing sth

Kelime yapımı

İngilizcede kelime inşa etmenin bazı yolları.

Ön ekler

Ön eklerin anlamlarını değiştirmek için kelimelerin başlangıçlarına eklenir. Bu kitabın sonundaki eklerde sıkça rastlanan ön eklerin bir listesi vardır. Zıt ve genellikle de olumsuz anlam vermek için sıfatlardan önce kullanılan ön eklerden sıkça rastlanan bazıları:

dis- dissimilar **il-** illegal **im-** impossible **in-** inexpensive **ir-** irregular **un-** unhappy	Yeni bir sıfat önerdiğinizde zıttı bir ön ekle oluşturulmuş mu bulmaya çalışın ve iki kelimeyi yazın, örneğin: **happy unhappy**

Un- ve **dis-** ön ekleri, fiilin eyleminin zıttını oluşturmak için fiillerle birleşir:
▸ *She appeared from behind a door.*   ▸ *He **disappeared** through the window.*
▸ *I covered the food with a cloth.*   ▸ *They brushed away the dirt to **uncover** a box.*

1 Yeni kelimeler yapmak için ön ekleri soldaki sıfatlar ve sağdaki fiillerle eşleştirin.

1 un-   4 im-   lock   legal
2 dis-   5 ir-   responsible   agree
3 il-   possible

2 Şimdi de yaptığınız kelimeleri aşağıdaki cümlelerdeki boşlukları doldurmak için kullanın.

1 Which key do I need to ___ this door?
2 The tide is so strong it's ___ to swim against it.
3 It is ___ to drive without a licence.
4 I ___ with her views on immigration.
5 Leaving the children alone was a very ___ thing to do.

3 İngilizcede diğer birçok ön ek kullanılmaktadır. Soldaki ön ekleri sağdaki kullanım ile eşleştirin. Ardından da her bir ön ekle birleşecek uygun kelimeyi kutudan seçerek yeni kelimeler yapın.

1 multi-   a half
2 semi-   b in favour of
3 anti-   c former (not now)
4 pro-   d not enough
5 ex-   e many
6 post-   f against
7 over-   g after
8 under-   h too much

president war
cooked   racial
graduate   worked
circle
democracy

Son ekler

Son ekler kelimelerin sonlarında kullanılır. Bu kitabın sonundaki eklerde sıkça rastlanan son eklerin bir listesi vardır. Bazı sıkça rastlanan örnekler:

-er **-or**	■ aktivite yapanlar ve belirli bir işlevi olan şeyler için	worker, swimmer, golfer, driver, actor, sailor, conductor; tin opener, screwdriver, hanger, projector
-ist	■ belirli inançları olanlar için ■ müzik aletleri çalanlar için ■ bazı meslekler için	Buddhist, socialist violinist, pianist, guitarist journalist, pharmacist, artist
-ness	sıfatlardan isimler yapmak için	happiness, sadness, rudeness
-(t)ion	fiillerden isimler yapmak için	education, television, pollution
-ment	fiillerden isimler yapmak için	improvement, government

Not: Bir kelimeye son ek ilave edilmesi bazen onun söylenişini değiştirir.
Bu kelimelerdeki vurgunun nasıl değiştiğine bakınız:

photograph → pho**tog**rapher   **ed**ucate → edu**ca**tion

İsim, fiil, sıfat?

Son eklerin çoğunluğu bir kelimenin isim, fiil veya sıfat mı olduğunu size söyleyebilir.
Bu tablo bazı sıkça rastlananları gösteriyor:

sıfatlar	-able, -al, -ful, -ible, -ive, -less, -ous, -y	washable, natural, beautiful, flexible, active, helpless, adventurous, happy
isimler	-al -ance, -(t)ion, -ence, -hood, -ity, -ment, -ness, -ship	performance, reduction, independence, parenthood, similarity, enjoyment, politeness, friendship, arrival
fiiller	-en, -ify, -ize	harden, solidify, modernize

Not: -al isimler, örneğin arrival, ve sıfatlar, örneğin comical, yapmak için kullanılabilir

4 Aşağıdaki sıfatlar ve fiilleri isimlere çevirmek için son ekler kullanın.

1 rude   4 ignorant
2 create   5 hilarious
3 prefer   6 develop

Sayılar

Sayıların söylenmesi

Yüzlerden sonra 'and' demeyi unutmayın:
- 569 _five hundred and sixty-nine_
- 7,892 _seven thousand, eight hundred and ninety-two_
- 4,680,022 _four million, six hundred and eighty thousand and twenty-two_

Sayıların kısımları: Ondalıklar ve kesirler

Ondalıklarda noktadan (.) sonraki her sayıyı ayrı söylüyoruz:
- 2.5 _two point five_
- 3.65 _three point six five_
- 22.33 _twenty-two point three three_

Kesirlerde şöyle söylüyoruz:
- 2¼ _two and a quarter_
- ⅕ _one fifth_
- 5¾ _five and three quarters_

Kesirlerin çoğu için sıra sayıları kullandığımızı ancak bunun ½, ¼, ¾ olmadığını hatırlayın:
- ⅜ _three eighths_
- ⅓ _a third or one third_
- ¹⁄₁₂ _a twelfth or one twelfth_

Yüzdelikler ve diğer simgeler

Sayılarla kullanılan sembollerden diğer bazıları:

% percent	45%	_forty-five percent_
° degree	22°C	_twenty-two degrees Celsius_
	70°F	_seventy degrees Fahrenheit_
+ addition	$6+2=8$	_six plus two is/equals eight_
− subtraction	$6-2=4$	_six minus two is/equals four_
× multiplication	$6\times3=18$	_six times three/six multiplied by three is/equals eighteen_
÷ division	$24\div4=6$	_twenty-four divided by four is/equals six_

0'ın söylenmesi

'0' farklı şekillerde söylenebilir. Genellikle 'oh' veya 'zero' ('zero' özellikle Amerikan İngilizcesinde kullanılır) olarak söylenir. 0'ın söylemenin bazı yolları:

MATHS: 0.65 (UK): _nought point six five_, (US): _zero point six five_
FOOTBALL: 6–0 (UK): _six nil_, (US): _six to zero_
TENNIS: 15–0 _fifteen love_
TELEPHONE NUMBER: 965703 _nine six five seven oh three_
(Amerikan İngilizcesinde de _seven zero three_)

Ölçüler

Metrik ve emperyal ölçüler

Uluslar arası metrik ölçü birimleri sistemi ABD'de kullanılmaz.
Bu Britanya'da kullanılıyor olmakla beraber birçok kişi halen pounds, ayak ve galon gibi
eski emperyal birimler sistemini kullanmaktadır.

Britanya ve ABD'de bazı birimlerin isimleri aynı olmakla beraber farklı miktar
anlamlarına gelmektedir.

EMPERYAL	METRİK	EMPERYAL	METRİK
1 inch (in)	2.5 centimetres (cm)	1 ounce (oz)	28 gram (g)
1 foot (ft)	30 centimetres	1 pound (lb)	450 gram
	(100 cm = 1 metre (m))		
1 yard (yd)	90 centimetres	1 pint	(UK) 0.6 litres (US) 0.5 litres
1 mile (m)	2.2 kilometres (km)	1 gallon	(UK) 4.5 litres (US) 3.8 litres

Boyunuzun uzunluğunu söylemek

Britanya ve ABD'de çoğu kişi boylarını emperyal birimlerle söylerler.
▶ *I'm six feet tall.*   ▶ *I'm five foot seven.* (sıklıkla 5' 7" olarak yazılır)

Ağırlığınızı söylemek

Britanya'da çoğu kişi ağırlığını pound ve stone olarak söyler.
Bir stone'da on dört pound vardır.
▶ *I weigh nine stone three.* ('pounds' demek zorunda olmadığınızı not edin.)
▶ *I weigh seven and a half stone.*

ABD'de kişiler ağırlıklarını genellikle pound olarak söyler.
▶ *I weigh 160 pounds.*

Ölçüler hakkında konuşmak

Ölçüler hakkında konuşmak veya soru sormak için normalde sıfatları kullanırız:
▶ *The box is 30cm long.*   ▶ *How tall is David?*

İsimleri de kullanabiliriz fakat bunlar daha resmidir:
▶ *The length of the box is 30cm.* ▶ *What is David's height?*

height	deep	length	width	depth	high	long	wide

1 Kutudaki kelimelere bakın. Hangilerinin sıfat, hangilerinin isim olduğuna karar verin.
Bunları aşağıdaki tabloyu doldurmak için kullanın.

SORU	YANIT	RESMİ
1 How wide is it?	It's 5m ___ .	The ___ of the x is 5m.
2 How ___ is it?	It's 50m long.	The length of the x is 50m.
3 How deep is it?	It's 10m deep.	The ___ of the x is 10m.
4 How ___ is it?	It's 70m ___ .	The height of the x is 70m.

Söyleyiş

İngilizce kelimelerin söyleyişi zor olabilir. Sıklıkla kelimeler söylendikleri gibi yazılmazlar. Sözlükteki her kelimeden sonra gelen ses bilgisi simgeleri o kelimeyi nasıl söyleyeceğinizi gösterir. Bu simgelerin tümünün açıklamaları arka kapağın içinde bulunmakta olup söyleyiş sistemi hakkında daha fazla bilgi de sayfa xvı'dadır.

Simgelerin bazıları benzedikleri harfle aynı şekilde söylenir, örneğin /b/ 'bad'deki 'b' gibi gelir. Diğer tümü sözlükteki her sayfanın dibinde açıklanmıştır.

1 Bu kelimelere bakın ve söyleyişleri ile eşleştirin.

1	cough	a	/'sɪnəmə/
2	throw	b	/θruː/
3	through	c	/sɪŋ/
4	cup	d	/kɒf/
5	cinema	e	/θrəʊ/
6	sing	f	/kʌp/

2 Bu kelimelerin tümü hayvan isimleridir. Hayvanın ismini ses bilgisi simgelerinin yanına yazın.

1 /məʊɪ/   3 /hɔːs/   5 /laɪən/
2 /dʒɪˈraːf/   4 /ʃiːp/   6 /tʃɪmp/

Okunmayan (sessiz) harfler

İngilizcedeki birçok kelime söylenmeyen harfler içerir, örneğin 'listen' daki 't' /lɪsn/.

3 Bu kelimelerdeki harflerden hangileri okunmayan harflerdir?

1 know   3 island   5 two
2 honest   4 wrong   6 talk

Kelime vurgusu

Kelimenin doğru kısmını vurgulamak İngilizcede çok önemlidir.
/'/ simgesi ana vurguyu nerede yapacağınızı gösterir. (Bazı kelimelerin daha az önemli olan başka vurgusu da vardır.)

purple /'pɜːpl/   **important** /ɪmˈpɔːtənt/   **difficult** /'dɪfɪkəlt/

4 Her kelimenin ana vurgusunun olduğu kısmı daire içine alın.

1 brother   3 photographer   5 computer
2 education   4 below   6 necessary

Noktalama

	Kullanımlar	Örnekler
büyük harf / capital letter	■ bir cümlenin ilk harfi	Football is very popular in Britain.
	■ ülkeler, milliyetler, diller, dinler, kişi isimleri, yer isimleri, etkinlikler, kurumlar, ticari markalar, günler, aylar için	Portugal, Africa, Russian, Islam, Joanne, John, Dubai, Geneva, the World Trade Fair, Jaguar, the Internet, Sunday, February, Mr / Mrs / Ms / Dr / Professor
	■ kitap ve film v.b. isimleri için	Matrix Reloaded
	■ kısaltmalar için	OPEC, AIDS, WWF
nokta/ (full stop UK/ period US)	■ cümle sonu	I'm going for a walk.
	■ bazen bir kısaltmadan sonra	Marton Rd./Mrs. White/Dr. Evans
soru işareti/ question mark	■ doğrudan bir sorudan sonra	What's your name?
Ünlem/exclamation mark	■ sürprize uğrama, şok olma v.b. belirtiyi ifade etmek için cümle sonunda	I can't believe it!
	■ yüksek bir sesi işaret etmek için	Ouch! Yes!
virgül/comma	■ bir listedeki maddeler arasında	I need some peas, butter, sugar and eggs.
	■ uzun bir cümlede duraklamayı göstermek için	They didn't want to eat before I'd arrived, but I was an hour late.
	■ ekstra bilgi eklemek istediğinizde	The woman, who I'd met last week, waved as she went past.
tepeden virgül /apostrophe	■ eksik harfler için	don't, I'll, it's (it is)
	■ iyelikler için	Paul's bike
	■ Not: 's' ile biten kelimelere bir 's' daha eklemeye gerek yoktur	James' house
iki nokta üst üste/ colon	■ cümlede bir liste veya alıntı vermek için	You need the following: paint, brushes, water, cloths.
noktalı virgül / semi-colon	■ cümlenin iki kısmını ayırmak için	I spoke to Linda on Monday; she can't come to the meeting tomorrow.
kısa çizgi / hyphen	■ iki kelimeyi birleştirmek için	blue-black
	■ bir kelimenin bölündüğünü ve bir sonraki satırda devam ettiğini göstermek için	Everyone in the room was horrified by the news.
uzun çizgi / dash	cümlenin kısımlarını ayırmak için	The car – the one with the broken window – was parked outside our house.
tırnak işaretleri/ UK aynı zamanda ters virgüller / quotation marks/ UK also inverted commas	konuşulan kelimeleri göstermek için kelimeleri aslında başkasının yazdığını göstermek için	'I'm tired,' she said. 'Let's go,' he suggested. She had described the school as 'not attracting the best pupils'.

Heceleme

İngilizce dilinde, tarihinden dolayı basit heceleme kuralları yoktur. Kelimeler sıklıkla söylendiği gibi yazılmazlar, dolayısıyla da her kelimenin hecelenişini kontrol edip, doğru şekilde yazmak önemlidir.

10 en çok yapılan heceleme hataları

Bunlar *Cambridge Learner Corpus*'da bulunan ve PET (the Preliminary English Test) ve FCE (the First Certificate in English) gibi sınavlara giren orta seviye öğrencileri tarafından 10 en çok yapılan heceleme hatalarıdır.

1	accommodation	çift c ve çift m
2	restaurant	t'den sonra iki ünlü harfi (au) hatırlayın
3	advertisement	(-isement)'ın ortasındaki e'yi unutmayın
4	because	c'den sonra au'yu hatırlayın
5	which	w'dan sonraki h'yi hatırlayın
6	beautiful	b'den sonra üç ünlü harfi (eau) hatırlayın
7	different	çift f ve ikinci f'den sonra e'yi hatırlayın
8	environment	–ment'den önce n'yi hatırlayın
9	especially	bu kelime esp ile başlar
10	opportunity	çift p ve ikinci r'den sonra t'yi hatırlayın

Düzenli çekimler

Hecelemenize yardımcı olacak öğrenebileceğiniz birçok kural vardır. Düzenli çekim kurallarını (örneğin çoğullar, geçmiş zamanlar) açıklayan sayfa xvıı'ye bakın.

1 Bu isimlerin çoğullarını yazın.

1 house   2 watch   3 brick   4 minute   5 fax   6 loss

Kelime başlangıçları

Bazen bir kelimenin ilk harfini bile tahmin etmek zor olabilir.
c c ile başlayan bazı kelimeler s ile başlıyormuş gibi gelir.
▶ *cell, centre, circle*

ps ps ile başlayan bazı kelimeler s ile başlıyormuş gibi gelir.
▶ *pseudonym, psychiatrist*

ph ph ile başlayan bazı kelimeler f ile başlıyormuş gibi gelir.
▶ *philosophy, phone, physical*

Aynı veya benzer ses, farklı heceleme

İngilizcedeki bazı kelimeler aynı veya benzer seslere sahip olmakla beraber farklı hecelenir.

2 Boşlukları doldurmak için sağdaki çiftlerden doğru olan kelimeyi seçin.

1 I don't know ___ he will come.   weather/whether
2 It's ___ a long way to my brother's house.   quite/quiet
3 ___ of these pictures do you like best?   Which/Witch
4 They didn't have ___ coats with them.   their/there
5 We stayed in a cottage by the ___.   see/sea

İkili ünsüzler

-er ile karşılaştırmalı biçim ve **–est** ile üstünlük derecesi biçimi oluşturduklarında bazı sıfatların sonlarında ikileyen ünsüz vardır. Bu olduğunda bu sıfatların girişlerinde açıkça gösterilmiştir.

> ○ **big**[1] /bɪg/ *adjective* **bigger, biggest 1** SIZE large in size or amount **büyük, kocaman, iri** *I come from a big family.* ○ *We're looking for a bigger house.*

Geniş zaman sıfat fiili veya geçmiş zaman ve geniş zaman fiili yaptıklarında bazı fiillerde iki ünsüz vardır. Bu da bu fiillerin girişlerinde açıkça gösterilmiştir.

> **acquit** /əˈkwɪt/ *verb* [T] **acquitting**, *past* **acquitted** If someone is acquitted of a crime, a court of law decides that they are not guilty. **temize çıkarmak, aklanmak, beraat etmek** [often passive] *Both men were acquitted of murder.*

l ile biten fiillerin çoğunun (örneğin travel, level) UK İngilizcesinde iki ünsüzü, US İngilizcesinde tek ünsüzü vardır. Bu da bu fiillerin girişlerinde açıkça gösterilmiştir.

3 Aşağıdaki cümlelerdeki boşlukları kelimenin sağdaki listede bulunan doğru çekimi ile doldurun. Ünsüzü doğru olmayan yerde ikilememeye dikkat edin.

1 It's usually ___ than this in the summer.   (hot)
2 The use of mobile phones is ___ on aircraft.   (ban)
3 The concert was the ___ I've ever been to.   (loud)
4 I'm ___ to find my way around the city.   (begin)
5 I'm tired of ___ ten hours a day.   (work)

Britanya ve Amerika'daki çocuklar hecelemelerine yardımcı olması için bu tekerlemeyi öğrenirler:

'E 'den önce **I gelir C** 'den sonrası hariç'.

▶ *friend, receive*

Web ve İnternet

The Web veya World Wide Web (www) İnterneti kullanarak bakabileceğiniz tüm websitelerine (= elektronik belgeler) gönderme yapar. The Internet veya the Net dünyadaki tüm bilgisayarları birbirlerine bağlayan ve bilgisayar kullanıcılarının web sitelerine bakmalarına izin veren sistemdir. İnternet birçok kişinin yaşamının bir parçası olmuş ve yeni kelimeler yaratmıştır. Bunlardan önemli olan bazıları:

Çevrim içi
Online olmak İnternete bağlanmış veya İnternette müsait olmaktır.
Go online bilgisayarınızın İnternet bağlanmasını başlatmaktır.

Modemler
Modem bir kablo veya telefon hattıyla bir bilgisayardan bilgi göndermenizi sağlayan bir cihazdır.

www.'da gezinmek
Farklı bir web sitesine gitmek veya bir sitenin başka bir kısmına geçmek için links'lere (=İnternetteki belge veya bölgeler bağlantılar arasındaki bağlantılar) tıklamak üzere mouse'unuzu kullanabilirsiniz.

Web siteleri
Web siteleri genellikle bir seri web pages'den oluşur. Bir web sitesindeki ana sayfaya homepage denir. Bir web sitesinin web address veya URL'sini biliyorsanız ekranın üst tarafına yazabilirsiniz. Aksi takdirde bir search engine kullanabilirsiniz. Arama motoru, bir veya iki kelime yazarak İnternette bilgi aramanızı sağlayan yazılımdır. Surf veya to surf the Web çoğunlukla bir sonra nereye gideceğini veya ne aradığını bilmeden farklı birçok siteye bakmaktır.

Bloglar
Blog web sitesinin, bir kişinin her gün neler yaptığını veya farklı konularda neler düşündüğünü anlattığı kısmıdır. Blogger blog yazan kişidir.

Podcastlar
Podcast İnternetten yapılan ve bilgisayar veya MP3 çalarınızda dinleyebileceğiniz kayıttır. Ayrıca bir podcast'a sign up to (=yazılmak istediğinizi söylemek) yapabilirsiniz ki bu da MP3 çalarınızı bilgisayarınıza bağladığınızda İnternet yoluyla güncellenir (=üzerine yeni bilgi eklenir).

İndirme ve yükleme
Bir resim, video, müzik v.b.yi download yaparsınız, İnterneti kullanarak bilgisayarınıza kopyalarsınız. Upload bilgisayarınızdan bir şeyi birçok kişinin kullanabilmesi için İnternet yoluyla bir web sitesine veya başka bir yere kopyalamaktır.

Dosya paylaşımı
Filesharing bir dosyayı diğer kişilerin İnternet yoluyla kopyalayabilmeleri, bakabilmeleri veya kullanabilmeleri için bilgisayarınızda özel bir yere koyma aktivitesidir.

Eposta ve mesaj yollamak

Emails genellikle mektuplardan daha kısa ve daha az resmi olup kişiler bazen içlerinde
kısaltma ve gülen yüzler kullanır. **Smileys** ('**emoticons**' da denir) yandan baktığınızda
yüze benzeyen resimlerdir. Bunlar klavye simgeleri kullanılarak yapılır ve duyguları ifade
etmek için kullanılır. Metin mesajları daha da kısa ve daha da az resmi olup genellikle
kısaltmalar kullanılır.
Sık sık kullanılan gülen yüzler ve kısaltmalar:

Gülen yüzler

:-)	Mutluyum veya gülümsüyorum
:-(	Mutsuz veya kızgınım
:-D	Gülüyorum
>:-(	Çok kızgınım
:-I	Sıkıldım
:-o	Sürprize uğradım veya bağırıyorum
:-@	Çığlık atıyorum
:-*	Sana öpücük gönderiyorum
;-)	Sadece şaka yapıyorum
:-p	Sırıtıyorum (= hoş olmayan veya nezaketsiz şekilde gülümsemek)
:-b	Sana dil çıkarıyorum

Abbreviations

AFAIK	as far as I know	IMHO	in my humble opinion
ASAP	as soon as possible	IOU	I owe you
B4	before	LOL	laughing out loud
B4N	bye for now	L8R	later
BRB	be right back	MSG	message
BTW	by the way	PLS	please
C	see	R	are
CU	See you!	SPK	speak
CUL8R	See you later!	TAFN	that's all for now
FYI	for your information	THX	thanks
GR8	great	2DAY	today
GSOH	good sense of humour	2MORO	tomorrow
GTG	got to go	2NITE	tonight
ILU	I love you	U	you
		WAN2	want to
		WKND	weekend
		X	kiss

UK ve US İngilizcesi

UK ve US'daki İngilizce çok benzer olmakla beraber kelime dağarcığı, heceleme, dil bilgisi ve söyleyişte birçok farklar vardır.

Bu sözlük size nerelerde farklar olduğunu gösterir.
UK ve US etiketlerinin tam açıklaması için sayfa xv'e bakın.

Kelime dağarcığı

Her gün gördüğümüz veya kullandığımız sıkça rastlanan maddeler için olan kelimeler UK ve US İngilizcelerinde farklıdır.

1 Soldaki kelimeler UK İngilizcesidir. Her birini soldaki listede bulunan US kelimesi ile eşleştirin.

1 aubergine	4 windscreen	a elevator	d eggplant
2 wardrobe	5 queue	b truck	e closet
3 lift	6 lorry	c windshield	f line

Resmi olmayan dilde UK ve US İngilizceleri arasında birçok farklar vardır.

2 Her cümledeki <u>altı çizilmiş</u> olan kelime sadece UK İngilizcesinde kullanılır.
Sağdaki listeden, hem UK hem de US İngilizcesinde anlaşılacak bir kelime ile değiştirin.

1 I got it from a <u>bloke</u> at work.	a complaining
2 I'm feeling rather <u>poorly</u> today.	b man
3 I wish he'd stop <u>whingeing</u> and do some work.	c weak
4 I was <u>gutted</u> when I heard I hadn't got the job.	d disappointed
5 My brother's too <u>weedy</u> to climb that tree.	e ill

Heceleme

3 Kelime çiftlerine bakın. Hangisi UK hecelemesi, hangisi US hecelemesidir?

1 labour/labor	3 offence/offense	5 metre/meter
2 center/centre	4 color/colour	6 traveller/traveler

Söyleyiş

Bu sözlükte, UK ve US İngilizcelerinde çok farklı söylenen kelimelerin her iki söylenişleri de kelimede gösterilmiştir.
US söyleyişleri Ⓤ simgeyi takip eder.

4 Bu kelimelerin hangilerinin söyleyişleri UK ve US İngilizcelerinde farklıdır?

1 peach	4 ballet
2 schedule	5 zebra
3 colour	6 bicycle

> **albino** /æl'bi:nəʊ/ Ⓤ /æl'baɪnəʊ/ *noun* [C] a person or animal with white skin, white hair or fur, and pink eyes **beyaz tenli, kıllı ve pembe gözlü hayvan veya insan, albino**

Mektup yazmak

Resmi mektuplar

```
                                          47 Abrahams Rd
                                              Cambridge
                                               CB4 3AL
                                        20 January 2009

Ms R Perry
Evening News
107 Wolfs Way
Newtown
NT7 0PE

Dear Ms Perry ❶

I am ❸ writing to enquire about ❷ the possibility of holiday
work with your company this summer. I am very interested in
gaining some experience working for a newspaper.

For the last two years I have been editor of the student
magazine at my school. Next year I am planning to do a
one-year course in newspaper journalism.

I have good computer skills and accurate written English.

I very much hope you have a vacancy for me. I enclose a
copy of my CV and look forward to hearing from you soon. ❹

Yours sincerely, ❶

Anna Thompson
```

❶ Mektup yazdığınız kişinin ismini biliyorsanız fakat mektup resmiyse mektubu şöyle bitirin: *Yours sincerely.*

Mektup yazdiginiz kisinin ismini bilmiyorsaniz mektuba söyle baslayin: *Dear Sir/Madam* ve söyle bitirin: *Yours faithfully.*

❷ Resmi bir mektuba başlamanın diğer yolları:
- ▶ *I am writing to inform you of/that ...*
- ▶ *I am writing to complain about ...*
- ▶ *I am writing regarding your advertisement ...*
- ▶ *Please send me ...*
- ▶ *Further to my letter of June 1st ...*

❸ Resmi mektupta kısaltmalar (örneğin I'm, I'd) kullanmamalısınız.

❹ Resmi bir mektubu bitirmenin diğer yolları:
- ▶ *Thank you in advance for your help.*
- ▶ *Wishing you all the best for the future.*

Resmi olmayan mektuplar

47 Abrahams Rd
Cambridge
CB4 3AL

20 January 2009

Dear Julia,

It was lovely to chat to you the other day. **❶** It seems ages since we last met. We're so excited that you're finally coming over to see us. In fact, John's going to take those two weeks off work so he can spend more time with us.

By the way, could you bring some photos of your family?

I'd love to see them.

We're both really looking forward to seeing you. **❷**

Love, **❸**

Anna

---

❶ Resmi olmayan bir mektuba başlamanın diğer yolları:
▶ *Thanks for your letter.*
▶ *How are you?*
▶ *I hope you're well.*
▶ *Sorry it's been so long since I last wrote.*
▶ *It was lovely to hear from you.*

❷ Resmi olmayan bir mektubu bitirmenin diğer yolları:
▶ *Drop me a line soon.*
▶ *Write soon.*
▶ *Take care.*
▶ *Do keep in touch.*
▶ *Give my love to Paul.*
▶ *Hope to hear from you soon.*

❸ İsminizden önce şunu yazarsınız:

yakın arkadaşlarınıza:
▶ *love from*
▶ *all my love*
▶ *lots of love*

daha az yakın olan arkadaşlarınıza:
▶ *best wishes*
▶ *all the best*
▶ *yours*
▶ *kind regards*

Eş dizimli/kelime ortağı nedir?

Eş dizimli, ana dilini konuşanların sık sık birlikte söyledikleri veya yazdıkları iki veya daha fazla kelimedir. Bu sözlüğün a-z kısmındaki kutularda bunlara '**kelime ortakları**' diyoruz. Bunlar İngilizce'nin doğallığı için önemlidir. Örneğin ana dili İngilizce olan birisi şöyle der:
He made a mistake.

Fakat şöyle **demez**:
He did a mistake.

Bunun nedeni **mistake, make** ile eş dizimlilik oluşturur fakat **do** ile oluşturmaz.

Doğal bir İngilizce konuşmak istiyorsanız, konuşma ve yazmanızda doğru kelimeleri bir araya getirebilmeniz için önemli eş dizimlerini hatırlamanız gereklidir. Bu, İngilizcenizi daha kolay anlaşılır kılacaktır.

Ne tip eş dizimler vardır?

Fiiller ve isimler
Fiil + isim eş dizimleri vardır. Örneğin:

take a photo	**have** fun	**make** a decision

Veya isim + fiil eş dizimleri vardır. Örneğin:

an accident **happens**	disaster **strikes**	a problem **arises**

Sıfatlar ve isimler
Sıfat + isim eş dizimleri vardır. Örneğin:

heavy traffic	a **written** agreement	a **useful** skill

İsimler ve ilgeçler
İsim + ilgeç eş dizimleri vardır. Örneğin:

an answer **to** sth	an argument **with** sb	a choice **between** sth and sth

Veya ilgeç + isim eş dizimleri vardır. Örneğin:

by mistake	**in** pain	be **of** interest

Eş dizimler bazen aynı konudaki birçok kelimeyle kullanılır. Örneğin 'clothes' konusunda 'wear' eş dizimi, 'jeans', 'skirt', 'shirt' v.b. gibi kelimelerle kullanılır.

Aynı eş dizimlerin birçok farklı kelimeyle kullanıldığı on iki konu aşağıdadır. Takip eden sayfalarda bu konular için en önemli olan eş dizimlerini bulacaksınız. Bunlar öğrenilmesi çok yararlı eş dizimlerdir.

1	Yaş	7	Yemekler
2	Giysiler	8	Aylar
3	Suçlar	9	Müzik aletleri
4	Haftanın günleri	10	Mevsimler
5	Hastalıklar	11	Yazılım
6	Diller	12	Eğitim konuları

1 Yaş

- be [15/30/50, etc.] **years old**
  *She's only four **years old**.*

- be **in your** [30s/40s/50s, etc.]
  *Many women now have children **in their** thirties.*

- *formal* [32/57/70, etc.] **years of age**
  *The prices apply to children between 2 and 15 **years of age**.*

- [a man/woman/daughter, etc] **of** [20/30/65, etc.]
  *She has a son **of** 10 and a daughter **of** 8.*

- **about** [17/40/65, etc.]
  *Their son must be **about** 25 now.*

- **approaching/nearly** [50/60/70, etc.]
  *I would think he's **approaching** 70. • She's **nearly** twenty and still lives with her parents.*

- **over /under** [18/35/80, etc.]
  *You have to be **over** 21 to get into the club. • People **under** 18 are not allowed to drive.*

- **over the age of/under the age of**
  *You must be **over the age of** 16 to buy cigarettes. • We don't sell alcohol to anyone **under the age of** 18.*

- *humorous* **be the wrong side of** [40/50/60, etc.] = be older than 40, 50, 60, etc.
  *She's **the wrong side of** 50 but she's still attractive.*

2 Giysiler

- **wear** [jeans/a skirt/a shirt, etc.]
  *I **wear** a uniform for work.*

- **in** sth/be **dressed in** sth/**wearing** sth
  *He was **dressed in** a grey suit. • She was **wearing** a green dress. • a woman **in** a red coat*

- **have** [a dress/skirt/T-shirt, etc.] **on**
  *I only **had** a thin shirt **on**.*

- **put on/take off** [your dress/jeans/coat, etc.]
  *Put your hat **on** – it's cold. • She **took off** her coat.*

- **do up/fasten/undo/unfasten** [your skirt/belt/coat, etc.]
  ***Fasten** your coat. • She **undid** her jacket and took it off.*

- **loose/tight** [jeans/T-shirt, etc.]
  *He was wearing a pair of **tight** black jeans. • Wear **loose** clothes in hot weather.*

3 Suçlar

- be **accused of/charged with** (doing) sth
  *He appeared in court, **accused of** stabbing a man. • He has been **charged with** the murder of a 10-year-old girl.*

- **face charges of** [murder/burglary, etc.]
  *He arrived in the country to **face charges** of theft and kidnapping.*

- **confess to/admit** (doing) sth
  *She **confessed to** the murder. • He **admitted** driving while drunk.*

- **deny** (doing) sth
*He has **denied** murdering his girlfriend.*

- be **convicted of/found guilty of** (doing) sth
*Jenkins was **convicted of** murdering his mother in 1998. • Bates was **found guilty of** assault.*

- be **arrested for/jailed for** (doing) sth
*She was **arrested for** shoplifting. • He was **jailed for** stealing cars.*

- **investigate** [a murder/assault, etc.]
*Police are **investigating** the murder of a young mother.*

- the [murder/rape, etc.] **of** sb
*The murder **of** the 85-year-old woman has shocked everyone.*

- a [crime/murder/rape, etc.] **victim**
*The organization offers help to rape **victims**.*

- a [murder/rape, etc.] **inquiry/investigation**
*Police have a launched a murder **inquiry** after a woman's body was found.*

- a [murder/rape, etc.] **case**
*The police still have 110 unsolved rape **cases**.*

- a **brutal** [murder/attack/rape, etc.]
*He was jailed for the **brutal** rape of a teenage girl.*

4 Haftanın günleri

- **on** [Monday/Tuesday, etc.]
*I'm going to London **on** Friday.*

- **on** [Mondays/Tuesdays, etc.] (= every Monday, Tuesday, etc.)
*She works **on** Wednesdays and Fridays.*

- **every** [Saturday/Tuesday, etc.]
*I have a piano lesson **every** Saturday.*

- **last/next** [Wednesday/Thursday, etc.]
*The meeting was **last** Monday. • It's my birthday **next** Tuesday.*

- **the following** [Tuesday/Friday, etc.]
*She went into hospital on Friday for an operation **on the following** Monday.*

- [Monday/Friday, etc.] **afternoon/evening/morning/night**
*I have to work on Monday **morning**. • I'm going to a party on Friday **night**.*

5 Hastalıklar

- **have (got)/suffer from** [a cold/cancer, etc.]
*I've got a really bad cold. • He was **suffering from** flu.*

- be **diagnosed with** [asthma/a brain tumour/cancer, etc.]
*In 2001, she **was diagnosed with** breast cancer.*

- **catch** [a cold/chickenpox/measles, etc.]
*I **caught** chickenpox from one of the children.*

- **develop** [cancer/an infection/asthma, etc.]
*People who smoke are more likely to **develop** cancer.*

- **go down with** [flu/a stomach upset, etc.]
*He **went down with** flu two days before we were due to leave.*

- **shake off** [a cold, flu, etc.]
*I've had a cold for two weeks now and I can't **shake** it **off**.*

- **cure/treat** [a cold/infection/cancer, etc.]
*Scientists are searching for a drug to **cure** colds. • Antibiotics can be used to **treat** some throat infections.*

- [hay fever/asthma/cancer, etc.] **sufferers**
*The drug offers new hope to cancer **sufferers**.*

6 Diller

- **speak** [French/Italian/Arabic, etc.]
*She **speaks** very good Russian.*

- **learn/study** [Cantonese/Urdu/Spanish, etc.]
*I'm **learning** German at school. • She wants to study Icelandic at university.*

- **in** [Danish/Mandarin/Portuguese, etc.]
*All the signs were **in** French.*

- **fluent/be fluent in** [German/Japanese/Russian, etc.]
*He speaks **fluent** Italian. • Anna is **fluent in** Japanese.*

- **broken** (= not good and full of mistakes) [French/Italian/Spanish, etc.]
*I tried to make myself understood in **broken** French.*

- a [French/Latin/Russian, etc.] **teacher**
*She's a Spanish **teacher** at the local school.*

7 Yemekler

- **eat/have** [breakfast/lunch, etc.]
*More workers are **eating** lunch at their desks. • He was sitting in a café **having** lunch.*

- **make/prepare** [breakfast/lunch, etc.]
*He was in the kitchen **making** lunch. • She'd **prepared** a lovely meal for us.*

- **have** sth **for** [lunch/dinner, etc.]
*I **had** toast **for** breakfast. • What did you **have for** dinner?*

- serve [breakfast/lunch, etc.]
*Breakfast is **served** in the hotel restaurant between 7 and 9.30am.*

- **skip** [breakfast/lunch, etc.] (= not eat breakfast, lunch, etc.)
*I was late for school so I had to **skip** breakfast.*

- a **big/light** [breakfast/lunch, etc.]
*He always eats a **big** breakfast. • I usually have a **light** lunch.*

- an **early/late** [breakfast/lunch, etc.]
*We had an **early** lunch and then set off. • I got up at 11am and had a **late** breakfast.*

- a **leisurely/quick** [breakfast/lunch, etc.]
*They enjoyed a **leisurely** lunch on the hotel terrace. • We set off early after a **quick** breakfast.*

- **at/over** [lunch/dinner, etc.]
*He didn't say a word **at** breakfast.* • *We discussed it **over** dinner.*

8 Aylar

- **in** [December/March, etc.]
*My birthday's **in** July.*

- **on** [August 24th/May 12th, etc.]
*Her birthday's **on** August 24th.*

- **early/mid/late** [January/June, etc.]
*The weather is usually very nice in **early** July.* • *By **late** May, the situation had improved.*

- **the beginning of/the end of** [May/October, etc.]
*The work should be finished by **the beginning of** April.* • *He's coming at **the end of** November.*

- **last/next** [May/June, etc.]
*They got married **last** December.* • *The elections will be held **next** June.*

9 Müzik aletleri

- **play the/play** [guitar/piano, etc.]
*He **plays** saxophone in a band.* • *She was **playing the** violin.*

- **learn (to play) the** [flute/violin, etc.]
*John's **learning** the clarinet.*

- **on the/on** [drums/violin, etc.]
*Sam was **on the** trumpet and Jim was **on the** saxophone.*

- a [piano/guitar, etc.] **lesson/player/teacher**
*I'm having piano **lessons**.* • *He's a great guitar **player**.*

10 Mevsimler

- **during the/in the/in** [spring/summer, etc.]
*We're very busy **during the** summer.* • *The park is open for longer **in** summer.* • *It often snows **in the** winter.*

- **through the/throughout the** [summer/winter, etc.]
*The plant produces flowers **throughout the** summer.*

- **early/late** [autumn/spring, etc.]
*Sow the seeds in **early** spring.* • *It was a cold night in **late** autumn.*

- **last/next** [winter/summer, etc.]
*The book was published **last** autumn.* • *They're getting married **next** summer.*

- **the depths of winter/the height of spring/summer**
*He never wears a coat, even in **the depths of** winter.* • *It was **the height of summer** and very hot.*

- **the** [spring/summer, etc.] **of** [1995/2004, etc.]
*He had a heart attack in **the** summer **of** 2002.*

- **the** [summer/winter, etc.] **months**
*In the **winter** months, people visit the area to ski.*

11 Yazılım

- **download** [files/music/software, etc.]
*You can just **download** the software from the Internet.*

- **install/uninstall** [a program/software, etc.]
*Follow the on-screen instructions to **install** the program.* • ***Uninstall** the software if you want to free up more disk space.*

- **run** [a program, etc.]
*Click on the icon to **run** the program.*

- **copy/paste** [a file, etc.]
***Copy** the file onto the C-drive.*

- **develop** [software/a program, etc.]
*The software was **developed** in the US.*

12 Eğitim konuları

- **do/study** [physics/German, etc.]
*I'm **doing** French and German this year.* • *Amy's **studying** law at Cambridge University.*

- **have a degree in** [French/history/law, etc.]
*She **has a degree in** chemistry.*

- a [geography/history/maths, etc.] **class/course/lesson**
*He fell asleep in the geography **class**.* • *The college offers language and computer **courses**.*
• *She's having French **lessons**.*

- a [history/maths, etc.] **lecturer/student/teacher**
*Our English **teacher** is called Mrs Jackson.* • *She's a maths **lecturer** at the university.*

Doğal konuşmak
1: farklı durumlar için dil

Bu sayfalar doğal olarak konuşmanıza yardımcı olacaktır. Bunlar size birçok farklı durumlarda ihtiyacınız olan deyimler (=sıklıkla birlikte kullanılan kelime grupları) vermektedir. Bu deyimleri öğrenmeye çalışın.

1	Merhaba demek	4	Bir şeyi yapabileceğinizi sormak	6	Bir şey sunmak
2	Hoşça kal demek			7	Birisine yardım sunmak
3	Birisi üzgünüm dediğinde	5	Bir şeyi alabileceğinizi sormak	8	Birisini davet etmek
				9	Birisi size teşekkür ettiğinden ne denir

1 Merhaba demek

Merhaba demenin alışılmış olan 'Hello' veya 'Hello, how are you?' dışında da şekilleri vardır. İşte bunlardan birkaç tanesi:

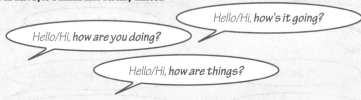

Hello/Hi, how's it going?

Hello/Hi, how are you doing?

Hello/Hi, how are things?

İyi veya mutluysanız yanıt vermek

İyi veya mutlu değilseniz yanıt vermek

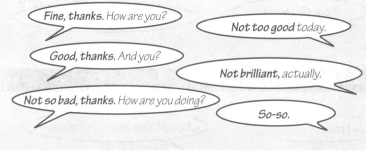

Fine, thanks. How are you?

Not too good today.

Good, thanks. And you?

Not brilliant, actually.

Not so bad, thanks. How are you doing?

So-so.

2 Hoşça kal demek

Arkadaşlarınıza ve ailenize 'goodbye' demenin diğer şekilleri:

Bye. Catch you later!

Bye. See you later!

See you!

3 Birisi üzgünüm dediğinde

Birisi yaptığı bir şeyden dolayı üzgün olduğunu söylerse şunlardan birisini söyleyebilirsiniz:

> It doesn't matter.

> That's all right!

> Don't worry about it!

4 Bir şeyi yapabileceğinizi sormak

> Is it all right if I open a window?

> Do you mind if I smoke?

> May I sit here?

'Evet' demek   'Hayır' demek

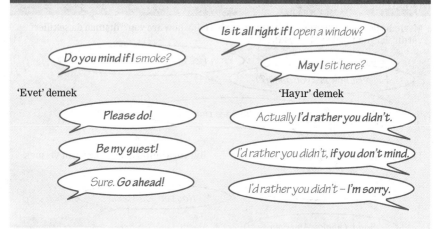

> Please do!

> Be my guest!

> Sure. Go ahead!

> Actually I'd rather you didn't.

> I'd rather you didn't, if you don't mind.

> I'd rather you didn't – I'm sorry.

5 Bir şeyi alıp alamayacağınızı sormak

> May I take this chair?

> Could I have a hand-out, please?

'Evet' demek   'Hayır' demek

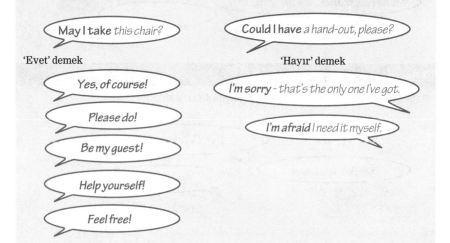

> Yes, of course!

> Please do!

> Be my guest!

> Help yourself!

> Feel free!

> I'm sorry - that's the only one I've got.

> I'm afraid I need it myself.

6 Bir şey sunmak

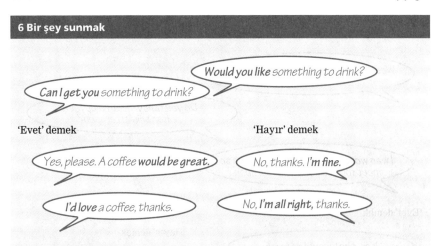

Would you like something to drink?

Can I get you something to drink?

'Evet' demek   'Hayır' demek

Yes, please. A coffee **would be great.**   *No, thanks.* **I'm fine.**

I'd love a coffee, thanks.   *No,* **I'm all right,** thanks.

7 Birisine yardım sunmak

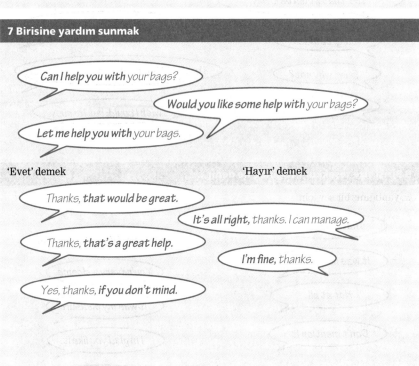

Can I help you with your bags?

Would you like some help with your bags?

Let me help you with your bags.

'Evet' demek   'Hayır' demek

Thanks, **that would be great.**

It's all right, thanks. I can manage.

Thanks, **that's a great help.**

I'm fine, thanks.

Yes, thanks, **if you don't mind.**

8 Birisini davet etmek

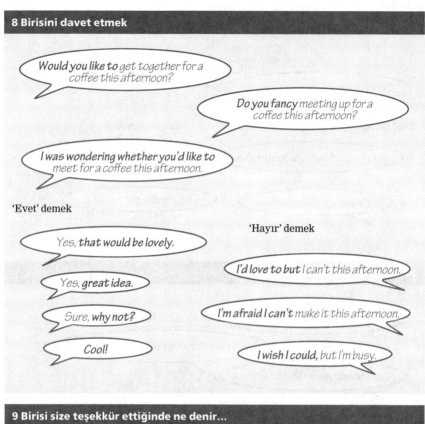

> Would you like to get together for a
> coffee this afternoon?

> Do you fancy meeting up for a
> coffee this afternoon?

> I was wondering whether you'd like to
> meet for a coffee this afternoon.

'Evet' demek

> Yes, **that would be lovely.**

> Yes, **great idea.**

> Sure, **why not?**

> Cool!

'Hayır' demek

> **I'd love to but** I can't this afternoon.

> **I'm afraid I can't** make it this afternoon.

> **I wish I could,** but I'm busy.

9 Birisi size teşekkür ettiğinde ne denir...

... yaptığınız bir şey için:

> That's all right.

> It was no trouble.

> Not at all.

> Don't mention it.

... onlara verdiğiniz bir şey için:

> You're very welcome.

> It was my pleasure.

> I'm glad you like it.

> Don't mention it.

Doğal konuşmak
2: konuşma alıştırmaları

Bu sayfalar farklı durumlarda yapılan on iki tane daha uzun konuşma içermektedir.
Konuşmalarda boşluklar vardır. Her konuşmanın altında bazı deyimler (=sıklıkla birlikte
kullanılan kelime grupları) vardır. Boşlukları doldurmak için doğru deyimleri bulmaya
çalışın. Ardından da bu deyimleri öğrenmeye çalışın. Yine, bunlar da İngilizcenizin kulağa,
İngilizceyi ana dilleri olanlarınki gibi doğal gelmesine yardımcı olacaktır.

1 Randevu almak	7 Birisine ailesinin nasıl olduğunu sormak
2 Telefon etmek	8 Geldiğiniz yer hakkında konuşmak
3 Davetler	9 Planlarınız (hafta sonu veya tatiliniz için)
4 Özür dilemek (üzgün	hakkında konuşmak
olduğunuzu söylemek)	10 Geçen hafta sonu hakkında konuşmak
5 Lokantada	11 Bir düzenlemeyi iptal etmek
6 Birisinin evini ziyaret etmek	12 Birisi size bir haber (iyi veya kötü) verdiğinde

1 Randevu almak

Karşılıklı konuşmaları aşağıdaki deyimlerle tamamlayın:

Doktordan randevu almak
Mark: I'd like to (1) _____ Dr Parker, please.
Receptionist: Right, let me see. The first appointment available is 3.30, Wednesday.
Mark: I'm afraid Wednesday is no good. (2) _____ on Friday?
Receptionist: 4.20 on Friday?
Mark: Yes, that's fine - (3) _____
Receptionist: What's the name, please?
Mark: Mark Klein, (4) _____ K-L-E-I-N.
Receptionist: So, that's 4.20 on Friday with Dr Parker.

a. I'll take that
b. make an appointment to see
c. Do you have anything
d. that's spelt

2 Telefon etmek

Karşılıklı konuşmaları aşağıdaki deyimlerle tamamlayın:

Resmi olmayan bir telefon görüşmesi
Su: Hello.
Anna: Hello, can I speak to Jane, please?
Su: I'm afraid she's not here at the moment. (1) _____
Anna: Yes, please. It's Anna Morris calling. Could you ask her to call me
when she gets back?
Su: Sure. (2) _____
Anna: I think so but I'll give it to you anyway. It's 0209 435876.
Su: Ok, (3) _____
Anna: Thanks very much.
Su: Bye.
Anna: Goodbye.

Bir iş görüşmesi
Receptionist: Good morning. Smith and Dawson. (4)_____
John: Hello. Could I speak to Sylvie Roberts, please?
Receptionist: Certainly. (5)_____
John: It's John Wilson.
Receptionist: OK. (6)_____

a. I'll just put you through.
b. Does she have your number?
c. I'll ask her to call you when she gets in.
d. How can I help you?
e. Could I ask who's calling, please?
f. Can I take a message?

3 Davetler

Karşılıklı konuşmaları aşağıdaki deyimlerle tamamlayın:

Bir davete 'evet' demek
Sasha: I was wondering whether you'd like to come over for dinner one evening.
Nihal: Yes, thank you (1)_____
Sasha: Are you free on Thursday evening?
Nihal: Yes. (2)_____
Sasha: About 7 o'clock?
Nihal: Yes, thanks, that would be great. (3)_____
Sasha: OK, see you on Thursday, then.
Nihal: (4)_____

a. I'll put it in my diary.
b. What sort of time?
c. I'd love to.
d. I'll look forward to it.

Bir davete kibarca 'hayır' demek
Tomas: Suki, would you like to join us for dinner this evening?
Suki: I'd love to but (1)_____ - I'm meeting a friend.
Tomas: That's a shame.
Suki: Yes, (2)_____
Tomas: Maybe another time, then?
Suki: (3)_____

a. I'd love to have come otherwise.
b. Definitely.
c. I'm afraid I can't

4 Özür dilemek (üzgün olduğunuzu söylemek)

Karşılıklı konuşmaları aşağıdaki deyimlerle tamamlayın:

Vikram: Maria, (1)_____ I said I'd call you last night, and I completely forgot.
Maria: Oh, (2)_____. It doesn't matter. I know you're really busy.
Vikram: (3)_____ - it just completely slipped my mind.
Maria: Really, Vikram, it doesn't matter. (4)_____

a. Don't give it another thought.
b. Don't worry about it.
c. I owe you an apology.
d. I feel really bad about it

5 Lokantada

Karşılıklı konuşmaları aşağıdaki deyimlerle tamamlayın:

Yemekten önce
Waiter: Good evening.
Alexandra: Good evening. (1)_____
Waiter: (2)_____
Alexandra: Non-smoking, please.
Waiter: Take a seat near the window.
Alexandra: Thanks. (3)_____ and wine list, please?

a. Smoking or non-smoking?
b. Could we see the menu, please?
c. A table for two, please.

Yemek ısmarlarken
Waiter: Are you (1)_____
Alexandra: Yes, I think so. (2)_____ salmon, please.
Waiter: And for you, madam?
Danielle: Do you have (3)_____
Waiter: Yes, we have several dishes without meat, at the bottom of the menu.
Danielle: Ah yes, I'll have the mushroom tart, please.
Waiter: Okay. (4)_____
Danielle: Yes, one mixed salad, please.
Waiter: (5)_____
Danielle: A bottle of house red and some mineral water, please.
Waiter: (6)_____
Danielle: Sparkling, please.
Waiter: (7)_____
Danielle: Yes, thank you.

a. a vegetarian option?
b. I'll have the
c. Any side dishes with that?
d. And to drink?
e. ready to order?
f. Is that everything?
g. Sparkling or still?

Yemek sırasında
Waiter: (1)_____
Alexandra: Yes, thanks. (2)_____bread, please?
Waiter: Certainly. And (3)_____wine?
Alexandra: No thanks, but could we have another bottle of sparkling mineral water?

a. Could we have some more
b. Is everything all right for you?
c. can I get you any more

Yemekten sonra
Waiter: (1)_____
Danielle: Yes, thanks. It was lovely.
Waiter: Good. (2)_____More coffee?
Danielle: No thanks. (3)_____
Waiter: Of course.

a. Would you like anything else?
b. Could we have the (*UK*) bill/(*US*) check, please?
c. Did you enjoy your meal?

6 Birinin evini ziyaret etmek

Karşılıklı konuşmaları aşağıdaki deyimlerle tamamlayın:
Ethan akşam yemeği için Lidia'nın evine gelir.

Birini karşılamak
Lidia: Hello. (1)_____
Ethan: Hello. (2) _____
Lidia: Not at all. Perfect timing. (3)_____
Ethan: Thank you.
Lidia: (4)_____
Ethan: No, not at all. We've brought you these flowers.
Lidia: Oh, (5)_____ They're beautiful – thank you!

a. I'm sorry we're late.
b. Did you have any problems finding us?
c. Lovely to see you.
d. you shouldn't have!
e. Let me take your coats.

Hoşça kal demek
Ethan: It's been a lovely evening. (1)_____
Lidia: Not at all. (2)_____ Thank you for coming.
Ethan: We'll see you soon. (3)_____
Lidia: That would be great. See you soon. (4)_____
Ethan: Thanks. Bye!
Lidia: Bye!

a. You must come over to us next time.
b. Thank you very much for having us.
c. It's been a pleasure.
d. Drive carefully.

7 Birisine ailesinin nasıl olduğunu sormak

Karşılıklı konuşmaları aşağıdaki deyimlerle tamamlayın:

Luis: Juan, hello!
Juan: Hello Luis, how are you?
Luis: (1)_____, thanks, and you?
Juan: Fine. How's the family?
Luis: (2)_____, thanks. Julia has just been promoted at work.
Juan: (3)_____
Luis: Yes, she's very pleased.
Juan: Do (4)_____
Luis: Yes, I will. By the way, (5)_____, how is your father these days?
Juan: He's much better, thank you.
Luis: That's good. (6)_____ ,won't you?
Juan: Yes, I will. Thanks. (7)_____
Luis: Nice to see you too.

a. They're doing well
b. tell her I was asking after her.
c. Not too bad
d. Good for her!
e. Give him my regards when you see him
f. I was meaning to ask you
g. Nice to see you.

8 Geldiğiniz yer hakkında konuşmak

Karşılıklı konuşmaları aşağıdaki deyimlerle tamamlayın:

Jude: So (1)_____, Thomas?
Thomas: I'm from Germany.
Jude: (2)_____ in Germany?
Thomas: From the north – Osnabrück. Do you know it?
Jude: No, I've been to Karlsruhe but I don't know the north of Germany at all.
Thomas: (3)_____ Where are you from?
Jude: (4)_____ Edinburgh but I live in London now.
Thomas: (5)_____ London?
Jude: North London – a place called Hampstead . (6)_____
Thomas: Yes, I know the name but I've never been there.

a. Have you heard of it?
b. What about you?
c. Where are you from
d. I'm originally from
e. Whereabouts
f. Which part of

9 Planlarınız hakkında konuşmak

Karşılıklı konuşmaları aşağıdaki deyimlerle tamamlayın:

...hafta sonu için
Akbar: (1)_____ this weekend?
Carolina: (2)_____ Just having (3)_____ at home. How about you?
Akbar: We're going to visit my brother in Paris.
Carolina: Paris? That'll be nice.(4)_____
Akbar: Yes, it should be good.

a. a quiet weekend
b. What are you doing
c. Are you looking forward to it?
d. Nothing special.

...tatiliniz, (*UK*) holiday (*US*) vacation, için
Georgia: (1)_____this summer?
Leo: Yes, we're going camping in France. How about you?
Georgia: (2)_____yet but (3)_____Switzerland for a couple of weeks.
Leo: Switzerland. We went there last year and really enjoyed it. (4)_____

a. I think you'll like it.
b. we're thinking of going to
c. Are you going away
d. We haven't booked anything

10 Geçmiş hafta sonu hakkında konuşmak

Karşılıklı konuşmaları aşağıdaki deyimlerle tamamlayın:

Ava: (1)_____
Owen: Yes, thanks - very good. Did you?
Ava: Yes, it was nice.
Owen: Did you (2)_____
Ava: No not really – we just (3)_____ How about you?
Owen: We went to the coast on Saturday.
Ava: (4)_____
Owen: It was really nice. The weather was perfect.
Ava: (5)_____

a. Sounds great!
b. Did you have a good weekend?
c. do anything special?
d. had a quiet one.
e. How was that?

11 Bir düzenlemeyi iptal etmek

Karşılıklı konuşmaları aşağıdaki deyimlerle tamamlayın:

Marta: I'm really sorry , Michel, but (1)_____dinner tonight. (2)_____
Michel: Oh what a shame. (3)_____
Marta: Can we arrange it for another time?
Michel: Yes, (4)_____
Marta: Next week sometime would be great. (5)_____
Michel: Don't worry about it – it's not a problem.

a. Something's come up.
b. I'm going to have to cancel
c. I'm free most evenings next week.
d. Never mind.
e. I'm really sorry about tonight.

12 Birisi size bir haber verdiğinde

Karşılıklı konuşmaları aşağıdaki deyimlerle tamamlayın:

İyi haberler
James: I've just heard that I've got the job.
Erin: (1)_____
James: Thank you!
Erin: Well done! (2)_____
James: Yes, I am. It's really good news.
Erin: I'm so pleased for you, James – you deserve it.
James: Thank you – (3)_____

Kötü haberler
Conor: I'm afraid I won't be able to make it to the party tonight.
 I've got to work.
Patrice: Oh no, (4)_____ You were really looking forward to it.
Conor: Yes, I'm really disappointed.
Patrice: (5)_____ Is there no way round it?

a. You must be really pleased.
b. what a shame!
c. that's very kind.
d. Congratulations!
e. I bet you are.

© Cambridge University Press 2009

Yanıt anahtarı

Çalışmanızı kontrol etmek

1 1 The new rule affects everyone.
  2 What time is it?
  3 It's quite hot in here.
  4 He made/gave an interesting speech.
2 1 do **2** take **3** of **4** feeling
3 The name of this place is Milan, and it is one of the most important Italian cities. You will find Milan in the north of Italy and you can get there by car, train, or plane, but **I think/in my opinion**, travelling by car is the best solution. I suggest **visiting/you visit** Milan, not only because it's full of people but also for its historical buildings.
  I decided to go **to** Milan because **I wanted to** see the Duomo and the Castello Sforsesco, and I must **tell you** that they are **incredible**. I hope that you decide to go to Milan **next summer**.
  I look forward to **seeing** you very soon, with love, Luca PS Besides, in Milan there are **a lot of** pubs and discos where I know many interesting **people**.

Sayılabilen ve sayılamayan isimler

1 1 homework **2** sand **3** ✓
  4 ✓ **5** luggage
2 1 an **2** —, a **3** a **4** — **5** —
3 1 fly **2** furniture **3** luggage **4** day
  5 accidents
4 1 a lot of **2** much **3** many **4** much
  5 duck, ice cream, lipstick, pizza

Yardımcı fiiller

1 7
2 1 b **2** d **3** a **4** e **5** c
3 1 d **2** e **3** b **4** c **5** a

Öbek fiiller

1 1 drag: 3 **2** hand: 5 **3** pack: 3
  4 make: 12
2 1 on **2** off **3** up **4** over
3 your own answers
4 1 for **2** with **3** on **4** about **5** on

Deyimler

1 1 neck: b **2** nail: e **3** battle: a **4** end: c
  5 face: d
2 1 leg **2** head **3** arm **4** ear **5** face

Fiil kalıpları

1 1 T **2** I,T **3** I,T **4** I,T **5** T **6** I,T
  7 T **8** I,T **9** I **10** T
2 1 c **2** e **3** d **4** a **5** b
3 your own answers

Kelime yapımı

1 1 unlock **2** disagree **3** illegal
  4 impossible **5** irresponsible
2 1 unlock **2** impossible **3** illegal
  4 disagree **5** irresponsible
3 1 e, multiracial **2** a, semicircle
  3 f, anti-war **4** b, pro-democracy
  5 c, ex-president **6** g, postgraduate
  7 h, overworked **8** d, under-cooked
4 1 rudeness **2** creation **3** preference
  4 ignorance **5** hilarity **6** development

Ölçüler

1 wide, width **2** long **3** depth
4 high, high

Söyleyiş

1 1 d **2** e **3** b **4** f **5** a **6** c
2 1 mole **2** giraffe **3** horse **4** sheep
  5 lion **6** chimp
3 1 k **2** h **3** s **4** w **5** w **6** l
4 1 **bro**ther **2** edu**ca**tion **3** pho**tog**rapher
  4 be**low** **5** com**pu**ter **6** ne**ce**ssary

Heceleme

1 1 houses **2** watches **3** bricks
  4 minutes **5** faxes **6** losses
2 1 whether **2** quite **3** which **4** their
  5 sea
3 1 hotter **2** banned **3** loudest
  4 beginning **5** working

UK ve US İngilizcesi

1 1 d **2** e **3** a **4** c **5** f **6** b
2 1 b **2** e **3** a **4** d **5** c
3 in each case, UK comes first
  1 labour/labor **2** centre/center
  3 offence/offense **4** colour/color
  5 metre/meter **6** traveller/traveler
4 schedule, ballet, zebra

Doğal konuşmak
2: konuşma alıştırmaları

1 **1** b **2** c **3** a **4** d
2 **Resmi olmayan bir telefon görüşmesi**
 1 f **2** b **3** c
 Bir iş görüşmesi
 4 d **5** e **6** a
3 **Bir davete 'evet' demek**
 1 c **2** b **3** a **4** d
 Bir davete kibarca 'hayır' demek
 1 c **2** a **3** b
4 **1** c **2** b **3** d **4** a
5 **Yemekten önce**
 1 c **2** a **3** b
 Yemek ısmarlarken
 1 e **2** b **3** a **4** c **5** d **6** g **7** f
 Yemek sırasında
 1 b **2** a **3** c
 Yemekten sonra
 1 c **2** a **3** b
6 **Birisini karşılamak**
 1 c **2** a **3** e **4** b **5** d
 Hoşça kal demek
 1 b **2** c **3** a **4** d
7 **1** c **2** a **3** d **4** b **5** f **6** e **7** g
8 **1** c **2** e **3** b **4** d **5** f **6** a
9 **Bu hafta sonu için**
 1 b **2** d **3** a **4** c
 Tatiliniz, (UK) holiday (US) vacation, için
 1 c **2** d **3** b **4** a
10 **1** b **2** c **3** d **4** e **5** a
11 **1** b **2** a **3** d **4** c **5** e
12 **İyi haberler**
 1 d **2** a **3** c
 Kötü haberler
 4 b **5** e

lous research. ● **meticulously** *adverb* **çok dikkatli bir şekilde, itina ile**

me time /'mi:taɪm/ *noun* [U] *informal* time when you can do exactly what you want **kendine ayrılan zaman**

o⌐**metre** *UK* (*US* **meter**) /'mi:tə^r/ *noun* **1** [C] (*written abbreviation* **m**) a unit for measuring length, equal to 100 centimetres **metre, 100 cm'ye eşit uzunluk ölçü birimi** *Our bedroom is five metres wide.* ○ *She finished third in the women's 400 metres* (= running race). **2** [C, U] a pattern of rhythm in poetry **vezin**

metric /'metrɪk/ *adjective* The metric system of measurement uses units based on the gram, metre, and litre. **metrik**

,metric 'ton *noun* [C] a unit for measuring weight, equal to 1000 kilograms **1000 kilograma eşit ağırlık ölçü birimi; metrik ton**

metro[1] /'metrəʊ/ *noun* [C] an underground railway system in a large city **metro; yeraltı raylı sistem** *the Paris metro*

metro[2] /'metrəʊ/ *adjective* [always before noun] *US informal* relating to a large city and the towns around it **büyük şehir ve kentlerle ilgili; şehirsel** *the New York metro area*

metropolis /mə'trɒpəlɪs/ *noun* [C] a very large city, often the capital of a country or region **büyük şehir**

metropolitan /ˌmetrə'pɒlɪt²n/ *adjective* [always before noun] relating to a large city **büyük şehire ilişkin** *a metropolitan area/council*

mg *written abbreviation for* milligram (= a unit for measuring weight) **miligram'ın kısa yazılışı**

miaow *UK* (*US* **meow**) /miː'aʊ/ *noun* [C] the sound that a cat makes **miyav, kedi sesi**

mice /maɪs/ *plural of* mouse **fareler**

mickey /'mɪki/ **take the mickey (out of sb)** *UK informal* to laugh at someone and make them seem silly **dalga geçmek, alay etmek**

micro- /maɪkrəʊ-/ *prefix* very small **çok ufak anlamında ön ek; mikro** *a microchip* ○ *microscopic* (= very small)

microbe /'maɪkrəʊb/ *noun* [C] a very small organism, often a bacterium that causes disease **mikrop**

microchip /'maɪkrəʊtʃɪp/ *noun* [C] a very small part of a computer or machine which does calculations or stores information **mikroçip; bilgisayarda veya bir makinada hesaplamaları yapan ve bilgiyi depolayan küçük parça**

microcosm /'maɪkrəʊˌkɒz²m/ *noun* [C] *formal* a place, group of people, or situation that has the same characteristics as a larger one **mini evren, küçük topluluk, mikrokozmoz, model** *The town is a microcosm of French culture.*

microphone /'maɪkrəfəʊn/ *noun* [C] a piece of electrical equipment for recording or broadcasting sounds, or for making sounds louder **mikrofon**

microprocessor /ˌmaɪkrəʊ'prəʊsesə^r/ ⓤ /'maɪkrəʊ-ˌprɑːsesər/ *noun* [C] the part of a computer that controls all the other parts **mikroişlemci; bilgisayarda tüm diğer parçaları kontrol eden birim**

⌐⌐⌐ *microscope* .... İLE BİRLİKTE KULLANILAN KELİMELER

under a microscope ● **through** a microscope

microscope /'maɪkrəskəʊp/ *noun* [C] a piece of scientific equipment which uses lenses (= pieces of curved glass) to make very small objects look bigger **mikroskop**

microscopic /ˌmaɪkrə'skɒpɪk/ *adjective* extremely small and needing a microscope to be seen, or using a microscope to see something **mikroskopik; sadece mikroskopla görülebilen** *microscopic organisms/particles*

microwave[1] /'maɪkrəʊweɪv/ *noun* [C] **1** (*also* micro-,wave 'oven) an electric oven that uses waves of energy to cook or heat food **mikrodalga fırın** ⮕Orta kısımdaki renkli sayfalarına bakınız. **2** a very short wave similar to a radio wave that is used for sending information and cooking **mikrodalga**

microwave[2] /'maɪkrəʊweɪv/ *verb* [T] to cook or heat food using a microwave oven **mikrodalga fırında pişirmek**

mid- /mɪd-/ *prefix* among or in the middle of **ortasında/ arasında anlamında ön ek** *mid-March* ○ *mid-after-noon*

mid-air /ˌmɪd'eə^r/ *noun* **in mid-air** in the air or sky **havada, gökyüzünde** *She jumped up and caught the ball in mid-air.* ● **mid-air** *adjective* [always before noun] *a mid-air collision* **havada asılı**

midday /ˌmɪd'deɪ/ *noun* [U] 12 o'clock in the middle of the day, or the period around this time **gün ortası** *the heat of the midday sun*

o⌐**middle**[1] /'mɪdl/ *noun* **1 the middle** the central part, position, or point in time **(zaman, konum vs.) ortası, ortasında** *We used to live just outside Boston but now we live right* (= exactly) *in the middle.* ○ *The letter should arrive by the middle of next week.* **2 be in the middle of doing sth** to be busy (tam) ...iken/ortasındayken/ile uğraşırken/meşgulken *I can't talk now - I'm in the middle of cooking a meal.* **3 your middle** *informal* your waist, or your waist and stomach **bel bölgesi; bel/ mide/karın boşluğu** *He wrapped the towel round his middle.* **4 in the middle of nowhere** a long way from places where people live **dağ başında, ıssız bir yerde, neresi olduğu bilinmeyen bir yerin ortasında** *His car broke down in the middle of nowhere.*

o⌐**middle**[2] /'mɪdl/ *adjective* [always before noun] **1** in a central position **ortasında, merkezde** *The middle layer is made of plastic.* ○ *Our company rents the middle warehouse.* **2** neither very high nor low in importance or amount **orta, vasat, şöyle böyle; ne iyi ne kötü** *middle managers*

middle-aged /ˌmɪdl'eɪdʒd/ *adjective* in the middle of your life before you are old **orta yaşlı** *a middle-aged couple/man/woman*

the ,Middle 'Ages *noun* the period in European history between the end of the Roman Empire and the start of the Renaissance **Orta Çağlar; Avrupa tarihinde Roma İmparatorluğu'nun sonu ve Rönesans'ın başlamasını kapsayan dönem**

,middle 'class *noun* [group] a social group that consists of well-educated people, such as doctors, lawyers, and teachers, who have good jobs and are neither very rich nor very poor **orta sınıf** ● **middle-class** /ˌmɪdl'klɑːs/

microscope

M

adjective belonging or relating to the middle class sınıfa ait/ile ilgili *a middle-class suburb*

the ˌMiddle ˈEast *noun* a group of countries in the area where Africa, Asia, and Europe meet **Orta Doğu** • **Middle Eastern** *adjective* relating to the Middle East **Orta Doğu'ya ilişkin** *Middle Eastern cuisine*

middleman /ˈmɪdlmæn/ *noun* [C] *plural* **middlemen** someone who buys goods from one person and sells them to someone else for a higher price **aracı, komisyoncu; birinden alıp başkasına satan kişi** *Selling direct from the factory cuts out the middleman.*

ˌmiddle ˈname *noun* [C] an extra name between someone's first and family names **orta isim**

ˈmiddle ˌschool *noun* [C] a school in the US for children usually between the ages of 11 and 14 **ortaokul; (ABD) 11-14 yaşları arasında çocukların devam ettiği okul**

midget /ˈmɪdʒɪt/ *noun* [C] someone who is very small **cüce**

the Midlands /ˈmɪdləndz/ *noun* the central area of England which includes several large industrial cities **İngiltere'de bir çok büyük sanayi şehrinin yeraldığı orta bölge**

ˌmid-life ˈcrisis *noun* [C] *plural* **mid-life crises** a period in the middle of your life when you lose confidence in your abilities and worry about the future **kendine güvenin kaybolduğu ve gelecekten endişe duyulan yaşamın tam ortasında hissedilen kriz**

midnight /ˈmɪdnaɪt/ *noun* [U] 12 o'clock at night **gece yarısı** *He died shortly after midnight.*

midriff /ˈmɪdrɪf/ *noun* [C] the front of your body between your chest and waist **göğüsle karın arasındaki bölge**

midst /mɪdst/ *noun* **1 in the midst of sth** in the middle of something, usually an event or activity **tam ortasında/arasında; bir olay veya faaliyetin tam ortasında/esnasında** [+ of + doing sth] *Can I phone you back? I'm in the midst of cooking dinner.* **2 in your midst** among the group of people that you belong to **...ın/in arasında/ortasında/esnasında** *Residents are protesting about a convicted murderer living in their midst.*

midsummer /ˌmɪdˈsʌməʳ/ *noun* [U] the longest day of the year, or the period around this **yaz ortası**

midway /ˌmɪdˈweɪ/ *adverb* **1 midway between sth and sth** at the middle point between two places or things **yolun yarısında, yarı yolda, ...ın/in ortasında** *Leeds is midway between London and Edinburgh.* **2 midway through sth** at the middle point of an activity or a period of time **tam yarısında, bir eylemin/zamanın tam ortasında** *He scored the third goal midway through the second half.*

midweek /ˌmɪdˈwiːk/ *noun* [U] the middle of the week, usually from Tuesday to Thursday **hafta ortası** • **midweek** *adjective, adverb* [always before noun] in the middle of the week **hafta ortasında** *a midweek game/match* ○ *Flights are cheaper if you travel midweek.*

the Midwest /ˌmɪdˈwest/ *noun* the northern central area of the United States **ABD'nin kuzey orta bölgesi; Ortabatı** • **Midwestern** *adjective* [always before noun] relating to the Midwest **Ortabatıya ait/ilişkin**

midwife /ˈmɪdwaɪf/ *noun* [C] *plural* **midwives** /ˈmɪdwaɪvz/ a nurse who has had special training to help women give birth **doğum hemşiresi, ebe**

midwifery /mɪdˈwɪfʳri/ *noun* [U] the work of a midwife **doğum hemşireliği, ebelik**

midwinter /ˌmɪdˈwɪntəʳ/ *noun* [U] the shortest day of the year, or the period around this **kış ortası**

oᵃ**might¹** /maɪt/ *modal verb* **1** used to talk about what will possibly happen **olasılık/ihtimal bildiren yardımcı fiil;** ...a/e bilir; olması mümkün *It might be finished by Thursday.* ○ *She might not come.* **2** used to talk about what is possibly true **olabilir, olması muhtemeldir; olasılık dahilindedir** *I think Isabel might be pregnant.* ○ *The rain might have stopped by now.* **3 you might like/want to** UK *formal* used to politely suggest something ...a/e bilirsin; ...ya/yı yapmayı düşünebilirsin; nazik öneride bulunmada kullanılır *You might want to try a different approach next time.* ⊃See study page Modal verbs on page Centre 22.

might² /maɪt/ *noun* [U] *formal* great strength or power **büyük güç/kuvvet** *economic/military might* ○ *She pushed the door with all her might* (= with as much force as possible).

mightn't /ˈmaɪtⁿnt/ *mainly UK formal short for* might not **olumsuz olasılık bildiren 'might not' yardımcı fiilinin kısa yazılışı** *It mightn't be true.*

might've /ˈmaɪtəv/ *short for* might have **geçmişte olan ve hâlen etkisi devam eden olasılığı bildiren yardımcı fiilin kısa yazılışı** *The children might've seen her in the park.*

mighty¹ /ˈmaɪti/ *adjective* very powerful or successful **çok güçlü ve başarılı, kudretli, haşmetmeap** *In their next game they're playing the mighty Redskins.*

mighty² /ˈmaɪti/ *adverb* mainly US *informal* very **çok** *It's mighty tempting to stay in bed on a rainy morning.*

migraine /ˈmaɪgreɪn/ *noun* [C, U] a very bad pain in the head, often one that makes you vomit **migren**

migrant /ˈmaɪgrⁿnt/ *noun* [C] someone who goes to live in a different place in order to find work **göçmen** *migrant labour/workers*

migrate /maɪˈgreɪt/ ⓤ /ˈmaɪgreɪt/ *verb* [I] **1** When birds, fish, or animals migrate, they travel from one place to another at the same time each year. **(kuşlar, balıklar, hayvanlar) göç etmek** *Many birds migrate from Europe to African forests for the winter.* **2** When people migrate, they move to another place, often a different country, in order to find work and a better life. **(insanlar) göçmek, göç etmek** *Between 1900 and 1914, 3.1 million people migrated to the US from central Europe.* • **migration** /maɪˈgreɪʃⁿn/ *noun* [C, U] **göç**

migratory /ˈmaɪgreɪtʳri/ ⓤ /ˈmaɪgrətɔːri/ *adjective* [always before noun] relating to birds, fish, or animals that migrate **göçmen, göç eden (kuşlar, balıklar, hayvanlar)**

mike /maɪk/ *noun* [C] *informal short for* microphone **mikrofon**

mild /maɪld/ *adjective* **1** WEATHER When weather is mild, it is less cold than you would expect. **(hava) yumuşak, ılıman** *a mild winter* **2** ILLNESS When an illness is mild, it is not as serious as it could be. **(hastalık) hafif, sarsmayan, ciddi olmayan** *My doctor said I had a mild form of pneumonia.* **3** WEAK not having a strong effect **zayıf, fazla etkili olmayan** *a mild taste* ○ *a mild detergent* **4** KIND calm and gentle **sakin, nazik, yumuşak, mülayim** *He has a very mild manner.*

mildly /ˈmaɪldli/ *adverb* **1** slightly **hafifçe, yumuşakça, biraz** *I find his films mildly amusing.* **2 to put it mildly** something you say when an opinion is not expressed as strongly as it should be **en hafif deyimiyle söylemek** *The building is unsafe, to put it mildly.*

oᵃ**mile** /maɪl/ *noun* [C] a unit for measuring distance, equal to 1609 metres or 1760 yards **mil** *The nearest station is two miles from here.* ○ *It's a five-mile walk to the next village.* ○ *The latest high-speed trains can travel at 140 miles per hour.* ⊃See study page Measurements on page Centre 31. **2 miles** a very long distance çok uzun mesafe, millerce *We drove for miles along dusty roads.* ○ *Her cottage is miles from the nearest village.*

mileage /'maɪlɪdʒ/ *noun* 1 [DISTANCE] [C, U] the number of miles that a vehicle has travelled since it was new **bir aracın yapmış olduğu mil** *low mileage* 2 [FUEL] [C, U] the number of miles a vehicle can travel using a particular amount of fuel **belli oranda yakıtla bir aracın kaç mil gideceği; yapılan mil** 3 [ADVANTAGE] [U] *informal* an advantage got from something **fayda, kâr, elde edilen avantaj** *There's no mileage in taking your employer to court.*

milestone /'maɪlstəʊn/ *noun* [C] an important event in the history or development of something or someone **önemli olay, dönüm noktası; kilometre taşı** *Passing my driving test was an important milestone for me.*

militant¹ /'mɪlɪtᵊnt/ *adjective* expressing strong support for a political or social idea, and willing to use extreme or violent methods to achieve it **militan, mücadeleci** *a militant group/organization* ● **militancy** /'mɪlɪtᵊnsi/ *noun* [U] when someone is militant **militanlık**

militant² /'mɪlɪtᵊnt/ *noun* [C] a militant person **militan**

o‑**military¹** /'mɪlɪtri/ *adjective* relating to the army, navy, or air force **askeri** *military action/service*

the military² /'mɪlɪtri/ *noun* a country's army, navy, and air force **ordu, silahlı kuvvetler**

militia /mɪˈlɪʃə/ *noun* [C] a group of people who have been trained as soldiers but are not part of a country's official army **milis, halk ordusu** ● **militiaman** *noun* [C] *plural* **militiamen** a member of a militia **milis/halk ordusu mensubu**

o‑**milk¹** /mɪlk/ *noun* [U] a white liquid produced by women and other female animals, such as cows, for feeding their babies **süt** *a carton of milk* ○ *breast milk* ⊃See also: **skimmed milk**.

milk² /mɪlk/ *verb* [T] 1 to get as much money or as many advantages as possible from a person or situation **iliğini kurutmak, sömürmek, sağmak; (argo) sağmal inek gibi kullanmak** *She milked her grandfather for all his savings.* 2 to take milk from a cow using your hands or a machine **süt sağmak**

milkman /'mɪlkmən/ *noun* [C] *plural* **milkmen** a man whose job is bringing milk to people's homes early in the morning **sütçü**

milkshake /'mɪlkʃeɪk/ *noun* [C, U] a sweet drink made of milk and chocolate or fruit **süt çikolata veya meyve karışımı** *a banana milkshake*

milky /'mɪlki/ *adjective* 1 containing milk, often a lot of it **sütlü, sütten yapılmış mamül** *milky coffee/tea* 2 similar to milk **süte benzer, süt gibi** *a milky liquid*

the Milky Way /ˌmɪlkiˈweɪ/ *noun* the group of very many stars which includes the sun **Samanyolu**

mill¹ /mɪl/ *noun* [C] 1 [FLOUR] a machine for crushing grain into flour, or a building with this machine **değirmen** *a flour mill* 2 [POWDER] a small machine used in the kitchen for crushing things such as coffee beans into a powder **el değirmeni, öğütme makinası** *a coffee/pepper mill* 3 [MATERIAL] a factory where one material or substance is made **fabrika** *a cotton/woollen mill* ○ *a paper/steel mill*

mill² /mɪl/ *verb* [T] to use a machine to crush something into a powder **öğütmek, değirmende çekmek** *freshly milled black pepper*

mill about/around (sth) *phrasal verb* When people mill around, they come together in a place, usually to wait for someone or something. **bir yerde toplaşıp bekleşmek; dönüp dolaşıp durmak**

millennium /mɪˈleniəm/ *noun* [C] *plural* **millennia** 1 a period of 1000 years, often calculated from the date when Christ is thought to have been born **binyıl, binyıllık dönem** 2 **the Millennium** the change from the year 1999 to 2000 in the Western calendar **Binyıl, Milenyum** *Where did you celebrate the Millennium?*

milli- /mɪli-/ *prefix* a thousandth **bininci anlamında ön ek** *a millisecond*

milligram /'mɪlɪɡræm/ (*written abbreviation* **mg**) *noun* [C] a unit for measuring weight, equal to 0.001 grams **miligram**

millilitre *UK* (*US* **milliliter**) (*written abbreviation* **ml**) /'mɪlɪˌliːtər/ *noun* [C] a unit for measuring liquid, equal to 0.001 litres **mililitre**

millimetre *UK* (*US* **millimeter**) (*written abbreviation* **mm**) /'mɪlɪˌmiːtər/ *noun* [C] a unit for measuring length, equal to 0.001 metres **milimetre**

o‑**million** /'mɪljən/ 1 the number 1,000,000 **milyon** 2 **millions** *informal* a lot **milyonlarca, çok fazla, epeyce** *I've seen that film millions of times.*

millionaire /ˌmɪljəˈneər/ *noun* [C] a very rich person who has money and possessions to the value of at least one million pounds or dollars **milyoner**

millionth¹ /'mɪljənθ/ 1,000,000th written as a word **milyonuncu**

millionth² /'mɪljənθ/ *noun* [C] one of a million equal parts of something; ¹/₁,₀₀₀,₀₀₀; .000001 **milyonda bir**

mime /maɪm/ *verb* [I, T] to act or tell a story without speaking, using movements of your hands and body, and expressions on your face **mimik ve hareketlerle anlatmak** *Pop stars often mime (= pretend to sing while their song is played) on TV.* ● **mime** *noun* [C, U] *a mime artist* **taklit**

mimic¹ /'mɪmɪk/ *verb* [T] **mimicking**, *past* **mimicked** 1 to copy the way someone talks and behaves, usually to make people laugh **taklidini yapmak, taklit etmek; mimiklerini taklit etmek** *He's always getting into trouble for mimicking his teachers.* 2 to have the same behaviour or qualities as something else **aynı özelliklere sahip olmak; benzer özellikler taşımak** *The drug mimics the effects of a natural hormone.*

mimic² /'mɪmɪk/ *noun* [C] someone who is good at mimicking other people **taklitçi**

mince¹ /mɪns/ *UK* (*US* **ground beef**) *noun* [U] meat, usually from a cow, which has been cut into very small pieces by a machine **kıyma (et)**

mince² /mɪns/ *verb* [T] to cut food into small pieces in a machine **kıyma yapmak/çekmek (et)** *minced beef/onions*

mincemeat /'mɪnsmiːt/ *noun* [U] 1 a spicy, sweet mixture of apples, dried fruit, and nuts, which have been cut into small pieces **baharatlı elma, kuru meyve ve fındık karışımı** 2 **make mincemeat of sb** *informal* defeat someone very easily **kolayca alt etmek/yenmek; kısa yoldan halletmek**

ˌmince ˈpie *noun* [C] *UK/US* a small pastry filled with mincemeat that is eaten mainly at Christmas **Noel pastası/çöreği/kurabiyesi**

o‑**mind¹** /maɪnd/ *noun* [C] 1 someone's memory or their ability to think, feel emotions, and be aware of things **beyin, akıl, zihin, kafa** *For some reason her words stuck in my mind.* ○ *She has a very logical mind.* 2 **have sth on your mind** to think or worry about something **kafasında bir şeyler olmak; bir şeyler tasarlamak/düşünmek; bir şeylerden endişe duymak** *Jim has a lot on his mind at the moment.* 3 **bear/keep sb/sth in mind** to remember someone or something that may be useful in the future **aklında tutmak,** unutmamak, hatırlamak *I'll keep you in mind if another job comes up.* ○ [+ (that)] *Bear in mind that there's a bank holiday next week.* **4 make your mind up** to make a decision **karar vermek** [+ question word] *I haven't made up my mind whether to go yet.* **5 change your mind** to change a decision or opinion **fikrini değiştirmek, kararından vazgeçmek** *We've changed our minds about selling the house.* **6 come/spring to mind** If an idea comes to mind, it is the first thing you think of. **(birden) aklına gelmek** *I was thinking about who might be suitable for this job, and your name came to mind.* **7 put your mind to sth** to give your full attention to something **dikkatini/kafasını bir şeye vermek; üzerinde yoğunlaşmak** *You could win if you put your mind to it.* **8 be out of your mind** *informal* to be crazy or very stupid **kendinden geçmek, çılgına dönmek 9 be out of your mind with worry/grief**, etc to be very worried or upset **endişeden/üzüntüden/kederden deliye dönmek/allak bullak olmak/kaygılanmak 10 blow your mind** *informal* If something blows your mind, you are very excited or surprised by it. **aklını başından almak; şaşırmak; şaşkına dönmek; heyecandan deliye dönmek** *There was one scene in the film that really blew my mind.* **11 cross your mind** If an idea crosses your mind, you think about it for a short time. **çok kısa bir süre düşünmek; şöyle bir düşünmek** [+ (that)] *It never crossed my mind* (= I never thought) *that she might be married.* **12 be in two minds** *UK* (*US* be of two minds) to have difficulty making a decision **zar zor karar vermek; karar vermekte zorlanmak, kararsız olmak** *I'm in two minds about accepting his offer.* **13 put/set sb's mind at rest** to say something to someone to stop them worrying **rahatlatmak; yatıştırmak; kafasına takmamasını sağlamak; teskin etmek** *I was really worried about the tests, but talking to the doctor put my mind at rest.* **14 read sb's mind** to know what someone is thinking **15 slip your mind** If something slips your mind, you forget it. **unutmak 16 speak your mind** to say exactly what you think without worrying if it will upset anyone **aklından geçeni olduğu gibi söylemek; dobra dobra konuşmak** *She has very strong opinions and she's not afraid to speak her mind.* **17 take your mind off sth** to stop you thinking about something unpleasant *Talking to him took my mind off the pain.* ⊃See also: at/in the **back²** of your mind, **frame¹** of mind, give sb **a piece¹** of your mind, a **weight** off your mind.

○✺**mind²** /maɪnd/ *verb* **1** BE ANNOYED [I, T] to be annoyed or worried by something **önemsemek, alınmak, aldırmak, rahatsız olmak, sakıncalı bulmak** *Do you think he'd mind if I borrowed his book?* ○ [+ doing sth] *Tim won't mind lending you his car.* ○ *He doesn't seem to mind doing all the driving.* ○ *I don't mind taking her* (= I am willing to take her) *if you're too busy.* **2** LOOK AFTER [T] to look after someone or something **bakmak, göz kulak olmak, ilgilenmek** *Who's minding the baby?* **3 do you mind/would you mind** something you say when politely asking someone to do something **(birinden bir şeyi nazikçe yapmasını isterken) '...mahsuru var mı?', 'Ne dersiniz?' '...a/ebilir miydiniz?'** *Do you mind not smoking in here, please?* ○ *Would you mind if I borrowed your phone?* **4** BE CAREFUL [T] something you say when telling someone to be careful with something dangerous **(birine uyarıda bulunurken) 'Dikkat et!'** *Mind the iron - it's still very hot!* **5 never mind a** DO NOT WORRY something that you say to tell someone that something is not important **'Aldırma!', 'Zararı yok!', 'Önemi yok!', 'Üzülme!', 'Sağlık olsun!'** *"I forgot to bring any money." "Never mind, you can pay me next week."* **b** IMPOSSIBLE something you say to emphasize that something is impossible **Hele o, mümkün değil!', 'Asla olamaz!'** *I can't afford to buy a bike,*

never mind a car! **6 mind you** something you say before saying the opposite of what you have just said **(daha fazla bilgi vermek ve bir noktaya dikkat çekmek için) bununla beraber, ama (unutulmasın ki)** *We had a lovely holiday in France. Mind you, the weather was appalling.*

Mind out! *phrasal verb UK* something you say to warn someone about a danger or to tell them to move **'Aman dikkat (et)!', 'Aman dikkatli ol!'** *Mind out - this plate's very hot!*

mind-boggling /'maɪnd,bɒglɪŋ/ *adjective informal* difficult to accept, imagine, or understand **kabul edilmesi/hayal edilmesi/anlaşılması çok zor, inanması zor** *The amount of information available on the Internet is mind-boggling.*

-minded /'maɪndɪd/ ⊃See absent-minded, narrow-minded, open-minded, single-minded.

minder /'maɪndə'/ *noun* [C] *UK* someone who physically protects a famous, important, or very rich person **koruma, muhafız, koruyucu, bekçi, bakıcı**

mindless /'maɪndləs/ *adjective* stupid and done without a good reason **akılsız/ahmak, düşüncesiz, zihinsel faaliyet gerektirmeyen** *mindless violence*

○✺**mine¹** /maɪn/ *pronoun* the things that belong or relate to the person who is speaking or writing **benimki** *I borrowed them from a friend of mine.* *"Whose book is this?" "It's mine."* ○ *Can I use your pen? Mine's not working.*

○✺**mine²** /maɪn/ *noun* [C] **1** an underground system of holes and passages where people dig out coal or other minerals **maden, maden ocağı 2** a bomb hidden in the ground or water which explodes when it is touched **mayın** ⊃See also: gold mine.

mine³ /maɪn/ *verb* **1** [I, T] to dig out of the ground minerals such as coal, metals, or valuable stones **kazmak, (kömür, metal, değerli taş vs.) kazıp çıkarmak** *Tin was mined in this area for hundreds of years.* ○ *He made his fortune mining for gold and diamonds.* **2** [T] to put mines (= bombs) in the ground or water **mayın döşemek** *The southern coast was heavily mined during the war.*

minefield /'maɪnfi:ld/ *noun* [C] **1** a situation with many complicated problems **içinden çıkılmaz/sorunlu/tehlikeli durum** *a legal minefield* **2** an area of land or sea where bombs have been hidden **mayın tarlası; mayınlı bölge/arazi**

miner /'maɪnə'/ *noun* [C] someone who works in a mine **madenci** *a coal miner*

mineral /'mɪn²rªl/ *noun* [C] **1** a valuable or useful substance that is dug out of the ground **mineral, maden** *The region's rich mineral deposits include oil, gold, and aluminium.* **2** a chemical that your body needs to stay healthy **vücudun ihtiyacı olan mineral**

'mineral ,water *noun* [C, U] water which is taken from the ground and contains chemicals that are good for your health **maden suyu**

mingle /'mɪŋgl/ *verb* **1** [I, T] to mix, or be mixed **karıştırmak; karıştırılmak** *The smell of fresh coffee mingled with cigarette smoke.* **2** [I] to meet and talk to a lot of people at a party or similar event **katılmak, karışmak, kaynaşmak** *The party will be a good opportunity to mingle with the other students.*

mini- /mɪnɪ-/ *prefix* small **küçük anlamında ön ek** *a miniskirt* (= very short skirt) ○ *a minibus*

miniature¹ /'mɪnətʃə'/ *adjective* [always before noun] extremely small **son derece küçük/ufak, minyatür** *a miniature camera*

miniature² /ˈmɪnətʃə^r/ *noun* **1** [C] a very small copy of an object bir şeyin çok küçük örneği, minyatür *You can buy miniatures of the statue in the museum shop.* **2 in miniature** If something is in miniature, it is a very small copy of something else. minyatürü; çok küçük örneği

minibus /ˈmɪnɪbʌs/ *noun* [C] a small bus with seats for about ten people minibüs

MiniDisk /ˈmɪnɪdɪsk/ *noun* [C] *trademark* a very small plastic disc on which high-quality sound, especially music, is recorded

minimal /ˈmɪnɪməl/ *adjective* very small in amount asgari düzeyde; çok az miktarda; düşük seviyede *Damage to the building was minimal.* ● **minimally** *adverb* küçük miktarda

minimize (*also* UK **-ise**) /ˈmɪnɪmaɪz/ *verb* [T] to make the amount of something that is unpleasant or not wanted as small as possible asgari düzeye indirmek; mümkün olan ölçüde azaltmak *Airport staff are trying to minimize the inconvenience caused to passengers.*

o⌐**minimum¹** /ˈmɪnɪməm/ *adjective* [always before noun] The minimum amount of something is the smallest amount that is allowed, needed, or possible. en az, asgari, en aşağı, minimum *How much is the minimum wage?* ○ *There is a minimum charge of $5 for postage.* ⊃Opposite maximum.

minimum ...... İLE BİRLİKTE KULLANILAN KELİMELER

a minimum of [5/2%, etc] ● keep sth to a minimum ● an absolute/bare minimum ● with the minimum of sth

o⌐**minimum²** /ˈmɪnɪməm/ *noun* [no plural] the smallest amount that is allowed, needed, or possible asgari/en az/en düşük miktar *The judge sentenced him to a minimum of five years in prison.* ○ *Please keep noise to an absolute minimum.*

mining /ˈmaɪnɪŋ/ *noun* [U] the industrial process of digging coal or other minerals out of the ground madencilik

miniscule /ˈmɪnɪskjuːl/ *adjective* a common spelling of 'minuscule' that is not correct 'minuscule' sözcüğünün yanlış yazılışı

miniskirt /ˈmɪnɪˌskɜːt/ *noun* [C] a very short skirt mini etek ⊃Orta kısımdaki renkli sayfalarına bakınız.

minister /ˈmɪnɪstə^r/ *noun* [C] **1** a politician who is responsible for a government department or has an important position in it bakan; kabine üyesi *a finance/health minister* **2** a priest in some Christian churches papaz *a Baptist/Methodist minister* ⊃See also: prime minister.

ministerial /ˌmɪnɪˈstɪəriəl/ *adjective* relating to a government minister bakanlıkla ilgili; bakanlığa ilişkin *a ministerial job/post*

ministry /ˈmɪnɪstri/ *noun* **1** [C] a government department which is responsible for a particular subject bakanlık *the Ministry of Defence* ○ *a Foreign Ministry spokesman* **2 the ministry** the job of being a priest papazlık mesleği

minivan /ˈmɪnɪvæn/ *noun* [C] *US* a people carrier (= large, high car for many people) minibüs otomobil arası çok kişi taşıyabilen araba; küçük kamyonet

mink /mɪŋk/ *noun* [C, U] a small animal with valuable fur which is used to make expensive coats, or the fur from this animal vizon, vizon kürkü, mink *a mink coat*

minor¹ /ˈmaɪnə^r/ *adjective* **1** not important or serious önemsiz, basit, ciddi olmayan, küçük, ufak *a minor offence* ○ *Most of the passengers suffered only minor in-*

juries. **2** [always before noun] in music, belonging to a key (= set of musical notes) that often produces a sad sound minör ⊃Opposite major.

minor² /ˈmaɪnə^r/ *noun* [C] *formal* someone who is too young to have the legal responsibilities of an adult reşit olmayan; ergin olmayan

minority ...... İLE BİRLİKTE KULLANILAN KELİMELER

be **in** a minority ● a sizeable/small/substantial/tiny minority ● a minority **of** sth

o⌐**minority** /maɪˈnɒrəti/ *noun* **1** [no plural] a part of a group which is less than half of the whole group, often much less azınlıkta olan grup, küçük grup *The violence was caused by a small minority of football supporters.* ○ *I voted to accept the proposal, but I was in the minority.* ⊃Opposite majority. **2** [C] a group of people whose race is different from the race of most of the people where they live azınlık *ethnic minorities*

mint¹ /mɪnt/ *noun* **1** SWEET [C] a sweet with a fresh, strong taste nane şekeri **2** HERB [U] a plant whose leaves are used to add flavour to food and drinks nane **3** FACTORY [C] a factory which produces coins for the government darphane

mint² /mɪnt/ *verb* [T] to produce a coin for the government madeni para basmak

minus¹ /ˈmaɪnəs/ *preposition* **1** used when the second of two numbers should be taken away from the first eksi *Five minus three is two.* **2** *informal* without something that should be there ...sız/siz *She arrived at the meeting minus her briefcase.*

minus² /ˈmaɪnəs/ *adjective* **1** [always before noun] A minus number is less than zero. eksi, sıfırın altında *The temperature last night was minus ten.* **2 A minus/B minus, etc** used with scores given to written work meaning 'slightly lower than' A eksi (A-), B eksi (B-) vs. *I got an A minus for my last essay.*

minus³ /ˈmaɪnəs/ *noun* [C] **1** (*also* 'minus ˌsign) the sign which shows that the second of two numbers should be taken away from the first, or that a number is less than zero, shown by the symbol '-' eksi işareti **2** a problem or difficulty sorun, güçlük; eksi/olumsuz durum *It isn't easy having a child but the pluses outweigh the minuses.*

minuscule /ˈmɪnəskjuːl/ *adjective* extremely small çok küçük, ufacık, minnacık *The cost of vaccination is minuscule compared to the cost of treating the disease.*

o⌐**minute¹** /ˈmɪnɪt/ *noun* [C] **1** 60 SECONDS a period of time equal to 60 seconds dakika *She was ten minutes late for her interview.* ○ *"Did you have a good holiday?" "Yes, thanks. I enjoyed every minute of it."* ○ *a thirty-minute journey* **2** SHORT TIME a very short period of time an, lahza, çok kısa müddet *It'll only take a minute to call him.* ○ *I'll be with you in a minute.* ○ *She died within minutes of* (= very soon after) *the attack.* **3 (at) any minute** very soon neredeyse, her an, şimdi; çok yakında; hemen *Her train should be arriving any minute.* **4 the last minute** the latest time possible son anda/dakikada *The concert was cancelled at the last minute.* **5 the minute (that)** as soon as derhal, hemen; ...sır/maz *I'll tell you the minute we hear any news.* **6 Wait/Just a minute; Hold on a minute. a** WAIT used when asking someone to wait for a short time 'Bir dakika!', 'Biraz bekle!', 'Az bekle!' *Just a minute - I've left my coat in the restaurant.* **b** DISAGREEING used when you disagree with something that someone has said or done 'Dur hele!', 'Bir dakika!', 'Hop hop!', 'Az dinle bir kez!' *Hold on a minute, Pete! I never said you could borrow my car.*

M

minute² /maɪˈnjuːt/ *adjective* **1** extremely small **çok küçük, ufacık, minnacık** *a minute amount/quantity* **2** [always before noun] done in great detail **ayrıntılı, çok ince, çok detaylı** *He explained everything in minute detail.*

the minutes /ˈmɪnɪts/ *noun* [plural] an official record of what is said and decided during a meeting **tutanaklar, zabıt; toplantı kayıtları** *Michael has kindly agreed to take the minutes* (= write them down).

miracle /ˈmɪrəkl/ *noun* [C] **1** something that is very surprising or difficult to believe **mucize, harika bir olay** *an economic miracle* ○ [+ (that)] *It's a miracle that he's still alive.* ○ *a miracle cure* **2** an event which should be impossible and cannot be explained by science **mucize, imkansız olay**

miraculous /mɪˈrækjələs/ *adjective* very surprising or difficult to believe **mucizevi, hayret verici** *John's made a miraculous recovery from his illness.* ● **miraculously** *adverb* **inanılması zor**

mirage /ˈmɪrɑːʒ/ Ⓤⓢ /mɪˈrɑːʒ/ *noun* [C] when hot air produces an image of water in a desert or on a road **serap, ılgın**

⚬ᵐ**mirror¹** /ˈmɪrəʳ/ *noun* [C] a piece of glass with a shiny metallic material on one side which produces an image of anything that is in front of it **ayna** *a bathroom mirror* ○ *He looked at his reflection in the mirror.* ➡Orta kısımdaki renkli sayfalarına bakınız ➡See also: **rear-view mirror, wing mirror.**

mirror² /ˈmɪrəʳ/ *verb* [T] to be similar to or represent something **yansıtmak, göstermek; ...ın/in aynısı olmak** *Our newspaper mirrors the opinions of ordinary people.*

mirth /mɜːθ/ *noun* [U] *formal* laughter or happiness **kahkaha, neşe, sevinç, mutluluk, bol bol gülme**

mis- /mɪs-/ *prefix* not or badly **olumsuzluk/kötü/ uygun değil anlamında ön ek** *mistrust* ○ *to misbehave*

misadventure /ˌmɪsədˈventʃəʳ/ *noun* **1** [U] *UK formal* when someone is killed by accident and no one is legally responsible for the death **kim vurduya gitme; faili meçhul kaza** *The coroner recorded a verdict of death by misadventure.* **2** [C] an unlucky event **aksilik, terslik, talihsizlik, kaza**

misanthrope /ˈmɪsᵊnθrəup/ *noun* [C] *formal* someone who hates people in general and avoids being with them **insanlardan nefret eden ve birlikte olmak istemeyen kişi**

misapprehension /ˌmɪsæprɪˈhenʃᵊn/ *noun* [C] *formal* a idea or opinion about someone or something that is wrong **yanlış anlama** [+ that] *He was labouring under the misapprehension* (= wrongly believed) *that she loved him.*

misbehave /ˌmɪsbɪˈheɪv/ *verb* [I] to behave badly **yaramazlık, terbiyesizlik** ● **misbehaviour** *UK (US* misbehavior) *noun* [U] bad behaviour **edepsizlik, yaramazlık, terbiyesizlik**

misc *written abbreviation for* miscellaneous **türlü türlü, çeşit çeşit, muhtelif**

miscalculate /ˌmɪsˈkælkjəleɪt/ *verb* [I, T] **1** to make a mistake when calculating something **yanlış hesap etmek** *I think I've miscalculated how much wine we'll need for the party.* **2** to make a bad decision because you do not completely understand a situation **yanlış yargıya varmak; hatalı hüküm vermek;** *If she thinks Mike will support her plan, then she's seriously miscalculated.* ● **miscalculation** /ˌmɪskælkjəˈleɪʃᵊn/ *noun* [C, U] **yanlış hesaplama**

miscarriage /ˈmɪsˌkærɪdʒ/ *noun* [C, U] **1** when a baby is born too early and dies because it has not developed enough **çocuk düşürme, düşük yapma, düşük** *She had a miscarriage after her car accident.* **2 miscarriage of justice** when a court makes a wrong or unfair decision **adli hata**

miscarry /mɪˈskæri/ *verb* [I, T] to give birth to a baby too early so that it dies **çocuk düşürmek; düşük yapmak**

miscellaneous /ˌmɪsᵊlˈeɪniəs/ *adjective* [always before noun] consisting of a mixture of several different things **türlü türlü, çeşit çeşit, muhtelif** *The plumber tried to charge me fifty pounds for miscellaneous items.*

mischief /ˈmɪstʃɪf/ *noun* [U] behaviour, usually of a child, which is slightly bad but not serious **muziplik, yaramazlık, afacanlık, şeytanlık; muzırlık**

mischievous /ˈmɪstʃɪvəs/ *adjective* behaving in a way that is slightly bad but not serious **yaramaz, afacan, muzip, hınzır** *a mischievous grin* ○ *a mischievous five-year-old* ● **mischievously** *adverb* **haylazca**

misconceived /ˌmɪskənˈsiːvd/ *adjective* If a plan is misconceived, it is not suitable or has not been thought about carefully. **yanlış tasarlanmış, hatalı**

───────────────

misconception .... İLE BİRLİKTE KULLANILAN KELİMELER

be **based on** a misconception ● a **common/popular** misconception ● a misconception **about** sth

───────────────

misconception /ˌmɪskənˈsepʃᵊn/ *noun* [C] when your understanding of something is wrong **yanlış kanı/ anlama/yorumlama** [+ that] *It's a common misconception that older workers cannot learn to use new technology.*

misconduct /mɪˈskɒndʌkt/ *noun* [U] *formal* when someone in a position of responsibility behaves in a way that is morally wrong or breaks rules while doing their job **kötü davranış/hareket/yönetim; yolsuzluk** *professional misconduct*

misdemeanour *UK (US* misdemeanor) /ˌmɪsdɪˈmiːnəʳ/ *noun* [C] **1** behaviour that is bad or not moral **kabahat, kusur** *political/sexual misdemeanours* **2** *US* a crime which is not serious **hafif/önemsiz suç**

misdirect /ˌmɪsdɪˈrekt/ *verb* [T] to use money or people's skills in a way that is not suitable **kötü idare etmek/ yönlendirmek/sevketmek; beceriksizce kullanmak; birinin yeteneklerini doğru kullanmamak** [often passive] *Large quantities of money and expertise have been misdirected.*

miserable /ˈmɪzᵊrəbl/ *adjective* **1** [SAD] unhappy **çok mutsuz, bedbaht, perişan** *I just woke up feeling miserable.* **2** [NOT PLEASANT] very unpleasant or bad, and causing someone to feel unhappy **kötü, berbat, pis** *Some families are living in miserable conditions.* **3** [NOT ENOUGH] *informal* A miserable amount is too small to be acceptable. **biraz azcık, avuç içi kadar, çok az, yetersiz** *She offered me a miserable £50 for my old computer.*

miserably /ˈmɪzᵊrəbli/ *adverb* **1** in a way that causes disappointment or suffering **üzgün** *miserably low wages* ○ *Every job application that I've made has failed miserably* (= has been extremely unsuccessful). **2** in a very unhappy way **mutsuz/umutsuz şekilde; bedbaht halde** *"I feel so ill,"* said Rachel *miserably.*

misery /ˈmɪzᵊri/ *noun* [C, U] **1** great suffering or unhappiness **bedbahtlık, mutsuzluk, sefalet, perişanlık** *The war brought misery to millions of people.* ○ *Her husband's drinking is making her life a misery.* **2 put sb out of their misery** to stop someone worrying by telling them what they want to know **birini sıkıntıdan/ endişeden kurtarmak; söyleyerek/anlatarak rahatlatmak/ferahlatmak**

misfire /mɪsˈfaɪəʳ/ *verb* [I] When something that you do misfires, it does not have the result that you intended.

başarısızlığa uğramak; sonuç alamamak; suya düşmek; boşa çıkmak; gerçekleşmemek *His joke misfired badly, and he was forced to make a public apology.*

misfit /'mɪsfɪt/ *noun* [C] someone with strange or unusual behaviour who is not accepted by other people sıradışı/uyumsuz/uygunsuz kişi *a social misfit*

misfortune /mɪs'fɔːtʃuːn/ *noun* [C, U] bad luck, or an unlucky event talihsizlik, aksilik, kötü talih, terslik [+ to do sth] *He had the misfortune to fall in love with a married woman.*

misgiving ...... İLE BİRLİKTE KULLANILAN KELİMELER

express/have misgivings • grave/serious/strong misgivings • misgivings **about** sth

misgiving /mɪs'gɪvɪŋ/ *noun* [C] a feeling of doubt or worry about a future event endişe, korku, kaygı [usually plural] *She has serious misgivings about giving birth at home.*

misguided /mɪs'gaɪdɪd/ *adjective* not likely to succeed because of a bad judgment or understanding of a situation yanlış, hatalı; yanılgıya düşmüş *The government's policy seems to me completely misguided.*

mishandle /mɪs'hændl/ *verb* [T] to deal with a problem or situation badly sorunu ve durumu yanlış ele almak; eline yüzüne bulaştırmak; gerektiği gibi ilgilenememek *The murder investigation was mishandled from the beginning.*

mishap /'mɪshæp/ *noun* [C, U] an accident or unlucky event which usually is not serious aksilik, talihsizlik, terslik *They suffered a series of mishaps during the trip.*

misinform /ˌmɪsɪn'fɔːm/ *verb* [T] to give someone false information yanlış bilgilendirmek; hatalı bilgi vermek [often passive] *I'm afraid you've been misinformed about your exam results.*

misinterpret /ˌmɪsɪn'tɜːprɪt/ *verb* [T] to understand something in the wrong way yanlış yorumlamak/ anlam vermek/çıkarmak [often passive] *He claims his speech was deliberately misinterpreted by journalists.*

misjudge /mɪs'dʒʌdʒ/ *verb* [T] **1** to form a wrong opinion about a person or situation yanlış yargıya/ kanaate varmak; yanlış fikir edinmek *We believe that the government has seriously misjudged the public mood.* **2** to guess an amount or distance wrongly yanlış tahminde bulunmak; hatalı hesaplamak

misjudgment (*also UK* misjudgement) /mɪs'dʒʌdʒmənt/ *noun* [C, U] when you form a wrong opinion or make a wrong guess yanlış hüküm/yargı/fikir *Her outspoken criticism of her boss was a serious misjudgment.*

mislay /mɪs'leɪ/ *verb* [T] *past* mislaid *formal* to lose something for a short time by forgetting where you put it koyduğu yeri unutmak; nereye koyduğunu/bıraktığını hatırlamamak *I seem to have mislaid my car keys.*

mislead /mɪs'liːd/ *verb* [T] *past* misled /mɪs'led/ to make someone believe something that is untrue by giving them information that is wrong or not complete yanıltmak, aldatmak [often passive] *She claims the public was misled by the government.*

misleading /mɪs'liːdɪŋ/ *adjective* making someone believe something that is untrue yanıltma, aldatma *misleading information/statements*

mismanage /ˌmɪs'mænɪdʒ/ *verb* [T] to control or organize something badly kötü idare etmek/yönetmek *He accused the government of mismanaging the crisis.* • **mismanagement** *noun* [U] when something is badly organized or controlled kötü yönetim, idare

misnomer /mɪs'nəʊməʳ/ *noun* [C] a name which is not suitable for the person or thing that it refers to yanlış isim, yanıltıcı ad [usually singular] *It's a misnomer to call young car thieves 'joyriders'.*

misogynist /mɪ'sɒdʒ⁽ᵊ⁾nɪst/ *noun* [C] a man who dislikes women very much kadınlardan nefret eden adam; kadın düşmanı erkek • **misogynistic** /mɪˌsɒdʒ⁽ᵊ⁾n-'ɪstɪk/ (*also* misogynist) *adjective* expressing a great dislike of women kadınlardan nefret eden; kadın düşmanı *a misogynistic attitude/writer*

misogyny /mɪ'sɒdʒɪni/ *noun* [U] a great dislike of women kadınlardan aşırı nefret

misplaced /mɪ'spleɪst/ *adjective* If you have a misplaced feeling or belief, it is wrong because you have not understood the situation correctly. yersiz, anlamsız, yanlış anlama; yanlış kanıya kapılma *misplaced loyalty/ trust*

misprint /'mɪsprɪnt/ *noun* [C] a mistake made in the printing of a newspaper or book dizgi/baskı hatası *The article is full of misprints.*

misread /mɪs'riːd/ *verb* [T] *past* misread /mɪs'red/ **1** to make a mistake when you are reading something yanlış okumak *He misread the cooking instructions on the packet.* **2** to not understand something correctly yanlış anlamak/yorumlamak/anlam çıkarmak *She completely misread the situation.*

misrepresent /ˌmɪsreprɪ'zent/ *verb* [T] to say things that are not true about someone or something çarpıtarak anlatmak; yanıltıcı biçimde söylemek *He claims that the article misrepresented his views.* • **misrepresentation** /ˌmɪsreprɪzen'teɪʃ⁽ᵊ⁾n/ *noun* [C, U] yanlış beyan açıklama

o▪**miss¹** /mɪs/ *verb* **1** FEEL SAD [T] to feel sad about someone that you do not see now or something that you do not have or do not now özlemek, hasretini çekmek *I'll miss you when you go.* ○ [+ doing sth] *He misses having a room of his own.* **2** NOT GO TO [T] to not go to something kaçırmak; yetişememek *I missed my class this morning.* **3** NOT SEE/HEAR [T] to not see or hear something or someone kaçırmak; anlayamamak; duyamamak *Sorry, I missed that, could you repeat it please?* ○ *We missed the first five minutes of the film.* **4** NOT HIT [I, T] to not hit or catch something as you intended ıskalamak, kaçırmak *It should have been such an easy goal and he missed.* **5** TOO LATE [T] to arrive too late to get on a bus, train, or aircraft (otobüs, tren, uçak vs.) kaçırmak; yetişememek *If I don't leave now, I'll miss my train.* **6** NOT NOTICE [T] to not notice someone or something farketmemek; gözden kaçırmak; görememek *It's the big house on the corner - you can't miss it.* **7 miss a chance/opportunity** to not use an opportunity to do something bir şansı/fırsatı kaçırmak *You can't afford to miss a chance like this.* **8 miss the point** to not understand something correctly asıl noktayı kaçırmak/anlayamamak; esas manayı yaklayamamak ⊃See also: miss the boat.

miss sb/sth out *phrasal verb UK* to not include someone or something atlamak, gözden kaçırmak

miss out *phrasal verb* to not do or have something that you would enjoy or something that other people do or have kaçırmak, kaybetmek *I got there late and missed out on all the fun.*

miss² /mɪs/ *noun* **1** [C] when you do not hit or catch something as you intended ıskalama **2 give sth a miss** *UK informal* to not do an activity boş vermek, geçmek *I think I'll give aerobics a miss this evening.* • **3 a near miss** something bad which does not happen but almost happens kılpayı kurtulma durumu; ramak kalma hâli o-**Miss** /mɪs/ *noun* a title for a girl or woman who is not married, used before her family name or full name **bayan, hanım, küçük hanım** *Miss Olivia Allenby* ○ *Tell Miss Russell I'm here.*

misshapen /mɪsˈʃeɪpᵊn/ *adjective* not the correct or normal shape **biçimsiz, şekilsiz, çarpık çurpuk**

missile /ˈmɪsaɪl/ ⑤ /ˈmɪsəl/ *noun* [C] **1** an explosive weapon which can travel long distances through the air **füze** *nuclear missiles* ○ *a missile attack* **2** an object which is thrown through the air to hit someone or something **füze**

go missing ● **report sb missing** ● **missing from sth**

o-**missing** /ˈmɪsɪŋ/ *adjective* **1** If someone or something is missing, you cannot find them because they are not in their usual place. **kayıp, yok** *Have you found those missing documents?* ○ *Her daughter went missing a week ago.* **2** not included in something **eksik, noksan, olmayan** *There are a couple of things missing from the list.*

mission /ˈmɪʃᵊn/ *noun* [C] **1** [JOB] an important job, usually travelling somewhere **görev, vazife** *I'll be going on a fact-finding mission to Paris next week.* **2** [GROUP] an official group of people who are sent somewhere, usually to discover information about something **heyet, delegasyon, misyon** *a trade mission* **3** [JOURNEY] an important journey which a spacecraft or military aircraft goes on **(uzay aracı, askerî jet vs.) önemli görev 4** [PURPOSE] someone's duty or purpose in life **görev, misyon** *Her mission in life was to help the poor.*

missionary /ˈmɪʃᵊnᵊri/ *noun* [C] someone who travels to another country to teach people about the Christian religion **Hıristiyan misyoner; misyonerlik**

missive /ˈmɪsɪv/ *noun* [C] *literary* a letter or message **mektup, name, ileti**

misspell /mɪsˈspel/ *verb* [T] *past* **misspelled** or *UK* **misspelt** to spell something wrongly **yanlış hecelemek/yazmak**

mist¹ /mɪst/ *noun* [C, U] small drops of water in the air which make it difficult to see objects which are not near **pus, sis** *Gradually the mist cleared and the sun began to shine.*

mist² /mɪst/ *verb*
　mist over/up *phrasal verb* If a glass surface mists over, it becomes covered with very small drops of water so that you cannot see through it easily. **puslanmak**

correct/make/repeat a mistake ● a **big/costly/fatal/serious/terrible** mistake ● **by mistake**

o-**mistake¹** /mɪˈsteɪk/ *noun* [C] **1** something that you do or think which is wrong **hata, yanlış, kusur** *a spelling mistake* ○ *He made a lot of mistakes in his written test.* ○ [+ to do sth] *It would be a big mistake to leave school.* ○ [+ of + doing sth] *She made the mistake of giving him her phone number.* **2 by mistake** If you do something by mistake, you do it without intending to. **kazara, yanlışlıkla, kasıtsız** *I picked up someone else's book by mistake.*

Error kelimesi bir alternatif olarak kullanılabilir. *He admitted that he'd made an error.* ● *The letter contained a number of typing errors.*
Aptalca yapılmış bir hata **blunder** olarak ifade edilebilir. *The company was struggling after a series of financial blunders.*
Karmaşaya sebep olan bir hata **mix-up** olarak ifade

edilebilir. *There was a mix-up with the bags at the airport.*
Kişinin konuşurken istem dışı yaptığı ve utanmasına sebebiyet veren durumların ifadesi için **gaffe** kullanılabilir. *I made a real gaffe by calling her `Emma' which is the name of his previous girlfriend.*
Oversight kelimesi kişinin bir şeyi yapmayı unutmasından dolayı ortaya çıkan hatanın ifadesinde kullanılır. *The payment was delayed because of an oversight in the accounts department.*

mistake² /mɪˈsteɪk/ *verb* [T] *past tense* **mistook**, *past participle* **mistaken** to not understand something correctly **yanlış anlamak, yanılmak** *I think you mistook my meaning.*
　mistake sb/sth for sb/sth *phrasal verb* to confuse someone or something with someone or something else **birini birisiyle karıştırmak; benzetmek; sanmak** *People sometimes mistake him for a girl.*

mistaken /mɪˈsteɪkᵊn/ *adjective* If you are mistaken, or you have a mistaken belief, you are wrong about something. **hatalı, kusurlu, yanılmış, yanlış** *If you think you can behave like that, you are mistaken.* ● **mistakenly** *adverb* *I mistakenly* (= wrongly) *thought he had left.* **yanlışlıkla**

Mister /ˈmɪstər/ *noun* [U] *US informal* used when calling or talking to a man that you do not know **Bay, Bayım; Beyefendi** *Hey Mister, you forgot your suitcase!*

mistletoe /ˈmɪsltəʊ/ *noun* [U] a plant with white berries (= small, round fruit) which is often used as a decoration at Christmas **ökseotu**

mistook /mɪˈstʊk/ *past tense of* mistake **'yanlış anlamak', 'yanılmak' fiilinin geçmiş zaman hâli**

mistreat /mɪsˈtriːt/ *verb* [T] to treat a person or animal in a bad or cruel way **kötü/acımasız/kaba davranmak** *A local farmer has been accused of mistreating horses.* ● **mistreatment** *noun* [U] when people or animals are badly or cruelly treated **kötü muamele; kaba davranış**

mistress /ˈmɪstrəs/ *noun* [C] a woman who has a sexual relationship with a man who is married to someone else **metres; sevgili; evli erkekle cinsel ilişki kuran kadın**

mistrust /mɪsˈtrʌst/ *noun* [U] when you do not believe or have confidence in someone or something **güvensizlik, kuşku, itimatsızlık** *They have a deep mistrust of strangers.* ● **mistrust** *verb* [T] **güvenmemek**

misty /ˈmɪsti/ *adjective* If the weather is misty, there is a cloud of small drops of water in the air, which makes it difficult to see objects which are not near. **puslu** *a cold and misty morning*

misunderstand /ˌmɪsʌndəˈstænd/ *verb* [T] *past* **misunderstood 1** to not understand someone or something correctly **yanlış/ters anlamak** *He misunderstood the question completely.* **2 be misunderstood** If someone is misunderstood, other people do not understand that they have good qualities. **yanlış anlaşılmak; iyi/doğru anlaşılmamak**

misunderstanding /ˌmɪsʌndəˈstændɪŋ/ *noun* **1** [C, U] when someone does not understand something correctly **yanlış anlama** *There must have been a misunderstanding.* **2** [C] a slight disagreement **anlaşmazlık, uyuşmazlık, ihtilaf**

misuse /ˌmɪsˈjuːz/ *verb* [T] to use something in the wrong way or for the wrong purpose **yanlış/hatalı kullanmak; kötü amaçlar için kullanmak; suistimal** *He misused his position to obtain money dishonestly.* ● **misuse** /ˌmɪsˈjuːs/ *noun* [C, U] *the misuse of drugs/power* **yanlış kullanım**

mite /maɪt/ *noun* [C] **1** an extremely small insect with eight legs **sekiz ayaklı oldukça küçük böcek; mayt** *dust mites* **2** *informal* a small child **küçük çocuk, bıcırık** *You're so cold, you poor little mite!* **3** a mite *mainly UK informal* slightly **hafifçe, farkedilmez biçimde** *He seemed a mite embarrassed.*

mitigate /'mɪtɪɡeɪt/ *verb* [T] to reduce the harmful effects of something **hafifletmek; azaltmak; dindirmek** ● **mitigation** /ˌmɪtɪ'ɡeɪʃⁿn/ *noun* [U] **azaltma**

mitigating /'mɪtɪɡeɪtɪŋ/ *adjective* **mitigating circumstances/factors** facts that make something bad that someone has done seem less bad or less serious **(kötü durum/şey) hafifleten/azaltan şartlar/unsurlar**

mitt /mɪt/ *noun* [C] a thick leather glove (= cover for the hand) used for catching a baseball **beyzbol eldiveni** ➝Orta kısımdaki renkli sayfalarına bakınız.

o-**mix**[1] /mɪks/ *verb* **1** [COMBINE SUBSTANCES] [I, T] If two or more substances mix, they combine to make one substance, and if you mix two or more substances, you combine them to make one substance. **karışmak, karıştırmak; birleşmek, birleştirmek** *Mix the powder with water to form a paste.* ○ *Put the chocolate, butter, and egg in a bowl and mix them all together.* ○ *Oil and water don't mix.* **2** [COMBINE QUALITIES ETC] [I, T] to have or do two or more qualities, styles, activities, etc at the same time **karıştırmak, karmak** *a feeling of anger mixed with sadness* **3** [MEET] [I] to meet and talk to people **kaynaşmak, karışmak; anlaşmak** *She enjoys going to parties and mixing with people.*
mix sth/sb up *phrasal verb* to confuse two people or things by thinking that one person or thing is the other person or thing **(kişi, şey vs.) karıştırmak, yanılmak; bir şeyi diğeri ile karıştırmak** *People often mix them up because they look so similar.*
mix sth up *phrasal verb* to cause a group of things to be untidy or badly organized **birbirine karıştırmak** *The books were all mixed up in a box.*

🔲 **mix** .... İLE BİRLİKTE KULLANILAN KELİMELER

a mix of sth ● an **ethnic/racial/social** mix

mix[2] /mɪks/ *noun* **1** [C] a combination of things or people, often in a group **karışma, dahil olma, kaynaşma** [usually singular] *There's a good mix of nationalities in the class.* **2** [C, U] a powder to which you add liquid in order to make something **karışım** *cake mix*

mixed /mɪkst/ *adjective* **1** made of a combination of different people or things **karışık** *a racially mixed area* ○ *a mixed salad* **2 mixed feelings** If you have mixed feelings about something, you are pleased and not pleased at the same time. **karmaşık duygular; içinden çıkılmaz hisler** ➝See also: a mixed **blessing**.

mixed-race /mɪkst'reɪs/ *adjective* describes a person whose parents are of different races (= the groups that people are divided into according to their physical characteristics) **karma ırk**

ˌ**mixed 'up** *adjective informal* **1** confused **kafası karışık; zihni karma karışık** *I got a bit mixed up and thought we were supposed to be there at eight.* **2 be mixed up in sth** to be involved in an activity that is bad or illegal **kötü veya yasa dışı bir eyleme karışmış/bulaşmış olmak** **3 be mixed up with sb** to be involved with someone who has a bad influence on you **kötü etkisi olan kişiyle ilişkide/ilişkisi olmak/ düşüp kalkmak** *Her son got mixed up with the wrong people.*

mixer /'mɪksər/ *noun* [C] a machine that mixes things **karıştırıcı, mikser** *an electric mixer*

o-**mixture** /'mɪkstʃər/ *noun* **1** [C, U] a substance made of other substances that have been combined **karışım**

Add milk to the mixture and stir until smooth. **2** [no plural] when there is a combination of two or more ideas, qualities, styles, etc **(fikir, nitelik ve tarz vs.) karışım, çeşit** *Their house is decorated in a mixture of styles.*

mix-up /'mɪksʌp/ *noun* [C] *informal* when there is a mistake because things are confused **karışıklık, karmaşa, düzensizlik** [usually singular] *There was a mix-up with the bags at the airport.*

ml *written abbreviation for* millilitre (= a unit for measuring liquid) **mililitrenin kısa yazılışı**

mm *written abbreviation for* millimetre (= a unit for measuring length) **milimetrenin kısa yazılışı**

moan /məʊn/ *verb* [I] **1** to complain or speak in a way that shows you are unhappy **homurdanmak; yakınmak, sızlanmak, şikayet etmek; feryat figan etmek** *She's always moaning about something.* **2** to make a low sound, especially because you are in pain **inlemek** *He lay on the floor moaning.* ● **moan** *noun* [C] **sızlanma**

mob[1] /mɒb/ *noun* [C] a large group of people that is often violent or not organized **taşkın kalabalık, azgın topluluk, güruh** *an angry mob*

mob[2] /mɒb/ *verb* [T] **mobbing**, *past* **mobbed** If a group of people mob someone, they get close to them, often to get their photograph or signature. **başına üşüşmek, toplaşmak, etrafını sarmak** [often passive] *She was mobbed by photographers.*

mobile[1] /'məʊbaɪl/ ⓤ /'məʊbəl/ *adjective* able to move or be moved easily **hareketli; hareket ettirilebilir** *a mobile home* ➝Opposite **immobile**.

o-**mobile**[2] /'məʊbaɪl/ ⓤ /'məʊbiːl/ *noun* [C] **1** a mobile phone **cep telefonu** **2** a decoration made of objects on threads that hang down and move in the air **havada asılı dönerdurur süs**

o-**mobile 'phone** *noun* [C] a telephone that you can carry everywhere with you **cep telefonu**

mobile phone

mobilize (*also UK* -ise) /'məʊbɪlaɪz/ *verb* **1** [T] to organize a group of people so that they support or oppose something or someone **harekete geçirmek, organize etmek** *He's trying to mobilize support for the strike.* **2** [I, T] *formal* to prepare for a war **seferber etmek/olmak** *The forces were fully mobilized for action.* ● **mobilization** /ˌməʊbɪlaɪ'zeɪʃⁿn/ *noun* [U] **seferber etme**

mock[1] /mɒk/ *verb* [I, T] to laugh at someone or something in an unkind way **alay etmek, maskara etmek, dalga geçmek** *The older kids mocked him whenever he made a mistake.*

mock[2] /mɒk/ *adjective* [always before noun] not real but appearing or pretending to be exactly like something **sahte, yapmacık, taklit** *a mock exam* ○ *mock surprise* ○ *mock leather*

mockery /'mɒkⁿri/ *noun* [U] **1** when someone laughs at someone or something in an unkind way **alay, istihza** **2 make a mockery of sth** to make something seem stupid **gülünç duruma düşürmek, küçük düşürmek** *The latest outbreak of fighting makes a mockery of the peace process.*

modal verb /'məʊdⁿl,vɜːb/ (*also* modal) *noun* [C] a verb, for example 'can', 'might', or 'must', that is used before another verb to show that something is possible, necessary, etc **can', 'might', 'must' benzeri çekimsiz yardımcı fiil** ➝See study page **Modal verbs** on page Centre 22.

mode /məʊd/ *noun* [C] *formal* **1** a way of doing something **bir şeyi yapma biçimi/şekli/tarzı/yolu** *a mode of transport* **2** the number or value which appears most often in a particular set

○–**model**[1] /'mɒdəl/ *noun* [C] **1** PERSON someone whose job is to wear fashionable clothes, be in photographs, etc in order to advertise things **manken, model** *a fashion model* **2** COPY a smaller copy of a real object, often used to show how something works or what it looks like **maket, model 3** EXAMPLE someone or something that is an example for others to copy **numune, örnek, model** *a model of good behaviour* **4** DESIGN a design of machine or car that is made by a particular company **(araba, makina) model, örnek** *I think her car is a slightly older model.* ◑See also: role model.

model[2] /'mɒdəl/ *verb* [I, T] *UK* **modelling**, *past* **modelled**, *US* **modeling**, *past* **modeled** to wear clothes in fashion shows, magazines, etc as a model **mankenlik yapmak; giyim teşhir etmek**
be modelled on sth *phrasal verb* to be based on the design of something else **bir başka şeye dayalı modellemek/tasar(lan)mak/yap(ıl)mak** *The house is modelled on a 16th century castle.*
model yourself on sb *phrasal verb* to try to make yourself very similar to someone else **kendini birine çok benzetmeye çalışmak; birini kendine örnek olarak almak** *He models himself on Mohammed Ali.*

modem /'məʊdem/ *noun* [C] a piece of equipment that is used to send information from a computer through a telephone line, cable or other link **modem; bilgisayardan telefon/kablo veya diğer hatlarla bilgi göndermek** ◑See study page **Web and the Internet** on page Centre 36.

moderate[1] /'mɒdərət/ *adjective* **1** average in size or amount and not too much **vasat, orta** *Eating a moderate amount of fat is healthy.* **2** not extreme, especially relating to political opinions **ılımlı** *a moderate political group* ● **moderately** *adverb* **makul bir miktarda**

moderate[2] /'mɒdərət/ *noun* [C] someone who does not have extreme political opinions **ılımlı insan; orta yolcu**

moderate[3] /'mɒdəreɪt/ *verb* [T] to make something less extreme **hafifletmek, yumuşatmak, yatıştırmak** *He's trying to moderate his drinking.*

moderation /,mɒdə'reɪʃən/ *noun* **1 in moderation** If you do something in moderation, you do not do it too much. **ölçülü, aşırılığa kaçmadan, ılımlı** *I only drink alcohol in moderation now.* **2** [U] when you control your feelings or actions and stop them from becoming extreme **ılımlı, ölçülü olma**

○–**modern** /'mɒdən/ *adjective* **1** relating to the present time and not to the past **yeni, çağdaş, modern** *modern society* ○ *the stresses of modern life* **2** using the newest ideas, design, technology, etc and not traditional **yeni, modern, alışılmışın dışında** *modern art/architecture* ○ *modern medicine* ● **modernity** /mɒd'ɜːnəti/ *noun* [U] *formal* when something is modern **yenilik, çağdaşlık, modernlik**

modern-day /'mɒdəndeɪ/ *adjective* [always before noun] relating to the present time and not to the past **günümüze ait/ilişkin, zamanımız** *a modern-day version of Shakespeare*

modernize (*also UK* -ise) /'mɒdənaɪz/ *verb* [I, T] to make something more modern or to become more modern **yenileştirmek, çağdaşlaştırmak; modernleştirmek** *We really need to modernize our image.* ● **modernization** /,mɒdənaɪ'zeɪʃən/ *noun* [U] **modernleştirme**

,**modern 'languages** *noun* [plural] languages that are spoken now such as Spanish or German **çağdaş/modern diller**

modest /'mɒdɪst/ *adjective* **1** not large in size or amount, or not expensive **az, cüz'i, mütevazı** *a modest amount of money* ○ *Their house is quite modest in size.* **2** If you are modest, you do not talk in a proud way about your skills or successes. **alçak gönüllü, mütevazı** *He's very modest about his achievements.* ● **modestly** *adverb* **mütevazi bir miktarda, şekilde**

modesty /'mɒdɪsti/ *noun* [U] when you do not talk in a proud way about your skills or successes **alçak gönüllülük, mütevazılık, utangaçlık**

modicum /'mɒdɪkəm/ *noun formal* **a modicum of sth** a small amount of something **az miktar, bir nebze** *a modicum of success*

modification /,mɒdɪfɪ'keɪʃən/ *noun* [C, U] a small change to something **değişiklik** *We've made a few modifications to the system.*

modifier /'mɒdɪfaɪər/ *noun* [C] in grammar, a word that describes or limits the meaning of another word **küçük değişiklik yapan; dilbilgisinde bir sözcüğün anlamını sınırlayan/tanımlayan sözcük**

modify /'mɒdɪfaɪ/ *verb* [T] **1** to change something in order to improve it **değişiklik yapmak** [often passive] *The plans will have to be modified to reduce costs.* ○ *genetically modified food* **2** In grammar, a word that modifies another word describes or limits the meaning of that word. **küçük değişiklik yapmak; dilbilgisinde bir sözcüğün anlamını sınırlayan/tanımlayan sözcük** *Adjectives modify nouns.*

module /'mɒdjuːl/ *noun* [C] **1** *UK* a part of a university or college course **ünite, birim, modül 2** a part of an object that can operate alone, especially a part of a spacecraft **özellikle bir uzay aracının tek başına çalışabilen bir parçası**

mogul /'məʊgəl/ *noun* [C] an important, powerful person **önemli güçlü bir kişi** *media/movie moguls*

Mohammed /mə'hæmɪd/ *noun* the main prophet of Islam, who revealed the Koran (= the Islamic holy book) **Hz. Muhammed; İslâm dininin temelleri O'nun hayatı ve öğretileri üzerine kurulan Peygamber**

moist /mɔɪst/ *adjective* slightly wet **nemli, rutubetli** *Keep the soil moist but not wet.* ○ *It was a lovely, moist cake.* ● **moisten** /'mɔɪsən/ *verb* [I, T] to make something slightly wet, or to become slightly wet **nemlen(dir)mek**

moisture /'mɔɪstʃər/ *noun* [U] very small drops of water in the air or on a surface **nem, rutubet**

moisturizer (*also UK* -iser) /'mɔɪstʃəraɪzər/ *noun* [C, U] a substance which you put on your skin to make it less dry **nemlendirici madde** ● **moisturize** (*also UK* -ise) /'mɔɪstʃəraɪz/ *verb* [T] to put moisturizer on your skin **cildi nemlendirmek**

molasses /mə'læsɪz/ (*also UK* treacle) *noun* [U] a sweet, thick, dark liquid used in sweet dishes **pekmez**

mold /məʊld/ *noun, verb US spelling of* mould **küf; kalıp; şekil vermek, kalıba sokmak, biçimlendirmek**

moldy /'məʊldi/ *adjective US spelling of* mouldy **küflü, küflenmiş**

mole /məʊl/ *noun* [C] **1** SKIN a small, dark mark on the skin **ben; derideki küçük siyah iz 2** ANIMAL a small animal with black fur that digs holes in the soil and lives under the ground **köstebek 3** PERSON *informal* someone who gives other organizations or governments secret information about the organization where they work **casus, köstebek 4** MEASUREMENT a unit of measurement of the amount of a substance

molecule /'mɒlɪkjuːl/ *noun* [C] the smallest unit of a substance, consisting of one or more atoms **molekül**

molehill /'məʊlhɪl/ *noun* [C] ➔See make a **mountain** out of a molehill.

molest /məʊ'lest/ *verb* [T] to hurt or attack someone in a sexual way **sarkıntılık etmek, taciz etmek** *He was accused of molesting children.* ● **molestation** /ˌməʊles'teɪʃən/ *noun* [U] **sarkıntılık, taciz**

mom /mɒm/ *US* (*UK* **mum**) *noun* [C] *informal* mother **anne** *My mom phoned last night.* ○ *Can we go now, Mom?*

o▸**moment** /'məʊmənt/ *noun* **1** [C] a very short period of time **saniye** *I'll be back in a moment.* ○ *For a moment I thought it was Anna.* ○ *Could you wait a moment?* **2** [C] a point in time **an, lahza, çok kısa süre** *Just at that moment, the phone rang.* **3 at the moment** now **şu anda, şimdi** *I'm afraid she's not here at the moment.* **4 for the moment** If you do something for the moment, you are doing it now but might do something different in the future. **şimdilik, şimdi 5 the moment (that)** as soon as *...ar/er...maz/mez; ...ınca/ince* **derhal** *I'll call you the moment I hear anything.* **6 have a senior, blond etc moment** *informal* to behave, for a short time, in a way which shows you are old, silly, etc **kısa bir süre aptal/saf/yaşlıymış gibi davranmak** *I've just had a senior moment – I couldn't remember why I'd gone into the kitchen.* ➔See also: on the **spur²** of the moment.

momentarily /'məʊmənt^ər^əli/ *adverb* for a very short time **bir an için** *I momentarily forgot his name.*

momentary /'məʊmənt^əri/ *adjective* lasting for a very short time **bir anlık, geçici, anlık, anî** *a momentary lapse of memory*

momentous /məʊ'mentəs/ *adjective* A momentous decision, event, etc is very important because it has a big effect on the future. **çok önemli, son derece ciddi**

▒▒▒ *momentum* ...... İLE BİRLİKTE KULLANILAN KELİMELER

gain/gather/lose momentum ● **keep up/maintain** the momentum ● the momentum **for/of** sth

momentum /məʊ'mentəm/ *noun* [U] **1** when something continues to move, increase, or develop **kuvvet, güç, hız, gelişme** *to gain/gather momentum* ○ *The players seemed to lose momentum halfway through the game.* **2** in science, the force that makes something continue to move **hız, ivme, moment**

momma /'mɒmə/ *noun* [C] *US another word for* mommy **anne**

mommy /'mɒmi/ *US* (*UK* **mummy**) *noun* [C] *informal* a word for 'mother', used especially by children **çocuk dilinde anne** *I want my mommy!* ○ *Can I have some candy, Mommy?*

Mon *written abbreviation for* Monday **Pazartesi**

monarch /'mɒnək/ *noun* [C] a king or queen **hükümdar, kral, kraliçe, imparator**

monarchy /'mɒnəki/ *noun* **1** [U, no plural] when a country is ruled by a king or queen **mutlakiyet, monarşi 2** [C] a country that is ruled by a king or queen **monarşi, krallık**

monastery /'mɒnəst^əri/ *noun* [C] a building where men live as a religious group **manastır**

monastic /mə'næstɪk/ *adjective* relating to a monk (= religious man) or a monastery **manastır/keşiş/rahip ile ilgili**

o▸**Monday** /'mʌndeɪ/ (*written abbreviation* **Mon**) *noun* [C, U] the day of the week after Sunday and before Tuesday **Pazartesi, pazartesi günü**

monetary /'mʌnɪt^əri/ *adjective* relating to money **parasal, mali, paraya ait**

▒▒▒ *money* ...... İLE BİRLİKTE KULLANILAN KELİMELER

borrow/earn/lend/pay/raise/save/spend money

o▸**money** /'mʌni/ *noun* [U] the coins or banknotes (= pieces of paper with values) that are used to buy things **para, nakit** *How much money have you got?* ○ *He spends all his money on clothes and CDs.* ○ *The company's not making* (= earning) *any money at the moment.* ➔See also: pocket **money.**

money ˌorder *US* (*UK* **postal order**) *noun* [C] an official piece of paper bought at a post office that you can send instead of money **posta çeki**

mongrel /'mʌŋɡr^əl/ *noun* [C] a dog that is a mix of different breeds **melez/kırma köpek**

monies /'mʌniz/ *noun* [plural] *formal* amounts of money **paralar, nakitler; (argo) mangırlar**

monitor¹ /'mɒnɪtə^r/ *noun* [C] **1** SCREEN a screen that shows information or pictures, usually connected to a computer **bilgisayar ekranı** *a colour monitor* ➔**Orta** **kısımdaki renkli sayfalarına bakınız. 2** MACHINE a machine, often in a hospital, that measures something such as the rate that your heart beats **(kalp atışı vb.) ölçüm cihazı** *a heart monitor* **3** PERSON someone who watches something to make sure that it is done correctly or fairly **denetleyen, gözeten, kontrol eden, izleyen** *a human rights monitor*

monitor² /'mɒnɪtə^r/ *verb* [T] to watch something carefully and record your results **denetlemek, kontrol etmek, izlemek, bulguları kaydetmek** *to monitor progress*

monk /mʌŋk/ *noun* [C] a member of a group of religious men living apart from other people **keşiş, rahip**

monkey /'mʌŋki/ *noun* [C] a hairy animal with a long tail that lives in hot countries and climbs trees **maymun**

mono- /mɒnəʊ-/ *prefix* one or single **bir/tek/yekpare anlamında ön ek** *monolingual* ○ *a monologue*

monochrome /'mɒnəkrəʊm/ *adjective* A monochrome image is only in black, white, and grey and not in colour. **siyah beyaz ve gri imge/görüntü/resim; tek renk imge**

monogamy /mə'nɒɡəmi/ *noun* [U] when someone has a sexual relationship with only one person **tek eşlilik** ● **monogamous** *adjective* relating to monogamy **tek eşli** *a monogamous relationship*

monolingual /ˌmɒnəʊ'lɪŋɡw^əl/ *adjective* using only one language **tek dilli** *monolingual dictionaries*

monolithic /ˌmɒnəʊ'lɪθɪk/ *adjective* large and powerful **muazzam ve güçlü; iktidar ve güç sahibi olan**

monologue (*also US* **monolog**) /'mɒn^əlɒɡ/ *noun* [C] a long speech by one person, often in a performance **tek taraflı konuşma, monolog**

mononucleosis /ˌmɒnəʊˌnjuːkli'əʊsɪs/ *US* (*UK* **glandular fever**) *noun* [U] an infectious disease that makes your glands (= small organs in your body) swell and makes you feel tired **enfeksiyöz mononükleoz veya pfieffer hastalığı, kan hastalıklarından lösemiye benzer kötü huylu olmayan hastalık**

monopolize (*also UK* **-ise**) /mə'nɒp^əlaɪz/ *verb* [T] to control a situation by being the only person or organization involved in it **tekeline almak, tekelleştirmek**

monopoly /mə'nɒp^əli/ *noun* [C] **1** when a company or organization is the only one in an area of business or activity and has complete control of it **tekel** *They have a monopoly on the postal service.* **2** a company or other

M

organization that has a monopoly in a particular industry **tekelcilik, tekel düzeni**

monosyllabic /ˌmɒnəʊsɪˈlæbɪk/ *adjective* using only short words such as 'yes' or 'no', usually because you do not want to talk **tek heceli**

monotonous /məˈnɒtᵊnəs/ *adjective* If something is monotonous, it is boring because it stays the same. **sıkıcı, yavan, tekdüze, monoton** *a monotonous voice* ○ *monotonous work* ● **monotonously** *adverb* **sıkıcı/monoton bir şekilde**

monsoon /mɒnˈsuːn/ *noun* [C] the season when there is heavy rain in Southern Asia **muson yağmurları, muson**

monster /ˈmɒnstəʳ/ *noun* [C] an imaginary creature that is large, ugly, and frightening **canavar**

monstrous /ˈmɒnstrəs/ *adjective* **1** very bad or cruel **iğrenç, kaba, korkunç** *a monstrous crime* **2** like a monster **koskocaman, heyula gibi, dev gibi, muazzam**

⚬**month** /mʌnθ/ *noun* [C] **1** one of the twelve periods of time that a year is divided into **ay; yılın ayları** *last/next month* ○ *Your birthday's this month, isn't it?* **2** a period of approximately four weeks **ay** *I saw him about three months ago.*

monthly /ˈmʌnθli/ *adjective, adverb* happening or produced once a month **aylık, aylık olarak; ayda bir olan** *a monthly meeting* ○ *a monthly magazine*

monument /ˈmɒnjəmənt/ *noun* [C] **1** a building or other structure that is built to make people remember an event in history or a famous person **abide, anıt** *a national monument* ○ *They built the statue as a monument to all the soldiers who died.* **2** an old building or place that is important in history **tarihi yapı/eser** *an ancient monument*

monumental /ˌmɒnjəˈmentᵊl/ *adjective* very large **anıtsal, abidevî, çok büyük, muazzam** *a monumental task*

moo /muː/ *noun* [C] the sound that a cow makes **böğürmek, inek sesi** ● **moo** *verb* [I] **mooing**, *past* **mooed böğürmek**

⬚ *mood* ...... İLE BİRLİKTE KULLANILAN KELİMELER

be **in** a [bad/confident/foul/good, etc] **mood** ● mood **changes/swings** ● a **bad/foul/good** mood

⚬**mood** /muːd/ *noun* **1** [C, U] the way someone feels at a particular time **ruh hâli, ruhsal durum, mizaç** *to be in a good/bad mood* ○ *The public mood changed dramatically after the bombing.* **2 be in a mood** to not be friendly to other people because you are feeling angry **heyheyleri üstünde olmak; aksiliği üzerinde olmak; (deyim) burnundan kıl aldırmamak; öfkeli sabırsız ve kızgın olmak 3 be in the mood for sth/to do sth** to want to do or have something **bir şeyi yapma/elde etme isteğinde olmak** *I'm not really in the mood for shopping at the moment.* **4 be in no mood for sth/to do sth** to not want to do something with someone else, often because you are angry with them **bir şeye/bir şeyi yapmaya istekli olmamak/istememek; kızgın olduğu için yapmaya yanaşmamak 5** [C] in grammar, one of the different ways a sentence is being used, for example to give an order, express a fact, etc **dilbilgisinde cümlelerin emir vermek/bir gerçeği belirtmek vb. gibi durumlarda farklı kullanımlarından biri; cümlenin anlam bağlamı** *the indicative/imperative mood*

moody /ˈmuːdi/ *adjective* If someone is moody, they are often unfriendly because they feel angry or unhappy. **huysuz, aksi, ters, mutsuz, küskün; günü gününe**

uymayan ● **moodily** *adverb* **aksi bir şekilde** ● **moodiness** *noun* [U] **aksilik**

⚬**moon** /muːn/ *noun* **1 the moon** the round object that shines in the sky at night and moves around the Earth **ay, kamer 2 crescent/full/new moon** the shape made by the amount of the moon that you can see at a particular time **hilâl/dolunay/yeni ay; ayın şekilleri 3** [C] a round object like the moon that moves around another planet **uydu 4 once in a blue moon** rarely **ayda yılda bir; kırk yılda bir; (argo) ölme eşeğim ölme** *We only go out once in a blue moon.* ● **5 be over the moon** UK to be very pleased about something **çok sevinçli olmak; ayakları yerden kesilmek; çok mutlu olmak; keyfine diyecek olmamak** *"I bet she was pleased with her results." "She was over the moon."*

moonlight /ˈmuːnlaɪt/ *noun* [U] light that comes from the moon **mehtap, ay ışığı** *In the moonlight she looked even more beautiful.* ● **moonlit** *adjective* [always before noun] with light from the moon **mehtaplı**

moor /mɔːʳ/ *noun* [C] an open area in the countryside that is covered with rough grass and bushes **fundalık, fundalık arazi; çalılık** [usually plural] *the Yorkshire Moors*

moose /muːs/ *noun* [C] *plural* **moose** a large deer that comes from North America **Kanada geyiği**

moot point /ˌmuːtˈpɔɪnt/ *noun* [C] a subject that people cannot agree about **tartışmalı konu; üzerinde uzlaşılamayan husus**

mop¹ /mɒp/ *noun* [C] a piece of equipment used for cleaning floors that has a long handle and thick strings at one end **püsküllü paspas**

mop² /mɒp/ *verb* [T] **mopping**, *past* **mopped** to use a mop **paspas çekmek; paspaslamak** *to mop the floor* **mop sth up** *phrasal verb* to use a cloth or mop to remove liquid from a surface **paspasla/yer beziyle silmek/silip temizlemek**

⚬**moral¹** /ˈmɒrᵊl/ *adjective* **1** [always before noun] relating to beliefs about what is right or wrong **ahlâk değerleriyle ilgili** *moral standards/values* ○ *a moral issue* **2** behaving in a way that most people think is correct and honest **ahlâkî, manevî, vicdani** *He's a very moral person.* ⊃Opposite immoral ⊃Compare amoral. ● **morally** *adverb* **morally wrong ahlaki olarak**

moral² /ˈmɒrᵊl/ *noun* [C] something you learn from a story or event about how to behave **kıssadan hisse; çıkarılan/alınan ders** *The moral of the story is never lie.*

⬚ *morale* ...... İLE BİRLİKTE KULLANILAN KELİMELER

boost/damage/improve/raise/undermine morale ● **high/low** morale

morale /məˈrɑːl/ *noun* [U] the amount of confidence or hope for the future that people feel **maneviyat, moral** *The pay increase should help to improve* staff *morale.*

morality /məˈræləti/ *noun* [U] ideas and beliefs about what is right or wrong **edep, ahlak, terbiye, ahlakî değerlere uygunluk**

morals /ˈmɒrᵊlz/ *noun* [plural] principles of good behaviour **ahlakî değerler manzumesi/bütünü/ilkeleri** *He doesn't care what he does, he has no morals at all.*

moral su'pport *noun* [U] help and encouragement **yardım ve yüreklendirme; moral destek** *Roz has said she'll come with me for moral support.*

morbid /ˈmɔːbɪd/ *adjective* showing too much interest in unpleasant things such as death **marazi, hastalıklı, anormal, sapkın** *a morbid fascination with death*

⚬**more¹** /mɔːʳ/ *quantifier* **1** something in addition to what you already have **daha, daha da** *Would anyone like* *some more food?* ○ *I need a bit more money.* **2** a greater number or amount of people or things **daha, daha çok, daha fazla** *There are a lot more people here today than yesterday.* ○ *He knows more about computers than I do.* **3 more and more** an increasing number **giderek/gittikçe/git gide daha çok,** *More and more people are choosing not to get married.* ➲See also: **any more.**

o╾**more²** /mɔːʳ/ *adverb* **1 more beautiful/difficult/interesting, etc** used to show that someone or something has a greater amount of a quality than someone or something else **daha güzel/zor/ilginç vs. gibi ifadelerle mukayeselerde kullanılır** *It's more expensive than the others.* ○ *She's far more intelligent than her sister.* **2** used to show that something happens a greater number of times than before **daha çok, daha fazla** *We eat out a lot more than we used to.* **3 more or less** almost **aşağı yukarı, yaklaşık olarak, hemen hemen, az çok** *We've more or less finished work on the house.* **4 more and more** more as time passes **gittikçe** *It's becoming more and more difficult to pass the exam.* ➲See also: **any more.**

moreover /mɔːrˈəʊvəʳ/ *adverb formal* also **üstelik, ayrıca, bundan başka** *It is a cheap and, moreover, effective way of dealing with the problem.*

morgue /mɔːg/ *noun* [C] a building or room where dead bodies are kept and prepared before a funeral **morg**

Mormon /ˈmɔːmən/ *adjective* belonging or relating to a Christian group that was started in the US by Joseph Smith **ABD'de Joseph Smith tarafından başlatılan Hıristiyan bir gruba ait/ilişkin; Mormon** ● **Mormon** *noun* [C] **Mormon**

o╾**morning** /ˈmɔːnɪŋ/ *noun* [C, U] **1** the first half of the day, from the time when the sun rises or you wake up until the middle of the day **sabah** *Friday morning* ○ *tomorrow morning* ○ *I got up late this morning.* **2 in the morning a** during the early part of the day **sabahleyin, sabah vakti, sabah** *I listen to the radio in the morning.* **b** tomorrow morning **ertesi sabah; sabahleyin** *I'll pack my bags in the morning.* **3 3/4/, etc o'clock in the morning** 3/4, etc o'clock in the night **sabahın üçünde/dördünde vs.; sabaha karşı** *My car alarm went off at 3 o'clock in the morning.* **4 (Good) morning.** used to say hello to someone in the morning **Günaydın!', 'iyi/Hayırlı sabahlar!',**

moron /ˈmɔːrɒn/ *noun* [C] *informal* a very stupid person **ahmak/budala/kuş beyinli kimse; (argo) kaz kafalı kimse** ● **moronic** /mɔːˈrɒnɪk/ *adjective informal* stupid **ahmak, budala, kuş beyinli; (argo) kaz kafalı**

morose /məˈrəʊs/ *adjective* If someone is morose, they are not friendly or happy and they talk very little. **huysuz, suratsız, ters, geçimsiz**

morphine /ˈmɔːfiːn/ *noun* [U] a powerful drug that is used to reduce pain **kuvvetli ağrı kesici, uyuşturucu, morfin**

morsel /ˈmɔːsəl/ *noun* [C] a small piece of something **ufak bir parça, küçük bir yiyecek parçası; kırıntı** *a morsel of food*

mortal¹ /ˈmɔːtəl/ *adjective* **1** not living forever **fani, ölümlü** ➲Opposite **immortal. 2 mortal danger/fear/terror, etc** extreme danger/fear/terror, etc, because you could die **öldürücü/ölümcül tehlike/korku/terör vs.** ● **mortally** *adverb* **mortally wounded** **ölümlü olan**

mortal² /ˈmɔːtəl/ *noun* [C] *literary* a human being **fani, insan, ölümlü**

mortality /mɔːˈtæləti/ *noun* [U] **1** the number of deaths at a particular time or in a particular place **can kaybı, ölü sayısı** *infant mortality* ○ *the mortality rate* **2** the way that people do not live forever **ölümlülük, fanilik** *Her death made him more aware of his own mortality.*

mortar /ˈmɔːtəʳ/ *noun* **1** [C] a heavy gun that fires explosives high into the air **havan, havan topu** *a mortar attack/bomb* **2** [U] a mixture of substances, for example sand and water, that is used between bricks or stones to keep them together **harç**

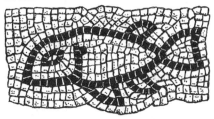

🧩 **mortgage** .... İLE BİRLİKTE KULLANILAN KELİMELER

get/have/pay off/take out a mortgage ● a mortgage **payment**

mortgage /ˈmɔːɡɪdʒ/ *noun* [C] money that you borrow to buy a home **gayrimenkul ipoteği/ipotek karşılığı alınan kredi/para** *a monthly mortgage payment*

mortified /ˈmɔːtɪfaɪd/ *adjective* very embarrassed **mahcup olmuş, incinmiş, utanmış, küçük düşmüş**

mortify /ˈmɔːtɪfaɪ/ *verb* **be mortified** to feel very embarrassed or upset about something **incitmek, küçük düşürmek, mahcup etmek, utandırmak** *I told her she'd upset John and she was mortified.*

mortuary /ˈmɔːtʃuəri/ *noun* [C] a building or room where dead bodies are prepared and kept before a funeral **morg**

mosaic

mosaic /məʊˈzeɪɪk/ *noun* [C, U] a picture or pattern that is made with small pieces of coloured stone, glass, etc **mozaik**

Moslem /ˈmɒzləm/ *noun* [C] *another spelling of* Muslim (= someone who believes in Islam) **Müslüman; İslâm dinine inanan** ● **Moslem** *adjective* **Müslüman**

mosque /mɒsk/ *noun* [C] a building where Muslims say their prayers **cami, Müslümanların ibadethanesi**

mosquito /mɒsˈkiːtəʊ/ *noun* [C] *plural* **mosquitoes** a small flying insect that sucks your blood, sometimes causing malaria (= a serious disease) **sivrisinek** *mosquito bites*

moss /mɒs/ *noun* [C, U] a very small, green plant that grows on the surface of rocks, trees, etc **yosun**

o╾**most¹** /məʊst/ *adverb* **1 the most attractive/important/popular, etc** used to show that someone or something has the greatest amount of a quality **en çekici/önemli/meşhur vs.** *She's the most beautiful girl I've ever seen.* ○ *There are various reasons but this is the most important.* **2** more than anyone or anything else **her şeyden çok, en çok, en fazla** *Which subject do you like most?* ○ *Sam enjoyed the swings most of all.*

o╾**most²** /məʊst/ *quantifier* **1** almost all of a group of people or things **çoğu, büyük bir kısmı, hemen hemen tümü** *Most people think he's guilty.* ○ *Most of our students walk to school.* **2** a larger amount than anyone or anything else **en çok, en fazla** *This one costs the most.* ○ *Which of you earns most?* **3 the most** the largest number or amount possible **azami, maksimum** *That's the most I can pay you.* **4 make the most of sth** to take full advantage of something because it may not last long **en iyi biçimde faydalanmak; azami ölçüde yararlanmak; ziyadesiyle tadını çıkarmak** *We should make the most of this good weather.* **5 at (the) most** not more than a particular amount or number **olsa olsa, en çok, en fazla** *The journey will take an hour at the most.*

⚬**mostly** /ˈməʊstli/ *adverb* mainly or most of the time **çoğunlukla, genellikle, daha çok** *She reads mostly romantic novels.*

motel /məʊˈtel/ *noun* [C] a hotel for people who are travelling by car **şehir dışında otel, motel**

moth /mɒθ/ *noun* [C] an insect with large wings that often flies at night and is attracted to light **güve, pervane** ➾See picture at **insect**.

⚬**mother** /ˈmʌðəʳ/ *noun* [C] **1** your female parent **anne, ana** *a single mother* ○ *My mother and father are divorced.* **2 Mother** the title of an important nun (= woman who lives in a female religious group) **Ana, Aziz; baş rahibeye verilen ünvan** *Mother Teresa* ➾See also: **surrogate mother**.

motherhood /ˈmʌðəhʊd/ *noun* [U] when someone is a mother **annelik, analık**

mother-in-law /ˈmʌðərɪnˌlɔː/ *noun* [C] *plural* **mothers-in-law** the mother of your husband or wife **kayınvalide; kaynana**

motherly /ˈmʌðəli/ *adjective* A motherly woman is like a mother, usually because she is kind and looks after people. **anne gibi, ana şefkati gösteren, ana gibi, anaç**

'**Mother's ,Day** *noun* [C, U] a Sunday in the spring when people give their mothers presents to show their love **Anneler Günü**

'**mother ,tongue** *noun* [C] the first language that you learn when you are a child **ana dil**

motif /məʊˈtiːf/ *noun* [C] a small design used as a decoration on something **desen, motif** *a floral motif*

motion¹ /ˈməʊʃən/ *noun* **1** [MOVEMENT] [U] when or how something moves **hareket** *The motion of the boat made him feel sick.* **2** [ACTION] [C] a single action or movement **hareket** *She made a motion with her hand.* **3** [SUGGESTION] [C] a suggestion that you make in a formal meeting or court of law **önerge, teklif** *to propose/oppose a motion* **4 set sth in motion** to make something start to happen **harekete geçirmek, eyleme dönüştürmek** **5 go through the motions** to do something that you have to do without enthusiasm **âdet yerini bulsun diye yapmak; lâf olsun diye yapmak** ➾See also: **slow motion**.

motion² /ˈməʊʃən/ *verb* **motion (for/to) sb to do sth** to make a movement as a sign for someone to do something **birine bir şeyi göstererek yaptırmak/yapmasını sağlamak** *She motioned him to sit down.*

motionless /ˈməʊʃənləs/ *adjective* not moving **hareketsiz, kımıldamayan, durgun** *He stood motionless in the middle of the road.*

motivate /ˈməʊtɪveɪt/ *verb* [T] **1** to make someone enthusiastic about doing something **harekete geçirmek, sevketmek, dürtülemek, güdülemek, motive etmek** [+ to do sth] *Teaching is all about motivating people to learn.* **2** to cause someone to behave in a particular way **gayrete getirmek, heveslendirmek, yönlendirmek, şevk vermek** [often passive] *Some people are motivated by greed.* ● **motivated** *adjective a racially motivated crime* ○ *a very motivated student* (= one who works hard and wants to succeed) **motive olmuş**

sb's **main/primary** motivation ● the motivation **behind/for** sth

motivation /ˌməʊtɪˈveɪʃən/ *noun* **1** [U] enthusiasm for doing something **güdü, dürtü, coşku, istek, heves,**

şevk *There is a lack of motivation among the staff.* **2** [C] the need or reason for doing something **gereksinim, sebep, neden** *What was the motivation for the attack?*

motivational /ˌməʊtɪˈveɪʃənəl/ *adjective* [always before noun] giving you encouragement to do something **güdüleyen, dürtüleyen, heveslendiren, coşku/istek uyandıran** *a motivational speaker*

have a motive ● an **ulterior/underlying** motive ● the motive **behind/for** sth

motive /ˈməʊtɪv/ *noun* [C] a reason for doing something **neden, sebep, dürtü** *The police don't yet know the motive for the killing.*

motor¹ /ˈməʊtəʳ/ *noun* [C] the part of a machine or vehicle that changes electricity or fuel into movement and makes it work **motor** *an electric motor*

motor² /ˈməʊtəʳ/ *adjective* [always before noun] relating to cars **arabalarla ilgili, arabalara ilişkin** *motor racing*

motorbike /ˈməʊtəbaɪk/ *noun* [C] a vehicle with two wheels and an engine **motosiklet**

motorcycle /ˈməʊtəˌsaɪkl/ *noun* [C] a motorbike **motosiklet**

motoring /ˈməʊtərɪŋ/ *adjective* [always before noun] UK relating to driving **sürüşle ilgili, otomobil sürme, araba kullanma** *a motoring offence*

motorist /ˈməʊtərɪst/ *noun* [C] someone who drives a car **sürücü, otomobil sürücüsü**

'**motor ,racing** *noun* [U] the sport of driving extremely fast and powerful cars around a track **araba yarışı**

motorway /ˈməʊtəweɪ/ *noun* [C] UK (US **freeway, expressway, interstate**) a long, wide road, usually used by traffic travelling fast over long distances **otoyol, şehirlerarası yol, otoban**

mottled /ˈmɒtld/ *adjective* A mottled pattern has a mixture of dark and light areas. **benekli, alacalı bulacalı** *mottled skin*

motto /ˈmɒtəʊ/ *noun* [C] a short phrase that expresses someone's purpose or beliefs **parola, slogan** *Her motto is, "Work hard, play hard".*

mould¹ UK (US **mold**) /məʊld/ *noun* **1** [U] a green or black substance that grows in wet places or on old food **küf 2** [C] a container that is used to make something in a particular shape **kalıp** *a chocolate mould* **3 break the mould** to do something differently after it has been done in the same way for a long time **alışılmış usulde yapmamak; farklı bir şekilde yapmak**

mould² UK (US **mold**) /məʊld/ *verb* [T] to make a soft substance a particular shape **şekil vermek, biçimlendirmek, kalıba dökmek** *moulded plastic*

mouldy UK (US **moldy**) /ˈməʊldi/ *adjective* covered with mould **küflü, küflenmiş** *mouldy cheese*

mound /maʊnd/ *noun* [C] **1** a large pile of something **yığın, küme** *a mound of clothes waiting to be ironed* **2** a higher area of soil, like a small hill **tümsek, tepecik** *an ancient burial mound*

Mount /maʊnt/ *noun* [C] used in the names of mountains **dağ; ...dağı** *Mount Everest*

mount /maʊnt/ *verb* **1 mount a campaign/challenge/ protest, etc** to arrange a series of organized activities that will achieve a particular result **bir kampanyayı/ mücadeleyi/protestoyu başlatmak/harekete geçirmek 2** [INCREASE] [I] to increase in amount or level **artmak, yükselmek** *Tension in the room was mounting.* **3 mount sth on/to, etc** to fix an object onto something **tutturmak, koymak, yerleştirmek, monte etmek** *They've mounted a camera on the wall by the door.*

4 [GO UP] [T] to go up something **çıkmak, tırmanmak** *to mount the stairs* **5** [RIDE] [T] to get on a horse or bicycle **ata/bisiklete binmek** ⊃Opposite **dismount.**

mount up *phrasal verb* to gradually become a large amount **azar azar artmak, çoğalmak** *My homework is really mounting up this week.*

o⌐**mountain** /'maʊntɪn/ **mountain**
noun [C] **1** a very high
hill **dağ** *to climb a*
mountain ○ *a*
mountain range
2 *informal* a large pile
of something **dağ gibi**
bir şey, büyük yığın/
küme *There's a*
mountain of papers on
my desk. **3 make a**
mountain out of a

molehill to deal with a small problem as if it were a big problem **pireyi deve yapmak, habbeyi kubbe yapmak; gereksiz büyütmek**

'**mountain ,bike** *noun* [C] a bicycle with thick tyres, originally made for people to ride on hills and rough ground **dağ bisikleti**

mountainous /'maʊntɪnəs/ *adjective* A mountainous area has a lot of mountains. **dağlık**

mourn /mɔːn/ *verb* [I, T] to feel very sad because someone has died **matem tutmak, yas tutmak** *He mourned for his dead son every day.*

mourner /'mɔːnər/ *noun* [C] someone at a funeral **yaslı kimse, ölünün yakınları; cenazeye katılanlar**

mournful /'mɔːnfəl/ *adjective* very sad **kederli, yaslı, acılı** *a mournful voice* ● **mournfully** *adverb* **keyifsiz bir şekilde**

mourning /'mɔːnɪŋ/ *noun* [U] when someone mourns the death of someone else **yas, matem** *a period of mourning* ○ *She's in mourning for her husband.*

mouse

mouse /maʊs/ *noun* [C] *plural* **mice 1** a small piece of equipment connected to a computer that you move with your hand to control what the computer does **(bilgisayar) kumanda aleti, mouse 2** a small animal with fur and a long, thin tail **fare**

'**mouse ,mat** *noun* [C] a flat piece of material on which you move the mouse of your computer **(bilgisayar) mouse altlığı**

mousse /muːs/ *noun* [C, U] **1** a soft, cold food that is often sweet and usually has eggs or cream in it **kaymak ve yumurtayı çırparak yapılan tatlı krema; mus** *chocolate mousse* **2** a substance that you put in your hair so that it stays in a particular shape **saç jölesi; saça şekil vermek için kullanılan madde**

moustache (*also US* **mustache**) /məˈstɑːʃ/ ⓤ /ˈmʌstæʃ/ *noun* [C] a line of hair that some men grow above their mouths **bıyık**

moustache

mousy (*also* **mousey**) /ˈmaʊsi/ *adjective* **1** Mousy hair is light brown. **açık kahverengi 2** A mousy person is shy and not very interesting. **utangaç ve sıkıcı**

`mouth` .... İLE BİRLİKTE KULLANILAN KELİMELER

close/open your mouth ● **in** your mouth

o⌐**mouth** /maʊθ/ *noun* [C] **1** the part of the face that is used for eating and speaking **ağız** ⊃Orta kısımdaki renkli sayfalarına bakınız. **2 mouth of a cave/tunnel, etc** the opening or entrance of a cave/tunnel, etc **mağara/ tünel ağzı/girişi 3 mouth of a river** where a river goes into the sea **nehir ağzı** ⊃See also: **butter¹** wouldn't melt in sb's mouth.

mouthful /ˈmaʊθfʊl/ *noun* [C] the amount of food or drink that you can put into your mouth at one time **ağız dolusu**

mouthpiece /ˈmaʊθpiːs/ *noun* [C] a person, newspaper, etc that expresses the opinions of the government or a political group **sözcü, sahibinin sesi**

mouthwash /ˈmaʊθwɒʃ/ *noun* [U] a liquid used to make your mouth clean and fresh **gargara**

movable /ˈmuːvəbl/ *adjective* able to be moved **taşına-bilir, hareket ettirilebilir**

o⌐**move¹** /muːv/ *verb* **1** [CHANGE PLACE] [I] If a person or an organization moves, they go to a different place to live or work. **taşınmak** *Eventually, he moved to Germany.* ○ *She's moving into a new apartment.* ○ *Our children have all moved away.* **2** [POSITION] [I, T] to change place or position, or to make something change place or position **yer değiş(tir)mek, hareket et(tir)mek** *We moved the chairs to another room.* ○ *Someone was moving around upstairs.* **3 move ahead/along/for-ward, etc** to make progress with something that you have planned to do **ilerlemek, belirli bir yöne doğru ilerlemek/hareket etmek** *The department is moving ahead with changes to its teaching programme.* **4** [ACTION] [I] to take action **eyleme geçmek, harekete geçmek** [+ to do sth] *The company moved swiftly to find new products.* **5** [TIME] [T] to change the time or order of some-thing **zamanın veya bir şeyin düzenini değiştirmek** *We need to move the meeting back a few days.* **6** [FEELING] [T] to make someone have strong feelings of sadness or sympathy **duygulandırmak, müteessir etmek, dokunmak** [often passive] *I was deeply moved by his speech.* ○ *Many people were moved to tears* (= were so sad they cried). ⊃Compare **unmoved. 7 move house** *UK* to leave your home in order to live in a new one **evden taşınmak; başka bir eve taşınmak 8 get moving** *informal* to hurry **acele etmek; telaşlanmak**

move in *phrasal verb* to begin living in a new home **yeni bir yere taşınmak** *She's just moved in with her boyfriend.* ○ *They want to move in together before they get married.*

move out *phrasal verb* to stop living in a particular home **ayrılmak, çıkmak, başka yere taşınmak**

move on *phrasal verb* **1** [NEW PLACE] to leave the place where you are staying and go somewhere else **terket-mek, ayrılmak, başka bir yere gitmek** *After three days in Madrid we thought we'd move on.* **2** [NEW ACTIVITY] to start doing a new activity ...a/e geçmek; ...a/e **devam etmek** *I'd done the same job for ten years and felt it was time to move on.* **3** NEW SUBJECT to change from one subject to another when you are talking or writing (yazıda, konuşmada) **konuyu değiştirmek; bir konudan diğerine geçmek** *Let's move on to the next topic.*

move over *phrasal verb* to change the place where you are sitting or standing so that there is space for someone else to sit or stand **yer açmak; yer vermek; kaymak; ilerlemek**

move² /muːv/ *noun* [C] **1** ACTION something that you do in order to achieve something or to make progress in a situation **hareket, girişim, adım** *"I've told her she's got to find somewhere else to live." " Good move!"* ○ *The latest policies are clearly a move towards democracy.* ○ *a good career move* **2** NEW HOME/OFFICE when you go to live or work in a different place **taşınma** *The move will cost us a lot of money.* **3 make a move** a MOVE to change from one place or position to another **hareket etmek; bir yerden/durumdan diğerine geçmek** *He made a move as if to leave.* **b** LEAVE *UK informal* to leave somewhere **ayrılmak, terketmek, çıkmak, uzaklaşmak** *I'd better make a move or I'll be late.* **4 get a move on** *informal* to hurry **acele etmek, çabuk olmak** *Come on, get a move on!*

◦━**movement** /'muːvmənt/ *noun* **1** GROUP [C] a group of people with the same beliefs who work together to achieve something **hareket, eylem, girişim** *the women's movement* ○ *the labour movement* **2** CHANGE [C] a change or development in the way people think or behave **gelişme, değişim, hareket, eylem** *a movement towards democracy* **3** POSITION [C, U] a change of position or place **hareket** *His movements were rather clumsy.* **4** MUSIC [C] a part of a piece of music **bölüm, kısım** *The symphony opens with a slow movement.* **5 sb's movements** what someone is doing during a particular period of time **yaptığı işler, faaliyetler, eylemler, yaptıkları** *I don't know his movements this week.*

━━━━━━━━━━━━━━━━━━━━━━━━━━━━━
🧩 **movie** .... İLE BİRLİKTE KULLANILAN KELİMELER
━━━━━━━━━━━━━━━━━━━━━━━━━━━━━
make/see/watch a movie ● **in** a movie

◦━**movie** /'muːvi/ *noun* [C] **1** a film **film 2 the movies** *US* (*UK* **the cinema**) a cinema, or group of cinemas **sinema** *What's playing at the movies?* ○ *Why don't we go to the movies tonight?*

'**movie ,star** *noun* [C] a famous movie actor or actress **film yıldızı**

'**movie ,theater** *US* (*UK* **cinema**) *noun* [C] a building where you go to watch films **sinema salonu**

moving /'muːvɪŋ/ *adjective* **1** causing strong feelings of sadness or sympathy **dokunaklı, duygulandırıcı, acıklı** *a moving tribute* **2** [always before noun] A moving object is one that moves. **hareket edebilen, hareketli, oynar** *a moving target*

mow /məʊ/ *verb* [T] *past tense* **mowed**, *past participle* **mown** or **mowed** to cut grass using a machine **çim biçmek/kesmek** *to mow the lawn*

mower /'məʊəʳ/ (*also* **lawn mower**) *noun* [C] a machine that you use to cut grass **çim biçme makinası**

MP /ˌemˈpiː/ *noun* [C] *abbreviation for* Member of Parliament: someone who has been elected to the government of the United Kingdom **Parlamento Üyesi, milletvekili**

MP3 /empiːˈθriː/ *noun* [C, U] a computer file (= collection of information) which stores good-quality sound in a small amount of space, or the technology that makes this possible **küçük alanda kaliteli ses dosyalarını**

saklayabilen bilgisayar bilgi toplama dosyası veya bunu sağlayan teknoloji; MP3

MP'3 ,player *noun* [C] a piece of electronic equipment or a computer program for playing music that has been stored as MP3 files (= collections of information) **MP3 çalar**

mph *written abbreviation for* miles per hour: a unit for measuring speed **mil cinsinden sürat ölçme birimi; mil saat** *a 30 mph speed limit*

MPV /ˌempiːˈviː/ *UK* (*US* **minivan**) *noun* [C] *abbreviation for* multi-purpose vehicle: a large, high car which can carry more people than a normal car **çok amaçlı araç**

◦━**Mr** /'mɪstəʳ/ *noun* a title for a man, used before his family name or full name **Bay** *Good morning, Mr Smith.* ○ *This package is addressed to Mr Gordon Harper.*

MRI /ˌemɑːrˈaɪ/ *noun* [C] *abbreviation for* magnetic resonance imaging: a system that produces electronic pictures of the organs inside a person's body **Manyetik Titreşim Görüntüleme (MTG); insan bedenindeki organların elektronik resimlerini çeken sistem**

◦━**Mrs** /'mɪsɪz/ *noun* a title for a married woman, used before her family name or full name (evli) **Bayan, Bn.; soyadı/tam isimden önce kullanılan ünvan** *Hello, Mrs. Jones.* ○ *Please send your application to the finance director, Mrs Laura Fox.*

MRSA /ˌemɑːresˈeɪ/ *noun abbreviation for* Methicillin Resistant Staphylococcus Aureus: a type of bacteria (= very small living things that cause disease) that is often found in hospitals and can make people very ill **hastane mikrobu; hasatanelerde üreyen ve hastalıklara sebep olan bir tür bakteri**

◦━**Ms** /mɪz/ *noun* a title for a woman, used before her family name or full name **Bayan, Bn.; evli olup olmadığı bilinmeyen bayanlara hitap şekli** *Ms Holly Fox*

MS /ˌemˈes/ *noun* [U] *abbreviation for* multiple sclerosis (= a serious disease that gradually makes it difficult for a person to see, speak, or move) **çoğul/katmerli doku sertleşmesi**

MSc *UK* /ˌemesˈsiː/ (*US* **MS**) *noun* [C] *abbreviation for* Master of Science: a higher university qualification in a science subject **fen bilimlerinde yapılan Yüksek Lisans/Master**

MTV /ˌemtiːˈviː/ *noun* [U] *abbreviation for* Music Television: an organization that broadcasts pop music around the world **müzik televizyonu**

◦━**much¹** /mʌtʃ/ *quantifier* **1** QUESTION In questions, 'much' is used to ask about the amount of something. (sorularda) **çok, fazla** *Was there much food there?* ○ *How much money will I need for the taxi?* **2** NEGATIVE In negative sentences, 'much' is used to say that there is not a large amount of something. (olumsuz cümlelerde) **çok, fazla, yeterince** *She doesn't earn much money.* ○ *Pete didn't say much at dinner.* ○ *"Is there any coffee left?" "Not much."* **3 too much/so much** a large amount of something, often more than you want **çok fazla, haddinden fazla, ziyadesiyle** *I'd love to come, but I've got too much work.* ○ *We were having so much fun, I didn't want to go home.* **4** A LOT OF a large amount of **çok fazla** *Much of his evidence was unreliable.* **5 not much of a sth** used when you want to say that a person or thing is not a good example of something **...pek iyi değil; ...kadar iyi değil** *I'm not much of a cook.* **6 not be up to much** *UK informal* to be of bad quality **pek bir şeye benzemiyor olmak; pek bir işe yarıyor olmamak; (argo) bir halt etmemek; bir halta benzememek** *Her latest novel isn't up to much.*

much or many?

Unutmayın! Much sayılamayan isimler ile kullanılır. (örnek: para, trafik, bilgi): *There is too much traffic in the city centre.* Çoğul hali olan isimler için **many** kullanılır. **Much** değil!: ~~The concert hall was too small for so much people.~~ Yanlış cümle örneği

The concert hall was too small for so many people.

o─**much²** /mʌtʃ/ *adverb* **more**, **most 1** often or a lot **fazla, çok** *Do you go to London much?* ○ *I don't like curry very much.* **2** used before comparative adjectives (= adjectives like 'better' and 'smaller', that are used to compare things) to mean 'a lot' **çok daha...** *Their old house was much bigger.* ○ *That's a much more sensible idea.* ○ *"Is her new car faster than her old one?" "Oh yes, much."*

muck¹ /mʌk/ *noun* [U] *informal* dirt **pislik, kir pas** *You've got muck on your shoes.*

muck² /mʌk/ *verb*

muck about/around *phrasal verb mainly UK informal* to behave stupidly and waste time **bir amacı olmadan oyalanmak, vakti boşa geçirmek; dalga geçmek** *Stop mucking around, will you!*

muck sth up *phrasal verb informal* to do something badly, or to spoil something **berbat etmek, bozmak, yanlış yapmak, yüzüne gözüne bulaştırmak** *I mucked up the interview.*

mucus /ˈmjuːkəs/ *noun* [U] a thick liquid produced inside the nose and other parts of the body **sümük, sümüksü salgı, balgam**

o─**mud** /mʌd/ *noun* [U] a thick liquid mixture of soil and water, or this mixture after it has dried **çamur** *He'd been playing football and was covered in mud.*

be/get **in** a muddle ● a muddle **over/with** sth

muddle¹ /ˈmʌdl/ *noun* [C, U] a situation of confusion or bad organization **karışıklık, kargaşa, dağınıklık, arbede** *There was a big muddle over who was buying the tickets.* ○ *I'm in such a muddle with these bills.*

muddle² /ˈmʌdl/ *verb* **get sb/sth muddled up** to think that a person or thing is someone or something else **karıştırmak, yanılmak; birini/bir şeyi başkasına/başka bir şeye benzetmek** *I often get Jonathan and his brother muddled up.*

muddle through (sth) *phrasal verb* to manage to do something although you do not know how to do it well **bilmemesine rağmen yapmayı başarmak; üstesinden gelmek; bir şekilde halletmek** *None of us has any formal training but somehow we muddle through.*

muddle sth up *phrasal verb* to arrange things in the wrong order **karma karışık etmek; karıştırmak, dağıtmak, düzenini berbat etmek** *Please don't muddle up those books - I've just sorted them out.*

muddled /ˈmʌdld/ *adjective* **1** A person who is muddled is confused. **şaşırmış, zihni/aklı karışmış** *He became increasingly muddled as he grew older.* **2** Things that are muddled are badly organized. **dağınık, karma karışık, tertipsiz düzensiz, karışık** *He left his clothes in a muddled pile in the corner.*

muddy /ˈmʌdi/ *adjective* covered by or containing mud (= mixture of soil and water) **çamurlu** *a muddy stream* ○ *muddy boots*

mudguard /ˈmʌdɡɑːd/ *UK* (*US* **fender**) *noun* [C] a curved piece of metal or plastic fixed above a wheel of a bicycle or motorcycle to prevent water or dirt from hitting the person's legs **çamurluk**

muesli /ˈmjuːzli/ *noun* [U] a mixture of grains, dried fruit and nuts that people eat with milk as part of the first meal of the day **içinde tahıl taneleri, kuru meyve/yemiş olan ve sütle yanilen karışım; müsli**

muffin

muffin *UK*, English muffin *US*

muffin

muffin /ˈmʌfɪn/ *noun* [C] **1** a small, sweet cake **küçük tatlı kek; mufin kek** *a blueberry muffin* **2** *UK* (*US* English muffin) a small, round, flat bread that is often eaten hot with butter **çörek, bazlama** *toasted muffins*

muffle /ˈmʌfl/ *verb* [T] to make a noise quieter and less clear **(ses) boğmak, azaltmak, düşürmek** *The pillow muffled her screams.* ● **muffled** *adjective* Muffled sounds cannot be heard clearly. **(ses) boğuk, kısık, açık seçik duyulmayan** *a muffled sound/voice* ○ *a muffled scream/cry*

muffler /ˈmʌflər/ *US* (*UK* silencer) *noun* [C] a part of a vehicle that reduces noise **(araba) susturucu, seskes**

mug¹ /mʌɡ/ *noun* [C] **1** a large cup with straight sides usually used for hot drinks **kulplu büyük bardak, maşrapa** *a coffee mug* ○ *a steaming mug of tea* **2** *informal* someone who is stupid and easily deceived **avanak, safdil, saftirik, bön kimse** *I was such a mug to think he'd pay me back.*

mug² /mʌɡ/ *verb* [T] **mugging**, *past* **mugged** to attack and rob someone in a public place **saldırıp soymak; parasını gaspetmek** (*often passive*) *He was mugged as he walked across the park.* ● **mugger** *noun* [C] someone who mugs people **insanlara saldırıp soyan kimse, saldırgan**

mugging /ˈmʌɡɪŋ/ *noun* [C, U] when someone is attacked in a public place and money, etc stolen from them **saldırı, soygun, gasp**

muggy /ˈmʌɡi/ *adjective* When the weather is muggy, it is unpleasantly warm and the air contains a lot of water. **bunaltıcı derecede sıcak ve nemli, yapış yapış** *a muggy afternoon*

Muhammad /məˈhæmɪd/ *noun another spelling of* Mohammed (= the main prophet of Islam) **Hz. Muhammed; İslâm dininin temelleri O'nun hayatı ve öğretileri üzerine kurulan Peygamber**

mule /mjuːl/ *noun* [C] an animal whose mother is a horse and whose father is a donkey (= animal like a small horse) **katır**

mules /mjuːlz/ *noun* [plural] women's shoes that have no back **sıpıdık, arkalıksız bayan ayakkabısı/terlik** ⊃Orta kısımdaki renkli sayfalarına bakınız.

mull /mʌl/ *verb*

mull sth over *phrasal verb* to think carefully about something over a long period, often before you make a decision **uzun uzadıya düşünmek, düşünüp taşınmak;** enine boyuna değerlendirmek

mullah /'mʌlə/ *noun* [C] a Muslim religious teacher or leader **Müslüman din adamı; dinî önder**

multi- /mʌlti-/ *prefix* many **çok anlamında ön ek** *a multi-millionaire* ○ *a multi-storey car park*

multicultural /ˌmʌlti'kʌltʃ°r°l/ *adjective* including people of different races and religions **çok kültürlü; değişik din ve ırkları bünyesinde barındıran** *a multicultural society*

multilingual /ˌmʌlti'lɪŋgwəl/ *adjective* using or speaking more than two languages **çok dilli**

multimedia /ˌmʌlti'mi:diə/ *adjective* [always before noun] Multimedia computers and programs use sound, pictures, film, and text. **ses, resim, film ve yazıyı kullanan program ve bilgisayarlar; multimedya** *multimedia software/technology*

multinational¹ /ˌmʌlti'næʃ°n°l/ *adjective* active in several countries, or involving people from several countries **çok uluslu** *a multinational company/corporation*

multinational² /ˌmʌlti'næʃ°n°l/ *noun* [C] a large company that produces goods or services in several countries **bir çok ülkeye hizmet ve mal götüren büyük şirket**

multiple¹ /'mʌltɪpl/ *adjective* with several parts **çoklu, muhtelif, çok** *multiple injuries*

multiple² /'mʌltɪpl/ *noun* [C] a number that can be divided by another number an exact number of times **kat, çarpım katları** *Nine is a multiple of three.*

multiple 'choice *adjective* A multiple choice exam or question gives you different answers and you choose the correct one. **çoktan seçmeli**

multiple sclerosis /ˌmʌltɪplsklə'rəʊsɪs/ *noun* [U] a serious disease that gradually makes it difficult for a person to see, speak, or move **çoğul/katmerli doku sertleşmesi**

multiplex /'mʌltipleks/ *noun* [C] a cinema which has separate screens and shows different films at the same time **bir çok sinema salonunun bulunduğu alan/bina/yer**

multiplication /ˌmʌltɪplɪ'keɪʃ°n/ *noun* [U] the process of multiplying a number with other numbers **çarpma işlemi**

multiply /'mʌltɪplaɪ/ *verb* 1 [I, T] to increase by a large number, or to cause something to increase by a large number **art(ır)mak, çoğal(t)mak** *In warm weather, germs multiply rapidly.* 2 [T] to add one number to itself a particular number of times **çarpmak, çarpma işlemi yapmak** *Three multiplied by six equals eighteen.*

multi-purpose /ˌmʌlti'pɜːpəs/ *adjective* describes something that can be used in many different ways **çok amaçlı**

multiracial /ˌmʌlti'reɪʃ°l/ *adjective* involving people from different races **çok ırklı** *a multiracial society*

multi-storey /ˌmʌlti'stɔːri/ *UK* (*US* multistory) *adjective* describes a building that has many floors **çok katlı** *UK: a multi-storey car park/US: a multistory office building*

multitasking /ˌmʌlti'tɑːskɪŋ/ *noun* [U] the ability of a person to do more than one thing at a time **aynı anda birden fazla iş yapabilen kimse** *Women are often very good at multitasking.*

multitude /'mʌltɪtjuːd/ *noun* [C] *formal* a large number of people or things **bir sürü/bir yığın/çok fazla/kalabalık/kişi veya şey** *a multitude of problems/questions*

◦▴**mum** /mʌm/ *UK* (*US* mom) *noun* [C] *informal* mother **anne** *I asked my mum but she said no.* ○ *Can we go now, Mum?*

mumble /'mʌmbl/ *verb* [I, T] to speak too quietly and not clearly enough for someone to understand you **mırıldanmak, ağzında gevelemek; belli belirsiz konuşmak** *He mumbled something about it being a waste of time.*

mummy /'mʌmi/ *noun* [C] 1 *UK informal* (*US* mommy) a word for 'mother', used especially by children **çocuk dilinde anne** *Come here, Mummy!* ○ *My mummy and daddy came too.* 2 a dead body covered in cloth, especially from ancient Egypt **mumya**

mumps /mʌmps/ *noun* [U] an illness that children get which makes the throat and neck swell **kabakulak** *to have mumps*

munch /mʌnʃ/ *verb* [I, T] to eat something in a noisy way **döke saça/hatur hutur yemek** *She was sitting on the lawn munching an apple.*

mundane /mʌn'deɪn/ *adjective* ordinary, or not interesting **sıradan, basmakalıp, sıkıcı, olağan** *a mundane task/life*

municipal /mjuː'nɪsɪp°l/ *adjective* [always before noun] relating to the government of a town or city **belediye ile ilgili; yerel yönetime ilişkin** *a municipal council/election*

munitions /mjuː'nɪʃ°nz/ *noun* [plural] bombs, guns, and other military equipment **cephane, mühimmat** *a munitions factory*

mural /'mjʊər°l/ *noun* [C] a picture that is painted on a wall **duvar resmi, fresk**

┌─────────────────────────────────────
│ **murder** ...... İLE BİRLİKTE KULLANILAN KELİMELER
└─────────────────────────────────────

commit (a) murder ● the murder of sb ● a murder **charge/investigation/victim/weapon**

◦▴**murder¹** /'mɜːdə/ *noun* [C, U] 1 the crime of intentionally killing someone **cinayet** *to commit murder* ○ *She was charged with attempted murder.* ○ *a murder charge/trial* 2 **be murder** *informal* to be unpleasant or cause difficulty **çok kötü/zor/çetin/berbat olmak** *Driving in Chicago at rush hour is murder.*

◦▴**murder²** /'mɜːdə/ *verb* [T] to kill someone intentionally and illegally **cinayet işlemek, öldürmek** [often passive] *He was murdered by a former employee.*

murderer /'mɜːd°rə/ *noun* [C] someone who has committed murder **katil** *a convicted murderer*

murderous /'mɜːd°rəs/ *adjective* [always before noun] likely to kill someone, or wanting to kill them **ölüm saçan, kanlı, ölümcül, gözünü kan bürümüş** *a murderous dictator/regime*

murky /'mɜːki/ *adjective* 1 secret, and involving dishonest or illegal activities **gizli, şüpheli; saman altından su yürüten; kapalı kapılar ardında dümen çeviren** *He has a murky past as an arms dealer.* ○ *the murky world of drug dealing* 2 dirty and dark **bulanık, karanlık, pis, iğrenç** *murky water*

murmur¹ /'mɜːmə/ *verb* [I, T] to speak quietly so that you can only be heard by someone near you **mırıldanmak** *"Go to sleep now," she murmured.* ○ *He murmured a few words of sympathy.*

murmur² /'mɜːmə/ *noun* [C] the sound of something being said quietly **mırıltı, mırıldanma** *I could hear the low murmur of voices from behind the door.*

◦▴**muscle¹** /'mʌsl/ *noun* 1 [C, U] one of many pieces of tissue in the body that are connected to bones and which produce movement by becoming longer or shorter **kas, adele** *aching joints and muscles* ○ *stomach/thigh muscles* ○ *I think I may have pulled* (= injured) *a*

muscle. 2 [U] the ability to control or influence people **güç, kuvvet, kudret, etki** *political/military muscle*

muscle² /'mʌsl/ *verb* **muscle in** *phrasal verb informal* to force yourself into an activity in which other people do not want you to be involved **zorla/cebren girmek, gücünü kullanarak kendini kabul ettirmek** *How can we stop him muscling in on this project?*

muscular /'mʌskjələʳ/ *adjective* **1** having firm, strong muscles **adeleli, kaslı, güçlü, iri kıyım** *muscular legs/arms* **2** relating to muscles **kaslara ilişkin, adele ile ilgili** *muscular aches/pains*

muse /mju:z/ *verb* [I] *formal* to think carefully about something for a long time **derin düşünmek, uzun uzun düşünmek; üzerinde kafa yormak** *I was just musing about relationships.*

o⚬**museum** /mju:'zi:əm/ *noun* [C] a building where you can look at important objects connected with art, history, or science **müze** *a museum of modern art*

mush /mʌʃ/ *noun* [U] *informal* food that is unpleasantly soft and wet, usually because it has been cooked for too long **lapa, pelte, çok pişmiş**

mushroom¹ /'mʌʃru:m/ *noun* [C] a type of fungus (= organism like a plant) with a short stem and a round top, some types of which can be eaten **mantar** *pasta with wild mushrooms*

mushroom² /'mʌʃru:m/ *verb* [I] to increase or develop very quickly **mantar gibi artmak, hızla büyüyüp gelişmek** *mushrooming costs*

mushroom

music ...... İLE BİRLİKTE KULLANILAN KELİMELER

compose/listen to/play music ● a piece of music ● dance/pop/classical music ● put on some music

o⚬**music** /'mju:zɪk/ *noun* [U] **1** a pattern of sounds that is made by playing instruments or singing, or a recording of this **müzik, musiki** *pop/dance music* ○ *classical music* ○ *He likes listening to music.* ○ *Could you put on some music?* ○ *a music festival* ○ *a music lesson/ teacher* **2** written signs which represent sounds that can be sung or played with instruments **nota** *I never learnt to read music* (= understand written music). **3 face the music** to accept punishment or criticism for something bad that you have done **ceremesini çekmek, cezaya/eleştiriye razı olmak/katlanmak** ⊃See also: chamber music, country music, folk music.

musical¹ /'mju:zɪkəl/ *adjective* **1** [always before noun] relating to music **müzik, müzikle ilgili** *a musical instrument* **2** good at playing music **musikî kabiliyet/müzik yeteneği olan** *She comes from a very musical family.* ● **musically** *adverb* **müzikal açıdan**

musical² /'mju:zɪkəl/ *noun* [C] a play or film in which singing and dancing tell part of the story **müzikli oyun, müzikal** *a Broadway/Hollywood musical*

musician /mju:'zɪʃən/ *noun* [C] someone who plays a musical instrument, often as a job **müzisyen** *a talented jazz/classical musician*

Muslim (*also* **Moslem**) /'mʊzlɪm/ ⑤ /'mʌzləm/ *noun* [C] someone who believes in Islam **Müslüman** ● **Muslim** *adjective* **Müslüman** *a Muslim family*

muslin /'mʌzlɪn/ *noun* [U] a very thin cotton cloth **pamuklu ince kumaş**

mussel /'mʌsəl/ *noun* [C] a small sea creature that has a black shell in two parts and that can be eaten **midye**

o⚬**must¹** *strong form* /mʌst/ *weak forms* /məst, məs/ *modal verb* [NECESSARY] used to say that it is necessary that something happens or is done **gereklilik/zorunluluk bildiren yardımcı fiil;** ...**malı/meli** *The meat must be cooked thoroughly.* ○ *You mustn't show this letter to anyone else.* ○ *I must get some sleep.* **2** [LIKELY] used to show that you think something is very likely or certain to be true **güçlü olasılık bildirir;** ...**malı/meli** *You must be exhausted.* ○ *She must be very wealthy.* **3** [SUGGEST] used to show that you think it is a good idea for someone to do something **birini bir şeyi yapmasını önermeyi bildirir;** ...**malı/meli** *You must come and stay with us some time.* ⊃See study page **Modal verbs** on page Centre 22.

must² /mʌst/ *noun* **be a must** *informal* If something is a must, it is very important to have or do it. **zorunlu/ mecburî olmak; yapılması şart olmak** *The restaurant has become so popular that reservations are a must.*

mustache /mə'stɑːʃ/ ⑤ /'mʌstæʃ/ *noun* [C] *another US spelling of* moustache (= a line of hair above the mouth) **bıyık**

mustard /'mʌstəd/ *noun* [U] a thick, spicy, yellow or brown sauce often eaten in small amounts with meat **hardal** *a teaspoon of mustard*

muster /'mʌstəʳ/ (*also* **muster up**) *verb* [T] to get enough support, bravery, or energy to do something difficult **cesaret/destek/enerji toplamak; zoru başarmak için bütün gücünü toplamak** *I hope she musters the courage to invite him for dinner.*

o⚬**mustn't** /'mʌsᵊnt/ *short for* must not 'must not' **yardımcı fiilinin kısa yazılışı** *You mustn't let her know I'm coming.*

musty /'mʌsti/ *adjective* smelling old and slightly wet in an unpleasant way **küflü, küf kokulu** *a musty room* ○ *the musty smell of old books*

mutant /'mju:tᵊnt/ *noun* [C] an organism or cell that is different from others of the same type because of a change in its genes **başkalaşmış/değişime uğramış canlı; mutasyona uğramış varlık** *a mutant virus*

mutation /mju:'teɪʃᵊn/ *noun* [C, U] a permanent change in the genes of an organism, or an organism with such a change **değişim, dönüşüm, mutasyon** *The disease is caused by a mutation in a single gene.*

mute /mju:t/ *adjective* **1** expressed in thoughts but not in speech or writing **sessiz, suskun** *The president has remained mute about whether he will resign.* ○ *I gazed at her in mute admiration.* **2** unable to speak for physical or mental reasons **dilsiz, ahraz** *a school for deaf and mute children*

muted /'mju:tɪd/ *adjective* **1** [FEELING] not strongly expressed **(duygu, tepki) bastırılmış, yumuşak** *a muted response/reaction* ○ *muted criticism* **2** [SOUND] A muted sound is quieter than usual. **(ses) yumuşak** *muted voices* **3** [COLOUR] [always before noun] A muted colour is not bright or easily noticed. **(renk) uçuk, solgun**

mutilate /'mju:tɪleɪt/ *verb* [T] to damage someone's body violently and severely, often by cutting off a part of it **doğramak, parça parça etmek** *a mutilated body/corpse* ● **mutilation** /ˌmju:tɪ'leɪʃᵊn/ *noun* [C, U] **parçalama**

mutiny /'mju:tɪni/ *noun* [C, U] when a group of people, usually soldiers or sailors, refuse to obey orders, often because they want to be in control themselves **ayak-**

M

lanma, isyan ● **mutiny** *verb* [I] to take part in a mutiny **isyan çıkarmak/etmek, ayaklanmak**

mutt /mʌt/ *noun* [C] *informal* a dog that is a mixture of different breeds (= types) **kırma/cins/melez köpek**

mutter /'mʌtər/ *verb* [I, T] to speak quietly so that your voice is difficult to hear, often when complaining about something **mırıldanmak, homurdanmak, alçak sesle yakınmak/dertlenmek** *She walked past me, muttering to herself.* ○ *He muttered something about the restaurant being too expensive.* ● **mutter** *noun* [C] **homurdanma**

mutton /'mʌtªn/ *noun* [U] **1** meat from an adult sheep **koyun eti** *a leg/shoulder of mutton* **2 mutton dressed as lamb** *UK informal* an older woman who wears clothes that would be more suitable for a young woman **kokona, kart taze, kart piliç**

mutual /'mju:tʃuəl/ *adjective* **1** When two or more people have a mutual feeling, they have the same opinion about each other. **karşılıklı** *mutual admiration/ respect* ○ *He doesn't like her, and I suspect the feeling's mutual.* **2** When two or more people have a mutual friend or interest, they have the same one. **müşterek, ortak** *Andrew and Jean were introduced to each other by a mutual friend.*

mutually /'mju:tʃuəli/ *adverb* You use mutually before an adjective when the adjective describes all sides of a situation. **karşılıklı olarak** *a mutually dependent relationship* ○ *Being attractive and intelligent are not mutually exclusive* (= someone can be attractive and intelligent).

muzzle¹ /'mʌzl/ *noun* [C] **1** the mouth and nose of a dog, or a covering put over these to prevent the dog biting **(hayvan) ağız burun, ağızlık 2** the open end of the long cylindrical part of a gun **namlu ağzı**

muzzle² /'mʌzl/ *verb* [T] **1** to put a muzzle on a dog **bir köpeğe ağızlık takmak 2** to prevent someone expressing their own opinions **sansürlemek, baskılamak, baskı kurmak**

o▪**my** /maɪ/ *determiner* belonging to or relating to the person who is speaking or writing **benim** *Tom's my older son.* ○ *It's not my fault.* ○ *My house is near the station.*

MYOB *informal internet abbreviation for* mind your own business: used in emails and text messages to say rudely that you do not want to talk about something **Sen Kendi İşine Bak: e-posta ve yazılı iletilerde konuşmak istemediğini kaba bir üslupla belirtmede kullanılır**

myriad /'mɪriəd/ *adjective literary* very many **çok, epey, pek fazla, çok sayıda; sürüyle, tonla** *myriad problems* ● **myriad** *noun* [C] *literary* Digital technology resulted in *a myriad of* (= many) *new TV channels.* **çok fazla sayıda**

o▪**myself** /maɪ'self/ *pronoun* **1** the reflexive form of the pronouns 'me' or 'I' **kendimi, kendime** *I've bought myself a new coat.* ○ *I looked at myself in the mirror.* **2** used to emphasize the pronoun 'I', especially when the speaker wants to talk about their actions and not someone else's **kendim, bizzat kendim** *I'll tell her myself.* ○ *Jack always drinks red wine but I prefer white myself.* **3 (all) by myself** alone or without anyone else's help **tek başıma, bizzat kendim/şahsım, yalnız** *I live by myself in a small flat.* ○ *Mummy, I got dressed all by myself.* **4 (all) to myself** for my use only **kendime, sadece kendim için, tek başıma, şahsî kullanıma** *I'll have the flat all to myself this weekend.*

mysterious /mɪ'stɪəriəs/ *adjective* **1** strange or unknown, and not explained or understood **esraren-** giz, tuhaf, acayip, esrarlı, anlaşılmaz *a mysterious stranger* ○ *the mysterious death of her son* **2** refusing to talk about something and behaving in a secretive way **ketum, sır çıkmaz, gizemli** *Nick is being so mysterious about where he's going on holiday.* ● **mysteriously** *adverb to disappear/vanish mysteriously* **bilinmedik bir şekilde**

◇◇◇ **mystery** .... İLE BİRLİKTE KULLANILAN KELİMELER

explain/solve/unravel a mystery ● the mystery surrounding sth ● an unexplained/unsolved mystery ● the mystery of sth ● be a mystery to sb

mystery¹ /'mɪstªri/ *noun* **1** [C, U] something strange or unknown that cannot be explained or understood **giz, sır, esrar, muamma, gizem** *an unsolved mystery* ○ *He never gave up hope that he would solve the mystery of his son's disappearance.* ○ *He's out of work, so how he pays his rent is a mystery to me* (= I cannot explain it). **2** [C] a story, often about a crime, in which the strange events that happen are explained at the end **esrar, muamma** *a murder mystery*

mystery² /'mɪstªri/ *adjective* [always before noun] A mystery person or thing is one who is unknown. **gizli, bilinmeyen, esrarengiz, tuhaf** *I saw her with a mystery man in a restaurant last night.*

mystic /'mɪstɪk/ *noun* [C] someone who attempts to be united with God through prayer **mutasavvıf, sufi, mistik**

mystical /'mɪstɪkªl/ (*also* **mystic**) *adjective* **1** relating to the religious beliefs and activities of mystics **dinî inançlara ve mistik faaliyetlere ilişkin 2** involving magical or spiritual powers that are not understood **efsanevî, efsanelerde olan**

mysticism /'mɪstɪsɪzªm/ *noun* [U] the religious beliefs and activities of mystics **tasavvuf, mistisizm**

mystify /'mɪstɪfaɪ/ *verb* [T] If something mystifies someone, they cannot understand or explain it because it is confusing or complicated. **hayrete düş(ür)mek; hayretler içinde kalmak** [often passive] *I was mystified by the decision.*

mystique /mɪ'sti:k/ *noun* [U] a mysterious quality that makes a person or thing seem interesting or special **gizem, esrar, ilginçlik, mistik** *the mystique of the princess*

◇◇◇ **myth** .... İLE BİRLİKTE KULLANILAN KELİMELER

debunk/dispel/explode a myth (= show that an idea is not true) ● a common/popular myth ● the myth of sth

myth /mɪθ/ *noun* [C] **1** an ancient story about gods and brave people, often one that explains an event in history or the natural world **efsane** *a Greek myth* **2** an idea that is not true but is believed by many people **söylenti, uydurma şey** *It's a myth that men are better drivers than women.*

mythical /'mɪθɪkªl/ (*also* **mythic**) *adjective* **1** existing in a myth **efsanevî, efsanelerde olan** *a mythical character* **2** imaginary or not true **hayali, uydurma, gerçek olmayan**

mythology /mɪ'θɒlədʒi/ *noun* [U] myths, often those relating to a single religion or culture **efsane, söylencebilim, mitoloji** *classical mythology* ○ *the mythology of the ancient Greeks* ● **mythological** /ˌmɪθªl'ɒdʒɪkªl/ *adjective* **mitolojik**

N

N, n /en/ the fourteenth letter of the alphabet **alfabenin ondördüncü harfi**

N/A (*also US* **NA**) *written abbreviation for* not applicable: used on official forms to show that you do not need to answer a question **cevaplamayınız; resmi formlarda cevaplanmaması gereken soruyu belirtir**

naff /næf/ *adjective UK informal* silly and not fashionable **zevksiz, rüküş, sıradan** *naff lyrics*

nag /næg/ *verb* [I, T] **nagging**, *past* **nagged** to keep criticizing or giving advice to someone in an annoying way **başının etini yemek, dır dır etmek, sürekli eleştirmek** *They keep nagging me about going to university.* **nag (away) at sb** *phrasal verb* If doubts or worries nag at you, you think about them all the time. **beynini kemirmek, devamlı rahatsız etmek** *The same thought has been nagging away at me since last week.*

nagging /'nægɪŋ/ *adjective* [always before noun] Nagging doubts or worries make you worried and you cannot forget them. **sürekli rahatsızlık veren, beyni kemiren** *a nagging doubt*

o⊷**nail¹** /neɪl/ *noun* [C] **1** a thin piece of metal with a sharp end, used to join pieces of wood together **çivi** *a hammer and nails* **2** the hard surface at the end of your fingers and toes **tırnak** *fingernails/ toenails* ○ *to cut your nails* ○ *nail clippers/ scissors* ○ *Stop biting your nails.* **3 hit the nail on the head** to describe exactly what is causing a situation or problem **tam üstüne basmak, tam isabet ettirmek; taşı gediğine koymak** ● **4 the final nail in the coffin** an event which causes the failure of something that had already started to fail **bardağı taşıran damla; son noktayı koyan bir hadise** *This latest evidence could be the final nail in the coffin for Jackson's case.*

nail

nail² /neɪl/ *verb* **1 nail sth down/on/to, etc** to fasten something with nails **çivilemek, çiviyle tutturmak** *There was a 'private property' sign nailed to the tree.* **2** [T] *mainly US informal* to catch someone who has committed a crime **suç işleyen bir kişiyi yakalamak** *They eventually nailed him for handling stolen goods.* **nail sb down** *phrasal verb* to make someone give you exact details or a decision about something **söyletmek, ağzından almak, zorlamak, mecbur etmek** **nail sth down** *phrasal verb US* to understand something completely, or to describe something correctly **tamamen anlamak; açık seçik tanımlamak** *We haven't been able to nail down the cause of the fire yet.*

'nail ,brush *noun* [C] a small brush, used for cleaning your nails **tırnak fırçası** ⊃Orta kısımdaki renkli sayfalarına bakınız.

'nail ,polish (*also UK* **'nail ,varnish**) *noun* [U] paint that you put on your nails **oje; tırnak cilâsı**

naive /naɪ'iːv/ *adjective* If someone is naive, they believe things too easily and do not have enough experience of the world. **saf, deneyimsiz, toy** *I was much younger then, and very naive.* ● **naively** *adverb I naively believed that we would be treated as equals.* **saf, toy bir şekilde**

● **naivety** /naɪ'iːvəti/ *noun* [U] the quality of being naive **saflık, toyluk**

🧩 **naked** .... İLE BİRLİKTE KULLANILAN KELİMELER
buck /stark naked ● **half** naked

o⊷**naked** /'neɪkɪd/ *adjective* **1** not wearing clothes or not covered by anything **çıplak** *a naked thigh/shoulder* ○ *He was stark naked* (= completely naked). **2** [always before noun] A naked feeling or quality is not hidden, although it is bad. **apaçık, düpedüz, gözle görülür, aşikâr** *naked aggression* **3 the naked eye** If something can be seen by the naked eye, it is big enough to be seen without special equipment. **çıplak göz, çıplak gözle görülebilir, görülmesi kolay**

o⊷**name¹** /neɪm/ *noun* **1** [C] the word or group of words that is used to refer to a person, thing, or place **ad, isim** *What's your name?* ○ *My name's Alexis.* ○ *I can't remember the name of the street he lives on.* ○ *He didn't mention her by name* (= he did not say her name). **2 in the name of sth** If bad things are done in the name of something, they are done in order to help that thing succeed. *...ın/in* **adına/namına/hesabına** *So much blood has been spilt in the name of religion.* **3 a bad/ good name** If things or people have a bad/good name, people have a bad/good opinion of them. **iyi/kötü isim/ad/ün/nam/şöhret** *Their behaviour gives us all a bad name.* **4 call sb names** to use impolite or unpleasant words to describe someone **sövüp saymak, ağzına geleni söylemek, kötü sözler söylemek** **5 make a name for yourself** to become famous or respected by a lot of people **isim yapmak, adını duyurmak** ● **6 the name of the game** the main purpose or most important part of an activity **asıl sorun, asıl mesele** *Popularity is the name of the game in television.* ⊃See also: brand name, Christian name, family name, first name, last name, maiden name, middle name.

o⊷**name²** /neɪm/ *verb* [T] **1** [GIVE A NAME] to give someone or something a name **isim vermek, adlandırmak** [+ two objects] *We named our first son Mike.* ○ *A young boy named Peter answered the phone.* **2** [SAY NAME] to say what the name of someone or something is **adını/ ismini söylemek** [often passive] *The dead man has been named as John Kramer.* ○ *She cannot be named for legal reasons.* **3** [ANNOUNCE] to announce who has got a new job or won a prize **ismini/adını anons etmek** [+ two objects] *She has been named manager of the new Edinburgh branch.* **4 you name it** something that you say which means anything you say or choose **Sen de ki!', 'Adını sen koy!', 'Diyelim ki!'** *I've never seen such a wide selection. You name it, they've got it.* **5 name and shame** *UK* to publicly say that a person or business has done something wrong **kişi ya da işin/şirketin yaptığı yanlışları ilan etmek/duyurmak** **name sb after sb** *phrasal verb* to give someone the same name as someone else **adını vermek; ismini koymak** *We named him after my wife's brother.*

nameless /'neɪmləs/ *adjective* If someone or something is nameless, they have no name or their name is not known. **isimsiz, adsız, meçhul** *a nameless soldier* ⊃Compare unnamed.

namely /'neɪmli/ *adverb* a word used when you are going to give more detail about something you have just said **yani..., şöyle ki...** *She learned an important* *lesson from failing that exam, namely that nothing is ever certain.*

namesake /'neɪmseɪk/ *noun* [C] **your namesake** someone who has the same name as you **adaş**

nan /næn/ *noun* [C] *UK informal* grandmother **büyükanne**

nanny /'næni/ *noun* [C] someone whose job is to look after a family's children **dadı**

nano- /nænəʊ-/ *prefix* **1** extremely small **son derece küçük anlamında ön ek** *nanotechnology* **2** one billionth (= a thousand millionth) **bir milyarıncı anlamında ön ek** *a nanosecond*

nap /næp/ *noun* [C] a short sleep **şekerleme, kısa uyku** *He likes to have/ take a nap after lunch.* ● **nap** *verb* [I] **napping,** *past* **napped kısa uyku, şekerleme**

nape /neɪp/ *noun* [C] the back of your neck **ense**

napkin /'næpkɪn/ (*also UK* **serviette**) *noun* [C] a piece of cloth or paper used when you eat to keep your clothes clean and to clean your mouth and hands **peçete** *a paper napkin*

nappy /'næpi/ *UK* (*US* **diaper**) *noun* [C] a thick piece of paper or cloth worn by a baby on its bottom **çocuk bezi** *disposable nappies* ○ *to change a nappy*

narcissism /'nɑ:sɪsɪzᵊm/ *noun* [U] *formal* great interest in and pleasure at your own appearance and qualities **kendini sevme/beğenme** ● **narcissistic** /,nɑ:sɪ'sɪstɪk/ *adjective* If people or their actions are narcissistic, they show narcissism. **kendini seven/beğenen**

narcotic /nɑ:'kɒtɪk/ *noun* [C] a drug that stops you feeling pain or makes you sleep, and that is addictive (= difficult to stop using) **narkotik, uyuşturucu, uyuşturucu madde**

narrate /nə'reɪt/ *verb* [T] *formal* to tell the story in a book, film, play, etc **anlatmak, söylemek** *'Peter and the Wolf,' narrated by actress Glenn Close* ● **narration** /nə'reɪʃᵊn/ *noun* [U] *formal* **anlatım, tasvir**

narrative /'nærətɪv/ *noun* [C] *formal* a story or description of a series of events **anlatım, öykü, hikaye**

narrator /nə'reɪtəʳ/ *noun* [C] the person who tells the story in a book, film, play, etc **anlatan, öykücü, öyküleyen**

narrow

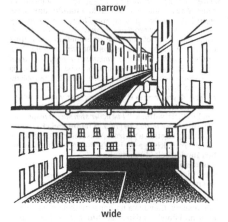

wide

ᵒ⁼**narrow**[1] /'nærəʊ/ *adjective* **1** Narrow things measure a small distance from one side to the other. **dar** *a narrow lane/street* ○ *a narrow tie* **2** including only a small number **sınırlı, yetersiz, dar** *He has very narrow interests.*

3 a narrow defeat/victory If you have a narrow defeat/victory, you only just lose/win. **kılpayı/ucu ucuna mağlubiyet/zafer 4 a narrow escape** If you have a narrow escape, you only just avoid danger. **kılpayı kurtulma; tehlikeyi zar zor atlatma**

narrow[2] /'nærəʊ/ *verb* [I, T] **1** to become less wide or to make something less wide **daral(t)mak** *The road has been narrowed to one lane.* **2** to become less or to make something become less **azal(t)mak, küçül(t)mek** *to narrow the gap between rich and poor*
narrow sth down *phrasal verb* to make something, for example a list or a choice, smaller and clearer by removing the things that are less important **(liste, seçenek vs.) sınırlamak, tahdit koymak; indirmek** *We've managed to narrow the list down to four.*

narrowly /'nærəʊli/ *adverb* only by a small amount **ucu ucuna, kıl payı** *A tile fell off the roof, narrowly missing my head.*

narrow-minded /,nærəʊ'maɪndɪd/ *adjective* not willing to accept new ideas or opinions different from your own **dar kafalı, bağnaz, dar görüşlü**

nasal /'neɪzᵊl/ *adjective* relating to the nose **buruna ait, burunla ilgili** *the nasal passages*

nascent /'næsᵊnt/, /'neɪsᵊnt/ *adjective formal* starting to develop **gelişmeye başlayan, gelişen, gelişme gösteren** *a nascent democracy*

nasty /'nɑ:sti/ *adjective* **1** [BAD] very bad **çok kötü, iğrenç, pis** *a nasty shock/surprise* ○ *a nasty smell/ taste* ○ *a nasty cut/burn* **2** [UNKIND] unkind **kaba, terbiyesiz** *She's always being nasty to her little brother.* **3** [ANGRY] very angry or violent **tehlikeli, ciddi, çok kızgın** *When I asked for the money, he turned really nasty.* ● **nastiness** *noun* [U] **hoşa gitmeyen, çirkin**

nation .... İLE BİRLİKTE KULLANILAN KELİMELER
a **civilized/industrialized/poor/powerful** nation ● **govern/lead** a nation ● **across** the nation ● **a nation of sth**

ᵒ⁼**nation** /'neɪʃᵊn/ *noun* [C] a country or the people living in a country **millet, ulus, halk** *Asian nations* ○ *industrial nations* ○ *The entire nation mourned her death.* ○ *a nation of dog lovers.* ⊃See also: **the United Nations.**

ᵒ⁼**national**[1] /'næʃᵊnᵊl/ *adjective* **1** relating to the whole of a country **(toplum) millî, ulusal** *to threaten national security* ○ *a sense of national identity* ○ *a national newspaper* ○ *national elections* ○ *His income is way above the national average.* ○ *Gambling is a national pastime* (= many people do it) *here.* **2** [always before noun] connected with the traditions of a particular nation **(örf, âdet) millî, ulusal** *national dress/customs* ● **nationally** *adverb* **ulusal**

national[2] /'næʃᵊnᵊl/ *noun* [C] someone who officially belongs to a particular country **vatandaş, yurttaş, millet**

national 'anthem *noun* [C] the official song of a country, played at public events **millî/ulusal marş**

the ,National 'Health Service *noun* the system providing free medical services in the UK **(Birleşik Krallık) Ulusal Sağlık Hizmeti**

national 'holiday (*also US* **federal holiday**) *noun* [C] a day when most people in a country do not have to work **millî bayram**

National In'surance *noun* [U] the system in the UK in which people regularly pay money to the government in order to help people who are ill or have no work **(Birleşik Krallık) ulusal sigorta kurumu**

nationalism /'næʃⁿnᵊlɪzᵊm/ *noun* [U] **1** a feeling of pride in your own country **milliyetçilik 2** the belief that a particular area should have its own government **vatanperverlik, milletseverlik, ulusal bağımsızlık yandaşlığı** *Welsh nationalism*

nationalist /'næʃⁿnᵊlɪst/ *noun* [C] someone who wants a particular area to have its own government **milliyetçi, milliyetçi kimse**

nationalistic /ˌnæʃⁿn'lɪstɪk/ *adjective* having a lot of pride, often too much pride, in your own country **milliyetçi** *nationalistic fervour*

nationality /ˌnæʃⁿn'æləti/ *noun* [C, U] If you have American/British/Swiss, etc nationality, you are legally a member of that country. **milliyet, uyruk, tabiiyet** *What nationality is she?* ○ *She has dual nationality* (= nationality of two countries).

nationalize /'næʃⁿnᵊlaɪz/ *verb* [T] If private companies are nationalized, the government takes control of them. **devletleştirmek, millileştirmek ● nationalization** /ˌnæʃⁿnlaɪ'zeɪʃⁿn/ *noun* [U] **kamulaştırma**

ˌnational 'park *noun* [C] a large area of park for use by the public, usually an area of special beauty **milli park**

ˌnational 'service *noun* [U] the period of time young people in some countries have to spend in the army **askerlik hizmeti, askerlik**

nationwide /ˌneɪʃⁿn'waɪd/ *adjective, adverb* including all parts of a country **ülke çapında** *a nationwide campaign* ○ *Surveys have been carried out nationwide.*

native¹ /'neɪtɪv/ *adjective* **1** [BORN IN] [always before noun] Your native town or country is the place where you were born. **asıl..., ana..., doğum yeri olan** *It was a custom in his native Algeria.* ○ *She is a native-born Texan.* **2** [LANGUAGE] [always before noun] Your native language is the first language you learn. **ana ... (dil) 3** [PEOPLE] [always before noun] relating to the people who lived in a country first, before other people took control of it **yerli** *the native inhabitants/population* **4** [ANIMALS AND PLANTS] Native animals or plants live or grow naturally in a place, and have not been brought from somewhere else. **yerli ... (hayvan, bitki vs.); ...da/de yetişen/yaşayan** *a large bird native to Europe*

native² /'neɪtɪv/ *noun* [C] **1** someone who was born in a particular place **...da/de doğan (kişi), yerli/yerel, lı/li** *He's a native of Texas.* **2** an old-fashioned and often offensive word for a person who lived in a country, for example an African country, before Europeans went there **(küçültücü, aşağılayıcı eski sözcük) ilkel, yerli**

ˌNative A'merican *adjective* relating or belonging to the original group of people who lived in North America **Amerika'nın yerli halkı, Kızılderili ● Native American** *noun* [C] **Kuzey Amerika'da yaşayan**

ˌnative 'speaker *noun* [C] someone who speaks a language as their first language **bir dili ana dili olarak konuşan kimse**

NATO (*also UK* **Nato**) /'neɪtəʊ/ *noun abbreviation for* North Atlantic Treaty Organization: an international military organization formed in 1949 to improve the defence of Western Europe **Kuzey Atlantik Antlaşma Paktı; Batı Avrupa'nın savunması amacıyla 1949 yılında kurulan askerî teşkilat**

natter /'nætər/ *verb* [I] *mainly UK informal* to talk about things that are not important **çene çalmak, gevezelik etmek; yarenlik etmek; sohbet etmek ● natter** *noun* [no plural] *UK to have a natter* **gevezelik**

o⊶**natural** /'nætʃrᵊl/ *adjective* **1** [NATURE] Something that is natural exists or happens because of nature, not because it was made or done by people. **doğal, tabii** *natural gas/resources* ○ *natural beauty* ○ *to die of*

natural causes (= because you are ill or old) ○ *This product contains only natural ingredients.* **2** [NORMAL] normal or expected **normal, beklenen, olması gereken, doğal** *a natural impulse/instinct* ○ *It's perfectly natural to feel nervous.* ⊃Opposite **unnatural. 3** [FROM BIRTH] If you have a natural characteristic, it is something you have been born with. **doğuştan, Allah vergisi** *a natural talent* ○ *She's a natural athlete/blonde.* **● naturalness** *noun* [U] **doğallık**

ˌnatural 'gas *noun* [U] a gas that is found under the ground and is used for cooking and heating **doğal gaz**

ˌnatural 'history *noun* [U] the study of animals and plants **tabiat/doğa bilgisi, doğabilim**

naturalist /'nætʃᵊrᵊlɪst/ *noun* [C] someone who studies animals and plants **tabiat/doğa bilimci**

naturalistic /ˌnætʃᵊrᵊ'lɪstɪk/ *adjective* Naturalistic art, writing, or acting tries to show things as they really are. **doğal (sanat, yazı, oyun vs.)**

naturalize /'nætʃᵊrᵊlaɪz/ *verb* **be naturalized** to officially become a member of another country **resmen vatandaş olmak** *a naturalized US citizen* **● naturalization** /ˌnætʃᵊrᵊlaɪ'zeɪʃⁿn/ *noun* [U] **alıştırma**

naturally /'nætʃᵊrᵊli/ *adverb* **1** [AS EXPECTED] as you would expect **tabii ki, elbette, doğal olarak** *Naturally, he was very disappointed.* **2** [NORMALLY] in a normal way **normal olarak, doğal yoldan** *Relax and try to behave naturally.* **3** [FROM BIRTH] having been born with a characteristic **doğuştan, yaradılıştan** *naturally aggressive/funny/slim* **4** [NATURE] Something that exists or happens naturally is part of nature and not made or done by people. **tabii yoldan, doğal, yapmacık olmayan, kendinden** *Organic tomatoes are grown naturally without chemical fertilizers.*

ˌnatural 'sciences *noun* [plural] sciences that relate to the physical world such as biology, chemistry, and physics **doğa bilimleri**

ˌnatural se'lection *noun* [U] the way that plants and animals die when they are weak or not suitable for the place where they live, while stronger ones continue to exist **doğal eleme yöntemi; zayıfın yok olup, güçlünün var olduğu tabii sonuç**

┌─ *nature* ...... İLE BİRLİKTE KULLANILAN KELİMELER
in sb's nature ● [happy/optimistic, etc.] by nature

o⊶**nature** /'neɪtʃər/ *noun* **1** [PLANTS AND ANIMALS] [U] all the plants, creatures, substances, and forces that exist in the universe, which are not made by people **tabiat, doğa** *the laws of nature* ○ *I like to get out and enjoy nature.* ○ *a nature trail* **2** [CHARACTER] [no plural] someone's character **mizaç, huy, karakter, doğuştan var olan özellik, yaradılış** *I didn't think it was in his nature to behave like that.* **3** [TYPE] [no plural] *formal* type **tür, çeşit, tip, hususiyet, özellik** *What exactly is the nature of your business?* ○ *I don't like hunting and things of that nature.* ⊃See also: **human nature, second nature.**

'nature reˌserve *noun* [C] a place where animals and plants live and are protected **doğal/tabii koruma alanı**

naught *old-fashioned* (*also UK* **nought**) /nɔːt/ *noun* [U] nothing **hiçbir şey**

naughty /'nɔːti/ *adjective* **1** If a child is naughty, they behave badly. **yaramaz, haşarı, saygısız, kaba, düşüncesiz** *a naughty little boy/girl* **2** a word used humorously to describe things that are sexual **açık saçık, ahlâka aykırı** *naughty films/magazines*

nausea /'nɔːziə/ *noun* [U] the unpleasant feeling of wanting to vomit **bulantı, kusma hissi** *She was hit by a sudden wave of nausea.*

nauseating /'nɔːsieɪtɪŋ/ *adjective* If something is nauseating, it makes you want to vomit. **mide bulandıran/bulandırıcı** *a nauseating smell*

nauseous /'nɔːsiəs/ *adjective* If you feel nauseous, you feel like you might vomit, and if something is nauseous, it makes you want to vomit. **midesi bulanan, mide bulandırıcı**

nautical /'nɔːtɪkəl/ *adjective* relating to boats or sailing **denizcilik ve gemilerle ilgili** *a nautical mile*

naval /'neɪvəl/ *adjective* [always before noun] relating to the navy **deniz kuvvetlerine ait** *a naval base/officer*

navel /'neɪvəl/ *noun* [C] the small, round, and usually hollow place on your stomach, where you were connected to your mother before birth **göbek deliği/çukuru**

navigable /'nævɪgəbl/ *adjective* If an area of water is navigable, it is wide, deep, and safe enough to sail a boat on. **gemilerin işlemesine/çalışmasına elverişli**

navigate /'nævɪgeɪt/ *verb* 1 [WITH MAP] [I, T] to find the right direction to travel by using maps or other equipment **rota beilrleyerek doğru yolda ilerlemek; rotasında götürmek** *He navigated the ship back to Plymouth.* ○ *We navigated using a map and compass.* ○ *I drive and he navigates.* 2 [BOAT] [T] to successfully sail along an area of water **başarıyla seyretmek; ilerlemek** 3 [DIFFICULT JOURNEY] [T] to find your way through a difficult place **yolunu bulmak, yolculuk yapmak, geçmek** *We had to navigate several flights of stairs.* 4 [SYSTEM] [T] to successfully use a complicated system **karmaşık bir sistemi başarıyla kullanmak** *to navigate a website* ● **navigation** /ˌnævɪ'geɪʃən/ *noun* [U] **geminin dolaşımı, seyri** ● **navigator** *noun* [C] a person who navigates **rota görevlisi/sorumlusu, seyrüseferci**

navy /'neɪvi/ *noun* 1 **the Navy** ships and soldiers used for fighting wars at sea **Deniz Kuvvetleri, Donanma** *to be in the navy* 2 [U] (*also* ˌnavy 'blue') a very dark blue colour **lacivert, koyu mavi** ○Orta kısımdaki renkli sayfalarına bakınız.

Nazi /'nɑːtsi/ *noun* [C] someone who supported the ideas of Hitler in Germany in the 1930s and 1940s **Nazi, 1930-1940 yılları arasında Almanya'da Hitler'in fikirlerini destekleyen kimse** *Nazi propaganda*

nb, NB /ˌen'biː/ *used to tell the reader that a particular piece of information is very important* **özel/önemli not, dikkat**

ᴼ⁴**near**¹ /nɪər/ *adverb, preposition* 1 [DISTANCE] not far away in distance **yakın, yakında, uzak olmayan** *Could you come a bit nearer, please?* ○ *I stood near the window.* ○ *Are you going anywhere near the post office?* 2 **be/come near to doing sth** to almost achieve or do something **bir şeyi yapmaya/başarmaya çok yakın olmak; yapmak üzere olmak** *This is the nearest I've ever got to winning anything.* ○ *He came near to punching him.* 3 [STATE] If something or someone is near a particular state, they are almost in that state. **hemen hemen, neredeyse, yakında** *She looked near exhaustion.* ○ *She was near to tears* (= almost crying) *when I told her.* 4 [TIME] not far away in time **(zaman) uzakta değil, yakında, hemen hemen** *She shouldn't be partying so near her exams.* ○ *We can decide nearer the time.* 5 [SIMILAR] similar **hemen hemen aynısı, tıpatıp benzeri** *The feelings I had were near hysteria.* ○ *He is Russia's nearest thing to a rock legend.* 6 **nowhere near** not close in distance, amount, time, or quality **(mesafe, miktar, zaman, nitelik vs.) yanından bile geçmemiş, hiç alakası bile yok; eline su dökemez** *It wasn't me - I was nowhere near him.* ○ *That's nowhere near enough for six people.* ○ *It was nowhere as dif-*

ficult as I thought it would be. 7 **near enough** almost **yeterince yakın, hemen hemen, neredeyse** *The books were ordered near enough alphabetically.*

ᴼ⁴**near**² /nɪər/ *adjective* 1 not far away in distance or time **yakın, uzak değil** *The school's very near.* ○ *The nearest garage is 10 miles away.* ○ *The baby's due date was getting nearer.* 2 **in the near future** at a time that is not far away **yakın gelecekte** *Space travel may become very common in the near future.* ⊃See also: a near miss².

near³ /nɪər/ *verb* to get close to something in distance or time **yaklaşmak, yakınlaşmak; zaman daralmak** *The building work is nearing completion at last.*

nearby /ˌnɪə'baɪ/ *adjective, adverb* not far away **civardaki, civarda, çevrede, yörede, mahalde** *a nearby town/village*

ᴼ⁴**nearly** /'nɪəli/ *adverb* 1 almost **hemen hemen, neredeyse** *It's nearly three weeks since I last saw her.* ○ *Nearly all the food had gone when I arrived.* ○ *She nearly drowned when she was eight.* ○ *I'll be with you in a minute - I've nearly finished.* 2 **not nearly (as/so)** a lot less **kadar değil, çok daha az** *It's not nearly as expensive as I thought.*

nearsighted /ˌnɪə'saɪtɪd/ *US* (*UK* short-sighted) *adjective* If you are nearsighted, you cannot see things very well if they are too far away. **miyop, uzağı göremeyen**

neat /niːt/ *adjective* 1 [TIDY] tidy and clean **düzgün, düzenli, intizamlı, derli toplu, tertipli** *He always looks very neat and tidy.* 2 [GOOD] *US informal* good **iyi, güzel** *That's really neat.* ○ *What a neat idea.* 3 [ALCOHOL] A neat alcoholic drink is drunk on its own, and not mixed with any other liquid. **sek, sade**

neatly /'niːtli/ *adverb* in a tidy way **düzgün şekilde, derli toplu olarak** *neatly dressed* ○ *a neatly folded pile of clothes*

necessarily /ˌnesə'serəli/ *adverb* **not necessarily** not for certain **zaruri/kesin/mutlak olmayan** *That's not necessarily true.* ○ *I know she doesn't say much, but it doesn't necessarily mean she's not interested.*

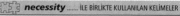
necessary ...... BAŞKA BİR DEYİŞLE

Need, require fiilleri ve **must** modalitesi gereklilik ifadesinde kullanılır. *The meat must be cooked thoroughly.* ● *Does she have the skills needed/required for work of that sort?*

Eğer bir şey önemli ve gerekli ise, durumu belirtmede **essential, fundamental** ve **indispensable** sıfatları kullanılır. *Some understanding of grammar is essential/fundamental to learning a language.* ● *This book is an indispensable resource for teachers.*

Be a must ifadesi resmi olmayan durumlarda yapılmasının gerekli olmadığı şeylerin tanımlamasında kullanılır. *If you live in the country a car is a must.*

ᴼ⁴**necessary** /'nesəsəri/ *adjective* needed in order to achieve something **gerekli, elzem, zaruri** [+ to do sth] *Is it really necessary to give so much detail?* ○ *Does he have the necessary skills and experience?* ○ *The police are prepared to use force, if necessary.* ⊃Opposite unnecessary.

necessitate /nə'sesɪteɪt/ *verb* [T] *formal* to make something necessary **gerektirmek, zaruri hale getirmek, gerekli kılmak**

necessity ...... İLE BİRLİKTE KULLANILAN KELİMELER

out of necessity ● **the** necessity **for/of** sth ● **financial** necessity

necessity /nə'sesəti/ *noun* 1 [U] the need for something **gereklilik, zorunluluk, mecburiyet, zaruret** *There's* *no financial necessity for her to work.* ○ *Sewing is something I do out of necessity, not for pleasure.* **2** [C] something you need **ihtiyaç, gereksinim** *Most people seem to consider a car a necessity, not a luxury.*

o╾**neck** /nek/ *noun* [C] **1** the part of the body between your head and your shoulders **boyun** *He was wearing a gold chain around his neck.* ○Orta kısımdaki renkli sayfalarına bakınız. **2** the part of a piece of clothing that goes around your neck **yaka** *a polo-neck/V-neck jumper* **3 be breathing down sb's neck** to watch what someone does all the time in a way that annoys them **daima ensesinde olmak, gözünü üstünden ayırmamak, nefes aldırmamak** *The last thing I want is a boss breathing down my neck.* ● **4 neck and neck** If two people who are competing are neck and neck, they are very close and either of them could win. **başa baş, kafa kafaya** ● **5 be up to your neck (in sth)** to be very busy **çok meşgul olmak, başını kaşıyacak zamanı olmamak** ○See also: **polo neck,** by the **scruff** of the/your neck**.**

necklace /'nekləs/ *noun* [C] a piece of jewellery that you wear around your neck **kolye, gerdanlık** *a pearl necklace* ○See picture at **jewellery.**

neckline /'neklaɪn/ *noun* [C] the shape made by the edge of a dress or shirt at the front of the neck **yaka çizgisi** *a low neckline*

nectar /'nektə^r/ *noun* [U] a sweet liquid produced by plants and collected by bees **çiçek özü, nektar**

nectarine /'nekt^əri:n/ *noun* [C] a soft, round fruit which is sweet and juicy and has a smooth red and yellow skin **nektarin**

née /neɪ/ *adjective* [always before noun] a word used to introduce the family name that a woman had before she got married **kızlık soyadıyla, evlenmeden önceki soyadı** *Margaret Hughes, née Johnson*

o╾**need**¹ /ni:d/ *verb* [T] **1** If you need something, you must have it, and if you need to do something, you must do it. **ihtiyacı olmak; gereksinim duymak; gerekmek; icap etmek** *I need some new shoes.* ○ *The country still desperately needs help.* ○ [+ to do sth] *If there's anything else you need to know, just give me a call.* ○ *We need you to look after the children for us.* **2 don't need to do sth/ needn't do sth** used in order to say that someone does not have to do something or should not do something **yapılmamalı; yapılmasına gerek yok; ...mamalı/ memeli; mayabilir/meyebilir** *You didn't need to come all this way.* ○ *You don't need to be frightened.* ○ *She needn't have taken him to the hospital.* **3** If something needs something to be done to it, that thing should be done in order to improve it. **gereksinimi olmak, yapılması gerekli olmak** *Do the clothes on this chair need washing?* ○ *The car needs to be serviced.* **4 There needs to be sth** used to say that something is necessary **olmalı, olması gerekli,** *There needs to be more funding for education in this country.*

identify a need ● **meet** a need (= provide what is needed) ● a need **for** sth

o╾**need**² /ni:d/ *noun* **1** [no plural] something that is necessary to have or do **gereksinim, ihtiyaç** *There's an urgent need for more medical supplies.* ○ [+ to do sth] *Is there any need to change the current system?* ○ *There's really no need for that sort of behaviour.* **2 be in need of sth** to need something **ihtiyacında olmak, gereksinim/ihtiyaç duymak; yapılması zaruri olmak** *My car's in desperate need of repair.*

needle /'ni:dl/ *noun* [C] **needle**
1 [MEDICAL] the thin, sharp, metal part of a piece of medical equipment used to take blood out of the body, or to put medicine or drugs in **iğne, şırınga** **2** [SEWING] a thin, pointed metal object with a small hole at one end for thread, used in sewing **dikiş iğnesi** *a needle and thread* **3** [MEASURING] a thin, pointed piece of metal or plastic that moves to point to numbers on equipment used for measuring things **ibre, gösterge ibresi** ○See also: **pins and needles.**

needless /'ni:dləs/ *adjective* not necessary **gereksiz, lüzumsuz, boşuna, beyhude** *a needless expense* ○ *Needless to say* (= as you would expect), *it rained the whole time we were there.* ● **needlessly** *adverb* **gereksizce**

o╾**needn't** /'ni:d^ənt/ *short for* need not **'need not' fiil yapısının kısa yazılışı** *You needn't have come.*

needs /ni:dz/ *noun* [plural] the things you need in order to have a good life **ihtiyaçlar, gereksinimler** *her emotional needs* ○ *The city is struggling to meet the needs of its homeless people.*

needy /'ni:di/ *adjective* Needy people do not have enough money. **muhtaç, yoksul, fakir** *The mayor wants to establish permanent housing for the needy.*

negate /nɪˈgeɪt/ *verb* [T] *formal* to make something lose its effect or value **geçersiz kılmak, boşa çıkarmak, etkisiz kılmak** ● **negation** /nɪˈgeɪʃ^ən/ *noun* [U] *formal* **değer kaybı**

o╾**negative**¹ /'negətɪv/ *adjective* **1** [NO ENTHUSIASM] not having enthusiasm or positive opinions about something **olumsuz, menfi, kötümser** *negative feelings* ○ *Many people have a negative attitude towards ageing.* **2** [BAD] A negative effect is bad and causes damage to something. **olumsuz, negatif** *Terrorist threats have had a very negative impact on tourism.* **3** [MEDICINE] If the result of a test to prove if someone is pregnant or ill is negative, that person is not pregnant or ill. **(tıp) olumsuz; hasta/hamile vs. değil 4** [NUMBERS] A negative number is less than zero. **(rakam) eksi, sıfırdan küçük 5** [GRAMMAR] In language, a negative word or phrase expresses the meaning 'no' or 'not'. **dilde cümleye 'no', 'not' gibi sözcükler kullanarak olumsuz anlam veren; olumsuz**

negative² /'negətɪv/ *noun* [C] **1** a piece of film from which a photograph can be produced, where dark areas look light and light areas look dark **banyo yapılmış/işlenmiş fotoğraf filmi; negatif 2** a word or phrase which expresses the meaning 'no' or 'not' **olumsuzluk ifade eden sözcük veya ifadeler**

negatively /'negətɪvli/ *adverb* **1** without enthusiasm or positive opinions **olumsuz olarak, olumsuzca** *to react/respond negatively* **2** with a bad effect **kötü şekilde, menfi şekilde** *negatively affected*

negativity /ˌnegəˈtɪvəti/ *noun* [U] when you do not feel enthusiastic or positive about things **olumsuzluk, menfilik, kötümserlik**

neglect¹ /nɪˈglekt/ *verb* [T] **1** to not give enough care or attention to something or someone **ihmal etmek, önemsememek, göz ardı etmek** *to neglect your appearance/the garden* ○ [often passive] *Some of these kids have been badly neglected in the past.* ○ *neglected children* **2 neglect to do sth** to not do something, often intentionally **ihmal etmek, boşlamak, sermek**

N

He neglected to mention the fact that we could lose money on the deal.

neglect² /nɪˈglekt/ noun [U] when you do not give enough care or attention to something or someone **ihmal, boşlama** *to suffer years of neglect*

negligence /ˈneglɪdʒəns/ noun [U] when you are not careful enough in something you do, especially in a job where your actions affect other people **ihmalkârlık, dikkatsizlik** *Her parents plan to sue the surgeon for medical negligence.*

negligent /ˈneglɪdʒənt/ adjective not giving enough care or attention to a job or activity, especially where your actions affect someone else **ihmalkâr, dikkatsiz** *The report found him negligent in his duties.*

negligible /ˈneglɪdʒəbl/ adjective small and not important **önemsiz, ehemmiyetsiz, az miktarda** *a negligible effect/result*

negotiable /nɪˈgəʊʃiəbl/ adjective If something is negotiable, it is not completely fixed, and can be changed after discussion. **tartışmaya/pazarlığa açık, tartışılabilir** *The January deadline is not negotiable.*

negotiation .... İLE BİRLİKTE KULLANILAN KELİMELER

enter into/be in negotiations • negotiations break down/fail • negotiations about/on/over sth • negotiations with sb • negotiations between sb and sb

negotiate /nɪˈgəʊʃieɪt/ verb 1 [I, T] to try to make or change an agreement by discussion **müzakere etmek, konuşarak anlaşmaya varmak, pazarlık etmek** *to negotiate with employers about working conditions* 2 [T] to successfully move around, through, or past something **başarıyla aşmak/geçmek** *to negotiate your way around/through a city* • **negotiator** noun [C] *a peace negotiator* **arabulucu**

negotiation /nɪˌgəʊʃiˈeɪʃᵊn/ noun [C] when people try to make or change an agreement by discussion **müzakere, görüşme, pazarlık** *Peace negotiations are due to start.*

Negro /ˈniːgrəʊ/ noun [C] plural **Negroes** old-fashioned a word that means a black person, which some people think is offensive **zenci**

o•**neighbour** UK (US **neighbor**) /ˈneɪbər/ noun [C] 1 someone who lives very near you, especially in the next house **komşu** *Our next-door neighbours are always arguing.* 2 someone or something that is near or next to someone or something else **yakındaki, yanıbaşındaki şey/kimse** *The French make more films than their European neighbours.*

neighbourhood UK (US **neighborhood**) /ˈneɪbəhʊd/ noun [C] an area of a town or city that people live in **semt, muhit, mahalle, çevre** *I grew up in a very poor neighbourhood.* ○ *Are there any good restaurants in the neighbourhood* (= in this area)?

neighbouring UK (US **neighboring**) /ˈneɪbᵊrɪŋ/ adjective [always before noun] near or next to somewhere **yakın, yakındaki, civardaki, komşu** *neighbouring countries/villages*

o•**neither¹** /ˈnaɪðər, ˈniːðər/ adverb used to say that a negative fact is also true of someone or something else **hiç biri, hiç birisi** *Jerry doesn't like it, and neither do I.* ○ *Her family wouldn't help her and neither would anyone else.* ○ *She's not very tall and neither is her husband.*

o•**neither²** /ˈnaɪðər, ˈniːðər/ pronoun, determiner not either of two people or things **hiç biri, (ikisinde) hiç biri, ...in/her ikisi de** *Luckily, neither child was hurt in the accident.* ○ *Neither of us had ever been to London before.* ○ *They gave us two keys, but neither worked.*

o•**neither³** /ˈnaɪðər, ˈniːðər/ conjunction **neither ... nor** used when a negative fact is true of two people or things or when someone or something does not have either of two qualities **ne...ne; ne...ne de** *Neither he nor his mother would talk to the police.* ○ *Their performance was neither entertaining nor educational.*

neo- /niːəʊ-/ prefix new **yeni anlamında ön ek** *neo-facists*

neon /ˈniːɒn/ noun [U] a gas that produces bright, colourful light when electricity passes through it, often used in signs (formula Ne) **neon, neon gazı/ışığı** *neon lights/signs*

nephew /ˈnefjuː/ noun [C] the son of your brother or sister, or the son of your husband's or wife's brother or sister **erkek yeğen**

Neptune /ˈneptjuːn/ noun [no plural] the planet that is eighth from the Sun, after Uranus and before Pluto **Neptün; Güneş sisteminde Pluto ve Uranüs arasındaki 8. gezegen**

nerd /nɜːd/ noun [C] informal someone, especially a man, who is not fashionable and who is interested in boring things **(bilhassa erkek) tekdüze/sıkıcı şeylerden hoşlanan kimse; güne/çağa uymayan kimse** • **nerdy** adjective informal boring and not fashionable **sıkıcı ve tekdüze**

nerve /nɜːv/ noun 1 [PART OF THE BODY] [C] one of the threads in your body which carry messages between your brain and other parts of the body **sinir, âsap** *the optic nerve* ○ **nerve cells/endings** 2 [BEING BRAVE] [no plural] the quality of being brave **cesaret, yüreklilik** [+ to do sth] *I haven't got the nerve to tell him I'm leaving.* ○ *He lost his nerve and couldn't go through with it.* 3 [RUDENESS] [no plural] the rudeness necessary to do something you know will upset someone **cüret; ...acak/ecek kadar yüzsüzlük/utanmazlık/arsızlık** *You've got a nerve, coming here!* ○ [+ to do sth] *I can't believe she had the nerve to talk to me after what happened.* 4 **hit/touch a (raw) nerve** to upset someone by talking about a particular subject **sinirlendirmek, âsabını bozmak**

nerve-racking /ˈnɜːvˌrækɪŋ/ adjective If an experience is nerve-racking, it makes you very nervous. **sinirlendirici, can sıkıcı, âsap bozucu, sinirleri geren** *a nerve-racking experience*

nerves .... İLE BİRLİKTE KULLANILAN KELİMELER

suffer from nerves • calm/settle/steady your nerves

nerves /nɜːvz/ noun [plural] 1 the state of being nervous **sinirli, asabî** *I need something to calm my nerves.* ○ *I always suffer from nerves before a match.* 2 **steady/strong nerves** the ability to be calm in difficult situations **güçlü/sağlam sinirler** *You need a cool head and steady nerves for this job.* 3 **get on sb's nerves** to annoy someone, especially by doing something again and again **sinirine dokunmak, âsabını bozmak** *If we spend too much time together we end up getting on each other's nerves.*

o•**nervous** /ˈnɜːvəs/ adjective 1 worried and anxious **endişeli, kaygılı, asabı, sinirli** *a nervous cough/laugh* ○ *She's very nervous about her driving test.* 2 [always before noun] relating to the nerves in the body **sinirsel, sinirlerle ilgili** *a nervous disorder*

nervous ˈbreakdown noun [C] a short period of mental illness when people are too ill to continue with their normal lives **sinir krizi**

nervously /ˈnɜːvəsli/ adverb in a worried and anxious way **sinirli sinirli, tedirgin biçimde** *to giggle/laugh nervously* • **nervousness** noun [U] **gerginlik, endişe**

'nervous ,system noun [C] your brain and all the nerves in your body which control your feelings and actions **sinir sistemi** a disease of the central nervous system

nest¹ /nest/ noun [C] a home built by birds for their eggs and by some other creatures to live in **kuş yuvası, yuva** a birds'/wasps' nest

nest² /nest/ verb [I] to live in a nest or build a nest **yuvada yaşamak, yuva yapmak**

nestle /'nesl/ verb **1 nestle (sth) against/in/on, etc** to rest yourself or part of your body in a comfortable, protected position **yaslanmak, dayanmak** The cat was nestling in her lap. **2 nestle beneath/between/in, etc** If a building, town, or object nestles somewhere, it is in a protected position, with bigger things around it. **gizlenmek, korunmak, etrafı sarıp sarmalanmak** a village nestled in the Carpathian mountains

net

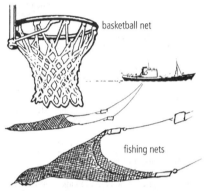

basketball net

fishing nets

net¹ /net/ noun **1** [U] material made of crossed threads with holes between them **ağ 2** [C] something made with a piece of net, for example for catching fish or insects, or for sports **ağ, file** a fishing net ○ a tennis/basketball net **3 the Net** short for the Internet **internet** ⊃See also: **safety net.**

net² (also UK **nett**) /net/ adjective A net amount of money has had costs such as tax taken away from it. **net, safı** a net income/profit of £10,000

net³ /net/ verb [T] **netting,** past **netted 1** to get an amount of money as profit **kâr sağlamak/etmek** One trader netted a bonus of £1 million. **2** to hit, throw, or kick a ball into a net **topu ağa/fileye temas ettirmek** He netted a great penalty.

netball /'netbɔːl/ noun [U] a game usually played by teams of women, where a ball is thrown from player to player and goals are scored by throwing the ball through a high net **netbol**

netting /'netɪŋ/ noun [U] material made of crossed threads or wires with holes between them **kafes** wire netting

nettle /'netl/ noun [C] a wild plant whose leaves hurt you if you touch them **ısırgan otu**

network ...... İLE BİRLİKTE KULLANILAN KELİMELER

build/create/establish/form a network ● a network of sth ● a **rail/road** network

network¹ /'netwɜːk/ noun [C] **1** [SYSTEM] a system or group of connected parts **ağ, örgü** a rail/road network ○ a network of cables/tunnels **2** [PEOPLE] a group of people who know each other or who work together a

large network of friends **3** [COMPANY] a large television or radio company that broadcasts programmes in many areas **tv radyo yayın şirketi/ağı**

network² /'netwɜːk/ verb **1** [I] to use social events to meet people who might be useful for your business **insanlarla iş yapmak amacıyla tanışmak için sosyal faaliyetleri kullanmak; tanışma fırsatları yaratmak 2** [T] to connect computers together so that they can share information and programs **bilgisayar ağı kurmak**

networking /'netwɜːkɪŋ/ noun [U] **1** when you use social events to meet people who might be useful for your business **iş amaçlı sosyal topalantılar düzenleme 2** when you connect computers together so that they can share programs and information **bilgisayar ağı kurma**

neural /'njʊərᵊl/ adjective [always before noun] relating to the nerves in your body **sinirsel, sinir hücresiyle ilgili** neural activity

neurology /njʊəˈrɒlədʒi/ noun [U] the study of the system of nerves in people's bodies **sinirbilim, nöroloji**
● **neurological** /ˌnjʊərəˈlɒdʒɪkᵊl/ adjective Neurological illnesses affect the nerves in people's bodies. **sinirbilimine ait, sinirsel hastalıklarla ilgili, nörolojik**
● **neurologist** /njʊəˈrɒlədʒɪst/ noun [C] a doctor who deals with neurological illnesses **sinirsel hastalıklar hekimi, nörolojist**

neuron /'njʊərɒn/ noun [C] a nerve cell which carries messages between your brain and other parts of your body **beyin hücresi, sinir, nöron**

neurosis /njʊəˈrəʊsɪs/ noun [C] plural **neuroses** /njʊəˈrəʊsiːz/ a mental illness, often causing you to worry too much about something **nevroz, bir tür sinir hastalığı**

neurotic /njʊəˈrɒtɪk/ adjective If you are neurotic, you worry about things too much. **nörotik, takıntılı, evhamlı, sinir hastası**

neuter /'njuːtəʳ/ adjective in some languages, belonging to a group of nouns or adjectives that have the same grammatical behaviour. The other groups are 'masculine' and 'feminine'. **eril/dişil olmayan, cinsiyetsiz, nötr**

neutral¹ /'njuːtrᵊl/ adjective **1** independent and not supporting any side in an argument, fight, or competition **tarafsız, yansız, taraf/yan tutmayan, bitaraf** neutral ground/territory ○ He decided to remain neutral on the issue. **2** Neutral colours are not strong or bright. **soluk, parlak renkli olmayan, kurşuni, soluk gri**

neutral² /'njuːtrᵊl/ noun [U] In driving, neutral is the position of the gears (= parts of a vehicle that control how fast the wheels turn) when they are not connected. **vites boşta** to be in neutral

neutrality /njuːˈtræləti/ noun [U] the state of being independent and not supporting any side in an argument, war, etc **tarafsızlık, yansızlık, bitaraflık** political neutrality

neutron /'njuːtrɒn/ noun [C] a part of an atom which has no electrical charge (= the electricity something stores or carries) **nötron, atomun elektrik taşımayan parçası**

○People **never** /'nevəʳ/ adverb **1** not ever, not one time **asla, hiç** bir zaman, hiç "Have you ever been to Australia?" "No, never." ○ I've never even thought about that before. ○ She'll never be able to have children. ○ He just walked out of the door one day and never came back. **2** used to emphasize something negative **hiç, hiç bir şekilde** I never knew you lived around here.

N

never-ending /ˌnevˈrˈendɪŋ/ *adjective* If something is never-ending, it continues for ever. **bitmez tükenmez, aralıksız, sonu gelmeyen** *The housework in this place is just never-ending.*

nevertheless /ˌnevəðəˈles/ *adverb* despite that **yine de, bununla beraber, buna rağmen, mamafih** *I knew a lot about the subject already, but her talk was interesting nevertheless.*

✺**new** /njuː/ *adjective* **1** DIFFERENT different from before **yeni** *I need some new shoes.* ○ *Have you met Fiona's new boyfriend?* ○ *He's starting his new job on Monday.* ○ *We're always looking for new ways to improve our services.* **2** RECENTLY MADE recently made **yeni, hiç kullanılmamış** *Their house is quite new - it's about five years old.* ○ *The factory will provide hundreds of new jobs for the area.* **3** NOT KNOWN BEFORE not known before **tanınmamış, başka, yeni, görülmemiş** *to discover a new gene/star* **4 be new to sb** If a situation or activity is new to you, you have not had experience of it before. **yeni/yabancı olmak 5 be new to sth** If you are new to a situation or activity, you have only recently started experiencing it. **yeni/çiçeği burnunda olmak** *I'm new to the job.* ⊃See also: a whole new **ball game**, new **blood**, **brand new**, break new **ground**[1], new **heights**, turn over a new **leaf**[1], give sb/sth a new **lease**[1] of life.

newborn /ˌnjuːˈbɔːn/ *adjective* [always before noun] A newborn baby has just been born. ● **newborn** *noun* [C] a newborn baby **yeni doğmuş bebek**

newcomer /ˈnjuːˌkʌmərˈ/ *noun* [C] someone who has only recently arrived or started doing something **yeni gelen/katılan kişi** *He's a relative newcomer to the area.*

new-found /ˈnjuːˌfaʊnd/ *adjective* [always before noun] A new-found quality or ability has started recently. **yeni keşfedilmiş, yeni edinilmiş** *This success is a reflection of their new-found confidence.*

newly /ˈnjuːli/ *adverb* recently **yeni, yakınlarda, son zamanlarda** *a newly married couple* ○ *newly built houses*

🧩 **news** ...... İLE BİRLİKTE KULLANILAN KELİMELER

the latest news ● hear/listen to/see/watch the news ● in/on the news

✺**news** /njuːz/ *noun* [U] **1 the news** the announcement of important events on television, radio, and in newspapers **haberler** *the local/national news* ○ *to watch the 6 o'clock news* ○ *Did you see that report about child labour on the news last night?* ○ *a news bulletin/report* **2** new information **haber** *Have you had any news about your job yet?* ○ *I've got some good news for you.* ○ *Any news from John?* **3 be news to sb** *informal* to be a surprise to someone **birisi için yeni/haber olmak** *He's leaving? Well that's certainly news to me.* **4 be bad/good news for sb** to affect someone badly/well **kötü/iyi haber olmak; iyi/kötü etkilemek** *This weather is bad news for farmers.*

newsagent /ˈnjuːzˌeɪdʒˈnt/ *noun* [C] *UK* **1 newsagent's** a shop that sells newspapers, magazines, and things like sweets and cigarettes **gazete büfesi 2** someone who owns or works in a newsagent's **gazete bayii**

newscast /ˈnjuːzkɑːst/ *noun* [C] *US* a television or radio broadcast of the news **haber ajansı, haber bülteni** *the evening newscast*

newscaster /ˈnjuːzkɑːstərˈ/ *noun* [C] someone who reads the news on the radio or television **haber spikeri**

newsgroup /ˈnjuːzgruːp/ *noun* [group] a collection of messages on the Internet that people write about a particular subject **haber grubu** *a political newsgroup*

newsletter /ˈnjuːzˌletərˈ/ *noun* [C] a regular report with information for people who belong to an organization or who are interested in a particular subject **haber bülteni; haber postası, bülten** *a monthly newsletter about business and the environment*

✺**newspaper** /ˈnjuːsˌpeɪpərˈ/ ⑤ /ˈnuːzˌpeɪpərˈ/ *noun* **1** [C] large, folded sheets of paper which are printed with the news and sold every day or every week **gazete** *a local/national newspaper* ○ *I read about his death in the newspaper.* ○ *a newspaper article/headline* **2** [U] paper from newspapers **gazete sayfası, okunmuş gazete kağıdı** *The cups were wrapped in newspaper.*

newsprint /ˈnjuːzprɪnt/ *noun* [U] cheap, low quality paper used to print newspapers **gazete kağıdı**

newsreader /ˈnjuːzˌriːdərˈ/ *noun* [C] *UK* someone who reads the news on the radio or television **haber okuyan spiker**

newsstand /ˈnjuːzstænd/ *noun* [C] *US* a small shop in a public area of a building or station, or part of a bigger shop, where newspapers and magazines are sold **gazete büfesi/tezgâhı/standı**

newsworthy /ˈnjuːzˌwɜːði/ *adjective* interesting or important enough to be included in the news **haber değeri olan**

the ˌNew ˈTestament *noun* the part of the Bible (= holy book) written after the birth of Jesus Christ **Yeni Ahit, İncil; Hz. İsa'nın doğumundan sonra yazılan İncil'in bir bölümü**

ˌnew ˈwave *noun* [C] people who are doing activities in a new and different way **yeni akım/dalga** *the new wave of wine producers*

ˌnew ˈyear (*also* New Year) *noun* [C] the period in January when another year begins **yeni yıl** *Happy New Year!* ○ *We're going away in the new year.*

ˌNew ˌYear's ˈDay *noun* [C, U] 1 January, the first day of the year and a public holiday in many countries **Yılbaşı**

ˌNew ˌYear's ˈEve *noun* [C, U] 31 December, the last day of the year **Yılbaşı Gecesi**

✺**next**[1] /nekst/ *adjective* **1 next week/year/Monday, etc** the week/year/Monday, etc that follows the present one **gelecek/önümüzdeki/ertesi hafta/ay/yıl vs.** *I'm planning to visit California next year.* ○ *Are you doing anything next Wednesday?* ○ *Next time, ask my permission before you borrow the car.* **2** The next time, event, person, or thing is the one nearest to now or the one that follows the present one. **sonraki, sıradaki, gelecek** *What time's the next train to London?* ○ *We're going to be very busy for the next few months.* **3** The next place is the one nearest to the present one. **yakın, yandaki, bitişiğindeki** *She only lives in the next village.* ○ *Turn left at the next roundabout.* **4 the next best thing** the thing that is best, if you cannot have or do the thing you really want **en iyi ikinci/bir diğer şey; en uygun olan şey** *Coaching football is the next best thing to playing.* **5 the next thing I knew** used to talk about part of a story that happens in a sudden and surprising way **hatırladığım/bildiğim tek şey** *A car came speeding round the corner, and the next thing I knew I was lying on the ground.*

✺**next**[2] /nekst/ *adverb* **1** immediately after ...**dan/den hemen sonra gelen, bir sonraki** *You'll never guess what happened next.* ○ *Where shall we go next?* **2** The time when you next do something is the first time you do it again. **ikinci kez, tekrar, yine** *Could you get some coffee when you next go to the supermarket?*

✺**next**[3] /nekst/ *preposition* **next to sth/sb** very close to something or someone, with nothing in between ...**ın/in yanına/yanında/bitişiğine/bitişiğinde** *Come and* sit next to me. ○ *The factory is right next to a residential area.*

o─**next⁴** /nekst/ *pronoun* **1** the person or thing that follows the present person or thing **sıradaki, sırası gelen, bir sonraki** *Who's next to see the nurse?* ○ *Blue roses? Whatever next?* (= What other strange things might happen?) **2 the weekend/week/Thursday, etc after next** the weekend/week/Thursday, etc that follows the next one **öbür hafta sonu/hafta/perşembe vs.**

,next '**door** *adjective, adverb* in the next room, house, or building **kapı komşusu olan; bitişikteki, yandaki, kapı komşusu** *What are your next-door neighbours like?* ○ *That's the old man who lives next door to Paul.*

,next of '**kin** *noun* [C] *plural* next of kin *formal* the person you are most closely related to **en yakın akraba** *The names of the dead cannot be released until their next of kin have been notified.*

the NHS /,enetʃ'es/ *noun abbreviation for* the National Health Service: the system providing free medical services in the UK **(Birleşik Krallık) Ulusal Sağlık Hizmeti'nin kısa yazılışı** *Did she get it done privately or on the NHS?*

nib /nɪb/ *noun* [C] the pointed end of a pen, where the ink comes out **uç, kalem ucu**

nibble /'nɪbl/ *verb* [I, T] to eat something by taking very small bites or to bite something gently **azar azar ısırıp yemek, dişlemek, kemirmek** *He was nibbling a biscuit.* ○ *She nibbled playfully at his ear.*

nice ...... BAŞKA BİR DEYİŞLE

Eğer kişi diğer insanlara olan nazik davranışlarından dolayı iyi olarak nitelendiriliyorsa, bu kişilerin tanımlanmasında **kind** veya **sweet** ifadeleri kullanılabilir. *She's a very kind person.* ● *Thank you so much for the card - it was very sweet of you!*
Eğer yaptığınız bir şey iyi veya güzel ise, durum **fun**, **enjoyable** veya **lovely** ifadeleriyle tanımlanabilir. *We had a really lovely day at the beach.* ● *You'd have liked the party - it was fun.*
Eğer bir şey bakılacak kadar güzel ise, **attractive**, **beautiful, pleasant, lovely,** ve **pretty** ifadeleri kullanılabilir. *There's some beautiful countryside in Yorkshire.* ● *That's a pretty dress you're wearing.*
Eğer yediğimiz yemeğin tadı güzel ise, **delicious** veya **tasty** sıfatları durumun tanımlanmasında kullanılabilir. *This chicken soup is absolutely delicious.*

o─**nice** /naɪs/ *adjective* **1** pleasant **iyi, hoş** *They live in a nice old house on Market Street.* ○ *We could go to the coast tomorrow, if the weather's nice.* ○ [+ to do sth] *It was very nice to meet you.* ○ [+ doing sth] *Nice talking to you.* **2** kind and friendly **nâzik, samimi** *He seems like a really nice guy.* ○ *She's always been very nice to me.* **3 nice and sth** *informal* used to emphasize a positive quality **güzel ve aynı zamanda ...** *nice and clean* ○ *This chair's nice and comfy.*

nicely /'naɪsli/ *adverb* **1** well **pekiyi, pekala, çok iyi** *That table would fit nicely in the bedroom.* ○ *His business is doing very nicely.* **2** in a pleasant way **kibarca, nazikçe** *nicely dressed*

niche /niːʃ/ ⓤ /nɪtʃ/ *noun* [C] **1** a job or activity that is very suitable for someone **uygun yer/iş/mevki** *After years of job dissatisfaction, he's at last found his niche in financial services.* **2** a hollow space cut into a wall **duvarda bulunan oyuk, niş**

,niche '**market** *noun* [C] a small number of people who buy a particular product or service, especially an unusual or expensive one **tek bir alanda hizmet veya ürün sunan mağaza** *They make luxury cars for a small but significant niche market.*

nick¹ /nɪk/ *verb* [T] **1** STEAL *UK informal* to steal something **çalmak, aşırmak, yürütmek, araklamak** *She got caught nicking CDs from Smith's.* **2** CATCH *UK informal* If the police nick someone, they catch that person because they have committed a crime. **enselemek, yakalamak, ele geçirmek** [often passive] *He got nicked for handling stolen goods.* **3** CUT to make a small cut in something without intending to **çentik açmak, hafifçe kesmek, çizmek** *He nicked himself shaving.*

nick² /nɪk/ *noun* **1** [C] *mainly UK informal* a prison or police station **hapishane, mahpus, karakol, nezarethane** *They spent the night in the nick.* **2** [C] a small cut **çentik, çizik** *He has a little nick on his cheek.* **3 in bad/good nick** *UK informal* in bad/good condition **kötü/iyi durumda 4 in the nick of time** just before it was too late **son anda, ucu ucuna, son dakikada, tam sırasında** *The ambulance arrived in the nick of time.*

nickel /'nɪkl/ *noun* **1** [C] a US or Canadian coin with a value of 5 cents **(ABD, Kanada) 5 sente eşit madenî para 2** [U] a silver-white metal that is often mixed with other metals (formula Ni) **nikel**

nickname /'nɪkneɪm/ *noun* [C] a name used informally instead of your real name **lakap, takma ad** *His behaviour has earned him the nickname 'Mad Dog'.* ● **nickname** *verb* [+ two objects] *They nicknamed her 'The Iron Lady'.* **takma isim**

nicotine /'nɪkətiːn/ *noun* [U] a poisonous chemical substance in tobacco **nikotin; tütünde bulunan zehirli kimyasal**

niece /niːs/ *noun* [C] the daughter of your brother or sister, or the daughter of your husband's or wife's brother or sister **kız yeğen**

nifty /'nɪfti/ *adjective informal* well-designed and effective **çekici, zarif, iyi tasarlanmış, etkin** *a nifty piece of software*

nigger /'nɪɡəʳ/ *noun* [C] *offensive* a very offensive word for a black person **zenciler için aşağılayıcı bir söz**

niggle /'nɪɡl/ *verb* **1** [I, T] to worry or annoy someone slightly for a long time **uzun süre sıkıntı ve rahatsızlık vermek, endişe duymak** *a niggling injury* **2 niggle about/over, etc** *UK* to complain about things which are not very important **pireyi deve yapmak, incir çekirdeğini doldurmayacak konuda şikayet etmek; önemsiz şeylerden yakınmak** *She kept niggling about the extra work.* ● **niggle** *noun* [C] **titizlik**

nigh /naɪ/ *adverb* **1** *literary* near **yakın, yakında** *The end of the world is nigh.* **2 well nigh/nigh on** *old-fashioned* almost **hemen hemen, neredeyse** *Our family has lived here well nigh two hundred years.*

night ...... İLE BİRLİKTE KULLANILAN KELİMELER

spend the night ● **at** night ● **in** the night ● the **middle of** the night ● **last** night

o─**night** /naɪt/ *noun* [C, U] **1** DARK the time in every 24 hours when it is dark and people usually sleep **gece** *I didn't get any sleep last night.* ○ *It's warm during the day, but it can get quite cold at night.* ○ *The phone rang in the middle of the night.* ○ *We stayed up almost all night talking.* ○ *Tim's working nights this week.* **2** EVENING the period from the evening to the time when you go to sleep **gece, akşam** *Did you have a good time last night?* ○ *Are you doing anything on Friday night?* **3** SAYING THE TIME used to describe the hours from the evening until just after 12 midnight **gece, gece yarısına kadar olan süre** *They're open from 7 in the morning until 10 o'clock at night.* **4 have an early/a late night** to go to bed early/late **erken/geç yatmak 5 a night out** an evening spent away from home doing something enjoyable **eğlenmek için dışarıda geçiri-**

len *gece a night out at the theatre* **6 Good night.** You say 'Good night' to someone who is going to bed. **'İyi geceler!', 'İyi uykular!', 'Allah rahatlık versin!'** *Good night, sleep well.* ➲See also: the **dead**³ of night/winter.

nightclub /'naɪtklʌb/ *noun* [C] a place where you can dance and drink at night **gece kulübü**

nightdress /'naɪtdres/ *noun* [C] *mainly UK* a loose dress that women wear in bed **gecelik**

nightfall /'naɪtfɔːl/ *noun* [U] the time in the evening when it gets dark **akşam vakti, akşam karanlığı**

nightgown /'naɪtgaʊn/ *noun* [C] a loose dress that women wear in bed **gecelik**

nightie /'naɪti/ *noun* [C] a loose dress that women wear in bed **gecelik**

nightingale /'naɪtɪŋgeɪl/ *noun* [C] a small brown bird which sings very well **bülbül**

nightlife /'naɪtlaɪf/ *noun* [U] entertainment for the night such as bars, restaurants, and theatres **gece hayatı/yaşamı** *What's the nightlife like around here?*

nightly /'naɪtli/ *adjective* [always before noun], *adverb* happening every night **her gece olan/yapılan** *the nightly news* ○ *The show, lasting ninety minutes, will be broadcast nightly from Monday to Friday.*

🧩 **nightmare** ...... İLE BİRLİKTE KULLANILAN KELİMELER

an **absolute/complete/living/total** nightmare ● be sb's **worst** nightmare ● the nightmare **of** (doing) sth ● a nightmare **for** sb

nightmare /'naɪtmeə/ *noun* [C] **1** a very unpleasant experience **kâbus, berbat bir deneyim** *The traffic can be a real nightmare after 4.30.* **2** a frightening dream **kâbus, karabasan, korkulu rüya**

'night ,school *noun* [U] classes for adults that are taught in the evening **akşam/gece okulu/kursları**

nightstick /'naɪtstɪk/ *US* (*UK* truncheon) *noun* [C] a short stick that police officers carry to use as a weapon **cop, sopa**

night-time /'naɪttaɪm/ *noun* [U] the period of time when it is dark at night **gece, gece vakti**

nil /nɪl/ *noun* [U] **1** *UK* In sports results, nil means 'zero'. **sıfır, hiç** *Germany beat England three nil* (= 3-0). **2** not existing **sıfır, var olmayan** *The chances of that happening are virtually nil.*

nimble /'nɪmbl/ *adjective* able to move quickly and easily **çevik, atik, kıvrak** *nimble fingers*

☞**nine** /naɪn/ the number 9 **dokuz**

☞**nineteen** /ˌnaɪn'tiːn/ the number 19 **ondokuz** ● **nineteenth** 19th written as a word **ondokuzuncu**

nine-to-five /ˌnaɪntə,faɪv/ *adjective, adverb* describes work that begins at nine o'clock in the morning and ends at five o'clock, which are the hours that people work in many offices from Monday to Friday **dokuzbeş çalışma/mesai saatleri** *She's tired of working nine-to-five.* ● **nine-to-five** /ˌnaɪntə'faɪv/ *noun* [C] **Saat 9'dan 5'e çalışma**

☞**ninety** /'naɪnti/ **1** the number 90 **doksan 2 the nineties** the years from 1990 to 1999 **doksanlı yıllar 3 be in your nineties** to be aged between 90 and 99 **doksanlı yaşlarda olmak** ● **ninetieth** 90th written as a word **doksanıncı**

ninth¹ /naɪnθ/ 9th written as a word **dokuzuncu**

ninth² /naɪnθ/ *noun* [C] one of nine equal parts of something; ¹/₉; **dokuzda bir**

nip /nɪp/ *verb* nipping, *past* nipped **1** nip **down/out/up, etc** *UK informal* to go somewhere quickly and for a short time **acele girmek, bir koşu gitmek** *I'm just nip-*

ping down the road to get a paper. **2** [T] If something nips you, it gives you a small, sharp bite. **hafifçe ısırmak, çimdiklemek, dişlemek, makas almak** *His parrot nipped him on the nose.* ➲See also: nip sth in the **bud.**

nipple /'nɪpl/ *noun* [C] the small, circular area of slightly darker, harder skin in the centre of each breast in women, or on each side of the chest in men **meme başı, meme ucu**

nirvana /nɪə'vɑːnə/ *noun* [U] a state of perfection **mükemmellik, eşsizlik**

nitrate /'naɪtreɪt/ *noun* [C, U] a chemical containing nitrogen and oxygen that is used on crops to make them grow better **nitrat, besleyici kimyasal gübre**

nitrogen /'naɪtrədʒən/ *noun* [U] a gas that has no colour or smell and is the main part of air (symbol **N**) **nitrojen**

the nitty-gritty /ˌnɪti'grɪti/ *noun* the important details of a subject or activity **asıl mesele, konunun özü, önemli ayrıntılar** *English teachers should concentrate on the nitty-gritty of teaching grammar.*

☞**no**¹ /nəʊ/ *exclamation* **1** something that you say in order to disagree, give a negative answer, or say that something is not true **hayır** *"Have you seen Louise?" "No, I haven't."* ○ *"Have you ever been to Ireland?" "No."* ○ *"Can I have some more cake?" "No, you'll be sick."* ○ *"He's really ugly." "No he isn't!"* **2** something that you say to agree with something that is negative **hayır** *"He's not very bright, is he?" "No, I'm afraid not."* **3 Oh no!** something that you say when you are shocked and upset **A, hayır!** *Oh no! It's gone all over the carpet!*

☞**no**² /nəʊ/ *determiner* **1** not any **yok, hayır** *There were no signposts anywhere.* ○ *I had no difficulty getting work.* ○ *There was no mention of money.* **2** a word used to say that something is forbidden **hayır** *No smoking.* ○ *There was no talking in her classes.* **3 There's no doing sth** something that you say when an action is impossible **Yapacak birşey olmamak; ...yapmak faydasız/olanaksız; ...maz/mez; ...ması/mesi yararsız** *There's no pleasing some people* (= nothing that you do will make them happy).

no³ /nəʊ/ *adverb* **no ... than** not any ...**dan/den** ...**başka** *The work should be done no later than Friday.* ○ *There were no more than ten people there.*

no. *written abbreviation for* number **numara**

nobility /nəʊ'bɪləti/ *noun* **1 the nobility** [group] the people from the highest social group in a society **soylular sınıfı, aristokrasi 2** [U] the quality of being noble **asalet, soyluluk**

noble¹ /'nəʊbl/ *adjective* **1** honest, brave, and kind **dürüst, soylu, cesur, kibar** *a noble gesture* **2** belonging to the highest social group of a society **soylu, asil, yüce, yüksek**

noble² /'nəʊbl/ *noun* [C] a person of the highest social group in some countries **asiller sınıfından kimse**

nobleman, noblewoman /'nəʊblmən, 'nəʊbl,wʊmən/ *noun* [C] *plural* **noblemen** or **noblewomen** someone belonging to the highest social group in some countries **asiller sınıfından bayan/erkek; asilzâde**

nobly /'nəʊbli/ *adverb* in a brave or generous way **cesur ve cömertçe** *She nobly offered to sell her jewellery.*

☞**nobody** /'nəʊbədi/ *pronoun* no person **hiç kimse, kimse** *There was nobody I could talk to.* ○ *Nobody's listening.* ○ *Sally helped me, but nobody else bothered.*

no-brainer /ˌnəʊ'breɪnə/ *noun* [C] *informal* something that is very simple to do or to understand, or a decision that is very easy to take

nocturnal /nɒk'tɜːnᵊl/ *adjective* **1** Nocturnal animals and birds are active at night. **gece faal olan (kuşlar/**

hayvanlar) 2 happening at night **gece olan, geceleyin vuku bulan** *nocturnal activities/habits*

nod /nɒd/ *verb* [I, T] nodding, *past* nodded to move your head up and down as a way of agreeing, to give someone a sign, or to point to something **başını sallayarak olumlu cevap vermek; başıyla tasdik etmek/onaylamak** *They nodded enthusiastically at the proposal.* ○ *Barbara nodded in approval.* ● **nod** *noun* [C] *He gave a nod of approval.* **kabul etme anlamında başını öne doğru sallama**
nod off *phrasal verb informal* to start sleeping **oturduğu yerde uykuya dalmak; uyurken başı önüne düşmek**

nodule /ˈnɒdjuːl/ *noun* [C] a small lump, especially on a plant or someone's body **yumru, ur, şişlik**

no-fault /ˈnəʊfɔːlt/ *adjective* [always before noun] US No-fault laws or systems are ones where it is not important who is responsible for what has happened. **(yasa, sistem) sorumlusu/müsebbibi belli olmayan** *no-fault insurance*

‚no-go ˈarea *noun* [C] *mainly UK* an area, usually in a city, where it is too dangerous to go because there is a lot of violent crime there **girilmez bölge; girilmesi sakıncalı bölge/mahal**

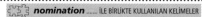 **noise** .... İLE BİRLİKTE KULLANILAN KELİMELER
background noise ● a **deafening/faint/loud/strange** noise ● **hear/make** a noise

o⊶**noise** /nɔɪz/ *noun* [C, U] a sound, often a loud, unpleasant sound **gürültü, ses** *a deafening/loud noise* ○ *Stop making so much noise!* ○ *The engine's making funny noises.* ○ *There is some **background noise** on the recording.* ○ *I had to shout above the noise of the party.*

ˈnoise polˌlution *noun* [U] noise, often from traffic, which upsets people where they live or work **gürültü kirliliği**

o⊶**noisy** /ˈnɔɪzi/ *adjective* Noisy people or things make a lot of noise. **gürültülü** *A crowd of noisy protesters gathered in the square.* ○ *We've had problems with noisy neighbours.* ● **noisily** *adverb* **gürültülü bir şekilde**

nomad /ˈnəʊmæd/ *noun* [C] a member of a group of people who move from one place to another instead of living in the same place all the time **göçebe, göçer, bedevî** ● **nomadic** /nəʊˈmædɪk/ *adjective* Nomadic people move from place to place. **göçebe**

ˈno-man's ˌland *noun* [U, no plural] an area of land which no one owns or controls, especially in a war **savaş zamanı hiç kimsenin kontrolünde olmayan bölge/alan**

nominal /ˈnɒmɪnəl/ *adjective* **1** existing officially, but not in reality **sözde, itibarî, bir tek kağıt üzerinde varolan** *a nominal leader* **2** A nominal sum of money is a small amount of money. **az, sembolik, önemsiz, cüz'î** *a nominal charge/fee*

nominally /ˈnɒmɪnəli/ *adverb* officially but not in reality **sözde/itibarî olarak** *nominally Catholic areas*

nominate /ˈnɒmɪneɪt/ *verb* [T] **1** to officially suggest a person for a job or a position in an organization, or to suggest a person or their work for a prize **aday göstermek** [often passive] *Judges are nominated by the governor.* ○ *The film was nominated for an Academy Award.* ○ *He was nominated as best actor.* **2** to choose someone for a job or to do something **resmî olarak seçmek, atamak** *He has nominated his brother as his heir.* ○ [+ to do sth] *Two colleagues were nominated to attend the conference.*

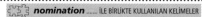 **nomination** .... İLE BİRLİKTE KULLANILAN KELİMELER
make/receive/seek/win a nomination ● a nomination **as/for** sth

nomination /ˌnɒmɪˈneɪʃən/ *noun* [C, U] **1** the act of officially suggesting a person for a job or their work for a prize **adaylık, aday göster(il)mek** *to seek/win a nomination for mayor of Chicago.* ○ *She has just received her fourth Oscar nomination.* **2** the choice of someone for a job or to do something **atama/atanma, tayin, seçme/seçilme** *They did everything they could to defeat his nomination to be surgeon general.*

nominee /ˌnɒmɪˈniː/ *noun* [C] a person or a piece of work which has been nominated **aday, namzet**

non- /nɒn-/ *prefix* not or the opposite of ...**sız/siz/suz/süz; ...olmayan/gayri veya ters, aksi manasında ön ek** *non-alcoholic drinks* ○ *non-smokers*

non-alcoholic /ˌnɒnælkəˈhɒlɪk/ *adjective* describes a drink that does not contain alcohol **alkolsüz**

nonchalant /ˈnɒnʃələnt/ ⓤ /ˌnɑːnʃəˈlɑːnt/ *adjective* calm and not worried **kayıtsız, umursamaz, pervasız** *a nonchalant shrug* ● **nonchalantly** *adverb* **umursamaz bir şekilde**

noncommittal /ˌnɒnkəˈmɪtəl/ *adjective* not showing your opinion about something **fikrini açıkça belirtmeyen, suya sabuna dokumayan; rengini belli etmeyen, politik** *a noncommittal expression/response*

nondescript /ˈnɒndɪskrɪpt/ *adjective* not interesting **sıradan, kişiliksiz, ruhsuz, renksiz, ne olduğu belli olmayan, tuhaf** *a nondescript building/man*

o⊶**none** /nʌn/ *quantifier* **1** not any **hiç, hiçbir; hiç kimse, hiç bir** *None* of them smoke. ○ *In 1992, the company had 2,700 part-time workers. Today is has none.* ○ *There were only three births here in March and none at all in April.* ○ *He asked if there was any hope. I told them frankly that there was none.* **2** none too **clean/clever/pleased, etc** not at all **clean/clever/pleased, etc hiç de ...clean/clever ... değil** *His handkerchief was none too clean.* **3** none the **happier/poorer/wiser, etc** not any happier/poorer/wiser, etc than before **öncekinden/olduğundan hiç de daha mutlu/fakir/akıllı vs. değil** *She must have explained the theory three times, but I'm still none the wiser.*

nonetheless /ˌnʌnðəˈles/ *adverb* despite what has just been said **yine de, bununla beraber, buna rağmen** *He was extremely rude in meetings. Nonetheless, his arguments found some support.*

non-event /ˌnɒnɪˈvent/ *noun* [no plural] *informal* an event that was not as exciting or interesting as you expected it to be **umulduğu kadar ilginç veya heyecan verici olmayan şey; hayal kırıklığı yaratan şey** *Her party was a bit of a non-event.*

non-existent /ˌnɒnɪgˈzɪstənt/ *adjective* not existing **yok, var olmayan, gayri mevcut** *We knew our chances of success were non-existent.*

nonfiction /ˌnɒnˈfɪkʃən/ *noun* [U] writing about things which are true **gerçekleri anlatan yazı; hayal ürünü/kurgusal olmayan yazı** *nonfiction books/titles*

no-no /ˈnəʊnəʊ/ *noun* [C] *informal* something that is forbidden or not socially acceptable **yasak; toplumca kabul görmeyen** *Cardigans are a fashion no-no this season.*

no-nonsense /ˌnəʊˈnɒnsəns/ *adjective* [always before noun] not having or allowing others to have any silly ideas or behaviour **mantıklı, kararlı, pratik ve etkin; başkalarının saçma sapan düşüncelere kapılmasını engelleyen** *a no-nonsense approach to child rearing*

nonplussed /ˌnʌnˈplʌst/ *adjective* extremely surprised **şaşkın, çok şaşırmış**

non-profit-making /ˌnʌnˈprɒfɪtˌmeɪkɪŋ/ *UK* (*US* **nonprofit**) *adjective* A non-profit-making organization does not make money from its activities. **kâr amacı taşımayan/gütmeyen**

🧩 ***nonsense*** .... İLE BİRLİKTE KULLANILAN KELİMELER

talk nonsense ● absolute/complete/utter nonsense ● a **load of** nonsense

nonsense /ˈnɒnsᵊns/ *noun* [U] **1** If something someone has said or written is nonsense, it is silly and not true. **anlamsız/boş söz; safsata, lakırdı, saçma, zırva** *She talks such nonsense sometimes.* ○ *That's **a load of nonsense.*** ○ *It's nonsense to suggest they could have cheated.* **2** silly behaviour **saçmalık, zırvalık, aptallık** *Will you stop this childish nonsense!* **3 make a nonsense of sth** *UK* to spoil something or make it seem stupid **berbat/rezil etmek, mahvetmek, bozmak** *Cuts to the text made a nonsense of the play.*

non-smoker /ˌnʌnˈsməʊkəʳ/ *noun* [C] a person who does not smoke **sigara içmeyen kimse**

non-smoking /ˌnʌnˈsməʊkɪŋ/ *adjective* A non-smoking area is one where people are not allowed to smoke. **sigara içilmeyen (yer, mekân, alan)**

non-starter /ˌnʌnˈstɑːtəʳ/ *noun* [C] *informal* something that will not be successful **(plan, fikir, tasarı, kişi) baştan kaybeden/başarı şansı olmayan, umutsuz, boş şey** *The amount of money needed makes his project a non-starter.*

non-stop /ˌnʌnˈstɒp/ *adjective, adverb* without stopping or resting **durmadan, aralıksız, durmaksızın, aralıksız, kesintisiz, sürekli, ara vermeden; biteviye** ***non-stop flights** from Britain to the West Indies* ○ *We've been **talking non-stop** the whole way.*

non-violent /ˌnʌnˈvaɪələnt/ *adjective* not using violent methods **şiddet içermeyen, şiddete vaşvurmayan, zor kullunmayan** *non-violent action/protests* ○ *non-violent crimes/offenders*

noodles /ˈnuːdlz/ *noun* [plural] thin pieces of pasta (= food made from flour, eggs, and water) **erişte, şehriye**

nook /nʊk/ *noun* **every nook and cranny** every part of a place **köşe bucak, en ücra köşe/yer** *I know every nook and cranny of this place.*

noon /nuːn/ *noun* [U] 12 o'clock in the middle of the day **öğle, öğle vakti** *He has until noon to act.* ○ *The service will be held at 12 noon.*

o⁻**no ˌone** *pronoun* no person **kimse, hiç kimse** *No one bothered to read the report.* ○ *No one knows where he is now.* ○ *There was no one there.* ○ *No one else makes puddings like my Mum.*

noose /nuːs/ *noun* [C] a piece of rope tied in a circle, used to catch animals or to hang (= kill) people **ilmek**

o⁻**nor** /nɔːʳ/ *adverb, conjunction* **1 neither...nor...** used after 'neither' to introduce the second thing in a negative sentence **ne...ne; ne...ne** *Strangely, neither James nor Emma saw what happened.* ○ *He neither spoke nor moved.* **2 nor can I/nor do you, etc** *mainly UK* used after something negative to say that the same thing is true for someone or something else **olumsuz cümlelerden sonra aynı düşünceye katıldığını göstemek için kullanılır; ben de...; sen de...; o da...** *"I don't like cats." "Nor do I." ○ "I won't get to see him tomorrow." "Nor will Tom." ○ She couldn't speak a word of Italian and nor could I.*

Nordic /ˈnɔːdɪk/ *adjective* from or relating to the North European countries of Sweden, Denmark, Norway, Finland, and Iceland **İsveç, Danimarka, Norveç, Finlandiya ve İzlanda gibi Kuzey Avrupa ülkelerine ilişkin/ülkelerden**

norm /nɔːm/ *noun* **1 the norm** the usual way that something happens **düstur, ölçü, kural, âdet, norm** *Short-term job contracts are the norm nowadays.* **2** [C] an accepted way of behaving in a particular society **belli toplumlarda kabul edilmiş davranışlar bütünü/manzumesi** [usually plural] *cultural/social norms*

🧩 ***normal*** .... İLE BİRLİKTE KULLANILAN KELİMELER

be back to/return to normal ● perfectly normal

o⁻**normal** /ˈnɔːmᵊl/ *adjective* usual, ordinary, and expected **beklenen, her zamanki gibi, normal** *to lead a normal life* ○ *It's perfectly normal to feel some degree of stress at work.* ○ *It's normal for couples to argue now and then.* ○ *Now that trains are running again things are back to normal.*

normality /nɔːˈmæləti/ (*also US* **normalcy** /ˈnɔːmᵊlsi/) *noun* [U] a situation in which everything is happening normally **tabiîlik, normallik** *a return to normality*

o⁻**normally** /ˈnɔːməli/ *adverb* **1** usually **genellikle, normalde, normal olarak** *Normally, I start work around nine o'clock.* **2** in the ordinary way that you would expect **beklenilen şekilde; normal/tabii bir şekilde, alışıldığı gibi** *Both lungs are now functioning normally.*

north

o⁻**north, North** /nɔːθ/ *noun* [U] **1** the direction that is on your left when you face towards the rising sun **kuzey yönü; Kuzey** *The stadium is to the north of the city.* **2 the north** the part of an area that is further towards the north than the rest **kuzeyde, kuzey bölgesi** *She's from the north of England.* ● **north** *adjective* *a north wind* **Kuzey** ● **north** *adverb* towards the north **kuzeye doğru, kuzey yönünde** *I live north of the river.* ○ *We're going to visit Paul's family up north.*

northbound /ˈnɔːθbaʊnd/ *adjective* going or leading towards the north **kuzeye giden**

northeast, Northeast /ˌnɔːθˈiːst/ *noun* [U] **1** the direction between north and east **güneydoğu yönünde; Güneydoğu 2 the northeast** the northeast part of a country **kuzeydoğusu** ● **northeast, Northeast** *adjective, adverb* **Kuzeydoğu**

northeastern, Northeastern /ˌnɔːθˈiːstən/ *adjective* in or from the northeast **kuzeydoğu'dan, kuzeydoğu'da; Kuzeydoğu**

northerly /ˈnɔːðᵊli/ *adjective* **1** towards or in the north **kuzeyde; kuzeye doğru** *Canada's most **northerly***

point 2 A northerly wind comes from the north. kuzeye ait, kuzeyden gelen/esen

o⁻**northern, Northern** /'nɔːðⁿn/ *adjective* in or from the north part of an area **kuzeyden, kuzeyde; kuzey'den** *Northern England* ○ *a northern accent*

northerner, Northerner /'nɔːðⁿnaʳ/ *noun* [C] someone from the north part of a country **kuzeyli kimse; kuzeyli**

northernmost /'nɔːðənməʊst/ *adjective* The northernmost part of an area is the part furthest to the north. **en kuzeyde; en kuzeyi**

north-facing /'nɔːθ͵feɪsɪŋ/ *adjective* [always before noun] positioned towards the north **kuzeye dönük/yönelik** *a north-facing slope*

the ͵North 'Pole *noun* the point on the Earth's surface which is furthest north **Kuzey Kutbu**

northward, northwards /'nɔːθwəd, 'nɔːθwədz/ *adverb* towards the north **kuzeye doğru, kuzey yönünde** ● **northward** *adjective a northward direction* **kuzeye doğru**

northwest, Northwest /͵nɔːθ'west/ *noun* [U] **1** the direction between north and west **kuzeybatı yönünde; kuzeybatı 2 the northwest** the northwest part of a country **kuzeybatısı** ● **northwest, Northwest** *adjective, adverb* **kuzeybatı**

northwestern, Northwestern /͵nɔːθ'westən/ *adjective* in or from the northwest **kuzeybatıdan, kuzeybatıda; kuzeybatılı**

o⁻**nose**[1] /nəʊz/ *noun* [C] **1** the part of your face through which you breathe and smell **burun** *a big/broken nose* ○ *She paused to* **blow her nose** (= breathe out hard to empty it into a piece of cloth). ⊃Orta kısımdaki renkli sayfalarına bakınız. **2 get up sb's nose** *UK informal* to annoy someone **kızdırmak, sinirlendirmeki gıcık etmek** ● **3 poke/stick your nose into sth** *informal* to show too much interest in a situation that does not involve you **başkasının işine burnunu sokmak, karışmak** *You shouldn't go sticking your nose into other people's business.* ● **4 thumb your nose at sth/sb** to show that you do not respect rules, laws, or powerful people **kurallara/yasalara/güçlü kimselere saygı duymadığın göstermek; önemsememek; umursamamak** ● **5 turn your nose up at sth** *informal* to not accept something because you do not think it is good enough for you **burun kıvırmak** *He turned his nose up at my offer of soup, saying he wanted a proper meal.* ● **6 under your nose** If something bad happens under your nose, it happens close to you but you do not notice it. **burnunun dibinde, gözünün önünde**

nose[2] /nəʊz/ *verb* **nose about/around (sth)** *phrasal verb informal* to look around a place, often in order to find something **aramak, araştırmak, kolaçan etmek** *I caught him nosing around in my office.*

nosebleed /'nəʊzbliːd/ *noun* [C] **have a nosebleed** to have blood coming from your nose **burnu kanamak**

nosedive /'nəʊzdaɪv/ *verb* [I] to fall very quickly in value **baş aşağı düşmek/dalmak, tepe taklak olmak** *The economy nosedived after the war.* ● **nosedive** *noun* [C] **değerde ani düşüş**

nosey /'nəʊzi/ *another spelling of* nosy **fazla meraklı, işgüzar, her şeye burnunu sokan**

nostalgia /nɒs'tældʒə/ *noun* [U] a feeling of happiness mixed with sadness when you think about things that happened in the past **geçmişe duyulan aşırı özlem, nostalji** *his nostalgia for his college days*

nostalgic /nɒs'tældʒɪk/ *adjective* feeling both happy and sad when you think about things that happened in the past **geçmiş özlemi, nostaljik** *Talking about those holidays has made me feel quite nostalgic.*

nostril /'nɒstrⁿl/ *noun* [C] one of the two holes at the end of your nose **burun deliği** ⊃Orta kısımdaki renkli sayfalarına bakınız.

nosy /'nəʊzi/ *adjective* always trying to find out private things about other people **fazla meraklı, işgüzar, her şeye burnunu sokan** *nosy neighbours* ○ *Don't be so nosy!*

o⁻**not** /nɒt/ *adverb* **1** used to form a negative phrase after verbs like 'be', 'can', 'have', 'will', 'must', etc, usually used in the short form 'n't' in speech **yardımcı fiilleri olumsuz yapmak için kullanılır; kısa yazılışı 'n't'; **...ma/me** *I won't tell her.* ○ *I can't go.* ○ *He hasn't eaten yet.* ○ *Don't you like her?* ○ *It isn't difficult* (= It is easy). ○ *The service isn't very good* (= it is bad). ○ *You're coming, aren't you?* ○ *I will not tolerate laziness.* **2** used to give the next word or group of words a negative meaning **yardımcı fiillerle olumsuzluk anlamı vermek için kullanılır; kısa yazılışı 'n't'; **...değil/yok** *I told you not to do that.* ○ *I like most vegetables but not cabbage.* ○ *"Come and play football, Dad." "Not now, Jamie."* ○ *"Whose are these?" "Not mine."* **3** used after verbs like 'be afraid', 'hope', 'suspect', etc in short, negative replies **'be afraid', 'hope', 'suspect' vb. fiillerden sonra kısaca olumsuz yanıt vermek için kullanılır** *"Do you think it's going to rain?" "I hope not."* ○ *"Have you finished?" "I'm afraid not."* **4 certainly/hopefully not** used after an adverb in short, negative replies **bir zarftan sonra olumsuz cevap için kullanılır: kesinlikle/ümit ederim ki öyle değil** *"She's not exactly poor, is she?" "Certainly not."* ○ *"We won't need much money, will we?" "Hopefully not."* **5 not at all** used instead of 'no' or 'not' to emphasize what you are saying **'hayır', 'asla', 'kat'iyen', 'hiç de öyle değil'** *"I hope this won't cause you any trouble." "No, not at all."* ○ *I'm not at all happy about it.* **6 Not at all.** used as a polite reply after someone has thanked you **'Bir şey değil!', 'Rica ederim!' 'Ne demek!', 'Estağfurullah!'** *"Thanks for all your help." "Not at all."* **7 if not** used to say what the situation will be if something does not happen **eğer öyle olmasaydı; öyle değilse** *I hope to see you there but, if not, I'll call you.* **8 or not** used to express the possibility that something might not happen **...yoksa mı/mi ...** *Are you coming or not?* **9 not a/one** used to emphasize that there is nothing of what you are talking about **tek bir kişi/kimse bile ...** *Not one person came to hear him talk.* ○ *"You haven't heard from Nick, have you?" "Not a word."*

notable /'nəʊtəbl/ *adjective* If someone or something is notable, they are important or interesting. **dikkate/kayda değer, önemli, ilginç**

notably /'nəʊtəbli/ *adverb* used to emphasize an important example of something **özellikle, bilhassa** *Florida is well known for many of its fruits, notably oranges and avocados.*

notation /nəʊ'teɪʃⁿn/ *noun* [U] a system of written symbols used especially in mathematics or to represent musical notes **işaret veya rakamlarla gösterme, nota sistemi**

notch[1] /nɒtʃ/ *noun* [C] **1** a level of quality or amount **derece, seviye, basamak** *Interest rates have moved up another notch.* **2** a cut in the shape of the letter V on the edge or surface of something **V-şeklinde kesik**

notch[2] /nɒtʃ/ *verb* **notch up sth** *phrasal verb* to achieve something **başarmak, kazanmak, elde etmek** *He has notched up a total of 34 goals this season.*

leave/scribble/send/write a note • a note for/from
sb • get sb's note

⚬**note**[1] /nəʊt/ noun **1** LETTER [C] a short letter **not, pusula**
He left a note on her desk. ○ *Did you get my note?*
2 INFORMATION [C] words that you write down to help you
remember something **not** *She studied her notes before
the exam.* ○ *Let me make a note of* (= write) *your phone
number.* ○ *The doctor took notes* (= wrote information)
while I described my symptoms. **3** EXPLANATION [C] a short
explanation or an extra piece of information that is
given at the bottom of a page or at the back of a book
not, dipnot *See note 3, page 37.* **4** FEELING [no plural] a particular feeling or mood **his, ruhsal durum, hava,
atmosfer** *a sad/serious/positive note* ○ *His speech
had just the right note of sympathy.* **5** MUSIC [C] a single
musical sound or the symbol that represents it **nota**
6 MONEY [C] UK (US bill) a piece of paper money **kâğıt
para, banknot** *a ten-pound note* **7 take note (of sth)**
to pay careful attention to something **önemsemek,
bütün dikkatini vermek** *Make sure you take note of
what she says.* **8 sb/sth of note** *formal* someone or
something famous or important **meşhur, önemli
kimse/şey** *A medieval church is the only monument of
note in the town.* **9 compare notes** If two people compare notes, they tell each other what they think about
something that they have both done. **bilgi ve görüş
alışverişinde bulunmak; fikir alışverişi yapmak**
We compared notes about our experiences in China.

note[2] /nəʊt/ verb [T] **1** to notice something **dikkat
etmek, fark etmek** *She noted a distinct chill in the air.*
○ [+ (that)] *We noted that their idea had never been tried.*
2 to say or write something **söylemek veya yazmak** *In
the article, she notes several cases of medical incompetence.*
note down sth *phrasal verb* to write something so that
you do not forget it **not almak; not tutmak, bir yere
kaydetmek** *I noted down the telephone number for the
police.*

notebook /'nəʊtbʊk/ noun [C] **1** a book with empty
pages that you can write in **defter, not defteri 2** a
small computer that can be carried around and used
anywhere **taşınabilir küçük bilgisayar**

noted /'nəʊtɪd/ adjective important or famous **önemli,
tanınmış, ünlü, saygın, seçkin** *a noted artist* ○ *He
was noted for his modern approach to architecture.*

'**notepad (com,puter)** noun [C] a very small computer
which you can carry easily **taşınabilir çok küçük bilgisayar; cep bilgisayarı**

notepaper /'nəʊt,peɪpər/ noun [U] paper that you write
letters on **mektup kâğıdı**

noteworthy /'nəʊt,wɜːði/ adjective If someone or something is noteworthy, they are important or interesting.
önemli, dikkate değer, göze çarpan, ilginç *a noteworthy example*

⚬**nothing** /'nʌθɪŋ/ pronoun **1** not anything **hiçbir şey**
I've had nothing to eat since breakfast. ○ *He claimed
that he did nothing wrong.* ○ *He had nothing in his
pockets.* ○ *There was nothing else* (= no other thing) *I
could do to help.* ○ *She did nothing but criticize* (= criticized a lot). **2** not something important or of value **hiçbir şey, hiçbir, solda sıfır** *He's a dangerous person -
human life means nothing to him.* ○ *A thousand pounds
is nothing to a woman of her wealth.* **3 for nothing** without a successful result **boşu boşuna, boş yere, nafile
yere** *I've come all this way for nothing.* **4 be nothing to
do with sb** If something is or has nothing to do with
you, you have no good reason to know about it or be
involved with it. **ilgisi olmamak, ...ile hiç bir alakâsı**

olmamak *I wish he wouldn't offer advice on my marriage - it's nothing to do with him.* **5 have nothing to
do with sb/sth** to have no connection or influence with
someone or something **alıp vereceği olmamak, işi
olmamak, ilişkisi olmamak** *He made his own decision
- I had nothing to do with it.* **6 to say nothing of sth**
used to emphasize other problems you have not talked
about **bir yana, şöyle dursun, üstelik** *Most wild otters
have disappeared from populated areas, to say nothing of
wilderness areas.* **7 nothing of the sort** used to emphasize that something is not true **hiç öyle şey değil,
hiç de ilgisi yok** *He said that he was a legitimate businessman - in fact, he was nothing of the sort.* **8 It was
nothing.** a polite reply to someone who has thanked
you for doing something **'Hiç önemli değil!', 'Bir şey
değil!', 'Rica ederim!'** **9 be nothing if not sth** used to
emphasize a quality **son derece, ziyadesiyle** *The senator was nothing if not honest* (= he was very honest).
• **10 stop at nothing** to be willing to do anything in
order to achieve something **ne olursa olsun başarmayı istemek; asla vazgeçmemek, hiçbir şey kendini durduramamak** *He will stop at nothing to get
what he wants.*

nothingness /'nʌθɪŋnəs/ noun [U] a state where nothing exists **yokluk, hiçbir şeyin olmama durumu,
çaresizlik,**

⚬**notice**[1] /'nəʊtɪs/ verb [I, T] to see something and be
aware of it **farketmek, farkına varmak, gözüne ilişmek** *If the sign's too small, no one will notice it.* ○ *I
noticed that he walked with a limp.*

display/put up a notice • a notice says sth • a notice
about sth • on a notice

notice[2] /'nəʊtɪs/ noun **1** SIGN [C] a sign giving information about something **duyuru, ilan** *The notice said that
the pool was closed for repairs.* ○ *Have you seen any notices about the new sports club?* **2** WARNING [U] a warning
that something will happen **uyarı, ihtar, ihtarname,
tebligat** *I had to give my landlord a month's notice before
moving.* **3 at short notice** UK (US on short notice) only a
short time before something happens **hemen, birdenbire, kısa sürede 4** ATTENTION [U] attention **ehemmiyet,
dikkat, ilgi, alaka** *I didn't take any notice of* (= give
attention to) *his advice.* ○ *It has come to our notice* (= we
became aware) *that you are being overcharged for your
insurance.* **5 hand/give in your notice** to tell your employer that you are going to stop working for them **işten
ayrılacağını bildirmek; sözleşmesinin yenilenme-
yeceğini duyurmak** *I handed in my notice yesterday.*

noticeable /'nəʊtɪsəbl/ adjective easy to see or be aware
of **kolay görülebilen, belirgin, göze çarpan, dikkate
değer** *There was a noticeable difference in his behaviour
after the injury.* • **noticeably** adverb **belirgin bir
şekilde**

noticeboard /'nəʊtɪsbɔːd/ UK (US bulletin board) noun
[C] a board on a wall where you put advertisements
and announcements **ilan tahtası, duyuru panosu** *I
saw the ad on the noticeboard.* ⊃Orta kısımdaki renkli sayfalarına bakınız.

notify /'nəʊtɪfaɪ/ verb [T] formal to officially tell someone
about something **resmi yoldan bildirmek, haber vermek, tebliğ etmek** *You should notify the police if you
are involved in a road accident.* ○ [+ (that)] *The court notified her that her trial date had been postponed.* • **notifi-
cation** /,nəʊtɪfɪ'keɪʃən/ noun [C, U] **bildirme**

notion /'nəʊʃən/ noun [C] an idea or belief **kavram, inanış, fikir, nosyon** *The notion of sharing is unknown to
most two-year-olds.*

notoriety /ˌnəʊtˈrʌɪəti/ *noun* [U] when someone is famous for something bad **kötü şöhret/ün, dillere düşmüşlük** *He gained notoriety for his racist speeches.*

notorious /nəʊˈtɔːriəs/ *adjective* famous for something bad **adı kötüye çıkmış, kötü ünlü/namlı** *a notorious criminal* ○ *She was notorious for her bad temper.*
● **notoriously** *adverb* *Mount Everest is a notoriously difficult mountain to climb.* **kötü üne sahip bir şekilde**

notwithstanding /ˌnɒtwɪθˈstændɪŋ/ *adverb, preposition formal* despite **...a/e karşı, rağmen, bununla birlikte, her ne kadar...ise de** *Injuries notwithstanding, he won the semi-final match.*

nought /nɔːt/ *noun* [C, U] *UK* the number 0 **sıfır 2** *old-fashioned* (*mainly US* **naught**) nothing **hiçbir şey, sıfır, boş**

o⌐**noun** /naʊn/ *noun* [C] a word that refers to a person, place, object, event, substance, idea, feeling, or quality. For example the words 'teacher', 'book', 'development', and 'beauty' are nouns. **isim** ⊃See also: **countable noun, proper noun, uncountable noun.**

nourish /ˈnʌrɪʃ/ *verb* [T] *formal* to provide living things with food in order to make them grow or stay healthy **beslemek, büyütmek, bakmak, yedirip içirmek** *Mammals provide milk to nourish their young.*

nourishing /ˈnʌrɪʃɪŋ/ *adjective* Nourishing food makes you healthy. **besleyici, sağlıklı, besin değeri yüksek**

nourishment /ˈnʌrɪʃmənt/ *noun* [U] *formal* the food that you need to stay alive and healthy **besleme, besin, yiyecek, gıda**

Nov *written abbreviation for* November **Kasım, kasım ayı**

novel   İLE BİRLİKTE KULLANILAN KELİMELER

read/write a novel ● a novel by sb ● a novel about sth ● in a novel

novel¹ /ˈnɒvəl/ *noun* [C] a book that tells a story about imaginary people and events **roman** *Have you read any good novels lately?* ● **novelist** *noun* [C] someone who writes novels **romancı**

novel² /ˈnɒvəl/ *adjective* new or different from anything else **yeni, değişik, alışılmışın dışında**

novelty /ˈnɒvəlti/ *noun* 1 QUALITY [U] the quality of being new or unusual **yenilik** *The fashion industry relies on novelty, and photographers are always looking for new faces.* 2 NEW THING [C] an object, event, or experience that is new or unusual **alışılmamış şey, yeni şey** *Tourists are still a novelty on this remote island.* 3 CHEAP TOY [C] a cheap toy or unusual object, often given as a present (**hediye olarak verilen**) **yeni çıkmış şey/oyuncak vs.; alışılmamış şey**

o⌐**November** /nəʊˈvembər/ (*written abbreviation* **Nov**) *noun* [C, U] the eleventh month of the year **Kasım, yılın onbirinci ayı**

novice /ˈnɒvɪs/ *noun* [C] someone who is beginning to learn how to do something **acemi, yeni; çömez, deneyimsiz** *I've never used a computer before - I'm a complete novice.*

o⌐**now¹** /naʊ/ *adverb* 1 AT PRESENT at the present time **şimdi, şimdilerde, şu günlerde** *She's finished her degree and now she teaches English.* ○ *Do you know where Eva is right now?* (= at this moment)? 2 IMMEDIATELY immediately **şimdi, hemen, şu an** *Come on, Andreas, we're going home now.* ○ *I don't want to wait - I want it now!* 3 LENGTH OF TIME used to show the length of time that something has been happening, from the time it began until the present **...o zamandan şu ana kadar/değin/şimdiye dek** *I've lived in Cambridge for two years now.* 4 IN SPEECH used when you start to tell some-

one something 'Haydi bakalım...', 'Hadi görelim...', 'Hadi hadi...', 'Öyleyse...', 'Buna göre...' *Now, I have been to Glasgow many times before.* ○ *Now then, would anyone else like to ask a question?* 5 **just now** a very short time ago **hemen şimdi, az evvel, tam şimdi** *When I came in just now, everyone was laughing.* ○ *Who was that woman who was speaking just now?* 6 **(every) now and then/again** If something happens now and then, it happens sometimes but not very often. **arada bir, ara sıra, bazen, zaman zaman** *I love chocolate, but I only eat it now and then.* 7 **any day/minute/time, etc now** used to say that something will happen very soon **her an** *We're expecting our second child any day now.*

o⌐**now²** /naʊ/ (*also* **now that**) *conjunction* as a result of a new situation **madem ki; şu durumda; mevcut durum itibariyle; görüldüğü gibi** *Now that I've got a car I can visit her more often.* ○ *You should help in the house more, now you're older.*

o⌐**now³** /naʊ/ *pronoun* the present time or moment **şu an, şu zaman dilimi, içinde bulunduğumuz zaman; şu ana değin, şimdiye kadar** *Now isn't a good time to speak to him.* ○ *She'd kept calm until now.* ○ *I'll be more careful from now on* (= from this moment and always in the future).

nowadays /ˈnaʊədeɪz/ *adverb* at the present time, especially when compared to the past **bu/şu günlerde, şu sıralar, zamanımızda, günümüzde** *Everything seems more expensive nowadays.*

o⌐**nowhere** /ˈnəʊweər/ *adverb* 1 not anywhere **hiçbir yer/yerde** *The room was very crowded - there was nowhere to sit.* ○ *We had nowhere else to go.* 2 **out of nowhere** If someone or something appears out of nowhere, it appears suddenly or unexpectedly. **ansızın, kaşla göz arasında, birdenbire, nasıl olduğu anlaşılmadan** *The car came out of nowhere and we had to swerve to miss it.* 3 **get/go nowhere** *informal* to fail to make any progress or achieve anything **hiç bir yere varamamak, bir arpa boyu mesafe alamamak, bir ilerleme kaydetmemek; başaramamak, sonuca ulaşmamak** *They're getting nowhere on this project.* ● 4 **get you nowhere** If something gets you nowhere, it does not help you to succeed. **başarıya götürmemek; hiç bir kazanç/yarar sağlamamak, hiç bir faydası olmamak, yararı dokunmamak** *Bad manners will get you nowhere.*

noxious /ˈnɒkʃəs/ *adjective* [always before noun] *formal* poisonous or harmful **zehirli, zararlı, tehlikeli** *noxious fumes/gases*

nozzle /ˈnɒzl/ *noun* [C] a narrow, hollow object which is fixed to a tube and which helps you to control the liquid or air that comes out **hortum başlığı/ağızlığı/ucu**

o⌐**n't** /ənt/ *short for* not **olumsuzluk eki 'not' sözcüğünün kısa yazılışı** *She isn't* (= is not) *going.* ○ *I can't* (= cannot) *hear you.* ○ *They didn't* (= did not) *believe me.*

nuance /ˈnjuːɑːns/ *noun* [C] a very slight difference in meaning, appearance, sound, etc **ince ayrıntı, küçük fark, detay, nüans** *a subtle nuance* ○ *Linguists explore the nuances of language.*

o⌐**nuclear** /ˈnjuːkliər/ *adjective* [always before noun] 1 relating to the energy that is released when the nucleus (= central part) of an atom is divided **nükleer** *nuclear weapons/waste* ○ *a nuclear power plant* 2 relating to the nucleus (= central part) of an atom **atom çekirdeğinin merkezine ilişkin** *nuclear physics*

nuclear reˈactor *noun* [C] a large machine which uses nuclear fuel to produce power **nükleer reaktör**

nucleus /ˈnjuːkliəs/ *noun* [C] *plural* **nuclei** /ˈnjuːkliaɪ/ 1 the central part of an atom or cell **atom çekirdeğinin merkezi, nükleon 2** the central or most important part of a group or idea **bir şeyin/bir fikrin çekirdeği/ özü/esası** *Senior coaches handpicked the nucleus of the team.*

nude¹ /njuːd/ *adjective* not wearing any clothes **çıplak** *Our children were running around the garden **in the nude** (= not wearing any clothes).*

nude² /njuːd/ *noun* [C] a painting or other piece of art that shows a nude person **çıplak vücut resmi, nü**

nudge /nʌdʒ/ *verb* [T] to gently push someone or something **hafifçe dürtmek/itmek/dürtüklemek** *She nudged me towards the door.* • **nudge** *noun* [C] *I gave him a nudge.* **iteleme**

nudism /ˈnjuːdɪzəm/ *noun* [U] when someone wears no clothes when they are outside with other people, etc **çıplaklık** • **nudist** *noun* [C] someone who practices nudism **çıplaklığı/çıplak olmayı yeğleyen/kabuleden, nudist**

nudity /ˈnjuːdəti/ *noun* [U] when you are wearing no clothes **çıplaklık** *Some people are offended by nudity.*

nugget /ˈnʌɡɪt/ *noun* [C] **1** a small amount of something good **iyi bir şeyin küçük parçası** *nuggets of wisdom* **2** a small, round piece of a solid substance **külçe, parçacık, parça** *gold nuggets*

nuisance /ˈnjuːsəns/ *noun* [C] **1** a person, thing, or situation that annoys you or causes problems for you **baş belası şey, çekilmez kimse/dert, musibet** *Not being able to use my computer is a real nuisance.* **2 make a nuisance of yourself** to annoy someone or cause problems for them **baş belâsı olmak, başına belâ kesilmek**

nullify /ˈnʌlɪfaɪ/ *verb* [T] *formal* **1** to make something lose its effect **etkisini yok etmek, bertaraf etmek; etkisiz hâle getirmek** *Advances in medicine have nullified the disease's effect.* **2** to say officially that something has no legal power **resmî olarak ortadan kaldırmak; artık yasal bir etkisi olmadığını bildirmek** *The judge could nullify the entire trial.*

numb /nʌm/ *adjective* **1** If a part of your body is numb, you cannot feel it. **uyuşmuş, hissizleşmiş** *My fingers and toes were numb with cold.* **2** If you are numb with a bad emotion, you are so shocked that you are not able to think clearly. **sersemlemiş, sereme dönmüş; kendinden geçmiş, (acı ve kederden dolayı) hiç bir şey hissedemez hâle gelmiş** *I was numb with grief after his death.*

๐ⁿ**number¹** /ˈnʌmbər/ *noun* **1** [SYMBOL] [C] a symbol or word used in a counting system or used to show the position or order of something **numara, sayı, rakam** *Think of a number smaller than 100.* ○ *The Prime Minister lives at number 10, Downing Street.* ○ *Look at item number three on your agenda.* **2** [GROUP OF NUMBERS] [C] a group of numbers that represents something **(telefon vs.) numara** *What's your phone number?* ○ *Each person receives a membership number when they join.* **3** [AMOUNT] [C] an amount **miktar, sayı, adet** *a small number of* (= a few) ○ *a large number of* (= many) ○ *There are a number of* (= several) *soldiers present at the rally.* ○ *Scientists have noticed a drop in the number of song birds in Britain.* ⊃See also: **cardinal number, ordinal number, phone number, telephone number.**

number² /ˈnʌmbər/ *verb* [T] **1** to give something a number **numaralandırmak, numara vermek, sayı belirtmek** [often passive] *Each volume was numbered and indexed.* **2** If people or things number a particular amount, there are that many of them. **...a/e varmak; toplamı ...ı/i bulmak** *Our company's sales force numbered over 5,000.*

'**number ˌplate** *UK* (*US* **license plate**) *noun* [C] an official metal sign with numbers and letters on the front and

back of a car **(araç) plaka** ⊃Orta kısımdaki renkli sayfalarına bakınız.

numeral /ˈnjuːmərəl/ *noun* [C] a symbol used to represent a number **rakam** ⊃See also: **Roman numeral.**

numerical /njuːˈmerɪkl/ *adjective* [always before noun] relating to or expressed by numbers **sayısal** *The exams were filed in numerical order.*

numerous /ˈnjuːmərəs/ *adjective formal* many **pek çok, çok fazla, sayısız** *He is the author of numerous articles.*

nun /nʌn/ *noun* [C] a member of a group of religious women living apart from other people **rahibe**

๐ⁿ**nurse¹** /nɜːs/ *noun* [C] someone whose job is to care for ill and injured people **hemşire**

nurse² /nɜːs/ *verb* [T] **1** [CARE FOR] to care for a person or animal that is ill **bakmak, hemşirelik etmek** *We nursed the injured sparrow back to health.* **2** [FEED] US to feed a baby milk from its mother's breast **emzirmek, süt vermek** *She nursed her son until he was a year old.* **3** [INJURY] to try to cure an illness or injury by resting **tedavi etmek, bakmak, ilgilenmek** *He was nursing a broken nose.* **4** [EMOTION] to think about an idea or an emotion for a long time **(fikir, duygu vb.) beslemek, gönlünde yaşatmak** *She nursed a great hatred towards her older sister.*

nursery /ˈnɜːsəri/ *noun* [C] **1** a place where babies and young children are looked after without their parents **çocuk yuvası, kreş 2** a place where plants are grown and sold **fidanlık**

'**nursery ˌrhyme** *noun* [C] a short poem or song for young children **çocuk şarkısı/şiiri, tekerleme**

'**nursery ˌschool** *noun* [C] a school for very young children **ana okulu, çocuk yuvası**

nursing /ˈnɜːsɪŋ/ *noun* [U] the job of being a nurse **hemşirelik, hasta bakıcılık**

'**nursing ˌhome** *noun* [C] a place where old people live to receive medical care **huzurevi, bakımevi**

nurture /ˈnɜːtʃər/ *verb* [T] *formal* **1** to encourage or support the development of someone or something **destek olmak, gelişmesine yardımcı olmak, teşvik etmek** *He was an inspiring leader who nurtured the talents of his colleagues.* **2** to look after, feed, and protect young children, animals, or plants **bakmak, büyütmek, ilgilenmek, beslemek, yetiştirmek** *The rains nurtured the newly planted crops.*

๐ⁿ**nut** /nʌt/ *noun* [C] **1** [FOOD] the dry fruit of some trees which grows in a hard shell, and can often be eaten **(ceviz fındık vb.) sert kabuklu meyve; kuruyemiş** *a brazil/cashew nut* **2** [METAL] a piece of metal with a hole in it through which you put a bolt (= metal pin) to hold pieces of wood or metal together **somun, civata somunu** ⊃See picture at **tool. 3** [KEEN] *informal* a person who is keen on a particular subject or hobby **tek bir konuya/şeye düşkün kimse** *She's a real sports nut.* **4 the nuts and bolts** the basic parts of a job or an activity **bir işin/mesleğin en ince ayrıntıları; mesleğin cilveleri** *Law school can teach you theory, but it can't teach you the nuts and bolts of the profession.*

nutrient /ˈnjuːtriənt/ *noun* [C] *formal* any substance that animals need to eat and plants need from the soil in order to live and grow **besleyici şey/besin/gıda** *A healthy diet should provide all your essential nutrients.*

nutrition /njuːˈtrɪʃən/ *noun* [U] the food that you eat and the way that it affects your health **beslenme, besin** *Good nutrition is essential for growing children.* • **nutritional** *adjective* relating to nutrition **besin/beslenmeye dair/ilişkin** *Some snacks have little nutritional value.*

nutritionist /njuːˈtrɪʃᵊnɪst/ *noun* [C] someone who gives advice on the subject of nutrition **beslenme uzmanı; diyetisyen**

nutritious /njuːˈtrɪʃəs/ *adjective* Nutritious food contains substances that your body needs to stay healthy. **besleyici** *a nutritious meal*

nuts /nʌts/ *adjective informal* **1** crazy **kaçık, deli, fıttırık, kafadan kontak, çılgın** *They thought I was nuts to go parachuting.* **2 go nuts** to become very excited, angry, or upset **deliye dönmek; tepesi atmak; fıttırmak** *If I don't have a holiday soon, I'll go nuts.*

nutshell /ˈnʌtʃel/ *noun* **in a nutshell** something that you say when you are describing something using as few words as possible **özet olarak, kısaca, esasen, hulâsa** *The answer, in a nutshell, is yes.*

nutty /ˈnʌti/ *adjective* **1** *informal* crazy **deli, budala, aptal, çılgın** *nutty ideas* **2** Something nutty tastes of nuts. **fındık veya ceviz tadında**

nylon /ˈnaɪlɒn/ *noun* [U] a strong, artificial material used to make clothes, ropes, etc **naylon** *nylon stockings* ○ *a nylon shirt/bag*

nymph /nɪmf/ *noun* [C] in Greek and Roman stories, a spirit in the form of a young girl who lives in trees, rivers, mountains, etc **Yunan ve Roma hikayelerinde ağaçlarda, nehirlerde, dağlarda vb. yerlerde genç kız görünümünde yaşayan ruh**

N

O

O, o /əʊ/ the fifteenth letter of the alphabet **alfabenin on beşinci harfi**

oak /əʊk/ *noun* [C, U] a large tree found in northern countries, or the wood of this tree **meşe, meşe ağacı**

OAP /ˌəʊeɪˈpiː/ *noun* [C] *UK abbreviation for* old-age pensioner: a person who regularly receives money from the state because they are too old to work **yaşlılık aylığı alan kişi**

oar /ɔːʳ/ *noun* [C] **1** a long pole with a wide, flat end that you use to move a boat through water **kayık küreği 2 stick/put your oar in** *UK informal* to involve yourself in a discussion or situation when other people do not want you to **bir tartışmaya/duruma burnunu sokmak/karışmak; istenmediği halde bulaşmak/karışmak**

oasis /əʊˈeɪsɪs/ *noun* [C] *plural* **oases** /əʊˈeɪsiːz/ **1** a place in the desert where there is water and where plants grow **vaha 2** a place that is much calmer and more pleasant than what is around it **cennet gibi bir yer; çok hoş bir mahal** *The cafe was an oasis in the busy, noisy city.*

oath /əʊθ/ *noun* **1** [C] a formal promise **söz, yemin, ant** *an oath of allegiance* ○ *They refused to **take an oath** of* (= promise) *loyalty to the king.* **2 under oath** If someone is under oath, they have promised to tell the truth in a law court. **yemin etmiş, ant içmiş** *He denied under oath that he was involved in the crime.*

oats /əʊts/ *noun* [plural] grain which people eat or feed to animals **yulaf**

obedience /əʊˈbiːdiəns/ *noun* [U] when someone is willing to do what they are told to do **itaat, boyun eğme** *He demanded complete obedience from his soldiers.* ⊃Opposite **disobedience.** ● **obedient** /əʊˈbiːdiənt/ *adjective* willing to do what you are told to do **itaatkâr, rıza gösteren** *an obedient child/dog* ⊃Opposite **disobedient.**

obese /əʊˈbiːs/ *adjective* extremely fat **çok şişman, obez** ● **obesity** *noun* [U] when someone is obese **çok şişmanlık, obezlik**

o~**obey** /əʊˈbeɪ/ *verb* [I, T] to do what you are told to do by a person, rule, or instruction **itaat etmek, söz dinlemek, uymak** *He gave the command, and we obeyed.* ⊃Opposite **disobey.**

obfuscate /ˈɒbfʌskeɪt/ *verb* [T] *formal* to make something harder to understand or less clear **karıştırmak, şaşırtmak, anlaşılmaz hâle getirmek**

obituary /əʊˈbɪtʃʊəri/ *noun* [C] a report in a newspaper that gives details about a person who has recently died **vefat/ölüm ilanı**

o~**object¹** /ˈɒbdʒɪkt/ *noun* **1** [C] a thing that you can see or touch but that is usually not alive **nesne, cisim, eşya, şey** *a bright, shiny object* **2 the object of sth** the purpose of something **bir şeyin amacı/maksadı/gayesi** *The object of the game is to score more points than the opposing team.* **3 the object of sb's affection/desire, etc** the cause of someone's feelings **birinin hislerinin sebebi/hedefi** *He's the object of my affection.* **4** in grammar, the person or thing that is affected by the action of the verb **nesne, tümleç** ⊃See also: **direct object, indirect object.**

object² /əbˈdʒekt/ *verb* [I] to feel or say that you do not like or do not approve of something or someone **itiraz etmek, karşı çıkmak** *We objected to his unreasonable*

demands. ○ *Would anyone object if I were to leave early?* ⊃See also: **conscientious objector.**

lodge/make/raise/voice an objection ● have no objections ● a serious/strong objection ● an objection **to** sth

objection /əbˈdʒekʃʰn/ *noun* [C, U] when someone says that they do not like or approve of something or someone **itiraz, karşı çıkma** *Our main objection to the new factory is that it's noisy.* ○ *I have no objections, if you want to stay an extra day.*

objectionable /əbˈdʒekʃʰnəbl/ *adjective formal* very unpleasant **tatsız, hoş olmayan, sakıncalı, mahzurlu**

objective¹ /əbˈdʒektɪv/ *noun* [C] something that you are trying to achieve **hedef, amaç, gaye, maksat** *His main objective was to increase profits.*

objective² /əbˈdʒektɪv/ *adjective* only influenced by facts and not by feelings **tarafsız, nesnel, objektif** *I try to be objective when I criticize someone's work.*

feel/have an obligation to do sth ● carry out/fulfil/meet an obligation ● be **under** an obligation

obligation /ˌɒblɪˈgeɪʃʰn/ *noun* [C, U] something that you do because it is your duty or because you feel you have to **yükümlülük, mecburiyet, görev, boyun borcu, zorunluluk** *a moral/legal obligation* ○ *to fulfil an obligation* ○ *He was under no obligation to answer any questions.* ○ [+ to do sth] *Parents have an obligation to make sure their children receive a proper education.*

obligatory /əˈblɪgətʰri/ *adjective* If something is obligatory, you must do it because of a rule, or because everyone else does it. **zorunlu, mecburi** *obligatory military service*

oblige /əˈblaɪdʒ/ *verb* **1 be obliged to do sth** to be forced to do something **bir şeyi yapmak zorunda olmak; mecbur olmak, mecbur etmek** *Sellers are not legally obliged to accept the highest offer.* **2** [I, T] *formal* to be helpful **yardımsever olmak, isteğini yerine getirmek** *The manager was only too happy to oblige.*

obliged /əˈblaɪdʒd/ *adjective* **1 feel obliged to do sth** to think that you must do something **kendini mecbur hissetmek** *They helped us when we moved so I feel obliged to do the same.* **2** *formal old-fashioned* grateful or pleased **minnettar, müteşekkir** *Thank you, I'm much obliged to you.*

oblique /əˈbliːk/ *adjective formal* not expressed in a direct way **dolaylı, üstü kapalı, ima yollu** *an oblique comment* ● **obliquely** *adverb formal* **direkt olmayan bir şekilde, dolambaçlı olarak**

obliterate /əˈblɪtʰreɪt/ *verb* [T] to destroy something completely **yerle bir etmek, tarumar etmek, tamamen yok etmek** [often passive] *The town was obliterated by bombs.*

oblivion /əˈblɪviən/ *noun* [U] **1** when someone or something is not remembered **unutulma, unutulup gitme, tarihe karışma** *to disappear into oblivion* **2** when you are not aware of what is happening around you **far-**

kında olmama, dünyadan haberi olmama *He drank himself into oblivion.*

oblivious /ə'blɪviəs/ *adjective* not aware of something **dünyadan habersiz, ilgisiz, kayıtsız** *She seemed completely oblivious to what was happening around her.*

obnoxious /əb'nɒkʃəs/ *adjective* very unpleasant or rude **sevimsiz, çirkin, kaba, nahoş, iğrenç** *He was loud and obnoxious.*

obscene /əb'siːn/ *adjective* **1** relating to sex in a way that is unpleasant or shocking **müstehcen, açık saçık, edebe/ahlaka aykırı** *an obscene gesture* ○ *obscene language* **2** An obscene amount of something is morally wrong because it is too large. **fahiş, aşırı, ahlaken gereğinden fazla/büyük; ahlak dışı** *obscene profits*

obscenity /əb'senəti/ *noun* **1** [U] when something is sexually shocking **müstehcenlik, edebe/ahlaka aykırılık** *obscenity laws/trials* **2** [C] a sexually shocking word or expression **edebsiz dil, açık saçık kelime/söz; müstehcen kelime/hareket** [usually plural] *He was shouting obscenities at people walking by.*

obscure¹ /əb'skjʊər/ *adjective* **1** not known by many people **tanınmamış, pek bilinmeyen** *an obscure figure/writer* **2** difficult to understand **anlaşılması güç, karmaşık, kafa karıştıran** *His answers were obscure and confusing.*

obscure² /əb'skjʊər/ *verb* [T] **1** to prevent something from being seen or heard **gizlemek, gözden ırak tutmak, örtmek; duyulmasını/görülmesini önlemek** [often passive] *The moon was partially obscured by clouds.* **2** to make something difficult to understand **anlaşılmaz hâle getirmek; anlaşılmasını güçleştirmek;** *He deliberately obscured details of his career in the army.*

obscurity /əb'skjʊərəti/ *noun* [U] when something or someone is not known by many people **kenarda kalmışlık; unutulmuşluk; fazla tanınmazlık** *to fade into obscurity* ○ *He rose from relative obscurity to worldwide recognition.*

obsequious /əb'siːkwiəs/ *adjective formal* too willing to praise or obey someone **dalkavukluk yapan; aşırı derecede öven; gereğinden fazla itaatkâr**

observance /əb'zɜːvəns/ *noun* [C, U] *formal* when someone obeys a law or follows a religious custom **itaat, uyma, riayet** *strict observance of the law* ○ *religious observances*

observant /əb'zɜːvənt/ *adjective* good or quick at noticing things **dikkatli, gözlemleyen** *He's very observant.*

☞ *observation* ..... İLE BİRLİKTE KULLANILAN KELİMELER
careful/close observation ● observation **of** sth ● **under** observation ● **powers of** observation

observation /ˌɒbzə'veɪʃən/ *noun* **1** [U] when someone watches someone or something carefully **inceleme, gözlem, müşahede** *The doctor wants to keep him under observation for a week.* ○ *to have good powers of observation* (= to be good at noticing things) **2** [C] a remark about something that you have noticed **gözlem, bulgu** *He made an interesting observation.*

observatory /əb'zɜːvətri/ *noun* [C] a building that is used by scientists to look at stars and planets **gözlemevi, rasathane**

observe /əb'zɜːv/ *verb* [T] 1 [WATCH] to watch someone or something carefully **dikkatle gözlemek/incelemek/tetkik etmek** *Children learn by observing adults.* **2** [NOTICE] *formal* to notice something **dikkat etmek; farketmek; farkına varmak 3** [SAY] *formal* to make a remark about something you have noticed **işaret etmek, demek, söylemek, yorumda bulunmak** *"It's*

still raining," he observed. **4** [OBEY] to obey a law, rule, or religious custom **(kanuni kural, dini gelenek vs.) uymak, itina göstermek, saygılı olmak, riayet etmek** *to observe the law*

observer /əb'zɜːvər/ *noun* [C] **1** someone who watches people and events as a job **gözlemci** *a UN observer* ○ *a political observer* **2** someone who sees something **gören/fark eden/farkına varan kimse** *a casual observer*

obsess /əb'ses/ *verb* [I, T] If something or someone obsesses you, or if you obsess about something or someone, you think about them all the time. **takıntılı olmak; hiç aklından çıkmamak; kafaya takmak; gözünün önünden gitmemek; saplantı haline getirmek** *She used to obsess about her weight.*

obsessed /əb'sest/ *adjective* be obsessed by/with sb/ sth to think about someone or something all the time **birine/bir şeye kafayı takmak; ...ile takıntılı olmak; ...dan/den başka bir şey düşünememek** *to be obsessed with money/sex*

obsession /əb'seʃən/ *noun* [C, U] someone or something that you think about all the time **saplantı, takıntı, tutku, sabit fikir** *an unhealthy obsession with death* ○ *a lifelong/national obsession*

obsessive /əb'sesɪv/ *adjective* thinking too much about something, or doing something too much **takıntılı, saplantılı, tutkun, sabit fikirli** *obsessive behaviour* ○ *He's obsessive about his health.* ● **obsessively** *adverb* **takıntılı bir şekilde**

obsolete /'ɒbsəliːt/ *adjective* not used now **artık mevcut olmayan, tarihe karışmış** *obsolete equipment* ○ *Will books become obsolete because of computers?*

☞ *obstacle* ...... İLE BİRLİKTE KULLANILAN KELİMELER
face/overcome an obstacle ● **the biggest/the main/a major** obstacle ● an obstacle **to** sth

obstacle /'ɒbstəkl/ *noun* [C] something that makes it difficult for you to go somewhere or to succeed at something **engel, mâni** *to overcome an obstacle* ○ *His refusal to talk is the main obstacle to peace.*

obstetrician /ˌɒbstə'trɪʃən/ *noun* [C] a doctor who looks after pregnant women and helps in the birth of children **kadın doğum uzmanı/doktoru; jinekolog**

obstinate /'ɒbstɪnət/ *adjective* not willing to change your ideas or behaviour although you are wrong **inatçı, dediğim dedikçi, dik kafalı, söz dinlemez, bildiğini okuyan** *He's a very rude and obstinate man.*

obstruct /əb'strʌkt/ *verb* [T] **1** to be in a place that stops someone from moving or stops someone from seeing something **engel/mani olmak; tıkamak, kapamak** *to obstruct the traffic* ○ *There was a pillar obstructing our view.* **2** to try to stop something from happening or developing **engellemek, mâni olmak, sekte vurmak** *to obstruct a police investigation* ● **obstruction** /əb'strʌkʃən/ *noun* [C, U] *Your car's causing an obstruction.* ○ *the obstruction of justice* **mâni olma**

obtain /əb'teɪn/ *verb* [T] *formal* to get something **elde etmek, edinmek, kazanmak** *to obtain permission* ○ *He obtained a law degree from the University of California.* ● **obtainable** *adjective* If something is obtainable, you can get it. **elde edilebilir, kazanılabilir** *This information is easily obtainable on the Internet.*

☞ **obvious** /'ɒbviəs/ *adjective* easy to understand or see **açık, aşikâr, belli, apaçık, gün gibi ortada** *an obvious choice/answer* ○ [+ (that)] *It's obvious that he doesn't really care about her.*

obviously /ˈɒbviəsli/ *adverb* in a way that is easy to understand or see **açıkça, besbelli, belli ki** *They're obviously in love.* ○ *Obviously we want to start as soon as possible.*

occasion /əˈkeɪʒⁿn/ *noun* **1** [C] a time when something happens **uygun durum, vesile, münasip zaman, fırsat** *a previous/separate occasion* ○ *We met on several occasions to discuss the issue.* **2** [C] an important event or ceremony **özel gün/kutlama/tören; önemli gün** *a special occasion* ○ *She bought a new dress for the occasion.* **3 on occasion(s)** sometimes, but not often **ara sıra, bazen, fırsat düştükçe** *I only drink alcohol on occasion.*

occasional /əˈkeɪʒⁿnˀl/ *adjective* not happening often **ara sıra olan, fırsat düştükçe yapılan, seyrek** *He still plays the occasional game of football.* ● **occasionally** *adverb* *They only meet occasionally.* **ara sıra**

the occult /ˈɒkʌlt/ *noun* the study of magic or mysterious powers **doğa üstü güçler bilimi; gizli güçler bilimi; sihir bilimi**

occupant /ˈɒkjəpənt/ *noun* [C] *formal* someone who lives or works in a room or building **yaşayan/oturan/çalışan kimse** *the occupant of No. 46*

occupation /ˌɒkjəˈpeɪʃⁿn/ *noun* **1** [JOB] [C] *formal* your job **iş güç, meslek, sanat, uğraşı** *You have to give your name, age, and occupation on the application form.* **2** [CONTROL] [U] when an army moves into a place and takes control of it **zaptetme, işgal, ele geçirme** *a military occupation* **3** [HOBBY] [C] *formal* something that you do in your free time **uğraşı, hobi, meşgale, uğraş**

occupational /ˌɒkjəˈpeɪʃⁿnˀl/ *adjective* relating to your job **mesleki, iş veya meslekle ilgili** *an occupational hazard*

occupied /ˈɒkjəpaɪd/ *adjective* **1** being used by someone **dolu/meşgul/işgal edilmiş/tutulmuş olmak** *All of these seats are occupied.* ↪Opposite **unoccupied**. **2** busy doing something or thinking about something **meşgul** *There was enough to keep us occupied.*

occupier /ˈɒkjəpaɪəʳ/ *noun* [C] *UK* someone who lives or works in a room or building **bir yerde yaşayan/oturan/çalışan kimse**

occupy /ˈɒkjəpaɪ/ *verb* [T] **1** [FILL] to fill a place or period of time **işgal etmek, doldurmak, yer kaplamak** *His book collection occupies most of the room.* ○ *The baby seems to occupy all our time.* **2** [LIVE] to live or work in a room or building **yaşamak, ikâmet etmek, oturmak** *They occupy the second floor of the building.* **3** [CONTROL] to move into a place and take control of it **işgal etmek, ele geçirmek, zapt etmek** *The troops eventually occupied most of the island.*

occur /əˈkɜːʳ/ *verb* [I] **occurring**, *past* **occurred 1** *formal* to happen, often without being planned **meydana gelmek, olmak, vuku bulmak** *According to the police, the shooting occurred at about 12.30 a.m.* **2 occur in/among, etc sth/sb** to exist or be present in a particular place or group of people **belli bir yerde/bir grup içinde yer almak/bulunmak/olmak/var olmak** *Minerals occur naturally in the Earth's crust.* ○ *The disease mainly occurs in women over 40.*
occur to sb *phrasal verb* If something occurs to you, you suddenly think of it **birden düşünmek; aklına düşmek; akla gelmek; hatıra gelmek** [+ (that)] *It had never occurred to me that he might be lying.*

occurrence ...... İLE BİRLİKTE KULLANILAN KELİMELER
a **common/everyday/rare/regular** occurrence

occurrence /əˈkʌrⁿns/ *noun* [C] something that happens **olay, vaka, hadise** *a common/everyday occurrence*

ocean /ˈəʊʃⁿn/ *noun* **1** [no plural] the sea **okyanus, deniz** *to swim in the ocean* **2** [C] one of the five main areas that the sea is divided into **okyanus** *the Pacific Ocean*

o'clock /əˈklɒk/ *adverb* **one/two/three, etc o'clock** used after the numbers one to twelve to mean exactly that hour when you tell the time **saat bir/iki/üç vs.** *It was ten o'clock when we got home.*

Oct *written abbreviation for* October **ekim, ekim ayı**

octagon /ˈɒktəgən/ *noun* [C] a flat shape with eight equal sides **sekizgen**

octave /ˈɒktɪv/ *noun* [C] the space between two musical notes that are eight notes apart **oktav**

October /ɒkˈtəʊbəʳ/ (*written abbreviation* Oct) *noun* [C, U] the tenth month of the year **ekim, ekim ayı**

octopus /ˈɒktəpəs/ *noun* [C] a sea creature with eight long arms **ahtapot**

octopus

odd /ɒd/ *adjective* **1** [STRANGE] strange or unusual **alışılmamış, garip, tuhaf, acayip** *I always thought there was something odd about her.* ○ *It's a bit odd that he didn't come.* **2** [NOT OFTEN] [always before noun] not happening often **nadiren olan; sık olmayan** *He does odd jobs here and there.* **3** [SEPARATED] [always before noun] being one of a pair when the other item is missing **tek, diğer teki kaybolmuş** *an odd sock* **4** [APPROXIMATELY] used after a number to mean approximately **yaklaşık, tahminen** *There are thirty odd kids in the class.* **5** [NUMBER] An odd number does not produce a whole number when it is divided by two. **(rakam, sayı) tek**

oddity /ˈɒdɪti/ *noun* [C] someone or something that is strange or unusual **tuhaflık, acayiplik, gariplik**

oddly /ˈɒdli/ *adverb* in a strange way **tuhaf/acayip biçimde/şekilde** *He's been behaving very oddly lately.* ○ *Oddly enough, business was good during the bad weather months.*

odds ...... İLE BİRLİKTE KULLANILAN KELİMELER
the odds **of/on** sth happening ● the odds are **(stacked) against** sb

odds /ɒdz/ *noun* [plural] **1** the probability that something will happen **ihtimal, şans** *What are the odds of winning the top prizes?* ○ *I'm afraid the odds are against us.* **2 against all (the) odds** If you do or achieve something against all the odds, you succeed although you were not likely to. **her şeye rağmen, bütün zorluklara karşın, tüm güçlüklere rağmen** *We won the game against all odds.* **3 be at odds with sb/sth** to not agree with someone or something **arası açılmış/bozuşmuş olmak; anlaşmazlığa düşmüş olmak** *His remark was at odds with our report.* **4 odds and ends** *informal* a group of small objects of different types which are not valuable or important **ufak tefek şeyler, önemsiz ve değersiz şeyler**

odious /ˈəʊdiəs/ *adjective formal* very unpleasant **iğrenç, nefret verici** *an odious little man*

odour *UK* (*US* odor) /ˈəʊdəʳ/ *noun* [C] a smell, often one that is unpleasant **koku, keskin koku** *body odour*

odyssey /'ɒdɪsi/ *noun* [C] *literary* a long, exciting journey **uzun heyacan verici yolculuk/seyahat**

oestrogen UK (US **estrogen**) /'iːstrəʊdʒ³n/ ⓊⓈ /'estrə-dʒən/ *noun* [U] a chemical substance in a woman's body which prepares her eggs for fertilization (= joining with the male seed to make a baby) **östrojen hormonu**

o-•**of** *strong form* /ɒv/ *weak form* /əv/ *preposition* **1** BELONG belonging or relating to someone or something **...nın/nin; bir şeye birine ilişkin/ait olmayı belirtir** *a friend of mine* ○ *the colour of her hair* ○ *part of the problem* **2** AMOUNT used after words which show an amount **miktar belirten sözcüklerden sonra kullanılır** *a kilo of apples* ○ *both of us* ○ *a handful of raisins* **3** NUMBER used with numbers, ages and dates **rakam, yaş ve tarihlerle kullanılır** *a boy of six* ○ *a decrease of 10%* ○ *the 14th of February 2005* **4** CONTAIN containing **içeren** *a glass of milk* ○ *sacks of rubbish* **5** MADE made or consisting of **...dan/den yapılmış/ibaret** *dresses of lace and silk* **6** ADJECTIVE/VERB used to connect particular adjectives and verbs with nouns **belli sıfat ve fiilleri isimlerle birleştirmek için kullanılır** *frightened of spiders* ○ *smelling of garlic* **7** SHOW showing someone or something **bir şeyi, birini göstermede kullanılır** *a map of the city centre* **8** CAUSE showing a reason or cause **...dan/den meydana gelmek; ...sebebiyle/nedeniyle** *He died of a heart attack.* **9** POSITION showing position or direction **...nın/nin konumu/yönünü göstermede** *the front of the queue* ○ *a small town north of Edinburgh* **10** ACTION/FEELING used after nouns describing actions or feelings to mean 'done to' or 'experienced by' **...dan/den meydana gelen; ...ın/in ...** *the destruction of the rain forest* ○ *the suffering of millions* **11** WRITTEN written or made by **...tarafından yapılan/yazılan** *the collected works of William Shakespeare*

o-•**of course** /əv'kɔːs/ *adverb* **1** used to say 'yes' and emphasize your answer **elbette, tabii, evet** *'Can you help me?' 'Of course!'* **2** used to show that what you are saying is obvious or already known **şüphesiz ki, elbette ki** *The rain meant, of course, that the match was cancelled.* ○ *Of course, the Olympics are not just about money.* **3 of course not** used to say 'no' and emphasize your answer **elbette hayır, tabii ki hayır** *'Do you mind if I borrow your pen?' 'Of course not.'*

o-•**off**[1] /ɒf/ *adverb, preposition* **1** NOT TOUCHING not touching or connected to something or not on a surface **...dan/den öteye/uzağa** *Keep off the grass!* ○ *A button came off my coat.* **2** AWAY away from a place or position **...dan/den uzakta/ötede/ayrı** *He ran off to find his friend.* ○ *I'll be off* (= will go) *soon.* **3** NOT OPERATING not operating or being used **serbest, boş, çalışmaz** *Make sure you switch your computer off.* **4** NEAR near to a building or place **bir yere/binaya yakın; yakınında** *an island off the coast of Spain* **5** PRICE If a price has a certain amount of money off, it costs much less than the usual price. **...dan/den dah düşük fiyata/ucuz/aşağı/aşağıda** *These jeans were $10 off.* **6** DISTANCE/TIME far in distance or time **...dan/den uzakta/ötede; zamanından uzakta/ötede** *My holidays seem a long way off.* **7 go off sth/sb** UK to stop liking something or someone **soğumak, uzaklaşmak, artık sevmemek** *I've gone off meat.* **8** NOT AT WORK not at work **izinde, çalışmıyor, boş, mesaide değil** *I had 6 months off when my son was born.* ⊃See also: off the **cuff, on**[2] and off.

off[2] /ɒf/ *adjective* [never before noun] **1** NOT CORRECT not correct **yanlış, eksik, doğru değil** *Our sales figures were off by ten percent.* **2** FOOD If food or drink is off, it is not now fresh and good to eat or drink. **bayat, eskimiş, yenilmez, bozuk** *This milk smells off.* **3** NOT AT WORK not at work **izinli, çalışmayan, boş** *He's off today - I think he's ill.* ⊃See also: **off-chance.**

offal /'ɒf³l/ *noun* [U] organs from the inside of animals that are killed for food **sakatat**

,**off 'balance** *adjective, adverb* If someone or something is off balance, they are in a position where they are likely to fall or be knocked down. **dengesini kaybetmiş, dengesiz, düşmek üzere, dengesiz şekilde** *to knock/throw someone off balance*

off-chance /'ɒftʃɑːns/ *noun* UK *informal* **on the off-chance** hoping that something may be possible, although it is not likely **ümidiyle, beklentisiyle, varsayımıyla, belki ...dır/dir diye; pek olası değil ama** *I went to the station on the off-chance that she'd be there.*

,**off 'duty** *adjective* When an official such as a police officer is off duty, they are not working. **izin gününde, izinli, çalışmayan, görevde olmayan**

offence .... İLE BİRLİKTE KULLANILAN KELİMELER
cause/give/take offence ● **grave** offence

o-•**offence** UK (US **offense**) /ə'fens/ *noun* **1** [U] when something rude makes someone upset or angry **darıltma, gücendirme** *to cause/give offence* ○ *Many people take offence at swearing.* **2** [C] a crime **suç, kabahat, cürüm** *a criminal offence* ○ *He committed several serious offences.*

o-•**offend** /ə'fend/ *verb* **1** [T] to make someone upset or angry **kırmak, gücendirmek, darıltmak, küstürmek** [often passive] *I was deeply offended by her comments.* **2** [I] *formal* to commit a crime **suç/cürüm işlemek** *If she offends again, she'll go to prison.*

offender /ə'fendə'/ *noun* [C] someone who has committed a crime **suçlu, suç işleyen kimse** *a sex offender* ○ *a young offender*

o-•**offense** /ə'fens/ *noun* US spelling of offence **suç, kabahat, cürüm**

offensive[1] /ə'fensɪv/ *adjective* **1** likely to make people angry or upset **kırıcı, gücendirici** *an offensive remark* ⊃Opposite **inoffensive. 2** used for attacking **saldırı/hücum/taarruz amaçlı** *an offensive weapon* ● **offensively** *adverb* **kırıcı bir tarzda**

offensive[2] /ə'fensɪv/ *noun* [C] an attack **saldırı, hücum, taarruz** *It's time to launch a major offensive against terrorism.*

o-•**offer**[1] /'ɒfə'/ *verb* **1** ASK [+ two objects] to ask someone if they would like something **teklif etmek, sunmak** *They offered me a job.* **2** SAY YOU WILL DO [I, T] to say that you are willing to do something **önermek, teklif etmek** [+ to do sth] *He offered to get me a cab.* **3** AGREE TO PAY [T] to say that you will pay a particular amount of money **teklif sunmak, vermek, yapmak, bulunmak** [+ two objects] *He offered me £500 for the car.* ○ *Police have offered a $1,000 reward for information.* **4** PROVIDE [T] to give or provide something **vermek, sağlamak, sunmak** *to offer advice* ○ *The hotel offers a wide range of facilities.*

offer .... İLE BİRLİKTE KULLANILAN KELİMELER
accept/make/receive/turn down an offer ● **a generous/tempting** offer ● **an offer of** sth

o-•**offer**[2] /'ɒfə'/ *noun* [C] **1** ASK when you ask someone if they would like something **teklif, sunma, verme** *an offer of help* ○ *a job offer* ○ *to accept/refuse an offer* **2** PAYMENT an amount of money that you say you will pay for something **teklif, öneri** *The highest offer anyone has made so far is £150.* **3** CHEAP a cheap price or special arrangement for something **indirim, fırsat, ucuz teklif, düşük fiyat** *This special offer ends on Friday.* **4 on offer a** CHEAP at a cheaper price than usual **daha ucuz fiyat teklifi, satılık, satışa çıkarılmış, indirimde** *Are these jeans still on* *offer*? **b** [AVAILABLE] available to do or have **var olan, satışta, mevcut** *We were amazed at the range of products on offer.*

offering /'ɒfᵊrɪŋ/ *noun* [C] something that you give to someone **sunulan şey, verilen şey, ortaya konulan şey** *a peace offering*

offhand¹ /ˌɒf'hænd/ *adjective* not friendly or polite **nezaketsiz, laubali, cıvık, kaba** *He was a bit offhand with me.*

offhand² /ˌɒf'hænd/ *adverb* immediately, without thinking about something **düşünmeden, anında, hemencecik, hazırlıksız** *I don't know offhand how much it will cost.*

●***office** /'ɒfɪs/ *noun* **1** [PLACE] [C] a room or building where people work **iş yeri, büro, yazıhane** *an office worker* ○ *I never get to the office before nine.* ⊃Orta kısımdaki renkli sayfalarına bakınız. **2** [INFORMATION] [C] a room or building where you can get information, tickets, or a particular service **yazıhane, büro, ofis** *a ticket office* ○ *the tourist office* **3** [JOB] [U] an important job in an organization **makam, görev, iş, mevki, memuriyet** *Some people think he has been in office for too long.* ○ *She held the office of mayor for eight years.* ⊃See also: box office, the Oval Office, post office, register office, registry office.

'**office ˌbuilding** (*also UK* office block) *noun* [C] a large building which contains offices **iş yeri, çalışma binası**

'**office ˌhours** *noun* [plural] the hours during the day when people who work in offices are usually at work **çalışma saatleri**

officer /'ɒfɪsər/ *noun* [C] **1** [MILITARY] someone with an important job in a military organization **subay** *an army/naval officer* **2** [GOVERNMENT] someone who works for a government department **görevli, memur, devlet memuru** *a customs officer* ○ *a prison officer* **3** [POLICE] a police officer **polis, polis memuru** *a uniformed officer* ⊃See also: probation officer.

●***official¹** /ə'fɪʃᵊl/ *adjective* **1** [APPROVED] approved by the government or someone in authority **resmî** *the official language of Singapore* ○ *an official document* **2** [JOB] [always before noun] relating to the duties of someone in a position of authority **resmî** *the official residence of the ambassador* ○ *an official visit* **3** [KNOWN] known by the public **herkesçe bilinen, malum** *It's official - they're getting married!* **4** [NOT TRUE] [always before noun] An official explanation or statement is one that is given, but which may not be true. **(beyanat, bildiri) resmî** *The official reason for the delay is bad weather.* ⊃Opposite unofficial. ● **officially** *adverb* *The new hospital was officially opened yesterday.* **resmî olarak**

official² /ə'fɪʃᵊl/ *noun* [C] someone who has an important position in an organization such as the government **üst düzey bürokrat, yüksek dereceli memur** *a senior official* ○ *a UN official*

offing /'ɒfɪŋ/ *noun* **be in the offing** If something is in the offing, it will happen or be offered soon. **olması yakın, eli kulağında, yakında, ufukta** *He thinks there might be a promotion in the offing.*

off-licence /'ɒfˌlaɪsᵊns/ *UK* (*US* liquor store) *noun* [C] a shop that sells alcoholic drink **alkollü içki dükkânı, içki bayii**

offline (*also* off-line) /ɒf'laɪn/ *adjective, adverb* A computer is offline when it is not connected to a central system, or not connected to the Internet. **(bilgisayar) bağlı olmayan; sistem dışı**

off-peak /ˌɒf'pi:k/ *adjective* not at the most popular and expensive time **az işlek, durgun, çok fazla istenmeyen zamanda, çok az kullanılan zamanda** *an off-peak phone call*

offset /ɒf'set/ *verb* [T] offsetting, *past* offset If one thing offsets another thing, it has the opposite effect and so creates a more balanced situation. **dengelemek, dengede tutmak/olmak** [often passive] *The costs have been offset by savings in other areas.*

offsetting /ɒf'setɪŋ/ *noun* [U] trying to stop the damage caused by activities that produce carbon by doing other things to reduce it, such as planting trees **mahsup etmek**

offshore /ˌɒf'ʃɔːr/ *adjective* [always before noun] **1** in the sea and away from the coast **kıyıdan açıkta, sahile yakın, açıkta** *an offshore island* **2** An offshore bank or bank account is based in another country and so less tax has to be paid. **ülke sınırları dışında olan; başka ülke sınırları içindeki** *an offshore account/trust*

offside /ɒf'saɪd/ (*also US* offsides) *adjective* [always before noun] In sports such as football, a player who is offside is in a position that is not allowed. **ofsayt**

offspring /'ɒfsprɪŋ/ *noun* [C] *plural* offspring *formal* the child of a person or animal **evlat, yavru, döl** *to produce offspring*

off-the-cuff /ˌɒfðə'kʌf/ *adjective* An off-the-cuff remark is one that is not planned. **düşünmeden sarf edilen, ağızdan kaçan, rastgele söylenen**

●***often** /'ɒfᵊn, 'ɒftᵊn/ *adverb* **1** many times or regularly **sık sık, sıklıkla, genellikle** *I often see her there.* ○ *He said I could visit as often as I liked.* ○ *How often* (= How many times) *do you go to the gym?* ○ *I don't see her very often.* **2** If something often happens or is often true, it is normal for it to happen or it is usually true. **ekseriyetle, çoğunlukla, çok defa** *Headaches are often caused by stress.* ○ *Brothers and sisters often argue.*

ogre /'əʊɡər/ *noun* [C] an unpleasant, frightening person **dev, umacı, öcü**

●***oh** /əʊ/ *exclamation* **1** used before you say something, often before replying to what someone has said 'A...!', 'Ya...!', 'Ooo...!' 'Ian's going." "Oh, I didn't realize." ○ *"I'm so sorry." "Oh, don't worry."* **2** used to show an emotion or to emphasize your opinion about something 'Aaa...!', 'Aah...!', 'Yaa...!', 'Of...!', 'Vay...!' *Oh, no! I don't believe it!* ○ *"I don't think I can come." "Oh, that's a shame."* ○ *Oh, how sweet of you!*

●***oil** /ɔɪl/ *noun* [U] **1** a thick liquid that comes from under the Earth's surface that is used as a fuel and for making parts of machines move smoothly **petrol** *an oil company* ○ *an oil well* **2** a thick liquid produced from plants or animals that is used in cooking **yemeklik yağ, sıvı yağ** *vegetable oil* ⊃See also: crude oil, olive oil.

oilfield /'ɔɪlˌfiːld/ *noun* [C] an area under the ground where oil is found **petrol yatağı/sahası** *an offshore oilfield*

'**oil ˌpainting** *noun* [C] a picture made using paint which contains oil **yağlı boya resim/tablo**

'**oil ˌspill** *noun* [C] when oil has come out of a ship and caused pollution **petrol sızıntısı**

oily /'ɔɪli/ *adjective* containing a lot of oil or covered with oil **yağlı, yağ kaplı, yağ içinde** *oily fish* ○ *oily hands*

oink /ɔɪŋk/ *noun* [C] the sound that a pig makes **domuz sesi, domuzun çıkardığı ses**

ointment /'ɔɪntmənt/ *noun* [C, U] a smooth, thick substance that is used on painful or damaged skin **merhem, pomad**

okay¹ (*also* OK) /əʊ'keɪ/ *exclamation* **1** used when agreeing to do something or when allowing someone to do something 'Tamam!', 'Pekâlâ!', 'Oldu!', 'Tabi ki!', 'Hay hay'! *"Let's meet this afternoon." "Okay."* ○ *"Can I use the car?" "Okay."* **2** used before you start speaking, especially to a group of people 'Pekâlâ!', 'Evet!',

'**Şimdi!', 'Tamam!'** *Okay, I'm going to start by showing you a few figures.*

⊶**okay**² *informal* (*also* **OK**) /əʊˈkeɪ/ *adjective, adverb* **1** GOOD good or good enough **iyi, güzel, uygun; iyice, fena değil** *Is your food okay?* ○ *It was okay, but it wasn't as good as his last film.* **2** SAFE safe or healthy **güvenli, sağlıklı, sıhhatli, merak edilecek bir durum yok** *Is your grandmother okay now?* **3** ALLOWED allowed or acceptable **onay, uygun bulma, kabul edilebilir** *Is it okay if I leave early today?* ○ [+ to do sth] *Is it okay to smoke in here?*

⊶**old** /əʊld/ *adjective* **1** LIVED LONG having lived or existed for a long time **yaşlı, ihtiyar, eski** *an old man/woman* ○ *an old house* ○ *We're all getting older.* ○ *Children should show some respect for the old.* **2** USED A LOT having been used or owned for a long time **eski, kullanılmış, eskimiş, yıpranmış** *You might get dirty so wear some old clothes.* **3** AGE used to describe or ask about someone's age **yaş, yaşında** *How old are you?* ○ *She'll be 3 years old this month.* **4 an old friend/enemy, etc** someone who has been your friend/enemy, etc for a long time **eski arkadaş/düşman/hasım vs.** *I met an old friend who I was at college with.* **5** BEFORE [always before noun] used before or in the past **eski, önceden var olan/kullanılan, önceki** *I think the old system was better in many ways.*

,**old 'age** *noun* [U] the period of time when you are old **yaşlılık**

,**old-age 'pension** *noun* [U] UK money that people receive regularly from the government when they are old and have stopped working **emekli aylığı/maaşı**

,**old-age 'pensioner** *noun* [C] UK someone who gets an old-age pension **emekli aylığı/maaşı alan kimse; emekli**

olden /ˈəʊldᵊn/ *adjective* **in the olden days/in olden times** a long time ago **çok önceden, uzun süre önce; eskiden; çok önceden**

⊶**old-fashioned** /ˌəʊldˈfæʃᵊnd/ *adjective* not modern **modası geçmiş, eski moda; günümüzde kullanılmayan** *old-fashioned clothes/furniture*

oldie /ˈəʊldi/ *noun* [C] *informal* an old song or film, or an old person **eski bir şarkı/film veya yaşlı kimse** *a golden oldie*

old-style /ˈəʊldstaɪl/ *adjective* [always before noun] used or done in the past **eski usul/tarz** *old-style politics*

the ,Old 'Testament *noun* the part of the Bible (= holy book) written before the birth of Jesus Christ **Tevrat; İncil'in Hz. İsa'nın doğumundan önce yazılan bölümü**

the 'Old ,World *noun* Asia, Africa, and Europe **Eski Dünya; Asya, Afrika, Avrupa**

olive /ˈɒlɪv/ *noun* **1** [C] a small green or black fruit with a bitter taste that is eaten or used to produce oil **zeytin** **2** [U] (*also* ,**olive 'green**) a colour that is a mixture of green and yellow **zeytin yeşili** ● **olive** (*also* **olive-green**) *adjective* **zeytin**

'**olive ,oil** *noun* [U] oil produced from olives, used for cooking or on salads **zeytinyağı**

-ology /-ɒlədʒi/ *suffix* makes a noun meaning 'the study of something' **...bilimi anlamında son ek; -loji** *psychology* (= the study of the mind) ○ *sociology* (= the study of society)

the Olympic Games /əˈlɪmpɪkˌɡeɪmz/ (*also* **the Olympics**) *noun* [plural] an international sports competition that happens every four years **Olimpiyat Oyunları** ● **Olympic** *adjective* [always before noun] relating to the Olympic Games **Olimpik, olimpik oyunlarla ilgili** *She broke the Olympic record.*

ombudsman /ˈɒmbʊdzmən/ *noun* [C] *plural* **ombudsmen** someone who deals with complaints that people make against the government or public organizations **kamu denetçisi, halkın şikâyetleriyle ilgilenmekle görevli kamu görevlisi/devlet memuru**

omelette /ˈɒmlət/ (*also* US **omelet**) *noun* [C] a food made with eggs that have been mixed and fried, often with other foods added **omlet** *a cheese omelette*

omen ...... İLE BİRLİKTE KULLANILAN KELİMELER

a bad/good/lucky omen ● an omen of [death/disaster/good fortune,etc] ● an omen for sb/sth

omen /ˈəʊmən/ *noun* [C] a sign of what will happen in the future **işaret, belirti, iz** *a good/bad omen*

ominous /ˈɒmɪnəs/ *adjective* making you think that something bad is going to happen **uğursuz, kötü, hayra alamet olmayan, meşum** *an ominous sign* ○ *ominous clouds*

omission ...... İLE BİRLİKTE KULLANILAN KELİMELER

a glaring/serious/surprising omission ● sb/sth's omission from sth ● the omission of sb/sth

omission /əʊˈmɪʃᵊn/ *noun* [C, U] when something has not been included but should have been **ihmal edilmiş/atlanmış/unutulmuş/dahil edilmemiş şey** *There are some serious omissions in the book.*

omit /əʊˈmɪt/ *verb* **omitting**, *past* **omitted** **1** [T] to not include something **atlamak, dahil etmemek, yanlışlıkla unutmak, çıkarmak, dışında bırakmak** [often passive] *He was omitted from the team because of his behaviour.* **2 omit to do sth** *mainly UK formal* to not do something **ihmal etmek, yapmamak** *She omitted to mention she was going.*

⊶**on**¹ /ɒn/ *preposition* **1** SURFACE on a surface of something **üstüne, üstünde** *We put all of our medicine on a high shelf.* **2** PLACE in a particular place **...da/de** *the diagram on page 22* ○ *I met her on a ship.* **3** RECORDING/PERFORMANCE used to show the way in which something is recorded or performed (tv. vs.) **...da/de** *What's on television tonight?* **4** TOUCHING used to show what happens as a result of touching something **...ile; kullanımında** *I cut myself on a knife.* **5** SUBJECT about **hakkında, ...da/de/dair; ...ile ilgili** *a book on pregnancy* **6** MONEY/TIME used to show what money or time is used for **(zaman ve para sarfetmede) ...da/de** *I've wasted too much time on this already.* ○ *She refuses to spend more than £20 on a pair of shoes.* **7** NEXT TO next to or along the side of something **...da/de** *The post office is on Bateman Street.* **8** DATE/DAY used to show the date or day when something happens **(gün ve tarih belirtmede) ...tarihinde; ...gününde; ...da/de** *He's due to arrive on 14 February.* ○ *I'm working on my birthday.* **9** USING using something **(telefon vs.)...da/de** *I spoke to Mum on the phone.* **10** AFTER happening after something and often because of it **...da/de** *The Prince was informed on his return to the UK.* **11** TRANSPORT used to show some methods of travelling **(araç, vasıta vs.) ...ile; ...da/de** *Did you go over on the ferry?* ○ *Sam loves travelling on buses.* **12** FOOD/FUEL/DRUGS used to show something that is used as food, fuel, or a drug **(yiyecek, yakıt, ilaç vs.) ...ile; kullanarak** *This radio runs on batteries.* ○ *I can't drink wine because I'm on antibiotics.* **13 be on a committee/panel, etc** to be a member of a group or organization **kurul/jüri/komite üyesi olmak** *She's on the playgroup committee.* **14 have/carry sth on you** to have something with you **yanında/üstünde bulundurmak/taşımak** *Do you have your driving licence on you?* **15 be on him/her, etc** *informal* used to show who is paying for something **parası/ödemesi benden/ ondan vs. olmak** *This meal is on me.*

o╍**on²** /ɒn/ *adverb* **1** ‾CONTINUE‾ used to show that an action or event continues **devamlı; süren/devam eden eylem ve olayları belirtmede** *The old tradition lives on.* ○ *It was a complicated situation that dragged on for weeks.* **2** ‾WEAR‾ If you have something on, you are wearing it. **üzerinde/giyiyor olmada** *She's got a black coat on.* ○ *Why don't you put your new dress on?* **3** ‾WORKING‾ working or being used **çalışıyor/kullanılıyor olmada** *The heating has been on all day.* **4** ‾TRAVEL‾ into a bus, train, plane, etc **(otobüs, tren, uçak vs.) ...da/de, ... ile** *Amy got on in Stamford.* **5** ‾HAPPENING‾ happening or planned **olan, planlanan** *I've got a lot on at the moment.* ○ *Have you checked what's on at the cinema?* **6 on and off** (*also* **off and on**) If something happens on and off during a period of time, it happens sometimes. **zaman zaman, aralıklarla** *They've been seeing each other on and off since Christmas.*

o╍**once¹** /wʌns/ *adverb* **1** ‾ONE TIME‾ one time **bir defa, bir kez** *It's only snowed once or twice this year.* ○ *I go swimming once a week* (= one time every week)*.* **2** ‾NOT NOW‾ in the past, but not now **bir zamanlar, eskiden** *This house once belonged to my grandfather.* **3 once again** again **yine, bir daha, tekrar** *Once again I'm left with all the washing up.* **4 all at once** suddenly **aniden, birden bire** *All at once he stood up and walked out of the room.* **5 at once a** ‾IMMEDIATELY‾ immediately **derhal, hemen** *I knew at once that I would like it here.* **b** ‾AT SAME TIME‾ at the same time **aynı zamanda, hep bir anda** *They all started talking at once.* **6 once in a while** sometimes but not often **zaman zaman, arada sırada, bazen** *He plays tennis once in a while.* **7 once and for all** If you do something once and for all, you do it now so that it does not have to be dealt with again. **ilk ve son defa/olarak, son olarak; bir daha ...mamak/memek üzere** *Let's get to the bottom of this matter once and for all!* **8 once more** one more time **yine, bir daha, yeniden** *If you say that once more, I'm going to leave.* **9 for once** used to mean that something is happening that does not usually happen **bir defalık, bu seferlik** *For once, I think I have good news for him.* **10 once upon a time** used at the beginning of a children's story to mean that something happened a long time ago **bir zamanlar, eskiden; evvel zaman içinde; bir varmış bir yokmuş** ⊃See also: once in a blue **moon.**

o╍**once²** /wʌns/ *conjunction* as soon as **...ar/er ... maz/mez; yapar yapmaz, olur olmaz, gelir gelmez vs.** *Once I've found somewhere to live, I'll send you my new address.* ○ *We'll send your tickets once we've received your cheque.*

oncoming /'ɒn,kʌmɪŋ/ *adjective* [always before noun] Oncoming vehicles are coming towards you. **karşıdan gelen, karşıdan yaklaşmakta olan**

o╍**one¹** /wʌn/ the number 1 **bir** ⊃See also: back to **square¹** one.

o╍**one²** /wʌn/ *pronoun* **1** used to refer to a particular person or thing in a group that has already been talked about **bir şey/kişi** *I've just made some scones, do you want one?* ○ *Throw those gloves away and get some new ones.* ○ *Chris is the one with glasses.* **2** *formal* any person in general **biri, herhangi biri** *One ought to respect one's parents.* **3 one at a time** separately **ayrı ayrı, birer birer, aynı anda bir tek şeyi yapmayı belirtir** *Eat them one at a time.* **4 one by one** separately, with one thing happening after another **birer birer, teker teker** *One by one the old buildings have been demolished.* **5 one another** each other **biri diğerine, birbirlerine** *How can they reach an agreement if they won't talk to one another?* **6 (all) in one** combined into a single thing **bir arada; hepsi bir arada** *It's a vacation and art course all in one.*

o╍**one³** /wʌn/ *determiner* **1** ‾PARTICULAR PERSON/THING‾ used to refer to a particular person or thing in a group **bir, biri, tek, yalnız** *One drawback is the cost of housing in the area.* ○ *One of our daughters has just got married.* **2** ‾FUTURE TIME‾ used to refer to a time in the future which is not yet decided **(bilinmeyen) bir (gün, hafta vs.)** *We must have a drink together one evening.* **3** ‾TIME IN PAST‾ at a particular time in the past **(geçmişte bilinmeyen) bir (gün, hafta vs.)** *I first met him one day in the park.* **4** ‾ONLY‾ only **tek, sadece, yalnız, bir** *He's the one person you can rely on in this place.* **5** ‾WITH ADJECTIVE‾ mainly US used to emphasize an adjective **sıfatları vurgulamak için kullanılır; bir, yalnız tek** *That's one big ice cream you've got there!* **6 one or two** a few **bir iki, bir kaç, bir en fazla iki, cüzi** *I'd like to make one or two suggestions.* ⊃See also: put sth to one **side¹**, be one **step¹** ahead (of sb).

one-man /,wʌn'mæn/ *adjective* [always before noun] with only one person doing something **tek kişi; tek kişinin yaptığı** *a one-man show*

,one-night 'stand *noun* [C] when two people have sex just after they meet but do not then have a relationship **bir gecelik sevişme; tek gecelik aşk; bir gecelik birliktelik**

one-off /,wʌn'ɒf/ *adjective* [always before noun] UK only happening once **bir defalık, bir defaya mahsus** *a one-off payment* ● **one-off** *noun* [C] UK something that only happens once **bir kerelik şey; bir defalık olan şey** *His Olympic victory was not just a one-off.*

one-on-one /,wʌnɒn'wʌn/ *adjective, adverb mainly US* only including two people **iki kişilik, iki kişiyle yapılan; sadece çift kişiyle**

onerous /'əʊnʳrəs/ *adjective formal* difficult and needing a lot of effort **zahmetli, külfetli, ağır** *an onerous task*

oneself /wʌn'self/ *pronoun formal* the reflexive form of the pronoun 'one' when it refers to the person speaking or people in general **kendi, kendisi, kendine** *How else should one protect oneself and one's family?*

one-sided /,wʌn'saɪdɪd/ *adjective* **1** If a competition is one-sided, one team or player is much better than the other. **tek taraflı; tek yönlü** *a one-sided contest/game* **2** only considering one opinion in an argument in a way that is unfair **yanlı, tek taraflı** *a one-sided view*

one-time /'wʌntaɪm/ *adjective* [always before noun] A one-time position or job is one that you had or did in the past, but not now. **geçmiş, eski** *a one-time friend/minister*

one-to-one /,wʌntə'wʌn/ *adjective, adverb mainly UK* only including two people **ferdî olarak, bireysel şekilde** *She's having private lessons on a one-to-one basis.*

one-way /,wʌn'weɪ/ *adjective* If a road is one-way, you can only drive on it in one direction. **tek yönlü** *a one-way street*

,one-way 'ticket US (UK **single**) *noun* [C] A one-way ticket for a journey can only be used to travel in one direction and not for returning. **gidşi bileti**

ongoing /'ɒn,gəʊɪŋ/ *adjective* [always before noun] still happening **hâlâ olan, devam eden, süren** *an ongoing process/investigation*

onion /'ʌnjən/ *noun* [C, U] a round vegetable with layers that has a strong taste and smell **soğan** ⊃Orta kısımdaki renkli sayfalarına bakınız ⊃See also: spring **onion.**

o╍**online** /,ɒn'laɪn/ *adjective, adverb* connected to a system of computers, especially the Internet **(bilgisayar) bağlantılı; internete bağlı** *online services* ○ *to go online* (= start using the Internet) ○ *Most newspapers are now available online.* ⊃See study page The Web and the Internet on page Centre 36.

onlooker /ˈɒnˌlʊkəʳ/ *noun* [C] someone who watches something happening without becoming involved in it **seyirci, seyreden, temaşacı** *a crowd of onlookers*

o⁻**only¹** /ˈəʊnli/ *adverb* **1** NOT MORE not more than a particular size or amount **yalnız, yalnızca, sadece** *It'll only take a few minutes.* ○ *She's only fifteen.* **2** NO ONE/NOTHING ELSE not anyone or anything else **sadece, yalnızca, bir tek** *The offer is available to UK residents only.* **3** RECENTLY used to mean that something happened very recently **daha, henüz** *She's only just finished writing it.* **4 not only ... (but) also** used to say that one thing is true and another thing is true too, especially a surprising thing **...sadece değil ... aynı zamanda ...da/de/dahi; sadece o değil aynı zamanda öteki de** *Not only did he turn up late, he also forgot his books.*

o⁻**only²** /ˈəʊnli/ *adjective* [always before noun] used to mean that there are not any others **yegâne, bir tek, yalnızca** *This could be our only chance.* ○ *You're the only person here I know.*

only³ /ˈəʊnli/ *conjunction* used to introduce a statement which explains why something you have just said cannot happen or is not completely true **yalnız, ancak** *I'd phone him myself only I know he's not there at the moment.*

'**only ˌchild** *noun* [C] *plural* **only children** someone who has no brothers or sisters **tek çocuk, hiç kardeşi olmayan çocuk**

on-screen /ˈɒnskriːn/ *adjective, adverb* appearing on a computer or television screen **(bilgisayar, tv. vs.) ekranda, ekranda görünen**

onset /ˈɒnset/ *noun* **the onset of sth** the beginning of something, usually something unpleasant **(hoş olmayan şey) başlangıç, ortaya çıkış** *the onset of cancer*

> 🔧 **onslaught** ...... İLE BİRLİKTE KULLANILAN KELİMELER
>
> **launch/mount** an onslaught ● an onslaught **against/on** sb

onslaught /ˈɒnslɔːt/ *noun* [C] when someone attacks or criticizes someone or something **şiddetli saldırı, müthiş taarruz, hücum**

o⁻**onto** (*also* on to) /ˈɒntuː/ *preposition* **1** used to show movement into or on a particular place **...ın/in üzerine/üstüne** *The sheep were loaded onto trucks.* ○ *Can you get back onto the path?* **2 hold/grip, etc onto sth** to hold something **bir şeyi sıkı sıkıya tutmak; tutunmak** *Hold onto my hand before we cross the road.* **3** used to show that you are starting to talk about a different subject **(başka bir konuya) ...ya/ye geçiş** *Can we move onto the next item on the agenda?* **4 be onto sb** to know that someone has done something wrong or illegal **hatasını/yasa dışı yapılanları bilmek; haberdar olmak; peşinde olmak** *She knows we're onto her and she's trying to get away.* ○ *Who put the police onto* (= told the police about) *her?* **5 be onto sth** to know or discover something useful or important **faydalı/önemli bir şeyi keşfetmek/bilmek** *Researchers think they may be onto something big.* ○ *Can you put me onto* (= tell me about) *a good dentist?*

the onus /ˈəʊnəs/ *noun formal* the responsibility for doing something **sorumluluk, yükümlülük, vazife, görev** *The onus is on parents to make sure their children attend school.*

onward /ˈɒnwəd/ (*also* onwards) *adverb* **1 from the 1870s/March/6.30 pm, etc onwards** beginning at a time and continuing after it **...dan/den başlayarak/itibaren sonrasında devam eden 2** If you move onwards, you continue to go forwards. **ileriye doğru, ileri**

oops /uːps/ *exclamation* something you say when you make a mistake or have a slight accident '**Aah!**', '**Aay!**', '**Aman!**', '**Eyvah!**', '**Ey!**' *Oops! I've spilled my coffee.*

ooze /uːz/ *verb* **1** [I, T] If a liquid oozes from something or if something oozes a liquid, the liquid comes out slowly. **sızmak, sızdırmak** *Blood was oozing out of the wound.* **2** [T] *informal* to show a lot of a quality **abartıyla göstermek, yansıtmak, dışarı vurmak** *to ooze charm*

opaque /əʊˈpeɪk/ *adjective* **1** If an object or substance is opaque, you cannot see through it. **saydam olmayan, ışık geçirmeyen 2** *formal* difficult to understand **zor anlaşılan, anlaşılması güç, kolay anlaşılmayan**

op-ed /ɒpˈed/ *US* (*UK* **editorial**) *adjective* [always before noun] describes a piece of writing in a newspaper in which a writer gives an opinion about a subject **gazete baş yazısına benzer fikir yazısı şeklinde; yorum** *an op-ed article/page*

open

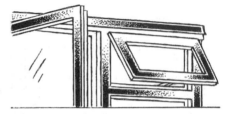

The window is open.

The book is open.

o⁻**open¹** /ˈəʊp³n/ *adjective* **1** NOT CLOSED not closed or fastened **açık** *an open door/window* ○ *Someone had left the gate wide open.* ○ *Is there a bottle of wine already open?* ○ *A magazine was lying open on her lap.* **2** DOING BUSINESS A shop or business is open during the time it is available for business or serving customers. **(mağaza, işyeri) açık** *Most shops are open on Sundays now.* **3** COMPUTERS If a computer document or program is open, it is ready to be read or used. **(bilgisayar dökümanı) açık; kullanıma/okunmaya hazır 4** WITHOUT BUILDINGS [always before noun] An open area of land has no buildings on it or near it. **açık arazi/alan** *large open spaces* **5** NOT COVERED [always before noun] without a roof or cover **üstü açık, çatısız, tepesi kapalı olmayan** *an open courtyard* **6** FOR EVERYONE If a place or event is open, everyone can go to it or become involved in it. **herkese açık; kamuya açık; ücretsiz; giriş serbest** *an open debate* ○ *Are the gardens open to the public?* **7** HONEST An open person is honest and does not hide their feelings. **samimi, dürüst, açık sözlü/yürekli 8** NOT HIDDEN [always before noun] Open feelings, usually negative ones, are not hidden. **saklanmayan, gizli olmayan, açık** *open hostility/rivalry* **9** NOT DECIDED If a decision or question is open, it has not yet been decided. **açık, karar verilmemiş, kararlaştırılmamış** *We don't have to make a firm arrangement now. Let's* *leave it open.* **10 have/keep an open mind** to wait until you know all the facts before you form an opinion about something or judge someone **yargıya varmadan önce zihnini açık tutmak; karar vermeden önce fikirlere açık olmak** *The cause of the fire is still unclear and we are keeping an open mind.* **11 open to discussion/suggestions, etc** willing to consider a discussion/ suggestions, etc **tartışmaya/önerilere açık olmak** *This is only a proposal. I'm open to suggestions.* **12 open to abuse/criticism, etc** likely to be abused/ criticized, etc **istismara/eleştiriye açık olmak** *The system is wide open to abuse.* ⊃See also: with your eyes (**eye¹**) open.

o⚬**open²** /ˈəʊpᵊn/ *verb* **1** NOT CLOSED [I, T] If something opens, it changes to a position that is not closed, and if you open it, you make it change to a position that is not closed. **açmak, açılmak** *to open a door/window* ○ *The gate won't open.* ○ *Don't open your eyes yet.* **2** REMOVE COVER [T] to remove part of a container or parcel so that you can see or use what it contains **kapağını açmak/kaldırmak** *Karen opened the box and looked inside.* ○ *Why don't you open the envelope?* ○ *I can't open this bottle.* **3** PREPARE FOR USE [I, T] If an object opens, the parts that are folded together move apart, and if you open it, you make the parts that are folded together move apart. **açmak** *Shall I open the umbrella?* ○ *Open your books at page 22.* **4** START WORK [I] If a shop or office opens at a particular time of day, it starts to do business at that time. **açılmak, açık olmak** *What time does the bank open?* **5** COMPUTERS [T] to make a computer document or program ready to be read or used (**bilgisayar dökümanını**) **açmak, kullanıma sunmak 6** START OFFICIALLY [I, T] If a business or activity opens, it starts officially for the first time, and if you open it, you make it start officially for the first time. (**yeni iş/iş yeri**) **açmak, açılmak** *That restaurant's new - it only opened last month.* ○ *Several shops have opened up in the last year.* **7** MAKE AVAILABLE [T] to allow people to use a road or area (**yol, bölge, alan, saha**) **açmak, açık tutmak, kullanıma sunmak** *They opened up the roads again the day after the flooding.* **8 open an account** to make an arrangement to keep your money with a bank **hesap açmak** *Have you opened a bank account yet?* ⊃See also: open the floodgates.

open (sth) up *phrasal verb* **1** to create a new opportunity or possibility **yeni bir fırsat/olasılık yaratmak; fırsat sunmak** *A teaching qualification can* **open up** *many more career* **opportunities.** **2** to open the lock on the door of a building **kilidi açmak** *The caretaker opens up the school every morning at seven.*

open up *phrasal verb* to start to talk more about yourself and your feelings **kendisi ve hisleri hakkında eskiye oranla daha fazla konuşmaya başlamak** *I've tried to get him to* **open up to** *me, but with no success.*

the open /ˈəʊpᵊn/ *noun* **1 in the open** outside **açık havada, dışarıda, açıkta** *We spent the night in the open.* **2 bring sth out into the open** to tell people information that was secret **bütün kirli çamaşırları ortaya dökmek; gizli sırları ifşa etmek; meydana çıkarmak** [often passive] *It's time this issue was brought out into the open.*

open-air /ˌəʊpən'eəʳ/ *adjective* [always before noun] An open-air place does not have a roof. **açık hava** *an* **open-air swimming pool**

ˈopen ˌday *noun* [C] UK A day when people can visit a school or organization to see what happens there **ziyaret günü, halk günü, halka açık gün**

open-ended /ˌəʊpən'endɪd/ *adjective* An open-ended activity or situation does not have a planned ending. **açık uçlu** *We are not willing to enter into* **open-ended discussions.**

opener /ˈəʊpənəʳ/ *noun* [C] **1 bottle/can/tin, etc opener** a piece of kitchen equipment used to open bottles/cans, etc **şişe/konserve/teneke kutu açacağı 2** someone or something that begins a series of events, usually in sports (**sporda**) **bir eylemi ilk başlatan kişi/şey** ⊃See also: eye-opener.

opening¹ /ˈəʊpənɪŋ/ *noun* [C] **1** HOLE a hole or space that something or someone can pass through **delik, açıklık, yarık** *We found an opening in the fence and climbed through.* **2** START the beginning of something **başlangıç** *The opening of the opera is quite dramatic.* **3** CEREMONY a ceremony at the beginning of an event or activity **açış, açılış, başlangıç** *I've been invited to the opening of the new exhibition on Tuesday.* **4** OPPORTUNITY a job or an opportunity to do something **açık iş, boş/ münhal kadro/iş** *There's* **an opening for** *an editorial assistant in our department.*

opening² /ˈəʊpənɪŋ/ *adjective* [always before noun] happening at the beginning of an event or activity **açılışta olan, açılış** *the* **opening night** ○ *her* **opening remarks**

openly /ˈəʊpᵊnli/ *adverb* without hiding any of your thoughts or feelings **açıkça, alenen, açık açık, açıktan** *He talks quite openly about his feelings.*

open-minded /ˌəʊpən'maɪndɪd/ *adjective* willing to consider ideas and opinions that are new or different to your own **açık fikirli, açık görüşlü**

openness /ˈəʊpᵊnnəs/ *noun* [U] when someone is honest about their thoughts and feelings **açık yüreklilik, dürüstlük, açıklık** *I appreciated his openness.*

open-plan /ˌəʊpᵊn'plæn/ *adjective* describes a room or a building without many walls **açık planlı, duvarları olmayan** *an* **open-plan office**

opera /ˈɒpᵊrə/ *noun* [C, U] a musical play in which most of the words are sung **opera** *to go to the opera* ○ *opera singers* ○ *an* **opera house** (= building for opera) ● **operatic** /ˌɒpᵊr'ætɪk/ *adjective* relating to opera **operaya ilgili** *an operatic society*

o⚬**operate** /ˈɒpᵊreɪt/ *verb* **1** ORGANIZATION [I, T] If an organization or business operates, it is working, and if you operate it, you manage it and make it work. **işlemek, işletmek, faaliyet göstermek, faaliyette bulunmak** *Our company is operating under very difficult conditions at present.* **2** MACHINE [I, T] If a machine operates, it does what it is designed to do, and if you operate it, you make it do what it is designed to do. **çalışmak, çalıştırmak, işlemek, işletmek** *You have to be trained to operate the machinery.* **3** TREATMENT [I] to treat an illness or injury by cutting someone's body and removing or repairing part of it **ameliyat yapmak** *Did they have to* **operate on** *him?*

ˈoperating ˌroom US (UK operating theatre) *noun* [C] a room in a hospital where doctors do operations **ameliyathane**

ˈoperating ˌsystem *noun* [C] computer software that controls how different parts of a computer work together **bilgisayar yazılım sistemi**

ˈoperating ˌtheatre UK (US operating room) *noun* [C] a room in a hospital where doctors do operations **ameliyathane**

🧩 ***operation*** .... İLE BİRLİKTE KULLANILAN KELİMELER
have/undergo an operation ● **do/perform** an operation ● an operation **on** sb/sb's [knee/hand,etc] ● a **major/minor** operation

o⚬**operation** /ˌɒpᵊr'eɪʃᵊn/ *noun* [C] **1** MEDICAL TREATMENT when a doctor cuts someone's body to remove or repair part of it **ameliyat** *a heart/lung operation* ○ *a* **major/ minor operation** ○ *My son's got to* **have an operation.** **2** ORGANIZATION an organization or business **şirket,**

işletme *a large commercial operation* **3** [ACTIVITY] an activity that is intended to achieve a particular purpose **eylem, faaliyet** *a military/peacekeeping operation* ○ *a joint operation by French and Spanish police* **4 in operation** If a machine or system is in operation, it is working or being used. **faal, işler/çalışır durumda, yürürlükte** *The new rail link is now in operation.* ○ *Most of the machines are now back in operation.*

operational /ˌɒpəˈreɪʃᵊnᵊl/ *adjective* **1** If a system is operational, it is working. **işler hâlde, faal, kullanıma hazır** *The service becomes fully operational next June.* **2** [always before noun] relating to a particular activity **belli bir eyleme/faaliyete ilişkin** *operational control/responsibility*

operative¹ /ˈɒpᵊrətɪv/ *adjective formal* working or being used **faal, işler/çalışır durumda, yürürlükte** *The agreement will not become operative until all members have signed.*

operative² /ˈɒpᵊrətɪv/ *noun* [C] *mainly US* someone who does secret work for a government or other organization **gizli görevli/ajan, devlet veya bir kurum adına gizli işler yapan kimse** *a former CIA operative*

operator /ˈɒpəreɪtəʳ/ *noun* [C] **1** [TELEPHONE] someone who helps to connect people on a telephone system **santral görevlisi/memuru, operatör** *Why don't you call the operator?* **2** [MACHINE] someone whose job is to use and control a machine or vehicle **bir makine/aleti kullanan kimse** *a computer operator* **3** [BUSINESS] a company that does a particular type of business **işletme, şirket, firma, kuruluş** *a tour operator*

opinion .... İLE BİRLİKTE KULLANILAN KELİMELER

express/hold/voice an opinion ● a favourable/low/personal/poor/strong opinion ● in sb's opinion ● sb's opinion about/on sth

○ᴗ**opinion** /əˈpɪnjən/ *noun* **1** [C] a thought or belief about something or someone **fikir, düşünce, kanı, kanaat** *What's your opinion about/on the matter?* ○ *He has fairly strong opinions on most subjects.* ○ *In my opinion* (= I think) *he's the best football player we have in this country.* **2 public opinion** the thoughts and beliefs that most people have about a subject **kamuoyu** *Eventually, the government will have to take notice of public opinion.* **3 have a high/low opinion of sb/sth** to think that someone or something is good/bad **birisinin/birinin iyi/kötü olduğunu düşünmek; iyi/kötü düşünceye sahip olmak** *He has a low opinion of doctors.*

opinionated /əˈpɪnjəneɪtɪd/ *adjective* being too certain that your strong opinions are correct **dik kafalı, inatçı, fikrinden caymaz, bildiğinden şaşmaz**

o'pinion ˌpoll *noun* [C] when people are asked questions to discover what they think about a subject **kamuoyu araştırması/yoklaması, anket** *The latest opinion poll shows that the president's popularity has improved.*

opium /ˈəʊpiəm/ *noun* [U] a drug made from the seeds of a poppy (= a red flower) **afyon**

opponent /əˈpəʊnənt/ *noun* [C] **1** someone who you compete against in a game or competition **rakip** *He beat his opponent six games to two.* **2** someone who disagrees with an action or belief and tries to change it **muhalif, muhalefet eden kimse** *an opponent of slavery* ○ *a political opponent*

opportune /ˈɒpətjuːn/ *adjective formal* **an opportune moment/time** a good time for something to happen **uygun/münasip/müsait an/zaman** *His letter arrived at an opportune moment.*

opportunist /ˌɒpəˈtjuːnɪst/ *noun* [C] someone who tries to get power or an advantage in every situation **fırsatçı; fırsat düşkünü kimse** ● **opportunistic**

/ˌɒpətjuːˈnɪstɪk/ *adjective* using a situation to get power or an advantage **fırsat düşkünü**

opportunity .... İLE BİRLİKTE KULLANILAN KELİMELER

create/have/miss/offer/provide/seize an opportunity ● a golden/good/great/unique/wasted opportunity ● at every opportunity ● an opportunity for sth

○ᴗ**opportunity** /ˌɒpəˈtjuːnəti/ *noun* **1** [C, U] a situation in which it is possible for you to do something, or a possibility of doing something **fırsat, uygun zaman, vesile** *a unique opportunity* ○ *a golden* (= very good) *opportunity* ○ [+ to do sth] *Everyone will have an opportunity to comment.* ○ *There are plenty of opportunities for research.* ○ *Don't miss this opportunity to win a million pounds.* ○ *She talks about her boyfriend at every opportunity.* **2** [C] the chance to get a job **fırsat, olanak** [usually plural] *opportunities for young graduates* ○ *job/employment opportunities* **3 take the opportunity to do sth** to use an occasion to do or say something **istifade etmek, fırsattan yararlanmak** *I'd like to take this opportunity to thank all of you.*

○ᴗ**oppose** /əˈpəʊz/ *verb* [T] to disagree with a plan or activity and to try to change or stop it **karşı çıkmak, muhalefet etmek** *The committee opposed a proposal to allow women to join the club.*

opposed /əˈpəʊzd/ *adjective* **1 be opposed to sth** to disagree with a plan or activity **karşı/muhalif olmak** *We're not opposed to tax increases.* **2 as opposed to** to say that two things are very different ...**ın/in aksine/tersine; karşı** *I'm talking about English football, as opposed to European football.*

opposing /əˈpəʊzɪŋ/ *adjective* **1 opposing teams/players, etc** Opposing teams/players, etc are competing against each other. **rakip takımlar/oyuncular** **2 opposing ideas/beliefs, etc** Opposing ideas/beliefs, etc are completely different. **karşı fikirler/inançlar** *The book presents two opposing views.*

○ᴗ**opposite¹** /ˈɒpəzɪt/ *adjective* **1** in a position facing something or someone but on the other side **karşısında, karşı tarafında** *on the opposite page* ○ *in the opposite corner* ○ *We live on opposite sides of the city.* ○ *I noticed a gate at the opposite end of the courtyard.* **2** completely different **tamamen farklı/ayrı/değişik** *Police attempts to calm the violence had completely the opposite effect.*

○ᴗ**opposite²** /ˈɒpəzɪt/ *adverb, preposition* in a position facing something or someone but on the other side **karşı, zıt, aksi** *The couple sat down opposite her.* ○ *UK She lives opposite* (= on the other side of the road). ○ *Is there a bakery opposite your house?*

○ᴗ**opposite³** /ˈɒpəzɪt/ *noun* [C] someone or something that is completely different from another person or thing **öteki, öbür, karşı** *They're complete opposites.* ○ *He's the exact opposite of my father.*

the ˌopposite 'sex *noun* someone who is male if you are female, or female if you are male **karşı cins** *It's not always easy to meet members of the opposite sex* .

○ᴗ**opposition** /ˌɒpəˈzɪʃᵊn/ *noun* **1** [U] strong disagreement **karşı çıkma, karşı olma, uyuşmazlık** *Is there much opposition to the proposed changes?* ○ *There has been strong opposition from local residents.* **2 the Opposition/opposition** political parties that are not in government **Muhalefet/muhalefet partileri**

oppress /əˈpres/ *verb* [T] **1** to treat a group of people in an unfair way, often by limiting their freedom **baskı yapmak, zulmetmek, eziyet etmek** [often passive] *Women were oppressed by a society which considered* *them inferior.* **2** to make someone feel anxious **sıkıntı vermek, içini sıkmak/daraltmak, bunaltmak**

oppressed /ə'prest/ *adjective* treated in an unfair way **baskı ve zulüm gören, mazlum** *oppressed minorities*

oppression /ə'preʃᵊn/ *noun* [U] when people are treated in a way that is unfair and that limits their freedom **baskı, zulüm, eziyet** *political oppression* ○ *the oppression of women*

oppressive /ə'presɪv/ *adjective* **1** [UNFAIR] cruel and unfair **acımasız, zalim, insafsız, adaletsiz** *an oppressive government/regime* **2** [HOT] If the weather or heat is oppressive, it is too hot and there is no wind. **bunaltıcı, ağır, sıkıcı, sıkıntılı** *oppressive heat* **3** [NOT RELAXING] not relaxing or pleasant **can sıkıcı, sıkıntı veren** *an oppressive silence*

oppressor /ə'presər/ *noun* [C] someone who treats people in an unfair way, often by limiting their freedom **acımasız/zalim/insafsız/adaletsiz kimse**

opt /ɒpt/ *verb* **opt for sth; opt to do sth** to choose something or to decide to do something **seçmek, bir şeyi yapmaya karar vermek** *Mike opted for early retirement.* ○ *Most people opt to have the operation.*
opt out *phrasal verb* to choose not to be part of an activity or to stop being involved in it **çıkmak, çekilmek, karışmamak, dahil olmamak** *He's decided to opt out of the company's pension scheme.*

optical /'ɒptɪkᵊl/ *adjective* relating to light or the ability to see **görme ve ışıkla ilgili** *optical equipment/instruments*

optical i'llusion *noun* [C] something that you think you see, but which is not really there **göz yanılması, optik yanılsama**

optician /ɒp'tɪʃᵊn/ *noun* [C] **1** someone whose job is to make eye glasses **gözlükçü 2** *UK* a shop where you can have your eyes tested and have your glasses made **gözlük mağazası, gözlük evi**

🔲 *optimism* ...... İLE BİRLİKTE KULLANILAN KELİMELER

express optimism • **cautious/renewed** optimism • **cause for/grounds for/reason for** optimism • optimism **about** sth

optimism /'ɒptɪmɪzᵊm/ *noun* [U] when you believe good things will happen **iyimserlik** *a mood/spirit of optimism* ○ *There is cause/reason for optimism.* ○ *He expressed cautious optimism about the future.* ⊃Opposite pessimism.

optimist /'ɒptɪmɪst/ *noun* [C] someone who always believes that good things will happen **iyimser**

optimistic /ˌɒptɪ'mɪstɪk/ *adjective* always believing that good things will happen **iyimser** *He's optimistic about our chances of success.* ○ [+ (that)] *I'm not optimistic that we'll reach an agreement.* ⊃Opposite pessimistic.

optimum /'ɒptɪməm/ *adjective* [always before noun] *formal* best or most suitable **en elverişli, en iyi, en uygun** *the optimum temperature*

🔲 *option* ...... İLE BİRLİKTE KULLANILAN KELİMELER

consider/examine the options • **be given/have** the option **of** doing sth • an **attractive/viable** option • an option **for** sb

option /'ɒpʃᵊn/ *noun* **1** [C] a choice **seçenek, alternatif** *That's an option you might like to consider.* ○ *We don't have many options.* ○ [+ of + doing sth] *You always have the option of not attending.* **2 have no option (but to do sth)** to not have the possibility of doing something else **başka seçenek şansı/çaresi/imkânı olmamak**

We didn't want to dismiss him, but we had no option. **3 keep/leave your options open** to wait and not make a decision or choice yet **beklemek ve henüz bir seçim yapmamak/karar vermemek** ⊃See also: soft option.

optional /'ɒpʃᵊnᵊl/ *adjective* If something is optional, it is available but you do not have to have it. **tercihli, isteğe bağlı, ihtiyari, seçmeli** *an optional extra*

opulent /'ɒpjələnt/ *adjective* Opulent things are expensive and give a feeling of luxury. **gösterişli, zengin görünüşlü, görkemli** *an opulent bathroom*

or *strong form* /ɔːr/ *weak form* /ər/ *conjunction* **1** [BETWEEN POSSIBILITIES] used between possibilities, or before the last in a list of possibilities **veya, yoksa** *Would you like toast or cereal?* ○ *Is that a boy or a girl?* ○ *You can have beer, wine, or mineral water.* ○ *The house will take two or three years to complete.* **2** [CHANGE] used to change or correct something you have said **veya, veyahut, ya da** *We told the truth, or most of it.* **3** [REASON] used to give a reason for something you have said **yoksa, aksi takdirde/hâlde** *She must love him or she wouldn't have stayed with him all these years.* **4** [NOT EITHER] used after a negative verb between a list of things to mean not any of those things or people **veya...de** *Tim doesn't eat meat or fish.*

oral¹ /'ɔːrᵊl/ *adjective* **1** spoken **sözlü** *an oral examination* ○ *an oral agreement* **2** relating to or using the mouth **ağızdan söylenen, şifahi** *oral medication* • **orally** *adverb* **sözel olarak**

oral² /'ɔːrᵊl/ *noun* [C] an examination that is spoken, usually in a foreign language **sözlü sınav**

orange¹ /'ɒrɪndʒ/ *adjective* being a colour that is a mixture of red and yellow **turuncu rengi, portakal renginde** *a deep orange sunset* ⊃Orta kısımdaki renkli sayfalarına bakınız.

orange² /'ɒrɪndʒ/ *noun* **1** [FRUIT] [C] a round, sweet fruit with a thick skin and a centre that is divided into many equal parts **portakal** *orange juice* ⊃Orta kısımdaki renkli sayfalarına bakınız. **2** [COLOUR] [C, U] a colour that is a mixture of red and yellow **turuncu, portakal rengi** ⊃Orta kısımdaki renkli sayfalarına bakınız. **3** [DRINK] [U] *UK* a drink made with oranges **portakallı içecek** *Would you like some orange?*

'orange juice *noun* [U] a drink made from the juice of oranges **portakal suyu**

orator /'ɒrətər/ *noun* [C] *formal* someone who gives good speeches **hatip** *a brilliant orator*

oratory /'ɒrətᵊri/ *noun* [U] *formal* when people give good speeches **hatiplik, belagat** *political oratory*

orbit /'ɔːbɪt/ *noun* [C, U] the circular journey that a spacecraft or planet makes around the sun, the moon, or another planet **yörünge** *the Earth's orbit* ○ *Two satellites are already in orbit.* ○ *It was the first spacecraft to go into orbit around Jupiter.* • **orbit** *verb* [I, T] *The moon orbits the Earth.* **yörüngede dönmek**

orchard /'ɔːtʃəd/ *noun* [C] a piece of land where fruit trees are grown **meyve bahçesi** *an apple/cherry orchard*

orchestra /'ɔːkɪstrə/ *noun* [C] **1** a large group of musicians who play different instruments together **orkestra, müzik topluluğu** *a symphony orchestra* ○ *a youth orchestra* **2** *US* (*UK* the stalls) the seats on the main floor near the front of a theatre or cinema **sinema ve tiyatroda sahneye yakın koltuklar** • **orchestral** /ɔː'kestrᵊl/ *adjective* [always before noun] Orchestral music is played by or written for an orchestra. **orkestra tarafından çalınmak için yazılmış**

orchestrate /'ɔːkɪstreɪt/ *verb* [T] to intentionally organize something in order to achieve what you want **titiz-**

likle düzenlemek; başarmak için özenle yapmak *a carefully orchestrated demonstration of support*

orchid /ˈɔːkɪd/ *noun* [C] a plant with flowers which are an unusual shape and beautiful colours **orkide**

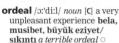
orchid

ordain /ɔːˈdeɪn/ *verb* [T] to officially make someone a Christian priest **kilise görevlisi/papaz olarak atamak/atanmak** [often passive] *Dr Coker was ordained by the Bishop of London in 1986.*

ordeal /ɔːˈdiːl/ *noun* [C] a very unpleasant experience **bela, musibet, büyük eziyet/sıkıntı** *a terrible ordeal* ○ *They feared he would not survive the ordeal.* ○ *She went through the ordeal of being interviewed by a panel of ten people.*

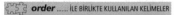
order ...... İLE BİRLİKTE KULLANILAN KELİMELER

follow/give/ignore/issue/obey orders ● **clear/strict** orders

o⌐**order**[1] /ˈɔːdəʳ/ *noun* 1 [ARRANGEMENT] [C, U] the arrangement of a group of people or things in a list from first to last **sıra, düzen** *in alphabetical order* ○ *in the right/wrong order* ○ *We ranked the tasks in order of importance.* 2 [INSTRUCTION] [C] an instruction that someone must obey **talimat, emir, direktif** *to obey orders* ○ *to give orders* 3 **under orders** If you are under orders, someone has told you to do something. **emir altında, emir almış, emredilmiş** [+ to do sth] *Team members are under orders to behave well.* ○ *They claimed they were under orders from the president.* 4 [REQUEST] [C] a request for food or goods in return for payment **sipariş, ısmarlama** *Can I take your order now?* 5 [TIDINESS] [U] a situation in which everything is in its correct place **tertip, düzen, biçim** *It's nice to see some order around here for a change.* ○ *I want to put all my things in order before I go away.* ⊃Opposite **disorder.** 6 **out of order a** [MACHINE] If a machine or system is out of order, it is not working as it should. **bozuk, çalışmaz, işlemiyor, çalışmıyor** *The coffee machine's out of order.* **b** [BEHAVIOUR] If someone's behaviour is out of order, it is not acceptable. **yakışıksız, yersiz, usule aykırı, usulsüz** *What he did was completely out of order.* 7 **in order to do/for sth to do sth** with the purpose of achieving something ...**mak/mek için** *She worked all summer in order to save enough money for a holiday.* 8 [NO TROUBLE] [U] a situation in which people obey laws and there is no trouble **düzen, intizam, asayiş, dirlik** *The army was brought in to restore order to the troubled province.* ⊃Opposite **disorder.** 9 **economic/political/social order** the way that the economy, politics, or society is organized **ekonomik/siyasi/sosyal düzen/nizam** *a threat to the established social order* 10 [GROUP] [C] a religious group who live together and have the same rules **tarikat, mezhep** *an order of nuns* ○ *a monastic order* ⊃See also: **mail order, postal order, standing order.**

o⌐**order**[2] /ˈɔːdəʳ/ *verb* 1 [TELL] [T] to give someone an instruction that they must obey **emretmek, emir vermek; direktif vermek; istemek, buyurmak** [+ to do sth] *He ordered them to leave.* 2 [REQUEST] [I, T] to ask for food, goods, etc **sipariş vermek/etmek, ısmarlamak** *to order a drink/pizza* ○ *to order tickets* ○ *We've ordered new lights for the kitchen.* ○ [+ two objects] *Can I order you a drink?* 3 [ARRANGE] [T] to arrange a group of people or things in a list from first to last **sıraya koymak,**

düzenlemek, liste yapmak; listelemek *Have you ordered the pages correctly?*

order sb about/around *phrasal verb* to tell someone what they should do all the time **emirler yağdırmak; talimatlar vermek** *You can't just come in here and start ordering people around.*

orderly[1] /ˈɔːdəli/ *adjective* tidy or organized **muntazam, düzenli, tertipli, sistemli** *an orderly pile* ○ *Please form an orderly queue.* ⊃Opposite **disorderly.**

orderly[2] /ˈɔːdəli/ *noun* [C] a hospital worker who has no special skills or training **hastane hademesi**

ordinal number /ˌɔːdɪnˈəl ˈnʌmbəʳ/ (*also* **ordinal**) *noun* [C] a number such as 1st, 2nd, 3rd, etc that shows the order of things in a list **sıra sayısı**

ordinance /ˈɔːdɪnəns/ *noun* [C] *mainly US* a law or rule which limits or controls something **yasa, yönetmelik** *a tax ordinance*

ordinarily /ˈɔːdɪnˈərəli/ *adverb* usually **genellikle, umumiyetle, normal olarak** *These are people who would not ordinarily carry guns.*

o⌐**ordinary** /ˈɔːdɪnʳri/ *adjective* 1 not special, different, or unusual in any way **normal, orta, vasat, özelliği olmayan** *ordinary life* ○ *an ordinary day* ○ *I had a very ordinary childhood.* 2 Ordinary people are not rich or famous and do not have special skills. **sıradan, vasat, orta direk, orta halli; hiçbir meziyeti olmayan** *ordinary people/citizens* ○ *an ordinary man/woman* 3 **out of the ordinary** unusual or different **görülmemiş, olağanüstü, fevkalade, müstesna** *Their relationship was a little out of the ordinary.* ○ *The investigation revealed nothing out of the ordinary.*

ore /ɔːʳ/ *noun* [U] rock or soil from which metal can be obtained **cevher, maden filizi/cevheri** *iron ore*

.org /dɒtˈɔːg/ *internet abbreviation for* organization: used in some Internet addresses **internet adreslerinde 'kurum/kuruluş' anlamında kısaltılmış uzantı** *You can search Cambridge dictionaries online at www. dictionary.cambridge.org*

organ /ˈɔːgən/ *noun* [C] 1 a part of an animal or plant that has a special purpose **belli amaç taşıyan hayvan/bitki organı/uzvu** *reproductive/sexual organs* ○ *The liver is a vital organ* (= you need it to stay alive). ○ *an organ donor/transplant* 2 a large musical instrument that has keys like a piano and produces different notes when air is blown through pipes of different lengths **org** *a church organ*

organic /ɔːˈɡænɪk/ *adjective* 1 [FARMING] not using artificial chemicals when keeping animals or growing plants for food **suni kimyasallar kullanmayan; organik; doğal; hormonsuz** *organic farming/farmers* ○ *organic food/vegetables* 2 [CHEMISTRY] In chemistry, 'organic' describes chemicals that contain carbon. **kimyada karbon ihtiva eden kimyasallar; organik** *organic compounds* 3 [LIVING] from a living organism **canlı organizmadan olan; canlı, organik** *organic matter/material* ⊃Opposite **inorganic.** ● **organically** *adverb* **organik bir şekilde** *organically grown* vegetables

organism /ˈɔːgənɪzəm/ *noun* [C] a living thing, often one that is extremely small **organizma** *Plants, animals, bacteria, and viruses are organisms.*

organist /ˈɔːgənɪst/ *noun* [C] someone who plays the organ (= an instrument like a piano) **orgcu, org çalan kimse** *a church organist*

organization ...... İLE BİRLİKTE KULLANILAN KELİMELER

a **charitable/international/voluntary** organization ● **join/set up** an organization

○***organization** (*also UK* **-isation**) /ˌɔːgᵊnaɪˈzeɪʃᵊn/ *noun*
1 [GROUP] [C] an official group of people who work together for the same purpose **teşkilat, kurum, kuruluş, yapı, bünye** *a charitable/voluntary organization* **2** [ARRANGEMENT] [U] the way that parts of something are arranged **düzenleme, tertip, teşkil** *Better organization of the office would improve efficiency.* **3** [PLAN] [U] the planning of an activity or event **düzenleme, organizasyon** *Who was responsible for the organization of the conference?* ● **organizational** *adjective* **organizational skills örgütsel, kurumsal**

○***organize** (*also UK* **-ise**) /ˈɔːgᵊnaɪz/ *verb* [T] to plan or arrange something **planlamak, düzenlemek, tertiplemek, hazırlamak** *to organize a meeting/wedding*

organized (*also UK* **-ised**) /ˈɔːgᵊnaɪzd/ *adjective* **1** An organized person plans things well and does not waste time or effort. **düzenli, tertipli, planlı, organize** ⊃Opposite **disorganized. 2** [always before noun] involving a group of people who have planned to do something together **düzenli, tertipli, organize, örgütlenmiş** *organized crime/religion* ⊃See also: **well-organized.**

organizer (*also UK* **-iser**) /ˈɔːgᵊnaɪzəʳ/ *noun* [C] someone who plans an event or activity **düzenleyici, düzenleyen, organizatör** *conference/exhibition organizers*

orgasm /ˈɔːgæzᵊm/ *noun* [C, U] the time of greatest pleasure and excitement during sex **sekste doyuma ulaşma, cinsel doyum, orgazm** *to have an orgasm*

orgy /ˈɔːdʒi/ *noun* [C] **1** a noisy party at which people have a lot of sex, alcohol, or illegal drugs (**seks, uyuşturcu, alkol bulunan) çılgın parti 2 an orgy of sth** a period when there is too much of an often bad activity **aşırılık, ifrat** *an orgy of destruction*

Oriental /ˌɔːriˈentᵊl/ *adjective* relating or belonging to the countries of east Asia **Doğu Asya ülkelerine ait** *Oriental art*

orientated /ˈɔːriᵊnteɪtɪd/ *UK* (*UK/US* **oriented**) *adjective* directed towards or interested in something **yönelik, meyilli, yönelmiş**

orientation /ˌɔːriᵊnˈteɪʃᵊn/ *noun* **1** [C, U] the type of beliefs that a person has **inanç, inanış** *He's very secretive about his political orientation.* **2** [U] training or preparation for a new job or activity **oryantasyon; yeni işe alışma; giriş eğitimi** *an orientation session*

oriented /ˈɔːriᵊntɪd/ *(also UK* **orientated**) *adjective* directed towards or interested in something **yönelik, meyilli, yönelmiş** *His new TV series is oriented towards teenage viewers.* ○ *He's very family oriented.*

the Orient /ˈɔːriᵊnt/ *noun old-fashioned* the countries of east Asia **Doğu Asya ülkeleri**

▨▨▨ **origin** .... İLE BİRLİKTE KULLANILAN KELİMELER

sth has its origins in sth ● the origin(s) of sth ● be [Chinese/French, etc] in origin

origin /ˈɒrɪdʒɪn/ *noun* [C, U] **1** the cause of something, or where something begins or comes from **kaynak, köken, başlangıç** *the origin of the universe* ○ *This dish is Greek in origin.* **2** the country, race, or social class of a person's family **asıl, soy, köken, kök** *ethnic origin* ○ *She's of Irish origin.*

○***original**¹ /əˈrɪdʒᵊnᵊl/ *adjective* **1** special and interesting because of not being the same as others **özgün, tek, kendine özgü, özel ve ilginç** *Her essay was full of original ideas.* ○ *He's a highly original thinker.* **2** [always before noun] existing since the beginning, or being the earliest form of something **orijinal, kendine has, özgün, yeni** *His original plan was to stay for a week, but he ended up staying for a month.* ○ *Do you still have the original version of this document?*

original² /əˈrɪdʒᵊnᵊl/ *noun* [C] something that is in the form in which it was first created and has not been copied or changed **ilk, asıl, eski, orijinal** *If the painting were an original, it would be very valuable.*

originality /əˌrɪdʒᵊnˈæləti/ *noun* [U] the quality of being interesting and different from everyone or everything else **özgünlük, gerçeklik, farklılık, orijinallik** *The judges were impressed by the originality of his work.*

○***originally** /əˈrɪdʒᵊnᵊli/ *adverb* at the beginning or before any changes **başlangıçta, aslında, aslen; özgün olarak** *The bathroom was originally a bedroom.*

originate /əˈrɪdʒᵊneɪt/ *verb* [I] **originate from/in/with, etc** to come from a particular place or person, or to begin during a particular period **...dan/de/ile başlamak; kaynaklanmak, çıkmak, başlamak** *Citrus fruits originated in China and Southeast Asia.*

originator /əˈrɪdʒᵊneɪtəʳ/ *noun* [C] *formal* The originator of an idea is the person who first thought of it. **ilk ortaya atan/koyan, yaratıcı**

ornament /ˈɔːnəmənt/ *noun* [C] an attractive object that is used as a decoration in a home or garden **süs, süs eşyası, biblo** ⊃Orta kısımdaki renkli sayfalarına bakınız.

ornamental /ˌɔːnəˈmentᵊl/ *adjective* used for decoration and having no other purpose **süsleyici, süs olarak kullanılan**

ornate /ɔːˈneɪt/ *adjective* decorated with a lot of complicated patterns **süslü, süslü püslü, şatafatlı** *ornate wooden doors*

ornithology /ˌɔːnɪˈθɒlədʒi/ *noun* [U] the scientific study of birds **kuş bilimi, ornitoloji** ● **ornithologist** *noun* [C] a scientist who studies birds **kuş bilimci, ornitolojist**

orphan¹ /ˈɔːfᵊn/ *noun* [C] **1** a child whose parents are dead **öksüz, yetim 2** in printing, the first line of a paragraph, separated from the rest which is on the next page

orphan² /ˈɔːfᵊn/ *verb* **be orphaned** When a child is orphaned, both their parents die. **öksüz/yetim kalmak/olmak** *She was orphaned at the age of six.*

orphanage /ˈɔːfᵊnɪdʒ/ *noun* [C] a home for children whose parents are dead **öksüzler yurdu; yetimhane**

orthodox /ˈɔːθədɒks/ *adjective* **1** keeping the traditional beliefs and customs of Judaism or some types of Christianity **sofu, dindar, sıkı sıkıya eskiye bağlı, ortodoks** *an orthodox Jewish family* ○ *the Russian/Greek Orthodox Church* **2** If ideas or methods are orthodox, most people think they are correct, usually because they have existed for a long time. **geçerli, yaygın, alışılmış, herkesçe kabul gören; alışılmış, geleneksel** *orthodox medicine* ⊃Opposite **unorthodox.**

orthodoxy /ˈɔːθədɒksi/ *noun* [C, U] *formal* an idea of a society, religion, political party, or subject that most people believe is correct, or a set of such ideas **geleneksel/yerleşik/yaygın kabul gören inanış/fikir**

orthopaedic *UK* (*US* **orthopedic**) /ˌɔːθəˈpiːdɪk/ *adjective* [always before noun] relating to the treatment or study of bones that have been injured or have not grown correctly **ortopedik** *an orthopaedic surgeon*

Oscar /ˈɒskəʳ/ *noun* [C] *trademark* one of several prizes given to actors and people who make films every year in Hollywood in the US **Oskar Ödülü** *Who won the Oscar for best actress this year?*

oscillate /ˈɒsɪleɪt/ *verb* [I] *formal* to move repeatedly between two positions or opinions **sallanmak, salınmak; bocalamak, tereddüt etmek, kararsız kalmak** *an oscillating fan* ○ *The story oscillates between* *comedy and tragedy.* ● **oscillation** /ˌɒsɪˈleɪʃᵊn/ *noun* [C, U] duraksama, gidip gelme

ostensibly /ɒsˈtensɪbli/ *adverb* If something is ostensibly the reason for something else, people say it is the reason, although you do not believe it. görünüşe bakılırsa; görünüş olarak; sözde olarak; zahirî bir şekilde *He was discharged from the army, ostensibly for medical reasons.*

ostentatious /ˌɒstenˈteɪʃəs/ *adjective* intended to attract attention or admiration, often by showing money or power gösterişli, görkemli, göz alıcı, gösteriş meraklısı *an ostentatious display of wealth* ● **ostentatiously** *adverb* şatafatlı bir şekilde

osteopath /ˈɒstiəʊpæθ/ *noun* [C] someone who treats injuries to bones and muscles by moving and rubbing them kırık çıkıkçı ● **osteopathy** *noun* [C] osteopati

osteoporosis /ˌɒstiəʊpəˈrəʊsɪs/ *noun* [U] a disease which makes bones weak and makes them break easily kemik erimesi hastalığı

ostracize (*also UK* -ise) /ˈɒstrəsaɪz/ *verb* [T] When a group of people ostracizes someone, they refuse to talk to or do things with that person. dışlamak, toplum dışına itmek; afaroz etmek; toplu tepki koymak [often passive] *He was ostracized by the other children at school.*

ostrich /ˈɒstrɪtʃ/ *noun* [C] a very large bird from Africa which cannot fly but can run very fast devekuşu

ostrich

o-* **other**¹ /ˈʌðəʳ/ *adjective, determiner* 1 MORE used to refer to people or things which are similar to or in addition to those you have talked about diğer, başka, diğeri, öteki *I don't like custard - do you have any other desserts?* ○ *I don't think he's funny, but other people do.* 2 PART OF SET used to talk about the remaining members of a group or items in a set diğer, öbür, öteki/ötekiler *Mario and Anna sat down to watch the other dancers.* ○ *I found one shoe - have you seen the other one?* 3 DIFFERENT different from a thing or person which you have talked about başka, diğer *Ask me some other time, when I'm not so busy.* 4 **the other side/end (of sth)** the opposite side/end of something bir şeyin diğer yanı/öbür ucu vs. *Our house is on the other side of town.* 5 **the other day/week, etc** used to mean recently, without giving a particular date geçen gün/hafta *I asked Kevin about it just the other day.* 6 **every other day/week, etc** happening one day/week, etc but not the next gün aşırı, hafta aşırı *Alice goes to the gym every other day.* 7 **other than** except ...dan/den başka; ...ın/in dışında; hariç; bunun dışında *The form cannot be signed by anyone other than the child's parent.* ○ [+ to do sth] *They had no choice other than to surrender.* 8 **other than that** *informal* except for the thing you have just said bundan başka; bundan manada; bunu dikkate almazsak/saymazsak *My arm was a bit sore - other than that I was fine.*

o-* **other**² /ˈʌðəʳ/ *pronoun* 1 used to refer to a person or thing which belongs to a group or set that you have already talked about diğeri, diğerinde, ötekine, ötekinde *Hold the racket in one hand, and the ball in the other.* ○ *Some of the pieces were damaged, others were missing.* 2 **others** used to refer to people or things that are similar to people or things you have already talked

about başka *This is broken - do you have any others?* ➔See also: each other.

o-* **others** /ˈʌðəz/ *pronoun* [plural] other people başkaları; ötekileri, diğerleri *Don't expect others to do your work for you.*

otherwise¹ /ˈʌðəwaɪz/ *adverb* 1 except for what has just been referred to yoksa; ...nın/nin dışında *She hurt her arm in the accident, but otherwise she was fine.* 2 different to what has just been stated başka türlü; ... dan/den farklı *I'll meet you there at 6 o'clock unless I hear otherwise.* ○ *I'd like to help you with any problems, financial or otherwise.*

otherwise² /ˈʌðəwaɪz/ *conjunction* used when saying what will happen if someone does not obey an order or do what has been suggested aksi takdirde, yoksa *You'd better phone home, otherwise your parents will start to worry.*

otter /ˈɒtəʳ/ *noun* [C] a small animal with short, brown fur and a long body that swims well and eats fish su samuru

ouch /aʊtʃ/ *exclamation* something you say when you experience sudden physical pain 'Ah!', 'Uff!', 'Aman!', 'Off!' *Ouch! This radiator's really hot.*

o-* **ought** /ɔːt/ *modal verb* 1 **ought to do sth** used to say or ask what is the correct or best thing to do ...malı/meli; yapılması gereken doğru ve en iyi olanı söylemek; istemek için kullanılır *You ought to see a doctor.* ○ *He ought to have told her the truth.* ○ *Ought I to phone her?* 2 **ought to be/do sth** used to say that you expect something to be true or that you expect something to happen ...olmalı/yapılmalı; bir şeyin doğru olduğunu/olmasının beklendiğini belirtmek için kullanılır *He ought to pass the exam this time.* ➔See study box Modal verbs on page Centre 22.

oughtn't /ˈɔːtᵊnt/ *formal short for* ought not 'ought not' yardımcı fiil yapısını kısa yazılışı *He oughtn't to have shouted at us.*

ounce /aʊns/ *noun* 1 [C] (*written abbreviation* oz) a unit for measuring weight, equal to 28.35 grams 28.35 grama eşit bir tür ağırlık ölçüm birimi; ons ➔See study page Measurements on page Centre 31. ➔See also: fluid ounce. 2 **not have an ounce of sth** to not have any of a quality or emotion zerre kadar kalite ve duyguya sahip olmamak *His new novel doesn't have an ounce of originality.* 3 **every ounce of sth** all of a quality or emotion that is available mevcut tüm duygu ve kalitesi *He deserves every ounce of support that we can give him.*

o-* **our** /aʊəʳ/ *determiner* belonging to or relating to the person who is speaking and one or more other people bizim, bizlerin *Janice is our youngest daughter.*

o-* **ours** /aʊəz/ *pronoun* the things that belong or relate to the person who is speaking and one or more other people bizimki, bizimkiler *Matt's a friend of ours.* ○ *That's their problem - not ours.*

o-* **ourselves** /ˌaʊəˈselvz/ *pronoun* 1 the reflexive form of the pronoun 'we' kendimizi, kendimize *We've promised ourselves a holiday abroad this year.* 2 used for emphasis with the pronoun 'we' or when referring to yourself and at least one other person biz, kendimiz *John and I arranged the wedding reception ourselves.* 3 **(all) by ourselves** alone or without anyone else's help kendimiz, kendi başımıza *It's a big garden but we manage to look after it by ourselves.* 4 **(all) to ourselves** for our use only sadece bize, kendimize *We arrived early and had the swimming pool all to ourselves.*

oust /aʊst/ *verb* [T] to force someone to leave a position of power or responsibility atmak, kovmak, defetmek;

görevden el çektirmek [often passive] *He was ousted from power by a military coup.*

✿**out¹** /aʊt/ *adjective, adverb* **1** [AWAY FROM] used to show movement away from the inside of a place or container **dışarı, dışarıya** *He dropped the bag and all the apples fell out.* ○ *She opened the window and stuck her head out.* **2** [OUTSIDE] outside a building or room **dışarda, dışında, açık havada** *Would you like to wait out here?* ○ *It's bitterly cold out today.* **3** [NOT THERE] not in the place where you usually live or work, especially for a short time **yerinde değil, dışarda** *I came round to see you this morning but you were out.* **4** [FIRE/LIGHT] A fire or light that is out is not burning or shining. **(ateş, ışık) yanmıyor, sönmüş, parlamıyor** *Bring some more wood, the fire's gone out.* **5** [AVAILABLE] available to buy or see **gösterimde, satışta, sunulma, çıkma** *When's the new Spielberg film out?* **6** [FASHION] no longer fashionable or popular **moda olmayan, eskisi gibi popüler değil** *Trousers like that went out years ago.* **7** [NOT ACCURATE] not accurate **doğru değil, yanlış, hatalı, eksik** *Your figures are out by £300.* **8** [GAME] no longer able to play or take part in a game or competition **yarış/yarışma/ oyun dışı kalma** *Two of the best players were out after ten minutes.* **9** [APPEAR] able to be seen **ortaya çıkma, gözükme, doğma, yükselme** *After a few minutes the sun came out.* **10** [NOT POSSIBLE] not possible or not acceptable **mümkün olmama, kabul görmeme** *Next weekend is out because we're going away.* **11 be out of sth** to have no more of something left **bit(ir)mek, tükenmek, tüketmek** *We're nearly out of petrol.* **12 be out for sth; be out to do sth** to intend to do something, especially for an unpleasant reason **istemeyerek bir şeyi yapma niyetinde olmak** *He's only out to impress the boss.* ⊃See also: **out of**.

out² /aʊt/ *verb* [T] to report to the public the secret that someone is homosexual **birinin eşcinsel olduğunu topluma ilan etmek/rapor etmek** [often passive] *He was outed by a tabloid newspaper.*

out- /aʊt-/ *prefix* more than or better than **daha fazla/ iyi anlamında önek** *to outgrow something* ○ *to outnumber* (= to outdo someone (= to show that you are better than someone)

out-and-out /ˌaʊtˈnˈaʊt/ *adjective* [always before noun] complete or in every way **tam, tamamen, her şekilde, katıksız** *an out-and-out lie*

the outback /ˈaʊtbæk/ *noun* the areas of Australia where few people live, especially the central desert areas **Avustralya'nın ortalarında çok az insanının yaşadığı çoğunluğu çöl ıssız/ücra bölge; kuş uçmaz kervan geçmez yer/bölge**

outbid /ˌaʊtˈbɪd/ *verb* [T] outbidding, *past* outbid to offer to pay more for something than someone else **daha fazla fiyat teklifi vermek** *She had to outbid two rivals to buy the business.*

out-box /ˈaʊtbɒks/ (outbox) *noun* [C] **1** the place on a computer which keeps copies of email messages which you have sent **bilgisayarda gönderilen iletilerin saklandığı yer/kutucuk 2** US (UK out-tray) a container where you keep letters and documents that you want to send to someone else **gönderilecek mektup ve belgelerin konulduğu/tutulduğu yer/kutu**

outbreak /ˈaʊtbreɪk/ *noun* [C] when something unpleasant and difficult to control starts, such as a war or disease **patlak verme, ortaya çıkma, baş gösterme** *an outbreak of flu/fighting*

outburst /ˈaʊtbɜːst/ *noun* [C] a sudden, forceful expression of emotion in words or actions **galeyana gelme, taşkınlık, feveran, aniden öfkelenme** *an angry outburst*

outcast /ˈaʊtkɑːst/ *noun* [C] someone who is not accepted by society because they are different to most other people **toplumdan dışlanmış kişi** *a social outcast*

🧩 **outcome** ...... İLE BİRLİKTE KULLANILAN KELİMELER

announce/await/determine the outcome ● the **eventual/final** outcome ● the outcome **of** sth

outcome /ˈaʊtkʌm/ *noun* [C] the final result of an activity or process **son, sonuç, netice, akıbet** *the outcome of an election*

outcrop /ˈaʊtkrɒp/ (also US outcropping) *noun* [C] a rock or group of rocks that sticks out above the surface of the ground **toprağın üstüne çıkan kaya ve kaya tabakası; kayalık alan** *a rocky outcrop*

🧩 **outcry** ...... İLE BİRLİKTE KULLANILAN KELİMELER

cause/provoke/spark an outcry ● an **international/national/public** outcry ● an outcry **against/ over** sth

outcry /ˈaʊtkraɪ/ *noun* [C] a strong public expression of anger and disapproval about a recent event or decision **toplumsal tepki, toplu feryat/çığlık, itiraz, protesto, şikâyet, bağırıp çağırma** *There has been a public outcry against the new road.*

outdated /ˌaʊtˈdeɪtɪd/ *adjective* not modern enough **modası geçmiş, artık kullanılmayan** *outdated equipment* ○ *an outdated idea*

outdo /ˌaʊtˈduː/ *verb* [T] *past tense* outdid, *past participle* outdone to do something better than someone else ... **dan/den daha iyi yapmak/olmak; geçmek; yenmek** *They are always trying to outdo each other with their jokes and funny stories.*

outdoor /ˌaʊtˈdɔːʳ/ *adjective* [always before noun] happening, used, or in a place that is outside and not inside a building **açık havada yapılan/olan; açıkta olan; dışarda yapılan** *outdoor activities* ○ *an outdoor concert* ○ *an outdoor swimming pool* ○ *outdoor clothing* ⊃Opposite indoor.

outdoors /ˌaʊtˈdɔːz/ *adverb* not inside a building **dışarda, açık havada** *If it's warm this evening, we could eat outdoors.* ⊃Opposite indoors.

the outdoors /ˌaʊtˈdɔːz/ *noun* countryside **kır, kırsal alan/bölge; şehir dışı** *He enjoys hunting, fishing, and the outdoors.*

outer /ˈaʊtəʳ/ *adjective* [always before noun] on the edge or surface of something **dış, dıştaki** *Remove the outer layers of the onion.* ⊃Opposite inner.

ˌouter ˈspace *noun* [U] the universe outside the Earth and its gases where other planets and stars are **uzay derinliği, atmosfer dışı, göklerin ötesi, uzay boşluğu**

the outfield /ˈaʊtfiːld/ *noun* the outer area of the playing field in sports such as cricket and baseball **kriket ve beyzbolda oyun sahası dışındaki alan; saha dışı, alan dışı** ● **outfielder** *noun* [C] a baseball player who stands in the outfield **saha dışında bekleyen beyzbol oyuncusu**

outfit¹ /ˈaʊtfɪt/ *noun* [C] **1** a set of clothes for a particular event or activity **(belirli amaçlar için) giysiler, elbiseler** *a cowboy outfit* **2** *informal* an organization, company, or any group of people who work together **takım, ekip, grup, kuruluş, şirket, teşkilat**

outfit² /ˈaʊtfɪt/ *verb* [T] outfitting, *past* outfitted US to provide equipment for something **malzeme/gereç temin etmek** [often passive] *My hotel room was small and outfitted with cheap wooden furniture.*

outgoing /ˌaʊtˈgəʊɪŋ/ ⓤⓢ /ˈaʊtgəʊɪŋ/ *adjective* **1** [FRIENDLY] Someone who is outgoing is friendly, talks a lot, and enjoys meeting people. **dost canlısı, cana yakın,**

sıcakkanlı, sempatik, hoş, kolay iletişim kurulabilen **2** LEAVING POWER [always before noun] leaving a position of power or responsibility **ayrılan; terk eden; çekilen, gidecek olan** *the outgoing president* **3** LEAVING A PLACE [always before noun] going to another place **başka bir yere giden; çıkan, gönderilen, iletilen, aktarılan** *outgoing calls/messages*

outgoings /'aʊtˌgəʊɪŋz/ *noun* [plural] *UK* money that you have to spend on rent, food, etc **harcama**

outgrow /ˌaʊt'grəʊ/ *verb* [T] *past tense* **outgrew,** *past participle* **outgrown 1** to grow too big for something **büyüdüğü için üzerine olmamak; küçülmek** *He's already outgrown these shoes.* **2** to develop so that something is not now suitable **büyümek/gelişmek ve mevcut konumuna uymamak; büyümek/gelişmek** *She's outgrown her current job and needs a new challenge.*

outing /'aʊtɪŋ/ *noun* **1** [C] when a group of people go on a short journey for pleasure or education **gezi, gezinti, kısa seyahat** *a family/school outing* ∘ *to go on an outing* **2** [U] when someone says publicly that someone else is homosexual **bir kimsenin eşcinsel olduğunu toplumna ilanı/duyurusu/açıklanması**

outlandish /ˌaʊt'lændɪʃ/ *adjective* very strange and unusual **çok garip, acayip, tuhaf, alışılmamış** *an outlandish story/idea* ∘ *outlandish behaviour/clothes*

outlast /ˌaʊt'lɑːst/ *verb* [T] to continue for longer than someone or something else **...dan/den daha uzun süre devam etmek/dayanmak/sürmek/ömürlü olmak**

outlaw¹ /'aʊtlɔː/ *verb* [T] to make something officially illegal **yasakla(n)mak; kanun dışı ilan etmek** *I think all handguns should be outlawed.*

outlaw² /'aʊtlɔː/ *noun* [C] *old-fashioned* a criminal **kanun kaçağı** *a dangerous outlaw*

outlay /'aʊtleɪ/ *noun* [C] an amount of money spent by a business or government **harcamalar, giderler, masraflar** *The project requires an initial outlay of $450,000.*

outlet /'aʊtlet/ *noun* [C] **1** SHOP In business, an outlet is a shop that sells one type of product or the products of one company. **tek tip ürüne dayalı fabrika satış mağazası 2** CHEAP SHOP *US* a shop that sells goods for a lower price than usual **indirim mağazası 3** EXPRESS a way for someone to express an emotion, idea, or ability **gösterecek/çıkış olabilecek olan şey; kindini/fikirlerini/duygularını anlatma/ifade etme** *She needs a job that will provide an outlet for her creative talent.* **4** WAY OUT a place where a liquid or gas can flow out of something **çıkış yeri, delik, ağız 5** CONNECTION *US* a place where you can connect a wire on a piece of electrical equipment **elektrik prizi; fişin takıldığı yer** *an electrical outlet*

outline¹ /'aʊtlaɪn/ *verb* [T] to describe only the most important ideas or facts about something **ana hatlarını açıklamak** *He outlined the department's plans for next year.*

outline² /'aʊtlaɪn/ *noun* [C] **1** a short description of the most important ideas or facts about something **kısa açıklama/tanım, taslak, ana hatlar** *He gave us a brief outline of the town's history.* **2** the shape made by the outside edge of something **silüet**

outlive /ˌaʊt'lɪv/ *verb* [T] to continue living or existing after someone or something else has died or stopped existing **...nın/nin ölümünden/yok olmasından sonra yaşamaya/var olmaya devam etmek; yaşamını sürdürmek** *She outlived both her children.*

outlook /'aʊtlʊk/ *noun* **1** [no plural] the likely future situation **muhtemel geleceği, genel gidişatı; genel görüntüsü** *The outlook for the economy next year is bleak.* **2** [C] the way a person thinks about something

hayata bakışı *Despite her illness, she has a very positive outlook on life.*

outlying /'aʊtˌlaɪŋ/ *adjective* [always before noun] far from towns and cities, or far from the centre of a place **çok uzak, çok uzaktaki** *outlying farms/villages*

outmanoeuvre *UK* (*US* **outmaneuver**) /ˌaʊtmə'nuːvəʳ/ *verb* [T] to do something clever that gives you an advantage over someone you are competing against **rakibini zekice bir manevrayla geçmek, alt etmek; ustalıkla bertaraf etmek** *She outmanoeuvred her opponents throughout the election campaign.*

outmoded /ˌaʊt'məʊdɪd/ *adjective* not modern enough **yeterince güncel olmayan, modası geçmiş, eski** *outmoded equipment*

outnumber /ˌaʊt'nʌmbəʳ/ *verb* [T] to be larger in number than another group **sayıca üstün olmak, sayı olarak geçmek** *Women now far outnumber men on language courses.*

out of /aʊt əv/ *preposition* **1** AWAY FROM used to show movement away from the inside of a place or container **dışında, dışına, sarkan, çıkan** *A bunch of keys fell out of her bag.* ∘ *She stepped out of the car and walked towards me.* **2** NO LONGER IN no longer in a place or situation **dışarda, orada değil, uzakta; ...da/de olmamak** *He's out of the country until next month.* ∘ *I've been out of work for the past year.* **3** MADE FROM used to show what something is made from **...dan/den yapılmış/üretilmiş/meydana getirilmiş** *The statue was carved out of a single block of stone.* **4** BECAUSE OF used to show the reason why someone does something **...dan/den dolayı, sebebiyle, gerkeçesiyle, nedeniyle; yüzü suyu hürmetine** *I only gave her the job out of pity.* **5** FROM AMONG from among an amount or number **...dan/den...sı/si** *Nine out of ten people said they preferred it.* **6** NOT INVOLVED no longer involved in something **dışında, artık orada olmayan, artık yer almayan** *He missed the practice session and now he's out of the team.*

out-of-court /ˌaʊtəv'kɔːt/ *adjective* [always before noun] agreed without involving a law court **mahkemeye gitmeden uzlaşılan; yargılama olmaksızın çözülen** *an out-of-court settlement*

out-of-date /ˌaʊtəv'deɪt/ *adjective* old and not useful or correct any more **modası geçmiş, eski, güncel olmayan, çağ dışı** *I do have a road map but I think it's out-of-date.*

out-of-town /ˌaʊtəv'taʊn/ *adjective* [always before noun] positioned or happening in the countryside or on the edge of a town **şehir dışında olan, kırsal bölgede bulunan/olan** *an out-of-town supermarket*

outpace /ˌaʊt'peɪs/ *verb* [T] to move or develop more quickly than someone or something else **çok daha hızlı ilerlemek/gelişme kaydetmek**

outpatient /'aʊtˌpeɪʃᵊnt/ *noun* [C] someone who is treated in a hospital but does not sleep there at night **ayakta tedavi gören hasta**

outperform /ˌaʊtpə'fɔːm/ *verb* [T] to do something better than someone or something else **...dan/den daha üstün başarı göstermek/daha iyi/mükemmel yapmak** *Girls are consistently outperforming boys at school.*

outplay /ˌaʊt'pleɪ/ *verb* [T] to play a game or sport better than another player or team **...dan/den daha iyi oynamak/daha başarılı bir oyun ortaya koymak**

outpost /'aʊtpəʊst/ *noun* [C] a small place that is far from large towns or cities, often where a government or company is represented **(hükümet, şirket) şehir dışındaki hizmet birimi/daha küçük idare merkezi**

outpouring /'aʊtˌpɔːrɪŋ/ *noun* [C] when an emotion is expressed a lot in public **içini dökme, açılma, duygularını dışa vurma; insanlar önünde duygularını**

açıklama *His death provoked a national **outpouring** of grief.*

output /'aʊtpʊt/ *noun* [U] **1** AMOUNT the amount of something that is produced üretim, verim, hasıla, çıktı, randıman *Over the past year the factory's output has fallen by 15%.* **2** INFORMATION information produced by a computer (bilgisayar) veri, çıktı, sonuç *You can look at the output on screen before you print it out.* **3** POWER the power or energy produced by an electrical or electronic system elektrik/elektronik çıkış enerjisi/akım gücü

💠 outrage ...... İLE BİRLİKTE KULLANILAN KELİMELER

cause/express/provoke/spark outrage ● moral/ public outrage ● outrage at/over sth

outrage¹ /'aʊtreɪdʒ/ *noun* **1** [U] a strong feeling of anger or shock hiddet, büyük öfke, müthiş şok, nefret *moral outrage* ○ *The scandal caused public outrage.* **2** [C] something that causes great anger or shock vahşet, gaddarlık, zulüm, infial *a terrorist outrage* ○ [+ (that)] *It's an outrage that these children don't have enough to eat.*

outrage² /'aʊtreɪdʒ/ *verb* [T] to make someone feel very angry or shocked fevkalade kızdırmak/öfkelendirmek, şoke etmek; çılgına çevirmek [often passive] *The audience was outraged by his racist comments.* ○ *Local people were outraged at the bombing.*

outrageous /ˌaʊt'reɪdʒəs/ *adjective* shocking or extreme korkunç, müthiş, cüretkâr; terbiyesiz, ahlaksız, öfke veren, rezilce *outrageous behaviour/ clothes* ○ *The prices in that restaurant were outrageous.* ● *adverb* **outrageously** expensive çok kötü bir şekilde

outran /ˌaʊt'ræn/ *past tense of* outrun 'outrun' fiilinin ikinci hâli

outreach /'aʊtriːtʃ/ *noun* [U] *mainly US* when an organization helps people with their social, medical, or educational problems eğitim, tıbbi, sosyal problemlerde yardım yapma *an outreach programme* ○ *an outreach worker*

outright /'aʊtraɪt/ *adjective* [always before noun] total, clear, and certain tam, açık, ortada, kesin, bütün *an outright ban on smoking* ○ *an outright victory* ● **outright** /ˌaʊt'raɪt/ *adverb* *She needs 51% of the vote to win outright.* ○ *He was killed outright* (= immediately) *when the car hit him.* net bir şekilde

outrun /ˌaʊt'rʌn/ *verb* [T] **outrunning**, *past tense* **outran**, *past part* **outrun** to move or develop faster or further than someone or something ...dan/den daha da hızlı ilerlemek/gelişmek/ileri gitmek

outscore /ˌaʊt'skɔːʳ/ *verb* [T] *mainly US* to score more points than another player or team daha fazla sayı kaydetmek; sayı olarak önde olmak

outshine /ˌaʊt'ʃaɪn/ *verb* [T] *past* outshone to be much better than someone else çok daha iyi olmak; daha parlak olmak *She easily outshone the other students on the course.*

○ᵐ**outside¹** /ˌaʊt'saɪd/ *(also US* outside of) *preposition* **1** not in a particular building or room, but near it dışarda, dışında *She waited outside his room for nearly two hours.* **2** not in dışında, dışarıda, dışta *a flat just outside Blackpool* ○ *You have to phone a different number outside office hours.*

○ᵐ**outside²** /ˌaʊt'saɪd/ *adverb* **1** not inside a building dış, dış mekân, dışarıda yapılan/olan *Go and play outside for a while.* ○ *It's cold outside today.* **2** not in a particular building or room, but near it dışarda olan, dışında bulunan/kalan *She knocked on his bedroom door and left the tray outside.*

outside³ /ˌaʊt'saɪd/ *adjective* [always before noun] **1** not in a building dış, dış mekân, dışarıda *an outside light* ○ *outside activities* **2** from a different organization or group of people dış, harici, başka bir kuruluş veya toplumdan *outside help* ○ *outside influences* ⊃See also: the outside world.

○ᵐ**the outside⁴** /ˌaʊt'saɪd/ *noun* the outer part or surface of something dışı, yüzeyi, dış yüzeyi/cephesi *The pie was cooked on the outside but cold in the middle.*

outside 'chance *noun* [no plural] when something is not likely to happen başka bir şans ;dışarıdan bir etki; bir şeyin gerçekleşme olasılığı olmadığında ortaya çıkan beklenmedik bir şans *She has an outside chance of reaching the final.*

outsider /ˌaʊt'saɪdəʳ/ *noun* [C] someone who does not belong to a particular group, organization, or place yabancı, herhangi bir gruba/kuruluşa/yere ait olmayan kimse *The villagers are very suspicious of outsiders.* ⊃Compare insider.

the ,outside 'world *noun* other people in other places dış dünya *When he was in prison, his radio was his only contact with the outside world.*

outsize /ˌaʊt'saɪz/ *(also* outsized) *adjective* [always before noun] larger than usual olması gerekenden daha büyük; normalden çok daha büyük *an outsize jumper*

the outskirts /'aʊtskɜːts/ *noun* the outer area of a city, town, or village kenar mahalleler, gecekondu bölgeleri *There are plans to build a new stadium on the outskirts of Liverpool.*

outspoken /ˌaʊt'spəʊkᵊn/ *adjective* expressing an opinion forcefully and not worrying about what other people think dobra, açık sözlü, sözünü esirgemeyen, lâfını sakınmayan *outspoken comments* ○ *He's an outspoken critic of nuclear energy.*

outstanding /ˌaʊt'stændɪŋ/ *adjective* **1** excellent and much better than most mükemmel, fevkalade, güzide, kalburüstü, harika *an outstanding achievement* **2** waiting to be paid or dealt with ödenmemiş, beklenen, askıda, sonuca varmamış; henüz yapılmamış, yarım kalmış *an outstanding debt*

outstandingly /ˌaʊt'stændɪŋli/ *adverb* used to emphasize how good something is fevkalade olarak, harika/mükemmel bir şekilde *outstandingly successful*

outstay /ˌaʊt'steɪ/ *verb* ⊃See outstay/overstay your welcome⁴.

outstretched /ˌaʊt'stretʃt/ *adjective* When a part of your body is outstretched, it is reaching out as far as possible. iki yana olabildiğince esneyen/açılan; uzatılmış, uzanmış *He ran towards me with his arms outstretched.*

outstrip /ˌaʊt'strɪp/ *verb* [T] **outstripping**, *past* **outstripped** When one amount outstrips another amount, it is much greater than it. miktar olarak çok üstünde/fevkinde olmak; sayı/miktar olarak daha büyük olmak *Demand for the toys far outstrips supply.*

outta /'aʊtə/ *informal short for* out of 'out of' ifadesinin sözlük kullanım biçimi *Let's get outta here!*

out-take /'aʊtteɪk/ *noun* [C] a short part of a film, television programme or music recording that was removed, usually because it contains mistakes **(film, tv. programı, müzik kaydı) çıkarılan hatalı bölümler; hatalı çekimler** *They showed a video with funny outtakes from famous films.*

outward¹ /ˈaʊtwəd/ *adjective* [always before noun] **1** showing on the outside **dış, harici** *He had a serious illness, but there was no outward sign of it.* **2 outward flight/ journey, etc** when you travel away from a place that you will return to **dış/harici uçuş/seyahat vs.** ➾Opposite inward.

outward² /ˈaʊtwəd/ (*also UK* **outwards**) *adverb* towards the outside or away from the centre **dışa/dışına doğru, dışarıya** *This door opens outward.*

outwardly /ˈaʊtwədli/ *adverb* If someone is outwardly calm, confident, etc, they seem to be calm, confident, etc, although they may not feel that way. **dışta, dıştan, görünüşte** *She was very nervous, but she remained outwardly calm.* ➾Opposite inwardly.

outweigh /ˌaʊtˈweɪ/ *verb* [T] to be greater or more important than something else **...dan/den daha büyük/önemli olmak; ağır basmak** *The benefits of this treatment far outweigh the risks.*

outwit /ˌaʊtˈwɪt/ *verb* [T] **outwitting**, *past* **outwitted** to get an advantage over someone by doing something clever and deceiving them **zekice davranarak/kandırarak altetmek, mat etmek; üstünlük sağlamak** *She outwitted her kidnappers and managed to escape.*

oval /ˈəʊvəl/ *adjective* in the shape of an egg or a slightly flat circle **oval, yumurta şeklinde** *an oval face* ○ *an oval table* ● **oval** *noun* [C] an oval shape **oval şekli** ➾See picture at **shape**.

the ˈOval ˌOffice *noun* the office of the president of the United States **Oval Ofis; ABD başkanının çalışma odası**

ovary /ˈəʊvəri/ *noun* [C] the part of a woman or female animal that produces eggs, or the part of a plant that produces seeds **yumurtalık** ● **ovarian** /əʊˈveəriən/ *adjective* [always before noun] relating to the ovaries **yumurtalıkla ilgili** *ovarian cancer*

ovation /əʊˈveɪʃᵊn/ *noun* [C] when a group of people clap for a long time to show that they approve of someone or something **coşkulu alkış, aşırı tazahürat** ➾See also: standing ovation.

oven /ˈʌvᵊn/ *noun* [C] a piece of kitchen equipment with a door which is used for cooking food **fırın** *an electric oven* ○ *a microwave oven* ➾Orta kısımdaki renkli sayfalarına bakınız.

⊶**over¹** /ˈəʊvəʳ/ *adverb, preposition* **1** [ABOVE] above or higher than something **üstünde, üzerinde, üzerine** *The sign over the door said "Private, No Entry".* ○ *A fighter plane flew over.* **2** [SIDE TO SIDE] If you walk, jump, climb, etc over an object or place, you go from one side of it to the other side. **(yürüme, tırmanma, atlama) üzeri, üzerinde, üzerinden** *We had to climb over large rocks to get to the beach.* **3** [AMOUNT] more than a particular amount, number, or age **(miktar, sayı, yaş vs.) ...dan/den fazla** *Over 5,000 Internet users contact our website every year.* ○ *Suitable for children aged 5 and over.* **4** [OPPOSITE SIDE] on or to the opposite side of a road, bridge, path, etc **karşısında/karşısına; çaprazında/çaprazına** *The station is over the bridge.* **5** [COVER] covering someone or something **üstüne, üzerine** *She placed the quilt over the bed.* **6** [DOWN] down from a higher to a lower position **aşağı, yere** *The little boy fell over and started to cry.* ○ *She tripped over the rug.* **7** [PLACE] to a particular place **buraya, burada/şuraya, şurada** *Could you bring the plates over here* (= bring them to this place). ○ *He was sent over there during the war.* **8** [TIME] during a particular period of time **boyunca,**

süresince, zamanında, döneminde *I was in Seattle over the summer.* **9** [ABOUT] connected with or about **...ile ilgili olarak; konusunda/hususunda** *It's stupid arguing over something so trivial.* **10** [NOT USED] not used **kalan, kullanılmamış olan; kullanılmamış/kalmış, bırakılmış** *There's some food left over from the party.* **11** [USING] using the radio or telephone **telefon/radyo kullanarak; telefon/radyo ile** *I made the booking over the phone.* **12 be/get over sth** to feel better after being ill or feeling unhappy about something **iyileşmek, kendine gelmek, toparlamak, daha mutlu olmak** *It took him months to get over splitting up with his girlfriend.* **13 do sth over** *US* to do something again from the beginning because you did not do it well the first time **bir şeyi yeni baştan yapmak** *You've ruined it! Now I'll have to do it over.* **14 (all) over again** again from the beginning **ta baştan, yeni baştan, bir daha** *It looks all messy. I'm going to have to do it all over again.* **15 over and over (again)** repeatedly **tekrar tekrar, defalarca** *He was whistling the same tune over and over.* **16 roll/turn, etc (sth) over** to move so that a different part is showing, or to make something do this **arkasını çevirmek; alt üst etmek; öteki tarafını döndürmek/çevirmek; ters yüz etmek/olmak** *She turned the page over.* **17** [CONTROL] in control of someone or something **kontrolünde, etkisinde, altında** *Her husband has a lot of influence over her.*

⊶**over²** /ˈəʊvəʳ/ *adjective* **1** [never before noun] finished **bitmiş, son bulmuş, tamam** *The exams will be over next week.* ○ *It was all over very quickly.* **2 get sth over (and done) with** to do something difficult or unpleasant as soon as you can so that you do not have to worry about it any more **üstesinden gelmek, halletmek, çözmek; zor ve nahoş bir şeyi halletmek; bir sorundan kurtulmak**

over- /ˈəʊvəʳ/ *prefix* too much **çok fazla anlamında önek** *to overeat* ○ *overpopulated*

overall /ˈəʊvᵊrɔːl/ *adjective* [always before noun] considering everything or everyone **tümü, hepsi, toplamı, geneli, tamamı** *the overall cost of the holiday* ○ *the overall effect* ● **overall** /ˌəʊvᵊrˈɔːl/ *adverb* How would you rate the school overall? **genel olarak, bütününe bakıldığında**

overalls /ˈəʊvᵊrɔːlz/ *noun* [plural] **1** *UK* (*US* **coveralls**) a piece of clothing that you wear over your clothes to keep them clean while you are working **iş önlüğü, gömlek, tulum 2** *US* (*UK* **dungarees**) trousers with a part that covers your chest and straps that go over your shoulders **iş tulumu, iş elbisesi**

overbearing /ˌəʊvəˈbeərɪŋ/ *adjective* trying to have too much control over other people **zorba, buyurgan, hükmünü zorla uygulayan; baskıcı** *an overbearing mother*

overblown /ˌəʊvəˈbləʊn/ *adjective* If something is overblown, it is made to seem more important or serious than it really is. **şişirilmiş, abartılmış, abartılı**

overboard /ˈəʊvəbɔːd/ *adverb* **1** over the side of a boat and into the water **gemiden/küpeşteden suya/denize** *to fall overboard* **2 go overboard** *informal* to do something too much, or to be too excited about something **abartmak, aşırı düşkünlük göstermek, hastası olmak** *I think people go overboard at Christmas.*

overburdened /ˌəʊvəˈbɜːdᵊnd/ *adjective* having too much to deal with **başını kaşıyacak zamanı olmayan; çok meşgul, çok işi olan** *overburdened with work*

overcame /ˌəʊvəˈkeɪm/ *past tense of* overcome 'overcome' fiilinin ikinci hâli

overcast /ˈəʊvəkɑːst/ *adjective* cloudy and dark **bulutlu, kapalı** *an overcast sky/day*

o

overcharge /ˌəʊvə'tʃɑːdʒ/ *verb* [I, T] to charge someone too much money for something **fazla para almak, kazıklamak** *The shop overcharged me by £5.*

overcoat /'əʊvəkəʊt/ *noun* [C] a long, warm coat **palto, manto**

overcome /ˌəʊvə'kʌm/ *verb past tense* **overcame,** *past participle* **overcome 1** [T] to deal with and control a problem or feeling **üstesinden gelmek, alt etmek, halletmek, çözmek, kurtulmak** *He's trying to overcome his drug addiction and find a job.* ○ *Let's hope she overcomes her shyness.* **2 be overcome by excitement/fear/sadness, etc** to suddenly have too much of a feeling **etkilenmek, etkisinde kalmak, kapılmak; birden kapılmak** *She was overcome by emotion.* **3 be overcome by smoke/fumes, etc** to become ill or weak because you have been breathing smoke or poisonous gas **dumandan/zehirli gazdan etkilenmek, boğulmak; duman altı olmak; boğulmak** *One worker died when he was overcome by chemical fumes.*

overcrowded /ˌəʊvə'kraʊdɪd/ *adjective* containing too many people or things **aşırı kalabalık, tıklım tıklım** *an overcrowded classroom/prison* ● **overcrowding** *noun* [U] **kalabalık**

overdo /ˌəʊvə'duː/ *verb* [T] *past tense* **overdid,** *past participle* **overdone** to do or use too much of something **aşırıya kaçmak, abartmak, ifrata kaçmak** *I went to the gym yesterday, but I think I overdid it a bit.*

overdone /ˌəʊvə'dʌn/ *adjective* cooked for too long **çok/aşırı pişmiş**

overdose /'əʊvədəʊs/ *noun* [C] too much of a drug taken at one time **aşırı doz** *Her daughter died of a drug overdose.* ● **overdose** /ˌəʊvə'dəʊs/ *verb* [I] **aşırı doz almak**

overdraft /'əʊvədrɑːft/ *noun* [C] If you have an overdraft, you have taken more money out of your bank account than you had in it. **hesabından fazla miktarda çekilen para; kredi** *a £250 overdraft*

overdrawn /ˌəʊvə'drɔːn/ *adjective* If you are overdrawn, you have taken more money out of your bank account than you had in it. **fazla çekilmiş, hesaba içeri girilmiş** *We've gone £200 overdrawn!*

overdue /ˌəʊvə'djuː/ *adjective* happening later than expected **gecikmeli, geç kalmış** *This decision is long overdue.*

overestimate /ˌəʊv°r'estɪmeɪt/ *verb* [I, T] to guess or think that something is bigger or better than it really is **gözünde büyütmek, gereğinden fazla önemsemek** *They overestimated her ability to do the job.* ⊃Opposite **underestimate**.

over-fishing /ˌəʊvə'fɪʃɪŋ/ *noun* [U] catching so many fish in a part of the sea that there are not many fish left there **aşırı avlanma, gereğinden fazla balık avlama** *low fish stocks caused by over-fishing*

overflow /ˌəʊvə'fləʊ/ *verb* **1** [I] If a container or a place overflows, the thing that is inside it starts coming out because it is too full. **taşırmak, taşırarak dökmek** *The bath overflowed, and there's water all over the floor!* ○ *The bin was overflowing with rubbish.* **2** [I, T] to come out of a container or a place because it is too full **taşmak, taşarak dökülmek** *The river overflowed its banks after the heavy rainfall.* **3 overflow with confidence/happiness/love, etc** to have a lot of a quality or emotion **(güven, mutluluk, aşk vs.) kabına sığmamak; coşmak, ayakları yerden kesilmek** ● **overflow** /'əʊvəfləʊ/ *noun* [C, U] **taşma**

overgrown /ˌəʊvə'grəʊn/ *adjective* covered with plants that have become too big **her tarafı ot bürümüş, bakımsız; ...ile kaplanmış** *an overgrown garden*

overhang /ˌəʊvə'hæŋ/ *verb* [T] *past* **overhung** to hang over something **üstünde bulunmak, üzerine sarkmak** *overhanging branches*

overhaul /ˌəʊvə'hɔːl/ *verb* [T] to examine a machine or a system carefully and improve it or repair it **baştan aşağı gözden/bakımdan geçirmek; bütünüyle bakım onarım yapmak** *to overhaul an engine* ● **overhaul** /'əʊvəhɔːl/ *noun* [C] **gözden geçirme, kontrol etme**

overhead /ˌəʊvə'hed/ *adjective, adverb* above you, usually in the sky **üstten, gökyüzünde, başı üstünde, tepeden** *overhead power cables* ○ *A police helicopter was hovering overhead.*

overheads /'əʊvəhedz/ *UK* (*US* **overhead**) *noun* [plural] money that a company spends on its regular and necessary costs, for example rent and heating **sabit/genel giderler; zaruri ödemeler**

overhear /ˌəʊvə'hɪər/ *verb* [T] *past* **overheard** to hear what someone is saying when they are not talking to you **kulak kabartmak, istemeden kulak misafiri olmak, duymak/işitmek** [+ doing sth] *I overheard him telling her he was leaving.*

overheat /ˌəʊvə'hiːt/ *verb* [I] to become too hot **aşırı/ fazla ısınmak, çok ısınmak/kızmak** *The engine keeps overheating.*

overhung /ˌəʊvə'hʌŋ/ *past of* overhang **'overhang' fiilinin geçmiş zaman hâli**

overjoyed /ˌəʊvə'dʒɔɪd/ *adjective* very happy **sevinçten havalara uçan, aşırı mutlu, mutluluktan etekleri zil çalan** [+ to do sth] *He was overjoyed to hear from his old friend.*

overkill /'əʊvəkɪl/ *noun* [U] when something is done too much **fazladan olan şey, gereksiz yapılan şey** *Should I add an explanation or would that be overkill?*

overlap /ˌəʊvə'læp/ *verb* [I, T] **overlapping,** *past* **overlapped 1** If two subjects or activities overlap, they are the same in some way. **örtüşmek, benzeşmek** *Although our job titles are different, our responsibilities overlap quite a lot.* **2** If two objects overlap, part of one covers part of the other. **birbiri üstüne binmek** ● **overlap** /'əʊvəlæp/ *noun* [C, U] **örtüşme**

overload /ˌəʊv°'l'əʊd/ *verb* [T] **1** to put too many people or things into or onto a vehicle **fazla yolcu almak; kapasitesinin üstünde yolcu yüklemek** [often passive] *The coach was overloaded with passengers.* **2** to give someone more work or problems than they can deal with **kaldırabileceğinden fazla yük/sorumluluk yüklemek/vermek**

overlook /ˌəʊvə'lʊk/ *verb* [T] **1** VIEW to have a view of something from above **tepeden bakmak/seyretmek** *a balcony overlooking the sea* **2** NOT NOTICE to not notice or consider something **gözden kaçırmak; (argo) es geçmek** *Two important facts have been overlooked in this case.* **3** FORGIVE to forgive or ignore someone's bad behaviour **görmezden gelmek; affetmek; göz yummak**

overly /'əʊv°li/ *adverb* in a way that is extreme or too much **oldukça, fevkalade, son derece** *overly optimistic* ○ *It wasn't overly expensive.*

overnight /ˌəʊvə'naɪt/ *adverb* **1** for or during the night **bir gecelik, gece boyunca, gece boyu** *Sometimes we would stay overnight at my grandmother's house.* **2** very quickly or suddenly **aniden, ansızın, birdenbire** *Change does not happen overnight.* ● **overnight** *adjective* [always before noun] *overnight rain* ○ *an overnight* (= sudden) *success* **bir gece içinde, aniden**

overpass /'əʊvəpɑːs/ *US* (*UK* **flyover**) *noun* [C] a bridge that carries a road over another road **üst geçit, üst yol**

overpower /ˌəʊvəˈpaʊəʳ/ *verb* [T] **1** to defeat someone by being stronger than they are **zor ve kuvvet kullanarak yenmek, hakkından gelmek, ezmek, boyun eğdirmek** [often passive] *The gunman was overpowered by two security guards.* **2** If a feeling, smell, etc overpowers you, it is very strong and makes you feel weak. **(his, koku vs.) etkilemek, güçsüzleştirmek, zora sokmak**

overpowering /ˌəʊvəˈpaʊərɪŋ/ *adjective* unpleasantly strong or powerful **çok güçlü, acı kuvveti olan** *an overpowering smell*

overpriced /ˌəʊvəˈpraɪst/ *adjective* too expensive **çok/aşırı pahalı; fahiş fiyatlı**

overran /ˌəʊvəʳˈræn/ *past tense of* overrun **'overrun' fiilinin ikinci hâli**

overrated /ˌəʊvəʳˈreɪtɪd/ *adjective* If something is overrated, it is considered to be better or more important than it really is. **abartılan, gözünde büyütülen, abartılmış; olduğundan fazla değer verilen**

overreact /ˌəʊvʳriˈækt/ *verb* [I] to react in a way that is more extreme than you should **aşırı tepki vermek** *She tends to overreact to criticism.*

override /ˌəʊvʳˈraɪd/ *verb* [T] *past tense* **overrode**, *past participle* **overridden** **1** If someone in authority overrides a decision or order, they officially decide that it is wrong. **kaale almamak, geçersiz saymak** *I don't have the power to override his decision.* **2** to be more important than something else **daha önemli/mühim olmak; baskın çıkmak** *His desire for money seems to override anything else.*

overriding /ˌəʊvʳˈraɪdɪŋ/ *adjective* [always before noun] more important than others **başlıca, en önde/başta gelen** *an overriding concern*

overrule /ˌəʊvʳˈruːl/ *verb* [T] If someone in authority overrules a decision or order, they officially decide that it is wrong. **kale almamak, geçersiz saymak, resmî olarak yanlış saymak** *Does the judge have the power to overrule the jury?*

overrun /ˌəʊvʳˈrʌn/ *verb* **overrunning**, *past tense* **overran**, *past participle* **overrun** **1** [T] If something unpleasant overruns a place, it fills it in large numbers. **istila etmek, ele geçirmek, kaplamak, sarmak** [often passive] *The house was overrun by rats.* ○ *Troops overran the city.* **2** [I] *UK* to continue for a longer time than planned **süresini aşmak, süresi geçmek** *Sorry I'm late, but the meeting overran by 20 minutes.*

overseas /ˌəʊvəˈsiːz/ *adjective* [always before noun] in, to, or from another country **denizaşırı ülkelerden gelen, yabancı, dış ülkelerden gelen** *an overseas student* ● **overseas** *adverb* to live/work overseas **başka bir ülkeden**

oversee /ˌəʊvəˈsiː/ *verb* [T] **overseeing**, *past tense* **oversaw**, *past participle* **overseen** to watch work as it is done in order to make cer`tain that it is done correctly **nezaret etmek, denetlemek, gözetmek** *A committee has been set up to oversee the project.*

overshadow /ˌəʊvəˈʃædəʊ/ *verb* [T] **1** to cause something to be less enjoyable **gölge düşürmek** [often passive] *The party was overshadowed by a family argument.* **2** to cause someone or something to seem less important or successful **gölgede bırakmak, önemsiz konuma getirmek**

oversight /ˈəʊvəsaɪt/ *noun* [C, U] a mistake that you make by not noticing something or by forgetting to do something **ehemmiyetsizlik, gözden kaçma, dikkatsizlik**

oversleep /əʊvəˈsliːp/ *verb* [I] *past* **overslept** to sleep longer than you had intended **uyuyup kalmak** *Sorry I'm late, I overslept.*

overstate /ˌəʊvəˈsteɪt/ *verb* [T] to talk about something in a way that makes it seem more important than it really is **mübalağa etmek, abartmak**

overstep /ˌəʊvəˈstep/ *verb* **overstepping**, *past* **overstepped overstep the mark** to behave in a way that is not allowed or not acceptable **haddini aşmak, sınırı/haddini aşmak, ölçüyü kaçırmak**

overt /əʊˈvɜːt/ *adjective* done or shown publicly and not hidden **aleni/açık/ortada/meydanda yapılan** *overt criticism* ● **overtly** *adverb* overtly racist remarks **açık bir şekilde yapılan**

overtake /ˌəʊvəˈteɪk/ *verb past tense* **overtook**, *past participle* **overtaken 1** [T] to become more successful than someone or something else **daha da başarılı olmak** *Tobacco has overtaken coffee to become the country's leading export.* **2** [I, T] to go past a vehicle or person that is going in the same direction **devirmek, düşürmek**

over-the-counter /ˌəʊvəðəˈkaʊntəʳ/ *adjective* [always before noun] Over-the-counter medicines can be bought in a shop without first visiting a doctor. **(ilaç) reçetesiz, tezgâh üstünde satılan** ● **over-the-counter** *adverb* Most of these tablets can be **bought over-the-counter.** **doktora gitmeden satın alınabilen ilaçlar**

overthrow /ˌəʊvəˈθrəʊ/ *verb* [T] *past tense* **overthrew**, *past participle* **overthrown** to remove someone from power by using force **devirmek, düşürmek; zorla devirmek/alaşağı etmek** *They were accused of plotting to overthrow the government.* ● **overthrow** /ˈəʊvəθrəʊ/ *noun* [no plural] **devirme (kişi, hükümet)**

overtime /ˈəʊvətaɪm/ *noun* [U] extra time that you work after your usual working hours **fazla mesai/çalışma zamanı** *unpaid overtime* ● **overtime** *adverb* fazla **mesai yapılmış şekilde**

overtones /ˈəʊvətəʊnz/ *noun* [plural] ideas that seem to be expressed but that are not stated directly **sezdirme, iz, belirti, dolaylı anlatım** *His speech had political overtones.*

overtook /ˌəʊvəˈtʊk/ *past tense of* overtake **'overtake' fiilinin ikinci hâli**

overture /ˈəʊvətjʊəʳ/ *noun* [C] a piece of classical music that introduces another longer piece such as an opera **giriş müziği**

overturn /ˌəʊvəˈtɜːn/ *verb* **1** overturn a conviction/ruling/verdict, etc to officially change a legal decision **yasal bir sonucu resmî olarak değiştirmek 2** [I, T] If something overturns or if you overturn something, it turns over onto its top or onto its side. **devirmek, devrilmek, altüst etmek/olmak** *She overturned her car in the accident.*

 overview .... İLE BİRLİKTE KULLANILAN KELİMELER

give/provide an overview ● a **brief/broad/comprehensive/general** overview ● an overview **of** sth

overview /ˈəʊvəvjuː/ *noun* [C] a short description giving the most important facts about something **genelini anlama/tanımlama** *I'll just give you an overview of the job.*

overweight /ˌəʊvəˈweɪt/ *adjective* too heavy or too fat **aşırı kilolu, çok şişman** *He's still a few pounds overweight.* ➔Opposite **underweight.**

overwhelm /ˌəʊvəˈwelm/ *verb* [T] If a feeling or situation overwhelms you, it has an effect that is too strong or extreme. **(duygu, durum) kapılmak, etkisi altına almak; gark etmek, boğmak** [often passive] *She was overwhelmed by the excitement of it all.*

overwhelming /ˌəʊvəˈwelmɪŋ/ *adjective* very strong in effect or large in amount **ezici, üstün, ağır basan, karşı konulamayan** *an overwhelming feeling of sad-*

ness ○ *They won by an overwhelming majority.*
● **overwhelmingly** *adverb* karşı koyulamaz, kuvvetli bir şekilde

overworked /ˌəʊvə'wɜːkt/ *adjective* Someone who is overworked has to work too much. çok fazla çalışan, aşırı iş yapan; çok çalıştırılan *We're overworked and underpaid.*

overwrite /ˌəʊvə'raɪt/ *verb* [T] If you overwrite a computer file, you replace it with a different one.

ovulate /'ɒvjəleɪt/ *verb* [I] When a woman ovulates, her body produces eggs. (kadın) yumurtalamak

ᴏ⇥**owe** /əʊ/ *verb* [T] **1** to have to pay money back to someone borçlu olmak, borcu olmak [+ two objects] *You still owe me money.* ○ *He owes about £5000 to the bank.* **2 owe sb an apology/favour/drink, etc** to have to give something to someone because they deserve it birine özür/iyilik/içki vs. borcu olmak *I think I owe you an apology.* **3 owe your existence/success, etc to sb/sth** to have something or achieve something because of someone or something else varlığını/başarısını birine/bir şeye borçlu olmak *The museum owes much of its success to the present generation of young British artists.*

owing to /əʊɪŋ tuː/ *preposition* because of ...dan/den dolayı, yüzünden, sebebiyle, nedeniyle *The concert has been cancelled owing to lack of support.*

owl /aʊl/ *noun* [C] a bird
that has large eyes and
hunts small animals at
night baykuş

owl

ᴏ⇥**own**[1] /əʊn/ *adjective,
pronoun, determiner*
1 belonging to or done
by a particular person
or thing kendi,
kendisi *Each
student has their own
dictionary.* ○ *Petra
makes all her own
clothes.* ○ *"Is that your
mum's car?" "No, it's my own* (= it belongs to me).*"* **2 of your own** belonging to someone or something sadece kendisine ait *I'll have a home of my own* (= home belonging only to me) *someday.* **3 (all) on your own a** alone kendi başına, yalnız başına, yalnız *Jessica lives on her own.* **b** If you do something on your own,

you do it without any help from other people. tek başına, yardımsız, hiç kimseden yardım almadan *She's raised three kids on her own.* **4 come into your/ its own** to be very useful or successful çok faydalı/başarılı olmak *By the 1970s, Abrams was starting to come into his own as a soloist.* ● **5 get your own back (on sb)** *UK* to do something unpleasant to someone because they have done something unpleasant to you öcünü/intikamını almak ● **6 hold your own** to be as successful as other people or things başkaları kadar başarılı olmak *She could always hold her own in political debates.*

ᴏ⇥**own**[2] /əʊn/ *verb* [T] to have something that legally belongs to you sahip olmak *The University owns a lot of the land around here.*

own up *phrasal verb* to admit that you have done something wrong üstüne almak, üstlenmek [+ to + doing sth] *No one has owned up to breaking that window.*

🧩 **owner** .... İLE BİRLİKTE KULLANILAN KELİMELER

the **current/original/previous** owner ● the owner **of** sth

---

ᴏ⇥**owner** /əʊnə^r/ *noun* [C] someone who legally owns something sahip, malik *a property owner* ● **ownership** *noun* [U] mülkiyet sahiplik, mülkiyet

ox /ɒks/ *noun* [C] *plural* **oxen** a large, male cow, used especially in the past to pull farm vehicles öküz

oxygen /'ɒksɪdʒən/ *noun* [U] a gas that is in the air and that animals need to live (formula O) oksijen

oxymoron /ˌɒksɪ'mɔːrɒn/ *noun* [C] two words used together, which mean two different or opposite things, such as 'bitter-sweet' or 'smart casual' iki ayrı ve farklı şeyi ifade eden birlikte kullanılan ikili/birleşik ifade

oyster /'ɔɪstə^r/ *noun* [C] a sea creature that lives in a flat shell and is eaten as food istiridye

oz *written abbreviation for* ounce (= a unit for measuring weight) ons, bir tür ağırlık ölçüm birimi *an 8 oz steak*

ozone /'əʊzəʊn/ *noun* [U] a form of oxygen that has a powerful smell (formula O$_3$) ozon

the 'ozone ˌlayer *noun* the layer of ozone high above the Earth's surface that prevents the sun from harming the Earth ozon tabakası; güneşin zararlı ışınlarından koruyan, yeryüzünü saran tabaka

P, p /piː/ the sixteenth letter of the alphabet **alfabenin onaltıncı harfi**

p. 1 *written abbreviation for* page **sayfa'nın kısa yazılışı** *See diagram on p.135.* **2** *abbreviation for* penny or pence (= units of British money) **İngiliz madeni parası** *a 20p coin*

PA /piːˈeɪ/ *UK abbreviation for* personal assistant: a person who organizes letters, meetings and telephone calls for someone with an important job **yardımcı, sekreter, asistan**

🧩 **pace** ...... İLE BİRLİKTE KULLANILAN KELİMELER

quicken/slow your pace ● **at** a [blistering/brisk/leisurely, etc] pace ● **the pace of** sth

pace¹ /peɪs/ *noun* **1** [no plural] the speed at which someone or something moves or does something **hız, sürat** *We started to walk at a much faster pace.* ○ *the **pace** of life* **2** [C] a step **adım** *Every few paces I stopped to listen.* **3 keep pace with sb/sth** to move or develop at the same speed as someone or something else **ayak uydurmak, aynı hızda gelişmek/ilerleme kaydetmek** *We have to keep pace with the changing times.* ⊃See also: at a snail's pace.

pace² /peɪs/ *verb* **1 pace about/up and down, etc** to walk around because you are worried or excited about something **huzursuzca gezinmek, sinirli sinirli dolanmak** *He kept pacing up and down, glancing at his watch.* **2 pace yourself** to be careful not to do something too quickly so that you do not get too tired to finish it **hızını/süratini kendine/çalışmasına göre ayarlamak**

pacemaker /ˈpeɪsˌmeɪkər/ *noun* [C] a small piece of medical equipment in someone's heart that makes it work at the correct speed **kalp atışlarını düzenleyen aygıt**

pacifier /ˈpæsɪfaɪər/ *US* (*UK* **dummy**) *noun* [C] a small rubber object that you give to a baby to suck in order to make it calm **emzik, bebek emziği**

pacifism /ˈpæsɪfɪzᵊm/ *noun* [U] the belief that war or fighting of any type is wrong **savaş aleyhtarlığı, barışçılık** ● **pacifist** /ˈpæsɪfɪst/ *noun* [C] someone who believes in pacifism **savaş aleyhtarı, barış yanlısı**

pacify /ˈpæsɪfaɪ/ *verb* [T] to do something in order to make someone less angry or upset **yatıştırmak, sakinleştirmek, teskin etmek** *She smiled at Jamie to pacify him.*

oPeople**pack¹** /pæk/ *verb* **1** [I, T] to put your things into bags or boxes when you are going on holiday or leaving the place where you live **eşyalarını toplamak; valize/bavula yerleştirmek; toplanmak** *I've got to go home and pack.* ○ *to **pack** your bags* ⊃Opposite unpack. **2** [T] If people pack a place, there are so many of them in it that it is very crowded. **toplanmak, doluşmak, tıka basa doluşmak/doldurmak** *Thousands of fans packed the club.*

pack sth in *phrasal verb* **1** *informal* to stop doing something **vazgeçmek, bırakmak** *If this job doesn't get any better I'm going to **pack it in**.* **2** to manage to do a lot of things in a short period of time **kısa zaman diliminde çok iş yapmak; iki arada bir derede bir çok şey yapmayı başarmak** *We were only there four days but we packed so much in.*

pack sb off *phrasal verb informal* to send someone away **göndermek; (argo) sepetlemek** *We were **packed off to** our grandparents' for the summer holidays.*

pack (sth) up *phrasal verb* to collect all your things together when you have finished doing something **toplanmak, derli toplu hale getirmek** *I'm about to **pack my things up** and go home.*

pack² /pæk/ *noun* [C] **1** ⊞BOX *mainly US* a small box that contains several of the same thing **kutu, paket** *a pack of cigarettes* **2** ⊞BAG *mainly US* a bag that you carry on your back **sırt çantası, çanta** **3** ⊞ANIMALS a group of animals that live together, especially those of the dog family **köpek sürüsü** *a **pack** of wolves* **4** ⊞CARDS (*also US* **deck**) a set of playing cards **bir deste iskambil kağıdı** ⊃See also: fanny pack.

package

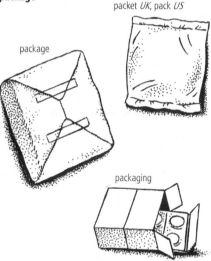

packet *UK*, pack *US*

package

packaging

package¹ /ˈpækɪdʒ/ *noun* [C] **1** ⊞PARCEL an object that is covered in paper, inside a box, etc, especially so that it can be sent somewhere **paket 2** ⊞GROUP OF THINGS a group of objects, plans, or arrangements that are sold or considered together **öneri paketi; birlikte satılan/değerlendirilen bir grup nesne/plan/düzenlemeler; paket** *a computer package* ○ *This ski package includes hotel, transport, and four days of skiing.* **3** ⊞BOX *US* a box or container in which something is put to be sold **paket, kutu,** *a package of raisins/cookies*

package² /ˈpækɪdʒ/ *verb* [T] **1** to put something into a box or container so that it can be sold **ambalaj yapmak, paketlemek** *It's neatly packaged in a blue and white box.* **2** to show someone or something in an attractive way so that people will like or buy them **albenisini ortaya çıkarmak; allayıp pullamak; yaldızlamak** *What's important is the way we package the programme.*

ˌpackage ˈholiday *UK* (*UK/US* **ˈpackage ˌtour**) *noun* [C] a holiday that is arranged for you by a travel company and for which you pay a fixed price before you go **paket tatil, turla yapılan tatil**

packaging /'pækɪdʒɪŋ/ noun [U] the paper, box, etc that something is inside so that it can be sold or sent somewhere **ambalaj, paketleme**

packed /pækt/ (also UK **packed out**) adjective very crowded **çok kalabalık, tıka basa dolu** The hall was packed.

packed 'lunch noun [C] UK food that you put in a bag or box and take to eat at work, school, etc **evden getirilen yemek; sefertası ile getirilen yemek; kumanya**

packet /'pækɪt/ UK (US **pack**) noun [C] a small container that contains several of the same thing **paket, kutu, torba, zarf** a packet of cigarettes/sweets

packing /'pækɪŋ/ noun [U] **1** when you put things into bags or boxes in order to take them somewhere **yerleştirme, toplanma, paketleme** I've got to do my packing because I'm going tomorrow. **2** paper, material, etc that you put around an object in a box so that it does not get damaged **ambalaj/paket yapma malzemesi**

━━━ **pact** ...... İLE BİRLİKTE KULLANILAN KELİMELER ━━━

have/make/sign a pact ● a pact between sb and sb ● a pact with sb

pact /pækt/ noun [C] an agreement between two people or groups **antlaşma, pakt** We have a pact never to talk about each other.

pad¹ /pæd/ noun [C] **1** (also US **tablet**) sheets of paper that have been fastened together at one edge, used for writing or drawing **bloknot; not kağıtları** There's a pad and pencil by the phone. **2** a small piece of soft material used to protect something or to make something more comfortable **tampon, ufak yastık, vadka, yumuşak destek** knee/shin pads

pad² /pæd/ verb **padding**, past **padded** **1 pad about/ around/down, etc** to walk somewhere with small, quiet steps **usul usul yürümek; aheste yürümek** He padded downstairs and out of the front door. **2** [T] to protect something or make something more comfortable by filling or surrounding it with soft material **etrafını yumuşak malzemelerle destekleyerek korumak/ daha rahat hale getirmek**
pad sth out phrasal verb to make a piece of writing or a speech longer by adding more information to it **uzatmak**

padding /'pædɪŋ/ noun [U] soft material that is used to fill or cover something to protect it or make it more comfortable **dolgu malzemesi**

paddle¹ /'pædl/ noun **1** [C] a short pole with one flat end that you use to make a small boat move through the water **kürek, kayık küreği 2** [no plural] UK when you walk in water that is not deep **sığ suda çıplak ayakla yürüyüş** to go for a paddle

paddle² /'pædl/ verb **1** BOAT [I, T] to move a small boat through water with a paddle **kürek çekmek 2** WALK [I] UK (US **wade**) to walk in water that is not deep **sığ suda çıplak ayakla yürümek 3** SWIM [I] US to swim using short, quick movements with your arms and legs **kısa hızlı kulaçlarla ve ayak hareketleriyle yüzmek**

paddock /'pædək/ noun [C] a small field where animals are kept, especially horses **atların bulunduğu çimenlik alan**

paddy field /'pædi,fiːld/ UK (UK/US **rice paddy**) noun [C] a field in which rice is grown **pirinç tarlası**

padlock /'pædlɒk/ noun [C] a metal lock with a U-shaped part that is used for fastening bicycles, doors, etc **asma kilit** ● **padlock** verb [T] **asma kilit vurmak**

paediatrician UK (US **pediatrician**) /ˌpiːdiə'trɪʃən/ noun [C] a children's doctor **çocuk doktoru**

paedophile UK (US **pedophile**) /'piːdəʊfaɪl/ noun [C] someone who is sexually interested in children **çocuklara cinsel istek duyan kimse**

pagan /'peɪɡ°n/ adjective relating to religious beliefs that do not belong to any of the main religions of the world **putperest** a pagan festival ● **pagan** noun [C] someone who has pagan religious beliefs **putperestlik**

━━━ **page** .... İLE BİRLİKTE KULLANILAN KELİMELER ━━━

turn a page ● the back/front page ● on page [25/36, etc.]

◦━**page¹** /peɪdʒ/ noun [C] **1** a piece of paper in a book, magazine, etc, or one side of a piece of paper **sayfa, yaprak** The article is on page 36. ○ I've only read 50 pages so far. **2** (also **web page**) one part of a website that you can see or print separately **internet sayfası** ⊃See also: **home page, the Yellow Pages.**

page² /peɪdʒ/ verb [T] **1** to call someone using a sound system in a public place **hoparlör vs. ile anons etmek 2** to send a message to someone's pager (= small piece of electronic equipment) **çağrı cihazına ileti göndermek**

pageant /'pædʒ°nt/ noun [C] a show that happens outside in which people dress and act as if they are from a time in history **temsili gösteri, şov, resmi geçit**

pageantry /'pædʒ°ntri/ noun [U] ceremonies in which there are a lot of people in special clothes **görkemli gösteri**

pager /'peɪdʒəʳ/ noun [C] a small piece of electronic equipment that you carry which makes a noise or movement when someone sends a message **çağrı cihazı**

pagoda /pə'ɡəʊdə/ noun [C] a tall religious building in Asia with many levels, each of which has a curved roof **Asya'da büyük dini tapınak**

paid /peɪd/ past of pay **pay' fiilinin geçmiş zaman hâli**

pail /peɪl/ noun [C] a container with an open top and a handle used for carrying liquids **kova, bakraç**

━━━ **pain** .... İLE BİRLİKTE KULLANILAN KELİMELER ━━━

excruciating/severe/sharp/unbearable pain ● ease/inflict/relieve/suffer pain ● in pain

◦━**pain¹** /peɪn/ noun **1** [C, U] an unpleasant physical feeling caused by an illness or injury **ağrı, sızı** chest/stomach pains ○ Are you in pain? ○ I felt a sharp pain in my foot. **2** [U] sadness or mental suffering caused by an unpleasant event **acı, keder, elem** I can't describe the pain I suffered when he died. **3 be a pain (in the neck)** informal to be annoying **can sıkıcı şey/kimse; baş belası** My brother can be a real pain in the neck sometimes. **4 be at pains to do sth; take pains to do sth** to make a lot of effort to do something **çok uğraşmak, didinmek, büyük çaba sarfetmek, çırpınmak** He was at great pains to explain the reasons for his decision.

pain² /peɪn/ verb [T] formal If something pains you, it makes you feel sad or upset. **acı vermek, üzmek, kederlendirmek** [+ to do sth] It pained him to see animals being treated so cruelly.

pained /peɪnd/ adjective appearing to be sad or upset **üzülmüş, kızgın, gücenmiş** a pained expression

◦━**painful** /'peɪnf°l/ adjective **1** causing physical pain **ağrılı, sızılı, acıyan, acı veren** Recovery from the operation is a slow and painful process. **2** making you feel sad or upset **ıstırap/acı veren** a painful memory

painfully /ˈpeɪnᵊli/ adverb **1** in a painful way **üzücü, acılı, can sıkıcı, zor, zahmetli** He landed painfully on his elbow. **2 painfully clear/obvious, etc** If a problem is painfully clear/obvious, etc, it is embarrassing because it is so clear/obvious, etc. **ıstırap/utanç verici şekilde belirgin/açık** It was painfully obvious that she didn't like him. **3** used to emphasize an unpleasant situation or quality **can sıkıcı şekilde** She's painfully thin.

painkiller /ˈpeɪnˌkɪləʳ/ noun [C] a drug which reduces pain **ağrı kesici**

painless /ˈpeɪnləs/ adjective **1** causing no physical pain **ağrısız, ağrı vermeyen** a painless death **2** causing no problems or difficulties **sorunsuz, güçlük çıkarmayan, sorun yaratmayan, zahmetsiz** There is no painless way of learning a language. ● **painlessly** adverb **acısız bir şekilde**

painstaking /ˈpeɪnzˌteɪkɪŋ/ adjective done with a lot of care **özenle/itinayla yapılan; dikkatli, titiz** It took months of painstaking research to write the book. ● **painstakingly** adverb **özenle yapılmış bir şekilde**

o⃘**paint¹** /peɪnt/ noun [C, U] a coloured liquid that you put on a surface to decorate it **boya** a gallon of blue paint ○ The door needs another **coat** (= layer) **of paint**.

o⃘**paint²** /peɪnt/ verb **1** [T] to cover a surface with paint in order to decorate it **boyamak** We've painted the kitchen yellow. **2** [I, T] to produce a picture of something or someone using paint **yağlı boya resim yapmak** These pictures were all painted by local artists. ⊃See also: paint a bleak/rosy, etc picture¹ of sth.

paintbrush /ˈpeɪntbrʌʃ/ noun [C] a brush that is used for painting pictures or for painting surfaces such as walls and doors **boya fırçası** ⊃See picture at brush.

painter /ˈpeɪntəʳ/ noun [C] **1** someone who paints pictures **ressam, yağlı boya resim yapan 2** someone whose job is to paint surfaces, such as walls and doors **boyacı** a painter and decorator

---
🧩 painting .... İLE BİRLİKTE KULLANILAN KELİMELER
---

do a painting ● a painting of sth/sb ● a painting by sb

o⃘**painting** /ˈpeɪntɪŋ/ noun **1** [C] a picture that someone has painted **yağlı boya tablo/resim 2** [U] the activity of painting pictures or painting surfaces **ressamlık, yağlı boya işi yapma** ⊃See also: oil painting.

o⃘**pair¹** /peəʳ/ noun [C] TWO THINGS two things that look the same and that are used together **çift** a pair of socks/shoes **2** TWO PARTS something that is made of two parts that are joined together **iki parçadan oluşan bir şey** a pair of scissors ○ a new pair of jeans/trousers **3** TWO PEOPLE two people who are doing something together **ikili, çift** For the next exercise, you'll need to work **in pairs**.

pair² /peəʳ/ verb
pair off phrasal verb If two people pair off, they begin a romantic or sexual relationship. **eşleşmek, romantik ve cinsellik içeren ilişkiye başlamak**
pair sb off with sb phrasal verb to introduce one person to another because you hope they will begin a romantic relationship **romantik bir ilişkiyi başlatmak için bir kimseyi diğerine tanıştırmak** Caroline tried to pair me off with her sister.
pair up phrasal verb to join another person for a short time in order to do something **ortak çalışma yapmak, işbirliği yapmak** I paired up with Chris for the last dance.

pajamas /pəˈdʒɑːməz/ noun [plural] US spelling of pyjamas (= shirt and trousers that you wear in bed) **pijama**

pal /pæl/ noun [C] informal a friend **arkadaş, dost, ahbap** He's an old pal of mine.

---

pair

a pair of trousers   a pair of scissors

a pair of gloves

o⃘**palace** /ˈpælɪs/ noun [C] a large house where a king or queen lives **saray** Buckingham Palace

palatable /ˈpælətəbl/ adjective formal **1** If food or drink is palatable, it has a pleasant taste. **lezzetli, tadı hoş** a palatable local wine **2** If an idea or plan is palatable, it is acceptable. **hoş, kabul edilebilir, hoş karşılanan** They need to make the project more palatable to local people. ⊃Opposite unpalatable.

palate /ˈpælət/ noun [C] **1** the top part of the inside of your mouth **damak 2** the ability to judge and enjoy good food and drink **damak tadı**

o⃘**pale** /peɪl/ adjective **1 pale blue/green/red, etc** light blue/green/red, etc **uçuk/açık mavi/yeşil/kırmızı** a pale yellow dress **2** If your face is pale, it has less colour than usual because you are ill or frightened. **uçuk, solgun, donuk**

pall¹ /pɔːl/ verb [I] to become less interesting and enjoyable **bıktırmak, tadı kaçmak, sıkıcı olmak, usandırmak** The pleasure of not having to work soon began to pall.

pall² /pɔːl/ noun **1 a pall of dust/smoke, etc** a thick cloud of dust/smoke, etc **yoğun duman/toz vs. bulutu 2 cast a pall over sth** If an unpleasant situation or piece of news casts a pall over an event, it spoils it. **gölge düşürmek; mahvetmek** The news of Nick's accident cast a pall over the celebrations.

palm¹ /pɑːm/ noun [C] **1** the inside surface of your hand **avuç içi, aya** ⊃Orta kısımdaki renkli sayfalarına bakınız. **2** a palm tree **palmiye, palmiye ağacı**

palm² /pɑːm/ verb
palm sb off phrasal verb to tell someone something that is not true so that they will stop asking questions **kandırmak, yalanla geçiştirmek** He palmed me off with an excuse about why he couldn't pay.
palm sth off as sth phrasal verb to deceive people by saying that something has a particular quality or value that it does not have **yalan dolanla elden çıkarmak; kandırmak, hileyle kabul ettirmek**
palm sth off on sb phrasal verb to give or sell something to someone because you want to get rid of it **kandırarak satmak/vermek; üçkâğıda getirmek** He palmed his old computer off on me.

Palm /pɑːm/ noun [C] trademark a small computer that you can carry with you **taşınabilir küçük bilgisayar**

'palm, tree *noun* [C] a tall tree with long leaves at the top which grows in hot countries **palmiye ağacı**

palpable /ˈpælpəbl/ *adjective* very obvious **apaçık, belli, aşikâr** *There was a palpable sense of tension in the crowd.*

paltry /ˈpɔːltri/ *adjective* A paltry amount of something, especially money, is very small. **hiç denecek kadar az, önemsiz** *a paltry sum of money*

pamper /ˈpæmpər/ *verb* [T] to treat someone in a kind way and give them everything they want **şımartmak, yüz vermek** *She pampered herself with a trip to the beauty salon.*

pamphlet /ˈpæmflɪt/ *noun* [C] a very thin book with a paper cover that gives information about something **kitapçık, broşür** *The tourist office gave me a pamphlet about places to visit in the city.*

pan¹ /pæn/ *noun* [C] a metal container with a handle that is used for cooking food in **tencere, tava** ➾See also: a **flash²** in the pan, **frying pan.**

pan² /pæn/ *verb* [T] **panning,** *past* **panned** *informal* to criticize something severely **acımasızca eleştirmek** [often passive] *His last novel was panned by the critics.*
pan out *phrasal verb* to develop in a particular way **belli bir biçimde gelişmek** *Not all his ideas had panned out in the way he would have liked.*

panacea /ˌpænəˈsiːə/ *noun* [C] something that people believe can solve all their problems **insanların bütün dertlerine çare olduğuna inandığı şey; her derde deva şey**

panache /pəˈnæʃ/ *noun* [U] a confident and attractive way of doing things **gösteriş, caka, çalım, hava atma** *The orchestra played with great panache.*

pancake /ˈpænkeɪk/ *noun* [C] a thin, flat food made from flour, milk, and egg mixed together and cooked in a pan **krep, gözleme, ince çörek**

panda /ˈpændə/ *noun* [C] a large, black and white animal that lives in forests in China **panda**

pandemonium /ˌpændəˈməʊniəm/ *noun* [U] when there is a lot of noise and confusion because people are angry or excited about something that has happened **karışıklık, velvele, curcuna** *Pandemonium broke out in the courtroom as they took him away.*

pander /ˈpændər/ *verb*
pander to sb/sth *phrasal verb* to do what someone wants although it is wrong **yanlış olmasına rağmen birşeye/birinin arzularına/isteklerine boyun eğmek** *He said he would not pander to public pressure.*

P&P /ˌpiːˈnpiː/ *noun* [U] *UK abbreviation for* postage and packing **posta ve ambalaj**

pane /peɪn/ *noun* [C] a flat piece of glass in a window or door **pencere camı**

panel /ˈpænl/ *noun* [C] **1** PIECE a flat, rectangular piece of wood, metal, etc that forms the surface of a door, wall, etc **levha, panel, pano 2** PEOPLE a group of people who are chosen to discuss something or make a decision about something **panel, kurul, heyet; tartışma/münazaraheyeti/kurulu** *a panel of experts* **3** CONTROLS the part of a car, aircraft, etc that the controls are fixed to **gösterge panosu** ➾See also: **solar panel.**

panelling *UK* (*US* **paneling**) /ˈpænəlɪŋ/ *noun* [U] flat, rectangular pieces of wood that form the surface of the

walls, doors, etc **lâmbri, ahşap kaplamalı, kaplama** *carved oak panelling*

panellist *UK* (*US* **panelist**) /ˈpænəlɪst/ *noun* [C] one of a group of people who are chosen to discuss something or make a decision about something **panel/heyet/kurul üyesi**

pang /pæŋ/ *noun* [C] a sudden, strong feeling of an unpleasant emotion **ani ve şiddetli sancı, ağrı, spazm** *Bernard felt a sharp pang of jealousy.*

panhandle /ˈpænˌhændl/ *verb* [I] *US* to ask people for money in a public place **sokakta para toplamak; dilenmek ● panhandler** *noun* [C] *US* **dilenci**

panic ...... İLE BİRLİKTE KULLANILAN KELİMELER
be **in** a panic ● panic **breaks out** ● **absolute/blind** panic ● panic **about/over** sth ● do sth **in** panic ● a panic **attack**

panic¹ /ˈpænɪk/ *noun* [C, U] a sudden, strong feeling of worry or fear that makes you unable to think or behave calmly **panik, büyük korku** *He was in a panic about his exams.* ○ *She had a panic attack* (= suddenly felt extreme panic) *in the supermarket.*

panic² /ˈpænɪk/ *verb* [I, T] **panicking,** *past* **panicked** to suddenly feel so worried or frightened that you cannot think or behave calmly, or to make someone feel this way **paniğe/korkuya kapılmak; çok korkmak** *Don't panic, we've got plenty of time.*

panic-stricken /ˈpænɪkˌstrɪkən/ *adjective* extremely frightened **korkuya/paniğe kapılmış**

panorama /ˌpænərˈɑːmə/ *noun* [C] a view of a wide area **genel/görünüm manzara**

panoramic /ˌpænəˈræmɪk/ *adjective* A panoramic view is very wide. **panoramik** *a panoramic view of the city*

pansy /ˈpænzi/ *noun* [C] a small garden flower with round petals which can be many different colours **hercaî menekşe**

pant /pænt/ *verb* [I] to breathe quickly and loudly because it is hot or because you have been running, etc **soluk soluğa kalmak, derin derin nefes almak; nefes nefese kalmak**

panther /ˈpænθər/ *noun* [C] a large, black, wild cat **panter**

panties /ˈpæntiz/ *mainly US* (*UK* **knickers**) *noun* [plural] women's underwear that covers the bottom **kadın külotu** ➾Orta kısımdaki renkli sayfalarına bakınız.

pantomime /ˈpæntəmaɪm/ *noun* [C, U] a funny play performed in the UK around Christmas, based on traditional children's stories **geleneksel çocuk hikâyeleri üzerine kurulu Birleşik Krallık'da Noel zamanı gösterilen komik oyun; peri masalı oyunu**

pantry /ˈpæntri/ *noun* [C] a small room where food is kept **kiler**

pants /pænts/ *noun* [plural] **1** *US* (*UK/US* **trousers**) a piece of clothing that covers the legs and has a separate part for each leg **pantolon** ➾Orta kısımdaki renkli sayfalarına bakınız. **2** *UK* (*US* **underpants**) underwear that covers the bottom **don, külot** ➾Orta kısımdaki renkli sayfalarına bakınız.

'pant ˌsuit *US* (*UK* **trouser suit**) *noun* [C] a woman's jacket and trousers made of the same material **bayan ceket etek (takım)**

pantyhose /ˈpæntihəʊz/ *US* (*UK* **tights**) *noun* [plural] a piece of women's clothing made of very thin material that covers the legs and bottom **külotlu çorap**

papa /pəˈpɑː/ *noun* [C] *old-fashioned another word for* father **baba**

the papacy /'peɪpəsi/ *noun* the position or authority of the Pope (= leader of the Roman Catholic Church) papalık; Roma Katolik Kilisesi lideri Papa'nın yetki ve makamı

papal /'peɪpəl/ *adjective* relating to the Pope (= leader of the Roman Catholic Church) papaya ilişkin/ait

paparazzi /ˌpæpə'rætsi/ *noun* [plural] photographers whose job is to follow famous people and take photographs of them for newspapers and magazines paparazzi

o⌐**paper**[1] /'peɪpəʳ/ *noun* 1 [MATERIAL] [U] thin, flat material used for writing on, covering things in, etc kâğıt *a piece/sheet of paper* 2 [NEWSPAPER] [C] a newspaper gazete 3 [EXAM] [C] *UK* an examination sınav kâğıdı *Candidates must answer two questions from each paper.* 4 [WRITING] [C] a piece of writing about a particular subject written by someone who has been studying that subject yazılı çalışma/ödev; yazıya dökülmüş araştırma, inceleme *She's just published a paper on language acquisition.* ⊃See also: blotting paper, carbon paper, toilet paper, White Paper, wrapping paper.

paper[2] /'peɪpəʳ/ *verb* [T] to decorate the walls of a room by covering them with paper duvar kâğıdı yapmak; duvar kâğıdı ile kaplamak

paperback /'peɪpəbæk/ *noun* [C] a book that has a soft paper cover karton kapak

'**paper ˌclip** *noun* [C] a small piece of metal used to hold several pieces of paper together ataş, kağıt tutacağı/ raptiyesi ⊃Orta kısımdaki renkli sayfalarına bakınız.

papers /'peɪpəz/ *noun* [plural] official documents belgeler, resmi evraklar *My papers are safely locked away.*

'**paper ˌweight** *noun* [C] a small, heavy object that you put on top of pieces of paper to stop them from moving kâğıtların dağılmasını önlemek için üzerine konulan küçük ağır cisim

paperwork /'peɪpəwɜːk/ *noun* [U] the part of a job that involves writing letters, organizing information, etc yazışmalar; kâğıt/evrak işleri

par /pɑːʳ/ *noun* 1 **be on a par with sb/sth** to be the same as or equal to someone or something eşit derecede/ aynı ölçüde olmak; başabaş, aynı düzeyde 2 **below par** not as good as usual her zamanki kadar iyi olmamak *I'm feeling a bit below par today.* 3 **be par for the course** If a type of behaviour, event, or situation is par for the course, it is not good but it is normal or as you would expect. idare eder durumda olmak; çok iyi olmasa da kabul edilir derecede olmak *"Simon was late." "That's just par for the course, isn't it?"*

parable /'pærəbl/ *noun* [C] a short story, especially in the Bible, that shows you how you should behave mesel, kıssa, dini ve ahlaki öykü/hikâye

paracetamol /ˌpærə'siː-təmɒl/ *noun* [C, U] a common drug used to reduce pain and fever ağrı kesici ve ateş düşürücü bir tür ilaç

parachute /'pærəʃuːt/ *noun* [C] a large piece of cloth which is fixed to your body by strings and helps you to drop safely from an aircraft paraşüt ● **parachute**

parachute

verb [I] to jump from an aircraft using a parachute paraşütle atlayış yapmak

parade[1] /pə'reɪd/ *noun* [C] a line of people or vehicles that moves through a public place as a way of celebrating an occasion geçit töreni, resmi geçit , tören, alay *a victory parade*

parade[2] /pə'reɪd/ *verb* 1 **parade down/past/through sth** to walk as a group, usually to show disagreement about something protesto yürüyüşü/gösterisi yapmak *Thousands of workers paraded through the streets.* 2 **parade around/up and down, etc** to walk somewhere so that people will see and admire you dikkat çekmek için aşağı yukarı yürümek *The kids were parading around in their new clothes.* 3 [T] to try to make someone notice something that you are proud of, especially how rich you are or how much you know gösteriş yapmak, sergilemek, caka satmak

paradigm /'pærədaɪm/ *noun* [C] *formal* a typical example or model of something kendi türünün yegane örneği; tipik numune; model *Career women are establishing a new paradigm of work and family life.*

paradise /'pærədaɪs/ *noun* 1 [no plural] in some religions, a place where good people go after they die cennet 2 [C, U] a perfect place or situation cennet misali yer/mekan; rahat, ferah, iç açıcı yer *a tropical paradise* ○ *a shoppers' paradise*

paradox /'pærədɒks/ *noun* [C] a situation that seems very strange or impossible because of two opposite qualities or facts içinden çıkılmaz/anlaşılmaz çelişki; ● **paradoxical** /ˌpærə'dɒksɪkᵊl/ *adjective* involving a paradox ciddi çelişkili, içinden çıkılmaz olan, mantık dışı olan ● **paradoxically** *adverb* çelişkili bir şekilde

paraffin /'pærəfɪn/ *UK* (*US* kerosene) *noun* [U] oil used for heating and lights gaz yağı, parafin

paragraph /'pærəgrɑːf/ *noun* [C] a part of a text that contains at least one sentence and starts on a new line paragraf

parallel[1] /'pærəlel/ *adjective* 1 If two or more lines are parallel, the distance between them is the same along all their length. paralel *The streets are parallel.* 2 similar and happening at the same time benzer, paralel, aynı anda olan *Parallel experiments are being conducted in both countries.*

⟨⟨⟨ *parallel (noun)* ...... İLE BİRLİKTE KULLANILAN KELİMELER

draw a parallel ● a clear/close/strong parallel ● a parallel between sth and sth ● a parallel with sth

parallel[2] /'pærəlel/ *noun* [C] a similarity paralellik, benzerlik, ortak özellikler *There are a number of parallels between our two situations.* ○ *People are drawing parallels* (= describing similarities) *between the two cases.*

the Paralympic Games /ˌpærəˌlɪmpɪk'geɪmz/ (*also* Paralympics) *noun* [plural] an international sports competition for people who have a disability (= a condition that makes it difficult for a person to do the things that other people do) Özürlüler Olimpiyat Oyunları ● **Paralympic** *adjective* engelliler için düzenlenmiş spor müsabakaları ● **Paralympian** *noun* [C] engelliler için düzenlenmiş spor müsabakaları

paralyse *UK* (*US* paralyze) /'pærᵊlaɪz/ *verb* [T] 1 to make someone unable to move all or part of their body felç etmek, sakat bırakmak; kötürüm bırakmak [often passive] *He was paralysed from the waist down by polio.* 2 to make something stop working çalışmasını engellemek, felç etmek, felce uğratmak *Rail strikes have paralysed the city's transport system.*

P

pain

paralysed UK (US **paralyzed**) /'pærəlaızd/ adjective **1** unable to move all or part of your body because of an injury or illness felç olmuş, felç inmiş, inme inmiş **2** unable to move or speak because you are so frightened korkudan konuşamayan hareket edemeyen; geçici felç durumu yaşayan to be paralysed with fear

paralysis /pə'ræləsıs/ noun [U] **1** being unable to move all or part of your body because of injury or illness felç, inme muscular paralysis **2** not being able to take action hareket edememe, felce uğrama political paralysis

paralyze /'pærəlaız/ verb [T] US spelling of paralyse felç etmek, sakat bırakmak; kötürüm bırakmak

paramedic /,pærə'medık/ noun [C] someone who is trained to give medical treatment to people who are injured or very ill, but who is not a doctor or nurse sağlık memuru

parameter /pə'ræmıtər/ noun [C] a limit that controls the way that you can do something sınırlayıcı unsurlar [usually plural] Before we can start the research we need to set some parameters (= decide some limits).

paramilitaries /,pærə'mılıtºriz/ noun [plural] people who belong to paramilitary organizations milis güçleri

paramilitary /,pærə'mılıtºri/ adjective [always before noun] organized like an army, but not belonging to an official army milis a paramilitary organization/group

paramount /'pærəmaunt/ adjective formal more important than anything else en önemli/üstün/yüce Safety, of course, is paramount. ○ Communication is of paramount importance.

paranoia /,pærə'nɔıə/ noun [U] **1** when you wrongly think that other people do not like you and are always criticizing you başkalarının kendisini sevmediğini ve sürekli eleştirildiği konusunda yanlış kanı sahibi olma; paranoya Do you think his boss really hates him or is it just paranoia? **2** a mental illness that makes people wrongly think that other people are trying to harm them evham hastalığı; başkalarının kensine zarar vereceğini düşünme hastalığı; paranoya ● **paranoid** /'pærºnɔıd/ adjective when you have paranoia evhamlı, paranoyak Stop being so paranoid - no one's talking about you.

paraphernalia /,pærəfº'neılıə/ noun [U] all the objects used in a particular activity kişisel ufak tefek eşya, öteberi, ıvır zıvır the painter's paraphernalia of brushes, paints, and pencils

paraphrase /'pærəfreız/ verb [I, T] to express something that has been said or written in a different way, usually so that it is clearer başka sözcüklerle anlatmak; yorumlamak ● **paraphrase** noun [C] izah

parasite /'pærəsaıt/ noun [C] **1** a plant or animal that lives on or inside another plant or animal in order to get food asalak, parazit **2** a lazy person who expects other people to give them money and food her şeyi başkalarından bekleyen

paratrooper /'pærətru:pər/ noun [C] a soldier who is trained to be dropped from an aircraft using a parachute (= large piece of cloth fixed to the body by strings) hava indirme askeri/personeli

o=**parcel** /'pɑːsºl/ noun [C] something that is covered in paper so that it can be sent by post paket, koli ⊃See also: part¹ and parcel.

parched /pɑːtʃt/ adjective **1 be parched** informal to be very thirsty çok susamış olmak, kupkuru olmak I'm going to get a drink - I'm parched. **2** very dry kupkuru, çoraklaşmış, kavrulmuş, yanmış a parched desert/land

pardon¹ /'pɑːdºn/ exclamation **1** (also US **pardon me**) a polite way of asking someone to repeat what they have just said Affedersiniz!', 'Anlayamadım!', 'Efendim?', 'Pardon?' "You'll need an umbrella." "Pardon?" "I said you'll need an umbrella." **2 Pardon me.** used to say 'sorry' after you have done something rude, for example after burping (= letting air from your stomach out of your mouth) Efendim?!', 'Affedersiniz!', 'Özür dilerim!', 'Bağışlayın lütfen!', 'Çok affedersiniz

pardon² /'pɑːdºn/ noun **1** [C] when someone who has committed a crime is officially forgiven and allowed to be free af, bağışlama, affetme, özgür/serbest bırakma **2 I beg your pardon.** formal spoken **a** used for saying 'sorry' when you have made a mistake or done something wrong Affedersiniz!', 'Özür dilerim!', 'Bağışlayın lütfen!', 'Çok affedersiniz I beg your pardon - I thought you were speaking to me. **b** used to show that you strongly disagree or that you are angry about something that someone has said Affedersiniz ama...!', 'Özür dilerim ama...!', 'Sizinle aynı kanaatte değilim!', 'Lütfen!', 'Çok rica ederim!' I beg your pardon, young man - I don't want to hear you speak like that again!

pardon³ /'pɑːdºn/ verb [T] to officially forgive someone who has committed a crime and allow them to be free affetmek, bağışlamak;

o=**parent** /'peºrºnt/ noun [C] your mother or father anne baba, ebeveyler Her parents live in Oxford. ● **parental** /pə'rentºl/ adjective relating to a parent anne babaya ilişkin parental responsibility

'parent ,company noun [C] a company which controls other smaller companies ana şirket; asıl kuruluş

parentheses /pə'renθəsi:z/ (also UK **brackets**) noun [plural] two curved lines ( ) used around extra information or information that should be considered as separate from the main part parantez işareti '( )' The age of each student is listed in parentheses.

parenthood /'peºrºnthʊd/ noun [U] being a parent annelik babalık; anne baba olma, ana babalık the demands of parenthood ○ single parenthood

parenting /'peºrºntıŋ/ noun [U] the things that you do during the time when you take care of your baby or child annelik babalık etme; bakım, ilgi, çocuk yetiştirme

parish /'pærıʃ/ noun [C] an area that has its own church kilise bölgesi

parishioner /pə'rıʃºnər/ noun [C] someone who lives in a parish and often goes to church kilise bölgesinde yaşayan ve kilise müdavimi olan kimse

parity /'pærəti/ noun [U] formal equality, usually relating to the money people earn or their position eşitlik The union has also asked for wage parity with similar public-sector workers. ⊃Opposite disparity.

o=**park¹** /pɑːk/ noun [C] a large area of grass, often in a town, where people can walk and enjoy themselves park We went for a walk in the park. ⊃See also: amusement park, car park, industrial park, national park, theme park, trailer park.

o=**park²** /pɑːk/ verb [I, T] to leave a vehicle in a particular place for a period of time aracı park etmek I parked the car near the old bridge. ○ You can park outside the school.

parking /'pɑːkıŋ/ noun [U] leaving a vehicle in a particular place for a period of time araç park etme, araç parkı free/underground parking

'parking ,lot US (UK **car park**) noun [C] a place where vehicles can be parked park yeri/alanı

'parking ,meter noun [C] a device next to a road that you pay so that you can park your vehicle on that road **parkmetre**

'parking ,ticket noun [C] a piece of paper that tells you that you must pay money because you have parked your car where you should not **park fişi**

---
parliament ...... İLE BİRLİKTE KULLANILAN KELİMELER

dissolve/elect a parliament ● **enter** parliament ● **in** parliament
---

➔**parliament** /'pɑːləmənt/ noun [C, U] in some countries, a group of people who make the laws for the country **millet meclisi, parlamento** *the Russian parliament* ● **parliamentary** /ˌpɑːlə'mentˤri/ adjective [always before noun] relating to a parliament **meclise/parlamentoya ait** *a parliamentary candidate/election* ➔See also: **Houses of Parliament, Member of Parliament.**

parlour UK (US **parlor**) /'pɑːlər/ noun [C] a shop that provides a particular type of goods or services **tek tip ürün satan veya bir alanda hizmet sunan dükkan/işyeri** *a beauty/pizza parlour*

parody /'pærədi/ noun [C, U] a film, book, etc that copies someone else's style in a way that is funny **parodi** *It's a parody of a low-budget 1950's horror movie.* ● **parody** verb [T] **parodi**

parole /pə'rəʊl/ noun [U] when someone is allowed to leave prison early but is only allowed to remain free if they behave well **şartlı tahliye** *He's hoping to get released* **on parole.**

parrot /'pærət/ noun [C] a tropical bird with a curved beak and colourful feathers that can be taught to copy what people say **papağan**

parsimonious /ˌpɑːsɪ'məʊniəs/ adjective formal not willing to spend money or give something **cimri, eli sıkı, pinti**

parsley /'pɑːsli/ noun [U] a herb that is added to food to give it flavour **maydanoz**

parsnip /'pɑːsnɪp/ noun [C] a long, cream-coloured root that is eaten as a vegetable **yabani havuç**

➔**part¹** /pɑːt/ noun **1** NOT ALL [C, U] one of the things that, with other things, makes the whole of something **kısım, parça, bölüm** *Part of this form seems to be missing.* ○ *I did French as part of my degree course.* ○ *It's all part of growing up.* ○ *You're part of the family.* **2 take part (in sth)** to be involved in an activity with other people **iştirak etmek, katılmak, yer almak** *She doesn't usually take part in any of the class activities.* **3** FILM/PLAY [C] a person in a film or play **film veya oyundaki kişi** *He plays the part of the father.* **4 have/play a part in sth** to be one of the people or things that are involved in an event or situation **rolü olmak, etkisi olmak, yeri/katkısı olmak** *Alcohol plays a part in 60 percent of violent crime.* **5** MACHINE [C] a piece of a machine or vehicle **(makina, araç) parça, yedek parça** *aircraft parts* ○ *spare parts* **6** HAIR [C] US (UK **parting**) the line on your head made by brushing your hair in two different directions **saçın ayrıldığı bölüm/yer 7 the best/better part of sth** most or nearly all of time ...**ın/in büyük bir bölümü/çoğu/ekseriyeti** *It took the better part of the afternoon to put those shelves up.* **8 in part** formal partly **kısmen, bir ölçüde, bir dereceye kadar; bir nebze** *He is in part to blame for the accident.* **9 for the most part** mostly or usually **ekseriyetle, genellikle, çoğunlukla, çoğu zaman** *I enjoyed it for the most part.* **10 look the part** to look suitable for a particular situation **uygun/münasip olmak** *If you're going to be a successful businesswoman, you've got to look the part.* ● **11 part and parcel** If something is part and parcel of an experience, it is a necessary part of that experience and cannot be avoided. **esas/temel/ana bölüm/kısım; temel unsur** *Stress is part and parcel of the job.*

part² /pɑːt/ adverb not completely **kısmen, belli bir bölüm** *She's part Irish and part English.*

part³ /pɑːt/ verb **1** SEPARATE [I, T] If two sides of something part, they become separated, and if you part them, you make them separate. **ayrılmak, uzaklaşmak; ayırmak, uzaklaştırmak** *Slowly her lips parted and she smiled.* **2** LEAVE [I, T] formal If two people part, or if one person parts from another, they leave each other. **ayrılmak, terketmek; ilişkilerini kesmek** *That summer, after six years of marriage, we parted.* ○ *Even after we* **parted company**, *we remained in contact.* **3** HAIR [T] to brush your hair in two directions so that there is a straight line showing on your head **saçlarına bir taraftan ayırmak** *In my school days, I had long hair parted in the middle.*

part with sth phrasal verb to give something to someone else, often when you do not want to **gözden çıkarmak, ayrılmak, vazgeçmek** *You know how hard it is to get Simon to part with his money.*

partial /'pɑːʃˤl/ adjective **1** not complete **kısmî, sınırlı** *He made a partial recovery.* **2 be partial to sth** If you are partial to something, you like it. **düşkün/tutkun olmak, hoşlanmış/yanlı olmak** *I'm rather partial to red wine myself.*

partially /'pɑːʃˤli/ adverb not completely **kısmen, sınırlı olarak** *partially cooked*

---
participant ...... İLE BİRLİKTE KULLANILAN KELİMELER

an **active/unwilling** participant ● a participant **in** sth
---

participant /pɑː'tɪsɪpˤnt/ noun [C] someone who is involved in an activity **katılımcı, iştirakçi, katılan kimse** *All participants finishing the race will receive a medal.*

participate /pɑː'tɪsɪpeɪt/ verb [I] to be involved with other people in an activity **katılmak, iştirak etmek, yer almak, içinde bulunmak** *She rarely participates in any of the discussions.* ● **participation** /pɑːˌtɪsɪ'peɪʃˤn/ noun [U] Both shows encourage **audience participation.** **katılım**

participle /pɑː'tɪsɪpl/ ⓤ /'pɑːtɪsɪpl/ noun [C] the form of a verb that usually ends with '-ed' or '-ing' and is used in some verb tenses or as an adjective **(dilbilgisi) sıfatfiil, ortaç; '-ed' veya '-ing' ile biten ve bazı fiil çekimlerinde veya sıfat olarak kullanılan fiil şekli** ➔See also: **past participle, present participle.**

particle /'pɑːtɪkl/ noun [C] **1** a very small piece of something **zerre, tanecik, parçacık** *particles of dust* **2** a very small part of an atom, for example an electron or a proton

➔**particular** /pə'tɪkjələr/ adjective **1** ONE PERSON/THING [always before noun] used to talk about one thing or person and not others **belli, belirli, muayyen** *Is there any particular restaurant you'd like to go to?* ○ *"Why did you ask?" "No particular reason."* **2** SPECIAL [always before noun] special **belli, özel, hususi, müstesna** *"Was anything important said at the meeting?" "Nothing of particular interest."* **3** NOT EASILY SATISFIED [never before noun] choosing things carefully and not easily satisfied **titiz, zor beğenen, müşkülpesent, seçici** *Teenagers are very particular about the clothes they'll wear.* **4 in particular** especially **özellikle, bilhassa** *Are you looking for anything in particular?*

➔**particularly** /pə'tɪkjələr/ adverb especially **özellikle, bilhassa** *She didn't seem particularly interested.* ○ *"Was the food good?" "Not particularly."*

particulars /pə'tɪkjələz/ *noun* [plural] *formal* details about something or someone **ayrıntılar, detaylar, bilgi** *There's a form for you to note down all your particulars.*

parting¹ /'pɑːtɪŋ/ *noun* **1** [C, U] *formal* when you are separated from another person, often for a long time **ayrılma, veda, vedalaşma** *The pain of parting gradually lessened over the years.* **2** [C] *UK* (*US* **part**) the line on your head made by brushing your hair in two different directions **kafada saçların ayrılma çizgisi**

parting² /'pɑːtɪŋ/ *adjective* **parting glance/words, etc** something that you do or say as you leave **veda bakışı/sözleri**

partisan¹ /ˌpɑːtɪ'zæn/ ⓤ /'pɑːrtɪzən/ *adjective* showing support for a particular political system or leader **yandaş, taraftar, partizan** *partisan politics* ○ *a partisan crowd*

partisan² /ˌpɑːtɪ'zæn/ ⓤ /'pɑːrtɪzən/ *noun* [C] **1** someone who supports a particular political system or leader **partizan, belli bir siyasî partiyi lideri destekleyen kimse 2** a member of a group that secretly fights against soldiers who are controlling their country **partizan, çeteci, gerillâ**

partition /pɑː'tɪʃ°n/ *noun* **1** [C] a wall that divides a room into two parts **bölme, ara duvar 2** [U] when a country divides into two or more countries or areas of government **(ülke) bölünme, ayrılma ● partition** *verb* [T] **duvar ile bölme**

○━**partly** /'pɑːtli/ *adverb* used to show that something is true to some degree but not completely **kısmen, sınırlı olarak** *The house is partly owned by her father.* ○ *He was partly responsible.*

○━**partner¹** /'pɑːtnər/ *noun* [C] **1** [RELATIONSHIP] someone that you are married to or having a sexual relationship with **eş, karı kocadan biri, sevgili** *sexual partners* ○ *Are partners invited to the office dinner?* **2** [SPORTS/DANCING] someone that you are dancing or playing a sport or game with **oyun veya takım arkadaşı; eş, kavalye, dam 3** [BUSINESS] someone who owns a business with another person **ortak; iş ortağı** *a junior/senior partner* ○ *He's a partner in a law firm.* **4** [COUNTRY] a country that has an agreement with another country **ortak devlet/ülke; antlaşmaya imza koyan devlet/ülke** *a trading partner* ○ *Britain and its European partners*

partner² /'pɑːtnər/ *verb* [T] to be someone's partner in a dance, sport, or game **(oyun, spor vb.) eş olmak; kavalye/dam olmak; eşlik etmek;** *He looks certain to partner him again in the finals.*

partnership .... İLE BİRLİKTE KULLANILAN KELİMELER

enter into/go into partnership ● be in partnership with sb ● a partnership between sb and sb

partnership /'pɑːtnəʃɪp/ *noun* **1** [C, U] when two people or organizations work together to achieve something **ortaklık, işbirliği; ortak iş yapma** *She's gone into partnership* (= started to work together) *with an ex-colleague.* **2** [C] a company which is owned by two or more people **şirket, ortaklık**

part-time /ˌpɑː'taɪm/ *adjective, adverb* working or studying only for part of the day or the week **yarı zamanlı; yarı zamanlı çalışan** *a part-time job* ○ *He works part-time as a waiter.*

party .... İLE BİRLİKTE KULLANILAN KELİMELER

go to/have/throw a party ● a birthday/Christmas party ● be at a party

○━**party¹** /'pɑːti/ *noun* [C] **1** [EVENT] an event where people enjoy themselves by talking, eating, drinking, and dancing **eğlence, cümbüş, parti** *a birthday party* ○ *We're*

having a party to celebrate the occasion. **2** [POLITICS] an organization that shares the same political beliefs and tries to win elections **siyasi parti** *a political party* **3** [GROUP] a group of people who are working or travelling together **grup, ekip, takım; çalışma/seyahat grubu** *a party of tourists* **4** [LEGAL] one of the sides in a legal agreement or disagreement **(antlaşma ve anlaşmazlık) taraf, taraflar** *the guilty party* ○ *We hope to provide a solution that is acceptable to both parties.* ⊃See also: the Conservative Party, the Democratic Party, the Green Party, the Labour Party, toe the (party) line¹, the Republican Party, search party, slumber party, third party.

party² /'pɑːti/ *verb* [I] to enjoy yourself by talking, eating, drinking, and dancing with a group of people **eğlence düzenlemek, parti vermek** *They were out partying till five o'clock in the morning.*

○━**pass¹** /pɑːs/ *verb* **1** [GO PAST] [I, T] (*also* **pass by**) to go past something or someone **geçmek, geçip gitmek** *She passed me this morning in the corridor.* ○ *Cars kept passing us on the motorway.* **2** **pass (sth) over/through, etc** to go in a particular direction, or to cause something to go in a particular direction **geçmek, geçirmek** *Another plane passed over our heads.* ○ *We pass through your village on the way home.* **3** [GIVE] [T] to give something to someone **vermek, uzatmak** *Could you pass the salt, please?* ○ *He passed a note to her in the meeting.* **4** [TIME] [I] If a period of time passes, it happens. **geçmek, geçip gitmek, bitmek, sona ermek, tükenmek** *Four years have passed since that day.* **5** **pass (the) time** to spend time doing something **zaman geçirmek; bir şeyler yaparak zamanı geçirmek** *She was eating only to pass the time.* **6** [EXAM] [I, T] to succeed at a test or an exam, or to decide that someone has been successful **(sınav, test) geçmek, başarmak, geçirmek, başarılı saymak** *I passed my driving test the first time.* **7** [BE MORE THAN] [T] to be more than a particular level **...ın/in üstüne çıkmak; geçmek; aşmak** *Donations have passed the one million mark.* **8** [SPORTS] [I, T] in sports, to throw or kick a ball to someone else **pas vermek, pas atmak** *Edwards passes to Brinkworth.* **9** **pass a law/motion, etc** to officially approve of something and make it into a law or rule **kanunlaştırmak, kabul etmek, onaydan geçirmek** *They passed a law banning the sale of alcohol.* **10** [GO AWAY] [I] If a feeling passes, it goes away. **(his) geçmek, yok olmak, geride kalmak, geçip gitmek** *I know he's angry now but it'll pass.* **11** **pass judgment** to judge someone's behaviour **yargılamak 12** **pass sentence** If a judge passes sentence, they state what the criminal's punishment will be. **karar vermek, hüküm vermek 13** **let sth pass** to decide not to criticize someone when they say something unpleasant or they make a mistake **eleştirmemek, kendi hâline bırakmak; üzerinde durmamak** ⊃See also: pass the buck¹.

pass sth around/round *phrasal verb* to offer something to each person in a group of people **tek tek teklif etmek; herkese ayrı ayrı sunmak** *Take a copy for yourself and pass the rest around.*

pass as/for sth/sb *phrasal verb* If someone or something passes as or for someone or something else, they appear like that person or thing. **...gibi görünmek; ...a/e benzemek; ...hissini vermek; sanılmasına meydan vermek** *She's fifteen but could easily pass for eighteen.*

pass away *phrasal verb* to die **vefat etmek; ölmek** *She passed away peacefully in her sleep.*

pass sth down *phrasal verb* to teach or give something to someone who will be alive after you have died **kendisinden sonra gelene öğretmek/bırakmak; babadan oğula geçmek** [often passive] *Folk tales have been passed down from generation to generation.*

pass sth/sb off as sth/sb *phrasal verb* to pretend that something or someone is different from what they really are **kendini...imiş süsü verip yutturmak; kendini...diye tanıtmak** *He tried to pass himself off as some sort of expert.*

pass on *phrasal verb* to die **geçip gitmek, vefat etmek, ölmek**

pass sth on *phrasal verb* 1 TELL to tell someone something that someone else has told you **iletmek, aktarmak, başkalarına söylemek** *Did you pass on my message to him?* 2 GIVE to give something to someone else **vermek, teslim etmek** *Could you pass it on to Laura when you've finished reading it?* 3 DISEASE to give a disease to another person **geçmek, bulaşmak** *The virus can be passed on through physical contact.*

pass out *phrasal verb* to become unconscious **bayılmak, kendinden geçmek** *I don't remember any more because I passed out at that point.*

pass sth up *phrasal verb* to not use an opportunity to do something **fırsatı değerlendirmemek, kaçırmak, yararlanmamak** *It's a great opportunity - you'd be a fool to pass it up.*

pass² /pɑːs/ *noun* [C] 1 TEST a successful result in a test or a course **başarılı** *A pass is above 60%.* 2 DOCUMENT an official document that allows you to do something **izin belgesi** *a bus/rail pass* ○ *You need a pass to get into the building.* 3 SPORTS in sports, when you throw or kick a ball to someone else **pas, pas verme, topu verme** 4 PATH a narrow path between two mountains **geçit** *a mountain pass* ➔See also: **boarding pass.**

passage /ˈpæsɪdʒ/ *noun* 1 SPACE [C] (*also* passageway /ˈpæsɪdʒweɪ/) a long, narrow space that connects one place to another **geçit, dehliz** *There's a passage to the side of the house, leading to the garden.* 2 WRITING/MUSIC [C] a short part of a book, speech, or piece of music **parça, bölüm, pasaj** *She can quote whole passages from the novel.* 3 TUBE [C] a tube in your body that allows air, liquid, etc to pass through it **yol, kanal, tüp** *the nasal/respiratory passages* 4 PROGRESS [U, no plural] the movement or progress from one stage or place to another **geçiş, ilerleme** *It's a difficult passage from boyhood to manhood.* 5 **the passage of time** *literary* the way that time passes **geçiş, akış, ilerleyiş** *Love changes with the passage of time.*

passenger /ˈpæsⁿndʒəʳ/ *noun* [C] someone who is travelling in a vehicle, but not controlling the vehicle **yolcu** *a front-seat passenger*

passer-by /ˌpɑːsəˈbaɪ/ *noun* [C] *plural* **passers-by** someone who is walking past something by chance **yoldan gelip geçen kimse** *Police were alerted by a passer-by who saw the accident.*

passing¹ /ˈpɑːsɪŋ/ *adjective* [always before noun] lasting only for a short time and not important **geçici, kısa süren, ömrü kısa olan, gelip geçici** *a passing interest*

passing² /ˈpɑːsɪŋ/ *noun* 1 **the passing of time/years** the way that time passes (**yıllar/zaman**) **geçme** *With the passing of time their love had changed.* 2 **in passing** If you say something in passing, you talk about one thing briefly while talking mainly about something else. **iki arada bir derede, ayak üstü; aklına gelmişken** *She mentioned in passing that she'd seen Stuart.*

passion /ˈpæʃⁿn/ *noun* 1 [U] a strong, sexual feeling for someone **ihtiras, şehvet** *She saw the passion in his eyes.* 2 [C, U] a strong belief in something or a strong feeling about a subject **tutku, düşkünlük, merak** *She spoke with passion about the injustice.* 3 **a passion for sth** when you like something very much **bir şeye tutku/düşkünlük; aşırı merak** *a passion for football*

passionate /ˈpæʃⁿnət/ *adjective* 1 having a strong, sexual feeling for someone **ihtiraslı, şehvetli** *a passionate affair/lover* 2 showing a strong belief in something or a strong feeling about a subject **tutkulu, düşkün, meraklı** *a passionate speaker* • **passionately** *adverb* **ihtiraslı bir şekilde**

passive /ˈpæsɪv/ *adjective* 1 letting things happen to you and not taking action **pasif, hareketsiz** *Women at that time were expected to be passive.* 2 A passive verb or sentence is one in which the subject does not do or cause the action but is affected by it. For example 'He was released from prison.' is a passive sentence. (**dilbilgisi) edilgen, edilgen çatı**

the passive /ˈpæsɪv/ (*also* the ˌpassive ˈvoice) *noun* the passive form of a verb **fiilin edilgen yapısı**

ˌpassive ˈsmoking *noun* [U] breathing in smoke from other people's cigarettes **pasif içicilik**

Passover /ˈpɑːsˌəʊvəʳ/ *noun* [U] the Jewish period of religious celebration held in March or April **mart veya nisan ayında Musevilikte dinî kutlamalar dönemi**

┌─────────────────────────────────────┐
│ 🧩 **passport** .... İLE BİRLİKTE KULLANILAN KELİMELER │
└─────────────────────────────────────┘
apply for a passport • **have/hold** a [British/Japanese, etc] passport • a **valid** passport

passport /ˈpɑːspɔːt/ *noun* 1 [C] an official document, often a small book, that you need to enter or leave a country **pasaport** *a British passport* 2 **a passport to sth** something that allows you to achieve something else **başarmak için araç, anahtar, yol** *Education is a passport to a better life.*

┌─────────────────────────────────────┐
│ 🧩 **password** .... İLE BİRLİKTE KULLANILAN KELİMELER │
└─────────────────────────────────────┘
enter/put in your password • a **secret** password • **forget** a password • **change** a password

password /ˈpɑːswɜːd/ *noun* [C] a secret word that allows you to do something, such as use your computer **parola, şifre**

past¹ /pɑːst/ *adjective* 1 BEFORE NOW [always before noun] having happened or existed before now **geçmiş, geçmişe ait** *past relationships* ○ *I know this from past experience.* 2 UNTIL NOW [always before noun] used to refer to a period of time before and until the present **geçen, geçtiğimiz** *It's been raining for the past three days.* 3 FINISHED [never before noun] Something that is past has now finished. **geçmiş, bitmiş** *My student days are past.* 4 **past tense** the form of the verb which is used to show what happened in the past **geçmiş zaman**

past² /pɑːst/ *noun* 1 **the past a** the time before the present and all the things that happened then **geçmiş** *In the past people would bathe once a month.* **b** the form of the verb which is used to show what happened in the past **fiilin geçmiş zaman hâli** 2 **sb's past** all of the things that someone has done in their life **bir kimsenin geçmişi** *I knew nothing about his past.*

past³ /pɑːst/ *adverb, preposition* 1 FURTHER further than **geçince, sonra; ...dan/den sonra; ...ın/in ötesinde/ilerisinde** *I live on Station Road, just past the Post Office.* 2 UP TO AND FURTHER up to and further than someone or something **geçip giderek, geçme** *Three boys went past us on mountain bikes.* ○ *I've just seen the bus go past.* 3 AFTER HOUR used to say 'after' the hour when you are saying what time it is (**saat) geçe** *It's five past three.* 4 AFTER LIMIT after a particular time or age limit **zamanı geçmiş, eskimiş, kullanım tarihi geçen; zaman aşımı** *This bacon is past its sell-by date.* 5 **past it** *informal* too old to do something **bir şeyi yapmak için çok yaşlı olmak** 6 **I wouldn't put it past sb (to do sth)** *informal* used to say that you would not be surprised if someone did something, especially something bad, because it is a typical thing for them to do **bekle-nir/beklenirdi; tam onun yapacağı türden şey; bunu ancak o yapardı** *I wouldn't put it past him to sell her jewellery.*

pasta /ˈpæstə/ ⑮ /ˈpɑːstə/ *noun* [U] a food that is made from flour, water, and sometimes eggs and is made in many different shapes **makarna** ⊃Orta kısımdaki renkli sayfalarına bakınız.

paste¹ /peɪst/ *noun* [C, U] **1** a soft, wet, sticky substance that is used to stick things together **zamk, macun, yapıştırıcı** *wallpaper paste* **2** a soft food that spreads easily **salça, macun, ezme** *tomato/almond paste*

paste² /peɪst/ *verb* **1** [T] to stick a piece of paper to another piece of paper **yapıştırmak** *The cuttings had been pasted into a scrapbook.* **2** [I, T] to move a piece of text to a particular place in a computer document **bilgisayarda bir yazıyı bir yerden başka bir yere taşımak** ⊃See also: **cut and paste.**

pastel /ˈpæstəl/ ⑮ /pæsˈtel/ *adjective* A pastel colour is light. **soluk renkli, pastel** *pastel colours/shades* ○ *pastel pink* ● **pastel** *noun* [C] *The bedroom is decorated in pastels* (= pale colours). **pastel**

pastime /ˈpɑːstaɪm/ *noun* [C] an activity that you enjoy doing when you are not working **hobi, meşgale, eğlenceli şey** *Shopping is one of her favourite pastimes.*

pastor /ˈpɑːstəʳ/ *noun* [C] a priest in some Protestant churches **Protestan kilisesi papazı, pastör**

pastoral /ˈpɑːstərəl/ *adjective* **1** related to giving advice and looking after people **insanlarla ilgilenme ve öğüt vermeye ilişkin** *the teacher's pastoral role* **2** [always before noun] *literary* relating to life in the country **kır hayatıyla ilgili** *a pastoral song/tradition*

‚past par'ticiple UK (US ‚past 'participle) *noun* [C] the form of a verb that usually ends with '-ed' and can be used in the perfect tense, the passive tense, or as an adjective. For example 'baked' is the past participle of 'bake'. **geçmiş zaman ortacı**

the ‚past 'perfect (*also* the pluperfect) *noun* the form of a verb that is used to show that an action had already finished when another action happened. In English, the past perfect is made with 'had' and a past participle. (dilbilgisi) **iki farklı eylemden bahsederken bir eylem olduğunda önceki eylemin çoktan bitmiş olduğunu gösteren fiil çekimi**

pastry /ˈpeɪstri/ *noun* **1** [U] a mixture of flour, fat, and water that is cooked, usually used to cover or contain other food **hamur** **2** [C] a small cake that is made with pastry **börek çörek**

pasture /ˈpɑːstʃəʳ/ *noun* [C] an area of land with grass where animals can feed **çayır, otlak, mera**

pat¹ /pæt/ *verb* [T] patting, *past* patted to touch a person or animal with a flat hand in a gentle, friendly way **sıvazlamak, hafifçe vurmak** *She stopped to pat the dog.*

pat² /pæt/ *noun* **1** [C] when you pat a person or animal **sıvazlama, hafif dokunuş, okşama** *He gave her an encouraging pat on the shoulder.* **2 a pat on the back** praise for something good that someone has done **sırtını sıvazlama** *I got a pat on the back for all my hard work.*

patch¹ /pætʃ/ *noun* [C] **1** [AREA] a small area that is different from the area around it **leke, parça, kısım** *a bald patch.* ○ *There are icy patches on the road.* **2** [MATERIAL] a piece of material that you use to cover a hole in your clothes or in other material **yama, yamalık** *He had leather patches sewn on the elbows of his jacket.* **3** [EYE] a small piece of material used to cover an injured eye **göz bağı** **4** [LAND] a small area of land used for a particular purpose **belli bir amaçla kullanılan arazi** *a cabbage/*

vegetable patch **5 a bad/rough, etc patch** a difficult time **zor/kötü/çetin zaman/dönem** *I think their marriage is going through a bad patch.* **6 not be a patch on sb/sth** UK *informal* to not be as good as someone or something else **boy ölçüşememek, eline su dökememek** *Her cooking is okay but it's not a patch on yours.*

patch² /pætʃ/ *verb* [T] to repair a hole in a piece of clothing or other material by sewing a piece of material over it **yamamak, yama yapmak, yama yaparak kapatmak** *to patch your trousers*

patch sth up *phrasal verb* **2** to try to improve your relationship with someone after you have had an argument **tatlıya bağlamak, aradaki buzları eritmek, yatıştırmak, arayı bulmak** *Has he managed to patch things up with her?*

patchwork /ˈpætʃwɜːk/ *noun* **1** [U] a type of sewing in which a lot of small pieces of different material are sewn together **parçalı desen, yama/parça işi** *a patchwork quilt* **2 a patchwork of sth** something that seems to be made of many different pieces **farklı parçaların bir araya getirilerek oluşturulduğu şey** *We flew over a patchwork of fields.*

patchy /ˈpætʃi/ *adjective* **1** not complete or not good in every way **bölük börçük, derme çatma, gelişigüzel** *patchy knowledge of Spanish* **2** existing only in some areas **parça parça, dalga dalga, leke leke** *patchy clouds/fog*

patent¹ /ˈpeɪtnt, ˈpætnt/ *noun* [C] a legal right that a person or company receives to make or sell a particular product so that others cannot copy it **patent, buluş tescil belgesi; imtiyaz/hak sahibi beratı** ● **patent** *verb* [T] to get a patent for something **buluş tescil belgesi almak, patentini almak**

patent² /ˈpeɪtnt, ˈpætnt/ *adjective formal* **patent lie/nonsense** something that is obviously false **bariz/açıkça/belirgin yanlış, yalan** *The explanation he gave - that was patent nonsense.* ● **patently** *adverb formal Her claims are patently* (= obviously) *false.* **imtiyazlı bir şekilde**

paternal /pəˈtɜːnəl/ *adjective* **1** like a father **babacan, baba gibi** *paternal affection* **2** [always before noun] A paternal relative is part of your father's family. **baba tarafıyla ilgili** *He was my paternal grandfather.*

paternity /pəˈtɜːnəti/ *noun* [U] the state of being a father **babalık, baba olma hâli**

pa'ternity ‚leave *noun* [U] a period of weeks or months that a father spends away from his usual job so that he can look after his baby or child **babalık izni**

path /pɑːθ/ *noun* [C] **1** [GROUND] a long, narrow area of ground for people to walk along **patika, dar yol/geçit, keçi yolu** *There's a path through the forest.* ○ *a garden path* **2** [DIRECTION] the direction that a person or vehicle moves in **yol, hat, rota** *a flight path* **3** [CHOOSING] a particular way of doing something over a period of time **belli bir süreçten sonra bir şeyi yapma şekli/biçimi; hal tarzı; izlenen yol** *a career path* ○ *Whichever path we choose, we'll have difficulties.*

pathetic /pəˈθetɪk/ *adjective* **1** *informal* showing no skill, effort, or bravery **beceri/çaba/yürek sergilemeyen; beceriksiz; çaba göstermeyen; zayıf, değersiz** *He made a rather pathetic attempt to apologize.* ○ *You're too frightened to speak to her? Come on, that's pathetic!* ○ *It was a pathetic performance.* **2** sad and weak **acıklı, dokunaklı, zayıf, güçsüz, çelimsiz** *Four times the pathetic little creature fell to the ground.* ● **pathetically** *adverb a pathetically small amount of money* **acınacak halde**

pathological /ˌpæθəˈlɒdʒɪkəl/ *adjective* **1** Pathological behaviour or feelings are extreme and cannot be controlled. **hastalık derecesinde, anormal, mantıksız** *a pathological liar* ○ *pathological hatred* **2** relating to pathology (= the study of disease) **hastalık ilmi/patoloji ile ilgili**

pathologist /pə'θɒlədʒɪst/ *noun* [C] a doctor who has studied pathology, especially one who tries to find out why people have died **patolog**

pathology /pə'θɒlədʒi/ *noun* [U] the scientific study of disease and causes of death **hastalık ilmi, patoloji**

pathos /'peɪθɒs/ *noun* [U] *literary* a quality in a situation that makes you feel sympathy and sadness **dokunaklı hâl; dokunaklılık**

---

patience .... İLE BİRLİKTE KULLANILAN KELİMELER

have/run out of patience ● **lose** (your) patience ● **test/try** sb's patience ● **sth takes** patience ● patience **with** sb/sth

---

o▲**patience** /'peɪʃ³ns/ *noun* [U] **1** the quality of being able to stay calm and not get angry, especially when something takes a long time **sabırlılık, sabır, tahammül** *Finally, I lost my patience and shouted at her.* ○ *Making small scale models takes a lot of patience.* ⊃Opposite **impatience. 2** *UK* (*US* **solitaire**) a card game for one person **tek kişilik iskambil oyunu, pasiyans**

o▲**patient¹** /'peɪʃ³nt/ *adjective* having patience **sabırlı, tahammüllü** *You need to be patient with children.* ● **patiently** *adverb* ⊃Opposite **impatient. sabırlı bir şekilde**

o▲**patient²** /'peɪʃ³nt/ *noun* [C] someone who is being treated by a doctor, nurse, etc **hasta** *a cancer patient*

patio /'pætiəʊ/ *noun* [C] an outside area with a stone floor next to a house, where people can sit to eat and relax **teras, taraça, veranda**

patriot /'peɪtriət/ *noun* [C] someone who loves their country and is proud of it **vatansever/yurtsever kimse**

patriotic /ˌpeɪtri'ɒtɪk/ *adjective* showing love for your country and pride in it **vatansever, yurtsever** *patriotic duty* ○ *a patriotic song* ● **patriotism** /'peɪtriətɪzm/ *noun* [U] when you love your country and are proud of it **vatanseverlik, yurtseverlik**

patrol¹ /pə'trəʊl/ *noun* **1** [C, U] the act of looking for trouble or danger around an area or building **devriye** *We passed a group of soldiers on patrol.* ○ *a patrol boat/car* **2** [C] a group of soldiers or vehicles that patrol an area or building **askerî devriye, devriye araçları** *a border patrol* ○ *an armed patrol*

patrol² /pə'trəʊl/ *verb* [I, T] **patrolling**, *past* **patrolled** to look for trouble or danger in an area or around a building **devriyeye çıkmak, devriye gezmek/atmak** *Police patrol the streets night and day.*

patron /'peɪtr³n/ *noun* [C] **1** someone who supports and gives money to artists, writers, musicians, etc **patron; koruyucu, hami** *a generous patron* ○ *a patron of the arts* **2** a customer at a bar, restaurant, or hotel **(bar, lokanta, otel vb.) müşteri**

patronize (*also UK* -ise) /'pætr³naɪz/ *verb* [T] **1** to speak or behave towards someone as if you were better than them **büyüklük/patronluk/üstünlük taslamak** *Don't patronize me! I know what I'm doing.* **2** *formal* to go to a store, business, etc, especially if you go regularly **devamlı müşterisi olmak; müdavimi olmak**

,**patron 'saint** *noun* [C] a saint (= a special, famous Christian) who is believed to help a particular place, person, or activity **koruyucu aziz** *St. Christopher is the patron saint of travellers.*

---

pattern .... İLE BİRLİKTE KULLANILAN KELİMELER

alter/establish/fall into/follow a pattern ● a **consistent/familiar/traditional** pattern

---

o▲**pattern** /'pæt³n/ *noun* [C] **1** WAY a particular way that something is often done or repeated **biçim, şekil, tarz** *behaviour patterns* **2** DESIGN a design of lines, shapes, colours, etc **desen, motif, tasarım 3** SHAPE a drawing or shape that helps you to make something **örnek çizim, taslak tasarım, patron** *a dress pattern*

o▲**pause** /pɔːz/ *verb* [I] to stop doing something for a short time **ara/fasıla vermek, durmak, duraklamak** *She paused for a moment and looked around her.* ● **pause** *noun* [C] *There was a short pause before he spoke.* **duraklama**

pave /peɪv/ *verb* [T] to cover a path or road with flat stones, bricks, concrete, etc **yola taş/tuğla/beton döşemek**

pavement /'peɪvmənt/ *noun* [C] **1** *UK* (*US* **sidewalk**) a path by the side of a road that people walk on **yaya kaldırımı, kaldırım** *It's illegal to park on the pavement.* **2** *US* the hard surface of a road **yer/zemin kaplama, kaldırım**

pavement

pavilion /pə'vɪljən/ *noun* [C] **1** TENT a large tent that is used for outside events **büyük çadır 2** SPORTS *UK* a building next to a sports field where players can change their clothes **spor alanı yanındaki soyunma binası 3** BUILDING *US* one of a group of related buildings, such as a hospital **aynı amaçla kullanılan binalardan birisi**

paw /pɔː/ *noun* [C] the foot of certain animals, such as cats and dogs **pençe** ● **paw** (*also* **paw at**) *verb* [T] to touch something with a paw **pençe atmak, pençe ile dokunmak** *I could hear the dog pawing at the door.*

pawn¹ /pɔːn/ *noun* [C] **1** in the game of chess, the smallest piece and the one that has the lowest value **piyon 2** someone who does not have power and is used by other people **piyon, maşa, oyuncak; başkalarınca kullanılan zayıf kimse**

pawn² /pɔːn/ *verb* [T] to leave something with a pawnbroker, who gives you money for it and will sell it if you do not pay the money back **rehine vermek/bırakmak** *She pawned her wedding ring to pay the rent.*

pawnbroker /'pɔːnˌbrəʊkər/ *noun* [C] someone who lends you money in exchange for items that they will sell if you cannot pay the money back **tefeci, rehinci, faizci**

o▲**pay¹** /peɪ/ *verb past* **paid 1** BUY [I, T] to give money to someone because you are buying something from them, or because you owe them money **ödemek, vermek** *Helen paid for the tickets.* ○ *Did you pay the telephone bill?* ○ *You can pay by cash or credit card.* **2** WORK [I, T] to give someone money for the work that they do **yapılan iş karşılığı ücret ödemek/vermek** *She gets paid twice a month.* ○ *People work for them because they pay well.* ○ *We paid them £600 for the work.* ○ *a paid job* **3** ADVANTAGE [I] to be a good thing to do because it gives you money or an advantage **para getirmek, kazandırmak, karşılığını vermek** *Crime doesn't pay.* **4** SUFFER [I, T] to suffer because of something bad you have done **cezasını ödemek, çekmek, katlanmak, ödemek** *He's certainly paying for his mistakes.* **5 pay attention** to look at or listen to someone or something carefully **dikkat etmek** *I missed what she* *was saying because I wasn't paying attention.* **6 pay sb a compliment** to tell someone that you admire something about them **iltifat etmek 7 pay tribute to sb/sth** to thank someone or say that you admire someone or something, especially in public **saygı göstermek, toplum önünde teşekkür etmek** *He paid tribute to his former teacher.* **8 pay sb/sth a visit; pay a visit to sb/sth** to visit a place or a person, usually for a short time **ziyaret etmek, kısa ziyarette bulunmak**

pay sb/sth back *phrasal verb* to pay someone the money that you owe them **geri ödemek** *Only borrow money if you're sure you can pay it back.* ○ *I lent him £10 last month and he still hasn't paid me back.*

pay sth off *phrasal verb* to pay all of the money that you owe **tüm borcunu kapatmak/ödemek** *I'm planning to pay off my bank loan in five years.*

pay (sth) out *phrasal verb* to spend a lot of money on something, or to pay a lot of money to someone **bir şeye çok para harcamak; birine çok para ödemek** *I've just paid out £700 to get the car fixed.*

pay up *phrasal verb informal* to give someone all of the money that you owe them, especially when you do not want to **borcunu ödemek; tamamen kapatmak** *Come on, pay up!*

a pay **cheque/cut/raise/rise** ● **rates of** pay

pay² /peɪ/ *noun* [U] the money you receive from your employer for doing your job **maaş, ücret, ödeme** *UK a pay rise/ US a pay raise* ○ *good rates of pay*

payable /ˈpeɪəbl/ *adjective* **1** describes something to be paid **ödenmesi gereken, ödenecek, ödenebilir** *Rent is payable monthly.* **2** If a cheque (= a piece of paper printed by a bank that you use to pay for things) is payable to a person, that person's name is written on the cheque and the money will be paid to them. **hami-line/isme yazılı**

pay-as-you-go /ˌpeɪəzjəˈgəʊ/ *adjective* [always before noun] describes a system in which you pay for a service before you use it **ön ödemeli** *a pay-as-you-go mobile phone* ● **pay-as-you-go** *noun* [U] **alacağınız servis için önceden ödeme yapma**

'pay ˌchannel *noun* [C] a television channel (= a broadcasting company) that you pay money to watch **öde-meli kanal** *Most of the best football matches are on the pay channels.*

'pay ˌcheck *noun* [C] *US pay cheque* **maaş/ücret çeki**

'pay ˌcheque *noun* [C] the amount of money a person earns **maaş/ücret çeki**

payday /ˈpeɪdeɪ/ *noun* [C] the day on which a worker is paid **maaş/ödeme günü**

make/receive payment ● a **form/method** of payment ● payment **for/of** sth

o→**payment** /ˈpeɪmənt/ *noun* **1** [U] the act of paying **ödeme** *They will accept payment by credit card.* **2** [C] the amount of money that is paid **maaş, ücret, ödenti** *monthly payments* ⊃See also: balance of payments, down payment.

pay-per-view /ˌpeɪpəˈvjuː/ *noun* [U] a system in which you choose particular television programmes and then pay to watch them **seyret-öde sistemi** *pay-per-view television/channels*

'pay ˌphone *noun* [C] a telephone in a public place that you pay to use **ankesörlü telefon**

PC¹ /ˌpiːˈsiː/ *noun* [C] **1** a personal computer **kişisel bil-gisayar 2** *UK abbreviation for* police constable (= a police officer of the lowest rank) **polis, polis memuru**

PC² /ˌpiːˈsiː/ *adjective abbreviation for* politically correct (= careful to speak or behave in a way which is not offensive to women, people of a particular race, or people who have physical or mental problems) **incelikli, ustruplu, diplomatik**

PDA /ˌpiːdiːˈeɪ/ *noun* [C] *abbreviation for* personal digital assistant: a small computer that you can carry with you **taşınabilir kişisel bilgisayar**

PDF /ˌpiːdiːˈef/ **1** [U] *abbreviation for* portable document format: a system for storing and moving documents between computers that usually only allows them to be looked at or printed **taşınabilir belge/doküman formatı; bilgisayarlar arası belgelerin taşınıp depolanmasına olanak tanıyan sistem 2** [C] a document using the PDF system **taşınabilir belge forma-tını kullanan doküman**

PE /ˌpiːˈiː/ *noun* [U] *abbreviation for* physical education: classes at school where children do exercise and play sport **beden eğitimi**

pea /piː/ *noun* [C] a small, round, green seed that people eat as a vegetable **bezelye**

bring about/establish/restore peace ● **keep the** peace ● the peace **process** ● a peace **agreement/initiative/treaty**

o→**peace** /piːs/ *noun* [U] **1** when there is no war, violence, or arguing **barış, sulh** *peace talks* ○ *a peace agreement/treaty* ○ *There seems little hope for world peace.* ○ *The UN sent troops to the region to keep the peace.* **2** when there is quiet and calm **huzur, sükûnet, sessizlik, rahatlık** *a feeling of peace* ○ *After a busy day, all I want is peace and quiet.* ○ *I wish you'd stop complaining and leave me in peace!* **3 peace of mind** a feeling that you do not need to worry about anything **gönül rahatlığı, zihinsel huzur** *We lock our doors and windows at night for peace of mind.* ⊃See also: Justice of the Peace.

o→**peaceful** /ˈpiːsfˀl/ *adjective* **1** without violence **şiddet-siz, barış dolu, sulh hâkim olan** *a peaceful protest* **2** quiet and calm **sakin, sessiz, huzur dolu** *The churchyard was empty and peaceful.* ● **peacefully** *adverb* *He died peacefully at home.* **barış içinde**

peacekeeping /ˈpiːsˌkiːpɪŋ/ *adjective* [always before noun] relating to the activity of preventing war and violence **barışı koruyan; sulhu sağlayan** *peacekeeping forces/troops* ○ *a peacekeeping effort/operation* ● **peacekeeper** /ˈpiːsˌkiːpəʳ/ *noun* [C] someone, usually a soldier, who tries to prevent war and violence in countries where there is trouble **barış koruma askeri; barış gücü askeri** *UN peacekeepers*

peacetime /ˈpiːstaɪm/ *noun* [U] a time when a country is not at war **barış/sulh zamanı/dönemi**

peach /piːtʃ/ *noun* [C] a soft, sweet, round fruit with red and yellow skin **şeftali**

peacock /ˈpiːkɒk/ *noun* [C] a large, male bird with long tail feathers that it can lift up to show a lot of colours **tavus kuşu**

peak¹ /piːk/ *noun* [C] **1** the highest level or value of something **en yüksek düzey, en üst seviye; en değerli konum** *Here we see an athlete at the peak of fitness.* ○ *The price of gold reached its peak during the last recession.* ○ *peak travel times* **2** the top of a mountain, or the mountain itself **zirve, en üst nokta, tepe** *snow-covered/mountain peaks*

peak² /piːk/ *verb* [I] to reach the highest level or value of something **en üst düzeye/seviyeye çıkmak** *Her singing career peaked in the 1990s.*

peak

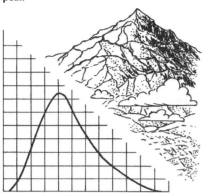

peanut /ˈpiːnʌt/ *noun* [C] an oval-shaped nut with a soft, brown shell **yer fıstığı** *salted peanuts* ○ *peanut oil* ⊃Orta kısımdaki renkli sayfalarına bakınız.

peanut 'butter *UK* (*US* 'peanut ˌbutter) *noun* [U] a pale brown food made by crushing peanuts **yer fıstığı ezmesi** *a peanut butter and jelly sandwich*

pear /peəʳ/ *noun* [C] an oval-shaped, pale green or yellow fruit **armut** ⊃Orta kısımdaki renkli sayfalarına bakınız.

pear

pearl /pɜːl/ *noun* [C] a hard, white, round object that is made inside the shell of an oyster (= a sea creature) and that is used to make jewellery **inci** *a string of pearls* ○ *a pearl necklace* ○ *pearl earrings*

pear-shaped /ˈpeəʃeɪpt/ *adjective* **go pear-shaped** *UK informal* If a plan goes pear-shaped, it fails. **(plan vs.) suya düşmek, başarısız olmak**

peasant /ˈpezᵊnt/ *noun* [C] a poor person who works on the land, usually in a poor country **köylü, rençber, çiftçi** *a peasant farmer*

peat /piːt/ *noun* [U] a dark brown soil made from decaying plants that you can burn as fuel or that you can put around living plants to help them grow **bitki gübresi, turba**

pebble /ˈpebl/ *noun* [C] a small stone **çakıl, çakıl taşı**

pecan /ˈpiːkæn/ ⓤ /pɪˈkɑːn/ *noun* [C] a nut that grows on a tree, or the tree itself **ceviz, ceviz ağacı** *chopped pecans* ○ *pecan pie*

peck[1] /pek/ (*also* peck at) *verb* [T] If a bird pecks something, it lifts or hits it with its beak. **gagalamak** *chickens pecking at corn*

peck[2] /pek/ *noun* [C] **1 give sb a peck on the cheek** to give someone a quick, gentle kiss on the face **öpücük kondurmak 2** when a bird pecks something **gagalama**

peckish /ˈpekɪʃ/ *adjective* *UK* slightly hungry **acıkmış, aç, karnı zil çalan**

peculiar /pɪˈkjuːliəʳ/ *adjective* **1** strange, often in an unpleasant way **acayip, tuhaf, garip** *The wine had a peculiar, musty smell.* **2 peculiar to sb/sth** belonging to or relating to a particular person or thing **nev'i şahsına münhasır; birine/bir şeye özgü/has/mahsus** *Her accent is peculiar to the region.*

peculiarity /pɪˌkjuːliˈærəti/ *noun* [C] **1** something that is typical of a person, place, or thing **özellik, hususiyet, kendine mahsusluk** *Each college has its own traditions and peculiarities.* **2** a strange or unusual characteristic **gariplik, tuhaflık, acayiplik** *My mother always hummed - it was one of her little peculiarities.*

peculiarly /pɪˈkjuːliəli/ *adverb* **1** in a way that is typical of someone or something **tipik, özellikle** *a peculiarly American sense of humour* **2** in a strange way **acayip/tuhaf bir şekilde** *The birds were peculiarly quiet just before the earthquake.*

pedagogue /ˈpedəɡɒɡ/ *noun* [C] *formal* a teacher, usually a very strict one **pedagog**

pedal /ˈpedᵊl/ *noun* [C] a part of a machine that you press with your foot to operate or move the machine **pedal** *bicycle pedals* ○ *a gas/brake pedal*

pedant /ˈpedᵊnt/ *noun* [C] someone who thinks too much about details and rules **gereksiz ayrıntılara önem veren kimse, ayrıntıcı; detaycı; kılı kırk yaran; ayrıntılarda boğulan kimse** ● **pedantic** /pɪˈdæntɪk/ *adjective* thinking too much about details and rules **ayrıntılara önem veren, gelenekçi** *I hate to be pedantic, but Freud was actually Austrian, not German.*

peddle /ˈpedl/ *verb* [T] to sell things, especially drugs or things of bad quality **uyuşturucu madde satmak** *The shops on the pier peddled cheap souvenirs to the tourists.* ○ *He was arrested for peddling drugs.*

pedestal /ˈpedɪstᵊl/ *noun* [C] **1** the base for a statue (= model of a person or animal) **taban, kaide, altlık, temel 2 put sb on a pedestal** to believe that someone is perfect **birinin mükemmel olduğuna inanmak, başına taç etmek; aşırı değer vermek**

pedestrian[1] /pɪˈdestriən/ *noun* [C] a person who is walking and not travelling in a vehicle **yaya** *Many streets are reserved for cyclists and pedestrians.* ○ *a pedestrian precinct/crossing*

pedestrian[2] /pɪˈdestriən/ *adjective* *formal* ordinary or not interesting **sıkıcı, sıradan, yavan** *pedestrian ideas* ○ *a pedestrian speech*

peˌdestrian 'crossing *UK* (*US* crosswalk) *noun* [C] a special place on a road where traffic must stop if people want to cross **yaya geçidi**

pediatrician /ˌpiːdiəˈtrɪʃᵊn/ *noun* [C] *US spelling of* paediatrician **çocuk doktoru**

pedicure /ˈpedɪkjʊəʳ/ *noun* [C, U] treatment to make your feet look attractive **ayak bakımı, pedikür** ⊃Compare manicure.

pedigree[1] /ˈpedɪɡriː/ *noun* [C] **1** a list of the parents and other relatives of an animal **(hayvan) soy, nesep, 2** someone's family history, or their education and experience **şecere, soy ağacı; soy, nesep**

pedigree[2] /ˈpedɪɡriː/ *adjective* [always before noun] A pedigree animal has parents and other relatives all from the same breed and is thought to be of high quality. **safkan, cins, soylu** *a pedigree dog*

pedophile /ˈpiːdəʊfaɪl/ *noun* [C] *US spelling of* paedophile **çocuklara cinsel istek duyan kimse; cinsi sapık; cinsel sapkın kimse; padofil**

pee /piː/ *verb* [I] **peeing**, *past* **peed** *informal* to urinate **çiş yapmak** ● **pee** *noun* [no plural] *informal Do I have time for a pee before we go?* **idrar**

peek[1] /piːk/ *verb* [I] to look at something for a short time, often when you do not want other people to see you **gizlice bakmak, dikizlemek, gözlemek** *I peeked out the window to see who was there.*

peek[2] /piːk/ *noun* **have/take a peek** to look at something for a short time **göz gezdirmek, göz atmak**

peel¹ /pi:l/ verb 1 [T] to remove the skin of fruit or vegetables **kabuğunu soymak** *Peel and chop the onions.* 2 [I, T] If you peel something from a surface, you remove it and if something peels, it comes away from a surface. **kabuğunu soymak; kabuğu soyulmak** *The paint is starting to peel off where the wall is damp.* ⊃See also: keep your eyes (**eye¹**) open/peeled (for sb/sth).

peel sth off *phrasal verb* to take off clothes, especially wet or tight clothes **soymak, çekip çıkarmak, çıkarıp/soyup atmak** *We peeled off our muddy socks and left them outside.*

peel² /pi:l/ noun [U] the skin of fruit or vegetables, especially after it has been removed **kabuk, meyve sebze kabuğu** *Combine nuts, sugar, and orange peel in a small bowl.*

peep /pi:p/ verb [I] 1 **peep at/ through/out, etc** to look at something for a short time, often when you do not want other people to see you **bir şeye gizlice bakmak, dikizlemek, gözlemek** *She peeped at them through the fence.* 2 **peep through/over/out from, etc** to appear but not be seen completely **yavaş yavaş ortaya çıkmak, hafiften görünmek** *The sun peeped out from behind the clouds.* ● **peep** *noun* [no plural] *She took a peep at herself in the mirror.* **dikizleme**

peer¹ /pɪər/ noun [C] 1 someone who is the same age, or who has the same social position or abilities as other members of a group **yaşıt, akran** *Most teenagers want to be accepted by their peers.* 2 in the UK, a person who has a title and a high social position **lord, Britanya asilzadesi**

peer² /pɪər/ verb **peer at/into/through, etc** to look carefully or with difficulty **merakla/dikkatle bakmak, görmeye çalışmak; gözlerini kısarak görmek için bakmak** *She peered at me over her glasses.*

'peer ,group noun [C] a group of people of about the same age, social position, etc **yaşıt/akran/emsal grubu; yaşıtlar, emsaller** *He was the first of his peer group to get married.*

'peer ,pressure noun [U] strong influence on a member of a group to behave in the same way as other members in the group, although that behaviour is not good **grup/akran/emsalbaskısı** *Many teenagers take drugs because of boredom or peer pressure.*

peg¹ /peg/ noun [C] 1 [ON WALL] an object on a wall or door that you hang things on **askı, askı çengeli** 2 [ON ROPE] (*also* **clothes peg**) UK a short piece of wood, plastic, etc that is used to hold clothes on a rope while they dry **askı, askı çengeli** 3 [STICK] a stick made of metal or wood that has a sharp end and which is used to fix something somewhere **mandal** *a tent peg*

peg² /peg/ verb [T] **pegging,** *past* **pegged** to fix the cost of borrowing money or the value of a country's money at a particular level **mandallamak, mandalla tutturmak** [often passive] *Interest rates were pegged at 8.2 %.*

pellet /'pelɪt/ noun [C] a small, hard ball of metal, grain, etc **topak, yumak, saçma** *shotgun/feed pellets*

pelvic /'pelvɪk/ adjective [always before noun] relating to the area below your waist and above your legs **leğen kemiği**

pelvis /'pelvɪs/ noun [C] the group of bones that forms the area below your waist and above your legs and to which your leg bones are joined **vücudun leğen kemiği bölgesi**

o▪**pen¹** /pen/ noun [C] 1 a long, thin object that you use to write or draw in ink **dolma kalem** ⊃Orta kısımdaki renkli sayfalarına bakınız. 2 a small area with a fence around it that you keep animals in **ağıl, hayvan barınağı** *a pig/sheep pen* ⊃See also: ballpoint pen, felt-tip pen, fountain pen.

pen² /pen/ verb [T] **penning,** *past* **penned** *literary* to write something **dolma kalemle yazmak** *sonnets penned by Shakespeare*

pen sb/sth in/up *phrasal verb* to keep people or animals in a small area **bir yerde tutmak, bir yere kapatmak; tık(ıl)mak, kapat(ıl)mak** [often passive] *The soldiers were penned up in their barracks.*

penal /'pi:nᵊl/ adjective [always before noun] relating to the punishment of criminals **cezaî, ceza ile ilgili** *a penal code/system*

penalize (*also* UK **-ise**) /'pi:nᵊlaɪz/ verb [T] 1 to cause someone a disadvantage **ceremesini ödetmek, cezalandırmak** *The present tax system penalizes poor people.* 2 to punish someone for breaking a law or a rule **cezalandırmak, ceza vermek** *He was penalized early in the match for dangerous play.*

penalty ...... İLE BİRLİKTE KULLANILAN KELİMELER
face a penalty ● a heavy/severe/stiff penalty ● a penalty for (doing) sth

penalty /'penᵊlti/ noun [C] 1 a punishment for doing something which is against a law or rule **ceza** *There's a £50 penalty for late cancellation of tickets.* 2 in sports, an advantage given to a team when the opposing team has broken a rule **penaltı** *They won a penalty in the first five minutes of the game.* ○ *a penalty goal/kick* ⊃See also: death penalty.

penance /'penᵊns/ noun [C, U] an act that shows you are sorry for something that you have done **kefaret**

pence /pens/ noun plural of British penny; p **peni**

penchant /'pɒnʃɒŋ/ @ /'pentʃənt/ noun **have a penchant for sth** *formal* to like something very much **düşkün olmak, tutkusu olmak, aşırı sevmek** *Miguel has a penchant for fast cars.*

o▪**pencil** /'pensᵊl/ noun [C, U] a long, thin wooden object with a black or coloured point that you write or draw with **kurşun kalem** ⊃Orta kısımdaki renkli sayfalarına bakınız.

'pencil ,sharpener noun [C] a tool that you use to make pencils sharp **kalem açacağı** ⊃Orta kısımdaki renkli sayfalarına bakınız.

pendant /'pendᵊnt/ noun [C] a piece of jewellery on a chain that you wear around your neck **kolye, pandantif**

pending¹ /'pendɪŋ/ preposition *formal* used to say that one thing must wait until another thing happens **başka bir şey bitinceye/oluncaya kadar bekletilen, askıda, muallakta** *Several employees have been suspended pending an investigation.*

pending² /'pendɪŋ/ adjective *formal* not decided or finished **kararlaştırılmamış, askıda olan, sürüncemede kalan; sümen altı edilmiş olan, bekletilen** *Their court case is still pending.*

pendulum /'pendjᵊləm/ noun [C] a heavy object on a chain or stick that moves from side to side, especially inside a large clock **sarkaç**

penetrate /'penɪtreɪt/ verb 1 [I, T] If something penetrates an object, it moves into that object. **batmak, saplanmak, girmek** *The bullet penetrated his skull.* 2 [T] If someone penetrates a place or a group, they succeed in moving into or joining it. **girmek, sızmak, içine girmek, yer almak** *No one in our industry has successfully penetrated the Asian market.* ● **penetration** /ˌpenɪ'treɪʃᵊn/ noun [U] **nüfuz etme**

penetrating /'penɪtreɪtɪŋ/ adjective 1 intelligent and full of careful thought **zeki, akıllı, etkileyici, akıl dolu** *a penetrating discussion/mind* ○ *She wrote a penetrating analysis of Shakespeare's Hamlet.* 2 a pene-

trating gaze/look/stare, etc If someone gives you a penetrating look, you feel as if they know what you are thinking. **içe işleyen/ne düşünüldüğünü anlayan bakış/dikiz/göz atma 3** If a sound is penetrating, it is very strong and unpleasant. **tiz, keskin ve şiddetli** *a penetrating voice/scream*

penguin /'peŋgwɪn/ *noun* [C] a large, black and white sea bird that swims and cannot fly **penguen**

penicillin /ˌpenɪ'sɪlɪn/ *noun* [U] a type of medicine that kills bacteria and is used to treat illness **penisilin**

peninsula /pə'nɪnsjələ/ *noun* [C] a long, thin piece of land which has water around most of it **yarımada** *the Korean peninsula*

penis /'piːnɪs/ *noun* [C] the part of a man's or male animal's body that is used for urinating and having sex **erkeğin cinsel organı; penis**

peninsula

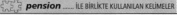

penitentiary /ˌpenɪ'tenʃʳri/ *noun* [C] a prison in the US (ABD) **cezaevi, hapishane**

pennant /'penənt/ *noun* [C] a long, pointed flag **büyük uzun bayrak/flama**

penniless /'penɪləs/ *adjective* having no money **kuruş-suz, beş parasız, meteliksiz; (argo) züğürt**

penny /'peni/ *noun* [C] *plural* **pence** or **p** or **pennies 1** a coin or unit of money with a value of ¹/₁₀₀ of a pound (= UK unit of money); p **peni** *There are 100 pence in a pound.* ○ *fifty pence/50p* **2** a coin with a value of one cent (= ¹/₁₀₀ of a dollar) **peni,** *and always let us have his pennies to buy candy.* **3 every penny** all of an amount of money **her bir kuruşu** *He seemed intent on spending every penny of his salary.*

get/be on/receive a pension ● a pension **fund/plan/scheme** ● a **state/private** pension

pension¹ /'penʃⁿn/ *noun* [C] money that is paid regularly by the government or a private company to a person who has stopped working because they are old or ill **emekli maaşı/aylığı** *a state/private pension* ○ *a pension plan/scheme* ● **pensioner** *noun* [C] *mainly UK* someone who receives a pension **emekli** ⊃See also: old-age pension, old-age pensioner.

pension² /'penʃⁿn/ *verb*
pension sb off *phrasal verb mainly UK* If an organization pensions someone off, it forces that person to leave their job but pays them a pension. **zorla emekli etmek/emekliye ayırmak**

the Pentagon /'pentəgɒn/ *noun* the department of the US government that controls the army, navy, etc, or the building where it is **Pentagon; ABD Savunma Bakanlığı/Genel Kurmay Başkanlığı** *The Pentagon refused to comment on potential military targets.*

penthouse /'penthaʊs/ *noun* [C] *plural* **penthouses** /'penthaʊzɪz/ an expensive apartment at the top of a building **lüks çatı katı**

pent-up /ˌpent'ʌp/ *adjective* [always before noun] Pent-up feelings are feelings that you have not expressed for a

long time. **(duygular) bastırılmış, uzun süre baskı-lanmış/gizlenmiş/dışa vurulmamış** *pent-up anger*

penultimate /pə'nʌltɪmət/ *adjective* [always before noun] *formal* next to the last **sondan bir önceki** *Y is the penultimate letter of the alphabet.*

o—**people¹** /'piːpl̩/ *noun* **1** [plural] more than one person **insanlar, halk, kişiler** *Our company employs over 400 people.* ○ *People live much longer than they used to.* **2 the people** all the ordinary people in a country **halk, ahali** *The rebels have gained the support of the people.* **3** [C] *formal* all the people of a race **millet, ırk, halk, toplum** *Europe is made up of many different peoples.*

people² /'piːpl̩/ *verb*
be peopled by/with sb *phrasal verb literary* to be filled with a particular kind of person **insanlarla doldur-mak; iskân etmek, belli insanlarla doldurmak** *His novels are peopled with angry young men.*

'people ˌcarrier *UK* (*US* minivan) *noun* [C] a large, high car which can carry more people than a normal car **halk arabası; insan taşımak için kullanılan büyük araç**

pepper¹ /'pepəʳ/ *noun* **1** [U] a black, grey, or red powder that is made from crushed seeds, used to give food a slightly spicy flavour **biber, toz biber** *salt and pepper* **2** [C] a hollow green, red, or yellow vegetable **yeşil/kır-mızı/sarı biber** *green/red pepper* ⊃Orta kısımdaki renkli sayfalarına bakınız.

pepper² /'pepəʳ/ *verb*
pepper sth with sth *phrasal verb* to include a lot of something **bir çok şeyi içermek; birden fazla şeyi bir arada bulundurmak/sunmak/vermek** [often passive] *His speech was peppered with quotations.*

peppermint /'pepəmɪnt/ *noun* **1** [U] oil from a plant that is added to food to give it a strong, fresh taste, or the taste itself **nane** *peppermint tea* **2** [C] a small, hard sweet that tastes like peppermint **nane şekeri**

per *strong form* /pɜːʳ/ *weak form* /pəʳ/ *preposition* for each **her biri, her biri için; başına** *Our hotel room costs $60 per night.* ○ *The speed limit is 100 kilometres per hour.* ○ *The wedding dinner will cost £30* **per head** (= for each person).

per annum /pɜːr'ænʌm/ *adverb formal* every year **her yıl, yılda** *a salary of $19,000 per annum*

per capita /pɜː'kæpɪtə/ *adjective, adverb formal* for each person **her bir fert/birey için; kişi başına** *This county has the lowest per capita income in the country.* ○ *Belgians eat more chocolate per capita than any other nation in Europe.*

perceive /pə'siːv/ *verb* [T] *formal* **1** to think of something or someone in a particular way **sezmek, farkına var-mak, algılamak, düşünmek** [often passive] *The British are often perceived as being very formal.* **2** to notice something that is not easy to notice **algılamak, gör-mek, tanımak** *We perceived a faint light in the distance.*

o—**percent** (*also* **per cent**) /pə'sent/ *adjective, adverb* for or out of every 100, shown by the symbol % **yüzde; yüzde olarak; ...lik** *a 40 percent increase in prices* ● **percent** (*also* **per cent**) *noun* [C] *Nearly 70 percent of all cars in the UK are less than five years old.* **oran**

a **high/large/small** percentage ● the percentage **of** sth

percentage /pə'sentɪdʒ/ *noun* [C] an amount of something, expressed as a number out of 100 **yüzde oranı; yüzde, nispet** *The percentage of women who work has risen steadily.* ○ *The percentage of people who are left-handed is small - only about 10%.*

perceptible /pə'septəbl/ *adjective formal* just able to be noticed **farkedilebilir, görülebilir, hissedilebilir** *a perceptible difference* in colour ○ *His pulse was barely perceptible.*

perception /pə'sepʃᵊn/ *noun* **1** [C] what you think or believe about someone or something **algılama, sezgi, görme** *The public perception of him as a hero is surprising.* **2** [U] the ability to notice something **fark etme, farkına varma, tanıma, görme** *Alcohol reduces your perception of pain.*

perceptive /pə'septɪv/ *adjective* quick to notice or understand things **anlayışlı, kavrayışlı** *a perceptive writer*

perch¹ /pɜːtʃ/ *verb* **1 perch (sth) on/in/above, etc** to be in a high position or in a position near the edge of something, or to put something in this position **tünemek, oturmak, durmak; tünetmek, oturtmak, koymak** [often passive] *The village was perched on the side of a mountain.* ○ *She wore glasses perched on the end of her nose.* **2 perch on/in, etc** to sit near the edge of something **konmak, tünemek, oturmak** *The children perched on the edges of their seats.*

perch² /pɜːtʃ/ *noun* [C] a place where a bird sits, especially a stick inside a cage **tünek; kuşların üzerinde tünediği dal vs.**

percussion /pə'kʌʃᵊn/ *noun* [U] musical instruments that make a sound when you hit them with a stick or your hand **vurmalı çalgılar** *Drums, tambourines, and cymbals are percussion instruments.*

perennial¹ /pᵊr'eniəl/ *adjective* happening again and again, or continuing for a long time **sürekli/daimi olan; süregelen; ezelî** *the perennial problem of unemployment*

perennial² /pᵊr'eniəl/ *noun* [C] a plant that lives for several years **bir kaç yıllık ömrü olan bitki**

perfect ...... BAŞKA BİR DEYİŞLE

Eğer bir şey hiçbir hata içermediğinden dolayı mükemmel ise, **faultless, flawless, immaculate** veya **impeccable** sıfatları kullanılabilir. *They gave a faultless/immaculate performance.* ● *His English is impeccable.* ● *She has a flawless complexion.*
Ideal ve **tailor-made** sıfatları birşeyin belirli bir amaç için çok uygun olduğunun ifadesinde kullanılır. *The book is ideal for children aged between four and six.* ● *It sounds as if she's tailor-made for the job.*
Resmiyet gerektirmeyen ortamlarda, eğer tam size göre olduğunu düşündüğünüz bir ev veya işten bahsetmek istiyorsanız, **dream job** veya **dream house** ifadelerini kullanabilirsiniz. *A pretty cottage in the Suffolk countryside - that would be my dream home.*

⊶**perfect¹** /'pɜːfɪkt/ *adjective* **1** WITHOUT FAULT without fault, or as good as possible **mükemmel, kusursuz; tam istendiği gibi** *James is a perfect husband and father.* ○ *Her performance was perfect.* **2** SUITABLE exactly right for someone or something **uygun, biçilmiş kaftan, ideal, tam isabetli** *You'd be perfect for the job.* ○ *The weather's just perfect for a picnic.* **3** TO EMPHASIZE [always before noun] used to emphasize a noun **(isimlerden önce) tam, tamamen** *His suggestion makes perfect sense.*

perfect² /pə'fekt/ *verb* [T] to make something as good as it can be **mükemmelleştirmek, kusursuz hâle getirmek** *I've spent hours perfecting my speech.*

the perfect /'pɜːfɪkt/ (*also* the ˌperfect 'tense) *noun* the form of the verb that is used to show an action that has happened in the past or before another time or event. In English, the perfect is made with 'have' and a past participle. **has, have, had' ve geçmiş zaman orta-**

cıyla kurulan fiil zamanı ↪See also: the future perfect, the past perfect, the present perfect.

perfection /pə'fekʃᵊn/ *noun* [U] when someone or something is perfect **mükemmellik, kusursuzluk; eşsizlik** *She strives for perfection in everything she does.* ○ *chicken legs cooked to perfection*

perfectionist /pə'fekʃᵊnɪst/ *noun* [C] someone who wants everything to be perfect **mükemmeliyetçi**

⊶**perfectly** /'pɜːfɪktli/ *adverb* **1** used to emphasize the word that follows it **tamamen, kesinlikle; her bakımdan** *To be perfectly honest, I don't care any more.* ○ *I made it perfectly clear to him what I meant.* **2** in a perfect way **mükemmel/kusursuz bir şekilde** *The jacket fits perfectly, the skirt not so well.*

perforated /'pɜːfəreɪtɪd/ *adjective* **1** Perforated materials such as paper have small holes in them so that they can be torn or liquid can pass through them. **delikli, delik delik, gözenekli 2** If an organ of your body is perforated, it has a hole in it. **gözenekli, delikleri olan** *a perforated eardrum* ● **perforate** *verb* [T] **delik açmak**

⊶**perform** /pə'fɔːm/ *verb* **1** [I, T] to entertain people by acting, singing, dancing, etc **eğlendirmek, (müzik, dans, tiyatro vs.) gösteri yapmak** *She has performed all over the world.* ○ *The orchestra will perform music by Mozart.* **2** [T] *formal* to do a job or a piece of work **yapmak, icra etmek, sergilemek** *In the future, many tasks will be performed by robots.* ○ *Surgeons performed the operation in less than two hours.* **3 perform well/badly, etc** If something performs well, badly, etc, it works that way. **iyi/kötü çalışmak** *These cars perform poorly at high speeds.*

performance ...... İLE BİRLİKTE KULLANILAN KELİMELER

give/put on a performance ● a **brilliant/virtuoso/ wonderful** performance

⊶**performance** /pə'fɔːməns/ *noun* **1** [C] acting, singing, dancing, or playing music to entertain people **gösteri, oyun, temsil, gösteri programı** *a performance of Shakespeare's Hamlet* **2** [U] how successful someone or something is **başarı, performans** *The company's performance was poor for the first two years.* ○ *Some athletes take drugs to improve their performance.*

performer /pə'fɔːmər/ *noun* [C] someone who entertains people **sanatçı, oyuncu, icracı, müzisyen**

the perˌforming 'arts *noun* [plural] types of entertainment that are performed in front of people, such as dancing, singing, and acting **gösteri/sahne sanatları**

perfume /'pɜːfjuːm/ *noun* [C, U] a liquid with a pleasant smell that women put on their skin **parfüm, güzel koku** ● **perfumed** *adjective* containing perfume **parfümlü, güzel kokulu**

⊶**perhaps** /pə'hæps/ *adverb* **1** possibly **belki, muhtemelen** *Perhaps I'll go to the gym after work.* ○ *Ben won't be coming but perhaps it's better that way.* **2** used when you want to suggest or ask someone something **belki de; ne dersin vb.** ifadelerle birine bir şey önerirken veya ricada bulunurken kullanılabilir *Perhaps you should leave now.*

peril /'perᵊl/ *noun* [C, U] *formal* extreme danger **büyük tehlike** *A shortage of firefighters is putting lives in peril.* ○ *His book describes the perils of war.*

perilous /'perᵊləs/ *adjective formal* very dangerous **çok tehlikeli; korkutucu, ürkütücü** *a perilous journey* ● **perilously** *adverb* **tehlikeli bir şekilde**

perimeter /pə'rɪmɪtər/ *noun* [C] the outer edge of an area **(alan, yer, bölge) çevre, çevresi, sınır** *the perimeter of the airport* o⌐**period** /'pɪəriəd/ *noun* [C] **1** [TIME] a length of time **süre, dönem, devre, çağ** *a 24-hour period* ○ *a period of four months* **2** [SCHOOL/SPORTS] one of the equal parts of time that a school day or sports game is divided into **ders, ders saati, devre 3** [WOMEN] when blood comes out of a woman's uterus each month **(kadın) aybaşı, âdet dönemi, regl 4** [MARK] *US (UK* **full stop)** a mark (.) used at the end of a sentence, or to show that the letters before it are an abbreviation **nokta** ⊃See study page **Punctuation** on page Centre 33.

periodic /,pɪəri'ɒdɪk/ *adjective* happening regularly **belli aralıklarla olan, fasılalı, periyodik** *Our sales team makes periodic trips to Asia.* ● **periodically** *adverb* **düzenli aralıklarla**

periodical /,pɪəri'ɒdɪkᵊl/ *noun* [C] a magazine about a particular subject **dergi, mecmua**

peripheral¹ /pə'rɪfᵊrᵊl/ *adjective* not as important as someone or something else **diğerleri kadar önemli olmayan; göreceli olarak, çevresel**

periphery /pə'rɪfᵊri/ *noun* [C] the outer edge of an area **çevre, kenar bölge** *The soldiers were camped on the periphery of the village.*

perish /'perɪʃ/ *verb* [I] *literary* to die **can vermek, yok olmak, telef olmak, ölmek, ölüp gitmek** *Hundreds of people perished in the flood.*

perishable /'perɪʃəbl/ *adjective* Food that is perishable goes bad very quickly. **çabuk/kolay bozulan**

perjury /'pɜːdʒᵊri/ *noun* [U] the crime of telling a lie in a court of law **mahkemede yalan ifade verme suçu; yalan beyan, yalancı tanıklık** *The witness was accused of committing perjury.*

perk¹ /pɜːk/ *noun* [C] an advantage, such as money or a car, that you are given because of your job **artı avantajlar; ek yararlar/kazanç** [usually plural] *A mobile phone is one of the perks of the job.*

perk² /pɜːk/ *verb*
perk (sb) up *phrasal verb informal* to start to feel happier, or to make someone feel happier **keyiflen(dir)mek; içini açmak; içi açılmak; neşelen(dir)mek; canlan(dır)mak** *A cup of coffee always perks me up in the morning.*

perm /pɜːm/ *noun* [C] the use of chemicals on someone's hair to make it have curls for several months, or the hairstyle that is made in this way **perma, permalı saçlar** *I'm thinking of having a perm.* ● **perm** *verb* [T] **perma yaptırmak**

permanence /'pɜːmᵊnəns/ *noun* [U] when something continues forever or for a long time **süreklilik, daimilik, devamlılık, kalıcılık**

o⌐**permanent** /'pɜːmᵊnənt/ *adjective* continuing forever or for a long time **kalıcı, uzun süreli** *permanent damage* ○ *a permanent job* ● **permanently** *adverb* *He moved here permanently in 1992.* **sürekli olarak**

permeate /'pɜːmieɪt/ *verb* [T] *formal* to move gradually into every part of something **yavaş yavaş içine işlemek; her yere nüfuz etmek; yayılmak** *The pungent smell of vinegar permeated the air.* ○ *Drug dealers have permeated every level of society.*

permissible /pə'mɪsəbl/ *adjective formal* allowed by the rules **izin verilebilir, müsaade edilebilir; yasaların izin verdiği** [+ to do sth] *It is not permissible to smoke inside the building.*

permission .... İLE BİRLİKTE KULLANILAN KELİMELER
ask for/give/grant/obtain/receive/refuse/seek permission ● permission **for** sth

o⌐**permission** /pə'mɪʃᵊn/ *noun* [U] when you allow someone to do something **izin, müsaade** *She gave him per-*

mission *without asking any questions.* ○ [+ to do sth] *He has permission to stay in the country for one more year.* ○ *They even have to* **ask for permission** *before they go to the toilet.* ○ *He took the car* **without permission**.

permissive /pə'mɪsɪv/ *adjective* allowing people to behave in ways which other people may not approve of **çok müsamahakâr, aşırı hoşgörülü, mezhebi geniş, özgürlükçü, sıkmayan** *permissive attitudes*

permit¹ /pə'mɪt/ *verb* **permitting**, *past* **permitted 1** [T] *formal* to allow something **izin vermek, müsaade etmek** [often passive] *Photography is not permitted inside the museum.* ○ [+ to do sth] *He permitted them to leave.* **2** [I] to make something possible **izin/imkân vermek; mümkün kılmak** *The match starts at 3 p.m., weather permitting.*

permit² /'pɜːmɪt/ *noun* [C] an official document that allows you to do something **izin belgesi, ruhsat, permi** *a work permit* ○ *You need a permit to park your car here.*

pernicious /pə'nɪʃəs/ *adjective formal* very harmful **çok zararlı, muzır, hınzır**

perpendicular /,pɜːpᵊn'dɪkjʊləʳ/ *adjective* at an angle of 90 degrees to something **dik, dikey, dik açılı, dimdik**

perpetrate /'pɜːpɪtreɪt/ *verb* [T] *formal* to do something very bad **çok berbat/kötü şeyler yapmak; her türlü kötülüğü uygulamak** [often passive] *They heard of torture perpetrated by the army.*

perpetrator /'pɜːpɪtreɪtəʳ/ *noun* [C] *formal* someone who has done something very bad **zulüm/vahşet/kötülük yapan** *There is great public pressure to bring the perpetrators of these crimes to justice.*

perpetual /pə'petʃuəl/ *adjective* never ending **sürekli, ardı arkası kesilmez; uzadıkça uzayan** *He seems to be in a perpetual state of confusion.* ● **perpetually** *adverb* **sonlanmayan bir şekilde**

perpetuate /pə'petʃueɪt/ *verb* [T] *formal* to make something continue, especially something bad **devam ettirmek, sürekli hâle getirmek** *People think of him as a cruel man, an image perpetuated by the media.*

perplexed /pə'plekst/ *adjective* confused **zihni karışmış, şaşkın, şaşırmış, afallamış** *He seemed a little perplexed by the question.* ● **perplex** *verb* [T] **kafası karışmak**

perplexing /pə'pleksɪŋ/ *adjective* confusing **zihin bulandıran, şaşırtan, afallatan, şaşırtıcı** *a perplexing problem*

persecute /'pɜːsɪkjuːt/ *verb* [T] to treat someone unfairly or cruelly because of their race, religion, or beliefs **(ırk, din, inançlardan vs. dolayı) eziyet etmek, zulmetmek; rahat vermemek; dünyayı dar etmek** [often passive] *He was persecuted for his religious beliefs.* ● **persecution** /,pɜːsɪ'kjuːʃᵊn/ *noun* [U] *political/religious persecution* **zulüm**

persecutor /'pɜːsɪkjuːtəʳ/ *noun* [C] someone who persecutes people **zalim, zulmeden, işkenceci, cani**

perseverance /,pɜːsɪ'vɪərᵊns/ *noun* [U] when you persevere **azim, sebat, dayanma gücü, yılmayan kimse** *Hard work and perseverance do pay off in the end.*

persevere /,pɜːsɪ'vɪəʳ/ *verb* [I] to continue to try to do something although it is difficult **sebat etmek, dayanmak, azim göstermek; yılmamak, yılgınlık göstermemek** *Despite the difficulties, I decided to persevere with the project.*

persist /pə'sɪst/ *verb* [I] **1** If an unpleasant feeling or situation persists, it continues to exist. **devam etmek, sürmek** *If symptoms persist, consult a doctor.* **2** to continue to do something although it is annoying other people ısrar etmek, inat etmek, ayak diremek *He persists in calling me Jane, even though I've corrected him twice.*

persistence /pə'sɪst^əns/ *noun* [U] when someone or something persists ısrar, sebat, dayanma, sürme

persistent /pə'sɪst^ənt/ *adjective* **1** Something unpleasant that is persistent continues for a long time or is difficult to get rid of. devam eden, süregelen, bir türlü yaka sıyrılamayan *a persistent cough* **2** A persistent person continues to do something although other people do not want them to. inatçı, ısrarcı, dayatan, direten *He can be very persistent sometimes.* ● **persistently** *adverb He has persistently lied to us.* ısrarlı bir şekilde

◦╸**person** /'pɜːs^ən/ *noun plural* **people 1** [C] a human being kişi, birey, şahıs, kimse *You're the only person I know here.* ○ *He is a very dangerous person.* **2 in person** If you do something in person, you go somewhere to do it yourself. şahsen, bizzat *If you can't be there in person the next best thing is watching it on TV.* ⊃See also: **the first person, the second person, the third person.**

persona /pə'səʊnə/ *noun* [C] *plural* **personae** or **personas** the way your character seems to other people kişilik, karakter *He's trying to improve his public persona.*

◦╸**personal** /'pɜːs^ən^əl/ *adjective* **1** [RELATING TO A PERSON] [always before noun] relating to or belonging to a particular person kişisel, şahsî *I can only speak from my own personal experience.* ○ *Please ensure you take all personal belongings with you when you leave the train.* ○ *This is a personal view and not that of the government.* **2** [PRIVATE] relating to the private parts of someone's life, including their relationships and feelings şahsî, özel, hususî, mahrem, kişisel *He's got a few personal problems at the moment.* ○ *She prefers to keep her personal and professional lives separate.* **3** [FOR ONE PERSON] [always before noun] designed for or used by one person kişiye ait, şahsen kullanılan; hususî olarak tasarlanmış *a personal computer/stereo* ○ *a personal loan/pension* **4** [RUDE] rude about or offensive towards someone kişileri hedef alan *I know you're upset, but there's no need to get personal* (= start making offensive remarks). **5** [BODY] [always before noun] relating to your body bedensel, bedenî, vücutla ilgili *personal hygiene*

personal ˌdigital aˈssistant (*abbreviation* **PDA**) *noun* [C] a small computer that you can carry with you taşınabilir kişisel bilgisayar

╠╣ *personality* .... İLE BİRLİKTE KULLANILAN KELİMELER

a bubbly/forceful/outgoing/warm personality

◦╸**personality** /ˌpɜːs^ən'æləti/ *noun* **1** [CHARACTER] [C] the way you are as a person kişilik, şahsiyet, karakter *She's got a lovely, bubbly personality.* **2** [FAMOUS] a famous person tanınmış kişi, ünlü şahsiyet, şöhret *a well-known TV personality* **3** [INTERESTING] [U] the quality of having a very strong or interesting character renkli kişilik, güçlü ve ilginç kişilik *Sales people need a lot of personality.*

personalized (*also UK* **-ised**) /'pɜːs^ən^əlaɪzd/ *adjective* A personalized object has someone's name on it, or has been made for a particular person. üzerinde ismi veya isminin baş harfleri yazılı; kişi özel tasarlanmış; özel *a personalized fitness plan* ● **personalize** (*also UK* **-ise**) *verb* [T] kişileştirmek

personally /'pɜːs^ən^əli/ *adverb* **1** done by you and not someone else şahsen, bizzat, kendi, bizatihi olarak *I'd like to personally apologize for the delay.* **2** used when you are going to give your opinion bana göre, şahsi kanaatime göre, kanımca *Personally, I'd rather stay at home and watch TV.* **3 take sth personally** to think that someone is criticizing you when they are not

üstüne alınmak; alınganlık göstermek *You mustn't take everything so personally.*

ˌpersonal ˈorganizer *noun* [C] a small book or computer containing a calendar, address book, etc kişisel ajanda veya bilgisayar ⊃See **PDA.**

ˌpersonal ˈpronoun *noun* [C] a word that is used to refer to a person in speech or in writing. For example the words 'I', 'you', and 'they' are personal pronouns. (dilbilgisi) kişi/şahıs zamiri

ˌpersonal ˈtrainer *noun* [C] a person whose job is to help you improve the shape of your body by showing you what exercises to do şahsi/özel eğitmen/öğretici

personify /pə'sɒnɪfaɪ/ *verb* [T] If someone personifies a particular quality, they are a perfect example of that quality. timsali/simgesi olmak; ...ın/in canlı örneği olmak *She seems to personify honesty and goodness.* ● **personified** *adjective* [always after noun] *Tom has always been laziness personified.* şahsileştirilmiş, örnek oluşturulmuş ● **personification** /pə,sɒnɪfɪ'keɪ^ən/ *noun* [U] kişiselleştirme

personnel /ˌpɜːs^ən'el/ *noun* **1** [plural] the people who work for an organization çalışanların tümü, kadro, personel, görevliler, çalışan elemanlar *military personnel* **2** [U] the department of an organization that deals with finding people to work there, keeping records about them, etc personel müdürlüğü; personel işleri daire başkanlığı *I need to speak to someone in Personnel.* ○ *the personnel manager*

╠╣ *perspective* .... İLE BİRLİKTE KULLANILAN KELİMELER

from sb's perspective ● from a [historical/political, etc] perspective ● perspective on sth

perspective /pə'spektɪv/ *noun* **1** [C] the way you think about something bakış/görüş açısı; perspektif *Being unemployed has made me see things from a different perspective.* **2** [U] When things are drawn so that they appear to be at a realistic size and in a realistic position çizim, perspektif; üç boyutlu çizim/taslak **3 put sth in/into perspective** If something puts a problem into perspective, it makes you understand how unimportant that problem is. bir sorunu bütün yönleriyle ortaya koymak

perspicacious /ˌpɜːspɪ'keɪʃəs/ *adjective formal* quick in noticing, understanding, or judging things accurately süratle düşünüp/değerlendirip yargıya/sonuca varabilen; zeki ve kolay kavrayan

perspiration /ˌpɜːspə'reɪʃ^ən/ *noun* [U] *formal* the liquid that comes out of your skin when you get hot ter

perspire /pə'spaɪə^r/ *verb* [I] *formal* to produce liquid through your skin because you are hot or nervous terlemek

◦╸**persuade** /pə'sweɪd/ *verb* [T] to make someone agree to do something by talking to them a lot about it ikna etmek, razı etmek, inandırmak [+ to do sth] *We managed to persuade him to come with us.* ○ [+ (that)] *I persuaded her that it was the right thing to do.* ⊃Opposite **dissuade.**

persuasion /pə'sweɪʒ^ən/ *noun* **1** [U] when you persuade someone ikna, inandırma *I'm sure she'll agree, she just needs a little gentle persuasion.* **2** [C] *formal* a political, religious, or moral belief inanç, itikât *There were people of all persuasions there.*

persuasive /pə'sweɪsɪv/ *adjective* able to make people agree to do something inandırıcı, ikna edici *It's a very persuasive argument.* ● **persuasively** *adverb* ikna edici bir şekilde

pertain /pə'teɪn/ verb
pertain to sth phrasal verb formal to relate to something ait/ilgili olmak; ...a/e dair olmak Some important evidence pertaining to the case has been overlooked.

pertinent /'pɜːtmənt/ adjective formal relating directly to a subject doğrudan bir konuyla bağlantılı/alakalı/ilgili; ilişkili, ilişkin a pertinent question

perturbed /pə'tɜːbd/ adjective worried or upset kaygılı, tedirgin, endişeli He seemed slightly perturbed by the news. • **perturb** verb [T] tedirgin etmek

peruse /pə'ruːz/ verb [T] formal to look at or read something in order to find what interests you dikkatle bakmak/okumak/incelemek

pervade /pə'veɪd/ verb [T] formal to move gradually through every part of something yayılmak, kaplamak, sinmek Cheap perfume and tobacco pervaded the room.

pervasive /pə'veɪsɪv/ adjective formal moving into or through everywhere or everything yaygın, herkesi/herşeyi kapsayan; şümullü a pervasive smell ○ the pervasive influence of television

perverse /pə'vɜːs/ adjective strange and not what most people would expect or enjoy aksi, huysuz, mantıksız, münasebetsiz, çarpık In a perverse way, I enjoy going to the dentist. • **perversely** adverb ters bir şekilde

perversion /pə'vɜːʃªn/ noun [C, U] **1** getting sexual pleasure in a way that seems strange or unpleasant cinsel sapıklık, sapkınlık, ahlaki değerleri zorlayan cinsel eğilimler **2** when something that is right is changed into something that is wrong saptırma, çarpıtma the perversion of justice

pervert[1] /'pɜːvɜːt/ noun [C] someone who gets sexual pleasure in a strange or unpleasant way cinsi sapıklığı olan kimse; sapık

pervert[2] /pə'vɜːt/ verb [T] to change something that is right into something that is wrong saptırmak, çarpıtmak, bozmak They were charged with conspiracy to pervert the course of justice.

perverted /pə'vɜːtɪd/ adjective relating to getting sexual pleasure in a strange or unpleasant way sapık, sapkın

pessimism /'pesɪmɪzªm/ noun [U] when you believe bad things will happen kötümserlik, karamsarlık ⊃Opposite optimism.

pessimist /'pesɪmɪst/ noun [C] someone who always believes that bad things will happen kötümser/karamsar kimse Don't be such a pessimist!

pessimistic /ˌpesɪ'mɪstɪk/ adjective always believing that bad things will happen kötümser, karamsar He was feeling pessimistic about the future. ⊃Opposite optimistic.

pest /pest/ noun [C] **1** an animal that causes damage to plants, food, etc haşere; tarım ürünlerine zarar veren böcek Most farmers think foxes are pests. **2** informal an annoying person baş belası kimse

pester /'pestər/ verb [T] to annoy someone by asking them something again and again rahatsız etmek, başının etini yemek, musallat olmak [+ to do sth] He's been pestering me to go out with him all week.

pesticide /'pestɪsaɪd/ noun [C, U] a chemical that is used to kill insects which damage plants haşere ilacı

pet[1] /pet/ noun [C] an animal that someone keeps in their home ev/süs hayvanı my pet rabbit

pet[2] /pet/ verb [T] petting, past petted **1** to touch an animal because you feel affection for it (hayvan) sevmek, okşamak **2** to touch someone in a sexual way öpüşüp koklaşmak, sıkıp okşamak

petal /'petªl/ noun [C] one of the thin, flat, coloured parts on the outside of a flower taç yaprak, petal rose petals

peter /'piːtər/ verb
peter out phrasal verb to gradually stop or disappear yavaş yavaş sona ermek/gözden kaybolmak; hızı kesilmek The track petered out after a mile or so.

,pet 'hate UK (US ,pet 'peeve) noun [C] something that annoys you a lot can sıkıcı/başbelası şey; sıkıntı; mustarip olunan şey That's one of my pet hates - people who smoke while other people are eating.

petite /pə'tiːt/ adjective A petite woman is small and thin in an attractive way. (kadın) ufak tefek, çıtı pıtı; minyon

petition[1] /pə'tɪʃªn/ verb [I, T] to officially ask someone in authority to do something dilekçe vermek [+ to do sth] They are petitioning the government to increase funding for the project.

▨▨ **petition** .... İLE BİRLİKTE KULLANILAN KELİMELER

launch/organize/sign a petition • a petition against/(calling) for sth

petition[2] /pə'tɪʃªn/ noun [C] a document that has been signed by a lot of people officially asking someone in authority to do something dilekçe Will you sign this petition against experiments on animals?

petrified /'petrɪfaɪd/ adjective extremely frightened ödü kopmuş, taş kesilmiş, korkudan dona kalmış; korkudan küçük dilini yutmuş I'm petrified of spiders.

o▬**petrol** /'petrªl/ UK (US gas) noun [U] a liquid fuel used in cars benzin unleaded petrol

petroleum /pə'trəʊliəm/ noun [U] thick oil found under the Earth's surface which is used to produce petrol and other substances petrol

'petrol ,station UK (US gas station) noun [C] a place where you can buy petrol benzin istasyonu

petticoat /'petɪkəʊt/ noun [C] a thin piece of women's clothing worn under a dress or skirt iç/astar eteklik; kombinezon

petty /'peti/ adjective **1** [always before noun] unimportant or not serious önemsiz, ehemmiyetsiz, küçük, ufak; incir çekirdeğini doldurmayan petty crime **2** [never before noun] complaining too much about unimportant things pireyi deve yapan, küçük şeyleri sorun hâline getiren You can be so petty sometimes!

petulant /'petʃələnt/ adjective behaving in an angry, silly way like a child huysuz, hırçın, ters; çocukça davranan

pew /pjuː/ noun [C] a long seat in a church arkalıklı kilise sırası

pewter /'pjuːtər/ noun [U] a blue-grey metal kurşun ve kalay alaşımı

phantom[1] /'fæntəm/ noun [C] the spirit of a dead person hayalet, hortlak

phantom[2] /'fæntəm/ adjective [always before noun] imagined, not real hayalî, hayal ürünü olan phantom pains

pharaoh /'feərəʊ/ noun [C] a king of ancient Egypt eski Mısır'da kıral; Farah

pharmaceutical /ˌfɑːmə'sjuːtɪkªl/ adjective relating to the production of medicines eczacılığa ait, ilaç yapımıyla ilgili a pharmaceutical company ○ the pharmaceutical industry • **pharmaceuticals** noun [plural] medicines ilaçlar

pharmacist /'fɑːməsɪst/ noun [C] someone who is trained to prepare or sell medicines eczacı

pharmacy /ˈfɑːməsi/ *noun* **1** [C] a shop or part of a shop that prepares and sells medicines **eczane 2** [U] the study of the preparation of medicines **eczacılık**

⁂ phase ...... İLE BİRLİKTE KULLANILAN KELİMELER

enter/go through a phase • a passing phase • a phase of sth

phase¹ /feɪz/ *noun* [C] a stage or period which is part of a longer period **evre, aşama, safha, kademe** *The first phase of the project is scheduled for completion next year.* ○ *My younger daughter is going through a phase of only wearing black.*

phase² /feɪz/ *verb*
phase sth in *phrasal verb* to gradually start using a new system, process, or law **yavaş yavaş başlatmak; aşama aşama uygulamaya koymak; kademe kademe ilerlemek** *The new tax will be phased in over five years.*
phase sth out *phrasal verb* to gradually stop using something **yavaş yavaş devreden çıkarmak; aşama aşama sona erdirmek**

PhD /ˌpiːeɪtʃˈdiː/ *noun* [C] an advanced university qualification, or a person who has this qualification **doktora, (bilimsel alanda) doktor** *a PhD course/programme* ○ *Maria has a PhD in mathematics.*

pheasant /ˈfezᵊnt/ *noun* [C] *plural* **pheasants** or **pheasant** a bird with a long tail that is shot for food **sülün**

phenomenal /fɪˈnɒmɪnᵊl/ *adjective* extremely successful or showing great qualities or abilities **olağanüstü** *The film has been a phenomenal success.* • **phenomenally** *adverb* **olağandışı, inanılmaz bir şekilde**

phenomenon /fɪˈnɒmɪnən/ *noun* [C] *plural* **phenomena** something that exists or happens, usually something unusual **olay, olgu, fenomen** *storms, lightning, and other natural phenomena* ○ *Road rage seems to be a fairly recent phenomenon.*

phew (*also* **whew**) /fjuː/ *exclamation* used when you are happy that something is not going to happen, or when you are tired or hot **Ohh!', 'Üüh!', 'Üf!'**

philanthropist /fɪˈlænθrəpɪst/ *noun* [C] someone who gives money to people who need help **hayırsever kimse, hayır sahibi kişi**

-phile /-faɪl/ *suffix* makes a noun meaning 'enjoying or liking something' **seven/hoşlanan anlamında sonek** *a Francophile* (= someone who loves France) ○ *a bibliophile* (= someone who loves books)

philosopher /fɪˈlɒsəfər/ *noun* [C] someone who studies or writes about the meaning of life **filozof, düşünür**

philosophical /ˌfɪləˈsɒfɪkᵊl/ *adjective* **1** relating to the study or writing of philosophy **felsefi, felsefeyle ilgili, filozofça** *a philosophical problem/question* **2** accepting unpleasant situations in a calm and wise way **sakin, sabırlı, kalender, mütevekkil** *She seems fairly philosophical about the failure of her marriage.* • **philosophically** *adverb* **filozofik açıdan**

philosophy /fɪˈlɒsəfi/ *noun* **1** [C, U] the study or writing of ideas about the meaning of life, or a particular set of ideas about the meaning of life **felsefe** *Descartes is considered by many to be the father of modern philosophy.* **2** [C] a way of thinking about what you should do in life **yaşam felsefesi, ilke, prensip, temel düşünce; felsefe** *My philosophy has always been to give those with ability the chance to progress.*

phishing /ˈfɪʃɪŋ/ *noun* [U] the practice of sending emails to people to trick them into giving information that would let someone take money from their Internet bank account (= an arrangement with your bank to keep your money there and take it out when you need

it) **bilişim suçları kapsamında çeşitli hile ve yalanlarla internet bankacılığına ait bilgileri elde etme ve hesapların içini boşaltma eylemi**

phlegm /flem/ *noun* [U] a thick liquid produced in your lungs, throat, and nose when you have a cold (= common illness that makes you sneeze) **balgam**

phlegmatic /flegˈmætɪk/ *adjective formal* Someone who is phlegmatic is calm and does not get excited easily. **serin/ağır kanlı, aldırmaz, sakin; vurdum duymaz, kayıtsız**

-phobe /-fəʊb/ *suffix* someone who hates something **bir şeyden nefret eden kişi anlamında son ek** *a commitment-phobe* (= a person who hates commitment)

phobia /ˈfəʊbiə/ *noun* [C] an extreme fear of something **korku, yılgı, fobi** *My mum's got a phobia about birds.*

⁂ phone ...... İLE BİRLİKTE KULLANILAN KELİMELER

answer/pick up the phone • put the phone down • a phone rings • by/over the phone • a phone bill/company /conversation

phone¹ /fəʊn/ (*also* **telephone**) *noun* **1** SYSTEM [U] a communication system that is used to talk to someone who is in another place **telefon** *We'll contact you by phone when we get the results.* **2** EQUIPMENT [C] a piece of equipment that is used to talk to someone who is in another place **telefon** *Would someone please answer the phone?* ○ *I could hear the phone ringing.* **3 on the phone a** USING PHONE using the phone **telefonda, telefonla konuşmakta** *She's been on the phone all night.* **b** HAVING A PHONE *UK* when you have a phone **telefonu olan; telefonla aranan** ⊃See also: cellular phone, mobile phone, pay phone.

phone² /fəʊn/ (*also* **phone up**) *verb* [I, T] to communicate with someone by telephone **telefon etmek; telefonla aramak** *I tried to phone her last night, but she was out.* ○ *I'm going to phone for a taxi.*

'phone ˌbook *noun* [C] a book that contains the telephone numbers of people who live in a particular area **telefon defteri**

'phone ˌbox *UK* (*US* **'phone ˌbooth**) *noun* [C] a small structure containing a public telephone **telefon kulübesi** ⊃See picture at **telephone.**

'phone ˌcall *noun* [C] when you use the telephone **telefonla arama** *Will you excuse me, I've got to make a phone call.*

'phone ˌcard *noun* [C] a small piece of plastic used to pay for the use of some telephones **telefon kartı**

phone-in /ˈfəʊnɪn/ *UK* (*US* **call-in**) *noun* [C] a television or radio programme in which the public can ask questions or give opinions over the telephone **(tv. radyo programını vs.) telefonla arama/katılma**

'phone ˌnumber *noun* [C] the number of a particular telephone **telefon numarası**

phonetic /fəʊˈnetɪk/ *adjective* relating to the sounds you make when you speak **sesle ilgili, fonetik** *the international phonetic alphabet* • **phonetically** *adverb* **sesler ile ilgili**

phonetics /fəˈnetɪks/ *noun* [U] the study of the sounds made by the human voice in speech **ses bilgisi, fonetik**

phoney¹ *UK* (*US* **phony**) /ˈfəʊni/ *adjective informal* not real **sahte, uydurma, düzmece, yapmacık** *He gave the police a phoney number.*

phoney² *UK* (*US* **phony**) /ˈfəʊni/ *noun* [C] *informal* someone who is not sincere **sahtekâr, düzenbaz** • **phoney** *UK* (*US* **phony**) *adjective informal* a phoney smile **suni, yapay**

phosphate /ˈfɒsfeɪt/ *noun* [C, U] a chemical that is used in cleaning products and to help plants grow **fosfat**

o▪**photo** /ˈfəʊtəʊ/ *noun* [C] a picture produced with a camera **fotoğraf** *a black-and-white/colour photo* ○ *I took a photo of Jack lying on the beach.*

photocopier /ˈfəʊtəʊˌkɒpiəʳ/ *noun* [C] a machine which produces copies of documents by photographing them **fotokopi makinası** ➔Orta kısımdaki renkli sayfalarına bakınız.

photocopy /ˈfəʊtəʊˌkɒpi/ *noun* [C] a copy of a document made with a photocopier **fotokopi** *I made a photocopy of my letter before sending it.* ● **photocopy** *verb* [T] **kopyalamk**

photogenic /ˌfəʊtəʊˈdʒenɪk/ *adjective* Someone who is photogenic has the type of face that looks attractive in a photograph. **fotoğrafta iyi görünen/çıkan; fotojenik**

o▪**photograph¹** /ˈfəʊtəɡrɑːf/ *noun* [C] a picture produced with a camera **fotoğraf** *a black-and-white/colour photograph* ○ *He took a lovely photograph of the children in the garden.*

photograph² /ˈfəʊtəɡrɑːf/ *verb* [T] to take a photograph of someone or something **fotoğraf çekmek** *They were photographed leaving a nightclub together.*

photographer /fəˈtɒɡrəfəʳ/ *noun* [C] someone whose job is to take photographs **fotoğrafçı**

photographic /ˌfəʊtəˈɡræfɪk/ *adjective* [always before noun] relating to photographs **fotoğraf/fotoğrafçılıkla ilgili** *photographic equipment/film* ○ *photographic evidence*

photography /fəˈtɒɡrəfi/ *noun* [U] the activity or job of taking photographs **fotoğrafçılık sanatı/mesleği**

phrasal verb /ˌfreɪzəlˈvɜːb/ *noun* [C] a verb together with an adverb or preposition which has a different meaning to the meaning of its separate parts. For example 'look up' and 'carry on' are phrasal verbs. **takım fiil, deyim özelliği taşıyan fiil takımı** ➔See study page Phrasal verbs on page Centre 24 ➔Orta kısımdaki renkli sayfalarına bakınız.

o▪**phrase¹** /freɪz/ *noun* [C] a group of words which are often used together and have a particular meaning **sözcük takımı**

phrase² /freɪz/ *verb* [T] to express something by choosing to use particular words **ifade etmek; belli bir şekilde dile getirmek** *It might have been better if he had phrased it differently.*

o▪**physical¹** /ˈfɪzɪkəl/ *adjective* **1** relating to the body **bedenle ilgili, bedensel** *physical fitness/strength* ○ *People put too much emphasis on physical appearance* (= what you look like). **2** [always before noun] relating to real things that you can see and touch **fiziki; maddi** *There was no physical evidence linking Jones to Shaw's murder.*

physical² /ˈfɪzɪkəl/ *US* (*UK medical*) *noun* [C] an examination of your body by a doctor to find out if you are healthy **bedensel muayene**

physically /ˈfɪzɪkəli/ *adverb* in a way that relates to the body **fiziki olarak** *physically attractive/fit*

physical ˈtherapist *US* (*UK/US physiotherapist*) *noun* [C] someone whose job is to give people physical therapy **fizyoterapist; fizik tedavi uzmanı**

physical ˈtherapy *US* (*UK/US physiotherapy*) *noun* [U] treatment for illness or injury in which you practise moving parts of your body **fizik tedavi; fizyoterapi**

physician /fɪˈzɪʃən/ *noun* [C] *formal* a doctor **doktor, hekim**

physicist /ˈfɪzɪsɪst/ *noun* [C] someone who studies physics **fizikçi**

physics /ˈfɪzɪks/ *noun* [U] the scientific study of natural forces, such as energy, heat, light, etc **fizik, fizik bilimi**

physio /ˈfɪziəʊ/ *noun* [C, U] *UK informal short for* physiotherapy or physiotherapist **fizyoterapi, fizyoterapist**

physiological /ˌfɪziəˈlɒdʒɪkəl/ *adjective* relating to how the bodies of living things work **bedenle ilgili, fizyolojik; fizik tedavi ile ilgili**

physiology /ˌfɪziˈɒlədʒi/ *noun* [U] the scientific study of how the bodies of living things work **fizyoloji; bedenin çalışma biçiminin bilimsel çalışması**

physiotherapist /ˌfɪziəʊˈθerəpɪst/ (*also US* **physical therapist**) *noun* [C] someone whose job is to give people physiotherapy **fizyoterapist; fizik tedavi uzmanı**

physiotherapy /ˌfɪziəʊˈθerəpi/ (*also US* **physical therapy**) *noun* [U] treatment for illness or injury in which you practise moving parts of your body **fizyoterapi; fizik tedavi**

physique /fɪˈziːk/ *noun* [C] the shape and size of your body **beden/vücut yapısı; fizik** *He has a very muscular physique.*

pianist /ˈpiːənɪst/ *noun* [C] someone who plays the piano **piyanist**

piano /piˈænəʊ/ *noun* [C] a large wooden musical instrument with strings inside and black and white bars that produce sounds when you press them **piyano** ➔See also: grand piano.

piano

o▪**pick¹** /pɪk/ *verb* [T] **1** [CHOOSE] to choose something or someone **seçmek** *Do you want to help me pick some numbers for my lottery ticket?* ○ *I was never picked for the school football team.* **2** [FLOWERS/FRUIT, ETC] If you pick flowers, fruit, etc, you take them off a tree or out of the ground. **toplamak; koparmak** *I picked some apples this morning.* **3** [REMOVE] to remove small pieces from something with your fingers **ayıklamak, seçmek, parmaklarla almak** *You'll have to let the glue dry and then you can pick it off.* **4 pick a fight/argument** to start a fight or argument with someone **kavgayı/tartışmayı başlatmak 5 pick sb's pocket** to steal something from someone's pocket **aşırmak, çarpmak, çalmak, soymak** ➔See also: have a **bone¹** to pick with sb.

pick at sth *phrasal verb* **1** to only eat a small amount of your food because you are worried or ill **isteksiz ve nazlanarak yemek** *He picked at his food but had no appetite.* **2** to remove small pieces from something with your fingers **parmaklarıyla ayıklamak/küçük parçaları almak** *If you keep picking at that scab it'll never heal.*

pick on sb *phrasal verb* to choose a person and criticize or treat them unfairly **takmak, sürekli kusur bulmak; eleştirmek, sataşmak, uğraşmak** *He just started picking on me for no reason.*

pick sth/sb out *phrasal verb* to choose someone or something from a group of people or things **seçmek, ayırt etmek, belirlemek, ayırmak** *She picked out a red shirt for me to try on.*

pick sth/sb up *phrasal verb* **1** to lift something or someone by using your hands **eğilip almak, tutup kaldırmak** *He picked his coat up off the floor.* ○ *Just pick up the phone and call him.* ➔Orta kısımdaki renkli sayfalarına bakınız.

2 to collect someone who is waiting for you, or to collect something that you have left somewhere **birini/bir şeyi gidip almak/alıp getirmek** *Can you pick me up from the airport?*

pick sth up *phrasal verb* **1** GET to get something **almak, satın almak** *She picked up some real bargains in the sale.* **2** LEARN to learn a new skill or language by practising it and not by being taught it **kulaktan kaparak öğrenmek, kapmak, edinmek; (beceri/dil) uygulayarak öğrenmek** *He hadn't done any skiing before the holiday, but he picked it up really quickly.* **3** ILLNESS to get an illness from someone or something **kapmak, hastalığa yakalanmak; hastalık kapmak** *She picked up a nasty stomach bug while she was on holiday.* **4** SIGNAL If a piece of equipment picks up a signal, it receives it. **sinyal almak** *Antennas around the top of the ship picked up the radar signals.* **5** NOTICE to notice something **(koku vb.) almak, farketmek** *Police dogs picked up the scent of the two men from clothes they had left behind.*

pick sb up *phrasal verb* **1** to start talking to someone in order to try to begin a romantic relationship with them **...ile tanışmak, tavlamak, yakınlık kurmaya başlamak 2** If the police pick someone up, they take that person to the police station. **birini alıp karakola götürmek, yakalamak; durdurup sorguya çekmek**

pick up *phrasal verb* **1** If a business or social situation picks up, it improves. **toparlanmak, iyiye gitmek, gelişmek, düzelmek** *Business is really starting to pick up now.* **2** If the wind picks up, it becomes stronger. **rüzgâr gittikçe şiddetlenmek/hız kazanmak**

pick up sth *phrasal verb* If a vehicle picks up speed, it starts to go faster. **hızını arttırmak, süratlenmek**

pick² /pɪk/ *noun* **1** [C] a sharp metal stick used to break hard ground or rocks **murç, kazma 2 the pick of sth** the best of a group of things or people **en iyisi; en gözde olanı; en çok bilineni 3 have/take your pick** to choose what you want **seçimini yapmak; tercihini yapmak** *We've got tea, coffee, or hot chocolate - take your pick.*

picket /'pɪkɪt/ *(also* 'picket ˌline) *noun* [C] a group of people who stand outside a building in order to show their anger about something and to try to stop people going inside **grev gözcüleri ● picket** *verb* [I, T] *Protesters picketed cinemas across the whole country.* **grev yapan kişilerin ayakta dikilmeleri**

ˌpicket 'fence *noun* [C] *US* a low fence made from a row of flat sticks that are pointed at the top **alçak çit**

pickle /'pɪkl/ *noun* **1** [C, U] *UK* food which has been put into vinegar or salt water for a long time and has a sour taste **turşu** *cold meat and pickles* **2** [C] *US* a small cucumber (= a green, cylindrical vegetable) that has been put in vinegar or in a liquid containing salt and spices **kornişon turşu, salatalık turşusu ● pickled** *adjective* *pickled onions* **turşu içeren**

pickpocket /'pɪkˌpɒkɪt/ *noun* [C] someone who steals things from people's pockets **yankesici**

pickup /'pɪkʌp/ *(also* 'pickup ˌtruck) *noun* [C] *US* a small, open truck **küçük kamyonet, pikap**

picky /'pɪki/ *adjective informal* Someone who is picky does not like many things. **müşkülpesent, zor seçen** *a picky eater*

picnic /'pɪknɪk/ *noun* [C] a meal that you make and take with you somewhere to eat outside **piknik** *We're going to have a picnic down by the lake.* **● picnic** *verb* [I] **picnicking,** *past* **picnicked piknik yapmak**

pictorial /pɪk'tɔːriəl/ *adjective* relating to pictures or shown using pictures **resimli**

---

picture .... İLE BİRLİKTE KULLANILAN KELİMELER

draw/paint a picture ● take a picture ● a picture of sb/sth ● in a picture

○━**picture¹** /'pɪktʃər/ *noun* [C] **1** DRAWING ETC a drawing, painting, or photograph of something or someone **resim** *to draw/paint a picture* ○ *She's got pictures of pop stars all over her bedroom wall.* ○ *Did you take many pictures* (= photograph many things) *while you were in Sydney?* ⊃Orta kısımdaki renkli sayfalarına bakınız. **2** IDEA an idea of what something is like **tasvir, betimleme** [usually singular] *I've got a much clearer picture of what's happening now.* **3** TV the image on a television screen **görüntü** *I'm afraid it's not a very good picture.* **4** FILM a film **film, sinema filmi** *Could this be the first animated film to win a best picture award?* **5 the pictures** *old-fashioned* the cinema **sinema** *I really fancy going to the pictures tonight.* **6 get the picture** *informal* used to say that someone understands a situation **kavramak, anlamak, çakmak** *Oh right, I get the picture.* **● 7 paint a bleak/rosy, etc picture of sth** to describe something in a particular way **bir şeyi belli bir şekilde tasvir etmek/betimlemek/resmetmek** *She paints a rosy* (= happy) *picture of family life.* **● 8 put/keep sb in the picture** *informal* to explain to someone what is happening **olup biteni birine en ayrıntısıyla anlatmak** *Jim had no idea what was going on till I put him in the picture.*

picture² /'pɪktʃər/ *verb* [T] **1** to imagine something in a particular way **düşünmek, tasavvur etmek, hayal etmek** *The house isn't at all how I had pictured it.* **2** to show someone or something in a picture **resmini yapmak** [often passive] *They were pictured holding hands on the beach.*

'picture ˌmessaging *noun* [C] sending and receiving pictures on a mobile phone **cep telefonunda resimli ileti gönderip almak**

picturesque /ˌpɪktʃər'esk/ *adjective* A picturesque place is attractive to look at. **çok çekici/canlı, tablo gibi güzel, pitoresk** *a picturesque cottage on the edge of the Yorkshire Moors*

pie /paɪ/ *noun* [C, U] a type of food made with meat, vegetables, or fruit which is covered in pastry and baked **börek, tart** *apple/meat pie* ⊃See also: mince pie.

pie

○━**piece¹** /piːs/ *noun* [C] **1** AMOUNT/PART an amount of something, or a part of something **parça** *a piece of paper/wood* ○ *She cut the flan into eight pieces.* ○ *Some of the pieces seem to be missing.* ○ *These shoes are falling to pieces* (= breaking into pieces). ⊃Orta kısımdaki renkli sayfalarına bakınız. **2** ONE one of a particular type of thing **parça, kısım** *a useful piece of equipment* **3** SOME some of a particular type of thing **parça kısım, bölüm** *a piece of news/information* ○ *Can I give you a piece of advice?* **4** ART/WRITING, ETC an example of artistic, musical, or written work **yapıt, parça, eser** *There was an interesting piece on alternative medicine in the paper yesterday.* **5 ten-/twenty-, etc pence piece** a coin with a value of ten/twenty, etc pence (= British money) **on/yirmi pens; madeni para 6 be a piece of cake** *informal* to be very easy **çok kolay olmak; çocuk oyuncağı olmak** *The test was a piece of cake.* **● 7 give sb a piece of your mind** *informal* to speak angrily to someone because they have done something wrong **fırçalamak, akıl vermek, hatasını azarlayarak yüzüne vurmak ● 8 go/fall**

to pieces If someone goes to pieces, they become so upset that they cannot control their feelings or think clearly. **kendini kaybetmek/dağıtmak, kendinden geçmek** *He went to pieces when his mother died.* ᗧSee also: **set-piece.**

piece[2] /piːs/ *verb*
piece sth together *phrasal verb* to try to understand something or discover the truth about something by collecting different pieces of information **yavaş yavaş anlamak/kavramak; parçalar yerine oturmak** *Police are trying to piece together a profile of the murderer.*

piecemeal /ˈpiːsmiːl/ *adjective, adverb* happening very gradually **parça parça, bölük börçük, azar azar** *The land is being sold in a piecemeal fashion over a number of years.*

pier

pier /pɪəʳ/ *noun* [C] a long structure that is built from the land out over the sea and sometimes has entertainments, restaurants, etc on it **iskele**

pierce /pɪəs/ *verb* [T] **1** to make a hole in something using a sharp point **delmek, delik açmak** *I'd like to have my ears pierced.* **2** *literary* If a light or a sound pierces something, it is suddenly seen or heard. **delip geçmek; (ışık) süzülmek; (ses) duyulmak/işitilmek** *A few rays of sunlight pierced the bedroom shutters.*

piercing /ˈpɪəsɪŋ/ *adjective* **1** A piercing noise, light, etc is very strong and unpleasant. **keskin, titiz, acı** *I heard a loud, piercing scream.* **2** Piercing eyes seem to look at you very closely. **(gözler, bakış) delip geçen, içine işleyen**

piety /ˈpaɪəti/ *noun* [U] a strong belief in religious morals **dindarlık, sofuluk**

o-ᴬ**pig**[1] /pɪg/ *noun* [C] **1** a large pink, brown, or black farm animal that is kept for its meat **domuz 2** *informal* someone who is very unpleasant, or someone who eats a lot **domuz gibi kimse; hayvan gibi yiyen/somuran kimse** *He's an ignorant pig.* ᗧSee also: **guinea pig.**

pig[2] /pɪg/ *verb* **pigging,** *past* **pigged**
pig out *phrasal verb informal* to eat too much **domuz gibi/hayvan gibi tıkınmak/yemek; somurmak** *We pigged out on the cakes and pastries.*

pigeon /ˈpɪdʒən/ *noun* [C] a grey bird which often lives on buildings in towns **güvercin**

pigeonhole[1] /ˈpɪdʒənhəʊl/ *noun* [C] one of a set of small open boxes in which letters or messages are left, especially in an office or hotel **göz, bölme, mektup kutusu**

pigeonhole[2] /ˈpɪdʒənhəʊl/ *verb* [T] If you pigeonhole someone, you unfairly decide what type of person they are. **yanlış kanıya kapılmak; yanlış tanımak**

piggyback /ˈpɪgibæk/ *(also* **'piggyback ˌride)** *noun* [C] a way of carrying someone on your back in which they put their arms and legs around you **sırtta taşıma, omuzda taşıma**

piggy bank /ˈpɪgiˌbæŋk/ *noun* [C] a small container, often in the shape of a pig, used by children to keep money in **kumbara, domuz şeklinde kumbara**

pigheaded /ˌpɪgˈhedɪd/ *adjective* refusing to change your opinion or the way you are doing something although it would be better if you did **inatçı, nakıs, dikbaşlı; keçi gibi inatçı**

piglet /ˈpɪglət/ *noun* [C] a baby pig **domuz yavrusu**

pigment /ˈpɪgmənt/ *noun* [C, U] a substance that gives something colour **boya maddesi, pigment ● pigmentation** /ˌpɪgmənˈteɪʃᵊn/ *noun* [U] the natural colour of a living thing **doğal renk**

pigsty /ˈpɪgstaɪ/ *(also US* **pigpen** /ˈpɪgpen/) *noun* [C] a place where pigs are kept **domuz ahırı/ağılı**

pigtail /ˈpɪgteɪl/ *noun* [C] a hairstyle in which the hair is twisted together and tied **saç örgüsü, örgülü saç** [usually plural] *A little girl in pigtails presented the flowers.*

pike /paɪk/ *noun* [C, U] *plural* **pike** a large river fish with sharp teeth, or the meat of this fish **turna balığı**

Pilates /pɪˈlɑːtiːz/ *noun* [U] a system of physical exercise involving controlled movements, stretching and breathing

pile .... İLE BİRLİKTE KULLANILAN KELİMELER
a pile of sth ● be in/put sth into a pile

o-ᴬ**pile**[1] /paɪl/ *noun* **1** [C] an amount of a substance in the shape of a small hill or a number of objects on top of each other **yığın, küme** *a pile of books/bricks* ○ *a pile of sand/rubbish* ○ *The clothes were arranged in piles on the floor.* **2** a pile of sth *informal* a lot of something **pek çok, bir yığın, bir sürü, yığınla** *It's all right for him, he's got piles of money.*

pile[2] /paɪl/ *verb*
pile in/out *phrasal verb informal* to enter/leave a place quickly and not in an organized way **bir yere doluşmak; ahırdan çıkar gibi çıkmak** *She opened the door and we all piled in.*
pile sth up *phrasal verb* to make a lot of things into a pile by putting them on top of each other **yığmak, istiflemek, istif etmek, üstüste yığmak** *Just pile those books up over there.*
pile up *phrasal verb* If something unpleasant piles up, you get more of it. **yığılmak, birikmek** *My work's really starting to pile up.*

pile-up /ˈpaɪlʌp/ *noun* [C] an accident involving several cars **zincirleme trafik kazası**

pilfer /ˈpɪlfəʳ/ *verb* [I, T] to steal things that do not have much value **yükte ağır pahada hafif şeyleri çalmak**

pilgrim /ˈpɪlgrɪm/ *noun* [C] someone who travels to a place which is important in their religion **hacı**

pilgrimage /ˈpɪlgrɪmɪdʒ/ *noun* [C, U] a journey to a place which has religious importance **hac yolculuğu/seyahati** *to go on a pilgrimage to Mecca*

pill /pɪl/ *noun* **1** [C] a small, hard piece of medicine that you swallow **hap, ilaç, tablet** *a vitamin pill* ○ *I've taken a couple of pills, but my headache still hasn't gone.* ᗧSee picture at **medicine. 2 the pill** a pill which prevents a woman from becoming pregnant **doğum kontrol hapı** ᗧSee also: **sleeping pill.**

pillar /'pɪlər/ noun [C] **1** a tall structure made of stone, wood, etc which supports something above it **sütun, direk** *The new bridge will be supported by 100 concrete pillars.* **2 a pillar of sth** someone or something who is very important to a place, organization, etc **temel direk, asıl unsur, esas kişi ya da şey** *He was a pillar of the local community.*

pillow /'pɪləʊ/ noun [C] a soft object which you rest your head on in bed **yastık**

pillowcase /'pɪləʊkeɪs/ noun [C] a cloth cover for a pillow **yastık kılıfı**

pilot /'paɪlət/ noun [C] someone who flies an aircraft **pilot** ● **pilot** verb [T] **yol göstermek**

pimp /pɪmp/ noun [C] someone who controls the work and money of a prostitute (= person who has sex for money) **pezevenk, beyaz kadın taciri; genelev patronu/patroniçesi**

pimple /'pɪmpl/ noun [C] a small spot on your skin **sivilce** ● **pimply** adjective **sivilceli** ⊃See also: goose pimples.

pin¹ /pɪn/ noun [C] **1** a thin piece of metal with a sharp point used to fasten pieces of cloth, etc together **dikiş iğnesi** *She pricked her finger on a pin.* **2** a thin piece of metal, wood, plastic, etc that holds or fastens things together **toka** *He's had a metal pin put in his leg so that the bones heal properly.* ⊃See also: drawing pin, pins and needles, rolling pin, safety pin.

pin² /pɪn/ verb [T] **pinning, past pinned 1** to fasten something with a pin **iğneyle tutturmak, iğnelemek** *We're not allowed to pin anything on these walls.* ○ *She had a red ribbon pinned to her collar.* **2 pin sb to/against/under, etc** to force someone to stay in a position by holding them **mecbur etmek, zorlamak; ...yapmak zorunda bırakmak** *They pinned him to the ground.* ⊃See also: pin your hopes (hope²) on sb/sth.

pin sb down phrasal verb **1** to make someone give you details or a decision about something **(birini) sıkıştırmak, zorlamak, cebren yaptırmak** *I've been trying to get a decision from Jim, but he's very difficult to pin down.* **2** to force someone to stay in a horizontal position by holding them **kişiyi mıhlamak, çivilemek** *They pinned him down on the floor.*

pin sth down phrasal verb to discover exact details about something **belirlemek, saptamak, gerçek ayrıntılarını keşfetmek** *Investigators are trying to pin down the cause of the fire.*

pin sth on sb phrasal verb informal to blame someone for something they did not do **masum olduğu halde suçlamak; suçu üstüne yıkmak** *They tried to pin the murder on the dead woman's husband.*

pin sth up phrasal verb to fasten something to a wall using a pin **toplu iğne ile tutturmak** *The exam results have been pinned up on the noticeboard.*

PIN /pɪn/ (also 'PIN ˌnumber) noun [C] abbreviation for Personal Identification Number: the secret number that allows you to use a bank card in a machine **Kişisel Kimlik Numarası (KKN); banka kartı ile makinadan para çekerken kullanılan gizli şifre**

pinafore /'pɪnəfɔːr/ UK (US jumper) noun [C] a loose dress with no sleeves that is worn over other clothes such as a shirt **askılı kolsuz entari, önlük**

pincer /'pɪnsər/ noun [C] one of a pair of curved hand-like parts of an animal such as a crab (= round, flat sea animal with ten legs) **kerpeten**

pinch¹ /pɪnʃ/ verb [T] **1** to press someone's skin tightly between your thumb and first finger, sometimes causing pain **çimdiklemek** *One of the kids had been pinching her and she was crying.* **2** mainly UK informal to steal something that does not have much value **arak-**

lamak, çalmak, aşırmak, yürütmek *Who's pinched my ruler?*

pinch² /pɪnʃ/ noun [C] **1** a small amount of a substance that you pick up between your thumb and your first finger **bir tutam** *a pinch of salt* **2** when you press part of the body or an area of skin tightly between your thumb and first finger **çimdik 3 at a pinch** UK (US **in a pinch**) If something can be done at a pinch, it is possible but it is difficult. **icabında, gerekirse, mecburiyet hâsıl olduğunda** *We can fit ten round the table, at a pinch.* **4 feel the pinch** to have problems because you do not have enough money **sıkışık durumda olmak, para sıkıntısı çekmek** ⊃See also: take sth with a pinch of salt¹.

pinched /pɪnʃt/ adjective A pinched face looks thin and ill. **(yüz) süzülmüş, solgun, bitkin**

pine¹ /paɪn/ noun **1** [C, U] (also 'pine ˌtree) a tall tree with long, thin leaves shaped like needles **çam ağacı 2** [U] the pale coloured wood from this tree **çam kerestesi**

pine² /paɪn/ (also pine away) verb [I] to be sad because you want someone or something that has gone away **hasretini/özlemini çekmek; karalar bağlamak** *He's pining for his ex-girlfriend.*

pineapple /'paɪnæpl/ noun [C, U] a large fruit with thick skin and sharp leaves sticking out of the top which is sweet and yellow inside **ananas**

pineapple

pinecone /'paɪnˌkəʊn/ noun [C] a hard, brown, oval object that grows on pine and fir trees (= tall trees which stay green all winter) **kozalak**

ping /pɪŋ/ verb [I] to make a short, high noise like a bell **tın/vın sesi çıkarmak; tiz ses çıkarmak; çınlamak, vınlamak** *They could hear the microwave pinging in the kitchen.* ● **ping** noun [C] **çınlama gibi bir ses çıkarma**

pink /pɪŋk/ adjective being a pale red colour **pembe** *pretty, pink flowers* ● **pink** noun [C, U] **pembe** ⊃Orta kısımdaki renkli sayfalarına bakınız.

pinnacle /'pɪnəkl/ noun [no plural] the highest or best part of something **zirve, doruk, en yüksek derece** *At 35, she is at the pinnacle of her career.*

pinpoint /'pɪnpɔɪnt/ verb [T] to say exactly what or where something is **tam olarak saptamak, kesin olarak belirlemek; parmak basmak** *It is difficult to pinpoint the exact time of death.*

ˌpins and 'needles noun **have pins and needles** to feel slight sharp pains in a part of your body when you move it after keeping it still for a period of time **karıncalanmak, uyuşmak**

pint /paɪnt/ noun [C] **1** (written abbreviation pt) a unit for measuring liquid, equal to 0.568 litres in the UK and 0.473 litres in the US **(Birleşik Krallık) 0.473 (ABD) 0.568 litereye eşit sıvı ölçüm birimi** ⊃See study page Measurements on page Centre 31. **2** UK informal a pint of beer **büyük bira**

pin-up /'pɪnʌp/ noun [C] an attractive, famous person who is often in big photographs which people stick to their walls, or the photograph of that person **(genellikle güzel kadın) duvara asılan resim**

pioneer /ˌpaɪəˈnɪəʳ/ *noun* [C] someone who is one of the first people to do something **öncü** *one of the pioneers of modern science* ● **pioneer** *verb* [T] *He pioneered the use of lasers in surgery.* **öncü olmak, en iyisi olmak**

pioneering /ˌpaɪəˈnɪərɪŋ/ *adjective* [always before noun] starting the development of something important **öncülük eden** *pioneering work/research on atomic energy*

pious /ˈpaɪəs/ *adjective* having strong religious beliefs, and living or behaving in a way which shows these beliefs **dindar, sofu**

pip¹ /pɪp/ *noun* [C] UK a small seed inside fruit such as apples and oranges **meyve çekirdeği**

pip² /pɪp/ *verb* [T] **pipping,** *past* **pipped** UK informal to beat someone by a very small amount **çok az bir farkla yenmek; kıl payı mağlup etmek**

---
pipe ...... İLE BİRLİKTE KULLANILAN KELİMELER

a pipe **leads/runs** [from/to, etc] sth ● a pipe **bursts/leaks** ● **through** a pipe

---

pipe¹ /paɪp/ *noun* [C] **1** a long tube which liquid or gas can move through **boru** *A water pipe had burst, flooding the basement.* **2** a tube with a bowl-shaped part at one end, used to smoke tobacco **pipo** *to smoke a pipe* ⊃See also: **exhaust pipe.**

pipe² /paɪp/ *verb* [T] to send something through a pipe **boruyla taşımak** *Water is piped from a spring to houses in the local area.*
 pipe down *phrasal verb informal* to stop making noise and become quieter **gürültüyü kesmek ve gittikçe sakinleşmek/sessizleşmek**
 pipe up *phrasal verb informal* to suddenly say something **aniden söylemek; hemen söyleyivermek** *Then Lydia piped up with her view of things.*

pipeline /ˈpaɪplaɪn/ *noun* [C] **1** a series of pipes that carry liquid or gas over a long distance **boru hattı 2 be in the pipeline** If a plan is in the pipeline, it is being developed and will happen in the future. **eli kulağında olmak, yolda, hazırlanmakta** *We have several projects in the pipeline.*

piping /ˈpaɪpɪŋ/ *noun* [U] a piece of pipe **borular, boru şebekesi, boru ağı** *copper piping*

piping 'hot *adjective* Piping hot food is very hot. **çok sıcak, dumanı üstünde**

piquant /ˈpiːkənt/ *adjective formal* having a pleasant, spicy taste **hafif acılı, baharatlı**

pique¹ /piːk/ *noun* [U] *formal* when someone is annoyed **gücenmiş olma, kırgınlık, incinme**

pique² /piːk/ *verb* **piquing,** *past* **piqued pique sb's curiosity/interest, etc** to make someone interested in something **ilgisini çekmek, ilgilenmesini sağlamak**

piqued /piːkt/ *adjective* annoyed **gücenmiş, alınmış, kızmış, kırılmış**

piracy /ˈpaɪərəsi/ *noun* [U] **1** attacking and stealing from ships **korsanlık 2** the illegal activity of copying and selling music, films, etc **(film, müzik, kitap vs.) korsan baskı/üretim/kopya** *software/video piracy*

pirate¹ /ˈpaɪrət/ *noun* [C] **1** someone who attacks ships and steals from them **korsan 2** someone who illegally copies and sells music, films, etc **korsan üretim/baskı yapan**

pirate² /ˈpaɪrət/ *verb* [T] to illegally copy and sell music, films, etc **korsan baskı/üretim/çoğaltım yapmak**

pirate³ /ˈpaɪrət/ *adjective* [always before noun] illegally copied **korsan olarak çoğaltılmış** *a pirate CD/DVD*

Pisces /ˈpaɪsiːz/ *noun* [C, U] the sign of the zodiac which relates to the period of 20 February - 20 March, or a person born during this period **Balık Burcu** ⊃See picture at **zodiac.**

piss¹ /pɪs/ *verb* [I] *very informal* a very impolite word meaning to pass urine from the body **çiş yapmak**
 piss sb off *phrasal verb very informal* to annoy someone **rahatsız etmek, canını sıkmak, sıkıntı vermek**

piss² /pɪs/ *noun* **take the piss** UK *very informal* an impolite phrase meaning to make jokes about someone **utandırmak; mahcup etmek; şaka ile rezil etmek**

pissed /pɪst/ *adjective very informal* **1** *mainly UK* an impolite way of describing someone who has drunk too much alcohol **ayyaş, sarhoş, rezil, kafayı bulmuş, berduş 2** *US* an impolite way of describing someone who is angry **zıvanadan çıkmış, küplere binmiş, kızmış**

,pissed 'off *adjective very informal* an impolite way of describing someone who is angry **kızmış, bıkmış, gına gelmiş, tepesi atmış**

pistol /ˈpɪstəl/ *noun* [C] a small gun **tabanca**

piston /ˈpɪstən/ *noun* [C] a part of an engine that moves up and down and makes other parts of the engine move **piston**

pit¹ /pɪt/ *noun* [C] **1** HOLE a large hole which has been dug in the ground **çukur, delik 2** SEED *US (UK* stone) a large, hard seed that grows inside some types of fruit and vegetables **meyve/sebze çekirdeği 3** COAL *(also US* 'pit ,mine)* a place where coal is dug out from under the ground **maden ocağı; kömür madeni 4 the pits** UK *(US* the pit) the place where racing cars stop to be repaired or filled with fuel during a race **pistte yarış arabalarının bakımının yapıldığı cep, pit 5 be the pits** *informal* to be very bad **en berbat/en kötüsü olmak** *Our hotel was the absolute pits.*

pit² /pɪt/ *verb* **pitting,** *past* **pitted**
 pit sb/sth against sb/sth *phrasal verb* to make someone or something compete against someone or something else **kapıştırmak, boy ölçüştürmek** *Chelsea will be pitted against Manchester United in the fourth round of the tournament.*

pitch¹ /pɪtʃ/ *verb* **1** LEVEL [T] to make something suitable for a particular level or group of people **ayarlamak, düzenlemek** [often passive] *His talk was pitched at slightly too high a level for the audience.* **2** PERSUADE [I, T] *mainly US* to try to persuade someone to do something **ikna etmek, kafasına girmek, yapması için elinden geleni yapmak** *They are pitching for new business at the moment.* **3 pitch (sb/sth) forward/into, etc** to suddenly move in a particular direction, or to make someone or something suddenly move in a particular direction **belli bir yöne aniden hamle yap(tır)mak/hareket et(tir)mek** *He braked too hard and the car pitched forward.* **4 pitch a tent** to choose a place for a tent and put it there **çadır kurmak 5** BALL [I, T] in baseball, to throw the ball towards the person who is going to hit it **beyzbolda topu vurması için fırlatmak/atmak** *He used to pitch for the Chicago White Sox.* **6** SOUND [T] to make sound at a particular level **belli bir seviyede ses çıkarmak** *The tune was pitched much too high for me.*
 pitch in *phrasal verb informal* to help a group of people to do some work that needs to be done **yardım için işe koyulmak; yardım etmek; katkıda bulunmak** *If we all pitch in, we'll get this kitchen cleaned up in no time.*

pitch² /pɪtʃ/ *noun* **1** SPORT [C] UK an area of ground where a sport is played **spor sahası/alanı** *a cricket/football pitch* **2** THROW [C] in baseball, a throw towards the person who is going to hit the ball **beyzbolda oyuncunun vurması için topu fırlatma/atma** *He struck* *out two batters with six pitches.* **3** SOUND [U] how high or low a sound is **ses perdesi 4** PERSUADING [C, U] the things someone says in order to persuade you to do something **ikna sözcükleri/çabaları; dil dökme; yalvarış/ yakarma** *I wasn't very impressed by his sales pitch.* ⊃See also: **fever pitch.**

pitch-black /ˌpɪtʃˈblæk/ (*also* pitch-dark) *adjective* very dark **zifirî karanlık** *Outside it was pitch-black.*

pitcher /ˈpɪtʃəʳ/ *noun* [C] **1** in baseball, someone who throws the ball at the person who is going to hit it **beyzbolda topu fırlatan oyuncu** ⊃Orta kısımdaki renkli sayfalarına bakınız. **2** *US* a container for holding and pouring out liquids **maşrapa, sürahi, testi** *a pitcher of water*

pitfall /ˈpɪtfɔːl/ *noun* [C] a likely mistake or problem in a situation **beklenmedik tehlike, tuzak** *the pitfalls of buying a house*

pithy /ˈpɪθi/ *adjective* A pithy remark expresses something in a very clear and direct way. **kısa ve özlü, anlamlı, veciz**

pitiful /ˈpɪtɪfˀl/ *adjective* **1** making you feel pity **hazin, acılı, yürek burkan, yürekler acısı** *I didn't recognize him, he looked so pitiful.* **2** very bad **berbat, çok kötü, iğrenç** *a pitiful excuse* ● **pitifully** *adverb* **acınacak halde**

pittance /ˈpɪtˀns/ *noun* [no plural] a very small amount of money **çok az para, sadaka gibi ücret** *She works very long hours and yet she earns a pittance.*

━━━ **pity** .... İLE BİRLİKTE KULLANILAN KELİMELER ━━━

feel pity ● take pity on sb ● pity for sb

๐⁓**pity**[1] /ˈpɪti/ *noun* **1 It's a pity...** used to say that something is disappointing **çok yazık, vah vah; maalesef, üzücü** *It's a pity you're not staying longer.* **2** [U] a feeling of sympathy for someone **acıma, merhamet** *I was hoping someone would take pity on me* (= help me in a difficult situation) *and give me a lift home.* ⊃See also: self-pity.

pity[2] /ˈpɪti/ *verb* [T] to feel sorry for someone **acımak, merhamet etmek, üzülmek** *She doesn't want people to pity her.*

pivot /ˈpɪvət/ *noun* [C] **1** a fixed point on which something balances or turns **mil, eksen 2** the most important part of something **en önemli öge, temel direk, asıl önemli bölüm** ● **pivot** *verb* [I, T] **mil üstüne koymak**

pivotal /ˈpɪvətˀl/ *adjective* having a very important influence on something **önemli ölçüde etkileyen, çok fazla etkisi olan** *He has played a pivotal role in the negotiations.*

pixel /ˈpɪksˀl/ *noun* [C] a small point that forms part of the image on a computer screen **bilgisayar ekranında görüntüyü oluşturan küçük noktacıklar**

pixie /ˈpɪksi/ *noun* [C] a small imaginary person who can do magic things **peri, cin**

pizza /ˈpiːtsə/ *noun* [C, U] a food made from a flat, round piece of bread covered with cheese, vegetables, etc and cooked in an oven **pizza** ⊃Orta kısımdaki renkli sayfalarına bakınız.

placard /ˈplækɑːd/ *noun* [C] a large sign with writing that someone carries, often to show that they disagree with something **yafta, pankart, afiş, duvar ilanı**

placate /pləˈkeɪt/ ⑤ /ˈpleɪkeɪt/ *verb* [T] *formal* to make someone less angry about something **teskin etmek, yatıştırmak, sakinleştirmek**

๐⁓**place**[1] /pleɪs/ *noun* SOMEWHERE [C] a position, building, town, area, etc **yer, mahal, konum, bina, şehir, bölge vs.** *His leg's broken in two places.* ○ *Edinburgh would be*

a nice place to live. ○ *What a stupid place to park.* **2 take place** to happen **vuku bulmak, meydana gelmek, olmak** *The meeting will take place next week.* **3 in place a** CORRECT POSITION in the correct position **yerli yerinde, tam yerinde** *The chairs are all in place.* **b** EXISTING If a rule, system, etc is in place, it has started to exist. **işlemekte, yürürlükte, uygulamada** *There are new laws in place to prevent this from happening.* **4 out of place c** WRONG POSITION not in the correct position **her zamanki yerinde olmayan** *Why are my files all out of place?* **d** NOT SUITABLE not right or suitable for a particular situation **yersiz, yakışıksız, uygunsuz** *Everyone else was wearing jeans and I felt completely out of place in my office clothes.* **5 all over the place** in or to many different places **her tarafta, her yerde; her tarafa, her yere** *There was blood all over the place.* **6 in place of sth** instead of something **yerine** *Try adding fruit to your breakfast cereal in place of sugar.* **7** HOME [C] *informal* someone's home **ev, mekân, yuva** *They've just bought a place in Spain.* **8** OPPORTUNITY [C] an opportunity to take part in something **durum, fırsat, yer ve zaman** *She's got a place at Liverpool University to do Spanish.* **9 in first/second/third, etc place** If you are in first/second, etc place in a race or competition, that is your position. **(yarışta, yarışmada vs.) birinci/ ikinci/üçüncü vs.** *He finished in fifth place.* **10 fall into place** When events or details that you did not understand before fall into place, they become easy to understand. **taşlar yerine oturmak; her şey yerli yerine oturmak; başta anlaşılmayanları zamanla anlaşılmaya başlamak** ● **11 in the first place** used to refer to the time when something started **ilk önce, herşeyden önce, bir kere** *How did this error happen in the first place?* ● **12 put sb in their place** to let someone know that they are not as important as they think they are **layık olduğu değeri vermek; herkese yerini bildirmek** ⊃See also: decimal place, have/take pride[1] of place.

place[2] /pleɪs/ *verb* **1 place sth in/on, etc** to put something somewhere carefully **özenle/itina ile yerleştirmek/koymak** *She placed a large dish in front of me.* **2** [T] to cause someone to be in a situation **sokmak, ...durumuna getirmek; ...konumunda bırakmak** *One stupid action has placed us all at risk.* **3 can't place sb** to not be able to remember who someone is or where you have met them **tanıyamamak, hatırlayamamak, çıkaramamak** *I recognize her face, but I can't quite place her.* **4 place an advertisement/bet/order, etc** to arrange to have an advertisement/bet/order, etc **ilan/ sipariş vermek, bahis oynamak 5 place emphasis/ importance, etc on sth** to give something emphasis/ importance, etc **önem vermek; vurgu yapmak** *They place a lot of importance on qualifications.*

placement /ˈpleɪsmənt/ *noun* **1** [C] *UK* a position that someone has with an organization for a short time in order to learn about the work that is done there **iş, kadro, mevkî** *He got a month's placement on a national newspaper.* **2** [U, no plural] when you put something or someone somewhere **yerleştirme, sınıflandırma; yerini/düzeyini tespit etme** *the placement of additional police on the streets*

placid /ˈplæsɪd/ *adjective* A placid person is calm and does not often get angry or excited. **sakin, uysal, halim selim; kendi halinde** ● **placidly** *adverb* **durgun bie şekilde**

plagiarism /ˈpleɪdʒˀrɪzˀm/ *noun* [U] when someone copies someone else's work or ideas **aşırma, eser hırsızlığı** *He was accused of plagiarism.*

plagiarize (*also* UK -ise) /ˈpleɪdʒˀraɪz/ *verb* [I, T] to copy someone else's work or ideas **aşırmak; eserlerden alıntı hırsızlığı yapmak** ● **plagiarist** /ˈpleɪdʒˀrɪst/

noun [C] someone who plagiarizes **aşıran; eser hırsızlığı yapan**

plague¹ /pleɪg/ *noun* [C] **1** a serious disease that spreads quickly and kills a lot of people **salgın hastalık 2** a **plague of sth** a large number of something unpleasant that causes a lot of damage **felâketler zinciri; bir çok zarara yol açan sıkıntılar/dertler/hastalıklar** *a plague of rats*

plague² /pleɪg/ *verb* [T] **plaguing**, *past* **plagued** to make someone suffer for a long time **musallat olmak, rahatsız etmek, başına belâ kesilmek** [often passive] *He's been plagued by bad luck ever since he bought that house.*

plaid /plæd/ *noun* [C, U] *US* cloth with a pattern of different coloured squares and crossing lines **ekose, kareli kumaş** *a plaid dress*

o▪**plain** /pleɪn/ *adjective* **1** SIMPLE simple and not complicated **sade, gösterişsiz** *plain food* **2** NOT MIXED not mixed with other colours, substances, etc **düz, desensiz, tek renkli** *a plain blue carpet* ○ *plain yoghurt* **3** PERSON A plain person is not attractive to look at. **sıradan, sade, sevimsiz, çirkin 4** OBVIOUS obvious and clear **açık, belli, ortada, kolay anlaşılır** [+ (that)] *It's quite plain that she doesn't want to talk to me about it.* ⊃See also: be plain **sailing**.

plain² /pleɪn/ *adverb informal* **plain stupid/wrong, etc** completely stupid/wrong, etc **tamamen yanlış, tümüyle aptal** *That's just plain stupid!*

plain³ /pleɪn/ *noun* [C] a large area of flat land **ova**

plainclothes /ˌpleɪnˈkləʊðz/ *adjective* [always before noun] Plainclothes police wear normal clothes and not a uniform. **sivil kıyafet**

plainly /ˈpleɪnli/ *adverb* **1** in a simple way that is not complicated **basitçe, açıkça, açık seçik bir şekilde** *plainly dressed* **2** in a clear and obvious way **açıkça, belli ki, anlaşılıyor ki, hiç kuşkusuz** *This is plainly wrong.*

plaintiff /ˈpleɪntɪf/ *noun* [C] someone who takes legal action against someone else in a court of law **davacı**

plaintive /ˈpleɪntɪv/ *adjective* sounding sad **ağlamaklı, üzgün, hüzünlü, acıklı** *a plaintive cry*

plait /plæt/ *UK* (*US* braid) *verb* [T] to twist three pieces of hair, rope, etc together so that they form one long piece **örmek, örgü yapmak ● plait** *UK* (*US* braid) *noun* [C] *She wore her hair in plaits.* **saç örgüsü**

announce/approve/implement/oppose/outline/unveil a plan ● an ambitious/controversial/strategic plan

o▪**plan¹** /plæn/ *noun* [C] **1** an arrangement for what you intend to do or how you intend to do something **plân** *the country's economic plan* ○ *Do you have any plans for the weekend?* ○ *The plan is that we'll buy a car once we're there.* ○ *There's been a change of plan and we're going on Wednesday instead.* ○ *Luckily, everything went according to plan* (= happened the way it was planned). **2** a drawing that shows how something appears from above or will appear from above when it is built **plân, proje, taslak, çizim** *a street plan.* ○ *We had a designer draw up a plan for the yard.*

o▪**plan²** /plæn/ *verb* **planning**, *past* **planned 1** to think about and decide what you are going to do or how you are going to do something **plânlamak, tasarlamak, yapmayı düşünmek** *We're just planning our holidays.* ○ *As a manager, you've got to plan ahead.* ○ *I'd planned the meeting for Friday.* **2 plan to do sth** to intend to do something **yapmaya niyet etmek; yapmayı tasarlamak** *He plans to go to college next year.* **3** [T] to decide

how something will be built **plân/proje çizmek, plânlamak** *We got an architect to help us plan our new kitchen.*

plan

Dikkat! Fiil sonlarını kontrol ediniz. Çoğu Türk öğrenci, **plan** fiilini geçmiş zamanda kullanırken hata yapmaktadır. **Plan** fiilinin 2. ve 3. halleri **planned** şeklindedir. Fiilin -ing formu planning şeklindedir.

plan on doing sth *phrasal verb* to intend to do something **bir şeyi yapmaya niyetli olmak; yapmayı düşünmek; niyet etmek** *We're planning on catching the early train.*

plan sth out *phrasal verb* to think about and decide what you are going to do or how you are going to do something **ayrıntılarıyla plânlamak/tasarlamak** *Have you planned out your journey?* ○ *I'm just planning out my day.*

board/catch/get on/get off a plane ● a plane gets in/lands/takes off ● on a plane ● by plane

o▪**plane¹** /pleɪn/ *noun* [C] **1** FLYING a vehicle that flies and has an engine and wings **uçak** *What time does her plane get in* (= arrive)? ○ *He likes to watch the planes taking off and landing.* ○ *a plane crash* **2** TOOL a tool that you use to make wood smooth **büyük elektrikli rende aleti 3** SURFACE in mathematics, a flat surface **(matematik) düz, düzey**

plane² /pleɪn/ *verb* [T] to make a piece of wood smooth using a tool called a plane **plânya ile düzleştirmek, rendelemek**

planet /ˈplænɪt/ *noun* [C] a large, round object in space that moves around the sun or another star **gezegen** *Jupiter is the largest planet of our solar system.* **● planetary** *adjective* relating to planets **gezegenlere ait**

planetarium /ˌplænɪˈteəriəm/ *noun* [C] *plural* **planetariums** or **planetaria** a building that has a machine for showing the positions and movements of the stars and planets **plânetaryum, yıldız gözlem evi**

plank /plæŋk/ *noun* [C] a long, flat piece of wood **kalas** *wooden planks*

plankton /ˈplæŋktən/ *noun* [U] very small plants and animals in the sea that are eaten by fish and other sea creatures **plankton**

planner /ˈplænəʳ/ *noun* [C] someone whose job is to plan things, especially which buildings are built in towns **plânlamacı** *urban planners*

planning /ˈplænɪŋ/ *noun* [U] **1** the activity of thinking about and deciding what you are going to do or how you are going to do something **plânlama, tasarlama** *Events like these take months of careful planning.* **2** control over which buildings are built in an area **kent plânlaması** *town planning* ⊃See also: family **planning**.

o▪**plant¹** /plɑːnt/ *noun* [C] **1** a living thing that grows in the soil or water and has leaves and roots, especially one that is smaller than a tree **bitki** *Have you watered the plants?* ○ *tomato plants* **2** a large factory where an industrial process happens **fabrika, atelye, imalâthane, santral, reaktör** *a nuclear power plant.* ⊃See also: potted **plant**.

plant² /plɑːnt/ *verb* [T] **1** SEEDS/PLANTS to put seeds or plants in the ground so that they will grow **dikmek, ekmek** *to plant bulbs/seeds/trees* **2** SECRETLY to secretly put something in a place that will make someone seem guilty **gizlice koymak/sokmak/yerleştirmek** *She insisted that the drugs had been planted on her*

P

without her knowledge. **3 plant a bomb** to put a bomb somewhere so that it will explode there **bomba koymak/yerleştirmek 4 plant sth in/next/on, etc** to put something firmly in a particular place **koymak, kondurmak, yerleştirmek** *He planted himself next to me on the sofa.* **5** [IDEA/DOUBTS] to make someone start thinking something **düşünmeye başlamasını sağlamak** *I was confident till you planted doubts in my mind.*

plantation /plæn'teɪʃ°n/ *noun* [C] **1** an area of land in a hot country where a crop is grown **büyük çiftlik, plantasyon** *a banana/cotton/sugar plantation* **2** an area of land where trees are grown to produce wood **koru, fidanlık**

plaque /plɑːk/ *noun* **1** [C] a flat piece of metal or stone with writing on it which is fixed to a wall, often in order to make people remember a dead person **plâka, levha, tabelâ 2** [U] a harmful substance that forms on your teeth **diş üstünde oluşan tabaka; diş kiri/pası; pesek**

plasma /'plæzmə/ *noun* [U] the clear liquid part of blood which contains the blood cells **plâzma**

'**plasma ,screen** *noun* [C] a screen for showing very clear words or pictures which uses special gases pressed between two flat pieces of glass **plâzma ekran**

plaster[1] /'plɑːstəʳ/ *noun* **1** [U] a substance that is spread on walls in order to make them smooth **sıva 2** [C] *UK* (*US* Band-Aid *trademark*) a small piece of sticky material that you put on cuts on your body **yara bandı 3 be in plaster** *UK* (*US* be in a cast) If your arm or leg is in plaster, it is covered in a hard, white substance to protect a broken bone. **alçıda olmak, alçıya almak; alçıyla sarmak**

plaster[2] /'plɑːstəʳ/ *verb* [T] **1** to cover most of a surface with something **sarmak, örtmek, kaplamak, yapıştırmak** *My boots were plastered with mud.* **2** to cover a wall with a substance in order to make it smooth **sıvamak, sıva yapmak**

plastered /'plɑːstəd/ *adjective informal* very drunk **körkütük sarhoş, zom, küfelik**

☞**plastic** /'plæstɪk/ *noun* [C, U] a light, artificial substance that can be made into different shapes when it is soft and is used in a lot of different ways **plastik** *Most children's toys are made of plastic.* ● **plastic** *adjective a plastic bag* **plastik**

plasticity /plæs'tɪsəti/ *noun* [U] *formal* the quality of being soft enough to make into many different shapes **plastik, her türlü şekle girebilme**

,**plastic 'surgery** *noun* [U] operations on someone's face or body to make them more attractive **plastik cerrahi** *to have plastic surgery*

'**plastic ,wrap** *US* (*UK* clingfilm) *noun* [U] thin, transparent plastic used for wrapping or covering food **plastik geçirgen ambalaj malzemesi**

☞**plate** /pleɪt/ *noun* **1** [FOOD] [C] a flat, round object which is used for putting food on **tabak, sahan** *a dinner plate* ○ *a plate of biscuits* **2** [METAL/GLASS] [C] a flat piece of metal or glass **tabaka, levha, plâka** *I had a metal plate put in my knee after the accident.* **3** [U] **gold/silver plate** metal with a thin layer of gold or silver on top **altın/gümüş kaplama 4** [PICTURE] [C] a picture in a book **kitaptaki resim** ➔See also: L-plate, license plate, number plate.

plateau /'plætəʊ/ ⓤ /plæ'təʊ/ *noun* [C] *plural UK* **plateaux** or *also US* **plateaus 1** a large area of high, flat land **yayla, plâto 2** a period when the level of something stays the same **duraklama dönemi, durgunluk süresi** [usually singular] *Sales are still good but they've reached a plateau.*

platform /'plætfɔːm/ *noun* [C] **1** [RAISED SURFACE] a raised surface for people to stand on, especially when they are speaking to a lot of people **kürsü, podyum, sahne** *The speakers all stood on a platform.* **2** [TRAIN] the area in a railway station where you get on and off the train **peron, tren istasyonu platformu** *The train for London, Paddington, will depart from platform 12.* **3** [POLITICS] all the things that a political party promises to do if they are elected **parti programı, platform** *They campaigned on a platform of low taxation.* **4** [FOR OPINIONS] a way of telling the public about your opinions **fikirlerini aktarma biçimi; fikirlerini toplumla paylaşma şekli/yöntemi** *Basically, he uses the newspaper as a platform for airing his political views.*

platinum /'plætɪnəm/ ⓤ /'plætnəm/ *noun* [U] a silver-coloured metal that is very valuable (symbol Pt) **plâtin**

platitude /'plætɪtjuːd/ *noun* [C] something that is boring because it has been said many times before **basmakalıp söz, beylik lâf**

platonic /plə'tɒnɪk/ *adjective* A platonic relationship is friendly and not sexual. **plâtonik**

platoon /plə'tuːn/ *noun* [C] a small group of soldiers **takım, müfreze**

platter /'plætəʳ/ *noun* [C] a large plate used for serving food **servis tabağı**

plaudit /'plɔːdɪt/ *noun* [C] *formal* praise **övgü, methiye** [usually plural] *He has earned/won plaudits* (= been praised) *for his latest novel.*

plausible /'plɔːzɪbl/ *adjective* If something that someone says or writes is plausible, it could be true. **akla yatkın, akıllıca, mâkul** *a plausible excuse/explanation* ➔Opposite implausible. ● **plausibility** /ˌplɔːzɪ'bɪləti/ *noun* [U] when something is plausible **akla yatkınlık; mâkul olma; akla uygunluk**

☞**play**[1] /pleɪ/ *verb* **1** [SPORTS/GAMES] [I, T] When you play a sport or game, you take part in it. **oynamak, karşılaşmak** *You play tennis, don't you Sam?* ○ *We often used to play cards.* ○ *I used to play netball for my school.* ○ *I'm playing Tony* (= playing against Tony) *at squash tonight.* ○ *Newcastle are playing against Arsenal tonight.* **2** [CHILDREN] [I, T] When children play, they enjoy themselves with toys and games. **oyun oynamak** *She likes playing with her dolls.* **3** [MUSIC] [I, T] to make music with a musical instrument **müzik aleti/enstrüman çalmak** *Tim was playing the piano.* **4** [RECORD/RADIO] [I, T] If a radio, record, etc plays, it produces sounds, or if you play a radio, record, etc you make it produce sounds. **(müzik, radyo, plak vs.) çalmak** *A radio was playing in the background.* ○ *He plays his records late into the night.* **5** [ACTING] [T] to be a character in a film or play **filmde/oyunda bir karakteri oynamak/canlandırmak** *Morgan played the father in the film version.* **6 play a joke/trick on sb** to deceive someone as a joke **birine oyun oynamak; hile yapmak, kandırmak; şaka yapmak, dalga geçmek** *I played a trick on her and pretended we'd eaten all the food.* ➔See also: play it by ear, play games (game[1]), play (it) safe[1], play for time[1], play truant.

play about/around *phrasal verb* to behave in a silly way **aptalca davranmak; avanakça hareket etmek** *Stop playing around and get on with your homework!*

be playing at sth *phrasal verb UK* If you ask what someone is playing at, you are angry because they are doing something silly. **laf olsun diye yapmak, eğlenmek** *What do you think you're playing at!*

play sth back *phrasal verb* to listen to sounds or watch pictures that you have just recorded **(kaydedilmiş film/müzik) göstermek, çalmak** *When I played back our conversation, I realized I hadn't made myself clear.*

play sth down *phrasal verb* to try to make people think that something is less important or bad than it really is **ciddiye almamak, ehemmiyet vermemek, önemse-**

memek *The government have tried to play down the seriousness of the incident.*

play on sth *phrasal verb* to use someone's fears in order to make that person do or believe what you want **yararlanmak, istismar etmek; zayıf anından çıkar sağlamak** *A lot of marketing strategies just play on your fears and insecurities.*

play up *phrasal verb UK* **1** If a child plays up, he or she behaves badly. **yaramazlık/terbiyesizlik etmek; haşarı davranmak 2** If a machine plays up, it does not work as it should. **başa dert açmak; düzgün çalışmamak; randımanlı çalışmamak**

play (about/around) with sth *phrasal verb* **1** to think about or try different ways of doing something **yeni fikirler/şeyler üzerinde çalışmak; farklı şeyler aramak** *We've been playing around with ideas for a new TV show.* **2** to keep touching or moving something, often when you are bored or nervous **sıkıntıdan/sinirden bir yerleriyle oynamak/kalem çevirmek/tesbih çekmek; sinirden oraya buraya dokunmak** *Stop playing with your hair!*

🧩 play (noun) .... İLE BİRLİKTE KULLANILAN KELİMELER

perform/put on/write a play ● **in** a play ● a play **about** sth

play² /pleɪ/ *noun* **1** [THEATRE] [C] a story that is written for actors to perform, usually in a theatre **oyun, tiyatro oyunu** *We saw a play at the National Theatre.* ○ *Most schools usually put on a play* (= perform a play) *at Christmas.* **2** [SPORTS/GAMES] [U] the activity of taking part in a sport or a game **müsabaka, karşılaşma, oyun** *Rain stopped play in the Hingis-Davenport match.* **3** [CHILDREN] [U] when children enjoy themselves with toys and games **oyun, çocukların oynadığı oyun, eğlence** *a play area* **4 fair play** behaviour that is fair, honest, and does not take advantage of people **adil davranma; dürüst olma** ● **5 a play on words** a joke using a word or phrase that has two meanings **kelimelerle oynama; kelime oyunu** ➔See also: **foul play, role-play.**

playboy /'pleɪbɔɪ/ *noun* [C] a rich man who spends his time enjoying himself and has relationships with a lot of beautiful women **hovarda, sefa düşkünü**

♦**player** /'pleɪəʳ/ *noun* [C] **1** someone who plays a sport or game **oyuncu** *football/tennis players* **2** someone who plays a musical instrument **sanatçı, herhangi bir müzik aleti çalan** *a piano player* ➔See also: **cassette player, CD player, record player.**

playful /'pleɪfʰl/ *adjective* funny and not serious **şen, şakacı, samimi** *a playful mood/remark* ● **playfulness** *noun* [U] **şakacı olma durumu** ● **playfully** *adverb* **şakacı bir şekilde**

playground /'pleɪgraʊnd/ *noun* [C] an area of land where children can play, especially at school **oyun sahası, çocuk bahçesi**

playgroup /'pleɪgruːp/ *noun* [C] a place where small children go during the day when they are too young to go to school **anaokulu**

'**playing ˌcard** *noun* [C] one of a set of 52 small pieces of stiff paper with numbers and pictures on, used for playing games **iskambil kâğıdı**

'**playing ˌfield** *noun* [C] **1** an area of land used for sports such as football **futbol/oyun sahası 2 a level playing field** a situation in which everyone has the same chance of succeeding **herkesin eşit başarı şansının olduğu durum**

playoff /'pleɪɒf/ *noun* [C] a game between two teams that have equal points in order to decide which is the winner **son maç, karar maçı**

playpen /'pleɪpen/ *noun* [C] a small structure with net or bars around the sides that young children are put into so that they can play safely **(bebek, küçük çocuk) oyun bahçesi**

playroom /'pleɪruːm/ *noun* [C] a room in a house for children to play in **oyun odası**

PlayStation /'pleɪˌsteɪʃˀn/ *noun* [C] *trademark* a machine that you use to play games on your television **televizyon oyun aleti; PlayStaytion**

plaything /'pleɪθɪŋ/ *noun* [C] someone who is treated without respect and is forced to do things for someone else's enjoyment **başkasının eğlencesi için kendisiyle oyuncak gibi oynanan kimse**

playtime /'pleɪtaɪm/ *noun* [C, U] *UK* a period of time when children at school can play outside **oyun vakti**

playwright /'pleɪraɪt/ *noun* [C] someone who writes plays **oyun yazarı**

plaza /'plɑːzə/ *noun* [C] *US* **1** an open, public area in a city or town **açık umumî alan, plaza** *Mexico City's main plaza is called the Zocalo.* **2** a group of buildings with shops, often including an open, public area **açık alan etrafında bulunan ve alış veriş yapılan mağazalar bölgesi, plaza** *a shopping plaza*

plc, PLC /ˌpiːel'siː/ *noun* [C] *abbreviation for* Public Limited Company: used after the name of a large company in Britain whose shares (= equal parts of its total value) can be bought and sold by the public **Anonim Şirket; A.Ş.**

🧩 plea .... İLE BİRLİKTE KULLANILAN KELİMELER

issue/make/reject a plea ● a **desperate/emotional/ impassioned** plea ● a plea **for** sth ● a plea **from** sb

plea /pliː/ *noun* [C] **1** when someone says in a court of law if they are guilty or not guilty of the crime they have been accused of **(mahkeme) davalı beyanı** *a plea of guilty/not guilty* **2** a strong request **yalvarma, yakarma, rica** *an emotional plea for forgiveness*

plead /pliːd/ *verb past* **pleaded** or *also US* **pled 1** [LEGAL] [T] to say in a court of law if you are guilty or not guilty of the crime you have been accused of **(mahkeme) iddia etmek, beyan etmek, öne sürmek, söylemek** *He pleaded not guilty to five felony charges.* **2** [ASK] [I] to ask for something in a strong and emotional way **yalvarmak, rica etmek, dilemek** *He pleaded with her to come back.* ○ *She pleaded for mercy.* **3** [EXCUSE] [T] to say something as an excuse **mazeret göstermek; bahaneler üretmek/yaratmak** *You'll just have to plead ignorance* (= say you did not know). **4 plead sb's case/cause** to say something to try to help someone get what they want or avoid punishment **(mahkeme) savunmak**

♦**pleasant** /'plezˀnt/ *adjective* **1** enjoyable or attractive **zevkli, hoş, çekici** *pleasant weather/surroundings* ○ *We had a very pleasant evening.* **2** A pleasant person has a friendly character. **tatlı, hoş, cana yakın, dost canlısı** ➔Opposite **unpleasant.** ● **pleasantly** *adverb* *I was pleasantly surprised.* **hoş bir şekilde**

pleasantry /'plezˀntri/ *noun* [C] a polite thing that you say when you meet someone **hoş/güzel söz, takılma, lâtife, şaka** [usually plural] *They exchanged pleasantries about the weather.*

♦**please¹** /pliːz/ *exclamation* **1** something that you say to be polite when you are asking for something or asking someone to do something **Lütfen!'** *Could you fill in the form, please?* ○ *Please may I use your telephone?* **2 Yes, please.** used to accept something politely **Evet, lütfen!'** *"Would you like a lift home?" "Oh yes, please."*

please[2] /pliːz/ *verb* **1** [I, T] to make someone happy **mutlu/memnun etmek** *the desire to please* ○ *I only got married to please my parents.* ➔Opposite **displease**. **2 anything/as/what/whatever, etc you please** used to say that someone can have or do anything they want **Nasıl istersenizi!', 'Dilediğiniz gibi!', 'Keyfinize göre!', 'Her nasıl dilerseniz!'** *Feel free to talk about anything you please.* ○ *He can come and go as he pleases.* **3 Please yourself.** a slightly rude way of telling someone that you do not care what they choose to do **Siz bilirsiniz!', 'Nasıl istersenizi!', 'Her nasıl tensip buyurursanız!'** *"I don't want anything to eat." "Please yourself."*

o=**pleased** /pliːzd/ *adjective* **1** happy or satisfied **mutlu, memnun, mesut, tatmin olmuş** *I wasn't very pleased about having to pay.* ○ [+ to do sth] *I'm pleased to be back in England.* ○ [+ (that)] *He was pleased that she had come back.* ○ *I'm really pleased with the quality of his work.* **2 Pleased to meet you.** a polite way of greeting someone you are meeting for the first time **Tanıştığımıza memnun oldum!', 'Sizi tanıdığıma memnun oldum!'**

pleasing /ˈpliːzɪŋ/ *adjective* Something that is pleasing gives pleasure. **memnuniyet verici, hoş, tatlı** *the most pleasing aspect of her work* ○ *These buildings are very pleasing to the eye.*

pleasurable /ˈpleʒ°rəbl/ *adjective* enjoyable **keyif verici, hoş, zevkli** *a pleasurable experience*

⚃ **pleasure** ...... İLE BİRLİKTE KULLANILAN KELİMELER

derive/express/give pleasure ● take pleasure in sth ● enormous/great/perverse/pure/sheer pleasure

o=**pleasure** /ˈpleʒəʳ/ *noun* **1** [HAPPINESS] [U] a feeling of happiness or enjoyment **zevk, haz, sevinç, mutluluk** *His visits used to give us such pleasure.* ○ *She seemed to take pleasure in* (= enjoy) *humiliating people.* ○ *It gives me great pleasure to introduce our next guest.* ➔Opposite **displeasure**. **2** [ENJOYABLE EXPERIENCE] [C, U] an enjoyable activity or experience **zevk, sevinç, keyif** *Food is one of life's great pleasures.* ○ *I once had the pleasure of sharing a taxi with her.* **3** [NOT WORK] [U] If you do something for pleasure, you do it because you enjoy it and not because it is your job. **zevkine yapılan, keyif alınan şey, zevk** *reading for pleasure* **4 It's a pleasure.; My pleasure.** a polite way of replying to someone who has thanked you **Rica ederim!', 'Benim için bir zevkti!', 'Her zaman!', 'Bir şey değil!'** *"Thank you for a wonderful evening." "My pleasure."*

pleated /ˈpliːtɪd/ *adjective* A pleated piece of clothing or piece of cloth has regular, vertical folds in it. **plili, kıvrımlı** *a pleated skirt*

pled /pled/ *US past of* plead **plead' fiilinin geçmiş zaman hâli**

⚃ **pledge (noun)** ...... İLE BİRLİKTE KULLANILAN KELİMELER

break/fulfil/make a pledge ● a pledge on sth

pledge[1] /pledʒ/ *noun* [C] a serious promise **taahhüt, söz, namus sözü, ant, yemin** [+ to do sth] *a pledge to create jobs* ○ *He made a solemn pledge to the American people.*

pledge[2] /pledʒ/ *verb* [T] to promise seriously to do something or give something **söz vermek, vaat etmek, ant içmek, yemin etmek** *Foreign donors have pledged $550 million.* ○ *He pledged his support to Mandela.* ○ [+ to do sth] *He pledged to cut government salaries.*

plentiful /ˈplentɪf°l/ *adjective* If something is plentiful, there is a lot of it available. **bol, pek çok, ziadesiyle** *a plentiful supply of meat*

o=**plenty** /ˈplenti/ *quantifier* **1** easily as much or as many as you need **bol, çok, yeterli, kâfi derecede** *Don't bring any food - we've got plenty.* ○ *There is plenty of evidence to support her claims.* ○ *There's plenty of room.* ○ *Help yourself to food - there's plenty more.* **2 plenty big/large/wide, etc enough** easily as big/large/wide, etc as you need something to be **yeterince, oldukça, gereğinden bile fazla** *This house is plenty big enough for two families.* **3** a lot **çok, pek çok** *I know plenty of unemployed musicians.* ○ *There's plenty for you to do.*

plethora /ˈpleθ°rə/ *noun* **a plethora of sth** *formal* a large number of something **yığınla, pek fazla, bir hayli** *There is a confusing plethora of pension plans.*

pliers /plaɪəz/ *noun* [plural] a tool for holding or pulling small things like nails or for cutting wire **kerpeten, pense, karga burun** *a pair of pliers* ➔See picture at **tool**.

plight /plaɪt/ *noun* [no plural] *formal* an unpleasant or difficult situation **zor ve nahoş bir durum, dram, acıklı durum** *the plight of the sick and the poor*

plod /plɒd/ *verb* plodding, *past* plodded **plod along/on/through, etc** to walk with slow, heavy steps **zar zor yürümek** *We plodded through the mud.*

plonk[1] /plɒŋk/ *verb UK informal* **plonk sth down/in/on, etc** to put something somewhere quickly and without care **pat diye bırakmak, küt diye sertçe koymak; alelusul koymak** *She plonked her bag on the floor.*
plonk yourself down *phrasal verb* to sit down quickly and without care **gelişigüzel pat diye bütün ağırlığı ile oturmak; kendini olanca ağırlığıyla bırakıvermek**

plonk[2] /plɒŋk/ *noun* [U] *UK informal* cheap wine **ucuz şarap; (argo) garip öldüren şarap**

plop[1] /plɒp/ *noun* [C] the sound made by an object when it falls into water **(suya düşerken çıkan ses) cup, foş, pıt**

plop[2] /plɒp/ *verb* plopping, *past* plopped *US informal* **plop (sth) down/onto, etc** to put something somewhere quickly and without care **pat diye bırakmak, küt diye sertçe koymak; alelusul koymak** *She plopped down next to me.*

plot[1] /plɒt/ *noun* [C] **1** [STORY] the things that happen in a story **olay örgüsü, konu, plan, olaylar dizisi** *I don't like movies with complicated plots.* **2** [PLAN] a plan to do something bad **komplo, haince yapılan plan** [+ to do sth] *a plot to blow up the embassy* **3** [LAND] a piece of land, often for growing food or for building on **arsa, parsel, arazi, yer** *a building plot*

plough *UK*, **plow** *US*

plot² /plɒt/ *verb* **plotting**, *past* **plotted 1** [I, T] to plan to do something bad **haince/kötü amaçlar için plan yapmak** [+ to do sth] *They plotted to bring down the government.* ○ *He fired all those accused of plotting against him.* **2** [T] to make marks on a map, picture, etc to show the position or development of something **haritada göstermek, işaretlemek, yerini belirlemek** *This chart plots the position of all aircraft.*

plough¹ *UK* (*US* **plow**) /plaʊ/ *noun* [C] a large tool used by farmers to turn over the soil before planting crops **kara saban, pulluk**

plough² *UK* (*US* **plow**) /plaʊ/ *verb* [I, T] to turn over soil with a plough **çift sürmek, toprağı sürmek**
plough sth back *phrasal verb* to spend the money that a business has earned on improving that business **yatırmak, yatırım yapmak, gelirleri işi geliştirmek için harcamak** *All profits are ploughed back into the company.*
plough into sth *phrasal verb* to hit something with great force **hızla çarpmak, şiddetle vurmak** *My car ploughed straight into the car in front.*
plough on *phrasal verb* to continue doing something, although it is difficult or boring **güçlükle ilerlemek, zorlukla yapmaya çalışmak**
plough through sth *phrasal verb* to finish what you are reading, eating, or working on, although there is a lot of it **çok olmasına rağmen ne yapıp edip bitirmek** *I had to plough through the whole report.*

plow /plaʊ/ *noun*, *verb US* spelling of plough **saban, pulluk; sürmek; toprağı alt üst etmek**

--- **ploy** ...... İLE BİRLİKTE KULLANILAN KELİMELER ---
use a ploy ● a ploy **backfires/works** ● a **clever/cunning/cynical/deliberate** ploy ● a ploy **by sb**

ploy /plɔɪ/ *noun* [C] a slightly dishonest method used to try to achieve something **ayak oyunu, manevra, numara** [+ to do sth] *The phone call was just a ploy to get rid of her.*

PLS *informal written abbreviation for* please: used in emails and text messages **lütfen sözcüğünün kısa yazılışı**

pluck /plʌk/ *verb* **1 pluck sth/sb from/out, etc** to quickly pull something or someone from the place where they are **kuvvetle çekmek, almak; çekip çıkarmak** *A helicopter plucked him from the sea.* **2** [BIRD] [T] to pull all the feathers out of a bird before cooking it **yolmak, almak 3** [MUSIC] [T] If you pluck the strings of a musical instrument, you pull them with your fingers to make a sound. **(müzik aleti) parmakla çalmak 4** [PLANT] [T] *literary* to pick a flower or part of a plant **(çiçek, bitki) toplamak, yolmak, koparmak 5 pluck your eyebrows** to pull hairs out of your eyebrows (= lines of hair above your eyes) to make them look tidy **kaşlarını almak** ○See also: pluck up the **courage** (to do sth).

plug¹ /plʌg/ *noun* [C] **1** [ELECTRICITY] a plastic or rubber object with metal pins, used to connect electrical equipment to an electricity supply **fiş, elektrik fişi** *I need to change the plug on my hairdryer.* **2** [HOLE] something you put in a hole to block it **tapa, tıkaç, tıpa** *a bath plug* **3** [ADVERTISEMENT] when someone talks about a new book, film, etc in public to advertise it **(kitap, film vs.) reklâm, tanıtım, tanıtım toplantısı; bilgilendirme** *She managed to get in a plug for her new book.* **4 pull the plug** to prevent an activity from continuing **fişini çekmek, eyleme son vermek, yarıda kesmek, durdurmak** *They have pulled the plug on jazz broadcasts.* ○See also: spark plug.

plug² /plʌg/ *verb* [T] **plugging**, *past* **plugged 1 plug a gap/hole** *mainly UK* to solve a problem by supplying something that is needed **bir boşluğu doldurarak/**

plug

gereksinimi gidererek sorunu çözmek; halletmek; bir gediği kapamak; eksiği gidermek *The new computer system will help to plug the gap in the county's ability to collect taxes.* **2** to talk about a new book, film, etc in public in order to advertise it **reklâmını/tanıtımını yapmak** *He was on TV, plugging his new book.* **3** to block a hole **tıpamak, tıkamak, tıkaçla kapamak**
plug away *phrasal verb informal* to work hard at something for a long time **üzerinde çalışmak/uğraşmak; büyük emek harcamak** *I'm still plugging away at my article.*
plug sth in *phrasal verb* to connect a piece of electrical equipment to an electricity supply **prize takmak** *Could you plug the iron in for me?* ○Opposite unplug.
plug sth into sth *phrasal verb* to connect one piece of electrical equipment to another **elektrikli aletleri birbirine fiş ile bağlamak** *You need to plug the speakers into the stereo.*

plughole /ˈplʌɡhəʊl/ (*also US* **drain**) *noun* [C] the hole in a bath or sink (= place in a kitchen where dishes are washed) where the water flows away **küvet deliği**

plug-in (*also* **plugin**) /ˈplʌɡɪn/ *noun* [C] a small computer program that makes a larger one work faster or be able to do more things **daha büyük bir bilgisayarın hızını artıran bilgisayar programı**

plum /plʌm/ *noun* [C] a soft, round fruit with red, yellow, or purple skin and a stone in the middle **erik**

plumage /ˈpluːmɪdʒ/ *noun* [U] a bird's feathers **kuş tüyü**

plumber /ˈplʌmər/ *noun* [C] someone whose job is to repair or connect water pipes and things like toilets and baths **sıhhî tesisatçı, muslukçu, su tesisatçısı**

plumbing /ˈplʌmɪŋ/ *noun* [U] the water pipes in a building **su tesisatı**

plume /pluːm/ *noun* **1 a plume of dust/smoke, etc** a tall, thin amount of dust/smoke, etc rising into the air. **toz/duman buzurğu 2** [C] a large feather, often worn for decoration **kuş tüyü, telek**

plummet /ˈplʌmɪt/ *verb* [I] to fall very quickly in amount or value **ansızın düşmek, birden azalmak; tepe taklak olmak** *Temperatures plummeted to minus 20.*

plump¹ /plʌmp/ *adjective* **1** quite fat **tombul, tıknaz, etine dolgun** *a plump child* **2** pleasantly round or full **semiz** *nice plump cloves of garlic*

plump² /plʌmp/ *verb*
plump for sth *phrasal verb UK* to choose something, especially after thinking about it for a time **düşündük-**

ten sonra seçmek/oy vermek *I plumped for the salmon.*

plunder /'plʌndə^r/ *verb* [I, T] to steal, especially during a war **yağmalamak, yağma/talan etmek** *Many of the region's churches had been plundered.* ● **plunder** *noun* [U] **yağmalama**

plunge¹ /plʌndʒ/ *verb* **1 plunge down/into, etc** to fall or move down very quickly and with force **hızla ve süratle düşmek** *The car came off the road and plunged down the hillside.* **2** [I] to become lower in temperature, value, etc very suddenly and quickly **(ısı, değer vs.) aniden düşmek; birdenbire azalmak; düşüş göstermek** *Temperatures plunged below zero.*

plunge sth into sth *phrasal verb* to push something very hard into something else **daldırmak, batırmak, saplamak, sokuşturmak, tıkmak** *He plunged the knife into the man's stomach.*

plunge sb/sth into sth *phrasal verb* to make someone or something suddenly be unhappy or in an unpleasant situation **ansızın mutsuz/huzursuz etmek; huzursuzluğa/kaosa girmek** [often passive] *The country had been plunged into chaos.*

plunge into sth *phrasal verb* to start doing something with a lot of energy **dalmak, girişmek, koyulmak** *Trying to forget about her, he plunged into his work.*

🧩 plunge ...... İLE BİRLİKTE KULLANILAN KELİMELER

take a plunge ● a plunge in sth ● a **stock market** plunge

plunge² /plʌndʒ/ *noun* **1** [C] a sudden and quick decrease in the value, amount, or level of something **düşüş, azalma, aşağı inme, değer/miktar/seviye kaybetme** *Prices have taken a plunge* (= suddenly become less). **2 take the plunge** to do something important or difficult, especially after thinking about it for a long time **gözünü karartmak; tehlikeye atılmak, riske girmek** *We're finally going to take the plunge and buy a house.*

the pluperfect /,plu:'pɜ:fɪkt/ (*also* the past perfect) *noun* the form of the verb that is used to show that an action had already finished when another action happened. In English, the pluperfect is made with 'had' and a past participle. **had + geçmiş zaman ortacı' ile oluşan fiil kipi; geçmişte bitmiş zaman kipi**

plural /'plʊər^əl/ *noun* [C] a word or part of a word which shows that you are talking about more than one person or thing. For example 'babies' is the plural of 'baby'. **çoğul** ● **plural** *adjective* 'Cattle' and 'trousers' are plural nouns. **çoğul**

pluralism /'plʊər^əlɪz^əm/ *noun* [U] the existence in a society of many different types of people with many different beliefs and opinions **çoğulculuk** *political pluralism* ● **pluralist** (*also* pluralistic /,plʊər^əl'ɪstɪk/) *adjective* relating to pluralism **çoğulculuğa ilişkin** *a pluralist society*

o⁼**plus¹** /plʌs/ *preposition* **1** added to **artı** *Five plus three is eight.* **2** and also **ilaveten, artı olarak; fazladan** *You've won their latest CD plus two tickets for their concert.*

plus² /plʌs/ *adjective* **40 plus, 150 plus, etc** more than the amount stated **40 ve üstü, 150 ve üstü vs.** *temperatures of 40 plus*

plus³ /plʌs/ *conjunction informal* and also **ayrıca, ilave olarak, ilaveten** *Don't go there in August. It'll be too hot, plus it'll be really expensive.*

plus⁴ /plʌs/ *noun* [C] **1** *informal* an advantage **artı, ilave** *Well, the apartment has a garden so that's a plus.* **2** (*also* 'plus ,sign) the symbol +, used between two numbers to show that they are being added together **(+) işareti**

plush /plʌʃ/ *adjective* Plush furniture, buildings, rooms, etc are very expensive and comfortable. **lüks, ihtişamlı pahalı, gösterişli** *a plush red carpet*

Pluto /'plu:təʊ/ *noun* [no plural] a dwarf planet (= an object in space like a small planet) that comes after Neptune in space and distance from the sun. Pluto was considered to be a proper planet until 2006, when it was officially decided that it was a dwarf planet. **Pluto, Neptün'den sonra gelen ve Güneş'e en uzak gezegen**

plutonium /plu:'təʊniəm/ *noun* [U] a chemical element that is used in the production of nuclear power and nuclear weapons (symbol Pu) **plutonyum**

ply /plaɪ/ *verb* **1 ply across/between, etc** *old-fashioned* to often make a particular journey **düzenli sefer yapmak, gidip gelmek, işlemek** *fishing boats plying across the harbour* **2 ply your trade** to work at your job, especially selling things **işinde çalışma, icra etmek**

ply sb with sth *phrasal verb* **1** to give someone a lot of something again and again **tekrar tekrar vermek; sürekli verip durmak; yağdırmak; boğmak** *They plied me with food and drink.* **2** to ask someone a lot of questions **sürekli soru sormak; soru yağmuruna tutmak; ...ile bunaltmak** *They plied him with questions about where he had been.*

plywood /'plaɪwʊd/ *noun* [U] wood that is made by sticking several thin layers of wood together **kontrapläk**

o⁼**p.m.** (*also* pm) /,pi:'em/ used when you are referring to a time after 12 o'clock in the middle of the day, but before 12 o'clock in the middle of the night **(saat) post meridium kısaltması; öğleden sonra** *Opening hours: 9 a.m. - 6 p.m.*

PM /,pi:'em/ *noun* [C] *abbreviation for* prime minister: the leader of an elected government in some countries **Başbakan**

pneumatic /nju:'mætɪk/ *adjective* filled with air, or operated using air **hava basınçlı, hava basıncı ile çalışan** *pneumatic tyres*

pneumonia /nju:'məʊniə/ *noun* [U] a serious illness in which your lungs fill with liquid and it is difficult to breathe **zatürre, akciğer iltihabı**

poach /pəʊtʃ/ *verb* **1** [COOK] [T] to cook something, especially an egg without its shell, by putting it into liquid that is gently boiling **(yumurta kabuğunu kırıp) suda pişirmek 2** [ANIMALS] [I, T] to illegally catch or kill animals, especially by going onto land without the permission of the person who owns it **kaçak avlanmak; özel arazide izinsiz avlanmak 3** [PERSON] [I, T] to persuade someone to leave a company or team in order to work or play for yours **(müşteri, çalışan) ayartmak, kandırmak; ikna etmek** *They can poach experienced people easily because they offer higher salaries.*

poacher /'pəʊtʃə^r/ *noun* [C] someone who illegally catches or kills animals **kaçak avcı**

o⁼**pocket¹** /'pɒkɪt/ *noun* [C] **1** [BAG] a small bag that is sewn or fixed onto or into a piece of clothing, a bag, the back of a seat, etc **cep, göz** *a coat/shirt/trouser pocket* ○ *He was asked to empty his pockets.* ○ *Safety instructions are in the pocket on the seat in front of you.* **2** [SMALL AREA/AMOUNT] a small area or small amount of something that is different from what is around it **kısım, kesim, taraf, küme, bölge** *There was real poverty in some pockets of the country.* ○ *small pockets of air trapped inside the glass* **3** [MONEY] the amount of money that you have for

pocket

spending **harçlık, cep harçlığı** *I shouldn't have to pay for travel out of my own pocket* (= with my own money). **4 be out of pocket** to have less money than you should have because you have paid for something **az parası kalmak, harçlığı azalmak; olması gerekenden daha az parası olmak** *The holiday company cancelled our trip and we were left hundreds of pounds out of pocket.*

pocket² /ˈpɒkɪt/ *verb* [T] **1** to take something, especially money, which does not belong to you **cebe indirmek, aşırmak, iç etmek** *His plan was to pocket the money from the sale of the business and leave the country.* **2** to put something in your pocket **cebine koymak** *Juan pocketed the knife and walked away.*

pocket³ /ˈpɒkɪt/ *adjective* [always before noun] small enough to fit in your pocket **cebe sığabilen/girebilen, küçük, cepte taşınabilir** *a pocket dictionary*

pocketbook /ˈpɒkɪtbʊk/ *noun* [C] *US* **1** a woman's bag **para cüzdanı 2** Someone's pocketbook is their ability to pay for something. **gelir, kazanç, cüzdan** *The sales tax hits consumers in the pocketbook.*

pocketful /ˈpɒkɪtfʊl/ *noun* [C] the amount you can fit in a pocket **cep dolusu** *a pocketful of coins*

pocketknife /ˈpɒkɪtnaɪf/ *noun* [C] *plural* **pocketknives** a small knife that folds into a case **çakı**

'pocket ,money *noun* [U] an amount of money given regularly to a child by its parents **cep harçlığı**

pod /pɒd/ *noun* [C] the long, flat part of some plants that has seeds in it **fasulye, tohum zarfı** *a pea pod*

podcast /ˈpɒdkɑːst/ *noun* [C] a recording that you can listen to on your computer or MP3 player from a website. You can also sign up to (= say that you want to receive) a podcast which is then updated (= new information is added to it) through the Internet when you plug your MP3 player into a computer. **bir web sitesi vasıtasıyla bilgisayarda ya da MP3 te dinlenebilen kayıt** ⊃See study page **The Web and the Internet** on page Centre 39.

podiatrist /pəˈdaɪətrɪst/ *US* (*UK* chiropodist) *noun* [C] someone whose job is to treat problems with people's feet **ayaklardaki rahatsızlıklarla uğraşan hekim/ kimse**

podium /ˈpəʊdiəm/ *noun* [C] a small, raised area, sometimes with a tall table on it, that someone stands on when they are performing or speaking **podyum**

read/recite/write a poem ● in a poem ● a poem about sth ● a poem by sb ● a love poem

o~**poem** /ˈpəʊɪm/ *noun* [C] a piece of writing, especially one that has short lines and uses words that sound the same **şiir** *love/war poems*

poet /ˈpəʊɪt/ *noun* [C] someone who writes poems **şair**

poetic /pəʊˈetɪk/ *adjective* **1** Something that is poetic makes you feel strong emotions because it is so beautiful. **şiirsel, şiir gibi güzel** *To him, life seemed poetic.* **2** relating to poetry **şiirle ilgili** *poetic language*

o~**poetry** /ˈpəʊɪtri/ *noun* [U] poems in general, or the writing of poetry **şiir** *I enjoy all kinds of poetry, especially love poetry.*

poignant /ˈpɔɪnjənt/ *adjective* making you feel sad **dokunaklı, üzücü, acıklı** *It's a poignant story about a poor family's struggle to survive.* ● **poignancy** /ˈpɔɪnjənsi/ *noun* [U] when something is poignant **dokunaklılık, acıklılık** ● **poignantly** *adverb* **üzücü bir şekilde**

illustrate/make/prove/raise a point ● take sb's point ● a point about sth

o~**point¹** /pɔɪnt/ *noun* **1** OPINION [C] an opinion, idea, or fact which someone says or writes (**düşünce**) **nokta, husus, mesele, gaye, maksat** *Could I make a point about noise levels?* ○ *I take your point* (= I agree with you) *about cycling, but I still prefer to walk.* **2** IMPORTANT OPINION [no plural] an opinion or fact that deserves to be considered seriously, or which other people agree is true (**önemli husus**) **sorun, husus, nokta** *"She's always complaining that the office is cold." "Well, she's got a point."* ○ *"How are we going to get there if there are no trains?" "Good point."* **3 the point** the most important part of what has been said or written **önemli ve haklı nokta, üzerinde durulması gereken husus** *I thought he was never going to get to the point.* ○ *The point is, if you don't claim the money now you might never get it.* ○ *To say his art is simplistic is missing the point* (= not understanding the most important thing about it). **4** SHARP [C] the thin, sharp end of something (**keskin**) **uç, sivri uç** *the point of a needle* **5** PLACE [C] a particular place (**yer**) **nokta, yer, durak** *a stopping/fuelling point* ○ *the point where the pipes enter the building* **6** TIME [C] a particular time in an event or process (**zaman**) **zaman, zamanda belli bir nokta** *At this point, people started to leave.* ○ *It has got to the point where I can hardly bear to speak to him.* **7 be at/on the point of doing sth** to be going to do something very soon **bir şeyi yapmak üzere olmak; tam yapma aşamasında olmak** *Amy was on the point of crying.* **8** REASON [no plural] the reason for or purpose of something **yarar, amaç, neden, sebep** *What's the point of studying if you can't get a job afterwards?* ○ *There's no point inviting her - she never comes to parties.* **9 beside the point** not important or not connected with what you are talking about **yersiz, önemli olmayan şey, başka bir şey, konuyla alakası olmayan** *The fact that he doesn't want to come is beside the point - he should have been invited.* **10 make a point of doing sth** to be certain that you always do a particular thing **özen göstermek, üzerinde durmak** *He made a point of learning all the names of his staff.* **11 to the point** If something someone says or writes is to the point, it expresses the most important things without extra details. **özü, esası, tam noktası; konuya direkt temas eden** *His report was short and to the point.* **12 up to a point** partly **bir noktaya/dereceye kadar** *What he says is true up to a point.* **13** GAME [C] a unit used for showing who is winning in a game or competition **puan, sayı** *With 3 games still to play, Manchester United are 5 points ahead.* **14** MEASUREMENT [C] a unit used in some systems of measuring and comparing things (**ölçüm**) **puan, nokta** *The stock exchange fell by five points.* **15 boiling/freezing/melting point** the temperature at which a substance boils, freezes, or melts **kaynama/donma/erime noktası 16** QUALITY [C] a quality which someone has **iyi yönleri, özellikleri/ hususları, yan, taraf, nokta** *I know she's bossy, but she has lots of good points too.* ○ *Chemistry never was my strong point* (= I was never good at it). **17** MATHEMATICS [C] (*also* decimal point) the mark (.) that is used to separate the two parts of a decimal (**.**) **nokta** *One mile equals one point six* (= 1.6) *kilometres.* **18** DIRECTION [C] one of the marks on a compass (= object used for showing directions) (**pusula**) **nokta, kerte, bölme 19** LETTERS [C] a unit of measurement of the size of letters, used in printing and on computers ⊃See also: **breaking point**, a **case** in **point**, **decimal point**, **focal point**, **moot point**, **point of view**, **starting-point**, **turning point**, **vantage point**.

point² /pɔɪnt/ *verb* **1** SHOW [I] to show where someone or something is by holding your finger or a thin object towards it **işaret etmek, göstermek** *She pointed at/ to a bird flying overhead.* **2** AIM [T] to hold something so that it faces towards something else **çevirmek, doğrultmak, yöneltmek** *She pointed her camera at them.* **3** FACE [I] to face towards a particular direction **belli bir yöne doğru dönmek, yönelmek; yönünü çevirmek** *The solar panels were pointing away from the sun.*

point sb/sth out *phrasal verb* to make a person notice someone or something **dikkat çekmek, işaret etmek, hatırlatmak, belirtmek** *I didn't think about the disadvantages until you pointed them out to me.*

point sth out *phrasal verb* to tell someone a fact **bildirmek, işaret etmek, anlatmak, söylemek, belirtmek** *If he makes a mistake I always think it's best to point it out immediately.*

point to/towards sth *phrasal verb* to show that something probably exists, is happening, or is true **bir sonuca götürmek; belli bir hususa işaret etmek** *All the evidence points to suicide.*

point-blank /ˌpɔɪntˈblæŋk/ *adjective, adverb* **1** If you refuse point-blank, you refuse completely and will not change your decision. **açıkça, dobra dobra, ağzında gevelemeden, evirip çevirmeden 2 at point-blank range** If someone is shot at point-blank range, they are shot from a very short distance away. **yakın mesafeden**

pointed /ˈpɔɪntɪd/ *adjective* **1** If someone says something in a pointed way, they intend to criticize someone. **iğneleyerek, imâ yollu, anlamlı, maksatlı, kinayeli** *He made some pointed references to her history of drug problems.* **2** A pointed object has a thin, sharp end. **sivri, sivri uçlu** *a pointed chin/beard*

pointer /ˈpɔɪntər/ *noun* [C] **1** a piece of information which can help you understand a situation or do something better **öğüt, ipucu, salık, öneri, faydalı bilgi** *I asked for some pointers on applying for jobs.* **2** an object that you use to point at something **işaret çubuğu**

pointless /ˈpɔɪntləs/ *adjective* Something that is pointless has no purpose. **amaçsız, faydasız, beyhude, boşuna, yararsız** *pointless arguments/conflict* ○ [+ to do sth] *It would be pointless to argue with him.* ● **pointlessly** *adverb* **manasızca**

point of view ...... İLE BİRLİKTE KULLANILAN KELİMELER

from sb's point of view ● from a [political/financial, etc] point of view

point of 'view *noun* [C] *plural* **points of view 1** a way of thinking about a situation **görüş/bakış açısı** *From a medical point of view, there was no need for the operation.* **2** an opinion **düşünce, fikir, yorum, kanı, kanaat** *You have to be willing to see other people's points of view.*

poise /pɔɪz/ *noun* [U] **1** when you behave in a calm and confident way **ağırbaşlılık, öz güven, temkin, ölçülülük** *Recovering his poise, he congratulated his opponent.* **2** when you move or stand in a careful, pleasant way **duruş, figür, salınış, hareket**

poised /pɔɪzd/ *adjective* **1** READY [never before noun] ready to do something **harekete geçmeye hazır, eyleme hazır beklemede, kalkmış ayakta; darbeye/eylem/ harekete hazır** [+ to do sth] *They have three hundred ships, all poised to attack.* **2** POSITION [never before noun] in a particular position or situation, ready to move or change **...a/e hazır; üstünde; beklemede; harekete hazır** *a helicopter poised above the crowd* CALM calm and confident **temkinli, ağırbaşlı, dengeli, ölçülü** *a poised performance*

poison¹ /ˈpɔɪzən/ *noun* [C, U] a substance that can make you ill or kill you if you eat or drink it **zehir** *Someone had put poison in her drink.*

poison² /ˈpɔɪzən/ *verb* [T] **1** KILL to try to kill someone by giving them a dangerous substance to drink or eat **zehirlemek** *He tried to poison his wife.* **2** MAKE DANGEROUS to put poison or a dangerous substance in something **zehir koymak/katmak** *They poisoned the city's water supply.* **3** SPOIL to make something very unpleasant **zehir etmek, bozmak, mahvetmek, berbat etmek** *These arguments were poisoning his life.* **4 poison sb's mind** to make someone think bad things about someone or something **kötü fikirler aşılamak, aklını çelmek, kafasını yemek, zihnini bulandırmak** *Her father had poisoned her mind against me.* ● **poisoned** *adjective* **zehirlenmiş**

poisoning /ˈpɔɪzənɪŋ/ *noun* [U] an illness caused by eating, drinking, or breathing a dangerous substance **zehirlenme** *alcohol/lead poisoning* ➔See also: food poisoning.

poisonous /ˈpɔɪzənəs/ *adjective* **1** containing poison **zehirli** *poisonous gas* **2** A poisonous animal uses poison in order to defend itself. **zehirli** *a poisonous snake*

poke

She poked her head out of the window.

She poked him.

poke¹ /pəʊk/ *verb* **1** [T] to quickly push your finger or other pointed object into someone or something **dürtmek, sokmak, dürtüklemek, batırarak delik açmak** *Nell kept poking me in the arm.* ○ *He poked the fire with his stick.* **2 poke (sth) round/out/through, etc** to appear through or from behind something, or to make something do this **bir şeyin arkasından gözükmek/görünmek; görünmesini/gözükmesini sağlamak** *Grace poked her head round the door.* ➔See also: poke/stick your nose¹ into sth.

poke about/around *phrasal verb informal* to look for something by moving other things **karıştırarak/yoklayarak aramak** *I was poking around in the garage, looking for a paintbrush.*

poke² /pəʊk/ *noun* [C] when you quickly push your finger or other pointed object into someone or something **dürtme, itme, dürtükleme** *I gave him a poke in the back.*

poker /ˈpəʊkər/ *noun* **1** [U] a game played with cards in which people try to win money from each other **poker oyunu, bir tür iskambil oyunu 2** [C] a long, metal stick used for moving the coal or wood in a fire so that it burns better **ocak süngüsü**

poker-faced /'pəʊkə,feɪst/ *adjective* not showing on your face what you are really thinking or feeling **hiç renk vermeyen; ne düşündüğü anlaşılmayan; yüzünden okunmayan**

poky (*also* **pokey**) *informal* /'pəʊki/ *adjective* **1** A room or house that is poky is unpleasant because it is too small. **küçücük, daracık, kutu gibi, küçük 2** *US* too slow **kaplumbağa gibi yavaş, çok ağır**

polar /'pəʊləʳ/ *adjective* relating to the North or South Pole **kutup, kutba ait**

'polar ,bear *noun* [C] a large, white bear that lives in the Arctic (= most northern part of the Earth) **kutup ayısı**

Polaroid /'pəʊlˀrɔɪd/ *noun* [C] *trademark* a camera that prints a photograph immediately after you have taken it, or a picture taken with this type of camera **çekbas kamera, Polaroid; çekilip anında basılan fotoğraf**

pole /pəʊl/ *noun* **1** [C] a long, thin stick made of wood or metal, often used to hold something up **direk, sırık** *tent poles* **2 the North/South Pole** the part of the Earth that is furthest North/South **Kuzey/Güney Kutbu 3 be poles apart** to be complete opposites **zıt kutuplar olmak**

polemic /pəˈlemɪk/ *noun* [C, U] *formal* writing or speech that strongly criticizes or defends an idea, a belief, etc **şiddetli tartışma**

'pole ,vault *noun* [no plural] a sport in which you use a very long stick to jump over a high bar **yüksek atlama**

🧩 **police** ...... İLE BİRLİKTE KULLANILAN KELİMELER

call the police ● report sb/sth to the police ● police arrest/question sb

---

◦ **police¹** /pəˈliːs/ *noun* [plural] the official organization that makes people obey the law and that protects people and places against crime, or the people who work for this organization **polis teşkilâtı; emniyet güçleri** *I heard a gun shot and decided to call the police.* ○ *A 30-year-old taxi driver is being interviewed by police.* ○ *a police investigation*

police² /pəˈliːs/ *verb* [T] to make sure that people obey the law in a particular place or when they are doing a particular activity **emniyeti/düzeni/huzuru/güvenliği sağlamak** *Clubs have to pay for the cost of policing matches.*

po,lice 'constable *noun* [C] in the UK, a police officer of the lowest rank **(Birleşik Krallık) polis memuru**

po'lice de,partment *noun* [C] in the US, the police force in an area or city **(ABD) bölge/şehir polis teşkilatı; emniyet merkezi**

po'lice ,force *noun* [C] the police in a country or area **emniyet güçleri; polis teşkilâtı**

policeman, policewoman /pəˈliːsmən, pəˈliːs,wʊmən/ *noun* [C] *plural* **policemen** *or* **policewomen** a man/woman who is a member of the police **erkek/bayan polis memuru/memuresi**

po'lice ,officer *noun* [C] someone who is a member of the police **polis, polis memuru/memuresi)**

po'lice ,state *noun* [C] a country in which the people are not free to do what they want because the government controls them **polis devleti; her şeyin kontrolünün devlette olduğu ülke**

po'lice ,station *noun* [C] the office of the police in a town or part of a city **karakol, polis merkezi**

🧩 **policy** ...... İLE BİRLİKTE KULLANILAN KELİMELER

adopt/formulate/implement/pursue a policy ● a policy on sth ● a policy of (doing) sth ● company policy ● foreign policy

---

policy /'pɒləsi/ *noun* **1** [C, U] a set of ideas or a plan of what to do in particular situations that has been agreed by a government, business, etc **siyaset, politika, tutum, hareket tarzı** *foreign policy* ○ *It is company policy to help staff progress in their careers.* **2** [C] an agreement that you have with an insurance company (= company that pays the costs if you are injured, etc) **poliçe, sigorta senedi**

polio /'pəʊliəʊ/ *noun* [U] a serious disease that sometimes makes it impossible for you to move your muscles **çocuk felci, kas hastalığı**

polish¹ /'pɒlɪʃ/ *noun* **1** [C, U] a substance that you rub on something in order to make it clean and shiny **cilâ 2** [no plural] when you rub something in order to make it clean and shiny **cilâlama, parlatma** *Just give the table a polish.* ⊃See also: **nail polish.**

polish² /'pɒlɪʃ/ *verb* [T] to rub something with a cloth in order to make it clean or to make it shine **cilâlamak, parlatmak** *to polish your shoes*
polish sth off *phrasal verb informal* to finish something quickly **çarçabuk halletmek, hızla bitirivermek** *I gave him a bowl of ice cream which he soon polished off.*

polished /'pɒlɪʃt/ *adjective* **1** clean and shiny after polishing **pırıl pırıl, parlak, cilâlı, tertemiz** *a polished floor* **2** done with skill and style **mükemmel, kusursuz** *He gave a highly polished performance.*

---

polite ...... BAŞKA BİR DEYİŞLE

Courteous, respectful ve well-mannered sıfatları kişinin diğerlerine karşı kibar ve saygılı olduğunu gösteren ifadelerdir. *Although she often disagreed with me, she was always* courteous. ● *They were quiet,* well-mannered *children.*
Bir bayana karşı kibar davranan erkek chivalrous olarak tanımlanabilir. *He held open the door in that* chivalrous *way of his.*
Politically correct ifadesi ve bunun kısaltması olan PC kişinin gerek bayanlara gerekse farklı din veya ırktan insanlara kibar davrandığını gösterir. *'Fireman' has been replaced by the* politically-correct *term 'firefighter'.* ● *Calling them 'ladies' - that's not very* PC *of you.*
Kibarlıkla ve sakin bir şekilde yapılan sohbet civilized olarak tanımlanır. *Let's discuss this in a* civilized *manner.*

◦ **polite** /pəˈlaɪt/ *adjective* behaving in a way that is not rude and shows that you do not only think about yourself **kibar, nazik, terbiyeli, edebli** *She was too polite to point out my mistake.* ● **politely** *adverb* *He thanked them politely.* **kibarca** ● **politeness** *noun* [U] **kibarlık**

◦ **political** /pəˈlɪtɪkˀl/ *adjective* relating to or involved in politics **siyasî, siyasal, poltikayla ilgili** *There are two main political parties in my country.* ○ *The church has a strong political influence.* ● **politically** *adverb* **politik açıdan**

po,litical a'sylum *noun* [U] protection given by a government to someone whose political activities have made it too dangerous for them to live in their own country **siyasi sığınma**

po,litically co'rrect *adjective* careful to speak or behave in a way which is not offensive to women, people of a particular race, or people who have physical or mental problems **siyaseten doğru konuşan ve davranan; toplumun hassas çizgilerine dokunmayan** *It's* *not politically correct to call women 'girls'.* • **political correctness** *noun* [U]

po,litical 'prisoner *noun* [C] someone who is in prison because their political activities or opinions oppose the government **siyasî tutuklu**

○▪**politician** /ˌpɒlɪˈtɪʃᵊn/ *noun* [C] someone who works in politics, especially a member of the government **siyasetçi, politikacı**

politicize (*also UK* -ise) /pəˈlɪtɪsaɪz/ *verb* [T] to make something or someone become more involved with politics **siyasileştirmek, politikayla ilgilendirmek; siyasetin içine sokmak** [often passive] *The whole issue has been politicized.* ○ *a highly politicized debate*

📝 **politics** ...... İLE BİRLİKTE KULLANILAN KELİMELER

enter/go into/be involved in politics • domestic/international/local politics

○▪**politics** /ˈpɒlətɪks/ *noun* **1** [ACTIVITIES] [U] ideas and activities relating to how a country or area is governed **politika, siyaset** *He has little interest in local politics.* **2** [JOB] [U] a job in politics **siyaset, politika mesleği/uğraşı** *She's planning to retire from politics next year.* **3** **sb's politics** someone's opinions about how a country or area should be governed **siyasi görüşler; politik düşünceler** *I don't know what his politics are, but he strongly disagreed with the decision.* **4** [RELATIONSHIPS] [plural] the relationships in a group which allow particular people to have power over others **görüş, düşünce, ortak tavır, anlayış** *I try not to get involved in office politics.*

polka /ˈpɒlkə/ *noun* [C] a type of dance, or a piece of music used for this type of dance **polka dansı, polka müziği**

polka-dot /ˈpɒlkəˌdɒt/ *adjective* [always before noun] having a regular pattern of small, round spots **puantiyeli; küçük nokta desenli** *a polka-dot bikini*

📝 **poll** ...... İLE BİRLİKTE KULLANILAN KELİMELER

carry out/conduct a poll • a poll indicates/reveals/shows/suggests sth • a poll of sb

poll¹ /pəʊl/ (*also* **opinion poll**) *noun* [C] when people are asked questions to discover what they think about a subject **kamu oyu araştırması, nabız yoklaması, anket** *A recent poll indicated that 77 percent of Americans supported the president.*

poll² /pəʊl/ *verb* [T] **1** to ask someone's opinion as part of a study on what people think about a subject **anket yapmak, kamu oyu araştırması yapmak** [often passive] *Most students polled said they preferred the new system.* **2** to receive a particular number of votes in an election **oy almak/kazanmak/toplamak/elde etmek** *Labour polled only 45 percent of the Scottish vote.*

pollen /ˈpɒlən/ *noun* [U] a powder produced by flowers, which is carried by insects or the wind and makes other flowers produce seeds **polen, çiçek tozu**

'pollen ,count *noun* [C] the measurement of the amount of pollen in the air **polen sayımı**

'polling ,day *UK* (*US* **election day**) *noun* [C] the day when people vote in an election **seçim günü**

'polling ,station *UK* (*US* **'polling ,place**) *noun* [C] a building where people go to vote in an election **seçim merkezi/yeri/sandığı**

the polls /pəʊlz/ *noun* [plural] voting in an election **oy verme işlemi, seçim** *The country will go to the polls* (= vote) *on 13 September.*

pollster /ˈpəʊlstə*ʳ*/ *noun* [C] someone who tries to discover what most people think about a subject by asking questions **anketör, kamu oyu araştırmacısı**

pollute /pəˈluːt/ *verb* [T] to make water, air, soil, etc dirty or harmful **kirletmek, pisletmek** *We need a fuel that won't pollute the environment.* • **pollutant** *noun* [C] a substance that pollutes water, air, etc **kirletici/pisletici/zararlı madde**

pollution /pəˈluːʃᵊn/ *noun* [U] damage caused to water, air, etc by harmful substances or waste **kirlilik** *The book shows simple things you can do to reduce pollution from your car.*

polo /ˈpəʊləʊ/ *noun* [U] a game played between two teams who ride horses and hit a ball with long, wooden hammers **polo oyunu; at üstünde takımlarla uzun bir sopa ile topa vurmaya dayalı oyun**

'polo ,neck *UK* (*US* turtleneck) *noun* [C] a piece of clothing that covers the top part of the body and has a tube-like part covering the neck **polo yaka, yuvarlak yaka; balıkçı yaka** *a black polo neck sweater*

polo neck

polo neck *UK,* turtleneck *US*

'polo ,shirt *noun* [C] a cotton shirt with short sleeves, a collar, and buttons at the front **önden düğmeli polo gömlek**

poly- /pɒli-/ *prefix* many **çok, çok sayıda anlamında ön ek** *polygamy* (= having more than one husband or wife at the same time) ○ *a polygon* (= a shape with many sides)

polyester /ˌpɒliˈestə*ʳ*/ *noun* [U] a type of artificial cloth used for making clothes **suni kumaş, polyester** *a polyester shirt/skirt*

polystyrene /ˌpɒliˈstaɪriːn/ *UK* (*US* **Styrofoam**) *noun* [U] a light plastic material that is wrapped around delicate objects to protect them, and around hot things to keep them hot **polistiren; hafif plastik madde** *polystyrene packaging/polystyrene cups*

polytechnic /ˌpɒliˈteknɪk/ *noun* [C] a college where students study scientific and technical subjects **teknik okul**

polythene /ˈpɒliθiːn/ *UK* (*US* **polyethylene** /ˌpɒli-ˈeθəliːn/) *noun* [U] a thin, soft plastic, often used for making bags **polietilen; ince yumuşak plastik**

pomp /pɒmp/ *noun* [U] *formal* special clothes, decorations, and music at an official ceremony **tantanalı/debdebeli/görkemli tören**

pompous /ˈpɒmpəs/ *adjective* Someone who is pompous is too serious and thinks they are more important than they really are. **kibirli, böbürlenen, gösterişli; kendini beğenmiş** • **pompously** *adverb* **kibirli bir şekilde** • **pomposity** /pɒmˈpɒsəti/ *noun* [U] when someone is pompous **büyüklük taslama; kibirlilik**

pond /pɒnd/ *noun* [C] a small area of water, especially one that has been made artificially in a park or garden **gölcük, gölet**

ponder /ˈpɒndə*ʳ*/ *verb* [I, T] *literary* to think carefully about something **üzerinde kafa patlatmak, düşünüp taşınmak** [+ question word] *He pondered what might have happened if he hadn't gone home.*

ponderous /ˈpɒndᵊrəs/ *adjective* **1** Ponderous speech or writing is boring or too serious. **(konuşma, yazı) sıkıcı, çok ciddi, ağır 2** slow because of being very heavy or large **hantal, çok ağır ● ponderously** *adverb* **sıkıcı bir şekilde**

pony /'pəʊni/ *noun* [C] a small horse **midilli, midilli atı**

ponytail /'pəʊnieɪl/ *noun* [C] hair tied at the back of your head so that it hangs down like a horse's tail **kuyruğu yapılmış saç**

ponytail

poodle /'puːdl/ *noun* [C] a type of dog with thick, curly hair **kaniş, kaniş cinsi köpek**

pool¹ /puːl/ *noun* 1 ⟨SWIM⟩ [C] (*also* **swimming pool**) an area of water that has been made for people to swim in **yüzme havuzu** *The hotel has two outdoor pools.* 2 ⟨LIQUID⟩ [C] a small area of water or a small amount of liquid on a surface **havuz, su birikintisi** *We dipped our feet in a shallow pool by the rocks.* ○ *a pool of blood* 3 ⟨GAME⟩ [U] a game in which two people use long, thin sticks to hit coloured balls into holes around the edge of a table **bilardo** 4 ⟨COLLECTION⟩ [C] a collection of money, people, or equipment which is shared by a group of people **ortak kullanım için bir araya getirme/birleştirmek; ortak kullanım** *a car pool for company business*

pool² /puːl/ *verb* [T] If a group of people pool their money, knowledge, or equipment, they collect it together so that it can be shared or used for a particular purpose. **birleştirmek, bir araya getirmek, toplamak, ortak kullanım için biriktirmek** *Several villages pooled their resources to set up a building project.*

the pools /puːlz/ *noun* [plural] in Britain, a game in which people try to win a lot of money by guessing the results of football matches **spor toto**

ˢ⁻**poor** /pɔːʳ/ ⟨US⟩ /pʊr/ *adjective* 1 ⟨NO MONEY⟩ having very little money or few possessions **yoksul, fakir, fukara, zavallı** *Most of these people are desperately poor.* ○ *Modern fertilizers are too expensive for poorer countries to afford.* ○ *housing for the poor* 2 ⟨BAD⟩ of very low quality **kötü, fena, yetersiz, düşük kaliteli** *poor health* ○ *Last year's exam results were poor.* ○ *a poor harvest* ○ *The meeting went smoothly but attendance was poor* (= not many people came). 3 ⟨NO SKILL⟩ not having much skill at a particular activity **zayıf, yetersiz, kıt** *She's always been poor at spelling.* 4 ⟨SYMPATHY⟩ [always before noun] used to show sympathy for someone **zavallı, biçare** *That cold sounds terrible, you poor thing.* 5 **be poor in sth** If something is poor in a particular substance, it has very little of the substance. **zayıf/yetersiz/kıt olmak** *Avoid foods which are high in calories but poor in nutrients.*

poorly¹ /'pɔːli/ *adverb* badly **kötü bir şekilde, yetersizce** *poorly educated*

poorly² /'pɔːli/ *adjective* UK *informal* ill **hasta, rahatsız** *Rosie was feeling poorly so I put her to bed.*

pop¹ /pɒp/ *verb* **popping**, *past* **popped** 1 [I, T] to make a short sound like a small explosion, or to make something do this by breaking it **patla(t)mak** *The music played and champagne corks popped.* 2 **pop in/out/over, etc** *informal* to go to a particular place **uğramak, belli bir yere gitmek** *Doug's just popped out for a few minutes.* ○ *I'll pop into the supermarket on my way home.* 3 **pop sth in/into/on, etc** *informal* to quickly put something in a particular place **atıvermek, bırakıvermek, koyuvermek** *Can you pop the pizza in the oven?* 4 **pop out/up** to move quickly and suddenly, especially out of something **yerinden fırlamak; ok gibi fırlayıp çıkmak**

pop up *phrasal verb informal* to suddenly appear or happen, often unexpectedly **birdenbire çıkıvermek, aniden ortaya çıkıvermek** *A message just popped up on my screen.*

pop² /pɒp/ *noun* 1 ⟨MUSIC⟩ [U] (*also* '**pop ˌmusic**) modern music with a strong beat which is popular with young people **pop müziği, çağdaş popüler müzik** 2 ⟨SOUND⟩ [C] a short sound like a small explosion **pop' sesi; küçük patlama sesi** 3 ⟨DRINK⟩ [U] *informal* (*also US* **soda**) a sweet drink with bubbles **gazoz** 4 ⟨FATHER⟩ [no plural] *US informal* father **baba**

popcorn /'pɒpkɔːn/ *noun* [U] yellow seeds of grain that break open when heated and are eaten with salt, sugar, or butter **patlamış mısır**

Pope /pəʊp/ *noun* [C] the leader of the Roman Catholic Church **Papa** *Pope John Paul II* ○ *The Pope was due to visit Paraguay in May.*

poplar /'pɒpləʳ/ *noun* [C, U] a tall tree with branches that grow up to form a thin, pointed shape **kavak, kavak ağacı**

popper /'pɒpəʳ/ *noun* [C] UK (*US* **snap**) a metal or plastic object used to fasten clothing, made of two parts which fit together with a short, loud sound **çıtçıt**

poppy /'pɒpi/ *noun* [C] a red flower with small, black seeds **gelincik**

populace /'pɒpjələs/ *noun* [group] *formal* all the people who live in a particular country or place **halk, ahâli, toplum**

ˢ⁻**popular** /'pɒpjələʳ/ *adjective* 1 ⟨LIKED⟩ liked by many people **çok beğenilen, tutulan, popüler** *'Jack' was the most popular boy's name.* ○ *The North African coast is becoming increasingly popular with British tourists.* ⊃Opposite **unpopular.** 2 ⟨GENERAL⟩ [always before noun] for or involving ordinary people and not specialists or people who are very educated **halka hitap eden, halk tipi; fazla tanınmış olmayan** *The issue was given full coverage in the popular press.* 3 ⟨MANY PEOPLE⟩ [always before noun] A popular belief, opinion, etc is one that many people have. **yaygın, genel; umuma ait, popüler** *The allegations are false, contrary to popular belief.*

popularity ⟨...⟩ İLE BİRLİKTE KULLANILAN KELİMELER

gain popularity ● be **growing in/increasing in** popularity ● sb's/sth's popularity **increases/soars/wanes** ● the popularity **of** sth ● sb/sth's popularity **with** sb

popularity /ˌpɒpjə'lærəti/ *noun* [U] the quality of being liked by many people **tutulma, rağbet, beğenilme; popülarite** *the increasing popularity of organic produce* ⊃Opposite **unpopularity.**

popularize (*also UK* **-ise**) /'pɒpjəl°raɪz/ *verb* [T] to make something become known or liked by many people **herkesin seveceği bir hâle getirmek; topluma tanıtmak; herkesçe tanınmasını sağlamak** *It was the World Cup which popularized professional soccer in the United States.* ● **popularization** (*also UK* **-isation**) /ˌpɒpjəl°raɪˈzeɪʃ°n/ *noun* [U] **kişilerin beğeneceği şekilde tanıtma**

popularly /'pɒpjələli/ *adverb* **popularly believed/called/known, etc** believed/called, etc by most people **herkesçe/toplumun büyük bölümünce inanılan/bilinen/adlandırılan** *Los Angeles is popularly known as 'LA'.*

populate /'pɒpjəleɪt/ *verb* **be populated** If an area is populated by people or animals, they live in that area. **insan yerleştirilmiş/iskân edilmiş olmak** *The countryside is densely/sparsely populated* (= there are many/few people). ○ *The forest was populated by rare and colourful birds.*

population ...... İLE BİRLİKTE KULLANILAN KELİMELER

have a population of [50 million, etc] • population **growth**

⚬**population** /ˌpɒpjəˈleɪʃᵊn/ noun **1** [C, U] the number of people living in a particular area **nüfus, insan sayısı** *What's the population of Brazil?* **2** [group] all the people living in a particular area, or all the people or animals of a particular type **nüfus, sayı, miktar** *a 9% rise in the prison population*

populous /ˈpɒpjələs/ *adjective formal* A populous area has a lot of people living in it. **kalabalık, tıklım tıklım; çok nüfuslu** *It's one of the world's most populous cities.*

pop-up /ˈpɒpʌp/ *adjective* [always before noun] **1** A pop-up book is a book which has pictures that stand up from the pages when the book is opened. **içinden resimler çıkan kitap 2** A pop-up menu is a list of choices on a computer screen which is hidden until you choose to look at it. **bilgisayar ekranında birden kendiliğinden ortaya çıkan seçenekler listesi** *Select the option you want from the pop-up menu.*

porcelain /ˈpɔːsᵊlɪn/ noun [U] a hard, shiny, white substance used to make cups, plates, etc, or the cups and plates themselves **porselen** *a porcelain dish* ○ *a fine collection of porcelain*

porch /pɔːtʃ/ noun [C] a covered area built onto the entrance to a house **veranda**

pore¹ /pɔːʳ/ noun [C] a very small hole in your skin that sweat (= salty liquid) can pass through **gözenek**

pore² /pɔːʳ/ *verb*
pore over sth *phrasal verb* to study or look carefully at something, especially a book or document **didik didik etmek, özenle incelemek; dikkatle çalışmak/bakmak** *Jeremy spent the afternoon poring over his exam notes.*

pork /pɔːk/ noun [U] meat from a pig **domuz eti** *pork chops*

pornography /pɔːˈnɒgrəfi/ (*also* porn *informal*) noun [U] magazines and films showing naked people or sexual acts that are intended to make people feel sexually excited **pornografi; açık saçık resimlerin/görüntülerin bulunduğu dergiler/filmler** • **pornographic** /ˌpɔːnəˈgræfɪk/ *adjective* relating to pornography **pornografik** *pornographic images/videos*

porous /ˈpɔːrəs/ *adjective* allowing liquid or air to pass through **gözenekli, delikli, kevgir gibi** *porous rock*

porridge /ˈpɒrɪdʒ/ noun [U] a soft, white food made of oats (= type of grain) and water or milk **yulaf lapası**

port /pɔːt/ noun **1** [SHIPS] [C] a town or an area of a town next to water where ships arrive and leave from **liman, liman şehri** *a fishing port* ○ *the Belgian port of Zeebrugge* **2** [DRINK] [U] a sweet, strong, red wine which is made in Portugal **porto/Portekiz şarabı 3** [LEFT] [U] the left side of a ship or aircraft **iskele, iskele tarafı, sol taraf** *the port side*

portable /ˈpɔːtəbl/ *adjective* able to be carried **taşınabilir** *a portable computer*

portal /ˈpɔːtᵊl/ noun [C] a page on the Internet with links to many other pages or websites that people use to start searching the World Wide Web **internette arama yapmak için kullanılan sayfa; portal**

porter /ˈpɔːtəʳ/ noun [C] someone whose job is to carry other people's bags in hotels, stations, etc **taşıyıcı, hamal**

portfolio /ˌpɔːtˈfəʊliəʊ/ noun [C] **1** a collection of designs, pictures, documents, etc that represents a person's work, or the large, flat container that it is carried in **çalışmaların bir arada toplandığı dosya/klasör/koleksiyon 2** a collection of accounts, money, etc that is owned by a person or organization **kişi veya kuruluşun sahip olduğu hesaplar/para vs. yekünü/toplamı** *a stock portfolio*

porthole /ˈpɔːthəʊl/ noun [C] a small, round window in the side of a ship or aircraft **lomboz; uçak/gemi küçük pencere**

portion /ˈpɔːʃᵊn/ noun [C] **1** a part of something **parça, bölüm, miktar** *A large portion of their profits goes straight back into new projects.* **2** the amount of food served to one person, especially in a restaurant **bir defada verilen yemek, porsiyon**

portly /ˈpɔːtli/ *adjective humorous* quite fat **şişman, iri, oldukça tombul** *a portly gentleman*

portrait /ˈpɔːtrɪt/ noun **1** [C] a painting, drawing, or photograph of someone **portre** *a portrait of the princess* ○ *a portrait gallery/painter* **2** a portrait of sb/sth a film or book which describes someone or something in detail **birinin/bir şeyin portresi/ayrıntılı tanıtımı** *His latest film is a portrait of life in the 1920s.* ➭See also: self-portrait.

portray /pɔːˈtreɪ/ *verb* [T] **1** If a book or film portrays someone or something, it describes or shows them. **betimlemek, anlatmak/yazmak, resmetmek, tasvir etmek** *Both novels portray the lives of professional athletes.* ○ *In the film he's portrayed as a hero.* **2** to act the part of a character in a film or play **canlandırmak; ...rolünüde oynamak; karakteri yansıtmak** • **portrayal** noun [C, U] when you portray someone or something **canlandırma; ...rolünü yapma** *He won several awards for his portrayal of the dictator.*

pose¹ /pəʊz/ *verb* **1** pose a danger/problem/threat, etc to cause a problem **tehlike/sorun/tehdit yaratmak/çıkarmak/yol açmak/neden olmak** *A lot of these chemicals pose very real threats to our health.* **2** [I] to stay in a particular position so that someone can paint or photograph you **poz vermek, modellik etmek** *The two leaders posed for photographs outside the White House.* **3** [I] *mainly UK* to try to make people notice and admire you, especially by looking fashionable **caka satmak, hava atmak, poz yapmak** *Pascal was posing in his new sunglasses.* **4** pose a question *formal* to ask a question **soru sormak, sual etmek; ortaya atmak; ileri sürmek**
pose as sb *phrasal verb* to pretend that you are someone else **kendine...süsü vermek, ...gibi gözükmek, ... diye geçinmek; lık/lik taslamak** *He got into her house by posing as an electrician.*

pose² /pəʊz/ noun **1** [C] the position that you stay in while someone photographs or paints you **poz verme, modellik etme, poz** *an elegant pose* **2** [no plural] when someone pretends to be more clever or interesting than they really are **numara; gibi görünme; sahte tavır, yapmacıklık** *She's not really interested in art, it's just a pose.*

posh /pɒʃ/ *adjective* **1** expensive and used or owned by rich people **şık, lüks, pahalı ve gösterişli** *a posh hotel/restaurant* **2** *UK* from a high social class **yüksek tabakadan; toplumun üst katmanından; kodaman takımından** *a posh voice*

⚬**position¹** /pəˈzɪʃᵊn/ noun **1** [SITTING/STANDING] [C, U] the way someone is sitting, lying, or standing, or if something is pointing up or down, etc **durum, konum, yön, taraf** *a kneeling position* ○ *I go to sleep on my back but I always wake up in a different position.* ○ *Make sure your chair is in the upright position.* **2** [SITUATION] [C] the situation that someone is in **konum, durum, hâl** [usually singular] *She's in a very difficult position.* **3** be in a position to do sth to be able to do something because of your situation **bir şeyi yapabilecek durumda/konumda/ yerde olmak** *I'm not in a position to talk about this at the moment.* **4** [PLACE] [C] the place where someone or something is **yer, konum, mevki, pozisyon** *I'm trying to find our position on the map.* ○ *You're* **in a good position** *next to the window.* **5 be in position** If someone or something is in position, they are in the place that they should be in. **olması gerektiği yerde olmak; hak ettiği yerde bulunmak; bulunması gereken yer ve durumda olmak 6 in first/second/third, etc position** in first/second/third, etc place in a race or other competition **yarışmada** 1., 2., 3., **konumda** *She finished the race in third position.* **7** [JOB] [C] *formal* a job **iş, görev, memuriyet** *to apply for a position in a company* **8** [OPINION] [C] *formal* a way of thinking about a subject **tavır, tutum, görüş, düşünce, fikir, konum, durum, bakış** *What's the company's* **position** *on recycling?* **9** [GAME] [C] the part that someone plays in a game such as football **oyunda oynadığı yer/pozisyon/konum** *What* **position** *does he play?* **10** [IMPORTANCE] [C] your level of importance in society **mevki, yer, konum, durum, önem, itibar** *the position of women in society*

position² /pə'zɪʃᵊn/ *verb* [T] to put someone or something in a place for a reason **yerleştirmek, koymak** [often reflexive] *I positioned myself as far away from her as possible.*

o--**positive** /'pɒzətɪv/ *adjective* **1** [HAPPY] feeling happy about your life and your future **olumlu, müsbet, iyimser** *a positive attitude* ○ *I'm feeling much more positive about things now.* **2** [ENCOURAGING] Something that is positive makes you feel better about a situation. **olumlu, yapıcı, pozitif** *We've shown people samples of the product and had a very positive response.* **3** [CERTAIN] [never before noun] certain that something is true **kesin, kat'i** *"Are you sure you saw him?" "Absolutely positive."* ○ [+ (that)] *I'm positive that I switched it off.* **4** [PROOF] [always before noun] showing without any doubt that something is true **emin, kuşkusu olmayan** *positive proof* **5** [MEDICAL TEST] If a medical test is positive, it shows that the person being tested has a disease or condition. **müspet, pozitif** *She did a pregnancy test and it was positive.* **6** [NUMBER] In mathematics, a positive number is greater than zero. **pozitif, sıfırdan büyük 7 positive charge** the electrical charge that is carried by protons (= parts of atoms) **artı uç; akım taşıyan kablo**

positively /'pɒzətɪvli/ *adverb* **1** in a good way that makes you feel happier **olumlu şekilde, yapıcı olarak** *Most children* **respond positively** *to praise and encouragement.* **2** used to emphasize something that you say, especially when it is surprising **kuşkusuz, kesinlikle** *Our waiter was positively rude.*

possess /pə'zes/ *verb* **1** [T] *formal* to have or own something **sahip olmak; ...ın/in sahibi olmak** *He was found guilty of possessing an illegal weapon.* **2 what possessed her/him/you, etc?** something that you say when someone has done something stupid **Ne etkiledi de...?', 'Ne oldu da...?'; sevk etmek; ...a/e kapılmak; egemen olmak** [+ to do sth] *What possessed you to tell him?*

possessed /pə'zest/ *adjective* controlled by evil spirits **elegeçirilmiş, kötülüklerin esiri olmuş**

┌─┐ *possession* ...... İLE BİRLİKTE KULLANILAN KELİMELER

sb's **prized/most treasured** possessions ● **material/ personal** possessions

possession /pə'zeʃᵊn/ *noun* **1** [C] a thing that you own **sahip olunanlar; mal mülk** [usually plural] *personal possessions* ○ *He was happy to discover that all his possessions had been stolen.* **2** [U] *formal* when you have or own something **sahip olma, elinde bulundurma** *I have in*

my possession *a photograph which may be of interest to you.* ○ *He was caught* **in possession of** *explosives.*

possessive /pə'zesɪv/ *adjective* **1** wanting someone to love and spend time with you and no one else **sahipkâr, sahiplenen, başkalarıyla paylaşmak istemeyen 2** In grammar, a possessive word or form of a word shows who or what something belongs to. For example the words 'mine' and 'yours' are possessive pronouns. (dilbilgisi) **iyelik belirten sözcük, iyelik hâli**

┌─┐ *possibility* ...... İLE BİRLİKTE KULLANILAN KELİMELER

consider/discuss/raise/rule out a possibility ● a **distinct/real/strong** possibility ● possibility **of** doing sth

o--**possibility** /,pɒsə'bɪləti/ *noun* **1** [C, U] a chance that something may happen or be true **olasılık, ihtimal** *Is there any* **possibility** *of changing this ticket?* ○ [+ (that)] *There is a* **strong** *possibility that she was lying.* **2** [C] something that you can choose to do **olasılık, olanak, imkân** *Have you considered the* **possibility** *of flying?* ↪Opposite **impossibility.**

o--**possible** /'pɒsəbl/ *adjective* **1** If something is possible, it can happen or be done. **mümkün, olabilir, imkân dahilinde** [+ to do sth] *Is it possible to speak to the manager please?* ○ *The operation will make it possible for her to walk without crutches.* ○ *I'll send it today, if possible.* ↪Opposite **impossible. 2** If something is possible, it might or might not exist or be true. **muhtemel, olası** *possible safety problems* ○ [+ (that)] *It's possible that the tapes were stolen.* **3 as much/quickly/soon, etc as possible** as much/quickly/soon, etc as something can happen or be done **mümkün olduğu kadar çok/çabuk/ yakın vs.** *I'll go as soon as possible.* **4 the best/cheapest/worst, etc possible** the best/cheapest/worst, etc that can happen or exist **olabilecek en iyi/en ucuz/en kötü vs.** *the shortest possible time*

o--**possibly** /'pɒsəbli/ *adverb* **1** [NOT CERTAIN] used when something is not certain **belki, belki de, ihtimal, herhalde** *Someone, possibly Tom, had left the window open.* **2** [EMPHASIS] used with 'can' or 'could' for emphasis **can', 'could' ile vurgu amaçlı 'mümkün olduğunca/ elverdiğince' anlamında kullanılır** *We'll do everything we possibly can to help.* ○ *I couldn't possibly ask you to do that.* **3** [QUESTIONS] used in polite questions **mümkünse, acaba, ne dersiniz?, olası mı? gibi nezaket içeren sorularda kullanılır** *Could I possibly borrow your bike?*

o--**post¹** /pəʊst/ *noun* **1** [SYSTEM] [no plural] *UK* (*US* **mail**) the system for sending letters, parcels, etc **posta, posta teşkilâtı** *Your letter is in the post.* ○ *I'm sending the documents* **by post.** **2** [LETTERS] [U] *UK* (*US* **mail**) letters, parcels, etc that you receive or send **posta, gönderiler** *Has the* **post arrived/come** *yet?* **3** [JOB] [C] *formal* a job **iş, görev, makam, mevki, memuriyet** *a part-time post* ○ *a teaching post* **4** [POLE] [C] a long, vertical piece of wood or metal fixed into the ground at one end **direk, kazık, sopa** *I found the dog tied to a post.* **5** [PLACE] [C] a place where someone stands to guard something **nöbet yeri, nöbetçi kulübesi, karakol, nokta, mevki**

o--**post²** /pəʊst/ *verb* [T] **1** *UK* (*US* **mail**) to send a letter or parcel by post **postalamak, posta ile göndermek** *Did you post my letter?* **2** to leave a message on a website **web sitesine ileti bırakmak** *I posted a query about arthritis treatment.* **3 be posted to France/London/Singapore, etc** to be sent to France/London/Singapore, etc to work, usually for the government or army **Fransa'ya, Londra'ya, Singapura (resmi/askerî) atanmak/ atanmak, görevlendir(il)mek, tayin etmek/edilmek 4 post a notice/sign, etc** to put a notice/sign, etc

[P]

somewhere **ilan/duyuru/not asmak/yapıştırmak** *He posted the message on the noticeboard.* **5 keep sb posted** to make certain that someone always knows what is happening **sürekli haberdar etmek/bilgilendirmek** *Keep me posted on anything that happens while I'm away.*

postage /'pəʊstɪdʒ/ *noun* [U] money that you pay to send a letter or parcel **posta/gönderi ücreti** *first-class postage* ○ *postage and packing*

postage and packing (*US* shipping and 'handling) *noun* [U] money that you pay so that a company will send you something through the post **paketleme ve taşıma ücreti**

postage stamp *noun* [C] *formal* a small, official piece of paper that you buy and stick onto a letter or parcel before you post it **posta pulu**

postal /'pəʊstəl/ *adjective* [always before noun] relating to the system of sending letters and parcels **posta ile ilgili** *the postal service/system*

postal order *UK* (*US* money order) *noun* [C] an official piece of paper bought at a post office that you can send instead of money **posta havalesi**

post box *UK* (*US* mailbox) *noun* [C] a large, metal container in a public place where you can post letters **posta kutusu**

postcard /'pəʊstkɑːd/ *noun* [C] a card with a picture on one side that you send without an envelope **resimli posta kartı, kartpostal** *Send me a postcard.*

postcode /'pəʊstkəʊd/ *noun* [C] a group of letters and numbers that comes at the end of someone's address in the UK **posta kodu** ⊃Compare zip code.

poster /'pəʊstər/ *noun* [C] a large, printed picture or notice that you put on a wall, in order to decorate a place or to advertise something **afiş, poster**

posterity /pɒs'terəti/ *noun* [U] the people who will be alive in the future **gelecek kuşaklar, ileriki nesiller** *These works of art should be preserved for posterity.*

postgraduate /ˌpəʊst'grædʒuət/ (*US* graduate) (*also* postgrad *informal*) *noun* [C] a student who has one degree and now studies at a university for a more advanced degree **lisanüstü eğitim yapan öğrenci** ● **postgraduate** *adjective a postgraduate degree in mathematics* **master eğitimi görmüş**

posthumous /'pɒstjʊməs/ *adjective* happening after someone's death **ölümünden sonra** *the posthumous publication of her letters* ● **posthumously** *adverb* **bir kişinin ölümünden sonra olan bir şekilde**

posting /'pəʊstɪŋ/ *noun* [C] *mainly UK* when you are sent to work in another place **atama, tayin, görevlendirme** *a posting to Madrid*

Post-it (note) /'pəʊstɪtˌnəʊt/ *noun* [C] *trademark* a small piece of paper that you can write on and then stick to other papers or surfaces **as-oku; yapışkanlı not kağıdı**

postman /'pəʊstmən/ *UK* (*US* mailman, letter carrier) *noun* [C] *plural* **postmen** a man who takes and brings letters and parcels as a job **postacı**

postmark /'pəʊstmɑːk/ *noun* [C] an official mark on a letter or parcel, showing the place and time it was sent **posta damgası**

post-mortem /ˌpəʊst'mɔːtəm/ *noun* [C] a medical examination of a dead body to find out why the person died **otopsi**

post office *noun* [C] a place where you can buy stamps and send letters and parcels **posta idaresi; postahane**

postpone /pəʊst'pəʊn/ *verb* [T] to arrange for something to happen at a later time **ertelemek, tehir**

etmek *The trip to the museum has been postponed until next week.*

postscript /'pəʊstskrɪpt/ *noun* [C] extra information at the end of a letter or email, usually added after writing the letters 'PS' **not, dip not**

posture /'pɒstʃər/ *noun* [U] the position of your back, shoulders, etc when you are standing or sitting **duruş, salınma; vaziyet, poz** *She has very good posture.*

postwar /'pəʊstwɔːr/ *adjective* happening or existing in the period after a war **savaş sonrası** *postwar Europe*

pot¹ /pɒt/ *noun* **1** [C] a round container, usually used for storing things or cooking **çömlek, tencere, kap** *a flower pot* ○ *a pot of coffee/tea* ○ *pots and pans* **2 go to pot** to be damaged or spoilt because no effort has been made **boşa gitmek; zarar görmek, bozulmak** *My diet's gone to pot since the holidays.* ⊃See also: melting pot.

pot² /pɒt/ *verb* [T] **potting**, *past* **potted** to put a plant into a pot filled with soil **saksıya dikmek**

potassium /pə'tæsiəm/ *noun* [U] a chemical element that combines easily with other elements, often used to help plants grow well (symbol K) **potasyum**

o*potato /pə'teɪtəʊ/ *noun* [C, U] *plural* **potatoes** a round vegetable with a brown, yellow, or red skin that grows in the ground **patates** *boiled/fried potatoes* ○ *mashed potato* ⊃Orta kısımdaki renkli sayfalarına bakınız ⊃See also: couch potato, jacket potato, sweet potato.

potato chip *US* (*UK* crisp) *noun* [C] a very thin, dry, fried slice of potato **patates gevreği**

potent /'pəʊtənt/ *adjective* very powerful or very effective **etkili, güçlü** *a potent drug/weapon* ● **potency** /'pəʊtənsi/ *noun* [U] when something is potent **etki, güç, iktidar, azamet**

potential¹ /pə'tenʃəl/ *adjective* [always before noun] A potential problem, employer, partner, etc may become one in the future, although they are not one now. **olası, muhtemel, potansiyel** *a potential danger/threat* ○ *a potential customer* ○ *A number of potential buyers have expressed interest in the building.* ● **potentially** *adverb a potentially fatal condition* **olma olasılığı yüksek bir şekilde**

potential ...... İLE BİRLİKTE KULLANILAN KELİMELER

have [enormous/great, etc] potential ● achieve/fulfil/reach/realize your (full) potential ● see/spot sb's/sth's potential ● sb's/sth's potential as sth

potential² /pə'tenʃəl/ *noun* **1** [U] qualities or abilities that may develop and allow someone or something to succeed **güç, yetenek, özellik, potansiyel** *to achieve your full potential* **2 potential for sth/doing sth a** the possibility that something may happen **olması olası/muhtemel** *There is the potential for some really interesting research.* **b** the difference in voltage (= how strong an electrical current is) between two points

pothole /'pɒthəʊl/ *noun* [C] a hole in the surface of a road **yoldaki çukur, köstebek çukuru, kasis**

potted /'pɒtɪd/ *adjective* **1** planted in a container **dikili** *potted plants/flowers* ○ *a potted palm* **2 potted history/version, etc of sth** *UK* a story or report that has been changed to make it shorter and more simple **kısaltılmış, basitleştirilmiş** *a potted version of Shakespeare*

potted plant (*also UK* 'pot plant) *noun* [C] a plant that is grown in a container, and usually kept inside **saksı çiçeği/bitkisi**

potter¹ /'pɒtər/ *noun* [C] a person who makes plates, bowls, etc from clay **çömlekçi**

potter² /'pɒtər/ *verb*
potter about/around (sth) *phrasal verb mainly UK* to spend time in a pleasant, relaxed way, often doing

small jobs in your house **(ufak tefek şeylerle) vakit geçirmek, oyalanmak**

pottery /ˈpɒt³ri/ noun 1 OBJECTS [U] plates, bowls, etc that are made from clay **toprak kaplar, çanak, çömlek vs.** 2 ACTIVITY [U] the activity of making plates, bowls, etc from clay **çömlekçilik** 3 PLACE [C] a place where plates, bowls, etc made from clay are made or sold **çömlekçi, çömlek yapımevi, çömlekhane**

potty¹ /ˈpɒti/ noun [C] a small toilet that young children use **lazımlık, çocuk tuvaleti, oturak**

potty² /ˈpɒti/ adjective UK informal crazy or stupid **aptal, çılgın, fıttırık, çatlak, ahmak, akılsız**

pouch /paʊtʃ/ noun [C] 1 a small, soft bag made of leather or cloth **kese, cep** 2 a pocket of skin in which some female animals carry their babies **hayvanların yavrularını taşıdıkları kese**

poultry /ˈpəʊltri/ noun 1 [plural] chickens and other birds that people breed for meat and eggs **kümes hayvanları** 2 [U] the meat of chickens and other birds eaten as food **kümes hayvanı eti**

pounce /paʊns/ verb [I] to suddenly move towards a person or animal that you want to catch **üstüne atlayıp/çullanıp yakalamak** The police were waiting to pounce when he arrived at the airport.
pounce on sth/sb phrasal verb to immediately criticize a mistake **hemen farkedip üstüne gitmek/eleştirmek; hatayı anında tenkit etmek**

o→**pound¹** /paʊnd/ noun [C] 1 the unit of money used in the UK **sterlin, pound; Birleşik Krallık para birimi** a hundred pounds/£100 ○ a **pound coin** 2 (written abbreviation **lb**) a unit for measuring weight, equal to 453.6 grams or 16 ounces **453.6 gram veya 16 onsa eşit ağırlık ölçüm birimi** a pound of potatoes ○ The baby weighed just four pounds when she was born ⊃See study page Measurements on page Centre 31.

pound² /paʊnd/ verb 1 [I, T] to hit something many times using a lot of force **pat pat vurmak, yumruklamak; ardarda darbe indirmek** Someone was pounding on the door. 2 [I] If your heart pounds, it beats very quickly. **(kalp) hızla çarpmak, küt küt atmak** My heart was pounding as I walked out onto the stage. 3 **pound along/down/up, etc** to run somewhere with quick, loud steps **hızlı ve ağır adımlarla koşmak; paldır küldür koşmak/gitmek/çıkmak vs.** He pounded up the stairs.

o→**pour** /pɔːʳ/ verb 1 LIQUID   **pour** [T] to make a liquid flow from or into a container **dökmek, doldurmak, koymak, akıtmak, boşaltmak** I poured the milk into a jug. ○ [+ two objects] Can I pour you a drink? 2 RAIN [I] (also UK **pour down**) to rain, producing a lot of water **bardaktan boşanırcasına yağmak; sağanak şeklinde yağmak** We can't go out in this weather - it's pouring! 3 **pour into/out/from, etc** a LIQUID to flow quickly and in large amounts **(sıvı) fışkırmak; oluk oluk akmak** Blood was pouring from my leg. **b** PEOPLE to enter or leave a place in large numbers **doluşmak; bir yere sürü halinde girmek; bir yerden kalabalıklar halinde çıkmak** The crowd poured out into the street.
pour sth out phrasal verb If you pour out your feelings or thoughts, you talk very honestly about what is making you sad. **içini dökmek, açılmak, açığa**

vurmak She listened quietly while he **poured out** his troubles.

pout /paʊt/ verb [I] to push your lips forward because you are annoyed or because you want to look sexually attractive **dudak kıvırmak/bükmek; seksi görünmek için dudaklarını büzmek** ● **pout** noun [C] **dudaklarını buruşturma**

⬙ **poverty** ...... İLE BİRLİKTE KULLANILAN KELİMELER

die in/live in poverty ● **alleviate/fight/tackle** poverty ● **abject/extreme** poverty

poverty /ˈpɒvəti/ noun [U] when you are very poor **yoksulluk, fakirlik, sefalet, yokluk** live in poverty

poverty-stricken /ˈpɒvətiˌstrɪkⁿn/ adjective A poverty-stricken area or person is very poor. **fukara, sefalet/yokluk içinde; çok yoksul**

POW /ˌpiːəʊˈdʌbljuː/ noun [C] abbreviation for prisoner of war: a soldier who is caught by enemy soldiers during a war **savaş mahkumu/esiri/tutsağı/suçlusu**

powder /ˈpaʊdəʳ/ noun [C, U] a dry substance made of many small, loose grains **pudra, un** curry powder ○ face powder ● **powdered** adjective in the form of a powder **toz, pudra, toz hâlindeki** powdered milk/sugar ⊃See also: talcum powder.

⬙ **power** ...... İLE BİRLİKTE KULLANILAN KELİMELER

come to/devolve/seize/take/wield power ● **considerable/enormous** power

o→**power¹** /paʊəʳ/ noun 1 CONTROL [U] control or influence over people and events **güç, yetki, kudret** He likes to have power over people. 2 POLITICS [U] political control in a country **siyasi güç, iktidar, yönetim** They have been in power too long. ○ When did this government come to power (= start to control the country)? 3 ENERGY [U] energy, usually electricity, that is used to provide light, heat, etc **elektrik enerjisi** Turn off the power at the main switch. 4 COUNTRY [C] a country that has a lot of influence over others **güçlü devlet; süper güç** a major world power 5 OFFICIAL RIGHT [U] an official or legal right to do something **yetki, selâhiyet, güç** [+ to do sth] It's not in my power to stop him publishing this book. 6 STRENGTH [U] strength or force **güç, kuvvet** economic/military power 7 ABILITY [U] a natural ability **doğal yetenek** to lose the power of speech 8 **do everything in your power to do sth** to do everything that you are able and allowed to do **gücünün yettiği/yetkili olduğu herşeyi yapmak; yekisini/gücünü kullanmak** I've done everything in my power to help him. 9 **the powers that be** important people who have authority over others **güçlü kimseler; iktidarda olanlar; etkili/yetkili/güçlü şahsiyetler** ⊃See also: balance of power.

power² /paʊəʳ/ verb [T] to supply energy to a machine and make it work **enerji vermek, çalıştırmak, güç sağlamak** [often passive] The clock was powered by two small batteries.

power cut (also US **power outage**) noun [C] when the supply of electricity suddenly stops **elektrik kesintisi**

o→**powerful** /ˈpaʊəfˀl/ adjective 1 CONTROL A powerful person is able to control and influence people and events. **kudretli, güçlü, kuvvetli** a powerful man/woman 2 STRENGTH having a lot of strength or force **güçlü, kuvvetli** a powerful engine/weapon 3 EFFECT having a strong effect on people **etkili, güçlü, kuvvetli, etkileyen** a powerful effect/influence ● **powerfully** adverb **güçlü bir şekilde**

powerless /ˈpaʊələs/ adjective not able to control events **güçsüz, kuvvetsiz, etkisiz** [+ to do sth] The police were powerless to stop the fighting.

power outage /ˈpaʊərˌaʊtɪdʒ/ US (UK/US **power cut**) noun [C] when the supply of electricity suddenly stops **ani elektrik kesintisi**

'power ˌstation (also US **'power ˌplant**) noun [C] a place where electricity is produced **elektrik santralı**

'power ˌtool noun [C] a tool that uses electricity **elektrikli alet**

pp written abbreviation for pages **sayfaların kısa yazılışı** See pp 10 - 12 for more information.

PR /ˌpiːˈɑːr/ noun [U] abbreviation for public relations: writing and activities that are intended to make a person, company, or product more popular **halkla ilişkiler** good/bad PR ○ a PR campaign

practicable /ˈpræktɪkəbl/ adjective formal able to be done successfully **uygulanabilir, yapılabilir, uygun** It's just not practicable to travel in this weather.

◦→**practical¹** /ˈpræktɪkəl/ adjective **1** REAL relating to real situations or actions and not to thoughts or ideas **pratik, gerçekçi** practical experience ○ They can offer practical help. **2** SUITABLE suitable or useful for a situation which may involve some difficulty **uygulanabilir, mümkün, yapılabilir** practical clothes/shoes ○ Pale carpets just aren't practical if you have kids. **3** POSSIBLE able to be done successfully **başarıyla yapılabilir** a practical solution ○ The plan is simply not practical. **4** GOOD AT PLANNING Someone who is practical is good at planning things and dealing with problems. **makûl, sağduyulu, aklıbaşında, hesabını kitabını bilen** She has a lot of interesting ideas but she's not very practical. **5** GOOD WITH HANDS good at repairing and making things **becerikli, elinden her iş gelen**

practical² /ˈpræktɪkəl/ noun [C] a lesson or examination in which you do or make something instead of only writing **uygulamaya dayalı ders veya sınav**

practicalities /ˌpræktɪˈkælətiz/ noun [plural] real situations or facts **gerçekler, gerçek uygulamalar; gerçek durumlar** the practicalities of running your own business

practicality /ˌpræktɪˈkæləti/ noun [U] **1** the possibility that something can be done successfully **başarıyla gerçekleştirilebilirlik; işlerlik** I like the idea but I'm not sure about the practicality of it. **2** how suitable or useful something is for a situation which may involve some difficulty **elverişlilik, kullanışlılık, uygulanabilirlik**

ˌpractical 'joke noun [C] a trick using actions and not words to make people laugh **eşek şakası, ağır şaka** to play a practical joke on someone

practically /ˈpræktɪkəli/ adverb **1** almost **hemen hemen, neredeyse, âdeta, sanki** It's practically impossible to get there. ○ We see her practically every day. **2** in a suitable or useful way **pratik olarak** We need to think practically.

◦→**practice** /ˈpræktɪs/ noun **1** REPEATING [U] when you repeat an activity to improve your ability **çalışma, idman, pratik, antreman** We need a bit more practice before the concert. ○ I've got basketball practice tonight. **2** ACTIVITY [C, U] what people do or how they do it **uygulama, âdet, alışkanlık, gelenek** business/working practices ○ [+ of + doing sth] the illegal practice of copying CDs ○ [+ to do sth] It is common practice to bury waste in landfills. **3** WORK [C] a business in which several doctors or lawyers work together, or the work that they do **avukatlık veya doktorluk vb. mesleklerde bir araya gelerek çalışma; muayenehane, büro** a legal/medical practice **4** **in practice** If something is true in practice, this is the real situation. **uygulamada, gerçekte** In practice, the new laws have had little effect. **5** **be out of practice** to not do something

well because you have not done it recently **antremansız, pratiksiz, pratiğini kaybetmiş, idmansız; hamlamış** **6** **put something into practice** to try a plan or idea **uygulamaya/yürürlüğe koymak; hayata geçirmek** Next month we will have a chance to put these ideas into practice.

◦→**practise** UK (US **practice**) /ˈpræktɪs/ verb **1** REPEAT [I, T] to repeat something regularly in order to improve your ability **alıştırma/pratik yapmak** You need to practise your pronunciation. ○ They're practising for tomorrow's concert. **2** WORK [I, T] to work as a doctor or a lawyer **hekimlik/avukatlık yapmak** to practise medicine/law **3** CUSTOM/RELIGION [T] to do something regularly according to a custom, religion, or a set of rules **(gelenek, din, kurallar) gereklerini yerine getirmek, uygulamak** to practise a religion **4** **practise what you preach** to behave as well as you often tell other people they should behave **sözüyle özü bir olmak; davranışları sözlerine uymak; olduğu gibi görünüp, göründüğü gibi olmak** I'd have more respect for him if he practised what he preached.

practised UK (US **practiced**) /ˈpræktɪst/ adjective very good at doing something because you have done it so often **usta, tecrübeli, deneyimli** She answered the questions with practised ease.

practising UK (US **practicing**) /ˈpræktɪsɪŋ/ adjective a **practising Catholic/Jew/Muslim, etc** someone who follows the rules of a religion **Katolik/Musevilik/müslümanlık kurallarını harfiyen uygulayan kimse**

practitioner /prækˈtɪʃənər/ noun [C] formal someone who works as a doctor or a lawyer **doktor, avukat** a medical practitioner ⊃See also: general practitioner.

pragmatic /prægˈmætɪk/ adjective doing things in a practical and realistic way and not using only ideas **pratik, yararcı, gerçekci** a pragmatic approach to a problem

pragmatism /ˈprægmətɪzəm/ noun [U] when someone is pragmatic **uygulamacılık, pragmatizm** ● **pragmatist** noun [C] someone who is pragmatic **yararcı/gerçekci/uygulama taraftarı olan kimse**

prairie /ˈpreəri/ noun [C] a large, flat area of land in North America that is usually covered in grass **step, geniş çayırlık arazi; Kuzey Amerika'daki geniş stepler**

◦→**praise¹** /preɪz/ verb [T] **1** to say that you admire someone or something, or that they are very good **övmek, methiyeler düzmek, yüceltmek, methetmek** He praised the team's performance. ○ Residents praised the firemen for their swift action. **2** to give respect and thanks to a god **Allah'a methiye düzmek; yüceliğine övgüler söylemek** Praise God, no one was hurt.

praise ...... İLE BİRLİKTE KULLANILAN KELİMELER

deserve/earn/be singled out for/win praise ● **be full of** praise **for/have nothing but** praise **for** sb/sth ● **glowing/high** praise ● praise **for** sb/sth ● **in** praise **of** sth

praise² /preɪz/ noun [U] words you say to show that you admire someone or something **övgü, methiye, yüceltme** They deserve praise for their achievements. ○ Her first novel won a lot of praise from the critics.

praiseworthy /ˈpreɪzˌwɜːði/ adjective formal deserving praise **övgüye değer, methedilmeyi hakeden**

pram /præm/ noun [C] mainly UK a small vehicle with four wheels for carrying a baby **bebek arabası**

prance /prɑːns/ verb [I] to walk or dance in a proud way, often because you want people to look at you **kırıtmak, kırıta kırıta yürümek, caka satmak, fiyaka yap-**

mak; dikkati çekmek için hoplayıp zıplamak *She was **prancing around** in a bikini.*

prank /præŋk/ *noun* [C] a trick that is intended to be funny **muziplik, şaka, oyun, şeytanlık, cingözlük**

prat /præt/ *noun* [C] *UK very informal* a stupid person **avanak, aptal, salak**

prawn /prɔːn/ *noun* [C] a small sea animal which you can eat, and which has a shell and ten legs **karides**

pray /preɪ/ *verb* [I, T] **1** to speak to a god in order to show your feelings or to ask for something **dua etmek** *Let us pray for all the sick children.* ○ [+ that] *She prayed that God would forgive her.* **2** to hope very much that something will happen **çok istemek, içtenlikle arzu etmek** *We're just praying for rain.*

prayer /preər/ *noun* **1** [C] the words you say to a god **dua etmek** *Shall we say a prayer for him?* **2** [U] when you say words to a god **dua etme** *They knelt in prayer.*

preach /priːtʃ/ *verb* **1** [I, T] to talk to a group of people about a religious subject, usually as a priest in a church **vaaz vermek** *to preach the gospel* **2** [I] to try to persuade people to believe or support something, often in an annoying way **telkin etmek, ısrarla telkinde bulunmak** ⊃See also: practise what you preach.

preacher /ˈpriːtʃər/ *noun* [C] someone who speaks in public about a religious subject, especially someone whose job is to do this **vaiz**

preamble /ˈpriːæmbl/ *noun* [C] *formal* an introduction to a speech or piece of writing **giriş, başlangıç, ön söz**

precarious /prɪˈkeəriəs/ *adjective* **1** A precarious situation is likely to become worse. **tehlikeli, güvenliksiz, rizikolu, nazik** *Many illegal immigrants are in a precarious position.* **2** not fixed and likely to fall **sağlam değil, sallantılı, güvenilir olmayan** *That shelf looks a bit precarious.* • **precariously** *adverb Her cup was balanced precariously on the arm of the chair.* **kötüye giden bir şekilde**

┌───┐
│ ◌◌◌ **precaution** ...... İLE BİRLİKTE KULLANILAN KELİMELER │
└───┘
take [adequate/extra/necessary, etc] precautions • as a precaution • a sensible/wise precaution • a safety precaution • a precaution **against** sth

precaution /prɪˈkɔːʃən/ *noun* [C] something that you do to prevent bad things happening in the future **önlem, tedbir** *Driving alone at night can be dangerous, so always take precautions.* ○ *They called the doctor as a precaution.* ○ [+ of + doing sth] *He took the precaution of locking the door.* • **precautionary** *adjective* **önlemsel a precautionary measure/step** something that you do in order to prevent something bad from happening

precede /priːˈsiːd/ *verb* [T] *formal* to happen or exist before something else ...**dan/den önce gelmek/ olmak; önden gelmek, önünde/önden gitmek** [often passive] *The formal ceremony was preceded by a parade.* • **preceding** *adjective* [always before noun] happening or coming before **önce/önden gelen; önce/önünde olan** *the preceding months*

precedence /ˈpresɪdəns/ *noun* [U] when someone or something is considered more important than another person or thing ...**dan/den daha önce olmak/daha önemli olmak** *to give precedence to something* ○ *Quality should take precedence over cost.*

precedent /ˈpresɪdənt/ *noun* [C, U] an action or decision that is used as an example when someone wants to do a similar thing in the future **örnek, emsal, gelenek** *This decision has set an important legal precedent for other countries.*

precinct /ˈpriːsɪŋkt/ *noun* **1** **a pedestrian/shopping precinct** *UK* an area in a town where there are shops

and no cars are allowed **araç trafiğine kapalı alışveriş alanı; mağazalar bölgesi 2** [C] *US* an area in a city that a particular group of police are responsible for, or the building in which they work **semt, bölge, merkez, saha, mıntıka; polis sorumluluk sahası; polis merkezi** *the 45th precinct*

precincts /ˈpriːsɪŋkts/ *noun* [plural] the area of land around a building, especially a large church **bina çevresindeki alan; kilise sahası/bahçesi** *the cathedral precincts*

precious¹ /ˈpreʃəs/ *adjective* **1** very important to you **çok önemli, emsalsiz** *His books are his most precious possessions.* **2** rare and very valuable **nadir, çok değerli, kıymetli** *a precious vase* ○ *a precious metal/ stone*

precious² /ˈpreʃəs/ *adverb* **precious few/little** very little or very few of something **ender bulunan, nadide, çok az olan** *We have precious little money at present.*

precipice /ˈpresɪpɪs/ *noun* [C] **1** a dangerous situation that could lead to failure or harm **sonu kötü bitebilecek/başarısız olabilecek tehlikeli durum** *The two countries stood on the precipice of war.* **2** a steep side of a mountain or high area of land **uçurum, yar, sarp yamaç**

precipitate /prɪˈsɪpɪteɪt/ *verb* [T] *formal* to make something happen **oldurmak, yol açmak, hızlandırmak; ...a/e neden olmak** [often passive] *The war was precipitated by an invasion.*

precipitation /prɪˌsɪpɪˈteɪʃən/ *noun* [U] In science, precipitation is rain or snow that falls to the ground.

precis /ˈpreɪsiː/ *noun* [C, U] *formal* a report giving the main ideas of a piece of writing or speech **özet**

o–**precise** /prɪˈsaɪs/ *adjective* **1** exact and accurate **tam, kesin, kat'i** *precise details/instructions* ⊃Opposite imprecise. **2 to be precise** used to give exact details about something **tam olarak, kesin olarak; tam ve doğru ayrıntıları veren** *We met in 1994 - October first to be precise.* **3** [always before noun] used to emphasize something that you are referring to **tam, doğru** *At that precise moment, the door opened.*

precisely /prɪˈsaɪsli/ *adverb* **1** [EXACTLY] exactly **tam, tam olarak** *at 6 o' clock precisely* **2** [EMPHASIS] used to emphasize something **kesinlikle, tamamen** *This is precisely the kind of thing I was hoping to avoid.* **3** [AGREEMENT] used to agree with what someone else says **Haklısınız!', 'Doğru!', 'Kesinlikle!', 'Evet, öyle!'** *" It's not the shape I dislike, it's the colour. " "Precisely!"*

precision /prɪˈsɪʒən/ *noun* [U] when something is very exact and accurate **doğruluk, tamlık, hassaslık** *She parked the car with great precision.*

preclude /prɪˈkluːd/ *verb* [T] *formal* to prevent something from happening **önüne geçmek, önlemek, engel olmak, meydan vermemek** [+ from + doing sth] *His illness precludes him from taking part in any sports.*

precocious /prɪˈkəʊʃəs/ *adjective* Children who are precocious have the confidence or skill of an adult. **büyümüş küçülmüş, yaşına göre erken gelişmiş** *A precocious child, she went to university at the age of 15.*

preconceived /ˌpriːkənˈsiːvd/ *adjective* Preconceived ideas are decided before the facts of a situation are known. **ön yargılı, peşin hükümlü** *preconceived ideas*

preconception /ˌpriːkənˈsepʃən/ *noun* [C] what you believe before you know the facts of a situation **ön yargı, peşin hüküm** *People have so many preconceptions about unmarried mothers.*

precondition /ˌpriːkənˈdɪʃən/ *noun* [C] *formal* what must happen before something else can happen **ön**

P

koşul, ilk şart, gerekli koşul *The ceasefire is a precondition for peace talks.*

precursor /ˌpriːˈkɜːsəʳ/ *noun* [C] *formal* something which happens or exists before something else and influences its development **öncü, haberci, müjdeci** *Infection with HIV is a precursor to AIDS.*

predate /ˌpriːˈdeɪt/ *verb* [T] to exist or happen before something else **önceden olan; önceleri varolan** *The drinking of alcohol predates the Greeks and Romans.*

predator /ˈpredətəʳ/ *noun* [C] an animal that kills and eats other animals **yırtıcı hayvan**

predatory /ˈpredətᵊri/ *adjective* **1** A predatory person tries to get things from other people in a way that is unfair. **yırtıcı; zorba 2** A predatory animal kills and eats other animals. **yırtıcı**

predecessor /ˈpriːdɪˌsesəʳ/ ⑤ /ˈpredəsesər/ *noun* [C] **1** the person who was in a job or position before **aynı görevi önceden yapmış kimse** *He seems a lot better than his predecessor.* **2** something that existed before another, similar thing **bir önceki benzer şey** *The predecessors to these computers were much larger and heavier.*

predetermined /ˌpriːdɪˈtɜːmɪnd/ *adjective formal* decided before **önceden saptanmış/kararlaştırılmış/belirlenmiş** *They met at a predetermined time and place.*

predeterminer /ˌpriːdɪˈtɜːmɪnəʳ/ *noun* [C] a word that is used before a determiner to give more information about a noun. For example 'all' in 'all these children' is a predeterminer. **(dilbilgisi) ön belirteç**

predicament ...... İLE BİRLİKTE KULLANILAN KELİMELER

face a predicament ● **explain** your predicament ● be in a predicament

predicament /prɪˈdɪkəmənt/ *noun* [C] a problem or a difficult situation **açmaz, müşkül, zor/güç durum** *I sympathize with your predicament.*

predicate /ˈpredɪkət/ *noun* [C] the part of a sentence which gives information about the subject. In the sentence 'We went to the airport.', 'went to the airport' is the predicate. **yüklem, yüklem öbeği**

predicative /prɪˈdɪkətɪv/ *adjective* A predicative adjective comes after a verb. In the sentence 'She is happy.', 'happy' is a predicative adjective. **yüklemsel, fiilden sonra gelen** ⟳Compare **attributive**.

predict /prɪˈdɪkt/ *verb* [T] to say what you think will happen in the future **tahmin etmek, önceden kestirmek/söylemek** *Companies are predicting massive profits.* ○ [+ (that)] *They predicted that the temperature would reach 80 degrees today.*

predictable /prɪˈdɪktəbl/ *adjective* happening or behaving in a way that you expect and not unusual or interesting **önceden tahmin edilebilir/kestirilebilir** *a predictable result* ○ *She's so predictable.* ⟳Opposite **unpredictable**. ● **predictably** *adverb* tahmin edilebilir bir şekilde

prediction .... İLE BİRLİKTE KULLANILAN KELİMELER

make a prediction ● an **accurate/gloomy** prediction ● a prediction **about** sth ● a prediction **of** [disaster/an improvement, etc]

prediction /prɪˈdɪkʃⁿn/ *noun* [C, U] when you say what you think will happen in the future **tahmin, önceden kestirme** *I wouldn't like to make any predictions about the result of this match.*

preˌdictive ˈtexting *noun* [U] when your mobile phone suggests words automatically while you use it to write a text message (= a written message sent from one mobile

phone to another) **hazır ileti örnekleri; cep telefonunun otomatik olarak yazılı ileti metni için sözcük önerileri sunması**

predilection /ˌpriːdɪˈlekʃⁿn/ *noun* [C] *formal* when you like something very much **aşırı düşkünlük/tutkunluk** *She has a predilection for chocolate.*

predisposed /ˌpriːdɪˈspəʊzd/ *adjective* **be predisposed to sth** to be more likely than other people to have a medical problem or to behave in a particular way **yatkın olmak; daha çok meyilli/eğilimli olmak** *Some people are predisposed to addiction.* ● **predisposition** /ˌpriːdɪspəˈzɪʃⁿn/ *noun* [C] when you are likely to have a medical problem or to behave in a particular way **eğilim, yatkınlık, meyillilik, temayül, istidat** *people with a predisposition to heart disease*

predominant /prɪˈdɒmɪnənt/ *adjective* more important or noticeable than others **egemen, üstün, baskın, hâkim** *He has played a predominant role in these talks.* ● **predominance** /prɪˈdɒmɪnəns/ *noun* [U] when something is more important or noticeable than others **ağırlık, ağır basma durumu, üstünlük** *the predominance of English on the Internet*

predominantly /prɪˈdɒmɪnəntli/ *adverb* mostly or mainly **çoğunlukla, ekseriya, daha çok** *a predominantly Asian community*

predominate /prɪˈdɒmɪneɪt/ *verb* [I] to be the largest in number or the most important **sayıca çok/üstün olmak; daha çok göze çarpar/batar olmak; çoğunlukta olmak; ağır basmak** *Olive trees predominate in this area.*

pre-eminent /ˌpriːˈemɪnənt/ *adjective* more important or better than others **en üstün, seçkin, en başta gelen** *a pre-eminent artist/scholar* ● **pre-eminence** /ˌpriːˈemɪnəns/ *noun* [U] when someone or something is much more important or better than others **seçkinlik, üstünlük, güzidelik**

pre-empt /ˌpriːˈempt/ *verb* [T] to do something before something else happens in order to prevent it or reduce its effect **önceden tedbir almak; yapılması gerekenleri önceden yapmak; önceden önlem almak** ● **pre-emptive** *adjective* preventing something else from happening **önleyici, önleyen; önüne geçen; engelleyen; engelleyici** *to take pre-emptive action*

preen /priːn/ *verb* [I, T] **1** If a bird preens or preens itself, it makes its feathers clean and tidy. **gaga ile tüylerini düzeltip temizlemek 2** to try to look attractive **özenle giyinip kuşanmak; süslenmek; çekici görünmeye çalışmak** [often reflexive] *The actors preened themselves in the dressing room.*

pre-existing /ˌpriːɪgˈzɪstɪŋ/ *adjective* existing before something else **önceden varolan** *a pre-existing medical condition*

prefabricated /ˌpriːˈfæbrɪkeɪtɪd/ *adjective* **a prefabricated building/home/house, etc** a building that has already been partly built when it is put together **perfabrike bina/ev/yapı vs.**

preface /ˈprefɪs/ *noun* [C] a piece of writing at the beginning of a book that explains why it was written **ön söz**

prefect /ˈpriːfekt/ *noun* [C] in the UK, an older student in a school who has special duties and some authority **(Birleşik Krallık) öğrenci kıdemlisi/temsilcisi**

o▪ **prefer** /prɪˈfɜːʳ/ *verb* [T] **preferring**, *past* **preferred 1** to like someone or something more than another person or thing **tercih etmek, yeğlemek** *I prefer dogs to cats.* ○ [+ doing sth] *She prefers watching tennis to playing.* **2 would prefer** used to say what you want or ask someone what they want **istemek, tercih etmek, arzu etmek** [+ to do sth] *I'd prefer to go alone.* ○ *Would you prefer red or white wine?*

preferable /'prefᵊrəbl/ *adjective* better or more suitable **daha iyi/uygun; tercih olunur, yeğlenir** *Staying at home is **preferable** to going out with someone you don't like.*

preferably /'prefᵊrəbli/ *adverb* if possible **tercihen, şayet mümkünse; mümkün olursa** *Serve the pudding with ice cream, preferably vanilla.*

preference .... İLE BİRLİKTE KULLANILAN KELİMELER

express/have a preference ● a clear/marked preference ● a personal preference ● a preference for sth

preference /'prefᵊrᵊns/ *noun* **1** [C, U] when you like something or someone more than another person or thing **tercih, yeğleme** *personal preferences* ○ *We have white and brown bread. Do you **have a preference**?* ○ *I have a **preference for** dark-haired men.* **2 give preference to sb** to give special treatment to someone **tercih hakkı vermek; önceliği vermek** *Hospitals must give preference to urgent cases.*

preferential /,prefᵊr'enʃᵊl/ *adjective* **preferential treatment** If you are given preferential treatment, you are treated in a better way than other people. **ayrıcalıklı, imtiyazlı** *There were complaints that some guests had been given preferential treatment.*

prefix /'pri:fɪks/ *noun* [C] a group of letters that you add to the beginning of a word to make another word. In the word 'unimportant', 'un-' is a prefix. **ön ek** ○Compare **suffix** ⟳See study page **Word formation** on page Centre 28.

pregnancy /'pregnənsi/ *noun* [C, U] when a woman is pregnant **gebelik, hamilelik** *a teenage pregnancy*

o⚬**pregnant** /'pregnənt/ *adjective* **1** A pregnant woman has a baby developing inside her uterus. **hamile, gebe** *to **get pregnant*** ○ *She's five months pregnant.* **2 a pregnant pause/silence** a pause or silence full of meaning that is not said in words **anlamlı sessizlik; manidar ara**

preheat /pri:'hi:t/ *verb* [T] to heat an oven to a particular temperature before putting food in it **önceden ısıtma** *Preheat the oven to 180 degrees.*

prehistoric /,pri:hɪ'stɒrɪk/ *adjective* relating to a time in the past before there were written records of events **tarih öncesi** *prehistoric remains*

prejudice .... İLE BİRLİKTE KULLANILAN KELİMELER

encounter/experience/face prejudice ● prejudice against sb

prejudice¹ /'predʒədɪs/ *noun* [C, U] when someone dislikes a group of people or treats them unfairly because they are a different race, sex, religion, etc **önyargı, peşin hüküm** *racial prejudice* ○ *prejudice against women*

prejudice² /'predʒədɪs/ *verb* [T] **1** to influence someone in an unfair way so that they have a bad opinion of someone or something **olumsuz yönde etkilemek, başkaları hakkında olumsuz kanıya sahip olmasına neden olmak; önyargılı olmasına neden olmak** *Her comments may have **prejudiced** the voters **against** him.* **2** to have a harmful effect on a situation **zarar vermek; zarara uğratmak** *Newspaper reports have prejudiced the trial.*

prejudiced /'predʒədɪst/ *adjective* feeling dislike for a group of people or treating them unfairly because they are a different race, sex, religion, etc **önyargılı, peşin hükümlü** *Are the police **prejudiced against** black people?*

preliminary /prɪ'lɪmɪnᵊri/ *adjective* [always before noun] done or happening in order to prepare for the main event or activity **başlangıç, ilk, ön, giriş** *a preliminary*

discussion/meeting ● **preliminary** *noun* [C] something that you do at the start of an event or activity **hazırlık; giriş/başlangıç için yapılanlar**

prelude /'prelju:d/ *noun* **1 a prelude to sth** something that happens before another event or activity, usually as an introduction to it **başlangıç, giriş** *There are hopes that the talks are a prelude to an agreement.* **2** [C] a short piece of music that introduces the main piece **giriş parçası**

premature /'premətʃᵊr/ ⓤ /,pri:mə'tʊr/ *adjective* happening too soon or before the usual time **vaktinden önce, vakitsiz** *premature ageing/death* ○ *a premature baby* ○ [+ to do sth] *It seems a bit premature to start talking about it already.* ● **prematurely** *adverb He died prematurely of cancer.* **zamanından önce oluşan şekliyle**

premeditated /,pri:'medɪteɪtɪd/ *adjective* If a crime is premeditated, it is planned. **kasıtlı, önceden tasarlanmış** *premeditated murder* ○ *a premeditated attack*

premenstrual /,pri:'menstruəl/ *adjective* related to the time just before a woman's period (= monthly blood from the uterus) **âdet öncesi olan; regl öncesi olan** *premenstrual syndrome/tension*

premier¹ /'premiəʳ/ ⓤ /prɪ'mɪr/ *noun* [C] the leader of a government **hükümetin başı/lideri; başbakan** *the Chinese premier* ● **premiership** *noun* [U] the period in which someone is premier **başbakanlık, hükümet başkanlığı dönemi**

premier² /'premiəʳ/ ⓤ /prɪ'mɪr/ *adjective* [always before noun] best or most important **en iyi ve en önemli olan; ilk, baş, birinci, asıl** *the city's premier hotel*

premiere /'premieəʳ/ ⓤ /prɪ'mɪr/ *noun* [C] the first public performance of a film, play, etc **ilk gösterim, gala, prömiyer** *a film premiere* ○ *the world premiere* ● **premiere** *verb* [I, T] [often passive] *The opera was premiered in Paris.* **film veya oyunun galasını yapmak**

the Premiership /'premiəˌʃɪp/ *noun* the group of the best English football teams who compete against each other **İngiliz futbol takımlarının en iyilerinin birbirleriyle karşılaşması; prömiyer takımlar**

premise /'premɪs/ *noun* [C] *formal* an idea that you use to support another theory **başka bir kuramı desteklemek için kullanılan fikir/düşünce; varsayım, faraziye, hipotez**

premises /'premɪsɪz/ *noun* [plural] the land or buildings used by an organization **konut alanı, yer, mahal, bina** *We're moving to new premises.* ○ *Smoking is not allowed anywhere **on the premises**.*

premium¹ /'pri:miəm/ *noun* **1** [C] an amount of money you pay for insurance (= payments for an accident or illness) **prim, ek ödeme** *How much is the monthly premium?* **2** [C] an amount or rate that is higher than average **ortalamanın üstünde oran/miktar** *You pay a premium for apartments in the city centre.* **3 be at a premium** If something useful is at a premium, there is not enough of it. **çok aranan, çok rağbette** *Time is at a premium just before the start of exams.* **4 place/put a premium on sth** to consider a quality or achievement as very important **çok önem vermek, büyük değer vermek, özendirmek** *She puts a premium on honesty.*

premium² /'pri:miəm/ *adjective* [always before noun] A premium product is of a higher quality or value than others. **çok değerli/üstün kaliteli; türünün en iyi kalitesinde olan** *premium beer/cigars*

premonition /,premə'nɪʃᵊn/ *noun* [C] a feeling that something, especially something unpleasant, is going to happen **önsezi, kötü his, iç sıkıntısı** *to **have a premonition*** ○ *a **premonition** of disaster*

P

prenatal /ˌpriːˈneɪtᵊl/ *US* (*UK* antenatal) *adjective* relating to pregnant women before their babies are born **doğum öncesi** *prenatal care*

preoccupation /priːˌɒkjəˈpeɪʃᵊn/ *noun* **1** [C, U] when you think or worry about something so much that you do not think about other things **takıntı, aklını takma, zihin meşguliyeti** *a preoccupation with death/food* **2** [C] something that you think or worry about a lot **tasa, dert, gaile, kaygı, endişe** *His main preoccupations are football and women.*

preoccupied /priːˈɒkjəpaɪd/ *adjective* thinking or worrying about something a lot **dalgın, zihni meşgul, gözü bir şey görmeyen, düşünceli** *She's been very preoccupied recently.* ○ *He's far too preoccupied with his own problems to notice mine.* ● **preoccupy** /priːˈɒkjəpaɪ/ *verb* [T] If something preoccupies you, you think or worry about it a lot. **zihnini meşgul etmek, kafasını kurcalamak**

prepaid /priːˈpeɪd/ *adjective* If something is prepaid, you pay for it before a particular time. **ön ödeme, peşinat** *Susan just got prepaid tickets for the show next weekend.*

○ **preparation** /ˌprepᵊrˈeɪʃᵊn/ *noun* [U] the things that you do or the time that you spend preparing for something **hazırlama, hazırlanma, hazırlık** *Did you do much preparation for your interview?* ○ *He's been painting the outside of the house in preparation for winter.* ○ *the preparation of the document*

preparations ...... İLE BİRLİKTE KULLANILAN KELİMELER
begin/finalize/make preparations ● final/last-minute preparations ● preparations are underway ● preparations for sth

preparations /ˌprepərˈeɪʃᵊnz/ *noun* [plural] things that you do to get ready for something **hazırlıklar, düzenlemeler, hazırlık** *wedding preparations* ○ *We've been making preparations for the journey.* ○ *I've been busy with last-minute preparations for our trip.*

preparatory /prɪˈpærətᵊri/ *adjective* done in order to get ready for something **hazırlık, hazırlayıcı** *preparatory work*

pre'paratory ˌschool *noun* [C] *formal* a prep school **hazırlık okulu**

○ **prepare** /prɪˈpeᵊr/ *verb* **1** [I, T] to get someone or something ready for something that will happen in the future **hazırlamak** *They're preparing for the big match.* ○ *We're preparing the students for their end-of-year exam.* ○ [+ to do sth] *I was busy preparing to go on holiday.* **2 prepare yourself** to make yourself ready to deal with a difficult situation **kendini hazırlamak** *Prepare yourself for a shock.* **3** [T] to make food ready to be eaten **yemek hazırlamak** *to prepare lunch*

prepared /prɪˈpeəd/ *adjective* **1** ready to deal with a situation **hazır, hazırlıklı, hazırlanmış, istekli** *I wasn't prepared for the cold.* **2 be prepared to do sth** to be willing to do something **bir şeyi yapmaya hazır/istekli/arzulu/hevesli olmak** *You must be prepared to work hard.*

preponderance /prɪˈpɒndᵊrᵊns/ *noun formal* **a preponderance of sth** when there is a larger amount of one thing than of others **üstünlük, ağır basma, çoğunluk, ağırlık** *There is a preponderance of older people in this area.*

preposition /ˌprepəˈzɪʃᵊn/ *noun* [C] a word or group of words that is used before a noun or pronoun to show place, direction, time, etc. For example 'on' in 'Your keys are on the table.' is a preposition. **edat**

preposterous /prɪˈpɒstᵊrəs/ *adjective* extremely stupid **saçma, mantıksız, akla sığmaz, gülünç** *That's a preposterous idea!*

prep school /ˈprepskuːl/ *noun* [C] **1** in the UK, a private school for children aged between 8 and 13 **hazırlık okulu**; (Birleşik Krallık) 8-13 yaşları arasındaki çocuklar için özel okul **2** in the US, a private school which prepares students for college **(ABD) öğrenciler yüksek öğrenime hazırlayan özel okul, hazırlık okulu**

prerequisite /ˌpriːˈrekwɪzɪt/ *noun* [C] *formal* something that is necessary in order for something else to happen or exist **ön koşul, ön şart, ilk şart** *Trust is a prerequisite for any sort of relationship.*

prerogative /prɪˈrɒgətɪv/ *noun* [C] *formal* something that you have the right to do because of who you are **ayrıcalık, imtiyaz** *Alex makes the decisions - that's his prerogative as company director.*

Presbyterian /ˌprezbɪˈtɪəriən/ *adjective* belonging or relating to a type of Christian church with elected groups of local members involved in the official organization of local churches **Presbiteryan** ● **Presbyterian** *noun* [C] **kilise sistemi ile ilgili**

pre-school /ˈpriːskuːl/ *adjective* [always before noun] relating to children who are too young to go to school **okul öncesine ilişkin** *pre-school children/education* ● **pre-school** *noun* [C] a school for children younger than five years old **okul öncesi, ana okulu**

prescribe /prɪˈskraɪb/ *verb* [T] **1** to say what medical treatment someone needs **reçete yazmak, tedavi şeklini söylemek** [often passive] *Painkillers are the most common drugs prescribed by doctors in Britain.* **2** *formal* to say officially what people must do **emretmek, buyurmak, bildirmek, beyan etmek** *rules prescribed by law*

prescription /prɪˈskrɪpʃᵊn/ *noun* **1** [C] a piece of paper saying what medicine someone needs or the medicine itself **reçete** *a doctor's prescription* **2 on prescription** *UK* (*US* by prescription) If you get a medicine on prescription, you only get it if you have a written instruction from your doctor. **reçeteyle**

prescriptive /prɪˈskrɪptɪv/ *adjective formal* saying exactly what must happen *The government's homework guidelines are too prescriptive.*

presence ...... İLE BİRLİKTE KULLANILAN KELİMELER
the presence of sb/sth ● in the presence of sb/sth

presence /ˈprezᵊns/ *noun* **1** [IN A PLACE] [U] when someone or something is in a place **hazır bulunma, huzur** *She signed the document in the presence of two witnesses.* **2** [POLICE/SOLDIERS] [no plural] a group of police or soldiers who are watching or controlling a situation **(polis, asker) birlik; denetim kontrol grubu/müfrezesi/birliği** *a strong police presence* **3** [QUALITY] [U] a quality that makes people notice and admire you **kişilik, görünüş, tavı, edâ 4 presence of mind** the ability to deal with a difficult situation quickly and effectively **soğukkanlılık; ağır başlılık, pratik zekâ** *She had the presence of mind to press the alarm.* **5 make your presence felt** to have a strong effect on other people **varlığını hissettirmek, kendini göstermek, kendini saydırmak** *The new police chief has really made his presence felt.*

○ **present¹** /ˈprezᵊnt/ *adjective* **1 be present** to be in a particular place **orada olmak, mevcut olmak** *The whole family was present.* **2** [always before noun] happening or existing now **mevcut, var olan** *the present situation* ○ *What is your present occupation?* **3 present tense** the form of the verb which is used to show what happens or exists now **geniş zaman**

present ...... İLE BİRLİKTE KULLANILAN KELİMELER

buy/get/give sb/**wrap (up)** a present • a present **for/from** sb • a **birthday/wedding** present

o--**present**[2] /'prezᵊnt/ noun 1 **the present** a the period of time that is happening now bugün, şu an; içinde bulunulan an The play is set in the present. b the form of the verb which is used to show what happens or exists now şu an varolan veya olan eylemleri göstermek için kullanılan fiil biçimi 2 [C] something that you give to someone, usually for a particular occasion hediye, armağan a birthday/wedding present ○ to give someone a present 3 **at present** now şu an, şimdi At present she's working abroad.

present[3] /prɪ'zent/ verb   **present** [T] 1 [GIVE] to give something to someone, often at a formal ceremony sunmak, vermek, takdim etmek to present a prize ○ They presented her with a bouquet.

2 [INFORMATION] to give people information in a formal way bilgi vermek; bilgilendirmek He presented the report to his colleagues. 3 **present a danger/threat/problem, etc** to cause a danger/threat/problem, etc tehlike/tehdit/sorun vs. yaratmak/arzetmek The final exam may present some problems. 4 [TV/RADIO] UK (US host) to introduce a television or radio programme tv./radyo programı sunmak He presents a weekly sports quiz. 5 [PLAY/FILM] to show a new play or film yeni bir oyun/film göstermek The school is presenting 'West Side Story' this term. 6 [INTRODUCE] to introduce someone formally tanıştırmak, takdim etmek May I present my daughters? 7 [OPPORTUNITY] If an opportunity presents itself, it becomes possible. (ortaya) çıkmak, olmak, düşmek, zuhur etmek; mümkün hâle gelmek I'd be happy to go to New York, if the opportunity presented itself.

presentable /prɪ'zentəbl/ adjective looking clean and tidy enough eli yüzü düzgün, toplum içine çıkabilir; düzgün/temiz pak görünen He was looking quite presentable in his jacket and tie.

presentation /ˌprezᵊn'teɪʃᵊn/ noun 1 [SHOW] [U] the way something is arranged or shown to people sergileme, sunuş, teşhir Presentation is important if you want people to buy your products. 2 [TALK] [C] a talk giving information about something sunum, konuşma, konferans a sales presentation ○ She gave an excellent presentation. 3 [CEREMONY] [C] a formal ceremony at which you give someone something resmî tören, sunum töreni, tören a presentation ceremony

present-day /ˌprezᵊnt'deɪ/ adjective existing now bugünkü, çağdaş, şuan varolan present-day attitudes

presenter /prɪ'zentər/ UK (US host) noun [C] someone who introduces a radio or television programme program sunucu

presently /'prezᵊntli/ adverb 1 formal now şimdi, şu anda He's presently living with his parents. 2 old-fashioned soon or after a short time az sonra, birazdan, neredeyse I'll be back presently.

present par'ticiple UK (US ˌpresent 'participle) noun [C] the form of a verb that ends with '-ing' şimdiki zaman ortacı

the ˌpresent 'perfect noun the form of the verb that is used to show actions or events that have happened in a

period of time up to now. The sentence 'I have never been to Australia.' is in the present perfect. geçmişte başlayan ve eylemin konuşulduğu âna dek geçen süre içinde olan eylemleri belirten fiil şekli/çekimi

preservation /ˌprezə'veɪʃᵊn/ noun [U] when you keep something the same or prevent it from being damaged or destroyed koruma, muhafaza the preservation of peace ○ the preservation of wildlife

preservative /prɪ'zɜ:vətɪv/ noun [C, U] a substance used to prevent decay in food or in wood koruyucu madde, katkı maddesi

preserve[1] /prɪ'zɜ:v/ verb [T] 1 to keep something the same or prevent it from being damaged or destroyed korumak, muhafaza etmek; bozulmasını önlemek to preserve peace ○ to preserve the environment 2 to add substances to something so that it stays in good condition for a long time katkı maddesi ilave etmek; koruyucu madde ilave etmek to preserve food/wood

preserve[2] /prɪ'zɜ:v/ noun 1 [FOOD] [C, U] UK (US preserves) a sweet food made from fruit, sugar, and water reçel apricot/strawberry preserve 2 [ACTIVITY] [no plural] an activity which only a particular group of people can do sadece bir grup insanın yapabileceği eylem Sport used to be a male preserve. ○ Owning racehorses is **the preserve of the rich**. 3 [AREA] [C] mainly US an area where wild animals and plants are protected yabanî hayvanları koruma alanı

preside /prɪ'zaɪd/ verb [I] to be officially responsible for a formal meeting or ceremony resmî tören ve toplantılardan resmen sorumlu olmak; yönetmek An elderly priest presided at the marriage ceremony. **preside over sth** phrasal verb to be in charge of a situation, especially a formal meeting or legal trial yönetmek, başkanlık etmek The case was presided over by a senior judge.

presidency /'prezɪdᵊnsi/ noun 1 [C] the period when someone is president cumhur başkanlığı/başkanlık dönemi Her presidency lasted seven years. 2 **the presidency** the job of being president cumhurbaşkanlığı He won the presidency by a wide margin.

o--**president** /'prezɪdᵊnt/ noun [C] 1 the highest political position in some countries, usually the leader of the government başkan, cumhurbaşkanı President Obama 2 the person in charge of a company or organization başkan ⊃See also: vice president.

presidential /ˌprezɪ'denʃᵊl/ adjective relating to the president of a country cumhurbaşkanlığına/başkanlığa ilişkin a presidential campaign

o--**press**[1] /pres/ verb 1 [PUSH] [I, T] to push something firmly basmak, bastırmak Press the button to start the machine. ○ He pressed his face against the window. 2 [PERSUADE] [I, T] to try hard to persuade someone to do something ısrar etmek, üstelemek, zorlamak [+ to do sth] The committee pressed him to reveal more information. ○ We pressed him for an answer but he refused. 3 **press charges** to complain officially about someone in a court of law ...da/de bulunmak; ...isnat etmek; ...iddia etmek; şikâyete bulunmak The family decided not to press charges against him. 4 [MAKE SMOOTH] [T] to make clothes smooth by ironing them ütülemek I need to press these trousers. 5 [MAKE FLAT] [T] to make something flat by putting something heavy on it for a long time düzleştirmek to press fruit/flowers 6 **press a case/claim** to try to make people accept your demands isteklerini kabul ettirmeye çalışmak; ısrar etmek; bastırmak; mücadele etmek

press ahead/forward/on phrasal verb to continue to do something in a determined way kararlı bir şekilde yapmaya devam etmek They're determined to press ahead with their plans despite opposition.

press² /pres/ noun **1 the press** newspapers and magazines, or the people who write them **basın, matbuat, gazeteler** *the local/national press* ○ *press reports* **2 good/bad press** praise or criticism from newspapers, magazines, television, etc **televizyon/dergiler/gazetelerde vs. yer alan eleştiri ve övgüler** *She's had a lot of bad press recently.* **3** [BUSINESS] [C] a business that prints and sells books **matbaa** *Cambridge University Press* **4** [PRINT] [C] (*also* printing press) a machine used to print books, newspapers, and magazines **matbaa makinası 5** [MAKE FLAT] [no plural] when you make cloth flat and smooth with a piece of equipment **ütüleme, presleme, düzleştirme** *Can you give these trousers a press?*

press ,conference noun [C] a meeting at which someone officially gives information to the newspapers, television, etc **basın toplantısı** *to call/hold a press conference*

pressed /prest/ adjective **be pressed for time/money** to not have much time/money **para/zaman sıkıntısı içinde olmak; darda olmak; zor şarlarda olmak**

pressing /'presɪŋ/ adjective A pressing problem or situation needs to be dealt with immediately. **ivedi, acil, acele** *a pressing need for housing*

press re,lease noun [C] an official piece of information that is given to newspapers, television, etc **basın bildirisi/duyurusu/bülteni**

press-up /'presʌp/ *UK* (*US* push-up) noun [C] a physical exercise in which you lie facing the floor and use your hands to push your body up **şınav**

pressure .... İLE BİRLİKTE KULLANILAN KELİMELER

face/feel pressure ● be under/come under pressure
● pressure on sb ● pressure from sb ● pressure for sth

o⁻**pressure¹** /'preʃəʳ/ noun **1** [MAKE SOMEONE DO] [U] when someone tries to make someone else do something by arguing, persuading, etc **baskı, tazyik, zorlama** *public/political pressure* ○ [+ to do sth] *Teachers are under increasing pressure to work longer hours.* ○ *The government is facing pressure from environmental campaigners.* **2** [PROBLEMS] [C, U] difficult situations that make you feel worried or unhappy **baskı, sıkıntı, stres, zor durum** *the pressures of work* ○ *He's been under a lot of pressure recently.* **3** [LIQUID/GAS] [C, U] the force that a liquid or gas produces when it presses against an area **basınç** *water pressure* **4** [PUSH] [U] the force that you produce when you push something **baskı, basma, basınç 5 put pressure on sb** to try to force someone to do something **baskı/tazyik uygulama; zorlamak; baskılamak; zor kullanarak yaptırmak** [+ to do sth] *They're putting pressure on me to make a decision.* ⊃See also: blood pressure, peer pressure.

pressure² /'preʃəʳ/ (*also UK* pressurize, -ise /'preʃʳraɪz/) verb [T] to try to force someone to do something **zorlamak, baskı uygulayarak yaptırmaya çalışmak** [often passive, + into + doing sth] *We will not be pressured into making a decision.*

pressure ,cooker noun [C] a pan with a lid which you use to cook food quickly in steam **düdüklü tencere**

pressure ,group noun [C] a group of people who try to influence what the public or the government think about something **lobi, baskı grubu**

pressurize *UK* (*also* -ise) /'preʃʳraɪz/ verb [T] to try to force someone to do something **zorlamak, baskı uygulayarak yaptırmaya çalışmak, sıkıştırmak** [often passive, + into + doing sth] *He was pressurized into signing the agreement.*

pressurized (*also UK* -ised) /'preʃəraɪzd/ adjective containing air or gas that is kept at a controlled pressure **basınçlı, tazyikli** *a pressurized container*

prestige /pres'tiːʒ/ noun [U] when people feel respect and admiration for you, often because you are successful **itibar, saygınlık, prestij** *His company has gained international prestige.* ● **prestigious** /pres'tɪdʒəs/ adjective respected and admired, usually because of being important **itibarlı, saygın, prestijli** *a prestigious award* ○ *a prestigious university*

presumably /prɪ'zjuːməbli/ adverb used to say what you think is the likely situation **galiba, tahminen, herhalde** *Presumably he just forgot to send the letter.*

presume /prɪ'zjuːm/ verb **1** [T] to think that something is likely to be true, although you are not certain **varsaymak, tahmin etmek, sanmak, farzetmek** [+ (that)] *I presume that you've done your homework.* **2 be presumed dead/innocent, etc** If someone is presumed dead/innocent, etc, it seems very likely that they are dead/innocent, etc. **ölmüş/suçlu vs. kabul edilmek/farzedilmek/sayılmak/sanılmak 3 presume to do sth** *formal* to do something that you do not have the right or the skills to do properly **yapmak zorunda olmak; yeterli olmadığı/hakkı olmadığı hâlde yapmak** *I certainly wouldn't presume to tell you how to do your job.*

presumption /prɪ'zʌmpʃʳn/ noun **1** [C] when you believe that something is true without any proof **varsayım, tahmin, ihtimal** [+ (that)] *I object to the presumption that young people are only interested in pop music.* **2** [U] behaviour that is rude and does not show respect **saygısız/kaba davranış, küstahlık**

presumptuous /prɪ'zʌmptʃuəs/ adjective Someone who is presumptuous confidently does things that they have no right to do. **küstah, haddini bilmez, arsız, saygısız** *It was a bit presumptuous of her to take the car without asking.*

presuppose /ˌpriːsə'pəʊz/ verb [T] *formal* If an idea or situation presupposes something, that thing must be true for the idea or situation to work. **öngörmek, önceden farzetmek**

pre-teen /priː'tiːn/ noun [C] a boy or girl between the ages of 9 and 12 **ergenlik öncesi 9 ve 12 arası yaştaki kız/erkek** *a magazine for pre-teens* ● **pre-teen** adjective *pre-teen fashions* **9-12 yaş arası olan**

pretence *UK* (*US* pretense) /prɪ'tens/ noun **1** [U] when you make someone believe something that is not true **sahte tavır, numara, yapmacık, kandırmaca** *I can't keep up the pretence* (= continue pretending) *any longer.* ○ *They made absolutely no pretence of being interested.* **2 under false pretences** If you do something under false pretences, you do it when you have lied about who you are or what you are doing. **hile ile, sahtekârlıkla, numara yaparak** *The police charged him with obtaining money under false pretences.*

o⁻**pretend** /prɪ'tend/ verb [I, T] to behave as if something is true when it is not **numara yapmak, gibi görünmek; ...mış gibi görünmek** [+ (that)] *I can't pretend that I like him.* ○ [+ to do sth] *Were you just pretending to be interested?*

pretense /prɪ'tens/ noun *US spelling of* pretence **sahte tavır, numara, yapmacık, kandırmaca**

pretension /prɪ'tenʃʳn/ noun [C, U] when you try to seem better or more important than you really are **gösteriş, caka, fiyaka yapma** [usually plural] *He seems to be without pretensions of any sort.*

pretentious /prɪ'tenʃəs/ adjective trying to seem more important or clever than you really are **iddialı, gösterişli, kendini beğenmiş** *a pretentious film*

pretext /'pri:tekst/ *noun* [C] a false reason that you use to explain why you are doing something **bahane, kulp, uyduruk neden** *I called her* **on the pretext of** *needing some information.*

o⇥**pretty**¹ /'prɪti/ *adverb informal* **1** quite, but not extremely **oldukça, epey, bir hayli** *The traffic was pretty bad.* ○ *I'm pretty sure they'll accept.* **2 pretty much/well** almost **hemen hemen, neredeyse** *We've pretty much finished here.*

o⇥**pretty**² /'prɪti/ *adjective* **1** If a woman or girl is pretty, she is attractive. **güzel, hoş, sevimli, tatlı, çekici** *Your daughter is very pretty.* **2** If a place or an object is pretty, it is pleasant to look at. **güzel, hoş, sevimli, tatlı** *a pretty little village*

prevail /prɪ'veɪl/ *verb* [I] *formal* **1** to get control or influence **baskın çıkmak, üstün gelmek, etkin olmak** *We can only hope that* **common sense** *will* **prevail.** **2** to be common among a group of people **yaygın olmak, egemen olmak, hâkim olmak** *The use of guns prevails among the gangs in this area.*

prevail on/upon sb to do sth *phrasal verb formal* to persuade someone to do something that they do not want to do **ikna etmek, baskın çıkarak zorlamak, istemediği hâlde yapması için zorlamak** *He was eventually prevailed upon to accept the appointment.*

prevailing /prɪ'veɪlɪŋ/ *adjective* [always before noun] **1** existing a lot in a particular group, area, or at a particular time **yaygın, hüküm süren, sürekli varolan** *a prevailing attitude/mood* **2** a **prevailing wind** a wind that usually blows in a particular place **düzenli, her zaman esen**

prevalent /'prevələnt/ *adjective* existing a lot in a particular group, area, or at a particular time **yaygın/ hâkim olan; geçerli olan** *These diseases are more prevalent among young children.* ● **prevalence** /'prevələns/ *noun* [U] something that exists a lot in a particular group, area, or at a particular time **yaygınlık, hâkimiyet, üstünlük, geçerlilik** *the prevalence of smoking among teenagers*

o⇥**prevent** /prɪ'vent/ *verb* [T] to stop something happening or to stop someone doing something **önlemek, engel olmak, önüne geçmek** *to prevent accidents/crime* ○ [+ from + doing sth] *Members of the public were prevented from entering the building.* ● **preventable** *adjective* If something is preventable, it can be prevented. **önlenebilir, önüne geçilebilir**

preventative /prɪ'ventətɪv/ *adjective* another word for preventive **önleyici, engelleyici**

prevention /prɪ'venʃ°n/ *noun* [U] when you stop something happening or stop someone doing something **önlem, tedbir** *crime prevention* ○ *the* **prevention of** *diseases*

preventive /prɪ'ventɪv/ (*also* preventative) *adjective* Preventive action is intended to stop something before it happens. **önleyici, engelleyici** *preventive measures* ○ *preventive medicine*

preview /'pri:vju:/ *noun* [C] **1** an opportunity to see a film, play, etc before it is shown to the public **özel gösterim** **2** a short film that advertises a film or television programme **kısa film reklamı; ön gösterim** ● **preview** *verb* [T] **Önizlemek**

o⇥**previous** /'pri:viəs/ *adjective* existing or happening before something or someone else **önceki, geçmişe ait** *the previous day/year* ○ *a previous attempt* ○ *his previous marriage* ● **previously** *adverb* *He previously worked as a teacher.* **önceki**

prey¹ /preɪ/ *noun* **1** [U] an animal that is hunted and killed by another animal **av, kurban, yem** **2 fall prey to sth** to be hurt or deceived by something or someone

bad *...*ın/in eline düşmek; ağına düşmek ⊃See also: **bird of prey.**

prey² /preɪ/ *verb*
prey on sth *phrasal verb* If an animal preys on another animal, it catches and eats it. **avlanarak beslenmek** *Spiders prey on flies and other small insects.*
prey on/upon sb *phrasal verb* to hurt or deceive people who are weak and easy to deceive **zayıf ve kolay kandırılabilen kişileri incitmek/kandırmak; kolay avlamak; kolay av olmak** *These young thieves prey on the elderly.*

🧩 **price** .... İLE BİRLİKTE KULLANILAN KELİMELER

charge/increase/**pay**/put up prices ● prices **fall** ● an average/exorbitant/high/low/reasonable price

o⇥**price**¹ /praɪs/ *noun* **1** [C] the amount of money that you pay to buy something **fiyat high/low prices** ○ *House prices are falling/rising.* ○ *The price of fuel has gone up again.* **2** [no plural] the unpleasant results that you must accept or experience for getting or doing something **bedel, karşılık** *Suspension from the club was* **a high/ small price to pay** (= very bad/not very bad thing to experience) *for his mistake.* **3 at a price** If you can get something at a price, you have to pay a lot of money for it. **bir bedel karşılığında, belirli bir bedel ödeyerek** *False passports are available, at a price.* **4 at any price** If you want something at any price, you will do anything to get it. **ne pahasına olursa olsun; neye malolursa olsun** *She wanted the job at any price.*

price² /praɪs/ *verb* [T] to say what the price of something is **fiyatlandırmak, fiyat biçmek** [often passive] *The book is priced at $40.*

priceless /'praɪsləs/ *adjective* **1** very valuable **paha biçilmez** *a priceless antique/painting* **2** very important or useful **çok önemli, son derece yararlı, yeri doldurulamaz** *A trip round the world is a priceless opportunity.*

price ,tag (*also* 'price ,ticket) *noun* [C] a piece of paper attached to a product that shows the amount a product costs **fiyat etiketi**

pricey (*also* pricy) /'praɪsi/ *adjective informal* expensive **pahalı** *That jacket's a bit pricey!*

prick /prɪk/ *verb* [T] to make a very small hole in something with a sharp object **delmek, delik açmak, batırmak, kesici bir aletle oymak** *Prick the potatoes all over before baking.* ○ *I pricked my finger on a pin.* ● **prick** *noun* [C] *The injection won't hurt - you'll just feel a slight prick.* **batırmak, iğnelemek**

prickle¹ /'prɪk°l/ *noun* [C] a sharp point on the surface of some plants or the skin of some animals **diken, sivri uç**

prickle² /'prɪk°l/ *verb* [I] If part of your body prickles, it feels as if a lot of sharp points are touching it because you are frightened or excited. **ürpermek, tüyleri diken diken olmak, karıncalanmak** *a prickling sensation*

prickly /'prɪkli/ *adjective* **1** covered with prickles **dikenli, iğneli** *a prickly bush* **2** *informal* A prickly person or relationship is unfriendly or difficult to deal with. **huysuz, geçimsiz, sinirli, hırçın, hödük, cinleri tepesinde**

pricy /'praɪsi/ *adjective another spelling of* pricey **pahalı, tuzlu; (argo) kazık**

🧩 **pride** .... İLE BİRLİKTE KULLANILAN KELİMELER

take pride **in** sth ● a sense/source of pride ● great pride ● sb's pride **at/in** sth

⚬ **pride**[1] /praɪd/ *noun* [U] **1** [SATISFACTION] a feeling of satisfaction at your achievements or the achievements of your family or friends **gurur, kıvanç, iftihar, övünç** *She felt a great sense of pride as she watched him accept the award.* ○ *The whole community **takes pride in** (= feels proud about) the school.* **2** [RESPECT] the respect that you feel for yourself **haysiyet, onur, gurur, özsaygı, izzeti nefis** *Defeat in the World Cup has badly damaged national pride.* **3** [IMPORTANCE] the belief that you are better or more important than other people **kibir, gurur, kendini üstün görme, kendini beğenmişlik** *His pride prevented him from asking for help.* **4 sb's pride and joy** something or someone that is very important to you **önemli kişi/şey; değer verdiği kişi/şey** *He spends hours cleaning that motorcycle - it's his pride and joy.* **5 have/take pride of place** If something takes pride of place, you put it in the best position so that it can be seen easily. **layık olduğu/hak ettiği yeri almak; şeref köşesine/baş köşeye koymak/yerleştirmek** *A photo of her grandchildren took pride of place on the wall.* ● **6 swallow your pride** to decide to do something although it will embarrass you **gururunu ayaklar altına almak; gururunu yenmek/bir tarafa bırakmak** *He swallowed his pride and asked if he could have his old job back.*

pride[2] /praɪd/ *verb*
pride yourself on sth/doing sth *phrasal verb* to feel satisfaction at a quality or skill that you have **iftihar etmek, kendisiyle gurur duymak; övünç duymak** *The company prides itself on having the latest technology.*

priest /priːst/ *noun* [C] someone who performs religious duties and ceremonies **papaz**

the priesthood /ˈpriːsthʊd/ *noun* the job of being a priest **papazlık**

prim /prɪm/ *adjective* Someone who is prim behaves in a very formal way and is easily shocked by anything rude. **soğuk ve resmî, fazla ciddi, kolay alınan, kırılgan; çabuk etkilenen** *Sarah wouldn't find that funny - she's far too prim and proper* (= shocked by anything rude). ● **primly** *adverb* **çok resmi bir şekilde**

prima donna /ˌpriːməˈdɒnə/ *noun* [C] someone who behaves badly and expects to get everything they want because they think that they are very important **baş kadın oyuncu**

primal /ˈpraɪmᵊl/ *adjective formal* very basic, or relating to the time when human life on Earth began **temel, ilk insanlar ait, insanlığın doğuşuna ait; ilkel** *primal instincts*

primarily /praɪˈmerᵊli/ *adverb* mainly **başlıca; esas olarak; ana ilke olarak** *She's known primarily as a novelist but she also writes poetry.*

primary[1] /ˈpraɪmᵊri/ *adjective* [always before noun] most important **ana, temel, asıl, esas,** *Her primary responsibility is to train new employees.*

primary[2] /ˈpraɪmᵊri/ *noun* [C] a vote in which people in a political party in the US choose the person who will represent them in an election **önseçim, aday adayı seçimi**

primary colour *UK (US* **primary color**) *noun* [C] one of the three colours, which in paint, etc are red, blue, and yellow, that can be mixed together to make any other colour **ana renk; kırmızı, mavi, sarı renklerden biri**

primary school (*also US* **elementary school**) *noun* [C] a school for children aged 5 to 11 **ilkokul**

primate /ˈpraɪmeɪt/ *noun* [C] a member of the group of animals which includes monkeys and people, which have large brains and hands and feet developed for climbing **insanları ve maymunları içeren hayvanlar grubu üyesi; ilk yaratıklar**

prime[1] /praɪm/ *adjective* [always before noun] **1** main, or most important **asıl, esas, ana, baş** *the prime suspect in a murder investigation* **2** of the best quality **seçkin, en nitelikli, en iyi** *The hotel is in a prime location in the city centre.* **3 a prime example** a very good example of something **esas örnek, en iyi misal/örnek**

prime[2] /praɪm/ *noun* [no plural] the period in your life when you are most active or successful **insan hayatının en verimli ve başarılı dönemi** *At 35, she's in her prime.* ○ *the prime of life*

prime[3] /praɪm/ *verb* [T] to prepare someone for an event or situation, often by giving them the information that they need **hazırlamak, yetiştirmek, gerekli bilgilerle donatmak** *The president had been well primed before the debate.*

prime minister *noun* [C] the leader of an elected government in some countries **başbakan**

prime time *noun* [U] the time in the evening when the largest number of people watch television **televizyonun en çok izlendiği zaman dilimi** *prime-time television*

primeval /praɪˈmiːvᵊl/ *adjective* belonging to a very early period in the history of the world **ilk çağ, eski çağlara ait** *primeval forest*

primitive /ˈprɪmɪtɪv/ *adjective* **1** relating to human society at a very early stage of development, with people living in a simple way without machines or a writing system **ilkel; ilk çağlara/ilk insanlara ait** *primitive man* ○ *primitive societies* **2** very basic or old-fashioned **ilkel, iptidaî** *The conditions at the campsite were rather primitive.*

primrose /ˈprɪmrəʊz/ *noun* [C] a wild plant with pale yellow flowers **çuha çiçeği**

prince /prɪns/ *noun* [C] **1** the son of a king or queen, or one of their close male relatives **prens** *Prince Edward* **2** the male ruler of a small country **prens**

princely /ˈprɪnsli/ *adjective* **a princely sum** a large amount of money **yüklü, pek çok, çok, bir hayli** *It cost the princely sum of £2 million.*

princess /prɪnˈses/ ⓤˢ /ˈprɪnsəs/ *noun* [C] **1** the daughter of a king or queen, or one of their close female relatives **prenses 2** the wife of a prince **prenses, prensin eşi**

principal[1] /ˈprɪnsəpᵊl/ *adjective* [always before noun] main, or most important **ana, asıl, esas, en önemli** *Her principal reason for moving is to be nearer her mother.*

principal[2] /ˈprɪnsəpᵊl/ *noun* [C] the person in charge of a school or college **müdür**

principality /ˌprɪnsɪˈpæləti/ *noun* [C] a country ruled by a prince **prenslik**

principally /ˈprɪnsəpᵊli/ *adverb* mainly **başlıca, genellikle, çoğunlukla, özellikle** *The advertising campaign is aimed principally at women.*

principle ...... İLE BİRLİKTE KULLANILAN KELİMELER

stick to your principles ● a guiding principle ● be against sb's principles ● be a matter of principle

⚬ **principle** /ˈprɪnsəpl/ *noun* **1** [C, U] a rule or belief which influences your behaviour and which is based on what you think is right **ilke, prensip** *He must be punished - it's a matter of principle.* **2** [C] a basic idea or rule which explains how something happens or works **ilke, prensip, genel kural ve uygulamalar** *The organization works on the principle that all members have the same rights.* **3 in principle** If you agree with something in principle, you agree with the idea or plan although you do not know the details or you do not know if it will be possible. **ilke olarak, prensipte, prensip itiba-riyle, temelde** *They have approved the changes in principle.* **4 on principle** If you refuse to do something on principle, you refuse to do it because you think it is morally wrong. **ilke olarak, prensipte, prensip itiba-riyle** *She doesn't wear fur on principle.*

principled /'prɪnsəpld/ *adjective* showing strong beliefs about what is right and wrong **ilkeli, ilke/prensip sahibi, prensipli**

o⇥**print¹** /prɪnt/ *verb* 1 WRITING/IMAGES [T] to produce writing or images on paper or other material with a machine **basmak** *The instructions are printed on the side of the box.* **2** BOOKS/NEWSPAPERS [T] to produce books, newspapers, magazines, etc, usually in large quantities, using machines **yayımlamak** *Fifty thousand booklets have been printed for the exhibition.* **3** INCLUDE [T] to include a piece of writing in a newspaper or magazine **basmak, yayımlamak, yazmak** *They printed his letter in Tuesday's paper.* **4** WRITE [I, T] to write words without joining the letters together **kitap harfiyle yazmak** *Please print your name and address clearly using capitals.* **5** PATTERN [T] to produce a pattern on material or paper **kalıp baskıyla basmak**
print sth out *phrasal verb* to produce a printed copy of a document that has been written on a computer **çıktı almak, kağıda dökmek; kağıda yazdırmak** *Can you print out a copy of that letter for me?*

print² /prɪnt/ *noun* 1 WORDS [U] words, letters, or numbers that are produced on paper by a machine **baskı** **2 in/out of print** If a book is in print, it is possible to buy a new copy of it, and if it is out of print, it is not now possible. **stokta/satışta mevcut; baskısı tükenmiş** **3** PICTURE [C] a copy of a picture made using photography or by pressing paper onto a design covered in ink **resim nüshası/kopyası; baskı tekniği kullanarak resim, şekil vb. üretme** *a print of Van Gogh's 'Sunflowers'* **4** PHOTOGRAPH [C] a photograph that is produced on paper **resim baskısı, filmden elde edilen resim** **5** PATTERN [C] a pattern that is produced on material or paper **baskı, kâğıt veya herhangi bir madde üzerinde yapılan baskı** *a floral print* **6** HAND [C] (*also* fingerprint) a mark that is left on a surface where someone has touched it **(el, parmak) iz, işaret** *His prints were found all over the house and he was arrested the next day.* **7** MARK [C] a mark that is left on a surface where someone has walked **ayak izi** *The dog left prints all over the kitchen floor.* ⊃See also: small print.

printer /'prɪntər/ *noun* [C] 1 a machine which is connected to a computer and which produces writing or images on paper **yazıcı** *a laser printer* 2 a person or company that prints books, newspapers, magazines, etc **matbaacı, basım yapan kimse**

printing /'prɪntɪŋ/ *noun* [U] when writing or images are produced on paper or other material using a machine **baskı, basım işi**

'**printing ,press** *noun* [C] a machine that prints books, newspapers, magazines, etc **matbaa makinası; baskı makinaları**

printout /'prɪntaʊt/ *noun* [C] information or a document that is printed from a computer **yazıcı çıktısı** *He asked for a printout of the year's sales figures.*

prior /praɪər/ *adjective formal* 1 [always before noun] existing or happening before something else **...dan/den önce/evvel** *The course requires no prior knowledge of Spanish.* 2 **prior to sth** before a particular time or event **önceden, öncesinde** *the weeks prior to her death*

prioritize (*also* UK **-ise**) /praɪ'ɒrɪtaɪz/ *verb* [I, T] to decide which of a group of things are the most important so that you can deal with them first **öncelik vermek; ön sıralara yerleştirmek; önem sırasına göre önceli-**

ğini belirlemek *You must learn to prioritize your work.*

priority /praɪ'ɒrəti/ *noun* 1 [C] something that is very important and that must be dealt with before other things **öncelik, önceliği olan** *My first/top priority is to find somewhere to live.* 2 **give priority to sth** to consider that something is more important than other things and deal with it first **öncelik vermek/tanımak, ehemmiyet vermek** 3 **have/take priority (over sth)** to be more important than other things and to be dealt with first **...dan/den daha önemli/öncelikli olmak** *His job seems to take priority over everything else.*

prise /praɪz/ *verb* UK **prise sth apart/off/open, etc** to use force to move, remove, or open something **kanırtmak, kanırtarak açmak; zorlayarak açmak** *I prised the lid off with a spoon.*

prism /'prɪzəm/ *noun* [C] an object made of clear glass which separates the light that passes through it into different colours **prizma**

prison ...... İLE BİRLİKTE KULLANILAN KELİMELER

go to/be sent to prison ● be released from prison **● in/out of prison ● a prison sentence**

o⇥**prison** /'prɪzən/ *noun* [C, U] a place where criminals are kept as a punishment **hapishane, mahpushane** *He's spent most of his life in prison.* ○ *She was sent to prison for two years.*

o⇥**prisoner** /'prɪzənər/ *noun* 1 [C] someone who is being kept in prison as a punishment, or because they have been caught by an enemy **mahkûm, hükümlü 2 hold/keep/take sb prisoner** to catch someone and guard them so that they cannot escape **esir almak; tutsak etmek; gözaltında tutmak** ⊃See also: political prisoner.

,**prisoner of 'war** *noun* [C] *plural* **prisoners of war** a soldier who is caught by enemy soldiers during a war **savaş esiri/tutsağı** *a prisoner of war camp*

pristine /'prɪstiːn/ *adjective* in very good condition, as if new **yepyeni, gıpgıcır, tertemiz** *Her car is in pristine condition.*

privacy /'prɪvəsi/ ⑤ /'praɪvəsi/ *noun* [U] when you are alone and people cannot see or hear what you are doing **gizlilik, mahremiyet, özel hayat** *I hate sharing a bedroom - I never get any privacy.*

o⇥**private¹** /'praɪvɪt/ *adjective* 1 NOT EVERYONE only for one person or group and not for everyone **hususi, özel, kişisel, şahsi** *Each room has a balcony and a private bathroom.* ○ *You can't park here - this is private property.* 2 NOT GOVERNMENT controlled by or paid for by a person or company and not by the government **özel** *Charles went to a private school.* 3 SECRET If information or an emotion is private, you do not want other people to know about it. **gizli, özel** *This is a private matter - it doesn't concern you.* 4 **in private** If you do something in private, you do it where other people cannot see or hear you. **özel olarak, yalnız** *I need to talk to you in private.* 5 **sb's private life** someone's personal relationships and activities and not their work **özel hayat; mahrem yaşam** 6 QUIET A place which is private is quiet and there are no other people there to see or hear what you are doing. **yalnız, özel, sakin, sessiz, gözlerden uzak, sıra** *Is there somewhere private where we can talk?* ● **privately** *adverb* **özel olarak**

private² /'praɪvɪt/ *noun* [C] a soldier of the lowest rank in the army **er (askeriye)**

the 'private ,sector *noun* businesses and industries that are not owned or controlled by the government **özel sektör**

privatize (*also* UK **-ise**) /'praɪvɪtaɪz/ *verb* [T] If an industry or organization owned by the government is privatized, it is sold to private companies. **özelleştirmek** ● **privatization** /ˌpraɪvɪtaɪˈzeɪʃᵊn/ *noun* [U] **özelleştirme**

privilege /ˈprɪvᵊlɪdʒ/ *noun* **1** [C, U] an advantage that only one person or group has, usually because of their position or because they are rich **ayrıcalık, imtiyaz 2** [no plural] an opportunity to do something special or enjoyable **imtiyaz, ayrıcalık** [+ of + doing sth] *I had the privilege of meeting the Queen.* ● **privileged** *adjective* having a privilege **ayrıcalıklı, imtiyazlı** *to be in a privileged position*

privy /ˈprɪvi/ *adjective formal* **privy to sth** knowing information that is not known by many people **haberdar, haberli, bilgi sahibi**

prize ...... İLE BİRLİKTE KULLANILAN KELİMELER

be awarded/win a prize ● first/second/the runner's-up/the top prize ● a prize for sth ● a prize of [£500/a car, etc] ● prize money/winner

○•**prize¹** /praɪz/ *noun* [C] something valuable that is given to someone who wins a competition or who has done good work **ödül, mükâfat** *to win a prize* ○ *first/second prize* See also: **booby prize.**

prize² /praɪz/ *adjective* [always before noun] A prize animal or vegetable is good enough to win a competition. **ödül kazanabilecek olan**

prize³ /praɪz/ *verb* [T] to think that something is very valuable or important **itibar etmek, önem/değer vermek** *His car is his prized possession.*

prize-winning /ˈpraɪzˌwɪnɪŋ/ *adjective* [always before noun] having won a prize **ödül kazanmış** *a prize-winning author*

pro /prəʊ/ *noun* [C] **1** *informal* someone who earns money for playing a sport **spordan para kazanan kimse; profesyonel sporcu** *a golf/tennis pro* **2 the pros and cons** the advantages and disadvantages of something **olumlu ve olumsuz yönleri; avantaj ve dezavantajları** [+ of + doing sth] *We discussed the pros and cons of buying a bigger house.*

pro- /prəʊ-/ *prefix* supporting or approving of something **desteleyen/onaylayan/taraftarı olan anlamında önek** *pro-European* ○ *pro-democracy demonstrations* ⊃Compare **anti-**.

proactive /ˌprəʊˈæktɪv/ *adjective* taking action by causing change and not only reacting to change when it happens **zamanından önce değişiklik yaparak önlem alınan; önceden davranılan**

probability /ˌprɒbəˈbɪləti/ *noun* **1** [C, U] how likely it is that something will happen **ihtimal, olasılık** [+ of + doing sth] *What's the probability of winning?* ○ [+ (that)] *There's a high probability that he'll get the job.* **2 in all probability** used to mean that something is very likely **büyük bir olasılıkla/ihtimalle** *She will, in all probability, have left before we arrive.*

probable /ˈprɒbəbl/ *adjective* likely to be true or to happen **olası, muhtemel** *The probable cause of death was heart failure.* ○ [+ (that)] *It's highly probable that he'll lose his job.*

○•**probably** /ˈprɒbəbli/ *adverb* used to mean that something is very likely **muhtemelen, olasılıkla** *I'll probably be home by midnight.*

probation /prəʊˈbeɪʃᵊn/ *noun* [U] **1** a period of time when a criminal must behave well and not commit any more crimes in order to avoid being sent to prison **şartlı salıverme/tahliye; sınamalı olma hâli** *to be on probation* **2** a period of time at the start of a new job when you are watched and tested to see if you are suitable for the job **deneme/sınama süresi** ● **proba-**

tionary *adjective* relating to probation **deneme/sınama süresi** *a probationary period*

pro'bation ˌofficer *noun* [C] someone whose job is to watch and help criminals who have been put on probation **şartlı tahliye görevlisi**

probe¹ /prəʊb/ *verb* [I, T] to ask a lot of questions in order to discover information about something or someone **araştırmak, soruşturmak, tetkik etmek** *The interviewer probed deep into her private life.* ○ *probing questions*

probe² /prəʊb/ *noun* [C] **1** when you try to discover information about something by asking a lot of questions **araştırma, soruşturma, tetkik, inceleme** *an FBI probe into corruption* **2** a long, thin, metal tool used by doctors to examine parts of the body **sonda**

problem ...... İLE BİRLİKTE KULLANILAN KELİMELER

cause/face/have/tackle/pose a problem ● a problem arises ● a big/major/real/serious problem

problem ...... BAŞKA BİR DEYİŞLE

Difficulty kelimesi **problem** kelimesine alternatif olarak kullanılır. *The company is having some financial difficulties at the moment.*
Resmi olmayan konuşmalarda, küçük ve geçici bir problem **hitch** ve **hiccup** ifadeleriyle tanımlanabilir. *The ceremony went without a hitch.* ● *I'm afraid there's been a slight hiccup with the arrangements.*
Glitch bir şeyin düzenli çalışmasını engelleyen bir problem anlamında kullanılır. *We've had a few technical glitches, but I'm confident we'll be ready on time.*
İlerleme kaydetmek için başa çıkmanız gereken bir problem **hurdle** veya **obstacle** kelimeleriyle tanımlanabilir. *Getting a work permit is the first hurdle/obstacle.*
Bir durumda meydana gelebilecek problem **pitfall** ifadesiyle tanımlanabilir. *It's just one of the pitfalls of buying a house.*
Bir şeyin gerekenden daha uzun bir zamanda olmasına sebep olan problemin tanımlanması için **setback** ifadesi kullanılabilir. *The project has suffered a series of setbacks this year.*

○•**problem** /ˈprɒbləm/ *noun* **1** DIFFICULT SITUATION [C] a situation that causes difficulties and that needs to be dealt with **sorun, mesele, problem** *health problems* ○ *I'm having problems with my computer.* ○ *Drugs have become a serious problem in the area.* **2** MATHEMATICS [C] a question that you use mathematics to solve **problem 3 have a problem with sth/sb** to find something or someone annoying or offensive **sorunu/meselesi olmak** *Yes, she can smoke in the house - I don't have a problem with that.* **4 No problem. a** AFTER QUESTION something that you say to mean you can or will do what someone has asked you to do **Tabii!', 'Elbette!', 'Lafı mı olur!', 'Hiç dert etmeyin!** *"Can you get me to the airport by 11.30?" "No problem."* **b** AFTER THANKS something that you say when someone has thanked you for something **Rica ederim!', 'Hiç önemli değil!', 'Bir şey değil!', 'Her zaman!'** *"Thanks for taking me home." "No problem."*

problematic /ˌprɒbləˈmætɪk/ *adjective* full of problems or difficulties **sorunlu, problemli** *He has a very problematic relationship with his father.*

procedure ...... İLE BİRLİKTE KULLANILAN KELİMELER

follow a procedure ● correct/proper/standard procedure ● a procedure for (doing) sth

procedure /prəʊˈsiːdʒəʳ/ *noun* [C, U] the official or usual way of doing something **yol, yöntem, usül, prosedür**

*The company has new **procedures** for dealing with complaints.*

proceed /prəʊˈsiːd/ *verb* [I] *formal* **1** to continue as planned **planlandığı/tasarlandığı gibi devam etmek/ilerlemek** *His lawyers have decided not to proceed with the case.* **2 proceed to do sth** to do something after you have done something else **...dan/den sonra ...a/e devam etmek/ilerlemek/geçmek** *She sat down and proceeded to tell me about her skiing trip.* **3 proceed along/down/to, etc** *formal* to move or travel in a particular direction **ilerlemek, devam etmek** *Passengers for Sydney should proceed to gate 21.*

proceedings /prəˈsiːdɪŋz/ *noun* [plural] **1** legal action against someone **yasal işlemler, kovuşturma, takibat** *The bank is threatening to start legal proceedings against him.* **2** a series of organized events or actions **olup bitenler, olaylar** *The chairman opened the proceedings with a short speech.*

proceeds /ˈprəʊsiːdz/ *noun* [plural] the money that is earned from an event or activity **gelir, kazanç** *All proceeds from the concert will go to charity.*

o┅**process**[1] /ˈprəʊses/ ⓤ /ˈprɑːses/ *noun* [C] **1** a series of actions that you take in order to achieve a result **işlem, yol, metod, usül** *Buying a house can be a long and complicated process.* **2** [C] a series of changes that happen naturally **doğal olarak meydana gelen değişimler dizisi; işlem/olgu** *the ageing process* **3 in the process** If you are doing something, and you do something else in the process, the second thing happens as a result of doing the first thing. **bu sırada, bu esnada** *She stood up to say hello and spilled her drink in the process.* **4 be in the process of doing sth** to have started doing something **...yapmakta/sürecinde olmak** *We're in the process of painting our apartment.*

process[2] /ˈprəʊses/ ⓤ /ˈprɑːses/ *verb* [T] **1** [CHEMICALS] to add chemicals to a substance, especially food, in order to change it or make it last longer **işleme tâbi tutmak, işlemek; kimyasal katkı maddeleri katmak; işlemden geçirmek** *processed food* **2** [INFORMATION] to deal with information or documents in an official way **üzerinde çalışmak; işleme tâbi tutmak, bilgisayar kulanarak ve resmî şekilde ele almak; işleme sokmak** *Visa applications take 28 days to process.* **3** [COMPUTER] When a computer processes data (= information), it does things to it so that it can be used and understood ● **processing** *noun* [U] *data processing* **işlem**

procession /prəˈseʃən/ *noun* [C] a line of people or vehicles that moves forward slowly as part of a ceremony or public event **kafile, alay, tören kıtası; yürüyüş kolu** *a funeral procession*

processor /ˈprəʊsesər/ *noun* [C] the main part of a computer that controls all the other parts **bilgi işlemci; işlemci** ➔See also: **food processor, word processor**.

proclaim /prəʊˈkleɪm/ *verb* [T] *formal* to announce something officially or in public **ilân etmek; resmen duyurmak** ● **proclamation** /ˌprɒkləˈmeɪʃən/ *noun* [C] an official announcement about something important **ilân, duyuru**

procrastinate /prəʊˈkræstɪneɪt/ *verb* [I] *formal* to wait a long time before doing something that you must do **bir eylemi uyumaya bırakmak; bekletmek/beklemek; sümen altı etmek; (argo) bir horoz ötüm süresi beklemek/bekletmek** *I know I've got to deal with the problem at some point - I'm just procrastinating.*

procure /prəˈkjʊər/ *verb* [T] *formal* to obtain something that is difficult to get **elde etmek, sağlamak, temin etmek**

prod /prɒd/ *verb* **prodding**, *past* **prodded** **1** [I, T] to push someone or something with your finger or with a

pointed object **dürtmek, dürtüklemek** *He prodded me in the back and told me to hurry up.* **2** [T] to encourage someone to do something **yüreklendirmek, dürtmek, sıkıştırmak** [+ into + doing sth] *We need to prod him into making a decision.* ● **prod** *noun* [C] [usually singular] to **give someone a prod** **itme**

prodigious /prəˈdɪdʒəs/ *adjective formal* extremely great in size or ability **muazzam, çok büyük, hayret verici** *a prodigious talent* ○ *a prodigious appetite*

prodigy /ˈprɒdɪdʒi/ *noun* [C] a young person who is very good at something **dâhi, harika çocuk** *A child prodigy, she entered university at the age of eleven.*

o┅**produce**[1] /prəˈdjuːs/ *verb* [T] **1** [MAKE] to make or grow something **yapmak, üretmek, yaratmak** *The factory produces about 900 cars a year.* ○ *This plant will produce small yellow flowers in the spring.* **2** [CAUSE] to cause a particular reaction or result **neden olmak, olmasını sağlamak** *Nuts produce an allergic reaction in some people.* **3** [SHOW] to take an object from somewhere so that people can see it **ortaya koymak, göstermek** *One of the men suddenly produced a gun from his pocket.* **4** [FILM/PLAY] to control how a film, play, programme, or musical recording is made **(müzik, film, oyun, program vb.) yapmak, üretmek, meydana getirmek, ortaya koymak** *He's produced some of the top Broadway shows.* ➔See also: mass-produce.

produce[2] /ˈprɒdjuːs/ *noun* [U] food that is grown or made in large quantities to be sold **ürün, mahsul** *dairy produce*

producer /prəˈdjuːsər/ *noun* [C] **1** a company, country, or person that makes goods or grows food **üretici firma/ülke/kimse** *Australia is one of the world's main producers of wool.* **2** someone who controls how a film, play, programme, or musical recording is made **yapımcı, prodüktör** *a film/record producer*

o┅**product** /ˈprɒdʌkt/ *noun* [C] **1** something that is made or grown to be sold **ürün, mahsul** *They have a new range of skin-care products.* ○ *Does she eat dairy products* (= things made from milk)? **2 product of sth** someone or something that is the result of a particular experience or process **sonuç, hasıla, ortaya çıkan ürün** *His lack of confidence is the product of an unhappy childhood.* ➔See also: by-product, end-product.

┄┄ **production** ┄┄┄┄ İLE BİRLİKTE KULLANILAN KELİMELER
sth goes into production ● production of sth

o┅**production** /prəˈdʌkʃən/ *noun* **1** [MAKING] [U] when you make or grow something **üretme, yetiştirme** *Sand is used in the production of glass.* ○ *The new model goes into production* (= starts being made) *next year.* **2** [AMOUNT] an amount of something that is made or grown **üretim, verim, istihsal** *We need to increase production by 20%.* **3** [PERFORMANCE] [C] a performance or series of performances of a play or show **yapım, prodüksiyon, sahneye koyma** *a school production of 'Romeo and Juliet'* **4** [ORGANIZING FILM/PLAY] [U] when someone controls how a film, play, programme, or musical recording is made **yapım, yapıt, eser, prodüksiyon** *She wants a career in TV production.*

productive /prəˈdʌktɪv/ *adjective* **1** producing a good or useful result **verimli, yararlı, iyi sonuç veren** *We had a very productive meeting and sorted out a lot of problems.* **2** producing a large amount of goods, food, work, etc **üretken, verimli** *productive land* ○ *a productive worker*

productivity /ˌprɒdʌkˈtɪvəti/ *noun* [U] the rate at which goods are produced **üretkenlik, verimlilik, prodütivite** *We need to increase productivity by 50%.*

Prof /prɒf/ *noun* [C] *short for* professor **Prof., profesör** *Prof Susan Nishio*

profane /prəˈfeɪn/ *adjective formal* showing no respect for God or for religious or moral rules **Allah'a/kutsal değerlere/ahlâk ilkelerine karşı saygısız davranan; değertanımaz** *profane language* ● **profanity** /prəˈfænəti/ *noun* [U] *formal* **din, ahlaki konular ve Tanrı'ya karşı saygısızlık**

profess /prəˈfes/ *verb* [T] *formal* to express a quality or belief, often when it is not true **açıkça belirtmek, ileri sürmek; ifade etmek** [+ to do sth] *She professes to hate shopping, but she's always buying new things.*

profession /prəˈfeʃᵊn/ *noun* **1** [C] a type of work that needs special training or education **meslek, uğraşı** *He's working in a restaurant, but he's a teacher by profession* (= he trained to be a teacher). **2** [group] the people who do a type of work considered as a group **meslek grubu** *The medical profession has expressed concern about the new drug.*

ᴏ̴**professional**[1] /prəˈfeʃᵊnᵊl/ *adjective* **1** [JOB] [always before noun] relating to a job that needs special training or education **mesleki, profesyonel** *You should get some professional advice about your finances.* **2** [EARNING MONEY] Someone is professional if they earn money for a sport or activity which most people do as a hobby. **profesyonel (sporcu vb.)** *a professional athlete/musician* ᴄ⟲Opposite amateur. **3** [SKILL] showing skill and careful attention **ustalıklı, profesyonel, işini iyi yapan kişi** *a professional attitude* ○ *He looks very professional in that suit.* ᴄ⟲Opposite unprofessional.

professional[2] /prəˈfeʃᵊnᵊl/ *noun* [C] **1** [TRAINED] someone who does a job that needs special training or education **özel eğitim ve bilgi gerektiren bir işi yapan kimse, profesyonel 2** [WITH EXPERIENCE] someone who has done a job for a long time and who does it with a lot of skill **meslek erbabı, profesyonel, ustalıkla yapan kimse** *She dealt with the problem like a true professional.* **3** [SPORTS] someone who earns money for doing a sport or activity which most other people do as a hobby **profesyonel sporcu, profesyonel** *a rugby professional* ᴄ⟲Opposite amateur.

professionalism /prəˈfeʃᵊnᵊlɪzᵊm/ *noun* [U] the skill and careful attention which trained people are expected to have **ustalık, profesyonellik** *He complained about the lack of professionalism in the company.*

professionally /prəˈfeʃᵊnᵊli/ *adverb* **1** [WORK] in a way that relates to your work **mesleki olarak, profesyonel biçimde** *I know him professionally, but he's not a close friend.* **2** [WITH TRAINING] Work that is done professionally is done by someone who has had special training. **ustalıkla yapılarak, profesyonelce yapılan** *Their house has been professionally decorated.* **3** [HIGH STANDARDS] in a way that shows high standards or skill **ustalıkla, profesyonelce** *He dealt with the situation very professionally.* **4** [SPORT] If someone does an activity or sport professionally, they earn money for doing it. **profesyonelce oynayarak; sporu meslek olarak yaparak** *He's good enough at football to play professionally.*

professor /prəˈfesəʳ/ *noun* [C] the highest rank of teacher in a British university, or a teacher in an American university or college **profesör; (ABD) üniversite öğretim görevlisi/üyesi** *a professor of history at Oxford* ○ *Professor Blackman.*

proffer /ˈprɒfəʳ/ *verb* [T] *formal* to offer something to someone **teklif etmek, önermek, sunmak** *to proffer advice*

proficiency /prəˈfɪʃᵊnsi/ *noun* [U] when you can do something very well **yeterlik** *The job requires proficiency in written and spoken English.*

proficient /prəˈfɪʃᵊnt/ *adjective* very good at something **yeterli, usta, mahir, becerikli, yetenekli** *She's proficient in two languages.* ○ *I've become quite proficient at repairing bicycles.*

build up/create a profile ● a profile **of** sb/sth

profile[1] /ˈprəʊfaɪl/ *noun* [C] **1** [DESCRIPTION] a short description of someone's life, character, work, etc **kısa yaşam öyküsü/biyografi 2** [HEAD] a side view of someone's face or head **profilden/yandan görünüş** *The picture shows him in profile.* **3** [ATTENTION] the amount of attention that something receives **dikkatleri üzerine toplama; çekilen dikkat** *We need to increase our company's profile in Asia.* **4 high profile** important and noticeable **önemli, göze çarpan, dikkate değer** *a high-profile job* **5** a description of yourself and your interests on a website **6 keep a low profile** to try not to be noticed **göze çarpmamak/batmamak; gözden uzan olmak; (argo) etliye sütlüye karışmamak**

profile

profile[2] /ˈprəʊfaɪl/ *verb* [T] to describe someone's life, character, work, etc **kısa yaşam öyküsü yazmak; kısaca tanımlamak**

boost/increase profits ● **make** a profit ● profits **fall/rise** ● an **annual/big/gross/healthy/large/small** profit

ᴏ̴**profit**[1] /ˈprɒfɪt/ *noun* [C, U] money that you get from selling goods or services for more than they cost to produce or provide **kâr, kazanç** *a profit of $4.5 million* ○ *It's very hard for a new business to make a profit in its first year.*

profit[2] /ˈprɒfɪt/ *verb*

profit from sth *phrasal verb* to earn a profit or get an advantage from something **yararlanmak, istifade etmek; kâr elde etmek** *Investors have profited from a rise in interest rates.*

profitable /ˈprɒfɪtəbl/ *adjective* **1** making or likely to make a profit **kârlı, kazançlı** *a profitable business* **2** useful or likely to give you an advantage **faydalı, kâr sağlayan, yararlı, değerli** *a profitable discussion* ● **profitability** /ˌprɒfɪtəˈbɪlɪti/ *noun* [U] **karlılık** ● **profitably** *adverb* **karlı bir şekilde**

profound /prəˈfaʊnd/ *adjective* **1** [EFFECT] If an effect is profound, it is extreme. **çok büyük, derin, esaslı** *The war had a profound impact on people's lives.* **2** [FEELING] If a feeling is profound, you feel it very strongly. **derin, derinden gelen, esaslı, güçlü** *a profound sense of sadness* **3** [UNDERSTANDING] If an idea or piece of work is profound, it shows intelligence or a great ability to understand. **çok inceleme gerektiren, anlaşılması zor; anlaşılması zekâ ve büyük kabiliyet gerektiren** *a profound question* ○ *His theories were simple, but profound.* ● **profoundly** *adverb* **çok büyük, engin bir şekilde**

profusely /prəˈfjuːsli/ *adverb* a lot **çok, bol bol, çok fazla** *He apologized profusely for being late.*

profusion /prəˈfjuːʒᵊn/ *noun* [U, no plural] *formal* an extremely large amount of something **bolluk, çokluk,**

fazlalık *a profusion of wild flowers* ○ *Bacteria grow in profusion in the warm, wet soil.*

prognosis /prɒgˈnəʊsɪs/ *noun* [C] *plural* **prognoses** /prɒgˈnəʊsiːz/ *formal* **1** a judgment that a doctor makes about an ill person's chance of becoming healthy **hastalığın seyri ile ilgili tahmin; ...nın/nin geleceği hakkında tahminde bulnma; öngörüler belirleme 2** an opinion about the future of someone or something *...nın/nin geleceğine ilişkin fikir yürütme/tahminde bulunma The prognosis for economic growth is good.*

o⁻**program**¹ /ˈprəʊɡræm/ *noun* [C] **1** a set of instructions that you put into a computer to make it do something **program** *to write a computer program* **2** *US spelling of* programme **program**

program² /ˈprəʊɡræm/ *verb* [T] **programming**, *past* **programmed 1** If you program a computer, you give it a set of instructions to do something. **(bilgisayar) programlamak 2** *US spelling of* programme **program yapmak**

o⁻**programme**¹ UK (*US* **program**) /ˈprəʊɡræm/ *noun* [C] **1** TELEVISION/RADIO a show on television or radio **radyo/tv. programı** *a TV programme* ○ *Did you see that programme about spiders last night?* **2** PLAN a plan of events or activities with a particular purpose **belli bir amaç için düşünülen eylem ve faaliyetler planı; program** *a health education programme* **3** THIN BOOK a thin book that you buy at a theatre, sports event, etc which tells you who or what you are going to see **tiyatro/spor program kitapçığı/broşürü**

programme² UK (*US* **program**) /ˈprəʊɡræm/ *verb* [T] If you programme a machine, you give it a set of instructions to do something. **bir aleti/makinayı programlamak** [+ to do sth] *I've programmed the video to start recording at 10 o'clock.*

programmer /ˈprəʊɡræməʳ/ *noun* [C] someone who writes computer programs as a job **bilgisayar programcısı ● programming** *noun* [U] when someone writes computer programs **bilgisayar programı yazma; programlama**

[ILE BİRLİKTE KULLANILAN KELİMELER] **progress** ....

halt/impede/make/monitor progress **● rapid/real/significant/slow/steady** progress **●** progress **on/toward** sth

o⁻**progress**¹ /ˈprəʊɡres/ Ⓤ /ˈprɒɡres/ *noun* [U] **1** development and improvement of skills, knowledge, etc **ilerleme, gelişme** *slow/rapid progress* ○ *technological progress* ○ *He has made good progress in French this year.* **2 in progress** *formal* happening or being done now **sürmekte, devam etmekte, yapılmakta, olmakta; işlem görmekte** *Quiet please - Exams in progress.* **3** movement towards a place **bir yöne doğru ilerleme/hareket**

progress² /prəʊˈɡres/ *verb* [I] **1** to improve or develop in skills, knowledge, etc **gelişmek, ilerlemek, bilgi/beceri sahibi olmak** *Technology has progressed rapidly in the last 100 years.* **2** to continue gradually **devam etmek, süregelmek, yavaş yavaş ilerlemek** *I began to feel more relaxed as the evening progressed.*

progression /prəʊˈɡreʃᵊn/ *noun* [C, U] when something or someone changes to the next stage of development **ilerleme, gelişme** *a logical/natural progression* ○ *Drugs can stop the progression of the disease.*

progressive /prəʊˈɡresɪv/ *adjective* **1** thinking or behaving in a new or modern way **aydın, ileriyi gören; modern görüşlü; ileri düşünen** *progressive ideas/attitudes* **2** developing or happening gradually **aşama aşama, derece derece** *a progressive disease*

● progressively *adverb* gradually **gittikçe, giderek** *My headaches are getting progressively worse.*

the progressive /prəʊˈɡresɪv/ *noun* the form of the verb that is used to show that an action is continuing. In English, the progressive is made with 'be' and the present participle. **fiilin şimdiki zaman hâli**

prohibit /prəʊˈhɪbɪt/ *verb* [T] *formal* to officially forbid something **yasaklamak, menetmek** [often passive] *Smoking is prohibited on most international flights.* ○ [+ doing sth] *The new law prohibits people from drinking alcohol in the street.* ○ *a prohibited substance* **● prohibition** /ˌprəʊhɪˈbɪʃᵊn/ *noun* [U] when something is prohibited **yasaklayıcı yasa/kural/hüküm**

prohibitive /prəʊˈhɪbətɪv/ *adjective* If the cost of something is prohibitive, it is too expensive for many people. **aşırı, fahiş, çok yüksek, yanına yaklaşılmaz** *The cost of flying first class is prohibitive for most people.* **● prohibitively** *adverb* **prohibitively expensive** yüksek maliyetli

o⁻**project**¹ /ˈprɒdʒekt/ *noun* [C] **1** a carefully planned piece of work that has a particular purpose **proje, tasarı** *a research project* ○ *The new building project will cost $45 million.* **2** a piece of school work that involves detailed study of a subject **okul projesi, ödev** *We're doing a class project on the environment.*

project² /prəʊˈdʒekt/ *verb* **1** CALCULATE [T] to calculate an amount or make a guess about the future based on information that you have **tasarlamak, planlamak, projelendirmek** [often passive, + to do sth] *As people live longer, the demand for health care is projected to increase dramatically.* ○ *projected costs/growth* **2** IMAGE [T] to show a film or other image on a screen or a wall **görüntüyü bir perdeye/duvara yansıtmak; aksettirip göstermek** *Laser images were projected onto a screen.* **3** QUALITY [T] If you project a particular quality, that quality is what most people notice about you. **bir yönüyle öne çıkmak/dikkat çekmek** *She projected an image of strong leadership.* **4 project from/into/out, etc** *formal* to stick out **çıkmak, çıkıntı yapmak, fırlamak; ucu görünmek; dışarı doğru çıkmak**

projection /prəʊˈdʒekʃᵊn/ *noun* **1** [C] a calculation or guess about the future based on information that you have **tasarlama, tasarım, tahmin** *government projections of population growth* **2** [U] when a film or an image is projected onto a screen or wall **yansıma, gösterim, projeksiyon**

projector /prəʊˈdʒektəʳ/ *noun* [C] a machine that projects films, pictures or words onto a screen or a wall **gösterim/yansıtma aygıtı, projektör**

proliferate /prəʊˈlɪfᵊreɪt/ *verb* [I] *formal* to increase in number very quickly **hızla artmak/çoğalmak; birden yığınla artmak**

proliferation /prəʊˌlɪfᵊrˈeɪʃᵊn/ *noun* [U] when something increases in number very quickly **hızlı artış; sürekli çoğalma, beklenmedik meblağa ulaşma** *the proliferation of new TV channels*

prolific /prəʊˈlɪfɪk/ *adjective* producing a lot of something **üretken, verimli, çok çalışkan; hep bir şeyler üreten** *a prolific writer/composer*

prologue /ˈprəʊlɒɡ/ *noun* [C] an introduction to a book, film, or play **önsöz, giriş**

prolong /prəʊˈlɒŋ/ *verb* [T] to make something last longer **ömrünü uzatmak; uzun süre devam ettirmesini sağlamak** *Eating a good diet can prolong your life.*

prolonged /prəʊˈlɒŋd/ *adjective* continuing for a long time **uzun süre devam eden; hep süregelen** *a prolonged illness*

prom /prɒm/ *noun* [C] in the US, a formal dance party for older students held at the end of the school year (**ABD**) yılsonu partisi/eğlencesi *a school prom*

promenade /ˌprɒmə'nɑːd/ *noun* [C] a wide path by the sea deniz kıyısında gezinti yolu

prominence /'prɒmɪnəns/ *noun* [U] when someone or something is important or famous şan, şöhret, ün, nam, şöhretlilik, ünlülük; ön planda olma *He first came to prominence as a singer in the 1980s.*

prominent /'prɒmɪnənt/ *adjective* **1** important or famous önemli, ünlü, meşhur, herkesçe bilinen, topluma malolmuş *a prominent figure* **2** very easy to see or notice göze çarpan, çok kolay görülebilen *a prominent feature* • **prominently** *adverb* önemli ve ünlü olarak

promiscuous /prə'mɪskjuəs/ *adjective* Someone who is promiscuous has sex with a lot of people. önüne gelenle cinsel ilişkiye giren • **promiscuity** /ˌprɒmɪ'skjuːəti/ *noun* [U] when someone is promiscuous önüne gelenle cinsel ilişkiye girme

°ↄ**promise¹** /'prɒmɪs/ *verb* **1** [I, T] to say that you will certainly do something or that something will certainly happen söz vermek, vaatte bulunmak [+ to do sth] *She promised to write to me every week.* ○ [+ (that)] *Paul promised me that he'd cook dinner tonight.* **2** [+ two objects] to say that you will certainly give something to someone vaat etmek, sözünü vermek; ümit vermek *They promised us a reward.* **3** **promise to be sth** If something promises to be good, exciting, etc, people expect that it will be good, exciting, etc. ...olacağını vaat etmek; ...sözünü vermek; heyecan verici/iyi gibi görenmek/olacağa benzemek

promise ...... İLE BİRLİKTE KULLANILAN KELİMELER
break/keep/make/renege on a promise • a broken/rash/solemn/vague promise

°ↄ**promise²** /'prɒmɪs/ *noun* **1** [C] when you say that you will certainly do something söz, vaat, taahhüt *I'm not sure I can do it so I won't make any promises.* **2** **keep/break a promise** to do/not do what you said that you would do sözünü tutmak/tutmamak **3** **show promise** If someone or something shows promise, they are likely to be successful. ümit vaat etmek; başarı/gelecek göstermek *As a child, he showed great promise as an athlete.*

promising /'prɒmɪsɪŋ/ *adjective* likely to be very good or successful in the future ümit veren/verici, geleceği parlak, yetenekli *a promising student* ○ *a promising start to the game*

promo /'prəʊməʊ/ *noun* [C] informal an advertisement, especially a short film reklâm, reklâm filmi

promote /prə'məʊt/ *verb* [T] **1** [ENCOURAGE] to encourage something to happen or develop olmasına/gelişmesine destek vermek; yüreklendirmek; cesaret vermek *to promote good health/peace* **2** [ADVERTISE] to advertise something reklâmını yapmak, tanıtmak *The band is promoting their new album.* **3** [JOB] to give someone a more important job in the same organization terfi ettirmek, yükseltmek; rütbe vermek [often passive] *She's just been promoted to manager.*

promoter /prə'məʊtə'/ *noun* [C] **1** someone who organizes a large event büyük bir eylemi/işi düzenleyen kimse, organizatör *a concert promoter* **2** someone who tries to encourage something to happen or develop bir şeyin olmasını gelişmesine çaba sarfeden/güç veren kimse *a promoter of sexual equality*

promotion ...... İLE BİRLİKTE KULLANILAN KELİMELER
gain/get/be given a promotion • promotion to sth

promotion /prə'məʊʃᵊn/ *noun* **1** [ADVERTISEMENT] [C, U] activities to advertise something reklâm yapma, tanıtma, promosyon; reklâm kampanyası *a sales promotion* ○ *They're giving away free T-shirts as a special promotion.* **2** [JOB] [C, U] when someone is given a more important job in the same organization yükseltme, terfi, yükselme *She was given a promotion in her first month with the company.* **3** [ENCOURAGE] [U, no plural] when you encourage something to happen or develop geliştirme, yükseltme, artırma, promosyon *the promotion of a healthy lifestyle*

promotional /prə'məʊʃᵊnᵊl/ *adjective* Promotional items or activities are used to advertise something. tanıtımla ilgili olan; reklâm yapmaya yönelik eylemlere ilişkin *a promotional campaign*

prompt¹ /prɒmpt/ *verb* [T] **1** to cause something harekete geçirmek; teşvik etmek, zorlamak; ...a/e neden olmak *His remarks prompted a lot of discussion.* **2** **prompt sb to do sth** to cause someone to do sth bir şeyi yapmasına sebep olmak; cesaretlendirmek, teşvik etmek; zorlamak *What prompted him to leave?* **3** to help someone, often an actor, remember what they were going to say or do sufle yapmak; bir oyuncuya söyleyeceklerini/rolünü hatırlatmak

prompt² /prɒmpt/ *adjective* done or acting quickly and without waiting, or arriving at the correct time ivedi, acil, tez, çabuk; vakit geçirmeden yapılan *a prompt reply* ○ *prompt payment* • **promptly** *adverb* çok çabuk bir şekilde

prone /prəʊn/ *adjective* **1** **be prone to sth/doing sth** to often do something or suffer from something, especially something bad bir şeye/bir şeyi yapmaya duyarlı/eğilimli/yatkın olmak; kolay maruz kalabilmek *I'm prone to headaches.* **2** **accident-/injury-, etc prone** often having accidents/injuries, etc kazaya/yaralanmaya maruz kalmak/eğilimli olmak ⊃See also: accident-prone.

°ↄ**pronoun** /'prəʊnaʊn/ *noun* [C] a word that is used instead of a noun which has usually already been talked about. For example the words 'she', 'it', and 'mine' are pronouns. zamir, adıl ⊃See also: personal pronoun, relative pronoun.

pronounce /prə'naʊns/ *verb* [T] **1** to make the sound of a letter or word telâffuz etmek, sesletmek *How do you pronounce his name?* **2** **pronounce sb/sth dead/a success, etc** formal to state that something is true in an official or formal way ilân etmek, resmen açıklamak *Doctors pronounced him dead at 12.23 a.m.*

pronounced /prə'naʊnst/ *adjective* very easy to notice belirgin, belli, açık, bariz, ortada *She spoke with a pronounced American accent.*

pronouncement /prəʊ'naʊnsmənt/ *noun* [C] formal an official announcement resmi, açıklama, karar, hüküm, ilân *to make a pronouncement*

pronunciation /prəˌnʌnsi'eɪʃᵊn/ *noun* [C, U] how words are pronounced telâffuz, sesletim *There are two different pronunciations of this word.*

proof ...... İLE BİRLİKTE KULLANILAN KELİMELER
have/provide proof • conclusive/positive/scientific proof • proof of sth

°ↄ**proof** /pruːf/ *noun* [U] a fact or a piece of information that shows something exists or is true kanıt, delil *She showed us her passport as proof of her identity.* ○ [+ (that)] *My landlord has asked for proof that I'm employed.*

-proof /pruːf/ *suffix* used at the end of words to mean 'protecting against' or 'not damaged by' ...geçirmez/işlemez/...a/e dayanıklı anlamında sonek *a bulletproof vest* ○ *a waterproof jacket*

prop¹ /prɒp/ *verb* **propping,** *past* **propped prop sth against/on,** *etc* to put something somewhere so that it is supported on or against something **dayamak, yaslamak; payanda yapmak** *He propped the ladder against the wall.*
prop sth up *phrasal verb* **1** to lift and give support to something by putting something under it **yaslamak, dayamak** *We had to prop up the bed with some bricks.* **2** to help something to continue **destek vermek; yardım etmek; yardımcı olmak** *For years the industry was propped up by the government.*

prop² /prɒp/ *noun* [C] an object used in a film or play **film ve oyunlarda kullanılan aksesuar** *a stage prop*

propaganda /ˌprɒpə'gændə/ *noun* [U] information or ideas, which are often false, that an organization prints or broadcasts to make people agree with what it is saying **propaganda** *political propaganda* • **propagandist** *noun* [C] someone who creates, prints, or broadcasts propaganda **propagandacı, propaganda yapan kimse**

propagate /'prɒpəgeɪt/ *verb formal* **1** [I, T] If you propagate plants, you help them to produce new plants, and if plants propagate, they produce new plants. **çoğal(t)mak, üre(t)mek; artmak/artırmak 2** [T] to tell your ideas or opinions to a lot of people in order to make them agree with what you are saying **propaganda yapmak, yaymak, nakletmek** *to propagate lies/rumours* • **propagation** /ˌprɒpə'geɪʃ°n/ *noun* [U] *formal* **üretme**

propel /prə'pel/ *verb* [T] **propelling,** *past* **propelled 1** **propel sb into/to sth** to cause someone to do an activity or be in a situation **sürüklemek, itmek, zorla yaptırmak, hareket ettirmek, sevketmek** *The film propelled him to international stardom.* **2** to push or move something somewhere, often with a lot of force **itmek, zorlamak, zorla hareket etmesini sağlamak** *a rocket propelled through space*

propeller /prə'pelə^r/ *noun* [C] a piece of equipment made of two or more flat metal pieces that turn around and cause a ship or aircraft to move **pervane**

propensity /prə'pensəti/ *noun* [C] *formal* If someone has a propensity for something or to do something, they often do it. **doğal eğilim, istek, meyil, temayül** *to have a propensity for violence* ○ *a propensity to talk too much*

propeller

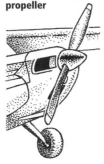

o--**proper** /'prɒpə^r/ *adjective* **1** CORRECT [always before noun] correct or suitable **uygun, doğru, yerinde** *the proper way to do something* ○ *Please put those books back in the proper place.* **2** REAL [always before noun] *mainly UK* real and satisfactory **gerçek ve tatminkâr** *his first proper job* ○ *You should eat some proper food instead of just sweets.* **3** ACCEPTABLE socially acceptable **uygun, yaraşır, hoşagiden, toplumca kabul edilebilen** *It's not proper to interrupt someone when they're speaking.* **4** MAIN [always after noun] referring to the main or most important part of something **ortasında; merkezinde; göbeğinde** *I live outside Cambridge - I don't live in the city proper.*

o--**properly** /'prɒp°li/ *adverb* correctly, or in a satisfactory way **uygun şekilde, gerektiği gibi, doğru olarak, hakkıyla** *She doesn't eat properly.*

,**proper 'noun** *noun* [C] a word or group of words that is the name of a person or place and always begins with a capital letter. For example 'Tony' and 'London' are proper nouns. **özel isim**

┌───┐
│ **property** ...... İLE BİRLİKTE KULLANILAN KELİMELER │
└───┘
private property • property **prices** • a property **developer**

o--**property** /'prɒpəti/ *noun* **1** BUILDING [C, U] a building or area of land **binave arazisi; mülk ve arsası; gayrimenkulu ve sahip olunan arazi** *There are several properties for sale in this area.* ○ *Private property - no parking.* ○ *a property developer* **2** OBJECT [U] objects that belong to someone **mal, mülk** *The police recovered a large amount of stolen property.* **3** QUALITY [C] a quality of something **nitelikler, özellikler** *the medicinal properties of wild plants* ⊃ See also: **lost property.**

the 'property ˌladder *noun* a process in which you buy a small house and then sell it to buy a bigger house when you have more money **mevcut küçük evini satarak daha büyük bir ev alma işlemi** *When house prices are high, it is hard for buyers to* **move up the** *property ladder.*

prophecy /'prɒfəsi/ *noun* [C, U] when someone says that something will happen in the future **kehanet, gaipten haber verme** • **prophesy** /'prɒfəsaɪ/ *verb* [I, T] to say that you believe something will happen in the future **kehanette bulunmak**

prophet /'prɒfɪt/ *noun* [C] someone sent by God to tell people what to do, or to say what will happen in the future **peygamber**

prophetic /prə'fetɪk/ *adjective* saying what will happen in the future **kâhince, kehanet gibi** *a prophetic dream/vision* ○ *Her warnings proved prophetic.*

proponent /prə'pəʊnənt/ *noun* [C] *formal* someone who supports a particular idea or plan of action **taraftar, destekleyici, savunucu** *a proponent of nuclear energy*

proportion /prə'pɔːʃ°n/ *noun* **1** [C] a part of a total number or amount **oran, nispet, miktar** *Children make up a large proportion of the world's population.* ○ *The class consists of both men and women in roughly* **equal proportions. 2 out of proportion** If something is out of proportion, it is much bigger or smaller than it should be, when compared to other things. **gereğinden büyük, abartılı, oran dışı, orantısız; aşırı** *The punishment is completely out of proportion to the crime.* **3 in proportion** If something is in proportion, it is the right size or shape when compared to other things. **oranında, nispetinde, orantılı 4 in proportion to** If something changes in proportion to another thing, it changes to the same degree as that thing. **...a/e oranla/göre/nazaran/kıyasla** *Your tax payment increases in proportion to your salary.* **5 blow/get sth out of proportion** to behave as if something that has happened is much worse than it really is **abartmak, büyütmek, mübalağa etmek**

proportional /prə'pɔːʃ°n°l/ *adjective* If two amounts are proportional, they change at the same rate so that the relationship between them does not change. **orantısal, orantılı** *Weight is proportional to size.*

pro,portional ˌrepresen'tation *noun* [U] a system of voting in which the number of a political party's elected representatives is related to the number of votes the party gets **nispi temsil**

proportionate /prə'pɔ:ʃᵊnət/ *adjective* If two amounts are proportionate, they change at the same rate so that the relationship between them does not change. **orantılı** *His success was proportionate to his efforts.* ⊃Opposite **disproportionate.** • **proportionately** *adverb* **oransal olarak**

proportions /prə'pɔ:ʃᵊnz/ *noun* [plural] the size, shape, or level of something **boyutlar, ölçütler, ebatlar** *Crime has increased to alarming proportions.*

proposal /prə'pəʊzᵊl/ *noun* [C] **1** a suggestion for a plan **öneri, teklif** [+ to do sth] *a proposal to raise taxes* ○ *The proposal for a new sports hall has been rejected.* **2** when someone asks someone to marry them **evlenme teklifi**

propose /prə'pəʊz/ *verb* **1** [T] to suggest a plan or action **önermek, teklif etmek** [+ (that)] *I propose that we delay our decision until we have more information.* ○ *proposed changes* **2 propose to do sth** to intend to do something **niyetinde olmak; niyet etmek, yeltenmek** *They propose to cycle across Europe.* **3** [I] to ask someone to marry you **evlenme teklif etmek** *He proposed to me on my birthday.*

proposition /ˌprɒpə'zɪʃᵊn/ *noun* [C] **1** OFFER an offer or suggestion, usually in business **teklif, öneri** *an attractive/interesting proposition* **2** IDEA an idea or opinion **önerme, sav, iddia** [+ that] *the proposition that all people are created equal* **3** PLAN in the US, a formal plan that people accept or refuse by voting **(ABD)** halk oyuna sunulan resmi plân/öneri

proprietary /prə'praɪətᵊri/ *adjective* [always before noun] *formal* owned or controlled by a company **patentli, tescilli, müseccel**

proprietor /prə'praɪətər/ *noun* [C] *formal* the owner of a business such as a hotel, shop, newspaper, etc **mal sahibi, sahip, iş yeri sahibi**

propriety /prə'praɪəti/ *noun* [U] *formal* socially acceptable behaviour **âdap, yol yordam, adabı muhaşeret; toplumsal kabul gören davranış**

propulsion /prə'pʌlʃᵊn/ *noun* [U] a force that pushes something forward **itici güç, itme kuvveti** *jet propulsion*

prosaic /prəʊ'zeɪk/ *adjective formal* ordinary and not interesting **sıradan, yavan, sıkıcı**

prose /prəʊz/ *noun* [U] ordinary written language that is not poetry **düz yazı, nesir** *He's a wonderful writer - readers love his clear and lively prose.*

prosecute /'prɒsɪkjuːt/ *verb* [I, T] to accuse someone of a crime in a law court **dava etmek/açmak; kovuşturma açmak** *No one has been prosecuted for the murders.*

prosecution /ˌprɒsɪ'kjuːʃᵊn/ *noun* **1 the prosecution** [group] the lawyers who are prosecuting someone in a court of law **iddia makamı; avukatlar** *The prosecution will begin presenting evidence today.* **2** [C, U] when someone is prosecuted **kovuşturma**

prosecutor /'prɒsɪkjuːtər/ *noun* [C] a lawyer who prosecutes people **davacı avukatı; savcı**

⚙ **prospect** ...... İLE BİRLİKTE KULLANILAN KELİMELER

face the prospect of sth • **with** the prospect of sth • **at** the prospect of sth

prospect /'prɒspekt/ *noun* **1** [C, U] the possibility that something good might happen in the future **olasılık, ihtimal, imkân, umut** *Is there any prospect of the weather improving?* **2** [no plural] the idea of something that will happen in the future **olasılık, ihtimal** [+ of + doing sth] *We face the prospect of having to start all over again.* ○ *I'm very excited at the prospect of seeing her again.* **3 sb's prospects** the possibility of being success-

ful at work **mesleğinde başarı şansı; işinde ilerleme olasılığı** *He's hoping the course will improve his career prospects.*

prospective /prə'spektɪv/ *adjective* **prospective buyers/employers/parents, etc** Prospective buyers, employers, parents, etc are not yet buyers, employers, parents, etc but are expected to be in the future. **beklenen, muhtemel, müstakbel alıcı/işçi/ebeveyn vb.**

prospectus /prə'spektəs/ *noun* [C] a book or magazine which gives information about a school, college, or business for future students or customers **broşür, tanıtım kitapçığı, prospektüs**

prosper /'prɒspər/ *verb* [I] to be successful, usually by earning a lot of money **çok para kazanarak başarılı ve zengin olmak; ilerlemek, gelişmek**

prosperity /prɒs'perəti/ *noun* [U] when someone is successful, usually by earning a lot of money **refah, başarı, zenginlik**

prosperous /'prɒspᵊrəs/ *adjective* successful, usually by earning a lot of money **başarılı, zengin, müreffeh, kalkınmış**

prostitute /'prɒstɪtjuːt/ *noun* [C] someone whose job is having sex with people **fahişe, orospu** • **prostitution** /ˌprɒstɪ'tjuːʃᵊn/ *noun* [U] **fuhuş**

prostrate /'prɒstreɪt/ *adjective* lying flat on the ground with your face pointing down **secdeye varmak, yerlere kapanmak**

protagonist /prəʊ'tægᵊnɪst/ *noun* [C] *formal* the main character in a play, film, or story **oyun/film ve hikayedeki baş karakter; (argo) iyi kişi; esas oğlan/kız**

ᵒᚸ **protect** /prə'tekt/ *verb* [I, T] to keep someone or something safe from something dangerous or bad **korumak, kol kanat germek, tehlikelerden uzak tutmak** *It's important to protect your skin from the harmful effects of the sun.* ○ *Vitamin C may help protect against cancer.* • **protection** /prə'tekʃᵊn/ *noun* [U] *This coat doesn't provide any protection against the rain.* **koruma**

protective /prə'tektɪv/ *adjective* **1** giving protection **koruyucu** *protective clothing* ○ *a protective mask* **2** wanting to protect someone from criticism, hurt, danger, etc because you like them **koruyucu, kol kanat geren** *She's fiercely protective of her children.*

protector /prə'tektər/ *noun* [C] someone or something that protects **koruyucu kişi/şey**

protein /'prəʊtiːn/ *noun* [U] food such as meat, cheese, fish, or eggs that is necessary for the body to grow and be strong **protein**

⚙ **protest** ...... İLE BİRLİKTE KULLANILAN KELİMELER

hold/stage a protest • **do** sth **as** a protest • **in** protest **at** sth • a protest **against/over** sth • a protest **by/from** sb

protest¹ /'prəʊtest/ *noun* [C, U] when people show that they disagree with something by standing somewhere, shouting, carrying signs, etc **protesto** *a protest against the war* ○ *a peaceful/violent protest*

protest² /prəʊ'test/ *verb* **1** protest (about/against/at sth) to show that you disagree with something by standing somewhere, shouting, carrying signs, etc **protesto etmek; itiraz etmek, karşı çıkmak** *Students were protesting about cuts to the education budget.* **2 protest sth** US to show that you disagree with something by standing somewhere, shouting, carrying signs, etc **bir şeyi protesto etmek** *Thousands gathered to protest the plan.* **3** [I, T] to say something forcefully or complain about something **kesinlikle iddia etmek; sürekli**

yakınmak/karşı çıkmak [+ that] *The girl was crying, protesting that she didn't want to leave her mother.*

Protestant /ˈprɒtɪstᵊnt/ *adjective* belonging or relating to the part of the Christian religion that separated from the Roman Catholic Church in the 1500s **Protestan** ● **Protestant** *noun* [C] **Protestan** ● **Protestantism** *noun* [U] the beliefs of the Protestant Churches **Protestanlık**

protestation /ˌprɒtesˈteɪʃᵊn/ *noun* [C] *formal* when someone says something forcefully or complains about something **itiraz, karşı çıkma, protesto, protesto etme** *He was arrested despite his protestations of innocence.*

protester (*also* **protestor**) /prəˈtestəʳ/ *noun* [C] someone who shows that they disagree with something by standing somewhere, shouting, carrying signs, etc **protestocu, karşı çıkanlar**

protégé /ˈprɒtəʒeɪ/ *noun* [C] a young person who is helped and taught by an older and usually famous person **hamilik yapılan/korunan/himaye edilen kişi**

protocol /ˈprəʊtəkɒl/ *noun* [C, U] the rules about what you must do and how you must behave in official or very formal situations **protokol, resmî ve ciddî durumlarda uygulanan kurallar** *royal protocol*

proton /ˈprəʊtɒn/ *noun* [C] a part of an atom with a positive electrical charge **proton**

prototype /ˈprəʊtəʊtaɪp/ *noun* [C] the first model or example of something new that can be developed or copied in the future **orijinal model, ilk örnek, prototip** *a prototype for a new car*

protracted /prəˈtræktɪd/ *adjective* If an unpleasant situation is protracted, it lasts a long time. **uzamış, uzayıp giden; (argo) temcit pilavı gibi özenen** *a protracted dispute/struggle*

protrude /prəˈtruːd/ *verb* [I] If something such as a part of the body protrudes, it comes out from the surface more than usual. **çıkıntı yapmak/oluşturmak, dışarı fırlamak, pırtlamak** *protruding ears/teeth*

proud ...... İLE BİRLİKTE KULLANILAN KELİMELER
fiercely/immensely/rightly proud ● **proud of sth/sb**

o⌐**proud** /praʊd/ *adjective* **1** feeling very pleased about something you have done, something you own, or someone you know **gurur duymuş, onurlanmış, kıvanç duymuş, iftihar eden; gururlu** *She was so proud of her son.* ○ [+ to do sth] *I'm very proud to be involved in this project.* **2 be too proud to do sth** to not be able to do something, especially ask for help, because you are too embarrassed **aşırı gururlanmak; gururuna yenik düşmek; gururunu alt edememek; mahcubiyetten yapmamak** *He's too proud to ask you for any money.* **3** feeling that you are more important than you really are **gururlu, kibirli, burnu büyük, mağrur, onurlu**

proudly /ˈpraʊdli/ *adverb* in a way that shows you are pleased about something you have done, something you own, or someone you know **gururla, iftiharla** *He proudly showed us a photo of his grandchildren.*

o⌐**prove** /pruːv/ *verb* [T] *past tense* **proved**, *past participle* **proved** or *mainly US* **proven** **1** to show that something is true **ispat etmek, kanıtlamak** *They knew who had stolen the money, but they couldn't prove it.* ○ [+ (that)] *Can you prove that you weren't there?* ➔Opposite **disprove**. **2 prove sth/to be sth** to show a particular quality after a period of time **çıkmak, anlaşılmak, görünmek/göstermek, bulunmak** *The new treatment has proved to be very effective.* **3 prove yourself** to show that you are good at something **kendini ispat etmek/kanıtlamak** *I wish he'd stop trying to prove himself all the time.*

proven /ˈpruːvᵊn/ *adjective* If something is proven, it has been shown to be true. **kanıtlanmış, ispatlanmış** *proven ability/skills*

proverb /ˈprɒvɜːb/ *noun* [C] a famous phrase or sentence which gives you advice **atasözü** *an ancient Chinese proverb* ● **proverbial** /prəˈvɜːbiəl/ *adjective* relating to a proverb **atasözüne ait; atasözleriyle ilgili**

o⌐**provide** /prəˈvaɪd/ *verb* [T] to supply something to someone **sağlamak, temin etmek, vermek, sunmak** *This booklet provides useful information about local services.* ○ *It's a new scheme to provide schools with free computers.* ● **provider** *noun* [C] someone who provides something **tedarikçi, temin eden kimse** *an Internet service provider*

provide for sb *phrasal verb* to give someone the things they need such as money, food, or clothes **gereksinimlerini/ihtiyaçlarını sağlamak/temin etmek; bakmak** *He has a wife and two young children to provide for.*

provided (that) /prəˈvaɪdɪd/ *conjunction* (*also* **providing (that)**) only if **eğer, yeter ki; ...mak/mek şartıyla** *He's welcome to come along, provided that he behaves himself.*

province /ˈprɒvɪns/ *noun* **1** [C] one of the large areas which some countries are divided into because of the type of government they have **eyalet, bölge** *the Canadian province of Alberta* **2 the provinces** the areas of a country that are not the capital city and so are not considered exciting or fashionable **taşra**

provincial /prəˈvɪnʃᵊl/ *adjective* **1** relating to a province **taşra, taşraya ait 2** relating to or typical of the provinces **taşralı, dar görüşlü, kaba görüşsüz** *a provincial town* ○ *provincial attitudes*

provision /prəˈvɪʒᵊn/ *noun* **1** [U, no plural] when something is provided for someone **sağlama, temin etme, temin, tedarik** *We need to increase the provision of health care for the elderly.* **2 make provision for sth** to make arrangements to deal with something **hazırlıklar/düzenlemeler yapmak; önlemler almak** *He hasn't made any provision for his retirement yet.* **3** [C] a rule that is part of a law or an agreement **madde, koşul, şart, hüküm, kayıt**

provisional /prəˈvɪʒᵊnᵊl/ *adjective* If a situation or arrangement is provisional, it is not certain and might change in the future. **geçici, muvakkat** *These dates are only provisional at the moment.* ● **provisionally** *adverb* **geçici olarak**

provisions /prəˈvɪʒᵊnz/ *noun* [plural] supplies of food and other necessary items **nevale, erzak, yiyecek, kumanya**

proviso /prəˈvaɪzəʊ/ *noun* [C] *formal* something that must happen as part of an agreement **madde, koşul, şart, hüküm, kayıt** *He was released from prison with the proviso that he doesn't leave the country.*

provocation /ˌprɒvəˈkeɪʃᵊn/ *noun* [C, U] when someone makes you angry **kışkırtma, tahrik, kızdırma, provokasyon** *He'll start a fight at the slightest provocation.*

provocative /prəˈvɒkətɪv/ *adjective* **1** causing an angry reaction, usually intentionally **kışkırtıcı, tahrik edici, kızdırıcı** *a provocative question/remark* **2** Provocative clothes, images, etc are sexually exciting. **kışkırtıcı, tahrik edici** ● **provocatively** *adverb* *She dresses very provocatively.* **kışkırtan bir tarzda**

provoke /prəˈvəʊk/ *verb* [T] **1** to cause a strong and usually angry reaction **neden olmak, yol açmak, uyandırmak, sevk etmek** *to provoke an argument* ○ *Her statement has provoked a public outcry.* **2** to intentionally make someone angry so that they react in an angry or violent way **kışkırtmak, tahrik**

P

etmek, kızdırmak, kasıtlı olarak damarına basmak *He claimed he was provoked by the victim.*

prowess /'praʊɪs/ *noun* [U] *formal* when you are good at doing something **olağan üstü yetenek, ustalık, maharet, beceriklilik** *athletic/sporting prowess*

prowl[1] /praʊl/ *verb* [I, T] to walk around somewhere slowly as if hunting someone or something **sinsi sinsi gezinmek, çevreyi kolaçan etmek; sessizce ve sinsizce avlamaya çalışmak** *to prowl the streets*

prowl[2] /praʊl/ *noun* **be on the prowl** to be hunting for someone or something **sinsi sinisi dolaşıyor olmak; etrafı kolaçan ediyor olmak**

proximity /prɒk'sɪməti/ *noun* [U] *formal* when something is near to something else **yakınlık** *What's good about this hotel is its proximity to the airport.*

proxy /'prɒksi/ *noun* **by proxy** using another person to do something instead of doing something yourself **vekâleten, başkasının yerine** *to vote by proxy*

Prozac /'prəʊzæk/ *noun* [U] *trademark* a drug that is used to make people feel happier and less worried **endişe giderici ve mutluluk verici bir ilaç; Prozak** *She's on Prozac because of her depression.*

prude /pruːd/ *noun* [C] someone who does not like to hear or see things relating to sex **namusluluk taslayan kişi, aşırı erdemlilik taslayan kimse** *Don't be such a prude.* ● **prudish** *adjective a prudish woman* **utangaç (cinsel konularda)**

prudent /'pruːdᵊnt/ *adjective formal* wise and careful **basiretli, sağduyulu, erdemli, dikkatli, ağırbaşlı** [+ to do sth] *I think it would be prudent to leave now before it starts raining.* ● **prudence** /'pruːdᵊns/ *noun* [U] *formal* **dikkat, ihtiyat** ● **prudently** *adverb* **ihtiyatlı bir şekilde**

prune[1] /pruːn/ *verb* [T] If you prune a tree or bush, you cut off some of the branches or flowers to help it grow better. **budamak**

prune[2] /pruːn/ *noun* [C] a dried plum (= type of fruit) **erik kurusu; kurutulmuş erik türü meyve**

pry /praɪ/ *verb* **1** [I] to try to discover private things about people **insanların özel yaşamlarını gizlice araştırmak; başkalarının işine gizlice burnunu sokmak** *to pry into someone's personal life.* ○ *She wanted a private holiday away from prying eyes.* **2 pry sth apart/loose/open, etc** to open something with difficulty **zorla açmak/gevşetmek/ayırmak** *She managed to pry open a window and escape.*

PS /ˌpiː'es/ used when you want to add extra information at the end of a letter or email **dipnot, eklenti, sonradan ilave edilen not** *PS Give my love to Emma.*

psalm /sɑːm/ *noun* [C] a song or poem from the Bible (= holy book) **ilahi**

pseudo- /sjuːdəʊ-/ *prefix* false **sözde, uydurma, sahte anlamında önek** *a pseudonym* (= a false name, especially by a writer) ○ *pseudo-academic*

pseudonym /'sjuːdənɪm/ *noun* [C] a name used by a writer instead of their own name **takma ad** *He writes under a pseudonym.*

psych /saɪk/ *verb*
psych yourself up *phrasal verb informal* to try to make yourself feel confident and ready to do something difficult **ruhunu/zihnini hazırlamak**

psyche /'saɪki/ *noun* [C] the human mind and feelings **benlik, zihin ve ruh** *the male psyche*

psychedelic /ˌsaɪkə'delɪk/ *adjective* **1** Psychedelic drugs make you see things that are not really there. **duyu kamçılayan ilaçlar; saykıdelik ilaçlar** **2** Psychedelic colours or patterns are very strong, bright, and strange. **duyuları kışkırtıcı renk ve şekiller**

psychiatrist /saɪ'kaɪətrɪst/ *noun* [C] a doctor who is trained in psychiatry **ruh doktoru; psikiyatr**

psychiatry /saɪ'kaɪətri/ *noun* [U] the study and treatment of mental illness **ruhbilim; psikiyatri** ● **psychiatric** /ˌsaɪki'ætrɪk/ *adjective* relating to psychiatry **ruhbilimi/psikiyatri ile ilgili** *a psychiatric disorder* ○ *a psychiatric nurse*

psychic /'saɪkɪk/ *adjective* having a special mental ability, for example so that you are able to know what will happen in the future or know what people are thinking **gizli güç sahibi, medyum, saykik** *psychic powers*

psycho /'saɪkəʊ/ *noun* [C] *informal* someone who is crazy and frightening **ruh hastası, deli**

psychoanalysis /ˌsaɪkəʊə'næləsɪs/ *noun* [U] the treatment of mental problems by studying and talking about people's dreams, fears, and experiences **ruhi çözümleme; psikanaliz** ● **psychoanalytic** /ˌsaɪkəʊˌænᵊl'ɪtɪk/ *adjective* relating to psychoanalysis **ruhi çözümleme/psikanaliz ile ilgili olan**

psychoanalyst /ˌsaɪkəʊ'ænᵊlɪst/ *noun* [C] someone who treats people using psychoanalysis **psikanalizci**

psychological /ˌsaɪk'ɒdʒɪkᵊl/ *adjective* relating to the human mind and feelings **ruhsal, psikolojik** *psychological problems* ● **psychologically** *adverb* **pisikolojik olarak**

psychologist /saɪ'kɒlədʒɪst/ *noun* [C] someone who has studied the human mind and feelings **ruh bilimci, psikolog**

psychology /saɪ'kɒlədʒi/ *noun* [U] **1** the study of the human mind and feelings **ruhbilim, psikoloji** *child psychology* ○ *He's studying psychology and philosophy.* **2** the way someone thinks and behaves **(kişi) psikoloji** *the psychology of serial killers*

psychopath /'saɪkəʊpæθ/ *noun* [C] someone who is very mentally ill and usually dangerous **ruh hastası, psikopat** ● **psychopathic** /ˌsaɪkəʊ'pæθɪk/ *adjective a psychopathic killer* **pisikopat**

psychosis /saɪ'kəʊsɪs/ *noun* [C] *plural* **psychoses** /saɪ'kəʊsiːz/ a mental illness that makes you believe things that are not real **gerçek olmayan şeylere inanmasına sebep olan ruhsal hastalık, psikoz**

psychotherapy /ˌsaɪkəʊ'θerəpi/ *noun* [U] the treatment of mental problems by talking about your feelings instead of taking medicine **psikoterapi** ● **psychotherapist** *noun* [C] someone who gives people psychotherapy **psikoterapist**

psychotic /saɪ'kɒtɪk/ *adjective* suffering from a mental illness that makes you believe things that are not true **hasta ruhlu, psikotik, psikozlu**

pâté /'pæteɪ/ ⓤ /pæt'eɪ/ *noun* [U] a soft food, usually made of meat or fish, that you spread on bread, etc **ezme, pate** *liver pâté*

pt *noun* [C] **1** *written abbreviation for* point (=a unit used for showing who is winning in a game or competition) **puan sözcüğünün kısa yazılışı** *Hill 81 pts, Villeneuve 68 pts* **2** *written abbreviation for* pint (= a unit for measuring liquid) **sıvı ölçüm birimi pint sözcüğünün kısa yazılışı**

PTO /ˌpiːtiː'əʊ/ *UK abbreviation for* please turn over: used at the bottom of a page of writing to show that there is more information on the other side **Lütfen Sayfayı Çevirin (LSÇ)**

pub /pʌb/ *noun* [C] a place where you can get drinks such as beer and usually food **birahane, meyhane; akşamcı yeri** *We're all going to the pub after work.*

P

puberty /'pjuːbəti/ noun [U] the time when children's bodies change and become like adults' bodies **ergenlik/buluğ çağı** to reach puberty

pubic hair /ˌpjuːbɪk'heə^r/ noun [U] the hair that grows around the sexual organs **kasıktaki kıllar; cinsel organ çevresindeki kıllar**

o╌**public**[1] /'pʌblɪk/ adjective **1 public awareness/health/ support, etc** the awareness/health/support, etc of all ordinary people **halk bilinci/farkındalığı/sağlığı/ desteği vs.** *Public opinion has turned against him.* ○ *Is it really **in the public interest** (= useful for people) to publish this information?* **2 public parks/toilets/ transport, etc** parks/toilets/transport, etc that are for everyone to use and are not private **umumî parklar/ tuvaletler; toplu taşım araçları** *Smoking should be banned in public places.* **3 a public announcement/ appearance/statement, etc** an announcement/appearance/statement, etc that can be seen or heard or known by everyone **umumî ilan/duyuru/görünüm/ açıklama, ifade vs.** *The Prime Minister is due to make a public statement later today.* **4 make sth public** to allow everyone to know about something **açıklamak, umumî efkâra duyurmak; kamuya ilan etmek** *The government does not plan to make its findings public.* **5 public funds/services/spending, etc** funds/services/spending, etc controlled or supplied by the government and not by a private company **kamu fonu/hizmetleri/harcamaları vs.**

o╌**public**[2] /'pʌblɪk/ noun [group] **1 the (general) public** all ordinary people **halk, kamu, umumi efkâr** *a member of the public* ○ *The public has a right to know about this.* ○ *The house is only open to the general public on Sundays.* **2 in public** where everyone can see you **açıkça, alenen, herkesin önünde** *He shouldn't behave like that in public.*

public ad'dress system (*also UK* tannoy) noun [C] a system of equipment used in public places that someone speaks into in order to make their voice loud enough to hear **kamuya açık nutuk çekme sistemi; herkesin dilediğince konuşabileceği umuma açık nutuk**

publication /ˌpʌblɪ'keɪʃ^ən/ noun **1** [U] when a book, newspaper, etc is printed and sold **yayınlama, yayın 2** [C] a book, newspaper, or magazine **yayın, neşriyat** *a monthly/weekly publication*

publicist /'pʌblɪsɪst/ noun [C] someone whose job is to make people know about someone or something by advertising or giving information in the newspaper, on television, etc **tanıtımcı, reklâmcı**

╔══ **publicity** ...... İLE BİRLİKTE KULLANILAN KELİMELER

attract/get/receive/seek publicity ● **adverse/bad/ good/negative** publicity ● publicity **about/for** sth ● publicity **surrounding** sth ● a publicity **campaign/stunt**

publicity /pʌb'lɪsəti/ noun [U] advertising or information about someone or something in the newspaper, on television, etc **tanıtma, reklâm** *a publicity campaign* ○ *to get bad/good publicity*

publicize (*also UK* -ise) /'pʌblɪsaɪz/ verb [T] to make people know about something by advertising or giving information in newspapers, on television, etc **tanıtmak, reklamını yapmak** *a highly/widely publicized event*

publicly /'pʌblɪkli/ adverb If you do something publicly, everyone can see it, hear it, or know about it. **açıkça, alenen**

public re'lations noun [U] *formal* PR (=writing and activities that are intended to make a person, company, or product more popular) **halkla ilişkiler**

public 'school (*US* 'public ˌschool) noun [C] **1** in the UK, a school that you pay to go to **(Birleşik Krallık) ücretli özel okul 2** (*UK* state school) in the US, a school that is free to go to because the government provides the money for it **(ABD) devlet okulu**

the ˌpublic 'sector noun [usually singular] businesses and industries that are owned or controlled by the government **kamu sektörü** *public sector workers*

public 'transport noun [U] a system of vehicles such as buses and trains which operate at regular times and that the public use **toplu taşım araçları**

public u'tility noun [C] an organization that supplies the public with water, gas, or electricity **havagazı/su/ elektrik dağıtım şirketi/kuruluşu**

o╌**publish** /'pʌblɪʃ/ verb [T] **1** PRINT to prepare and print a book, newspaper, magazine, article, etc so that people can buy it **yayımlamak, yayınlamak, basmak** [often passive] *This book is published by Cambridge University Press.* **2** WRITE to write something that is then printed in a book, newspaper, magazine, etc **yayımlatmak, yayınlamak, basmak, bastırmak** *He's published several short stories in national magazines.* **3** MAKE PUBLIC to make information available to the public **açıklamak, yayımlamak, duyurmak**

publisher /'pʌblɪʃə^r/ noun [C] a company or person who prepares and prints books, newspapers, magazines, etc **yayıncı**

publishing /'pʌblɪʃɪŋ/ noun [U] the business of preparing and printing books, newspapers, magazines, etc **yayımcılık, yayıncılık** *a career in publishing*

puck /pʌk/ noun [C] in ice hockey (= a sport), a small, hard disc that players hit with a stick **buz hokeyi diski/topu** ⊃Orta kısımdaki renkli sayfalarına bakınız.

pudding /'pʊdɪŋ/ noun **1** [C, U] in the UK, a sweet dish that is usually eaten as the last part of a meal **puding** *We've got apple pie for pudding.* **2** [U] in the US, a soft, sweet food made from milk, sugar, eggs, and sometimes flour **tatlı, puding** *chocolate/vanilla pudding*

puddle /'pʌdl/ noun [C] a pool of liquid on the ground, usually from rain **gölcük, su birikintisi**

puerile /'pjʊəraɪl/ Ⓤ /'pjuːərɪl/ adjective formal behaving in a silly way like a child **çocukça davranan, çocuksu; aptalca davranan**

puff[1] /pʌf/ verb **1** [I] to breathe fast and with difficulty, usually because you have been doing exercise **solumak, soluk soluğa kalmak, nefesi kesilmek 2** [I, T] to smoke something **içmek, tüttürmek** *to puff on a cigarette*

puff sth out phrasal verb to make your chest or your face become bigger by filling them with air **şişirmek, kabartmak; avurtlarını hava ile doldurup şişirmek**

puff up phrasal verb If part of your body puffs up, it becomes larger because it is infected or injured. **şişmek, apse yapmak, kabarmak**

puff[2] /pʌf/ noun [C] **1** a small amount of smoke, gas, powder, etc **az, biraz gaz/pudra/duman miktarı; esinti, püfürtü** *a puff of smoke/air* **2** when someone breathes in smoke from a cigarette **bir nefes** *to take a puff on a cigarette*

puffin /'pʌfɪn/ noun [C] a black and white sea bird with a large head and brightly coloured beak **büyük kafalı parlak gagalı siyah beyaz bir tür kuş, pafin**

puffy /'pʌfi/ adjective If the skin around your eyes is puffy, it is slightly swollen. **şişkin, kabarık** *His eyes were still puffy with sleep.*

puke

puke /pjuːk/ (*also* puke up) *verb* [I, T] *informal* to vomit **kusmak**

pull

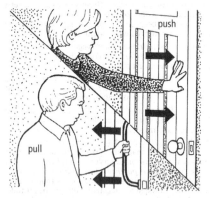

o͞=**pull¹** /pʊl/ *verb* **1** [I, T] to take hold of something and move it somewhere **çekmek** *If you keep pulling his tail, he'll bite you.* ○ *No wonder it's not working, someone's pulled the plug out.* ○ *He pulled off his boots.* ○ *She bent down and pulled up her socks.* **2 pull a muscle** to injure a muscle by stretching it too much **kaslarını incitmek 3 pull a gun/knife, etc on sb** to suddenly take out a weapon **silah çekmek** *He pulled a gun on us and demanded money.* ⊃See also: pull/tear your hair out, pull the plug¹, not pull any punches (punch²), pull out all the stops (stop²), pull strings (string¹), pull your weight.

pull sth apart *phrasal verb* **1** to destroy something by tearing it into pieces **yırtmak, param parça etmek 2** to say that something, usually a piece of work, is very bad **kötülemek, çamur atmak**

pull sb/sth apart *phrasal verb* to separate two things or people **iki şeyi ayırmak**

pull at sth *phrasal verb* to pull something several times, usually with quick, light movements **çekiştirmek, çekip durmak** *Stop pulling at my sleeve.*

pull away *phrasal verb* **1** If a vehicle pulls away, it starts moving. **hareket etmek** *I just managed to get on the bus before it pulled away.* **2** If you pull away from someone who is holding you, you suddenly move your body backwards, away from them. **kendini geri çekmek; elinden kurtulmak**

pull sth down *phrasal verb* to destroy a building because it is not wanted any more. **yıkmak, yerle bir etmek** *They've started pulling down the old cinema.*

pull in/into sth *phrasal verb* If a vehicle pulls in or pulls into somewhere, it moves in that direction and stops there. **yanaşıp/girip durmak** *They pulled in at the side of the road.*

pull sth off *phrasal verb* to succeed in doing or achieving something difficult **başarmak, üstesinden gelmek, halletmek, içinden çıkmak** *He is about to pull off his biggest deal yet.*

pull off *phrasal verb* UK If a vehicle pulls off, it starts moving. **hareket etmek** *The car pulled off and sped up the road.*

pull on sth *phrasal verb* to put on clothes quickly **çabucak giymek; üstüne bir şeyler almak** *I pulled on my jeans and ran downstairs.*

pull out *phrasal verb* If a vehicle pulls out, it starts moving onto a road or onto a different part of the road. **hareket etmek, ayrılmak** *That car pulled out right in front of me.*

pull over *phrasal verb* If a vehicle pulls over, it moves to the side of the road and stops. **kenara çekip durmak**

pull through *phrasal verb* to continue to live after you have been badly injured or very ill **iyileşmek, sağlığına kavuşmak**

pull yourself together *phrasal verb informal* to become calm and behave normally again after being angry or upset **toplamak, toparlanmak; sakinleşmek; kendine gelmek**

pull up *phrasal verb* **1** If a vehicle pulls up, it stops, often for a short time. **kısa bir süre durmak** *A car pulled up outside the bank and two men got out.* **2 pull up a chair** to move a chair nearer to something or someone *Why don't you pull up a chair and join us?*

pull² /pʊl/ *noun* [no plural] a strong force that causes something to move somewhere or be attracted to something **çekme, çekiş**

pull-down /ˈpʊldaʊn/ *adjective* [always before noun] A pull-down menu is a list of choices on a computer screen which is hidden until you choose to look at it. **istenince ortaya çıkan bilgisayar ekranında gizlenmiş seçenekler menüsü**

pulley /ˈpʊli/ *noun* [C] a wheel with a rope going round it which is used to lift things **makara, palanga**

pulley

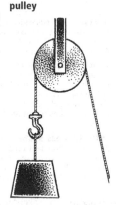

pullover /ˈpʊləʊvəʳ/ *noun* [C] a warm piece of clothing which covers the top of your body and is pulled on over your head **süveter, kazak** *a black woolly pullover*

pulp /pʌlp/ *noun* [U] **1** a soft, wet substance made from wood, which is used to make paper **kâğıt hamuru 2** the soft part inside a fruit or vegetable **meyvenin etli kısmı**

pulpit /ˈpʊlpɪt/ *noun* [C] the raised structure in a church where the priest stands when he or she speaks to everyone **(kilise) kürsü**

pulsate /pʌlˈseɪt/ ⑮ /ˈpʌlseɪt/ *verb* [I] to beat or move with a strong, regular rhythm **atmak, çarpmak** *The whole room was pulsating with music.*

pulse /pʌls/ *noun* [C] the regular movement of blood through your body when your heart is beating **nabız, nabız atışı** *She put her fingers on my wrist to take my pulse* (= count the number of beats per minute). ○ *My pulse rate is 70.*

pulses /pʌlsɪz/ *noun* [plural] UK seeds such as beans or peas which are cooked and eaten as food **bakliyat**

pump¹ /pʌmp/ *noun* [C] a piece of equipment which forces liquid or gas to move somewhere **pompa** *a gas/petrol pump* ○ *a water pump*

pump² /pʌmp/ *verb* [T] to force liquid or gas to move somewhere **pompalamak** *Your heart pumps blood around your body.* ○ *Firemen used powerful hoses to pump water into the building.*

pump sth into sth *phrasal verb* to give a lot of money to a plan or organization **çok fazla para yardımı yapmak, akıtmak, dökmek, sarfetmek** *They've pumped millions of pounds into the economy.*

pump

bicycle pump

petrol pump *UK*,
gas pump *US*

pump sth out *phrasal verb informal* to continuously produce a lot of something **sürekli üretmek; yağdırmak, akıtmak** *a radio pumping out music*
pump sth up *phrasal verb* to fill something with air using a pump **şişirmek, havayla doldurmak** *You should pump your tyres up.*

pumpkin /'pʌmpkɪn/ *noun* [C, U] a large, round vegetable with thick, orange skin **kabak, balkabağı**

pun /pʌn/ *noun* [C] a joke that you make by using a word that has two meanings **cinas, kelime oyunu**

punch¹ /pʌnʃ/ *verb* [T] **1** to hit someone or something with your fist (= closed hand) **yumruklamak, yumrukla vurmak, yumruk atmak** *He punched me twice in the stomach.* **2 punch a hole in sth** to make a hole in something with a special piece of equipment **bir aletle delik açmak**

╔══ **punch** ...... İLE BİRLİKTE KULLANILAN KELİMELER ══╗
aim a punch at sb • deliver/land/swing/throw a punch

punch² /pʌnʃ/ *noun* **1** [HIT] [C] when you hit someone or something with your fist (= closed hand) **yumruklama, yumruk atma** *a punch on the nose* **2** [DRINK] [U] a sweet, mixed drink made from fruit juice, spices, and usually alcohol **bir tür meyveli kokteyl** **3** [HOLE] [C] a piece of equipment that makes a hole in something **zımba, delik açma aleti, kopça aleti** **4 not pull any punches** to speak in an honest way without trying to be kind **açık sözlü olmak; dobra dobra konuşmak; lafını esirgememek; lafı eveleyip gevelemek**

punchline /'pʌntʃlaɪn/ *noun* [C] the last part of a joke that makes it funny **fıkraların en sonunda gülmeyi/düşünmeyi sağlayan en önemli bölüm**

punch-up /'pʌntʃʌp/ *noun* [C] *UK informal* a fight in which people hit each other with their fists (= closed hands) **yumruklaşma, kavga**

punctual /'pʌŋktʃuəl/ *adjective* arriving at the right time and not too late **dakik** • **punctuality** /ˌpʌŋktʃu'ælɪti/ *noun* [U] when you are punctual **dakiklik** • **punctually** *adverb* **dakik bir şekilde**

punctuate /'pʌŋktʃueɪt/ *verb* [T] to add punctuation marks to written words so that people can see when a sentence begins and finishes, that something is a question, etc **noktalama işaretlerini koymak**

punctuation /ˌpʌŋktʃu'eɪʃ°n/ *noun* [U] the use of punctuation marks in writing so that people can see when a sentence begins and finishes, that something is a ques-

tion, etc **noktalama, noktalama işaretleri** ↪See study page **Punctuation** on page Centre 33.

punctu'ation ˌmark *noun* [C] a symbol such as a full stop (.) or a question mark (?) used in writing to show where a sentence begins and finishes, etc. **noktalama işareti**

puncture¹ /'pʌŋktʃəʳ/ *noun* [C] **1** a small hole made by a sharp object **patlak, delik** **2** *UK* a hole in a tyre that makes the air come out **patlak lastik, lastikte delik** *to have a puncture*

puncture² /'pʌŋktʃəʳ/ *verb* [T] to make a hole in something **patlatmak, delmek** *The knife went through his ribs and punctured his lung.*

pundit /'pʌndɪt/ *noun* [C] someone who is an expert in a subject and often gives their opinions on television, radio, etc **bilgin, âlim, üstat** *a political pundit*

pungent /'pʌndʒ°nt/ *adjective* A pungent smell is very strong. **keskin koku, kötü koku** *the pungent smell of vinegar*

o⋆**punish** /'pʌnɪʃ/ *verb* [T] to make someone suffer because they have done something bad **cezalandırmak, ceza vermek** [often passive] *They must be severely punished for these crimes.*

punishable /'pʌnɪʃəbl/ *adjective* A crime that is punishable is one that you can be punished for. **cezalandırılabilir, cezayı hak eden** *Drug dealing is punishable by death in some countries.*

punishing /'pʌnɪʃɪŋ/ *adjective* very difficult and making you tired **yorucu, zor, çetin** *a punishing schedule*

╔══ **punishment** ...... İLE BİRLİKTE KULLANILAN KELİMELER ══╗
capital/corporal punishment • an appropriate/
cruel/harsh/severe punishment • deserve/
escape/impose/inflict/receive punishment

o⋆**punishment** /'pʌnɪʃmənt/ *noun* [C, U] when someone is punished **ceza, cezalandırma** *He had to stay in his bedroom as a punishment for fighting.* ↪See also: **capital punishment, corporal punishment,** be a **glutton** for punishment.

punitive /'pjuːnətɪv/ *adjective formal* given as a punishment or seeming like a punishment **cezalandırıcı, ceza mahiyetinde** *punitive action*

punk /pʌŋk/ *noun* **1** [STYLE] [U] (*also* ˌpunk 'rock) a style of music and fashion in the 1970s which was wild, loud, and violent **1970'lerin müziği, pank, pank müziği** **2** [PERSON] [C] someone who wears punk clothes and likes punk music **pank, pankçı** **3** [BAD MAN] [C] *US informal* a bad young man **kötü genç adam**

punt¹ /pʌnt/ *noun* [C] **1** a long boat with a flat bottom that you push along the river with a long pole **sırık ile yürütülen altı düz sandal** **2** in some sports, a powerful kick which causes the ball to go very far **bazı sporlarda topa hızlı vuruş**

punt² /pʌnt/ *verb* **1** [I, T] to go or take someone along a river in a punt **sandalla gitmek, götürmek** **2** [T] in some sports, to kick a ball after you have dropped it from your hands and before it touches the ground **topa yere düşmeden vurmak**

punter /'pʌntəʳ/ *noun* [C] *UK informal* someone who is buying something or making a bet (= risking money on a competition) **bahisçi, bahis oynayan kimse**

puny /'pjuːni/ *adjective* very small and weak **zayıf, çelimsiz, ufak tefek**

pup /pʌp/ *noun* [C] a young dog or other particular type of baby mammal **köpek yavrusu, enik, encik; yavru** *a seal pup*

pupil /'pjuːp°l/ *noun* [C] **1** a student at school **öğrenci** *The school has 1,100 pupils aged 11 to 18.* ↪Orta kısımdaki

P

renkli sayfalarına bakınız. **2** the black, round part in the centre of your eye **gözbebeği**

puppet /'pʌpɪt/ *noun* [C] **1** a toy in the shape of a person or animal that you can move with strings or by putting your hand inside **kukla** *a glove puppet* **2** someone who is controlled by someone else **başkaları tarafından kullanılan/kontrol edilen kimse, kukla** *a political puppet*

puppy /'pʌpi/ *noun* [C] a young dog **köpek yavrusu, enik, encik** *a litter of puppies*

purchase¹ /'pɜːtʃəs/ *verb* [T] *formal* to buy something **satın almak** *Tickets must be purchased two weeks in advance.*

purchase² /'pɜːtʃəs/ *noun formal* **1** [C, U] when you buy something **satın alma** *the illegal purchase of guns* **2** [C] something that you buy **satın alınan şey** *a major purchase*

☞**pure** /pjʊəʳ/ *adjective* **1** NOT MIXED A pure substance is not mixed with anything else. **saf, halis, has** *pure gold* ○ *pure wool* **2** EMPHASIS [always before noun] used to emphasize that a feeling, quality, or state is completely and only that thing **(duygu, kalite, durum) saf, katıksız, tertemiz, katkısız** *pure coincidence* ○ *Her face had a look of pure delight.* **3** CLEAN clean and healthy **temiz ve sağlıklı, duru, net** *pure air/water* **4 pure mathematics/physics, etc** the study of mathematics/physics, etc based only on ideas and not on practical use **kuramsal/teorik/nazarî matematik/fizik 5** GOOD completely good and not having any bad qualities or bad morals **tertemiz, saf, masum, lekesiz**

puree /'pjʊəreɪ/ ⓤ /pjʊə'reɪ/ *noun* [U] a thick, smooth, liquid food made by crushing and mixing fruit or vegetables **püre, ezme** *tomato puree*

purely /'pjʊəli/ *adverb* only **tamamen, sadece, tümüyle** *She married him purely for his money.*

purgatory /'pɜːgətᵊri/ *noun* [U] **1** in the Catholic religion, a very unpleasant place where you have to go and suffer before you go to heaven **Araf 2** a very unpleasant situation **cehennem, cehennem azabı, ıstırap** *This diet is purgatory.*

purge /pɜːdʒ/ *verb* [T] **1** to get rid of bad feelings that you do not want **tasfiye etmek, ayıklamak, temizlemek** [often reflexive] *She wanted to purge herself of guilt.* **2** to get rid of people from an organization because you do not agree with them **istenmeyen kişileri ayıklamak/çıkarmak; kurtulmak ● purge** *noun* [C] **istenmedik duygulardan arınma**

purify /'pjʊərɪfaɪ/ *verb* [T] to remove bad substances from something to make it pure **arıtmak, temizlemek, tasfiye etmek** *Plants help to purify the air.* ○ *purified water* ● **purification** /ˌpjʊərɪfɪ'keɪʃᵊn/ *noun* [U] **saflaştırma**

purist /'pjʊərɪst/ *noun* [C] someone who believes in and follows very traditional rules or ideas in a subject **fikirleri ve geleneksel kuralları harfiyen uygulayan/takip eden kimse**

puritanical /ˌpjʊərɪ'tænɪkᵊl/ *adjective* having severe religious morals and not wanting people to enjoy themselves **katı din kuralcı; aşırı tutucu; ahlaki değerlerden ödün vermeyen ● puritan** /'pjʊərɪtᵊn/ *noun* [C] a puritanical person **katı ahlak/din kuralcısı**

purity /'pjʊərəti/ *noun* [U] the quality of being pure **saflık, halislik, temizlik, katıksızlık** *air purity*

purple /'pɜːpl/ *adjective* being a colour that is a mixture of red and blue **mor** *purple pansies* ● **purple** *noun* [C, U] **mor** ➋Orta kısımdaki renkli sayfalarına bakınız.

purport /pə'pɔːt/ *verb*
purport to be/do sth *phrasal verb formal* to pretend to be or do something *...mış/miş gibi olmak/yapmak a man purporting to be a police officer*

defeat/have/fulfil/serve a purpose ● a **clear/good/primary/practical/useful** purpose ● the purpose **of** sth

☞**purpose** /'pɜːpəs/ *noun* **1** [C] why you do something or why something exists **neden, sebep, amaç, niyet** *The main purpose of the meeting is to discuss the future of the company.* ○ *The drug may be legalized for medical purposes.* **2** [U] the feeling of knowing what you want to do **amaç, maksat, gaye** *He seems to have lost all sense of purpose.* **3 on purpose** intentionally **kasten, bilerek, isteyerek, bile bile, mahsus** *I didn't do it on purpose, it was an accident.* **4 serve a purpose** to have a use **yararı olmak, işe yaramak; bir amacı olmak** *These small village shops serve a very useful purpose.* ➌See also: **cross purposes, to/for all intents (intent¹) (and purposes).**

purpose-built /ˌpɜːpəs'bɪlt/ *adjective mainly UK* A purpose-built building has been specially designed for the way it will be used. **belli bir amaç için inşa edilmiş; amaca uygun**

purposeful /'pɜːpəsfᵊl/ *adjective* showing that you know what you want to do **kararlı, azimli** *He has a quiet, purposeful air.* ● **purposefully** *adverb* **amaçlı**

purposely /'pɜːpəsli/ *adverb* intentionally **bile bile, kasten, bilerek** *I wasn't purposely trying to hurt you.*

purr /pɜːʳ/ *verb* [I] **1** CAT If a cat purrs, it makes a soft sound in its throat to show pleasure. **(kedi) mırlamak, mırıldamak 2** PERSON to talk in a soft, low voice **mırıldanmak, alçak ve yumuşak bir ses tonuyla konuşmak 3** CAR If a car purrs, its engine is very smooth and makes a soft sound. **(motor) vınlamak, düzenli/saat gibi çalışmak**

purse¹ /pɜːs/ *noun* [C] **1** *UK* a small container for money, usually used by a woman **para çantası, cüzdan** *a leather purse* **2** *mainly US* (*mainly UK* **handbag**) a bag, usually carried by a woman **bayan çantası, el çantası** *I always carry aspirin in my purse.*

purse² /pɜːs/ *verb* **purse your lips** to press your lips tightly together, often to show that you are angry **dudaklarını büzmek, bükmek; kızgınlıktan dudaklarını ısırmak**

pursue /pə'sjuː/ ⓤ /pər'suː/ *verb* [T] **pursuing,** *past* **pursued 1** If you pursue a plan, activity, or situation, you try to do it or achieve it, usually over a long period of time. **elde etmeye çalışmak, kovalamak** *She decided to pursue a career in television.* **2** to follow someone or something, usually to try to catch them **kovalamak, peşinden koşmak, takip etmek** *The car was pursued by helicopters.* **3 pursue a matter** to try to discover information about something **incelemek, araştırmak, bilgi toplamaya çalışmak** *We will not be pursuing this matter any further.*

pursuit /pə'sjuːt/ ⓤ /pər'suːt/ *noun* [U] **1** when you try to achieve a plan, activity, or situation, usually over a long period of time **vazgeçmeme, başarmaya çalışma, uzun süre başarmaya çalışma** *the pursuit of pleasure* ○ *He left his native country in pursuit of freedom.* **2** when you follow someone or something to try to catch them **peşinden koşmak, peşini bırakmama, elde etmeye çalışma** *The police are in pursuit of a 25-year-old murder suspect.*

pursuits /pə'sjuːts/ ⓤ /pər'suːts/ *noun* [plural] *formal* activities or hobbies **hobi ve etkinlikler** *He enjoys climbing and other outdoor pursuits.*

purveyor /pə'veɪəʳ/ *noun* [C] *formal* someone who sells or provides something **satıcı, tedarikçi** *a purveyor of antiques*

pus /pʌs/ *noun* [U] a yellow substance that is produced when part of your body is infected **irin, cerahat**

⚬**push**¹ /pʊʃ/ *verb* 1 [MOVE SOMETHING] [I, T] to move someone or something by pressing them with your hands or body **itmek** *She pushed the books aside and sat down on my desk.* ○ *We pushed the children down the slide.* ○ *He pushed me violently out of the door.* ○ *Someone pushed him into the river.* ⊃See picture at pull. 2 [MOVE YOURSELF] [I, T] to move somewhere by moving someone or something away from you **ite kaka ilerlemek, ite kaka yol açmak** *He pushed past me.* ○ *He pushed his way to the front of the crowd.* 3 [PRESS] [T] to press something **basmak, üzerine baskı uygulamak** *If you push this button, your seat goes back.* 4 **push (sb) for sth/to do sth** to try hard to achieve something or to make someone else do something **başarmaya çalışmak; zorla yaptırmak** *Local residents are pushing for the road to be made safer.* 5 [ENCOURAGE] [T] to try to make someone do something that they do not want to do **zorlamak, mecbur etmek, sıkıştırmak** [+ into + doing sth] *My mother pushed me into having ballet lessons.* 6 **push yourself** to make yourself work very hard to achieve something **kendini zorlamak, çok sıkı çalışmak** ⊃See also: push the **boat** out.

push sb about/around *phrasal verb* to tell someone what to do in a rude way **çok kaba bir şekilde emretmek, ne yapacağını söylemek** *I'm fed up with being pushed around.*

push ahead/forward *phrasal verb* to continue doing something, especially when this is difficult **bir şeyi yapmaya devam etmek; zor bir şeyi yapmayı sürdürmek** *They have decided to **push ahead with** legal action.*

push sth/sb aside *phrasal verb* to decide to forget about or ignore something or someone **birini birşeyi unutmaya/aklından çıkarmaya karar vermek; görmezden gelmek** *We can't just push these problems aside - we have to deal with them.*

push in *phrasal verb UK informal* to rudely join a line of people who are waiting for something by moving in front of some of the people who are already there **zorla sıradan araya girmek; kuyrukta araya girmek**

push on *phrasal verb* to continue doing something, especially when this is difficult **zorluğuna rağmen yapmaya devam etmek, vazgeçmemek**

push sb/sth over *phrasal verb* to push someone or something so that they fall to the ground **itip düşürmek**

push sth through *phrasal verb* to make a plan or suggestion be officially accepted **resmen kabul edilmesi için öneri getirmek/plan yapmak; kabul ettirmek, kabule zorlamak** *We're trying to push this deal through as quickly as possible.*

push sth up *phrasal verb* to increase the amount, number, or value of something **artırmak, çoğaltmak** *If you want to travel on Saturday, it will push the price up a bit.*

push² /pʊʃ/ *noun* 1 **a push for sth/to do sth** a big effort to achieve something or make someone do something **başarmak için itici güç/büyük çaba; yaptırmak; yapmaya zorlamak** *a push for higher standards in education* 2 [C] when you move someone or something by pressing them with your hands or body **itiş, kakış, itme, itekleme** [usually singular] *She gave him a little push towards the door.* 3 **give sb the push** *UK informal* to get rid of someone from a job or relationship **birini uzaklaştırmak; işten çıkarmak/atmak, yol vermek; (argo) sepetlemek** 4 [C] encouragement to make someone do something **yüreklendirme, cesaretlendirme, itme** [usually singular] *I'm sure he'll go, he just*

needs a little push that's all. 5 **at a push** *UK* If you can do something at a push, you can do it but it will be difficult. **gerekirse, zorda kalırsak; zorda olsa** 6 **if/when push comes to shove** *informal* If you say that something can be done if push comes to shove, you mean that it can be done if the situation becomes so bad that you have to do it. **bıçak kemiğe dayanırsa, zorda kalırsak; mecburiyet hasıl olursa** *If push comes to shove, we'll just have to sell the car.*

pushchair /'pʊʃtʃeəʳ/ *UK* (*US* **stroller**) *noun* [C] a chair on wheels which is used to move small children **puset, çocuk arabası**

pushed /pʊʃt/ *adjective UK informal* **be pushed for sth** to not have much of something **...sı/sı yok; ...ca/ce sıkıntıda; kıt, dar, sıkıntıda** *I can't stop, I'm a bit pushed for time.*

pusher /'pʊʃəʳ/ *noun* [C] someone who sells illegal drugs **uyuşturucu satıcısı**

push-up /'pʊʃʌp/ *US* (*UK* **press-up**) *noun* [C] a physical exercise in which you lie facing the floor and use your hands to push your body up **şınav** *I did forty push-ups yesterday.*

pushy /'pʊʃi/ *adjective* behaving in an unpleasant way by trying too much to get something or to make someone do something **elde etmek için her yolu deneyen, ısrarcı, girişken** *a pushy salesman*

⚬**put** /pʊt/ *verb* [T] **putting**, *past* **put** 1 **put sth down/in/on, etc** to move something to a place or position **koymak, yerleştirmek** *Where have you put the keys?* ○ *She put her bag on the floor.* ○ *You can put your coat in the car.* ○ *He put his arm around her.* 2 **put sb in a mood/position, etc** to cause someone or something to be in a particular situation **sokmak, koymak, düşürmek, yapmak** *They'd had an argument and it had put her in a bad mood.* ○ *This puts me in a very difficult position.* 3 to say something using particular words **belli kelimelerle söylemek** *I don't know quite how to put this, but I'm leaving.* 4 to write something **yazmak, kaleme almak** *Please put your name on the list by Monday evening.*

put sth across *phrasal verb* to explain or express something clearly so that people understand it easily **açılamak, ifade etmek**

put sth aside *phrasal verb* to save something so that you can use it later **saklamak, biriktirmek, kötü günler için saklamak, bir kenara koymak** *I've been putting a bit of money aside every month.*

put sth away *phrasal verb* to put something in the place where you usually keep it **her zamanki yerine koymak** *She folded the towels and put them away in the cupboard.* ⊃Orta kısımdaki renkli sayfalarına bakınız.

put sth back *phrasal verb* to put something where it was before it was moved **eski yerine koymak, yerleştirmek** *I put the book back on the shelf.*

put sth down *phrasal verb* 1 [STOP HOLDING] to put something that you are holding onto the floor or onto another surface **yere koymak, yere bırakmak** *I'll just put my bag down for a minute, it's rather heavy.* ⊃Orta kısımdaki renkli sayfalarına bakınız. 2 [TELEPHONE] *UK* If you put the phone down, you put the part of the telephone that you speak into back to its usual position. **telefonu yerine koymak; konuşmayı bitirmek** 3 [ANIMAL] to kill an animal, usually because it is suffering **itlaf etmek, ölmek üzere olan bir hayvanı öldürmek; can çekişen hayvanın fazla acı çekmesi için öldürmek**

put sb down *phrasal verb* 1 to make someone feel stupid or unimportant by criticizing them **küçük düşürmek, aşağılamak, alenen tenkit etmek** *I'm tired of him putting me down all the time.* 2 to write someone's name on a list or document, usually in order to arrange for them to do something **ismini listeye kaydetmek/**

P

yazmak *I've **put** you **down** for the trip to Rome next week.*

put sth down to sth *phrasal verb UK* to think that a problem or situation is caused by a particular thing **bir şeye yormak, bir neden yüklemek**

put sth forward *phrasal verb* to state an idea or opinion, or to suggest a plan, so that it can be considered or discussed **bir düşünceyi fikri ifade etmek; öneride bulunmak**

put sb/sth in sth *phrasal verb* to arrange for someone or something to go somewhere **gidişi ayarlamak/düzenlemek; koymak** *to put someone in prison* ○ *to put some money in the bank* ○ *I'd never put my mother in an old people's home.*

put sth in *phrasal verb* to fix something into a room or building **koymak, yerleştirmek, sabitlemek** *I've just had a new kitchen put in.*

put sth into sth/doing sth *phrasal verb* If you put time, work, or effort into something, you spend a lot of time or effort doing it. **zaman/çaba/emek harcamak, sarfetmek** *We've put a lot of effort into this project and we want it to succeed.*

put sth off *phrasal verb* to decide or arrange to do something at a later time **ertelemek, başka bir zaman bırakmak, tehir etmek** *I must talk to her about this, I can't put it off any longer.*

put sb off (sth) *phrasal verb* to make someone not like someone or something, or not want to do something **soğutmak, tiksindirmek, nefret ettirmek** *Jan was talking about her operation and it put me off my food.*

put sth on *phrasal verb* **1** CLOTHES to put clothes or shoes onto your body **giymek, giyinmek** *You'd better put your coat on, it's cold outside.* ⊃Orta kısımdaki renkli sayfalarına bakınız. **2** EQUIPMENT *mainly UK* to make a piece of equipment work by pressing a switch **çalıştırmak, açmak, düğmesine basmak** *Can you put the light on please?* **3** BEHAVIOUR to pretend to have a particular feeling, or to behave in a way which is not real or natural for you (tavır) takınmak; ...mış/miş gibi davranmak *He's not really upset, he's just putting it on.* **4** MUSIC/FILM to put a CD or other recording into a machine so that you can see or hear it **CD ve benzeri şey çalmak** *Why don't you put on some music?* **5 put on weight** *UK* to become fatter and heavier

put sth out *phrasal verb* **1** STOP SHINING *mainly UK* to make a light stop shining by pressing a switch **ışığı söndürmek, kapamak** *Please put the lights out when you leave.* **2** STOP BURNING to make something that is burning stop burning **ateşi söndürmek** *to put out a fire* **3** PUT OUTSIDE to put something outside the house **dışarı koymak; evin dışına çıkarmak** *to put out the rubbish/trash*

put sb out *phrasal verb* to cause trouble or extra work for someone **zahmet vermek, zora sokmak** *It would be great if you could help, but I don't want to put you out.*

be put out *phrasal verb* to be annoyed, often because of something that someone has done or said to you **üzülmek, canı sıkılmak; üzmek, canını sıkmak** *He seemed a bit **put out** at not having been invited.*

put sb through sth *phrasal verb* to make someone experience or do something unpleasant or difficult ... **a/e altına sokmak/uğratmak** *Why did they put themselves through this ordeal?*

put sb through *phrasal verb* to connect someone using a telephone to the person they want to speak to **telefonu birine irtibatlamak** *Can you put me through to customer services, please?*

put sth to sb *phrasal verb* **1** to suggest an idea or plan to someone so that they can consider it or discuss it **öne sürmek, önermek 2** to ask someone a question **soru sormak** *to put a question to someone*

put sth together *phrasal verb* **1** to put the parts of something into the correct place and join them to each

other **kurmak, bir araya getirmek, oluşturmak, monte etmek** *You buy it in a kit and then put it together yourself.* **2** to prepare a piece of work by collecting several ideas and suggestions and organizing them **düzenlemek, hazırlamak, yapmak** *to put together a plan/proposal*

put sth up *phrasal verb* **1** BUILD to build something **kurmak, inşa etmek, yapmak** *to put up a tent* ○ *We spent the weekend putting up a fence in the backyard.* **2** FASTEN to fasten something to a wall or ceiling **duvara veya tavana tutturmak/çakmak/monte etmek/asmak** *to put up shelves* ○ *I need to put up some curtains in the back bedroom.* **3** INCREASE *mainly UK* to increase the price or value of something **değerini/fiyatını artırmak/yükseltmek** *They're going to **put up the price** of fuel.*

put sb up *phrasal verb* to let someone stay in your home for a short period **kalmasına izin vermek, barındırmak, yatırmak, misafir etmek** *If you need somewhere to stay, we can put you up for the night.*

put up with sb/sth *phrasal verb* to accept unpleasant behaviour or an unpleasant situation, although you do not like it **tahammül etmek, dayanmak, katlanmak** *He's so rude, I don't know how you put up with him.*

putrid /'pjuːtrɪd/ *adjective* decaying and smelling bad **çürümüş, kötü kokan; çürük, bozuk, kokuşmuş** *a putrid smell*

putt /pʌt/ *verb* [I, T] in golf, to hit the ball gently when you are near the hole **golf oyununda deliğin yakınında iken topa hafifçe dokunmak; pıt diye vurmak** ● **putt** *noun* [C] **vuruş**

putty /'pʌti/ *noun* [U] a soft, grey substance that becomes hard when it is dry and is used to fasten glass into windows or to fill small holes in wood **cam macunu**

🧩 ***puzzle*** .... İLE BİRLİKTE KULLANILAN KELİMELER
resolve/solve a puzzle ● the puzzle **of** sth

puzzle¹ /'pʌzl/ *noun* [C] **1** a game or activity in which you have to put pieces together or answer questions using skill **bulmaca, bilmece** *to do/solve a puzzle* ○ *a crossword puzzle* ○ *a jigsaw puzzle* **2** a situation which is very difficult to understand **bilmece, muamma, sır** *Scientists have been trying to **solve** this **puzzle** for years.*

puzzle² /'pʌzl/ *verb* [T] to make someone confused because they do not understand something **şaşırtmak, kafasını karıştırmak, hayrete düşürmek** [often passive] *I was puzzled by what he said.*

puzzle over sth *phrasal verb* to try to solve a problem or understand a situation by thinking carefully about it **kafa yormak, çözmeye çalışmak, çok düşünmek; üzerinde kafa patlatmak**

puzzled /'pʌzld/ *adjective* confused because you do not understand something **şaşırmış, afallamış, şaşkın, hayrete düşmüş** *He had a puzzled look on his face.*

puzzling /'pʌzlɪŋ/ *adjective* If something is puzzling, it confuses you because you do not understand it. **şaşırtan, kafa karıştıran, içinden çıkılmaz hâle getiren**

PVC /ˌpiːviː'siː/ *noun* [U] a strong material similar to thick plastic **kalın plastiğe benzer sert madde/materyal**

pyjamas *UK* (*US* **pajamas**) /pɪ'dʒɑːməz/ *noun* [plural] shirt and trousers that you wear in bed **pijama** *a pair of blue pyjamas* ⊃Orta kısımdaki renkli sayfalarına bakınız.

pyjamas

pylon /'paɪlɒn/ *noun* [C] a tall structure which

supports electrical wires above the ground **elektrik direği**

pyramid /'pɪrəmɪd/ *noun* [C] a shape with a square base and four triangular sides that meet to form a point at the top **piramit** ➜See picture at **shape.**

pyre /paɪəʳ/ *noun* [C] a pile of wood on which a dead person is burned in some countries **ölü/ceset yakma töreninde kullanılan odun yığını**

python /'paɪθ°n/ *noun* [C] a large snake that kills other animals by putting itself tightly around them **piton, piton yılanı**

Q, q /kjuː/ the seventeenth letter of the alphabet **alfabenin onyedinci harfi**

QC /ˌkjuːˈsiː/ *noun* [C] *abbreviation for* Queen's Counsel: a lawyer of high rank in the UK **Birleşik Krallık'da üst düzey avukat** *Horace Rumpole QC*

qt *written abbreviation for* quart (= a unit for measuring liquid) **sıvı ölçü birimi kuart'ın kısa yazılışı**

quack /kwæk/ *noun* [C] the sound made by a duck (= water bird) **vak vak, ördek sesi** ● **quack** *verb* [I] **ördek gibi bağırmak**

quadruple /kwɒdˈruːpl/ *verb* [I, T] If an amount quadruples, it becomes multiplied by four, or if you quadruple it, you multiply it by four. **dört kat art(tır)mak, dört katına çıkmak/çıkartmak; dörtle çarp(ıl)mak**

quagmire /ˈkwɒɡmaɪər/ *noun* [C] **1** a difficult and unpleasant situation **zor müşkül bir durum** *a legal quagmire* **2** an area of wet ground that you can sink into **bataklık**

quail /kweɪl/ *noun* [C] *plural* **quail** or **quails** a small bird which is shot for food **bıldırcın**

quaint /kweɪnt/ *adjective* attractive or unusual in an old-fashioned way **eski tip, antika, eski moda ama hoş** *a quaint little village*

quake¹ /kweɪk/ *noun* [C] *US short for* earthquake (= when the Earth shakes) **deprem, zelzele**

quake² /kweɪk/ *verb* [I] to shake because you are frightened **korkudan zangır zangır/tir tir titremek**

🧩 ***qualification* .... İLE BİRLİKTE KULLANILAN KELİMELER**

an **academic/basic/formal/recognised** qualification ● **gain/get/have/need** a qualification ● a qualification **in** sth

qualification /ˌkwɒlɪfɪˈkeɪʃən/ *noun* **1** EXAMS [C] *mainly UK* what you get when you pass an exam or a course **yeterlik, yeterlik belgesi** [usually plural] *legal/medical qualifications* ○ *What qualifications do you need to be a nanny?* **2** SKILLS [C] the skills, qualities, or experience that you need in order to do something **nitelik, özellik, vasıf** *The only qualification needed for this job is an eye for detail.* **3** COMPETITION [U] success in getting into a competition **yeterli olmak; vasıfları/nitelikleri koşulları karşılama** *England's qualification for the World Cup* **4** ADDITION [C, U] an addition to something that is said that makes its meaning less certain **sınırlama, yeni şeyler ilave etme; kesinliğini azaltma**

qualified /ˈkwɒlɪfaɪd/ *adjective* **1** having passed exams or courses **yeterli, vasıflı, yetkin olan, sınavı/dersleri başarmış olan** *a newly qualified teacher* **2** **qualified to do sth** having the skills, qualities, or experience that you need in order to do something **bir şeyi yapmaya yetkin/kabiliyeti/deneyimi olmak; yeterli bulunmak** *I think John is the best qualified to make that decision.* **3** If something someone says is qualified, they have added something to it to make it less certain. **sınırlandırılmış** *The answer was a qualified yes.* ◆Opposite **unqualified.**

qualifier /ˈkwɒlɪfaɪər/ *noun* [C] **1** a game or competition which decides whether you can enter another competition **seçmeler, elemeler** **2** someone who has succeeded in getting into a competition **seçilmiş, kendini kanıtlamış, yeterli bulunmuş**

qualify /ˈkwɒlɪfaɪ/ *verb* **1** BE ALLOWED [I, T] If you qualify for something, you are allowed to do it or have it, and if something qualifies you for something, it allows you to do it or have it. **yeterli hâle gelmek/getirilmek; yeterli bulmak/bulunmak** *Foreign students no longer qualify for grants in the UK.* ○ *To qualify for the competition, you must be over 18.* ◆Opposite **disqualify.** **2** PASS EXAMS [I] *mainly UK* to pass exams so that you are able to do a job **başarılı olmak; başarmak; kendini kanıtlamak** *He's recently qualified as a doctor.* **3** GET INTO COMPETITION [I] to succeed in getting into a competition **katılmayı başarmak; hak kazanmak** *Nigeria were the first team to qualify for the World Cup.* **4** ADD [T] to add something to what you say to make its meaning less certain **sınırlandırmak, kapsamını daraltmak**

qualitative /ˈkwɒlɪtətɪv/ Ⓤ /ˈkwɑːlɪteɪtɪv/ *adjective formal* relating to how good something is and not how much of it there is **nitelik, niteliğe ait** ● **qualitatively** *adverb* **nitelikle ilgili**

🧩 ***quality* .... İLE BİRLİKTE KULLANILAN KELİMELER**

affect/enhance/improve/maintain quality ● **good/high/inferior/low/poor** quality

‒ **quality¹** /ˈkwɒləti/ *noun* **1** GOOD OR BAD [U] how good or bad something is **kalite, nitelik, vasıf** *good/high quality* ○ *poor/low quality* ○ *The air quality in this area is terrible.* ○ *All we are asking for is a decent quality of life.* ○ *The spokeswoman says a quality control system is being developed for next year.* **2** GOOD [U] when something is very good or well made **kalite** *A designer label isn't necessarily a guarantee of quality.* **3** CHARACTER [C] part of the character or personality of someone or something **vasıf, özellik, kişilik, nitelik, huy** *leadership qualities*

quality² /ˈkwɒləti/ *adjective* [always before noun] very good **çok üstün, çok iyi** *We only sell quality products in this store.*

'quality ˌtime *noun* [U] time that you spend with someone when you can give them all of your attention **birine ayrılan değerli zaman; tüm dikkatin verildiği zaman dilimi** *We've been too busy to give the children much quality time this week.*

qualm /kwɑːm/ *noun* [C] a worry or doubt about something **kuşku, endişe, kuruntu, huzursuzluk** *I would have no qualms about reporting her to the police.*

quandary /ˈkwɒndəri/ *noun* [no plural] a situation in which you are trying to make a difficult choice **kararsızlık, tereddüt, karar vermeme** *We're in a quandary over which school to send her to.*

quantifier /ˈkwɒntɪfaɪər/ *noun* [C] a word or group of words that is used before a noun to show an amount of that noun. For example the words 'many', 'some', and 'a lot of' are quantifiers. **nicelik sözcükleri/sıfatları**

quantify /ˈkwɒntɪfaɪ/ *verb* [T] to measure or state the amount of something **miktarını/niceliğini belirlemek/ölçmek/ifade etmek** *It is difficult to quantify the damage that this storm has caused.*

quantitative /ˈkwɒntɪtətɪv/ Ⓤ /ˈkwɑːntəteɪtɪv/ *adjective* relating to quantity **nicel, miktar ile ilgili; kantitatif**

quantity ...... İLE BİRLİKTE KULLANILAN KELİMELER

a **huge/large/small/sufficient/vast** quantity ● **in** [big/large, etc] quantities

o⊷**quantity** /'kwɒntəti/ *noun* **1** [C, U] the amount or number of something **nicelik, miktar, sayı, çokluk** *A vast quantity of information is available on the Internet.* ○ *They are now developing ways to produce the vaccine in large quantities and cheaply.* つOrta kısımdaki renkli sayfalarına bakınız. **2 an unknown quantity** someone or something that you do not know and so you cannot be certain about **anlaşılmayan/bilinmeyen şey/kimse; bilinmez, belirsiz, niceliği belli olmayan**

quantum leap /ˌkwɒntʌm'li:p/ *noun* [C] a sudden, large increase or improvement in something **çok büyük/çok önemli artış/gelişme** [usually singular] *a quantum leap in information technology*

quarantine /'kwɒrᵊnti:n/ *noun* [U] If an animal or person is put into quarantine, they are kept away from other animals or people because they have or might have a disease. **karantina**

quarrel ...... İLE BİRLİKTE KULLANILAN KELİMELER

have a quarrel ● a quarrel **about/over** sth ● a quarrel **with** sb ● a quarrel **between** sb and sb

quarrel¹ /'kwɒrᵊl/ *noun* **1** [C] an argument **tartışma, münakaşa, ağız kavgası, kavga** *She walked out after having a quarrel with her boss.* **2 have no quarrel with sb/sth** to not disagree with someone or something **itirazı olmamak, karşı çıkmamak** *We have no quarrel with either of those ideas.*

quarrel² /'kwɒrᵊl/ *verb* [I] *UK* **quarrelling**, *past* **quarrelled**, *US* **quarreling**, *past* **quarreled** to have an argument with someone **tartışmak, ağız dalaşına girmek, münakaşa etmek** *She'd been quarrelling with her mother all morning.*

quarry /'kwɒri/ *noun* [C] a place where stone is dug out of a large hole in the ground **taş ocağı** *a marble quarry* ● **quarry** *verb* [T] to dig stone out of a quarry **taş ocağında taş çıkarmak**

quart /kwɔ:t/ (*written abbreviation* qt) *noun* [C] a unit for measuring liquid, equal to 1.14 litres in the UK and 0.95 litres in the US **Birleşik Krallık'da 1.14 litreye ABD'de 0.95 litreye eşit bir sıvı ölçüm birimi; kuart**

o⊷**quarter** /'kwɔ:tər/ *noun*
1 EQUAL PART [C] (*also US* **fourth**) one of four equal parts of something; ¹⁄₄ **çeyrek, dörtte bir** *Three quarters of the island's residents speak English.* ○ *My house is one and three-quarter miles/a mile and three-quarters from here.* ○ *I waited a quarter of an hour for her.* **2** BEFORE AN HOUR [no plural] a period of 15 minutes before or after the hour **çeyrek kala/geçe** *It's (a) quarter to three* (= 2.45). ○ *also US It's a quarter of three* (= 2.45). ○ *We're leaving at (a) quarter past six* (= 6.15). ○ *also US We're leaving at (a) quarter after six* (= 6.15). **3** BUSINESS [C] one of four periods of time into which a year is divided for financial calculations such as profits or bills (= orders for payment) **yılın dörtte biri, üç aylık dönem** *I get an electricity bill every quarter.* **4** SCHOOL [C] *US* one of four periods of time into which a year at college or university is divided **üni-**

quarter

versite ve yüksekokulda yılllık dört dönemden her biri; **çeyrek dönem 5** SPORT [C] *US* one of four periods of time into which some sports games are divided **spor oyunlarında çeyrek periyod; oyunun dörtte biri 6** PART OF TOWN [C] a part of a town, often where people from a particular country or religion live **mahalle, semt, muhit** *the Jewish quarter* **7** COIN [C] a US or Canadian coin with a value of 25 cents, which is a quarter of a dollar **25 sent; doların dörtte biri**

quarterback /'kwɔ:təbæk/ *noun* [C] a player in American football who controls the attack **Amerikan futbolunda hücumu karşılayan oyuncu**

quarter-final /ˌkwɔ:tə'faɪnᵊl/ *noun* [C] the part of a competition when eight people or teams are left and there are four games to decide who will reach the semi-final (= when only four people or teams are left) **çeyrek final** *She was knocked out of the competition in the quarter-finals.*

quarterly /'kwɔ:tᵊli/ *adjective, adverb* produced or happening every three months **yılda dört kez olan; üç ayda bir olan** *Water and electricity bills are paid quarterly.* ○ *a quarterly magazine/report*

quarters /'kwɔ:təz/ *noun* [plural] rooms to live in or sleep in, usually for people in a military organization **kışla yatakhanesi; barakalar; asker yatakhanesi; lojman; asker misafirhanesi**

quartet /kwɔ:'tet/ *noun* [C] four people singing or playing music in a group **dört kişilik müzik grubu; dörtlü**

quartz /'kwɔ:ts/ *noun* [U] a mineral used to make watches and clocks accurate **kuvars; saat yapımında kullanılan mineral**

quash /kwɒʃ/ *verb* [T] **1** *formal* to officially change a legal decision so that it stops existing **(resmen) bozmak, iptal etmek feshetmek; yürürlükten kaldırmak** *His conviction was quashed last month.* **2** to stop something that you do not want to happen **durdurmak, engel olmak** *He appeared on television to quash rumours that he was seriously ill.*

quasi- /kweɪzaɪ-/ *prefix* partly **hemen hemen-; yarı-; sözde-; güya- anlamında önek** *quasi-religious ideas*

quay /ki:/ *noun* [C] a structure built next to water where ships stop and goods are taken on and off **rıhtım, iskele**

queasy /'kwi:zi/ *adjective* If you feel queasy, you feel slightly ill as if you might vomit. **rahatsız, midesi bulanan, iyi hissetmeyen**

o⊷**queen** /kwi:n/ *noun* [C] **1** FEMALE RULER a female ruler in some countries **kraliçe** *Queen Elizabeth II* ○ *God save the Queen!* **2** KING'S WIFE the wife of a king when he is the main ruler in a country **kraliçe; kralın eşi 3** PLAYING CARD a playing card with a picture of a queen on it **iskambilde bir kağıt, kız** *the queen of diamonds* **4** INSECT a large female insect which is the most important in a group and which produces all the eggs **ece, kraliçe; yumurtlayan büyük dişi böcek** *queen bee*

queer /kwɪər/ *adjective* **1** *informal* an offensive word meaning homosexual **eşcinsel 2** strange **acayip, garip, tuhaf**

quell /kwel/ *verb* [T] *formal* to stop something that you do not want to happen **zaptetmek, tutmak, bastırmak, önlemek** *to quell a riot* ○ *to quell rumours*

quench /kwenʃ/ *verb* **quench your thirst** to drink liquid so that you stop being thirsty **susuzluğunu gidermek/dindirmek**

query¹ /'kwɪəri/ *noun* [C] a question **soru, sual** *His job is to answer telephone queries about airline schedules.*

query² /'kwɪəri/ *verb* [T] to ask questions in order to check that something is true or correct **soru sormak**

[+ question word] *A few students have queried whether exam marks were added up correctly.*

quest /kwest/ *noun* [C] *formal* an attempt to get something or do something difficult **arama, arayış, araştırma** *the quest for truth* ○ [+ to do sth] *He has begun his quest to become the Conservative Party's first Asian MP.*

question ...... İLE BİRLİKTE KULLANILAN KELİMELER

ask/answer/pose/raise/reply to a question ● a question arises ● an awkward/fundamental/important/interesting/hypothetical question ● a question about sth

○~**question**[1] /'kwestʃən/ *noun* **1** SENTENCE [C] a sentence or phrase that asks you for information **soru, sual** *Is it OK if I ask you a few questions?* ○ *He refused to answer my question.* ○ *If you have any questions about the scheme, do ask me.* ○ *"So where's the money coming from?" " That's a good question"* (= I do not know). **2** SITUATION [C] a situation or problem that needs to be considered **sorun, mesele, problem** *This documentary raises important questions about the American legal system.* ○ *Two important questions arise from this debate.* **3** DOUBT [U] doubt **şüphe, kuşku** [+ that] *There is no question that this was an accidental fire.* ○ *His ability as a chef has never been in question.* ○ *She's the right person for the job." "Yes, absolutely, without question."* ○ *The report brings/calls into question* (= causes doubts about) *the safety of this drug.* **4 sb/sth in question** the person or thing that is being discussed **söz konusu olan/adı geçen/sözü edilen kimse/şey; bahse konu kişi/şey** *He claims that he was in the pub with his girlfriend on the night in question.* **5 be out of the question** If something is out of the question, it is not possible or not allowed. **olanaksız, imkânsız, söz konusu bile olamaz** ⊃See also: loaded question, rhetorical question.

question[2] /'kwestʃən/ *verb* [T] **1** to ask someone questions **soru sormak/yöneltmek** *Detectives were questioning a boy about the murder.* ○ [often passive] *Two out of three people questioned in the survey were non-smokers.* **2** to show or feel doubt about something **şüphe etmek, kuşku duymak; dan/den pek emin olamamak** *I'm not for a moment questioning your decision.* ○ [+ question word] *I'm just questioning whether we need the extra staff.*

questionable /'kwestʃənəbl/ *adjective* **1** possibly not true or correct **şüpheli, kuşku uyandıran** [+ question word] *It is highly questionable whether this drug has any benefits at all.* **2** not honest or not legal **şaibeli, kuşkulu; dürüst ve yasal olmayan** *He's being investigated for questionable business practices.*

questioning /'kwestʃənɪŋ/ *noun* [U] when the police ask someone questions about a crime **sorgulama, sorguya çekme** *She was taken in for questioning by police yesterday morning.*

'question ,mark *noun* [C] a mark (?) used at the end of a question **soru işareti** ⊃See study page Punctuation on page Centre 33.

questionnaire ...... İLE BİRLİKTE KULLANILAN KELİMELER

complete/fill in a questionnaire ● draw up a questionnaire ● a questionnaire asks sth ● a questionnaire about/on sth

questionnaire /ˌkwestʃə'neə^r/ *noun* [C] a set of questions asked of a large number of people to discover information about a subject **anket, sormaca** *Residents have been sent questionnaires about their homes and energy use.*

'question ,tag *noun* [C] a short phrase such as 'isn't it' or 'don't you' that is added to the end of a sentence to check information or to ask if someone agrees with you. In the sentence, 'It's hot, isn't it?', 'isn't it' is a question tag. **Değil mi' edatlı soru cümleciği**

queue ...... İLE BİRLİKTE KULLANILAN KELİMELER

form/be in/join a queue ● a queue stretches [for miles/around sth, etc] ● a big/long/short/small queue ● a queue of [cars/people, etc] ● a queue for sth

queue /kjuː/ *UK (US line) noun* [C] **1** a row of people waiting for something, one behind the other **kuyruk, sıra** *to join the queue* ○ *Are you in the queue?* **2 jump the queue** to move in front of people who have been waiting longer for something than you **sıranın önüne geçmek; sırayı/kuyruğu ihlal etmek** ● **queue (up)** *UK (US line up) verb* [I] to stand in a row in order to wait for something **kuyruk olmak, sıraya/kuyruğa girmek** [+ to do sth] *They're queueing up to get tickets.*

quibble /'kwɪbl/ *verb* **quibble about/over/with sth** to argue about something that is not important **incir çekirdeğini doldurmayan/önemsiz konu üzerinde tartışmak/münkaşa etmek** *They spend far too much time quibbling over details.* ● **quibble** *noun* [C] **baştan savma durumu**

quiche /kiːʃ/ *noun* [C, U] a dish made of a pastry base filled with a mixture of egg and milk and usually cheese, vegetables, or meat **kiş; yumurta,süt ve genellikle peynir, sebze veya etle yapılan tart**

○~**quick**[1] /kwɪk/ *adjective* **1** doing something fast or taking only a short time **çabuk, hızlı** *I tried to catch him but he was too quick for me.* ○ [+ to do sth] *Publishers were quick to realize that a profit could be made.* **2** lasting a short time **hemen yapılan, çabuk, tez, hızlı** *Can I ask you a quick question?*

quick[2] /kwɪk/ *adverb informal* fast **hızlı bir şekilde, süratle** *Come here, quick!*

quicken /'kwɪk^ən/ *verb* [I, T] to become faster or to cause something to become faster **çabuklaş(tır)mak, hızlan(dır)mak** *His breathing quickened.*

○~**quickly** /'kwɪkli/ *adverb* fast or in a short time **çabuk, çabuk, hızlıca, süratle** *I quickly shut the door.* ○ *These people need to be treated as quickly as possible.*

quid /kwɪd/ *noun* [C] *plural* **quid** *UK informal* a pound (= UK unit of money) **sterlin; Birleşik Krallık para birimi** *This bike's not bad for twenty quid.*

○~**quiet**[1] /kwaɪət/ *adjective* **1** NOT NOISY making little or no noise **sessiz, sakin** *Can you be quiet, please?* ○ *The children are very quiet.* **2** NOT BUSY without much noise or activity **gürültüsüz, sessiz, sakin** *I fancy a quiet night in tonight.* ○ *They found a table in a quiet corner of the restaurant.* **3** NOT TALKING MUCH If someone is quiet, they do not talk very much. **sessiz, fazla konuşmaz, sakin, yumuşak huylu** *He was a shy, quiet man.* **4 keep (sth) quiet** to not talk about something that is secret **susmak, gizli tutmak, hakkında konuşmamak** *It might be wise to keep this quiet for a while.*

quiet[2] /kwaɪət/ *noun* [U] when there is little or no noise **sessizlik, sükûnet** *She needs a bit of peace and quiet.*

quieten /'kwaɪət^ən/ *UK (US quiet) verb* [T] to make someone or something quiet **sakinleştirmek, susturmak, yatıştırmak**

quieten (sb/sth) down *phrasal verb UK* (*US* **quiet (sb/sth) down**) to become quieter or calmer, or to make a person or animal become quieter or calmer **susmak/susturmak; yatışmak/yatıştırmak**

◦⊷**quietly** /'kwaɪətli/ *adverb* **1** making little or no noise **sessizce** *"Don't worry," she said quietly.* **2** doing something without much noise or activity **farkettirmeden; sessizce, fazla gürültü yapmadan** *He sat quietly on the sofa, waiting for her to come home.*

quilt /kwɪlt/ *noun* [C] a cover for a bed which is filled with feathers or other warm material **yorgan**

quip /kwɪp/ *verb* [I, T] **quipping**, *past* **quipped** to say something in a funny and clever way **espri yapmak, nükteyle anlatmak** ● **quip** *noun* [C] **şaka**

quirk /kwɜːk/ *noun* **1** [C] a strange habit **garip davranış, acayip huy** *My aunt has a few odd quirks.* **2 quirk of fate** a strange and unexpected event **garip tesadüf, beklenmedik acayip olay** *By some quirk of fate, we came to live in the same town.* ● **quirky** *adjective* strange **garip, tuhaf, acayip** *a quirky sense of humour*

quit /kwɪt/ *verb* **quitting**, *past* **quit 1** [I, T] to leave your job or school permanently **iş veya okuldan uzun süreli ayrılmak, terketmek, istifa etmek** *She recently quit her job to spend more time with her family.* **2** [T] to stop doing something **yapmaktan vazgeçmek, bırakmak** *I quit smoking and put on weight.*

◦⊷**quite** /kwaɪt/ *adverb* **1** NOT COMPLETELY *UK* a little or a lot but not completely **bayağı, oldukça, epey** *I'm quite tired, but I'm happy to walk a little further.* ○ *He's quite attractive but not what I'd call gorgeous.* **2** VERY *US* very **çok, epeyce** *My sister and I are quite different.* **3** COMPLETELY completely **tam, tam olarak, tamamen** *The two situations are quite different.* ○ *Are you quite sure you want to go?* **4 not quite** almost but not completely **tam değil, yeteri kadar olmayan; gerektiği gibi değil** *I'm not quite sure that I understand this.* ○ *He didn't get quite enough votes to win.* **5 quite a bit/ a few/a lot, etc** a large amount or number **oldukça, bir hayli, neredeyse tamamen** *There are quite a few letters for you here.* ○ *He's changed quite a bit.*

YAYGIN HATALAR

quite or quiet?

Dikkat! Doğru kelimeyi seçin. Bu iki kelime aynıymış gibi görünebilir fakat hem yazılışları hem de anlamları birbirlerinden farklıdır. **Quite** bir hayli anlamındadır. Az veya hiç ses yapmak anlamında kullanmak istiyorsanız **quiet** kullanmanız gerekecektir.: ~~I need a~~

~~quite environment where I can study in peace.~~ Yanlış cümle örneği

I need a quiet environment where I can study in peace.

quiver /'kwɪvər/ *verb* [I] to shake slightly **titremek, ürpermek** ● **quiver** *noun* [C] **titreme**

quiz¹ /kwɪz/ *noun* [C] *plural* **quizzes 1** a game in which you answer questions **bilgi yarışması** *a television quiz show* **2** *US* a short test on a subject in school **küçük sınav**

quiz² /kwɪz/ *verb* [T] **quizzing**, *past* **quizzed** to ask someone questions about something **sorular sormak, sorguya çekmek** *A group of journalists quizzed them about/on the day's events.*

quizzical /'kwɪzɪk³l/ *adjective* A quizzical expression or look seems to ask a question without words. **sorgulayıcı, sorgulayan, şüpheci**

quota /'kwəʊtə/ *noun* [C] a limited amount of something that is officially allowed **kota, kontenjan** *an import quota*

quotation /kwəʊ'teɪʃ³n/ *noun* [C] **1** a sentence or phrase that is taken out of a book, poem, or play **alıntı, aktarma, iktibas** *a quotation from Shakespeare/the Bible* **2** the amount that a piece of work will probably cost **muhtemel maliyet/fiyat; olası fiyat** *Make sure you get a quotation for all the work before they start.*

quot'ation ˌmarks *noun* [plural] a pair of marks (" ") or (' ') used before and after a group of words to show that they are spoken or that someone else originally wrote them **tırnak işareti (" ") (' ')** ⟹See study page **Punctuation** on page Centre 33.

quote¹ /kwəʊt/ *verb* **1** REPEAT [I, T] to repeat what someone has said or written **alıntı yapmak, aktarmak** *I was quoting from Marx.* ○ *Witnesses were quoted as saying there were two gunmen.* **2** GIVE EXAMPLE [T] to give a fact or example in order to support what you are saying **örnek olarak alıntılarla söylediklerini desteklemek** *The minister quoted recent unemployment figures.* **3** COST [T] to say how much a piece of work will cost before you do it **fiyat vermek; maliyet çıkarmak**

quote² /kwəʊt/ *noun* [C] *short for* quotation **alıntı, aktarma, iktibas**

quotes /kwəʊts/ *noun* [plural] *short for* quotation marks **tırnak işaretleri**

the Qur'an /kɒr'ɑːn/ *noun another spelling of* the Koran (= the holy book of Islam) **Kur'anı Kerim; İslâm dininin esaslarını anlatan kutsal kitap; Allah Kelâmı**

Q

R

R, r /ɑːʳ/ the eighteenth letter of the alphabet **alfabenin onsekizinci harfi**

R *informal written abbreviation for* are: used in emails and text messages **are' yardımcı fiilinin e-posta ve yazılı iletilerde kullanılan kısa şekli**

rabbi /'ræbaɪ/ *noun* [C] a leader and teacher in the Jewish religion **Musevi dininde önder, öğretici; rabbi** *Rabbi Hugo Gryn*

rabbit /'ræbɪt/ *noun* [C] a small animal with fur and long ears that lives in a hole in the ground **tavşan**

rabble /'ræbl/ *noun* [no plural] a group of noisy, uncontrolled people **kuru kalabalık, güruh**

rabies /'reɪbiːz/ *noun* [U] a serious disease that people can get if they are bitten by an infected animal **kuduz, kuduz hastalığı**

🧩 **race** ...... İLE BİRLİKTE KULLANILAN KELİMELER

drop out of/lose/win a race ● **in** a race

o⁻**race¹** /reɪs/ *noun* **1** COMPETITION [C] a competition in which people run, ride, drive, etc against each other in order to see who is the fastest **yarış, yarışma, müsabaka, koşu** *a horse race* **2** PEOPLE [C, U] one of the groups that people are divided into according to their physical characteristics **ırk** *people of many different races* **3** FOR POWER [C] a situation in which people compete against each other for power or control **yarış, rekâbet, çekişme, yarışma** *the race for governor* **4 the races** an event when horses race against each other **at yarışları 5 a race against time/the clock** a situation in which something has to be done very quickly **zamana/saate karşı yarış** ⊃See also: **the human race, the rat race.**

race² /reɪs/ *verb* **1** [I, T] to compete in a race **yarışmak** *I'll race you to the end of the road.* ○ *I used to race against him at school.* **2 race along/down/over, etc** to move somewhere very quickly **koşmak, koşuşturmak** *I raced over to see what was the matter.* **3 race sb to/back, etc** to take someone somewhere very quickly **süratle götürmek; hızlıca alıp götürmek** *Ambulances raced the injured to a nearby hospital.* **4** [T] to put a horse, dog, etc in a race **yarıştırmak, yarışa sokmak**

racecourse /'reɪskɔːs/ *noun* [C] UK the place where horses, cars, etc race **yarış pisti/sahası; hipodrom; araba yarış pisti**

racehorse /'reɪshɔːs/ *noun* [C] a horse that has been trained to run in races **yarış atı**

race re'lations *noun* [plural] the relationship between people from different races who live together in the same place **ırklar arasındaki ilişkiler**

racetrack /'reɪstræk/ *noun* [C] the place where horses, cars, etc race **yarış pisti, hipodrom**

racial /'reɪʃ⁰l/ *adjective* relating to people's race **ırkî, ırkla ilgili** *a racial minority* ○ *racial discrimination/tension* ● **racially** *adverb* *a racially motivated crime* **ırk ile ilgili**

racing /'reɪsɪŋ/ *noun* [U] the activity or sport in which people, animals, or vehicles race against each other **yarış** *motor racing* ⊃See also: **horse racing.**

🧩 **racism** ...... İLE BİRLİKTE KULLANILAN KELİMELER

combat/encounter/face/tackle racism ● **a form of** racism ● racism **against** sb

racism /'reɪsɪz⁰m/ *noun* [U] the belief that other races of people are not as good as your own, or the unfair treatment of people because they belong to a particular race **ırkçılık**

racist /'reɪsɪst/ *noun* [C] someone who believes that other races of people are not as good as their own **ırkçı** ● **racist** *adjective* *a racist attack* **ırkçı**

rack¹ /ræk/ *noun* [C] a type of shelf that you can put things on or hang things from **raf** *a magazine/luggage rack*

rack² /ræk/ *verb* **1 be racked with pain/guilt, etc** If someone is racked with pain or an emotion, they suffer a lot because of it. **üzülmek, acı çekmek 2 rack your brain/brains** *informal* to think very hard, usually to try to remember something or solve a problem **kafa patlatmak/yormak, çok düşünmek**
rack up sth *phrasal verb informal* to get or achieve a lot of something **çok fazla olmak; gücünü aşacak kadar aşırı olmak** *He's racked up debts of over thirty thousand pounds.*

racket /'rækɪt/ *noun* **1** SPORT [C] (*also* racquet) a piece of equipment that you use to hit a ball in sports such as tennis **raket** ⊃Orta kısımdaki renkli sayfalarına bakınız. **2** ILLEGAL [C] *informal* an illegal activity that is used to make money **yasadışı yolla para kazanma** *a drugs smuggling racket* **3** NOISE [no plural] *informal* a loud noise **gürültü, patırtı** *The neighbours were making such a racket.*

radar /'reɪdɑːʳ/ *noun* [U] a system that uses radio waves to find out the position of something you cannot see **radar**

radiant /'reɪdiənt/ *adjective* **1** showing that you are very happy **neşe saçan, mutluluğu yüzünden okunan** *a radiant smile* **2** very bright **çok parlak, ışık saçan; parıldayan; ışıl ışıl** ● **radiance** /'reɪdiəns/ *noun* [U] **mutluluktan çıldırmak, parıldamak**

radiate /'reɪdieɪt/ *verb* **1 radiate from/out, etc** to spread out in all directions from a particular point **yayılmak, saçılmak** *A number of roads radiate out from the centre.* **2** [T] to show an emotion or quality in your face or behaviour **yüzünde ve davranışında göstermek/sergilemek/vermek/yaymak** *His face just radiates happiness.* **3** [T] to send out heat or light (ısı, ışık) yaymak, saçmak

radiation /ˌreɪdi'eɪʃ⁰n/ *noun* [U] **1** a form of energy that comes from a nuclear reaction and that in large amounts can be very dangerous **radyasyon, ışınım** *dangerously high levels of radiation* ○ *radiation sickness* **2** energy from heat or light that you cannot see **ışın, ısı** *solar/microwave radiation*

radiator /'reɪdieɪtəʳ/ *noun* [C] **1** a metal piece of equipment that is filled with hot water and is used to heat a room **radyatör, kalorifer peteği** ⊃Orta kısımdaki renkli sayfalarına bakınız. **2** a part of a vehicle engine that is used to make the engine cool **araç radyatörü**

radical¹ /'rædɪk⁰l/ *adjective* **1** A radical change is very big and important. **köklü, esaslı** *a radical reform* **2** believing that there should be big social and political changes **köklü toplumsal ve siyasi değişim olması gerektiğine inanan** *a radical group/movement* ○ *a radical proposal* ● **radically** *adverb* *The company has changed radically in recent years.* **derinden, kökten**

radical² /'rædɪkᵊl/ *noun* [C] someone who supports the idea that there should be big social and political changes **köktenci, radikal**

◦-**radio¹** /'reɪdiəʊ/ *noun* **1** [BROADCASTS] [C] a piece of equipment used for listening to radio broadcasts **radyo** *a car radio* **2 the radio** the programmes that you hear when you listen to the radio **radyo programları** *We heard him speaking on the radio this morning.* **3** [SYSTEM] [U] a system of sending and receiving sound through the air **telsiz, telsiz haberleşmesi** *local radio* ○ *a radio station* **4** [MESSAGES] [C] a piece of equipment for sending and receiving messages by sound **sesli iletileri gönderen alan alet; telsiz**

radio² /'reɪdiəʊ/ *verb* [I, T] **radioing**, *past* **radioed** to send a message to someone by radio **telsizle haberleşmek/haber göndermek** *They radioed for help.*

radioactive /ˌreɪdiəʊˈæktɪv/ *adjective* containing harmful radiation (= energy from a nuclear reaction) **radyoaktif** *radioactive waste*

radioactivity /ˌreɪdiəʊækˈtɪvəti/ *noun* [U] when something is radioactive **radyoaktivite**

radish /'rædɪʃ/ *noun* [C] a small, round, white or red vegetable with a slightly hot taste that you eat in salad **turp**

radius /'reɪdiəs/ *noun* [C] **radius**
plural **radii 1** a certain distance from a particular point in any direction **herhangi bir yöne belli bir noktadan uzaklık; yarıçaplık alan** *Most facilities lie within a two-mile radius of the house.* **2** the distance from the centre of a circle to its edge **yarıçap**

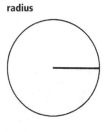

raffle /'ræfl/ *noun* [C] a competition in which people buy tickets with numbers on them and win a prize if any of their numbers are chosen **piyango; eşya piyangosu** *raffle tickets* ● **raffle** *verb* [T] to offer something as a prize in a raffle **piyangoda ödül olarak sunmak**

raft /rɑːft/ *noun* **1** [C] a small, flat boat made by tying pieces of wood together **sal; ağaçtan yapılma sal 2 a raft of sth/sb** a lot of things or people **bir sürü, çok, epey, bir hayli, çokça** *a raft of data*

rafter /'rɑːftə/ *noun* [C] one of the long pieces of wood that supports a roof **çatı kirişi/direği**

rag /ræg/ *noun* [C] **1** a piece of old cloth that you use to clean things **toz bezi 1 be like a red rag to a bull** *UK* If a particular subject is like a red rag to a bull, it always makes someone angry. **kızmak/hiddetlenmek; öfkeden deliye dönmek; kan beynine sıçramak**

rage¹ /reɪdʒ/ *noun* **1** [C, U] strong anger that you cannot control **öfke, hiddet, kızgınlık** *a jealous rage* ○ *He flew into a rage* (= suddenly became angry) *over the smallest mistake.* **2 be all the rage** *informal old-fashioned* to be very popular **çok ünlü olmak; adı herkesin dilinde olmak** ⊃See also: **road rage.**

rage² /reɪdʒ/ *verb* [I] **1** to continue with great force or violence **tüm şiddetiyle sürmek; ortalığı kasıp kavurmak** *The battle raged well into the night.* **2** to speak or behave in a very angry way **hiddetlenmek, öfkelenmek**

ragged /'rægɪd/   **ragged**
adjective **1** [CLOTHES] old and torn **eski püskü, yırtık pırtık** *ragged jeans* **2** [PERSON] wearing clothes that are old and torn **pejmürde kılıklı, yırtık pırtık giysili** *a ragged child* **3** [ROUGH] rough and not smooth **eski püskü, yırtık pırtık** *a ragged edge*

rags /rægz/ *noun* [plural] **1** clothes that are old and torn **yırtık pırtık/eski püskü giysiler** *an old man dressed in rags* **2 go from rags to riches** to start your life very poor and then later in life become very rich **sıfırdan zengin olmak; beş parasızken servet sahibi olmak**

🔲 **raid** ...... İLE BİRLİKTE KULLANILAN KELİMELER

carry out a raid ● a raid **on** sth ● an air raid ● a dawn raid

---

raid¹ /reɪd/ *noun* [C] **1** [SOLDIERS] a sudden attack on a place by soldiers **baskın, akın, saldırı** *an air raid* ○ *a dawn raid* **2** [POLICE] a sudden visit to a place by police in order to find someone or something **polis baskını, baskın** *a police raid to recover illegal weapons* **3** [STEAL] when people enter a place by force in order to steal from it **yağma, soygun** *a bank raid* ⊃See also: **air raid.**

raid² /reɪd/ *verb* [T] **1** [SOLDIERS] If soldiers raid a place, they suddenly attack it. **saldırı düzenlemek, baskın yapmak 2** [POLICE] If the police raid a place, they suddenly visit it in order to find someone or something. **baskın yapmak, basmak** *Police raided nine properties in search of the documents.* **3** [STEAL] to steal many things from somewhere **yağmalamak, baskın yapmak, basmak** *to raid the fridge*

rail /reɪl/

clothes rail

towel rail *UK,*
towel rack *US*

rail /reɪl/ *noun* **1** [FOR HANGING] [C] *UK* a horizontal bar on the wall that you hang things on **askılık; ...asacağı** *a curtain rail* **2** [FOR SUPPORTING] [C] a bar around or along something which you can hold to stop you from falling **trabzan, korkuluk, parmaklık** *a hand rail* **3** [TRAIN SYSTEM] [U] trains as a method of transport **demiryolu** *rail travel* ○ *a rail link* ○ *They sent the shipment by rail.* **4** [TRAIN] [C] the metal tracks that trains run on **raylar, tren rayları** ⊃See also: **towel rail.**

R

railing /ˈreɪlɪŋ/ noun [C] a fence made from posts and bars **demir parmaklık, demir parmaklıklı çit** *an iron railing*

ˈrailroad ˌtie *US* (*UK* **sleeper**) noun [C] a piece of wood that is used to support a railway track **demiryolu rayları altına döşenen ağaç kalaslar**

railway /ˈreɪlweɪ/ noun **1** [C] (*also US* **railroad** /ˈreɪlrəʊd/) the metal tracks that trains travel on **demiryolu** *Repairs are being carried out on the railway.* **2 the railway(s)** (*also US* **the railroad(s)**) the organizations connected with trains **demiryolları işletmesi** *He worked on the railways all his life.*

╬ **rain** ...... İLE BİRLİKTE KULLANILAN KELİMELER

rain **falls** ● **heavy/light/pouring/torrential** rain ● be **pouring with** rain ● a **drop of/spot of** rain ● **in the rain**

◦◦**rain¹** /reɪn/ noun **1** [U] water that falls from the sky in small drops **yağmur** *heavy rain* ○ *It looks like rain* (= as if it will rain). **2 the rains** in tropical countries, the time of year when there is a lot of rain **muson yağmurları dönemi** *They were waiting for the rains to come.* ➔See also: acid rain.

◦◦**rain²** /reɪn/ verb **it rains** If it rains, water falls from the sky in small drops. **yağmak, yağmur yağmak** *It was raining all weekend.*

be rained off phrasal verb *UK* (*US* **be rained out**) If a sport or outside activity is rained off, it cannot start or continue because it is raining. **yağmurdan dolayı ertele(n)mek; tehir etmek/edilmek**

rainbow /ˈreɪnbəʊ/ noun [C] a half circle with seven colours that sometimes appears in the sky when the sun shines through rain **gökkuşağı**

ˈrain ˌcheck noun [C] **1** *US* a piece of paper which allows you to buy something at a low price although that thing is now being sold at a higher price **sonradan bir malı daha ucuza almak için verilen belge/fiş/yazı/çek 2** *US* a ticket that allows you to see an event at a later time if bad weather stops that event from happening **tehir edilen bir gösteriyi sonradan izleme fırsatı veren bilet/fiş/yazı vs. 3** take a rain check on sth something you say when you cannot accept someone's invitation, but would like to do it at a later time **hakkının saklı kalmasını istemek**

raincoat /ˈreɪnkəʊt/ noun [C] a coat that you wear when it is raining **yağmurluk** ➔Orta kısımdaki renkli sayfalarına bakınız.

raindrop /ˈreɪndrɒp/ noun [C] a single drop of rain **yağmur damlası**

rainfall /ˈreɪnfɔːl/ noun [U] the amount of rain that falls in a particular place at a particular time **yağış miktarı; bir bölgenin/yerin aldığı yağış miktarı** *monthly rainfall* ○ *heavy rainfall*

rainforest /ˈreɪnˌfɒrɪst/ noun [C] a forest with a lot of tall trees where it rains a lot **yağmur ormanları** *a tropical rainforest*

rainy /ˈreɪni/ adjective raining a lot **yağmurlu** *a rainy afternoon*

◦◦**raise¹** /reɪz/ verb [T] **1** LIFT to lift something to a higher position **kaldırmak, yükseltmek** *to raise your hand* **2** INCREASE to increase an amount or level **artırmak, çoğaltmak** *to raise prices/taxes* **3** IMPROVE to improve something **geliştirmek** *to raise standards* **4** MONEY to collect money from other people (para) **toplamak** *They're raising money for charity.* **5** raise your voice to speak loudly and angrily to someone **sesini yükseltmek; azarlamak 6** raise hopes/fears/doubts, etc to cause emotions or thoughts **korkuların/şüphelerin/ümitlerin artmasına sebep olmak; uyandırmak;**

yol açmak *Her answers raised doubts in my mind.* **7** raise a question/subject, etc to start talking about a subject that you want other people to consider **ortaya atmak, ileri sürmek; gündeme getirmek 8** CHILD to look after and educate a child until they have become an adult **(çocuk) bakmak büyütmek; yetiştirmek; eğitimini üslenmek** *Their ideas on how to raise children didn't always agree.* **9** ANIMALS/CROPS to make an animal or crop grow **(ürün, hayvan) yetiştirmek, bakmak** *to raise chickens/sheep* ➔See also: raise the alarm¹.

raise² /reɪz/ *US* (*UK* **rise**) noun [C] an increase in the amount of money that you earn **maaş/gelir artışı** *We usually get a raise at the start of a year.*

raisin /ˈreɪzᵊn/ noun [C] a dried grape (= small round fruit) **kuru üzüm**

rake¹ /reɪk/ noun [C] a garden tool with a long handle that is used for moving dead leaves, grass, etc **tırmık**

rake² /reɪk/ verb [I, T] to use a rake to move dead leaves, grass, etc **tırmıklamak; tırmıkla temizlemek**
rake sth in phrasal verb informal to earn a large amount of money. **çok para kazanmak** *He's raking it in.*

╬ **rally** ...... İLE BİRLİKTE KULLANILAN KELİMELER

hold/organize/stage a rally ● a **mass** rally ● **at a** rally

rally¹ /ˈræli/ noun [C] **1** a large public meeting in support of something **toplantı, miting** *an election/campaign rally* **2** a car or motorcycle race **ralli; araba/motosiklet yarışı** *a rally driver*

rally² /ˈræli/ verb **1** [I, T] to come together or bring people together to support something **topla(n)mak; bir araya gelmek/getirmek; birleşmek/birleştirmek** *Her fans rallied behind her from the start.* **2** [I] to get stronger or better after being weak **toparlanmaya başlamak; iyileşmeye yüz tutmak** *The stock market rallied late in the day.*
rally around/round (sb) phrasal verb to help or give support to someone **yardımına koşmak, destek vermek** *If one of the family has a crisis we rally round them.*

ram¹ /ræm/ verb [T] **ramming**, past **rammed** to hit something or push something into something with great force **tıkmak, tıkıştırmak, zorla sokmak, ite kaka yerleştirmek** *He had to stop suddenly and a car rammed into him.*

ram² /ræm/ noun [C] a male sheep **koç**

RAM /ræm/ noun [U] abbreviation for random access memory: a computer's ability to immediately store information **ara bellek; bilgisayarın bilgiyi süratle depolama işlevi** ➔Compare ROM.

Ramadan /ˈræmədæn/ noun [U] the Muslim religious period in which Muslims do not eat or drink during the part of the day when it is light **Ramazan, Ramazan/oruç ayı**

ramble¹ /ˈræmbl/ verb **1** ramble along/through, etc to walk for a long time, especially in the countryside **kır bayır dolaşmak, gezinmek 2** (*also* ramble on) to talk for a long time in a boring and often confused way **abuk sabuk konuşmak; ipsiz sapsız sözler etmek; uzattıkça uzatmak** *He rambled on for hours about his time in the army.*

ramble² /ˈræmbl/ noun [C] a long walk in the countryside **kırda uzun yürüyüş/gezinti**

rambler /ˈræmblər/ noun [C] someone who walks in the countryside **kırda bayırda yürüyen kimse**

rambling /ˈræmblɪŋ/ adjective A rambling speech, letter, etc is very long and confused. **tutarsız/kendi içinde çelişkili ve karmaşık konuşma/mektup; dal-**

dan dala atlayan konuşma/yazı **2** A rambling build-ing is big and without a regular shape. **biçimsiz, şekil-siz**

ramifications /ˌræmɪfɪˈkeɪʃᵊnz/ noun [plural] the pos-sible results of an action **bir eylemin muhtemel/bek-lenen sonuçları**

ramp /ræmp/ noun [C] **1** a sloping surface that joins two places that are at different heights **farklı yükseklik-lerde iki şeyi birleştiren eğimli yüzey; rampa; eğik düzlem** *a wheelchair ramp* **2** US (UK slip road) a short road that is used to drive onto or off a large, fast road **sürüş rampası**

rampage¹ /ræmˈpeɪdʒ/ verb [I] to run around or through an area, making a lot of noise and causing damage **deliler gibi sağa sola koşuşturmak; etrafı yakıp yıkmak** *Angry citizens **rampaged through** the city.*

rampage² /ˈræmpeɪdʒ/ noun [no plural] when a group of people rampage **bilinçsizce sağa sola koşuşturma/saldırma/zarar verme** *Rioters **went on a rampage** through the city.*

rampant /ˈræmpənt/ adjective growing or spreading quickly, in a way that cannot be controlled **çok yayıl-mış, her tarafa dal budak salmış; yaygın** *rampant corruption/inflation*

ramshackle /ˈræmˌʃækl/ adjective A ramshackle build-ing is in very bad condition. **köhne, harap; külüstür, viran**

ran /ræn/ past tense of run **koşmak' fiilinin ikinci hâli**

ranch /rɑːnʃ/ noun [C] a large farm where animals are kept **hayvan üretme çiftliği, içinde malikâne bulu-nan büyük çiftlik** *a cattle/sheep ranch*

rancher /ˈrɑːnʃəʳ/ noun [C] someone who owns or works on a ranch **çiftlik sahibi**

rancid /ˈrænsɪd/ adjective Rancid fat, such as oil or but-ter, smells and tastes bad because it is not fresh. **ekş-imiş, acımış, kokmuş, bayat**

random /ˈrændəm/ adjective **1** done or chosen without any plan or system **rastgele, gelişigüzel, belli bir sıra düzen takip etmeyen** *random testing* ○ *a random selection* **2 at random** chosen by chance **rastgele şekilde gelişigüzel biçimde** *Winners will be chosen at random.* ● **randomly** adverb **rastgele**

rang /ræŋ/ past tense of ring² **zil çalmak' fiilinin ikinci hâli**

🧩 **range** .... İLE BİRLİKTE KULLANILAN KELİMELER

a full/wide range ● a range of sth

range¹ /reɪndʒ/ noun **1** OF THINGS [C] a group of different things of the same general type **çeşit, tür, sınıf, çeşit-lilik, dağılım** *a range of colours/patterns* ○ *We discus-sed a **wide range** of subjects.* **2** AMOUNT [C] the amount or number between a particular set of limits **sıra, dizi, silsile** [usually singular] *The **price range** is from $100 to $200.* ○ *The product is aimed at young people in the 18-25 **age range**.* **3** DISTANCE [U] the distance from which things can be seen, heard, or reached **menzil, erim** *The soldiers came **within firing range**.* ○ *He was shot **at close range** (= from very near).* **4** MOUNTAINS [C] a line of hills or mountains **sıralı (dağlar)** **5** SHOOTING [C] a place where you can practise shooting a gun **atış poli-gonu, atış sahası** *a rifle/shooting range*

range² /reɪndʒ/ verb **1 range from sth to sth** to have several different amounts or types **farklı miktar ve türler arasında değişmek** *Tickets range from $12 to $35.* ○ *Choose from 13 colours, ranging from classic white to antique blue.* **2** [I] to deal with a large number

of subjects **fazla sayıda konuyla/hususla ilgilenmek** *The discussion **ranged over** many topics.*

ranger /ˈreɪndʒəʳ/ noun [C] someone whose job is to look after a forest or a park **ormancı, orman muhafaza memuru, korucu, bekçi** *a forest ranger*

rank¹ /ræŋk/ noun **1** [C, U] a position in society or in an organization, for example the army **rütbe, mevki, makam** *He holds the rank of colonel.* **2 the ranks** the ordinary members of an organization, especially the army **rütbeler 3 break ranks** to publicly show that you disagree with a group that you belong to **ait olduğu grupla uyuşmadığını ilan etmek; genel tea-müllere aykırı hareket etmek; hiyerarşiye karşı çıkmak** ● **4 the rank and file** the ordinary members of an organization and not its leaders **sıradan bireyler, alt tabaka/kademeler** ⊃See also: taxi rank.

rank² /ræŋk/ verb [I, T] to have a position in a list which shows things or people in order of importance, or to give someone or something a position on such a list **dahil olmak/etmek; saymak/sayılmak; bir listede yer almak/yeri olmak** *He ranked number one in the world at the start of the competition.* ○ *The city's canals now **rank among** the world's dirtiest.*

ransom /ˈrænsᵊm/ noun [C, U] the money that is demanded for the return of someone who is being kept as a prisoner **fidye** *a ransom note/letter*

rant /rænt/ verb [I] to talk a lot about something in an excited or angry way **atıp tutmak; bol keseden atmak** *He was **ranting and raving** about the injustice of the situation.*

rap¹ /ræp/ noun **1** [U] a type of music in which the words are spoken and there is a strong beat **bir ritim eşli-ğinde sözcüklerin söylenmesiyle yapılan müzik** *a rap artist* **2** [C] a sudden, short sound made when some-one or something hits a hard surface **vuruş, darbe, ritmik tıklama/vuruş** *There was a rap on the window.* **3 a rap on/across/over the knuckles** a punishment that is not severe **uyarı, ikaz, çok ciddi olmayan ceza**

rap² /ræp/ verb rapping, past rapped **1** [I, T] to hit a hard surface to make a sudden, short noise **hafif hafif vur-mak, tık tık ses yapmak; kısa aralıklarla hafif dar-beler vurmak** *He **rapped on** the door.* **2** [I] to perform rap music **rep müzik yapmak**

rape /reɪp/ verb [T] to force someone to have sex when they do not want to **ırza geçmek, tecavüz etmek** ● **rape** noun [C, U] **tecavüz**

rapid /ˈræpɪd/ adjective happening or moving very quickly **hızlı, süratli, çok çabuk** *rapid change/growth* ● **rapidity** /rəˈpɪdəti/ noun [U] **hız** ● **rapidly** adverb **hızlıca**

rapids /ˈræpɪdz/ noun [plural] a part of a river where the water moves very fast **suyun hızlı aktığı yer**

rapist /ˈreɪpɪst/ noun [C] someone who forces another person to have sex when they do not want to **tecavüzcü, ırz düşmanı, ırza geçen adam**

rapper /ˈræpəʳ/ noun [C] someone who performs rap music (= a type of music in which the words are spoken and there is a strong beat) **rep müzik yapan kimse**

rapport /ræˈpɔːʳ/ noun [U, no plural] a good understanding of someone and ability to communicate with them **iyi ilişki, uyum, ahenk** *She has a good **rapport with** her staff.*

rapture /ˈræptʃəʳ/ noun [U] a feeling of extreme pleasure and excitement **coşku, kendinden geçme, aşırı heye-cana kapılma; ayakları yerden kesilme**

o→**rare** /reəʳ/ adjective **1** very unusual **nadir, az bulunur, nadide** *a rare disease/species* ○ [+ to do sth] *It's very*

R

rare to see these birds in England. **2** If meat is rare, it is still red because it has only been cooked for a short time. **az pişmiş** *a rare steak*

rarely /ˈreəli/ *adverb* not often **nadiren, ender olarak** *I rarely see her these days.*

raring /ˈreərɪŋ/ *adjective* **be raring to do sth** *informal* to be very enthusiastic about starting something **can atıyor olmak, üstüne atlamak**

rarity /ˈreərəti/ *noun* **1 be a rarity** to be unusual **az bulunur/nadir olmak** *Genuine enthusiasm is a rarity.* **2** [U] the fact that something is not common **az bulunur/nadir/ender rastlanan şey; nadirlik, nadidelik** *Precious stones are valued for their rarity.*

rascal /ˈrɑːskªl/ *noun* [C] **1** *humorous* a person who behaves badly, but who you still like **yaramaz, haşarı, kerata, afacan 2** *old-fashioned* a dishonest man **ahlaksız/dürüst olmayan kişi**

rash¹ /ræʃ/ *noun* **1** [C] a group of small, red spots on the skin **kızartı, isilik, kurdeşen** *an itchy rash* ○ *Certain foods give him a rash.* **2 a rash of sth** a group of unpleasant events of the same type, happening at the same time **aynı anda olan bir sürü olumsuzluk** *There has been a rash of burglaries in the area.*

rash² /ræʃ/ *adjective* done suddenly and without thinking carefully **ihtiyatsız, dikkatsiz, acele ve ehemmiyetsizce yapılan** *a rash decision/promise*

rasher /ˈræʃəʳ/ *noun* [C] *UK* a slice of bacon (= meat from a pig) **ince dilim domuz salamı/pastırması**

raspberry /ˈrɑːzbªri/ *noun* [C] a small, soft, red fruit that grows on bushes **ahududu, ağaç çileği**

rat /ræt/ *noun* [C] **1** an animal that looks like a large mouse and has a long tail **sıçan, iri fare; lağım faresi** *Rats carry disease.* **2** *informal* an unpleasant and, dishonest person **yüzsüz, hain/alçak kimse**

rat

rate ...... İLE BİRLİKTE KULLANILAN KELİMELER

a **cut in/drop in/increase in/rise in** the rate • **at** a rate (of) • **the** rate **for/of**

o•**rate¹** /reɪt/ *noun* [C] **1** [HOW MANY] how often something happens, or how many people something happens to **oran, nispet** *the birth rate* ○ *the rate of unemployment* **2** [MONEY] a fixed amount of money given for something **oran, rayiç** *the interest/exchange rate* ○ *rates of pay* **3** [SPEED] the speed at which something happens **hız, sürat** *the rate of progress* **4 at this rate** used before saying what will happen if a situation continues in the same way **bu gidişle, bu suretle, böyle giderse** *At this rate we're not going to be there till midnight.* **5 at any rate** used before saying one fact that is certain in a situation that you are generally not certain about **hiç değilse, hiç olmazsa, en azından** *Well, at any rate we need her to be there.* **6 first-/second-/third-rate** very good, bad, or very bad **çok iyi, kötü, çok kötü gibi düzeylerde/oranda/nispette** *a first-rate hotel* ⊃See also: birth rate, exchange rate.

rate² /reɪt/ *verb* [T] **1** to judge the quality or ability of someone or something **değerlendirmek, saymak, kabiliyet ve niteliğini belirlemek/değerlendirmek** *How do you rate her as a singer?* **2** to deserve something **hak etmek; ...a/e layık olmak** *The incident didn't even*

rate a mention (= was not written about) *in the local newspaper.*

o•**rather** /ˈrɑːðəʳ/ *adverb* **1** slightly or to a degree **biraz, az çok, oldukça** *I rather like it.* ○ *I find her books rather dull.* ○ *I find her books rather dull.* **2 rather than** instead of **yerine; ...dan/den ziyade/çok; ...-mektense/dense** *He saw his music as a hobby rather than a career.* **3 would rather** If you would rather do something, you would prefer to do that thing. **tercih etmek; yeğlemek** *I'd much rather go out for a meal than stay in and watch TV.* **4** used to change something you have just said and make it more correct **daha doğrusu, aslında** *I tried writing some drama, or rather comedy-drama, but it wasn't very good.*

ratify /ˈrætɪfaɪ/ *verb* [T] to make an agreement official **onaylamak, tasdik etmek** *Sixty-five nations need to ratify the treaty.*

rating ...... İLE BİRLİKTE KULLANILAN KELİMELER

give sb/sth/have a rating • sb's/sth's rating **drops/falls/improves/increases** • a **high/low** rating • a rating **of** [5/28%, etc]

rating /ˈreɪtɪŋ/ *noun* **1** [C] a measurement of how good or popular something or someone is **değerlendirme, puanlama, puan verme, derecelendirme** *A high percentage of Americans gave the President a positive rating.* **2 the ratings** a list of television and radio programmes showing how popular they are **izlenme/dinlenme sıralaması; reyting sıralaması; seyredilme/dinlenme oranı**

ratio /ˈreɪʃiəʊ/ *noun* [C] the relationship between two things expressed in numbers to show how much bigger one is than the other **oran, nispet** *The female to male ratio at the college is 2 to 1.*

ration¹ /ˈræʃªn/ *noun* [C] the amount of something that you are allowed to have when there is little of it available **pay, istihkak** *a food/petrol ration*

ration² /ˈræʃªn/ *verb* [T] to give people only a small amount of something because there is little of it available **vesika/karne ile dağıt(ıl)mak/ver(il)mek** *They might have to start rationing water.*

rational /ˈræʃªnªl/ *adjective* **1** based on facts and not affected by someone's emotions or imagination **gerçeklere dayalı, mantıksal; akıl/izan çerçevesinde olan** *a rational argument/debate/explanation* **2** able to make decisions based on facts and not be influenced by your emotions or imagination **akılcı, mantıklı, aklı başında, mâkul** *Look, we've got to try to be rational about this.* ⊃Opposite **irrational.** • **rationally** *adverb* **mantıklı olarak**

rationale /ˌræʃəˈnɑːl/ *noun* [C] a group of reasons for a decision or belief **gerekçe; temelinde/gerisinde/arkasında yatan asıl neden/sebep** *I don't understand the rationale behind the policy.*

rationalize (*also UK* -ise) /ˈræʃªnªlaɪz/ *verb* **1** [I, T] to try to find reasons to explain your behaviour or emotions **mazeret/geçerli neden bulmak, kılıf bulmak/uydurmak** *I can't rationalize the way I feel towards him.* **2** [T] *mainly UK* to improve the way a business is organized, usually by getting rid of people **verimli hâle getirmek/gelmek; rasyonel çalışır duruma sokmak; daha iyi işler hâle getirmek** • **rationalization** (*also UK* -isation) /ˌræʃªnªlaɪˈzeɪʃªn/ *noun* [C, U] **bir mantığa oturtma**

the 'rat ,race *noun informal* the unpleasant way that people compete against each other at work in order to succeed **acımasız rekabet/yarış/çekişme/mücadele; çirkin ayak oyunları; gereksiz/yersiz rekabet**

rattle¹ /ˈrætl/ *verb* **1** [I, T] to make a noise like something knocking repeatedly, or to cause something to make

this noise **takırda(t)mak, zangırda(t)mak** *The wind blew hard, rattling the doors and windows.* **2** [T] to make someone nervous **tedirgin etmek, huysuzlandırmak, sinirlendirmek, sinirlerini bozmak** [often passive] *He was clearly rattled by their angry reaction.*
rattle sth off *phrasal verb* to quickly say a list or something that you have learned **bir çırpıda hepsini söylemek; nefes almadan anlatmak/söylemek** *She can rattle off the names of all the players.*

rattle² /'rætl/ *noun* [C] a toy that a baby shakes to make a noise **çıngırak**

raucous /'rɔːkəs/ *adjective* loud and unpleasant **(ses) kaba, kulakları tırmalayan** *raucous laughter*

ravage /'rævɪdʒ/ *verb* [T] to damage or destroy something **tahrip/harap etmek; yerle bir etmek; yakıp yıkmak** [often passive] *The whole area has been ravaged by war.*

ravages /'rævɪdʒɪz/ *noun* [plural] **the ravages of disease/time/war, etc** the damaging effects of disease/time/war, etc **hastalık/zaman/savaş vs. yıkıcı/yokedici etkileri**

rave¹ /reɪv/ *verb* [I] **1** to talk about something that you think is very good in an excited way **çılgınca bağırıp çağırmak, heyecanlı heyecanlı anlatmak** *He went there last year and he's been raving about it ever since.* **2** to talk in an angry, uncontrolled way **deliler gibi konuşup durmak; zırvalamak, saçmalamak**

rave² /reɪv/ *noun* [C] an event where people dance to modern, electronic music **elektronik müzik eşliğinde çılgınca eğlenmek**

raven /'reɪvᵊn/ *noun* [C] a large, black bird **kuzgun, kara karga**

ravenous /'rævᵊnəs/ *adjective* very hungry **çok acıkmış, kurt gibi aç ● ravenously** *adverb* **aç bir şekilde**

ravine /rə'viːn/ *noun* [C] a narrow, deep valley with very steep sides **derin vadi**

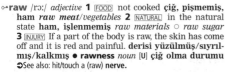
ravine

raving /'reɪvɪŋ/ *adjective informal* completely uncontrolled **kudurmuş, çileden çıkmış, gözü dönmüş, çılgın** *He was acting like a raving lunatic.*

ravings /'reɪvɪŋz/ *noun* [plural] the strange things that a crazy person says **zırva, deli saçması, saçma sapan sözler** *the ravings of a madman*

ravishing /'rævɪʃɪŋ/ *adjective* very beautiful **büyüleyici, çok güzel**

o⌐**raw** /rɔː/ *adjective* **1** FOOD not cooked **çiğ, pişmemiş, ham** *raw meat/vegetables* **2** NATURAL in the natural state **ham, işlenmemiş** *raw materials* ○ *raw sugar* **3** INJURY If a part of the body is raw, the skin has come off and it is red and painful. **derisi yüzülmüş/sıyrılmış/kalkmış ● rawness** *noun* [U] **çiğ olma durumu** ⊃See also: hit/touch a (raw) **nerve.**

ray /reɪ/ *noun* **1** [C] a narrow beam of light, heat, or energy **ışın, şua** *an ultraviolet ray* ○ *the rays of the sun* **2 a ray of hope/comfort, etc** a small amount of hope, etc **ışık, pırıltı; az bir ümit ışığı vs.** ⊃See also: **X-ray.**

razor /'reɪzəʳ/ *noun* [C] a piece of equipment with a sharp blade used for removing hair from the face, legs, etc **ustura, tıraş makinası** ⊃Orta kısımdaki renkli sayfalarına bakınız.

razor

'**razor ,blade** *noun* [C] a very thin, sharp blade that you put in a razor **jilet**

Rd *written abbreviation for* road **yol' sözcüğünün kısa yazılışı** *17, Lynton Rd*

re- /riː-/ *prefix* again **tekrar, yeniden anlamında ön ek** *remarry* ○ *a reusable container*

o⌐**reach¹** /riːtʃ/ *verb* **1** ARRIVE [T] to arrive somewhere **ulaşmak, varmak, erişmek** *We won't reach Miami till five or six o'clock.* **2** STRETCH [I, T] to stretch your arm and hand to touch or take something **uzanmak, uzatmak, erişmeye/almaya çalışmak** *She reached for a cigarette.* ○ *She reached down to stroke the dog's head.* ○ *He reached out and grabbed her arm.* **3 can reach (sth)** to be able to touch or take something with your hand **yetişebilmek, uzanmak, erişebilmek, dokunabilmek** *Could you get that book down for me - I can't reach.* **4** BE LONG ENOUGH [I, T] If something reaches, or reaches something, it is long enough to touch something. **uzanmak, uzatmak, erişmek, yetişmek** *The rope won't be long enough to reach the ground.* **5** LEVEL [T] to get to a particular level, situation, etc **belli bir seviyeye/duruma ulaşmak/erişmek** *We hope to reach our goal by May next year.* ○ *I've reached the point where I'm about to give up.* **6 reach a decision/agreement/conclusion, etc** to make a decision, agreement, etc about something **bir sonuca/anlaşmaya/karara v. varmak 7** TELEPHONE [T] to speak to someone on the telephone **telefonla ulaşmak/konuşmak** *You can reach him at home.*

reach² /riːtʃ/ *noun* **1 out of/beyond (sb's) reach** too far away for someone to take hold of **erişilemez, ulaşılamaz, el kol ulaşamayacak yerde** *I keep the medicines up here, out of the kids' reach.* **2 beyond (sb's) reach** not possible for someone to have **erişilemiyecek mesafede/yerde/konumda** *With all this money we can buy things previously beyond our reach.* **3 be within reach (of sth)** to be close enough to travel to **gidilebilecek mesafede/menzilde/uzaklıkta olmak** *You'll be within easy reach of London.* **4 be within (sb's) reach a** to be close enough for someone to take hold of **ulaşılabilecek mesafede/uzaklıkta olmak** *The gun lay within reach.* **b** possible for someone to achieve **başarılabilecek konumda olmak** *Winning the championship suddenly seemed within their reach.*

react /ri'ækt/ *verb* [I] **1** SAY/DO to say, do, or feel something because of something else that has been said or done **tepki göstermek, karşılık vermek** *He reacted angrily to her comments.* **2** BAD EFFECT to become ill because something that you have eaten or used on your body has had a bad effect on you **...dan/den dolayı tepki vermek/rahatsızlanmak/hastalanmak** *My skin reacts to most perfumes.* **3** SUBSTANCES In science, if a substance reacts with another substance, it changes. **tepkimek, reaksiyon göstermek** *Carbon reacts with oxygen to produce carbon dioxide.*
react against sth *phrasal verb* to do the opposite of what someone wants you to do because you do not like their rules or ideas **başkaldırmak, karşı gelmek**

R

reaction ...... İLE BİRLİKTE KULLANILAN KELİMELER

an adverse/angry/immediate/initial/instinctive/
negative/rapid reaction ● gauge/produce/provoke
a reaction ● a reaction to/towards sth

o⁻**reaction** /riˈækʃ°n/ noun 1 [CAUSED BY SOMETHING] [C, U]
something you say, feel, or do because of something
that has happened tepki, karşılık, reaksiyon What
was his reaction to the news? 2 **reactions** mainly UK
the ability to move quickly when something suddenly
happens tepki, ani davranışlar, reaksiyon; çabuk
karşılık verebilme, refleks Drivers need to have
quick reactions. 3 [CHANGE] [no plural] a change in the way
people behave or think because they do not agree with
the way people behaved or thought in the past gerici-
lik, irtica In art, there was a reaction against Realism.
4 [BAD EFFECT] [C] an unpleasant feeling or illness caused
by something you have eaten or used on your body
vücudun ortaya koyduğu tepki, reaksiyon A number of people have had a bad reaction to this drug.
5 [SUBSTANCES] [C] a change which happens when two substances are put together kimyasal tepkime, reaksiyon a chemical reaction ⊃See also: chain reaction.

reactionary /riˈækʃ°nªri/ adjective being against political or social progress gerici, mürteci;siyasi ve sosyal
ilerlemeye karşı olan ● **reactionary** noun [C] someone
who is against political or social progress gerici, mürteci;siyasi ve sosyal ilerlemeye karşı olan kimse

reactor /riˈæktər/ (also nuclear reactor) noun [C] a large
machine which uses nuclear fuel to produce power
nükleer santral, reaktör

o⁻**read¹** /riːd/ verb past read /red/ 1 [WORDS] [I, T] to look at
words and understand what they mean okumak What
was the last book you read? ○ I've been reading about
John F Kennedy. ○ [+ that] I've read that the economy is
going to improve by the end of the year. 2 [SAY] [I, T] to look
at words that are written and say them aloud for other
people to listen to sesli okumak Do you want me to read
it to you? ○ [+ two objects] I read him a story at bedtime.
3 [SIGNS] [T] to look at signs and be able to understand
them okuyup anlamak Can you read music?
4 [MEASUREMENT] [T] to show the temperature, time, etc on
a piece of measuring equipment (ısı, zaman vs.) göstermek The thermometer read 20 degrees this morning.
⊃See also: lip-read.

read sth into sth phrasal verb to believe that an action,
remark, etc has a particular meaning when it has not
anlam yüklemek, kendi yorumunu yapmak Don't
read too much into anything he says.

read sth out phrasal verb to read something and say the
words aloud so that other people can hear yüksek sesle
okumak He read out the names of all the winners.

read sth over/through phrasal verb to read something
from the beginning to the end, especially to find mistakes baştan sona dikkatlice okumak; düzeltme
okuması yapmak I read over my essay to check for
errors.

read² /riːd/ noun [no plural] 1 the act of reading something okuma It's not brilliant but it's worth a read. 2 a
good/easy, etc read something that is enjoyable, easy,
etc to read okuması zevkli/kolay vs.

readable /ˈriːdəbl/ adjective enjoyable and easy to read
kolay okunabilir; okuması zevkli

reader /ˈriːdər/ noun [C] someone who reads okuyucu
She's a slow reader.

readership /ˈriːdəʃɪp/ noun [no plural] the number and
type of people who read a particular newspaper, magazine, etc okuyucular, abone sayısı These magazines
have a very young readership.

readily /ˈredɪli/ adverb 1 quickly and easily kolayca,
çabucak, şıp diye Information is readily available
on the Internet. 2 willingly and without stopping to
think seve seve, isteyerek, bir an bile tereddüt etmeden He readily admits to having problems himself.

readiness /ˈredɪnəs/ noun [U] 1 when someone is willing to do something isteklilik, gönüllülük [+ to do sth]
They expressed a readiness to accept our demands.
2 when someone is prepared for something hazır
olma, hazırlıklı olma It was time to repair their shelters in readiness for the winter.

o⁻**reading** /ˈriːdɪŋ/ noun 1 [ACTIVITY] [U] the activity or skill
of reading books okuma I did a lot of reading on holiday. 2 [EVENT] [C] an event at which someone reads something to an audience okuma çalışması/eylemi/
seansı/gösterisi a poetry reading 3 [MEASUREMENT] [C]
the measurement that is shown on a piece of measuring
equipment ölçüm, sayı, derece, görülen rakam vs.
It's best to take a meter reading as soon as you move in.

readjust /ˌriːəˈdʒʌst/ verb 1 [I] to change in order to deal
with a new situation, such as a new job or home yeniden alışmak, adapte olmak, uymak The children will
have to readjust to a new school. 2 [T] to move something
slightly or make a small change to something ayarlamak, ufak tefek ayarlar/ayarlamalar yapmak He
readjusted his tie.

o⁻**ready** /ˈredi/ adjective 1 [never before noun] prepared for
doing something hazır Give me a call when you're ready.
○ [+ to do sth] Are you ready to go yet? ○ We're going at
eight, so you've got an hour to get ready. ○ The army was
ready for action. 2 [never before noun] prepared and
available to be eaten, drunk, used, etc yenilmeye/kul-
lanıma/içilmeye hazır Is dinner ready? ○ When will
the book be ready for publication? 3 be ready to do
sth to be willing to do something yapmaya hazır/
istekli olma We are ready to die for our country. ⊃See
also: rough¹ and ready.

ready-made /ˌrediˈmeɪd/ adjective made and ready to
use hazır yapım; kullanıma hazır ready-made
meals

'ready ,meal noun [C] a meal that has already been
cooked, that is bought at a shop but taken home to be
heated and eaten

o⁻**real¹** /rɪəl/ adjective 1 [NOT IMAGINED] existing and not imagined gerçek, sahici, hakiki Romance is never like
that in real life. 2 [TRUE] true and not pretended sahici,
doğru What was the real reason she didn't come? ○ Is
that your real name? 3 [NOT ARTIFICIAL] not artificial or
false sunî olmayan, gerçek real fur/leather ○ It's not
a toy gun, it's the real thing. 4 [FOR EMPHASIS] [always before
noun] used to emphasize a noun gerçek, hakiki, ciddi,
pek, tam tamına She was a real help. 5 Get real! informal used to tell someone that they are hoping for something that will never happen, or that they believe something that is not true Aptallık etme!', 'Gerçeği gör!',
'Gözünü aç!', 'Farkında değil misin?' ⊃See also: the real
McCoy.

real² /rɪəl/ adverb US informal very çok, gerçekten,
hakikaten It's real easy to get there from here.

'real es,tate noun [U] US buildings and land gayri menkul, emlâk, taşınmaz mal/mülk

'real estate ,agent US (UK estate agent) noun [C] someone who sells buildings and land as their job emlâkçı

realism /ˈrɪəlɪzªm/ noun [U] 1 when things and people in
art, literature, etc are shown as they are in real life
gerçekçilik, realizm 2 when you accept and deal
with the true facts of a situation and do not hope for
things that will not happen gerçekleri görme, gerçek-
cilik

realist /'rɪəlɪst/ *noun* [C] **1** someone who accepts the true facts of a situation and does not hope for things that will not happen **gerçekçi, realist 2** an artist or writer who shows people and things in their work as they are in real life **(ressam, yazar) gerçekçi, realist kimse**

realistic /ˌrɪə'lɪstɪk/ *adjective* **1** accepting the true facts of a situation and not basing decisions on things that will not happen **gerçekçi, realist; gerçekleri dikkate alan** *Let's be realistic - we're not going to finish this by Friday.* **2** showing things and people as they really are, or making them seem to be real **olduğu gibi gösteren/görünen** *realistic special effects in a film* ⊃Opposite **unrealistic**. ● **realistically** *adverb* **gerçekçi bir şekilde**

┌───┐
│ 🧩 *reality* ...... İLE BİRLİKTE KULLANILAN KELİMELER │
└───┘
face up to reality ● **turn** [an idea/dream, etc] **into** reality ● **lose touch with** reality ● **in** reality

reality /rɪ'æləti/ *noun* **1** [U] the way things or situations really are and not the way you would like them to be **gerçek, hakikât** *Sooner or later you have to face up to reality.* ○ *He may seem charming but in reality he's actually quite unpleasant.* **2 the reality/realities of sth** the truth about an unpleasant situation **hoş olmayan bir durumun gerçek şekli/gerçeği/hakikâti** *the harsh realities of life* **3 become a reality** to start to happen or exist **gerçekleşmek; olmaya/varolmaya başlamak** *New jobs could become a reality by next month.* ⊃See also: **virtual reality**.

reˌality TˈV *noun* [U] television programmes about ordinary people who are filmed in real situations **gerçek hayattan kesitler gösteren televizyon programları**

realization (*also UK* -isation) /ˌrɪəlaɪ'zeɪ∫ᵊn/ *noun* **1** [U, no plural] when you notice or understand something that you did not notice or understand before **idrak, anlama, farkında olma** [+ that] *There is a growing realization that education has benefits at many levels.* **2** [U] when you achieve something that you wanted **gerçekleştirme, sonunda elde etme; sahip olma** *the realization of an ambition*

o⋅**realize** (*also UK* -ise) /'rɪəlaɪz/ *verb* [T] **1** NOTICE to notice or understand something that you did not notice or understand before **farkına varmak; farketmek; idrak etmek** [+ question word] *I didn't realize how unhappy she was.* ○ *I suddenly realized I'd met him before.* ○ [+ (that)] *Some people just don't seem to realize that the world has changed.* **2 realize an ambition/dream/goal, etc** to achieve something that you have wanted for a long time **uzun süre istediği bir şeyi başarmak; bir tutkuyu/rüyayı/amacı gerçekleştirmek** *He had realized all his ambitions by the age of 30.* **3** SELL to sell things that you own *to realize your assets* **4** MAKE MONEY to be sold for a particular amount of money *The shares realized £1.4 million.*

o⋅**really** /'rɪəli/ *adverb* **1** very or very much **gerçekten, sahiden** *She's really nice.* ○ *I really don't want to go.* ○ *"Did you like it then?" "Er, not really."* (= no). **2** used when you are saying what is the truth of a situation **aslında, gerçekte** *She tried to hide what she was really thinking.* **3 Really?** used when you are surprised at what someone has just said **'Gerçekten mi?', 'Sahiden mi?', 'Ciddi misin?'** *"Apparently, he's leaving." "Really?"*

┌─────────────────────────────┐
│ **YAYGIN HATALAR** │
└─────────────────────────────┘
really
Dikkat! Sık yapılan kelime türetme hatası! Eğer bir sıfat **l** ile bitiyorsa, onu zarf haline dönüştürmek için

-**ly** ekleyin. **Realy** olarak yazmayın. Doğru hali **really** olarak kullanımıdır.

realm /relm/ *noun* [C] **1** *formal* an area of knowledge or activity **alan, saha;** ...**dünyası** *successes in the realm of foreign policy* **2** *literary* a country that has a king or queen **krallık**

realtor /'riːltər/ *US* (*UK* **estate agent**) *noun* [C] someone who sells buildings or land as their job **emlâkçı**

reap /riːp/ *verb* **1 reap the benefits/profits/rewards** to get something good by working hard for it **yararını/kârını/ödülünü görmek; istenilen sonucu elde etmek** *Sometimes, this approach can reap tremendous rewards.* **2** [I, T] to cut and collect a crop of grain **hasat etmek; mahsül kaldırmak/toplamak**

reappear /ˌriːə'pɪər/ *verb* [I] to appear again or return after a period of time **tekrar ortaya çıkmak, yeniden görünmek** *He reappeared later that day.* ● **reappearance** /ˌriːə'pɪərᵊns/ *noun* [C, U] **tekrardan ortaya çıkma**

rear¹ /rɪər/ *noun* **1 the rear** the back part of something **geri, arka** *First class accommodation is towards the rear of the train.* **2 bring up the rear** to be at the back of a group of people who are walking or running **en arkadan gelmek, en sonunda bulunmak** ● **rear** *adjective* [always before noun] *a rear window/wheel* **arka**

rear² /rɪər/ *verb* **1** [T] If you rear children or young animals, you care for them until they are adults. **büyütmek, bakmak, yetiştirmek** *In these waters they breed and rear their young.* **2** [I] (*also* **rear up**) If a horse rears, it stands on its back legs. **şahlanmak, şaha kalkmak** ⊃See also: **raise/rear its ugly head¹**.

rearrange /ˌriːə'reɪndʒ/ *verb* [T] **1** to change the order or position of things **(düzen) yeniden düzenlemek** *I've rearranged the furniture.* **2** to change the time of an event or meeting **(zaman) yeniden ayarlamak** *I've rearranged the meeting for Monday.*

ˌrear-view 'mirror *noun* [C] a small mirror inside a car which the driver looks in to see what is happening behind the car **dikiz aynası** ⊃Orta kısımdaki renkli sayfalarına bakınız.

┌───┐
│ 🧩 *reason* ...... İLE BİRLİKTE KULLANILAN KELİMELER │
└───┘
a **compelling/good/obvious/simple** reason ● **have/give/understand** a reason ● **the** reason **for sth** ● **the** reason **why sth happens**

o⋅**reason¹** /'riːzᵊn/ *noun* **1** WHY [C] the facts about why something happens or why someone does something **neden, sebep** *Is there any particular reason why he doesn't want to come?* ○ *He left without giving a reason.* ○ *That was the reason for telling her.* **2** RIGHT [C, U] something that makes it right for you to do something **gerekçe, neden, sebep** [+ to do sth] *There is every reason to believe the project will be finished on time.* **3** ABILITY [U] the ability to think and make good decisions **sağduyu, mantık, akılselim** *By this time he'd lost his powers of reason.* **4 within reason** If something is within reason, it is acceptable and possible. **mantık çerçevesinde, makul ölçüler içerisinde** *You can have as much as you like, within reason.* **5 it stands to reason** If it stands to reason that something happens or is true, it is what you would expect. **gayet açık ki; herkes bilir ki; son derece aşikar ki** *It stands to reason that a child who is constantly criticized will have little self-confidence.*

reason² /'riːzᵊn/ *verb* [T] to decide that something is true after considering the facts **muhakeme etmek, kara-**

R

rına varmak [+ that] *We reasoned that it was unlikely he would be a serious threat to the public.*

reason with sb *phrasal verb* to persuade someone not to do something stupid by giving them good reasons not to inandırmaya/ikna etmeye çalışmak

reasonable /ˈriːzᵊnəbl/ *adjective* **1** [FAIR] fair and showing good judgment **makul, akla yatkın, sağduyulu** [+ to do sth] *It's not reasonable to expect people to work those hours.* ⊃Opposite **unreasonable**. **2** [BIG ENOUGH] big enough or large enough in number, although not big or not many **uygun, makul, yerinde** *There were a reasonable number of people there.* **3** [GOOD ENOUGH] good enough but not the best **uygun, oldukça iyi, makul** *I'd say her work is of a reasonable standard.* **4** [CHEAP] not expensive **ne ucuz ne pahalı, makul** *reasonable prices*

reasonably /ˈriːzᵊnəbli/ *adverb* **1** in a fair way, showing good judgment **makul bir şekilde, akla uygun biçimde** *Why can't we discuss this reasonably, like adults?* **2 reasonably good/successful/well, etc** good/successful/well, etc enough but not very good or very well **oldukça, epeyce** *I did reasonably well at school but not as well as my sister.* **3 reasonably priced** not expensive **makul ölçüde fiyatlandırılmış; ne ucuz ne pahalı; tam değerinde**

reasoning /ˈriːzᵊnɪŋ/ *noun* [U] the process of thinking about something in order to make a decision **akıl süzgecinden geçirme, muhakeme,mantıklı düşünme** *I don't understand the reasoning behind this decision.*

reassure /ˌriːəˈʃʊəʳ/ *verb* [T] to say something to stop someone from worrying **içini rahatlatmak, güvenini pekiştirmek** [+ that] *He reassured me that I would be paid soon.* ● **reassurance** /ˌriːəˈʃʊərᵊns/ *noun* [C, U] something that you say to make someone stop worrying **güven verme, içini rahatlatma, güvence, teminat, garanti** *Despite my repeated reassurances that she was welcome, she wouldn't come.*

reassuring /ˌriːəˈʃʊərɪŋ/ *adjective* making you feel less worried **güven verici, iç rahatlatan,** *a reassuring smile/voice* ● **reassuringly** *adverb* **temin edercesine**

rebate /ˈriːbeɪt/ *noun* [C] an amount of money that is given back to you because you have paid too much **iade, iade edilen tutar/meblağ** *a tax/rent rebate*

rebel¹ /ˈrebᵊl/ *noun* [C] **1** someone who fights against the government in their country, especially a soldier **âsi, isyancı, başkaldıran kimse** *Rebels seized control of the airport.* **2** someone who does not like authority and refuses to obey rules **kurallara isyan eden/karşı çıkan/başkaldıran kimse**

rebel² /rɪˈbel/ *verb* [I] **rebelling,** *past* **rebelled 1** to fight against the government **devlete başkaldırmak/isyan etmek 2** to refuse to obey rules because you do not like authority **otoriteye/kurallara başkaldırmak/isyan etmek** *She rebelled against her family.*

🔲🔳🔲 **rebellion** ...... İLE BİRLİKTE KULLANILAN KELİMELER

launch/lead/quash/stage a rebellion ● a rebellion **against** sb/sth ● a rebellion **by** sb

rebellion /rɪˈbeliən/ *noun* [C, U] when people fight against the government in their country **isyan, ayaklanma, başkaldırı**

rebellious /rɪˈbeliəs/ *adjective* refusing to obey rules because you do not like authority **isyankâr, âsi, söz dinlemez** *a rebellious teenager*

rebirth /ˈriːbɜːθ/ *noun* [no plural] when something becomes popular or active for the second time **tekrar meşhur olan/ortaya çıkan/aktif olan** *the rebirth of the women's movement*

reboot /ˌriːˈbuːt/ *verb* [T, I] When a computer reboots, it switches off and then starts again immediately, and when you reboot a computer, you make it do this **yeniden açmak (bilgisayar)**

rebound¹ /rɪˈbaʊnd/ *verb* [I] to move back through the air after hitting something **çarpıp geri gelmek, çarpıp/vurup sekmek** *The ball rebounded off the post.*

rebound² /ˈriːbaʊnd/ *noun* **be on the rebound** to be unhappy because your romantic relationship has ended **romantik ilişkisi bittiğinden dolayı mutsuz olmak** *She was on the rebound when she met her second husband.*

rebuff /rɪˈbʌf/ *verb* [T] *formal* to refuse someone's suggestion or offer, especially in an unfriendly way **terslemek, kabaca reddetmek, geri çevirmek** *The company has rebuffed several buyout offers.* ● **rebuff** *noun* [C] **tersleme, kabul etmeme**

rebuild /ˌriːˈbɪld/ *verb* [T] *past* **rebuilt 1** to build something again after it has been damaged **yeniden inşa etmek, tekrar yapmak** *The cathedral was rebuilt after being destroyed by fire.* **2** to make a situation succeed again after something bad caused it to fail **düzeltmek, iyileştirmek, canlandırmak, eski hâline getirmek** *The country is still struggling to rebuild its economy.*

rebuke /rɪˈbjuːk/ *verb* [T] *formal* to speak angrily to someone because they have done something wrong **terslemek, azarlamak, çıkışmak, paylamak** ● **rebuke** *noun* [C] *formal* **azar**

recalcitrant /rɪˈkælsɪtrənt/ *adjective formal* not willing to obey or help someone **inatçı, huysuz, çekilmez, dik kafalı, boyun eğmeyen** *recalcitrant schoolchildren*

recall /rɪˈkɔːl/ *verb* [T] **1** to remember something **hatırlamak, anımsamak** *I don't recall arranging a time to meet.* **2** to order the return of someone or something **geri çağırmak, geri getirtmek** [often passive] *The ambassador was recalled to London.* ● **recall** /ˈriːkɔːl/ *noun* [U] **anımsatma**

recap /ˈriːkæp/ *verb* [I] **recapping,** *past* **recapped** to repeat the most important parts of what you have just said **en önemli bölümü tekrar söylemek, özetlemek; ana hatlarını tekrar söylemek** ● **recap** /ˈriːkæp/ *noun* [C] **toparlama, özetleme**

recapture /ˌriːˈkæptʃəʳ/ *verb* [T] **1** to catch a person or animal that has escaped **tekrar yakalamak, yeniden ele geçirmek 2** to experience or feel something from the past again **yeniden yaşa(t)mak; canlandırmak, yakalamak** *Some men try to recapture their youth by going out with younger women.*

recede /rɪˈsiːd/ *verb* [I] **1** [MOVE AWAY] to become further and further away **uzaklaşmak, yavaş yavaş kaybolmak** *The coastline receded into the distance.* **2** [LESS STRONG] If a memory or feeling recedes, it becomes less clear or strong. **gittikçe zayıflamak, etkisini kaybetmek, azalmak, solmak 3** [HAIR] If a man's hair recedes, it stops growing at the front of his head. **alnı açılmak, öndeki saçları dökülmek** *a receding hairline*

receipt /rɪˈsiːt/ *noun* **1** [C] a piece of paper that proves that you have received goods or money **fiş, makbuz** *Could I have a receipt?* ○ *Remember to keep receipts for any work done.* **2** [U] *formal* the act of receiving something **teslim alma** *Items must be returned within fourteen days of receipt.*

receipts /rɪˈsiːts/ *US* (*UK* **takings**) *noun* [plural] the amount of money that a business gets from selling things **hâsılat, gelir, kazanç** *box-office receipts*

o***receive** /rɪˈsiːv/ *verb* [T] **1** [GET] to get something that someone has given or sent to you **teslim almak, almak** *Occasionally, he receives letters from fans.* **2** [REACT] to react to a suggestion or piece of work in a particular way **bir öneriye veya bir işe tepki vermek, karşılamak** [often passive] *His first book was not well received* (= people did not like it). **3** WELCOME to formally welcome guests **kabul etmek, karşılamak** ⊃See also: be on/at the receiving **end**¹ of sth.

receive

Dikkat! Yazılışını kontrol edin. Receive Türk öğrencileri tarafından en çok yanlış yazılan 10 kelimeden biridir. Unutmayın! ie olarak yazmayın; **ei** olarak yazın.

receiver /rɪ'siːvəʳ/ *noun* [C] **1** TELEPHONE the part of a telephone that you hold in your hand and use for listening and speaking **ahize 2** RADIO/TV the part of a radio or television that receives signals from the air **alıcı; televizyon/radyo alıcısı 3** PERSON someone who officially deals with a company when it has to stop business because it cannot pay the money it owes **iflas etmiş bir şirketin yönetimine resmen el koyan ve yürüten kişi**

o⇥**recent** /'riːsᵊnt/ *adjective* happening or starting from a short time ago **yeni, son, geçenlerdeki** *a recent photo* ○ *In recent years, sales have decreased quite markedly.*

o⇥**recently** /'riːsᵊntli/ *adverb* not long ago **geçenlerde, son günlerde, yakınlarda** *Have you seen any good films recently?* ○ *Until recently he worked as a teacher.*

⊞ reception ...... İLE BİRLİKTE KULLANILAN KELİMELER

get/be given/receive a [cool/good, etc] reception ● a **cool/chilly/frosty/hostile** reception ● a **good/great/rapturous/warm** reception ● a **lukewarm/mixed** reception ● reception **from** sb

reception /rɪ'sepʃᵊn/ *noun* **1** HOTEL/OFFICE [no plural] the place in a hotel or office building where people go when they arrive **kayıt kabul yeri, resepsiyon** *Ask for me at reception.* ○ *a reception area/desk* **2** PARTY [C] a formal party that is given to celebrate a special event or to welcome someone **tören, davet, kabul resmi/töreni** *a wedding reception* **3** REACTION [no plural] the way people react to something or someone **karşılama, kabul, resepsiyon** *We were given a very warm reception.* **4** RADIO/TV [U] the quality of a radio or television signal **radyo/televizyon sinyal kalitesi**

receptionist /rɪ'sepʃᵊnɪst/ *noun* [C] someone who works in a hotel or office building, answering the telephone and dealing with guests **kabul görevlisi, resepsiyon memuru** *a hotel receptionist*

receptive /rɪ'septɪv/ *adjective* willing to think about and accept new ideas **kabule hazır/istekli** *She's generally very receptive to ideas and suggestions.*

recess /rɪ'ses/ *noun* **1** NOT WORKING [C, U] a time in the day or in the year when a parliament or law court is not working **meclis tatili, adlî tatil; mola; ara** *a parliamentary/congressional recess* ○ *The court is in recess for thirty minutes.* **2** SCHOOL [C, U] US (UK break) a period of free time between classes at school **teneffüs, ara, mola** *At recess the boys would fight.* **3** WALL [C] a part of a wall in a room that is further back than the rest of the wall **girinti, niş**

recession /rɪ'seʃᵊn/ *noun* [C, U] a time when the economy of a country is not successful **ekonomide durgunluk/gerileme** *The latest report confirms that the economy is in recession.*

recharge /ˌriː'tʃɑːdʒ/ *verb* [T] to fill a battery (= object that provides a machine with power) with electricity so that it can work again **doldurmak, şarj etmek**

recipe /'resɪpi/ *noun* **1** [C] a list of foods and a set of instructions telling you how to cook something

yemek tarifi *a recipe for carrot cake* **2 be a recipe for disaster/trouble/success,** etc to be likely to become a disaster, a success, etc **muhtemel felakete/soruna/başarıya vs. davetiye/yol/reçete/anahtar/hazırlayıcı olmak**

recipient /rɪ'sɪpiənt/ *noun* [C] someone who receives something **alıcı, alan kimse** *a recipient of an award*

reciprocal¹ /rɪ'sɪprək³l/ *adjective* involving two people or groups that agree to help each other in a similar way **karşılıklı, iki taraflı** *a reciprocal arrangement*

reciprocate /rɪ'sɪprəkeɪt/ *verb* [I, T] to do something for someone because they have done something similar for you **karşılık vermek, mukabele etmek**

recital /rɪ'saɪt³l/ *noun* [C] a performance of music or poetry **müzik, şiir dinletisi/resitali** *a piano recital*

recite /rɪ'saɪt/ *verb* [I, T] to say something aloud from memory **ezbere söylemek/okumak** *She can recite the whole poem.*

reckless /'rekləs/ *adjective* doing something dangerous and not caring about what might happen **atak, pervasız, kayıtsız, umursamaz, dikkatsiz, ihtiyatsız** *reckless driving* ● **recklessly** *adverb* **umursamazca**

reckon /'rekᵊn/ *verb* [T] **1** to think that something is probably true **sanmak, düşünmek** *I reckon he likes her.* ○ [+ (that)] *He reckons that he earns more in a week than I do in a month.* **2** to guess that a particular number is correct **ummak, tahminde bulunmak** *His fortune is reckoned at $5 million.* ⊃See also: a **force**¹ to be reckoned with.

reckon on sth/doing sth *phrasal verb* to think that something is going to happen and make it part of your plans **ummak, beklemek, bel bağlamak**

reckon with sb/sth *phrasal verb* to deal with someone or something difficult **hesaba katmak, göze almak; zoru başarmaya çalışmak**

reclaim /rɪ'kleɪm/ *verb* [T] **1** to get something back from someone **geri almak, geri istemek** *You can reclaim the tax at the airport.* **2** to make land good enough to be used for growing crops **tarıma elverişli/kullanışlı/kullanıma uygun hâle getirmek; toprağı ıslah etmek**

recline /rɪ'klaɪn/ *verb* **1** [I] to lie back with the upper part of your body in a horizontal position **yaslanmak, yaslanarak oturmak/yatmak** *I found him reclining on the sofa.* **2** [I, T] If a chair reclines, you can lower the back part so that you can lie in it, and if you recline a chair, you put it in this position. **arkalığı yatmak/yatırmak** *a reclining chair/seat*

recluse /rɪ'kluːs/ *noun* [C] someone who lives alone and does not like being with other people **münzevî, topluluktan kaçan kişi; içine kapanık kimse** ● **reclusive** *adjective* living alone and avoiding other people **yalnız yaşayan; münzevî bir yaşam süren; topluluktan kaçan**

⊞ recognition ...... İLE BİRLİKTE KULLANILAN KELİMELER

achieve/deserve/gain recognition ● **in** recognition **of** sth ● recognition **for** sth

recognition /ˌrekəg'nɪʃᵊn/ *noun* **1** ACCEPT [U, no plural] when you accept that something is true or real **tanıma** *There is a growing recognition of the scale of the problem.* ○ [+ that] *There is a general recognition that she's the best person for the job.* **2** HONOUR [U] when someone is publicly thanked for something good that they have done **takdir; toplum önünde takdir etme** *Ellen gained recognition for her outstanding work.* ○ *He was given a medal in recognition of his bravery.* **3** KNOW [U] when you know something or someone because you have seen or experienced them before **önceden gör-**

düğü denediğini tekrar tanıma/farketme *I waved at her, but she showed no sign of recognition.*

recognizable *(also UK -isable)* /'rekəgnaızəbl/ *adjective* able to be recognized (= able to be known) **tanınabilir, ayırt edilebilir** *Megan's voice is instantly recognizable.*
● **recognizably** *adverb* **farkedilir şekilde**

⚬**recognize** *(also UK -ise)* /'rekəgnaız/ *verb* [T] KNOW to know someone or something because you have seen or experienced them before **tanımak, bilmek** *I recognized her from her picture.* ○ *Doctors are trained to recognize the symptoms of disease.* **2** ACCEPT to accept that something is true or real **tanımak, kabul etmek, onaylamak** [+ (that)] *She recognized that she had been partly to blame.* ○ *Smoking is recognized as a leading cause of lung cancer.* **3** SHOW RESPECT to officially show respect for someone for an achievement **takdir etmek, başarıyı resmen takdir etmek** *He was recognized by the governor for his work with teenagers.*

recoil /rı'kɔıl/ *verb* [I] to react to something with fear or hate **ürkmek, irkilmek; ürküp geri çekilmek** *She recoiled in horror at the thought of touching a snake.*

recollect /ˌrekəl'ekt/ *verb* [T] to remember something **hatırlamak, anımsamak** *I didn't recollect having seen him.*

recollection /ˌrekəl'ekʃən/ *noun* [C, U] when you remember something **hatırlama, anımsama** *He had no recollection of the incident.*

⚬**recommend** /ˌrekə'mend/ *verb* [T] **1** to say that someone or something is good or suitable for a particular purpose **tavsiye etmek, önermek, salık vermek** *Can you recommend a good wine to go with this dish?* ○ *She has been recommended for promotion.* **2** to advise someone that something should be done **öğütlemek, salık vermek, tavsiye etmek** *The judge is likely to recommend a long jail sentence.* ○ [+ that] *The report recommended that tourists avoid the region.*

accept/follow/implement/make a recommendation ● a recommendation **for/on** sth

recommendation /ˌrekəmen'deıʃən/ *noun* **1** [C] a piece of advice about what to do in a particular situation **öğüt, tavsiye, salık** *The marketing department made several recommendations to improve sales.* ○ [+ that] *It's my recommendation that this factory be closed immediately.* **2** [C, U] a suggestion that someone or something is good or suitable for a particular purpose **öneri, tavsiye** *I bought this book on Andy's recommendation.*

recompense /'rekəmpens/ *noun* [U] *formal* payment that you give to someone when you have caused them difficulty or an injury **tazminat** *Angry soccer fans sought recompense for the cancelled match.* ● **recompense** *verb* [T] *formal He was recompensed for loss of earnings.* **ceza ödemek**

reconcile /'rekənsaıl/ *verb* [T] **1** to make two different ideas, beliefs, or situations agree or able to exist together **uzlaştırmak, bağdaştırmak** *It is sometimes difficult to reconcile science and religion.* ○ *How can you reconcile your love of animals with your habit of eating them?* **2 be reconciled (with sb)** to become friendly with someone after you have argued with them **barışmak, uzlaşmak, bağdaşmak**
reconcile yourself to sth *phrasal verb* to accept a situation although you do not like it **alışmak, kabullenmek, razı olmak, boyun eğdirmek** *Eventually he reconciled himself to living without her.*

reconciliation /ˌrekənˌsıli'eıʃən/ *noun* **1** [C, U] when two people or groups become friendly again after they have argued **barışma, uzlaşma** *to seek a reconciliation* **2** [U, no plural] the process of making two opposite ideas, beliefs, or situations agree **barışma/uzlaşma eylemi** *the reconciliation of facts with theory*

reconnaissance /rı'kɒnısəns/ *noun* [U] the process of getting information about a place or an area for military use **keşif, keşif çalışması**

reconsider /ˌri:kən'sıdər/ *verb* [I, T] to think again about a decision or opinion and decide if you want to change it **tekrar/yeniden gözden geçirmek** *We've been asked to reconsider the proposal.* ● **reconsideration** /ˌri:kən, sıdər'eıʃən/ *noun* [U] **tekrar gözden geçirme**

reconstruct /ˌri:kən'strʌkt/ *verb* [T] **1** to create a description of a past event using all the information that you have **yeniden canlandırmak/kurmak** *The police tried to reconstruct the crime using evidence found at the scene.* **2** to build something again after it has been damaged or destroyed **yeniden inşa etmek/yapmak**

reconstruction /ˌri:kən'strʌkʃən/ *noun* [C, U] **1** when you create a description of a past event using all the information that you have **yeniden canlandırma/kurma/teşkil/oluşturma** *A reconstruction of the crime was shown on TV.* **2** when you build something again after it has been damaged or destroyed **yeniden inşa etme/yapma; restorasyon**

have/keep a record ● records **indicate/reveal/show** sth ● a record of sth ● [the hottest/the lowest, etc] **on** record

⚬**record¹** /'rekɔ:d/ *noun* **1** STORED INFORMATION [C, U] information that is written on paper or stored on computer so that it can be used in the future **kayıt** *medical/dental records* ○ *My teacher keeps a record of my absences.* ○ *This has been the hottest summer on record* (= the hottest summer known about). **2** BEHAVIOUR [C] A person's or company's record is their behaviour or achievements. **kişi/şirket sicili/kayıtları** [usually singular] *She has an outstanding academic record* (= has done very well in school). ○ *Of all airlines they have the best safety record.* **3** BEST [C] the best, biggest, longest, tallest, etc **rekor; en iyi/büyük/uzun vs.** *to set/break a record* ○ *He holds the world record for 100 metres.* **4** MUSIC [C] a flat, round, plastic disc that music is stored on, used especially in the past **plak** *to play a record* **5 off the record** If you say something off the record, you do not want the public to know about it. **gizli, gayrî resmi olarak, açıklanmaması şartı ile 6 put/set the record straight** to tell people the true facts about a situation **düzeltmek, doğruyu ortaya koymak, tashih etmek 7** COMPUTER a collection of pieces of information in a computer database that is treated as one unit *You can sort the records on any field.* ⊃See also: **track record.**

⚬**record²** /rı'kɔ:d/ *verb* [T] **1** to write down information or store it on a computer so that it can be used in the future **bilgisayarda kaydetmek** *He recorded details of their conversation in his diary.* **2** [I, T] to store sounds or pictures using electronic equipment, a camera, etc so that you can listen to them or see them again **resim, müzik kaydetmek** *to record a new album* ○ *a recorded message*

record-breaking /'rekɔ:dˌbreıkıŋ/ *adjective* [always before noun] better, bigger, longer, etc than anything else before **rekor kıran** *record-breaking sales of the new video*

recorder /rı'kɔ:dər/ *noun* [C] **1** a machine for storing sounds or pictures **kayıt aleti/makinası/cihazı** *a video recorder* **2** a long, thin, hollow instrument that you play by blowing into it **blok flüt** ⊃See also: **cassette recorder, tape recorder.**

recording /rɪ'kɔːdɪŋ/ noun [C, U] sounds or moving pictures that have been recorded, or the process of recording kayıt, kayıt etme *a recording of classical music* ○ *a new system of digital recording*

'**record ,label** noun [C] a company that records and sells music **müzik kayıt şirketi/stüdyosu**

'**record ,player** noun [C] a machine that makes it possible to hear the music on a record (= a flat, round disc used especially in the past) **pikap, plâk çalar, gramofon, fonograf**

recount¹ /rɪ'kaʊnt/ verb [T] formal to tell a story or describe an event **söylemek, anlatmak, hikaye etmek, aktarmak** *He was recounting a story about a woman he'd met on a train.*

recount² /ˌriː'kaʊnt/ verb [T] to count something again **yeniden/tekrar saymak**

recount³ /'riːkaʊnt/ noun [C] a second count of votes in an election **seçimde oyların yeniden sayılması** *They demanded a recount.*

recoup /rɪ'kuːp/ verb [T] to get back money that you have lost or spent **(harcırah, harcama vs.) almak, geri almak** *to recoup your losses*

recourse /rɪ'kɔːs/ noun [U] formal someone or something that can help you in a difficult situation **yardım edilme** *For many cancer patients, surgery is the only recourse.* ○ *They solved their problem without recourse to* (= without using) *violence.*

o-= **recover** /rɪ'kʌvəʳ/ verb 1 [HEALTH] [I] to become healthy or happy again after an illness, injury, or period of sadness **yeniden sağlığına kavuşmak, iyileşmek, şifa bulmak** *It takes a long time to recover from surgery.* ○ *She never recovered from the death of her husband.* 2 [SITUATION] [I] If a system or situation recovers, it returns to the way it was before something bad happened. **toparlanmak, eski hâline gelmek** *The economy was quick to recover after the election.* 3 [BODY] [T] to be able to use or feel again part of your body which has been damaged **vücudun hasar görmüş kısımlarını yeniden kullanmaya başlamak** *He never fully recovered the use of his legs.* 4 [GET BACK] [T] to get something back that has been lost or stolen **yeniden elde etmek, tekrar kazanmak, bulmak** *Police recovered the stolen money.*

recovery ...... İLE BİRLİKTE KULLANILAN KELİMELER

make a recovery • a full/**miraculous/slow/speedy** recovery • recovery **from** sth

recovery /rɪ'kʌvəʳri/ noun 1 [HEALTH] [U, no plural] when you feel better or happier again after an illness, injury, or period of sadness **iyileşme, şifa bulma, sağlığına kavuşma** *She only had the operation last month but she's made a good recovery.* 2 [SITUATION] [U, no plural] when a system or situation returns to the way it was before something bad happened **düzelme, iyileşme** *economic recovery* ○ *The housing industry has made a remarkable recovery.* 3 [GET BACK] [U] when you get back something that was lost or stolen **tekrar elde etme, yeniden kavuşma, bulma** *the recovery of stolen jewels*

recreate /ˌriːkri'eɪt/ verb [T] to make something exist or happen again **yeniden canlandırmak, yaratmak** *They plan to recreate a typical English village in Japan.*

recreation /ˌrekri'eɪ[ə]n/ noun [C, U] activities that you do for enjoyment when you are not working **eğlence, dinlenme, hoşça vakit geçirme için yapılan aktiviteler** *Shopping seems to be her only form of recreation.* • **recreational** adjective **eğlence için yapılan**

recrimination /rɪˌkrɪmɪ'neɪ[ə]n/ noun [C, U] formal the things you say when you blame someone for something,

or the act of blaming someone for something **karşılıklı suçlayan söz ve davranışlar; karşılıklı suçlama**

recruit¹ /rɪ'kruːt/ verb [I, T] to try to persuade someone to work for a company or to join an organization **çalışmaya/katılmaya ikna etmek; yazmak, kaydetmek, almak, katmak** • **recruitment** noun [U] when you recruit people **yeniden üye alma/kaydetme; askere alma/kaydetme** *graduate recruitment*

recruit ...... İLE BİRLİKTE KULLANILAN KELİMELER

a **new** recruit • a recruit **to** sth

recruit² /rɪ'kruːt/ noun [C] someone who has recently joined an organization **yeni üye, acemi er** *a new recruit*

rectangle /'rektæŋgl/ noun [C] a shape with four 90° angles and four sides, with opposite sides of equal length and two sides longer than the other two **dikdörtgen** ⊃See picture at **shape.** • **rectangular** /rek'tæŋgjələʳ/ adjective shaped like a rectangle **dikdörtgen biçiminde** *a rectangular room*

rectify /'rektɪfaɪ/ verb [T] formal to correct something or change it so that it is acceptable **doğrultmak, düzeltmek; ...ı/i gidermek, ıslâh etmek** *The government has promised to rectify the situation.*

rector /'rektəʳ/ noun [C] a priest in some Christian churches **papaz**

rectum /'rektəm/ noun [C] the last part of the body that solid waste travels through before coming out of the bottom **kalın bağırsak; vücudun boşaltım sistemi**

recuperate /rɪ'kuːp[ə]reɪt/ verb [I] to become healthy again after an illness or injury **iyileşmek, sağlığına yeniden kavuşmak** *She's still recuperating from her injuries.* • **recuperation** /rɪˌkjuːp[ə]r'eɪ[ə]n/ noun [U] **sağlığına kavuşma, iyileşme**

recur /rɪ'kɜːʳ/ verb [I] **recurring**, past **recurred** to happen again or many times **tekrarlamak, yinelemek, tekerrür etmek** *The same ideas recur throughout her books.* • **recurrence** /rɪ'kʌrəns/ noun [C, U] when something recurs **tekrarlanma, yinelenme, nüksetme** *a recurrence of the disease*

recurring /rɪ'kɜːrɪŋ/ (also recurrent) adjective happening again or many times **tekrarlayan, yineleyen, nükseden** *a recurring dream*

recycle /ˌriː'saɪkl/ verb [I, T] to put used paper, glass, plastic, etc through a process so that it can be used again **yeniden kazanmak; tekrar kullanmak** *We recycle all our newspapers and bottles.* • **recyclable** /ˌriː'saɪkləbl/ adjective able to be recycled **yeniden kazanılabilir** *Glass is recyclable.*

recycled /ˌriː'saɪkld/ adjective Recycled paper, glass, plastic, etc has been used before and put through a process so that it can be used again. **önceden kullanılmış fakat yeniden kullanılabilir hale getirilmiş**

recycling /ˌriː'saɪklɪŋ/ noun [U] when paper, glass, plastic, etc is put through a process so that it can be used again **yeniden kazanma** *ways to encourage recycling* ○ *a recycling centre*

o-= **red¹** /red/ adjective or **redder** or **reddest** 1 [COLOUR] being the same colour as blood **kırmızı** *a red shirt* ⊃Orta kısımdaki renkli sayfalarına bakınız. 2 [HAIR] Red hair is an orange-brown colour. **kızıl 3 go red** UK (US **turn red**) If someone goes red, their face becomes red because they are embarrassed or angry. **kızarmak, mahcubiyetten yüzü kızarmak 4** [WINE] Red wine is made from black grapes (= small, round, purple fruits). **kırmızı** ⊃See also: be like a red **rag** to a bull.

o-= **red²** /red/ noun 1 [C, U] the colour of blood **al, kan kırmızısı, al renk** ⊃Orta kısımdaki renkli sayfalarına bakınız. **2 in**

the red If your bank account is in the red, you have spent more money than there was in it. borçlu, hesabından fazla para çekmiş, hesapta içeri girmiş **3 see red** to become very angry öfkeden çılgına dönmek, tepesi atmak, gözü dönmek

,red 'card *noun* [C] in football, a small red card which the referee (= someone who makes sure the players follow the rules) shows to a player to make him stop playing because he has broken a rule futbolda kırmızı kart

the ,red 'carpet *noun* special treatment that is given to an important person when they go somewhere kırmızı halı serme, önemli bir kişiye gösterilen hassasiyet, özenli davranış *She's given the red carpet treatment wherever she goes.*

redden /ˈredⁿn/ *verb* [I, T] to become red or to make something become red kızarmak, kızartmak *His face reddened with anger.*

redeem /rɪˈdiːm/ *verb* [T] **1** [IMPROVE] to make something seem less bad durumu kurtarmak, telâfi etmek; daha az kötü hâle getirmek *He tried to redeem his reputation by working extra hard.* ○ *a redeeming feature* **2 redeem yourself** to do something that makes people have a better opinion of you after you have done something bad kendini affettirmek, suçunu bağışlatmak *He was two hours late, but he redeemed himself by bringing presents.* **3** [GET SOMETHING] to exchange something for something else bir şeyi bir diğeri için değiştirmek **4** [RELIGION] to save someone from evil, especially according to the Christian religion kötülüklerden korumak/kurtarmak

redemption /rɪˈdempʃⁿn/ *noun* **1** [U] when someone is saved from evil, especially according to the Christian religion kurtulma, halâs, bağışlanma **2 be beyond redemption** to be too bad to be improved or saved iflâh olmaz olmak, bağışlanamaz olmak; korunamayacak kadar kötü olmak

redeploy /ˌriːdɪˈplɔɪ/ *verb* [T] to move employees, soldiers, equipment, etc to a different place or use them in a more effective way çalışan/asker/ekipman vs. yerini değiştirmek; daha verimli şekilde düzenlemek ● **redeployment** *noun* [C, U] when you redeploy someone or something yerini değiştirme, daha verimli şekilde düzenleme

redevelop /ˌriːdɪˈveləp/ *verb* [T] to make a place more modern by improving old buildings or building new ones yeniden imar etmek *There are plans to redevelop the city's waterfront area.* ● **redevelopment** *noun* [C, U] when a place is redeveloped yeniden imar etme

red-handed /ˌredˈhændɪd/ *adverb* **catch sb red-handed** *informal* to discover someone doing something wrong suçüstü yaklamak *He was caught red-handed trying to steal a car.*

redhead /ˈredhed/ *noun* [C] someone who has red hair kızıl kafa

,red 'herring *noun* [C] a fact or idea that takes your attention away from something that is important ilgiyi başka yöne çeken farklı konu

red-hot /ˌredˈhɒt/ *adjective* extremely hot kıpkırmızı kesilmiş, oldukça sıcak, öfkeli, kızmış

redirect /ˌriːdɪˈrekt/ *verb* [T] **1** to send something in a different direction farklı yöne sevketmek *Traffic should be redirected away from the city centre.* **2** to use money, energy, etc for a different purpose para/enerji vs. farklı amaçlar için kullanmak *Money spent on weapons could be redirected to hospitals and schools.*

redistribute /ˌriːdɪˈstrɪbjuːt/ *verb* [T] to share money, land, power, etc between people in a different way from before farklı şekilde dağıtmak, yeniden bölüşmek *to redistribute wealth* ● **redistribution**

/ˌriːdɪstrɪˈbjuːʃⁿn/ *noun* [U] the process of redistributing something farklı dağıtım, yeniden bölüşüm

,red 'meat *noun* [U] meat from animals and not birds or fish kırmızı et

redo /ˌriːˈduː/ *verb* [T] to do something again yeniden yapmak *I'm going to have to redo that report.*

redress[1] /rɪˈdres/ *verb* [T] *formal* to correct something that is wrong, unfair, or not equal düzeltmek, onarmak, telâfi etmek *laws aimed at redressing racial inequality*

redress[2] /rɪˈdres/ ⓤ /ˈriːdres/ *noun* [U] *formal* payment for an action or situation that is wrong or unfair düzeltme, tazminat, telâfi

,red 'tape *noun* [U] official rules that do not seem necessary and make things happen very slowly bürokrasi

•≁**reduce** /rɪˈdjuːs/ *verb* [T] **1** to make something less azaltmak, kısmak, indirmek *to reduce air pollution* ○ *The number of employees was reduced from 500 to 300.* **2** to add one or more electrons to a substance or to remove oxygen from a substance
reduce sb to sth/doing sth *phrasal verb* to make someone unhappy or cause them to be in a bad situation ... hâle getir(il)mek/sok(ul)mak/düşür(ül)mek *She was reduced to tears by his comments.*
reduce sth to sth *phrasal verb* to destroy something, especially something that has been built olmuş/yapılmış bir şeyi harap etmek/mahvetmek *The earthquake reduced the city to rubble.*

🌀 *reduction* ...... İLE BİRLİKTE KULLANILAN KELİMELER

a **dramatic/drastic/sharp/significant** reduction ● a reduction in sth

reduction /rɪˈdʌkʃⁿn/ *noun* [C, U] **1** when something is reduced kısma, indirim, azaltma, eksiltme *She refused to accept a reduction in wages.* ○ *price reductions* **2** the process of adding one or more electrons to a substance or removing oxygen from a substance

redundancy /rɪˈdʌndənsi/ *noun* **1** [C, U] *UK* when your employer makes you stop working because there is not enough work işten çıkarılma, ihtiyaç fazlası olma *There have been a lot of redundancies in the mining industry.* **2** [U] when something is not needed or used because there are other similar or more modern things fazlalık, gereksizlik

redundant /rɪˈdʌndənt/ *adjective* **1** [NOT WORKING] *UK* not working because your employer has told you there is not enough work işsiz, boş, ihtiyaç fazlası *Eight thousand people have been made redundant in Britain this year.* **2** [NOT NEEDED] *UK* not needed or any more because there are other similar or more modern things fazla, gereksiz, gereksinim duyulmayan *redundant weapons* **3** [TOO MUCH] more than is needed, especially extra words that mean the same thing gereksiz, lüzumsuz, fazla olan, aşırı

redwood /ˈredwʊd/ *noun* [C, U] a very tall tree that grows on the west coast of the US, or the wood of this tree kızılağaç

reed /riːd/ *noun* [C] a tall, stiff plant like grass that grows near water kamış, saz

reef /riːf/ *noun* [C] a line of rocks or sand near the surface of the sea sığ kayalık, resif *a coral reef*

reek /riːk/ *verb* [I] to have a very unpleasant smell fena kokmak; pis pis kokmak, leş gibi kokmak *The whole room reeked of sweat.* ● **reek** *noun* [no plural] pis koku

reel[1] /riːl/ *verb* [I] **1** to feel very shocked kafası karışmak, şaşırmak *She was still reeling from the news of his death.* **2** to walk in a way that looks as if you are

going to fall over **yalpalayarak yürümek, sendeleyerek gitmek** *He came reeling down the street like a drunk.*
reel sth off *phrasal verb* to say a long list of things quickly and without stopping **makineli tüfek gibi konuşmak; peşpeşe sıralamak; düşünmeden sayıp dökmek** *She reeled off a list of all the countries she'd been to.*

reel[2] /riːl/ *noun* [C] an object shaped like a wheel that you can roll film, thread, etc around **makara**

re-elect /ˌriːɪˈlekt/ *verb* [T] to elect someone again to a particular position **tekrar/yeniden seçmek**

re-election /ˌriːɪˈlekʃᵊn/ *noun* [C, U] when someone is elected again to the same position **yeniden seçilme** *She's* UK **standing for**/ US **running for** *re-election* (= she wants to be re-elected).

ref /ref/ *noun* [C] *informal short for* referee **hakem sözcüğünün kısa yazılışı**

refer /rɪˈfɜːʳ/ *verb* referring, *past* referred
refer to sb/sth *phrasal verb* **1** to talk or write about someone or something, especially briefly **söz etmek; ...a/e değinmek; kastetmek** *She didn't once refer to her son.* ○ *He always referred to his father as 'the old man'.* **2** If writing or information refers to someone or something, it relates to that person or thing. **belirtmek; kasdetmek; referans almak** *The sales figures refer to UK sales only.*
refer to sth *phrasal verb* to read something in order to get information **başvurmak; göz atmak; bakmak** *Please refer to your owner's manual for more information.*
refer sb/sth to sb/sth *phrasal verb* to send someone or something to a different place or person for information or help **yönlendirmek, göndermek, sevketmek** *My doctor referred me to a specialist.*

referee[1] /ˌrefᵊˈriː/ *noun* [C] someone who makes sure that players follow the rules during a sports game **hakem** ⊃*Orta kısımdaki renkli sayfalarına bakınız.*

referee[2] /ˌrefᵊˈriː/ *verb* [I, T] refereeing, *past* refereed to be the referee in a sports game **hakemlik yapmak**

reference /ˈrefᵊrᵊns/ *noun* **1** [SAY] [C, U] when you briefly talk or write about someone or something **söz etme, değinme, atıfta bulunma** *In his book, he makes several references to his time in France.* **2** **with/in reference to sth** *formal* relating to something **...ile ilgili olarak** *I am writing to you with reference to the job advertised in yesterday's newspaper.* **3** [LOOK AT] [C, U] when you look at information, or the thing that you look at for information **başvurma, danışma** *Please keep this handout for* **future reference** (= to look at in the future). **4** [LETTER] [C] a letter that is written by someone who knows you, to say if you are suitable for a job or course **referans, bonservis** ⊃*See also:* **cross reference.**

'reference ˌbook *noun* [C] a book that you look at in order to find information **başvuru kitabı, kaynak, referans**

referendum /ˌrefᵊˈrendəm/ *noun* [C] an occasion when all the people in a country can vote in order to show their opinion about a political question **halk oylaması, refrandum**

referral /rɪˈfɜːrᵊl/ *noun* [C, U] when someone or something is sent to a different place or person for information or help **başvuru, danışma, referans, yardım, ilişki**

refill /ˌriːˈfɪl/ *verb* [T] to fill something again **tekrar doldurmak** *He got up and refilled their glasses.* ● **refill** /ˈriːfɪl/ *noun* [C] **tekrardan doldurma**

refine /rɪˈfaɪn/ *verb* [T] **1** to make a substance pure by removing other substances from it **arıtmak, saflaştır-**

mak, rafine etmek **2** to improve an idea, method, system, etc by making small changes **geliştirmek, ıslah etmek** *The engineers spent months refining the software.*

refined /rɪˈfaɪnd/ *adjective* **1** [PURE] A refined substance has been made more pure by removing other substances from it. **saf, arıtılmış, rafine** *refined sugar* **2** [POLITE] very polite and showing knowledge of social rules **zarif, ince, kibar 3** [IMPROVED] improved by many small changes **geliştirilmiş, ıslah edilmiş** *a refined method*

refinement /rɪˈfaɪnmənt/ *noun* **1** [IMPROVEMENT] [C, U] a small change that improves something **geliştirme, ıslah, ilave özellik; küçük değişiklik** *Several refinements have been made to improve the car's performance.* **2** [POLITE] [U] polite behaviour and knowledge of social rules **incelik, kibarlık, zariflik, zerafet** *a woman of refinement* **3** [PURE] [U] the process of making a substance pure **saflaştırma, arıtma, arılaştırma**

refinery /rɪˈfaɪnᵊri/ *noun* [C] a factory where substances, such as sugar, oil, etc are made pure **arıtım tesisi, rafineri**

reflect /rɪˈflekt/ *verb* **1** [SHOW] [T] to show or be a sign of something **yansıtmak, belirtmek, göstermek** *The statistics reflect a change in people's spending habits.* **2** [SEND BACK] [T] If a surface reflects heat, light, sound, etc, it sends the light, etc back and does not absorb it. **yansıtmak, aksettirmek 3** [IMAGE] [I, T] If a surface such as a mirror or water reflects something, you can see the image of that thing in the mirror, water, etc. **yansı(t)mak, akset(tir)mak** *He saw himself reflected in the shop window.* **4** [THINK] [I] *formal* to think in a serious and careful way **iyice düşünüp taşınmak, kafa yormak, düşünmek** *In prison, he had plenty of time to reflect on the crimes he had committed.*
reflect on sb/sth *phrasal verb* If something reflects on someone or something, it affects other people's opinion of them, especially in a bad way. **kötü etkilemek; gölge düşürmek; ...izlenim vermek** *The whole affair reflects badly on the government.*

reflection

reflection /rɪˈflekʃᵊn/ *noun* **1** [C] the image of something in a mirror, on a shiny surface, etc **yansıma, görünüm, akis** *I saw my reflection in the window.* **2** [C, U] *formal* when you think in a serious and careful way **düşünme, düşünüş** *He paused for reflection before answering my question.* ○ **On reflection** (= after thinking again), *I think I was wrong.* **3 a reflection of sth** something that is a sign or result of a particular situation **görüntü, akis** *His poor job performance is a reflection of his lack of training.* **4 a reflection on sb/sth** something that makes people have a particular opinion about someone or something, especially a bad opinion **kötü izlenim, olumsuz etki, gölge düşürme** *Low test scores are a sad reflection on our school system.*

reflective /rɪˈflektɪv/ *adjective* **1** thinking carefully and quietly **dikkatli ve derinden düşünen; kılı kırk yaran** *a reflective mood* **2** A reflective surface is one that you can see easily when a light shines on it. **yansıtan, aksettiren** *a jacket made of reflective material*

reflex /ˈriːfleks/ *noun* [C] a physical reaction that you cannot control **tepki, tepke, refleks** *Shivering and blushing are reflexes.*

reflexes /ˈriːfleksɪz/ *noun* [plural] your ability to react quickly **refleksler; tepkiler** *A boxer needs to have good reflexes.*

reflexive /rɪˈfleksɪv/ *adjective* A reflexive verb or pronoun is used to show that the person who does the action is also the person who is affected by it. In the sentence 'I looked at myself in the mirror.', 'myself' is a reflexive pronoun. **(dilbilgisi) dönüşlü, dönüşlü fiil/zamir/yapı**

reflexology /ˌriːflekˈsɒlədʒi/ *noun* [U] the treatment of your feet by rubbing and pressing them in a special way in order to make the blood flow and help you relax **kan dolaşımını sağlayan ayak bakımı/masajı**

reform ...... İLE BİRLİKTE KULLANILAN KELİMELER

introduce/propose a reform ● a major/radical/sweeping reform ● reform in/of sth ● economic/political reform

reform¹ /rɪˈfɔːm/ *noun* [C, U] when changes are made to improve a system, organization, or law, or a change that is made **yenilik, ıslahat, reform** *economic/political reform*

reform² /rɪˈfɔːm/ *verb* **1** [T] to change a system, organization, or law in order to improve it **geliştirmek, değiştirmek, reform yapmak, ıslah etmek** *efforts to reform the education system* **2** [I, T] to change your behaviour and stop doing bad things, or to make someone else do this **adam etmek/etmek; düzel(t)mek, kendine çeki düzen vermek; ıslah etmek/olmak** *a programme to reform criminals* ○ *a reformed drug addict*

reformer /rɪˈfɔːməʳ/ *noun* [C] someone who tries to improve a system or law by changing it **yenilikçi, reformcu** *a social reformer*

refrain¹ /rɪˈfreɪn/ *verb* [I] *formal* to stop yourself from doing something **uzak durmak, sakınmak, kaçınmak, kendini tutmak/frenlemek** [+ doing sth] *Please refrain from talking during the performance.*

refrain² /rɪˈfreɪn/ *noun* [C] **1** *formal* a phrase or idea that you repeat often **nakarat, sık sık tekrarlanan** *'Every vote counts' is a familiar refrain in politics.* **2** a part of a song that you repeat **nakarat**

refresh /rɪˈfreʃ/ *verb* **1** [T] to make you feel less hot or tired **serinletmek, dinçleştirmek, dinlendirmek** *A cool drink should refresh you.* **2** [I, T] to make the most recent information on an Internet page appear on your computer **bilgisayarda en son bilginin görünmesini sağlamak; sayfayı en güncel hâle gitrmek** **3** refresh sb's memory to help someone remember something **hafızasını tazelemek, belleğini canlandırmak; hatırlatmak**

refreshing /rɪˈfreʃɪŋ/ *adjective* **1** different and interesting **farklı ve ilginç; yeni, alışılmışın dışında** *a refreshing change* ○ [+ to do sth] *It's refreshing to see a film that's so original.* **2** making you feel less hot or tired **serinletici, ferahlatıcı, canlandırıcı** *a refreshing shower/swim* ● **refreshingly** *adverb* **yeni ve ilginç bir şekilde**

refreshments /rɪˈfreʃmənts/ *noun* [plural] food and drinks that are available at a meeting, event, on a journey, etc **meşrubat ve yiyecekler** *Refreshments are available in the lobby.*

refrigerate /rɪˈfrɪdʒəˈreɪt/ *verb* [T] to make or keep food cold so that it stays fresh **soğutmak, taze kalmasını sağlamak** *You should refrigerate any leftover food immediately.* ● **refrigeration** /rɪˌfrɪdʒəˈreɪʃəⁿn/ *noun* [U] **soğutma, dondurma**

refrigerated /rɪˈfrɪdʒəreɪtɪd/ *adjective* **1** A refrigerated container or vehicle keeps the things inside it cold. **soğutmalı araç** **2** Refrigerated food or drink is cold because it has been kept in a refrigerator. **dondurulmuş gıda**

refrigerator /rɪˈfrɪdʒəˈreɪtəʳ/ *noun* [C] a large container that uses electricity to keep food cold **buzdolabı, soğutucu** ⊃Orta kısımdaki renkli sayfalarına bakınız.

refuel /ˌriːˈfjuːəl/ *verb* [I, T] to put more fuel into an aircraft, ship, etc so that it can continue its journey **yakıt ikmâli yapmak**

refuge /ˈrefjuːdʒ/ *noun* **1** [U] protection from danger or unpleasant conditions **sığınma, korunma, koruma** *We took refuge from the storm in an old barn.* **2** [C] a place where you are protected from danger **sığınak, barınak** *a refuge for homeless people*

refugee /ˌrefjʊˈdʒiː/ *noun* [C] someone who has been forced to leave their country, especially because of a war **sığınmacı, mülteci** *a refugee camp*

refund ...... İLE BİRLİKTE KULLANILAN KELİMELER

claim/give sb/get a refund ● a full refund ● a refund of sth

refund¹ /ˈriːfʌnd/ *noun* [C] an amount of money that is given back to you, especially because you are not happy with something you have bought **geri ödeme, iade, geri ödenen para** *The holiday company apologized and gave us a full refund.*

refund² /ˌriːˈfʌnd/ *verb* [T] to give back money that someone has paid to you **geri ödemek, iade etmek**

refurbish /ˌriːˈfɜːbɪʃ/ *verb* [T] *formal* to repair or improve a building **(bina) tadilat yapmak, onarmak, tamir ederek güzelleştirmek, yenilemek** ● **refurbishment** *noun* [C, U] the process of refurbishing a building **(bina) tadilat, tamirat, bakım onarım, yenileme** *The library was closed for refurbishment.*

refusal /rɪˈfjuːzᵊl/ *noun* [C, U] when someone refuses to do or accept something **ret, reddetmek, kabul etmeme** [+ to do sth] *his refusal to admit his mistake*

ᵒ⁻**refuse¹** /rɪˈfjuːz/ *verb* [I, T] to say that you will not do or accept something **reddetmek, kabul etmemek, geri çevirmek** *I asked him to leave but he refused.* ○ [+ to do sth] *Cathy refuses to admit that she was wrong.*

refuse² /ˈrefjuːs/ *noun* [U] *formal* waste **çöp, atık, süprüntü, döküntü** *a pile of refuse*

refute /rɪˈfjuːt/ *verb* [T] *formal* to say or prove that something is not true or correct **yalanlamak, çürütmek** *attempts to refute his theory* ○ *She angrily refuted their claims.*

regain /rɪˈɡeɪn/ *verb* [T] to get something back again **yeniden elde etmek/kavuşmak/almak; tekrar ele geçirmek** *Armed troops have regained control of the capital.* ○ *It was several hours before he regained consciousness.*

regal /ˈriːɡᵊl/ *adjective* very special and suitable for a king or queen **kral ve kraliçeye özgü/uygun; krallar gibi** *a regal dress*

regard¹ /rɪˈɡɑːd/ *verb* [T] **1** to think of someone or something in a particular way **...olarak kabul etmek; ...**

gözü ile bakmak; ...gibi değerlendirmek *She is generally* **regarded as** *one of the greatest singers this century.* ○ *The plans were* **regarded with** *suspicion.* **2** *formal* to look carefully at someone or something **dikkate almak, itina ile bakmak, özenle değerlendirmek**

regard² /rɪˈɡɑːd/ *noun* **1** [U] respect or admiration for someone or something **saygı, hürmet, itibar, takdir** *I* **have** *the greatest* **regard for** *her.* ➲Opposite **disregard.** **2 in/with regard to sth** *formal* relating to something **...hakkında; ...a/e dair/gelince; ...ile ilgili** *I am writing in regard to your letter of 24 June.*

regarding /rɪˈɡɑːdɪŋ/ *preposition formal* about or relating to **...konusunda/hususunda/hakkında; ...a/e ilişkin; ...ile ilgili olarak** *I am writing to you regarding your application dated 29 April.*

regardless /rɪˈɡɑːdləs/ *adverb* **1 regardless of sth** despite something **...hiç önem vermeyerek; ...a/e bakmayarak/umursamayarak** *She'll make a decision regardless of what we think.* **2** without thinking about problems or difficulties **her şeye rağmen, ne olursa olsun, gene de** *Mr Redwood claimed he would carry on with his campaign regardless.*

regards /rɪˈɡɑːdz/ *noun* [plural] friendly greetings **saygılar, selamlar, iyi dilekler** *Give/send my regards to your mother when you see her.*

regeneration /rɪˌdʒenəˈreɪʃən/ *noun* [U] the process of improving a place or system, especially to make it more active or successful **geliştirme, iyileştirme, güzelleştirme** *a programme of* **urban regeneration** • **regenerate** /rɪˈdʒenəreɪt/ *verb* [T] to improve a place or system **geliştirmek, iyileştirmek, güzelleştirmek; daha iyi hâle getirmek**

reggae /ˈreɡeɪ/ *noun* [U] a type of popular music from Jamaica with a strong beat **Jamaika müziği**

regime /reɪˈʒiːm/ *noun* [C] a system of government or other control, especially one that people do not approve of **yönetim, rejim, düzen, sistem** *the former Communist regime*

regiment /ˈredʒɪmənt/ *noun* [group] a large group of soldiers **alay** • **regimental** /ˌredʒɪˈmentəl/ *adjective* relating to a regiment **alaya ait, alay ile ilgili**

regimented /ˈredʒɪmentɪd/ *adjective* too controlled or organized **katı denetimli, sıkı disiplinli, sıkı kontrol altına alınmış** *a regimented lifestyle*

∘• **region** /ˈriːdʒən/ *noun* **1** [C] a particular area in a country or the world **bölge, yöre** *China's coastal region* **2** [C] an area of the body (vücut) **bölge, kısım** *pain in the lower abdominal region* **3 in the region of sth** approximately **civarında, aşağı yukarı, takriben, kadar** *It probably cost somewhere in the region of £900.*

regional /ˈriːdʒənəl/ *adjective* relating to a region (= particular area in a country) **bölgesel, yöresel** *a regional dialect/newspaper*

compile a register • **on** a register • a register **of** sth

register¹ /ˈredʒɪstər/ *noun* **1** [C] an official list of names **sicil, kütük, liste, kayıt** *a register of approved builders* ○ *the* **electoral register** **2** [C, U] the style of language, grammar, and words used in particular situations **belli durumlarda kullanılan sözcükler, dilbilgisi ve dil biçimi** *a formal/informal register* ➲See also: **cash register.**

register² /ˈredʒɪstər/ *verb* **1** ON A LIST [I, T] to put information about someone or something, especially a name, on an official list **kaydetmek, deftere/kütüğe işlemek, listelemek** *Is he registered with the authorities to sell alcohol?* ○ *Students need to* **register for** *the*

course by the end of April. ○ *a registered nurse* **2** SHOW A FEELING [T] to show an opinion or feeling **dışa vurmak, ifade etmek, belli etmek** *People gathered to* **register** *their opposition to the plans.* **3** SHOW AMOUNT [I, T] to show an amount on an instrument that measures something (ölçüm aletlerinde) **göstermek, belirtmek, yazı ile göstermek** *The earthquake registered 7.3 on the Richter scale.*

registered /ˈredʒɪstəd/ *adjective* **registered mail/post** a special service that records when a letter or parcel is sent and received **taahütlü mektup/posta**

'register ˌoffice *noun* [C] in Britain, a place where births, deaths, and marriages are officially recorded and where you can get married (Britanya'da) **nüfus/evlendirme memurluğu**

registrar /ˌredʒɪˈstrɑːr/ *noun* [C] **1** someone whose job is to keep official records, especially of births, deaths, and marriages, or of students at a university (sicil) **kayıt/ evrak memuru/memuresi; nüfus/evlendirme memuru/memuresi; öğrenci işleri/kayıt kabul işleri memuru/memuresi 2** *UK* a type of hospital doctor **hekim, doktor**

registration /ˌredʒɪˈstreɪʃən/ *noun* **1** [U] when a name or information is recorded on an official list **kayıt, kütüğe/sicile işleme, tescil 2** [C] (*also* regis'tration ˌnumber) *mainly UK* the official set of numbers and letters on the front and back of a vehicle **araç plakası**

registry /ˈredʒɪstri/ *noun* [C] a place where official records are kept **sicil dairesi, tescil bürosu; kayıt memurluğu** *the land registry*

'registry ˌoffice *noun* [C] in Britain, a place where births, deaths, and marriages are officially recorded and where you can get married (Britanya'da) **nüfus/ evlendirme memurluğu**

regress /rɪˈgres/ *verb* [I] *formal* to go back to an earlier, less advanced state **eski hâline dönmek, kötüye gitmek, kötüleşmek, bozulmak; kötü durumuna geri dönmek** • **regression** /rɪˈgreʃən/ *noun* [U] *formal* when someone or something regresses **kötüleşme, bozulma, eski kötü hâline dönme**

∘• **regret¹** /rɪˈgret/ *verb* [T] **regretting,** *past* **regretted 1** to feel sorry about a situation, especially something that you wish you had not done **pişman olmak, hayıflanmak, pişmanlık duymak; nedamet duymak** [+ doing sth] *I really regret leaving school so young.* ○ [+ (that)] *He began to regret that he hadn't paid more attention in class.* **2** *formal* used to say that you are sorry that you have to tell someone about a situation **üzülmek, esef etmek** [+ to do sth] *We regret to inform you that the application has been refused.*

express regret • **have (no)** regrets • sb's **biggest/ only** regret • **with** regret • regret **about/at/over** sth

∘• **regret²** /rɪˈgret/ *noun* [C, U] a feeling of sadness about a situation, especially something that you wish you had not done **pişmanlık, kişinin yaptığından dolayı duyduğu üzüntü** *We married very young but we've been really happy and I've* **no regrets.** ○ *It is* **with** *great* **regret** *that I announce Steve Adam's resignation.* • **regretful** *adjective* expressing regret **pişman, pişman olmuş, üzüntülü** • **regretfully** *adverb* **pişmanlıkla**

regrettable /rɪˈgretəbl/ *adjective* If something is regrettable, you wish it had not happened and you feel sorry about it. **üzücü, hoşa gitmeyen, müessif** *a deeply regrettable incident* • **regrettably** *adverb* **maalesef**

∘• **regular¹** /ˈreɡjələr/ *adjective* **1** SAME TIME/SPACE repeated with the same amount of time or space between one thing and the next **düzenli, muntazam, alışılmış,**

R

mutat *a regular pulse* ○ *Plant the seedlings at regular intervals.* **2** OFTEN happening or doing something often, especially at the same time every week, year, etc **daimi, düzenli** *a regular occurrence* ○ *We arranged to meet on a regular basis.* **3** USUAL *US* usual or normal **her zamanki, olağan, devamlı, mutat** *I couldn't see my regular dentist.* **4** SIZE *informal* being a standard size **standart ölçüde, aynı büyüklükte, her zamanki** *a burger and regular fries* **5** SHAPE Something that has a regular shape is the same on both or all sides. **düzenli, aynı ölçüde, aynı hizada, muntazam** *She's got lovely, regular teeth.* **6** GRAMMAR following the usual rules or patterns in grammar **(dilbilgisi) düzenli, kurallı** *'Talk' is a regular verb but 'go' is not.* ⊃Opposite **irregular**. • **regularity** /ˌreɡjəˈlærəti/ *noun* [U] when something is regular **düzenlilik, düzen, intizam**

regular² /ˈreɡjələr/ *noun* [C] *informal* someone who often goes to a particular shop, restaurant, etc **daimi müşteri, mutat müşteri, abone, müdavim, muvazzaf** *Mick was one of the regulars at the local pub.*

⚬**regularly** /ˈreɡjələli/ *adverb* **1** often **düzenli olarak, sık sık, her zaman** *Accidents occur regularly on this stretch of the road.* **2** at the same time each day, week, month, etc **her gün/hafta/ay vs. aynı zamanda; düzenli olarak** *They meet regularly - usually once a week.*

regulate /ˈreɡjəleɪt/ *verb* [T] **1** to control an activity or process, especially by using rules **düzenlemek, düzene sokmak, tanzim etmek** *laws regulating advertising* **2** to control the speed, temperature, etc of something **ayarlamak, ayarını yapmak** *Babies find it difficult to regulate their body temperature.*

🧩 *regulation* .... İLE BİRLİKTE KULLANILAN KELİMELER

breach/comply with/enforce/introduce regulations • regulations governing sth • strict/stringent/tough regulations • under a regulation

regulation /ˌreɡjəˈleɪʃᵊn/ *noun* **1** [C] an official rule that controls how something is done **tüzük, yönetmelik, kural, mevzuat** [usually plural] *building regulations* **2** [U] when a process or activity is controlled **denetim altına alma, kontrol altında tutma** *government regulation of interest rates*

regulator /ˈreɡjəleɪtər/ *noun* [C] **1** someone whose job is to make sure that a system works in a fair way **düzenleyen/sistemin iyi işleyişini sağlayan kimse** *the water industry regulator* **2** a piece of equipment that is used to control the temperature, speed, etc of something **düzenleyici alet; regülatör**

regulatory /ˈreɡjələtᵊri/ *adjective* controlling an activity or process, especially by using rules **kurallarla düzenleyen/düzene sokan**

rehab /ˈriːhæb/ *noun* [U] *informal* treatment to help someone stop drinking too much alcohol or taking drugs **tedavi altına alma; tedavi etme, rehabilitasyon** *He spent six months in rehab.*

rehabilitate /ˌriːhəˈbɪlɪteɪt/ *verb* [T] to help someone live a normal life again after they have had a serious illness or been in prison **eski haline tekrar kavuşmasına yardımcı olmak; rehabilite etmek; iyileşmesine katkı yapmak** *a programme to rehabilitate young offenders* • **rehabilitation** /ˌriːhəˌbɪlɪˈteɪʃᵊn/ *noun* [U] **rehabilitasyon**

rehearsal /rɪˈhɜːsᵊl/ *noun* [C, U] a time when all the people involved in a play, dance, etc practise in order to prepare for a performance **prova**

rehearse /rɪˈhɜːs/ *verb* [I, T] to practise a play, dance, etc in order to prepare for a performance **prova yapmak**

reign¹ /reɪn/ *noun* **1** [C] a period of time when a king or queen rules a country **hükümdarlık dönemi, saltanat süresi** *the reign of Henry VIII* **2** [no plural] a period of time when someone controls a sports team, an organization, etc **görev süresi; bir takımı/teşkilatı yönetme süresi** *Christie's reign as captain of the British athletics team* **3 reign of terror** a period of time when someone uses violence to control people **terör/anarşi/kargaşa dönemi**

reign² /reɪn/ *verb* [I] **1** to be the king or queen of a country **hükümdarlık etmek, saltanat sürmek** *Queen Victoria reigned for 64 years.* **2** *formal* to be the main feeling or quality in a situation **egemen/hâkim olmak, hüküm sürmek** *Chaos reigned as angry protesters hammered on the doors.*

reigning 'champion *noun* [C] the most recent winner of a competition **yarışmanın en son galibi**

reimburse /ˌriːɪmˈbɜːs/ *verb* [T] *formal* to pay money back to someone, especially money that they have spent because of their work **zararını telâfi etmek, giderini karşılamak, masrafını ödemek** *Employees will no longer be reimbursed for taxi fares.* • **reimbursement** *noun* [U] *formal* when you reimburse someone **tazminat, karşılama, ödeme, telâfi**

rein /reɪn/ *noun* **1** [C] a long, thin piece of leather that helps you to control a horse **dizgin** [usually plural] *Hold the reins in your left hand.* **2 free rein** the freedom to do or say what you want **aşırı özgürlük, serbestlik, hürriyet, başıboşluk** [+ to do sth] *The school gives teachers free rein to try out new teaching methods.* **3 keep a tight rein on sb/sth** to have a lot of control over someone or something **dizginleri sıkı tutmak, sıkı kontrol altına almak; göz açtırmamak** *We've been told to keep a tight rein on spending.*

reincarnation /ˌriːɪnkɑːˈneɪʃᵊn/ *noun* [U] the belief that a dead person's spirit returns to life in another body **ölümden sonra tekrar başka birinin bedeninde dünyaya gelme/yaratılma inancı**

reindeer /ˈreɪndɪər/ *noun* [C] *plural* **reindeer** a type of deer with large horns that lives in northern parts of Europe, Asia, and America **ren geyiği**

reinforce /ˌriːɪnˈfɔːs/ *verb* [T] **1** to make an existing opinion or idea stronger **güçlendirmek, desteklemek, daha güçlü hâle getirmek, pekiştirmek** *to reinforce a view/feeling* **2** to make something stronger **sağlamlaştırmak, güçlendirmek, takviye etmek** *a security door reinforced by steel bars* ○ *reinforced concrete* • **reinforcement** *noun* [C, U] when you reinforce something **sağlamlaştırma, güçlendirme, takviye**

reinforcements /ˌriːɪnˈfɔːsmənts/ *noun* [plural] soldiers who are sent to make an army stronger **takviye güç, destek kuvvet**

reinstate /ˌriːɪnˈsteɪt/ *verb* [T] **1** to give someone the job or position that they had before **görevine iade etmek** **2** to cause a rule, law, etc to exist again **tekrar yürürlüğe koymak/işleme sokmak** • **reinstatement** *noun* [C, U] when you reinstate someone or something **göreve iade**

reinvent /ˌriːɪnˈvent/ *verb* **1** [T] to produce something new that is based on something that already exists **yeniden üretmek/yapmak** *The story of Romeo and Juliet was reinvented as a Los Angeles gangster movie.* **2 reinvent yourself** to change the way you look and behave so that you seem very different **kendini yeniden baştan değiştirmek/yaratmak** ⊃See also: reinvent the wheel¹.

reiterate /riˈɪtᵊreɪt/ *verb* [T] *formal* to say something again so that people take notice of it **yeniden/tekrar**

ifade etmek/söylemek [+ that] *I must reiterate that we have no intention of signing this contract.* ● **reiteration** /rɪˌɪtəˈreɪʃən/ *noun* [C, U]

o--**reject**¹ /rɪˈdʒekt/ *verb* [T] **1** NOT ACCEPT to refuse to accept or agree with something **reddetmek, geri çevirmek** *The United States government rejected the proposal.* **2** JOB/COURSE to refuse to accept someone for a job, course, etc **kabul etmemek, reddetmek, işe/kursa almamak** *I applied to Cambridge University but I was rejected.* **3** PERSON to not give someone the love or attention they were expecting **gerekli sevgiyi/yakınlığı göstermemek/vermemek; reddetmek; istememek** *She felt rejected by her husband.*

reject² /ˈriːdʒekt/ *noun* [C] a product that is damaged or not perfect in some way **hatalı ürün, ıskarta mal**

rejection /rɪˈdʒekʃən/ *noun* **1** NOT ACCEPT [C, U] when you refuse to accept or agree with something **red, geri çevirme** *Their rejection of the peace plan is very disappointing for the government.* **2** JOB/COLLEGE [C] a letter that says you have not been successful in getting a job, a place at college, etc **red/kabul etmeme yazısı** **3** PERSON [U] when someone does not give someone else the love or attention they were expecting **sevgi göstermeme; itme, reddetme** *a feeling of rejection*

rejoice /rɪˈdʒɔɪs/ *verb* [I] *literary* to feel very happy because something good has happened **çok sevinmek, memnun olmak, büyük sevinç duymak**

rejoicing /rɪˈdʒɔɪsɪŋ/ *noun* [U] when people show that they are very happy because something good has happened **şenlik, bayram, mutluluk**

rejoin /rɪˈdʒɔɪn/ *verb* [T] to return to a person or place **tekrar katılmak; dönmek** *I was feeling better, so I rejoined the party.*

rejuvenate /rɪˈdʒuːvəneɪt/ *verb* [T] to make someone look or feel young and energetic again **gençleştirmek, dinçleştirmek** *You're supposed to come back from a holiday feeling rejuvenated.* ● **rejuvenation** /rɪˌdʒuːvəˈneɪʃən/ *noun* [U] **gençleştirme**

rekindle /ˌriːˈkɪndl/ *verb* [T] to make someone have a feeling that they had in the past **bazı duyguları tekrar/yeniden yaşatmak; tazelemek** *The trip seemed to rekindle their love for each other.*

relapse /rɪˈlæps/, /ˈriːlæps/ *noun* [C, U] **1** when someone becomes ill again after a period of feeling better **tekrar hastalanmak; yeniden kendini iyi hissetmemek** *I had a relapse last year and was off work for a month.* **2** when something or someone gets worse again after being better **tekrar fenalaşmak, nüksetmek, depreşmek** *The company's share prices have suffered a relapse this week.* ● **relapse** /rɪˈlæps/ *verb* [I] **nüksetmek**

relate /rɪˈleɪt/ *verb* **1** [I, T] to be connected, or to find or show the connection between two or more things **ilgili/bağlantılı olmak; ilişki/bağlantı kurmak** *How do the two proposals relate?* **2** [T] *formal* to tell a story or describe a series of events **anlatmak, nakletmek, bir dizi olayı tanımlamak**

relate to sb/sth *phrasal verb* to be connected to, or to be about someone or something **bağlantılı/ilişkili olmak; hakkında/hususunda olmak** *Please provide all information relating to the claim.*

relate to sb *phrasal verb* to understand how someone feels **ne hissettiğin anlamak; iyi ilişkiler kurmak; geçinmek** *Most teenagers find it hard to relate to their parents.*

related /rɪˈleɪtɪd/ *adjective* **1** connected **bağlantılı, ilgili, alakalı, ilişkili** *There's been an increase in criminal activity related to drugs.* **2** If two or more people are related, they belong to the same family. **akraba,** akraba olan, aile bağı ile bağlı *Did you know that I'm related to Jackie?* ➔Opposite **unrelated.**

relation /rɪˈleɪʃən/ *noun* **1** CONNECTION [C, U] a connection between two or more things **ilgi, ilişki, bağ, münasebet** *the relation between smoking and lung cancer* **2** FAMILY [C] someone who belongs to the same family as you **akraba** *He's called Ken Russell, no relation to* (= he is not from the same family as) *the film director.* **3** **in relation to sth** a COMPARED WITH when compared with something *...a/e göre/oranla;* *...ile kıyaslandığında/mukayese edildiğinde Salaries are low in relation to the cost of living.* **b** ABOUT about or relating to something *...a/e göre/nazaran I'd like to ask you something in relation to what you said earlier.*

relations /rɪˈleɪʃənz/ *noun* [plural] the way two people or groups feel and behave towards each other **münasebetler, ilişkiler** *It was an attempt to restore diplomatic relations between the two countries.* ➔See also: public relations, race relations.

‗‗‗ **relationship** ...... İLE BİRLİKTE KULLANILAN KELİMELER

a **close/intimate/personal/loving/stormy** relationship ● **end/forge/form/have** a relationship ● a relationship **between** sb and sb

o--**relationship** /rɪˈleɪʃənʃɪp/ *noun* **1** BEHAVIOUR [C] the way two people or groups feel and behave towards each other **ilişki, münasebet, dostluk, bağ, alâka** *He has a very good relationship with his older sister.* **2** ROMANTIC [C] a sexual or romantic friendship **cinsel veya romantik ilişki; sevgili olma** *I don't feel ready for a relationship at the moment.* **3** CONNECTION [C, U] a connection between two or more things **ilişki, bağlantı, münasebet, temas** *the relationship between sunburn and skin cancer*

o--**relative**¹ /ˈrelətɪv/ *noun* [C] a member of your family **akraba** *a party for friends and relatives*

relative² /ˈrelətɪv/ *adjective* **1** [always before noun] compared to other similar things or people **göreli, nispi, izafi** *the relative prosperity of the West* **2** **relative to sth** when compared to something else *...ile ilgili/alakalı; ...a/e ilişkin/göre; ...ile kıyaslandığında The economy has been declining relative to other countries.*

‚relative 'clause *noun* [C] a part of a sentence that is used to describe the noun which comes just before it. In the sentence, 'The woman who I saw yesterday wasn't his wife.', 'who I saw yesterday' is a relative clause. **sıfat/ilgi cümleciği; bağ-zamir cümleciği**

relatively /ˈrelətɪvli/ *adverb* quite, when compared to other things or people **nispeten, göreli olarak, bir dereceye kadar** *Eating out is relatively cheap.*

‚relative 'pronoun *noun* [C] a word such as 'that', 'which', or 'who' that is used to begin a relative clause **ilgi zamiri**

relax ...... BAŞKA BİR DEYİŞLE

chill fiili ve **chill out** deyimi resmi olmayan ortamlarda **relax** fiilinin anlamında kullanılabilir. *We spent the whole week chilling out on the beach.*

wind down deyimi ve **unwind** fiili zor bir işin bitiminde rahatlamaya başlama anlamında kullanılabilir. *It takes me a while to wind down when I get back from work.* ● *Music helps me to* **unwind.**

Eğer kişi çok enerji harcamamak için dinleniyorsa, **take it easy/take things easy** söylemleri kullanılabilir. *You'll need to spend a few days taking it easy/taking things easy after the operation.*

put your feet up ifadesi oturup dinlenmek anlamında kullanılır. *I'm going to make myself a cup of*

relax 610 ◦ᵃ Important words to learn

coffee and put my feet up *for half an hour.*

◦ᵃ**relax** /rɪˈlæks/ *verb* **1** PERSON [I, T] to become happy and comfortable because nothing is worrying you, or to make someone do this **dinlenmek, rahatla(t)mak, sakinleş(tir)mek** *I find it difficult to relax.* ○ *The wine had relaxed him and he began to talk.* **2** LESS STIFF [I, T] If a part of your body relaxes, it becomes less stiff, and if you relax it, you make it become less stiff. **gevşe(t) mek, yumuşa(t)mak, hafifle(t)mek** *Try these exercises to relax your neck muscles.* **3** RULES [T] to make laws or rules less severe **gevşetmek, yumuşatmak, hafifletmek** *The government has recently relaxed laws on bringing animals into Britain.* ● **relaxation** /ˌriːlækˈseɪʃᵊn/ *noun* [U] **rahatlama**

◦ᵃ**relaxed** /rɪˈlækst/ *adjective* **1** feeling happy and comfortable because nothing is worrying you **sakin, rahat, mutlu** *She seemed relaxed and in control of the situation.* **2** A relaxed situation is comfortable and informal. **rahat, huzurlu, iç açıcı, hoş, hafif** *There was a very relaxed atmosphere at the party.*

◦ᵃ**relaxing** /rɪˈlæksɪŋ/ *adjective* making you feel relaxed **sakin, huzur verici, dinlendirici** *a relaxing bath*

relay¹ /ˌriːˈleɪ/ *verb* [T] **1** to send a message from one person to another **söylemek, nakletmek, iletmek** *Cory had an idea which he relayed to his friend immediately.* **2** to broadcast radio or television signals **yayınlamak**

relay² /ˈriːleɪ/ *(also* 'relay ˌrace) *noun* [C] a race in which each member of a team runs or swims part of the race **bayrak yarışı**

◦ᵃ**release¹** /rɪˈliːs/ *verb* [T] **1** PRISONER to allow a prisoner to be free **tahliye etmek, serbest bırakmak, salıvermek** *Six hostages were released shortly before midday.* **2** STOP HOLDING to stop holding someone or something **bırakmak, salıvermek, koyvermek** *Release the handle.* **3** INFORMATION to let the public have news or information about something **yayınlamak** *Police have not released the dead woman's name.* **4** RECORD/FILM to make a record or film available for people to buy or see **gösterime sun(ul)mak, piyasaya sun(ul)mak/ çıkar(ıl)mak** *The album is due to be released in time for Christmas.* **5** SUBSTANCE to let a substance flow out from somewhere **akıtmak, akmasına meydan vermek, akıtmak, salmak, yaymak** *Dangerous chemicals were accidentally released into the river.*

⟦ **release** ...... İLE BİRLİKTE KULLANILAN KELİMELER
demand/secure sb's release ● release **from** sth

release² /rɪˈliːs/ *noun* **1** FROM PRISON [C] when someone is allowed to leave prison **kurtulma, serbest bırakılma, tahliye** *After his release from jail, Jackson found it difficult to find work.* **2** FILM/RECORD [C] a new film or record that you can buy **piyasaya çıkmış film/plak/CD/ kaset vs.** *Have you heard the group's latest release?* **3** SUBSTANCE [C, U] when a substance is allowed to flow out of somewhere **akma, çıkma, yayılma, salma** *a release of toxic gas from the factory* ⊃See also: press release.

relegate /ˈrelɪɡeɪt/ *verb* [T] to put someone or something in a less important position **(mevki, küme) indirmek, daha alt gruba/kademeye getirmek, düşürmek** [often passive] *He'd been relegated to the B team.* ● **relegation** /ˌrelɪˈɡeɪʃᵊn/ *noun* [U] **sürgün**

relent /rɪˈlent/ *verb* [I] to allow something that you refused to allow before **yumuşamak, merhamete/ insafa gelmek** *The security guard relented and let them through.*

relentless /rɪˈlentləs/ *adjective* never stopping or getting any less extreme **aman vermez, durup dinlen-**

meden, acımasız, insafsız *relentless criticism* ● **relentlessly** *adverb* **insafsızca**

relevance /ˈreləvᵊns/ *(also US* **relevancy** /ˈreləvᵊntsi/) *noun* [U] the degree to which something is related or useful to what is happening or being talked about **ilgi, ilişki, alâka, münasebet** *This point has no relevance to the discussion.*

relevant /ˈreləvᵊnt/ *adjective* related or useful to what is happening or being talked about **...ile ilgili, ...a/e uyan, faydalı, uygun** *relevant information* ○ *Education should be relevant to children's needs.* ⊃Opposite irrelevant.

reliable /rɪˈlaɪəbl/ *adjective* able to be trusted or believed **güvenilir, emin, itimat edilebilir** *a reliable car* ○ *reliable information* ○ *Andy's very reliable - if he says he'll do something, he'll do it.* ⊃Opposite unreliable. ● **reliability** /rɪˌlaɪəˈbɪləti/ *noun* [U] how reliable someone or something is **güvenilirlik, emniyet** ● **reliably** *adverb* *I am* **reliably** *informed that the concert has been cancelled.* **güvenilir bir şekilde**

reliance /rɪˈlaɪəns/ *noun* **reliance on sb/sth** when someone or something depends on someone or something else **birine/bir şeye bağlılık/güven/itimat/ emniyet** *our increasing reliance on computers*

reliant /rɪˈlaɪənt/ *adjective* **be reliant on sb/sth** to depend on someone or something **birine/bir şeye bağlı olmak/güvenmek/itimat etmek** *I don't want to be reliant on anybody.* ⊃See also: self-reliant.

relic /ˈrelɪk/ *noun* [C] a very old thing from the past **arta kalan eşya, hatıra, yadigar, kalıntı** *an Egyptian relic*

⟦ **relief** ...... İLE BİRLİKTE KULLANILAN KELİMELER
a big/great/tremendous relief ● **a sense** of relief ● **to** sb's relief

◦ᵃ**relief** /rɪˈliːf/ *noun* **1** EMOTION [U, no plural] the good feeling that you have when something unpleasant stops or does not happen **rahatlama, iç ferahlığı** *It'll be such a relief when these exams are over.* ○ *"James can't come tonight." "Well, that's a relief!"* **2** HELP [U] money, food, or clothes that are given to people because they need help **yardım, bağış** *an international relief operation* **3** PHYSICAL FEELING [U] when something stops hurting you **kurtulma, rahatlama** *I'd been trying to sleep to find relief from the pain.*

relieve /rɪˈliːv/ *verb* [T] **1** to make pain or a bad feeling less severe **azaltmak, hafifletmek, gidermek, geçirmek** *Breathing exercises can help to relieve stress.* **2** to allow someone to stop working by taking their place **serbest bırakmak, rahatlatmak** *The 7 a.m. team arrived to relieve the night workers.*

relieve sb of sth *phrasal verb formal* to take something away from someone **(yük, sorumluluk vb.) kurtarmak, uzaklaştırmak** *Let me relieve you of your luggage.*

relieved /rɪˈliːvd/ *adjective* feeling happy because something unpleasant did not happen or you are not worried about something any more **rahatlamış, ferahlamış** [+ (that)] *I'm just relieved that she's safe and well.* ○ [+ to do sth] *I heard a noise and was relieved to find that it was only a cat.*

⟦ **religion** ...... İLE BİRLİKTE KULLANILAN KELİMELER
believe in/practise a religion ● **a major** religion ● **be against** sb's religion

◦ᵃ**religion** /rɪˈlɪdʒᵊn/ *noun* [C, U] the belief in a god or gods, or a particular system of belief in a god or gods **din, inanç** *the Christian religion*

◦ᵃ**religious** /rɪˈlɪdʒəs/ *adjective* **1** relating to religion **dinî, dinle ilgili, din ile ilgili** *religious paintings* **2** having a strong belief in a religion **dindar, dini bütün, sofu** *He's a very religious man.*

religiously /rɪ'lɪdʒəsli/ *adverb* **1** regularly **titizlikle, düzenli olarak, itinayla, özenle** *He visited the old woman religiously every weekend.* **2** in a religious way **dinî bir görev gibi, ibadet yapar gibi; dinî olarak**

relinquish /rɪ'lɪŋkwɪʃ/ *verb* [T] *formal* to allow something to be taken away from you **bırakmak, terketmek, vazeçmek** *At 80 he still refuses to relinquish control of the company.*

relish¹ /'relɪʃ/ *verb* [T] to enjoy something **çok hoşlanmak, büyük zevk almak, tadını çıkarmak** *I don't relish the thought of a twelve-hour flight.*

relish² /'relɪʃ/ *noun* **1** [U] enjoyment **zevk, keyf, hoşlanma, haz** *He had baked a cake which the children now ate with relish.* **2** [C] a sauce that you put on food to give it more taste **sos, salça**

relive /ˌriː'lɪv/ *verb* [T] to remember something so clearly that you feel as if it is happening now **kafasında yeniden yaşamak/canlandırmak; tekrar yaşar gibi olmak**

relocate /ˌriːləʊ'keɪt/ ⑤ /ˈriː'ləʊˌkeɪt/ *verb* [I, T] to move to another place **başka bir yere taşı(n)mak/yerleş(tir)mek** *The company relocated to Tokyo.* ● **relocation** /ˌriːləʊ'keɪʃⁿn/ *noun* [U] **relocation costs** yeniden yerleştirme

reluctant /rɪ'lʌktᵊnt/ *adjective* not wanting to do something **isteksiz, gönülsüz, kerhen** [+ to do sth] *Many victims of crime are reluctant to go to the police.* ● **reluctance** /rɪ'lʌktᵊns/ *noun* [U] when someone does not want to do something **isteksizlik, gönülsüzlük** [+ to do sth] *a reluctance to accept changes* ● **reluctantly** *adverb* **istjust**

o—**rely** /rɪ'laɪ/ *verb*
rely on sb/sth *phrasal verb* **1** to need someone or something in order to be successful, work correctly, etc **bağlı/tabi olmak, bel bağlamak, eline bakmak, muhtaç olmak** *Families rely more on wives' earnings than before.* **2** to trust someone or something **güvenmek, itimat etmek, bel bağlamak** [+ to do sth] *I know I can rely on you to help me.*

o—**remain** /rɪ'meɪn/ *verb* **1** [I] to continue to exist when everything or everyone else has gone **kalmak** *Only a few hundred of these animals remain today.* **2 remain calm/open, etc; remain a secret/mystery/prisoner, etc** to continue to be in the same state **sakin/açık vs. kalmak; bir sır/gizem/mahkum vs. kalmak** *The exact date of the wedding remains a secret.* **3 remain at/in/with, etc** *formal* to stay in the same place **aynı durumda/konumda kalmak** *She will remain at her mother's until I return.*

remainder /rɪ'meɪndəʳ/ *noun* [no plural] the things or people that are left when everything or everyone else has gone or been dealt with **artan, geri kalan, bakiye** *He drank the remainder of his coffee and got up to leave.*

remaining /rɪ'meɪnɪŋ/ *adjective* [always before noun] continuing to exist when everything or everyone else has gone or been dealt with **kalan, hâlâ var olan, geride kalan** *Mix in half the butter and keep the remaining 50g for later.*

remains /rɪ'meɪnz/ *noun* [plural] **1** the parts of something, especially a building, that continue to exist when the rest of it has been destroyed **kalıntılar, harabeler** *the remains of a Buddhist temple* **2** *formal* someone's body after they have died **ceset, ceset kalıntısı**

remake /'riːmeɪk/ *noun* [C] a film that is the same as one that has been made before **tekrar yapım/çevirim/versiyon** *a remake of 'King Kong'* ● **remake** /ˌriː'meɪk/ *verb* [T] *past* **remade** yeniden yapmak

remand¹ /rɪ'mɑːnd/ *noun* **on remand** *UK* in prison before your trial (= when a law court decides if you are guilty or not) **tutuklu/tutuksuz yargılanmayı bekleyen** *He spent two weeks on remand in Bullingdon prison.*

remand² /rɪ'mɑːnd/ *verb* **be remanded in custody** *UK* to be kept in prison on remand **yargılanmak üzere hapiste tutulmak** *He was charged with murder and remanded in custody.*

⟪ **remark** ...... İLE BİRLİKTE KULLANILAN KELİMELER ⟫

make a remark ● a remark **about/on** sth

remark¹ /rɪ'mɑːk/ *noun* [C] something that you say **söz, lâf, beyan** *He made a remark about her clothes.*

remark² /rɪ'mɑːk/ *verb* [I] to say something **söylemek, demek** [+ that] *He remarked that she was looking thin.* **remark on/upon sth** *phrasal verb* to say something about something that you have just noticed **söylemek, yorumda bulunmak, belirtmek** *He remarked on how well you were.*

remarkable /rɪ'mɑːkəbl/ *adjective* very unusual or noticeable in a way that you admire **dikkate değer, olağanüstü** *a remarkable woman* ○ *He has a remarkable memory.* ⊃Opposite **unremarkable**.

remarkably /rɪ'mɑːkəbli/ *adverb* in a way that makes you feel surprised **dikkat çekecek şekilde; şaşırtıcı biçimde** *She has remarkably good skin for her age.*

remarry /ˌriː'mæri/ *verb* [I] to get married again **tekrar/yeniden evlenmek** *His wife died in 1970 and he never remarried.*

remedial /rɪ'miːdiəl/ *adjective* [always before noun] **1** intended to help people who are having difficulty learning something **geliştirici, yetiştirici, yardımcı** *remedial English classes* **2** *formal* intended to improve something **iyileştirici, tedavi edici, şifa verici, düzeltici** *Remedial action is needed.*

remedy¹ /'remədi/ *noun* [C] **1** something that makes you better when you are ill **ilâç, deva, derman, çare** *a flu remedy* **2** something that solves a problem **çare, çıkar yol, çözüm** *The remedy for the traffic problem is to encourage people to use public transport.*

remedy² /'remədi/ *verb* [T] to solve a problem, or to improve a bad situation **çözmek, düzeltmek, iyileştirmek** *They were able to remedy the problem very easily.*

⟪ **remember** ...... BAŞKA BİR DEYİŞLE ⟫

Daha resmi olan kullanımları **recall** ve **recollect** ifadeleridir. *I don't recall arranging a time to meet.* ● *I didn't recollect having seen him.*
Remind fiili kişiye bir şey hatırlatmak veya birşeyi yapmasını hatırlatmak anlamında kullanılır. *Every time we meet he reminds me about the money he lent me.* ● *Will you remind me to buy some eggs?*
Kişinin aniden bir şey hatırladığı durumlarda **come back to** ve **come to** deyimleri kullanılabilir. *I'd forgotten his name but it's just come (back) to me.*
Geçmişte olan güzel olaylardan bahsetmek anlamında **reminisce** fiili kullanılabilir. *We were just reminiscing about our school days.*
Gelecekte yararlı olabilecek bir kişi veya şeyin hatırlandığı durumlar için **bear something in mind** söylemi kullanılabilir. *When you book, bear in mind that Christmas is the busiest period.*

o—**remember** /rɪ'membəʳ/ *verb* [I, T] **1** If you remember a fact or something from the past, you keep it in your mind, or bring it back into your mind. **hatırlamak, anımsamak** *I can't remember his name.* ○ [+ doing sth] *I don't remember signing a contract.* ○ [+ (that)] *Just as the door closed he remembered that his keys were inside the room.* **2** to not forget to do something **unutmamak, akla gelmek, hatırlamak** [+ to do sth] *I must remember to send Carol a birthday card.*

remembrance /rɪˈmembrᵊns/ *noun* [U] when you remember and show respect for someone who has died **yâd etme, hatıra, anımsama, anma** *They erected a statue in remembrance of him.*

∘ᐞ**remind** /rɪˈmaɪnd/ *verb* [T] to make someone remember something, or remember to do something **hatırla(t)mak, anımsa(t)mak** *Every time we meet he reminds me about the money he lent me.* ○ [+ to do sth] *Will you remind me to buy some eggs?*

remind sb of sth/sb *phrasal verb* to make someone think of something or someone else **anımsatmak, hatırlatmak; aklına düşürmek** *Harry reminds me of my father.* ○ *This song reminds me of our trip to Spain.*

┇┇┇ reminder .... İLE BİRLİKTE KULLANILAN KELİMELER

need/serve as a reminder • a constant/gentle/timely reminder • a grim/poignant/sharp/stark reminder • a reminder of sth

reminder /rɪˈmaɪndər/ *noun* [C] something that makes you remember something else **katırlatıcı şey, hatırlatma** *For me, ice cream is a reminder of happy childhood holidays at the seaside.*

reminisce /ˌremɪˈnɪs/ *verb* [I] to talk about pleasant things that happened in the past **yâdetmek, geçmişi anmak, anıları tazelemek** *We were just reminiscing about our school days.* • **reminiscence** *noun* [C, U] when you reminisce **hatırat, hatıralar, anılar**

reminiscent /ˌremɪˈnɪsᵊnt/ *adjective* **reminiscent of sth/sb** making you think of someone or something that is similar **anımsatan, hatırlatan, çağrıştıran, ...kanısını uyandıran** *a smell reminiscent of an old church*

remission /rɪˈmɪʃᵊn/ *noun* **be in remission** to be in a period of time when a serious illness is better **iyileşme sürecinde olmak, iyi durumda olmak, toparlamak** *He is in remission at the moment.*

remit¹ /ˈriːmɪt/ *noun* [no plural] *UK* the things that you are responsible for in your job **sorumluluğunda olan şeyler**

remit² /rɪˈmɪt/ *verb* [T] **remitting,** *past* **remitted** *formal* to send money to someone **para göndermek, para havalesi yapmak**

remnant /ˈremnənt/ *noun* [C] a piece of something that continues to exist when the rest of that thing has gone **artık, kalıntı, bakiye** *the remnants of last night's meal*

remorse /rɪˈmɔːs/ *noun* [U] the feeling that you are sorry for something bad that you have done **vicdan azabı, pişmanlık, nedamet** *He has shown no remorse for his actions.* • **remorseful** *adjective* feeling remorse **pişmanlık dolu, vicdan azabı çeken**

remorseless /rɪˈmɔːsləs/ *adjective* **1** *UK* never stopping **aman vermem, hiç durmayan** *remorseless pressure to succeed* **2** cruel **acımasız, vicdansız** • **remorselessly** *adverb* **durmadan**

remote /rɪˈməʊt/ *adjective* **1** PLACE far away **uzak, uzakta, ırak** *It was a remote mountain village with no electricity supply.* **2** TIME far in time **uzak in the remote past** **3** SLIGHT slight **uzak, pek zayıf, çok az** *There is a remote possibility that it could be cancer.* • **remoteness** *noun* [U] **uzaklık**

re,mote con'trol *noun* **remote control**
1 [C] (*also* **remote**) a piece of equipment that is used to control something such as a television from a distance **uzaktan kumanda aleti** ⊃Orta kısımdaki renkli sayfalarına bakınız. **2** [U] the use of radio waves to control something such as a television from a distance **uzaktan kumanda**

remotely /rɪˈməʊtli/ *adverb* **not remotely interested/surprised/possible, etc** not at all interested, surprised, etc **uzaktan yakından ilgisi olmayan; çok ufak ölçüde, pek küçük derecede** *I'm not remotely interested in football.*

removal /rɪˈmuːvᵊl/ *noun* **1** [U] when you remove something **çıkarma, yok etme, temizleme** *stain removal* **2** [C, U] *UK* when you move everything from one house to take to another **taşıma, nakliye, nakil** *a removals firm*

∘ᐞ**remove** /rɪˈmuːv/ *verb* [T] **1** TAKE AWAY to take something away **taşımak, kaldırmak, alıp götürmek** *An operation was needed to remove the bullets from his chest.* **2** TAKE OFF to take something off **çıkarmak, temizlemek** *Carefully remove the lid, then stir the paint.* **3** JOB *formal* to make someone stop doing their job **at(ıl)mak, çıkar(ıl)mak, uzaklaştır(ıl)mak** [often passive] *He had been removed from his job on medical grounds.* **4 be far removed from sth** to be very different from something **...dan/den uzak olmak/farklı olmak; ilgisi/alâkası olmamak** *The princess's world was far removed from reality.*

remuneration /rɪˌmjuːnᵊrˈeɪʃᵊn/ *noun* [U] *formal* when someone is paid for work they have done **ödeme, ücret ödeme; bir iş karşılığı yapılan ödeme**

renaissance /rəˈneɪsᵊns/ ⓤⓢ /ˌrenəˈsɑːns/ *noun* [no plural] a time when something becomes popular or fashionable again **yenilik, yeniden popüler/moda olma** *The British film industry is enjoying a renaissance.*

the Renaissance /rəˈneɪsᵊns/ ⓤⓢ /ˌrenəˈsɑːns/ *noun* the period during the 14th, 15th, and 16th centuries in Europe when there was a lot of interest and activity in art, literature, ideas, etc **Rönesans**

rename /ˌriːˈneɪm/ *verb* [T] to give something a new name **yeniden isim vermek/ad koymak** [+ two objects] *Siam was renamed Thailand in 1939.*

render /ˈrendər/ *verb* [T] *formal* **1** to cause something or someone to be in a particular state or condition **haline getirmek; etmek, yapmak** *She was rendered speechless upon hearing the news.* **2** to give someone a decision, opinion, help, etc **karar/fikir/yardım vs. vermek/sunmak** *payment for services rendered*

rendering /ˈrendᵊrɪŋ/ *noun* [C] the way that something is performed, written, drawn, etc **yorumlama, icra, oynama** *a child's rendering of a house*

rendezvous /ˈrɒndɪvuː/ *noun* [C] *plural* **rendezvous** an arrangement to meet someone, or the place you have arranged to meet them **randevu, buluşma** • **rendezvous** *verb* [I] **randevulaşmak**

rendition /renˈdɪʃᵊn/ *noun* [C] the way in which a song, piece of music, etc is performed **yorumlama, icra, oynama, sunma**

renegade /ˈrenɪɡeɪd/ *noun* [C] someone who changes and joins a group that is against their own group **dönek kimse, dönme** *a group of renegade soldiers*

renege /rə'neɪɡ/ ⓤⓢ /rə'nɪɡ/ *verb*
renege on sth *phrasal verb formal* to not do what you said you were going to do **sözünü tutmamak, vaadini yerine getirmemek** *to renege on a promise*

renew /rɪ'njuː/ *verb* [T] **1** OFFICIAL AGREEMENT to arrange to continue an official agreement that was going to end soon **resmî antlaşmayı yenilemek, uzatmak, temdit etmek** *I've decided not to renew my golf club membership this year.* **2** BUY *UK* to get a new one of something that is old **eski bir şeyi yenilemek, yenisini almak** *A car isn't the sort of thing you renew every year.* **3** DO AGAIN to start to do something again **yeniden yapmaya başlamak, canlandırmak, yenileştirmek** *The next morning enemy war planes renewed their bombing.* ● **renewal** *noun* [C, U] when you renew something **yenileme**

renewable /rɪ'njuːəbl/ *adjective* **1** A renewable form of energy can be produced as quickly as it is used. **yenilenebilir (enerji)** *a renewable energy source such as wind power* **2** A renewable official agreement is one that you can arrange to continue when the time limit is reached. **(antlaşma, evrak vb.) uzatılabilir, yenilenebilir** *a 6-month renewable contract*

renewables /rɪ'njuːəblz/ *noun* [plural] types of energy such as wind power and power from the sun that can be replaced as quickly as they are used **(rüzgâr, güneş enerjisi vb.) yenilenebilir enerji türleri**

renewed /rɪ'njuːd/ *adjective* starting again in a stronger way than before **yenilenmiş, daha güçlü hâle gelmiş, gelişmiş, tazelenmiş** *He sang now with renewed confidence.*

renounce /rɪ'naʊns/ *verb* [T] to officially say that you do not have the right to something any more, or that you do not want to be involved in something any more **feragat etmek, vazgeçmek, bırakmak** *They had renounced all rights to ownership of the land.*

renovate /'renəveɪt/ *verb* [T] to repair and decorate a building that is old and in bad condition **onarmak, yenileştirmek, restore etmek** ● **renovation** /ˌrenə'veɪʃ³n/ *noun* [C, U] **yenileme**

renowned /rɪ'naʊnd/ *adjective* famous **meşhur, ünlü, namlı, şöhretli, tanınmış** *The Lake District is renowned for its beauty.*

rent¹ /rent/ *verb* **1** HOME [I, T] to pay money to live in a building that someone else owns **kiralamak, kira ile tutmak** *He'll be renting an apartment until he can find a house to buy.* **2** PAY TO USE [T] *US* (*UK* hire) to pay money to use something for a short time **kiralamak, para ile tutmak** *We could rent a car for the weekend.* **3** RECEIVE MONEY [T] (*also* rent out) to allow someone to pay you money to live in your building **kiraya vermek** *I rented out my house and went travelling for a year.*

┌─────────────────────────────────────┐
│ 🧩 **rent** ...... İLE BİRLİKTE KULLANILAN KELİMELER │
└─────────────────────────────────────┘
pay the rent ● the rent **on** sth

rent² /rent/ *noun* [C, U] the amount of money that you pay to live in a building that someone else owns **kira, kira gideri** *They couldn't afford the rent.*

rental /'rent³l/ *noun* [C, U] an arrangement to rent something, or the amount of money that you pay to rent something **kiralık, kiralanan; kira, kira bedeli** *The price includes flights and car rental.*

rented /'rentɪd/ *adjective* describes something that you rent **kiralanmış, kiralık** *rented accommodation*

renter /'rentəʳ/ *noun* [C] *US* someone who pays money to live in a house or an apartment that someone else owns **kiracı; kiralayan**

renunciation /rɪˌnʌnsi'eɪʃ³n/ *noun* [U, no plural] when you say that you do not want something or believe in

something any more **feragat, vazgeçme, bırakma** *a renunciation of violence*

reorganize (*also UK* -ise) /ˌriː'ɔːɡənaɪz/ *verb* [I, T] to organize something again in order to improve it **yeniden düzenle(n)mek, reorganize etmek, ıslah etmek** *He's completely reorganized his schedule for the week.* ● **reorganization** /ˌriːˌɔːɡ³naɪ'zeɪʃ³n/ *noun* [C, U] **tekrar organize etme**

rep /rep/ *noun* [C] *informal* someone whose job is to sell things for a company **satıcı, firma temsilcisi** *the UK sales rep*

repaid /ˌriː'peɪd/ *past of* repay **geri vermek' fiilinin geçmiş zaman hâli**

┌─────────────────────────────────────┐
│ **repair** ...... BAŞKA BİR DEYİŞLE │
└─────────────────────────────────────┘
Fix ve **mend** fiilleri sıklıkla kullanılan alternatiflerdir. *I must get my bike fixed.* ● *Can you mend that hole in my trousers?*
Kişinin birşeyi tamir edip iyi duruma getirdiğinin ifadesinde **do up** ve **fix up** deyimleri sıklıkla kullanılır. *Nick loves fixing up old cars.* ● *They're planning to buy an old cottage and do it up.*
Service fiili arabaların veya diğer makinelerin tamirinin ifadesinde kullanılır. *I'm taking the car to the garage to have it serviced this afternoon.*

o͙**repair¹** /rɪ'peəʳ/ *verb* [T] **1** to fix something that is broken or damaged **onarmak, tamir etmek, elden geçirmek** *I must get my bike repaired.* **2** to improve a bad situation **iyileştirmek, düzeltmek, daha iyi hâle getirmek** *It will take a long time to repair relations between the two countries.*

┌─────────────────────────────────────┐
│ 🧩 **repair (noun)** ...... İLE BİRLİKTE KULLANILAN KELİMELER │
└─────────────────────────────────────┘
carry out/do repairs ● **be in need of** repair ● **extensive/major/minor** repairs ● the repair **of** sth

repair² /rɪ'peəʳ/ *noun* **1** [C, U] something that you do to fix something that is broken or damaged **tamirat, onarım, bakım onarım** [usually plural] *The repairs cost me £150.* **2 be in good/bad repair** to be in good/bad condition **iyi/kötü/fena hâlde/tamir ister durumda olmak**

repatriate /ˌriː'pætrieɪt/ ⓤⓢ /ˌriː'peɪtrieɪt/ *verb* [T] to send someone back to their own country **ülkesine geri göndermek, sınır dışı etmek** ● **repatriation** /ˌriːˌpætri'eɪʃ³n/ ⓤⓢ /ˌriːˌpeɪtri'eɪʃ³n/ *noun* [U] **ülkesine iade**

repay /ˌriː'peɪ/ *verb* [T] *past* **repaid 1** to pay back money that you have borrowed **ödemek, geri vermek** *to repay a loan* **2** to do something kind for someone who has done something to help you **bir iyiliği karşılıksız bırakmamak; karşılığını vermek; altında kalmamak** *What can I do to repay you for your kindness?* ● **repayment** /rɪ'peɪmənt/ *noun* [C, U] when you repay someone or the money that you pay back **geri ödeme**

repeal /rɪ'piːl/ *verb* [T] to officially make a law end **yürürlükten kaldırmak, feshetmek, lağvetmek**

o͙**repeat¹** /rɪ'piːt/ *verb* [T] **1** to say or do something more than once **tekrar etmek, yinelemek** *He repeated the number.* ○ *The test must be repeated several times.* **2** to tell someone something that someone else has told you **tekrar söylemek, aktarmak** *I've got some news for you but you mustn't repeat it to anyone.*

repeat² /rɪ'piːt/ *noun* **1** [no plural] when something happens or is done more than once **tekrar, yineleme, tekrar etme** *Everything is being done to avoid a repeat of the tragedy.* **2** [C] *UK* (*US* rerun) a television or radio programme that is broadcast again **tekrar yanıtlama**

repeated /rɪ'piːtɪd/ *adjective* [always before noun] done or happening more than once **tekrar edilen, tekrarla-**

repel

nan *He has refused repeated requests to be interviewed.* ● **repeatedly** *adverb The victim was stabbed repeatedly.* tekrarlanarak

repel /rɪ'pel/ *verb* [T] **repelling**, *past* **repelled 1** to make someone or something move away or stop attacking you püskürtmek, uzaklaştırmak, defetmek *a smell that repels insects* **2** If someone or something repels you, you think they are extremely unpleasant. iğrendirmek, tiksindirmek, nefret uyandırmak

repellent¹ /rɪ'pelᵊnt/ *adjective* extremely unpleasant itici, uzaklaştırıcı, iğrenç, tiksindirici, nefret uyandırıcı *I find his views utterly repellent.*

repellent² /rɪ'pelᵊnt/ *noun* [C, U] **insect/mosquito repellent** a substance that you use to keep insects away böcek/sivrisinek kovucu

repent /rɪ'pent/ *verb* [I, T] *formal* to say that you are sorry for doing something bad pişman olmak, pişmanlık duymak, nedamet duymak ● **repentance** *noun* [U] *formal* when someone repents pişmanlık, nedamet, pişman olma

repentant /rɪ'pentənt/ *adjective formal* feeling sorry about something bad that you have done pişman, pişmanlık duyan ⊃Opposite unrepentant.

repercussions /ˌriːpə'kʌʃᵊnz/ *noun* [plural] the effects that an action or event has on something, especially bad effects (kötü) etki, tepki, yankı, aks, sonuç *Any decrease in tourism could have serious repercussions for the local economy.*

repertoire /'repətwɑː/ *noun* [C] all the songs, plays, etc that someone can perform repertuar

repertory /'repᵊtᵊri/ *noun* **1** [C, U] when a group of actors performs several different plays during a period of time bir kaç oyunu birden oynama; repertuar tiyatrosu yapma *They have four plays in repertory this season.* ○ *a repertory company/theatre* **2** [C] all the songs, plays, etc that someone can perform oyun/ şarkıların tümü; repertuar

repetition /ˌrepɪ'tɪʃᵊn/ *noun* [C, U] when something is repeated tekrar, yineleme *We don't want a repetition of last year's disaster.*

repetitive /rɪ'petətɪv/ (*also* **repetitious** /ˌrepɪ'tɪʃəs/) *adjective* doing or saying the same thing several times, especially in a way that is boring tekrarlamalı, tekrarlı *a repetitive job* ● **repetitively** *adverb* tekrarlanarak

re,petitive 'strain ,injury ⊃See RSI.

◦**replace** /rɪ'pleɪs/ *verb* [T] **1** USE INSTEAD to start using another thing or person instead of the one that you are using now ...ın/in yerine yenisini koymak; ...ile değiştirmek *We're thinking of replacing our old TV with a fancy new one.* **2** BE USED INSTEAD to start to be used instead of the thing or person that is being used now...ın/in yerine yenisini konulmak; ...ile değiştirilmek *This system will replace the old one.* **3** GET SOMETHING NEW to get something new because the one you had before has been lost or damaged yenisini almak *We'll have to replace this carpet soon.* **4** PUT BACK *formal* to put something back in the place where it usually is yerine koymak, eski yerine yerleştirmek *She picked up the books and carefully replaced them on the shelf.*

replacement /rɪ'pleɪsmənt/ *noun* **1** [C] the thing or person that replaces something or someone yerine geçen kişi/şey *It's not going to be easy to find a replacement for you.* **2** [U] when something or someone is replaced yerine koyma/geçme; yerini alma

replay /'riːpleɪ/ *noun* [C] **1** an important part of a sports game or other event on television that is shown again immediately after it has happened tekrar/yeniden gösterme/yayınlama **2** *UK* a game of sport that is played again yeniden/tekrar oynama ● **replay** /ˌriː'pleɪ/ *verb* [T] ⊃See also: action replay *UK*, instant replay *US*. tekrar gösterilen maç

replenish /rɪ'plenɪʃ/ *verb* [T] *formal* to fill something or make it complete again yeniden doldurmak, tamamlamak *to replenish supplies* ● **replenishment** *noun* [U] *formal* when you fill something or make it complete again yeniden doldurma, tamamlama

replica /'replɪkə/ *noun* [C] something that is made to look almost exactly the same as something else eş, örnek, kopya, suret *a replica of the White House*

replicate /'replɪkeɪt/ *verb* [T] *formal* to make or do something again in exactly the same way aynısını yapmak, kopyasını çıkarmak; tıpkısını üretmek ● **replication** /ˌreplɪ'keɪʃᵊn/ *noun* [C, U] tekrar

◦**reply¹** /rɪ'plaɪ/ *verb* [I, T] to answer cevap vermek, yanıtlamak *"I don't understand," she replied.* ○ *He didn't reply to my email.* ○ [+ that] *Henry replied that he had no idea what I was talking about.*

reply (noun) .... İLE BİRLİKTE KULLANILAN KELİMELER

give/make/send a reply ● get/have/receive a reply ● a reply to sth ● in reply

◦**reply²** /rɪ'plaɪ/ *noun* [C, U] an answer cevap, yanıt, karşılık *Her reply was short and unfriendly.* ○ *Have you had a reply to your letter?* ○ *She sent me an email in reply* (= as an answer).

◦**report¹** /rɪ'pɔːt/ *noun* [C] **1** a description of an event or situation rapor, eylem/durum raporu *a police report* ○ *an annual report on the economy* **2** *UK* (*US* re'port ,card) when teachers write about a child's progress at school for their parents (okul/öğrenci) gelişim raporu, karne, not karnesi

◦**report²** /rɪ'pɔːt/ *verb* **1** DESCRIBE [I, T] to describe a recent event or situation, especially on television, radio, or in a newspaper bilgi vermek; açılamada bulunmak *Jo Smith reports on recent developments.* ○ [+ that] *She reported that the situation had changed dramatically.* ○ [+ doing sth] *A woman outside the shop reported seeing the gun.* **2** TELL [T] to tell someone in authority that something has happened, especially an accident or crime rapor etmek, bildirmek *He should have reported the accident immediately.* ○ *Have you reported the fault to a technician?* **3** COMPLAIN [T] to complain about someone's behaviour to someone in authority. şikayet etmek, yanlışı rapor etmek *I'm going to report him to the police.* ○ *Duncan's been reported for smoking.*

report to sb/sth *phrasal verb* to go to someone or a place and say that you have arrived dönüşünü/varışını bildirmek/rapor etmek *All visitors please report to reception.*

reportedly /rɪ'pɔːtɪdli/ *adverb* If something has reportedly happened or is reportedly a fact, people say it has happened or is true. söylenenlere bakılırsa; söylendiğine göre; güya *Two students were reportedly killed and several wounded.*

re,ported 'speech *noun* [U] speech or writing that is used to report what someone has said, but not using exactly the same words dolaylı aktarım/anlatım

reporter /rɪ'pɔːtə/ *noun* [C] someone whose job is to discover information about news events and describe them on television, radio, or in a newspaper muhabir, haber muhabiri/spikeri, sunucu

repossess /ˌriːpəˈzes/ *verb* [T] to take back someone's house, car, furniture, etc because they cannot finish paying for them **ipotekli ev/araba/mobilyayı geri almak; borcu ödenmediği için el koymak ● repossession** /ˌriːpəˈzeʃ³n/ *noun* [C, U] when someone repossesses something, or the thing that is repossessed **yeniden elde etme, geri alma; yeniden elde edilen/geri alınan**

reprehensible /ˌrepriˈhensəbl/ *adjective formal* Reprehensible behaviour is extremely bad. **azarlanmayı hak eden, çok ayıp/kötü/çirkin**

o⌐**represent** /ˌrepriˈzent/ *verb* [T] **1** BE to be equal to something **anlamına gelmek, ...ile eşit olmak; örneğini oluşturmak, göstermek** *In practice the figure represents a 10% pay cut.* ○ *The cancellation of the new road project represents a victory for protesters.* **2** SPEAK FOR to officially speak or do something for someone else because they have asked you to **temsil etmek; ...ın/in adına hareket etmek** *The union represents over 200 employees.* **3** COMPETITION to be the person from a country, school, etc that is in a competition **yarışmalarda bir ülkeyi temsil etmek 4** SIGN to be a sign or symbol of something **sembolize etmek; ...ın/in simgesi olmak** *The crosses on the map represent churches.* **5** SHOW to show someone or something in a particular way **göstermek, sunmak, açıklamak, bildirmek**

representation /ˌreprizenˈteiʃ³n/ *noun* **1** [U] speaking or doing something officially for another person **resmî olarak temsil edilme** *Can he afford legal representation?* **2** [C, U] the way someone or something is shown **tasvir, resim, suret** *an accurate representation of country life* ⊃See also: **proportional representation.**

representative¹ /ˌrepriˈzentətiv/ *noun* [C] someone who speaks or does something officially for another person **temsilci, delege, temsil eden** ⊃See also: **House of Representatives.**

representative² /ˌrepriˈzentətiv/ *adjective* the same as other people or things in a particular group **temsil, örnek, tipik, karakteristik** *Are his views representative of the rest of the department?*

repress /riˈpres/ *verb* [T] **1** to stop yourself from showing your true feelings **bastırmak, zaptetmek, tutmak, gem vurmak, dizginlemek** *Brigitta repressed a sudden desire to cry.* **2** to control what people do, especially by using force **güç kullanarak baskı altında tutmak, ezmek, baskılamak, boyun eğdirmek ● repression** /riˈpreʃ³n/ *noun* [U] when you repress something **baskı, engelleme, zaptetme, frenleme, zaptetme**

repressed /riˈprest/ *adjective* **1** unable to show your true feelings and emotions **duygularına gem vuran/frenleyen; her şeyi içine atan** *a lonely, repressed man* **2** A repressed feeling or emotion is one that you do not show. **frenlenmiş, baskılanmış, baskı altına alınmış** *repressed anger*

repressive /riˈpresiv/ *adjective* cruel and not allowing people to have freedom **baskı uygulayan/altında tutan; özgürlüğünü engelleyen/engelleyici** *a repressive military regime*

reprieve /riˈpriːv/ *noun* [C] **1** an official order that stops a prisoner from being killed as a punishment **idam cezasını iptâl/erteleme emri 2** when something happens to stop a bad situation **geçici rahatlık/ferahlık/soluk alma; erteleme; kötü bir duruma engel olma ● reprieve** *verb* [T] **tecil etmek**

reprimand /ˈreprimɑːnd/ *verb* [T] to tell someone in an official way that they have done something wrong **tekdir etmek, kınamak, azarlamak, paylamak** [+ **for + doing sth**] *Watts has already been reprimanded for*

disclosing confidential information. **● reprimand** *noun* [C] **azar**

reprint /riːˈprint/ *verb* [T, I] to print a book again **yeniden/tekrar basmak**

---

reprisal ⋯⋯⋯ İLE BİRLİKTE KULLANILAN KELİMELER

fear reprisals ● in reprisal **for** sth **●** a reprisal **against/from** sb

---

reprisal /riˈpraiz³l/ *noun* [C, U] something violent or unpleasant that is done to punish an enemy for something they have done **misilleme, kısas** *The attack was in reprisal for police raids.* ○ *He did not wish to be filmed because he feared reprisals.*

reproach¹ /riˈprəʊtʃ/ *noun* [C, U] criticism of someone, especially for not being successful or not doing what is expected **sitem, serzeniş, kınama** *There was a hint of reproach in his voice.* ○ *The article gave the impression that the teachers were above/beyond reproach* (= could not be criticized). **● reproachful** *adjective* showing criticism **sitemkâr, sitem dolu, kınayan** *a reproachful look* **● reproachfully** *adverb* **kınayıcı bir şekilde**

reproach² /riˈprəʊtʃ/ *verb* [T] to criticize someone for not being successful or not doing what is expected **sitem etmek, serzenişte bulunmak, kınamak** [often reflexive] *You've no reason to reproach yourself.*

reproduce /ˌriːprəˈdjuːs/ *verb* **1** [T] to make a copy of something **kopyasını yapmak, taklit etmek** *The diagram is reproduced by permission of the original author.* **2** [I] *formal* If people, animals, or plants reproduce, they produce babies or young animals or plants. **üremek, çoğalmak, yavrulamak**

reproduction /ˌriːprəˈdʌkʃ³n/ *noun* **1** [U] the process of producing babies or young animals and plants **üreme, çoğalma, yavrulama 2** [C] a copy of something, especially a painting **kopya, taklit, reprodüksiyon**

reproductive /ˌriːprəˈdʌktiv/ *adjective* [always before noun] relating to the process of producing babies or young animals and plants **üreme/yavrulama; üremeyle/yavrulamayla ilgili** *the reproductive organs*

reptile /ˈreptail/ *noun* [C] an animal whose body is covered with scales (= pieces of hard skin), and whose blood changes temperature, for example a snake **sürüngen ● reptilian** /repˈtiliən/ *adjective* like a reptile, or relating to reptiles **sürüngen gibi, sürüngenlerle ilgili**

republic /riˈpʌblik/ *noun* [C] a country with no king or queen but with an elected government **cumhuriyet**

republican /riˈpʌblikən/ *noun* [C] **1** someone who supports the principles of a republic **cumhuriyetçi 2 Republican** someone who supports the Republican Party in the US (ABD) **Cumhuriyetçi Parti taraftarı** *the Republican candidate* **● republican** *adjective* relating to a republic **cumhuriyete ilişkin**

the Republican ˌParty *noun* [group] one of the two main political parties in the US (ABD) **Cumhuriyetçi Parti**

repudiate /riˈpjuːdieit/ *verb* [T] *formal* to refuse to accept or agree with something **reddetmek, tanımamak, kabul etmemek** *Cousteau repudiated the criticism/claims.* **● repudiation** /riˌpjuːdiˈeiʃ³n/ *noun* [U] *formal* **reddetme**

repugnant /riˈpʌɡnənt/ *adjective formal* extremely unpleasant **çirkin, tiksindirici, iğrenç** *She thought the idea morally repugnant.* **● repugnance** /riˈpʌɡnəns/ *noun* [U] *formal* when something or someone is repugnant **çirkinlik, tiksinti, iğrençlik, iticilik**

repulse /rɪ'pʌls/ *verb* [T] **1** If someone or something repulses you, you think they are extremely unpleasant. **tiksinti duymak, iğrenmek** *The smell of him repulsed her.* **2** to successfully stop a military attack **püskürtmek, askerî bir saldırıyı başarıyla engellemek** [often passive] *The enemy attack was quickly repulsed.*

repulsion /rɪ'pʌlʃᵊn/ *noun* [U, no plural] a strong feeling that someone or something is extremely unpleasant **nefret, iğrenme, tiksinti**

repulsive /rɪ'pʌlsɪv/ *adjective* extremely unpleasant, especially to look at **iğrendiren/iğrenç, tiksinti veren/tiksindirici** *a repulsive man with long, greasy hair*

reputable /'repjətəbl/ *adjective* known to be good and honest **saygıdeğer, tanınmış, muteber** *a reputable organization* ⊃Opposite disreputable.

🧩 *reputation* ..... İLE BİRLİKTE KULLANILAN KELİMELER

have a reputation ● a reputation for sth ● a bad/good reputation ● acquire/establish/get a reputation ● damage/destroy/ruin sb's reputation

◦▪**reputation** /ˌrepjə'teɪʃᵊn/ *noun* [C] the opinion that people have about someone or something based on their behaviour or character in the past **ün, şöhret, nam** *Both hotels have a good reputation.* ○ *He has a reputation for efficiency.*

reputed /rɪ'pjuːtɪd/ *adjective formal* believed by most people to be true ...**sayılan, sözde, güya;** ...**olduğu söylenmek/sanılmak** [+ to do sth] *The ghost of a young woman is reputed to haunt the building.* ● **reputedly** *adverb* **şöhtetli bir şekilde**

◦▪**request¹** /rɪ'kwest/ *noun* [C, U] when you politely or officially ask for something **rica, istek, dilem, dilek, talep** *His doctor made an urgent request for a copy of the report.* ○ *An application form is available on request* (= if you ask for it). ○ *A clause was added to the contract at his request* (= because he asked).

◦▪**request²** /rɪ'kwest/ *verb* [T] to politely or officially ask for something **rica etmek, talep etmek, dilemek, istemek** *We've requested a further two computers.* ○ [+ that] *They requested that no photographs be taken in the church.*

requiem /'rekwiəm/ *noun* [C] a Christian ceremony where people pray for someone who has died, or a piece of music written for this ceremony **Hıristiyan dininde cenaze merasiminde yapılan dua/müzik; cenaze marşı**

◦▪**require** /rɪ'kwaɪər/ *verb* [T] **1** to need or demand something **istemek, gerekmek; gereksinim duymak; talep etmek** *Training to be a doctor requires a lot of hard work.* ○ [+ that] *A recent law requires that all programmes are censored.* **2 require sb to do sth** to officially demand that someone does something **resmen talep etmek/istemek/zorunda olmak/mecbur olmak** [often passive] *You are required by law to produce a valid passport.*

requirement /rɪ'kwaɪəmənt/ *noun* [C] something that is needed or demanded **gereklilik, koşul, icap, şart** *college entrance requirements* ○ *Valid insurance is a legal requirement.*

requisite /'rekwɪzɪt/ *adjective* [always before noun] *formal* needed for a particular purpose **gerekli, lüzumlu, lâzım (olan)** *I felt that he lacked the requisite skills for the job.*

re-release /ˌriːrɪ'liːs/ *verb* [T] to make a record or film available for people to buy or see for a second time **(film, plâk, CD vs.) tekrar piyasaya çıkarmak/ satışa sunmak**

rerun /'riːrʌn/ *US* (*UK* repeat) *noun* [C] a television or radio programme or film that is broadcast again **yeniden yayınlamak**

reschedule /riː'ʃedjuːl/ ⑤ /riː'skedʒuːl/ *verb* [T] to agree a new and later date for something to happen **yeniden kararlaştırmak; tekrar başka bir tarih belirlemek**

rescue¹ /'reskju:/ *verb* [T] **rescuing**, *past* **rescued** to save someone from a dangerous or unpleasant situation **kurtarmak** *Fifty passengers had to be rescued from a sinking ship.* ● **rescuer** *noun* [C] **kurtarıcı, kurtaran**

rescue² /'reskju:/ *noun* **1** [C, U] when someone is saved from a dangerous or unpleasant situation **kurtarma, yardım** *an unsuccessful rescue attempt* **2 come to the/ sb's rescue** to help someone who is in a difficult situation **yardımına koşmak, imdadına yetişmek** *I forgot my purse but Anna came to the rescue and lent me some money.*

🧩 *research* ..... İLE BİRLİKTE KULLANILAN KELİMELER

carry out/conduct/do research ● research indicates/proves/reveals/suggests sth ● research into sth ● a research assistant/institute/programme/ project

◦▪**research¹** /rɪ'sɜːtʃ/ *noun* [U] when someone studies a subject in detail in order to discover new information **araştırma, inceleme, tetkik** *research into language development* ○ *They are doing research into the effects of passive smoking.* ○ *a research project* ⊃See also: market research.

research² /rɪ'sɜːtʃ/ *verb* [I, T] to study a subject in detail in order to discover new information about it **araştırmak, incelemek, tetkik etmek** *He spent several years researching a rare African dialect.* ● **researcher** *noun* [C] **araştırmacı**

resemblance /rɪ'zembləns/ *noun* [C, U] a similarity between two people or things, especially in their appearance **benzeyiş, benzerlik** *There's a striking resemblance between Diane and her mother.* ○ *He bears a resemblance to* (= looks like) *someone I used to know.*

resemble /rɪ'zembl/ *verb* [T] to look like or be like someone or something **benzemek** *She resembles her father.*

resent /rɪ'zent/ *verb* [T] to feel angry and upset about a situation or about something that someone has done **içerlemek, kırılmak, kızmak** [+ doing sth] *I resent having to work late.* ○ *He resents the fact that she gets more money than he does.*

resentful /rɪ'zentfᵊl/ *adjective* angry and upset about a situation that you think is unfair **içerlemiş, kızgın, buruk** *He was bitterly resentful of his brother's success.* ● **resentfully** *adverb* **kızgın bir şekilde** ● **resentfulness** *noun* [U] **kızgınlık**

resentment /rɪ'zentmənt/ *noun* [U] a feeling of anger about a situation that you think is unfair **içerleme, kırılma, kızma**

reservation /ˌrezə'veɪʃᵊn/ *noun* **1** [C] an arrangement that you have to have a seat on an aircraft, a room in a hotel, etc **yer ayırtma, rezervasyon** *I'd like to make a reservation for Friday evening.* **2** [C, U] a doubt or a feeling that you do not agree with something completely **kuşku, şüphe** *I still have reservations about her ability to do the job.*

reserve¹ /rɪ'zɜːv/ *verb* [T] **1** to arrange to have a seat on an aircraft, a room in a hotel, etc **ayırmak, tahsis etmek, rezerve yapmak/etmek** *I'd like to reserve two seats on the 9.15 to Birmingham.* **2** to not allow people to use something because it is only for a particular person or for a particular purpose **ayırmak, yer ayırmak,**

tahsis etmek *This seat is reserved for elderly or disabled passengers.*

reserve² /rɪˈzɜːv/ *noun* **1** [SUPPLY] [C] a supply of something that you keep until it is needed **yedek, ihtiyat** *emergency cash reserves* **2 in reserve** ready to be used if you need it **yedek olarak, yedekte, gerektiğinde kullanılmak üzere, ihtiyaten** *I always keep a little money in reserve.* **3** [QUALITY] [U] when someone does not show what they are thinking or feeling **hislerini açığa vurmama, düşündüklerini belli etmeme, itidalli olma 4** [SPORT] [C] in sport, an extra player who is ready to play if one of the other players has an injury **yedek oyuncu 5** [AREA] [C] an area of land where animals and plants are protected **koruma alanı/bölgesi/arazisi** ➔See also: nature reserve.

reserved /rɪˈzɜːvd/ *adjective* not wanting to show what you are thinking or feeling **hislerini gizleyen, duygularını açığa vurmayan, itidalli** *a quiet, reserved woman*

reservoir /ˈrezəvwɑːʳ/ *noun* [C] an artificial lake where water is stored before it goes to people's houses **gölet, bent, baraj gölü**

'reset ,(button) *noun* [C] a button or switch on a computer that allows the user to turn the computer off and then on again when a program does not work correctly **bilgisayarda herhangi program düzgün çalışmadığında açma kapama tuşu; kurulum tuşu**

reshuffle /ˌriːˈʃʌfl/ *noun* [C] when people in an organization, especially a government are given different jobs to do **başka bir işle görevlendirme** *a government reshuffle* ● **reshuffle** *verb* [T] **tekrardan düzenlemek**

reside /rɪˈzaɪd/ *verb formal* **reside in/with, etc** to live somewhere **ikamet etmek, yaşamak** *My sister currently resides in Seattle.*

residence /ˈrezɪdəns/ *noun formal* **1** [C] a building where someone lives **konut, ikametgâh** *the Queen's official residence* **2** [U] when someone lives somewhere **ikamet, yaşama, oturma** *He took up residence* (= started to live) *in St. Louis.* **3 in residence** living or working somewhere **çalışma, oturma, yaşama, kalma** *He was writer in residence with a professional theatre company.* ➔See also: hall of residence.

resident¹ /ˈrezɪdənt/ *noun* [C] **1** someone who lives in a particular place **sakin, oturan/yaşayan kişi, yerli** *complaints from local residents* **2** *US* a doctor who is working in a hospital to get extra training in a particular area of medicine **ihtisas yapan hekim**

resident² /ˈrezɪdənt/ *adjective* living in a place **oturan, yaşayan, sakin** *She has been resident in Britain for most of her life.*

residential /ˌrezɪˈdenʃəl/ *adjective* **1** A residential area has only houses and not offices or factories. **yaşam/oturma için ayrılmış 2** *UK* A residential job or course is one where you live at the same place as you work or study. **yatılı (iş, kurs)**

residual /rɪˈzɪdjuəl/ *adjective* remaining **tortulaşmış, kalan, artan, çöken, artık** *residual value*

residue /ˈrezɪdjuː/ *noun* [C] something that remains after most of a substance has gone or been removed **çökelti, tortu, kalıntı, telve**

resign /rɪˈzaɪn/ *verb* [I, T] to officially tell your employer that you are leaving your job **istifa etmek, çekilmek, ayrılmak** *She resigned as headteacher.* ○ *Mr Aitken has resigned from the company.*
resign yourself to sth *phrasal verb* to make yourself accept something that you do not like because you cannot easily change it **boyun eğmek, razı olmak, katlanmak, kabullenmek** *He resigned himself to living alone.*

resignation ...... İLE BİRLİKTE KULLANILAN KELİMELER
accept/call for sb's resignation ● announce/hand in/tender your resignation ● the resignation of sb ● sb's resignation as [manager/chairman, etc] ● a letter of resignation

resignation /ˌrezɪɡˈneɪʃən/ *noun* **1** [C, U] when someone tells their employer that they are leaving their job **istifa, çekilme, görevden ayrılma** *a letter of resignation* ○ *I handed in my resignation yesterday.* **2** [U] when you accept something that you do not like because you cannot easily change it **boyun eğme, tevekkül, teslimiyet**

resilient /rɪˈzɪliənt/ *adjective* strong enough to get better quickly after damage, illness, shock, etc **çabuk iyileşen, kendini çabuk toparlayabilen** *Growth figures show that the economy is still fairly resilient.* ● **resilience** /rɪˈzɪliəns/ *noun* [U] **çabuk iyileşme kabiliyeti**

resin /ˈrezɪn/ *noun* [C, U] **1** a thick, sticky substance that is produced by some trees **reçine, çam sakızı 2** a substance that is used for making plastics **yapay reçine**

resist /rɪˈzɪst/ *verb* [I, T] **1** [AVOID] to stop yourself from doing something that you want to do **direnç göstermek, kendini tutmak, karşı koymak** *I can't resist chocolate.* ○ [+ doing sth] *I just can't resist reading other people's mail.* **2** [NOT ACCEPT] to refuse to accept something and try to stop it from happening **karşı çıkmak, muhalefet etmek** *The President is resisting calls for him to resign.* **3** [FIGHT] to fight against someone or something that is attacking you **karşı koymak, direnmek, mukavemet etmek** *British troops resisted the attack for two days.*

resistance /rɪˈzɪstəns/ *noun* [U, no plural] **1** [DISAGREE] when people disagree with a change, idea, etc and refuse to accept it **karşı koyma, muhalefet, direnç, direnme** *resistance to political change* **2** [FIGHT] when someone fights against someone who is attacking them **karşı koyma, mücadele etme, direnç gösterme, dayanma** *She didn't put up much resistance* (= fight). **3** [ILLNESS] the ability of your body to not be affected by illnesses **vücut direnci, hastalıklara karşı koyma** *Cold weather may lower the body's resistance to infection.*

resistant /rɪˈzɪstənt/ *adjective* **1** not wanting to accept something, especially changes or new ideas **karşı koyan/çıkan, direnen, muhalefet eden** *They're resistant to change.* **2** not harmed or affected by something **dirençli, dayanıklı, bağışık** *a water-resistant cover* ○ *Bacteria can become resistant to antibiotics.*

resolute /ˈrezəluːt/ *adjective formal* determined not to change what you do or believe because you think that you are right **kararlı, azimli** *a resolute opponent of the war* ● **resolutely** *adverb* **azimli bir şekilde**

resolution /ˌrezəˈluːʃən/ *noun* **1** [DECISION] [C] an official decision that is made after a group or organization have voted **teklif, öneri, önerge** *Congress passed a resolution in support of the plan* (= voted to support it). **2** [PROMISE] [C] a promise to yourself to do something **sıkı /ciddi/samimi karar** *My New Year's resolution is to do more exercise.* **3** [SOLUTION] [U, no plural] *formal* the solution to a problem **karar, önerge, bir sorunun çözümü** *a successful resolution to the crisis* **4** [DETERMINATION] [U] *formal* the quality of being determined **azim, azimlilik, kararlılık**

resolve¹ /rɪˈzɒlv/ *verb* **1** [T] to solve or end a problem or difficulty **bir sorunu çözmek, güçlüğü çözmek, sonlandırmak, halletmek** *an attempt to resolve the dispute* **2** [I, T] *formal* to decide that you will do something and be determined to do it **karar vermek, azmetmek, aklına koymak** [+ to do sth] *I have resolved to keep my bedroom tidy.*

resolve² /rɪ'zɒlv/ noun [U] formal when you are very determined to do something **azim, karar, niyet, istek**

resonant /'rezᵊnənt/ adjective A resonant sound is loud and clear. **çınlayan, çın çın öten, yankılanan** a deep, resonant voice ● **resonance** /'rezᵊnəns/ noun [U] **titreşim**

resonate /'rezᵊneɪt/ verb [I] to make a loud, clear sound **çınlamak, yankılanmak, çın çın ötmek**

resort¹ /rɪ'zɔːt/ noun [C] a place where many people go for a holiday **tatil beldesi, sayfiye yeri** a ski resort **2 a last resort** something that you do because everything else has failed **son çare, yapılacak başka bir şey kalmadığında yapılan eylem** Soldiers were given the authority to shoot, but only as a last resort.

resort² /rɪ'zɔːt/ verb
resort to sth/doing sth phrasal verb to do something that you do not want to do because you cannot find any other way of achieving something **son çare olmak/olarak başvurmak/yapmak** They should be able to control the riots without resorting to violence.

resound /rɪ'zaʊnd/ verb [I] to make a loud sound, or to be filled with a loud sound **çınlamak, yankılanmak, sesle dolu olmak** The whole hall resounded with applause.

resounding /rɪ'zaʊndɪŋ/ adjective [always before noun] **1** very loud **çınlayan, yankılanan, çok yüksek sesli** resounding applause **2 a resounding success/victory/failure, etc** a very great success, victory, etc **çok büyük/müthiş başarı/zafer/başarısızlık vs.**

resource /rɪ'zɔːs/, /'riːsɔːrs/ noun [C] something that a country, person, or organization has which they can use **kaynak, olanak, imkân** [usually plural] natural resources ⊃See also: human resources.

resourceful /rɪ'zɔːsfᵊl/ adjective good at finding ways to solve problems **becerikli, maharetli, açıkgöz** ● **resourcefulness** noun [U] **problem çözme becerisi**

⟦⟧ respect ...... İLE BİRLİKTE KULLANILAN KELİMELER
command respect ● have/show [great/no, etc] respect for sb ● treat sb/sth with respect

●⁻**respect¹** /rɪ'spekt/ noun **1** [POLITE] [U] when you are polite to someone, especially because they are older or more important than you **saygı, hürmet** You should show more respect for your parents. **2** [ADMIRATION] [U] when you admire someone because of their knowledge, skill, or achievements **saygı, hayranlık** She's an excellent teacher and I have the greatest respect for her. **3** [SHOW IMPORTANCE] [U] when you show by your behaviour that you think something is important or needs to be dealt with carefully **önem, ehemmiyet, itina** Electricity can be dangerous and should always be treated with respect. **4 in this respect/many respects** in a particular way, or in many ways **bir çok bakımdan/açıdan; bu açıdan/manada** The school has changed in many respects. **5 with respect to sth; in respect of sth** formal relating to a particular thing **...ile ilgili olarak; ...hususunda/konusunda** I am writing with respect to your letter of 24 June. **6 pay your respects a** [VISIT SOMEONE] formal to visit someone or go to talk to them **ziyaret etmek; hal hatır sormak için uğramak b** [GO TO FUNERAL] (also pay your last respects) to go to someone's funeral **cenaze törenine katılmak; son görevini yerine getirmek** ⊃See also: self-respect.

●⁻**respect²** /rɪ'spekt/ verb [T] **1** to admire someone because of their knowledge, achievements, etc **saygı duymak, hayran olmak, hürmet etmek** I respect him for his honesty. **2** If you respect someone's rights, customs, wishes, etc you accept their importance and

are careful not to do anything they would not want. **saygı göstermek, hürmet etmek, dikkate almak,**

respectable /rɪ'spektəbl/ adjective **1** behaving in a socially acceptable way or looking socially acceptable **saygın, saygı değer, muhterem, hürmete lâyık** a respectable family ○ a respectable hotel **2** large enough or good enough **bir hayli, hatırı sayılır, oldukça, tatminkâr** a respectable income ● **respectably** adverb **saygılı bir şekilde** ● **respectability** /rɪˌspektə'bɪləti/ noun [U] **saygınlık**

respected /rɪ'spektɪd/ adjective admired by people because of your knowledge, achievements, etc **hürmete değer, saygın, hayranlık uyandıran** a highly respected doctor

respectful /rɪ'spektfᵊl/ adjective showing respect for someone or something **saygılı, hürmetkâr** ● **respectfully** adverb **saygılı bir şekilde**

respective /rɪ'spektɪv/ adjective [always before noun] relating to each of the people or things that you have just talked about **kendi, herkes kendi, ayrı ayrı** members of staff and their respective partners

respectively /rɪ'spektɪvli/ adverb in the same order as the people or things you have just talked about **sırasıyla, her biri ayrı ayrı olarak** Mr Ewing and Mr Campbell gave £2000 and £250 respectively.

respiration /ˌrespᵊr'eɪʃᵊn/ noun [U] the process of breathing **solunum, nefes alma, teneffüs**

respiratory /rɪ'spɪrᵊtᵊri/ ⑤ /'respərətɔːri/ adjective [always before noun] relating to the process of breathing **solunuma ilişkin** respiratory illnesses

respite /'respaɪt/ ⑤ /'respɪt/ noun [U, no plural] a short period of rest from something difficult or unpleasant **kısa bir dinlence, nefes alma, kısa rahatlama** The weekend was a brief respite from the pressures of work.

●⁻**respond** /rɪ'spɒnd/ verb [I] **1** to say or do something as an answer or reaction to something **cevap/karşılık vermek** [+ by + doing sth] The government has responded by sending food and medical supplies to the region. ○ How quickly did the police respond to the call? **2** to improve as the result of a particular medical treatment **tedaviye cevap vermek** She's responding well to drug treatment.

respondent /rɪ'spɒndᵊnt/ noun [C] someone who has answered a request for information **cevaplayan, cevap veren** [usually plural] More than half the respondents were opposed to the new tax.

⟦⟧ response ...... İLE BİRLİKTE KULLANILAN KELİMELER
in response to sth ● sb's response to sth ● draw/elicit/provoke a response ● sb's immediate/initial/instinctive response

●⁻**response** /rɪ'spɒns/ noun [C, U] an answer or reaction to something that has been said or done **cevap, yanıt, tepki** The President's comments provoked an angry response from students. ○ I'm writing in response to your letter of 14 February.

⟦⟧ responsibility ...... İLE BİRLİKTE KULLANILAN KELİMELER
abdicate/accept/assume/claim/take/shirk responsibility ● collective/heavy/huge/total responsibility ● responsibility for sth

●⁻**responsibility** /rɪˌspɒnsə'bɪləti/ noun **1** [C, U] something that it is your job or duty to deal with **sorumluluk, mesuliyet** The head of the department has various additional responsibilities. ○ [+ to do sth] It is your responsibility to make sure that your homework is done on time.

2 take/accept/claim responsibility for sth to say that you have done something or caused something to happen, especially something bad **sorumluluğu kabul etmek/üstüne almak** *No one has yet claimed responsibility for yesterday's bomb attack.*

o→**responsible** /rɪˈspɒnsəbl/ *adjective* **1 be responsible for sb/sth/doing sth** to be the person whose duty is to deal with someone or something **bir şeyden/şeyi yapmaktan dolayı sorumlu/mesul olmak** *I'm responsible for looking after the children in the evenings.* **2 be responsible for sth/doing sth** to be the person who caused something to happen, especially something bad **olumsuz bir şeyin sorumlusu/sebebi olmak; sorumlu olmak** *Who was responsible for the accident?* **3** showing good judgment and able to be trusted **güvenilir, sorumluluk duygusu taşıyan** *a responsible attitude* ⊃Opposite **irresponsible.** **4** A responsible job is important because you have to make decisions that affect other people. **sorumluluk gerektiren 5 be responsible to sb** If you are responsible to someone at work, they are in a higher position than you and you have to tell them what you have done. **sorumlu olmak, amiri/üstü olmak**

responsibly /rɪˈspɒnsəbli/ *adverb* in a way that shows you have good judgment and can be trusted **sorumluluğunun bilincinde; itimada layık bir şekilde** *to behave/act responsibly*

responsive /rɪˈspɒnsɪv/ *adjective* listening to someone or something and having a positive and quick reaction to them **duyarlı, hassas, hemen karşılık veren** *a wonderfully responsive audience* ○ *They have not been very responsive to the needs of disabled customers.* ● **responsiveness** *noun* [U] **tepkide bulunan, cevap veren**

o→**rest**[1] /rest/ *noun* **1 the rest** the part of something that remains, or the others that remain **kalanlar, arta kalanlar, geri kalan kısmı, diğerleri** *I'm not sure I want to spend the rest of my life with him.* ○ *She was slightly older than the rest of us.* **2** [C, U] a period of time when you relax or sleep **dinlenme, istirahat** *Why don't you have a rest?* ○ *I must get some rest.* **3 come to rest** to stop moving **durmak** ⊃See also: put/set sb's **mind**[1] at rest.

o→**rest**[2] /rest/ *verb* **1** [I] to relax or sleep because you are tired after doing an activity or because you are ill **dinlenmek, istirahat etmek** *Pete's resting after his long drive.* **2 rest your eyes/feet/legs, etc** to stop using your eyes/feet, etc for a while because they are tired **gözlerini/ayaklarını/bacaklarını dinlendirmek 3 rest (sth) on/against, etc** If something rests somewhere, or if you rest it somewhere, it is supported by something else. **yasla(n)mak, daya(n)mak** *She rested her elbows on the table.* ⊃See also: rest on your **laurels.**
rest on/upon sth *phrasal verb formal* to depend on something **dayanmak, bağlı olmak** *The whole future of the team rests on his decision.*

restart /ˌriːˈstɑːt/ *verb* [T] **1** to start something again that had stopped **yeniden/tekrar başlatmak** *They want to restart the talks.* **2** If you restart a computer, you turn it off and then on again

go to a restaurant ● **manage/own/run** a restaurant ● a restaurant **offers/serves/specializes in** sth ● **at/in** a restaurant

o→**restaurant** /ˈrestərɒnt/ *noun* [C] a place where you can buy and eat a meal **lokanta, restaurant** *an Italian/vegetarian restaurant* ○ *We had lunch at/in a/restaurant near the station.*

restaurant
Dikkat! Yazılışını kontrol edin. **Restaurant** Türk öğrencileri tarafından en çok yanlış yazılan 10 kelimeden biridir. Unutmayın! Doğru yazılışında kelimenin ortasında **au** vardır.

restaurateur /ˌrestərəˈtɜː/ *noun* [C] someone who owns a restaurant **lokanta/restaurant sahibi/işletmecisi**

restive /ˈrestɪv/ *adjective formal* unable to be quiet and calm **huzursuz, huysuz, aksi, sabırsız, yerinde duramaz**

restless /ˈrestləs/ *adjective* **1** unable to be still or relax because you are bored or nervous **huzursuz, sabırsız, rahatsız** *The audience was getting restless.* **2** not satisfied with what you are doing now and wanting something new **tatminsiz, sahip olduğu ile yetinmeyen** *After a while in the same relationship I start to get restless.* ● **restlessly** *adverb* **huzursuz bir şekilde** ● **restlessness** *noun* [U] **huzursuzluk**

restore /rɪˈstɔː/ *verb* [T] **1** MAKE EXIST to make something good exist again **eski yerine/durumuna/hâline vb. getirmek** *Three wins in a row helped restore the team's confidence.* ○ *Peace has now been restored in the region.* **2** REPAIR to repair something old **onarmak, yenileştirmek** *to restore antiques* **3** RETURN *formal* to give something back to the person it was stolen from or who lost it **geri vermek, iade etmek** *The painting was restored to its rightful owner.* ● **restoration** /ˌrestəˈreɪʃən/ *noun* [C, U] *The building is now closed for restoration* (= repair work). ○ *the restoration* (= return) *of the former government* **onarım**

restrain /rɪˈstreɪn/ *verb* [T] **1** to stop someone doing something, sometimes by using force **zaptetmek, engel olmak, frenlemek, alıkoymak, mâni olmak** *He became violent and had to be physically restrained.* ○ [+ doing sth] *I had to restrain myself from shouting at him.* **2** to limit something **sınırlamak, gem vurmak, dizginlemek** *to restrain arms sales*

restrained /rɪˈstreɪnd/ *adjective* calm and not showing emotions **sakin, duygularını belli etmeyen, ölçülü** *I was expecting him to be furious but he was very restrained.* ⊃Opposite **unrestrained.**

restraint /rɪˈstreɪnt/ *noun* **1** [U] showing control over your feelings **ölçülülük, itidal, soğukkanlılık 2** [C] control over something **sınırlama, kısıtlama, tahdit** *wage restraints*

restrict /rɪˈstrɪkt/ *verb* [T] to limit something **sınırlamak, yasaklamak, kısmak, azaltmak** *They've brought in new laws to restrict the sale of cigarettes.* ○ *I restrict myself to one cup of coffee a day.*

restricted /rɪˈstrɪktɪd/ *adjective* controlled or limited **sınırlı, kısıtlı, mahdut, yasak** *They do good food but the choice is fairly restricted.*

restriction /rɪˈstrɪkʃən/ *noun* [C, U] a rule or law that limits what people can do **kısıtlama, sınırlama, tahdit** *There are restrictions on how many goods you can bring into the country.* ○ *parking restrictions*

restrictive /rɪˈstrɪktɪv/ *adjective* limiting activities too much **kısıtlayıcı, sınırlayıcı, tahdit edici** *restrictive practices*

restroom /ˈrestruːm/ *noun* [C] *US* a room with toilets that is in a public place, for example in a restaurant **tuvalet, umumi tuvalet**

restructure /ˌriːˈstrʌktʃə/ *verb* [I, T] to organize a system or organization in a new way **yeniden düzenle-**

R

mek, çeki düzen vermek, düzeltmek ● **restructuring** *noun* [U] **yeniden yapılandırma**

the result **of** sth ● **as a result of** sth ● **with the result that** ● **with** catastrophic/disastrous, etc results ● **excellent/good/disappointing/disastrous** results

o━**result**[1] /rɪ'zʌlt/ *noun* **1** [HAPPEN] [C, U] something that happens or exists because something else has happened **sonuç, netice** *Unemployment has risen as a direct result of new economic policies.* ○ *Most accidents are the result of human error.* **2** [COMPETITION] [C] the score or number of votes at the end of a competition or election **yarışma/seçim sonucu/puanı** *The election results will be known by Sunday.* **3** [INFORMATION] [C] information that you get from something such as an exam, a scientific experiment, or a medical test **sınav/bilimsel deney/tıbbi test sonucu** *She's waiting for the results of a blood test.*

result[2] /rɪ'zʌlt/ *verb* [I] to happen or exist because something else has happened **...dan/den kaynaklanmak/ileri gelmek; ...ın/in sonucu olmak** *There was a food shortage resulting from the lack of rainfall.*
result in sth *phrasal verb* to be the reason something happens **...ile sonuçlanmak; yol açmak** *The improvements in training resulted in increased wins.*

resultant /rɪ'zʌltⁿnt/ *adjective formal* happening as a result of something else **sonuç olarak ortaya çıkan, sonuçtaki; ...ın/in neticesinde**

resume /rɪ'zju:m/ *verb* [I, T] *formal* If an activity resumes, or if you resume it, it starts again. **yeniden başla(t)mak, tekrar devam et(tir)mek** *The talks are due to resume today.* ● **resumption** /rɪ'zʌmpʃⁿn/ *noun* [no plural] **yeniden başlama**

resurface /ˌriː'sɜːfɪs/ *verb* [I] to appear again after having been lost or forgotten **tekrar gün ışığına çıkmak; görünmek; ortaya çıkmak; unutulmaya yüz tutmuşken tekrar gözükmek** *The story resurfaced in the news again last week.*

resurgence /rɪ'sɜːdʒəns/ *noun* [no plural] when something starts to happen again or people become interested in something again **yeniden canlanma/güç kazanma** *There has been a resurgence of interest in the game.* ● **resurgent** /rɪ'sɜːdʒənt/ *adjective* happening again **tekrar olan; yeniden meydana gelen**

resurrect /ˌrezⁿr'ekt/ *verb* [T] to make something exist again which has not existed for a long time **yeniden canlandırmak; tekrar ortaya çıkarmak** *With this film Dykes hopes to resurrect his career.*

resurrection /ˌrezⁿr'ekʃⁿn/ *noun* [U] **1** when something starts to exist again which has not existed for a long period **yeniden ortaya çıkma, tekrar canlanma** *the resurrection of a fashion* **2** in the Christian religion, Jesus Christ's return to life after he was killed **Hıristiyanlık'ta Hz. İsa'nın ölümünden sonra tekrar canlanacağı inancı**

resuscitate /rɪ'sʌsɪteɪt/ *verb* [T] to make someone breathe again when they have stopped breathing **ayıltmak, hayata döndürmek, diriltmek** ● **resuscitation** /rɪˌsʌsɪ'teɪʃⁿn/ *noun* [U] **diriltme, canlandırma**

retail[1] /'riːteɪl/ *noun* [U] when products are sold to customers from shops **perakende satış** *jobs in retail*

retail[2] /'riːteɪl/ *verb* **retail at/for** £50/$100, etc to be sold to the public for a particular price **belli bir fiyata satılmak** *This computer retails at $2,000.*

retailer /'riːteɪləʳ/ *noun* [C] someone who sells products to the public **perakende satıcı**

retailing /'riːteɪlɪŋ/ *noun* [U] the business of selling products to customers in shops **perakende satış işi**

retain /rɪ'teɪn/ *verb* [T] to continue to keep something **muhafaza etmek, tutmak, elinden kaçırmamak** *The council will retain control of the school.*

retaliate /rɪ'tælieɪt/ *verb* [I] to do something bad to someone because they have done something bad to you **misilleme yapmak, yapılan bir kötülüğe kötülükle cevap vermek** *They have threatened to retaliate against any troops that attack.* ● **retaliation** /rɪˌtæli'eɪʃⁿn/ *noun* [U] *They bombed the hotel in retaliation for the arrests.* **misilleme** ● **retaliatory** /rɪ'tæliətⁿri/ *adjective* *retaliatory measures* **misilleme olarak yapılan**

retention /rɪ'tenʃⁿn/ *noun* [U] when something continues to be kept **muhafaza, tutma, alıkoyma; öğrenip özümleme; zihinde/akılda kalma**

rethink /ˌriː'θɪŋk/ *verb* [I, T] *past* **rethought** to change what you think about something or what you plan to do **yeniden düşünmek, üzerinde tekrar kafa yormak, tekrar gözden geçirmek** *We've had to rethink our strategy.* ● **rethink** /'riːθɪŋk/ *noun* [no plural] *The whole issue needs a fundamental rethink.* **tekrar düşünme**

reticent /'retɪsⁿnt/ *adjective* saying little about what you think or feel **az konuşur, ketum, ağzı sıkı, suskun; düşündükleri hakkında fazla konuşmayan** *He was reticent about his private life.* ● **reticence** /'retɪsⁿns/ *noun* [U] **suskun**

retina /'retɪnə/ *noun* [C] a part at the back of the eye, which is affected by light and sends messages to the brain **retina**

o━**retire** /rɪ'taɪəʳ/ *verb* [I] **1** to leave your job and stop working, usually because you are old **emekli olmak, emekliye ayrılmak** *She retired from the company in 1990.* **2** *formal* to go to another place where you can be alone or more private **yalnız, tek başına kalabileceği bir yere gitmek; inzivaya çekilmek; gitmek; gözden uzak kalmak** *After dinner, he retired to his bedroom.*

retired /rɪ'taɪəd/ *adjective* having stopped working, often because you are old **emekli olan; emekli, tekaüt** *a retired farmer/teacher*

retiree /rɪ'taɪriː/ *noun* [C] *US* someone who has stopped working, usually because they are old **emekli, emekli olmuş kimse**

take early retirement ● **in** retirement ● retirement **from** sth ● retirement **age**

retirement /rɪ'taɪəmənt/ *noun* [C, U] **1** when you leave your job and stop working, usually because you are old **emeklilik, tekaütlük** *He's taking early retirement.* **2** the period of your life after you have stopped working **emeklilik yaşamı, tekaüt hayatı** *We wish you a long and happy retirement.*

retiring /rɪ'taɪərɪŋ/ *adjective* shy and quiet **çekingen, utangaç, mahcup, sıkılgan**

retort /rɪ'tɔːt/ *verb* [T] *formal* to answer someone quickly in an angry or funny way **sert cevap/karşılık vermek** *"That doesn't concern you," she retorted sharply.* ● **retort** *noun* [C] *formal* **sert, sinirli bir biçimde karşılık verme**

retrace /rɪ'treɪs/ *verb* **retrace your steps** to go back somewhere the same way that you came **geldiği yerden geri gitmek** *I was lost so I retraced my steps.*

retract /rɪ'trækt/ *verb* [I, T] *formal* to admit that something you said before was not true **söylediğini geri almak, caymak, dönmek, yaptığının yanlış oldu-**

ğunu kabul etmek *Several key witnesses have retracted their* **statements/claims/allegations**.

retrain /ˌriːˈtreɪn/ *verb* [T] to learn a new skill so you can do a different job **yeni bir beceri kazanmak, yeni şeyler öğrenmek** *Owen used to be an actor but now he's retraining as a teacher.*

retraining /ˌriːˈtreɪnɪŋ/ *noun* [U] when someone learns new skills so they can do a different job **yeni şeyler öğrenme, yeni beceriler kazanma**

retreat¹ /rɪˈtriːt/ *verb* [I] **1** When soldiers retreat, they move away from the enemy, especially to avoid fighting. **geri çekilmek; cephe hattından çekilmek; mücadeleden/savaştan vazgeçmek; uzaklaşmak, geri gitmek** *The army was forced to retreat.* **2 retreat to/into, etc** to go away to a place or situation which is safer or quieter **daha güvenli ve sakin bir yere gitmek; gizlenmek/saklanmak** *She retreated into the bathroom for some peace and quiet.*

retreat² /rɪˈtriːt/ *noun* **1** MOVE [U, no plural] a move away, especially to a place or situation which is safer or quieter **daha güvenli yere/bölgeye gerileme/çekilme/ hareket etme/intikal etme** *He saw the dog coming towards him and beat a hasty retreat* (= moved quickly away). **2** MILITARY [C, U] a move back by soldiers or an army, especially to avoid fighting **cephe hattından geri çekilme; çekilme; savaştan/mücadeleden vazgeçme** *a strategic retreat* **3** PLACE [C] a quiet place where you can go to rest or be alone **tenha/kafa dinlenecek yer, inziva köşesi, sığınak** *a mountain retreat*

retrial /ˌriːˈtraɪəl/ *noun* [C] a new trial for a crime that has already been judged in a law court **yeniden yargılama** *The judge ordered a retrial.*

retribution /ˌretrɪˈbjuːʃⁿn/ *noun* [U] *formal* punishment for something morally wrong that was done alone **ahlaki hataya verilen ceza, cezalandırma** *They're seeking retribution for the killings.*

retrieve /rɪˈtriːv/ *verb* [T] to get something after first finding it **bulup çıkarmak, almak; gidip almak** *I've just retrieved the ball from the bottom of the pond.* ○ *computer tools for retrieving information* ● **retrieval** *noun* [U] when something is retrieved **çıkarma, alma, elde etme**

retriever /rɪˈtriːvər/ *noun* [C] a large dog with thick black or light brown hair **siyah veya açık kahverengi kıllı büyük köpek**

retro /ˈretrəʊ/ *adjective* looking or sounding like something from the past **geçmişe ait hissi veren; eski/geçmişe ait gibi görünen** *His clothes had a retro look.*

retrospect /ˈretrəʊspekt/ *noun* **in retrospect** thinking now about something in the past **geçmişte, geriye dönüp bakıldığında** *In retrospect, I should probably have told her.*

retrospective¹ /ˌretrəʊˈspektɪv/ *noun* [C] a show of work done by an artist over many years **geçmişe ait eserler sergisi; eskiyi/geçmiş kapsayan eserler**

retrospective² /ˌretrəʊˈspektɪv/ *adjective* If a law or decision is retrospective, it affects situations in the past as well as in the future. **geçmişi de kapsayan, geriye dönük, geçmişe ait** ● **retrospectively** *adverb* **geriye dönük**

☞ **return¹** /rɪˈtɜːn/ *verb* **1** GO BACK [I] to go or come back to a place where you were before **geri gitmek/gelmek** *She returned to America in 1954.* ○ *I won't return from my holiday till May.* **2** GIVE BACK [T] to give, send, or put something back where it came from **bir şeyi geri vermek/ göndermek/koymak** *He immediately returned the records to the files.* **3 return to sth a** START AGAIN to start doing an activity again or talking about something again **dönmek, tekrar ele almak** *I returned to*

work three months after Susie was born. **b** AS BEFORE to go back to a previous condition **önceki duruma geri dönmek; tekrar…a/e dönmek** *Life has begun to return to normal now that the war is over.* **4** HAPPEN AGAIN [I] If something returns, it happens again. **tekrar olmak/meydana gelmek** *If the pains return phone the doctor.* **5** DO THE SAME [T] to react to something that someone does or says by doing or saying the same **karşılık vermek; cevap olarak yapmak, mukabele etmek** *I must return Michael's call* (= telephone him because he telephoned me earlier). **6 return a verdict/sentence** to announce if someone is guilty or not guilty or what punishment the person will be given in a law court **karar vermek; nihaî kararı açıklamak/ilan etmek** *The jury returned a verdict of guilty.* **7** SPORTS [T] to hit or throw a ball back to someone when playing a sport **topu geri göndermek, tekrar pas verme/topa vurmak**

return² /rɪˈtɜːn/ *noun* **1** GOING BACK [no plural] when someone goes or comes back to a place where they were before **geri gelme/dönme** *On his return to Sydney, he started up a business.* **2** GIVING BACK [no plural] when something is given back, put back, or sent back **geri verme/ koyma/gönderme; iade etme** *the return of the stolen goods* **3** ACTIVITY [no plural] when someone starts an activity again **tekrar başlama/başlatma** *This film marks his return to acting.* **4** HAPPENING AGAIN [no plural] when something starts to happen or be present again **dönüş, başlama, olma** *What we are seeing here is a return to traditional values.* **5** TICKET [C] *UK* (*US* round-trip ticket) a ticket that lets you travel to a place and back again, for example on a train **gidiş-dönüş bileti** **6** PROFIT [C, U] the profit that you get from an investment **kâr, kazanç, gelir** *This fund has shown high returns for the last five years.* **7 in return** in exchange for something or as a reaction to something **karşılık olarak; mukabilinde, karşılığında** *I'd like to give them something in return for everything they've done for us.* **8** SPORTS [C] when a ball is thrown or hit back to another player in a sports match **(spor) pas verme** *She hit an excellent return.* **9** COMPUTER [U] a key on a computer keyboard that is used to make the computer accept information or to start a new line in a document **bilgisayar klavyesinde bilgiyi kabul/tamam ve satır atlatma tuşu** *Type in the password and press return.* ⊃See also: **day return.**

returnable /rɪˈtɜːnəbl/ *adjective* If something is returnable, it can be taken or given back. **geri verilebilir/ alınabilir** *a returnable deposit*

reunification /ˌriːjuːnɪfɪˈkeɪʃⁿn/ *noun* [U] when a country that was divided into smaller countries is joined together again as one country **yeniden bir araya gelme; tekrar birleşme; tek bir devlet olma** *the reunification of Germany*

---

have/go to a reunion ● an **emotional** reunion ● a reunion of sb ● sb's reunion **with** sb ● a **family/ school** reunion

---

reunion /ˌriːˈjuːniən/ *noun* [C] an occasion when people who have not met each other for a long time meet again **birleşme, kavuşma, yeniden bir araya gelme toplantısı** *a family/school reunion*

reunite /ˌriːjuːˈnaɪt/ *verb* [I, T] to meet again after being apart for a long time, or to bring people together who have been apart for a long time **yeniden birleş(tir) mek; tekrar bir araya gelmek/getirmek** [often passive] *Years later, he was reunited with his brother.*

reuse /ˌriːˈjuːz/ *verb* [T] to find a new use for something so that it does not have to be thrown away **yeniden**

R

kullanmak; tekrar işe yaramak *Businesses are finding new ways to reuse materials.* ● **reusable** *adjective* **tekrardan kullanılabilen**

Rev *written abbreviation for* Reverend (= title of Christian official) **Muhterem, Saygıdeğer; Aziz** *Rev Jo Harding*

rev /rev/ (*also* rev up) *verb* [I, T] revving, *past* revved to increase the engine speed of a vehicle **hızını artırmak/yükseltmek; hızlandırmak** *He revved the engine and drove off.*

revamp /ˌriː'væmp/ *verb* [T] to change something in order to make it better **daha iyi olması için değiştirmek, iyiye götürmek** *They're revamping the restaurant.*

Revd *written abbreviation for* Reverend (= title of Christian official) **Muhterem, Saygıdeğer; Aziz** *the Revd Laurie Clow*

o﹣**reveal** /rɪ'viːl/ *verb* [T] 1 to give someone a piece of information that is surprising or that was previously secret **açıklamak, ifşa etmek** [+ that] *It was revealed in this morning's papers that the couple intend to marry.* 2 to allow something to be seen that, until then, had been hidden **meydana çıkarmak, gözler önüne sermek, göstermek** *His shirt came up at the back, revealing an expanse of white skin.*

revealing /rɪ'viːlɪŋ/ *adjective* 1 showing someone's true character or the true facts about someone or something **gerçekleri ve gerçek karakterinin gösteren; gözler önüne seren** *a revealing biography/remark* 2 If clothes are revealing, they show a lot of your body. **gösteren, vücudun büyük bölümünü açıkta bırakan**

revel /'revᵊl/ *verb* UK revelling, *past* revelled, US reveling, *past* reveled
revel in sth *phrasal verb* to enjoy a situation or activity very much **çok hoşlanmak, büyük keyf almak** *He revelled in his role as team manager.*

revelation /ˌrevᵊl'eɪʃᵊn/ *noun* 1 [C] a piece of information that is discovered although it was intended to be kept secret **ifşaat, açılama, açığa vurma** *He resigned following revelations about his private life.* 2 be a revelation to be an extremely pleasant surprise **büyük bir sürpriz/beklenmedik şey olmak** *Anna's boyfriend was a revelation.*

revenge ...... İLE BİRLİKTE KULLANILAN KELİMELER

get/plot/seek/take revenge ● in revenge for sth ● revenge against/on sb ● an act of revenge

revenge /rɪ'vendʒ/ *noun* [U] something that you do to punish someone who has done something bad to you **öç, intikam, kan davası** *He's made life very difficult for me but I'll get/take my revenge.* ○ *He was shot in revenge for the murder.*

revenue /'revᵊnjuː/ (*also* revenues) *noun* [U] large amounts of money received by a government as tax, or by a company **vergi, toplanan vergi gelirleri**

reverberate /rɪ'vɜːbᵊreɪt/ *verb* [I] If a sound reverberates, it is heard for a long time as it is sent back from different surfaces. **yankılanmak, aksetmek, yankı yapmak** *The sound of the shots reverberated around the building.*

revere /rɪ'vɪər/ *verb* [T] *formal* to respect and admire someone very much **saygı duymak, hürmet etmek** *a revered religious leader*

reverence /'revᵊrᵊns/ *noun* [U] *formal* a strong feeling of respect and admiration **büyük saygı, sonsuz hürmet**

Reverend /'revᵊrᵊnd/ *adjective* used as a title before the name of some Christian officials **Muhterem, Saygıdeğer; Aziz** *the Reverend Alan Pringle*

reverie /'revᵊri/ *noun* [C] *formal* a pleasant state in which you are thinking of something else, not what is happening around you **dalıp gitme, hülyalara dalma, kendiyle meşgul olup etrafıyla ilgilenmeme**

reversal /rɪ'vɜːsᵊl/ *noun* [C] when something changes to its opposite **tersine/aksine çevirme/dönme; aksi/ tersi olma** *In a reversal of traditional roles, Paul stayed at home to look after the baby and Clare went out to work.*

reverse[1] /rɪ'vɜːs/ *verb* 1 [I, T] to drive a vehicle backwards **geri geri sürmek/gitmek** *I hate reversing into parking spaces.* 2 [T] to change a situation or change the order of things so that it becomes the opposite **tersine/ aksine çevirmek/döndürmek; aksi/tersi olmak; değiştirmek** *It is unlikely that the judge will reverse his decision.*

reverse[2] /rɪ'vɜːs/ *noun* 1 the reverse the opposite of what has been suggested **aksi, tersi** *"So, is he happier?" "Quite the reverse - I've never seen him look so miserable."* 2 [U] (*also* reᵊverse 'gear) the method of controlling a vehicle that makes it go backwards **geri vites, geri geri gitme** *Put the car into reverse.* 3 in reverse in the opposite order or way **aksi düzende; tersine; sondan başa doğru; aksine** *Do the same steps but this time in reverse.*

reverse[3] /rɪ'vɜːs/ *adjective* [always before noun] opposite to the usual way or to the way you have just described **ters, zıt, aksi, karşıt, bilinenin aksine; söylenenin tersine** *I'm going to read out the names of the winners in reverse order.*

reversible /rɪ'vɜːsəbl/ *adjective* 1 If something is reversible, it can be changed back to what it was before. **değiştirilebilir, eski hâline dönebilir/gelebilir/ dönüşebilir; eski şeklini alabilir** *Most of the damage done to the cells is reversible.* ⊃Opposite irreversible. 2 Reversible clothes can be worn so that the inside is the outside. **çift taraflı; değiştirilebilir, çift tarafıda kullanılabilir** *a reversible jacket*

revert /rɪ'vɜːt/ *verb*
revert to sth/doing sth *phrasal verb* to go back to how something was before **eski hâline dönmek/dönüş yapmak; önceden yaptığı şeye geri dönmek/başlamak** *For a while I ate low-fat food but then I reverted to my old eating habits.* ● **reversion** /rɪ'vɜːʃᵊn/ *noun* [U, no plural] **tersine dönüş**

review ...... İLE BİRLİKTE KULLANILAN KELİMELER

carry out a review ● a review of sth ● be under review

review[1] /rɪ'vjuː/ *noun* 1 [C, U] the process of considering something again in order to make changes to it **gözden geçirme, tekrar ele alma** *a review of teachers' pay* ○ *The policy is now under review* (= being considered). 2 [C] a report in a newspaper, magazine, or programme that gives an opinion about a new book, film, etc **gazete/dergi/programlarda yapılan kitap, film vb. eleştirisi** *a book review* ○ *The film has had mixed reviews* (= some good, some bad).

review[2] /rɪ'vjuː/ *verb* 1 CONSIDER [T] to consider something again in order to decide if changes should be made **gözden geçirmek, tekrar ele almak** *The courts will review her case.* 2 REPORT [T] to give your opinion in a report about a film, book, television programme, etc **eleştirmek, görüşlerini dile getirmek** *He reviews films for the Times.* 3 STUDY [I, T] US (UK revise) to study a subject before you take a test **sınavdan önce tekrar yapmak/gözden geçirmek**

reviewer /rɪ'vjuːər/ *noun* [C] someone who writes reviews of a film, book, etc **eleştirmen**

reviled /rɪ'vaɪld/ *adjective* hated **nefret edilen, iğrenilen, hiç sevilmeyen** *He is possibly the most reviled man in Britain.*

revise /rɪ'vaɪz/ *verb* **1** [T] to change something so that it is more accurate **elden geçirmek, gözden geçirmek** *a revised edition of the book* **2** [I, T] *UK* (*US* review) to study a subject before you take a test **sınavdan önce göz atmak/tekrar yapmak**

revision /rɪ'vɪʒ°n/ *noun* **1** [C, U] when you change something so that it is more accurate **gözden geçirme, değişiklik yapma, revizyon** *a downward revision of prices* **2** [U] *UK* when you study a subject before taking a test **sınav öncesi tekrar/gözden geçirme**

revitalize (*also UK* -ise) /,ri:'vaɪt°laɪz/ *verb* [T] to make something more active or exciting **canlandırmak, diriltmek, daha aktif hâle getirmek** *attempts to revitalize the city*

revival /rɪ'vaɪv°l/ *noun* **1** [C, U] when something becomes more active or popular again **canlanma, tekrar rağbet bulma/beğenilme** *a revival in folk music* ○ *Yoga is enjoying a revival.* **2** [C] a performance of a play, opera, etc that has not been performed for a long time **oyun, opera vb. gösteriyi tekrar sahneleme/oynama/sergileme**

revive /rɪ'vaɪv/ *verb* **1** [EXIST AGAIN] [T] to make something from the past exist again **eskide kalmış şeyi tekrar canlandırmak; hayat vermek, tekrar yaşam alanına sokmak** *to revive memories* ○ *A lot of traditional skills are currently being revived.* **2** [CONSCIOUS] [I, T] to become conscious again or make someone conscious again **canlandırmak, hayat vermek, hayata döndürmek** *A police officer tried unsuccessfully to revive her.* **3** [FEEL BETTER] [I, T] to start to feel healthier and more active again, or to make someone feel this way **yeniden sağlığına/eski hâline kavuşmak/kavuşturmak; tekrar yeniden zinde/aktif olmak** *A cup of tea and something to eat might revive you.*

revoke /rɪ'vəʊk/ *verb* [T] *formal* to stop someone having official permission to do something, or to change an official decision **geri almak, feshetme, iptal etmek; yürürlükten kaldırmak; iznini iptal etmek** *His work permit was revoked after six months.*

revolt¹ /rɪ'vəʊlt/ *noun* [C, U] when people try to change a government, often using violence, or when they refuse to accept someone's authority **isyan, ayaklanma, başkaldırı** *a slave/peasant revolt*

revolt² /rɪ'vəʊlt/ *verb* **1** [I] to try to change a government, often using violence, or to refuse to accept someone's authority **isyan etmek, ayaklanmak, başkaldırmak** *Many were killed when nationalists revolted against the new government.* **2 be revolted by sth** to think that something is extremely unpleasant **son derece kötü/iğrenç olduğunu düşünmek; tiksinmek; nefret etmek**

revolting /rɪ'vəʊltɪŋ/ *adjective* extremely unpleasant **iğrenç, tiksindirici, nefret verici**

revolution /,rev°l'u:ʃ°n/ *noun* **1** [POLITICS] [C, U] a change in the way a country is governed, usually to a different political system and often using violence or war **ihtilâl, devrim** *the French Revolution* **2** [CHANGE] [C] a very important change in the way people think or do things **büyük değişim, devrim** *the technological revolution* ○ *This discovery caused a revolution in medicine.* **3** [CIRCLE] [C, U] one whole circular movement around a central point, for example one whole movement of a wheel **devir**

revolutionary¹ /,rev°l'u:ʃ°n°ri/ *adjective* **1** completely different from what was done before **devrim yapan; büyük değişim gösteren** *The twentieth century has*

brought about **revolutionary changes** in our lifestyles. **2** relating to a political revolution **siyasi devrime ilişkin; büyük değişime dair** *a revolutionary movement*

revolutionary² /,rev°l'u:ʃ°n°ri/ *noun* [C] someone who tries to cause or take part in a political revolution **devrimci, ihtilâlci**

revolutionize (*also UK* -ise) /,rev°l'u:ʃ°naɪz/ *verb* [T] to change something in every way so that it is much better **devrim yaratmak, büyük değişim yapmak** *This will revolutionize the way we do business.*

revolve /rɪ'vɒlv/ *verb* [I] to move in a circle around a central point **dönmek, devir yapmak** *A fan was revolving slowly.* ● **revolving** *adjective* [always before noun] *a revolving door* **dönen**

revolve around/round sth/sb *phrasal verb* to have as the only interest or subject **bir konu/bir tek şey etrafında dönüp durmak** *Her whole life revolves around her children.*

revolver /rɪ'vɒlvə°/ *noun* [C] a small gun **toplu tabanca**

revue /rɪ'vju:/ *noun* [C] a show in a theatre with jokes, songs, and dancing **şaka şarkı ve danslardan oluşan gösteri, revü**

revulsion /rɪ'vʌlʃ°n/ *noun* [U] a strong feeling that something is very unpleasant **tiksinme, iğrenme**

get/receive a reward ● **a big/handsome/substantial reward** ● **a reward for** sb/sth ● **a reward of** [$500/$300, etc]

o▄**reward¹** /rɪ'wɔːd/ *noun* **1** [C, U] something good that you get or experience because you have worked hard, behaved well, etc **ödül, armağan, karşılık; büyük çaba/alın teri karşılığı** *There'll be a reward for whoever finishes first.* **2** [C] money that the police give to someone who gives them information about a crime **para ödülü; suçluların yakalanmasını sağlayanlara verilen ödül**

reward² /rɪ'wɔːd/ *verb* [T] to give a reward to someone **ödül/armağan vermek** *She was rewarded for her bravery.*

rewarding /rɪ'wɔːdɪŋ/ *adjective* making you feel satisfied that you have done something well **karşılığını veren, ödüllendiren, tatmin edici** *Teaching is hard work but it's very rewarding.*

rewind /,ri:'waɪnd/ *verb* [I, T] *past* **rewound** to make a sound or television recording go back to the beginning **geri sarmak**

rework /,ri:'wɜːk/ *verb* [T] to change a piece of music or writing in order to improve it or make it more suitable **(beste, müzik, yazı vb.) daha iyi yapabilmek için yeniden düzenlemek/yapmak; üzerinde yeniden kafa yormak** *Elton John reworked his 1974 hit, 'Candle in the Wind', for Princess Diana's funeral.*

rewrite /,ri:'raɪt/ *verb* [T] *past tense* **rewrote**, *past participle* **rewritten** to write something again in order to improve it **yeniden yazmak** *I had to rewrite my essay.*

rhapsody /'ræpsədi/ *noun* [C] a piece of music for instruments **enstrümanla çalınan müzik, rapsodi**

rhetoric /'ret°rɪk/ *noun* [U] language that is intended to make people believe things, often language that is not sincere **iyi konuşma/yazma; hitabet, belâgat** *It was the usual political speech, full of empty rhetoric.* ● **rhetorical** /rɪ'tɒrɪk°l/ *adjective* **düşündürücü ama cevap alma amaçlı olmayan soru** ● **rhetorically** *adverb* **düşündürücü ama cevap alma amaçlı olmayan soru şekliyle**

rhe,torical 'question /rɪ,tɒrɪk°l'kwestʃən/ *noun* [C] a question that is not intended to be used as a real question because you do not expect anyone to answer it **cevap beklenmeyen ama sadece ifadeyi güçlendirmek için sorulan soru; konuşmayı/yazıyı akıcı kılan soru**

rheumatism /ˈruːmətɪzᵃm/ *noun* [U] a disease in which there is swelling and pain in the joints (= parts of the body where bones join) **romatizma**

rhino /ˈraɪnəʊ/ *noun* [C] *short for* rhinoceros **gergedan**

rhinoceros /raɪˈnɒsᵃrəs/ *noun* [C] a large animal from Africa or Asia that has thick skin and one or two horns on its nose **gergedan**

rhubarb /ˈruːbɑːb/ *noun* [U] a plant that has long, red stems that can be cooked and eaten as a fruit **ravent bitkisi; uzun kırmızı kökleri olan pişirilip yenilebilen bir tür meyve**

rhyme¹ /raɪm/ *verb* [I] If a word rhymes with another word, the end part of the words sound the same. **kafiyeli olmak** *'Moon' rhymes with 'June'.*

rhyme² /raɪm/ *noun* 1 [POEM] [C] a short poem that has words that rhyme at the end of each line **kafiyeli kısa şiir** 2 [STYLE] [U] a style of writing or speaking that uses words which rhyme **kafiyeli konuşma/yazma** *The story was written entirely in rhyme.* 3 [WORD] [C] a word that rhymes with another word **kafiye, uyak** ⊃See also: nursery rhyme.

rhythm /ˈrɪðᵃm/ *noun* [C, U] a regular, repeating pattern of sound **ritim, uyum, ahenk** *You need a sense of rhythm to be a good dancer.* ● **rhythmic** /ˈrɪðmɪk/ *adjective* with rhythm **ritmik, uyumlu, ahenkli** ● **rhythmically** *adverb* **ritmik bir şekilde**

rib /rɪb/ *noun* [C] one of the curved bones in the chest **kaburga kemiği, kaburga**

ribbon /ˈrɪbᵃn/ *noun* [C] a long, narrow piece of cloth that is used for tying things or used for decoration **şerit, kurdele**

'rib ˌcage *noun* [C] the structure of ribs (= curved bones) in the chest **göğüs kafesi**

०॰**rice** /raɪs/ *noun* [U] small grains from a plant that are cooked and eaten **pirinç** ⊃Orta kısımdaki renkli sayfalarına bakınız.

'rice ˌpaddy (*also UK* paddy field) *noun* [C] a field in which rice is grown **pirinç tarlası**

rich   BAŞKA BİR DEYİŞLE

wealthy ve **well-off** sıfatları **rich** sıfatının alternatifleri olarak kullanılabilirler. *Oliver's parents are very wealthy/well-off.*

Eğer kişi çok zengin ise, resmi olmayan durumlarda, kişinin durumunu belirtmede **loaded** veya **be rolling in it** ifadeleri kullanılabilir. *They don't have any money worries - they're* **loaded.** ● *If he can afford a yacht, he must* **be rolling in it.**

Eğer kişi eskiye göre daha zengin ise, **better-off** sıfatı kullanılabilir. *We're a lot* **better-off** *now that Jane's working again.*

affluent ve **prosperous** sıfatları kişilerin zengin olduğu alanları gösterir. *It's a very* **affluent** *neighbourhood.* ● *In a* **prosperous** *country like this, no-one should go hungry.*

०॰**rich** /rɪtʃ/ *adjective* 1 [MONEY] having much more money than most people, or owning things that could be sold for a lot of money **zengin, varlıklı** *She's the third richest woman in Britain.* ○ *These cars are only for the rich.* 2 [CONTAINING A LOT] containing a lot of something that is important or valuable **zengin, önemli ve değerli şeyleri içeren** *rich soil* ○ *Both foods are* **rich** *in Vitamin C.* 3 [FOOD] Rich food has a lot of butter, cream, or eggs in it. **zengin, besleyici, içinde bir çok şey olan (yiyecek); kuvvetli ağır, kalorisi yüksek** *a rich sauce* 4 [STRONG] A rich sound is low and strong, and a rich colour is deep

and strong. **(ses, renk vb.) canlı, baskın, ağır, koyu, parlak, göz kamaştıran, güçlü** ● **richness** *noun* [U] **zenginlik**

riches /ˈrɪtʃɪz/ *noun* [plural] *literary* a lot of money or valuable objects **zenginlik, varlık** ⊃See also: go from rags to riches.

richly /ˈrɪtʃli/ *adverb* 1 **be richly decorated/furnished, etc** to have a lot of beautiful or expensive decoration, furniture, etc **adam akıllı döşenmiş/dekore edilmiş olmak; çok görkemli/şaşalı olmak; göz alıcı ve zengin döşenmiş/süslenmiş olmak** *a richly decorated church* 2 **be richly rewarded** to be paid a lot of money **tam anlamıyla/hakkıyla ödüllendirilmiş olmak** 3 **richly deserve** to very much deserve something **bir hayli hak etmek; ziyadesiyle hak etmek** *Later that year he received the award he so richly deserved.*

rickety /ˈrɪkəti/ *adjective* likely to break soon **çürük, eften püften, elde kalacakmış gibi olan** *a rickety wooden chair*

ricochet /ˈrɪkəʃeɪ/ *verb* [I] to hit a surface and then be sent back through the air **sekmek, sekerek zıplamak, seke seke gitmek** *The bullet ricocheted off the wall.*

०॰**rid¹** /rɪd/ *adjective* 1 **get rid of sth a** to throw something away or give something to someone because you do not want it now **kurtulmak, başından defetmek/atmak** *We must get rid of some of those old books.* **b** to end something unpleasant **son vermek, kesip atmak; yakasını kurtarmak** *I can't seem to get rid of this headache.* 2 **get rid of sb** to make someone leave **uzaklaştırmak, başından atmak; defetmek; yollamak, gitmeye zorlamak** *She was useless at her job so we had to get rid of her.* 3 **be rid of sb/sth** to be without someone or something that you do not like or want **sevilmeyen birinden/birşeyden kurtulmak/onsuz olmak;** *I'd do anything to be rid of him.*

rid² /rɪd/ *verb* ridding, past rid
rid sth of sth *phrasal verb* to remove something unpleasant from somewhere **kurtarmak; arındırmak** *to rid the world of nuclear weapons*
rid yourself of sth *phrasal verb* to remove something that you do not want **kurtulmak, arınmak, uzaklaştırmak** *to rid yourself of a reputation*

riddance /ˈrɪdᵃns/ *noun* **Good riddance!** used to express pleasure when you have got rid of something or someone that you do not want **'Şükürler olsun!', 'Nihayet!', 'Hele şükür kurtulduk!'**

ridden /ˈrɪdᵃn/ *past participle of* ride **binmek' fiilinin üçüncü hâli**

riddle /ˈrɪdl/ *noun* [C] 1 a strange and difficult question that has a clever and often funny answer **bilmece** 2 a situation or event that you cannot understand **muamma, esrar, sır, bilmece** *Scientists may have solved the riddle of Saturn's rings.*

riddled /ˈrɪdld/ *adjective* **be riddled with sth** to contain a large number of something bad **dopdolu olmak, delik deşik olmak; her tarafı kaplamış olmak** *The wall was riddled with bullets.*

०॰**ride¹** /raɪd/ *verb* past tense rode, past participle ridden 1 [I, T] to travel by sitting on a horse, bicycle, or motorcycle and controlling it **(at, bisiklet, motosiklet) binmek, sürmek** *I ride my bike to work.* ○ *She taught me to ride* (= to ride a horse). 2 [T] *US* to travel in a vehicle as a passenger **gitmek, binmek** *I've told her not to ride the subway at night.*
ride on sth *phrasal verb* If something important rides on a situation, it will succeed or fail depending on the situation. **bağlı olmak,** *There was $600,000 riding on the outcome of the deal.*

ride out sth *phrasal verb* to continue to exist during a bad situation **devam etmek, süregelmek, olmaya devam etmek** *to ride out a recession*

🔲 **ride (noun)** ...... İLE BİRLİKTE KULLANILAN KELİMELER

go for/hitch a ride • a ride in/on sth • give sb a ride

ride² /raɪd/ *noun* [C] **1** VEHICLE a journey in a vehicle or train (tren vb.) **gitme, seyahat etme, binme** *Can I give you a ride to the station?* **2** BICYCLE a journey riding a bicycle, motorcycle, or horse (bisiklet, motosiklet, at vb.) **binme, sürme, kullanma** *He's gone out for a ride on his bike.* **3** PLAYING a machine at a fair (= event outdoors) which moves people up and down, round in circles, etc as they sit in it **dönme dolap**

rider /'raɪdər/ *noun* [C] someone who rides a horse, bicycle, or motorcycle **binici, sürücü, kullanan** ➔Orta kısımdaki renkli sayfalarına bakınız.

ridge /rɪdʒ/ *noun* [C] **1** a long, narrow piece of high land, especially along the top of a mountain **sırt, bayır, yamaç, kenar** *a mountain ridge* **2** a narrow, raised line on a flat surface **sırt, yükselti, kabartı, kabarık çizgi/hat**

ridicule¹ /'rɪdɪkjuːl/ *verb* [T] to make people laugh at someone in an unkind way **alay etmek, dalga geçmek, tiye almak, komik duruma düşürmek** *I was ridiculed for saying they might win.*

ridicule² /'rɪdɪkjuːl/ *noun* [U] when people laugh at someone in an unkind way **alay, eğlenme, dalga geçme**

ridiculous /rɪ'dɪkjələs/ *adjective* very silly **saçma, aptalca, gülünç, komik** *I've never heard anything so ridiculous.* • **ridiculously** *adverb* ridiculously expensive **aptalca bir şekilde**

riding /'raɪdɪŋ/ *noun* [U] the sport or activity of riding horses **at binme, binicilik sporu**

rife /raɪf/ *adjective* [never before noun] Something unpleasant that is rife is very common. **yaygın, çok rastlanan, salgın, gırla** *Rumours were rife that the band would split up.*

rifle¹ /'raɪfl/ *noun* [C] a long gun that you hold against your shoulder when you shoot **tüfek**

rifle² /'raɪfl/ *(also rifle through) verb* [T] to quickly search through things, often in order to steal something **soyup soğana çevirmek, soygun amaçlı her şeyi altına üstüne getirmek** *I caught him rifling through my drawers.*

🔲 **rift** ...... İLE BİRLİKTE KULLANILAN KELİMELER

create/heal a rift • a deep/growing/huge/serious rift • a rift with sb • a rift between sb and sb • a rift over sth

rift /rɪft/ *noun* [C] **1** a serious disagreement **sürtüşme, anlaşmazlık, tatsızlık, ara bozukluğu** *the deepening rift between the government and the unions* **2** a very large hole that separates parts of the Earth's surface **açıklık, yarık, çatlak, gedik**

rig¹ /rɪg/ *verb* [T] **rigging**, *past* **rigged** to arrange an election, competition, etc so that the results are not fair or true **şike yapmak, hile katmak/karıştırmak; hileli bir biçimde yapmak** *He accused the government of rigging the elections.*

rig sth up *phrasal verb* to quickly make a piece of equipment from any materials you can find **derme çatma yapmak, hemen bir şeyler uydurmak, yapıvermek**

rig² /rɪg/ *noun* [C] a large structure for removing gas or oil from the ground or the sea (petrol, gaz vb.) **platform, kuyu, techizat, donatım, tesisat** *an oil rig*

rigging /'rɪgɪŋ/ *noun* [U] a system of ropes and chains used to support a ship's masts (= poles) **gemide ip ve halatlar, donanım, teçhizat**

o⤴ **right¹** /raɪt/ *adjective* **1** CORRECT correct or true **doğru** *He only got half the answers right.* ○ *You're right about Alison - she's incredible!* ○ *"You came here in 1979, didn't you?" "That's right."* **2** DIRECTION [always before noun] on or towards the side of your body that is to the east when you are facing north **sağ, sağ tarafta** *your right hand* ○ *There's a tree on the right side of the house.* **3** SUITABLE suitable or best in a particular situation **uygun, tamam, en iyi, haklı, doğru, yerinde, isabetli** *I'm not sure she's the right person for the job.* ○ *Are we going in the right direction?* **4** ACCEPTABLE fair or morally acceptable **doğru, adil, ahlaken kabuledilebilir, doğruluk, dürüstlük** *It's not right to criticize him behind his back.* **5 put sth right** to solve a problem **çözmek, halletmek** **6** COMPLETE [always before noun] *UK informal* used for emphasizing when something is bad **oldukça, tamamen, baştan sona, gerçek, tam** *His house is a right mess.* ➔See also: all right.

o⤴ **right²** /raɪt/ *adverb* **1** EXACTLY exactly in a place or time **tam, tamı tamına** *He's right here with me.* ○ *I fell asleep right in the middle of her speech.* **2** CORRECTLY correctly **doğru olarak, tam olarak, doğru şekilde** *He guessed right most of the time.* **3** DIRECTION to the right side **sağ tarafa, sağ tarafta** *Turn right after the bridge.* **4 right away/now/after** immediately **derhal, hemen, şimdi, çarçabuk, vakit geçirmeden** *Do you want to start right away?* **5** ALL all the way **tamamen, bütünüyle** *Did you read it all the way through to the end?* **6** IN SPEECH *UK* used at the beginning of a sentence to get someone's attention or to show you have understood someone **peki, tamam, pekâla, oldu** *Right, who's turn is it to tidy up?* ○ *Right, so Helen's coming tomorrow and Trevor on Thursday.* **7 Right** used in the UK as part of the title of some politicians and Christian officials **Saygın, Saygıdeğer** *Right Honourable/Reverend* **8 It serves her/him/you right!** *informal* something you say about a bad thing which has happened to a person and which they deserve **'Bunu hak etti!', 'O buna müstahak!', 'Hak ettiğini buldu!'** *So she left him, did she? Serves him right!* • **rightness** *noun* [U] ➔See also: be right up sb's alley, be right up sb's street. **doğruluk**

o⤴ **right³** /raɪt/ *noun* **1** LAW [C] something that the law allows you to do **yasal hak, hak** *the right to free speech* ○ *[+ to do sth] the right to vote* **2** DIRECTION [U] the right side of your body, or the direction towards this side **sağ, sağ taraf** *You'll find her in the second room on the right.* **3** BEHAVIOUR [U] morally correct behaviour **doğruluk, dürüstlük, adalet, haklılık** *I've tried to teach them the difference between right and wrong.* **4 have a/no right to do sth** to have, or not have, a good reason for something **yapmaya hakkı olmak/olmamak** *He has a right to be angry.* ○ *She had no right to speak to me like that.* **5 the Right/right** political groups which support capitalism (= a system in which industries and companies are owned by people and not the government) **Sağcılar, sağ kanat** *The right campaigned against the president.*

right⁴ /raɪt/ *verb* [T] **1** to put something back in a vertical position, or to return to a vertical position **düzel(t)mek, doğrul(t)mak, dik konuma getirmek, dikleştirmek** [often reflexive] *The boat righted itself and I rowed us back to the shore.* **2 right a wrong** to do something good to make an unfair situation seem better **bir yanlış düzeltmek; bir kusur/hatayı gidermek** *How can we right the wrongs of the past?*

'right ‚angle *noun* [C] a 90 degree angle of the type that is in a square **dik açı**

ˌright 'click *verb* [I] to press the button on the right of a computer mouse (= a small piece of equipment that you move with your hand to control what the computer does) **sağ tuşu tıklamak**

righteous /ˈraɪtʃəs/ *adjective* morally right and for good moral reasons **doğru, dürüst, âdil** *righteous anger/ indignation* ● **righteousness** *noun* [U] ⊃See also: self-righteous. **dürüstlük**

rightful /ˈraɪtfºl/ *adjective* [always before noun] legally or morally correct **yasal, meşru, kanunî, yasalarca ve ahlâken doğru** *The wallet was returned to its **rightful** owner.*

right-hand /ˌraɪtˈhænd/ *adjective* [always before noun] **1** on the right of something **sağda, sağa, sağ taraftaki, sağdaki** *On the **right-hand** side you'll see a sign.* **2** sb's **right-hand man/woman** the person that you most trust and depend on, especially at work **sağ kolu/en güvenilen kadın/erkek/kimse**

right-handed /ˌraɪtˈhændɪd/ *adjective* Someone who is right-handed uses their right hand to do most things. **sağ elini kullanan, sağlak**

rightly /ˈraɪtli/ *adverb* in a correct way **haklı olarak, doğru olarak** *He is **rightly** concerned about the situation.*

rights /raɪts/ *noun* [plural] freedom to do and say things without fear of punishment **haklar, özgürlükler; yapma söyleme özgürlüğü** ⊃See also: civil rights, human rights.

right-wing /ˌraɪtˈwɪŋ/ *adjective* supporting the ideas of parties on the political right **sağ kanat, muhafazakâr kanat** *a right-wing newspaper* ● **right-winger** *noun* [C] **sağ taraflı düşünceyi savunan**

rigid /ˈrɪdʒɪd/ *adjective* **1** not able to change or be changed easily **sert, katı** *I found the rules a little too rigid.* **2** not able to bend or move easily **eğilmez, bükülmez, sert, katı** *a rigid structure* ● **rigidly** *adverb* **katı ve ser bir şekilde, değişmez** ● **rigidity** /rɪˈdʒɪdəti/ *noun* [U] being unable to bend or change easily **sertlik, katılık, bükülmezlik, eğilmezlik**

rigorous /ˈrɪɡºrəs/ *adjective* careful to look at or consider every part of something to make sure it is correct or safe **dikkatli, titiz, özenle yapılan** *rigorous testing* ○ *a rigorous medical examination* ● **rigorously** *adverb* **titizlikle**

rigour UK (US **rigor**) /ˈrɪɡəʳ/ *noun* [U] when you look at or consider every part of something to make sure it is correct or safe **dikkat, özen, itina** *His arguments lack intellectual rigour.*

rigours UK (US **rigors**) /ˈrɪɡəz/ *noun* **the rigours of sth** the difficult conditions of a particular situation **meşakkat, cefa,güçlük, zor şartlar** *the rigours of a harsh winter*

rim /rɪm/ *noun* [C] the edge of something round **kenar** *the rim of a wheel*

rind /raɪnd/ *noun* [C, U] the thick skin of fruits such as oranges and lemons and other foods, for example cheese **(limon, portakal vb.) kabuk, dış kabuk**

o▪**ring¹** /rɪŋ/ *noun* [C] **1** [JEWELLERY] a round piece of jewellery that you wear on your finger **yüzük, alyans** *a wedding ring* ○ *a gold ring* ⊃See picture at jewellery. **2** [CIRCLE] something that is the shape of a circle **halka, daire** *The children sat in a ring around the teacher.* **3** [SOUND] the sound a bell makes **zil, zil sesi** *The ring of the doorbell woke him up.* **4** a crime/drug/spy, etc **ring** a group of people who are involved in an illegal activity together **suç/uyuşturucu/casus vb. şebekesi, çetesi** **5** a **boxing/circus ring** an area with seats around it where boxers (= people fighting) or people in a circus (= show) perform **boks ringi, sirk gösteri alanı, güreş minderi, arena**

6 give sb a **ring** UK to telephone someone **telefon etmek, telefonla aramak** *If you want anything, just give me a ring.* ⊃See also: key ring.

o▪**ring²** /rɪŋ/ *verb past tense* **rang**, *past participle* **rung** **1** [SOUND] [I, T] If something rings, it makes the sound of a bell, or if you ring a bell, you cause it to make a sound. **zil sesi çıkarmak, zil çalmak; çın sesi çıkarmak** *The phone's ringing.* ○ *I rang the doorbell.* **2** [TELEPHONE] [I, T] UK (UK/US **call**) to telephone someone **telefon etmek, telefonla aramak** *Have you rung your mother?* ○ *I've rung for a taxi.* **3** [EARS] [I] If your ears are ringing, you can hear a loud sound after the sound has stopped. **çınlamak, kulak çınlamak** ⊃See also: ring a bell, ring true.

ring (sb) back *phrasal verb* UK (UK/US **call (sb) back**) to telephone someone a second time, or to telephone someone who rang you earlier **geri aramak, tekrar aramak** *I'm a bit busy - can I ring you back later?*

ring off *phrasal verb* UK (UK/US **hang up**) to end a telephone conversation and put down the part of the telephone that you speak into **telefonda konuşmayı sonlandırmak; ahizeyi yerine koymak** *She'd rung off before I could say goodbye.*

ring³ /rɪŋ/ *verb* [T] to make a circle around something **daire içine almak, etrafına yuvarlak çizmek** *Dozens of armed police ringed the building.*

ringleader /ˈrɪŋˌliːdəʳ/ *noun* [C] the leader of a group who are doing something harmful or illegal **çete başı, elebaşı, şebeke lideri** *the ringleader of a gang of drug smugglers*

'ring ˌroad *noun* [C] UK a road built to take traffic around the outside of a city **çevre yolu, otoban, şehir dışından dolaşan şehirlerarası yol**

ringtone /ˈrɪŋtəʊn/ *noun* [C] the sound that a telephone makes, especially a mobile phone, when someone is calling it **zil sesi, telefon sesi**

rink /rɪŋk/ *noun* [C] a large, flat surface made of ice or wood where you can skate (= move wearing boots with wheels or a piece of metal) **pist, buz pateni pisti** *a roller skating rink* ⊃See also: ice rink.

rinse¹ /rɪns/ *verb* [T] to wash something in clean water in order to remove dirt or soap **durulamak, temiz suyla yıkamak** *Rinse the beans with cold water.*

rinse sth out *phrasal verb* to quickly wash the inside of something with clean water **çalkalamak, gargara yapmak** *I'll just rinse these glasses out and leave them to dry.*

rinse² /rɪns/ *noun* [C] **1** when you wash something in clean water to remove dirt or soap **durulama, temiz suyla yıkama, sudan geçirme** *Give it a **quick rinse**, then squeeze it dry.* **2** a liquid that is used for changing the colour of someone's hair **geçici saç boyası** *a dark brown rinse*

riot .... İLE BİRLİKTE KULLANILAN KELİMELER

quell/spark a riot ● **a riot breaks out**

riot¹ /raɪət/ *noun* **1** [C] angry, violent behaviour by a crowd of people **gösteri, kargaşa, ayaklanma** *a race riot* ○ *Riots started in several cities.* **2** **run riot** to behave in a noisy, violent, or wild way without being controlled **azıtmak, kontrolden çıkmak, taşkınlık yapmak, çığırından çıkmak** *They allow their kids to run riot.*

riot² /raɪət/ *verb* [I] to take part in a riot **ayaklanmak, isyan çıkarmak** *People were rioting in the streets.* ● **rioter** *noun* [C] **isyancı**

rioting /ˈraɪətɪŋ/ *noun* [U] when a crowd of people riots **ayaklanma, isyan, kontrolden çıkma** *There was widespread rioting.*

riotous /ˈraɪətəs/ *adjective* **1** wild and not controlled by anyone **coşkulu, heyecanlı, gürültülü, ele avuca**

sığmaz, kontrolden çıkmış *a riotous party* **2** *formal* violent and not controlled **çılgın, huzur bozan, kargaşa çıkaran** *He was charged with riotous behaviour and jailed for six months.*

rip¹ /rɪp/ *verb* **ripping**, *past* **ripped** **1** [I, T] to tear quickly and suddenly, or to tear something quickly and suddenly **yırtmak, yırtılmak, paramparça etmek** *She ripped her dress getting off her bike.* ○ *He ripped open the parcel.* **2 rip sth out/off/from, etc** to remove something by pulling it away quickly **yırtarak çekip çıkarmak; parçalayarak çıkarmak** *Hedges had been ripped out to make larger fields.* **3** [T] to copy information from a CD onto an MP3 player (= a piece of electronic equipment or a computer program for storing music) **CD'den MP3'e kopyalamak/aktarmak**

rip sb off *phrasal verb informal* to cheat someone by making them pay too much money for something **kazık atmak, soymak, kazıklamak** *We were ripped off by the first taxi driver.*

rip sth off *phrasal verb* to remove a piece of clothing very quickly and carelessly **hızlıca çıkarıp atmak; çabuk çabuk çıkarmak; parçalayıp çıkarmak** *I ripped off my clothes and jumped in the shower.*

rip through sth *phrasal verb* to move through a place or building, destroying it quickly **yıkarak ilerlemek, yıkıp geçmek** *The bomb ripped through the building, killing six people.*

rip sth up *phrasal verb* to tear something into small pieces **parça parça etmek, yırtarak küçük parçalara ayırmak** *He ripped up all her letters.*

rip² /rɪp/ *noun* [C] a hole in the shape of a line when cloth or paper has been torn **yırtık, yarık**

ripe /raɪp/ *adjective* **1** developed enough and ready to be eaten **olmuş, olgun, hazır** *ripe bananas* **2 ripe for sth** developed enough to be ready for something **hazır, gelişmiş, olgunlaşmış** *The country is ripe for change.* ○ *The time is ripe for* (= It is the right time for) *investing in new technology.*

ripen /ˈraɪpᵊn/ *verb* [I, T] to become ripe, or to make something become ripe **olgunlaş(tır)mak** *The peaches had ripened in the sun.*

rip-off /ˈrɪpɒf/ *noun* [C] *informal* something that costs far too much money **soygun, fahiş, fazla pahalı, kazık** *The drinks here are a complete rip-off.*

ripple¹ /ˈrɪpl/ *verb* [I, T] to move in small waves, or to make something move in small waves **küçük dalgalar oluşmak/oluşturmak; hafifçe dalgalan(dır)mak** *A field of wheat rippled in the breeze.*

ripple² /ˈrɪpl/ *noun* [C] **1** a small wave or series of small waves on the surface of water **çırpıntı, ufak dalga, küçük dalgalanma** *She dived in, sending ripples across the pool.* **2** something that spreads through a place in a gentle way **hafif hafif yayılma/dağılma** *a ripple of applause/laughter*

o┅rise¹ /raɪz/ *verb* [I] *past tense* **rose**, *past participle* **risen 1** [INCREASE] to increase in level **artmak, çoğalmak, yükselmek** *rising temperatures* ○ *Prices rose by 10 percent.* **2** [GO UP] to move up **yükselmek, yukarı doğru çıkmak** *The balloon rose slowly into the air.* **3** [STAND] to stand, especially after sitting **kalkmak, yükselmek, doğrulmak, ayağa kalkmak** *He rose from his seat.* **4 rise to/through, etc** to become important, successful, or rich **yükselmek, önemli/başarılı/zengin hâle gelmek** *He quickly rose to stardom.* **5** [STRENGTH] to become stronger or louder **artmak, daha kuvvetli/gürültülü hâle gelmek** *The wind is rising.* **6** [HIGH] to be high above something **yükselmek, yüksekte olmak; üstte olmak** *The bridge rose almost 600 feet above the water.* **7** [APPEAR] When the sun or moon rises, it appears in the sky. **doğmak, çıkmak, yükselmek** *The sun rises in the*

East. **8 rise to the occasion/challenge, etc** to deal with a difficult job or opportunity successfully **halletmek, çözmek, başa çıkmak, üstesinden gelmek**

rise above sth *phrasal verb* to succeed in not allowing something harmful or bad to affect or hurt you **etkilemesine izin vermemek, yenmek, zararını/kötü etkilerini bertaraf etmek**

rise up *phrasal verb* to try to defeat and change a government **ayaklanmak, isyan etmek**

> **rise** ...... İLE BİRLİKTE KULLANILAN KELİMELER
>
> a **big/dramatic/massive/sudden** rise ● a rise **in** sth ● be **on** the rise ● the rise **and fall of** sb/sth ● a **pay/price** rise

o┅rise² /raɪz/ *noun* **1** [C] an increase in the level of something **artış, yükselme, çoğalma, artma** *a tax rise* ○ *a rise in interest rates* **2 sb's rise to fame/power, etc** when someone becomes very famous or powerful **birinin meşhur/güçlü olması; ünlülük, güçlülük 3 give rise to sth** to cause something **neden olmak, yol açmak, davetiye çıkarmak, sebebiyet vermek** *The bacteria live in the human body but do not give rise to any symptoms.* **4** [C] *UK* (*US* **raise**) an increase in the amount of money that you earn **gelir/kazanç artışı; maaş artışı/yükselmesi** *a pay rise*

> **risk** ...... İLE BİRLİKTE KULLANILAN KELİMELER
>
> **carry/increase/pose/minimize/reduce/take** a risk ● **run** the risk **of** sth ● a **great/high/serious/slight/small** risk ● the risk **of** sth ● **at** risk

o┅risk¹ /rɪsk/ *noun* **1** [C, U] the possibility of something bad happening **tehlike, risk, riziko** *the risk of heart disease* ○ *People in the Northeast face the highest risk of being burgled.* ○ [+ (that)] *There is a slight risk that the blood could have become infected.* **2** [C] something bad that might happen **tehlike, zarar** *There are more health risks when older women get pregnant.* **3 at risk** being in a situation where something bad is likely to happen **tehlikede, tehlike altında** *Releasing these prisoners into the community puts the public at risk.* **4 at your own risk** If you do something at your own risk, you are completely responsible for anything bad that might happen because of it. **sorumluluk kendinize ait olmak üzere/şartıyla/koşuluyla 5 run the risk of sth** to do something although something bad might happen because of it **tehlikesini/riskini göze almak** *I think I'll run the risk of hurting her feelings, and tell her the truth.* **6 take a risk** to do something although something bad might happen because of it **tehlikeyi göze almak; risk almak, riske girmek** *This time I'm not taking any risks - I'm going to get insured.*

o┅risk² /rɪsk/ *verb* [T] **1** If you risk something bad, you do something although that bad thing might happen. **...ı/i göze almak; tüm olumsuzlukları göğüslemek, denemek, kalkışmak** [+ doing sth] *I'd like to help you, but I can't risk losing my job.* **2** If you risk something important, you cause it to be in a dangerous situation where you might lose it. **tehlikeye sokmak, riske atmak** *He risked his life to save me.*

risky /ˈrɪski/ *adjective* dangerous because something bad might happen **tehlikeli, riskli** *Investing in shares is always a risky business.*

rite /raɪt/ *noun* [C] a traditional ceremony in a particular religion or culture **âyin, dinî tören** *initiation/funeral rites*

ritual /ˈrɪtʃuəl/ *noun* [C] an activity or a set of actions that are always done in the same way or at the same time, sometimes as part of a religion **usül, kural, âdet, töre, örf; dinî gelenek/görenek** *Coffee and the paper are part of my morning ritual.* ● **ritualistic**

/ˌrɪtjuᵊl'ɪstɪk/ *adjective* done as a ritual **törensel, geleneksel, dinî örf anane ve örfe ait**

rival¹ /'raɪvᵊl/ *noun* [C] someone or something that is competing with another person or thing **rakip, rakibe** *business/political rivals* ● **rival** *adjective* [always before noun] *a rival company/gang* **rakip** ● **rivalry** *noun* [C, U] when two people or things are rivals **rekâbet, çekişme, yarışma** *There is intense rivalry between the two teams.*

rival² /'raɪvᵊl/ *verb* [T] *UK* **rivalling**, *past* **rivalled**, *US* **rivaling**, *past* **rivaled** to be good enough to compete with someone or something else **...ile boy ölçüşmek/yarışmak/aşık atmak; ...ın/in dengi olmak** *Australian wine can now rival the best from France.*

oᵐ**river** /'rɪvəʳ/ *noun* [C] a long, natural area of water that flows across the land and into a sea, lake, or another river **nehir, ırmak** *the River Thames*

riverside /'rɪvəsaɪd/ *noun* [no plural] the area of land at the side of a river **nehir kenarı, ırmak kıyısı** *a riverside path*

rivet¹ /'rɪvɪt/ *verb* **be riveted** to give something all of your attention because it is so interesting or important **hayran bırakmak/kalmak; kendini alamamak; tüm dikkatini vermek** *Her eyes were riveted on/to his face.*

rivet² /'rɪvɪt/ *noun* [C] a metal pin used to fasten pieces of metal together **perçin**

riveting /'rɪvɪtɪŋ/ *adjective* extremely interesting or exciting **son derece ilginç, müthiş, heyecan verici** *I found the film absolutely riveting.*

roach /rəʊtʃ/ *noun* [C] *plural* **roach** or **roaches** *US* a cockroach (= large insect that sometimes breeds in houses) **hamam böceği**

oᵐ**road** /rəʊd/ *noun* **1** [C, U] a long, hard surface built for vehicles to drive on **yol** *Be careful when you cross the road.* ○ *The journey takes about three hours by road* (= in a car, bus, etc). ○ *Follow the main road* (= large road) *till you come to a church.* **2 Road** (*written abbreviation* **Rd**) used in the name of a road as part of an address *...yolu; sokak, cadde 142 Park Road* **3 along/down/up the road** a distance away on the same road **yol üstünde/boyunca; yolun aşağısında; yolun yukarısında** *There's a supermarket just down the road.* **4 over the road** *UK* (*UK/US* **across the road**) on the other side of the road **yolun/caddenin/sokağın öte tarafında/karşısında** *Who lives in that big house over the road?* **5 on the road** driving or travelling, usually over a long distance **yolda, trafikte, seyahatte, turda** *We'd been on the road for 48 hours.* **6 down the road** If an event is a particular period of time down the road, it will not happen until that period has passed. **ötede, uzakta, daha vakti varken** *Why worry about something that's 10 years down the road?* **7 go down that road** to decide to do something in a particular way **bir şeyi yapmaya karar vermek, kararlaştırmak** *I don't think we want to go down that road.* ⊃See also: **ring road, slip road, trunk road.**

roadblock /'rəʊdblɒk/ *noun* [C] something that is put across a road to stop people who are driving down it **yol kapama, barikat, yol engeli** *The police had set up a roadblock and were checking identity papers.*

'road ˌmap *noun* [C] a plan for achieving something **yol haritası, hareket tarzı** *the road map for peace in the Middle East*

'road ˌrage *noun* [U] anger and violence between drivers **trafikte/yolda kavga/ağız dalaşı/sürtüşme** *a road rage incident*

roadshow /'rəʊdʃəʊ/ *noun* [C] a radio or television programme broadcast from a public place **sokaktan yapılan naklen yayın**

roadside /'rəʊdsaɪd/ *noun* [C] the area next to a road **yol kenarı** [usually singular] *They found an injured cat lying by the roadside.*

roadway /'rəʊdweɪ/ *noun* [C] the part of the road that the traffic drives on **trafiğin aktığı yol/cadde; taşıt yolu**

roadworks /'rəʊdwɜːks/ *noun* [plural] *UK* repairs being done to the road **yol çalışması/inşaatı**

roadworthy /'rəʊdˌwɜːði/ *adjective* If a car is roadworthy, it is in good enough condition to be safe to drive. **(taşıt) yola çıkabilecek durumda, iyi durumda, sağlam**

roam /rəʊm/ *verb* [I, T] to move around a place without any purpose **gezinmek, avare avare dolaşmak** *gangs of youths roaming the street at night*

roar¹ /rɔːʳ/ *verb* **1** [I] to make a loud, deep sound **uğuldamak, gürüldemek, gümbürdemek; kükremek** *We could hear a lion roaring from the other side of the zoo.* ○ *She roared with laughter.* **2 roar past/down, etc** If a vehicle roars somewhere, it moves fast making a loud noise. **gümbürtüyle/gürültüyle geçmek/geçip gitmek** *A huge motorcycle roared past.* **3** [I, T] to say something in a very loud voice **avaz avaz bağırmak, bağırarak söylemek** *"Stop that!" he roared.*

roar² /rɔːʳ/ *noun* [C] a loud, deep sound **gürüldeme, gümbürdeme, kükreme** *a lion's roar* ○ *the roar of a jet engine*

roaring /ˈrɔːrɪŋ/ *adjective* [always before noun] **1** A roaring fire or wind is very powerful. **uğuldayan, gürüldeyen, kükreyen 2** *informal* used to emphasize a situation or state **çok büyük, müthiş, muhteşem, ses getiren** *The party was a roaring success.*

roast¹ /rəʊst/ *verb* [I, T] If you roast food, you cook it in an oven or over a fire, and if food roasts, it is cooked in an oven or over a fire. **kızartmak, kızarmak** *Roast the lamb in a hot oven for 35 minutes.* ● **roast** *adjective* [always before noun] *roast beef/pork* ⊃See picture at **cook. kavrulmuş**

roast² /rəʊst/ *noun* [C] a piece of roasted meat **kızartma, kızartma et**

rob /rɒb/ *verb* [T] **robbing**, *past* **robbed 1** to steal from someone or somewhere, often using violence **soymak, zorla soymak; soyup soğana çevirmek** *to rob a bank* ○ *Two tourists were robbed at gunpoint in the city centre last night.* **2 rob sb of sth** to take something important away from someone **yoksun bırakmak, mahrum etmek** *The war had robbed them of their innocence.*

robber /'rɒbəʳ/ *noun* [C] someone who steals **soyguncu, hırsız** *a bank robber* ○ *a gang of armed robbers*

┌─────────────────────────────────────┐
│ **robbery** ...... İLE BİRLİKTE KULLANILAN KELİMELER │
└─────────────────────────────────────┘

commit/take part in a robbery ● an **armed/ attempted** robbery ● a **bank** robbery

robbery /'rɒbᵊri/ *noun* [C] the crime of stealing from someone or somewhere **soygun, hırsızlık** *a bank robbery* ○ *an armed robbery* ○ *to commit a robbery*

robe /rəʊb/ *noun* [C] a long, loose piece of clothing, often something that is worn for ceremonies or special occasions **cübbe, sabahlık, bornoz**

robin /'rɒbɪn/ *noun* [C] a small, brown bird with a red chest **ardıç kuşu, nar bülbülü, kızıl gerdan**

robot /'rəʊbɒt/ *noun* [C] a machine controlled by a computer, which can move and do other things that people can do **robot** ● **robotic** /rəʊ'bɒtɪk/ *adjective* relating to or like a robot **robota ilişkin, robot gibi**

robust /rəʊˈbʌst/ *adjective* strong and healthy **sağlam, gürbüz, güçlü, sağlıklı** *He looks robust enough.* ○ *a robust economy*

o→**rock**¹ /rɒk/ *noun* **1** [SUBSTANCE] [U] the hard, natural substance which forms part of the Earth's surface **kaya** *a layer of volcanic rock* **2** [LARGE PIECE] [C] a large piece of rock or stone **kayalık, kaya, taş** *Huge waves were crashing against the rocks.* **3** [MUSIC] [U] loud, modern music with a strong beat, often played with electric guitars and drums **rock müziği** *hard/soft rock* ○ *rock music* ○ *a rock band/singer* **4 on the rocks a** [RELATIONSHIP] If a relationship is on the rocks, it has problems and is likely to end soon. **sallantıda, çıkmazda, iyi gitmeyen, kopmak üzere olan; sorunlu b** [DRINK] If a drink is on the rocks, it is served with ice in it. **buzlu içki, buzlu soğuk içecek**

rock² /rɒk/ *verb* **1** [I, T] to move backwards and forwards or from side to side, or to make someone or something do this **salla(n)mak, sars(ıl)mak, öne arkaya sağa sola hareket etmek** *She rocked back and forth on her chair.* ○ *He gently rocked the baby to sleep.* **2** [T] to shock a large number of people **sarsmak, şaşkınlığa uğratmak şok etmek** [often passive] *The country has been rocked by a series of drug scandals.* ⊃See also: rock the boat.

rock 'bottom *noun informal* **hit/reach rock bottom** to reach the lowest level possible **mümkün olan en alt seviyeye ulaşmak; dibe vurmak** *The president's popularity has hit rock bottom.*

rocket¹ /ˈrɒkɪt/ *noun* [C] **1** a tube-shaped vehicle for travelling in space **roket, füze 2** a tube-shaped weapon that carries a bomb **füze, bomba**

rocket² /ˈrɒkɪt/ *verb* [I] **1** to quickly increase in value or amount **fırlamak, hızlı artış göstermek, aniden yükselmek** *House prices have rocketed this year.* **2** to make quick progress **hızlı gelişme göstermek** *She rocketed to stardom after modelling for Vogue last year.*

rock 'n' roll /ˌrɒkən'rəʊl/ *noun* [U] (*also* ˌrock and 'roll) a type of dance music that was especially popular in the 1950s **1950'lerde meşhur olan bir dans müziği 2 be the new rock 'n' roll** to now be the most fashionable and popular activity **en meşhur ve bilinen faaliyet hâline gelmek**

'rock ˌstar *noun* [C] a famous rock musician **rock yıldızı**

rocky /ˈrɒki/ *adjective* with lots of rocks **kayalık** *a rocky beach*

rod /rɒd/ *noun* [C] a thin, straight pole **çubuk, değnek** *a fishing rod* ○ *The concrete is strengthened with steel rods.*

rode /rəʊd/ *past tense of* ride **'binmek' fiilinin ikinci hâli**

rodent /ˈrəʊdᵊnt/ *noun* [C] an animal with long, sharp teeth, such as a mouse or rabbit **kemirgen hayvan**

rodeo /ˈrəʊdiəʊ/ *noun* [C] a competition in which people show their skill at riding wild horses and catching cows **rodeo; yabani hayvan sırtında sığır yakalama yarışması**

roe /rəʊ/ *noun* [U] fish eggs **balık yumurtası**

rogue /rəʊg/ *adjective* [always before noun] not behaving in the way that is expected or wanted **dolandırıcı, düzenbaz, namussuz, sahtekâr, alçak** *a rogue state* ○ *rogue cells*

o→**role** /rəʊl/ *noun* [C] **1** the job someone or something has in a particular situation **görev, rol, yer** *This part of the brain **plays an** important **role in** learning.* **2** a part in a play or film **rol, oyunda görev** *In his latest film, he **plays the role of** a violent gangster.* ⊃See also: title role.

'role ˌmodel *noun* [C] someone you try to behave like because you admire them **örnek model/timsal** *Jane is such a good role model for her younger sister.*

role-play /ˈrəʊlˌpleɪ/ *noun* [C, U] pretending to be someone else, especially as part of learning a new skill **öğrenme aşamasında rol-yapma çalışmaları**

roll¹ /rəʊl/ *verb* **1 roll (sth) across/around/over, etc** to move somewhere by turning in a circular direction, or to make something move this way **yuvarlanarak/döne döne ilerlemek/ilerletmek/dökmek/dökülmek** ○ *She rolled over onto her side.* **2 roll down/in/off, etc** to move somewhere smoothly **dökülmek, sağa sola sapmadan düz bir şekilde ilerlemek/hareket etmek** *Tears rolled down her face.* **3** [T] to turn something around itself to make the shape of a ball or tube **yuvarlanmak/yuvarlamak** *to roll a cigarette* **4 roll your eyes** to move your eyes so that they are looking up, usually to show surprise or disapproval **gözleri fal taşı gibi açılmak; hayretten gözleri parlamak 5 be rolling in it** *informal* to be very rich **çok zengin/varlıklı olmak, para içinde yüzmek** ⊃See also: set/start the ball rolling.

roll in *phrasal verb* to arrive in large numbers **doluşmak, oluk gibi akmak, yağmak** *She only set up the business last year and already the money's rolling in.*

roll sth up *phrasal verb* to fold something around itself to make the shape of a ball or tube, or to make a piece of clothing shorter **rulo/yumak/topak yapmak, yuvarla(n)mak, sarmak, sarıp sarmalamak** *to roll up your sleeves/trouser legs* ○ *to roll up a carpet* ⊃Opposite **unroll.**

roll up *phrasal verb informal* to arrive somewhere, usually late **arzı endam etmek, geç gelmek/varmak** *By the time Jim rolled up, the party had almost finished.*

roll

roll of film   roll

roll² /rəʊl/ *noun* [C] **1** [ROUND OBJECT] something that has been turned around itself into a round shape like a tube **top, rulo, bobin, makara, tomar** *a roll of film* ○ *a roll of toilet paper* **2** [BREAD] a small loaf of bread for one person **(yuvarlak) sandviç ekmek** *Would you like a roll and butter with your soup?* **3** [LIST] a list of names **isim listesi** *the electoral roll* **4** [SOUND] a long, deep sound **gümbürtü, gürleme** *a roll of thunder* ○ *a drum roll* **5 be on a roll** *informal* to be having a successful period **iyi bir dönem geçiriyor olmak; iyi/başarılı durumda olmak** *We were on a roll, winning our fourth game in a row.* ⊃See also: rock 'n' roll, toilet roll.

roller /ˈrəʊləʳ/ *noun* [C] a piece of equipment in the shape of a tube which is rolled around or over something **makara, merdane; bigudi** *She uses rollers to curl her hair.*

R

Rollerblades /ˈrəʊləbleɪdz/ *noun* [plural] *trademark* (*also* in-line skates) boots with a single line of wheels on the bottom, used for moving across the ground **paten ayakkabısı/botları** ● **rollerblading** *noun* [U] *Lots of people go rollerblading in Central Park.* ⊃Orta kısımdaki renkli sayfalarına bakınız. **tekerlekli ayakkabılar**

roller coaster /ˌrəʊləˈkəʊstəʳ/ *noun* [C] an exciting entertainment which is like a fast train that goes up and down very steep slopes **eğlence treni**

'**roller** ˌ**skate** *noun* [C] a boot with wheels on the bottom, used for moving across the ground **tekerlekli paten ayakkabısı/botları** ● **roller skating** *noun* [U] **tekerlekli patenle kayma**

'**rolling** ˌ**pin** *noun* [C] a kitchen tool shaped like a tube that you roll over pastry to make it thinner before cooking **oklava** ⊃Orta kısımdaki renkli sayfalarına bakınız.

Roman[1] /ˈrəʊmən/ *adjective* relating to ancient Rome or its empire **eski Roma'ya/Roma imparatorluğuna ait/ilişkin** *Roman remains*

Roman[2] /ˈrəʊmən/ *noun* [C] someone who lived in ancient Rome or its empire **Romalı**

ˌ**Roman** '**Catholic** *adjective* related to the part of the Christian religion that has the Pope (= a very important priest) as its leader **Katolik** ● **Roman Catholic** *noun* [C] **Katolik** ● **Roman Catholicism** *noun* [U] the beliefs of the Roman Catholic religion **Katoliklik**

---

romance ...... İLE BİRLİKTE KULLANILAN KELİMELER

find/look for romance ● a romance **blossoms** ● a **whirlwind** romance ● a **holiday** romance ● the romance **between** sb and sb ● sb's romance **with** sb

---

romance /rəʊˈmæns/ *noun* 1 [LOVE] [C, U] an exciting relationship of love between two people, often a short one **aşk, aşk macerası** *They got married last September after a whirlwind romance.* 2 [STORY] [C] a story about love **aşk hikâyesi/romanı** 3 [EXCITEMENT] [U] a feeling of excitement or exciting danger **aşk, macera, heyacan** *the romance of the sea*

ˌ**Roman** '**numeral** *noun* [C] a letter that represents a number in the Roman system in which I is 1, II is 2, V is 5, etc **Romen rakamı** *My watch has Roman numerals.*

romantic[1] /rəʊˈmæntɪk/ *adjective* 1 [LOVE] relating to exciting feelings of love **aşka ait, aşk heyecanına ilişkin, romantik** *a romantic dinner for two* 2 [STORY] relating to a story about love **aşk hikâyesine dair, romantik** *romantic fiction* ○ *a romantic comedy* 3 [IDEAS] thinking that things are better than they really are, and that things are possible which are not **hayali, romantik, duygusal** *a romantic view of the world* ● **romantically** *adverb* **romantik bir şekilde**

romantic[2] /rəʊˈmæntɪk/ *noun* [C] someone who thinks that things are better than they really are, and that things are possible which are not **hayalperest, romantik**

romanticize (*also* UK **-ise**) /rəʊˈmæntɪsaɪz/ *verb* [T] to make something seem much better or exciting than it really is **idealize etmek; romantikleştirmek** *a romanticized image of married life*

romp /rɒmp/ *verb* **romp around/in/through, etc** to run around in a happy, energetic way **haşarılık etmek, mutlu biçimde koşup zıplamak** *The children were romping around in the garden.* ● **romp** *noun* [C] **sıçrayıp oynama**

○**roof** /ruːf/ *noun* 1 [C] the surface that covers the top of a building or vehicle **çatı, tavan** *a flat/sloping roof* ○ *He climbed onto the roof.* 2 **the roof of your mouth** the top part of the inside of your mouth **damak; tavan** 3 **a roof**

over your head somewhere to live **başını sokacak bir yer, oturacak/yaşayacak bir yer** 4 **go through the roof** If the level of something, especially a price, goes through the roof, it increases very quickly. **(fiyat, ücret) tavan yapmak, hızla yükselmek, süratle artmak** 5 **hit the roof** *informal* to become very angry and start shouting **tepesi atmak, küplere binmek, çok kızmak, köpürmek** *If I'm late again he'll hit the roof.*

roof

roofing /ˈruːfɪŋ/ *noun* [U] material used to make a roof **çatı kaplama malzemesi**

rooftop /ˈruːftɒp/ *noun* [C] the top of a roof **çatı tepesi, dam üstü** *a view across the city rooftops*

rook /rʊk/ *noun* [C] a large, black bird that lives in Europe **ekin kargası**

rookie /ˈrʊki/ *noun* [C] *mainly US* someone who has only recently started doing a job or activity and so has no experience **acemi çaylak, yeni, tecrübesiz kimse** *a rookie cop*

---

room ...... İLE BİRLİKTE KULLANILAN KELİMELER

leave/make room ● **take up** room ● room **for** sb/sth

○**room**[1] /ruːm/, /rʊm/ *noun* 1 [C] a part of the inside of a building, which is separated from other parts by walls, floors, and ceilings **oda, bölme** *a hotel room* 2 [U] space for things to fit into **yer, alan, bölüm, oda, odacık** *Is there enough room for all of us in your car?* ○ *Can everyone move up a bit to make room for these people?* ○ [+ to do sth] *There's hardly enough room to move in here.* 3 **room for sth** a possibility for something to happen **fırsat, şans, olanak, olasılık** *His work isn't bad but there's still some room for improvement.* ⊃See also: changing room, chat room, dining room, drawing room, dressing room, elbow room, emergency room, living room, locker room, men's room, operating room, sitting room, waiting room.

room[2] /ruːm/, /rʊm/ *verb* **room with sb** *US* to share a bedroom with someone, usually at college **bir odayı paylaşmak, aynı odada yaşamak**

roommate /ˈruːmmeɪt/ *noun* [C] 1 someone who you share a room with **oda arkadaşlığı** 2 *US* (*UK* **housemate/flatmate**) someone who you share your home with **oda arkadaşı**

'**room** ˌ**service** *noun* [U] in a hotel, room service is when someone serves you food and drink in your room **oda servisi**

roomy /ˈruːmi/ *adjective* having a lot of space **geniş, ferah, serbest** *It looks small, but it's really quite roomy inside.*

roost /ruːst/ *noun* [C] 1 a place where birds go to rest or sleep **tünek, kuş yuvası** 2 **rule the roost** to be the person who makes all the decisions in a group **sözünü geçiren kimse olmak; astığı astık kestiği kestik olmak, dediğim dedikçi olmak, lider/söz sahibi olmak**

rooster /ˈruːstəʳ/ *noun* [C] a male chicken **horoz**

○**root**[1] /ruːt/ *noun* [C] 1 the part of a plant that grows under the ground and gets water and food from the soil **kök, çil** 2 the part of a hair or tooth that is under the skin **saç/diş kökü** 3 **the root of sth** the cause of something, usually something bad **neden, kaynak, köken, asıl, esas** *the root of all evil* ⊃See also: grass roots.

root² /ruːt/ *verb*
  root about/around (sth) *phrasal verb* to search for something, especially by looking through other things **kökünü/temelini araştırmak; aslını astarını aramak** *She was rooting around in her drawer for a pencil.*
  root for sb *phrasal verb informal* to show support for someone who is in a competition or who is doing something difficult **desteklemek, arka çıkmak; yardım etmek, destek vermek** *Good luck! We're all rooting for you.*
  be rooted in sth *phrasal verb* to be based on something or caused by something **bir şeye dayalı olmak; ...dan/den kaynaklanmak; ...nedeniyle zuhur etmek** *Most prejudices are rooted in ignorance.*
  root sth/sb out *phrasal verb* to find and get rid of the thing or person that is causing a problem **kökünü kazımak/kurutmak, kökten halletmek** *It is our aim to root out corruption.*

roots /ruːts/ *noun* [plural] where someone or something originally comes from **kökleri, kökeni, aslı esası; çıktığı/doğduğu/geldiği yer** *the roots of modern jazz*

rope¹ /rəʊp/ *noun* [C, U] **1** very thick string made from twisted thread **halat, ip, urgan 2 be on the ropes** *mainly US* to be doing badly and likely to fail **başarısızlığa yüz tutmak, çaresiz durumda olmak** *His career is on the ropes.* **3 learn/know the ropes** to learn/know how to do a job or activity **nasıl yapılacağını öğrenmek/bilmek; ...konusunda bilgi sahibi olmak** ⊃See also: at the **end¹** of your tether, **jump rope, skipping rope.**

rope² /rəʊp/ *verb* [T] to tie things together with rope **iple/halatla/urganla bağlamak**
  rope sb in *phrasal verb informal* to persuade someone to help you with something, especially when they do not want to **ikna etmek, kandırmak**

rosé /ˈrəʊzeɪ/ Ⓤ /rəʊˈzeɪ/ *noun* [U] pink wine **pembe şarap**

rosary /ˈrəʊzəri/ *noun* [C] a string of beads (= small, round balls) that is used to count prayers in the Catholic religion **tespih**

rose¹ /rəʊz/ *noun* [C] a flower with a pleasant smell and thorns (= sharp points on the stem), that grows on a bush **gül**

rose² /rəʊz/ *past tense of* rise **yükselmek' fiilinin ikinci hâli**

rosemary /ˈrəʊzmˀri/ *noun* [U] a herb that grows as a bush with thin, pointed leaves **biberiye**

rosette /rəʊˈzet/ *noun* [C] **1** *UK* (*US* ribbon) a decoration made of coloured cloth, which is given as a prize **rozet 2** *UK* a decoration made of coloured cloth in the shape of a rose, worn to show political support for someone **siyasi destek amaçlı takılan kumaştan yapılmış gül şeklinde rozet; renkli kurdelelerden yapılmış rozet**

⋯ roster ...... İLE BİRLİKTE KULLANILAN KELİMELER
  draw up/organize a roster ● a roster of sth ● on a roster

roster /ˈrɒstəʳ/ *noun* [C] **1** a plan which shows who must do which jobs and when they must do them **görev listesi, nöbet çizelgesi, görev cetveli** *a staff roster* **2** a list of names of people who belong to a team or organization **takım oyuncu listesi**

rostrum /ˈrɒstrəm/ *noun* [C] a raised surface which someone stands on to make a speech or receive a prize **konuşma kürsüsü, podyum**

rosy /ˈrəʊzi/ *adjective* **1** Rosy faces are a healthy pink colour. **kırmızı yanaklı, yanaklarından sıhhat fışkıran** *rosy cheeks* **2** very positive and happy **çok olumlu ve mutlu, umut verici, parlak** *The future looks rosy.*

rot¹ /rɒt/ *verb* [I, T] rotting, *past* rotted If vegetable or animal substances rot, they decay, and if something rots them, it makes them decay. **çürümek, kokmak, çürütmek** *Sugar rots your teeth.* ○ *the smell of rotting fish*

rot² /rɒt/ *noun* [U] **1** decay **çürüme, çürütmek, kokma** *There was rot in the woodwork.* **2 the rot sets in** *UK* If the rot sets in, a situation starts to get worse. **işler sarap sarmak/tersine gitmek; işler kötüye gitmek/içinden çıkılmaz bir hâl almak 3 stop the rot** *UK* to do something to prevent a situation from continuing to get worse **daha kötüye gitmesine engel olmak; işlerin sarpa sarmasına mani olmak**

rota /ˈrəʊtə/ *noun* [C] *UK* (*UK/US* roster) a plan which shows who must do which jobs and when they must do them **görev çizelgesi, nöbet/sıra listesi, liste**

rotary /ˈrəʊtˀri/ *adjective* [always before noun] moving in a circular direction **bir eksen eterafında dönen, döner**

rotate /rəʊˈteɪt/ *verb* [I, T] **1** to turn in a circular direction, or to make something turn in a circular direction **bir eksen etrafında dönmek/döndürmek** *The television rotates for viewing at any angle.* **2** to change from one person or thing to another in a regular order **dönüşümlü yapmak, sıra ile yapmak; rotasyonla yapmak** *Farmers usually rotate their crops to improve the soil.* ● **rotation** /rəʊˈteɪʃˀn/ *noun* [C, U] *the rotation of the Earth* ○ *crop rotation* **deveran**

rotten /ˈrɒtˀn/ *adjective* **1** Rotten vegetable or animal substances are decaying. **çürümüş, çürük, bozuk, kokmuş** *rotten eggs* **2** *informal* very bad **iğrenç, berbat, çok fena, rezil** *rotten weather*

rottweiler /ˈrɒtwaɪləʳ/ *noun* [C] a type of large, powerful dog **büyük güçlü cins köpek, rotveyler**

o▪**rough¹** /rʌf/ *adjective* **1** NOT SMOOTH A rough surface is not smooth. **pürüzlü, pütürlü, engebeli** *rough hands* ○ *rough ground* **2** APPROXIMATE approximate **kabaca, yaklaşık, şöyle böyle, takribi, aşağı yukarı** *a rough estimate* ○ *Can you give me a rough idea of the cost?* **3** FORCEFUL If the sea or weather is rough, there is a lot of strong wind and sometimes rain. **(deniz, hava) sert, rüzgarlı, kaba dalgalı, fırtınalı** *The boat sank in rough seas off the Swedish coast.* **4** ILL [never before noun] *UK* ill **keyifsiz, rahatsız, bozuk, pek iyi hissetmeyen** *I feel a bit rough after last night.* **5** DIFFICULT difficult or unpleasant **güç, çetin, sıkıntılı zor, nahoş** *She's having a rough time at work.* **6** DANGEROUS dangerous or violent **tehlikeli ve şiddetli; riskli** *a rough part of town* ○ *Hockey can be quite a rough game.* **7** NOT PERFECT quickly done and not perfect **kaba saba yapılmış, derme çatma yapılmış** *These are just rough sketches.* **8 rough and ready a** NOT PREPARED produced quickly without preparation **aceleyle yapılmış, özen gösterilmemiş, yasak savma kabilinden b** NOT POLITE not very polite or well-educated **kaba, eğitimsiz, görgüsüz, sıradan ● roughness** *noun* [U] **sert ve pürüzlü olması, tehlikeli, kaba saba**

rough² /rʌf/ *noun* **take the rough with the smooth** *UK* to accept the unpleasant parts of a situation as well as the pleasant parts **bir şeyi eğrisiyle doğrusuyla kabul etmek; hayatın iyi yönlerinin yanısıra olumsuz yönlerini de kabul etmek; gülü sevmek için dikenine katlanmak**

rough³ /rʌf/ *adverb* **live/sleep rough** *UK* to live and sleep outside because you have nowhere else to live **sokakta yatmak/yaşamak; evsizler gibi sokaklarda/parklarda yaşamak**

rough⁴ /rʌf/ *verb* **rough it** to live in a way that is simple and not comfortable **hiç bir lüksü olmayan sıradan bir yaşam sürmek; hayatı idame şartlarında yaşa-**

R

mak, çok yoksul bir hayat sürmek, sefalet içinde yaşamak

roughage /'rʌfɪdʒ/ *noun* [U] a substance in fruit and vegetables that helps you to get rid of waste from the body **lifli meyve ve sebzeler**

roughen /'rʌfⁿn/ *verb* [I, T] to become rough or to make something become rough **sertleş(tir)mek, pürüzleş(tir)mek** *Years of housework had roughened her hands.*

roughly /'rʌfli/ *adverb* **1** approximately **takriben, yaklaşık olarak, hemen hemen, aşağı yukarı, kabataslak** *There's been an increase of roughly 30% since last year.* **2** forcefully or violently **haşince, hoyratça, şiddetle, zorla** *He pushed us roughly out of the door.*

roulette /ruː'let/ *noun* [U] a game in which a small ball moves around a dish with numbers on it, and people try to win money by guessing where the ball will stop **rulet, bir tür kumar oyunu**

o•**round**¹ /raʊnd/ *adjective* **1** in the shape of a circle or ball **yuvarlak, toparlak** *a round table/window* ○ *round eyes* ○ *a round face* **ⵙSee picture at flat. 2 round figures/ numbers** numbers given to the nearest 10, 100, 1000, etc and not as the exact amounts **10,100, 1000 gibi yaklaşık/yuvarlak rakamlar**

o•**round**² /raʊnd/ *UK* (*UK/US* around) *adverb, preposition* **1** ⌐IN A CIRCLE⌐ on all sides of something **çevresine/çevresinde, etrafında/etrafına çepeçevre** *We sat round the table.* ○ *She had a scarf round her neck.* **2** ⌐DIRECTION⌐ to the opposite direction **arkasına, tersine, öteki yanında/ yanına, diğer yanına** *She looked round.* ○ *Turn the car round and let's go home.* **3** ⌐TO A PLACE⌐ to or in different parts of a place **çevresini, çevresi, etraf, etrafını, her tatafını, farklı yerleri/yönleri, baştan başa** *He showed me round the flat.* **4** ⌐SEVERAL PLACES⌐ from one place or person to another **elden ele, birinden diğerine, herkese, oradan oraya** *Could you pass these forms round, please?* **5** ⌐VISIT⌐ to someone's home **ziyarete, eve, bize/ onlara vs., birini ziyarete/görmeye** *Wendy's coming round this afternoon.* **6** ⌐NEAR⌐ near an area **çevre, civarda, yakınlarda** *Do you live round here?* **7 round about** at approximately a time or approximately an amount **aşağı yukarı, yaklaşık olarak, şöyle böyle, tahminen** *We'll be there round about 10 o'clock.* **8 round and round** moving in a circle without stopping **daireler çizerek dönen, fırıl fırıl dönen** *We drove round and round trying to find the hotel.*

round³ /raʊnd/ *noun* [C] **1 first/second/third/etc, round** a part of a competition **birinci/ikinci/üçüncü vs. raunt** *He was beaten in the first round.* **2** ⌐EVENTS⌐ a group of events that is part of a series **dizi, seri, raunt** *a round of interviews* ○ *a new round of talks between the two countries* **3** ⌐VISITS⌐ *UK* regular visits to a group of people or houses to give them something or to see them **düzenli ziyaretler, mutat ziyaret/uğrama; tur, dolaşma, uğrama** *a milk/newspaper round* **4** ⌐DRINKS⌐ drinks that you buy for a group of people **içki ısmarlama** *It's your turn to buy the next round.* **5 round of applause** when people clap their hands, büyük alkış **alkış tufanı, büyük alkış** *The crowd gave him a huge round of applause.* **6** ⌐BULLETS⌐ a bullet or a set of bullets to be fired at one time from a gun **atım, atış, el, mermi atımı 7 round of golf** a game of golf (golf) **parti, maç, oyun**

round⁴ /raʊnd/ *verb* [T] to go around something **virajı dönmek, viraja girmek, dönmek** *They rounded the corner at high speed.*

round sth down *phrasal verb* to reduce a number to the nearest whole or simple number **en yakın aşağıdaki rakama yuvarlamak, yekün hâline getirmek**

round sth off *phrasal verb* to end an activity in a pleasant way **güzel bir şekilde sona erdirmek/bitirmek; iyi sonlandırmak** *We rounded off the lesson with a quiz.*
round sb/sth up *phrasal verb* to find and bring together a group of people or animals **bir araya toplamak/ getirmek** *The police are rounding up the usual suspects.*
round sth up *phrasal verb* to increase a number to the nearest whole or simple number **yuvarlamak, bir üst yeküne tamamlamak; yüksek bütüne tamamlamak**

roundabout

roundabout *UK*, traffic circle *US*

roundabout

roundabout¹ /'raʊndə‚baʊt/ *noun* [C] **1** *UK* (*US* traffic circle) a circular place where roads meet and where cars drive around until they arrive at the road that they want to turn into **kavşak, göbek (yol)** *to go round a roundabout* **2** *UK* an entertainment which goes round and round while children sit on it **atlı karınca; döner tabla**

roundabout² /'raʊndə‚baʊt/ *adjective* [always before noun] A roundabout way of doing something or going somewhere is not the direct way. **dolaylı, dolambaçlı, dolaşık**

rounded /'raʊndɪd/ *adjective* smooth and curved **yuvarlak, toparlak** *a table with rounded corners*

rounders /'raʊndəz/ *noun* [U] a British game in which you try to hit a small ball and then run round all four sides of a large square **Britanya'da oynanan bir tur beyzbol**

roundly /'raʊndli/ *adverb* If you criticize someone or something roundly, you do it very strongly. **(eleştiri) acımasızca, sertçe, şiddetle** *The action was roundly condemned by French and German leaders.*

round-the-clock /‚raʊndðə'klɒk/ *adjective* all day and all night **24 saat, gece gündüz, gün ve gece boyunca** *round-the-clock nursing care*

‚round 'trip *noun* [C] a journey from one place to another and back to where you started **gidiş dönüş yolculuğu**

‚round-trip 'ticket *US* (*UK* return) *noun* [C] a ticket that lets you travel to a place and back again, for example on a train **gidiş dönüş bileti**

round-up /'raʊndʌp/ *noun* [C] **1** when a group of people or animals are found and brought together **bir araya toplama, toplanma** *a police round-up* **2** a short report of all the facts or events relating to a subject **her şeyi içeren kısa rapor, özet, hülâsa** *a news round-up*

R

rouse /raʊz/ *verb* [T] **1** to cause a feeling or emotion in someone **tahrik etmek, harekete geçirmek, gayrete getirmek** *This issue is rousing a lot of public interest.* **2** *formal* to wake someone up **uyanmak, uyandırmak** *He was roused from a deep sleep.*

rousing /'raʊzɪŋ/ *adjective* making people feel excited and proud or ready to take action **uyarıcı, kışkırtıcı, tahrik edici** *a rousing speech*

rout /raʊt/ *verb* [T] to defeat someone completely **yenmek, bozguna uğratmak, hezimete uğratmak** ● **rout** *noun* [C] *an election rout* **birisini yenme**

▛▜ **route** ...... İLE BİRLİKTE KULLANILAN KELİMELER

follow/take a route ● plan/work out a route ● along/on a route ● a route between/from/to

o⊶**route** /ruːt/ ⓤⓢ /ruːt/, /raʊt/ *noun* [C] **1** the roads or paths you follow to get from one place to another place **yol, güzergâh** *an escape route* ○ *Crowds gathered all along the route to watch the race.* **2** a method of achieving something **usül, tarz, yöntem, yol** *A university education is seen by many as the best route to a good job.* ↪See also: **en route.**

▛▜ **routine** ...... İLE BİRLİKTE KULLANILAN KELİMELER

get into/have/settle into a routine ● sb's daily/normal routine ● a routine of doing sth

routine¹ /ruː'tiːn/ *noun* **1** [C, U] the things you regularly do and how and when you do them **mutat, hergünkü, rütin** *a daily routine* ○ *He longed to escape the routine of an office job.* **2** [C] a regular series of movements, jokes, etc used in a performance **bir gösteride ortaya konulan her zamanki hareketler/şakalar/fıkralar vs.** *a dance routine*

routine² /ruː'tiːn/ *adjective* **1** done regularly and not unusual **alışılmış, herzamanki, mutat** *a routine procedure* ○ *routine checks* **2** done regularly and very boring **sıkıcı, bıkkınlık veren, angarya, hep yapılan** *His job is very routine.*

routinely /ruː'tiːnli/ *adverb* regularly or often **düzenli olarak, sık sık**

roving /'rəʊvɪŋ/ *adjective* [always before noun] moving around from one place to another place **başıboş, aylak aylak, avare, amaçsız** *a roving reporter*

o⊶**row**¹ /rəʊ/ *noun* **1** [C] a straight line of people or things **sıra, dizi** *a row of chairs/houses* ○ *My students sit at desks in rows for most of the time.* **2** [C] a line of seats **sıralar, koltuk sırası** *to sit on the back/front row* ○ *Isn't that Sophie sitting in the row behind us?* **3** **in a row** one after another without a break **üst üste, ardı ardına, arka arkaya** *He's just won the tournament for the fifth year in a row.* ↪See also: **death row.**

row² /rəʊ/ *verb* [I, T] to move a boat or move someone in a boat through the water using oars (= poles with flat ends) **kürek çekerek götürmek/gitmek** ● **rowing** *noun* [U] **kürek çekçe**

▛▜ **row (=argument)** ...... İLE BİRLİKTE KULLANILAN KELİMELER

have a row ● an almighty/blazing/heated row ● a row about/over sth ● a row with sb ● a row between sb and sb

row³ /raʊ/ *noun* UK **1** ⎡LOUD ARGUMENT⎤ [C] a loud, angry argument **yaygara, ağız dalaşı/kavgası, hırgür, tartışma, atışma** *a blazing row* ○ *The couple next door are always having rows.* **2** ⎡DISAGREEMENT⎤ [C] a disagreement about a political or public situation **anlaşmazlık, kavga, gürültü, uyuşmazlık, çıkmaz** *A row has erupted over defence policy.* **3** ⎡NOISE⎤ [no plural] very loud noise

şamata, gürültü, patırtı *The kids were making a terrible row upstairs.*

rowdy /'raʊdi/ *adjective* loud and uncontrolled **şamatacı, tantanacı, gürültücü, gürültülü** *rowdy behaviour* ○ *rowdy football fans*

'row ˌhouse *US* (*UK* terraced house) *noun* [C] one of a row of houses that are joined together **sıra evlerden biri**

'rowing ˌboat *UK* (*US* rowboat /'rəʊbəʊt/) *noun* [C] a small boat moved by oars (= poles with flat ends) **tekne, kürekle kullanılan kayık, sandal**

o⊶**royal**¹ /'rɔɪəl/ *adjective* **1** relating to a queen or king and their family **kraliyet, kırallığa ait** *the British royal family* ○ *a royal visit* **2** **Royal** used in the UK as part of the title of a royal person (**İng.**) **Kraliyet asalet ünvanı** *His Royal Highness, the Duke of York*

royal² /'rɔɪəl/ *noun* [C] *informal* a member of a royal family **kraliyet ailesi üyesi** *a book about the royals*

royalist /'rɔɪəlɪst/ *noun* [C] someone who supports the principle of having a King or Queen **kralcı, kral taraftarı** ● **royalist** *adjective* **kraliyet/kral taraftarı**

royalties /'rɔɪəltiz/ *noun* [plural] money that is paid to a writer, actor, etc each time their work is sold or performed **telif hakkı, telif hakkı ücreti** *He could receive as much as $1 million in royalties over the next six years.*

royalty /'rɔɪəlti/ *noun* [U] the members of the royal family **kraliyet ailesi üyeleri**

RSI /ˌɑːres'aɪ/ *noun* [C] *abbreviation for* repetitive strain injury: a painful medical condition which can damage the hands, arms and backs of people, especially people who use computers **daha çok bilgisayar kullanan kişilerde görülen ve ellerde, kollarda ve sırtta sık sık tekrar eden ağrılar; Hareketsizliğe bağlı Mafsal Ağrıları (HMA)**

résumé /'rezəmeɪ/ *US* (*UK* CV) *noun* [C] a document which describes your qualifications and the jobs that you have done, which you send to an employer that you want to work for **özgeçmiş**

RSVP /ˌɑːresviː'piː/ used at the end of a written invitation to mean 'please answer' **Lütfen Cevap Veriniz (LCV)** *RSVP by October 9th*

rub¹ /rʌb/ *verb* **rubbing**, *past* **rubbed** **1** [T] to press your hand or a cloth on a surface and move it backwards and forwards **ovmak, ovalamak, ovuşturmak** *She rubbed her hands together to warm them.* ○ *Rub the stain with a damp cloth.* **2** **rub sth into/on, etc** to move a substance backwards and forwards over a surface so that it covers it and goes into it **sürmek, yaymak** *I rubbed some suntan oil on her back.* ○ *Rub the butter into the flour.* **3** [I, T] to touch and move against something, often causing pain or damage **sürmek, sürtmek** *My new boots are rubbing against my toes.* **4** **rub it in** *informal* to upset someone by talking to them about something which you know they want to forget **unutulması istenilen bir şeyi sürekli hatırlatmak, ısrarla tekrarlamak, küllenmiş koru alevlendirmek** ↪See also: rub shoulders (**shoulder**¹) with sb, rub sb up the wrong **way**¹.

rub off *phrasal verb* If a quality or characteristic of a particular person rubs off, other people begin to have it because they have been with that person. **bulaşmak, geçmek, etkilenmek, aynı özellikleri kapmak** *His enthusiasm is starting to rub off on the rest of us.*

rub sth out *phrasal verb* UK to remove writing from something by rubbing it with a piece of rubber or a cloth **silmek, silerek temizlemek**

rub² /rʌb/ *noun* [C] when you rub something **kaşıma, sürme, sürtme** [usually singular] *Give it a rub and it'll feel better.*

rubber /ˈrʌbəʳ/ *noun* **1** [U] a strong material that bends easily, originally produced from the juice of a tropical tree, and used to make tyres, boots, etc **lastik, kauçuk 2** [C] *UK* (*US* **eraser**) a small object which is used to remove pencil marks from paper **silgi, kurşun kalem silgisi** ℈Orta kısımdaki renkli sayfalarına bakınız.

rubber 'band (*also UK* **elastic band**) *noun* [C] a thin circle of rubber used to hold things together **lastik bant**

rubber 'boot *noun* [C] *US* (*UK* **wellies** [plural]) a large shoe made of rubber that covers your foot and part of your leg **lastik bot**

rubber-stamp /ˌrʌbəˈstæmp/ *verb* [T] to officially approve a decision or plan without thinking very much about it **incelemeden kabul etmek/onaylamak; düşünüp araştırmadan tasdik etmek**

rubbery /ˈrʌbəri/ *adjective* feeling or bending like rubber **lastik gibi, kauçuğa benzer** *a rubbery piece of meat*

⊶**rubbish¹** /ˈrʌbɪʃ/ *noun* [U] *mainly UK* **1** [WASTE] things that you throw away because you do not want them **çöp, süprüntü** *Our rubbish gets collected on Thursdays.* ○ *a rubbish dump/bin* **2** [NONSENSE] something that is nonsense or wrong **saçma, anlamsız, saçmalık, zırva** *Ignore him, he's talking rubbish.* **3** [BAD QUALITY] *informal* something that is of bad quality **berbat, kötü, değersiz** *There's so much rubbish on TV.*

rubbish² /ˈrʌbɪʃ/ *verb* [T] to criticize someone or something **tenkit etmek, eleştirmek, yermek** *I wish you wouldn't rubbish everything about the concert - I really enjoyed it!*

rubble /ˈrʌbl/ *noun* [U] pieces of broken bricks from a building that has been destroyed **moloz, yıkıntı, tuğla kiremit kalıntısı** *a pile of rubble*

rubella /ruːˈbelə/ (*also German measles*) *noun* [U] a disease which causes red spots on your skin **kızamıkçık, kızamık**

rubric /ˈruːbrɪk/ *noun* [C] a set of instructions or an explanation, especially in an examination paper or book **açıklama, talimat, izah, bilgilendirme**

ruby /ˈruːbi/ *noun* [C] a valuable red stone which is used in jewellery **yakut**

rucksack /ˈrʌksæk/ *noun* [C] *UK* a bag that you carry on your back **sırt çantası** ℈See picture at **bag**.

rudder /ˈrʌdəʳ/ *noun* [C] a piece of equipment that changes the direction of a boat or aircraft **dümen**

ruddy /ˈrʌdi/ *adjective* A ruddy face is red. **kırmızı, al al** *ruddy cheeks*

rude ...... BAŞKA BİR DEYİŞLE

Eğer kişi biraz kaba ise ve komik görünen bir şekilde saygısızca davranıyorsa, bu kişiyi **cheeky** kelimesiyle tanımlayabiliriz. *You asked your teacher how old she was? That was a bit cheeky!*
rude kelimesine alternatif olarak **impolite** kelimesi kullanılabilir. *She asks direct questions without being in any way* **impolite**.
Eğer kişi kendinden daha yaşlı veya daha üst bir makamda olan bir kişiye saygısızca davranıyorsa, **impertinent, insolent** sıfatlarıyla tanımlanabilirler. *It was clear that they found his questions* **impertinent**.
abrasive sıfatı kişinin hal ve hareketleri saygısızca ve arkadaşça olmadığı zaman kullanılabilir. *I found him rather* **abrasive**.
Kaba ve saygısız kişiler **uncouth** ifadesiyle tanımlanabilirler. *She found him loud-mouthed and* **uncouth**.
Kişinin vücudu ile ilgili kullanılan kaba kelimeler için **vulgar** veya **crude** ifadeleri kullanılabilir. *He*

told a rather **vulgar** *joke over dinner.*

⊶**rude** /ruːd/ *adjective* **1** behaving in a way which is not polite and upsets other people **kaba, nezaketsiz, saygısız** *a rude remark* ○ *He complained that a member of staff had been* **rude** *to him.* ○ [+ to do sth] *It would be* **rude** *to leave without saying goodbye.* **2** Rude words or jokes relate to sex or going to the toilet. **edepsiz, açık saçık, ayıp** ● **rudely** *adverb* **kaba bir şekilde** ● **rudeness** *noun* [U] **kabalık** ℈See also: a rude **awakening**.

rudiments /ˈruːdɪmənts/ *noun formal* **the rudiments of sth** the most basic parts or principles of something **temel bilgiler, esaslar** ● **rudimentary** /ˌruːdɪˈmentʳri/ *adjective formal* very basic **basit, ilkel, gelişmemiş, temel**

rueful /ˈruːfʳl/ *adjective* showing slight sadness about something but not in a serious way **pişman, pişmanlık duyan; nadim** *a rueful smile* ● **ruefully** *adverb* **pişmanlıkla**

ruffle /ˈrʌfl/ *verb* [T] If someone ruffles your hair, they rub it gently. **(saç) karıştırmak, bozmak; nazikçe dokunmak** *He ruffled my hair and kissed me.*

rug /rʌg/ *noun* [C] **1** a soft piece of material used to cover the floor **yaygı, halı, kilim** *The dog was lying on the rug in front of the fire.* ℈Orta kısımdaki renkli sayfalarına bakınız. **2** *UK* a soft cover that keeps you warm or comfortable **battaniye, örtü**

rug

rugby /ˈrʌgbi/ *noun* [U] a sport played by two teams with an oval ball and H-shaped goals **ragbi** *a rugby player* ℈Orta kısımdaki renkli sayfalarına bakınız.

rugged /ˈrʌgɪd/ *adjective* **1** If an area of land is rugged, it looks rough and has lots of rocks. **engebeli, kayalık** *a rugged coastline* **2** If a man looks rugged, his face looks strong and attractive. **set, haşin, kaya gibi set** *a rugged face*

ruin¹ /ˈruːɪn/ *verb* [T] **1** to spoil or destroy something **harap etmek, yıkmak, mahvetmek** [often passive] *They were late and the dinner was ruined.* **2** to cause someone to lose all their money or their job **(maddî olarak) mahvetmek, yıkıma sebep olmak, batırmak, iflâs ettirmek** *If the newspapers get hold of this story they'll ruin him.*

ruin² /ˈruːɪn/ *noun* **1** [DESTRUCTION] [U] the destruction of something **enkaz, harabe** *Fonthill Abbey fell into ruin 10 years after it was built.* **2** [BROKEN BUILDING] [C] the broken parts that are left from an old building or town **tarihî kalıntı, ören yeri** *Thousand of tourists wander around these* **ancient ruins** *every year.* **3** [LOSING EVERYTHING] [U] when someone loses everything such as all their money or their job **iflas, mahvolma, her şeyini kaybetme, yıkım** *The collapse of the bank has left many people in financial* **ruin**. **4** **be/lie in ruins** to be in a very bad state **harap/viran olmak; mahvolmak** *The war left one million people dead and the country in ruins.*

rule ...... İLE BİRLİKTE KULLANILAN KELİMELER

apply/break/enforce/establish a rule ● **a rule forbids/prohibits sth** ● **a strict/unwritten rule** ● **a rule against sth**

⊶**rule¹** /ruːl/ *noun* **1** [INSTRUCTION] [C] an official instruction about what you must or must not do **kural, kaide, talimat, nizam** *to break* (= not obey) *the rules.* ○ *to obey/follow the rules* ○ *You can't smoke at school, it's against the rules* (= allowed). **2** [LEADER] [U] when someone is

in control of a country **yönetme, idare, yönetim, egemenlik** *military rule* ○ *There have been reports of
immense human suffering under his rule.* **3** USUAL WAY
[no plural] the usual way something is **âdet, yerleşmiş
ilke, kural, kaide** *an exception to the rule* ○ *Workers
in the North are, as a rule, paid less than those in the
South.* **4** PRINCIPLE [C] a principle of a system, such as a
language or science (**dil, ilim**) **kural, usül, esas** *the
rules of grammar* **5 a rule of thumb** a way of calculating something, which is not exact but which will help
you to be correct enough **üstünkörü ölçme, parmak
kesabıyla ölçme; göz kararı ölçme 6 bend/stretch
the rules** to allow someone to do something which is
not usually allowed **kuralları gevşetmek/yumuşat-
mak; kuralı ihlâl etmesine göz yummak** *We don't
usually let students take books home, but I'll bend the
rules on this occasion.* ○See also: ground rules.

rule² /ruːl/ *verb* [I, T] **1** to make an official legal decision
karar vermek, hüküm vermek [+ (that)] *The judge
ruled that it was wrong for a 16-year-old girl to be held
in an adult prison.* **2** to be in control of somewhere,
usually a country **yönetmek, hüküm sürmek, idare
etmek** [often passive] *They were ruled for many years by a
dictator.* ○ *the ruling party* ○See also: rule the roost.

rule sb/sth out *phrasal verb* to decide that something or
someone is not suitable for a particular purpose, or to
decide that something is impossible **ihtimalini ortadan kaldırmak, izin vermemek, hesaba katmamak,
hariç tutmak, bertaraf etmek** *The police have not
ruled him out as a suspect.*

ruler /ˈruːləʳ/ *noun* [C] **1** the leader of a country **hükümdar, yönetici, idareci 2** a flat, straight stick which is
used to measure things **cetvel** ○Orta kısımdaki renkli sayfalarına bakınız.

ruling /ˈruːlɪŋ/ *noun* [C] an official legal decision, usually
made by a judge **yargı, karar, hüküm, hukukî sonuç**

rum /rʌm/ *noun* [C, U] a strong, alcoholic drink made
from sugar **rom, bir tür sert alkollü içki**

rumble /ˈrʌmbl/ *verb* [I] to make a deep, long sound
gümbürdemek, gürüldemek, gürültü yapmak *The
smell of cooking made his stomach rumble.* ● **rumble**
noun [no plural] *the distant rumble of thunder* **gürültü,
gümbürtü**

rumbling /ˈrʌmblɪŋ/ *noun* [C] a deep, long sound **gümbürdeme, gürüldeme, gürültü** *the rumbling of a train
passing by*

rumblings /ˈrʌmblɪŋz/ *noun* [plural] signs that people
are angry about something **iz, işaret, belirti, alâmet,
gösterge** *rumblings of discontent*

rummage /ˈrʌmɪdʒ/ *verb* **rummage around/in/
through, etc** to search inside something and move
things around **didik didik ederek aramak; altını
üstüne getirerek aramak, alt üst etmek; içini
dışına çıkararak aramak** *I found him rummaging
through my drawers.*

'**rummage ,sale** *US* (*UK* jumble sale) *noun* [C] a sale of old
items, especially clothes, usually to make money for an
organization **yardım amaçlı eski eşya satışı; bit
pazarı satışı**

◇◇◇ *rumour* .... İLE BİRLİKTE KULLANILAN KELİMELER

fuel/spark/spread/start rumours ● **deny/dismiss/
hear** rumours ● a rumour **circulates/goes around**
● a **persistent/strong/unconfirmed** rumour ● a
rumour **about/of** sth

rumour¹ *UK* (*US* rumor) /ˈruːməʳ/ *noun* [C] a fact that a
lot of people are talking about although they do not
know if it is true **dedikodu, söylenti, şayia** *to spread*

rumours ○ *to deny rumours* ○ [+ (that)] *I heard a
rumour that you were leaving.*

rumour² *UK* (*US* rumor) /ˈruːməʳ/ *verb* **be rumoured** If a
fact is rumoured, people are talking about it although
they do not know if it is true. **dedikodu çıkarmak;
asılsız bir şeyi yaymak; söylenti çıkarmak; yayılmak; dilden dile/kulaktan kulağa ulaşmak** [+ (that)]
*It's rumoured that the company director is about to
resign.* ○ [+ to be sth] *The company is rumoured to be in
financial difficulty.*

rump /rʌmp/ *noun* [C] the area above an animal's back
legs **but; hayvanların arka ayaklarının üst kısmı**

rumpled /ˈrʌmpld/ *adjective* Rumpled clothes or sheets
are untidy because they have folds in them. **buruş
buruş olmuş, buruşmuş, buruşuk**

o--**run¹** /rʌn/ *verb* **running**, *past tense* **ran**, *past participle* **run
1** MOVE FAST [I, T] to move on your feet at a faster speed
than walking **koşmak, seğirtmek** *He ran away when I
tried to pick him up.* ○ [+ to do sth] *We had to run to catch
up with him.* ○ *I run about three miles every morning.*
2 ORGANIZE [T] to organize or control something **yönetmek, idare etmek, işletmek, çalıştırmak, çekip
çevirmek** *She ran her own restaurant for five years.*
3 run sb/sth to/down, etc to take someone or something somewhere, usually by car **arabayla götürmek**
Could you run me to the station this afternoon? **4** WORKING
[I, T] If a piece of equipment is running, it is switched on
and working, and if you run it, you switch it on and
make it work. **işle(t)mek, çalış(tır)mak, faaliyette
olmak, faaliyete geçirmek** *The engine is running
more smoothly now.* **5** USE COMPUTER [T] If you run a computer program, you use it on your computer. **bilgisayar
programı çalıştırmak** *Did you run a virus check this
morning?* **6** TRAVELLING [I] If trains or buses are running,
they are available to travel on. **işlemek, çalışmak, gitmek, sefer yapmak, sefere çıkmak** *The buses only
run until 11 p.m.* **7** LIQUID [I] If liquid runs somewhere,
it flows. **akmak, dökülmek, boşalmak** *Tears ran
down her face.* **8** PUBLISH [T] to publish something in a
newspaper or magazine **basmak, yayınlamak** *All the
papers are running this story on the front page.* **9 run a
bath** *UK* to fill a bath with water so that it is ready to use
**küveti doldurmak 10 run sth along/over/through,
etc sth** to move something along, over, or through
something else **gezdirmek, hareket ettirmek, karıştırmak** *She ran her fingers through her hair.* **11 run
through/down/along, etc** If something long and narrow runs somewhere, it is in that position. **geçmek,
döşenmiş olmak** *There are wires running across the
floor.* **12** CONTINUE [I] If a play, film, etc runs for a period
of time, it continues that long. (**oyun, film vb.**) **oynamak, gösterimde olmak 13 run in sb's/the family** If a
quality, ability, disease, etc runs in the family, many
members of the family have it. **hâkim olmak, var
olmak, bulunmak, sahip olmak, kişide/ailede
hâkim olmak** *A love of animals runs in our family.*
14 COLOUR [I] If a colour runs, it comes out of some material when it is washed. (**boya**) **çıkmak, akmak, solmak, rengini kaybetmek 15 be running at sth** to be
at a particular level **civarında seyretmek; belli bir
düzeyde olmak** *Inflation is now running at 5.8%.* ○See
also: cast/run your/an eye¹ over sth, run the gauntlet, run riot¹, run
out of steam¹, run wild¹.

run across sb *phrasal verb* to meet someone you know
when you are not expecting to **karşılaşmak, rastlamak, rast gelmek, tesadüf etmek** *I ran across Jim in
town the other day.*

run after sb/sth *phrasal verb* to chase someone or something that is moving away from you **peşinden koş-
mak/gitmek; takip etmek**

run around *phrasal verb* to be very busy doing a lot of different things **koşuşturmak, çok meşgul olmak, yapacak çok işi olmak** *I'm exhausted, I've been running around all morning.*

run away *phrasal verb* to secretly leave a place because you are unhappy there **gizlice kaçmak, sıvışmak, çekip gitmek, ayrılmak** *to run away from home*

run sth by sb *phrasal verb* to tell someone about something so that they can give their opinion about it **istişare etmek, anlatmak, bilgi vermek, bir fikri paylaşmak, tartışmak** *Can I run something by you, Sam?*

run sb/sth down *phrasal verb informal* to criticize someone or something, often unfairly **kötülemek, yermek, aleyhinde konuşmak, eleştirmek**

run for sth *phrasal verb* to compete in an election **seçimde yarışmak, seçime girmek, aday olmak** *He's running for mayor again this year.*

run into sb *phrasal verb* to meet someone you know when you are not expecting to **tesadüf etmek, rastgelmek, karşılaşmak, ansızın karşı karşıya gelmek** *I ran into Emma on my way home.*

run into sth *phrasal verb* **1** [HIT] to hit something while you are driving a vehicle **arabayla çarpmak/vurmak** *He skidded and ran into a tree.* **2** [REACH A LEVEL] If an amount runs into thousands, millions, etc, it reaches that level. **...a/e varmak/ulaşmak; ...ı/i bulmak 3** [PROBLEMS] If you run into difficulties, you begin to experience them. **(güçlük, sorun) yüz yüze gelmek, karşılaşmak; yaşamak; tecrübe etmek** *to run into trouble*

run off *phrasal verb informal* to leave somewhere unexpectedly **kaçmak, basıp gitmek, sıvışmak; aniden kalkıp gitmek** *He ran off with all my money.*

run on sth *phrasal verb* If a machine runs on a supply of power, it uses that power to work. **...ile çalışmak/işlemek/faaliyete geçmek** *The scanner runs on mains electricity and batteries.*

run out *phrasal verb* **1** to use all of something so that there is none left **bitirmek, tüketmek** *I've nearly run out of money.* **2** If a supply of something runs out, there is none left because it has all been used. **bitmek, tükenmek, suyunu çekmek** *Come on, time is running out.*

run sb/sth over *phrasal verb* to hit someone or something with a vehicle and drive over them, injuring or killing them **araçla çarparak ezmek/öldürmek/yaralamak/zarar vermek; çiğnemek** *He was run over by a bus as he crossed the road.*

run through sth *phrasal verb* to repeat something in order to practise it or to make sure that it is correct **tekrarlamak, prova etmek; gözden geçirmek, değinmek** *I just need to run through my speech one more time.*

run sth up *phrasal verb* If you run up a debt, you do things which cause you to owe a large amount of money. **borçlanmak, borç altına girmek**

run up against sth *phrasal verb* If you run up against problems or difficulties, you begin to experience them. **karşılaşmak, yüz yüze gelmek; tecrübe etmek, zorlukla/güçlükle karşılaşmak**

✎**run²** /rʌn/ *noun* **1** [MOVING] [C] when you move on your feet at a speed faster than walking as a sport **koşu** [usually singular] *to go for a run* **2** [SCORING] [C] in cricket or baseball, a single point **kriket ve beyzbolda tek puan** *to score a run* **3 a dummy/practice/trial run** when you do something to practise it before the real time **çalışma, uygulama, egzersiz 4 a run of sth** when something happens several times without something different happening during that period **defalarca olan, yapılan, olan, meydana gelen** *a run of 10 games without a win* ○ *a run of good/bad luck* **5** [PERFORMANCES] [C] a period of performances of a play, film, etc **sürekli oynama, afişte kalma** (film, oyun)

6 be on the run to be trying to avoid being caught, especially by the police **firarda olmak; sürekli kaçıyor olmak 7 make a run for it** *informal* to suddenly run fast in order to escape from somewhere **kaçıp kurtulmak, firar etmek, aniden kaçmak 8 in the long/short run** at a time that is far away or near in the future **uzun/kısa vadede/sürede**

runaway¹ /'rʌnəˌweɪ/ *adjective* [always before noun] **1 a runaway success/victory/winner, etc** something good that happens very quickly or easily **önlenemez, engellenemez, son anda olan; hızlı ve çabuk gelişen 2** A runaway vehicle is moving away from somewhere without anyone controlling it. **(araç) kontrolden çıkmış, kontrolsüz, sürücüsü olmayan** *a runaway car/train*

runaway² /'rʌnəˌweɪ/ *noun* [C] someone who has secretly left a place because they are unhappy there **firarî, firar etmiş kimse** *teenage runaways*

run-down /ˌrʌn'daʊn/ *adjective* Run-down buildings or areas are in very bad condition. **harap, yıkık, köhne** *a run-down housing estate*

rundown /'rʌndaʊn/ *noun* [no plural] a report of the main facts relating to a subject **kısa açıklama, özet, rapor, bildiri** *He gave us a rundown on what happened at the meeting.*

rung¹ /rʌŋ/ *noun* **1** [C] one of the horizontal parts across a ladder (= structure for climbing up) **seyyar merdiven basamağı 2 the first/highest/next, etc rung of the ladder** the first, highest, next, etc position, especially in society or in a job **ilk/en yüksek/sonraki vs. derece, basamak, seviye, kademe, durum, konum** *She's on the bottom rung of the management ladder.*

rung² /rʌŋ/ *past participle of* ring² **zil çalmak' fiilinin ikinci hâli**

run-in /'rʌnɪn/ *noun* [C] *informal* an argument **münakaşa, tartışma, ağız dalaşı** *to have a run-in with someone*

runner /'rʌnər/ *noun* **1** [C] someone who runs, usually in competitions **koşucu** *a long-distance runner* **2 drug/gun runner** someone who takes drugs or guns illegally from one place to another **uyuşturucu/silah kaçakçısı** ⊃See also: front-runner.

runner 'bean UK (US 'runner ˌbean) *noun* [C] a long, flat, green bean **çalı fasulyesi**

runner-up /ˌrʌnər'ʌp/ *noun* [C] *plural* **runners-up** someone who finishes in second position in a competition **yarışmada ikinci gelen müsabık/yarışmacı**

running¹ /'rʌnɪŋ/ *noun* [U] **1** the sport of moving on your feet at a speed faster than walking **koşu yarışı** *I go running three times a week.* ○ *running shoes* ⊃Orta kısımdaki renkli sayfalarına bakınız. **2** the activity of controlling or looking after something **idare, yönetim, işletme** *He has recently handed over the day-to-day running of the museum to his daughter.* ○ *running costs*

running² /'rʌnɪŋ/ *adjective* **1** [always before noun] continuing for a long time **uzun süre devam eden, süregelen, sürekli, devamlı, aralıksız** *a running battle* ○ *a running joke* **2 second/third, etc day/week, etc running** If something happens for the second/third, etc day/week, etc running, it happens on that number of regular occasions without changing. **ardarda, arka arkaya, üst üste, peş peşe, sürekli** *He's won the Championship for the fifth year running.* **3 running water** If a place has running water, it has a working water system. **akar, akan, musluktan akan**

runny /'rʌni/ *adjective* **1** A runny substance is more liquid than usual. **sulu, cıvık, vıcık vıcık** *runny egg* **2 runny nose** If you have a runny nose, your nose is producing liquid all the time. **akan burun, burun akıntısı**

run-of-the-mill /ˌrʌnəvðə'mɪl/ *adjective* ordinary and not special or exciting in any way **sıradan, alelâde, olağan; hiç bir özelliği olmayan** *He gave a fairly run-of-the-mill speech.*

run-up /'rʌnʌp/ *noun* **the run-up to sth** *UK* the period of time before an event ...**arifesinde;** ...**öncesi;** ...**dan/den hemen bir süre önce** *Sales increased by 15% in the run-up to Christmas.*

runway /'rʌnweɪ/ *noun* [C] a large road that aircraft use to land on or to start flying from **uçuş pisti**

rupture /'rʌptʃə'/ *verb* [I, T] If you rupture something, you break or tear it, and if something ruptures, it breaks or tears. **kes(il)mek, yırt(ıl)mak, kır(ıl)mak, parçala(n)mak** *He fell and ruptured a ligament in his knee.* ● **rupture** *noun* [C] **koparma, parçalama**

rural /'rʊər'l/ *adjective* relating to the countryside and not to towns **kırsal, kıra ait, kırsal yaşama ilişkin** *a rural area*

ruse /ruːz/ *noun* [C] a way of deceiving someone so that they do something that you want them to do **hile, düzen, üç kağıt, dolap, alavere dalavere, oyun** [+ to do sth] *The story was just a ruse to get her out of the house.*

o▪**rush¹** /rʌʃ/ *verb* **1** [I, T] to hurry or move quickly somewhere, or to make someone or something hurry or move quickly somewhere **koşmak, koşturmak, atılmak, fırlamak, acele etmek** *We rushed out into the street to see what all the noise was.* ○ *The UN has rushed medical supplies to the war zone.* ○ [+ to do sth] *We had to rush to catch the bus.* **2 rush to do something** to do something quickly and enthusiastically **acele etmek, koşturmak, heyecanla yapmak** *His friends rushed to congratulate him after the ceremony.* **3** [T] to make someone do something more quickly than they want to do it **koşturmak, acele ettirmek, zorlamak, baskı yapmak, sık boğaz etmek** [+ into + doing sth] *I refuse to be rushed into making a decision.*

rush ...... İLE BİRLİKTE KULLANILAN KELİMELER

a frantic/headlong/last-minute/mad rush ● a rush for sth

rush² /rʌʃ/ *noun* [no plural] **1** MOVEMENT when something suddenly moves somewhere quickly **acele, telâş, hücum, akın** *a rush of air* **2** ACTIVITY a lot of things happening or a lot of people trying to do something **izdiham, telâş, acele, sıkışıklık** [+ to do sth] *There was a mad rush to get tickets for the concert.* **3** HURRY when you

have to hurry or move somewhere quickly **acele etme, telâşlanma, hücum** *I'm sorry I can't talk now, I'm in a rush.*

rushes /rʌʃɪz/ *noun* [plural] tall plants that grow near water **saz, hasır bitkisi**

'rush ˌhour *noun* [C, U] the time when a lot of people are travelling to or from work and so roads and trains are very busy **işe gidiş/iş çıkış saatleri; trafiğin en yoğun olduğu saatler** *the morning/evening rush hour*

rust /rʌst/ *noun* [U] a dark orange substance that you get on metal when it has been damaged by air and water **pas** ● **rust** *verb* [I, T] **paslanmak**

rustic /'rʌstɪk/ *adjective* simple and old-fashioned in style in a way that is typical of the countryside **kaba saba, kırsal, kırsala ait, rustik**

rustle /'rʌsl/ *verb* [I, T] If things such as paper or leaves rustle, or if you rustle them, they move about and make a soft, dry sound. **hışırda(t)mak, hışırtı sesi çıkarmak; hışır hışır etmek** *Outside, the trees rustled in the wind.*

rustle up sth *phrasal verb* to produce something very quickly **çabucak hazırlamak, bulup buluşturmak; uydurmak** *I managed to rustle up a meal from the bits and pieces I found in his fridge.*

rusty /'rʌsti/ *adjective* **1** Rusty metal has rust (= an orange substance) on its surface. **paslı, pas tutmuş** *rusty nails* **2** If a skill you had is now rusty, it is not now good because you have forgotten it. **(bilgi, beceri) körelmiş, eski özelliğini kay betmiş, pas tutmuş, işe yaramaz, eskisi kadar iyi olmayan** *My French is a bit rusty.*

rut /rʌt/ *noun* **1 in a rut** in a bad situation where you do the same things all the time, or where it is impossible to make progress **dar bir çevreye sıkışıp kalmış; sürekli kendini tekrar eden; hiç bir gelişme gösteremeyen** *He seems to be stuck in a rut at the moment.* **2** [C] a deep, narrow mark in the ground made by a wheel **tekerlek izi**

ruthless /'ruːθləs/ *adjective* not caring if you hurt or upset other people when you try to get what you want **merhametsiz, acımasız, zalim** *ruthless ambition* ○ *a ruthless dictator* ● **ruthlessly** *adverb* **acımasızca** ● **ruthlessness** *noun* [U] **acımasızlık**

rye /raɪ/ *noun* [U] a plant that has grains which are used to make things such as bread and whisky (= strong alcoholic drink) **çavdar** *rye bread*

S, s

638   ꝏ Important words to learn

S

S, s /es/ the nineteenth letter of the alphabet **alfabenin ondokuzuncu harfi**

the Sabbath /'sæbəθ/ *noun* a day of the week that many religious groups use for prayer and rest **Şabat günü; bazı dinî grupların haftanın belli bir günü ibadet edip dinlendiği gün**

sabbatical /sə'bætɪkəl/ *noun* [C, U] a period when a university teacher does not do their usual work and instead travels or studies **bir üniversite hocasının normal işi dışında araştırma yaparak ve seyahat ederek geçirdiği dönem** *He was on sabbatical last year.*

sabotage /'sæbətɑːʒ/ *verb* [T] **1** to damage or destroy something in order to prevent an enemy from using it **sabotaj yapmak; düşmanın kullanımını engellemek için yok etmek/yıkmak/zarar vermek** *Rebels sabotaged the roads and bridges.* **2** to spoil someone's plans or efforts in order to prevent them from being successful **baltalamak, sabote etmek** *She tried to sabotage my chances of getting the job.* ● **sabotage** *noun* [U] *an act of sabotage* **sabotaj**

sac /sæk/ *noun* [C] a part in an animal or plant that is like a small bag

saccharin /'sækərɪn/ *noun* [U] a sweet, chemical substance that is used in food instead of sugar **sakarin; şeker yerine kullanılan suni tatlandırıcı**

sachet /'sæʃeɪ/ ⓤ /sæ'ʃeɪ/ *noun* [C] a small bag containing a small amount of something **poşet, torba** *sachets of sugar and coffee powder*

sack[1] /sæk/ *noun* **1** [C] a large bag made of paper, plastic, or cloth and used to carry or store things **çuval, büyük torba 2 the sack** UK When someone gets the sack or is given the sack, they are told to leave their job. **kov(ul)ma, işten at(ıl)ma, çıkar (ıl)ma** *He got the sack from his last job.*

 sack

sack[2] /sæk/ *verb* [T] UK to tell someone to leave their job, usually because they have done something wrong **kov (ul)mak, işten at(ıl)mak, çıkar(ıl)mak, yol ver(il) mek** *He was sacked for being late.*

sacrament /'sækrəmənt/ *noun* [C] an important religious ceremony in the Christian Church **dinî tören, ayîn** *the sacrament of marriage*

sacred /'seɪkrɪd/ *adjective* **1** relating to a religion or considered to be holy **kutsal, mukaddes, mübarek, ulu** *sacred music* ○ *a sacred object* **2** too important to be changed or destroyed **değiştirilemeyecek/yok edilemeyecek kadar önemli/değerli; kutsal** *I don't work at weekends - my private time is sacred.*

sacrifice ...... İLE BİRLİKTE KULLANILAN KELİMELER

make (great/huge) sacrifices ● sacrifices **for** sb/sth ● the sacrifice **of** sth

sacrifice[1] /'sækrɪfaɪs/ *noun* [C, U] **1** something valuable that you give up in order to achieve something, or the act of giving it up **fedakârlık, özveri** *Sometimes you have to make sacrifices to succeed.* **2** something offered to a god in a religious ceremony, especially an animal that is killed, or the act of offering it **kurban olma, kurban etme** ⊃See also: self-sacrifice.

sacrifice[2] /'sækrɪfaɪs/ *verb* [T] **1** to give up something that is valuable to you in order to achieve something **feda etmek; ...uğrunda harcamak** *There are thousands of men ready to sacrifice their lives for their country.* **2** to kill an animal and offer it to a god in a religious ceremony **kurban etmek, adamak**

sacrilege /'sækrɪlɪdʒ/ *noun* [U, no plural] when you treat something that is holy or important without respect **dini konularda saygısızlık**

sacrosanct /'sækrəʊsæŋkt/ *adjective formal* too important to be changed or destroyed **çok kutsal, dokunulmaz, eleştirilemez** *Human life is sacrosanct.*

sad ...... BAŞKA BİR DEYİŞLE

Unhappy ve **miserable** kelimeleri **sad** kelimesiyle aynı anlamda kullanılabilir. *She'd had a very* **unhappy** *childhood.* ● *I just woke up feeling* **miserable.**
Kişi olan kötü bir olaydan dolayı mutsuz ise, duygusu **Upset** ifadesiyle tanımlanabilir. *They'd had an argument and she was still* **upset** *about it.* ● *Mike got very* **upset** *when I told him the news.*
Eğer kişinin bir sevdiği onunla olan ilişkisini bitirdiyse, terkedilen kişinin hislerinin ifadesi için **broken-hearted** veya **heartbroken** söylemleri kullanılabilir. *She was* **broken-hearted** *when Richard left.*
Eğer kişi çok keyifsiz ve üzgün ise, durumun ifadesi için **devastated** veya **distraught** kelimeleri kullanılabilir. *She was* **devastated** *when he died.* ● *The missing child's* **distraught** *parents made an emotional appeal for information on TV.*
Depressed sıfatı kişinin uzun süreli mutsuzluğunu dile getirmede kullanılır. *She became deeply* **depressed** *after her husband died.*

ꝏ**sad** /sæd/ *adjective* **sadder, saddest 1** NOT HAPPY unhappy or making you feel unhappy **üzgün, üzücü, tasalı, neşesiz, kederli, gamlı** *I was very sad when our cat died.* ○ *a sad book/movie* ○ [+ that] *It's a bit sad that you'll miss our wedding.* ○ [+ to do sth] *I was sad to see him go.* **2** NOT SATISFACTORY [always before noun] not pleasant or satisfactory **hoş/tatminkâr olmayan, hoşa gitmeyen, tatsız** *The sad truth is that we've failed.* **3** NOT FASHIONABLE UK *informal* boring or not fashionable **sıkıcı, hoşa gitmeyen, uygunsuz** *You enjoy reading timetables? You sad man!* ● **sadness** *noun* [U] **keder, üzüntü**

sadden /'sædⁿn/ *verb* [T] *formal* to make someone feel sad or disappointed **üzmek, keyfini kaçırmak, kederlendirmek** [often passive] *We were saddened by his death.*

saddle[1] /'sædl/ *noun* [C] **1** a leather seat that you put on a horse so that you can ride it **eyer; semer** ⊃Orta kısımdaki renkli sayfalarına bakınız. **2** a seat on a bicycle or motorcycle **bisiklet motosiklet oturağı**

 saddle

saddle² /'sædl/ (*also* **saddle up**) *verb* [I, T] to put a saddle on a horse **eyerlemek; semerlemek**
saddle sb with sth *phrasal verb* to give someone a job or problem which will cause them a lot of work or difficulty **yüklemek, yük yüklemek, sorumluluk/görev vermek; angarya yüklemek**

saddo /'sædəʊ/ *noun* [C] *UK informal* someone, especially a man, who is boring and not fashionable and has no friends **sıkıcı, hiç dostu olmayan kimse**

sadistic /sə'dɪstɪk/ *adjective* getting pleasure from being cruel or violent **sadistçe davranan; başkalarına zarar vermekten/eziyet etmekten zevk almak** *sadistic behaviour* ○ *a sadistic murderer* ● **sadist** /'seɪdɪst/ *noun* [C] someone who gets pleasure from being cruel or violent **sadist, eziyet etmekten zevk alan kimse** ● **sadism** /'seɪdɪzᵊm/ *noun* [U] **sadistlik**

sadly /'sædli/ *adverb* **1** [NOT HAPPY] in a sad way **üzgün şekilde, üzücü olarak** *She shook her head sadly.* **2** [NOT SATISFACTORY] in a way that is not satisfactory **yetersiz/kifayetsiz** *Enthusiasm has been sadly lacking these past few months at work.* **3** [SORRY] used to say that you are sorry something is true **ne yazık ki, maalesef** *Sadly, the marriage did not last.*

sae, SAE /ˌes eɪ'iː/ *noun* [C] *UK abbreviation for* stamped addressed envelope or self-addressed envelope: an envelope that you put a stamp and your own address on and send to someone so that they can send you something back **posta pulu yapıştırılmış; Posta Ücreti Ödenmiş (PÜÖ)**

safari /sə'fɑːri/ *noun* [C, U] a journey, usually to Africa, to see or hunt wild animals **safari, Afrika'da yabanî hayvan avı** *She is on safari in Kenya.*

o▸**safe¹** /seɪf/ *adjective* **1** [NOT DANGEROUS] not dangerous or likely to cause harm **emin, güvenli, sağlam, emniyetli, tehlikesiz** *a safe driver* ○ *Air travel is generally quite safe.* ○ *We live in a safe neighbourhood.* ○ [+ to do sth] *Is it safe to drink the water here?* ⊃Opposite **unsafe.** **2** [NOT HARMED] not harmed or damaged **sağ salim, kazasız belasız** *She returned safe and sound* (= not harmed in any way). **3** [NOT IN DANGER] not in danger or likely to be harmed **emniyette, kurtulmuş, selâmette** *During the daylight hours we're safe from attack.* **4 safe to say** If it is safe to say something, you are sure it is correct. **yerinde, doğru, uygun, mâkul** *I think it's safe to say that he'll be the next president.* **5 a safe place; somewhere safe** a place where something will not be lost or stolen **emin bir yer, güvenilir mahal, emniyetli mekân** *It's very valuable so put it somewhere safe.* **6 play (it) safe** *informal* to be careful and not take risks **dikkatli olmak ve riske/tehlikeye girmemek** ● **safely** *adverb* *Make sure you drive safely.* ○ *I can safely say* (= I am certain) *I have never met anyone as rude as him.* ⊃See also: **a safe bet².** **güvenli bir şekilde**

safe² /seɪf/ *noun* [C] a strong metal box or cupboard with locks where you keep money, jewellery, and other valuable things **kasa**

safeguard¹ /'seɪfgɑːd/ *verb* [T] to protect something from harm **korumak, güvence/garanti altına almak; muhafaza etmek** *a plan to safeguard public health*
safeguard against sth *phrasal verb* to do things that you hope will stop something unpleasant from happening **bir şeye karşı önlem/tedbir almak; ...dan/den korumak** *A good diet will safeguard against disease.*

safeguard² /'seɪfgɑːd/ *noun* [C] a law, rule, or system that protects people or things from being harmed or lost **güvence, emniyet, garanti, ihtiyat**

safe 'haven *noun* [C] a place where someone is safe from danger **korunaklı/güvenli/emniyetli yer**

safe 'sex *noun* [U] when people have sex using a condom (= a thin rubber covering that a man wears on his penis) so that they do not catch a disease **güvenli cinsel ilişki; korunmalı seks**

🔲 *safety* ...... **İLE BİRLİKTE KULLANILAN KELİMELER**

ensure/guarantee sb's safety ● safety **is paramount**

---

o▸**safety** /'seɪfti/ *noun* [U] **1** when you are safe **güvenlik, emniyet** *food/road safety* ○ *The hostages were led to safety* (= to a safe place). ○ *a safety valve* **2** how safe something is **güvenlilik, emniyetlilik** *Safety at the factory has been improved.*

'safety ,belt *noun* [C] a piece of equipment that keeps you fastened to your seat when you are travelling in a vehicle **emniyet kemeri** *Please fasten your safety belt for take-off.*

'safety ,net *noun* [C] **1** a plan or system that will help you if you get into a difficult situation **güvence; güvence kaynağı/planı/sistemi** *Legal aid provides a safety net for people who can't afford a lawyer.* **2** a net that will catch someone if they fall from a high place **emniyet ağı/filesi**

'safety ,pin *noun* [C] a pin with a round cover that fits over the sharp end **çengelli iğne, firkete**

saffron /'sæfrən/ *noun* [U] a yellow powder that is used as a spice **safran; safran tozu**

sag /sæg/ *verb* [I] *sagging, past* **sagged** **1** to sink or bend down **batmak, eğilmek, bel vermek, sarkmak** *Our mattress sags in the middle.* **2** *informal* to become weaker or less successful **gittikçe zayıflamak; daha az başarılı olmak** *a sagging economy*

saga /'sɑːgə/ *noun* [C] a long story about a lot of people or events **destan, öykü, hikaye, olaylar dizisi**

sagacious /sə'geɪʃəs/ *adjective literary* having or showing understanding and the ability to make good decisions and judgments **iyi kararlar verebilen; mâkul yargılarda bulunabilen; aklı başında; mâkul**

sage /seɪdʒ/ *noun* **1** [U] a herb whose leaves are used to give flavour to food **ada çayı 2** [C] *literary* a wise person **bilge kişi, ekâbir, işin piri**

Sagittarius /ˌsædʒɪ'teəriəs/ *noun* [C, U] the sign of the zodiac which relates to the period of 22 November - 22 December, or a person born during this period **Yay Burcu** ⊃See picture at **zodiac.**

said /sed/ *past of* say **söylemek' fiilinin geçmiş zaman hâli**

sail¹ /seɪl/ *verb* **1** [TRAVEL] [I] to travel in a boat or a ship **gemiyle teknenyle yol almak/gitmek/seyahat etmek** *We sailed to Malta.* **2** [CONTROL BOAT] [I, T] to control a boat that has no engine and is moved by the wind **yelkenli kullanmak, yelkenle yol almak** *She sailed the small boat through the storm.* **3** [START JOURNEY] [I] When a ship sails, it starts its journey, and if people sail from a particular place or at a particular time, they start their journey. **deniz yolculuğu yapmak, sefere çıkmak, denizde seyahat etmek/yol almak** *This ship sails weekly from Florida to the Bahamas.* **4 sail over/past, etc** to move quickly through the air **havada hızla hareket etmek; uçup gitmek** *The ball sailed past me.*
sail through (sth) *phrasal verb* to succeed very easily, especially in a test or competition **kolayca halletmek; bir çırpıda çözmek; hemen hakkından gelivermek** *She sailed through her exams.*

sail² /seɪl/ *noun* **1** [C] a large piece of material that is fixed to a pole on a boat to catch the wind and make the boat move **yelken 2 set sail** to start a journey by boat or ship **sefere çıkmak, yelken açmak, yelkenliyle hareket etmek**

sailboat /ˈseɪlbəʊt/ *noun* [C] *US* a small boat with sails **yelkenli tekne**

sailing /ˈseɪlɪŋ/ *noun* [U] **1** a sport using boats with sails **yelken sporu, yelkencilik** *UK a sailing boat* **2 be plain sailing** to be very easy **çok kolay olmak, çocuk oyuncağı olmak; tereyağından kıl çeker gibi kolay olmak**

sailor /ˈseɪlər/ *noun* [C] someone who sails ships or boats as their job or as a sport **gemici, denizci**

saint /seɪnt/ *noun* [C] **1** a dead person who has been officially respected by the Christian church for living their life in a holy way **aziz, azize** *Catherine of Siena was made a saint in 1461.* **2** a very kind or helpful person **çok kibar ve yardımsever kimse, melek gibi insan** ⊃See also: **patron saint.**

saintly /ˈseɪntli/ *adjective* very good and kind **evliya gibi, çok iyi ve kibar; melek gibi**

sake /seɪk/ *noun* **1 for the sake of sth** for this reason or purpose **uğruna; ...için; ...sun diye** *For the sake of convenience, they combined the two departments.* **2 for the sake of sb** in order to help or please someone **uğruna, hatırına; mutlu olsun diye** *He begged her to stay for the sake of the children.* **3 for God's/goodness/heaven's, etc. sake** something you say when you are angry about something 'Allah aşkına!', 'Allah'ını seversen!' *For heaven's sake, stop moaning!*

○⁻**salad** /ˈsæləd/ *noun* [C, U]   **salad** a cold mixture of vegetables that have not been cooked, usually eaten with meat, cheese, etc **salata** *I made a big salad for lunch.* ⊃Orta kısımdaki renkli sayfalarına bakınız.

salami /səˈlɑːmi/ *noun* [C, U] a spicy sausage (= tube of meat and spices) that is usually eaten cold in slices **salam**

salaried /ˈsæləʳrid/ *adjective* receiving a fixed amount of money from your employer, usually every month **maaşlı, ücretli, aylıklı**

S

⟨⟩ **salary** ...... İLE BİRLİKTE KULLANILAN KELİMELER

earn a salary ● a **good/high/top** salary ● an **annual** salary ● a salary **cut/increase/rise**

○⁻**salary** /ˈsæləri/ *noun* [C, U] a fixed amount of money that you receive from your employer, usually every month **maaş, aylık, ücret**

○⁻**sale** /seɪl/ *noun* **1** [SELLING THINGS] [U, no plural] the act of selling something, or the time when something is sold **satış yapma** *The sale of alcohol is now banned.* ○ *to make a sale* **2 (up) for sale** available to buy **satılık** *For sale: ladies' bicycle - good condition.* ○ *The house next to mine is up for sale.* **3 on sale a** [AVAILABLE] *UK* available to buy in a shop **satışta, satışa sunulmuş/arzedilmiş** *The video and book are now on sale.* **b** [CHEAP] available for a lower price than usual **indirimde, indirim** *This album was on sale for half price.* **4** [EVENT] [C] an event where things are sold **satış** *a sale of used books* **5** [CHEAP PRICE] [C] a time when a shop sells goods at a lower price than usual **indirimli satışlar** *UK I bought this dress in the sale.* ⊃See also: car boot sale, jumble sale.

saleable /ˈseɪləbl/ *adjective* Something that is saleable can be sold easily. **kolay satılabilir** *He's painted some very saleable landscapes.*

sales /seɪlz/ *noun* [plural] **1** the number of items sold **satış, sürüm miktarı/sayısı** *Our sales have doubled this year.* **2** the part of a company that deals with selling things **satış bölümü** *I used to work in sales.* ○ *a sales department*

'sales as,sistant (*also US* 'sales ,clerk) *noun* [C] someone whose job is selling things in a shop **tezgâhtar, satış görevlisi**

salesman, saleswoman /ˈseɪlzmən/, /ˈseɪlz,wʊmən/ *noun* [C] *plural* **salesmen** or **saleswomen** someone whose job is selling things **(bayan, erkek) satıcı**

salesperson /ˈseɪlz,pɜːsən/ *noun* [C] *plural* **salespeople** someone whose job is selling things **satıcı, satış yapan kimse**

'sales ,rep (*formal* sales representative) *noun* [C] someone who travels to different places trying to persuade people to buy their company's products or services **satış temsilcisi**

salient /ˈseɪliənt/ *adjective formal* The salient facts about something or qualities of something are the most important things about them. **göze çarpan, belirgin, belli başlı, en önemli**

saline /ˈseɪlaɪn/ /ˈseɪliːn/ *adjective formal* containing salt **tuzlu, tuz içeren** *saline solution*

saliva /səˈlaɪvə/ *noun* [U] the liquid that is made in your mouth **salya**

sallow /ˈsæləʊ/ *adjective* Sallow skin is slightly yellow and does not look healthy. **soluk, sararmış**

salmon /ˈsæmən/ *noun* [C, U] *plural* **salmon** a large, silver fish, or the pink meat of this fish **somon balığı** *fresh/smoked salmon*

salmonella /ˌsælməˈnelə/ *noun* [U] a type of bacteria which can make you very ill, sometimes found in food that is not cooked enough **salmonela bakterisi; zehirlenmeye neden olan bir tür bakteri**

salon /ˈsælɒn/ *noun* [C] a shop where you can have your hair cut or have your appearance improved **traş/güzellik salonu, salon** *a hair salon* ⊃See also: beauty salon.

saloon /səˈluːn/ *noun* [C] **1** *UK* (*US* sedan) a large car with a separate, closed area for bags **sedan/büyük araba** **2** *US old-fashioned* a public bar **bar, meyhane**

salsa /ˈsælsə/ *noun* [U] **1** a cold, spicy sauce **soğuk acı sos** **2** a type of dance and music from Latin America **salsa, bir tür Latin Amerika dansı ve müziği** *a salsa club*

○⁻**salt¹** /sɔːlt/, /sɒlt/ *noun* [U] **1** a white substance used to add flavour to food **tuz** *salt and pepper* **2 take sth with a pinch of salt** *UK* (*US* take sth with a grain of salt) to not completely believe something that someone tells you **ihtiyatla yaklaşmak; hemen balıklama atlamamak, temkinli davranmak**

salt² /sɔːlt/, /sɒlt/ *verb* [T] to add salt to food **tuzlamak, tuz koymak**

'salt ,cellar *UK* (*US* 'salt ,shaker) *noun* [C] a small container with holes in for shaking salt on food **tuzluk**

saltwater /ˈsɔːlt,wɔːtəʳ/ *adjective* [always before noun] living in or containing water that has salt in it **tuzlu suda yaşayan, suyu tuzlu** *a saltwater fish*

salty /ˈsɔːlti/ *adjective* tasting of or containing salt **tuzlu** *Is the soup too salty?*

salute¹ /səˈluːt/ *noun* [C] a sign of respect to someone of a higher rank in a military organization, often made by raising the right hand to the side of the head **asker selâmı** *to give a salute*

salute² /səˈluːt/ *verb* [I, T] to give a salute to someone of a higher rank in a military organization **selâm vermek; selâmlamak**

salvage¹ /ˈsælvɪdʒ/ *verb* [T] **1** to save things from a place where other things have been damaged or lost **geriye kalanları kurtarmak** *gold coins salvaged from a shipwreck* **2** to try to make a bad situation better **kurtarmak** *an attempt to salvage her reputation*

salvage² /ˈsælvɪdʒ/ *noun* [U] when things are saved from being damaged, or the things that are saved **kurtarma** *a salvage company*

salvation /sælˈveɪʃᵊn/ *noun* [U] **1** in the Christian religion, when God saves someone from the bad effects of evil **(Hıristiyanlıkta) kurtuluş, halâs, selâmet 2** something or someone that saves you from harm or a very unpleasant situation **kurtarıcı, imdada yetişen kimse** *Getting a dog was Dad's salvation after Mum died.*

salwar kameez (shalwar kameez) /ˌsalwɑːkəˈmiːz/ *noun* [C] a type of suit, worn especially by women in India, with loose trousers and a long shirt **Hindistan'da kadınların giydiği bol pantolon ve üzerine giyilen uzun gömlek** ⊃Orta kısımdaki renkli sayfalarına bakınız.

o←**same¹** /seɪm/ *adjective, pronoun* **1 the same a** exactly alike **aynı, benzer, tıpkısı** *He's the same age as me.* ○ *We arrive at the same speed.* ○ *Cars cost the same here as they do in Europe.* **b** not another different thing or situation **aynı** *They met at the same place every week.* ○ *You meet the same people at all these events.* **c** not changed **aynı, hiç değişmemiş, tıpkısının aynısı** *She's the same lively person she's always been.* ○ *He looks exactly the same as he did ten years ago.* **2 all/just the same** despite what has just been said **yine de, buna rağmen, bununla birlikte** *He doesn't earn much. All the same, he ought to pay for some of his own drinks.* **3 Same here.** *informal* something that you say when something another person has said is also true for you **'Al benden de o kadar!', 'Benim için de aynı!', 'Söyledikleri tıpa tıp doğru!', 'Söylediklerine tamamen katılıyorum!'** *"I think she's awful." "Same here."* **4 the same old arguments/faces/story, etc** *informal* something or someone you have seen or heard many times before **aynı tartışmalar/yüzler/hikaye vs. 5 same old same old** *informal* used to say that a situation or someone's behaviour remains the same, especially when it it boring or annoying **hep aynı şeyler, git gel aynı şey; aynı tas aynı hamam** *Most people just keep on doing the same old same old every day.* ⊃See also: be in the same **boat**, in the same **vein**, be on the same **wavelength.**

same

Unutmayın! Same -the kelimesini takip eder. same olarak kullanmayın. Doğru kullanımı the same şeklindedir:: ~~My sister is in same class as me.~~ Yanlış cümle örneği

My sister is in the same class as me.

o←**same²** /seɪm/ *adverb* **the same** in the same way **eşit olarak, aynı şekilde** *We treat all our children the same.*

sample ILE BIRLIKTE KULLANILAN KELIMELER

analyse/collect/take/test a sample ● a sample of sth

sample¹ /ˈsɑːmpl/ *noun* [C] **1** SHOW a small amount of something that shows you what it is like **örnek, numune** *a free sample of chocolate* ○ *She brought in*

some *samples of her work.* **2** EXAMINE a small amount of a substance that a doctor or scientist collects in order to examine it **tıbbi tetkik numunesi/örneği** *a blood/urine sample* **3** NUMBER a small number of people from a larger group that is being tested **örnek grup** *a sample of 500 male drivers*

sample² /ˈsɑːmpl/ *verb* [T] **1** to taste a small amount of food or drink to decide if you like it **tadına bakmak, tadmak** *We sampled eight different cheeses.* **2** to experience a place or an activity, often for the first time **ilk defa görmek/denemek/yapmak/yaşamak; deneyerek tanımak** *an opportunity to sample the local night life*

sanatorium (*also US* sanitarium) /ˌsænəˈtɔːriəm/ *noun* [C] *plural* **sanatoriums** or **sanatoria** a hospital where people go to rest and get well after a long illness **sanatoryum**

sanction ILE BIRLIKTE KULLANILAN KELIMELER

impose/lift sanctions ● tough sanctions ● sanctions against/on sb ● economic/trade sanctions

sanction¹ /ˈsæŋkʃᵊn/ *noun* **1** [C] a punishment for not obeying a rule or a law **yaptırım** *economic/trade sanctions against a country* **2** [U] official approval or permission **resmî izin, onay**

sanction² /ˈsæŋkʃᵊn/ *verb* [T] to formally approve of something **resmî izin vermek, onaylamak** *He refused to sanction the publication of his private letters.*

sanctity /ˈsæŋktəti/ *noun formal* **the sanctity of life/marriage, etc** when something is very important and deserves respect **evliliğin/yaşamın kutsallığı/kutsiyeti**

sanctuary /ˈsæŋktʃʊəri/ *noun* **1** QUIET [C, U] a quiet and peaceful place **sessiz ve huzur dolu yer** *After a busy day, I like to escape to the sanctuary of my garden.* **2** PROTECTION [C, U] a place that provides protection **korunak, barınak** *to seek sanctuary* **3** ANIMALS [C] a place where animals are protected and cannot be hunted **hayvan barınağı; korunak, barınak** *a bird/wildlife sanctuary*

o←**sand¹** /sænd/ *noun* [U] a substance that is found on beaches and in deserts, which is made from very small grains of rock **kum** *a grain of sand*

sand² /sænd/ *verb* [T] to make wood smooth by rubbing it with sandpaper (= strong paper with a rough surface) **zımparalamak**

sandal /ˈsændᵊl/ *noun* [C] a light shoe with straps that you wear in warm weather **sandalet** ⊃Orta kısımdaki renkli sayfalarına bakınız.

sandcastle /ˈsændˌkɑːsl/ *noun* [C] a model of a castle made of wet sand, usually built by children on a beach **kumdan kale**

'sand ˌdune *noun* [C] a hill of sand in the desert or on the coast **kum tepesi/tepecikler**

sandpaper /ˈsændˌpeɪpər/ *noun* [U] strong paper with a rough surface that is rubbed against wood to make it smooth **zımpara, zımpara kâğıdı**

sands /sændz/ *noun* [plural] a large area of sand **kumsal**

sandstone /ˈsændstəʊn/ *noun* [U] rock made of sand **kum taşı**

o←**sandwich¹** /ˈsænwɪdʒ/ *noun* [C] two slices of bread with meat, cheese, etc between

sandwich

them **ekmek arası; sandviç** *a cheese/tuna sandwich*
➔Orta kısımdaki renkli sayfalarına bakınız.

sandwich² /'sænwɪdʒ/ *verb*
  be sandwiched between sth/sb *phrasal verb informal*
  to be in a small space between two people or things **iki
  şey/kişi arasına sıkışmak/sıkıştırmak; arada sıkışıp kalmak** *Andorra is a small country sandwiched between Spain and France.*

sandy /'sændi/ *adjective* covered with or containing
  sand **kumlu** *a sandy beach*

sane /seɪn/ *adjective* **1** not suffering from mental illness
  akıllı, aklı başında 2 [always before noun] showing good
  judgment **akla uygun, mantıklı, mâkul** *a sane atti-
  tude/decision* ➔Opposite insane.

sang /sæŋ/ *past tense of* sing **şarkı söylemek' fiilinin
  ikinci hâli**

sanguine /'sæŋgwɪn/ *adjective formal* positive and full
  of hope **iyimser, ümitli, hayata olumlu bakan** *The
  director is sanguine about the company's prospects.*

sanitarium /ˌsænɪ'teəriəm/ *noun* [C] *plural* **sanitariums**
  or **sanitaria** *another US spelling of* sanatorium (= a hospital where people rest and get well after a long illness)
  sanatoryum hastanesi

sanitary /'sænɪt³ri/ *adjective* relating to preventing disease by removing dirt and waste **sıhhî, sağlık, hijyenik** *sanitary conditions*

'sanitary ˌtowel *UK* (*US* ˌsanitary 'napkin) *noun* [C] a
  thick piece of soft paper that a woman wears to absorb
  blood from her period (= monthly blood from the
  uterus) **âdet bezi, hijyenik bağ**

sanitation /ˌsænɪ'teɪʃ³n/ *noun* [U] a system for protecting people's health by removing dirt and waste **sağlık
  koruma, hıfzısıhha, hijyen**

sanity /'sænəti/ *noun* [U] **1** the quality of behaving
  calmly and showing good judgment **sağduyu, akıl
  fikir, sağlam muhakeme** *Jogging helps me keep my
  sanity.* **2** when you have a healthy mind and are not
  mentally ill **akıl sağlığı, aklı başında olma akıllılık**
  ➔Opposite insanity.

sank /sæŋk/ *past tense of* sink **batmak' fiilinin ikinci
  hâli**

Santa /'sæntə/ (*also* Santa Claus /'sæntəklɔːz/) *noun* [no
  plural] a kind, fat, old man in red clothes who people
  say brings presents to children at Christmas **Noel
  Baba**

sap¹ /sæp/ *verb* [T] **sapping**, *past* **sapped** to gradually
  make something weak **zayıflatmak, tüketmek, bitir-
  mek** *Ten years of war had sapped the country's
  strength.*

sap² /sæp/ *noun* [U] the liquid inside plants and trees
  özsu, besi suyu

sapling /'sæplɪŋ/ *noun* [C] a young tree **fidan**

sapphire /'sæfaɪə'/ *noun* [C] a bright blue, transparent
  stone **safir, gök yakut**

sarcasm /'sɑːkæz³m/ *noun* [U] when you say the opposite of what you mean to insult someone or show them
  that you are annoyed **gizli ve ince alay, dokunaklı
  söz, iğneleme** *"Oh, I am sorry," she said, her voice
  heavy with sarcasm.*

sarcastic /sɑː'kæstɪk/ *adjective* using sarcasm **alaycı,
  alay eden, iğneleyici** *a sarcastic comment/remark*
  ○ *Are you being sarcastic?* ● **sarcastically** *adverb* alaycı
  bir şekilde

sardine /sɑː'diːn/ *noun* [C] a small sea fish that you can
  eat **sardalye, sardalye balığı**

sari (*also* saree) /'sɑːri/ *noun* [C] a dress, worn especially
  by women from India and Pakistan, made from a very

long piece of thin cloth **Hintli/Pakistanlı kadın kıyafeti, sari**

SARS /sɑːz/ *noun* [U] *abbreviation for* Severe Acute
  Respiratory Syndrome: a serious disease that makes it
  difficult to breathe **Ciddi Akut Solunum Yetmezliği
  Sendromu (CASYS)**

SASE /ˌeseɪes'iː/ *noun* [C] *US abbreviation for* self-
  addressed stamped envelope: an envelope that you put
  a stamp and your own address on and send to someone
  so that they can send you something back **Adresli
  Pullu İade Zarfı (APİZ)**

sash /sæʃ/ *noun* [C] a long, narrow piece of cloth that is
  worn around the waist or over the shoulder, often as
  part of a uniform **kuşak; üniforma kuşağı/kemeri**

sassy /'sæsi/ *adjective US informal* **1** very energetic and
  confident **çok canlı ve kendinden emin** *a smart, sassy
  young woman* **2** slightly rude, but not offensive **saygısız, kaba, itici** *a sassy remark*

sat /sæt/ *past of* sit **oturmak' fiilinin ikinci hâli**

Sat *written abbreviation for* Saturday **cumartesi, Cumartesi günü**

Satan /'seɪt³n/ *noun* [no plural] the Devil (= the enemy of
  God) **Şeytan**

satanic /sə'tænɪk/ *adjective* relating to the Devil (= the
  enemy of God) **şeytani** *a satanic cult/ritual*

satchel /'sætʃ³l/ *noun* [C] a large bag with a strap that
  goes over your shoulder, often used for carrying school
  books **okul sırt çantası** ➔Orta kısımdaki renkli sayfalarına
  bakınız.

satellite /'sæt³laɪt/ *noun* [C] **1** a piece of equipment that
  is sent into space around the Earth to receive and send
  signals or to collect information **(yapay) uydu** *a spy/
  weather satellite* **2** a natural object that moves around a
  planet in space **uydu, gezegen** *The moon is the Earth's
  satellite.*

'satellite ˌdish *noun* [C] a round piece of equipment that
  receives television and radio signals broadcast from
  satellites **uydu anteni**

ˌsatellite 'television (*also* ˌsatellite T'V) *noun* [U] television programmes that are broadcast using a satellite
  uydu yayın yapan televizyon

satin /'sætɪn/ *noun* [U] a smooth, shiny cloth **saten,
  atlas**

satire /'sætaɪə'/ *noun* **1** [U] when you use jokes and
  humour to criticize people or ideas **taşlama, yerme,
  hicvetme** *political satire* **2** [C] a story, film, etc that
  uses satire **(oyun, film) taşlama, yergi, hiciv** ● **satirist**
  /'sæt³rɪst/ *noun* [C] someone who uses satire **taşlayan/
  yeren/hicveden kimse**

satirical /sə'tɪrɪk³l/ *adjective* using satire **taşlayan, hic-
  veden, yeren** *a satirical magazine/novel*

⚙ satisfaction .... İLE BİRLİKTE KULLANILAN KELİMELER

derive/get satisfaction **from** sth ● sth **gives** sb satisfaction ● **deep/immense** satisfaction ● **a sense of**
satisfaction ● **job** satisfaction
---

satisfaction /ˌsætɪs'fækʃ³n/ *noun* [U] **1** the pleasant
  feeling you have when you get something that you
  wanted or do something that you wanted to do **tatmin,
  memnuniyet, memnunluk** *job satisfaction* ○ *She
  smiled with satisfaction.* ○ [+ of + doing sth] *I had the
  satisfaction of knowing that I'd done everything I could.*
  2 to sb's satisfaction as well as someone wants **...ı/i
  memnun edecek şekilde; tatmin edecek biçimde** *He
  won't get paid until he completes the job to my satisfaction.* ➔Opposite dissatisfaction.

satisfactory /ˌsætɪsˈfæktᵊri/ *adjective* good enough **tatminkâr, memnuniyet verici** *We hope very much to find a satisfactory solution to the problem.* ⊃Opposite unsatisfactory. ● **satisfactorily** *adverb* **tatmin edici bir şekilde**

satisfied /ˈsætɪsfaɪd/ *adjective* **1** pleased because you have got what you wanted, or because something has happened in the way that you wanted **tatmin olmuş, memnun, memnunluk duyan** *Are you satisfied with the new arrangement?* ⊃Opposite dissatisfied. **2 be satisfied that** If you are satisfied that something is true, you believe it. **inanmış/tatmin olmuş/kanaat getirmiş olmak** *The judge was satisfied that she was telling the truth.* ⊃See also: self-satisfied.

satisfy /ˈsætɪsfaɪ/ *verb* **1** [T] to please someone by giving them what they want or need **tatmin etmek, doyurmak, karşılamak, gidermek** *They sell 31 flavours of ice cream - enough to satisfy everyone!* **2 satisfy conditions/needs/requirements, etc** to have or provide something that is needed or wanted **şartları/gereksinimleri/gereklilikleri karşılamak/gidermek/tatmin etmek** *She satisfies all the requirements for the job.* **3 satisfy sb that** to make someone believe that something is true **ikna etmek, inandırmak, için rahat ettirmek, tatmin etmek** *I satisfied myself that I had locked the door.*

satisfying /ˈsætɪsfaɪɪŋ/ *adjective* making you feel pleased by providing what you need or want **tatmin edici, memnunluk verici, doyurucu** *a satisfying meal* ○ *My work is very satisfying.*

SATNAV /ˈsætnæv/ *noun* [U] *abbreviation for* satellite navigation: a system of computers and satellites (= equipment that is sent into space around the Earth to receive and send signals), used in cars and other places to tell a user where they are or where something is **Uydudan Seyrüsefer (UYSEY); bilgisayarlar ve uydular aracılığı ile araçlarda ve diğer yerlerde kullanıcıya saklamak yeri bildiren sistem**

saturate /ˈsætʃᵊreɪt/ *verb* **1 be saturated with sth** to be filled with a lot or too much of something **doyurmak** *The city is saturated with cheap restaurants* **2** [T] to make something completely wet **ıslatmak, sırılsıklam etmek** *Heavy rain had saturated the playing field.* **3** to put as much of a substance that dissolves into a solution as is possible **emdirmek** ● **saturation** /ˌsætʃᵊrˈeɪʃᵊn/ *noun* [U] **emmek**

ˌsaturated ˈfat *noun* [C, U] a fat found in meat, milk, and eggs, which is thought to be bad for your health **doymuş yağ** ⊃Compare unsaturated fat.

o⚬**Saturday** /ˈsætədeɪ/ *(written abbreviation* Sat) *noun* [C, U] the day of the week after Friday and before Sunday **cumartesi, cumartesi günü**

YAYGIN HATALAR

Saturday

Unutmayın! Haftanın günleri her zaman büyük harf ile yazılır. **saturday** olarak yazmayın. Doğru yazılımı **Saturday** şeklindedir. ~~The festival began at midday on saturday.~~ Yanlış cümle örneği

The festival began at midday on Saturday.

Saturn /ˈsætən/ *noun* [no plural] the planet that is sixth from the Sun, after Jupiter and before Uranus **Satürn, güneş sisteminde Jüpiter'den sonra Uranüs'ten önce gelen altıncı gezegen**

o⚬**sauce** /sɔːs/ *noun* [C, U] a hot or cold liquid that you put on food to add flavour **sos, salça** *pasta with tomato sauce* ⊃See also: soy sauce.

saucepan /ˈsɔːspən/ *noun* [C] a deep, metal pan, usually with a long handle and a lid, that is used to cook food in **saplı tencere** ⊃Orta kısımdaki renkli sayfalarına bakınız.

saucer /ˈsɔːsəʳ/ *noun* [C] a small plate that you put under a cup **fincan/çay tabağı** *a cup and saucer*

saucy /ˈsɔːsi/ *adjective* slightly rude, or referring to sex in a funny way **arsız, sulu, sırnaşık, haddini bilmez** *a saucy postcard/joke*

sauna /ˈsɔːnə/ *noun* [C] **1** a room that is hot and filled with steam where people sit to relax or feel healthy **sauna** *a gym with a pool and a sauna* **2 have a sauna** to spend time inside a sauna **saunaya girmek**

saunter /ˈsɔːntəʳ/ *verb* **saunter into/over/through, etc** to walk in a slow and relaxed way **sallana sallana/salına salına yürümek** *He sauntered through the door two hours late.*

sausage /ˈsɒsɪdʒ/ *noun* [C, U] a mixture of meat and spices pressed into a long tube **sosis**

sausage

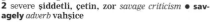
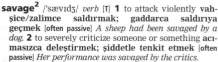

sauté /ˈsəʊteɪ/, /ˈsəʊˈteɪ/ *verb* [T] to fry food quickly in a small amount of hot oil **sote**

savage¹ /ˈsævɪdʒ/ *adjective* **1** extremely violent **vahşi, zalim, gaddar** *a savage attack* **2** severe **şiddetli, çetin, zor** *savage criticism* ● **savagely** *adverb* **vahşice**

savage² /ˈsævɪdʒ/ *verb* [T] **1** to attack violently **vahşice/zalimce saldırmak; gaddarca saldırıya geçmek** [often passive] *A sheep had been savaged by a dog.* **2** to severely criticize someone or something **acımasızca deleştirmek; şiddetle tenkit etmek** [often passive] *Her performance was savaged by the critics.*

savage³ /ˈsævɪdʒ/ *noun* [C] *old-fashioned* an offensive word for a person from a country at an early stage of development **vahşi kimse**

o⚬**save¹** /seɪv/ *verb* **1** MAKE SAFE [T] to stop someone or something from being killed or destroyed **kurtarmak, korumak** *He was badly injured, but the doctors saved his life.* ○ *She saved the children from drowning.* ○ *I had to borrow money to save his business.* **2** MONEY [I, T] *(also* save up) to keep money so that you can buy something with it in the future **biriktirmek, tasarruf yapmak** *We've saved almost $900 for our wedding.* ○ *Michael's saving up for a new computer.* **3** KEEP [T] to keep something to use in the future **saklamak, biriktirmek, ayırmak, bir kenara koymak** *I've saved some food for you.* **4 save money/space/time, etc** to reduce the amount of money/space/time, etc that you have to use **para/yer/zaman vs. tasarruf etmek 5 save sb (from) doing sth** to help someone avoid having to do something **kurtarmak** *We'll eat in a restaurant - it'll save you having to cook.* **6 save files/work, etc** to store work or information electronically on or from a computer **çalışmaları/dosyaları vs. bilgisayar ortamında saklamak; hafızaya kaydetmek 7 save a goal** to prevent a player from scoring a goal **gol olmasına engel olmak; kurtarmak** *He saved two goals in the last minute of the game.* ⊃See also: save the day, lose/save face¹.

save on sth *phrasal verb* to avoid using something so that you do not have to pay for it **bir konuda tasarruf etmek; saklamak; kullanmamak** *She walks to work to save on bus fares.*

S

save² /seɪv/ *noun* [C] when someone prevents a goal from being scored in a sport **gol kurtarma** *The goalkeeper made a great save.*

saver /'seɪvə^r/ *noun* [C] someone who saves money in a bank **tasarruf yapan kimse, tasarrufçu**

saving /'seɪvɪŋ/ *noun* [C] *UK* (*US* **savings**) when you pay less money than you would usually have to **kazanç, tasarruf** [usually singular] *a saving of £20.*

savings /'seɪvɪŋz/ *noun* [plural] money that you have saved, usually in a bank **birikimler, tasarruflar, birikmiş para** *I spent all my savings on a new kitchen.* ○ *a savings account*

savings and 'loan associ,ation *US* (*UK* **building society**) *noun* [C] a bank that is owned by the people who keep their money in it and that lets them borrow money to buy a house **tasarruf ve kredi ortaklığı; sahibi müşteriler olan ve kredi alınabilen banka**

saviour *UK* (*US* **savior**) /'seɪvjə^r/ *noun* **1** [C] someone who saves someone or something from harm or difficulty **kurtarıcı 2 the Saviour** in Christianity, Jesus Christ **Hz. İsa, Mesih**

savour *UK* (*US* **savor**) /'seɪvə^r/ *verb* [T] to enjoy food or a pleasant experience as much and as slowly as possible **tadını/zevkini çıkarmak, zevkine varmak** *to savour a meal* ○ *We savoured our moment of victory.*

savoury *UK* (*US* **savory**) /'seɪvʰri/ *adjective* Savoury food is not sweet. **tuzlu, baharatlı, lezzetli** *savoury biscuits*

savvy /'sævi/ *noun* [U] *informal* practical knowledge and ability **pratik bilgi ve kabiliyet** *business/political savvy* ● **savvy** *adjective informal* having knowledge and ability **pratik bilgi ve kabiliyetli** *a savvy consumer*

saw¹ /sɔː/ *noun* [C] a tool with a sharp edge that you use to cut wood or other hard material **testere** ⊅See picture at **tool.** ● **saw** *verb* [I, T] *past tense* **sawed**, *past participle* **sawn** or *mainly US* **sawed** to use a saw **testere ile kesmek** *They sawed the door in half.*

saw² /sɔː/ *past tense of* see **görmek' fiilinin ikinci hâli**

sawdust /'sɔːdʌst/ *noun* [U] very small pieces of wood and powder that are produced when you cut wood with a saw **talaş, testere talaşı, bıçkı tozu**

saxophone /'sæksəfəʊn/ (*also* **sax** *informal*) *noun* [C] a metal musical instrument that you play by blowing into it and pressing keys to produce different notes **saksafon** ● **saxophonist** /sæk'sɒfʰnɪst/ (US) /'sæksəfəʊnɪst/ *noun* [C] someone who plays the saxophone **saksafoncu**

○•**say¹** /seɪ/ *verb* [T] **says**, *past* **said 1** WORDS to speak words **söylemek, demek** *"I'd like to go home," she said.* ○ *I couldn't hear what they were saying.* ○ *How do you say this word?* **2** TELL to tell someone about a fact, thought, or opinion **söylemek, belirtmek, ifade etmek** [+ question word] *Did she say where she was going?* ○ [+ (that)] *The jury said that he was guilty.* **3** INFORMATION to give information in writing, numbers, or signs **bilgi vermek, göstermek, belirtmek** *My watch says one o'clock.* ○ *What do the papers say about the election?* **4 say sth to yourself** to think something but not speak **düşünmek, kendi kendine demek** *"I hope she likes me," he said to himself.* **5** SHOW to show what you think without using words **demek istemek, göstermek, söylemek, ifade etmek, açıklamak** *His smile seemed to say that I was forgiven.* **6 (let's) say...** used to introduce a suggestion or possible example of something **diyelim ki...** *Say you were offered a better job in another city - would you take it?* **7 You can say that again!** *informal* used to show that you completely agree with something that someone has just said **Tamamen katılıyorum!', 'Seninle/sizinle aynı fikirdeyim!', 'Doğru söylüyorsunuz!'** *"That was a very bad movie!" "You can say that*

again!" **8 it goes without saying** If something goes without saying, it is generally accepted or understood. **hiç bir söze gerek yok, elbette, şurası muhakkak ki, hiç kuşkusuz** *It goes without saying that smoking is harmful to your health.* ⊃See also: Say **cheese!**, easier (easy²) said than done.

🧩 **say (noun)** ...... İLE BİRLİKTE KULLANILAN KELİMELER

be given/have [a/no/some, etc] say ● **the final say** ● say **in/on** sth

say² /seɪ/ *noun* [U] **1** when you are involved in making a decision about something **söz hakkı** *We had some say in how our jobs would develop.* **2 have your say** to give your opinion about something **söyleyeceğini söylemek, fikrini belirtmek;** *We can't vote yet - Christina hasn't had her say.*

saying /'seɪɪŋ/ *noun* [C] a famous phrase that people use to give advice about life **atasözü, ata sözü, deyiş, özlüsöz** *Have you heard the saying, "misery loves company"?*

sb *written abbreviation for* somebody **birisi' sözcüğünün kısa yazılışı** ● **sb's** *written abbreviation for* somebody's **birisinin' sözcüğünün kısa yazılışı**

scab /skæb/ *noun* [C] a layer of dried blood that forms to cover a cut in the skin **kabuk, yara kabuğu**

scaffolding /'skæfʰldɪŋ/ *noun* [U] a temporary structure made of flat boards and metal poles used to work on a tall building **iskele, inşaat iskelesi**

scald /skɔːld/ *verb* [T] to burn something or someone with very hot liquid or steam **buharla/suyla haşlamak** *She scalded her mouth on the hot soup.*

🧩 **scale** ...... İLE BİRLİKTE KULLANILAN KELİMELER

on a [grand/large/massive/small, etc] scale ● **the scale of** sth

scale¹ /skeɪl/ *noun* **1** SIZE [no plural] the size or level of something **boyut, ölçüt, derece, kapsam, çap** *We don't yet know the scale of the problem.* ○ *Nuclear weapons cause destruction on a massive scale* (= cause a lot of destruction). **2 large-/small-scale** A large-/small-scale event or activity is large/small in size. **büyük-/küçük- ölçekte/çapta/ölçüde/çapta** *a large-scale investigation* **3** MEASURING SYSTEM [C] the set of numbers, amounts, etc used to measure or compare the level of something **derece, ölçü, ölçek, cetvel** *How would you rate her work on a scale of 1-10?* **4** EQUIPMENT [C] *US* (*UK* **scales** [plural]) a piece of equipment for measuring weight **tartı, terazi** *a bathroom/kitchen scale* ⊃Orta kısımdaki renkli sayfalarına bakınız. **5** COMPARISON [C, U] how the size of things on a map, model, etc relates to the same things in real life **ölçü, mikyas** *a map with a scale of one centimetre per ten kilometres* **6** MUSIC [C] a series of musical notes that is always played in order and that rises gradually from the first note **gam 7** SKIN [C] one of the flat pieces of hard material that covers the skin of fish and snakes (balık, yılan) **pul, kabuk**

scale² /skeɪl/ *verb* [T] to climb something that is high or steep **tırmanmak** *to scale a wall*
scale sth back *phrasal verb mainly US* (*UK/US* **scale** sth **down**) to make something smaller than it was or smaller than it was planned to be **küçül(t)mek**

scales /skeɪlz/ *noun* [plural] *UK* (*US* **scale** [C]) a piece of equipment for measuring weight **terazi** *bathroom/kitchen scales* ⊃Orta kısımdaki renkli sayfalarına bakınız.

scallion /'skæliən/ *US* (*UK* **spring onion**) *noun* [C] a small onion with a white part at the bottom and long, green leaves which is eaten in salads **yeşil soğan**

S

scallop /'skæləp/ *noun* [C] a small sea creature that lives in a shell and is eaten as food **midye; bir tür deniz yaratığı**

scalp /skælp/ *noun* [C] the skin on the top of your head under your hair **kafa derisi**

scalpel /'skælpᵊl/ *noun* [C] a small, sharp knife that doctors use to cut through skin during an operation **neşter, bistüri**

scalper /'skælpər/ *US* (*UK* **tout**) *noun* [C] someone who unofficially sells tickets outside theatres, sports grounds, etc **karaborsa bilet satan kimse**

scaly /'skeɪli/ *adjective* If your skin is scaly, it is rough and falls off in small, dry pieces. **pul pul, kabuk kabuk**

scam /skæm/ *noun* [C] *informal* an illegal plan for making money **şike**

scamper /'skæmpər/ *verb* **scamper away/down/off, etc** to run quickly and with small steps, like a child or a small animal (**çocuk, hayvan**) **seğirtmek, kaçışmak, sağa sola dağılmak**

scampi /'skæmpi/ *noun* [U] prawns (= small sea creatures) that have been fried **kızarmış kerevit, skampi**

scan¹ /skæn/ *verb* **scanning,** *past* **scanned 1** [T] to examine something with a machine that can see inside an object or body **aletle taramak** *Airports use X-ray machines to scan luggage for weapons.* **2** [COMPUTER] [T] to use a piece of equipment that copies words or pictures from paper into a computer **resim ve yazıları bilgisayara aktarmak için taramak** *to scan photos into a computer* **3** [LOOK] [T] to look around an area quickly to try to find a person or thing **iyice incelemek, inceden inceye araştırmak** *She scanned the crowd for a familiar face.* **4** [READ] [T] (*also* **scan through**) to quickly read a piece of writing to understand the main meaning or to find a particular piece of information **hızlıca okumak/göz gezdirmek** *I scanned the travel brochures looking for a cheap holiday.*

scan² /skæn/ *noun* [C] a medical examination in which an image of the inside of the body is made using a special machine **tarama** *a brain scan*

scandal ...... İLE BİRLİKTE KULLANILAN KELİMELER

a scandal **breaks/erupts** ● be **at the centre of/involved in** a scandal ● a scandal **surrounding** sth ● **a sex** scandal

scandal /'skændᵊl/ *noun* [C, U] something that shocks people because they think it is morally wrong **rezalet, kepazelik, skandal** *a sex scandal*

scandalous /'skændᵊləs/ *adjective* shocking or morally wrong **utanç verici, rezil, kepazelik çıkaran, çirkin, rezil** *a scandalous waste of money*

Scandinavian /ˌskændɪˈneɪviən/ *adjective* from or relating to the countries of Sweden, Denmark, Norway, and sometimes Finland and Iceland **İskandinav ülkelerinden gelen, oraya ait** ● **Scandinavian** *noun* [C] **İskandinav**

scanner /'skænər/ *noun* [C] **1** a piece of equipment that copies words or pictures from paper into a computer **tarayıcı alet/makina 2** a piece of medical equipment used to examine images of the inside of someone's body **tıbbî tarama cihazı/aygıtı**

scant /skænt/ *adjective* [always before noun] very little and not enough **az, kıt, yetersiz, sınırlı** *His work has received only scant attention outside this country.*

scantily /'skæntɪli/ *adverb* **scantily clad/dressed** not wearing many clothes and showing a lot of the body **açık saçık giyinmiş, orası burası görünen**

scanty /'skænti/ *adjective* very small in size or quantity **az, dar, yetersiz, kifayetsiz, seyrek** *scanty clothing*

scapegoat /'skeɪpgəʊt/ *noun* [C] someone who is blamed for a bad situation, although they have not caused it **günah keçisi, şamar oğlan** *He was made a scapegoat for the disaster.*

scar /skɑːr/ *noun* [C] **1** a permanent mark left on the body from a cut or other injury **yara izi 2** damage done to a person's mind by a very unpleasant event or situation (**zihinde**) **iz, etki, tesir, yara** *a psychological scar* ● **scar** *verb* [T] **scarring,** *past* **scarred** to cause a scar **yara izi bırakmak/kalmak** [often passive] *He was scarred for life by the accident.*

scarce /skeəs/ *adjective* rare or not available in large amounts **nadir, yetersiz, az, kıt** *scarce resources*

scarcely /'skeəsli/ *adverb* **1** only just **ancak, hemen hemen hiç, henüz** *They had scarcely finished eating when the doorbell rang.* **2 can scarcely do sth** If you say you can scarcely do something, you mean it would be wrong to do it. **yalnızca ...yapabilir; sadece şunu/bunu yapabilir** *He's only two - you can scarcely blame him for behaving badly.*

scarcity /'skeəsəti/ *noun* [C, U] when there is not enough of something **nadirlik, kıtlık, darlık, azlık** *a scarcity of food/affordable housing*

scare¹ /skeər/ *verb* [T] **1** to frighten a person or animal **korkutmak** *Sudden, loud noises scare me.* **2 scare the hell/life/living daylights, etc out of sb** *informal* to make someone feel very frightened **ödünü patlatmak/koparmak, çok korkutmak; aklını başından almak** ⊃ See also: scare/frighten sb out of their **wits.**

scare sb/sth away/off *phrasal verb* to make a person or an animal so frightened that they go away **korkutup/ürkütüp kaçırmak** *She scared off her attacker by screaming.*

scare sb away/off *phrasal verb* to make someone worried about doing something so that they decide not to do it **kaçırmak, ürkütmek, endişelendirip uzaklaştırmak** *The recent bomb attacks have scared away the tourists.*

scare ...... İLE BİRLİKTE KULLANILAN KELİMELER

give sb/**have/suffer** a scare ● a **food/health** scare

scare² /skeər/ *noun* [C] **1** a sudden feeling of fear or worry **korku, ürperti, endişe, ürküntü** *The earthquake gave us a scare.* **2** a situation that worries or frightens people **panik, korkutucu/ürkütücü durum** *a food/health scare*

scarecrow /'skeəkrəʊ/ *noun* [C] a model of a person that is put in a field to frighten birds and stop them from eating the plants **bostan korkuluğu**

scared ...... BAŞKA BİR DEYİŞLE

Afraid ve **frightened** sıfatları scared sıfatına alternatif olarak kullanılabilir. *Don't be frightened. The dog won't hurt you.* ● *Gerry has always been afraid of heights.*

Eğer kişi gerçekten çok korktuysa, durumu belirtmek için **petrified, terrified, panic-stricken,** veya çok gayri resmi olarak **scared to death** söylemleri kullanılabilir. *I'm petrified/terrified of spiders.* ● *She was panic-stricken when her little boy disappeared.* ● *He's scared to death of having the operation.*

Eğer kişi bir endişesinden dolayı korkuyorsa, **afraid** veya **worried** sıfatları kullanılabilir. *I'm afraid/worried that something will go wrong.*

o--scared /skeəd/ *adjective* frightened or worried **korkmuş, tedirgin** *Robert's scared of heights.* ○ *I was scared to death* (= very frightened)*.* ○ [+ (that)] *We were scared that we'd be killed.*

scarf¹ /skɑːf/ *noun* [C] *plural* **scarves** /skɑːvz/ or **scarfs** a piece of cloth that you wear around your neck, head, or shoulders to keep warm or for decoration **atkı, eşarp, kaşkol** つOrta kısımdaki renkli sayfalarına bakınız.

scarf² /skɑːf/ (*also* scarf down) *verb* [T] *US informal* (*UK* scoff) to eat a lot of something quickly **tıkınmak, abur cubur yemek, tıka basa yemek** *Who scarfed all the cookies?*

scarlet /'skɑːlət/ *noun* [U] a bright red colour **parlak kırmızı, al** ● **scarlet** *adjective* **parlak kırmızı**

scary /'skeəri/ *adjective informal* frightening **korkutucu, ürkütücü, tedirgin eden** *a scary place/woman*

scathing /'skeıðıŋ/ *adjective* criticizing very strongly **sert, kırıcı, iğneleyici, eleştirel** *He was scathing about the report.*

scatter /'skætər/ *verb*
1 [T] to throw objects over an area so that they land apart from each other **dağıtmak, saçmak, yaymak, serpmek** *He scattered some flower seeds in the garden.* **2** [I] to suddenly move apart in different directions **sağa sola dağılmak, darma dağınık olmak, dağılmak** *The crowd scattered at the sound of gunshots.*

scatter

scattered /'skætəd/ *adjective* covering a wide area **dağılmış, saçılmış, yayılmış, dağınık** *His toys were scattered all over the floor.* ○ *There will be scattered showers* (= separate areas of rain) *today.*

scattering /'skætərıŋ/ *noun* [no plural] a small number of separate things, especially in a large area **serpinti, az miktar şey** *a scattering of houses*

scavenge /'skævındʒ/ *verb* [I, T] to search for food or for useful things that have been thrown away **çöp/süprüntü karıştırmak, çöplük karıştırarak yiyecek aramak** ● **scavenger** *noun* [C] a person or animal who scavenges **yiyeceğini çöplükten sağlayan kimse/hayvan**

scenario /sı'nɑːriəʊ/ *noun* [C] a description of a situation, or of a situation that may develop in the future **senaryo** **2 worst-case scenario** the worst situation that you can imagine **tahmin edilebilen en kötü durum**

scene /siːn/ *noun* **1** [PART OF FILM] [C] a short part of a film, play, or book in which the events happen in one place **sahne, bölüm** *a love scene* ○ *the final scene* **2** [VIEW] [C] a view or picture of a place, event, or activity **manzara, görüntü, görünüm** *scenes of everyday life* **3** [PLACE] [C] a place where an unpleasant event has happened **bir hadisenin meydana geldiği yer, mahal; olay mahalli** *the scene of the crime* **4 the club/gay/music, etc scene** all the things connected with a particular way of life or activity **yaşam/faaliyet alanı/manzarası/görüntüsü** **5** [ARGUMENT] [C] when people have a loud argument or show strong emotions in a public place **hadise, olay, kazağı, tatsızlık, patırtı** [usually singular] *She made a scene when I told her she couldn't come with us.* **6 behind the scenes** If something happens behind the scenes, it happens secretly. **saman altından, el altından, gizlice, perde arkasından** **7 set the scene for sth** to make an event or situation possible or likely to happen **mümkün kılmak, ortamı yaratmak, gerçekleştirmek, sağlamak**

scenery /'siːnəri/ *noun* [U] **1** the attractive, natural things that you see in the countryside **manzara, doğa görünümü** *The Grand Canyon is famous for its spectacular scenery.* **2** the large pictures of buildings, countryside, etc used on a theatre stage **sahne dekoru**

scenic /'siːnık/ *adjective* having views of the attractive, natural things in the countryside **güzel manzaralı** *a scenic route* ○ *an area of great scenic beauty*

scent /sent/ *noun* **1** [SMELL] [C] a pleasant smell **hoş/güzel koku** *the sweet scent of orange blossoms* **2** [LIQUID] [C, U] a pleasant smelling liquid that people put on their skin **parfüm, koku** **3** [ANIMAL] [C, U] the smell of an animal or a person that is left somewhere **hayvan/insan kokusu**

scented /'sentıd/ *adjective* having a pleasant smell **kokulu, hoş/güzel kokulu** *a scented candle*

sceptic *UK* (*US* skeptic) /'skeptık/ *noun* [C] someone who doubts that a belief or an idea is true or useful **kuşkucu/şüpheci kimse**

sceptical *UK* (*US* skeptical) /'skeptıkᵊl/ *adjective* doubting that something is true or useful **şüpheci, kuşkucu, kuşkulu, şüphe duyan** *Scientists remain sceptical about astrology.* ○ *She was sceptical of the new arrangement.*

scepticism *UK* (*US* skepticism) /'skeptısızᵊm/ *noun* [U] when you doubt that something is true or useful **şüphecilik, kuşkuculuk** *There was some scepticism about her ability to do the job.*

schedule¹ /'ʃedjuːl/ ⑥ /'skedʒuːl/ *noun* **1** [C, U] a plan that gives events or activities and the times that they will happen or be done **plân, program** *I have a very busy schedule today.* ○ *Will the work be completed on schedule* (= at the expected time)? ○ *The project was finished ahead of schedule* (= earlier than planned). **2** [C] *mainly US* a list of times when buses, trains, etc arrive and leave **otobüs/tren vb. programı**

schedule² /'ʃedjuːl/ ⑥ /'skedʒuːl/ *verb* [T] to arrange that an event or an activity will happen at a particular time **plânlamak, programlamak, programa almak** [often passive] *Your appointment has been scheduled for next Tuesday.* ○ *a scheduled flight*

┌───┐
│ **scheme** ⋯⋯ İLE BİRLİKTE KULLANILAN KELİMELER │
└───┘
come up with/devise a scheme ● **implement/introduce/launch/unveil** a scheme ● a scheme **for** doing sth

◦ **scheme¹** /skiːm/ *noun* [C] **1** *mainly UK* an official plan or system **tasarı, proje** *an insurance/savings scheme* ○ *a training scheme for teenagers* **2** a plan for making money, especially in a dishonest way **plan kurma, entrika/dolap çevirme** *a scheme to steal money from investors*

scheme² /skiːm/ *verb* [I] to make a secret plan in order to get an advantage, usually by deceiving people **entrika çevirmek, dolap çevirmek, gizli plan yapmak**

schizophrenia /ˌskıtsəʊ'friːniə/ *noun* [U] a serious mental illness in which someone cannot understand what is real and what is imaginary **şizofreni hastalığı** ● **schizophrenic** /ˌskıtsəʊ'frenık/ *noun* [C] someone who suffers from schizophrenia **şizofren kimse/hastası**

schizophrenic /ˌskıtsəʊ'frenık/ *adjective* relating to schizophrenia **şizofrenik** *schizophrenic patients/symptoms*

schmooze /ʃmuːz/ *verb* [I, T] *informal* to talk to someone in a friendly, informal way so that they will like you or do something for you **dil dökmek, sevimli görünmek,**

sempatik görünmeye çalışmak *politicians schmoozing with journalists*

scholar /'skɒlər/ *noun* [C] someone who has studied a subject and knows a lot about it **bilgin, âlim, ilim adamı** *a legal scholar*

scholarly /'skɒləli/ *adjective* **1** A scholarly article or book is a formal piece of writing by a scholar about a particular subject. **bilimsel 2** If someone is scholarly, they study a lot and know a lot about what they study. **bilgili, bilgince, âlimane**

scholarship /'skɒləʃɪp/ *noun* **1** [C] an amount of money given to a person by an organization to pay for their education, usually at a college or university **burs 2** [U] when you study a subject for a long time **ilim tahsili, bilim, derin bilgi, ilim irfanı**

scholastic /skə'læstɪk/ *adjective* [always before noun] relating to school and education **akademik, eğitimle ilgili** *scholastic achievements*

school .... İLE BİRLİKTE KULLANILAN KELİMELER

go to school ● **at** school ● a school **holiday** ● a school **year** ● school **children/kids**

o⁻**school** /skuːl/ *noun* **1** [PLACE] [C] a place where children go to be educated **okul, mektep** *Which school do you go to?* ○ *I ride my bike to school.* **2** [TIME] [U] the time that you spend at school **eğitim/tahsil süresi** *I like school.* ○ *We're going shopping after school.* **3** [PEOPLE] [no plural] all the students and teachers at a school **öğrenciler ve öğretmenler; eğitim ordusu** *The whole school took part in the project.* **4 a dance/language/riding, etc school** a place where you can study a particular subject **dans/dil/binicilik vs. okulu 5** [PART] [C] a part of a college or university **fakülte/yüksekokul** *the University of Cambridge Medical School* **6** [UNIVERSITY] [C, U] *US informal* in the US, any college or university, or the time you spend there **(ABD) fakülte/yüksekokul; eğitim süresi** *Which schools did you apply for?* **7** [FISH] [C] a group of fish or other sea animals **balık sürüsü 8 school of thought** the ideas and beliefs shared by a group of people **görüş, teori, ekol** ➲See also: **boarding school, elementary school, grade school, grammar school, high school, junior high school, junior school, middle school, night school, nursery school, prep school, preparatory school, primary school, public school, secondary school, state school.**

schoolboy /'skuːlbɔɪ/ *noun* [C] a boy who goes to school **erkek öğrenci**

schoolchild /'skuːltʃaɪld/ *noun* [C] *plural* **schoolchildren** a child who goes to school **öğrenci, okul çocuğu**

schooldays /'skuːldeɪz/ *noun* [plural] *UK* the period in your life when you go to school **okul günleri**

schoolgirl /'skuːlgɜːl/ *noun* [C] a girl who goes to school **kız öğrenci**

schooling /'skuːlɪŋ/ *noun* [U] education at school **eğitim, öğrenim/öğretim**

schoolteacher /'skuːlˌtiːtʃər/ *noun* [C] someone who teaches children in a school **öğretmen, hoca**

o⁻**science** /'saɪəns/ *noun* **1** [U] the study and knowledge of the structure and behaviour of natural things in an organized way **bilim, müspet ilim 2** [C, U] a particular type of science **dal, bölüm** *computer science* ○ *Chemistry, physics, and biology are all sciences.* ➲See also: **natural sciences, social science.**

,**science 'fiction** *noun* [U] stories about life in the future or in other parts of the universe **bilim kurgu**

o⁻**scientific** /ˌsaɪən'tɪfɪk/ *adjective* relating to science, or using the organized methods of science **bilimsel; ilmî** *scientific experiments/research* ● **scientifically** *adverb* a scientifically proven fact **bilimsel açıdan**

o⁻**scientist** /'saɪəntɪst/ *noun* [C] someone who studies science or works in science **bilim insanı**

sci-fi /'saɪˌfaɪ/ *noun* [U] *informal short for* science fiction **bilim kurgu**

scintillating /'sɪntɪleɪtɪŋ/ *adjective* very interesting or exciting **ilginç ve heyecan verici** *a scintillating performance*

scissors /'sɪzəz/ *noun* [plural] a tool for cutting paper, hair, cloth, etc that you hold in your hand and that has two blades that move against each other **makas** *a pair of scissors*

scissors

scoff /skɒf/ *verb* **1** [I] to laugh at someone or something, or criticize them in a way that shows you do not respect them **alay etmek, dalga geçmek** *The critics scoffed at his work.* **2** [I, T] *UK informal (US scarf)* to eat a lot of something quickly **tıkınmak, yalayıp yutmak** *Who scoffed all the chocolates?*

scold /skəʊld/ *verb* [T] *old-fashioned* to speak angrily to someone because they have done something wrong **azarlamak, paylamak, çıkışmak**

scone /skɒn/, /skəʊn/ *noun* [C] a small, round cake **küçük yuvarlak çörek/kek** *tea and buttered scones*

scoop[1] /skuːp/ *verb* [T] to remove something from a container using a spoon, your curved hands, etc **kaşıkla oymak/içini çıkarmak** *She scooped the ice cream into the dishes.*

scoop sth/sb up *phrasal verb* to lift someone or something with your hands **elle kaldırmak/havaya kaldırmak**

scoop[2] /skuːp/ *noun* [C] **1** a large, deep spoon for lifting and moving an amount of something, or the amount that can be held in it **kürek, bakkal küreği** *an ice cream scoop* ○ *a scoop of ice cream* **2** a piece of news discovered and printed by one newspaper before it appears anywhere else **sadece bir gazetede yayınlanan önemli haber**

scoot /skuːt/ *verb informal* **scoot along/down/over, etc** to go somewhere quickly **süratle gitmek, hızla ilerlemek/gitmek**

scooter /'skuːtər/ *noun* [C] **1** a small motorcycle **hafif motosiklet 2** a child's vehicle that has two wheels fixed to the ends of a long board and a long handle **tornet**

scope .... İLE BİRLİKTE KULLANILAN KELİMELER

expand/extend/limit/widen the scope **of** sth ● be **beyond/outside/within** the scope of sth

scope /skəʊp/ *noun* **1** [no plural] how much a subject or situation relates to **kapsam** *Do we know the full scope of the problem yet?* **2** [U] the opportunity to do something **fırsat** *There is plenty of scope for improvement.*

scorch /skɔːtʃ/ *verb* [T] to damage something with fire or heat **yakmak, kavurmak**

scorched /skɔːtʃt/ *adjective* slightly burnt, or damaged by fire or heat **yanmış, kavrulmuş** *scorched earth/fields*

scorching /'skɔːtʃɪŋ/ *adjective* very hot **çok sıcak, kavurucu** *a scorching hot day*

---

score İLE BİRLİKTE KULLANILAN KELİMELER

keep score ● even/level the score ● the final/latest score ● a score of sth ● a high/low score

---

०=**score**[1] /skɔːʳ/ *noun* **1** [C] the number of points someone gets in a game or test **sonuç, puan, sayı** *a high/low score* ○ *What's the score?* **2 scores of sth** a large number of people or things **çok sayıda insan ve şey** *Scores of teenage girls were waiting to get his autograph.* **3** [C] a printed piece of music **partisyon 4 on that/this score** about the thing or subject which you have just discussed **bu/o yüzden, bu/o konuda** *The company will pay your travel expenses, so don't worry on that score.*

०=**score**[2] /skɔːʳ/ *verb* [I, T] to get points in a game or test **puan kazanmak, üstünlük sağlamak** *He scored just before half-time to put Liverpool 2-1 ahead.*

scoreboard /'skɔːbɔːd/ *noun* [C] a large board which shows the score of a game **puan tabelası/tahtası**

scorer /skɔːrəʳ/ *noun* [C] a player who scores points in a game **golcü, puan kazandıran oyuncu, skorer** *Domingo was Italy's top scorer.*

scorn /skɔːn/ *noun* [U] *formal* the feeling that something is stupid and does not deserve your respect **küçümseme, aşağılama, hor görme, azarlama ● scorn** *verb* [T] *formal* to show scorn for someone or something **hor görmek, küçümsemek, aşağılamak, tenezzül etmemek** *You scorned all my suggestions.*

scornful /'skɔːnfᵊl/ *adjective formal* showing that you think something is stupid and does not deserve your respect **küçümseyen/küçümseyici; aşağılayan/aşağılayıcı; hor gören/görücü** *I'm very scornful of any findings that lack proper scientific data.* ● **scornfully** *adverb* **hakaret içeren şekilde**

Scorpio /'skɔːpiəʊ/ *noun* [C, U] the sign of the zodiac which relates to the period of 23 October - 21 November, or a person born during this period **Akrep Burcu** ⊃See picture at **zodiac**.

scorpion /'skɔːpiən/ *noun* [C] a small, insect-like creature with a curved, poisonous tail **akrep**

Scotch /skɒtʃ/ (*also* ‚Scotch 'whisky) *noun* [C, U] a type of whisky (= strong alcoholic drink) **bir tür viski**

‚Scotch 'tape *US trademark* (*UK trademark* **Sellotape**) *noun* [U] clear, thin tape used for sticking things, especially paper, together **bant, yapıştırıcı bant** ⊃Orta kısımdaki renkli sayfalarına bakınız.

the Scots /skɒts/ *noun* [plural] the people of Scotland **İskoç halkı**

Scottish /'skɒtɪʃ/ *adjective* relating to Scotland **İskoçya'ya ait** *Scottish history*

scour /skaʊəʳ/ *verb* [T] **1** to search for something very carefully, often over a large area **karış karış aramak, didik didik etmek, arayıp taramak** *The police scoured the surrounding countryside for possible clues.* **2** to clean something by rubbing it with something rough **ovmak, ovarak temizlemek**

scourge /skɜːdʒ/ *noun formal* **the scourge of sth** something which causes a lot of suffering or trouble **belâ, musibet, kötülük, âfet, felâket** *Drug-related crime is the scourge of modern society.*

scout[1] /skaʊt/ *noun* **1** [C] (*also* Boy Scout) a member of an organization for young people which teaches them practical skills and encourages them to be good members of society **izci 2 the Scouts** an organization for young people which teaches them practical skills and encourages them to be good members of society **izcilik teşkilatı 3** [C] someone whose job is to find good musi-

cians, sports people, etc to join an organization **organizatör** *a talent scout*

scout[2] /skaʊt/ (*also* scout around) *verb* [I] to try to find something by looking in different places **bulmaya çalışmak, aramak** *I'm scouting around for somewhere to park.*

scowl /skaʊl/ *verb* [I] to look at someone angrily **kaş çatmak, suratını ekşitmek, yüzünü buruşturmak** *He scowled at me from behind his paper.* ● **scowl** *noun* [C] **kaşlarını çatarak bakma**

scrabble /'skræbl/ *verb*
scrabble about/around *phrasal verb* to use your fingers to quickly find something that you cannot see **el yordamıyla aramak/bulmak/bulmaya çalışmak** *She scrabbled around in her bag, trying to find her keys.*

scramble /'skræmbl/ *verb* **1 scramble down/out/up, etc** to move or climb quickly but with difficulty, often using your hands **ellerin yardımıyla güçlükle tırmanmak** *We scrambled up the hill.* **2** [I] to compete with other people for something which there is very little of **çabalamak, az olan bir şeyi kapmak için yarışmak** [+ to do sth] *New teachers scramble to get jobs in the best schools.* ● **scramble** *noun* [no plural] *There was a mad scramble for places near the front.* **kapışma**

‚scrambled 'eggs *noun* [plural] eggs which are mixed together and then cooked **çırpılıp yağda pişirilmiş yumurta**

scrap[1] /skræp/ *noun* **1** SMALL PIECE [C] a small piece or amount of something **parça, kırıntı** *He wrote his phone number on a scrap of paper.* ○ *I've read every scrap of information I can find on the subject.* **2** OLD [U] old cars and machines that are not now needed but have parts which can be used to make other things **hurdalık, hurdalar, demir yığını** *scrap metal* ○ *The car was so badly damaged we could only sell it as scrap.* **3** FIGHT [C] *informal* a fight or an argument, usually not very serious **hırgür, ağız dalaşı, münakaşa, kavga, dövüş** *He was always getting into scraps at school.*

scrap[2] /skræp/ *verb* [T] **scrapping**, *past* **scrapped 1** *informal* to not continue with a plan or idea **devam etmemek, vazgeçmek** *That project has now been scrapped.* **2** to get rid of something which you do not now want **ıskartaya çıkarmak, atıp kurtulmak, hurdaya çıkarmak**

scrapbook /'skræpbʊk/ *noun* [C] a book with empty pages where you can stick newspaper articles, pictures, etc, that you have collected and want to keep **yapıştırma albümü**

scrape[1] /skreɪp/ *verb* [T] **1** to damage the surface of something by rubbing it against something rough **kazımak, sıyırmak** *Jamie fell over and scraped his knee.* **2** to remove something from a surface using a sharp edge **kazıyarak çıkarmak, sıyırmak, kazımak** *The next morning I had to scrape the ice off the car.* **3 scrape a win/draw/pass** *UK* to succeed in a test or competition but with difficulty **zorluklara rağmen sınav ya da yarışmada başarılı olmak** *France scraped a 3-2 win over Norway.*
scrape by *phrasal verb* to manage to live when you do not have enough money **kıt kanaat geçinmek**
scrape through (sth) *phrasal verb* to succeed in something but with a lot of difficulty **güç bela başarmak, kıl payı ile geçmek** *I scraped through my exams* (= just passed).
scrape sth together *phrasal verb* to manage with a lot of difficulty to get enough of something, often money **güçlükle biriktirmek, dişinden tırnağından artırarak biriktirmek** *I finally scraped together enough money for a flight home.*

scrape² /skreɪp/ *noun* [C] **1** the slight damage caused when you rub a surface with something rough **sür-tünme izi, yara bere, çizik, sıyrık** *He suffered a few cuts and scrapes but nothing serious.* **2** *informal* a difficult or dangerous situation which you cause yourself **sıkıntı, belâ, musibet, müşkül durum, varta** *She's always getting into scrapes.*

scrappy /'skræpi/ *adjective* **1** *UK* untidy or organized badly **düzensiz, darma dağınık, allak bullak** *They won but it was a scrappy match.* **2** *US* determined to win or achieve something **kararlı, azimli** *a scrappy competitor*

scratch¹ /skrætʃ/ *verb* **1** RUB SKIN [I, T] to rub your skin with your nails, often to stop it itching (= feeling unpleasant) **kaşımak, çizmek, sıyırmak, hafifçe yırtmak** *He scratched his head.* **2** HURT/DAMAGE [T] to make a slight cut or long, thin mark with a sharp object **çizmek, tırmalamak, sivri bir şeyle çizerek yaralamak** *The surface was all scratched.* ○ *I scratched myself on the roses.* **3** RUB SURFACE [I, T] to rub a hard surface with a sharp object, often making a noise **kazımak, kazıyarak çıkarmak** *I could hear the cat scratching at the door.*

scratch² /skrætʃ/ *noun* **1** [C] a slight cut or a long, thin mark made with a sharp object **çizik, sıyrık, hafif yırtık** *I've got all these scratches on my arm from the cat.* **2** [no plural] when you rub your skin with your nails, often to stop it itching (= feeling unpleasant) **kaşıma** *Could you give my back a scratch?* **3 from scratch** If you do something from scratch, you do it from the beginning. **sıfırdan, ilk başından 4 not be/come up to scratch** *informal* to not be good enough **yeterli düzeyde olmamak** *She told me my work wasn't up to scratch.*

scrawl /skrɔːl/ *verb* [T] to write something quickly so that it is untidy **karalamak, çiziktirmek, kargacık burgacık yazmak** *She scrawled a note, but I couldn't read it.* • **scrawl** *noun* [C, U] **karalama**

scrawny /'skrɔːni/ *adjective* too thin **sıska, bir deri bir kemik, iskelet gibi** *a scrawny neck*

o-<**scream¹** /skriːm/ *verb* [I, T] to make a loud, high noise with your voice, or to shout something in a loud, high voice because you are afraid, hurt, or angry **çığlık atmak, feryat etmek, acı acı bağırmak, haykırmak** *She screamed for help.* ○ *I could hear a woman screaming, "Get me out of here!"*

🧩 **scream** ...... İLE BİRLİKTE KULLANILAN KELİMELER

let out a scream • a **blood-curdling/piercing/shrill** scream • a scream **of** [horror/pain/shock, etc]

scream² /skriːm/ *noun* **1** [C] when someone screams **çığlık, feryat, haykırma** *We heard screams coming from their apartment.* ○ *We heard a blood curdling scream.* **2 be a scream** *informal* to be very funny **komik olmak, matraklık yapmak** *You'd love Amanda - she's a scream.*

screech /skriːtʃ/ *verb* **1** [I, T] to make an unpleasant, high, loud sound **tiz ve keskin ses çıkarmak; bağırmak, feryat etmek** *A car came screeching around the corner.* ○ *She was screeching at him at the top of her voice.* **2 screech to a halt/stop** If a vehicle screeches to a halt, it suddenly stops, making a loud sound. **acı fren sesi çıkararak durmak** • **screech** *noun* [C] *We could hear the screech of brakes.* **çığlık**

o-<**screen¹** /skriːn/ *noun* **1** COMPUTER/TV [C] the part of a television or computer which shows images or writing **ekran, perde** *I spend most of my day working in front of a computer screen.* **2 on screen** using a computer **bilgisayar kullanma** *Do you work on screen?* **3** FILM SURFACE [C] a large, flat surface where a film or an image is shown **sinema perdesi 4** CINEMA [U, no plural]

screen

cinema screen *UK,* movie screen *US*

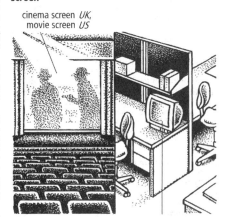

computer screen

cinema films **sinema filmleri** *an actor of stage and screen* (= theatre and films) ○ *She first appeared on screen in 1965.* **5** NET [C] a wire net which covers a window or door and is used to stop insects coming in **sineklik 6** SEPARATE [C] a vertical structure which is used to separate one area from another **ara bölme, perde, paravana**

screen² /skriːn/ *verb* [T] **1** MEDICAL to find out if people have an illness by doing medical tests on them **tıbbî testlerle hastalığı teşhis etmek** *Babies are routinely screened for the condition.* **2** GET INFORMATION to find out information about someone in order to decide if they are suitable for a particular job **soruşturmak, soruşturma yapmak, araştırmak** *Applicants are screened to ensure that none of them is a security risk.* **3** SHOW to show something on television or at a cinema **televizyonda sinemada göstermek/oynatmak** [often passive] *The first episode will be screened tonight.*

screen sth off *phrasal verb* to separate one area from another using a vertical structure **perde ile bölmek, paravana ile ayırmak** *Part of the room is screened off and used as an office.*

screenplay /'skriːnpleɪ/ *noun* [C] a story that is written for television or for a film **senaryo, oyun**

'screen ˌsaver (**screensaver**) *noun* [C] a program to protect a computer screen that automatically shows a moving image if the computer is not used for a few minutes **ekran koruyucu**

screw¹ /skruː/ *noun* [C] a small, pointed piece of metal that you turn round and round to fix things together, especially pieces of wood **vida** ➔See picture at **tool.**

screw² /skruː/ *verb* **1 screw sth down/to/onto, etc** to fasten something with a screw **vidalamak, vidayla tutturmak** *You need to screw the cabinet to the wall.* **2 screw sth on/down/together, etc** to fasten something by turning it round until it is tight, or to be fastened this way **çevirerek sıkmak, dönerek sıkmak** *The lid is screwed on so tight I can't get it off.* ➔Opposite **unscrew. 3 screw up your eyes/face** to move the muscles of your face so that your eyes become narrow **gözlerini kırpıştırmak, yüzünü buruşturmak** *He screwed up his eyes in the bright sunlight.*

screw (sth) up *phrasal verb informal* to make a mistake, or to spoil something **bozmak, berbat etmek, yüzüne gözüne bulaştırmak** *I screwed up my exams last year.*

screw sth up *phrasal verb* to twist and crush a piece of paper with your hands **elleriyle kağıdı buruşturmak** *She screwed the letter up and threw it in the bin.*

screwdriver /'skru:,draɪvəʳ/ *noun* [C] a tool for turning screws **tornavida** ⊃See picture at **tool.**

screwed-up /,skru:d'ʌp/ *adjective informal* If someone is screwed-up, they are unhappy and anxious because they have had a lot of bad experiences. **mutsuz, endişeli, kötü günler geçirmiş, hayatı altüst olmuş**

scribble /'skrɪbl/ *verb* [I, T] to write or draw something quickly and carelessly **çalakalem yazmak, çiziktirmek, karalamak** *She scribbled some notes in her book.* ● **scribble** *noun* [C, U] something that has been scribbled **karalama, kargacık burgacık yazı, çalakalem yazı**

script /skrɪpt/ *noun* **1** [C] the words in a film, play, etc **senaryo, film/oyun metni** *He wrote a number of film scripts.* **2** [C, U] a set of letters used for writing a particular language **yazı, alfabe** *Arabic/Roman script*

scripted /'skrɪptɪd/ *adjective* A scripted speech or broadcast has been written before it is read or performed. **yazılı, metin hâline getirilmiş**

scripture /'skrɪptʃəʳ/ *(also* the scriptures*) noun* [U] the holy books of a religion **kutsal kitaplar**

scriptwriter /'skrɪpt,raɪtəʳ/ *noun* [C] someone who writes the words for films or radio or television programmes **(film, radyo, televizyon) metin yazarı**

scroll¹ /skrəʊl/ *noun* [C] a long roll of paper with writing on it, used especially in the past **üzerinde yazılar olan kağıt rulo/tomar**

scroll² /skrəʊl/ *verb* **scroll up/down/through, etc** to move text or an image on a computer screen so that you can look at the part that you want **bilgisayar ekranında metni taramak**

scrollbar /'skrəʊlbɑ:ʳ/ *noun* [C] on a computer screen, a thin rectangle on the side or bottom that you use to move text or an image **bilgisayar ekranında tarama çubuğu**

scrooge /skru:dʒ/ *noun* [C] *informal* someone who spends very little money **eli sıkı/tutumlu kimse**

scrounge /skraʊndʒ/ *verb* [I, T] *informal* to get something from someone else instead of paying for it yourself **ondan bundan dilenmek, beleşçilik yapmak, bedavaya konmak** *He's always scrounging money off you.*

scrub¹ /skrʌb/ *verb* [I, T] **scrubbing**, *past* **scrubbed** to clean something by rubbing it hard with a brush **ovmak/ovalamak, fırçalayarak/ovalayarak temizlemek/çıkarmak** *to scrub the floor*

scrub² /skrʌb/ *noun* **1** [U] bushes and small trees that grow in a dry area **çalılık, fundalık 2** [no plural] when you clean something by rubbing it with a brush **ovalama, fırçalama, temizleme** *I gave my hands a scrub.*

scruff /skrʌf/ *noun* **by the scruff of the/your neck** by the back of the neck **ensesinden, ense kökünden** *She picked the cat up by the scruff of its neck.*

scruffy /'skrʌfi/ *adjective* dirty and untidy **pis, pasaklı, pejmurde, bakımsız** *scruffy jeans* ○ *I don't like to look scruffy.*

scruple /'skru:pl/ *noun* [C] a belief that something is wrong which stops you from doing that thing **vicdan azabı, iç sızlaması, suçluluk duygusu** [usually plural] *She has no scruples about accepting bribes.*

scrupulous /'skru:pjələs/ *adjective* **1** very careful and giving great attention to details **titiz, çok dikkatli, en ince ayrıntıyı bile kaçırmayan, kılı kırk yaran** *He's very scrupulous about making sure that all the facts are checked.* **2** always honest and fair **adil, dürüst, vicdanlı** ⊃Opposite **unscrupulous.**

scrutinize *(also UK* -ise*)* /'skru:tɪnaɪz/ *verb* [T] to examine something very carefully **iyice incelemek, dikkatle gözden geçirmek** *The evidence was carefully scrutinized.*

be under/come under scrutiny ● **careful/close/ rigorous** scrutiny ● **public** scrutiny

scrutiny /'skru:tɪni/ *noun* [U] when you examine something carefully **inceleme, araştırma, tetkik** *Every aspect of her life came under public scrutiny.*

scuba diving /'sku:bə,daɪvɪŋ/ *noun* [U] a sport in which you swim under water using special equipment for breathing **tüplü dalış, dalma sporu**

scuff /skʌf/ *verb* [T] to make a mark on your shoes by rubbing them against something rough **ayaklarını sürümek**

scuffle /'skʌfl/ *noun* [C] a short fight in which people push each other **itiş kakış, arbede, dövüş, kavga, boğuşma** *A scuffle broke out* (= started) *behind the courtroom.*

sculptor /'skʌlptəʳ/ *noun* [C] someone who makes sculpture **heykeltraş**

sculpture /'skʌlptʃəʳ/ *noun* **1** [C, U] a piece of art that is made from stone, wood, clay, etc **heykeltraşlık, heykelcilik** *a wooden sculpture* ○ *modern sculpture* **2** [U] the art of making objects from stone, wood, clay, etc **heykeltraşlık sanatı** *She teaches sculpture at an art school.*

scum /skʌm/ *noun* **1** [U, no plural] an unpleasant, thick substance on the surface of a liquid **sıvı üstünde kirli tabaka, birikinti, köpük, kir tabakası 2** [U] *informal* an offensive way of referring to a very bad person **pislik/ayaktakımı kişi; (argo) boktan/beş para etmez kimse**

scurry /'skʌri/ *verb* **scurry along/around/away, etc** to walk quickly or run because you are in a hurry **telaşla koşmak, aceleyle gitmek**

scuttle /'skʌtl/ *verb* **scuttle across/along/away, etc** to run quickly using short steps **kısa adımlarla hızlı hızlı koşmak** *A beetle scuttled across the floor.*

scythe /saɪð/ *noun* [C] a tool with a long handle and a curved blade that is used to cut tall grass and crops **tırpan**

⚬⁺**sea** /si:/ *noun* **1** [C, U] a large area of salt water **deniz** *I'd like to live by the sea.* ○ *It was our third day at sea* (= travelling on the sea). ○ *It's cheaper to send parcels by sea* (= on a ship). **2 Sea** a particular area of salt water ... **Denizi** *the North Sea* ○ *the Black Sea* **3** a sea of sth a large number of something **yığın, küme, kalabalık** *He looked across the room and saw a sea of faces.*

seabed /'si:bed/ *noun* [no plural] the floor of the sea **deniz tabanı**

seafood /'si:fu:d/ *noun* [U] animals from the sea that are eaten as food, especially animals that live in shells **deniz mahsulü/ürünü**

seafront /'si:frʌnt/ *noun* [C] *UK* a part of a town that is next to the sea **kasaba rıhtımı** [usually singular] *We walked along the seafront.*

seagull /'si:gʌl/ *noun* [C] a grey and white bird that lives near the sea **martı**

seagull

seahorse /'si:hɔ:s/ *noun* [C] a small fish that has a head and neck the same shape as a horse's **denizatı**

seal¹ /si:l/ *noun* [C] **1** ANIMAL an animal with smooth fur that eats fish and lives near the sea **ayı balığı 2** ON A CONTAINER a piece of paper or plastic on a container that you break in order to open it **bir şeyin kullanılmadığını ve açılmadığını gösteren kâğıt veya plastik kapak/sargı/bant vs. 3** OFFICIAL MARK an official mark made of wax, paper, or metal that is put on important documents **mühür, damga, kaşe 4** STOP LIQUID/AIR an object or substance that stops liquid or air from leaving or entering a container **kapak, tıpa, mantar**

seal² /si:l/ *verb* [T] **1** (*also* **seal up**) to close an entrance or container so that air or liquid cannot enter or leave it **kapamak, tıpamak, ağzını tıkamak** *She quickly sealed up the bottle.* **2** to close a letter or parcel by sticking the edges together **zarf/paket ağzını yapıştırarak kapamak** *to seal an envelope*
seal sth off *phrasal verb* to prevent people from entering an area or building, often because it is dangerous **giriş çıkışı engellemek, tecrit etmek, tehlikeden ötürü giriş çıkışa izin vermemek** *Police immediately sealed off the streets.*

'sea ,level *noun* [U] the level of the sea's surface, used to measure the height of an area of land **deniz seviyesi**

'sea ,lion *noun* [C] a large seal (= sea animal) **deniz aslanı**

seam /si:m/ *noun* [C] **1** a line of sewing where two pieces of cloth have been joined together **dikiş, dikiş yeri 2** a long, thin layer of coal under the ground **taş kömürü tabakası, katmanı, damarı**

seaman /'si:mən/ *noun* [C] *plural* **seamen** a sailor **denizci**

seance /'seɪɒns/ *noun* [C] a meeting at which people try to communicate with spirits of dead people **ruh çağırma toplantısı, seans**

o▪**search¹** /sɜ:tʃ/ *verb* **1** TRY TO FIND [I, T] to try to find someone or something **araştırmak, aramak** *I've searched my bedroom but I can't find my watch.* ○ *Police are still searching the woods for the missing girl.* **2** POLICE [T] If the police search someone, they look in their clothes and bags to see if they are hiding anything illegal, such as drugs. **(polis) aramak, arama yapmak** *They were searched at the airport.* **3** FIND ANSWER [I] to try to find an answer to a problem **cevabını aramak, bulmaya çalışmak** *Doctors are still searching for a cure.*

search (noun) ...... İLE BİRLİKTE KULLANILAN KELİMELER
carry out/conduct/make/mount a search ● **abandon/call off** a search ● a **desperate/frantic/painstaking** search ● a search **for** sb/sth ● **in search of** sb/sth

o▪**search²** /sɜ:tʃ/ *noun* **1** [C] when you try to find someone or something **arama tarama, araştırma** [usually singular] *Police are continuing their search for the missing girl.* ○ *They went off in search of* (= to find) *a bar.* **2** [no plural] when you try to find an answer to a problem **cevabını arama** *the search for happiness*

'search ,engine *noun* [C] a computer program which finds information on the Internet by looking for words which you have typed in **bilgisayar arama motoru** ➋See study page **The Web and the Internet** on page Centre 36.

searching /sɜ:tʃɪŋ/ *adjective* A searching question or look is intended to discover the truth about something. **araştırıcı, sorgulayıcı**

'search ,party *noun* [C] a group of people who look for someone who is lost **arama ekibi/grubu**

'search ,warrant *noun* [C] an official document that allows the police to search a building **arama izni/emri**

searing /sɪərɪŋ/ *adjective* [always before noun] extreme and unpleasant **şiddetli, acı veren, sızlayan** *searing pain/heat*

'sea ,shell *noun* [C] the empty shell of some types of sea animals **deniz kabuğu**

the seashore /'si:ʃɔ:r/ *noun* the area of land along the edge of the sea **sahil, deniz kıyısı**

seasick /'si:sɪk/ *adjective* feeling ill because of the way a boat is moving **deniz tutmuş**

the seaside /'si:saɪd/ *noun* an area or town next to the sea **kıyı, sahil, deniz kenarı/kıyısı** *We had a picnic at the seaside.* ○ *a seaside resort/community*

o▪**season¹** /'si:zən/ *noun* [C] **1** PART OF YEAR one of the four periods of the year; winter, spring, summer, or autumn **mevsim 2** SPECIAL TIME a period of the year when a particular thing happens **mevsim, sezon** [usually singular] *the holiday season* ○ *the rainy/dry season* ○ *the football season* **3 in season a** FRUIT/VEGETABLES If vegetables or fruit are in season, they are available and ready to eat. **mevsimi, mevsiminde b** ANIMALS If a female animal is in season, she is ready to mate. **(dişi hayvan) çiftleşme mevsimi 4 out of season c** FRUIT/VEGETABLES If vegetables or fruit are out of season, they are not usually available at that time. **mevsimi değil, mevsim dışı, mevsimsiz d** FEW PEOPLE If you go somewhere out of season, you go during a period of the year when few people are there. **sezon dışı, sezon sonrası**

season² /'si:zən/ *verb* [T] to add salt or spices to food that you are cooking **yemeklere tuz ve baharat katmak; çeşnilendirmek**

seasonal /'si:zənəl/ *adjective* happening or existing only at a particular time of the year **mevsimlik** *a seasonal worker* ○ *the seasonal migration of birds*

seasoned /'si:zənd/ *adjective* [always before noun] having a lot of experience of doing something **deneyimli, tecrübeli, kurt, usta, görmüş geçirmiş** *a seasoned traveller*

seasoning /'si:zənɪŋ/ *noun* [C, U] salt or spices that you add to food **çeşni, baharat**

'season ,ticket *UK* (*US* ,season 'ticket) *noun* [C] a ticket that you can use many times without having to pay each time **abonman bileti**

seat ...... İLE BİRLİKTE KULLANILAN KELİMELER
have/take a seat ● **in/on** a seat ● the **back/driver's/front/passenger** seat

seat¹ /si:t/ *noun* [C] **1** SIT something that you sit on **oturacak yer, sandalye, koltuk, oturak** *Please, have/take a seat* (= sit down). ○ *I've booked three seats for the cinema tonight.* ○ *the back/front seat of a car* **2** PART the flat part of a chair, bicycle, etc that you sit on **sandalyenin, bisikletin vs. oturacak yeri 3** POLITICS a position in a parliament or other group that makes official decisions **parlamentoda sandalye, koltuk, temsilci** *a seat in parliament* ○ *a congressional seat*

seat² /si:t/ *verb* **1 seat yourself in/on/next to, etc** to sit somewhere **oturmak** *I seated myself next to the fire.* **2 be seated a** to be sitting down **oturmuş, oturuyor olmak** *The director was seated on his right.* **b** used to politely ask a group of people to sit down **'Lütfen oturunuz!'** *Would the people at the back please be seated.* **3 seat 4/12/200, etc** If a building, room, or vehicle seats a particular number of people, that many people can sit in it. **kişilik, kişi kapasiteli; ...koltuklu**

S

'seat ˌbelt

'seat ˌbelt noun [C] a strap that you fasten across your body when travelling in a vehicle **emniyet kemeri** to *fasten your seat belt* ➾Orta kısımdaki renkli sayfalarına bakınız.

seating /'si:tɪŋ/ noun [U] the seats in a public place, or the way that they are arranged **oturma yerleri, oturma düzeni**

seaweed /'si:wi:d/ noun [U] a plant that you find on the beach and that grows in the sea **deniz yosunu**

sec /sek/ noun [C] informal a very short time **saniye** *Just a sec - I'm nearly ready.*

secluded /sɪ'klu:dɪd/ adjective If a place is secluded, it is quiet and not near people. **gözden ırak, kuytu, tenha, köşe** *a secluded beach/garden*

seclusion /sɪ'klu:ʒn/ noun [U] when someone lives alone, away from other people **yalnızlık, inziva, gözlerden uzak olma** *He lived in seclusion for the rest of his life.*

⚬▪**second¹** /'sekənd/ adjective, pronoun **1** referring to the person, thing, or event that comes immediately after the first **ikinci** *You're second on the list.* ○ *This is my second piece of chocolate cake.* ○ *She didn't win but she did come second (= was the one after the winner) in one race.* **2** 2nd written as a word **ikinci** ➾See also: second best, second-hand, second language, second nature, the second person, second-rate, second thought, second wind.

⚬▪**second²** /'sekənd/ noun [C] **1** [TIME] one of the 60 parts a minute is divided into **saniye** **2** [SHORT TIME] informal a very short period of time **an, saniye** *I'll be back in just a second.* **3** [PRODUCT] something that is sold cheaply because it is damaged or not in perfect condition **defolu/özürlü mallar/eşyalar** [usually plural] *Some of those towels are seconds.*

second³ /'sekənd/ verb [T] to formally support an idea at a meeting **desteklemek, destek vermek** [often passive] *The chairperson's proposal was seconded by Ms Jones.*

second⁴ /sɪ'kɒnd/ verb [T] UK to send someone to another job for a fixed period of time **geçici göreve ata(n)mak/gönder(il)mek** [often passive] *He was seconded from the police to the Department of Transport.*

secondary /'sekəndəri/ adjective **1** relating to the education of students aged between 11 and 18 **orta öğretim** *secondary education* **2** less important than something else **ikinci derecede, ikinci derecede olan** *What matters is the size of the office. The location is of secondary importance.*

'secondary ˌschool noun [C] mainly UK a school for students aged between 11 and 18 **lise/orta öğretim**

ˌsecond 'best adjective not the best but the next best **ikinci en iyi** *the second best candidate* ● **second best** noun [U] **ikinci en iyi**

second-class /ˌsekənd'klɑ:s/ adjective **1** [TRAVEL] relating to the less expensive way of travelling in a train, aircraft, etc, that most people use **ikinci mevki** *a second-class carriage/ticket* **2** [NOT IMPORTANT] less important than other people **ikinci sınıf** *Women are still treated as second-class citizens.* **3** [UNIVERSITY] A second-class university degree is a good degree but not the best possible. **iyi derece üniversite diploması** ● **second class** adverb *We always travel second class.* **ikinci sınıf, ikinci kalite**

second-guess /ˌsekənd'ges/ verb [T] to guess what someone will do in the future **tahminde bulunmak, gelecekle ilgili yorum yapmak**

second-hand /ˌsekənd'hænd/ adjective, adverb If something is second-hand, someone else owned or used it before you. **kullanılmış, ikinci el, elden düşme**

second-hand *books/clothes* ○ *She buys a lot of clothes second-hand.*

ˌsecond 'language noun [C] a language that you speak that is not the first language you learned as a child **ikinci dil**

secondly /'sekəndli/ adverb used for introducing the second reason, idea, etc **ikinci olarak** *I want two things: firstly, more money, and secondly, better working hours.*

ˌsecond 'nature noun [U] something that you can do easily because you have done it many times before **meleke, kazanılmış yeti** *After a few years, teaching became second nature to me.*

the ˌsecond 'person noun the form of a verb or pronoun that is used when referring to the person being spoken or written to. For example 'you' is a second person pronoun **(dilbilgisi) ikinci şahıs**

second-rate /ˌsekənd'reɪt/ adjective of bad quality **ikinci derecede/sınıf; bir alt kalitede olan, aşağı derecede** *a second-rate writer*

ˌsecond 'thought noun **1 on second thoughts** UK used when you want to change a decision you have made **iyice düşündükten sonra, yeniden gözden geçirerek, kararını bir kez daha düşünerek** *I'll have tea, please - on second thoughts, make that coffee.* **2 without a second thought** If you do something without a second thought, you do it without first considering if you should do it or not. **tereddütsüz, hiç tereddüt etmeden, hiç kuşkusuz** *She'll spend a hundred pounds on a dress without a second thought.* **3 have second thoughts** to change your opinion about something or start to doubt it **kararsız olmak, pek emin olamamak, şüphesi olmak, tereddütlü olmak** [+ about + doing sth] *I've been having second thoughts about doing the course.*

ˌsecond 'wind noun [no plural] a return of energy that makes it possible to continue an activity **enerjik hissetme, kendine gelme, gücünü toplama, bir şevk gelmesi** *I was feeling tired, but I got my second wind after lunch.*

⊞ **secrecy** .... İLE BİRLİKTE KULLANILAN KELİMELER

be shrouded in secrecy ● do sth in secrecy ● absolute/strict secrecy ● the secrecy of/surrounding sth

secrecy /'si:krəsi/ noun [U] when something is kept secret **gizlilik, mahremiyet** *Politicians criticized the secrecy surrounding the air attack.*

⚬▪**secret¹** /'si:krət/ adjective **1** If something is secret, other people are not allowed to know about it. **gizli, mahrem** *a secret affair/meeting* ○ *I'll tell you but you must keep it secret.* **2 secret admirer/drinker, etc** someone who does something or feels something without telling other people about it **gizli hayran; saklı gizli içki içen** ● **secretly** adverb *He secretly taped their conversation.* ➾See also: top-secret. **gizlice**

⊞ **secret** .... İLE BİRLİKTE KULLANILAN KELİMELER

keep a secret ● let sb in on/reveal/tell sb a secret ● a big/closely-guarded/well-kept secret

⚬▪**secret²** /'si:krət/ noun [C] **1** something that you tell no one about or only a few people **sır, esrar** *I'm having a party for him but it's a secret.* ○ *Can you keep a secret?* **2 the secret** the best way of achieving something **sır** *So what's the secret of your success?* **3 in secret** without telling other people **gizlice, el altından, gizli olarak** *For years they met in secret.*

ˌsecret 'agent noun [C] someone who tries to find out secret information, especially about another country **gizli ajan**

secretarial /ˌsekrəˈteəriəl/ adjective relating to the work of a secretary (= office worker who types letters, etc) **sekreterlik, sekreterlikle ilgili** *secretarial skills*

o--**secretary** /ˈsekrətˤri/ noun [C] **1** someone who works in an office, typing letters, answering the telephone, and arranging meetings, etc **sekreter 2** (also **Secretary**) an official who is in charge of a large department of the government **bakan** *the Secretary of State*

secrete /sɪˈkriːt/ verb [T] to produce a substance **salgılamak, çıkarmak** *A mixture of substances are secreted by cells within the stomach.* ● **secretion** /sɪˈkriːʃˤn/ noun [C, U] **salgı**

secretive /ˈsiːkrətɪv/ adjective not willing to tell people what you know or what you are doing **ağzı sıkı, sır saklayan, ketum** *He's very secretive about his relationships.* ● **secretively** adverb **ağzı sıkı, sır tutar şekilde**

,**Secret 'Service** noun [no plural] **1** in the UK, a department of the government that tries to find out secret information about foreign countries (**İng.**) **gizli servis 2** in the US, a government organization that protects the president (**ABD**) **başkanın gizli koruma teşkilâtı**

sect /sekt/ noun [C] a group of people with a set of religious or political beliefs, often extreme beliefs **mezhep, tarikat, cemaat, fırka**

sectarian /sekˈteəriən/ adjective relating to the differences between religious groups **mezhepçilik/tarikatçılık/ayrılıkçı/hiziple ilgili** *sectarian violence*

o--**section** /ˈsekʃˤn/ noun [C] **1** one of the parts that something is divided into **bölüm, kısım** *a non-smoking section in a restaurant* ○ *the business section of a newspaper* ○ *the tail section of an aircraft* **2** a model or drawing of something that shows how it would look if it were cut from top to bottom and seen from the side **kesit** ⊃See also: **cross-section**.

sector /ˈsektər/ noun [C] **1** one part of a country's economy **sektör** *the private/public sector* ○ *the financial/manufacturing sector* **2** one of the parts that an area is divided into **kesim, bölüm** *the British sector of the North Sea*

secular /ˈsekjələr/ adjective not religious or not controlled by a religious group **dinî olmayan, laik, dinin kontrolünde olmayan** *secular education* ○ *a secular state*

secure¹ /sɪˈkjʊər/ adjective **1** [NOT FAIL] not likely to fail or be lost **güvenli, emniyette, emin, garantili** *a secure investment/job* **2** [SAFE] safe from danger **güvenli, emniyetli, sağlam** *I don't feel that the house is secure.* **3** [CONFIDENT] confident about yourself and the situation that you are in **güvencesi olan, güvenceli** *I need to feel secure in a relationship.* **4** [FIXED] firmly fastened and not likely to fail or break **sağlam, emniyetli, güvende, sıkı sıkıya bağlanmış, iyi tutturulmuş** *Check that all windows and doors are secure.* ⊃Opposite **insecure**.

secure² /sɪˈkjʊər/ verb [T] **1** [ACHIEVE] to achieve something, after a lot of effort **elde etmek, ele geçirmek, temin etmek, başarmak** *to secure the future of hostages* **2** [FASTEN] to fasten something firmly **sıkıca tutturmak, bağlamak, emniyete almak** *He secured the bike to the gate.* **3** [MAKE SAFE] to make something safe **güvenli hâle getirmek, korumak, güven altına almak**

securely /sɪˈkjʊəli/ adverb If something is securely fastened, it will not fall or become loose. **sağlam şekilde, güvenli biçimde, sağlam olarak**

security ...... İLE BİRLİKTE KULLANILAN KELİMELER

lax/tight security ● security **arrangements/checks** ● a security **breach/guard/lapse/operation/risk** ● **national** security

security /sɪˈkjʊərəti/ noun [U] **1** [BEING SAFE] the things that are done to keep someone or something safe **güvenlik, emniyet** *airport/national security* ○ *a security alarm* **2** [SAFE SITUATION] when something is not likely to fail or be lost **sağlamlık, emniyette olma, güvende olma** *financial security* ○ *job security* **3** [CONFIDENCE] confidence about yourself and the situation that you are in **güvence, kendine güven** ●Opposite *the security of a long-term relationship.* ⊃Opposite **insecurity**. **4** [BORROWING] something valuable that you offer to give someone when you borrow money if you cannot pay the money back **güvence, garanti** ⊃See also: **social security**.

sedan /sɪˈdæn/ *US* (*UK* **saloon**) noun [C] a large car with a separate, closed area for bags **sedan araba; bagaj bölümü ayrı araç**

sedate¹ /sɪˈdeɪt/ adjective calm and slow **sakin, sessiz, ağırbaşlı, vakarlı** *walking at a sedate pace*

sedate² /sɪˈdeɪt/ verb [T] to give a person or animal a drug to make them feel calm **sakinleştirmek, yatıştırmak** ● **sedation** /sɪˈdeɪʃˤn/ noun [U] *She had to be put under sedation.* **sakinleştirme**

sedative /ˈsedətɪv/ noun [C] a drug used to sedate a person or an animal **sakinleştirici, ağrı kesici, müsekkin**

sedentary /ˈsedˤntˤri/ adjective spending a lot of time sitting down or not being active **hareketsiz, durgun, oturarak zaman geçiren** *a sedentary job/lifestyle*

sediment /ˈsedɪmənt/ noun [C, U] a solid substance that forms a layer at the bottom of a liquid **tortu, çökelti**

seduce /sɪˈdjuːs/ verb [T] **1** to persuade someone to have sex with you, especially someone young **ayartmak, iğfal etmek, baştan çıkartmak 2** to persuade someone to do something they would not normally do **kandırmak, ayartmak, aklını çelmek; ikna etmek** *I wouldn't have bought it but I was seduced by the low prices.*

seductive /sɪˈdʌktɪv/ adjective **1** sexually attractive **baştan çıkartıcı, kışkırtıcı, çekici, cazibeli, cilveli, oynak, fingirdek** *a seductive smile/voice* **2** making you want to have or do something **çekici, cazip, akıl çelici, ayartıcı** *the seductive power of money*

o--**see** /siː/ verb **seeing**, past tense **saw**, past participle **seen 1** [EYES] [I, T] to notice people and things with your eyes **görmek** *Have you seen Jo?* ○ *Turn the light on so I can see.* **2** [UNDERSTAND] [I, T] to understand something **anlamak, kavramak, farkına varmak** *I see what you mean.* ○ *I don't see why I should go.* **3** [MEET] [T] to meet or visit someone **görüşmek, ziyaret etmek, görmek** *I'm seeing Peter tonight.* ○ *You should see a doctor.* **4** [WATCH] [T] to watch a film, television programme, etc **seyretmek, bakmak, izlemek** *Did you see that film last night?* **5** [INFORMATION] [T] to find out information **öğrenmek, bilgi edinmek, bulup öğrenmek** [+ question word] *I'll see what time the train gets in.* **6** [IMAGINE] [T] to imagine or think about something or someone in a particular way **hayal etmek, görmek, kabul etmek** *I just can't see him as a father.* **7** [BELIEVE] [T] to believe that something will happen **inanmak, olacağına inanmak** *I can't see us finishing on time.* **8** [HAPPEN] [T] to be the time or place where something happens **tanık olmak, olmak, görmek** *This decade has seen huge technological advances.* **9 see that** If you ask someone to see that something happens, you ask them to make sure it happens. **bak gör, işte bak, farketmek, hissetmek** *Could you see that* *everyone gets a copy of this letter?* **10 see sb home/to the station, etc** to go somewhere with someone, especially to make sure they are safe **güvende olduğunu görmek, güven/emniyet içinde birini bir yere bırakmak** *Let me see you home.* **11 I'll/we'll see** used to say that you will make a decision about something later **'Hele bakalım/bakayım!', 'Dur bakalım/bakayım!', 'Bir düşüneyim/düşünelim!'** *"Dad, can I have a guitar?" "We'll see."* **12 see you** *informal* used for saying goodbye **'Görüşürüz!', 'Hadi hoşçakal!', 'Görüşmek üzere!'** ⊃See also: be glad/happy, etc to see the back² of sb/sth, see eye¹ to eye (with sb), see red².

see about sth/doing sth *phrasal verb* to deal with something, or arrange for something to be done **icabına bakmak, gerekeni yapmak, halletmek, çözümlemek** *You should see about getting your hair cut.*

see in sb/sth *phrasal verb* to believe that someone or something has a particular quality **birinde bir yeteneği/kabiliyeti görmek/keşfetmek** *I can't understand what you see in her* (= why you like her).

see sb off *phrasal verb* to go to the place that someone is leaving from in order to say goodbye to them **uğurlamak, yolcu etmek, uğurlamaya gitmek** *My parents came to the airport to see me off.*

see sb out *phrasal verb* to take someone to the door of a room or building when they are leaving **geçirmek, kapıya kadar geçirmek; yolcu etmek, uğurlamak** *Don't worry, I'll see myself out* (= leave the room/building by myself).

see through sb/sth *phrasal verb* to understand that someone is trying to deceive you **iç yüzünü anlamak, gerçek niyetini anlamak, içini/aklından geçenleri okumak, aslını esasını anlamak, hakkındaki gerçeği görmek** *I saw through him at once.*

see to sth *phrasal verb* to deal with something **icabına bakmak, gerekeni/gereğini yapmak; bakmak, ilgilenmek, meşgul olmak** *Don't worry, I'll see to everything while you're away.*

seed¹ /siːd/ *noun* **1** [C, U] a small round or oval object produced by a plant that a new plant can grow from **tohum, çekirdek** *Sow the seeds* (= plant them) *near the surface.* **2 (the) seeds of sth** the beginning of something **çekirdeği, başlangıcı, esası, özü** *the seeds of hope/change* ⊃See also: sesame seed.

seed² /siːd/ *verb* **1** [T] to plant seeds in the ground **tohum ekmek, ekim yapmak 2 be seeded first/second, etc** in tennis, to be the first/second, etc on a list of players expected to succeed in a competition **teniste başarılı olabilecek oyuncular listesinde birinci/ikinci vb. olmak**

seedless /ˈsiːdləs/ *adjective* without seeds **çekirdeksiz** *seedless grapes*

seedling /ˈsiːdlɪŋ/ *noun* [C] a young plant that has been grown from a seed **fide**

seedy /ˈsiːdi/ *adjective informal* looking dirty or in bad condition and likely to be involved in immoral activities **köhne, kılıksız, pejmurde** *a seedy bar/hotel*

,seeing 'eye dog *US* (*UK/US* guide dog) *noun* [C] a dog that is trained to help blind people **görme özürlülere yardım eden köpek**

seek /siːk/ *verb* [T] *past* sought **1** to try to find or get something **aramak, bulmaya/almaya çalışmak** *to seek advice/a solution* **2** to try to do something **yapmaya çalışmak** [+ to do sth] *They are seeking to change the rules.* ○ *to seek re-election* ⊃See also: hide-and-seek.

○ᴬ **seem** /siːm/ *verb* **seem happy/a nice person, etc; seem like/as if, etc** to appear to be a particular thing or to have a particular quality **...gibi görünmek; mış/miş gibi olmak; sanki ...imiş gibi görünmek** *She seemed happy enough.* ○ *It seemed like a good idea at the time.*

○ *There doesn't seem to be any real solution.* ○ [+ (that)] *It seems that the bars close early here.* ○ *It seems to me* (= I think) *that she's in the wrong job.*

seemingly /ˈsiːmɪŋli/ *adverb* appearing to be something without really being that thing **görünüşe bakılırsa, görünürde** *a seemingly harmless comment*

seen /siːn/ *past participle of* see **'görmek' fiilinin üçüncü hâli**

seep /siːp/ *verb* **seep from/into/through, etc** to flow very slowly through something **sızmak, sızarak akmak** *Water was seeping through the walls.*

seesaw

seesaw /ˈsiːsɔː/ (*also US* teeter-totter) *noun* [C] a long board that children play on by sitting at each end and using their feet on the ground to push the board up and down **tahterevalli**

seethe /siːð/ *verb* [I] to be very angry, often without showing it **için için kızmak, sinirini sürekli içine atmak** *I left him seething with anger.*

segment /ˈsegmənt/ *noun* [C] one of the parts that something can be divided into **dilim, bölüm, parça, kısım, kesim** *a segment of the population/market* ○ *an orange segment*

segregate /ˈsegrɪgeɪt/ *verb* [T] to separate one group of people from another, especially one sex or race from another **ayırmak** *At school the girls were segregated from the boys.* ● **segregation** /ˌsegrɪˈgeɪʃ⁰n/ *noun* [U] *racial segregation* **ayırım**

seismic /ˈsaɪzmɪk/ *adjective* relating to or caused by an earthquake (= when the earth shakes) **sismik, depremin sebep olduğu; depremle ilgili** *seismic activity*

seize /siːz/ *verb* [T] **1** HOLD to take hold of something quickly and firmly **tutmak, kavramak, yakalamak** *She seized my arm and pulled me towards her.* **2** OPPORTUNITY to do something quickly when you have the opportunity **fırsat varken alelacele süratle yapmak** *You need to seize every opportunity.* **3** PLACE to take control of a place suddenly by using military force **ele geçirmek, zapt etmek** *Troops seized control in the early hours of the morning.* **4** DRUGS ETC to take away something that is illegal, for example drugs **ele geçirmek, yakalamak** *Officials seized 2.7 tons of cocaine from the ship.*

seize on/upon sth *phrasal verb* to quickly use something that will give you an advantage **benimsemek, kabullenmek, tutmak, el atmak, hemen yararlanmak** *Her story was seized upon by the press.*

seize up *phrasal verb* If part of your body or a machine seizes up, it stops moving or working in the normal way. **takılmak, durmak, tıkelemek, tutulmak** *His right leg suddenly seized up during the race.*

seizure /ˈsiːʒəʳ/ *noun* **1** CONTROL [U] when someone takes control of a country, government, etc **el koyma, müsa-**

dere, ele geçirme, zaptetme *a seizure of power* **2** ⌐DRUGS ETC⌐ [C] when someone in authority takes away something that is illegal, for example drugs **yakalama, el koyma, ele geçirme** *a seizure of heroin* **3** ⌐ILLNESS⌐ [C] a sudden attack of an illness **nöbet, havale, kriz** *an epileptic seizure*

seldom /'seldəm/ *adverb* not often **nadiren, seyrek, pek az** *We seldom go out in the evenings.*

select¹ /sɪ'lekt/ *verb* [T] to choose something or someone **seçmek, ayıklamak** *We've selected three candidates.*

select² /sɪ'lekt/ *adjective* consisting of only a small group of people who have been specially chosen **seçkin, seçme, güzide, elit, üstün nitelikli** *a select group*

⌐ **selection** ...... İLE BİRLİKTE KULLANILAN KELİMELER

a **good/wide** selection ● a selection of sth

selection /sɪ'lekʃᵊn/ *noun* **1** [U] when someone or something is chosen **seçme, seçilme** *the selection process* **2** [C] a group of people or things that has been chosen **seçilen/belirlenen bir grup insan/kimse** *We have a wide selection of imported furniture.* ⊃See also: **natural selection.**

selective /sɪ'lektɪv/ *adjective* **1** careful about what you choose **seçici, seçmeye özen gösteren** *He's very selective about the people he spends time with.* **2** involving only people or things that have been specially chosen **ayrıcalıklı, özel, seçilmiş** *selective breeding*

self /self/ *noun* [C, U] *plural* **selves** /selvz/ your characteristics, including your personality, your abilities, etc **kendi, kendine, öz, kendiliğinden** *his true self*

self-assured /ˌselfə'ʃʊəd/ *adjective* confident about yourself **kendine güvenli, kendinden emin, öz güvenli**

self-catering /ˌself'keɪtᵊrɪŋ/ *adjective UK* describes a holiday in which you have a kitchen so that you can cook meals for yourself **yemeksiz, kendi yemeğini kendin yapman** *We decided to stay in self-catering accommodation rather than in a hotel.*

self-centred *UK* (*US* **self-centered**) /ˌself'sentəd/ *adjective* interested only in yourself **bencil, egoist, hotbin, ben merkezci**

self-confident /ˌself'kɒnfɪdᵊnt/ *adjective* feeling sure about yourself and your abilities **kendinden emin, özgüvenli** ● **self-confidence** *noun* [U] being self-confident **kendine güven**

self-conscious /ˌself'kɒnʃəs/ *adjective* too aware of what other people are thinking about you and your appearance **utangaç, sıkılgan, çekingen** ● **self-consciously** *adverb* **kendi görüntüsünü çok düşünen** ● **self-consciousness** *noun* [U] **özbilinç**

self-contained /ˌselfkən'teɪnd/ *adjective UK* If a flat is self-contained, it has its own kitchen, bathroom, and entrance. **her şeyi olan/içeren; yeterli; her şeyi barındıran; bağımsız, müstakil**

self-control /ˌselfkən'trəʊl/ *noun* [U] the ability to control your emotions and actions although you are very angry, upset, etc **kendine hakimiyet, soğukkanlılık**

self-defence *UK* (*US* **self-defense**) /ˌselfdɪ'fens/ *noun* [U] when you protect yourself from someone who is attacking you by fighting **meşru müdafaa, kendini savunma** *He claimed he had acted in self-defence.*

self-destructive /ˌselfdɪ'strʌktɪv/ *adjective* A self-destructive action harms the person who is doing it. **kendi kendini yok eden; kendine zarar veren**

self-discipline /ˌself'dɪsɪplɪn/ *noun* [U] the ability to make yourself do things that you do not want to do **öz disiplin, kendini kontrol etme**

self-employed /ˌselfɪm'plɔɪd/ *adjective* working for yourself and not for a company or other organization **kendi işini yapan** ● **self-employment** /ˌselfɪm'plɔɪmənt/ *noun* [U] **serbest meslek**

⌐ **self-esteem** ...... İLE BİRLİKTE KULLANILAN KELİMELER

boost/build/damage/raise self-esteem ● **high/low** self-esteem

self-esteem /ˌselfɪ'stiːm/ *noun* [U] confidence in yourself and a belief in your qualities and abilities **öz saygı, kendine saygı** *She suffers from low self-esteem.*

self-evident /ˌself'evɪdᵊnt/ *adjective* obviously true and not needing to be explained **apaçık, besbelli, meydanda, aşikâr**

self-explanatory /ˌselfɪk'splænətᵊri/ *adjective* easy to understand and not needing to be explained **açıklama gerektirmeyen, açık**

self-help /ˌself'help/ *adjective* A self-help book, activity, organization, etc is designed to help you deal with your problems on your own. **yardımcı, yardım eden; kendilerine yardım eden** *a self-help group for alcoholics*

self-indulgent /ˌselfɪn'dʌldʒᵊnt/ *adjective* doing or having things that you like although they are not necessary or are bad for you **sırf kendi zevkini düşünen; sadece kendini eğlendiren; keyfine/rahatına düşkün** ● **self-indulgence** /ˌselfɪn'dʌldʒᵊns/ *noun* [C, U] **isteklerine düşkün olma durumu**

self-inflicted /ˌselfɪn'flɪktɪd/ *adjective* If an injury or a problem is self-inflicted, you have caused it yourself. **kendi kendini yaralayan/inciten**

self-interest /ˌself'ɪntrəst/ *noun* [U] interest in what will help you and not what will help other people **bencillik, egoizm, menfaatçilik**

selfish /'selfɪʃ/ *adjective* caring only about yourself and not other people **bencil, hep kendini düşünen, egoist** *It's very selfish of him.* ● **selfishly** *adverb* **bencilce** ● **selfishness** *noun* [U] **bencillik**

selfless /'selfləs/ *adjective* caring about other people and not about yourself **kendini düşünmeyen, bencil olmayan, özverili, feragatli, fedakâr**

self-made /ˌself'meɪd/ *adjective* rich because you have earned a lot of money yourself **kendi kendini yetiştirmiş, kendi çabasıyla zengin olmuş, sıfırdan başlamış** *a self-made millionaire*

self-pity /ˌself'pɪti/ *noun* [U] sadness for yourself because you think you have suffered so much, especially when this is not true **kendine acıma, yerinme, acındırma, sürekli acınaklı**

self-portrait /ˌself'pɔːtreɪt/ *noun* [C] a picture that you draw or paint of yourself **oto portre**

self-reliant /ˌselfrɪ'laɪənt/ *adjective* able to do things yourself without depending on other people **kendi kendine yeten, iki ayağının üzerinde durabilen**

self-respect /ˌselfrɪ'spekt/ *noun* [U] the feeling of pride in yourself and your character **özsaygı, onur, haysiyet, izzetinefis** ● **self-respecting** *adjective* **özüne saygılı**

self-righteous /ˌself'raɪtʃəs/ *adjective* believing that you are morally better than other people **kendi erdemine inânan, kendini ahlaken üstün gören**

self-sacrifice /ˌself'sækrɪfaɪs/ *noun* [U] when you do not have or do something so that you can help other people **özveri, fedakârlık, feragat**

self-satisfied /ˌself'sætɪsfaɪd/ *adjective* too pleased with yourself and what you have achieved **kendini beğenmiş, kendini kaf dağında gören, burnu havada olan**

S

self-service /ˌselfˈsɜːvɪs/ *adjective* A self-service restaurant or shop is one in which you serve yourself and are not served by the people who work there. **kendin al kendin ye sistemiyle çalışan**

self-sufficient /ˌselfsəˈfɪʃᵊnt/ *adjective* having everything that you need yourself and not needing help from others **kendi kendine yeterli, başkalarına muhtaç olmayan**

◦**sell** /sel/ *verb past* **sold 1** [FOR MONEY] [I, T] to give something to someone who gives you money for it **satmak** *He sold his guitar for £50.* ○ *I sold my bike to Claire.* ○ [+ two objects] *I'm hoping she'll sell me her car.* **2** [OFFER] [T] to offer something for people to buy **satışa sunmak, satmak** *Excuse me, do you sell newspapers?* **3 sell for/at sth** to be available for sale at a particular price **satılmak; ...fiyata gitmek** *The shirts are selling for £30 each.* **4** [A LOT] [I, T] to be bought in large numbers **büyük miktarlarda satılmak/satmak** *His last book sold eight million copies.* **5** [MAKE YOU WANT] [T] to make someone want to buy something **sattırmak** *Scandal sells newspapers.* **6** [IDEA/PLAN] [T] to persuade someone that an idea or plan is good **fikir/plan satmak** *I'm currently trying to sell the idea to my boss.*

sell sth off *phrasal verb* to sell all or part of a business **tümünü satmak, hepsini elden çıkarmak, tasfiye etmek**

sell out *phrasal verb* If a shop sells out of something, it sells all of that thing. **tümünü satmak, hepsini satıp bitirmek** *They'd sold out of bread by the time I got there.*

sell up *phrasal verb UK* to sell your house or company in order to go somewhere else or do something else **nesi var nesi yok satmak, satıp savmak, tasfiye etmek**

'sell-by ˌdate *noun* [C] *UK* the date printed on a food or drink container after which it should not be sold **son satış tarihi**

seller /ˈselər/ *noun* [C] **1** someone who sells something **satıcı** *a flower seller* **2** a product that a company sells **satışa sunulan ürün; ticari mal** *Our biggest sellers are the calendars.*

Sellotape /ˈseləʊteɪp/ *UK* (*US* Scotch tape) *noun* [U] clear, thin material with glue on it, used to stick things together, especially paper **şeffaf bant, seloteyp** ➔Orta kısımdaki renkli sayfalarına bakınız.

sellout /ˈselaʊt/ *noun* [no plural] **1** a performance or event where all of the tickets have been sold **bütün biletleri satılmış gösteri/olay; yok satan gösteri/ouyn vs. 2** *informal* when someone does something that is against their beliefs in order to get money or power **satış, satışa gelme/getirilme; satma**

selves /selvz/ *plural of* self **kendi' sözcüğünün çoğul hâli**

semantic /sɪˈmæntɪk/ *adjective* connected with the meaning of language **anlamla ilgili olan/bağlantılı**

semblance /ˈsembləns/ *noun* **semblance of normality/order, etc** a small amount of a quality, but not as much as you would like **görünüm, hava** *Our lives have now returned to some semblance of normality.*

semen /ˈsiːmən/ *noun* [U] the liquid that is produced by the male sex organs, that contains sperm (= cells that join with female eggs to make new life) **meni, ersuyu, döl**

semester /sɪˈmestər/ *noun* [C] *mainly US* one of the two time periods that a school or college year is divided into **öğrenimde yarıyıl, sömestri, akademik yarıyıl**

semi- /semi-/ *prefix* half or partly **yarı.../yarım... anlamında önek** *a semicircle* ○ *semifrozen*

semicircle

semicircle /ˈsemɪˌsɜːkl/ *noun* [C] half a circle **yarım daire**

semicolon /ˌsemɪˈkəʊlən/ ⑤ /ˈsemɪˌkəʊlən/ *noun* [C] a mark (;) used to separate parts of a sentence, or items in a list which already has commas **noktalı virgül (;)** ➔See study page Punctuation on page Centre 33.

semi-detached /ˌsemɪdɪˈtætʃt/ *adjective UK* A semi-detached house has one wall that is joined to another house. **ortak duvarlı, duvarı ortak olan (bina)**

semifinal /ˌsemɪˈfaɪnᵊl/ *noun* [C] one of the two games in a sports competition that are played to decide who will play in the final game **yarı final**

seminar /ˈsemɪnɑːr/ *noun* [C] a meeting of a group of people with a teacher or expert for training, discussion, or study of a subject **seminer**

Semitic /sɪˈmɪtɪk/ *adjective* relating to the Jewish or Arab races, or their languages **Yahudi/Arap ırkına veya dillerine ilişkin**

the Senate /ˈsenɪt/ *noun* [group] a part of a government in some countries **Senato**

senator /ˈsenətər/ *noun* [C] someone who has been elected to the Senate **senatör** *Senator Moynihan*

◦**send** /send/ *verb* [T] *past* **sent 1** to arrange for something to go or be taken somewhere, especially by post **postalamak, göndermek, yollamak** [+ two objects] *Send him a letter last week.* ○ *Do you think we should send flowers?* **2** to make someone go somewhere **yollamak, göndermek** *I sent him into the house to fetch some glasses.* **3 send sb to sleep** to cause someone to start sleeping **uyutmak** ➔See also: drive/send sb round the bend².

send sth back *phrasal verb* to return something to the person who sent it to you, especially because it is damaged or not suitable **geri göndermek, iade etmek** *I had to send the shirt back because it didn't fit me.*

send for sb *phrasal verb* to send someone a message asking them to come to see you **çağırmak, getirtmek** *Do you think we should send for a doctor?*

send (off/away) for sth *phrasal verb* to write to an organization to ask them to send you something **sipariş etmek, istemek** *I've sent off for a catalogue.*

send sth in *phrasal verb* to send something to an organization **göndermek, sunmak** *Viewers were asked to send in photographs of their pets.*

send sb in *phrasal verb* to send soldiers, police, etc to a place in order to deal with a dangerous situation **asker/polis sevketmek/göndermek**

send sth off *phrasal verb* to send a letter, document, or parcel by post **mektup/belge/paket göndermek, postalamak**

send sb off *phrasal verb UK* to order a sports player to leave the playing area because they have done something wrong **oyundan çıkarmak, oyun dışı bırakmak**

send sth out *phrasal verb* **1** to send something to a lot of different people **bir çok kişiye göndermek** *to send out invitations* **2** to produce light, sound, etc **ışık/ses vb. yaymak, çıkarmak**

send sb/sth up *phrasal verb UK* to make someone or something seem stupid by copying them in a funny way **taklit etmek, taklidini yaparak alaya almak**

send-off /ˈsendɒf/ *noun* [C] when a group of people say goodbye to someone at the same time **topluca uğurlama; hoşçakal deme** *I got a good send-off at the station.*

senile /ˈsiːnaɪl/ *adjective* confused and unable to remember things because of old age **bunamış, bunak** • **senility** /sɪˈnɪləti/ *noun* [U] the state of being senile **bunaklık, bunamışlık**

senior¹ /ˈsiːniər/ *adjective* **1** [MORE IMPORTANT] having a more important job or position than someone else **üst, kıdemli** *a senior executive* ○ *We work in the same team but she's senior to me.* **2** [OLDER] older **yaşça büyük, daha yaşlı** *senior students* **3** [NAME] mainly US (written abbreviation **Sr**) used at the end of a man's name to show that he is the older of two men in the same family who have the same name **ailede aynı isimde olup ta yaşça büyük olan** *Hello, may I speak to Ken Griffey Senior, please?*

senior² /ˈsiːniər/ *noun* **1 be 20/30, etc years sb's senior** to be 20/30, etc years older than someone **birinden 20/30 yaş daha büyük olmak** *She married a man 20 years her senior.* **2** [C] *US* a student who is in the last year of high school or college **son sınıf öğrencisi**

senior 'citizen *noun* [C] an old person **emekli, emekli kimse**

seniority /ˌsiːniˈɒrəti/ *noun* [U] the state of being older or of having a more important position in an organization **kıdem, mevki, kıdemlilik**

sensation /senˈseɪʃən/ *noun* **1** [PHYSICAL] [C, U] a physical feeling, or the ability to physically feel things **his, duygu** *a burning sensation* ○ *Three months after the accident she still has no sensation in her right foot.* **2** [FEELING] [C] a strange feeling or idea that you can not explain **acayip duygu/fikir, izlenim** *I had the strangest sensation that I had met him before.* **3** [EXCITEMENT] [no plural] a lot of excitement, surprise, or interest, or the person or event that causes these feelings **sansasyon, büyük heyecan/ilgi; garip duygu** *Their affair caused a sensation.*

sensational /senˈseɪʃənəl/ *adjective* **1** done in a way that is intended to shock people **büyük heyecan/ilgi yaratan, sansasyonel** *sensational journalism* **2** very exciting or extremely good **müthiş, harika, olağanüstü** *a sensational performance*

sensationalism /senˈseɪʃənəlɪzəm/ *noun* [U] when a story is told in a way that is intended to shock people **sansasyon yaratan/şok edici anlatım/hikaye**

sense ...... İLE BİRLİKTE KULLANILAN KELİMELER

have the sense to do sth • **good** sense

o--**sense¹** /sens/ *noun* **1** [GOOD JUDGMENT] [U] good judgment, especially about practical things **akıl, zekâ, muhakeme, dirayet** *He had the good sense to book a seat in advance.* **2** [ABILITY] [no plural] the ability to do something **anlayış, takdir** *a sense of direction* ○ *good business sense* **3** [NATURAL ABILITY] [C] one of the five natural abilities of sight, hearing, touch, smell, and taste **duyu** *I have a very poor sense of smell.* **4 a sense of humour** *UK* (*US*

sense of humor) the ability to understand funny things and to be funny yourself **mizah/espri anlayışı; mizahtan/nikteden anlama 5 a sense of loyalty/responsibility/security, etc** the quality or feeling of being loyal, responsible, safe, etc **bağlılık/sorumluluk/güven vs. duygusu** *He has absolutely no sense of loyalty.* **6** [MEANING] [C] the meaning of a word, phrase, or sentence **anlam, mâna 7 in a sense/in some senses** thinking about something in a particular way **bir bakıma/anlamda; bazı bakımdan** *In a sense, he's right.* **8 make sense a** [CLEAR MEANING] to have a meaning or reason that you can understand **anlaşılır/kavranılabilir olmak** *He's written this note but it doesn't make any sense.* **b** [SHOULD DO] to be a good thing to do **akla uygun olmak, akıllıca/makul olmak** [+ to do sth] *It makes sense to buy now while prices are low.* **9 make sense of sth** to understand something that is difficult to understand **anlamak, anlam çıkarmak, anlamını sökmek** *I'm trying to make sense of this document.* **10 come to your senses** to start to understand that you have been behaving stupidly **aklı başına gelmek, aklını başına getirmek** ᴑSee also: common sense.

sense² /sens/ *verb* [T] to understand what someone is thinking or feeling without being told about it **sezmek, hissetmek, farkına varmak; anlamak** [+ (that)] *I sensed that you weren't happy about this.*

senseless /ˈsensləs/ *adjective* **1** happening or done without a good reason **anlamsız, manasız, saçma** *senseless violence* **2** not conscious **şuurunu yitirmiş, baygın, bayılmış, kendinden geçmiş** *He was beaten senseless.*

sensibility /ˌsensɪˈbɪləti/ *noun* [C, U] *formal* someone's feelings, or the ability to understand what other people feel **duyarlık, sezgi**

sensible /ˈsensɪbl/ *adjective* **1** showing good judgment **makul, aklı başında, mantıklı** *a sensible decision* ○ [+ to do sth] *Wouldn't it be more sensible to leave before the traffic gets bad?* **2** having a practical purpose **pratik, uygun, makul, uygulanabilir** *sensible shoes/clothes* • **sensibly** *adverb* to eat/behave sensibly **makul, mantıklı bir şekilde**

sensitive /ˈsensɪtɪv/ *adjective* **1** [KIND] able to understand what people are feeling and deal with them in a way that does not upset them **duyarlı, hassas** *I want a man who's kind and sensitive.* **2** [EASILY UPSET] easily upset by the things people say or do **duyarlı, alıngan, buluttan nem kapan** *He was always sensitive to criticism.* ○ *She's very sensitive about her weight.* **3** [SUBJECT] A sensitive subject or situation needs to be dealt with carefully in order to avoid upsetting people. **nazik, hassas, itina edilmesi gereken, dikkatle ele alınması gereken** *Gender is a very sensitive subject.* **4** [EASILY DAMAGED] easily damaged or hurt **duyarlı, hassas, çabuk etkilenen** *sensitive eyes/skin* **5** [EQUIPMENT] Sensitive equipment is able to measure very small changes. **hassas, dakik** ᴑOpposite insensitive. • **sensitively** *adverb* *I think she dealt with the problem very sensitively.* **duyarlı bir şekilde** • **sensitivity** /ˌsensɪˈtɪvəti/ *noun* [U] when someone or something is sensitive **duyarlık, hassaslık; hassasiyet, duyarlılık**

sensor /ˈsensər/ *noun* [C] a piece of equipment that can find heat, light, etc **almaç, sensör** *Sensors detect movement in the room.*

sensual /ˈsensjuəl/ *adjective* relating to physical pleasure, often sexual pleasure **şehvetli, şehvet uyandıran; tensel, bedensel** *a sensual experience* ○ *a sensual mouth* • **sensuality** /ˌsensjuˈæləti/ *noun* [U] being sensual **bedensel zevklere hitap etme, tensellik**

sensuous /'sensjʊəs/ *adjective* giving physical pleasure **duyulara hitap eden, insan ruhunu okşayan; bedensel zevk veren** *the sensuous feel of silk sheets*

sent /sent/ *past of* send **göndermek' fiilinin geçmiş zaman hâli**

⟦ᵈ⟧ **sentence** ...... İLE BİRLİKTE KULLANILAN KELİMELER

impose/receive/serve a sentence ● a **jail/prison** sentence ● a sentence **for sth**

๑•**sentence¹** /'sentəns/ *noun* **1** [C] a group of words, usually containing a verb, that expresses a complete idea **cümle 2** [C, U] a punishment that a judge gives to someone who has committed a crime **ceza, hüküm** *a 30-year sentence*

sentence² /'sentəns/ *verb* [T] to give a punishment to someone who has committed a crime **mahkûm etmek, hüküm giydirmek, ceza vermek** [often passive] *She was sentenced to six months in prison.*

sentiment /'sentɪmənt/ *noun* **1** [C, U] an opinion that you have because of the way you feel about something **düşünce, kanı, fikir; görüş** *nationalist/religious sentiments* **2** [U] emotional feelings such as sympathy, love, etc, especially when they are not considered to be suitable for a situation **duyarlılık, hassasiyet, sempati, sevgi** *I find her writing full of sentiment.*

sentimental /ˌsentɪ'mentᵊl/ *adjective* **1** showing kind feelings such as sympathy, love, etc, especially in a silly way **aşırı duygusal, çok hassas** *a sentimental song* ○ *The British are very sentimental about animals.* **2** related to feelings and memories and not related to how much money something costs **duygusal, duygulu** *It wasn't an expensive ring but it had great sentimental value.* ● **sentimentality** /ˌsentɪmen'tæləti/ *noun* [U] **duygusallık**

sentry /'sentri/ *noun* [C] a soldier who stands outside a building in order to guard it **nöbetçi, nöbetçi er, nizamiye/kapı nöbetçisi**

separable /'sepᵊrəbl/ *adjective* able to be separated **ayrılabilir** ⊃ Opposite **inseparable.**

๑•**separate¹** /'sepᵊrət/ *adjective* **1** [NOT JOINED] not joined or touching anything else **ayrı, ayrılmış, müstakil** *a separate compartment* ○ *I try to keep meat separate from other food.* **2** [NOT AFFECTING] not affecting or related to each other **etkilenmeyen, ayrı** *I've asked him to turn his music down on three separate occasions.* ○ *I have my professional life and my private life and I try to keep them separate.* **3** [DIFFERENT] different **ayrı, farklı, değişik** *Use a separate sheet of paper.* ● **separately** *adverb* **ayrı bir şekilde**

๑•**separate²** /'sepᵊreɪt/ *verb* **1** [DIVIDE] [I, T] to divide into parts, or to make something divide into parts **böl(ün)mek, ayırmak, ayrılmak** *I separated the class into three groups.* **2** [MOVE APART] [I, T] to move apart, or to make people move apart **ayırmak, ayrılmak, ayrı tutmak** *I shall separate you two if you don't stop talking.* **3** [HUSBAND/WIFE] [I] to start to live in a different place from your husband or wife because the relationship has ended **ayrı yaşamak** *My parents separated when I was four.*

separation /ˌsepᵊr'eɪʃᵊn/ *noun* **1** [C, U] when people or things are separate or become separate from other people or things **ayırma, ayrılma** *the separation of church and state* ○ *Their working in different countries meant long periods of separation.* **2** [C] a legal agreement when two people stay married but stop living together **ayrılık, ayrı yaşama**

๑•**September** /sep'tembər/ (*written abbreviation* **Sept**) *noun* [C, U] the ninth month of the year **eylül, eylül ayı**

septic /'septɪk/ *adjective* infected by poisonous bacteria (= small living things which cause disease) **mikrop kapmış, mikroplu, enfeksiyonlu**

sequel /'siːkwᵊl/ *noun* [C] a film, book, etc that continues the story from an earlier one **devam, arka**

⟦ᵈ⟧ **sequence** ...... İLE BİRLİKTE KULLANILAN KELİMELER

in a sequence ● a sequence **of** sth ● be **out of** sequence ● a **logical** sequence

sequence /'siːkwəns/ *noun* **1** [C] a series of related events or things that have a particular order **dizi, zincir, silsile** *the sequence of events that led to his death* **2** [U] the order that events or things should happen or be arranged in **sıra, dizi, ardışıklık** *I got my slides mixed up and they appeared out of sequence.*

sequin /'siːkwɪn/ *noun* [C] a small, flat, shiny circle that is sewn onto clothes for decoration **pul**

serenade /ˌserə'neɪd/ *noun* [C] a song, usually about love **aşk şarkısı, serenat**

serendipity /ˌserᵊn'dɪpəti/ *noun* [U] *literary* when you are lucky and find something interesting or valuable by chance **şanslılık, şans, şans eseri bulma**

serene /sɪ'riːn/ *adjective* calm and quiet **sakin, huzurlu, asude, dingin** *a serene face/smile* ● **serenely** *adverb* **sakin bir biçimde**

sergeant /'sɑːdʒᵊnt/ *noun* [C] **1** an officer of low rank in the police **çavuş; polis teşkilatında rütbe 2** a soldier of middle rank in the army or air force **astsubay çavuş**

serial /'sɪəriəl/ *noun* [C] a story in a magazine or on television or radio that is told in separate parts over a period of time **dizi, seri**

'**serial ,killer** *noun* [C] someone who has murdered several people over a period of time **seri katil**

'**serial ,number** *noun* [C] one of a set of numbers that is put on an item that is made in large quantities, such as computers, televisions, paper money, etc, so that you can tell one item from another **seri numarası**

๑•**series** /'sɪəriːz/ *noun* [C] *plural* **series 1** several things or events of the same type that come one after the other **dizi, seri** *a series of lectures* **2** a group of television or radio programmes that have the same main characters or deal with the same subject **dizi** *a four-part drama series*

๑•**serious** /'sɪəriəs/ *adjective* **1** [BAD] A serious problem or situation is bad and makes people worry. **ciddî, endişe verici, vahim** *a serious accident/illness* ○ *This is a serious matter.* **2** [NOT JOKING] thinking or speaking sincerely about something and not joking **ciddî** *I'm being serious now - this is a very real problem.* ○ *Are you serious about changing your job?* **3** [QUIET] A serious person is quiet and does not laugh often. **ciddî, ağırbaşlı, vakur** *a serious child* ● **seriousness** *noun* [U] **ciddiyet**

๑•**seriously** /'sɪəriəsli/ *adverb* **1** in a serious way **ciddî bir şekilde** *seriously injured* ○ *Smoking can seriously damage your health.* **2** used to show that what you are going to say is not a joke **cidden, gerçekten, doğrusu, şaka bir yana** *Seriously though, you mustn't say that.* **3 take sb/sth seriously** to believe that someone or something is important and that you should pay attention to them **ciddiye almak, önemsemek, ehemmiyet vermek** *The police have to take any terrorist threat seriously.*

sermon /'sɜːmən/ *noun* [C] a religious speech given by a priest in church **vaaz, dinî konuşma** *to deliver/give a sermon*

serotonin /ˌserə'təʊnɪn/ *noun* [U] a chemical in your brain which controls your moods **beyinde ruhsal durumu kontrol eden salgı; seratonin**

serpent /ˈsɜːpᵊnt/ *noun* [C] *literary* a snake **yılan**

serrated /sɪˈreɪtɪd/ *adjective* A serrated edge, usually of a knife, has sharp triangular points along it. **testere dişli, tırtıllı, tırtıklı**

serrated

serum /ˈsɪərəm/ *noun* [U] a clear liquid in blood that contains substances that stop infection **serum**

servant /ˈsɜːvᵊnt/ *noun* [C] someone who works and lives in someone else's house doing their cooking and cleaning, especially in the past **hizmetçi, uşak, hizmetkâr** ⊃See also: civil servant.

o⊶**serve¹** /sɜːv/ *verb*
1 FOOD/DRINK [I, T] to give someone food or drink, especially guests or customers in a restaurant or bar **hizmet etmek, servis yapmak, görev yapmak** *We're not allowed to serve alcohol to anyone under 18.* **2** SHOP [I, T] to help customers and sell things to them in a shop **hizmet vermek, bakmak, hizmet sunmak** *Are you being served?* **3** WORK [I, T] to do work that helps society, for example in an organization such as the army or the government **görev yapmak/etmek, görev almak** *to serve in the army* ○ *to serve on a committee/jury* ○ *He served as mayor for 5 years.* **4** BE USEFUL [I, T] to be useful as something **işe yaramak, faydalı olmak** *It's a very entertaining film but it also serves an educational purpose.* ○ *The spare bedroom also serves as a study.* ○ [+ to do sth] *He hopes his son's death will serve to warn others about the dangers of owning a gun.* **5** PRISON [T] to be in prison for a period of time **hapiste yatmak, ceza çekmek** *Williams, 42, is serving a four-year jail sentence.* **6** SPORT [I] in a sport such as tennis, to throw the ball up into the air and then hit it towards the other player **servis atmak/kullanmak 7 serves one/two/four, etc** If an amount of food serves a particular number, it is enough for that number of people. **yeterli olmak; ... lık/lik olmak** ⊃See also: It serves her/him/you **right²**!.

serve² /sɜːv/ *noun* [C] in sports such as tennis, when you throw the ball up into the air and hit it towards the other player **(teniste) servis, atış, servis kullanma**

server /ˈsɜːvəʳ/ *noun* [C] a computer that is used only for storing and managing programs and information used by other computers **ana bilgisayar** *an email/Internet server*

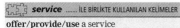

service .... İLE BİRLİKTE KULLANILAN KELİMELER

offer/provide/use a service

o⊶**service¹** /ˈsɜːvɪs/ *noun* **1** SHOP [U] when people help you and bring you things in a place such as a shop, restaurant, or hotel **hizmet, servis, bakıma, ilgilenme** *The food was nice, but the service wasn't very good.* **2** SYSTEM [C] a system that supplies something that people need **servis, hizmet** *financial/medical services* ○ *electricity/water services* ○ *They provide a free bus service from the station.* **3** WORK [U] the time you spend working for an organization **çalışma süresi, hizmet yılı** *He retired last week after 25 years' service.* **4** CEREMONY [C] a religious ceremony **dinî tören, ayin** *They held a memorial service for the victims of the bombing.* **5** CAR/MACHINE [C] when a car or machine is examined for faults and repaired **tamir/bakım/araç servisi 6** SPORT [C] when you

throw a ball up into the air and hit it towards the other player in sports such as tennis **(sporda) servis** ⊃See also: the Civil Service, community service, lip-service, the National Health Service, national service, secret service.

service² /ˈsɜːvɪs/ *verb* [T] to examine and repair a car or machine **araç/makina bakım tamir yapmak**

serviceable /ˈsɜːvɪsəbl/ *adjective* able to be used, but not very good or attractive **yararlı, faydalı, işe yarar** *I have some old but serviceable chairs.*

'service ˌcharge *noun* [C] an amount of money that is added to what you pay in a restaurant for being helped and brought things **servis ücreti** *a 10% service charge*

serviceman /ˈsɜːvɪsmən/ *noun* [C] *plural* **servicemen** a man who is in the army or navy **asker, silâhlı kuvvetler mensubu**

the services /ˈsɜːvɪsɪz/ *noun* [plural] the military forces such as the army or navy **silâhlı kuvvetler**

'service ˌstation *noun* [C] a place at the side of a road where you can buy fuel for cars, and food **benzin istasyonu, benzinlik, servis istasyonu**

serviette /ˌsɜːviˈet/ *UK* (*UK/US* napkin) *noun* [C] a piece of cloth or paper used when you eat, to keep your clothes clean and to clean your mouth and hands **peçete**

servile /ˈsɜːvaɪl/ ⑤ /ˈsɜːrvᵊl/ *adjective* too willing to do things for other people **dalkavuk, gurursuz, gereksiz yere köle gibi hizmet eden**

serving /ˈsɜːvɪŋ/ *noun* [C] an amount of food for one person to eat **porsiyon** *a large serving of rice*

sesame seed /ˈsesəmiˌsiːd/ *noun* [C] a small seed that is used to add a taste to food **susam**

session /ˈseʃᵊn/ *noun* **1** [C] a period during which you do one activity **dönem** *a weekly aerobics session* ○ *We're having a training session this afternoon.* **2** [C, U] a meeting of an official group of people such as in a court or in the government **oturum, celse, toplantı** *The court is now in session.*

o⊶**set¹** /set/ *verb* **setting**, *past* **set 1** A TIME [T] to arrange a time when something will happen **kurmak, ayarlamak, zamanı belirlemek** [often passive] *The next meeting is set for 6 February.* **2** LEVEL [T] to decide the level of something **saptamak, belirlemek, tespit etmek** *The interest rate has been set at 5%.* **3** MACHINE [T] to press switches on a machine so that it will start when you want it to **ayarlamak, kurmak** *I've set the alarm for 6.30.* ○ [+ to do sth] *Can you set the video to record 'Neighbours' please?* **4 set an example/a record/a standard, etc** to do something in a way that people will copy or try to improve on **örnek teşkil etmek; numune olmak** *She's set a new world record with that jump.* **5 set fire to sth; set sth on fire** to make something start burning **ateşe vermek, tutuşturmak, yakmak 6 set sb free** to allow someone to leave prison, or to allow a person or animal to escape **salıvermek, serbest bırakmak, tahliye etmek 7 set sth alight** to make something start burning **yakmak, tutuşturmak 8 set the table** to put plates, knives, forks, etc on the table before you have a meal **masayı kurmak/hazırlamak 9** SUN [I] When the sun sets, it moves down in the sky so that it cannot be seen. **batmak** *The sun rises in the East and sets in the West.* **10** BECOME SOLID [I] If a liquid substance sets, it becomes solid. **katılaşmak, tutmak, sertleşmek 11** SCHOOL WORK [T] *UK* If you set work or an exam at a school or college, you ask the students to do it. **vermek, belirlemek** [+ two objects] *Mr Harley forgot to set us any maths homework.* **12 set sth down/on, etc** to put something somewhere **koymak, yerleştirmek** *She set the vase down on the table.* **13** BOOK/FILM/PLAY [T] If a book, play, or film is set in a place or period of time, the story happens there or at that time. **geçmek, olmak, meydana gelmek, yaşanmış olmak** [often passive] *It's a historical adventure set in India in the 1940s.* **14 set to work** to start working **işe koyulmak, çalışmaya başlamak**

set about sth/doing sth *phrasal verb* to start doing something, especially something that uses a lot of time or energy **başlamak, girişmek, koyulmak** *I got home and immediately set about cleaning the house.*

be set against sth/doing sth *phrasal verb* to not want to do or have something **karşı olmak; istememek** *He is dead set against the move.*

set sb/sth apart *phrasal verb* If a quality sets someone or something apart, it makes them different from and usually better than others of the same type. ...dan/den **ayırmak** *It's their intelligence which sets them apart from other rock bands.*

set sth aside *phrasal verb* to save something, usually time or money, for a special purpose **ayırmak, bir kenara koymak**

set sb/sth back *phrasal verb* to make something happen more slowly or later than it should **geciktirmek, geriye atmak, geri bırakmak** *The heavy traffic set us back about half an hour.*

set sb back (sth) *phrasal verb informal* to cost someone a large amount of money **pahalıya malolmak/patlamak** *A car like that will probably set you back about £12,000.*

set in *phrasal verb* If something unpleasant sets in, it begins and seems likely to continue. **gelip çatmak, başlamak, ortaya çıkmak, etkisini belli etmek** *This rain looks as if it has set in for the rest of the day.*

set off *phrasal verb* to start a journey **yola çıkmak, yolculuğa başlamak, seyahate gitmek üzere yola çıkmak** *What time are you setting off tomorrow morning?*

set sth off *phrasal verb* to cause something to begin or happen, especially a loud noise or a lot of activity **başlatmak, başlamasına neden olmak; devreye sokmak/girmek** *He's always burning the toast and setting off the smoke alarm.*

set sb/sth on/upon sb *phrasal verb* to make a person or animal attack someone **kışkırtmak, saldırtmak, saldırmasını sağlamak, salmak, göndermek** *If you come any closer, I'll set the dog on you.*

set out *phrasal verb* **1** to start doing something when you have already decided what you want to achieve ... **maya/meye koyulmak, girişmek, kalkışmak** [+ to do sth] *I'd done what I set out to do.* **2** to start a journey **yola çıkmak, yolculuğa başlamak, seyahate gitmek üzere yola çıkmak**

set sth out *phrasal verb* to give all the details of something, or to explain something clearly, especially in writing **bir bir açıklamak, sıra ile anlatmak** *Your contract will set out the terms of your employment.*

set sth up *phrasal verb* **1** to start a company or organization **oluşturmak, yapmak, kurmak** *A committee has been set up to investigate the problem.* **2** to arrange for something to happen **düzenlemek, kurmak, oluşturmak** *I've set up a meeting with him for next week.*

set sb up *phrasal verb* to trick someone in order to make them do something, or in order to make them seem guilty of something that they have not done **kara çalmak, iftira atmak, çamur atmak**

set (sth) up *phrasal verb* to get all the necessary equipment ready for an activity **yapmak, oluşturmak, halletmek** *I need one or two people to help me set up the display.*

⚬**set²** /set/ *noun* [C] **1** GROUP a group of things which belong together **takım** *a set of instructions/rules* ○ *a set of keys/tools* **2** FILM/PLAY the place where a film or play is performed or recorded, and the pictures, furniture, etc that are used **set, dekor, sahne** *They first met on the set of 'Star Wars'.* **3** TENNIS one part of a tennis match **tenis maçında set** *Agassi is leading by four games to one in the third set.* **4** TV/RADIO a television or radio **alıcı, cihaz** *a TV set* **5** MUSIC a group of songs or tunes that go together to make a musical performance **repertuar, müzik dinletisini oluşturan şarkılar** **6** MATHS a group of numbers or things

set³ /set/ *adjective* **1** fixed and never changing **sabit, değişmez** *Most people work for a set number of hours each week.* ○ *I have no set routine.* **2** **be all set** to be ready **tamamen hazır olmak** [+ to do sth] *We were all set to go when the phone rang.* ⊃See also: On your marks (**mark¹**). Get set. Go!.

╠┅╣ **setback** ...... İLE BİRLİKTE KULLANILAN KELİMELER

suffer a setback ● a **major/serious** setback ● a setback **for** sb ● a setback **in/to** sth

setback /'setbæk/ *noun* [C] a problem that makes something happen later or more slowly than it should **aksilik, terslik, engel** *The project has suffered a series of setbacks this year.*

set-piece /ˌset'piːs/ *noun* [C] a speech or set of actions that has been carefully planned and practised **önceden planlanmış ve çalışılmış konuşma ve bir grup faaliyet**

settee /set'iː/ *UK (UK/US* **sofa***) noun* [C] a large, comfortable seat for more than one person **kanepe**

setting /'setɪŋ/ *noun* [C] **1** the place where something is or where something happens, often in a book, play, or film **sahne, dekor, set, yer, çevre, ortam, mahal** *The house provided the setting for the TV series 'Pride and Prejudice'.* **2** a position on the controls of a piece of equipment **ayar, derece** *Set the oven at the lowest setting.*

settle /'setl/ *verb* **1** ARGUMENT [T] If you settle an argument, you solve the problem and stop arguing. **halletmek, çözmek, çözüm yolu bulmak, halletmek, karara bağlamak** *to settle a dispute* **2** LIVE [I] to start living somewhere that you are going to live for a long time **yerleşmek, yaşamaya başlamak** *He travelled around Europe for years before finally settling in Vienna.* **3** DECIDE [T] to decide or arrange something **karar vermek, düzenlemek** [often passive] *Right, that's settled. We're going to Spain.* **4** RELAX [I, T] to relax into a comfortable position **istirahat etmek, dinlenmek** [often reflexive] *She settled herself into the chair opposite.* **5** PAY [T] If you settle a bill or a debt, you pay the money that you owe. **borcu/faturayı ödemek 6** MOVE DOWN [I] to move down towards the ground or the bottom of something and then stay there **oturmak, çökmek** *Do you think the snow will settle?* ⊃See also: the **dust¹** settles.

settle down *phrasal verb* **1** to start living in a place where you intend to stay for a long time, usually with a partner **bir yere yerleşmek, ikâmet etmeye başlamak; ev bark edinip yerleşmek** *Do you think he'll ever settle down and have a family?* **2** to start to feel happy and confident with a new situation **memnun olmak, güven duymak, ısınmak, kabullenmeye başlamak** *Has she settled down in her new job?*

settle (sb) down *phrasal verb* to become quiet and calm, or to make someone become quiet and calm **sakinleşmek, yatışmak, durulmak; sakinleştirmek, yatıştırmak** *Come on children, stop chatting and settle down please!*

settle for sth *phrasal verb* to accept something, especially something that is not exactly what you want **yetinmek, razı olmak, çaresiz kabullenmek** *He wants a full refund and he won't settle for anything less.*

S

settle in *phrasal verb* to begin to feel relaxed and happy in a new home or job **alışmak, ısınmak, intibak etmek** *Are you settling in OK?*

settle on/upon sth *phrasal verb* to agree on a decision **karar vermek/kılmak, üzerinde anlaşmak** *We still haven't settled on a place to meet.*

settle up *phrasal verb* to pay someone the money that you owe them **hesabı ödemek/kapatmak/temizlemek** *I need to settle up with you for the tickets.*

settled /'setld/ *adjective* **1 be settled** to feel happy and relaxed in a place or situation **alışmak, ısınmak, yabancılık çekmemek, yerlisi gibi olmak** *He seems quite settled now.* **2** regular and not often changing **değişmez, yerleşmiş, oturmuş, yerleşik** *The weather's a lot more settled at this time of year.* ⊃Opposite **unsettled.**

╬╬ settlement ..... İLE BİRLİKTE KULLANILAN KELİMELER

agree/negotiate/reach a settlement ● a settlement **between** sb and sb ● a settlement **over** sth ● a **peace** settlement

settlement /'setlmənt/ *noun* [C] **1** an official agreement that finishes an argument **sözleşme, antlaşma** *a peace settlement* **2** a town or village which people built to live in after arriving from somewhere else **yeni yerleşim bölgesi; yerleşim alanı, meskün mahal** *a Jewish settlement*

settler /'setlə^r/ *noun* [C] someone who moves to a new place where there were not many people before **yeni gelen, göçmen** *The first European settlers arrived in Virginia in 1607.*

set-top box /'settɒp,bɒks/ *noun* [C] a piece of electronic equipment that allows you to watch digital broadcasts (= television sounds and pictures sent as signals in the form of numbers) on an ordinary television **dijital kanal göstergesi; dijital tv alıcısı**

set-up /'setʌp/ *noun* [C] *informal* **1** the way that something is arranged or organized **düzen, yapı, durum, vaziyet, organizasyon** *It took me a while to get used to the set-up in my new job.* **2** a plan that is dishonest and is intended to trick someone **tuzak, oyun, hile, aldatma**

oᴖ**seven** /'sev^ən/ the number 7 **yedi, yedi rakam**

oᴖ**seventeen** /,sev^ən'ti:n/ the number 17 **on yedi, on yedi rakamı** ● **seventeenth** 17th written as a word **on yedinci**

seventh¹ /'sev^ənθ/ 7th written as a word **yedinci**

seventh² /'sev^ənθ/ *noun* [C] one of seven equal parts of something; $1/7$ **yedide bir, bir bölü yedi**

oᴖ**seventy** /'sev^ənti/ **1** the number 70 **yetmiş, yetmiş rakamı** **2 the seventies** the years from 1970 to 1979 **yetmişler, yetmişli yıllar 3 be in your seventies** to be aged between 70 and 79 **yetmişlerinde olmak** ● **seventieth** 70th written as a word **yetmişinci**

sever /'sevə^r/ *verb* [T] **1** to cut through something, especially a part of the body **koparmak, bölmek, ikiye ayırmak** *to sever an artery* ○ [often passive] *Two of her fingers were severed in the accident.* **2 sever links/ties, etc with sb** to end a relationship with someone **ilişkiyi kesmek/bitirmek/kesmek/sona erdirmek**

oᴖ**several** /'sev^ər^əl/ *pronoun, determiner* some, but not a lot **bir kaç** *Several people have complained about the scheme.* ○ *Several of my friends studied in Manchester.*

severance /'sev^ərəns/ *noun* [U] when an employer forces an employee to leave a job **işten ayrılmaya/çıkmaya zorlama** *severance pay*

severe /sɪ'vɪə^r/ *adjective* **1** BAD extremely bad **çok kötü, ağır, ciddi, vahim** *a severe headache* ○ *severe weather conditions* **2** NOT KIND not kind or gentle **hoşgörüsüz,**

sert, katı, haşin *a severe punishment* **3** PERSON A severe person looks unfriendly or very strict. **ciddi, sert, tavizsiz, sevimsiz** ● **severely** *adverb* to be severely injured* ○ *She has been severely criticized for the speech.* **kötü bir şekilde**

severity /sɪ'verəti/ *noun* [U] how severe something is **ciddiyet, sertlik**

sew /səʊ/ *verb* [I, T] *past tense* **sewed**, *past participle* **sewn** or **sewed** to join things together with a needle and thread **dikmek** *I need to sew a button on my shirt.*

sew sth up *phrasal verb* **1** to close or repair something by sewing the edges together **dikerek tamir etmek/ kapatmak; dikip birleştirmek 2 have sth sewn up** *informal* to be certain to win or succeed at something

sewage /'su:ɪdʒ/ *noun* [U] waste water and waste from toilets **pis su, lağım suyu, kanalizasyon suyu** *a sewage treatment plant*

sewer /suə^r/ *noun* [C] a large underground system of pipes that carries away sewage **lağım**

sewing /'səʊɪŋ/ *noun* [U] **1** the activity of joining pieces of cloth together or repairing them with a needle and thread **dikiş 2** the pieces of cloth that you are joining together or repairing with a needle and thread **dikiş, dikilen şey**

'sewing ma,chine *noun* [C] a machine that joins pieces of cloth together with a needle and thread **dikiş makinası**

sewn /səʊn/ *past participle of* sew **'dikmek' fiilinin geçmiş zaman hâli**

oᴖ**sex¹** /seks/ *noun* **1** [U] sexual activity between people **cinsiyet** *to have sex with someone* ○ *sex education* **2** [U] the fact of being male or female **cinsiyet, cins** *Do you know what sex the baby is?* ○ *sex discrimination* **3 the female/male/opposite, etc sex** people who are female/male/the other sex from you, etc **dişi/erkek/ karşı vb. cins/cinsiyet**

sex² /seks/ *verb*

sex sth up *phrasal verb UK informal* to make something seem more exciting than it really is **heyecanlandırmak; heyecan verici hâle getirmek; heyecan uyandırmak** *It was said that the government had sexed up the report.*

sexism /'seksɪz^əm/ *noun* [U] when someone is treated unfairly because they are a woman or because they are a man **cinsiyet ayırımı/ayırımcılığı** ● **sexist** *adjective* sexist attitudes/jokes **cinsiyet ayırımı yapan**

'sex ,life *noun* [C] a person's sexual activities and relationships **cinsel yaşam**

oᴖ**sexual** /'sekʃʊəl/ *adjective* **1** relating to the activity of sex **cinsel, seksüel** *sexual experiences* ○ *sexual organs* **2** relating to being male or female **cinsel, cinsî; erkek/ dişi olmakla ilgili** *sexual discrimination* ○ *sexual equality*

sexual 'intercourse *noun* [U] *formal* when a man puts his penis into a woman's vagina **cinsel ilişki, seks, sevişme**

sexuality /,sekʃu'æləti/ *noun* [U] the way you feel about sexual activity and the type of sex you prefer **cinsel ilişki isteği, cinsellik, cinsel tercih**

sexually /'sekʃʊəli/ *adverb* in a way that relates to the activity of sex **cinsel yönden/olarak** *sexually attractive* ○ *a sexually transmitted disease*

sexy /'seksi/ *adjective* attractive or exciting in a sexual way **seksi, cinsel çekiciliği olan; cinsel cazibeli; şuh, çekici** *sexy underwear* ○ *He's very sexy.*

SGML /esdʒi:em'el/ *noun* [U] *abbreviation for* standard generalized markup language: a system for organizing different parts of a computer document **standart**

S

genellenmiş marka lisan (SGML); bilgisayar belgelerinin farklı parçalarını düzenleyen sistem

sh (also **shh**) /ʃ/ exclamation used to tell someone to be quiet 'Şşşş!', 'Sessiz ol!', 'Sakin ol!'

shabby /'ʃæbi/ adjective **1** looking untidy and in bad condition **eski püskü, kılıksız, pejmurde, yıpranmış** shabby clothes/furniture **2** Shabby behaviour or treatment is bad and unfair. **haksız, kötü, berbat, adi, aşağılık** ● **shabbily** adverb shabbily dressed ○ shabbily treated **pejmürde bir şekilde**

shack¹ /ʃæk/ noun [C] a small simple building that has been badly built **derme çatma kulübe, baraka**

shack² /ʃæk/ verb
shack up with sb phrasal verb very informal to start living in the same house as someone you are having a romantic relationship with **birlikte yaşamaya başlamak**

shackle /'ʃækl/ verb [T] **1** to fasten a prisoner's arms or legs together with chains **zincirlemek, prangaya vurmak, kelepçelemek 2 be shackled by sth** to be prevented from doing what you want to do by something **engellenmek, kösteklenmek**

shackles /'ʃæklz/ noun [plural] chains used to fasten together prisoners' arms or legs **pranga, kelepçe, zincirler**

shade

shade   shadow

shade¹ /ʃeɪd/ noun **1** NO SUN [U] an area where there is no light from the sun and so it is darker and not as hot **gölge** I'd prefer to sit **in the shade**. **2** COLOUR [C] a colour, especially when referring to how dark or light it is **(açık, koyu) renk tonu** a pale/dark shade of grey ○ pastel shades **3** COVER [C] a cover that stops too much light coming from the sun or from an electric light **gölgelik** a lamp shade **4 a shade** a small amount **birazcık, az miktarda, azıcık** He's perhaps a shade taller. **5 a shade of meaning/opinion, etc** a slight difference in the meaning of something **nüans, ince ayrıntı, küçük fark; anlam/görüş farkı/ayrıntısı/nüansı**

shade² /ʃeɪd/ verb [T] to cover something in order to protect it from the sun **gölgelemek, gölge yapmak/etmek** He shaded his eyes with his hand.

shades /ʃeɪdz/ noun [plural] informal sunglasses (= dark glasses that protect your eyes from the sun) **güneş gözlüğü**

🧩 **shadow** .... İLE BİRLİKTE KULLANILAN KELİMELER

sth **casts** a shadow ● a shadow **crosses/falls across** sth ● sth is **in** shadow ● the shadow **of** sth

shadow¹ /'ʃædəʊ/ noun **1** [C, U] a dark area made by something that is stopping the light **gölge, loşluk, yarı karanlık** The tree had cast (= made) a long shadow. ⟳ See picture at **shade**. **2 beyond/without a shadow of a doubt** If something is true beyond a shadow of a doubt, it is certainly true. **zerre kadar bir şüphe olmayan; hiç su götürmeyen; en ufak bir kuşku içermeyen; kesinlikle doğru** ● **3 cast a shadow over sth** to spoil a good situation with something unpleasant **gölge düşürmek, berbat etmek** The bombing has cast a shadow over the Queen's visit.

shadow² /'ʃædəʊ/ verb [T] to follow someone secretly in order to see where they go and what they do **izlemek, gölge gibi takip etmek** [often passive] He was being shadowed by a private detective.

shadowy /'ʃædəʊi/ adjective **1** dark and full of shadows **gölgeli, loş, karanlık** in a shadowy corner **2** secret and mysterious **gizemli, bilinmeyen, gizli** the shadowy world of espionage

shady /'ʃeɪdi/ adjective **1** A shady place is protected from the sun and so it is darker and cooler. **gölgeli** We found a shady spot to sit in. **2** informal dishonest and illegal **karanlık, sahtekâr ve yasadışı** shady deals

shaft /ʃɑːft/ noun [C] **1** a long, vertical hole that people or things can move through, either inside a building or in the ground **dikey boşluk, yarık, çukur** a mine shaft ○ a ventilation shaft **2** the handle of a tool or weapon **kabza, tutamak, sap 3 a shaft of light** a beam of light **ışın/şua demeti**

shake¹ /ʃeɪk/ verb past tense **shook**, past part **shaken 1** MOVE [I, T] to make quick, short movements from side to side or up and down, or to make something or someone do this **sarsmak, silkelemek, sallamak** He was shaking with nerves. ○ Shake the bottle. **2 shake hands** to hold someone's hand and move it up and down when you meet them for the first time, or when you make an agreement with them **el sıkışmak** The two leaders smiled and shook hands for the photographers. ○ I shook hands with him. **3 shake your head** to move your head from side to side to mean 'no' **kafasını sallamak; başını hayır anlamında sallamak 4** SHOCK [T] to shock or upset someone **sarsmak, perişan etmek, allak bullak etmek** [often passive] No one was injured in the crash, but the driver was badly shaken. **5** VOICE [I] If your voice shakes, you sound very nervous or frightened. **sesi titremek**

shake

shake sth off phrasal verb to get rid of an illness or something that is causing you problems **...dan/den kurtulmak/paçasını kurtarmak; atlatmak** I hope I can shake off this cold before the weekend.

shake sb off phrasal verb to succeed in escaping from someone who is following you **atlatmak, kurtulmak, yakayı sıyırmak**

shake sth out phrasal verb to hold something that is made of cloth at one end and move it up and down in order to get rid of dirt **silkelemek**

shake sb up *phrasal verb* If an unpleasant experience shakes someone up, it makes them feel shocked and upset. **sarsmak, şok etmek, üzmek, canını sıkmak** *The accident really shook him up.*

shake² /ʃeɪk/ *noun* [C] **1** when you shake something **sallama, sarsıntı, çalkalama, sarsma** *Give it a good shake before you open it.* **2** (*also* **milkshake**) a sweet drink made of milk and chocolate or fruit **süt çikolata veya şuyu ile yapılan tatlı içecek**

shake-up /'ʃeɪkʌp/ *noun* [C] when big changes are made to a system or an organization **yeniden yapılanma/örgütlenme** *This is the biggest shake-up in the legal system for fifty years.*

shaky /'ʃeɪki/ *adjective* **1** [MOVING] making quick, short movements from side to side or up and down **tir tir titreyen, ayaklarının bağı çözülmüş** *shaky hands* **2** [NOT STRONG] not physically strong because you are nervous, old, or ill **zayıf, kötü, cılız, ayakta duracak hâli olmayan, güçsüz** *I felt a bit shaky when I stood up.* **3** [LIKELY TO FAIL] not working well and likely to fail **neredeyse başarısız, çok iyi olmayan, doğru dürüst çalışmayan, istikrarsız** *They managed to win the game, despite a very shaky start.*

○━**shall** *strong form* /ʃæl/ *weak form* /ʃəl/ *modal verb* **1 shall I/we...? a** used to make an offer or suggestion **...yım/lım mı?** *Shall I cook dinner tonight?* ○ *We'll ask him later; shall we?* **b** used to ask someone what to do **...ım/im mi?** *What restaurant shall we go to?* ○ *Who shall I ask?* **2 I/we shall...** *formal* used to say what you are going to do in the future **...eceğim/acağım/eceğiz/acağız** *I shall be talking to her tomorrow.* ○ *I shan't forget to tell them.* ⊃See study page **Modal verbs** on page Centre 22.

shallot /ʃə'lɒt/ *noun* [C] a vegetable like a small onion **küçük soğana benzer sebze**

○━**shallow** /'ʃæləʊ/ *adjective* **1** not deep **sığ, derin olmayan** *shallow water* ○ *a shallow dish* ⊃See picture at **deep**. **2** not showing any interest in serious ideas **yüzeysel, derinliği olmayan, ciddi düşünceden yoksun, üstünkörü**

the shallows /'ʃæləʊz/ *noun* [plural] areas of shallow water **sığlık, sığ yerler**

sham /ʃæm/ *noun* [no plural] something that is not what it seems to be and is intended to deceive people **düzmece, sahte** *Newspapers have described their marriage as a sham.*

shambles /'ʃæmblz/ *noun* **be a shambles** *informal* to be very badly organized **çok kötü düzenlenmiş olmak; dağınık, savaş alanı gibi olmak** *The performance was a complete shambles.*

🧩 **shame** ...... İLE BİRLİKTE KULLANILAN KELİMELER

bring shame **on** sb/sth ● a **sense of** shame ● the shame **of** (doing) sth

shame¹ /ʃeɪm/ *noun* **1 a shame** If you describe something as a shame, you are disappointed that it has happened. **yazık, ayıp, günah, utanç verici şey** [+ to do sth] *It's a real shame to waste all this food.* ○ [+ (that)] *What a shame that they had to destroy such a beautiful building.* **2** [U] when you feel embarrassed and guilty about something bad that you have done or said **utanç, mahcubiyet, yüz karası, leke, şerefsizlik** *to be filled with shame* **3 have no shame** to not feel embarrassed or guilty about doing bad or embarrassing things **utanç duymamak, hiç yüzü kızarmamak; yüzüne tükürsen yağmur yağıyor sanmak; utanmamak; hiç mahcup olmamak** **4 put sb/sth to shame** to be much better than someone or something else **çok daha iyi olmak; fevkalâde olmak** *Your cooking puts mine to shame.*

shame² /ʃeɪm/ *verb* [T] to make someone feel embarrassed and guilty about something **utandırmak, mahcup etmek** [+ into + doing sth] *His children are trying to shame him into giving up smoking.*

shameful /'ʃeɪmfºl/ *adjective* Something shameful is bad and should make you feel embarrassed and guilty. **utanç verici, yüz kızartıcı, ayıp, çirkin** *shameful scenes* ● **shamefully** *adverb* **utanılası bir şekilde**

shameless /'ʃeɪmləs/ *adjective* without feeling embarrassed or guilty although you should **utanmaz, arsız, yüzsüz** *shameless behaviour/lies* ● **shamelessly** *adverb* **utanmaz bir şekilde**

shampoo /ʃæm'puː/ *noun* [C, U] a liquid substance that you use to wash your hair **şampuan** *a bottle of shampoo* ● **shampoo** *verb* [T] **shampooing**, *past* **shampooed** **şampuan**

○━**shan't** /ʃɑːnt/ *mainly UK short for* shall not **shall not'** **yardımcı fiilinin kısa hâli** *I was invited to the party, but I shan't be going.*

shanty town /'ʃænti,taʊn/ *noun* [C] an area on the edge of a town where poor people live in very simply built houses **gecekondu bölgesi**

🧩 **shape** ...... İLE BİRLİKTE KULLANILAN KELİMELER

an **irregular/pleasing/strange/unusual** shape ● **change** shape ● **in** the shape **of** sth

shapes

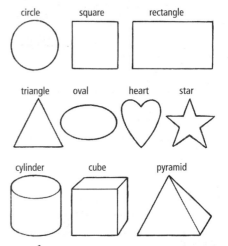

circle   square   rectangle

triangle   oval   heart   star

cylinder   cube   pyramid

○━**shape¹** /ʃeɪp/ *noun* **1** [C, U] the physical form of something made by the line around its outer edge **şekil, biçim** *a circular/rectangular shape* ○ *You can recognize trees by the shape of their leaves.* **2 in good/bad/great, etc shape** in good/bad, etc health or condition **iyi/kötü/harika vs.durumda** *She runs every day so she's in pretty good shape.* **3 out of shape** not healthy or physically strong **sağlıksız, zayıf, kötü, şekilsiz** **4 keep in shape** to stay healthy and physically strong **formunu korumak; sağlığına ve fiziğine iyi bakmak 5 take shape** to start to develop and become more clear or certain **şekil almak, bir şeye benzemeye başlamak** *The project is slowly beginning to take shape.* **6 all shapes and sizes** many different types of people or things **bir çok farklı türde insan ve nesneler** *We saw people there of all shapes and sizes.*

S

shape² /ʃeɪp/ *verb* [T] **1** to influence the way that something develops **biçim vermek, etkilemek, şekillendirmek** [often passive] *Their attitudes were shaped during the war.* **2** to make something become a particular shape **biçimlendirmek, şekil/biçim vermek** *Combine the meat and egg and shape the mixture into small balls.*

shape up *phrasal verb informal* to develop or improve **geliş(tir)mek, gitmek, sürmek** *Things at work seem to be shaping up quite nicely.*

-shaped /ʃeɪpt/ *suffix* used after nouns to mean 'having a particular shape' **...-şeklinde/biçiminde anlamında sonek** *a heart-shaped cake* ⊃See also: pear-shaped.

shapeless /'ʃeɪpləs/ *adjective* not having a clear or well designed shape **şekilsiz, biçimsiz** *a shapeless dress*

shapely /'ʃeɪpli/ *adjective* having an attractive shape **güzel, düzgün, biçimli, çekici, hoş** *shapely legs*

o▪**share¹** /ʃeəʳ/ *verb* **1** [I, T] to have or use something at the same time as someone else **paylaşmak, bölüşmek** *She shares a house with Paul.* **2** [I, T] to divide something between two or more people **paylaştırmak, bölüştürmek** *We shared a pizza and a bottle of wine.* ○ *We shared the cost of the wedding between us.* **3 share an interest/opinion, etc** to have the same interest/opinion, etc as someone else **aynı fikri/ilgi alanını vb. paylaşmak** *They share a love of gardening.* **4 share your problems/thoughts/ideas, etc** to tell someone your problems/thoughts, etc **sorun/düşünce/fikirlerini vb. biriyle paylaşmak**

share sth out *phrasal verb* to divide something into smaller amounts and give one amount to each person in a group **pay etmek, küçük parçacıklara ayırmak, paylaştırmak, bölüştürmek** *Profits are shared out equally among members of the group.*

🧩 share (noun) ...... İLE BİRLİKTE KULLANILAN KELİMELER

buy/have/sell shares ● shares **in** sth ● share **prices**

share² /ʃeəʳ/ *noun* [C] **1** one of the equal parts that the value of a company is divided into when it is owned by a group of people **hisse, pay** *to buy/sell shares* ○ *We own shares in a number of companies.* ○ *Share prices have fallen for the third day running.* **2** a part of something that has been divided **pay, hisse, parça, bölüm, kısım** [usually singular] *When am I going to get my share of the money?* **3 have your (fair) share of sth** to have a lot of something and enough of it, usually something bad **payına düşeni yeterince almak; kendi hissesine düşeni almak** *We've had our fair share of rain already this summer.*

shareholder /'ʃeə,həʊldəʳ/ *noun* [C] someone who owns shares in a company **hissedar** *a shareholders' meeting*

shareware /'ʃeəweəʳ/ *noun* [U] software that you get from the Internet that you can use free for a short time without paying for it **ücretsiz kullanılan yazılım programı**

Sharia /ʃəˈriːə/ *noun* [U] the holy law of Islam **Şarya, İslâm'ın kutsal yasası/kuralı**

shark /ʃɑːk/ *noun* [C] a large fish with very sharp teeth **köpek balığı**

shark

o▪**sharp¹** /ʃɑːp/ *adjective* **1** [ABLE TO CUT] having a very thin or pointed edge that can cut things **keskin, sivri, sivri uçlu** *a sharp knife* ○ *sharp claws/teeth* **2 a sharp rise/increase/drop, etc** a sudden and very large increase or reduction in something **net/belirgin/**

bariz yükselme/artış/düşüş vs. **3 a sharp contrast/difference/distinction, etc** a very big and noticeable difference between two things **gözle görülebilir/besbelli tezat/farklılık/ayrım vs. 4** [QUICK] quick to notice and understand things **(zekâ) keskin, zehir gibi, çabuk kavrayan, hızlı anlayan** *a sharp mind* **5 a sharp pain** a sudden, short, strong pain **ani kısa, keskin/şiddetli/sert ağrı/acı 6** [SEVERE] severe and not gentle **şiddetli, keskin, sert** *sharp criticism* ○ *She can be a bit sharp with people sometimes.* **7 a sharp bend/turn, etc** a sudden large change in the direction you are travelling **keskin kavşak/viraj 8** [SOUR] A sharp taste is slightly sour. **ekşi, keskin tadı olan, mayhoş, buruk 9** [CLEAR] A sharp image is very clear. **net, açık, pürüzsüz, belirgin, resim gibi** *a photograph in sharp focus* **10 a sharp wit** the ability to say things that are funny and clever **kıvrak zekâlı, zeki, keskin zekâlı 11 a sharp tongue** If you have a sharp tongue, you often upset people by saying unkind things to them. **sivri dilli, düşünmeden konuşan, sözünü esirgemeyen 12** [FASHIONABLE] If a piece of clothing or a style is sharp, it is fashionable and tidy. **gösterişli, modaya uygun, göze batan, güzel, hoş** *young men in sharp suits* **13 C sharp/F sharp, etc** the musical note that is between the note C, F, etc and the note above it **diyez (müzikte nota) 14** [TOO HIGH] A sharp musical note sounds unpleasant because it is slightly higher than it should be. **tiz** ● **sharply** *adverb* **keskince, modaya uygun olan, ekşi tadı olan** ● **sharpness** *noun* [U] **keskinlik**

sharp² /ʃɑːp/ *adverb* **3 o'clock/8.30 p.m., etc sharp** at exactly 3 o'clock, 8.30 p.m., etc **tam, dakikası dakikasına, tam vaktinde**

sharp³ /ʃɑːp/ *noun* [C] a musical note that is between one note and the note above it **diyezden, bir üst perdeden**

sharpen /'ʃɑːpⁿn/ *verb* [T] to make something sharper **bilemek, keskinleştirmek, sivriltmek, yontmak** *to sharpen a knife/pencil*

shatter /'ʃætəʳ/ *verb* **1** [I, T] to break into very small pieces, or to make something break into very small pieces **param parça etmek/olmak, tuzla buz etmek/olmak** *Someone threw a stone at the car, shattering the windscreen.* **2** [T] to destroy something good, such as your confidence, hopes, or belief in something **(güven, ümit, inanç) yıkmak, parçalamak, yok etmek, mahvetmek** *The accident completely shattered her confidence.*

shattered /'ʃætəd/ *adjective* **1** very upset **yıkılmış, sarsılmış, perişan olmuş, param parça olmuş 2** UK *informal* very tired **yorgun, bitkin, bitmiş, tükenmiş**

shave¹ /ʃeɪv/ *verb* [I, T] to cut hair off your face or body **tıraş olmak** *to shave your head/legs* ○ *shaving cream/foam*

shave

shave sth off *phrasal verb* to cut a very thin piece off a surface **yontmak, kesmek, kazımak, traşlamak**

shave² /ʃeɪv/ *noun* **1** [C] when a man shaves the hair growing on his face **tıraş 2 a close shave** a situation when something unpleasant or dangerous almost happens **kıl payı, ramak kala, az kalsın, neredeyse**

shaven /'ʃeɪvⁿn/ *adjective* A shaven part of the body has had the hair cut off it. **tıraşlı, traş edilmiş** *a gang of youths with shaven heads*

shaver /ˈʃeɪvəʳ/ *noun* [C] a piece of electrical equipment used to cut hair off the head or body **elektrikli traş makinası**

shavings /ˈʃeɪvɪŋz/ *noun* [plural] very thin pieces that have been cut off something **yonga, talaş** *wood shavings*

shawl /ʃɔːl/ *noun* [C] a piece of cloth that is worn by a woman around her shoulders or used to cover a baby **şal, atkı**

o→**she** *strong form* /ʃiː/ *weak form* /ʃi/ *pronoun* used as the subject of the verb when referring to someone female who has already been talked about **(bayan)** o *"When is Ruth coming?" "She'll be here soon."*

sheaf /ʃiːf/ *noun* [C] *plural* **sheaves** /ʃiːvz/ **1** several pieces of paper held together **deste, tomar** *a sheaf of papers* **2** several pieces of wheat or corn (= plant for grain) tied together **deste, demet**

shear /ʃɪəʳ/ *verb* [T] *past tense* **sheared**, *past part* **sheared** or **shorn** to cut the wool off a sheep **kırkmak, yününü kırkmak/kesmek**

shears /ʃɪəz/ *noun* [plural] a cutting tool with two large blades, like a large pair of scissors **yün kırkma makası, bahçıvan makası** *a pair of garden shears*

sheath /ʃiːθ/ *noun* [C] a cover for the sharp blade of a knife **bıçak kını, kılıf**

o→**she'd** /ʃiːd/ **1** *short for* she had **she had' fiil yapısının kısa hâli** *By the time I got there, she'd fallen asleep.* **2** *short for* she would **she would' fiil yapısının kısa hâli** *She knew that she'd be late.*

shed¹ /ʃed/ *noun* [C] a small building used to store things such as tools **baraka, sundurma, müştemilat** *a garden shed*

shed² /ʃed/ *verb* [T] **shedding**, *past* **shed 1 shed leaves/skin/hair, etc** to lose something because it falls off **yaprak/deri/saç vs. Dökülmek** *A lot of trees shed their leaves in the autumn.* **2** to get rid of something that you do not want or need **atmak;** ...**dan/den kurtulmak** *A lot of companies are shedding jobs.* **3 shed tears** to cry **göz yaşı dökmek/akıtmak, ağlamak 4 shed blood** to kill or injure someone **kan dökmek, cana kıymak, öldürmek, yaralamak** ⊃See also: cast/shed **light¹** on sth.

sheen /ʃiːn/ *noun* [no plural] a smooth shine on a surface **parlaklık, parıltı**

sheep /ʃiːp/ *noun* [C] *plural* **sheep** a farm animal whose skin is covered with wool **koyun** *a flock of sheep*

sheepish /ˈʃiːpɪʃ/ *adjective* slightly embarrassed, usually because you have done something stupid **sıkılgan, mahcup, utangaç, şaşkın** *a sheepish grin/look* ● **sheepishly** *adverb* **utangaç, mahcup bir şekilde**

sheer /ʃɪəʳ/ *adjective* **1** [EXTREME] [always before noun] used to emphasize how strong a feeling or quality is **katıksız, safi, tam, tamamen** *a look of sheer delight/joy* o *sheer determination/hard work* **2** [LARGE] [always before noun] used to emphasize the large size or amount of something **sırf, düpedüz, yalnız, bütün bütün** *The delays are due to the sheer volume of traffic.* **3** [STEEP] very steep **dik, dimdik, sarp** *a sheer cliff face* **4** [CLOTH] Sheer cloth is very thin and you can see through it. **incecik, çok ince, şeffaf** *sheer tights/nylons*

sheet /ʃiːt/ *noun* [C] **1** a large piece of cloth put on a bed to lie on or under **çarşaf, yatak çarşafı** *a double fitted sheet* o *to change the sheets* **2 a sheet of paper/glass/metal, etc** a flat piece of paper/glass, etc **bir tabaka/yaprak/levha kağıt/cam/metal** *a sheet of yellow paper* ⊃See also: balance sheet.

sheet

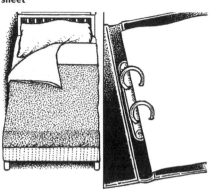

sheets on a bed   sheet of paper

sheeting /ˈʃiːtɪŋ/ *noun* [U] a large flat piece of material, usually used as a cover **metal kaplama** *plastic sheeting*

Sheikh (*also* Sheik) /ʃeɪk/ *noun* [C] an Arab leader **Şeyh**

shelf /ʃelf/ *noun* [C] *plural* **shelves** /ʃelvz/ a flat, horizontal board used to put things on, often fixed to a wall or inside a cupboard **raf** *a book shelf* o *on the top/bottom shelf*

'shelf ˌlife *noun* [C] *plural* **shelf lives** A product's shelf life is the length of time it stays in good condition and can be used. **dayanma süresi, kullanım süresi** [usually singular] *Fresh fruit has a very short shelf life.*

o→**she'll** /ʃiːl/ *short for* she will **she will' fiil yapısının kısa hâli** *She'll be away until Tuesday.*

shell¹ /ʃel/ *noun* [C] **1** the hard outer covering of some creatures and of eggs, nuts, or seeds **kabuk, deniz kabuğu** *a snail's shell* o *an egg shell* **2** a bomb fired from a large gun **mermi, gülle, mermi kovanı** ⊃See also: sea shell.

shell

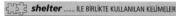

shell² /ʃel/ *verb* [T] to attack a place with bombs **bombardıman etmek, bomba yağdırmak**

shell out (sth) *phrasal verb informal* to pay or give money for something, especially when you do not want to **istemeye istemeye para harcamak, vermek**

shell

shellfish /ˈʃelfɪʃ/ *noun* [U] sea creatures that live in shells and are eaten as food **su kabuklusu, deniz yumuşakçası**

shelter¹ /ˈʃeltəʳ/ *noun* **1** [C] a place that protects you from bad weather or danger **barınak, sığınak** *a bomb shelter* **2** [U] protection from bad weather or danger **koruma, sığınma** *We took shelter from the rain in a doorway.*

shelter² /'ʃeltər/ *verb* **1 shelter from/in/under, etc** to go under a cover or inside a building to be protected from bad weather or danger **barınmak, sığınmak, korunmak** *They went under a tree to shelter from the rain.* **2** [T] to provide cover or protection for someone **korumak, muhafaza etmek, yataklık etmek** *Many households are already sheltering refugees.*

sheltered /'ʃeltəd/ *adjective* **1** covered or protected from bad weather or danger **korunaklı** *a sheltered spot by the wall* **2 a sheltered existence/life/upbringing, etc** If you have a sheltered life, you are protected too much and experience very little danger or excitement. **emin ve rahat, ihtimam görmüş, korunmuş 3 sheltered accommodation/housing** *UK* houses for old and ill people in a place where help can be given if it is needed **koruma/bakım evi; düşkünler yurdu**

shelve /ʃelv/ *verb* [T] to decide not to continue with a plan **ertelemek, rafa kaldırmak, sümen altı etmek** [often passive] *The project had to be shelved when they ran out of money.*

shelves /ʃelvz/ *plural of* shelf **raflar**

shenanigans /ʃɪ'nænɪɡənz/ *noun* [plural] *informal* secret or dishonest behaviour **gizli ve saygısız davranış, entrika, dolap, düzen** *political/sexual shenanigans*

shepherd¹ /'ʃepəd/ *noun* [C] someone whose job is to look after sheep **çoban**

shepherd² /'ʃepəd/ *verb* [T] to go somewhere with someone in order to guide them or protect them **göz kulak olmak, eşlik etmek** *children shepherded to school by their parents*

sheriff /'ʃerɪf/ *noun* [C] an elected law officer in the US **şerif**

sherry /'ʃeri/ *noun* [C, U] a strong Spanish wine that is drunk before a meal **bir tür İspanyol şarabı, şeri**

o▪**she's** /ʃi:z/ **1** *short for* she is **she is' fiil yapısının kısa hâli** *She's a very good student.* **2** *short for* she has **she has' fiil yapısının kısa hâli** *She's been working very hard.*

shh /ʃ/ *exclamation* used to tell someone to be quiet **'Şşşş!', sessiz olmayı belirten ünlem**

Shia /'ʃi:ə/ *noun* [C] a Shiite **Şii**

shield¹ /ʃi:ld/ *noun* [C] **1** a large, flat object that police officers and soldiers hold in front of their bodies to protect themselves **kalkan 2** a person or thing used as protection **kalkan, siper, koruyucu** *The hostages are being used as human shields.*

shield² /ʃi:ld/ *verb* [T] to protect someone or something from something dangerous or unpleasant **korumak, siper olmak** *to shield your eyes from the sun*

─── **shift** ...... İLE BİRLİKTE KULLANILAN KELİMELER

a **dramatic/fundamental/gradual/major** shift ● a shift **(away) from/towards** sth ● a shift **in** sth

shift¹ /ʃɪft/ *noun* [C] **1** a change in something **değişim, değişme** *There has been a dramatic shift in public opinion on this matter.* **2** a period of work in a place such as a factory or hospital **vardiya, posta** *afternoon/night shift* ○ *He works an eight-hour shift.*

shift² /ʃɪft/ *verb* **1** [CHANGE] [I, T] to change something **değiştirmek, hafif değişiklik yapmak** *We are trying to shift the emphasis from curing illness to preventing it.* **2** [MOVE STH] [T] to move something to another place **yerini değiştirmek** *We need to shift all these boxes into the other room.* **3** [MOVE YOURSELF] [I, T] to move into a different position **yer/yön değiştirmek** *He shifted uncomfortably in his seat.* **4** [CHANGE SPEED] [T] (*also* shift into) *US* to change the position of the gears (= parts that control

how fast the wheels turn) in a vehicle **vites değiştirmek** *to shift gears*

'shift ˌkey *noun* [C] the key on a computer keyboard which allows you to create a capital letter (= a large letter of the alphabet at the beginning of sentences and names) **bilgisayarda büyük harf tuşu/değiştirme tuşu**

shifty /'ʃɪfti/ *adjective informal* Someone who looks shifty looks dishonest. **hilekâr, kalleş, tilki gibi**

Shiite (*also* Shi'ite) /'ʃi:aɪt/ *noun* [C] a member of a large group within the Islamic religion **Şiiler, Şiilik ● Shiite** (*also* Shi'ite) *adjective* describing the Shiites or their type of Islam **Şiilere/Şiiliğe ilişkin**

shilling /'ʃɪlɪŋ/ *noun* [C] a unit of money used in the past in the UK **şiling**

shimmer /'ʃɪmər/ *verb* [I] to shine gently and seem to be moving slightly **titrek titrek parıldamak** *The trees shimmered in the moonlight.*

shin /ʃɪn/ *noun* [C] the front part of a leg between the knee and the foot **incik kemiği, kaval kemiği** ⊃Orta kısımdaki renkli sayfalarına bakınız.

shine¹ /ʃaɪn/ *verb past* shone *or* shined **1** [PRODUCE LIGHT] [I] to produce bright light **parlamak, ışık saçmak** *The sun was shining brightly through the window.* **2** [POINT LIGHT] [I, T] to point a light somewhere **ışık tutmak, bir bölgeyi aydınlatmak** *The car's headlights shone right into my eyes.* **3** [REFLECT] [I, T] If a surface shines, it reflects light, and if you shine it, you make it reflect light. **parlamak, parlatmak** *She polished her shoes until they shone.* **4** [EYES/FACE] [I] If your eyes or face shine, you look happy, healthy, or excited. **sağlıklı/mutlu/heyecanlı gözükmek; gözleri parlamak** *His eyes were shining with excitement.* **5** [DO WELL] [I] to do something very well, usually better than other people. **parlamak, kendini göstermek, çok üstün olmak**

shine² /ʃaɪn/ *noun* **1** [no plural] when something is bright from reflected light on its surface **parlaklık, parlama, parıltı** *hair with body and shine* **2 take a shine to sb** *informal* to like someone immediately **birden kanı ısınmak, kısa sürede sevmek, hemen hoşlanmak** *I think he's taken a bit of a shine to you.* ● **3 take the shine off sth** to spoil something pleasant **berbat etmek, gölge düşürmek, mahvetmek**

shingle /'ʃɪŋɡl/ *noun* [U] *UK* a lot of very small pieces of stone on a beach **çakıl, çakıl taşı**

shiny /'ʃaɪni/ *adjective* A shiny surface is bright because it reflects light. **parlak, parlayan** *shiny hair*

o▪**ship¹** /ʃɪp/ *noun* [C] a large boat that carries people or goods by sea **gemi** *a cargo ship*

ship² /ʃɪp/ *verb* [T] **shipping,** *past* shipped to send something from one place to another **göndermek, yollamak, sevketmek** [often passive] *These vegetables have been shipped halfway around the world.*

shipment /'ʃɪpmənt/ *noun* **1** [C] an amount of goods sent from one place to another **yükleme** *The first shipments of food arrived this month.* **2** [U] when something is sent from one place to another **gemi ile nakil, sevk, gönderme** *the shipment of nuclear waste*

ˌshipping and 'handling *noun* [U] *US* postage and packing **nakliye ve ambalaj**

shipwreck¹ /'ʃɪprek/ *noun* [C] an accident in which a ship is destroyed at sea **deniz/gemi kazası**

shipwreck² /'ʃɪprek/ *verb* **be shipwrecked** If someone is shipwrecked, the ship they are in is destroyed in an accident. **deniz kazasına uğramak**

shipyard /'ʃɪpjɑːd/ *noun* [C] a place where ships are built or repaired **tersane**

shirk /ʃɜːk/ verb [I, T] to avoid doing something because it is difficult or unpleasant **kaytarmak, kaçmak, yan çizmek** to shirk your duties/responsibilities

o→**shirt** /ʃɜːt/ noun [C] a piece of clothing worn on the top part of the body, often made of thin material like cotton and fastened with buttons down the front **gömlek** ⊃Orta kısımdaki renkli sayfalarına bakınız ⊃See also: **polo shirt, T-shirt**.

shish kebab /ˈʃɪʃkəˌbæb/ noun [C] small pieces of meat or vegetables cooked on a long, thin stick **şiş kebap**

shit¹ /ʃɪt/ exclamation very informal a very impolite word used to show surprise, anger, disappointment, etc **Lanet!', 'Boktan şey!', 'Kahretsin!' (argo) 'Hassiktir!'**

shit² /ʃɪt/ noun [U] very informal a very impolite word for waste from the body of a person or animal that comes out of their bottom **dışkı, bok**

shiver /ˈʃɪvəʳ/ verb [I] to shake because you are cold or frightened **titremek, ürpermek** She shivered with cold. ● **shiver** noun [C] He felt a shiver run down his spine (= He felt afraid). **titreme**

shoal /ʃəʊl/ noun [C] a large group of fish swimming together **balık sürüsü/akını**

shock ...... İLE BİRLİKTE KULLANILAN KELİMELER
come as a shock ● get/have a shock ● a big/nasty/real shock ● a shock to sb ● be in shock

shock¹ /ʃɒk/ noun 1 [SURPRISE] [C, U] a big, unpleasant surprise **şok, sarsıntı** We got a nasty shock when he gave us the bill. ○ Her death came as a terrible shock to him. ○ They are still in shock (= feeling the effect of a shock) from the accident. 2 [ILLNESS] [U] a medical condition when someone is extremely weak because of damage to their body **şoka girme, şok, travma** He went into shock and nearly died. 3 [ELECTRICITY] [C] (also electric shock) a sudden, painful feeling that you get when electricity flows through your body **elektrik şoku** 4 [MOVEMENT] [C] a sudden movement caused by an explosion, accident, etc **şok, travma, geçici şuur kaybı** ⊃See also: **culture shock**.

shock² /ʃɒk/ verb [I, T] to surprise and upset someone **sarsmak, şok etmek, çok etkilemek** [often passive] Many people were shocked by the violent scenes in the film. ● **shocked** adjective [+ to do sth] We were shocked to find rat poison in our hotel room. **şaşırmış**

shocking /ˈʃɒkɪŋ/ adjective 1 very surprising and upsetting or immoral **üzücü, şok edici, hayrete düşürücü** shocking news ○ This report contains scenes that some people may find shocking. 2 UK very bad **berbat, çok kötü, iğrenç** My memory is shocking. ● **shockingly** adverb **şaşırtıcı bir şekilde**

shoddy /ˈʃɒdi/ adjective very bad quality **kalitesiz, kötü, bayağı, sıradan** shoddy goods ○ shoddy work/workmanship/treatment

o→**shoe** /ʃuː/ noun [C] 1 a strong covering for the foot, often made of leather **ayakkabı, pabuç** a pair of shoes ○ to put your shoes on/take your shoes off 2 **be in sb's shoes** informal to be in the same situation as someone else, especially an unpleasant situation **aynı durumda olmak, benzer şartları yaşamak** What would you do if you were in my shoes?

shoelace /ˈʃuːleɪs/ noun [C] a long, thin piece of material used to fasten shoes **ayakkabı bağcığı**

shoestring /ˈʃuːstrɪŋ/ noun **on a shoestring** If you do something on a shoestring, you do it using very little money. **çok az para ile, çok ucuza**

shone /ʃɒn/ ⓤⓢ /ʃəʊn/ past of shine **'parlamak' fiilinin geçmiş zaman hâli**

shoo /ʃuː/ verb **shooing, past shooed shoo sb away/off/out, etc** to make a person or animal leave a place by chasing them or shouting 'shoo' at them **kış kışlamak, 'Hoşt, hoşt!' diye kovalamak** ● **shoo** exclamation **Kış Kış!**

shook /ʃʊk/ past tense of shake **'sarsmak' fiilinin ikinci hâli**

o→**shoot¹** /ʃuːt/ verb past shot 1 [INJURE] [T] to injure or kill a person or animal by firing a bullet from a gun at them **ateş etmek, kurşun yağdırmak; silahla vurmak** [often passive] He was robbed and then shot in the stomach. ○ An innocent bystander was shot dead in the incident. 2 [FIRE BULLET] [I, T] to fire a bullet from a gun **ateş edip vurmak; silahı ateşlemek** Don't shoot! 3 [SPORT] [I] to try to score points in sports such as football by hitting, kicking, or throwing the ball towards the goal **gol atmak** 4 **shoot across/out/up, etc** to move somewhere very quickly **aniden fırlamak, ok gibi atılmak; hızlıca hareket etmek** She shot across the road without looking. 5 [FILM] [T] to use a camera to record a film or take a photograph **resim çekmek, kamera ile çekim yapmak** [often passive] Most of the film was shot in Italy.

shoot sb/sth down phrasal verb to destroy an aircraft or make it fall to the ground by firing bullets or weapons at it **ateş ederek düşürmek, vurup düşürmek; vurulup düşmek**

shoot up phrasal verb If a number or amount shoots up, it increases very quickly. **sürate artmak, hızla yükselmek** Prices have shot up by 25%.

shoot² /ʃuːt/ noun [C] 1 a new branch or stem growing on a plant **sürgün, filiz, fışkın** bamboo shoots 2 when someone takes photographs or makes a film **resim çekme; film çekme** a fashion shoot

shooting /ˈʃuːtɪŋ/ noun 1 [C] when someone is injured or killed by a bullet from a gun **vurulma, yaralanma, silahla öldürülme** a fatal shooting 2 [U] the sport of firing bullets from guns, sometimes to kill animals **atıcılık, avcılık, av partisi**

o→**shop¹** /ʃɒp/ (also US store) noun [C] a building or part of a building where you can buy things **dükkân, mağaza** a book shop ○ a shoe shop ○ to go to the shops ○ a shop window ⊃See also: **charity shop**.

o→**shop²** /ʃɒp/ verb [I] shopping, past shopped to buy things in shops **alışveriş yapmak** I'm shopping for baby clothes. ○ I usually go shopping on Saturday.

shop around phrasal verb to compare the price and quality of the same thing from different places before deciding which one to buy **dükkân dükkân dolaşmak** to shop around for a computer

shop asˌsistant UK (US sales clerk) noun [C] someone whose job is selling things in a shop **tezgâhtar, satış elemanı**

shop ˈfloor noun [no plural] the part of a factory where things are made and not the part where the managers' offices are **imalât bölümü**

shopkeeper /ˈʃɒpˌkiːpəʳ/ noun [C] someone who owns or manages a small shop **dükkân sahibi, esnaf**

shoplifting /ˈʃɒplɪftɪŋ/ noun [U] stealing things from a shop **mağaza hırsızlığı, dükkândan mal yürütmek** ● **shoplifter** noun [C] **dükkan hırsızlığı** ● **shoplift** verb [I] **dükkândan hırsızlık yapmak**

shopper /ˈʃɒpəʳ/ noun [C] someone who is buying things from shops **alışveriş yapanlar, müşteriler**

shopping ...... İLE BİRLİKTE KULLANILAN KELİMELER
a shopping spree/trip ● to go shopping

o→**shopping** /ˈʃɒpɪŋ/ noun [U] 1 when you buy things from shops **alışveriş** I love shopping. ○ a shopping basket/

trolley **2** the things that you buy from a shop or shops **alışverişte alınan şeyler** *Can you help me unpack the shopping?* ○ *a shopping bag* ⊃See also: **window shopping**.

'shopping ,basket *noun* [C] a place on a website where you collect things that you plan to buy from the website **internette alışveriş sepeti** ⊃See **basket**.

'shopping ,centre *UK* (*US* **shopping center**) *noun* [C] a place where a lot of shops have been built close together **alışveriş merkezi**

'shopping ,mall *noun* [C] a large, covered shopping area **kapalı alışveriş merkezi**

shore[1] /ʃɔːr/ *noun* [C, U] the area of land along the edge of the sea or a lake **sahil, kıyı, deniz kenarı** *They had to abandon the boat and swim back to shore.*

shore[2] /ʃɔːr/ *verb*
shore sth up *phrasal verb* to help or improve something that is likely to fail **desteklemek, takviye etmek, güçlendirmek**

shorn /ʃɔːn/ *past participle of* shear **kırkmak' fiilinin geçmiş zaman hâli**

o~**short**[1] /ʃɔːt/ *adjective* **1** [DISTANCE] having a small distance from one end to the other **kısa** *short, brown hair* ○ *short legs* ○ *a short skirt* **2** [TIME] continuing for a small amount of time **az, kısa** *a short visit* ○ *There's a short break for coffee between classes.* **3** [BOOK] A short book or other piece of writing has few pages or words. **kısa/ az metin içeren** *a short article/story* **4** [PERSON] A short person is not as tall as most people. **kısa (kişi)** *She's short and slim with dark hair.* **5** [NOT HAVING ENOUGH] not having enough of something **yetersiz, az, biraz** *I'm a bit short of money at the moment.* ○ *Would you like to play? We're a couple of people short.* ○ *He seemed a bit short of breath* (= having difficulty breathing). **6 be short for sth** to be a shorter way of saying the same thing **kısa yazılışı/söylenişi olmak; kısa şekli olmak** *'Mick' is short for 'Michael'.* **7 be short with sb** to talk to someone quickly in an angry or rude way **azarlamak, nezaketsiz/kaba/sert davranmak** ● **shortness** *noun* [U] ⊃See also: in the long/short run[2]. **kısalık**

short[2] /ʃɔːt/ *adverb* **1 short of doing sth** without doing something **hariç; ...dan/den başka; dışında** *He did everything he could to get the money, short of robbing a bank.* **2 stop short of sth/doing sth** to almost do something but decide not to do it **vazgeçmek, yapmamaya karar vermek** *She stopped short of accusing him of lying.* **3 fall short of sth** to not reach a particular level, but only by a small amount **beklenenin altına düşmek, istenilen düzeye ulaşmamak** *Sales for the first half of this year fell just short of the target.* **4 cut sth short** to have to stop doing something before it is finished **kısa kesmek, yarıda kesmek; sözünü kesmek** *They had to cut the holiday short when her mother was taken ill.*

short[3] /ʃɔːt/ *noun* **1 in short** in a few words **kısacası, sözün özü, özetle** *In short, we need more staff.* **2** [C] a short film **kısa film 3** [C] *UK* A small amount of a strong alcoholic drink like whisky **az içki, küçük şişelerde sunulan içki**

┌─────────────────────────────────────┐
│ **shortage** .... İLE BİRLİKTE KULLANILAN KELİMELER │
└─────────────────────────────────────┘

an **acute/chronic/desperate/serious** shortage ● a shortage **of** sth

shortage /ʃɔːtɪdʒ/ *noun* [C] when there is not enough of something **darlık, kıtlık, sıkıntı** *a shortage of nurses* ○ *food shortages*

shortbread /ʃɔːtbred/ *noun* [U] a hard, sweet cake **kurabiye**

short-circuit /ʃɔːtsɜːkɪt/ *noun* [C] a fault in an electrical connection **kısa devre** ● **short-circuit** *verb* [I, T] **kısa devre yapmak**

shortcoming /ʃɔːtkʌmɪŋ/ *noun* [C] a fault **kusur, eksik, noksan** [usually plural] *I like him despite his shortcomings.*

shortcut (*also UK* ,short 'cut) /ʃɔːtkʌt/ *noun* [C] **1** a quicker and more direct way of getting somewhere or doing something **kestirme, kestirme/kısa yol** *I took a shortcut through the car park.* **2** In computing, a shortcut is a quick way to start or use a computer program. **(bilgisayar) kısayol; bir programı başlatmak ve kullanmak için oluşturulan kısayol** *a shortcut key*

shorten /ʃɔːtən/ *verb* [I, T] to become shorter or to make something shorter **kısal(t)mak** *Smoking shortens your life.*

shortfall /ʃɔːtfɔːl/ *noun* [C] the difference between the amount that is needed and the smaller amount that is available **açık, eksik, noksan, yetmezlik** *a shortfall in government spending*

shorthand /ʃɔːthænd/ *noun* [U] a fast way of writing using abbreviations and symbols **steno, stenografi**

short-haul /ʃɔːthɔːl/ *adjective* travelling a short distance **kısa mesafe seyahat** *a short-haul flight*

shortlist /ʃɔːtlɪst/ *noun* [C] *UK* A list of people who are competing for a prize, job, etc, who have already been chosen from a larger list **son eleme aday listesi** *to be on the shortlist* ● **shortlist** *verb* [T] *UK* shortlisted candidates **son elemeye kalmak**

short-lived /ʃɔːtlɪvd/ *adjective* only lasting for a short time **kısa ömürlü/süreli, geçici**

shortly /ʃɔːtli/ *adverb* **1** If something is going to happen shortly, it will happen soon. **hemen, az sonra, yakında, kısa bir süre sonra** *Our plans for the next year will be announced shortly.* **2 shortly after/before sth** a short time after or before something **...dan/den kısa bir süre sonra/önce** *He left here shortly after midnight.*

short-range /ʃɔːtreɪndʒ/ *adjective* intended to go a short distance **kısa menzilli/mesafeli** *a short-range missile*

shorts /ʃɔːts/ *noun* [plural] **1** a very short pair of trousers that stop above the knees **şort, kısa pantolon** *T-shirt and shorts* ○ *cycling shorts* **2** *US* men's underwear to wear under trousers **erkek külotu** ⊃See also: **boxers**.

short-sighted /ʃɔːtsaɪtɪd/ *adjective* **1** not able to see far without wearing glasses **miyop; uzağı göremeyen 2** not thinking enough about how an action will affect the future **ileriyi göremeyen, geleceği yorumlayamayan, kısa/dar görüşlü; sağduyusuz** *a short-sighted policy*

short-term /ʃɔːttɜːm/ *adjective* lasting a short time **kısa vadeli** *short-term memory*

short-wave /ʃɔːtweɪv/ *noun* [U] a system used to broadcast radio signals around the world **kısa dalga; kısa dalgadan yayın** *short-wave radio*

shot[1] /ʃɒt/ *noun* [C] **1** [GUN] when a bullet is fired from a gun **atış, atım, el, silâh atımı** *Three shots were fired.* **2** [SPORT] when someone tries to score points in sports such as football by hitting or throwing the ball **şut, vuruş, gol** *Good shot!* **3** [PHOTOGRAPH] a photograph **resim, fotograf, enstantane** *I got a good shot of them leaving the hotel together.* **4 give sth a shot; have/take a shot at sth** *informal* to try to do something, often for the first time **yapmaya çalışmak, girişmek, başlamak, girişimde bulunmak, denemek, tecrübe etmek** *I've never played football, but I'll give it a shot.* **5** [MEDICINE] an amount of medicine put into the body with a special needle **aşı, iğne 6** ⟨DRINK⟩ a small amount of a strong alcoholic drink **bir yudum/duble içki** *a shot of whisky* **7 like a shot** If someone does something like a shot, they do it quickly and enthusiastically. **hemen, derhal, hiç vakit kaybetmeden ● 8 a shot in the dark** an attempt to guess something when you have no information or knowledge about it **tahmin, atma, rastgele tahmin/yorum** ⇒See also: long shot.

shot² /ʃɒt/ *past of* shoot **ateş etmek' fiilinin geçmiş zaman hâli**

shotgun /'ʃɒtɡʌn/ *noun* [C] a long gun that fires small, metal balls **av tüfeği, çifte**

o┅**should** *strong form* /ʃʊd/ *weak form* /ʃəd/ *modal verb*
1 ⟨BEST⟩ used to say or ask what is the correct or best thing to do ...**malı/meli; yapılması gerekeni istemeden/sormada kullanılır** *He should have gone to the doctor.* ○ *Should I apologize to her?* ○ *You shouldn't be so angry with him.* **2** ⟨EXPECT⟩ used to say that you expect something to be true or that you expect something to happen ...**malıydı/meliydi (ama olmadı); bir şeyin olmasını ümit etmede kullanılır** *She should be feeling better by now.* ○ *The letter should arrive by Friday.* **3** ⟨POSSIBLE⟩ *formal* used to refer to a possible event in the future ...**acak/ecek olursa; ...sa/se; gelecekte muhtemel eylemlere değinmede kullanılır** *Should you have any further queries, please do not hesitate to contact me.* **4 why should/shouldn't...?** used to ask or give the reason for something, especially when you are surprised or angry about it **Neden ...malıyım/meliyim; Neden ... mamalıyım/memeliyim?'** özellikle **kızgınlıkta ve şaşırdığında belli bir nedeni söylemede kullanılır** *He told me to forgive her, but why should I?* ⇒See study page **Modal verbs** on page Centre 22.

o┅**shoulder¹** /'ʃəʊldəʳ/
noun **1** [C] where your arm joins your body next to your neck **omuz** *He put his arm around my shoulder.* ⇒Orta kısımdaki renkli sayfalarına bakınız. **2** [C] *US* (*UK* hard shoulder) the area on the edge of a main road, where a car can stop in an emergency (otoyol) **cep, acil durum cebi 3 rub shoulders with sb** to spend time with famous people **meşhur kimselerle arkadaşlık kurmak; tanışıp görüşmek ● 4 a shoulder to cry on** someone who gives you sympathy when you are upset **dert ortağı, içini dökeceği biri; omuzuna yaslanıp ağlayabileceği kimse** ⇒See also: have a **chip¹** on your shoulder.

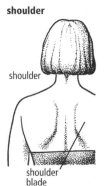

shoulder

shoulder

shoulder blade

shoulder² /'ʃəʊldəʳ/ *verb* **shoulder the blame/burden/ responsibility, etc** to accept that you are responsible for something difficult or bad **yüklenmek, kabullenmek, üstüne almak, üstlenmek**

'**shoulder ,bag** *noun* [C] a bag with a long strap that you hang from your shoulder **omuz çantası**

'**shoulder ,blade** *noun* [C] a large, flat bone on each side of your back below your shoulder **kürek kemiği**

shoulder-length /'ʃəʊldələŋθ/ *adjective* If your hair is shoulder-length, it goes down as far as your shoulders. **omuzlara kadar uzun olan**

o┅**shouldn't** /'ʃʊdᵊnt/ *short for* should not **should not' fiil yapısının kısa yazılışı** *I shouldn't have said that.*

o┅**should've** /'ʃʊdəv/ *short for* should have **should have' fiil yapısının kısa yazılışı** *She should've finished by now.*

o┅**shout¹** /ʃaʊt/ *verb* [I, T] to say something very loudly **bağırmak, haykırmak** *"Look out!" she shouted.* ○ *I was angry and I shouted at him.* ○ *I shouted out her name but she didn't hear me.*

shout (noun) .... İLE BİRLİKTE KULLANILAN KELİMELER

give a shout ● a shout of [anger, etc] ● an **angry** shout

shout² /ʃaʊt/ *noun* [C] when you say something very loudly or make a very loud sound with your voice **bağırma, haykırma** *He was woken by a loud shout.*

shove /ʃʌv/ *verb* [I, T] **1** to push someone or something in a rough way **itmek, itip kakmak** *He wouldn't move, so I shoved him out of the way.* **2 shove sth into/in/under, etc** to put something somewhere in a quick, careless way **rastgele koymak; gelişigüzel koymak; ativermek** *She shoved the suitcase under the bed.* ● **shove** *noun* [C] *to give someone a shove* ⇒See also: if/when **push²** comes to shove. **iteleme**

shovel /'ʃʌvᵊl/ *noun* [C] a tool with a long handle, used for digging or moving things such as soil or snow **kürek ● shovel** *verb* [I, T] *UK* **shovelling,** *past* **shovelled,** *US* **shoveling,** *past* **shoveled kürekle temizlemek**

o┅**show¹** /ʃəʊ/ *verb past tense* **showed,** *past part* **shown**
1 ⟨PROVE⟩ [T] If numbers, results, facts, etc show something, they prove that it is true. **göstermek [+ (that)]** *Research shows that 40% of the programme's viewers are aged over 55.* ○ *Sales figures showed a significant increase last month.* **2** ⟨LET SOMEONE SEE⟩ [T] to let someone look at something **göstermek, gezdirmek [+ two objects]** *Show me your photos.* ○ *Show your passport to the officer.* **3 show sb what to do/how to do sth** to teach someone how to do something by explaining it or by doing it yourself while they watch **göstermek, öğretmek; ne ve nasıl yapılacağını öğretmek** *She showed me how to use the new computer system.* ○ *Have you shown him what to do?* **4** ⟨EXPRESS⟩ [T] to express a feeling so that other people are able to notice it **göstermek, belli etmek** *He hasn't shown any interest so far.* ○ *If she was upset, she certainly didn't show it.* **5** ⟨EASY TO SEE⟩ [I, T] to be easy to see, or to make something easy to see **görünmek, gözükmek; göstermek, görünmesini sağlamak** *The sadness really shows on her face.* ○ *Light-coloured carpets show the dirt.* **6 show sb into/around/round, etc** to take someone to or round a place **gezdirmek, dolaştırmak, göstermek** *She showed me round the factory.* **7** ⟨IMAGE⟩ [T] If a picture, film, map, etc shows something, that thing can be seen in the picture, film, etc. **göstermek, ortaya koymak, belli etmek; bildirmek** *A diagram shows the amount of rainfall in different parts of the country.* **8** ⟨FILM⟩ [I, T] If a cinema shows a film or a film is showing somewhere, you can go and see it there. **oynamak, gösterimde olmak, oynamak, oynatmak**

show off *phrasal verb* to try to make people admire your abilities or achievements in a way which other people find annoying **gösteriş yapmak, hava atmak, caka satmak, fiyaka yapmak** *He was the kind of kid who was always showing off to his classmates.*

show sb/sth off *phrasal verb* to show something or someone you are proud of to other people **gururlanmak, gurur duyduğu şeyi kimseyi göstermek; onunla gurur duymak** *I couldn't wait to show off my new ring.*

S

show up *phrasal verb informal* to arrive somewhere **varmak, gelmek, ortaya çıkmak, gözükmek, görünmek** *I waited for nearly half an hour, but he didn't show up.*

show sb up *phrasal verb* to behave in a way that makes someone you are with feel embarrassed **utandırmak, rezil etmek, mahcup etmek** *I didn't want my parents there, showing me up in front of all my friends.*

---

show (noun) ...... İLE BİRLİKTE KULLANILAN KELİMELER

host/present a show ● a show is **broadcast/screened** ● be **on** a show

---

show² /ʃəʊ/ *noun* **1** [C] a television or radio programme or a theatre performance **gösteri, temsil, oyun** *He's got his own show on Channel 5.* **2** [C] an event at which a group of similar things are brought together for the public to see **sergi, sergileme** *a fashion show* **3 a show of sth** an expression of a feeling which can be clearly seen by other people **gösteri** *Crowds gathered in the central square in a show of support for the government.* **4 for show** for looking at only, and not for using **sadece gösteri için, gösteri amaçlı; sergileme amaçlı** *The cakes are just for show - you can't eat them.* **5 on show** being shown to the public **gösterimde, sergide, gösterilmekte, sergilenmekte** *Her designs are currently on show at the Museum of Modern Art.* ⊃See also: **chat show, game show, talk show.**

'show ‚business (*also* **show biz** *informal*) *noun* [U] the entertainment industry, including films, television, theatre, etc **gösteri dünyası; eğlence endüstrisi**

showcase /ʃəʊkeɪs/ *noun* [C] an event which is intended to show the best qualities of something **vitrin, sergi vitrini, sergileme, ortaya koyma, gösterime sunma** *The exhibition acts as a showcase for British design.*

---

showdown ...... İLE BİRLİKTE KULLANILAN KELİMELER

face/be heading for a showdown ● a showdown **between** sb and sb ● a showdown **with** sb

---

showdown /ʃəʊdaʊn/ *noun* [C] an argument or fight that is intended to end a period of disagreement **hesaplaşma, kartları açma; her şeyi ortaya koyma** *Opponents of the changes are heading for a showdown with party leaders.*

○ᴹ**shower¹** /ʃaʊəʳ/ *noun* [C] **1** WASH If you have or take a shower, you wash your whole body while standing under a flow of water. **duş alma** *I got up, had a shower and got dressed.* **2** BATHROOM EQUIPMENT a piece of bathroom equipment that you stand under to wash your whole body **duş** *He likes to sing in the shower.* ⊃Orta kısımdaki renkli sayfalarına bakınız. **3** RAIN a short period of rain **sağanak 4 a shower of sth** a lot of small things in the air, especially falling through the air **yağmur gibi şey, sağanak şeklinde yağma** *a shower of glass*

shower² /ʃaʊəʳ/ *verb* [I] to wash standing under a shower **duş almak; banyo yapmak**

shower sb with sth *phrasal verb* to give a lot of something to someone **yağmur gibi yağdırmak, boğmak** *I was showered with gifts.*

showing /ʃəʊɪŋ/ *noun* **1** [C] a broadcast of a television programme at a particular time or of a film at a cinema **gösterim, yayın** *There's a repeat showing of Wednesday's episode on Saturday morning.* **2 a good/poor/strong, etc showing** how successful someone is in a

competition, election, etc **iyi/kötü/güçlü vb. gösteri** *She made a good showing in the world championships.*

showman /ʃəʊmən/ *noun* [C] *plural* **showmen** someone who is very good at entertaining people **gösteri yapan/eğlendiren kimse**

shown /ʃəʊn/ *past participle of* show **göstermek' fiilinin geçmiş zaman hâli**

show-off /ʃəʊɒf/ *noun* [C] someone who tries to make other people admire their abilities or achievements in a way which is annoying **gösterişçi kimse, şakacı/fiyakacı kişi**

showroom /ʃəʊruːm/ *noun* [C] a large room where you can look at large items for sale, such as cars or furniture **sergi/teşhir salonu**

shrank /ʃræŋk/ *past tense of* shrink **çekmek, küçülmek' fiilinin geçmiş zaman hâli**

shrapnel /ʃræpnəl/ *noun* [U] small, sharp pieces of metal which fly through the air when a bomb explodes **şarapnel**

shred¹ /ʃred/ *noun* [C] **1** a very small piece that has been torn from something **parça, lime, dilim** [usually plural] *She tore the letter to shreds.* **2 not a shred of sth** not the smallest amount of something **en ufak parça/kırıntı/zerre değil** *There is not a shred of evidence to support his story.*

shred² /ʃred/ *verb* [T] **shredding,** *past* **shredded** to tear or cut something into small, thin pieces **lime lime etmek, ufak ufak doğramak** *shredded cabbage*

shrewd /ʃruːd/ *adjective* good at judging situations and making decisions which give you an advantage **kurnaz, zeki, açıkgöz, cin fikirli, akıllı** *a shrewd businessman* ○ *a shrewd investment* ● **shrewdly** *adverb* **kurnazca**

shriek /ʃriːk/ *verb* [I, T] to make a sudden, loud, high noise because you are afraid, surprised, excited, etc **çığlık atmak, acı acı bağırmak, feryat etmek** *to shriek with laughter* ○ *"It's about to explode!" she shrieked.* ● **shriek** *noun* [C] **feryat**

shrill /ʃrɪl/ *adjective* A shrill sound is very high, loud, and often unpleasant. **acı, keskin, tiz** *a shrill voice*

shrimp /ʃrɪmp/ *noun* [C] a small, pink, sea animal that you can eat, with a curved body and a shell **karides**

shrine /ʃraɪn/ *noun* [C] a place where people go to pray because it is connected with a holy person or event **tapınak, türbe, kutsal yer, yatır**

shrink¹ /ʃrɪŋk/ *verb* [I, T] *past tense* **shrank,** *past part* **shrunk** to become smaller, or to make something smaller **daral(t)mak, çek(tir)mek, küçül(t)mek** *My shirt shrank in the wash.* ○ *Its forests have shrunk to almost half the size they were 10 years ago.*

shrink from sth/doing sth *phrasal verb* to avoid doing something that is difficult or unpleasant **kaçınmak, çekinmek, uzak durmak, es geçmek** *We will not shrink from using force.*

shrink² /ʃrɪŋk/ *noun* [C] *informal* a doctor trained to help people with mental or emotional problems **zihinsel ve duygusal problemleri çözmek için eğitilmiş hekim; ruh hekimi**

shrivel /ʃrɪvəl/ *verb* [I] *UK* **shrivelling,** *past* **shrivelled,** *US* **shriveling,** *past* **shriveled** If something shrivels, it becomes smaller, dryer, and covered in lines, often because it is old. **buruşmak, kuruyup büzülmek** ● **shrivelled** *adjective* *There were a few shrivelled apples at the bottom of the bowl.* **büzülmüş**

shroud¹ /ʃraʊd/ *noun* [C] a cloth used to cover the body of a dead person **kefen**

shroud² /ʃraʊd/ *verb* **1 be shrouded in darkness/fog/mist** to be hidden or covered by the dark/fog, etc **karanlık/sis/pus ile/içine kaplanmak/sarılmak/gizlenmek** *The island was shrouded in sea mist.* **2 be**

shrouded in mystery/secrecy to be difficult to find out about or to know the truth about **(gizem, gizlilik vs.) gömülmek, bürünmek, gizlenmek** *Details of the president's trip remain shrouded in secrecy.*

shrub /ʃrʌb/ *noun* [C] a large plant, smaller than a tree, that has several main stems **çalı, funda**

shrubbery /'ʃrʌbªri/ *noun* **1** [C, U] an area of a garden with shrubs in it **çalılık, fundalık 2** [U] US shrubs considered as a group **çalı/funda kümesi, grubu**

shrug /ʃrʌg/ *verb* [I, T] **shrugging**, *past* **shrugged** to move your shoulders up and down to show that you do not care about something or that you do not know something **omuz silkmek** *I told him we weren't happy with it but he just shrugged his shoulders.* ● **shrug** *noun* [C] **omuz silkme**

shrug sth off *phrasal verb* to not worry about something and treat it as not important **umursamamak, aldırmamak, omuz silkmek, önemsiz saymak** *The team manager shrugged off criticism.*

shrunk /ʃrʌŋk/ *past participle of* shrink **çekmek, daralmak' fiilinin geçmiş zaman hâli**

shrunken /'ʃrʌŋkən/ *adjective* having become smaller or having been made smaller **küçülmüş, çekmiş, daralmış, kısalmış** *a shrunken old man*

shudder /'ʃʌdəʳ/ *verb* [I] to shake, usually because you are thinking of something unpleasant **ürpermek, tir tir titremek** *I still shudder at the thought of the risks we took.* ○ *She shuddered with horror.* ● **shudder** *noun* [C] **ürperti**

shuffle /'ʃʌfl/ *verb* **1** [WALK] [I] to walk slowly without lifting your feet off the floor **ayaklarını sürümek, ayaklarını sürüyerek yürümek** *I heard him shuffling around downstairs.* **2** [ARRANGE] [I, T] If you shuffle papers or cards, you mix them or arrange them in a different order. **kağıtları/iskambil kağıtlarını karıştırmak 3** [MOVE] [I, T] to move your body or feet a little because you feel nervous or uncomfortable. **ayaklarını sürtüp durmak, huzursuzca kımıldayıp durmak** *People started shuffling their feet and looking at their watches.*

shun /ʃʌn/ *verb* [T] **shunning**, *past* **shunned** to avoid or ignore someone or something **uzak durmak, kaçınmak, sakınmak, gözardı etmek** *He was shunned by colleagues and family alike.* ○ *She has always shunned publicity.*

shunt /ʃʌnt/ *verb* [T] to move someone or something from one place to another, usually because they are not wanted **bir tarafa/yana çekmek, aktarmak** *As a teenager he was shunted between different children's homes.*

o→**shut¹** /ʃʌt/ *verb* [I, T] **shutting**, *past* **shut 1** to close something, or to become closed **örtmek, kapamak, örtülmek, kapatılmak** *Shut the door.* ○ *He lay back and shut his eyes.* ○ *The lid shut with a bang.* **2** UK (UK/US **close**) When a shop, restaurant, etc shuts, it stops serving customers and does not allow people to enter. **kapamak, kapanmak** *The museum shuts at 4 o'clock on a Friday.* ○ *Several schools were shut because of the bad weather.*

shut sb/sth away *phrasal verb* to put someone or something in a place from which they cannot leave or be taken away **bir yere kapatmak, hapsetmek, saklamak, muhafaza altına almak**

shut (sth) down *phrasal verb* If a business or a large piece of equipment shuts down or someone shuts it down, it stops operating. **kapatmak, kapanmak** *Many factories have been forced to shut down.*

shut sb/sth in (sth) *phrasal verb* to prevent someone or something from leaving a place by shutting a door or gate **kilit altında tutmak, kapatmak, gitmesine/çık-**

masına engel olmak *We normally shut the dog in the kitchen when we go out.*

shut sth off *phrasal verb* to stop a machine working, or to stop the supply of something **(makina) kapatmak, durdurmak** *Shut the engine off.* ○ *Oil supplies have been shut off.*

shut sth/sb out *phrasal verb* to stop someone or something from entering a place or from being included in something **girmesine engel olmak, dışarıda tutmak; hariç tutmak, dahil etmemek** *The curtains shut out most of the light from the street.*

shut (sb) up *phrasal verb informal* to stop talking or making a noise, or to make someone do this **sus(tur)mak, konuş(tur)mamak** *Just shut up and get on with your work!*

shut sb/sth up *phrasal verb* to keep a person or animal somewhere and prevent them from leaving **birini/bir hayvanı bir yere kapatmak/kilitlemek/hapsetmek** *You can't keep it shut up in a cage all day.*

shut² /ʃʌt/ *adjective* [never before noun] **1** closed **kapalı** *Her eyes were shut and I thought she was asleep.* **2** UK (UK/US **closed**) When a shop, restaurant, etc is shut, it has stopped serving customers and does not allow people to enter it. **(dükkân, lokanta vb.) kapalı**

shutdown /'ʃʌtdaʊn/ *noun* [C] when a business or a large piece of equipment stops operating, usually for a temporary period **kapama, iş yerini kapama, işi durdurma**

shutter /'ʃʌtəʳ/ *noun* [C] **1** a wooden or metal cover on the outside of a window **kepenk, panjur 2** the part at the front of a camera which opens quickly to let in light when you take a photograph **mercek kapağı/perdesi, objektif kapağı**

shuttle¹ /'ʃʌtl/ *noun* [C] **1** a bus, train, plane etc which travels regularly between two places, usually a short distance **iki kısa mesafe arasında karşılıklı sefer yapan otobüs, tren, uçak vb.** *the London-Glasgow shuttle* ○ *There's a shuttle service between the airport and the city centre.* **2** (also '**space ˌshuttle**) a spacecraft which can go into space and return to Earth more than once **uzay mekiği**

shuttle² /'ʃʌtl/ *verb* [I, T] to travel or take people regularly between the same two places **iki nokta arasında mekik seferi yapmak** *He shuttles between Ireland and England.*

shuttlecock /'ʃʌtlkɒk/ (also US **birdie**) *noun* [C] a small object with feathers that is used like a ball in badminton (= sport like tennis) **badminton topu**

shy¹ /ʃaɪ/ *adjective* or **shyer** or **shyest** not confident, especially about meeting or talking to new people **mahcup, utangaç, sıkılgan, çekingen, ürkek** *He was too shy to say anything to her.* ● **shyly** *adverb* *She smiled shyly.* **utangaç bir şekilde** ● **shyness** *noun* [U] **utangaçlık**

shy² /ʃaɪ/ *verb* [I] If a horse shies, it moves backwards suddenly because it has been frightened by something. **ürkmek**

shy away from sth *phrasal verb* to avoid doing something, usually because you are not confident enough to do it **çekinmek, kaçınmak** *He tends to shy away from public speaking.*

sibling /'sɪblɪŋ/ *noun* [C] *formal* a sister or brother **kardeş**

sic /sɪk/ *adverb* (**sic**) used in writing after a word that you have copied to show that you know it has been spelt or used wrongly **başka bir kaynaktan kopyalanan bir kelimenin yazılışından sonra yanlış hecelendiğini veya yanlış kullanıldığını göstermek için kullanılır**

S

oꞥ**sick¹** /sɪk/ *adjective* **1** ill **hasta, rahatsız** *He was off work sick for most of last week.* ○ *They provide care for the sick.* **2 be sick** If you are sick, food and drink comes up from your stomach and out of your mouth. **midesi bulanmak** *The baby was sick all down his shirt.* **3 feel sick** to feel that the food or drink in your stomach might soon come up through your mouth **midesi bulanmak; kusacak gibi hissetmek** *I was so nervous I felt quite sick.* **4 be sick of sth** *informal* to be bored with or annoyed about something that has been happening for a long time **bıkmış/bezmiş/usanmış/canına tak etmiş olmak** *I'm sick of people telling me how to run my life.* **5 It makes me sick.** *informal* something you say when you are jealous of someone **'Canımı sıkıyor.', 'Kafamı kızdırıyor.', 'Beni hasta ediyor.'** *She looks fantastic whatever she wears - it makes me sick.* **6** cruel and unpleasant **ürkütücü, iğrenç, tiksindirici, korkunç** *He's got a sick mind.* ○ *a sick joke*

sick² /sɪk/ *noun* [U] *UK informal* food or liquid that has come up from someone's stomach and out of their mouth **kusma, kusmuk**

sicken /'sɪkᵊn/ *verb* [T] to shock someone and make them very angry **tiksindirmek, iğrendirmek, nefret ettirmek, midesini bulandırmak, kızdırmak** *Sickened by the violence, she left.*

sickening /'sɪkᵊnɪŋ/ *adjective* causing shock and anger **kızdırıcı, mide bulandırıcı, şok edici, tiksindirici** *a sickening act of violence*

sickle /'sɪkl/ *noun* [C] a tool with a round blade used to cut long grass or grain crops **orak**

'**sick ˌleave** *noun* [U] when you are away from your work because you are ill **hastalık izni; rapor**

sickly /'sɪkli/ *adjective* **1** weak and often ill **hastalıklı, zayıf ve sağlıksız** *a sickly child* **2** unpleasant and making you feel slightly ill **mide bulandırıcı, tiksindirici** *a sickly smell*

sickness /'sɪknəs/ *noun* **1** [ILL] [U] when you are ill **hastalık, rahatsızlık** *She's had three weeks off for sickness this year.* **2** [VOMIT] [U] when the food or drink in your stomach come up through your mouth, or a feeling that this might happen **bulantı, kusma** *morning/travel sickness* **3** [ILLNESS] [C, U] a particular illness **hastalık; belli bir rahatsızlık** *radiation sickness*

---
side ...... İLE BİRLİKTE KULLANILAN KELİMELER

on the [right/left] **side** ● **the side of** sth
---

oꞥ**side¹** /saɪd/ *noun* [C] **1** [PART OF SOMETHING] one of the two parts that something would divide into if you drew a line down the middle **yan, taraf, kenar** *In most countries people drive on the right side of the road.* ○ *Which side of the bed do you sleep on?* **2** [SURFACE] a flat, outer surface of an object, especially one that is not its top, bottom, front, or back **kenar** *The ingredients are listed on the side of the box.* ○ *The side of the car was badly scratched.* **3** [EDGE] one edge of something **yan, kenar** *A square has four sides.* ○ *There were chairs round the sides of the room.* **4** [NEXT TO SOMETHING] the area next to something **taraf, yüz** *trees growing by the side of the road* **5** [PAPER/COIN ETC] either of the two surfaces of a thin, flat object such as a piece of paper or a coin **kenar, yan** *Write on both sides of the paper.* **6** [ARGUMENT] one of the people or groups who are arguing, fighting, or competing **taraf** *Whose side is he on?* ○ *Whenever we argue he always takes Alice's side* (= gives support to Alice). **7** [TEAM] *UK* the players in a sports team **oyuncular, sporcular** *He's been selected for the national side.* **8** [PART OF A SITUATION] part of a situation that can be considered or dealt with separately **bölüm, cephe, yön, taraf** *She looks after the financial side of things.* **9** [CHARACTER] a part of someone's character **karakteri-**

nin bir tarafı/yanı *She has a very practical side.* **10** [BODY] the two areas of your body from under your arms to the tops of your legs **vücudun yan tarafı** *Stand with your arms by your sides.* ○ *She lay on her side.* **11** [STORY] Someone's side of a story is the way in which they explain how something happened. **birinin anlatacakları, hikâyesi, hikayenin bir tarafı** *I thought I'd better listen to Clare's side of the story.* ○ *So far they'd only heard the story from the wife's side.* **12** [TELEVISION/RADIO] *UK* a number on a television or radio that you can choose in order to receive a broadcast tv. **/radyo istasyon/kanal numarası** *Which side is the film on?* **13 from side to side** If something moves from side to side, it moves from left to right and back again repeatedly. **soldan sağa, sağa sola** *swinging from side to side* **14 side-by-side** If two things or people are side-by-side, they are next to each other. **yan yana** *sitting side-by-side on the sofa* **15** [RELATIVES] the part of your family who are either your mother's relatives or your father's relatives **anne/baba tarafı** *They tend to be tall on my mother's side of the family.* **16 err on the side of caution** to be very careful instead of taking a risk or making a mistake **risk almamak/hata yapmak yerine dikkatli olmak; itinalı/özenli/dikkatli olmak** **17 on the side** in addition to your main job **fazladan, ayrıca, ek olarak; ek iş olarak** *She does a bit of bar work on the side.* **18 put sth to one side** to not use or deal with something now, but keep it for a later time **bir kenara koymak, saklamak, ileride kullanmak için bir yerde tutmak** ⊃See also: the flip side.

side² /saɪd/ *verb*

side with sb *phrasal verb* to support one person or group in an argument **...ın/in tarafını tutmak; ...a/e arka çıkmak** *If ever there was any sort of argument, she'd always side with my father.*

sideboard /'saɪdbɔːd/ *noun* [C] a piece of furniture with a flat top and low cupboards and drawers, used for storing dishes and glasses, etc in the room you eat in **mutfak dolabı, büfe**

sideburns /'saɪdbɜːnz/ *noun* [plural] hair that grows on the sides of a man's face in front of the ear **(saç) her iki yandaki favoriler**

side effect /'saɪdɪfekt/ *noun* [C] **1** another effect that a drug has on your body in addition to the main effect for which the doctor has given you the drug **yan etki** *Headaches are one side effect of this drug.* **2** an unexpected result of a situation **yan etki, hesapta olmadan ortaya çıkan durum, beklenmeyen sonuç**

sidekick /'saɪdkɪk/ *noun* [C] someone who helps, or is friends with, a more powerful and important person **arka yardım eden kimse, destek veren kişi**

sideline¹ /'saɪdlaɪn/ *noun* [C] a job or business in addition to your main job or business **ek uğraş, ikinci iş** *He works in a bank but teaches English as a sideline.*

sideline² /'saɪdlaɪn/ *verb* [T] to stop someone from being included in an activity that they usually do, especially a sport **takım dışında bırakmak, listeye dahil etmemek, yedekte tutmak** [often passive] *He's broken his ankle and could be sidelined for weeks.*

sidelines /'saɪdlaɪnz/ *noun* [plural] **1** the outside edge of the playing area of a sport such as football **kenar çizgileri** *The coach was shouting instructions from the sidelines.* **2 on the sidelines** not really involved in something **arka plânda, geride, fazla ortada görünmeyen**

sidelong /'saɪdlɒŋ/ *adjective* **a sidelong glance/look** a very short look at someone, moving your eyes to the side, and not looking at them directly **yan yan göz atma, göz ucuyla bakış**

'side ˌmirror *US* (*UK* **wing mirror**) *noun* [C] a small mirror on the side of a car or truck **yan ayna** ⊃Orta kısımdaki renkli sayfalarına bakınız.

sideshow /'saɪdʃəʊ/ *noun* [C] an event or activity that is considered less important than another event or activity **giriş gösterisi; daha önemsiz faaliyet/olay; ısınma faaliyeti**

sidestep /'saɪdstep/ *verb* [T] **sidestepping,** *past* **side-stepped** to avoid talking about a subject, especially by starting to talk about something else **yan çizmek, kaçınmak, lafı değiştirmek, konuya girmemek,** *She neatly* **sidestepped questions** *about her recent divorce.*

sidetrack /'saɪdtræk/ *verb* [T] to make someone forget what they were doing or speaking about and start doing or speaking about something different **konuyu dağıt-mak, dikkatini dağıtıp yapacağını unutturmak** [often passive] *Sorry, I was talking about staffing and I got sidetracked.*

sidewalk /'saɪdwɔːk/ *US* (*UK* **pavement**) *noun* [C] a path with a hard surface by the side of a road that people walk on **yaya kaldırımı**

sideways /'saɪdweɪz/ *adverb* in a direction to the left or right, not forwards or backwards **yanlamasına, uzun-lamasına** *He glanced sideways.*

siding /'saɪdɪŋ/ *noun* **1** [C] a short railway track, con-nected to a main track, where trains are kept when they are not being used **yan yol, yan manevra hattı, barınma hattı 2** [U] *US* material which covers the out-side walls of a building, usually in layers **dış cephe kaplaması**

sidle /'saɪdl/ *verb* **sidle along/over/up, etc** to walk towards someone, trying not to be noticed **gizlice sokulmak, sinsice yanaşmak, farkedilmeden yanaşmak** *He sidled up to her and whispered something in her ear.*

SIDS /sɪdz/ *noun* [U] *US abbreviation for* sudden infant death syndrome: the sudden death of a sleeping baby for no obvious reason **anî bebek ölümü sendromu, uyuyan bebeklerin belli bir nedeni olmaksızın ölümü** ⊃See **cot death.**

siege /siːdʒ/ *noun* [C, U] when an army or the police stand around a building or city to stop supplies from entering it, in order to force the people inside to stop fighting **kuşatma, muhasara** *The city is* **under siege** *from rebel forces.*

siesta /si'estə/ *noun* [C] a short period of rest or sleep in the afternoon **öğle uykusu, kestirme, şekerleme**

sieve /sɪv/ *noun* [C] a piece of kitchen equipment with a wire or plastic net which separates large pieces of food from liquids or powders **süzgeç, elek, kalbur** *Pass the sauce through a sieve to remove any lumps.* ⊃Orta kısımdaki renkli sayfalarına bakınız. ● **sieve** *verb* [T] **elek-ten geçirmek**

sift /sɪft/ *verb* [T] **1** to put flour, sugar, etc through a sieve (= wire net shaped like a bowl) to break up large pieces **elemek, süzgeçten/kalburdan geçirmek** *Sift the flour into a large bowl.* **2** (*also* **sift through**) to carefully look at every part of something in order to find some-thing **dikkatle incelemek, gözden geçirmek, tek tek ayıklamak** *to sift through evidence*

sigh /saɪ/ *verb* [I, T] to breathe out slowly and noisily, often because you are annoyed or unhappy **iç çekmek** *He sighed deeply and sat down.* ● **sigh** *noun* [C] *a sigh of relief* **iç çekiş**

o~**sight¹** /saɪt/ *noun* **1** [ABILITY] [U] the ability to use your eyes to see **görme gücü** *Doctors managed to save his sight.* **2 the sight of sb/sth** when you see someone or some-thing **birinin/bir şeyin görünümü/görüntüsü** *The

sight of so much blood had shocked him. ○ *informal I* **can't stand the sight of** *her* (= I hate her). **3** [AREA SEEN] [U] the area that it is possible for you to see **görünüm, görünüş, manzara** *I looked for her but she was nowhere* **in sight.** ○ *I was able to park* **within sight** *of the house.* ○ *Security guards were waiting* **out of sight** (= where they could not be seen). **4** [VIEW] [C] something which you see, especially something interesting **görüntü** *the* **sights and sounds** *of the market* **5 at first sight** when you first see or hear about something or someone **ilk görüşte/bakışta** *It may, at first sight, seem a surprising choice.* **6 the sights** the beautiful or interesting places in a city or country, that a lot of people visit **görülecek yerler, manzaralar** *He took me around New York and showed me the sights.* **7 lose sight of sth** to forget about an important idea or fact because you are thinking too much about other, less important things **unutmak, dikkate almamak; ... dan/den uzaklaşmak; önemsiz şeylerle uğraşırken önemli hususları unutmak** *We mustn't lose sight of the original aims of this project.* **8 set your sights on sth** to decide to achieve something **amaçlamak, başarmaya karar vermek** *She's set her sights on becoming an actress.*

sight² /saɪt/ *verb* [T] to see something that it is difficult to see or that you have been looking for **görmek, kavuşmak** [often passive] *The ship was last sighted off the French coast at 8 o'clock yesterday evening.*

-sighted /'saɪtɪd/ used after a word describing a per-son's ability to see **...gören/görüşlü anlamında söz-cük** *long-/short-sighted* ○ *partially-sighted*

sighted /'saɪtɪd/ *adjective* A sighted person is able to see. **görebilen, kör/âmâ olmayan**

sighting /'saɪtɪŋ/ *noun* [C] when you see something that is rare or unusual **görme, görülme, görünme, rast-lama** *UFO sightings*

🧩 **sightseeing** ...... İLE BİRLİKTE KULLANILAN KELİMELER

do some/go sightseeing ● a sightseeing **tour/trip**

sightseeing /'saɪtsiːɪŋ/ *noun* [U] the activity of visiting places which are interesting because they are histori-cal, famous, etc **şehir turu, ilginç yerleri gezip görme** *a* **sightseeing tour** *of London* ● **sightseer** /'saɪtˌsiːəʳ/ *noun* [C] a person who goes sightseeing **gezi/tur yapan kimse, turist**

🧩 **sign** ...... İLE BİRLİKTE KULLANILAN KELİMELER

see/take sth **as a sign** ● **show** (no) **signs of** sth ● a **clear/sure sign** ● a **sign of** sth

o~**sign¹** /saɪn/ *noun* [C] **1** [PROOF] something which shows that something is happening **işaret, iz, simge, im, sembol** *Flowers are the first sign of Spring.* ○ *It's a sign that things are improving.* ○ *Staff are* **showing signs of** *strain.* **2** [NOTICE] a symbol or message in a public place which gives information or instructions **tabelâ, sembol, işaret, ileti, duyuru, levha** *a road sign* ○ *a 'no-smoking' sign* **3** [SYMBOL] a symbol which has a parti-cular meaning **belli bir anlamı olan işaret/tabelâ** *a dollar/pound sign* ○ *the sign of the cross* **4** [MOVEMENT] a movement you make to give someone information or tell them what to do **hareket, işaret, belirti, ikaz** ⊃See also: **star sign.**

o~**sign²** /saɪn/ *verb* [I, T] to write your name on something to show that you wrote/painted, etc it or to show that you agree to it **imzalamak, imza koymak** *He signs his letters 'Prof. James D. Nelson'.* ○ *to* **sign a contract/ treaty**

sign for sth *phrasal verb UK* If a player signs for a foot-ball team, he signs a formal agreement saying that he

signal

will play for that team. **mutabakat/sözleşme imzalamak; kontrat yapmak/imzalamak**

sign (sb) in *phrasal verb* to write your name or someone else's name in a book when you arrive at a building such as an office or hotel **isim kaydı yapmak, ismini kaydetmek**

sign on *phrasal verb* **1** to sign a document saying that you will work for someone **işe giriş kontratı/sözleşmesi imzalamak** *She's signed on with a temp agency.* **2** *UK* to sign a form at a government office to say that you do not have a job and that you want to receive money from the government **işsizlik/muhtaçlık belgesi imzalamak**

sign (sb) out *phrasal verb* to write your name or someone else's name in a book when leaving a building such as an office or factory **iş/işyeri çıkışında imza atmak**

sign up *phrasal verb* to arrange to do an organized activity **sözleşme/kontrat imzalamak** *I've signed up for evening classes at the local college.*

signal¹ /'sɪgnᵊl/ *noun* [C] **1** ACTION a movement, light, or sound which gives information, or tells people what to do **işaret, sinyal** *Don't move until I give the signal.* **2** WAVE a series of light waves or sound waves which are sent to a radio or television **radyo/televizyon sinyali 3** PROOF something which shows that something else exists or is likely to happen **gösterge, işaret, belirti, emare** *The changing colour of the leaves on the trees is a signal that it will soon be autumn.* **4** TRAINS a piece of equipment which tells trains to stop or to continue **demiryolu sinyalizasyon sistemi 5** VEHICLES/PEOPLE *US* a piece of equipment that shows people or vehicles when to stop, go, or move carefully **trafik işaretleri** *a traffic signal*

signal² /'sɪgnᵊl/ *verb* [I, T] *UK* **signalling**, *past* **signalled**, *US* **signaling**, *past* **signaled 1** to make a movement which gives information or tells people what to do **işaret etmek, işaretle bildirmek, sinyal vermek** *He signalled for them to be quiet.* ○ [+ to do sth] *He signalled the driver to stop.* **2** to show that you intend or are ready to do something **işaret vermek, göstermek, işaretini vermek, hazır olduğu işaretini göstermek** [+ (that)] *The US signalled that they were ready to enter talks.*

signatory /'sɪgnətᵊri/ *noun* [C] *formal* a person or country that signs an official document **imza koyan kişi/ülke; imza sahibi ülke/kişi**

signature /'sɪgnətʃər/ *noun* [C] your name written in your own way which is difficult for someone else to copy **imza**

significance ...... İLE BİRLİKTE KULLANILAN KELİMELER

play down /realize/understand the significance **of** sth ● **have** significance **for** sb ● be **of** [great/little/major/no] significance

significance /sɪg'nɪfɪkᵊns/ *noun* [U] the importance or meaning of something **önem, kıymet, anlam** *I still don't understand the significance of his remark.*

o↝**significant** /sɪg'nɪfɪkᵊnt/ *adjective* important or noticeable **önemli, değerli, anlamlı, mühim** *These measures will save a significant amount of money.* ○ *It is significant that Falkner did not attend the meeting himself.* ○Opposite **insignificant.** ● **significantly** *adverb* **önemli ve gözle görülebilir şekilde**

signify /'sɪgnɪfaɪ/ *verb* [T] to be a sign of something **bildirmek, belirtmek, anlamına gelmek** *Red signifies danger.*

signing /'saɪnɪŋ/ *noun* [C] **1** *UK* a player who has joined a sports team or a musician who has joined a record company **futbol takımına katılan oyuncu; plâk şirketine katılan müzisyen 2** the act of signing something

imzalama, imza koyma, imza töreni [usually singular] *the signing of the declaration*

'sign ,language *noun* [C, U] a system of communication using hand movements, used by people who are deaf (= cannot hear) **işaret dili**

signpost /'saɪmpəʊst/ *noun* [C] a sign by the side of the road that gives information about routes and distances **(yol) işaret levhası**

Sikh /siːk/ *noun* [C] someone who believes in an Indian religion based on belief in a single god and on the teachings of Guru Nanak **Sih, Guru Nanak öğretileri üzerine kurulu ve tek Tanrı inancına dayalı Hint dinine inanan kimse** ● **Sikh** *adjective* a Sikh temple **Hindistan'daki dine dair inanç** ● **Sikhism** *noun* [U] **Hindistan'daki dine dair**

silence .... İLE BİRLİKTE KULLANILAN KELİMELER

in silence ● **deafening/stunned** silence ● **break the** silence ● **lapse into** silence ● silence **falls/descends/ensues**

o↝**silence¹** /'saɪləns/ *noun* **1** NO SOUND [U] when there is no sound **sessizlik, sükût** *The three men ate in silence.* ○ *No sound broke the silence of the wintry landscape.* **2** NO TALKING [U] when someone says nothing about a particular subject **susma, suskunluk, sessiz kalma** *She ended her silence yesterday and spoke to a TV reporter about the affair.* **3** PERIOD OF TIME [C] a period of time when there is no sound or no talking **sessizlik, sükûnet, dinginlik** *an awkward/embarrassed silence*

silence² /'saɪləns/ *verb* [T] **1** to stop something making a sound or stop someone from talking, often about a particular subject **susturmak** *He silenced the alarm.* ○ *Opponents of the government would be silenced or thrown into prison.* **2** to stop people from criticizing you by giving a good argument to support your opinion **tartışmada karşı tarafı bastırmak; susturmak; ağzının payını vermek** *He seems to have silenced his critics.*

silencer /'saɪlənsər/ *noun* [C] **1** *UK* (*US* **muffler**) a part of a vehicle that reduces noise **susturucu 2** a piece of equipment that you use on a gun to reduce the sound of it firing **(silah, tabanca vs.) susturucu**

o↝**silent** /'saɪlənt/ *adjective* **1** NO SOUND without any sound **sessiz, sakin, suskun** *The building was dark and silent.* ○ *At last the guns fell silent.* **2** NO TALKING without talking **sessiz, ses çıkarmayan** *He remains silent about his plans.* **3** LETTER If a letter in a word is silent, it is not pronounced. **sessiz harf, telaffuz edilmeyen harf** *The 'p' in 'receipt' is silent.* ● **silently** *adverb* sessizce

silhouette /ˌsɪlu'et/ *noun* [C, U] the shape of something when the light is behind it so that you cannot see any details **siluet, gölge görüntü** *He saw a woman in silhouette.* ● **silhouetted** *adjective* the roofs silhouetted *against the night sky* **silüeti / şekli çıkmış**

silicon /'sɪlɪkən/ *noun* [U] a chemical element used in making electronic equipment such as computers, and materials such as glass and concrete (symbol Si) **silikon** *a silicon chip*

silk /sɪlk/ *noun* [U] a type of cloth which is light and smooth **ipek** *a silk dress/shirt*

silken /'sɪlkᵊn/ *adjective literary* soft and smooth, like silk **pürüzsüz ve yumuşak, ipek gibi** *her silken skin*

silky /'sɪlki/ *adjective* soft and smooth, like silk **ipeğimsi, ipek gibi, yumuşacık** *a large, silky, grey cat*

o↝**silly** /'sɪli/ *adjective* **1** stupid **aptal, şaşkın, sersem** *silly games/hats* ○ *I feel silly in this hat.* ○ *It's a bit silly spending all that money on something we don't need.* **2** small and not important **küçük, önemsiz, değersiz** *She gets upset over such silly things.* ● **silliness** *noun* [U] **aptallık**

silt /sɪlt/ *noun* [U] sand and clay that has been carried along by a river and is left on land **mil, alüvyon**

o⚬**silver¹** /'sɪlvər/ *noun* **1** METAL [U] a valuable, shiny, grey-white metal used to make coins and jewellery (symbol Ag) **gümüş** *silver and gold* ○ *a solid silver ring* **2** OBJECTS [U] objects made of silver **gümüş eşyalar 3** PRIZE [C] a silver medal (= a small, round disc given to someone for finishing second in a race or competition) **gümüş madalya**

o⚬**silver²** /'sɪlvər/ *adjective* **1** made of silver **gümüşten yapılmış, gümüş** *a silver coin* ○ *a silver necklace* **2** being the colour of silver **gümüşi, gümüş renginde** *a silver sports car*

,**silver 'medal** *noun* [C] a small, round disc given to someone for finishing second in a race or competition **gümüş madalya**

silverware /'sɪlvəweər/ *noun* [U] US (UK cutlery) knives, forks, spoons, etc that are used for eating **gümüş kaşık çatal bıçak takımı**

,**silver 'wedding anniversary** *noun* [C] the date that is 25 years after the day that two people married **25. evlilik yıl dönümü**

silvery /'sɪlvəri/ *adjective* shiny and pale like silver **gümüş gibi, gümüşi** *a silvery light*

sim card /'sɪm kɑːd/ *noun* [C] a plastic card in a mobile phone that contains information about you and makes you able to use the phone **cep telefonu kartı; simkart, telefon şebeke kartı**

o⚬**similar** /'sɪmɪlər/ *adjective* Something which is similar to something else has many things the same, although it is not exactly the same. **benzer, aynı türden** *The two houses are remarkably similar.* ○ *The style of cooking is similar to that of Northern India.* ↻Opposite **dissimilar**.

similarity /ˌsɪmɪˈlærəti/ *noun* [C, U] when two things or people are similar, or a way in which they are similar **benzerlik** *There are a number of similarities between the two systems.* ○ *He bears a striking similarity to his grandfather.*

similarly /'sɪmɪləli/ *adverb* in a similar way **aynı, aynı şekilde, bunun gibi**

simile /'sɪmɪli/ *noun* [C] a phrase which compares one thing to something else, using the words 'like' or 'as', for example 'as white as snow' **teşbih, benzetme**

simmer /'sɪmər/ *verb* [I, T] to gently cook a liquid or something with liquid in it so that it is very hot, but does not boil **hafif ateşte pişmek/pişirmek**

o⚬**simple** /'sɪmpl/ *adjective* **1** EASY not difficult to do or to understand **basit, kolay** [+ to do sth] *It's very simple to use.* ○ *Just mix all the ingredients together - it's as simple as that.* **2** NOT COMPLICATED not complicated or containing details which are not necessary **yalın, süssüz, sade** *a simple life* ○ *a simple black dress* (= dress without decoration) **3** IMPORTANT used to describe the one important fact, truth, etc **sıradan, basit, kolay** *We chose her for the simple reason that she's the best person for the job.*

simplicity /sɪmˈplɪsəti/ *noun* [U] **1** when something is not complicated and has few details or little decoration **basitlik, sadelik, yalınlık** *I admire the simplicity of his designs.* **2** when something is easy to understand **basitlik**

simplify /'sɪmplɪfaɪ/ *verb* [T] to make something less complicated or easier to do or to understand **basitleştirmek, sadeleştirmek, yalınlaştırmak** *We need to simplify the instructions.* ● **simplification** /ˌsɪmplɪfɪˈkeɪʃən/ *noun* [C, U] **basitleştirme**

simplistic /sɪmˈplɪstɪk/ *adjective* making something complicated seem simple by ignoring many of the details **sadeleştirilmiş, basitleştirilmiş, basite indirgenmiş** *a simplistic explanation*

simply /'sɪmpli/ *adverb* **1** EMPHASIS used to emphasize what you are saying **gerçekten, hâkikaten** *We simply don't have the time.* **2** ONLY only **yalnızca, sırf, sadece, ancak** *A lot of people miss out on this opportunity simply because they don't know about it.* **3** NOT COMPLICATED in a way which is not complicated or difficult to understand **kolay anlaşılır biçimde, sade bir şekilde, basitçe** *simply prepared food*

simulate /'sɪmjəleɪt/ *verb* [T] to do or make something which behaves or looks like something real but which is not real **benzetmek, taklidini yapmak, yalandan yapmak, yapıyormuş gibi görünmek** *The company uses a computer to simulate crash tests of its new cars.* ● **simulation** /ˌsɪmjəˈleɪʃən/ *noun* [C, U] **benzetim**

simulator /'sɪmjəleɪtər/ *noun* [C] a machine on which people can practise operating a vehicle or an aircraft without having to drive or fly **herhangi bir aracın çalıştırılması veya çalışması alıştırılmasının yapıldığı birebir aynı özellikleri taşıyan makina; simülatör** *a flight simulator*

simultaneous /ˌsɪmºlˈteɪniəs/ *adjective* If two or more things are simultaneous, they happen or exist at the same time. **aynı anda olan, eş zamanlı** *simultaneous translation* ● **simultaneously** *adverb* *It was broadcast simultaneously in Britain and France.* **aynı anda olan**

sin ┈┈┈ İLE BİRLİKTE KULLANILAN KELİMELER

commit a sin ● the sin **of** [pride/greed, etc.]

sin¹ /sɪn/ *noun* **1** [C, U] something which is against the rules of a religion **günah** *the sin of pride* **2** [no plural] *informal* something that you should not be doing because it is morally wrong **ahlaka aykırı şey, günah** *You've only got one life and it's a sin to waste it.*

sin² /sɪn/ *verb* [I] **sinning**, *past* **sinned** to do something that is against the rules of a religion **günah işlemek, günaha girmek** ● **sinner** *noun* [C] someone who does something against the rules of a religion **günahkâr**

o⚬**since¹** /sɪns/ *adverb, preposition* from a time in the past until a later time or until now **...dan/den beri** *They've been waiting since March.* ○ *The factory had been closed since the explosion.* ○ *I've felt fine ever since.*

o⚬**since²** /sɪns/ *conjunction* **1** from a time in the past until a later time or until now **...dan/den beri; o zamandan beri** *He's been much happier since he started his new job.* ○ *I've known Tim since he was seven.* **2** because **çünkü; ...dığı/diği için** *He drove quite slowly since we had plenty of time.*

sincere /sɪnˈsɪər/ *adjective* **1** honest and saying or showing what you really feel or believe **samimi, candan, içten, yürekten** *He seems to be sincere.* ↻Opposite **insincere**. **2** **sincere apologies/thanks, etc** *formal* used to add emphasis when you are expressing a feeling **samimi/içten özürler/teşekkürler vs.** *The family wishes to express their sincere thanks to all the staff at the hospital.* ● **sincerity** /sɪnˈserəti/ *noun* [U] *No one doubted his sincerity.* **içtenlik**

sincerely /sɪnˈsɪəli/ *adverb* **1** in a sincere way **içtenlikle, samimi olarak** *I sincerely hope that this never happens again.* **2** **Yours sincerely** *formal* used at the end of formal letters where you write the name of the person you are writing to **'En derin saygılarımla...!', 'En içten hürmetlerimle...!'**

---

sinful /ˈsɪnf³l/ *adjective* against the rules of a religion or morally wrong **günahkâr, günah işlemiş** *sinful thoughts*

o▪**sing** /sɪŋ/ *verb* [I, T] *past tense* **sang**, *past participle* **sung** to make musical sounds with your voice **şarkı söylemek** *They all sang 'Happy Birthday' to him.* ○ *She sings in the church choir.*

singer /ˈsɪŋəʳ/ *noun* [C] someone who sings **şarkıcı** *a jazz singer*

singing /ˈsɪŋɪŋ/ *noun* [U] the activity of singing **şarkıcılık, şarkı söyleme**

o▪**single¹** /ˈsɪŋgl/ *adjective* **1** ONE [always before noun] only one **tek, bir** *There was a single light in the corner of the room.* **2 every single** used to emphasize that you are talking about each one of a group or series **her bir, tek tek** *I call him every single day.* **3** MARRIAGE not married **bekâr, evlenmemiş** *He's young and single.* **4** PARENT [always before noun] looking after your children alone without a partner or the children's other parent **tek başına (tek ebeveyn olarak)** *a single mother* ○ *a single-parent family* **5** FOR ONE [always before noun] for only one person **tek kişilik** *a single bed*

single² /ˈsɪŋgl/ *noun* [C] **1** a record or CD which includes only one main song **tekli plâk, 45'lik 2** *UK* (*US* **one-way ticket**) a ticket for a journey that is from one place to another but not back again **sadece gidiş** *Could I have a single to London, please?*

single³ /ˈsɪŋgl/ *verb*
single sb/sth out *phrasal verb* to choose one person or thing from a group to criticize or praise them **seçip ayırmak; sadece bir kişi ya da nesneyi ön plana çıkarmak/belirlemek** *The report singled him out for special criticism.*

single-handedly /ˌsɪŋglˈhændɪdli/ (*also* **single-handed**) *adverb* on your own, without anyone's help **tek başına olarak, yalnız bir şekilde** *After his partner left, he kept the business going single-handedly.* ● **single-handed** /ˌsɪŋglˈhændɪd/ *adjective* [always before noun] *a single-handed round-the-world yacht race* **tek başına yapılmış olan**

single-minded /ˌsɪŋglˈmaɪndɪd/ *adjective* very determined to achieve something **kararlı, başarı için tek amacı olan, başarma azminde olan** *She had a single-minded determination to succeed in her career.*

single parent (*UK* **lone parent**) *noun* [C] someone who has a child or children but no husband, wife or partner that lives with them **tek ana/baba, tek ebeveyn**

singles /ˈsɪŋglz/ *noun* [U] a game in sports such as tennis, in which one person plays against another (**spor oyunları**) **tekler** *He won the men's singles title two years running.*

singly /ˈsɪŋgli/ *adverb* separately or one at a time **yalnız başına, tek başlarına, birer birer, teker teker** *We don't sell them singly, only in packs of four or ten.*

singular /ˈsɪŋgjələʳ/ *adjective* **1** The singular form of a word is used to talk about one person or thing. For example 'woman' is the singular form of 'women'. **tekil 2** *formal* very special, or found only in one person or situation **eşsiz, görülmemiş, müstesna** *a landscape of singular beauty*

the singular /ˈsɪŋgjələʳ/ *noun* the singular form of a word **bir sözcüğün tekil hâli**

singularly /ˈsɪŋgjələli/ *adverb* *formal* very **çok, fevkalâde, olağanüstü, fazla** *Fulbright was singularly uninterested in his comments.*

sinister /ˈsɪnɪstəʳ/ *adjective* making you feel that something bad or evil might happen **uğursuz, meşum, netameli** *a sinister figure dressed in black*

o▪**sink¹** /sɪŋk/ *verb past* **sank** *or also US* **sunk**, *past participle* **sunk 1** WATER [I, T] to go down or make something go down below the surface of water and not come back up **batmak** *The Titanic sank after hitting an iceberg.* ⊃See picture at **float. 2** SOFT SUBSTANCE [I, T] to go down, or make something go down, into something soft **batmak, batırmak** *My feet keep sinking into the sand.* **3** MOVE DOWN [I] to move down slowly **yavaş yavaş batmak** *The sun sank below the horizon.*
sink in *phrasal verb* If an unpleasant or surprising fact sinks in, you gradually start to believe it and understand what effect it will have on you. **anlaşılmak, iyice kavranmak** *It still hasn't sunk in that I'll never see her again.*
sink sth into sth *phrasal verb* to spend a large amount of money in a business or other piece of work **çok para yatırmak; epey harcama yapmak; büyük yatırım yapmak** *Millisat has already sunk $25 million into the Hong Kong project.*
sink into sth *phrasal verb* to slowly move into a sitting or lying position, in a relaxed or tired way **yorgunluktan veya istirahat amaçlı yavaş yavaş oturmak/yatmak** *I just want to go home and sink into a hot bath.*

sink² /sɪŋk/ *noun* [C] a bowl that is fixed to the wall in a kitchen or bathroom that you wash dishes or your hands, etc in **evye, lâvabo** ⊃Orta kısımdaki renkli sayfalarına bakınız.

sinus /ˈsaɪnəs/ *noun* [C] one of the spaces inside the head that are connected to the back of the nose **sinüs**

sip /sɪp/ *verb* [I, T] **sipping**, *past* **sipped** to drink, taking only a small amount at a time **yudumlamak, yudum yudum içmek** *She sipped her champagne.* ● **sip** *noun* [C] *He took a sip of his coffee and then continued.* **yudum**

siphon¹ /ˈsaɪf³n/ *noun* [C] a piece of equipment for moving liquid from one place to another **sifon**

siphon² /ˈsaɪf³n/ *verb* [T] **1** to remove liquid from a container using a siphon **sifon çekmek, sifonla akıtmak 2** (*also* **siphon off**) to dishonestly take money from an organization or other supply over a period of time **sahtekârca bir kurum ya da kaynaktan para almak/aktarmak; hesabına geçirmek**

sir /sɜːʳ/ *noun* (*also* **Sir**) **1** You call a man 'sir' when you are speaking to him politely. **beyefendi, bayım** *Excuse me, sir, is this seat taken?* **2** You write 'Sir' at the beginning of a formal letter to a man when you do not know his name. **'Sayın...', 'Saygıdeğer...'** *Dear Sir, I am writing to...* **3 Sir** a title used in the UK before the name of a man who has been officially respected or who has a high social rank (**İng.**) **Sör; bir asâlet ünvanı** *Sir Cliff Richard*

siren ...... İLE BİRLİKTE KULLANILAN KELİMELER
a siren **goes off/sounds** ● a siren **blares/wails** ● a **police** siren

siren /ˈsaɪərən/ *noun* [C] a piece of equipment that makes a loud sound as a warning **siren, (ambulans, itfaiye vb.) ikaz düdüğü** *a police siren*

o▪**sister** /ˈsɪstəʳ/ *noun* [C] **1** RELATIVE a girl or woman who has the same parents as you **kız kardeş** *an older/younger sister* ○ *my big/little sister* **2** RELIGION (*also* **Sister**) a nun (= woman who lives in a female religious group) **rahibe, hemşire** *Sister Bridget* **3** NURSE (*also* **Sister**) a female nurse in the UK who is responsible for a hospital ward (= an area of a hospital containing beds for ill people) **hemşire 4** MEMBER a woman who is a member of the same race, religious group, organization, etc **kar-**

deş, hemşire; aynı kuruluşun/dini örgütün/kurumun vs. üyesi bayan

sister-in-law /'sɪstᵊrɪnlɔː/ *noun* [C] *plural* **sisters-in-law** the woman married to your brother, or the sister of your husband or wife **görümce, baldız, yenge**

sisterly /'sɪstəli/ *adjective* experienced by or for a sister **kız kardeş gibi sevecen, kız kardeşe yakın, kız kardeşçe** *sisterly love*

o-**sit** /sɪt/ *verb* **sitting**, *past* **sat 1** BODY POSITION [I] to be in a position with the weight of your body on your bottom and the top part of your body up, for example, on a chair **oturmak** *Emma was **sitting on** a stool.* ○ *The children **sat at** the table by the window.* ○ *We **sat by** the river and had a picnic.* **2** MOVE BODY [I] (*also* **sit down**) to move your body into a sitting position after you have been standing **oturmak** *She came over and **sat beside** him.* ○ *She **sat down on** the grass.* ➲Orta kısımdaki renkli sayfalarına bakınız. **3 sit sb down/at/in, etc** to make someone sit somewhere **oturtmak, oturmasını sağlamak** *She sat me down and told me the bad news.* ○ *I thought we'd sit the children at the end of the table.* **4** STAY [I] to stay in one place for a long time and not be used **kalmak, beklemek, uzun süre orada olmak** *He hardly ever drives the car. It just sits in the garage.* **5** MEETING [I] If a court, parliament, etc sits, it has a meeting to do its work. **toplanmak, oturum yapmak, toplantı/oturum hâlinde olmak** *The board will be sitting next week.* **6** TEST/EXAM [T] *UK* to take a test or exam **sınava girmek** *The changes will affect many students sitting their exams this summer.* ➲See also: sit on the **fence**[1].

sit about/around *phrasal verb* to spend time sitting down and doing very little **boş boş oturmak, çok az çalışmak; vaktinin çoğunu oturarak geçirmek** [+ doing sth] *He just sits around all day watching television.*

sit back *phrasal verb* **1** to relax in a chair so that your back is against the back of the chair **sırtını yaslayarak oturmak; rahatına bakmak; keyif çatmak** *Just sit back and enjoy the show.* **2** to wait for something to happen without making any effort to do anything yourself **oturup beklemek; hiç bir girişimde bulunmadan beklemek** *You can't just sit back and expect someone else to deal with the problem.*

sit in *phrasal verb* to go to a meeting or class to watch **sadece oturup izlemek, dinleyici olmak; gözlem yapmak;** *I **sat in on** a couple of classes before choosing a course.*

sit sth out *phrasal verb* **1** to not do an activity such as a game or dance because you are tired or have an injury **yorgunluktan veya geçici sakatlıktan dolayı hiç bir faaliyete katılmamak** *I think I'll sit out the next dance.* **2** to wait for something unpleasant to finish before you do anything **sabırla oturup beklemek; sonuna kadar dayanmak** *The government is prepared to sit out the strike rather than agree to union demands.*

sit through sth *phrasal verb* to stay until the end of a meeting, performance, etc that is very long or boring **sonuna kadar kalmak, sabırla sonuna dek beklemek** *We had to sit through two hours of speeches.*

sit up *phrasal verb* **1** to move your body to a sitting position after you have been lying down **doğrulup/dikilip oturmak** *I sat up and opened my eyes.* **2** to stay awake and not go to bed although it is late **geç vakte kadar yatmadan/uyumadan oturmak** [+ doing sth] *We sat up talking all night.*

sitcom /'sɪtkɒm/ *noun* [C, U] a funny television programme that is about the same group of people every week in different situations **televizyonda her hafta ayrı bir konunun işlendiği güldürü dizisi/programı**

site[1] /saɪt/ *noun* **1** HISTORY [C] the place where something important happened in the past **yer, mevkî, mahal** *a **historic site*** ○ *the site of a battle* **2** AREA [C] an area that is used for something or where something happens **alan, arazi, yer, mevkî** *a **building site*** **3 on site** inside a factory, office building, etc **fabrika, işyeri vb. içinde; alan dahilinde; çalışma mekânında** *There are two restaurants on site.* ○ *They provide on-site childcare facilities for employees.* **4** INTERNET [C] *short for* website (= an area on the Internet where information about a particular subject, organization, etc can be found) **web sitesi; internette kullanılan alan/site**

site[2] /saɪt/ *verb formal* **site sth in/on, etc** to build something in a particular place **yapmak, inşa etmek, site kurmak** [often passive] *The company's head office is sited in Geneva.*

sitter /'sɪtə^r/ *noun* [C] *mainly US* a babysitter (= someone who looks after children when their parents go out) **çocuk bakıcısı**

sitting /'sɪtɪŋ/ *noun* [C] **1** a meeting of a parliament, court, etc **(meclis, mahkeme vb.) oturum, celse, toplantı** *a late-night sitting of parliament* **2** one of the times when a meal is served to a large group of people who cannot all eat at the same time **yemek servisi, yemek servis zamanı, yemek servis postası**

'sitting ˌroom *noun* [C] *UK* the room in a house where people sit to relax and, for example, watch television **oturma odası**

situated /'sɪtjueɪtɪd/ *adjective formal* **be situated in/on/by, etc** to be in a particular place **belli bir yerde olmak, bulunmak, konuşlanmak** *a hotel situated by Lake Garda*

situation ...... İLE BİRLİKTE KULLANILAN KELİMELER

bring about/rectify/improve a situation • a situation **arises/deteriorates/worsens** • a **complicated/dangerous/difficult/stressful** situation • **in** a situation

o-**situation** /ˌsɪtju'eɪʃᵊn/ *noun* [C] **1** the set of things that are happening and the conditions that exist at a particular time and place **hâl, durum, vaziyet, keyfiyet** *the economic/political situation* ○ *He's **in a** difficult **situation**.* **2** *formal* the position of a town, building, etc **konum, yer, mevkî, mahal, çevre, muhit, durum, yöre** *The park's situation was perfect.*

o-**six** /sɪks/ the number 6 **altı rakamı**

o-**sixteen** /ˌsɪk'stiːn/ the number 16 **onaltı rakamı** • **sixteenth** 16th written as a word **onaltıncı**

sixth[1] /sɪksθ/ 6th written as a word **altıncı**

sixth[2] /sɪksθ/ *noun* [C] one of six equal parts of something; 1/6 **altıda bir; altı bölü bir**

'sixth ˌform *noun* [C] in Britain, the part of a school for students between the ages of 16 and 18 **(Britanya'da) lise son sınıf**

o-**sixty** /'sɪksti/ **1** the number 60 **altmış rakamı 2 the sixties** the years from 1960 to 1969 **altmışlı yıllar 3 be in your sixties** to be aged between 60 and 69 **altmışlarında olmak** • **sixtieth** 60th written as a word **altmışıncı**

sizable /'saɪzəbl/ *adjective another spelling of* sizeable **oldukça büyük, epey çok sayıda**

size ...... İLE BİRLİKTE KULLANILAN KELİMELER

take/wear a size [10/39, etc] • **come in** [all/different/various, etc] sizes

o-**size**[1] /saɪz/ *noun* **1** [C, U] how big or small something is **büyüklük, boyut, ebat, hacim** *It's an area about the size of Oxford.* ○ *The size of some of those trees is incre-*

S

dible (= they are very large). **2** [C] one of the different measurements in which things, for example clothes, food containers, etc are made **ölçü, beden, numara** *a size 10 skirt* ○ *What size shoes do you take?* ○ *I usually buy the 1.5 litre size.* ⊃See also: all shapes (**shape**¹) and sizes.

size² /saɪz/ *verb*
size sb/sth up *phrasal verb* to look at someone or think about something carefully before making a judgment **ölçüp biçmek, tartmak, değerlendirmek** *I could see her trying to size me up.*

sizeable (*also* sizable) /'saɪzəbl/ *adjective* quite large **oldukça büyük, epey çok sayıda** *a sizeable crowd*

-sized /saɪzd/ *suffix* used at the end of a word to mean 'of a particular size' **...-ölçüde/bedende anlamında sonek** *a medium-sized pizza* ○ *a good-sized bedroom*

sizzle /'sɪzl/ *verb* [I] to make the sound of food cooking in hot oil **cızırdamak**

skanky /'skæŋki/ *adjective informal* very unpleasant or dirty **çok berbat ve pis, iğrenç, kötü**

skate¹ /skeɪt/ *noun* [C] **1** (*also* roller skate) a boot with wheels on the bottom, used for moving across the ground **tekerlekli paten** *a pair of skates* **2** (*also* ice skate) a boot with a metal part on the bottom, used for moving across ice **buz pateni ayakkabısı** ⊃Orta kısımdaki renkli sayfalarına bakınız. **3 get/put your skates on** UK informal used to tell someone to hurry 'Acele et!', 'Çabuk ol!'

skate² /skeɪt/ *verb* [I] to move using skates **paten yapmak, patenle kaymak** ● **skater** *noun* [C] **paten yapan kişi** ● **skating** *noun* [U] **paten (spor)**

skateboard /'skeɪtbɔːd/ *noun* [C] a board with wheels on the bottom, that you stand on and move forward by pushing one foot on the ground **kaykay** ⊃Orta kısımdaki renkli sayfalarına bakınız.

skateboarding /'skeɪtbɔːdɪŋ/ *noun* [U] the activity of moving using a skateboard **kaykay yapma** ⊃Orta kısımdaki renkli sayfalarına bakınız.

skeletal /'skelɪtᵊl/ *adjective* like a skeleton, or relating to skeletons **iskelet, iskelete ait**

skeleton /'skelɪtᵊn/ *noun* **1** [C] the structure made of all the bones in the body of a person or animal **iskelet 2 a skeleton crew/staff/service** the smallest number of people that you need to keep an organization working **çekirdek kadro; bir işyerinin bel kemiğini oluşturan personel 3 have a skeleton in the cupboard** UK (US have a skeleton in the closet) to have an embarrassing or unpleasant secret about something that happened in the past **utanç veren bir sırrı olmak**

skeptic /'skeptɪk/ *noun* [C] US spelling of sceptic **kuşkucu/şüpheci kimse**

skeptical /'skeptɪkᵊl/ *adjective* US spelling of sceptical **şüpheci, kuşkucu, kuşkulu, şüphe duyan**

skepticism /'skeptɪsɪzᵊm/ *noun* [U] US spelling of scepticism **şüphecilik, kuşkuculuk**

sketch¹ /sketʃ/ *noun* [C] **1** [PICTURE] a picture that you draw quickly and with few details **taslak, kroki, eskiz** *He did a quick sketch of the cat.* **2** [ACTING] a short piece of acting about a funny situation **skeç 3** [DESCRIPTION] a short description of something without many details **kısa tanımlama; basit betimleme**

sketch² /sketʃ/ *verb* [T] to draw a sketch **taslak/kroki/eskiz çizmek** *I sketched a map for him on a scrap of paper.*
sketch sth out *phrasal verb* to give a short description with few details, especially of an idea or plan **kısa bir tanımlamasını yapmak, ana hatlarıyla anlatmak, kısaca açıklamak** *I've sketched out some ideas for my new book.*

sketchy /'sketʃi/ *adjective* with few details **kabataslak, yarım yamalak, üstünkörü, ayrıntısız** *Reports about the accident are still sketchy.*

ski¹ /skiː/ *noun* [C] *plural* skis one of a pair of long, thin pieces of wood or plastic that you wear on the bottom of boots to move over snow **kayak** ⊃Orta kısımdaki renkli sayfalarına bakınız.

ski² /skiː/ *verb* [I] skiing, *past* skied to move over snow wearing skis **kayak yapmak** ● **skier** *noun* [C] **kayak yapan kişi** ● **skiing** *noun* [U] *I'd like to go skiing in Switzerland.* **kayak (spor)** ⊃See also: water-skiing ⊃Orta kısımdaki renkli sayfalarına bakınız.

skid /skɪd/ *verb* [I] skidding, *past* skidded If a vehicle skids, it slides along a surface and you cannot control it. **patinaj yapmak, kaymak** *The car skidded on ice and hit a tree.* ● **skid** *noun* [C] **kızak**

skies /skaɪz/ *noun* [plural] the sky in a particular place or in a particular state **gökyüzü** *beautiful, clear, blue skies*

skilful UK (US skillful) /'skɪlfᵊl/ *adjective* **1** good at doing something **maharetli, becerikli, usta, hünerli, mahir** *a skilful artist* **2** done or made very well **ustaca, usta işi** *skilful use of language* ● **skilfully** *adverb* UK **beceriyle**

acquire/develop/learn/master/require a skill ● consummate/great skill ● a basic/necessary/useful skill ● skill at/in sth

o╼**skill** /skɪl/ *noun* [C, U] the ability to do an activity or job well, especially because you have practised it **beceri, hüner, marifet, ustalık** *You need good communication skills to be a teacher.*

skilled /skɪld/ *adjective* **1** having the abilities needed to do an activity or job well **usta, becerikli, marifetli** *a highly skilled* (= very skilled) *photographer* ○ *He has become skilled in dealing with the media.* **2** Skilled work needs someone who has had special training to do it. **ustalık isteyen, beceri gerektiren, vasıflı, nitelikli** ⊃Opposite unskilled.

skillet /'skɪlɪt/ *noun* [C] mainly US a large, heavy pan with a long handle, used for frying food **uzun saplı büyük ağır tava**

skillful /'skɪlfᵊl/ *adjective* US spelling of skilful **maharetli, becerikli, usta, hünerli**

skim /skɪm/ *verb* skimming, *past* skimmed **1** [MOVE OVER] [I, T] to move quickly, and almost or just touch the surface of something **yalayarak geçek, sıyırıp geçmek** *Birds skimmed the surface of the pond.* **2** [REMOVE] [T] (*also* skim off) to remove something from the surface of a liquid **sıyırıp almak** *Skim off any excess fat before serving.* **3** [READ QUICKLY] [T] (*also* skim through) to read or look at something quickly without looking at the details **hızlıca okumak/gözden geçirmek** *She began skimming through the reports on her desk.*

skimmed 'milk (*also* US 'skim ,milk) *noun* [U] milk that has had the fat removed from it **kaymağı alınmış süt**

skimp /skɪmp/ *verb*
skimp on sth *phrasal verb* to not spend enough time or money on something, or not use enough of something **cimrilik/pintilik etmek; cimrice/pintice davranmak** *We've got plenty of cheese so don't skimp on it.*

skimpy /'skɪmpi/ *adjective* Skimpy clothes show a lot of your body. **açık saçık, az, yetersiz, kıt, belli belirsiz** *skimpy bikini/dress*

dark/fair/olive skin ● dry/oily/sensitive skin

o↩**skin¹** /skɪn/ *noun* [C, U] **1** BODY the outer layer of a person or animal's body **deri, cilt** *dark/fair skin* **2** ANIMAL the outer layer of a dead animal used as leather, fur, etc **deri, post, pösteki** *a leopard skin rug* **3** FRUIT the outer layer of a fruit or vegetable **(meyve, sebze) kabuk, deri, zar** *a banana/potato skin* **4** LIQUID a thin, solid layer that forms on the top of a liquid **kabuk, üstteki tabaka** *A skin had formed on the top of the milk.* **5** COMPUTERS the particular way that information is arranged and shown on a computer screen **bilgisayar ekranında bilginin düzenlendiği ve gösterildiği biçim 6 do sth by the skin of your teeth** *informal* to only just succeed in doing something **kıl payı başarmak; güç belâ halletmek; sıyırmak; paçayı zar zor kurtarmak** *They held on by the skin of their teeth to win 1-0.* ● **7 have (a) thick skin** to not care if someone criticizes you **umursamamak, aldırmamak, kılını kıpırdatmamak, oralı bile olmamak**

skin² /skɪn/ *verb* [T] **skinning,** *past* **skinned 1** to remove the skin from something **derisini yüzmek 2** (*also UK* **graze**) to injure your skin by rubbing it against something **rough sıyırmak, sıyırtmak** *Mary fell and skinned her knees.*

skinhead /'skɪnhed/ *noun* [C] a man who has extremely short hair, especially one who behaves in a violent way **dazlak**

skinny /'skɪni/ *adjective* Someone who is skinny is too thin. **cılız, bir deri bir kemik, kaknem, sıska, çiroz gibi**

skip¹ /skɪp/ *verb* **skipping,** *past* **skipped 1** MOVE FORWARD [I] to move forward, jumping quickly from one foot to the other **sekmek, seke seke gitmek** *She watched her daughter skipping down the street.* **2** JUMP [I] (*US* ˌskip 'rope) to jump over a rope while you or two other people move it over and then under your body again and again **ip atlamak** *I skip for ten minutes every day to keep fit.* **3** NOT DO [T] to not do something that you usually do or that you should do **atlamak, es geçmek, boş vermek** *I think I'll skip lunch today - I'm not very hungry.* **4** AVOID [T] (*also* **skip over**) to avoid reading or talking about something by starting to read or talk about the next thing instead **atlamak, başka bir konuya geçmek, atlatmak** *I usually skip the boring bits.*

skip² /skɪp/ *noun* [C] **1** *UK* (*US* **Dumpster** *trademark*) a very large, metal container for big pieces of rubbish **moloz bidonu/kasası; inşaat sandığı; çöp bidonu 2** when you jump quickly from one foot to the other **sek sek**

skipper /'skɪpəʳ/ *noun* [C] *informal* the leader of a team, an aircraft, a ship, etc **kaptan, reis, lider, öncü**

'**skipping ˌrope** *UK* (*US* **jump rope**) *noun* [C] a rope that you move over your head and then jump over as you move it under your feet **atlama ipi**

skirmish /'skɜːmɪʃ/ *noun* [C] a small fight **çatışma, çarpışma, müsademe; atışma, takışma**

skirt¹ /skɜːt/ *noun* [C] a piece of women's clothing that hangs from the waist and has no legs **etek** ⊃*Orta kısımdaki renkli sayfalarına bakınız.*

skirt² /skɜːt/ (*also* **skirt around**) *verb* [T] **1** to avoid talking about something **değinmekten kaçınmak, geçiştirmek, kaçınmak** *I deliberately skirted the question of money.* **2** to move around the edge of something **etrafından dolanmak, kenarından geçip gitmek** *We skirted around the edge of the field.*

skittle /'skɪtl/ *noun* **1** [C] one of a set of bottle-shaped objects that you try to knock down with a ball as a game **kuka 2 skittles** [U] a game in which you try to knock down bottle-shaped objects with a ball **dokuz kuka oyunu**

skive /skaɪv/ (*also* **skive off**) *verb* [I, T] *UK* to not go to school or work when you should, or to leave school or work earlier than you should **kaytarmak, işten kaçmak; okulu/işi kırmak** ● **skiver** *noun* [C] *UK informal* someone who skives **kaytarmacı, işten kaçan kimse**

skulk /skʌlk/ *verb* **skulk about/behind/in, etc** to hide somewhere or move around quietly in a way that makes people think you are going to do something bad **gizlenmek, saklanmak, gizli gizli hareket etmek** *I saw a man skulking behind the shed.*

skull /skʌl/ *noun* [C] the part of your head that is made of bone and which protects your brain **kafatası**

'**skull ˌcap** *noun* [C] a small round hat worn especially by some religious men **takke**

skunk /skʌŋk/ *noun* [C] a black and white animal that produces a very unpleasant smell in order to defend itself **kokarca**

🧩 **sky** .... İLE BİRLİKTE KULLANILAN KELİMELER

the sky **darkens/lightens** ● in the sky ● a **clear/ cloudy/overcast** sky

o↩**sky** /skaɪ/ *noun* [U, no plural] the area above the Earth where you can see clouds, the sun, the moon, etc **gök, gökyüzü** *a beautiful, blue sky* ○ *The sky suddenly went dark.* ⊃*See also:* **skies.**

skydiving /'skaɪˌdaɪvɪŋ/ *noun* [U] the sport of jumping out of an aircraft with a parachute (= large piece of cloth that allows you to fall slowly to the ground) **paraşütle atlama sporu**

skylight /'skaɪlaɪt/ *noun* [C] a window in the roof of a building **tepe/çatı penceresi**

skyline /'skaɪlaɪn/ *noun* [C] the pattern that is made against the sky by tall buildings **uzun binaların oluşturduğu ufuk çizgisi/silüet** *the New York skyline*

'**sky ˌmarshal** *noun* [C] a person whose job is to carry a gun and protect the passengers on an aircraft **silahlı hava koruması; uçak koruması**

skyscraper /'skaɪˌskreɪpəʳ/ *noun* [C] a very tall building **gökdelen**

skyline

slab /slæb/ *noun* [C] a thick, flat piece of something, especially stone **plaka, tabaka, kalın dilim, levha** *a slab of concrete*

slack¹ /slæk/ *adjective* **1** LOOSE loose or not tight **gevşek, sarkık, lâçka** *Suddenly the rope became slack.* **2** BUSINESS If business is slack, there are not many customers. **durgun, sönük, kesat, hareketsiz, ölü 3** LAZY not trying hard enough in your work **gevşek, ilgisiz, kayıtsız** *slack management*

slack² /slæk/ *informal* (*also US* **slack off**) *verb* [I] to work less hard than usual **gevşek çalışmak, sıkı çalışmamak** *I'm afraid I haven't been to the gym recently - I've been slacking.*

slacken /'slækªn/ *verb* [I, T] **1** to become slower or less active, or to make something become slower or less active **yavaşla(t)mak, tavsa(t)mak, azal(t)mak** *Economic growth is slackening.* **2** to become loose, or to make something become loose **gevşe(t)mek** *As you get older your muscles slacken.*

slacks /slæks/ *noun* [plural] *mainly US* trousers **bol pantolon**

slag /slæg/ *verb* **slagging**, *past* **slagged**
slag sb/sth off *phrasal verb UK informal* to criticize someone or something in an unpleasant way **yermek, alaycı bir dille eleştirmek, kabaca tenkit etmek**

slain /sleɪn/ *past participle of* slay **katletmek' fiilinin geçmiş zaman hâli**

slalom /ˈslɑːləm/ *noun* [C] a race in which you go forwards by moving from side to side between poles **slalom**

slam /slæm/ *verb* **slamming**, *past* **slammed 1** [I, T] to close with great force, or to make something close with great force **çarparak kapatmak, çarpıp kapatmak; çarpıp kapanmak** *Kate heard the front door slam.* **2 slam sth down/onto/into, etc** to put something somewhere with great force **pat' diye bırakmak; fırlatıp atmak, çarpmak** *She slammed the phone down.* ● **slam** *noun* [C] [usually singular] *the slam of a car door* **sert bir şekilde kapatma**

slander /ˈslɑːndəʳ/ *noun* [C, U] the crime of saying bad things about someone that are not true **iftira, karalama, kara çalma** ● **slander** *verb* [T] **iftira atmak** ● **slanderous** /ˈslɑːndʳrəs/ *adjective* saying bad things about someone that are not true **iftira atan, karalayan, kara çalan; yalan yanlış şeyler söyleyen**

slang /slæŋ/ *noun* [U] informal language, often language that is only used by people who belong to a particular group **argo** *prison slang*

slant¹ /slɑːnt/ *verb* [I, T] to slope in a particular direction, or to make something slope in a particular direction **meyilli olmak, eğmek, eğik olmak, yana yat(ır)mak** *Pale sunlight slanted through the curtain.*

slant² /slɑːnt/ *noun* [no plural] **1** a position that is sloping **eğim, meyil, yokuş** *The road is on/at a slant.* **2** a way of writing about something that shows who or what you support **ön yargılı/taraflı görüş/yazı** *a political slant* ○ *It's certainly a new slant on the subject.*

slap¹ /slæp/ *verb* [T] **slapping**, *past* **slapped** to hit someone with the flat, inside part of your hand **tokatlamak, tokat atmak, şamar atmak** *She slapped him across the face.*
slap sth on *phrasal verb* to quickly put or spread something on a surface **sürüvermek, koyuvermek, çalmak** *I'll just slap some make-up on.*

slap² /slæp/ *noun* [C] **1** a hit with the flat, inside part of your hand **tokat, şamar, tokat atma 2 a slap in the face** something someone does that insults or upsets you **suratına bir şamar, tersleme, hakaret** *After all that hard work, losing my job was a real slap in the face.*

slapdash /ˈslæpdæʃ/ *adjective* done quickly and without being careful **üstünkörü, alelacele, uyduruktan, rastgele** *Her work has been a bit slapdash recently.*

slapstick /ˈslæpstɪk/ *noun* [U] when actors do funny things like falling down, which is funny and done to make people laugh **şaklabanlık; şaklabanlığa dayalı ucuz komedi; âdi komedi**

slap-up /ˈslæpˌʌp/ *adjective* **slap-up meal/dinner, etc** *UK informal* a large and very good meal **mükellef/ enfes bir yemek**

slash¹ /slæʃ/ *verb* [T] **1** to cut something by making a quick, long cut with something very sharp **yarmak, derince kesmek** *His throat had been slashed.* **2** to reduce the amount of something by a lot **indirmek, düşürmek, azaltmak** *to slash prices*

slash² /slæʃ/ *noun* [C] **1** a long, deep cut **yarık, kesik 2** a mark (/) used in writing to separate words or numbers, often to show a choice or connection **(/) eğri çizgi**

slate¹ /sleɪt/ *noun* [C, U] a dark grey rock that can easily be cut into thin pieces, or a small, flat piece of this used to cover a roof **kayağan taş, arduvaz, kayrak**

slate² /sleɪt/ *verb* **1** [T] *UK* to criticize someone or something severely **acımasızca eleştirmek; şiddetle tenkit etmek** [often passive] *The film had been slated by critics.* **2 be slated** *US* to be expected to happen in the future, or to be expected to be or do something in the future **olmasını ummak; olması beklenmek; yapılması umulmak** [+ to do sth] *Filming is slated to begin next spring.*

slaughter¹ /ˈslɔːtəʳ/ *verb* [T] **1** ANIMAL to kill an animal for meat **kesmek 2** PEOPLE to kill a lot of people in a very cruel way **kesmek, katliam yapmak, topluca öldürmek, kıyım yapmak 3** DEFEAT *informal* to defeat someone very easily **kolayca yenmek/altetmek; hakkından gelmek**

slaughter² /ˈslɔːtəʳ/ *noun* [U] when a lot of people or animals are killed in a cruel way **toplu katliam, kıyım**

slaughterhouse /ˈslɔːtəhaʊs/ *noun* [C] *plural* **slaughterhouses** /ˈslɔːtəhaʊzɪz/ a place where animals are killed for meat **mezbaha, kesimhane**

slave¹ /sleɪv/ *noun* **1** [C] someone who is owned by someone else and has to work for them **esir, köle, tutsak** *He treats his mother like a slave.* **2 be a slave to sth** to be completely controlled or influenced by something **kölesi olmak; etkisi altına almak, tamamen onun kontrolünde olmak** *You're a slave to fashion.*

slave² /sleɪv/ *(also* slave away) *verb* [I] *informal* to work very hard **çok çalışmak, köle gibi çalışmak** *Giorgio was slaving away at his homework.*

slavery /ˈsleɪvʰri/ *noun* [U] the system of owning slaves, or the condition of being a slave **kölelik**

slay /sleɪ/ *verb* [T] *past tense* **slew**, *past part* **slain** *literary* to kill someone in a very violent way **hunharca öldürmek, katletmek**

sleaze /sliːz/ *noun* [U] political or business activities that are morally wrong **ahlaksızlık, rüşvet, yozlaşma**

sleazy /ˈsliːzi/ *adjective* unpleasant and morally wrong, often in a way that relates to sex **pis, salaş, köhne, pepaye, karanlık** *He spent the night drinking in a sleazy bar.*

sledge¹ /sledʒ/ *UK (US* sled /sled/) *noun* [C] a vehicle that is used for travelling on snow **kızak**

sledge² /sledʒ/ *UK (US* sled /sled/) *verb* [I] to travel on snow using a sledge **kızak kaymak, kızakla gitmek**

sleek /sliːk/ *adjective* **1** Sleek hair is smooth and very shiny. **düzgün ve parlak, düz ve ipek gibi 2** A sleek car is attractive and looks expensive. **şık ve kalantor görünümlü**

✪ **sleep¹** /sliːp/ *verb past* **slept 1** [I] to be in the state of rest when your eyes are closed, your body is not active, and your mind is unconscious **uyumak** *Did you sleep well?* **2 sleep four/six, etc** If a place sleeps four, six, etc, it is big enough for that number of people to sleep in. **çok kişinin uyuyabileceği/kalabileceği yer 3 sleep on it** to wait until the next day before making a decision about something important so that you can think about it carefully **karar vermeden önce düşünmek, düşünüp taşınmak** ⊃ See also: not sleep a wink².
sleep in *phrasal verb* to sleep longer in the morning than you usually do **uzun süre uyumak, uyuya kalmak**
sleep sth off *phrasal verb* to sleep until you feel better, especially after drinking too much alcohol **(içkiden sonra) etkisini uyuyarak gidermek**
sleep over *phrasal verb* to sleep in someone else's home for a night **başkasının evinde kalmak/yatmak/uyumak** *After the party, I slept over at Tom's house.*
sleep through sth *phrasal verb* to continue to sleep although there is noise **gürültüye rağmen uyumaya**

devam etmek/uyanmamak *I don't know how you slept through the storm.*
sleep with sb *phrasal verb informal* to have sex with someone **yatmak, cinsel ilişkide bulunmak, sevişmek**

> **sleep (noun)** ...... İLE BİRLİKTE KULLANILAN KELİMELER
> get [no/some, etc] sleep ● get to/go to sleep ● have a sleep ● a **good night's** sleep ● in your sleep

o-**sleep²** /sliːp/ *noun* **1** [U, no plural] the state you are in when you are sleeping, or a period of time when you are sleeping **uyku** *I haven't had **a good night's sleep*** (= a long sleep at night) *for weeks.* ○ *You need to go home and get some sleep.* ○ *It took me ages to get to sleep* (= to succeed in sleeping). ○ *He died peacefully in his sleep.* **2 go to sleep a** to begin to sleep **uykuya dalmak, uyumak** *Babies often go to sleep after a feed.* **b** *informal* If part of your body goes to sleep, you cannot feel it. **uyuşmak, hissizleşmek** *I'd been sitting on my feet and they'd gone to sleep.* **3 put sth to sleep** to kill an animal that is very old or ill **uyutmak, uyutarak öldürmek 4 could do sth in your sleep** to be able to do something very easily **kolayca yapabilmek, kolay bir şekilde halledebilmek 5 lose sleep over sth** to worry about something **uykuları kaçmak, endişelenmek**

sleeper /ˈsliːpəʳ/ *noun* **1 a light/heavy sleeper** someone who wakes up easily/does not wake up easily **uykusu ağır/hafif kimse 2** TRAIN [C] a train or a part of a train that has beds in it **yataklı/kuşetli tren; yataklı vagon 3** SUPPORT [C] *UK (US railroad tie)* a piece of wood that is used to support a railway track (= the thing a train moves along on) **travers 4** JEWELLERY [C] *UK* a small gold or silver ring worn in the ear **altın veya gümüş halka küpe**

'sleeping ˌbag *noun* [C] a long bag made of thick material that you sleep inside **uyku tulumu**

sleeping bag

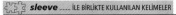

'sleeping ˌpill *noun* [C] a medicine that you take to help you sleep **uyku hapı**

sleepless /ˈsliːpləs/ *adjective* **sleepless night** a night when you are not able to sleep **uykusuz geçen gece** *He'd spent a sleepless night worrying about his exam.* ● **sleeplessness** *noun* [U] **uykusuzluk**

sleep-over /ˈsliːpəʊvəʳ/ *noun* [C] a party when a group of young people stay at a friend's house for the night **evde parti gecesi**

sleepwalk /ˈsliːpˌwɔːk/ *verb* [I] to get out of bed and walk around while you are sleeping **uykuda gezmek, uykuda dolaşmak ● sleepwalker** *noun* [C] **uyur gezer**

sleepy /ˈsliːpi/ *adjective* **1** feeling tired and wanting to go to sleep **uykulu, uykusu gelmiş, uyku basmış** *The heat had made me sleepy.* **2** quiet and with little activity **sakin, hareketsiz** *a sleepy little town ● **sleepily** *adverb* **uykulu bir şekilde ● sleepiness** *noun* [U] **uyku hali**

sleet /sliːt/ *noun* [U] a mixture of snow and rain **sulu sepken ● sleet** *verb* [I] *It was sleeting when I looked outside.* **sulu kar yağması**

> **sleeve** ...... İLE BİRLİKTE KULLANILAN KELİMELER
> long/short sleeves ● roll up your sleeves

sleeve /sliːv/ *noun* **1** [C] the part of a jacket, shirt, etc that covers your arm **yen, elbise kolu** *He rolled up*

his *sleeves* to do the dishes. ⊃See picture at **jacket**. **2 have sth up your sleeve** *informal* to have a secret plan **gizli plânı olmak, bir bildiği olmak, kozu olmak, bir şeytanlık düşünmek** *They were worried he might have another nasty surprise up his sleeve.*

-sleeved /sliːvd/ *suffix* **short-sleeved/long-sleeved** having short/long sleeves **kısa/uzun kollu** *a short-sleeved shirt*

sleeveless /ˈsliːvləs/ *adjective* describes a piece of clothing with no sleeves **kolsuz** *a sleeveless dress*

sleigh /sleɪ/ *noun* [C] a large vehicle that is pulled by animals and used for travelling on snow **kızak**

slender /ˈslendəʳ/ *adjective* thin in an attractive way **incecik, nârin, fidan gibi** *a slender woman with long, red hair*

slept /slept/ *past of* sleep **uyumak' fiilinin geçmiş zaman hâli**

sleuth /sluːθ/ *noun* [C] *old-fashioned* a police officer whose job is to discover who has committed a crime **dedektif, hafiye**

slew /sluː/ *past tense of* slay **katletmek' fiilinin geçmiş zaman hâli**

slice¹ /slaɪs/ *noun* **1** [C] a flat piece of food that has been cut from a larger piece **dilim** *a slice of bread/cake/meat* ⊃Orta kısımdaki renkli sayfalarına bakınız. **2 a slice of sth** a part of something that is being divided **kısım, bölüm, parça** *a large slice of the profits* ⊃See also: **fish slice**.

slice² /slaɪs/ *verb* **1** [T] *(also slice up)* to cut food into thin, flat pieces **dilimlemek, dilmek, dilim dilim kesmek** *Could you slice the tomatoes?* **2 slice into/off/through, etc** [I, T] to cut into or through something with a knife or something sharp **kesmek, yarmak, dilim dilim etmek** *I almost sliced my finger off.* ⊃See also: **the best/greatest thing** since sliced bread.

slick /slɪk/ *adjective* **1** done with a lot of skill **ustalıkla, maharetle** *a slick presentation* **2** attractive but in a way that is not sincere or honest **akıl çelen, cerbezeli, yüze gülücü, kandırıcı, görünüşte güzel** *He was a bit slick - I didn't trust him.*

slide¹ /slaɪd/ *verb past* slid **1 slide (sth) across/down/along, etc** to move smoothly over a surface, or to make something move smoothly over a surface **kaymak, kaydırmak** *He slid the letter into his pocket.* **2 slide (sth) into/out of/through, etc** to move somewhere quietly, or to make something move quietly **kaymak, kayıp gitmek, kaydırmak, kayar gibi geçip gitmek** *She slid out of the room, being careful not to wake Alan.*

slide² /slaɪd/ *noun* **1** PHOTOGRAPH [C] a small piece of film that you shine light through in order to see a photograph **slayt, diapozitif 2** GAME [C] a large object that children climb and slide down as a game **kaydırak 3** GLASS [C] a small piece of glass that you put something on when you want to look at it under a microscope (= equipment used to make things look bigger) **lâm 4** LESS/WORSE [no plural] when the level or quality of something gets less or worse **düşüş, kötüleşme, azalma** *a price slide*

o-**slight¹** /slaɪt/ *adjective* **1** small and not important **ufak, az, hafif, belli belirsiz, zayıf** *slight differences in colour* ○ *We're having a slight problem with our computer system.* **2** Someone who is slight is thin. **incecik, narin**

slight² /slaɪt/ *noun* [C] an action or remark that insults someone **küçümseme, horlama, hiçe sayma**

slighted /ˈslaɪtɪd/ *adjective* **be/feel slighted** to feel insulted because someone has done or said something which shows that they think you are not important **küçük düşmek, mahcup hissetmek; horlanmış his-**

slightest

setmek *Annie felt slighted because she hadn't been invited to the meeting.*

slightest /'slaɪtɪst/ *adjective* **1 the slightest** [always before noun] the smallest **en küçük, en az, en önemsiz** *The slightest movement will disturb these shy animals.* **2 not in the slightest** not at all **hiç mi hiç, hiç de, bir nebze bile değil, bir parça bile değil** *"Do you mind if I open the window?" "Not in the slightest."*

◦-**slightly** /'slaɪtli/ *adverb* a little **birazcık, azıcık** *I think I did slightly better in my exams this time.* ○ *I find it slightly worrying.*

slim¹ /slɪm/ *adjective* **slimmer, slimmest 1** Someone who is slim is thin in an attractive way. **incecik, fidan gibi, nârin 2** small and not as much as you would like **az, zayıf** *There's a slim chance he'll succeed.*

slim² /slɪm/ *verb* [I] **slimming,** *past* **slimmed** *UK* to eat less in order to become thinner **zayıflamak, kilo vermek slim down** *phrasal verb* to become thinner **incelmek, zayıflamak, incecik olmak slim sth down** *phrasal verb* to reduce the size of something **azaltmak, ebadını küçültmek, küçültmek** *It is not our intention to slim down the workforce.*

slime /slaɪm/ *noun* [U] a thick, sticky liquid that is unpleasant to touch **sümük, sümüksü madde**

slimy /'slaɪmi/ *adjective* **1** covered in slime **balçık/çamur/sümük/sümüğümsü madde ile kaplı 2** *informal* too friendly in a way that is not sincere **yağcı, yaltakçı, görünürde dost**

sling¹ /slɪŋ/ *noun* [C] **1** a piece of cloth that you wear around your neck and put your arm into to support it when it is injured **askı, kol askısı 2** a piece of cloth or a strap that you tie around your body to carry things in **askılı çanta, askı, bel çantası** *She had her baby in a sling.*

sling² /slɪŋ/ *verb* *past* **slung 1 sling sth over/around/on, etc** to put something in a position where it hangs loosely **asıp sallandırmak** *He slung his bag over his shoulder.* **2 sling sth into/onto/under, etc** to throw something somewhere in a careless way **fırlatıp atmak, rastgele koymak** *She slung her coat onto the bed.*

slingshot /'slɪŋʃɒt/ *US* (*UK* **catapult**) *noun* [C] a Y-shaped object with a piece of elastic across it used by children to shoot small stones **sapan**

slink /slɪŋk/ *verb* *past* **slunk slink away/off/out, etc** to move somewhere quietly so that no one will notice you **sıvışmak, farkedilmeden gitmek, süzülmek** *I caught him slinking out of the meeting.*

slip¹ /slɪp/ *verb* **slipping,** *past* **slipped 1** [FALL] [I] to slide by accident and fall or almost fall **kaymak, kayıp düşmek** *She slipped on the ice and broke her ankle.* **2** [OUT OF POSITION] [I] to slide out of the correct position (kazara elinden) **kaymak, kayıp yerinden çıkmak** *The photo had slipped from the frame.* **3 slip away/out/through, etc** to go somewhere quietly or quickly **usulca ve sessizce gidivermek; süzülüvermek; çaktırmadan gitmek** *I'll slip out of the room if I get bored.* **4 slip sth into/through, etc** to put something somewhere quickly or secretly **gizlice ve çaktırmadan koymak; çabucak gizlemek** *She slipped the letter into an envelope and sealed it.* **5** [GIVE SECRETLY] [+ two objects] *informal* to give something to someone secretly **gizlice vermek, tutuşturuvermek** *I slipped her a five pound note.* **6** [GET LESS/WORSE] [I] to get less or worse in level or quality **düşmek, düşüş göstermek, kötüleşmek, azalmak** *His school grades have slipped recently.* **7 let sth slip** to forget that something is a secret and tell someone about it **ağzından kaçırmak** ⊃See also: slip your mind¹.

slip into sth *phrasal verb* to quickly put on a piece of clothing **giyivermek, üstüne geçirivermek**

slip sth off *phrasal verb* to quickly take off a piece of clothing **çıkarıvermek, üstünden çıkarıp etivermek** *Slip your shirt off and I'll listen to your heart.*

slip sth on *phrasal verb* to quickly put on a piece of clothing **giyivermek, üstüne geçirivermek** *I'll just slip my shoes on.*

slip out *phrasal verb* If a remark slips out, you say it without intending to. **söyleyivermek, ağzından kaçmak, dili sürçmek** *I didn't mean to tell anyone you were getting married - it just slipped out.*

slip out of sth *phrasal verb* to quickly take off a piece of clothing **çıkarıvermek, üstünden çıkarıp atıvermek**

slip up *phrasal verb* to make a mistake **yanılmak, hata yapmak**

slip² /slɪp/ *noun* [C] **1** [PAPER] a small piece of paper **fiş, pusula** *He wrote the number on a slip of paper.* **2** [FALL] when you slide by accident and fall or almost fall **kayma, sendeleme, düşüverme, kayış 3** [WOMEN'S CLOTHING] a piece of clothing that a woman wears under a dress or skirt **kombinezon 4** [MISTAKE] a small mistake **hata, kusur, yanılgı, ufak bir hata 5 give sb the slip** *informal* to escape from someone you do not want to be with **kaçmak, sıvışmak, uzak durmak 6 a slip of the tongue** a mistake made by using the wrong word **dil sürçmesi**

slipper /'slɪpər/ *noun* [C] a soft, comfortable shoe that you wear in the house **terlik** ⊃Orta kısımdaki renkli sayfalarına bakınız.

slippery /'slɪpəri/ *adjective* **1** smooth and wet and difficult to hold or walk on **kaygan** *Be careful - the floor's slippery.* **2** a slippery slope a bad situation that is likely to get worse **gittikçe kötüleşme olasılığı olan kötü durum, çıkmaz/açmaz durum**

'slip ,road *UK* (*US* **ramp**) *noun* [C] a short road that is used to drive onto or off a motorway (= wide, fast road) **hızlı araç kullanılabilecek otoyol**

slit¹ /slɪt/ *noun* [C] a long, narrow cut or hole in something **uzun kesik, yarık** *Make a slit in the pastry to allow the steam to escape.*

slit² /slɪt/ *verb* [T] **slitting,** *past* **slit** to make a long, narrow cut in something **uzunlamasına kesmek, yarmak** *She slit her wrists.*

slither /'slɪðər/ *verb* [I] to move smoothly by twisting and sliding **kıvrılarak ve sürünerek gitmek, yılan gibi ilerlemek**

sliver /'slɪvər/ *noun* [C] a thin piece of something that has come off a larger piece **ufak ince parça, kıymık** *slivers of glass*

slob /slɒb/ *noun* [C] *informal* a lazy or dirty person **çok tembel/miskin/pasaklı/uyuşuk kimse**

slog¹ /slɒg/ *verb* **slogging,** *past* **slogged** *informal* **slog up/down/through, etc** to move forward with difficulty **güçlükle ilerlemek/yürümek/inmek/çıkmak/hareket etmek** *We slogged up the hill in silence.* **slog away** *phrasal verb* to work very hard for a long time **didinmek, sebatla/azimle çalışmak; dur suruk bilmeden çalışmak** *I've been slogging away at this for hours and I'm exhausted.*

slog² /slɒg/ *noun* [U, no plural] *UK informal* a period of hard work **zahmetli iş, ağır görev** *Studying for all the exams was a hard slog.*

sth **bears/carries** a slogan ● a slogan **of** sth ● an **advertising** slogan

slogan /'sləʊgən/ noun [C] a short phrase that is easy to remember and is used to make people notice something **slogan** an *advertising slogan*

slop /slɒp/ verb **slopping**, past **slopped slop (sth) about/around/into, etc** If liquid slops about, it moves around or over the edge of its container, and if you slop it about, you make it move around or over the edge of its container. **dökülüp saçılmak, döküp saçmak** *Her hand shook, making her tea slop into the saucer.*

slope¹ /sləʊp/ noun [C] a surface or piece of land that is high at one end and low at the other **yamaç, yokuş, bayır** *There's a steep slope to climb before we're at the top.* ⊃See also: a **slippery** slope.

slope² /sləʊp/ verb [I] to be high at one end and low at the other **eğimli/meyilli olmak** *The field slopes down to the river.*

sloppy /'slɒpi/ adjective **1** [CARELESS] not done carefully **dikkatsiz, özensiz, yarım yamalak** *His work was sloppy and full of spelling mistakes.* **2** [CLOTHES] Sloppy clothes are loose and untidy. **salaş, bakımsız, dikkatsiz, özensiz** *a girl wearing a sloppy sweater and torn jeans* **3** [TOO WET] A sloppy substance has too much liquid in it. **vıcık vıcık, su içinde ● sloppily** adverb **dikkatsiz bir şekilde, yarım yamalak, pasaklı ● sloppiness** noun [U] **dikkatsizlik**

slosh /slɒʃ/ verb **slosh against/over/around, etc** If liquid sloshes, it moves against or over the edge of its container. **dökülüp saçılmak, döküp saçmak** *Water sloshed over the edge of the pool as the swimmers dived in.*

sloshed /slɒʃt/ adjective informal drunk **sarhoş, zom**

slot¹ /slɒt/ noun [C] **1** a long, narrow hole that you put something into, especially money **yarık, delik 2** a period of time that you allow for something in a plan **zaman aralığı, süre, ayrılan zaman** *The programme is being moved to a later slot.*

slot² /slɒt/ verb [I, T] **slotting**, past **slotted** to fit into a slot, or to make something fit into a slot **yerine yerleş(tir) mek; yerine otur(t)mak**
slot sb/sth in phrasal verb to find time for someone or something in a period of time that has already been planned **bir araya sıkıştırmak, zaman bulmak** *Dr O'Neil can slot you in around 9.30.*

sloth /sləʊθ/ noun **1** [C] an animal that moves very slowly and lives in Central and South America **Orta ve Güney Amerika'da yaşayan yakalı tembel hayvan 2** [U] literary when someone is lazy **tembellik, miskinlik, uyuşukluk**

'slot ma‚chine noun [C] a machine that you put money into in order to try to win money **kumar makinası**

slouch¹ /slaʊtʃ/ verb [I] to stand, sit, or walk with your shoulders forward so that your body is not straight **başı öne düşmüş omuzları çökmüş yürümek/oturmak/dikilmek** *Stop slouching and stand up straight.*

slouch

slouch² /slaʊtʃ/ noun **1** [no plural] the position your body is in when you slouch **kamburu çıkmış/başı öne düşmüş pozisyon 2 be no slouch** informal to work very hard and be good at something **çok çabalamak; çok iyi olmak; başarılı olmak** *He's no slouch when it comes to cooking.*

slovenly /'slʌvºnli/ adjective lazy, untidy, and dirty **tembel, savruk, pis, özensiz, rüküş, derbeder** *slovenly habits* ● **slovenliness** noun [U] **pasaklı olma durumu**

o⊸**slow¹** /sləʊ/ adjective **1** [NOT FAST] moving, happening, or doing something without much speed **yavaş, ağır** *I'm making slow progress with the painting.* ○ *He's a very slow reader.* **2 be slow to do sth; be slow in doing sth** to take a long time to do something **yavaş hareket etmek/yapmak; bir şeyi yaparken ağırdan almak** *The government has been slow to react to the problem.* ○ *The ambulance was very slow in coming.* **3** [CLOCK] If a clock is slow, it shows a time that is earlier than the correct time. **(saat) geri, geri kalmış 4** [BUSINESS] If business is slow, there are few customers. **(iş) hareketsiz, yavaş, satış yapamayan, cansız 5** [NOT CLEVER] not quick at learning and understanding things **öğrenmede ve anlamada yavaş, yavaş öğrenen 6** [NOT EXCITING] not exciting **hareketsiz, cansız, heyecansız** *I find his films very slow.*

slow² /sləʊ/ verb [I, T] to become slower or to make something become slower **yavaşla(t)mak, ağırlaş(tır)mak** *The car slowed to a halt* (= moved more and more slowly until it stopped).
slow (sth) down phrasal verb to become slower or to make something become slower **yavaşla(t)mak, ağırlaş(tır)mak; hız/hızını kesmek** *Slow down, Claire, you're walking too fast!*
slow down phrasal verb If someone slows down, they become less active. **yavaşlamak, daha az hareket etmek; ağırdan almak** *The doctor told me I should slow down and not work so hard.*

slowdown /'sləʊdaʊn/ noun [C] when business activity becomes slower **düşüş, yavaşlama, azalma, etkisini yitirme, müşteri kaybetme** *an economic slowdown* ○ *The figures show a slowdown in retail sales.*

o⊸**slowly** /'sləʊli/ adverb at a slow speed **yavaş yavaş, ağır ağır** *Could you speak more slowly, please?*

‚slow 'motion noun [U] a way of showing pictures from a film or television programme at a slower speed than normal **ağır çekim** *They showed a replay of the goal in slow motion.*

sludge /slʌdʒ/ noun [U] soft, wet soil, or a substance that looks like this **katı/koyu çamur; balçık**

slug¹ /slʌg/ noun [C] **1** a small, soft creature with no legs that moves slowly and eats plants **sümüklü böcek** ⊃See picture at **snail**. **2** a small amount of a drink, especially an alcoholic drink **bir yudum, az miktarda içki** *He took a slug of whisky from the bottle.*

slug² /slʌg/ verb [T] **slugging**, past **slugged** informal to hit someone with your fist (= closed hand) **yumruk atmak/vurmak/patlatmak/indirmek**
slug it out phrasal verb informal to fight, argue, or compete with someone until one person wins **taraflardan biri galip gelinceye kadar mücadele etmek/tartışmak/yarışmak** *Federer and Hewitt slugged it out for a place in the final.*

sluggish /'slʌgɪʃ/ adjective moving or working more slowly than usual **uyuşuk, miskin, yorgun, ağır kanlı, bezgin** *a sluggish economy* ○ *I felt really sluggish after lunch.*

slum /slʌm/ noun [C] a poor and crowded area of a city where the buildings are in a very bad condition **gece-**

S

---

kondu bölgesi *He grew up in the slums of Mexico City.* ○ *slum areas*

slumber /ˈslʌmbər/ *noun* [C, U] *literary* sleep **uyku** *She lay down on the bed and fell into a deep slumber.* ● **slumber** *verb* [I] *literary* **uyuklamak**

ˈslumber ˌparty *noun* [C] *US* a party when a group of children spend the night at one child's house **bir grup çocuğun birinin evinde yaptıkları parti ;çocuk partisi**

slump¹ /slʌmp/ *verb* **1** [I] If a price, value, or amount slumps, it goes down suddenly. **aniden büyük ölçüde düşmek; dibe vurmak** *Sales have slumped by 50%.* **2 slump back/down/over, etc** to fall or sit down suddenly because you feel tired or weak **çökmek, yığılıp kalmak; dizlerinin bağı çözülmek** *She slumped back in her chair, exhausted.*

slump (noun) .... İLE BİRLİKTE KULLANILAN KELİMELER

a **dramatic/severe** slump ● a slump **in** sth

slump² /slʌmp/ *noun* [C] **1** a sudden fall in prices or sales **fiyat ve satışlarda ani düşüş** *a slump in world oil prices* **2** a period when there is very little business activity and not many jobs **ekonomik durgunluk/ kriz; çöküntü, bunalım** *It's been the worst economic slump for 25 years.*

slung /slʌŋ/ *past of* sling **asıp sallandırmak' fiilinin geçmiş zaman hâli**

slunk /slʌŋk/ *past of* slink **sıvışmak' fiilinin geçmiş zaman hâli**

slur¹ /slɜːr/ *verb* [I, T] *slurring, past* **slurred** to speak without separating your words clearly, often because you are tired or drunk **dili dolaşmak, konuştukları/ne dediği anlaşılmamak** *He'd drunk too much and was slurring his words.*

slur .... İLE BİRLİKTE KULLANILAN KELİMELER

cast slurs ● a slur **against/on** sb/sth

slur² /slɜːr/ *noun* [C] a criticism that will make people have a bad opinion of someone or something **iftira, kara çalma, çamur atma, leke, küçültücü söz** *a racial slur* ○ *She regarded it as a slur on her character.*

slurp /slɜːp/ *verb* [I, T] *informal* to drink in a noisy way **höpürdeterek içmek; höpürdetmek, şapırdatmak** *He slurped his tea.* ● **slurp** *noun* [C] *informal* **şapırdatarak içme**

slush /slʌʃ/ *noun* [U] snow that has started to melt **erimeye başlamış/sulu kar/yumuşamış kar**

sly /slaɪ/ *adjective* **slyer, slyest 1** deceiving people in a clever way to get what you want **sinsi, şeytanî, şeytanca, hınzır 2 sly smile** a smile that shows you know something that other people do not **sinsi sinsi gülümseme; hınzırca sırıtma; bıyık altından gülme** *"I know why Chris didn't come home yesterday," she said with a sly smile.* ● **slyly** *adverb* **kurnazca**

smack¹ /smæk/ *verb* **1** [T] to hit someone with the flat, inside part of your hand **şaplak atmak, tokat vurmak** *Do you think it's right to smack children when they're naughty?* **2 smack sth against/onto/down, etc** to hit something hard against something else **sertçe çarpmak, hızlıca vurmak** *Ray smacked the ball into the net.*

smack of sth *phrasal verb* If something smacks of an unpleasant quality, it seems to have that quality. **andır-mak, anımsatmak, hatırlatmak** *a policy that smacks of racism*

smack² /smæk/ *noun* [C] a hit with the flat, inside part of your hand **şamar, tokat** *Stop shouting or I'll give you a smack!*

smack³ /smæk/ *informal (also UK* **'smack ˌbang**) *(also US* **ˌsmack 'dab**) *adverb* **1** exactly in a particular place **tam, tastamam, doğruca** *She lives smack in the middle of Edinburgh.* **2** suddenly and with a lot of force **aniden ve zorla** *He braked too late and ran smack into the car in front.*

small .... BAŞKA BİR DEYİŞLE

Little sıfatı small sıfatına alternatif olarak kullanılabilir ve bunun yanısıra kişi veya cansız şeyleri tanımlamada kullanılabilir. *I'll just have a little piece of cake.* ● *She's so* little.
Eğer kişi bedensel olarak çok küçükse, **tiny** veya **minute** sıfatları kullanılabilir. Eğer cansız bir şey ölçüm olarak çok küçükse **microscopic** veya **minuscule** sıfatları kullanılabilir. *Inside the pram was a* tiny *baby.* ● *The phone he pulled out of his pocket was* minute. ● *The cost of vaccination is* minuscule *compared to the cost of treatment.*
Dwarf ve **miniature** sıfatları normal boyuttan daha küçük olan şeylerin tanımlanmasında kullanılır. *There were* dwarf *fir trees in pots on the patio.* ● *It's a* miniature *bath for the doll's house.*
Eğer küçük bir kız veya bir bayan çekici bir şekilde ufak tefek ise, **dainty** veya **petite** sıfatları kullanılabilir. *She had* dainty *feet.* ● *Like all his girlfriends, Emma was dark and* petite.
Çok küçük olan bir bölge veya odadan bahsetmek için gayri resmi ortamlarda **poky** sıfatı kullanılabilir. *They live in a* poky *little flat in south London.*
Küçük ve çok önemli olmayan soyut şeylerin tanımlanmasında **slight** sıfatı kullanılabilir. *There was a* slight *difference in colour.*

small¹ /smɔːl/ *adjective* **1** [LITTLE] little in size or amount **küçük, ufak** *They live in a small apartment near Times Square.* ○ *We teach the children in small groups.* **2** [YOUNG] A small child is very young. **(çocuk) küçük, ufak** *a woman with three small children* **3** [NOT IMPORTANT] not important or serious **önemsiz, cüzi, ufak, az** *a small mistake* **4 feel small** to feel stupid or unimportant **aptal ve önemsiz hissetmek; kendini değersiz his-setmek** *Simon was always trying to make me feel small.*

small² /smɔːl/ *adverb* in a small size **küçük ölçüde/ ebatta; küçük, dar** *Emma knitted the sweater far too small.*

ˈsmall ˌad *noun* [C] *UK* a small advertisement that you put in a newspaper if you want to buy or sell something **küçük ilân**

ˌsmall 'change *noun* [U] coins that have little value **bozuk para**

ˈsmall ˌfry *noun* [U] *informal* people or activities that are not considered important **önemsiz kimse; ufak tefek şeyler** *Compared to companies that size we're just small fry.*

ˌsmall 'print *noun* [U] the part of a written agreement that is printed smaller than the rest and that contains important information **anlaşma metninde küçük yazılmış önemli maddeler; ek maddeler, ayrıntılar** *Make sure you read the small print before you sign.*

small-scale /ˌsmɔːlˈskeɪl/ *adjective* A small-scale activity or organization is not big and involves few people. **küçük ölçekli**

ˈsmall ˌtalk *noun* [U] polite conversation between people at social events **davetlerde ayaküstü yapılan muhabbet; şundan bundan konuşma** *He's not very good at making small talk.*

small-time /ˈsmɔːl,taɪm/ adjective [always before noun] informal not important or successful **önemsiz ve başarısız** a small-time criminal

smart[1] /smɑːt/ adjective 1 INTELLIGENT intelligent **zeki, akıllı** Rachel's one of the smartest kids in the class. 2 TIDY If you look smart or your clothes are smart, you look clean and tidy. **şık, zarif** a smart, blue suit ○ I need to look a bit smarter for my interview. 3 FASHIONABLE fashionable and expensive **şık, zarif, sosyetik, lüks** a smart, new restaurant 4 MACHINE/WEAPON A smart machine, weapon, etc uses computers to make it work. **akıllı, bilgisayar destekli** smart bombs • **smartly** adverb **akıllıca**

smart[2] /smɑːt/ verb [I] 1 to feel upset because someone has said or done something unpleasant to you **incinmek, üzülmek, üzüntü duymak** The team are still smarting from last week's defeat. 2 If part of your body smarts, it hurts with a sharp, burning pain. **yanmak, sızlamak, acımak** The smoke from the fire made her eyes smart.

'smart ,card noun [C] a small, plastic card that contains a very small computer and can be used to pay for things or to store personal information **akıllı kart**

smarten /ˈsmɑːtᵊn/ verb
smarten (sb/sth) up phrasal verb to make a person or place look more clean and tidy **süslemek, güzelleştirmek, şıklaştırmak** plans to smarten up the city centre

smash[1] /smæʃ/ verb
1 [I, T] to break into a lot of pieces with a loud noise, or to make something break into a lot of pieces with a loud noise **ezmek, paramparça etmek, kırıp parçalamak** Thieves smashed the shop window and stole $50,000 worth of computer equipment. 2 **smash (sth) against/into/through, etc** to hit a hard object or surface with a lot of force, or to make something do this **şiddetle çarpmak/vurmak** The car skidded and smashed into a tree. ○ He smashed the glass against the wall. 3 [T] to destroy a political or criminal organization **ortadan kaldırmak, yok etmek, mahvetmek, canına okumak; kökünü kazımak** attempts to smash a drug smuggling ring
smash sth up phrasal verb to damage or destroy something **parça parça etmek; yok etmek** They were arrested for smashing up a hotel bar.

smash

smash[2] /smæʃ/ (also ,smash 'hit) noun [C] a very successful film, song, play, etc **büyük sükse yapan/başarı kazanan film/şarkı/oyun vb.** the smash hit movie 'Titanic'

smashing /ˈsmæʃɪŋ/ adjective UK old-fashioned extremely good or attractive **müthiş, şahane, mükemmel, harika; çekici, cezbedici** We had a smashing time at Bob and Vera's party.

smear[1] /smɪəʳ/ verb [T] 1 to spread a thick liquid or sticky substance over something **sürmek, sıvamak** His shirt was smeared with paint. ○ He smeared sun cream over his face and neck. 2 to say unpleasant and untrue things about someone in order to harm them,

especially in politics **leke sürmek, kara çalmak, çamur atmak, iftira etmek**

smear[2] /smɪəʳ/ noun [C] 1 a dirty mark **leke, kir izi** There was a smear of oil on his cheek. 2 an unpleasant and untrue story about someone that is meant to harm them, especially in politics **iftira, çamur, leke, karalama** a smear campaign

∘ᐧ**smell**[1] /smel/ verb past **smelled** or also UK **smelt** 1 smell of/like, smell delicious/horrible, etc to have a particular quality that people notice by using their nose ...**gibi kokmak; ...kokusunu vermek** I've been cooking, so my hands smell of garlic. ○ That soup smells delicious - what's in it? 2 NOTICE [T] to notice something by using your nose **koklamak, kokusunu almak** I think I can smell something burning. 3 UNPLEASANT [I] to have an unpleasant smell **pis/kötü/iğrenç kokmak** Your running shoes really smell! 4 PUT YOUR NOSE NEAR [T] to put your nose near something and breathe in so that you can notice its smell **koklamak, koku almak** Come and smell these flowers. 5 ABILITY [I] to have the ability to notice smells **koku alabilmek; koklayabilmek; kokusunu alabilmek** Dogs can smell much better than humans.

∘ᐧ**smell**[2] /smel/ noun 1 QUALITY [C] the quality that something has which you notice by using your nose **koku** The smell of roses filled the room. ○ There was a delicious smell coming from the kitchen. 2 UNPLEASANT [C] an unpleasant smell **kötü/pis koku** I wish I could get rid of that smell in the bathroom. 3 ABILITY [U] the ability to notice smells **koklama, koku alma** Smoking can affect your sense of smell.

smelly /ˈsmeli/ adjective having an unpleasant smell **pis/kötü kokulu** smelly feet

smelt /smelt/ UK past of smell **koklamak' fiilinin geçmiş zaman hâli**

∘ᐧ**smile**[1] /smaɪl/ verb [I] to make a happy or friendly expression in which the corners of your mouth curve up **gülümsemek, tebessüm etmek** She smiled at me.

╔═══════════════════════════════════╗
smile (noun) ...... İLE BİRLİKTE KULLANILAN KELİMELER
╚═══════════════════════════════════╝

a **beaming / faint / radiant / rueful / wry** smile • **break into/force/give/wear** a smile • a smile **broadens/flickers across sb's face/fades**

∘ᐧ**smile**[2] /smaɪl/ noun [C] a happy or friendly expression in which the corners of your mouth curve up **gülümseme, tebessüm** "I passed my driving test," she said with a smile.

smiley /ˈsmaɪli/ noun [C] an image such as :-) which looks like a face when you look at it from the side, made using keyboard symbols and used in emails to express emotions :-) **mesajlarda kullanılan gülümseme işareti** ➲See study page Emailing and texting on page Centre 37.

smirk /smɜːk/ verb [I] to smile in an annoying or unkind way **sırıtmak, pis pis gülümsemek; alay ederek gülümsemek** What are you smirking at? • **smirk** noun [C] **sırıtma**

smitten /ˈsmɪtᵊn/ adjective [never before noun] loving someone or liking something very much **düşkün, çok seven, aşırı sevgi duyan** He's absolutely smitten with this Carla woman.

smog /smɒg/ noun [U] air pollution in a city that is a mixture of smoke, gases, and chemicals **hava kirliliğine sebep olan dumanlı sis**

∘ᐧ**smoke**[1] /sməʊk/ noun 1 [U] the grey or black gas that is produced when something burns **duman** 2 [no plural] when someone smokes a cigarette **sigara içen** I'm just going outside for a smoke.

∘ᐧ**smoke**[2] /sməʊk/ verb 1 CIGARETTE [I, T] to breathe smoke into your mouth from a cigarette **sigara içmek** Do you

S

mind if I smoke? ○ *She smokes thirty cigarettes a day.*
2 MEAT/FISH [T] to give meat or fish a special taste by hanging it over burning wood **tütsülemek (et/balık)** *smoked ham/salmon* **3** PRODUCE SMOKE [I] to produce or send out smoke **tütmek, duman çıkarmak** *smoking chimneys* ⊃See also: **chain-smoke.**

smoker /'sməʊkə^r/ *noun* [C] someone who smokes cigarettes regularly **sigara tiryakisi, sigara içen kimse** *He used to be a heavy smoker* (= someone who smokes a lot). ⊃Opposite **non-smoker.**

give up/stop/quit smoking ● **ban** smoking ● **heavy** smoking ● the **dangers/effects** of smoking

o▪**smoking** /'sməʊkɪŋ/ *noun* [U] when someone smokes a cigarette or regularly smokes cigarettes **sigara içme** *The new law will restrict smoking in public places.* ⊃See also: **passive smoking.**

smoky /'sməʊki/ *adjective* **1** filled with smoke **dumanlı, duman dolu** *a smoky bar/room* **2** having the smell, taste, or appearance of smoke **dumanlı, duman gibi** *That ham has a delicious, smoky flavour.*

smolder /'sməʊldə^r/ *verb* [I] *US spelling of* smoulder **için için yanmak**

o▪**smooth**¹ /smuːð/ *adjective* **1** SURFACE having a regular surface that has no holes or lumps in it **düz, düzgün, pürüzsüz** *soft, smooth skin* ○ *a smooth wooden table* **2** SUBSTANCE A substance that is smooth has no lumps in it. **kabarcıksız, topaksız** *Mix the butter and sugar together until smooth.* **3** MOVEMENT happening without any sudden movements or changes **rahat ve sarsıntısız** *The plane made a smooth landing.* **4** PROCESS happening without problems or difficulties **sakin, problemsiz, sorunsuz, olaysız** *Her job is to help students make a smooth transition from high school to college.* **5** PERSON too polite and confident in a way that people do not trust **kuşku yaratacak şekilde kibar/kendinden emin** *a smooth salesman* ● **smoothness** *noun* [U] ⊃See also: take the **rough**² with the smooth. **yumuşaklık, pürüzsüz olma**

smooth² /smuːð/ *(also smooth down/out, etc) verb* [T] to move your hands across something in order to make it flat **eliyle düzlemek/düzeltmek; düzleştirmek** *He straightened his tie and smoothed down his hair.*
smooth sth over *phrasal verb* to make a disagreement or problem seem less serious, especially by talking to the people involved in it **yumuşatmak, hafifletmek; arayı bulmak** *Would you like me to smooth things over between you and Nick?*

smoothie /'smuːði/ *noun* [C, U] a thick cold drink made mainly from fruit, sometimes with milk, cream or ice cream (= cold, sweet food) **süt, meyve, krema ve dondurma ile yapılan bir tür içecek**

smoothly /'smuːðli/ *adverb* **1 go smoothly** to happen without any problems or difficulties **çok iyi gitmek; her şey yolunda olmak; sorunsuz ve sıkıntısız olmak** *Everything was going smoothly until Darren arrived.* **2** without any sudden movements or changes **pürüzsüzce, sorunsuzca, düzgün bir şekilde, tıkır tıkır** *The car accelerated smoothly.*

smother /'smʌðə^r/ *verb* [T] **1** KILL to kill someone by covering their face with something so that they cannot breathe **boğmak, boğarak öldürmek 2** LOVE to give someone too much love and attention so that they feel they have lost their freedom **(sevgiyle, ilgiyle) boğmak, sıkboğaz etmek, bunaltmak; bıktırmak; usandırmak** *I try not to smother him.* **3** PREVENT to prevent something from happening **önlemek, bastırmak, kontrol altında tutmak; mani olmak** *I tried to smot-*

her my cough. **4** FIRE to make a fire stop burning by covering it with something **üstünü örterek söndürmek**
smother sth in/with sth *phrasal verb* to cover something completely with a substance **tamamen örtmek, her yerini kapamak** *She took a slice of chocolate cake and smothered it in cream.*

smoulder *UK* (*US* **smolder**) /'sməʊldə^r/ *verb* [I] **1** to burn slowly, producing smoke but no flames **için için yanmak** *a smouldering bonfire* **2** to have a strong feeling, especially anger, but not express it **için için kızmak; gizliden gizliye sürmek/devam etmek** *I could see he was smouldering with anger.*

SMS /esem'es/ *noun* [U] *abbreviation for* short message service: a system for sending written messages from one mobile phone to another **Kısa İleti Servisi (KİS), cep telefonları arasında gönderilen ileti sistemi** ● **SMS** *verb* [T, I] **cep telefonundan mesaj göndermek**

smudge¹ /smʌdʒ/ *noun* [C] a dirty mark **pis leke, sıvanmış leke** *a smudge of ink*

smudge² /smʌdʒ/ *verb* [I, T] If ink, paint, etc smudges, or if it is smudged, it becomes dirty or not clear because someone has touched it. **kirletmek, bulaştırmak, lekelemek** *Be careful you don't smudge the drawing.*

smug /smʌg/ *adjective* too pleased with your skill or success in a way that annoys other people **kendini pek beğenmiş, kendisiyle övünen/gurur duyan; sürekli böbürlenen** *a smug smile* ● **smugly** *adverb* *"I've never lost a match yet," she said smugly.* **kendini beğenmiş bir şekilde**

smuggle /'smʌgl/ *verb* [T] to take something into or out of a place in an illegal or secret way **kaçakçılık yapmak; kaçak olarak sokmak/çıkarmak** *He was arrested for smuggling cocaine into Britain.* ● **smuggler** *noun* [C] *drug smugglers* **kaçakçı** ● **smuggling** *noun* [U] **kaçakçılık**

have a snack ● a **light** snack

snack¹ /snæk/ *noun* [C] a small amount of food that you eat between meals **ara öğün, atıştırma; hafif yemek** *Do you want a quick snack before you go out?* ○ *snack food*

snack² /snæk/ *verb* [I] *informal* to eat a snack **atıştırmak, hafif yemek yemek** *I've been snacking on chocolate and biscuits all afternoon.*

hit a snag ● the **(only)** snag **is** ● a snag **in/with** sth

snag¹ /snæg/ *noun* [C] *informal* a problem or difficulty **kusur, bit yeniği, sorun, pürüz, ufak sorun** *I'd love to come - the only snag is I have to be home by 3 o'clock.*

snag² /snæg/ *verb* [T] **snagging**, *past* **snagged 1** If you snag something, it becomes stuck on a sharp object and tears. **takmak, takıp yırtmak** *I snagged my coat on the wire.* **2** *US informal* to get, catch, or win something **almak, yakalamak, kazanmak** *She managed to snag a seat in the front row.*

snail /sneɪl/ *noun* [C] **1** a small creature with a

snail

snail

slug

long, soft body and a round shell **salyangoz 2 at a snail's pace** very slowly **son derece yavaş; ağır ağır** *There was so much traffic that we were travelling at a snail's pace.*

'snail ,mail *noun* [U] *humorous informal* letters or messages that are not sent by email but by post **posta gönderileri**

snake[1] /sneɪk/ *noun* [C] a long, thin creature with no legs that slides along the ground **yılan**

snake[2] /sneɪk/ *verb* **snake across/around/through, etc** to follow a route that has a lot of bends **kıvrıla kıvrıla gitmek/ilerlemek** *The river snakes through some of the most spectacular countryside in France.*

snap[1] /snæp/ *verb* **snapping,** *past* **snapped 1** BREAK [I, T] If something long and thin snaps, it breaks making a short, loud sound, and if you snap it, you break it, making a short, loud sound. **aniden kopmak/koparmak** *The twigs snapped as we walked on them.* **2 snap (sth) open/shut/together, etc** to suddenly move to a particular position, making a short, loud noise, or to make something do this **şırak diye kapanmak/kapatmak** *The suitcase snapped open and everything fell out.* **3** SPEAK ANGRILY [I, T] to say something suddenly in an angry way **ters ters konuşmak, paylamak, azarlamak, terslemek** *I was snapping at the children because I was tired.* **4** LOSE CONTROL [I] to suddenly be unable to control a strong feeling, especially anger **kendini tutamamak, kendine hakim olamamak, birden parlamak; öfkesini dizginleyememek** *She asked me to do the work again and I just snapped.* **5** PHOTOGRAPH [T] *informal* to take a photograph of someone or something **şipşak resim çekmek** *Photographers snapped the Princess everywhere she went.* **6** ANIMAL [I] If an animal snaps, it tries to bite someone. **birden kapmak, ısırmaya çalışmak** *The dog was barking and snapping at my ankles.* ⊃See also: snap your fingers (**finger**[1]).

snap out of sth *phrasal verb informal* to force yourself to stop feeling sad, angry, upset etc **birdenbire sıyrılmak/kurtulmak, kendine gelmek** *He's in a bad mood now but he'll soon snap out of it.*

snap sth up *phrasal verb informal* to buy or get something quickly because it is cheap or exactly what you want **havada kapmak; düşünmeden satın almak; sanki bedavaymış gibi saldırmak; görünce almak** *The dress was perfect, so I snapped it up.*

snap sb up *phrasal verb informal* to immediately accept someone's offer to join your company or team because you want them very much **hemen işe almak, havada kapmak; hemen kabul etmek** *She was snapped up by a large law firm.*

snap[2] /snæp/ *noun* **1** SOUND [no plural] a sudden, short, loud sound like something breaking or closing **ani kırılma/çarpma sesi; çıt sesi; çatırtı** *I heard a snap as I sat on the pencil.* **2** PHOTOGRAPH [C] *UK informal* (*UK/US* **snapshot**) a photograph **şipşak resim** *holiday snaps* **3** FASTENING [C] *US* (*UK* **popper**) a metal or plastic object made of two parts which fit together with a short, loud sound, used to fasten clothing **çıt çıt 4** GAME [U] a card game in which you say "snap" when you see two cards that are the same (**iskambil**) **pişti oyunu 5 be a snap** *US informal* to be very easy **çok kolay olmak; çocuk oyuncağı olmak** *The French test was a snap.*

snap[3] /snæp/ *adjective* **snap decision/judgment** A snap decision or judgment is made very quickly and without careful thought. **aceleyle verilmiş karar; düşünmeden varılan yargı**

snappy /'snæpi/ *adjective* **1** written or spoken in a short and interesting way **ilginç ve kısa olarak yazılan/söylenen** *a snappy title* **2** Snappy clothes are fashionable. **modaya uygun, canlı, gösterişli** *a snappy new*

suit **3 make it snappy** *informal* used to tell someone to hurry **acele etmek, çabuk olmak; acele et, çabuk ol**

snapshot /'snæpʃɒt/ *noun* [C] a photograph that you take quickly without thinking **şipşak resim**

snare[1] /sneər/ *noun* [C] a piece of equipment used to catch animals **tuzak, kapan**

snare[2] /sneər/ *verb* **1** to catch an animal using a snare **tuzak kurmak, kapan kurmak; tuzakla/kapanla hayvan yakalamak 2** to trick someone so that they cannot escape from a situation **tuzağa düşürmek, kapana kıstırmak** *She's trying to snare a rich husband.*

snarl /snɑːl/ *verb* **1** [I, T] to speak angrily **hırlamak, hırlar gibi konuşmak, kızgın kızgın konuşmak, homurdanmak** *"Go away!" he snarled.* ○ *She snarled at me.* **2** [I] If an animal snarls, it shows its teeth and makes an angry sound. **hırlamak** ● **snarl** *noun* [C] **sinirlenme**

snatch[1] /snætʃ/ *verb* [T] **1** to take something or someone quickly and suddenly **kapmak, kapıp kaçmak** *Bill snatched the telephone from my hand.* ○ *The child was snatched from his bed.* **2** to do or get something quickly because you only have a short amount of time **ele geçirmek, yakalamak; çabucak almak/yapmak** *I managed to snatch some lunch.*

snatch[2] /snætʃ/ *noun* [C] a short part of a conversation, song, etc that you hear **parça, bölüm** *I keep hearing snatches of that song on the radio.*

sneak[1] /sniːk/ *verb past* **sneaked** or *also US* **snuck 1 sneak into/out/around, etc** to go somewhere quietly because you do not want anyone to hear you **belli etmeden gizlice girmek, çaktırmadan sokulmak, süzülmek, sıvışmak** *I sneaked into his bedroom while he was asleep.* **2 sneak sth into/out of/through, etc** to take something somewhere without anyone seeing you **gizlice sokmak, çaktırmadan götürmek, aşırmak, yürütmek** *We tried to sneak the dog into the hotel.* **3 sneak a look/glance at sb/sth** to look at someone or something quickly and secretly **gizlice belli etmeden bakmak, dikizlemek, çaktırmadan gözlemek** *I sneaked a look at the answers.*

sneak up *phrasal verb* to move close to someone without them seeing or hearing you **usulca yanına sokulmak; gizlice yanaşmak** *Don't sneak up on me like that - you scared me!*

sneak[2] /sniːk/ *noun* [C] *informal UK* someone who you do not like because they tell people when someone else has done something bad **ispiyoncu, gammaz, muhbir**

sneaker /'sniːkər/ *US* (*UK* **trainer**) *noun* [C] a soft sports shoe **yumuşak spor ayakkabısı** ⊃Orta kısımdaki renkli sayfalarına bakınız.

sneaking /'sniːkɪŋ/ *adjective* **1 have a sneaking feeling/suspicion** to think that something is true but not be sure **emin olmadığı halde doğru olduğunu düşünmek; doğru olduğundan şüphe duymak** [+ (that)] *I have a sneaking feeling that the English test is going to be very difficult.* **2 have a sneaking admiration/fondness for sb** *UK* to like someone secretly, especially when you do not want to **gizlice sevmek; farkında olmadan hoşlanmak; gizli gizli hayranlık duymak**

sneaky /'sniːki/ *adjective* doing things in a secret and unfair way **gizli, sinsi, yılan gibi, kurnaz**

sneer /snɪər/ *verb* [I] to talk about, or look at someone or something in a way that shows you do not approve of them **dudak bükmek, küçümsemek, alay etmek** *Carlos sneered at my attempts to put the tent up.* ● **sneer** *noun* [C] **alay**

S

sneeze /sni:z/ *verb* [I] When you sneeze, air suddenly comes out through your nose and mouth. **hapşırmak, aksırmak** *He had a cold and was sneezing a lot.* ● **sneeze** *noun* [C] **esneme**

snicker /'snɪkə^r/ *US* (*UK* snigger) *verb* [I] to laugh quietly in a rude way **alaycı/bıyık altından gülmek; çirkin çirkin gülmek; alaya almak** ● **snicker** *noun* [C] **alaylı gülüş**

snide /snaɪd/ *adjective* A snide remark criticizes someone in an unpleasant way. **küçültücü, alçaltıcı, kirici, inciten**

sniff /snɪf/ *verb* **1** [I] to breathe air in through your nose in a way that makes a noise **burnunu çekmek** *Sam had a cold and she kept sniffing.* **2** [I, T] to breathe air in through your nose in order to smell something **burnunu çekerek kutlamak** *She sniffed the flowers.* ● **sniff** *noun* [C] **burnunu çekme**

snigger /'snɪgə^r/ *UK* (*US* snicker) *verb* [I] to laugh quietly in a rude way **kıs kıs gülmek, bıyık altından/alay ederek gülmek** *The boys were sniggering at the teacher.* ● **snigger** *noun* [C] **bıyık altından gülme**

snip¹ /snɪp/ *verb* [I, T] **snipping**, *past* **snipped** to cut something using scissors (= tool with two flat blades) with quick, small cuts **makasla kesmek, kırpmak** *She snipped the article out of the magazine.*

snip² /snɪp/ *noun* **1** [C] a small, quick cut with scissors (= tool with two flat blades) **makasla kesilmiş parça, kırpıntı 2 be a snip** *UK informal* to be very cheap **kelepir/çok ucuz olmak; kuruşluk şey olmak**

snipe /snaɪp/ *verb* [I] **1** to criticize someone in an unpleasant way **eleştirmek, saldırmak, tenkit etmek** *I hate the way politicians snipe at each other.* **2** to shoot people from a place that they cannot see **pusudan/siperden ateş etmek; gizlice vurmak** *Rebels were indiscriminately sniping at civilians.* ● **sniping** *noun* [U] **eleştiri**

sniper /'snaɪpə^r/ *noun* [C] **1** someone who shoots at people from a place they cannot see **keskin nişancı 2** on a website, someone who makes an offer for an item just before the end of an auction (= a sale in which things are sold to the person who offers the most money) **internette açık artırmada en son teklifi veren kişi**

snippet /'snɪpɪt/ *noun* [C] a small piece of information, news, conversation, etc **parça, bölüm, fragman** *I kept hearing snippets of conversation.*

snob /snɒb/ *noun* [C] someone who thinks they are better than other people because they are in a higher social position **züppe kişi, kendini beğenmiş/burnu havada kimse** ● **snobbery** /'snɒb^əri/ *noun* [U] behaviour and opinions that are typical of a snob **züppelik, ukalâlık, kendini beğenmişlik**

snobbish /'snɒbɪʃ/ (*also* snobby) *adjective* like a snob **züppece, kibirli, burnu yere düşse almayacak olan** *a snobbish attitude*

snog /snɒg/ *verb* [I, T] **snogging**, *past* **snogged** *UK informal* If two people snog, they kiss each other for a long time. **okşayıp öpüşmek, uzun süre öpüşmek, öpüşüp koklaşmak, sarılıp öpüşmek** ● **snog** *noun* [C] *UK informal* **öpücük, öpüşme**

snooker /'snu:kə^r/ *noun* [U] a game in which two people use long sticks to hit coloured balls into holes at the edge of a table **bir tür bilardo oyunu, sunuker**

snoop /snu:p/ *verb* [I] to look around a place secretly in order to find out information about someone **gizlice araştırmak, hafiyelik yapmak** *I found her snooping around in my bedroom.* ● **snoop** *noun* [no plural] **izin olmadan alma**

snooty /'snu:ti/ *adjective* Someone who is snooty behaves in an unfriendly way because they think they

are better than other people. **mağrur, kibirli, burnu havada, tepeden bakan, küçük gören**

snooze /snu:z/ *verb* [I] *informal* to sleep for a short time, especially during the day **kestirmek, şekerleme yapmak** *Grandpa was snoozing in his chair.* ● **snooze** *noun* [C] *informal* *Why don't you have a snooze?* **kestirme (uyku)**

snore /snɔ:^r/ *verb* [I] to breathe in a very noisy way while you are sleeping **horlamak** *I couldn't sleep because my brother was snoring.* ● **snore** *noun* [C] **horlama**

snorkel¹ /'snɔ:k^əl/ *noun* [C] a tube that you use to help you breathe if you are swimming with your face under water **şnorkel**

snorkel² /'snɔ:k^əl/ *verb* [I] *UK* **snorkelling**, *past* **snorkelled**, *US* **snorkeling**, *past* **snorkeled** to swim using a snorkel **şnorkelle yüzmek**

snort /snɔ:t/ *verb* [I, T] to breathe out noisily through your nose, especially to show that you are annoyed or think something is funny **homurda(n)mak, bunundan solumak** *"Stupid man!" he snorted.* ○ *Rosie started snorting with laughter.* ● **snort** *noun* [C] **homurtu**

snot /snɒt/ *noun* [U] *informal* the thick liquid that is produced in your nose **sümük**

snout /snaʊt/ *noun* [C] the long nose of some animals, such as pigs **uzun hayvan burnu**

snow **falls/melts** ● a snow **flurry/shower** ● **deep/ heavy** snow ● [**walk/tramp**, etc] **through** the snow

๑ᴥ**snow¹** /snəʊ/ *noun* [U] soft white pieces of frozen water that fall from the sky when the weather is cold **kar** *children playing in the snow*

๑ᴥ**snow²** /snəʊ/ *verb* **1 it snows** If it snows, snow falls from the sky. **kar yağmak** *It snowed all day yesterday.* **2 be snowed in** to be unable to leave a place because there is too much snow **karda mahsur kalmak** *We were snowed in for two days.* **3 be snowed under** to have too much work **işi çok/işi başından aşkın olmak** *I'm snowed under with homework.*

snowball¹ /'snəʊbɔ:l/ *noun* [C] a ball made from snow that children throw at each other **kartopu**

snowball² /'snəʊbɔ:l/ *verb* [I] If a problem, idea, or situation snowballs, it quickly grows bigger or more important. **gittikçe artmak, çığ gibi büyümek** *The whole business idea snowballed from one phone call.*

snowboard /'snəʊbɔ:d/ *noun* [C] a large board that you stand on to move over snow **kar kayağı** ⊃Orta kısımdaki renkli sayfalarına bakınız.

snowboarding /'snəʊbɔ:dɪŋ/ *noun* [U] a sport in which you stand on a large board and move over snow **kar kayağı sporu** ● **snowboarder** *noun* [C] **kar üzerinde yapılan kayak sporu** ⊃Orta kısımdaki renkli sayfalarına bakınız.

snowdrift /'snəʊdrɪft/ *noun* [C] a deep pile of snow that the wind has blown **kar yığını**

snowdrop /'snəʊdrɒp/ *noun* [C] a small, white flower that you can see at the end of winter **kardelen, kardelen çiçeği**

snowfall /'snəʊfɔ:l/ *noun* [C, U] the snow that falls at one time, or the amount of snow that falls **kar yağması** *a heavy snowfall* (= a lot of snow)

snowflake /'snəʊfleɪk/ *noun* [C] a small piece of snow that falls from the sky **kar tanesi**

snowman /'snəʊmæn/ *noun* [C] *plural* **snowmen** something that looks like a person and is made from snow **kardan adam** *The kids made a snowman in the garden.*

snowplough UK (US **snowplow**) /'snəʊplaʊ/ noun [C] a vehicle used for moving snow off roads and railways **kar temizleme aracı**

snowstorm /'snəʊstɔːm/ noun [C] a storm when a lot of snow falls **kar fırtınası**

snowy /'snəʊi/ adjective snowing or covered with snow **karlı** a cold, snowy day

Snr UK (UK/US **Sr**) written abbreviation for senior (= the older of two men in a family with the same name) **ailede aynı isimde yaşça büyük olan erkek** Thomas Smith, Snr

snub /snʌb/ verb [T] **snubbing**, past **snubbed** to be rude to someone, especially by not speaking to them **hor görmek, hiçe saymak, önemsememek, yokmuş gibi davranmak** ● **snub** noun [C] **kabalaşma, küçük görme**

snuck /snʌk/ US past of sneak 'gizlice gözlemek' fiilinin geçmiş zaman hâli

snuff¹ /snʌf/ noun [U] tobacco powder that people breathe in through their noses, especially in the past **endiye, burun otu**

snuff² /snʌf/ verb
snuff sth out phrasal verb **1** informal to suddenly end something **aniden sona erdirmek, bir anda bitirmek** England's chances were snuffed out by three brilliant goals from the Italians. **2** to stop a candle flame from burning by covering it or pressing it with your fingers **mum ışığını söndürmek**

snug /snʌg/ adjective **1** warm and comfortable **sıcak ve rahat, konforlu** a snug little house **2** Snug clothes fit tightly. **(kıyafet) üstüne tam oturan, tam gelen** a pair of snug brown shoes ● **snugly** adverb **rahat bir şekilde, üzerine sıkı sıkı yapışan (giysi)**

snuggle /'snʌgl/ verb **snuggle up/down/into, etc** to move into a warm, comfortable position **sıcacık sokulmak, yanaşmak, sokulup yatmak** I snuggled up to him on the sofa.

o--so¹ /səʊ/ adverb **1** VERY used before an adjective or adverb to emphasize what you are saying, especially when there is a particular result **öyle, öyle...ki, o kadar, bu kadar** I was so tired when I got home. ○ [+ (that)] I was so upset that I couldn't speak. **2** ANSWER used to give a short answer to a question to avoid repeating a phrase **ifadeyi tekrar etmemek için kısa cevaplarda kullanılır; öyle; aynı** "Is Ben coming to the party?" "I hope so." **3 so did we/so have I/so is mine, etc** used to say that someone else also does something or that the same thing is true about someone or something else **biz de öyle; ben de öyle; benimki de öyle** "We saw the new Star Trek movie last night." "Oh, so did we." **4** GET ATTENTION used to get someone's attention when you are going to ask them a question or when you are going to start talking **yani, demek ki, desene** So, when are you two going to get married? **5** SHOW SOMETHING used with a movement of your hand to show someone how to do something or show them the size of something **böyle, şöyle, bu şekilde, şu şekilde** The box was so big. ○ For this exercise, you have to put your hands like so. **6 so it is/so they are, etc** used to agree with something that you had not noticed before **işte, aha, işte bu, işte şu** "The cat's hiding under the chair." "So it is." **7 or so** used after a number or amount to show that it is not exact **vesaire vesaire (vs.), ve benzerleri (vb.); ...kadar falan/filan** "How many people were at the party?" "Fifty or so, I guess." **8 I told you so** used to say that you were right and that someone should have believed you 'Sana söylemiştim!', 'Beni dinlemeliydin!' **9 So (what)?** used to say that you do not think something is important, especially in a rude way 'Yani?', 'Ne olmuş yani?', 'Niye bu kadar önemli

ki?' "She might tell Emily." "So what?" **10 and so on/forth** used after a list of things to show that you could have added other similar things **vesaire vesaire (vs.), ve benzerleri (vb.)** She plays a lot of tennis and squash and so on. **11 so as (not) to do sth** used to give the reason for doing something ...(ma)sın diye; ...ebil (me)mek için He went in very quietly so as not to wake the baby. **12 only so much/many** used to say that there are limits to something **sadece bu kadar/bu sayıda** There's only so much help you can give someone. **13 so much for...** informal used to say that something has not been useful or successful 'Bu kadar... yeter!', '...işi yetti artık!' "The computer's crashed again." "So much for modern technology."

o--so² /səʊ/ conjunction **1** used to say that something is the reason why something else happens **bu nedenle, bu yüzden, bu bakımdan** I was tired so I went to bed. ○ Greg had some money so he bought a bike. **2 so (that)** in order to make something happen or be possible ...sın/sin diye; ...ması/mesi için He put his glasses on so that he could see the television better. **3** used at the beginning of a sentence to connect it with something that was said or happened previously **yani, şu demek oluyor ki,** So we're not going away this weekend after all?

so³ /səʊ/ adjective **be so** to be correct or true **doğru olmak; gerçek olmak** "Apparently, she's moving to Canada." " Is that so?"

soak /səʊk/ verb [I, T] **1** If you soak something, or let it soak, you put it in a liquid for a period of time. **ıslanmak, ıslatmak** He left the pan in the sink to soak. ○ Soak the bread in the milk. **2** If liquid soaks somewhere or soaks something, it makes something very wet. **ıslatmak, sırılsıklam etmek** The rain soaked my clothes. ○ The ink soaked through the paper onto the table.
soak sth up phrasal verb If a dry substance soaks up a liquid, the liquid goes into the substance. **emmek, çekmek** Fry the potatoes until they soak up all the oil.

soaked /səʊkt/ adjective completely wet **ıslanmış, sırılsıklam olmuş** My shirt was soaked.

soaking /'səʊkɪŋ/ adjective completely wet **çok ıslak, sırılsıklam** Why didn't you take an umbrella? ○ The dog was soaking wet.

so-and-so /'səʊəndsəʊ/ noun [C] **1** used to talk about someone or something without saying a particular name **falanca filanca, falan filan; bilmem kim** It was the usual village news - so-and-so got married to so-and-so, and so-and-so's having a baby. **2** informal someone who you do not like **ismi lâzım değil; hınzır; Allah'ın cezası** He's a lazy so-and-so.

o--soap /səʊp/ noun **1** [U] a substance that you use for washing **sabun** a bar of soap ○ soap powder ⊃Orta kısımdaki renkli sayfalarına bakınız. **2** [C] (also 'soap ˌopera) a television programme that about the lives of a group of people that is broadcast several times every week **bir grup insanın hayatlarını anlatan ve her hafta yayınlanan televizyon programı**

'soap ˌopera (informal **soap**) noun [C] a series of television or radio programmes that continues over a long period and is about the lives of a group of characters **pembe dizi, melodram dizisi**

soapy /'səʊpi/ adjective containing soap, or covered with soap **sabunlu** soapy hands

soar /sɔːʳ/ verb [I] **1** to increase to a high level very quickly **birden fırlamak, aniden yükselmek** House prices have soared. **2** to move quickly and smoothly in the sky, or to move quickly up into the sky **fırlamak, çıkmak, yükselmek; yüksekten uçmak; yüksellerde uçmak** The birds were soaring high above. ● **soaring** adjective **yükselen**

sob /sɒb/ *verb* [I] **sobbing**, *past* **sobbed** to cry in a noisy way hıçkıra hıçkıra ağlamak; içini çekerek ağlamak ● **sob** *noun* [C] hıçkırma

sober¹ /'səʊbəʳ/ *adjective* **1** [NOT DRUNK] Someone who is sober is not drunk. ayık, sarhoş değil **2** [SERIOUS] Someone who is sober is serious and thinks a lot. ılımlı, ölçülü, ağırbaşlı, ciddi *He was in a sober mood.* **3** [NOT BRIGHT] Clothes or colours that are sober are plain and not bright. yalın, sade, gösterişsiz *a sober, grey dress* ● **soberly** *adverb* hıçkırırcasına

sober² /'səʊbəʳ/ *verb*

sober (sb) up *phrasal verb* to become less drunk or to make someone become less drunk ayıl(t)mak *You'd better sober up before you go home.*

sobering /'səʊbərɪŋ/ *adjective* making you feel serious ciddiyete davet eden, aklını başına getiren *a sobering thought*

so-called /ˌsəʊ'kɔːld/ *adjective* [always before noun] used to show that you think a word that is used to describe someone or something is wrong sözde, sözüm ona, güya *My so-called friend has stolen my girlfriend.*

soccer /'sɒkəʳ/ (*also UK* **football**) *noun* [U] a game in which two teams of eleven people kick a ball and try to score goals futbol ⊃Orta kısımdaki renkli sayfalarına bakınız.

sociable /'səʊʃəbl/ *adjective* Someone who is sociable enjoys being with people and meeting new people. hoşsohbet, arkadaş canlısı, sokulgan, sosyal

○ **social** /'səʊʃ°l/ *adjective* **1** relating to society and the way people live toplumsal, sosyal *social problems* ○ *social and political changes* **2** relating to the things you do with other people for enjoyment when you are not working sosyal; eğlence kabilinden *I have a very good social life.* ● **socially** *adverb* ⊃Compare anti-social. sosyal olarak

socialism /'səʊʃ°lɪz°m/ *noun* [U] a political system in which the government owns important businesses and industries, and which allows the people to share the money and opportunities equally sosyalizm

socialist /'səʊʃ°lɪst/ *noun* [C] someone who supports socialism sosyalist ● **socialist** *adjective* socialist principles sosyalist

socialize (*also UK* **-ise**) /'səʊʃ°laɪz/ *verb* [I] to spend time enjoying yourself with other people ahbaplık etmek, dostça vakit geçirmek, sohbet etmek *The cafe is a place where students can socialize with teachers.*

ˌsocial 'science *noun* [C, U] the study of society and the way people live sosyal bilim

ˌsocial se'curity *noun* [U] money that the government gives to people who are old, ill, or not working sosyal güvenlik

'social ˌworker *noun* [C] someone whose job is to help people who have problems because they are poor, old, have difficulties with their family, etc sosyal hizmetler görevlisi/uzmanı ● **social work** *noun* [U] sosyal yardım uzmanı

a democratic/free/modern/multicultural/secular society

○ **society** /sə'saɪəti/ *noun* **1** [C, U] a large group of people who live in the same country or area and have the same laws, traditions, etc toplum, cemiyet *The US is a multicultural society.* **2** [C] an organization for people who have the same interest or aim dernek, cemiyet, klüp *the London Zoological Society* ⊃See also: building society

socio- /ˌsəʊʃiəʊ-/ *prefix* relating to society topluma ilişkin; sosyo- anlamında önek *socio-economic*

sociology /ˌsəʊʃi'ɒlədʒi/ *noun* [U] the study of society and the relationship between people in society toplumbilim, sosyoloji ● **sociologist** /ˌsəʊʃi'ɒlədʒɪst/ *noun* [C] someone who studies society toplumbilimci; sosyolog

sociopath /'səʊʃiəʊpæθ/ *noun* [C] someone who is completely unable to behave in a way that is acceptable to society toplumda kabul gören kuralların aksine davranan kimse

sock /sɒk/ *noun* [C] *plural* **socks** or *also US* **sox** something that you wear on your foot inside your shoe çorap [usually plural] *a pair of black socks* ⊃Orta kısımdaki renkli sayfalarına bakınız.

socket /'sɒkɪt/ *noun* [C] **1** the place on a wall where you connect electrical equipment to the electricity supply priz **2** a hollow place where one thing fits inside another thing yuva, oyuk, çukur *Your eyeball is in your eye socket.*

soda /'səʊdə/ *noun* **1** [U] (*also* 'soda ˌwater) water with bubbles in it that you mix with other drinks soda **2** [C, U] *US* (*also* 'soda ˌpop) a sweet drink with bubbles gazoz *a can of soda*

sodden /'sɒd°n/ *adjective* extremely wet sırılsıklam, su içinde *Your shoes are sodden!*

sodium /'səʊdiəm/ *noun* [U] a chemical element that is found in salt and food (symbol Na) sodyum *a low-sodium diet*

○ **sofa** /'səʊfə/ *noun* [C] a large, comfortable seat for more than one person sofa, kanape, sedir ⊃Orta kısımdaki renkli sayfalarına bakınız.

sofa

○ **soft** /sɒft/ *adjective* **1** [NOT HARD] not hard, and easy to press yumuşak *a soft cushion* ○ *Cook the onion until it's soft.* **2** [SMOOTH] smooth and pleasant to touch düz, pürüzsüz, yumuşak *soft hair/skin* **3** [SOUND] A soft sound is very quiet. (ses) yumuşak, alçak, tatlı *He spoke in a soft voice.* **4** [COLOUR/LIGHT] A soft colour or light is not bright. yumuşak, tatlı, hoş *soft lilac paint* **5** [PERSON] too kind and not angry enough when someone does something wrong müşfik, yumuşak, nazik, sevecen; hoş görülü, mülâyim *The kids are naughty because she's too soft on them.* **6** [DRUGS] Soft drugs are illegal drugs that some people think are not dangerous. daha az tehlikeli, hafif; tehlikeli olduğu düşünülmeyen (uyuşturucu ilaç) ● **softness** *noun* [U] ⊃See also: have a soft spot¹ for sb. yumuşaklık

softball /'sɒftbɔːl/ *noun* [U] a game that is like baseball but played with a larger and softer ball beyzbola benzeyen bir oyun, softbol

ˌsoft 'drink *UK* (*US* 'soft ˌdrink) *noun* [C] a cold, sweet drink that does not have alcohol in it alkolsüz içecek; meşrubat

soften /'sɒf°n/ *verb* [I, T] **1** to become softer or to make something become softer yumuşamak, yumuşatmak *Heat the butter until it softens.* **2** to become more gentle or to make someone or something become more gentle yumuşa(t)mak, yatış(tır)mak, teskin olmak/etmek *Her voice softened.*

softly /'sɒftli/ *adverb* in a quiet or gentle way yavaşça, tatlılıkla *"Are you OK?" she said softly.*

,soft 'option *noun* [C] *UK* a choice that is easier than other choices **kolay yol, kolay seçenek, kolay seçim** *The cookery course is not a soft option.*

soft-spoken /ˌsɒftˈspəʊkᵊn/ *adjective* having a quiet, gentle voice **tatlı dilli, hoş/yumuşak sesli** *a small, soft-spoken man*

software /ˈsɒftweəʳ/ *noun* [U] programs that you use to make a computer do different things **yazılım programları** *educational software*

soggy /ˈsɒgi/ *adjective* very wet and soft **cıvık cıvık, su içinde** *soggy ground*

soil¹ /sɔɪl/ *noun* [C, U] the top layer of earth that plants grow in **toprak** *clay/sandy soil*

soil² /sɔɪl/ *verb* [T] *formal* to make something dirty **kirletmek, pisletmek ● soiled** *adjective* dirty **kirli, pis, toz toprak olmuş** *soiled clothes*

solace /ˈsɒləs/ *noun* [U, no plural] *formal* comfort when you are feeling sad **avuntu, teselli** *Music was a great solace to me.*

solar /ˈsəʊləʳ/ *adjective* relating to, or involving the sun **güneşle ilgili, güneş enerjisi sağlayan** *solar panels*

,solar 'energy *noun* [U] energy that uses the power of the sun **güneş enerjisi**

,solar 'panel *noun* [C] a piece of equipment that changes light from the sun into electricity **güneş paneli**

the 'solar ,system *noun* the sun and planets that move around it **güneş sistemi**

sold /səʊld/ *past of* sell **satmak' fiilinin geçmiş zaman hâli**

o•►**soldier** /ˈsəʊldʒəʳ/ *noun* [C] a member of an army **asker, er**

sole¹ /səʊl/ *adjective* [always before noun] **1** only **tek, yegâne, biricik** *the sole survivor* **2** not shared with anyone else **tek, tek başına; kimseyle paylaşılmayan** *She has sole responsibility for the project.*

sole² /səʊl/ *noun* **1** [C] the bottom part of your foot that you walk on **taban 2** ⌐SHOE⌐ [C] the part of a shoe that is under your foot **taban, alt, pençe 3** ⌐FISH⌐ [C, U] a small, flat fish that you can eat **dil balığı**

solely /ˈsəʊlli/ *adverb* only, and not involving anyone or anything else **yalnız, yalnızca, sadece, sırf** *I bought it solely for that purpose.*

solemn /ˈsɒləm/ *adjective* **1** serious or sad **vakur, ciddi, ağırbaşlı** *solemn music* **2** A solemn promise, warning, etc is serious and sincere. **ciddi, samimi ● solemnly** *adverb* **Ciddi bir şekilde ● solemnity** /səˈlemnəti/ *noun* [U] **ağırbaşlı olma**

solicit /səˈlɪsɪt/ *verb* **1** [T] *formal* to ask someone for money, information, or help **rica etmek, talep etmek** *to solicit donations for a charity* **2** [I] to offer sex for money, usually in a public place **para karşılığı cinsel ilişki teklifinde bulunmak**

soliciting /səˈlɪsɪtɪŋ/ *noun* [U] when someone offers to have sex for money **para karşılığı ilişki teklif etme**

solicitor /səˈlɪsɪtəʳ/ *noun* [C] in Britain, a lawyer who gives legal advice and help, and who works in the lower courts of law **(Britanya'da) avukat, hukuk danışmanı/müşaviri**

o•►**solid¹** /ˈsɒlɪd/ *adjective* **1** ⌐HARD/FIRM⌐ hard and firm without holes or spaces, and not liquid or gas **katı** *solid ground* ○ *solid food* **2** ⌐STRONG⌐ strong and not easily broken or damaged **katı, set** *solid furniture* **3** solid gold/silver/wood, etc gold/silver/wood, etc with nothing added **saf/som altın/gümüş/ahşap** *a solid silver bracelet* **4** ⌐TIME⌐ continuing for a period of time without stopping **aralıksız, süregelen** *The noise continued for two solid hours/two hours solid.* **5** ⌐INFORMATION⌐ [always before

noun] Solid information, proof, etc is based on facts and you are certain that it is correct. **güvenilir; gerçek, elle tutulur, kayda değer, inandırıcı** *This provides solid evidence that he committed the crime.* **6** ⌐PERSON⌐ honest and able to be trusted **sağlam karakterli, güvenilir, saygıdeğer ● solidity** /səˈlɪdəti/ *noun* [U] **katılaşma ● solidly** *adverb* **katı bir şekilde**

solid² /ˈsɒlɪd/ *noun* [C] **1** a substance or object that is not a liquid or a gas **katı madde/cisim 2** a shape that has length, width, and height, and is not flat **üç boyutlu cisim**

solidarity /ˌsɒlɪˈdærəti/ *noun* [U] agreement and support between people in a group who have similar aims or beliefs **dayanışma, birlik, yekvücut olma**

solidify /səˈlɪdɪfaɪ/ *verb* [I] If a liquid solidifies, it becomes solid. **katılaşmak**

solids /ˈsɒlɪdz/ *noun* [plural] food that is not liquid **katı yiyecekler** *Three weeks after the operation he still couldn't eat solids.*

solipsism /ˈsɒlɪpsɪzᵊm/ *noun* [U] the belief that in life you can only really know yourself and your own experiences **sadece kendini ve kendi deneyimlerini tanımak üzerine kurulu inanç; tekbencilik**

solitaire /ˌsɒlɪˈteəʳ/ ⓤⓢ /ˈsɒləteər/ *US* (*UK* patience) *noun* [U] a card game for one person **tek kişilik iskambil oyunu**

solitary /ˈsɒlɪtᵊri/ *adjective* **1** A solitary person or thing is the only person or thing in a place. **yalnız, tek başına** *a solitary figure/walker* **2** A solitary activity is done alone. **yalnız** *solitary walks*

,solitary con'finement *noun* [U] when a prisoner is kept in a room alone as a punishment **hücre hapsi** *He was kept in solitary confinement for ten days.*

solitude /ˈsɒlɪtjuːd/ *noun* [U] being alone **yalnızlık, tek başınalık** *He went upstairs to read the letter in solitude.*

solo¹ /ˈsəʊləʊ/ *adjective, adverb* done alone by one person only **solo, tek kişilik yapılan** *a solo performance* ○ *to perform solo*

solo² /ˈsəʊləʊ/ *noun* [C] a piece of music for one person or one instrument **solo müzik/enstrüman**

soloist /ˈsəʊləʊɪst/ *noun* [C] a musician who performs a solo **solist**

solstice /ˈsɒlstɪs/ *noun* [C] the longest day or the longest night of the year **yılın en uzun gün ve gecesi** *the summer/winter solstice*

soluble /ˈsɒljəbᵊl/ *adjective* If a substance is soluble, it will dissolve in water. **eriyebilir, çözünebilir** *soluble vitamins* ○ *These tablets are soluble in water.*

┌───┐
│ ⌐ⁿ **solution** .... İLE BİRLİKTE KULLANILAN KELİMELER │
│ **find/offer/provide/seek** a solution ● a **diplomatic/** │
│ **good/long-term/peaceful/simple/workable** solu- │
│ tion ● a solution **to sth** │
└───┘

o•►**solution** /səˈluːʃᵊn/ *noun* [C] **1** the answer to a problem **çözüm, çözüm yolu** *There's no easy solution to this problem.* **2** a liquid which a substance has been dissolved into **eriyik, solüsyon**

o•►**solve** /sɒlv/ *verb* [T] to find the answer to something **çözmek, cevabını bulmak** *to solve a problem* ○ *to solve a mystery/puzzle* ○ *Police are still no nearer to solving the crime.*

solvent¹ /ˈsɒlvᵊnt/ *noun* [C] a liquid which is used to dissolve other substances **çözücü, solvent**

solvent² /ˈsɒlvᵊnt/ *adjective* having enough money to pay your debts **ödeme gücü olan, vadesi geldiğinde borcunu ödeyebilen**

S

sombre UK (US **somber**) /'sɒmbə^r/ adjective **1** sad and serious **hüzünlü, karamsar, vahim, ciddi, kötümser** a sombre expression/mood **2** dark and without bright colours **karanlık, donuk, kasvetli** a sombre colour

ᴏ▸**some^1** strong form /sʌm/ weak form /s^{ə}m/ pronoun, quantifier **1** [UNKNOWN AMOUNT] used to refer to an amount of something without saying exactly how much or how many **biraz, bir miktar** You'll need a pair of scissors and some glue. ○ I can't eat all this chocolate, would you like some? ○ Could I have some more (= an extra amount of) paper, please? **2** [NOT ALL] used to refer to part of a larger amount or number of something and not all of it **az, biraz, bir kaç, bir kısım, bir parça** In some cases it's possible to fix the problem right away. ○ Some of the children were frightened. **3** [UNKNOWN NAME] used to refer to someone or something when you do not know the name of it or exact details about it **(herhangi) biri/bir, birisi, bir şey** Some girl phoned for you, but she didn't leave a message. **4** some time/distance, etc a large amount of time, distance, etc **bir miktar zaman/mesafe vb.** I'm afraid it'll be some time before it's ready.

some^2 strong form /sʌm/ weak form /s^{ə}m/ adverb used before a number to show that it is not the exact amount **yaklaşık, aşağı yukarı, takriben** He died some ten years ago.

ᴏ▸**somebody** /'sʌmbədi/ pronoun another word for someone **biri, birisi**

someday /'sʌmdeɪ/ adverb US at an unknown time in the future **günün birinde, bir gün** We plan to get married someday.

ᴏ▸**somehow** /'sʌmhaʊ/ adverb in a way which you do not know or do not understand **her nasılsa, bir yolunu bulup, bir şekilde** Don't worry, we'll fix it somehow. ○ Somehow or other (= I do not know how) they managed to get in.

ᴏ▸**someone** /'sʌmwʌn/ (also **somebody**) pronoun **1** used to refer to a person when you do not know who they are or when it is not important who they are **birisi, bir kimse** There's someone at the door. ○ Will someone please answer the phone? **2** someone else a different person **herhangi biri/bir kimse** Sorry, I thought you were talking to someone else.

someplace /'sʌmpleɪs/ adverb US used to refer to a place when you do not know where it is or when it is not important where it is **herhangi bir yer/yere** They live someplace in the South. ○ If they don't like it here, they can go someplace else (= to a different place).

somersault /'sʌməsɔːlt/ noun [C] when you roll your body forwards or backwards so that your feet go over your head and come back down to the ground again **takla, perende ● somersault** verb [I] **takla atmak**

ᴏ▸**something** /'sʌmθɪŋ/ pronoun **1** used to refer to a thing when you do not know what it is or when it is not important what it is **bir şey** As soon as I walked in, I noticed that something was missing. ○ We know about the problem and we're trying to do something about it. ○ It's not something that will be easy to change. ○ There's something else (= another thing) I wanted to tell you. **2 or something (like that)** used to show that what you have just said is only an example or you are not certain about it **onun gibi bir şey; falan; ona benzer şey** Why don't you go to a movie or something? **3 something like** similar to or approximately ...gibi bir şey He paid something like $2000 for his car. **4 be something** informal to be a thing which is important, special, or useful **bir değeri/özelliği/faydası olan şey olmak** The President visiting our hotel - that would really be something. **5 something of a sth** used to describe a person or thing in a way which is partly true but not completely

or exactly ...dan/den meydana gelen şey/kişi; ...ın/in sonucu olan bir şey/kişi It came as something of a surprise. **6 be/have something to do with sth/sb** to be related to something or a cause of something but not in a way which you know about or understand exactly **biriyle/bir şeyle yapacak bir şeyi olmak; ...ile ilgili/ilgisi/alakası olmak** It might have something to do with the way it's made.

sometime /'sʌmtaɪm/ adverb used to refer to a time when you do not know exactly what it is or when it is not important what it is **bir ara** sometime before June ○ You must come over and visit sometime.

ᴏ▸**sometimes** /'sʌmtaɪmz/ adverb on some occasions but not always or often **bazen, ara sıra** He does cook sometimes, but not very often. ○ Sometimes I feel like no one understands me.

somewhat /'sʌmwɒt/ adverb formal slightly **oldukça, az çok, az buçuk** We were somewhat disappointed with the food.

ᴏ▸**somewhere** /'sʌmweə^r/ adverb **1** used to refer to a place when you do not know exactly where it is or when it is not important exactly where it is **bir yere, bir yerde, bir yere** They had difficulties finding somewhere to live. ○ He comes from somewhere near London. ○ Can you think of somewhere else (= a different place) we could go? **2 somewhere around/between, etc** approximately **tahminen buralarda bir yerde; yaklaşık bu arada bir yerde** He earns somewhere around £50,000 a year. **3 get somewhere** to achieve something or to make progress **bir yere varmak; başarmak, ilerleme kaydetmek** Right, that's the printer working. Now we're getting somewhere!

ᴏ▸**son** /sʌn/ noun [C] your male child **erkek çocuk**

sonar /'səʊnɑː^r/ noun [U] a system, used especially on ships, which uses sound waves to find the position of things in the water **sonar, sonar cihazı**

sonata /sə'nɑːtə/ noun [C] a piece of music written to be played on a piano or on another instrument and the piano together **sonat**

song ...... İLE BİRLİKTE KULLANILAN KELİMELER

sing/write a song ● a song about sth ● a love song

ᴏ▸**song** /sɒŋ/ noun [C] words that go with a short piece of music **şarkı** a folk/love song ○ to sing a song

songwriter /'sɒŋˌraɪtə^r/ noun [C] someone who writes songs **şarkı sözü yazarı**

sonic /'sɒnɪk/ adjective relating to sound **sesle/ses dalgalarıyla ilgili**

son-in-law /'sʌnɪnlɔː/ noun [C] plural **sons-in-law** your daughter's husband **damat**

sonnet /'sɒnɪt/ noun [C] a poem with 14 lines, written in a particular pattern **sone; 14 mısralı şiir** Shakespeare's sonnets

ᴏ▸**soon** /suːn/ adverb **1** after a short period of time **birazdan, biraz sonra, yakında, çok geçmeden** I've got to leave quite soon. ○ It's too soon to make a decision. ○ He joined the company soon after leaving college. **2 as soon as** at the same time or a very short time after ...**ar/er... maz/mez; olur olmaz, yapar yapmaz vs.** As soon as I saw her, I knew there was something wrong. ○ They want it as soon as possible. **3 sooner or later** used to say that you do not know exactly when something will happen, but you are sure that it will happen **er geç, er ya da geç** Sooner or later they'll realize that it's not going to work. **4 would sooner** would prefer **tercih etmek, yeğlemek** I'd sooner spend a bit more money than take chances with safety. **5 no sooner ... than** used to show that something happens immediately after something else ...**ar/ır**

er ... maz/mez *No sooner had we got home than the phone rang.*

soot /sʊt/ *noun* [U] a black powder produced when coal, wood, etc is burnt **kurum, is**

soothe /suːð/ *verb* [T] **1** to make something feel less painful **hafifletmek, dindirmek, azaltmak** *I had a long, hot bath to soothe my aching muscles.* **2** to make someone feel calm or less worried **yatıştırmak, rahatlatmak, teskin etmek, sakinleştirmek** *to soothe a crying baby* ● **soothing** *adjective* making you feel calm or in less pain **hafifletici, dinlendirici, azaltıcı** *soothing music* ○ *a soothing effect/voice*

sophisticated /səˈfɪstɪkeɪtɪd/ *adjective* **1** well-educated and having experience of the world or knowledge of culture **kültürlü, düzeyli, görmüş geçirmiş 2** A sophisticated machine or system is very advanced and works in a clever way. **ileri teknoloji ürünü, karmaşık** *a sophisticated computer system* ● **sophistication** /səˌfɪstɪˈkeɪʃᵊn/ *noun* [U] **incelik, duyarlılık, eğitimli ve kültürlü olma**

sophomore /ˈsɒfəmɔːʳ/ *noun* [C] US a student studying in the second year of a course at a US university or high school (= school for students aged 15 to 18) **(ABD) üniversite veya lise 2. sınıf öğrencisi**

soprano /səˈprɑːnəʊ/ *noun* [C] a female singer who sings the highest notes **soprano**

sordid /ˈsɔːdɪd/ *adjective* unpleasant, dirty, or immoral **pis, sefil, rezil, iç karartıcı, aşağılık** *a sordid affair*

sore¹ /sɔːʳ/ *adjective* **1** painful, especially when touched **ağrıyan, ağrılı, sızlayan** *a sore throat/knee* ○ *Her eyes were red and sore.* **2 sore point/spot/subject** a subject which causes disagreement or makes people angry when it is discussed **hassas bir konu, nâzik bir husus; tartışmaya/anlaşmazlığa neden olan husus** *Money is a bit of a sore point with him at the moment.* ➲See also: stick/stand out like a sore **thumb¹**.

sore² /sɔːʳ/ *noun* [C] an area of skin which is red and painful because of an infection **yara**

sorely /ˈsɔːli/ *adverb formal* very much **çok, şiddetli, dehşetli** *to be sorely disappointed/tempted* ○ *He will be sorely missed by everyone.*

sorrow /ˈsɒrəʊ/ *noun* [C, U] *formal* when someone feels very sad **keder, elem, üzüntü** ● **sorrowful** *adjective formal* **hazin**

o⌐**sorry** /ˈsɒri/ *adjective* **1 (I'm) sorry** something that you say to be polite when you have done something wrong, or when you cannot agree with someone or accept something **'Özür dilerim!', 'Üzgünüm!', 'Affedersiniz!' 'Pardon!'** *Sorry I'm late.* ○ *Oh, I'm sorry. I didn't see you there.* ○ *Tom, I'm so sorry about last night - it was all my fault.* ○ *I'm sorry, but I just don't think it's a good idea.* **2** used to show sympathy or sadness for a person or situation **üzgün, mütessir** *I feel sorry for the children - it must be very hard for them.* ○ *I was sorry to hear about your brother's accident.* ○ *[+ (that)] I'm sorry that things didn't work out for you.* **3 Sorry?** mainly UK used as a polite way to say that you did not hear what someone has just said **'Pardon?', 'Efendim?', 'Özür dilerim, anlayamadım?', 'Ne demiştiniz?'** *Sorry? What was that?* **4** used to say that you wish something in the past had not happened or had been different **üzgün, pişman, mütessir** *[+ (that)] I'm sorry that I ever met him.* **5 a sorry sight/state/tale** a bad condition or situation **berbat bir durum/şart/ koşul** *Her car was in a sorry state after the accident.*

o⌐**sort¹** /sɔːt/ *noun* **1** [C] a type of something **tür, çeşit, cins, nevi** *We both like the same sort of music.* ○ *What sort of shoes does she wear?* ○ *I'm going to have a salad of some sort.* **2 all sorts of sth** many different types of

something **tüm çeşitleri, her neviden şeyler; farklı türde bir çok şey 3 sort of** *informal* used to describe a situation approximately **sanki, adeta, bir tür, bir cins, bir nevi** *It's a sort of pale orange colour.* **4 (and) that sort of thing** *informal* used to show that what you have just said is only an example from a larger group of things **gibi bir şey, bir tür, öyle bir şey** *They sell souvenirs, postcards, that sort of thing.* **5 of sorts** *informal* used to describe something which is not a typical example **sıradan, öylesine, sözüm ona** *He managed to make a curtain of sorts out of an old sheet.*

o⌐**sort²** /sɔːt/ *verb* **1** [T] to arrange things into different groups or types or into an order **sınıflamak, tasnif etmek, ayırmak** *They sort the paper into white and coloured for recycling.* ○ *The names are sorted alphabetically.* **2 be sorted/get sth sorted** UK *informal* If something is sorted or you get something sorted, you successfully deal with it and find a solution or agreement. **halletmek, çözümlemek, halledilmek, çözüm bul (un)mak** *Did you manage to get everything sorted?* **sort sth out** *phrasal verb* to successfully deal with something, such as a problem or difficult situation **halletmek, düzenlemek, düzeltmek, çözüme ulaştırmak, başetmek, başarıyla sonuçlandırmak** *Have you sorted out your schedule yet?* **sort through sth** *phrasal verb* to look at a number of things to organize them or to find something **elden geçirmek, gözden geçirmek** *I had the sad task of sorting through her papers after she died.*

so-so /ˈsəʊsəʊ/ *adjective informal* not very good, but not bad **şöyle böyle, eh işte, pek iyi değil, orta karar** *"Are you feeling better today?" "So-so."*

soufflé /ˈsuːfleɪ/ ⓤ /suːˈfleɪ/ *noun* [C, U] a light food made by baking the white part of eggs **sufle** *chocolate/ cheese soufflé*

sought /sɔːt/ *past of* seek **aramak' fiilinin geçmiş zaman hâli**

sought-after /ˈsɔːtˌɑːftəʳ/ *adjective* wanted by lots of people, but difficult to get **aranan, rağbet gören, çok talebi olan; çok aranılan** *a house in a sought-after location*

soul /səʊl/ *noun* **1** [SPIRIT] [C] the part of a person which is not their body, which some people believe continues to exist after they die **ruh, duygu, hissiyat 2** [MUSIC] [U] (*also* 'soul ˌmusic) popular music which expresses deep feelings, originally performed by Black Americans **Amerikalı siyahîlerin yaptığı bir müzik türü 3** [PERSON] [C] *informal* a person **kişi, kimse, şahıs, adam** *I didn't see a soul when I went out.* ➲See also: heart and soul.

soulful /ˈsəʊlfᵊl/ *adjective* expressing deep feelings, often sadness **içli, duygulu, hisli, duygusal** *soulful eyes*

soulless /ˈsəʊlləs/ *adjective* without any interesting or attractive characteristics **ruhsuz, cansız, duygusuz** *a soulless housing estate*

soul-searching /ˈsəʊlˌsɜːtʃɪŋ/ *noun* [U] when you think very carefully about something to decide if it is the right thing to do **kılı kırk yarma; inceden inceye düşünme; kardardan önce uzun süre düşünme** *After much soul-searching, he decided to leave his job.*

⌐⌐⌐ **sound** .... İLE BİRLİKTE KULLANILAN KELİMELER

emit/make/produce a sound ● **hear/listen to** a sound ● **the sound of** sth

o⌐**sound¹** /saʊnd/ *noun* **1** [C, U] something that you hear or that can be heard **ses** *I could hear the sounds of the city through the open window.* ○ *She stood completely still, not making a sound.* ○ *Can you turn the sound up*

(= make a radio, television, etc louder)? **2 the sound of sth** *informal* how something seems to be, from what you have been told or heard **izlenim, etki, anlaşıldığı kadarıyla** *I like the sound of the beef in red wine sauce.* ○ *He's really enjoying college,* **by the sound of it.**

℗**sound**[2] /saʊnd/ *verb* **1 sound good/interesting/ strange, etc** to seem good/interesting/strange, etc, from what you have heard or read **iyi/ilginç/acayip vb. görünmek/gibi gelmek** *Your job sounds really interesting.* **2 sound like/as if/as though** to seem like something, from what you have heard or read **sanki, güya** *That sounds like a really good idea.* **3 sound angry/happy/rude, etc** to seem angry/happy/rude, etc when you speak **kızgın/mutlu/kaba görünmek/ gibi gelmek** *You don't sound too sure about it.* **4** [I, T] to make a noise **ses yapmak, ses çıkarmak** *It looks and sounds like a real bird.* ○ *If the alarm sounds, you must leave the building immediately.*

sound[3] /saʊnd/ *adjective* good or safe and able to be trusted **emin, emniyetli, güvenilir** *sound advice/ judgment* ○ *The building is quite old, but still* **structurally sound.** ⊃Opposite **unsound.**

sound[4] /saʊnd/ *adverb* **sound asleep** in a deep sleep **deliksiz uyku, mışıl mışıl uyku**

soundbite /'saʊndbaɪt/ *noun* [C] a short statement which is easy to remember, usually used by a politician to get attention on television, in newspapers, etc **canalıcı ifade/sözcük; televizyonda/gazetede siyasetçilerce kullanılan önemli/slogan türü ifade**

'sound ˌcard *noun* [C] a small piece of electronic equipment inside a computer that makes it able to record and play sound **ses kartı**

soundly /'saʊndli/ *adverb* **1 sleep soundly** to sleep well **mışıl mışıl uyumak, deliksiz uyumak 2 soundly beaten/defeated** beaten/defeated easily and by a large amount **adamakıllı mağlup edilen/bozguna uğratılan; tamamen bertaraf edilen**

soundtrack /'saʊndtræk/ *noun* [C] the music used in a film **film müziği**

℗**soup** /suːp/ *noun* [U] a hot, liquid food, made from vegetables, meat, or fish **çorba** *chicken/tomato soup* ⊃Orta kısımdaki renkli sayfalarına bakınız.

sour[1] /saʊər/ *adjective* **1** having a sharp, sometimes unpleasant, taste or smell, like a lemon, and not sweet **ekşi, mayhoş** *These plums are a bit sour.* **2** very unfriendly or unpleasant **huysuz, geçimsiz, dost hatırı bilmeyen, ters, aksi** *Their relationship suddenly* **turned sour.**

sour[2] /saʊər/ *verb* [T] to make something unpleasant or unfriendly **kötüleştirmek, berbat olmak/etmek; araya soğukluk sokmak; arayı bozmak** *This affair has* **soured relations** *between the two countries.*

┌───┐
│ **source** ...... İLE BİRLİKTE KULLANILAN KELİMELER │
└───┘
a [good/important/major, etc] source of sth

source /sɔːs/ *noun* [C] **1** where something comes from **kaynak, memba, köken** *a source of income/information* ○ *Oranges are a good* **source** *of vitamin C.* **2** someone who gives information to the police, newspapers, etc **haber kaynağı**

℗**south, South** /saʊθ/ *noun* [U] **1** the direction that is on your right when you face towards the rising sun **güney yönü, Güney yönü 2 the south** the part of an area that is further towards the south than the rest **güney** ● **south** *adjective the south side of the house* **güney** ● **south** *adverb* towards the south **güneye doğru** *Birds fly south in winter.*

southbound /'saʊθbaʊnd/ *adjective* going or leading towards the south **güney giden; güneye uzanan**

southeast, Southeast /ˌsaʊθ'iːst/ *noun* [U] **1** the direction between south and east **güneydoğu/Güneydoğu 2 the southeast** the southeast part of a country **güneydoğu bölgesi/bölümü** ● **southeast, Southeast** *adjective, adverb* **güneydoğu**

southeastern, Southeastern /ˌsaʊθ'iːstən/ *adjective* in or from the southeast **güneydoğudan/da; Güneydoğudan/da**

southerly /'sʌðəli/ *adjective* **1** towards or in the south **güneye doğru** *We continued in a southerly direction.* **2** A southerly wind comes from the south. **güneyden gelen**

℗**southern, Southern** /'sʌðən/ *adjective* in or from the south part of an area **güneyden/de; Güneyden/de** *the southern half of the country*

southerner, Southerner /'sʌðənər/ *noun* [C] someone from the south part of a country **güneyli; Güneyli kimse**

southernmost /'sʌðənməʊst/ *adjective* The southernmost part of an area is the part furthest to the south. **güneyde en uç noktada**

south-facing /'saʊθˌfeɪsɪŋ/ *adjective* [always before noun] positioned towards the south **güneye bakan** *a south-facing garden/window*

the ˌSouth 'Pole *noun* a point on the Earth's surface which is furthest south **Güney Kutbu**

southward, southwards /'saʊθwəd/, /'saʊθwədz/ *adverb* towards the south **güneye doğru** ● **southward** *adjective a southward direction* **güneye doğru**

southwest, Southwest /ˌsaʊθ'west/ *noun* [U] **1** the direction between south and west **güneybatı yönü, Güneybatı yönü 2 the southwest** the southwest part of the country **güneybatı** ● **southwest, Southwest** *adjective, adverb* **güneybatı**

southwestern, Southwestern /ˌsaʊθ'westən/ *adjective* in or from the southwest **güneybatıda/dan, Güneybatıda/dan**

souvenir /ˌsuːvən'ɪər/ *noun* [C] something which you buy or keep to remember a special event or holiday **hatıra, hediyelik eşya** *a souvenir shop* ○ *I kept the ticket as a* **souvenir** *of my trip.*

sovereign[1] /'sɒvərɪn/ *adjective* A sovereign country or state is completely independent. **müstakil, bağımsız** ● **sovereignty** /'sɒvərɪnti/ *noun* [U] the power of a country to control its own government **hükümranlık, egemenlik, hâkimiyet**

sovereign, Sovereign[2] /'sɒvərɪn/ *noun* [C] *formal* a king or queen **kral/kraliçe/hükümdar; Kral/Kraliçe/Hükümdar**

sow[1] /səʊ/ *verb* [T] *past tense* **sowed**, *past participle* **sown** or **sowed** to put seeds into the ground **ekmek, tohum ekmek** *to sow seeds/crops*

sow[2] /saʊ/ *noun* [C] a female pig **dişi domuz**

soya bean /'sɔɪəˌbiːn/ *UK* (*US* **soybean** /'sɔɪbiːn/) *noun* [C] a bean used to produce oil, and which is used in many foods **soya fasulyesi**

soy sauce /ˌsɔɪ'sɔːs/ *noun* [U] a dark brown sauce made from soya beans, used in Chinese and Japanese cooking **soya sosu**

spa /spɑː/ *noun* [C] a place where people go to improve their health by exercising or by having baths in special water **kaplıca, ılıca** *a health spa* ○ *a spa town*

┌───┐
│ **space** ...... İLE BİRLİKTE KULLANILAN KELİMELER │
└───┘
create/make space ● fill a/occupy a/take up space
● space for sb/sth ● an open space

o⊶**space**[1] /speɪs/ *noun* **1** [C, U] an empty area which is available to be used **yer, alan, mahal, boşluk** *a parking space* ○ *We need more open spaces for children to play in.* ○ *There wasn't enough space for everyone.* ○ [+ to do sth] *We don't have the space to store it all.* **2** [U] the area outside the Earth **uzay, feza** *They plan to send another satellite into space.* ○ *space travel* **3 in the space of six weeks/three hours, etc** during a period of six weeks/ three hours, etc **altı haftalık/üç saatlik vs. zaman zarfında** *It all happened in the space of 10 minutes.* ⊃See also: breathing space, outer space.

space[2] /speɪs/ *verb* [T] to arrange things so that there is some distance or time between them **aralıklarla veya zaman aralığı ile sıraya koymak/dizmek/düzenlemek** [often passive] *They will have to be spaced at least two metres apart.*

spacecraft /'speɪskrɑːft/ *noun* [C] *plural* **spacecraft** a vehicle which can travel outside the Earth and into space **uzay aracı**

spaceship /'speɪsˌʃɪp/ *noun* [C] a vehicle which can travel outside the Earth and into space, especially one which is carrying people **uzay gemisi**

'**space ˌshuttle** *noun* [C] a vehicle in which people travel into space (= the area outside the Earth) and back again **uzay mekiği**

spacious /'speɪʃəs/ *adjective* large and with a lot of space **geniş, ferah, açıklık** *a spacious apartment/office*

spade /speɪd/ *noun* [C]
1 a tool with a long handle and a flat, metal part at one end used for digging **bel, bahçıvan beli/küreği 2 spades** playing cards with black leaf shapes on them **(iskambilde) maça** *the ace of spades*

spade

spaghetti /spə'geti/ *noun* [U] long, thin pieces of pasta **spageti**

spam /spæm/ *noun* [U] emails that you do not want, usually advertisements **istenmeyen e-postalar; reklâmlar ● spam** *verb* [T] **gereksiz bir çok e-mail mesajı almak ● spammer** *noun* [C] a person who sends spam **istenmeyen e-postaları/reklâmları gönderen kişi**

span /spæn/ *noun* [C] **1** the period of time that something exists or happens **süre, zaman, zaman aralığı** *a short attention span* ○ *an average life span of seventy years* **2** the length of something from one end to the other **açıklık, ara, mesafe, uzaklık** *a wing span of five metres ● span* *verb* [T] **spanning**, *past* **spanned** to exist or continue for a particular distance or length of time **sürmek, kapsamak** *Her acting career spanned almost forty years.*

spaniel /'spænjəl/ *noun* [C] a dog with long hair and long ears **uzun killi ve kulaklı köpek, spanyel**

spank /spæŋk/ *verb* [T] to hit someone, usually a child, on their bottom **poposuna vurmak (genellikle çocuklara)**

spanner /'spænər/ *UK* (*US* **wrench**) *noun* [C] a tool with a round end that is used to turn nuts and bolts (= metal objects used to fasten things together) **somun anahtarı, İngiliz anahtarı** ⊃See picture at **tool.**

spar /spɑːr/ *verb* [I] **sparring**, *past* **sparred** to fight or argue with someone in a friendly way **dostane tartışmak, kızmadan kavga etmeden münakaşa etmek**

o⊶**spare**[1] /speər/ *adjective* **1** If something is spare, it is available to use, because it is extra and not being used. **yedek** *a spare bedroom* ○ *spare cash* ○ *spare parts*

2 spare time time when you are not working **boş vakit, çalışmadan geçirilen zaman** *I enjoy gardening in my spare time.*

spare[2] /speər/ *noun* [C] an extra thing which is not being used and which can be used instead of a part which is broken, lost, etc **yedek eşya/nesne/parça**

spare[3] /speər/ *verb* **1** [T] to give time or money to someone **para/zaman ayırmak/vermek** *I have to go soon, but I can spare a few minutes.* ○ [+ **two objects**] *Can you spare me some change?* **2** [+ **two objects**] to prevent someone from having to experience something unpleasant **kurtarmak, korumak, esirgemek** [often passive] *I was spared the embarrassment of having to sing in front of everybody.* **3 to spare** If you have time, money, etc to spare, you have more than you need. **(zaman, para) harcamak; boşa harcayacak parası/zamanı olmak** *I arrived at the station with more than an hour to spare.* **4 spare no effort/expense, etc** to use a lot of effort/ expense, etc to do something **hiç bir çaba ve masraftan kaçınmamak** [+ to do sth] *We will spare no effort to find out who did this.* **5 spare sb's life** to not kill someone **hayatını bağışlamak, öldürmemek** ⊃See also: spare a **thought**[1] for sb.

sparingly /'speərɪŋli/ *adverb* carefully using only a very small amount of something **idareli/tutumlu olarak/bir şekilde** *to eat/drink sparingly ● sparing adjective* **tutumlu**

spark[1] /spɑːk/ *noun* [C] **1** [FIRE] a very small, bright piece of burning material **kıvılcım** *The fire was caused by a spark from a cigarette.* **2** [ELECTRICITY] a small flash of light caused by electricity **kıvılcım, ateş, çakım 3** [START] a small idea or event which causes something bigger to start **kıvılcım, işaret, belirti, iz, fikir, olay** *a spark of hope/inspiration*

spark[2] /spɑːk/ (*also* **spark off**) *verb* [T] to cause an argument, fight, etc to start happening **başlatmak, alevlendirmek** *to spark a debate/protest* ○ *to spark criticism/fears*

sparkle[1] /'spɑːkl/ *verb* [I] **1** to shine brightly because of reflected light **parlamak, parıldamak, ışıldamak** *water sparkling in the sun* ○ *Her eyes sparkled with excitement.* **2** to do something in a special or exciting way **seçkinleşmek, temayüz etmek ,göze çarpmak** *The concert gave her an opportunity to sparkle.*

sparkle[2] /'spɑːkl/ *noun* **1** [C, U] the light from something reflecting on a shiny surface **pırıltı, ışıltı 2** [U] the quality of being special or exciting **hususiyet, temayüz etme, seçkinlik** *The performance lacked a bit of sparkle.*

sparkling /'spɑːklɪŋ/ *adjective* **1** shining brightly because of reflected light **parlayan, parıl parıl, parlak 2** special or exciting **göze çarpan, özel, heyecan veren** *a sparkling performance* ○ *sparkling conversation* **3 sparkling water/wine** water/wine with bubbles in it **köpüklü şarap/su**

'**spark ˌplug** *noun* [C] a part in an engine that makes the fuel burn **buji**

sparrow /'spærəʊ/ *noun* [C] a small, brown bird which is common in towns and cities **serçe**

sparse /spɑːs/ *adjective* **1** existing only in small amounts over a large area **seyrek, dağınık, kıt** *sparse population/vegetation* **2** A room that is sparse contains little furniture and does not seem very comfortable. **boş, az mobilyalı, seyrek döşenmiş ● sparsely** *adverb* **sparsely populated/furnished** **seyrek bir şekilde**

spartan /'spɑːtən/ *adjective* very simple and not comfortable or luxurious **sade, basit, yalın, konforsuz, ilkel** *The rooms were clean but spartan.*

S

spasm /'spæzᵊm/ *noun* [C, U] when a muscle suddenly gets tight in a way that you cannot control **kasılma, spazm** *a back/muscle spasm* ○ *to go into spasm*

spasmodic /spæz'mɒdɪk/ *adjective* happening suddenly for short periods of time and not in a regular way **gelip giden, ara sıra ,gayri muntazam, zaman zaman**

spat /spæt/ *past of* spit **tükürmek' fiilinin geçmiş zaman hâli**

spate /speɪt/ *noun* **a spate of accidents/crimes/thefts, etc** a large number of bad things which happen at about the same time **yığınla/diz boyu/pek çok kaza/suç/ hırsızlık vb.; dalga, silsile**

spatial /'speɪʃᵊl/ *adjective* relating to the position, area, and size of things **mekânsal, boyutsal, konumsal; fiziksel** ● **spatially** *adverb* **yer veya ölçüyle ilgili**

spatter /'spætər/ *verb* [T] to cover someone or something with small drops of liquid without intending to **sıçratmak, sıçramak** [often passive] *His shirt was spattered with blood.*

spatula /'spætjələ/ *noun* [C] a tool with a wide flat blade, used in cooking for mixing, spreading, or lifting food **spatula, mablak** ➲ *Orta kısımdaki renkli sayfalarına bakınız.*

spawn /spɔːn/ *verb* [T] to cause a lot of other things to be produced or to exist **neden olmak, yol açmak, ...ı/i doğurmak; sebebiyet vermek** *Her death spawned several films and books.*

☞**speak** /spiːk/ *verb past tense* **spoke,** *past participle* **spoken 1** [I] to say something using your voice **konuşmak** *to speak loudly/quietly* ○ *There was complete silence - nobody spoke.* **2 speak to sb** *mainly UK (mainly US* **speak with sb)** to talk to someone **biriyle konuşmak** *Could I speak to Mr Davis, please?* ○ *Have you spoken with your new neighbors yet?* **3 speak about/of sth** to talk about something **bir şey hakkında konuşmak** *He refused to speak about the matter in public.* **4 speak English/French/German, etc** to be able to communicate in English/French/German, etc **yabancı dil konuşmak** *Do you speak English?* **5** [I] to make a speech to a large group of people **konuşma yapmak** *She was invited to speak at a conference in Madrid.* **6 speak for/ on behalf of sb** to express the feelings, opinions, etc of another person or of a group of people **birisi adına konuşmak** *I've been chosen to speak on behalf of the whole class.* **7 generally/personally, etc speaking** used to explain that you are talking about something in a general/personal, etc way **genel/kişisel anlamda** *Personally speaking, I don't like cats.* **8 so to speak** used to explain that the words you are using do not have their usual meaning **tâbiri caizse, deyim yerindeyse, neredeyse, âdeta, sanki** ➲See also: speak/talk of the **devil,** speak your **mind**[1].

speak out *phrasal verb* to give your opinion about something in public, especially on a subject which you have strong feelings about **açıkça söylemek, dobra dobra konuşmak, çekinmeden söylemek** *He decided to speak out against the bombing.*

speak up *phrasal verb* **1** to say something in a louder voice so that people can hear you **sesini yükseltmek, yüksek sesle konuşmak** *Could you speak up a bit? I can't hear you.* **2** to give your opinion about something, especially about a problem or to support someone else **bir konuda fikrini söylemek; birini destekler şeklinde konuşmak** *It's getting bad - it's time someone spoke up about it.*

speaker /'spiːkər/ *noun* [C] **1** the part of a radio, CD player, etc which the sound comes out of **hoparlör** ➲ *Orta kısımdaki renkli sayfalarına bakınız.* **2 an English/ French/German, etc speaker** someone who can speak English/French, etc **yabancı dil konuşabilen**

kişi 3 someone who makes a speech to a group of people **konuşmacı, konuşma yapan kimse** *a guest speaker*

spear /spɪər/ *noun* [C] a long weapon with a sharp point at one end used for hunting **mızrak, zıpkın**

spearhead /'spɪəhed/ *verb* [T] to lead an attack or series of actions **öncülük etmek, önayak olmak; hareketin lideri olmak** *to spearhead a campaign*

spearmint /'spɪəmɪnt/ *noun* [U] a type of mint (= a herb used as a flavour for sweets) **bahçe nanesi** *spearmint chewing gum*

<table><tr><td>**special** ...... BAŞKA BİR DEYİŞLE</td></tr></table>

Eğer bir kişi veya şey normalde bulunandan daha iyiyse, **exceptional** veya **outstanding** olarak tanımlanabilirler. *Their standard of acting was very high but there was one* exceptional/outstanding *performance.* **Extraordinary** sıfatı şaşırtıcı bir şekilde özel olan kişi veya cansız şeyler için kullanılır. *Her capacity to remember things is* extraordinary. ● *She has an* extraordinary *talent.* **Deluxe** ve **superior** sıfatları yüksek kalitesinden dolayı satın alabileceğiniz ve özellikleri olan şeylerin tanımında kullanılır. *The shop assistant tried to sell us the* deluxe/superior *model.* **Rare** ve **unique** sıfatları lağan dışı anlamında kullanıldığında **special** kelimesinin yerine kullanılabilir. *This is a* rare/unique *opportunity to see inside the building.* Eğer bir şey çok yüksek kalitesinden dolayı özel ise, **out of this world** olarak tanımlanabilir. *Their chocolate cake is just* out of this world.

☞**special**[1] /'speʃᵊl/ *adjective* **1** better or more important than usual things **özel, hususi** *a special friend* ○ *something special for her birthday.* **2 special attention/care/treatment** treatment that is better than usual **özel ilgi/dikkat/muamele/ihtimam 3 special offer** *UK* a price which is lower than usual **özel teklif** *I bought them because they were on special offer.* **4** different from normal things, or used for a particular purpose **özel, özgü, has, mahsus** *You need to use a special kind of paint.*

special[2] /'speʃᵊl/ *noun* [C] **1** a television programme made for a particular reason or occasion and not part of a series **özel (TV programı)** *The Christmas special had 24.3 million viewers.* **2** a dish in a restaurant which is not usually available **özel (yemek)** *Today's specials are written on the board.*

,special ef'fects *noun* an unusual type of action in a film, or an entertainment on stage, created by using special equipment **özel efektler** *The new Harry Potter film includes some very frightening special effects.*

<table><tr><td>**specialist** ...... İLE BİRLİKTE KULLANILAN KELİMELER</td></tr></table>

a **leading** specialist ● a specialist **in** sth ● specialist **knowledge**

specialist /'speʃᵊlɪst/ *noun* [C] someone who has a lot of experience, knowledge, or skill in a particular subject **uzman, mütehassıs** *a cancer/software specialist* ○ *He's a specialist in childhood illnesses.*

speciality /,speʃi'æləti/ *UK (US* **specialty** /'speʃᵊlti/) *noun* [C] a product, skill, etc that a person or place is especially known for **uzmanlık, uzmanlık alanı, ihtisas sahası** *We tasted a local speciality made from goat's cheese.*

specialize (*also UK* -ise) /'speʃᵊlaɪz/ *verb* [I] to spend most of your time studying one particular subject or doing one type of business **uzmanlaşmak, ihtisas yapmak** *She works for a company specializing in busi-*

ness law. ● **specialization** /ˌspeʃ³laɪ'zeɪʃ³n/ *noun* [U] **uzmanlik, ihtisas**

specialized (*also UK* -ised) /'speʃəlaɪzd/ *adjective* relating to a particular subject or activity and not general **uzmanlaşmış, ihtisas görmüş** *specialized equipment/language*

o-**specially** /'speʃəli/ *adverb* for a particular purpose **özellikle, bilhassa, özel olarak** *They searched the building with specially trained dogs.* ○ *I made this specially for you.*

‚**special 'needs** *adjective* describes something that is intended for people who have an illness or condition that makes it difficult for them to do the things that other people do **özel gereksinimler** *a special needs school*

species /'spiːʃiːz/ *noun* [C] *plural* **species** a group of plants or animals which share similar characteristics **tür, cins** *a rare species of bird*

specific /spə'sɪfɪk/ *adjective* **1** used to refer to a particular thing and not something general **belli, belirli, özel** *a specific purpose/reason* ○ *Could we arrange a specific time to meet?* **2** exact or containing details **ayrıntı, teferruat** *Could you be more specific about the problem?*

specifically /spə'sɪfɪk³li/ *adverb* **1** for a particular reason, purpose, etc **özellikle, bilhassa** *They're designed specifically for children.* ○ [+ to do sth] *She bought it specifically to wear at the wedding.* **2** exactly or in detail **tam olarak, tüm ayrıntılarıyla** *I specifically told them that she doesn't eat meat.*

specification /ˌspesɪfɪ'keɪʃ³n/ *noun* [C] *formal* a detailed description of how something should be done, made, etc **şartname, yapılması gerekenlerin tümünü içeren belge, tarifname, teknik şartname; mukavele şartnamesi** *They are made exactly to the customer's specifications.*

specifics /spə'sɪfɪks/ *noun* [plural] exact details about something **ayrıntılar, teferruat** *I can't comment on the specifics of the case.*

specify /'spesɪfaɪ/ *verb* [T] to say or describe something in a detailed way **açıkça belirtmek, kesinlikle açıklamak** [+ question word] *They didn't specify what colour they wanted.*

specimen /'spesəmɪn/ *noun* [C] **1** an animal, plant, etc used as an example of its type, especially for scientific study **örnek, numune, göstermelik, mostra** *This is one of the museum's finest specimens.* **2** a small amount of a substance, such as blood, that is used for a test **örnek, numune**

speck /spek/ *noun* [C] a very small spot or a very small amount of something **nokta, zerre, ufacık benek, küçücük leke** *a speck of dirt/dust* ○ *I watched the car until it was just a tiny speck in the distance.*

speckled /'spekld/ *adjective* covered in a pattern of very small spots **benekli, çilli, alacalı** *a speckled egg*

specs /speks/ *noun* [plural] *informal* short for spectacles **gözlük**

spectacle /'spektəkl/ *noun* [C] **1** an event that is exciting or unusual to watch **görülmedik şey, ilginç durum 2 make a spectacle of yourself** to do something that makes you look stupid and that makes other people look at you **kendini rezil etmek, gülünç duruma düşmek; başkalarını kendine güldürmek** *He got drunk and made a real spectacle of himself.*

spectacles /'spektəklz/ *noun* [plural] *old-fashioned* glasses **gözlük** *a pair of spectacles*

spectacular /spek'tækjələr/ *adjective* extremely good, exciting, or surprising **hârikulâde, göz alıcı, muhteşem, şahane, nefes kesici, hayret verici** *a spectacular success* ○ *a spectacular view* ○ *spectacular scenery* ● **spectacularly** *adverb* *a spectacularly beautiful country* **harika bir şekilde**

spectator /spek'teɪtər/ *noun* [C] someone who watches an event, sport, etc **izleyici, seyirci** *They won 4-0 in front of over 40,000 cheering spectators.* ● **spectate** /spek'teɪt/ *verb* [I] to watch an event, sport, etc **seyretmek, izlemek**

spectre *UK* (*US* specter) /'spektər/ *noun* **1 the spectre of sth** the idea of something unpleasant that might happen in the future **korkunç hayal, kâbus** *This attack raises the spectre of a return to racial violence.* **2** [C] *literary* a ghost (= dead person's spirit) **hayalet**

spectrum /'spektrəm/ *noun* [C] *plural* **spectra 1** all the different ideas, opinions, possibilities, etc that exist **yelpaze, spektrum** *He has support from across the whole political spectrum.* **2** the set of colours into which light can be separated **tayf**

speculate /'spekjəleɪt/ *verb* [I, T] to guess possible answers to a question when you do not have enough information to be certain **tahminde bulunmak, tahmin yürütmek, mütalâa etmek** *The police refused to speculate about the cause of the accident.* ○ [+ that] *The newspapers have speculated that they will get married next year.*

speculation /ˌspekjə'leɪʃ³n/ *noun* [U] when people guess about something without having enough information to be certain **tahmin yürütme, spekülasyon, kurgu, nazariye** [+ that] *She has dismissed the claims as pure speculation.*

speculative /'spekjələtɪv/ *adjective* based on a guess and not on information **tahmine dayanan, kuramsal, tahminî, spekülatif** *The article was dismissed as highly/purely speculative.* ● **speculatively** *adverb* **tahmini olarak**

sped /sped/ *past of* speed **hız yapmak' fiilinin geçmiş zaman hâli**

speech .... İLE BİRLİKTE KULLANILAN KELİMELER

careful/continuous/human/normal speech ● **slur** your speech

o-**speech** /spiːtʃ/ *noun* **1** [U] someone's ability to talk, or an example of someone talking **konuşma biçimi, lehçe, ağız** *His speech was very slow and difficult to understand.* ○ *These changes can be seen in both speech and writing.* **2** [C] a formal talk that someone gives to a group of people **konuşma** *I had to make a speech at my brother's wedding.* **3 free speech/freedom of speech** the right to say or write what you want **konuşma/ifade özgürlüğü** ⊃See also: figure of speech, reported speech.

speechless /'spiːtʃləs/ *adjective* unable to speak because you are so angry, shocked, surprised, etc **dili tutulmuş, nutku tutulmuş** *I couldn't believe what he was telling me - I was speechless.*

speed .... İLE BİRLİKTE KULLANILAN KELİMELER

gain/gather/pick up speed ● **lower /reduce** sb's/ sth's speed ● **reach** a speed of [100kph/70mph, etc] ● **at** a speed of [100kph/70mph, etc]

o-**speed¹** /spiːd/ *noun* **1** [C, U] how fast something moves or happens **hız, sürat** *high/low speed* ○ *He was travelling at a speed of 90 mph.* **2** [U] very fast movement **hız, sürat** *He put on a sudden burst of speed.* **3 up to speed** having all the most recent information about a subject or activity **en son bilgiye/malumata sahip olma;**

S

tüm ayrıntıya hakim olma *The course should bring you up to speed with the latest techniques.*

speed² /spi:d/ *verb past* **sped** or **speeded 1 speed along/down/past, etc** to move somewhere or happen very fast **sürate/hızla gitmek/olmak** *The three men jumped into a car and sped away.* **2 be speeding** to be driving faster than you are allowed to **hız sınırını ihlal ederek araba kullanıyor olmak**

speed (sth) up *phrasal verb* to move or happen faster, or to make something move or happen faster **hızlan(dır)-mak, hızını art(ır)mak** *Can you try to speed up a bit please?*

speedboat /'spi:dbəʊt/ *noun* [C] a small, fast boat with an engine **sürat motoru**

'speed ,dating *noun* [U] a way to meet people for possible romantic relationships, in which you talk with lots of people for a short amount of time to see if you like them **kısa süre içinde bir çok kişiyle görüşerek arkadaş seçme şekli; hızlı tanışma**

'speed ,dial *noun* [U] a feature on a telephone that makes it possible for you to call a number by pressing only one button ● **speed dial** *verb* [I, T] **tek bir numaraya basarak istediğiniz kişiyi telefonla aramak**

speeding /'spi:dɪŋ/ *noun* [U] driving faster than you are allowed to **hız yapma** *They were stopped by the police for speeding.*

'speed ,limit *noun* [C] the fastest speed that a vehicle is allowed to travel on a particular road **hız sınırı** *to break the speed limit*

speedometer /spi:'dɒmɪtə'/ *noun* [C] a piece of equipment in a vehicle that shows how fast it is moving **hız göstergesi, hızölçer; kilometre saati** ⊃*Orta kısımdaki renkli sayfalarına bakınız.*

speedy /'spi:di/ *adjective* done quickly **hızlı, süratli, çabuk, seri** *a speedy recovery* ● **speedily** *adverb* **çabuk bir şekilde**

o➤**spell¹** /spel/ *verb past* **spelled** or *also UK* **spelt 1** [T] to write down or tell someone the letters which are used to make a word **hecelemek, harf harf söylemek** *How do you spell that?* ○ *Her name's spelt S-I-A-N.* **2** [I] If you can spell, you know how to write the words of a language correctly. **yazım kurallarına göre yazmak** *My grammar's all right, but I can't spell.* **3 spell disaster/ trouble, etc** If something spells disaster, trouble, etc, you think it will cause something bad to happen in the future. **felâket/sorun/kötülük getirmek; kötülüğe neden olmak; berbat etmek** *The new regulations could spell disaster for small businesses.*

spell sth out *phrasal verb* to explain something in a very clear way with details **ayrıntıyla açıklamak, açıkça anlatmak** *They sent me a letter, spelling out the details of the agreement.*

spell² /spel/ *noun* [C] **1** a period of time **dönem, süre, vakit, devre, müddet, dalga** *a short spell in Australia* ○ *a spell of dry weather* **2** a magic instruction **tılsım, büyü, sihir, efsun** *The witch cast a spell over him and he turned into a frog.*

spell-check (*also* spellcheck) /'speltʃek/ *verb* [T] to use a computer program to make certain that the words in a document have the correct letters in the correct order **(bilgisayarda) yazım/heceleme kontrol programı** ● **spell-check** *noun* [C] *to run a spell-check* **bir belgedeki yazı, heceleme kontrolü**

o➤**spelling** /'spelɪŋ/ *noun* **1** [C] how a particular word is spelt **heceleme** *There are two possible spellings of this word.* ○ *spelling mistakes* **2** [U] someone's ability to spell words **heceleme yeteneği** *My spelling is terrible.*

spelt /spelt/ *UK past of* spell **hecelemek' fiilinin geçmiş zaman hâli**

spend ...... BAŞKA BİR DEYİŞLE

En sıklıkla kullanılan alternatif **pay** fiilidir. *When you booked the tickets, how much did you pay?* ● *I paid an extra £30 to get a double room.*

Invest fiili bir kişinin kar amacıyla birşeye yatırım yapması durumunda kullanılır. *She's invested all her savings in the business.*

Eğer kişi bir tek şey için çok para harcıyorsa, **pay out** deyimi kullanılabilir. *I've just paid out £700 to get the car fixed.*

Eğer kişi istediği fakat ihtiyacı olmayan bir şey için çok para harcıyorsa, **splash out** deyimi kullanılabilir. *We've just splashed out £12,000 on a new kitchen.*

Kişi bir süredir sakladığı bir paranın bir bölümünü harcıyorsa, **dip into** deyimi kullanılabilir. *We had to dip into our savings to pay for the repairs.*

Eğer kişi istemediği birşeye para harcıyorsa, bu durumda **fork out** ve **shell out** deyimleri sıklıkla kullanılır. *We had to shell out two thousand pounds to get the roof fixed.* ● *I'm not going to fork out another five hundred quid for their tickets.*

o➤**spend** /spend/ *verb* [T] *past* **spent 1** to use money to buy or pay for something **para harcamak** *The company has spent £1.9 million on improving its computer network.* ○ *She spends too much money on clothes.* ○ *How much did you spend?* **2** to use time doing something or being somewhere **zaman harcamak/geçirmek** *He spent 18 months working on the project.* ○ *He's planning to spend some time at home with his family.* ○ *How long did you spend in Edinburgh?*

spending /'spendɪŋ/ *noun* [U] the money which is used for a particular purpose, especially by a government or organization **harcamalar, giderler** *government spending on health* ○ *spending cuts*

spent¹ /spent/ *adjective* already used, so not useful or effective any more **harcanmış, sarfedilmiş, kullanılmış** *spent bullets*

spent² /spent/ *past of* spend **para harcamak' fiilinin geçmiş zaman hâli**

sperm /spɜ:m/ *noun* [C] *plural* **sperm** a small cell produced by a male animal which joins an egg from a female animal to create a baby **meni, sperm**

spew /spju:/ (*also* spew out) *verb* [I, T] If something spews liquid or gas, or liquid or gas spews from something, it flows out or rises in large amounts. **fışkır(t)mak, püskür(t)-mek** *The factory spews out clouds of black smoke.*

SPF /,espi:'ef/ *noun* [C] *abbreviation for* sun protection factor: the letters and numbers on a bottle of sunscreen (= a substance which protects your skin in the sun) which shows how effective the sunscreen is **güneş koruma faktörü (GKF)**

sphere ...... İLE BİRLİKTE KULLANILAN KELİMELER

in a sphere ● a sphere of **activity/influence/life**

sphere /sfɪə'/ *noun* [C] **1** a subject or area of knowledge, work, etc **çalışma/bilgi alanı/sahası** *the political sphere* **2** a round object shaped like a ball **küre, yuvarlak**

spice¹ /spaɪs/ *noun* **1** [C, U] a substance made from a plant, which is used to give a special taste to food **baharat, bahar** *herbs and spices* **2** [U] something that makes something else more exciting **çeşni, lezzet, heyecan, canlılık** *A scandal or two adds a little spice to office life.*

spice² /spaɪs/ *verb* [T] to add spice to something **baharat koymak/eklemek** [often passive] *The apples were spiced with nutmeg and cinnamon.*

spice sth up *phrasal verb* to make something more interesting or exciting **heyecan katmak, hareket ve canlılık getirmek** *You can always spice up a talk with a few pictures.*

spicy /'spaısi/ *adjective* containing strong flavours from spice **baharatlı** *spicy food* ○ *a spicy sauce*

spider /'spaıdə^r/ *noun* [C] a small creature with eight long legs which catches insects in a web (= structure like a net) **örümcek**

spidery /'spaıdəri/ *adjective* thin and often untidy, looking like a spider **ince ve birbirine girmiş, örümcek gibi** *spidery handwriting*

spike /spaık/ *noun* [C] a long, thin piece of metal, wood, etc with a sharp point at one end **sivri uçlu metal çubuk** ● **spiky** *adjective* covered with spikes or having that appearance **sivri uçlu, diken gibi, diken diken, dikenli** *spiky hair*

o-**spill** /spıl/ *verb* [T] *past* **spilled** or *also UK* **spilt** to pour liquid somewhere without intending to **dökmek** *Someone at the party spilled red wine on the carpet.* ● **spill** *noun* [C] *an oil spill* **dökme**
spill out *phrasal verb* 1 to flow or fall out of a container **taşmak, dökülmek** *The contents of the truck spilled out across the road.* 2 If people spill out of a place, large numbers of them move out of it. **boşalmak; sel gibi akmak; (argo) ağıldan çıkar gibi çıkmak** *The crowd spilled out onto the street.*
spill over *phrasal verb* If a bad situation spills over, it begins to have an unpleasant effect on another situation or group of people. **etkilemek, sıçramak, sirayet etmek, bulaşmak, yayılmak** *There are fears that the war could spill over into neighbouring countries.*

o-**spin**¹ /spın/ *verb* [I, T] *spinning, past* **spun** 1 If something spins or you spin something, it turns around and around quickly. **dönmek, döndürmek** *The car spun across the road.* 2 to make thread by twisting together cotton, wool, etc **(yün, pamuk) eğirmek**
spin (sb) around/round *phrasal verb* If you spin around, or someone spins you around, your body turns quickly to face the opposite direction. **kensi ekseninde dönmek; etrafında dönmek**
spin sth out *phrasal verb* to make something such as a story or an activity last as long as possible **uzattıkça uzatmak, gereksiz yere uzatmak**

spin² /spın/ *noun* 1 [TURN] [C, U] the movement of something turning round very quickly **dönme, döndürme** *The skater did a series of amazing spins and jumps.* 2 [IDEA] [no plural] when an idea is expressed in a clever way that makes it seem better than it really is, especially in politics **zekice ifade etme; iyice anlatma** *This report puts a different spin on the issue.* 3 [CAR] [no plural] *informal* a short journey by car **araçla kısa gezinti/seyahat**

spinach /'spınıtʃ/ *noun* [U] a vegetable with large, dark green leaves and a strong taste **ıspanak**

spinal /'spaın°l/ *adjective* relating to the spine **bel kemiğine ait, omurgayla ilgili** *a spinal injury*

'spin ,doctor *noun* [C] *informal* someone whose job is to make ideas, events, etc seem better than they really are, especially in politics **bilhassa siyasette fikirleri ve olayları olduğundan farklı gösteren kişi; politika cambazı**

spine /spaın/ *noun* [C] 1 the long structure of bones down the centre of your back, which supports your body **bel kemiği, omurga** 2 the narrow part of a book cover where the pages are joined together and which you can see when it is on a shelf **(kitap) sırt**

spineless /'spaınləs/ *adjective* A spineless person has a weak personality and is frightened easily. **ödlek, omurgasız, tabansız, yüreksiz, korkak**

spin-off /'spınɒf/ *noun* [C] a product that develops from another more important product **yan ürün**

spinster /'spınstə^r/ *noun* [C] *old-fashioned* a woman who has never married **evde kalmış yaşlı kız, evlenmemiş yaşlı bayan; kalık, geçkin**

spiral /'spaıər°l/ *noun* [C] 1 a shape made by a curve turning around and around a central point **sarmal, spiral, helezon** *a spiral staircase* 2 a downward spiral a situation which is getting worse very quickly, and which is difficult to control **gittikçe kötüye giden ve kontrolden çıkan durum**

spiral

spire /spaıə^r/ *noun* [C] a tall, pointed tower on the top of a building such as a church **kule külâhı, kule ucu/ tepesi**

spirit¹ /'spırıt/ *noun* 1 [FEELING] [no plural] the way people think and feel about something **ruh, can** *a spirit of optimism* ○ *Everyone soon got into the spirit of* (= started to enjoy) *the carnival - singing, dancing, and having fun.* 2 **community/team**, etc spirit when you feel enthusiasm about being part of a group **toplum/takım vs. ruhu** 3 **in good/high/low spirits** feeling good/excited/unhappy **iyi/yüksek/düşük ruh hâlinde; iyi/ heyecanlı/mutsuz hissetme** 4 [NOT BODY] [C] the part of a person which is not their body, which some people believe continues to exist after they die **ruh** 5 [NOT ALIVE] [C] something which people believe exists but does not have a physical body, such as a ghost **ruh, hayalet** *evil spirits* 6 the spirit of the law/an agreement, etc the intended meaning of the law/an agreement, etc and not just the written details **kasdedilen anlam/mana/öz** 7 [DRINK] [C] a strong alcoholic drink, such as whisky or vodka **alkollü içki** [usually plural] *I don't often drink spirits.*

spirit² /'spırıt/ *verb* **be spirited away/out/to**, etc to be moved somewhere secretly **gizlice uzaklaştırmak/ götürmek** *He was spirited away to a secret hide-out in Mexico.*

spirited /'spırıtıd/ *adjective* enthusiastic and determined, often in a difficult situation **canlı, ateşli, coşkulu, kararlı** *a spirited performance*

spiritual /'spırıtʃuəl/ *adjective* relating to deep feelings and beliefs, especially religious beliefs **manevî, tinsel** *a spiritual leader*

spiritualism /'spırıtʃu°lız°m/ *noun* [U] the belief that living people can communicate with people who are dead **ispiritizma** ● **spiritualist** *noun* [C] someone who is involved with spiritualism **ispiritizmacı**

spit¹ /spıt/ *verb* [I, T] *spitting, past* **spat** or *also US* **spit** 1 to force out the liquid in your mouth **tükürmek** *I don't like to see people spitting in public.* ○ *He took a mouthful of coffee and then spat it out.* 2 **Spit it out!** *informal* used to tell someone to say more quickly what it is they want to say **'Dökül bakalım!', 'Kus bakalım!', 'Hadi konuş!'** *Spit it out!*

spit² /spıt/ *noun* 1 [U] *informal* the liquid that is made in your mouth **tükürük** 2 [C] a long, thin stick used for cooking meat over a fire **şiş, kebap şişi**

spite /spaıt/ *noun* 1 **in spite of sth** although something exists or happens **...a/e rağmen/karşın** *He still smokes, in spite of all the health warnings.* 2 [U] a feeling of anger towards someone that makes you want to hurt

S

or upset them **kin, garaz, nispet** *He hid my new jacket out of spite.*

spiteful /ˈspaɪtᵊl/ *adjective* intentionally hurting or upsetting someone **kin dolu, kindar** *That was a very spiteful thing to do.* ● **spitefully** *adverb* **kindarlık hissiyle**

splash¹ /splæʃ/ *verb* [I, T] **1** If a liquid splashes or you splash a liquid, drops of it hit or fall on something. **sıçramak** *The paint splashed onto his new shirt.* ○ *She splashed some cold water on her face.* **2 splash about/around/through, etc** to move in water so that drops of it go in all directions **suda sıçratarak hareket etmek, sıçratmak** *The children splashed about in the puddles.* **3 be splashed across/all over sth** to be the main story in a newspaper, usually on the front page, which many people will see **ön sayfa haberi olmak** *His picture was splashed across the front pages of all the newspapers the next morning.*

splash out (sth) *phrasal verb UK* to spend a lot of money on something which you want but do not need **savurganlık yapmak, müsriflik etmek; gereksiz yere para harcamak; hovardaca harcamak, para saçmak** *He splashed out on the best champagne for the party.*

splash² /splæʃ/ *noun* [C] **1** a drop of liquid which has fallen on something, or the mark made by it **damla, leke** *There were several small splashes of paint on the carpet.* **2** the sound of something falling into or moving in water **suya çarpma sesi** *They sat listening to the splash of raindrops on the lake.* **3 a splash of colour** a small area of colour which makes something look brighter **renklerin daha parlak göründüğü alan/yer** *The flowers added a splash of colour to the room.* **4 make a splash** *informal* to get a lot of public attention **dikkatleri üzerine çekmek, göz önünde olmak** *The film made quite a splash in the US.*

splatter /ˈsplætᵊr/ *verb* [I, T] If a liquid splatters or you splatter it, it falls onto a surface, often in many small drops. **sıçra(t)mak, dağılmak** [often passive] *His clothes were splattered with blood.*

splendid /ˈsplendɪd/ *adjective* very good or very beautiful, special, etc **şahane, harika, enfes, mükemmel** *a splendid idea* ○ *a splendid view* ● **splendidly** *adverb* **harika bir biçimde**

splendour *UK (US splendor)* /ˈsplendᵊr/ *noun* [C, U] when something is extremely beautiful or luxurious **görkem, ihtişam** *Tourists marvelled at the splendour of the medieval cathedral.*

splinter /ˈsplɪntᵊr/ *noun* [C] **1** a small, sharp piece of wood, glass, etc which has broken from a large piece **kıymık, parça** *I've got a splinter in my finger.* **2 a splinter group** a small group of people that forms after leaving a larger organization, such as a political party **siyasi partiden ayrılıp oluşturulan grup** ● **splinter** *verb* [I] to break into small, sharp pieces **küçük parçalara ayrılmak, dağılmak, paramparça olmak**

๐ⁿ**split¹** /splɪt/ *verb* **splitting**, *past* **split 1** BREAK [I, T] If something splits or if you split it, it tears so that there is a long, thin hole in it. **böl(ün)mek, parçala(n)mak, ayırmak, ayrılmak, yar(ıl)mak** *He split his trousers when he bent over.* ○ *Her shoes were splitting apart at the sides.* **2** DIVIDE [I, T] *(also split up)* to divide into smaller parts or groups, or to divide something into smaller parts or groups **küçük parçalara/gruplara ayırmak/ayrılmak** *The children split up into three groups.* **3** SHARE [T] to share something by dividing it into smaller parts **paylaşmak, bölüşmek, üleşmek** *The cost of the wedding will be split between the two families.* **4** DISAGREE [I, T] If a group of people splits, or something splits them, they disagree and form smaller groups. **böl**

(ün)mek, ayırmak, ayrılmak, hipleş(tir)mek [often passive] *The government is split on the issue of hunting.* ⊃See also: split hairs (hair).

split up *phrasal verb* If two people split up, they end their relationship. **ayrılmak, bozuşmak, ilişkiye son vermek** *She split up with her boyfriend.*

┌─────────────────────────────────────┐
split (noun) ...... İLE BİRLİKTE KULLANILAN KELİMELER

cause/create a split ● a split **develops** ● a split **between** sb and sb ● a split **in** sth ● a split **on/over** sth
└─────────────────────────────────────┘

split² /splɪt/ *noun* [C] **1** BREAK a long, thin hole in something where it has broken apart **yarık, çatlak, yırtık** *There's a split in my trousers.* **2** DISAGREEMENT when a group of people divides into smaller groups because they disagree about something **hizpleşme, ayrılık, ayrılmak, bölünme** *This issue is likely to cause a major split in the party.* **3** RELATIONSHIP when a marriage or relationship ends **ayrılık, boşanma, bozuşma** *Very few of their friends were surprised when they announced their split last week.*

split³ /splɪt/ *adjective* **a split second** a very short period of time **çok kısa bir zaman dilimi, saniyenin onda biri kadar bir zaman** *It was all over in a split second.* ○ *a split second decision*

splitting ˈheadache *noun* [C] a very bad pain in your head **şiddetli/müthiş/başı çatlatan baş ağrısı** *I've got a splitting headache.*

splurge /splɜːdʒ/ *verb* [I, T] to spend a lot of money on something which you want but do not need **düşüncesizce para harcamak; boş yere harcamak; gereksiz masraf yapmak; hoyratça harcamak** *We could either save the money or splurge on a new car.* ● **splurge** *noun* [C] **savurganlık**

┌─────────────────────────────────────┐
spoil ...... BAŞKA BİR DEYİŞLE

Ruin fiili **spoil** fiiline sıklıkla alternatif olarak kullanılır. *I put too much salt in the sauce and ruined it.*
Eğer kişi birşeyin görüntüsünü üzerine yazı yazarak veya resim çizerek bozuyorsa, **deface** fiili kullanılabilir. *Many of the library books had been defaced.*
Kişinin fiziksel görünümü bozulduğu zamanlarda **disfigure** fiili kullanılabilir. *Her face was disfigured by the scar.*
Eğer bir şey varolan bir ilişki veya arkadaşlığı bozuyorsa **sour** veya **poison** fiilleri kullanılabilir. *The long dispute has poisoned/soured relations between the two countries.*
Bir şeyin mahvolduğunu gayri resmi olarak dile getirmek istediğinizde **mess up** ve **screw up** deyimleri kullanılabilir. *Laurie's illness has completely messed up all our holiday plans.* ● *That new software has really screwed up my computer.*
└─────────────────────────────────────┘

๐ⁿ**spoil** /spɔɪl/ *verb past* **spoiled** or **spoilt 1** MAKE BAD [T] to stop something from being enjoyable or successful **bozmak, berbat etmek, içine etmek** *The picnic was spoiled by the bad weather.* **2** CHILD [T] If you spoil a child, you let them have anything they want or do anything they want, usually making them badly behaved. **şımartmak, yüz vermek 3** TREAT WELL [T] to treat someone very well, buying them things or doing things for them **kayırmak, torpil yapmak** *He's always sending flowers - he absolutely spoils me!* **4** FOOD [I] *formal* If food spoils, it starts to decay and you cannot eat it. **bozulmak, çürümek, ekşimek, kokmak**

spoils /spɔɪlz/ *noun* [plural] *formal* things which are taken by the winners of a war **ganimet** *the spoils of war*

spoilt /spɔɪlt/ *adjective UK (US spoiled* /spɔɪld/*)* badly behaved because you are always given what you want or allowed to do what you want **şımarık, yüz bulmuş** *He was behaving like a spoilt child.*

spoke¹ /spəʊk/ noun [C] one of the thin pieces of metal which connects the middle of a wheel to the outside edge, for example, on a bicycle **tekerlek parmağı, jant teli**

spoke² /spəʊk/ past tense of speak **konuşmak' fiilinin ikinci hâli**

spoken /'spəʊkᵊn/ past participle of speak **konuşmak' fiilinin üçüncü hâli**

spokesman, spokeswoman /'spəʊksmən/, /'spəʊks-ˌwʊmən/ noun [C] plural **spokesmen** or **spokeswomen** a man/woman who is chosen to speak officially for a group or organization **(kadın/erkek) sözcü** A spokesman for the company refused to comment on the reports.

spokesperson /'spəʊksˌpɜːsᵊn/ noun [C] plural **spokespeople** someone who is chosen to speak officially for a group or organization **sözcü**

sponge /spʌndʒ/ noun [C, U] **1** a soft substance full of small holes, which absorbs liquid very easily and is used for washing things **sünger 2** (also 'sponge ˌcake) a soft, light cake **hafif yumuşak kek**

sponge

spongy /'spʌndʒi/ adjective soft and full of small holes **emici**

sponsor¹ /'spɒnsər/ verb [T] to give money to someone to support an activity, event, or organization, sometimes as a way to advertise your company or product **desteklemek, finanse etmek, himaye etmek** The event is sponsored by First National Bank. ○ UK a sponsored walk (= a walk for charity) ● **sponsorship** noun [U] when someone gives money to support something **mali destek, para yardımı, finanse etme**

sponsor² /'spɒnsər/ noun [C] a person or organization that gives money to support an activity, event, etc **finansör, sponsor**

spontaneous /spɒn'teɪniəs/ adjective happening naturally and suddenly and without being planned **kendiliğinden olan, içten gelen, doğal** a spontaneous reaction ○ The crowd broke into spontaneous applause. ● **spontaneity** /ˌspɒntə'neɪəti/ noun [U] when something is spontaneous **kendilğinden olma, doğal davranış, içten gelen davranış** ● **spontaneously** adverb **önceden planlanmadan, o an olan**

spoof /spuːf/ noun [C] a funny television programme, film, article, etc that copies the style of a real programme, film, article, etc **parodi** They did a spoof of the Oscars, giving awards for the worst films of the year.

spooky /'spuːki/ adjective informal strange and frightening **ürkütücü, tüyleri diken diken eden, acayip** There's something spooky about that place.

◦- **spoon** /spuːn/ noun [C] an object with a handle and a round, curved part at one end, used for eating and serving food **kaşık** knives, forks, and spoons ● **spoon** verb [T] to move or serve food using a spoon **kaşıkla almak/koymak/yemek** Spoon the sauce over the fish.

spoonful /'spuːnfʊl/ noun [C] the amount of something which can be held on a spoon **kaşık dolusu** Then add a spoonful of yoghurt.

sporadic /spə'rædɪk/ adjective not happening regularly or happening in different places **ara sıra olan, seyrek, tek tük, münferit** sporadic violence ● **sporadically** adverb **tek tük bir şekilde**

do/play a sport ● **spectator/team** sports

◦- **sport¹** /spɔːt/ noun **1** [C] a game or activity which people do to keep healthy or for enjoyment, often competing against each other **spor** winter sports ○ **team sports** ⟳Orta kısımdaki renkli sayfalarına bakınız. **2** [U] UK all types of physical activity which people do to keep healthy or for enjoyment **spor hareketleri** ⟳See also: blood sport.

sport² /spɔːt/ verb [T] humorous to wear something, especially something which people notice **giymek, takmak, sürmek** He turned up sporting a bright red baseball cap and sunglasses.

sporting /'spɔːtɪŋ/ adjective relating to sports **spor ile ilgili, spor yapmaya yarayan, spor için kullanılan** a sporting hero

'**sports ˌcar** noun [C] a car designed to go very fast, often with only two seats and an open roof **spor araba**

'**sports ˌcentre** UK (US sports center) noun [C] a building with places where you can play different sports **spor merkezi**

sportsman, sportswoman /'spɔːtsmən/, /'spɔːts-ˌwʊmən/ noun [C] plural **sportsmen** or **sportswomen** a man/woman who is good at sport **sporcu, sportmen, bayan sporcu**

sportsmanship /'spɔːtsmənʃɪp/ noun [U] behaviour in sport which is fair and shows respect for other players **sportmenlik** We hope to teach children good sportsmanship.

sportswear /'spɔːtsweər/ noun [U] clothes, shoes, etc for people to wear when they play sports **spor kıyafeti** a sportswear shop

sporty /'spɔːti/ adjective **1** Sporty cars, clothes, etc are attractive, comfortable, and stylish. **çekici, rahat, lüks, moda 2** Sporty people are good at sports. **sporcu, sportmen, sporda iyi olan**

◦- **spot¹** /spɒt/ noun [C] **1** [ROUND MARK] a small, round mark which is a different colour to the surface it is on **benek, nokta, leke** a blue shirt with white spots ○ I noticed a small spot of oil on my jacket. **2** [SKIN] UK (US pimple) an unpleasant, small, red mark on your skin **leke, sivilce, ben** He suffered badly with spots as a teenager. **3** [PLACE] a place **yer, mahal** We found a good spot to sit and have our picnic. **4 a spot of sth** UK old-fashioned a small amount of something **azıcık, biraz** a spot of lunch/shopping **5 on the spot a** [TIME] immediately **derhal, hemen, cecik, şipşak** I accepted the job on the spot. **b** [PLACE] in the place where something happens **yerinde, mahallinde, oracıkta** The police were called and they were on the spot within three minutes. **6 have a soft spot for sb** to like someone a lot …**a/e düşkün olmak/zaafı olmak; çok hoşlanmak** I've always had a soft spot for her. ● **7 put sb on the spot** to ask someone a question which is difficult or embarrassing to answer at that time **köşeye sıkıştırmak, zora sokmak, zor durumda bırakmak** ⟳See also: beauty spot, blind spot.

spot² /spɒt/ verb [T] **spotting**, past **spotted** to see or notice something or someone **görmek, tanımak, seçmek, ayırt etmek** They were spotted together in London last week. ○ She soon spotted the mistake.

spotless /'spɒtləs/ adjective completely clean **lekesiz, tertemiz, pırıl pırıl** By the time I'd finished, the whole room was spotless. ● **spotlessly** adverb **spotlessly clean tertemiz bir şekilde**

be under/come under the spotlight ● **the spotlight falls on/is on** sb/sth ● **put/turn** the spotlight **on** sb/

S

sth ● **in/out of** the spotlight ● the **media/public** spotlight

spotlight /'spɒtlaɪt/ *noun* **1** [C] a strong light which can be pointed in different directions **sahne ışığı, projektör, spot 2 the spotlight** when someone gets public attention by being on television, in the newspapers, etc **genel ilgi, kamu oyunun ilgisi** *to be in the spotlight* ○ *She's rarely out of the media spotlight these days.* ● **spotlight** *verb* [T] *past* **spotlighted** or **spotlit ilgi çekmek**

,**spot 'on** *adjective* [never before noun] UK exactly correct **yüzde yüz doğru, tamamen doğru, yüzde yüz haklı** *Her imitation of Ann was spot on.*

spotty /'spɒti/ *adjective* **1** [SKIN] UK having a lot of unpleasant, small, red marks on your skin **sivilceli** *a spotty young man with greasy hair* **2** [PATTERN] UK with a pattern of round marks **benek benek, lekeli** *a spotty dress* **3** [NOT GOOD/REGULAR] US (UK **patchy**) If an action, quality, supply, etc is spotty, it is not all good or regular. **düzensiz, iyi değil, eksik, parça parça** *Sales of tickets for the concert have been spotty.*

spouse /spaʊs/ *noun* [C] *formal* your husband or wife **eş, karı veya koca**

spout[1] /spaʊt/ *noun* [C] an opening of a container, in the shape of a tube which liquid flows out through **emzik, ağız, uç** *the spout of a teapot*

spout[2] /spaʊt/ *verb* [I, T] **1** If a liquid spouts or if something makes it spout, it flows out of something with force. **fışkır(t)mak, püskür(t)mek 2** *informal* to talk a lot about something, often when other people are not interested **sıkıcı biçimde sürekli aynı şeyleri söylemek; habire konuşmak; döktürmek; parçalamak** *He was spouting his usual rubbish about politics.*

sprain /spreɪn/ *verb* [T] to injure part of your body by twisting it, but not so badly that it breaks **burkmak, incitmek** *I slipped on the ice and sprained my ankle.* ● **sprain** *noun* [C] **burkulma**

sprang /spræŋ/ *past tense of* spring **sıçramak' fiilinin geçmiş zaman hâli**

sprawl /sprɔ:l/ *verb* [I] **1** (*also* sprawl out) to sit or lie in a relaxed, untidy position with your arms and legs stretched out **yayılıp oturmak, kaykılmak, sere serpe oturmak/yatmak, yayılmak** *He sprawled out on the sofa.* **2** to cover a large area, often in a way which is not tidy or not planned **yayılmak, uzanmak** *sprawling suburbs* ● **sprawl** *noun* [U] *urban sprawl* **çok rahat bir şekilde uzanma, yayılma**

spray[1] /spreɪ/ *noun* **1** [C, U] liquid in a container which forces it out in small drops **sprey** *hair spray* ○ *spray paint* **2** [U] many small drops of liquid blown through the air **serpinti, su zerreciği** *sea spray*

spray[2] /spreɪ/ *verb* **1** [T] to force liquid out of a container in many small drops **püskürtmek, sıkmak** *The fields are sprayed with pesticides.* ○ *She sprayed a little perfume on her wrists.* **2** [I, T] If small pieces of something spray somewhere or if something sprays them, they are sent through the air in all directions. **püskürmek, fışkırmak** *A brick shattered the window, spraying the room with pieces of broken glass.*

⊶**spread**[1] /spred/ *verb* *past* **spread 1** spread sth **across/over/through, etc** to arrange something so that it covers a large area **yaymak, dağıtmak** *He spread the cards out on the table.* **2** [TIME] [T] (*also* spread out) to arrange for something to happen over a period of time and not at once **zamana yaymak** *The payments will be spread over two years.* **3** [INCREASE] [I] to increase, or move to cover a larger area or affect a larger number of people **yayılma, dağılmak, bulaşmak, artmak** *The virus is spread by rats.* **4** [SURFACE] [T] to move a soft substance across a surface so that it covers it **sürmek, yaymak** *What I really like is hot buttered toast spread with strawberry jam.* ○ *He spread a thin layer of glue on the paper.* **5** [INFORMATION] [I, T] If information spreads or if someone spreads it, it is communicated from one person to another. **yayılmak, yaymak, dağılmak, dağıtmak** *News of his death spread quickly.*

spread out *phrasal verb* If people spread out, they move from being close together in a group to being in different places across a larger area. **yayılmak, dağılmak** *They spread out to search the whole area.*

⠿⠿ **spread (noun)** ...... İLE BİRLİKTE KULLANILAN KELİMELER

the spread **of** sth ● **control/halt/limit/prevent** the spread of sth

spread[2] /spred/ *noun* **1** [MOVEMENT] [U] when something moves to cover a larger area or affect a larger number of people **yayılma, dağılma** *They are looking for ways to slow down **the spread** of the disease.* **2** [FOOD] [C, U] a soft food which you put on bread **ekmeğe sürülen ezme** *cheese spread* **3** [NEWSPAPER] [C] an article which covers one or more pages of a newspaper or magazine **özel sayfa** *a double-page spread*

spreadsheet /'spredʃi:t/ *noun* [C] a computer program which helps you to do business calculations and planning **(bilgisayarda) tablolama/grafik ve hesaplama programı**

spree /spri:/ *noun* a **shopping/spending**, etc spree a short period when someone does a lot of shopping/spending, etc **alışveriş/harcama çılgınlığı**

sprig /sprɪg/ *noun* [C] a small piece of a plant with leaves **filiz, sürgün** *a sprig of parsley*

sprightly /'spraɪtli/ *adjective* A sprightly person is able to move about easily and quickly although they are old. **canlı, hareketli, şen, neşeli**

⠿⠿ **spring** ...... İLE BİRLİKTE KULLANILAN KELİMELER

in (the) spring ● **early/late** spring ● **last/next** spring

⊶**spring**[1] /sprɪŋ/ *noun* **1** [SEASON] [C, U] the season of the year between winter and summer, when the weather becomes warmer and plants start to grow again **ilkbahar** *I'm starting a new course in the spring.* ○ *spring flowers/weather* **2** [METAL] [C] a piece of metal which curves round and round and which returns to its original shape after being pushed or pulled **yay** *bed springs* **3** [WATER] [C] a place where water comes out of the ground **kaynak, memba, pınar** *hot springs* **4** [MOVEMENT] [C, U] when someone or something suddenly moves or jumps somewhere **ani sıçrama, hareket**

spring[2] /sprɪŋ/ *verb* *past* **sprang** or *also* US **sprung**, *past part* **sprung 1** spring back/forward/out, etc to jump or move somewhere suddenly **aniden hareket etmek, sıçramak** *The cat sprang onto the sofa.* ○ *I tried to shut the door, but it kept springing open.* **2 spring to life** to suddenly become very active **birden harekete geçmek, aniden aktif hâle gelmek** *After about 8 o'clock, the city springs to life.* **3 spring to mind** If a word or idea springs to mind, you suddenly think of it. **aniden/birden aklına gelmek** *He asked if I knew any good places to go, but nothing sprang to mind.*

spring from sth *phrasal verb* to come from or be the result of something **...dan/den kaynaklanmak; ...sonucunda olmak** *Many of his problems spring from his strict religious upbringing.*

spring sth on sb *phrasal verb* to suddenly tell or ask someone something when they do not expect it **birden söylemek, pat diye açıklamak/söylemek** *I'm sorry to spring this on you, but could you give a talk at tomorrow's meeting?*

spring up *phrasal verb* to appear suddenly **baş göstermek, hızla yayılmak, mantar gibi çoğalmak; birden çıkıvermek** *A lot of new hotels have sprung up along the coast recently.*

,spring 'clean *UK (UK/US* ,spring 'cleaning) *noun* [no plural] when you clean a place more carefully and using more effort than usual **bahar temizliği** *I gave the kitchen a spring clean at the weekend.* ● **spring clean** *verb* [I, T] *UK* **çok detaylı temizlik yapmak**

,spring 'onion *UK (US* scallion) *noun* [C, U] a small onion with a white part at the bottom and long, green leaves, which is eaten in salads **yeşil soğan**

sprinkle /'sprɪŋkl/ *verb* **sprinkle** [T] to gently drop small pieces of something over a surface **saçmak, serpmek, ekmek, serpiştirmek** *Sprinkle the cake with sugar before serving.*
● **sprinkling** *noun* [no plural] a small amount of a powder or liquid that has been sprinkled on a surface **bir tutam, tek tük, az sayıda** *a sprinkling of pepper/snow*

sprinkler /'sprɪŋklə'/ *noun* [C] a piece of garden equipment which automatically spreads drops of water over grass and plants **fıskiye, püskürtücü, yağmurlama fıskiyesi, püskürteç**

sprint /sprɪnt/ *verb* [I] to run very fast for a short distance **kısa mesafe son sürat koşmak** *She sprinted along the road to the bus stop.* ● **sprinter** *noun* [C] someone who runs short distances in competitions **kısa mesafe sürat koşucusu** ● **sprint** *noun* [C] *a 100m sprint* **hızlı koşu**

sprout¹ /spraʊt/ *verb* [I, T] If a plant sprouts, or if it sprouts something, it begins to produce leaves, flowers, etc. **çimlenmek, tomurcuklanmak, filiz vermek, filizlenmek** *The seeds I planted are just beginning to sprout.*
sprout up *phrasal verb* If a large number of things sprout up, they suddenly appear or begin to exist. **hızla çoğalmak/üremek, türemek, mantar gibi çoğalmak** *New buildings are sprouting up all over the city.*

sprout² /spraʊt/ *noun* [C] **1** *(also* brussel sprout) a small, green vegetable which is round and made of leaves **Brüksel lahanası 2** a part of a plant that is just beginning to grow **filiz, sürgün, tomurcuk**

spruce /spruːs/ *verb*
spruce sb/sth up *phrasal verb* to make someone or something cleaner or more tidy **derli toplu hâle getirmek, aklayıp paklamak, tertemiz etmek; kendine çeki düzen vermek** *(often* reflexive) *I'd like to spruce myself up a bit before we go out.*

sprung /sprʌŋ/ **1** *past participle of* spring **sıçramak' fiilinin geçmiş zaman hâli 2** *US past tense of* spring **sıçramak' fiilinin geçmiş zaman hâli**

spun /spʌn/ *past tense of* spin **eğirmek' fiilinin geçmiş zaman hâli**

spur¹ /spɜː'/ *(also* spur on) *verb* [T] **spurring,** *past* **spurred** to encourage someone to do something or something to happen **teşvik etmek, özendirmek, yüreklendirmek** *Spurred on by his fans, he won the next three games easily.*

spur² /spɜː'/ *noun* [C] **1** a sharp, pointed piece of metal fixed to the boot of someone riding a horse **mahmuz 2 on the spur of the moment** If you do something on

the spur of the moment, you do it suddenly, without planning it. **birden, aniden, düşünmeden, hemen**

spurious /'spjʊəriəs/ *adjective formal* false and not based on the truth **sahte, aldatıcı**

spurn /spɜːn/ *verb* [T] *formal* to not accept someone or something **reddetmek, geri çevirmek, tepmek** *He spurned my offer/suggestion.* ○ *a spurned lover*

spurt¹ /spɜːt/ *verb* **1** [I, T] *(also* spurt out) If something spurts liquid or fire, or if liquid or fire spurts from somewhere, it flows out suddenly with force. **fışkır(t) mak, püskür(t)mek** *Blood was spurting out of his stomach.* **2 spurt ahead/into/past, etc** to increase your speed, effort, or activity **hamle yapmak, atağa kalkmak, hızlanmak** *She spurted ahead in the final lap.*

spurt² /spɜːt/ *noun* [C] **1** a sudden, short increase in speed, effort, or activity **atılım, hamle, ani gelişme, patlama, atak** *He works in short spurts.* **2** a sudden, powerful flow of liquid **fışkırma, püskürme** *The water came out of the tap in spurts.*

sputter /'spʌtə'/ *verb* [I] to make several quick, explosive sounds **tıslamak** *The car sputtered to a halt.*

spy¹ /spaɪ/ *noun* [C] someone who secretly tries to discover information about a person, country, etc **casus**

spy² /spaɪ/ *verb* **1** [I] to secretly try to discover information about a person, country, etc **casusluk yapmak 2** [T] *literary* to see someone or something, often from a distance **gizlice gözetlemek; uzaktan izlemek** *I spied him on the dance floor.*
spy on sb *phrasal verb* to secretly watch someone **birini gizlice gözetlemek** *He spied on her through the keyhole.*

sq *written abbreviation for* square in measurements **metrekare** *an area of 70 sq km* (= square kilometres)

squabble /'skwɒbl/ *verb* [I] to argue about something that is not important **atışmak, dalaşmak, hırgür yapmak, ağız kavgası yapamak** *They're always squabbling over money.* ● **squabble** *noun* [C] **kavga**

squad /skwɒd/ *noun* [C] **1 bomb/drug/fraud, etc squad** a group of police officers who have special skills to deal with particular problems **ekip, tim 2 death/firing/hit, etc squad** a group of people who are trained to kill, usually with guns **manga, müfreze 3** a sports team **spor ekibi/takımı** *the England rugby squad*

squadron /'skwɒdr°n/ *noun* [C] a group of soldiers, ships, aircraft etc in a military organization **filo** *a squadron of fighter jets*

squalid /'skwɒlɪd/ *adjective* **1** very dirty and unpleasant **kir pas içinde, çok pis ve bakımsız, sefil** *squalid conditions* **2** morally bad **ahlaken kötü, karaktersiz** *a squalid affair*

squall /skwɔːl/ *noun* [C] a sudden storm with strong winds **ani ve kuvvetli fırtına**

squalor /'skwɒlə'/ *noun* [U] extremely dirty and unpleasant conditions **pislik, sefalet, bakımsızlık, derbederlik** *They were found living in absolute squalor.*

squander /'skwɒndə'/ *verb* [T] to waste time, money, etc **saçıp savurmak, israf etmek, çarçur etmek, boş yere harcamak** *He squandered all his money on alcohol and drugs.*

o⁻**square¹** /skweə'/ *noun* [C] SHAPE a shape with four equal sides and four 90° angles **kare** ○See picture at shape. **2** PLACE an open area with buildings around it, often in the centre of a town **meydan, alan** *Trafalgar Square* **3** NUMBER a number that results from multiplying a number by itself **(matematik) karesi** *The square of 3 is 9.* **4 back to square one** back to the beginning of a long process or piece of work **başlanılan noktaya geri dönüş, sil baştan, işin başına gelme**

None of the applicants were suitable, so we had to go back to square one and advertise the job again. ➌See also: **fair³** and **square.**

ᴏ⁀**square²** /skweə*/ *adjective* **1** having the shape of a square **kare şeklinde** *a square room* ○ *He has broad shoulders and a square jaw.* **2 square centimetre/ metre/mile, etc** the area of a square with sides that are a centimetre/metre/mile, etc long **santimetre/ metre/mil vs.** *kare 3000 square feet of office space* **3 a square meal** a big, healthy meal **dört başı mamur yemek, doyurucu yemek** *You need three square meals a day.*

square³ /skweə*/ *verb* **2/3/4, etc squared** 2/3/4, etc multiplied by itself **2/3/4 vb. karesi** *Four squared is sixteen.*

square off *phrasal verb US* to prepare to fight, compete, or argue with someone **birisiyle tartışmaya/yarış- maya/kavgaya hazırlanmak** *The two teams will square off in the finals next Saturday.*

square up *phrasal verb UK* **1** to prepare to fight, com- pete, or argue with someone **birisiyle tartışmaya/ yarışmaya/kavgaya hazırlanmak** *The players squa- red up to each other and started shouting.* **2** *informal* to pay someone the money that you owe them **borcunu kapatmak/ödemek** *If you pay for it now, I'll square up with you later.*

square with sth *phrasal verb* to match or to agree with something **uymak/uydurmak; bağdaşmak/bağdaş- tırmak** *Her story doesn't quite square with the evidence.*

squarely /ˈskweəli/ *adverb* directly **dosdoğru** *I looked him squarely in the eye.* ○ *The report put the blame squa- rely on the police.*

,**square 'root** *noun* **the square root of 16/64/144, etc** the number you multiply by itself to get 16/64/144, etc **16/64/144'ün karekökü** *The square root of 144 is 12.*

squash¹ /skwɒʃ/ *noun* **1** [SPORT] [U] a sport in which two people hit a small rubber ball against the four walls of a room **duvar tenisi, skuaş** *a game of squash* ○ *a squash court/racket* **2 it's a squash** *UK* used to say that there are too many people or things in a small space **sıkış tıkış, konserve gibi, altalta üstüste, çok kalabalık, mahşeri kalabalık; sıkışıklık, kalabalık** *We mana- ged to get in but it was a squash.* **3** [DRINK] [U] *UK* a sweet drink that tastes like fruit **konsantre meyve suyu** **4** [VEGETABLE] [C, U] a fruit with hard skin, a soft inside, and large seeds, that you cook and eat as a vegetable **kabak**

squash² /skwɒʃ/ *verb* **1** [T] to crush something into a flat shape **ezmek** *I stepped on a spider and squashed it.* **2** [I, T] to push someone or something into a small space **zorla sokmak, tıkıştırmak, sıkıştırmak** [often passive] *The kids were all squashed into the back seat.*

squat¹ /skwɒt/ *verb* [I] **squatting,** *past* **squatted 1** (*also* **squat down**) to bend your legs so that you are sitting with your bottom very close to the ground **çömelmek** *He squatted down beside me.* **2** to live in an empty buil- ding without the owner's permission **izinsiz yerleş- mek, boş bir binada yaşamaya başlamak; işgal etmek**

squat² /skwɒt/ *adjective* short and wide **bodur, tıknaz** *a squat little man*

squat³ /skwɒt/ *noun* [C] a building that people are living in without the owner's permission **virane, sahipsiz bina, yersiz yurtsuzların kaldığı bina**

squatter /ˈskwɒtə*/ *noun* [C] someone who lives in a building without the owner's permission **izinsiz yerle- şen kimse, işgalci**

squawk /skwɔːk/ *verb* [I] If a bird squawks, it makes a loud, unpleasant noise. **acı acı ötmek, ciyaklamak, viyaklamak** ● **squawk** *noun* [C] **acı, inleyen bağırtı**

squeak /skwiːk/ *verb* [I] to make a short, high sound **gıcırdamak, cik ciklemek, kısa ve tiz ses çıkarmak** *His shoes squeaked loudly as he walked.* ● **squeak** *noun* [C] **gıcırdama**

squeaky /ˈskwiːki/ *adjective* **1** making short, high sounds **gıcırtılı 2 squeaky clean** very clean **çok temiz, pırıl pırıl**

squeal /skwiːl/ *verb* [I] to make a loud, high sound, often because of fear or excitement **acı acı bağırmak, fer- yat etmek, ciyaklamak** *She squealed with delight.* ● **squeal** *noun* [C] *squeals of laughter* **haykırış**

squeamish /ˈskwiːmɪʃ/ *adjective* If you are squeamish about something such as blood, you find it very unplea- sant and it makes you feel ill. **midesi tutan, kolay iğrenen, çabuk tiksinen, midesi hemen bulanıve- ren**

ᴏ⁀**squeeze¹** /skwiːz/ *verb* **1** [T] to press something firmly **sıkmak, sıkıştırmak** *She squeezed his hand and said goodbye.* **2 squeeze into/through/past, etc** to move somewhere where there is very little space **sıkışmak, sıkıştırmak** *She squeezed through a narrow gap in the wall.* **3 squeeze a lemon/orange, etc** to press a lemon/ orange, etc to get juice from it **limon/portakal vb. sık- mak, sıkıp suyunu çıkarmak** *freshly squeezed orange juice*

squeeze sth/sb in *phrasal verb* to manage to do some- thing or see someone when you are very busy **bir araya sıkıştırmak; çok meşgulken bile zaman ayırmak** *The doctor will try to squeeze you in this afternoon.*

squeeze² /skwiːz/ *noun* **1** [C] when you press something firmly **sıkma, sıkıştırma** *He gave her hand a little squeeze.* **2 it's a squeeze** used to say that there are too many people or things in a small space **sıkışıklık, izdiham, kalabalık, ana baba günü** *We all got in, but it was a tight squeeze.* **3 a squeeze of lemon/orange, etc** a small amount of juice from a lemon/orange, etc **bir sıkımlık limon/portakal vb.**

squid /skwɪd/ *noun* [C] *plural* **squid** a sea creature with a long body and ten long arms **kalamar, mürekkep balığı**

squiggle /ˈskwɪɡl/ *noun* [C] *informal* a short, curly line **eğri büğrü çizgi** *Her signature just looks like a squiggle.*

squint /skwɪnt/ *verb* [I] to look at something with your eyes partly closed **gözlerini kısarak bakmak** *She was squinting at her computer screen.*

squirm /skwɜːm/ *verb* [I] to twist your body because you are embarrassed, nervous, etc **kıvranmak**

squirrel /ˈskwɪrəl/ ⓊⓈ /ˈskwɜːrəl/ *noun* [C] a small animal with a big, fur tail that climbs trees and eats nuts **sincap**

squirrel

squirt /skwɜːt/ *verb* **1** [I, T] If liquid squirts, it comes out suddenly and with force, and if you squirt liquid, you make it come out suddenly and with force. **fışkırmak, fışkırtmak** *Water squirted out all over the floor.* **2 squirt sb with sth** to hit someone with a liquid **fışkırtmak, fışkırtarak ıslatmak**

Sr (*also UK* **Snr**) *written abbreviation for* senior (= the older of two men in a family with the same name) **ailede aynı ismi taşıyan erkeklerin yaşlı olanı** *Joseph Kennedy, Sr.*

St 1 *written abbreviation for* street (= a road in a town or city that has houses or other buildings) **cadde'nin kısa**

yazılışı *42 Oxford St* **2** *written abbreviation for* saint (= a dead person who has been officially respected by the Christian Church for living their life in a holy way) *aziz sözcüğünün kısa yazılışı St Patrick*

stab¹ /stæb/ *verb* [T] **stabbing**, *past* **stabbed** to push a knife into someone **bıçaklamak, bıçak saplamak** *He was stabbed several times in the chest.*

stab² /stæb/ *noun* [C] **1** the act of pushing a knife into someone **bıçaklama** *He had a deep stab wound in his neck.* **2 a stab of guilt/jealousy/regret, etc** a sudden, unpleasant emotion **ani ve keskin bir duygu, bıçak saplanır gibi bir his; ani suç/kıskançlık/pişmanlık vb. duygusu** *She felt a stab of guilt.* **3 have a stab at sth/doing sth** *informal* to try to do something, or to try an activity that you have not done before **denemek, teşebbüs etmek** *She had a stab at solving the problem.*

stabbing /ˈstæbɪŋ/ *noun* [C] when someone stabs someone **bıçaklama** *Where were you on the night of the stabbing?* ○ *US a stabbing death*

ˈstabbing ˌpain *noun* [C] a sudden, strong pain **ani ve bıçak gibi keskin ağrı/acı**

stability /stəˈbɪləti/ *noun* [U] when something is not likely to change or move **kararlılık, istikrar** *political/financial stability* ➔Opposite **instability.**

stabilize (*also UK* -ise) /ˈsteɪbᵊlaɪz/ *verb* [I, T] If you stabilize something, or if something stabilizes, it stops changing or moving. **istikrara kavuşmak/kavuşturmak; sürekli değişiklik göstermemek** *The economy has finally stabilized.* ● **stabilization** /ˌsteɪbᵊlaɪˈzeɪʃᵊn/ *noun* [U] **istikrar**

stable¹ /ˈsteɪbl/ *adjective* **1** SITUATION not likely to change or end suddenly **değişmez, dengeli, istikrarlı** *a stable relationship* ○ *The doctor said his condition was stable.* **2** OBJECT fixed or safe and not likely to move **sabit, yıkılmaz, sağlam** *Be careful! That chair isn't very stable.* **3** PERSON mentally calm and not easily upset **sakin, kolay etkilenmeyen** ➔Opposite **unstable.**

stable² /ˈsteɪbl/ *noun* [C] a building where horses are kept **at ahırı**

stack¹ /stæk/ *noun* [C] **1** a tidy pile of things **yığın, küme, istif** *a stack of books/CDs* **2 stacks of sth** *informal* a lot of something **yığınla, bir sürü** *There are stacks of studies linking salt to high blood pressure.*

stack² /stæk/ (*also* stack up) *verb* [T] to arrange things in a tidy pile **istif etmek, istiflemek, yığmak, üst üste koymak** *Can you help me stack these chairs?*

stadium /ˈsteɪdiəm/ *noun* [C] a large, open area with seats around it, used for playing and watching sports **stadyum** *a football/baseball stadium*

◦⚬**staff¹** /stɑːf/ *noun* [group] the people who work for an organization **kadro, personel, çalışanlar, elemanlar** *The company has a staff of over 500 employees.* ○ *Please talk to a member of staff.*

staff² /stɑːf/ *verb* [T] to provide workers for an organization **personel sağlamak, eleman bulmak** [often passive] *The charity was staffed by volunteers.*

stag /stæg/ *noun* [C] a male deer **erkek geyik**

◦⚬**stage¹** /steɪdʒ/ *noun* **1** [C] a period of development, or a particular time in a process **evre, aşama, safha** *an early stage in his career* ○ *Our project is in its final stages.* ○ *I'm not prepared to comment at this stage.* **2** [C] the raised area in a theatre where actors perform **sahne** *He's on stage for most of the play.* **3 the stage** performances in theatres **tiyatro dünyası, sahne** *He's written plays for television and the stage.* **4 set the stage for sth** to make something possible or likely to happen **mümkün kılmak, ortam yaratmak/hazırlamak** *The meeting set the stage for future cooperation between the companies.*

stage² /steɪdʒ/ *verb* **1 stage a demonstration/protest, etc** to organize and take part in a public meeting to complain about something **gösteri/protesto gösterisi vb. düzenlemek/yapmak/hazırlamak** **2 stage a concert/show, etc** to organize and produce a performance of music or a play, etc **konser/gösteri vb. düzenlemek/sahneye koymak** *They staged a free concert in Central Park.*

stagger /ˈstæɡəʳ/ *verb* **1** [I] to walk as if you might fall **sanki düşecekmiş gibi yürümek, sendelemek, sendeleyerek yürümek, yalpalamak** *He staggered drunkenly towards the door.* **2** [T] to arrange events so that they do not happen at the same time **farklı zamanlarda düzenlemek; ayrı ayrı zamanlarda yapmak** *We stagger our lunch breaks at work.*

staggered /ˈstæɡəd/ *adjective* [never before noun] very shocked or surprised **şaşırmış, şaşkınlığa düşmüş, afallamış; sersemlemiş; şok olmuş** *I was staggered at the prices.*

staggering /ˈstæɡərɪŋ/ *adjective* very shocking and surprising **şaşırtan, sersemleten, afallatan, şok eden; şaşkınlık yaratan** *He earns a staggering amount of money.*

stagnant /ˈstæɡnənt/ *adjective* **1** Stagnant water or air does not flow and becomes dirty and smells unpleasant. **akmaz, durgun, dingin, sakin** *a stagnant pond* **2** A stagnant economy, society, or organization does not develop or grow. **durgun, hareketsiz, sönük**

stagnate /stæɡˈneɪt/ ⓤ /ˈstæɡneɪt/ *verb* [I] to stay the same and not grow or develop **durgunlaşmak, hareketsizleşmek** *He expects the economy to stagnate and unemployment to rise.* ● **stagnation** /stæɡˈneɪʃᵊn/ *noun* [U] **durgunluk**

ˈstag ˌnight *noun* [C] a night when a group of men go out just before one of them gets married **bekârlığa veda gecesi** ➔Compare **hen night.**

staid /steɪd/ *adjective* serious and old-fashioned **ciddî ve eski kafalı, ağır başlı, muhafazakâr** *a staid, middle-aged man*

stain¹ /steɪn/ *noun* **1** [C] a dirty mark on something that is difficult to remove **leke** *a blood/grass stain* ○ *a stain on the carpet* **2** [C, U] a dark liquid that you put on wood to make it darker **astar boya** *wood stain*

stain² /steɪn/ *verb* **1** [I, T] to leave a dirty mark on something which is difficult to remove, or to become dirty in this way **lekelemek, leke yapmak** *That wine I spilt has stained my shirt.* **2** [T] to paint a wooden surface with a thin paint in order to change its colour **astar**

S

boya yapmak *She stained the bookcase to match the desk.*

,stained 'glass *noun* [U] coloured glass that is used to make pictures in windows **vitray** *a stained-glass window*

stainless steel /ˌsteɪnləsˈstiːl/ *noun* [U] a type of steel (= strong metal) that is not damaged by water **paslanmaz çelik**

stair /steə^r/ *noun* [C] one of the steps in a set of steps **basamak, merdiven basamağı**

staircase /ˈsteəkeɪs/ *noun* [C] a set of stairs and the structure around them **merdiven** *a spiral staircase*

stairs .... İLE BİRLİKTE KULLANILAN KELİMELER

climb/fall down/go down/go up the stairs ● the bottom of/foot of the stairs ● the head of/top of the stairs ● on the stairs ● a flight of stairs

o➤**stairs** /steəz/ *noun* [plural] a set of steps from one level in a building to another **merdiven** *to climb the stairs* ○ *a flight* (= set) *of stairs*

stairway /ˈsteəweɪ/ *noun* [C] a set of stairs and the structure around them **merdiven**

stake¹ /steɪk/ *noun* 1 be at stake If something is at stake, it is in a situation where it might be lost or damaged. **tehlikede, riske girmiş, riskte** *We have to act quickly - people's lives are at stake.* 2 [C] a part of a business that you own, or an amount of money that you have invested in a business **hisse, pay** *He has a 30 percent stake in the company.* 3 [C] a strong stick with a pointed end that you push into the ground **kazık** *a wooden stake*

stake² /steɪk/ *verb* stake a/your claim to say that you want something and that you should have it **hak iddia etmek, sahip çıkmak**
stake sth on sth *phrasal verb* to risk something on the result of a competition or situation **tehlikeye atmak, riske sokmak; yarışmada ortaya para koymak; bahis oynamak** *He has staked his reputation on the film's success.*
stake sth out *phrasal verb* to watch a place in order to catch criminals or to see a famous person **bir suçluyu yakalamak/meşhur birini görmek için bir yeri gözetlemek** *The police are staking out the house where the terrorists are hiding.*

stakes /steɪks/ *noun* [plural] money or other advantages that you may get or lose in a competition or situation **bahis/yarışmada elde edilen/kaybedilen para ve çıkarlar** *People get very competitive because the stakes are so high.*

stale /steɪl/ *adjective* 1 old and not fresh **bayat, eskimiş, bayatlamış** *stale bread* ○ *Cake goes stale quickly if it's not covered.* 2 boring or bored, and not producing or feeling excitement or enthusiasm like before **sıkıcı, sıkılmış, yorgun, bitkin, tükenmiş** *I'd been too long in the same job and was getting stale.*

stalemate /ˈsteɪlmeɪt/ *noun* [C, U] a situation in which neither side in an argument can win **açmaz, çıkmaz, müşkül durum** *The talks ended in a stalemate.*

stalk¹ /stɔːk/ *verb* 1 [T] to follow a person or animal closely and secretly, often to try to catch or attack them **peşine düşmek, gizli gizli izlemek; sinsice yaklaşmak** *She claimed that the man had been stalking her for a month.* 2 stalk out/off, etc to walk in an angry or proud way **kasıla kasıla yürümek; azametle/çalım satarak yürümek** *She stalked out of the restaurant.*

stalk² /stɔːk/ *noun* [C] the main stem of a plant **sap**

stalker /ˈstɔːkə^r/ *noun* [C] someone who follows a person or animal closely and secretly, often to try to catch or attack them **takip eden kimse, gizlice izleyen kimse**

stall¹ /stɔːl/ *noun* [C]
1 mainly UK a small

stall

shop with an open front or a table from which goods are sold **satıcı sergisi, tezgâh, tabla; seyyar satıcı tablası** *a market stall* 2 US a small area in a room for washing or using the toilet **oda köşesindeki lavabo tuvalet** *a shower stall*

stall² /stɔːl/ *verb* 1 [ENGINE] [I, T] If an engine stalls, or if you stall it, it stops working suddenly. **(motor) aniden durmak/durdurmak** *The car stalled when I stopped at the traffic lights.* 2 [STOP] [I] to stop making progress **oyalamak, savsaklamak, atlatmak; ilerlemesine engel olmak** *The peace talks have stalled over the issue of nuclear weapons.* 3 [MORE TIME] [T] to intentionally make someone wait or make something happen later so that you have more time **kasden bekletmek/savsaklamak/atlatmak** *She wanted an answer immediately, but I managed to stall her.*

stallion /ˈstæljən/ *noun* [C] an adult male horse **yetişkin erkek at; aygır**

the stalls /stɔːlz/ *UK* (*US* orchestra) *noun* [plural] the seats on the main floor near the front of a theatre or cinema **sinema ve tiyatrodaki ön koltuklar** *a seat in the stalls*

stalwart /ˈstɔːlwət/ *noun* [C] someone who supports an organization, team, etc in a very loyal way **sadık ve çalışkan; güvenilir, sağlam** ● **stalwart** *adjective* **taraftar olan**

stamina .... İLE BİRLİKTE KULLANILAN KELİMELER

have stamina ● build up/improve/increase stamina ● mental/physical stamina ● stamina for sth ● a test of stamina

stamina /ˈstæmɪnə/ *noun* [U] the physical or mental energy that allows you to do something for a long time **dayanma gücü, dayanıklılık, tahammül** *Marathon runners need a lot of stamina.*

stammer /ˈstæmə^r/ *verb* [I] to pause a lot and repeat sounds because of a speech problem or because you are nervous **kekelemek, kekeleyerek konuşmak** *He blushed and began to stammer.* ● **stammer** *noun* [C] *He has a stammer.* **kekeme olma durumu**

o➤**stamp¹** /stæmp/ *noun* [C] 1 (*also* postage stamp) a small, official piece of paper that you buy and stick onto a letter or parcel before you post it **pul, posta pulu** 2 a tool for putting a special ink mark on something, or the mark made by it **damga, kaşe, ıstampa, mühür** *a stamp in a passport* 3 **stamp of approval** official, public approval **onaylama/kabul damgası/mührü** *The president has put his stamp of approval on the proposal.*

stamp² /stæmp/ *verb* 1 [T] to make a mark on something with a tool that you put ink on and press down **damgalamak, mühürlemek** *She stamped the date on the invoice.* 2 [I, T] to put your foot down on the ground hard and quickly, often to show anger **tepinmek, ayaklarını hızla yere vurmak** *"No!" she shouted, stamping her foot.* ➲See also: rubber-stamp.
stamp sth out *phrasal verb* to get rid of something that is wrong or harmful **yok etmek, kökünü kurutmak, son vermek** *a campaign to stamp out racism*

stampede /stæm'pi:d/ *noun* [C] when a large group of animals or people suddenly move in an uncontrolled way, often in the same direction **ürküp kaçma, panik, bozgun; panik halinde kaçışma** *Gunfire caused a stampede in the marketplace.* • **stampede** *verb* [I]

stance ...... İLE BİRLİKTE KULLANILAN KELİMELER

take a stance • change your stance • a hardline/ tough stance • a stance against sb/sth • sb's stance on sth

stance /stæns/ *noun* [C] **1** an opinion or belief about something, especially if you say it in public **tutum, davranış** [usually singular] *What's their stance on nuclear energy?* ○ *They are taking a very tough stance against drugs.* **2** *formal* the way that someone stands **duruş, duruş biçimi** [usually singular] *an awkward stance*

o─**stand**[1] /stænd/ *verb past* **stood 1** [ON FEET] [I] to be in a vertical position on your feet **ayakta durmak, dikilmek** *We'd been standing for hours.* **2** [RISE] [I] (*also* **stand up**) to rise to a vertical position on your feet from sitting or lying down **ayağa kalkmak, dikilmek** *I get dizzy if I stand up too quickly.* ○ *Please stand when the bride arrives.* ↻Orta kısımdaki renkli sayfalarına bakınız. **3 stand in line** *US* (*UK* queue) to wait for something as part of a line of people **sırada durmak/beklemek, sıraya girmek** *We stood in line all afternoon.* **4 stand (sth) in/against/by, etc sth** to be in or to put something in a particular place or position **bir yerde durmak/olmak; dik koymak/ dayamak/yaslamak** *His walking stick stood by the door.* ○ *You'll have to stand the sofa on its end to get it through the door.* **5 can't stand sb/sth** *informal* to hate someone or something **tahammül edememek, dayanamamak; nefret etmek** *I can't stand him.* ○ [+ doing sth] *She can't stand doing housework.* **6** [ACCEPT] [T] to be able to accept or deal with a difficult situation **dayanmak, kabul etmek, dayanmak** *She couldn't stand the pressures of the job.* **7 stand at sth** to be at a particular level, amount, height, etc **belli bir düzeyde/miktarda/yükseklikte vb. durmak/olmak** *Inflation currently stands at 3 percent.* **8 where you stand on sth** what your opinion is about something **bir meselede/ konuda nerede olduğu; fikrinin ne olduğu; duruşunu gösterme** *We asked the senator where she stood on gun control.* **9 where you stand (with sb)** what someone thinks about you, how they expect you to behave, and how they are likely to behave **tutum, tavır, nerede olduğu; hangi konumda olduğu; neyin/kimin tarafında/yanında olduğu** *She said she will never leave her husband, so now at least I know where I stand.* **10** [OFFER] [I] If an offer still stands, it still exists. **geçerli olmak; devam ediyor olmak, yürürlükte olmak; muteber olmak** *You're welcome to visit any time - my invitation still stands.* **11 as it stands** something is now, without changes in it **olduğu gibi, her zaman olduğu şekliyle** *The law as it stands is very unclear.* **12 stand trial** If someone stands trial, they appear in a law court where people decide if they are guilty of a crime. **duruşmaya çıkmak, mahkemeye çıkmak, yargılanmak** *to stand trial for murder* **13 stand to gain/lose sth** to be in a situation where you can get/lose money or an advantage **bir şeyi kazanma/kaybetme konumunda olmak; ...mak/ mek/mamak/memek olasılığı olmak** *He stands to gain a fortune if the company is sold.* **14** [ELECTION] [I] *UK* (*US* run) to compete in an election for an official position **aday olmak, katılmak** *to stand for office* ↻See also: stand your ground[1], not have a leg to stand on, it stands to reason[1], stand on your own two feet (foot[1]), stand sb in good stead.

stand about/around *phrasal verb* to spend time standing somewhere and doing very little **oyalanmak, bek-**

lemek, zaman geçirmek *They stood around waiting for the store to open.*

stand aside *phrasal verb* to leave a job or position so that someone else can do it instead **kenara çekilmek; hakkından ferâgat etmek**

stand back *phrasal verb* to move a short distance away from something or someone **geri çekilmek, geride durmak** *Stand back while I light the fire.*

stand by *phrasal verb* **1** to be ready to do something or to help someone **hazır beklemek; bekleme listesinde olmak** *Doctors were standing by to treat the injured passengers.* **2** to do nothing to prevent something unpleasant from happening **seyirci kalmak; kılını bile kıpırdatmamak, aldırış etmemek, bir şeyler yapmamak; kayıtsız kalmamak** *We can't stand by while millions of people starve.*

stand by sb *phrasal verb* to continue to support someone when they are in a difficult situation **desteklemeye devam etmek, desteğini sürdürmek; arka çıkmaya devam etmek** *She stood by him throughout his troubled career.*

stand by sth *phrasal verb* If you stand by an agreement, decision, etc, you do not change it. **desteklemek, arkasında durmak; sadık/bağlı kalmak** *The government stood by its promise to improve education.*

stand down *phrasal verb UK* to leave a job or position so that someone else can do it instead **çekilmek, istifa etmek; ...1/i bırakmak** *He stood down as party leader.*

stand for sth *phrasal verb* **1** If a letter stands for a word, it is used to represent it. **...1/i temsil etmek; demek olmak, anlamına gelmek; ...ın/in kısa biçimi olmak** *UFO stands for 'unidentified flying object'.* **2** If a group of people stand for a set of ideas, they support those ideas. **temsil etmek, savunmak, desteklemek, yansıtmak** *The party stands for low taxes and individual freedom.* **3 not stand for sth** If you will not stand for something, you will not accept a situation or someone's behaviour. *He can't speak to me like that - I won't stand for it!*

stand in *phrasal verb* to do something that someone else was going to do because they cannot be there **yerini almak, yerine geçmek; görevini üstlenmek, vekâlet etmek** *She stood in for me when I was sick.*

stand out *phrasal verb* **1** to be very easy to see or notice **hemen göze çarpmak, gözden kaçmamak** *The bright blue letters really stand out on the page.* **2** to be better than other similar things or people **temayüz etmek, sivrilmek, göze çarpmak** *His application stood out from all the rest.* ↻See also: stick/stand out like a sore thumb[1].

stand up *phrasal verb* If an idea or some information stands up, it is proved to be correct. **doğru/haklı çıkmak; doğru kabul edilmek, yeterli bulunmak**

stand sb up *phrasal verb* to fail to meet someone when you said you would **atlatmak, randevuya gitmemek, ekmek** *He's stood me up twice now.*

stand up for sth/sb *phrasal verb* to support an idea or a person who is being criticized **desteklemek, savunmak, müdafaa etmek, tarafını tutmak** [often reflexive] *Never be afraid to stand up for yourself.*

stand[2] /stænd/ *noun* **1** [SHOP] [C] a small shop with an open front or a table from which goods are sold **tezgâh, sergi, tabla, seyyar satıcı tezgâhı** *a hot dog stand* ○ *Visit our stand at the trade fair.* **2** [SPORT] [C] *UK* (*US* stands) a structure in a sports ground where people can stand or sit to watch an event **tribün 3** [FURNITURE] [C] a piece of furniture for holding things **altlık, destek, sehpa, askı** *a music/hat stand* **4 the (witness) stand** (*UK also* the dock) the place in a law court where people sit or stand when they are being asked questions **tanık dinleme yeri** *The judge asked her to take the stand* (= go into the witness stand). **5** [OPINION] [C] an opinion or belief about something, especially if you say it in public **genel görüş/fikir/düşünce/inanç** [usually singular] *What's the President's **stand on gun control?*** **6 take a stand** to express your opinion about something publicly **açıkça fiirlerini belirtmek; tavır koymak** *He refuses to take a stand on this issue.* **7 make a stand** to publicly defend something or stop something from happening **ayak diremek, kafa tutmak, ulu orta desteklemek/engellemek**

---

standard ...... İLE BİRLİKTE KULLANILAN KELİMELER

come up to standard ● **below/(not) up to** standard ● **set** standards ● **comply with/conform to/meet** standards ● **exacting/high/low/rigorous** standards ● **standards of** sth

---

○•**standard**[1] /ˈstændəd/ *noun* [C] **1** a level of quality, especially a level that is acceptable **standart, kriter; ölçüt, kıstas** *a **high standard** of service* ○ *low **safety standards*** ○ *His work was **below standard*** (= not acceptable). ○ *She sets very **high standards** for herself.* **2** a level of behaviour, especially a level that is acceptable **standart, ilke, prensip, değer yargısı** [usually plural] *high moral standards* ⊃See also: **double standard**.

standard[2] /ˈstændəd/ *adjective* usual and not special **normal, olağan, standart, genel** *standard procedure/practice*

standardize (*also* UK **-ise**) /ˈstændədaız/ *verb* [T] to change things so that they are all the same **standart hâle getirmek, standartlaştırmak** *I wish someone would standardize clothing sizes.* ● **standardization** /ˌstændədaɪˈzeɪʃⁿn/ *noun* [U] *the standardization of computer terms* **standard hale getirme**

standard of ˈliving *noun* [C] *plural* **standards of living** how much money and comfort someone has **yaşam standardı; yaşam düzeyi** *a high standard of living*

standby /ˈstændbaɪ/ *noun* [C] *plural* **standbys 1** someone or something extra that is ready to be used if needed **yedek, yedekte olan kimse/nesne; stok** *We kept our old TV as a standby in case the new one broke.* **2 be on standby** to be ready to do something or to be used if needed **yedekte olmak, yedek olmak** *Police were on standby in case there was any trouble after the game.*

stand-in /ˈstændɪn/ *noun* [C] someone who does what another person was going to do because the other person cannot be there **vekâlet, yerini alma, yerine geçme; vekil, yardımcı**

standing[1] /ˈstændɪŋ/ *noun* [U] Your standing is the opinion that other people have of you. **saygınlık, itibar, şöhret, fikir, düşünce** *Last week's speech has improved the Prime Minister's standing in the polls.*

standing[2] /ˈstændɪŋ/ *adjective* [always before noun] **1** permanent and not only created when necessary **daimî, kalıcı, sürekli, değişmeyen** *a standing committee* ○ *He has a standing invitation to stay at our house.* **2 a standing joke** a situation that a group of people often make jokes about **beylik şaka, şaka konusu, fıkra konusu; genel alay konusu; ne zaman anılsa alaya alınan konu** *The poor quality of his work has become a standing joke in the office.* ⊃See also: **long-standing**.

standing ˈorder *noun* [C] UK an instruction to a bank to pay someone a fixed amount of money at regular times from your account **düzenli ödeme emri; otomatik virman talimâtı**

standing oˈvation *noun* [C] when people stand while clapping to show that they have enjoyed a performance very much **ayakta alkış** *She got a standing ovation for her speech.*

stand-off UK (US **standoff**) /ˈstændɒf/ *noun* [C] when an argument or fight stops for a period of time because no

one can win or get an advantage **tartışmaya/savaşa ara verme; geçici durdurma**

standpoint /ˈstændpɔɪnt/ *noun* [C] a particular way of thinking about a situation or problem **bakış açısı, görüş, değerlendirmek, görüş noktası** *to look at something from a political/religious standpoint*

standstill /ˈstændstɪl/ *noun* [no plural] a situation in which all movement or activity has stopped **durma, duraklama, sekte; durağanlık** *The traffic came to a standstill in the thick fog.*

stand-up /ˈstændʌp/ *adjective* [always before noun] A stand-up comedian is someone who stands in front of a group of people and tells jokes as a performance. **stand-up, ayakta, seyirci önünde (komedi, güldürü)** *stand-up comedy*

stank /stæŋk/ *past tense of* stink **kötü kokmak' fiilinin geçmiş zaman hâli**

staple[1] /ˈsteɪpl/ *adjective* [always before noun] A staple food, product, etc is basic and very important. **ana, temel, asıl, esas** *a staple diet of rice and fish*

staple[2] /ˈsteɪpl/ *noun* [C] a small piece of wire that you put through pieces of paper to join them together **tel raptiye, zımba teli** ● **staple** *verb* [T] to join pieces of paper together with staples **zımbalamak, zımba ile tutturmak**

stapler /ˈsteɪpləʳ/ *noun* [C] a piece of equipment used for putting staples through paper **tel zımba**

---

star ...... İLE BİRLİKTE KULLANILAN KELİMELER

become/make sb a star ● **a big** star ● **a pop** star

---

star

○•**star**[1] /stɑːʳ/ *noun* [C] **1** SKY a ball of burning gases that you see as a small point of light in the sky at night **yıldız 2** FAMOUS PERSON a famous singer, actor, sports person, etc **meşhur şarkıcı/aktör/sporcu vb.** *a pop star* **3** BEST PERSON someone in a group of people who is the best at doing something **grubun en iyisi/yıldızı** *Baggio is one of our star players.* **4** SHAPE a shape that has five or more points **yıldız, yıldız şekli** ⊃See picture at shape. **5 two-star/three-star, etc** used to show how good a restaurant or hotel is **iki/üç vs. yıldızlı** *a five-star hotel* **6 sb's stars/the stars** UK informal something you read that tells you what will happen to you based on the position of the stars in the sky **yıldızı/yıldız falı, yıldızları** *My stars said it would be a good month for romance.* ⊃See also: **co-star, film star, rock star**.

star[2] /stɑːʳ/ *verb* [I, T] **starring,** *past* **starred** If a film, play, etc stars someone, or if someone stars in a film, play, etc, they are the main person in it. **yıldız yapmak, yıldızlaşmak, yıldızı parlamak** *a film starring Meg Ryan*

○ Tom Hanks **starred in** 'Sleepless in Seattle'. ⊃See also: co-star.

starboard /ˈstɑːbəd/ noun [U] the right side of a ship or aircraft **sancak, sağ tarafı**

starch /stɑːtʃ/ noun **1** [C, U] a substance in foods such as rice, bread, and potatoes **nişasta 2** [U] a substance used to make cloth stiff **kola** ● **starchy** adjective containing a lot of starch **nişastalı**

stardom /ˈstɑːdəm/ noun [U] when someone is very famous for acting, singing, etc **şöhret, yıldız, yıldızlık**

stare /steəʳ/ verb [I] to look at someone or something for a long time and not move your eyes **dik dik bakmak, gözünü dikip bakmak, bakakalmak** Sean was staring at me. ● **stare** noun [C] **gözlerini dikerek bakma**

stark¹ /stɑːk/ adjective **1** unpleasantly clear and obvious **çıplak, sade, yalın, belirgin, apaçık** His death is a stark warning to other people about the dangers of drugs. **2** stark **difference/contrast** a total difference **tamamen farklı/tezat** Jerry is very lazy, in stark contrast to his sister who works very hard. **3** with a very plain and simple appearance and not very attractive **açık, yalın, çıplak, süssüz, sade** a stark, snowy landscape ● **starkly** adverb **yalın bir şekilde**

stark² /stɑːk/ adverb **stark naked** wearing no clothes **çırılçıplak, anadan doğma**

starry /ˈstɑːri/ adjective A starry sky or night is one in which you can see a lot of stars. **yıldızlı, yıldızlarla kaplı, yıldız dolu**

'star ˌsign UK (US sign) noun [C] one of the twelve signs that are based on star positions when you are born, which some people believe shows what type of person you are **yıldız burçları** "What star sign are you?" "I'm Capricorn."

∘⌐**start¹** /stɑːt/ verb **1** [BEGIN DOING] [I, T] to begin doing something **başlamak** [+ doing sth] He started smoking when he was eighteen. ○ [+ to do sth] Maria started to laugh. ○ We start work at nine o'clock. **2** [BEGIN HAPPENING] [I, T] to begin to happen or to make something begin to happen **başlamak, başlatmak** The programme starts at seven o'clock. ○ Police believe the fire started in the kitchen. **3** [BUSINESS] [I, T] (also start up) If a business, organization, etc starts, it begins to exist, and if you start it, you make it begin to exist. **kurmak, açmak, başlamak, başlatmak, faaliyete başlamak** She started her own computer business. ○ A lot of new restaurants have started up in the area. **4** [CAR] [I, T] (also start up) If a car or engine starts, it begins to work, and if you start it, you make it begin to work. **(araç) çalış(tır)mak, başla(t)mak** The car won't start. ○ Start up the engine. **5** to start with a [SITUATION] used to talk about what a situation was like at the beginning before it changed **başlangıçta, başta, ilk başta;** ...ile başlamak I was happy at school to start with, but later I hated it. **b** [LIST] used before saying the first thing in a list of things **ilk olarak, ilk başta, başlangıçta** To start with, we need better computers. Then we need more training. **6** [MOVE SUDDENLY] [I] to move suddenly because you are frightened or surprised **ürkmek, irkilmek, ürküp sıçramak** ⊃See also: set/start the **ball** rolling, get/start off on the wrong **foot¹**.

start (sth) off phrasal verb to begin by doing something, or to make something begin by doing something **ile başlamak/başlatmak; söze ...ile başlamak** She started off the meeting with the monthly sales report.

start on sth phrasal verb to begin doing something **başlamak; bir şeyi yapmaya koyulmak** Have you started on your homework yet?

start out phrasal verb to begin your life or the part of your life when you work, in a particular way **hayata vb. başlamak, yola çıkmak** My dad started out as a sales assistant in a shop.

start over phrasal verb US to begin something again **yeniden başlamak, tekrar başlamak** If you make a mistake, you'll have to start over.

start .... İLE BİRLİKTE KULLANILAN KELİMELER

at the start ● from the start ● the start of sth

∘⌐**start²** /stɑːt/ noun **1** [BEGINNING] [C] the beginning of something **başlama** [usually singular] Our teacher checks who is in class at the start of each day. ○ Ivan has been involved in the project from the start. ○ The meeting got off to a bad start (= began badly). **2** make a start mainly UK to begin doing something **bir başlangıç yapmak** I'll make a start on the washing-up. **3** for a start UK used when you are giving the first in a list of reasons or things **öncelikle, ilk olarak** I won't be going - I've got too much homework for a start. **4** [ADVANTAGE] [C] an advantage that you have over someone else when you begin something **üstünlük, avantaj** [usually singular] I'm grateful for the start I had in life. **5** the start the place where a race begins **başlangıç noktası; yarış başlama çizgisi 6** [SUDDEN MOVEMENT] [no plural] a sudden movement that you make because you are frightened or surprised **ürkme, irkilme** Kate sat up with a start. ⊃See also: false start.

starter /ˈstɑːtəʳ/ noun **1** [C] UK (US appetizer) something that you eat as the first part of a meal **başlangıç, başlangıç yemeği 2** [C] US in sports, a member of a team who is involved in a competition from the beginning **yarışmanın başından beri yarışmalarda olan takım** At only 20, he's the team's youngest starter. **3** for starters informal used to say that something is the first in a list of things **ilk baştakiler; listenin en üstündekiler** Try this exercise for starters. ⊃See also: non-starter.

starting-point /ˈstɑːtɪŋpɔɪnt/ noun [C] an idea, subject, etc that you use to begin a discussion or process **başlangıç noktası**

startle /ˈstɑːtl/ verb [T] to suddenly surprise or frighten someone **korkutmak, ürkütmek, aklını başından almak** The sound startled me. ● **startled** adjective a startled expression **irkilmiş**

startling /ˈstɑːtlɪŋ/ adjective making you feel very surprised **şaşırtıcı, ürkütücü, hayrete düşürücü** startling news

start-up /ˈstɑːtʌp/ adjective [always before noun] relating to starting a business **iş kurma ile ilgili** start-up costs

starve /stɑːv/ verb [I, T] to become ill or die because you do not have enough food, or to make someone ill or die because they do not have enough food **açlık çekmek, açlıktan ölmek** Many people have starved to death in parts of Africa. ● **starvation** /stɑːˈveɪʃən/ noun [U] Children were dying of starvation. **açlık**

starved /stɑːvd/ adjective **1** be starved of sth UK (US starved for sth) to not have enough of something that you need very much **hasret kalmak, hasretini/özlemini çekmek; yoksun kalmak** a child starved of love **2** mainly US informal very hungry **aç, acıkmış**

starving /ˈstɑːvɪŋ/ adjective **1** dying because there is not enough food **açlıktan ölen** starving people **2** informal very hungry **açlık çeken, acıkmış** I'm absolutely starving.

stash¹ /stæʃ/ (also stash away) verb [T] informal to keep a lot of something in a safe, secret place **gizlemek, saklamak** His money was stashed away in a cupboard.

stash² /stæʃ/ noun [C] informal a lot of something that you keep in a safe, secret place **saklanan/gizlenen şeyler** He had a stash of whisky under the bed.

∘⌐**state¹** /steɪt/ noun **1** [CONDITION] [C] the condition that something or someone is in **durum, vaziyet, hâl** the state of the economy ○ The building is in a terrible state.

2 in/into a state *informal* very upset or nervous **sinirli, endişeli, canı sıkkın** *Ben was in a real state before the exam.* **3** [PART OF COUNTRY] [C] (*also* **State**) one of the parts that some countries such as the US are divided into **eyalet** *Washington State* ○ *Alaska is the largest state in the US.* **4** [COUNTRY] [C] a country **devlet, ülke** *a union of European states* **5 the state** the government of a country **hükümet, devlet** *financial help from the state* **6 state visit/occasion, etc** an important visit/occasion, etc involving the leader of a government **devlet ziyareti, resmî ziyaret; devletler arası görüşmeler/ilişkiler 7 the States** the United States of America **Amerika Birleşik Devletleri** ⊃See also: **police state, welfare state.**

state² /steɪt/ *verb* [T] to officially say or write something (resmî olarak) **söylemek, bildirmek, ifade etmek, açıklamak, belirtmek** [+ (that)] *Two medical reports stated that he was mentally ill.*

stately /'steɪtli/ *adjective* formal and slow **resmî ve yavaş** *a stately procession through the streets*

stately 'home *noun* [C] a big, old house in the countryside that people pay to visit in Britain **malikâne, köşk, konak**

▨▨▨ **statement** ...... İLE BİRLİKTE KULLANILAN KELİMELER

issue/make/prepare/release a statement • a false/joint/public/sworn statement • a statement about/on sth

o-**statement** /'steɪtmənt/ *noun* [C] **1** something that someone says or writes officially **ifade, beyan, söz** *The pop star is expected to make a statement about his involvement with drugs.* **2** (*also* bank statement) a piece of paper that shows how much money you have put into your bank account and how much you have taken out **hesap cüzdanı, hesap özeti**

state of a'ffairs *noun* [no plural] a situation **genel durum** *a sad state of affairs*

state of 'mind *noun* [C] *plural* **states of mind** how you are feeling at a particular time **ruh hâli, ruhsal durum** *to be in a positive state of mind*

state-of-the-art /ˌsteɪtəvðiˈɑːt/ *adjective* using the newest ideas, designs, and materials **yeni fikir/tasarı ve malzemeleri kullanan** *a computer system that uses state-of-the-art technology*

state 'school *UK* (*US* public school) *noun* [C] a school that is free to go to because the government provides the money for it **devlet okulu**

statesman /'steɪtsmən/ *noun* [C] *plural* **statesmen** an important politician, especially one who people respect **devlet adamı**

static¹ /'stætɪk/ *adjective* not moving or changing **durgun, durağan, hareketsiz, statik** *The number of students on the course has remained static.*

static² /'stætɪk/ *noun* [U] **1** (*also* ˌstatic elec'tricity) electricity that you get when two surfaces rub together **statik, akım hâlinde olmayan, iki yüzeyin birbirine sürtünmesiyle oluşan elektrik 2** noise on a radio or television that is caused by electricity in the air **parazit (radyo/televizyon)**

o-**station¹** /'steɪʃᵊn/ *noun* [C] **1** [TRAINS] a building where trains stop so that you can get on or off them **istasyon** *Dad met me at the station.* **2 bus station** (*also* UK coach station) a building where a bus starts or ends its journey **otobüs terminali, otogar 3** [SERVICE] a building where a particular service is based **istasyon, benzinlik** *UK a petrol station/ US a gas station* **4** [RADIO/TV] a company that broadcasts television or radio programmes **TV/radyo yayın istasyonu** *a classical music station* ⊃See

also: filling station, fire station, police station, polling station, power station, service station.

station² /'steɪʃᵊn/ *verb* **be stationed at/in, etc** If someone such as a soldier is stationed somewhere, they are sent there to work for a period of time. **görevlendirilmek; yerleştirilmek; atanmak** *US soldiers stationed in Germany*

stationary /'steɪʃᵊnᵊri/ *adjective* not moving **sabit, hareketsiz** *stationary cars*

stationer's /'steɪʃənəz/ *noun* [C] *UK* a shop where you can buy pens, paper, and other things for writing **kırtasiye**

stationery /'steɪʃᵊnᵊri/ *noun* [U] things that you use for writing, such as pens and paper **kırtasiye malzemesi**

'station ˌwagon *US* (*UK* estate car) *noun* [C] a big car with a large space for bags behind the back seat **arkası yüksek ve geniş araç; büyük araç**

▨▨▨ **statistic** ...... İLE BİRLİKTE KULLANILAN KELİMELER

collect/gather statistics • statistics confirm/indicate/reveal/show sth • according to statistics • statistics on sth

statistic /stəˈtɪstɪk/ *noun* [C] a fact in the form of a number that shows information about something **istatistik** [usually plural] *Statistics show that skin cancer is becoming more common.* • **statistical** *adjective* relating to statistics **istatistikle ilgili** *statistical evidence* • **statistically** *adverb* **istatistiki olarak**

statistics /stəˈtɪstɪks/ *noun* [U] the subject that involves collecting and studying numbers to show information about something **istatistik, istatistik bilimi**

statue /'stætʃuː/ *noun* [C] a model that looks like a person or animal, usually made from stone or metal **heykel**

stature /'stætʃər/ *noun* [U] *formal* **1** the importance that someone has because of their work **önem, kişilik, şöhret, nam, ün** *a scientist of international stature* **2** your height **boy, boy hos, endam** *a man of small stature*

status /'steɪtəs/ *noun* [U] **1** the position that you have in relation to other people because of your job or social position **sosyal mevki, statü** *The pay and status of nurses has improved.* **2** the legal position of someone or something **resmî mevkî, konum; yasal konum** *What's your marital status* (= are you married or not)?

the status quo /ˌsteɪtəsˈkwəʊ/ *noun* *formal* the situation that exists now, without any changes **yürürlükteki/süregelen durum, statüko** *They only want to maintain the status quo.*

'status ˌsymbol *noun* [C] something that someone owns that shows they have a high position in society **sosyal mevkî sembolü**

statute /'stætʃuːt/ *noun* [C] *formal* a law or rule **yasa, kanun, nizam, tüzük**

statutory /'stætjətᵊri/ *adjective formal* decided or controlled by law **yasal, kanunî** *a statutory minimum wage*

staunch /stɔːnʃ/ *adjective* [always before noun] very loyal in your support for someone or your belief in something **sadık, vefalı, bağlı** *a staunch supporter of the Communist party*

stave /steɪv/ *verb*
stave sth off *phrasal verb* to stop something bad from happening now although it may happen later **durdurmak, önlemek, önüne geçmek** *He had a bar of chocolate to stave off his hunger.*

o-**stay¹** /steɪ/ *verb* **1** [NOT LEAVE] [I] to continue to be in a place, job, etc and not leave **kalmak** *The weather was* *bad so we stayed at home.* ○ *Do you want to stay in teaching?* **2** [IN A STATE] [T] to continue to be in a particular state kalmak *The supermarket stays open late.* ○ *I was tired and couldn't stay awake.* **3** [VISIT] [I, T] to spend a short period of time in a place geçirmek, kalmak, harcamak *We stayed in a hotel.* ○ *We're going to stay with my grandmother.* **4 stay put** *informal* to continue to be in the same place kalmaya devam etmek; hâlâ aynı yerde kalmak *He told me to stay put while he fetched the car.*

stay
Unutmayın! Stay fiilinin ardından isim kullanılmaz. Stay a place yanlış kullanımdır. Stay at/in a place şeklinde kullanılmalıdır.: ~~We stayed the Royal Hotel in Lampton.~~ Yanlış cümle örneği
We stayed at the Royal Hotel in Lampton.

stay behind *phrasal verb* to not leave a place when other people leave geride kalmak *I stayed behind after class to speak to the teacher.*
stay in *phrasal verb* to stay in your home evde kalmak, dışarı çıkmamak *Let's stay in tonight and watch a video.*
stay on *phrasal verb* to continue to be in a place, job, or school after other people have left ...da/de kalmak *I stayed on an extra two years at school.*
stay out *phrasal verb* to not go home at night, or to go home late eve gelmemek, eve geç gelmek; geç vakte kadar dışarıda kalmak *He stayed out all night.*
stay out of sth *phrasal verb* to not become involved in an argument or discussion dışında kalmak, dahil olmamak, bulaşmamak, katılmamak *It's better to stay out of their arguments.*
stay up *phrasal verb* to go to bed later than usual geç vakitte yatmak [+ to do sth] *She stayed up to watch a film.*

stay² /steɪ/ *noun* [C] a period of time that you spend in a place kalma, kalış, bulunma, ziyaret *Did you enjoy your stay in Tokyo?*

stead /sted/ *noun* **stand sb in good stead** to be useful to someone in the future faydalı olmak, işe yaramak; faydası dokunmak *The course will stand you in good stead.*

steadfast /'stedfɑːst/ *adjective formal* refusing to change your beliefs or what you are doing sarsılmaz, değişmez, sabit *He is steadfast in his support for political change.* ● **steadfastly** *adverb* değişmeyen bir şekilde

steady¹ /'stedi/ *adjective* **1** [GRADUAL] happening at a gradual, regular rate devamlı, sürekli, düzenli *steady economic growth* ○ *He has had a steady flow/stream of visitors.* **2** [STILL] still and not shaking sabit, sarsılmaz, oynamaz *You need steady hands to be a dentist.* ◑Opposite **unsteady. 3** [NOT CHANGING] not changing değişmez, sabit *She drove at a steady speed.* **4 steady job/work** a job that is likely to continue for a long time and pay you regular money devamlı/daimî görev/iş ● **steadily** *adverb* düzenli olarak ● **steadiness** *noun* [U] sabit olma durumu

steady² /'stedi/ *verb* **1** [T] to make something stop shaking or moving sabitlemek, sabit tutmak, dengede tutmak, dengelemek *He managed to steady the plane.* **2 steady yourself** to stop yourself from falling kendini dengede tutmak, kontrol etmek *She grabbed hold of the rail to steady herself.*

steak /steɪk/ *noun* [C, U] a thick, flat piece of meat or fish biftek *steak and chips*

---

o~**steal** /stiːl/ *verb past tense* **stole,** *past participle* **stolen 1** [I, T] to secretly take something that does not belong to you, without intending to return it çalmak, aşırmak, yürütmek *Burglars broke into the house and stole a computer.* ○ *stolen cars* **2 steal away/in/out,** etc to move somewhere quietly and secretly sıvışmak, usulca ve gizlice girmek/çıkmak/uzaklaşmak

stealth /stelθ/ *noun* [U] secret, quiet behaviour gizlilik, sessiz ve hissettirmeden yapılan davranış ● **stealthy** *adjective* behaving in a secret, quiet way gizli, sinsi, el altından, çaktırmadan ● **stealthily** *adverb* gizli bir şekilde

o~**steam¹** /stiːm/ *noun*
1 [U] the gas that water produces when you heat it buhar, istim
2 let off steam to get rid of your anger, excitement, etc by being noisy or using a lot of energy söylenip içini boşaltmak; bağırıp çağırarak rahatlamak, boşalmak **3 run out of steam** to not have enough energy to finish doing something gücü tükenmek, bitirecek enerjiyi kendinde bulamamak; (argo) pili bitmek

 **steam**

steam² /stiːm/ *verb* **1** [T] to cook something using steam buğulamak, buharla pişirmek *steamed rice* **2** [I] to produce steam buhar çıkarmak *a steaming bowl of soup*
steam (sth) up *phrasal verb* If glass steams up, or if you steam it up, it becomes covered in steam. buğulanmak, buğu yapmak

steamer /stiːməʳ/ *noun* [C] **1** a pan used for cooking food using steam düdüklü tencere **2** a ship that uses steam power buhar gücüyle çalışan gemi

steamy /'stiːmi/ *adjective* **1** hot and full of steam buharlı, buharla kaplı, buhar içinde, buğulu *a steamy kitchen* **2** sexually exciting cinsel heyecan uyandıran *a steamy love story*

steel¹ /stiːl/ *noun* [U] a very strong metal made from iron, used for making knives, machines, etc çelik ◑See also: **stainless steel.**

steel² /stiːl/ *verb* **steel yourself** to prepare yourself to do something difficult or unpleasant muhtemel olumsuzluklara karşı kendini hazırlamak *He was steeling himself for an argument.*

steely /'stiːli/ *adjective* [always before noun] very strong and determined güçlü ve kararlı *a steely determination to succeed*

o~**steep¹** /stiːp/ *adjective* **1** [SLOPE] A steep slope, hill, etc goes up or down very quickly. dik, sarp, yalçın *The hill was too steep to cycle up.* **2** [CHANGE] A steep increase or fall in something is very big and quick. büyük, önemli, aşırı, haddinden fazla *a steep rise in prices* **3** [PRICE] *informal* very expensive fahiş, kazık, pahalı *Hotel prices are steep at $300 for a room.* ● **steeply** *adverb* *Food prices have risen steeply.* dik bir biçimde, ani bir şekilde ● **steepness** *noun* [U] dik olma durumu

steep² /stiːp/ *verb* **be steeped in sth** to have a lot of something around or to be strongly influenced by something dopdolu olmak, ağzına kadar dolu olmak; çok fazla etkilenmiş olmak *The town is steeped in history.*

S

steeple /'sti:pl/ *noun* [C] a church tower that has a point at the top **kilise kulesi; çan kulesi**

steer /stɪə^r/ *verb* **1** [I, T] to control the direction of a vehicle **seyretmek, sürmek, kullanmak, yönetmek; direksiyonda/dümende olmak** *I tried to steer the boat away from the bank.* **2** [T] to influence the way a situation develops **yönlendirmek, yön vermek; gelişmeyi etkilemek** *I managed to steer the conversation away from my exam results.* **3 steer sb into/out of/ towards, etc** to guide someone somewhere, especially by putting your hand on their back **elinden tutup götürmek, öncülük etmek, yol göstermek** *He steered me towards the door.* ⊃See also: steer **clear**³ of sb/sth.

steering /'stɪərɪŋ/ *noun* [U] the parts of a vehicle that control its direction **direksiyon, dümen**

'steering ˌwheel *noun* [C] a wheel that you turn to control the direction of a vehicle **direksiyon, dümen** ⊃Orta kısımdaki renkli sayfalarına bakınız.

stem¹ /stem/ *noun* [C] the long, thin part of a plant that the leaves and flowers grow on **sap**

stem² /stem/ *verb* [T] **stemming**, *past* **stemmed** to stop something from continuing or increasing **durdurmak, engel olmak, önlemek, artışını engellemek** *The new procedures are intended to stem the flow of drugs into the country.*

stem from sth *phrasal verb* to develop as the result of something ...**dan/den kaynaklanmak/doğmak/ ileri gelmek** *Her problems stem from childhood.*

'stem ˌcell *noun* [C] a cell, especially one taken from a person or animal in a very early stage of development, that can develop into any other type of cell **kök hücre**

stench /stenʃ/ *noun* [C] a very unpleasant smell **pis koku** *the stench of rotten fruit*

stencil /'stensəl/ *noun* [C] a piece of paper or plastic with patterns cut into it, that you use to paint patterns onto a surface **şablon** ● **stencil** *verb* [I, T] *UK* **stencilling**, *past* **stencilled**, *US* **stenciling**, *past* **stenciled** to use a stencil to paint patterns onto a surface **şaplonla çizmek/boyamak/yazmak**

[step (noun)] İLE BİRLİKTE KULLANILAN KELİMELER

take steps to do sth ● a **big/important/major** step ● the **first/next** step ● a step **towards** sth ● a step **in** (doing) sth

o*-**step**¹ /step/ *noun* [C] **1** [MOVEMENT] one of the movements you make with your feet when you walk **adım** *She took a few steps forward and then started to speak.* **2** [METHOD] one of the things that you do to achieve something **basamak, adım, hamle** *This meeting is the first step towards a peace agreement.* ○ *The company has taken steps to improve its customer service.* **3** [STAIR] one of the surfaces that you walk on when you go up or down stairs **basamak 4 in step (with sb/sth)** having the same ideas, opinions, etc as other people **izinde; aynı düşünce ve fikirleri taşıyan** *This time, Britain is in step with the rest of Europe.* **5 out of step (with sb/sth)** having different ideas, opinions, etc from other people **farklı fikir ve düşüncede olan** *Her views are out of step with government policy.* **6 be one step ahead (of sb)** to have done something before someone else **bir adım önde olmak; ileride olmak 7 watch your step a** [WALKING] used to tell someone to be careful about where they are walking 'Bastığın yere dikkat et!', 'Adımlarına dikkat et! **b** [BEHAVIOUR] to be careful about what you say and do **Ayağını denk al!', 'Dikkatli ol!'**

step² /step/ *verb* **stepping**, *past* **stepped 1 step back/ forward/over, etc** to move somewhere by lifting your foot and putting it down in a different place **geri/ileri/ üzerinden adım atmak** *She stepped carefully over the dog.* **2 step on/in sth** to put your foot on or in something **üstüne basmak** *I accidentally stepped on her foot.*

step down *phrasal verb* to leave an important job **çekilmek, istifa etmek, görevi bırakmak** *He stepped down as manager of the Italian team.*

step in *phrasal verb* to become involved in a difficult situation in order to help **karışmak, müdahale etmek, araya girmek** [+ to do sth] *A Japanese bank stepped in to provide financial help.*

step sth up *phrasal verb* to increase what you are doing to try to achieve something **artırmak, hızlandırmak, çoğaltmak** *Police have stepped up their efforts to find the man.*

stepbrother /'step.brʌðə^r/ *noun* [C] not your parent's son but the son of the person your parent has married **üvey erkek kardeş**

step-by-step /ˌstepbaɪ'step/ *adjective* [always before noun] A step-by-step method, plan, etc, deals with one thing and then another thing in a fixed order. **adım adım, aşama aşama, merhale merhale** *a step-by-step guide to buying a house*

'step ˌchange *noun* [C] when a very big change happens **büyük değişim** *There is a step change taking place in communications technology.*

stepchild /'steptʃaɪld/ *noun* [C] *plural* **stepchildren** the child of your husband or wife from an earlier marriage **üvey evlat**

stepdaughter /'step.dɔːtə^r/ *noun* [C] the daughter of your husband or wife from an earlier marriage **üvey kız evlat**

stepfather /'step.fɑːðə^r/ *noun* [C] the man who has married your mother but is not your father **üvey baba**

stepmother /'step.mʌðə^r/ *noun* [C] the woman who has married your father but is not your mother **üvey anne**

stepping-stone /'stepɪŋstəʊn/ *noun* [C] **1** an event or experience that helps you achieve something else **sıçrama taşı, başarı yolu, basamak, vasıta** *Education is a stepping-stone to a good job.* **2** one of several stones that you walk on to cross a stream **suda üzerine basılarak geçilen taşlardan her biri**

stepsister /'step.sɪstə^r/ *noun* [C] not your parent's daughter but the daughter of the person your parent has married **üvey kız kardeş**

stepson /'stepsʌn/ *noun* [C] the son of your husband or wife from an earlier marriage **üvey oğul**

stereo /'steriəʊ/ *noun* **1** [C] a piece of equipment for playing CDs, listening to the radio, etc that has two speakers (= parts where sound comes out) **müzik seti** *a car stereo* ⊃Orta kısımdaki renkli sayfalarına bakınız. **2** [U] a system for hearing music, speech, etc through two speakers (= parts where sound comes out) **stereo** *The concert was broadcast in stereo.* ○ *stereo sound*

[stereotype] İLE BİRLİKTE KULLANILAN KELİMELER

challenge/fit a stereotype ● a **negative** stereotype ● a stereotype **of** sth ● a **racial** stereotype

stereotype¹ /'steriəʊtaɪp/ *noun* [C] a fixed idea that people have about what a particular type of person is like, especially an idea that is wrong **basmakalıp tip, kalıplaşmış örnek, klişe** *racial stereotypes* ● **stereotypical** /ˌsteriəʊ'tɪpɪkəl/ *adjective* having the qualities that you expect a particular type of person to have **basmakalıp, kalıplaşmış örnek olan, klişeleşmiş** *a stereotypical person*

stereotype² /'steriəʊtaɪp/ *verb* [T] to have a fixed idea about what a particular type of person is like, especially an idea that is wrong **belli bir kalıba oturtmak; kli-**

şeleştirmek [often passive] *Young people are often stereotyped as being lazy.*

sterile /'steraɪl/ *adjective* **1** [CLEAN] completely clean and without any bacteria **temiz, bakterisiz, mikropsuz, steril** *a sterile needle* **2** [NO CHILDREN] unable to produce children **kısır, çocuğu olmayan 3** [NO IDEAS] not having enough new ideas **verimsiz, kısır, semeresiz, yeni fikirleri olmayan** *a sterile discussion* ● **sterility** /stə'rɪləti/ *noun* [U] **mikrop olmaması durumu, kısırlık, verimli olmama**

sterilize (*also UK* -**ise**) /'ster°laɪz/ *verb* [T] **1** to make something clean and without bacteria **mikroplardan arındırmak, sterilize etmek** *a sterilized needle* **2** to perform a medical operation on someone to make them unable to have children **kısırlaştırmak** ● **sterilization** /,ster°laɪ'zeɪʃ°n/ *noun* [U] **mikroptan arındırma**

sterling /'stɜːlɪŋ/ *noun* [U] British money **sterlin; Büyük Britanya para birimi**

stern¹ /stɜːn/ *adjective* very serious and without any humour **ciddi, acımasız, haşin, mizahtan yoksun, katı** *a stern expression/face* ○ *stern criticism* ● **sternly** *adverb* **katı, sert bir biçimde**

stern² /stɜːn/ *noun* [C] the back part of a ship **pupa, kıç, arka taraf**

steroid /'steroɪd/ *noun* [C] a drug for treating injuries that some people use illegally in sport to make their muscles stronger **steroid, hormon, doping**

stethoscope /'steθəskəʊp/ *noun* [C] a piece of equipment that a doctor uses to listen to your heart and breathing **hasta dinleme cihazı, steteskop**

stew /stjuː/ *noun* [C, U] a dish made of vegetables and meat cooked together slowly in liquid **yahni** *beef/lamb stew* ● **stew** *verb* [T] to cook food slowly in liquid **ağır ateşte sıvı içinde pişirmek; yahni yapmak** *stewed fruit*

steward /'stjuːəd/ *noun* [C] **1** a man who looks after people on an aircraft, boat, or train **kabin memuru, kamarot** *an air steward* **2** someone who helps to organize a race or big event **düzenleyici, organizatör**

stewardess /'stjuːədɪs/ *noun* [C] a woman who looks after people on an aircraft, boat, or train **hostes, kadın kamarot** *an air stewardess*

sth *written abbreviation for* something **bir şey' sözcüğünün kısa yazılışı** ● **sth's** *written abbreviation for* something's **bir şeyin' sözcüğünün kısa yazılışı**

◦⁻**stick**¹ /stɪk/ *verb past* **stuck 1** [I, T] to become joined to something else or to make something become joined to something else, usually with a substance like glue **yapıştırmak** *Anne stuck a picture of her boyfriend on the wall.* ○ *The stamp wouldn't stick to the envelope.* **2 stick sth in/on/under, etc** *informal* to put something somewhere **bir yerlere koymak, atıvermek** *Just stick your bag under the table.* **3 stick (sth) in/into/through, etc** If something sharp sticks into something, it goes into it, and if you stick something sharp somewhere, you push it into something. **bat(ır)mak, sok(ul)mak, sapla(n)mak** *She stuck the needle into his arm.* **4** [I] to become fixed in one position and not be able to move **takılmak, saplanmak** *This drawer has stuck - I can't*

stick

The boy stuck his tongue out.

open it. **5 can't stick sb/sth** *UK informal* to not like someone or something **katlanamamak, tahammül edememek; hoşlanmamak** *I can't stick her.* ➔See also: stick to your guns (**gun**¹), poke/stick your **nose**¹ into sth, stick/put your **oar** in.

stick around *phrasal verb informal* to stay somewhere for a period of time **oyalanmak, beklemek, zaman geçirmek** *Stick around after the concert and you might meet the band.*

stick at sth *phrasal verb* to continue trying hard to do something difficult **sebat etmek, yılmamak, ısrarla devam etmek** *I know it's hard learning to drive but stick at it.*

stick by sb *phrasal verb* to continue to support someone when they are having problems **kötü gün dostu olmak; yanında olmak, yalnız bırakmamak, desteklemeye devam etmek**

stick out *phrasal verb* **1** If part of something sticks out, it comes out further than the edge or surface. **çıkmak, taşmak, çıkıntı yapmak** *His ears stick out a bit.* **2** to be very easy to notice **kolay farkedilmek, çok belirgin olmak, aşikâr olmak** *She certainly sticks out in a crowd.* ➔See also: stick/stand out like a sore **thumb**¹.

stick sth out *phrasal verb* to make part of your body come forward from the rest of your body **(dışarı) çıkarmak, uzatmak** *The little boy stuck his tongue out.*

stick it out *phrasal verb informal* to continue doing something that is boring, difficult, or unpleasant **dayanmak, katlanmak, sebat etmek, ısrarla devam etmek, dişini sıkmak**

stick to sth *phrasal verb* to continue doing or using something and not change to anything else **...dan/den vazgeçmemek; ...a/e sadık kalmak** *I'll stick to lemonade - I'm driving.*

stick together *phrasal verb* If people stick together, they support and help each other. **kenetlenmek, birbirine yaslanmak, yakın olmak**

stick up *phrasal verb* to point up above a surface and not lie flat **dimdik durmak** *I can't go out with my hair sticking up like this.*

stick up for sb/sth *phrasal verb informal* to support someone or something when they are being criticized **arka çıkmak, kuvvetle savunmak, tarafını tutmak**

stick with sb/sth *phrasal verb* to continue using someone or doing something and not change to anyone or anything else **bırakmamak, beraber olmak, bağlı kalmak; ...dan/den ayrılmamak** *He's a good builder - I think we should stick with him.*

◦⁻**stick**² /stɪk/ *noun* [C] **1** a long, thin piece of wood, usually broken or fallen from a tree **sopa, değnek 2 walking/hockey, etc stick** a long, thin piece of wood that you use when you are walking/playing hockey, etc **baston, yürüme değneği, hokey sopası 3** a long, thin piece of something **çubuk, sopa** *a stick of candy/celery* ➔See also: carrot and stick, get (hold of) the wrong **end**¹ of the stick.

sticker /'stɪkər/ *noun* [C] a piece of paper or plastic with writing or a picture on it that you stick onto a surface **çıkartma, etiket** *a car sticker* ➔See also: bumper sticker.

sticky /'stɪki/ *adjective* **1** made of or covered with a substance that can stick to other things **yapışkan, yapış yapış** *sticky fingers* ○ *sticky tape* **2** Sticky weather is unpleasantly hot. **yapış yapış, sıcak ve rutubetli, bunaltıcı ve nemli 3** a sticky moment/problem/ situation, etc *informal* a moment/problem/situation, etc that is difficult or embarrasses you **zor/güç/tatsız/berbat an/sorun/durum vb.**

◦⁻**stiff**¹ /stɪf/ *adjective* **1** [HARD] hard and difficult to bend **sert, katı, eğilemez, bükülemez** *stiff material* **2** [NOT MOVING] A door, drawer, etc that is stiff does not move as easily as it should. **sıkışmış, kolayca kapanmayan, tutukluk yapan 3** [HURTING] If a part of your

S

body is stiff, it hurts and is difficult to move. **kaskatı, sert, tutulmuş** *I've got a stiff neck.* **4** [SEVERE] very severe or difficult **güç, zor, şiddetli, ciddi** *stiff competition/ opposition* ○ *We need stiffer penalties for drink driving.* **5** [FORMAL] behaving in a way that is formal and not relaxed **ciddi, resmî davranış 6** [THICK] A stiff substance is thick and does not move around easily. **katı, sert, koyu, hantal, ağır** *Whip the cream until it is stiff.* **7 stiff drink/whisky/vodka, etc** a strong alcoholic drink **sert içki** *I need a stiff brandy.* **8 stiff wind/breeze** a wind that is quite strong **sert rüzgâr** ● **stiffly** *adverb* **bükülmesi zor bir şekilde, katılaşmış, sertleşmiş** ● **stiffness** *noun* [U] **sert olma durumu**

stiff² /stıf/ *adverb* **bored/scared/worried, etc stiff** extremely bored, worried, etc **çok, pek, son derece sıkılmış/endişeli** vb. *The lecture was awful - I was bored stiff.*

stiffen /'stıfªn/ *verb* **1** [I, T] to become stiff or to make something become stiff **sertleş(tir)mek, katılaş(tır) mak 2** [I] to suddenly stop moving because you are frightened or angry **kaskatı kesilmek, donup kalmak** *She stiffened at the sound of the doorbell.*

stifle /'staıfl/ *verb* [T] to stop something from happening or continuing **bastırmak, tutmak, sürüp gitmesine engel olmak** *to stifle a sneeze/yawn* ○ *Large supermarkets stifle competition.*

stifling /'staıflıŋ/ *adjective* extremely hot **boğucu** *a stifling summer in Rome*

sth carries a stigma ● the stigma attached to/surrounding sth ● sth loses its stigma ● a social stigma ● the stigma of (doing) sth

stigma /'stıgmə/ *noun* [C, U] when people disapprove of something, especially when this is unfair **leke, damga, rezalet, yüz kızartıcı durum** *There is still a stigma attached to being mentally ill.* ● **stigmatize** (*also UK* -ise) *verb* [T] to treat someone or something unfairly by disapproving of them **damgalamak, toplum dışına itmek; kötü şöhret sahibi olmasına neden olmak** [often passive] *Unmarried mothers are stigmatized by society.*

stiletto /stı'letəʊ/ *noun* [C] a shoe with a very high, pointed heel (= part at the bottom and back of a shoe) **sivri topuklu ayakkabı** *a pair of stilettos*

o=**still¹** /stıl/ *adverb* **1** [CONTINUING] used to say that something is continuing to happen now or that someone is continuing to do something now **hâlâ** *He's still here if you want to speak to him.* ○ *Do you still play basketball?* **2** [POSSIBLE] used to say that something continues to be possible **daha, hâlâ** *We could still catch the train if we leave now.* **3** [EMPHASIS] used to emphasize that you did not expect something to happen because something else makes it surprising **daha da** *He didn't do much work but still came top of the class.* ○ *The weather was terrible. Still, we had a good holiday.* **4 better/harder/worse, etc still** better/harder/worse, etc than something else **katı, sert, koyu, hantal, ağır** vs.

o=**still²** /stıl/ *adjective* **1 stand/stay/sit, etc still** to stand, stay, sit, etc without moving **hareketsizce/kıpırdamadan ayakta durmak/kalmak/oturmak** vs. *Sit still so I can brush your hair.* **2** A still place is calm and quiet. **durgun, sakin** *It was night and the whole village was still.* **3** *UK* A still drink does not have any bubbles in it. **gazsız (içecek)** ● **stillness** *noun* [U] **sükunet, kabarcıklı olmayan (içecek)**

still³ /stıl/ *noun* [C] a photograph from one moment in a film **sinema/film fotoğraf karesi**

stillborn /,stıl'bɔ:n/ (US /'stıl,bɔ:n/ *adjective* born dead **ölü doğmuş** *a stillborn baby*

stilt /stılt/ *noun* [C] **1** one of two long poles that you can stand on and use to walk above the ground **cambaz değneği** [usually plural] *a clown on stilts* **2** one of several poles that support a building above the ground **bina sütunu/ayağı; temel destek direkleri** [usually plural] *a house on stilts*

stilted /'stıltıd/ *adjective* talking or writing in a formal way that does not sound natural **yapmacıklı; yapay, doğal olmayan** *a stilted conversation*

stimulant /'stımjələnt/ *noun* [C] a drug that makes you feel more active and awake **uyarıcı** *Coffee contains caffeine which is a stimulant.*

stimulate /'stımjəleıt/ *verb* [T] **1** to make something happen or develop more **uyarmak, harekete geçirmek, canlandırmak** *It stimulates the production of red blood cells.* **2** to make someone feel interested and excited **heves uyandırmak, gayrete getirmek; heyecanlandırmak** *Colourful pictures can stimulate a child.* ● **stimulation** /,stımjə'leıʃªn/ *noun* [U] **geliştirme, uyarma**

stimulating /'stımjəleıtıŋ/ *adjective* interesting and making you think **ilginç, heyecanlı** *a stimulating discussion*

act as/provide a stimulus ● a stimulus for/to sth

stimulus /'stımjələs/ *noun* [C, U] *plural* **stimuli** /'stımjəlaı/ something that makes something else happen, grow, or develop more **harekete geçirici/teşvik edici şey** *The report provided the stimulus for more studies.*

sting¹ /stıŋ/ *verb past* **stung 1** [CAUSE PAIN] [T] If an insect, plant, etc stings you, it causes pain by putting poison into your skin. **sokmak** *He was stung by a wasp.* **2** [FEEL PAIN] [I, T] If your eyes, skin, etc sting, or if something makes them sting, you feel a sudden, burning pain. **yanmak, acımak, sızlamak, yakmak, acıtmak, sızlatmak** *That shampoo really made my eyes sting.* **3** [UPSET] [T] to upset someone **incitmek, üzmek, kırmak, iğnelemek; yüreğini sızlatmak** [often passive] *She was clearly stung by his criticism.*

sting² /stıŋ/ *noun* **1** [WOUND] [C] a painful wound that you get when an insect, plant, etc puts poison into your skin **sızı, acı, sokma** *a wasp/bee sting* **2** [PAIN] [no plural] a sudden, burning pain in your eyes, skin, etc **yanma, acı, sızlama 3** [UPSET] [no plural] the feeling of being upset by something **incinme, üzülme, kırılma, yüreği sızlama** *the sting of defeat*

stingy /'stındʒi/ *adjective informal* not generous **cimri, hasis, pinti, eli sıkı** *He's too stingy to buy any drinks.*

stink¹ /stıŋk/ *verb* [I] *past* **stank** or *also US* **stunk**, *past participle* **stunk 1** to smell very bad **çok pis kokmak, leş gibi kokmak** *The kitchen stinks of fish.* **2** *informal* to be very bad and dishonest **kokuşmak, mide bulandırıcı olmak, bozulmak** *If you ask me, the whole affair stinks.*

stink² /stıŋk/ *noun* **1 make/cause/create, etc a stink** *informal* to complain about something in a forceful way **şiddetle şikâyet etmek, sürekli sert bir şekilde dertlenmek 2** [no plural] a very bad smell **çok kötü koku**

stint /stınt/ *noun* [C] a period of time spent doing something **belli süreli iş; süre, müddet** *He had a two-year stint as a teacher in Spain.*

stipulate /'stıpjuleıt/ *verb* [T] *formal* to say exactly what must be done **koşul öne sürmek, şart koşmak; yapılması gerekeni tam olarak söylemek** [+ (that)] *The* *rules stipulate that smoking is not allowed.* ● **stipulation** /ˌstɪpjəˈleɪʃᵊn/ *noun* [C] şart

o╍**stir¹** /stɜːʳ/ *verb* **stirring,** *past* **stirred 1** [MIX] [T] to mix food or liquid by moving a spoon round and round in it **karıştırmak** *Stir the mixture until it is smooth.* **2** [MOVE] [I, T] to move slightly or make someone move slightly **kımıldamak, kımıldatmak** *The baby stirred in its sleep.* **3** [FEEL] [T] to make someone feel a strong emotion **coşturmak, harekete geçirmek, uyandırmak** *The case has stirred great anger among the public.*
stir sth up *phrasal verb* **1** to cause arguments or bad feelings between people, often intentionally **ortalığı karıştırmak, kışkırtmak, yaratmak, çıkartmak; (argo) kepçelik yapmak** *I think she just likes to stir up trouble.* **2** If something stirs up memories, it makes you remember events in the past. **uyanmak, depreşmek, belirmek, ortaya çıkmak** *The photographs stirred up some painful memories.*

stir² /stɜːʳ/ *noun* **1 cause/create a stir** to make people excited or surprised **heyecanlandırmak, şaşırtmak, ortalığı karıştırmak** *Her new book has caused quite a stir.* **2** [no plural] when you mix food or liquid with a spoon **karıştırma** *Could you give the soup a stir?*

stir-fry /ˈstɜːˌfraɪ/ *verb* [T] to fry small pieces of vegetable, meat, etc very quickly while mixing them around **karıştırarak kızartmak** ● **stir-fry** *noun* [C] **kızgın yağda pişirme**

stirring /ˈstɜːrɪŋ/ *adjective* making people feel excitement or other strong emotions **heyecanlandıran, güçlü duygular uyandıran, harekete geçiren, canlılık katan** *a stirring performance/speech*

stirrup /ˈstɪrəp/ *noun* [C] one of the two metal parts that support your feet when you are riding a horse **üzengi**

stitch¹ /stɪtʃ/ *noun* **1** [THREAD] [C] a short line of thread that is sewn through a piece of material **dikiş 2** [WOUND] [C] one of the small pieces of thread that is used to sew together a cut **ameliyat ipliği, yara dikiş ipliği** *She made 50 stitches in her head.* **3** [WOOL] [C] one of the small circles of wool that you make when you are knitting (= making something from wool) **ilmek 4** [PAIN] [no plural] a sudden pain that you get in the side of your body when you exercise too much **sancı, vücuttaki acı** *to get a stitch* **5 in stitches** laughing a lot **gülme krizine tutulmuş, katıla katıla gülme** *He had the whole audience in stitches.*

stitch² /stɪtʃ/ *verb* [I, T] to sew two things together or to repair something by sewing **dikmek, dikerek onarmak** *I need to get my shoes stitched.*
stitch sth up *phrasal verb* to sew together the two parts of something that have come apart **dikmek, dikiş atmak** *The nurse stitched up my finger.*

stock¹ /stɒk/ *noun* **1** [SHOP] [U] all the goods that are available in a shop **stok; bir dükkandaki tüm mallar** *We're expecting some new stock in this afternoon.* **2 be in stock/out of stock** to be available/not available in a shop **mevcut olmak/mevcudu tükenmek; stokta olmak/olmamak 3** [SUPPLY] [C] a supply of something that is ready to be used **stok, birikim, mevcut** [usually plural] *stocks of food/weapons* **4** [COMPANY] [C, U] the value of a company, or a share in its value **hisse senedi, tahvil** *to buy/sell stock* ○ *falling/rising stock prices* **5** [LIQUID] [U] a liquid made by boiling meat, bones, or vegetables and used to make soups, sauces, etc **et/kemik/sebze suyu** *chicken/vegetable stock* **6 take stock (of sth)** to think carefully about a situation before making a decision **değerlendirme yapmak, durum değerlendirmesinde bulunmak** ⊃See also: laughing stock.

stock² /stɒk/ *verb* [T] to have something available for people to buy **doldurmak, yığmak, istiflemek, depo etmek** *They stock a wide range of books and magazines.*

stock up *phrasal verb* to buy a lot of something **depolamak, stok yapmak** *We'd better stock up on food for the holiday.*

stock³ /stɒk/ *adjective* **stock answer/phrase, etc** an answer/phrase, etc that is always used and so is not really useful **beylik söz/ifade; hazır cevap; basmakalıp söz/laf/ifade**

stockbroker /ˈstɒkˌbrəʊkəʳ/ *noun* [C] someone whose job is to buy and sell stocks and shares in companies for other people **borsacı, borsa simsarı, komisyoncu**

the ˈstock exˌchange (*also* the ˈstock ˌmarket) *noun* **1** the place where stocks and shares in companies are bought and sold **menkul kıymetler borsası 2** the value of stocks and shares being bought and sold **borsa**

stocking /ˈstɒkɪŋ/ *noun* [C] a very thin piece of clothing that covers a woman's foot and leg **ince çorap** *a pair of stockings*

stockpile /ˈstɒkpaɪl/ *verb* [T] to collect a lot of something, usually so that it can be used in the future **biriktirmek, yığmak, toplamak, stok yapmak** *to stockpile food* ● **stockpile** *noun* [C] *a stockpile of weapons* **stok**

stocky /ˈstɒki/ *adjective* having a wide, strong, body **tıknaz** *a short, stocky man*

stoic /ˈstəʊɪk/ *adjective formal* dealing with pain, problems, etc, but never complaining **asla dertlenmeyen, problemlerle başa çıkıp şikayet etmeyen** ● **stoically** *adverb* hiç şikayet etmeden ● **stoicism** /ˈstəʊɪsɪzᵊm/ *noun* [U] **Stoacılık**

stole /stəʊl/ *past tense of* steal **çalmak' fiilinin 2. hâli**

stolen /ˈstəʊlᵊn/ *past participle of* steal **çalmak' fiilinin 3. hâli**

stolid /ˈstɒlɪd/ *adjective* calm and not showing emotion or excitement **duygularını belli etmeyen, kayıtsız görünen, soğuk**

o╍**stomach¹** /ˈstʌmək/ *noun* [C] *plural* **stomachs 1** the organ inside your body where food goes after it has been eaten and where it starts to be digested **mide 2** the front part of your body just below your chest **karın, karın boşluğu** *He punched me in the stomach.* ⊃Orta kısımdaki renkli sayfalarına bakınız. **3 have no stomach for sth** to not feel brave enough to do something unpleasant **kötülük yapmaya cesaret edememek; kalkışmaya cesaret edememek** ⊃See also: have butterflies (**butterfly**) (in your stomach).

stomach² /ˈstʌmək/ *verb informal* **can't stomach sth** to be unable to deal with, watch, etc something unpleasant **dayanamamak, kaldıramamak, katlanamamak, sineye çekmemek, tahammül edememek** *I can't stomach horror movies.*

ˈstomach ˌache *noun* [C, U] pain in your stomach **mide/karın ağrısı** *I've got terrible stomach ache.*

stomp /stɒmp/ *verb* [I] to put your foot down on the ground hard and quickly, or to walk with heavy steps, usually because you are angry **sert adımlarla yürümek, ayaklarını pat pat vurarak yürümek** *He stomped off to his room.*

o╍**stone¹** /stəʊn/ *noun* **1** [SUBSTANCE] [U] a hard, natural substance that is found in the ground **taş** *a stone wall* **2** [ROCK] [C] a small rock or piece of rock **taş, taş parçası 3** [JEWEL] [C] a hard, valuable substance that is often used in jewellery **değerli taş** *precious stones* **4** [WEIGHT] [C] *plural* **stone** UK a unit for measuring weight, equal to 6.35 kilograms or 14 pounds **6.35 kilograma veya 14 pounda eşit bir ağırlık ölçüm birimi; ston** *I gained two stone when I was pregnant.* ⊃See study page Measurements on page Centre 31. **5** [SEED] [C] the hard seed that is at the centre of some fruits **çekirdek** *a cherry stone* ⊃See also: stepping-stone.

stone² /stəʊn/ *verb* [T] to kill or hurt someone by throwing stones (= small rocks) at them, usually as a punishment **taşlamak, taş atarak öldürmek/yaralamak, taşa tutmak** [often passive] *Two men were stoned to death by the crowd.*

stoned /stəʊnd/ *adjective informal* **1** relaxed or excited because of the effect of drugs **zil zurna sarhoş; kafası kıyak/dumanlı 2** drunk **şarhoş, zil zurna sarhoş, kör kütük sarhoş, zom olmuş**

stonemason /'stəʊn,meɪsᵊn/ *noun* [C] someone who makes things from stone **taşçı, duvar ustası**

stony /'stəʊni/ *adjective* **1** covered with or containing stones (= small rocks) **taşlı, taşlık** *a stony path/road* **2** not friendly, usually because you are angry **soğuk, buz gibi, taş gibi, donuk** *a stony silence*

stood /stʊd/ *past of* stand **ayakta durmak' fiilinin geçmiş zaman hâli**

stool /stuːl/ *noun* [C] a seat that does not have a back or arms **tabure, oturak** *a piano/bar stool*

stool

stoop¹ /stuːp/ *verb* [I] to bend the top half of your body forward and down **kamburunu çıkarmak** *He stooped to pick up the letter.*

stoop to sth/doing sth *phrasal verb* to do something bad that will give you an advantage **alçalmak, tenezzül etmek, şerefsizleşmek** *I can't believe he would stoop to blackmail.*

stoop² /stuːp/ *noun* **1** [no plural] when the upper part of your body is bent forwards **kambur** *He has a slight stoop.* **2** [C] *US* a raised area in front of the door of a house, with steps leading up to it **eşik, merdiven yükseltisi, kapı önü eşiği**

ᴏ▪**stop¹** /stɒp/ *verb* **stopping**, *past* **stopped 1** [FINISH] [I, T] to finish doing something that you were doing **durmak, bırakmak, bitirmek, son vermek** [+ doing sth] *Stop laughing - it's not funny.* ○ *He started to say something and then stopped.* ○ *I'm trying to work but I keep having to stop to answer the phone* (= stop so that I can answer the telephone). **2** [FOR A SHORT TIME] [I] to stop a journey or an activity for a short time **ara vermek, durdurmak, bırakmak** *He stopped at a pub for lunch.* **3** [NOT OPERATE] [I, T] to not continue to operate, or to make something not continue to operate **çalışmamak, çalıştırmamak, durmak, durdurmak, işlememek, işletmemek** *My watch has stopped.* ○ *Can you stop the video for a minute?* **4** [FINISH MOVING] [I, T] to not move any more, or make someone or something not move any more **durmak/durdurmak, hareket etmek/ettirmemek** *A car stopped outside the house.* ○ *I stopped someone in the street to ask for directions.* **5** [BUS/TRAIN] [I] If a bus, train, etc stops at a particular place, it pauses at that place so that people can get on and off. **(otobüs, tren vb.) durmak; durakta durmak** *Does this train stop at Cambridge?* **6** [END] [T] to make something end **sona erdirmek, son vermek** *We must find a way to stop the war.* **7** [PREVENT] [T] to prevent something from happening or someone from doing something **engellemek, engel olmak; ...a/e son vermek; ...ı/i durdurmak** [+ from + doing sth] *Health workers are trying to stop the disease from spreading.* **8 Stop it/that!** used to tell someone to finish doing something, usually something annoying **'Kes şunu!', 'Bırak onu!', 'Durdur şunu!'** *Stop it! I can't concentrate if you keep making a noise.* **9 stop a cheque** *UK* (*US* **stop a check**) to prevent money from being paid from a cheque (= a piece of paper that you sign to pay for things)

ödemeyi durdurmak ➭See also: stop at **nothing**, stop the **rot²**.

stop by (sth) *phrasal verb* to visit a person or place for a short time **kısa ziyarette bulunmak** *If you're passing our house, why don't you stop by sometime?*

stop off *phrasal verb* to visit a place for a short time when you are going somewhere else **uğramak, ziyaret etmek** *We stopped off in Paris for a couple of days before heading south.*

ᴏ▪**stop²** /stɒp/ *noun* [C] **1** a place where a bus or train stops so that people can get on or off **durak, istasyon** *We need to get off at the next stop.* **2 put a stop to sth** to end something unpleasant **bir son vermek; ...ı/i durdurmak** *We must put a stop to the violence.* **3** a place where you stop on a journey, or the time that you spend there **durak, mola, ara** *We had an overnight stop in Singapore.* **4 come to a stop** to stop moving **durmak, kesilmek, dinmek** *The car came to a stop in front of an old cottage.* **5 pull out all the stops** to do everything you can to make something succeed **elinden geleni yapmak, canla başla çalışmak, dişini tırnağına takmak** ➭See also: bus **stop**, full **stop**.

stoplight /'stɒplaɪt/ *noun* [C] *US* a set of red, green, and yellow lights that is used to stop and start traffic **trafik ışıkları**

stopover /'stɒp,əʊvəʳ/ *noun* [C] a short stop between parts of a journey, especially a plane journey **mola**

stoppage /'stɒpɪdʒ/ *noun* [C] when people stop working because they are angry about something their employers have done **iş bırakma, grev**

stopwatch /'stɒpwɒtʃ/ *noun* [C] a watch that can measure exactly how long it takes to do something and is often used in sports activities **kronometre**

storage /'stɔːrɪdʒ/ *noun* [U] when you put things in a safe place until they are needed **depolama, depo etme** *We had to put our furniture into storage.*

ᴏ▪**store¹** /stɔːʳ/ *noun* [C] **1** *mainly US* a shop **dükkan, mağaza** *a book store* ○ *She works at a men's clothing store.* **2** a supply of something that you are keeping to use later **stok, depolanan mal, saklanan eşya** *a store of grain* **3 be in store (for sb)** If something is in store for you, it will happen to you in the future. **bekleyen, ileride olacak olan** *There's a surprise in store for you!* **4 set great store by sth** *UK* to believe that something is very important **büyük önem vermek, çok gerekli olduğunu düşünmek** *Martina sets great store by physical strength and fitness.* ➭See also: chain **store**, convenience **store**, department **store**, liquor **store**.

ᴏ▪**store²** /stɔːʳ/ *verb* [T] **1** (*also* **store away**) to put something somewhere and not use it until you need it **depolamak, stok yapmak, saklamak, depo etmek** *We have a lot of old clothes stored in the attic.* **2** to keep information on a computer **bilgiyi bilgisayara yüklemek; saklamak** *All the data is stored on diskettes.*

storeroom /'stɔːruːm/ *noun* [C] a room where goods are kept until they are needed **ardiye, depo**

storey *UK* (*US* **story**) /'stɔːri/ *noun* [C] a level of a building **kat** *a three-storey house*

stork /stɔːk/ *noun* [C] a large, white bird with very long legs which walks around in water to find its food **leylek**

┌───┐
│ 🕮 **storm** ...... İLE BİRLİKTE KULLANILAN KELİMELER │
└───┘
an **approaching/gathering** storm ● a **fierce/severe/violent** storm ● a storm **breaks** ● a storm **abates/passes**

ᴏ▪**storm¹** /stɔːm/ *noun* [C] **1** very bad weather with a lot of rain, snow, wind, etc **fırtına** *a snow/thunder storm* **2 a storm of controversy/protest, etc** a strong, negative reaction to something that has been said or done **büyük tepki, öfke, kıyamet**

storm² /stɔːm/ *verb* **1** [T] to attack a building, town, etc, using violence **saldırmak, hücum etmek** *Armed police stormed the embassy and arrested hundreds of protesters.* **2 storm into/out of, etc** to enter or leave a place in a very noisy way because you are angry **hışımla girmek/çıkmak; fırtına gibi/hiddetle girmek/çıkmak/basmak** *He stormed out of the meeting.*

'**storm ˌsurge** *noun* [C] when a lot of water is pushed from the sea onto the land, usually caused by a hurricane (= a violent storm with very strong winds) **fırtınanın/tayfunun/kasırganın/hortumun neden olduğu sel baskını**

stormy /ˈstɔːmi/ *adjective* **1** If it is stormy, the weather is bad with a lot of wind and rain. **fırtınalı** *a stormy night* ○ *stormy seas* **2** A stormy relationship or situation involves a lot of anger and arguments. **fırtınalı, şiddetli, gürültülü** *a stormy relationship* ○ *a stormy meeting/debate*

> 🧩 ***story*** ⋯⋯ İLE BİRLİKTE KULLANILAN KELİMELER
> **read/listen** to a story ● **tell** sb a story ● a story **about/of** sth

◦┅**story** /ˈstɔːri/ *noun* [C] **1** [DESCRIPTION] a description of a series of real or imaginary events which is intended to entertain people **hikaye, masal, öykü** *a horror/detective story* ○ *the story of the revolution* ○ *Tell us a story, Mum.* ○ *She reads stories to the children every night.* **2** [REPORT] a report in a newspaper, magazine, or news programme **hikaye, öykü, rapor, makale, haber** *Today's main story is the hurricane in Texas.* **3** [EXPLANATION] an explanation of why something happened, which may not be true **olay hikayesi/öyküsü** *Did he tell you the same story about why he was late?* **4** [BUILDING] *US spelling of* storey **kat**

stout¹ /staʊt/ *adjective* **1** quite fat **oldukça şişman, toplu, kilolu** *a short, stout man* **2** If shoes or other objects are stout, they are strong and thick. **kalın ve sağlam**

stout² /staʊt/ *noun* [C, U] a very dark beer **siyah bira**

stove /stəʊv/ *noun* [C] **1** a piece of equipment that you cook on **ocak** *I've left some soup on the stove for you.* ⊃Orta kısımdaki renkli sayfalarına bakınız. **2** a piece of equipment that burns coal, gas, wood, etc and is used for heating a room **soba**

stow /stəʊ/ (*also* stow away) *verb* [T] to put something in a particular place until it is needed **yerleştirmek, koymak** *Our camping equipment is stowed away in the loft.*

stowaway /ˈstəʊəˌweɪ/ *noun* [C] someone who hides on a ship or aircraft so that they can travel without paying **kaçak yolcu**

straddle /ˈstrædl/ *verb* [T] **1** to sit or stand with one leg on either side of something **bacaklarını açarak oturmak/durmak** *He straddled the chair.* **2** to be on both sides of a place **her iki yakada ayağı olmak** *Niagara Falls straddles the Canadian border.*

straggle /ˈstrægl/ *verb* [I] **1** to move more slowly than other members of a group **gruptan ayrılmak; daha yavaş hareket etmek/ağırdan almak** *Some runners are straggling a long way behind.* **2** to grow or spread out in an untidy way **düzensiz biçimde büyümek, yayılmak; dağınık olmak** *I could see a line of straggling bushes.*

straggly /ˈstrægli/ *adjective* growing or spreading out in an untidy way **dağınık, düzensiz** *a straggly beard*

◦┅**straight¹** /streɪt/ *adjective* **1** [NOT CURVED] not curved or bent **düz, dümdüz, doğru, dosdoğru** *a straight road*

○ *straight hair* **2** [LEVEL] in a position that is level or vertical **düz, doğru, dik** *That shelf's not straight.* **3** [IN A SERIES] [always before noun] one after another **iki, ikili, çift** *They've won five straight games so far.* **4** [HONEST] honest **dürüst, açık, dobra dobra** *a straight answer* **5** [DRINK] An alcoholic drink that is straight is not mixed with water, ice, etc. **sek, katışıksız** **6 get sth straight** to make sure that you completely understand a situation **tamamen anladığından emin olmak; tümüyle anlamak, açıklık kazandırmak** *Let me get this straight - am I paying for this?* **7** [NOT HOMOSEXUAL] *informal* not homosexual **eşcinsel olmayan; cinsel tercihlerinde sapkınlık göstermeyen** ⊃See also: keep a straight face¹.

◦┅**straight²** /streɪt/ *adverb* **1** in a straight line **dosdoğru, dümdüz, düz** *It's straight ahead.* ○ *He was looking straight at me.* **2** immediately **doğruca, hemen, derhal, dosdoğru** *I went straight back to sleep.* **3 sit up/stand up straight** to sit or stand with your body vertical **dik oturmak, dik durmak** **4 not think straight** If you cannot think straight, you are not thinking clearly about something. **mantıklı düşünememek, açık seçik bir düşünce ortaya koyamamak** *I was so tired, I couldn't think straight.* **5 tell sb straight (out)** to tell someone the truth in a clear way **doğrudan/dobra dobra/yüzüne söylemek,** *I told him straight that he wasn't getting a pay increase.* **6 straight away** immediately **derhal, hemen, hiç vakit kaybetmeden** *Go there straight away.*

straighten /ˈstreɪtⁿn/ *verb* [I, T] to become straight or to make something straight **düzelmek, düzeltmek, düzleştirmek, düz hâle getirmek**
straighten sth out *phrasal verb* to successfully deal with a problem or a confusing situation **bir meseleyi başarıyla halletmek; çözmek; ustalıkla üstesinden gelmek** *We need to straighten a few things out.*
straighten sth up *phrasal verb* to make a place tidy **düzeltmek, düzenlemek** *Could you straighten up your room?*
straighten up *phrasal verb* to stand so that your back is straight **doğrulmak, ayağa kalkmak, düz durmak**

straightforward /ˌstreɪtˈfɔːwəd/ *adjective* **1** easy to do or understand **anlaşılması kolay, basit, açık seçik** *The task looked fairly straightforward.* **2** saying clearly and honestly what you think **açık ve dürüst, gizlisi saklısı olmayan, düşündüğünü dürüstçe söyleyen** *She's very straightforward.*

> 🧩 ***strain*** ⋯⋯ İLE BİRLİKTE KULLANILAN KELİMELER
> **feel** the strain ● be **under** strain ● the strain **of** doing sth

strain¹ /streɪn/ *noun* **1** [FEELING] [C, U] when you feel worried and nervous about something **gerginlik, gerilme, stres** *The strain of the last few months had exhausted her.* **2 put a strain on sb/sth** to cause problems for someone or to make a situation difficult **sorun çıkarmak, belâ olmak; gittikçe kötüye götürmek** *Children put tremendous strains on a marriage.* **3** [INJURY] [C, U] an injury to part of your body that is caused by using it too much **incitme, burkma, zorlama; incinme, zorlanma, burkulma** *back strain* **4** [STRETCH] [U] when something is pulled or stretched too tightly **zorlama, çekme, germe** *The rope broke under the strain.* **5** [DISEASE/PLANT] [C] a type of disease or plant **bir tür hastalık veya bitki** *a new strain of virus*

strain² /streɪn/ *verb* **1** [TRY HARD] [I, T] to try hard to do something, usually to see or hear something **büyük çaba harcamak, zorlamak, çok fazla güç sarfetmek** [+ to do sth] *I had to strain to hear the music.* **2** [INJURE] [T] to injure part of your body by using it too much **incitmek, zorlamak, burkmak** *I think I've strained a muscle.*

3 [CAUSE PROBLEMS] [T] to cause problems for a situation or relationship **sorunlara neden olmak, ilişkiyi kötüye götürmek, zora sokmak** *The incident has strained relations between the two countries.* **4** [MONEY] [T] to cause too much of something to be used, especially money **çok fazla masraf etmek/açmak; harcamaları artırmak** *The war is straining the defence budget.* **5** [SEPARATE] [T] to separate solids from a liquid by pouring the mixture into a container with small holes in it **elemek, süzgeçten geçirmek** *Strain the sauce to remove the seeds and skins.*

strained /streɪnd/ *adjective* **1** showing that someone is nervous or anxious **sinirli, endişeli, gergin** *We had a rather strained conversation.* **2** If a relationship is strained, problems are spoiling that relationship. **soğuk, gergin, sorunlu, çıkmazda, iyi gitmeyen** *Relations are still strained between the two countries.* ○ *They have a rather strained relationship.*

strait /streɪt/ *noun* [C] a narrow area of sea that connects two large areas of sea **boğaz** [usually plural] *the straits of Florida*

strait-jacket /'streɪt,dʒækɪt/ *noun* [C] a special jacket used for mentally ill people that prevents them from moving their arms **deli gömleği**

strand /strænd/ *noun* [C] **1** a thin piece of hair, thread, rope, etc **tel, iplik** *She tucked a strand of hair behind her ear.* **2** one part of a story, situation, idea, etc **bölüm, kısım, parça** *There are a number of different strands to the plot.*

stranded /'strændɪd/ *adjective* unable to leave a place **mahsur kalmış, saplanıp kalmış, karaya oturmuş** *We were stranded at the airport for ten hours.*

ᵒ°**strange** /streɪndʒ/ *adjective* **1** If something is strange, it is surprising because it is unusual or unexpected. **acayip, garip ,tuhaf** [+ (that)] *It's strange that she hasn't called.* ○ *It's midnight and he's still at work - that's strange.* ○ *What a strange-looking man.* **2** A strange person or place is one that you are not familiar with. **yabancı, tanınmayan, bilinmeyen** *I was stuck in a strange town with no money.* ● **strangely** *adverb* *She's been behaving very strangely* (= in an unusual way) *recently.* **ilginç, garip bir şekilde**

Strange kelimesinin yerine **odd, bizarre** ve **weird** kelimeleri kullanılabilir. *I always thought there was something a bit* **odd** *about her.* ● *I had a really* **bizarre/ weird** *dream last night.*

Eğer bir şey beklentilerinizin dışında bir şekilde ise, bu durumda **curious, funny** veya **peculiar** sıfatları kullanılabilir. *This lemonade tastes* **funny.** ● *The chicken had a* **peculiar** *smell.* ● *A* **curious** *thing happened to me yesterday.*

Eğer kişi sürekli olarak ilginç davranışlarda bulunuyorsa, **eccentric** ifadesiyle tanımlanabilir. *The whole family are* **eccentric.**

stranger /'streɪndʒəʳ/ *noun* [C] **1** someone you have never met before **yabancı, tanımadık biri, bilinmedik kimse** *I can't just walk up to a complete stranger and start speaking to them.* **2 be no stranger to sth** to have a lot of experience of something **yabancısı olmamak, işin yabancısı/acemisi olmamak** *He's no stranger to hard work himself.*

strangle /'stræŋgl/ *verb* [T] **1** to kill someone by pressing their throat with your hands, a rope, wire, etc **boğmak, boğazını sıkarak öldürmek** [often passive] *Police believe the victim was strangled.* **2** to prevent something from developing **gelişmesine mani olmak; boğmak, engellemek; sekteye uğratmak** *High-level corruption is strangling the economy.*

stranglehold /'stræŋglhəʊld/ *noun* [no plural] a position of complete control that prevents something from developing **aşırı baskı/kontrol; yıldırıcı/boğucu hâkimiyet** *Two major companies have a stranglehold on the market.*

strap /stræp/ *noun* [C] a narrow piece of material used to fasten two things together or to carry something **kayış, askı, şerit, bant** *a watch strap* ○ *a bra strap* ○ *I want a bag with a shoulder strap.* ● **strap** *verb* [T] **strapping,** *past* **strapped** to fasten something using a strap **kayışla bağlamak**

strategic /strə'ti:dʒɪk/ *adjective* **1** [PLAN] helping to achieve a plan, usually in business or politics **stratejik, taktiksel** *strategic planning* **2** [WAR] related to fighting a war **stratejik, savaşta mücadeleye ilişkin; savaş taktiğine dair** *strategic weapons* **3** [POSITION] If something is in a strategic position, it is in a useful place for achieving something. **önemli, elverişli, stratejik** ● **strategically** *adverb* **stratejik olarak**

adopt/develop/have a strategy ● a strategy **for** doing sth ● the strategy **of** doing sth ● an **economic** strategy ● a **long-term/short-term** strategy ● a **sales** strategy

strategy /'strætədʒi/ *noun* **1** [C] a plan that you use to achieve something **strateji, plan, taktik** *a an economic strategy* ○ *a long-term strategy* **2** [U] the act of planning how to achieve something **planlama, taktik yapmak, strateji** *a military strategy*

straw /strɔ:/ *noun* **1** [U] the long, dried stems of plants such as wheat (= plant for grain), often given to animals for sleeping on and eating **saman** *a straw hat* **2** [C] a thin plastic or paper tube that you use for drinking through **kamış, pipet 3 the final/last straw** the last in a series of unpleasant events which finally makes you stop accepting a bad situation **bardağı taşıran son damla, sabrın tükenme noktası** *Last week he came home drunk at five in the morning, and that was the last straw.*

strawberry /'strɔ:bᵊri/ *noun* [C] a small, red fruit with a green leaf at the top and small, brown seeds on its surface **çilek**

stray¹ /streɪ/ *verb* [I] **1** to move away from the place where you should be, without intending to **farkında olmadan uzaklaşmak; kaybolmak** *I suddenly realized that I had strayed far from the village.* **2** to start thinking or talking about a different subject from the one you should be giving attention to **konudan sapmak/uzaklaşmak; zihni başka tarafa kaymak** *We seem to have strayed from the original subject.*

stray² /streɪ/ *adjective* [always before noun] **1** A stray animal is lost or has no home. **başıboş, sahipsiz** *a stray dog* **2** A stray piece of something has become separated from the main part. **etrafa saçılmış, ,tek tük etrafa dağılmış** *a stray hair*

stray³ /streɪ/ *noun* [C] an animal that is lost or has no home **başıboş/sahipsiz hayvan**

streak¹ /stri:k/ *noun* [C] **1** a thin line or mark **uzun çizgi, uzunlamasına leke, şerit** *She has a streak of white hair.* **2** a quality in someone's character, especially a bad one **(olumsuz) yan, yön, nitelik, özellik; karakter olumsuzluğu; damar, huy** *Tom has a mean/ruthless streak.* **3 a winning/losing streak** a period of always winning/losing a game **kazanma/ kaybetme dönemi/süresi/müddeti** *I'm on a winning streak.*

streak² /stri:k/ *verb* **1 streak across/down/through,** etc to move quickly **hızlıca hareket etmek** *The plane streaked across the sky.* **2 be streaked with sth** to have thin lines of a different colour farklı renklerde çizgilerden oluşmak; gölgeli/çizgili/yol yol olmak *His dark hair was lightly streaked with grey.*

stream

stream   stream of water

stream¹ /striːm/ *noun* [C] **1** a small river dere, çay **2 a** stream of sth **a** a line of people or vehicles moving in the same direction akım, sel gibi kalabalık; aynı yöne giden araç veya insan sırası/seli *a constant stream of traffic* **b** a large number of similar things that happen or appear one after another bir biri ardısıra olan, akan, akış, sel, yağmur *He has produced a steady stream of books.* **c** a moving line of liquid, gas, smoke, etc akış, akıntı, akım *A stream of smoke was coming from the chimney.*

stream² /striːm/ *verb* **1** stream down/in/through, etc to move or flow continuously in one direction bir yönde akmak/hareket etmek/ilerlemek *Tears were streaming down her face.* **2** [T] to listen to or watch something on a computer directly from the Internet internet aracılığıyla bilgisayarda bir şeyi izlemek/dinlemek

streamer /ˈstriːməʳ/ *noun* [C] a long, narrow piece of coloured paper that you use to decorate a room or place for a party uzun ince süs kağıdı, serpantin, grapon kağıdı

streamline /ˈstriːmlaɪn/ *verb* [T] **1** to make an organization or process simpler and more effective bir sistemi/işlemi daha basit ve etkin hâle getirmek; etkinleştirmek *We need to streamline our production procedures.* **2** to give a vehicle a smooth shape so that it moves easily through air or water aerodinamik şekil vermek

o-**street** /striːt/ *noun* [C] **1** a road in a town or city that has houses or other buildings cadde *We live on the same street.* ○ *a street map* **2 the man/person, etc in the street** a typical, ordinary person sokaktaki adam; halk adamı; sıradan kimse, alelâde insan **3 be right up sb's street** UK informal (US be right up sb's alley) to be exactly the type of thing that someone knows about or likes to do ilgi alanı içinde olmak; çok iyi bilinen olmak; tam şenlik/onluk/benlik olmak *I've got a little job here which should be right up your street.* **4 be streets ahead (of sb/sth)** UK to be much better or more advanced than someone or something else çok önde/üstün olmak; fersah fersah ilerde olmak *American film companies are streets ahead of their European rivals.* ⊃See also: high street, Wall Street.

streetcar /ˈstriːtkɑːʳ/ US (UK/US tram) *noun* [C] an electric vehicle for carrying passengers, mostly in cities, which runs along metal tracks in the road tramvay

ˈstreet ˌlight (also 'street ˌlamp) *noun* [C] a light on a tall post next to a street sokak lambası ⊃See picture at light.

streetwise /ˈstriːtwaɪz/ (US also street-smart) *adjective* Someone who is streetwise knows how to manage dangerous or difficult situations in big towns or cities. büyük şehir yaşamını ve tehlikeleri savuşturmayı bilen; sokakların adamı olan

strength ...... İLE BİRLİKTE KULLANILAN KELİMELER
full/great/superhuman strength ● draw/have/muster/regain/sap strength

o-**strength** /streŋθ/ *noun* **1** STRONG [U] when someone or something is strong güç, kuvvet, tâkat *upper-body strength* ○ *A good boxer needs skill as well as strength.* **2** INFLUENCE [U] the power or influence that an organization, country, etc has güç, kuvvet, etki, yaptırım gücü *economic strength* **3** BEING BRAVE [U] when you are brave or determined in difficult situations cesaret, kararlılık, dayanıklılık, mukavemet *I think she showed great strength of character.* **4** GOOD QUALITIES [C] a good quality or ability that makes someone or something effective etkinlik, güçlülük, kalite, yetenek, güç *We all have our strengths and weaknesses.* ○ *The great strength of this arrangement is its simplicity.* **5** STRONG FEELING [U] how strong a feeling or opinion is güçlü duygu, kuvvetli fikir; güç *There is great strength of feeling against tax increases.* **6** VALUE [U] the value of a country's money değer, alımgücü, güç *The strength of the dollar has traders worried.* **7 at full strength** with the necessary number of people tam güç, tam kadro, tam mevcut *Our team is now at full strength.* **8 on the strength of sth** If you do something on the strength of facts or advice, you do it because of them. ...a/e güvenerek/dayanarak; ...ın/in yardımıyla/etkisiyle/gücüyle *On the strength of this year's sales figures, we've decided to expand the business.* **9 go from strength to strength** UK to continue to become more successful aşama aşama gücünü artırmak/ilerlemek; adım adım yükselmek; gittikçe başarılı olmak ⊃See also: a tower¹ of strength.

strengthen /ˈstreŋθən/ *verb* [I, T] to become stronger or make something become stronger güçlen(dir)mek, sağlamlaş(tır)mak, desteklemek, kuvvet vermek *exercises to strengthen the leg muscles*

strenuous /ˈstrenjuəs/ *adjective* using or needing a lot of effort güç, ağır, yorucu, çaba isteyen, çetin *strenuous exercise*

stress ...... İLE BİRLİKTE KULLANILAN KELİMELER
be under stress ● cope with/deal with/handle stress ● alleviate/combat/reduce/relieve stress ● stress levels

o-**stress¹** /stres/ *noun* **1** WORRY [C, U] feelings of worry caused by difficult situations such as problems at work gerilim, stres, baskı, sıkıntı *work-related stress* ○ *She's been under a lot of stress recently.* **2** IMPORTANCE [U] special importance that you give to something önem verme, vurgulama, bilhassa belirtme *At school, they laid great stress on academic achievement.* **3** PHYSICAL FORCE [C, U] physical force on something basınç, tazzik *Jogging puts a lot of stress on your knee joints.* **4** STRONG PART [U] when you say one part of a word more strongly vurgulama, tonlama, vurgulu söyleme *In the word 'blanket', the stress is on the first syllable.*

stress² /stres/ *verb* **1** [T] to emphasize something in order to show that it is important vurgulamak, üze-

S

rinde durmak, altını çizerek belirtmek [+ (that)] *I stressed that this was our policy.* **2** [I] *US informal* to be worried **strese girmek, baskı altında hissetmek, endişelenmek** *Stop stressing about tonight - it'll be fine.*

stressed /strest/ (*also* **stressed out**) *adjective* worried and not able to relax **endişeli, stresli, baskı altında olan** *Tanya's really stressed out about her exams.*

stressful /ˈstresfʊl/ *adjective* making you stressed **stresli, sıkıntılı, gerilimli** *a stressful job*

○▪**stretch**[1] /stretʃ/ *verb* **1** [I, T] to become longer or wider, or to pull something so that it becomes longer or wider **uzanmak, yayılmak, uzatmak, yaymak** *Don't pull my sweater - you'll stretch it.* **2** [I, T] to make your body or part of your body straighter and longer **gerinmek, germek** *Stretch your arms above your head.* **3 stretch away/into, etc** to cover a large area **büyük bir alanı kaplamak, uzanmak, yayılmak** *The fields stretched away into the distance.* **4 stretch into/over, etc** to continue for a long period of time **uzun bir süre devam etmek; sürmek** *The discussions will probably stretch into next month.* つSee also: stretch your legs (**leg**), bend/stretch the rules (**rule**[1]).
stretch out *phrasal verb* to lie with your legs and arms spread out in a relaxed way **uzanıp yatmak, kolları bacakları açık yatmak**

stretch[2] /stretʃ/ *noun* [C] **1** LAND/WATER an area of land or water **alan, saha, bölüm, kısım** *a stretch of coastline* **2** TIME a continuous period of time **süre, zaman, müddet, aralık** *He often worked ten hours at a stretch.* **3** BODY when you stretch part of your body **gerinme** *I always do a few stretches before I go jogging.* **4 not by any stretch of the imagination** used to say that something, often a description, is certainly not true **yanından bile geçmez; hiç alâkası bile yok** *She was never a great player, not by any stretch of the imagination.*

stretcher /ˈstretʃər/ *noun* [C] a flat structure covered with cloth which is used to carry someone who is ill or injured **sedye**

stricken /ˈstrɪkən/ *adjective* suffering from the effects of something bad, such as illness, sadness, etc **kapılmış, uğramış, tutulmuş, yakalanmış** *a child stricken by fear* つSee also: panic-stricken, poverty-stricken.

stretcher

○▪**strict** /strɪkt/ *adjective* **1** PERSON A strict person makes sure that children or people working for them behave well and does not allow them to break any rules. **katı, sert, disiplinli, hoşgörüsüz** *a strict teacher* ○ *My parents were very strict with us.* **2** RULE If a rule, law, etc is strict, it must be obeyed. **sıkı, sert, katı, ödünsüz** *She gave me strict instructions to be there by ten.* **3** BEHAVIOUR [always before noun] always behaving in a particular way because of your beliefs **koyu, katı, tam** *a strict Muslim* **4** EXACT exactly correct **tam, kesinlikle, mutlak, harfi harfine** *a strict translation of a text*

strictly /ˈstrɪktli/ *adverb* **1** exactly or correctly **tamamen, kesinlikle** *That's not strictly true.* ○ *Strictly speaking* (= The rules say), *we're not allowed to give you any advice.* **2** done or existing for a particular person or purpose **sadece, yalnızca; bir tek** *Her visit is strictly business.* **3 strictly forbidden/prohibited** used to emphasize that something is not allowed **kesinlikle yasaklanmış**

stride[1] /straɪd/ *verb past* **strode** stride across/down/into, etc to walk somewhere with long steps **çabuk ve uzun adımlarla yürümek** *She strode across the stage.*

stride[2] /straɪd/ *noun* [C] **1** a long step when walking or running **uzun adım** **2 get into your stride** *UK* (*US* hit your stride) to start to do something well and with confidence because you have been doing it for a period **(uzun süre yaptığı bir işin) havasına girmek** *Once I get into my stride, I'm sure I'll work much faster.* **3 take sth in your stride** *UK* (*US* take sth in stride) to calmly deal with something that is unpleasant and not let it affect what you are doing **mesele yapmamak, sakince üstesinden gelmek; telaşa kapılmadan halletmek** *There are often problems at work but she seems to take it all in her stride.*

strident /ˈstraɪdᵊnt/ *adjective* **1** expressed in a strong way **keskin, tiz, acı, rahatsız edici** *strident criticism* **2** loud and unpleasant **yaygaracı, tantanacı, şirret, ağzı pis** *a strident voice*

strife /straɪf/ *noun* [U] *formal* trouble or disagreement between people **kavga, çekişme, mücadele, uyuşmazlık**

○▪**strike**[1] /straɪk/ *verb past* **struck 1** HIT [T] to hit someone or something **vurmak** *His car went out of control and struck a tree.* ○ *I've never heard of anyone being struck by lightning.* **2** THINK [T] If a thought or idea strikes you, you suddenly think of it. **birden düşünmek, şıp diye düşünüvermek, aklına gelivermek; zihninde şimşek gibi çakmak** [+ (that)] *It struck me that I'd forgotten to order the champagne.* **3 strike sb as sth** If someone strikes you as having a particular quality, they seem to have that quality. **...gibi gelmek; ...izlenimini uyandırmak** *He didn't strike me as a passionate man.* **4** NOT WORK [I] to stop working for a period of time because you want more money, etc **greve gitmek, grev yapmak** *Bus drivers are threatening to strike.* **5** EFFECT [T] If something bad strikes something or someone, it affects them strongly and quickly. **çabucak ve güçlü şekilde etkile(n)mek** *The hurricane struck the coast at about eight in the morning.* **6** ATTACK [I] to attack suddenly **saldırmak, hücuma geçmek** *The marines will strike at dawn.* **7** CLOCK [I, T] If a clock strikes, a bell rings to show what the time is. **(saat) çalmak, göstermek; vurmak 8 strike gold, oil, etc** to find a supply of gold, oil, etc in the ground **altın/petrol vb. bulmak/ damarına rastlamak 9 strike a match** to light a match in order to produce fire **kibrit yakmak 10 strike a balance** to give two things the same amount of attention **denge kurmak, dengeyi sağlamak** *It's important to strike a balance between spending and saving.* **11 strike a deal** If two people strike a deal, they promise to do something for each other which will give them both an advantage. **karşılıklı iyilik yapmaya söz vermek** *The book's author has struck a deal with a major film company.* つSee also: strike a **chord** (with sb), be struck **dumb**.
strike back *phrasal verb* to attack someone who has attacked you **karşı saldırıya geçmek**
strike out *phrasal verb* **1** to start moving towards somewhere in a determined way **kararlı bir şekilde bir tarafa yönelmek; azimle başlamak** *She struck out for the opposite bank.* **2** *US informal* to fail at something **başarısızlığa uğramak; bir şeyi başaramamak** *I really struck out with her - she wouldn't even let me kiss her goodbye.*
strike sth out *phrasal verb* to draw a line through something wrong that you have written **üstünü çizmek/ karalamak**
strike up sth *phrasal verb* to start a conversation or relationship with someone **sohbeti/dostluğu başlat-**

mak; dostluk kurmak/başlatmak *I struck up a conversation with a guy who worked behind the bar.*

strike (noun) .... İLE BİRLİKTE KULLANILAN KELİMELER
be on/go on strike ● a strike over sth ● strike action

strike² /straɪk/ *noun* **1** [C, U] a period of time when people are not working because they want more money, etc grev *Teachers are planning to go on strike next month.* **2** [C] a sudden military attack askerî hücum/saldırı *an air strike* ➡See also: hunger strike.

striker /ˈstraɪkəʳ/ *noun* [C] **1** someone who is on strike grevci **2** a football player whose job is to try to score goals golcü futbolcu

striking /ˈstraɪkɪŋ/ *adjective* **1** easily noticed göze çarpan, kolayca görülebilen *There's a striking resemblance between them.* **2** very attractive çarpıcı, çok güzel/yakışıklı/çekici *She's very striking.*

string¹ /strɪŋ/ *noun* **1** [C, U] very thin rope used for tying things ip, sicim, kınnap *a ball of string* **2** [C] a piece of wire that is part of a musical instrument tel, yay, kiriş *guitar strings* **3** a string of beads/pearls a set of decorative things joined together on a thread, worn as jewellery boncuk/inci kolye/süs **4** a string of sth a number of similar things dizi, sıra *a string of questions* ○ *As a writer, she's enjoyed a string of successes.* **5** no strings (attached) If there are no strings attached to an offer or arrangement, there is nothing that is unpleasant that you have to accept. koşulsuz, şartsız, sınırlanmamış, sınırlayıcı koşullar içermeyen *I'll drive you home - no strings attached.* ● **6** pull strings to secretly use the influence that you have over important people to get something or to help someone torpil yaptırmak, iltimas geçmesini istemek

string² /strɪŋ/ *verb* [T] *past* **strung** to hang something somewhere with string asmak, dizmek *They had strung flags across the entrance to welcome us home.*
string sb along *phrasal verb* to deceive someone for a long time about what you are intending to do kandırmak, aldatmak
be strung out *phrasal verb* If a group of things or people are strung out somewhere, they are in a line with spaces between them. sıra sıra dizilmek, sırala(n)mak *There were chairs strung out across the room.*

stringent /ˈstrɪndʒənt/ *adjective* Stringent controls, rules, etc are very strict or extreme. sıkı, sert, katı

the strings /strɪŋz/ *noun* [plural] the people in a musical group who play instruments with strings on them such as the violin yaylı sazlar, telli sazlar

strip¹ /strɪp/ *verb* stripping, *past* stripped **1** [I, T] (*also UK* strip off) to remove all your clothes, or to remove all someone else's clothes soymak, soyunmak; kıyafetlerini çıkarmak/soymak *She was stripped and searched by the guards.* ○ *He stripped off his clothes and ran into the sea.* **2** (*also* strip off) to remove a covering from the surface of something soymak *to strip paint/wallpaper off the wall*
strip sb of sth *phrasal verb* to take something important away from someone as a punishment ceza vermek amacıyla sahip olduğunu elinden almak *He was stripped of his gold medal.*

strip² /strɪp/ *noun* [C] **1** PIECE a long, narrow piece of something şerit *a strip of paper/plastic* **2** AREA a long, narrow area of land or water uzun ve dar alan/parça **3** REMOVING CLOTHES entertainment in which someone takes off their clothes in a sexually exciting way soyunarak tahrik etme, striptiz *a strip club/show* ➡See also: comic strip.

stripe /straɪp/ *noun* [C] a long, straight area of colour şerit, yol, çizgi, çubuk *white with blue stripes* ➡See picture at horizontal.

striped /straɪpt/ *adjective* with a pattern of stripes çizgili, şeritli, yollu *a striped shirt*

stripey /ˈstraɪpi/ *adjective* another spelling of stripy şeritli, çizgili

stripper /ˈstrɪpəʳ/ *noun* [C] someone who takes off their clothes in a sexually exciting way to entertain people striptizci

striptease /ˈstrɪptiːz/ *noun* [C, U] entertainment in which someone takes off their clothes in a sexually exciting way soyunarak tahrik etme

stripy (*also* stripey) /ˈstraɪpi/ *adjective* with a pattern of stripes şeritli, çizgili *stripy trousers*

strive /straɪv/ *verb* [I] *past* **strove** or **strived**, *past part* **striven** or **strived** *formal* to try very hard to do or achieve something çabalamak, gayret etmek, çalışmak *to strive for happiness/peace* ○ [+ to do sth] *We are constantly striving to improve our service.*

strode /strəʊd/ *past of* stride çabuk ve uzun adımlarla yürümek' fiilinin geçmiş zaman hâli

stroke¹ /strəʊk/ *noun* **1** ILLNESS [C] a sudden problem in your brain that changes the flow of blood and makes you unable to move part of your body felç, inme *to have/suffer a stroke* **2** MOVEMENT [C] a movement that you make against something with your hand, a pen, brush, etc darbe vuruş *a brush stroke* **3** SWIMMING [C] a style of swimming bir yüzme şekli, vuruş, kulaç, kürek çekme **4** SPORT [C] when you move your arm and hit the ball in sports such as tennis, golf, etc vuruş **5** a stroke of luck something good that happens to you by chance beklenmedik, şans, umulmadık talih *He had exactly the part that I needed so that was a stroke of luck.*

stroke² /strəʊk/ *verb* [T] to gently move your hand over a surface okşamak, sıvazlamak *to stroke a cat/dog* ○ *He stroked her hair.*

stroll /strəʊl/ *verb* **stroll along/down/through, etc** to walk somewhere in a slow and relaxed way sallana sallana yürümek, gezinmek, dolaşmak *They strolled along the beach.* ● **stroll** *noun* [C] *Shall we go for a stroll around the garden?* gezinti

stroller /ˈstrəʊləʳ/ *US* (*UK* pushchair) *noun* [C] a chair on wheels that is used to move small children çocuk arabası, puset

○━strong /strɒŋ/ *adjective* **1** PHYSICALLY POWERFUL A strong person or animal is physically powerful. güçlü, kuvvetli *Are you strong enough to lift this table on your own?* **2** NOT BREAK A strong object does not break easily or can support heavy things. sağlam, dayanıklı, güçlü *a strong box/chair* **3** QUALITY of a good quality or level and likely to be successful iyi, güçlü, kuvvetli, şansı yüksek *a strong competitor/team* ○ *a strong economy* **4** FEELING A strong feeling, belief, or opinion is felt in a very deep and serious way. güçlü, kaliteli, başarılı, mükemmel *a strong sense of pride* **5** NOTICEABLE If a taste, smell, etc is strong, it is very noticeable. keskin, farkedilebilen, güçlü *There's a strong smell of burning.* **6** PERSONALITY If a person or their personality is strong, they are confident and able to deal with problems well. güçlü, kişilikli, kuvvetli, kendinden emin, gözükara, azimli **7** ALCOHOL containing a lot of alcohol (içki) sert, koyu, demli *a strong drink* **8** RELATIONSHIP If a friendship, relationship, etc is strong, it is likely to last for a long time. sağlam, güçlü, kuvvetli **9** strong chance/possibility, etc something that is very likely to happen kuvvetli olasılık/şans *There's a strong possibility of rain this afternoon.* **10** strong

opposition/support, etc a lot of opposition/support, etc **güçlü muhalefet/destek 11 strong language** words that some people might consider to be offensive **kaba/sert dil; kaba sözcükler 12 sb's strong point** something that someone is very good at **en güçlü noktası; en iyi olduğu konu** *Cooking is not my strong point.* **13 be still going strong** continuing to be successful after a long time **hâlâ dimdik ayakta olmak, etkin olmak; cami yıkılmış ama mihrap yerinde olmak**

strongly /'strɒŋli/ *adverb* very much or in a very serious way **tamamıyla, çok ciddi biçimde** *He is strongly opposed to violence of any sort.* ○ *I strongly believe that we should take action.*

strong-willed /ˌstrɒŋ'wɪld/ *adjective* very determined to do what you want to do **kararlı, azimli, bildiğini okuyan**

stroppy /'strɒpi/ *adjective UK informal* angry or arguing a lot **aksi, huysuz, keçi inatlı, dik kafalı** *a stroppy teenager*

strove /strəʊv/ *past tense of* strive **çabalamak' fiilinin geçmiş zaman hâli**

struck /strʌk/ *past of* strike **vurmak' fiilinin geçmiş zaman hâli**

structural /'strʌktʃ°r°l/ *adjective* relating to the structure of something **yapısal, yapıya ait** *structural damage* ○ *The last five years have seen big structural changes in the company.* ● **structurally** *adverb* **yapısal olarak**

⚬⊷**structure¹** /'strʌktʃə°/ *noun* **1** [C, U] the way that parts of something are arranged or put together **yapı, bünye, çatı, strüktür** *cell structure* ○ *grammatical structure* **2** [C] a building or something that has been built **yapı, bina**

structure² /'strʌktʃə°/ *verb* [T] to arrange something in an organized way **itinalı bir şekilde düzenlemek** *How is the course structured?*

⚬⊷**struggle¹** /'strʌgl/ *verb* [I] **1** to try very hard to do something difficult **çaba sarfetmek, uğraşmak, mücadele etmek** [+ to do sth] *He's struggling to pay off his debts.* **2** to fight someone when they are holding you **çırpınmak, debelenmek** *She struggled but couldn't break free.*
struggle on *phrasal verb* to continue doing something that is difficult **çabalamaya devam etmek, mücadeleyi sürdürmek, canını dişine takmak**

🧩   **struggle (noun)** .... İLE BİRLİKTE KULLANILAN KELİMELER

a **constant/ongoing/uphill** struggle ● a struggle **for** [justice/survival, etc]

⚬⊷**struggle²** /'strʌgl/ *noun* [C] **1** when you try very hard to do something difficult **uğraşma, mücadele, savaş** *It was a real struggle to stay awake during the film.* **2** a fight between people **kavga, boğuşma, mücadele**

strum /strʌm/ *verb* [I, T] **strumming**, *past* **strummed** to move your fingers across the strings of a guitar **tıngırdatmak, çalmak**

strung /strʌŋ/ *past of* string **asmak, dizmek' fiilinin geçmiş zaman hâli**

strut /strʌt/ *verb* **strutting**, *past* **strutted strut along/ around/down, etc** to walk somewhere with big steps in a proud way **kasılarak yürümek, caka satarak yürümek** ⟴See also: strut your stuff¹.

stub¹ /stʌb/ *noun* [C] the short, end piece of something such as a cigarette or pencil that is left after it has been used **izmarit, dip, koçan** *There were cigarette stubs all over the floor.*

stub² /stʌb/ *verb* **stubbing**, *past* **stubbed stub your toe** to hit your toe against a hard surface by accident **kazara çarpıp incitmek**
stub sth out *phrasal verb* to stop a cigarette from burning by pressing the burning end against a hard surface **bastırıp söndürmek**

stubble /'stʌbl/ *noun* [U] **1** very short, stiff hairs, usually on a man's face **kirli sakal, hafif uzamış sakal 2** the short bits of dried plant stems left in a field after it has been cut **anız**

stubborn /'stʌbən/ *adjective* determined not to change your ideas, plans, etc, although other people want you to **inatçı, dik başlı, dik kafalı ● stubbornly** *adverb* **inatçılıkla ● stubbornness** *noun* [U] **inatçılık**

stubby /'stʌbi/ *adjective* short and thick **küt** *stubby legs/fingers*

stuck¹ /stʌk/ *adjective* [never before noun] **1** not able to move anywhere **sıkışıp kalmış, takılmış, sıkışmış** *My car got stuck in a ditch.* ○ *We were stuck at the airport for twelve hours.* **2** not able to continue reading, answering questions, etc because something is too difficult **takılmış, çaresiz kalmış, içinden çıkılmaz durumda kalmış** *I keep getting stuck on difficult words.* **3 be stuck with sb/sth** to have to deal with someone or something unpleasant because no one else wants to **istemediği halde ilgilenmek zorunda olmak, başına kalmak** *Whenever we eat out, I always get stuck with the bill.*

stuck² /stʌk/ *past of* stick **'yapıştırmak' fiilinin geçmiş zaman hâli**

stud /stʌd/ *noun* [C] **1** [JEWELLERY] a small, metal piece of jewellery that is put through a part of your body such as your ear or nose **küpe, geçmeli küpe, hızma** ⟴See picture at **jewellery**. **2** [DECORATION] a small piece of metal that is fixed to the surface of something, usually for decoration **metal düğme, süs, kabara, çivi 3** [ANIMALS] *(also* **'stud ˌfarm)** a place where horses are kept for breeding **damızlık hayvan harası**

⚬⊷**student** /'stjuːd°nt/ *noun* [C] someone who is studying at a school or university **öğrenci, talebe** *a law student* ○ *a foreign student* ⟴See also: mature student.

studio /'stjuːdiəʊ/ *noun* [C] **1** [ART] a room where an artist or photographer works **stüdyo 2** [TV/RADIO] a room where television/radio programmes or musical recordings are made **tv/radyo/müzik stüdyosu 3** [FILMS] a film company or a place where films are made **film stüdyosu**

studious /'stjuːdiəs/ *adjective* spending a lot of time studying **çalışkan, çalışmayı seven, gayretli ● studiously** *adverb* **çalışkanlıkla**

⚬⊷**study¹** /'stʌdi/ *verb* **1** [I, T] to learn about a subject, usually at school or university **okumak, öğrenmek, çalışmak** *I studied biology before going into medicine.* ⟴See Common learner error at **learn. 2** [T] to look at something very carefully **dikkatlice çalışmak** *He studied his face in the mirror.*

🧩   **study (noun)** .... İLE BİRLİKTE KULLANILAN KELİMELER

carry out/conduct/undertake a study ● a study **examines/focuses on** sth ● a study **concludes/ finds/shows/suggests** sth ● a study **into** sth

---

study² /'stʌdi/ *noun* **1** [FINDING OUT INFORMATION] [C] when someone studies a subject in detail in order to discover new information **çalışma, araştırma, öğrenme** *For years, studies have shown the link between smoking and cancer.* **2** [LEARNING] [U] when you learn about a subject, usually at school or university **öğrenme, çalışma, araştırma, inceleme** *the study of English literature*

3 [ROOM] [C] a room in a house where you can read, write, etc **çalışma odası** ➸See also: **case study.**

o⊷**stuff**¹ /stʌf/ noun [U] informal **1** used to refer to a substance or a group of things or ideas, etc without saying exactly what they are **şey, madde, nesne** *There's some sticky stuff on the carpet.* ○ *They sell bread and cakes and stuff like that.* ○ *Can I leave my stuff at your house?* **2 know your stuff** informal to know a lot about a subject, or to be very good at doing something **işini iyi bilmek; konusuna hâkim olmak** *She's an excellent teacher - she really knows her stuff.* **3 strut your stuff** humorous informal to dance **dans etmek**

stuff² /stʌf/ verb [T] **1 stuff sth in/into/behind, etc** to push something into a small space, often quickly or in a careless way **tıkmak, tıkıştırmak** *He stuffed the papers in his briefcase and left.* **2** [FILL] to completely fill a container with something **doldurmak, tıka basa doldurmak** *an envelope stuffed with money* **3** [FOOD] to fill meat, vegetables, etc with a mixture of food before you cook them **dolma yapmak, içini doldurmak** *stuffed peppers* **4** [DEAD ANIMAL] to fill the body of a dead animal with special material so that it looks as if it is still alive **(ölü hayvan) içini doldurmak**

stuffing /'stʌfɪŋ/ noun [U] **1** a mixture of food which is put into meat, vegetables, etc before they are cooked **iç, dolma içi 2** material which is used to fill the inside of things such as soft chairs, beds, toys, etc **dolgu maddesi, kıtık**

stuffy /'stʌfi/ adjective **1** If a room or a building is stuffy, it is hot and unpleasant and the air is not fresh. **havasız ve sıcak 2** old-fashioned, formal and boring **eski kafalı, gelenekçi, resmî** *a stuffy club for wealthy old men*

stumble /'stʌmbl/ verb [I] **1** to step badly and almost fall over **tökezlemek** *Mary stumbled on the loose rocks.* **2** to make a mistake, such as pausing or repeating a word, while speaking or performing **duraksamak, dili sürçmek, dili takılmak** *He kept stumbling over the same word.*

stumble across/on/upon sth/sb phrasal verb to discover something by chance, or to meet someone by chance **...a/e rastgelmek; rastlamak, tesadüf etmek** *I stumbled across these photographs while I was cleaning out my desk.*

'**stumbling ,block** noun [C] a problem which makes it very difficult to do something **engel, mânia, zorluk, güçlük** *Lack of money has been the main stumbling block.*

stump¹ /stʌmp/ noun [C] **1** the short part of something that is left after most of it has been removed **kalıntı, kütük, kalan parça** *a tree stump* **2** one of the three vertical wooden sticks that you throw a ball at in the game of cricket **krikette kale çubuğu** ➸Orta kısımdaki renkli sayfalarına bakınız.

stump² /stʌmp/ verb **1 be stumped by sth** informal to not be able to answer a question or solve a problem because it is too difficult **aklını karıştırmak, içinden çıkılmaz duruma sokmak** *Scientists are completely stumped by this virus.* **2** [I] US to travel to different places to get political support **siyasi destek almak amacıyla şehir şehir/kasaba kasaba dolaşmak**

stump (sth) up phrasal verb UK informal to provide money for something, especially when you do not want to **istemeyerek para vermek**

stun /stʌn/ verb [T] **stunning, stunned 1** to shock or surprise someone very much **şaşırtmak, afallamak, şaşkına dönmek** [often passive] *Friends and family were stunned by her sudden death.* **2** to make a person or animal unconscious, usually by hitting them on the head **sersemletmek, bayıltmak**

stung /stʌŋ/ past of sting **sokmak' fiilinin geçmiş zaman hâli**

stunk /stʌŋk/ **1** past participle of stink **pis kokmak' fiilinin geçmiş zaman hâli 2** US past tense of stink **kokuşmak' fiilinin geçmiş zaman hâli**

stunning /'stʌnɪŋ/ adjective very beautiful **çok güzel, fevkalâde, şahane, mükemmel** *stunning views over the city* ○ *She's stunning.* • **stunningly** adverb *a stunningly beautiful woman* **çok alıcı bir şekilde**

stunt¹ /stʌnt/ noun [C] **1** when someone does something dangerous that needs great skill, usually in a film **tehlikeli film sahnesi/numarası** *He always does his own stunts.* **2** something that is done to get people's attention **hüner, gösteri, ustalık, numara** *Their marriage was just a cheap publicity stunt.*

stunt² /stʌnt/ verb [T] to stop the normal growth or development of something **büyümesini önlemek, gelişmesine mani olmak** *They say that smoking stunts your growth.*

stupefied /'stju:pɪfaɪd/ adjective so shocked, tired, etc that you cannot think **şok olmuş, yorgun, kafası durmuş, sersemlemiş, aptallaşmış, bunalmış** • **stupefying** adjective making you stupefied **şok eden, sersemleten, aptallaştıran, bunaltan** • **stupefy** verb [T] **çok şaşırtmak, aptallaşmak**

stupendous /stju:'pendəs/ adjective extremely good or large **muazzam, çok büyük, harikulâde** *a stupendous performance* • **stupendously** adverb stupendously successful **muazzam bir şekilde**

o⊷**stupid** /'stju:pɪd/ adjective **1** silly or not intelligent **aptal, budala, ahmak, akılsız** *That was a really stupid thing to do.* ○ *How could you be so stupid?* **2** [always before noun] informal used to show that you are annoyed about something which is causing a problem **saçma, aptalca** *I can never get this stupid machine to work!* • **stupidity** /stju:'pɪdəti/ noun [U] **aptallık** • **stupidly** adverb **aptalca**

stupor /'stju:pəʳ/ noun [no plural] when someone is almost unconscious and cannot think clearly, especially because they have drunk too much alcohol **sersemleme, baygınlık, bilinç yitimi** *He staggered into the room in a drunken stupor.*

sturdy /'stɜ:di/ adjective very strong and solid **sağlam, güçlü, kuvvetli, dayanıklı** *sturdy walking boots*

stutter /'stʌtəʳ/ verb [I, T] to repeat the first sound of a word several times when you talk, usually because you have a speech problem **kekelemek, pepelemek** *"C-c-can we g-go now?" she stuttered.* • **stutter** noun [no plural] *He has a really bad stutter.* **kekeleme**

[style ...... İLE BİRLİKTE KULLANILAN KELİMELER]

a distinctive style • in a style • a style of doing sth

o⊷**style**¹ /staɪl/ noun **1** [WAY] [C, U] a way of doing something that is typical of a particular person, group, place, or period **tip, stil, tarz, biçim, teknik** *a style of painting/writing* **2** [DESIGN] [C, U] a way of designing hair, clothes, furniture, etc **tasarım, tarz, biçim, zevk, tavır, usul** *She's had her hair cut in a really nice style.* **3** [QUALITY] [U] the quality of being attractive and fashionable or behaving in a way which makes people admire you **şıklık ve kibarlık, zerafet ve incelik** *She's got style.* **4 do sth in style** to do something in a way that people admire, usually because it involves spending a lot of money *bir şeyi çok para harcayarak çok güzel bir tasarımla yapmak* *If we ever get married we'll do it in style.* **5 cramp sb's style** to prevent someone from enjoying themselves, especially by going somewhere with them **eğlencenin içine etmek; berbat etmek; keyfini bozmak, eğlenmesine mani olmak**

S

style² /staɪl/ *verb* [T] to shape or design hair, clothes, furniture, etc in a particular way **şekil vermek, biçimlendirmek, tasarlamak** *He spends hours in the bathroom styling his hair.*

-style /staɪl/ *suffix* used at the end of words to mean 'looking or behaving like something or someone' ...**tarzında/biçiminde/benzeri anlamında sonek** *antique-style furniture* ○ *Japanese-style management* ➌See also: old-style.

stylish /ˈstaɪlɪʃ/ *adjective* fashionable and attractive **şık, zarif, modaya uygun, çekici** *a stylish, black suit* • **stylishly** *adverb* *stylishly dressed* **modaya uygun bir şekilde**

Styrofoam /ˈstaɪrəfəʊm/ *noun* [U] *trademark* polystyrene (= light plastic material used to protect objects when they are packed)

suave /swɑːv/ *adjective* If someone, especially a man, is suave, they are polite and confident in a way that is attractive but may be false. **hoş ve nazik, kibar ve tatlı** *suave and sophisticated*

sub- /sʌb-/ *prefix* **1** under or below **altında/aşağısında...** **anlamında önek** *substandard workmanship* **2** less important or a smaller part of a larger whole **daha az önemli/daha küçük.. anlamında önek** *a subsection*

subconscious¹ /sʌbˈkɒnʃəs/ *adjective* Subconscious thoughts and feelings influence your behaviour without you being aware of them. **bilinçaltında olan, şuuraltındaki** *a subconscious fear* • **subconsciously** *adverb* **bilinç altından gelen**

subconscious² /sʌbˈkɒnʃəs/ *noun* [no plural] the part of your mind which contains thoughts and feelings that you are not aware of but which influence your behaviour **bilinçaltı, şuuraltı** *The memory was buried deep within my subconscious.*

subcontract /ˌsʌbkənˈtrækt/ *verb* [T] to pay someone else to do part of a job that you have agreed to do **alt sözleşme yapmak**

subculture /ˈsʌbˌkʌltʃər/ *noun* [C] a group of people with beliefs, interests, etc that are different from the rest of society **alt kültür**

subdivide /ˌsʌbdɪˈvaɪd/ *verb* [T] to divide something into smaller parts **küçük parçalara bölmek/ayırmak** [often passive] *Each chapter is subdivided into smaller sections.* • **subdivision** /ˌsʌbdɪˈvɪʒⁿn/ *noun* [C, U] **alt bölüm**

subdue /səbˈdjuː/ *verb* [T] **subduing**, *past* **subdued** to start to control someone or something, especially by using force **boyun eğdirmek, kontrol altına almak, bastırmak**

subdued /səbˈdjuːd/ *adjective* **1** quiet because you are feeling sad or worried **(üzüntü ve endişeden dolayı) suskun, neşesiz, keyifsiz, sessiz** *She seemed a bit subdued.* **2** Subdued lights or colours are not bright. **loş, belli belirsiz, kısık, solgun, parlak olmayan** *subdued lighting*

---

subject ...... İLE BİRLİKTE KULLANILAN KELİMELER

bring up/broach/raise a subject • **get onto** a subject • **change/drop/get off** a subject • **on** the subject (of sth)

ᴼ⁻**subject**¹ /ˈsʌbdʒɪkt/ *noun* [C] **1** WHAT what someone is writing or talking about **konu, mevzu** *I'm not sure whether the subject matter is suitable for children.*

grammes on the subject of homelessness **2** STUDY an area of knowledge studied in school or university **ders, konu, çalışma alanı** *Chemistry is my favourite subject.* **3** GRAMMAR the person or thing which performs the action described by the verb. In the sentence 'Bob pho-

---

ned me yesterday.', 'Bob' is the subject. **özne 4** PERSON someone who is from a particular country, especially a country with a king or queen **vatandaş, uyruk** *a British subject*

subject² /ˈsʌbdʒɪkt/ *adjective* **1 subject to sth** a often affected by something, especially something unpleasant **maruz kalabilir, uğrayabilir, karşı karşıya** *Departure times are subject to alteration.* **b** only able to happen if something else happens ...**a/e bağlı olarak/göre** *The pay rise is subject to approval by management.*

subject³ /səbˈdʒekt/ *verb* **subject sb/sth to sth** *phrasal verb* to make someone or something experience something unpleasant **mecbur tutmak, maruz bırakmak, mahkûm etmek** *In prison, he was subjected to beatings and interrogations.*

subjective /səbˈdʒektɪv/ *adjective* influenced by someone's beliefs or feelings, instead of facts **öznel, subjektif** *a subjective judgment* • **subjectively** *adverb* **başkasının fikrinden etkilenmiş olarak** • **subjectivity** /ˌsʌbdʒekˈtɪvəti/ *noun* [U] when someone or something is influenced by beliefs or feelings instead of facts **öznellik, subjektiflik**

'subject ˌmatter *noun* [U] what is being talked or written about **konu, mevzuu, asıl husus** *I'm not sure whether the subject matter is suitable for children.*

subjunctive /səbˈdʒʌŋktɪv/ *noun* [no plural] the form of the verb which is used to express doubt, possibility, or wish. In the sentence 'I wish I were rich.', 'were' is in the subjunctive. **dilek/istek/şart kipi** • **subjunctive** *adjective* **Fiilin istek, şüphe ve olasılık belirten hali**

sublime /səˈblaɪm/ *adjective* extremely good, beautiful, or enjoyable **harikulâde, olağanüstü, çok güzel, pek hoş** *sublime scenery* • **sublimely** *adverb* **heybetli ve asil bir şekilde**

submarine /ˌsʌbməˈriːn/ *noun* [C] a boat that travels under water **denizaltı**

submerge /səbˈmɜːdʒ/ *verb* [I, T] to cause something to be under the surface of water, or to move below the surface of water **bat(ır)mak, dal(dır)mak** *The floods destroyed farmland and submerged whole villages.* • **submerged** *adjective* **batırılmış**

submission /səbˈmɪʃⁿn/ *noun* **1** [U] when you accept that someone has complete control over you **boyun eğme, kendini teslim etme, razı olma; hizaya/yola gelme** *They tried to starve her into submission.* **2** [C, U] when you send a document, plan, etc to someone so that they can consider it, or the document, plan, etc that you send **sunma, teklif, sunuş, arz** *The deadline for submissions is 29 April.*

submissive /səbˈmɪsɪv/ *adjective* always doing what other people tell you to do **itaatkâr, uysal, söz dinler** *a quiet, submissive wife*

submit /səbˈmɪt/ *verb* **submitting**, *past* **submitted 1** [T] to send a document, plan, etc to someone so that they can consider it **sunmak, arzetmek, göndermek, vermek** *Applications must be submitted before 31 January.* **2** [I] to accept that someone has control over you and do what they tell you to do **uymak, yumuşak başlı olmak, razı olmak, boyun eğmek** *He was forced to submit to a full body search.*

subordinate¹ /səˈbɔːdⁿnət/ *adjective* less important or lower in rank **ast, ast rütbede olan** *a subordinate position/role* ○ *An individual's needs are subordinate to those of the group.*

subordinate² /səˈbɔːdⁿnət/ *noun* [C] someone who has a less important position than someone else in an organization **alt kademede, ikinci, daha az önemli, tali**

subordinate³ /səˈbɔːdɪneɪt/ *verb* [T] *formal* to put someone or something in a less important position **daha**

az önemli konuma getirmek, ...dan/den değersiz görmek; önemsememek ● subordination /səˌbɔːdɪˈneɪʃ^ən/ *noun* [U] **itaat**

sub͵ordinate 'clause *noun* [C] in grammar, a clause which cannot form a separate sentence but adds information to the main clause **yan/yardımcı cümlecik**

subpoena /səbˈpiːnə/ *noun* [C] a legal document ordering someone to go to court **mahkeme celbi, çağrı pusulası ● subpoena** *verb* [T] to give someone a subpoena **mahkeme celbi tebliğ etmek; celp pusulası vermek**

subscribe /səbˈskraɪb/ *verb* [I] to pay money to an organization so that you regularly receive a service or product, such as a magazine or newspaper **abone olmak** *to subscribe to a magazine/an internet service* **● subscriber** *noun* [C] **üye**
subscribe to sth *phrasal verb formal* to agree with an opinion, belief, etc **kabul etmek, razı olmak, onaylamak** *I certainly don't subscribe to the view that women are morally superior to men.*

subscription ...... İLE BİRLİKTE KULLANILAN KELİMELER
cancel/pay/take out a subscription ● a subscription to sth ● an **annual** subscription

subscription /səbˈskrɪpʃ^ən/ *noun* [C] an amount of money that you pay regularly to receive a product or service or to be a member of an organization **abonelik ücreti** *an* **annual** *subscription*

subsequent /ˈsʌbsɪkwənt/ *adjective* [always before noun] happening after something else **sonraki, müteakip, takip eden, sonra gelen** *The mistakes were corrected in a subsequent edition of the book.* **● subsequently** *adverb* **sonuç olarak**

subservient /səbˈsɜːviənt/ *adjective* always doing what other people want you to do **başkalarının söylediğini düşünmeden yapan, köle ruhlu, körü körüne hizmet eden**

subside /səbˈsaɪd/ *verb* [I] **1** to become less strong or extreme **hafiflemek, azalmak, yatışmak** *The violence seems to be subsiding at last.* **2** If a building subsides, it sinks down to a lower level. **çökmek, batmak, alçalmak**

subsidence /səbˈsaɪd^əns/ *noun* [U] when buildings subside or land sinks down to a lower level **çökme, çöküntü, alçalma**

subsidiary /səbˈsɪdi^əri/ *noun* [C] a company which is owned by another larger company **yan şirket, alt kuruluş**

subsidize (*also UK* -ise) /ˈsʌbsɪdaɪz/ *verb* [T] If a government or other organization subsidizes something, it pays part of the cost of it, so that prices are reduced. **mali destek sağlamak, sübvanse etmek** *We have a subsidized restaurant at work.*

subsidy /ˈsʌbsɪdi/ *noun* [C] money given by a government or other organization to pay part of the cost of something **yardım, ek ödeme, ödenek, sübvansiyon; destek ödeneği** *housing subsidies for the poor*

subsist /səbˈsɪst/ *verb* [I] to manage to live when you only have a very small amount of food or money **çok az para ve yiyecekle yaşamak; hayatını idame etmek; yaşamını sürdürmek; idare etmek ● subsistence** *noun* [U] **geçim (parası)**

substance ...... İLE BİRLİKTE KULLANILAN KELİMELER
a **dangerous/hazardous/toxic** substance ● a **powdery/sticky/waxy** substance

o▄substance /ˈsʌbst^əns/ *noun* **1** [C] a solid, liquid, or gas **madde, cisim** *a dangerous substance* ○ *illegal sub-*

stances (= illegal drugs) **2** [U] truth or importance **gerçek ve önemlilik, değer, anlam** *There's no substance to the allegations.* **3 the substance of sth** the most important part of what someone has said or written **özü, esası, ana fikir, hülâsa**

substandard /sʌbˈstændəd/ *adjective* Something that is substandard is not as good as it should be. **düşük standartlı, daha düşük kaliteli** *substandard conditions/housing*

substantial /səbˈstænʃ^əl/ *adjective* **1** large in amount **esaslı, yüklü, muazzam, önemli, büyük** *a substantial change/increase* ○ *a substantial amount of money/time* **2** large and strong **büyük ve sağlam** *a substantial building* ⊃Opposite **insubstantial**.

substantially /səbˈstænʃ^əli/ *adverb* by a large amount **büyük miktarda önemli derecede** *House prices are substantially higher in the south.*

substantiate /səbˈstænʃieɪt/ *verb* [T] *formal* to provide facts which prove that something is true **doğrulamak, doğruluğunu kanıtlamak, ispat etmek** *His claims have never been substantiated.*

substantive /ˈsʌbst^əntɪv/ *adjective formal* important or serious **önemli ve ciddi** *a substantive issue*

substitute¹ /ˈsʌbstɪtjuːt/ *noun* [C] someone or something that is used instead of another person or thing **vekil, yedek** *Margarine can be used as a substitute for butter.* ○ *a substitute teacher*

substitute² /ˈsʌbstɪtjuːt/ *verb* **1** [T] to use someone or something instead of another person or thing **yerine koymak, yerine kullanmak** *You can substitute pasta for the rice, if you prefer.* **2 substitute for sb** to do someone's job because they are not there **vekâlet etmek, yerine geçmek, yerini almak** *I'm substituting for her while she's on holiday.* **● substitution** /ˌsʌbstɪˈtjuːʃ^ən/ *noun* [C, U] **yedek**

subsume /səbˈsjuːm/ *verb* [T] *formal* to include someone or something as part of a larger group **içermek, içine almak, kapsamak, dahil etmek** [often passive] *The company has been subsumed by a large US bank.*

subterfuge /ˈsʌbtəfjuːdʒ/ *noun* [C, U] *formal* a trick or a dishonest way of achieving something **hile, şerefsizlik, kurnazlık, aldatmaca** *They obtained the information by subterfuge.*

subterranean /ˌsʌbt^ərˈeɪniən/ *adjective* under the ground **yer altı** *subterranean passages*

subtitles /ˈsʌbˌtaɪtlz/ *noun* [plural] words shown at the bottom of a cinema or television screen to explain what is being said **alt yazılar** *It's a French film with English subtitles.*

subtle /ˈsʌtl/ *adjective* **1** NOT OBVIOUS not obvious or easy to notice **kolay farkedilmeyen/anlaşılmayan; aşikâr olmayan, ince, girift, gözle çarpmayan** *a subtle change/difference* ○ *a subtle hint* **2** NOT STRONG A subtle flavour, colour, etc is delicate and not strong or bright. **belli belirsiz; kolay farkedilmeyen 3** CLEVER clever in a way that does not attract attention **kurnaz, cin fikirli, ustalıklı, ustaca** *a subtle way of solving the problem* **● subtly** *adverb* **farkedilmesi kolay olmayan bir şekilde, sinsilikle**

subtlety /ˈsʌtlti/ *noun* **1** [U] the quality of being subtle **incelik, nüans, küçük ayrıntı 2** [C] something that is subtle **kolay farkedilmeyen şey; zor açıklanır olan şey**

subtract /səbˈtrækt/ *verb* [T] to take a number or amount away from another number or amount **çıkarmak, çıkarma yapmak** *You need to subtract 25% from the final figure.* **● subtraction** /səbˈtrækʃ^ən/ *noun* [C, U] **çıkarma**

suburb /'sʌbɜːb/ *noun* [C] an area where people live out-side the centre of a city **dış mahalle, banliyö, varoş, gecekondu** *a suburb of New York* ● **suburban** /sə'bɜː-bən/ *adjective* relating to a suburb **banliyöye ilişkin, dış mahalleye dair** *a suburban area/home*

suburbia /sə'bɜːbiə/ *noun* [U] the suburbs of towns and cities generally **banliyö, dış semtler/mahalleler**

subversive /səb'vɜːsɪv/ *adjective* trying to destroy the authority of a government, religion, etc **yıkıcı, zayıfla-tıcı, güçsüzleştirici** *subversive literature* ● **subversive** *noun* [C] someone who is subversive **yıkıcı/bozguncu/bölücü/münafık/karşı duran kimse**

subvert /sʌb'vɜːt/ *verb* [T] *formal* to try to destroy the authority of a government, religion, etc **yıkmak, boz-mak, altüst etmek** *a plot to subvert the government* ● **subversion** /səb'vɜːʃⁿn/ *noun* [U] *formal* **devirme, yıkma**

subway /'sʌbweɪ/ *noun* [C] **1** UK (UK/US **underpass**) a passage under a road or railway for people to walk through **alt geçit, yeraltı geçidi 2** US (UK **underground**) a system of trains that travel underground **metro, tünel** *We can take the subway to Grand Central Station.*

sub-zero /'sʌb,zɪərəʊ/ *adjective* Sub-zero temperatures are temperatures below zero degrees. **sıfırın altında olan**

○←**succeed** /sək'siːd/ *verb* **1** [I] to achieve what you are try-ing to achieve **başarmak, muvaffak olmak, üstesin-den gelmek** *She has the skill and determination to suc-ceed.* ○ [+ in + doing sth] *He has finally succeeded in passing his exams.* **2** [T] to take an official job or position after someone else **halefi olmak, ...ın/in yerini almak/yerine geçmek** *The Queen was succeeded by her eldest son when she died.*

achieve/have success ● **the key to/secret of** success ● success **in** (doing) sth ● **without** success

○←**success** /sək'ses/ *noun* **1** [U] when you achieve what you want to achieve **başarı, muvaffakiyet** *Her success is due to hard work and determination.* **2** [C] something that has a good result or that is very popular **başarı, temayüz, popülerlik** *His first film was a great success.*

○←**successful** /sək'sesfⁿl/ *adjective* **1** ACHIEVEMENT achieving what you want to achieve **başarılı, muvaffak** *If the operation is successful, she should be walking within a few months.* **2** WORK having achieved a lot or made a lot of money through your work **çok para kazanmış, başarılı olmuş, zengin olmuş** *a successful business-man* **3** POPULAR very popular **çok popüler, iyi tanınan, başarılı, bilinen** *a successful book/film* ⊃Opposite **unsuc-cessful.** ● **successfully** *adverb* **başarılı bir şekilde**

successful

Dikkat' Kelimenin yazılışına dikkat edin! **Successful** Türk öğrencileri tarafından en çok yanlış yazılan 10 kelimeden biridir. Dikkat! Doğru yazılışında **cc ss** ve tek bir **l** var.

succession /sək'seʃⁿn/ *noun* **1** [no plural] a number of similar events or people that happen, exist, etc after each other **art arda gelen, peşi sıra olan** *to suffer a succession of injuries* ○ *a succession of boyfriends* **2 in quick/rapid succession** If several things happen in quick/rapid succession, they happen very quickly after each other. **hızlı/süratli art arda gelen/peş peşe olan** *She had her first three children in quick suc-cession.* **3** [U] when someone takes an official position or

job after someone else **yerine geçme, halefi olma; görevi devralma**

successive /sək'sesɪv/ *adjective* happening after each other **art arda gelen, peş peşe olan, üst üste gelen** *He has just won the World Championship for the third successive year.*

appoint/choose/find a successor ● a **natural/worthy** successor ● a successor **to** sb

successor /sək'sesər/ *noun* [C] **1** someone who has a position or job after someone else **halef, vâris** *He is her most likely successor.* **2** an organization, product, etc that follows and takes the place of an earlier one **öncekinin yerine geçen ürün/kuruluş vb.**

succinct /sək'sɪŋkt/ *adjective* said in a very clear way using only a few words **özlü, kısa, veciz** *a succinct ex-planation* ● **succinctly** *adverb* **kısa ve öz bir şekilde**

succulent /'sʌkjələnt/ *adjective* If food is succulent, it is good to eat because it has a lot of juice. **sulu ve lezzetli** *a succulent piece of meat*

succumb /sə'kʌm/ *verb* [I] *formal* **1** to not be able to stop yourself doing something **dayanamamak, kapılmak, yenilmek; kendini alıkoyamamak** *I succumbed to temptation and had some cheesecake.* **2** to die or suffer badly from an illness **acı çekerek ölmek, çok çekmek, yakalanmak, tutulmak, yenik düşmek; boyun eğmek, teslim olmak**

○←**such** /sʌtʃ/ *pronoun, determiner* **1** used to refer to some-thing or someone that you were just talking about, or something or someone of that type **böyle, bu gibi, bunun gibi** *It's difficult to know how to treat such cases.* **2** used to emphasize a quality of someone or something **bu kadar, o kadar, öylesine** *She's such a nice person.* ○ *It's such a shame that he's leaving.* **3 such as** for example **örneğin, meselâ, söz gelimi, benzeri** *She can't eat dairy products, such as milk and cheese.* **4 as such** used after a word or phrase in negative statements to mean in the exact meaning of that word or phrase **aslında, esasında, başlı başına** *There are no rules as such, just a few guidelines.* **5 such...that** used to talk about the result of something **öylesine ... ki; oka-dar ...ki** *The whole thing was such a worry that I began to lose sleep over it.* **6 there's no such thing/person (as)...** used to say that something or someone does not exist **(gibi) böyle bir şey/kimse yok** *There's no such thing as ghosts.*

such-and-such /'sʌtʃⁿnsʌtʃ/ *determiner informal* used instead of referring to a particular or exact thing **falan filan** *If they tell you to arrive at such-and-such a time, get there a couple of minutes before.*

suck /sʌk/ *verb* **1** [I, T] to have something in your mouth and use your tongue, lips, etc to pull on it or to get liquid, air, etc out of it **emmek** *to suck a sweet/lollipop* ○ *to suck your thumb* **2 suck sth in/under/up, etc** to pull something somewhere using the force of moving air, water, etc **emerek içine çekmek** *He was sucked under the boat and drowned.* **3 be sucked into sth** to become involved in something bad when you do not want to **bulaşmak, müdahil olmak, karışmak, çekilmek** **4 he/it/this, etc sucks!** US *very informal* If someone or something sucks, they are bad or unpleasant. **Ber-bat/kötü/iğrenç biri/birşey!'**

suck up to sb *phrasal verb very informal* to try to make someone who is in authority like you by doing and say-ing things that will please them **yalakalık yapmak, yağ çekmek, yağcılık yapmak**

sucker /'sʌkər/ *noun* [C] **1** *informal* someone who believes everything that you tell them and is easy to deceive **enayi/saf/alık/budala kimse 2** something that helps an animal or object stick to a surface **vantuz**

suction /'sʌkʃᵊn/ *noun* [U] when something is forced into a container or space by removing air **emme, emiş**

◦┅**sudden** /'sʌdᵊn/ *adjective* **1** done or happening quickly and unexpectedly **ani, beklenmedik, apansız, ansızın** *a sudden change/increase* ○ *His sudden death was a great shock to us all.* **2 all of a sudden** unexpectedly **ansızın, aniden, beklenmedik bir şekilde, birdenbire** *All of a sudden she got up and walked out.* ● **suddenness** *noun* [U] **aniden olma durumu**

ˌsudden ˌinfant 'death ˌsyndrome *noun* [U] SIDS **Anî Bebek Ölümü Sendromu (ABÖS)**

◦┅**suddenly** /'sʌdᵊnli/ *adverb* quickly and unexpectedly **beklenmedik ve hızlı bir şekilde; birden, birdenbire, ansızın** *I suddenly realized who she was.* ○ *It all happened so suddenly that I can't remember much about it.*

Sudoku (also **Su Doku**) /suː'dɒkuː/ *noun* [C, U] a number game in which you have to write a number between 1 and 9 in each small box of a 9x9 square **Sudoku, 9 harfin 9 ayrı kareye yazılmasıyla oynanan bir rakam oyunu**

suds /sʌdz/ *noun* [plural] small bubbles made from soap and water **sabun köpüğü**

sue /suː/ *verb* [I, T] **suing**, *past* **sued** to take legal action against someone and try to get money from them because they have harmed you **dava etmek/açmak; mahkemeye vermek; kanun önünde hesaplaşmak** *He's threatening to sue the newspaper for slander.*

suede /sweɪd/ *noun* [U] leather that has a slightly rough surface **süet, süet deri**

◦┅**suffer** /'sʌfər/ *verb* **1** [I, T] to experience pain or unpleasant emotions **acı çekmek, ıstırap duymak, katlanmak, mustarip olmak** *I can't bear to see animals suffering.* **2 suffer from sth** to have an illness or other health problem **sıkıntı çekmek, çekmek; ...dan/den acı çekmek/çok çekmek** *She suffers from severe depression.* **3 suffer a broken leg/a heart attack, etc** to experience an injury or other sudden health problem **kırık bacak/kalp krizi vs. acı çekmek/mustarip olmak** *He suffered a serious neck injury in the accident.* **4 suffer damage/defeat/loss, etc** to experience something bad such as damage/defeat/loss, etc **kayıp/mağlubiyet/zarar ziyandan vs. mustarip olmak/çok çekmek/etkilenmek 5** [I] to become worse in quality **kaliteyi yitirmek, etkilenmek, kötüye gitmek** *If you're tired all the time your work tends to suffer.*

sufferer /'sʌfᵊrər/ *noun* [C] someone who suffers from an illness or other health problem **hasta, acı çeken, mustarip, rahatsız** *AIDS/cancer sufferers*

░░░ *suffering* ┅┅ İLE BİRLİKTE KULLANILAN KELİMELER

create/endure/relieve suffering ● **human** suffering ● **unnecessary/unspeakable** suffering ● **the suffering of** sb

suffering /'sʌfᵊrɪŋ/ *noun* [U] when someone experiences pain or unpleasant emotions **acı, ıstırap, keder, elem, dert, tasa** *human suffering*

suffice /sə'faɪs/ *verb* [I] *formal* to be enough **yeterli olmak, yetmek, kâfi gelmek** *You don't need to give a long speech - a few sentences will suffice.*

sufficient /sə'fɪʃᵊnt/ *adjective* as much as is necessary **yeterli, kâfi** *She didn't have sufficient time to answer all the questions.* ↪Opposite **insufficient**. ● **sufficiently** *adverb* **yeterli miktarda** *I was sufficiently close to hear what they were saying.* ↪See also: **self-sufficient**. **yeterli miktarda**

suffix /'sʌfɪks/ *noun* [C] a group of letters that you add to the end of a word to make another word. In the word 'slowly', '-ly' is a suffix. **son ek** ↪Compare **prefix** ↪See study page **Word formation** on page Centre 28.

suffocate /'sʌfəkeɪt/ *verb* [I, T] to die because you cannot breathe or to kill someone by stopping them from breathing **boğmak, nefessiz bırakıp öldürmek, nefessiz kalıp ölmek, boğulmak** *He suffocated her with a pillow.* ● **suffocation** /ˌsʌfə'keɪʃᵊn/ *noun* [U] **nefessizlikten meydana gelen ölüm**

◦┅**sugar** /'ʃʊgər/ *noun* **1** [U] a very sweet substance used to give flavour to food and drinks **şeker** *coffee with milk and sugar* **2** [C] a spoon of sugar in a cup of tea or coffee **şeker** *He likes two sugars in his tea.*

◦┅**suggest** /sə'dʒest/ *verb* [T] **1** IDEA to express an idea or plan for someone to consider **önermek, teklif etmek** [+ (that)] *I suggest that we park the car here and walk into town.* ○ [+ doing sth] *He suggested having the meeting at his house.* **2** ADVICE to say that someone or something is suitable for something **tavsiye etmek, salık vermek** *to suggest someone for a job* ○ *Can you suggest a good hotel?* **3** SEEM TRUE to make something seem likely to be true **fikrini uyandırmak, izlenimini vermek** *All the evidence suggests that she did it.*

░░░ *suggestion* ┅┅┅ İLE BİRLİKTE KULLANILAN KELİMELER

bristle at/deny/make/reject/welcome a suggestion ● an **alternative/constructive/helpful/ridiculous/sensible** suggestion ● **at sb's** suggestion

░░░ *suggestion* ┅┅┅ BAŞKA BİR DEYİŞLE

Ne yapılacağı konusunda verilen bir teklif **thought** veya **idea** ifadeleriyle tanımlanabilir. *Rebecca has a few ideas about how we could improve things.* ● *I've had a thought about what we might do this summer.* Eğer kişi özellikle iş hayatı içinde bir plan veya fikir ortaya koyuyorsa, **proposal** veya **proposition** kelimeleri kullanılabilir. *The proposal for a new sports hall has been rejected.* ● *He wrote to me with a very interesting business proposition.*

◦┅**suggestion** /sə'dʒestʃᵊn/ *noun* **1** [C] an idea or plan that someone suggests **öneri, teklif** *to make a suggestion* ○ *Have you got any suggestions for improvements?* **2 a suggestion of/that sth** something that makes something seem likely to be true **belli belirsiz, iz, eser, az miktar** *There's no suggestion of any connection between the two men.* **3 at sb's suggestion** following the advice that someone has given you **...nın/nin tavsiyesi üzerine/önerisini dikkate alarak** *We went to that restaurant at Paul's suggestion.*

suggestive /sə'dʒestɪv/ *adjective* **1** making you think about sex **seks imalı, açık saçık, ayıp şeyler çağrıştıran** *suggestive comments/remarks* **2 suggestive of** sth *formal* similar to something and making you think about it **telkin edici, fikir verici** *The shapes are suggestive of human forms.* ● **suggestively** *adverb* **müstehcen bir şekilde**

suicidal /ˌsuːɪ'saɪdᵊl/ *adjective* **1** so unhappy that you want to kill yourself **intihar eğilim olan** *to feel suicidal* **2** likely to have an extremely bad result **çok tehlikeli, intihar sayılabilecek** *a suicidal decision*

suicide /'suːɪsaɪd/ *noun* **1** [C, U] when you intentionally kill yourself **intihar, cana kıyma** *He committed suicide after a long period of depression.* **2** [U] when you do something that will have an extremely bad result for you **intihar, risk, tehlike** *political suicide*

'suicide ˌbomber *noun* [C] a person who has a bomb hidden on their body and who kills themselves in the attempt to kill others **intihar bombacısı, canlı bomba**

S

o▪**suit¹** /suːt/ *noun* [C] **1** a jacket and trousers or a jacket and skirt that are made from the same material **takım elbise, kostüm, tayyör, kıyafet** *She wore a dark blue suit.* ➍Orta kısımdaki renkli sayfalarına bakınız. **2** one of the four types of cards with different shapes on them in a set of playing cards **iskambilde aynı şekilde kağıtlar grubu/takımı 3 follow suit** to do the same as someone else has just done **başkasının yaptığının aynısını yapmak; yapılanı takip etmek** *If other shops lower their prices, we will have to follow suit.* ➍See also: **bathing suit, pant suit, trouser suit, wet suit.**

o▪**suit²** /suːt/ *verb* [T] **1** to make someone look more attractive **daha çekici yapmak, uygun olmak, güzelleştirmek, uymak, çok iyi gitmek** *Green really suits you.* **2** to be acceptable or right for someone **uygun olmak, eşverişli olmak, doğru ve kabul edilebilir olmak** *It would suit me better if we left a bit earlier.* **3 be suited to/ for sth** to be right for someone or something **...a/e/için uygun/yerinde olmak** *These plants are better suited to a warm climate.* ➍See also: **suit sb down to the ground¹.**

suitable ...... BAŞKA BİR DEYİŞLE

Suitable sıfatına alternatif olarak **appropriate** sıfatı kullanılabilir. *Is this film* **appropriate** *for young children?* ● *You should bring* **appropriate** *footwear.*
Eğer bir davranış şekli belirli bir durum için uygunsa, **apt** veya **fitting** sıfatları kullanılabilir. *'Unusual', yes, that's a very* **apt** *description.* ● *The promotion was a* **fitting** *reward for all his hard work.*
Kişinin veya cansız bir şeyin bir duruma uygunluğunu belirtmek için **right** sıfatı kullanılabilir. *I'm not sure that she's the* **right** *person for the job.* ● *Is this the* **right** *way to do it?*
Eğer bir kişi veya şey bir duruma çok uygun ise, **perfect** sıfatı ile tanımlanabilir. *It's a* **perfect** *day for a picnic.* ● *She'd be* **perfect** *for the job.*
In keeping with söylemi bir şeyin belirli bir adet veya geleneğe uygunluğunu gösterir. *The antique desk was very much* **in keeping with** *the rest of the furniture in the room.*

o▪**suitable** /ˈsuːtəbl/ *adjective* acceptable or right for someone or something **uygun, elverişli, münasip** *a suitable time to call* ○ *This film is* **suitable** *for children.* ➍Opposite **unsuitable.** ● **suitably** *adverb* **suitably** *dressed* **uygun bir şekilde**

suitcase /ˈsuːtkeɪs/ *noun* [C] a rectangular case with a handle that you use for carrying clothes when you are travelling **bavul, valiz** *to pack your suitcase* ➍See picture at **luggage.**

suite /swiːt/ *noun* [C] **1** several pieces of furniture which go together **takım, mobilya takımı** *a bedroom suite* **2** a set of hotel rooms which are used together **daire, süit** ➍See also: **en suite.**

suitor /ˈsuːtər/ *noun* [C] *old-fashioned* a man who wants to marry a particular woman **tâlip, istekli, evlenmeye gönüllü kimse**

sulfur /ˈsʌlfər/ *noun* [U] *US spelling of* sulphur **kükürt, sülfür**

sulk /sʌlk/ *verb* [I] to look unhappy and not speak to anyone because you are angry about something **somurtmak, surat asmak, küsmek** *He's upstairs sulking in his bedroom.* ● **sulky** *adjective a sulky teenager* **suratını asan**

sullen /ˈsʌlən/ *adjective* in an unpleasant mood and not smiling or speaking to anyone **somurtkan, buz dolabı gibi, yüzü gülmez, küskün, ters, aksi**

sulphur *UK* (*US* sulfur) /ˈsʌlfər/ *noun* [U] a yellow chemical element that has an unpleasant smell (symbol S) **kükürt, sülfür**

sultan /ˈsʌltən/ *noun* [C] a ruler in some Muslim countries **sultan**

sultana /sʌlˈtɑːnə/ *noun* [C] *UK* a dried grape (= small round fruit) often used in cakes **(çekirdeksiz) kuru üzüm**

sultry /ˈsʌltri/ *adjective* **1** If a woman is sultry, she behaves in a sexually attractive way. **şuh, ihtiraslı, ateşli, baştan çıkarıcı, fettan** *a sultry voice* **2** If the weather is sultry, it is hot and wet. **yapış yapış ve bunaltıcı; aşırı sıcak ve nemli** *a sultry summer night*

o▪**sum¹** /sʌm/ *noun* [C] **1** MONEY an amount of money **toplam, tutar, yekûn, meblağ** *a large/small sum of money* **2** MATHS *UK* a simple mathematical calculation such as adding two numbers together **toplama** *Kids these days can't* **do sums** *without a calculator.* **3** TOTAL the total amount that you get when you add two or more numbers together **toplam, sonuç, yekûn** *The sum of six and seven is thirteen.* ➍See also: **lump sum.**

sum² /sʌm/ *verb* **summing,** *past* **summed**
sum (sth/sb) up *phrasal verb* to describe briefly the important facts or characteristics of something or someone **özetlemek, ana hatlarıyla belirtmek** *The purpose of a conclusion is to sum up the main points of an essay.*
sum sth/sb up *phrasal verb* to quickly decide what you think about something or someone **düşüncesini özetlemek, hızlıca karar vermek, toparlamak, hüküm vermek** *I think she summed up the situation very quickly.*

summarize (*also UK* -ise) /ˈsʌməraɪz/ *verb* [I, T] to describe briefly the main facts or ideas of something **özetlemek**

summary (noun) ...... İLE BİRLİKTE KULLANILAN KELİMELER

give/produce/provide a summary ● a **brief/quick/short** summary ● a summary **of** sth

summary¹ /ˈsʌməri/ *noun* [C] a short description that gives the main facts or ideas about something **özet, hülasa** *He gave a brief summary of what happened.*

summary² /ˈsʌməri/ *adjective* [always before noun] *formal* decided or done quickly, without the usual discussions or legal arrangements **seri, alelacele, anında yapılan, üstünkörü** *a summary arrest/execution*

summer ...... İLE BİRLİKTE KULLANILAN KELİMELER

in (the) summer ● **last/next** summer ● **early/late** summer ● the summer **months**

o▪**summer** /ˈsʌmər/ *noun* [C, U] the season of the year between spring and autumn, when the weather is warmest **yaz, yaz mevsimi** *We usually go away* **in the summer.** ○ *a long, hot summer* ● **summery** *adjective* typical of or suitable for summer **yaza uygun/mahsus; yazın özelliğinden olan**

summer holiday (*US* summer vacation) *noun* [C] the time during the summer when you do not have to go to school **yaz tatili**

'summer ,school *noun* [C] an educational course that happens during the summer when other courses have finished **yaz öğretimi, yaz okulu**

summertime /ˈsʌmətaɪm/ *noun* [U] when it is summer **yazın, yaz, yaz mevsimi** *In the* **summertime,** *we often eat outside.*

summit /ˈsʌmɪt/ *noun* [C] **1** an important meeting between the leaders of two or more governments **zirve/doruk, zirve/doruk toplantısı** *a two-day summit* ○ *a summit meeting* **2** the top of a mountain **zirve, doruk** *The climbers hope to* **reach the summit** *before nightfall.*

summon /'sʌmən/ *verb* [T] **1** *formal* to officially order someone to come to a place **çağırmak, resmî olarak davet etmek, celp etmek** *He was summoned to a meeting.* **2 summon (up) the courage/strength, etc** to make a great effort to do something **bir şeyi yapmak için bütün cesaretini/gücünü toplamak/toparlamak** [+ to do sth] *He tried to summon up the courage to speak to her.*

summons /'sʌmənz/ *noun* [C] an official order saying that you must go to a court of law **davet, çağrı, çağrı belgesi, celp kağıdı**

Sun *written abbreviation for* Sunday **pazar, pazar günü**

✏ **sun**[1] /sʌn/ *noun* **1 the sun** the large, bright star that shines in the sky during the day and provides light and heat for the Earth **güneş 2** [U, no plural] the light and heat that comes from the sun **güneş ışığı/ısısı** *I can't sit in the sun for too long.*

sun[2] /sʌn/ *verb* **sunning**, *past* **sunned sun yourself** to sit or lie in the sun **güneşte yatıp uzanmak; güneşlenmek** *She was sitting on the deck sunning herself.*

sunbathe /'sʌnbeɪð/ *verb* [I] to sit or lie in the sun so that your skin becomes brown **güneş banyosu** ● **sunbathing** *noun* [U] **güneşlenme**

sunbed /'sʌnbed/ (*US* **tanning bed**) *noun* [C] a piece of equipment with a flat area like a bed and a strong light, which you lie on in order to make your skin go darker **güneş yatağı, solaryum**

sunblock /'sʌnblɒk/ *noun* [C, U] sunscreen **güneşlik**

sunburn /'sʌnbɜːn/ *noun* [U] when your skin becomes painful and red from being in the sun too long **güneş yanığı** ● **sunburnt** (*also* **sunburned**) *adjective* **güneş yanığından dolayı acısı olan**

sundae /'sʌndeɪ/ *noun* [C] a sweet dish made of ice cream with fruit and nuts **meyve, fındık ve dondurma ile yapılan bir tatlı**

✏ **Sunday** /'sʌndeɪ/ (*written abbreviation* **Sun**) *noun* [C, U] the day of the week after Saturday and before Monday **pazar, pazar günü**

sundry /'sʌndri/ *adjective* **1** [always before noun] of different types **çeşitli, türlü, muhtelif** *sundry items* **2 all and sundry** *UK informal* (*US* **various and sundry**) everyone **herkes, cümle âlem** *I don't want all and sundry knowing about my problems.*

sunflower /'sʌnflaʊəʳ/ *noun* [C] a tall, yellow flower with a large, black centre full of seeds **ayçiçeği**

sung /sʌŋ/ *past participle of* sing **şarkı söylemek' fiilinin üçüncü hâli**

sunglasses /'sʌnˌglɑːsɪz/ *noun* [plural] dark glasses that you wear to protect your eyes from the sun **güneş gözlüğü** ⊃Orta kısımdaki renkli sayfalarına bakınız.

sunk /sʌŋk/ **1** *past participle of* sink **batmak' fiilinin üçüncü hâli 2** *US past tense of* sink **batmak' fiilinin ikinci hâli (ABD)**

sunken /'sʌŋkən/ *adjective* [always before noun] **1** at a lower level than the surrounding area **çökük, çukurlaşmış** *a sunken bath* **2** having fallen down to the bottom of the sea **batık, batmış** *a sunken ship* **3 sunken eyes/cheeks** eyes or cheeks that make you look ill because they go too far into your face **çökük gözler/ avurtlar/yanaklar**

sunlight /'sʌnlaɪt/ *noun* [U] the light from the sun **güneş/gün ışığı**

sunlit /'sʌnlɪt/ *adjective* [always before noun] A sunlit place is bright because of light from the sun. **güneşli, aydınlık** *a sunlit room*

sun ˌlotion *noun* [C, U] sunscreen **güneş kremi**

Sunni /'sʊni/ *noun* [C] a member of a large group within the Islamic religion **Sünnî, İslâm dininde Sünnî mezhebinden olan kimse** ● **Sunni** *adjective* describing the Sunni or their type of Islam **Sünnî, Sünnî mezhebinden olan**

sunny /'sʌni/ *adjective* **1** bright because of light from the sun **güneşli** *a lovely sunny day* **2** behaving in a happy way **yüzünde güller açan, mutlu, sevinçli** *a sunny smile/personality*

sunrise /'sʌnraɪz/ *noun* [C, U] when the sun appears in the morning and the sky becomes light **gün doğması**

sunroof /'sʌnruːf/ *noun* [C] part of a roof of a car which you open to allow air and light from the sun to come in **açık tavan**

sunscreen /'sʌnskriːn/ *noun* [C, U] a substance that protects your skin in the sun **güneşlik**

sunset /'sʌnset/ *noun* [C, U] when the sun disappears in the evening and the sky becomes dark **gün batması**

sunshine /'sʌnʃaɪn/ *noun* [U] the light from the sun **güneş/gün ışığı** *Let's sit over there in the sunshine.*

sunstroke /'sʌnstrəʊk/ *noun* [U] an illness caused by spending too much time in the sun **güneş çarpması, başa güneş geçmesi**

suntan /'sʌntæn/ (*also* **tan**) *noun* [C] when your skin is brown from being in the sun **bronzlaşma** *suntan oil* ● **suntanned** (*also* **tanned**) *adjective* **bronzlaşmış**

super /'suːpəʳ/ *adjective, adverb* informal old-fashioned very good **olağanüstü, süper, çok iyi** *We had a super time.*

super- /suːpəʳ-/ *prefix* extremely or more than usual **sonderece/çok fazla/süper/üstün... anlamında önek** *a supermodel* ○ *super-rich*

superb /suːˈpɜːb/ *adjective* excellent **mükemmel** *a superb performance/restaurant* ● **superbly** *adverb* **harika bir şekilde**

superbug /'suːpəbʌg/ *noun* [C] a type of bacteria (= very small living things that cause disease) that is very difficult to destroy **kötü bir bataklığa neden olan bakteri**

superficial /ˌsuːpəˈfɪʃəl/ *adjective* **1** [NOT SERIOUS] If someone is superficial, they never think about things that are serious or important. **özen göstermeyen, baştan savmacı, özensiz 2** [NOT COMPLETE] not complete and involving only the most obvious things **yüzeysel,üstünkörü, yarım yamalak** *superficial knowledge* ○ *a superficial resemblance* **3** [NOT DEEP] only on the surface of something **yüzeysel, serinliksiz, görünen** *superficial damage/injuries* ● **superficially** *adverb* **yüzeysel olarak**

superfluous /suːˈpɜːfluəs/ *adjective* not needed, or more than is needed **gereksiz, lüzumsuz, yersiz** *superfluous details/information*

superhuman /ˌsuːpəˈhjuːmən/ *adjective* **superhuman effort/strength, etc** more effort/strength, etc than a normal human being **insanüstü çaba/güç/kuvvet**

superimpose /ˌsuːpərɪmˈpəʊz/ *verb* [T] to put an image, text, etc over something so that the thing under it can still be seen **üstüste bindirmek, üstüne koymak, üzerine oturtmak**

superintendent /ˌsuːpərɪnˈtendənt/ *noun* [C] **1** in Britain, a police officer of high rank **(Britanya'da) polis şefi, polis müfettişi 2** in the US, an official responsible for a place, event, etc **(ABD) yönetici, memur, idare memuru, resmî sorumlu**

superior[1] /suːˈpɪəriəʳ/ *adjective* **1** better than other things **daha üstün/yüksek/iyi** *superior quality* ○ *This car is far superior to the others.* **2** thinking that

S

you are better than other people **üstünlük taslayan, mağrur, kibirli, kendini beğenmiş** *She has a very superior manner.*

superior² /suːˈpɪəriəʳ/ *noun* [C] someone in a higher position than you at work **âmir, üst** *I will have to report this to my superiors.*

superiority /suːˌpɪəriˈɒrəti/ *noun* [U] **1** when something is better than other things **üstünlük, kalitelilik, iyilik** *the superiority of modern design* **2** when you think that you are better than other people **kibirlilik, üstünlük, mağrurluk** *She has an air of superiority.*

superlative /suːˈpɜːlətɪv/ *noun* [C] the form of an adjective or adverb that is used to show that someone or something has more of a particular quality than anyone or anything else. For example 'best' is the superlative of 'good' and 'slowest' is the superlative of 'slow'. **en üstünlük derecesi** ⊃Compare **comparative**.

○ⁱ**supermarket** /ˈsuːpəˌmɑːkɪt/ *noun* [C] a large shop that sells food, drink, products for the home, etc **büyük bakkal, süpermarket**

supermodel /ˈsuːpəˌmɒdəl/ *noun* [C] a very famous model (= someone whose job is to wear fashionable clothes for photographs) **meşhur manken, süper model**

the supernatural /ˌsuːpəˈnætʃərəl/ *noun* things that cannot be explained by our knowledge of science or nature **doğaüstü güçler/varlıklar** ● **supernatural** *adjective supernatural forces/powers* **doğaüstü**

superpower /ˈsuːpəˌpaʊəʳ/ *noun* [C] a country that has great military and political power in the world **süper güç, süper devlet, cihan devleti**

supersede /ˌsuːpəˈsiːd/ *verb* [T] to take the place of someone or something that went before **yerini almak, yerine geçmek** [often passive] *Records were superseded by CDs.*

supersonic /ˌsuːpəˈsɒnɪk/ *adjective* faster than the speed of sound **sesten hızlı, süpersonik** *supersonic aircraft*

superstar /ˈsuːpəstɑːʳ/ *noun* [C] a very famous singer, performer, etc **çok meşhur sanatçı/şarkıcı; süperstar; as**

superstition /ˌsuːpəˈstɪʃən/ *noun* [C, U] when someone believes that particular actions or objects are lucky or unlucky **batıl inanç/itikat, boş inanç**

superstitious /ˌsuːpəˈstɪʃəs/ *adjective* believing that particular objects or events are lucky or unlucky **batıl inançlı/itikatlı** *Are you superstitious about the number 13?*

superstore /ˈsuːpəstɔːʳ/ *noun* [C] a very large shop that sells many different things, often outside a town **büyük mağaza, alışveriş merkezi**

supervise /ˈsuːpəvaɪz/ *verb* [I, T] to watch a person or activity and make certain that everything is done correctly, safely, etc **denetlemek, nezaret etmek, yönetmek, idare etmek** *Students must be supervised by a teacher at all times.* ● **supervisor** *noun* [C] someone who supervises **âmir, müfettiş, nezaretçi, danışman**

be **under** supervision ● **close/constant** supervision ● **the supervision of** sb/sth

supervision /ˌsuːpəˈvɪʒən/ *noun* [U] when you supervise someone or something **denetleme, nezaret, idare, denetim** *He needs constant supervision.*

supper /ˈsʌpəʳ/ *noun* [C] a meal that you eat in the evening **akşam yemeği** *What are we having for supper?*

supplant /səˈplɑːnt/ *verb* [T] *formal* to take the place of someone or something **yerini almak, yerine geçmek**

supple /ˈsʌpl/ *adjective* able to bend or move easily **esnek, yumuşak, eğilir, bükülür** *a supple body*

supplement /ˈsʌplɪmənt/ *noun* [C] an extra amount or part added to something **ek, katkı, ilâve** *to take a vitamin supplement* ○ *a newspaper with a colour supplement* ● **supplement** /ˈsʌplɪment/ *verb* [T] *She works part-time to supplement her pension.* **takviye etmek**

supplementary /ˌsʌplɪˈmentəri/ (*also US* **supplemental**) *adjective* added to something **ek, ilâve, tamamlayıcı, ekstra** *supplementary materials*

supplier /səˈplaɪəʳ/ *noun* [C] someone who provides things that people want or need, often over a long period of time **tedarikçi, satıcı, mal sağlayıcı**

supplies /səˈplaɪz/ *noun* [plural] the food, equipment, etc that is needed for a particular activity, holiday, etc **erzak, levazım malzemesi, techizat, gereçler**

○ⁱ**supply¹** /səˈplaɪ/ *verb* [T] to provide things that people want or need, often over a long period of time **sağlamak, tedarik etmek, vermek** *to supply food/drugs to people* ○ *This lake supplies the whole town with water.*

a supply **of** sth ● a **constant/endless/plentiful** supply

○ⁱ**supply²** /səˈplaɪ/ *noun* **1** [C] an amount of something that is ready to be used **stok, arz, mal, donanım, mevcut** *a supply of water* ○ *food supplies* **2 in short supply** If something is in short supply, there is little of it available. **yetersiz, kıt, az 3** [C] the system of supplying something to people **tedarik, sağlama, verme, arz** *Someone has turned off the electricity supply.*

○ⁱ**support¹** /səˈpɔːt/ *verb* [T] **1** AGREE to agree with an idea, group, or person **desteklemek, destek vermek** *Do you support their views on nuclear weapons?* **2** PROVE to help to show that something is true **doğrulamak, teyit etmek** *There's no evidence to support his story.* **3** HOLD to hold the weight of someone or something **desteklemek, tutmak, çekmek, taşımak** *Is this ladder strong enough to support me?* **4** PAY to look after someone by paying for their food, clothes, etc **yardım etmek, desteklemek, bakmak, bakımını üstlenmek** *She has three children to support.* **5** SPORT *mainly UK* to like a particular sports team and want them to win **takım desteklemek, taraftar olmak** *Who do you support?*

enlist/express/give/lose/rally support ● **overwhelming/public/strong/tacit/widespread** support ● support **for** sb/sth

○ⁱ**support²** /səˈpɔːt/ *noun* **1** AGREEMENT [U] agreement with an idea, group, or person **destek, arka çıkma, uyuşma** *Is there much public support for the death penalty?* **2 in support of** sb/sth agreeing with someone or something **destekleyici biçimde, lehinde** *The minister spoke in support of military action.* **3** HELP [U] help or encouragement **destek, yardım, yüreklendirme, arka çıkma** *emotional/financial support* **4** OBJECT [C] an object that can hold the weight of something **payanda, destek, dayak** ⊃See also: **child support, income support, moral support**.

a **keen/loyal/staunch/strong** supporter ● a supporter **of** sth

supporter /sə'pɔːtəʳ/ *noun* [C] **1** someone who supports a particular idea, group, or person **destekçi, taraftar, arka çıkan** *a strong supporter of the government* **2** *mainly UK* someone who likes a particular sports team and wants them to win **taraftar, destekleyici** *English football supporters*

supportive /sə'pɔːtɪv/ *adjective* giving help or encouragement **destekleyici, arka çıkan** *a very supportive friend*

o-- **suppose** /sə'pəʊz/ *verb* **1 be supposed to do sth a** to be expected or intended to do something, especially when this does not happen **gerekmek, beklenmek; ...ması/mesi lazım; ...acak/ecek olmak** *These drugs are supposed to reduce the pain.* ○ *He was supposed to be here by nine.* **b** If you are supposed to do something, the rules say that you should do it. **...mak/mek zorunda olmak; ...malı/meli** *You're supposed to pay by the end of the month.* ○ *You're not supposed to* (= you should not) *smoke in here.* **2 be supposed to be sth** to be considered by many people to be something **...olduğu dikkate alınmalı; ...mış/miş olduğu değerlendirilmek** *The scenery is supposed to be fantastic.* **3** [T] to think that something is likely to be true **farzetmek, zannetmek, sanmak, var saymak** [+ (that)] *I suppose that you've already heard the news?* **4 suppose/supposing (that)** used to introduce an idea for someone to consider **eğer, ya, diyelim ki, farzedelim ki** *Suppose he phones tonight. What should I say?* **5 I suppose** used to show that you are not certain or not completely happy about something **Herhalde!', 'Galiba!', 'Zannedersem!'** *It was quite interesting, I suppose.* **6 I suppose so** used to show agreement to something when you do not really want to **Galiba!', 'Başka yolu yok!', 'Başka çare yok!', 'Herhalde!'** *"Can I come with you?" "I suppose so."*

supposed /sə'pəʊzɪd/ *adjective* [always before noun] used to show that you do not believe that someone or something really is what many people consider them to be **sözde, iddia edilen, ileri sürülen, kabul edilen** *a supposed genius* ● **supposedly** /sə'pəʊzɪdli/ *adverb* *The building is supposedly in good condition.* **Güya!**

supposition /ˌsʌpə'zɪʃᵊn/ *noun* [C, U] *formal* when someone believes that something is true although there is no proof **varsayım, faraziye**

suppress /sə'pres/ *verb* [T] **1** [FEELINGS] to control feelings so that they do not show **bastırmak, sindirmek, durdurmak** *I could barely suppress my anger.* **2** [INFORMATION] to prevent information from being known **gizli tutmak, örtbas etmek, saklamak** *to suppress evidence/news* **3** [FIGHT] to stop someone or something by using force **zorla durdurmak, zaptetmek** [often passive] *The rebellion was suppressed by government forces.* ● **suppression** /sə'preʃᵊn/ *noun* [U] **bastırma (duygu)**

supremacy /suː'preməsi/ *noun* [U] when a country or group of people is more powerful, successful, etc than anyone else **üstünlük** *a battle/struggle for supremacy*

supreme /suː'priːm/ *adjective* **1** of the highest rank or greatest importance **yüce, yüksek** *the supreme ruler* **2** very great **en büyük, en yüksek, çok büyük** *supreme confidence/effort* ● **supremely** *adverb* very **fevkalâde, epey, bir hali** *supremely confident*

the su,preme 'court *noun* the court of law that has the most authority in a state or country **yargıtay, en üst mahkeme**

surcharge /'sɜːtʃɑːdʒ/ *noun* [C] an extra amount of money that you have to pay for something **ek ücret, ilave ödeme, fazla ödeme** *There is a surcharge for single rooms.*

o-- **sure** /ʃɔːʳ/ *adjective* **1** [never before noun] certain **emin** [+ (that)] *I'm sure that he won't mind.* ○ [+ question word]

She's **not sure** *what she's going to do next.* ○ *I'm quite* **sure about** *the second answer.* ⊃Opposite unsure. **2 make sure (that)** to take action so that you are certain that something happens, is true, etc **sağlamak, temin etmek** *Make sure that you close all the windows before you leave.* **3 be sure of sth** to be confident that something is true **...dan/den emin olmak** *He'll win, I'm sure of it.* **4** for sure without any doubts **muhakkak, kesinlikle, su götürmez, kesin** *I think he's from Korea but don't know for sure.* **5 be sure of yourself** to be confident of your own abilities, qualities, etc **kendinden emin olmak; kendine güvenmek** *She's always been very sure of herself.* **6 be sure to do sth a** If you are sure to do something, it is certain that you will do it. **yapacağından emin olmak; kesinlikle yapacak olmak** *He's sure to go back there again.* **b** used to tell someone what they must remember to do **yapmayı unutmamak, yapacağından emin olmak; muhakkak yapmak** *Be sure to tell her I called.* **7 a sure sign of/that sth** something that makes something seem certain to be true **kesin işaret/delil; doğruluğunu gösteren kesin işaret/delil 8 a sure thing** something that is certain to happen **tabii, elbette** *Death is the one sure thing about life.* **9 sure** (*also US* **sure thing**) used to show agreement **kesin, muhakkak, su götürmez** *"Can I borrow your pen please?" "Sure."* **10 sure enough** as expected **nitekim de, gerçekten de, nitekim** *He said the book was on his desk, and sure enough, there it was.*

o-- **surely** /'ʃɔːli/ *adverb* used to express surprise that something has happened or is going to happen **elbette, kesinlikle, şüphesiz, muhakkak** *You surely didn't tell him, did you?* ○ *Surely you're not going to go out dressed like that?*

surf[1] /sɜːf/ *verb* **1** [I] to ride on a wave in the sea using a special board **sörf yapmak 2 surf the Internet/Net/ Web** to look at information on the Internet by moving from one page to another using electronic links (= connections) **internette/nette/web'de gezinmek** ⊃See study page **The Web and the Internet** on page Centre 36. ● **surfer** *noun* [C] someone who surfs **sörfçü, sörf yapan kimse** ● **surfing** *noun* [U] **sörf**

surf[2] /sɜːf/ *noun* [U] the top of the waves in the sea as it moves onto the coast **sörf, köpüklü kırılan dalga**

surface .... İLE BİRLİKTE KULLANILAN KELİMELER

a flat/hard/level/smooth/uneven surface ● cover the surface ● above/below/beneath/on the surface

o-- **surface**[1] /'sɜːfɪs/ *noun* **1** [C] the top or outside part of something **yüz, yüzey, satıh** *the Earth's surface* ○ *The sun was reflected on the surface of the water.* **2** [no plural] what someone or something seems to be like when you do not know much about them **görünüş, görünüm, yüzey** *On the surface he seemed very pleasant.* ⊃See also: **work surface.**

surface[2] /'sɜːfɪs/ *verb* **1** [APPEAR] [I] to appear or become public, often after being hidden **ortaya çıkmak, gözükmek, görünmek** *This problem first surfaced about two weeks ago.* ○ *So when did these allegations surface?* **2** [RISE] [I] to rise to the surface of water **su yüzüne çıkmak; yüzeye çıkak** *The submarine surfaced a few miles off the coast.* **3** [COVER] [T] to cover a road with a hard substance **yol kaplamak, kaplama yapmak, yüzeyini kaplamak**

'surface ,mail *noun* [U] letters, parcels, etc that are sent by road, sea, or train and not by aircraft **kara/deniz yoluyla gönderilen posta**

surfboard /'sɜːfbɔːd/ *noun* [C] a long piece of wood or plastic that you use to ride on waves in the sea **sörf tahtası, sörf kayağı**

S

surfeit /'sɜ:fɪt/ *noun* [no plural] *formal* too much of something **aşırılık, ölçüyü kaçırma, bolluk** *We've had a surfeit of applications from women for this job.*

surfing /'sɜ:fɪŋ/ *noun* [U] **1** the sport of riding on a wave on a special board **sörf yapma, sörf sporu 2** the activity of looking at a lot of different things on the Internet **internette gezinme/sörf yapma**

surge¹ /sɜ:dʒ/ *verb* **1 surge forward/into/through, etc** to move somewhere with great strength **birden hamle yapmak, atılmak, fırlamak, sökün etmek, akın etmek; hücum etmek** *The crowd surged against the barriers.* **2** [I] to increase very quickly **süratle artmak, çoğalmak** *Prices surged on the stock exchange.*

surge² /sɜ:dʒ/ *noun* [C] **1** a large increase in something **artış, kabarma, büyük miktarda artış** *a surge in spending* **2** a sudden movement forward **hücum, atak, ani hareket**

surgeon /'sɜ:dʒ³n/ *noun* [C] a doctor who does medical operations **cerrah, operatör** ⊃See also: **veterinary surgeon.**

surgery /'sɜ:dʒ³ri/ *noun* **1** [U] when a doctor cuts your body open and repairs or removes something **ameliyat, operasyon** *to have surgery* ○ *heart/knee surgery* **2** [C] *UK* a place where doctors or other medical workers treat people **muayenehane** ⊃See also: plastic surgery.

surgical /'sɜ:dʒɪk³l/ *adjective* relating to medical operations **cerrahi, cerrahlık veya ameliyatla ilgili** *surgical instruments/gloves* • **surgically** *adverb* **ameliyat ile ilgili**

surly /'sɜ:li/ *adjective* unfriendly and rude **asık suratlı, somurtkan, huysuz, hırçın** *a surly teenager*

surmount /sə'maʊnt/ *verb* [T] *formal* to deal successfully with a problem **üstesinden gelmek, halletmek, altından kalkmak, yenmek**

surname /'sɜ:neɪm/ *noun* [C] the name that you and other members of your family all have **soyisim** *His surname is Walker.*

surpass /sə'pɑ:s/ *verb* [T] *formal* to be or do better than someone or something else **üstün olmak, geçmek, baskın çıkmak, bastırmak, aşmak** *The book's success surpassed everyone's expectations.*

surplus /'sɜ:pləs/ *noun* [C, U] an amount of something that is more than you need **fazlalık, artık, fazla** *Every year we produce a huge surplus of meat.* • **surplus** *adjective* **surplus wheat artan, fazlalık**

surprise ...... İLE BİRLİKTE KULLANILAN KELİMELER

come as a surprise • a big/nice/unpleasant surprise • a surprise to sb • a surprise party

๐▪**surprise¹** /sə'praɪz/ *noun* **1** [C] an event that you did not expect to happen **sürpriz, şaşkınlık** *I didn't know that my parents were coming - it was a lovely surprise.* ○ *Her resignation came as a complete surprise* (= was very surprising). ○ *a surprise party* **2** [U] the feeling that you get when something happens that you did not expect **hayret, şaşkınlık, sürpriz** *He agreed to everything, much to my surprise.* **3 take/catch sb by surprise** to be unexpected and make someone feel surprise **şaşırtmak, gafil avlamak, hayrete düşürmek** *I wasn't expecting her to be so angry - it took me by surprise.*

surprise ...... BAŞKA BİR DEYİŞLE

Hoş olmayan bir sürpriz **shock** ifadesiyle tanımlanabilir. *We got a nasty shock when he gave us the bill.* • *His death came as a terrible shock.*

Kişiyi üzüntüye ve hayal kırıklığına sürükleyen bir olay **blow** olarak tanımlanabilir. *Losing his job was a terrible blow to him.*

İnanılması güç ve sürpriz bir şekilde gelişen bir olay **miracle** ifadesiyle tanımlanabilir. *It's a miracle that she survived the accident.* • *If I pass this exam it'll be a miracle.*

Kişi eğer hiç beklemediği bir şekilde acı gerçeği öğreniyorsa, bu durum için **a rude awakening** söylemi kullanılabilir. *She'll be in for a rude awakening when she has to pay her own bills.*

Eğer olayların hiç beklenmedik bir şekilde gerçekleştiğini söylemek isitiyorsanız, **be news to** ifadesi kullanılabilir. *Sarah is leaving? Well that's news to me.*

surprise² /sə'praɪz/ *verb* [T] **1** to make someone feel surprise **şaşırtmak, hayrete düşürmek** *I didn't tell her I was coming home early - I thought I'd surprise her.* **2** to find or attack someone when they are not expecting it **ani baskın yapmak; aniden bulmak/yakalamak**

๐▪**surprised** /sə'praɪzd/ *adjective* feeling surprise because something has happened that you did not expect **şaşırmış, hayrete düşmüş; (argo) apışıp kalmış** [+ to do sth] *I'm surprised to see you here.* ○ *She wasn't surprised at his decision.* ○ [+ (that)] *I'm surprised that you've decided to leave.*

๐▪**surprising** /sə'praɪzɪŋ/ *adjective* not expected and making someone feel surprised **şaşırtıcı, hayret verici, acayip** *It's not surprising you're putting on weight, the amount you're eating!* • **surprisingly** *adverb* **surprisingly good şaşırtıcı olarak**

surreal /sə'rɪəl/ (*also* surrealistic /sə,rɪə'lɪstɪk/) *adjective* strange and not real, like something in a dream **gerçeküstü; acayip ve gerçek dışı** *His paintings have a surreal quality.*

surrender /s³r'end³r/ *verb* **1** [I] to stop fighting and admit that you have been beaten **teslim olmak, yenik düşmek, boyun eğmek** *Rebel troops are refusing to surrender.* **2** [T] *formal* to give something to someone else because you have been forced or officially asked to give it to them **teslim etmek** *He was released on the condition that he surrendered his passport.* • **surrender** *noun* [C, U] **teslimiyet**

surreptitious /,sʌrəp'tɪʃəs/ *adjective* done secretly so that other people do not see **gizli, el altından, kaçamak** *surreptitious glances at the clock* • **surreptitiously** *adverb* **gizlice**

surrogate /'sʌrəgɪt/ *adjective* [always before noun] used instead of someone or something else **vekil, yerine geçen** *Twenty years older than her, he effectively became a surrogate father.* • **surrogate** *noun* [C] someone or something that is used instead of someone or something else **vekil, yerine kullanılan şey/kimse** *He seemed to regard her as a surrogate for his dead mother.*

surrogate 'mother *noun* [C] a woman who has a baby for a woman who is not able to have a baby herself **kiralık anne, başkası yerine doğum yapan kadın**

๐▪**surround** /sə'raʊnd/ *verb* [T] **1** to be or go everywhere around something or someone **çevirmek, sarmak, kuşatmak** *The house is surrounded by a large garden.* ○ *The police have surrounded the building.* ○ *the surrounding countryside* **2 be surrounded by sb/sth** to have a lot of people or things near you **kuşatılmak, sarılmak, çevrelenmek** *She's surrounded by the people she loves.* **3** If a feeling or situation surrounds an event, it is closely connected with it. **etrafını sarmak, kuşat-**

mak; ilgisi olmak; ilişkisi olmak *Mystery still sur-rounds the exact circumstances of his death.*

surroundings /sə'raʊndɪŋz/ *noun* [plural] the place where someone or something is and the things that are in it **civar, çevre, muhit, etraf, havali** *Have you got used to your new surroundings?*

surveillance /sɜː'veɪləns/ *noun* [U] when someone is watched carefully, especially by the police or army, because they are expected to do something wrong **gözetleme, keşif, gözetim, gözaltı, nezaret** *The police have kept the man under strict surveillance.*

survey ...... İLE BİRLİKTE KULLANILAN KELİMELER

carry out/conduct/take part in a survey ● a survey finds/reveals/shows/suggests sth ● a survey of sth ● in a survey ● according to a survey ● a recent survey

survey¹ /'sɜːveɪ/ *noun* [C] **1** QUESTIONS an examination of people's opinions or behaviour made by asking people questions **anket, inceleme, tenkit** *Holidays in the UK are becoming more popular, according to a recent survey.* **2** BUILDING *UK* an examination of the structure of a building in order to find out if there is anything wrong with it **muayene, ekspertiz, keşif** *The bank have refused a loan until we've had a survey done on the property.* **3** LAND when an area of land is looked at, and its measurements and details recorded, especially in order to make a map **yer ölçme, haritasını çıkarma**

survey² /sə'veɪ/ *verb* [T] **1** EXAMINE to look at or examine something carefully **iyice incelemek, ekspertiz yapmak** *I got out of the car to survey the damage.* **2** QUESTION to ask people questions in order to find out about their opinions or behaviour **anket yapmak, araştırma yapmak** *75% of midwives surveyed were in favour of home births.* **3** LAND to measure and record the details of an area of land **ölçüm yapmak, kadastro yapmak, ölçüp biçmek 4** BUILDING *UK* to examine the structure of a building in order to find out if there is anything wrong with it **bina incelemesi yapmak; binada teknik ölçüm yapmak**

surveyor /sə'veɪəʳ/ *noun* [C] *UK* someone whose job is to examine the structure of buildings **bina eksperi, 2** someone whose job is to measure and record the details of an area of land **kadastro memuru, tekniker, ölçüm memuru**

survival /sə'vaɪvᵊl/ *noun* [U] when someone or something continues to live or exist, especially after a difficult or dangerous situation **hayatta kalma, yaşama** *Flood victims had to fight for survival.*

○⁺**survive** /sə'vaɪv/ *verb* [I, T] **1** NOT DIE to continue to live after almost dying because of an accident, illness, etc **hayatta kalmak, hayatı idame etmek, yaşamını sürdürmek** *He was born with a heart problem and only survived ten days.* ○ *No one survived the plane crash.* **2** EXIST [I, T] to continue to exist after being in a difficult or dangerous situation **varlığını sürdürmek, ayakta kalmak** *Only two buildings survived the earthquake.* **3** LIVE LONGER [T] If you survive someone, you continue to live after they have died. **neslini devam ettirmek, soyunu yaşatmak**

survivor /sə'vaɪvəʳ/ *noun* [C] someone who continues to live after almost dying because of an accident, illness, etc **sağ kalan kişi, kurtulan kimse, kazazede** *Rescuers have given up hope of finding any more survivors.*

susceptible /sə'septəbl/ *adjective* easily influenced or harmed by something **çabuk etkilenen, duyarlı, hassas** *Older people are more susceptible to the virus.* ○ *a susceptible young teenager* ● **susceptibility** /sə,septə-'bɪləti/ *noun* [U] when someone is susceptible **duyarlılık, hassaslık, çabuk etkilenme**

sushi /'suːʃi/ *noun* [U] Japanese food made of cold rice and fish which has not been cooked **suşi, çiğ balık** *a sushi bar*

suspect ...... İLE BİRLİKTE KULLANILAN KELİMELER

the chief/main/prime suspect ● a suspect for/in sth

suspect¹ /'sʌspekt/ *noun* [C] **1** someone who may have committed a crime **şüpheli, sanık** *He's the prime suspect* (= the most likely suspect) *in the murder case.* **2** the usual suspects the people you would expect to be present somewhere or doing a particular thing **her zamanki kişiler; bilinen kimseler** *"Who was at the party?" "Oh, Adrian, John, Dave - the usual suspects."*

○⁺**suspect²** /sə'spekt/ *verb* [T] **1** CRIME to think that someone may have committed a crime or done something bad **şüphelenmek, şüphe duymak, kuşkulanmak** *He was suspected of drug dealing.* ○ *suspected terrorists* **2** THINK LIKELY to think that something is probably true, or is likely to happen **ihtimal vermek, tahmin etmek** [+ (that)] *They suspected that he was lying.* **3** NOT TRUST to not trust someone or something **güvenmemek, kuşku duymak, şüphelenmek** *She suspected his motives for offering to help.*

suspect³ /'sʌspekt/ *adjective* difficult to trust or believe **şüpheli, kuşkulu** *His explanation was highly suspect.*

suspend /sə'spend/ *verb* [T] **1** to stop something happening for a short time **ertelemek, tehir etmek, tatil etmek, askıya almak, dondurmak** *The semi-final was suspended because of bad weather.* **2 suspend sth from/between, etc** to hang something from somewhere **asmak, asılı durmak, sarkıtmak** [often passive] *A light bulb was suspended from the ceiling.* **3** to not allow someone to go to work or school for a period of time because they have done something wrong **geçici olarak men etmek, bir süre kovmak, okula/işe gitmesine izin vermemek** [often passive] *She was suspended from school for fighting.*

suspenders /sə'spendəz/ *noun* [plural] **1** *UK* (*US* **garters**) pieces of elastic fixed to a belt that hold up a woman's stockings (= very thin pieces of clothing that cover a woman's foot and leg) **çorap jartiyeri 2** *US* (*UK* **braces**) two straps fixed to a pair of trousers that go over your shoulders and stop the trousers from falling down **pantolon askısı**

suspense /sə'spens/ *noun* [U] the feeling of excitement that you have when you are waiting for something to happen **merak, merakla bekleme, belirsizlik durumu** *What's your answer then? Don't keep me in suspense.*

suspension /sə'spenʃᵊn/ *noun* **1** STOP [U] when someone stops something happening for a period of time **erteleme, durdurma, askıya alma, kesme** *an immediate suspension of all imports and exports* **2** JOB/SCHOOL [C, U] when someone is not allowed to go to work or school for a period of time **geçici bir süre işten el çektirme, kovma, yasaklama, belli bir süre askıya alma 3** VEHICLE [C, U] equipment which is fixed to the wheels of a vehicle in order to make it move more smoothly **süspansiyon donanımı**

suspicion ...... İLE BİRLİKTE KULLANILAN KELİMELER

have a suspicion ● confirm sb's suspicion ● a deep/sneaking/strong suspicion

suspicion /sə'spɪʃᵊn/ *noun* **1** [C, U] a feeling or belief that someone has done something wrong **kuşku, şüphe, vesvese** *They were arrested on suspicion of drug dealing.* ○ *Several members of staff are under suspicion of stealing money.* **2** [C] an idea that something may be true önsezi, içe doğuş [+ (that)] *I had a sneaking suspicion that the two events might be connected.*

suspicious /sə'spɪʃəs/ *adjective* **1** making you feel that something is wrong or that something bad or illegal is happening **kuşkulu, şüpheli, şüphe duyulan** *suspicious behaviour/circumstances* ○ *I called airport security after noticing a **suspicious package**.* **2** not trusting someone **şüphe uyandıran, kuşkulandıran, güven vermeyen** *Many of them remain **suspicious** of journalists.* ● **suspiciously** *adverb She's been acting very suspiciously lately.* **şüpheci bir şekilde**

sustain /sə'steɪn/ *verb* [T] **1** to cause or allow something to continue for a period of time **sürdürmek, devam ettirmek** *The team may not be able to sustain this level of performance.* **2** to support someone or something so that they can live or exist **güç/umut/cesaret vermek, tahammül gücü vermek** *The money he received was hardly enough to sustain a wife and five children.* **3 sustain damage/injuries/losses** *formal* If someone or something sustains injuries/damage/losses, etc, they are injured/damaged, etc. **yaralı/hasarlı/kayıpları olmak**

sustainable /sə'steɪnəbl/ *adjective* **1** able to continue over a period of time **sürdürülebilir, devam ettirilebilir** *sustainable development/growth* **2** causing little or no damage to the environment and therefore able to continue for a long time

sustained /sə'steɪnd/ *adjective* continuing for a period of time without getting weaker **devamlı, uzun süreli, ardı arkası kesilmeyen** *a sustained attack* ○ *sustained pressure*

SUV /,esju:'vi:/ *noun* [C] *abbreviation for* sports utility vehicle: a large vehicle with an engine that supplies power to all four wheels, so that the vehicle can travel easily over rough ground **dörtçeker araç; Güçlendirilmiş Dörtçeker Araç (GDA)**

svelte /svelt/ *adjective* thin in an attractive way **çekici ve zarif; ince ve çekici**

swab /swɒb/ *noun* [C] a small piece of material used for cleaning an injury or for taking a small amount of a substance from someone's body so that it can be tested **eczalı pamuk/bez**

swagger /'swægər/ *verb* [I] to walk in a way that shows that you are confident and think that you are important **caka satarak yürümek; kasılarak yürümek** *A group of young men swaggered around in leather jackets.* ● **swagger** *noun* [no plural] **kendine çok güvenme ve övünme**

◦**swallow**[1] /'swɒləʊ/ *verb* **1** FOOD OR DRINK [T] to move your throat in order to make food or drink go down **yutmak** *The snake swallowed the bird whole.* **2** THROAT [I] to make a movement with your throat as if you are eating, sometimes because you are nervous **yutkunmak** *Claire swallowed hard, opened the door and stepped inside.* **3** ACCEPT [T] to accept something unpleasant **yutmak, kanmak, kabullenmek** *They found the final decision **hard to swallow**.* **4** BELIEVE [T] *informal* to believe something, usually something which is not true **yutmak, katlanmak, sineye çekmek** *I told him we were journalists and he seemed to swallow it.* ➔See also: swallow your pride[1].

swallow sth up *phrasal verb* to make something disappear **yok etmek, yutmak, silip süpürmek, mahvetmek, tüketmek** *Many small businesses are being swallowed up by large international companies.*

swallow[2] /'swɒləʊ/ *noun* [C] **1** a small bird with long, pointed wings and a tail with two points **kırlangıç** **2** the movement of swallowing **yutma**

swam /swæm/ *past tense of* swim **yüzmek' fiilinin 2. hâli**

swamp[1] /swɒmp/ *noun* [C, U] an area of very wet, soft land **bataklık, batak**

swamp[2] /swɒmp/ *verb* [T] **1** to give someone more of something than they can deal with **fazla yük yüklemek, bir şeye boğmak, hücumuna uğratmak** [often passive] *The company was **swamped with** calls about its new service.* ○ *The market has been **swamped by** cheap imports.* **2** If an area is swamped, it becomes covered with water. **bataklığa dönmek** *Heavy rain has swamped many villages in the region.*

swan /swɒn/ *noun* [C] a large, white bird with a long neck which lives on lakes and rivers **kuğu**

swap /swɒp/ *verb* [I, T] **swapping**, *past* **swapped** to give something to someone and get something from them in return **değiş tokuş etmek, trampa etmek** *Would you mind if Dave **swapped** places **with** you for a bit?* ● **swap** *noun* [C] *We'll **do a swap**.* **değiş tokuş**

swarm[1] /swɔːm/ *noun* [C] a large group of things, usually insects, moving together **kalabalık, yığın, küme, sürü** *a swarm of bees*

swarm[2] /swɔːm/ *verb* [I] to move in a large group **akın etmek, akın akın gitmek, sürü halinde gitmek/hareket etmek** *TV reporters swarmed outside the pop star's home.*

swarm with sb/sth *phrasal verb* If a place is swarming with people, insects, etc, there are a lot of them moving around it. **dolup taşmak, mahşer yerine dönmek, kum gibi kaynamak** *The house was swarming with police.*

swarthy /'swɔːði/ *adjective* having dark skin **esmer, kara yağız**

swat /swɒt/ *verb* [T] **swatting**, *past* **swatted** to hit something, especially an insect, with a flat object **böceği bir nesneyle vurarak ezmek** *He swatted a fly with his newspaper.*

sway /sweɪ/ *verb* **1** [I] to move slowly from one side to the other **sallanmak** *The trees swayed gently in the wind.* **2** [T] to persuade someone to change their opinion or decision **etkilemek, ikna etmek, inandırmak** *I think I was swayed by what James said.*

◦**swear** /sweər/ *verb past tense* **swore**, *past participle* **sworn** **1** BAD LANGUAGE [I] to use language which people think is rude or offensive **küfretmek, sövmek** *He was sent home because he **swore at** the teacher.* **2** PROMISE [I, T] to make a serious promise **yemin etmek, ant içmek, söz vermek** [+ to do sth] *I swear to tell the truth.* ○ [+ (that)] *She swore that she was at home at the time of the accident.* **3** TRUE [T] used to say that you are sure something is true **yeminle/ısrarla söylemek** [+ (that)] *I could have sworn that she said she lived in Canterbury (= I was sure she lived in Canterbury, but now I have found that it is not true).*

swear by sth *phrasal verb* to believe strongly that something is useful or effective **çok güvenmek, yürekten inanmak** *Have you tried using vinegar to clean windows? My Mum swears by it.*

swear sb in *phrasal verb* to make someone such as a president, judge, etc officially promise to be honest and responsible when they start their job **yemin ettirip görev vermek/işe başlatmak/görevi devralmak; bağlılık yemini ettirmek** [often passive] *Mr Stein was sworn in as City Council president yesterday.*

swearing /'sweərɪŋ/ *noun* [U] using rude or offensive language **küfür, sövgü, kaba ve iğrenç söz** *He was always getting into trouble for swearing.*

'swear ,word *noun* [C] a word which people think is rude or offensive **küfür**

sweat /swet/ *verb* [I] to produce liquid through your skin because you are hot or nervous **terlemek** *I'd been running and I was sweating.* ● **sweat** *noun* [U] *The sweat was running down his face.* **ter**

sweat it out *phrasal verb informal* to wait nervously for an unpleasant situation to improve or end **endişeyle beklemek** *I don't get my exam results till the end of June so I'll just have to sweat it out till then.*

sweat over sth *phrasal verb* to work hard at something **canla başla çalışmak, ter dökmek, çok çalışmak** *She's been sweating over the preparations for the party all weekend.*

sweater /'swetə^r/ (*also UK* jumper) *noun* [C] a warm piece of clothing which covers the top of your body and is pulled on over your head **örgü kazak, süveter** ⊃Orta kısımdaki renkli sayfalarına bakınız.

sweats /swets/ *noun* [plural] *US* a sweatshirt and sweatpants (= loose, comfortable trousers), often worn for exercising **eşofman** ⊃Orta kısımdaki renkli sayfalarına bakınız.

sweatshirt /'swetʃɜːt/ *noun* [C] a piece of clothing made of soft cotton which covers the top of your body and is pulled on over your head **eşofman üstü** ⊃Orta kısımdaki renkli sayfalarına bakınız.

sweatshop /'swetʃɒp/ *noun* [C] a small factory where workers are paid very little and work many hours in very bad conditions **çalışanların az ücretle çok kötü şartlarda uzun saatler çalıştırıldığı küçük fabrika/imâlathane**

sweaty /'sweti/ *adjective* covered in sweat **terli, terden sırılsıklam olmuş** *He was hot and sweaty from working in the garden.*

swede /swiːd/ *noun* [C, U] *UK* a round, yellow vegetable which grows in the ground **sarı şalgam, şalgam**

sweep¹ /swiːp/ *verb past* swept **1** [I, T] (*also* sweep up) to clean the floor using a brush **süpürmek, silmek** *She's just swept the floor.* ○ *He swept up the pieces of broken glass* (= removed them from the floor with a brush). **2 be swept along/away, etc** to be pushed or carried along, often by something strong which you cannot control **sürüklenmek, alıp götürülmek, önüne katıp götürülmek; silinmek; süpürülmek** *Many trees were swept away in the flood.* **3** [I, T] to quickly affect a large area **süratle yayılmak, çarçabuk etkisi altına almak** *The disease is sweeping the country.* ○ *Panic swept through the crowd.* **4 sweep along/into/past, etc** to move quickly, especially in a way that shows you think you are important **bir hışımla hareket etmek/kalkmak; çalımla geçmek** *She swept past me in the corridor.*

sweep² /swiːp/ *noun* [C] **1** a long movement **uzun bir hareket** [usually singular] *With a sweep of his arm, he gestured towards the garden.* **2** something shaped in a long curve **kavis; eğrilik** *a long sweep of sandy beach* ⊃See also: **chimney sweep.**

sweeping /'swiːpɪŋ/ *adjective* **1** [always before noun] affecting many things or people **her şeyi herkesi etkisi altına alan** *sweeping changes/reforms* **2 a sweeping statement/generalization** when someone says something that is very general and has not been carefully thought about **düşünmeden genelleme; yüzeysel ele alma**

sweepstake /'swiːpsteɪk/ *UK* (*US* sweepstakes) *noun* [C] a type of betting (= risking money on a competition) in which the winner receives all the money **bütün parasını bahse koyma; tüm parasına iddiaya girme**

◦━**sweet¹** /swiːt/ *adjective* **1** [TASTE] with a taste like sugar **tatlı** *It was covered in a very sweet chocolate sauce.* **2** [ATTRACTIVE] attractive, often because of being small **hoş, sevimli, şirin, tatlı** *Look at that kitten - isn't she*

sweet? **3** [KIND] kind and friendly **nazik, tatlı, dost canlısı** *It was really sweet of you to come.* **4** [SMELL/SOUND] A sweet smell or sound is pleasant. **hoş, latif, güzel** ● **sweetness** *noun* [U] **tatlı olma durumu**

sweet² /swiːt/ *UK* (*US* candy) *noun* [C] a small piece of sweet food, often made of sugar or chocolate **şekerleme, bonbon** *You shouldn't eat so many sweets - they're bad for your teeth.*

sweetcorn /'swiːtkɔːn/ *UK* (*US* corn) *noun* [U] the sweet, yellow seeds of maize (= a plant) which are eaten as a vegetable **mısır** ⊃Orta kısımdaki renkli sayfalarına bakınız.

sweeten /'swiːtᵊn/ *verb* [T] to make something sweeter, for example by adding more sugar **tatlandırmak** *She gave me a hot lemon drink, sweetened with honey.*

sweetener /'swiːtᵊnə^r/ *noun* [C] **1** something which is used to make something taste sweeter **tatlandırıcı** *an artificial sweetener* **2** something that is used to persuade someone to do something **gönül alıcı/ikna edici şey; bir tür rüşvet**

sweetheart /'swiːthɑːt/ *noun* [C] You call someone 'sweetheart' to show affection or to be friendly. **sevgili, sevdiği, sevdalısı** *Come here, sweetheart.*

sweetly /'swiːtli/ *adverb* in an attractive or kind way **hoş, sevimli, çekici şekilde, nazikçe** *She smiled sweetly.*

sweet po'tato *UK* (*US* 'sweet po,tato) *noun* [C, U] *plural* **sweet potatoes** a long, red vegetable like a potato but that tastes slightly sweet **yer elması, tatlı patates**

swell¹ /swel/ *verb past tense* swelled, *past participle* swollen or swelled **1** [I] (*also* swell up) to increase in size **şişmek, kabarmak** *One side of his face had swollen up where he'd been stung.* **2** [I, T] to increase in amount because more things are added **çoğalmak, miktarı artmak** *The population of the region was swollen by refugees from across the border.*

swell² /swel/ *noun* **1** [C] the movement of waves in the sea, or the waves themselves **hava akımı, hava dalgası** *ocean swells* **2** [C] an increase **artış, artma**

swell³ /swel/ *adjective US old-fashioned* good or pleasant **iyi, hoş, güzel** *Everyone's having a swell time.*

swelling /'swelɪŋ/ *noun* [C, U] a part of your body which has become bigger because of illness or injury **şişme, şişkinlik, ödem** *The doctor gave me drugs to reduce the swelling in my ankle.*

sweltering /'sweltərɪŋ/ *adjective* so hot that you feel uncomfortable **bunaltıcı/boğucu sıcak** *It was a sweltering afternoon in August.*

swept /swept/ *past of* sweep **'süpürmek' fiilinin geçmiş zaman hâli**

swerve /swɜːv/ *verb* [I] to change direction suddenly, especially when you are driving a vehicle **aniden direksiyon kırmak; birden yön değiştirmek** *He swerved to avoid a cyclist and hit another car.*

swift /swɪft/ *adjective* happening or moving quickly **çabuk, tez, hızlı** *a swift response* ● **swiftly** *adverb* **süratli bir şekilde**

swig /swɪɡ/ *verb* [T] swigging, *past* swigged *informal* to drink something, taking a lot of liquid into your mouth at a time **bir nefeste içmek, yuvarlamak; bir dikişte içmek** ● **swig** *noun* [C] *He took a swig of his beer and carried on with the story.* **bir anda çok büyük miktar yudumlama**

swill¹ /swɪl/ *verb* [T] **1** (*also* swill out) to clean something by making liquid move around it **bol su ile yıkamak** *The dentist handed me a glass of water to swill my mouth out.* **2** to quickly drink a large amount of something, especially alcohol **(içki) bir dikişte içmek; bir hamlede yuvarlamak**

S

swill² /swɪl/ *noun* [U] waste food that is fed to pigs **domuzlara verilen yiyecek artığı; bir tür yal**

o←**swim¹** /swɪm/ *verb* **swimming**, *past tense* **swam**, *past participle* **swum 1** THROUGH WATER [I, T] to move through water by moving your body **yüzmek** *I learnt to swim when I was about 5 years old.* ○ *I swim thirty lengths of the pool most mornings.* ⟳Orta kısımdaki renkli sayfalarına bakınız. **2** HEAD [I] If your head swims, you feel confused and are unable to see or think clearly. **başı dönmek, fırıl fırıl dönmek 3** SEEM TO MOVE [I] to seem to move about **hareket ediyor gibi gözükmek; zemin ayaklarının altından kayıyor gibi gelmek; başı dönmek** *I got up suddenly and the room started swimming.* ● **swimming** *noun* [U] *I usually go swimming about twice a week.* **yüzme** ● **swimmer** *noun* [C] *I'm not a very strong swimmer.* **yüzücü**

swim² /swɪm/ *noun* [C] a time when you swim **yüzme** *I went for a swim before breakfast.*

'**swimming ˌcostume** *UK* (*US* **bathing suit**) *noun* [C] a piece of clothing that you wear to go swimming **mayo, yüzme kıyafeti** ⟳Orta kısımdaki renkli sayfalarına bakınız.

'**swimming ˌpool** *noun* [C] an area of water that has been made for people to swim in **yüzme havuzu**

'**swimming ˌtrunks** *noun* [plural] a piece of clothing that boys and men wear when they swim **erkeklerin giydiği şort-mayo** ⟳Orta kısımdaki renkli sayfalarına bakınız.

swimsuit /'swɪmsuːt/ *noun* [C] a piece of clothing that girls and women wear to go swimming **bayan mayosu, mayo** ⟳Orta kısımdaki renkli sayfalarına bakınız.

swindle /'swɪndl/ *verb* [T] to get money from someone by cheating or deceiving them **dolandırmak** [often passive] *She was swindled out of thousands of dollars.* ● **swindle** *noun* [C] *a multi-million-pound swindle* **dolandırma** ● **swindler** *noun* [C] **dolandırıcı**

swine /swaɪn/ *noun* **1** [plural] *formal* pigs **domuzlar 2** [C] *informal* an unpleasant person **nefret uyandıran kimse**

swing¹ /swɪŋ/ *verb past* **swung 1** BACKWARDS/FORWARDS [I, T] to move smoothly backwards and forwards, or to make something do this **sallamak, sallanmak** *She really swings her arms when she walks.* **2** CURVE [I, T] to move smoothly in a curve, or to make something do this **savurmak, savrulmak, döndürmek** *The door swung shut.* ○ *Watch the ball as you swing the bat.* **3** CHANGE [I] If someone's opinion or their feelings swing, they suddenly change. **aniden fikrinden dönmek, caymak, fikri değişmek** *Her moods swing with absolutely no warning.*

swing around/round *phrasal verb* to turn around quickly **birden dönmek, dönüvermek**

swing at sb *phrasal verb informal* to try to hit someone **yumruk savurmak/sallamak/atmak**

swing² /swɪŋ/ *noun* [C] **1** FOR CHILDREN a chair hanging on two ropes that children sit on and swing backwards and forwards **salıncak 2** HIT an attempt to hit someone **vurma, darbe, saldırma, savurma** *Isn't that the boy Mark took a swing at* (= tried to hit)? **3** CHANGE a sudden change **anî değişim, beklenmedik başkalaşım** *He suffered terrible mood swings.* **4 be in full swing** If an event is in full swing, everything has started and there is a lot of activity. **en hengâmeli zamanında olmak, en civcivli/hareketli anında olmak; başını kaşıyamayacak durumda olmak** *By ten o'clock, the party was in full swing.*

swipe¹ /swaɪp/ *verb* [T] **1** (*also* swipe at) to move your arm in order to try to hit someone or something **savurmak, kolunu sallayıp vurmaya çalışmak 2** *informal* to steal something **araklamak, çalmak, aşırmak, yürütmek**

swipe² /swaɪp/ *noun* [C] an attempt to hit someone **vurmaya çalışma, darbe indirmeye teşebbüs etme**

'**swipe ˌcard** *noun* [C] *UK* a small piece of plastic that contains electronic information, used to open doors, etc **elektronik bilgi içeren kapı kartı**

swirl /swɜːl/ *verb* [I, T] to move around and around quickly, or to make something do this **anafor yap(tır) mak, fırıl fırıl dön(dür)mek** *The mist swirled round the castle.* ● **swirl** *noun* [C] **kıvrılma, kıvırma**

swish /swɪʃ/ *verb* [I, T] to move quickly through the air making a soft sound, or to make something do this **hışırda(t)mak; hışırdayarak hareket et(tir)mek; havada hisleyerek hareket et(tir)mek** ● **swish** *noun* [C] *the swish of curtains closing* **ıslık sesi**

o←**switch¹** /swɪtʃ/ *verb* [I, T] **1** to change from one thing to another **dönmek, geçiş yapmak** *We're trying to encourage people to switch from cars to bicycles.* ○ *He's just switched jobs.* **2** to exchange something with someone else **değiştirmek, değişmek** *After a couple of months we switched roles.*

switch (sth) off *phrasal verb* to turn off a light, television, etc by using a switch **tv.ışık vb. kapamak/söndürmek** *Have you switched the computer off?*

switch off *phrasal verb UK* to stop giving your attention to someone or something **ilgisini yitirmek, hevesi geçmek/kaybolmak** *I'm afraid I just switch off when she starts telling me about her problems.*

switch (sth) on *phrasal verb* to turn on a light, television, etc by using a switch **tv.ışık vb. açmak/yakmak**

switch over *phrasal verb* **1** *UK* to change from one television or radio station to another **istasyon/kanal değiştirmek 2** to change from doing one thing to another **bir işten öbürüne geçmek** *We've decided to switch over to low fat milk.*

⟨⟨⟨ *switch* ...... İLE BİRLİKTE KULLANILAN KELİMELER

flick/press a switch ● the **on/off** switch

o←**switch²** /swɪtʃ/ *noun* [C] **1** a small object that you push up or down with your finger to turn something electrical on or off **anahtar, düğme 2** a change **değişim, değişme, değişiklik** *There has been a switch in policy.*

switchboard /'swɪtʃbɔːd/ *noun* [C] a piece of equipment that is used to direct all the telephone calls made from and to a building **telefon santralı**

swivel /'swɪvªl/ (*also* swivel around) *verb* [I, T] *UK* **swivelling**, *past* **swivelled**, *US* **swiveling**, *past* **swiveled** to turn round, or to make something turn round **dönmek, döndürmek**

swollen¹ /'swəʊlən/ *adjective* bigger than usual **şişmiş, şişik, apse yapmış** *a swollen wrist/ankle* ○ *swollen rivers*

swollen² /'swəʊlən/ *past participle* of swell **'şişmek' fiilinin geçmiş zaman hâli**

swoop /swuːp/ *verb* [I] **1** to suddenly move very quickly down through the air **aniden dalmak, pike yapmak** *Huge birds swoop down from the sky.* **2** to suddenly attack **ansızın saldırmak, saldırıya geçmek** *The day before police had swooped on his home.* ● **swoop** *noun* [C] **saldırı**

swop /swɒp/ *verb* [I, T] **swopping**, *past* **swopped** *another UK spelling of* swap (= to give something to someone and get something from them in return) **değiş tokuş etmek**

sword /sɔːd/ *noun* [C] a weapon with a long, metal blade and a handle, used especially in the past **kılıç**

swordfish /'sɔːdfɪʃ/ *noun* [C, U] *plural* **swordfish** a large fish with a long, pointed part at the front of its head, that can be eaten as food **kılıç balığı**

swore /swɔːʳ/ *past tense of* swear **yemin etmek' fiilinin 2. hâli**

sworn¹ /swɔːn/ *adjective* **1 sworn statement/testimony, etc** something that you have officially said is true **yeminli ifade/şahitlik 2 sworn enemies** two people, or two groups of people who are completely against each other **can düşmanları, ezeli düşmanlar, kanlılar, kanlı bıçaklı düşmanlar**

sworn² /swɔːn/ *past participle of* swear **yemin etmek' fiilinin 3. hâli**

swot¹ /swɒt/ *noun* [C] *UK informal* someone who studies too much **çok çalışan kimse, hafızlayan kişi; (argo) inek kimse**

swot² /swɒt/ *UK informal* (*US* cram) *verb* [I] **swotting**, *past* **swotted** to study a lot **çok çalışmak, hafızlamak, sabahlara kadar çalışmak** *I'm swotting for tomorrow's exam.*
swot up (on sth) *phrasal verb* to learn as much as you can about a subject, especially before an examination **sınav öncesi öğrenebildiği kadar öğrenmek/çalışa bildiği kadar çalışmak**

swum /swʌm/ *past participle of* swim **yüzmek' fiilinin 3. hâli**

swung /swʌŋ/ *past of* swing **sallanmak' fiilinin geçmiş zaman hâli**

sycamore /'sɪkəmɔːʳ/ *noun* [C, U] a tree with leaves that are divided into five parts and with seeds that turn around as they fall **çınar ağacı**

sycophantic /ˌsɪkəʊ'fæntɪk/ *adjective formal* Someone who is sycophantic praises people in authority in a way that is not sincere, especially in order to get an advantage for themselves. **yağcı, sürekli yağ yakan; menfaati için başkalarını öven; yalaka; saykofantik ● sycophant** /'sɪkəfænt/ *noun* [C] **dalkavuk, yağcı**

syllable /'sɪləbl/ *noun* [C] a word or part of a word that has one vowel sound **hece** *'But' has one syllable and 'apple' has two syllables.*

syllabus /'sɪləbəs/ *noun* [C] *plural* **syllabuses** or **syllabi** a list of the subjects that are included in a course of study **müfredat programı**

∘ᵸ**symbol** /'sɪmbᵊl/ *noun* [C] **1** a sign or object that is used to represent something **imge, işaret, im, sembol** *A heart shape is the symbol of love.* **2** a number, letter, or sign that is used instead of the name of a chemical substance, another number, etc **kimyasal vb. sembol/imgeler/simgeler** *The symbol for oxygen is O.* ⊃See also: **status symbol.**

symbolic /sɪm'bɒlɪk/ *adjective* representing something else **simgesel, sembolik** *The blue, white and red of the French flag are symbolic of liberty, equality and fraternity.* ● **symbolically** *adverb* **sembolik olarak**

symbolism /'sɪmbᵊlɪzᵊm/ *noun* [U] the use of signs and objects in art, films, etc to represent ideas **sembolizm, simgecilik**

symbolize (*also UK* -ise) /'sɪmbᵊlaɪz/ *verb* [T] to represent something **simgelemek, sembolize etmek** *The lighting of the Olympic torch symbolizes peace and friendship among the nations of the world.*

symmetrical /sɪ'metrɪkᵊl/ (*also* **symmetric**) *adjective* having the same shape or size on both halves **bakışımlı, simetrik; aynı ölçü ve ebatlarda olan** *Faces are roughly symmetrical.*

symmetry /'sɪmətri/ *noun* [U] when something is symmetrical **bakışım, simetri**

∘ᵸ**sympathetic** /ˌsɪmpə'θetɪk/ *adjective* **1** showing that you understand and care about someone's problems **cana yakın, dost canlısı, sempatik** *My boss is very sympathetic about* my situation. **2** agreeing with or supporting someone's ideas or actions **olumlu/iyi bakan; cana yakın, sıcak, katılan, paylaşan, sempati duyan; aynı fikir/duygu/düşünceleri taşıyan** *He was sympathetic to their views.* ⊃Opposite **unsympathetic.** ● **sympathetically** *adverb* **anlayışlı bir şekilde**

sympathize (*also UK* -ise) /'sɪmpəθaɪz/ *verb* [I] **1** to understand and care about someone's problems **acımak, yakınlık göstermek, acısını paylaşmak** *It's a really bad situation - I do sympathize with her.* **2** to agree with or support someone's ideas or actions **halden anlamak; uyuşmak; desteklemek; yanında olmak; anlayışla karşılamak; katılmak** *I sympathize with the general aims of the party.*

sympathizer (*also UK* -iser) /'sɪmpəθaɪzəʳ/ *noun* [C] someone who supports a particular political organization, or believes in a particular set of ideas **taraftar, yandaş, sempatizan** *a communist sympathizer*

sympathy ...... İLE BİRLİKTE KULLANILAN KELİMELER

have/express/feel [every/little/no, etc] sympathy for sb ● look for sympathy ● deep/great/heartfelt sympathy ● words of sympathy

∘ᵸ**sympathy** /'sɪmpəθi/ *noun* [U] **1** when you show that you understand and care about someone's problems **halden anlama, çelebice davranma, anlayış gösterme, merhamet, sempati** *I have no sympathy for people who say they can't find work but are really just too lazy to look.* **2** agreement with or support for someone's ideas or actions **katılma, aynı şeyleri hissetme, destekleme; uyuşma** *Scott was in sympathy with this view.*

symphony /'sɪmfəni/ *noun* [C] a long piece of music for an orchestra (= large group of different musicians) **senfoni**

symptom /'sɪmptəm/ *noun* [C] **1** a physical feeling or problem which shows that you have a particular illness **hastalık belirtisi, işaret, semptom** *The inability to sleep is often a symptom of some other illness.* **2** a problem that is caused by and shows a more serious problem **belirti, gösterge, işaret** *The drinking was just a symptom of his general unhappiness.* ● **symptomatic** /ˌsɪmptə'mætɪk/ *adjective* relating to a symptom **belirtisi/göstergesi/işareti olan**

synagogue /'sɪnəgɒg/ *noun* [C] a building in which Jewish people pray **sinagog, havra; Musevi ibadethanesi**

sync /sɪŋk/ *noun informal* **1 be in sync** to be happening at the same time **eşzamanlı olmak; ayna zamanda meydana geliyor olmak 2 be out of sync** to not be happening at the same time **aynı anda olmamak, eş zamanlı olmamak**

synchronize (*also UK* -ise) /'sɪŋkrənaɪz/ *verb* [T] **1** to make something happen at the same time as something else **eş zamanlı olmasını sağlamak, senkronize etmek** *We had a problem synchronizing the music and the images.* **2 synchronize watches** to make two or more watches show exactly the same time **saatleri aynı zamana ayarlamak** ● **synchronization** /ˌsɪŋkrənaɪ'zeɪʃᵊn/ *noun* [U] **uyum**

syndicate /'sɪndɪkət/ *noun* [C] a group of people or companies who join together in order to achieve something **sendike** *a bank syndicate* ∘ *a crime syndicate*

syndrome /'sɪndrəʊm/ *noun* [C] a combination of physical problems that often go together in a particular illness **sendrom**

synergy /'sɪnədʒi/ *noun* [C, U] when two companies or groups work together and achieve more success than they would separately **sinerji; ortak çalışma; ortak başarı** *a synergy between the two software companies*

synonym /'sɪnənɪm/ *noun* [C] a word or phrase that means the same as another word or phrase **eş anlamlı/anlamdaş sözcük**

synonymous /sɪ'nɒnɪməs/ *adjective* **1** If one thing is synonymous with another, they are very closely connected with each other in people's minds. **aynı şeyi çağrıştıran; benzer şeyleri ortaya koyan; özdeşleşen** *It is a country where wealth is synonymous with corruption.* **2** If one word is synonymous with another, they have the same meaning. **eş anlamlı, anlamdaş**

synopsis /sɪ'nɒpsɪs/ *noun* [C] *plural* **synopses** a short description of a book, film, etc **(kitap, film vb.) kısa tanım, özet**

syntax /'sɪntæks/ *noun* [U] the grammatical arrangement of words in a sentence **söz dizimi, cümle bilgisi**

synthesis /'sɪnθəsɪs/ *noun* [C, U] *plural* **syntheses** /'sɪnθəsiːz/ *formal* the mixing of several things to make another whole new thing **sentez, bireşim, terkip**

synthesize (*also UK* **-ise**) /'sɪnθəsaɪz/ *verb* [T] to mix several things in order to make something else **sentez yaparak yeni bir şey elde etmek; birleştirerek yeni bir şekle sokmak**

synthesizer (*also UK* **-iser**) /'sɪnθəsaɪzəʳ/ *noun* [C] an electronic musical instrument that can copy the sounds made by other musical instruments **diğer aletlerin sesini kaydedebilen elektronik müzik âleti**

synthetic /sɪn'θetɪk/ *adjective* not made from natural substances **yapay, sunî, sentetik** *synthetic rubber* ● **synthetically** *adverb* **doğal maddelerden yapılmamış bir şekilde**

syphilis /'sɪfɪlɪs/ *noun* [U] a serious disease caught during sex that spreads slowly from the sex organs to all parts of the body **frengi, frengi hastalığı**

syringe /sɪ'rɪndʒ/ *noun* **syringe** [C] a piece of medical equipment used to push liquid into or take liquid out of someone's body **şırınga, enjektör**

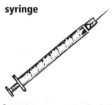

syrup /'sɪrəp/ *noun* [U] a very sweet liquid made from sugar and water **şurup, şerbet**

o⊶**system** /'sɪstəm/ *noun* [C] **1** METHOD a way or method of doing things **düzen, yol, metod, yöntem, sistem** *the American legal system* ○ *the public transport system* **2** EQUIPMENT a set of connected pieces of equipment that operate together **tertibat, düzenek, sistem, kurulum** *They've had an alarm system installed at their home.* **3** BODY parts of the body that work together in order to make something happen **vücudun çalışma düzeni** *the body's immune system* **4 the system** the laws and rules of a society **yasal düzen, sistem; bir toplumun kanun ve kuralları; kanunlar ve kurallar bütünü** **5 get sth out of your system** to get rid of a strong feeling or a need to do something, especially by expressing that feeling or doing the thing you want to do **içini döküp/derdini söyleyip rahatlamak/kurtulmak; boşaltmak; içinden atmak; sıkıntılarından kurtulup arınmak** *It's not a bad idea to travel before getting a job - that way you get it out of your system.* ⊃See also: immune system, nervous system, operating system, public address system, the solar system.

systematic /ˌsɪstə'mætɪk/ *adjective* done using a fixed and organized plan **düzenli ve sistemli bir şekilde olan; sistematik, sistemli; belli bir plan/düzen dahilinde olan** *the systematic collection and analysis of information* ● **systematically** *adverb* **sistemli bir şekilde**

T

T, t /tiː/ the twentieth letter of the alphabet **alfabenin yirminci harfi**

ta /tɑː/ *exclamation UK informal* thank you **Sağol!', 'Teşekkür!'**

tab /tæb/ *noun* [C] **1** a small piece of paper, metal, etc that is fixed to something and that you use to open it or find out information about it **kulp, halka, açma halkası, şerit, uç** *Pull tab to open.* **2** an amount of money that you owe for something you have bought or for a service you have used **hesap, fatura, ödeme** *Officials said the tab for the new bridge would be $8 million.* **3 pick up the tab** to pay for something, especially a meal in a restaurant **hesabı ödemek 4 keep tabs on sb/sth** *informal* to watch someone or something carefully to check they do nothing wrong **ensesinde olmak, izlemek, gözetlemek**

tabby /'tæbi/ *noun* [C] a cat that has stripes in its fur **tekir kedi**

'tab ˌkey *noun* [C] the key on a computer keyboard which allows you to move the cursor (= a symbol which shows you where you are working) forward a few spaces **bilgisayar klavyesindeki boşluk/tab tuşu; uzun tuş**

∘⁃**table¹** /'teɪbl/ *noun* [C] **1** FURNITURE a piece of furniture with four legs, used for eating off, putting things on, etc **masa** *the kitchen table* **2 lay the table** *UK* (*UK/US* **set the table**) to put plates, knives, forks, etc on the table to prepare for a meal **masayı hazırlamak** **3** NUMBERS/WORDS a set of numbers or words written in rows that go across and down the page **tablo, çizelge, cetvel, liste** *The table below shows the results of the experiment.* **4** COMPUTER a collection of a particular kind of information in a database **5 turn the tables on sb** to change a situation so that you have an advantage over someone who before had an advantage over you **durumu kendi lehine/başkasının aleyhine çevirmek** ⊃See also: put/lay your cards (**card**) on the table, **coffee table, dressing table.**

table

table² /'teɪbl/ *verb* [T] **1** *UK* to formally suggest that a particular subject is discussed **müzakereye sunmak, masaya koymak, tartışmaya açmak 2** *US* to decide to discuss something later **sonraya bırakmak, daha sonra müzakereye bırakmak**

tablecloth /'teɪblklɒθ/ *noun* [C] a piece of material that covers a table, especially during a meal **masa örtüsü**

tablespoon /'teɪblspuːn/ *noun* [C] a large spoon used for measuring or serving food, or the amount this spoon can hold **büyük kaşık, yemek kaşığı**

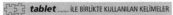
tablet ...... İLE BİRLİKTE KULLANILAN KELİMELER

take a tablet • a tablet **for** sth • **sleeping** tablets • **headache** tablets

tablet /'tæblət/ *noun* [C]
1 MEDICINE a small, round object containing medicine that you swallow **hap, tablet** ⊃See picture at **medicine. 2** STONE a square piece of stone that has words cut into it **üzeri kazınarak yazılmış taş, tablet, levha,**

tablet

plâket 3 PAPER *US* (*UK/US* **pad**) sheets of paper that have been fastened together at one edge, used for writing or drawing **bloknot; bir ucu tutturulmuş not/çizim için kağıt bloku**

'table ˌtennis *noun* [U] a game in which two or four people hit a small ball over a low net on a large table **masa tenisi, pinpon**

tabloid /'tæblɔɪd/ *noun* [C] a small newspaper with a lot of pictures and short, simple news stories **sadece basit ve sıradan hikâyeleri çokça resimlerle basan magazin gazetesi**

taboo /tə'buː/ *noun* [C, U] something that you should not say or do because people generally think it is morally wrong, unpleasant, or embarrassing **tabu, yasak** *Sex is a taboo in this country.* • **taboo** *adjective Suicide is a taboo subject.* **yasak**

tacit /'tæsɪt/ *adjective formal* understood without being said **söylenmeden anlaşılan, üstü kapalı** *a tacit agreement*

taciturn /'tæsɪtɜːn/ *adjective formal* saying very little and not seeming friendly **az konuşan, sessiz, suskun; için için kuran**

tack¹ /tæk/ *noun* **1 take/try a different tack** to try to deal with a problem in a different way **ayrı/başka bir yol denemek; farklı bir tarz/hareket tarzı denemek** *I've tried being nice to her and it doesn't work so I might take a different tack.* **2** [C] a small, sharp nail with a flat top **tepesi düz küçük çivi, raptiye** *carpet tacks* **3** [C] *US* (*UK* **drawing pin**) a short pin with a flat, round top, used for fastening pieces of paper to the wall **raptiye**

tack² /tæk/ *verb* [T] **1** to fasten something to a wall with a tack **raptiyelemek, tutturmak 2** to sew something loosely **alelacele dikmek, tutturuvermek**

tack sth on *phrasal verb* to add something that you had not planned to add in a different way **ekleyivermek, acele ile ilave etmek**

tackle¹ /'tækl/ *verb* [T] **1** DEAL WITH to try to deal with a problem **hemen ilgilenmek, ele almak, çaresine bakmak** *new ways to tackle crime* **2** SPEAK TO *UK* to speak to someone about something bad that they have done **nazik bir konuyu/yapılan kötü bir şeyi biriyle paylaşmak/konuşmak** *I decided to tackle him about his absences.* **3** BALL to try to get the ball from someone in a game such as football **futbolda topu birinin ayağından almak/çalmak, topu kesmek/kapmak**

tackle² /'tækl/ *noun* **1** [C] an attempt to get the ball from someone in a game such as football **futbolda topu kapma/çalma/ayağından alma 2** [U] all the things you need for a particular activity **gerekli olan her şey; tüm gereksinimler** *fishing tackle*

tacky /'tæki/ *adjective* **1** *informal* cheap and of bad quality **ucuz, düşük kalite, zevksiz, sıradan** *tacky holiday souvenirs* **2** slightly sticky **yapışkan**

tact /tækt/ *noun* [U] the ability to talk to people about difficult subjects without upsetting them **davranış inceliği, zarafet, görgü, diploması**

tactful /'tæktf⁰l/ *adjective* careful not to say or do anything that could upset someone **incelikli, düşünceli, zarif, diplomatça** • **tactfully** *adverb* **kimseyi incitmemek için çok dikkatli davranmak**

🧩 **tactic** ...... İLE BİRLİKTE KULLANILAN KELİMELER

adopt/employ/use tactics ● a change of tactics
● bullying/underhand tactics

tactic /ˈtæktɪk/ *noun* [C] a way of doing something that you plan in order to achieve what you want **taktik, yöntem, strateji** [usually plural] *These bomb attacks represent a change of tactics by the terrorists.*

tactical /ˈtæktɪkᵊl/ *adjective* relating to tactics, or done in order to achieve something **taktik/yöntem/strate- jiyle ilgili** *tactical voting* ○ *a tactical error* ● **tactically** *adverb* **taktiksel olarak**

tactless /ˈtæktləs/ *adjective* not being careful about say- ing or doing something that could upset someone **pata- vatsız, vurdum duymaz, zarafetsiz, kaba, düşünce- siz**

tad /tæd/ *noun informal* **a tad** a little **biraz, azıcık** *It was a tad expensive, I thought.*

tadpole /ˈtædpəʊl/ *noun* [C] a small, black animal that lives in water and will become a frog (= green jumping animal) **kurbağa yavrusu, iribaş**

taffeta /ˈtæfɪtə/ *noun* [U] a stiff, shiny cloth used in women's formal dresses **tafta, bir tür sert parlak kumaş**

TAFN *internet abbreviation for* that's all for now: used at the end of an email or message **Şimdilik Bu Kadar (ŞBK); e-posta veya iletiler sonunda kullanılan ifade**

tag¹ /tæg/ *noun* [C] a small piece of paper or plastic with information on it that is fixed to something **etiket** *a price tag*

tag² /tæg/ *verb* [T] **tagging**, *past* **tagged** to put a tag on something **etiketlemek, etiket yapıştırmak**

tag along *phrasal verb informal* to go somewhere with someone, especially when they have not asked you to **peşine takılmak; ...ile gitmek/gelmek**

t'ai chi /taɪˈtʃiː/ *noun* [U] a form of Chinese exercise that involves a series of slow movements **taiçi; yavaş hare- ketlerden oluşan bir tür çin sporu**

tail¹ /teɪl/ *noun* [C] **1** the long, narrow part that sticks out at the back of an animal's body **kuyruk** *The dog's pleased to see you - he's wagging his tail.* **2** the back part of something long, such as a plane **uç kısım, kuyruk** **3** the tail end of sth the last part of something **en son bölümü** *the tail end of the eighties*

tail

tail² /teɪl/ *verb* [T] to secretly follow someone, especially because you think they have done something wrong **gizlice takip etmek; sezdirmeden peşine takılmak**

tail off *phrasal verb* to gradually become quieter, smal- ler, less frequent, etc **gittikçe etkisini kaybetmek; gün geçtikçe azalarak kaybolmak/yok olmak** *His voice tailed off.*

tailback /ˈteɪlbæk/ *noun* [C] *UK* a line of cars that have stopped or are moving very slowly because of an acci- dent or other problem on the road in front of them **kuy- ruk olma; peşpeşe yığılma; sıra sıra dizilme**

tailcoat /ˈteɪlˌkəʊt/ *noun* [C] a formal coat that has a short front part and a long back part that is divided in two **frak, önü kısa arkası uzun bir tür tören giysisi**

tailgate /ˈteɪlgeɪt/ *verb* [I, T] to drive too closely to the car in front of you **tampon tampona araç kullanmak; öndeki arabayı yakından takip etmek** ● **tailgating** *noun* [U] **öndeki arabayı tam arkasından takip etmek**

'tail ˌlight *noun* [C] *US* one of the two red lights on the back of a car **arka lambalar; park lambaları; stop lambaları** ➲Orta kısımdaki renkli sayfalarına bakınız.

tailor¹ /ˈteɪləʳ/ *noun* [C] someone whose job is to make or repair clothes, especially men's clothes **terzi**

tailor² /ˈteɪləʳ/ *verb* [T] to make or change something so that it is suitable **yeni bir biçim vererek veya deği- şiklik yaparak uygun hâle getirmek** *The kitchen can then be tailored exactly to the customer's needs.*

tailor-made /ˌteɪləˈmeɪd/ *adjective* **1** perfect for a parti- cular person or purpose **biçilmiş kaftan; tıpatıp uyan; çok uygun** *It sounds as if you're tailor-made for the job.* **2** Tailor-made clothes are made by a tailor. **terzi yapımı, özel sipariş/dikiş**

tailpipe /ˈteɪlpaɪp/ *US* (*UK* **exhaust pipe**) *noun* [C] the pipe that waste gas from a vehicle's engine flows through **egzoz, egzoz borusu; araç duman tahliye borusu** ➲Orta kısımdaki renkli sayfalarına bakınız.

tails /teɪlz/ *noun* [plural] **1** the side of a coin that does not have someone's head on it **madeni paranın yazı bölümü; yazı** *Let's toss a coin - heads or tails?* **2** a for- mal coat that has a short front part and a long back part that is divided in two **frak**

taint /teɪnt/ *verb* [T] **1** to spoil people's opinion of someone **başkası hakkında kötü düşünülmesine neden olmak; dedikodu ile birini yıpratmak** [often **passive**] *a government tainted by scandal* **2** to spoil some- thing, especially food or blood, by adding a harmful substance **bozmak, kötü madde katarak berbat etmek**

o▴**take** /teɪk/ *verb* [T] *past tense* **took**, *past participle* **taken** **1** CARRY to get and carry something with you when you go somewhere **almak, götürmek** *I always take my mobile phone with me.* **2** GO to go somewhere with someone, often paying for them or being responsible for them **biriyle gitmek, birini götürmek** *I took the kids to the park.* **3** WITHOUT PERMISSION to remove some- thing without permission **izinsiz almak/götürmek** *Someone's taken my coat.* **4** GET HOLD to get hold of some- thing and move it **alıp götürmek** *He reached across and took the glass from her.* **5** ACCEPT to accept something **kabul etmek, almak, kabullenmek** *So, are you going to take the job?* ○ *Do you take credit cards?* **6** NEED If some- thing takes a particular amount of time, or a particular quality, you need that amount of time or that quality in order to be able to do it. **almak, gerektirmek, gerek- mek** [+ to do sth] *It's taken me three days to get here.* ○ *It takes a lot of courage to stand up and talk in front of so many people.* **7** MEDICINE to swallow or use medicine **ilaç almak; hap yutmak** *Take two tablets, three times a day.* **8** MEASURE to measure something **ölçüsünü almak, ölç- mek** *Have you taken her temperature?* **9** CLOTHES to wear a particular size of clothes **belli bedende bir kıyafet giymek** *I take a size 12 in trousers.* **10** SPACE to have enough space for a particular number of people or things **(belli sayıda insan ve eşya) almak, kaldır- mak, taşımak** *There's six of us and the car only takes five.* **11** TRAVEL to travel somewhere by using a bus, train, car, etc, or by using a particular road **otobüs, tren, otomobil vb araçla gitmek/seyahat etmek** *Are you taking the train to Edinburgh?* **12** take a break/rest, etc to stop working for a period **ara ver- mek, teneffüs yapmak, bir süre dinlenmek; mola vermek; nefes almak** **13** take pleasure/pride/an interest, etc to have a particular, good feeling about something that you do **zevk almak, gurur duymak; ilgi duymak** *I take great pleasure in cooking.* ○ *These women take their jobs very seriously* (= think their jobs are very important). **14** take a look to look at some- thing **bir göz atmak, şöyle bir bakmak** *Take a look at these photos.* **15** UNDERSTAND to understand something in a particular way **anlamak, gerektiği gibi anlamak** *Whatever I say she'll take it the wrong way.* **16 I take it (that)** used when you think that what you say is probably true **Sanırım!, Farzediyorum!, Zannediyorum!'** *I take it you're not coming with us.* **17 can't take sth** to not be able to deal with an unpleasant situation **kaldıramamak, artık dayanamamak; daha fazla güç bulamamak** *We argue all the time - I really can't take it any more.* **18 take it from me** accept that what I say is true, because I know or have experienced it **sözünü dinlemek; tecrübe ve bilgisine itibar etmek; söylediğine güvenmek; 'inan ki!'** *You could be doing a much less interesting job, take it from me.* **19 take sth as it comes** to deal with something as it happens, without planning for it **nasılsa öyle ilgilenmek; planlamadan ilgilenmek; işi oluruna bırakmak 20** [BY FORCE] to get control of something by force **ele geçirmek, zorla elde etmek, zorla almak** *By morning they had taken the city.*

take after sb *phrasal verb* to be similar to an older member of your family **birine benzemek; özelliklerini çekmek; ...a/e çekmek** *Peter's very tall - he takes after his father.*

take sth apart *phrasal verb* to separate something into its different parts **sökmek, parçalara ayırmak** *He spent the whole afternoon taking his bike apart.*

take sth away *phrasal verb* **1** to remove something **alıp götürmek** *The waitress took our plates away.* ○ *Supermarkets are taking business away from small local shops.* **2** to subtract a number **bir sayıyı çıkarmak** *Take 3 away from 20.*

take sb away *phrasal verb* to make someone leave a place and go with you **birini zorla götürmek; çıkmaya ve gelmeye zorlamak**

take sth back *phrasal verb* **1** to return something to the place you borrowed or bought it from **geri götürmek/ vermek; iade etmek 2** to admit that your opinion was wrong **sözünü geri almak, yanlış olduğunu kabul etmek** *You're right, he's nice - I take back everything I said about him.*

take sth down *phrasal verb* **1** to write something **yazmak, kaydetmek** *Did you take down the telephone number?* **2** to remove something that is on a wall or something that is temporary **sökmek** *I've taken the pictures down.*

take sth in *phrasal verb* **1** [UNDERSTAND] to understand something **anlamak, kavramak** *It was an interesting lecture but there was just too much to take in.* **2** [FILM/BUILDING ETC] to go to see a film, visit an interesting building, etc for enjoyment **zevk için yapmak, eğlenmek, keyfi için yapmak** *I thought we might get something to eat and then take in a movie.* **3** [CLOTHES] to make a piece of clothing narrower **daraltmak, küçültmek**

take sb in *phrasal verb* **1** If the police take someone in, they take that person to the police station. **içeri almak, karakola götürmek 2** to let someone stay in your house **eve almak, eve götürmek, misafir etmek** *You could earn some extra cash by taking in foreign students.* **3 be taken in** to be deceived by someone

take sth off *phrasal verb* **1** to remove something **çıkarmak** *If you're hot, take your jacket off.* ➔*Orta kısımdaki renkli sayfalarına bakınız.* **2** to spend time away from your work **izin almak** *I'm taking Friday off to get some things done around the house.*

take off *phrasal verb* **1** [AIRCRAFT] If an aircraft takes off, it begins to fly. **kalkmak, havalanmak 2** [SUCCESSFUL] to suddenly become successful **beklenmedik anda başarıyı yakalamak** *Her career had just taken off.* **3** [LEAVE] to suddenly leave without telling anyone where you are going **aniden gitmek, birden ayrılmak** *He took off in the middle of the night.*

take sth on *phrasal verb* to accept a responsibility **üstüne almak, sorumluluğu kabul etmek, üstlenmek, yüklenmek** *I don't want to take on too much work.* **take sb on** *phrasal verb* **1** to begin to employ someone **iş vermek, işe almak, adam çalıştırmak, tutmak** *We'll be taking on two new members of staff.* **2** to compete against someone **yarışmak, kapışmak, mücadeleye tutuşmak, rekâbete girmek** *I might take you on at tennis sometime.*

take on sth *phrasal verb* to begin to have a particular quality **kazanmak, bürünmek, girmek; ...gibi olmaya başlamak** *Her voice took on a tone of authority.*

take sth out *phrasal verb* to remove something from somewhere **çıkarmak** *He reached into his bag and took out a book.*

take sb out *phrasal verb* to go somewhere with someone and pay for them **gezmeye götürmek, dışarı çıkarmak** *Are you taking her out for her birthday?*

take sth out on sb *phrasal verb* to unfairly treat someone badly because you are upset **acısını başkasından çıkarmak; hıncını başkasından almak; ...a/e ödetmek** *Don't take it out on me!*

take (sth) over *phrasal verb* to get control of or responsibility for something **ele geçirmek, yönetimi/kontrolü ele geçirmek; hâkim olmak** *They've recently been taken over by a larger company.* ○ *Who'll be taking over from Cynthia when she retires?*

take sb through sth *phrasal verb* to explain something to someone **birine bir şeyi izah etmek/açıklamak**

take to sb/sth *phrasal verb* to start to like someone or something **kanı ısınmak, görür görmez hoşlanmak, sevivermek, cana yakın bulmak** *For some reason, I just didn't take to him.*

take to sth/doing sth *phrasal verb* to start doing something **âdet edinmek, alışkanlık hâline getirmek** *Dad's taken to swimming every morning.*

take sth up *phrasal verb* **1** to start doing a particular job or activity **...a/e başlamak; iş yapmaya başlamak; bir şeye koyulmak/kalkışmak** *I thought I might take up cycling.* **2** to use an amount of time or space **kaldığı yerden devam etmek; bıraktığı yerden başlamak** *This desk takes up too much space.*

take sb up on sth *phrasal verb* to accept an offer **kabul etmek** *Could I take you up on your offer of a ride home?*

take sth up with sb *phrasal verb* to discuss something with someone **enine boyuna tartışmak, şikayet etmek; işi ...a/e götürmek** *You'll have to take the matter up with your manager.*

takeaway /ˈteɪkəweɪ/ UK (US **takeout** /ˈteɪkaʊt/) *noun* [C] a meal that you buy in a restaurant but eat at home, or a shop that sells this type of meal **hazır yemek; al götür yemek; hazır yemekçi**

take-off /ˈteɪkɒf/ *noun* **1** [C, U] when an aircraft leaves the ground and begins to fly **kalkış, havalanma 2** [C] a film, book, etc that copies someone else's style in a way that is funny **bir başka tarzda bir filmi/kitabı vb. alaya alma/komik şekilde anlatma**

takeover /ˈteɪkˌəʊvər/ *noun* [C] when a company gets control of another company **yönetimi ele geçirme, devralma**

takings /ˈteɪkɪŋz/ UK (US **receipts**) *noun* [plural] all the money that a business gets from selling things **hâsılat, kazanç, gelir**

talcum powder /ˈtælkəmˌpaʊdər/ (*also* **talc**) *noun* [U] white powder that you put on your skin after a bath **talk pudrası**

tale /teɪl/ *noun* [C] a story, especially one which is not true or is difficult to believe **öykü, hikâye, masal** *My grandfather used to tell us tales of his time as a pilot during the war.* ➔See also: **fairy tale.**

have/show a talent for sth ● a natural talent ● sb's talent as sth

∘*talent /'tælənt/ noun [C, U] a natural ability to do something yetenek, kabiliyet, istidat *She showed an early talent for drawing.* ● talented *adjective* showing natural ability in a particular area yetenekli, kabiliyetli, istidatlı *a talented young musician*

talisman /'tælɪzmən/ noun [C] plural talismans an object that people think will make them lucky tılsım, uğur

En sıklıkla kullanılan alternatifler speak ve say fiilleridir. *Could you speak more quietly, please?* ● *I couldn't hear what they were saying.*

chat fiili veya have a chat söylemi iki kişinin arkadaşça bir ortamda sohbet ettiklerini belirtir. *We were just chatting about the party on Saturday.* ● *Give me a call and we'll have a chat.*

Eğer kişiler önemli olmayan konularda uzun süreyle konuşuyorlarsa, chatter, natter (gayri resmi), ve have a natter ifadeleri kullanılabilir. *She spent the morning chattering away to her friends.* ● *We had a long natter over coffee.*

Eğer kişi bir olay hakkında çok uzun süreyle artık bıktırıcı bir şekilde konuşuyorsa, go on deyimi kullanılabilir. *He's always going on about how much he hates his work.*

Eğer kişi bir şey hakkında şikayet ettiğinden dolayı kısık sesle konuşuyorsa, mumble ve mutter fiilleri kullanılabilir. *She walked past me, muttering to herself.* ● *He mumbled something about it being a waste of time.*

Eğer kişi diğer insanların duymaması için çok kısık sesle konuşuyorsa, whisper fiili kullanılabilir. *What are you two girls whispering about?*

∘*talk¹ /tɔːk/ verb 1 [I] to say things to someone konuşmak *We were just talking about Simon's new girlfriend.* ○ *It was nice talking to you.* ○ *(US) It was nice talking with you.* 2 [I] to discuss something with someone, often to try to find a solution to a disagreement görüşmek, tartışmak *The two sides have agreed to talk.* 3 talk about sth/doing sth to think about or make plans to do something in the future gelecekle ilgili planlar yapmak; detayıyla düşünmek *They're talking about building a new fire station just up the road.* 4 talk business/politics, etc to discuss a particular subject iş/siyaset vs. Konuşmak *I don't like to talk business over lunch.* 5 talking of sth UK (US speaking of sth) used when you are going to start talking about something that is related to what has just been said ...dan/den söz açılmışken *Talking of holidays, did you hear about Lesley's skiing trip?* ⇒See also: speak/talk of the devil.

talk at sb phrasal verb to talk to someone without letting them say anything or without listening to them sürekli konuşmak; karşısındakini dinlemeden sürekli talimatlar veren/azarlayan şekilde konuşmak

talk back phrasal verb If a child talks back to an adult, they answer them rudely. karşılık vermek; saygısızca cevap vermek

talk down to sb phrasal verb to talk to someone in a way that shows you think they are not intelligent or not important aşağılayıcı biçimde konuşmak; tepeden bakarak konuşmak; hor görmek; küçük görmek

talk sb into/out of (doing) sth phrasal verb to persuade someone to do or not do something konuşarak ikna etmek; dil dökmek *We managed to talk Lisa into doing the cooking.*

talk sth over phrasal verb to discuss something with someone, often to find out their opinion or to get advice before making a decision görüşmek, müzakere etmek

have a talk ● a talk with sb ● a talk about sth ● a long/serious talk

∘*talk² /tɔːk/ noun 1 CONVERSATION [C] a conversation between two people, often about a particular subject konuşma, görüşme *I had a long talk with Chris at the weekend about going to university.* 2 PEOPLE [U] when people talk about what might happen or be true görüş, düşünce, konuşma, fikir *There's been some talk of possible job losses.* 3 TO A GROUP [C] when someone speaks to a group of people about a particular subject konuşma, konferans *Someone's coming to the school to give a talk about road safety.* 4 be all talk (and no action) If someone is all talk, they never do the brave or exciting things they often say they will do. gürleyip yağmamak; sürekli laf yapıp eyleme geçmemek ⇒See also: small talk.

talkative /'tɔːkətɪv/ adjective A talkative person talks a lot. konuşkan/geveze/çenesi düşük kimse

attend/have/hold/resume talks ● talks break down/take place ● lengthy/secret/urgent talks ● talks about/on sth

talks /tɔːks/ noun [plural] formal meetings, especially between political leaders, to discuss a problem and to try to reach an agreement müzakereler, görüşmeler *peace talks* ○ *US officials are holding talks with EU leaders over trade.*

'talk ,show US (UK chat show) noun [C] an informal television or radio programme where people are asked questions about themselves and their lives sohbet programı

∘*tall /tɔːl/ adjective 1 having a greater than average height. uzun, uzun boylu *He's tall and thin.* ○ *It's one of the tallest buildings in the city.* 2 used to describe or ask about the height of someone or something ...uzunluğunda; ...boyunda *How tall is she?* ○ *He's almost 2 metres tall.*

tally¹ /'tæli/ noun [C] the number of things you have achieved, used, won, etc until now çetele, kayıt, hesap *This adds to his tally of 12 race wins so far this year.*

tally² /'tæli/ verb 1 [I] If two numbers or stories tally, they are the same. uymak, uyuşmak, birbirini tutmak 2 [T] (also tally up) to find out the total number toplam rakamı bulmak

the Talmud /'tælmʊd/ noun the ancient Jewish written laws and traditions Talmud, yazılı eski Musevi yasalar ve gelenekler

talon /'tælən/ noun [C] a sharp nail on the foot of a bird that it uses to catch animals pençe tırnağı, pençe

tambourine /ˌtæmbəˈriːn/ noun [C] a musical instrument with a wooden ring and small metal discs loosely fixed to it which you play by shaking or hitting tef, zilli tef

tame¹ /teɪm/ adjective 1 If an animal is tame, it is not wild and not frightened of people. evcil, ehil, evcilleştirilmiş 2 too controlled and not exciting aşırı kontrollü, sıkıcı, yavan, sönük *His TV show is very tame in comparison with his live performances.*

tame² /teɪm/ verb [T] to make a wild animal tame evcilleştirmek, ehlileştirmek

tamper /'tæmpər/ *verb*
tamper with sth *phrasal verb* to touch or make changes to something which you should not, often in order to damage it **tahrif etmek, kurcalamak, değiştirmek, üzerinde oynamak**

tampon /'tæmpɒn/ *noun* [C] a small roll of cotton which a woman puts in her vagina to absorb her monthly flow of blood **tampon, kadın bağı**

tan¹ /tæn/ (*also* **suntan**) *noun* [C] when your skin is brown from being in the sun **bronz rengi, güneş yanığı**

tan² /tæn/ *verb* [I, T] **tanning**, *past* **tanned** to become brown from the sun, or to make a person or body part become brown *I tan quite easily.* **bronzlaşmak**

tan³ /tæn/ *adjective* **1** being a pale yellow-brown colour **hâki renk** *a tan jacket* **2** *US* (*UK/US* **tanned**) having darker skin because you have been in the sun **yanık, bronzlaşmış, güneş yanığı**

tandem /'tændəm/ *noun* **1 in tandem (with sb)** If someone does something in tandem with someone else, they do it together or at the same time. **beraberce, birlikte 2** [C] a bicycle for two people **iki kişilik bisiklet**

tangent /'tændʒ³nt/ *noun* [C] **1** a straight line which touches but does not cross a curve **teğet 2 go off at/ on a tangent** to suddenly start talking about a different subject **konuyu değiştirmek**

tangerine /ˌtændʒ³r'iːn/ *noun* [C] a fruit like a small orange **mandalina**

tangible /'tændʒəbl/ *adjective* Something which is tangible is real and can be seen, touched, or measured. **somut, elle tutulur, açık, kesin** *tangible benefits/ evidence* ↗Opposite **intangible**.

tangle¹ /'tæŋgl/ *noun* [C] several things which have become twisted together in an untidy way **düğüm, içinden çıkılmaz durum; arapsaçı** *a tangle of hair/ wires*

tangle² /'tæŋgl/ *verb* [I, T] to become twisted together, or to make things become twisted together **düğüm olmak/etmek, dolaş(tır)mak, arapsaçına dön(dür) mek; karma karışık olmak/etmek** ↗Opposite **disentangle, untangle**.

tangled /'tæŋgld/ *adjective* **1** (*also* **tangled up**) twisted together in an untidy way **karma karışık olmuş; kör düğüm olmuş, arapsaçına dönmüş** *The wires are all tangled.* **2** confused and difficult to understand **karma karışık, anlaşılması güç** *tangled finances* **3 be tangled up in/with sth** to be involved in something unpleasant or complicated that is difficult to escape from **dolanmak/dolaştırmak; dolandırmak/dolaşmak**

tango /'tæŋgəʊ/ *noun* [C] a South American dance **tango**

tangy /'tæŋi/ *adjective* having a strong, sharp but pleasant taste or smell **keskin kokulu, keskin tadı olan** *a tangy lemon drink* ● **tang** *noun* [no plural] **acı tat veya koku**

tank /tæŋk/ *noun* [C] **1** a large container for storing liquid or gas **tank, depo, sarnıç** (*UK*) *a petrol tank/ (US) a gas tank* ○ *a hot-water tank* **2** a large, strong military vehicle with a gun on it which moves on wheels inside large metal belts **tank** ↗See also: **think tank**.

tanker /'tæŋkər/ *noun* [C] a ship or truck used to carry large amounts of liquid or gas **tanker** *an oil tanker*

tanned /tænd/ (*also US* **tan**) *adjective* having darker skin because you have been in the sun **yanmış, bronzlaşmış**

'tanning ˌbed *noun* [C] *US* a sun bed **bronzlaşma/ güneş yatağı**

tannoy /'tænɔɪ/ *UK trademark* (*UK/US* **public address system**) *noun* [no plural] a system of equipment used in public places that someone speaks into in order to make their voice loud enough to hear **ses sistemi, hoparlör**

tantalizing (*also UK* **-ising**) /'tæntəlaɪzɪŋ/ *adjective* Something that is tantalizing is very attractive and makes you want it, although often you cannot have it. **umutlandıran, boşuna ümit veren, çekici, baştan çıkarıcı** *a tantalizing glimpse of blue sea*

tantamount /'tæntəmaʊnt/ *adjective* **be tantamount to sth** to be almost as bad as something else **nerdeyse aynı oranda kötü olmak; hemen hemen aynı olmak; eşdeğerde olmak** *Resignation would be tantamount to admitting he was guilty.*

tantrum /'tæntrəm/ *noun* [C] when someone, especially a child, suddenly shows that they are very angry, usually because they cannot have something **öfke nöbeti, huysuzluk krizi** *Tom threw a tantrum in the middle of the supermarket.*

🧩 **tap** ...... İLE BİRLİKTE KULLANILAN KELİMELER

turn on/turn off a tap ● a tap is **dripping/running** ● the **cold/hot** tap ● **under** the tap ● **tap water**

tap¹ /tæp/ *noun* [C]
1 [WATER] *mainly UK* (*also US* **faucet**) the part at the end of a pipe which controls the flow of water **musluk** *the cold/hot tap* ○ *to turn a tap on/off* ○ *She rinsed the cup under the tap.* **2** [KNOCK] a gentle knock or touch, or the noise made by knocking something gently **tıkırdı, hafif hafif vurma** *I felt a tap on my shoulder.* ○ *There was a tap at the door.* **3** [TELEPHONE] a small piece of equipment that can be fixed to someone's telephone in order to listen to their telephone calls **telefon dinleme cihazı 4 on tap** easily available **kolay elde edilebilir; hazırda** *They have all that sort of information on tap.*

tap *UK*, **faucet** *US*

tap² /tæp/ *verb* **tapping**, *past* **tapped 1** [KNOCK] [I, T] to knock or touch something gently **hafif hafif vurmak, tıngırdatmak, takırdatmak** *I tapped on the window to try and get her attention.* **2** [A SUPPLY] [T] If you tap a supply of something, you use what is available. **yararlanmak, faydalanmak** *There are immense natural resources here waiting to be tapped.* **3** [TELEPHONE] [T] to use a special piece of equipment to listen to someone's telephone calls **telefon dinleme cihazı yerleştirerek dinlemek** [often passive] *I think the phone's been tapped.*
tap into sth *phrasal verb* to use part of a large supply of something for your own advantage **yararına kullanmak; ıkarı doğrultusunda kullanmak**

'tap ˌdancing *noun* [U] a type of dancing where the dancer wears special shoes with pieces of metal on the bottom which make a noise **ayakları vurarak yapılan dans** ● **tap dance** *verb* [I] **ayak topuklarının yere vurularak yapıldığı dans** ● **tap dancer** *noun* [C] **ayak topuklarının yere vurularak yapıldığı dansı yapan kişi**

tape¹ /teɪp/ *noun* **1** [RECORDING] [C, U] a long, thin piece of plastic which is used to store sound, pictures, or information, or a plastic box containing it **teyp, kaset, kayıt teybi** *I've got the match on tape.* **2** STICKY [U] a thin piece of plastic which has glue on one side and is used for sticking things together **seloteyp** *adhesive/ sticky tape* **3** MATERIAL [C, U] a long, thin piece of material used, for example, in sewing or to tie things together **şerit, bant** ➲See also: **red tape, Scotch tape.**

tape² /teɪp/ *verb* **1** [T] to record something onto tape **kaydetmek** *I often tape programmes and watch them later.* **2 tape sth to/onto, etc** to stick something somewhere using tape **seloteyple yapıştırmak/tutturmak**

'**tape ˌmeasure** *noun* [C] a long, thin piece of cloth, metal, or plastic used to measure lengths **mezura, şerit metre**

taper /'teɪpəʳ/ *verb* [I, T] to become gradually narrower at one end **gittikçe incelmek, giderek sivrilmek, gittikçe daralmak** ● **tapered** *adjective* **sivrilmiş (ucu)** **taper off** *phrasal verb* to become gradually smaller or less frequent **giderek azalmak/küçülmek** *Sales have gradually tapered off.*

'**tape reˌcorder** *noun* [C] a machine used to record sound onto tape **kasetçalar** ● **tape recording** *noun* [C] something which has been recorded on tape **ses kaydı**

tapestry /'tæpɪstri/ *noun* [C] a picture or pattern created by sewing different coloured threads onto heavy cloth **goblen, işleme**

'**tap ˌwater** *noun* [U] water which comes out of a tap (= part at the end of a pipe) **musluk suyu**

tar /tɑːʳ/ *noun* [U] **1** a thick, black substance that is sticky when hot and is used to cover roads **asfalt, katran 2** a black, sticky substance that is produced when tobacco burns **katran** ● **tar** *verb* [T] **tarring,** *past* **tarred** to cover something with tar **katranla kaplamak**

tarantula /təˈræntjələ/ *noun* [C] a large, hairy spider that is often poisonous **tarantula, zehirli örümcek**

🧩 **target** ...... İLE BİRLİKTE KULLANILAN KELİMELER

attack/hit/miss/strike a target ● an **obvious/prime** target ● a target **for** sth

target¹ /'tɑːgɪt/ *noun* [C] **1** ATTACK something or someone that you attack, shoot at, try to hit, etc **hedef** *It's very difficult to hit a moving target.* ○ *Foreign businesses in the region have become a target for terrorist attacks.* **2** ACHIEVE something that you intend to achieve **hedef, amaç, gaye, maksat** *I'm hoping to save £3,000 by June - that's my target.* ○ *If you want to lose weight, you have to set yourself* (= decide) *a target.* **3** BLAME the person or thing that people are criticizing or blaming for something **hedef kimse; hedefteki kişi** *Such extreme views have recently made him the target of criticism.* **4 be on target** to have made enough progress in order to achieve something that you intended to achieve **gerekli gelişmeyi sağlamış olmak; hedefte ilerlemek; amaçlandığı gibi devam etmek** [+ to do sth] *We're on target to finish the project in June.* **5 target audience/market, etc** the group of people that a programme, product, etc is aimed at **hedef kitle**

target² /'tɑːgɪt/ *verb* [T] **1** to aim an attack at a particular person or place **hedeflemek, nişan almak; saldırı amaçlamak** *They mostly targeted military bases.* **2** to aim advertising, criticism, or a product at someone **hedefini tespit etmek; hedefine koymak** [often passive] *The products are targeted at people in their late twenties.*

tariff /'tærɪf/ *noun* [C] **1** an amount of money that has to be paid for goods that are brought into a country **gümrük vergisi** *import tariffs* **2** a list of prices **fiyat listesi**

tarmac /'tɑːmæk/ *noun trademark* **1** [U] *UK* (*US* **asphalt**) a thick, black substance that is sticky when hot and is

used to cover roads **kaba asfalt 2 the tarmac** the area at an airport where aircraft land and take off **uçuş pisti; asfalt pist**

tarnish /'tɑːnɪʃ/ *verb* **1** [T] to spoil the way in which people think of someone so that they do not respect them **lekelemek, kirletmek** *to tarnish someone's image/ reputation* **2** [I, T] If a metal tarnishes or something tarnishes it, it becomes less bright and shiny. **karar(t) mak, parlaklığını kaybet(tir)mek; donuklaş(tır) mak**

tarpaulin /tɑːˈpɔːlɪn/ (*also US* **tarp**) *noun* [C, U] a large piece of plastic or cloth that water cannot go through which is used to cover and protect things **katranlı muşamba**

tart¹ /tɑːt/ *noun* [C] **1** an open pastry case with a sweet filling, often of fruit **turta, reçelli/ meyveli pasta** *an apple tart* **2** *UK very informal* a woman who dresses or behaves in a way to attract a lot of attention from men **erkeklerin dikkatini çekmek için giyinen kadın; şuh/çekici kadın**

tart² /tɑːt/ *adjective* having a sour, bitter taste **ekşi, acı, buruk tad veren**

tart

tartan /'tɑːtᵊn/ *noun* [C, U] cloth with a pattern of different coloured squares and crossing lines **ekose kumaş** *a tartan kilt*

o‑**task** /tɑːsk/ *noun* [C] a piece of work, especially something unpleasant or difficult **iş, görev, vazife** [+ of + doing sth] *I was given the task of sorting out all the stuff in the garage.*

taskbar /'tɑːskbɑːʳ/ *noun* [C] on a computer screen, a set of symbols that shows the programs you are using and allows you to change them **bilgisayar ekranında çeşitli ikonların bulunduğu çubuk; görev çubuğu**

'**task ˌforce** *noun* [C] a group of people, often a military group, who are brought together in order to do a particular job **görev gücü/kuvveti**

tassel /'tæsᵊl/ *noun* [C] a decoration made of a group of short threads tied together which is hung on curtains, furniture, etc **püskül**

🧩 **taste** ...... İLE BİRLİKTE KULLANILAN KELİMELER

disguise/improve/like/spoil a taste ● a **bitter/pleasant/strong/unpleasant/unusual** taste

o‑**taste¹** /teɪst/ *noun* **1** FOOD [C, U] the flavour of a particular food in your mouth **tat, lezzet** *a sweet/bitter taste* ○ *It's got quite a strong taste.* **2** ABILITY [U] the ability to feel different flavours in your mouth **tat, tat alma, lezzet** *When you've got a cold you often lose your sense of taste.* **3 a taste** a small amount of food that you have in order to try it **tadımlık, yudum** *Could I have just a taste of the sauce?* **4** WHAT YOU LIKE [C, U] the particular things you like, such as styles of music, clothes, decoration, etc **zevk, haz, hoşlanma** *I don't like his taste in music.* ○ *It's okay, but it's not really to my taste.* **5** ART/STYLE ETC [U] the ability to judge what is attractive or suitable, especially in things related to art, style, beauty, etc **beğeni, zevk, tad alma, haz duyma** *Everything in his house is beautiful - he's got very good taste.* **6 be in good taste** to be acceptable in a way that will not upset or anger people **uygun/hoş/güzel olmak 7 be in bad/poor taste** to be unacceptable in a way that will upset or anger people **uygunsuz/tatsız/ iğrenç olmak** *He told a joke about a plane crash which I thought was in rather poor taste.* **8 a taste for sth** when you like or enjoy something **hoşlanma, zevk** *I've developed a bit of a taste for opera.* **9 taste of sth** when you do or experience something new for a short time **yeni bir zevk/tat/beğeni** *That was my first taste of Mexican culture.*

∘ᐳ**taste²** /teɪst/ *verb* **1 taste funny/nice/sweet, etc** If food tastes a particular way, it has that flavour. ...**tadında** *This sauce tastes strange.* ○ *It tastes of chocolate.* **2 can taste sth** to be able to experience a particular flavour in a food **tadabilmek; tadını alabilmek** *You can really taste the garlic in it.* **3** [T] to put food or drink in your mouth to find out what its flavour is like **tatmak, tadına bakmak** *I always taste food while I'm cooking it.*

'taste ,buds *noun* [plural] the cells on your tongue that allow you to taste different foods **tat alma duygusu**

tasteful /'teɪstf°l/ *adjective* attractive and chosen for style and quality **zarif, zevkli, hoş, enfes** *a tasteful beige suit* ● **tastefully** *adverb* tastefully dressed/decorated **zevkli bir şekilde**

tasteless /'teɪstləs/ *adjective* **1** [UGLY] ugly or without style **zevksiz, yavan, tatsız, çirkin, biçimsiz** **2** [OFFENSIVE] likely to upset or anger people **tatsız, nahoş** *a tasteless joke* **3** [FOOD] having no flavour **lezzetsiz, tatsız, yavan** *The meat was dry and tasteless.*

tasty /'teɪsti/ *adjective* Food which is tasty has a good flavour and is nice to eat. **lezzetli, tadı güzel**

tattered /'tætəd/ *adjective* old and badly torn **yırtık, buruşmuş, kırışık; eski püskü, yırtık pırtık** *tattered clothes*

tatters /'tætəz/ *noun* **in tatters** badly torn, damaged, or spoilt **paramparça, paçavra; berbat halde, yıpranmış** *The yacht finally made it to the harbour, its sails in tatters.* ○ *His reputation is in tatters.*

tattoo /tæt'u:/ *noun* [C] a design on someone's skin that is put on using ink and a needle **dövme** ● **tattoo** *verb* [T] past **tattooed** **dövme yaptırmak**

tattoo

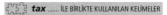

tatty /'tæti/ *adjective UK informal* untidy and in bad condition **düzensiz, eski püskü, kötü durumda; berbat** *He turned up wearing a pair of tatty old jeans.*

taught /tɔ:t/ *past of* teach **'öğretmek' fiilinin geçmiş zaman hâli**

taunt /tɔ:nt/ *verb* [T] to repeatedly say unkind things to someone in order to upset them or make them angry **sataşmak, laf atmak, kötü söz söylemek, alay etmek, damarına basmak, kızdırmak, üstüne gitmek** *He was taunted by his classmates because of his size.* ● **taunt** *noun* [C] **alay**

Taurus /'tɔ:rəs/ *noun* [C, U] the sign of the zodiac which relates to the period of 21 April - 22 May, or a person born during this period **Boğa Burcu** ⊃See picture at zodiac.

taut /tɔ:t/ *adjective* stretched very tight **çok gergin, iyice gerilmiş** *My skin feels taut.*

tavern /'tæv°n/ *noun* [C] *mainly US* a place where people go to drink alcohol **taverna, meyhane**

tawdry /'tɔ:dri/ *adjective* **1** unpleasant and immoral **adî, ahlaksız, çirkin, nahoş 2** cheap and of bad quality **ucuz ve kötü, berbat**

tawny /'tɔ:ni/ *adjective* being a light yellow-brown colour **sarımsı/açık kahverengi**

⧈ **tax** ...... İLE BİRLİKTE KULLANILAN KELİMELER

deduct/increase/pay tax ● **high/low** taxes ● a tax **on** sth ● **after/before** tax

∘ᐳ**tax¹** /tæks/ *noun* [C, U] money that you have to pay to the government from what you earn or when you buy things **vergi** *They're putting up the tax on cigarettes.* ○ *Do you have to pay tax on that?* ⊃See also: income tax.

tax² /tæks/ *verb* [T] **1** to make someone pay a tax **vergilendirmek, vergi almak, vergiye bağlamak, vergiye tâbi tutmak** *Goods such as clothes are taxed at 15%.* **2** to need a lot of effort **çok fazla çabaya gerek duymak; ağır koşul/yük gerektirmek** *It's only a short report - it shouldn't tax me too much.*

taxable /'tæksəbl/ *adjective* If something is taxable, you have to pay tax on it. **vergiye tâbi, vergilendirilebilir** *taxable income*

taxation /tæk'seɪʃ°n/ *noun* [U] the system of making people pay taxes **vergilendirme**

tax-free /ˌtæks'fri:/ *adjective* If something is tax-free, you do not pay tax on it. **vergiden muaf**

⧈ **taxi** ...... İLE BİRLİKTE KULLANILAN KELİMELER

call/get/hail/order/take a taxi ● a taxi **driver/ fare/firm**

∘ᐳ**taxi** /'tæksi/ *noun* [C] a car with a driver who you pay to take you somewhere **taksi** *a taxi driver* ○ *I'll take a taxi to the airport.*

taxing /'tæksɪŋ/ *adjective* difficult and needing a lot of thought or effort to do or understand **yorucu, güç, zor, çetin**

'taxi ,rank *UK* (*US* 'taxi ,stand) *noun* [C] a place where you can go to get a taxi **taksi durağı**

taxpayer /'tæksˌpeɪəʳ/ *noun* [C] a person who pays tax **vergi mükellefi**

TB /ˌti:'bi:/ *noun* [U] *abbreviation for* tuberculosis (= a serious infectious disease of the lungs) **verem sözcüğünün kısa yazılışı**

tbsp *written abbreviation for* tablespoonful: the amount that can be held by a large spoon used for measuring food **kaşık dolusu sözcüğünün kısa yazılışı**

∘ᐳ**tea** /ti:/ *noun* [C, U] **1** [DRINK] a hot drink that you make by pouring water onto dried leaves, or the leaves that you use to make this drink **çay, çay bitkisi** *herbal teas* ○ *Would you like a cup of tea or coffee?* **2** [AFTERNOON MEAL] *UK* A small afternoon meal of cakes, biscuits, etc and tea to drink **ikindi kahvaltısı** *They invited us for afternoon tea.* **3** [EVENING MEAL] *UK* a word used by some people for the meal that is eaten in the evening **akşam atıştırması; çayla yapılan akşam kahvaltısı**

teabag /'ti:bæg/ *noun* [C] a small paper bag with dried leaves inside, used for making tea **poşet çay**

∘ᐳ**teach** /ti:tʃ/ *verb* past **taught 1** [GIVE LESSONS] [I, T] to give lessons in a particular subject at a school, university, etc **öğretmek, ders vermek** *She taught at Harvard University for several years.* ○ *He teaches history.* **2** [SHOW HOW TO] [T] to show or explain to someone how to do something **öğretmek** [+ to do sth] *My dad taught me to drive.* ○ *Can you teach me how to knit?* **3** [GET KNOWLEDGE] [T] If a situation teaches you something, it gives you new knowledge or helps you to understand something. **ders vermek** [+ to do sth] *The whole experience taught him to be more careful with money.* ⊃See Common learner error at learn ⊃See also: teach sb a **lesson**.

∘ᐳ**teacher** /'ti:tʃəʳ/ *noun* [C] someone whose job is to teach in a school, college, etc **öğretmen** *a history/science teacher* ⊃Orta kısımdaki renkli sayfalarına bakınız

T

teaching /'tiːtʃɪŋ/ *noun* [U] the job of being a teacher **öğretim, öğretmenlik, ders verme** *He decided to go into teaching* (= become a teacher).

teachings /'tiːtʃɪŋz/ *noun* [plural] the ideas or beliefs of someone, such as a political or religious leader **öğretiler, doktrin** *the teachings of Martin Luther King*

teacup /'tiːkʌp/ *noun* [C] a cup that you drink tea from **çay fincanı**

---

team .... İLE BİRLİKTE KULLANILAN KELİMELER

be **in/on** a team ● **join/play for** a team ● team **captain/coach/member**

---

o━**team¹** /tiːm/ *noun* [group] **1** a group of people who play a sport or game together against another group of players **takım, ekip, tim** *a basketball/football team* **2** a group of people who work together to do something **ekim, takım, grup, tim** *a management team* ○ *a team of advisers*

team² /tiːm/ *verb*

team up *phrasal verb* to join someone else and work together with them to do something **ekip oluşturmak, grup kurmak, bir araya gelmek** *I teamed up with Brendan for the doubles tournament.*

teammate /'tiːmmeɪt/ *noun* [C] a member of your team **takım/ekip arkadaşı**

teamwork /'tiːmwɜːk/ *noun* [U] when a group of people work well together **ekip/takım çalışması**

teapot /'tiːpɒt/ *noun* [C] a container used for making and serving tea, which has a lid, a handle, and a spout (= tube that liquid comes out of) **çaydanlık** Orta kısımdaki renkli sayfalarına bakınız.

teapot

tear¹ /teə'/ *verb past tense* **tore**, *past participle* **torn 1** [T] to pull paper, cloth, etc into pieces, or to make a hole in it by accident **yırtmak, yırtılmak** *The nail had torn a hole in my skirt.* **2** [I] If paper, cloth, etc tears, it becomes damaged because it has been pulled. **yırtılmak, yırtmak, paramparça etmek 3 tear sth out of/off/down, etc** to remove something by pulling it quickly and violently **yırtarak almak/çıkarmak; yırtmak** *She tore his picture down from the wall.* **4 tear along/ about/past,** etc *informal* to move somewhere very quickly **hızlıca hareket etmek** *The kids were tearing around the house.* **5 be torn between sth and sth** to be unable to decide between two choices **iki şey arasında karar verememek; seçenekler arasında seçim yapamamak** *I'm torn between the apple pie and the chocolate mousse.* See also: pull/tear your hair out.

tear

tear sth apart *phrasal verb* **1** to make a group of people argue or fight with each other **aralarını bozmak; kavga etmeye sebep olmak; bölmek, parçalamak** *The country was torn apart by 12 years of civil war.* **2** to destroy something **paramparça etmek; yırtmak** *The building was torn apart by the bomb blast.*

tear sb apart *phrasal verb* to make someone very unhappy **ziyadesiyle üzmek; perişan etmek; mutsuz etmek**

tear sb away *phrasal verb* to make someone stop doing something that they enjoy, in order to do something else **zorla ayırmak/yarıda bıraktırmak/koparmak** *I'll bring Ian, if I can tear him away from his computer games.*

tear sth down *phrasal verb* to intentionally destroy a building or structure **yıkmak, yerle bir etmek** *They tore down the old hospital and built some offices.*

tear sth off *phrasal verb* to quickly remove your clothes **yırtar gibi çıkarmak; çekip çıkarmak, alelacele çıkarmak** *He tore off his shirt and jumped into the stream.*

tear sth up *phrasal verb* to tear paper into a lot of small pieces **küçük küçük parçalara ayırmak; bölüp parçalamak** *He tore up her photograph.*

tear² /teə'/ *noun* [C] a hole in a piece of cloth, paper, etc where it has been torn **yırtık, yarık**

o━**tear³** /tɪə'/ *noun* [C] a drop of water that comes from your eye when you cry **göz yaşı** *Suddenly he burst into tears* (= started crying). ○ *I was in tears* (= crying) *by the end of the film.* ● **tearful** *adjective* crying **ağlayan, gözleri dolan, göz yaşı döken** *a tearful goodbye* ● **tearfully** *adverb* See also: in floods (flood²) of tears. **gözleri yaşlı bir şekilde**

'tear ˌgas *noun* [U] a gas that makes people's eyes hurt, used by the police or army to control violent crowds **göz yaşartıcı bomba**

tease /tiːz/ *verb* [I, T] to laugh at someone or say unkind things to them, either because you are joking or because you want to upset them **takılmak, eğlenmek, kızdırmak** *They were teasing Dara about her new haircut.* ○ *Don't get upset, I'm only teasing.*

teaspoon /'tiːspuːn/ *noun* [C] a small spoon that is used for mixing drinks and measuring small amounts of food, or the amount this spoon can hold **çay kaşığı**

teatime /'tiːtaɪm/ *noun* [C, U] UK the time in the evening when people have a meal **akşam yemeği vakti**

'tea ˌtowel UK (US dishtowel) *noun* [C] a cloth that is used for drying plates, dishes, etc **bulaşık kurulama bezi**

tech¹ /tek/ *adjective mainly US short for* technical¹ **teknik sözcüğünün kısa yazılışı** *online tech support*

tech² /tek/ *noun mainly US* **1** [U] *short for* technology **teknoloji sözcüğünün kısa yazılışı** *high/low tech* ○ *tech stocks* **2** [C] *informal short for* technician **teknisyen/tekniker sözcüğünün kısa yazılışı** *Bill was a lab tech at NYU.*

techie /'teki/ *noun* [C] *informal* someone who has a strong interest in technology, usually computers **teknoloji/bilgisayar düşkünü**

o━**technical** /'teknɪkᵊl/ *adjective* **1** SCIENCE/INDUSTRY relating to the knowledge, machines, or methods used in science and industry **teknik** *We're having a few technical problems.* **2** SPECIALIZED relating to the knowledge and methods of a particular subject or job **teknik** *There are a few technical terms here that I don't understand.* **3** PRACTICAL SKILL relating to practical skills and methods used in a particular activity **teknik, yöntem** *As a dancer she had great technical skill.*

technicalities /ˌteknɪ'kælətiz/ *noun* [plural] the exact details of a system or process **teknik ayrıntılar** *the technicalities of photography*

technicality /ˌteknɪ'kæləti/ *noun* [C] a small detail of a law or rule **teknik ayrıntı**

technically /'teknɪkªli/ *adverb* **1** relating to the knowledge, machines, or methods used in science and industry **teknik olarak, teknik açıdan** *technically advanced weapons* **2** according to the exact details of a rule, law, or fact **esasında; formalite açısından, resmi bakımdan** *Irvine is technically British but lives in Dublin and races for the Irish team.*

technician /tek'nɪʃªn/ *noun* [C] someone whose job involves practical work with scientific or electrical equipment **teknisyen, tekniker** *a lab technician*

o--**technique** /tek'ni:k/ *noun* [C, U] a particular or special way of doing something **teknik, usul, yöntem** [+ for + doing sth] *Scientists have developed a new technique for taking blood samples.*

techno /'teknəʊ/ *noun* [U] UK a type of electronic dance music **bir tür elektronik dans müziği**

techno- /teknəʊ-/ *prefix* relating to technology **teknolojiye ilişkin/tekno' anlamında önek** *a technophile* (= a person who loves technology)

technology ...... İLE BİRLİKTE KULLANILAN KELİMELER

advanced/cutting-edge/modern technology • develop/harness technology

o--**technology** /tek'nɒlədʒi/ *noun* [C, U] knowledge, equipment, and methods that are used in science and industry **teknoloji** *computer technology* • **technological** /ˌteknə'lɒdʒɪkªl/ *adjective* relating to, or involving technology **teknolojik, teknolojiye ilişkin** *technological developments* • **technologically** *adverb* ⊃See also: information technology **teknolojik olarak**

teddy bear /'tedi,beəʳ/ (*also UK* teddy) *noun* [C] a soft, toy bear **oyuncak ayı**

tedious /'ti:diəs/ *adjective* boring **sıkıcı, bıktırıcı, usandırıcı, bezdiren** *a tedious job* • **tediously** *adverb* **sıkıcı bir şekilde**

tee /ti:/ *noun* [C] a small stick that is used for holding a golf ball **golf topunun üzerine konulduğu küçük çubuk**

teem /ti:m/ *verb*
be teeming with sb/sth *phrasal verb* to contain large numbers of people or animals **kaynamak, çokça olmak; dolu olmak**

teeming /'ti:mɪŋ/ *adjective* full of people **dolu, kalabalık, kaynayan, arı kovanı gibi** *the teeming city*

teen[1] /ti:n/ *noun* [C] mainly US short for teenager **ergen, genç, yeni yetme**

teen[2] /ti:n/ *adjective* [always before noun] informal relating to, or popular with people who are between 13 and 19 years old **ergenle ilgili; gençlere ilişkin** *a teen idol*

teenage /'ti:neɪdʒ/ *adjective* [always before noun] aged between 13 and 19 or suitable for people of that age **ergen, genç; 13-19 yaş arası** *a teenage daughter* ○ *a teenage disco*

o--**teenager** /'ti:n,eɪdʒəʳ/ *noun* [C] someone who is between 13 and 19 years old **13-19 yaş arası kimse, ergenlik dönemindeki kişi**

teens /ti:nz/ *noun* [plural] the part of your life between the age of 13 and 19 **13-19 arası yaş dönemi; ergenlik dönemi** *Her youngest daughter is still in her teens.*

'tee ,shirt *noun* [C] another spelling of T-shirt (= a piece of cotton clothing for the top part of the body with short sleeves and no collar) **yakasız kısa kollu pamuklu giysi; tişört**

teeter /'ti:təʳ/ *verb* **1 be teetering on the brink/edge of sth** to be in a situation where something bad might happen very soon *...a/e çok yakın olmak; tehlike/ olumsuzluk içinde olmak; ha oldu ha olacak*

olmak *The economy is teetering on the brink of collapse.* **2 teeter about/across/around, etc** to look as if you are going to fall **sendelemek, yalpalamak, düşecek gibi olmak** *She teetered around the room in six-inch heels.*

teeter-totter /ˌti:tə'tɒtəʳ/ *US* (UK/US seesaw) *noun* [C] a long board that children play on by sitting at each end and using their feet on the ground to push the board up and down **tahterevalli**

teeth /ti:θ/ *plural of*
tooth **dişler**

teethe /ti:ð/ *verb* **1** be **teething** If a baby is teething, it is getting its first teeth. **diş çıkarıyor olmak** **2 teething problems/ troubles** problems that happen because something is new and has not been done before **başlangıçtaki sorunlar; daha işin başındaki güçlükler**

teetotal /ˌti:'təʊtªl/ *adjective* never drinking any alcohol **hiç alkol kullanmayan** • **teetotaller** UK (US teetotaler) *noun* [C] someone who never drinks alcohol **alkol kullanmayan kimse**

TEFL /'tefl/ *noun* [U] abbreviation for Teaching English as a Foreign Language **İngilizce'nin Yabancı Dil olarak Öğretimi (İYDÖ)**

tel *written abbreviation for* telephone number **tel. no.** *Tel 0113 246369*

tele- /telɪ-/ *prefix* **1** TELEPHONE done using a telephone **telefonla yapılan' anlamında ön ek** *telesales* **2** TELEVISION connected with television **televizyonla ilgili' anlamında ön ek** *telecast* (= something that is broadcast on television) **3** DISTANCE over a long distance **uzun mesafeli' anlamında ön ek** *telephoto lens* (= a camera lens that makes distant objects look nearer)

telecommunications /ˌtelɪkəˌmju:nɪ'keɪʃªnz/ *noun* [U, group] the process or business of sending information or messages by telephone, radio, etc **telekominikasyon; iletişim işleri**

telecommuting /ˌtelɪkə'mju:tɪŋ/ US (UK teleworking) *noun* [U] working at home, while communicating with your office by computer and telephone **hem ofis hem mesken** • **telecommuter** *noun* [C] US **bilgisayar aracılığıyla ofise bağlanarak evden çalışma**

telecoms /'telɪkɒmz/ *noun* [U] short for telecommunications **telekominikasyon; iletişim işleri**

teleconference /ˌtelɪ'kɒnfªrªns/ *noun* [C] when people in different places have a meeting using computers, telephones, televisions, etc to allow them to talk to each other and see each other **telekonferans; uydu aracılığıyla uzaktan verilen konferans**

telegram /'telɪgræm/ *noun* [C] a message that is sent by telegraph and printed on paper **telgraf**

telegraph /'telɪgrɑːf/ *noun* [U] an old-fashioned system of sending messages using radio or electrical signals **telgraf**

telemarketing /'telɪˌmɑːkɪtɪŋ/ (*also UK* telesales) *noun* [U] the selling of goods or services by telephone **telepazarlama; telefonla satış/pazarlama**

telepathy /tɪ'lepəθi/ *noun* [U] the ability to know what someone is thinking or to communicate thoughts without speaking or writing **telepati; altıncı his; önsezi** • **telepathic** /ˌtelɪ'pæθɪk/ *adjective* having or involving telepathy **telepati yapabilen; telepatik**

telephone

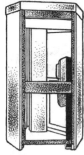

telephone

telephone box *UK*,
telephone booth *US*

mobile phone

o⁻**telephone¹** /'telɪfəʊn/ (*also* phone) *noun* **1** [U] a communication system that is used to talk to someone who is in another place **telefon** *a telephone call* ○ *I'm sorry, he's on the telephone* (= using the telephone) *at the moment.* **2** [C] a piece of equipment that is used to talk to someone who is in another place **telefon** *The telephone rang and she hurried to pick it up.* ○ *Could you answer the telephone?*

telephone² /'telɪfəʊn/ (*also* phone) *verb* [I, T] *formal* to communicate with someone by telephone **telefon etmek; telefonla iletişim kurmak**

'**telephone di,rectory** *noun* [C] a book that contains the telephone numbers of people who live in a particular area **telefon rehberi**

'**telephone ,number** (*also* phone number) *noun* [C] the number of a particular telephone **telefon numarası**

telesales /'telɪseɪlz/ *UK* (*UK/US* telemarketing) *noun* [U] the selling of goods or services by telephone **telefonla satışlar**

telescope /'telɪskəʊp/ *noun* [C] a piece of equipment, in the shape of a tube, that makes things which are far away look bigger or nearer **teleskop**

telescope

Teletext /'telɪˌtekst/ *noun* trademark a system that gives written information on many subjects, such as news, on a television screen **teleteks; tv ekranında bilginin yazı ile sunulduğu sistem**

televise /'telɪvaɪz/ *verb* [T] to show something on television **televizyonda yayınlamak/göstermek** *The concert will be televised live around the world.*

o⁻**television** /'telɪvɪʒ³n/ *noun* **1** [EQUIPMENT] [C] a piece of equipment in the shape of a box, with a screen on the front, used for watching programmes **televizyon**

2 [PROGRAMMES] [U] the programmes that are shown on a television **televizyon programları** *I mostly watch television in the evening.* ○ *I saw it on television.* ○ *a television programme* **3** [SYSTEM] [U] the system or business of making and broadcasting programmes for television **televizyonculuk işi/sistemi** ⊃See also: closed-circuit television, satellite television.

teleworking /'telɪˌwɜːkɪŋ/ *UK* (*US* telecommuting) *noun* [U] working at home, while communicating with your office by computer and telephone **bilgisayar ve telefonla işini evden yönetme** • **teleworker** *noun* [C] *UK* **bilgisayar aracılığla ofise bağlanarak evden çalışma**

o⁻**tell** /tel/ *verb past* told **1** [SAY] [T] to say something to someone, usually giving them information **söylemek, demek, anlatmak** *He told me about his new school.* ○ [+ (that)] *Sally told me that the play didn't start until 9 o'clock.* ○ [+ question word] *Can you tell me what time the next bus leaves?* **2 tell sb to do sth** to order someone to do something **emretmek, söylemek** *I told you to stay here.* **3 can tell** to know or recognize something from what you hear, see, etc **ayırtedebilmek, bilebilmek, farkedebilmek** [+ (that)] *You could tell that he was tired.* ○ [+ question word] *You can never tell whether Hajime's being serious or not.* ○ *I can't tell the difference between them.* **4** [UNDERSTAND FROM] [T] If something tells you something, it gives you information. **anlatmak, söylemek, haber vermek** *What does the survey tell us about the lives of teenagers?* **5 (I'll) tell you what** used to suggest a plan **Bak ne diyeceğim?', 'Ne diyorum, biliyor musun?** *Tell you what, let's go swimming and then get a pizza.* **6** [EFFECT] [I] to have a bad effect on someone **kötü etkisi olmak; kötü/olumsuz etkilemek** *The worry of the last few months was starting to tell on him.* **7 (I) told you so!** *informal* used when someone has caused problems for themselves by doing something that you told them not to **Sana söylemiştim!', 'Dememiş miydim ben sana?', 'Yaa ben sana söylemiştim!** ⊃See also: tell sb's fortune.

tell sb/sth apart *phrasal verb* to be able to see the difference between two things or people that are very similar **ayırt etmek, ayırmak, farkına varmak** *It's impossible to tell the twins apart.*

tell sb off *phrasal verb* to tell someone that they have done something wrong and that you are angry about it **azarlamak, paylamak, ağzına geleni söylemek, fırçalamak** [+ for + doing sth] *Darren got told off for talking in class.* ⊃Orta kısımdaki renkli sayfalarına bakınız.

teller /'telər/ *noun* [C] *US* someone who works in a bank and gives out or takes in money **veznedar** ⊃See also: fortune-teller.

telling /'telɪŋ/ *adjective* showing the truth about a situation, or showing what someone really means **açığa vuran, belli eden, gösteren** *a telling comment*

telltale /'telteɪl/ *adjective* [always before noun] showing something that someone is trying to keep secret **açığa vuran, ortaya çıkaran, belli eden** *She was showing all the telltale signs of pregnancy.*

telly /'teli/ *noun* [C, U] *UK informal* short for television **televizyon**

temp /temp/ *noun* [C] someone who works in an office for a short time while someone else is away, ill, etc **geçici görevle çalışan kişi; yerine bakan kimse; geçici çalışan** • **temp** *verb* [I] to work as a temp in an office **geçici olarak çalışmak**

temper¹ /'tempər/ *noun* **1** [C, U] when someone becomes angry very easily **öfke, kızgınlık, çabuk sinirlenme** *He's got a really bad temper.* **2 be in a bad/foul, etc temper** to be feeling angry **kızmak, hiddetlenmek, kendini kaybetmek** *I'd avoid her if I were you - she's* *in a foul temper.* **3 lose your temper (with sb)** to suddenly become very angry **kendini kaybedip öfkelenmek, kendini tutamayıp hiddetlenmek** *I lost my temper with the children this morning.* **4 keep your temper** to succeed in staying calm and not becoming angry **kendine/sinirlerine hâkim olmak; sakin kalmayı becerebilmek; kolay kolay sinirlenmemek**

temper² /'tempər/ *verb* [T] to make something less strong, extreme, etc **yumuşatmak, hafifletmek** *I learnt to temper my criticism.*

temperament /'tempərəmənt/ *noun* [C, U] the part of your character that affects your moods and the way you behave **huy, yaradılış, tabiat, mizaç** *I don't think he's got the right temperament to be a teacher.*

temperamental /ˌtempərə'mentəl/ *adjective* **1** becoming angry or upset very often and suddenly **değişken mizaçlı, saati saatine uymayan; günü gününü tutmayan 2** A machine, vehicle, etc that is temperamental does not always work correctly. **(araç, makina) randımanlı çalışmayan; sık sık arıza yapan; günü gününe uymayan**

temperate /'tempərət/ *adjective formal* having weather that is not very hot and not very cold **ılıman, mutedil** *a temperate climate*

temperature .... İLE BİRLİKTE KULLANILAN KELİMELER

average/extreme/high/low temperatures ● temperatures drop/fall/rise/soar

o- **temperature** /'temprətʃər/ *noun* **1** [C, U] how hot or cold something is **sıcaklı, ısı** *The room's kept at a temperature of around 20°C.* **2 sb's temperature** how hot or cold someone's body is **vücudunun sıcaklığı; vücut sıcaklığı** *The doctor examined him and took his temperature* (= measured his temperature). **3 have a temperature** to be hotter than usual because you are ill **ateşi olmak**

template /'templeɪt/ *noun* [C] **1** a metal, plastic, etc pattern that is used for making many copies of a shape **kalıp, şablon 2** a system that helps you arrange information on a computer screen **bilgisayar ekranında bilgiyi düzenlemeye yarayan sistem**

temple /'templ/ *noun* [C] **1** a building where people in some religions go to pray or worship **mâbet, tapınak** *a Buddhist temple* **2** the area on each side of your head in front of the top of your ear **şakak**

tempo /'tempəʊ/ *noun* **1** [U, no plural] the speed at which an activity happens **hız, tempo** *The tempo of the game increased in the second half.* **2** [C, U] *formal* the speed of a piece of music **(müzik) tempo**

temporary .... BAŞKA BİR DEYİŞLE

For now söylemi bir şeyin şu an yapılması veya olması gerektiğini fakat ileride değiştirilebileceğini belirtir. *Just put everything on the table* **for now** - *I'll sort it all out later.*

Disposable sıfatı kısa süreli kullanılacak ve daha sonra atılacak şeyler için kullanılan bir sıfattır. *I bought a* **disposable** *camera at the airport.*

Eğer bir şey geçici ve düşük kalitede ise, **makeshift** ifadesi kullanılabilir. *We built a* **makeshift** *shelter under the trees.*

Short-lived sıfatı birşeyin kısa süreli olduğunu belirtmede **temporary** kelimesinin yerine kullanılabilir. *I had a few relationships at college, most of which were fairly* **short-lived.**

Acting manager/chairman ifadesi kişinin kısa bir süreyle görevdeki kişi orada olmadığı için onun görevini üstlendiğini belirtir. *He'll be the* **acting** *director until they appoint a permanent one.*

temporary /'tempərəri/ *adjective* existing or happening for only a short or limited time **geçici** *a temporary job* ○ *temporary accommodation/housing* ● **temporarily** *adverb* **geçici olarak**

tempt /tempt/ *verb* [T] to make someone want to have or do something, especially something that they do not need or something that is wrong **özendirmek, teşvik etmek, imrendirmek** [+ to do sth] *She's trying to tempt me to go shopping with her.*

temptation .... İLE BİRLİKTE KULLANILAN KELİMELER

avoid/resist (the) temptation ● give in to/succumb to temptation ● a strong temptation ● the temptation of doing sth

temptation /temp'teɪʃən/ *noun* **1** [C, U] a feeling that you want to do or have something, although you know you should not do something **karşı konulamaz istek, şeytana uyma, tahrik** [+ to do sth] *I resisted the temptation to* (= I did not) *have another piece of chocolate cake.* **2** [C] something that makes you want to do or have something although you know you should not **cezbeden şey, baştan çıkarıcı şey** *He knew crime was wrong but the money was too great a temptation.*

tempting /'temptɪŋ/ *adjective* Something that is tempting makes you want to have or do it. **cazip, baştan çıkarıcı, iştah kabartıcı** *a tempting invitation/offer*

o- **ten** /ten/ the number 10 **on rakamı**

tenacious /tɪ'neɪʃəs/ *adjective* very determined to do something and not wanting to stop **azimli, inatçı, vazgeçmez** ● **tenaciously** *adverb* **azimli** ● **tenacity** /tɪ'næsəti/ *noun* [U] **inatçılık, azim**

tenancy /'tenənsi/ *noun* [C, U] the period of time when someone rents a room, house, etc **kiracılık, icarcılık**

tenant /'tenənt/ *noun* [C] someone who pays rent to live in a room, house, etc **kiracı, icarcı**

o- **tend** /tend/ *verb* **1 tend to do sth** to often do a particular thing or be likely to do a particular thing **eğiliminde/meyilli/istekli/temayüllü olmak** *I tend to wear dark colours.* ○ *July and August tend to be our busiest months.* **2** [T] (*also* tend to) *formal* to look after someone or something **ilgilenmek, çok iyi bakmak, bakım göstermek** *He spends most afternoons tending his vegetable garden.*

tendency /'tendənsi/ *noun* [C] something that someone often does, or something that often happens **eğilim, meyil, istek, temayül** [+ to do sth] *She has a tendency to talk for too long.* ○ *There is a growing tendency for companies to employ people on short contracts.*

tender¹ /'tendər/ *adjective* **1** GENTLE kind and gentle **şefkatli, sevgi dolu** *a tender kiss/look* **2** FOOD Tender meat or vegetables are soft and easy to cut. **yumuşak, kesimi kolay (et, sebze) 3** PAINFUL If part of your body is tender, it is painful when you touch it. **hassas, kolay etkilenen, dokununca acıyan, ağrılı 4 at the tender age of 8/17/25, etc** *literary* at the young age of 8/17/25, etc **8/17/25 vb. hassas yaşlarda** ● **tenderness** *noun* [U] **yumuşaklık, hassasiyet**

tender² /'tendər/ *verb formal* **1** [I] to make a formal offer to do a job or to provide a service **teklif vermek; teklif mektubu sunmak 2** [T] *formal* to formally offer a suggestion, idea, money, etc **para/fikir/öneri vb. teklifinde bulunmak** *He tendered his resignation* (= offered to leave his job).

tender³ /'tendər/ *noun* [C, U] a formal offer to do some work **teklif mektubu; öneri paketi** *The work has been put out to tender* (= people have been asked to make offers to do the work).

tenderly /'tendəli/ *adverb* in a kind and gentle way **şef-kat/sevgi dolu biçimde; nazikçe, nezaketle; hassas bir şekilde** *He looked at her tenderly.*

tendon /'tendən/ *noun* [C] a strong piece of tissue in your body that connects a muscle to a bone **tendon**

tenement /'tenəmənt/ *noun* [C] a large building that is divided into apartments, usually in a poor area of a city **şehrin yoksul bölgelerinde bir çok ailenin yaşayabileceği dairelerin bulunduğu büyük bina**

tenet /'tenɪt/ *noun* [C] a principle or belief of a theory or religion **ilke, prensip, inanç** *one of the basic tenets of Islam*

tenner /'tenəʳ/ *noun* [C] *UK informal* a piece of paper money that has a value of £10 **onluk, on sterlinlik kâğıt para**

tennis /'tenɪs/ *noun* [U] a sport in which two or four people hit a small ball to each other over a net **tenis, tenis sporu** ➔Orta kısımdaki renkli sayfalarına bakınız ➔See also: **table tennis**.

tenor /'tenəʳ/ *noun* [C] a male singer with a high voice **tenor**

tense¹ /tens/ *adjective* **1** FEELING nervous, worried, and not able to relax **gergin, sinirli, huzursuz** *The students looked tense as they waited for their exam results.* **2** SITUATION A tense situation makes you feel nervous and worried. **gergin, sinirleri bozan, huzursuz** *There were some tense moments in the second half of the game.* **3** MUSCLE A tense muscle feels tight and stiff. **gergin, sertleşmiş**

tense² /tens/ (*also* **tense up**) *verb* [I, T] If your muscles tense, they become tight and stiff, and if you tense them, you make them do this. **kasları ger(il)mek/sertleş(tir)mek**

tense³ /tens/ *noun* [C, U] the form of a verb which shows the time at which an action happened. For example 'I sing' is in the present tense and 'I will sing' is in the future tense. **fiil zamanı, kip**

🧩 **tension** ...... İLE BİRLİKTE KULLANILAN KELİMELER

create/defuse/ease tension ● tension **mounts** ● **growing/increased/mounting** tension ● tension **between** sb and sb ● **ethnic/racial** tensions
---

tension /'tenʃ°n/ *noun* **1** NO TRUST [C, U] a feeling of fear or anger between two groups of people who do not trust each other **gerginlik, gerilim, tansiyon; iplerin gerilmiş olması** *ethnic/racial tension* ○ *There are growing* **tensions between** *the two countries.* **2** BEING NERVOUS [U] a feeling that you are nervous, worried, and not relaxed **gerginlik, gerilim; endişe** *You could feel the tension in the room as we waited for her to arrive.* **3** TIGHT [U] when a muscle, rope, etc, is tight or stiff **kasılma, gerilme, kaskatı kesilme; gerginlik**

tent /tent/ *noun* [C] a structure made of metal poles and cloth which is fixed to the ground with ropes and used as a cover or to sleep under **çadır** *It only took twenty minutes to* **put the tent up** (= make it ready to use).

tent

tentacle /'tentəkl/ *noun* [C] one of the long, arm-like parts of some sea creatures **deniz hayvanı kolu**

tentative /'tentətɪv/ *adjective* **1** A tentative idea, plan, agreement, etc is not certain. **geçici, kesin olmayan** *The two companies have announced a tentative deal.* **2** doing something in a way that shows you are not confident **tereddüt eden, dikkatli ve ürkek, çekingen** *a child's tentative first steps* ● **tentatively** *adverb* **geçici olarak**

tenth¹ /tenθ/ 10th written as a word **onuncu**

tenth² /tenθ/ *noun* [C] one of ten equal parts of something; $1/10$; 0.1 **onda bir**

tenuous /'tenjuəs/ *adjective* A tenuous connection, idea, or situation is weak and possibly does not exist. **zayıf, güçsüz, uzun sürmez, yetersiz** *The court is unlikely to accept such tenuous evidence.* ● **tenuously** *adverb* **narin bir biçimde**

tenure /'tenjəʳ/ *noun* [U] **1** BUILDING/LAND the legal right to live in a building or use a piece of land for a period **kullanma hakkı 2** TIME the period of time when someone has an important job **önemli görev/memuriyet süresi** *his tenure as president* **3** PERMANENT If you have tenure in your job, your job is permanent. **geçici görev süresi; geçici görev dönemi**

tepid /'tepɪd/ *adjective* A tepid liquid is slightly warm. **ılık**

○= **term¹** /tɜːm/ *noun* **1** WORD [C] a word or phrase that is used to refer to a particular thing, especially in a technical or scientific subject **terim, deyim, tâbir** *a legal/technical term* **2** TIME [C] the fixed period of time when someone does an important job or is in a particular place **dönem, süre, devre** *a prison term* ○ *The government has been elected for another four-year term.* **3** SCHOOL [C] one of the periods of time that the school or university year is divided into **dönem, sömestr** *We've got a test at the* **end of term**. **4** in the **long/short, etc term** a long/short, etc period of time from now **uzun/kısa vadede** ➔See also: **half-term**.

term² /tɜːm/ *verb* [T] *formal* to use a particular word or phrase to describe something **adlandırmak, demek, tanımlamak** *Critics termed the movie a 'disaster'.*

terminal¹ /'tɜːmɪn°l/ *noun* [C] **1** a building where you can get onto an aircraft, bus, or ship **terminal** *a terminal building* **2** a screen and keyboard with which you can use a computer **terminal, bilgisayar ekran ve klavyesi**

terminal² /'tɜːmɪn°l/ *adjective* A terminal illness will cause death. **ölümcül, tedavisi imkânsız** *terminal cancer* ● **terminally** *adverb* **terminally** *ill* **ölümcül**

terminate /'tɜːmɪneɪt/ *verb* [I, T] *formal* If something terminates, it ends, and if you terminate something, you make it end. **bit(ir)mek, sona er(dir)mek** *His contract has been terminated.* ● **termination** /ˌtɜːmɪ'neɪʃ°n/ *noun* [C, U] **sonlanma**

terminology /ˌtɜːmɪ'nɒlədʒi/ *noun* [C, U] the special words and phrases that are used in a particular subject **terimler, terminoloji** *medical/scientific terminology*

terminus /'tɜːmɪnəs/ *noun* [C] the place where a train or bus finishes its journey **son istasyon/durak**

🧩 **terms** ...... İLE BİRLİKTE KULLANILAN KELİMELER

agree terms ● **break/meet** the terms of sth ● **under** the terms of sth
---

terms /tɜːmz/ *noun* [plural] **1** the rules of an agreement **koşullar, şartlar** *Under the terms of their contract, employees must give 3 months notice if they want to leave.* **2 be on good/bad/friendly, etc terms** to have a good/bad, etc relationship with someone **araları/ilişkileri iyi/kötü/dostâne vb. olmak; ...ilişkileri ... olmak 3 not be on speaking terms** to not speak to someone because you have argued with them **dargın olmak, konuşmamak, küs olmak; suskunluk döneminde olmak 4 in ... terms** (*also* **in terms of sth**) used to explain which part of a problem or situation you are referring to ...açı(sın)dan, ...bakım(ın)dan; ...yönünden/cihetinden *In financial terms, the project was not a success.* **5 in no uncertain terms** in a direct and often angry way **doğrudan ve kesin bir dille; kızarak ve yüzüne; doğrudan yüzüne** *I told him to go away in no uncertain terms.* **6 come to terms with sth** to accept a sad situation **kabullenmek** *He still hasn't come to terms with his brother's death.* ⊃See also: a **contradiction** in terms.

terrace /'terɪs/ *noun* [C] **1** a flat area outside a house, restaurant, etc where you can sit **teras; bahçe, yeşillik açık alan 2** *UK* a row of houses that are joined together **sıra evler**

,**terraced 'house** *UK* (*US* **row house**) *noun* [C] one of a row of houses that are joined together **bitişik nizam/sıralanmış evler**

the terraces /'terɪsɪz/ *noun* [plural] in the UK, wide, concrete steps where people stand to watch a football game (**İng.**) **tribün basamakları**

terrain /tə'reɪn/ *noun* [C, U] a particular type of land **arazi, alan, yer** *rough terrain*

terrestrial /tə'restriəl/ *adjective formal* relating to the Earth, not space **yeryüzüne ilişkin**

o-***terrible** /'terəbl/ *adjective* very bad, of low quality, or unpleasant **korkunç, dehşet verici, müthiş** *a terrible accident* ○ *The weather was terrible.*

terribly /'terəbli/ *adverb* **1** very **çok; korkunç** *She seemed terribly upset.* **2** very badly **korkunç derecede, fevkalâde, çok kötü bir şekilde** *I slept terribly last night.*

terrier /'teriə^r^/ *noun* [C] a type of small dog **terier, bir tür küçük köpek**

terrific /tə'rɪfɪk/ *adjective* **1** excellent **şahane, mükemmel, olağanüstü** *a terrific opportunity* ○ *I thought she looked terrific.* **2** [always before noun] very large, great, or serious **büyük, muazzam, müthiş** *a terrific increase in prices* ○ *a terrific storm* ● **terrifically** *adverb* **harika bir şekilde**

terrified /'terəfaɪd/ *adjective* very frightened **ödü kopmuş, dehşete düşmüş** *I'm terrified of flying.* ○ *Maggie was terrified that her parents would discover the truth.*

terrify /'terəfaɪ/ *verb* [T] to make someone feel very frightened **ödünü patlatmak, dehşete düşürmek; çok korkutmak; yüreğini ağzına getirmek** *The idea of parachuting out of an aircraft terrifies me.* ● **terrifying** *adjective* *a terrifying experience* **korkunç**

territorial /,terɪ'tɔːriəl/ *adjective* relating to the land that is owned or controlled by a particular country **ülkeye ait; ülkenin toprakları ile ilgili** *a territorial dispute*

territory /'terɪt^ə^ri/ *noun* **1** [LAND] [C, U] land that is owned or controlled by a particular country **toprak, bölge, ülke, vatan toprağı** *Spanish territory* **2** [PERSON/ANIMAL] [C, U] an area that an animal or person thinks belongs to them **arazi, bölge, toprak, mıntıka** *Cats like to protect their territory.* **3** [AREA OF KNOWLEDGE] [U] an area of knowledge or experience **bilgi/deneyim alanı sahası; uzmanlık alanı** *With this project we'll be moving into unknown territory.*

terror /'terə^r^/ *noun* [U] a feeling of being very frightened **terör, dehşet** *There was a look of terror on his face.* ⊃See also: **reign**[1] of terror.

terrorism /'ter^ə^rɪz^ə^m/ *noun* [U] the use of violence for political purposes, for example putting bombs in public places **terörizm** *an act of terrorism*

terrorist /'terərɪst/ *noun* [C] someone who is involved in terrorism **terörist** *a terrorist attack*

terrorize (*also UK* -ise) /'ter^ə^raɪz/ *verb* [T] to make someone feel very frightened by saying that you will hurt or kill them **dehşet saçmak, yıldırmak, sindirmek; öldürmekle tehdit etmek** *A gang of young men with knives were terrorizing local people.*

terse /tɜːs/ *adjective* said or written in a few words, often showing that you are annoyed **kısa ve öz** ● **tersely** *adverb* **kısa ve net bir şekilde**

tertiary /'tɜːʃ^ə^ri/ *adjective UK formal* Tertiary education is education at university or college level. **üniversite ayarında eğitim** *a tertiary institution*

TESOL /'tiːsɒl/ *noun* [U] *abbreviation for* Teaching English to Speakers of Other Languages **Diğer Dilleri Konuşanlara İngilizce Öğretimi (DDKİÖ)**

$\square$ **test** .... İLE BİRLİKTE KULLANILAN KELİMELER

do/sit/take a test ● **fail/pass** a test ● a test **on** sth

o-***test**[1] /test/ *noun* [C] **1** [EXAM] a set of questions to measure someone's knowledge or ability **sınav, imtihan, test** *a driving test* ○ *You have to take a test.* ○ *Only two students in the class failed the test.* ○ *Did you pass the biology test?* **2** [MEDICAL] a short medical examination of part of your body **sağlık için yapılan test** *an eye test* ○ *a pregnancy test* **3** [EXPERIMENT] something that you do to discover if something is safe, works correctly, etc **deneme, test** *a safety test* **4** [SITUATION] a situation that shows how good something is **test** *This will be a real test of his ability.*

o-***test**[2] /test/ *verb* [T] **1** [EXPERIMENT] to do something in order to discover if something is safe, works correctly, etc **denemek, test etmek, denemeden geçirmek** *None of our products are tested on animals.* **2** [MEDICAL] to do a medical examination of part of someone's body **tıbbi testler yapmak; tetkik yapmak** *I'm going to get my hearing tested.* **3** [EXAM] to give someone a set of questions, in order to measure their knowledge or ability **sınav yapmak, test etmek** *You'll be tested on all the things we've studied this term.* **4** [SITUATION] If a situation tests someone, it proves how good, strong, etc they are. **denemek, imtihan etmek**

testament /'testəmənt/ *noun* a **testament to sth** *formal* proof of something good **bir şeyin kanıtı/delili** *It's a testament to Jane's popularity that so many people are celebrating with her today.* ⊃See also: **the New Testament, the Old Testament.**

testicle /'testɪkl/ *noun* [C] one of the two round, male sex organs that produce sperm **testis**

testify /'testɪfaɪ/ *verb* [I] to say what you know or believe is true in a law court **tanıklık yapmak, şahitlik etmek** [+ that] *Elliott testified that he had met the men in a bar.*

testimony /'testɪməni/ *noun* **1** [C, U] a formal statement about what someone knows or believes is true, especially in a law court **tanıklık, şahitlik, ifade, beyan** *the testimony of a witness* **2** **testimony to sth** *formal* proof of something good **bir şeyin kanıtı/delili/göstergesi** *The book's continued popularity is testimony to the power of clever marketing.*

'**test ,tube** *noun* [C] a glass tube that is open at one end and used in scientific experiments **deney tüpü**

tetanus /'tet^ə^nəs/ *noun* [U] a serious disease that makes your muscles stiff and is caused by an infection that gets into the body through a cut **tetanoz**

tether /'teðə^r^/ *verb* [T] to tie an animal to something so that it cannot move away **direğe/ağaca bağlamak** ● **tether** *noun* [C] ⊃See also: at the **end**[1] of your tether. **yular**

T

•►**text¹** /tekst/ *noun* **1** [WRITING] [C, U] the written words in a book, magazine, etc, not the pictures **metin, yazı** *a page of text* **2** [BOOK/DOCUMENT] [C] a book or piece of writing that you study as part of a course **ders, ders kitabı, yazı, metin 3** [MESSAGE] a written message, usually containing words with letters left out, sent from one mobile phone to another **yazılı ileti**

text² /tekst/ *verb* [I, T] to send a text message (= written message from a mobile phone) **yazılı ileti göndermek**

textbook /'tekstbʊk/ *noun* [C] a book about a particular subject, written for students **ders kitabı** *a chemistry/ French textbook* ➔*Orta kısımdaki renkli sayfalarına bakınız.*

textile /'tekstaɪl/ *noun* [C] any type of cloth that is made by weaving (= crossing threads under and over each other) **tekstil, mensucat**

text message .... İLE BİRLİKTE KULLANILAN KELİMELER

get/send a text message • a text message **saying** sth • a text message **from/to** sb

'text ,message *noun* [C] a written message, usually containing words with letters left out, sent from one mobile phone to another **yazılı ileti** • **text messaging** *noun* [U] **cep telefonundan yollanan mesaj**

texture /'tekstʃər/ *noun* [C, U] the way that something feels when you touch it **doku, yapı** *wood with a rough texture*

•►**than** *strong form* /ðæn/ *weak form* /ðᵊn/ *preposition, conjunction* used to compare two different things or amounts **...dan/den** *Susannah's car is bigger than mine.* ○ *Tom's a bit taller than Sam.* ○ *It cost less than I expected.*

[YAYGIN HATALAR]

than or then?

Dikkat: Doğru kelimeyi seçin. Bu iki kelime benzer görünmelerine rağmen, hem yazılışları hem de anlamları farklıdır. Belirli bir zamandan bahsetmek için veya daha sonra ne olduğundan bahsetmek için **then** kullanılmalıdır: ~~I did the washing up and than I went to bed.~~ Yanlış cümle örneği

I did the washing up and then I went to bed.

•►**thank** /θæŋk/ *verb* [T] **1** to tell someone that you are grateful for something they have done or given you **teşekkür etmek** *I haven't thanked her for her present yet.* ○ [+ for + doing sth] *Yu Yin thanked the boys for helping her.* **2 thank God/goodness/Heavens, etc** something that you say when you are happy because something bad did not happen **Allah'a şükürler olsun!', 'Çok şükür!', 'Şükürler olsun!'** *Thank goodness you're okay - I was really worried.*

thankful /'θæŋkfᵊl/ *adjective* pleased or grateful about something **minnettar, memnun, müteşekkir** [+ that] *We were thankful that none of the children saw the accident.*

thankfully /'θæŋkfᵊli/ *adverb* used at the beginning of a sentence to show that you are pleased or grateful about something **Çok şükür ki...!', 'Ne mutlu ki ...!'** *Thankfully, nobody was hurt.*

thankless /'θæŋkləs/ *adjective* A thankless job is difficult or unpleasant and no one thanks you for doing it. **iyilik bilmez, nankör, değeri bilinmeyen** *Nursing can be a thankless job.*

thanks¹ /θæŋks/ *exclamation informal* **1** used to tell someone that you are grateful because they have given you something or done something for you **Teşekkürler!'** *Can you pass me the book? Thanks very much.* ○ *Thanks for all your help.* **2 thanks/no, thanks** used to accept or refuse someone's offer **Teşekkürler!'**

'Hayır, teşekkür ederim!' *"Would you like a cup of coffee?" "No, thanks."*

•►**thanks²** /θæŋks/ *noun* [plural] **1** words that show you are grateful for something someone has given to you or done for you **Teşekkürler!'** *He sent a message of thanks.* **2 thanks to sb/sth** because of someone or something **...ın/in sayesinde/yüzünden; ...dan/den dolayı; ...ın/in nedeniyle** *I passed my driving test, thanks to the extra help my Dad gave me.*

Thanksgiving /ˌθæŋks'gɪvɪŋ/ *noun* [C, U] a holiday in the autumn in the US and Canada, when families have a big meal together **Şükran Günü**

•►**thank ,you** *exclamation* **1** used to tell someone that you are grateful because they have given you something or done something for you **Size teşekkür ederim/teşekkürler!'** *Thank you very much for the birthday card.* ○ *"Here's the money I promised you." "Thank you."* **2 thank you/no, thank you** used to accept or refuse someone's offer **Teşekkür ederim!'** *"Would you like something to eat?" "No, thank you."*

•►**thank-you** /'θæŋkju/ *noun* [C] something that you say or do to thank someone for doing something **teşekkür** [+ for + doing sth] *I bought Emma some chocolates as a thank-you for looking after the dog.* ○ *a thank-you present*

•►**that¹** /ðæt/ *determiner plural* **those 1** used to refer to something or someone that has already been talked about or seen **şu, o** *Did you know that woman in the post office?* ○ *How much are those shoes?* **2** used to refer to something or someone that is not near you **şu, o, oradaki, uzaktaki** *He went through that door.* ○ *Have you seen that man over there?* ➔*See Common learner error at this.*

•►**that²** /ðæt/ *pronoun plural* **those 1** [ALREADY DISCUSSED/SEEN] used to refer to something that has already been talked about or seen **şu, o** *That looks heavy.* ○ *You can't possibly wear those!* **2** [NOT NEAR] used to refer to something that is not near you **şu, o, oradaki, uzaktaki** *What's that in the corner?* **3 that's it a** [CORRECT] used to say that something is correct **işte o kadar; işte bu kadar** *You need to push the two pieces together. That's it.* **b** [ENDED] used to say that something has ended **söyleyecek başka şey yok; hepsi bu kadar; yapacak başka bir şey yok** *Well that's it then, we've finished.* **4 that's that** used to say that something has happened or a decision has been made and there is nothing more to say or do **mesele kapanmıştır; işte o kadar** *I won't agree to it and that's that.* **5 that is (to say)** used to correct something you have said or give more information about something **yani ...; yani demek oluyor ki...; yani demek isteniyor ki...** *Everybody was at the meeting, well everyone except Jeanne, that is.*

•►**that³** *strong form* /ðæt/ *weak form* /ðət/ *conjunction* **1** used after some verbs, nouns, and adjectives to introduce a new part of a sentence **...ki; ...diğini/dığını** *He said that he'd collect it later.* ○ *Is it true that she's pregnant?* **2** used instead of 'who' or 'which' at the beginning of a relative clause **ki o ...; ...en/an** *Have you eaten all the cake that I made yesterday?*

that⁴ /ðæt/ *adverb* **1** used when describing the size, amount, or state of something or someone **o kadar; bu kadar; bu denli** *I've never seen a fish that big before.* **2 not (all) that big/good/warm, etc** not very big/good/warm, etc **pek fazla/ okadar/öylesine büyük, iyi, sıcak vs. Değil** *It hasn't been all that cold this winter.*

thatched /θætʃt/ *adjective* A thatched building has a roof that is made of straw (= dried grass-like stems).

sazla kaplı, kamıştan yapılmış; sazlıklı; hasırla kaplı *a thatched cottage*

thaw /θɔː/ *verb* **1** [I, T] (*also* **thaw out**) If something that is frozen thaws, it becomes warmer and softer or changes to liquid, and if you thaw something that is frozen, you make it do this. **eri(t)mek; çöz(ül)mek** *Allow the meat to thaw before cooking it.* **2** [I] If a relationship between people thaws, it becomes more friendly after being bad. **aradaki buzlar erimek; aradaki sorunları gidermek/halletmek; soğukluğu ortadan kaldırmak** ● **thaw** *noun* [C] **buzların erimesi, çözülmesi**

o⇥**the** *strong form* /ðiː/ *weak forms* /ði/, /ðə/ *determiner* **1** [ALREADY KNOWN] used before nouns to refer to particular things or people that have already been talked about or are already known **bilinen veya hakkında konuşulan nesne ve insanları belirtmede isimlerden önce kullanılır** *Can you pass the salt?* ○ *I'll pick you up at the station.* ○ *That's the new restaurant I told you about.* **2** [ONLY ONE] used before nouns when only one of something exists **sadece bir tane olan isimlerden önce** *Have you seen the Eiffel Tower?* ○ *I'd love to travel round the world.* **3** [SINGULAR NOUN] used before a singular noun to refer to all the things or people described by that noun **bir grubu niteleyen tekil bir isimde önce** *The tiger has become extinct in many countries.* **4** [ADJECTIVE] used before some adjectives to make them into nouns **bazı sıfatları isim yapmak için sıfatlardan önce getirilir** *a home for the elderly* ○ *relatives of the deceased* **5** [COMPARE] used before each of two adjectives or adverbs to show how one thing changes depending on another **ne kadar ... o kadar ...** *The longer we live here, the more we like it.* **6** [EACH] used with units or measurements to mean each or every **her, her biri anlamında ölçümlerde veya birimlerde kullanılır** *How many Belgian francs to the pound?* **7** [BODY] used when referring to a part of the body **vücudun bir uzvundan bahsederken** *He held her tightly by the arm.* **8** [TIME] used before numbers which refer to dates or periods of time **tarih ve zaman dilimini belirten rakamlardan önce** *the sixties* ○ *Thursday the 29th of April* **9** [MUSIC] used with the names of musical instruments or dances to mean the type of instrument or dance in general **belirli müzik aletleri ve dans isimlerinden önce** *Can you play the violin?*

┌──────────────────────────────────────┐
│ **theatre** ...... İLE BİRLİKTE KULLANILAN KELİMELER │
└──────────────────────────────────────┘

go to the theatre ● at the theatre ● **musical** theatre ● **street** theatre ● a theatre **company/director**

o⇥**theatre** UK (US **theater**) /ˈθɪətəʳ/ *noun* **1** [BUILDING WITH STAGE] [C] a building with a stage where people go to watch plays **tiyatro binası** *the Arts Theatre* **2** [BUILDING FOR FILMS] [C] US a building where people go to watch films **sinema binası/salonu** *a movie theater* **3** [WORK] [U] the work of writing, acting in, and producing plays **tiyatro** **4** [MEDICAL] [C, U] UK a room in a hospital where doctors do operations **ameliyathane**

theatrical /θiˈætrɪkʰl/ *adjective* **1** [always before noun] relating to the theatre **tiyatroya ilişkin/özgü** *theatrical make-up* **2** doing and saying things in a very obvious way that is intended to make people notice you **abartılı, gösterişli, yapmacık**

theft /θeft/ *noun* [C, U] the action or crime of stealing something **hırsızlık** *car theft*

o⇥**their** /ðeəʳ/ *determiner* **1** belonging to or relating to a group of people, animals, or things that have already been talked about **onların** *It was their problem, not mine.* **2** used to refer to what belongs to or relates to a person when you want to avoid saying 'his' or 'her' or when you do not know if the person is male or female

(emin olmayan durumlarda) onların *Did this person give their name?*

o⇥**theirs** /ðeəz/ *pronoun* the things that belong or relate to a group of people, animals, or things that have already been talked about **onlarınki, onların** *I think she's a relation of theirs.*

o⇥**them** *strong form* /ðem/ *weak form* /ðəm/ *pronoun* **1** used after a verb or preposition to refer to a group of people, animals, or things that have already been talked about **onları, onlara** *I'm looking for my keys - have you seen them?* **2** used after a verb or preposition to refer to a person when you want to avoid saying 'him' or 'her' or when you do not know if the person is male or female (emin olmayan durumlarda) **onları, onlara** *When each passenger arrives we ask them to fill in a form.*

┌──────────────────────────────────────┐
│ **theme** ...... İLE BİRLİKTE KULLANILAN KELİMELER │
└──────────────────────────────────────┘

a theme **runs through** sth ● the **central/main** theme ● a **recurring** theme ● the theme of sth ● **on the** theme of sth

theme /θiːm/ *noun* **1** [C] the subject of a book, film, speech, etc **tema, konu** *The theme of loss runs through most of his novels.* **2** theme **music/song/tune** the music that is played at the beginning and end of a particular television or radio programme **tanıtım müziği**

'**theme ˌpark** *noun* [C] a park with entertainments, such as games, machines to ride on, restaurants, etc, that are all based on one idea **eğlence parkı; belli bir fikir üzerine kurulu içinde eğlence mekânları, oyuncaklar, lokantalar bulunan park**

o⇥**themselves** /ðəmˈselvz/ *pronoun* **1** the reflexive form of the pronoun 'they' **kendileri, kendilerine, kendilerini** *They're both 16 - they're old enough to look after themselves.* **2** used to emphasize the pronoun 'they' or the particular group of people you are referring to **kendileri** *They've decided to run the club themselves.* **3** (**all**) **by themselves** alone or without anyone else's help **bizzat kendileri; kendi kendilerine; kendi başlarına** *The kids arranged the party all by themselves.* **4** (**all**) **to themselves** for their use only **kendileri için; sadece onların kendisi için** *They had the whole campsite to themselves.*

o⇥**then**[1] /ðen/ *adverb* **1** [TIME] at that time **o zaman, o vakit** *Call me tomorrow - I'll have time to speak then.* ○ *Tim and I were at school together, but I haven't seen him since then.* **2** [NEXT] next, or after something has happened **sonra, ondan sonra, daha sonra, ardından** *She trained as a teacher and then became a lawyer.* ○ *Let me finish my drink, then we'll go.* **3** [SO] so or because of that **böylece, böylelikle, o zaman, o takdirde** *Have a rest now, then you won't be tired this evening.* ○ *"My interview's at 9 o'clock." "You'll be catching an early train, then?"* **4** [IN ADDITION] used in order to add something to what you have just said **ayrıca, buna ilave olarak, ardından** *I've got two essays to write and then my science project to finish.* **5** **now then/right then/okay then** used to introduce a question or a suggestion **pekâla; o halde; tamam o zaman** *Right then, what do you want to drink?*

then[2] /ðen/ *adjective* [always before noun] used to refer to something which was true in the past but which is not true now **o zaman ki** *the then Prime Minister Margaret Thatcher*

thence /ðens/ *adverb formal* from there **oradan** *The oil is shipped to Panama and thence to Texan refineries.*

theology /θiˈɒlədʒi/ *noun* [U] the study of religion and religious belief **ilâhiyat; din bilimi** ● **theological** /ˌθiː əˈlɒdʒɪkʰl/ *adjective theological college* **ilahiyat ile ilgili**

theoretical /θɪə'retɪkᵊl/ *adjective* **1** based on the ideas that relate to a subject, not the practical uses of that subject **kuramsal, teorik** *theoretical physics* **2** related to an explanation that has not been proved **varsayıma dayanan, teorik**

theoretically /θɪə'retɪkᵊli/ *adverb* in a way that obeys some rules but is not likely **kuramsal olarak, teorik olarak; görünüşe bakılırsa** *It is theoretically possible.*

theorist /'θɪərɪst/ *noun* [C] someone who develops ideas about the explanation for events **kuramcı, teorist** *a political theorist*

theorize (*also UK* -ise) /'θɪəraɪz/ *verb* [I, T] to develop a set of ideas about something **kuram tasarlamak, teori öne sürmek** [+ that] *Investigators theorized that the crash was caused by engine failure.*

---

  theory ...... İLE BİRLİKTE KULLANILAN KELİMELER

challenge/formulate/prove/test a theory ● a popular/plausible/new theory ● a theory about sth

---

o→**theory** /'θɪəri/ *noun* **1** [C] an idea or set of ideas that is intended to explain something **kuram, teori** *Darwin's theory of evolution* **2** [U] the set of principles on which a subject is based **kuram, teori** *economic theory* **3** **in theory** If something is possible in theory, it should be possible but often it does not happen this way. **kuramsal olarak, teorik olarak**

therapeutic /ˌθerə'pju:tɪk/ *adjective* **1** helping to cure a disease or improve your health **iyileştirici, tedavi edici** *the therapeutic benefits of massage* **2** helping you to feel happier and more relaxed **rahatlatıcı, ferahlatıcı** *I find gardening very therapeutic.*

therapist /'θerəpɪst/ *noun* [C] someone whose job is to treat a particular type of mental or physical illness **rahatlatıcı, ferahlatıcı** *a speech therapist*

therapy /'θerəpi/ *noun* [C, U] the work of treating mental or physical illness without using an operation **tedavi, terapi** *cancer therapy* ○ *She's now in therapy to help her deal with her alcohol problem.* ➾See also: **physical therapy**

o→**there¹** *strong form* /ðeər/ *weak form* /ðər/ *pronoun* **There is/are/was, etc** used to show that something exists or happens **var, vardı, mevcut, mevcuttu vb.** *There are three pubs in the village.* ○ *There's not much room in the back of the car.* ○ *There have been a lot of accidents on this road.* ○ *Is there any milk?*

o→**there²** /ðeər/ *adverb* **1** [PLACE] in or at a particular place **orada** *We live in York because my wife works there.* ○ *I went to the party but I didn't know anyone there.* ○ *We'll never get there* (= arrive) *in time!* **2** [DIRECTION] used when you are pointing or looking at something in order to make someone look in the same direction **bak orada, orada, burada** *Put them in that box there.* ○ *Your bag's over there by the door.* **3** [AVAILABLE] present or available **var, mevcut, elde, hazır** *They were all there - Mark, Jill, and the three kids.* ○ *That money is there for you if you need it.* **4** [POINT] at a particular point in a process or activity **bir işlemin/eylemin belli bir yerinde/noktasında** *Do you want to play another game or do you want to stop there?* ○ *Keep on trying - you'll get there* (= succeed) *in the end.* **5** **there and then** If you do something there and then, you do it immediately. **hemen, anında, derhal, hemen oracıkta** *I showed James the ring I liked and he bought it there and then.* **6** **There you are/go. a** [GIVING] İşte!', 'Buyrun!', 'Buyrun alın!', 'işte, buyrun!' *Do you want a tissue? There you are.* **b** [EMPHASIZING] used to emphasize that you were right **Al işte, ben demiştim!', 'Ben dememiş miydim!', 'işte gördün mü!'** *There you go - I told you you'd win!*

thereabouts /'ðeərəbaʊts/ *adverb mainly UK* near the number, amount, or time that has just been given **oralara, oralarda, o civarda** *For this recipe you'll need 1kg of tomatoes, or thereabouts.*

thereafter /ˌðeə'rɑ:ftər/ *adverb formal* after a particular amount, time, or event **ondan sonra** *Faxes cost $1.20 for the first page, and 60 cents for each page thereafter.*

thereby /ˌðeə'baɪ/ *adverb formal* as a result of a particular action or event **böylece, bu yüzden, bu nedenle** *The new dam will improve the water supply and thereby reduce hunger and disease.*

o→**therefore** /'ðeəfɔ:r/ *adverb* for that reason **onun için, bu nedenle, bu yüzden** *The region has suffered severe flooding and tourists are therefore advised not to travel there.*

therein /ˌðeə'rɪn/ *adverb formal* **1** in a particular document or place **orada, o yerde, onun içindeki** *We recommend that you study the report and the proposals contained therein.* **2** **therein lies sth** because of the reason that has just been given **belirtilen nedenden dolayı, bu sebep yüzünden** *But the medicines are expensive, and therein lies the problem.*

thereof /ˌðeə'rɒv/ *adverb formal* relating to what has just been said **...ile ilgili; ...ile benzer şeyler; söylenenlere ilişkin** *It's gospel music, traditional country, jazz, and some strange combinations thereof.*

thermal /'θɜ:mᵊl/ *adjective* [always before noun] **1** relating to heat **ısıyla ilgili, termal** *thermal energy* **2** Thermal clothes are made to keep you warm. **sıcak tutan, ısıtan** *thermal underwear*

thermo- /'θɜ:məʊ-/ *prefix* relating to heat or temperature **sıcakla/ısıyla ilgili- anlamında önek** *a thermostat* (= a piece of equipment that controls temperature) ○ *a thermometer*

thermometer /θə'mɒmɪtər/ *noun* [C] a piece of equipment that measures the temperature of the air or of your body **termometre**

thermometer

Thermos /'θɜ:mɒs/ *noun* [C] *trademark* a container that keeps hot liquids hot or cold liquids cold **termos** *(UK) a Thermos flask/ (US) a Thermos bottle* ➾See picture at **flask.**

thermostat /'θɜ:məstæt/ *noun* [C] a piece of equipment that controls the temperature of something or of a place **termostat; ısıyı kontrol eden cihaz**

thesaurus /θɪ'sɔ:rəs/ *noun* [C] a book in which words with similar meanings are put together in groups **eşanlamlı kelimeler sözlüğü**

o→**these** /ði:z/ *pronoun, determiner plural of* this **bunlar** ➾See Common learner error at **this.**

YAYGIN HATALAR

these or this?

Bir çok Türk öğrenci **these** kullanımında hata yapmaktadır. Unutmayın! **These**-**this** söyleminin çoğul halidir. Bir şeye gönderme yapmak isityorsanız, **this** kullanmanız gerekir: ~~These hotel is very popular with tourists.~~

Yanlış cümle örneği

This hotel is very popular with tourists.

---

thesis /'θi:sɪs/ *noun* [C] *plural* **theses** /'θi:si:z/ **1** a long piece of writing that you do as part of an advanced university course **tez** *a master's/PhD thesis* **2** *formal* a theory that is suggested and can then be argued with or agreed with **tez, sav, iddia** *That is the central thesis of the book.*

o⌐**they** /ðeɪ/ *pronoun* **1** GROUP used as the subject of the verb when referring to a group of people, animals, or things that have already been talked about **onlar** *I saw Kate and Nigel yesterday - they came over for dinner.* ○ *"Have you seen my car keys?" "They're on the kitchen table."* **2** PERSON used to refer to a person when you want to avoid saying 'he' or 'she' or when you do not know if the person is male or female **Someone I met at a party said they knew you.** **3** PEOPLE people in general **insanlar, onlar; kişiler** *They say that breaking a mirror brings you seven years' bad luck.*

o⌐**they'd** /ðeɪd/ *short for* they had **They had' fiil yapısının kısa hâli** *They'd just moved in when I saw them.* **2** *short for* they would **They would' fiil yapısının kısa hâli** *They'd like to take us out to dinner.*

o⌐**they'll** /ðeɪl/ *short for* they will **They will' fiil yapısının kısa hâli** *They'll be in Scotland next week.*

o⌐**they're** /ðeəʳ/ *short for* they are **They are' fiil yapısının kısa hâli** *They're both from Washington.*

they've /ðeɪv/ *short for* they have **They have' fiil yapısının kısa hâli** *They've got three children - two girls and a boy.*

o⌐**thick¹** /θɪk/ *adjective* **1** DISTANCE Something that is thick is larger than usual between its opposite sides. **kalın** *a thick slice of meat* ○ *a thick layer of snow* **2 10cm/2m, etc thick** being 10cm/2m, etc thick **10cm/2m vs. Kalınlıkta** *a piece of wood 2cm thick* **3** LARGE AMOUNT growing very close together and in large amounts **sık, gür, kesif, yoğun** *thick, dark hair* **4** SMOKE Thick smoke, cloud, or fog is difficult to see through. **koyu, kalın, yoğun** *Thick, black smoke was pouring out of the chimney.* **5** LIQUID A thick substance or liquid has very little water in it and does not flow easily. **koyu, kalın, peltemsi** *Stir the sauce over a low heat until thick.* **6** STUPID *informal* not intelligent **pek akıllı omayan, anlam güçlüğü çeken** **7 be thick with sth** If something is thick with a particular substance, it is covered in or full of that substance. **...ile dolu/kaplı** *The air was thick with petrol fumes.* **8 thick and fast** quickly and in large numbers **süratle ve çok sayıda, birbiri ardı sıra** *Calls were coming in thick and fast by the end of the programme.* ➔See also: have (a) thick **skin¹**.

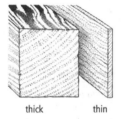

thick

thick   **thin**

thick² /θɪk/ *noun* **1 be in the thick of sth** to be involved in a situation at the point where there is most activity **...ın/in tam ortasında; ...en civcivli yerinde; tam ortasında** *He loves being in the thick of the action.* **2 through thick and thin** If you support or stay with someone through thick and thin, you always support or stay with them in easy and difficult situations. **iyi günde kötü günde; her güçlüğü göğüsleyerek; sadakatle** *She'd stuck by (= stayed with) Neil through thick and thin.*

thicken /ˈθɪkᵊn/ *verb* [I, T] to become thicker, or to make something thicker **koyulaş(tır)mak; kalınlaş(tır)mak; yoğunlaş(tır)mak** *Boil the sauce until it thickens.*

thickly /ˈθɪkli/ *adverb* in thick pieces, or in a thick layer **kalın bir şekilde; kalın tabakalar/dilimler şeklinde** *toast thickly spread with butter*

thickness /ˈθɪknəs/ *noun* [C, U] the distance between the opposite sides of something **kalınlık, sıklık, koyuluk, yoğunluk**

thick-skinned /ˌθɪkˈskɪnd/ *adjective* If someone is thick-skinned, they do not get upset when other people criticize them. **vurdumduymaz, aldırmaz, pişkin, kalın derili**

thief /θiːf/ *noun* [C] *plural* **thieves** /θiːvz/ someone who steals things **hırsız** *a car thief* ○ *Thieves stole $500,000 worth of computer equipment.*

thigh /θaɪ/ *noun* [C] the top part of your leg above your knee **uyluk, but** ➔Orta kısımdaki renkli sayfalarına bakınız.

thimble /ˈθɪmbl/ *noun* [C] a small metal or plastic object that you use to protect your finger when you are sewing **yüksük**

o⌐**thin¹** /θɪn/ *adjective* **thinner, thinnest** **1** DISTANCE Something that is thin is smaller than usual between its opposite sides. **ince** *a thin slice of ham* ○ *The walls are very thin.* ➔See picture at **thick**. **2** PERSON A thin person or animal has very little fat on their body. **ince, zayıf** **3** LIQUID A thin substance or liquid has a lot of water in it and flows easily. **sıvı sulu, koyu değil** *thin soup* **4** AMOUNT having only a small number of people or a small amount of something **seyrek, kalabalık değil** *His hair is going thin on top.* **5** AIR Thin air does not have enough oxygen in it. **hafif, az oksijenli** **6 wear thin a** ANNOYED If your patience wears thin, you become less and less patient with someone who is annoying you. **sabrı tükenmek, dayanamamak; sabrı taşmak** **b** REPEATED If a joke or explanation wears thin, it becomes less effective because it has been used too much. **ilginçliğini yitirmek, eskimek** ➔See also: disappear/vanish into thin **air¹**, be thin on the **ground¹**, through **thick²** and thin.

thin² /θɪn/ *verb* [T] **thinning**, *past* **thinned** to make a substance less thick, often by adding a liquid to it **incel(t) mek, seyrel(t)mek**

thin out *phrasal verb* If a large number of people or things thins out, they become fewer in number. **azalmak, küçülmek, incelmek, seyrelmek**

o⌐**thing** /θɪŋ/ *noun* **1** OBJECT [C] used to refer to an object without saying its name **şey, nesne** *How do I switch this thing off?* ○ *I need to get a few things in town.* **2** PERSON [C] used to refer to a person or animal when you are expressing your feelings towards them **şey (insan, hayvan)** *You silly thing, you poor thing.* **3** IDEA [C] used to refer to an idea, event, or activity **şey, şeyi (fikir, olay, faaliyet)** *I can't believe Nick would say such a thing!* ○ *Meeting Nina was the best thing that's ever happened to me.* **4 for one thing** used to give a reason for something **bir kere, her şeyden önce, en azından** *You can't give Amy that shirt - for one thing it's too small for her.* **5 the thing** *informal* used to introduce a problem which relates to something that you have just said **esas olan şey şudur ki...; ancak, gerçek şu ki ...; mesele şu ki** *I'd love to go out tonight, but the thing is, I've got to finish my report.* **6 a thing** used instead of 'anything' in order to emphasize what you are saying **hiç bir şey** *I haven't got a thing to wear!* **7 have a thing about sth/sb** *informal* to like or dislike something or someone very much **birini/bir şeyi çok sevmek/nefret etmek** *He's got a thing about blonde women.* **8 it's a good thing** *informal* If it is a good thing that something happened, it is lucky that it happened. **iyi bir şey; ne şans ki, iyiki de; ne şey ki** *It's a good thing that Jo was there to help you.* **9 first/last thing** *informal* at the beginning/end of the day **ilk ve son şey olarak** *I'll phone him first thing and tell him I can't come.* ○ *She likes a glass of milk last thing at night.* **10 be sb's thing** *informal* If an activity or subject is someone's thing,

T

they are very interested in it and like doing it. **birinin asıl işi/uğraşı olmak; çok sevdiği şey olmak** *Jogging's just not my thing - I prefer team sports.* **11 the best/greatest thing since sliced bread** *humorous* extremely good **fevkalâde iyi, çok mükemmel, harikulade; olabilecek en iyi şey olmak** *When I first got this computer I thought it was the best thing since sliced bread.*

things /θɪŋz/ *noun* [plural] **1** what is happening in your life **yaşam, durumlar, işler, gidişat, keyifler** *Don't worry - things will get better soon.* **2** the objects that you own **kişisel eşyalar, giysiler; sahip olduklar vs.** *I'll just gather my things and then I'll be ready.* **3 be hearing/seeing things** to imagine that you can hear or see things that do not exist **hayali şeyler görüyor duyuyor olmak; hayal etmek**

thingy /ˈθɪŋi/ *noun* [C] *UK informal* used to refer to something or someone when you cannot remember their name **gibi/benzeri şey/şeyi; ...imsi/ımsı şey** *We ate that beef thingy for lunch.*

⊶**think**[1] /θɪŋk/ *verb past* **thought 1** OPINION [I, T] to have an opinion about something or someone **sanmak, farzetmek, düşünmek** *Do you think it's going to rain?* ○ [+ (that)] *I don't think that Emma will get the job* (= I believe she will not get it). ○ *What did you think of the film?* ○ *What do you think about modern art?* **2** CONSIDER [I] to consider an idea or a problem **düşünmek, akla vurmak** *He thought for a few seconds before answering.* ○ *You should think about where you want to live.* **3** EXPECT [I, T] to believe that something is true, or to expect that something will happen, although you are not sure **sanmak, farzetmek, inanmak** *I think she's called Joanna.* ○ *"Does this train stop at Oxford?" "Yes, I think so."* ○ [+ (that)] *I never thought that I would see Steven again.* **4 think about/of doing sth** to consider doing something **hakında/yapmayı düşünmek** *I'm thinking of moving to Sydney. We thought about getting married, but decided not to.* **5 think about/of sb/sth** to use your mind to imagine a situation **düşünmek, hatırlamak, anımsamak, akla getirmek; düşünüp taşınmak; planlamak, niyeti olmak** *I'm sorry I can't be at the wedding, but I'll be thinking of you.* **6 think of sth** to use your imagination and intelligence to produce an idea, a solution to a problem, or an answer to a question **bir fikir/çözüm/cevap düşünmek; akıl etmek, aklına gelmek** *When did you first think of the idea?* **7 think a lot of sb/sth** to admire someone, or to believe that something is good quality **hayran olmak; çok düşünmek, iyi olduğuna inanmak** *Simon thinks a lot of you, you know.* **8 not think much of sb/sth** to not like someone, or to believe that something is not good quality **fazla düşünmemek, üzerinde durmamak; pek önemsememek; olumsuz düşünmek** *I don't think much of the food here.* **9 I think** used to introduce a suggestion or explanation in order to be polite **Sanırım...', 'Kanımca...', Sanıyorum...', Zannedersem...'** [+ (that)] *It's getting late - I think that we should go.* **10 Who would have thought...?** used to express how surprising something is **Kim bilebilirdi ki?', 'Kim akıl edebilirdi ki?' 'Kim düşünebilirdi ki?'** [+ (that)] *Who would have thought that buying a house could take so long?* ⊃See also: think the **world**[1] of sb. **11 think outside the box** to use new ideas instead of traditional ideas when you think about something **alışılmışın dışında düşünmek; eski fikirlere itibar etmemek; yeni şeyler düşünmek**

think back *phrasal verb* to remember something that happened in the past **hatırlamaya çalışmak** *I thought back to the time when I was living in Toronto.*

think sth out *phrasal verb* to consider all the possible details of something **tasarlamak, planlamak; her**

ayrıntıyı dikkate almak; enine boyuna düşünmek *The scheme was well thought out.*

think sth over *phrasal verb* to consider an idea or plan carefully before making a decision **iyice düşünüp taşınmak; dikkatle gözden geçirmek**

think sth through *phrasal verb* to carefully consider the possible results of doing something **en ince ayrıntısına kadar düşünmek; enine boyuna düşünmek**

think sth up *phrasal verb* to produce a new idea or plan **bulmak, keşfetmek; düşünüp bulmak** *I don't want to go tonight and I'm trying to think up an excuse.*

think[2] /θɪŋk/ *noun UK* **have a think** to consider something carefully **dikkatle düşünmek; itinayla değerlendirmek** *Have a think about it and then tell me what you've decided.*

thinker /ˈθɪŋkər/ *noun* [C] someone who considers important subjects or produces new ideas **düşünür, filozof** *a political/religious thinker*

thinking /ˈθɪŋkɪŋ/ *noun* [U] **1** when you use your mind to consider something **düşünce, fikir, düşünme** *This problem requires careful thinking.* **2** someone's ideas or opinions **düşünce, fikir** *The book discusses the impact of Christian thinking on western society.* ⊃See also: wishful thinking.

ˈthink ˌtank *noun* [C] a group of people who advise the government or an organization about particular subjects and who suggest new ideas **düşünce kulübü; âkıl insanlar grubu**

thinly /ˈθɪnli/ *adverb* **1** in thin pieces, or in a thin layer **ince parçalar hâlinde; ince tabakalar biçiminde** *She sliced the bread thinly.* **2** with only a small number of people or things **küçük bir grup insanla/şeylerle** *thinly populated areas*

third[1] /θɜːd/ 3rd written as a word **üçüncü**

⊶**third**[2] /θɜːd/ *noun* [C] **1** one of three equal parts of something; 1/3 **üçte bir 2 a third** in the UK, one of the lowest exam results you can achieve at the end of a university course **(ing.) anılabilecek en düşük notlardan biri**

thirdly /ˈθɜːdli/ *adverb* used in order to introduce the third thing in a list **üçüncü olarak**

ˌthird ˈparty *noun* [C] someone who is not one of the two main people or groups that are involved in a situation **üçüncü kişi**

the ˌthird ˈperson *noun* the form of a verb or pronoun that is used when referring to the person or thing being spoken about or described. For example 'she' and 'they' are third person pronouns. **(dilbilgisi) üçüncü şahıs**

the ˌThird ˈWorld *noun* the countries in Africa, Asia, and South America, which do not have well-developed economies **Üçüncü Dünya Ülkeleri (Afrika, Asya ve Güney Amerika**

thirst /θɜːst/ *noun* **1** [U, no plural] the feeling that you want to drink something **susuzluk, susama, susamışlık** *I had a long, cold drink to quench my thirst* (= stop me feeling thirsty). **2 a thirst for sth** a strong wish for something **bir şeye susamışlık, şiddetli istek, tutku** *a thirst for adventure*

⊶**thirsty** /ˈθɜːsti/ *adjective* wanting or needing a drink **susamış** *I felt really hot and thirsty after my run.* ● **thirstily** *adverb* **susamış bir biçimde**

⊶**thirteen** /θɜːˈtiːn/ the number 13 **onüç** ● **thirteenth** 13th written as a word **onüçüncü**

⊶**thirty** /ˈθɜːti/ **1** the number 30 **otuz 2 the thirties** the years from 1930 to 1939 **otuzlu yıllar 3 be in your thir-**

ties to be between the ages of 30 and 39 **otuzlu yaşlarda olmak • thirtieth** 30th written as a word **otuzuncu**

⚬**this¹** /ðɪs/ *determiner plural* **these 1** ALREADY TALKED ABOUT used to refer to something that you have already talked about **bu** *Most people don't agree with this decision.* ○ *How did you hear about this course?* **2** NEAR used to refer to something or someone that is near you or that you are pointing to **bu (yakınında, işaret edilen)** *How much does this CD cost?* ○ *David gave me these earrings for my birthday.* **3** TIME used to refer to the present week, month, year, etc or the one that comes next **bu (hafta, ay, yıl vb.)** *I'll see you this evening.* ○ *Kate and Nigel are getting married this June.* **4** NOW TALKING ABOUT *informal* used to refer to a particular person or thing that you are going to talk about **bu (belli bir şey/kişi)** *We went to this really great club last night.* ⊃See also: be out of this **world¹**.

this or these?

Birçok Türk öğrenci **this** kullanımında hata yapmaktadır. Unutmayın! **This** tekil isimlerle kullanılır. Birşeyden fazlasına gönderme yapmak istiyorsanız **these** kullanmanız gerekir: ~~After all this problems, I was glad to get home.~~ Yanlış cümle örneği

After all these problems, I was glad to get home.

⚬**this²** /ðɪs/ *pronoun plural* **these 1** ALREADY TALKED ABOUT used to refer to something that you have already talked about **bu (bahsedilen şey)** *When did this happen?* ○ *This is the best news I've heard all week!* **2** NEAR used to refer to something or someone that is near you or that you are pointing to **bu (yakınında, işaret edilen)** *Try some of this - it's delicious.* ○ *Are these your keys?* ○ *This is my girlfriend, Beth.* **3** SAY/ASK WHO used to say or ask who someone is when speaking on the telephone, radio, etc **bu, kim, şu (telefon/radyoda vb. konuşan kişi)** *"Hello, is this Julie Hawkins?" "Yes, who's this?"* **4 this and that** different things which are not very important **şunu bunu, şundan bundan; önemsiz şeyler** *"What are you doing today?" "Oh, just this and that."*

⚬**this³** /ðɪs/ *adverb* used when describing the size, amount, or state of something or someone **bu kadar, şu kadar (ebat, miktar, durum vs. ifade etmede)** *I need a piece of wood this big.* ○ *I've never seen her this angry.*

thistle /ˈθɪsl/ *noun* [C] a wild plant with purple flowers and sharp points **deve dikeni**

THNQ *informal written abbeviation for* thank you: used in emails and text messages **teşekkür ederim/teşekkürler (tşk) anlamında kısa ve e-posta iletilerinde kullanılan kısaltma**

thong /θɒŋ/ *noun* [C] **1** a piece of underwear or the bottom part of a bikini (= two parts of clothing with two parts that women wear for swimming) which does not cover the bottom **bikini altı 2** *US* a flip flop **terlik/ayakkabı, parmak arası terlik/ayakkabı**

thorn /θɔːn/ *noun* [C] a small, sharp point on the stem of a plant **diken**

thorny /ˈθɔːni/ *adjective* **1** covered in thorns **dikenli 2** A thorny problem, question, subject, etc is difficult to deal with. **zor, güç, çetin, belâlı**

thorough /ˈθʌrə/ ⓤ /ˈθɜːrəʊ/ *adjective* careful and covering every detail **dikkatli ve her ayrıntıyı kapsayan** *The government has promised a thorough investigation of the matter.* • **thoroughness** *noun* [U] **çok detaylı olma durumu**

thoroughbred /ˈθʌrəbred/ *noun* [C] a horse especially bred for racing **damızlık at**

thoroughly /ˈθʌrəli/ *adverb* **1** very carefully **tamamen, adamakıllı, çok dikkatlice** *Wash the spinach thoroughly before cooking.* **2** very, or very much **tam anlamıyla, bütün, büsbütün** *We thoroughly enjoyed ourselves.*

⚬**those** /ðəʊz/ *pronoun, determiner plural of* that **şunlar** ⊃See Common learner error at **this.**

⚬**though¹** /ðəʊ/ *conjunction* **1** used to introduce a fact or opinion that makes the other part of the sentence seem surprising **...dığı/diği halde; ...sa/se de; her ne kadar** *And though she's quite small, she's very strong.* ○ *Nina didn't phone, even though she said she would.* **2** but **ama, bununla beraber** *They're coming next week, though I don't know when.* ○ *The restaurant serves good, though extremely expensive, food.*

though² /ðəʊ/ *adverb* used to add a new fact or opinion which changes what you have just said **ancak, mamafih** *Okay, I'll come to the party - I'm not staying late though.*

give sth **some thought • have** a **thought • a secret/ sobering/terrible thought**

⚬**thought¹** /θɔːt/ *noun* **1** IDEA [C] an idea or opinion **düşünce, fikir** *Do you have any thoughts about/on where you want to spend Christmas?* ○ [+ of + doing sth] *The thought of seeing her again filled him with happiness.* ○ *informal "Why don't we invite Ben?" " That's a thought* (= That's a good idea.)*."* **2** THINKING [U] the activity of thinking, or when you think about something carefully **düşünme** *She sat staring at the picture, deep in thought.* ○ *You'll need to give the matter some thought.* **3** CARE [no plural] when you do something that shows you care about someone **incelik, düşünceli davranış, düşünce, davranış, jest** *Thanks for the card - it was a really kind thought.* **4** SET OF IDEAS [U] a set of ideas about a particular subject **düşünceler, fikirler** *The book examines his influence on recent political thought.* **5 spare a thought for sb** to think about someone who is in a bad situation **zor durumda olanları düşünmek; bir nebze düşünmek** *Spare a thought for all the people who have lost their homes.* ⊃See also: **school** of thought, **second thought.**

thought² /θɔːt/ *past of* think **düşünmek' fiilinin geçmiş zaman hâli**

thoughtful /ˈθɔːtfᵊl/ *adjective* **1** quiet because you are thinking about something **düşünceli, düşünceye dalmış** *You look thoughtful.* **2** kind and always thinking about how you can help other people **düşünceli, anlayışlı, nazik, saygılı** *Thank you for the card - it was very thoughtful of you.* • **thoughtfully** *adverb* *She gazed thoughtfully into the distance.* **düşüncelere dalmış bir şekilde • thoughtfulness** *noun* [U] **düşünceli olma durumu**

thoughtless /ˈθɔːtləs/ *adjective* not considering how your actions and words might upset someone else **incelikten yoksun, bencil, düşüncesiz, kaba, saygısız** *I should have called her to say we'd be late - it was a bit thoughtless of me.* • **thoughtlessly** *adverb* **düşüncesizce**

thought-provoking /ˈθɔːtprəˌvəʊkɪŋ/ *adjective* making you think a lot about a subject **düşünmeye sevkeden; düşündüren** *a thought-provoking book/film*

⚬**thousand** /ˈθaʊzᵊnd/ **1** the number 1000 **bin 2 thousands** *informal* a lot **binlerce** *She tried on thousands of dresses but didn't like any of them.*

thousandth¹ /ˈθaʊzᵊndθ/ 1000th written as a word **bininci**

thousandth² /ˈθaʊzᵊndθ/ *noun* [C] one of a thousand equal parts of something; ¹/₁₀₀₀; **.001 binde bir** *a thousandth of a second*

thrash /θræʃ/ *verb* **1** [HIT] [T] to hit a person or animal several times as a punishment **dövmek, dayak atmak, döverek cezalandırmak 2** [MOVE] [I] to move from side to side in a violent way **çırpınmak, kıvranmak, debelenmek** *He was screaming in pain and thrashing around on the floor.* **3** [DEFEAT] [T] *informal* to win against someone very easily **ağır yenilgiye uğratmak**

thrash sth out *phrasal verb* to discuss a plan or problem in detail until you reach an agreement or find a solution **enine boyuna tartışıp karara bağlamak**

thrashing /ˈθræʃɪŋ/ *noun* [C] **1** *informal* when you win against someone very easily **galibiyet, kazanma, yenme; bozguna uğratma 2** *old-fashioned* when someone hits a person or animal several times as a punishment **dayak, cezalandırma**

thread¹ /θred/ *noun* **1** [C, U] a long, thin piece of cotton, wool, etc that is used for sewing **iplik** *a needle and thread* **2** [C] the connection between different events or different parts of a story or discussion **rabıta, mecra, bağlantı** *By that point I'd lost the thread of the conversation.* **3** a group of pieces of writing on the Internet in which people discuss one subject

thread² /θred/ *verb* [T] **1 thread a needle** to push thread through the hole in a needle **iğneye iplik geçirmek 2 thread your way through/between, etc** to move carefully through a crowded place, changing direction in order to avoid people or things **kendine yol açıp ilerlemek; zorlukla yol bulup ilerlemek; yararak/yol açıp geçmek**

threadbare /ˈθredbeəʳ/ *adjective* Threadbare material or clothes are very thin because they have been used too much. **çok eskimiş, elek gibi, çok yıpranmış** *a threadbare carpet*

threat ...... İLE BİRLİKTE KULLANILAN KELİMELER

a threat to sb/sth • pose a threat • a potential threat • a growing/serious threat • a security/terrorist threat

o⁻**threat** /θret/ *noun* **1** [HARM] [C] when someone says they will kill or hurt you, or cause problems for you if you do not do what they want **tehdit, gözdağı** *a death threat* ○ *I was scared he would carry out his threat* (= do what he said he would do). **2** [DAMAGE] [C] someone or something that is likely to cause harm or damage **tehlike, thlike kaynağı, tehdit** [usually singular] *a threat to the environment* ○ *Smoking poses* (= is) *a serious threat to your health.* **3** [POSSIBILITY] [no plural] the possibility that something bad will happen **tehlike, tehdit, risk** *the threat of invasion*

o⁻**threaten** /ˈθretᵊn/ *verb* **1** [HARM] [T] to tell someone that you will kill or hurt them, or cause problems for them if they do not do what you want **korkutmak, gözdağı vermek, tehdit etmek** *He threatened the staff with a gun and demanded money.* ○ **[+ to do sth]** *He threatened to report her to the police.* **2** [DAMAGE] [T] to be likely to cause harm or damage to something or someone **tehlikeye sokmak, tehdit etmek, tehdit unsuru oluşturmak** *His knee problem is threatening his cycling career.* **3** [HAPPEN] [I] If something bad threatens to happen, it is likely to happen. **tehlikeli olmak; tehdit oluşturmak, tehditi altında kalmak** **[+ to do sth]** *The conflict threatened to spread to neighbouring countries.* • **threatening** *adjective* **threatening behaviour** **tehditkar** • **threateningly** *adverb* **tehdit edercesine**

o⁻**three** /θriː/ the number 3 **üç, üç rakamı**

three-dimensional /ˌθriːdɪˈmenʃᵊnᵊl/ (*also* 3-D /θriːˈdiː/) *adjective* having length, depth, and height **üç boyutlu** *three-dimensional computer graphics*

threshold /ˈθreʃhəʊld/ *noun* **1** [C] the level at which something starts to happen **eşik, giriş, ilk basamak** *He had a low boredom threshold.* **2 on the threshold of sth** at the start of a new and important time or development **...ın/in başlangıcında/eşiğinde** *We're on the threshold of a new era in European relations.* **3** [C] the floor of an entrance **eşik, giriş, kapı önü**

threw /θruː/ *past tense of* throw **'fırlatmak' fiilinin geçmiş zaman hali**

thrift /θrɪft/ *noun* [U] careful use of money so that you do not spend too much **tasarruf, tutum, idare, ekonomi** • **thrifty** *adjective* **tutumlu**

'thrift ˌshop US (UK charity shop) *noun* [C] a shop which sells goods given by the public, especially clothes, to make money for a particular charity **toplanan eşyaları yardım amaçlı satan dükkan**

thrill ...... İLE BİRLİKTE KULLANILAN KELİMELER

feel a thrill • get a thrill from/out of doing sth • a big/great thrill • the thrill of (doing) sth • a thrill seeker

thrill¹ /θrɪl/ *noun* [C] a strong feeling of excitement and pleasure **büyük heyecan/zevk/korku** *It was a big thrill meeting the stars of the show.* ○ **[+ of + doing sth]** *the thrill of winning a competition*

thrill² /θrɪl/ *verb* [T] to make someone feel excited and happy **heyecanlandırmak, büyük zevk vermek** *Ballesteros thrilled the golf world with his performance.*

thrilled /θrɪld/ *adjective* very excited and pleased **çok zevk almış, büyük heyecan duymuş** *She was thrilled with your present.*

thriller /ˈθrɪləʳ/ *noun* [C] a book or film with an exciting story, often about crime **heyecan ve macera dolu film/kitap**

thrilling /ˈθrɪlɪŋ/ *adjective* very exciting **çok heyecanlı ve zevkli** *a thrilling game*

thrive /θraɪv/ *verb* [I] to grow very well, or to become very healthy or successful **gelişmek, serpilmek, başarılı ve mutlu olmak** *The business is thriving.* ○ *He seems to thrive on hard work.* • **thriving** *adjective* a thriving economy **başarmış, zenginleşmiş**

throat /θrəʊt/ *noun* [C] **1** the back part of your mouth and the passages inside your neck **boğaz** *a sore throat* **2** the front of your neck **gırtlak, boğaz** *He grabbed her round the throat.* **3** **clear your throat** to cough once so that you can speak more clearly **boğazını temizlemek**

throb /θrɒb/ *verb* [I] **throbbing**, *past* **throbbed 1** If a part of your body throbs, you feel pain in it in a series of regular beats. **zonklamak, hızlı hızlı çarpmak, küt küt atmak** *My head was throbbing.* **2** to make a strong, regular sound or movement **düzenli aralıklarla çarpmak/vurmak** *The whole house throbbed with the music.* • **throb** *noun* [C] *the throb of the engine* **zonklama, çok ağrıma**

throes /θrəʊz/ *noun* **in the throes of sth** in a difficult or unpleasant situation **...ile boğuşan/uğraşan; zor ve nahoş durumda olan** *a country in the throes of war*

throne /θrəʊn/ *noun* **1** [C] the special chair that a king or queen sits on **taht 2 the throne** the position of being king or queen **taht, saltanat** *He came to the throne in 1936.*

throng¹ /θrɒŋ/ *noun* [C] *literary* a large group of people **büyük kalabalık, insan seli**

throng² /θrɒŋ/ verb [I, T] to be or go somewhere in very large numbers **akın akın gitmek, üşüşmek, dolmak** *drunken people thronging the streets* ○ *The street was thronged with shoppers and tourists.*

throttle¹ /'θrɒtl/ verb [T] to press someone's throat tightly so they cannot breathe **boğmak, gırtlaklamak, gırtlağına çökmek**

throttle² /'θrɒtl/ noun [C] the part of a vehicle that controls how much fuel or power goes to the engine **gaz pedalı, yakıt valfı, kelebek**

○▪**through¹** /θruː/ preposition 1 ONE SIDE TO ANOTHER from one end or side of something to the other ...ın/in içinden; ...dan/den geçerek *The River Seine flows through Paris.* ○ *The sun was shining through the window.* ○ *She cut through the wire.* 2 START TO END from the start to the end of something **boyunca; başından sonuna dek; süresince** *He worked through the night.* ○ *The phone rang halfway through the programme.* 3 BECAUSE OF because of someone or something, or with someone's help ...ın/in sonucu olarak; ...nedeniyle/yüzünden; **sayesinde** *I got the job through my mum's friend.* ○ *He became ill through eating undercooked meat.* 4 UNTIL US (UK **to**) from a particular time until and including another time ...dan/den ... a/e kadar *The store is open Monday through Friday.*

○▪**through²** /θruː/ adverb 1 from one end or side to another **arasından, içinden; ortasından, bir yandan öbür yana** *He opened the door and walked through.* 2 read/think/talk, etc sth through to read/think/talk, etc very carefully to someone about something from the start to the end **başından sonuna kadar dikkatli bir şekilde okumak/düşünmek/konuşmak** *I've thought it through and decided not to take the job.* 3 connected to someone by telephone (telefon) **bağlanma, ile ulaşarak; bağlantı yoluyla** *I tried to phone David but I couldn't **get through**.* ○ *Can you put me **through** to the manager, please?*

through³ /θruː/ adjective 1 be through with sth *informal* to have finished using something or doing something **işi bitmek, işi bitirmek** *Let me know when you're through with the iron.* 2 be through (with sb) *informal* to not have a relationship with someone any more (**artık onunla**) **işi olmamak, ilişkisini kesmek; konuşmamak** 3 [always before noun] UK A through train goes all the way from one place to another place without the passenger having to change trains. **direk, aktarmasız**

○▪**throughout** /θruː'aʊt/ adverb, preposition 1 in every part of a place **her tarafı, her tarafında** *The same laws apply throughout much of Europe.* ○ *The house was painted pink throughout.* 2 during the whole of a period of time **süresince, boyunca** *He yawned throughout the performance.*

○▪**throw¹** /θrəʊ/ verb [T] past tense **threw**, past participle **thrown** 1 THROUGH THE AIR to make something move through the air by pushing it out of your hand **atmak, fırlatmak** *Amy threw the ball to the dog.* ○ *He threw the book at the wall.* ○ [+ two objects] *Throw me a chocolate.*

○ *How far can you throw?* 2 throw sth in/on, etc to put something somewhere quickly and without thinking about it **atmak, fırlatmak, bırakmak, koymak** *He threw his clothes on the floor and got into bed.* 3 throw sth around/down/on, etc to suddenly and quickly move your body or a part of your body **vücudunu veya bir parçasını aniden ve hızla hareket ettirmek** *She threw her arms around the child.* ○ *Gabriela threw herself onto the bed and started to cry.* 4 throw sb from/forward, etc to make someone move somewhere suddenly or fall down **itmek, kakmak, düşürmek; aniden fırlatmak/sarsmak** [often passive] *The bus suddenly stopped and we were thrown forward.* 5 CONFUSE to make someone feel shocked or confused **afallatmak, neye uğradığına şaşırtmak, sersemletmek; kafasını karıştırmak** *It threw me completely when he asked me to marry him.* 6 LIGHT make light or shadows (= dark shapes) appear on something **ışık/gölge yapmak; gölge/ışık oluşturmak/vermek/yansıtmak** *The trees threw shadows across the road.* ⊃See also: throw **caution¹** to the wind, throw sb in at the deep **end¹**, throw down the **gauntlet**, throw in the **towel**, throw your **weight** around.

throw sth away *phrasal verb* 1 to get rid of something that you do not want any more **atmak, atıp kurtulmak, çöpe atmak** *He read the magazine and then threw it away.* ⊃Orta kısımdaki renkli sayfalarına bakınız. 2 to waste a skill or opportunity **ziyan etmek, heba etmek; çarçur etmek; boşa harcamak** *You've spent three years studying - don't throw it all away.*

throw sth in *phrasal verb* to add something extra when you sell something and not increase the price **fazladan/cabadan/eşantiyon olarak vermek; ekstradan vermek** *They're selling computers with a free printer thrown in.*

throw sth out *phrasal verb* to get rid of something that you do not want any more **atmak, atıp kurtulmak, çöpe atmak** *I must throw some of my old clothes out.*

throw sb out *phrasal verb* to force someone to leave **atmak, kapı dışarı etmek** *He was thrown out of school for taking drugs.*

throw (sth) up *phrasal verb informal* to vomit **kusmak, çıkarmak**

throw sth up *phrasal verb* to produce new problems or ideas **ortaya koymak, çıkarmak, üretmek** *The meeting threw up some interesting ideas.*

throw² /θrəʊ/ noun [C] when you throw something **atma, atış** *a throw of the dice*

throwback /'θrəʊbæk/ noun [C] something that is like something of the same type in the past **andırma; ...gibi olma** *Her style of playing is **a throwback** to the early days of jazz.*

thru /θruː/ adjective, adverb, preposition mainly US informal another spelling of through, used in signs and advertisements **thru' sözcüğünün işaretlerde ve reklamlarda kullanılan kısa hâli**

thrust¹ /θrʌst/ verb past **thrust thrust sth behind/into/through, etc** to push something somewhere suddenly and with force **itmek, sokmak, sürmek** *She thrust a letter into my hand and told me to read it.*

thrust sth on/upon sb *phrasal verb* to force someone to accept or deal with something **zorlamak, zorla ilgilenmesini/kabul etmesini sağlamak** [often passive] *Fatherhood had been thrust on him.*

thrust² /θrʌst/ noun 1 [C, U] a strong push or the power used to push something forward **itiş, itme, sokma, dürtme, hamle, darbe** 2 the thrust of sth the main part or ideas of what someone says or does **ana, esas, öz, asıl amaç** *The main thrust of our work involves helping victims of crime.*

throw

T

thud /θʌd/ *noun* [C] the sound that is made when something heavy falls or hits something else **pat, güm, tak' sesi** *There was a thud as he fell on the floor.* ● **thud** *verb* [I] **thudding,** *past* **thudded** güm diye ses çıkarmak

thug /θʌg/ *noun* [C] an unpleasant person who behaves violently **haydut, eşkiya**

thumb¹ /θʌm/ *noun* [C] **1** the short, thick finger on the side of your hand that can touch the top of all your other fingers **baş parmak** ⊃Orta kısımdaki renkli sayfalarına bakınız. **2 have a green thumb** US (UK **have green fingers**) to be good at gardening and making plants grow well **bitki ve bahçe işlerinde iyi/becerikli olmak; bahçıvanlıkta başarılı olmak ● 3 be under sb's thumb** If you are under someone's thumb, they control you completely. **tamamen birinin kontrolünde olmak; emri/boyunduruğu altında olmak ● 4 stick/stand out like a sore thumb** to be very different from all the other people or things around them **farklı olmak; farkedilir olmak** *I was the only one in uniform and I stuck out like a sore thumb.* ⊃See also: a **rule¹** of thumb.

thumb² /θʌm/ *verb* ⊃See thumb your **nose¹** at sth/sb.
thumb through sth *phrasal verb* to quickly turn the pages of a book or magazine **karıştırmak, sayfaları hızlıca çevirmek**

thumbtack /'θʌmtæk/ *US* (UK **drawing pin**) *noun* [C] a pin with a wide, flat top, used for fastening pieces of paper to a wall **raptiye**

thump /θʌmp/ *verb* **1** [HIT] [T] *UK* to hit someone with your fist (= closed hand) **yumruklamak, yumruk vurmak 2** [NOISE] [I, T] to hit something and make a noise **vurmak ve 'güm' diye ses çıkarmak** *She thumped the tambourine.* **3** [HEART] [I] If your heart thumps, it beats very quickly because you are excited or frightened. **korkudan/heyecandan kalbi güm güm atmak/hızla çarpmak ● thump** *noun* [C] **vurma**

a clap/crack/crash/roll/rumble of thunder ● thunder rumbles/rolls ● thunder and lightning

thunder¹ /'θʌndər/ *noun* [U] the loud noise in the sky that you hear during a storm **gök gürlemesi** *thunder and lightning*

thunder² /'θʌndər/ *verb* **1 it thunders** When it thunders during a storm, a loud noise comes from the sky. **gök gürlüyor 2 thunder along/down/through, etc** to move in a way that makes a deep, loud, continuous sound **uğultuyla hareket etmek/ilerlemek** *Traffic thunders through the village all day.*

thunderous /'θʌndərəs/ *adjective* extremely loud **gök gürültüsü gibi çıkan, kulakları sağır eden** *the thunderous roar of the aircraft's engine*

thunderstorm /'θʌndəstɔ:m/ *noun* [C] a storm that has thunder (= loud noise) and lightning (= sudden flashes of light in the sky) **gök gürültülü ve şimşekle beraber sağanak yağışlı hava**

o⁻**Thursday** /'θɜ:zdeɪ/ (*written abbreviation* **Thur, Thurs**) *noun* [C, U] the day of the week after Wednesday and before Friday **perşembe, perşembe günü**

thus /ðʌs/ *adverb formal* **1** used after saying a fact to introduce what then happened as a result **böylece, bu nedenle, bunun için, bu yüzden** *The guard fell asleep, thus allowing Bates to escape.* **2** in this way **böyle, şöyle, bu şekilde/tarzda** *They limit the number of people allowed into the forest, thus preventing damage to the trails.*

thwart /θwɔ:t/ *verb* [T] to prevent someone from doing what they have planned to do **engel olmak, boşa çıkarmak, bozmak**

thyme /taɪm/ *noun* [U] a herb used in cooking **kekik**

thyroid /'θaɪrɔɪd/ *noun* [C] an organ in the neck that produces a substance that helps your body to grow and develop **tiroid bezi; büyüme ve gelişmeyi sağlayan organ**

TIA *internet abbreviation for* thanks in advance: used in an email when you have asked someone for something **Peşinen Teşekkür Ederim (PTE)!', 'Şimdiden teşekkürler!' anlamında e-posta iletilerinde kullanılır**

tick¹ /tɪk/ *noun* [C] **1** [CLOCK] the sound that some clocks or watches make every second **tik tak sesi 2** [MARK] *UK* (*US* **check**) a mark (√) that shows something is correct or has been done (√) **tik işaret 3** [INSECT] a small insect that sucks the blood of animals **kene 4** [TIME] *UK informal* a short time **dakika, saniye, kısa zaman dilimi** *Wait a tick!*

tick² /tɪk/ *verb* **1** [I] If a clock or watch ticks, it makes a sound every second. **(saat) tik sesi çıkararak çalışmak; tiklemek; tik sesi çıkarmak 2** [T] *UK* to mark something with a tick **işaretlemek, kontrol etmek 3 what makes sb tick** *informal* the reasons for someone's behaviour **davranışlarının sebebi; neden öyle davrandığının gerekçesi**
tick away/by *phrasal verb* If seconds or minutes tick away or by, they pass. **(saniyeler/dakikalar) geçmek, ilerlemek, akıp gitmek** *With the final seconds ticking away, Milan scored a goal.*
tick sth off *phrasal verb UK* (*US* **check sth off**) to put a small mark next to something on a list to show that you have dealt with it **Kontrol edildi' işareti koymak**
tick sb off *phrasal verb* **1** *UK informal* to tell someone that they have done something wrong and that you are angry about it **azarlamak, paylamak, haşlamak** *I got ticked off for not going to the meeting.* **2** *US informal* to annoy someone **rahatsız etmek; canını sıkmak**
tick over/along *phrasal verb UK* If a business or system ticks over, it continues to work but makes little progress. **ağır ağır işlemek; ağır ağır çalışmaya devam etmek; rölantide gitmek/çalışmak** *Carlton managed to keep the business ticking over.*

book/buy/get/purchase a ticket ● a ticket for sth

o⁻**ticket** /'tɪkɪt/ *noun* [C] **1** a small piece of paper that shows you have paid to do something, for example travel on a bus, watch a film, etc **bilet** *a lottery ticket* ○ *plane tickets* **2** a piece of paper that orders you to pay money because you have put your car in an illegal place, driven too fast, etc **trafik cezası** *a parking ticket* ⊃See also: round-trip ticket, season ticket.

tickets

tickle /'tɪkl/ *verb* **1** [TOUCH LIGHTLY] [T] to touch someone lightly with your fingers, in order to make them laugh **gıdıklamak 2** [PART OF THE BODY] [I, T] If a part of your body tickles, or if something tickles it, it feels uncomfortable and you want to rub it. **kaşın(dır)mak; huylan(dır)mak** *My nose is tickling.* **3** [AMUSE] [T] to make someone smile or laugh **gıdıklayarak güldürmek; eğlendirmek, memnun etmek** *I was very tickled by his comments.* ● **tickle** *noun* [C] **gıdıklama**

tidal /'taɪdəl/ *adjective* relating to the regular rising and falling of the sea **gelgitle ilgili; gelgitli**

'**tidal** ,**wave** *noun* [C] a very large wave that destroys things, often caused by an earthquake (= when the Earth shakes) **(okyanusta/denizde deprem sonrası oluşan) deprem dalgası**

tidbit *US* (*UK* **titbit**) /'tɪdbɪt/ *noun* [C] a small piece of nice food, or an interesting piece of information **çok leziz bir yemek; çok ilginç bir bilgi**

🧩 **tide** ...... İLE BİRLİKTE KULLANILAN KELİMELER

the tide **comes in/goes out** ● the tide is **in/out** ● at **high/at low** tide

tide[1] /taɪd/ *noun* **1** [C] the regular rise and fall in the level of the sea **gelgitle ilgili; gelgitli** *high/low tide* **2** [no plural] an increase in something that is developing **büyük miktar, artış** *the rising tide of drug-related deaths*

tide[2] /taɪd/ *verb*
tide sb over (sth) *phrasal verb* to help someone through a difficult time, especially by giving them money **sıkıntıyı bir süreliğine gidermesine/atlatmasına yardımcı olmak; ...a/e kadar idare etmesine imkân vermek**

tidy[1] /'taɪdi/ *adjective* **1** having everything in the right place and arranged in a good order **düzenli, tertipli, derli toplu** *Her room was clean and tidy.* **2** liking to keep things in the correct place and arranged in a good order **yerli yerinde, düzenli, derli toplu** *I'm afraid I'm not very tidy.* ➲Opposite **untidy.** ● **tidily** *adverb* **düzenli bir şekilde** ● **tidiness** *noun* [U] **düzenlilik**

tidy[2] /'taɪdi/ (*also* **tidy up**) *verb* [I, T] *UK* to make a place tidy **çeki düzen vermek, düzenlemek, derleyip toparlamak** *I'm tidying up before our guests arrive.*
tidy sth away *phrasal verb* *UK* to put things back in drawers, cupboards, etc after you have used them **ortalığı toparlamak, ortadan kaldırmak; ayak altından kaldırmak**

tie

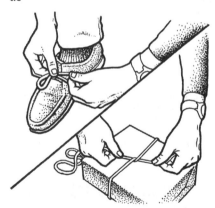

o--**tie**[1] /taɪ/ *verb* **tying**, *past* **tied 1 tie sth to/together/ around, etc** to fasten something with string, rope, etc **bağlamak** *The dog was tied to a tree.* **2** [T] to make a knot in a piece of string, rope, etc **düğümlemek, bağlamak** *She tied the scarf.* ➲Opposite **untie. 3** [I] to have the same score as someone else at the end of a competition or game **aynı sayıda/sonuçta/skorda beraber olmak; berabere olmak** *Sweden tied with France in the winter sports competition.* ➲See also: tie the **knot**[1].
tie sb down *phrasal verb* to limit someone's freedom **özgürlüğünü sınırlamak/kısıtlamak; ayak bağı**

olmak; sınırlama koymak *I don't want to be tied down by having children.*
tie in *phrasal verb* If one idea or statement ties in with another one, they have some of the same information in them. **...ile ilişkisi/bağlantısı olmak/bulunmak** *His story ties in with what Gemma told me.*
tie sb/sth up *phrasal verb* to tie a part of someone's body with a rope or something similar so they cannot move **sıkıca bağlamak** ➲Opposite **untie.**
tie sth up *phrasal verb* to fasten something together using string, rope, etc **bağlamak, bağlayıp düğümlemek**
be tied up *phrasal verb* to be very busy and unable to speak to anyone, go anywhere, etc **çok meşgul olmak**

🧩 **tie** ...... İLE BİRLİKTE KULLANILAN KELİMELER

create/forge ties ● **cut/sever** (all) ties ● **have** ties **with** sb/sth ● **close/strong** ties ● ties **between** sb **and** sb ● ties **to/with** sb/sth

tie[2] /taɪ/ *noun* [C] **1** CLOTHES a long, thin piece of cloth that a man wears round his neck with a shirt **kıravat** ➲Orta kısımdaki renkli sayfalarına bakınız. **2** CONNECTION a relationship that connects you with a place, person, etc **bağ, bağlar** [usually plural] *The two countries have close ties with each other.* **3** GAME/COMPETITION when a game or competition ends with two people or teams having the same score **berabere** ➲See also: bow tie.

tie-break /'taɪbreɪk/ *noun* [C] an extra part that is played when a game or competition ends in a tie, to decide who is the winner **berabere biten maçlardan sonra galibi belirlemek için oynanan ilave bölüm**

tier /tɪər/ *noun* [C] one of several rows or layers **sıra, dizi, kat** *the upper tier of seats in a stadium*

tiger /'taɪɡər/ *noun* [C] a large wild cat that has yellow fur with black lines on it **kaplan**

o--**tight**[1] /taɪt/ *adjective* **1** FIRM firm and difficult to move **sıkı, dar** *Make sure the knot is tight.* **2** CLOTHES fitting your body very closely **sımsıkı, bedene sıkıca oturan; bedeni sımsıkı saran** *a tight skirt* **3** CONTROLLED controlled and obeying all rules completely **sıkı sıkıya bağlı; titizlikle uyan** *tight security* ○ *They kept tight control of the school budget.* **4** STRAIGHT If cloth, wire, skin, etc is tight, it has been pulled so that it is straight or smooth. **gergin, gerili, gerilmiş 5** NOT MUCH If money, time, or space is tight, there is only just enough of it. **kıt kanaat, sadece ihtiyacı karşılayan; ucu ucuna** *We should get six people into the car but it will be tight.* ● **tightly** *adverb* **sıkı sıkıya, ancak yetecek kadar** ● **tightness** *noun* [U] ➲See also: keep a tight **rein** on sb/sth. **sıkışıklık, sıkı olma durumu**

tight[2] /taɪt/ *adverb* very firmly or closely **sıkıca, sıkı sıkıya, sımsıkı** *He held her tight.*

tighten /'taɪtᵊn/ *verb* [I, T] to become tighter or to make something become tighter **sıkmak, sıkılmak** *His hand tightened around her arm.* ➲See also: tighten your **belt**[1].
tighten sth up *phrasal verb* to make something firmer and less easy to move **iyice sıkıştırmak** *Tighten up the screws.*
tighten (sth) up *phrasal verb* to make a rule, system, or law more difficult to avoid **sıkılaştırmak; etkinleştirmek; daha sıkı hâle getirmek** *I think they should tighten up the laws on gun ownership.*

tightrope /'taɪtrəʊp/ *noun* [C] a rope high above the ground that a performer walks along at a circus (= show) **cambaz ipi, gerilmiş ip**

tights /taɪts/ *UK* (*US* **pantyhose**) *noun* [plural] a piece of women's clothing made of very thin material that covers the legs and bottom **tayt; bacakları va basen bölgesini sımsıkı saran bayan giysisi** *a pair of black tights* ➲Orta kısımdaki renkli sayfalarına bakınız.

T

tile /taɪl/ *noun* [C] one of the flat, square pieces that are used for covering roofs, floors, or walls **kiremit, fayans, çini** ● **tile** *verb* [T] *a tiled kitchen* **fayans döşemek**

till¹ /tɪl/ *preposition, conjunction* until ... **a/e kadar** *The supermarket is open till midnight.* ○ *I lived with my parents till I was twenty.*

till² /tɪl/ *noun* [C] **1** *UK* a machine that holds the money in a shop and shows how much you have to pay **kasa, ödeme makinası/noktası 2** *US* a drawer where money is kept in a store **para çekmecesi, kasa**

tilt /tɪlt/ *verb* [I, T] to move into a position where one end or side is higher than the other, or to make something move into this position **yana yat(ır)mak, eğmek/eğilmek** *He tilted backwards on his chair.* ● **tilt** *noun* [no plural] **yana yatma, eğme**

timber /'tɪmbə'/ *noun* **1** [WOOD] [U] *UK* (*US* **lumber**) wood that is used for building **kereste 2** [TREE] [U] *US* trees that are grown to provide wood for building **kerestelik ağaçlar 3** [PIECE OF WOOD] [C] *UK* a large piece of wood **kalas** *The roof was supported by timbers.*

o━**time¹** /taɪm/ *noun* **1** [HOURS/YEARS ETC] [U] Time is what we measure in minutes, hours, days, etc. **zaman** *He wants to spend more time with his family.* ○ *Time seems to pass so slowly when you're unhappy.* **2** [PARTICULAR POINT] [C, U] a particular point in the day or night **zaman, vakit** *What time is it?* ○ *What time do you leave for school in the mornings?* ○ *Can you tell me the times of the trains to London, please?* **3 it's time (for/to do sth)** used to say that something should happen or be done now **tam vakti/zamanı** *It's time to get up.* **4 in (good) time** early or at the right time **vaktinden önce veya tam vaktinde** *We arrived in time to catch the train.* **5 on time** not early or late **tam zamanında** *I got to school on time.* **6 can tell the time** to be able to know what time it is by looking at a clock or watch **zamanı söyleyebilmek 7** [PERIOD] [no plural] a period of minutes, hours, years, etc **zaman** *I lived in Switzerland for a long time.* ○ *It takes time* (= takes a long time) *to make friends at a new school.* **8 have time** to have enough time to do something **yeterli vakti olmak** *Do you have time for a cup of coffee?* ○ [+ **to do sth**] *I never have time to eat breakfast.* **9 in no time** very soon **çok yakında, az sonra, hemen şimdi** *We'll be home in no time.* **10** [OCCASION] [C] an occasion when something happens **fırsat, zaman** *Give me a call the next time you're in Seattle.* ○ *I can't remember the last time we went away.* ○ *How many times have you been to Germany?* **11 at the same time** If two things happen at the same time, they happen together. **aynı zamanda** *We arrived at the same time.* **12 one/two/six, etc at a time** one/two/six, etc on one occasion (**her defasında; bir seferde**) **birer, ikişer, altışar vb.** *He carried the chairs, three at a time.* **13 time after time** again and again on repeated occasions **defalarca; tekrar tekrar 14 all the time a** [OFTEN] very often **hep, boyuna, çok sık** *"She's been late twice this week." "It happens all the time."* **b** [WHOLE TIME] during the whole of a period of time **tüm bu süre zarfında; bu süre içinde** *He was ill all the time we were in Spain.* **15 three/eight/nine, etc times** used to say how much bigger, better, worse, etc one thing is than another thing **üç/sekiz/dokuz vb. kez/defa daha** *Ben earns three times more than me.* **16 in a day's/two months', etc time** a day/two months, etc from now **bir günlük/iki aylık vb. zaman sonra/geçince** *I have to go to the doctor again in a month's time.* **17 at times** sometimes **zaman zaman, bazen** *At times, I wish I didn't have to go to school.* **18 for the time being** for now but not permanently **şimdilik, kısa bir süre için, geçici olarak** *I'm living with my parents for the time being.* **19** [IN THE PAST] [C] a period of time in the past **geçirilen**

zaman; o zamanları *Did you enjoy your time in Japan?* **20 at one time** at a time in the past **eskiden, vaktiyle, bir zamanlar** *At one time, you could drive without taking a driving test.* **21 before sb's time** before someone was born ...**dan/den önce**; ...**doğmadan önce 22 from time to time** sometimes, but not often **arada bir, ara sıra** *I still see my ex-boyfriend from time to time.* **23** [RACE] [C] the amount of time that someone takes in a race **yarışta geçirilen zaman/süre** *a winning time of three minutes* **24** [IN A PLACE] [U] the time in a particular place ...**ın/in zamanına; yerel saat/zaman** *The plane arrives at 20.50, New York time.* **25 be ahead of your time** to have new ideas a long time before other people think that way **çağın ilerisinde/çağdaşlarının önünde olmak** ● **26 behind the times** not fashionable or modern **çağın gerisinde, modası geçmiş, köhne, eski** *Dad's a bit behind the times.* ● **27 bide your time** to wait for an opportunity to do something **fırsatını kollamak, uygun zamanı beklemek; anını kollamak; sabırla beklemek** *She was biding her time until she could get her revenge.* ● **28 give sb a hard time** to criticize someone and make them feel guilty about something they have done **zor anlar yaşatmak, suçlamak; emdiği sütü burnundan getirmek** *Ever since I missed the goal, the other players have been giving me a hard time.* ● **29 have no time for sb/sth** to have no respect for someone or something **hiç saygı duymamak, hiç hazzetmemek, hoşlanmamak, tahammül edememek; azarlamak, aşağılamak; hiç tahammülü olmamak** *I have no time for people who are racist.* ● **30 kill time** to do something while you are waiting for something else **zaman öldürmek, zamanı boşa geçirmek** *I went shopping to kill some time before my job interview.* ● **31 play for time** *UK* to try to make something happen more slowly because you want more time or because you do not want it to happen **ağırdan almak; işi yavaşlatmak; gönülsüz yapmak** ● **32 take your time** to do something without hurrying **acele etmemek** ⊃See also: **half-time, local time, in the nick² of time, night-time, prime time, a race¹ against time/the clock.**

time² /taɪm/ *verb* [T] **1** to decide that something will happen at a particular time **zamanlamak, ayarlamak** *They timed production of the CD so it was in the shops just before Christmas.* ○ *Her comment was well timed.* **2** to measure how long it takes for something to happen or for someone to do something **zamanını ölçmek, saat tutmak** *It's a good idea to time yourself while you do the exercises.* ⊃See also: **two-time.**

time-consuming /'taɪmkənˌsjuːmɪŋ/ *adjective* needing a lot of time **vakit alan, oyalayıcı** *The legal process was time-consuming and expensive.*

'time ˌframe ⊃See timescale.

time-honoured *UK* (*US* **time-honored**) /'taɪmˌɒnəd/ *adjective* [always before noun] A time-honoured tradition or way of doing things is one that has been used for a long time. **köklü, yerleşmiş; nesilden nesile geçen**

'time ˌlag *noun* [C] a period of time between two things happening **zaman aralığı, boşluk, ara, gecikme**

timeless /'taɪmləs/ *adjective* not changing because of time or fashion **modası geçmeyen, çağları aşan, değişmeyen, sonsuz, ebedî** *Her clothes have a timeless quality.* ○ *a timeless classic*

timely /'taɪmli/ *adjective* happening or done at exactly the right time **tam vaktinde olan; tam zamanında yapılan** ⊃Opposite **untimely.**

time-out /ˌtaɪm'aʊt/ *noun* [C] a short period during a sports game in which players can rest **mola, ara**

timer /'taɪmə'/ *noun* [C] a piece of equipment that measures time **saat, sayaç, zaman göstergesi**

times /taɪmz/ *preposition* used to say that one number is multiplied by another number **kere, çarpı** *Two times three is six.*

timescale /ˈtaɪmskeɪl/ (*also* **time frame**) *noun* [C] the amount of time that something takes or during which something happens **oluş süreci, meydana gelme süresi**

━━━━━━━━━━━━━━━━━━━━━━━━━━━━━━━━━━━
    timetable ...... İLE BİRLİKTE KULLANILAN KELİMELER
━━━━━━━━━━━━━━━━━━━━━━━━━━━━━━━━━━━
draw up/give/keep to/set a timetable ● a timetable **for** (doing) sth
━━━━━━━━━━━━━━━━━━━━━━━━━━━━━━━━━━━

timetable /ˈtaɪmˌteɪbl/ *noun* [C] **1** (*also US* **schedule**) a list of times when buses, trains, etc arrive and leave (otobüs, tren vb.) **zaman çizelgesi, tarife 2** a list of dates and times that shows when things will happen **program** ⊃Orta kısımdaki renkli sayfalarına bakınız.

ˈtime ˌzone *noun* [C] one of the areas of the world that has a different time from all the other areas **zaman aralığı, zaman boşluğu; bölgeler arası zaman farklılığı** *London and New York are five time zones apart.*

timid /ˈtɪmɪd/ *adjective* shy and easily frightened **korkak, ürkek, çekingen, sıkılgan** *a timid little boy* ● **timidly** *adverb* **utangaç bir şekilde** ● **timidity** /tɪˈmɪdəti/ *noun* [U] **utangaçlık**

timing /ˈtaɪmɪŋ/ *noun* [U] **1** the time when something happens **zamanlama, zaman ayarlama** *the timing of the announcement* **2** the ability to do something at exactly the right time **tam zamanında yapma** *You need great timing to be a good football player.*

tin /tɪn/ *noun* **1** [METAL CONTAINER] [C] *UK* (*UK/US* **can**) a metal container in which food is sold **teneke kutu** *a tin of beans/soup* ⊃See picture at **container**. **2** [CONTAINER WITH LID] [C] *UK* a metal container with a lid that you keep food or other substances in **konserve kutusu** *a biscuit tin* ○ *a paint tin* **3** [COOKING EQUIPMENT] [C] (*US* **pan**) a flat pan that you use to cook food in **yayvan tava** *a roasting tin* **4** [METAL] [U] a soft, silver metal that is often combined with other metals or used to cover them (symbol **Sn**) **teneke**

tinfoil /ˈtɪnfɔɪl/ *noun* [U] metal made into very thin sheets like paper and used mainly for covering food **alüminyum folyo**

tinge /tɪndʒ/ *noun* [C] a small amount of a sad feeling or colour **bir nebze, çok az, tın parça** *"Goodbye," he said, with a tinge of sadness.* ● **tinged** *adjective Her dark hair is now tinged with grey.* **az miktarda boyanmış**

tingle /ˈtɪŋgl/ *verb* [I] If a part of your body tingles, the skin feels slightly uncomfortable. **sızlamak, yanmak, karıncalanmak** *My hands are starting to tingle with the cold.* ● **tingle** *noun* [C] **sızı, ağrı**

tinker /ˈtɪŋkər/ *verb* [I] to make small changes to something in order to improve or repair it **ufak tefek onarmalar yapmak; kurcalamak, oynamak** *Tim loves tinkering with car engines.*

tinkle /ˈtɪŋkl/ *verb* [I] to make a soft, high, ringing sound **çıngırdamak, çınlamak, çınlatmak** ● **tinkle** *noun* [C] **çınlama**

tinned /tɪnd/ *UK* (*UK/US* **canned**) *adjective* Tinned food is sold in metal containers. **konserve**

ˈtin ˌopener *noun UK* (*UK/US* **can opener**) *noun* [C] a piece of kitchen equipment for opening metal food containers **konserve açacağı** ⊃Orta kısımdaki renkli sayfalarına bakınız.

tinsel /ˈtɪnsəl/ *noun* [U] long, shiny, coloured string, used as a decoration at Christmas (= a Christian holiday) **metal süs ipliği, duvak teli**

tint¹ /tɪnt/ *noun* [C] a particular colour **hafif renk, gölge, ton** *the yellow and red tints of autumn*

tint² /tɪnt/ *verb* [T] to add a small amount of a colour to something **rengini açmak, renk vermek** *Do you think he tints his hair?*

tinted /ˈtɪntɪd/ *adjective* Tinted glass has colour added to it. **renklendirilmiş, soluk renkli** *tinted sunglasses*

∘⌐**tiny** /ˈtaɪni/ *adjective* extremely small **minicik, ufacık, küçücük** *a tiny baby* ○ *a tiny little room*

━━━━━━━━━━━━━━━━━━━━━━━━━━━━━━━━━━━
    tip ...... İLE BİRLİKTE KULLANILAN KELİMELER
━━━━━━━━━━━━━━━━━━━━━━━━━━━━━━━━━━━
give/pass on/pick up tips ● a **handy/helpful/hot/ useful** tip ● tips **for/on** sth
━━━━━━━━━━━━━━━━━━━━━━━━━━━━━━━━━━━

tip¹ /tɪp/ *noun* [C] **1** [END] the end of something long and narrow **uç** *the tips of your fingers* **2** [ADVICE] a piece of useful advice **faydalı öğüt, yararlı tavsiye, ipucu** *gardening tips* ○ *Emma was giving me some tips on how to grow tomatoes.* **3** [MONEY] an extra amount of money that you give to a driver, someone working in a restaurant, etc to thank them **bahşiş** *We left a tip because the waiter was so friendly.* **4** [WASTE] *UK* (*UK/US* **dump**) a place where people take things that they want to get rid of **hurdalık, eski eşyaların atıldığı yer** *We took our old fridge to the tip.* **5** [UNTIDY PLACE] *UK informal* (*UK/US* **dump**) a place that is dirty and untidy **çöplük, mezbele** *His bedroom is an absolute tip.* **6 be on the tip of your tongue** If a word is on the tip of your tongue, you want to say it but cannot remember it. **dilinin ucunda olmak** ● **7 be the tip of the iceberg** to be a small part of a very big problem **sadece buz dağının görünen kısmı olmak; esas sorun daha geride olmak**

tip² /tɪp/ *verb* **tipping**, *past* **tipped 1** [I, T] to move so that one side is higher than the other side, or to make something move in this way **eğmek, yana yatırmak** *The table tipped and all the drinks fell on the floor.* **2 tip sth into/onto/out of sth** to make the contents of a container fall out by holding the container in a position where this happens **tıra çevirip boşaltmak** *She tipped the contents of her purse onto the table.* **3** [I, T] to give an extra amount of money to a driver, someone working in a restaurant, etc to thank them **bahşiş vermek 4 be tipped as/to do/for sth** *UK* If someone is tipped to achieve something, most people say it will happen. **cesaretlendirilmek; yüreklendirilmek; desteklenmek, teşvik edilmek; ummak, olacak gözüyle bakmak** *Christie was tipped to win the race.*

tip sb off *phrasal verb* to warn someone secretly about something so that they can take action or prevent it happening **gizli bilgi vermek, tüyo vermek; gizlice uyarmak** ● **tip-off** /ˈtɪpɒf/ *noun* [C] a piece of information that you give someone secretly, so that they can take action or prevent something happening

tip (sth) over *phrasal verb* If something tips over, or if you tip it over, it falls onto its side. **devrilmek; devirmek**

tiptoe¹ /ˈtɪptəʊ/ *noun* **on tiptoe** standing on your toes with the rest of your feet off the ground **ayak parmaklarının ucunda**

tiptoe² /ˈtɪptəʊ/ *verb* **tiptoe across/down/through, etc** to walk quietly on your toes **sessizce ayak parmaklarının ucuna basarak yürümek**

tire¹ /taɪər/ *noun* [C] *US spelling of* **tyre** **lâstik, araba lâstiği** ⊃Orta kısımdaki renkli sayfalarına bakınız.

tire² /taɪər/ *verb* [I, T] to become tired or to make someone become tired **yorulmak, yormak** *He tires easily.*

tire of sth/doing sth *phrasal verb* to become bored with something **bıkmak, usanmak, gına gelmek** *He never tires of playing games on his computer.*

tire sb out *phrasal verb* to make someone very tired **yormak, yorgun düşürmek, canını çıkarmak**

tired ...... BAŞKA BİR DEYİŞLE

Eğer kişi çok yorgun ise, bunu belirtmede **exhausted**, **worn-out** veya resmi olmayan durumlarda **shattered** ifadesi kullanılabilir. *I'm too exhausted to take the dog for a walk tonight.* ● *By the time I got home, I was absolutely* **shattered**.

Uzun zamandır çok çalışıp yorulan bir kişiyi tanımlamada **burnt-out**, ve **drained** sıfatları kullanılabilir. *He was completely burnt-out after a full week of performances.* ● *I'd worked a twelve-hour day and was absolutely* **drained**.

Eğer kişi çok yorgunsa ve uyumak istiyorsa, durumu belirtmek için **drowsy** veya **sleepy** ifadeleri kullanılabilir. *The heat had made me* **drowsy**/**sleepy**.

⚬ᐧ**tired** /taɪəd/ *adjective* **1** feeling that you want to rest or sleep **yorgun, bitkin** *He was tired out* (= very tired) *by the end of the day.* ○ *She never seems to get tired.* **2 tired of doing sth** bored or annoyed by something that has happened too often **bir şeyi yapmaktan bıkmış, usanmış, gına gelmiş** *I'm tired of listening to her problems.* ● **tiredness** *noun* [U] **yorgunluk**

tireless /ˈtaɪələs/ *adjective* working very hard at something and not stopping **yorulmaz, yorulmak bilmez** *He was a tireless campaigner/worker for children's organizations.* ○ *I want to thank James for his tireless efforts on behalf of the company.*

tiresome /ˈtaɪəsəm/ *adjective formal* making you feel annoyed or bored **yorucu, sıkıcı, bıktırıcı, usandırıcı, bezdirici, sinir bozucu** *a tiresome little boy*

tiring /ˈtaɪərɪŋ/ *adjective* making you feel tired **yorucu** *a long and tiring day*

tissue /ˈtɪʃuː/ *noun* **1** [ANIMAL/PLANT] [C, U] the material that animals and plants are made of **doku** *human brain tissue* **2** [FOR YOUR NOSE] [C] a soft piece of paper that you use for cleaning your nose **kâğıt mendil 3** [FOR WRAPPING] [U] *(also* '**tissue** ˌpaper)* soft, thin paper that you cover things with in order to protect them **ince kâğıt, ipek kâğıt**

tit /tɪt/ *noun* [C] **1** *very informal* a woman's breast **göğüs, meme 2 tit for tat** *informal* when you do something bad to someone because they have done something bad to you **misilleme**

titbit *UK (US* **tidbit)** /ˈtɪtbɪt/ *noun* [C] a small piece of nice food, or an interesting piece of information **tadımlık lokma, meze; flaş haber; önemli bilgi**

title ...... İLE BİRLİKTE KULLANILAN KELİMELER

defend/lose/retain/take/win the title ● the world title

⚬ᐧ**title** /ˈtaɪtl/ *noun* [C] **1** [BOOK/FILM ETC] the name of a book, film, etc **ad, isim, başlık 2** [SPORTS] what you get if you win an important sports competition **ünvan, san, şampiyonluk ünvanı** *He won the 1999 world motor racing title.* **3** [SOMEONE'S NAME] a word such as 'Lord', 'Dr', etc that is used before someone's name **ünvan, rütbe, meslek adı**

titled /ˈtaɪtld/ *adjective* having a title such as 'Lord', 'Lady', or 'Duke' that shows you have a high social position **soyluluk ünvanı olan**

title-holder /ˈtaɪtlˌhəʊldər/ *noun* [C] someone who has won a sports competition **şampiyonluk, şampiyonluk ünvanını elinde bulunduran kimse veya takım; rekoru elinde tutan** *the World Grand Prix title-holder*

'**title ˌrole** *noun* [C] the person in a play or film who has the same name as the play's or film's title **bir film veya oyuna adını veren karakterin rolü; başrol**

titter /ˈtɪtər/ *verb* [I] to laugh in a nervous way **kıkırdamak, kıkır kıkır gülmek** ● **titter** *noun* [C] **kıkırdama**

T-junction /ˈtiːˌdʒʌŋkʃən/ *UK (US* intersection) *noun* [C] a place where two roads join and make the shape of the letter 'T' **T şeklinde kavşak**

⚬ᐧ**to¹** /tə/ **1** used with a verb to make the infinitive ...mak/mek *I want to learn Spanish.* ○ *He forgot to feed the cat.* **2** used to give the reason for doing something ...mak/mek için *I'm just going out to get some milk.*

⚬ᐧ**to²** *strong form* /tuː/, *weak forms* /tʊ/, /tə/ *preposition* **1** [DIRECTION] in the direction of somewhere ...a/e doğru; ...ya/ye *Dimitri is going to Germany next week.* ○ *I ran to the door.* **2** [ANOTHER PERSON] used to show who receives something or experiences an action ...a/e; ...ya/ye *Could you give these keys to Pete?* ○ *Anna was speaking to her mother on the phone.* ○ *I lent my bike to Tom.* **3** [POSITION] almost touching or facing something ... a/e yaslanarak/dokunarak/dönük *She stood with her back to the window.* **4 from ... to ...** a [TIME/DISTANCE] used to give information about periods of time and distances ...dan/den ... a/e kadar *The museum is open from Monday to Saturday.* ○ *The bus goes from London to Cambridge.* **b** [INCLUDING] including ...dan/den ... a/e kadar; içeren/kapsayan *The book deals with everything from childhood to old age.* **5** [BEFORE] used to say 'before' the hour when you are saying what time it is ...a/e; kala *It's five to three.* **6** [COMPARE] used to compare two things ...ı/i ... a/e tercihte kullanılır *I prefer football to cricket.* **7** [UNTIL] until a particular time or state ... a/e; belli bir duruma veya zamana kadar *It's only two weeks to my birthday.* ○ *She nursed him back to health.* **8** [SOMEONE'S OPINION] used to say what someone's opinion is ...için; birinin fikrinin ne olduğunu belli etmek için *Fifty pounds is nothing to Matthew* (= he would not think it was a lot of money). **9 to sb's disappointment/relief/surprise, etc** used to say that someone feels disappointed/relieved/surprised, etc by something **duygusal tepkileri ifade ederken; bir de bakmış ki; öylesine şaşırmış ki** *To Pierre's disappointment, Monique wasn't at the party.* **10** [MEASUREMENT] used to say how many parts make up a whole unit of measurement or money **ölçümlerde kullanılır;** ... da/de *There are 100 pence to the British pound.* **11** [BELONGING] belonging to or connected with **ait olan veya ...ı ile bağlantılı olarak anlamında;** ...nın/nin *Can you give me the keys to the car?*

YAYGIN HATALAR

to or too?

Dikkat! Doğru kelimeyi seçin. Bu iki kelime benzer görünmelerine rağmen, hem yazılışları hem de anlamları farklıdır. Eğer izin verilenden veya gerekenden fazla anlamını vermek istiyorsanız, **too** kullanmanız gerekir.: ~~She didn't want to go outside because it was too hot.~~ Yanlış cümle örneği

She didn't want to go outside because it was too hot.

to³ /tuː/ *adverb* **1** *UK* If you push or pull a door to, you close it. **açmak/kapamak için kullanılır 2 to and fro** backwards and forwards **şuraya buraya; öteye beriye; ileri geri; sağa sola; öne arkaya** *The sign was swinging to and fro in the wind.*

toad /təʊd/ *noun* [C] a small, brown animal with long back legs for swimming and jumping **kara kurbağası**

toadstool /ˈtəʊdstuːl/ *noun* [C] a poisonous fungus (= organism like a plant) with a short stem and a round top **zehirli şapkalı mantar**

toast¹ /təʊst/ *noun* **1** [U] bread that has been heated to make it brown **kızarmış ekmek dilimi** *a slice of toast* **2** [C] a time when people lift their glasses and drink because they want someone to be successful, happy, etc şerefe/sağlığa/kutlama amaçlı kadeh kaldırma *At the wedding, there was a **toast to** the happy couple.*

toast² /təʊst/ *verb* [T] **1** to lift your glass and drink with other people because you want someone to be successful, happy, etc kadeh kaldırmak; şerefe içmek **2** to heat bread so that it becomes brown ekmek kızartmak

toaster /'təʊstə^r/ *noun* [C] a machine that heats bread so that it becomes brown ekmek kızartma/tost makinası ➲Orta kısımdaki renkli sayfalarına bakınız.

toasty /'təʊsti/ *adjective* warm and comfortable sıcak ve rahat *It's nice and toasty near the fire.*

tobacco /tə'bækəʊ/ *noun* [U] dried leaves that are inside cigarettes tütün, tütün yaprağı

toboggan /tə'bɒgᵊn/ *noun* [C] a board that you sit or lie on, used for going down a hill on a surface of snow kıvrık burunlu kızak

ᴏ⁻ᴡ**today** /tə'deɪ/ *noun* [U], *adverb* **1** this day, or on this day bugün *It's Johann's birthday today.* ○ *Today is Friday.* **2** the period of time that is happening now or in this period of time günümüz, bugünün, zamanımızın, çağımızın *More young people smoke today than in the past.*

toddle /'tɒdl/ *verb* **toddle down/off/to, etc** *informal* to walk somewhere tıpış tıpış yürümek; paytak paytak yürümek *Sophie said goodbye and toddled off towards the station.*

toddler /'tɒdlə^r/ *noun* [C] a child who has just learned to walk yeni yürümeye başlayan çocuk

toe¹ /təʊ/ *noun* [C] **1** one of the five separate parts at the end of your foot ayak parmağı *your big toe* (= largest toe) ○ *your little toe* (= smallest toe) ➲Orta kısımdaki renkli sayfalarına bakınız. **2** the part of a shoe or sock that covers your toes ayakkabı/çorap ayak ucu **3 keep sb on their toes** to make sure that someone gives all their attention to what they are doing and is ready for anything that might happen tetikte tutmak; bütün dikkatini vermesini sağlamak

toe² /təʊ/ *verb* ➲See toe the (party) line¹.

toenail /'təʊneɪl/ *noun* [C] one of the hard, flat parts on top of the end of your toes ayak tırnağı ➲Orta kısımdaki renkli sayfalarına bakınız.

toffee /'tɒfi/ *noun* [C, U] a sticky sweet, made by boiling sugar and butter together karamelâ; şekerleme

tofu /'təʊfuː/ (*also* bean curd) *noun* [U] a soft pale food made from the soya bean plant soya fasulyesinden yapılan bir tür yiyecek

ᴏ⁻ᴡ**together¹** /tə'geðə^r/ *adverb* **1** [WITH SOMEONE] with each other beraber, birlikte *We went shopping together.* ○ *They live together.* **2** [CONNECTED] used to say that two or more things are joined to each other, mixed with each other, etc beraber, yanyana, birlikte *She tied the two pieces of rope together.* **3** [SAME PLACE] in the same place or close to each other yanyana, birbirine çok yakın *We all sat together.* **4** [SAME TIME] at the same time aynı zamanda, birlikte *We'll deal with the next two items on the list together.* **5 together with sth** in addition to something *...ile birlikte/beraber She sent some flowers together with a card.* ➲See also: get your act² together, get-together.

together² /tə'geðə^r/ *adjective informal* Someone who is together thinks clearly and organizes their life well. birlikte; ..ile; ...bir arada

togetherness /tə'geðənəs/ *noun* [U] a feeling of friendship birliktelik, bağlılık, samimiyet, sıcaklık

toil /tɔɪl/ *verb* [I] *literary* to do difficult work for a long time çok çalışmak, didinmek; üzerinde uğraş ver-

mek ● **toil** *noun* [U] *literary* zahmet, yorulma, zor iş yapma

be on/go to/flush/need the toilet ● toilet **facilities** ● **a** toilet **seat**

ᴏ⁻ᴡ**toilet** /'tɔɪlɪt/ *noun* [C] **1** a bowl that you sit on or stand near when you get rid of waste substances from your body klozet ➲Orta kısımdaki renkli sayfalarına bakınız. **2** *UK* (*US bathroom*) a room with a toilet in it tuvalet

'**toilet ,paper** *noun* [U] paper used for cleaning your body after you have used the toilet tuvalet kâğıdı ➲Orta kısımdaki renkli sayfalarına bakınız.

toiletries /'tɔɪlɪtriz/ *noun* [plural] things such as soap, toothpaste (= substance for cleaning teeth), etc that you use for making yourself clean tuvalet malzemesi

'**toilet ,roll** *noun* [C] *UK* paper for cleaning your body after using the toilet that is folded around a tube tuvalet kağıdı rulosu ➲Orta kısımdaki renkli sayfalarına bakınız.

token¹ /'təʊkᵊn/ *noun* [C] **1** [LOVE/THANKS] something that you give to someone in order to show them how you feel, to thank them, etc hatıra, yadigâr, işaret,simge *I gave Helen some chocolates as **a token of** thanks for all her help.* **2** [INSTEAD OF MONEY] a round piece of metal or plastic that you put in some machines instead of money jeton, marka, fiş *You need a token to get out of the car park.* **3** [PAPER] *UK* (*US gift certificate*) a piece of paper that you give someone which they can exchange for a book, CD, etc kupon *a book/record/gift token*

token² /'təʊkᵊn/ *adjective* [always before noun] **1** A token person is chosen so that an organization can pretend that they care about that type of person. göstermelik, yapmacık *a token woman* **2** A token action is small or unimportant and may show your future intentions or may only pretend to. sembolik, cüzi, göstermelik *He made a **token effort** to find a job.*

told /təʊld/ *past of* tell anlatmak' fiilinin geçmiş zaman hâli

tolerable /'tɒlᵊrəbl/ *adjective* acceptable but not excellent dayanılabilir, katlanılabilir; tolere edilebilir *The food was just about tolerable but the service was terrible.* ➲Opposite intolerable. ● **tolerably** *adverb* kabul edilebilir bir şekilde

show tolerance ● tolerance **of/towards** sb/sth ● sb's tolerance **level** ● **racial/religious** tolerance

tolerance /'tɒlᵊrᵊns/ *noun* [U] the quality of allowing people to do or believe what they want although you do not agree with it hoşgörü, tolerans *religious/racial tolerance* ➲See also: zero tolerance.

tolerant /'tɒlᵊrᵊnt/ *adjective* allowing people to do what they want especially when you do not agree with it hoşgörülü, toleranslı *a tolerant attitude* ○ *I think we're becoming more **tolerant of** children in public places.* ➲Opposite intolerant.

tolerate /'tɒlᵊreɪt/ *verb* [T] **1** to accept or allow something although you do not like it katlanmak, hoşgörmek, tolere etmek *We will not tolerate racism of any sort.* **2** to be able to deal with something unpleasant and not be harmed by it dayanmak, tahammül etmek *These plants can tolerate very low temperatures.* ● **toleration** /ˌtɒlᵊr'eɪʃᵊn/ *noun* [U] hoşgörü

toll¹ /təʊl/ *noun* **1** [C] money that you pay to use a bridge, road, etc (köprü, yol vb.) geçiş/giriş ücreti **2** [no plural] the number of people who are killed or injured (yaralı, ölü) sayı, adet **3 take its toll** to have a bad effect on

toll

someone or something, especially over a long period of time **hasara sebep olmak, kayıp verdirmek; etkisini göstermek; kendini belli etmek** *The stress was starting to take its toll on him.* ⊃See also: **death toll.**

toll² /təʊl/ *verb* [I] When a bell tolls, it rings slowly, especially because someone has died. **(zil, çan vb.) çalmak**

toll-free /ˌtəʊlˈfriː/ *US* (*UK* **freephone**) *adjective* A toll-free number is a telephone number that you can connect to without paying. **(telefon) ücretsiz, araması bedava**

o=**tomato** /təˈmɑːtəʊ/ ⑤ /təˈmeɪtəʊ/ *noun* [C, U] *plural* **tomatoes** a soft, round, red fruit eaten in salad or as a vegetable **domates** ⊃Orta kısımdaki renkli sayfalarına bakınız.

tomb /tuːm/ *noun* [C] a place where a dead person is buried, usually with a monument (= stone structure) **türbe, kabir, mezar**

tomboy /ˈtɒmbɔɪ/ *noun* [C] a young girl who behaves and dresses like a boy **erkek Fatma; erkek gibi giyinen genç kız**

tombstone /ˈtuːmstəʊn/ *noun* [C] a stone that shows the name of a dead person who is buried under it **mezar taşı**

tomcat /ˈtɒmkæt/ *noun* [C] a male cat **erkek kedi**

o=**tomorrow** /təˈmɒrəʊ/ *noun* [U], *adverb* **1** the day after today or on the day after today **yarın** *It's my birthday tomorrow.* ○ *Tomorrow is Friday.* **2** the future, or in the future **gelecek, gelecekte** *the children of tomorrow*

ton /tʌn/ *noun* [C] *plural* **tons** or **ton** **1** a unit for measuring weight, equal to 1016 kilograms in the UK and 907 kilograms in the US **ton; İngiltere'de 1016 kg'a ABD'de 907 kg'a eşit ağırlık ölçüm birimi** ⊃Compare **tonne 2 tons of sth** *informal* a lot of something **tonlarca, çokca, epey, bir ton** *We've got tons of cheese left.* **3 weigh a ton** *informal* to be very heavy **çok ağır olmak, bir ton çekmek**

tone¹ /təʊn/ *noun* **1** SOUND QUALITY [C, U] the quality of a sound, especially of someone's voice **ses tone** *I knew by her tone of voice that she was serious.* **2** FEELING/STYLE [U, no plural] the general feeling or style that something has **tarz** *Then the director arrived and the whole tone of the meeting changed.* **3** TELEPHONE [C] an electronic sound made by a telephone **telefonda çevir sesi** *a dialling tone/an engaged tone* **4** COLOUR [C] one of the many types of a particular colour **renk tonu**

tone² /təʊn/ (*also* **tone up**) *verb* [T] to make your muscles or skin firmer and stronger **kaslarını güçlendirmek/sıkılaştırmak** *Try these exercises to tone up your stomach muscles.*
tone sth down *phrasal verb* to make a piece of writing, a speech, etc less offensive or rude **yumuşatmak, hafifletmek** *The show was toned down for television.*

tone-deaf /ˌtəʊnˈdef/ ⑤ /ˈtəʊndef/ *adjective* unable to sing the correct musical notes or hear the difference between musical notes **müzik kulağı zayıf olan; sesleri ayırt edemeyen**

tongs /tɒŋz/ *noun* [plural] a tool used for picking things up, that has two pieces joined together at one end **maşa**

o=**tongue** /tʌŋ/ *noun* **1** MOUTH [C] the soft thing inside your mouth that you move and use for tasting and speaking **dil 2** FOOD [C, U] the tongue of some animals that you can eat as meat **yenilebilir hayvan dili, dil eti 3** LANGUAGE [C] *formal* a language **lisan, dil** *Japanese is her native tongue* (= the language she learnt to speak as a child). ⊃See also: **mother tongue,** a **slip²** of the tongue, be on the **tip¹** of your tongue.

tongue-in-cheek /ˌtʌŋɪnˈtʃiːk/ *adjective, adverb* said or done as a joke **şaka yollu, biraz alaylı; içten olmayan; samimi olmayan, şakacı**

tongue-tied /ˈtʌŋtaɪd/ *adjective* unable to say anything because you are nervous **dili tutulmuş; sinirden konuşamayan**

'tongue ˌtwister *noun* [C] a phrase or sentence that is difficult to say quickly because it has many similar sounds in it **tekerleme**

tonic /ˈtɒnɪk/ *noun* **1** [C, U] (*also* **'tonic ˌwater**) a drink with bubbles in it that has a bitter taste and is often added to alcoholic drinks **tonik 2** [no plural] something that makes you feel better **tonik, kuvvet ilacı; güç verici/canlandırıcı şey** *Spending time with Leo is always a tonic.*

o=**tonight** /təˈnaɪt/ *noun, adverb* [U] the night of this day, or during the night of this day **bu gece, bu gecede, bu akşam** *What are you doing tonight?* ○ *I'm looking forward to tonight.*

tonne /tʌn/ *noun* [C] *plural* **tonnes** or **tonne** *UK* a metric ton (= unit for measuring weight, equal to 1000 kilograms) **ton** ⊃Compare **ton.**

tonsil /ˈtɒnsᵊl/ *noun* [C] one of the two small, soft parts at the back of your mouth **bademcik**

tonsillitis /ˌtɒnsᵊlˈaɪtɪs/ *noun* [U] an illness that makes your tonsils very painful **bademcik iltihabı**

o=**too** /tuː/ *adverb* **1 too adjective/heavy/much, etc** used before adjectives and adverbs to mean 'more than is allowed, necessary, possible, etc' **çok fazla/epeyce küçük/ağır/çok vb.; gereğinden fazla, çok aşırı** *The film is also far too long.* ○ *There are too many cars on the roads these days.* ○ [+ to do sth] *I decided it was too early to get up and went back to sleep.* **2** also **de, de, dahi** *Do you know Jason too?* ○ *I'll probably go there next year too.* **3 not too** used before adjectives and adverbs to mean 'not very' **çok fazla/fena ... değil; eh şöyle böyle** *"How was your exam?" "Not too bad, I suppose."* ○ *I didn't play too well today.*

YAYGIN HATALAR

too or very?

Dikkat! Doğru zarf kullanımını seçin. **Too** izin verilen veya gerekenden çok anlamına gelir. Bir sıfata daha kuvvetli bir anlam katmak için **very** veya **so** kullanmak gerekmektedir.: ~~My host family were too kind to me.~~ Yanlış cümle örneği

My host family were very kind to me.

took /tʊk/ *past tense of* take **almak' fiilinin ikinci hâli**

o=**tool** /tuːl/ *noun* [C] **1** a piece of equipment that you use with your hands in order to help you do something **âlet, takım 2** something that helps you to do a particular activity **âlet, edevat** *Computers are an essential tool for modern scientists.* ⊃See also: **power tool.**

toolbar /ˈtuːlbɑːʳ/ *noun* [C] on a computer screen, a row of icons (= small pictures that you choose in order to make the computer do something) **bilgisayar ekranında kumut vermek için kullanılan küçük işaretlerin oluşturduğu çubuk; işlev seçim çubuğu**

'tool ˌbox *noun* [C] a container in which you keep and carry small tools **alet çantası**

toot /tuːt/ *UK* (*UK/US* **honk**) *verb* **toot your horn** If a driver toots their horn, they make a short sound with the horn (= thing you press to make a warning noise). **korna çalmak ● toot** *noun* [C] **düdük çalma**

tools

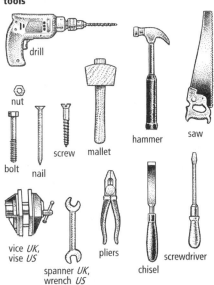

drill

nut

screw mallet

bolt nail

hammer

saw

vice *UK*, vise *US*

pliers

spanner *UK*, wrench *US*

chisel

screwdriver

tooth ...... İLE BİRLİKTE KULLANILAN KELİMELER
brush/clean your teeth • your **back/front** teeth • have a tooth **removed/taken out** • a **set of** teeth

o⁻**tooth** /tuːθ/ *noun* [C] *plural* **teeth 1** one of the hard, white objects in your mouth that you use for biting and crushing food **diş** *You should brush your teeth twice a day.* **2** one of the row of metal or plastic points that stick out from a tool such as a comb (= thing used to make your hair tidy), or saw (= thing used to cut wood) **tarak/testere vb. dişi 3 grit your teeth** to accept a difficult situation and deal with it in a determined way **dişlerini sıkmak, sabretmek; sabırla ve azimle devam etmek** ⊃See also: a **kick²** in the teeth, do sth by the **skin¹** of your teeth, **wisdom tooth.**

toothache /ˈtuːθeɪk/ *noun* [U] a pain in one of your teeth **diş ağrısı**

toothbrush /ˈtuːθbrʌʃ/ *noun* [C] a small brush that you use to clean your teeth **diş fırçası**

toothbrush

toothpaste /ˈtuːθpeɪst/ *noun* [U] a substance that you use to clean your teeth **diş macunu** ⊃Orta kısımdaki renkli sayfalarına bakınız.

toothpick /ˈtuːθpɪk/ *noun* [C] a small, thin stick that you use to remove pieces of food from between your teeth **kürdan**

top ...... İLE BİRLİKTE KULLANILAN KELİMELER
reach the top • at the top • on top • the top of sth

o⁻**top¹** /tɒp/ *noun* **1** [HIGHEST PART] [C] the highest part of something **tepe, en üst/tepe** *They were waiting for him at the top of the stairs.* ○ *I want a cake with cherries*

on top. **2** [SURFACE] [C] the flat, upper surface of something **tepe, üst, zirve** *the table top* **3** [LID] [C] the lid or cover of a container, pen, etc **kapak** *Put the top back on the bottle.* **4** [CLOTHING] [C] a piece of women's clothing worn on the upper part of the body **(elbise) üst, üst parçası/kısmı 5** [TOY] [C] a toy that turns round and round when you move its handle up and down **topaç 6 the top** the most important position in a company, team, etc **en üst mevki, üst düzey** *At forty he was already at the top of his profession.* **7 at the top of your voice** *UK* (*US* **at the top of your lungs**) shouting very loudly **çok yüksek sesle; en üst perdeden; bağırarak; haykırarak 8 from top to bottom** completely **tepeden tırnağa kadar; tamamen** *I've searched the house from top to bottom and still can't find it.* • **9 get on top of sb** *UK* If a difficult situation gets on top of someone, it upsets them. **bunaltmak; ...a/e çok fazla gelmek; ...ı/i aşmak; ...ın/in üstüne yığılmak • 10 off the top of your head** *informal* If you say a fact off the top of your head, you say it immediately, from memory. **fazla/hiç düşünmeden; kafadan atarak; rastgele** *"What date is their wedding?" "I couldn't tell you off the top of my head." • 11 on top of sth a* [IN ADDITION] in addition to something else that is bad **üstüne üstlük; ek olarak; ayrıca; bu yetmiyormuş gibi** *And then, on top of everything else, her car was stolen.* **b** [IN CONTROL] able to deal with or in control of something **başarıyla yürüten, hakkından gelen, üstesinden gelebilen** *I'm not at all sure that he's on top of the situation.* • **12 be on top of the world** *informal* to be very happy **dünyalar onun olmak; çok mutlu olmak** • **13 over the top** *mainly UK informal* too extreme and not suitable **abartılı, aşırı, uygun değil; kabul edilemez** *I thought her performance was way over the top.*

o⁻**top²** /tɒp/ *adjective* [always before noun] **1** the best, most important, or most successful **en iyi/önemli/başarılı** *He's one of the country's top athletes.* **2** at the highest part of something **en üst, tepe** *I can't reach the top shelf.*

top³ /tɒp/ *verb* [T] **topping,** *past* **topped 1** to be better or more than something **en iyisi/en üste olmak; ...dan/den daha üstün olmak** *I don't think film makers will ever top 'Gone With The Wind'.* **2 be topped with sth** to be covered with something **kaplanmış olmak, üstüne sürülmüş olmak** *lemon tart topped with cream*
top sth off *phrasal verb informal* to finish something in an enjoyable or successful way **başarıyla bitirmek; üstesinden gelmek; keyifle halletmek**
top sth up *phrasal verb UK* (*US* **top sth off**) **1** to add more liquid to a container in order to make it full **üstünü doldurarak tamamlamak; sıvı ilave etmek 2** to add more of something, especially money, to an existing amount to create the total you need *Can I top up my mobile phone here?*

top 'hat *UK* (*US* **'top ,hat**) *noun* [C] a tall, black or grey hat worn by men on some formal occasions **silindir şapka**

topic ...... İLE BİRLİKTE KULLANILAN KELİMELER
cover/discuss/raise a topic • a **controversial/hot** topic • the **(main)** topic of sth • a topic of **conversation /discussion**

topic /ˈtɒpɪk/ *noun* [C] a subject that you talk or write about **konu, mevzu**

topical /ˈtɒpɪkəl/ *adjective* relating to things that are happening now **güncel, aktüel**

topless /ˈtɒpləs/ *adjective* without clothes on the upper part of your body **üstsüz**

topmost /ˈtɒpməʊst/ *adjective* [always before noun] highest **en üst, en yüksek** *the topmost branches of a tree*

topography /tə'pɒɡrəfi/ *noun* [U] the shape and other physical characteristics of a piece of land **bir arazinin fizikî şekil ve yapısı; topoğrafya**

topping /'tɒpɪŋ/ *noun* [C, U] food that is put on top of other food in order to give it more flavour, or to make it look attractive **tabaka, sos, krema**

topple /'tɒpl/ *verb* **1** [I, T] to fall, or to make something or someone fall **devrilmek/devirmek; yık(ıl)mak; tepe taklak olmak/etmek 2** [T] to make a leader lose their position of power **alaşağı etmek; indirmek; tepe taklak etmek; devirmek, düşürmek**

top-secret /ˌtɒp'siːkrət/ *adjective* Top-secret information is very important and must not be told to anyone. **çok gizli**

topsy-turvy /ˌtɒpsi'tɜːvi/ *adjective informal* confused or badly organized **karman çorman, karmakarışık; arap saçına dönmüş; altüst olmuş**

'top-up ˌcard *noun* [C] a card you can buy which gives you a special number so that you can use your mobile phone for longer

the Torah /'tɔːrə/ *noun* the holy books of the Jewish religion, especially the first five books of the Bible **Tevrat; Museviliğin kutsal kitabı; İncil'in ilk beş kitabı**

torch¹ /tɔːtʃ/ *noun* [C] *UK* (*US* **flashlight**) a small electric light that you hold in your hand **el feneri 2** a long stick with material that burns tied to the top of it **meşale**

torch² /tɔːtʃ/ *verb* [T] *informal* to destroy something by burning it **yakmak, ateşe vermek** *A number of houses were torched.*

tore /tɔːr/ *past tense of* tear **yırtmak' fiilin ikinci hâli**

torment¹ /tɔː'ment/ *verb* [T] to make someone suffer or worry a lot **eziyet etmek, azap çektirmek, işkence etmek** *All evening the question tormented her.* ● **tormentor** *noun* [C] **eziyet eden**

torment² /'tɔːment/ *noun* [C, U] extreme unhappiness or pain **eziyet, acı, dert, sorun, çile, keder; büyük acı**

torn /tɔːn/ *past participle of* tear **yırtmak' fiilinin geçmiş zaman hâli**

tornado /tɔː'neɪdəʊ/ (*also US* **twister**) *noun* [C] *plural* **tornados** or **tornadoes** an extremely strong and dangerous wind that blows in a circle and destroys buildings as it moves along **hortum, kasırga, siklon**

torpedo /tɔː'piːdəʊ/ *noun* [C] *plural* **torpedoes** a long, thin bomb that is fired from a ship and moves under water to destroy another ship **torpido; deniz altından atılan bomba**

torrent /'tɒrənt/ *noun* [C] **1 a torrent of sth** a lot of something unpleasant **sel gibi, yığınla; heyula gibi, yağmur gibi** *a torrent of abuse* **2** a large amount of water that is moving very fast **sel**

torrential /tə'renʃəl/ *adjective* Torrential rain is very heavy rain. **sel gibi**

torso /'tɔːsəʊ/ *noun* [C] the main part of a human body without its arms, legs, or head **gövde**

tortilla /tɔː'tiːə/ *noun* [C] a type of thin round Mexican bread **ince yuvarlak Meksika ekmeği; tortilla**

tortoise /'tɔːtəs/ *noun* [C] an animal with a thick, hard shell that it can move its head and legs into for protection **kara kaplumbağası**

tortoise

tortuous /'tɔːtʃuəs/ *adjective formal* **1** very complicated or difficult **karmaşık ve zor; içinden çıkılmaz** *Gaining permission to build was a long and tortuous process.* **2** A tortuous road has

many turns in it. **dolambaçlı, bol virajlı** *a tortuous path/route*

torture¹ /'tɔːtʃər/ *verb* [T] to cause someone severe pain, often in order to make them tell you something **işkence etmek, eziyet etmek,** ● **torturer** *noun* [C] **işkence eden**

torture² /'tɔːtʃər/ *noun* [C, U] **1** when someone is tortured **işkence, eziyet 2** a very unpleasant experience **çok büyük sıkıntı; çekilen eziyet** *I had to sit there listening to her for two whole hours - it was torture!*

Tory /'tɔːri/ *noun* [C] someone who supports the Conservative Party in the UK **İngiltere'de Muhafazakâr Parti yandaşı/destekçisi/üyesi** *a Tory voter*

toss¹ /tɒs/ *verb* **1 toss sth away/into/on, etc** to throw something somewhere carelessly **atmak, fırlatıp atmak** *He read the letter quickly, then tossed it into the bin.* **2** [I, T] (*also* **toss up**) to throw a coin in the air and guess which side will land facing upwards as a way of deciding something **yazı tura atmak**

toss² /tɒs/ *noun* **1 a toss of a coin** when you throw a coin in the air and guess which side will land facing upwards as a way of deciding something **yazı tura 2 a toss of your head/hair** when you move your head quickly backwards **hızla başını/saçlarını geriye atma**

tot /tɒt/ *noun* [C] *informal* **1** a small child **ufaklık, bıcırık, bızdık, küçük çocuk 2** *UK* a small amount of strong alcohol **yudum, fırt**

o═**total¹** /'təʊtl/ *adjective* [always before noun] **1** including everything **toplam; tam, tamam** *The total cost of the work was $800.* **2** extreme or complete **tam, mutlak** *The whole evening was a total disaster.*

sth **brings/takes the total to** [500/4000, etc] ● **reach** a total of [500/4000, etc] ● **the final/overall/sum** total ● [500/4000, etc] in total

o═**total²** /'təʊtl/ *noun* [C] the amount you get when you add several smaller amounts together **toplam, yekûn, tutar** *In total we made over £3,000.*

total³ /'təʊtl/ *verb* [T] *UK* **totalling**, *past* **totalled**, *US* **totaling**, *past* **totaled** to add up to a particular amount **toplamak, toplam tutarı bulmak**

totalitarian /təʊˌtælɪ'teəriən/ *adjective* belonging to a political system in which the people in power have complete control and do not allow anyone to oppose them **totaliter; gücü elinde bulunduran bir gruba ait; baskıcı gruba ait olan** ● **totalitarianism** *noun* [U] **içinde serbestlik barındırmayan, korku yayan politik sistem**

o═**totally** /'təʊtli/ *adverb* completely **tamamen** *They look totally different.* ○ *I totally disagree.*

tote bag /'təʊtˌbæɡ/ *noun* [C] *US* a large bag with handles and an open top **alışveriş poşeti**

totter /'tɒtər/ *verb* [I] to walk in a way that looks as if you are going to fall **sendelemek, yalpalamak, sendeleyerek yürümek** *She tottered around the dance floor.*

o═**touch¹** /tʌtʃ/ *verb* **1** [HAND] [T] to put your hand on something **dokunmak, el sürmek, değmek** *You can look at them but please don't touch them.* **2** [GET CLOSE] [I, T] If two things touch, they are so close to each other that there is no space between them. **sürtünmek, dokunmak, temas etmek, değmek** *These two wires must not touch.* **3** [EMOTION] [T] If something kind that someone says or does touches you, it makes you feel pleased or a little sad. **etkilemek, duygulandırmak, dokunmak, üzmek** [often passive] *I was deeply touched by her letter.* **4 not touch sth** to not eat or drink something **hiç bir şey yememek, hiç bir şeye dokunmamak 5 not**

touch sb/sth to not harm someone or not damage something **hiç kimseye/birşeye zarar vermemek/dokunmamak** ⮞See also: touch/cover all the bases (**base**¹), hit/touch a (raw) **nerve**.

touch down *phrasal verb* When a plane touches down, it lands. **yere inmek, konmak**

touch on sth *phrasal verb* to briefly talk about something **değinmek** *We only touched on the subject.*

touch sth up *phrasal verb* to improve something by making small changes **el atmak, geliştirmek; ufak tefek değişiklikler yapmak**

touch² /tʌtʃ/ *noun* **1** [HAND] [no plural] when you put your hand on something **dokunma, dokunuş, elleme, temas** *I felt the touch of his hand on my face.* **2** [ABILITY] [U] the ability to feel things by putting your hand on them **dokunma, temas; dokunma duyusu** *It was cold to the touch* (= when I touched it). **3** [DETAIL] [C] a small detail that makes something better **ayrıntı, detay** *Having flowers on the tables was a nice touch.* **4 a touch** a little **az miktarda** *Add a little olive oil and a touch of vinegar.* **5 be/get/keep, etc in touch** to communicate or continue to communicate with someone by telephoning, or writing to them **temasta/temas hâlinde olmak; temasa geçmek; bağlantı kurmak; ilgi duymak; ilgisini sürdürmek 6 lose touch** to stop communicating with someone, usually because they do not live near you now **teması kaybetmek; izini kaybetmek; teması/iletişimi kesmek 7 be out of touch** to know little about what has recently happened **tam haberdar olmamak; fazla bilgisi olmamak**

touchdown /'tʌtʃdaʊn/ *noun* **1** [C, U] when an aircraft lands **inme, yere konma 2** [C] when the ball is carried or thrown over a line in order to score points in rugby or American football **rugbi ve Amerikan futbolunda puan almak için topun çizgi ötesine taşınması/atılması**

touched /tʌtʃt/ *adjective* pleased or a little sad because someone has done something kind **duygulanmış, etkilenmiş, minnettar** *She was touched that he had remembered her birthday.*

touching /'tʌtʃɪŋ/ *adjective* making you feel sadness or sympathy **dokunaklı, etkileyen, dokunan, duygulandıran** *a touching performance*

'touch ˌscreen *noun* [C] a screen that works when you touch it **dokunmatik ekran**

touchstone /'tʌtʃstəʊn/ *noun* [no plural] something that other things can be judged against **mihenk taşı**

touchy /'tʌtʃi/ *adjective* **1** easily upset **alıngan, aşırı duygusal, çabuk küsen** *Why are you so touchy today?* **2 touchy subject/issue, etc** a subject that you have to talk about carefully because it is likely to upset someone **hassas/nazik/özene ele alınması gereken konu/husus/sorun**

∘**tough** /tʌf/ *adjective* **1** [DIFFICULT] difficult **zor** *He's had a tough time at work recently.* ○ *We've had to make some tough decisions.* **2** [SEVERE] Tough rules are severe. **sert, katı** *tough new laws on noise pollution* **3** [STRONG THING] not easily damaged, cut, etc **dayanıklı, kolay etkilenmeyen** *Children's shoes have to be tough.* ○ *This meat's very tough.* **4** [STRONG PERSON] physically strong and not afraid of violence **güçlü, dayanıklı, sağlam** *a tough guy* **5** [DETERMINED] determined and not easily upset **kararlı, kolay etkilenmeyen** *You have to be tough to survive in politics.* **6** [UNFAIR] unfair or unlucky **şanssız, çok fena** *It can be tough on kids when parents get divorced.*

toughen /'tʌfªn/ (*also* **toughen up**) *verb* [I, T] to become stronger, or to make something or someone stronger **katılaş(tır)mak; sertleş(tir)mek; dayanıklı hâle gelmek/getirmek** *School tends to toughen kids up.*

toupee /'tuːpeɪ/, /ˌtuːpˈeɪ/ *noun* [C] a piece of artificial (= not natural) hair worn by a man to cover part of his head where there is no hair **yarım peruk, takma saç**

$$ \text{❝❞ tour} \text{....... İLE BİRLİKTE KULLANILAN KELİMELER} $$

be on/go on a tour ● a **guided/sightseeing/world** tour ● a tour **of** sth

∘**tour**¹ /tʊəʳ/ *noun* [C, U] a visit to and around a place, area, or country **gezi, seyahat** *a tour of Europe* ○ *We went on a guided tour of the cathedral.* ○ *The band are on tour* (= travelling and performing in different places).

tour² /tʊəʳ/ *verb* [I, T] to travel around a place for pleasure **gezmek, dolaşmak, seyahat etmek** *to tour the States*

tourism /'tʊərɪzªm/ *noun* [U] the business of providing services for tourists, including organizing their travel, hotels, entertainment, etc **turizm, turizm işi**

∘**tourist** /'tʊərɪst/ *noun* [C] someone who visits a place for pleasure and does not live there **turist**

$$ \text{❝❞ tournament} \text{...... İLE BİRLİKTE KULLANILAN KELİMELER} $$

host/play in/pull out of/take part in/win a tournament ● **in** a tournament ● a **major** tournament ● a **round/stage** of a tournament

tournament /'tʊənəmənt/ *noun* [C] a competition with a series of games between many teams or players, with one winner at the end **turnuva**, *a golf/tennis tournament*

tourniquet /'tʊənɪkeɪ/ ⑤ /'tɜːrnɪkɪt/ *noun* [C] a long piece of cloth that you tie tightly around an injured arm or leg to stop the blood coming out **turnike**

tousled /'taʊsld/ *adjective* Tousled hair is untidy. **dağınık, karmakarışık**

tout¹ /taʊt/ *verb* **1** [T] to praise someone or something in order to make people think that they are important **övmek, göklere çıkarmak; önemli olduğunu göstermek için övgü dolu sözler etmek** [often passive] *He is being touted as the next big star.* **2** [I, T] to try to persuade people to buy something **müşteri toplamak, satmaya çalışmak, almaya ikna etmek** *Drug dealers were seen touting for business outside schools.*

tout² /taʊt/ *UK* (*US* **scalper**) *noun* [C] someone who unofficially sells tickets outside theatres, sporting events, etc **korsan bilet satıcısı**

tow¹ /təʊ/ *verb* [T] to pull a car, boat, etc, using a rope or chain connected to another vehicle **(araba, tekne vb.) çekmek** *His car was towed away by the police.*

tow² /təʊ/ *noun informal* **in tow** If you have someone in tow, you have them with you. **peşinde, ardında, beraberinde** *Shopping can be very stressful with young children in tow.*

∘**towards** /təˈwɔːdz/ *mainly UK* (*mainly US* **toward**) *preposition* **1** [DIRECTION] in the direction of someone or something **...a/e doğru; ...istikametinde** *She stood up and walked towards him.* **2** [POSITION] near to a time or place ... **a/e doğru/sularında/dolaylarında** *Your seats are towards the back of the theatre.* ○ *He only became successful towards the end of his life.* **3** [FEELING] used when talking about feelings about something or someone ...**a/e karşı/hakkında/ilişkin** *His attitude towards work needs to improve.* **4** [PURPOSE] for the purpose of buying or achieving something ...**için/amacıyla/maksadıyla** *We're asking people for a contribution towards the cost.* ○ *This piece of work counts towards your final mark.*

∘**towel** /taʊəl/ *noun* [C] **1** a soft piece of cloth or paper that you use for drying yourself or for drying something **havlu** *a bath/beach towel* ○ *a paper towel* ⮞Orta kısımdaki renkli sayfalarına bakınız. **2 throw in the towel** to stop trying to do something because you do not think you can succeed **pes etmek, vazgeçmek** ➩See also: **sanitary towel, tea towel.**

'towel ,rail UK (US **'towel ,rack**) noun [C] a horizontal bar on the wall that you hang towels on **havluluk** ➩See picture at **rail.**

tower¹ /taʊəʳ/ noun [C] **1** a very tall, narrow building, or part of a building **kule** *a church tower* ○ *the Eiffel Tower* **2 a tower of strength** someone who helps you a lot during a difficult time **güç veren kişi; dayanak noktası kimse**

tower² /taʊəʳ/ verb **tower over/above sb/sth** to be much taller or higher than someone or something else **...dan/den çok daha yüksek/uzun olmak** *David towers over his mother.*

'tower ,block noun [C] UK a very tall building divided into apartments or offices **blok apartman, kule bina; yaşam ve iş yerlerinin bulunduğu dev blok/ bina**

towering /'taʊərɪŋ/ adjective [always before noun] very tall **çok yüksek/uzun, heybetli** *towering mountains/ trees*

town ...... İLE BİRLİKTE KULLANILAN KELİMELER

go into town ● in town ● a part of/side of town ● (UK) the town centre

o▪**town** /taʊn/ noun **1** [C] a place where people live and work, usually larger than a village but smaller than a city **kasaba, ilçe, şehir** *It's a small town in the north of England.* **2** [U] the central area of a town where the shops are **şehir merkezi, alışveriş merkezi** *I usually go into town on a Saturday.* ○ *Shall I meet you in town?* **3 go to town (on sth)** to spend a lot of money or time doing something in order to make it special **aşırıya kaçmak, abartmak, bol para harcamak** *They've really gone to town on the decorations.* ● **4 out on the town** informal enjoying yourself in bars, restaurants, etc in the evening **şehirde eğlenmiş, içki alemi yapmış; gece hayatına takılma** ➩See also: **ghost town, shanty town.**

,town 'hall noun [C] a large building where local government is based **hükümet konağı, belediye binası**

township /'taʊnʃɪp/ noun [C] in South Africa, an area where only black people live **Güney Afrika'da yerlilerin yaşadığı bölge**

toxic /'tɒksɪk/ adjective poisonous **zehirli** *toxic chemicals/fumes* ○ *toxic waste* (= poisonous waste materials produced by industry) ● **toxicity** /tɒk'sɪsəti/ noun [U] formal how poisonous a substance is **zehirlilik oranı**

toxin /'tɒksɪn/ noun [C] formal a poisonous substance **zehir, toksin, zehirli madde**

o▪**toy¹** /tɔɪ/ noun [C] an object for children to play with **oyuncak** *a toy car/train* ○ *He was happily playing with his toys.*

toy² /tɔɪ/ verb

toy with sth phrasal verb **1** to briefly think about doing something, but not really intend to do it **oynayıp durmak, yapmaktan çok düşünüp durmak** *I've toyed with the idea of going to work abroad.* **2** to move something around in your hands without any clear purpose **elinde oynayıp durmak; kendini oyalamak; bir şeylerle oyalanıp durmak** *He sat toying with his empty glass.*

trace¹ /treɪs/ verb [T] **1** [FIND] to find someone or something that was lost **izini bulmak, ortaya çıkarmak** *Police have so far failed to trace the missing woman.* **2** [ORIGIN] to find the origin of something **kökenini/**

aslını bulmak *She's* **traced** *her family* **back** *to the sixteenth century.* ○ *They were able to* **trace** *the* **call** (= find out the number of the telephone used). **3** [DEVELOPMENT] to describe the way something has developed over time **izini sürmek; izini sürerek bir şeyin gelişimini anlatmak** *The book traces the development of women's art since the start of the century.* **4** [COPY] to copy a picture by putting transparent paper on top and following the outer line of the picture with a pen **kopyasını çıkarmak** *tracing paper*

trace ...... İLE BİRLİKTE KULLANILAN KELİMELER

find no/leave no trace (of sth) ● disappear without/ vanish without trace

trace² /treɪs/ noun **1** [C, U] proof that someone or something was in a place **iz, işaret, belirti, kalıntı, emare, eser** *There was* **no trace** *of her anywhere.* ○ *Ships have* **disappeared without trace** (= completely). **2** [C] a small amount of something **zerre, azıcık miktar** *They found traces of blood on his clothing.*

track¹ /træk/ noun **1** [PATH] [C] a narrow path or road **dar toprak yol, patika, keçi yolu** *We followed a dirt track off the main road.* **2** [RAILWAY] [C] the long metal lines which a train travels along **raylar, demir yolu hattı** (UK) *a railway track/* (US) *a railroad track* **3** [RACE] [C] a path, often circular, used for races **pist, koşu yolu** *a race track* ○ *track events* **4** [U] US the sport of running in races around a wide circular path made for this sport **koşu pistinde yapılan koşu/atletizm sporu 5** [MUSIC] [C] one song or piece of music on a CD, record, etc **müzik parçası 6 keep track** to continue to know what is happening to someone or something **izini kaybetmemek; ...ile haberleşmeyi sürdürmek/teması kesmemek; haberdar olmak** *He changes jobs so often - I find it hard to keep track of what he's doing.* **7 lose track** to not know what is happening to someone or something any more **izini kaybetmek; ...ile haberleşmeyi/teması kesmek; haberdar olmak** *I've lost track of how much we've spent.* **8 on track** making progress and likely to succeed **gelişme gösteren, başarma olasılığı yüksek olan** [+ to do sth] *A fighter from Edinburgh is on track to become world heavyweight boxing champion.* **9 a fast track (to sth)** a very quick way of achieving or dealing with something **bir şeyle ilgilenmenin/başarmanın en hızlı şekli/yolu** *These intensive courses claim to offer a fast track to wealth and success.* ● **10 off the beaten track** in a place where few people go **sapa/ücra/ıssız yerde**

track² /træk/ verb [T] **1** to follow a person or animal by looking for proof that they have been somewhere, or by using electronic equipment **izini sürmek/takip etmek** *The wolves are tracked by using radio collars.* **2** to record the progress or development of something over a period **başarının/gelişmelerin kaydını tutmak/izlemek** *The project tracks the effects of population growth on the area.*

track sth/sb down phrasal verb to find something or someone after looking for them in a lot of different places **uzun uğraşı ve araştırmalar sonucu bulmak** *The man was finally tracked down by French police.*

,track and 'field US (UK **athletics**) noun [U] the sports which include running, jumping, and throwing **atletizm** ➩Orta kısımdaki renkli sayfalarına bakınız.

,track 'record UK (US **'track ,record**) noun [C] how well or badly you have done in the past **sicil, başarı çizelgesi; gelişim kayıtları, performans** *This company has an impressive track record in completing projects on time.*

tracks /træks/ noun [plural] the marks left on the ground by a person, animal, or vehicle **izler, emareler, belirtiler** *We followed their tracks in the snow.*

tracksuit /'træksu:t/ *noun* [C] *UK* loose, comfortable clothes, usually trousers and a top, especially worn for exercising **eşofman** ⊃Orta kısımdaki renkli sayfalarına bakınız.

tract /trækt/ *noun* [C] **1** a system of connected tubes in someone's body which has a particular purpose **birbirine bağlı organlar sistemi; meselâ solunum/sindirim sistemi** *the* **digestive/respiratory tract 2** a large area of land **geniş arazi parçası, geniş alan**

tractor /'træktə^r/ *noun* [C] a strong vehicle with large back wheels used on farms for pulling things **traktör**

trade (noun) ...... İLE BİRLİKTE KULLANILAN KELİMELER

trade **agreement/deal/policy** ● trade **between** [two countries/regions] ● trade **with** [a country] ● trade **in** sth ● a trade **dispute**

o~**trade**¹ /treɪd/ *noun* **1** BUYING AND SELLING [U] the buying and selling of large numbers of goods or services, especially between countries **ticaret, alışveriş** *a* **trade** **agreement/dispute** ○ *They rely heavily on* **trade** *with Europe.* ○ *The laws ban the international* **trade** *in ivory.* **2** BUSINESS [C] a particular area of business or industry **ticaret, iş** *the building/tourist trade* **3** JOB [C] someone's job, especially one which needs skill in using their hands **zanaat, meslek, iş, sanat** *He's a builder by trade.*

trade² /treɪd/ *verb* **1** [I] to buy and sell goods or services, especially between countries **ticaret yapmak** *This will increase costs for companies* **trading** *with Asia.* **2** [T] *mainly US* to give something to someone and receive something else in exchange **değiş tokuş etmek, takas etmek** *He* **traded** *his guitar for a leather jacket.* ● **trading** *noun* [U] **ticaret**
trade sth in *phrasal verb* to give something as part of your payment for something else **fiyat farkını verip eskiyi yenisiyle değiştirmek** *He* **traded** *his old car in for a new model.*

trademark /'treɪdmɑ:k/ *noun* [C] the name of a particular company or product which cannot be used by anyone else **marka, ticarî marka**

trade-off /'treɪdɒf/ *noun* [C] a situation where you accept something bad in order to have something good **değiş tokuş yapma** *There's always* **a trade-off** *between speed and quality.*

tradesman /'treɪdzmən/ *noun* [C] *plural* **tradesmen** *UK* someone who works in trade or in a trade which needs skill in using their hands, usually in the building industry **esnaf, ticaret erbabı kimse**

,trade 'union (*also US* labor union) *noun* [C] an organization that represents people who do a particular job **işçi sendikası**

tradition ...... İLE BİRLİKTE KULLANILAN KELİMELER

break **with/follow/revive/uphold** a tradition ● an **ancient/old/proud/rich/strong** tradition

o~**tradition** /trə'dɪʃ°n/ *noun* [C, U] a custom or way of behaving that has continued for a long time in a group of people or a society **gelenek, görenek, anane** *There is a* **strong tradition** *of dance in St Petersburg.* ○ *We decided to* **break with tradition** (= not behave as usual) *this year and go away for Christmas.*

o~**traditional** /trə'dɪʃ°n°l/ *adjective* following the customs or ways of behaving that have continued in a group of people or society for a long time **geleneksel, göreneksel, ananevî** *traditional Hungarian dress* ○ *traditional farming methods* ● **traditionally** *adverb* **geleneksel olarak**

traditionalist /trə'dɪʃ°n°lɪst/ *noun* [C] someone who believes in traditional ideas and ways of doing things **gelenekçi kimse, muhafazakâr kimse**

traffic ...... İLE BİRLİKTE KULLANILAN KELİMELER

reduce/ease/divert/slow down traffic ● **bad/heavy** traffic ● be **stuck in** traffic ● a traffic **accident**

o~**traffic** /'træfɪk/ *noun* [U] **1** CARS ETC the cars, trucks, etc using a road **trafik, kara trafiği** *Traffic is heavy* (= there are a lot of cars, etc) *in both directions.* ○ *a traffic accident* ○ *Sorry we're late - we got* **stuck in traffic.** **2** PLANES AND SHIPS the planes or ships moving around an area **trafik, deniz/hava trafiği** *air traffic control* **3** ILLEGAL the illegal buying and selling of goods, such as drugs, weapons, etc **kaçakçılık, yasadışı mal ticareti** *the traffic in illegal drugs*

'traffic ,circle *US* (*UK* roundabout) *noun* [C] a circular place where roads meet and where cars drive around until they arrive at the road that they want to turn into **kavşak** ⊃See picture at **roundabout.**

'traffic ,jam *noun* [C] a line of cars, trucks, etc that are moving slowly or not moving at all **trafik sıkışıklığı/tıkanıklığı** *They got stuck in a traffic jam.*

trafficking /'træfɪkɪŋ/ *noun* [U] the activity of illegally buying and selling goods, such as drugs or weapons **kaçakçılık yapma; yasadışı yollarla mal satma** *arms/drug trafficking* ● **trafficker** *noun* [C] **uyuşturucu alıp satan**

'traffic ,light *noun* (*also* lights [plural]) a set of red, green, and yellow lights that is used to stop and start traffic **trafik ışıkları** [usually plural] *Turn left at the traffic lights.* ⊃See picture at **light.**

'traffic ,warden *noun* [C] *UK* someone whose job is to make sure that people do not leave their cars in illegal places **trafik park kontrolörü/görevlisi**

tragedy /'trædʒədi/ *noun* **1** [C, U] an event or situation which is very sad, often involving death **facia, felaket, trajedi** *the tragedy of their daughter's death* **2** [C] a play with a sad end **trajedi, tragedya** *a Greek tragedy*

tragic /'trædʒɪk/ *adjective* very sad, often relating to death and suffering **feci, korkunç, trajik** *a tragic accident/death* ● **tragically** *adverb* *He was tragically killed in a flying accident at the age of 25.* **üzücü bir şekilde**

trail¹ /treɪl/ *noun* [C] **1** a line of marks that someone or something leaves behind as they move **iz, belirti** *He left a trail of muddy footprints across the kitchen floor.* **2** a path through the countryside, often where people walk **keçi yolu, patika** *a nature trail*

trail² /treɪl/ *verb* **1** FOLLOW [T] to follow someone, especially without them knowing, in order to watch or catch them **izini sürmek, takip etmek** *He suspected he was being trailed by undercover police.* **2** HANG DOWN [I, T] *UK* to hang down and touch the ground, or to make something do this **sürüklemek, sürüklenmek** *Your coat's trailing in the mud.* **3** LOWER SCORE [I, T] to have a lower score than someone else, especially in a sporting event **sporda daha düşük puanı/skoru olmak; arkadan gelmek** *City were trailing United 2-1 at half time.*

trail away/off *phrasal verb* If someone's voice trails away or off, it gradually becomes quieter until it stops. **giderek azalıp sona ermek; giderek yavaşlayıp bitmek**

trailer /'treɪlə^r/ *noun* [C] **1** CONTAINER a container with wheels that can be pulled by a car or a truck **römork, treyler 2** HOUSE *mainly US* a house on wheels which can be pulled by a car **karavan 3** FILM short parts of a film or television programme which are shown in order to advertise it **fragman**

'trailer ,park *noun* [C] US a place where trailers (= vehicles that people live in) can park **karavan/tır parkı**

o•**train¹** /treɪn/ *noun* **1** [C] a long, thin vehicle which travels along metal tracks and carries people or goods **tren** *a train journey* ○ *We could go by train.* ○ *You'll have to catch/get the next train.* **2 train of thought/ events** a series of connected thoughts, ideas, or events which come or happen one after the other **düşünce zinciri** *I was interrupted and lost my train of thought.*

o•**train²** /treɪn/ *verb* **1** TEACH [T] to teach someone how to do something, usually a skill that is needed for a job **eğitmek, öğretmek** *We are training all our staff in how to use the new computer system.* ○ [+ to do sth] *The aid workers trained local people to give the injections.* **2** LEARN [I] to learn the skills you need to do a job **eğitim görmek, eğitilmek** *He trained as a lawyer in Vienna.* ○ *I'm trained in basic first aid.* **3** SPORT [I, T] to practise a sport or exercise, often in order to prepare for a sporting event, or to help someone to do this **antreman yapmak, hazırlanmak; idman yaptırmak; hazırlamak** *He's been training hard for the race for several weeks now.*

trainee /ˌtreɪ'niː/ *noun* [C] someone who is learning how to do something, especially a job **kursiyer, stajyer** *a trainee accountant/teacher*

trainer /'treɪnəʳ/ *noun* [C] **1** PERSON someone who trains people **koç, antrenör; eğitici** *a fitness trainer* **2** ANIMALS a person who trains animals **hayvan terbiyecisi/eğiticisi** *a racehorse trainer* **3** SHOE UK (US sneaker) a soft sports shoe **spor ayakkabısı** *a pair of trainers* Ɔ*Orta kısımdaki renkli sayfalarına bakınız.*

training ……… İLE BİRLİKTE KULLANILAN KELİMELER

have/receive/undergo training • give sb/provide training • training in/on sth • a training course/ day/programme/session

o•**training** /'treɪnɪŋ/ *noun* [U] **1** the process of learning the skills you need to do a particular job or activity **eğitim, öğretim, öğrenim** *a training course* ○ *computer/ management training* **2** preparation for a sport or competition **idman, antreman** *weight training* ○ *He's in training for the big match next month.*

trait /treɪt/ *noun* [C] a quality, good or bad, in someone's character **kişisel özellik; karakter niteliği; kişilik hasletleri** *a family trait*

traitor /'treɪtəʳ/ *noun* [C] someone who is not loyal to their country or to a group which they are a member of **hain, vatan haini**

trajectory /trə'dʒektəri/ *noun* [C] *formal* the curved line that something follows as it moves through the air **havada çizilen/oluşan kavis; mermi yolu, kavis yörünge**

tram /træm/ *noun* [C] an electric vehicle for carrying passengers, mostly in cities, which moves along metal lines in the road **tramvay**

tramp¹ /træmp/ *noun* [C] someone who has no home, job, or money and who lives outside **serseri, berduş, evsiz barksız kimse; avare**

tramp² /træmp/ *verb* [I, T] to walk a long way, or to walk with heavy steps because you are tired **ağır ve yorgun adımlarla yürümek** *We spent all day tramping around the city looking for somewhere cheap to stay.*

trample /'træmpl/ (*also* trample on) *verb* [T] to walk on something, usually damaging or hurting it **çiğnemek, ayağı altında ezmek** *She shouted at the boys for tramp-* ling on her flowers. ○ Two people were **trampled to death** in the panic.

trampoline /'træmpəliːn/ *noun* [C] a piece of sports equipment that you jump up and down on, made of a metal structure with a piece of strong material fixed to it **trampolin**

trance /trɑːns/ *noun* [C] a condition in which you are not completely conscious of what is happening around you or able to control what you are doing **kendinden geçme, trans** *He sat staring out of the window as if in a trance.*

tranquil /'træŋkwɪl/ *adjective* calm and quiet **sessiz, sakin, asude** *a tranquil garden* ● **tranquility** (*also* tranquility) /træŋ'kwɪləti/ *noun* [U] *I love the tranquility of the woods.* **sükunet**

tranquilizer (*also* UK -iser) /'træŋkwɪˌlaɪzəʳ/ *noun* [C] a drug which is used to make people or animals sleep or to make them calm **yatıştırıcı, müsekkin**

trans- /træns-/, /trænz-/ *prefix* **1** across ın/in bir ucundan öbürüne/ötesinde… **anlamında önek** *transatlantic flights* **2** showing a change **değişim gösteren/ değişken… anlamında ön ek** *to transform* ○ *to translate*

transaction /træn'zækʃªn/ *noun* [C] *formal* when someone buys or sells something, or when money is exchanged **iş, işlem, muamele** *a business/financial transaction*

transatlantic /ˌtrænzət'læntɪk/ *adjective* crossing the Atlantic **Atlantik aşırı/ötesi** *a transatlantic flight/ phone call*

transcend /træn'send/ *verb* [T] *formal* to be better or more important than something else **aşmak, geçmek, üstün olmak** *Somehow her appeal transcends class barriers.*

transcribe /træn'skraɪb/ *verb* [T] to make a written record of something you hear, such as speech or music **yazılı biçimde çevirmek, kopya etmek, suret çıkarmak** *I later transcribed the tapes of the interviews.* ● **transcription** /træn'skrɪpʃªn/ *noun* [C, U] a written record of speech, music, etc, or the process of making it **konuşma/müzik yazılı kaydı; yazılı kaydını yapma**

transcript /'trænskrɪpt/ *noun* [C] an exact written record of speech, music, etc **yazılı kopya, suret**

transfer /træns'fɜːʳ/ *verb* **transferring**, *past* **transferred** **1** MOVE [T] to move someone or something from one place to another **nakletmek, aktarmak, transfer etmek** *She was later transferred to a different hospital.* ○ *I'll transfer some money into my other account.* **2** CHANGE JOB/TEAM ETC [I, T] to change to a different job, team, place of work, etc, or to make someone do this **transfer olmak/etmek; geçmek/geçirmek** *After a year he transferred to University College, Dublin.* **3** CHANGE OWNER [T] to change who owns or controls something **atamak, tayin etmek; atanmak/tayin olmak** *We had all the documents transferred to my name.* ● **transfer** /'trænsfɜːʳ/ *noun* [C, U] *I'm hoping for a transfer to the Brussels office.* **transfer**

transfixed /træns'fɪkst/ *adjective* unable to move or stop looking at something because you are so interested, surprised, or frightened **donup/çakılıp/mıhlanıp kalmak; kala kalmak** *We all sat in silence, transfixed by what we saw on the screen.*

transform /træns'fɔːm/ *verb* [T] to change something completely, usually to improve it **değiştirmek, dönüştürmek, çevirmek** *Within weeks they had transformed the area into a beautiful garden.* ● **transformation** /ˌtrænsfə'meɪʃªn/ *noun* [C, U] a complete change **değişim, dönüşüm, tamamıyla değişme** *The com-*

pany has **undergone** a dramatic **transformation** in the past five years.

transformer /træns'fɔːmə^r/ noun [C] a piece of equipment that changes the strength of an electrical current akım değiştirici/dönüştürücü; adaptör; dönüşüm aygıtı

transfusion /træns'fjuːʒ^ən/ (also blood transfusion) noun [C] when blood is put into someone's body **kan verme/nakli/aktarımı**

transgress /trænz'gres/ verb [I, T] formal to do something which is against a law or rule **ihlâl etmek, bozmak, uymamak** ● **transgression** /trænz'greʃ^ən/ noun [C] **kanuna karşı gelme**

transient¹ /'trænziənt/ adjective formal 1 lasting only for a short time **geçici, kısa süren/süreli** transient pleasures 2 staying in one place only for a short time **kısa süreli kalan/ikâmet eden**

transient² /'trænziənt/ noun [C] US someone who has no home and stays in a place for only a short time **evsiz ve hep başka yerlerde kalan kimse**

transistor /træn'zɪstə^r/ noun [C] a small piece of electrical equipment used in radios, televisions, etc **transistör**

transit /'trænsɪt/ noun [U] formal the movement of goods or people from one place to another **taşıma, nakliye** Some things got damaged in transit (= while they were being moved).

transition /træn'zɪʃ^ən/ noun [C, U] formal when something changes from one system or method to another, often gradually **geçiş, değişim, intikal** The country is in the process of making the transition from military rule to democracy. ● **transitional** adjective a transitional period/phase ○ a transitional government **geçiş yapılabilecek olan**

transitive /'trænsətɪv/ adjective A transitive verb always has an object. In the sentence 'I'll make a drink.', 'make' is a transitive verb. **geçişli; nesne alan** ⊃See study page Verb patterns on page Centre 27. ⊃Compare intransitive.

transitory /'trænsɪt^əri/ adjective formal lasting only for a short time **geçici, gelip geçici** the transitory nature of life

translate /trænz'leɪt/ verb [I, T] 1 to change written or spoken words from one language to another **çevirmek, tercüme etmek** The book has now been translated from Spanish into more than ten languages. 2 formal If an idea or plan translates into an action, it makes it happen. **dönüşmek, dönüştürmek** So how does this theory translate into practical policy?

translation /trænz'leɪʃ^ən/ noun [C, U] something which has been translated from one language to another, or the process of translating **çeviri, tercüme**

translator /trænz'leɪtə^r/ noun [C] someone whose job is to change written or spoken words from one language to another **çevirmen, tercüman**

translucent /trænz'luːs^ənt/ adjective If something is translucent, light can pass through it and you can almost see through it. **yarı saydam, yarı şeffaf** translucent fabric

transmission /trænz'mɪʃ^ən/ noun 1 BROADCAST [C, U] the process of broadcasting something by radio, television, etc, or something which is broadcast **yayınlama; yayın; yayın yapma** radio/satellite transmission 2 SPREADING [U] formal the process of passing something from one person or place to another **geçirme, iletme, gönderme, yayma** There is still a risk of transmission of the virus through infected water. 3 CAR [U] the system in a car that moves power from its engine to its wheels

şanzıman, vites kutusu automatic/manual transmission

transmit /trænz'mɪt/ verb [T] transmitting, past transmitted 1 to broadcast something, or to send out signals using radio, television, etc **yayın yapmak, göndermek, yayınlamak** [often passive] The information is transmitted electronically to the central computer. 2 formal to pass something from one person or place to another **geçirmek, yaymak, dağıtmak** The disease is transmitted by mosquitoes. ● **transmitter** noun [C] a radio/television transmitter **yayın yapan yer, sinyal yayan**

transparency /træn'spær^ənsi/ noun [C] a photograph or picture printed on plastic which you can see on a screen by shining a light through it **slayt, diyapozitif**

transparent /træn'spær^ənt/ adjective If a substance or material is transparent, you can see through it. **saydam, şeffaf, geçirgen** transparent plastic

transpire /træn'spaɪə^r/ verb formal 1 It transpires that If it transpires that something has happened, that fact becomes known. **belli etmek, meydana çıkarmak/çıkmak** It later transpired that he had known about the plan from the beginning. 2 [I] to happen **olmak, meydana gelmek, vuku bulmak**

---

transplant ...... İLE BİRLİKTE KULLANILAN KELİMELER

have/perform/undergo a transplant ● a transplant donor/operation/patient/surgeon

---

transplant /'trænsplɑːnt/ noun [C] an operation in which a new organ is put into someone's body **doku/organ nakli; transplantasyon** a heart/kidney transplant ● **transplant** /træn'splɑːnt/ verb [T] to remove an organ or other body part from one person and put it into someone else's body **doku/organ nakli yapmak**

---

transport ...... İLE BİRLİKTE KULLANILAN KELİMELER

provide/arrange/improve transport ● free/cheap transport ● public transport ● the transport system

---

o⌐**transport¹** /'trænspɔːt/ noun [U] 1 a vehicle or system of vehicles, such as buses, trains, aircraft, etc for getting from one place to another **taşıt, ulaştırma aracı; toplutaşım araçları** He can't drive so he has to rely on public transport. ○ The city's transport system 2 when people or goods are moved from one place to another **nakil, taşıma** the transport of live animals

transport² /træn'spɔːt/ verb [T] to move people or goods from one place to another **taşımak, nakletmek**

transportation /ˌtrænspɔː'teɪʃ^ən/ noun [U] 1 US (UK transport) a vehicle or system of vehicles, such as buses, trains, etc for getting from one place to another **taşıma/nakliye araçları; taşıma sistemi** 2 when people or goods are moved from one place to another **taşıma** transportation costs

transvestite /trænz'vestaɪt/ noun [C] someone, especially a man, who likes to wear the clothes of someone of the opposite sex **karşı cinsin elbiselerini giymeyi seven erkek**

trap¹ /træp/ noun [C] 1 a piece of equipment for catching animals **tuzak, kapan** a mouse trap 2 a dangerous or unpleasant situation which is difficult to escape from **tuzak, kurtulması zor ve tehlikeli durum** [usually singular] Such families get caught in the poverty trap. ⊃See also: booby trap.

trap² /træp/ verb [T] trapping, past trapped 1 CANNOT ESCAPE If someone or something is trapped, they cannot move or escape from a place or situation. **tuzağa düşmek, kapana kısılmak, faka basmak** The car turned over, trapping the driver underneath. 2 ANIMAL to catch an animal using a trap **tuzak kurup**

yakalamak 3 TRICK to trick someone into doing or saying something that they do not want to **tuzağa düşürmek, kapana kıstırmak, faka bastırmak**

trap 'door *noun* [C] a small door that you cannot see in a floor or ceiling **kapak şeklinde kapı, dam kapağı; yer kapağı**

trappings /'træpɪŋz/ *noun* [plural] things that you usually get when you are rich and successful, such as a big house and car (**zenginlik/başarı**) **göstergeler; mal mülk, süs, ziynet, varlık** *the trappings of success/power*

trash[1] /træʃ/ *noun* [U] *US* (*UK* **rubbish**) things that you throw away because you do not want them **çöp 2** *informal* something that is of bad quality **değersiz/kalitesiz şey** *It's better than the trash she usually reads.*

trash[2] /træʃ/ *verb* [T] *informal* to destroy something **mahvetmek; berbat etmek; yıkıp dökmek** *Vandals broke in and trashed the place.*

'trash ,can *noun* [C] *US* a container for waste, often one that is kept outdoors **çöp tenekesi** ⊃Orta kısımdaki renkli sayfalarına bakınız.

trashy /'træʃi/ *adjective informal* of very bad quality **değersiz, kalitesiz** *a trashy novel/movie*

trauma /'trɔːmə/ *noun* [C, U] severe shock caused by an unpleasant experience, or the experience which causes this feeling **ciddi şok, darbe, acı olay, çok üzücü/ kahredici hadise; travma** *the trauma of marriage breakdown*

traumatic /trɔː'mætɪk/ *adjective* If an experience is traumatic, it makes you feel very shocked and upset. **acı veren, pek üzücü, derinden sarsıcı; travmatik** *His parents split up when he was eight, which he found very traumatic.*

traumatized (*also UK* -**ised**) /'trɔːmətaɪzd/ *adjective* very shocked and upset for a long time **derinden sarsılmış; çok olmuş, üzüntüye gark olmuş** *The violence that she witnessed left him traumatized.*

◦ᴸ**travel**[1] /'trævᵊl/ *verb UK* **travelling**, *past* **travelled**, *US* **traveling**, *past* **traveled 1** [I, T] to make a journey **yolculuk etmek, seyahat etmek, gezmek** *I spent a year travelling around Asia.* ○ *He has to travel abroad a lot on business.* **2** [I] If light, sound, or news travels, it moves from one place to another. **gitmek, yayılmak, ulaşmak** *News of the accident travelled fast.*

travel[2] /'trævᵊl/ *noun* [U] the activity of travelling **yolculuk, seyahat** *air/rail travel* ○ *travel expenses/ insurance* **2** *sb's* **travels** someone's journey **seyahati, yolculuğu** *I meet all kinds of interesting people on my travels.*

'travel ,agency (*also* **'travel ,agent's**) *noun* [C] a company or shop that makes travel arrangements for people **seyahat acentesi**

'travel ,agent *noun* [C] someone whose job is making travel arrangements for people **turizmci, seyahat acentesi**

traveller /'trævᵊlə*r*/ *noun* [C] **1** (*also US* **traveler**) someone who is travelling or who often travels **yolcu, gezgin, seyyah** *We're doing a survey of business travellers.* **2** *UK* another word for gypsy (= a member of a race of people who travel from place to place, especially in Europe) **çingene, göçer**

'traveller's ,cheque *UK* (*US* **traveler's check**) *noun* [C] a special piece of paper which you buy at a bank and exchange for local money when you are in another country **seyahat çeki**

traverse /trə'vɜːs/ *verb* [T] *formal* to move across something **geçmek, aşmak**

travesty /'trævəsti/ *noun* [C] *formal* If something is a travesty, it is very badly done or unfair and does not represent how that thing should be. **kötü/berbat taklit, gülünç taklit** *She described the trial as a travesty of justice.*

trawl /trɔːl/ *verb*
trawl through sth *phrasal verb mainly UK* to look through a lot of things in order to find something **bir çok şeyi karıştırarak aramak/bulmaya çalışmak** *to trawl through data*

trawler /'trɔːlə*r*/ *noun* [C] a large ship which is used for catching fish by pulling a large net through the sea **behind it trol balıkçı gemisi**

tray /treɪ/ *noun* [C] a flat object with higher edges, used for carrying food and drinks **tepsi** *She came back carrying a tray of drinks.*

treacherous /'tretʃᵊrəs/ *adjective* **1** very dangerous, especially because of bad weather conditions (**hava koşulları**) **çok tehlikeli** *Ice had made the roads treacherous.* **2** *formal* If someone is treacherous, they deceive people who trust them. **güvenilmez, hain, iki yüzlü**

treachery /'tretʃᵊri/ *noun* [U] *formal* when a person deceives someone who trusts them **kalleşlik, hainlik, iki yüzlülük**

treacle /'triːkl/ *UK* (*UK/US* **molasses**) *noun* [U] a sweet, thick, dark liquid used in sweet dishes **şeker pekmezi**

tread[1] /tred/ *verb past tense* **trod**, *past participle* **trodden 1** [I, T] *mainly UK* to put your foot on something or to press something down with your foot **basmak, basıp ezmek, çiğnemek** *I trod on a piece of broken glass.* ○ *David trod in some paint.* ○ *The kids were treading cake crumbs into the carpet.* **2 tread carefully/gently/ lightly, etc** to be careful what you say so that you do not upset someone **dikkatli/nazik/hafifçe davranmak/ söylemek/hareket etmek 3 tread water** to float vertically in the water by moving your arms and legs up and down **suda dikey olarak yüzmek/hareket etmek; suda dik durmak**

tread[2] /tred/ *noun* [C, U] **1** the pattern of lines on the surface of a tyre **tırnak, lastik dişi 2** [no plural] the sound of someone putting their feet down when walking **ayak sesi**

treadmill /'tredmɪl/ *noun* [C] **1** a machine with a moving part which you walk or run on for exercise **yürüyüş/koşu bandı 2** a job which is boring because you have to repeat the same thing again and again **sıkıcı iş; hep tekrarlanan iş**

treason /'triːzᵊn/ *noun* [U] the crime of doing something that harms your country or government, especially by helping its enemies **vatan ihanet, vatana ihanet suçu**

treasure[1] /'treʒə*r*/ *noun* **1** [U] a collection of gold, silver, jewellery and valuable objects, especially in children's stories **hazine, define, gömü** *buried treasure* **2** [C] a very valuable object **hazine, çok değerli şey** [usually plural] *art treasures*

treasure[2] /'treʒə*r*/ *verb* [T] If you treasure something, it is very important to you and gives you a lot of pleasure. **çok büyük değer vermek; gözünün içine bakmak; çok değerli saymak; üzerine titremek** *I shall treasure those memories of her.*

treasurer /'treʒᵊrə*r*/ *noun* [C] someone who is responsible for the money of an organization **kasadar, sayman, muhasip, veznedar**

treasury /'treʒᵊri/ *noun* [C] the government department which controls a country's money supply and economy **Maliye Bakanlığı; hazine**

◦ᴸ**treat**[1] /triːt/ *verb* [T] **1** DEAL WITH to behave towards or deal with someone in a particular way **davranmak,**

muamele etmek *He treats her really **badly**.* ○ *She felt she'd been **unfairly** treated by her employer.* ○ *They treat her **like** one of their own children.* **2** CONSIDER to consider something in a particular way **ele almak, belli şekilde dikkate almak** *He treated my suggestion as a joke.* **3** ILLNESS/INJURY to give medical care to someone for an illness or injury **tedavi etmek, bakmak, iyileştirmek** *He's being **treated for** cancer at a hospital in Manchester.* **4** SPECIAL to do or buy something special for someone **birine bir şey almak; birisi için bir şey yapmak; ısmarlamak** *I'm going to **treat** her to dinner at that nice Italian restaurant.* **5** PROTECT to put a substance on something in order to protect it **kaplamak, işlemek, işleme tâbi tutmak** *The wood is then **treated with** a special chemical to protect it from the rain.*

treat² /triːt/ *noun* [C] something special which you buy or do for someone else **ikram, ısmarlama, sunma** *a birthday treat* ○ *As a **special treat** I'm taking him out for dinner.* ○ *Annie, put your money away, this is **my treat** (= I am paying).* ◆See also: **Trick or treat!**.

treatise /ˈtriːtɪz/ *noun* [C] a formal piece of writing that examines a particular subject **inceleme raporu; değerlendirme yazısı**

---
treatment ...... İLE BİRLİKTE KULLANILAN KELİMELER

get/have/receive/undergo treatment ● **give/provide** treatment ● **respond to** treatment ● treatment **for** sth
---

o~**treatment** /ˈtriːtmənt/ *noun* **1** [C, U] something which you do to try to cure an illness or injury, especially something suggested or done by a doctor **tedavi, bakım** *She's receiving **treatment** for a lung infection.* **2** [U] the way you deal with or behave towards someone or something **davranış, muamele** *There have been complaints about the treatment of prisoners.*

---
treaty ...... İLE BİRLİKTE KULLANILAN KELİMELER

draw up/ratify/sign a treaty ● the **terms of** a treaty ● **under** a treaty ● a treaty **between** sb and sb ● a treaty **on** sth ● a **peace** treaty ● an **international** treaty
---

treaty /ˈtriːti/ *noun* [C] a written agreement between two or more countries **antlaşma, muahede** *a peace treaty* ○ *an international treaty*

treble /ˈtrebl/ *verb* [I, T] to increase three times in size or amount, or to make something do this **üç misli artmak/artırmak**

o~**tree** /triː/ *noun* [C] a tall plant with a thick stem which has branches coming from it and leaves **ağaç** ◆See also: Christmas tree, family tree, palm tree.

trek /trek/ *noun* [C] a long, difficult journey that you make by walking **yaya olarak yapılan uzun dağ/kır yürüyüşü/gezisi** *They started out on the long trek across the mountains.* ● **trek** *verb* [I] **trekking,** *past* **trekked uzun ve zor bir yürüyüş yapmak**

trellis /ˈtrelɪs/ *noun* [C] a wooden structure fixed to a wall for plants to grow up **duvara tutturulmuş sarmaşık vb. bitkiler için ahşap parmaklık/kafes**

tremble /ˈtrembl/ *verb* [I] to shake slightly, especially because you are nervous, frightened, or cold **tir tir titremek** *My hands were trembling so much I could hardly hold the pen.*

tremendous /trɪˈmendəs/ *adjective* **1** extremely good **müthiş, olağanüstü, şahane, harika** *I think she's doing a tremendous job.* **2** very large, great, strong, etc **çok büyük, kocaman, muazzam** *a tremendous amount of money* ● **tremendously** *adverb* very much **çok, son derece**

tree

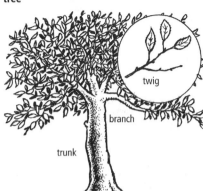

twig

branch

trunk

tremor /ˈtremər/ *noun* [C] **1** a slight earthquake (= when the Earth shakes) **hafif yer sarsıntısı, ufak deprem** **2** a slight shaking of part of your body which you cannot control **ürperti, titreme, ürperme**

trench /trenʃ/ *noun* [C] a long, narrow hole dug into the ground **hendek, siper**

trenchant /ˈtrenʃənt/ *adjective formal* expressing strong criticism **acımasız, yerici, sert** *trenchant criticism/views*

trenchcoat /ˈtrenʃˌkəʊt/ *noun* [C] a long coat that does not let water through, similar in style to a military coat **yağmurluk; trençkot**

trend /trend/ *noun* [C] a general development or change in a situation **eğilim, yön, gidiş, değişiklik** *There's a **trend towards** more locally produced television programmes.* ○ *I'm not familiar with the latest **trends** in teaching methodology.*

trendy /ˈtrendi/ *adjective informal* fashionable at the moment **son moda, modaya uygun**

trepidation /ˌtrepɪˈdeɪʃ³n/ *noun* [U] *formal* fear or worry about something you are going to do **korku, endişe** *It was with trepidation that I accepted Klein's invitation.*

trespass /ˈtrespəs/ *verb* [I] to go on someone's land without their permission **(başkasının arazisine) izinsiz girmek/geçmek** ● **trespasser** *noun* [C] **başkasının tarlasına/alanına izinsiz girş yapan**

tri- /traɪ-/ *prefix* three **üç... anlamında ön ek** *a triangle* ○ *a tripod*

---
trial ...... İLE BİRLİKTE KULLANILAN KELİMELER

be on/stand trial (for sth) ● **be awaiting/be facing** trial ● a trial **court/date/judge**
---

o~**trial** /traɪəl/ *noun* [C, U] **1** a legal process to decide if someone is guilty of a crime **yargılama, duruşma, mahkeme** *The two men are now **on trial** for attempted murder.* ○ *He will be taken to the US to **stand trial**.* **2** a test of something new to find out if it is safe, works correctly, etc **deneme, tecrübe** *The drug is currently undergoing **clinical trials**.* **3 trial and error** a way of learning the best way to do something by trying different methods **deneme/sınama yanılma** *There aren't any instructions with it - it's just a matter of trial and error.*

trials /traɪəlz/ *noun* [plural] **1** a sports competition to find out how good a player is **seçmeler, seçme müsabakaları** **2** **trials and tribulations** problems and suffering baştan geçenler; zorluk ve sıkıntılar; çekilenler *the trials and tribulations of growing up*

triangle /ˈtraɪæŋgl/ *noun* [C] **1** a flat shape with three sides üçgen ○See picture at **shape. 2** a small musical instrument made of a piece of metal with three sides which you hit with a metal bar **metal çubukla çalınan üçgen şeklinde müzik aleti ● triangular** /traɪˈæŋgjələʳ/ *adjective* shaped like a triangle **üçgen şeklinde üç köşeli**

tribe /traɪb/ *noun* [C] a group of people who live together, usually in areas far away from cities, and who share the same culture and language and still have a traditional way of life **kabile, aşiret, boy, klân** *Native American tribes* **● tribal** *adjective* relating to a tribe **kabile ile ilgili; kabileye ait** *a tribal dance*

tribulations /ˌtrɪbjəˈleɪʃⁿnz/ *noun* [plural] ○See **trials** and **tribulations.**

tribunal /traɪˈbjuːnⁿl/ *noun* [C] an official court or group of people whose job is to deal with a particular problem or disagreement **yargıçlar kurulu** ○See also: **industrial tribunal.**

tributary /ˈtrɪbjətʳri/ *noun* [C] a river or stream which flows into a larger river **ırmak/dere kolu/ayağı**

tribute /ˈtrɪbjuːt/ *noun* [C, U] **1** something which you do or say to show that you respect and admire someone, especially in a formal situation **övgü, takdir, güzel söz** *The concert was organized as **a tribute** to the singer who died last year.* ○ *The President **paid tribute to** (= expressed his admiration for) the brave soldiers who had defended the country.* **2 be a tribute to sb/sth** to show how good someone or something is **eseri olmak; olumlu sonuç/iyi eser olmak** *It's a tribute to Mark's hard work that the project is finished.*

'tribute ˌband *noun* [C] a group of musicians who play the music of a famous pop group and pretend to be that group **başkasının müzik ve hareketlerini benzeterek yapmaya çalışan taklit bandosu/orkestrası** *a Rolling Stones tribute band*

---

trick .... İLE BİRLİKTE KULLANILAN KELİMELER

play a trick (on sb) **●** a **cheap/cruel/dirty/sneaky** trick **●** a trick **question**

---

trick¹ /trɪk/ *noun* [C] **1** DECEIVE something you do to deceive or cheat someone, or to make someone look stupid as a joke **aldatmaca, hile, oyun, kandırma, el çabukluğu** *a trick question* ○ *I wasn't really ill - it was just a trick.* ○ *My little brother liked to **play tricks on** me* (= do things to deceive me as a joke). **2** METHOD an effective way of doing something **ustalık, marifet, numara** *What's the **trick to** pulling out this sofa bed?* **3** MAGIC something that is done to entertain people and that seems to be magic **oyun, numara, el çabukluğu, muziplik, hile** *a card trick* **4 do the trick** If something does the trick, it solves a problem or has the result you want. **işi bitirmek, istenilen sonucu sağlamak; zor bir işin üstesinden gelmek; amaca hizmet etmek** *If I've got a headache, a couple of aspirins usually do the trick.* ○See also: **hat trick.**

trick² /trɪk/ *verb* [T] to deceive someone **aldatmak, kandırmak, oyuna getirmek, faka bastırmak** [+ into + doing sth] *They tricked him into signing the papers.*

trickery /ˈtrɪkʳri/ *noun* [U] the use of tricks to deceive or cheat people **hile, hilekârlık, üçkağıtçılık, dolap çevirme**

trickle /ˈtrɪkl/ *verb* **1 trickle down/from/out of, etc** If liquid trickles somewhere, it flows slowly and in a thin line. **sızmak, ip gibi akmak; ince ince sızıp akmak** *She could feel the sweat trickling down her back.* **2 trickle in/into/out, etc** to go somewhere slowly in small num-

bers **küçük gruplar halinde/üçer beşer gitmek** *People began to trickle into the classroom.* **● trickle** *noun* [C] *a trickle of blood* **damlama**

ˌTrick or 'treat! 1 something that children say on Halloween (= a holiday on 31 October), when they dress to look frightening and visit people's houses to ask for sweets **Ya kanarsın ya bakarsın!'; Cadılar Bayramı'nda çocukların korkutucu kıyafetler giyerek ve kapı kapı dolaşarak şeker/çikolata isterken söyledikleri ifade 2 go trick or treating** If children go trick or treating, they visit people's houses on Halloween to ask for sweets. **Cadılar Bayramı'nda 'Ya kanarsın ya bakarsın!' oyunu oynamak**

tricky /ˈtrɪki/ *adjective* difficult to deal with or do **zor, güç, uğraşılması zor** *a tricky question/situation*

tricycle /ˈtraɪsɪkl/ *noun* [C] a bicycle with one wheel at the front and two at the back **üç tekerlekli bisiklet**

trifle /ˈtraɪfl/ *noun* **1 a trifle** *formal* slightly **biraz, azıcık bir dereceye kadar** *It does seem a trifle odd.* **2** [C, U] *UK* a cold, sweet dish that has layers of cake, fruit, custard (= sweet, yellow sauce), and cream **meyveli ve kremalı bir tür tatlı 3** [C] *formal* something silly or unimportant **önemsiz/değersiz şey, uyduruk şey; ıvır zıvır**

trigger¹ /ˈtrɪgəʳ/ (*also* trigger off) *verb* [T] to make something begin to happen **tetiklemek, başlatmak, harekete geçirmek** *His arrest triggered mass protests.*

trigger² /ˈtrɪgəʳ/ *noun* [C] **1** the part of a gun that you pull when you shoot **tetik 2** an event or situation that makes something else happen **bir şeyi başlatan olay/durum/hadise** *Stress can be a trigger for many illnesses.*

trillion /ˈtrɪljən/ the number 1,000,000,000,000 **trilyon**

trilogy /ˈtrɪlədʒi/ *noun* [C] a series of three books, plays, etc with the same characters or subject **üçlü yapıt/eser**

trim¹ /trɪm/ *verb* [T] **trimming**, *past* **trimmed 1** (*also* trim off) to cut a small amount from something to make it tidy or to remove parts that you do not need **kesip düzeltmek, kırkmak, uçlarını almak** *I've had my hair trimmed.* ○ *Trim the fat off the meat.* **2** to reduce something **azaltmak, kısmak, kırpmak** *to trim costs* **3 be trimmed with sth** to be decorated with something around the edges **süslemek, dekore etmek; süslerle bezemek** *a silk dress trimmed with lace*

trim² /trɪm/ *noun* **1** [no plural] when you cut something to make it tidy **kesip düzeltme, kırpma, düzenli hâle getirme** *The hedge needs a trim.* **2** [U, no plural] decoration that is added to something such as clothes or a car **süs, takı, süslü şeyler, biye** *The car has a stereo, sunroof, and leather trim.*

trim³ /trɪm/ *adjective* looking thin and healthy **ince ve zarif, sağlıklı, derli toplu**

trimester /trɪˈmestəʳ/ ⓤ /traɪˈmestər/ *noun* [C] *mainly US* one of the periods of time that the school or university year is divided into **dönem; üçlü dönemli eğitim öğretim yapan üniversite ve okullardaki dönemlerden biri**

trimming /ˈtrɪmɪŋ/ *noun* [C, U] decoration on the edge of something such as a piece of clothing **süs, aksesuar, biye**

trimmings /ˈtrɪmɪŋz/ *noun* [plural] extra dishes that are often eaten with a main dish **garnitür** *a roast dinner with all the trimmings*

the Trinity /ˈtrɪnəti/ *noun* the existence of God in three forms, Father, Son, and Holy Spirit, in the Christian religion **(Hıristiyanlıkta) teslis; Baba, Oğul ve Kutsal Ruh**

trio /'triːəʊ/ *noun* [C] a group of three things or people, especially three musicians who play together **üçlü grup**

⬚ *trip* ······ İLE BİRLİKTE KULLANILAN KELİMELER

go on/take a trip ● a **day/two-day/weekend** trip ● **on** a trip ● a trip **around/to** sth ● a **business** trip

---

◦┄**trip¹** /trɪp/ *noun* [C] a journey in which you visit a place for a short time and come back again **gezinti, gezi, yolculuk, seyahat** *a business trip* ○ *a day trip to Paris* ○ *We might **take a trip** to Spain later in the summer.* ⊃See also: round trip.

trip² /trɪp/ *verb* **tripping**, *past* **tripped 1** [I] to fall or almost fall because you hit your foot on something when you are walking or running **tökezlemek, ayağı sürçmek, takılmak, ayağı takılmak, takılıp düşmek** *Careful you don't **trip** over the cat!* ○ *He tripped on a stone and hurt his ankle.* **2** [T] to make someone fall by putting your foot in front of their foot **çelme takmak, çelme atmak, çelmelemek**
trip (sb) up *phrasal verb* **1** *UK* to fall because you hit your foot on something, or to make someone fall by putting your foot in front of their foot **tökezlemek, tökezletmek 2** to make a mistake, or to cause someone to make a mistake **hata yapmak, tökezlemek; hata yaptırmak;** *I tripped up on the last question.*

triple¹ /'trɪpl/ *adjective* having three parts of the same type, or happening three times **üçlü, üç kez** *a triple world champion*

triple² /'trɪpl/ *verb* [I, T] to increase three times in size or amount, or to make something do this **üçe katlamak; üçe katlanmak** *Sales have tripled in the past five years.*

triplet /'trɪplət/ *noun* [C] one of three children who are born to the same mother at the same time **üçüz**

tripod /'traɪpɒd/ *noun* [C] a piece of equipment with three legs, used for supporting a camera or a container in a science laboratory **üç ayaklı fotoğraf makinesi sehpası**

trite /traɪt/ *adjective* A trite remark, idea, etc does not seem sincere or true because it has been used so much before or is too simple. **bayat, eskimiş, özgün olmayan; çok kullanılmış; espri özelliğini yitirmiş**

triumph¹ /'traɪəmf/ *noun* **1** [C] an important success, achievement, or victory **zafer, başarı, galibiyet** *Barcelona's 2-0 triumph over Manchester United* **2** [U] the feeling of happiness that you have when you win something or succeed **zafer sevinci/şarhoşluğu/neşesi**

triumph² /'traɪəmf/ *verb* [I] to win or succeed **başarmak, yenmek, zafer kazanmak** *The Democrats once again triumphed in recent elections.*

triumphant /traɪ'ʌmfənt/ *adjective* feeling very pleased because you have won something or succeeded **muzaffer; zafer sarhoşu** *the President's triumphant return to the White House* ● **triumphantly** *adverb* **başarılı ve galip gelmiş bir şekilde**

trivia /'trɪviə/ *noun* [U] small facts or details that are not important **önemsiz/basit şeyler**

trivial /'trɪviəl/ *adjective* small and not important **önemsiz, değersiz, sıradan** *a trivial matter/offence*

trivialize (*also UK* **-ise**) /'trɪviᵊlaɪz/ *verb* [T] to make something seem less important or serious than it really is **önemini/değerini azaltmak; sıradanlaştırmak; küçültmek** *I don't mean to trivialize the problem.*

trod /trɒd/ *past tense of* tread **çiğnemek' fiilinin 2. hâli**

trodden /'trɒdᵊn/ *past participle of* tread **çiğnemek' fiilinin 3. hâli**

trolley

supermarket trolley *UK*, shopping cart *US*

luggage trolley *UK*, luggage cart *US*

trolley /'trɒli/ *noun* [C] **1** *UK* (*US* **cart**) a metal structure on wheels that is used for carrying things **el arabası; alışveriş arabası; tekerlekli servis arabası** *a supermarket trolley* ○ *a luggage trolley* **2** *US* (*UK/US* **tram**) an electric vehicle for carrying passengers, mostly in cities, which runs along metal tracks in the road **tramvay; troleybüs 3 off your trolley** *informal* mad

trombone /trɒm'bəʊn/ *noun* [C] a metal musical instrument that you play by blowing into it and sliding a tube up and down **trombon**

troop¹ /truːp/ *noun* [C] a group of people or animals **topluluk, grup, sürü**

troop² /truːp/ *verb informal* **troop into/through/out of, etc** to walk somewhere in a large group **büyük gruplar halinde gitmek/yürümek** *We all trooped into the hall in silence.*

trooper /'truːpəʳ/ *noun* [C] a police officer in the US state police force (**ABD**) **polis memuru**

troops /truːps/ *noun* [plural] soldiers **askerler; askeri birlikler** *UN troops have been sent to help in the rescue effort.*

trophy /'trəʊfi/ *noun* [C] a prize, such as a silver cup, that you get for winning a race or competition **ödül, kupa**

trophy

tropical /'trɒpɪkᵊl/ *adjective* from or in the hottest parts of the world **tropikal** *a tropical climate*

the tropics /'trɒpɪks/ *noun* [plural] the hottest parts of the world, near to the Equator (= imaginary line around the Earth's middle) **tropikal kuşak**

trot¹ /trɒt/ *verb* **trotting**, *past* **trotted 1** [I] If a horse trots, it runs slowly with short steps. **tırıs gitmek 2 trot down/up/along, etc** to walk with quick, short steps **hızlı ve küçük adımlarla yürümek** *The little boy trotted along behind his father.*
trot sth out *phrasal verb informal* to say something that has been said many times before and does not seem sincere **aynı şeyleri defalarca tekrarlayıp durmak** *They always trot out the same old statistics.*

trot² /trɒt/ *noun* **1** [no plural] the speed that a horse moves when it trots **tırıs 2 on the trot** If you do several things on the trot, you do them one after the other. **aralıksız, arka arkaya** *They won three games on the trot.*

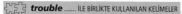

trouble ...... İLE BİRLİKTE KULLANILAN KELİMELER

have trouble **with** sth ● **get into/run into** trouble ● **the** trouble **is** ● **without** any trouble

o⌐**trouble¹** /'trʌbl/ *noun* **1** PROBLEMS [C, U] problems, difficulties, or worries **sorunlar, güçlükler, endişeler** [+ doing sth] *We had trouble finding somewhere to park.* ○ *She's been having a lot of trouble with her boss recently.* ○ *I'd like to go to the party, but the trouble is my parents won't let me.* **2 the trouble with sb/sth** used to say what is wrong with someone or something **Neyi var?', 'Derdi ne?', 'Ne oldu?'** *The trouble with a white floor is that it gets dirty so quickly.* **3** NOT WORKING [U] a problem that you have with a machine or part of your body **sorun, dert, tasa** *back trouble* ○ *car trouble* **4** FIGHTING [U] a situation in which people are fighting or arguing **maraza, kavga, karışıklık, belâ, anlaşmazlık** *The trouble started after a group of drunken football fans started to throw bottles.* **5** DIFFICULT SITUATION [U] a difficult or dangerous situation **zor teklikeli bir durum** *The company was in trouble and had huge debts.* **6** PUNISHMENT [U] when you have done something wrong and are likely to be punished **zorluk, sıkıntı, hata, kusur, dert, sorun** *Her children are always in trouble.* ○ *They got into trouble with the police.* **7** EXTRA WORK [U] when you use extra time or energy to do something **belâ, sıkıntı, çaba, zorluk** [+ to do sth] *He took the trouble to write to each of them personally.*

trouble² /'trʌbl/ *verb* [T] **1** If something troubles you, you think about it a lot and it makes you worry. **canını sıkmak, üzmek** *The situation has been troubling me for a while.* **2** *formal* used to ask someone politely to help you **sıkıntı vermek, zahmet verme, rahatsız etmek** *I'm sorry to trouble you, but could you tell me how to get to the station?*

troubled /'trʌbᵊld/ *adjective* worried or having a lot of problems **kederli, üzgün, perişan** *You look troubled.*

troublemaker /'trʌbl,meɪkəʳ/ *noun* [C] someone who intentionally causes problems **baş belâsı kimse; sürekli maraza çıkaran kimse; ortalık karıştıran kişi**

troublesome /'trʌblsəm/ *adjective* causing a lot of problems, especially over a long period of time **baş belâsı, sorun yaratan, musibet** *a troublesome knee injury*

trough /trɒf/ *noun* [C] **1** a long, narrow container that animals eat or drink from **hayvan yalağı/yemlik 2** *formal* a low point in a series of high and low points **en alt düzey, en düşük seviye** *peaks and troughs*

troupe /truːp/ *noun* [C] a group of singers, dancers, etc who perform together **sanat topluluğu**

o⌐**trousers** /'traʊzəz/ (*also US* pants) *noun* [plural] a piece of clothing that covers the legs and has a separate part for each leg **pantolon** *a pair of trousers* ⊃Orta kısımdaki renkli sayfalarına bakınız.

'trouser ,suit *UK* (*US* pant suit) *noun* [C] a woman's jacket and trousers made of the same material **(bayan)pantolon ceket takım**

trout /traʊt/ *noun* [C, U] *plural* trout a type of river fish, or the meat from this fish **alabalık**

truant /'truːənt/ *noun* [C] **1** a child who stays away from school without permission **okul kaçağı; okulu kıran öğrenci; dersi asan öğrenci 2 play truant** *UK* to stay away from school without permission **okulu kırmak/asmak; okuldan kaçmak; dersi asmak/kırmak** ● **truancy** /'truːənsi/ *noun* [U] when children are truants **okulu kırma/asma; okuldan kaçma; dersi asma/kırma**

---

truce ...... İLE BİRLİKTE KULLANILAN KELİMELER

agree/call/offer a truce ● a **fragile/uneasy** truce ● a truce **between** sb and sb ● a truce **with** sb

truce /truːs/ *noun* [C] an agreement between two enemies to stop fighting for a period of time **ateşkes, mütareke**

o⌐**truck** /trʌk/ (*also UK* lorry) *noun* [C] a large road vehicle for carrying goods from place to place **kamyon** ⊃See picture at **vehicle**.

trucker /'trʌkəʳ/ *noun* [C] *mainly US* someone whose job is driving trucks **kamyon şoförü**

trudge /trʌdʒ/ *verb* **trudge along/through/up, etc** to walk slowly with heavy steps, especially because you are tired **yorgun argın yürümek, zar zor yürümek** *We trudged back up the hill.*

o⌐**true** /truː/ *adjective* **1** based on facts and not imagined **gerçek, doğru** *a true story* ○ [+ (that)] *Is it true that Martin and Sue are getting married?* ⊃Opposite **untrue 2** [always before noun] real **hakikî, gerçek** *a true friend* ○ *true love* **3 come true** If a dream or hope comes true, it really happens. **gerçekleşmek, doğru çıkmak 4 be true to sb/sth** to be loyal and sincere even in a difficult situation **dürüst/ilkeli/bağlı/samimi/sadık olmak** *It's important to be true to your principles.* **5 ring true** to seem to be the truth **gerçek gibi gözükmek** *Something about the story didn't ring true.*

truffle /'trʌfl/ *noun* [C] **1** a soft sweet that is made with chocolate **çikolatalı yumuşak tatlı 2** a fungus (= organism like a plant) that you can eat, which grows under the ground **bir tür mantar**

truly /'truːli/ *adverb* **1** NOT FALSE used to emphasize that something is true in every way **gerçekten, hakikaten, tam anlamıyla** *The project was truly a team effort.* **2** VERY used to emphasize a description of something **tam anlamıyla, gerçekten** *It's truly amazing to watch a baby being born.* **3** SINCERE used to emphasize that something is sincere or honest **içtenlikle, samimiyetle** *I truly believe that he is innocent.*

trump /trʌmp/ *noun* **1** [C] a card that has a higher value than other cards in some card games **(iskambil) koz 2 come/turn up trumps** *UK* to be successful, or provide something that is needed, especially when people do not expect you to **başarılı olmak; elindeki kozları kullanarak başarmak** *He's really come up trumps with this latest book.*

'trump ,card *noun* [C] an advantage that will help you succeed, especially one that other people do not know about **koz, önemli üstünlük**

trumpet /'trʌmpɪt/ *noun* [C] a metal musical instrument that you play by blowing into it and pressing buttons to make different notes **trompet, boru** ● **trumpeter** *noun* [C] **borazan çalan**

trumpet

truncheon /'trʌnʃᵊn/ *UK* (*US* nightstick) *noun* [C] a short stick that police officers carry to use as a weapon **cop, polis sopası/cobu**

truncheon

trundle /'trʌndl/ *verb* **trundle (sth) along/**

down/up, etc to move slowly on wheels, or to push something slowly on wheels **(araçla) ağır ağır ilerlemek; kaplumbağa hızıyla gitmek; ağır ağır sürmek/gitmek** *The bus trundled along the lane.*

trunk /trʌŋk/ *noun* [C] **1** TREE the thick stem of a tree that the branches grow from **gövde, ağaç gövdesi** ⊃See picture at **tree**. **2** CAR *US* (*UK* **boot**) a closed space at the back of a car for storing things in **bagaj** ⊃Orta kısımdaki renkli sayfalarına bakınız. **3** NOSE the long nose of an elephant (= large, grey animal) **fil hortumu 4** CONTAINER a large box with a lid that you store things in **sandık 5** BODY the main part of your body, not your head, legs, or arms **gövde, insan gövdesi**

'trunk ,road *noun* [C] *UK* a main road across a country or area **ana yol**

trunks /trʌŋks/ *noun* [plural] **1** (*also* **swimming trunks**) a piece of clothing that boys and men wear when they swim **erkek mayosu 2** underwear worn by men **erkek içgiyim** ⊃Orta kısımdaki renkli sayfalarına bakınız.

o--**trust¹** /trʌst/ *verb* **1** [T] to believe that someone is good and honest and will not harm you **güvenmek, güven duymak, itimat etmek** *My sister warned me not to trust him.* ⊃Opposite **distrust, mistrust**. **2 trust sb to do sth** to be sure that someone will do the right thing or what they should do **inanmak, güvenmek, itimat etmek** *I trust them to make the right decision.* **3 trust sb with sb/sth** to allow someone to look after someone or something because you believe they will be careful **güvenerek vermek/söylemek, emniyet etmek** *I wouldn't trust him with my car.* **4 Trust sb (to do sth)!** *mainly UK informal* used to say that it is typical of someone to do something stupid **...yapacağını adı gibi bilmek** *Trust Chris to leave the tickets at home!* **5 I trust (that)** *formal* used to say that you hope something is true **Eminim ki...', 'Biliyorum ki...', 'Umuyorum ki...'** *I trust that you had an enjoyable stay.*

trust (noun) ...... İLE BİRLİKTE KULLANILAN KELİMELER

have/show trust **in** sb ● **earn/gain/win** sb's trust ● **betray** sb's trust ● trust **between** [two people]

o--**trust²** /trʌst/ *noun* **1** [U] the belief that you can trust someone or something **itimat, güven** *a marriage based on love and trust* ○ *They showed a lot of trust in me right from the beginning.* ⊃Opposite **distrust, mistrust**. **2** [C, U] a legal arrangement that allows a person or organization to control someone else's money **mutemetlik antlaşması; yeddi eminlik belgesi; vesayet antlaşması**

trustee /trʌs'tiː/ *noun* [C] someone who has legal control over someone else's money or possessions **emanetçi, yeddi emin, mutemet**

trusting /'trʌstɪŋ/ *adjective* always believing that other people are good or honest and will not harm or deceive you **herkese itimat eden, kolay inanan**

trustworthy /'trʌst,wɜːði/ *adjective* Someone who is trustworthy can be trusted. **güvenilir, emin, sağlam, itimada şayan**

truth ...... İLE BİRLİKTE KULLANILAN KELİMELER

tell the truth ● **discover/find out/learn/uncover** the truth ● the truth **comes out/emerges** ● the **awful/honest/simple** truth ● the truth **about** sb/sth

o--**truth** /truːθ/ *noun plural* **truths** /truːðz/ **1 the truth** the real facts about a situation **gerçek, hakikat** *Do you think he was telling the truth?* ○ *I don't think we'll ever know the truth about what really happened.* **2** [U] the quality of being true **gerçeklik, doğruluk** *There may be some truth in their claim.* **3** [C] a fact or idea

that people accept is true **gerçek, esas, hakikat, doğru** *moral/religious truths* ⊃Opposite untruth.

truthful /'truːθf°l/ *adjective* honest and not containing or telling any lies **doğrucu, doğru sözlü** *a truthful answer* ● **truthfully** *adverb* **dürüstçe** ● **truthfulness** *noun* [U] **dürüstlük, gerçekçilik**

o--**try¹** /traɪ/ *verb* **1** ATTEMPT [I] to attempt to do something **çalışmak, kalkışmak, girişmek, teşebbüs etmek** [+ to do sth] *I tried to open the window but couldn't.* ○ *Try not to drop anything this time.* **2** TEST [T] to do, test, taste, etc something to discover if it works or if you like it **denemek, tecrübe etmek** *I tried that recipe you gave me last night.* ○ *Why don't you try using a different shampoo?* **3** LAW [T] to examine facts in a court of law to decide if someone is guilty of a crime **yargılamak, yargılanmak** [often passive] *He was tried for attempted murder.*

try sth on *phrasal verb* to put on a piece of clothing to discover if it fits you or if you like it **elbiseyi denemek, prova etmek** *Could I try this dress on, please?*

try sth out *phrasal verb* to use something to discover if it works or if you like it **yaparak sınamak, uygulayarak denemek** *We're going to try out that new restaurant tonight.*

try² /traɪ/ *noun* **1** [C] an attempt to do something **kalkışma, girişme, teşebbüs, deneme** *She suggested I should have a try.* **2 give sth a try** to do something in order to find out if it works or if you like it **bir kez denemek, çalışıp çalışmadığına bakmak; deneyerek anlamak 3** [C] when a team scores points in rugby (= game played with an oval ball) by putting the ball on the ground behind the other team's goal line **(rugby oyununda) puan, skor, sayı**

trying /'traɪɪŋ/ *adjective* annoying and difficult **yorucu, bıktırıcı, sabır taşıran, can sıkıcı** *I've had a very trying day/time.*

tsar *UK* (*UK/US* **czar**) /zɑːʳ/ *noun* [C] **1** a male Russian ruler before 1917 **çar; Rus imparatoru 2** a powerful official who makes important decisions for the government about a particular activity **hükümet adına kararları veren güçlü yetkili**

T-shirt (*also* **tee shirt**) /'tiː.ʃɜːt/ *noun* [C] a piece of cotton clothing for the top part of the body with short sleeves and no collar **yakasız kısa kollu pamuklu giysi; T-gömlek veya Tömlek; tişört** ⊃Orta kısımdaki renkli sayfalarına bakınız.

tsp *written abbreviation for* teaspoonful: the amount that can be held by a small spoon used for measuring food **çay kaşığı dolusu/ölçüsünde**

tub /tʌb/ *noun* [C] **1** LARGE CONTAINER a large, round container with a flat base and an open top **küvet, çamaşır leğeni** *Outside was a stone patio with tubs of flowering plants.* **2** FOOD CONTAINER a small, plastic container with a lid, used for storing food **plastik kutu** *a tub of ice cream/margarine* ⊃See picture at **container**. **3** BATH *US* (*UK* **bath**) a large container that you fill with water and sit in to wash **küvet, banyo teknesi** ⊃Orta kısımdaki renkli sayfalarına bakınız.

tuba /'tjuːbə/ *noun* [C] a large, metal musical instrument that produces low notes, and is played by blowing into it **tuba**

tube /tjuːb/ *noun* **1** [C] a pipe of glass, plastic, metal, etc, especially for liquids or gases to flow through **boru, tüp, kanal, boru 2** [C] a long, thin container for a soft substance, that you press to get the substance out **tüp** *a tube of toothpaste* ⊃See picture at **container**. **3 the Tube** the system of railways under the ground in London **metro, tünel** *I got the Tube to Oxford Circus.* ⊃See also: test **tube**.

tuberculosis /tjuːˌbɜːkjəˈləʊsɪs/ (*abbreviation* **TB**) *noun* [U] a serious infectious disease of the lungs **verem, tüberküloz**

tubing /ˈtjuːbɪŋ/ *noun* [U] a long piece of metal, plastic, etc in the shape of a tube **borular** *steel tubing*

tubular /ˈtjuːbjələʳ/ *adjective* in the shape of a tube **tüp/ boru şeklinde/biçiminde**

tuck /tʌk/ *verb* **1 tuck sth into/behind/under, etc** to push a loose piece of clothing or material somewhere to make it tidy **sokmak; sokuşturmak** *Tuck your shirt in.* **2 tuck sth behind/under/in, etc** to put something in a small place so that it is safe and cannot move **sokmak, koymak, yerleştirmek** *I found an old letter tucked in the back of the book.*

tuck sth away *phrasal verb* to put something in a safe place **saklamak, gizlemek, güvenilir bir yere koymak** *Helen tucked the money away in her purse.*

be tucked away *phrasal verb* to be in a place that is hidden, or in a place that few people go to **sakla(n) mak; gizle(n)mek; gözlerden uzak yerde olmak/ konulmak** *He lives in a cottage tucked away in the Suffolk countryside.*

tuck in/tuck into sth *phrasal verb UK informal* to start eating something, especially with enthusiasm **iştahla yemek/atıştırmak** *I was just about to tuck into a huge bowl of pasta.*

tuck sb in/up *phrasal verb* to make someone, especially a child, comfortable in bed by putting the covers around them **üstünü örtmek, yerleştirmek, yatırmak ve üstünü itina ile örtmek**

⚬ʌ**Tuesday** /ˈtjuːzdeɪ/ (*written abbreviation* **Tue, Tues**) *noun* [C, U] the day of the week after Monday and before Wednesday **salı, salı günü**

tuft /tʌft/ *noun* [C] a small group of hairs, grass, etc **tutam, demet**

tug[1] /tʌg/ *verb* [T] **tugging**, *past* **tugged** to pull something suddenly and strongly **kuvvetle asılmak, şiddetle çekmek** *Tom tugged at his mother's arm.*

tug[2] /tʌg/ *noun* [C] **1** a sudden, strong pull on something **kuvvetli çekiş, asılma 2** (*also* **tugboat** /ˈtʌgbəʊt/) a boat used for pulling larger ships **römorkör**

get/be given/offer/receive tuition ● **expert** tuition ● **individual/one-to-one/private** tuition ● tuition **in** sth

tuition /tjuˈɪʃ^ən/ *noun* [U] **1** the teaching of one person or of a small group of people **özel ders, öğretim, öğretme** *French tuition* **2** *mainly US* money that you pay for being taught, especially at college or university **okul ücreti; eğitim ücreti**

tulip /ˈtjuːlɪp/ *noun* [C] a brightly coloured spring flower in the shape of a cup **lâle**

tumble /ˈtʌmbl/ *verb* [I] **1** to suddenly fall **tepe taklak yuvarlanmak; paldır küldür düşmek** *He tumbled down the stairs.* **2** If the price or value of something tumbles, it suddenly becomes lower. **(ücret, fiyat, değer) tepe yaklak olmak; düşmek; birden inmek** *Share prices tumbled by 20%.* ● **tumble** *noun* [C] **düşüş**

ˌ**tumble ˈdryer** *UK* (*US* **dryer**) *noun* [C] a machine that dries clothes **çamaşır kurutma makinası**

tumbler /ˈtʌmbləʳ/ *noun* [C] a glass that you drink out of, that has straight sides and no handle **su bardağı**

tummy /ˈtʌmi/ *noun* [C] *informal* stomach **mide**

tumour *UK* (*US* **tumor**) /ˈtjuːməʳ/ *noun* [C] a group of cells in someone's body which are not growing normally **tümör, kanserli hücre**

tumultuous /tjuˈmʌltjuəs/ *adjective* full of noise and excitement **gürültülü, patırtılı** *tumultuous applause* ○ *a tumultuous reception/welcome*

tuna /ˈtjuːnə/ *noun* [C, U] *plural* **tuna** a large sea fish, or the meat from this fish **ton balığı, orkinos**

hum/play/sing/whistle a tune ● a **catchy** tune

tune[1] /tjuːn/ *noun* **1** [C] a series of musical notes that are pleasant to listen to **ezgi, melodi, nağme** *He was humming a tune as he dried the dishes.* **2 in tune** singing or playing the right notes **doğru notada, akortlu 3 out of tune** singing or playing the wrong notes **yanlış notada, akortsuz** *The piano is out of tune.* **4 change your tune** to suddenly change your opinion about something **tavır/ağız/fikir değiştirmek** ● **5 be in tune with sb** to be able to understand what someone wants or needs **uyumlu/ahenkli/uygun/uyum sağlayan/uyum içinde olmak** *The government is not in tune with the voters.*

tune[2] /tjuːn/ *verb* [T] **1** to make slight changes to a musical instrument so that it plays the right notes **akort etmek 2** to make changes to a television or radio so that it receives programmes from a particular company **istasyon/kanal ayarlamak/ayarı yapmak** *Stay tuned for* (= continue watching or listening for) *more details.* ○ *The radio is tuned to Radio 5.*

tune in *phrasal verb* to watch or listen to a particular television or radio programme **belli bir tv. programı izlemek; radyo kanalını dinlemek** *Be sure to tune in to next week's show.*

tune (sth) up *phrasal verb* to make slight changes to a musical instrument before you play it so that it produces the right notes **akort yapmak; bir enstrümanı akort etmek** *The orchestra were tuning up.*

tunic /ˈtjuːnɪk/ *noun* [C] a loose piece of clothing that covers the top part of your body **tunik**

tunnel[1] /ˈtʌn^əl/ *noun* [C] a long passage under the ground or through a mountain **tünel** *The train went into the tunnel.* ⊃See also: **light**[1] at the end of the tunnel.

tunnel

tunnel[2] /ˈtʌn^əl/ *verb* [I, T] *UK* **tunnelling**, *past* **tunnelled**, *US* **tunneling**, *past* **tunneled** to dig a tunnel **tünel kazmak/açmak**

turban /ˈtɜːbən/ *noun* [C] a long piece of cloth that men from some religions fold around their heads **türban, sarık**

turbine /ˈtɜːbaɪn/ *noun* [C] a large machine that produces power by using gas, steam, etc to turn a wheel **türbin**

turbulent /ˈtɜːbjələnt/ *adjective* **1** A turbulent situation, time, etc is one in which there are a lot of sudden changes, arguments, or violence. **çalkantılı, karışık, başıboş** *a turbulent relationship* **2** Turbulent air or water moves very strongly and suddenly. **(su, hava) anaforlu, çalkantılı, ● turbulence** /ˈtɜːbjələns/ *noun* [U] **çalkantı, sallantı**

turf[1] /tɜːf/ *noun* [U] short, thick grass and the soil it is growing in **çim, çimen**

turf[2] /tɜːf/ *verb*

turf sb out *phrasal verb UK informal* to make someone leave **kovmak, defetmek, çıkartmak**

turkey /ˈtɜːki/ *noun* [C, U] a bird that looks like a large chicken, or the meat of this bird **hindi**

be in/be thrown into turmoil • a state of turmoil
• emotional/political turmoil • the turmoil of
(doing) sth

turmoil /'tɜːmɔɪl/ noun [U, no plural] a situation in which
there is a lot of trouble, confusion, or noise **karışıklık,
keşmekeş, karmaşa** *The whole region is in turmoil.*

o͞ **turn¹** /tɜːn/ verb **1** MOVE YOUR BODY [I] to move your body
so that you are facing a different direction **dönmek,
çevirmek** *Ricky turned and saw Sue standing in the
doorway.* **2** CHANGE DIRECTION [I, T] to change direction
when you are moving, or to make a car do this **dönmek, döndürmek** *Turn left at the traffic lights.*
3 CHANGE POSITION [T] to move something round so that it
faces a different direction **döndürmek; yönünü değiştirmek** *Ella turned the cup to hide the crack in it.*
4 GO ROUND [I, T] to move around a central point in a
circle, or to make something do this **dönmek, etrafında dönmek/döndürmek** *Turn the steering wheel
as quickly as you can.* **5 turn blue/cold/sour, etc** to
become blue, cold, etc **maviye dönmek; soğumak;
ekşileşmek vb.** *The sky turned black and it started to
rain.* **6 turn 16/21, etc** to become a particular age **belli
bir yaşa gelmek** *He turned 18 last May.* **7 turn a page**
to move a page in a book or magazine in order to see the
next one **sayfayı çevirmek** ⊃See also: turn your **back²** on sb/
sth, turn/put the **clock¹** back, turn a blind **eye¹** (to sth), turn over a
new **leaf¹**, turn your **nose¹** up at sth, turn the tables (**table¹**) on sb,
come/turn up trumps (**trump**), turn sth **upside down¹**.

turn sb away *phrasal verb* to not allow someone to
enter a place **geri çevirmek; girmesine izin vermemek; kabul etmemek** *By 10 o'clock the club was
already full and they were turning people away.*

turn (sb) back *phrasal verb* to return in the direction
you have come from, or to make someone do this **geri
dönmek; geriye döndürmek** *They had to turn back
because of the bad weather.*

turn sb/sth down *phrasal verb* to refuse an offer or
request **reddetmek; geri çevirmek; kabul etmemek**
They did offer me the job, but I turned it down.

turn sth down *phrasal verb* to reduce the level of sound
or heat that a machine produces (**ısı, ses**) **kısmak,
azaltmak** *Could you turn the radio down, please?*

turn (sb/sth) into sb/sth *phrasal verb* to change and
become someone or something different, or to make
someone or something do this **dönmek/dönüşmek/
çevirmek; dönüştürmek/çevrilmek** *There are plans
to turn his latest book into a film.*

turn off (sth) *phrasal verb* to leave the road you are
driving along and drive on a different road **sapmak,
yön değiştirmek**

turn sth off *phrasal verb* to move the switch on a
machine, light, etc so that it stops working, or to stop
the supply of water, electricity, etc **kapatmak, söndürmek, kesmek, bitirmek** *How do you turn the computer
off?* ⊃Orta kısımdaki renkli sayfalarına bakınız.

turn sth on *phrasal verb* to move the switch on a
machine, light, etc so that it starts working, or to start
the supply of water, electricity, etc **açmak, çalıştırmak**
Ben turned the TV on. ⊃Orta kısımdaki renkli sayfalarına bakınız.

turn out *phrasal verb* **1** to happen in a particular way,
or to have a particular result **olmak, gitmek, belli bir
sonuca ulaşmak** *The bomb warning turned out to be a
false alarm.* ○ [+ (that)] *I got talking to her and it turned
out that we'd been to the same school.* **2** If people turn out
for an event, they go to be there or watch. **toplanmak,
bir araya gelmek; toplaşmak** *Over 800 people turned
out for the protest.*

turn sth out *phrasal verb* **1** to produce something **yapmak, üretmek, imâl etmek** *The factory turns out more*

than 600 vehicles a month. **2** to move the switch on a
light so that it stops working **kapatmak, söndürmek,
kesmek**

turn (sth) over *phrasal verb UK* to change to a different
television station **kanal değiştirmek** *Are you watching this or can I turn over?*

turn to sb *phrasal verb* to ask someone for help or
advice **yardımını istemek, başvurmak** *Eventually
she turned to her aunt for help.*

turn to sth *phrasal verb* **1** to find a page in a book
kitapta sayfayı bulmak *Turn to page 105.* **2** to start to
do something bad, especially because you are unhappy
başlamak; kötü alışkanlık edinmek *She turned to
drugs after the break-up of her marriage.*

turn up *phrasal verb* **1** *informal* to arrive **varmak, gelmek, ortaya çıkmak, görünmek** *Fred turned up late
again.* **2** If something that you have been looking for
turns up, you find it. **olmak, ortaya çıkmak, bulmak;
sonunda kavuşmak**

turn sth up *phrasal verb* to increase the level of sound
or heat that a machine produces **açmak, çoğaltmak,
(ses, ısı) artırmak** *I'm cold, could you turn the heating
up please?*

turn² /tɜːn/ noun **1** TIME [C] the time when you can or
must do something, usually before or after someone
else **sıra** [+ to do sth] *It's your turn to feed the rabbit - I
did it yesterday.* ○ *You'll have to be patient and wait your
turn.* **2 take turns** (*also UK* take it in turns) If two or more
people take turns, one person does something, then
another person does something, etc. **sırayla yapmak,
dönüşümlü olarak yapmak** [+ doing sth] *They all took
turns carrying the suitcase.* ○ [+ to do sth] *The children
took it in turns to hold the baby.* **3 in turn** one after another **sırayla** *He spoke to the three boys in turn.*
4 CHANGE DIRECTION [C] a change in the direction in which
you are moving or facing **değişme, değişim** *a right/
left turn* **5** BEND [C] a bend or corner in a road, river, etc
viraj, dönemeç, kavşak *Take the next turn on the right.*
6 turn of events the way in which a situation develops,
especially a sudden or unexpected change **olaylarda
âni değişim; yön değiştirme; beklenmedik gelişme**
7 take a turn for the better/worse to become better or
worse suddenly **ansızın daha da iyi/kötü hâle gelmek 8 do sb a good turn** to do something to help someone **yardım etmek için bir şeyler yapmak 9 the turn
of the century** the start of a new century **yeni yüzyıl
başlangıcı; yeni asrın başlaması** ⊃See also: U-turn.

turnaround /'tɜːnəraʊnd/ noun [C] when a bad situation changes into a good one **iyiye gidiş, iyiye doğru
değişim; dönemeç**

turning /'tɜːnɪŋ/ noun [C] *UK* a corner where one road
meets another **dönemeç** *Take the second turning on
the left.*

mark/prove/reach a turning point • the turning
point came • be at a turning point • the turning
point in/of sth • the turning point for sb • a cru-
cial/important/major/real turning point

'**turning ,point** noun [C] a time when an important
change begins to happen **dönüm noktası** *This event
marked a turning point in the country's history.*

turnip /'tɜːnɪp/ noun [C, U] a large, round, pale yellow
vegetable that grows under the ground **şalgam**

turn-off /'tɜːnɒf/ noun **1** [C] a place where you can leave
a main road to go onto another road **dönemeç, yol
ayrımı 2** [no plural] *informal* something which you dislike or which makes you feel less interested, especially
sexually **(cinsel olarak) iticilik, tiksinti uyandırma,
şevk söndürme** *Greasy hair is a real turn-off.*

turnout /'tɜːnaʊt/ *noun* [C] the number of people at an event, such as a meeting or election **katılanlar, toplananlar, katılımcılar** [usually singular] *They blamed the low turnout on the bad weather.*

turnover /'tɜːnˌəʊvər/ *noun* **1** [no plural] how much money a business earns in a period of time **ciro, iş hacmi 2** [U, no plural] the rate at which workers leave an organization and new workers join it **kadro değişimi, eleman giriş çıkışı** *a high turnover of staff*

'**turn ,signal** *US* (*UK* **indicator**) *noun* [C] a light that flashes on a vehicle to show that the driver intends to turn right or left **sağ/sol sinyali, dönüş sinyali** ⊃Orta kısımdaki renkli sayfalarına bakınız.

turnstile /'tɜːnstaɪl/ *noun* [C] a gate that only allows one person to go through it at a time **turnike; sıralı geçiş sistemi**

turpentine /'tɜːpᵊntaɪn/ (*also UK* **turps** /tɜːps/) *noun* [U] a clear liquid that has a strong smell and is used for removing paint **terebentin, neft yağı**

turquoise /'tɜːkwɔɪz/ *noun* [U] a blue-green colour **turkuaz, turkuaz rengi** ● **turquoise** *adjective* **turkuvaz**

turret /'tʌrɪt/ *noun* [C] a small tower that is part of a building **küçük kule, kulecik**

turtle /'tɜːtl/ *noun* [C] an animal with four legs and a hard shell that lives mainly in water **deniz/su kaplumbağası**

turtleneck /'tɜːtlnek/ *US* (*UK* **polo neck**) *noun* [C] a piece of clothing that covers the top part of the body and has a tube-like part covering the neck **boğazlı/balıkçı yaka giysi** *a turtleneck sweater* ⊃See picture at **polo neck**.

tusk /tʌsk/ *noun* [C] one of the two long, pointed teeth that come out of the mouth of some animals **fildişi; uzun diş**

tussle /'tʌsl/ *noun* [C] a fight or argument, especially between two people who want the same thing **kavga, mücadele, sert çekişme**

tut /tʌt/ (*also* **tut-tut**) *exclamation* a sound you make when you do not approve of something **Cık cık!'**

tutor /'tjuːtər/ *noun* [C] **1** someone who teaches one person or a very small group of people **özel öğretmen/hoca; danışman öğretmek** *a private tutor* **2** *UK* a university teacher who is responsible for a small group of students **üniversite hocası** ● **tutor** *verb* [T] **öğretmek, ders vermek**

tutorial /tjuːˈtɔːriəl/ *noun* [C] **1** a class in which a small group of students talks about a subject with their tutor, especially at a British university **ders, danışmanlık saati; (Britanya) belli bir konuda grup çalışması 2** a set of instructions and exercises that teaches you how to use a computer program **bilgisayar programını kullanmayı öğreten talimatlar ve alıştırmalar bütünü**

tux /tʌks/ *noun* [C] *US short for* tuxedo **smokin' sözcüğünün kısa yazılışı**

tuxedo /tʌkˈsiːdəʊ/ *US* (*UK* **dinner jacket**) *noun* [C] a black or white jacket that a man wears on a very formal occasion **smokin** ⊃See picture at **dinner jacket**.

o→**TV** (*also* **tv**) /ˌtiːˈviː/ *noun* [C, U] *abbreviation for* television **televizyon** *What's on TV tonight?* ○ *We could stay in and watch TV.* ⊃Orta kısımdaki renkli sayfalarına bakınız.

twang /twæŋ/ *noun* [C] the sound that is made by pulling a tight string or wire **tınlamak, tın sesi çıkartmak** ● **twang** *verb* [I, T] **tın sesinin çıkması**

tweak /twiːk/ *verb* [T] **1** to change something slightly to try to improve it **gelistirmek için küçük değişiklikler yapmak 2** to pull or twist something quickly and suddenly **ansızın çimdikleyip çekmek, çekiştirmek**

Dad sat there tweaking his beard. ● **tweak** *noun* [C] **ayar yapmak, geliştirmek**

tweed /twiːd/ *noun* [U] a thick, rough cloth made of wool **iskoç kumaşı, tüvit**

tweezers /'twiːzəz/ *noun* [plural] a small tool with two narrow pieces of metal joined at one end, used for picking up or pulling out very small things **cımbız**

tweezers

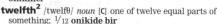

twelfth¹ /twelfθ/ 12th written as a word **onikinci**

twelfth² /twelfθ/ *noun* [C] one of twelve equal parts of something; 1/12 **onikide bir**

o→**twelve** /twelv/ the number 12 **oniki**

o→**twenty** /'twenti/ **1** the number 20 **yirmi 2 the twenties** the years from 1920 to 1929 **1920'li yıllar 3 be in your twenties** to be aged between 20 and 29 **yirmilerinde olmak** ● **twentieth** 20th written as a word **yirminci**

o→**twice** /twaɪs/ *adverb* two times **iki kez, iki defa, iki kere** *I've been there twice.* ○ *I have to take the tablets twice a day.*

twiddle /'twɪdl/ *verb* [I, T] to move your fingers around, or turn something around many times, especially because you are bored **sıkıntıdan parmaklarıyla oynamak; döndürmek, bir şeyle oynamak** *Karen just sat there twiddling with her hair.*

twig /twɪg/ *noun* [C] a small, thin branch on a tree **sürgün, ince dal** ⊃See picture at **tree**.

twilight /'twaɪlaɪt/ *noun* [U] the time just before it becomes completely dark in the evening **alaca karanlık**

a set of twins ● sb's twin brother/sister ● identical twins

twin¹ /twɪn/ *noun* [C] one of two children who are born to the same mother at the same time **ikiz** ⊃See also: **identical twin**.

twin² /twɪn/ *adjective* [always before noun] used to describe two similar things that are a pair **çift, ikiz, eş** *twin beds*

twin³ /twɪn/ *verb UK* **be twinned with sth** If a town in one country is twinned with a town in another country, the two towns have a special relationship. **kardeş şehir olmak** *Leeds in England is twinned with Dortmund in Germany.*

twinge /twɪndʒ/ *noun* [C] **1** a sudden, slight emotion **anî üzüntü duygusu, azap** *a twinge of guilt* **2** a sudden, slight pain **bıçak saplanır gibi bir ağrı; anî ve keskin bir acı; spazm**

twinkle /'twɪŋkl/ *verb* [I] **1** If light twinkles, it shines and seems to be quickly flashing on and off. **pırıldamak, parıldamak, ışıldamak** *The lights of the town twinkled in the distance.* **2** If someone's eyes twinkle, they look bright and happy. **gözleri parıldamak; ışıl ışıl yanmak** ● **twinkle** *noun* [C] **parıldamak (ışık), gözün kırpması**

twirl /twɜːl/ *verb* [I, T] to turn around and around quickly, or to make something do this **fırıl fırıl dönmek/döndürmek** ● **twirl** *noun* [C] **kıvırma, kıvrılma**

twist[1] /twɪst/ *verb*
1 [TURN] [T] to turn something using your hand **döndürmek, dönmek** *She sat there nervously twisting the ring around on her finger.* **2** [BEND] [T] to bend and turn something many times and change its shape **bükmek, kıvırmak, burkmak, bükülmek** *The wheels of the bike had been twisted in the accident.*
3 [TURN YOUR BODY] [I, T] to turn part of your body to face a different direction **döndürmek; dönmek; başka bir yöne dönmek** *She twisted her head so she could see what was happening.*
4 [CHANGE DIRECTION] [I] If a road, river, etc twists, it has a lot of bends in it. **(yol, nehir) kıvrılmak, dönmek,** *The path twisted and turned up the side of the mountain.* **5** [INJURE] [T] If you twist a part of your body, such as your knee, you injure it by turning it suddenly. **burkmak, bükmek 6** [CHANGE MEANING] [T] to unfairly change the meaning of something that someone has said **çarpıtmak, saptırmak;** *Journalists had twisted his remarks.* ➔See also: twist sb's **arm**[1].

twist[2] /twɪst/ *noun* [C] **1** [UNEXPECTED CHANGE] a sudden change in a story or situation that you do not expect **beklenmedik değişim/gelişme** *The story has an unusual twist at the end.* **2** [MOVEMENT] when you twist something **burkma, bükme, çevirme, döndürme 3** [PART] a part of something that is twisted **kıvrım, bükülme, eğiklik** *There's a twist in the wire.* **4** [SHAPE] a shape that is made by twisting something **büklüm, kıvrım** *Finally, add a twist of lemon for decoration.* **5** [RIVER/ROAD] a bend in a river, road, etc **kıvrım, dönemeç, dolambaç**

twisted /ˈtwɪstɪd/ *adjective* **1** Something that is twisted is bent a lot of times and does not have its usual shape. **kıvrımlı, bükülmüş 2** strange and slightly unpleasant or cruel **tuhaf, acayip, sapkın, kaba, acımasız** *He'd become bitter and twisted.*

twister /ˈtwɪstər/ *noun* [C] *US another word for* tornado (= an extremely strong and dangerous wind that blows in a circle) **hortum, bora** ➔See also: tongue twister.

twit /twɪt/ *noun* [C] *informal* a silly person **aptal, budala**

twitch /twɪtʃ/ *verb* [I] If a part of your body twitches, it suddenly makes a slight movement in a way that you cannot control. **seğirmek, titremek; ani hareket etmek** *His face twitched nervously.* ● **twitch** *noun* [C] **seğirme, tik**

twitter /ˈtwɪtər/ *verb* [I] If a bird twitters, it makes a series of short, high sounds. **cıvıl cıvıl ötmek, cıvıldamak**

o-***two** /tuː/ **1** the number 2 **iki, iki rakamı 2 in two** into two pieces **iki parça** *She broke the chocolate in two.* **3 put two and two together** to guess the truth from details that you notice about a situation **düşünerek bir sonuca varmak/sonuç çıkarmak; parçaları birleştirerek bir sonuca ulaşmak** *She didn't tell me she was pregnant - I just put two and two together.* ➔See also: the lesser of two evils, be in two minds (**mind**[1]), stand on your own two feet (**foot**[1]).

two-time /ˌtuːˈtaɪm/ *verb* [T] *informal* If someone two-times their partner, they secretly have a romantic relationship with someone else. **eşini aldatmak**

twist

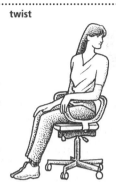

two-way /ˈtuːˌweɪ/ *adjective* moving, or allowing something to move or work in two directions **iki yönlü, çift yönlü** *a two-way street*

tycoon /taɪˈkuːn/ *noun* [C] someone who is very successful and powerful in business and has a lot of money **çok varlıklı ve nüfuzlu iş adamı; ...ın/in kralı; kodaman, büyük işadamı** *a media tycoon* ○ *a property/shipping tycoon*

tying /ˈtaɪɪŋ/ *present participle of* tie **bağlama**

Tylenol /ˈtaɪlənɒl/ *noun* [C, U] *trademark* a common drug used to reduce pain and fever **ağrı kesici ve ateş düşürücü ilaç**

∷ **type** .... İLE BİRLİKTE KULLANILAN KELİMELER

of this type ● all types of sth ● different/various types

o-***type**[1] /taɪp/ *noun* [C] **1** a person or thing that is part of a group of people or things that have similar qualities, or a group of people or things that have similar qualities **tip, tür, cins, çeşit** *They sell over 20 different types of cheese.* ○ *Illnesses of this type are very common in children.* **2** someone who has particular qualities or interests **tip; kendine özgü özellikleri ve ilgileri olan kimse** *He's the outdoor type* (= enjoys being outside). **3 not be sb's type** *informal* to not be the type of person that someone thinks is attractive **tipi olmamak; içi ısınmamak** *I like Bertrand but he's not really my type.* ➔See also: blood type.

type[2] /taɪp/ *verb* [I, T] to write something using a keyboard **daktiloyla/bilgisayarla yazmak ● typing** *noun* [U] **daktiloda/bilgisayarda yazı yazma**

typewriter /ˈtaɪpˌraɪtər/ *noun* [C] a machine with keys that you press to produce letters and numbers on paper **daktilo ● typewritten** /ˈtaɪpˌrɪtən/ *adjective* printed using a typewriter **daktilo edilmiş; bilgisayarda yazılmış** *a typewritten letter*

typhoid /ˈtaɪfɔɪd/ *noun* [U] a serious infectious disease that is caused by dirty water or food **tifo**

typhoon /taɪˈfuːn/ *noun* [C] a violent storm with very strong winds **tayfun**

o-***typical** /ˈtɪpɪkəl/ *adjective* having all the qualities you expect a particular person, object, place, etc to have **karakteristik, tipik** *typical German food* ○ *This style of painting is typical of Monet.*

typically /ˈtɪpɪkəli/ *adverb* **1** used for saying that something is typical of a person, thing, place, etc **tipik olarak, genelde** *behaviour that is typically English* **2** used for saying that what usually happens **tipik/belirgin biçimde** *Schools in the area typically start at 8.30.*

typify /ˈtɪpɪfaɪ/ *verb* [T] to be a typical example or quality of something **temsil etmek, simgelemek, tipik örneği olmak** *Emma's opinions typify the attitude of many young people.*

typist /ˈtaɪpɪst/ *noun* [C] *old-fashioned* someone who types (= writes using a machine) **daktilo, daktilo yazan kimse; yazıcı**

tyranny /ˈtɪrəni/ *noun* [U] when a leader or government has too much power and uses that power in a cruel and unfair way **zorbalık, zulüm, eziyet ● tyrannical** /tɪˈrænɪkəl/ *adjective* using or involving tyranny **acımasız, zulmeden, zalim, gaddar, zorba**

tyrant /ˈtaɪərənt/ *noun* [C] someone who has total power and uses it in a cruel and unfair way **zorba, zalim, zulmeden kimse**

tyre *UK* (*US* tire) /taɪər/ *noun* [C] a thick, round piece of rubber filled with air, that fits around a wheel **lâstik, teker, araç lâstiği** *It's got a flat tyre* (= tyre with no air in it). ➔Orta kısımdaki renkli sayfalarına bakınız.

T

U

U, u /ju:/ the twenty-first letter of the alphabet **alfabenin yirmibirinci harfi**

uber- /'u:bə^r-/ *prefix humorous* used before nouns to mean 'extreme' or 'extremely good or successful' **son derece, son derece iyi/başarılı... anlamında ön ek** *uber-billionaire*

ubiquitous /ju:'bɪkwɪtəs/ *adjective formal* seeming to be in all places **her yerde hazır ve nazır, her yerde mevcut/görülen** *the ubiquitous security cameras*

udder /'ʌdə^r/ *noun* [C] the part of a female cow, goat, etc that hangs under its body and produces milk **(hayvan) meme**

UFO /ˌju:ef'əʊ/ *noun* [C] *abbreviation for* unidentified flying object: something strange that you see in the sky that could be from another part of the universe **Tanımlanamayan Uçan Cisim (TUC)**

ugh /ʌɡ/ *exclamation* used to show that you think something is very unpleasant **Üff!, Iğğ!, Ööö!, Öff!'** *Ugh! What a smell!*

ugly /'ʌɡli/ *adjective* **1** unpleasant to look at **çirkin** *an ugly city* **2** An ugly situation is very unpleasant, usually because it involves violence. **tatsız, çirkin, kötü, nahoş** *There were ugly scenes outside the stadium.* ● **ugliness** *noun* [U] ⊃See also: raise/rear its ugly head¹. **çirkinlik**

uh *US* (*UK* **er**) /ə/ *exclamation* something that you say when you are thinking what to say next **Iıı, Aaa, Ha, Haa, Hı hı'** *It's not too far - it's about, uh, five miles from here.*

UK /ˌju:'keɪ/ *noun abbreviation for* United Kingdom **Birleşik Krallık**

ulcer /'ʌlsə^r/ *noun* [C] a painful, infected area on your skin or inside your body **ülser** *a mouth/stomach ulcer*

ulterior /ʌl'tɪəriə^r/ *adjective* **ulterior motive/purpose, etc** a secret purpose or reason for doing something **gizli dürtü/amaç vb.**

ultimate¹ /'ʌltɪmət/ *adjective* [always before noun] **1** better, worse, or greater than all similar things **en büyük/yüksek/önemli/güçlü; asıl** *Climbing Mount Everest is the ultimate challenge.* ○ *the ultimate insult* **2** final or most important **en son, nihai** *the ultimate aim/solution*

ultimate² /'ʌltɪmət/ *noun* **the ultimate in sth** the best or greatest example of something **...ın/in en büyüğü; ...yönünden en iyisi; ...bakımından en gelişmişi** *It describes the hotel as 'the ultimate in luxury'.*

ultimately /'ʌltɪmətli/ *adverb* **1** finally, after a series of things have happened **sonunda, nihayetinde, eninde sonunda** *a disease that ultimately killed him* **2** used to emphasize the most important fact in a situation **temelde, aslında, esasında** *Ultimately, he'll have to decide.*

ultimatum ...... İLE BİRLİKTE KULLANILAN KELİMELER
deliver/give sb/**issue** an ultimatum ● an ultimatum **demands** sth ● an ultimatum **from/to** sb

ultimatum /ˌʌltɪ'meɪtəm/ *noun* [C] when someone says they will do something that will affect you badly if you do not do what they want **ültimatom, emir** *The children were given an ultimatum - finish their work quietly or stay behind after class.*

ultra- /ʌltrə-/ *prefix* extremely **son derece... anlamında ön ek** *ultra-modern architecture* ○ *ultra-careful*

ultrasonic /ˌʌltrə'sɒnɪk/ *adjective* involving ultrasound **sesötesi/sesten hızlı**

ultrasound /'ʌltrəsaʊnd/ *noun* **1** [U] very high sound waves, especially those that are used in medical examinations to produce an image of something inside your body **ultrason** *an ultrasound scan* **2** [C] a medical examination which produces an image of something that is inside the body, using sound waves *An ultrasound revealed a perfectly healthy baby.*

ultraviolet /ˌʌltrə'vaɪələt/ *adjective* Ultraviolet light makes your skin become darker. **ultraviyole, morötesi**

umbilical cord /ʌm'bɪlɪklˌkɔ:d/ *noun* [C] the tube that connects a baby to its mother before it is born **göbek bağı**

umbrella /ʌm'brelə/ *noun* [C] **1** a thing that you hold above your head to keep yourself dry when it is raining **şemsiye 2 umbrella group/organization, etc** a large organization that is made of many smaller organizations **genel; geniş/ana grup/kurum vb.**

umbrella

umpire /'ʌmpaɪə^r/ *noun* [C] someone whose job is to watch a sports game and make sure that the players obey the rules **hakem** *a tennis/cricket umpire* ● **umpire** *verb* [I, T] **hakemlik yapmak**

umpteen /ʌm'ti:n/ *quantifier informal* very many **sayısız, bir sürü, sayılamayacak kadar çok** *I've been there umpteen times and I still can't remember the way.* ● **umpteenth** *I drank my umpteenth cup of coffee.* **çok**

the UN /ˌju:'en/ *noun abbreviation for* the United Nations: an international organization that tries to solve world problems in a peaceful way **Birleşmiş Milletler**

un- /ʌn-/ *prefix* not or the opposite of **sız/siz; aksi/ters... anlamında ön ek** *unhappy* ○ *unfair* ○ *to unfasten*

unable /ʌn'eɪbl/ *adjective* **be unable to do sth** to not be able to do something **yapamamak, becerememek, üstesinden gelememek** *Some days he is unable to get out of bed.*

unabridged /ˌʌnə'brɪdʒd/ *adjective* An unabridged book, play, etc is in its original form and has not been made shorter. **kısaltılmamış, sadeleştirilmemiş (kitap, oyun)**

unacceptable ...... İLE BİRLİKTE KULLANILAN KELİMELER
find sth unacceptable ● **completely/totally/wholly** unacceptable ● unacceptable **to** sb

unacceptable /ˌʌnək'septəbl/ *adjective* too bad to be allowed to continue **kabul edilemez,** *The water contains unacceptable levels of pollution.* ○ *I find that sort of behaviour completely unacceptable.* ● **unacceptably** *adverb* **kabul edilemez bir şekilde**

unaccompanied /ˌʌnə'kʌmpənid/ *adjective* not having anyone with you when you go somewhere **yalnız, tek başına, refakatsiz** *Unaccompanied children are not allowed in the museum.*

unaccountable /ˌʌnə'kaʊntəbl/ *adjective* **1** impossible to explain **izah edilemez, açıklanamaz, anlatılamaz** *For some unaccountable reason, I've got three copies of the same book.* **2** not having to give reasons for your actions or decisions **açıklanamaz, izah edilemez, sebebi anlaşılamayan** ● **unaccountably** *adverb* **anlaşılmaz bir şekilde**

unadulterated /ˌʌn'dʌltᵊreɪtɪd/ *adjective* **1** complete **tam, büsbütün** *I've never heard such unadulterated nonsense in all my life!* **2** pure and with nothing extra added **arı, saf, katışıksız, halis** *People using drugs can never be sure that they're using unadulterated substances.*

unaffected /ˌʌnə'fektɪd/ *adjective* not changed by something **etkilenmez, etkilenmemiş** *Smaller colleges will be unaffected by the new regulations.*

unaided /ʌn'eɪdɪd/ *adjective, adverb* without help **yardımsız, desteksiz, yardım görmeden** *He's now well enough to walk unaided.*

unanimous /juː'nænɪməs/ *adjective* agreed by everyone **oy birliği ile üzerinde uzlaşılan; herkesçe kabul edilen; genel kabul gören** *The jury was unanimous in finding him guilty.* ● **unanimity** /ˌjuːnə'nɪməti/ *noun* [U] when everyone agrees about something **genel/toplumsal uzlaşı; oy birliği ile anlaşma; genel kabul; fikir birliği** ● **unanimously** *adverb* *The members unanimously agreed to the proposal.* **oy birliği ile kabul edilmiş**

unannounced /ˌʌnə'naʊnst/ *adjective, adverb* without telling anyone first **habersiz, kimseye haber vermeden** *an unannounced visit*

unappealing /ˌʌnə'piːlɪŋ/ *adjective* not attractive or enjoyable **hiç bir çekiciliği/cazibesi/albenisi olmayan; sıkıcı; albenisiz** *Five hours on a train with Mike is a fairly unappealing prospect.* ○ *an unappealing character*

unarmed /ʌn'ɑːmd/ *adjective* not carrying a weapon **silâhsız**

unashamedly /ˌʌnə'ʃeɪmɪdli/ *adverb* in a way that shows you are not embarrassed or worried about what other people think of you **utanmaz/yüzsüz/arsız biçimde** *Galliano is unashamedly romantic.*

unassuming /ˌʌnə'sjuːmɪŋ/ *adjective* not wanting to be noticed **alçakgönüllü, mütevazı** *a shy, unassuming man*

unattached /ˌʌnə'tætʃt/ *adjective* not married or having a romantic relationship **bekâr, ilişkisi olmayan, evli olmayan**

unattended /ˌʌnə'tendɪd/ *adjective* not being watched or looked after **yalnız, tek başına, refakatsiz, kimsesiz; sahipsiz; başıboş; kendi hâlinde** *Passengers should not leave bags unattended.*

unattractive /ˌʌnə'træktɪv/ *adjective* **1** not beautiful or nice to look at **cazibesiz, çekici olmayan** *I felt old and unattractive.* **2** not interesting or useful **ilgi çekmeyen, enteresan olmayan, faydasız, gereksiz, yersiz** *an unattractive proposition*

unauthorized (*also UK* **-ised**) /ʌn'ɔːθᵊraɪzd/ *adjective* done without official permission **izinsiz, müsadesiz, yetkisiz** *an unauthorized use of company money*

unavailable /ˌʌnə'veɪləbl/ *adjective* **1** not able to talk to someone or meet them, especially because you are doing other things **meşgul, ulaşılamaz, görüşülemez; yerinde olmayan; makamında olmayan** *The manager was unavailable for comment.* **2** impossible to buy or get **satın alınamaz, elde edilemez; bulunmaz; alınmaz** *The book is unavailable in Britain.*

unavoidable /ˌʌnə'vɔɪdəbl/ *adjective* impossible to avoid or prevent **kaçınılmaz, önüne geçilemez, çaresiz, önlenemez** *an unavoidable delay*

🧩 **unaware** ...... İLE BİRLİKTE KULLANILAN KELİMELER

blissfully/completely/seemingly/totally unaware ● **unaware of** sth

unaware /ˌʌnə'weəʳ/ *adjective* [never before noun] not knowing about something **haberdar olmayan, habersiz, bilgisiz** *He seems totally unaware of the problem.*

unawares /ˌʌnə'weəz/ *adverb* **catch/take sb unawares** If something catches or takes you unawares, it happens when you do not expect it to. **gafil avlamak, habersiz yakalamak, şaşırtmak, şaşkınlığa uğratmak** *The rain caught me unawares and I didn't have my umbrella.*

unbalanced /ʌn'bælənst/ *adjective* **1** slightly mentally ill **dengesiz, hafif kaçık 2** false and not fair **taraflı, yanlı, tarafsızlığını yitirmiş, adil olmayan** *He gave an unbalanced view of the situation.*

unbearable /ʌn'beərəbl/ *adjective* too painful or unpleasant for you to continue to experience **dayanılmaz, çekilmez, tahammül edilemez** *The heat was almost unbearable.* ● **unbearably** *adverb* **dayanılmaz bir şekilde**

unbeatable /ʌn'biːtəbl/ *adjective* much better than everyone or everything else **mağlup edilemez, üstesinden gelinemez, fevkalâde, olağanüstü, üstüne yok, yenilmez, kıyas kabul etmez, rakipsiz** *We aim to sell the best products at unbeatable prices.*

unbeaten /ʌn'biːtᵊn/ *adjective* in sports, having won every game **namağlup, yenilmez, hiç mağlup olmamış** *Manchester United remain unbeaten this season.*

unbelievable /ˌʌnbɪ'liːvəbl/ *adjective* **1** extremely bad or good and making you feel surprised **inanılmaz, hayret verici, şaşırtıcı, fevkalâde** *It's unbelievable how lucky she's been.* **2** not probable and difficult to believe **olasılık dışı, inanması güç, akla sığmaz, akıl kârı olmayan** ● **unbelievably** *adverb* **inanılmaz bir şekilde**

unborn /ʌn'bɔːn/ *adjective* not yet born **doğmamış, henüz dünyaya gözlerini açmamış** *the unborn child*

unbreakable /ˌʌn'breɪkəbl/ *adjective* impossible to break **kırılmaz, sağlam, zarar verilemez** *unbreakable glass/plastic*

unbridled /ʌn'braɪdld/ *adjective* An unbridled feeling is one that you do not try to hide or control. **gizlenemez, saklanamaz, açık seçik** *unbridled enthusiasm/passion*

unbroken /ʌn'brəʊkᵊn/ *adjective* continuous and with no pauses **aralıksız, nefes aldırmayan, sürekli, kesintisiz** *unbroken sunshine*

unbutton /ʌn'bʌtᵊn/ *verb* [T] to open the buttons on a piece of clothing **düğmeleri açmak/çözmek** *He unbuttoned his jacket.*

uncalled for /ʌn'kɔːldfɔːʳ/ *adjective* If an action or remark is uncalled for, it is unfair or unkind. **yersiz, gereksiz, lüzumsuz, haksız, insafsız** *That was uncalled for, Tess - apologize to your brother.*

U

uncanny /ʌnˈkæni/ adjective strange and impossible to explain **tuhaf, acayip, anlaşılmaz, esrarengiz** *an uncanny resemblance* ● **uncannily** adverb **esrarengiz bir şekilde**

uncaring /ʌnˈkeərɪŋ/ adjective without sympathy for people with problems **ilgisiz, aldırmaz, kayıtsız, umursamaz** *victims of an uncaring society*

uncertain /ʌnˈsɜːtᵊn/ adjective **1** not sure or not able to decide about something **kararsız, belirsiz, kesin olmayan; mütereddit, ne yapacağını bilmeyen** *Bridie was uncertain about meeting him.* **2** not known, or not completely certain **belirsiz, muğlak, şüpheli, belli olmayan** *The museum faces an uncertain future.* ● **uncertainly** adverb **belirsizlik içinde** ● **uncertainty** noun [C, U] **belirsizlik**

---

uncertainty .... İLE BİRLİKTE KULLANILAN KELİMELER

face uncertainty ● the uncertainty **surrounding** sth ● uncertainty **about/as to/over** sth ● **continuing/great/growing** uncertainty ● the uncertainty **of** sth

---

uncertainty /ʌnˈsɜːtᵊnti/ noun [C, U] when something is uncertain **belirsizlik, muğlaklık** *Life is full of uncertainties.*

unchanged /ʌnˈtʃeɪndʒd/ adjective staying the same **değişmemiş, aynı kalmış** *The area has remained virtually unchanged in fifty years.*

uncharacteristic /ˌʌnkærəktərˈɪstɪk/ adjective not typical ...a/e özgü olmayan; ...dan/den umulmayan; tipik olmayan ● **uncharacteristically** adverb **alışılagelmişin dışında**

unchecked /ʌnˈtʃekt/ adjective If something bad continues unchecked, it is not stopped. **kontrolsüz, kontrol edilmemiş, önü alınamamış**

o⚬**uncle** /ˈʌŋkl/ noun [C] the brother of your mother or father, or the husband of your aunt **amca, dayı**

unclean /ʌnˈkliːn/ adjective morally bad, as described by the rules of a religion **dinen mekruh, ahlâken kötü**

unclear /ʌnˈklɪər/ adjective **1** not easy to understand **karışık, zor anlaşılır, anlaşılması güç** *The situation at the moment is unclear.* ○ [+ question word] *It's unclear what actually happened that night.* **2** If you are unclear about something, you do not understand it exactly. **emin değil, tam olarak anlaşılmış değil** *I'm unclear about exactly who's doing what.*

uncomfortable /ʌnˈkʌmftəbl/ adjective **1** not feeling comfortable and pleasant, or not making you feel comfortable and pleasant **rahatsız, rahat olmayan, konforsuz** *These shoes are really uncomfortable.* **2** slightly embarrassed, or making you feel slightly embarrassed **sıkılmış, rahatsız edici, huzursuz** *an uncomfortable silence* ● **uncomfortably** adverb **rahatsız bir şekilde**

uncommon /ʌnˈkɒmən/ adjective unusual **nadir, ender rastlanır, alışılmamış** [+ for + to do sth] *It's not uncommon for people to become ill* (= they often become ill) *when they travel.* ● **uncommonly** adverb **olağan dışı bir şekilde**

uncompromising /ʌnˈkɒmprəmaɪzɪŋ/ adjective determined not to change your ideas or decisions **uzlaşmaz, uyuşmaz, burnunun dikine giden, anlaşmaya yanaşmaz** *an uncompromising attitude*

unconcerned /ˌʌnkənˈsɜːnd/ adjective not worried by something **ilgisiz, aldırmaz, lâkayt, kayıtsız, umursamaz; aldırış etmez** *The baby seemed unconcerned by all the noise.*

unconditional /ˌʌnkənˈdɪʃᵊnᵊl/ adjective done or given without any limits and without asking for anything for

yourself **koşulsuz, kayıtsız, şartsız** *unconditional love* ● **unconditionally** adverb **koşulsuz olarak**

unconfirmed /ˌʌnkənˈfɜːmd/ adjective An unconfirmed report or story may not be true because there is no proof yet. **doğrulanmamış, teyit edilmemiş**

unconnected /ˌʌnkəˈnektɪd/ adjective If two or more things are unconnected, there is no connection between them. **bağlantısız, ilişkisiz, bağlantılı olmayan, bağlı olmayan** *The stomach ailment was unconnected with his cancer.*

unconscious¹ /ʌnˈkɒnʃəs/ adjective **1** in a state as though you are sleeping, for example because you have been hit on the head **baygın, bayılmış, kendinde değil** *She was knocked unconscious.* **2** An unconscious thought or feeling is one that you do not know you have. **habersiz, farkında değil** *an unconscious fear* ● **unconsciousness** noun [U] **kendinden geçmiş durumda olma**

unconscious² /ʌnˈkɒnʃəs/ noun [no plural] the part of your mind that contains feelings and thoughts that you do not know about, and that influences the way you behave **bilinçaltı, şuuraltı**

unconsciously /ʌnˈkɒnʃəsli/ adverb If you do something unconsciously, you do it without knowing that you are doing it. **bilinçsizce, şuursuzca, farkına varmaksızın**

unconstitutional /ˌʌnˌkɒnstɪˈtjuːʃᵊnᵊl/ adjective not allowed by the rules of an organization or political system **anayasaya aykırı, yasalara muhalif**

uncontrollable /ˌʌnkənˈtrəʊləbl/ adjective unable to be controlled **zaptedilemez, kontrol edilemez, bastırılamayan, tutulamaz** *uncontrollable anger* ○ *an uncontrollable desire to cry* ● **uncontrollably** adverb **kontrol edilemez bir şekilde**

unconventional /ˌʌnkənˈvenʃᵊnᵊl/ adjective doing things in a way that is different from most people **toplumsal âdet ve davranışlara uymayan, teamüle aykırı** *an unconventional lifestyle*

unconvincing /ˌʌnkənˈvɪntsɪŋ/ adjective not seeming true or real **inandırıcı olmayan, gerçek gibi görünmeyen** *an unconvincing explanation*

uncool /ʌnˈkuːl/ adjective embarrassing and not stylish or fashionable **mahcup edici, modası geçmiş**

uncountable noun /ʌnˌkaʊntəbᵊlˈnaʊn/ (also **uncount noun**) noun [C] a noun which does not have a plural form and cannot be used with 'a' or 'one'. For example 'music' and 'furniture' are uncountable nouns. **sayılamayan isim** ⊃See study page **Countable and uncountable nouns** on page Centre 20.

uncouth /ʌnˈkuːθ/ adjective behaving in a rude, unpleasant way **kaba saba, incelikten yoksun, yol yordam bilmez, nezaketsiz**

---

uncover .... İLE BİRLİKTE KULLANILAN KELİMELER

uncover **evidence/a plot/a secret/the truth** ● an **investigation** uncovers sth

---

uncover /ʌnˈkʌvər/ verb [T] **1** to discover something that had been secret or hidden **açığa çıkarmak, meydana çıkarmak; açmak, gün yüzüne çıkarmak** *The inspectors uncovered evidence of corruption.* **2** to remove a cover from something **örtüsünü açmak, üstünü açmak, ortaya çıkarmak**

undaunted /ʌnˈdɔːntɪd/ adjective not frightened to do something that is difficult or dangerous **cesur, gözüpek, yürekli** *Keiko spoke, undaunted by the crowd.*

undecided /ˌʌndɪˈsaɪdɪd/ adjective If you are undecided about something, you have not made a decision yet.

kararsız, mütereddit *I'm still undecided about whether to apply for the job.*

undefeated /ˌʌndɪˈfiːtɪd/ *adjective* in sports, having won every game **mağlup edilemez, yenilemez, namağlup, hep kazanan** *Both teams remain undefeated in the final weeks of the season.*

undeniable /ˌʌndɪˈnaɪəbl/ *adjective* certainly true **inkâr edilemez, kesinlikle doğru, yadsınamaz** *an undeniable fact* ● **undeniably** *adverb* **yadsınmaz bir şekilde**

∘⁼**under¹** /ˈʌndəʳ/ *preposition* **1** [BELOW] below something **altında** *She pushed her bag under the table.* ○ *The children were sitting under a tree.* **2** [BELOW THE SURFACE] below the surface of something **altında, yüzeyin altında** *He could only keep his head under the water for a few seconds.* **3** [LESS THAN] less than a number, amount, or age **altında, aşağısına, daha aza** *You can buy the whole system for just under $2000.* ○ *We don't serve alcohol to anyone under 18.* **4** [CONTROLLED BY] controlled or governed by a particular person, organization, etc **yönetiminde, idaresinde, liderliğinde; kontrolünde** *a country under military rule* ○ *The restaurant is under new management.* **5** [RULE/LAW] according to a rule, law, etc ...a/e **göre; gereğince** *Under the new law, all new buildings must be approved by the local government.* **6** [IN A PARTICULAR STATE] in a particular state or condition **durumunda, halinde, altında** *The President is under pressure to resign.* ○ *Students are allowed to miss school under certain circumstances.* **7** [IN PROGRESS] used to say that something is happening at the moment but is not finished **devam eden, süregelen, henüz bitmemiş** *A new 16-screen cinema is under construction.* ○ *Several different plans are under discussion.* **8** [NAME] using a particular name, especially one that is not your usual name **başka isim altında; müstehar isimle** *He also wrote several detective novels under the name, Edgar Sandys.* **9** [PLACE IN LIST] used to say which part of a list, book, library, etc you should look in to find something **başlığı altında** *Books about health problems are under 'Medicine'.*

under² /ˈʌndəʳ/ *adverb* **1** below the surface of something **altına, yüzeyin altına** *The child was swimming and suddenly started to go under.* **2** less than a particular number, amount, or age **aşağısında, daha azına, daha ucuza** *I want a computer that is £2000 or under.*

under- /ʌndəʳ-/ *prefix* **1** not enough **yetersiz, az, kifayetsiz...** **anlamında ön ek** *undercooked potatoes* **2** below **alt, iç...anlamında ön ek** *underwear* ○ *an underpass*

under-age /ˌʌndərˈeɪdʒ/ *adjective* younger than the legal age when you are allowed to do something **reşit olma yaşının altında olan; reşit olmayan** *under-age drinking/sex*

undercover /ˌʌndəˈkʌvəʳ/ *adjective, adverb* working secretly in order to get information for the police or government **gizli, gizli yapılan, gizli çalışan** *an undercover police officer*

undercut /ˌʌndəˈkʌt/ *verb* [T] **undercutting**, *past* **undercut** to sell something at a lower price than someone else **fiyat kırmak, daha ucuza satmak**

the underdog /ˈʌndədɒg/ *noun* the person or team that is expected to lose a race or competition **başarma olasılığı zayıf kişi/takım/ekip**

underestimate /ˌʌndəʳˈestɪmeɪt/ *verb* [T] **1** to not understand how large, strong, or important something is **gerçek değerinin altında değer biçmek; eksik tahmin etmek** *Many people underestimate the cost of owning a car.* **2** to not understand how powerful or clever someone is **küçümsemek, hafife almak; değersizmiş gibi davranmak** *I thought it would be an easy*

game but I had underestimated my opponent. ⊃**Opposite** **overestimate.**

underfoot /ˌʌndəˈfʊt/ *adverb* under your feet as you walk **ayak altındaki, basılan, yerdeki** *Several people were trampled underfoot in the rush to escape.*

undergo /ˌʌndəˈgəʊ/ *verb* [T] **undergoing**, *past tense* **underwent**, *past participle* **undergone** to experience something, especially a change or medical treatment **maruz kalmak, geçirmek, başından geçmek, uğramak, katlanmak** *The country is currently undergoing major political change.* ○ *He is undergoing surgery for a heart problem.*

undergraduate /ˌʌndəˈgrædʒuət/ (*also* **undergrad** /ˈʌndəgræd/ *informal*) *noun* [C] a student who is studying for their first university degree (= qualification) **üniversite öğrencisi**

underground¹ /ˈʌndəgraʊnd/ *adjective, adverb* **1** under the surface of the ground **yer altı, yer altında** *underground caves* ○ *an animal that lives underground* **2** Underground political activities are secret and illegal. **yer, altı, gizli, gizliden gizliye** *an underground political organization*

take the underground ● on the underground ● an underground station /train

underground² /ˈʌndəgraʊnd/ *UK* (*US* **subway**) *noun* [no plural] a system of trains that is built under a city **metro, tünel** *the London Underground*

undergrowth /ˈʌndəgrəʊθ/ *noun* [U] short plants and bushes that grow around trees **ağaç altı bitki ve çalılar, fazla büyümeyen bitkiler**

underhand /ˌʌndəˈhænd/ (*also* **underhanded**) *adjective* secret and not honest **el altından, gizlice, gizli olarak** *underhand business deals*

underline /ˌʌndəˈlaɪn/ *verb* [T] **1** to draw a line under a word or sentence **altını çizmek 2** to emphasize the importance or truth of something **vurgulamak, önemini belirtmek** *The report underlines the need for more teachers in schools.*

underlying /ˌʌndəˈlaɪɪŋ/ *adjective* [always before noun] An underlying reason or problem is the real reason or problem, although it is not obvious. **altında yatan, gerçek, belli başlı, esas** *We need to look at the underlying reasons for ill health.*

undermine /ˌʌndəˈmaɪn/ *verb* [T] to make someone less confident or make something weaker **ürkütmek, zayıflatmak, baltalamak, sabote etmek, sarsmak** *A series of scandals have undermined people's confidence in the government.*

underneath¹ /ˌʌndəˈniːθ/ *adverb, preposition* under something **altında** *Florian was wearing a jacket with a red shirt underneath.* ○ *Deborah pushed her shoes underneath the bed.*

the underneath² /ˌʌndəˈniːθ/ *noun* the bottom part of something **alt taraf, alt kısım**

underpaid /ˌʌndəˈpeɪd/ *adjective* not earning enough for your work **düşük ücretli, az kazançlı**

underpants /ˈʌndəpænts/ *noun* [plural] a piece of underwear that covers the area between your waist and the top of your legs **külot** ⊃**Orta** kısımdaki renkli sayfalarına bakınız

underpass /ˈʌndəpɑːs/ *noun* [C] a road or path that goes under another road **alt geçit**

underprivileged /ˌʌndəˈprɪvəlɪdʒd/ *adjective* poor and having fewer opportunities than most people **ikinci**

sınıf, ortadirek; ayrıcalıksız; imkânları kıt olan *underprivileged families*

underrate /ˌʌndəˈreɪt/ *verb* [T] to think that someone or something is not as good as they really are **olduğundan daha az değer vermek, hafife almak, küçümsemek** *Critics have continued to underrate Sampras.*
● **underrated** *adjective* **küçümsenmiş** *I think he's really underrated as an actor.* ↪Opposite **overrated**.

underscore /ˌʌndəˈskɔːʳ/ *verb* [T] mainly US to emphasize the importance of something **önemini vurgulamak, değerini belirtmek**

undershirt /ˈʌndəʃɜːt/ US (UK **vest**) *noun* [C] a piece of underwear that you wear under a shirt **atlet, fanila, içgiyim**

the underside /ˈʌndəsaɪd/ *noun* the bottom surface of something **alt kısım, alt taraf, alt yüz** *There was some damage to the underside of the car.*

○_→**understand** /ˌʌndəˈstænd/ *verb* [I, T] *past* **understood**
1 [KNOW MEANING] to know the meaning of something that someone says **anlamak, kavramak** *I don't understand half of what he says.* ○ *She didn't understand so I explained it again.* **2** [KNOW WHY/HOW] to know why or how something happens or works **anlamak, anlam vermek** [+ question word] *We still don't fully understand how the brain works.* **3** [KNOW FEELINGS] to know how someone feels or why they behave in a particular way **anlamak, anlayış göstermek** *I don't understand James sometimes.* ○ [+ question word] *I understand why she's so angry.* **4 I/we understand (that)...** *formal* used to say that you believe something is true because someone has told you it is **Anlıyorum ki...', 'Anlıyoruz ki...'** *I understand that the school is due to close next year.* **5 make yourself understood** to say something to someone in a way that they understand **meramını anlatmak** *I had a little difficulty making myself understood.*

understandable /ˌʌndəˈstændəbl/ *adjective* An understandable feeling or action is one that you would expect in that particular situation. **anlaşılabilir** *It's understandable that he's angry.* ● **understandably** *adverb* *She's understandably upset.* **anlaşılabilir, beklenen bir şekilde**

┌───┐
│ **understanding** ...... İLE BİRLİKTE KULLANILAN KELİMELER │
│ **develop/gain/have** an understanding (**of** sth) ● a **better/clear** understanding ● an understanding **of** sth │
└───┘

understanding¹ /ˌʌndəˈstændɪŋ/ *noun* **1** [KNOWLEDGE] [U, no plural] knowledge about a subject, situation, etc or about how something works **anlayış, anlama, kavrama** *We now have a better understanding of this disease.* **2** [AGREEMENT] [C] an informal agreement between two people **anlaşma, uzlaşma** [usually singular, + that] *We have an understanding that we don't discuss the subject in front of his mother.* **3** [SYMPATHY] [U] sympathy **anlayış, hoşgörü** *Thank you for your understanding.* **4 my/her/his, etc understanding** what you thought to be true **anlayış, yorum** *It was my understanding that she was coming alone.* **5** [ABILITY] [U] the ability to learn or think about something **öğrenme, anlama, kavrama**

understanding² /ˌʌndəˈstændɪŋ/ *adjective* showing sympathy for someone's problems **anlayışlı, hoşgörülü** *Fortunately, my girlfriend is very understanding.*

understated /ˌʌndəˈsteɪtɪd/ *adjective* simple and attractive in style **basit ama çekici, gösterişsiz ama fiyakalı** *an understated black dress*

understatement /ˌʌndəˈsteɪtmənt/ *noun* [C, U] when you say that something is less extreme than it really is **olduğundan daha az/hafif vb. gösterme, azım-**

sama, azımsama ifadesi *'Quite big', did you say? That's an understatement - he's enormous!*

understood /ˌʌndəˈstʊd/ *past of* understand **anlamak' fiilinin geçmiş zaman hâli**

understudy /ˈʌndəˌstʌdi/ *noun* [C] an actor in the theatre who learns the words and actions of another character so that they can perform it the usual actor is ill **yedek aktör/aktris/oyuncu**

undertake /ˌʌndəˈteɪk/ *verb past tense* **undertook**, *past participle* **undertaken** *formal* **1** [T] to start work on something that will take a long time or be difficult **üstlenmek, yüklenmek, yapmayı kabul etmek** *Max has undertaken the task of restoring an old houseboat.* **2 undertake to do sth** to promise to do something **söz vermek, vaad etmek, taahhüt etmek**

undertaker /ˈʌndəˌteɪkəʳ/ *noun* [C] someone whose job is to organize funerals and prepare dead bodies to be buried or burned **cenaze işleri yapan kimse; cenaze levazımatçısı**

┌───┐
│ **undertaking** ...... İLE BİRLİKTE KULLANILAN KELİMELER │
│ **give/sign** an undertaking ● a **written** undertaking ● an undertaking **by/from** sb │
└───┘

undertaking /ˈʌndəˌteɪkɪŋ/ *noun* [C] **1** a difficult or important piece of work, especially one that takes a long time **zor/önemli iş/görev/girişim/teşebbüs** [usually singular] *Building your own house is a major undertaking.* **2** UK a legal or official promise to do something **yasal/resmî vaad/taahhüt/söz/antlaşma** [usually singular] *The newspaper has given an undertaking not to print the story.*

undertone /ˈʌndətəʊn/ *noun* [C] a feeling or quality that exists but is not obvious **çağrışım, imâ, saklı duygu, gizli anlam** *an article with worrying political undertones*

undertook /ˌʌndəˈtʊk/ *past tense of* undertake **üstlenmek' fiilinin geçmiş zaman hâli**

undervalued /ˌʌndəˈvæljuːd/ *adjective* If someone or something is undervalued, they are more important or useful than people think they are. **kıymeti bilinmeyen, hak ettiği değer verilmeyen; küçümsenen; azımsanan**

underwater /ˌʌndəˈwɔːtəʳ/ *adjective, adverb* under the surface of water **su altı, su altında** *an underwater camera* ○ *Seals can hear very well underwater.*

underwear /ˈʌndəweəʳ/ *noun* [U] the clothes that you wear next to your skin, under your other clothes **içgiyim, iç çamaşırı**

underweight /ˌʌndəˈweɪt/ *adjective* too light **zayıf, hafif, kilosu normalden az**

underwent /ˌʌndəˈwent/ *past tense of* undergo **maruz kalmak' fiilinin geçmiş zaman hâli**

underworld /ˈʌndəwɜːld/ *noun* [no plural] criminals and their activities **yeraltı dünyası** *the criminal underworld* ○ *the London underworld*

undesirable /ˌʌndɪˈzaɪərəbl/ *adjective formal* Something that is undesirable is not wanted or is bad or unpleasant. **istenmeyen, hoş karşılanmayan, arzu edilmeyen, hoşa gitmeyen** *an undesirable influence*

undeveloped /ˌʌndɪˈveləpt/ *adjective* Undeveloped land has no buildings on it and is not used for anything. **gelişmemiş, geri kalmış**

undid /ʌnˈdɪd/ *past tense of* undo **çözmek, açmak' fiilinin geçmiş zaman hâli**

undisclosed /ˌʌndɪsˈkləʊzd/ *adjective* If official information is undisclosed, it is secret. **gizli** *The meeting is taking place at an undisclosed location.*

undisputed /ˌʌndɪˈspjuːtɪd/ *adjective* If something is undisputed, everyone agrees about it. **kuşkusuz, kesin, su götürmez, tartışmasız, kesin, mutlak** *an undisputed fact* ○ *the undisputed champion/master*

undisturbed /ˌʌndɪˈstɜːbd/ *adjective* not interrupted or changed in any way **rahatsız edilmemiş, kesilmemiş, araya girilmemiş; değiştirilmemiş** *undisturbed sleep*

undivided /ˌʌndɪˈvaɪdɪd/ *adjective* **undivided attention/loyalty/support, etc** complete attention/support, etc **tam, bütün, tüm, sürekli; tam destek/dikkat vb.** *There, now you can have my undivided attention.*

undo /ʌnˈduː/ *verb* [T] **undoing**, *past tense* **undid**, *past participle* **undone** **1** to open something that is tied or fastened **çözmek, açmak** *I took off my hat and undid my coat.* **2** to get rid of the effects of something that has been done before **etkisini ortadan kaldırmak; etkilerinden kurtulmak** *Some of the damage caused by pollution cannot be undone.*

undoing /ʌnˈduːɪŋ/ *noun* **be sb's undoing** to be the thing that makes someone fail **felâket sebebi olmak, mahvolma nedeni olmak; başarısızlık nedeni olmak** *It was a policy that proved to be the President's undoing.*

undone /ʌnˈdʌn/ *adjective* **1** not fastened or tied **açık, çözülmüş** *Her coat was undone.* **2** not done **yapılmamış, bitmemiş** *I don't think I've left anything undone.*

undoubted /ʌnˈdaʊtɪd/ *adjective* [always before noun] used to emphasize that something is true **şüphe götürmez, su götürmez, kesin, mutlak, şüphesiz** *The project was an undoubted success.* ○ *her undoubted ability/talent*

undoubtedly /ʌnˈdaʊtɪdli/ *adverb* used to emphasize that something is true **hiç şüphesiz, şüphesiz ki; kesinlikle** *Stress has undoubtedly contributed to her illness.*

undress /ʌnˈdres/ *verb* [I, T] to remove your clothes or someone else's clothes **soyunmak, soymak** ● **undressed** *adjective I got undressed and went to bed.* **soyunmuş**

undue /ʌnˈdjuː/ *adjective* [always before noun] *formal* more than is necessary **aşırı, gereğinden çok, yersiz, aşırı** *I don't want to cause undue alarm.*

undulating /ˈʌndjəleɪtɪŋ/ *adjective formal* having slight slopes or curves, or moving slightly up and down **hafifçe meyilli, hafif kıvrımlı/eğimli; aşağı yukarı hareket eden** *undulating roads*

unduly /ʌnˈdjuːli/ *adverb formal* more than necessary **aşırı derecede, gereğinden fazla, çok** *She didn't seem unduly concerned/worried.*

unearth /ʌnˈɜːθ/ *verb* [T] **1** to find something in the ground **bulmak, keşfetmek, ortaya çıkarmak, gün ışığına çıkarmak** [often passive] *Thousands of dinosaur bones have been unearthed in China.* **2** to find something that has been secret or hidden **gizli/saklı bir şeyi bulmak/keşfetmek** *Reporters unearthed evidence of criminal activity.*

unearthly /ʌnˈɜːθli/ *adjective* strange and frightening **acayip, tuhaf, ürkütücü** *an unearthly light/beauty*

unease /ʌnˈiːz/ *noun* [U] when you feel worried because you think something bad might happen **huzursuzluk, tedirginlik, gerginlik**

uneasy /ʌnˈiːzi/ *adjective* worried because you think something bad might happen **huzursuz, tedirgin, endişeli, rahatsız** *I feel a bit uneasy about her travelling alone.*

uneconomic /ʌnˌiːkəˈnɒmɪk/ *(also uneconomical) adjective* **1** using too much money, fuel, time, etc **ekonomik/iktisadî olmayan** *a car that is uneconomic to run* **2** not making enough profit **yeterli kazanç sağlamayan; kârlı olmayan, kâr getirmeyen, verimsiz** *plans to close uneconomic factories*

unemployed /ˌʌnɪmˈplɔɪd/ *adjective* not having a job **işsiz, boşta gezen, boşta** *I've been unemployed for six months.* ○ *The government is helping to create jobs for the unemployed.*

unemployment ...... İLE BİRLİKTE KULLANILAN KELİMELER

unemployment **drops/falls/increases/rises** ● **high/low/rising/soaring** unemployment ● the unemployment **rate** ● a **drop/fall/increase/rise** in unemployment

unemployment /ˌʌnɪmˈplɔɪmənt/ *noun* [U] **1** the number of people who are unemployed **işsizlik sayısı** *a rise/fall in unemployment* ○ *The unemployment rate has increased to 20 percent.* **2** when you do not have a job **işsizlik**

unending /ʌnˈendɪŋ/ *adjective* seeming to continue forever **hiç bitmeyen, bitmez tükenmez, sürekli, devamlı** *an unending series of problems*

unequal /ʌnˈiːkwəl/ *adjective* **1** different in size, level, amount, etc **eşit olmayan, farklı** **2** unfair **ayrımcı, haksız, adil olmayan** *the unequal distribution of wealth* ● **unequally** *adverb* eşit olmayan bir şekilde

unequivocal /ˌʌnɪˈkwɪvəkəl/ *adjective formal* clear and certain **açık ve seçik, şüpheye mahal vermeyen; açık ve kesin** *an unequivocal answer* ● **unequivocally** *adverb* net bir şekilde

unethical /ʌnˈeθɪkəl/ *adjective* morally bad **ahlaksızca, gayri ahlâkî** *unethical business methods*

uneven /ʌnˈiːvən/ *adjective* not level or smooth **pürüzlü, eğri büğrü, engebeli** *an uneven floor* ● **unevenly** *adverb* pürüzlü

uneventful /ˌʌnɪˈventfəl/ *adjective* without problems and without anything exciting happening **sorunsuz, olaysız, sakin, hadisesiz** *The journey itself was fairly uneventful.*

unexpected /ˌʌnɪkˈspektɪd/ *adjective* Something that is unexpected surprises you because you did not know it was going to happen. **beklenmedik, umulmadık, âni** *His death was completely unexpected.* ● **unexpectedly** *adverb* beklenmedik bir şekilde

unfailing /ʌnˈfeɪlɪŋ/ *adjective* An unfailing quality or ability is one that someone always has. **bitmez, tükenmez, hiç eksilmeyen, sürekli** *unfailing support/courtesy* ● **unfailingly** *adverb* tükenmeyen (beceri)

unfair /ʌnˈfeəʳ/ *adjective* **1** not treating people in an equal way **taraflı, tarafgir, haksız, eşitlik gözetmeyen** *an unfair system* ○ *The test was unfair because some people had seen it before.* **2** not true and morally wrong **haksız, ahlâken doğru olmayan, yanlış** [+ to do sth] *It's unfair to blame Frank for everything.* ● **unfairly** *adverb* haksızca ● **unfairness** *noun* [U] haksızlık

unfaithful /ʌnˈfeɪθfəl/ *adjective* having sex with someone who is not your wife, husband, or usual sexual partner **aldatan, sadakatsiz, ihanet eden** *She was unfaithful to me.*

unfamiliar /ˌʌnfəˈmɪljəʳ/ *adjective* **1** not known to you **yabancı, tanıdık olmayan; aşina olunmayan** *an unfamiliar face* ○ *His name was unfamiliar to me.* **2** **be unfamiliar with sth** to not have any knowledge or experience of something **aşina olmamak; yabancısı olmak; alışık olmamak** *Many older people are unfamiliar with computers.*

U

unfashionable /ʌnˈfæʃˠᵊnəbl/ *adjective* not fashionable or popular at a particular time **modası geçmiş, eski moda, demode**

unfasten /ʌnˈfɑːsˠn/ *verb* [T] to open something that is closed or fixed together **çözmek, açmak** *to unfasten a seat belt*

unfavourable *UK* (*US* **unfavorable**) /ʌnˈfeɪvˠrəbl/ *adjective* **1** negative and showing that you do not like something **olumsuz, elverişsiz, uygun olmayan** *unfavourable publicity* **2** not good and likely to cause problems **olumsuz, menfi, negatif; sorun çıkaran** *unfavourable weather conditions* ● **unfavourably** *adverb* **uygun olmayan şekilde**

unfeeling /ʌnˈfiːlɪŋ/ *adjective* not having sympathy for other people **hissiz, duygusuz, başkalarını düşünmeyen, katı yürekli, zalim**

unfettered /ʌnˈfetəd/ *adjective formal* not limited by rules **kuralsız, özgür, başıboş, dizginsiz** *The UN inspectors were given unfettered access to all nuclear sites.*

unfinished /ʌnˈfɪnɪʃt/ *adjective* not completed **bitmemiş, tamamlanmamış, eksik** *an unfinished novel/portrait*

unfit /ʌnˈfɪt/ *adjective* **1** not suitable or good enough **elverişsiz, uygun değil, yetersiz** *The food was judged unfit for human consumption.* **2** *UK* not healthy because you do too little exercise **idmansız, formsuz, antremansız**

unflattering /ʌnˈflætˠrɪŋ/ *adjective* making someone look less attractive or seem worse than usual **rencide edici, hoşa gitmeyen, övgü içermeyen, berbat** *an unflattering photo/dress/colour*

unfold /ʌnˈfəʊld/ *verb* **1** [I] If a situation or story unfolds, it develops or becomes known. **meydana çıkmak, anlaşılmak, gelişmek** *The nation watched on TV as the tragic events unfolded.* **2** [I, T] to become open and flat, or to make something become open and flat **açılmak, açmak; düzleşmek; düzleştirmek** *I unfolded the map.*

unforeseen /ˌʌnfɔːˈsiːn/ *adjective* not expected **beklenmedik, umulmadık** *The concert was cancelled due to unforeseen circumstances.*

unforgettable /ˌʌnfəˈɡetəbl/ *adjective* Something that is unforgettable is so good, interesting, etc that you remember it for a long time. **unutulmaz, uzun süre hatırdan çıkmayan** *Seeing Niagara Falls was an unforgettable experience.*

unfortunate /ʌnˈfɔːtʃˠnət/ *adjective* **1** used to show that you wish something was not true or had not happened **talihsiz, esef verici, üzücü** *an unfortunate mistake* ○ [+ (that)] *It was unfortunate that she lost her job just as her husband became ill.* **2** unlucky **şanssız, bahtsız, kadersiz** *One unfortunate person failed to see the hole and fell straight into it.*

unfortunately /ʌnˈfɔːtʃənətli/ *adverb* used to say that you wish something was not true or that something had not happened **maalesef, ne yazık ki, korkarım ki** *I'd love to come, but unfortunately I have to work.*

unfounded /ʌnˈfaʊndɪd/ *adjective* not based on facts **asılsız, aslı astarı olmayan, gerçeklere dayanmayan** *unfounded allegations/rumours*

unfriendly /ʌnˈfrendli/ *adjective* not friendly **düşmanca, dostça olmayan, soğuk**

unfulfilled /ˌʌnfʊlˈfɪld/ *adjective* **1** An unfulfilled wish, hope, promise, etc is one that has not happened or not been achieved. **yerine getirilmemiş, tatmin edilmemiş, gerçekleşmemiş** *an unfulfilled ambition/dream* ○ *unfulfilled potential* **2** unhappy because you think you should be achieving more in your life

mutsuz, istediklerini başaramamış, dileklerini gerçekleştirememiş

ungainly /ʌnˈɡeɪnli/ *adjective* moving in a way that is not attractive **hantal, beceriksiz, kaba, biçimsiz** *an ungainly walk*

ungrateful /ʌnˈɡreɪtfˠl/ *adjective* not thanking or showing that you are pleased with someone who has done something for you **nankör, iyilik bilmez, değer bilmez**

unhappy ...... BAŞKA BİR DEYİŞLE
Sad ve miserable sıfatları **unhappy** anlamına gelmektedir. *I felt so sad after he left.* ● *I just woke up feeling miserable.*
Upset sıfatı kötü olan bir olaydan dolayı kişinin mutsuz olduğunu gösterir. *They'd had an argument and she was still upset about it.* ● *Mike got very upset when I told him the news.*
Eğer kişinin bir sevdiği onunla olan ilişkisini bitirdiyse, terkedilen kişinin hislerinin ifadesi için **broken-hearted** veya **heartbroken** söylemleri kullanılabilir. *She was broken-hearted when Richard left.*
Eğer kişi çok mutsuz ve üzgün ise, **devastated** veya **distraught** kelimeleri kullanılır. *She was devastated when he died.* ● *The missing child's distraught parents made an emotional appeal for information on TV.*
Depressed sıfatı kişinin uzun süreli mutsuzluğunu dile getirmede kullanılır. *She became deeply depressed after her husband died.*

☞**unhappy** /ʌnˈhæpi/ *adjective* **1** sad **mutsuz, üzüntülü, mahzun** *an unhappy childhood* **2** not satisfied **tatminsiz, memnun olmayan, memnuniyet duymayan** *Giorgio was unhappy with his test results.* ○ *I'm unhappy about the situation.* ● **unhappily** *adverb* **mutsuz bir şekilde** ● **unhappiness** *noun* [U] **mutsuzluk**

unharmed /ʌnˈhɑːmd/ *adjective* [never before noun] not harmed or damaged **zarar görmemiş, sağ sağlam** *Both children escaped unharmed from the burning building.*

unhealthy /ʌnˈhelθi/ *adjective* **1** [CAUSE ILLNESS] likely to damage your health **sağlığa zararlı, sağlıklı olmayan** *Eating too much is unhealthy.* **2** [ILL] not strong, and likely to become ill **sağlıksız, sıhhatsiz, kolay rahatsızlanan** *She looks pale and unhealthy.* **3** [NOT NORMAL] not normal and slightly unpleasant **normal olmayan; hoş olmayan, kabul görmeyen** *an unhealthy interest in weapons*

unheard /ʌnˈhɜːd/ *adjective* not listened to or considered **duyulmamış, kulak arkası edilmiş; dikkate alınmamış** *Her cries went unheard.*

un'heard ˌof *adjective* [never before noun] never having happened before **eşi görülmemiş, işitilmemiş, olağan dışı, eşine rastlanmayan; ne duyulmuş ne görülmüş** *Thirty years ago the disease was unheard of.*

unhelpful /ʌnˈhelpfʊl/ *adjective* **1** not improving a situation **yararsız, yardımı dokunmayan, işe yaramayan** *an unhelpful remark* **2** not wanting to help someone, in a way that seems unfriendly **yardım etmek istemeyen** *The taxi driver was rude and unhelpful.*

unhurt /ʌnˈhɜːt/ *adjective* not harmed **yarasız beresiz, sağ salim**

unicorn /ˈjuːnɪkɔːn/ *noun* [C] an imaginary white horse with a horn growing from the front of its head **tek boynuzlu efsane at**

unidentified /ˌʌnaɪˈdentɪfaɪd/ *adjective* not recognized **tanımlanmayan, kimliği belirsiz, kimliği meçhul** *The body of an unidentified woman was found in a field last night.*

unification /ˌjuːnɪfɪˈkeɪʃᵊn/ *noun* [U] when two or more countries join together and become one country **birleşme, birleştirme** *the unification of East and West Germany*

uniform¹ /ˈjuːnɪfɔːm/ *noun* [C, U] a special set of clothes that are worn by people who do a particular job or people who go to a particular school **üniforma, forma** *a school uniform* ○ *a nurse's uniform* ○ *Tom looks completely different in uniform* (= wearing a uniform).
● **uniformed** *adjective uniformed police officers* **üniforma giymiş**

uniform² /ˈjuːnɪfɔːm/ *adjective* being the same size, shape, amount, etc **bir örnek, aynı tipte, değişmeyen, aynı** *a row of houses of uniform height* ● **uniformity** /ˌjuːnɪˈfɔːməti/ *noun* [U] **benzerlik** ● **uniformly** *adverb* **benzer bir şekilde**

unify /ˈjuːnɪfaɪ/ *verb* [T] to join together two or more countries or groups to make a single one **birleştirmek** *We need a leader who can unify the party.* ● **unified** *adjective Many people want a more unified Europe.* **birleştirilmiş**

unilateral /ˌjuːnɪˈlætᵊrᵊl/ *adjective* A unilateral action or decision is done or made by one country, group, etc without waiting for others to agree. **tek yanlı, tek taraflı** *unilateral nuclear disarmament* ● **unilaterally** *adverb* **tek taraflı bir biçimde**

unimaginable /ˌʌnɪˈmædʒɪnəbl/ *adjective* Something that is unimaginable is difficult to imagine because it is so bad, good, big, etc. **düşünülemez, tasavvur edilemez, akıl almaz** *unimaginable pain/wealth* ● **unimaginably** *adverb* **hayal edilemeyecek kadar güzel bir şekilde**

unimportant /ˌʌnɪmˈpɔːtᵊnt/ *adjective* not important **önemsiz, değersiz**

uninhabitable /ˌʌnɪnˈhæbɪtəbl/ *adjective* too cold, dangerous, etc to live in **oturulamaz, yaşanamaz**

uninhabited /ˌʌnɪnˈhæbɪtɪd/ *adjective* If a place is uninhabited, no one lives there. **ıssız, boş, gayri meskûn, oturulmayan** *an uninhabited island*

uninhibited /ˌʌnɪnˈhɪbɪtɪd/ *adjective* feeling free to behave in any way that you want without worrying about other people's opinions **doğal, içinden geldiği gibi davranan, serbest, çekingen olmayan**

uninstall /ˌʌnɪnˈstɔːl/ *verb* [T] to remove a computer program from a computer **bilgisayarda bilgisayar programını kurulumdan çıkarmak**

unintelligible /ˌʌnɪnˈtelɪdʒəbl/ *adjective* impossible to understand **anlaşılmaz, anlaşılması imkânsız**

unintentional /ˌʌnɪnˈtentʃᵊnᵊl/ *adjective* not planned or intended **kasıtsız, kasdi olmayan, istenmeyerek yapılan** *If I did offend her it was entirely unintentional.*

uninterested /ʌnˈɪntrəstɪd/ *adjective* not interested **ilgisiz, kayıtsız, ilgilenmeyen** *He's completely uninterested in politics.*

uninterrupted /ˌʌnˌɪntᵊrˈʌptɪd/ *adjective* continuous **kesintisiz, sürekli, aralıksız, devamlı** *I want a radio station that offers uninterrupted music.*

union ...... İLE BİRLİKTE KULLANILAN KELİMELER

join a union ● a union **member/official/leader/representative**

union /ˈjuːnjən/ *noun* **1** [C] (*also* **trade union**) (*also US* **labor union**) an organization that represents people who do a particular job **sendika** *a teachers'/firefighters' union* **2** [U, no plural] when two or more countries, groups, etc join together to make one country, group, etc **birlik** *a move towards full economic union of EU countries* ⊃See also: **the European Union.**

Union 'Jack (Union flag) *noun* [C] the red, white and blue flag of the United Kingdom **Birleşik Krallığın kırmızı, beyaz ve mavi renklerden oluşan bayrağı**

unique /juːˈniːk/ *adjective* **1** different from everyone and everything else **biricik, tek, eşsiz** *Everyone's fingerprints are unique.* **2** unusual and special **alışılmışın dışında, özgü, müstesna, nadir, emsalsiz** *a unique opportunity* **3** be unique to sb/sth to exist in only one place, or be connected with only one person or thing *...özgü/has/mahsus olmak It's a method of education that is unique to this school.* ● **uniquely** *adverb* **herşeyden farklı, tek olarak, çok özel** ● **uniqueness** *noun* [U] **yeganelik**

unisex /ˈjuːnɪseks/ *adjective* for both men and women **her iki cinse uygun/ait** *unisex clothes* ○ *a unisex hairdresser*

unison /ˈjuːnɪsᵊn/ *noun* **in unison** If people do something in unison, they all do it at the same time. **hep beraber, birlikte, ortak**

unit /ˈjuːnɪt/ *noun* [C] **1** GROUP a group of people who are responsible for a particular part of an organization **birim, tim, ekip, grup** *an anti-terrorist unit* **2** MEASURE a measure used to express an amount or quantity **birim, ölçü birimi** *The kilogram is a unit of weight.* **3** SINGLE a single, complete thing that may be part of a larger thing **birim** *a French course book with ten units* **4** FURNITURE a piece of furniture that fits together with other pieces **ünite** *kitchen units* **5** MACHINE a small machine, or part of a machine, that has a particular purpose **ünite, blok, tertibat** *a computer's central processing unit* **6** BUILDING a single apartment, office, etc in a larger building **bölüm, blok, ünite**

unite /juːˈnaɪt/ *verb* [I, T] to join together as a group, or to make people join together as a group **birleşmek, bir araya gelmek, birleştirmek, bir araya getirmek** *We need a leader who can unite the party.*

united /juːˈnaɪtɪd/ *adjective* **1** If people are united, they all agree about something. **fikir birliği etmiş, birleşmiş, anlaşmış** *On the issue of education the party is united.* **2** joined together **birleşik, birleşmiş** *a united Germany*

the Un,ited 'Nations *noun* [group] an international organization that tries to solve world problems in a peaceful way **Birleşmiş Milletler**

unity ...... İLE BİRLİKTE KULLANILAN KELİMELER

achieve/maintain/restore unity ● unity **among/between** sb ● **a show of** unity

unity /ˈjuːnəti/ *noun* [U] when everyone agrees with each other or wants to stay together **birlik, beraberlik, bütünlük, uyum** *national unity* ○ *family unity*

universal /ˌjuːnɪˈvɜːsᵊl/ *adjective* relating to everyone in the world, or to everyone in a particular group **evrensel, genel, üniversal** *Kittens and puppies have an almost universal appeal.* ● **universally** *adverb It's a style of music that is universally popular.* **evrensel bir şekilde**

the universe /ˈjuːnɪvɜːs/ *noun* everything that exists, including stars, space, etc **kâinat, evren** *Many people believe that there is life elsewhere in the universe.*

university ...... İLE BİRLİKTE KULLANILAN KELİMELER

go to university ● at university ● a university course

o⊸**university** /ˌjuːnɪˈvɜːsəti/ *noun* [C, U] a place where students study at a high level to get a degree (= type of qualification) **üniversite** *the University of Cambridge* ○ *I applied to three universities.* ○ (*mainly UK*) *Sarah studied chemistry at university.* ○ (*mainly UK*) *I want to go to university when I finish school.*

unjust /ʌn'dʒʌst/ *adjective* not fair **haksız, adaletsiz, insafsız** *unjust treatment/laws/sanctions* ● **unjustly** *adverb* **haksız bir şekilde**

unjustified /ʌn'dʒʌstɪfaɪd/ *adjective* done without a reason and not deserved **mantıksız, haksız, mazur görülemez** *unjustified criticism*

unkempt /ʌn'kempt/ *adjective* untidy **düzensiz, dağınık, hırpani, bakımsız, derbeder** *Her hair was long and unkempt.*

unkind /ʌn'kaɪnd/ *adjective* slightly cruel **nazik olmayan, hatır kırıcı, düşmanca** *I didn't tell her the truth because I thought it would be unkind.* ● **unkindly** *adverb* **acımasızca** ● **unkindness** *noun* [U] **acımasızlık**

unknown¹ /ʌn'nəʊn/ *adjective* **1** not known **blinmeyen, tanınmayan, yabancı, meçhul** *The cause of his death is still unknown.* **2** not famous **meşhur olmayan, bilinmeyen, tanınmayan** *an unknown actor* ⊃See also: an unknown quantity.

unknown² /ʌn'nəʊn/ *noun* **1 the unknown** things that you have not experienced and know nothing about **bilinmeyen/meçhul şey** *It's normal to fear the unknown.* **2** [C] someone who is not famous **meşhur olmayan kimse, bilinmeyen/tanınmayan kişi** *The game was won by a complete unknown.*

unlawful /ʌn'lɔːf°l/ *adjective formal* illegal **yasadışı, kanunsuz** *unlawful possession of guns* ● **unlawfully** *adverb* **kanuna aykırı bir şekilde**

unleaded /ʌn'ledɪd/ *adjective* Unleaded fuel does not contain lead (= a metal). **kurşunsuz**

unleash /ʌn'liːʃ/ *verb* [T] to suddenly cause a strong reaction **anî ve sert tepkilcre neden olmak** *The newspaper report unleashed a storm of protest from readers.*

o-**unless** /ən'les/ *conjunction* except if ...**dıkça/mıkça**; ...**madıkça/medikçe**; ...**mazsa/mezse**; **meğer ki** *I won't call you unless there are any problems.*

unlike /ʌn'laɪk/ *preposition* **1** different from someone or something ...**dan/den farklı olarak**; ...**ın/in aksine**; ...**ın/in tersine** *Jackie's really clever, unlike her sister.* ○ *The furniture was unlike anything she had ever seen.* **2** not typical of someone or something **farklı, benzemez, ayrı** *It's unlike her to be quiet - was there something wrong?*

o-**unlikely** /ʌn'laɪkli/ *adjective* **1** not expected to happen **olası olmayan, muhtemel olmayan, ihtimal dışı** [+ (that)] *It's unlikely that I'll be able to come to the party.* ○ [+ to do sth] *He's unlikely to arrive before midday.* **2** probably not true **muhtemelen doğru olmayan, inanması zor** *an unlikely explanation*

unlimited /ʌn'lɪmɪtɪd/ *adjective* without any limits **sınırsız, sonsuz, pek çok, hadsiz, hesapsız** *a service that offers unlimited Internet access*

unload /ʌn'ləʊd/ *verb* **1** [I, T] to remove things from a vehicle **boşaltmak, indirmek** *Can you help me unload the car?* **2** [I] If a ship, aircraft, etc unloads, goods are taken off it. **boşaltma yapmak**

unlock /ʌn'lɒk/ *verb* [T] to open something which is locked using a key **açmak, kilidini açmak**

unlucky /ʌn'lʌki/ *adjective* having or causing bad luck **talihsiz, şanssız, bahtsız** [+ to do sth] *The team played well and was unlucky to lose.* ○ *Some people think it's unlucky to walk under ladders.* ● **unluckily** *adverb* **şanssız bir şekilde**

unmarked /ʌn'mɑːkt/ *adjective* having no signs or words that show what something is **işaretsiz, işaret konmamış** *an unmarked grave*

unmarried /ʌn'mærɪd/ *adjective* not married **evlenmemiş, bekâr**

unmatched /ʌn'mætʃt/ *adjective* better than anyone or anything else **kıyaslanamaz, karşılaştırılamaz** *Horses have an athletic beauty unmatched by any other animal.*

unmistakable /ˌʌnmɪ'steɪkəbl/ *adjective* Something that is unmistakable is very obvious and cannot be confused with anything else. **apaçık, kendini belli eden** *an unmistakable look of disappointment* ● **unmistakably** *adverb* **karıştırılması imkansız bir şekilde**

unmoved /ʌn'muːvd/ *adjective* not feeling any emotion **duygulanmamış, etkilenmemiş, heyecanlanmamış** *It's impossible to remain unmoved by pictures of starving children.*

unnamed /ʌn'neɪmd/ *adjective* An unnamed person or thing is talked about but their name is not said. **adı geçmeyen/söylenmeyen, adından söz edilmeyen** *The money was given by an unnamed businessman.*

unnatural /ʌn'nætʃ°r°l/ *adjective* not normal or right **anormal, tuhaf, garip** *an unnatural interest in death* ● **unnaturally** *adverb* **unnaturally thin doğal olmayan bir şekilde**

unnecessary /ʌn'nesəs°ri/ *adjective* **1** not needed **gereksiz, lüzumsuz** *You don't want to make any unnecessary car journeys in this weather.* **2** unkind **kaba, hiç gerekmeyen, anlamsız, saçma** *Why did she say that? That was unnecessary.* ● **unnecessarily** /ʌn'nesəs°r°li/ *adverb* **gereksizce**

unnerve /ʌn'nɜːv/ *verb* [T] to make someone feel nervous or frightened **korkutmak, ürkütmek**

unnerving /ʌn'nɜːvɪŋ/ *adjective* making you feel nervous or frightened **korkutucu, ürkütücü** *He kept looking at me which I found unnerving.*

unnoticed /ʌn'nəʊtɪst/ *adjective* without being seen or noticed **göze çarpmadan, farkedilmeden** *We managed to slip away unnoticed.*

unobtrusive /ˌʌnəb'truːsɪv/ *adjective* not attracting attention **dikkat çekmeyen, göze çarpmaz** *He was quiet and unobtrusive.* ● **unobtrusively** *adverb* **hiç dikkat çekmeden**

unoccupied /ʌn'ɒkjəpaɪd/ *adjective* An unoccupied building, room, seat, etc has no one in it. **boş, tutulmamış, oturulmayan, içinde oturulmayan**

unofficial /ˌʌnə'fɪʃ°l/ *adjective* not said or done by the government or someone in authority **resmi olmayan, gayri resmî** *Unofficial reports suggest the death toll from the earthquake is around 600.* ● **unofficially** *adverb* **gayri resmi bir şekilde**

unorthodox /ʌn'ɔːθədɒks/ *adjective* unusual and different from most people's opinions, methods, etc **alışılmışın dışında, genel temayüle uymayan** *unorthodox ideas/views* ○ *an unorthodox style of teaching*

unpack

unpack /ʌn'pæk/ *verb* [I, T] to take things out of a bag, box, etc **açmak, açıp içini boşaltmak, boşaltmak** *Bella unpacked her suitcase.* ○ *I haven't had time to unpack yet.*

unpaid /ʌn'peɪd/ *adjective* **1** An unpaid debt, tax, etc has not been paid. **ödenmemiş,**

ödenmeyi bekleyen **2** working without getting any money **parasız, ücretsiz** *unpaid work*

unpalatable /ʌnˈpælətəbl/ *adjective formal* shocking and difficult to accept **sarsıcı, kabul edilmesi güç, şok eden** *an unpalatable fact*

unparalleled /ʌnˈpærəleld/ *adjective formal* better, greater, worse, etc than anything else **emsalsiz, eşsiz, kıyas kabul etmez (iyi veya kötü olarak)** *an act of unparalleled cruelty*

unplanned /ʌnˈplænd/ *adjective* not planned or expected **plansız, planlanmamış** *an unplanned pregnancy*

unpleasant /ʌnˈpleznt/ *adjective* **1** not enjoyable or pleasant **berbat, iğrenç, tatsız, nahoş, çirkin** *an unpleasant experience/smell* **2** rude and angry **kaba, sürekli kızgın, hır gür çıkaran** *The waiter got quite unpleasant with us.* ● **unpleasantly** *adverb* **hoş olmayan bir şekilde**

unplug /ʌnˈplʌg/ *verb* [T] to stop a piece of electrical equipment being connected to an electricity supply by pulling its plug (= object with pins) out of the wall **fişi çekmek, fişi prizden çıkarmak**

unpopular /ʌnˈpɒpjələr/ *adjective* disliked by most people **toplumca sevilmeyen, kimsenin istemediği; nefret edilen** *an unpopular idea* ○ *an unpopular teacher* ● **unpopularity** /ʌnˌpɒpjəˈlærəti/ *noun* [U] **benimsenmeyen, beğenilmeyen**

unprecedented /ʌnˈpresɪdəntɪd/ *adjective* never having happened before **eşsiz, emsalsiz, hiç rastlanmamış,** *The Internet has given people unprecedented access to information.*

unpredictable /ˌʌnprɪˈdɪktəbl/ *adjective* changing so much that you do not know what will happen next **tahmin edilemeyen, kestirilemeyen, sağı solu belli olmayan** *unpredictable weather conditions* ● **unpredictability** /ˌʌnprɪˌdɪktəˈbɪləti/ *noun* [U] **tahmin edilemez**

unprofessional /ˌʌnprəˈfeʃənl/ *adjective* behaving badly at work **profesyonel olmayan; çalışma koşul ve kurallarının aksine davranan; iş yaşamı ilkelerine uymayan** *an unprofessional attitude*

unprovoked /ˌʌnprəˈvəʊkt/ *adjective* An unprovoked attack is one in which the person who is attacked has done nothing to cause it. **nedensiz, sebepsiz, durup dururken yapılan**

unqualified /ʌnˈkwɒlɪfaɪd/ *adjective* **1** without the qualifications or knowledge to do something **niteliksiz, vasıfsız, belgesiz, diplomasız** [+ to do sth] *She was totally unqualified to look after children.* **2** [always before noun] *formal* total and not limited in any way **tam, kesin, mutlak** *an unqualified success*

unquestionably /ʌnˈkwestʃənəbli/ *adverb* in a way that is obvious and causes no doubt **hiç şüphe yok ki, kuşkusuz bir şekilde** *She is unquestionably the best person for the job.*

unravel /ʌnˈrævəl/ *verb* [I, T] UK **unravelling,** *past* **unravelled,** US **unraveling,** *past* **unraveled 1** If you unravel a difficult situation or story, or if it unravels, it becomes clear and easier to understand. **çözmek, halletmek, açıklığa kavuşturmak** *No one has yet unravelled the mystery of his death.* **2** to stop being twisted together, or to move pieces of string, etc so that they are not twisted together **çözmek, açmak, çözülmek, açmak, sökülmek, açılmak**

unreal /ʌnˈrɪəl/ *adjective* Something that is unreal seems so strange that it is difficult to believe. **gerçek dışı, hayali** *For a while I couldn't believe she was dead - it all seemed unreal.* ● **unreality** /ˌʌnriˈæləti/ *noun* [U] **gerçek dışı**

unrealistic /ˌʌnrɪəˈlɪstɪk/ *adjective* not thinking about what is likely to happen or what you can really do **gerçekçi olmayan, pratiklikten yoksun** *She has a totally unrealistic view of life.* ○ [+ to do sth] *It's unrealistic to expect their decision before Tuesday.*

unreasonable /ʌnˈriːzənəbl/ *adjective* not fair **mantıksız, makul olmayan** *unreasonable demands/behaviour* ○ [+ to do sth] *It seems unreasonable to expect one person to do both jobs.* ● **unreasonably** *adverb* **mantıksız**

unrelated /ˌʌnrɪˈleɪtɪd/ *adjective* having no connection **ilişkisi olmayan, herhangi bir bağı olmayan** *Police said his death was unrelated to the attack.*

unrelenting /ˌʌnrɪˈlentɪŋ/ *adjective formal* never stopping or getting any less extreme **aman vermez, durmak dinlenmek bilmeyen** *unrelenting pressure* ○ *The heat was unrelenting.*

unreliable /ˌʌnrɪˈlaɪəbl/ *adjective* not able to be trusted or depended on **güvenilmez, itimat edilemez** *an unreliable witness* ○ *The trains were noisy, dirty, and unreliable.*

unremarkable /ˌʌnrɪˈmɑːkəbl/ *adjective* ordinary and not interesting **sıradan, söz etmeye değmez, kayda değer olmayan** *an unremarkable town*

unremitting /ˌʌnrɪˈmɪtɪŋ/ *adjective formal* never stopping or getting any less extreme **hiç durmayan, bitip tükenmeyen, aralıksız, aman vermeyen** *unremitting hostility/pressure* ○ *unremitting efforts*

unrepentant /ˌʌnrɪˈpentənt/ *adjective* not feeling sorry about something bad that you have done **pişmanlık/nedamet duymayan; pişman olmayan**

unreservedly /ˌʌnrɪˈzɜːvɪdli/ *adverb* completely **tamamen, büsbütün, bütünüyle** *The minister has apologized unreservedly.*

unresolved /ˌʌnrɪˈzɒlvd/ *adjective formal* If a problem or question is unresolved, there is still no solution or answer. **çözümsüz, hâl çaresi bulunamamış** *The question of who owns the land remains unresolved.*

🧩 **unrest** ...... İLE BİRLİKTE KULLANILAN KELİMELER

cause unrest ● **continuing/growing** unrest ● unrest **among** sb ● unrest **over** sth ● a **wave of** unrest ● **political/social** unrest

---

unrest /ʌnˈrest/ *noun* [U] when a lot of people are angry about something and are likely to become violent **huzursuzluk, rahatsızlık, karışıklık, karmaşa** *political/social unrest*

unrestrained /ˌʌnrɪˈstreɪnd/ *adjective* not limited or controlled **kontrolsüz, ölçüsüz, aşırı** *unrestrained anger*

unrivalled UK (US **unrivaled**) /ʌnˈraɪvəld/ *adjective* better than any other of the same type **rakipsiz, eşsiz, çok üstün** *The museum has an unrivalled collection of modern American paintings.* ○ *an unrivalled reputation*

unroll /ʌnˈrəʊl/ *verb* [T] to open something that was rolled into a tube shape and make it flat **yaymak, açmak, açarak sermek** *He unrolled the carpet.*

unruly /ʌnˈruːli/ *adjective* **1** behaving badly and difficult to control **idaresi zor, zaptolunmaz, ele avuca sığmaz, dik kafalı** *unruly children* **2** Unruly hair is difficult to keep tidy. **kolay şekil verilemeyen, muntazam tutulması zor**

unsafe /ʌnˈseɪf/ *adjective* **1** dangerous **emniyetsiz, tehlikeli, güven vermeyen** *The building is unsafe.* ○ [+ to do sth] *The water was dirty and unsafe to drink.* **2** If you feel unsafe, you feel that you are in danger. **tehlike**

U

içinde olan, emniyet içinde olmayan *Many women feel unsafe on the streets at night.*

unsatisfactory /ʌn‚sætɪs'fækt°ri/ *adjective* not good enough to be acceptable **tatminkâr olmayan, yetersiz, tatmin etmeyen** *Many school buildings are in an unsatisfactory condition.*

unsavoury UK (US **unsavory**) /ʌn'seɪv°ri/ *adjective* unpleasant and morally offensive **çirkin, çok kötü, rezil** *an unsavoury reputation/incident/character*

unscathed /ʌn'skeɪðd/ *adjective* [never before noun] not harmed **zarar görmemiş, yarasız beresiz, sağ salim, kazasız belasız** *The driver of the car was killed but both passengers escaped unscathed.*

unscrew /ʌn'skru:/ *verb* [T] **1** to remove something by twisting it **vidasını sökmek/açmak/gevşetmek** *I can't unscrew the lid.* **2** to remove something by taking the screws (= small, metal pieces) out of it **vidaları çıkararak sökmek**

unscrupulous /ʌn'skru:pjələs/ *adjective* behaving in a way that is dishonest or unfair in order to get what you want **vicdansız, insafsız, ahlaksız, ahlaki değerleri/kaygıları olmayan** *an unscrupulous financial adviser*

unseat /ʌn'si:t/ *verb* [T] to remove someone from a powerful position **gücünü elinden almak; etkisiz ve yetkisizleştirmek** *Kennedy has a good chance of unseating the President at the next election.*

unseen /ʌn'si:n/ *adjective, adverb* not seen or noticed **görünmeyen, göze çarpmayan; dikkatten kaçabilen** *an exhibition of previously unseen photographs*

unsettled /ʌn'setld/ *adjective* **1** changing often **sık sık değişen, karışık, belirsiz** *The weather continues to be unsettled.* **2** anxious and not able to relax or feel happy in a situation **endişeli, huzursuz, tedirgin** *Children tend to get unsettled if you keep changing their routine.*

unsettling /ʌn'setlɪŋ/ *adjective* making you feel anxious **endişelendiren, huzursuz eden, tedirgin eden** *an unsettling experience/feeling*

unsightly /ʌn'saɪtli/ *adjective* unpleasant to look at **göze hoş gelmeyen, çirkin, nahoş** *unsightly piles of litter*

unskilled /ʌn'skɪld/ *adjective* **1** without special skills or qualifications **vasıfsız, niteliksiz** *an unskilled labourer/worker* **2** Unskilled work does not need people with special skills or qualifications. **vasıf/nitelik gerektirmeyen**

unsociable /ʌn'səʊʃəbl/ *adjective* not wanting to be with other people **insanlardan kaçan, sosyal ortamlarda olmayı sevmeyen**

unsolicited /‚ʌnsə'lɪsɪtɪd/ *adjective* not asked for and often not wanted **istenmeden yapılan/verilen/gösterilen** *unsolicited advice/offer*

unsolved /ʌn'sɒlvd/ *adjective* having no answer or solution **çözümlenmemiş, aydınlığa kavuşmamış, nedeni belli olmayan** *an unsolved mystery/murder/crime*

unsound /ʌn'saʊnd/ *adjective* **1** based on ideas, facts, and reasons that are wrong **sağlam bir olguya dayanmayan, sağlıksız, hatalı** *an unsound practice* **2** in a bad condition **yıkık dökük, derme çatma, köhne, çürük, sağlam olmayan** *The bridge was structurally unsound.*

unspeakable /ʌn'spi:kəbl/ *adjective* extremely bad or shocking **berbat, çok kötü, müthiş, tarifsiz** *unspeakable crimes/suffering* ● **unspeakably** *adverb* **tarifsiz imkansız bir şekilde**

unspecified /ʌn'spesɪfaɪd/ *adjective* If something is unspecified, you are not told what it is. **açıkça belirtil-**

memiş *The court awarded her an unspecified amount of money.*

unspoiled (also UK **unspoilt**) /ʌn'spɔɪlt/ *adjective* An unspoiled place is beautiful because it has not been changed or damaged by people. **bozulmamış, henüz dokunulmamış, zarar/hasar görmemiş** *an island with clean, unspoiled beaches*

unspoken /ʌn'spəʊk°n/ *adjective* not said, but thought or felt **açığa vurulmamış, söylenmemiş** *unspoken doubts*

unstable /ʌn'steɪbl/ *adjective* **1** [CHANGE] likely to change or end suddenly **dengesiz, istikrarsız, kararsız** *an unstable situation* ○ *an unstable economy* **2** [PERSON] If someone is unstable, their moods and behaviour change suddenly, especially because they are mentally ill. **dengesiz, ne yapacağı belli olmayan** **3** [MOVE] not fixed or safe and likely to move **dengesiz, sabit olmayan** *That chair looks a bit unstable.*

unsteady /ʌn'stedi/ *adjective* moving slightly from side to side, as if you might fall **dengesiz, sallantılı, sallanan** *The alcohol had made her unsteady on her feet.*

unstuck /ʌn'stʌk/ *adjective* **1 come unstuck a** UK If something comes unstuck, it stops being fixed to something. **çıkmak, düşmek, dökülmek** *One of the photos has come unstuck.* **b** UK *informal* to experience difficulties and fail **başarısızlığa uğramak, başarısız olmak; güçlüklerin üstesinden gelemeyip başarısız olmak** *The negotiations came unstuck at a crucial stage.*

unsubscribe /‚ʌnsəb'skraɪb/ *verb* [I, T] to remove your name from an Internet mailing list (= a list of names and addresses that an organization sends information to) **(aboneliği) iptal emek**

unsuccessful /‚ʌnsək'sesf°l/ *adjective* not achieving what was wanted or intended **başarısız** *an unsuccessful attempt/effort* ● **unsuccessfully** *adverb* **başarısız bir biçimde**

unsuitable /ʌn'su:təbl/ *adjective* not acceptable or right for someone or something **elverişsiz, uygun/müsait olmayan** *My parents considered the programme unsuitable for children.*

unsung /ʌn'sʌŋ/ *adjective* not famous or praised although you have done something very well **kıymeti anlaşılmamış; değeri takdir edilmemiş; henüz keşfedilmemiş** *He was the unsung hero of the match.*

unsure /ʌn'ʃʊə°/ *adjective* **1** not certain or having doubts **şüphe duyan, emin olmayan** *I'm a bit unsure about what to do.* **2 unsure of yourself** without confidence **kendine güvenmeyen, güven duymayan, güvensiz**

unsuspecting /‚ʌnsə'spektɪŋ/ *adjective* [always before noun] not aware that something bad is happening **şüphelenmeyen, kuşkulanmayan** *In each case the unsuspecting victim had been invited into Cooper's home.*

unsustainable /‚ʌnsə'steɪnəb°l/ *adjective* **1** Something that is unsustainable cannot continue at the same rate **savunulamayacak** **2** causing damage to the environment by using more of something than can be replaced naturally **sürdürülemez** *unsustainable fishing methods*

unsympathetic /‚ʌnsɪmpə'θetɪk/ *adjective* **1** showing that you do not understand or care about someone's problems **sempatik olmayan, sevimsiz, soğuk** *I told him I'd got a cold but he was completely unsympathetic.* **2** not agreeing with or supporting someone's ideas or actions **ilgi duymayan, arka çıkmayan, sempati gelmeyen**

untangle /ʌn'tæŋgl/ *verb* [T] **1** to separate pieces of string, hair, wire, etc that have become twisted together **açmak, çözmek, düzeltmek** *I'm trying to untangle these wires.* **2** to understand the different parts of a situation that has become confused or very complicated anlamak, çözmek, en önemli sorunu halletmek *Historians have tried to untangle the complex issues behind the events.*

untapped /ʌnˈtæpt/ *adjective* not yet used **kullanılmamış, el değmemiş** *untapped potential*

untenable /ʌnˈtenəbl/ *adjective formal* If an argument, action, or situation is untenable, it cannot be supported or defended from criticism. **savunulamaz, tutulacak yanı olmayan, çürük** *an untenable position*

unthinkable /ʌnˈθɪŋkəbl/ *adjective* If something is unthinkable, it is so strange that you cannot imagine it will ever happen. **düşünülemez, tasavvur edilemez, imkânsız** *Thirty years ago a no-smoking restaurant would have been unthinkable.*

untidy

untidy /ʌnˈtaɪdi/ *adjective* not tidy **dağınık, düzensiz, karman çorman** *an untidy room* ○ *She's really untidy at home.*

untie /ʌnˈtaɪ/ *verb* [T]   **untie**
untying, *past* **untied** to open a knot or something that has been tied with a knot **çözmek, açmak** *I untied my shoelaces and kicked off my shoes.*

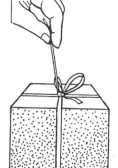

○━**until** /ˌⁿnˈtɪl/ (*also* till) *preposition, conjunction* **1** continuing to happen before a particular time or event and then stopping ...**a/e kadar;** ...**a/e dek, değin** *The show will be on until the end of the month.* ○ *Whisk the egg whites until they look white and fluffy.* **2** as far as ... **a/e kadar** *Carry on until you reach the traffic lights and turn right.* **3** not until not before a particular time or event ...**dan/den önce değil; ...madan/meden önce** *It doesn't open until 7.* ○ *We won't start until Jeanne arrives.*

untimely /ʌnˈtaɪmli/ *adjective* happening too soon **kısa sürede olan, çok kısa zamanda meydana gelen** *her untimely death from cancer*

untold /ʌnˈtəʊld/ *adjective* [always before noun] too much to be measured or counted **sayısız, tarifsiz, haddi hesabı olmayan** *untold riches* ○ *untold damage*

untouched /ʌnˈtʌtʃt/ *adjective* **1** not changed or damaged in any way **değişmemiş, el sürülmemiş, zarar görmemiş, bozulmamış** *Most of the island remains untouched by tourism.* **2** If food is untouched, it has not been eaten. **dokunulmamış, yenilmemiş**

untoward /ˌʌntəˈwɔːd/ *adjective formal* unexpected and causing problems **aksi, ters, uygunsuz, istenmedik** *If nothing untoward happens we should be there by midday.*

untrained /ʌnˈtreɪnd/ *adjective* **1** never having been taught the skills for a particular job **eğitimsiz, eğitilmemiş, deneyimsiz, acemi** *untrained staff* **2 the untrained eye** someone without the skill or knowledge to judge what they see **gözle karar vermeyen kimse; kestirme yeteneği/bilgisi olmayan kişi** *To the untrained eye, most fake diamonds look real.*

untried /ʌnˈtraɪd/ *adjective* not yet used or tested **kullanılmamış, denenmemiş** *new and untried technology*

untrue /ʌnˈtruː/ *adjective* false **sahte, yalan, gerçek dışı**

untruth /ʌnˈtruːθ/ *noun* [C] *formal* a lie, or something that is not true **yalan, uydurma, asılsız şey**

unused¹ /ʌnˈjuːzd/ *adjective* not used now or not used before now **kullanılmamış, kullanılmayan** *an unused room*

unused² /ʌnˈjuːst/ *adjective* **be unused to sth** to not have experience of something **alışmamış, alışık olmayan** *I was unused to city life.*

unusual /ʌnˈjuːʒuəl/ *adjective* different and not ordinary, often in a way that is interesting or exciting **ender, nadir, alışık olunmayan** *an unusual name* ○ [+ to do sth] *It's fairly unusual to keep insects as pets.*

unusually /ʌnˈjuːʒuəli/ *adverb* **1 unusually big/strong/good, etc** bigger/stronger/better, etc than is normal **olmadık şekilde, alışılmamış, olağanüstü şekilde** *unusually warm weather* **2 unusually for sb** in a way that is not usual for someone **anormal şekilde, yadırganacak biçimde, şaşılacak şekilde** *Unusually for me, I actually couldn't finish my meal.*

unveil /ʌnˈveɪl/ *verb* [T] **1** to tell the public about an idea or plan that was secret before **açıklamak, ortaya çıkarmak, kamu oyuna açıklamak** *The new policy is due to be unveiled later this month.* **2** to remove the cover from an object as part of an official ceremony **açmak, örtüsünü açmak**

unwanted /ʌnˈwɒntɪd/ *adjective* not wanted **istenmeyen** *an unwanted gift*

unwarranted /ʌnˈwɒrⁿntɪd/ *adjective formal* without a good reason **haksız, yersiz, sebepsiz** *unwarranted intrusion*

unwary /ʌnˈweəri/ *adjective* not aware of possible dangers **tedbirsiz, dikkatsiz, gâfil** *Unwary travellers can easily get lost in these parts.*

unwelcome /ʌnˈwelkəm/ *adjective* not wanted **istenmeyen, hoşa gitmeyen, tatsız, nahoş** *unwelcome publicity* ○ *an unwelcome visitor*

unwell /ʌnˈwel/ *adjective* [never before noun] *formal* ill **hasta, rahatsız, keyifsiz, iyi değil** *to feel/look unwell*

unwieldy /ʌnˈwiːldi/ *adjective* An unwieldy object is difficult to carry because it is heavy, large, or a strange shape. **hantal, havaleli, taşınması zor**

unwilling /ʌnˈwɪlɪŋ/ *adjective* not wanting to do something **isteksiz, gönülsüz** [+ to do sth] *A lot of people are unwilling to accept change.* ● **unwillingly** *adverb* **isteksizce** ● **unwillingness** *noun* [U] **isteksizlik**

unwind /ʌnˈwaɪnd/ *verb past* **unwound 1** [I] *informal* to relax, especially after working **dinlenmek, yorgunluğunu gidermek/atmak; rahatlamak** *Music helps me* *to unwind.* **2** [I, T] If you unwind something, or if something unwinds, it stops being curled round or twisted round something else and is made straight. **çözmek, açmak** *He unwound the bandage.*

unwise /ʌnˈwaɪz/ *adjective* stupid and likely to cause problems **akılsızca, aptalca, alıkca, düşüncesizce** *an unwise decision* ● **unwisely** *adverb* **aptalca**

unwittingly /ʌnˈwɪtɪŋli/ *adverb* without intending to do something **bilmeyerek, farkında olmadan, habersizce, istemeyerek; niyet etmeksizin** *I apologized for the chaos I had unwittingly caused.*

unworkable /ʌnˈwɜːkəbl/ *adjective* A plan that is unworkable is impossible. **gerçekleşmesi olanaksız, yapılması imkânsız** *The policy has been described as unworkable.*

unwrap /ʌnˈræp/ *verb* [T] **unwrapping**, *past* **unwrapped** to remove the paper, cloth, etc that is covering something **açmak, üstünü açmak, kabuğunu/dışını açmak** *She carefully unwrapped the present.*

unwrap

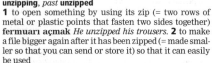

unwritten /ʌnˈrɪtⁿn/ *adjective* **an unwritten agreement/law/rule** an agreement/law, etc that is accepted and obeyed by most people but is not formally written **yazılmamış/yazılı olmayan/sözlü antlaşma/yasa/kural**

unzip /ʌnˈzɪp/ *verb* [T] **unzipping**, *past* **unzipped** **1** to open something by using its zip (= two rows of metal or plastic points that fasten two sides together) **fermuarı açmak** *He unzipped his trousers.* **2** to make a file bigger again after it has been zipped (= made smaller so that you can send or store it) so that it can easily be used

ᵒ٭**up¹** /ʌp/ *adverb, preposition* **1** [HIGHER PLACE] towards or in a higher place **yukarı, yukarıya, yukarıda** *He ran up the stairs.* ○ *Pick up your clothes and put them away.* ○ *She looked up and smiled at me.* **2** [VERTICAL] vertical or as straight as possible **dik olarak, doğrulmuş vaziyette, ayakta** *He stood up.* ○ *She opened her eyes and sat up.* **3** [INCREASE] to a greater degree, amount, volume, etc **...a/e kadar; ...a/e varan; (çoğaltma, artırma gibi eylemlerde kullanılır)** *Inflation keeps pushing prices up.* ○ *Can you turn up the heat? I'm freezing!* ○ *Please speak up* (= speak louder), *I can't hear you.* **4** [COMPLETELY] used to emphasize that someone completes an action or uses all of something **tamamını, hepsini, bütününü** *I used up all my money.* ○ *Eat up the rest of your dinner.* **5 up the road/street, etc** along or further along the street/road, etc **caddenin/yolun yukarısında/ilerisinde** *My best friend lives up the street from me.* ○ *He ran up the path and hugged her.* **6 go/walk, etc up to sb/sth** to walk directly towards someone or something until you are next to them **yürüyerek birinin/bir şeyin yanına kadar gitmek/sokulmak** *He walked straight up to me and introduced himself.* **7** [DIRECTION] in or towards a particular direction, usually north **kuzeye/kuzeyde; yukarıya/yukarıda** *We moved from London up to Scotland.* ○ *Chris lives up north.* **8 up and down** If something or someone moves up and down, they move repeatedly in one direction and then in the opposite direction. **bir aşağı bir yukarı; bir ileri bir geri** *The*

children were constantly running up and down the stairs. **9 up to 10/20, etc** any amount under 10/20, etc **...10'a, 20'ye vb. kadar** *We can invite up to 65 people.* **10 up to** until a particular time **belli bir zamana kadar** *You can call me up to midnight.* **11 up to sth** equal in quality or achievement **...a/e göre; ...nın/nin kadar; ... ın/in kalitesinde/başarı düzeyinde** *His work wasn't up to his usual standard.* **12 up to sth/doing sth** able to do something **...abilecek/ebilecek güçte; ...acak/ecek halde** *It'll be a while before I feel up to walking again.* **13 be up to (sth)** *informal* to be doing or planning something, often something secret and bad **gizlice bir şeyler çeviriyor/karıştırıyor olmak** *Joe, what are you up to?* **14 be up to sb** If an action or decision is up to someone, they are responsible for doing or making it. **...a/e kalmış; ...a/e bağlı** *I can't decide for you Jack, it's up to you.* ○ [+ to do sth] *It's up to her to decide whether she wants to enter the competition.* **15 be up against sb/sth** If you are up against a situation or a person, they make it very difficult for you to achieve what you want to achieve. **karşı karşıya kalmak; yüz yüze gelmek** *We were up against some of the best players in the world.*

ᵒ٭**up²** /ʌp/ *adjective* [never before noun] **1** [NOT IN BED] not in bed **ayakta, yatakta değil** *I was up all night with the baby.* ○ *Is she up yet?* **2 be up and around/about** to be well enough after an illness to get out of bed and move around **yeterince iyileşmek, ayaklanmak, kendine gelmek** **3** [FINISHED] If a period of time is up, it has ended. **zamanı bitti, süresi doldu** *My health club membership is up.* **4** [INCREASE] If a level or amount is up, it has increased. **artmak, yükselmek** *Profits are up by 26%.* **5** [ROAD] *UK* If a road is up, it is being repaired. **onarımda, tamirde** **6** [OPERATING] If a computer system is up, it is operating. **bilgisayar 'çalışıyor, işlem yapıyor'** **7** [SPORT] *US* In baseball and similar sports, if a player is up, they are taking a turn to play. **(beyzbol vb. sporlarda) 'sırada, sırası gelmiş, sırayla yapıyor'** **8 be up and running** If a system, organization, or machine is up and running, it is operating. **iyi gidiyor, iyi işliyor, tıkır tıkır/saat gibi çalışıyor; çalışır durumda olmak** **9 be up for sth** *informal* to want to do something **yapmak istemek** *We're going clubbing tonight if you're up for it.*

up³ /ʌp/ *verb* [T] **upping**, *past* **upped** to increase something **artırmak, yükseltmek, çoğaltmak** *Dad's upped my allowance by fifty cents a week.*

up-and-coming /ˌʌpənˈkʌmɪŋ/ *adjective* [always before noun] becoming popular and likely to achieve success **girişken, başarı vaat eden, geleceği parlak** *He's a young, up-and-coming DJ.*

upbeat /ˈʌpˌbiːt/ *adjective* *informal* positive and expecting a situation to be good or successful **iyimser, olumlu düşünen** *He remains upbeat about the future.*

upbringing /ˈʌpˌbrɪŋɪŋ/ *noun* [no plural] the way your parents treat you when you are growing up **yetişme, yetiştirme, terbiye, aile terbiyesi** *a middle-class/religious upbringing*

upcoming /ˈʌpˌkʌmɪŋ/ *adjective* [always before noun] An upcoming event will happen soon. **gelecekteki, yakında olan, bir sonraki** *the upcoming elections*

update¹ /ʌpˈdeɪt/ *verb* [T] **1** to add new information **güncelleştirmek, yeni bilgiler ilave etmek; güncel hâle getirmek** *We've just updated our website.* ○ *I'll update you on* (= tell you about) *any developments.* **2** to make something more modern **modernleştirmek, çağdaş hâle getirmek** *They need to update their image.*

U

update (noun) .... İLE BİRLİKTE KULLANILAN KELİMELER

get/give an update ● an update on sth ● an update from sb

update² /ˈʌpdeɪt/ *noun* [C] **1** new information **yeni/ güncel bilgi** *I'll need regular updates on your progress.* **2** a new form of something which existed at an earlier time **günümüze uyarlama, çağdaş/güncel forma sokma** *It's an update of an old 60's movie.*

upfront¹ /ˌʌpˈfrʌnt/ *adjective* **1** paid or obtained before work starts **avans olarak verilen/alınan; önceden ödenen/alınan** *an upfront payment/fee* **2** behaving in a way that makes your beliefs and intentions obvious to other people **aşikâr, açıkça belli eden, gizlemeyen** *She's very upfront about her dislike of men.*

upfront² /ˌʌpˈfrʌnt/ *adverb* If you pay someone upfront, you pay them before they work for you. **avans ödemek; ön ödeme yapmak**

upgrade /ʌpˈɡreɪd/ *verb* [T] to improve something so that it is of a higher quality or a newer model **yükseltmek, iyileştirmek, geliştirmek, ıslah etmek** *to upgrade a computer* ● **upgrade** /ˈʌpɡreɪd/ *noun* [C] **yükseltme, iyileştirme**

upheaval /ʌpˈhiːvəl/ *noun* [C, U] a very big change that causes difficulty or confusion **ani ve büyük değişiklik, kargaşa, karışıklık** *political/social upheaval*

uphill¹ /ʌpˈhɪl/ *adjective* **an uphill battle/struggle/task** something that is difficult to do and needs a lot of effort **çok zahmet isteyen/çaba gerektiren mücadele/ uğraş/görev** *I can lose weight but it's a real uphill struggle.*

uphill² /ʌpˈhɪl/ *adverb* towards the top of a hill **tepeye yukarı; yokuş/bayır yukarı** *We'd walked half a mile uphill.*

uphold /ʌpˈhəʊld/ *verb* [T] *past* **upheld** **1** to agree with a decision, especially a legal one, and say it was correct **uygun bulmak, onaylamak, kabul etmek** *The court upheld the ruling.* **2** to support a decision, principle, or law **arka çıkmak, desteklemek** *Police officers are expected to uphold the law.*

upholstery /ʌpˈhəʊlstəri/ *noun* [U] the material that covers chairs and other types of seats **döşemelik kumaş, döşeme malzemesi**

upkeep /ˈʌpkiːp/ *noun* [U] the process of keeping something in good condition, or of keeping a person or animal healthy **bakım, ihtimam, ilgilenme**

upland /ˈʌplənd/ *adjective* [always before noun] existing on a hill or mountain **yüksek, tepede, yükseklerdeki** *upland areas*

uplands /ˈʌpləndz/ *noun* [plural] high areas of land **yayla, plâto** *the uplands of Nepal*

uplifting /ʌpˈlɪftɪŋ/ *adjective* making you feel happy and full of good feelings **mutlu edici, ruhu okşayıcı, moral verici** *an uplifting film*

upload /ʌpˈləʊd/ *verb* [T] to copy computer programs or information electronically, usually from a small computer to a larger one or to the Internet **bilgisayar programlarını veya elektronik bilgiyi başka bir bilgisayara veya internete kopya etmek/yüklemek** ⊃Compare **download** ⊃See study page **The Web and the Internet** on page Centre 36.

upmarket /ʌpˈmɑːkɪt/ *UK* (*US* upscale) *adjective* expensive and used by people who are rich and from a high social class **şık, lüks, klas, kibar/seçkin kişilerin gittiği/olduğu/bulunduğu** *an upmarket hotel/restaurant*

upon /əˈpɒn/ *preposition formal* on **üzerine, üzerinde**

upper /ˈʌpər/ *adjective* [always before noun] **1** at a higher position **üst, üstteki** *an upper floor* ○ *the upper lip* ○ *the upper body* **2** of a higher social class **üst tabakadan, yüksek tabakadan, zenginler sınıfından** **3 the upper limit** the highest amount or level, or the longest time that something is allowed **en üst sınır; en üst zaman sınırı** ⊃See also: get/gain the upper **hand¹**.

,upper ˈcase *noun* [U] letters written as capitals **büyük harf**

,upper ˈclass *noun* [C] the highest social class of people **üst tabaka, yüksek tabaka, zenginler sınıfı** *members of the upper classes* ● **upper-class** *adjective* *an upper-class accent* **toplumda üst kademe**

uppermost /ˈʌpəməʊst/ *adjective* **1** highest **en üstteki, en yukarıdaki** *the building's uppermost floors* **2 be uppermost in sb's mind** to be the most important thing someone is thinking about **zihnindeki/kafasındaki en önemli şey olmak** *The safety of her children was uppermost in her mind.*

upright¹ /ˈʌpraɪt/ *adverb* vertical and as straight as possible **dik, dikine** *to sit/stand upright* ⊃See also: **bolt upright**.

upright² /ˈʌpraɪt/ *adjective* **1** straight up or vertical **dik, dimdik** *Please return your seat to an upright position and fasten your seat belt.* **2** honest and morally good **haysiyetli, doğru, dürüst, namuslu, ahlaklı** *an upright citizen*

uprising /ˈʌpˌraɪzɪŋ/ *noun* [C] when a large group of people try to make political changes or change the government by fighting **isyan, ayaklanma, sokağa dökülme** [usually singular] *a general/popular uprising*

uproar .... İLE BİRLİKTE KULLANILAN KELİMELER

cause/provoke (an) uproar ● be (UK) **in** (US) **in an** uproar ● uproar **among** sb ● uproar **at/over** sth

uproar /ˈʌprɔːr/ *noun* [U, no plural] when many people complain about something angrily **kargaşa, hengâme, gürültü patırtı, şamata; toplu yakınmalar** *The book caused an uproar in the United States.* ○ *Local residents are (UK) in uproar/(US) in an uproar over plans for the new road.*

uproot /ʌpˈruːt/ *verb* [T] **1** to pull a tree or plant out of the ground **kökünden sökmek** *Hundreds of trees were uprooted in the storm.* **2** to make someone leave a place where they have been living for a long time **yerinden yurdundan etmek, doğup büyüdüğü yerden kovmak/uzaklaştırmak** *The war has uprooted nearly half the country's population.*

ups and ˈdowns *noun* [plural] the mixture of good and bad things that happen to people **iniş çıkışlar; çalkantılar; iyi kötü gelişmeler** *Like most married couples, we've had our ups and downs.*

upscale /ˈʌpˌskeɪl/ *US* (*UK* upmarket) *adjective* expensive and used by people who are rich and from a high social class **pahalı, lüks, zenginlerin kullandığı; klas; üst tabaka insanlarının kullandığı** *an upscale restaurant/neighborhood*

o→**upset¹** /ʌpˈset/ *adjective* **1** unhappy or worried because something unpleasant has happened **üzgün, üzüntülü, keyfi kaçmış, canı sıkkın** *They'd had an argument and she was still upset about it.* ○ *Mike got very upset when I told him the news.* **2 upset stomach/ tummy** an illness in the stomach **mide fesadı, mide ağrısı; ağrıyan karın**

upset² /ʌpˈset/ *verb* [T] **upsetting**, *past* **upset** **1** to make someone feel unhappy or worried **üzmek, huzurunu bozmak, keyfini kaçırmak** *The phone call had clearly upset her.* **2** to cause problems for something **bozmak, altüst etmek, çorbaya çevirmek, mahvetmek,**

U

sorun çıkarmak *If I arrived later would that upset your plans?* **3 upset sb's stomach** to make someone feel ill in the stomach **midesini hasta etmek; midesini bozmak/ağrıtmak**

upset³ /'ʌpset/ *noun* [C] **1** when someone beats the player or team that was expected to win **bozgun, beklenmedik galibiyet** *After Harding won the second set, a major upset seemed likely.* **2 a stomach/tummy upset** *UK* an illness in the stomach **mide rahatsızlığı; karın ağrısı 3** a difficulty or problem **zorluk, güçlük, sorun, dert** *We had the usual upsets but overall the day went well.*

upsetting /ʌp'setɪŋ/ *adjective* making you feel unhappy or worried **üzücü, can sıkıcı, üzüntülü, bozulmuş; endişeli** *I found the programme very upsetting.*

the upshot /'ʌpʃɒt/ *noun* the final result of a discussion or series of events **sonuç, netice, nihai nokta, varılan sonuç** *The upshot is that we've decided to move to Sydney.*

upside down

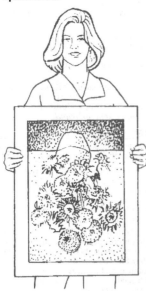

ˌupside 'down¹ *adverb* **1** turned so that the part that is usually at the top is now at the bottom **baş aşağı, tepe taklak, ters** *One of the pictures had been hung upside down.* ○ *Turn the jar upside down and shake it.* **2 turn sth upside down a** to make a place very untidy while looking for something **altüst etmek, her şeyi karman çorman etmek; altını üstüne getirmek b** to change someone's life or a system completely **hayatını/sistemi altüst etmek; her şeyi değiştirmek; hayatını baştan sona değiştirmek** *Their lives were turned upside down when their son was arrested.*

ˌupside 'down² *adjective* turned so that the part that is usually at the top is now at the bottom **baş aşağı/tepe taklak olmuş** *Why is this box upside down?*

upstage /ʌp'steɪdʒ/ *verb* [T] to do something that takes people's attention away from someone or something and gives it to you instead **dikkatleri başkasının/birinin üzerinden kendi üstüne çekmek** *You mustn't upstage the bride.*

upstairs /ʌp'steəz/ *adverb* on or to a higher level of a building **üst kata, üst katta** *He ran upstairs to answer*

the phone. ● **upstairs** *adjective* an upstairs bedroom **yukarı**

upstart /'ʌpstɑːt/ *noun* [C] someone who has just started a job but already thinks they are very important **hiç deneyimi olmamasına rağmen kendini çok önemli ve vazgeçilmez zannetme**

upstate /ˌʌp'steɪt/ *adjective* *US* in the northern part of a US state (= one of the parts into which the country is divided) **(ABD) kuzey eyaletlerinden** *upstate New York* ● **upstate** *adverb* *She's taken a trip upstate with some friends.* **merkez dışında, kuzey bölgesi**

upstream /ʌp'striːm/ *adverb* along a river in the opposite direction to the way that the water is moving **nehrin yukarısına, akıntıya karşı**

upsurge /'ʌpsɜːdʒ/ *noun* [C] a sudden increase **anî ve büyük artış/yükselme, fırlama, tırmanma** *an upsurge in violent crime*

uptake /'ʌpteɪk/ *noun informal* **be slow/quick on the uptake** to be slow/quick to understand something **anlayışı kıt/hızlı olmak; anlamakta/kavramakta yavaş/hızlı olmak**

uptight /ʌp'taɪt/ *adjective informal* worried or nervous and not able to relax **asabî, asabı bozuk, tedirgin, endişeli**

up-to-date /ˌʌptə'deɪt/ *adjective* **1** modern, and using the most recent technology or knowledge **çağdaş, son moda, zamana uygun 2** having the most recent information **en yeni bilgiye sahip, en son/güncel bilgilerden/gelişmelerden haberdar** *The Internet keeps us up-to-date.*

up-to-the-minute /ˌʌptəðə'mɪnɪt/ *adjective* most recent **en son, en yeni, en taze, en güncel** *up-to-the-minute news*

uptown /ʌp'taʊn/ *adjective, adverb* *US* in or to the northern part of a city **şehrin kuzeyinde/kuzeyine doğru** *She lives uptown.*

upturn /'ʌptɜːn/ *noun* [C] an improvement, especially in economic conditions or a business **düzelme, iyiye gitme, olumlu gelişme gösterme** *There's been a sharp upturn in sales.*

upturned /ʌp'tɜːnd/ *adjective* pointing up, or turned so the under side faces up **kalkık, yukarı doğru kıvrık** *an upturned boat*

upward /'ʌpwəd/ *adjective* [always before noun] moving towards a higher place or level **yukarıda** *an upward glance* ○ *an upward trend in sales*

upwards /'ʌpwədz/ *mainly UK* (*mainly US* **upward**) *adverb* **1** towards a higher place or level **yukarıya doğru** *House prices have started moving upwards again.* **2 upwards of sth** more than a particular amount **...dan/den fazla/daha çok** *Double rooms cost upwards of £70 a night.*

uranium /juə'reɪniəm/ *noun* [U] a heavy, grey metal that is used in the production of nuclear power (symbol U) **uranyum**

Uranus /'jʊərᵊnəs/ *noun* [no plural] the planet that is seventh from the Sun, after Saturn and before Neptune **Uranüs, güneş sisteminde yedinci gezegen**

urban /'ɜːbᵊn/ *adjective* belonging or relating to a town or city **kentsel, şehre/kente/modern yaşama dair/ait** *urban areas* ○ *urban development*

urbane /ɜː'beɪn/ *adjective* confident, relaxed, and polite **emin, rahat, nazik, kibar, görgülü, ince** *With his good looks and urbane manner, he was very popular.*

urge¹ /ɜːdʒ/ *verb* [T] **1 urge sb to do sth** to try to persuade someone to do something **ikna etmek, ısrar etmek, zorlamak, sıkıştırmak, üstelemek** *His parents urged him to go to university.* **2** *formal* to strongly

advise an action **ısrarla tavsiye etmek** *Financial experts are urging caution.*
urge sb on *phrasal verb* to encourage someone to do or achieve something **teşvik etmek, yüreklendirmek** *The crowd was cheering and urging her on.*

> **🧩 urge (noun) ...... İLE BİRLİKTE KULLANILAN KELİMELER**
> **feel/have/resist/satisfy** an urge • an **irresistible/ overwhelming/strong/sudden/uncontrollable** urge

urge² /ɜːdʒ/ *noun* [C] a strong wish or need **dürtü, büyük istek, büyük gereksinim** [+ to do sth] *I resisted a powerful urge to slap him.*

> **🧩 urgency ...... İLE BİRLİKTE KULLANILAN KELİMELER**
> a **matter of** urgency • a **sense of** urgency • the urgency **of** sth

urgency /ˈɜːdʒᵊnsi/ *noun* [U] when something is very important and needs you to take action immediately **âciliyet, ivedilik** *a matter of great urgency*

urgent /ˈɜːdʒᵊnt/ *adjective* very important and needing you to take action immediately **âcil, ivedi** *an urgent message* ○ *The refugees were in urgent need of food and water.* • **urgently** *adverb* *I need to speak to you urgently.* **acil bir şekilde**

urinate /ˈjʊərɪneɪt/ *verb* [I] to get rid of urine from your body **idrarını yapmak**

urine /ˈjʊərɪn/ *noun* [U] the liquid that comes out of your body when you go to the toilet **idrar**

URL /ˌjuːɑːrˈel/ *abbreviation for* uniform resource locator: a website address **Tektip Kaynak Belirleyici (TKB):** web sitesi adresi ⊃See study page **The Web and the Internet** on page Centre 36.

urn /ɜːn/ *noun* [C] **1** a round container that is used for plants or to store someone's ashes (= the powder that is left after a dead body has been burned) **yakılmış ceset kül kabı 2** a metal container that is used to make a large amount of coffee or tea and to keep it hot **semaver**

◦▪**us** *strong form* /ʌs/ *weak forms* /əs/, /s/ *pronoun* used after a verb or preposition to refer to the person who is speaking or writing and one or more other people **bizi, bize** *She gave us all a present.* ○ *Would you like to have dinner with us next Saturday?*

USA /ˌjuːesˈeɪ/ *noun abbreviation for* United States of America **ABD, Amerika Birleşik Devletleri**

usage /ˈjuːsɪdʒ/ *noun* **1** [C, U] the way that words are used **kullanım, kullanış** *a guide to English grammar and usage* **2** [U] the amount of something that is used, or the way that something is used **kullanılan miktar, kullanım şekli/biçimi** *restrictions on water usage*

◦▪**use¹** /juːz/ *verb* [T] *past* used **1** PURPOSE If you use something, you do something with it for a particular purpose. **kullanmak** *Can I use your pen?* ○ *She uses her car for work.* ○ [+ to do sth] *Nick used the money to buy a CD player.* **2** MAKE LESS to take an amount from a supply of something **almak, kullanmak** *A shower uses less water than a bath.* **3** PERSON to treat someone badly in order to get what you want **kullanmak, istismar etmek, sömürmek** *He was just using me to make his girlfriend jealous.* **4** WORD to say or write a particular word or phrase **kullanmak, yazmak, söylemek** *'Autumn' is used in British English and 'fall' in American English.* **5 could use sth** *mainly US informal* something that you say when you want or need something **ihtiyacı olmak, kullanmak istemek, kullanabileceğini söylemek** *I could use some help with these packages, please.*

use sth up *phrasal verb* to finish a supply of something **kullanarak bitirmek; tüketmek** *Someone's used up all the milk.*

◦▪**use²** /juːs/ *noun* **1** USING [U] when you use something, or when something is being used **kullanma, kullanım** *an increase in the use of mobile phones* ○ *Guests have free use of the hotel swimming pool.* ○ *Turn the machine off when it's not in use* (= being used). **2** PURPOSE [C] a purpose for which something is used **fayda, yarar** *A food processor has a variety of uses in the kitchen.* ○ *Can you find a use for this box?* **3 be (of) any/some use** to be useful **faydalı olm(ma)ak, işe yara(ma)mak** *Is this book of any use to you?* **4 be (of) no use** to not be useful **faydası olmamak, hiç bir işe yaramamak** *His advice was no use at all.* **5 be no use; be no use doing sth** used to say that trying to do something has no effect **hiç bir yararı olmamak; en küçük bir etkisi olmamak; faydasız/işe yaramaz olmak** *It was no use talking to him - he wouldn't listen.* **6** WORD [C] one of the meanings of a word, or the way that a particular word is used **(sözcük) kullanım; kullanım şekli** *Can you list all the uses of the verb 'go'?* **7 the use of sth** permission to use something, or the ability to use something **kullanım izni, kullanabilme** *Martin has offered me the use of his car.* **8 make use of sth** to use something that is available **yararlanmak, faydalanmak, kullanmak** *We were encouraged to make use of all the facilities.*

◦▪**used¹** /juːst/ *adjective* **used to sth/doing sth** If you are used to something, you have done it or experienced it many times before. **(eskiden) kullanmış olmak; denemiş olmak; yapmış olmak; alışkın/alışık olmak** *He's used to working long hours.* ○ *We've been living here for two years and we've (UK) got used to/ (US) gotten used to the heat.* ⊃Opposite **unused.**

used² /juːzd/ *adjective* Something that is used is not new and has been owned by someone else. **kullanılmış, eski, ikinci el** *a used car* ⊃Opposite **unused.**

◦▪**used to** /ˈjuːstuː/ *modal verb* **used to do/be sth** If something used to happen or a situation used to exist, it happened regularly or existed in the past but it does not happen or exist now. **(eskiden) yapılmış olmak; olmuş olmak (ama şimdi yapılmamak); ...a/e alışkın/alışık olmak** *I used to go out every night when I was a student.* ○ *He used to be a lot fatter.*

> **useful ...... BAŞKA BİR DEYİŞLE**
> Eğer bir şey birşeyi yapmanıza veya başarmanıza yarıyorsa, **helpful** veya **valuable** ifadeleriyle tanımlanabilir. *They gave us some really helpful advice.* ○ *He was able to provide the police with some valuable information.*
> **Invaluable** sıfatı çok faydalı (extremely useful) anlamına gelmektedir. *The Internet is an invaluable resource for teachers.*
> Çok çaba gerektiren fakat faydalı olan bir aktivite **worthwhile** olarak tanımlanabilir. *It's a difficult course but it's very worthwhile.*
> Kullanılmasının kolay oluşundan dolayı faydalı olan bir şey **handy** olarak tanımlanabilir. *That's a handy little gadget.*
> Eğer bir şeyin ileride faydalı olacağını düşünüyorsanız, **come in handy** ifadesi kullanılabilir. *Don't throw that away - it'll come in handy for the party.*
> Eğer bir yazı veya konuşma bir çok faydalı bilgi içeriyorsa, **informative** veya **instructive** olarak tanımlanabilir. *It's an interesting and highly informative book.*

◦▪**useful** /ˈjuːsfᵊl/ *adjective* **1** helping you to do or achieve something **faydalı, yararlı** *useful information* **2 come in useful** *UK* to be useful and help someone do or achieve something, especially when there is nothing

U

else to help them **faydası dokunmak, yararı olmak,** **işe yaramak** *You should keep that paint - it might come in useful.* ● **usefully** *adverb* **yararlı bir şekilde** ● **usefulness** *noun* [U] **yararlılık**

useful

Dikkat! Çok sık yapılan kelime türetme hatası Suffix **ful** ile biten sıfatlarda yalnızca bir tane **l** kullanılır. **Usefull** yazılışı doru değildir. **Useful** doğru yazılış şeklidir.

useless /'ju:sləs/ *adjective* **1** If something is useless, it does not work well or it has no effect. **faydasız, işe yaramaz, yararsız** *This umbrella's useless - there's a big hole in it.* ○ [+ doing sth] *It's useless arguing with her.* **2** *UK informal* having no skill in an activity **beceriksiz, yararsız, hiç bir becerisi/mahareti olmayan** *Dave's useless at football.*

user /'ju:zə^r/ *noun* [C] someone who uses a product, machine, or service **kullanıcı, kullanan kişi** *drug users* ○ *a new service for Internet users*

user-friendly /,ju:zə'frendli/ *adjective* A machine or system that is user-friendly is easy to use or understand. **kullanıcı dostu; kullanana yarar sağlayan; kolay kullanıma yatkın** *user-friendly software*

'user ,name (username) *noun* [C] a name or other word that you sometimes need to use together with a password (= secret word) before you can use a computer on the Internet **kullanıcı adı**

usher¹ /'ʌʃə^r/ *verb* **usher sb into/to/across, etc** to show someone where to go or sit **yer göstermek; teşrifatçılık yapmak; eşlik edip yerini göstermek** *She ushered me into her office.*

usher in sth *phrasal verb formal* to be at the start of a period when important changes happen, or to cause important changes to start happening **büyük değişiklikler döneminde olmak; önemli değişikliklerin başlamasına sebep olmak** *His presidency ushered in a new era of democracy.*

usher² /'ʌʃə^r/ *noun* [C] someone who shows people where to sit in a theatre or at a formal event **yer gösteren kişi**

○▲**usual** /'ju:ʒuəl/ *adjective* **1** normal and happening most often **alışılmış, her zamanki, olağan, mutat** *I went to bed at my usual time.* ○ *This winter has been much colder than usual.* ⊃Opposite **unusual.** **2 as usual** in the way that happens most of the time **her zaman olduğu gibi, alışılageldiği gibi, âdet olduğu üzere** *As usual, Ben was the last to arrive.*

○▲**usually** /'ju:ʒəli/ *adverb* in the way that most often happens **genellikle, çoğu kez, çoğunlukla, ekseriyetle** *I usually get home at about six o'clock.* ○ *Usually I just have a sandwich.*

usurp /ju:'zɜ:p/ *verb* [T] *formal* to take someone else's job or power when you should not **zorla almak, gasp etmek, el koymak**

utensil /ju:'tens^əl/ *noun* [C] a tool that you use for doing jobs in the house, especially cooking **âlet, kap kacak, mutfak eşyaları** *wooden cooking utensils* ⊃Orta kısımdaki renkli sayfalarına bakınız.

uterus /'ju:t^ərəs/ *noun* [C] the organ inside a woman's body where a baby grows **rahim, döl yatağı**

utilitarian /ˌju:tɪlɪ'teəriən/ *adjective* designed to be useful and not beautiful **yararcı, yarar güden** *utilitarian furniture*

utility /ju:'tɪləti/ (*also* public utility) *noun* [C] an organization that supplies the public with water, gas, or electricity (**İSKİ, ASKİ, BUSKİ vb. gibi) kamu hizmetleri kuruluşu**

utilize *formal* (*also UK -ise*) /'ju:tɪlaɪz/ *verb* [T] to use something in an effective way **yararlanmak, faydalanmak** *The vitamins come in a form that is easily utilized by the body.*

utmost¹ /'ʌtməʊst/ *adjective* [always before noun] *formal* used to emphasize how important or serious something is **son derece, pek çok, en fazla** *a matter of the utmost importance* ○ *The situation needs to be handled with the utmost care.*

utmost² /'ʌtməʊst/ *noun* **do your utmost** to try as hard as you can to do something **olanca gayreti göstermek, elinden geleni yapmak** [+ to do sth] *We did our utmost to finish the project on time.*

utopia /ju:'təʊpiə/ *noun* [C, U] an imaginary place where everything is perfect **yeryüzü cenneti, hayali mükemmel toplum, ütopya**

utopian /ju:'təʊpiən/ *adjective* A utopian idea or plan is based on the belief that things can be made perfect. **düşsel, hayalî, ütopik** *a utopian vision of society*

utter¹ /'ʌtə^r/ *adjective* [always before noun] used to emphasize something **tam, tüm, bütün, her şeyiyle, tam tamıyla** *She dismissed the article as utter nonsense.*

utter² /'ʌtə^r/ *verb* [T] *formal* to say something **söylemek, ifade etmek** *She left without uttering a word.*

utterance /'ʌt^ər^əns/ *noun* [C] *formal* something that you say **söz, söylenen/ifade edilen şey**

utterly /'ʌtəli/ *adverb* completely **tamamen, büsbütün, bütünüyle** *It's utterly ridiculous.*

U-turn /'ju:tɜ:n/ *noun* [C] **1** a change of direction that you make when driving in order to travel in the opposite direction **U-dönüşü** a complete change from one opinion or plan to an opposite one **geriye çark etme; 180 derecelik dönüş; tam aksi istikamete dönme** *the government's U-turn on economic policy*

U

V

V, v /viː/ the twenty-second letter of the alphabet **alfabenin yirmiikinci harfi**

V *written abbreviation for* volt (= a unit for measuring an electric current) **elektrik akım ölçme birimi volt'un kısa yazılışı** *a 9V battery*

v UK (UK/US vs) /viː/ *preposition abbreviation for* versus (= used to say that one team or person is competing against another) **karşı karşıya' anlamında sözcüğün kıza yazılışı** *Germany v France*

vacancy /'veɪkᵊnsi/ *noun* [C] **1** a room that is not being used in a hotel **boş oda, boş yer** *Do you have any vacancies?* **2** a job that is available for someone to do **iş, görev, hazır iş** *Tell me if you hear of any vacancies for secretaries.*

vacant /'veɪkᵊnt/ *adjective* **1** EMPTY Somewhere that is vacant is available because it is not being used. **açık, boş, tutulmamış, kullanılmıyor** *a vacant building* **2** JOB A vacant job is available for someone to do. (**iş**) **açık, boş, müsait 3** EXPRESSION A vacant expression on someone's face shows they are not thinking about anything. (**yüz ifadesi**) **anlamsız, boş boş • vacantly** *adverb* **kullanılmayan, boş durumda**

vacate /vəˈkeɪt/ ⑤ /'veɪkeɪt/ *verb* [T] *formal* to leave a room, building, chair, etc so that someone else can use it **boşaltmak, tahliye etmek**

o→**vacation**[1] /vəˈkeɪʃᵊn/ ⑤ /veɪˈkeɪʃᵊn/ *noun* [C, U] **1** US (UK **holiday**) a period of time when you are not at home but are staying somewhere else for enjoyment **tatil** *We're taking a vacation in Florida.* ○ *We met Bob and Wendi on vacation.* **2** *mainly US* a period of the year when schools or colleges are closed **tatil, yaz tatili, sömestr tatili** *the summer vacation* ○ *He's on vacation for three months.*

vacation[2] /vəˈkeɪʃᵊn/ ⑤ /veɪˈkeɪʃᵊn/ US (UK **holiday**) *verb* **vacation in/on/by, etc** to go on vacation **tatile çıkmak/gitmek** *Sam was vacationing in Guatemala.*

vaccinate /'væksɪneɪt/ *verb* [T] to give someone a vaccine to stop them from getting a disease **aşı yapmak** *Have you been vaccinated against polio?* • **vaccination** /ˌvæksɪˈneɪʃᵊn/ *noun* [C, U] **aşılama, aşı**

vaccine /'væksiːn/ *noun* [C, U] a substance that is given to people to stop them from getting a particular disease **aşı**

vacuum[1] /'vækjuːm/ *noun* **1** [C] a space that has no air or other gas in it **vakum 2** [no plural] when someone or something important is not now in your life and you are unhappy **boşluk, eksiklik, yokluk** *When her husband died, it left a big vacuum in her life.*

vacuum[2] /'vækjuːm/ *verb* [I, T] to clean somewhere using a vacuum cleaner **elektrik süpürgesiyle temizlemek**

'vacuum ˌcleaner (*also* UK **Hoover**) *noun* [C] an electric machine that cleans floors by sucking up dirt **elektrik süpürgesi**

vagaries /'veɪgəriz/ *noun* [plural] sudden changes that are not expected or known about before they happen **anî değişiklikler; beklenmedik gelişmeler** *the vagaries of the English weather*

vagina /vəˈdʒaɪnə/ *noun* [C] the part of a woman's body that connects her outer sex organs to the place where a baby grows **kadın cinsel organı, döl yatağı, vajina**

vagrant /'veɪgrᵊnt/ *noun* [C] *formal* someone who has no job and no home and who lives outside **serseri, boşta gezer, derbeder/başıboş kimse**

vague ...... İLE BİRLİKTE KULLANILAN KELİMELER

a vague **feeling/idea/impression/memory/promise**

vague /veɪg/ *adjective* **1** not clear or certain **belirsiz, bulanık, flu** *I have a vague idea of where the hotel is.* ○ *He was a bit vague about directions.* **2** showing that someone is not thinking clearly or does not understand **kafası dağınık, dalgın** *a vague expression* • **vaguely** *adverb I* **vaguely remember** (= slightly remember) *meeting her.* **net olmayan bir şekilde • vagueness** *noun* [U] **belirsizlik**

vain /veɪn/ *adjective* **1 in vain** without any success **boşuna, beyhude** *I tried in vain to start a conversation.* **2** vain attempt/effort/hope A vain attempt/effort, etc does not have the result you want. **faydasız/boşuna/beyhude teşebbüs/çaba/ümit 3** too interested in your own appearance and thinking you are very attractive **kendinden başkasını görmeyen, kendini beğenmiş, mağrur, kibirli • vainly** *adverb* **kibirli bir şekilde**

Valentine /'væləntaɪn/ (*also* 'Valentine ˌcard) *noun* [C] a card (= stiff, folded paper with a message inside) that you give someone on Valentine's Day **sevgililer günü kartı**

Valentine's Day /'væləntaɪnzˌdeɪ/ *noun* [C, U] 14 February, a day when you give a Valentine to someone you have a romantic relationship with or want a romantic relationship with **Sevgililer Günü**

valet /'væleɪ/ *noun* [C] **1** someone who parks your car when you arrive at a restaurant, hotel, or airport **vale, park görevlisi 2** a male servant who looks after a man's clothes and helps him to dress **şahsî uşak, hizmetçi (erkek)**

valiant /'væliənt/ *adjective formal* very brave **cesur, yiğit, gözükara** *a valiant effort* • **valiantly** *adverb* **cesurca**

valid /'vælɪd/ *adjective* **1** based on good reasons or facts that are true **mantıklı, akla uygun, makul** *a valid argument* **2** A valid ticket or document is legally acceptable. **geçerli, muteber, hâlâ kullanılabilir** *The ticket is valid for three months.* ⊃Opposite **invalid.** • **validity** /vəˈlɪdəti/ *noun* [U] **geçerlilik**

validate /'vælɪdeɪt/ *verb* [T] *formal* to prove that something is true **doğrulamak, teyit etmek, geçerli kılmak** • **validation** /ˌvælɪˈdeɪʃᵊn/ *noun* [C, U] **geçerlilik**

valley /'væli/ *noun* [C] an area of low land between hills or mountains **vadi**

valour UK *literary* (US **valor**) /'vælᵊr/ *noun* [U] when someone is very brave, especially during a war **yiğitlik, yüreklilik**

valuable ...... BAŞKA BİR DEYİŞLE

Eğer bir şey birşeyi yapmanıza veya başarmanıza yarıyorsa, **helpful** veya **useful** ifadeleriyle tanımlanabilir. *They gave us some really helpful advice.* ● *She made a really useful contribution to the project.*

Faydalı sonuçlar doğurduğu için değerli olan bir şey **constructive** veya **productive** olarak tanımlanabilir. *It was a very constructive discussion.* ● *We had a very productive meeting and sorted out a lot of problems.*

Faydalı olan fakat çok çaba gerektiren bir aktivite **worthwhile** olarak tanımlanabilir. *It's a difficult course but it's very worthwhile.*

Eğer bir yazı veya konuşma bir çok değerli bilgi içeriyorsa, **informative** veya **instructive** olarak tanımlanabilir. *It's an interesting and highly informative book.*

○►**valuable** /'væljuəbl/ *adjective* **1** Valuable objects could be sold for a lot of money. **(eşya) değerli, kıymetli** *valuable paintings and antiques* **2** Valuable information, help, advice, etc is very helpful. **(bilgi, yardım, tavsiye vb.) faydalı, kıymetli, değerli**

valuables /'væljuəblz/ *noun* [plural] small things that you own which could be sold for a lot of money **değerli şeyler, ziynet eşyaları** *valuables such as jewellery and watches*

valuation /ˌvælju'eɪʃᵊn/ *noun* [C, U] when someone judges how much money something could be sold for **değer, değer biçme, kıymet, kıymet takdiri, değerlendirme**

value ...... İLE BİRLİKTE KULLANILAN KELİMELER

the value **of** sth ● **of** [any/great/real] value ● values **go up/increase** ● values **decrease/go down** ● a **drop/fall/increase/rise** in value

○►**value**[1] /'vælju:/ *noun* **1** [C, U] how much money something could be sold for **değer, kıymet, eder** *The new road has affected the value of these houses.* ○ *Cars quickly go down in value.* **2** [U] how useful or important something is **önem, yarar** *a document of great historical value* **3** **good value (for money)** If something is good value, it is of good quality or there is a lot of it so you think the amount of money you spent on it was right. **verilen paraya değer** *The meal was very good value.* ➪See also: **face value.**

value[2] /'vælju:/ *verb* [T] **valuing,** *past* **valued 1** If you value something or someone, they are very important to you. **değer vermek, önemsemek, kıymetlisi olmak** *I always value his opinion.* **2** to judge how much money something could be sold for **değer biçmek, fiyat/değer belirlemek** *The ring was valued at $1000.*

values /'vælju:z/ *noun* [plural] your beliefs about what is morally right and wrong and what is most important in life **inançlar, değerler, değer yargıları; değerler/inançlar manzumesi**

valve /vælv/ *noun* [C] something that opens and closes to control the flow of liquid or gas **vana, valf, subap**

vampire /'væmpaɪə[r]/ *noun* [C] in stories, a dead person who bites people's necks and drinks their blood **vampir**

van /væn/ *noun* [C] a vehicle that is used for carrying things but which is smaller than a truck **kamyonet** ➪See picture at **vehicle.**

vandal /'vændᵊl/ *noun* [C] someone who intentionally damages things in public places **etrafı yakıp yıkma eğiliminde olan kimse** *Vandals had smashed the shop window.*

vandalism /'vændᵊlɪzᵊm/ *noun* [U] the crime of intentionally damaging things in public places **etrafı yakıp yıkma**

vandalize (*also* UK **-ise**) /'vændᵊlaɪz/ *verb* [T] to intentionally damage things in public places **bilerek ve isteyerek zarar vermek; sebepsiz yere kırıp dökmek/yakıp yıkmak**

vanguard /'vængɑːd/ *noun* **in the vanguard of sth** involved in the most recent changes in technology and understanding **teknolojideki en son yenilikleri ve anlayışın öncülüğünde** *Libraries are in the vanguard of the electronic revolution.*

vanilla /və'nɪlə/ *noun* [U] a substance that is used to give flavour to some sweet foods **vanilya** *vanilla ice cream*

vanish /'vænɪʃ/ *verb* [I] to disappear suddenly **aniden gözden kaybolmak** *The sun vanished behind the trees.* ○ *The report mysteriously vanished from the files.* ➪See also: disappear/vanish into thin air[1].

vanity /'vænəti/ *noun* [U] when someone thinks they are very attractive and is too interested in their own appearance **kendini beğenmişlik, kibir, gurur**

vantage point /'vɑːntɪdʒˌpɔɪnt/ *noun* [C] **1** the way you think about a subject when you are in a particular situation **bakış açısı, çıkış noktası, konuya hâkim olan nokta/eğilim** *From my vantage point, it is difficult to see how things can improve.* **2** a place from which you can see something very well **hâkim nokta**

vapour UK (US **vapor**) /'veɪpə[r]/ *noun* [U] many small drops of liquid in the air which look like a cloud **buhar**

variable[1] /'veəriəbl/ *adjective* changing often **sıkça değişen, değişken** *The sound quality on the recording is variable.* ● **variability** /ˌveəriə'bɪləti/ *noun* [U] **değişkenlik**

variable[2] /'veəriəbl/ *noun* [C] a number, amount, or situation which can change **değişken** *A patient's recovery time depends on so many variables, such as age, weight and general health.*

variance /'veəriəns/ *noun formal* **at variance with sb/sth** If two things or people are at variance with each other, they do not agree or are very different. **karşıt durumda, uyuşmazlık hâlinde, çelişkili, tutarsız** *The statement seems to be at variance with government policy.*

variant /'veəriənt/ *noun* [C] something that is a slightly different from the usual one **biraz değişik biçimi** *There are several variants of the virus.* ○ *spelling variants*

variation /ˌveəri'eɪʃᵊn/ *noun* **1** [C, U] a difference in amount or quality **değişiklik, fark** *variations in price* **2** [C] something that is slightly different from the usual form **değişim, değişme, değişiklik** *It's a variation on the standard apple pie.*

varied /'veərɪd/ *adjective* consisting of many different types of things **değişik, çeşitli, türlü türlü** *a long and varied career*

variety ...... İLE BİRLİKTE KULLANILAN KELİMELER

a **bewildering/great/infinite/wide** variety ● **offer/provide** variety

○►**variety** /və'raɪəti/ *noun* **1 a variety of sth/sb** many different types of things or people **çok çeşitli; muhtelif şekillerde; çeşit, tür** *Ben has done a variety of jobs.* **2** [C] a different type of something **çeşitlilik, değişiklik** *a new variety of potato* **3** [U] a lot of different activities, situations, people, etc **çeşit çeşit bir yığın, farklı farklı bir sürü** *I need more variety in my life.*

various /'veəriəs/ *adjective* many different **muhtelif, bir çok farklı biçim ve türlerde** *They have offices in various parts of the country.* ○ *I started learning Spanish for various reasons.*

variously /'veəriəsli/ *adverb* in many different ways **çok çeşitli şekilde, çok farklı olarak** *The event was variously described as "terrible", "shocking", and "unbelievable".*

varnish¹ /'vɑːnɪʃ/ *noun* [C, U] a clear liquid that you paint onto wood to protect it and make it shine **vernik** ⊃See also: **nail polish.**

varnish² /'vɑːnɪʃ/ *verb* [T] to put varnish on a surface **verniklemek, vernik sürmek**

vary /'veəri/ *verb* **1** [BE DIFFERENT] [I] If things of the same type vary, they are different from each other. **değişik olmak, farklı olmak** *Car prices vary greatly across Europe.* ○ *Roses vary widely in size and shape.* **2** [CHANGE] [I] to change **değişmek, değişim göstermek** *Temperatures vary depending on the time of year.* **3** [INTENTIONALLY CHANGE] [T] to often change something that you do **değiştirmek** *I try to vary what I eat.*

vase /vɑːz/ ⑤ /veɪs/ *noun* [C] a container that you put flowers in **vazo**

vase

vasectomy /və'sektəmi/ *noun* [C] a medical operation that is done to stop a man having children **erkeği kısırlaştırma ameliyatı**

vast /vɑːst/ *adjective* extremely big **çok geniş, çok büyük, uçsuz bucaksız, muazzam** *a vast amount of money* ○ *vast forest areas*

vastly /'vɑːstli/ *adverb* very much **çok, büyük çapta** *Life now is vastly different from 100 years ago.*

VAT /ˌviːeɪ'tiː/ *noun* [U] *abbreviation for* value added tax: a tax on goods and services in the UK **Katma Değer Vergisi (KDV)**

vault¹ /vɔːlt/ *noun* [C] **1** a special room in a bank where money, jewellery, and other valuable objects are kept **kasa dairesi 2** a room under a church where people are buried **(kilise) mezar odası**

vault² /vɔːlt/ *verb* [I, T] to jump over something by first putting your hands on it **sıçramak, atlamak** *Rick vaulted the gate and ran off.* ⊃See also: **pole vault.**

VCR /ˌviːsiːˈɑːʳ/ *mainly US* (*UK* video) *noun* [C] *abbreviation for* video cassette recorder: a machine that you use for recording television programmes and playing videos (= recorded films or programmes) **video kaydedici/oynatıcı** ⊃Orta kısımdaki renkli sayfalarına bakınız.

VDU /ˌviːdiːˈjuː/ *noun* [C] *UK abbreviation for* visual display unit: a machine with a screen that shows information from a computer **Görsel Sunum Ünitesi (GSÜ)**

've /v/ *short for* have **have' fiilinin kısa hâli** *I've already eaten.*

veal /viːl/ *noun* [U] meat from a very young cow **dana eti**

veer /vɪəʳ/ *verb* **veer across/off/towards, etc** to suddenly change direction **aniden istikamet değiştirmek, birden yön değiştirmek** *The car veered off the road and hit a tree.*

veg /vedʒ/ *noun* [C, U] *plural* **veg** *UK informal short for* vegetables **sebzeler** *fruit and veg*

vegan /'viːgən/ *noun* [C] someone who does not eat meat, fish, eggs, milk, or cheese **etyemez kimse; hayvansal gıdaları yemeyen kişi ● vegan** *adjective* **vejetaryen olan (peynir ürünleri dahil)**

o-*vegetable /'vedʒtəbl/ *noun* [C] a plant that you eat, for example potatoes, onions, beans, etc **sebze** ⊃Orta kısımdaki renkli sayfalarına bakınız.

vegetarian¹ /ˌvedʒɪ'teəriən/ *noun* [C] someone who does not eat meat or fish **etyemez kişi, vejeteryan kimse**

vegetarian² /ˌvedʒɪ'teəriən/ *adjective* not eating, containing, or using meat or fish **et ve et ürünleri içermeyen** *All her children are vegetarian.* ○ *a vegetarian restaurant/pizza*

vegetation /ˌvedʒɪ'teɪʃⁿn/ *noun* [U] the plants and trees that grow in a particular area **bitkiler, bitki örtüsü**

veggie /'vedʒi/ *noun* [C] *UK informal* a vegetarian **etyemez kimse' sözcüğünün kısa hâli ● veggie** *adjective* **vejetaryen**

vehement /'viːəmənt/ *adjective formal* showing strong, often negative, feelings about something **şiddetli, sert, hararetli, ateşli** *vehement criticism/opposition ● vehemently* *adverb* **şiddetli bir şekilde**

vehicles

van

bus

car

lorry *UK*, truck *US*

o-*vehicle /'viːɪkl/ *noun* **1** [C] *formal* something such as a car or bus that takes people from one place to another, especially using roads **araç, vasıta, taşıt, taşıt aracı, vesait 2 a vehicle for sth/doing sth** something that you use as a way of telling people your ideas or opinions **(fikirleri/düşünceleri aktarmada) araç, vasıta** *The paper was merely a vehicle for his political beliefs.*

veil /veɪl/ *noun* **1** [C] a thin piece of material that covers a woman's face **peçe, duvak 2 draw a veil over sth** to not talk any more about a subject because it could cause trouble or embarrassment **üstüne sünger çekmek, bir daha aynı konudan bahsetmemek, konuyu kapatmak; artık değinmemek**

veiled /veɪld/ *adjective* said so that the true meaning or purpose is not clear **üstü kapalı, dolaylı anlatılan, ima yollu ifade edilen** *veiled criticism*

vein /veɪn/ *noun* [C] **1** one of the tubes in your body that carries blood to your heart **damar, kan damarı 2** one of the thin lines on a leaf **damar 3 in the same vein** in

V

the same style of speaking or writing **aynı üslupta/ tarzda/stilde/havada vb.**

Velcro /'velkrəʊ/ noun [U] trademark material that consists of two pieces of cloth that stick together, used to fasten clothes **yapışkanlı naylon bant**

velocity /vɪ'lɒsəti/ noun [C, U] the speed at which something moves **hız, sürat**

velvet /'velvɪt/ noun [U] cloth that has a thick, soft surface on one side **kadife** a black velvet jacket

vendetta /ven'detə/ noun [C] when someone tries to do something bad to someone over a period of time because they have been treated badly by them **kan davası** He had a vendetta against the company after he lost his job.

vending machine /'vendɪŋmə,ʃiːn/ noun [C] a machine that sells drinks, cigarettes, etc **otomatik içecek, sigara vb. satan makina**

vendor /'vendɔːʳ/ noun [C] 1 someone who sells something outside **seyyar satıcı, işportacı, sokak satıcısı, büfeci** an ice cream vendor 2 formal a company that sells goods or services **mal veya hizmet satan şirket**

veneer /və'nɪəʳ/ noun 1 [C, U] a thin layer of wood that covers a piece of furniture that is made of a cheaper material **yaldızlı cilâ, yaldız, boya** 2 a veneer of sth formal a way of behaving that is not sincere and hides someone's real character or emotions **olduğundan farklı gözükme, aslını gizleme, iki yüzlülük** a thin veneer of calm/respectability

venerable /'venərəbl/ adjective old and very much respected **saygıdeğer, muhterem, aziz** a venerable institution/tradition

venetian blind /vən,iːʃən'blaɪnd/ noun [C] a covering for a window that is made from long, flat, horizontal pieces of metal or wood which you can move to let in light **jaluzi, pancur, Venedik pancuru**

vengeance /'vendʒəns/ noun 1 [U] when you do something bad to someone who has done something bad to you, or the feeling of wanting to do this **öç, intikam, hırs** an act of vengeance 2 with a vengeance If something happens with a vengeance, it happens a lot or in a very strong way. **olanca şiddetiyle, alabildiğine, son derece** The disease swept across the country with a vengeance.

vengeful /'vendʒfʰl/ adjective formal wanting vengeance **kin dolu, intikam hırsıyla yanıp tutuşan**

venison /'venɪsʰn/ noun [U] meat from a deer **geyik eti**

venom /'venəm/ noun [U] 1 poison that some snakes and insects produce **yılan/böcek zehiri** 2 a feeling of extreme anger or hate **garaz, kin, düşmanlık, öfke, hiddet, hınç** Much of his venom was directed at his boss. ● **venomous** adjective containing or involving venom **kin dolu, garaz taşıyan, zehir saçan**

vent[1] /vent/ noun [C] a hole in a wall or machine that lets air in and allows smoke or smells to go out **delik, ağız, havalık, hava deliği**

vent[2] /vent/ verb vent your anger/frustration, etc to do or say something to show your anger or another strong, bad feeling **kızgınlık/hayal kırıklığı vb. belirtmek/dışa vurmak/göstermek/hissettirmek**

ventilate /'ventɪleɪt/ verb [T] to let air come into and go out of a room or building **havalandırmak** ● **ventilation** /,ventɪ'leɪʃʰn/ noun [U] a ventilation system **havalandırma**

venture[1] /'ventʃəʳ/ noun [C] a new activity that may not be successful **riskli/tehlikeli/ne olacağı belli olmayan iş/girişim** a business venture ⊃See also: joint venture.

venture[2] /'ventʃəʳ/ verb formal 1 venture into/out/outside, etc to leave a safe place and go somewhere that may involve risks **tehlikeye atılmak, riske girmek, göze almak, kalkışmak** If the snow stops I might venture out. 2 [T] to be brave enough to say something that might be criticized **her şeye rağmen söylemek, cüret gösterip ifade etmek** I didn't dare venture an opinion.

venue /'venjuː/ noun [C] a place where a sports game, musical performance, or special event happens **yer, mahal**

Venus /'viːnəs/ noun [no plural] the planet that is second from the Sun, after Mercury and before the Earth **Venüs, Güneş sisteminde Dünya'dan önce Merkür'den sonra gelen gezegen**

veranda (also **verandah**) /ve'rændə/ noun [C] a room that is joined to the outside of a house and has a roof and floor but no outside wall **veranda, zemin balkon**

○- **verb** /vɜːb/ noun [C] a word that is used to say that someone does something or that something happens. For example the words 'arrive', 'make', 'be', and 'feel' are verbs. **fiil** ⊃See also: auxiliary verb, modal verb, phrasal verb.

verbal /'vɜːbʰl/ adjective 1 spoken and not written **sözlü** a verbal promise 2 relating to words or the use of words **sözlü, sözcüklerle ve kullanımıyla ilgili** verbal ability/skills ● **verbally** adverb **sözel olarak**

verbatim /vɜː'beɪtɪm/ adjective, adverb using the exact words that were originally used **kelimesi kelimesine aynı, noktasına virgülüne dokunmadan; tıpa tıp aynısını kullanan**

verdict ...... İLE BİRLİKTE KULLANILAN KELİMELER

deliver/reach/return a verdict ● a guilty/not guilty verdict

verdict /'vɜːdɪkt/ noun [C] 1 a decision in a court of law saying if someone is guilty or not **jüri kararı** a guilty verdict ○ The jury took nine hours to reach a verdict. 2 someone's opinion about something after experiencing it, often for the first time **kanı, düşünce, hüküm, karar, yargı** You tried out that Italian restaurant? What was the verdict?

verge[1] /vɜːdʒ/ noun [C] 1 UK the edge of a road or path that is usually covered in grass **yol kenarı** 2 be on the verge of sth/doing sth to be going to happen or to do something very soon **...ın/in eşiğinde olmak; ...a/e kıl payı kalmış olmak; yapma aşamasında/arefesinde olmak** a company on the verge of financial disaster

verge[2] /vɜːdʒ/ verb

verge on sth phrasal verb to almost be a particular state or quality **...a/e kadar varmak, yaklaşmak, sınırında olmak** His constant questions verged on rudeness.

verify /'verɪfaɪ/ verb [T] to prove that something is true, or do something to discover if it is true **doğrulamak, teyit etmek** It was impossible to verify her statement. ● **verification** /,verɪfɪ'keɪʃʰn/ noun [U] **doğrulama**

veritable /'verɪtəbl/ adjective [always before noun] formal used to emphasize how extreme something is **son derece, hakiki, gerçek** Their house was a veritable palace (= was very large).

vermin /'vɜːmɪn/ noun [plural] small animals that damage crops and can give people diseases **zararlı hayvanlar/böcekler**

versatile /'vɜːsətaɪl/ ⓤ /'vɜːrsətʰl/ adjective 1 having many different skills **elinden her iş gelen, becerikli; on parmağında on marifet olan** a versatile player/

performer 2 useful for doing a lot of different things **çok amaçlı, çok yönlü; birden çok faydası/kullanımı olan** *a versatile tool* ● **versatility** /ˌvɜːsəˈtɪləti/ *noun* [U] **beceriklilik**

verse /vɜːs/ *noun* 1 [C] one of the parts that a song or poem is divided into **kıta, beyit, mısra, dize, ayet, bölüm** *I only know the first verse.* 2 [U] words that are in the form of poetry **şiir, nazım** *The story was told in verse.*

⁙ **version** ..... İLE BİRLİKTE KULLANILAN KELİMELER

a new/the latest version ● a version of sth ● in a version

○ᐧ**version** /ˈvɜːʃᵊn/ *noun* [C] 1 one form of something that is slightly different to other forms of the same thing **değişik biçim** *I saw the original version of the film.* 2 someone's description of what has happened **yorum, kişisel anlatış, aktarma** *Bates gave his version of events to the police.*

versus /ˈvɜːsəs/ *preposition* 1 used to say that one team or person is competing against another ...**a/e karşı** *Tomorrow's game is Newcastle versus Arsenal.* 2 used to compare two things or ideas, especially when you have to choose between them ...**a/e karşı** *private education versus state education*

vertical /ˈvɜːtɪkᵊl/ *adjective* pointing straight up from a surface **dikey** *a vertical line* ● **vertically** *adverb* ⊃See picture at **horizontal**. **dikine bir şekilde**

vertigo /ˈvɜːtɪɡəʊ/ *noun* [U] when you feel slightly ill because you are in a high place and feel as if you might fall **baş dönmesi**

verve /vɜːv/ *noun* [U] *formal* energy and enthusiasm **coşku ve heyecan**

○ᐧ**very**¹ /ˈveri/ *adverb* 1 used to emphasize an adjective or adverb **çok** *She was very pleased.* ○ *Marie speaks very slowly.* ○ *Thank you very much.* 2 **not very good/tall/ happy, etc** not good/happy, etc **pek/çok** ...**değil** *The film wasn't very good.*

very² /ˈveri/ *adjective* [always before noun] used to emphasize a noun **kendi, asıl, gerçek** *This is the very house where you stayed.*

vessel /ˈvesᵊl/ *noun* [C] 1 *formal* a ship or large boat **gemi, tekne** 2 *old-fashioned* a container for liquids **kap** ⊃See also: **blood vessel**.

vest /vest/ *noun* [C] 1 *UK* (*US* **undershirt**) a piece of underwear that you wear under a shirt **iç gömleği, fanilâ** 2 *US* (*UK* **waistcoat**) a piece of clothing with buttons at the front and no sleeves, that you wear over a shirt **yelek** ⊃Orta kısımdaki renkli sayfalarına bakınız.

vested interest /ˌvestɪdˈɪntrest/ *noun* [C] If you have a vested interest in something, you want it to happen because it will give you advantages. **kazanılmış hak, müktesep hak**

vestige /ˈvestɪdʒ/ *noun* [C] a very small amount of something that still exists after most of it has gone **iz, eser, kırıntı, kalıntı** *There is still a vestige of hope that she might be found alive.*

vet¹ /vet/ *noun* [C] someone whose job is to give medical care to animals that are ill or hurt **veteriner, baytar**

vet² /vet/ *verb* [T] vetting, *past* vetted to look at details of someone's life, in order to make sure that they are suitable for a particular job **dikkatle araştırma yapmak** [often passive] *Applicants for the job are carefully vetted.*

veteran /ˈvetᵊrᵊn/ *noun* [C] 1 someone who has been in an army or navy during a war **savaş gazisi, eski asker** *a veteran of World War Two* 2 someone who has done a job or activity for a long time **mesleki deneyimi çok olan kimse; duayen, emektar** *a 20-year veteran of BBC news*

veterinarian /ˌvetᵊrɪˈneəriən/ *noun* [C] *US* a vet **veteriner**

veterinary /ˈvetᵊrɪnᵊri/ *adjectiveformal* relating to medical care given to animals that are ill or hurt **veterinerliğe ait**

veterinary surgeon *noun* [C] *UK formal* a vet **veteriner**

veto¹ /ˈviːtəʊ/ *verb* [T] vetoing, *past* vetoed If someone in authority vetoes something, they do not allow it to happen, although other people have agreed to it. **reddetmek, veto etmek** *The plan was vetoed by the President.*

veto² /ˈviːtəʊ/ *noun* [C, U] *plural* **vetoes** when someone in authority does not allow something to happen **veto, reddetme yetkisi/hakkı**

vexed /vekst/ *adjective* **vexed question/issue, etc** a situation that causes problems and is difficult to deal with **canı sıkılmış, sinirlenmiş, kızmış** *the vexed issue of unemployment*

via /vaɪə/ *preposition* 1 going through or stopping at a place on the way to another place ...**yolu ile;** ...**üzerinden;** ...**den geçerek** *The train to Utrecht goes via Amsterdam.* 2 using a particular machine, system, or person to send or receive something ...**aracılığı ile** *I receive all my work via e-mail.*

viable /ˈvaɪəbl/ *adjective* effective and able to be successful **uygulanabilir, pratik** *a viable alternative to nuclear power* ○ *an economically viable plan* ● **viability** /ˌvaɪəˈbɪləti/ *noun* [U] **tutarlılık, verimlilik**

viaduct /ˈvaɪədʌkt/ *noun* [C] a long, high bridge across a valley **viyadük; vadi köprüsü**

vibes /vaɪbz/ *noun* [plural] *informal* the way a person or place makes you feel **bir kişi ya da yerin uyandırdığı his/duygu** *I get bad/good vibes from her.*

vibrant /ˈvaɪbrənt/ *adjective* 1 full of excitement and energy **hareketli, canlı, coşkulu, enerji dolu, heyecan dolu** *a vibrant city* ○ *a vibrant, young performer* 2 A vibrant colour is very bright. **canlı ve parlak**

vibrate /vaɪˈbreɪt/ ⑤ /ˈvaɪbreɪt/ *verb* [I, T] to shake with small, quick movements or to make something shake this way **titremek** *The music was so loud that the floor was vibrating.* ● **vibration** /vaɪˈbreɪʃᵊn/ *noun* [C, U] **titreşim**

vicar /ˈvɪkər/ *noun* [C] a priest in some Christian churches **papaz**

vicarage /ˈvɪkᵊrɪdʒ/ *noun* [C] the house where a vicar lives **kilise papazının evi**

vicarious /vɪˈkeəriəs/ *adjective* [always before noun] A vicarious feeling is one you get from seeing or hearing about another person's experiences. **dolaylı, dolaylı olarak duyulan** *It gives me vicarious pleasure to watch him eat.*

vice /vaɪs/ *noun* 1 BAD HABIT [C] something bad that someone often does **zaaf, kusur, kişilik zayıflığı, karakter bozukluğu** *Smoking is his only vice.* 2 CRIME [U] crime that involves sex or drugs **ahlaksızlık, seks ve uyuşturucu içeren suç** 3 TOOL [C] *UK* (*US* **vise**) a tool used for holding something tightly while you cut it, make it smooth, etc **mengene** ⊃See picture at **tool**.

V

,vice 'president noun [C] 1 the person who is a rank lower than the president of a country başkan yardımcısı 2 US someone who is responsible for part of a company (şirket) genel müdür/başkan yardımcısı; ikinci ortak She's vice president of sales and marketing.

vice versa /,vaɪs'vɜ:sə/ adverb used for referring to the opposite of what you have just said aksine, tersine, ya da aksine, veya tersi Never use indoor lights outside and vice versa.

vicinity /vɪ'sɪnəti/ noun in the vicinity (of sth) formal in the area near a place civarda, çevrede, etrafta, mahalde A number of buildings in the vicinity of the fire were damaged.

vicious /'vɪʃəs/ adjective 1 violent and dangerous acımasız, insafsız a vicious attack on a child ○ a vicious dog 2 intended to upset someone kötü amaçlı, saldırgan, tehlikeli a vicious rumour ● viciously adverb vahşi ve tehlikeli bir şekilde

,vicious 'circle (also ,vicious 'cycle) noun [no plural] when one problem causes another problem which then makes the first problem worse kısır döngü

o- victim /'vɪktɪm/ noun [C] someone who has suffered the effects of violence, illness, or bad luck kurban victims of crime ○ hurricane/flood victims

victimize (also UK -ise) /'vɪktɪmaɪz/ verb [T] to treat someone unfairly because you do not like or approve of them zulmetmek, eziyet/mağdur etmek, Ben feels he has been victimized by his teacher.

victor /'vɪktər/ noun [C] formal the person who wins a fight or competition fatih, yarışı/mücadeleyi/savaşı kazanan kimse

Victorian /vɪk'tɔ:riən/ adjective from or relating to the period between 1837 and 1901 in Britain Kraliçe Viktorya döneminden/dönemine ait olan a Victorian house

victorious /vɪk'tɔ:riəs/ adjective having won a fight or competition muzaffer, galip, zafer kazanmış a victorious army

┌───┐
│ ⌨️ victory ...... İLE BİRLİKTE KULLANILAN KELİMELER │
└───┘

claim/secure victory ● a comfortable/easy/ impressive victory ● a victory for/over sb

victory /'vɪktəri/ noun [C, U] when you win a fight or competition zafer, galibiyet Phoenix managed a 135-114 victory over Denver.

o- video¹ /'vɪdiəʊ/ noun 1 [U] a film or television programme recorded on videotape video filmi 'Pride and Prejudice' has just come out on video. 2 [C] something that you have recorded on videotape using a video camera videoya kaydedilmiş olan şey Caroline and Yann showed us their wedding video last night. 3 [C] (also VCR) (also video recorder) a machine that you use for recording a television programme or watching a video video kamera ⊃Orta kısımdaki renkli sayfalarına bakınız.

video² /'vɪdiəʊ/ verb [T] videoing, past videoed 1 to record a television program using a video recorder videoya kaydetmek 2 to film something using a video camera video kamerayla filmini çekmek

'video ,camera noun [C] a piece of equipment used to record something onto videotape video kamera

'video ,clip noun [C] a short video recording kısa video filmi

'video ,game noun [C] a game in which you make pictures move on a screen video oyunu

videophone /'vɪdiəʊfəʊn/ noun [C] a telephone with a small screen so that you can see the person you are talking to

'video re,corder noun [C] a video machine video kayıt cihazı

videotape /'vɪdiəʊteɪp/ noun [C, U] a thin strip of material inside a plastic box that is used for recording television programmes and films video teybi

vie /vaɪ/ verb [I] vying, past vied to try hard to do something more successfully than someone else yarışmak, rekabet etmek The children were vying for attention. ○ [+ to do sth] Film crews were vying with each other to get the best pictures.

┌───┐
│ ⌨️ view ...... İLE BİRLİKTE KULLANILAN KELİMELER │
└───┘

express/have/hold a view ● strong views ● in sb's view ● sb's views about/on sth ● an exchange of views

o- view¹ /vju:/ noun 1 [OPINION] [C] your opinion görüş, düşünce, fikir We have different views about/on education. ○ In her view this is wrong. 2 [THINGS YOU SEE] [C] the things that you can see from a place manzara, görünüm, görünüş There was a lovely view of the lake from the bedroom window. 3 [ABILITY TO SEE] [no plural] how well you can see something from a particular place görüş, görme We had a great view of the procession. 4 [POSITION] [U] a position from which something can be seen görünüm, görüntü, görüş The house was hidden from view behind a wall. ○ He turned the corner and the harbour came into view. 5 in full view of sb happening where someone can easily see you biri tarafından açık seçik görülen, gözlerinin önünde/burnunun dibinde All this happened in full view of the cameras. 6 in view of sth formal because of yüzünden, ...dan/den dolayı; göz önünde tutarak In view of recent events, we have decided to cancel the meeting. 7 with a view to doing sth formal so that you can do something maksadıyla, amacıyla, niyetiyle He's doing some improvements on the house with a view to selling it. ⊃See also: point of view.

view² /vju:/ verb [T] formal 1 to have a particular opinion about someone or something kafasında olmak, tasarlamış olma In all three countries he is viewed as a terrorist. 2 to watch something bakmak They were able to view the city from a helicopter.

viewer /'vju:ər/ noun [C] someone who watches a television programme izleyici, seyirci

viewpoint /'vju:pɔɪnt/ noun [C] a way of thinking about a situation görüş/bakış açısı From his viewpoint the action seemed entirely justified.

vigil /'vɪdʒɪl/ noun [C, U] when people stay somewhere quietly in order to show that they support someone, disagree with someone, etc uyanık olma, başında bekleme, nöbet tutma an all-night vigil for peace

vigilant /'vɪdʒɪlənt/ adjective watching carefully and always ready to notice anything dangerous or illegal uyanık, tetikte, dikkatli, ihtiyatlı Police have asked people to be vigilant after yesterday's bomb attack. ● vigilance /'vɪdʒɪləns/ noun [U] tetikte olma, çok dikkatli olma

vigilante /,vɪdʒɪ'lænti/ noun [C] a member of a group of people who try to catch criminals and punish them without having any legal authority yasal yetkisi olmadan suçluları yakalayıp cezalandıran grubun üyesi; yasalar adına kendini yetkili kılan örgüt/çete üyesi

V

vigor /'vɪgə^r/ *noun* [U] *US spelling of* vigour enerji, canlılık, şevk

vigorous /'vɪg³rəs/ *adjective* **1** showing or needing a lot of physical energy canlı, dinç, enerjik *vigorous exercise* **2** showing strong, often negative, feelings about something sert, şiddetli, güçlü *a vigorous debate* ○ *He was a vigorous opponent of the government.* ● **vigorously** *adverb* Bates *vigorously denies* (= strongly denies) *murdering his wife.* gayretli bir şekilde

vigour UK (US vigor) /'vɪgə^r/ *noun* [U] strength and energy güç ve enerji *She set about her work with great vigour.*

vile /vaɪl/ *adjective* extremely unpleasant çok kötü, berbat, pis *a vile attack* ○ *The bathroom was vile.*

vilify /'vɪlɪfaɪ/ *verb* [T] *formal* to say bad things about someone so that other people will not like or approve of them kötülemek, aleyhinde konuşmak, başkalarının kötü intiba edinmesine sebep olmak

villa /'vɪlə/ *noun* [C] a large house, especially one used for holidays in a warm country villa

○⇀**village** /'vɪlɪdʒ/ *noun* [C] a place where people live in the countryside that includes buildings such as shops and a school but which is smaller than a town köy *She lives in a small village outside Oxford.* ○ *a village shop*

villager /'vɪlɪdʒə^r/ *noun* [C] someone who lives in a village köylü

villain /'vɪlən/ *noun* [C] a bad person in a film, book, etc kötü karakter

vindicate /'vɪndɪkeɪt/ *verb* [T] *formal* to prove that what someone said or did was right after people generally thought it was wrong haklı çıkarmak, doğruluğunu kanıtlamak ● **vindication** /ˌvɪndɪ'keɪʃ³n/ *noun* [C, U] *formal* doğruluğunu kanıtlama, şüpheleri yok etme

vindictive /vɪn'dɪktɪv/ *adjective* intending to harm or upset someone who has harmed or upset you kinci, kindar, kin güden

vine /vaɪn/ *noun* [C] a plant that grapes (= small, green or purple fruit used for making wine) grow on şarap

vinegar /'vɪnɪgə^r/ *noun* [U] a sour liquid that is used in cooking, often made from wine sirke

vineyard /'vɪnjəd/ *noun* [C] an area of land where someone grows grapes (= small, green or purple fruit) for making wine bağ, üzüm bağı

vintage¹ /'vɪntɪdʒ/ *adjective* **1** WINE Vintage wine is wine of a good quality that was made in a particular year. belli bir yıl veya bölgeye ait; iyi cins, kaliteli **2** VERY GOOD having all the best or most typical qualities of something, especially from the past bütün en iyi ve tipik özellikleri barındıran, klasik, geçmişten günümüze tüm özellikleri taşıyan; türüne emsal/örnek gösterilen *a vintage Hollywood movie* **3** CAR A vintage car was made between 1919 and 1930. klasik, belli bir döneme ait

vintage² /'vɪntɪdʒ/ *noun* [C] the wine that was made in a particular year rekolte *The 1993 vintage is one of the best.*

vinyl /'vaɪn³l/ *noun* [U] a type of very strong plastic vinil

viola /vi'əʊlə/ *noun* [C] a wooden instrument, larger than a violin, that you hold against your neck and play by moving a special stick across strings viyola

violate /'vaɪəleɪt/ *verb* [T] *formal* **1** to not obey a law, rule, or agreement ihlal etmek, bozmak, çiğnemek *Countries that violate international law will be dealt with severely.* **2** to not allow someone something that they should morally be allowed to have saygısızlık etmek, kutsallığını bozmak, kutsalına söz etmek

They were accused of violating human rights. ● **violation** /ˌvaɪə'leɪʃ³n/ *noun* [C, U] *a violation of privacy* ihlal

---

violence .... İLE BİRLİKTE KULLANILAN KELİMELER

erupt **into/renounce/use** violence ● **escalating/extreme/gratuitous** violence ● violence **against/towards sb**

○⇀**violence** /'vaɪəl³ns/ *noun* [U] **1** when someone tries to hurt or kill someone else şiddet, sertlik kaba kuvvet kullanma *an act of violence* ○ *A number of people were killed in the violence.* ○ *Violence against women has increased in recent years.* **2** extreme force and energy, especially of something causing damage şiddet, zor, zorbalık *Such was the violence of the explosion that three buildings collapsed.*

○⇀**violent** /'vaɪəl³nt/ *adjective* **1** ACTION involving violence şiddetli, zorlu, sert *a victim of violent crime* ○ *a violent protest* ○ *I don't like violent films* (= films that show violence). **2** PERSON likely to hurt or kill someone else tecavüzkâr, sert, saldırgan, zora başvuran *a violent criminal* **3** DAMAGE sudden and causing damage anî ve hasar veren, güçlü, şiddetli *a violent explosion/storm* **4** EMOTIONS showing very strong feelings, especially anger can yakan, acı veren, şiddet uygulayan; kızgınlık gösteren *violent emotions* ● **violently** *adverb* ⊃See also: non-violent. şiddetli bir şekilde

violet /'vaɪələt/ *noun* **1** [C] a small plant with a small, purple flower menekşe **2** [U] a pale purple colour menekşe rengi

violin /ˌvaɪə'lɪn/ *noun* [C]   **violin**
a wooden musical
instrument that you
hold against your neck
and play by moving a
bow (= special stick)
across strings keman
● **violinist** /ˌvaɪə'lɪnɪst/
noun [C] someone who
plays a violin kemancı;
keman sanatçısı

VIP /ˌviːaɪ'piː/ *noun* [C] *abbreviation for* very important person: someone who is famous or powerful and is treated in a special way Çok Önemli Zat (ÇÖZ) *The airport has a separate lounge for VIPs.*

viper /'vaɪpə^r/ *noun* [C] a small, poisonous snake engerek yılanı

viral /'vaɪr³l/ *adjective* caused by or relating to a virus (= infectious organism) virüsle ilgili/virüs tarafından neden olunan *a viral infection*

virgin¹ /'vɜːdʒɪn/ *noun* [C] someone who has never had sex bâkire

virgin² /'vɜːdʒɪn/ *adjective* Virgin land, forest, etc has not been used or damaged by people. bâkir, el değmemiş, işlenmemiş, kullanılmamış, keşfedilmemiş

virginity /və'dʒɪnəti/ *noun* [U] when someone has never had sex bâkirelik *Emma lost her virginity* (= had sex for the first time) *at sixteen.*

Virgo /'vɜːgəʊ/ *noun* [C, U] the sign of the zodiac which relates to the period of 23 August - 22 September, or a person born during this period Başak Burcu ⊃See picture at zodiac.

virile /'vɪraɪl/ (US) /'vɪr³l/ *adjective* A virile man is strong and has sexual energy. güçlü, kuvvetli, sekse düşkün, cinselliği yerinde ● **virility** /vɪ'rɪləti/ *noun* [U] erkeklik gücü ve cinsel enerjisi kuvvetli olma durumu

V

virtual /ˈvɜːtʃuəl/ *adjective* [always before noun] **1** almost a particular thing or quality **âdeta, gerçekte** *They played the game in virtual silence.* **2** using computer images and sounds that make you think an imagined situation is real **sanal** *a virtual art gallery*

virtually /ˈvɜːtʃuəli/ *adverb* almost **hemen hemen, neredeyse, âdeta** *They're virtually the same.* ○ *I've virtually finished.*

virtual reˈality *noun* [U] when a computer produces images and sounds that make you feel an imagined situation is real **sanal gerçek**

virtue /ˈvɜːtjuː/ *noun* **1** [ADVANTAGE] [C, U] an advantage or useful quality **üstünlük, avantaj** *The great virtue of having a small car is that you can park it easily.* **2** [GOOD QUALITY] [C] a good quality that someone has **erdem, fazilet** *Patience is not among his virtues.* **3** [MORAL BEHAVIOUR] [U] behaviour that is morally good **meziyet, haslet, takva, dürüstlük 4 by virtue of sth** *formal* because of something *...dan/den dolayı; ... yüzünden/nedeniyle She succeeded by virtue of hard work rather than talent.*

virtuoso /ˌvɜːtjuˈəʊsəʊ/ *noun* [C] someone who is extremely good at doing something, especially playing a musical instrument **üstât, virtüöz, usta**

virtuous /ˈvɜːtʃuəs/ *adjective* behaving in a good and moral way **namuslu, faziletli, doğru, dürüst, erdemli ● virtuously** *adverb* **erdemli bir şekilde**

virulent /ˈvɪrʊlənt/ *adjective* **1** A virulent disease or poison causes severe illness very quickly. **çok güçlü/tehlikeli/zararlı 2** *formal* criticizing or hating someone or something very much **sert, düşmanca, nefret dolu, eleştiren** *a virulent attack on the government*

🧩 **virus** …… İLE BİRLİKTE KULLANILAN KELİMELER

carry/contract/have/transmit a virus ● a deadly/ rare virus
---

oâ€¢**virus** /ˈvaɪərəs/ *noun* [C] **1** an infectious organism too small to be seen that causes disease, or an illness that it causes **virüs** *The doctor says I've got a virus.* **2** a program that is secretly put onto a computer in order to destroy the information that is stored on it **bilgisayar virüsü**

visa /ˈviːzə/ *noun* [C] an official mark in your passport (= document which proves your nationality) that allows you to enter or leave a particular country **vize** *She went to Miami on a tourist visa.*

vis-à-vis /ˌviːzəˈviː/ *preposition* relating to something, or in comparison with something *...a/e göre; ...ile karşılaştırıldığında I have to speak to James vis-à-vis the conference arrangements.*

vise /vaɪs/ *noun* [C] *US spelling of* vice (= a tool used for holding something tightly while you cut it, make it smooth, etc) **mengene** ➲See picture at **tool.**

visibility /ˌvɪzəˈbɪləti/ *noun* [U] how far or how well you can see because of weather conditions **görüş uzaklığı, görüş derecesi** *good/poor visibility* ○ *It was foggy and visibility was down to 50 metres.*

visible /ˈvɪzəbl/ *adjective* able to be seen **gözle görülebilir, görünür** *The fire was visible from five kilometres away.* ➲Opposite invisible. **● visibly** *adverb* *She was visibly upset.* **görünür bir şekilde**

vision /ˈvɪʒən/ *noun* **1** [IDEA] [C] an idea or image in your mind of what something could be like in the future **hayal gücü, hülya, sanı, düş, tasavvur, kuruntu** *a vision of a better society* **2** [SEE] [U] the ability to see **görme yeteneği, görüş** *He has poor vision in his left eye.* **3** [ABILITY TO PLAN] [U] the ability to make plans for the future that are imaginative and wise **ileri görüş, gele-**

---

ceği tasarlama, seziş *As a leader, he lacked vision.* **4** [RELIGION] [C] when you see someone or something that no one else can see as part of a religious experience **sanrı, vecit**

visionary /ˈvɪʒənəri/ *adjective* able to make plans for the future that are imaginative and wise **ileri görüşlü** *a visionary leader* **● visionary** *noun* [C] **hayali**

oâ€¢**visit¹** /ˈvɪzɪt/ *verb* [I, T] **1** [SEE A PERSON] to go to someone's home and spend time with them **ziyaret etmek** *We have friends coming to visit this weekend.* **2** [SEE A PLACE] to go to a place and spend a short amount of time there **ziyaret etmek, bulunmak, gezmek, görmek** *Did you visit St Petersburg while you were in Russia?* **3** [INTERNET] to look at a website **internet sitesine göz atmak/bakmak**

visit with sb *phrasal verb US* to spend time talking with someone who you know **konuşarak vakit geçirmek; yarenlik etmek** *Mom was visiting with our neighbor.*

🧩 **visit** …… İLE BİRLİKTE KULLANILAN KELİMELER

a visit to sth ● a visit from sb ● on a visit ● pay sb a visit ● have a visit from sb ● a brief/flying visit
---

oâ€¢**visit²** /ˈvɪzɪt/ *noun* [C] when you visit a place or a person **ziyaret** *the President's visit to Hong Kong* ○ *Why don't you pay him a visit* (= visit him)*?*

oâ€¢**visitor** /ˈvɪzɪtər/ *noun* [C] someone who visits a person or place **ziyaretçi** *The museum attracts large numbers of visitors.*

visor /ˈvaɪzər/ *noun* [C] **1** [PART OF HAT] the part of a helmet (= hard hat that protects your head) that you can pull down to cover your face **kask siperliği, siper 2** [HAT] (*also* ˈsun ˌvisor) a hat that has a curved part above your eyes to protect them from the sun **kasket, siperli şapka** ➲Orta kısımdaki renkli sayfalarına bakınız. **3** [CAR] the parts in the front window of a car that you pull down to protect your eyes from the sun **güneşlik, perde** ➲Orta kısımdaki renkli sayfalarına bakınız.

vista /ˈvɪstə/ *noun* [C] a view, especially a beautiful view that you look at from a high place **manzara, görüntü, panorama**

visual /ˈvɪʒuəl/ *adjective* relating to seeing **görsel** *The film has more powerful visual effects.* **● visually** *adverb* **visually appealing** **görünür bir şekilde**

visual ˈaid *noun* [C] something that helps you understand or remember information, such as a picture or film **görsel araç**

visualize (*also UK* -ise) /ˈvɪʒuəlaɪz/ *verb* [T] to create a picture in your mind of someone or something **göz önüne getirmek, hayalinde canlandırmak** *I was very surprised when I met Geoff - I'd visualized someone much older.* **● visualization** /ˌvɪʒuəlaɪˈzeɪʃən/ *noun* [U] **kafasında canlandırma**

vital /ˈvaɪtəl/ *adjective* **1** necessary **hayatî, çok önemli** *Tourism is vital to the country's economy.* ○ *[+ (that)] It's vital that you send off this form today.* **2** *formal* full of energy **enerji dolu, canlı, capcanlı**

vitality /vaɪˈtæləti/ *noun* [U] energy and strength **canlılık, dinamizm, zindelik** *At 48, he still projects an image of youth and energy.*

vitally /ˈvaɪtəli/ *adverb* in a very important way **hayatî derecede** *Safety at work is vitally important.*

vitamin /ˈvɪtəmɪn/ ⓤ /ˈvaɪtəmɪn/ *noun* [C] one of a group of natural substances in food that you need to be healthy **vitamin** *Oranges are full of vitamin C.*

vitriolic /ˌvɪtri'ɒlɪk/ *adjective formal* criticizing someone in a very severe and unpleasant way **dokunaklı, iğneleyici, kırıcı**

viva /'vaɪvə/ *noun* [C] *UK* a spoken examination at university **üniversitede sözlü sınav**

vivacious /vɪ'veɪʃəs/ *adjective* A vivacious person, especially a woman, is full of energy and enthusiasm. **şen şakrak, hayat dolu ve hoş, coşkulu, enerjik, neşeli**

vivid /'vɪvɪd/ *adjective* **1** Vivid descriptions or memories produce strong, clear images in your mind. **canlı ve ayrıntılı, sanki canlı gibi** *He gave a very vivid description of life in Caracas.* **2** A vivid colour is very bright. **canlı, parlak, pırıl pırıl** ● **vividly** *adverb* I *remember my first day at school very vividly.* **net, berrak şekilde olan**

vivisection /ˌvɪvɪ'sekʃᵊn/ *noun* [U] when living animals are used in scientific experiments, especially in order to discover the effects of new drugs **canlı hayvan deneyi; canlı hayvanlar üzerinde bilimsel deney yapma**

vixen /'vɪksᵊn/ *noun* [C] a female fox (= wild dog with red-brown fur) **dişi tilki**

V-neck /'viːnek/ *noun* [C] a V-shaped opening for your neck on a piece of clothing, or a sweater, dress, etc with this opening **v-yaka kıyafet** *a V-neck jumper* ● **V-necked** /viː'nekt/ *adjective* a *V-necked dress* **V-yaka bluz veya elbise**

▓▓▓ **vocabulary** ...... İLE BİRLİKTE KULLANILAN KELİMELER

a limited/wide vocabulary ● be in sb's vocabulary ● widen your vocabulary

vocabulary /vəʊ'kæbjələri/ *noun* **1** [WORDS] [C, U] all the words you know in a particular language **kelime hazinesi, sözcük dağarcığı** *Reading helps to widen your vocabulary.* **2** [LANGUAGE] [no plural] all the words that exist in a language, or that are used when discussing a particular subject **bir dildeki sözcüklerin tümü; belli bir konuyu tartışmada kullanılan sözcüklerin tamamı** *Computing has its own specialist vocabulary.* **3** [LIST] [no plural] a list of words and their meanings **sözcükler ve anlamlar listesi**

vocal /'vəʊkᵊl/ *adjective* **1** expressing your opinions in a strong way **görüş ve duygularını açıkça söyleyen; sesini yükselten, sözünü sakınmayan/esirgemeyen** *She is a vocal supporter of women's rights.* **2** involving or relating to the voice, especially singing **vokal; şarkıda ses içeren veya sesle ilgili** *vocal music*

'vocal ˌcords (*also* vocal chords) *noun* [plural] folds of skin at the top of your throat that make sounds when air from your lungs moves over them **ses telleri**

vocalist /'vəʊkᵊlɪst/ *noun* [C] the person who sings in a group of people who play popular music **vokalist**

vocals /'vəʊkᵊlz/ *noun* [plural] the part of a piece of music that is sung **vokal, şarkı söyleme**

vocation /vəʊ'keɪʃᵊn/ *noun* [C, U] a strong feeling that you are right for a particular type of work, or a job that gives you this feeling **yatkınlık, yetenek** *He knew that teaching was his true vocation.*

vocational /vəʊ'keɪʃᵊnᵊl/ *adjective* Vocational education and skills prepare you for a particular type of work. **mesleki** *The college offers both vocational and academic courses.*

vociferous /vəʊ'sɪfᵊrəs/ *adjective formal* expressing your opinions in a loud and strong way **bağırıp çağıran, yaygaracı, şamatacı** *She has become increasingly vociferous in her opposition to the scheme.*

vodka /'vɒdkə/ *noun* [C, U] a strong alcoholic drink that is popular in Russia and Poland **votka**

vogue /vəʊg/ *noun* [U, no plural] If there is a vogue for something, it is very fashionable. **moda, rağbet, revaç** *This period saw a vogue for Japanese painting.* ○ *Flat shoes are in vogue (= fashionable) this spring.*

▓▓▓ **voice** ...... İLE BİRLİKTE KULLANILAN KELİMELER

a deep/husky/low voice ● lose your voice ● lower/raise your voice ● in a [bored/stern, etc.] voice ● your tone of voice

o⁻**voice¹** /vɔɪs/ *noun* **1** [SOUNDS] [C] the sounds that you make when you speak or sing **ses** *I could hear voices in the next room.* ○ *Jessie has a beautiful singing voice.* ○ *Could you please keep your voices down* (= speak more quietly)? ○ *He raised his voice* (= spoke more loudly) *so that everyone could hear.* **2** lose your voice to become unable to speak, often because of an illness **sesini kaybetmek** *She had a bad cold and was losing her voice.* **3** [OPINION] [C] someone's opinion about a particular subject **fikir, düşünce** *The programme gives people the opportunity to make their voices heard.* **4** [PERSON] [no plural] someone who expresses the opinions or wishes of a group of people **sözcü, temsilci, konuşmacı** *It's important that students have a voice on the committee.* ◆See also: the passive.

voice² /vɔɪs/ *verb* [T] to say what you think about a particular subject **söylemek, ifade etmek, belirtmek, dile getirmek** *He has voiced concern about the new proposals.*

voice-activated /ˌvɔɪs'æktɪveɪtɪd/ *adjective* A machine that is voice-activated can recognize and follow low spoken instructions. **sesle çalışan**

'voice ˌmail *noun* [U] an electronic telephone answering system **sesli yanıt sistemi**

void¹ /vɔɪd/ *adjective* **1** [never before noun] not legally or officially acceptable **geçersiz, hükümsüz** *The contracts were declared void.* **2** be void of sth *formal* to be without something **boşluğu/yokluğu/eksikliği olmak** *His last statement was entirely void of meaning.*

void² /vɔɪd/ *noun* [no plural] **1** when someone or something important is not now in your life and you are unhappy **boşluk, eksiklik, yokluk** *Her husband's death left a void in her life.* **2** a large hole or empty space **oyuk, çukur, boşluk**

vol *written abbreviation for* volume **cilt' sözcüğünün kısa yazılışı**

volatile /'vɒlətaɪl/ ⑤ /'vɑːlᵊtᵊl/ *adjective* **1** A volatile person can suddenly become angry or violent. **dengesiz, havaî, kaypak, gelgeç** **2** A volatile situation might suddenly change. **dengesiz, kararsız, değişken** *a volatile political situation* ● **volatility** /ˌvɒlə'tɪləti/ *noun* [U] **sinirlenme, ani değişiklik gösterme**

volcano /vɒl'keɪnəʊ/ *noun* [C] *plural* **volcanoes** *or* **volcanos** a mountain with a large hole at the top which sometimes explodes and produces hot, melted rock and smoke

volcano

vole 810 Important words to learn

yanardağ, volkan ● volcanic /vɒlˈkænɪk/ *adjective* relating to a volcano **volkanik** *volcanic ash*

vole /vəʊl/ *noun* [C] a small animal like a mouse **tarla faresi**

volition /vəʊˈlɪʃ°n/ *noun* [U] *formal* the power to make your own decisions **istem, irade; kendiliğinden, kendi iradesiyle/isteğiyle** *He left the firm of his own volition* (= because he decided to).

volley¹ /ˈvɒli/ *noun* **1** [C] in sports, a kick or hit in which a player returns a ball before it touches the ground **vole 2 a volley of shots/gunfire, etc** when a lot of bullets are shot at the same time **yaylım ateşi** *A volley of bullets ripped through the floorboards.* **3 a volley of abuse/complaints, etc** a lot of insults/complaints, etc said at the same time **istismar/şikayet/yakınma bombardımanı/yaylım ateşi**

volley² /ˈvɒli/ *verb* [I, T] in sports, to return a ball by kicking or hitting it before it touches the ground **topa yere düşmeden vurmak, vole yapmak**

volleyball /ˈvɒlibɔːl/ *noun* [U] a game in which two teams use their hands to hit a ball over a net without allowing it to touch the ground **voleybol** ⊃Orta kısımdaki renkli sayfalarına bakınız.

volleyball

volt /vɒlt/ (*written abbreviation* V) *noun* [C] a unit for measuring the force of an electric current **volt**

voltage /ˈvəʊltɪdʒ/ *noun* [C, U] the force of an electric current, measured in volts **voltaj**

volume /ˈvɒljuːm/ *noun* **1** [SOUND] [U] the level of sound produced by a television, radio, etc **ses ayarı/seviyesi** *to turn the volume up/down* **2** [AMOUNT] [U] the number or amount of something, especially when it is large **yüklü sayı/miktar** *the volume of work involved* **3** [SPACE] [U] the amount of space inside an object **hacim** *Which of the bottles has the larger volume?* **4** [BOOK] [C] a book, especially one of a set **cilt** *a new dictionary in two volumes*

voluminous /vəˈluːmɪnəs/ *adjective formal* very large **çok büyük, uzun, sayfalar dolusu** *voluminous trousers*

voluntary /ˈvɒlənt°ri/ *adjective* **1** Voluntary work is done without being paid and usually involves helping people. **gönüllü** *She does voluntary work for the Red Cross.* ○ *voluntary organizations* **2** done or given because you want to and not because you have been forced to **isteğe bağlı, ihtiyarî** *voluntary contributions* ⊃Opposite **involuntary.** ● **voluntarily** /ˌvɒlənˈteər°li/ *adverb* She left voluntarily. **istekli bir şekilde**

volunteer¹ /ˌvɒlənˈtɪər/ *verb* **1** [OFFER] [I, T] to offer to do something without being asked or told to do it **gönüllü yapmak/olmak** [+ to do sth] *Rob volunteered to look after the kids.* **2** [ARMY] [I] to join the army, navy, etc without being officially told to join **orduya gönüllü kaydolmak/katılmak** *In 1939 he volunteered for active service.* **3** [INFORMATION] [T] to give information without being asked **istenilmeden bilgi vermek** *No one volunteered the truth.*

volunteer² /ˌvɒlənˈtɪər/ *noun* [C] **1** someone who does work without being paid, especially work that involves helping people **gönüllülük** *a Red Cross volunteer* **2** someone who does or gives something because they want to and not because they have been forced to

gönüllü, gönüllü kişi *Any volunteers to help me move these books?*

voluptuous /vəˈlʌptʃuəs/ *adjective* A voluptuous woman has a sexually attractive body, often with large breasts. **cinsel cazibeli, çekici, şehvet uyandıran, şehvetli**

vomit¹ /ˈvɒmɪt/ *verb* [I, T] If someone vomits, the food or liquid that was in their stomach comes up and out of their mouth. **kusmak, istifra etmek, çıkarmak** *She was vomiting blood.*

vomit² /ˈvɒmɪt/ *noun* [U] the food or liquid that comes from your mouth when you vomit **kusmuk**

voodoo /ˈvuːduː/ *noun* [U] a religion involving magic and praying to spirits **büyü ve ruhlara ibadet üzerine kurulu bir tür din; vudu**

voracious /vəˈreɪʃəs/ *adjective* wanting to do something a lot, especially wanting to eat a lot of food **doymak bilmez, pis boğaz, obur** *She has a voracious appetite.* ○ *a voracious reader of historical novels* ● **voraciously** *adverb* **aç gözlü bir biçimde** ● **voracity** /vəˈræsəti/ *noun* [U] **oburluk**

vote¹ /vəʊt/ *verb* [I, T] to show your choice or opinion in an election or meeting by writing a cross on an official piece of paper or putting your hand up **oy kullanmak/vermek** *Who did you vote for?* ○ *The unions voted against strike action.* ○ [+ to do sth] *Staff have voted to accept the pay offer.*

vote .... İLE BİRLİKTE KULLANILAN KELİMELER

cast your vote ● a vote **against/for** sb/sth ● a vote **on** sth

vote² /vəʊt/ *noun* [C] **1** [CHOICE] when someone shows their choice or opinion in an election or meeting by writing a cross on an official piece of paper or putting their hand up **oy** *He lost the election by twenty votes.* **2** [DECIDE] a way of making a decision by asking a group of people to vote **oylama** *We called a meeting in order to take a vote on the proposal.* **3 the vote a** [NUMBER OF VOTES] the total number of votes given or received in an election **oyların toplamı** *The Green party got 10% of the vote.* **b** [PERMISSION TO VOTE] when someone is officially allowed to vote **oy kullanma/verme hakkı** *In some countries women still don't have the vote.*

voter /ˈvəʊtər/ *noun* [C] someone who votes or who is officially allowed to vote **seçmen, oy kullanan kimse**

vouch /vaʊtʃ/ *verb* **vouch for sb/sth** *phrasal verb* to say that you know from experience that something is true or good, or that someone has a good character **güvence vermek, garanti etmek, doğrulamak, kefil olmak, teyit etmek**

voucher /ˈvaʊtʃər/ *noun* [C] a piece of paper that can be used instead of money to pay for goods or services **fiş, kupon** *a discount voucher*

vow¹ /vaʊ/ *verb* [T] to make a serious promise or decision **söz vermek, yemin etmek, ant içmek** [+ (that)] *She vowed that she would never leave the children again.* ○ [+ to do sth] *I've vowed never to go there again.*

vow² /vaʊ/ *noun* [C] a serious promise or decision **söz, yemin, ant, vaad** *marriage vows* ○ *I made a vow that I would write to him once a week.*

vowel /vaʊəl/ *noun* [C] a speech sound that you make with your lips and teeth open, shown in English by the letters 'a', 'e', 'i', 'o' or 'u' **ünlü/sesli harf**

voyage /ˈvɔɪɪdʒ/ *noun* [C] a long journey, especially by ship, or in space **deniz/uzay yolculuğu, sefer** *The ship sank on its maiden voyage* (= first journey).

vs (*also UK* **v**) *preposition written abbreviation for* versus (= used to say that one team or person is competing against another) ...a/e karşı' ifadesinin kısa yazılışı

vulgar /'vʌlgəʳ/ *adjective* **1** rude and likely to upset or anger people, especially by referring to sex and the body in an unpleasant way **kaba, terbiyesiz, nezaketten yoksun** *vulgar jokes/language* **2** not showing good judgment about what is suitable or pleasant to look at **zevksiz, görgüsüz, sıradan** *a vulgar shade of yellow* ● **vulgarity** /vʌl'gærəti/ *noun* [U] **kabalık**

vulnerable /'vʌlnᵊrəbl/ *adjective* easy to hurt or attack physically or emotionally **ruhsal ve fiziksel olarak kolaylıkla incinebilir/kırılabilir/yaralanabilir** *She was a vulnerable sixteen-year-old.* ○ *The troops are in a vulnerable position.* ○ *He's more vulnerable to infection because of his injuries.* ● **vulnerability** /ˌvʌlnᵊrə'bɪləti/ *noun* [U] **kırılganlık, kırılabilirlik**

vulture /'vʌltʃəʳ/ *noun* [C] a large bird with no feathers on its head or neck that eats dead animals **akbaba**

vying /'vaɪɪŋ/ *present participle of* vie **yarışan, rekâbet eden**

W

W, w /'dʌblju:/ the twenty-third letter of the alphabet alfabenin yirmiüçüncü harfi

W *written abbreviation for* watt (= a unit for measuring electrical power) **elektrik güç ölçüm birimi 'vat' sözcüğünün kısa yazılışı** *a 40W light bulb*

wacky /'wæki/ *adjective informal* unusual in a funny or surprising way **çılgın, uçuk kaçık** *a wacky sense of humour*

wad /wɒd/ *noun* [C] **1** a thick pile of pieces of paper, especially paper money **tomar, deste** *a wad of cash* **2** a piece of soft material in the shape of a ball **topak, tutam** *a wad of (UK) cotton wool/(US) cotton*

waddle /'wɒdl/ *verb* [I] A duck (= water bird) or fat person that waddles walks with short steps, moving from side to side. **paytak paytak yürümek**

wade /weɪd/ *verb* **wade across/through, etc** to walk through water **su içinde yürümek/yürüyerek geçmek** *He waded across the river.*

wade through sth *phrasal verb* to read a lot of boring or difficult information **zorla okuyup bitirmek, zar zor okuyup bitirmek**

wafer /'weɪfə'/ *noun* [C] a light, thin biscuit **gofret, kâğıt helva**

waffle¹ /'wɒfl/ *noun* **1** [U] *informal* speech or writing that says nothing important **abuk sabuk konuşma, zırvalama, boş boş konuşup durma 2** [C] a square, flat cake with a pattern of holes in it, eaten especially in the US **içinde küçük delikler olan ve daha çok ABD'de yenilen bir tür kek**

waffle² /'wɒfl/ *(also* **waffle on)** *verb* [I] *informal* to talk or write a lot and say nothing important **abuk sabuk konuşmak, zırvalamak, boş boş konuşup durmak**

waft /wɒft/ *verb* **waft from/through, etc** to gradually move through the air **havada yayılmak/dağılmak** *The smell of coffee wafted through the room.*

wag /wæg/ *verb* [I, T] **wagging,** *past* **wagged 1** If a dog wags its tail, it moves it from side to side. **(kuyruk) sağa sola sallamak 2** If you wag your finger, you move it from side to side, often to tell someone not to do something. **parmakla ikaz işareti yapmak**

 wage .... İLE BİRLİKTE KULLANILAN KELİMELER

earn a wage • a decent wage • a wage increase/rise
• the minimum wage

wage¹ /weɪdʒ/ *noun* [no plural] *(also* **wages** [plural]) the amount of money a person regularly receives for their job **ücret** *weekly wages* ○ *the minimum wage*

wage² /weɪdʒ/ *verb* **wage a battle/campaign/war, etc** to fight or organize a series of activities in order to achieve something **başarmak için bir dizi faaliyet düzenlemek; mücadele etmek; başlatıp sürdürmek; savaşmak** *They're currently waging a campaign to change the law.*

wager /'weɪdʒə'/ *verb* [T] to risk money on the result of a game, race, competition, etc **bahse para koymak; şans oyunlarına para yatırmak** • **wager** *noun* [C] **bahis**

wagon /'wægən/ *noun* [C] a large vehicle with four large wheels pulled by horses **yük arabası, at arabası**

wail /weɪl/ *verb* [I, T] **1** to cry loudly because you are very unhappy **hıçkıra hıçkıra/hüngür hüngür**

ağlamak; feryat etmek; yaygarayı basmak *"I've lost my mummy," she wailed.* **2** If a siren (= loud noise to warn of danger) wails, it makes a noise. **acı acı siren çalmak; feryat etmek** *Somewhere in the distance a police siren was wailing.* • **wail** *noun* [C] **feryat etme**

waist /weɪst/ *noun* [C] **1** the part around the middle of your body where you wear a belt **bel** *She had a 26 inch waist.* ⊃Orta kısımdaki renkli sayfalarına bakınız. **2** the part of a piece of clothing that fits round the waist **bel kısmı**

waist

waistband /'weɪstbænd/ *noun* [C] the strip of material at the top of a pair of trousers or a skirt that goes around the waist **kemer, kemer kısmı, bel yeri**

waistcoat /'weɪstkəut/ *UK (US* **vest)** *noun* [C] a piece of clothing with buttons at the front and no sleeves, that you wear over a shirt **yelek** ⊃Orta kısımdaki renkli sayfalarına bakınız.

waistline /'weɪstlaɪn/ *noun* [C] how big or small your waist is, or the part of a piece of clothing that goes around the waist **bel ölçüsü, bel çevresi**

◦⁓**wait¹** /weɪt/ *verb* [I] **1** to stay in a place until someone or something arrives or someone or something is ready for you **beklemek** *I'm **waiting** for Clive.* ○ *How long did you wait for a taxi?* ○ [+ to do sth] *I'm still waiting to use the phone.* **2** to not do something until something else happens **bir şeyin olmasını beklemek** *We'll wait till Jane gets here before we start eating.* **3 can't wait** *informal* used to say how excited you are about something that you are going to do **can atmak, çok istemek, sabırsızlanmak, bekleyememek** [+ to do sth] *I can't wait to see him.* **4 keep sb waiting** to be late so that someone has to wait for you **birini bekletmek** *I'm sorry to have kept you waiting.* **5 wait and see** to wait to discover what will happen **bekleyip görmek** *We'll wait and see what she says.* ⊃See also: be waiting in the wings.

YAYGIN HATALAR

wait

Wait fiilinin ardından isim gelmez. **For** edatını kullanmanız gerekir. **Wait something** değil **wait for something** kullanılmalıdır: *~~I will wait you in the hotel lobby.~~* Yanlış cümle örneği:

I will wait for you in the hotel lobby.

wait about/around *phrasal verb* to stay in a place and do nothing while you wait for someone to arrive or something to happen **oyalamak; oyalanmak**
wait in *phrasal verb* UK to stay at home because you are expecting someone to visit or telephone you **evde kalıp beklemek**
wait on sb *phrasal verb* to bring a meal to someone, especially in a restaurant **hizmet etmek, servis yapmak**

wait up *phrasal verb* to not go to bed at night until someone has come home **yatmayıp/uyumayıp beklemek** *I'll be quite late, so don't wait up for me.*

🧩 **wait** .... İLE BİRLİKTE KULLANILAN KELİMELER

face/have a wait ● an **agonizing/anxious/long** wait ● the wait **for** sth ● sth is (well) **worth the wait**

wait² /weɪt/ *noun* [no plural] when you stay in a place until someone or something arrives or someone or something is ready for you **bekleme** *We had a long wait at the airport.*

waiter /ˈweɪtəʳ/ *noun* [C] a man who works in a restaurant, bringing food to customers **erkek garson**

'waiting ,list *noun* [C] a list of people who are waiting until it is their time to have or do something **bekleme listesi, yedekler listesi** *a hospital waiting list*

'waiting ,room *noun* [C] a room in which people wait for something, for example to see a doctor or take a train **bekleme salonu/odası**

waitress /ˈweɪtrəs/ *noun* [C] a woman who works in a restaurant, bringing food to customers **bayan garson**

waive /weɪv/ *verb* [T] **1** to allow someone not to obey the usual rule or not to pay the usual amount of money **feragat etmek, iptal etmek, bırakmak** *He agreed to waive his fee to help us.* **2** to decide not to have something that you are allowed by law to have **vazgeçmek; yasal hakkından feragat etmek** *She waived her right to have a lawyer representing her.*

o-⁴**wake¹** /weɪk/ (*also* wake up) *verb* [I, T] *past tense* **woke**, *past participle* **woken** to stop sleeping or to make someone else stop sleeping **uyanmak** *I've only just woken up.* ○ *Could you wake me up before you go?* ○ *You woke me up making so much noise.* ⊃Orta kısımdaki renkli sayfalarına bakınız.

wake up to sth *phrasal verb* to start to understand something that is important **öneminin farkına varmak** *We need to wake up to the fact that the Earth's resources are limited.*

wake² /weɪk/ *noun* **1 in the wake of sth** after something has happened, and often because it has happened **...dan/den hemen sonra; ...ın/in hemen ardından/ peşinden** *Airport security was extra tight in the wake of last week's bomb attacks.* **2** [C] the waves behind a moving ship **geminin arkasında kalan dalgalar/iz/ dümen suyu 3** [C] when people come together to remember someone who has recently died **yakın zamanda ölen birinin ardından yasını tutmak için bir araya gelme**

'wake-up ,call *noun* [C] **1** a telephone call to wake you in the morning, especially when you are staying in a hotel **uyandırma araması/çağrısı 2** something bad that happens and shows you that you need to take action to change a situation **ikaz, uyarma, farkına varma**

o-⁴**walk¹** /wɔːk/ *verb* **1** [I, T] to move forward by putting one foot in front of the other and then repeating the action **yürümek** *She walks to school.* ○ *We walked twenty miles in all.* **2 walk sb home/to sth** to walk with someone in order to guide them or keep them safe **birini sağ salim eve kadar yürüyerek götürmek** *He walked me to my house.* **3 walk the dog** to walk with a dog to give the dog exercise **köpeği gezdirmek 4 walk all over sb** *informal* to treat someone badly **kötü muamele etmek, kaba davranmak**

walk into sth *phrasal verb* to get a job easily **kolayca iş sahibi olmak/işe girmek**

walk off with sth *phrasal verb* to win something easily **kolayca kazanmak** *She walked off with the top prize.*

walk out *phrasal verb* to leave a job, meeting, or performance because you are angry or do not approve of

something **kızarak/onaylamayarak terketmek; bırakıp gitmek, çekip gitmek** *He was so disgusted by the film he walked out.*

walk out on sb *phrasal verb* to suddenly leave your husband, wife, or partner and end your relationship with them **alıp başını gitmek; aniden terketmek; çekip gitmek; yüzüstü bırakmak** *He walked out on his wife and kids.*

🧩 **walk** .... İLE BİRLİKTE KULLANILAN KELİMELER

go for/take a walk ● a **brisk** walk ● a **long/short** walk

o-⁴**walk²** /wɔːk/ *noun* **1** [C] a journey that you make by walking, often for enjoyment **yürüyüş, gezinti** *We usually go for a walk on Sunday afternoons.* ○ *He took the dog for a walk.* **2 a short/ten-minute, etc walk** a journey that takes a short time/ten minutes, etc when you walk **kısa/on dakikalık vb. yürüyüş** *The station is just a five-minute walk from the house.* **3** [C] a path or route where people can walk for enjoyment **yürüyüş/ gezinti yolu/parkuru** *There are some lovely walks in the forest.* **4 walk of life** People from different walks of life have different jobs and different experiences in life. **toplumdaki yer, iş, meslek, sosyal mevki**

walker /ˈwɔːkəʳ/ *noun* [C] someone who walks for exercise or enjoyment **yürüyüş yapan kimse**

walkie talkie /ˌwɔːkiˈtɔːki/ *noun* [C] a radio that you carry with you and that lets you talk to someone else with a similar radio **el telsizi**

Walkman /ˈwɔːkmən/ *noun* [C] *trademark* a small piece of equipment with parts that you put in your ears which allows you to listen to music that no one else can hear **kulaklıkla dinlenebilen radyo/kaset çalabilen cihaz; volkmen**

o-⁴**wall** /wɔːl/ *noun* [C] **1** one of the vertical sides of a room or building **duvar** *There were several large paintings on the wall.* **2** a vertical structure made of brick or stone that divides areas that are owned by different people **duvar** *a garden wall* **3 drive sb up the wall** *informal* to make someone very angry **çok canını sıkmak, müthiş asabını bozmak** *She drives me up the wall.* See also: **fly²** on the wall, **be** banging your **head¹** against a brick wall.

walled /wɔːld/ *adjective* **walled garden/city** a garden/ city with walls around it **duvarlarla çevrili bahçe/ şehir**

wallet /ˈwɒlɪt/ (*also* US billfold) *noun* [C] a small, flat container for paper money and credit cards (= plastic cards used for paying with), usually used by a man **cüzdan, portföy**

wallop /ˈwɒləp/ *verb* [T] *informal* to hit someone or something hard **dövmek, patlatmak, pataklamak** ● **wallop** *noun* [no plural] *informal* **dayak, vurma, darbe**

wallow /ˈwɒləʊ/ *verb* [I] **1** to allow yourself to feel too much sadness in a way that stops people respecting you **kendini ...a/e kaptırmak; sürekli dövünerek insanları kendinden uzaklaştırmak** *There's no use wallowing in self-pity.* **2** to lie or move around in soil or water, especially for pleasure **yatıp yuvarlanmak**

wallpaper /ˈwɔːlˌpeɪpəʳ/ *noun* [C, U] paper, usually with a pattern, that you decorate walls with **duvar kâğıdı** ● **wallpaper** *verb* [T] **duvar kağıdı ile kaplamak**

'Wall ,Street *noun* the financial area of New York where shares (= small, equal parts of the value of a company) are bought and sold **New York Borsası** *The company's shares rose on Wall Street yesterday.*

wally /ˈwɒli/ *noun* [C] *UK informal* a silly person **aptal biri, salak kimse, şapşal insan**

walnut /'wɔːlnʌt/ noun 1 [C] a nut that is in two halves inside a brown shell, and whose surface has curves and folds in it ceviz 2 [U] the hard wood of the tree that produces walnuts, used to make furniture **ceviz ağacı**

walrus /'wɔːlrəs/ noun [C] a large sea animal that has two tusks (= long, pointed teeth that come out of the mouth) **deniz aygırı**

waltz¹ /wɒls/ noun [C] a dance for two partners performed to music that has a rhythm of three beats, or the music for the dance **vals, vals dansı**

waltz² /wɒls/ verb [I] 1 to dance a waltz **vals yapmak, vals dansı yapmak** 2 **waltz in/off, etc** to walk somewhere quickly and confidently, often in a way that annoys other people **başkalarını rahatsız etme derecesinde kendine güvenir bir şekilde yürümek** *You can't just waltz into my bedroom - it's private!*

wan /wɒn/ adjective pale and looking ill or tired **bitik, beti benzi atmış**

wand /wɒnd/ noun [C] a thin stick that someone who performs magic tricks holds in their hand **sihirbaz değneği, sihirli değnek**

wander /'wɒndə'/ verb 1 [I, T] to walk slowly about a place without any purpose **gezinip durmak, boş boş dolaşmak, amaçsızca gezinmek** *They wandered aimlessly around the town.* 2 [I] (also **wander off**) to walk away from the place where you should be **yürüyerek uzaklaşmak, ayrılmak, terketmek** *He was here a moment ago - he must have wandered off.* 3 **sb's attention/mind/thoughts, etc wander** If someone's attention/mind, etc wanders, they start thinking about one subject when they should be thinking about a different subject. **dağılmak, başka alemlere dalmak, asıl konudan uzaklaşmak, dalıp gitmek** *I was bored and my thoughts started to wander.*

wane /weɪn/ verb [I] to become less powerful, important, or popular **yavaş yavaş kaybolmak, gittikçe azalmak, küçülmek, önemini yitirmek** *Interest in the product is starting to wane.*

wangle /'wæŋgl/ verb [T] informal to succeed in getting something that a lot of people want, by being clever or tricking someone **ne yapıp edip elde etmek; (kurnazlık ve hileyle) koparmak; elde etmek** *He managed to wangle an invitation to the party.*

o➤**want¹** /wɒnt/ verb [T] 1 to hope to have or do something, or to wish for something **istemek, arzu etmek** *He wants a new car.* ○ [+ to do sth] *I don't want to talk about it.* ○ *You can't always do what you want.* ○ *We can go later if you want.* ○ *I want him to explain why.* 2 to need something **gereksinim duymak, gerekmek, istemek, ihtiyacı olmak** *This soup wants more salt.* 3 **want to do sth** UK informal used to give advice to someone **...malı/meli** *You want to go to bed earlier and then you won't be so tired.* 4 **be wanted** to be needed for a particular activity or in a particular place **aranmak** *You're wanted on the phone.*

want

Unutmayın! Want fiilinin ardından başka bir fiil geldiği zaman ikinci fiil mastar halinde -to yapısında olmalıdır. Want do something doğru bir kullanım değildir. Doğru şekli **want to do something** olarak kullanılır.: *I want thank you for your letter.* Yanlış cümle örneği

I want to thank you for your letter.

want² /wɒnt/ noun **want of sth** when there is not enough of something **eksiklik, noksanlık** *If we fail, it*

won't be for want of effort (= it is not because we have not tried).

wanted /'wɒntɪd/ adjective If someone is wanted, the police think they have committed a serious crime and are trying to find them. **aranan** *He is wanted for murder.*

wanton /'wɒntən/ adjective formal done in order to cause suffering or destruction but with no other reason **nedensiz, sebepsiz, maksatsız, gelişigüzel** *wanton cruelty/violence*

wants /wɒnts/ noun [plural] the things you want or need **eksikler, istenenler, gereksinim duyulanlar**

war ...... İLE BİRLİKTE KULLANILAN KELİMELER

all-out/full-scale war ● **declare/go to** war ● **wage** war **on** sb ● war **breaks out** ● war **against** sb

o➤**war** /wɔː'/ noun 1 [FIGHTING] [C, U] fighting, using soldiers and weapons, between two or more countries, or two or more groups inside a country **savaş** *They've been at war for the past five years.* ○ *He was only a child when the war broke out* (= started). ○ *If this country goes to war* (= starts to fight in a war), *thousands of people will die.* 2 [COMPETING] [C, U] when two or more groups are trying to be more successful than each other **savaş, kavga, mücadele** *a price war between supermarkets* 3 [TO STOP] [no plural] an attempt to stop something bad or illegal **mücadele, çaba, savaş, teşebbüs** *the war against crime/drugs* ⊃See also: civil war, prisoner of war, world war.

'war ˌcrime noun [C] a crime during a war that breaks the international rules of war **savaş suçu** ● **war criminal** noun [C] someone guilty of a war crime **savaş suçlusu**

ward¹ /wɔːd/ noun [C] a room in a hospital where people receiving treatment stay, often for the same type of illness **koğuş** *the maternity ward*

ward² /wɔːd/ verb

ward sth off phrasal verb to prevent something unpleasant happening **savuşturmak, atlatmak, önüne geçmek, önlemek** *I take vitamin C to ward off colds.*

-ward, -wards /-wəd/, /-wədz/ suffix makes an adverb meaning 'towards a direction or place' **...bir yöne/yere doğru' anlamında sonek** *inward* ○ *forward* ○ *homeward*

warden /'wɔːd°n/ noun [C] 1 US (UK **governor**) someone who is responsible for controlling a prison **hapishane müdürü** 2 UK someone who is responsible for looking after a particular place or the people in it **yönetici, bina yöneticisi** ⊃See also: traffic warden.

warder /'wɔːdə'/ noun [C] UK a prison guard **gardiyan**

wardrobe /'wɔːdrəʊb/ noun 1 [C] UK (US **closet**) a large cupboard for keeping clothes in **gardırop** 2 [no plural] all the clothes that you own **giysiler, gardırop**

warehouse /'weəhaʊs/ noun [C] plural **warehouses** /'weəhaʊzɪz/ a large building for storing goods that are going to be sold **ambar, depo**

wares /weəz/ noun [plural] literary goods that are for sale, especially not in a shop **satılık mal, eşya** *People were selling their wares at the side of the road.*

warfare /'wɔːfeə'/ noun [U] fighting in a war, especially using a particular type of weapon **savaş, harp** *chemical/modern warfare*

warhead /'wɔːhed/ noun [C] the part of a missile (= weapon) that explodes when it reaches the place it is aimed at **savaş başlığı, füze başlığı** *a nuclear warhead*

warlord /'wɔːlɔːd/ noun [C] a military leader who controls a particular area of a country **bir şehrin belli**

bir bölgesini kontrol altında tutan askeri lider/komutan

o⇠**warm¹** /wɔːm/ *adjective* **1** TEMPERATURE having a temperature between cool and hot **ılık, hafif sıcak** *It's nice and warm in here.* ○ *Are you warm enough?* ○ *Make sure you keep warm.* **2** CLOTHES Warm clothes or covers keep your body warm. **ısıtan, sıcak tutan** *a warm sweater* **3** FRIENDLY friendly and showing affection **sıcak, candan, sevecen, içten** *a warm smile/welcome*

warm² /wɔːm/ *verb* [I, T] to become warm or to make something become warm **ısınmak, ısıtmak** *She warmed her feet against his.* ○ *I'll warm the soup.*
warm to sb/sth *phrasal verb* to start to like a person or idea **ısınmak; kanı kaynamak, yakınlık duymaya başlamak**
warm up *phrasal verb* to do gentle exercises in order to prepare yourself for more energetic exercise **ısınmak, ısınma çalışması yapmak** *They were warming up before the match.* ● **warm-up** /'wɔːmʌp/ *noun* [C] **ısınma hareketleri (spor)**
warm (sb/sth) up *phrasal verb* to become warmer or to make someone or something warmer **ısınmak, ısıtmak** *The house soon warms up with the heating on.*

warmly /'wɔːmli/ *adverb* in a friendly way **samimiyetle, sıcak bir şekilde**

warmth /wɔːmθ/ *noun* [U] **1** the heat that is produced by something **sıcaklık, ılıklık, hararet** *the warmth of the fire* **2** when someone is friendly and shows affection **içtenlik, samimiyet, candanlık** *There was no warmth in his eyes.*

o⇠**warn** /wɔːn/ *verb* [T] **1** to tell someone that something bad may happen in the future, so that they can prevent it **uyarmak, ikaz etmek, uyarıp haberdar etmek** [+ that] *I warned you that it would be cold but you still wouldn't wear a coat.* ○ *I've been warning him for months.* **2** to advise someone not to do something that could cause danger or trouble **uyarmak, ikaz etmek, dikkatini çekmek, önerilerde bulunmak** [+ to do sth] *I warned you not to tell her.*

░░░ **warning** ...... İLE BİRLİKTE KULLANILAN KELİMELER

deliver/give/heed/ignore/issue　a warning　●　a blunt/final/stern warning　●　without warning

o⇠**warning** /'wɔːnɪŋ/ *noun* [C, U] something that tells or shows you that something bad may happen **ikaz, alarm** *All cigarette packets carry a warning.* ○ *The bombs fell completely without warning.*

warp /wɔːp/ *verb* **1** [I, T] to become bent into the wrong shape or to make something do this **eğril(t)mek, yamulup bozulmak, yamultup bozmak** *The window frames had warped.* **2** [T] If something makes your mind, it makes you strange and cruel. **etkileyip bozmak; zihnini allak bullak etmek; kontrolden çıkarmak**

warpath /'wɔːpɑːθ/ *noun* **be on the warpath** *informal* to be trying to find someone in order to be angry with them **çok kızmış/kavgaya hazır/patlamaya hazır olmak**

warped /wɔːpt/ *adjective* strange and cruel **çarpık, acayip ve kaba** *You've got a warped mind!*

warplane /'wɔːˌpleɪn/ *noun* [C] an aircraft for carrying bombs **savaş uçağı; bombardıman uçağı**

warrant¹ /'wɒrᵊnt/ *noun* [C] an official document that allows someone to do something, for example that allows a police officer to search a building **yetki/izin belgesi, tevkif müzekkeresi, arama emri** *The police have a warrant for his arrest.* ⊃See also: search warrant.

warrant² /'wɒrᵊnt/ *verb* [T] to make something necessary **gerekli kılmak, hak etmek, gerektirmek,**

layık olmak *None of her crimes is serious enough to warrant punishment.*

warranty /'wɒrᵊnti/ *noun* [C, U] a written promise made by a company to change or repair one of its products if it has a fault **garanti, garanti belgesi** *a five-year warranty*

warren /'wɒrᵊn/ (*also* 'rabbit ˌwarren) *noun* [C] a group of connected underground holes where rabbits live **yeraltı yuvaları**

warring /'wɔːrɪŋ/ *adjective* **warring factions/parties/sides, etc** groups that are fighting against each other **savaşan fraksiyonlar/hizipler/taraflar/gruplar**

warrior /'wɒriəʳ/ *noun* [C] a person who has experience and skill in fighting in a war, especially in the past **savaşçı, asker, muharip asker**

warship /'wɔːˌʃɪp/ *noun* [C] a ship with weapons, used in war **savaş gemisi, fırkateyn**

wart /wɔːt/ *noun* [C] a small, hard lump that grows on the skin **siğil**

wartime /'wɔːtaɪm/ *noun* [U] a period when a country is fighting a war **savaş/harp zamanı/dönemi**

war-torn /'wɔːˌtɔːn/ *adjective* damaged by war **savaşın mahvettiği/yıktığı/harap ettiği** *a war-torn country*

wary /'weəri/ *adjective* If you are wary of someone or something, you do not trust them completely. **tedbirli, ihtiyatlı, temkinli, dikkatli** *She's still wary of strangers.* ● **warily** *adverb* **güvenmeyen bir şekilde** ● **wariness** *noun* [U] **tedbirli olma**

was /wɒz/ *past simple I/he/she/it of* be **be' fiilinin geçmiş zaman tekil şahıs hâli**

o⇠**wash¹** /wɒʃ/ *verb* **1** [T] to make something clean using water, or water and soap **yıkamak** *Dad was washing the dishes.* **2** [I, T] to clean part of your body with water and soap **yıkamak, yıkanmak** *Have you washed your hands?* ○ *I got washed and dressed.* **3** **be washed away/out/up, etc** If something is washed away/out, etc, it is moved there by water. **yıkıp sürükleyip götür(ül)mek; yerle bir etmek/edilmek; silip süpür(ül)mek** *A lot of the waste is washed out to sea.* **4** **wash against/on, etc** If water washes somewhere, it flows there. **yıkmak, yıkıp götürmek, yerle bir etmek** *Waves washed against the base of the cliff.*
wash sth away *phrasal verb* If water washes something away, it removes that thing. **süpürüp götürmek; silip süpürüp alıp gitmek, yıkıp sürükleyip götürmek** *Floods washed away much of the soil.*
wash sth down *phrasal verb* to drink something with food or medicine to make it easier to swallow **su katarak içmek/yutmak** *I had a plate of sandwiches, washed down with a glass of cool beer.*
wash out *phrasal verb* If a colour or dirty mark washes out, it disappears when you wash something. **yıkayınca çıkarmak/temizlemek** *Most hair dye washes out after a few weeks.*
wash (sth) up *phrasal verb UK* to wash the dishes, pans, and other things you have used for cooking and eating **a meal bulaşıkları yıkamak** ⊃Orta kısımdaki renkli sayfalarına bakınız.
wash up *phrasal verb US* to wash your hands, especially before a meal **yemekten önce ellerini yıkamak** *Go and wash up - your dinner's ready.*

wash² /wɒʃ/ *noun* **1 a wash** when you wash a part of your body **yıkama, temizleme** *Have you had a wash?* **b** *mainly UK* when you wash something **temizlik, temizleme, yıkama** *Could you give the car a wash?* **2** [C, U] clothes, sheets, etc that are being washed together **çamaşır** *Your jeans are in the wash.*

washable /'wɒʃəbl/ *adjective* Something that is washable will not be damaged by being washed. **yıkanabilir**

washbasin /'wɒʃˌbeɪsᵊn/ UK (UK/US **sink**) noun [C] a bowl in a bathroom that water can flow into, used for washing your face or hands **lâvabo**

washcloth /'wɒʃklɒθ/ US (UK **flannel**) noun [C] a small cloth that you use to wash your face and body **lif, banyo lifi** ↪Orta kısımdaki renkli sayfalarına bakınız.

washed-out /ˌwɒʃt'aʊt/ adjective looking pale and tired **solgun, cansız**

washer /'wɒʃəʳ/ noun [C] **1** a thin, flat ring that is put between a nut and a bolt (= metal objects used to fasten things together) **rondelâ, pul 2** a machine that washes clothes **çamaşır makinası**

washing /'wɒʃɪŋ/ noun [U] clothes, sheets, and similar things that are being washed or have been washed, or when you wash these **çamaşır** *I'm doing the washing this morning.* ○ *He does his own washing and ironing.*

'washing ma,chine noun [C] a machine that washes clothes **çamaşır makinası**

'washing ,powder UK (US **laundry detergent**) noun [C] a soap in the form of a powder that is used to wash clothes **çamaşır tozu, çamaşır deterjanı**

washing-up /ˌwɒʃɪŋˈʌp/ noun [U] UK when you wash the dishes, pans, and other things you have used for cooking and eating a meal **bulaşık yıkama** *He was doing the washing-up.*

,washing-'up ,liquid UK (US **dish soap**) noun [C, U] a thick liquid soap used to wash pans, plates, knives and forks, etc **bulaşık deterjanı**

washout /'wɒʃaʊt/ noun [no plural] informal an event that fails badly **fiyasko, tam bir başarısızlık** *No one came to the fete - it was a complete washout.*

washroom /'wɒʃruːm/ noun [C] mainly US a room where you can go to the toilet or wash your hands and face **tuvalet, banyo**

wasn't /'wɒzᵊnt/ short for was not **was not' fiil yapısının kısa yazılışı** *I wasn't hungry this morning.*

wasp /wɒsp/ noun [C] a flying insect with a thin, black and yellow body **eşek arısı** *a wasp sting*

wastage /'weɪstɪdʒ/ noun [U] when you waste something **israf, savurganlık** *fuel wastage*

a waste **of** sth • a waste **of effort/money/time** • **household/nuclear/toxic** waste • waste **disposal** • **go to** waste

o▪**waste**¹ /weɪst/ noun **1** [U, no plural] a bad use of something useful, such as time or money, when there is a limited amount of it **israf, kayıp, ziyan** *Meetings are a* ***waste of time.*** ○ *They throw away loads of food - it's such a waste.* ○ *a waste of energy/resources* **2** [U] things that are not wanted, especially what remains after you have used something **artık, artık madde, döküntü, çöp** *household/nuclear waste* **3 go to waste** to not be used **boşa gitmek, ziyan olmak, heder olmak** *I hate to see good food go to waste.*

o▪**waste**² /weɪst/ verb [T] **1** to use too much of something or use something badly when there is a limited amount of it **israf etmek, boşa yere harcamak, çar çur etmek** *I don't want to waste any more time so let's start.* ○ *Why waste your money on things you don't need?* **2 be wasted on sb** to be clever or of high quality in a way that someone will not understand or enjoy **fazla olmak, ziyan olmak, değerini anlamaz olmak;** ...

dan/den yüksek olmak *Good coffee is wasted on Joe - he prefers instant.*

waste away phrasal verb to become thinner and weaker **giderek zayıflamak, eriyip gitmek, tükenmek**

waste³ /weɪst/ adjective [always before noun] Waste material is not now needed and can be got rid of. **atık** *waste paper*

wasteful /'weɪstfᵊl/ adjective using too much of something, or using something badly when there is a limited amount of it **savurgan, müsrif**

wasteland /'weɪstlænd/ noun [C, U] an area of land that cannot be used in any way **çorak/bomboş/işe yaramaz arazi**

'wastepaper ,basket UK (US **wastebasket**) noun [C] a container that is used inside buildings for putting rubbish such as paper into **çöp kutusu/kovası**

o▪**watch**¹ /wɒtʃ/ verb **1** LOOK AT [I, T] to look at something for a period of time **seyretmek, izlemek, bakmak** *I watched him as he arrived.* ○ *The kids are watching TV.* ○ *I want to watch the news* (= programme on television). **2** BE CAREFUL [T] to be careful about something **dikkatli olmak, göz kulak olmak, dikkat etmek** *She has to watch what she eats.* ○ *Watch how you cross the road!* **3** GIVE ATTENTION TO [T] to give attention to a situation which is changing **yakından izlemek, dikkatle takip etmek** *We'll be watching the case with interest.* ↪See also: bird-watching, watch your **step**¹.

watch out phrasal verb used to tell someone to be careful because they are in danger **dikkat etmek, dikkatli olmak** *Watch out! There's a car coming!* ○ *Drivers were told to watch out for black ice on the road.*

watch over sb phrasal verb to look after someone and protect them if it is necessary **bakmak, ilgilenmek, göz kulak olmak**

wear a watch • **glance at/look at** your watch

o▪**watch**² /wɒtʃ/ noun **1** [C] a small clock on a strap that you fasten round your wrist (= lower arm) **kol saati** *I don't* ***wear a watch.*** **2** [U, no plural] when you watch or give attention to something or someone, especially to make sure nothing bad happens **izleme, gözleme, takip etme** *We're* ***keeping a*** *close* ***watch*** *on the situation.*

watch

watchdog /'wɒtʃdɒg/ noun [C] an organization whose job is to make sure that companies behave legally and provide good services **(hukuk) denetçi, gözcü**

watchful /'wɒtʃfᵊl/ adjective careful to notice things and ready to deal with problems **dikkatli, uyanık, tetikte** *They were playing outside under the* ***watchful*** *eye of a teacher.*

watchword /'wɒtʃwɜːd/ noun [no plural] a word or phrase that describes the main ideas or most important part of something **parola, slogan** *As regards fashion, the watchword this season is simplicity.*

o▪**water**¹ /'wɔːtəʳ/ noun [U] **1** the clear liquid that falls from the sky as rain and that is in seas, lakes, and rivers **su** *hot/cold water* ○ *a drink of water* **2** (also **waters**) an area in the sea or in a river or lake **su, deniz, nehir; göl** *coastal waters* **3 be in deep water** to be in a difficult situation which is hard to deal with **başı belada olmak, sıkıntıda olmak, zor durumda olmak** *They* *tried to adopt a baby illegally and ended up in very deep water.* ● **4 be (like) water off a duck's back** If criticisms, insults, etc are like water off a duck's back to you, they do not affect you at all. **etki etmemek, tınmamak, aldırış etmemek, etkilememek; umurunda bile olmamak** *She calls him lazy and useless, but it's like water off a duck's back.* ⊃See also: **drinking water, mineral water, tap water.**

water² /'wɔːtəʳ/ *verb* **1** [PLANTS] [T] to pour water over plants **sulamak 2** [MOUTH] [I] If food makes your mouth water, it makes you want to eat it, sometimes making your mouth produce liquid. **ağzını sulandırmak** *The smells from the kitchen are making my mouth water.* **3** [EYES] [I] If your eyes water, they produce liquid because something is hurting them. **gözleri sulanmak** *The smoke was making my eyes water.*

water sth down *phrasal verb* **1** to add water to a drink, especially an alcoholic drink **su katmak, su ilave etmek, sulandırmak 2** to make a plan or idea less extreme, usually so that people will accept it **yumuşatmak, hafifletmek, etkisini azaltmak, sulandırmak**

watercolour *UK* (*US* **watercolor**) /'wɔːtəˌkʌləʳ/ *noun* [C] a type of paint that is mixed with water, or a picture made with this paint **suluboya**

'**water ˌcooler** *noun* [C] a machine for providing cool drinking water, usually in an office or other public place **soğuk su makinası; sebil**

watercress /'wɔːtəkres/ *noun* [U] a small, strong-tasting plant that is eaten in salads **su teresi**

waterfall /'wɔːtəfɔːl/ *noun* [C] a stream of water that flows from a high place, often to a pool below **şelale**

waterfront /'wɔːtəfrʌnt/ *noun* [C] a part of a town which is next to the sea, a lake, or a river **sahil, su kenarı, kıyı, yalı** *waterfront restaurants*

waterhole /'wɔːtəhəʊl/ *noun* [C] a small pool of water in a dry area where animals go to drink **su çukuru, su birikintisi**

'**watering ˌcan** *noun* [C] a container used for watering plants in the garden **süzgeçli kova, bahçe sulama tenekesi**

waterlogged /'wɔːtəlɒgd/ *adjective* Waterlogged land is too wet. **sularla kaplanmış, sular altında**

watermark /'wɔːtəmɑːk/ *noun* [C] a pattern or picture on paper, especially paper money, which you can only see when a strong light is behind it **filgran; kağıt paraların dokusunda bulunan ancak ışığa tutulunca görülebilen resim/şekil vb.**

watermelon /'wɔːtəˌmelən/ *noun* [C, U] a large, round, green fruit that is pink inside with a lot of black seeds **karpuz**

waterproof /'wɔːtəpruːf/ *adjective* Waterproof material or clothing does not let water through. **su geçirmez** *a waterproof sleeping bag*

waters /'wɔːtəz/ *noun* [plural] the part of a sea around the coast of a country that legally belongs to that country **kara suları**

watershed /'wɔːtəʃed/ *noun* [no plural] an important event after which a situation completely changes **dönüm noktası** *The discovery marked a watershed in the history of medicine.*

water-skiing /'wɔːtəskiːɪŋ/ *noun* [U] a sport in which someone is pulled behind a boat while standing on skis (= long, narrow pieces of wood or plastic fastened to the feet) **su kayağı**

watertight /'wɔːtətaɪt/ *adjective* **1** Something that is watertight prevents any water from entering it. **su geçirmez, su sızdırmaz 2** A watertight reason or excuse is one that no one can prove is false. **su götür-**

mez, **sağlam, mükemmel; aksi ispat edilemez** *a watertight alibi*

waterway /'wɔːtəweɪ/ *noun* [C] a river or canal (= river made by people, not nature) which people can use to travel along **su yolu, su kanalı**

watery /'wɔːtᵊri/ *adjective* **1** made with too much water **sulu** *watery soup* **2** Watery eyes are wet with tears. **gözü yaşlı, sulu**

watt /wɒt/ (*written abbreviation* **W**) *noun* [C] a unit for measuring electrical power **elektrik akımı ölçüm birimi, vat** *a 60 watt light bulb*

wave

a wave   She's waving.

o-**wave¹** /weɪv/ *verb* **1** [I] to raise your hand and move it from side to side in order to attract someone's attention or to say goodbye **el sallamak** *Wave goodbye to Grandma.* ○ *She waved at him.* **2 wave sb in/on/ through, etc** to show which way you want someone to go by moving your hand in that direction **el sallayarak işaret etmek/yönlendirmek/sevketmek** *The police waved him on.* **3** [I, T] (*also* **wave about/around**) to move from side to side in the air or make something move this way **sallamak, sallanmak** *The long grass waved in the breeze.* ○ *He started waving his arms about wildly.*

wave sth aside *phrasal verb* to refuse to consider what someone says **dikkate almamak, bir kenara itmek; terslemek** *She waved aside all my objections.*

wave sb off *phrasal verb* to wave to someone as they are leaving in order to say goodbye **el sallamak, el sallayarak yolcu etmek** *We went to the station to wave him off.*

o-**wave²** /weɪv/ *noun* [C] **1** [WATER] a line of higher water that moves across the surface of the sea or a lake **dalga** *I could hear the waves crashing against the rocks.* **2** [GROUP] a group of people or things that arrive or happen together or in a short period of time **(insan) dalga** *There has been a wave of kidnappings in the region.* ○ *Another wave of refugees is arriving at the border.* **3 a wave of hatred/enthusiasm/sadness, etc** when you suddenly feel an emotion **nefret/coşku/ üzüntü vb. dalgası** *She felt a sudden wave of sadness.* **4** [HAND] when you raise your hand and move it from side to side in order to attract someone's attention or say goodbye **el sallama** *She gave a little wave as the train left.* **5** [ENERGY] a piece of sound, light, or other energy that travels up and down in a curved pattern **(ses, ışık, enerji) dalga/dalgası** *a radio wave* ⊃See also: **new wave, tidal wave.**

wavelength /'weɪvleŋθ/ *noun* [C] **1** the length of radio wave used by a radio company for broadcasting its programmes **dalga boyu 2** the distance between one sound or light wave, etc and the next **dalga boyu 3 be on the same wavelength** If two people are on the same

W

wavelength, they have the same way of thinking and it is easy for them to understand each other. **aynı görüşte/kafada/anlayışta olmak**

waver /'weɪvər/ verb [I] **1** to start to be uncertain about a belief or decision **tereddüt etmek, kararsızlık göstermek, duraksamak** *Her support for him never wavered.* ○ *I'm wavering between the blue shirt and the red.* **2** to shake slightly or lose strength **sallanmak, titremek, kıpırdamak** *His voice wavered and I thought he was going to cry.*

wavy /'weɪvi/ adjective with slight curves **dalgalı, kıvrım kıvrım** *wavy hair*

wax¹ /wæks/ noun [U] a solid substance that becomes soft when warm and melts easily, often used to make candles **bal mumu**

wax² /wæks/ verb [T] **1** to put wax on something, especially to make it shiny **cilâlamak, cilâ sürmek** *They cleaned and waxed my car.* **2** If you wax your legs, you remove the hair from them by using wax. **ağda yapmak; bacaktaki kılları temizlemek**

○▪**way¹** /weɪ/ noun **1** [METHOD] [C] how you do something **yol, usül, yöntem** [+ to do sth] *I must find a way to help him.* ○ [+ of + doing sth] *We looked at various ways of solving the problem.* ○ [+ (that)] *It was the way that she told me that I didn't like.* **2** [ROUTE] [C] the route you take to get from one place to another **yol** [usually singular] *Is there another way out of here?* ○ *I must buy a paper on the way home.* ○ *Can you find your way back to my house?* ○ *I took the wrong road and lost my way* (= got lost). **3 make your way to/through/towards, etc** to move somewhere, often with difficulty **güçlükle yolunu açarak ilerlemek** *We made our way through the shop to the main entrance.* **4 be on her/my/its, etc way** to be arriving soon **yolda olmak, geliyor olmak** *Apparently she's on her way.* **5 in/out of the/sb's way** in/not in the area in front of someone that they need to pass or see through **önünde/yolunda ol(ma)mak** *I couldn't see because Bill was in the way.* ○ *Sorry, am I in your way?* ○ *Could you move out of the way, please?* **6 a third of the way/most of the way, etc** used to say how much of something is completed **üçte birinde/ çoğunda vb.** *A third of the way through the film she dies.* **7 get in the way of sth/sb** to prevent someone from doing or continuing with something **önüne geçmek, engellemek, mani olmak** *Don't let your new friends get in the way of your studies.* **8 be under way** to be already happening **devam etmekte/ilerlemekte olmak** *Building work is already under way.* **9 give way (to sb/sth) a** [ALLOW] to allow someone to get what they want, or to allow something to happen after trying to prevent it **teslim olmak, boyun eğmek, razı olmak** *The boss finally gave way when they threatened to stop work.* **b** [TRAFFIC] *(US yield) UK* to allow other vehicles to go past before you move onto a road **yol vermek 10 give way to sth** to change into something else **dönüşmek; ...a/e dönmek; değişmek; yol vermek** *Her excitement quickly gave way to horror.* **11 give way** If something gives way, it falls because it is not strong enough to support the weight on top of it. **kırılmak, kopmak, çökmek, bel vermek** *Suddenly the ground gave way under me.* **12 get sth out of the way** to finish something **bitirmek, tamamlamak, sona erdirmek** *I'll go shopping when I've got this essay out of the way.* **13** [DIRECTION] [C] a direction something faces or travels **yön, yol, taraf** *This bus is going the wrong way.* ○ *Which way up does this picture go* (= which side should be at the top)? ○ *(UK) He always wears his baseball cap the wrong way round* (= backwards). **14** [SPACE/TIME] [no plural] an amount of space or time **(zaman, mesafe) uzaklık** *We're a long way from home.* ○ *The exams are still a long way away/off.*

15 make way to move away so that someone or something can pass **yol vermek, yol açmak 16 make way for sth** If you move or get rid of something to make way for something new, you do so in order to make a space for the new thing. **yerine yeni bir şey yapmak için yer açmak/değişiklik yapmak** *They knocked down the old houses to make way for a new hotel.* **17 in a way/in many ways** used to say that you think something is partly true **bir bakıma, bir anlamda; bir çok bakımdan** *In a way his behaviour is understandable.* **18 in no way** not at all **hiç yolu yok, olmaz, hiçte** *This is in no way your fault.* **19 there's no way** informal If there is no way that something will happen, it is certainly not allowed or not possible. **ne yaparsan yap; ne olursa olsun; mutlaka** *There's no way that dog's coming in the house.* **20 No way!** informal certainly not **Kesinlikle hayır!', 'Hiç yolu yok!' ** *"Would you invite him to a party?" "No way!"* **21 get/have your (own) way** to get what you want, although it might upset other people **başkalarını üze de istediğini elde etmek** *She always gets her own way in the end.* **22 in a big/small way** informal used to describe how much or little you do a particular thing **büyük/küçük/ ufak çapta/ölçekte** *They celebrate birthdays in a big way.* **23 a/sb's way of life** the way someone lives **yaşam tarzı; hayat biçimi** *Violence has become a way of life there.* **24 by the way** used when you say something that does not relate to what is being discussed **aklıma gelmişken, bu arada, sırası gelmişken; haa** *Oh, by the way, my name's Julie.* ● **25 go out of your way to do sth** to try very hard to do something pleasant for someone **...zahmetine girmek; özel bir çaba sarfetmek** *In a week not of his way to make us feel welcome.* ● **26 rub sb up the wrong way** *UK (US rub sb the wrong way)* informal to annoy someone without intending to **istemeden birini rahatsız etmek/üzmek** ↪See also: the Milky Way.

way² /weɪ/ adverb informal used to emphasize how extreme something is **hayli, epey, oldukça** *The room was way too hot.* ○ *He's in second place and he's way behind/off.*

,way 'out noun [C] **1** *UK (UK/US exit)* a door that takes you out of a building **çıkış, çıkış kapısı 2** a way of avoiding doing something unpleasant **kaçış yolu, çıkış şekli, kurtuluş yolu** *I'm supposed to be going to this meeting at 2.00 and I'm looking for a way out.*

wayside /'weɪsaɪd/ noun **fall by the wayside** to fail to complete something or be completed **tamamlayamamak, başa çıkamamak, başarılı olamamak** *Many students fall by the wayside during their first year at college.*

wayward /'weɪwəd/ adjective literary behaving badly in a way that causes trouble for other people **ters, sağı solu belli olmayan, dik başlı, inatçı**

WC /,dʌblju:'si:/ noun [C] *UK abbreviation for* water closet: a toilet, especially in a public place **tuvalet**

○▪**we** strong form /wi:/ weak form /wi/ pronoun **1** used as the subject of the verb when the person speaking or writing is referring to themselves and one or more other people **biz** *My wife and I both play golf and we love it.* **2** people generally **biz** *The world in which we live is very different.*

○▪**weak** /wi:k/ adjective **1** [BODY] not physically strong **zayıf, güçsüz, mecalsiz** *He felt too weak to sit up.* ○ *The children were weak with/from hunger.* **2** [CHARACTER] not powerful, or not having a strong character **zayıf karakterli, zayıf, iradesiz, güçsüz** *a weak government/leader* **3** [LIKELY TO FAIL] likely to fail **zayıf, yetersiz** *a weak economy* ○ *a weak team* **4** [LIKELY TO BREAK] likely to break and not able to support heavy things **zayıf, güçsüz, dayanıksız, sağlam olmayan** *a weak bridge* **5** [TASTE] A weak drink has little

taste or contains little alcohol. **keskin değil, düşük alkollü** *weak coffee/beer* **6** REASON A weak reason or excuse is one that you cannot believe because there is not enough proof to support it. **inandırıcı olmayan, zayıf, desteksiz 7** NOT GOOD not good at something **zayıf, iyi değil** *She reads well but her spelling is weak.* **8** SLIGHT difficult to see or hear **zor duyulan, zar zor görülen, zayıf, belli belirsiz** *He spoke in a weak voice.*
○ *a weak light* ● **weakly** *adverb* **zayıf, güçsüz bir durumda**

weaken /'wiːkᵊn/ *verb* [I, T] **1** to become less strong or powerful, or to make someone or something less strong or powerful **zayıfla(t)mak, güçsüzleş(tir)mek** *A number of factors have weakened the economy.* **2** to become less certain or determined about a decision, or to make someone less determined **gittikçe önemini yitirmek, üzerinde fazla durmamak; ısrarcı olmamak** *I told him he wasn't having any more money but then I weakened.*

weakling /'wiːklɪŋ/ *noun* [C] someone who is physically weak **zayıf/cılız kimse, güçsüz kişi**

weakness /'wiːknəs/ *noun* **1** [U] when someone or something is not strong or powerful **zayıflık, düşkünlük, zaaf** *Asking for help is not a sign of weakness.* **2** [C] a particular part or quality of something or someone that is not good **zayıflık, yetersizlik, zaafiyet** *What do you think are your weaknesses as a manager?* ○ *There are a number of weaknesses in this proposal.* **3 have a weakness for sth/sb** to like a particular thing or person very much **...a/e karşı zaafı olmak; çok istemek; dayanamamak** *She has a real weakness for ice cream.*

wealth /welθ/ *noun* **1** [U] when someone has a lot of money or valuable possessions **zenginlik, varlık, servet** *He enjoyed his new wealth and status.* **2 a wealth of sth** a large amount of something good **bolluk, çokluk, zenginlik, birikim** *a wealth of experience/information*

wealthy /'welθi/ *adjective* rich **zengin, varlıklı, servet sahibi** *a wealthy businessman/nation* ○ *Only the very wealthy can afford to live here.*

wean /wiːn/ *verb* [T] to start to give a baby food to eat instead of its mother's milk **(bebeği) sütten kesmek, memeden kesmek; artık emzirmemek**
wean sb off sth *phrasal verb* to make someone gradually stop using something that is bad for them **yavaş yavaş vazgeçmesini sağlamak, giderek soğutmak** *I'm trying to wean myself off fatty food generally.*

weapon .... İLE BİRLİKTE KULLANILAN KELİMELER

biological/chemical/nuclear weapons ● deadly/lethal/offensive weapons ● carry/possess a weapon

◦⁻**weapon** /'wepən/ *noun* [C] a gun, knife, or other object used to kill or hurt someone **silâh** *nuclear weapons* ○ *Police have found the murder weapon.* ● **weaponry** *noun* [U] weapons **silâhlar, silahların tümü**

◦⁻**wear**[1] /weəʳ/ *verb* past tense **wore**, past participle **worn**
1 DRESS [T] to have a piece of clothing, jewellery, etc on your body **giymek, takmak** *I wear jeans a lot of the time.* ○ *She wears glasses.* ○ *I don't usually wear make-up for work.* **2** FACE [T] to show a particular emotion on your face. **(yüzüne ifade/his) takınmak** *He was wearing a smile/frown.* **3** HAIR [T] to arrange or grow your hair in a particular way **saçlarını belli tarzda kestirmek/taramak** *She usually wears her hair in a ponytail.* **4** SPOIL [I, T] to become thin and damaged after being used a lot, or to make this happen **yıpranmak, köhnemek, eskimek** *The carpet is already starting to wear in places.* ○ *He keeps wearing holes in his socks.* ⊃See also: wear thin¹.

wear (sth) away *phrasal verb* to disappear after a lot of time or use, or to make something disappear in this way **bir zaman sonra kaybolmak; kullanılarak zamanla gözden kaybetmek** *The words on the gravestone had worn away completely.*
wear sb down *phrasal verb* to make someone feel tired and less able to argue **yormak, bitirmek, tüketmek** *Their continual nagging just wears me down.*
wear off *phrasal verb* If a feeling or the effect of something wears off, it gradually disappears. **zamanla kaybolmak/etkisini yitirmek/azalmak** *The anaesthetic is starting to wear off.*
wear on *phrasal verb* If a period of time wears on, it passes, especially slowly. **ağır ağır geçmek/ilerlemek; geçmek bilmemek** *As time wore on she became more and more unhappy.*
wear sb out *phrasal verb* to make someone extremely tired **fazlasıyla yormak, canına okumak, tüketmek** *All this walking is wearing me out.*
wear (sth) out *phrasal verb* to use something so much that it is damaged and cannot be used any more, or to become damaged in this way **eskimek/eskitmek; yıpratmak** *He's already worn out two pairs of shoes this year.*

wear[2] /weəʳ/ *noun* [U] **1** (*also* **wear and tear**) damage that happens to something when it is used a lot **yıpranma, eskime** *The furniture is already showing signs of wear.* **2** how much you wear a piece of clothing **giyme, takma** *These clothes are not for everyday wear.* **3 be the worse for wear** to be in a bad state or condition **çok eskimiş/yıpranmış/bitkin/bitik olmak** *He looked a little worse for wear this morning.*

-wear /weəʳ/ *suffix* used at the end of words that describe a particular type of clothes **...giysisi/elbisesi anlamında sonek** *menswear/swimwear*

wearing /'weərɪŋ/ *adjective* making you tired or annoyed **yorucu, cansıkıcı**

weary /'wɪəri/ *adjective* **1** tired **yorgun, bitkin, bezgin** *You look weary, my love.* **2 weary of sth/sb** bored with something or someone **...dan/den yorulmak/bıkmak/bezmek; canına tak etmek** *She grew weary of the children and their games.* ● **wearily** *adverb* **bezgin bir şekilde** ● **weariness** *noun* [U] **yorgunluk**

weasel /'wiːzᵊl/ *noun* [C] a small animal with a long body that kills and eats other small animals **gelincik, sansar**

weather .... İLE BİRLİKTE KULLANILAN KELİMELER

bad/cold/good/hot/stormy/warm/wet weather ● weather brightens up/improves/worsens

◦⁻**weather**[1] /'weðəʳ/ *noun* [U] **1** the temperature or conditions outside, for example if it is hot, cold, sunny, etc **hava, hava durumu** *The flight was delayed because of bad weather.* **2 be/feel under the weather** to feel ill **keyifsiz/rahatsız/hasta olmak**

weather[2] /'weðəʳ/ *verb* [T] to deal with a difficult situation or difficult conditions **zor koşulları yenmek/atlatmak, halletmek, üstesinden gelmek** *to weather criticism/a recession*

weathered /'weðəd/ *adjective* looking rough and old **aşınmış, yıpranmış** *a weathered face*

'weather ,forecast *noun* [C] a description of what the weather will be like **hava tahmini**

weave /wiːv/ *verb* **1 weave in and out; weave through** *past* **weaved** to go somewhere by moving around a lot of things **zikzak yaparak ilerlemek, sağa sola çarparak gitmek** *to weave in and out of the traffic* ○ *to weave through the crowd* **2** [I, T] *past tense* **wove**, *past participle* **woven** to make cloth on a machine

w

by crossing threads under and over each other **doku-mak, örmek**

o~**web** /web/ *noun* [C] **1** a type of net made by a spider (= small creature with eight legs) to catch other insects **örümcek ağı** *a spider's web* **2 the Web** (*also* **the World Wide Web**) part of the Internet that consists of all the connected websites (= pages of text and pictures) **web; bağlı web sayfalarını içeren internet bölümü** ⊃See study page **The Web and the Internet** on page Centre 36.

'**web ad,dress** (*US* 'web ,address) *noun* [C] an email or website address **web adresi** ⊃See study page **The Web and the Internet** on page Centre 36.

'**web ,browser** *noun* [C] a computer program which allows you to look at pages on the Internet **internet tarayıcısı**

webcam /'webkæm/ *noun* [C] a camera which records moving pictures and sound and allows these to be shown on the Internet as they happen **bilgisayar kamerası**

webcast /'webkɑːst/ *noun* [C] a broadcast made on the Internet **internetten yayın**

'**web ,page** *noun* [C] a part of a website that can be read on a computer screen **internet sayfası** ⊃See study page **The Web and the Internet** on page Centre 36.

o~**website** /'websaɪt/ *noun* [C] an area on the Web (= computer information system) where information about a particular subject, organization, etc can be found **internet sitesi** ⊃See study page **The Web and the Internet** on page Centre 36.

o~**we'd** /wiːd/ **1** *short for* we had **we had' fiil yapısının kısa yazılışı** *By the time she arrived we'd eaten.* **2** *short for* we would **we would' fiil yapısının kısa yazılışı** *We'd like two tickets for the three o'clock show, please.*

Wed (*also* **Weds**) *written abbreviation for* Wednesday **çarşamba, çarşamba günü**

wedding ...... İLE BİRLİKTE KULLANILAN KELİMELER

go to/be invited to/plan a wedding ● at a wedding ● sb's wedding to sb ● sb's wedding day ● a wedding dress/guest/present/reception/ring

o~**wedding** /'wedɪŋ/ *noun* [C] an official ceremony at which a man and woman get married **düğün, nikâh töreni** *We're going to a wedding on Saturday.* ○ *a wedding dress/ring* ⊃See also: **golden wedding.**

wedge¹ /wedʒ/ *noun* [C] a piece of something that is thin at one end and thicker at the other **kama, takoz** *a big wedge of cheese*

wedge² /wedʒ/ *verb* [T] **1 wedge sth open/shut** to use a wedge or similar shaped object to keep a door or window firmly open or closed **araya takoz/kama koyarak açmak/kapamak** *The room was hot so I wedged the door open.* **2** to push something into a narrow space **sıkıştırmak, sabitleştirmek, tespit etmek** *I was wedged between Andy and Pete in the back of the car.*

o~**Wednesday** /'wenzdeɪ/ (*written abbreviation* **Wed, Weds**) *noun* [C, U] the day of the week after Tuesday and before Thursday **çarşamba, çarşamba günü**

wee¹ /wiː/ *noun* [no plural] *mainly UK informal* when you urinate **idrar, çiş** *to have a wee* ○ *I need a wee.* ● **wee** *verb* [I] **weeing,** *past* **weed** **idrar yapmak**

wee² /wiː/ *adjective* small, usually used by Scottish speakers **küçücük, azıcık, ufacık, minnacık** *a wee girl*

weed¹ /wiːd/ *noun* [C] a wild plant that you do not want to grow in your garden **yabani ot, zararlı ot, ayrık otu** *Dandelions are common weeds.*

weed² /wiːd/ *verb* [I, T] to remove wild plants from a garden where they are not wanted **yabani otları/ayrık otlarını temizlemek**

weed sb/sth out *phrasal verb* to get rid of people or things that you do not want from a group **ayıklamak, temizlemek, seçip ayırmak; atmak, çıkarmak** *The government plans to weed out bad teachers.*

weedy /'wiːdi/ *adjective UK informal* thin and weak **zayıf, sıska, bir deri bir kemik** *He looks too weedy to be an athlete.*

o~**week** /wiːk/ *noun* **1** [C] a period of seven days **hafta** *last week/next week* ○ *I've got three exams this week.* ○ *We get paid every week.* **2 the week** the five days from Monday to Friday when people usually go to work or school **iş günleri, çalışma günleri** *I don't go out much during the week.*

weekday /'wiːkdeɪ/ *noun* [C] one of the five days from Monday to Friday, when people usually go to work or school **iş günü** *This road is very busy on weekdays.*

o~**weekend** /ˌwiːk'end/ⓤ /'wiːkend/ *noun* [C] **1** Saturday and Sunday, the two days in the week when many people do not work **hafta sonu** *Are you doing anything this weekend?* ○ *I'm going home for the weekend.* **2 at the weekend** *UK* (*US* **on the weekend**) on Saturday or Sunday **hafta sonunda** *He's going to a football match at the weekend.*

weekly /'wiːkli/ *adjective, adverb* happening once a week or every week **haftada bir, haftada bir olan** *a weekly newspaper* ○ *We're paid weekly.*

weep /wiːp/ *verb* [I, T] *past* **wept** *literary* to cry, usually because you are sad **ağlamak, göz yaşı dökmek**

o~**weigh** /weɪ/ *verb* **1** weigh 200g/75 kg/10 stone, etc to have a weight of 200g/75 kg/10 stone, etc **...çekmek, ...gelme, ...ağırlığında olmak** *How much do you weigh?* **2** [T] to measure how heavy someone or something is **tartmak** *Can you weigh that piece of cheese for me?* ○ *She weighs herself every day.* **3** [T] (*also UK* **weigh up**) to consider something carefully, especially in order to make a decision **ölçüp biçmek, tartmak** *The jury must weigh the evidence.* ○ *He needs to weigh up the pros and cons of going to college.*

weigh sth against sth *phrasal verb* to judge which of two things is more important before making a decision **tartmak, kıyaslamak; birini diğeriyle tartmak** *The advantages have to be weighed against the possible disadvantages.*

be weighed down by/with sth *phrasal verb* **1** to be carrying or holding too much **çok fazla şey taşıyor/tutuyor olmak** *She was weighed down with shopping bags.* **2** to be very worried about something **kaygılanmak, endişe duymak, üzülmek** *be weighed down by problems/debts*

weigh on/upon sb/sth *phrasal verb* If a problem or responsibility weighs on you, it makes you worried or unhappy. **kaygılandırmak, üzmek, endişelendirmek** *Problems at work are weighing on me.*

weigh sth out *phrasal verb* to measure an amount of something **tartmak, tartıp ölçmek** *Weigh out 8 ounces of flour.*

weight ...... İLE BİRLİKTE KULLANILAN KELİMELER

gain/lose/put on weight ● carry/lift/support a weight ● average/excess/heavy/ideal/light weight

o~**weight** /weɪt/ *noun* **1** [AMOUNT] [U] how heavy someone or something is **ağırlık** *He's about average height and weight.* **2 lose weight** If someone loses weight, they become lighter and thinner. **kilo vermek** *I need to lose a bit of weight.* **3 put on/gain weight** If someone puts on weight or gains weight, they become heavier and fatter. **kilo almak, şişmanlamak 4** [HEAVINESS] [U, no plural] the quality of being heavy **ağırlık** *The shelf collapsed under the weight of the books.* **5** [OBJECT] [C] something that is heavy **yük, ağır şey** *You're not supposed to lift heavy weights after an operation.* **6 carry weight** to be considered important and effective in influencing someone **ağırlığı/önemi olmak; önemli/etkili olduğu değerlendirilmek** *His opinions carry a lot of weight with the scientific community.* ● **7 pull your weight** to work as hard as other people in a group **üzerine/payına düşeni yapmak** *The rest of the team complained that Sarah wasn't pulling her weight.* ● **8 throw your weight around** to behave as if you are more important or powerful than other people **otoritesini konuşturmak, efelik taslamak, gözdağı vermek** ● **9 a weight off your mind** when a problem which has been worrying you stops or is dealt with **iç ferahlaması; zihni meşgul eden sorunun ortadan kalkması ve rahatlama** *Finally selling that house was a weight off my mind.* ⟳See also: **paper weight.**

weighted /'weɪtɪd/ *adjective* **be weighted in favour of/towards/against sth** to give one group an advantage or disadvantage over other people ...**dan/den yana ağır basmak; avantaj vermek/vermemek** *The system is weighted in favour of families with young children.*

weights /weɪts/ *noun* [plural] heavy pieces of metal that you lift up and down to make your muscles stronger **ağırlıklar**

weighty /'weɪti/ *adjective* very serious and important **ağırlıklı, önemli ve ciddi** *The film deals with the weighty issues of religion and morality.*

weir /wɪəʳ/ *noun* [C] UK a low wall built across a river to control the flow of water **set, su bendi**

weird /wɪəd/ *adjective* very strange **çok acayip, garip, tuhaf** *I had a really weird dream last night.*

weirdo /'wɪədəʊ/ *noun* [C] *informal* a person who behaves strangely **acayip kişi, tuhaf insan**

welcome¹ /'welkəm/ *exclamation* used to greet someone who has just arrived somewhere **Hoş geldiniz!** *Welcome home!* ○ *Welcome to the UK.*

o⌐**welcome²** /'welkəm/ *verb* [T] **1** to greet someone who has arrived in a place **karşılamak, buyur etmek** *Both families were there to welcome us.* **2** to be pleased about something and want it to happen **hoşnut olmak, olmasını istemek/dilemek** *The decision was welcomed by everybody.* ○ *I would welcome your advice.*

welcome³ /'welkəm/ *adjective* **1** If something is welcome, people are pleased about it and want it to happen. **kabul gören, kabul edilen** *a welcome change* ○ *Your comments are very welcome.* ⟳Opposite **unwelcome.** **2 You're welcome.** used to be polite to someone who has thanked you **Rica ederim!', 'Bir şey değil!', 'Estağfurullah!', 'Teşekkür etmek yok!'** *"Thank you." "You're welcome."* **3 make sb (feel) welcome** to make a visitor feel happy and comfortable in a place by being kind and friendly to them **iyi karşılayıp memnun etmek, içtenlikle buyur etmek** *They made us very welcome in their home.* **4 be welcome to do sth** used to tell someone that they can certainly do something, if they want to **müsaade edilmiş olmak; izin verilmiş olmak; seve seve kabul edilmiş olmak** *Anyone who is interested is welcome to come along.* **5 be welcome to sth** used to tell someone that they can certainly have something, if they want it, because you do not **başının üstünde yeri olmak; memnuniyetle karşılıyor olmak**

welcome (noun) .... İLE BİRLİKTE KULLANILAN KELİMELER

get/be given a [big/friendly/warm, etc] welcome

welcome⁴ /'welkəm/ *noun* [no plural] **1** when someone is greeted when they arrive somewhere **karşılama** *He was given a warm* (= friendly) *welcome by his fans.* **2 outstay/overstay your welcome** to stay somewhere too long so that people want you to leave **misafirlikten öte geçmek; gereğinde fazla kalmak ve istenmemek; kendisine tanınan misafirlik süresini aşmak**

weld /weld/ *verb* [T] to join pieces of metal together by heating them until they almost melt and then pressing them together **kaynak yapmak**

welfare /'welfeəʳ/ *noun* [U] **1** Someone's welfare is their health and happiness. **sağlık afiyet; refah mutluluk; esenlik** *He is concerned about the welfare of young men in prison.* **2** US (UK social security) money paid by a government to people who are poor, ill, or who do not have jobs **sosyal yardım parası** *to be on welfare* (= getting welfare)

welfare 'state UK (US 'welfare ,state) *noun* [no plural] a system in which the government looks after and pays for people who are ill, old, or who cannot get a job **sosyal adaleti uygulayan devlet, toplumcu devlet; sosyal devlet düzeni; refah toplumunu savunan devlet**

o⌐**we'll** /wiːl/ *short for* we shall or we will **we shall veya we will** *fiil yapısının kısa yazılışı* *We'll be home on Friday.*

o⌐**well¹** /wel/ *adjective* [never before noun] better, best **1** healthy **sağlıklı, iyi** *to feel/look well* ○ *I'm not very well.* ○ *Are you feeling better now?* ⟳Opposite **unwell.** **2 all is well** everything is in a good or acceptable state **her şey çok güzel, her şey yolunda; tıkırında; saat gibi** *I hope all is well with Jack.* **3 be all very well** used to show that you do not agree with something or that you are annoyed about something **hepsi iyi de...; iyi güzel de...; iyi hoş da...; iyi hoş ama...** *It's all very well for her to say everything's fine, she doesn't have to live here.* **4 be (just) as well** used to say that something might be a good thing to do or happen **iyi olur, isabet olur; Allah'tan, iyi ki** [+ (that)] *It was just as well that you left when you did.* ⟳See also: be **alive and kicking/well.**

o⌐**well²** /wel/ *adverb* better, best **1** in a successful or satisfactory way **başarılı ve tatminkâr bir şekilde** *I thought they played well.* ○ *He's doing well at school/ work.* **2** in a complete way or as much as possible **adam akıllı, tamamen veya mümkün olduğu kadar; iyice** *I know him quite well.* ○ *Stir the mixture well.* **3 as well** also ...**da, ...de, ...dahi, aynı zamanda, ayrıca (da)** *Are you going to invite Steve as well?* **4 as well as sth** in addition to something **ilaveten, ayrıca, yanısıra; ...gibi...de; ...kadar...da** *They have lived in the United States as well as Britain.* **5 may/might do well do sth** If you may/might as well do something, it will not spoil the situation if you do that thing. ...**de (pek) fark (etmez)di; ...de (pek) fark (etmeye) cekti de** *If we're not waiting for Karen, we might as well go now.* **6 may/might/could well** used to say that something is likely to be true ...**abilir/ebilir** *He could well be at Michelle's house.* **7 well above/ahead/below, etc** above/ahead/below, etc by a large amount **çok çok üstünde, ziyadesiyle üstünde; fazla; oldukça** *It was well after seven o'clock when we got home.* **8 can't/ couldn't very well do sth** used to say that something is not a suitable or practical thing to do **uygun/münasip olmama durumu; ...edememe; yapması uygun olmama; yapamam** *I couldn't very well tell her while he was there.* **9 Well done!** used to tell someone how pleased you are about their success **Aferin!', 'Bravo!'** *"I passed my exams." "Well done!"*

o⌐**well³** /wel/ *exclamation* **1** used at the beginning of a sentence to pause slightly or to express doubt or disagreement **cümle başında kullanılan 'eee; şeyy' gibi duraksama veya tereddüt belirten ifadeler** *"You'll* go, won't you?" "Well, I'm not sure." ○ "You said the food was bad." "Well, I didn't exactly say that." **2** (also **well, well**) used to express surprise **Allah Allah!', 'Vay vay vaay!', 'Oooo!', 'Eeee!'** Well, well, I never expected that to happen. **3 oh well** used to say that a situation cannot be changed although it might be disappointing **her neyse!; eh ne yapalım; aldırma; boş ver; ne yaparsın'** gibi bir durumun değiştirilemeyeceğini belirten ifadeler Oh well, it doesn't matter, I can always buy another one.

well[4] /wel/ noun [C] a deep hole in the ground from which you can get water, oil, or gas **kuyu, artezyen**

well-balanced /,wel'bælənst/ adjective **1 a well-balanced diet/meal** food which includes all the different types of food that the body needs to be healthy **iyi düzenlenmiş/dengeli diyet/yemek 2** Well-balanced people are calm and have good judgment. **dengeli, mantıklı, aklı başında, makul**

well-behaved /,welbɪ'heɪvd/ adjective behaving in a polite and quiet way **terbiyeli, uslu** a well-behaved child

well-being /'wel,biːɪŋ/ noun [U] when someone is healthy, happy, and comfortable **sağlık ve mutluluk, esenlik**

well-built /,wel'bɪlt/ adjective having a large, strong body **güçlü kuvvetli, boylu boslu, iri yapılı**

well-connected /,welkə'nektɪd/ adjective having important or powerful friends **sağlam/iyi/önemli dostları/bağlantıları olan**

well-done /,wel'dʌn/ adjective Meat that is well-done has been cooked completely and is not pink inside. **iyi pişmiş**

well-dressed /,wel'drest/ adjective wearing attractive, good quality clothes **iyi giyimli, şık, kaliteli giyinen**

well-earned /,wel'ɜːnd/ adjective **well-earned break/holiday/rest, etc** a rest that you deserve because you have been working hard **hak edilmiş, hakkı olan**

well-educated /,wel'edʒʊkeɪtɪd/ adjective having had a good education **iyi eğitimli**

well-established /,welɪ'stæblɪʃt/ adjective having existed for a long time **iyi oturmuş; kökleşmiş; yer etmiş; uzun zamandır varolan** a well-established tradition

well-fed /,wel'fed/ adjective having eaten enough good food **iyi beslenen** a well-fed cat

well-heeled /,wel'hiːld/ adjective having a lot of money, expensive clothes, etc **zengin, varlıklı, paralı, komprador**

wellies /'weliz/ UK informal (US **rubber boots**) noun [plural] large rubber boots that you wear outside when the ground is wet and dirty **lastik çizme** a pair of wellies

well-informed /,welɪn'fɔːmd/ adjective knowing a lot of useful information **bilgili, bilgi sahibi**

wellingtons /'welɪŋtənz/ noun [plural] UK wellies **lastik çizme**

well-intentioned /,welɪn'tenʃ³nd/ adjective trying to be helpful and kind but not improving a situation **iyi niyetli**

well-kept /,wel'kept/ adjective **1 a well-kept secret** something that has been carefully and successfully kept secret **iyi gizlenmiş/muhafaza edilmiş sır** The recipe is a well-kept secret. **2** tidy and organized **bakımlı, düzenli ve tertipli** a well-kept kitchen

well-known /,wel'nəʊn/ adjective famous **meşhur, iyi bilinen, tanınan** a well-known actor

well-meaning /,wel'miːnɪŋ/ adjective trying to be helpful and kind but not improving a situation **iyi niyetli, kötü maksat gütmeyen** well-meaning friends

well-off /,wel'ɒf/ adjective having a lot of money **zengin, varlıklı, hâli vakti yerinde** His parents are very well-off.

well-organized (also UK -ised) /,wel'ɔːg³naɪzd/ adjective working in an effective and successful way because of good organization **iyi düzenlenmiş; iyi organize edilmiş; iyi ve verimli çalışan**

well-paid /,wel'peɪd/ adjective earning a lot of money **iyi kazandıran; iyi kazanan, çok kazanan**

well-placed /,wel'pleɪst/ adjective in a very convenient position or in a position that gives someone an advantage **iyi yerleşmiş/yerleştirilmiş; tam yerinde; avantajlı durumda** [+ to do sth] She's very well-placed to find out what's going on.

well-read /,wel'red/ adjective having read a lot of books on different subjects **iyi okumuş, çok okuyan/okumuş; bilgili kültürlü**

well-to-do /,weltə'duː/ adjective old-fashioned having a lot of money **varlıklı, hâli vakti yerinde** a well-to-do family

well-wisher /'wel,wɪʃə^r/ noun [C] someone who wants another person to be happy, successful, or healthy **iyilik dileyen kimse** A crowd of well-wishers gathered outside the hospital.

Welsh /welʃ/ noun [U] **1** a language that is spoken in some parts of Wales **Galler'in bazı bölgelerinde konuşulan dil 2 the Welsh** the people of Wales **Galler halkı**

went /went/ past tense of go **gitmek' fiilinin geçmiş zaman hâli**

wept /wept/ past of weep **ağlamak' fiilinin geçmiş zaman hâli**

o⊷**we're** /wɪə^r/ short for we are **we are' fiil yapısının kısa yazılışı** Hurry! We're late!

o⊷**were** /wɜː^r/ past simple you/we/they of be **be' fiilinin çoğul şahıslar için geçmiş zaman hâli**

o⊷**weren't** /wɜːnt/ short for were not **were not' fiil yapısının kısa yazılışı** They weren't there.

o⊷**west, West**[1] /west/ noun [U] **1** the direction that you face to see the sun go down **batı, Batı yönü 2 the west** the part of an area that is further towards the west than the rest **batısı, batıya, batı taraf, batı bölge 3 the West** the countries of North America and western Europe **Kuzey Amerika ve batı Avrupa ülkeleri ● west** adjective the west coast of Ireland **batı ● west** adverb towards the west **batıya doğru** They lived in a village four miles west of Oxford.

the ,West 'End noun a part of central London that has a lot of shops, theatres, restaurants, etc **Londra'nın alışveriş merkezleri, tiyatrolar ve lokantaların bulunduğu Batı Kıyısı/Ucu**

westerly /'west³li/ adjective **1** towards or in the west **batıya, batıda** Senegal is the most westerly country in Africa. **2** A westerly wind comes from the west. **batıdan, batı yönünden; batıdan esen** westerly breezes

o⊷**western, Western**[1] /'westən/ adjective [always before noun] **1** in or from the west part of an area **batıda, batıdan; Batıda, Batıdan** western France **2** related to the countries of North America and western Europe **Kuzey Amerika ve batı Avrupa ülkelerine ilişkin** a Western diplomat

western[2] /'westən/ noun [C] a film or story that happens in the west of the US at the time when Europeans started living there **ABD'nin batısında olan olayları işleyen hikâye ve filmler**

westerner, Westerner /'westənə^r/ *noun* [C] someone who is from a country in North America or western Europe **batılı; batı Avrupalı veya Kuzey Amerikalı**

westernized (*also UK* -**ised**) /'westənaɪzd/ *adjective* having a culture like North America and western Europe **batılılaşmış** *Some Asian countries are becoming increasingly westernized.*

¸West 'Indian *adjective* belonging or relating to the West Indies **Batı Hint Adaları'na ilişkin/ait** *a West Indian island* ● **West Indian** *noun* [C] someone from the West Indies **Batı Hint Adaları**

the ¸West 'Indies *noun* [plural] a group of islands in the Caribbean Sea **Karayip Denizi'nde bir grup ada**

westward, westwards /'westwəd/, /'westwədz/ *adverb* towards the west **batıya doğru** *They were travelling westward.* ● **westward** *adjective* **batıya doğru**

∘⚹**wet**¹ /wet/ *adjective* **wetter, wettest 1** ⌈WATER⌉ covered in water or another liquid **ıslak** *a wet towel* ○ *We got soaking wet in the rain.* ○ *(UK) Look at you - you're wet through* (= very wet)*!* **2** ⌈RAIN⌉ raining **yağmurlu** *a wet and windy day* **3** ⌈NOT DRY⌉ not dry yet **nemli** *wet paint* **4** ⌈PERSON⌉ *UK informal* Someone who is wet has a weak personality. **zayıf kişilikli**

wet² /wet/ *verb* [T] **wetting**, *past* **wet, wetted 1 wet the bed/your pants/yourself, etc** to urinate in your bed or in your underwear without intending to **altını ıslatmak 2** to make something wet **ıslatmak**

'wet ¸suit *noun* [C] a piece of clothing covering the whole body that keeps you warm and dry when you are under water **dalgıç giysisi**

∘⚹**we've** /wi:v/ *short for* we have **we have' fiil yapısının kısa yazılışı** *We've bought a house.*

whack /wæk/ *verb* [T] *informal* to hit someone or something in a quick, strong way **çarpmak, dövmek,yumruk indirmek** *She whacked him on the head with her book.* ● **whack** *noun* [C] *informal* **vurma, çarpma**

whale /weɪl/ *noun* [C] a very large animal that looks like a large fish, lives in the sea and breathes air through a hole at the top of its head **balina**

whale

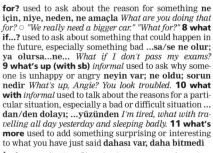

whaling /'weɪlɪŋ/ *noun* [U] hunting whales **balina avcılığı**

wharf /wɔːf/ *noun* [C] *plural* **wharves** /wɔːvz/ an area next to the sea or a river where goods can be put on or taken off ships **iskele, rıhtım**

∘⚹**what** /wɒt/ *pronoun*, *determiner* **1** ⌈INFORMATION⌉ used to ask for information about something **ne** *What's this?* ○ *What time is it?* ○ *What happened?* **2** ⌈THE THING⌉ used to refer to something without naming it **...dığı/dıkları (şeyi)** *I heard what he said.* ○ *Do you know what I mean?* ○ *What I like most about her is her honesty.* **3** ⌈NOT HEARD⌉ *informal* used when you have not heard what someone has said and you want them to repeat it. Some people think this use is not very polite. **(bir şey duyulmadığında, tekrar edilmesi istendiğinde) Ne?; Ne dedin?** *"Do you want a drink Tom?" "What?"* **4** ⌈REPLY⌉ *informal* used to ask what someone wants when they call you **ne, ne oldu; (kabaca) ne var** *"Hey Jenny?" "Yes, what?"* **5 what a/an ...** used to give your opinion, especially when you have strong feelings about something **ne kadar...; ne berbat..., ne...** *What a mess!* ○ *What an awful day!* **6** used to suggest something **ne dersin, '...maya/meye ne dersin, ... elim mi** *What about asking Martin to help?* **7 what ...**

for? used to ask about the reason for something **ne için, niye, neden, ne amaçla** *What are you doing that for?* ○ *"We really need a bigger car." "What for?"* **8 what if...?** used to ask about something that could happen in the future, especially something bad **...sa/se ne olur; ya olursa...ne...** *What if I don't pass my exams?* **9 what's up (with sb)** *informal* used to ask why someone is unhappy or angry **neyin var; ne oldu; sorun nedir** *What's up, Angie? You look troubled.* **10 what with** *informal* used to talk about the reasons for a particular situation, especially a bad or difficult situation **... dan/den dolayı; ...yüzünden** *I'm tired, what with travelling all day yesterday and sleeping badly.* **11 what's more** used to add something surprising or interesting to what you have just said **dahası var, daha bitmedi**

∘⚹**whatever** /wɒt'evə^r/ *adverb*, *pronoun*, *determiner* **1** ⌈ANYTHING⌉ anything or everything **ne her, ne olursa olsun** *Do whatever you want.* ○ *He eats whatever I put in front of him.* **2** ⌈NO DIFFERENCE⌉ used to say that what happens is not important because it does not change a situation **ne olursa olsun, her ne, hiç farketmez** *Whatever happens I'll still love you.* ○ *We'll support you, whatever you decide.* **3** ⌈QUESTION⌉ used to ask for information when you are surprised or angry about something **ne, nasıl bir şey, her ne ise** *Whatever do you mean?* **4** ⌈ANGRY⌉ *informal* something that you say when you are angry with someone who is asking you something **(kızgınlıkta) her neyse, hadi bakalım, tamam mı; oldu mu** *'Isabel, will you just listen when I'm talking to you?'* *'Whatever.'* **5 or whatever** or something similar **ya da ona benzer her hangi bir şey; veya benzeri şeyler** *The children are usually outside playing football or whatever.*

whatnot /'wɒtnɒt/ **and whatnot** *informal* and other things of a similar type **ve benzeri şeyler, aynı türden şeyler** *They sell cards and wrapping paper and whatnot.*

whatsoever /,wɒtsəʊ'evə^r/ (*also* **whatever**) *adverb* **no... whatsoever** none at all **hiç, hiç bir; hiç mi hiç, her-hangi bir** *There's no evidence whatsoever that she was involved.*

wheat /wiːt/ *noun* [U] a plant whose grain is used for making flour, or the grain itself **buğday**

∘⚹**wheel**¹ /wiːl/ *noun* **1** [C] a circular object fixed under a vehicle so that it moves smoothly over the ground **tekerlek, çark** *My bike needs a new front wheel.* **2 the wheel** a steering wheel (= circular object you turn to direct a vehicle) **direksiyon, direksiyon simidi** *You should drive with both hands on the wheel.* ○ *He fell asleep at the wheel* (= while driving). **3 reinvent the wheel** to waste time trying to create something that has been done before **önceden bilinen aynı şeyleri yaparak zaman kaybetmek** ⊃See also: Ferris wheel.

wheel² /wiːl/ *verb* **wheel sth around/into/to, etc** to push something that has wheels somewhere **tekerlekler üstünde gitmesini sağlamak; iterek bir yere götürmek** *He wheeled his bicycle into the garden.* **wheel around/round** *phrasal verb* to quickly turn around **birden çark etmek/dönmek** *She wheeled around to face him.*

wheelbarrow /'wiːl,bærəʊ/ *noun* [C] a big, open container with a wheel at the front and handles that is used to move things, especially around in a garden **el arabası**

wheelchair /'wiːlt͡ʃeə^r/ *noun* [C] a chair with wheels used by someone who cannot walk **tekerlekli sandalye**

wheeze /wiːz/ *verb* [I] to make a noisy sound when breathing because of a problem in your lungs **hırıltıyla solumak**

w

when 824 Important words to learn

o-**when**[1] /wen/ *adverb* used to ask at what time something happened or will happen **ne zaman** *When's your birthday?* ○ *When did he leave?* ○ *When are you going away?*

o-**when**[2] /wen/ *conjunction* **1** used to say at what time something happened or will happen **ne zaman, ne vakit** *I found it when I was cleaning out the cupboards.* ○ *We'll go when you're ready.* **2** although **rağmen; ... masına/mesine rağmen; ...dığı/diği/duğu halde** *Why are you doing this when I've asked you not to?*

whenever /wen'evə'/ *conjunction* every time or at any time **her zaman, her ne zaman, ne zaman olursa** *You can go whenever you want.* ○ *I try to help them out whenever possible.*

o-**where**[1] /weə'/ *adverb* used to ask about the place or position of someone or something **nerede** *Where does she live?* ○ *Where are my car keys?*

o-**where**[2] /weə'/ *conjunction* **1** at, in, or to a place or position **nereye, nereden, nerede** *He's not sure where they are.* ○ *I know where to go.* **2** relating to a particular part of a process or situation **...dığı/diği yer/yere/yerde** *We've now reached the point where we can make a decision.*

whereabouts[1] /,weərə'bauts/ *adverb* used to ask in what place or area someone or something is **nerelerde, nerelerde olduğu** *Whereabouts does he live?*

whereabouts[2] /'weərəbauts/ *noun* **sb's whereabouts** the place where someone or something is **birinin bulunduğu olduğu yer mahal** *His whereabouts are unknown.*

whereas /weə'ræz/ *conjunction* compared with the fact that **halbuki, oysa, ama** *His parents were rich, whereas mine had to struggle.*

whereby /weə'baı/ *adverb formal* by which **ki bununla, ki onun vasıtasıyla** *They've introduced a system whereby people share cars.*

wherein /weə'rın/ *adverb formal* in which **ki onun içinde, ...in bulunduğu**

whereupon /'weərəpɒn/ *conjunction formal* after which **bundan hemen sonra, bunun üzerine** *We decided to have a picnic, whereupon it started to rain.*

wherever[1] /weə'revə'/ *conjunction* **1** in or to any place or every place **her nereye/neresi/nerede** *You can sit wherever you like.* **2** **wherever possible** every time it is possible **her an mümkün** *We try to use natural fabrics wherever possible.*

wherever[2] /weə'revə'/ *adverb* used to ask in what situation or place something happened, especially when the person asking feels surprised **nereden, nasıl, ne şekilde, her nasıl, her nereden** *Wherever did you get that idea?*

wherewithal /'weəwıðɔːl/ *noun* **the wherewithal to do sth** the money, skills, or other things that are needed to do something **bir şeyin yapılması için gereken para, maharet ve diğer şeyler**

W o-**whether** /'weðə'/ *conjunction* **1** used to talk about a choice between two or more possibilities **iki veya daha çok olasılık arasındaki seçimden bahsederken; ...ıp/ip ...meyeceğin/mayacağını** *Someone's got to tell her, whether it's you or me.* ○ *I didn't know whether or not to go.* **2** if **eğer, şayet** *I wasn't sure whether you'd like it.*

whew /fju:/ *exclamation* used when you are happy that something is not going to happen, or when you are tired or hot **Üff!', 'Off!', 'Hay Allah!', 'Uf be!'**

o-**which** /wıtʃ/ *pronoun, determiner* **1** CHOICE used to ask or talk about a choice between two or more things **hangi, hangisi, hangisini** *Which of these do you like best?* ○ *Which way is it to the station?* ○ *I just don't know*

which one to choose. **2** REFERRING TO SOMETHING used at the beginning of a relative clause to show what thing is being referred to **ilgi zamiri olarak; ...ki** *These are principles which we all believe in.* **3** EXTRA INFORMATION used to give more information about something **ilave bilgi verirken bağımsız ara cümlecikle yine ilgi zamiri olarak kullanılır; ...ki** *The book, which includes a map, gives you all the information you need about Venice.* **4** GIVING OPINION used when you give an opinion about what you have just said **ilgi zamiri tamamının anlamına ilişkin fikir belirtirken; ...ki** *He took us both out for lunch, which I thought was very kind of him.*

whichever /wı'tʃevə'/ *pronoun, determiner* **1** used to say that what happens is not important because it does not change a situation **herhangi, hangi, her hangi, hangisi olursa olsun** *Whichever option we choose there'll be disadvantages.* ○ *It's a sad situation whichever way you look at it.* **2** any of a group of similar things **her hangisini, hangisi olursa, hangi** *Choose whichever bedroom you want.*

whiff /wıf/ *noun* [no plural] a smell which you only smell for a short time **hafif koku, esinti** *I just caught a whiff of garlic from the kitchen.*

o-**while**[1] /waıl/ (*also UK* **whilst** /waılst/) *conjunction* **1** DURING during the time that **iken, esnasında, sırasında** *I read a magazine while I was waiting.* ○ *I can't talk to anyone while I'm driving.* ○ *While you're away, I might decorate the bathroom.* **2** ALTHOUGH although ... **oysa; ...diği halde; ...e karşın** *And while I like my job, I wouldn't want to do it forever.* **3** COMPARING used to compare two different facts or situations **halbuki; iki farklı gerçeği/durumu kıyaslarken** *Tom is very confident while Katy is shy and quiet.*

while (noun) ...... İLE BİRLİKTE KULLANILAN KELİMELER

take/wait a while ● **after/for/in** a while ● **quite a** while ● **a short** while ● **a while ago**

o-**while**[2] /waıl/ *noun* **a while** a period of time **bir süre, biraz** *a long/short while* ○ *I'm going out for a while.*

while[3] /'waıl/ *verb*
while sth away *phrasal verb* to spend time in a relaxed way because you are waiting for something or because you have nothing to do **vakit geçirmek** *We played a few games to while away the time.*

whim /wım/ *noun* [C] when you suddenly want to do something without having a reason **geçici heves** *We booked the holiday on a whim.*

whimper /'wımpə'/ *verb* [I] to make quiet crying sounds because of fear or pain **mızıldamak, sızlanmak** *The dog was whimpering with pain.*

whimsical /'wımzık°l/ *adjective* unusual in a way that is slightly funny **(eğlenceli bir şekilde) garip, tuhaf, acayip** *a whimsical tale*

whine /waın/ *verb* [I] **1** to complain in an annoying way **sızlanmak, yakınmak, dertlenmek; dır dır etmek, mızmızlanmak** *She's always whining about something.* **2** to make a long, high, sad sound **inlemek** *The dog whined and scratched at the door.* ● **whine** *noun* [C] **şikayet, mızmızlanma**

whinge /wındʒ/ *verb* [I] **whingeing, whinging** *UK informal* to complain in an annoying way **sızlanıp/yakınıp/dertlenip durmak** *Oh, stop whingeing!* ● **whinge** *noun* [C] *UK He was just having a whinge.* **şikayet**

whip[1] /wıp/ *noun* [C] a long piece of leather fixed to a handle and used to hit an animal or person **kırbaç, kamçı**

whip[2] /wıp/ *verb* **whipping, past whipped 1** [T] to hit a person or animal with a whip **kırbaçlamak 2** [T] to make a food such as cream more solid by mixing it hard with a kitchen tool **çırpmak 3 whip (sth) away/off/out, etc** informal to move or make something move in a fast, sudden way **hızla/fırtına gibi çıkmak/çıkarmak; aniden fırlamak** *She opened the bag and whipped out her camera.*

whip up sth phrasal verb **1** to try to make people have strong feelings about something **kışkırtmak, kamçılamak, tahrik etmek** *to whip up enthusiasm/hatred* **2** to prepare food very quickly **çarçabuk hazırlayıvermek** *I could whip up a plate of spaghetti if you like.*

whir /wɜːʳ/ noun, verb whirring, past whirred US spelling of whirr **vınlama sesi, uğultu; vınlamak, uğuldamak**

whirl¹ /wɜːl/ verb [I, T] to move or make something move quickly round and round **fırıl fırıl dön(dür)mek**

whirl² /wɜːl/ noun [no plural] **1** when a lot of exciting or confusing things happen at the same time **telaş, hayhuy, baş dönmesi, zihin karışıklığı** *a whirl of activity* **2** a sudden turning movement **fırıl fırıl dönme, hızla dönme sesi 3 give sth a whirl** informal to try to do something, often for the first time **denemek, şans tanımak** *I've never danced salsa before but I'll give it a whirl.*

whirlpool /'wɜːlpuːl/ noun [C] an area of water that moves round and round very quickly **girdap, anafor, burgaç**

whirlwind¹ /'wɜːlwɪnd/ adjective **a whirlwind romance/visit/tour, etc** a relationship/visit, etc that only lasts a short time **çok kısa süren aşk/ziyaret/gezi**

whirlwind² /'wɜːlwɪnd/ noun **1 a whirlwind of sth** a lot of sudden activity, emotion, etc **aniden bindiren/gelişen faaliyet, duygu vb.** *a whirlwind of activity* **2** [C] a strong wind that moves round and round very quickly **hortum**

whirr UK (US whir) /wɜːʳ/ noun [no plural] a low, continuous sound **vınlama, vırlama, vızlama, parlama, uğultu** *the whirr of machinery* ● **whirr** UK (US whir) verb [I] **kısık fakat süregelen bir ses**

whisk¹ /wɪsk/ verb [T] **1 whisk sb away/off/into, etc** informal to take someone somewhere quickly **apar topar götürmek; derdest edip götürmek** *They whisked him off to the police station.* **2** to mix food such as eggs, cream, etc very quickly using a fork or whisk **çırpmak** *Whisk the mixture until smooth.*

whisk² /wɪsk/ noun [C] a kitchen tool made of wire that is used to mix eggs, cream, etc, or to make such food thicker **yumurta çırpacağı, çırpma teli** ⊃Orta kısımdaki renkli sayfalarına bakınız.

whisker /'wɪskəʳ/ noun [C] one of the long, stiff hairs that grows around the mouths of animals such as cats **bıyık, kedi bıyığı**

whiskers /'wɪskəz/ noun [plural] old-fashioned hairs growing on a man's face **sakal, bıyık**

whiskey /'wɪski/ noun [C, U] whisky in Ireland or the United States **viski**

whisky /'wɪski/ noun [C, U] a strong, alcoholic drink made from grain **viski**

o⊶**whisper** /'wɪspəʳ/ verb [I, T] to speak extremely quietly so that other people cannot hear **fısıldamak** *She whispered something to the girl sitting next to her.* ● **whisper** noun [C] **fısıltı**

whistle¹ /'wɪsl/ verb **1** [I, T] to make a sound by breathing air out through a small hole made with your lips or through a whistle **ıslık çalmak, ıslıkla söylemek** *Someone whistled at her as she walked past.* **2** [I] to produce a sound when air passes through a narrow space **ıslık çalmak, ıslık sesi çıkarmak, vınlamak** *He could hear the wind whistling through the trees.*

whistle² /'wɪsl/ noun [C] **1** a small, simple instrument that makes a high sound when you blow through it **düdük** *The referee blew the whistle to end the game.* **2** the sound made by someone or something whistling **ıslık, ıslık sesi**

o⊶**white¹** /waɪt/ adjective **1** COLOUR being the colour of snow or milk **beyaz** *a white T-shirt* ○ *white walls* ⊃Orta kısımdaki renkli sayfalarına bakınız. **2** PERSON Someone who is white has skin that is pale in colour. **solgun, beyaz** *He's described as a white man in his early thirties.* **3** OF WHITE PEOPLE relating to white people **beyazlara ilişkin** *the white community* **4** FACE having a pale face because you are ill or you are feeling shocked **(korkudan, şoktan) rengi kül gibi olmuş, sararmış; beti benzi atmış** *He was white with shock.* **5** COFFEE UK White coffee has milk or cream added to it. **sütlü** *Two coffees please, one black and one white.* **6** WINE White wine is a pale yellow colour. **(şarap) beyaz, beyaz şarap rengi** ● **whiteness** noun [U] ⊃See also: black¹ and white. **beyazlık**

o⊶**white²** /waɪt/ noun **1** COLOUR [C, U] the colour of snow or milk **beyaz renk** ⊃Orta kısımdaki renkli sayfalarına bakınız. **2** PERSON [C] a white person **beyaz, beyaz ırktan kimse** *For a long time, whites controlled the economy here.* **3** EGG [C] the part of an egg that is white when it is cooked **yumurta akı** *Mix the egg whites with the sugar.* ⊃See also: in black² and white.

whiteboard /'waɪtbɔːd/ noun [C] **1** (also interactive whiteboard) a white screen on which you can write with a special pen and which allows other people with computers to see what you have written **beyaz tahta 2** a large board with a white surface that teachers write on **beyaz tahta** ⊃Orta kısımdaki renkli sayfalarına bakınız.

white-collar /ˌwaɪtˈkɒləʳ/ adjective relating to work in an office or in a job that needs special knowledge and education **büroda çalışan, beyaz yakalı** *white-collar jobs/workers*

the 'White ˌHouse noun **1** the US president and government **Beyaz Saray; ABD başkanı ve hükümeti 2** the building that is the official home and offices of the US president **Beyaz Saray Binası** ● **White House** adjective *a White House spokesman* **Beyaz Saray**

ˌ**white 'lie** noun [C] a lie which is not important and is usually said to avoid upsetting someone **masum yalan, beyaz yalan, zararsız yalan**

ˌ**white 'meat** noun [U] a meat that is pale in colour, such as chicken **beyaz et**

whiten /'waɪtᵊn/ verb [I, T] to become white or to make something become white **beyazlamak, beyazlatmak**

ˌ**White 'Paper** noun [C] a government report in the UK giving information or suggestions on a subject **Parlamentoda sonradan tartışılmak üzere hazırlanmış resmi hükümet raporu** *a White Paper on employment*

whitewash /'waɪtwɒʃ/ noun [no plural] when the truth about a serious mistake, crime, etc is hidden from the public **gizleme, örtbas, hasıraltı** *The newspaper accused the government of a whitewash.* ● **whitewash** verb [T] **halktan saklamak, üstünü örtmek**

whizz (also whiz) /wɪz/ verb **whizz by/past/through, etc** informal to move somewhere very quickly **jet hızıyla**

whisper

harekét étmek; jet gibi gitmek *She whizzed down the street in her new sports car.*

whizzkid (*also* whizkid) /'wɪzˌkɪd/ *noun* [C] a young person who is very successful or good at doing something **harika çocuk, genç yetenek** *a computer whizzkid*

o⁻**who** /hu:/ *pronoun* **1** [NAME] used to ask about someone's name or which person or group someone is talking about **kim, kimi, kimler, kimleri** *Who told you?* ○ *Who's that?* **2** [WHICH PERSON] used at the beginning of a relative clause to show which person or group of people you are talking about **ki o...; ...an/en** *That's the man who I saw in the bank.* **3** [ADD INFORMATION] used to give more information about someone that you are talking about **ilgili daha fazla bilgi vermek için kullanılır** *My brother, who's only just seventeen, has already passed his driving test.*

o⁻**who'd** /hu:d/ **1** *short for* who had **who had' fiil yapısının kısa yazılışı** *I was reading about a man who'd sailed around the world.* **2** *short for* who would **Who would' fiil yapısının kısa yazılışı** *Who'd have thought we'd still be friends?*

whoever /hu:'evə^r/ *pronoun* **1** [WHICH PERSON] the person who **her kim/kimse** *Whoever broke the window will have to pay for it.* ○ *Could I speak to whoever is in charge please?* **2** [ANY PERSON] used to say that it is not important which person or group does something **her kimse, her kim olursa olsun** *Can whoever leaves last lock up, please?* **3** [SURPRISE] used to ask who a person is when expressing surprise **kim, kim olabilir** *Whoever could that be phoning at this time?* ○ *Whoever would believe such a ridiculous story?*

o⁻**whole¹** /həʊl/ *adjective* **1** [always before noun] complete, including every part **tüm, bütün, tümü, bütünü** *She spent the whole afternoon studying.* ○ *The whole family went to the show.* **2** [never before noun] as a single object and not in pieces **tümüyle, bütünüyle, bütünce** *The chick swallowed the worm whole.* つSee also: a whole new ball game, the whole world¹.

o⁻**whole²** /həʊl/ *noun* **1 the whole of sth** all of something **tamamı, tümü, bütünü** *His behaviour affects the whole of the class.* **2 as a whole** when considered as a group and not in parts **tüm olarak, bir bütün olarak** *The population as a whole is getting healthier.* **3 on the whole** generally **genel olarak, genellikle** *We've had a few problems, but on the whole we're very happy.*

wholefood /'həʊlfu:d/ *noun* [U] UK food that is as natural as possible, without artificial things added to it **tabi gıda, işlenip katkı maddesi katılmamış yiyecekler** *a wholefood shop*

wholehearted /ˌhəʊl'hɑːtɪd/ *adjective* **wholehearted agreement/approval/support, etc** complete agreement/approval/support, etc without any doubts **candan/içten/samimi antlaşma/onama/destek vb.** ● **wholeheartedly** *adverb* *I agree wholeheartedly.* **tüm kalbiyle**

wholemeal /'həʊlmiːl/ UK (UK/US whole wheat) *adjective* made using whole grains, or made from flour that contains whole grains **kepekli, kepekli undan yapılmış** *wholemeal bread/flour*

wholesale /'həʊlseɪl/ *adjective* **1** relating to products which are sold in large amounts, usually at a cheaper price **toptan, toptan satılan** *wholesale prices* **2** [always before noun] complete or affecting a lot of things, people, places, etc **geniş kapsamlı, toplu, büyük çapta, kökünden** *wholesale changes* ● **wholesale** *adverb* **toptan**

wholesaler /'həʊlˌseɪlə^r/ *noun* [C] a company that sells products in large amounts to shops which then sell them to customers **toptancı**

wholesome /'həʊls^əm/ *adjective* **1** Wholesome food is good for your health. **sağlıklı, sağlığa yararlı** **2** morally good **sağlıklı, yararlı, ahlâken iyi** *wholesome family entertainment*

whole ˌwheat (*also* UK wholemeal) *adjective* made using whole grains, or made from flour that contains whole grains **doygun tahıl, tam buğday** *whole wheat bread/flour*

o⁻**who'll** /hu:l/ *short for* who will **who will' fiil yapısının kısa yazılışı** *Who'll be at your party?*

wholly /'həʊlli/ *adverb* completely **tamamen, bütünüyle, bütün olarak** *His behaviour is wholly unacceptable.*

whom /hu:m/ *pronoun formal* used instead of 'who' as the object of a verb or preposition **kimi, kime** *I met a man with whom I used to work.*

whoop /wu:p/ *noun* [C] a loud, excited shout **bağırma, haykırma, çığlık atma** *He gave a loud whoop of delight.*

whooping cough /'hu:pɪŋˌkɒf/ *noun* [U] a serious children's disease in which a cough is followed by a 'whoop' noise **boğmaca**

whoops /wʊps/ *exclamation* used when you make a mistake or have or have a small accident **Eyvah!', 'Aman!' 'Ayy!', 'Hoop!'**

whopping /'wɒpɪŋ/ *adjective* [always before noun] *informal* extremely large **çok büyük, kocaman, okkalı** *a whopping 50 percent increase*

who're /'hu:ə^r/ *short for* who are **who are' fiil yapısının kısa yazılışı** *Who're the people we're going to see?*

whore /hɔː^r/ *noun* [C] an offensive word for someone whose job is having sex with people **fahişe, hayat kadını**

o⁻**who's** /hu:z/ **1** *short for* who is **who is' fiil yapısının kısa yazılışı** *Who's your new friend?* **2** *short for* who has **who has' fiil yapısının kısa yazılışı** *Who's been using my computer?*

o⁻**whose** /hu:z/ *pronoun, determiner* **1** used to ask who something belongs to or who someone or something is connected with **...an/en; ki onun** *Whose gloves are these?* ○ *Whose car shall we use?* **2** used to say that something or someone is connected with or belongs to a person **ilgi cümleciğinde bir şeyin/birinin bir kişiye ait olduğunu/bağlantısı olduğunu gösteren ilgi zamiri** *She has a brother whose name I can't remember.*

o⁻**who've** /hu:v/ *short for* who have **who have' fiil yapısının kısa yazılışı** *I know people who've bought their homes on the Internet.*

o⁻**why** /waɪ/ *adverb* **1** used to ask or talk about the reasons for something **neden, niçin, ne diye, ne sebepten, neden dolayı** *Why didn't you call me?* ○ *I wonder why he didn't come.* ○ *So that's the reason why he asked her!* **2 Why don't you?/Why not do sth?** used to make a suggestion **neden ...mıyorsun; niçin ... yapmıyorsun;** *Why don't you come with us?* ○ *Why not give it a try?* **3 why not?** *informal* used to agree with something that someone has suggested **neden olmasın; niçin; niye ... ki; ...sek ya** *"Let's have an ice cream." "Yes, why not?"*

wicked /'wɪkɪd/ *adjective* **1** [BAD] extremely bad and morally wrong **kötü, aşağılık, hain, ahlaksız, berbat** *a wicked man* **2** [AMUSING] funny or enjoyable in a way that is slightly bad or unkind **hınzır, muzip, şeytani** *a wicked sense of humour* **3** [GOOD] *very informal* extremely good **son derece iyi** *They sell some wicked clothes.*

wicker /'wɪkər/ *adjective* made from thin branches crossed over and under each other **sepet örgüsüyle yapılmış** *a wicker basket*

wicket /'wɪkɪt/ *noun* [C] in cricket, an arrangement of three long, vertical poles with two short poles across the top **kale, kriket kalesi**

o--**wide¹** /waɪd/ *adjective* **1** [LONG DISTANCE] measuring a long distance or longer than usual from one side to the other **geniş** *a wide river/road* ○ *I have very wide feet.* ⊃See picture at narrow. **2** **5 miles/3 inches/6 metres, etc** wide having a distance of 5 miles/3 inches/6 metres, etc from one side to the other **5 mil/3 inç/6 metre vb. geniş** *The swimming pool is five metres wide.* **3 a wide range/selection/variety, etc** a lot of different types of thing **geniş kapsamlı; çok, bol** *The library is a good source of a wide range of information.* **4** [EYES] If your eyes are wide, they are completely open. **geniş, açık; iyice açılmış** *Her eyes were wide with fear.* **5** [BALL] If a ball, shot, etc is wide, it does not go near enough to where it was intended to go. **hedefin/kalenin uzağına/açığına** ⊃See also: be wide of the **mark¹**.

o--**wide²** /waɪd/ *adverb* **1 wide apart/open** as far apart/open as possible **iyice, alabildiğine, adamakıllı, ardına kadar** *The window was wide open.* **2 wide awake** completely awake **tamamen uyanık**

wide-eyed /,waɪd'aɪd/ *adjective* with your eyes completely open because of surprise, fear, happiness, etc **gözleri fal taşı gibi açılmış** *The children looked on, wide-eyed with wonder.*

o--**widely** /'waɪdli/ *adverb* **1** including a lot of different places, people, subjects, etc **geniş ölçüde, adamakıllı, çok** *widely known* ○ *He has travelled widely in Europe.* **2 differ/vary widely** to be very different **çok/bir hayli farklı olmak** *Prices vary widely from shop to shop.*

widen /'waɪdən/ *verb* [I, T] **1** to become wider or make something become wider **genişlemek, genişletmek** *The road is being widened to two lanes.* **2** to increase or make something increase in number or degree **genişle(t)mek, art(ır)mak** *to widen choice*

wide-ranging /,waɪd'reɪndʒɪŋ/ *adjective* including a lot of subjects **geniş kapsamlı, her şeyi içeren, şümullü** *a wide-ranging discussion/interview*

widescreen /'waɪdskriːn/ *adjective* describes a very wide cinema or television screen which shows very clear pictures **geniş ekran** *widescreen TV*

widespread /'waɪdspred/ *adjective* affecting or including a lot of places, people, etc **büyük çapta, yaygın** *a widespread problem* ○ *widespread support*

widow /'wɪdəʊ/ *noun* [C] **1** a woman whose husband has died **dul kadın 2** in printing, the last line of a paragraph, separated from the rest which is on the page before

widowed /'wɪdəʊd/ *adjective* If someone is widowed, their husband or wife has died. **dul kalmış**

widower /'wɪdəʊər/ *noun* [C] a man whose wife has died **dul erkek**

the width of sth ● [1 metre/5 feet, etc] in width ● the full width of sth

width /wɪtθ/ *noun* **1** [C, U] the distance from one side of something to the other side **genişlik, en** *a width of 2 metres* ○ *height, length, and width* ⊃See picture at length. **2** [C] the distance across the shorter side of a swimming pool when you swim across it **havuz genişliği**

wield /wiːld/ *verb* [T] to hold a weapon or tool and look as if you are going to use it **tutmak; kullanmak üzere kavrayıp tutmak; kullanmaya hazır olmak** *They*

were confronted by a man wielding a knife. **2 wield influence/power, etc** to have a lot of influence or power over other people **etkisi olmak; nüfuzu olmak**

wiener /'wiːnər/ *noun* [C] US a long thin sausage (= tube of meat and spices) that is usually eaten in bread **sosis**

o--**wife** /waɪf/ *noun* [C] *plural* **wives** /waɪvz/ the woman that a man is married to **eş** *I've never met William's wife.*

wi-fi /'waɪfaɪ/ *noun* [U] a system for connecting electronic equipment such as computers and electronic organizers to the Internet without using wires **kablosuz (internet)**

wig /wɪg/ *noun* [C] a covering of real or artificial hair that you wear on your head **peruk** *She was wearing a blonde wig.*

wiggle /'wɪgl/ *verb* [I, T] to make small movements from side to side or to make something else move from side to side **oyna(t)mak, kıpırda(t)mak** *He was wiggling his hips to the music.* ● **wiggle** *noun* [no plural] **kımıldama**

o--**wild¹** /waɪld/ *adjective* **1** [ANIMAL] A wild animal or plant lives or grows in its natural environment and not where people live. **vahşi, yabanî** *a wild dog* ○ *wild flowers* **2** [LAND] Wild land is in a completely natural state. **vahşi doğa, doğal çevre** *a wild garden* **3** [ENERGETIC] very energetic and not controlled **azgın, sert, enerjik, kontrolden çıkmış, deli gibi çılgın, vahşi, delice, çılgınca** *a wild party* ○ *wild dancing* **4** [WEATHER] with a lot of wind, rain, etc **fırtınalı, yağmurlu** *a wild and stormy night* **5 a wild accusation/guess/rumour, etc** something that you say which is not based on facts and is probably wrong **gerçekten dayanmayan, mantıksız, gerçeklik payı olmayan 6 be wild about sth** *informal* to be very enthusiastic about something **çok sevmek, çılgına dönmek, yanıp tutuşmak; ...delisi olmak** *He's wild about jazz.* **7 run wild** If someone, especially a child, runs wild, they behave as they want to and no one controls them. **başı boş dolaşmak, başı boş büyümek** *Their nine-year-old son is left to run wild.* ● **wildness** *noun* [U] ⊃See also: beyond your wildest dreams (**dream¹**). **vahşilik**

wild² /waɪld/ *noun* **1 in the wild** in a natural environment **doğal çevrede, vahşi tabiatta** *Animals are better off in the wild than in a zoo.* **2 the wilds** an area which is far from where people usually live **ıssız bölgeler, yabani yerler, vahşi yerler** *the wilds of Alaska*

,**wild 'boar** *noun* [C] a wild pig **yaban domuzu**

'**wild ,card** *noun* [C] someone or something that you know nothing about **hakkında hiç bir şey bilinmeyen kişi/şey; tamamen yabancı kimse/şey** *a wildcard candidate* in the election

wildcard /'waɪld,kɑːd/ *noun* [C] a sign that is used to represent any letters, numbers, or symbols **bilgisayarda herhangi bir harfi ya da harf dizisini temsil eden işaret** *a wildcard search*

wilderness /'wɪldənəs/ *noun* [C] a place that is in a completely natural state without houses, industry, roads, etc **vahşi orman, el değmemiş tabiat** [usually singular] *a beautiful mountain wilderness*

wildlife /'waɪldlaɪf/ *noun* [U] animals, birds, and plants living in their natural environment **vahşi yaşam** *a wildlife park*

wildly /'waɪldli/ *adverb* **1** in a very energetic way and without control **vahşice, çılgınca** *They cheered wildly.* **2** extremely **bir hayli, alabildiğine** *It hasn't been wildly successful.*

wiles /waɪlz/ *noun* [plural] tricks or clever ways of making other people do what you want **hileler, dolaplar, düzenler, oyunlar** *I'll use my womanly wiles.*

wilful UK (US willful) /'wɪlfəl/ *adjective* doing what you want to do, although you are not allowed to or other

W

people tell you not to **kasıtlı, kasdî, bilerek yapılan** *wilful disobedience* ● **wilfully** *adverb* **kasten, umursamadan**

०►**will**¹ *strong form* /wɪl/ *weak forms* /wᵊl/, /ᵊl/ *modal verb*
1 [FUTURE] used to talk about what is going to happen in the future, especially things that you are certain about *...acek/ecak Claire will be five next month.* ○ *I'll see him on Saturday.* ○ *She'll have a great time.* **2** [ABLE/WILLING] used to talk about what someone or something is willing or able to do *...er/acak/ecek Ask Susie if she'll take them.* ○ *I've asked her but she won't come.* ○ *The car won't start.* **3** [ASK] used to ask someone to do something or to politely offer something to someone *...mısınız/misiniz Will you give me her address?* ○ *Will you have a drink with us, Phil?* **4** [IF] used in conditional sentences that start with 'if' and use the present tense **şart cümlelerinde geniş zaman manasında kullanılır** *If he's late again I'll be very angry.* **5** [HAPPENING OFTEN] used to talk about something that often happens, especially something annoying **ısrarla** *... ıyor Accidents will happen.* ○ *He will keep talking when I'm trying to concentrate.* **6 it/that will be** *mainly UK* used to talk about what is probably true *...malı/meli That will be Helen at the front door.* ○ *That will be his mother with him.* ⊃See study page Modal verbs on page Centre 22.

will .... İLE BİRLİKTE KULLANILAN KELİMELER

make/write a will ● **in** sb's will ● **leave** sb sth **in** your will

will² /wɪl/ *noun* **1** [MENTAL POWER] [C, U] the mental power to control your thoughts and actions or to succeed in doing something difficult **irade, azim** *She has a very strong will.* ○ [+ to do sth] *He lacks the will to win.* **2** [WANT] [no plural] what someone wants **istek, arzu** *She was forced to marry him against her will.* **3** [DOCUMENT] [C] a legal document that gives instructions about what should happen to your money and possessions after you die **vasiyet, vasiyetname** *She left me some money in her will.* ⊃See also: free will, ill will.

willful /'wɪlᵊl/ *adjective* US spelling of wilful **inatçı, dediği dedik, bildiğini okuyan; kasıtlı, kasdî, bilerek yapılan**

०►**willing** /'wɪlɪŋ/ *adjective* **1 be willing to do sth** to be happy to do something, if you need to **bir şeyi yapmaya hazır/istekli/can atıyor/gönüllü olmak** *He's willing to pay a lot of money for that house.* **2** wanting to do something **hazır, razı, istekli** *He is a very willing assistant.* ⊃Opposite unwilling. ● **willingly** *adverb He would willingly risk his life for her.* **isteyerek, gönüllü olarak** ● **willingness** *noun* [U] **istek**

willow /'wɪləʊ/ *noun* [C] a tree with long, thin leaves that grows near water **söğüt, söğüt ağacı**

willowy /'wɪləʊi/ *adjective* tall and attractively thin **uzun boylu ve çekici şekilde zarif/ince/hoş/alımlı** *a willowy blonde*

willpower /'wɪlpaʊəʳ/ *noun* [U] the ability to make yourself do difficult things or to stop yourself from doing enjoyable things that are bad for you **irade gücü** *It takes great willpower to lose weight.*

wilt /wɪlt/ *verb* [I] If a plant wilts, it starts to bend because it is dying or needs water. **solmak, boynunu bükmek, canlılığını yitirmek**

wily /'waɪli/ *adjective* good at getting what you want, especially by deceiving people **kurnaz, cin fikirli, şeytan**

wimp /wɪmp/ *noun* [C] *informal* someone who is not brave and tries to avoid dangerous or difficult situations **zayıf/korkak/kendine güvenmeyen/kaçak**

kimse *I'm too much of a wimp to go rock climbing.* ● **wimpy** *adjective informal* **korkak, mızıldanan**

०►**win**¹ /wɪn/ *verb* **winning**, *past* **won 1** [COMPETITION] [I, T] to get the most points in a competition or game, or the most votes in an election **kazanmak, yenmek, galip gelmek** *Barcelona won the game 6-0.* ○ *Who do you think will win the election?* **2** [ARGUMENT] [I, T] to be successful in a war, fight, or argument **savaşı/kavgayı/tartışmayı kazanmak/başarılı olmak** *Protesters have won their battle to stop the road being built.* **3** [PRIZE] [T] to get a prize in a game or competition **ödül kazanmak** *He won $500.* ○ *She won a gold medal at the Olympics.* **4 win approval/respect/support, etc** to get approval/respect/support, etc because of your skill and hard work **onay/saygı/destek kazanmak** *Her plans have won the support of many local people.* **5 sb can't win** *informal* used to say that nothing someone does in a situation will succeed or please people **dört dörtlük olmaz, herkesi memnun etmek zor** *Whatever I do seems to annoy her - I just can't win.*

win sb over *phrasal verb* to persuade someone to support you or agree with you **ikna etmek, kazanmak, kendi tarafına çekmek**

win (noun) .... İLE BİRLİKTE KULLANILAN KELİMELER

a **comfortable/convincing/emphatic** win ● a win **against/over** sb ● a win **for** sb

win² /wɪn/ *noun* [C] when someone wins a game or competition **kazanma, galibiyet** *The Jets have only had three wins this season.*

wince /wɪns/ *verb* [I] to suddenly look as if you are suffering because you feel pain or because you see or think about something unpleasant **ürkmek, geri kaçmak, irkilmek; yüzünü buruşturmak; suratını ekşitmek** *It makes me wince just to think about eye operations.*

winch /wɪnʃ/ *noun* [C] a machine with a thick chain, used for lifting heavy things **vinç** ● **winch** *verb* [T] to lift someone or something with a winch **vinçle kaldırmak/çekmek** *The injured climber was winched to safety by a helicopter.*

wind .... İLE BİRLİKTE KULLANILAN KELİMELER

the wind **blows** ● a **gust** of wind ● a **biting/light/strong** wind ● **high** winds ● **in** the wind

०►**wind**¹ /wɪnd/ *noun* **1** [C, U] a natural, fast movement of air **rüzgâr, yel** *The weather forecast said there would be strong winds and rain.* **2** [U] *UK* (*US* gas) gas or air in your stomach that makes you feel uncomfortable and sometimes makes noises **hava, gaz, gurultu, guruldama 3 get wind of sth** to discover something that is intended to be a secret **...dan/den haberdar olmak; ...ı/i duymak; ...ın/in kokusunu almak** *Dad got wind of our plans for a party.* **4 get your wind (back)** to breathe easily again, for example after you have been running **tekrar normal nefes alabilmek** ⊃See also: throw caution¹ to the wind, second wind.

wind² /wɪnd/ *verb* [T] to make someone have difficulty breathing, often by hitting them in the stomach **nefesini kesmek**

wind³ /waɪnd/ *verb* *past* **wound 1 wind sth around/round, etc** sth to turn or twist something long and thin around something else several times **(ip, urgan vb.) dolamak, sarmak, sarmalamak** *She wound the rope around the tree.* ⊃Opposite unwind. **2 wind (up) a clock/toy/watch, etc** to make a clock/toy/watch, etc work by turning a small handle or button several times **(saat, oyuncak vb.) kurmak** *Did you remember to wind the alarm clock?* **3 wind along/down/through, etc** If a river, road, etc winds somewhere, it bends a lot

and is not straight. **kıvrıla kıvrıla gitmek, dönemeçler yapmak** *The path winds along the edge of the bay.*
wind (sth) down *phrasal verb* to gradually end, or to make something gradually end **yavaş yavaş sona er(dir)mek/bit(ir)mek** *to wind down a business*
wind down *phrasal verb* (*also* **unwind**) to gradually relax after doing something that has made you tired or worried **kafa dinlemek, dinlenmek**
wind up *phrasal verb* to finally be somewhere or do something, especially without having planned it **soluğu...almak, kendini...bulmak, gözünü...açmak** *If he carries on like this, he'll wind up in prison.* ○ [+ doing sth] *I wound up having to start the course from the beginning again.*
wind (sth) up *phrasal verb* to end, or to make something end **bitirmek, sona erdirmek, bitmek, sona ermek** *It's time to wind up the game now.*
wind sb up *phrasal verb UK informal* **1** to tell someone something that is not true, as a joke **şaka yapmak, dalga geçmek** *Have I really won or are you winding me up?* **2** to annoy someone **kızdırmak, rahatsız etmek, taciz etmek** *He keeps complaining and it really winds me up.*

windfall /'wɪndfɔːl/ *noun* [C] an amount of money that you get that you did not expect **devlet kuşu, düşeş, beklenmedik zamanda kazanılan para** *Investors each received a windfall of £1000.*

winding /'waɪndɪŋ/ *adjective* **a winding path/road/street, etc** a path/road, etc that bends a lot and is not straight **dolambaçlı/kıvrımlı yol/patika/cadde vb.**

'wind ,instrument *noun* [C] a musical instrument that you play by blowing into it **nefesli saz, üflemeli çalgı** *A flute is a wind instrument.*

windmill /'wɪndmɪl/ *noun* [C] a building with long parts at the top that turn in the wind, used for producing power or crushing grain **yel değirmeni**

windmill

o-***window** /'wɪndəʊ/ *noun* [C] **1** a space in the wall of a building or vehicle that has glass in it, used for letting light and air inside and for looking through **pencere** *Open the window if you're too hot.* ○ *I could see the children's faces at the window.* ○ *a window frame/ledge* ЭOrta kısımdaki renkli sayfalarına bakınız. **2** a separate area on a computer screen showing information and which you can move around **(bilgisayar) pencere** *to minimize/maximize a window* ЭSee also: **French windows.**

windowpane /'wɪndəʊpeɪn/ *noun* [C] a piece of glass in a window **pencere camı**

'window ,shopping *noun* [U] when you look at things in shops but do not buy anything **vitrinlere bakma, vitrin alışverişi**

windowsill /'wɪndəʊsɪl/ *noun* [C] a shelf at the bottom of a window **pencere eşiği, pencere kenarı/pervazı** ЭOrta kısımdaki renkli sayfalarına bakınız.

windpipe /'wɪndpaɪp/ *noun* [C] the tube that carries air from your throat to your lungs **nefes borusu**

windscreen /'wɪndskriːn/ *UK (US* **windshield** /'wɪndʃiːld/) *noun* [C] the window at the front end of a car, bus, etc **araçlarda ön cam** ЭOrta kısımdaki renkli sayfalarına bakınız.

'windscreen ,wiper *UK (US* **'windshield ,wiper)** *noun* [C] one of two long, metal and rubber parts that move against a windscreen to remove rain **silecek, cam sileceği** ЭOrta kısımdaki renkli sayfalarına bakınız.

windsurfing /'wɪndsɜːfɪŋ/ *noun* [U] a sport in which you sail across water by standing on a board and holding onto a large sail **rüzgâr sörfü** ● **windsurfer** *noun* [C] **denizde rüzgar sörfü sporu yapan**

windswept /'wɪndswept/ *adjective* **1** A windswept place often has strong winds. **rüzgâr alan, rüzgâra açık** *a remote, windswept hill* **2** looking untidy because you have been in the wind **darma dağınık, dağılmış** *windswept hair*

'wind ,turbine *noun* [C] a machine with long parts at the top that are turned by the wind, used to make electricity **rüzgar türbini**

windy /'wɪndi/ *adjective* with a lot of wind **rüzgârlı, esintili** *a windy day* ○ *Outside it was cold and windy.*

🧩 **wine** ...... İLE BİRLİKTE KULLANILAN KELİMELER
a bottle of/glass of wine ● dry/red/sparkling/ sweet/white wine

o-***wine** /waɪn/ *noun* [C, U] an alcoholic drink that is made from the juice of grapes (= small, green or purple fruit), or sometimes other fruit **şarap** *a glass of wine* ○ *red/ white wine*

wing

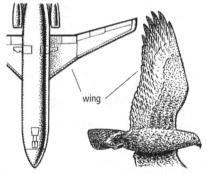

wing

o-***wing** /wɪŋ/ *noun* [C] **1** [CREATURE] one of the two parts that a bird or insect uses to fly **kanat** **2** [AIRCRAFT] one of the two long, flat parts at the sides of an aircraft that make it stay in the sky **uçak kanadı** **3** [CAR] *UK (US* **fender)** one of the parts at each corner of a car above the wheels **çamurluk** **4** [BUILDING] a part of a large building that is joined to the side of the main part **kanat, yan taraf** *Their offices are in the West wing.* **5** [POLITICS] a group of people in an organization or political party who have the same beliefs **aynı fikri/düşünceyi taşıyan kanat** *the nationalist wing of the party* **6** **take sb under your wing** to help and protect someone who is younger than you or who has less experience than you **kanatlarının altına almak, korumaya almak; hamisi olmak**

winged /wɪŋd/ *adjective* with wings **kanatlı** *a winged insect*

'wing ,mirror *UK (US* **side mirror)** *noun* [C] a small mirror on the side of a car or truck **yan ayna** ЭOrta kısımdaki renkli sayfalarına bakınız.

W

the wings /wɪŋz/ *noun* [plural] **1** the area behind the sides of a stage where actors wait just before they perform **kulis 2 be waiting in the wings** to be ready to do something or be used at any time **yapmaya/kullanılmaya hazır olmak**

wink

wink¹ /wɪŋk/ *verb* [I] to quickly close and then open one eye, in order to be friendly or to show that something is a joke **göz kırpmak** *She smiled and winked at me.*

wink² /wɪŋk/ *noun* [C] **1** when you wink at someone **göz kırpma** *He gave me a friendly wink.* **2 not sleep a wink** to not have any sleep **gözünü kırpmamak, hiç uyumamak** *I was so excited last night - I didn't sleep a wink.*

○-**winner** /'wɪnər/ *noun* [C] someone who wins a game, competition, or election **kazanan kişi, galip gelen kimse** *the winners of the World Cup*

winnings /'wɪnɪŋz/ *noun* [plural] money that you win in a competition **kazanç, kazanılan para**

winter .... İLE BİRLİKTE KULLANILAN KELİMELER
in (the) winter ● a **cold/severe** winter ● a **mild** winter ● **last/next** winter ● the winter **months**

○-**winter** /'wɪntər/ *noun* [C, U] the coldest season of the year, between autumn and spring **kış, kış mevsimi** *We went skiing last winter.* ○ *a mild winter* ● **wintry** /'wɪntri/ *adjective* cold and typical of winter **kış gibi** *wintry showers* (= snow mixed with rain) ⊃See also: the dead³ of night/winter.

win-win /'wɪnwɪn/ *adjective* A win-win situation is one in which something good happens to everyone. **herkesin lehine durum oluşması**

wipe¹ /waɪp/ *verb* [T] **1** to clean or dry something by moving a cloth across it **silmek** *I had a job wiping tables in a cafe.* ○ *She wiped her hands on the towel.* **2 wipe sth from/away/off, etc** to remove dirt, water, a mark, etc from something with a cloth or your hand **silmek, temizlemek, silip süpürmek; silip temizlemek** *He wiped a tear from his eye.* **wipe sth out** *phrasal verb* to destroy something completely **tümü ile yok etmek, silip süpürmek, tamamen ortadan kaldırmak** *The earthquake wiped out many villages.* **wipe sth up** *phrasal verb* to remove a substance, usually liquid, with a cloth **sıvı ile silip temizlemek** *Have you got something I could wipe this mess up with?*

wipe² /waɪp/ *noun* [C] **1** when you clean or dry something with a cloth **silme, kurulama, temizleme** *I'll give the table a wipe.* **2** a thin cloth or piece of paper used for cleaning **temizlik bezi, toz bezi** *baby wipes*

wiper /'waɪpər/ (*also* windscreen wiper) *noun* [C] a long, metal and rubber part that removes rain from the front window of a vehicle **silecek**

○-**wire¹** /waɪər/ *noun* **1** [C, U] thin, metal thread, used to fasten things or to make fences, cages, etc **tel 2** [C] a long, thin piece of metal thread, usually covered in plastic, that carries electricity **kablo, tel** *electrical wires* ⊃See also: barbed wire.

wire² /waɪər/ *verb* [T] **1** ELECTRICITY (*also* wire up) to connect wires so that a piece of electrical equipment will work **kablo çekmek, telleri bağlamak, kabloları bağlamak** *Do you know how to wire a burglar alarm?* **2** JOIN to join two things together using wire **telle/kabloya bağlamak 3** SEND *US* to send a message or money using an electrical communication system **telgraf çekmek, telgraf göndermek**

wireless /'waɪələs/ *adjective* without a cable **telsiz, kablosuz**

wiring /'waɪərɪŋ/ *noun* [U] the system of wires that carry electricity around a building **elektrik tesisatı/donanımı** *The fire was caused by faulty wiring.*

wiry /'waɪəri/ *adjective* **1** Someone who is wiry is strong but quite thin. **kuvvetli fakat incecik 2** Wiry hair is thick and stiff, like wire. **(saç) kaba ve sert, fırça gibi** *a wiry beard*

wisdom /'wɪzdəm/ *noun* **1** [U] the ability to use your knowledge and experience to make good decisions and judgments **akıl, akıllılık 2 the wisdom of sth/doing sth** If you doubt the wisdom of something, you think it is probably not a good plan. **akla uygunluğu; mantıklılığı; makul olması** *Many people have questioned the wisdom of spending so much money on weapons.*

'wisdom ,tooth *noun* [C] *plural* **wisdom teeth** one of the four teeth at the back of your mouth that are the last to grow **yirmi yaş dişi**

wise¹ /waɪz/ *adjective* **1** A wise decision or action shows good judgment and is the right thing to do. **akıllı** *I think we've made a wise choice.* ○ [+ to do] *It's always wise to see a doctor if you're worried about your health.* ⊃Opposite **unwise. 2** A wise person is able to use their knowledge and experience to make good decisions and give good advice. **makul, akıllı 3 be none the wiser** *informal* to still not understand something after someone has tried to explain it to you **pek anlamamış, hâlâ kavrayamamış; pek farkında olmayan; pek haberi olmayan** ● **wisely** *adverb* **akıllıca**

wise² /waɪz/ *verb* **wise up** *phrasal verb informal* to start to understand the truth about a situation **farkına varmak, anlamak, öğrenmek** *Employers are starting to wise up to the fact that people want flexible working hours.*

-wise /-waɪz/ *suffix* changes a noun into an adverb meaning 'relating to this subject' **...gibi/vari' anlamında sonek** *Weather-wise, the holiday was great.* ○ *How are we doing time-wise?*

○-**wish¹** /wɪʃ/ *verb* **1 wish (that)** to want a situation that is different from the one that exists **dilemek, istemek** *I wish that I didn't have to go to work.* ○ *I wish he would leave.* ○ *I wish I had been there.* **2 wish to do sth** *formal* to want to do something **yapmayı arzu etmek/dilemek** *I wish to speak to the manager.* **3 wish sb luck/success, etc** to say that you hope someone will be lucky/successful, etc **şans/başarı dilemek** *I wished him luck for his test.* **4 I/you wish!** *informal* used to say that you would like something to be true although you know it is not true **Keşke...!**" *"Have your exams finished yet?"* "*I wish!*"

YAYGIN HATALAR

wish or hope?

Unutmayın! Wish fiilinin ardından bir fiil geldiği zaman, geniş veya gelecek zamanda kullanılmamalıdır. Şimdi gelecekte olmasını istediğiniz bir şey için wish değil, hope kullanmanız gerekir: ~~I wish you will accept my invitation.~~ Yanlış cümle örneği
I hope you will accept my invitation.

---

wish (noun) ...... İLE BİRLİKTE KULLANILAN KELİMELER

ignore/respect sb's wishes ● get your wish ● have no wish to do sth ● according to/against sb's wishes

---

o-**wish²** /wɪʃ/ *noun* [C] **1** what you want to do or what you want to happen **istek, dilek, arzu** *The hospital always tries to respect the wishes of its patients.* ○ *I have no wish to travel the world.* **2** something that you say secretly to yourself about what you want to have or happen **dilek, dilek tutma** *She closed her eyes and made a wish.* **3** best wishes something you say or write at the end of a letter, to show that you hope someone is happy and has good luck **iyi şanslar!** *Please give her my best wishes when you see her.*

wishful thinking /ˌwɪʃfəl'θɪŋkɪŋ/ *noun* [U] when you want something to happen or be true but it is impossible **boş ümit, olmayacak arzu, hüsnü kuruntu**

wisp /wɪsp/ *noun* [C] **1 a wisp of cloud/smoke/steam** a small, thin line of cloud/smoke/steam **ince uzun bulut/duman/buhar demeti 2 a wisp of hair/grass, etc** a thin piece of hair/grass, etc **ince saç/çim parçası** ● **wispy** *adjective* in the form of wisps **tutam tutam, ince uzun parçalı** *wispy hair* ○ *a wispy cloud*

wistful /'wɪstfºl/ *adjective* slightly sad because you are thinking about something you cannot have **üzgün ve özlem dolu** *a wistful look/smile* ● **wistfully** *adverb* **düşünceli, dalgın bir şekilde**

wit /wɪt/ *noun* [U] the ability to say things that are funny and clever **nüktedanlık, nüktecilik** *a woman of great intelligence and wit*

witch /wɪtʃ/ *noun* [C] in stories, a woman who has magical powers that she uses to do bad or strange things **cadı**

witch

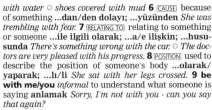

witchcraft /'wɪtʃkrɑːft/ *noun* [U] the use of magic to make bad or strange things happen **büyücülük**

witch-hunt /'wɪtʃhʌnt/ *noun* [C] when a group of people try to blame someone and punish them for something, in a way that is unfair **düzene karşı olanları yıldırma hareketi, cadı avı**

o-**with** /wɪð/ *preposition* **1** TOGETHER used to say that people or things are in a place together or are doing something together **ile, yanında, beraber, birlikte** *Emma lives with her boyfriend.* ○ *Hang your coat with the others.* **2** HAVING having or including something **ile, ...ile birlikte** *a house with a swimming pool* ○ *a woman with brown eyes* **3** USING using something **ile, ...kullanarak** *She hit him over the head with a tennis racket.* **4** HOW used to describe the way someone does something **...ile** *He plays with great enthusiasm.* ○ *She shut the drawer with a bang.* **5** WHAT used to say what fills, covers, etc something **...ile kaplı/dolu** *a bucket filled*

with water ○ shoes covered with mud **6** CAUSE because of something **...dan/den dolayı; ...yüzünden** *She was trembling with fear.* **7** RELATING TO relating to something or someone **...ile ilgili olarak; ...a/e ilişkin; ...hususunda** *There's something wrong with the car.* ○ *The doctors are very pleased with his progress.* **8** POSITION used to describe the position of someone's body **...olarak; yaparak; ...lı/li** *She sat with her legs crossed.* **9 be with me/you** *informal* to understand what someone is saying **anlamak** *Sorry, I'm not with you - can you say that again?*

withdraw /wɪð'drɔː/ *verb past tense* **withdrew**, *past participle* **withdrawn** **1** MONEY [T] to take money out of a bank account **hesaptan para çekmek** *She withdrew $50.* **2** REMOVE [T] to remove something, especially because of an official decision **çekmek, çekip almak** *This product has been withdrawn from sale.* ○ *He has threatened to withdraw his support.* **3** MILITARY [I, T] If a military force withdraws, or if someone withdraws it, it leaves the place where it is fighting. **geri çekmek/ çekilmek** *The President has ordered troops to be withdrawn from the area.* **4** COMPETITION [I] to decide that you will not now be in a race, competition, etc **(yarışma, yarış, müsabaka vb.) çekilmek, çekilmeye karar vermek** *Christie was forced to withdraw from the race because of injury.* **5** SOMETHING SAID [T] *formal* to say that you want people to ignore something you said before because it was not true **sözünü geri almak** *He admitted taking the money, but later withdrew his confession.*

withdrawal /wɪð'drɔːºl/ *noun* **1** MONEY [C] when you take money out of a bank account **para çekme** *This account allows you to make withdrawals whenever you want to.* **2** STOP [C, U] when someone stops doing something, for example helping someone or giving money **yapmama, geri çekilme, vazgeçme** [usually singular] *the withdrawal of financial support* **3** MILITARY [C, U] when a military force moves out of an area **(askerî birlik) çekilme, çekme** [usually singular] *the withdrawal of troops* **4** DRUGS [U] the unpleasant feelings that someone gets when they stop taking a drug that they have taken for a long time **bağımlılık yapan maddeleri kullanmayı bırakma** *withdrawal symptoms* **5** ALONE [U] when someone prefers to be alone and does not want to talk to other people **içine kapanma** *Withdrawal can be a symptom of depression.*

withdrawn /wɪð'drɔːn/ *adjective* [never before noun] quiet and not talking to other people **içine kapanık**

wither /'wɪðəʳ/ (*also* wither away) *verb* [I] If a plant withers, it becomes dry and starts to die. **sararıp solmak, kurumak**

withering /'wɪðərɪŋ/ *adjective* **withering attack/contempt/look** criticism or an expression that shows that someone strongly disapproves of someone or something **utandırıcı, yerin dibine sokan, yüzünü yer eden** *He published a withering attack on the government's policies.*

withhold /wɪð'həʊld/ *verb* [T] *past* **withheld** to not give someone the information, money, etc that they want **vermemek, alıkoymak, esirgemek, saklamak** *The company has decided to withhold payment until the job has been finished.*

o-**within¹** /wɪ'ðɪn/ *preposition* **1** TIME before a particular period of time has finished **içinde, dahilinde** *The ambulance arrived within 10 minutes.* ○ *Consume within two days of purchase.* **2** DISTANCE less than a particular distance from something **içinde, daha az mesafede** *She was born within 20 miles of New York.* ○ *The hotel is within easy reach of* (= near) *the airport.* **3** INSIDE inside an area, group, or system **içinde, dahilinde** *a dispute within the department* ○ *There's a pharmacy within the hospital building.* **4** LIMIT not outside the limits of something **sınırları içinde** *The project was completed well within budget.* **5 within the law/the rules/your rights, etc** allowed according to the law/the rules/your rights, etc **yasa/kurallar/hakları vb. dahilinde** *You're perfectly within your rights to complain.*

within² /wɪˈðɪn/ *adverb* inside someone or something **bir şeyin/birinin içinde** *The organization needs to change from within.*

⚬**without** /wɪˈðaʊt/ *preposition* **1** not having, using, or doing something **...sız/siz;** *...sızın I did the test without any problems.* ○ *I can't see without my glasses.* ○ *He went to school without eating any breakfast.* **2** when someone is not with someone else **...sız/siz; ...madan/ maksızın** *You can start the meeting without me.* **3 go/do without (sth)** to not have something important **...sız/ siz; ...madan/meden** *They went without sleep for three days.*

withstand /wɪðˈstænd/ *verb* [T] *past* **withstood** to not be damaged or broken by something **dayanmak, karşı koymak, direnmek** *a bridge designed to withstand earthquakes*

🧩 **witness** ...... İLE BİRLİKTE KULLANILAN KELİMELER

appeal for a witness ● a witness to sth ● a character/ key witness ● a witness account/testimony

⚬**witness¹** /ˈwɪtnəs/ *noun* [C] **1** COURT someone in a court of law who says what they have seen and what they know about a crime **tanık, şahit** *The witness was called to the stand.* **2** SEE someone who sees an accident or crime **tanık, şahit** *Police are appealing for witnesses to the shooting.* **3** DOCUMENT someone who signs their name on an official document to say that they were present when someone else signed it **şahitlik, tanıklık**

witness² /ˈwɪtnəs/ *verb* [T] **1** to see something happen, especially an accident or crime **görmek, şahit olmak** *Did anyone witness the attack?* **2** to sign your name on an official document to say that you were present when someone else signed it **tanıklık etmek**

'witness ,box *UK* (*UK/US* **'witness ,stand**) *noun* [C] the place in a court of law where a witness stands or sits when they are answering questions **tanık yeri, tanık kürsüsü/sandalyesi**

wits /wɪts/ *noun* [plural] **1** intelligence and the ability to think quickly **zekâ ve yetenek 2 keep/have your wits about you** to be ready to think quickly in a situation and react to things that you are not expecting **uyanık olmak, tetikte bulunmak, aklı başında olmak, telaşa kapılmamak, kendine hâkim olmak** *You have to keep your wits about you when you're cycling.* **3 be at your wits' end** to be very worried about something and not know what you should do next **ne yapacağını bilmemek, şaşkına dönmek; (argo) apışıp kalmak 4 scare/frighten sb out of their wits** to make someone very frightened **korkutmak, ürkütmek, aklını başından almak; (argo) çuvallatmak**

witty /ˈwɪti/ *adjective* using words in a funny and clever way **nükteli, nüktedan** *a witty comment* ○ *He was witty and charming.*

wives /waɪvz/ *plural of* wife **eşler, karılar, zevceler**

wizard /ˈwɪzəd/ *noun* [C] **1** MAGIC in stories, a man who has magical powers **sihirbaz, büyücü 2** SKILL *informal* someone who is very good at something or knows a lot about something **usta, her şeyi bilen kimse, sihirbaz** *a computer wizard* **3** COMPUTER a computer program that gives the user a series of questions or instructions to help them use a particular system

WMD /ˌdʌbəljuːemˈdiː/ *noun* [plural] abbreviation for weapons of mass destruction: weapons, such as nuclear

bombs, which cause a lot of damage and death when used **Toplu İmha Silahları (TİS)**

wobble /ˈwɒbl/ *verb* [I, T] If something wobbles or you make something wobble, it moves from side to side, often because it is not on a flat surface. **sallanmak, yalpalamak, dingildemek** *The ladder started to wobble.* ○ *Stop wobbling the table.* ● **wobbly** *adjective* likely to wobble **sallanan, yalpalayan, sallantılı** *a wobbly chair*

woe /wəʊ/ *noun* [U] *literary* sadness **elem, keder, ıstırap** *full of woe*

woeful /ˈwəʊfˀl/ *adjective* very bad and showing no skill **keder verici, çok üzüntülü, çok üzücü, çok acıklı** *a woeful attempt/performance* ● **woefully** *adverb* **üzücü bir şekilde**

woes /wəʊz/ *noun* [plural] *formal* **your woes** your problems and worries **dertleri, sorunları, endişeleri**

wok /wɒk/ *noun* [C] a large, bowl-shaped pan that is used for frying Chinese food **Çin mutfağında kullanılan kızartma tenceresi**

woke /wəʊk/ *past tense of* wake **uyanmak' fiilinin 2. hâli**

woken /ˈwəʊkˀn/ *past participle of* wake **uyanmak' fiilinin 3. hâli**

wolf¹ /wʊlf/ *noun* [C] *plural* **wolves** /wʊlvz/ a wild animal like a large dog **kurt**

wolf² /wʊlf/ (*also* **wolf down**) *verb* [T] *informal* to eat something very quickly **aç kurt gibi yemek** *I gave her a plate of pasta and she wolfed it down.*

⚬**woman** /ˈwʊmən/ *noun* [C] *plural* **women** /ˈwɪmɪn/ an adult female person **kadın, bayan, hanım** *a 30-year-old woman* ○ *There were two women at the bus stop.* ● **womanhood** *noun* [U] the state of being a woman **kadınlık**

womanly /ˈwʊmənli/ *adjective* having the qualities and appearance that people think a woman should have **kadınca, kadına özgü, kadına yakışır** *womanly charms*

womb /wuːm/ *noun* [C] the organ inside a woman's body where a baby grows **rahim, döl yatağı, vajina**

women /ˈwɪmɪn/ *plural of* woman **kadınlar, bayanlar**

won /wʌn/ *past of* win **kazanmak' fiilinin geçmiş zaman hâli**

⚬**wonder¹** /ˈwʌndəʳ/ *verb* **1** [I, T] to want to know something or to try to understand the reason for something **merak etmek** [+ question word] *I wonder what he's making for dinner.* ○ *I wonder why she left so suddenly.* **2 I/we wonder if/whether ...** used to politely ask someone for something or to suggest something **Acaba...'** *I wonder if you could help me?* ○ *We were wondering if you'd like to come over for a meal sometime.*

wonder² /ˈwʌndəʳ/ *noun* **1** [U] surprise and admiration **hayret, şaşkınlık** *The boys gazed in wonder at the shiny, red Ferrari.* **2** [C] something that makes you feel surprise or admiration **şaşılacak şey, mucize, hayranlık, hayret** [usually plural] *the wonders of modern medicine* **3 no wonder** used to say that you are not surprised about something **hiç de şaşılacak şey değil, normal, doğal, tevekkeli** *No wonder she failed the test if she didn't do any work.* **4 it's a wonder (that)** used to say that you are surprised about something **...mucize; şaşılacak şey** *It's a wonder he's still alive.*

⚬**wonderful** /ˈwʌndəfˀl/ *adjective* very good **şahane, harikulâde, çok güzel** *a wonderful idea* ○ *We had a wonderful time in Spain.* ● **wonderfully** *adverb* **harika bir şekilde**

wonderful

Dikkat! Çok sık yapılan kelime türetme hatası sonek **ful** ile biten sıfatlarda yalnızca bir tane **l** kullanılır. **Wonderfull** olarak yazmayın. **Wonderful** olarak yazılmalıdır.

o- **won't** /wəʊnt/ *short for* will not **will not'** fiil yapısını kısa yazılışı *I won't be home before midnight.*

woo /wuː/ *verb* [T] **wooing**, *past* **wooed** to try to persuade someone to support you or to use your business **kur yapmak, elde etmeye çalışmak; ikna etmeye çalışmak, desteğini kazanmaya çaba sarfetmek** *a political party trying to woo young voters*

o- **wood** /wʊd/ *noun* **1** [C, U] the hard material that trees are made of **odun** *a piece of wood* **2** [C] (*also* woods) a large area of trees growing near each other **ağaçlık, koru** *We went for a walk in the woods.*

wooded /'wʊdɪd/ *adjective* covered with trees **ağaçlı, ormanlık** *a wooded area*

wooden /'wʊdᵊn/ *adjective* made of wood **tahta, ağaç, ahşap** *a wooden chair*

woodland /'wʊdlənd/ *noun* [C, U] an area of land with a lot of trees **ağaçlık alan, ormanlık bölge**

woodwind /'wʊdwɪnd/ *noun* [U] the group of musical instruments that you play by blowing into them **ağaçtan yapılma bir grup müzik aleti** *woodwind instruments*

woodwork /'wʊdwɜːk/ *noun* [U] **1** the parts of a building that are made from wood **ağaç işleri, ahşap kısımlar, doğrama 2** the activity of making things from wood **ağaç işçiliği, marangozluk, doğramacılık**

woof /wʊf/ *noun* [C] the sound made by a dog **hav hav' sesi, havlama sesi**

o- **wool** /wʊl/ *noun* [U] **1** the soft, thick hair on a sheep **yün 2** thick thread or material that is made from the hair of a sheep **yün, yünlü** *a wool suit* ○ *a ball of wool* ⊃See also: cotton wool.

woollen UK (US woolen) /'wʊlən/ *adjective* made of wool **yün, yünlü** *woollen gloves*

woolly UK (US wooly) /'wʊli/ *adjective* made of wool, or made of something that looks like wool **yünlü, yün gibi** *a green woolly hat*

o- **word**[1] /wɜːd/ *noun* **1** [C] a group of letters or sounds that mean something, or a single letter or sound that means something **sözcük, kelime** *'Hund' is the German word for 'dog'.* ○ *He has difficulty spelling long words.* **2 not believe/understand/hear, etc a word** to not believe/understand/hear, etc anything **hiç bir şey anlamamak/inanmamak/işitmemek** vb. *I don't believe a word he says.* **3 a word of warning/advice/thanks,** etc something that you say to warn someone/give them advice/thank them, etc **ikaz/tavsiye/teşekkür** vb. **ifade eden sözler** *Just a word of warning - he doesn't like people being late.* **4 have a word with sb** to talk to someone for a short time **iki kelime etmek, kısa bir süre konuşmak** *I'll have a word with Ted and see if he wants to come.* **5 put in a good word for sb** to praise someone, often to someone who might be able to employ them **lehinde konuşmak/söylemek/bulunmak 6 give sb your word** to promise someone something **söz vermek, vaatte bulunmak** *He gave me his word that he wouldn't tell anyone.* **7 take sb's word for it** to believe what someone says without any proof **her söylediğine inanmak; sözlerine itibar etmek; sözüne güvenmek 8 in other words** used to explain what something means in a different way **yâni, diğer bir şekilde; bir başka deyişle** *He said he's too busy, in*

other words, he isn't interested. **9 in sb's words** used when you repeat what someone said **başkasının deyişiyle/ifadesiyle** *In the manager's words, the game was 'a total disaster'.* **10 word for word** using the exact words that were originally used **kelimesi kelimesine** *She repeated word for word what he had told her.* **11 have the last word** to say the last thing in a discussion or argument or make the final decision about something **son sözünü söylemek 12 not breathe a word** to not tell people a secret **tek kelime bile söylememek; ser verip sır vermemek** *Don't breathe a word about this to anyone.* **13 not get a word in edgeways** UK (US **not get a word in edgewise**) to be unable to say anything because someone else is talking so much **konuşma fırsatı elde edememek, araya laf sıkıştıramamak** ⊃See also: a play[2] on words, swear word.

word[2] /wɜːd/ *verb* [T] to choose the words you use when you are saying or writing something **kelimeleri seçmek; sözcüklerle ifade etmek** *How should I word this letter?*

change the wording ● the **exact** wording ● the wording **of** sth ● **a form of** wording

wording /'wɜːdɪŋ/ *noun* [U] the words that are used when someone says or writes something **anlatım, üslûp, yazılış tarzı**

word 'processor *noun* [C] a computer or computer program that you use for writing letters, reports, etc **yazı işlem bilgisayarı** ● **word processing** *noun* [U] **yazı programı (bilgisayar)**

wore /wɔːr/ *past tense of* wear **giymek' fiilinin geçmiş zaman hâli**

o- **work**[1] /wɜːk/ *verb* **1** [JOB] [I, T] to do a job, especially the job you do to earn money **çalışmak** *Helen works for a computer company.* ○ *He works as a waiter in an Italian restaurant.* ○ *My dad works very long hours* (= he works a lot of hours). **2** [MACHINE] [I] if a machine or piece of equipment works, it is not broken. **çalışmak, işlemek** *Does this radio work?* ○ *The washing machine isn't working.* **3** [SUCCEED] [I] if something works, it is effective and successful. **işe yaramak, başarılı olmak, yürümek** *Her plan to get rid of me didn't work.* **4 can work sth; know how to work sth** to know how to use a machine or piece of equipment **çalıştırabilmek; nasıl çalışacağını bilmek** *Do you know how to work the video recorder?* **5** [EFFORT] [I, T] to do something that needs a lot of time or effort, or to make someone do this **çalışmak, çabalamak, çalıştırmak** [+ to do sth] *He's been working to improve his speed.* ○ *Our teacher works us very hard.* **6 work your way around/through/up, etc sth** to achieve something gradually **yavaş yavaş başarmak** *I have a pile of homework to work my way through.*

work against sb *phrasal verb* to make it more difficult for someone to achieve something **aleyhinde çalışmak, engellemek, zararına çalışmak, ...ile mücadele etmek** *Age can work against you when you are looking for a job.*

work at sth *phrasal verb* to try hard to achieve something **başarmaya çalışmak, üstünde çalışmak** [+ doing sth] *You need to work at improving your writing.*

work on sth *phrasal verb* to spend time repairing or improving something **üzerinde çalışmak, uğraşmak** *Tim loves working on old cars.*

work sth out *phrasal verb* **1** to calculate an amount **çözmek, hesaplamak, bulmak, hâlletmek** *I'm trying to work out the total cost.* **2** to understand something or decide something after thinking very carefully **anlamak, çözmek, çözüm yolu bulmak, hâlletmek** [+ question word] *I haven't worked out what to do yet.*

work out *phrasal verb* **1** If a problem or difficult situation works out, it gradually becomes better. **işlemek, iyileşmek, olmak, gelişmek** *Don't worry - everything will work out in the end.* **2** to do exercises to make your body stronger **idman yapmak, spor yapmak, antreman yapmak, egzersiz yapmak** ⊃Orta kısımdaki renkli sayfalarına bakınız. **3 work out badly/well, etc** to happen or develop in a particular way *Changing schools worked out really well for me.* **4 work out at sth** to be the result when you calculate something *If we share the costs, it works out at $10 per person.*

work sb out *phrasal verb UK* to understand the reasons for someone's behaviour **birinin davranışlarına anlam vermek; nedenini anlamak** *I can't work him out at all.*

work up to sth *phrasal verb* to gradually prepare yourself for something difficult **kendini zor şeylere hazırlamak**

---
work .... İLE BİRLİKTE KULLANILAN KELİMELER

do/find/finish/have work ● **clerical/dirty/hard/part-time/pioneering** work ● **at** work

---

ᵒᴬ**work²** /wɜːk/ *noun* **1** [EFFORT] [U] when you use physical or mental effort to do something **iş, çaba, çalışma** *Decorating that room was hard work.* **2** [PLACE] [U] the place where you go to do your job **iş, işyeri, çalışma yeri** *He had an accident at work.* **3** [JOB] [U] something you do as a job to earn money **iş, uğraş, meslek** *Has she got any work yet?* ○ *Many young people are out of work* (= they do not have a job). **4** [ACTIVITY] [U] the activities that you have to do at school, for your job, etc **faaliyetler, uğraşılar, işler, görevler** *Have you got a lot of work to do?* ○ *The teacher said she was pleased with my work.* **5 get/set to work (on sth)** to start doing something **işe başlamak, işe koyulmak 6** [ART/MUSIC ETC] [C, U] a painting, book, piece of music, etc **eser, ürün, çalışma** *The exhibition includes works by Picasso and Klee.* ○ *the complete works of Shakespeare* **7 do sb's dirty work** to do something unpleasant or difficult for someone else because they do not want to do it themselves **başkasının kirli işlerini yapmak 8 have your work cut out** to have something very difficult to do **yapacak çok zor bir işi olmak, halletmesi gereken bir uğraşı olmak** *It's a demanding job - she's going to have her work cut out for her.* ⊃See also: **donkey work, work of art.**

workable /'wɜːkəbl/ *adjective* A workable plan or system can be used or done easily and is effective. **pratik, uygulanabilir** ⊃Opposite **unworkable.**

workaholic /ˌwɜːkə'hɒlɪk/ *noun* [C] *informal* someone who works too much and does not have time to do anything else **işkolik kimse, iş düşkünü kişi**

workbook /'wɜːkbʊk/ *noun* [C] a book with questions and exercises in it that you use when you are learning something **alıştırma kitabı**

,**worked 'up** *adjective* very nervous, angry, or excited **öfkelenmiş, sinirlenmiş, kızgın, heyecanlı**

worker /'wɜːkəʳ/ *noun* **1** [C] someone who works for a company or organization but does not have a powerful position **işçi, çalışan kişi/kimse** *an office worker* **2 a quick/slow/good, etc worker** someone who works quickly/slowly/well, etc **hızlı/yavaş/iyi vb. işçi** ⊃See also: **social worker.**

workforce /'wɜːkfɔːs/ *noun* [group] **1** all the people who work for a company or organization **iş gücü, çalışanlar 2** all the people in a country who are able to do a job **iş gücü, çalışanlar** *10% of the workforce are unemployed.*

working /'wɜːkɪŋ/ *adjective* [always before noun] **1** relating to your job **işe ilişkin; işle ilgili** *good working conditions* **2 a working man/woman, etc** someone who has

a job **çalışan erkek/kadın** *a working mother* **3 a working knowledge of sth** knowledge about something which is good enough to be useful **işe yarar/faydalı bilgi** *She has a working knowledge of German and Russian.* ⊃See also: **hard-working.**

,**working 'class** *noun* [C] the social class of people who have little money and who usually do physical work **işçi sınıfı; emekçi sınıfı** ● **working-class** /ˌwɜːkɪŋ'klɑːs/ *adjective* a working-class family **işçi sınıfı**

workings /'wɜːkɪŋz/ *noun* **the workings of sth** how something works **çalışma biçimi, işleme tarzı, hareket şekli** *the workings of the mind*

workload /'wɜːkləʊd/ *noun* [C] the amount of work that you have to do **iş yükü** *Nurses have a very heavy workload* (= they work hard).

workman /'wɜːkmən/ *noun* [C] *plural* **workmen** someone who does a physical job such as building **işçi**

workmanship /'wɜːkmənʃɪp/ *noun* [U] the skill that is used in making something **işçilik, sanatkârlık, zanaatkârlık**

,**work of 'art** *noun* [C] *plural* **works of art 1** a very beautiful and important painting, drawing, etc **başyapıt, şaheser** *They stole several valuable works of art.* **2 be a work of art** to be something which is beautiful or needed a lot of skill to create **şaheser/başyapıt olmak** *Have you seen the wedding cake? It's a work of art.*

workout /'wɜːkaʊt/ *noun* [C] when you do a series of exercises to make your body strong and healthy **antreman, egzersiz, idman** *a daily workout at the gym*

workplace /'wɜːkpleɪs/ *noun* [C] the place where you work **işyeri** *We are trying to get rid of bullying in the workplace.*

worksheet /'wɜːkˌʃiːt/ *noun* [C] a piece of paper with questions and exercises for students **alıştırma kâğıdı**

workshop /'wɜːkʃɒp/ *noun* [C] **1** when a group of people meet to learn more about something by discussing it and doing practical exercises **seminer, çalıştay** *a workshop on crime prevention* **2** a place where people use tools and machines to make or repair things **atelye, işyeri**

workstation /'wɜːkˌsteɪʃᵊn/ *noun* [C] a computer and the area around it where you work in an office **bilgisayar iş istasyonu; bilgi işlem odası; çalışma köşesi**

'**work ˌsurface** (*also* **worktop** /'wɜːktɒp/) *noun* [C] a flat surface for preparing food in a kitchen **mutfak tezgâhı** ⊃Orta kısımdaki renkli sayfalarına bakınız.

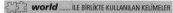

world .... İLE BİRLİKTE KULLANILAN KELİMELER

travel the world ● **in** the world ● **across/all over** the world

---

ᵒᴬ**world¹** /wɜːld/ *noun* **1 the world** the Earth and all the people, places, and things on it **dünya** *Everest is the highest mountain in the world.* ○ *She's travelled all over the world.* **2** [C] the people and things that are involved in a particular activity or subject **dünya, âlem** [usually singular] *the entertainment world* ○ *the world of politics* **3 the developing/industrialized/Western, etc world** a particular area of the Earth **gelişen/endüstrileşmiş/Batı vb. dünyası 4 the plant/animal, etc world** plants/animals, etc as a group **bitki/hayvan vb. dünyası 5 your whole world** your life and experiences **yaşam ve deneyimler** *His whole world fell apart when she left.* **6 do sb a/the world of good** *informal* to make someone feel much happier or healthier **çok iyi gelmek; çok yararı olmak; birini daha da mutlu/sağlıklı kılmak** *That swim has done me a world of good.* **7 be out of this world** *informal* to be of extremely good quality **son derece iyi kalitede olmak** *Their chocolate cake is just out of this world!* **8 think the world of sb** to like and admire someone very much **çok sevmek ve hayran olmak 9 the whole world** *informal* everyone **cümle âlem, herkes, tüm dünya** *The whole world knew she was getting married before I did.* つSee also: have the **best**³ of both worlds, not be the **end**¹ of the world, the Old World, the outside world, the Third World, be on **top**¹ of the world.

world² /wɜːld/ *adjective* [always before noun] relating to the whole world **tüm dünyaya ilişkin, dünya âlemi ilgilendiren** *world peace* ○ *the world championships*

world-class /ˌwɜːld'klɑːs/ *adjective* one of the best in the world **dünya çapında** *a world-class swimmer*

world-famous /ˌwɜːld'feɪməs/ *adjective* known by people everywhere in the world **dünyaca meşhur** *The Eiffel Tower is a world-famous landmark.*

worldly /'wɜːldli/ *adjective* **1 sb's worldly goods/possessions** everything that someone owns **dünyalıkları, mal mülk, tüm varlığı** *She lost all her worldly possessions in a fire.* **2** having had a lot of experience of life **görmüş geçirmiş** *a worldly woman*

,**world 'war** *noun* [C] a war in which several large or important countries fight **dünya savaşı**

worldwide /ˌwɜːld'waɪd/ *adjective, adverb* in all parts of the world **dünya çapında, bütün dünyada** *10 million copies have been sold worldwide.*

the ,World Wide 'Web *noun* all the websites (= pages of text and pictures) on the Internet **genel internet ağı (WWW)** つSee study page The Web and the Internet on page Centre 36.

worm¹ /wɜːm/ *noun* [C] a small creature with a long, thin, soft body and no legs **kurt, solucan** つSee also: a **can²** of worms.

worm² /wɜːm/ *verb* **worm your way into sth** to gradually get into a situation by making people like you and trust you, especially by deceiving them **sokulup girmek, güçlükle ilerlemek, kalabalığı yara yara ilerlemek** *He wormed his way into the family.*

worn¹ /wɔːn/ *adjective* Worn clothing or objects have been used a lot and show damage. **eskimiş, yıpranmış, lime lime olmuş** *a worn leather chair*

worn² /wɔːn/ *past participle of* wear **giymek' fiilinin geçmiş zaman hâli**

worn

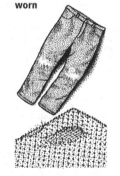

worn-out /ˌwɔːn'aʊt/ *adjective* **1** extremely tired **bitkin, tükenmiş, yorulmuş, mahvolmuş** *I was absolutely worn-out after all that dancing.* **2** Something that is worn-out is so old or has been used so much that it is damaged too much to repair. **eskimiş, yıpranmış, kullanılmaz hâle gelmiş** *a worn-out carpet*

◦–**worried** /'wʌrid/ *adjective* anxious because you are thinking about problems or unpleasant things that might happen **kaygılı, tedirgin, endişeli** *She's really worried about her son.* ○ [+ (that)] *I'm worried that she'll tell Maria.*

◦–**worry¹** /'wʌri/ *verb* **1** [I] to think about problems or unpleasant things that might happen in a way that makes you feel anxious **kaygılanmak, endişelenmek,**

merak etmek *Don't worry - she'll be all right.* ○ *She's always worrying about something.* ○ [+ (that)] *I worry that he might run away.* **2** [T] to make someone feel anxious because of problems or unpleasant things that might happen **kaygılandırmak, endişelendirmek, rahatsız etmek, canını sıkmak** *It worries me that he hasn't phoned yet.*

🖧🖧🖧 worry (noun) .... İLE BİRLİKTE KULLANILAN KELİMELER

allay/ease/express a worry ● a **constant/lingering/nagging/real** worry ● a worry **about/over** sth

worry² /'wʌri/ *noun* **1** [C] a problem that makes you feel anxious **sorun, dert, tasa** *health worries* **2** [U] when you are anxious about something **endişe, kaygı, merak** *She's been sick with worry.*

worrying /'wʌriɪŋ/ *adjective* making you feel anxious **kaygı verici, endişe uyandıran** *a worrying situation* ● **worryingly** *adverb* *She's worryingly thin.* **endişeli bir şekilde**

◦–**worse¹** /wɜːs/ *adjective* **1** *comparative of* bad: more unpleasant or difficult than something else that is also bad **daha kötü/zor** *The exam was worse than I expected.* ○ *We'll have to stop the game if the rain gets any worse.* **2** more ill **daha hasta/rahatsız** *The drugs aren't working, he just seems to be getting worse.* **3 be none the worse for sth** to not be harmed or damaged by something **hiç etkilenmemiş/zarar görmemiş olmak** *He seemed none the worse for the experience.* **4 worse luck** *UK informal* used to show that you are annoyed or unhappy about something **ne yazık ki** *I've got to work on Saturday, worse luck!*

worse² /wɜːs/ *noun* [U] **1** something that is more unpleasant or difficult **daha kötü/beter şey** *It was a nasty accident, although I've seen worse.* **2 for the worse** If a situation changes for the worse, it becomes worse. **daha da kötüye doğru**

worse³ /wɜːs/ *adverb comparative of* badly: less well **daha kötü olarak** *He was treated much worse than I was.*

worsen /'wɜːsᵊn/ *verb* [I, T] to become worse or to make something become worse **kötüleşmek, kötüleştirmek** *His condition suddenly worsened last week.*

,**worse 'off** *adjective* [never before noun] poorer or in a more difficult situation **daha kötü/berbat durumda** *If Rick loses his job we'll be even worse off.*

worship /'wɜːʃɪp/ *verb* **worshipping**, *past* **worshipped**, *also US* **worshiping**, *past* **worshiped 1** [I, T] to show respect for a god by saying prayers or performing religious ceremonies **ibadet etmek, dua etmek, tapınmak 2** [T] to love and respect someone very much **taparcasına sevmek, tapmak** *She worshipped her mother.* ● **worship** *noun* [U] *a place of worship* (= a religious building) **tapınma** ● **worshipper** *noun* [C] **tapınan**

◦–**worst¹** /wɜːst/ *adjective superlative of* bad: the most unpleasant or difficult **en kötüsü** *What's the worst job you've ever had?*

worst² /wɜːst/ *noun* **1 the worst** the most unpleasant or difficult thing, person, or situation **en kötü durum/şey/kişi/hâl** *I've made some mistakes in the past, but this is definitely the worst.* **2 at worst** used to say what the most unpleasant or difficult situation could possibly be **en kötü olasılıkla/ihtimalle/durumda** *At worst, we might lose our money.* **3 if the worst comes to the worst** *UK* (*US* if worse/worst comes to worst) if a situation develops in the most unpleasant or difficult way **çok sıkışırsak...; işler iyice berbat hâle gelirse...; en kötü şartlarda...**

worst³ /wɜːst/ *adverb superlative of* badly: the most badly **en kötü bir şekilde** *the worst affected area*

W

oⁿ**worth**¹ /wɜːθ/ *adjective* **1 be worth sth** to have a particular value, especially in money ...değerinde/ederinde olmak *Our house is worth about £600,000.* **2 be worth doing/seeing/trying, etc** to be useful or enjoyable to do/see/try, etc ...ya/ye değer olmak *It's not as good as his last book but it's definitely worth reading.* **3 be worth it** to be useful or enjoyable despite needing a lot of effort ...a/e değer olmak/değmek *It was a long climb up the mountain but the view was worth it.* ○ *Don't bother complaining - it's really not worth it.* **4 be worth your while** if it is worth your while doing something, it is useful or enjoyable despite needing a lot of effort ...ın/in zahmetine değer olmak *It isn't worth my while going all that way just for one day.*

oⁿ**worth**² /wɜːθ/ *noun* **1 £20/$100, etc worth of sth** the amount of something that you can buy for £20/$100, etc ...değerinde/kıymetinde *I've put £2 worth of stamps on the letter.* **2 a month's/year's, etc worth of sth** the amount of something that can be done or used in a month/year, etc değerinde *an hour's worth of free phone calls* **3** [U] how important or useful someone or something is değer, kadir, kıymet *She's finally proved her worth.*

worthless /'wɜːθləs/ *adjective* **1** not important or useful değersiz, yarasız, faydasız, işe yaramaz *He made me feel stupid and worthless.* **2** having no value in money kıymetsiz, değersiz *The painting's a fake - it's completely worthless.*

worthwhile /ˌwɜːθ'waɪl/ *adjective* useful and enjoyable, despite needing a lot of effort değer, değen *It's a difficult course but it's very worthwhile.*

worthy /'wɜːði/ *adjective* **1** deserving respect, admiration, or support lâyık, değer, yakışır *a worthy cause* ○ *a worthy champion* **2 be worthy of attention/respect, etc** to deserve attention/respect, etc dikkati/saygıyı hak ediyor olmak

oⁿ**would** *strong form* /wʊd/ *weak form* /wəd/ *modal verb* **1** [IF] used to say what might happen if something else happens bir şey olursa ondan sonra olabilecek şeyi anlatmada kullanılır (şart cümleciğinin 2. türünde) *What would you do if you lost your job?* **2** [SAID/THOUGHT] used as the past form of 'will' to talk about what someone has said or thought geçmiş zaman fiil yapısında 'will' yardımcı fiilinin 2. hâli olarak kullanılır *Sue promised that she would help.* ○ *They thought that she would never recover.* **3** [WILLING] used as the past form of 'will' to talk about what someone was willing to do or what something was able to do birinin bir şeyi önceden yapmaya istekli olduğunu veya bir şeyin neyi yapabileceğini belirtirken 'will' yardımcı fiilinin geçmiş hâli olarak kullanılır *I asked her to talk to him, but she wouldn't.* ○ *The car wouldn't start this morning.* **4 would like/love sth** used to say politely that you want something bir şeyi çok istemek/sevmek *I'd* (= I would) *like a cup of coffee, please.* **5 would you** used to politely ask someone something ...misiniz/mısınız *Would you like a drink?* ○ *Would you come with me, please?* **6** [IMAGINE] used to talk about a situation that you can imagine happening ne olabileceği hayal edilen durumla ilgili olarak konuşurken *It would be lovely to go to New York.* **7 I would imagine/think, etc** used to give an opinion in a polite way nazikçe bir konuda fikir beyan ederken kullanılır *I would imagine she'll discuss it with her husband first.* **8** [OFTEN] used to talk about things that happened often in the past geçmişte sıkça tekrarlanan şeyleri belirtirken kullanılır *He would always turn and wave at the end of the street.* **9 She/he/you would!** *mainly UK* used to show that you are not surprised by someone's annoying behaviour Beklenir!', 'Yapar!', 'Umulur!' gibi birinin yaptıklarından dolayı şaşır-

mamayı belirtirken kullanılır *Margot spent £200 on a dress for the occasion but she would, wouldn't she?* ⊃See study page **Modal verbs** on page Centre 22.

oⁿ**wouldn't** /'wʊdᵊnt/ *short for* would not **would not'** fiilinin kısa yazılışı *She wouldn't let us watch TV.*

⟨ 🧩 ⟩ **wound** (noun) .... İLE BİRLİKTE KULLANILAN KELİMELER

inflict/sustain a wound ● a wound **heals (up)** ● **bullet/gunshot/stab** wounds ● a wound **on/to** [sb's arm/back, etc] ● an **open** wound

wound¹ /wuːnd/ *noun* [C] an injury, especially one that is made by a knife or bullet yara

wound² /wuːnd/ *verb* [T] **1** to injure someone, especially with a knife or gun yaralamak [often passive] *He was badly wounded in the attack.* ○ *wounded soldiers* **2** to upset someone kalbini kırmak, incitmek [often passive] *She was deeply wounded by his rejection.*

wound³ /waʊnd/ *past of* wind³ kurmak' fiilinin 3. hâli

ˌ**wound 'up** *adjective* very nervous, worried, or angry aşırı sinirli/endişeli/kızgın *He gets very wound up before an important match.*

wove /wəʊv/ *past tense of* weave zikzak yaparak ilerlemek' fiilinin geçmiş zaman hâli

woven /'wəʊvᵊn/ *past participle of* weave örmek, dokumak' fiilinin geçmiş zaman hâli

wow /waʊ/ *exclamation informal* something that you say to show surprise, excitement, admiration, etc Vay be!', 'Vay canına"! *Wow! Look at that car!*

⟨ 🧩 ⟩ **wrangle** .... İLE BİRLİKTE KULLANILAN KELİMELER

be involved in/get into a wrangle ● a **bitter/legal** wrangle ● a wrangle **over** sth ● a wrangle **between** sb and sb ● a wrangle **with** sb

wrangle¹ /'ræŋgl/ *noun* [C] a long and complicated argument yaygara, münakaşa, kıyamet *a legal wrangle*

wrangle² /'ræŋgl/ *verb* [I] to argue with someone for a long time atışmak, kapışmak, tartışmak *They're still wrangling over money.*

wrap /ræp/ *verb* [T] **wrapping,** *past* **wrapped 1** (*also* wrap up) to cover someone or something with paper, cloth, etc sarmak, paket yapmak, sarıp sarmalamak *to wrap a present* ○ *They wrapped him in a blanket.* ⊃Opposite unwrap. **2 wrap sth around sb/sth** to fold paper, cloth, etc around something to cover it sarmak, sarıp sarmalamak *He wrapped a towel around his waist.* **3 wrap your arms/fingers, etc around sb/sth** to put your arms/fingers, etc around someone or something sarmak, dolamak *She wrapped her arms around my neck.*

wrap sth up *phrasal verb* **1** to fold paper, cloth, etc around something to cover it sarmak, sarmalamak *Have you wrapped up Jenny's present?* **2** to finish an activity successfully başarıyla tamamlamak, çözüp bitirmek, başarıyla sonuçlandırmak *We hope to have this deal wrapped up by Monday.*

wrap up *phrasal verb* to dress in warm clothes kalın giysilere bürünmek *Wrap up well - it's cold outside.*

be wrapped up in sth *phrasal verb* to give so much of your attention to something that you do not have time for other things or people kendini kaptırmak, bütün dikkatini ...a/e vermek *She's so wrapped up in her work that she hardly sees her kids.*

wrapper /'ræpər/ *noun* [C] a piece of paper or plastic that covers something that you buy, especially food ambalaj/paketleme kağıdı/naylonu vb. (UK) *sweet wrappers*/(US) *candy wrappers*

wrapping /'ræpɪŋ/ noun [C, U] paper or plastic that is used to cover and protect something **ambalaj, paket**

'wrapping ,paper noun [U] decorated paper that is used to cover presents **ambalaj/paketleme kağıdı**

wrath /rɒθ/ noun [U] literary extreme anger **öfke, gazap, hiddet**

wreak /riːk/ verb past **wrought** or **wreaked wreak havoc** to cause a lot of damage or harm **çok fazla zarar ve ziyana sebebiyet vermek** Floods have wreaked havoc in central Europe.

wreath /riːθ/ noun [C] plural **wreaths** /riːðz/ a large ring of leaves and flowers used as a decoration or to show respect for someone who has died **çelenk**

wreck¹ /rek/ verb [T] to destroy something completely **enkaza çevirmek, mahvetmek, perişan etmek** The explosion wrecked several cars and damaged nearby buildings.

wreck² /rek/ noun [C] 1 VEHICLE a car, ship, or aircraft that has been very badly damaged **enkaz 2** PERSON informal someone who is in a bad physical or mental condition **bitik, perişan, harap, sinirleri harap olmuş** [usually singular] I was a complete wreck by the end of my exams. **3** ACCIDENT mainly US a bad accident involving a car or train **kazaya uğrama, enkaz hâline gelme, enkaz** a car/train wreck

⋮⋮⋮ wreckage ...... İLE BİRLİKTE KULLANILAN KELİMELER

be **cut (free) from/pulled from/recovered from** the wreckage ● be **trapped in** the wreckage ● **a piece of** wreckage ● the **tangled** wreckage **of** sth

wreckage /'rekɪdʒ/ noun [U] the parts that remain of a car, ship, or aircraft that has been destroyed **enkaz, kazadan sonra kalan enkaz** Two survivors were pulled from the wreckage.

wren /ren/ noun [C] a very small, brown bird **çalı kuşu**

wrench¹ /renʃ/ verb [T] 1 **wrench sth from/off, etc sb/ sth** to pull something violently away from a fixed position **bükmek, çevirmek, zorla yerinden koparmak, şiddetle asılmak** The phone had been wrenched off the wall. 2 to injure part of your body by turning it suddenly **burkmak** I wrenched my right shoulder playing tennis.

wrench² /renʃ/ noun 1 [no plural] when you are very sad because you have to leave someone or something **ayrılık acısı** She found leaving home a real wrench. 2 [C] US (UK spanner) a tool with a round end that is used to turn nuts and bolts (= metal objects used to fasten things together) **ingiliz anahtarı** ⊃See picture at **tool**.

wrestle /'resl/ verb [I] to fight with someone by holding them and trying to push them to the ground **güreşmek, güreşe tutuşmak**

wrestle with sth phrasal verb to try very hard to deal with a difficult problem or decision **boğuşmak, uğraşmak** He's still wrestling with his conscience.

wrestling /'reslɪŋ/ noun [U] a sport in which two people fight and try to push each other to the ground **güreş, güreş sporu** ● **wrestler** noun [C] **güreşçi**

wretched /'retʃɪd/ adjective 1 UNHAPPY very unhappy or ill **perişan, berbat, çok mutsuz, aşırı hasta** I'd been feeling wretched all day so I went to bed early. 2 BAD very bad or of poor quality **berbat, çok kötü, adi, kalitesiz** The refugees were living in wretched conditions. 3 ANNOYED [always before noun] used to show that something or someone makes you angry **kör olasıca, lanet** This wretched phone won't work!

wriggle /'rɪgl/ verb [I, T] 1 to twist your body or move part of your body with short, quick movements **oynatıp durmak, durmadan kıpırdamak, kıpırdatmak** She wriggled her toes in the warm sand. 2 **wriggle out of sth/doing sth** to avoid doing something that you have agreed to do **kurtulmak, sıyrılmak** Are you trying to wriggle out of going to the meeting?

wring /rɪŋ/ (also wring out) verb [T] past **wrung** to twist a cloth or piece of clothing with your hands to remove water from it **sıkmak, sıkıp/büküp suyunu çıkarmak** He wrung out his socks and hung them up to dry. ⊃See also: **wring your hands (hand¹).**

wrinkle /'rɪŋkl/ noun [C] 1 a small line on your face that you get when you grow old **kırışıklık, buruşukluk** 2 a small fold in a piece of cloth **kabarma, buruşma, kırışma** ● **wrinkle** verb [I, T] a wrinkled face **buruşmak, kırışmak**

wrinkles

wrist /rɪst/ noun [C] the part of your body between your hand and your arm **bilek**

wristband /'rɪstbænd/ noun [C] 1 a piece of material which goes around the wrist (= the part of your body between your hand and your arm), for example to hold a watch **bileklik** 2 a piece of material in a particular colour which goes around the wrist and shows that the person wearing it supports a certain charity **bileğe takılan ve yardım kuruluşunu/yardımı simgeleyen bant**

wristwatch /'rɪstwɒtʃ/ noun [C] a watch which you wear on your wrist (= the part of your body between your hand and your arm) **kol saati**

writ /rɪt/ noun [C] a legal document that orders someone to do something **mahkeme emri, yazılı emir**

o⊷write /raɪt/ verb past tense **wrote**, past participle **written** 1 WORDS [I, T] to produce words, letters, or numbers on a surface using a pen or pencil **yazmak, yazıya dökmek** Write your name at the top of the page. ○ She can't read or write. 2 BOOK [I, T] to create a book, story, article, etc or a piece of music **kitap/hikaye/makale/şarkı sözü vb.** yazmak He's writing a book on Russian literature. ○ She writes for Time magazine. 3 LETTER [I, T] to send someone a letter **mektup yazmak** [+ two objects] I wrote her a letter last week. ○ Has Bill written to you recently? 4 DOCUMENT [T] (also write out) to put all the information that is needed on a document **bilgileri doldurmak/yazmak** He wrote out a cheque for £250.

YAYGIN HATALAR

write

Dikkat! Fiil sonlarına dikkat edin! Birçok Türk öğrenci **write** fiilini -ing formunda veya geçmiş zamanda kullanırken hata yapmaktadır. **Write** fiilinin -ing kullanımı **writing** şeklindedir ve bir **t** ile yazılır. **Write** fiilinin üçüncü halinde **tt** vardır. **Writen** veya **writed** olarak değil- **written** olarak yazılır.

write back phrasal verb to reply to someone's letter **mektuba cevap yazmak**

write sth down phrasal verb to write something on a piece of paper so that you do not forget it **not almak, not tutmak** Did you write Jo's phone number down?

write in phrasal verb to write a letter to a newspaper, television company, etc **gazete/tv. şirketi vb. mektup yazmak** Lots of people have written in to complain about the show.

write off *phrasal verb* to write a letter to an organization asking them to send you something **talep mektubu yazmak** *I've **written off** for an information pack.*

write sth off *phrasal verb* **1** to accept that an amount of money has been lost or will never be paid to you **silmek, gözden çıkarmak, üstüne soğuk su içmek** *to write off debts* **2** *UK* to damage a vehicle so badly that it cannot be repaired **bir aracı hurdaya çıkarmak/tamir edilemez hâle getirmek**

write sb/sth off *phrasal verb* to decide that someone or something is not useful or important **notunu vermek, defterini dürmek** *They had written him off before they even met him.*

write sth up *phrasal verb* to write something in a complete form, usually using notes that you made earlier **son şeklini vermek, temize çekmek** *Have you written up that report yet?*

write-off /'raɪtɒf/ *noun* [C] *UK* a vehicle that is damaged so badly in an accident that it cannot be repaired **hurda olmuş araba; hurdaya çıkmış araç** *I wasn't hurt, but the car was a complete write-off.*

o▪**writer** /'raɪtə^r/ *noun* [C] someone whose job is writing books, stories, articles, etc **yazar**

write-up /'raɪtʌp/ *noun* [C] an article in a newspaper or magazine in which someone gives their opinion about a performance, product, etc **ürün/gösteri vb. hakkında yazılan yorum/tanıtım yazısı** *The film got a very good write-up in yesterday's paper.*

writhe /raɪð/ *verb* [I] to twist your body in a violent way, often because you are in pain **acıdan kıvranmak, iki büklüm olmak** *She lay on her bed, writhing in agony.*

o▪**writing** /'raɪtɪŋ/ *noun* [U] **1** SKILL the skill or activity of producing words on a surface **yazı** *Teachers focus on reading and writing in the first year.* **2** WORDS words that have been written or printed **yazı, yazılı metin** *The writing was too small to read.* **3** STYLE the way that someone writes **yazı, yazı şekli/biçimi** *You've got very neat writing.* **4** BOOKS the books, stories, articles, etc written by a particular person or group of people **yazılar, yazılı eserler** *She's studying women's writing of the 1930s.* **5** JOB the activity or job of creating books, stories, or articles **yazma, yazarlık, yazma işi** **6 in writing** An agreement that is in writing is official because it has been written and not only spoken. **yazıyla, yazılı olarak** *Please confirm your reservation in writing.*

written¹ /'rɪt^ən/ *adjective* [always before noun] presented as a document on paper **yazılı** *a written statement/warning*

written² /'rɪt^ən/ *past participle of* write **yazmak' fiilinin 3. hâli**

o▪**wrong¹** /rɒŋ/ *adjective* **1** NOT CORRECT not correct **yanlış** *the wrong answer* ○ *We're going the wrong way.* **2 be wrong** to think or say something that is not correct **yanlış/hatalı olmak** *You were wrong about the party - it's today, not tomorrow.* **3 get sth wrong** to produce an answer or result that is not correct **yanlış anlamak; yanlış şeyler ortaya koymak** *I got most of the answers wrong.* **4** PROBLEM [never before noun] If something is wrong, there is a problem. **yanlış, hatalı, kusurlu** *There's something wrong with my computer.* ○ *What's*

wrong? **5** NOT MORAL [never before noun] morally bad **ahlâken kötü, hatalı, kusurlu** [+ to do sth] *It's wrong to tell lies.* **6** NOT SUITABLE not suitable **uygun olmayan, yanlış** *I think she's wrong for this job.* ⊃See also: get (hold of) the wrong end¹ of the stick, get/start off on the wrong foot¹, not put a foot¹ wrong, rub sb up the wrong way¹.

o▪**wrong²** /rɒŋ/ *adverb* **1** in a way that is not correct **yanlış/hatalı/kusurlu bir şekilde** *He always says my name wrong.* **2 go wrong** to develop problems **yanlış yapmak, yanılmak; hatalara sebep olmak** *Something's gone wrong with my computer.* **3 Don't get me wrong.** *informal* used when you do not want someone to think that you do not like someone or something **Beni yanlış anlama'** *Don't get me wrong, I like her, but she can be very annoying.*

wrong³ /rɒŋ/ *noun* **1** [C, U] when something is not morally right **kötülük, ahlâksızlık, hata, kusur** *She's old enough to know the difference between **right** and **wrong**.* **2 be in the wrong** to be responsible for a mistake or something bad that has happened **hatalı/kusurlu olmak**

wrong⁴ /rɒŋ/ *verb* [T] *formal* to treat someone unfairly **haksızlık etmek, günahına girmek** *a wronged man*

wrongdoing /'rɒŋduːɪŋ/ *noun* [C, U] *formal* when someone does something that is illegal or not honest **ahlâksızlık, yasadışı hareket**

wrongful /'rɒŋf^əl/ *adjective* **wrongful arrest/conviction/imprisonment, etc** when someone is accused of something or punished but there was something unfairly or illegally **haksız/hatalı tutuklama/yargılama/mahkumiyet vb.** ● **wrongfully** *adverb* **wrongfully arrested** **yanlış bir şekilde**

wrongly /'rɒŋli/ *adverb* **1** in a way that is not correct **hatalı olarak** *The letter was wrongly addressed.* **2 wrongly accused/convicted/imprisoned, etc** accused or punished unfairly or illegally **yanlışlıkla tutuklama/yargılama/mahkumiyet vb.** *She was wrongly convicted of drug smuggling.*

wrote /rəʊt/ *past tense of* write **yazmak' fiilinin 2. hâli**

wrought /rɔːt/ *past of* wreak **zarar vermek' fiilinin geçmiş zaman hâli**

,**wrought 'iron** *noun* [U] iron that can be bent into shapes and used to make gates, furniture, etc **demir dövme**

wrung /rʌŋ/ *past of* wring **sıkmak' fiilinin geçmiş zaman hâli**

wry /raɪ/ *adjective* A wry expression or remark shows your humour despite being in a difficult or disappointing situation. **muzip, hafif alaylı** *a wry smile* ● **wryly** *adverb* **alaycı bir şekilde**

www /,dʌblju:dʌblju:'dʌblju:/ *noun* abbreviation for World Wide Web (= part of the Internet that consists of all the connected websites) **internet adreslerinin başında yer alan uluslararası kullanılan 'Dünya Çapında internet Ağı' manasında sözcüklerin kısaltması** ⊃See study page **The Web and the Internet** on page Centre 36.

X, x /eks/ **1** [LETTER] the twenty-fourth letter of the alphabet **alfabenin yirmidördüncü harfi 2** [WRONG] used to show that an answer is wrong **cevabın yanlış olduğunu göstermek için kullanılır 3** [KISS] used to represent a kiss at the end of a letter **mektup sonunda öpücük anlamında kullanılır 4** [UNKNOWN] used to represent an unknown person or thing **bilinmeyen bir şeyi/kişiyi tanımlamada kullanılır**

xenophobia /ˌzenəʊˈfəʊbiə/ *noun* [U] extreme dislike or fear of people from other countries **yabancı/ yabancı ülke düşmanlığı ● xenophobic** /ˌzenəʊˈfəʊbɪk/ *adjective* **yabancı düşmanlığı**

XL /ˌeksˈel/ *abbreviation for* extra large: the largest size of clothes **çok büyük beden**

Xmas /ˈkrɪstməs/ *noun* [U] *informal* used as a short way of writing 'Christmas' (= a Christian holiday), mainly on signs or cards **Noel** *Happy Xmas!*

XML /ˌeksemˈel/ *noun trademark abbreviation for* extensible mark up language: a system of organizing information on computers **bilgisayar sistemine uygun olabilmesi için sembolleri yazıya dönüştürme şekli**

X-ray /ˈeksreɪ/ *noun* [C] **1** a photograph that shows the inside of your body **röntgen, x-ışını** *They took an X-ray of his leg.* **2** a wave of energy that can pass through solid materials **röntgen ışını ● X-ray** *verb* [T] to take a photograph that shows the inside of something **röntgen filmi çekmek**

xylophone /ˈzaɪləfəʊn/ *noun* [C] a musical instrument consisting of a row of flat, metal bars that you hit with sticks **zaylafon (müzik aleti)**

X

Y, y /waɪ/ the twenty-fifth letter of the alphabet **alfabenin yirmibeşinci harfi**

ya /jə/ *pronoun informal* you **sen/siz** *See ya later.*

yacht /jɒt/ *noun* [C] a large boat with sails used for pleasure or in races **yat, tekne** *a luxury yacht*

yacht

Yank /jæŋk/ *noun* [C] *informal* someone from the US, sometimes considered an offensive word **Amerikalı, Yanki**

yank /jæŋk/ *verb* [T] *informal* to pull something with a strong, sudden movement **asılmak, çekmek** *She yanked the drawer open.* ○ *He yanked at the rope.*

yap /jæp/ *verb* [I] **yapping**, *past* **yapped** If a small dog yaps, it makes a lot of short, high sounds. **acı acı havlamak**

●►**yard** /jɑːd/ *noun* [C] 1 UNIT (*written abbreviation* yd) a unit for measuring length, equal to 0.9144 metres or 3 feet **yarda; 0.9144 metre veya 3 fite eşit genişlik ölçüm birimi** *There's a bus stop a few hundred yards up the road.* ●See study page **Measurements** on page Centre 31. 2 HOUSE *US* (*UK* **garden**) an area of land in front of or behind a house **evin önündeki veya arkasındaki bahçe, alan; avlu** 3 AREA a small area of ground next to a building, often with a fence or wall around it **avlu, iç bahçe, binaya bitişik çevrili açıklık alan** *a school yard*

yardstick /'jɑːdstɪk/ *noun* [C] something that you use to judge how good or successful something else is **kıstas, ölçüt, kriter** *If popularity is the yardstick of success, he's done very well.*

yarn /jɑːn/ *noun* 1 [U] thread used for making cloth **dokuma/örgü ipliği** 2 [C] *informal* a long story that is probably not true **palavra, uydurma hikaye**

yawn /jɔːn/ *verb* [I] to take a deep breath with your mouth wide open, because you are tired or bored **esnemek** *She yawned and looked at her watch.* ● **yawn** *noun* [C] **esneyiş**

yawn

yawning /'jɔːnɪŋ/ *adjective* **a yawning gap** a very big gap (= space or difference) **alabildiğince açıklık/ farklılık**

yd *written abbreviation for* yard (= a unit for measuring length) **yarda' sözcüğünün kısa yazılışı**

yeah /jeə/ *exclamation informal spoken* yes (**ünlem**) **evet** *Yeah, I agree.*

year .... İLE BİRLİKTE KULLANILAN KELİMELER

each/every/last/next year ● the **past** year ● [2/5, etc] years **ago**

●►**year** /jɪəʳ/ *noun* [C] 1 a period of 12 months, or 365 or 366 days, especially from 1 January to 31 December **yıl** *last year/next year* ○ *He joined the company a year ago.* 2 **the academic/financial, etc year** the period of a year that is used by universities/businesses, etc to organize their activities **akademik/mali yıl** 3 **be two/ twelve/37, etc years old** to be a particular age ... **yaşında olmak** *Her son is six years old.* 4 **a two-/ twelve-/37-, etc year-old** someone who is a particular age ...**yaşında kimse** 5 *UK* a group of students who start college or a course together **aynı dönemde/yıllarda okulda olan bir grup öğrenci; devre** *He was in my year at school.* 6 **years** a long time **yıllarca; yıllar yılı** *I haven't seen Linda for years.* ●See also: for **donkey's years, leap year, new year.**

yearbook /'jɪəbʊk/ *noun* [C] a book produced every year by a school or organization, containing information about its activities, members, etc **yıllık olarak hazırlanan tanıtım kitabı**

yearly /'jɪəli/ *adjective, adverb* happening once a year or every year **yıllık, senelik, her yıl, yılda bir** *a yearly fee* ○ *Interest is paid yearly.*

yearn /jɜːn/ *verb* **yearn for sth; yearn to do sth** to want something very much with a feeling of sadness **can atmak, özlem duymak, gözünde tütmek, ...diye kıvranmak/yanıp tutuşmak** *They yearned for peace.* ○ *She yearned to get away.* ● **yearning** *noun* [C, U] **hasret**

yeast /jiːst/ *noun* [U] a substance used to make bread rise and to make beer and wine **maya**

yell /jel/ *verb* [I, T] to shout something very loudly **avaz avaz bağırmak, haykırmak, feryat etmek** *The policeman yelled at them to stop.* ● **yell** *noun* [C] **çığlık**

●►**yellow** /'jeləʊ/ *adjective* being the same colour as a lemon or the sun **sarı, sarı renkli** *a bright yellow tablecloth* ● **yellow** *noun* [C, U] the colour yellow **sarı renk** ●Orta kısımdaki renkli sayfalarına bakınız.

yellow 'card *noun* [C] in football, a small card shown to a player as a warning that the player has not obeyed a rule (**futbolda) sarı kart** ●Compare red card.

the ,Yellow 'Pages *UK trademark* (*US* the 'Yellow ,Pages) *noun* [**plural**] a big, yellow book containing telephone numbers of shops and businesses **telefon rehberindeki işyeri telefonlarını içeren sarı sayfalar**

yelp /jelp/ *verb* [I] If a dog yelps, it gives a sudden cry because of pain or shock. **kesik ve acı acı bağırmak; ciyaklamak; ciyak ciyak bağırmak**

yep /jep/ *exclamation informal spoken* yes **evet, hı hı,**

●►**yes**¹ /jes/ *exclamation* 1 AGREE used to agree with something, or to give a positive answer to something **evet, öyle** *"Can I borrow your pencil?" "Yes, of course."* ○ *"Are you feeling better?" "Yes, thanks."* ○ *"Coffee?" " Yes, please."* 2 ANSWER used as an answer when someone calls you **evet, buyurun, efendim** *"Jack!" "Yes?"* 3 DISAGREE used to disagree with a negative announcement (**olumsuz bir duyuruya katılımda) evet, öyle, katılıyorum, doğru, ...değil** *"He's not here yet." "Yes he is, I've just seen him."*

yes² /jes/ *noun* [C] a positive reaction or agreement with something **olumlu tepki veya uyuşma durumunda; evet, tabi, elbette, hay hay** *Was that a yes or a no?*

o→**yesterday** /ˈjestədeɪ/ *noun* [U], *adverb* the day before today **dün** *I went to see the doctor yesterday.* ○ *yesterday morning/afternoon*

o→**yet**[1] /jet/ *adverb* **1** before now or before that time **daha, şimdiden, henüz** *Have you read his book yet?* ○ *"Has he called?" "No, not yet."* **2** now or as early as this time **henüz, daha** *I don't want to go home yet.* **3 the best/worst, etc yet** the best/worst, etc until now **şu ana değin eniyisi/kötüsü vb.** *That was my worst exam yet.* **4 be/have yet to do sth** to not have done something that was expected before this time **daha yapacak bir şeyleri olmak; tamamlamamış olmak** *They have yet to make a decision.* **5 yet again/another/more, etc** used to show that you are surprised or annoyed that something is being repeated or increased **hâlâ yine/başka/daha da vs.** *He's given us yet more work to do.* **6 could/may/might, etc yet** used to say there is still a possibility that something will happen **hâlâ ... olabilirliği olmak** *He may win yet.*

yet[2] /jet/ *conjunction* used to add something that seems surprising because of what you have just said **ama, yine de** *simple yet effective*

yew /juː/ *noun* [C, U] a tree with dark, needle-shaped leaves, or the wood of this tree **porsuk ağacı**

┅┅┅ yield ┅┅┅ İLE BİRLİKTE KULLANILAN KELİMELER
yield **clues/information/a profit/a result**

yield[1] /jiːld/ *verb* **1** [T] to produce or provide something **ürün vermek, sağlamak, vermek** *to yield a profit* ○ *The investigation yielded some unexpected results.* **2 yield to demands/pressure, etc** to be forced to do something **kabul etmek, boyun eğmek, yapmaya zorlanmak 3** [I] *US (UK* **give way)** to stop in order to allow other vehicles to go past before you drive onto a bigger road **yol vermek; tâli yoldan ana yola girerken dikkatli/yavaş ve diğer araçları kollayarak girmek**

yield[2] /jiːld/ *noun* [C] the amount of something that is produced **ürün, gelir, kazanç**

yo /jəʊ/ *exclamation mainly US informal* used as a greeting **ooo, buyrun**

yob /jɒb/ *noun* [C] *UK informal* a rude or violent young man **serseri, holigan, hergele**

yoga /ˈjəʊgə/ *noun* [U] a set of exercises for the mind and body, based on the Hindu religion **yoga** *She does yoga three times a week.*

yoghurt *(also* **yogurt)** /ˈjɒgət/ Ⓤ /ˈjəʊgərt/ *noun* [C, U] a thick, liquid food with a slightly sour taste which is made from milk **yoğurt** *a low-fat strawberry yoghurt* ⊃Orta kısımdaki renkli sayfalarına bakınız.

yolk /jəʊk/ *noun* [C] the round, yellow part in the middle of an egg **yumurta sarısı**

Yom Kippur /ˌjɒmkɪˈpʊər/ *noun* [U] a Jewish holy day in September or October **Yahudi dininde kutsal bir gün, oruç günü**

yonder /ˈjɒndər/ *adverb, determiner literary* in that place or direction **şurada, şuradaki, ötede, ötedeki, orada, oradaki**

o→**you** *strong form* /juː/ *weak forms* /ju/, /jə/ *pronoun* **1** used to refer to the person or people you are talking to **sen, siz** *I love you.* ○ *You said I could go with you.* **2** people generally **sizler** *You learn to accept these things as you get older.*

o→**you'd** /juːd/ **1** *short for* you had **you had' fiil yapısının kısa yazılışı** *You'd better go home now.* **2** *short for* you would **you would' fiil yapısının kısa yazılışı** *I expect you'd like some lunch.*

o→**you'll** /juːl/ *short for* you will **you will' fiil yapısının kısa yazılışı** *I hope you'll come again.*

o→**young**[1] /jʌŋ/ *adjective* having lived or existed for only a short time and not old **genç** *young children/people* ○ *We were very young when we met.*

young[2] /jʌŋ/ *noun* [plural] **1 the young** young people generally **gençler** *It's the sort of music that appeals mainly to the young.* **2 sth's young** an animal's babies **yavrusu/yavruları**

youngster /ˈjʌŋstər/ *noun* [C] a young person, especially an older child **çocuk, genç, genç kimse** *He talked to the youngsters about the dangers of drugs.*

o→**your** *strong form* /jɔːr/ *weak form* /jər/ *determiner* **1** belonging or relating to the person or people you are talking to **senin, sizin** *Can I borrow your pen?* ○ *It's not your fault.* **2** belonging or relating to people in general **sizlerin** *You never stop loving your children.*

your or yours?
Dikkat! Doğru kelimeyi seçin. Bir mektubun sonunda, **Your** sincerely veya faithfully yazmayınız. Doğru şekli **Yours** sincerely veya faithfully şeklindedir.: ~~Your sincerely, D. Gilliver.~~ Yanlış cümle örneği
Yours sincerely, D. Gilliver.

o→**you're** /jɔːr/ *short for* you are **you are' fiil yapısının kısa yazılışı** *You're my best friend.*

o→**yours** /jɔːz/ *pronoun* **1** the things that belong to or relate to the person or people you are talking to **seninki, sizinki** *Is this pen yours?* ○ *Our tent's smaller than yours.* **2 Yours faithfully/sincerely, etc** used just before your name at the end of a polite or formal letter **en derin saygılarımla; en içten dileklerimle 3 yours truly** *humorous* I or me **saygılarımla, hürmetlerimle**

o→**yourself** /jɔːˈself/ *pronoun plural* **yourselves 1** the reflexive form of the pronoun 'you' **kendin, kendini, kendine; kendiniz, kendinizi, kendinize** *Don't cut yourself with that sharp knife.* **2** used to emphasize the pronoun 'you' when talking about the actions of the person you are speaking to **kendin, kendiniz** *Did you make the dress yourself?* **3 (all) by yourself/yourselves** alone or without anyone else's help **yalnız, tek başına/başlarına, kendi başına/kendilerine, kimseden yardım almadan** *I'm amazed you managed to move those boxes all by yourself.* **4 (all) to yourself** for your use only **sadece kendisine, kendisi için** *So you've got the whole house to yourself this weekend?*

┅┅┅ youth ┅┅┅ İLE BİRLİKTE KULLANILAN KELİMELER
recapture/relive your youth ● **in** sb's youth

youth /juːθ/ *noun* **1** YOUNG MAN [C] a young man **çocukluk, gençlik** *gangs of youths* **2** YOUNG PEOPLE [group] young people generally **gençlik, toyluk** *the youth of today* ○ *a youth club* **3 sb's youth** the period of time when someone is young **gençliği, gençlik yılları** *I was very shy in my youth.* **4** QUALITY [U] the quality of being young **genç, delikanlı**

youthful /ˈjuːθfʌl/ *adjective* typical of a young person **genç, dinamik, güçlü** *youthful energy/good looks*

youth hostel *noun* [C] a cheap, simple hotel, especially for young people who are travelling around **seyahat eden gençlerin kaldığı ucuz, basit otel; gençler pansiyonu, bekâr odaları**

o→**you've** /juːv/ *short for* you have **you have' fiil yapısının kısa yazılışı** *If you've finished your work, you can go.*

Y

yo-yo /ˈjəʊjəʊ/ *noun* [C] a small, round toy that you make go up and down on a string that you hang from your finger **yo-yo, oyuncak**

yuck /jʌk/ *exclamation informal* used to say that something looks or tastes very unpleasant **ööö; ıhhh; tiksinti belirten ünlem**

yum /jʌm/ (*also* ˌyum ˈyum) *exclamation informal* used to say that something tastes very good **hımm; tadına bakıldığında beğenildiğini belirten ünlem**

yummy /ˈjʌmi/ *adjective informal* If food or drink is yummy, it tastes very good. **nefis, enfes, leziz**

yuppie /ˈjʌpi/ *noun* [C] a young person who earns a lot of money and likes expensive things **pahalı şeylere düşkün ve başarılı genç adam/kadın**

Y

Z

Z, z /zed/ the twenty-sixth and last letter of the alphabet alfabenin yirmialtıncı harfi

zany /'zeɪni/ *adjective* funny in a strange way **garip ve gülünç** *zany humour*

zap /zæp/ *verb* [T] **zapping**, *past* **zapped** *informal* to attack or destroy something in a fast and powerful way **öldürmek, vurmak**

zeal /ziːl/ *noun* [U] extreme enthusiasm **fanatizm, aşırı düşkünlük, yüksek heyecan** *religious zeal*

zealous /'zeləs/ *adjective* extremely enthusiastic **çok gayretli aşırı düşkün, çok istekli** • **zealously** *adverb* **hevesli bir şekilde**

zebra /'zebrə/ ⑯ /'ziːbrə/ *noun* [C] an animal like a horse with black and white lines **zebra**

zebra 'crossing *noun* [C] *UK* a part of the road painted with black and white lines where people can cross over safely **yaya geçidi**

Zen /zen/ *noun* [U] a religion that developed from Buddhism **din; Budizm'den türeyen Zen tarikatı**

zenith /'zenɪθ/ ⑯ /'ziːnɪθ/ *noun* [no plural] *literary* the highest or most successful point of something **doruk noktası, zirve, en üst nokta** *The city reached its zenith in the 1980s.*

┌───┐
│ 🧩 **zero** ...... İLE BİRLİKTE KULLANILAN KELİMELER │
└───┘

sth drops to/falls to zero • **above/below zero**

zero /'zɪərəʊ/ the number 0 **sıfır**

zero 'tolerance *noun* [U] when you do not accept any bad behaviour, often by using laws to prevent it **sıfır hoşgörü/tolerans** *zero tolerance of crime*

zest /zest/ *noun* [U] **1** excitement and enthusiasm **merak, tutku, heves, şevk** *a zest for life* **2** the outer skin of a lemon or orange used to give flavour to food **lezzet/tat veren portakal/limon kabuğu**

zigzag /'zɪgzæg/ *noun* [C] a line that changes direction from left to right and back again at sharp angles **zikzak** • **zigzag** *verb* [I] **zigzagging**, *past* **zigzagged** to make a movement or pattern like a zigzag **zikzak çizmek**

zillion /'zɪljən/ *quantifier informal* a very large number **çok büyük bir sayı/rakam; sayılamayacak kadar** *a zillion times*

zinc /zɪŋk/ *noun* [U] a blue-white metal that is used to make or cover other metals (symbol **Zn**) **çinko**

zip¹ /zɪp/ *UK* (*US* **zipper**) *noun* [C] a thing for fastening clothes, bags, etc consisting of two rows of very small parts that connect together **fermuar** *Your zip's undone.*

zip² /zɪp/ *verb* **zipping**, *past* **zipped 1** [T] (*also* zip up) to fasten something with a zip **fermuarla kapatmak** *He zipped up his jacket.* **2** (*also* zip up) to reduce the size of a computer file (= collection of information) so that it uses less space and can be sent or stored more easily **bilgisayarda bilgiyi sıkıştırarak saklamak 3** **zip along/around/past, etc** *informal* to move somewhere very quickly **çok hızlıca hareket etmek**

zip ,code *noun* [C] a set of numbers that go after someone's address in the US **posta kodu** ⊃Compare **postcode**.

zip ,drive *noun* [C] a device used for copying large documents onto special disks **büyük belgelerin özel disk-**

lere kaydedilmesi için kullanılan bilgisayar programı; sıkıştırma sürümü ⊃See **Memory Stick**.

zip ,file *noun* [C] a computer file (= collection of information) that has been made smaller so that it uses less space **sıkıştırılmış dosya**

zipper /'zɪpəʳ/ *noun* [C] *US* a zip¹ **fermuar**

zodiac

Capricorn   Aquarius   Pisces

Aries   Taurus   Gemini

Cancer   Leo   Virgo

Libra   Scorpio   Sagittarius

the zodiac /'zəʊdiæk/ *noun* the twelve signs representing groups of stars which are thought by some people to influence your life and personality **burçlar kuşağı** *What sign of the zodiac are you?*

zombie /'zɒmbi/ *noun* [C] **1** a dead body that walks around because of magic **uyur gezer gibi hareket eden kişi, canlı cenaze gibi 2** *like a zombie informal* in a very tired, slow way **ölü gibi, cansız ve halsiz** *The day after the party I was walking around like a zombie.*

zone /zəʊn/ *noun* [C] an area where a particular thing happens **bölge, yer, mahal** *a war zone* ○ *a nuclear-free zone* ⊃See also: **buffer zone**.

zoo /zuː/ *noun* [C] a place where wild animals are kept and people come to look at them **hayvanat bahçesi**

zoological /ˌzəʊəʊ'lɒdʒɪkʰl/ *adjective* relating to the scientific study of animals **zoolojiyle ilgili**

zoology /zu'ɒlədʒi/ ⑯ /zəʊ'ɒlədʒi/ *noun* [U] the scientific study of animals and how they behave **hayvan bilimi, zooloji** • **zoologist** *noun* [C] someone who studies zoology **zoolog**

zoom /zuːm/ *verb informal* **zoom along/down/past, etc** to travel somewhere very fast, especially with a loud noise **bir yere doğru büyük ses çıkararak ilerlemek; rüzgâr gibi gitmek** **z**

zoom in *phrasal verb* to make something appear much closer and larger when using a camera or computer **çeşitli mercek/kamera kullanarak yakınlaştırıp büyütmek; zumlamak** *The TV cameras zoomed in on her face.*

'zoom ,lens *noun* [C] a lens (= part of a camera) that can make something appear much closer and larger **büyüteç mercekleri; mercek**

zucchini /zʊˈkiːni/ *US* (*UK* **courgette**) *noun* [C, U] *plural* **zucchini** or **zucchinis** a long, green vegetable which is white inside **sakız kabağı, kabak**

Z

Ekler

Anahtar kelimeleri – Türkçe-İngilizce

846

Turkish	English	Example
...ebilmeka bilmek	can	Can you drive?
...a/e doğru	towards *(moving towards)*	
...a/e kadar	until	The show will be on until the end of the month.
...dan/den	than	Susannah's car is bigger than mine.
...dan/den beri	since	
...gibi görünmek	seem	
...ın/in yerine	instead	
...malı/meli	must	
..e rağmen	although *(despite)*	
...e göre	according	
...sız	without	I've come out without my umbrella.
a	at	We met at the station.
acayip	strange	
acente	agent	The company has agents all over the world.
acımak	hurt	My eyes hurt.
açık	clear *(easy to understand)*	
açıkça	obviously	
açmak	open	Open your books.
ada	island	a Carribbean island
adam	man	a young man
adım	step *(noun)*	
adres	address	Her address is 1 Station Road, Cambridge.
Affedersiniz!	excuse me	Excuse me, I'd like to order.
afiş	poster	The children put up posters in the classroom.
Afrika	Africa	There are lots of animals in Africa.
ağaç	tree	The leaves were falling off the trees.
ağır	heavy	
ağırlık	weight	He's about average height and weight.
ağız	mouth	
ağlamak	cry	The child cried when he fell over.
ağrı	pain	I need some painkillers for my headache.
ağrımak	ache	My legs are aching after all that exercise.
Ağustos	August	August is in the summer.
aile	family	I'm from a big family.
akıl	mind *(someone's memory or their ability to think, feel emotions, and be aware of things)*	
akıllı	sensible	He is a sensible boy.
akşam	evening	Are you doing anything this evening?
akşam yemeği	dinner	We have dinner at six o'clock in the evening.
aktör	actor	Who's your favourite actor?
aktris	actress	Which actress do you like?
alfabe	alphabet	The English alphabet starts at A and ends at Z.
alış veriş	shopping	I love shopping.
alıştırma	exercise	For your homework, please do exercise 3 on page 24.
alkol	alcohol	Wine and beer contain alcohol.

847

almak	take	Take your umbrella, it's raining.
Alman	German	He is German.
Almanya	Germany	We live in Germany.
altı	six	I have six English books.
altın	gold	
altıncı	sixth	This is the sixth time I'm writing.
altında	under	Her bag is under the table.
altmış	sixty	There are sixty minutes in an hour.
altyazı	underline	Underline the words in the text.
amca	uncle	My uncle lives on a farm in Spain.
Amerika	America	My aunt lives in America.
Amerikalı	American	an American man
an	moment	I'm busy at the moment.
anahtar	key	
ancak	however	
anket	questionnaire	Please fill in this questionnaire.
anlamak	understand	I don't understand.
anlaşma	deal	
anlatmak	tell	He told me about his new school.
anne	mother	My mother is a nurse.
anne/baba	parents	Her parents live in Oxford.
anneanne	grandmother	Harry's grandmother is 65 years old.
antibiyotik	antibiotics	He is taking antibiotics for an ear infection.
aptal	stupid	That's a stupid thing to say.
ara	break	a coffee break
araba	car	Do you have a car?
araba kullanmak	drive	She's learning to drive.
Aralık	December	December is the last month of the year.
aramak	search	
arasında	between	The town is between Florence and Rome.
arıştırma	research (noun)	
arkadaş	friend	Sarah's my best friend.
arkasında	behind	Dan stood behind the chair.
art(ır)mak	increase	
artık	anymore	I don't teach Spanish any more.
asla	never	I never go to museums.
asmak	hang	
aşağıda	below (in a lower position than someone or something else)	
at	horse	Look at the horses. There's a black one and a white one.
ateş etmek	shoot	
atmak	throw	Amy threw the ball to the dog.
avantaj	advantage	
Avrupa	Europe	
Avrupalı	European	
avukat	lawyer	Tom is a lawyer.
Avustralya	Australia	Canberra is the capital of Australia.
Avustralyalı	Australian	Kangaroos are Australian.
ay	month	I'm going away next month.
ayak	foot	Many people go to work on foot.
ayakkabı	shoe	a pair of shoes
ayakta durmak	stand (verb)	
aynı	same	We treat all our children the same.
azaltmak	cut down	I really must cut down how much food I'm eating.

baba	father	What does your father do?
babaanne	grandmother	Harry's grandmother is 65 years old.
bacak	leg	My legs are tired after playing football.
bagaj	luggage	Do you have any luggage?
bağımsız	independent	
bahçe	garden	the front/back garden
bahşiş	tip	He gave me a good tip.
bakan	minister *(politician)*	
bakmak	look	Look at these pictures.
balık	fish	Do you like fish and chips?
balkon	balcony	Their house has a large balcony.
balta	axe	Sam used an axe to cut down the tree.
banka	bank	I asked the bank to lend me some money.
banka hesabı	bank account	
banyo	bathroom	Can I use the bathroom?
banyo yapmak	bath	I'll just have a quick bath.
bar	bar	Paul and Kate had something to drink in the bar.
bardak	glass	a glass of cola
basçın	pressure	
basın	press	the national press
basıt	simple	
baş	head	I've got a bad headache.
başaramamak	fail	I've just failed my driving test.
başarı	success	
Başbakan	prime minister	The British prime minister is visiting the USA.
başka	else	Would you like anything else to eat?
başka	another	I have another lesson now.
başkent	capital	Paris is the capital of France.
başlamak	start	I start work at nine o clock.
başlangıç	beginning	Read the notes at the beginning of the book.
başlıca	chief *(most important)*	
başlık	title	We need to think of a title for this book.
başvuru	application *(official form request)*	
batı	west	
batmak	sink *(ship)*	
bavul	suitcase	She packed her suitcase to go on holiday.
Bay	Mr	Good morning, Mr Smith.
Bayan	Mrs	
bayan	woman	a 30-year-old woman
baykuş	owl	a night owl
bazen	sometimes	He does cook sometimes, but not very often.
bebek	baby	a baby girl
becerikli	able	
bekar	single	Are you married or single?
beklemek	expect *(to think that something will happen)*	
beklemek	wait	I'm waiting for Guy.
belediye	council	Manchester Council
belki	maybe	Maybe we're too early.
bencil	selfish	He's a very selfish person.
beni / bana	me/to me	She gave me some money.
benim	my	Tom's my son.

benzer	similar	The two houses are remarkably similar.
beraber	together	Work together.
besteci	composer	Beethoven was a wonderful composer.
beş	five	I've been to London five times.
beşinci	fifth	I was fifth in the exam.
beyaz	white	a white T-shirt
bilet	ticket	a lottery ticket
bilgi	information	Do you have any information about English classes?
bilgisayar	computer	We've put all our records on computer.
bilim	science	We all study maths and science.
bilim-kurgu	science-fiction/sci-fi	My brother loves sci-fi films.
bilmek	know	Do you know how to ski?
bin	thousand	The painting cost thousands of pounds.
bina	building	The parliament building is next to the river.
binmek	ride	I ride my bike to work.
bir	a/an, one	an apple
bir kere	once	Do some exercise once a day.
bir şey	something	Would you like something to drink?
bir şey olmak	become	They became great friends.
bir yere	somewhere	
biraz	a bit, some	I'm a bit hungry.
birdenbire	suddenly	
biri	somebody	There's someone at the door.
birkaç	a few, several	
bisiklet	bicycle	Tom rides his bicycle to work every day.
bisküvi	biscuit	I ate three biscuits after lunch.
bit(ir)mek	end, finish	I finish work at five o'clock.
bitki	plant	Have you watered the plants?
biz	we	My wife and I both play golf and we love it.
bizim	our	Alice is our youngest daughter.
boğaz	throat	I've got a sore throat.
boş	empty	The office was empty.
boşanmış	divorced	He is divorced.
boyunca	along	We walked along the beach.
boyut	size	
Brezilya	Brazil	I'd like to go to Brazil next year.
Brezilyalı	Brazilian	Brazilian dancing is wonderful.
Britanya	Britain, the UK	It rains a lot in Britain.
Britanyalı	British	The British are friendly people.
bu	this	How much does this CD cost?
bu akşam	tonight	What are you doing tonight?
bugün	today	It's Johann's birthday today.
bulmak	find	I can't find my glasses and I've looked everywhere.
bulut	cloud	rain clouds
bulutlu	cloudy	a cloudy day
bunlar	these	Look at these photographs.
burada	here	Sign here please.
buzdolabı	fridge	I keep milk and meat in the fridge.
büfe	kiosk	I bought the newspaper from the kiosk.
büyük	big	That coat is very big.
büyümek	grow (to develop and become bigger or taller as time passes)	
caz	jazz	a jazz band
CD	CD	Do you have a lot of CDs?

CD çalar	(CD) player	
ceket	jacket	a leather jacket
cep telefonu	mobile phone	
cevap vermek	answer, reply	Did you answer Question 6?
ciddi	serious	
cömert	generous	It was very generous of you to buy her flowers.
Cuma	Friday	I don't go to work on Fridays.
Cumartesi	Saturday	Saturday is my favourite day of the week.
cumhurbaşkanı	president	the president of the United States
cuzdan	wallet	He carried money and cards in his wallet.
cümle	sentence	
çaba	effort (an attempt to do something)	
çağırmak	call	Call the police.
çakmak	lighter	a cigarette lighter
çalışmak	work	Work in pairs.
çamaşır makinası	washing machine	Can you empty the washing machine?
Çarşamba	Wednesday	What time do you go home on Wednesday?
çay	tea	They invited us for afternoon tea.
çek	cheque	Can I pay by cheque?
çekici	attractive	an attractive woman
çekingen	shy	He was too shy to say anything to her.
çekmek	pull	
çeyrek	quarter (to/past)	It's quarter to three (= 2.45).
çıkmak	leave	I leave work at 5 o'clock.
çiçek	flower	
çift	couple	a married couple
çift	double (having two parts of the same type or size)	
çift	pair	For the next exercise, you'll need to work in pairs.
çikolata	chocolate	a box of chocolates
Çin	China	I've never been to China.
Çinli	Chinese	Do you have any Chinese friends?
çirkin	ugly	an ugly building
çizgi	line (long thin mark)	
çizgi film	cartoon	My children love cartoons.
çizme	boots	I wore boots to work.
çizmek	draw	
çocuk	child	The child played in the garden.
çok	(a) lot (of),	There were a lot of people outside the building.
çok	many	I don't have many clothes.
çok	much (how much....)	
çok	very	She was very pleased.
çok fazla	too	It's too late.
çorap	socks	He wore red socks.
çorba	soup	chicken soup
çünkü	because	I'm calling because I need to ask you something.
da	also	She speaks French and also a little Spanish.
dağ	mountain	climb a mountain
daha	more	It's more expensive than the others.
daha	yet	I haven't finished my homework yet.
daha az	less	You should eat less.

daha iyi	better	Sara is a better singer than Clare.
daha sonra	later	See you later.
daire	apartment, flat	Mike lives in an apartment.
daire (apartman dairesi)	flat	a large block of flats
dakika	minute	I'll see you in a minute.
dans	dance	She's dancing with Steven.
davranış	behaviour	bad behaviour
dede	grandfather	Leah's grandfather lives in a small house.
değer	value	
değil	not	No, I'm not.
değişmek	change	She's changed a lot in the last few years.
demek	mean	What does this word mean?
demek	say	I'd like to go home, she said.
denemek	try	I tried to call you last night, but there was no one home.
deniz	sea	I'd like to live by the sea.
deniz mahsulleri	seafood	Good seafood
dergi	magazine	a fashion magazine
derin	deep	
ders	lesson	I am taking guitar lessons.
derslik	classroom	Our classroom is very small.
desteklemek	support	
devam et(tir)mek	continue	We'll have to continue this discussion tomorrow.
devasa	huge	
dışarda	out, outside	Do you want to go out tonight?
diğer	other	Do you know each other?
dijital	digital	a digital television
dikkat	attention *(care)*	
dikkatli	careful	Be careful, don't drop anything.
dil	language	How many languages do you speak?
dilemek	wish	
dinlemek	listen	Listen to the teacher.
dinlenmek	relax	I find it difficult to relax.
dinleyiciler	audience *(TV etc.)*	
dip	bottom	at the bottom of the sea
diş	teeth	He has very white teeth.
diş ağrısı	toothache	I have a terrible toothache.
diş hekimi	dentist	I've got an appointment at the dentist's (= where the dentist works) tomorrow.
dişi	female	There are two females and three males in my family.
dizi	series	
dizüstü	laptop	I take my laptop with me when I go away.
doğa	nature	
doğal	natural	
doğmak	born	She was born in London in 1973.
doğru	right	He only got half the answers right.
doğru	correct	Check that you have the correct information.
doğu	east	
doğum	birth	She gave birth to twins.
doğum günü	birthday	Her birthday is on March the 18th.
doksan	ninety	My grandfather is ninety years old.
doktor	doctor	You should see a doctor about that cough.

dokunmak	touch	
dokuz	nine	I've seen Star Trek nine times.
doldurmak	fill (in)	Please fill in this form.
dolu	full	
dönmek	return	Would you like a single ticket or a return?
dördüncü	fourth	Russ was fourth to arrive.
dört	four	There are four books on the table.
durmak	stop	A car stopped outside the house.
durum	situation	
duş	shower	I had a shower and got dressed.
duvar	wall	
duymak	hear	Can you hear the music?
duyurmak	announce	
düğün	wedding	We're going to a wedding on Saturday.
dün	yesterday	I went to see the doctor yesterday.
dünya	world	Everest is the highest mountain in the world.
düşmek	fall	She fell off her bike.
düştü	fall down	Daisy fell down at school.
düşük	low	low-fat diet
düşünce	thought	
düşünmek	think	Do you think it's going to rain?
düşürmek	drop (let something fall)	
düz	straight	
DVD	DVD	We watched a DVD last night.
eczane	chemist	Pippa bought cough medicine at the chemist.
eğer	if	We'll have a barbecue if the weather's good.
eğitim	education	
eğlence	fun	Did you have fun at the party?
Ekim	October	Halloween is in October.
ekmek	bread	a slice of bread
el	hand	Take your hands out of your pockets.
elbette	certainly, of course	'Could you pass the salt, please?' 'Certainly.'
elbise	dress	a dark blue dress
elektrik	electric	an electric heater
elli	fifty	My father is fifty years old.
elma	apple	Sophie likes apples.
emekli	retired	My father retired last year.
emin	sure	I'm sure that he won't mind.
emlakçı	estate agent	The estate agent sold our house.
en az	least	
en çok	most	She's the most beautiful girl I've ever seen.
en iyi	best	He's the best football player.
en önemli	main	We usually have our main meal in the evening.
en son	latest	She said to be there by 8 o'clock at the latest.
enerji	energy (the strength to be very active without becoming tired)	
enstrüman	instrument	musical instruments
epey	quite	I'm quite tired, but I'm happy to walk a little further.
e-posta	email	I got an email from Danielle yesterday.

erkek	male	The singer of the band is male.
erkek cocuk	boy	There are 13 boys in our class.
erken	early	the early 1980s
esas	basic *(being the main or most important part of something)*	The basic ınstrument of rock music is the guitar.
esasen	basically *(in the most important ways)*	
esnasında	while	
eşyalarını toplamak	pack	I've got to go home and pack.
et	meat	I don't eat red meat.
etek	skirt	a blue skirt
etki	effect *(a change, reaction, or result that is caused by something)*	
ev	house, home	a big house
ev kadını	housewife	I am a housewife.
ev ödevi	homework	Have you done your homework yet?
evet	yes	'Are you ready?' 'Yes?'
evlenmek	marry	Will you marry me?
evli	married	a married couple
Eylul	September	September is the ninth month of the year.
fakat	but	I'd drive you there, but I haven't got my car.
fakir	poor	He comes from a very poor family.
fark	difference	What's the difference between an ape and a monkey?
farketmek	notice	Notice the stress in this word.
farkında	aware	
farklı	different	We have eight different flavours of ice cream.
fatura	bill	Can I have the bill please?
favori	favourite	What's your favourite colour?
fazla	extra *(more, or more than usual)*	
fırıncı	baker	Our baker makes delicious bread.
fırsat	opportunity	
fikir	idea	What a good idea!
film	film	a romantic film
fincan	cup	a cup of tea
firma	business	He runs a small decorating business.
fiş	receipt	Could I have a receipt, please?
fiyat	price	high/low prices
form	form	Please fill in the form using black ink.
fotograf	photo	Have you got a photo of your family?
Fransa	France	Justin has been to France five times.
Fransız	French	Do you like French wine?
futbol	football	Carlos plays football every weekend.
garson	waiter/waitress	The waiter came to our table.
gazete	newspaper	I like reading a newspaper on the train.
gece	night	I slept really badly last night.
gece yarısı	midnight	The club closes at midnight.
geç	late	I was late for work this morning.
geçenlerdeki	recent *(happening or starting from a short time ago)*	Please supply a recent photo of yourself.
geçmek	pass	She passed all her exams.
geçmek (karşıdan karşıya)	cross *(cross the street)*	
gelecek	future	What do you want to do in the future?
gelmek	come	Come here.
gemi	boat	a fishing/sailing boat
genç	young	young people

genellikle	normally, usually	I normally start work at nine o'clock.
geniş	wide	
gerçek	true, real	a true story
gerçekten	really	Sara's really nice.
gerekli	necessary	It isn't necessary to work late today.
gerekmek	need	I need some new shoes.
geri	back	When do you go back to college?
getirmek	bring	Did you bring an umbrella with you?
gezi	sightseeing	a sightseeing tour of London
girmek	enter	Are you going to enter the photography competition?
gitar	guitar	an electric guitar
gitmek	go	Jane goes to bed at ten o'clock.
giymek	wear	I wear jeans most of the time.
göl	lake	We went sailing on the lake.
gömlek	shirt	a green shirt
göndermek	send	I sent him a letter last week.
görmek	see	I could see some houses in the distance.
görünen o ki	apparently *(used to say that you have read or been told something although you are not certain it is true)*	
görüntü	appearance	She's very worried about her appearance.
görüşme	interview	I had an interview last week for a job in London.
göstermek	show	Show me your photos.
götürmek	lead *(to show someone where to go, usually by taking them to a place or by going in front of them)*	Her father led them through the woods.
göz	eye	
gözükmek	appear *(to seem to be)*	
gram	gram	It weighs about 25 grams.
grev	strike	Teachers went on strike last month.
gri	grey	grey clouds
grup	band, group	a jazz band
güç	power *(control or influence over people and events)*	
güçlü	strong	You are very strong.
gül	rose	
gülmek	laugh	I dont know what you're laughing at.
gülümsemek	smile	
gün	day	the days of the week
güneş	sun	I can't sit in the sun for too long.
güneş banyosu	sunbathe	Nancy sunbathed every day on holiday.
güneşli	sunny	It was a lovely sunny day.
güney	south	The south is hotter than the north.
günlük	diary	She kept a diary of her trip to Egypt.
gürültü	noise	What's that noise?
gürültülü	noisy	The concert was great but it was too noisy.
güvenilir	reliable	a reliable car
güvenli	safe	She said that all the children were safe.
güvenmek	trust	
güzel	beautiful	a beautiful woman
haber	news	the local/national news
hafıza	memory *(your ability to remember)*	
hafta	week	What did you do last week?
hafta sonu	weekend	Are you doing anything this weekend?

hakkında	about	What was she talking about?
hala	still	I'm still hungry.
halı	carpet	We have a new carpet in the living room.
hamburger	burger	Polly likes burgers and chips.
hangi	which	Which of these do you like best?
hapishane	prison	He spent most of his life in prison.
harcamak	spend	I spent a lot of money last night.
hareket	action	
hariç	except	
harita	map	a road map
hasta	ill, sick	I'm feeling ill.
hastalık	disease, illness	heart disease / He has a serious illness.
hastane	hospital	
hata	mistake	Correct the mistakes.
hatırlamak	remember	I can't remember his name.
hava	air	air pollution
hava	weather	bad/good weather
hava limanı	airport	An international airport.
hayal etmek	imagine	
hayat	life	You have an exciting life.
hayran	fan	a soccer fan
hayvan	animal	Dogs are my favourite animals.
hazır	prepared, ready	
Haziran	June	There are thirty days in June.
heceleme	spelling	My spelling is terrible.
hediye	present	a birthday present
helikòpter	helicopter	The helicopter rescued them from the sea.
hemen	immediately	
hemen hemen	almost *(If something almost happens, it does not happen but it is very close to happening.)*	
hepsi	all	All animals have to eat.
her	every	He knows the name of every child in the school.
her şey	everything	
her zaman	always	I always walk to work.
herbiri	each	Each of the teams has four players.
herhangi bir yere/ yerde	anywhere	I can't find my glasses anywhere
herikisi	both	Both my brothers like football.
herkes	everybody	Everybody knows that!
heyecan verici	exciting	an exciting football match
hızlı	fast, quick	fast cars / It's a quick journey.
hızlıca,	quickly	I quickly shut the door.
hiçbir şey	anything	I haven't got anything to wear.
hiçbir şey	nothing	
hikaye	story	a horror story
Hindistan	India	The Taj Mahal is in India.
his	feeling	
hissetmek	feel	I feel sick.
hizmet	service	secret service
hoş	nice	He's a really nice person.
'Hoş geldiniz!'	welcome	Welcome home.
Hoşçakal!	goodbye	Goodbye, see you tomorrow.
hoşlanmak	enjoy	I hope you enjoy your meal.
hukuk	law	He studied law at university.

hücre	cell	
hükümet	government	
ılık	warm	It's usually warm in the spring.
ıslak	wet	a wet and windy day
ışık	light	bright light
iç	inside	
içeren	including	
için	for	Who do you work for?
içmek	drink	he drinks tea with breakfast
iddia	bet	
ifşa etmek	reveal (to give someone a piece of information that is surprising or that was previously secret)	
iki	two	I have two sisters.
iki kere	twice	I've been there twice.
ilaç	medicine	cough medicine
ile	with	Work with your partner.
ileri	forward	
ileri sürmek	claim (to say that something is true, although you have not proved it)	
ilgi	interest (the feeling of wanting to give attention to something or discover more about it)	She showed no interest in the film.
ilgili	interested	
ilginç	interesting	an interesting person
ilişki	relationship	He has a very good relationship with his older sister.
ilk	first	Ken was the first person to arrive.
ilkbahar	spring	Spring is my favourite season.
inanmak	believe (to think that something is true, or that what someone says is true)	
ince	thin	That girl is very thin.
indirim	sale	I bought this dress in the sale.
İngiliz	English	Do you speak English?
İngiltere	England	England is in Europe.
inşa etmek	build	
inşaatçı	builder	My brother is a builder.
irlanda	Ireland	I would like to go to Ireland next month.
isim	name	What's your name?
İskoçya	Scotland	Edinburgh is the capital of Scotland.
İspanya	Spain	Madrid is the capital of Spain
İspanyol	Spanish	I love Spanish food.
istasyon	station	a train station
istemek	want	He wants a new car.
iş	job	She got a job as a cleaner.
işaret	sign (something which shows that something is happening)	
işaret etmek	point	Point to the picture.
işlem	process (a series of actions that you take in order to achieve a result)	
işsiz	unemployed	I've been unemployed for six months.
İtalya	Italy	She's from Italy.
İtalyan	Italian	She speaks Italian fluently.
itiraf etmek	admit	He admitted taking my money.
iyi	good, fine	How are you? "I'm fine thanks. And you?"
iz	mark (an area of dirt, damage, etc that is left on something)	

izin vermek	allow	
Japon	Japanese	I can't speak any Japanese.
Japonya	Japan	Tokyo is the capital of Japan.
kablo	cable	cable TV
kabul etmek	accept	
kaçınmak	avoid *(stay away from)*	I think he's avoiding me.
kaçmak	miss	I missed the bus this morning.
kadro	staff *(employees)*	
kafe	café	Do you like the food in that café?
kağıt	paper	Have you got a piece of paper?
kahvaltı	breakfast	I have porridge for breakfast.
kahve	coffee	Do you want a cup of coffee?
kahve rengi	brown	
kalabalık	crowded	a crowded train
kalanlar	the rest	
kale	castle	
kalite	quality	
kalkmak	get up	I get up at seven o'clock.
kalmak	stay	The weather was bad so we stayed at home.
kalp	heart	My heart was beating fast.
kalp krizi	heart attack	He had a heart attack.
kamera	camera	Nancy got a digital camera for her birthday.
kamp yapmak	camp	We camped on the beach for two nights.
kampanya	campaign	
kan	blood	
Kanada	Canada	Have you ever been to Canada?
kanıt	evidence *(something that makes you believe that something is true or exists)*	
kanlı	bloody	
kanser	cancer	lung cancer
kapatmak	close	Jane closed the window.
kapı	door	Please shut the door behind you.
kaptan	captain	Who's the team captain?
kar	snow	It snowed all day yesterday.
karakter	character *(the combination of qualities and personality that makes one person or thing different from others)*	
karar	decision	
karar vermek	decide	She's decided to take the job.
kardeş (erkek)	brother	an older brother
kardeş (kız)	sister	an older/younger sister
karı	wife	I met my wife at university.
kârlı	snowy	a cold, snowy day
karşı	opposite	The bank is opposite the park.
karşı olma	against *(disagreeing)*	
karşı tarafta	across	There is a bank across the street from the school.
karşılamak	meet	My parents met me at the airport.
kart	card	a birthday card
kasap	butcher	I bought the sausages from the butcher.
Kasım	November	My birthday is in November.
kat	floor	the second/third floor
katılmak	agree	I agreed with him.
katılmak	join *(to become a member of a group or organization)*	

kaya	rock *(the hard, natural substance which forms part of the Earth's surface)*	
kayak yapmak	ski	Lets go skiing.
kaybetmek	lose	I'm always losing things.
kaybettim	lost	I lost my passport.
kaygılanmak	worry	
kayıp eşya	(lost) property	Maybe you'll find your camera at the lost property office.
kayıt	record	We kept a record of the meetings.
kaynak	source	
kaza	accident	I broke the plate by accident.
kaza	crash	a car/plane crash
kazak	jumper	a blue jumper
kazanan	winner	They are the winners of the competition.
kazanmak	win	He won £500!
kedi	cat	My aunt has four cats.
kel	bald	John started to go bald at an early age.
kelime	word	How many words do you know in English?
kelime hazinesi	vocabulary	Reading helps your vocabulary.
kenar	edge *(the part around something that is furthest from the centre)*	
kendi	herself / himself	He seems to be enjoying himself.
kendi	own	Paul has his own car.
kendileri	themselves	
kendimi, kendime	myself	
kendin	yourself	Don't cut yourself with that sharp knife.
kep	cap	a baseball cap
kesin	certain	
kesinlikle	definitely	
keskin	sharp	a sharp knife
kesmek	cut	
kırk	forty	My mother is forty years old.
kırmak	break	He broke my radio.
kırmızı	red	Red is my favourite colour.
kısa	short	a short visit
kısa pantolon	shorts	Jake always wears shorts in the summer.
kısım	part	Parts of the film were sad.
kışın	winter	We went skiing last winter.
kıyafetler	clothes	She was wearing her sister's clothes.
kıyaslamak	compare	The teachers are always comparing me with my sister.
kız	daughter	I have one son and one daughter.
kız	girl	Have you met Steve's new girlfriend?
kızarmış	fried	a fried egg
kızgın	angry	He's really angry with me because I was late.
kibar	polite	Be polite when talking to your teacher.
kilo	kilo	I bought two kilos of potatoes.
kim	who	Who told you?
kimin	whose	Whose gloves are these?
kimlik	identity card (ID)	I've lost my identity card.
kimse	anybody / anyone	I didn't know anyone at the party.
kimse	nobody	There was nobody in the office.
kira	rent	The rent is £600 a month.
kiralamak	hire	There is a car-hire company near where I live.

kirli	dirty	dirty clothes/dishes
kişi	person, people	You're the only person I know at this party. / How many people work here?
kişilik	personality	She's got a lovely warm personality.
kişisel	personal	a personal computer/stereo
kitap	book	I've just read a really good book.
kitapçı	bookshop	My sister works in a bookshop.
klasik müzik	classical music	I love classical music.
koca	husband	I married my husband in October.
kol	arm	She held the tiny baby in her arms.
kolay	easy	I'm going to take it easy this weekend.
kolayca	easily *(with no difficulty)*	
kolej	college *(private school)*	
koleksiyon	collection	
koltuk	armchair	There are two armchairs in my living room.
komedi	comedy	The film is described as a romantic comedy.
komik	funny	a funny story
konferans	conference	the annual sales conference
konforlu	comfortable	
konser	concert	a pop concert
kontrol etmek	check	Check your answers.
konu	matter	What's the matter?
konuşmak	speak	She speaks very quietly. / I'd like to speak to the manager.
konuşmak	talk	Talk to your partner.
kopyalamak	copy	She copied his answers.
korkmuş	afraid	
korku filmi	horror film	I don't like watching horror films.
korkunç	awful, terrible	an awful place
korumak	save *(protect)*	
koşmak	run	He can run very fast.
kot pantalonu	jeans	a pair of jeans
koymak	put	Where have you put the keys?
koyu renk	dark	dark blue/green
köpek	dog	Simon has two dogs.
köprü	bridge	We drove across the bridge.
köşe	corner	
kötü	bad	She's not a bad person.
köy	village	She lives in a small village outside Oxford.
kral	king	
kraliçe	queen	
kravat	tie	a pink tie
kredi	credit	We offer interest-free credit on all new cars.
kullanışlı	useful	useful information
kullanmak	use	Can I use your pen?
kulüp	club	a health club
kural	rule	if you break the rules you must pay a fine.
kuru	dry	Can you dry the dishes?
kuruluş	association *(organization)*	
kusura bakmayın	sorry	Sorry I'm late.
kuş	bird	There are a lot of birds in the park.
kutlamak	celebrate	We went out to celebrate Richard's promotion.

kutu	box	a cardboard box
kuzen	cousin	I have a lot of cousins.
kuzey	north	
küçük	little, small	a small mistake
lavabo	washbasin	I washed my face in the washbasin.
liste	list	a shopping list
lokanta	restaurant	an Italian restaurant
Lütfen!	please	Could I have a coffee, please?
maç	match	a football match
maden suyu	mineral water	I'd like a bottle of mineral water, please.
mağaza	shop	a shop assistant
mahkeme	court *(the place where a judge decides whether someone is guilty of a crime)*	
makale	article	I read an interesting article in the newspaper.
makine	machine	
malolmak	cost	Tickets cost £5.
manav	greengrocer	The greengrocer didn't have any oranges.
manken	model *(as in fashion model)*	
Mart	March	March is the beginning of spring.
masa	table	the kitchen table
mavi	blue	a dark blue jacket
Mayıs	May	May is the fifth month of the year.
Meksika	Mexico	Mexico is a beautiful country.
Meksikalı	Mexican	Mexican food is sometime quite hot.
mektup	letter	the letter K
mendil	tissue	Have you got a tissue?
menü	menu	a dinner menu
merhaba	hello, hi	Hello, Christina, how are you?
merkez	centre	in the city centre
mesaj	message	Did you get my message?
meslek	career	
meşgul	busy	Mum was busy in the kitchen.
metin	text	Read the text.
mevcut	available	This information is available free on the Internet.
mevsim	season	the holiday season
meydan	square	Is there a square in your town?
meyve	fruit	dried/fresh fruit
meyve suyu	juice	I have orange juice for breakfast.
mide	stomach	How's your stomach?
miktar	portion	The portions in the restaurant were very small.
milyon	million	He won a million pounds.
mobilya	furniture	I don't have much furniture in my apartment.
modern	modern	New York is a modern city.
motosiklet	motorbike	Ben goes to work on a motorbike.
muhasebeci	accountant	My father is an accountant.
muhtelif	various	
muhtemelen	probably	I'll probably be home by midnight.
mutfak	kitchen	My favourite room is the kitchen.
mutlu	happy	She looks very happy.
mutsuz	sad, unhappy	I was very sad when our cat died.
muz	banana	Tom had a banana for breakfast.
müdür	manager	The manager of the shop spoke to me.
mühendis	engineer	a mechanical engineer

mükemmel	excellent, great	That was an excellent meal.
mümkün	possible	I'm not sure if it's possible to see him now.
müsaade etmek	let	
müşteri	customer	A satisfied customer.
müze	museum	I love going to museums.
müzik	music	pop/dance music
müzisyen	musician	a jazz musician
nakit	cash	Do you want to pay by cash?
nasıl	how	How do you spell that?
ne	what	What do you do?
ne zaman	when	When's your birthday?
nefret etmek	hate	I hate cooking.
nehir	river	the River Thames
nerede	where	Where does she live?
neredeyse	nearly	We're nearly there.
nihayet	finally	
Nisan	April	April is the beginning of spring.
niye	why	Why didn't you call me?
nokta	spot *(noun)*	
normal	normal	a normal working day
not	note	He left a note on her desk.
numara	number	What's your phone number?
o zaman	then *(at that time)*	
Ocak	January	January is usually very cold.
oda	room	Your class is in room 4.
ofis	office	an office worker
oğlu	son	I have a son and a daughter
OK	OK	OK, I'll come with you.
okul	school	I like school.
okumak	read	What was the last book you read?
okumak	study	I studied biology at university.
olarak	as	She works as a waitress.
olasılık	chance *(the possibility that something will happen)*	
olay	event	
olmak	be	He is very rich.
on	ten	I've been to Spain ten times.
onaltı	sixteen	I live at number 16.
onbeş	fifteen	There are fifteen people on this bus.
onbir	eleven	My sister is eleven years old.
ondokuz	nineteen	I am ninteen. How old are you?
ondört	fourteen	I have fourteen cousins.
oniki	twelve	Today is May the twelfth.
onları, onlara	them	I'm looking for my keys - have you seen them?
onların	their	It was their problem, not mine.
onsekiz	eighteen	Suzy is 18 years old.
onun için	therefore	
onüç	thirteen	There are thirteen rooms in my house.
onyedi	seventeen	My brother is seventeen years old.
opera	opera	Do you like opera music?
opsiyon	option	You have several options.
orada	there	There are five questions.
ordu	army	He joined the army when he was 17.
orta	middle	I am sitting in the middle.
ortak	partner	Work with your partner.

otel	hotel	We stayed in a beautiful hotel.
otobus	bus	a school bus
oturmak	live	Where do you live?
oturmak	sit	Emma was sitting on a stool.
otuz	thirty	My thirtieth birthday is soon.
oynamak	play	You play tennis, don't you Sam?
oyun	game	a computer game
ödemek	pay	How can I pay?
ödül	prize	to win a prize
öğleden sonra	afternoon	I played tennis on Saturday afternoon.
öğlen yemeği	lunch	Shall we have lunch?
öğrenci	student	a law student
öğrenmek	learn	
öğretmen	teacher	a science teacher
öğün	meal	a three-course meal
öksürmek	cough	Paul has been coughing and sneezing all day.
öldürmek	kill	He killed a lot of people.
ölmek	die	She died of a heart attack.
ölü	dead	
ölüm	death	
ön	front	Write the address on the front of the envelope.
önce	ago	He left the house an hour ago.
önce, bir şeyden önce	before	He was a teacher before he became famous.
önceki	previous	I had been there on one previous occasion.
önde	ahead *(in front)*	
önemli	important	My family is very important to me.
öneri	suggestion	Phillip made a few suggestions.
önermek	suggest	I suggest that we park the car here.
örnek	example	Look at the first example.
örtmek	cover	They covered him with a blanket.
ötede	beyond	
öteye	further	
özel	private	What I do in my private life is my business.
özel	special	a special day
özellikle	especially *(more than other things or people, or much more than usual)*	
özgün	original	
pahalı	expensive	expensive jewellery
palto	coat	a winter coat
pantolon	trousers	a pair of trousers
para	money	How much money have you got?
paragraf	paragragh	Look at the first paragraph.
parça	piece	a piece of paper
park	park	We went for a walk in the park.
parlak	bright	her coat is bright red
parti	party	A New Year's Eve party.
pasaport	passport	a British passport
patates kızartması	chips	Do you like chips?
patron	boss	The boss of our company is very young.
paylaşmak	share	
pazar	market	Does your town have a market?
Pazar	Sunday	In the UK shops close early on Sunday.
Pazartesi	Monday	I start my new job on Monday.

pencere	window	Open the window if you're too hot.
performans	performance	A live performance.
Perşembe	Thursday	I'm going out this Thursday.
peynir	cheese	I love cheese and biscuits.
piknik	picnic	We're going to have a picnic down by the lake.
pil	battery	The battery in my Walkman is flat.
pilot	pilot	Brian is a pilot.
pirinç	rice	Do you like brown or white rice?
piyango	lottery	She won the lottery last year.
pizza	pizza	My favourite food is pizza.
plaj	beach	I went to the beach last weekend.
plan	plan *(an arrangement for what you intend to do or how you intend to do something)*	
polis	police officer	a police officer
polis	police	Have you called the police?
Polonya	Poland	Harry has never been to Poland.
Polonyalı	Polish	There are three Polish students in my class.
pop	pop (music)	I listened to pop music on the radio.
popüler	popular	'Jack' was the most popular boy's name.
portakal	orange	orange juice
posta kodu	postcode	What's your postcode?
postahane	post office	Can you take these letters to the post office?
pratik yapmak	practise	I'm quite good at tennis, but I need to practise.
profesyonel	professional	
program	programme	a TV programme
proje	project *(a carefully planned piece of work that has a particular purpose)*	
puan	score	a high/low score
pul	stamp	I'd like to buy two first class stamps.
radyo	radio	a car radio
rakamları toplamak	add	Have you added the numbers together?
rapor	report	Write a report about the trip.
reçel	jam	a jar of strawberry jam
referans	reference	My old headteacher said he would give me a good reference.
reklam	advert	a TV advert
reklam yapmak	advertise	Companies are not allowed to advertise cigarettes on television.
renk	colour	What's your favourite colour?
resim	picture	Look at the pictures.
resmi	official	
rutin	routine	a daily routine
rüzgar	wind	The wind blew her hat off.
rüzgarlı	windy	a windy day
rüya	dream	
saat	hour	working hours
saat	o'clock	I have lunch at one o'clock.
saat (kol saatı)	watch	I bought my watch in Switzerland.
sabah	morning	Friday morning
saç	hair	a girl with long, fair hair
sadece	only	There's only one hotel in the village.
sağ	alive *(living, not dead)*	
sağlık	health	Her health is very poor.
sağlıklı	healthy	a healthy diet

sağlıklı	well *(healthy)*	He didn't look well.
sağliksiz	unhealthy	Eating too much is unhealthy.
sahil	coast	the Black Sea coast
salata	salad	a mixed salad
Salı	Tuesday	I go swimming on Tuesdays.
salon	living room	Our living room is very small.
sanat	art	
sanayi	industry	
sandalye	chair	Sit on the chair.
sandviç	sandwich	a cheese sandwich
saniye	second	There are sixty seconds in a minute.
sarı	yellow	a bright yellow hat
sarışın	fair	a boy with fair hair
satıcı	seller	a ticket seller
satın almak	buy	I went to the shop to buy some milk.
satmak	sell	He's selling his house.
satranç	chess	I can't play chess, it's too difficult.
savaş	war	
savunmak	defend	
sayfa	page	The article is on page 36.
Sayın	dear	
saymak	count	Can you count to twenty in French?
sebep	cause, reason	Nobody knew the reason for the accident.
sebze	vegetable	vegetable soup
seçmek	choose , pick	Have you chosen a name for the baby?
sekiz	eight	There are eight students in my class.
sekreter	secretary	
seksen	eighty	My grandmother is eighty years old.
seksenli yıllar	eighties	Music was great in the eighties.
sel	flood	The flood destroyed thousands of homes.
sen	you	I love you.
senfoni	symphony	The orchestra played Beethoven's symphony.
senin	your	Can I borrow your pen?
sent	cent	A bottle of water costs 90 cents.
serbest	free *(without restriction)*	
sergi	exhibition	There's a new exhibition of sculpture on at the city gallery.
sert	hard *(firm and stiff, and not easy to press or bend)*	
ses	sound *(noun)*	
ses	voice	I heard a voice outside.
sessiz	quiet	Can you be quiet, please?
sevgili	darling	Would you like a drink, darling?
seviye	level	
sevmek	like, love	Do you like sport? / I love my family.
seyahat	trip	a business trip
seyahat etmek	travel	I travelled around Asia last year.
seyretmek	watch	I stayed in and watched TV that night.
sıcak	hot	a hot summer's day
sıcaklık	temperature	The temperature was 30 degrees.
sıfır	nought, zero	nought point five (0.5)
sık sık	often	I often see her there.
sıkıcı	boring	a boring job
sınav	exam, test	a maths exam
sınıf	class	We were in the same class at school.

865

sınıflamak	sort *(verb)*	
sır	secret	a secret agent
sıra	row	in the front row
sıradan	average *(usual. common)*	
sıralamak	put in order	
sigara	cigarette	Cigarettes are bad for you.
sigara içmek	smoke	Do you mind if I smoke?
sinema	cinema	I love going to the cinema.
sistem	system	
siyah	black	a black jacket
soğuk	cold	cold water/weather
sohbet	conversation	a telephone conversation
sokak	street	We live on the same street.
sol	left	I write with my left hand.
son	end	We all go home at the end of the day.
son	last	What did you do for your last birthday?
sonbahar	autumn	I'm starting a new job in the autumn.
sonra	after	H comes after G in the alphabet.
sonraki	next	Do the next exercise.
sonuç	result	
sonunda	eventually	
sormak	ask	I asked him about his hobbies.
soru	question	Answer the questions.
sorun	problem	no problem
sorunlar	trouble *(problems)*	
sosis	sausage	fried sausages
soyadı	surname	His surname is Walker.
soymak	rob	to rob a bank
söz vermek	promise	She promised to write to me every week.
sözleşme	contract	Tim signed a contract before he started work.
sözlük	dictionary	Use your dictionary to look up any words you don't understand.
spor	sport	Do you do a lot of sport?
spor ayakkabı	trainers	I wear trainers to play tennis.
spor salonu	gym	Nick goes to the gym three times a week.
standart	standard	
sterlin	pound	a hundred pounds
stil	style	
su	water	hot/cold water
suçlamak	accuse	
süpermarket	supermarket	Can you buy some apples in the supermarket?
sürpriz	suprise	What a lovely surprise!
sürücü	driver	a bus/train driver
süt	milk	a carton of milk
şahane	wonderful	The meal was wonderful.
şaka	joke	Ben told the joke to his friends.
şampiyon	champion	
şanslı	lucky	We're lucky to be alive.
şapka	hat	a red hat
şarap	wine	a glass of wine
şarkı söylemek	sing	They all sang 'Happy Birthday' to him.
şarkıcı	singer	a jazz singer
şaşırtan	amazing	
şehir	city, town	London is a big city. / Do you live in a big town?

şemsiye	umbrella	Take an unbrella with you.
şey	thing	That was an odd thing to say.
şimdi	now	I'm going now.
şirket	company	a software company
şişe	bottle	Can I have a bottle of milk, please?
şişman	fat	She eats all the time but never gets fat.
şu, o	that	How do you spell that?
Şubat	February	February is the second month of the year.
şunlar	those	These apples look much nicer than those.
şüphe	doubt *(when you are not certain about something, or do not trust someone or something)*	
tahmin etmek	guess	Guess how old he is.
tahta	board	The teacher wrote her name on the whiteboard.
takım	team	a football team
takım elbise	suit	She wore a dark blue suit.
takip etmek	follow	She followed me into the kitchen.
taksi	taxi	We caught a taxi home.
talimat	instruction, directions	Do you understand the instructions? / We stopped to ask for directions.
tamamen	exactly *(used when you are giving or asking for information that is completely correct)*	Where exactly did you go?
tamamiyle	absolutely	
tamamlamak	complete	Complete the sentence with one of the adjectives provided.
tanıtmak	introduce	He took me round the room and introduced me to everyone.
tarih	date	What's the date today?
tarih	history	He studied history at university.
tartışmak	discuss	Have you discussed this matter with anyone else?
taş	stone *(noun)*	
taşıma	transport	I use public transport every day.
taşımak	carry	
taşınmak	move	We moved the chairs to another room.
tatil	holiday	a skiing holiday
tatlı	sweet	You eat a lot of sweet things.
tavsiye,	advice	Steve gave me some good advice.
taze	fresh	
tebrikler	congratulations	I hear you're getting married. Congratulations!
tecrübe	experience	Do you have any experience of travelling alone?
tedavi	treatment	
tedirgin	concern *(worried)*	
tehlikeli	dangerous	It's dangerous to ride a motorcycle without a helmet.
teklif	offer	an offer of help
tekrar *(yine)*	again	Ask her again.
telefon	phone	What's your phone number?
televizyon	television, TV	I usually watch television in the evening.
televizyon sunucusu	TV presenter	The TV presenter spoke very slowly
temas	contact *(when you communicate with someone, especially by speaking to them)*	

tembel	lazy	My brother is very lazy.
temiz	clean	Your house is very clean.
temizlikçi	cleaner	Our cleaner comes once a week.
Temmuz	July	I went on holiday last July.
tenis	tennis	Can you play tennis?
tepe	hill	They climbed up the hill to get a better view.
tereyağ	butter	Will never puts butter on his bread.
teslim almak	receive *(to get something that someone has given or sent to you)*	
teşekkür etmek	thank	I want to thank you all for coming.
teyze / hala	aunt	My aunt is my brother's wife.
tırmanmak	climb	Slowly we climbed the hill.
tipik	typical	This is a typical meal from my country.
tişört	t-shirt	He's wearing a t-shirt and jeans.
tiyatro	theatre	the Arts Theatre
ton balığı	tuna	Would you like a tuna sandwich?
top	ball	He threw a golf ball at me.
toplam	total *(adj)*	
toplantı	meeting	We're having a meeting on Thursday to discuss the problem.
torba	bag	a paper bag
torun	granddaughter	Doris has two granddaughters.
trafik	traffic	The traffic is terrible in the city centre.
tramvay	tram	We took a tram to the city centre.
tren	train	The train was late.
turist	tourists	Many tourists come to the UK in the summer.
tutmak	catch	He caught the ball.
tutmak	hold	Can you hold my books for me?
tutmak	keep	Can I keep this pen?
tuvalet	toilet	This house has a toilet upstairs and downstairs.
tuz	salt	salt and pepper
tüm	whole	She spent the whole afternoon studying.
tür	kind, sort, type	What kind of music do you like? / They sell over 20 different types of cheese.
Türk	Turkish	Do you like Turkish food?
Türkiye	Turkey	She is from Turkey.
ucuz	cheap	a cheap flight
uçak	plane	What time does the plane arrive?
uçmak	fly	I'm flying to Bogotá tomorrow.
uçuş	flight	My flight goes from Heathrow airport.
uğraşmak	fight *(verb)*	
uluslar arası	international	an international language school.
ummak	hope	I hope the bus won't be late.
unutmak	forget	I've forgotten his name.
uyarmak	warn	
uyruk	nationality	What nationality is she?
uyumak	sleep	We had to sleep in the car that night.
uzak	far	The station isn't far from here.
uzakta	away	The nearest town is ten miles away.
uzun	long	long hair
uzun	tall	Your brother's very tall!
üç	three	I've got three brothers and sisters.
üçüncü	third	This is the third time I've read that book.
ülke	country	European countries
üniversite	university	Cambridge University

üniversite diploması	degree	She has a degree in physics.
ünlü	famous	a famous actress
üretmek	produce *(to make or grow something)*	
üst	top	There's a restaurant at the top of the hill.
üstünde	over	
üye	member *(a person who belongs to a group or an organization)*	
varmak	arrive	We arrived in Paris at midday.
ve	and	tea and coffee
vergi	tax	
veri	data *(data bank)*	
vermek	give	I gave her a bike for her birthday.
veya	or	Would you like tea or coffee?
video	video	a video recorder
vurmak	hit	
vücut	body	He had marks all over his body.
ya ... ya da	either ... or	
yabancı	foreign	a foreign language/student
yağ	oil	
yağmur	rain	It was raining all weekend.
yağmurlu	rainy	a rainy afternoon
yakın	near	The school's near here.
yakında	soon	I've got to leave quite soon.
yaklaşım	approach *(way of doing something)*	
yalnız	alone	She lives alone.
yan	side	
yangın	fire	
yanında	next to	
yanlış	wrong	That's the wrong answer.
yanlış	false	Which of these statements is true or false?
yapmak	make	Shall I make some coffee?
yardım etmek	help	Can you help me?
yardımcı	assistant	the assistant manager
yargıç	judge	
yarım	half	Over half of the population is female.
yarın	tomorrow	It's my birthday tomorrow.
yarış	race *(competition)*	
yarışma	competition	to enter a competition
yaş	age	People of all ages were there.
yaşam tarzı	lifestyle	She has a very unhealthy lifestyle.
yaşlı	old	How old are you?
yatak	bed	What time did you go to bed last night?
yatak odası	bedroom	There is a double bed in my bedroom.
yavaş	slow	The traffic was very slow.
yaygın	common *(widely spread)*	
yazar	writer	He is a famous writer.
yazık	shame	What a shame.
yazın	summer	We usually go away in the summer.
yazmak	write	Write your name on the paper.
yedi	seven	There are seven people in the class.
yemek	eat	Who ate all the cake?
yemek	food	Do you like Chinese food?
yemek pişirmek	cook	Who's cooking this evening?
yeni	new	I bought a new jacket yesterday.
yenmek	beat *(to defeat someone in a competition)*	

yer	place	Keep bread in a cool dark place.
yeşil	green	a green dress
yetenek	ability	
yeterli	enough *(as much as is necessary)*	
yeterlik	qualification	medical qualification
yetişebilmek	reach (can't)	Could you get that book down for me - I can't reach it.
yetişkin	adult	Children under 12 should be accompanied by an adult.
yetki	authority *(official power)*	
yetmiş	seventy	My grandfather is seventy years old.
yıl	year	We're going to Australia next year.
Yılbaşı gecesi	New Year's Eve	Where were you on New Year's Eve?
yıldız	star	
yıldönümü	anniversary	a wedding anniversary
yıllık	annual	the annual sales conference
yine de	anyway	Anyway, I think you are wrong.
yirmi	twenty	I am twenty years old.
yirmibeş	twenty-five	
yirmibir	twenty-one	He's twenty-one years old.
yirmidört	twenty-four	
yirmiki	twenty-two	
yirminci	twentieth	This is the twentieth time I've seen this film.
yirmiüç	twenty-three	
yok	no	There's no rice left.
yol	road	We live on a busy road.
yolcu	passenger	Passengers much check in before they fly.
yolculuk	journey	a train journey
yorgun	tired	I'm too tired to go out tonight.
yukarıda	above *(in or to a higher position than something else)*	
yukarıya	up	
yumurta	egg	a boiled/fried egg
yuvarlak	round *(shape)*	
yüksek	high	Some food is high in fat.
yükseltmek	raise *(to lift something to a higher position)*	
yürümek	walk	She walks to school.
yüz	face	
yüz	hundred	Over a hundred people were on the bus.
yüzmek	swim	I learnt to swim when I was 5 years old.
yüzük	ring	a wedding ring
yüzyıl	century	the twentieth century
zafer	victory	
zaman	time	Have you got time for a coffee?
zarar	injury	
zarf	envelope	There was no name on the envelope.
zaten	already *(before now)*	
zayıf	weak	I felt very weak.
zayıf	slim	She's very slim.
zeki	intelligent	She is very intelligent.
zengin	rich	He's the richest man in the world.
ziyaret etmek	visit	Visit me next time you're in town.
zor	difficult	Japanese is a difficult language to learn.

Sıkça rastlanan ilk isimler (ad'lar)

Parantez içindeki isimler, isimlerin kısa ve resmi olmayan şekilleridir.

Erkek isimleri

Adam /'ædəm/
Alan /'ælən/
Alexander /ˌælɪg'zɑːndər/
(Alex) /'ælɪks/
Andrew /'ændruː/
(Andy) /'ændi/
Anthony
UK /'æntəni/
US /'ænθəni/
(Tony) /'təʊni/
Benjamin /'bendʒəmɪn/
(Ben) /ben/
Charles /tʃɑːlz/
(Charlie) /'tʃɑːli/
Christopher /'krɪstəfər/
(Chris) /krɪs/
Daniel /'dænjəl/
(Dan) /dæn/
Darren /'dærən/
David /'deɪvɪd/
(Dave) /deɪv/
Edward /'edwəd/
(Ed) /ed/
(Ted) /ted/

Geoffrey /'dʒefri/
(Geoff) /dʒef/
George /dʒɔːdʒ/
Harry /'hæri/
Jack /dʒæk/
James /dʒeɪmz/
(Jim) /dʒɪm/
John /dʒɒn/
Jonathan /'dʒɒnəθən/
Joseph /'dʒəʊzɪf/
(Joe) /dʒəʊ/
Joshua /'dʒɒʃjuə/
(Josh) /dʒɒʃ/
Ian /'iːən/
Kevin /'kevɪn/
Liam /'liːəm/
Mark /mɑːk/
Martin /'mɑːtɪn/
Matthew /'mæθjuː/
(Matt) /mæt/
Michael /'maɪkəl/
(Mike) /maɪk/
(Mick) /mɪk/

Nicholas /'nɪkələs/
(Nick) /nɪk/
Patrick /'pætrɪk/
Paul /pɔːl/
Peter /'piːtə/
(Pete) /piːt/
Philip /'fɪlɪp/
(Phil) /fɪl/
Richard /'rɪtʃəd/
(Ricky) /'rɪki/
(Dick) /dɪk/
Robert /'rɒbət/
(Bob) /bɒb/
(Rob) /rɒb/
Samuel /'sæmjuəl/
(Sam) /sæm/
Simon /'saɪmən/
Thomas /'tɒməs/
(Tom) /tɒm/
Timothy /'tɪməθi/
(Tim) /tɪm/
William /'wɪljəm/
(Billy) /'bɪli/
(Will) /wɪl/

Kadın isimleri

Alice /'ælɪs/
Alison /'ælɪsən/
Amanda /ə'mændə/
(Mandy) /'mændi/
Amy /'eɪmi/
Ann/Anne /æn/
Bridget /'brɪdʒɪt/
Carol /'kærəl/
Caroline /'kærəlaɪn/
Catherine/Kathryn /'kæθrɪn/
(Kate) /keɪt/
(Katie) /'keɪti/
(Cath) /kæθ/
Charlotte /'ʃɑːlət/
Chloe /'kləʊi/
Christine /'krɪstiːn/
(Chris) /krɪs/
Clare/Claire /kleər/

Deborah /'debrə/
(Debbie) /'debi/
Diane /daɪ'æn/
Elizabeth /ɪ'lɪzəbəθ/
(Beth) /beθ/
(Liz) /lɪz/
Emily /'emɪli/
Emma /'emə/
Hannah /'hænə/
Helen /'helən/
Jane /dʒeɪn/
Jennifer /'dʒenɪfə/
(Jenny) /'dʒeni/
Joanne /dʒəʊ'æn/
(Jo) /dʒəʊ/
Julie /'dʒuːli/
Karen /'kærən/
Laura /'lɔːrə/

Linda /'lɪndə/
Lucy /'luːsi/
Margaret /'mɑːgərət/
(Maggie) /'mægi/
Mary /'meəri/
Rachel /'reɪtʃəl/
Rebecca /rɪ'bekə/
(Becky) /'beki/
Ruth /ruːθ/
Sarah /'seərə/
Sharon /'ʃærən/
Sophie /'səʊfi/
Susan /'suːzən/
(Sue) /suː/
Tracy /'treɪsi/
Valerie /'væləri/

Coğrafi isimler

Bu liste ülkeler, bölgeler ve kıtaların söyleyişlerini göstermektedir. Her ismi ilgili sıfat takip eder. Bu yerlerden gelen birisi hakkında konuşmak için çoğunlukla sıfatı kullanabilirsiniz. Bununla beraber bazı durumlarda 'Kişi' etiketi ile gösterilen sütunda verilmiş olan özel bir kelime kullanmak zorundasınız (örneğin, **Finland, Finnish, Finn**).

Belirli bir yerden olan birden fazla kişi hakkında konuşmak için aşağıdakiler haricinde 's' ekleyin:

* 'ese' veya 's' ile biten kelimelerde, ki bunlar aynı kalır (**Chinese, Swiss**)

* 'man' veya 'woman' ile biten kelimelerde, ki bunlar 'men' ve 'women' (**Irishman**) olarak değişir.

Bu liste sadece referans olması içindir. Bu listeye dâhil olmak egemen ulus statüsüne sahip olunduğunu ima etmez veya ileri sürmez.

İsim	Sıfat	Kişi (sıfattan farklıysa)
Afghanistan /æf'gænɪstæn/	Afghan /'æfgæn/	
Africa /'æfrikə/	African /'æfrikən/	
Albania /æl'beɪniə/	Albanian /æl'beɪniən/	
Algeria /æl'dʒɪəriə/	Algerian /æl'dʒɪəriən/	
Central America /ˌsentrəl ə'merɪkə/	Central American /ˌsentrəl ə'merɪkən/	
North America /ˌnɔːθ ə'merɪkə/	North American /ˌnɔːθ ə'merɪkən/	
South America /ˌsaʊθ ə'merɪkə/	South American /ˌsaʊθ ə'merɪkən/	
Andorra /æn'dɔːrə/	Andorran /æn'dɔːrən/	
Angola /æŋ'ɡəʊlə/	Angolan /æŋ'ɡəʊlən/	
Antigua and Barbuda /æn'tiːɡə æn bɑː'bjuːdə/	Antiguan /æn'tiːɡən/	
Argentina /ˌɑːdʒən'tiːnə/	Argentine /'ɑːdʒəntaɪn/	
Armenia /ɑː'miːniə/	Armenian /ɑː'miːniən/	
Asia /'eɪʒə/	Asian /'eɪʒən/	
Australia /ɒs'treɪliə/	Australian /ɒs'treɪliən/	
Austria /'ɒstriə/	Austrian /'ɒstriən/	
Azerbaijan /ˌæzəbaɪ'dʒɑːn/	Azerbaijani /ˌæzəbaɪ'dʒɑːni/	Azeri /ə'zeəri/
The Bahamas /ðə bə'hɑːməz/	Bahamian /bə'heɪmiən/	
Bahrain /bɑː'reɪn/	Bahraini /bɑː'reɪni/	
Bangladesh /ˌbæŋɡlə'deʃ/	Bangladeshi /ˌbæŋɡlə'deʃi/	
Barbados /bɑː'beɪdɒs/	Barbadian /bɑː'beɪdiən/	
Belarus /ˌbelə'ruːs/	Belorussian /ˌbelə'rʌʃən/	
Belgium /'beldʒəm/	Belgian /'beldʒən/	
Belize /be'liːz/	Belizian /bə'liːziən/	
Benin /be'niːn/	Beninese /ˌbenɪ'niːz/	
Bhutan /buː'tɑːn/	Bhutanese /ˌbuːtə'niːz/	
Bolivia /bə'lɪviə/	Bolivian /bə'lɪviən/	
Bosnia-Herzegovina /ˌbɒzniəˌhɜːzəɡɒ'vɪnə/	Bosnian /'bɒzniən/	
Botswana /bɒt'swɑːnə/	Botswanan /bɒt'swɑːnən/	Motswana /mɒt'swɑːnə/
Brazil /brə'zɪl/	Brazilian /brə'zɪliən/	
Brunei /bruː'naɪ/	Bruneian /bruː'naɪən/	
Bulgaria /bʌl'ɡeəriə/	Bulgarian /bʌl'ɡeəriən/	
Burkina Faso /bɜː'kiːnə 'fæseʊ/	Burkinabe /bɜː'kiːnəˌbei/	
Burundi /bʊ'rʊndi/	Burundi /bʊ'rʊndi/	Burundian /bʊ'rʊndiən/
Cambodia /ˌkæm'bəʊdiə/	Cambodian /ˌkæm'bəʊdiən/	

İsim	Sıfat	Kişi (sıfattan farklıysa)
Cameroon /ˌkæməˈruːn/	Cameroonian /ˌkæməˈruːniən/	
Canada /ˈkænədə/	Canadian /kəˈneɪdiən/	
Cape Verde /ˌkeɪp ˈvɜːd/	Cape Verdean /ˌkeɪp ˈvɜːdiən/	
The Central African Republic /ðə ˈsentrəl ˈæfrɪkən rɪˈpʌblɪk/	Central African /ˌsentrəl ˈæfrɪkən/	
Chad /tʃæd/	Chadian /ˈtʃædiən/	
Chile /ˈtʃɪli/	Chilean /ˈtʃɪliən/	
China /ˈtʃaɪnə/	Chinese /tʃaɪˈniːz/	
Colombia /kəˈlʌmbiə/	Colombian /kəˈlʌmbiən/	
Comoros /ˈkɒmərəʊz/	Comoran /kəˈmɔːrən/	
The Democratic Republic of Congo /ðə ˌdeməˈkrætɪk rɪˈpʌblɪk əv ˈkɒŋgəʊ/	Congolese /ˌkɒŋgəˈliːz/	
The Republic of Congo /ðə rɪˈpʌblɪk əv ˈkɒŋgəʊ/	Congolese /ˌkɒŋgəˈliːz/	
Costa Rica /ˌkɒstəˈriːkə/	Costa Rican /ˌkɒstəˈriːkən/	
Côte d'Ivoire /ˌkəʊt diːˈvwɑː/	Ivorian /aɪˈvɔːriən/	
Croatia /krəʊˈeɪʃə/	Croatian /krəʊˈeɪʃən/	Croat /ˈkrəʊæt/
Cuba /ˈkjuːbə/	Cuban /ˈkjuːbən/	
Cyprus /ˈsaɪprəs/	Cypriot /ˈsɪpriət/	
The Czech Republic /ðə tʃek rɪˈpʌblɪk/	Czech /tʃek/	
Denmark /ˈdenmɑːk/	Danish /ˈdeɪnɪʃ/	Dane /deɪn/
Djibouti /dʒɪˈbuːti/	Djiboutian /dʒɪˈbuːtiən/	
Dominica /ˌdəˈmɪnɪkə/	Dominican /dəˈmɪnɪkən/	
The Dominican Republic /ðə dəˈmɪnɪkən rɪˈpʌblɪk/	Dominican /dəˈmɪnɪkən/	
East Timor /iːst ˈtiːmɔːʳ/	East Timorese /iːst ˌtiːmɔːˈriːz/	
Ecuador /ˈekwədɔːʳ/	Ecuadorian /ˌekwəˈdɔːriən/	
Egypt /ˈiːdʒɪpt/	Egyptian /ɪˈdʒɪpʃən/	
El Salvador /ˌelˈsælvədɔːʳ/	Salvadoran /ˌsælvəˈdɔːrən/	
Equatorial Guinea /ˌekwətɔːriəl ˈgɪni/	Equatorial Guinean /ˌekwətɔːriəl ˈgɪniən/	
Eritrea /ˌerɪˈtreɪə/	Eritrean /ˌerɪˈtreɪən/	
Estonia /esˈtəʊniə/	Estonian /esˈtəʊniən/	
Ethiopia /ˌiːθiˈəʊpiə/	Ethiopian /ˌiːθiˈəʊpiən/	
Europe /ˈjʊərəp/	European /ˌjʊərəˈpiːən/	
Fiji /ˈfiːdʒiː/	Fijian /fɪˈdʒiːən/	
Finland /ˈfɪnlənd/	Finnish /ˈfɪnɪʃ/	Finn /fɪn/
France /frɑːnts/	French /frentʃ/	Frenchman /ˈfrentʃmən/
Gabon /gæbˈɒn/	Gabonese /ˌgæbənˈiːz/	
Gambia /ˈgæmbiə/	Gambian /ˈgæmbiən/	
Georgia /ˈdʒɔːdʒə/	Georgian /ˈdʒɔːdʒən/	
Germany /ˈdʒɜːməni/	German /ˈdʒɜːmən/	
Ghana /ˈgɑːnə/	Ghanaian /gɑːˈneɪən/	
Greece /griːs/	Greek /griːk/	
Greenland /ˈgriːnlənd/	Greenland /ˈgriːnlənd/	Greenlander /ˈgriːnləndəʳ/
Grenada /grəˈneɪdə/	Grenadian /grəˈneɪdiən/	
Guatemala /ˌgwɑːtəˈmɑːlə/	Guatemalan /ˌgwɑːtəˈmɑːlən/	
Guinea /ˈgɪni/	Guinean /ˈgɪniən/	
Guinea-Bissau /ˌgɪnibɪˈsaʊ/	Guinea-Bissauan /ˌgɪnibɪˈsaʊən/	
Guyana /gaɪˈænə/	Guyanese /ˌgaɪəˈniːz/	
Haiti /ˈheɪti/	Haitian /ˈheɪʃən/	
Honduras /hɒnˈdjʊərəs/	Honduran /hɒnˈdjʊərən/	
Hungary /ˈhʌŋgəri/	Hungarian /hʌŋˈgeəriən/	
Iceland /ˈaɪslənd/	Icelandic /aɪsˈlændɪk/	Icelander /ˈaɪsləndəʳ/
India /ˈɪndiə/	Indian /ˈɪndiən/	
Indonesia /ˌɪndəˈniːʒə/	Indonesian /ˌɪndəˈniːʒən/	
Iran /ɪˈrɑːn/	Iranian /ɪˈreɪniən/	
Iraq /ɪˈrɑːk/	Iraqi /ɪˈrɑːki/	

873

İsim	Sıfat	Kişi (sıfattan farklıysa)
Ireland /'aɪələnd/	Irish /'aɪrɪʃ/	Irishman /'aɪrɪʃmən/
Israel /'ɪzreɪl/	Israeli /ɪz'reɪli/	
Italy /'ɪtəli/	Italian /ɪ'tæliən/	
Jamaica /dʒə'meɪkə/	Jamaican /dʒə'meɪkən/	
Japan /dʒə'pæn/	Japanese /ˌdʒæpə'niːz/	
Jordan /'dʒɔːdn/	Jordanian /dʒɔː'deɪniən/	
Kazakhstan /ˌkæzæk'stɑːn/	Kazakh /kæ'zæk/	
Kenya /'kenjə/	Kenyan /'kenjən/	
Kiribati /ˌkɪrə'bæs/	Kiribati /ˌkɪrə'bæs/	
North Korea /ˌnɔːθ kə'riːə/	North Korean /ˌnɔːθ kə'riːən/	
South Korea /ˌsaʊθ kə'riːə/	South Korean /ˌsaʊθ kə'riːən/	
Kuwait /kuːweɪt/	Kuwaiti /kuːweɪti/	
Kyrgyzstan /ˌkɜːgɪ'stɑːn/	Kyrgyz /'kɜːgɪz/	
Laos /laʊs/	Laotian /'laʊʃən/	
Latvia /'lætviə/	Latvian /'lætviən/	
Lebanon /'lebənən/	Lebanese /ˌlebə'niːz/	
Lesotho /lə'suːtuː/	Basotho /bə'suːtuː/	Mosotho /mə'suːtuː/
Liberia /laɪ'bɪəriə/	Liberian /laɪ'bɪəriən/	
Libya /'lɪbiə/	Libyan /'lɪbiən/	
Liechtenstein /'lɪktənstaɪn/	Liechtenstein /'lɪktənstaɪn/	Liechtensteiner /'lɪktənstaɪnər/
Lithuania /ˌlɪθjuːeɪniə/	Lithuanian /ˌlɪθjuːeɪniən/	
Luxembourg /'lʌksəmbɜːg/	Luxembourg /'lʌksəmbɜːg/	Luxembourger /'lʌksəmbɜːgər/
Madagascar /ˌmædə'gæskər/	Malagasy /ˌmælə'gæsi/	
Malawi /mə'lɑːwi/	Malawian /mə'lɑːwiən/	
Malaysia /mə'leɪziə/	Malaysian /mə'leɪziən/	
The Maldives /ðə 'mɔːldiːvz/	Maldivian /mɔːl'dɪviən/	
Mali /'mɑːli/	Malian /'mɑːliən/	
Malta /'mɔːltə/	Maltese /mɔːl'tiːz/	
The Marshall Islands /ðə 'mɑːʃəl 'aɪləndz/	Marshallese /ˌmɑːʃə'liːz/	
Mauritania /ˌmɒrɪ'teɪniə/	Mauritanian /'mɒrɪ'teɪniən/	
Mauritius /mə'rɪʃəs/	Mauritian /mə'rɪʃən/	
Mexico /'meksɪkəʊ/	Mexican /'meksɪkən/	
Micronesia /ˌmaɪkrə'niːziə/	Micronesian /ˌmaɪkrə'niːziən/	
Moldova /mɒl'dəʊvə/	Moldovan /mɒl'dəʊvən/	
Monaco /'mɒnəkəʊ/	Monégasque /mɒneɪ'gæsk/	
Mongolia /mɒŋ'gəʊliə/	Mongolian /mɒŋ'gəʊliən/	
Morocco /mə'rɒkəʊ/	Moroccan /mə'rɒkən/	
Mozambique /ˌməʊzæm'biːk/	Mozambican /ˌməʊzæm'biːkən/	
Myanmar /'mjænmɑːr/	Burmese /bɜː'miːz/	
Namibia /nə'mɪbiə/	Namibian /nə'mɪbiən/	
Nauru /nɑː'uːruː/	Nauruan /nɑːuː'ruːən/	
Nepal /nə'pɔːl/	Nepalese /ˌnepəl'iːz/	
The Netherlands /ðə 'neðələnz/	Dutch /dʌtʃ/	Dutchman /'dʌtʃmən/
New Zealand /ˌnjuː'ziːlənd/	New Zealand /ˌnjuː'ziːlənd/	New Zealander /ˌnjuː'ziːləndər/
Nicaragua /ˌnɪkə'rɑːgwə/	Nicaraguan /ˌnɪkə'rɑːgwən/	
Niger /niː'ʒeə/	Nigerien /niː'ʒeəriən/	
Nigeria /naɪ'dʒɪəriə/	Nigerian /naɪ'dʒɪəriən/	
Norway /'nɔːweɪ/	Norwegian /nɔː'wiːdʒən/	
Oman /əʊ'mɑːn/	Omani /əʊ'mɑːni/	
Pakistan /ˌpɑːkɪ'stɑːn/	Pakistani /ˌpɑːkɪ'stɑːni/	
Palestine /'pæləstaɪn/	Palestinian /ˌpælə'stɪniən/	
Panama /'pænəmɑː/	Panamanian /ˌpænə'meɪniən/	
Papua New Guinea /'pæpuə njuː 'gɪni/	Papua New Guinean /'pæpuə njuː 'gɪniən/	
Paraguay /'pærəgwaɪ/	Paraguayan /ˌpærə'gwaɪən/	

İsim	Sıfat	Kişi (sıfattan farklıysa)
Peru /pə'ruː/	Peruvian /pə'ruːviən/	
The Philippines /ðə 'fɪlɪpiːnz/	Philippine /'fɪlɪpiːn/	Filipino /ˌfɪlɪ'piːnəʊ/
Poland /'pəʊlənd/	Polish /'pəʊlɪʃ/	Pole /pəʊl/
Portugal /'pɔːtʃəgəl/	Portuguese /ˌpɔːtʃə'giːz/	
Qatar /'kʌtɑːʳ/	Qatari /kʌ'tɑːri/	
Romania /rʊ'meɪniə/	Romanian /rʊ'meɪniən/	
Russia /'rʌʃə/	Russian /'rʌʃən/	
Rwanda /ru'ændə/	Rwandan /ru'ændən/	
Saint Kitts and Nevis	Kittsian /'kɪtsiən/	
/seɪnt kɪts ən 'nevɪs /		
Saint Lucia /seɪnt 'luːʃə/	Saint Lucian /seɪnt 'luːʃən/	
Saint Vincent and the Grenadines /	Vincentian /vɪn'sɪntiən/	
seɪnt 'vɪntsənt ən ðə ˌgrenə'diːnz/		
Samoa /sə'məʊə/	Samoan /sə'məʊən/	
San Marino /ˌsænmə'riːnəʊ/	Sanmarinese /ˌsænmærɪ'niːz/	
São Tomé and Príncipe	Sao Tomean /ˌsaʊ tə'meɪən/	
/ˌsaʊ tə'meɪ ən 'prɪnsɪpəɪ/		
Saudi Arabia /ˌsaʊdi ə'reɪbiə/	Saudi /'saʊdi/	
Scandinavia /ˌskændɪˌneɪviə/	Scandinavian /ˌskændɪˌneɪviən/	
Senegal /ˌsenɪ'gɔːl/	Senegalese /ˌsenɪgə'liːz/	
The Seychelles /ðə seɪ'ʃelz/	Seychelles /seɪ'ʃelz/	Seychellois /seɪʃel'wɑː/
Sierra Leone /si,erəli'əʊn/	Sierra Leonean /si'erə li'əʊniən/	
Singapore /ˌsɪŋə'pɔːʳ/	Singaporean /ˌsɪŋə'pɔːriən/	
Slovakia /slə'vækiə/	Slovak /'sləʊvæk/	
Slovenia /slə'viːniə/	Slovenian /slə'viːniən/	Slovene /'sləʊviːn/
The Solomon Islands	Solomon Islander	
/ðə 'sɒləmən 'aɪləndz/	/'sɒləmən 'aɪləndəʳ/	
Somalia /sə'mɑːliə/	Somali /sə'mɑːli/	
South Africa /ˌsaʊθ 'æfrɪkə/	South African /ˌsaʊθ 'æfrɪkən/	
Spain /speɪn/	Spanish /'spænɪʃ/	Spaniard /'spænjəd/
Sri Lanka /ˌsriː'læŋkə/	Sri Lankan /ˌsriː'læŋkən/	
Sudan /suː'dɑːn/	Sudanese /ˌsuːdə'niːz/	
Suriname /ˌsʊərɪ'næm/	Surinamese /ˌsʊərɪnæm'iːz/	
Swaziland /'swɑːzilænd/	Swazi /'swɑːzi/	
Sweden /'swiːdn/	Swedish /'swiːdɪʃ/	Swede /swiːd/
Switzerland /'swɪtsələnd/	Swiss /swɪs/	
Syria /'sɪriə/	Syrian /'sɪriən/	
Taiwan /ˌtaɪ'wɑːn/	Taiwanese /ˌtaɪwə'niːz/	
Tajikistan /tɑː'dʒiːkɪˌstɑːn/	Tajik /tɑː'dʒiːk/	
Tanzania /ˌtænzə'niːə/	Tanzanian /ˌtænzə'niːən/	
Thailand /'taɪlænd/	Thai /taɪ/	
Tibet /tɪ'bet/	Tibetan /tɪ'betn/	
Togo /'təʊgəʊ/	Togolese /ˌtəʊgə'liːz/	
Tonga /'tɒŋə/	Tongan /'tɒŋən/	
Trinidad and Tobago	Trinidadian /ˌtrɪnɪ'dædiən/	
/'trɪnɪdæd ən tə'beɪgəʊ/		
Tunisia /tjuː'nɪziə/	Tunisian /tjuː'nɪziən/	
Turkey /'tɜːki/	Turkish /'tɜːkɪʃ/	Turk /tɜːk/
Turkmenistan /tɜːkˌmenɪ'stɑːn/	Turkmen /'tɜːkmen/	
Tuvalu /tuː'vɑːluː/	Tuvaluan /ˌtuːvɑː'luːən/	
Uganda /juː'gændə/	Ugandan /juː'gændən/	
Ukraine /juː'kreɪn/	Ukrainian /juː'kreɪniən/	
The United Arab Emirates	Emirian /e'mɪriən/	
/ðə juː'naɪtɪd 'ærəb 'emɪrəts/		
The United Kingdom	British /'brɪtɪʃ/	Briton /'brɪtən/
/ ðə juː'naɪtɪd 'kɪŋdəm/		
The United States of America	American /ə'merɪkən/	
/ðə juː'naɪtɪd steɪts əv ə'merɪkə/		
Uruguay /'jʊərəgwaɪ/	Uruguayan /ˌjʊərə'gwaɪən/	
Uzbekistan /ʊzˌbekɪ'stɑːn/	Uzbek /'ʊzbek/	

İsim	Sıfat	Kişi (sıfattan farklıysa)
Vanuatu /ˌvænuˈɑːtuː/	Vanuatuan /ˌvænuɑːˈtuːən/	
Vatican City /ˈvætɪkən ˈsɪti/	Vatican /ˈvætɪkən/	
Venezuela /ˌvenɪˈzweɪlə/	Venezuelan /ˌvenɪˈzweɪlən/	
Vietnam /ˌviːetˈnæm/	Vietnamese /ˌviːetnəˈmiːz/	
Western Sahara /ˌwestən ˌsəˈhɑːrə/	Sahrawian /sɑːˈrɑːwɪən	
Yemen /ˈjemən/	Yemeni /ˈjeməni/	
Yugoslavia /ˌjuːgəʊˈslɑːviə/	Yugoslav /ˈjuːgəʊslɑːv/	
Zambia /ˈzæmbiə/	Zambian /ˈzæmbiən/	
Zimbabwe /zɪmˈbɑːbweɪ/	Zimbabwean /zɪmˈbɑːbwiən/	

Düzenli fiil zamanları

Yalın zamanlar The simple tenses

Geniş Zaman   Present Simple

Şimdiki zamanda var olan, her zaman doğru olan veya düzenli olarak yapılan şeyler ve görüşlerle inançlar için kullanılır

I/we/you/they   arrive (**do not** arrive)
he/she/it   arrives (**does not** arrive)

Di'li Geçmiş Zaman   Past Simple

tamamlanan eylemler ve geçmişteki olaylar için kullanılır

I/we/you/they   arrived (**did not** arrive)
he/she/it   arrived (**did not** arrive)

Gelecek Zaman   Future Simple

gelecekteki eylemler ve olaylar için kullanılır

I/we/you/they   **will** arrive (**will not** arrive)
he/she/it   **will** arrive (**will not** arrive)

Present Perfect

bir olayın şu andaki zamandan bir süre önce olduğunu veya o eylemin tamamlandığını göstermek için kullanılır

I/we/you/they   **have** arrived (**have not** arrived)
he/she/it   **has** arrived (**has not** arrived)

Miş'li Geçmiş Zaman   Past Perfect

geçmişteki belirli bir zamandan önce bir olayın olduğunu veya aksiyonun tamamlandığını göstermek için kullanılır

I/we/you/they   **had** arrived (**had not** arrived)
he/she/it   **had** arrived (**had not** arrived)

Gelecekte Bitmişlik   Future Perfect

bir şeyin gelecekteki belirli bir zamandan önce tamamlanacağını göstermek için kullanılır

I/we/you/they   **will have** arrived (**will not have** arrived)
he/she/it   **will have** arrived (**will not have** arrived)

Kesintisiz/ilerleyici zamanlar   The continuous/progressive tenses

Şimdiki Zaman   Present Continuous/Progressive

şimdi olan veya gelişen eylemler veya olaylar, gelecek planları veya bir olayın tekrarlandığını göstermek için kullanılır

	I **am** arriving (**am not** arriving)
we/you/they	**are** arriving (**are not** arriving)
he/she/it	**is** arriving (**is not** arriving)

Geçmiş Zamanda Süreklilik   Past Continuous/Progressive

Geçmişteki, henüz bitmemiş veya kesintiye uğramış eylemler veya olaylar için kullanılır

I	**was** arriving (**was not** arriving)
we/you/they	**were** arriving (**were not** arriving)
he/she/it	**was** arriving (**was not** arriving)

Gelecek Zamanda Süreklilik   Future Continuous/Progressive

Gelecekte olacak ve gelecekte devam edecek eylemler veya olaylar için kullanılır

I/we/you/they	**will be** arriving (**will not be** arriving)
he/she/it	**will be** arriving (**will not be** arriving)

Present Perfect Continuous/Progressive

geçmişte başlamış ve halen devam eden eylemler veya olaylar veya yakın zaman önce biten ve etkileri şimdi görülen geçmişteki eylemler için kullanılır

I/we/you/they	**have been** arriving (**have not been** arriving)
he/she/it	**has been** arriving (**has not been** arriving)

Past Perfect Continuous/Progressive

bir süre için olmuş fakat geçmişteki belirli bir zamandan önce tamamlanmış eylemler veya olaylar için kullanılır

I/we/you/they	**had been** arriving (**had not been** arriving)
he/she/it	**had been** arriving (**had not been** arriving)

Future Perfect Continuous/Progressive

Gelecekteki belirli bir zamanda hâlihazırda gerçekleşiyor olacak eylemler veya olaylar için kullanılır

I/we/you/they	**will have been** arriving (**will not have been** arriving)
he/she/it	**will have been** arriving (**will not have been** arriving)

Düzensiz fiiller

Bu liste fiilin mastar biçimini, geçmiş zamanını ve ardından da geçmiş zaman sıfat fiilini verir.

Eğer iki biçim verilmişse farklı anlamları olup olmadığını görmek için sözlüğü kullanın.

Mastar	Geçmiş Zaman	Geçmiş Zaman Sıfat Fiili	Mastar	Geçmiş Zaman	Geçmiş Zaman Sıfat Fiili
arise	arose	arisen	drink	drank	drunk
awake	awoke	awoken	drive	drove	driven
be	was/were	been	dwell	dwelt, dwelled	dwelt, dwelled
bear	bore	borne	eat	ate	eaten
beat	beat	beaten, (also US) beat	fall	fell	fallen
			feed	fed	fed
become	became	become	feel	felt	felt
befall	befell	befallen	fight	fought	fought
begin	began	begun	find	found	found
bend	bent	bent	flee	fled	fled
bet	bet, betted	bet, betted	fling	flung	flung
bid	bid, bade	bid, bidden	fly	flew	flown
bind	bound	bound	forbid	forbade	forbidden
bite	bit	bitten	forecast	forecast, forecasted	forecast, forecasted
bleed	bled	bled	foresee	foresaw	foreseen
blow	blew	blown	forget	forgot	forgotten
break	broke	broken	forgive	forgave	forgiven
breed	bred	bred	forgo	forwent	forgone
bring	brought	brought	forsake	forsook	forsaken
broadcast	broadcast, (also US) broadcasted	broadcast, (also US) broadcasted	freeze	froze	frozen
			get	got	got, (also US) gotten
build	built	built	give	gave	given
burn	burnt, burned	burnt, burned	go	went	gone
burst	burst	burst	grind	ground	ground
bust	(UK) bust, (US) busted	(UK) bust, (US) busted	grow	grew	grown
			hang	hung, hanged	hung, hanged
buy	bought	bought	have	had	had
cast	cast	cast	hear	heard	heard
catch	caught	caught	hide	hid	hidden
choose	chose	chosen	hit	hit	hit
cling	clung	clung	hold	held	held
come	came	come	hurt	hurt	hurt
cost	cost	cost	input	inputted, input	inputted, input
creep	crept	crept	keep	kept	kept
cut	cut	cut	kneel	knelt, kneeled	knelt, kneeled
deal	dealt	dealt	know	knew	known
dig	dug	dug	ay	laid	laid
dive	dived, (also US) dove	dived	lead	led	led
draw	drew	drawn	lean	leaned, (also UK) leant	leaned, (also UK) leant
dream	dreamed, dreamt	dreamed, dreamt			

Mastar	Geçmiş Zaman	Geçmiş Zaman Sıfat Fiili
leap	leapt, leaped	leapt, leaped
learn	learned, (also UK) learnt	learned, (also UK) learnt
leave	left	left
lend	lent	lent
let	let	let
lie	lay, lied	lain, lied
light	lit, lighted	lit, lighted
lose	lost	lost
make	made	made
mean	meant	meant
meet	met	met
mislay	mislaid	mislaid
mislead	misled	misled
misread	misread	misread
misspell	misspelled, (also UK) misspelt	misspelled, (also UK) misspelt
mistake	mistook	mistaken
misunderstand	misunderstood	misunderstood
mow	mowed	mown, mowed
outdo	outdid	outdone
outgrow	outgrew	outgrown
overcome	overcame	overcome
overdo	overdid	overdone
overhang	overhung	overhung
overhear	overheard	overheard
override	overrode	overridden
overrun	overran	overrun
oversee	oversaw	overseen
oversleep	overslept	overslept
overtake	overtook	overtaken
overthrow	overthrew	overthrown
pay	paid	paid
plead	pleaded, (also US) pled	pleaded, (also US) pled
prove	proved	proved, proven
put	put	put
quit	quit	quit
read	read	read
rebuild	rebuilt	rebuilt
repay	repaid	repaid
rethink	rethought	rethought
rewind	rewound	rewound
rewrite	rewrote	rewritten
rid	rid	rid
ride	rode	ridden
ring	rang	rung
rise	rose	risen
run	ran	run

Mastar	Geçmiş Zaman	Geçmiş Zaman Sıfat Fiili
saw	sawed	sawn, (also US) sawed
say	said	said
see	saw	seen
seek	sought	sought
sell	sold	sold
send	sent	sent
set	set	set
sew	sewed	sewn, sewed
shake	shook	shaken
shear	sheared	sheared, shorn
shed	shed	shed
shine	shone	shone
shoot	shot	shot
show	showed	shown, showed
shrink	shrank	shrunk
shut	shut	shut
sing	sang	sung
sink	sank	sunk
sit	sat	sat
slay	slew	slain
sleep	slept	slept
slide	slid	slid
sling	slung	slung
slink	slunk	slunk
slit	slit	slit
smell	smelled, (also UK) smelt	smelled, (also UK) smelt
sow	sowed	sown, sowed
speak	spoke	spoken
speed	sped, speeded	sped, speeded
spell	spelled, (also UK) spelt	spelled, (also UK) spelt
spend	spent	spent
spill	spilled, (also UK) spilt	spilled, (also UK) spilt
spin	spun	spun
spit	spat, (also US) spit	spat, (also US) spit
split	split	split
spoil	spoiled, spoilt	spoiled, spoilt
spread	spread	spread
spring	sprang	sprung
stand	stood	stood
steal	stole	stolen
stick	stuck	stuck
sting	stung	stung
stink	stank, (also US) stunk	stunk
stride	strode	strode
strike	struck	struck

Mastar	Geçmiş Zaman	Geçmiş Zaman Sıfat Fiili
string	strung	strung
strive	strove, strived	striven, strived
swear	swore	sworn
sweep	swept	swept
swell	swelled	swollen, swelled
swim	swam	swum
swing	swung	swung
take	took	taken
teach	taught	taught
tear	tore	torn
tell	told	told
think	thought	thought
throw	threw	thrown
thrust	thrust	thrust
tread	trod	trodden
undercut	undercut	undercut
undergo	underwent	undergone
understand	understood	understood
undertake	undertook	undertaken
undo	undid	undone
unwind	unwound	unwound
uphold	upheld	upheld
upset	upset	upset
wake	woke	woken
wear	wore	worn
weave	wove, weaved	woven, weaved
weep	wept	wept
wet	wet, wetted	wet, wetted
win	won	won
wind	wound	wound
withdraw	withdrew	withdrawn
withhold	withheld	withheld
withstand	withstood	withstood
wring	wrung	wrung
write	wrote	written

Kelime başlangıç ve sonları

İngilizce kelimelerin çoğunun anlamlarını sadece kelimenin başına veya sonuna bir grup harf ekleyerek değiştirebilirsiniz.

Ön ekler /Prefixes

Kelimenin başına eklenmiş bir grup harfe **prefix** denir. Aşağıda en sık rastlanan ön eklerle kullanılış biçimlerinin listesi vardır.

Anglo- relating to the UK or England *an Anglophile* (= someone who loves England)
anti- **1** opposed to or against *anti-racist laws* **2** preventing or destroying *an anti-aircraft missile*
astro- relating to stars or outer space *astronomer* • *astrophysics*
audio- relating to hearing or sound *audiotape*
auto- **1** operating without being controlled by humans *autopilot* (= a computer that directs an aircraft) **2** self *an autobiography* (= a book that someone writes about their own life)
bi- two *bilingual* (= speaking two languages) • *bimonthly* (= happening twice in a month or once every two months)
bio- relating to living things or human life *biodiversity* • *bioethics*
centi-, cent- hundred *a centimetre* • *a century*
co- with or together *a co-author* • *to coexist*
contra- against or opposite *to contradict* (= say the opposite) • *contraception* (= something that is used to prevent pregnancy)
counter- opposing or as a reaction to *a counter-attack* (= an attack on someone who has attacked you)
cross- **1** across *cross-border* **2** including different groups or subjects *a cross-party committee* (= one formed from many political parties) • *cross-cultural*
cyber- relating to electronic communications, especially the Internet *cyberspace*
de- to take something away *deforestation* (= when the trees in an area are cut down)
deca- ten *decade*
demi- half, partly *demitasse* (=a small coffee cup) • *demigod* (=a creature that is part god and part human)
dis- not or the opposite of *dishonest* • *disbelief* • *to disagree*
e- electronic, usually relating to the Internet *email* • *e-commerce*
eco- relating to the environment *eco-friendly tourism* (= tourism which does not damage the environment)
equi- equal, equally *equidistant* (=the same distance from two or more places)
Euro- relating to Europe *Europop* (= modern, young people's music from Europe)
ex- from before *an ex-boyfriend* • *an ex-boss*
extra- outside of or in addition to *extracurricular activities* (= activities that are in addition to the usual school work)
geo- of the earth *geothermal* (=of or connected with the heat inside the earth)
hydro- relating to water *hydroponic* (=a method of growing plants in water)
hyper- having a lot of or too much of a quality *hyperactive* • *hypersensitive* (= more than normally sensitive)

ill- in a way which is bad or not suitable *ill-prepared* • *an ill-judged remark*
in-, il-, im-, ir- not *incorrect* • *illegal* • *impossible* • *irregular*
inter- between or among *international* • *an interdepartmental meeting*
intra- within *an intranet*
kilo- a thousand *a kilometre* • *a kilogram*
macro- on a large scale *macroeconomics* (= the study of economics at a national or international level)
maxi- most, very large *maximum*
mega- **1** *informal* extremely *megarich* (= extremely rich) **2** one million *40 megabytes*
micro- very small *a microchip* • *microscopic* (= extremely small)
mid- in the middle of *mid-July* • *a man in his mid-forties* • *mid-afternoon/-morning*
milli- a thousandth *a millisecond*
mini- small *a miniskirt* (= very short skirt) • *a minibus*
mis- not or badly *mistrust* • *to misbehave*
mis- not or badly *mistrust* • *to misbehave*
mono- one or single *monolingual* • *a monologue*
multi- many *a multi-millionaire* • *a multi-storey car park*
nano- **1** one billionth *nanometre* **2** extremely small *nanotechnology*
neo- new *neo-fascists*
non- not or the opposite of *non-alcoholic drinks* • *non-smokers*
out- more than or better than *to outgrow* • *to outnumber* • *to outdo someone* (= to show that you are better than someone)
over- too much *to overeat* • *overpopulated*
poly- many *polygamy* (= having more than one husband or wife at the same time) • *a polygon* (= shape with many sides)
post- after or later than *postwar* • *a postgraduate*
pre- before or earlier than *pre-tax profits* • *pre-school*
pro- supporting *pro-democracy demonstrations*
pseudo- false *a pseudonym* (= false name used especially by a writer) • *pseudo-academic*
quasi- partly *quasi-religious ideas*
re- again *to remarry* • *a reusable container*
semi- half or partly *a semicircle* • *semi-frozen*
socio- relating to society *socio-economic*
sub- **1** under or below *subzero temperatures* **2** less important or a smaller part of a larger whole *a subsection*
super- extremely or more than usual *a supermodel* • *super-rich*
techno- relating to technology *technophile* (=a person who loves technology)

tele- 1 done using a telephone *telesales* **2** connected with television *telecast* (=something that is broadcast on television) **3** over a long distance *telephoto lens* (=a camera lens that makes distant objects look nearer)
thermo- relating to heat or temperature *a thermostat* (= piece of equipment that controls temperature) • *a thermometer*

trans- 1 across *transatlantic flights* **2** showing a change *to transform*• *to translate*
tri- three *a triangle* • *a tripod*
ultra- extremely *ultra-modern architecture* • *ultra-careful*
uber- *humorous* used before nouns to mean 'extreme' or 'extremely good or successful' *uber-billionare*
un- not or the opposite of *unhappy* • *unfair* • *to unfasten*

Son ekler /Suffixes

Suffix kelime sonunda olan ve kelimenin anlamını, sıklıkla da cümle öğesini değiştiren harfler grubudur. En sık rastlanan son ekler ve kullanım örnekleri.

-able,-ible changes a verb into an adjective meaning 'able to be' *avoid* → *avoidable* • *admire* → *admirable*
-age changes a verb into a noun meaning 'the action described by the verb or the result of that action' *marry* → *marriage* • *break* → *breakage* • *spill* → *spillage*
-aholic unable to stop doing or taking something *chocaholic* (=someone who cannot stop eating chocolate)
-al 1 changes a noun into an adjective meaning 'relating to' *culture* → *cultural* • *nation* → *national* • *nature* → *natural* **2** changes a verb into a noun meaning 'the action described by the verb' *approve* → *approval*
-an, -ian 1 makes a noun meaning 'a person who does something' *historian* • *politician* **2** makes an adjective meaning 'belonging somewhere' *American*
-ance, -ence, -ancy, -ency makes a noun meaning 'an action, state, or quality' *performance* • *independence*
-athon an event or activity that lasts a long time, usually to raise money for charity *a walkathon* (=a long walk)
-ation, -ion changes a verb into a noun meaning 'the process of the action described by the verb, or the result of that action' *educate* → *education* • *explain* → *explanation* • *connect* → *connection*
-ed makes an adjective meaning, 'having this thing or quality' *bearded* • *coloured* • *surprised*
-ee changes a verb into a noun meaning 'someone that something is done to' *employ* → *employee* • *interview* → *interviewee* • *train* → *trainee*
-en changes an adjective into a verb meaning 'to become or make something become' *thick* → *thicken* • *fat* → *fatten* • *soft* → *soften*
-ence, -ency See -ance
-er, -or changes a verb into a noun meaning 'the person or thing that does the activity' *dance* → *dancer* • *employ* → *employer* • *act* → *actor* • *cook* → *cooker* (= a machine for cooking) • *time* → *timer*
-ese of a place, the language spoken there *Lebanese* • *Chinese*
-esque in the style of *Kafka-esque* (= in the style of writer Franz Kafka)
-est makes superlative adjectives and adverbs *bravest* • *latest*
-ful changes a noun into an adjective meaning, 'having a particular quality' *beauty* → *beautiful* • *power* → *powerful* • *use* → *useful*
-hood makes a noun meaning 'the state of being something and the time when someone is something' *childhood* • *motherhood*
-ian See -an
-ible See -able
-ical changes a noun ending in -y or -ics into an adjective meaning 'relating to' *history* → *historical* • *politics* → *political*
-ify to produce a state or quality *simplify*
-in an activity in which many people take part a *sit- in*
-ing makes an adjective meaning 'making someone feel something' *interest* → *interesting* • *surprise* → *surprising*

-ion See -ation
-ise See -ize
-ish makes an adjective meaning **1** slightly *a greyish colour* • *a smallish* (= quite small) *house* **2** typical of or similar to *a childish remark* **3** approximately *fiftyish* (= about fifty)
-ist 1 makes a noun meaning 'a person who does a particular activity' *artist* • *novelist* • *scientist* **2** makes a noun and an adjective meaning 'someone with a particular set of beliefs' *communist* • *feminist*
-ive changes a verb into an adjective meaning 'having a particular quality or effect' *attract* → *attractive* • *create* → *creative* • *explode* → *explosive*
-ize, -ise changes an adjective into a verb meaning 'to make something become' *modern* → *modernize*
-less changes a noun into an adjective meaning 'without' *homeless people* • *a meaningless statement*
-let small, not very important *piglet*
-like changes a noun into an adjective meaning 'typical of or similar to' *childlike trust*• *a cabbage-like vegetable*
-ly 1 changes an adjective into an adverb describing the way that something is done *She spoke slowly.* • *Drive safely.* **2** makes an adjective and an adverb meaning 'happening every day, night, week, etc' *a daily newspaper* • *We hold the meeting weekly.* **3** changes a noun into an adjective meaning 'like that person or thing' *mother* → *motherly* • *coward* → *cowardly*
-ment changes a verb into a noun meaning 'the action or process described by a verb, or its result' *develop* → *development* • *disappoint* → *disappointment*
-ness changes an adjective into a noun meaning 'the quality or condition described by the adjective' *sweet* → *sweetness* • *happy* → *happiness* • *dark* → *darkness* • *ill* → *illness*
-ology makes a noun meaning 'the study of something' *psychology* (= the study of the mind) • *sociology* (= the study of society)
-or See -er
-ous changes a noun into an adjective meaning 'having that quality' *danger* → *dangerous* • *ambition* → *ambitious*
-phile makes a noun meaning 'enjoying or liking something' *a Francophile* (= someone who loves France) • *a bibliophile* (= someone who loves books)
-phobe makes a noun meaning who hates something *commitment-phobe* (= a person who hates commitment)
-ship makes a noun showing involvement between people *friendship* • *a relationship* • *partnership*
-ster a person who is associated with something *gangster*
-ward, -wards makes an adverb meaning 'towards a direction or place' *inward* • *forward* • *homeward*
-wise changes a noun into an adverb meaning 'relating to this subject' *Weather-wise, the holiday was great.* • *How are we doing time-wise?*
-y changes a noun into an adjective meaning 'having a lot of something (often something bad)' *noise* → *noisy* • *dirt* → *dirty* • *smell* → *smelly*

Kelime yapmak

881-882 sayfalarda bulunan ön ve son ekleri kullanarak kelime ailelerinin nasıl yapılacağını bilmek yararlı olup, bazı sınavlar için bunları bilmeniz gereklidir. Aşağıdaki listede, koyu yazılı ve yanlarında o—• simge olan kelimeler, çok sıkça rastlanıldıkları ve öğrenilmelerinin çok önemli olduğu anlamına gelmektedir. Her satırdaki diğer kelimeler aynı aileden olup genellikle ön ve son eklerle yapılmıştır veya bazen sadece cümlenin farklı öğeleridir (örneğin, isim ve fiildir). 'un-', 'im-', 'in-' or 'ir-' ile başlayan veya '-ly' veya '-ily' ile biten bazıları hariç, ki burada anlam her zaman devamlıdır, bu listedeki tüm kelimelerin sözlükte girişleri vardır. Bazen bir kelime ailesindeki bir kelime gruptaki diğerlerinden oldukça farklı anlama sahip olabilir, dolayısıyla anlamdan emin değilseniz her zaman sözlüğü kontrol etmelisiniz.

İsimler	Sıfatlar	Fiiller	Belirteçler
ability, disability, inability	**able**, unable, disabled	enable, disable	ably
acceptance	**acceptable**, unacceptable, accepted	**accept**	acceptably, unacceptably
accident	accidental		accidentally
accuracy, inaccuracy	**accurate**, inaccurate		accurately, inaccurately
accusation, the accused, accuser	accusing	**accuse**	accusingly
achievement, achiever	achievable	**achieve**	
act, action, inaction, interaction, reaction, transaction	acting	**act**	
activity, inactivity	**active**, inactive, interactive, proactive	activate	actively
addition	additional	**add**	additionally
admiration, admirer	admirable	**admire**	admirably
advantage, disadvantage	advantageous, disadvantaged		advantageously
advertisement, advertiser, **advertising**		advertise	
advice, adviser	advisable, inadvisable, advisory	**advise**	
agreement, disagreement	agreeable	**agree**, disagree	agreeably
aim	aimless	**aim**	aimlessly
amazement	amazed, **amazing**	amaze	amazingly
anger	**angry**	anger	angrily
announcement, announcer	unannounced	**announce**	unannounced
appearance, disappearance, reappearance		**appear**, disappear, reappear	
applicant, application	applicable, applied	**apply**	
appreciation	appreciable, appreciative	**appreciate**	appreciatively
approval, disapproval	approving, disapproving	**approve**, disapprove	approvingly
approximation	approximate	approximate	**approximately**
argument	arguable, argumentative	**argue**	arguably
arrangement		**arrange**, rearrange	
art, artist, artistry	artistic		artistically
shame	**ashamed**, unashamed, shameful, shameless	shame	shamefully, shamelessly
attachment	attached, unattached, detachable, detached	**attach**, detach	
attack, counter-attack, attacker		**attack**, counter-attack	
attention	attentive, inattentive	attend	attentively
attraction, attractiveness	**attractive**, unattractive	attract	attractively
authority, authorization	authoritarian, authoritative, unauthorized	authorize	

İsimler	Sıfatlar	Fiiller	Belirteçler
availability	**available**, unavailable		
avoidance	avoidable, unavoidable	**avoid**	
awareness	**aware**, unaware		unawares
base, the basics, basis	baseless, **basic**	**base**	**basically**
bearer	bearable, unbearable	**bear**	
beat, beating	unbeatable, unbeaten	**beat**	
beautician, **beauty**	**beautiful**		beautifully
beginner, **beginning**		**begin**	
behaviour/US **behavior**, misbehaviour/US misbehavior	behavioural/US behavioral	**behave**, misbehave	
belief, disbelief	believable, unbelievable	**believe**, disbelieve	unbelievably
block, blockage	blocked, unblocked	**block**, unblock	
blood, bleeding	bloodless, bloody	bleed	
the boil, boiler	boiling	**boil**	
bore, boredom	**bored, boring**	bore	boringly
break, outbreak, breakage	unbreakable, **broken**, unbroken	**break**	
breath, breather, breathing	breathless	**breathe**	breathlessly
brother, brotherhood	brotherly		
build, builder, **building**		**build**, rebuild	
burn, burner	burning, burnt	**burn**	
burial	buried	**bury**	
calculation, calculator	incalculable, calculated, calculating	**calculate**	
calm, calmness	**calm**	calm	calmly
capability	**capable**, incapable		capably
care, carer	careful, careless, caring, uncaring	**care**	carefully, carelessly
celebration, celebrity	celebrated, celebratory	**celebrate**	
centre/US **center**, centralization, decentralization	**central**, centralized	centre/US center, centralize, decentralize	centrally
certainty, uncertainty	**certain**, uncertain		certainly, uncertainly
challenge, challenger	challenging	challenge	
change	changeable, interchangeable, unchanged, changing	**change**	
character, characteristic, characterization	characteristic, uncharacteristic	characterize	characteristically
chemical, chemist, chemistry	chemical		chemically
circle, semicircle, circulation	circular	circle, circulate	
cleaner, cleaning, cleanliness	**clean**, unclean	**clean**	clean, cleanly
clarity, clearance, clearing	**clear**, unclear	**clear**	clear, **clearly**
close, closure	closed, closing	**close**	
closeness	**close**		**close**, closely
clothes, clothing	clothed, unclothed	clothe	
collection, collector	collected, collective	**collect**	collectively
colour/US **color**, colouring/US coloring	coloured/US colored, discoloured/US discolored, colourful/US colorful, colourless/US colorless	colour/US color	colourfully/US colorfully
combination	combined	**combine**	
comfort, discomfort	**comfortable**, uncomfortable, comforting	comfort	comfortably
commitment	noncommittal, committed	**commit**	
communication, communicator	communicative, uncommunicative	**communicate**	
comparison	comparable, incomparable, comparative	**compare**	comparatively
competition, competitor	competitive, uncompetitive	**compete**	competitively
completion, incompleteness	**complete**, incomplete	**complete**	**completely**, incompletely
complication	**complicated**, uncomplicated	complicate	

İsimler	Sıfatlar	Fiiller	Belirteçler
computer, computing, computerization		computerize	
concentration	concentrated	**concentrate**	
concern	**concerned**, unconcerned	**concern**	
conclusion	concluding, conclusive, inconclusive	conclude	conclusively
condition, precondition, conditioner, conditioning	conditional, unconditional	condition	conditionally, unconditionally
confidence	**confident**, confidential	confide	confidently, confidentially
confirmation	confirmed, unconfirmed	**confirm**	
confusion	confused, confusing	**confuse**	confusingly
connection	connected, disconnected, unconnected	**connect**, disconnect	
subconscious, unconscious, consciousness, unconsciousness	**conscious**, subconscious, unconscious		consciously, unconsciously
consequence	consequent, inconsequential		consequently
consideration	considerable, considerate, inconsiderate, considered	**consider**, reconsider	considerably, considerately
continent	continental, intercontinental		
continuation, continuity	continual, continued, **continuous**	**continue**, discontinue	continually, continuously
contribution, contributor	contributory	**contribute**	
control, controller	controlling, uncontrollable	**control**	uncontrollably
convenience, inconvenience	**convenient**, inconvenient	inconvenience	conveniently
	convinced, convincing, unconvincing	**convince**	convincingly
cook, cooker, cookery, **cooking**	cooked, uncooked	**cook**	
cool, coolness	**cool**	cool	coolly
correction, correctness	**correct**, incorrect, corrective	**correct**	correctly, incorrectly
count, recount	countable, uncountable, countless	**count**, recount	
cover, coverage, covering	undercover, uncovered	**cover**, uncover	undercover
creation, creativity, creator	creative, uncreative	**create**, recreate	creatively
crime, **criminal**, criminologist	criminal, incriminating	incriminate	criminally
critic, **criticism**	**critical**, uncritical	**criticize**	critically
crowd, overcrowding	**crowded**, overcrowded	crowd	
cruelty	**cruel**		cruelly
cry, outcry	crying	cry	
culture, subculture	cultural, cultured		culturally
cure	cured, incurable	**cure**	
custom, **customer**, customs	customary	accustom	customarily
cut, cutting	cutting	**cut**, undercut	
damage, damages	damaging	**damage**	
danger	endangered, **dangerous**	endanger	dangerously
dare, daring	daring	**dare**	daringly
dark, darkness	**dark**, darkened, darkening	darken	darkly
date	dated, outdated	date, predate	
day, midday	daily		daily
dead, **death**	**dead**, deadly, deathly	deaden	deadly, deathly
deal, dealer, dealings		**deal**	
deceit, deceiver, deception	deceitful, deceptive	**deceive**	deceptively
decision, indecision	decided, undecided, decisive, indecisive	**decide**	decidedly, decisively, indecisively
decoration, decorator	decorative	**decorate**	decoratively
deep, **depth**	**deep**, deepening	deepen	deeply
defeat, defeatism, defeatist	undefeated, defeatist	**defeat**	
defence/US **defense**, defendant, defender	defenceless/US defenseless, indefensible, defensive	**defend**	defensively
definition	**definite**, indefinite	define	**definitely**, indefinitely

886

İsimler	Sıfatlar	Fiiller	Belirteçler
demand, demands	demanding, undemanding	**demand**	
democracy, democrat	democratic, undemocratic		democratically
demonstration, demonstrator	demonstrable, demonstrative	**demonstrate**	demonstrably
denial	undeniable	**deny**	undeniably
dependant, dependence, independence, dependency	dependable, dependent, independent	**depend**	dependably, independently
description	describable, indescribable, nondescript, descriptive	**describe**	descriptively
desire	desirable, undesirable, desired, undesired	desire	
destroyer, destruction	indestructible, destructive	**destroy**	destructively
determination, determiner	**determined**, predetermined, indeterminate	determine	determinedly
developer, **development**, redevelopment	developed, undeveloped, developing	**develop**, redevelop	
difference, indifference, differentiation	**different**, indifferent	differ, differentiate	differently
directness, **direction**, directions, **director**	**direct**, indirect	**direct**, redirect	directly, indirectly
disagreement	disagreeable	**disagree**	disagreeably
disappointment	**disappointed**, disappointing	disappoint	disappointingly
disaster	disastrous		disastrously
disciplinarian, **discipline**	disciplinary, disciplined, undisciplined	discipline	
discoverer, **discovery**		**discover**	
distance	**distant**	distance	distantly
disturbance	disturbed, undisturbed, disturbing	**disturb**	disturbingly
divide, division, subdivision	divided, undivided, divisible, divisive	**divide**, subdivide	
divorce, divorcee	divorced	divorce	
do, doing	done, overdone, undone	**do**, outdo, overdo, redo, undo	
doubt, doubter	undoubted, doubtful, doubtless	**doubt**	undoubtedly, doubtfully
dream, dreamer	dream, dreamless, dreamy	**dream**	dreamily
dress, dresser, dressing	dressed, undressed, dressy	**dress**, redress, undress	
drink, drinker, drinking, drunk, drunkenness	**drunk**, drunken	**drink**	drunkenly
drive, **driver**, driving	driving	**drive**	
due, dues	**due**, undue		due, duly, unduly
earner, earnings		**earn**	
earth	earthy, earthly, unearthly	unearth	
ease, unease, easiness	**easy**, uneasy	ease	**easily**, uneasily, easy
east, easterner	east, easterly, eastern		east, eastward(s)
economics, economist, **economy**	**economic**, economical, uneconomic(al)	economize	economically
education	educated, uneducated, educational	educate	educationally
effect, effectiveness, ineffectiveness	**effective**, ineffective, ineffectual	effect	effectively, ineffectively
effort	effortless		effortlessly
election, re-election, elector, electorate	unelected, electoral	elect, re-elect	
electrician, **electricity**	**electric, electrical**	electrify	electrically
electronics	**electronic**		electronically
embarrassment	**embarrassed, embarrassing**	embarrass	embarrassingly
emotion	emotional, emotive		emotionally
emphasis	emphatic	**emphasize**	emphatically
employee, **employer**, **employment**, unemployment	unemployed	**employ**	
encouragement, discouragement	encouraged, encouraging, discouraging	**encourage**, discourage	encouragingly

887

İsimler	Sıfatlar	Fiiller	Belirteçler
end, ending	unending, endless	**end**	endlessly
energy	energetic	energize	energetically
enjoyment	enjoyable	**enjoy**	enjoyably
enormity	**enormous**		enormously
entrance, entrant, **entry**		**enter**	
entertainer, **entertainment**	entertaining	entertain	entertainingly
enthusiasm, enthusiast	**enthusiastic**, unenthusiastic	enthuse	enthusiastically, unenthusiastically
environment, environmentalist	environmental		environmentally
equality, inequality	**equal**, unequal	equalize	**equally**, unequally
escape, escapism	escaped, inescapable	**escape**	inescapably
essence, essentials	**essential**		essentially
estimate, estimation	estimated	**estimate**, overestimate, underestimate	
event, non-event	eventful, uneventful, eventual		eventfully, eventually
exam, examination, cross-examination, examiner		examine, cross-examine	
excellence	**excellent**	excel	excellently
excitement	excitable, **excited**, **exciting**, unexciting	excite	excitedly, excitingly
excuse	excusable, inexcusable	**excuse**	inexcusably
existence	non-existent, existing, pre-existing	**exist**, coexist	
expectancy, expectation	expectant, unexpected	**expect**	expectantly, unexpectedly
expenditure, **expense**, expenses	**expensive**, inexpensive	expend	expensively, inexpensively
experience, inexperience	**experienced**, inexperienced	experience	
experiment	experimental	experiment	experimentally
expert, expertise	expert, inexpert		expertly
explaining, **explanation**	unexplained, explanatory, explicable, inexplicable	**explain**	inexplicably
explosion, explosive	exploding, explosive	**explode**	explosively
exploration, explorer	exploratory	**explore**	
expression	expressive	**express**	expressively
extreme, extremism, extremist, extremity	**extreme**, extremist		**extremely**
fact	factual		factually
fail, failure	unfailing	**fail**	unfailingly
fairness	**fair**, unfair		**fairly**, unfairly
faith, faithfulness	faithful, unfaithful		faithfully
familiarity, **family**	**familiar**, unfamiliar	familiarize	familiarly
fame	famed, **famous**, infamous		famously, infamously
fashion	fashionable, unfashionable	fashion	fashionably, unfashionably
fat	**fat**, fattening, fatty	fatten	
fastener		**fasten**, unfasten	
fault	faultless, faulty	fault	faultlessly
fear	fearful, fearless, fearsome	fear	fearfully, fearlessly
feel, **feeling**, feelings	unfeeling	**feel**	
fiction, nonfiction	fictional		
fill, refill, filling	filling	**fill**, refill	
final, semifinal, finalist	**final**	finalize	**finally**
finish	finished, unfinished	**finish**	
firmness, infirmity	**firm**, infirm		firmly
fish, fishing	fishy	fish	fishily
fit, fittings	fitted, fitting	**fit**	fittingly
fix, fixation, fixture	fixed, transfixed, unfixed	**fix**	
flat	**flat**	flatten	flat, flatly
flower	flowered/flowery, flowering	flower	
fold, folder	folded, folding	**fold**, unfold	
follower, following	following	**follow**	
force	forceful, forcible	**force**	forcefully, forcibly

888

İsimler	Sıfatlar	Fiiller	Belirteçler
forest, deforestation, forestry	forested		
forgetfulness	forgetful, unforgettable	**forget**	forgetfully
forgiveness	forgiving, unforgiving	**forgive**	
form, formation, transformation, reformer, transformer	reformed	**form**, reform, transform	
formality	**formal**, informal	formalize	formally, informally
fortune	fortunate, unfortunate		**fortunately**, unfortunately
freebie, **freedom**	**free**	**free**	free, freely
freeze, freezer, freezing	freezing, frozen	**freeze**	
frequency, infrequency	**frequent**, infrequent	frequent	**frequently**, infrequently
freshness, refreshments	**fresh**, refreshing	freshen, refresh	freshly, refreshingly
friend, friendliness	friendly, unfriendly	befriend	
fright	**frightened, frightening**, frightful	**frighten**	frighteningly, frightfully
fruit, fruition	fruitful, fruitless, fruity		fruitfully, fruitlessly
fund, refund, funding	funded	fund, refund	
furnishings, **furniture**	furnished, unfurnished	furnish	
garden, gardener, gardening		garden	
generalization	**general**	generalize	**generally**
generosity	**generous**		generously
gentleness	**gentle**		gently
gladness	**glad**	gladden	gladly
glass, glasses	glassy		
good, goodies, goodness, goods	**good**		
government, governor	governmental, governing	govern	governmentally
gratitude, ingratitude	**grateful**, ungrateful		gratefully
greatness	**great**		greatly
green, greenery, greens	**green**		
ground, underground, grounding, grounds	groundless, underground	ground	underground
grower, **growth**, undergrowth	growing, grown, overgrown	**grow**, outgrow	
guilt, guiltiness	**guilty**		guiltily
habit	habitual		habitually
hair, hairiness	hairless, hairy		
hand, handful	underhand, handy	**hand**	
handle, handler, handling		**handle**	
hanger	hanging	**hang**, overhang	
happiness, unhappiness	**happy**, unhappy		happily, unhappily
hardship	**hard**	harden	**hard**, hardly
harm	unharmed, harmful, harmless	**harm**	harmlessly
head, heading	overhead, heady	head, behead	overhead
health	**healthy**, unhealthy		healthily, unhealthily
hearing	unheard, unheard of	**hear**, overhear	
heart	heartened, heartening, heartless, hearty		heartily, heartlessly
heat, heater, heating	heated, unheated	heat, overheat	heatedly
height, heights	heightened	heighten	
help, helper, helpfulness, helping	helpful, unhelpful, helpless	**help**	helpfully, helplessly
Highness	**high**		high, highly
historian, **history**	historic, prehistoric, historical		historically
hold, holder, holding		**hold**	
home	homeless, homely	home	**home**
honesty, dishonesty	**honest**, dishonest		honestly, dishonestly
hope, hopefulness, hopelessness	hopeful, hopeless	**hope**	**hopefully**, hopelessly
human, humanism, humanity, inhumanity	**human**, inhuman, superhuman, humane		humanly, humanely
hunger	**hungry**		hungrily

889

İsimler	Sıfatlar	Fiiller	Belirteçler
hurry	hurried, unhurried	**hurry**	hurriedly
hurt	unhurt, hurtful	**hurt**	hurtfully
ice, icicle, icing	icy	ice	icily
identification, identity	identifiable, unidentified	**identify**	
imagination	imaginable, unimaginable, imaginary, imaginative	**imagine**	unimaginably, imaginatively
importance	**important**, unimportant		importantly
impression	impressionable, impressive	impress	impressively
improvement	improved	**improve**	
increase	increased	**increase**	increasingly
credibility, incredulity	**incredible**, credible, incredulous		incredibly, incredulously
independence, independent	**independent**		independently
industrialist, industrialization, **industry**	**industrial**, industrialized, industrious		industrially, industriously
infection, disinfectant	infectious	infect, disinfect	infectiously
inflation	inflatable, inflated, inflationary	inflate, deflate	
informant, **information**, informer	informative, uninformative, informed, uninformed	inform, misinform	
injury	injured, uninjured	**injure**	
innocence	**innocent**		innocently
insistence	insistent	**insist**	insistently
instance, instant	**instant**, instantaneous		instantly, instantaneously
instruction, instructor	instructive	instruct	instructively
intelligence	**intelligent**, unintelligent, intelligible, unintelligible		intelligently
intent, **intention**	intended, unintended, intentional, unintentional	**intend**	intentionally, unintentionally
interest	**interested**, disinterested, uninterested, **interesting**	interest	interestingly
interruption	uninterrupted	**interrupt**	
interview, interviewee		interview	
introduction	introductory	**introduce**	
invention, inventiveness, inventor	inventive	**invent**, reinvent	inventively
invitation, invite	uninvited, inviting	**invite**	invitingly
involvement	**involved**, uninvolved	**involve**	
item	itemized	itemize	
joke, joker		joke	jokingly
journal, journalism, **journalist**	journalistic		
judge, **judg(e)ment**	judgmental	**judge**	
juice, juices	juicy		
keenness	**keen**		keenly
keep, keeper, keeping	kept	**keep**	
kill, overkill, killer, killing		**kill**	
kindness, unkindness	**kind**, unkind		kindly, unkindly
knowledge	knowing, knowledgeable, known, unknown	**know**	knowingly, unknowingly, knowledgeably
enlargement	**large**	enlarge	largely
laugh, **laughter**	laughable	**laugh**	laughably
law, **lawyer**, outlaw	lawful, unlawful	outlaw	lawfully, unlawfully
laziness	**lazy**		lazily
lead, **leader**, leadership	lead, leading	**lead**	
learner, learning	learned, unlearned	**learn**	
legality, illegality, legalization	**legal**, illegal	legalize	legally, illegally
length	lengthening, lengthy	lengthen	lengthily
liar, **lie**	lying	lie	
life	lifeless, lifelike, lifelong		lifelessly
light, lighter, lighting, lightness	**light**	light, lighten	lightly
dislike, liking	likeable	**like**, dislike	

İsimler	Sıfatlar	Fiiller	Belirteçler
likelihood	**likely**, unlikely		likely
limit, limitation, limitations	limited, unlimited	**limit**	
literature, literacy	literary, literate, illiterate		
liveliness, living	**live**, lively, living	**live**, outlive, relive	live
local, location, relocation	**local**	dislocate, relocate	locally
loser, **loss**	lost	**lose**	
	loud		aloud, loud/loudly
love, lover	lovable, unlovable, loveless, lovely, loving	**love**	lovingly
low	**low**, lower, lowly	lower	low
luck	**lucky**, unlucky		luckily, unluckily
machine, machinery, mechanic, mechanics, mechanism	mechanical, mechanized		mechanically
magic, magician	magic, magical		magically
make, remake, maker, making	unmade	**make**, remake	
man, manhood, mankind	manly, manned, unmanned	man	
management, manager	manageable, unmanageable, managerial	**manage**	
mark, marker, markings	marked, unmarked	**mark**	markedly
market, marketing	marketable	market	
marriage	**married**, unmarried	**marry**, remarry	
match	matching, unmatched	**match**	
material, materialism, materialist, materials	material, immaterial, materialistic	materialize	
meaning	meaningful, meaningless	**mean**	meaningfully
measure, **measurement**	measurable, immeasurable	**measure**	immeasurably
medical, medication, **medicine**	**medical**, medicated, medicinal		medically
memorial, **memory**	memorable	memorize	memorably
mentality	**mental**		mentally
method, methodology	methodical, methodological		methodically
militancy, militant, the military, militia	**military**, militant		militantly, militarily
mind, minder, reminder	mindless	**mind**, remind	mindlessly
minimum	minimal, **minimum**	minimize	minimally
miss	**missing**	**miss**	
mistake	mistaken, unmistakable	mistake	unmistakably, mistakenly
mix, mixer, **mixture**	mixed	**mix**	
modernity, modernization	**modern**	modernize	
moment	momentary, momentous		momentarily
mood, moodiness	moody		moodily
moral, morals, morality, immorality	**moral**, amoral, immoral		morally
mother, motherhood	motherly		
move, **movement**, removal, remover	movable, unmoved, moving	**move**, remove	movingly
murder, murderer	murderous	**murder**	murderously
music, musical, musician	musical, unmusical		musically
name	named, unnamed, nameless	**name**, rename	namely
nation, national, multinational, nationalism, nationalist, nationality, nationalization	**national**, international, multinational, nationalistic	nationalize	nationally, internationally
nature, naturalist, naturalization, naturalness the supernatural	**natural**, supernatural, unnatural, naturalistic	naturalize	naturally, unnaturally
necessity	**necessary**, unnecessary	necessitate	necessarily, unnecessarily
need, needs	needless, needy	**need**	needlessly
nerve, nerves, nervousness	**nervous**		nervously
news, renewal	**new**, renewable, renewed	renew	newly
night, midnight			overnight, nightly
noise	noisy		noisily

İsimler	Sıfatlar	Fiiller	Belirteçler
normality/US normalcy, abnormality	**normal**, abnormal		**normally**, abnormally
north, northerner	north, northerly, northern		north, northward(s)
notice	noticeable, unnoticed	**notice**	noticeably
number, numeral	innumerable, numerical, numerous	number, outnumber	
nurse, nursery, nursing		nurse	
obedience, disobedience	obedient, disobedient	**obey**, disobey	obediently, disobediently
occasion	occasional		occasionally
offence/US **offense**, offender, offensive	offensive, inoffensive	**offend**	offensively
office, officer, official	**official**, unofficial		officially, unofficially
the open, opener, opening, openness	**open**, opening	**open**	openly
operation, cooperation, operative, cooperative operator	operational, operative, cooperative	**operate**, cooperate	operationally
opposition, opposite	opposed, opposing, **opposite**	**oppose**	opposite
option	optional	opt	optionally
order, disorder	disordered, orderly, disorderly	**order**	
organization, disorganization, reorganization, organizer	organizational, organized, disorganized	**organize**, disorganize, reorganize	
origin, original, originality, originator	**original**, unoriginal	originate	**originally**
owner, ownership		**own**, disown	
pack, package, packaging, packet, packing	packed	**pack**, unpack, package	
pain	pained, **painful**, painless	pain	painfully, painlessly
paint, painter, **painting**		**paint**	
part, counterpart, parting, partition	partial, parting	part, partition	part, partially, **partly**
pass, overpass, underpass, passage, passing	passing	**pass**	
patience, impatience, **patient**	**patient**, impatient		patiently, impatiently
pay, **payment**, repayment	unpaid, underpaid	**pay**, repay	
peace	**peaceful**		peacefully
perfection, imperfection, perfectionist	**perfect**, imperfect	perfect	**perfectly**
performance, performer		**perform**	
permission, permit	permissible, impermissible, permissive	permit	
person, **personality**	**personal**, impersonal, personalized	personalize, personify	personally
persuasion	persuasive	**persuade**, dissuade	persuasively
photo, **photograph**, photographer, photography	photogenic, photographic	photograph	
picture	pictorial, picturesque	picture	
place, placement, displacement, replacement	misplaced	place, displace, replace	
plan, planner, planning	unplanned	**plan**	
plant, transplant, plantation		plant, transplant	
play, interplay, replay, **player**, playfulness	playful	**play**, outplay, replay	playfully
pleasantry, **pleasure**, displeasure	**pleasant**, unpleasant, **pleased**, displeased, pleasing, pleasurable	please, displease	pleasantly, unpleasantly
poem, poet, **poetry**	poetic		
point, pointer	pointed, pointless	**point**	pointlessly
politeness	**polite**, impolite		politely, impolitely
politician, **politics**	**political**, politicized	politicize	politically
popularity, unpopularity, popularization	**popular**, unpopular	popularize	popularly

İsimler	Sıfatlar	Fiiller	Belirteçler
population	populated, unpopulated, populous	populate	
possibility, impossibility, the impossible	**possible**, impossible		**possibly**, impossibly
post, postage	postal	**post**	
power, superpower	**powerful**, overpowering, powerless	power, empower, overpower powerfully	
practical, practicalities, practicality	practicable, **practical**, impractical		practically
practice, practitioner	practised/US practiced, practising/US practicing	**practise**/US **practice**	
precision	**precise**, imprecise		precisely
preference	preferable, preferential	**prefer**	preferably
preparation, preparations	prepared, unprepared, preparatory	**prepare**	
presence, **present**, presentation, presenter	**present**, presentable	present, represent	presently
press, **pressure**	pressed, pressing, pressurized	**press**, pressure/pressurize	
prevention	preventable, preventive/preventative	**prevent**	
price	overpriced, priceless, pricey/pricy	price	
print, printer, printing	printed	**print**	
prison, **prisoner**, imprisonment		imprison	
privacy, private, privatization	**private**	privatize	privately
probability	probable, improbable		**probably**, improbably
process, processing, procession, processor	processed	process	
produce, producer, **product**, **production**, reproduction, productivity	productive, counterproductive, reproductive, unproductive	**produce**, reproduce	
profession, professional, professionalism	**professional**, unprofessional		professionally
profit, profitability	profitable, unprofitable	profit	profitably
progress, progression	progressive	progress	progressively
proof	proven, unproven	prove, disprove	
protection, protector	protected, unprotected, protective	**protect**	protectively
provider, provision, provisions	provisional	**provide**	provisionally
public, publication, publicist, publicity	**public**	publicize	publicly
publisher, publishing	published, unpublished	**publish**	
punishment	punishable, punishing	**punish**	
purification, purist, purity, impurity	**pure**, impure	purify	purely
purpose	purposeful		purposefully, purposely
push, pusher	pushed, pushy	**push**	
qualification, disqualification, qualifier	qualified, unqualified	qualify, disqualify	
quarter, quarters	quarterly	quarter	quarterly
question, questioning	questionable, unquestionable	question	unquestionably
quiet, disquiet	**quiet**	quieten/quiet	quietly
race, racism, racist	racial, multiracial, racist		racially
rarity	**rare**		rarely
rate, rating	overrated, underrated	rate, underrate	
reaction, reactor	reactionary	**react**, overreact	
read, reader, readership, **reading**	readable, unreadable	**read**	
readiness	**ready**		readily
realism, realist, reality, unreality, realization	**real**, unreal, realistic, unrealistic	**realize**	real, **really**, realistically
reason, reasoning	reasonable, unreasonable	reason	reasonably, unreasonably
receipt, receipts, receiver, reception	receptive	**receive**	
recognition	recognizable, unrecognizable	**recognize**	recognizably
record, recorder, recording	recorded, unrecorded	**record**	

İsimler	Sıfatlar	Fiiller	Belirteçler
referee, reference, referral		**refer**, referee	
reflection	reflective	**reflect**	
regret	regrettable, regretful	**regret**	regrettably, regretfully
regular, regularity, irregularity	**regular**, irregular		**regularly**, irregularly
relation, relations, **relationship**, **relative**	**related**, unrelated, relative	relate	relatively
relaxation	**relaxed**, relaxing	**relax**	
reliability, reliance	**reliable**, unreliable, reliant	**rely**	reliably
religion	**religious**, irreligious		religiously
the remainder, remains	remaining	**remain**	
remark	remarkable, unremarkable	remark	remarkably
repair, disrepair	irreparable	**repair**	irreparably
repeat, repetition	repeated, repetitive/repetitious	**repeat**	repeatedly, repetitively
report, reporter	unreported	**report**	reportedly
representation, representative	representative, unrepresentative	**represent**	
reputation, disrepute	reputable, disreputable, reputed		reputedly
respect, disrespect, respectability	respectable, respected, respectful, disrespectful, respective	**respect**	respectably, respectfully, disrespectfully, respectively
respondent, **response**, responsiveness	responsive, unresponsive	**respond**	
responsibility, irresponsibility	**responsible**, irresponsible		responsibly, irresponsibly
rest, unrest, restlessness	restless	**rest**	restlessly
retiree, retirement	retired, retiring	**retire**	
reward	rewarding, unrewarding	reward	
riches, richness, enrichment	**rich**	enrich	richly
ride, rider, riding	overriding	**ride**, override	
right, rightness, rights, righteousness	right, righteous, rightful	right	**right**, rightly, rightfully
roll, roller		**roll**, unroll	
romance, romantic	**romantic**, unromantic, romanticized	romance, romanticize	romantically
rough, roughage, roughness	**rough**	rough, roughen	rough, **roughly**
round, rounders, roundness	**round**, rounded	round	**round**, roundly
royal, royalist, royalty	**royal**, royalist		royally
rudeness	**rude**		rudely
rule, ruler, ruling	ruling, unruly	rule, overrule	
run, rerun, runner, running	running, runny	**run**, outrun, overrun	
sadness	**sad**	sadden	sadly
safe, **safety**	**safe**, unsafe		safely
satisfaction, dissatisfaction	**satisfactory**, unsatisfactory, **satisfied**, dissatisfied, unsatisfied, satisfying	satisfy	satisfactorily, unsatisfactorily
save, saver, saving, savings, saviour/US savior		**save**	
	scared, scary	scare	
school, pre-school, schooling	pre-school		
science, **scientist**	**scientific**, unscientific		scientifically
score, scorer		**score**, outscore, underscore	
search, research, researcher	searching	**search**, research	
seat, seating	seated	seat, unseat	
secrecy, secret	**secret**, secretive		secretly, secretively
sense, nonsense, sensibility, sensitivity, insensitivity	**sensible**, senseless, sensitive, insensitive	sense	sensibly, sensitively, insensitively
separation	separable, inseparable, **separate**	**separate**	inseparably, separately
seriousness	**serious**		**seriously**
servant, serve, server, **service**, disservice, the services, serving	serviceable, servile	**serve**, service	

İsimler	Sıfatlar	Fiiller	Belirteçler
sex, sexism, sexuality	sexist, **sexual**, bisexual, sexy		sexually
shadow	shadowy	shadow, overshadow	
shake	shaky	**shake**	shakily
shape	shapeless, shapely	shape	
(pencil) sharpener, sharpness	**sharp**	sharpen	sharp, sharply
shine	shiny	**shine**, outshine	
shock	shocked, shocking	**shock**	shockingly
shop, shopper, **shopping**		shop	
short, shortage, shortness, shorts	**short**	shorten	short, shortly
shyness	**shy**	shy	shyly
sick, sickness	**sick**, sickening, sickly	sicken	sickeningly
sight, insight, oversight, sighting	sighted, unsightly	sight	
sign, **signal**, signatory, signature, signing	signed, unsigned	**sign**, signal	
significance, insignificance	**significant**, insignificant	signify	significantly, insignificantly
silence, silencer	**silent**	silence	silently
similarity	**similar**, dissimilar		similarly
simplicity, simplification	**simple**, simplistic	simplify	simply
singer, singing	unsung	**sing**	
single, singles	**single**, singular	single	singly
skill	skilful/US skillful, skilled, unskilled		skilfully/US skillfully
sleep, sleeper, sleepiness, sleeplessness	asleep, sleepless, sleepy	**sleep**	sleepily
slight	**slight**, slighted, slightest		**slightly**
slip, slipper	slippery	**slip**	
smoke, smoker, non-smoker, smoking	smoked, smoking, non-smoking, smoky	**smoke**	
smoothness	**smooth**	smooth	smoothly
society, sociologist, sociology	sociable, unsociable, **social**, anti-social, unsocial	socialize	socially
softness	**soft**	soften	softly
solid, solidarity, solidity, solids	**solid**	solidify	solidly
solution, solvent	soluble, insoluble, unsolved, solvent	**solve**	
south, southerner	south, southerly, southern		south, southward(s)
speaker, **speech**	unspeakable, speechless, outspoken, unspoken	**speak**	unspeakably
special, specialist, speciality/US specialty, specialization	**special**, specialized	specialize	**specially**
speed, speeding	speedy	speed	speedily
spelling		**spell**, misspell	
spoils	spoilt/spoiled, unspoiled/unspoilt	**spoil**	
sport	sporting, sporty	sport	
spot	spotted, spotless, spotty	spot	spotlessly
stand, standing	standing, outstanding	**stand**	outstandingly
standard, standardization	standard, substandard	standardize	
start, starter, non-starter		**start**, restart	
statement, understatement	understated	state, overstate	
steam, steamer	steamy	steam	
steepness	**steep**		steeply
sticker	sticky, stuck, unstuck	**stick**	
stiffness	**stiff**	stiffen	stiff, stiffly
stone	stoned, stony	stone	
stop, stoppage	non-stop	**stop**	non-stop
storm	stormy	storm	
	straight	straighten	**straight**
stranger	**strange**		strangely
strength	**strong**	strengthen	strongly

İsimler	Sıfatlar	Fiiller	Belirteçler
stress	stressed, stressful	stress	
strike, striker	striking	**strike**	
structure, restructuring	structural	structure, restructure	structurally
student, **study**	studious	**study**	studiously
stupidity	**stupid**		stupidly
style	stylish	style	stylishly
substance	substantial, insubstantial, substantive	substantiate	substantially
success, succession, successor	**successful**, unsuccessful, successive	**succeed**	successfully, unsuccessfully
suddenness	**sudden**		**suddenly**
sufferer, suffering	insufferable	**suffer**	insufferably
suggestion	suggestive	**suggest**	suggestively
summer, midsummer	summery		
supplier, supplies, **supply**		**supply**	
support, supporter	supportive	**support**	
supposition	supposed	**suppose**, presuppose	supposedly
surface		surface, resurface	
surprise	**surprised**, surprising	surprise	surprisingly
surroundings	surrounding	**surround**	
survival, survivor		**survive**	
suspect, suspicion	suspect, suspected, unsuspecting, suspicious	**suspect**	suspiciously
swearing	sworn	**swear**	
sweet, sweetener, sweetness	**sweet**	sweeten	sweetly
swim, swimmer, swimming		**swim**	
symbol, symbolism	symbolic	symbolize	symbolically
sympathy, sympathizer	**sympathetic**, unsympathetic	sympathize	sympathetically
system	systematic		systematically
takings, undertaking		**take**, overtake, undertake	
talk, talks	talkative	**talk**	
taste, distaste	tasteful, distasteful, tasteless, tasty	**taste**	tastefully, distastefully
tax, taxation	taxable, taxing	tax	
teacher, teaching, teachings		**teach**	
tear	tearful		tearfully
technicalities, technicality, technician, technique	**technical**		technically
technology	technological		technologically
thanks	thankful, thankless	**thank**	thankfully
theorist, **theory**	theoretical	theorize	theoretically
thick, thickness	**thick**	thicken	thickly
thinness	**thin**	thin	thinly
think, rethink, thinker, thinking	unthinkable	**think**, rethink	
thirst	**thirsty**		thirstily
thought, thoughtfulness	thoughtful, thoughtless		thoughtfully, thoughtlessly
threat	threatening	**threaten**	threateningly
tightness	**tight**	tighten	tight, tightly
time, overtime, timer, timing	timeless, timely, untimely	time	
tiredness	**tired**, tireless, tiresome, tiring	tire	tirelessly
title, subtitles	titled	entitle	
top, topping	**top**, topless, topmost	top	
touch	touched, untouched, touching, touchy	**touch**	touchingly
	tough	toughen	toughly
trade, trader, trading		trade	
tradition, traditionalist	**traditional**		traditionally
trainee, trainer, **training**, retraining	untrained	**train**	
transport, transportation		transport	
treat, **treatment**, mistreatment	untreated	**treat**, mistreat	

İsimler	Sıfatlar	Fiiller	Belirteçler
trick, trickery	tricky	trick	
trouble	troubled, troublesome	trouble	
trust, distrust, mistrust, trustee	trusting, trustworthy	**trust**, distrust, mistrust	
truth, untruth, truthfulness	**true**, untrue, truthful		truly, truthfully
try	trying, untried	**try**	
turn, upturn, turning	upturned	**turn**, overturn	
twist, twister	twisted	**twist**	
type	**typical**	typify	typically
understanding, misunderstanding	understandable, understanding, misunderstood	**understand**, misunderstand	understandably
upset	**upset**, upsetting	upset	
urgency	**urgent**		urgently
usage, **use**, disuse, misuse, usefulness, user	reusable, **used**, disused, unused, **useful**, **useless**	**use**, misuse, reuse	usefully
valuables, **value**, values	**valuable**, invaluable, undervalued	value, devalue	
variable, variance, variant, **variety**	variable, varied, **various**	vary	invariably, variously
view, overview, preview, review, viewer		view, preview, review	
violence	**violent**, non-violent	violate	violently
visit, **visitor**		**visit**, revisit	
vote, voter		**vote**	
want, wants	wanted, unwanted	**want**	
war, warfare, warrior	postwar, warring		
warmth	**warm**	warm	warmly
wash, washer, washing	washable, unwashed	**wash**	
wastage, **waste**	waste, wasteful	**waste**	wastefully
watch	watchful	**watch**	
water, waters	underwater, waterproof, watery	water	underwater
way, subway			midway
weakling, weakness	**weak**	weaken	weakly
wear, underwear	wearing, worn	**wear**	
week, midweek	weekly, midweek		weekly, midweek
weight, weights	overweight, underweight, weighted, weighty	**weigh,**	**outweigh**
welcome	welcome, unwelcome	**welcome**	
west, western, westerner	westerly, western		west, westward(s)
white, whiteness	**white**	whiten	
whole	**whole**, wholesome, unwholesome		
width	**wide**	widen	**wide**, **widely**
wild, wildness	**wild**		wildly
willingness, unwillingness	**willing**, unwilling		willingly, unwillingly
win, **winner**, winnings		**win**	
winter, midwinter	wintry		
wire, wireless, wiring	wiry	wire	
woman, womanhood	womanly		
wonder	**wonderful**	**wonder**	wonderfully
wood	wooded, wooden		
wool	woollen/US woolen, woolly/US wooly		
word, wording		word	
work, workaholic, worker, workings	workable, unworkable, overworked, working	**work**, rework	
world, underworld	world, worldly, unworldly, worldwide		worldwide
worry	**worried**, unworried, worrying	**worry**	worryingly

İsimler	Sıfatlar	Fiiller	Belirteçler
worth	**worth**, worthless, worthwhile, worthy, unworthy		
writer, **writing**	written, unwritten	**write**, rewrite	
wrong	**wrong**, wrongful	wrong	**wrong**, wrongly, wrongfully
year	yearly		yearly
young, youngster, youth	**young**, youthful		

Söyleyiş Simgeleri

ɪ	pit	ʊ	put	ɑː	arm
e	wet	ə	ago	ɔː	saw
æ	cat	i	cosy	uː	too
ʌ	run	u	influence	ɜː	her
ɒ	hot	iː	see		

eɪ	day	aʊ	how	ʊə	poor
aɪ	my	ɪə	near	aɪə	fire
ɔɪ	boy	eə	hair	aʊə	sour
əʊ	low				

b	bee	k	key	s	sun
d	do	l	led	t	ten
f	fat	m	map	v	van
g	go	n	name	w	wet
h	hat	p	pen	z	zip
j	yet	r	red		

dʒ	general	θ	thin	ʒ	measure
ŋ	hang	ʃ	ship	tʃ	chin
ð	that				

[ᵊ]   -sudden'da olduğu gibi /ˈsʌdᵊn/ söylenebilir veya söylenmez

[ʳ]   -teacher'ın UK İngilizcesinde söylendiği gibi /tiːʃəʳ/, bir ünlü ses takip ettiğinde söylenir ve bir ünsüz ses takip ettiğinde söylenmez. US İngilizcesinde her zaman söylenir.

[ˈ]   -Ana vurgu (kelimenin en çok vurguladığınız kısmı), above'da olduğu gibi /əˈbʌv/

[ˌ]   -İkincil vurgu (kelimenin yine vurguladığınız fakat ana vurgu kadar güçlü olmayan kısmı) abbreviation'da olduğu gibi /əˌbriːviˈeɪʃᵊn/